The Bill James Handbook 2011

Baseball Info Solutions

www.baseballinfosolutions.com

Published by ACTA Sports

A Division of ACTA Publications

Cover by Tom A. Wright
Front Cover Photo by Jamie Wisner
Back Cover Photo by Samara Pearlstein

First Edition: November 2010

Published by:
ACTA Sports, a division of ACTA Publications
4848 North Clark Street Chicago, IL 60640
(800) 397-2282
www.actasports.com www.actapublications.com

ISBN: 978-0-87946-439-4
ISSN: 1940-8668

Printed in the United States of America

Table of Contents

Dedication

This book is dedicated to my father, John Dewan Sr., who taught me so much, not the least of which is that being a White Sox fan is a life-long endeavor.

John Dewan

Introduction

We're the last man standing. Almost.

Thinking about what to write for this intro got me to thinking that this is the first year the Handbook will (eventually) be available in electronic format. Then thinking about electronic format got me to thinking about all the meat-and-potatoes, hold-them-in-your-hand statistical annuals that were available over the years.

Wanna see a list of extinct statistical baseball annuals that reside on my home bookshelf (in no order other than where they sit on my bookshelf)? The years are the ones I have:

The Baseball Weekly Almanac (1992-1996)
The Sporting News Major League Baseball Fact Book (1997-2006)
The Baseball Superstats 1989
The Baseball Sabermetric (1990-1993)
Baseball Insight (1994)
Major League Baseball 1992 Stat Book
1986 Red (AL) and Blue (NL) Boxscore Books

Then there's the John Benson Rotisserie library of books (1991-1998), the classic American League Red Books and National League Green Books (earliest I have is 1973 and latest is 1996), the controversial Baseball Player & Team Ratings books (1991-1994) by Mike Gimbel and, the greatly missed former industry standard Baseball Guide (born pre-1900, died 2006) and Baseball Register (born 1940, died 2007), done by Spalding and Reach in the early days and Sporting News since.

Let's not forget all the books I've been personally involved with, which I won't mention, and the Bill James Abstracts and Bill James Great American Stat Books, which kind of morphed into the Handbook.

Why did statistical annuals flourish in the 1990s? Because sabermetrics and fantasy baseball (attention all media, they're not the same thing) had a growth spurt and the internet was just getting started. It was the Golden Age of baseball books.

Every day some of my younger colleagues kid me about my reliance on what might soon be dinosaur bones – newspapers, books, even paper itself. But I can't help relive those fond memories of eagerly anticipating what old and new baseball book treasures would greet me with each trip to the non-virtual bookstore beginning in February and lasting sometimes all the way until the season began.

Here's to the 2011 Handbook, which I can literally add to that bookshelf with pages I can touch and turn with my fingers.

Steve Moyer
Baseball Info Solutions

2010 Team Statistics

Anyone can wake up in the morning and find updated standings in the newspaper or online, but you'd be hard-pressed to find more comprehensive extended standings, team records and team-by-team statistics than what follows in the next several pages.

While the basic standings are included, you can also find a wide variety of team information including information about the pennant race, team records based on the opponent (e.g. records vs. left-handed starters) and team records based on other factors such as game conditions (e.g. team record in day and night games). Want to know how many days the division-winning Giants spent in first place this year? You can find it here. (Answer: 35 days compared to 146 days for the San Diego Padres.)

Beyond win-loss records, there is an extensive amount of team statistics displayed in these pages. Broken out by league, there are complete batting, pitching, and fielding records for each team that go beyond standard team stats.

2010 American League Standings

Overall

EAST							CENTRAL							WEST						
Team	W-L	Pct	GB	D1	LD1	LLd	Team	W-L	Pct	GB	D1	LD1	LLd	Team	W-L	Pct	GB	D1	LD1	LLd
Tampa Bay Rays	96-66	.593	0.0	94	10/3	6.0	Minnesota Twins	94-68	.580	0.0	141	10/3	12.0	Texas Rangers	90-72	.556	0.0	153	10/3	11.0
New York Yankees*	95-67	.586	1.0	108	10/2	4.0	Chicago White Sox	88-74	.543	6.0	33	8/11	3.5	Oakland Athletics	81-81	.500	9.0	30	5/31	2.5
Boston Red Sox	89-73	.549	7.0	2	4/5	1.0	Detroit Tigers	81-81	.500	13.0	15	7/10	1.0	Los Angeles Angels	80-82	.494	10.0	4	6/7	0.5
Toronto Blue Jays	85-77	.525	11.0	8	4/15	1.0	Cleveland Indians	69-93	.426	25.0	0	-	0.0	Seattle Mariners	61-101	.377	29.0	2	4/21	0.0
Baltimore Orioles	66-96	.407	30.0	0	-	0.0	Kansas City Royals	67-95	.414	27.0	0	-	0.0							

* Clinched Wild Card Berth on 9/28. Division Clinch Dates: Minnesota 9/21, Texas 9/25, Tampa Bay 10/3.
D1 = Number of days a team had at least a share of first place of their division; LD1 = Last date the team had at least a share of first place; LLd = The largest number of games that a team led their division by.

East Division

	AT		VERSUS						CONDITIONS				GAME			MONTHLY						ALL-STAR	
Tm	Home	Road	East	Cent	West	NL	LHS	RHS	Day	Night	Grass	Turf	1-Rn	5+Rn	XInn	April	May	June	July	Aug	Sept	Pre	Post
TB	49-32	47-34	42-30	26-13	21-12	7-11	36-20	60-46	27-19	69-47	43-29	53-37	29-27	29-15	10-5	17-6	17-12	11-14	19-7	17-12	15-15	54-34	42-32
NYY	52-29	43-38	38-34	23-13	23-13	11-7	31-27	64-40	36-22	59-45	88-56	7-11	20-19	35-17	7-7	15-7	16-13	16-10	19-7	16-13	13-17	56-32	39-35
Bos	46-35	43-38	37-35	15-18	24-15	13-5	28-29	61-44	20-23	69-50	78-66	11-7	22-26	26-18	6-12	11-12	18-11	18-9	12-13	15-13	15-15	51-37	38-36
Tor	45-33	40-44	39-33	22-19	17-14	7-11	13-23	72-54	33-29	52-48	37-38	48-39	24-28	26-27	5-6	12-12	19-10	9-17	14-11	15-13	16-14	44-45	41-32
Bal	37-44	29-52	24-48	17-20	18-17	7-11	18-33	48-63	16-28	50-68	62-82	4-14	29-21	10-31	13-4	5-18	10-18	9-17	8-19	17-11	17-13	29-59	37-37

Central Division

	AT		VERSUS						CONDITIONS				GAME			MONTHLY						ALL-STAR	
Tm	Home	Road	East	Cent	West	NL	LHS	RHS	Day	Night	Grass	Turf	1-Rn	5+Rn	XInn	April	May	June	July	Aug	Sept	Pre	Post
Min	53-28	41-40	15-21	47-25	24-12	8-10	32-24	62-44	32-23	62-45	90-63	4-5	31-23	32-16	9-5	15-8	16-12	12-15	15-11	18-10	18-12	46-42	48-26
CWS	45-36	43-38	17-18	32-40	24-13	15-3	20-20	68-54	31-18	57-56	84-70	4-4	28-21	23-20	6-10	9-14	13-14	18-9	18-8	14-15	16-14	49-38	39-36
Det	52-29	29-52	17-22	38-34	15-18	11-7	26-21	55-60	35-28	46-53	79-75	2-6	16-26	22-21	7-8	14-10	15-12	15-12	11-15	15-16	14-14	48-38	33-43
Cle	38-43	31-50	17-24	34-38	13-18	5-13	18-28	51-65	17-35	52-58	66-87	3-6	23-21	21-29	6-6	9-13	9-18	12-16	13-14	10-18	16-14	34-54	35-39
KC	38-43	29-52	17-18	29-43	13-24	8-10	12-24	55-71	22-27	45-68	64-91	3-4	27-30	14-30	10-8	9-14	12-17	13-14	10-15	12-16	11-19	39-49	28-46

West Division

	AT		VERSUS						CONDITIONS				GAME			MONTHLY						ALL-STAR	
Tm	Home	Road	East	Cent	West	NL	LHS	RHS	Day	Night	Grass	Turf	1-Rn	5+Rn	XInn	April	May	June	July	Aug	Sept	Pre	Post
Tex	51-30	39-42	19-25	25-18	32-25	14-4	28-23	62-49	19-25	71-47	88-64	2-8	30-23	22-11	11-6	11-12	15-12	21-6	14-13	13-15	16-14	50-38	40-34
Oak	47-34	34-47	20-25	23-19	30-27	8-10	24-21	57-60	35-21	46-60	80-76	1-5	23-20	25-18	4-7	12-12	16-12	10-17	14-10	13-15	16-15	43-46	38-35
LAA	43-38	37-44	15-27	19-26	35-22	11-7	23-28	57-54	29-20	51-62	75-81	5-1	24-25	21-25	9-7	12-12	14-15	18-9	9-17	11-16	16-13	47-44	33-38
Sea	35-46	26-55	17-26	18-26	17-40	9-9	14-36	47-65	16-33	45-68	58-95	3-6	21-28	12-30	3-11	11-12	8-19	14-13	6-22	13-14	9-21	35-53	26-48

Team vs. Team Breakdown

	EAST					CENTRAL					WEST			
	TB	NYY	Bos	Tor	Bal	Min	CWS	Det	Cle	KC	Tex	Oak	LAA	Sea
Tampa Bay Rays	-	10	11	10	11	5	4	6	7	4	4	5	5	7
New York Yankees	8	-	9	8	13	4	4	4	6	5	4	9	4	6
Boston Red Sox	7	9	-	12	9	3	1	3	4	4	4	4	9	7
Toronto Blue Jays	8	10	6	-	15	6	5	4	4	3	7	4	3	3
Baltimore Orioles	7	5	9	3	-	3	4	5	3	2	6	3	6	3
Minnesota Twins	3	2	2	3	5	-	13	9	12	13	7	6	5	6
Chicago White Sox	3	2	6	3	3	5	-	8	9	10	4	4	7	9
Detroit Tigers	1	4	3	4	5	9	10	-	9	10	3	3	6	3
Cleveland Indians	2	2	4	6	3	6	9	9	-	10	2	3	5	3
Kansas City Royals	4	3	3	3	4	5	8	8	8	-	2	3	3	5
Texas Rangers	2	4	6	3	4	3	5	6	4	7	-	10	10	12
Oakland Athletics	4	1	5	3	7	3	5	3	6	6	9	-	8	13
Los Angeles Angels	4	4	1	6	0	2	2	4	4	7	9	11	-	15
Seattle Mariners	2	4	3	2	6	4	1	5	4	4	7	6	4	-

2010 National League Standings

Overall

EAST

Team	W-L	Pct	GB	D1	LD1	LLd
Philadelphia Phillies	97-65	.599	0.0	78	10/3	7.0
Atlanta Braves*	91-71	.562	6.0	105	9/11	7.0
Florida Marlins	80-82	.494	17.0	1	4/8	0.0
New York Mets	79-83	.488	18.0	7	5/1	1.0
Washington Nationals	69-93	.426	28.0	0	-	0.0

CENTRAL

Team	W-L	Pct	GB	D1	LD1	LLd
Cincinnati Reds	91-71	.562	0.0	110	10/3	8.0
St Louis Cardinals	86-76	.531	5.0	82	8/14	5.0
Milwaukee Brewers	77-85	.475	14.0	1	4/8	0.0
Houston Astros	76-86	.469	15.0	0	-	0.0
Chicago Cubs	75-87	.463	16.0	0	-	0.0
Pittsburgh Pirates	57-105	.352	34.0	4	4/8	0.0

WEST

Team	W-L	Pct	GB	D1	LD1	LLd
San Francisco Giants	92-70	.568	0.0	35	10/3	3.0
San Diego Padres	90-72	.556	2.0	146	9/25	6.5
Colorado Rockies	83-79	.512	9.0	1	4/5	0.0
Los Angeles Dodgers	80-82	.494	12.0	8	6/17	1.0
Arizona Diamondbacks	65-97	.401	27.0	1	4/5	0.0

* Clinched Wild Card Berth on 10/3. Division Clinch Dates: Philadelphia 9/27, Cincinnati 9/28, San Francisco 10/3.
D1 = Number of days a team had at least a share of first place of their division; LD1 = Last date the team had at least a share of first place; LLd = The largest number of games that a team led their division

East Division

Tm	Home	Road	East	Cent	West	AL	LHS	RHS	Day	Night	Grass	Turf	1-Rn	5+Rn	Xinn	April	May	June	July	Aug	Sept	Pre	Post
Phi	54-30	43-35	44-28	21-19	22-10	10-8	28-20	69-45	27-24	70-41	97-65	0-0	29-17	30-16	11-6	12-10	16-12	13-13	15-13	18-10	23-7	47-40	50-25
Atl	56-25	35-46	38-34	25-16	19-15	9-6	28-27	63-44	32-23	59-48	91-71	0-0	23-22	27-19	8-7	9-14	20-8	17-11	13-11	18-11	14-16	52-36	39-35
Fla	41-40	39-42	37-35	20-20	16-19	7-8	34-15	46-67	22-21	58-61	76-80	0-0	23-28	22-22	5-8	11-12	15-14	11-15	16-10	13-14	14-17	42-46	38-36
NYM	47-34	32-49	31-41	21-19	14-18	13-5	22-17	57-66	22-26	57-57	78-81	1-2	25-30	20-16	7-9	14-9	12-17	18-8	9-17	12-16	14-16	48-40	31-43
Was	41-40	28-53	30-42	19-20	15-18	5-13	17-23	52-70	26-31	43-62	69-93	0-0	20-28	19-30	3-10	13-10	13-16	8-19	12-13	11-18	12-17	39-50	30-43

Central Division

Tm	Home	Road	East	Cent	West	AL	LHS	RHS	Day	Night	Grass	Turf	1-Rn	5+Rn	Xinn	April	May	June	July	Aug	Sept	Pre	Post
Cin	49-32	42-39	17-15	49-30	17-19	8-7	33-22	58-49	31-26	60-45	91-71	0-0	27-27	27-16	11-8	12-11	18-11	14-13	14-12	19-8	14-16	49-41	42-30
StL	52-29	34-47	18-15	39-39	20-16	9-6	26-28	60-48	32-27	54-49	84-75	2-1	20-22	33-18	6-8	15-8	15-14	13-13	15-11	11-15	17-15	47-41	39-35
Mil	40-41	37-44	16-18	37-40	15-21	9-6	25-25	52-60	21-33	56-52	77-85	0-0	26-23	25-33	8-5	9-14	12-16	14-13	13-14	14-13	15-15	40-49	37-36
Hou	42-39	34-47	15-19	45-33	13-22	3-12	27-18	49-68	25-25	51-61	76-86	0-0	21-18	12-31	7-9	8-14	9-20	14-14	13-11	17-12	15-15	36-53	40-33
ChC	35-46	40-41	17-14	34-45	16-18	8-10	26-28	49-59	35-43	40-44	75-87	0-0	22-32	23-26	4-6	11-13	13-15	10-16	12-14	10-19	19-10	39-50	36-37
Pit	40-41	17-64	11-25	31-48	13-19	2-13	19-25	38-80	16-29	41-76	57-105	0-0	20-24	11-39	4-8	10-13	11-18	6-20	9-16	8-21	13-17	30-58	27-47

West Division

Tm	Home	Road	East	Cent	West	AL	LHS	RHS	Day	Night	Grass	Turf	1-Rn	5+Rn	Xinn	April	May	June	July	Aug	Sept	Pre	Post
SF	49-32	43-38	19-14	28-14	38-34	7-8	24-20	68-50	30-26	62-44	91-68	1-2	28-24	22-13	11-8	13-9	14-14	13-14	20-8	13-15	19-10	47-41	45-29
SD	45-36	45-36	16-18	27-14	38-34	9-6	31-20	59-52	31-25	59-47	88-71	2-1	28-22	25-14	7-7	15-8	16-12	15-12	14-10	16-13	14-17	51-37	39-35
Col	52-29	31-50	16-18	21-20	37-35	9-6	34-27	49-52	35-23	48-56	83-79	0-0	28-30	18-15	8-10	11-12	16-12	14-13	13-13	15-12	14-17	49-39	34-40
LAD	45-36	35-46	13-20	23-19	40-32	4-11	23-27	57-55	21-22	59-60	80-82	0-0	26-24	15-22	9-4	9-14	20-8	14-14	11-15	14-15	12-17	49-39	31-43
Ari	40-41	25-56	16-16	16-27	27-45	6-0	19-32	46-65	13-32	52-65	63-96	2-1	19-23	19-28	5-8	11-12	9-20	11-16	7-18	16-13	11-18	34-55	31-42

Team vs. Team Breakdown

	Phi	Atl	Fla	NYM	Was	Cin	StL	Mil	Hou	ChC	Pit	SF	SD	Col	LAD	Ari
Philadelphia Phillies	-	10	13	9	12	5	4	5	3	2	2	3	5	6	4	4
Atlanta Braves	8	-	11	11	8	3	2	5	5	4	6	4	4	2	5	4
Florida Marlins	5	7	-	12	13	2	3	4	3	2	6	2	3	4	4	3
New York Mets	9	7	6	-	9	2	3	2	4	4	6	3	3	3	4	1
Washington Nationals	6	10	5	9	-	3	3	2	4	2	5	2	3	3	3	4
Cincinnati Reds	2	2	5	4	4	-	6	11	10	12	10	3	2	2	5	5
St Louis Cardinals	4	6	2	3	3	12	-	7	5	6	9	3	4	4	4	5
Milwaukee Brewers	1	2	4	5	4	3	8	-	7	6	13	2	3	4	2	4
Houston Astros	4	1	3	3	4	5	10	8	-	11	11	2	2	4	2	3
Chicago Cubs	4	2	4	3	4	4	9	9	7	-	5	2	3	2	3	6
Pittsburgh Pirates	4	3	2	1	1	6	6	5	4	10	-	2	0	4	3	4
San Francisco Giants	3	3	5	4	4	4	3	5	7	5	4	-	6	9	10	13
San Diego Padres	2	2	6	3	3	4	3	4	5	5	6	12	-	6	10	10
Colorado Rockies	1	4	3	3	5	5	3	5	2	3	3	9	12	-	7	9
Los Angeles Dodgers	2	3	2	3	3	4	3	4	4	4	4	8	8	11	-	13
Arizona Diamondbacks	2	3	3	5	3	2	4	3	4	1	2	5	8	9	5	-

American League Batting

Tm	G	AB	H	2B	3B	HR	(Hm	Rd)	TB	R	RBI	TBB	IBB	SO	HBP	SH	SF	ShO	SB	CS	SB%	GDP	LOB	Avg	OBP	Slg
NYY	162	5567	1485	275	32	201	(115	86)	2427	859	823	662	36	1136	73	33	44	8	103	30	.77	124	1834	.267	.350	.436
Bos	162	5646	1511	358	22	211	(98	113)	2546	818	782	587	43	1140	47	29	46	4	68	17	.80	131	1769	.268	.339	.451
TB	162	5439	1343	295	37	160	(78	82)	2192	802	769	672	30	1292	57	39	57	9	172	47	.79	92	1728	.247	.333	.403
Tex	162	5635	1556	268	25	162	(93	69)	2360	787	740	511	37	986	45	53	54	5	123	48	.72	129	1845	.276	.338	.419
Min	162	5568	1521	318	41	142	(52	90)	2347	781	749	559	45	967	39	38	53	8	68	28	.71	159	1801	.273	.341	.422
Tor	162	5495	1364	319	21	257	(146	111)	2496	755	732	471	25	1164	55	16	34	8	58	20	.74	114	1537	.248	.312	.454
CWS	162	5484	1467	263	21	177	(111	66)	2303	752	710	467	23	922	79	50	38	5	160	74	.68	148	1657	.268	.332	.420
Det	162	5643	1515	308	32	152	(70	82)	2343	751	717	546	50	1147	41	41	41	10	69	30	.70	118	1840	.268	.335	.415
LAA	162	5488	1363	276	19	155	(69	86)	2142	681	656	466	28	1070	52	42	37	9	104	52	.67	125	1628	.248	.311	.390
KC	162	5604	1534	279	31	121	(60	61)	2238	676	640	471	25	905	35	45	53	8	115	50	.70	152	1817	.274	.331	.399
Oak	162	5448	1396	276	30	109	(46	63)	2059	663	619	527	16	1061	47	43	51	7	156	38	.80	129	1757	.256	.324	.378
Cle	162	5487	1362	290	20	128	(64	64)	2076	646	601	545	34	1184	64	36	33	15	91	33	.73	118	1775	.248	.322	.378
Bal	162	5554	1440	264	21	133	(72	61)	2145	613	577	424	32	1056	54	31	45	11	76	34	.69	154	1767	.255	.316	.386
Sea	162	5409	1274	227	16	101	(35	66)	1836	513	485	459	33	1184	39	42	40	15	142	39	.78	111	1665	.236	.298	.339
AL	1134	77467	20131	4016	368	2209	(1109	1100)	31510	10097	9600	7367	457	15214	727	538	626	122	1505	540	.74	1804	24420	.260	.327	.407

American League Pitching

Tm	G	CG	Rel	IP	BFP	H	R	ER	HR	SH	SF	HB	TBB	IBB	SO	WP	Bk	W	L	Pct.	ShO	Sv-Op	Hld	OAvg	OOBP	OSlg	ERA
Oak	162	7	423	1431.2	6011	1315	626	566	153	48	34	38	512	29	1070	42	8	81	81	.500	17	38-51	65	.245	.313	.379	3.56
TB	162	6	491	1453.2	6103	1347	649	611	175	25	37	46	478	34	1189	60	9	96	66	.593	12	51-67	80	.244	.308	.404	3.78
Min	162	9	465	1452.2	6106	1493	671	638	155	35	37	47	383	19	1048	41	4	94	68	.580	13	40-58	75	.266	.317	.417	3.95
Tex	162	7	481	1455.1	6213	1355	687	636	162	36	46	63	551	24	1181	56	4	90	72	.556	8	46-66	83	.246	.319	.390	3.93
NYY	162	3	430	1442.1	6102	1349	693	651	179	36	52	62	540	37	1154	69	6	95	67	.586	8	39-57	76	.249	.322	.399	4.06
Sea	162	11	358	1438.0	6091	1402	698	628	157	37	51	40	452	33	973	73	11	61	101	.377	10	38-55	36	.255	.313	.401	3.93
LAA	162	10	410	1449.1	6252	1422	702	651	148	41	42	46	565	33	1130	80	6	80	82	.494	9	39-56	63	.256	.327	.403	4.04
CWS	162	6	407	1446.1	6180	1471	704	658	136	38	36	34	490	41	1149	59	9	88	74	.543	11	43-57	57	.264	.325	.395	4.09
Tor	162	5	455	1440.2	6165	1407	728	676	150	21	37	60	539	35	1184	69	3	85	77	.525	11	45-61	69	.255	.326	.405	4.22
Det	162	6	416	1444.1	6198	1445	743	690	142	37	52	66	537	29	1056	75	9	81	81	.500	5	32-45	60	.262	.332	.400	4.30
Bos	162	3	443	1456.2	6267	1402	744	679	152	40	47	53	580	30	1207	58	3	89	73	.549	9	44-66	65	.253	.327	.399	4.20
Cle	162	10	470	1433.0	6224	1477	752	684	147	43	47	66	572	36	967	54	3	69	93	.426	4	34-50	73	.269	.342	.416	4.30
Bal	162	3	454	1436.1	6262	1508	785	733	186	47	43	59	520	45	1007	45	5	66	96	.407	7	35-62	72	.270	.336	.434	4.59
KC	162	7	441	1436.2	6333	1553	845	794	176	41	60	47	551	28	1035	55	7	67	95	.414	3	44-65	64	.276	.342	.435	4.97
AL	1134	93	6144	20217.0	86507	19946	10027	9295	2218	525	621	726	7270	453	15350	836	87	1142	1126	.504	127	568-816	938	.258	.325	.406	4.14

American League Fielding

Team	G	Inn	PO	Ast	OFAst	E	(Throw	Field)	TC	DP	GDP	SB	CS	SB%	CPkof	PPkof	PB	UER	UERA	FPct
New York	162	1442.1	4327	1522	32	69	(38	31)	5918	161	137	132	23	.85	1	4	12	42	0.26	.988
Minnesota	162	1452.2	4358	1710	34	78	(41	37)	6146	150	123	82	37	.69	0	5	8	33	0.20	.987
Tampa Bay	162	1453.2	4361	1499	21	85	(43	42)	5945	134	115	89	30	.75	0	3	9	38	0.24	.986
Toronto	162	1440.2	4322	1691	24	92	(57	35)	6105	172	148	69	35	.66	3	2	10	52	0.32	.985
Oakland	162	1431.2	4295	1704	26	99	(52	47)	6098	147	132	88	32	.73	0	12	8	60	0.38	.984
Chicago	162	1446.1	4339	1663	24	103	(53	50)	6105	158	140	105	39	.73	2	8	4	46	0.29	.983
Baltimore	162	1436.1	4309	1582	35	105	(33	72)	5996	141	116	83	27	.75	2	5	3	52	0.33	.982
Texas	162	1455.1	4366	1499	25	105	(44	61)	5970	133	119	116	35	.77	0	3	8	51	0.32	.982
Cleveland	162	1433.0	4299	1814	33	110	(44	66)	6223	179	159	125	58	.68	0	3	11	68	0.43	.982
Detroit	162	1444.1	4333	1668	40	109	(39	70)	6110	171	147	101	50	.67	0	3	11	53	0.33	.982
Seattle	162	1438.0	4314	1657	26	110	(42	68)	6081	145	124	73	29	.72	3	4	16	70	0.44	.982
Boston	162	1456.2	4370	1588	28	111	(56	55)	6069	132	116	169	42	.80	3	2	14	65	0.40	.982
Los Angeles	162	1449.1	4348	1562	36	113	(56	57)	6023	116	96	133	41	.76	4	7	16	51	0.32	.981
Kansas City	162	1436.2	4310	1588	21	121	(48	73)	6019	138	109	137	55	.71	0	5	11	51	0.32	.980
American League	1134	20217.0	60651	22747	405	1410	(646	764)	84808	2077	1781	1502	533	.74	18	66	141	732	0.33	.983

National League Batting

						BATTING														BASERUNNING					PERCENTAGES		
Tm	G	AB	H	2B	3B	HR	(Hm	Rd)	TB	R	RBI	TBB	IBB	SO	HBP	SH	SF	ShO	SB	CS	SB%	GDP	LOB	Avg	OBP	Slg
Cin	162	5579	1515	293	30	188	(102	86)	2432	790	761	522	34	1218	68	66	50	13	93	43	.68	113	1748	.272	.338	.436
Phi	162	5581	1451	290	34	166	(94	72)	2307	772	736	560	69	1064	63	44	43	11	108	21	.84	121	1788	.260	.332	.413
Col	162	5530	1452	270	54	173	(108	64)	2349	770	741	585	53	1274	47	56	47	10	99	42	.70	103	1759	.263	.336	.425
Mil	162	5606	1471	293	33	182	(100	82)	2376	750	710	546	35	1216	81	35	35	14	81	26	.76	116	1778	.262	.335	.424
Atl	162	5463	1411	312	25	139	(74	65)	2190	738	699	634	50	1140	51	69	35	13	63	29	.68	136	1818	.258	.339	.401
StL	162	5542	1456	285	18	150	(67	83)	2227	736	689	541	78	1027	50	66	40	13	79	41	.66	124	1752	.263	.332	.402
Fla	162	5531	1403	294	37	152	(69	83)	2227	719	686	514	42	1375	55	51	43	9	92	26	.78	108	1649	.254	.321	.403
Ari	162	5473	1366	301	34	180	(98	82)	2275	713	691	589	45	1529	39	41	41	11	86	41	.68	115	1667	.250	.325	.416
SF	162	5488	1411	284	30	162	(75	87)	2241	697	660	487	53	1099	50	76	41	16	55	32	.63	159	1644	.257	.321	.408
ChC	162	5512	1414	298	27	149	(74	75)	2213	685	658	479	32	1236	50	60	38	15	55	31	.64	124	1692	.257	.320	.401
LAD	162	5426	1368	270	29	120	(61	59)	2056	667	621	533	57	1184	46	85	50	17	92	50	.65	123	1730	.252	.322	.379
SD	162	5434	1338	236	24	132	(59	73)	2018	665	630	538	67	1183	50	79	46	12	124	50	.71	106	1697	.246	.317	.371
NYM	162	5465	1361	266	40	128	(63	65)	2091	656	625	502	53	1095	46	74	57	11	130	44	.75	101	1712	.249	.314	.383
Was	162	5418	1355	250	31	149	(74	75)	2114	655	634	503	36	1220	60	71	47	14	110	41	.73	125	1649	.250	.318	.390
Hou	162	5452	1348	252	25	108	(63	45)	1974	611	577	415	27	1025	33	75	29	13	100	36	.74	130	1610	.247	.303	.362
Pit	162	5386	1303	276	27	126	(64	62)	2011	587	570	463	28	1207	33	58	33	15	87	36	.71	119	1627	.242	.304	.373
NL	1296	87886	22423	4470	498	2404	(1245	1159)	35101	11211	10688	8411	759	19092	822	1006	675	207	1454	589	.71	1923	27320	.255	.324	.399

National League Pitching

HOW MUCH THEY PITCHED						WHAT THEY GAVE UP													THE RESULTS										
Tm	G	CG	Rel	IP	BFP	H	R	ER	HR	SH	SF	HB	TBB	IBB	SO	WP	Bk	W	L	Pct.	ShO	Sv-Op	Hld	OAvg	OOBP	OSlg	ERA
SD	162	2	499	1456.1	6058	1305	581	549	139	46	21	28	517	51	1295	29	5	90	72	.556	20	49-64	111	.240	.308	.368	3.39
SF	162	6	477	1461.0	6159	1279	583	546	134	64	41	51	578	58	1331	74	4	92	70	.568	17	57-73	65	.236	.313	.370	3.36
Atl	162	2	490	1439.1	6052	1326	629	569	126	67	34	49	505	64	1241	42	3	91	71	.562	9	41-58	77	.246	.314	.376	3.56
Phi	162	14	451	1456.1	6095	1402	640	594	168	67	30	57	416	42	1103	26	5	97	65	.599	21	40-59	61	.254	.311	.405	3.67
StL	162	7	455	1453.2	6137	1412	641	577	133	62	44	48	477	32	1094	42	4	86	76	.531	16	32-42	59	.256	.319	.387	3.57
NYM	162	8	491	1453.0	6245	1438	652	597	135	74	35	52	545	55	1106	48	5	79	83	.488	19	36-52	62	.260	.330	.394	3.70
Cin	162	4	502	1453.0	6182	1404	685	648	158	51	32	50	524	32	1130	48	6	91	71	.562	9	43-63	74	.254	.323	.396	4.01
LAD	162	4	475	1441.2	6141	1323	692	643	134	69	53	58	539	75	1274	59	8	80	82	.494	16	41-59	70	.244	.316	.378	4.01
Col	162	6	513	1442.0	6143	1405	717	663	139	59	44	56	525	54	1234	77	12	83	79	.512	12	35-56	82	.257	.326	.397	4.14
Fla	162	5	481	1438.1	6217	1433	717	652	134	70	46	51	549	42	1168	49	4	80	82	.494	17	39-64	86	.261	.331	.398	4.08
Hou	162	4	507	1439.1	6221	1446	729	654	140	53	38	40	548	39	1210	57	9	76	86	.469	11	45-60	82	.261	.330	.402	4.09
Was	162	2	494	1435.0	6214	1469	742	658	151	76	51	46	512	57	1068	33	7	69	93	.426	5	37-57	73	.266	.330	.410	4.13
ChC	162	1	482	1436.2	6298	1409	767	668	154	65	40	65	605	42	1268	46	6	75	87	.463	14	40-54	68	.255	.334	.398	4.18
Mil	162	3	495	1439.0	6324	1487	804	733	173	65	54	48	582	42	1258	71	3	77	85	.475	7	35-56	86	.267	.338	.427	4.58
Ari	162	3	454	1432.0	6260	1503	836	765	210	48	50	48	548	38	1070	82	4	65	97	.401	3	35-59	48	.271	.340	.448	4.81
Pit	162	1	517	1411.2	6300	1567	866	784	167	68	67	66	538	40	1026	56	10	57	105	.352	6	31-48	67	.282	.348	.449	5.00
NL	1296	72	7783	23088.1	99046	22608	11281	10300	2395	1019	680	823	8508	763	18956	839	95	1288	1304	.497	202	636-924	1171	.257	.326	.400	4.02

National League Fielding

							Fielding													
Team	G	Inn	PO	Ast	OFAst	E	(Throw	Field)	TC	DP	GDP	SB	CS	SB%	CPkof	PPkof	PB	UER	UERA	FPct
San Diego	162	1456.1	4369	1626	24	72	36	36	6067	141	110	79	39	.07	0	4	13	32	0.20	.988
Cincinnati	162	1453.0	4359	1608	25	72	31	41	6039	142	121	71	34	.68	3	4	4	37	0.23	.988
San Francisco	162	1461.0	4383	1485	33	73	38	35	5941	110	91	115	49	.70	1	2	6	37	0.23	.988
Philadelphia	162	1456.1	4369	1687	27	83	34	49	6139	158	132	84	31	.73	1	5	6	46	0.28	.986
New York	162	1453.0	4359	1665	34	87	45	42	6111	159	136	51	26	.66	1	3	10	55	0.34	.986
St Louis	162	1453.2	4361	1872	22	99	42	57	6332	172	152	53	38	.58	4	4	10	64	0.40	.984
Los Angeles	162	1441.2	4325	1590	17	98	44	54	6013	124	102	97	39	.71	4	5	6	49	0.31	.984
Colorado	162	1442.0	4326	1707	18	101	50	51	6134	182	155	81	43	.65	4	9	15	54	0.34	.984
Milwaukee	162	1439.0	4317	1516	29	101	50	51	5934	142	112	100	31	.76	0	0	5	71	0.44	.983
Arizona	162	1432.0	4296	1572	26	102	43	59	5970	142	125	115	36	.76	1	3	15	71	0.45	.983
Houston	162	1439.1	4318	1597	24	103	42	61	6018	135	113	89	44	.67	7	2	12	75	0.47	.983
Atlanta	162	1439.1	4318	1770	21	126	61	65	6214	167	139	102	44	.70	0	6	6	60	0.38	.980
Florida	162	1438.1	4315	1502	36	123	65	58	5940	130	103	111	44	.72	1	2	11	65	0.41	.979
Washington	162	1435.0	4305	1657	25	127	61	66	6089	148	126	103	35	.69	2	3	5	84	0.53	.979
Chicago	162	1436.2	4310	1550	22	126	56	70	5986	137	119	114	31	.79	0	2	6	99	0.62	.979
Pittsburgh	162	1411.2	4235	1654	31	127	57	70	6016	120	102	116	32	.78	1	5	11	82	0.52	.979
National League	1296	23088.1	69265	26058	414	1620	755	865	96943	2319	1946	1457	596	.71	30	59	141	981	0.38	.983

2010 Team Efficiency Summary

Bill James

They were still efficient; they just weren't very good.

As long as we have been measuring efficiency, the Los Angeles Angels of Anaheim, California, Disneyland and Mike Scioscia have been the most efficient team in the American League, if not all of baseball. They still were, in 2010; they weren't *good,* but they were still very *efficient.* In previous years their efficiency helped them to win. In 2010 it helped to disguise how bad they really were.

"Efficiency", as we measure it, consists of answering nine questions in order. Those questions are:

1) How many runs would we expect this team to score, based on their hits, walks, home runs, stolen bases, etc.?

2) How many runs did they actually score?

3) What is the ratio of (1) to (2)?

4) How many runs would we expect this team to allow, based on their hits, walks, home runs allowed, etc.?

5) How many runs did they actually score?

6) What is the ratio of (4) to (5)?

7) How many games would we expect this team to win, based on their runs scored and runs allowed?

8) How many games did they actually win?

9) What is the ratio of (7) to (8)?

The Angels in 2010 (and most other years) scored more runs than we would expect them to score, thus they were efficient in that way. They allowed fewer runs than we would expect them to allow, so they were efficient in that way. Even given the runs that they actually did score and the runs they actually did allow, they won more games (one more game) than we would expect them to win, so they were efficient in that way. They were, as they always are, highly efficient.

Mike Scioscia was out-sciosciaed, in 2010, by first-year manager Brad Mills of Houston. When Millsie took the job, I think I speak for most of us when I confess that we were whispering behind his back that, given the team he had to work with, he'd be lucky to get out of Houston with ten fingers and ten toes. Instead, he took a 65-win team and won 76 games—a nice start to his managerial career.

On the other end of that was the Rockies, who took a 93-win team and scratched and clawed their way to 83 wins. Which, I should add quickly, is not

necessarily the manager's fault. If a team doesn't hit in the clutch, this will be measured as inefficiency, but there's really not much the manager can do about it.

2010 American League Team Efficiency Summary

	RC	Runs	Hit Eff	Exp RA	RA	Pit Eff	Exp Wins	Wins	Runs Eff	Eff Wins	Wins	Overall Eff
Los Angeles Angels	649	681	105	733	702	104	79	80	102	71	80	112
Tampa Bay Rays	755	802	106	655	649	101	98	96	98	92	96	104
Chicago White Sox	743	752	101	695	704	99	86	88	102	86	88	102
Minnesota Twins	784	781	100	679	671	101	93	94	101	93	94	102
Baltimore Orioles	656	613	93	788	785	100	61	66	108	66	66	99
Toronto Blue Jays	745	755	101	692	728	95	84	85	101	87	85	98
Texas Rangers	797	787	99	688	687	100	92	90	98	93	90	97
Cleveland Indians	669	646	97	754	752	100	69	69	100	71	69	97
New York Yankees	860	859	100	679	693	98	98	95	97	100	95	95
Boston Red Sox	845	818	97	719	744	97	89	89	100	94	89	95
Kansas City Royals	730	676	93	829	845	98	63	67	106	71	67	95
Seattle Mariners	556	513	92	677	698	97	57	61	107	65	61	94
Oakland Athletics	681	663	97	635	626	101	86	81	95	87	81	94
Detroit Tigers	780	751	96	722	743	97	82	81	99	87	81	93

2010 National League Team Efficiency Summary

	RC	Runs	Hit Eff	Exp RA	RA	Pit Eff	Exp Wins	Wins	Runs Eff	Eff Wins	Wins	Overall Eff
Houston Astros	589	611	104	717	729	98	67	76	114	65	76	116
Pittsburgh Pirates	599	587	98	848	866	98	51	57	112	54	57	106
San Francisco Giants	689	697	101	616	583	106	95	92	97	90	92	102
San Diego Padres	649	665	102	593	581	102	92	90	98	88	90	102
Philadelphia Phillies	770	772	100	644	640	101	96	97	101	95	97	102
New York Mets	666	656	99	685	652	105	81	79	97	79	79	100
Chicago Cubs	690	685	99	741	767	97	72	75	104	75	75	100
Florida Marlins	712	719	101	718	717	100	81	80	98	80	80	100
Los Angeles Dodgers	657	667	101	637	692	92	78	80	103	84	80	96
Atlanta Braves	739	738	100	619	629	98	94	91	97	95	91	96
Cincinnati Reds	816	790	97	679	685	99	92	91	98	96	91	95
St Louis Cardinals	731	736	101	648	641	101	92	86	93	91	86	95
Milwaukee Brewers	793	750	95	781	804	97	75	77	102	82	77	94
Washington Nationals	669	655	98	730	742	98	71	69	97	74	69	93
Arizona Diamondbacks	723	713	99	826	836	99	68	65	95	70	65	93
Colorado Rockies	791	770	97	679	717	95	87	83	96	93	83	89

Daric Barton   Brett Gardner
Chase Utley   Michael Bourn
Evan Longoria   Ichiro Suzuki
Troy Tulowitzki
Yadier Molina
Mark Buehrle

THE FIELDING BIBLE AWARDS 2010

The Fielding Bible Awards 2010

John Dewan

We had our first unanimous winner in the five-year history of the Fielding Bible Awards this year. Each of our ten panelists awarded their first place vote to Yadier Molina, giving him the Fielding Bible Award at the catcher position for the 2010 season. That's Molina's fourth consecutive award. His only loss was to Pudge Rodriguez in the first year of the award, when Yadier finished second by six points.

Joining Molina as repeat winners are: Ichiro Suzuki (his third, second in a row), Mark Buehrle (his second, back to back), and Troy Tulowitzki (two also). We had a good number of first-time winners with Daric Barton, Chase Utley (finally!), Evan Longoria, Brett Gardner, and Michael Bourn.

Here's a short refresher course on how the awards are determined: We asked our panel of ten experts to rank 10 players at each position on a scale from one to ten. We then use the same voting technique as the Major League Baseball MVP voting. A first place vote gets 10 points, second place 9 points, third place 8 points, etc. Total up the points for each player and the player with the most points wins the award. A perfect score is 100.

One important distinction that differentiates our award from most other baseball awards, including the Gold Gloves, is that we only have one winner for all of Major League Baseball, instead of separate winners for each league. We also name the winners in left, right and center fields, instead of lumping all outfielders together (which has given an unfair advantage to center fielders in the Gold Glove voting). Our intention is to continue to stand up and say, "This is the best fielder at this position in the major leagues last season."

Here are the Fielding Bible Awards for the 2010 season:

First Base – Daric Barton, Oakland

For the first time, Albert Pujols didn't win this award. Daric Barton led all major league first basemen saving 20 runs defensively for the Oakland A's in 2010. The runner-up, Ike Davis of the Mets, was a distant second with 13 runs saved. Pujols was an average first baseman in 2010, neither saving nor costing his team any runs with his play at first base.

Previous Winners:

2009   Albert Pujols
2008   Albert Pujols
2007   Albert Pujols
2006   Albert Pujols

Second Base – Chase Utley, Philadelphia

Finally! After being atop the three-year Runs Saved leader board in each of the last four years, Chase Utley wins his first Fielding Bible Award in 2010. Utley has saved 60 runs with his defense for the Phillies in the last three years. Far behind him are Mark Ellis (33), Dustin Pedroia (30) and Aaron Hill (26). In the voting, Orlando Hudson gave Chase a run for his money, falling just six points short (80 points compared to 86 for Utley). Hudson did have three more runs saved than Utley in 2010 (17 to 14), but Chase's consistency over many years was rewarded by the voters. Now the question is, can Utley win his first Gold Glove award?

Previous Winners:

2009   Aaron Hill
2008   Brandon Phillips
2007   Aaron Hill
2006   Orlando Hudson

Third Base – Evan Longoria, Tampa Bay

This was our closest race. Evan Longoria prevented Ryan Zimmerman from winning his second consecutive award by a single point in the voting (92 to 91). Adrian Beltre continued his stellar defense after moving to the Red Sox and finished third in the voting. The leader in defensive runs saved, Chase Headley (21 runs saved), finished fourth. Longoria saved 13 runs for the 2010 Rays, giving him a total of 30 runs saved for the past two seasons.

Previous Winners:

2009 Ryan Zimmerman
2008 Adrian Beltre
2007 Pedro Feliz
2006 Adrian Beltre

Shortstop – Troy Tulowitzki, Colorado

Troy Tulowitzki's bat received a lot of attention this year as he led the Rockies in another near-miraculous end-of-season comeback. His 15 homers in the month of September was just short of Babe Ruth and Albert Belle's record of 17. Now his glove gets some attention as well. It's not the first time. In his rookie season in 2007, Tulo dazzled in the field, saving 30 runs for the Rockies with his glove and arm. He won the Fielding Bible Award that year. Now, in 2010, he saved 16 runs for the Rockies defensively and wins his second award.

Previous Winners:

2009 Jack Wilson
2008 Jimmy Rollins
2007 Troy Tulowitzki
2006 Adam Everett

Left Field – Brett Gardner, New York Yankees

An upset win for Brett Gardner and the Yankees. Gardner unseated three-time Fielding Bible Award winner Carl Crawford, giving the Yankees a victory over their season-long rival, the Tampa Bay Rays. Having a speedy and skillful player like Gardner cover the spacious left-field territory in Yankee Stadium is a real advantage for the Bronx Bombers. The voters recognized this important element and the voting wasn't that close (96 points for Gardner to 86 points for runner-up Crawford).

Previous Winners:

2009 Carl Crawford

2008   Carl Crawford
2007   Eric Byrnes
2006   Carl Crawford

Center Field – Michael Bourn, Houston

He is one of the fastest players in the game, and that pays off in spades patrolling center field for the Houston Astros. Michael Bourn won his first Fielding Bible Award for his spectacular defense in 2010. His defense saved 16 runs for the Astros, despite the fact that he missed 20-25 games with injury. Bourn topped two-time Fielding Bible Award winner Franklin Gutierrez by a comfortable margin in the voting (91 to 75).

Previous Winners:

2009   Franklin Gutierrez
2008   Carlos Beltran
2007   Andruw Jones
2006   Carlos Beltran

Right Field – Ichiro Suzuki, Seattle

Ichiro wins his third award in 2010. He saved 12 runs defensively for the 2010 Mariners. His three-year total of 39 runs saved ties him with Hunter Pence for the highest total in that time period. Ichiro made three home-run-saving catches last year, saving five runs for the Mariners.

Previous Winners:

2009   Ichiro Suzuki
2008   Franklin Gutierrez
2007   Alex Rios
2006   Ichiro Suzuki

Catcher – Yadier Molina, St. Louis

It was unanimous—for the first time in the five-year history of the Fielding Bible Awards. Yadier Molina was listed first on all ten ballots for a total of 100 points, the highest possible total in the voting. It's his fourth consecutive award, and nearly his fifth as he lost in 2006 by only six points. There is no question about it: Yadier is the best defensive catcher in all of baseball and it's not even close. He saved 12 runs for the Cardinals, based on the runs saved system presented in this book, but

when you factor in Misplays and Good Plays that Baseball Info Solutions tracks, he saved an additional 8 runs, the highest total for any player in all of baseball.

Previous Winners:

2009 Yadier Molina
2008 Yadier Molina
2007 Yadier Molina
2006 Ivan Rodriguez

Pitcher – Mark Buehrle, Chicago White Sox

Mark Buehrle won his second consecutive Fielding Bible Award as a pitcher, and it is well deserved. He made a statement with a defensive play that may have been the best fielding play of the entire season…and he did it on opening day. His back-turned-to-the-base, through-his-legs glove-flip from foul territory nipped a surprised Lou Marson at the first-base bag. But it's Buehrle's control of the running game that puts him head and shoulders over his competition. He only allowed six of 12 would-be base thieves to successfully steal against him, and he picked off six additional runners last year. That was good for five of his total of eight defensive runs saved for the 2010 White Sox.

Previous Winners:

2009 Mark Buehrle
2008 Kenny Rogers
2007 Johan Santana
2006 Greg Maddux

Background of the Fielding Bible Awards

While the first *The Fielding Bible* and *The Fielding Bible—Volume II* put a lot of emphasis on the numbers, especially Defensive Runs Saved and the Plus-Minus system, I feel that visual observation and subjective judgment are still very important parts of determining the best defensive players. Also, I think people have a right to know who is voting and all the players they are voting for. Therefore, in setting up the Fielding Bible Awards, we took the following steps:

1. *We appointed a panel of experts to vote.* We have a panel of ten experts plus three "tie-breaker" ballots. (See below.)

2. *We rate everybody in one group.* The Gold Glove vote is divided into National League and American League. We make ours different by putting everybody together. Besides, is playing shortstop in the American League one thing and playing shortstop in the National League a different thing, or are they really very much the same thing? Last year was a great example of this rule. Without the Fielding Bible Award, Jack Wilson won nada, because he switched teams in mid-year. According to our judges (and unlike the

Gold Glove judges), Jack was the best fielding shortstop in baseball in 2009. He deserved to be recognized for that.

3. *We use a ten-man ballot and a ten-point scale*. We use a ten-man ballot (I'm referring to the players listed, not the panel of experts). Then we give ten points for first place, nine points for second place, etc, down to one point for tenth place. We feel strongly that a ten-man ballot with weighted positions leads to more accurate outcomes.

4. *We defined the list of candidates*. Only players who actually were regulars at the position are candidates. This eliminates the possibility of a vote going to somebody who wasn't really playing the position.

5. *We are publishing the balloting*. We summarize the voting at each position, clearly identifying whom everybody voted for. Publishing the actual vote totals encourages the voters to take their votes more seriously. Also, we feel the public will have more respect for the voting if they have more insight into the process.

There is something cool about having 10 experts and a 10-man ballot and a 10-point scale, because that gives each position 100 possible points. If all 10 voters place one player first on their ballot, he scores 100. And look, it happened this year with Yadier Molina.

Here are the tie-breaker rules (which came into play in our very first year and did so again this year). They are applied one at a time until we have a winner:
1. Most first-place votes wins.
2. Count the tie-breaker ballots, highest point tally wins.
3. Award goes to player with the higher plus/minus rating.

Ballots were due on the Tuesday after the end of the regular season. Here is this year's panel:

Since you have this book, you probably know **Bill James**, a baseball writer and analyst published for more than thirty years. Bill is the Senior Baseball Operations Advisor for the Boston Red Sox.

The **BIS Video Scouts** at Baseball Info Solutions (BIS) study every game of the season, multiple times, charting a huge list of valuable game details.

The man who created Strat-O-Matic Baseball, **Hal Richman**, continues to lead his company's annual in-depth analysis of each player's season. Hal cautions SOM players that his voting on this ballot may or may not reflect the eventual fielding ratings for players in his game. Ballots were due prior to the completion of his annual research effort to evaluate player defense.

Named the best sports columnist in America by the Associated Press Sports Editors in 2003 and 2005, **Joe Posnanski** is a Senior Writer at *Sports Illustrated* and occasional columnist for the *Kansas City Star*. His website is joeposnanski.com.

For over twenty-five years, BIS owner **John Dewan** has collected, analyzed, and published in-depth baseball statistics and analysis. He wrote *The Fielding Bible* in 2006 and *The Fielding Bible—Volume II* in 2009.

Mat Olkin is a sabermetrics consultant to major league teams and has studied, analyzed, and written about baseball players for almost fifteen years.

Peter Gammons serves as on-air and online analyst for MLB Network, MLB.com and NESN (New England Sports Network). He is the 56th recipient of the J. G. Taylor Spink Award for outstanding baseball writing, given by the BBWAA (Baseball Writers Association of America).

Rob Neyer writes baseball for ESPN.com and appears regularly on ESPN radio and ESPNews.

Todd Radcliffe is Lead Video Scout at Baseball Info Solutions and brings 15 years of Major League Baseball scouting experience to the panel.

The **Tom Tango Fan Poll** represents the results of a poll taken at the website, Tango on Baseball (www.tangotiger.net). Besides hosting the website, Tom writes research articles devoted to sabermetrics.

Our three tie-breakers are **Steve Moyer**, president of Baseball Info Solutions, **Dan Casey**, veteran Video Scout at BIS, and **Dave Studenmund**, one of the founders of www.hardballtimes.com and *The Hardball Times Baseball Annual*.

The Fielding Bible Awards

Below we show the final point tally for The Fielding Bible Awards in the 2010 season. We asked a panel of experts to complete a ten-man ballot ranking the defensive ability of players from 1 to 10. We show the ranks in the tables below. We then awarded points in the same way as Major League Baseball's MVP voting: ten points for a first place vote, nine for second, etc., down to one point for tenth place. We cover all nine positions, looking at only their fielding work for the 2010 season. Non-pitchers are only eligible if they played at least 500 innings. Pitchers require a minimum of 100 innings pitched.

First Basemen

First Basemen	Bill James	BIS Video Scouts	Hal Richman	Joe Posnanski	John Dewan	Mat Olkin	Peter Gammons	Rob Neyer	Tango Fan Poll	Todd Radcliffe	Total Points
Daric Barton	2	1	6	1	1	1	1	1	6	4	86
Albert Pujols	5	3	2	2	4	3	3	5	2	5	76
Ike Davis	3	2	9	3	2	5	4	3		9	59
Mark Teixeira	1	6	1	6	9	6			1	6	52
Adrian Gonzalez	7	9	3	5		2	10	9	3	10	41
Kevin Youkilis	6	8	5	7	5	7	9		4	8	40
Justin Morneau		4			6	9	6	2		2	37
Lyle Overbay		7		8	3	8	8		8	1	34
Joey Votto		5		4			2	10	9		25
Casey Kotchman	9		4		8				7	3	24

Others receiving points: James Loney 19, Carlos Pena 17, Aubrey Huff 14, Todd Helton 13, Adam LaRoche 6, Derrek Lee 4, Lance Berkman 3

Second Basemen

Second Basemen	Bill James	BIS Video Scouts	Hal Richman	Joe Posnanski	John Dewan	Mat Olkin	Peter Gammons	Rob Neyer	Tango Fan Poll	Todd Radcliffe	Total Points
Chase Utley	1	2	10	1	1	2	1	1	3	2	86
Orlando Hudson	6	1	1	2	2	3	3	2	9	1	80
Mark Ellis	7	6	9	4	4	1	2	3	5	5	64
Brandon Phillips	2	5	3	7	8	5	7	4	1	6	62
Sean Rodriguez	3	4	7	6	3	8	4	8	6	3	58
Robinson Cano	5	3	2		9	4	6	9	7	4	50
Dustin Pedroia		8	6	8	7	9	5	5	2	8	41
Aaron Hill		10	4	3	5	6	9	7		9	35
Ian Kinsler	4	7		5	6		8	10	10	7	31
Freddy Sanchez				10				6	4		13

Others receiving points: Clint Barmes 6, David Eckstein 4, Martin Prado 4, Mike Aviles 3, Reid Brignac 3, Chone Figgins 3, Kelly Johnson 2, Adam Kennedy 2, Luis Valbuena 2, Ryan Theriot 1

Third Basemen

Third Basemen	Bill James	BIS Video Scouts	Hal Richman	Joe Posnanski	John Dewan	Mat Olkin	Peter Gammons	Rob Neyer	Tango Fan Poll	Todd Radcliffe	Total Points
Evan Longoria	1	2	2	2	2	1	2	3	1	2	92
Ryan Zimmerman	3	1	1	1	1	3	1	1	4	3	91
Adrian Beltre	5	4	4	4	4	2	5	2	5	6	69
Chase Headley	2	3		3	3	5	6	4		1	61
Scott Rolen	8	6	3	5	6	4	7	8	2	4	57
Placido Polanco	7	8	5	10		6		6	6	9	31
Jose Lopez	4	5		7	7	9	9			5	31
Casey Blake	6	10		8	5	8	3	9			28
Kevin Kouzmanoff	9	7	9	6	9		10	5		7	26
Brandon Inge	10		6			7	4		3	10	26

Others receiving points: Nick Punto 14, Ian Stewart 11, Felipe Lopez 4, Omar Vizquel 4, Alex Rodriguez 2, David Wright 2, Danny Valencia 1

Shortstops

Shortstops	Bill James	BIS Video Scouts	Hal Richman	Joe Posnanski	John Dewan	Mat Olkin	Peter Gammons	Rob Neyer	Tango Fan Poll	Todd Radcliffe	Total Points
Troy Tulowitzki	1	1	1	1	2	1	1	2	1	2	97
Brendan Ryan	6	2	5	2	1	6	2	1	3	1	81
Alexei Ramirez	3	6	9	3	4	2	3	3	5	3	69
Yunel Escobar		3	10	4	5	3		4	10	4	45
Jack Wilson	2	7	6	6	3		7	9		9	39
Elvis Andrus	4	8	2	9		7	4		4		39
Cliff Pennington	9	5		7		4	6	5	8	7	37
Alex Gonzalez	7	4		5	8	5	9	8		6	36
Jimmy Rollins		9			6	9		7	2	5	28
Cesar Izturis				8	7		8	10	7		15

Others receiving points: Alcides Escobar 14, Rafael Furcal 9, Ramon Santiago 9, Jason Bartlett 8, Asdrubal Cabrera 8, Erick Aybar 6, J.J. Hardy 5, Marco Scutaro 3, Orlando Cabrera 1, Wilson Valdez 1

Left Fielders

Left Fielders	Bill James	BIS Video Scouts	Hal Richman	Joe Posnanski	John Dewan	Mat Olkin	Peter Gammons	Rob Neyer	Tango Fan Poll	Todd Radcliffe	Total Points
Brett Gardner	1	2	2	1	1	1	1	1	2	2	96
Carl Crawford	5	1	1	2	2	2	7	2	1	1	86
Jose Tabata	2	3	10	4	6	7	5	3	5	3	62
Gerardo Parra	6	4	6	5	3	5	2	6	9	5	59
Matt Holliday	7	5		7	4	4	3	5		4	49
Josh Hamilton		6	3	6		3		4	4		40
David Murphy	3	10	5			6					20
Ryan Raburn	8			8	5		4	10			20
Juan Pierre			9	3	8	9	8		10		19
Carlos Gonzalez		8	4						3		18

Others receiving points: Ryan Braun 16, Corey Patterson 11, Lastings Milledge 11, Felix Pie 9, Melky Cabrera 6, Alfonso Soriano 5, Seth Smith 5, Scott Hairston 4, Michael Saunders 4, Pat Burrell 3, Travis Snider 3, Don Kelly 2, Juan Rivera 2

Center Fielders

Center Fielders	Bill James	BIS Video Scouts	Hal Richman	Joe Posnanski	John Dewan	Mat Olkin	Peter Gammons	Rob Neyer	Tango Fan Poll	Todd Radcliffe	Total Points
Michael Bourn	1	1	1	1	1	4	5	1	3	1	91
Franklin Gutierrez	10	5	2	2	4	1	2	5	1	3	75
Chris Young	2	3	6	3	3	7	4	4		8	59
Austin Jackson		2	3		2	8	3	10	4	2	54
Angel Pagan	7	4	4	5	8	5	1	6		7	52
Julio Borbon	3	8		10		3	9	2		4	38
Tony Gwynn		7	9	9	5	9	0	3	6	6	38
Curtis Granderson		6		4	10	2	10	8		6	31
Coco Crisp	4	9		7		10					14
Andres Torres			7						2	10	14

Others receiving points: Marlon Byrd 13, B.J. Upton 12, Shane Victorino 12, Cameron Maybin 11, Alex Rios 10, Adam Jones 6, Torii Hunter 5, Carlos Gomez 4, Aaron Rowand 4, Andrew McCutchen 3, Drew Stubbs 3, Nyjer Morgan 1

Right Fielders

Right Fielders	Bill James	BIS Video Scouts	Hal Richman	Joe Posnanski	John Dewan	Mat Olkin	Peter Gammons	Rob Neyer	Tango Fan Poll	Todd Radcliffe	Total Points
Ichiro Suzuki	5	2	1	1	2	1	3	1	1	1	92
Jay Bruce	2	3	5	2	1	2	1	3	2	2	87
Jason Heyward	3	1	6	3	6	9	4	4	7	3	64
Jeff Francoeur		4	7	6	3	4	6	2		6	50
Jayson Werth	1	5	10	8	4	3	8	5			44
Justin Upton	4	6		4			10	6		4	32
Shin-Soo Choo	8	7		7	9	5	2	7			32
Ben Zobrist		8		9		7	7	8	6	5	27
Mike Stanton	6	9		10	7		5	10	4		26
Hunter Pence			3	5	5					8	23

Others receiving points: J.D. Drew 17, Nick Markakis 16, Ryan Sweeney 10, Ryan Ludwick 8, Nelson Cruz 7, Will Venable 6, Tyler Colvin 3, Kosuke Fukudome 3, Andruw Jones 2, Brennan Boesch 1

Catchers

Catchers	Bill James	BIS Video Scouts	Hal Richman	Joe Posnanski	John Dewan	Mat Olkin	Peter Gammons	Rob Neyer	Tango Fan Poll	Todd Radcliffe	Total Points
Yadier Molina	1	1	1	1	1	1	1	1	1	1	100
Carlos Ruiz	4	4	6	4	2	2	2	3	7	2	74
Kurt Suzuki	5	5	4	5	3	5	3	2	9		58
Joe Mauer	2	8	2	3	8	3	10		2	8	53
Miguel Olivo	9	2	8	7	4	4		4		4	46
Yorvit Torrealba	3	3	7	2	7	8		7	10		41
Matt Wieters		7		8	6	7	5	6	3	9	37
Russell Martin			3	6	5		8	5		5	34
Humberto Quintero		6				6	6	9	6	3	30
Buster Posey		9	10		10		4	8	4	7	25

Others receiving points: Gerald Laird 18, Ivan Rodriguez 7, Alex Avila 5, Rod Barajas 5, Rob Johnson 4, Brian McCann 4, John Jaso 3, A.J. Pierzynski 3, Bengie Molina 2, Lou Marson 1

Pitchers

Pitchers	Bill James	BIS Video Scouts	Hal Richman	Joe Posnanski	John Dewan	Mat Olkin	Peter Gammons	Rob Neyer	Tango Fan Poll	Todd Radcliffe	Total Points
Mark Buehrle	2	1	1	1	1	1	4	1		1	86
Zack Greinke		3	3	2	2	4	5	2		4	63
Trevor Cahill		2	8	4	4		1	3		3	52
Rickey Romero	5	4		6	6		2	4		8	42
Bronson Arroyo	10	7	6	5	5		3	7		7	38
Jake Westbrook		5	7	3	3			5		9	34
Jon Garland		10	5	9	7	10		6	3	6	32
Chris Carpenter			4	7		6			5	2	31
Dallas Braden		6			8	2	7	9	4		30
Wade LeBlanc						7			1	5	20
Adam Wainwright	3		2	10					9		20
Tim Hudson	1	8			9	9	9	10			20

Others receiving points: R.A. Dickey 9, Javier Vazquez 9, Jonathon Niese 8, Shaun Marcum 8, Andy Pettitte 7, Johan Santana 6, David Price 5, Joe Saunders 5, Bruce Chen 4, Livan Hernandez 4, John Danks 3, Felix Hernandez 3, Carl Pavano 3, Clay Buchholz 3, Brian Matusz 2, Brad Bergesen 1, Scott Feldman 1, Wandy Rodriguez 1

Runs Saved and Plus/Minus Leaders

The Runs Saved and Plus/Minus leaders showcase baseball's best fielders from 2010 and over the past three years. The three-year leaders identify the best defensive players in baseball. Take a look at the top five at each position on the 3-Year Runs Saved and Plus/Minus Leaderboards and you get an excellent idea of the best defenders at each position.

Veteran *Handbook* readers are familiar with the Plus/Minus leaders and trailers in this section. The Plus/Minus System is a way to evaluate defensive range by measuring how often defenders turn grounders and fly balls into outs. A number greater than zero (plus "+") is above average. Below zero (minus "-") is below average. After making its debut in last year's book, the Runs Saved leaders and trailers return this year. Runs Saved combines Plus/Minus with our analysis of bunts, double plays, outfield arms, catchers' earned runs, catchers' stolen bases allowed, pitchers' stolen bases allowed, and home run saving catches to form a complete evaluation of a fielder.

Please see the Glossary for a more complete description of Plus/Minus and Runs Saved.

Infield Runs Saved Leaders

First Basemen 3-Year Leaders		Second Basemen 3-Year Leaders		Third Basemen 3-Year Leaders		Shortstops 3-Year Leaders	
Pujols,Albert	27	Utley,Chase	60	Beltre,Adrian	55	Ryan,Brendan	49
Barton,Daric	26	Ellis,Mark	33	Zimmerman,Ryan	53	Wilson,Jack	47
Votto,Joey	18	Pedroia,Dustin	30	Longoria,Evan	39	Escobar,Yunel	44
Youkilis,Kevin	18	Hill,Aaron	26	Rolen,Scott	27	Tulowitzki,Troy	27
Overbay,Lyle	17	Kinsler,Ian	23	Headley,Chase	22	Izturis,Cesar	27
Kotchman,Casey	17	Polanco,Placido	23	Kouzmanoff,Kevin	16	Rollins,Jimmy	20
Berkman,Lance	16	Hudson,Orlando	18	Blake,Casey	15	Hardy,J.J.	18
Teixeira,Mark	15	Barmes,Clint	16	Lopez,Jose	15	Ramirez,Alexei	16
Ishikawa,Travis	15	Rodriguez,Sean	16	Inge,Brandon	11	Andrus,Elvis	15
Davis,Ike	13	Phillips,Brandon	11	Jones,Chipper	10	Scutaro,Marco	13

First Basemen 3-Year Trailers		Second Basemen 3-Year Trailers		Third Basemen 3-Year Trailers		Shortstops 3-Year Trailers	
Dunn,Adam	-29	Castillo,Luis	-23	Young,Michael	-31	Betancourt,Yuniesky	-53
Fielder,Prince	-24	Uggla,Dan	-17	Teahen,Mark	-27	Cabrera,Orlando	-32
Giambi,Jason	-22	Schumaker,Skip	-15	Cantu,Jorge	-23	Cedeno,Ronny	-20
Konerko,Paul	-22	Matsui,Kaz	-14	Ramirez,Aramis	-23	Jeter,Derek	-20
Cabrera,Miguel	-15	Callaspo,Alberto	-13	Encarnacion,Edwin	-21	Renteria,Edgar	-19
Howard,Ryan	-15	Casilla,Alexi	-13	Gordon,Alex	-18	Crosby,Bobby	-17

First Basemen 2010 Leaders		Second Basemen 2010 Leaders		Third Basemen 2010 Leaders		Shortstops 2010 Leaders	
Barton,Daric	20	Hudson,Orlando	17	Headley,Chase	21	Ryan,Brendan	27
Davis,Ike	13	Rodriguez,Sean	17	Zimmerman,Ryan	20	Escobar,Yunel	19
Overbay,Lyle	9	Utley,Chase	14	Lopez,Jose	15	Gonzalez,Alex	16
Morneau,Justin	9	Hill,Aaron	9	Longoria,Evan	13	Ramirez,Alexei	16
Branyan,Russell	7	Ellis,Mark	8	Kouzmanoff,Kevin	13	Tulowitzki,Troy	16
Huff,Aubrey	6	Kinsler,Ian	8	Beltre,Adrian	10	Pennington,Cliff	9
Youkilis,Kevin	4	Cano,Robinson	7	Blake,Casey	10	Santiago,Ramon	8
Napoli,Mike	4	Rhymes,Will	7	Jones,Chipper	6	Wilson,Jack	8
Nady,Xavier	4	Valbuena,Luis	4	Encarnacion,Edwin	3	Rollins,Jimmy	7
Wallace,Brett	4	Pedroia,Dustin	4	Inge,Brandon	2	Hardy,J.J.	4

First Basemen 2010 Trailers		Second Basemen 2010 Trailers		Third Basemen 2010 Trailers		Shortstops 2010 Trailers	
Konerko,Paul	-17	Kendrick,Howie	-11	Betemit,Wilson	-13	Betancourt,Yuniesky	-21
Howard,Ryan	-14	Figgins,Chone	-11	Johnson,Chris	-13	Ramirez,Hanley	-16
Fielder,Prince	-13	Weeks,Rickie	-11	Young,Michael	-13	Cedeno,Ronny	-15
Jones,Garrett	-10	Uggla,Dan	-11	Alvarez,Pedro	-11	Jeter,Derek	-13
Glaus,Troy	-8	Guzman,Cristian	-10	Ramirez,Aramis	-10	Sanchez,Angel	-9
Dunn,Adam	-8	Walker,Neil	-9	Wright,David	-10	Scutaro,Marco	-7

Outfield Runs Saved Leaders

Left Fielders 3-Year Leaders		Center Fielders 3-Year Leaders		Right Fielders 3-Year Leaders	
Crawford,Carl	51	Gutierrez,Franklin	48	Pence,Hunter	39
Holliday,Matt	27	Gomez,Carlos	33	Suzuki,Ichiro	39
Parra,Gerardo	17	Bourn,Michael	32	Bruce,Jay	29
Rivera,Juan	15	Beltran,Carlos	24	Sweeney,Ryan	25
Gardner,Brett	13	Gwynn,Tony	24	Werth,Jayson	24
Hairston,Scott	9	Young,Chris	23	Cruz,Nelson	24
Raburn,Ryan	9	Rios,Alex	21	Upton,Justin	23
Jackson,Conor	8	Morgan,Nyjer	21	Ludwick,Ryan	22
Smith,Seth	8	Victorino,Shane	20	Winn,Randy	21
Pierre,Juan	7	Jones,Adam	17	Choo,Shin-Soo	18

Left Fielders 3-Year Trailers		Center Fielders 3-Year Trailers		Right Fielders 3-Year Trailers	
Young,Delmon	-27	Wells,Vernon	-28	Hawpe,Brad	-37
Lee,Carlos	-20	McLouth,Nate	-27	Ethier,Andre	-27
Lind,Adam	-18	McCutchen,Andrew	-18	Guillen,Jose	-20
Ramirez,Manny	-18	Fowler,Dexter	-13	Cuddyer,Michael	-12
Gomes,Jonny	-14	Kemp,Matt	-8	Abreu,Bobby	-10
Coghlan,Chris	-12	Ellsbury,Jacoby	-6	Hart,Corey	-9

Left Fielders 2010 Leaders		Center Fielders 2010 Leaders		Right Fielders 2010 Leaders	
Crawford,Carl	14	Jackson,Austin	21	Bruce,Jay	17
Parra,Gerardo	14	Bourn,Michael	16	Stanton,Mike	17
Gardner,Brett	13	Gutierrez,Franklin	14	Suzuki,Ichiro	12
Holliday,Matt	8	Rios,Alex	12	Choo,Shin-Soo	11
Tabata,Jose	6	Byrd,Marlon	11	Cruz,Nelson	11
Pie,Felix	6	Victorino,Shane	11	Heyward,Jason	10
Gordon,Alex	6	Gwynn,Tony	11	Pence,Hunter	9
Burroll,Pat	6	Young,Chris	10	Werth,Jayson	9
Raburn,Ryan	6	Span,Denard	9	Ross,Cody	8
Snider,Travis	6	Crisp,Coco	9	2 tied with	7

Left Fielders 2010 Trailers		Center Fielders 2010 Trailers		Right Fielders 2010 Trailers	
Lee,Carlos	-15	Kemp,Matt	-15	Quentin,Carlos	-19
Gomes,Jonny	-10	McLouth,Nate	-10	Ethier,Andre	-14
Podsednik,Scott	-10	McCutchen,Andrew	-10	Hart,Corey	-8
Rivera,Juan	-8	Upton,B.J.	-9	Hawpe,Brad	-6
Young,Delmon	-8	Davis,Rajai	-5	Cuddyer,Michael	-6
Ibanez,Raul	-6	Brantley,Michael	-4	Abreu,Bobby	-6

Pitcher/Catcher Runs Saved Leaders

Pitchers 3-Year Leaders		Catchers 3-Year Leaders	
Buehrle,Mark	23	Molina,Jose	21
Greinke,Zack	18	Molina,Yadier	20
Garland,Jon	14	Olivo,Miguel	17
Duke,Zach	13	Laird,Gerald	11
Arroyo,Bronson	12	Ruiz,Carlos	10
Westbrook,Jake	12	Quintero,Humberto	9
Cook,Aaron	11	Suzuki,Kurt	8
Cahill,Trevor	11	Mathis,Jeff	7
Vazquez,Javier	11	Barajas,Rod	7
Romero,Ricky	11	3 tied with	6

Pitchers 3-Year Trailers		Catchers 3-Year Trailers	
Santana,Ervin	-14	Posada,Jorge	-24
Lincecum,Tim	-13	Buck,John	-20
Penny,Brad	-10	Napoli,Mike	-20
Pavano,Carl	-10	Martinez,Victor	-18
Lackey,John	-9	Baker,John	-14
Niemann,Jeff	-8	Hernandez,Ramon	-12

Pitchers 2010 Leaders		Catchers 2010 Leaders	
Romero,Ricky	10	Olivo,Miguel	14
Westbrook,Jake	9	Molina,Yadier	12
Cahill,Trevor	9	Ruiz,Carlos	7
Buehrle,Mark	8	Torrealba,Yorvit	7
Greinke,Zack	7	Pierzynski,A.J.	6
Braden,Dallas	7	Wieters,Matt	5
Hudson,Tim	6	Posey,Buster	5
Garland,Jon	6	Quintero,Humberto	5
Arroyo,Bronson	6	Suzuki,Kurt	4
Dickey,R.A.	5	Martin,Russell	4

Pitchers 2010 Trailers		Catchers 2010 Trailers	
Santana,Ervin	-6	Hernandez,Ramon	-10
Lackey,John	-6	Posada,Jorge	-8
Bonderman,Jeremy	-5	Buck,John	-8
Garcia,Freddy	-5	Doumit,Ryan	-7
Hanson,Tommy	-5	Martinez,Victor	-7
Haren,Dan	-5	Hundley,Nick	-6

Infield Plus/Minus Leaders

First Basemen 3-Year Leaders		Second Basemen 3-Year Leaders		Third Basemen 3-Year Leaders		Shortstops 3-Year Leaders	
Pujols,Albert	+40	Utley,Chase	+76	Beltre,Adrian	+69	Escobar,Yunel	+59
Barton,Daric	+37	Ellis,Mark	+33	Zimmerman,Ryan	+62	Ryan,Brendan	+59
Overbay,Lyle	+33	Pedroia,Dustin	+31	Longoria,Evan	+49	Wilson,Jack	+58
Youkilis,Kevin	+27	Hudson,Orlando	+27	Rolen,Scott	+39	Izturis,Cesar	+36
Kotchman,Casey	+24	Hill,Aaron	+26	Headley,Chase	+26	Tulowitzki,Troy	+31
Teixeira,Mark	+22	Polanco,Placido	+22	Kouzmanoff,Kevin	+25	Hardy,J.J.	+29
Berkman,Lance	+18	Phillips,Brandon	+19	Lopez,Jose	+25	Rollins,Jimmy	+26
Votto,Joey	+17	Kinsler,Ian	+18	Blake,Casey	+17	Scutaro,Marco	+22
Ishikawa,Travis	+17	Barmes,Clint	+17	Inge,Brandon	+15	Ramirez,Alexei	+20
Morneau,Justin	+14	Rodriguez,Sean	+17	Stewart,Ian	+9	Andrus,Elvis	+16

First Basemen 3-Year Trailers		Second Basemen 3-Year Trailers		Third Basemen 3-Year Trailers		Shortstops 3-Year Trailers	
Dunn,Adam	-43	Schumaker,Skip	-26	Young,Michael	-33	Betancourt,Yuniesky	-66
Fielder,Prince	-33	Callaspo,Alberto	-25	Ramirez,Aramis	-32	Cabrera,Orlando	-41
Giambi,Jason	-31	Castillo,Luis	-21	Teahen,Mark	-30	Crosby,Bobby	-26
Konerko,Paul	-24	Matsui,Kaz	-20	Cantu,Jorge	-29	Cedeno,Ronny	-24
Howard,Ryan	-19	Uggla,Dan	-20	Encarnacion,Edwin	-27	Jeter,Derek	-22
Butler,Billy	-17	Figgins,Chone	-18	Wright,David	-26	Renteria,Edgar	-21

First Basemen 2010 Leaders		Second Basemen 2010 Leaders		Third Basemen 2010 Leaders		Shortstops 2010 Leaders	
Barton,Daric	+27	Hudson,Orlando	+23	Lopez,Jose	+25	Ryan,Brendan	+31
Davis,Ike	+14	Rodriguez,Sean	+20	Headley,Chase	+25	Escobar,Yunel	+22
Overbay,Lyle	+12	Utley,Chase	+16	Zimmerman,Ryan	+24	Ramirez,Alexei	+20
Morneau,Justin	+12	Kinsler,Ian	+10	Kouzmanoff,Kevin	+20	Tulowitzki,Troy	+16
Branyan,Russell	+10	Hill,Aaron	+8	Longoria,Evan	+17	Gonzalez,Alex	+16
Youkilis,Kevin	+7	Ellis,Mark	+8	Blake,Casey	+13	Santiago,Ramon	+11
Napoli,Mike	+7	Rhymes,Will	+8	Beltre,Adrian	+11	Pennington,Cliff	+10
Pujols,Albert	+6	Cano,Robinson	+7	Jones,Chipper	+9	Wilson,Jack	+10
Huff,Aubrey	+6	Theriot,Ryan	+5	Encarnacion,Edwin	+4	Bartlett,Jason	+6
Nady,Xavier	+5	Eckstein,David	+4	Rolen,Scott	+3	Hardy,J.J.	+6

First Basemen 2010 Trailers		Second Basemen 2010 Trailers		Third Basemen 2010 Trailers		Shortstops 2010 Trailers	
Konerko,Paul	-24	Figgins,Chone	-19	Johnson,Chris	-18	Ramirez,Hanley	-22
Fielder,Prince	-19	Kendrick,Howie	-15	McGehee,Casey	-16	Betancourt,Yuniesky	-20
Howard,Ryan	-18	Walker,Neil	-14	Betemit,Wilson	-15	Cedeno,Ronny	-18
Dunn,Adam	-15	Weeks,Rickie	-14	Alvarez,Pedro	-14	Jeter,Derek	-17
Jones,Garrett	-10	Schumaker,Skip	-12	Cantu,Jorge	-13	Sanchez,Angel	-12
Cabrera,Miguel	-10	Beckham,Gordon	-12	Wright,David	-13	Desmond,Ian	-9

Outfield Plus/Minus Leaders

Left Fielders 3-Year Leaders		Center Fielders 3-Year Leaders		Right Fielders 3-Year Leaders	
Crawford,Carl	+77	Gutierrez,Franklin	+62	Suzuki,Ichiro	+51
Holliday,Matt	+42	Gwynn,Tony	+45	Upton,Justin	+30
Parra,Gerardo	+24	Young,Chris	+43	Cruz,Nelson	+28
Smith,Seth	+19	Gomez,Carlos	+42	Sweeney,Ryan	+28
Pierre,Juan	+13	Bourn,Michael	+37	Bruce,Jay	+26
Hairston,Scott	+12	Morgan,Nyjer	+29	Winn,Randy	+24
Jackson,Conor	+10	Beltran,Carlos	+24	Pence,Hunter	+23
Rivera,Juan	+7	Rios,Alex	+24	Heyward,Jason	+23
Scott,Luke	+7	Crisp,Coco	+23	Swisher,Nick	+19
Gardner,Brett	+7	Span,Denard	+21	Schierholtz,Nate	+14

Left Fielders 3-Year Trailers		Center Fielders 3-Year Trailers		Right Fielders 3-Year Trailers	
Young,Delmon	-57	Wells,Vernon	-56	Hawpe,Brad	-58
Coghlan,Chris	-35	McLouth,Nate	-49	Abreu,Bobby	-51
Ibanez,Raul	-33	McCutchen,Andrew	-38	Ethier,Andre	-42
Lee,Carlos	-31	Kemp,Matt	-38	Cuddyer,Michael	-41
Gomes,Jonny	-27	Upton,B.J.	-30	Guillen,Jose	-31
Lind,Adam	-22	Jones,Adam	-28	Hart,Corey	-21

Left Fielders 2010 Leaders		Center Fielders 2010 Leaders		Right Fielders 2010 Leaders	
Crawford,Carl	+22	Jackson,Austin	+33	Bruce,Jay	+24
Parra,Gerardo	+19	Bourn,Michael	+24	Heyward,Jason	+23
Holliday,Matt	+14	Gutierrez,Franklin	+20	Stanton,Mike	+20
Tabata,Jose	+12	Gwynn,Tony	+19	Suzuki,Ichiro	+16
Diaz,Matt	+11	Rios,Alex	+17	Upton,Justin	+14
Snider,Travis	+10	Span,Denard	+14	Ludwick,Ryan	+13
Gardner,Brett	+9	Borbon,Julio	+13	Cruz,Nelson	+12
Braun,Ryan	+8	Crisp,Coco	+12	Ross,Cody	+12
Smith,Seth	+7	Morgan,Nyjer	+11	Pence,Hunter	+9
Gordon,Alex	+5	Young,Chris	+9	Swisher,Nick	+8

Left Fielders 2010 Trailers		Center Fielders 2010 Trailers		Right Fielders 2010 Trailers	
Young,Delmon	-20	Kemp,Matt	-23	Quentin,Carlos	-25
Gomes,Jonny	-18	McCutchen,Andrew	-21	Ethier,Andre	-21
Lee,Carlos	-17	Upton,B.J.	-18	Cuddyer,Michael	-17
Rivera,Juan	-16	McLouth,Nate	-14	Hart,Corey	-15
Morrison,Logan	-14	Jones,Adam	-12	Boesch,Brennan	-13
Cabrera,Melky	-12	Wells,Vernon	-10	Abreu,Bobby	-13

Pitcher Plus/Minus Leaders

Pitchers
3-Year Leaders

Westbrook,Jake	+15
Garland,Jon	+13
Buehrle,Mark	+13
Cahill,Trevor	+13
Greinke,Zack	+13
Bergesen,Brad	+13
Carmona,Fausto	+12
Dempster,Ryan	+11
Hernandez,Felix	+11
Arroyo,Bronson	+11

Pitchers
3-Year Trailers

Lee,Cliff	-12
Parra,Manny	-10
Santana,Ervin	-10
Garza,Matt	-10
Penny,Brad	-9
Jackson,Edwin	-8

Pitchers
2010 Leaders

Westbrook,Jake	+12
Cahill,Trevor	+10
Carmona,Fausto	+9
Romero,Ricky	+9
Dickey,R.A.	+7
Arroyo,Bronson	+7
Greinke,Zack	+7
Bergesen,Brad	+6
Hernandez,Felix	+5
Garland,Jon	+5

Pitchers
2010 Trailers

Bonderman,Jeremy	-7
Haren,Dan	-7
Sanchez,Anibal	-6
Porcello,Rick	-5
Lee,Cliff	-5
Lackey,John	-5

Career Register

We've added a new element to the career register this year: pronunciations. Our goal was not to provide pronunciations for every player, nor to annoy with pronunciations for established stars. If you don't know how to pronounce Tim Lincecum or Albert Pujols, chances are you're not buying this book anyway. Jhoulys Chacin and Eugenio Velez are more what we're after.

If a player led either the American or National League in a particular category, that number will appear in **boldface.**

Age is seasonal as of June 30, 2011.

For pitchers, BFP is Batters Facing Pitcher; TBB is Total Bases on Balls (or, Total Walks, intentional and unintentional); OP is Save Opportunities; Hld is Holds.

For the various levels of Class-A ball, we have used "A+" to indicate High A and "A-" to indicate Low A.

Regardless of whether their name at the time was Los Angeles, Anaheim, California, or Los Angeles of Anaheim, the abbreviation LAA denotes a reference to the Angels franchise.

For players who have appeared in fewer than three major league seasons, we included their full minor league statistics. For those players with three or more years in the big leagues who also spent time in the minor leagues in 2010 (for example, if they had a rehab assignment) we included only their 2010 minor league statistics—indicated by an asterisk. Those players who split time between the majors and the minors last season but have fewer than three years of major league experience will still have their full minor league stats included.

The Register also features Runs Created (RC) for hitters and Component ERA (ERC) for pitchers, in addition to the more traditional statistics. Developed by Bill James, Runs Created is a method of measuring every facet of a hitter's strengths and weaknesses, combining those factors into one number, indicative of a player's production. Component ERA estimates what a pitcher's ERA should have been based upon his raw pitching statistics and gives us a good indication of whether or not a pitcher actually deserved his ERA. An explanation of Bill's most-current formulas for both RC and ERC can be found in the Baseball Glossary at the end of the Handbook.

A player's total career numbers in the postseason appear on one line above his total regular season career numbers. Since we work hard to bring you this publication by November 1, 2010, postseason data from 2010 is not included.

David Aardsma

Pitches: R **Bats:** R **Pos:** RP-53 ARDZ-muh **Ht:** 6'3" **Wt:** 205 **Born:** 12/27/1981 **Age:** 29

			HOW MUCH HE PITCHED							WHAT HE GAVE UP												THE RESULTS							
Year	Team	Lg	G	GS	CG	GF	IP	BFP	H	R	ER	HR	SH	SF	HB	TBB	IBB	SO	WP	Bk	W	L	Pct	Sh	Sv-Op	Hld	ERC	ERA
2004	SF	NL	11	0	0	5	10.2	61	20	8	8	1	0	1	2	10	0	5	0	0	1	0	1.000	0	0-1	1	13.38	6.75
2006	ChC	NL	45	0	0	9	53.0	225	41	25	24	9	1	3	1	28	0	49	1	0	3	0	1.000	0	0-0	5	3.88	4.08
2007	CWS	AL	25	0	0	7	32.1	151	39	24	23	4	2	1	1	17	3	36	2	0	2	1	.667	0	0-3	3	5.93	6.40
2008	Bos	AL	47	0	0	7	48.2	228	49	32	30	4	3	2	5	35	2	49	3	0	2	2	.667	0	0-1	4	5.63	5.55
2009	Sea	AL	73	0	0	53	71.1	296	49	23	20	4	2	1	0	34	3	80	2	0	3	6	.333	0	38-42	6	2.34	2.52
2010	Sea	AL	53	0	0	43	49.2	202	33	19	19	5	7	1	2	25	5	49	2	0	0	6	.000	0	31-36	5	2.74	3.44
	6 ML YEARS		254	0	0	124	265.2	1163	231	131	124	27	15	9	11	149	13	268	10	0	13	15	.464	0	69-83	19	4.07	4.20

Fernando Abad

Pitches: L **Bats:** L **Pos:** RP-22 ah-BAHD **Ht:** 6'2" **Wt:** 207 **Born:** 12/17/1985 **Age:** 25

			HOW MUCH HE PITCHED							WHAT HE GAVE UP												THE RESULTS							
Year	Team	Lg	G	GS	CG	GF	IP	BFP	H	R	ER	HR	SH	SF	HB	TBB	IBB	SO	WP	Bk	W	L	Pct	Sh	Sv-Op	Hld	ERC	ERA
2007	Grnsvle	R+	17	4	0	6	50.0	210	47	29	23	6	3	2	2	12	0	54	2	3	6	4	.600	0	1--	-	3.36	4.14
2007	TriCity	A-	2	0	0	1	3.0	13	2	2	2	0	0	0	0	2	0	5	0	0	0	0	-	0	0--	-	2.54	6.00
2008	Lxngtn	A	45	0	0	27	76.1	325	78	31	28	9	4	3	4	13	3	94	1	2	2	7	.222	0	3--	-	3.47	3.30
2009	Lancst	A+	41	0	0	23	82.2	330	78	42	38	8	5	3	5	8	0	79	3	0	4	6	.400	0	6--	-	2.86	4.14
2009	CpChr	AA	3	3	0	0	14.0	57	12	7	5	1	0	0	0	3	0	13	1	0	1	0	1.000	0	0--	-	2.41	3.21
2010	CpChr	AA	14	4	0	0	39.2	167	48	16	11	3	3	1	0	6	1	33	2	1	4	3	.571	0	0--	-	4.12	2.50
2010	RdRck	AAA	5	0	0	1	6.1	26	5	1	1	1	0	0	0	2	0	9	0	0	0	0	-	0	0--	-	2.94	1.42
2010	Hou	NL	22	0	0	6	19.0	76	14	6	6	3	0	1	0	5	0	12	0	0	0	1	.000	0	0-0	6	2.49	2.84

Bobby Abreu

Bats: L **Throws:** R **Pos:** RF-93; LF-41; DH-17; PH-3 **Ht:** 6'0" **Wt:** 210 **Born:** 3/11/1974 **Age:** 37

			BATTING																			BASERUNNING				AVERAGES		
Year	Team	Lg	G	AB	H	2B	3B	HR	(Hm	Rd)	TB	R	RBI	RC	TBB	IBB	SO	HBP	SH	SF		SB	CS	SB%	GDP		Avg	OBP	Slg
1996	Hou	NL	15	22	5	1	0	0	(0	0)	6	1	1	1	2	0	3	0	0	1		0	0	-	1		.227	.292	.273
1997	Hou	NL	59	188	47	10	2	3	(3	0)	70	22	26	25	21	0	48	1	0	0		7	2	.78	0		.250	.329	.372
1998	Phi	NL	151	497	155	29	6	17	(10	7)	247	68	74	101	84	14	133	0	4	4		19	10	.66	6		.312	.409	.497
1999	Phi	NL	152	546	183	35	11	20	(13	7)	300	118	93	131	109	8	113	3	0	4		27	9	.75	13		.335	.446	.549
2000	Phi	NL	154	576	182	42	10	25	(14	11)	319	103	79	130	100	9	116	1	0	3		28	8	.78	12		.316	.416	.554
2001	Phi	NL	162	588	170	48	4	31	(13	18)	319	118	110	125	106	11	137	1	0	9		36	14	.72	11		.289	.393	.543
2002	Phi	NL	157	572	176	50	6	20	(8	12)	298	102	85	112	104	9	117	3	0	6		31	12	.72	11		.308	.413	.521
2003	Phi	NL	158	577	173	35	1	20	(11	9)	270	99	101	120	109	13	126	2	0	7		22	9	.71	13		.300	.409	.468
2004	Phi	NL	159	574	173	47	1	30	(13	17)	312	118	105	139	127	10	116	5	0	7		40	5	.89	5		.301	.428	.544
2005	Phi	NL	162	588	168	37	1	24	(15	9)	279	104	102	116	117	15	134	6	0	8		31	9	.78	7		.286	.405	.474
2006	2 Tms		156	548	163	41	2	15	(8	7)	253	98	107	123	124	6	138	3	2	9		30	6	.83	13		.297	.424	.462
2007	NYY	AL	158	605	171	40	5	16	(10	6)	269	123	101	101	84	0	115	3	0	7		25	8	.76	11		.283	.369	.445
2008	NYY	AL	156	609	180	39	4	20	(14	6)	287	100	100	108	73	2	109	1	0	1		22	11	.67	14		.296	.371	.471
2009	LAA	AL	152	563	165	29	3	15	(7	8)	245	96	103	109	94	7	113	1	0	9		30	8	.79	15		.293	.390	.435
2010	LAA	AL	154	573	146	41	1	20	(11	9)	249	88	78	91	87	3	132	2	0	5		24	10	.71	13		.255	.352	.435
06	Phi	NL	98	339	94	25	2	8	(5	3)	147	61	65	76	91	5	86	2	0	6		20	4	.83	8		.277	.427	.434
06	NYY	AL	58	209	69	16	0	7	(3	4)	106	37	42	47	33	1	52	1	2	3		10	2	.83	5		.330	.419	.507
	Postseason		20	67	19	6	0	1	(1	0)	28	9	9	11	12	3	15	0	0	0		2	1	.67	0		.284	.392	.418
	15 ML YEARS		2105	7626	2257	524	57	276	(150	126)	3723	1358	1265	1532	1341	107	1650	32	6	79		372	121	.75	147		.296	.400	.488

Tony Abreu

Bats: B **Throws:** R **Pos:** PH-37; 3B-20; SS-15; 2B-12; DH-1; PR-1 **Ht:** 5'9" **Wt:** 200 **Born:** 11/13/1984 **Age:** 26

			BATTING																			BASERUNNING				AVERAGES		
Year	Team	Lg	G	AB	H	2B	3B	HR	(Hm	Rd)	TB	R	RBI	RC	TBB	IBB	SO	HBP	SH	SF		SB	CS	SB%	GDP		Avg	OBP	Slg
2010	Reno*	AAA	24	94	33	7	1	0	(-	-)	48	17	21	18	4	0	21	2	1	1		2	0	1.00	2		.351	.386	.511
2007	LAD	NL	59	166	45	14	1	2	(0	2)	67	19	17	18	7	1	21	3	0	2		0	0	-	5		.271	.309	.404
2009	LAD	NL	6	8	2	0	0	0	(0	0)	2	0	1	2	3	0	2	0	0	0		0	1	.00	0		.250	.455	.250
2010	Ari	NL	81	193	45	11	1	1	(1	0)	61	16	13	12	4	0	47	0	0	4		2	1	.67	8		.233	.244	.316
	3 ML YEARS		146	367	92	25	2	3	(1	2)	130	35	31	32	14	1	70	3	0	6		2	2	.50	13		.251	.279	.354

Jeremy Accardo

Pitches: R **Bats:** R **Pos:** RP-5 uh-CAR-doe **Ht:** 6'1" **Wt:** 192 **Born:** 12/8/1981 **Age:** 29

			HOW MUCH HE PITCHED							WHAT HE GAVE UP												THE RESULTS							
Year	Team	Lg	G	GS	CG	GF	IP	BFP	H	R	ER	HR	SH	SF	HB	TBB	IBB	SO	WP	Bk	W	L	Pct	Sh	Sv-Op	Hld	ERC	ERA
2010	LsVgs*	AAA	42	0	0	41	44.0	193	52	22	17	1	3	4	1	15	2	26	0	0	3	2	.600	0	24--	-	4.37	3.48
2005	SF	NL	28	0	0	7	29.2	124	26	13	13	2	1	1	1	9	1	16	1	0	1	5	.167	0	0-1	4	2.87	3.94
2006	2 Tms		65	0	0	27	69.0	297	76	42	41	7	1	4	1	20	5	54	4	1	2	4	.333	0	3-8	10	4.17	5.35
2007	Tor	AL	64	0	0	48	67.1	275	51	19	16	4	0	1	2	24	2	57	0	1	4	4	.500	0	30-35	2	2.44	2.14
2008	Tor	AL	16	0	0	6	12.1	56	15	10	9	1	0	1	1	4	2	5	1	0	0	3	.000	0	4-6	2	4.88	6.57
2009	Tor	AL	26	0	0	5	24.2	107	23	8	7	2	0	2	2	17	1	18	0	0	0	0	-	0	1-1	4	5.26	2.55
2010	Tor	AL	5	0	0	0	6.2	34	12	6	6	0	0	1	0	3	0	3	2	0	0	1	.000	0	0-0	0	9.38	8.10
06	SF	NL	38	0	0	16	40.1	170	38	23	22	2	0	4	1	11	3	40	2	0	1	3	.250	0	3-6	8	2.88	4.91
06	Tor	AL	27	0	0	11	28.2	127	38	19	19	5	1	0	0	9	2	14	2	1	1	1	.500	0	0-2	2	6.25	5.97
	6 ML YEARS		204	0	0	95	209.2	893	203	98	92	16	2	9	6	77	11	153	8	2	7	17	.292	0	38-51	22	3.69	3.95

Alfredo Aceves

Pitches: R **Bats:** R **Pos:** RP-10   ah-SEVV-us   **Ht:** 6'3" **Wt:** 218 **Born:** 12/8/1981 **Age:** 29

Year Team	Lg		HOW MUCH HE PITCHED						WHAT HE GAVE UP											THE RESULTS						
		G	GS	CG	GF	IP	BFP	H	R	ER	HR	SH	SF	HB	TBB	IBB	SO	WP	Bk	W	L	Pct	Sh	Sv-Op	Hld	ERC	ERA
2010 S-WB*	AAA	3	2	0	0	3.2	23	4	4	3	0	0	1	2	5	0	4	0	0	0	0	-	0	0--	-	9.29	7.36
2010 Trntn*	AA	4	3	0	0	8.0	33	10	5	5	1	0	0	0	1	0	7	0	0	0	0	-	0	0--	-	4.75	5.63
2008 NYY	AL	6	4	0	1	30.0	120	25	8	8	4	0	0	0	10	0	16	1	0	1	0	1.000	0	0-0	0	3.23	2.40
2009 NYY	AL	43	1	0	10	84.0	337	69	36	33	10	1	2	5	16	2	69	0	0	10	1	.909	0	1-2	5	2.65	3.54
2010 NYY	AL	10	0	0	2	12.0	53	10	5	4	1	0	0	1	4	1	2	0	0	3	0	1.000	0	1-1	1	2.80	3.00
Postseason		4	0	0	1	4.1	20	5	2	2	0	1	0	0	3	1	2	1	0	0	1	.000	0	0-0	0	5.01	4.15
3 ML YEARS		59	5	0	13	126.0	510	104	49	45	15	1	2	6	30	3	87	1	0	14	1	.933	0	2-3	6	2.80	3.21

Manny Acosta

Pitches: R **Bats:** B **Pos:** RP-41   **Ht:** 6'4" **Wt:** 170 **Born:** 5/1/1981 **Age:** 30

Year Team	Lg		HOW MUCH HE PITCHED						WHAT HE GAVE UP											THE RESULTS						
		G	GS	CG	GF	IP	BFP	H	R	ER	HR	SH	SF	HB	TBB	IBB	SO	WP	Bk	W	L	Pct	Sh	Sv-Op	Hld	ERC	ERA
2010 Buffalo*	AAA	28	0	0	19	36.1	148	28	14	14	4	3	1	1	15	2	36	2	0	2	3	.400	0	5--	-	3.04	3.47
2007 Atl	NL	21	0	0	5	23.2	93	13	6	6	2	0	0	0	14	1	22	1	0	1	1	.500	0	0-0	4	2.39	2.28
2008 Atl	NL	46	0	0	22	53.0	226	48	25	21	7	4	1	1	26	5	31	5	0	3	5	.375	0	3-5	4	4.12	3.57
2009 Atl	NL	36	0	0	17	37.1	174	45	19	18	4	3	0	2	19	2	32	3	0	1	1	.500	0	0-0	2	5.90	4.34
2010 NYM	NL	41	0	0	12	39.2	157	30	13	13	4	1	1	0	18	1	42	3	0	3	2	.600	0	1-3	2	3.10	2.95
4 ML YEARS		144	0	0	56	153.2	650	136	63	58	17	8	2	3	77	9	127	12	0	8	9	.471	0	4-8	12	3.98	3.40

Mike Adams

Pitches: R **Bats:** R **Pos:** RP-70   **Ht:** 6'5" **Wt:** 190 **Born:** 7/29/1978 **Age:** 32

Year Team	Lg		HOW MUCH HE PITCHED						WHAT HE GAVE UP											THE RESULTS						
		G	GS	CG	GF	IP	BFP	H	R	ER	HR	SH	SF	HB	TBB	IBB	SO	WP	Bk	W	L	Pct	Sh	Sv-Op	Hld	ERC	ERA
2010 SnAnt*	AA	1	0	0	0	1.0	3	0	0	0	0	0	0	0	0	0	1	0	0	0	0	-	0	0--	-	0.00	0.00
2004 Mil	NL	46	0	0	13	53.0	225	50	21	20	5	5	2	2	14	2	39	2	0	2	3	.400	0	0 5	12	3.22	3.40
2005 Mil	NL	13	0	0	7	13.1	61	12	4	4	2	0	0	0	10	1	14	1	0	0	1	.000	0	1-2	5	5.12	2.70
2006 Mil	NL	2	0	0	0	2.1	13	4	3	3	1	0	0	0	2	0	1	0	0	0	0	-	0	0-0	0	13.74	11.57
2008 SD	NL	54	0	0	11	65.1	259	49	18	18	7	2	3	0	19	2	74	0	0	2	3	.400	0	0-2	10	2.38	2.48
2009 SD	NL	37	0	0	5	37.0	136	14	9	3	1	0	0	0	8	1	45	1	0	0	0	-	0	0-1	15	0.65	0.73
2010 SD	NL	70	0	0	3	66.2	268	48	14	13	2	0	0	0	23	2	73	0	0	4	1	.800	0	0-4	38	1.95	1.76
6 ML YEARS		222	0	0	39	237.2	962	177	69	61	18	9	5	2	76	8	246	4	0	8	8	.500	0	1-14	77	2.26	2.31

Jeremy Affeldt

Pitches: L **Bats:** L **Pos:** RP-53   AFF-felt   **Ht:** 6'5" **Wt:** 228 **Born:** 6/6/1979 **Age:** 32

Year Team	Lg		HOW MUCH HE PITCHED						WHAT HE GAVE UP											THE RESULTS						
		G	GS	CG	GF	IP	BFP	H	R	ER	HR	SH	SF	HB	TBB	IBB	SO	WP	Bk	W	L	Pct	Sh	Sv-Op	Hld	ERC	ERA
2010 SnJos*	A+	2	2	0	0	3.0	12	2	0	0	0	0	0	0	1	0	4	1	0	0	0	-	0	0--	-	1.57	0.00
2002 KC	AL	34	7	0	4	77.2	353	85	41	40	8	2	1	3	37	4	67	5	2	3	4	.429	0	0-1	1	4.97	4.64
2003 KC	AL	36	18	0	5	126.0	533	126	58	55	12	2	5	5	38	1	98	2	2	7	6	.538	0	4-4	3	3.82	3.93
2004 KC	AL	38	8	0	26	76.1	344	91	49	42	6	4	4	3	32	2	49	4	3	3	4	.429	0	13-17	0	5.26	4.95
2005 KO	AL	40	0	0	12	49.2	232	56	35	29	3	0	1	0	29	2	39	5	0	0	2	.000	0	0-0	12	5.08	5.26
2006 2 Tms		54	9	0	12	97.1	448	102	74	67	13	4	4	2	55	3	48	2	0	8	8	.500	0	1-3	5	5.21	6.20
2007 Col	NL	75	0	0	11	59.0	253	47	26	23	3	3	0	3	33	9	40	6	1	4	3	.571	0	0-4	9	3.19	3.51
2008 Cin	NL	74	0	0	20	78.1	335	78	36	29	9	7	0	3	25	0	80	6	1	1	1	.500	0	0-1	5	3.98	3.33
2009 SF	NL	74	0	0	8	62.1	248	42	14	12	3	0	1	3	31	3	55	5	0	2	2	.500	0	0-0	33	2.61	1.73
2010 SF	NL	53	0	0	14	50.0	228	56	25	23	4	7	1	3	24	5	44	4	0	4	3	.571	0	4-7	7	4.99	4.14
06 KC	AL	27	9	0	3	70.0	320	71	51	46	9	3	3	1	42	0	28	2	0	4	6	.400	0	0-0	2	5.18	5.91
06 Col	NL	27	0	0	9	27.1	128	31	23	21	4	1	1	1	13	3	20	0	0	4	2	.667	0	1-3	3	5.29	6.91
Postseason		7	0	0	0	5.1	10	3	1	1	1	0	0	0	1	0	4	0	0	0	0	-	0	0-0	2	1.70	1.69
0 ML YEARS		487	42	0	113	676.2	2974	683	358	320	61	29	23	25	304	29	526	39	8	32	33	.492	0	22-37	75	4.33	4.26

Jonathan Albaladejo

Pitches: R **Bats:** R **Pos:** RP-10   ahl-bah-lah-DAY-hoe   **Ht:** 6'5" **Wt:** 260 **Born:** 10/30/1982 **Age:** 28

Year Team	Lg		HOW MUCH HE PITCHED						WHAT HE GAVE UP											THE RESULTS						
		G	GS	CG	GF	IP	BFP	H	R	ER	HR	SH	SF	HB	TBB	IBB	SO	WP	Bk	W	L	Pct	Sh	Sv-Op	Hld	ERC	ERA
2010 S-WB*	AAA	57	0	0	54	63.1	248	38	10	10	3	0	4	2	18	0	82	6	1	4	2	.667	0	43--	-	1.52	1.42
2007 Was	NL	14	0	0	1	14.1	51	7	3	3	1	0	1	1	2	0	12	0	0	1	1	.500	0	0-1	2	1.10	1.88
2008 NYY	AL	7	0	0	2	13.2	58	15	6	6	1	1	0	0	6	0	13	0	0	0	1	.000	0	0-0	1	4.82	3.95
2009 NYY	AL	32	0	0	5	34.1	158	41	23	20	6	1	4	3	16	2	21	0	0	5	1	.833	0	0-1	1	6.41	5.24
2010 NYY	AL	10	0	0	5	11.1	50	9	5	5	1	0	1	2	8	1	8	0	0	0	0	-	0	0-0	0	4.73	3.97
4 ML YEARS		63	0	0	13	73.2	317	72	37	34	9	2	6	6	32	3	54	0	0	6	3	.667	0	0-2	4	4.61	4.15

Matt Albers

Pitches: R **Bats:** L **Pos:** RP-62   **Ht:** 6'1" **Wt:** 230 **Born:** 1/20/1983 **Age:** 28

Year Team	Lg		HOW MUCH HE PITCHED						WHAT HE GAVE UP											THE RESULTS						
		G	GS	CG	GF	IP	BFP	H	R	ER	HR	SH	SF	HB	TBB	IBB	SO	WP	Bk	W	L	Pct	Sh	Sv-Op	Hld	ERC	ERA
2006 Hou	NL	4	2	0	0	15.0	66	17	10	10	1	2	0	0	7	0	11	0	0	0	2	.000	0	0-0	0	4.97	6.00
2007 Hou	NL	31	18	0	2	110.2	508	127	77	72	18	6	8	7	50	6	71	7	0	4	11	.267	0	0-0	0	5.76	5.86
2008 Bal	AL	28	0	3	5	49.0	208	43	21	19	4	1	2	3	22	1	26	1	0	3	3	.500	0	0-2	6	3.62	3.49
2009 Bal	AL	56	0	0	13	67.0	309	80	43	41	3	5	2	2	36	3	49	3	0	3	6	.333	0	0-4	10	5.41	5.51
2010 Bal	AL	62	0	0	19	75.2	329	78	41	38	6	3	0	2	34	5	49	2	0	5	3	.625	0	0-2	7	4.35	4.52
5 ML YEARS		181	23	0	39	317.1	1420	345	192	180	32	17	13	13	149	15	206	13	0	15	25	.375	0	0-8	23	4.97	5.11

Cory Aldridge

Bats: L **Throws:** R **Pos:** RF-4; LF-1 **Ht:** 6'1" **Wt:** 225 **Born:** 6/13/1979 **Age:** 32

Year	Team	Lg	G	AB	H	2B	3B	HR	(Hm	Rd)	TB	R	RBI	RC	TBB	IBB	SO	HBP	SH	SF	SB	CS	SB%	GDP	Avg	OBP	Slg
1997	Braves	R	46	169	47	8	1	3	(-	-)	66	26	37	23	14	0	37	1	0	1	0	1	1.00	1	.278	.337	.391
1998	Danvle	R+	60	214	63	16	1	3	(-	-)	90	37	33	38	29	1	48	2	1	1	16	2	.89	3	.294	.382	.421
1999	Macon	A	124	443	111	19	4	12	(-	-)	174	48	65	55	33	2	123	6	1	5	9	6	.60	9	.251	.308	.393
2000	MrtlBh	A+	109	401	100	18	5	15	(-	-)	173	51	64	54	33	2	118	1	0	9	10	5	.67	0	.249	.302	.431
2001	Grnville	AA	131	452	111	19	2	19	(-	-)	191	57	56	64	48	1	139	5	0	3	12	6	.67	6	.246	.323	.423
2002	Braves	R	17	59	17	5	3	3	(-	-)	37	10	13	14	11	0	17	0	0	1	1	0	-	0	.288	.394	.627
2003	Grnville	AA	127	448	105	20	2	16	(-	-)	177	55	49	52	37	4	134	5	0	4	11	3	.79	5	.234	.298	.395
2004	Grnville	AA	39	132	32	5	2	2	(-	-)	47	17	13	12	6	0	47	0	0	0	1	2	.33	1	.242	.275	.356
2004	Wichta	AA	79	280	67	12	5	18	(-	-)	143	49	45	48	41	3	87	4	1	2	9	7	.56	1	.239	.343	.511
2005	Wichta	AA	98	388	106	20	4	27	(-	-)	215	66	77	70	29	4	94	2	1	3	9	4	.69	6	.273	.325	.554
2005	Omha	AAA	24	82	16	4	0	3	(-	-)	29	8	7	7	6	0	28	0	0	0	4	0	1.00	0	.195	.250	.354
2006	Norfolk	AAA	26	83	13	2	0	0	(-	-)	15	2	6	1	2	0	31	0	1	2	3	0	1.00	0	.157	.172	.181
2006	Brham	AA	84	293	84	17	4	4	(-	-)	121	34	30	43	29	2	85	2	0	4	7	6	.54	5	.287	.351	.413
2007	Brham	AA	124	421	109	33	5	9	(-	-)	179	60	58	70	70	5	118	3	0	6	5	3	.63	7	.259	.364	.425
2008	Newark	IND	62	230	84	17	4	7	(-	-)	130	43	54	55	33	1	49	0	0	3	0	0	-	3	.365	.440	.565
2008	NWArk	AA	49	167	45	6	1	10	(-	-)	83	23	40	30	25	2	37	0	1	2	2	4	.33	2	.269	.361	.497
2009	Omha	AAA	98	354	112	20	4	22	(-	-)	206	48	71	72	24	0	86	3	0	4	0	1	.00	6	.316	.361	.582
2010	Salt Lk	AAA	83	299	95	24	1	13	(-	-)	160	53	59	61	35	5	83	1	0	3	2	1	.67	3	.318	.388	.535
2001	Atl	NL	8	5	0	0	0	0	(	)	0	1	0	0	0	0	4	0	0	0	0	0	-	0	.000	.000	.000
2010	LAA	AL	5	13	1	0	1	0	(0	0)	3	0	1	0	0	0	5	0	0	0	0	0	-	0	.077	.077	.231
2 ML YEARS			13	18	1	0	1	0	(0	0)	3	1	1	0	0	0	9	0	0	0	0	0	-	0	.056	.056	.167

Eliezer Alfonzo

Bats: R **Throws:** R **Pos:** C-12; PH-1 ell-ee-AY-zer **Ht:** 5'11" **Wt:** 220 **Born:** 2/7/1979 **Age:** 32

Year	Team	Lg	G	AB	H	2B	3B	HR	(Hm	Rd)	TB	R	RBI	RC	TBB	IBB	SO	HBP	SH	SF	SB	CS	SB%	GDP	Avg	OBP	Slg
2010	Tacom*	AAA	48	174	44	9	2	9	(-	-)	84	23	23	25	8	0	48	4	0	2	0	1	.00	2	.253	.298	.483
2006	SF	NL	87	286	76	17	2	12	(3	9)	133	27	39	36	9	7	74	7	4	3	1	0	1.00	10	.266	.302	.465
2007	SF	NL	26	64	16	2	1	1	(1	0)	23	5	6	5	2	2	23	1	0	0	2	0	.00	2	.250	.284	.359
2008	SF	NL	5	11	1	0	0	0	(0	0)	1	0	1	0	0	0	4	0	0	0	0	0	-	2	.091	.091	.091
2009	SD	NL	37	114	20	3	0	2	(1	1)	29	6	8	4	3	0	34	0	0	0	0	0	-	0	.175	.197	.254
2010	Sea	AL	13	41	9	1	0	1	(0	1)	13	4	4	2	0	0	10	0	0	0	0	0	-	2	.220	.220	.317
5 ML YEARS			168	516	122	23	3	16	(5	11)	199	42	58	47	14	9	145	8	4	3	1	2	.33	16	.236	.266	.386

Brandon Allen

Bats: L **Throws:** R **Pos:** LF-14; PH-5; 1B-4 **Ht:** 6'2" **Wt:** 235 **Born:** 2/12/1986 **Age:** 25

Year	Team	Lg	G	AB	H	2B	3B	HR	(Hm	Rd)	TB	R	RBI	RC	TBB	IBB	SO	HBP	SH	SF	SB	CS	SB%	GDP	Avg	OBP	Slg
2004	Bristol	R+	58	185	38	9	1	3	(-	-)	58	17	23	16	16	1	60	4	0	2	2	3	.40	3	.205	.280	.314
2005	Gr Falls	R+	66	231	61	11	2	11	(-	-)	109	41	42	41	32	3	69	7	0	3	7	5	.58	7	.264	.366	.472
2006	Knapol	A	109	395	84	17	2	15	(-	-)	150	36	68	39	22	0	126	3	3	4	6	4	.60	8	.213	.257	.380
2007	Knapol	A	129	516	146	39	5	18	(-	-)	249	84	93	84	39	3	124	4	0	2	7	4	.64	4	.283	.337	.483
2008	WinSa	AA	89	319	89	26	4	15	(-	-)	168	57	44	64	41	2	83	6	0	0	14	3	.82	6	.279	.372	.527
2008	Brham	AA	41	153	42	6	2	14	(-	-)	94	30	32	33	19	0	41	1	0	0	3	1	.75	1	.275	.358	.614
2009	Brham	AA	62	241	70	12	3	7	(-	-)	109	39	35	41	30	3	47	2	0	1	1	2	.33	2	.290	.372	.452
2009	Charltt	AA	15	61	16	4	0	1	(-	-)	23	6	8	5	0	0	13	0	0	0	0	0	-	0	.262	.262	.377
2009	Reno	AAA	38	145	47	8	1	12	(-	-)	93	33	32	37	20	1	25	2	0	0	6	0	1.00	0	.324	.413	.641
2010	Reno	AAA	107	371	97	18	3	25	(-	-)	196	72	86	85	83	4	95	10	0	5	14	4	.78	5	.261	.405	.528
2009	Ari	NL	32	104	21	7	0	4	(1	3)	40	13	14	12	12	2	40	0	0	0	0	0	-	4	.202	.284	.385
2010	Ari	NL	22	45	12	3	0	1	(1	0)	18	5	6	7	10	1	20	0	0	1	0	0	-	0	.267	.393	.400
2 ML YEARS			54	149	33	10	0	5	(2	3)	58	18	20	19	22	3	60	0	0	1	0	0	-	4	.221	.320	.389

Yonder Alonso

Bats: L **Throws:** R **Pos:** PH-17; 1B-6 **Ht:** 6'2" **Wt:** 215 **Born:** 4/8/1987 **Age:** 24

Year	Team	Lg	G	AB	H	2B	3B	HR	(Hm	Rd)	TB	R	RBI	RC	TBB	IBB	SO	HBP	SH	SF	SB	CS	SB%	GDP	Avg	OBP	Slg
2008	Srsota	A+	6	19	6	1	0	0	(-	-)	7	1	2	3	5	0	5	0	0	1	0	0	-	0	.316	.440	.368
2009	Srsota	A+	49	175	53	13	0	7	(-	-)	87	21	38	33	24	0	30	0	0	2	0	1	.00	6	.303	.383	.497
2009	Carlina	AA	29	105	31	11	0	2	(-	-)	48	12	14	19	14	0	15	0	0	2	1	0	1.00	1	.295	.372	.457
2009	Reds	R	6	15	2	0	0	0	(-	-)	2	0	0	0	3	1	1	0	0	0	0	0	-	0	.133	.278	.133
2010	Carlina	AA	31	101	27	5	0	3	(-	-)	41	19	13	17	19	2	16	1	0	0	4	2	.67	5	.267	.388	.406
2010	Lsvlle	AAA	101	406	120	31	2	12	(-	-)	191	50	56	70	37	2	76	1	0	1	9	1	.90	12	.296	.355	.470
2010	Cin	NL	22	29	6	2	0	0	(0	0)	8	2	3	0	0	0	10	0	0	0	0	0	-	1	.207	.207	.276

Pedro Alvarez

Bats: L **Throws:** R **Pos:** 3B-94; PH-1 **Ht:** 6'3" **Wt:** 223 **Born:** 2/6/1987 **Age:** 24

Year	Team	Lg	G	AB	H	2B	3B	HR	(Hm	Rd)	TB	R	RBI	RC	TBB	IBB	SO	HBP	SH	SF	SB	CS	SB%	GDP	Avg	OBP	Slg
2009	Lynbrg	A+	66	243	60	14	1	14	(-	-)	118	38	55	42	37	4	70	0	0	4	1	1	.50	3	.247	.342	.486
2009	Altna	AA	60	222	74	18	0	13	(-	-)	131	42	40	53	34	5	59	0	0	2	1	0	1.00	4	.333	.419	.590
2010	Indy	AAA	66	242	67	15	4	13	(-	-)	129	42	53	46	32	2	68	2	0	2	4	4	.50	4	.277	.363	.533
2010	Pit	NL	95	347	89	21	1	16	(12	4)	160	42	64	50	37	1	119	0	0	2	0	0	-	8	.256	.326	.461

Hector Ambriz

Pitches: R Bats: L Pos: RP-34 AMM-brizz Ht: 6'2" Wt: 235 Born: 5/24/1984 Age: 27

Year	Team	Lg	G	GS	CG	GF	IP	BFP	H	R	ER	HR	SH	SF	HB	TBB	IBB	SO	WP	Bk	W	L	Pct	Sh	Sv-Op	Hld	ERC	ERA
2006	Msoula	R+	15	4	0	3	42.1	165	29	10	9	1	1	2	0	11	0	52	6	0	1	3	.250	0	3--	-	1.72	1.91
2007	Visalia	A+	28	26	2	1	150.0	640	137	79	68	12	3	12	6	50	1	133	14	0	10	8	.556	0	0--	-	3.30	4.08
2008	Mobile	AA	27	26	2	1	152.2	651	155	91	83	22	4	4	3	47	0	118	10	0	5	13	.278	0	0--	-	4.17	4.89
2009	Mobile	AA	5	5	0	0	29.0	109	18	7	7	1	3	0	0	6	0	32	0	0	3	2	.600	0	0--	-	1.33	2.17
2009	Reno	AAA	23	22	0	0	127.2	578	164	88	79	12	9	2	2	40	1	103	4	1	9	9	.500	0	0--	-	5.36	5.57
2010	Clmbs	AAA	7	0	0	0	8.0	35	9	1	1	0	0	1	0	1	0	15	1	0	0	0	-	0	0--	-	2.85	1.13
2010	Cle	AL	34	0	0	20	48.1	224	68	31	30	10	2	3	1	17	1	37	4	0	0	2	.000	0	0-0	0	7.30	5.59

Brett Anderson

Pitches: L Bats: L Pos: SP-19 Ht: 6'4" Wt: 235 Born: 2/1/1988 Age: 23

Year	Team	Lg	G	GS	CG	GF	IP	BFP	H	R	ER	HR	SH	SF	HB	TBB	IBB	SO	WP	Bk	W	L	Pct	Sh	Sv-Op	Hld	ERC	ERA
2007	Sbend	A	14	14	0	0	81.1	326	76	26	20	3	3	5	2	10	0	85	6	0	8	4	.667	0	0--	-	2.40	2.21
2007	Visalia	A+	9	9	0	0	39.0	174	50	23	21	6	1	0	1	11	0	40	1	2	3	3	.500	0	0--	-	5.79	4.85
2008	Stcktn	A+	14	13	0	0	74.0	311	68	35	34	5	1	2	4	18	0	80	5	1	9	4	.692	0	0--	-	2.98	4.14
2008	Mdland	AA	6	6	0	0	31.0	125	27	10	9	3	0	0	1	9	0	38	0	1	2	1	.667	0	0--	-	3.14	2.61
2010	Scrmto	AAA	3	3	0	0	13.1	61	19	6	6	0	0	0	1	3	0	12	0	0	1	0	1.000	0	0--	-	5.41	4.05
2010	As	R	2	2	0	0	6.0	25	11	2	2	0	0	1	0	0	0	6	0	0	0	0	-	0	0--	-	8.69	3.00
2009	Oak	AL	30	30	1	0	175.1	735	180	94	79	20	4	4	3	45	1	150	0	1	11	11	.500	1	0-0	0	3.84	4.06
2010	Oak	AL	19	19	0	0	112.1	470	112	41	35	6	3	2	7	22	2	75	4	2	7	6	.538	0	0-0	0	3.16	2.80
	2 ML YEARS		49	49	1	0	287.2	1205	292	135	114	26	7	6	10	67	3	225	4	3	18	17	.514	1	0-0	0	3.57	3.57

Bryan Anderson

Bats: L Throws: R Pos: C-8; PH-8 Ht: 6'1" Wt: 200 Born: 12/16/1986 Age: 24

Year	Team	Lg	G	AB	H	2B	3B	HR	(Hm	Rd)	TB	R	RBI	RC	TBB	IBB	SO	HBP	SH	SF	SB	CS	SB%	GDP	Avg	OBP	Slg
2005	JhsCty	R+	51	154	51	8	1	6	(-	-)	79	28	36	31	15	1	29	1	1	5	6	1	.86	3	.331	.383	.513
2006	QuadC	A	109	381	115	29	3	3	(-	-)	159	50	51	61	42	2	66	5	1	2	2	6	.25	13	.302	.377	.417
2007	Sprgfld	AA	103	389	116	15	1	6	(-	-)	151	51	53	55	32	1	77	2	2	6	0	1	.00	9	.298	.350	.388
2008	Sprgfld	AA	19	80	31	5	0	2	(-	-)	42	12	14	16	4	0	12	0	1	1	0	0	-	3	.388	.412	.525
2008	Memp	AAA	73	235	66	13	2	2	(-	-)	89	27	27	36	32	3	46	1	5	2	2	0	1.00	2	.281	.367	.379
2009	Memp	AAA	53	163	40	7	3	4	(-	-)	65	22	11	10	10	1	42	1	0	0	1	0	1.00	2	.245	.293	.399
2009	Cards	R	5	16	5	0	0	1	(-	-)	8	3	2	3	4	0	4	0	0	0	1	0	1.00	0	.313	.450	.500
2010	Memp	AAA	82	270	73	12	0	12	(-	-)	121	39	42	42	27	1	54	3	0	2	0	0	-	5	.270	.341	.448
2010	StL	NL	15	32	9	2	0	0	(0	0)	11	1	4	5	1	0	7	1	0	1	0	0	-	0	.281	.314	.344

Garret Anderson

Bats: L Throws: L Pos: PH-53; LF-27; RF-8 Ht: 6'3" Wt: 225 Born: 6/30/1972 Age: 39

Year	Team	Lg	G	AB	H	2B	3B	HR	(Hm	Rd)	TB	R	RBI	RC	TBB	IBB	SO	HBP	SH	SF	SB	CS	SB%	GDP	Avg	OBP	Slg
1994	LAA	AL	5	13	5	0	0	0	(0	0)	5	0	1	2	0	0	2	0	0	0	0	0	-	0	.385	.385	.385
1995	LAA	AL	106	374	120	19	1	16	(7	9)	189	50	69	63	19	4	65	1	2	4	6	2	.75	0	.321	.352	.505
1996	LAA	AL	150	607	173	33	2	12	(7	5)	246	79	72	68	27	5	84	0	5	3	7	9	.44	12	.285	.314	.405
1997	LAA	AL	154	624	189	36	3	8	(3	5)	255	76	92	80	30	6	70	2	1	5	10	4	.71	20	.303	.334	.409
1998	LAA	AL	156	622	183	41	7	15	(4	11)	283	62	79	88	29	8	80	1	3	3	8	3	.73	13	.294	.325	.455
1999	LAA	AL	157	620	188	36	2	21	(10	11)	291	88	80	92	34	8	81	0	0	6	3	4	.43	15	.303	.336	.469
2000	LAA	AL	159	647	185	40	3	35	(20	15)	336	92	117	95	24	5	87	0	0	9	7	6	.54	21	.286	.307	.519
2001	LAA	AL	161	672	194	39	2	28	(13	15)	321	83	123	97	27	4	100	0	0	5	13	6	.68	12	.289	.314	.478
2002	LAA	AL	158	638	195	56	3	29	(13	16)	344	93	123	108	30	11	80	0	0	10	4	6	.60	11	.306	.332	.539
2003	LAA	AL	159	638	201	49	4	29	(12	17)	345	80	116	114	31	10	83	0	0	4	6	3	.67	15	.315	.345	.541
2004	LAA	AL	112	442	133	20	1	14	(4	10)	197	57	75	70	29	6	75	1	0	3	2	1	.67	3	.301	.343	.446
2005	LAA	AL	142	575	163	34	1	17	(5	12)	250	68	96	82	23	8	84	0	0	5	1	1	.50	13	.283	.308	.435
2006	LAA	AL	141	543	152	28	2	17	(9	8)	235	63	85	75	38	11	95	0	0	7	1	0	1.00	8	.280	.323	.433
2007	LAA	AL	108	417	124	31	1	16	(11	5)	205	67	80	85	27	9	64	0	0	6	1	0	1.00	8	.297	.336	.492
2008	LAA	AL	145	557	163	27	3	15	(9	6)	241	66	84	86	29	6	77	1	0	6	7	4	.64	11	.293	.325	.433
2009	Atl	NL	135	496	133	27	0	13	(8	5)	199	52	61	50	27	2	73	2	0	9	1	0	1.00	11	.268	.303	.401
2010	LAD	NL	80	155	28	6	1	2	(0	2)	42	8	12	7	5	1	34	0	1	2	1	0	1.00	6	.181	.204	.271
	Postseason		36	147	36	5	1	5	(2	3)	58	17	22	14	5	0	20	0	0	2	0	1	.00	2	.245	.266	.395
	17 ML YEARS		2228	8640	2529	522	36	287	(136	151)	3984	1084	1365	1242	429	104	1224	8	13	87	80	47	.63	197	.293	.324	.461

Lars Anderson

Bats: L Throws: L Pos: 1B-18; PR-2 Ht: 6'4" Wt: 215 Born: 9/25/1987 Age: 23

Year	Team	Lg	G	AB	H	2B	3B	HR	(Hm	Rd)	TB	R	RBI	RC	TBB	IBB	SO	HBP	SH	SF	SB	CS	SB%	GDP	Avg	OBP	Slg
2007	Grnville	A	124	458	132	35	3	10	(-	-)	203	69	69	81	71	1	112	2	0	2	2	4	.33	10	.288	.385	.443
2007	Lancst	A+	10	35	12	2	0	1	(-	-)	17	13	9	9	11	0	9	0	0	1	0	0	-	0	.343	.489	.486
2008	Lancst	A+	77	306	97	19	1	13	(-	-)	157	58	50	65	46	1	64	3	0	3	0	0	-	10	.317	.408	.513
2008	Portlnd	AA	41	133	42	13	0	5	(-	-)	70	27	30	31	29	1	43	0	0	1	1	0	1.00	5	.316	.436	.526
2009	Portlnd	AA	119	447	104	23	0	9	(-	-)	154	50	51	55	63	4	114	1	0	1	2	0	1.00	8	.233	.328	.345
2010	Portlnd	AA	17	62	22	5	0	5	(-	-)	42	13	16	16	7	0	16	0	0	2	1	1	.50	0	.355	.408	.677
2010	Pwtckt	AAA	113	409	107	32	3	10	(-	-)	175	49	53	62	44	2	109	6	0	3	2	2	.50	10	.262	.340	.428
2010	Bos	AL	18	35	7	1	0	0	(0	0)	8	4	4	4	7	0	8	0	0	1	0	0	-	1	.200	.326	.229

Robert Andino

Bats: R **Throws:** R **Pos:** 2B-8; SS-7; 3B-6

Ht: 6'0" **Wt:** 195 **Born:** 4/25/1984 **Age:** 27

Year	Team	Lg	G	AB	H	2B	3B	HR	(Hm	Rd)	TB	R	RBI	RC	TBB	IBB	SO	HBP	SH	SF	SB	CS	SB%	GDP	Avg	OBP	Slg
2010	Norfolk*	AAA	132	546	144	30	4	13	(-	-)	221	72	76	71	29	0	110	4	2	7	16	3	.84	18	.264	.302	.405
2005	Fla	NL	17	44	7	4	0	0	(0	0)	11	4	1	1	5	1	8	0	1	0	1	0	1.00	2	.159	.245	.250
2006	Fla	NL	11	24	4	1	0	0	(0	0)	5	0	2	0	1	0	6	0	1	2	1	0	1.00	0	.167	.185	.208
2007	Fla	NL	7	13	5	1	0	0	(0	0)	6	0	0	1	0	0	2	0	0	0	0	0	-	0	.385	.385	.462
2008	Fla	NL	44	63	13	2	0	2	(1	1)	21	7	9	7	4	0	23	0	1	0	0	0	-	1	.206	.254	.333
2009	Bal	AL	78	198	44	7	0	2	(1	1)	57	31	10	11	15	1	47	0	0	2	3	3	.50	6	.222	.274	.288
2010	Bal	AL	16	61	18	4	0	2	(2	0)	28	6	6	4	3	0	13	1	0	1	1	1	.50	3	.295	.333	.459
6 ML YEARS			173	403	91	19	0	6	(4	2)	128	48	28	24	28	2	99	1	3	5	6	4	.60	12	.226	.275	.318

Elvis Andrus

Bats: R **Throws:** R **Pos:** SS-148; PH-3

ANN-druess

Ht: 6'0" **Wt:** 200 **Born:** 8/26/1988 **Age:** 22

Year	Team	Lg	G	AB	H	2B	3B	HR	(Hm	Rd)	TB	R	RBI	RC	TBB	IBB	SO	HBP	SH	SF	SB	CS	SB%	GDP	Avg	OBP	Slg
2005	Braves	R	46	166	49	6	1	3	(-	-)	66	26	20	26	19	0	28	4	0	2	7	4	.64	1	.295	.377	.398
2005	Danvle	R+	6	18	5	1	0	0	(-	-)	6	3	1	3	4	0	4	0	0	0	1	0	1.00	0	.278	.409	.333
2006	Rome	A	111	437	116	25	4	3	(-	-)	158	67	50	52	36	1	91	2	2	1	23	15	.61	8	.265	.324	.362
2007	MrtlBh	A+	99	385	94	20	3	3	(-	-)	129	59	37	48	44	0	88	6	3	2	25	7	.78	8	.244	.330	.335
2007	Bkrsfld	A+	27	110	33	2	0	2	(-	-)	41	19	12	15	10	0	19	2	1	0	15	8	.65	2	.300	.369	.373
2008	Frisco	AA	118	482	142	19	2	4	(-	-)	177	82	65	70	38	0	91	6	3	6	54	16	.77	17	.295	.350	.367
2009	Tex	AL	145	480	128	17	8	6	(3	3)	179	72	40	65	40	0	77	6	12	3	33	6	.85	4	.267	.329	.373
2010	Tex	AL	148	588	156	15	3	0	(0	0)	177	88	35	79	64	0	96	5	17	0	32	15	.68	6	.265	.342	.301
2 ML YEARS			293	1068	284	32	11	6	(3	3)	356	160	75	144	104	0	173	11	29	3	65	21	.76	10	.266	.336	.333

Rick Ankiel

Bats: L **Throws:** L **Pos:** CF-70; PH-5; PR-4

ANN-keel

Ht: 6'2" **Wt:** 205 **Born:** 7/19/1979 **Age:** 31

Year	Team	Lg	G	AB	H	2B	3B	HR	(Hm	Rd)	TB	R	RBI	RC	TBB	IBB	SO	HBP	SH	SF	SB	CS	SB%	GDP	Avg	OBP	Slg
2010	Omha*	AAA	18	67	17	6	0	4	(-	-)	35	8	9	9	1	0	19	0	0	0	0	0	-	1	.254	.265	.522
1999	StL	NL	9	10	1	0	0	0	(0	0)	1	0	0	0	0	0	3	0	1	0	0	0	-	0	.100	.100	.100
2000	StL	NL	33	68	17	1	1	2	(2	0)	26	8	9	0	4	0	20	0	1	0	0	0	-	0	.250	.292	.382
2001	StL	NL	6	8	0	0	0	0	(0	0)	0	1	0	0	1	0	5	0	1	0	0	0	-	0	.000	.111	.000
2004	StL	NL	5	1	0	0	0	0	(0	0)	0	0	0	0	1	0	1	0	0	0	0	0	-	0	.000	.500	.000
2007	StL	NL	47	172	49	8	1	11	(9	2)	92	31	39	32	13	0	41	0	1	4	1	0	1.00	3	.285	.328	.535
2008	StL	NL	120	413	109	21	2	25	(11	14)	209	65	71	60	42	3	100	5	0	3	2	1	.67	8	.264	.337	.506
2009	StL	NL	122	372	86	21	2	11	(4	7)	144	50	38	32	26	4	99	3	0	3	4	3	.57	5	.231	.285	.387
2010	2 Tms		74	211	49	13	1	6	(1	5)	82	31	24	22	26	2	71	2	0	1	3	1	.75	3	.232	.321	.389
10	KC	AL	27	92	24	7	0	4	(1	3)	43	14	15	11	7	0	29	1	0	1	1	0	1.00	2	.261	.317	.467
10	Atl	NL	47	119	25	6	1	2	(0	2)	39	17	9	11	19	2	42	1	0	0	2	1	.67	1	.210	.324	.328
Postseason			5	3	0	0	0	0	(0	0)	0	0	0	0	0	0	2	0	0	0	0	0	-	0	.000	.000	.000
8 ML YEARS			416	1255	311	64	7	55	(27	28)	554	186	181	146	113	9	340	10	4	11	10	5	.67	20	.248	.312	.441

J.P. Arencibia

Bats: R **Throws:** R **Pos:** C-8; DH-3

ah-renn-SEE-bee-ah

Ht: 6'1" **Wt:** 210 **Born:** 1/5/1986 **Age:** 25

Year	Team	Lg	G	AB	H	2B	3B	HR	(Hm	Rd)	TB	R	RBI	RC	TBB	IBB	SO	HBP	SH	SF	SB	CS	SB%	GDP	Avg	OBP	Slg
2007	Auburn	A-	63	228	58	17	1	3	(-	-)	86	31	25	27	14	1	56	5	0	2	0	0	-	3	.254	.309	.377
2008	Dnedin	A+	59	248	78	22	0	13	(-	-)	139	38	62	47	11	2	46	1	0	2	0	0	-	9	.315	.344	.560
2008	NHam	AA	67	262	74	14	0	14	(-	-)	130	32	43	39	7	0	55	2	0	4	0	0	-	7	.282	.302	.496
2009	LsVgs	AAA	116	466	110	32	1	21	(-	-)	207	67	75	60	26	0	114	6	0	2	0	1	.00	11	.236	.284	.444
2010	LsVgs	AAA	104	412	124	36	1	32	(-	-)	258	76	85	91	38	1	85	3	0	6	0	0	-	13	.301	.359	.626
2010	Tor	AL	11	35	5	1	0	2	(2	0)	12	3	4	4	2	0	11	0	0	0	0	0	-	0	.143	.189	.343

Joaquin Arias

Bats: R **Throws:** R **Pos:** 2B-38; PH-18; PR-12; 1B-5; SS-5; DH-3; LF-1

Ht: 6'1" **Wt:** 170 **Born:** 9/21/1984 **Age:** 26

Year	Team	Lg	G	AB	H	2B	3B	HR	(Hm	Rd)	TB	R	RBI	RC	TBB	IBB	SO	HBP	SH	SF	SB	CS	SB%	GDP	Avg	OBP	Slg
2010	Frisco*	AA	8	31	6	0	0	0	(-	-)	6	4	1	1	3	0	7	0	0	1	0	0	-	0	.194	.257	.194
2006	Tex	AL	6	11	6	1	0	0	(0	0)	7	4	1	3	1	0	0	0	0	0	0	1	.00	0	.545	.583	.636
2008	Tex	AL	32	110	32	7	3	0	(0	0)	45	15	9	15	7	0	12	2	1	0	4	1	.80	4	.291	.345	.409
2009	Tex	AL	3	8	0	0	0	0	(0	0)	0	0	0	0	0	0	3	0	1	0	0	0	-	0	.000	.000	.000
2010	2 Tms		72	128	33	6	1	0	(0	0)	41	23	13	10	4	0	23	0	2	0	1	0	1.00	2	.258	.280	.320
10	Tex	AL	50	98	27	5	1	0	(0	0)	34	18	9	8	2	0	17	0	1	0	1	0	1.00	2	.276	.290	.347
10	NYM	NL	22	30	6	1	0	0	(0	0)	7	5	4	2	2	0	6	0	1	0	0	0	-	0	.200	.250	.233
4 ML YEARS			113	257	71	14	4	0	(0	0)	93	42	23	28	12	0	38	2	4	0	5	2	.71	6	.276	.314	.362

Jose Arredondo

Pitches: R **Bats:** R **Pos:** P **Ht:** 6'0" **Wt:** 175 **Born:** 3/12/1984 **Age:** 27

Year Team	Lg	G	GS	CG	GF	IP	BFP	H	R	ER	HR	SH	SF	HB	TBB	IBB	SO	WP	Bk	W	L	Pct	Sh	Sv-Op	Hld	ERC	ERA
2004 Angels	R	8	0	0	4	12.1	56	14	10	4	1	1	0	1	4	0	14	2	0	0	0	-	0	1--	-	4.61	2.92
2005 Ark	AA	5	0	0	3	5.1	22	5	2	2	0	0	0	1	4	0	4	1	0	0	0	-	0	0--	-	4.84	3.38
2005 Orem	R+	15	13	0	0	68.2	295	76	34	32	4	1	1	6	20	0	60	6	0	5	0	1.000	0	0--	-	4.39	4.19
2006 RCuca	A+	15	15	0	0	90.0	360	62	28	23	4	1	5	6	35	0	115	6	0	5	6	.455	0	0--	-	2.36	2.30
2006 Ark	AA	11	11	1	0	60.2	280	80	47	44	8	2	3	1	22	0	48	6	0	2	3	.400	1	0--	-	6.09	6.53
2007 Ark	AA	23	0	0	18	25.0	102	16	10	7	2	1	2	0	12	0	28	1	0	0	1	.000	0	10--	-	2.35	2.52
2007 Salt Lk	AAA	2	0	0	1	3.0	13	2	1	1	0	1	1	0	2	0	1	0	0	0	0	-	0	0--	-	2.54	3.00
2008 Salt Lk	AAA	15	0	0	15	17.0	66	12	4	4	2	1	1	1	4	0	15	1	0	1	1	.500	0	10--	-	2.32	2.12
2009 Salt Lk	AAA	19	0	0	11	20.2	88	13	7	5	1	2	1	2	14	1	24	1	0	1	1	.500	0	1--	-	3.08	2.18
2008 LAA	AL	52	0	0	10	61.0	244	42	15	11	3	0	0	1	22	0	55	1	0	10	2	.833	0	0-7	16	2.08	1.62
2009 LAA	AL	43	0	0	15	45.0	202	47	30	30	6	3	1	0	23	2	47	5	1	2	3	.400	0	0-1	16	4.91	6.00
Postseason		3	0	0	1	3.2	15	2	0	0	0	0	0	0	2	0	4	0	0	0	0	-	0	0-0	0	1.65	0.00
2 ML YEARS		95	0	0	25	106.0	446	89	45	41	9	3	1	1	45	2	102	6	1	12	5	.706	0	0-8	32	3.19	3.48

Jake Arrieta

Pitches: R **Bats:** R **Pos:** SP-18 **Ht:** 6'4" **Wt:** 220 **Born:** 3/6/1986 **Age:** 25

Year Team	Lg	G	GS	CG	GF	IP	BFP	H	R	ER	HR	SH	SF	HB	TBB	IBB	SO	WP	Bk	W	L	Pct	Sh	Sv-Op	Hld	ERC	ERA
2008 Frdrck	A+	20	20	0	0	113.0	463	80	44	36	7	2	2	6	51	0	120	2	1	6	5	.545	0	0--	-	2.70	2.87
2009 Bowie	AA	11	11	2	0	59.0	244	45	21	17	4	0	1	4	23	0	70	2	0	6	3	.667	2	0--	-	2.82	2.59
2009 Norfolk	AAA	17	17	0	0	91.2	401	97	46	40	9	6	2	9	33	0	78	4	0	5	8	.385	0	0--	-	4.68	3.93
2010 Norfolk	AAA	12	11	0	0	73.0	293	48	18	15	3	3	0	2	34	0	64	1	0	6	2	.750	0	0--	-	2.31	1.85
2010 Bal	AL	18	18	0	0	100.1	449	106	57	52	9	4	2	4	48	3	52	5	0	6	6	.500	0	0-0	0	4.74	4.66

Bronson Arroyo

Pitches: R **Bats:** R **Pos:** SP-33 uh-ROY-oh **Ht:** 6'4" **Wt:** 194 **Born:** 2/24/1977 **Age:** 34

Year Team	Lg	G	GS	CG	GF	IP	BFP	H	R	ER	HR	SH	SF	HB	TBB	IBB	SO	WP	Bk	W	L	Pct	Sh	Sv-Op	Hld	ERC	ERA
2000 Pit	NL	20	12	0	1	71.2	338	88	61	51	10	5	2	4	36	6	50	3	1	2	6	.250	0	0-0	2	6.18	6.40
2001 Pit	NL	24	13	1	1	88.1	390	99	54	50	12	4	6	4	34	6	39	4	1	5	7	.417	0	0-0	2	5.09	5.09
2002 Pit	NL	9	4	0	1	27.0	123	30	14	12	1	1	1	0	15	3	22	0	0	2	1	.667	0	0-0	1	4.64	4.00
2003 Bos	AL	6	0	0	2	17.1	66	10	5	4	0	0	0	1	4	2	14	0	0	0	0	-	0	1-1	0	1.14	2.08
2004 Bos	AL	32	29	0	0	178.2	764	171	99	80	17	5	4	20	47	3	142	5	0	10	9	.526	0	0-0	0	3.65	4.03
2005 Bos	AL	35	32	0	1	205.1	878	213	116	103	22	4	4	14	54	3	100	5	1	14	10	.583	0	0-0	0	4.04	4.51
2006 Cin	NL	35	35	3	0	240.2	992	222	98	88	31	9	2	5	64	7	184	6	0	14	11	.560	1	0-0	0	3.37	3.29
2007 Cin	NL	34	34	1	0	210.2	921	232	109	99	28	10	7	13	63	6	156	4	0	9	15	.375	0	0-0	0	4.68	4.23
2008 Cin	NL	34	34	1	0	200.0	871	219	116	106	29	13	6	6	68	2	163	6	0	15	11	.577	0	0-0	0	4.83	4.77
2009 Cin	NL	33	33	3	0	220.1	923	214	101	94	31	9	5	9	65	6	127	1	0	15	13	.536	2	0-0	0	3.94	3.84
2010 Cin	NL	33	33	2	0	215.2	880	188	95	93	29	0	5	6	50	5	121	1	1	17	10	.630	0	0-0	0	3.21	3.88
Postseason		10	2	0	3	17.0	80	19	14	14	5	0	0	2	9	0	20	0	0	0	0	-	0	0-0	2	7.30	7.41
11 ML YEARS		295	259	11	6	1675.2	7146	1686	868	780	210	66	42	82	509	49	1118	35	4	103	93	.526	3	1-1	3	4.06	4.19

Scott Atchison

Pitches: R **Bats:** R **Pos:** RP-42, SP-1 **Ht:** 6'2" **Wt:** 200 **Born:** 3/29/1976 **Age:** 35

Year Team	Lg	G	GS	CG	GF	IP	BFP	H	R	ER	HR	SH	SF	HB	TBB	IBB	SO	WP	Bk	W	L	Pct	Sh	Sv-Op	Hld	ERC	ERA
2010 Pwtckt*	AAA	11	0	0	3	13.1	59	13	6	6	0	0	0	0	5	0	17	2	0	1	0	1.000	0	0--	-	3.01	4.05
2004 Sea	AL	25	0	0	8	30.2	133	29	12	12	4	2	1	0	14	2	36	2	0	2	3	.400	0	0-0	2	4.08	3.52
2005 Sea	AL	6	0	0	2	6.2	27	7	5	5	1	0	0	0	1	0	9	0	0	0	0	-	0	0-0	3	3.77	6.75
2007 SF	NL	22	0	0	4	30.2	131	32	14	14	5	1	2	1	10	0	25	2	0	0	0	-	0	0-1	5	4.65	4.11
2010 Bos	AL	43	1	0	8	60.0	253	58	37	30	9	1	2	1	19	2	41	4	0	2	3	.400	0	0-0	7	3.92	4.50
4 ML YEARS		96	1	0	22	128.0	544	126	68	61	19	4	5	2	44	4	111	8	0	4	6	.400	0	0-1	14	4.12	4.29

Luis Atilano

Pitches: R **Bats:** R **Pos:** SP-16 **Ht:** 6'2" **Wt:** 218 **Born:** 5/10/1985 **Age:** 26

Year Team	Lg	G	GS	CG	GF	IP	BFP	H	R	ER	HR	SH	SF	HB	TBB	IBB	SO	WP	Bk	W	L	Pct	Sh	Sv-Op	Hld	ERC	ERA
2003 Braves	R	12	12	1	0	54.0	225	61	25	23	5	3	0	3	7	0	24	3	1	3	2	.600	1	0--	-	3.96	3.83
2004 Danvle	R+	13	13	0	0	64.1	268	64	32	30	7	4	3	5	10	0	54	0	0	5	1	.833	0	0--	-	3.44	4.20
2005 Rome	A	24	24	1	0	136.0	574	138	77	63	17	2	5	7	32	0	66	6	0	8	9	.471	0	0--	-	3.88	4.17
2006 MrtlBh	A+	19	18	2	0	116.0	491	134	63	58	16	2	6	6	27	0	45	4	0	6	7	.462	0	0--	-	4.91	4.50
2007 Nats	R	1	0	0	0	1.1	7	1	1	1	0	0	0	1	1	0	2	1	0	0	0	-	0	0--	-	5.91	6.75
2008 Hgrstn	A	7	3	0	2	25.2	112	29	14	9	1	0	0	7	0	0	13	1	1	0	0	-	0	1--	-	3.81	3.16
2008 Ptomc	A+	15	11	0	1	62.0	239	50	21	16	5	4	1	2	14	0	39	1	1	5	2	.714	0	0--	-	2.53	2.32
2008 Hrsbrg	AA	2	1	0	0	6.0	25	6	3	1	0	1	2	0	2	0	3	0	0	1	0	1.000	0	0--	-	3.19	1.50
2009 Hrsbrg	AA	21	20	0	0	114.2	499	143	58	53	12	1	2	4	27	1	61	1	0	7	8	.467	0	0--	-	5.07	4.16
2009 Syrcse	AAA	2	2	0	0	11.0	43	11	3	3	2	0	0	1	1	0	5	1	0	2	0	1.000	0	0--	-	3.49	2.45
2010 Syrcse	AAA	3	3	0	0	13.1	59	17	7	7	1	1	2	0	5	0	9	0	1	2	1	.667	0	0--	-	5.54	4.73
2010 Was	NL	16	16	0	0	85.2	385	96	56	49	11	7	3	2	32	5	40	1	1	6	7	.462	0	0-0	0	4.77	5.15

Garrett Atkins

Bats: R **Throws:** R **Pos:** 1B-30; DH-9; PH-5   **Ht:** 6'3" **Wt:** 215 **Born:** 12/12/1979 **Age:** 31

Year	Team	Lg	G	AB	H	2B	3B	HR	(Hm	Rd)	TB	R	RBI	RC	TBB	IBB	SO	HBP	SH	SF	SB	CS	SB%	GDP	Avg	OBP	Slg
2003	Col	NL	25	69	11	2	0	0	(0	0)	13	6	4	2	3	0	14	1	0	0	0	0	-	1	.159	.205	.188
2004	Col	NL	15	28	10	2	0	1	(1	0)	15	3	8	8	4	0	3	0	0	1	0	0	-	0	.357	.424	.536
2005	Col	NL	138	519	149	31	1	13	(9	4)	221	62	89	74	45	1	72	5	0	4	0	2	.00	18	.287	.347	.426
2006	Col	NL	157	602	198	48	1	29	(15	14)	335	117	120	129	79	6	76	7	0	7	4	0	1.00	24	.329	.409	.556
2007	Col	NL	157	605	182	35	1	25	(10	15)	294	83	111	106	67	3	96	2	0	10	3	1	.75	16	.301	.367	.486
2008	Col	NL	155	611	175	32	3	21	(9	12)	276	86	99	76	40	0	100	3	0	10	1	1	.50	20	.286	.328	.452
2009	Col	NL	126	354	80	12	1	9	(4	5)	121	37	48	44	41	2	58	2	0	2	0	0	-	8	.226	.308	.342
2010	Bal	AL	44	140	30	7	0	1	(1	0)	40	5	9	8	12	0	30	0	0	0	0	0	-	7	.214	.276	.286
Postseason			15	53	10	5	0	1	(1	0)	18	6	5	5	5	1	8	1	0	0	0	0	-	0	.189	.271	.340
8 ML YEARS			817	2928	835	169	7	99	(49	50)	1315	399	488	447	291	12	449	20	0	34	8	4	.67	94	.285	.350	.449

Mitch Atkins

Pitches: R **Bats:** R **Pos:** RP-5   **Ht:** 6'3" **Wt:** 230 **Born:** 10/1/1985 **Age:** 25

Year	Team	Lg	G	GS	CG	GF	IP	BFP	H	R	ER	HR	SH	SF	HB	TBB	IBB	SO	WP	Bk	W	L	Pct	Sh	Sv-Op	Hld	ERC	ERA
2004	Cubs	R	10	8	0	0	29.2	146	42	33	26	0	0	2	4	14	0	20	8	1	2	2	.500	0	0--	-	6.55	7.89
2005	Boise	A-	15	15	0	0	73.1	337	85	45	41	8	4	2	9	30	0	59	6	4	3	6	.333	0	0--	-	5.60	5.03
2006	Peoria	A	25	25	0	0	138.1	570	110	47	37	10	1	6	3	53	0	127	4	3	13	4	.765	0	0--	-	2.83	2.41
2007	Dytona	A+	20	20	1	0	115.0	467	99	51	40	14	3	4	8	31	0	88	2	1	8	7	.533	0	0--	-	3.29	3.13
2007	Tenn	AA	7	4	0	0	26.0	119	30	18	16	5	2	0	2	11	0	18	2	0	1	1	.500	0	0--	-	6.07	5.54
2008	Tenn	AA	18	18	0	0	110.0	462	107	58	46	14	2	1	3	27	0	88	1	1	9	6	.600	0	0--	-	3.58	3.76
2008	Iowa	AAA	10	10	0	0	54.1	234	48	29	27	11	1	3	4	23	0	44	0	0	8	1	.889	0	0--	-	4.52	4.47
2009	Iowa	AAA	27	27	1	0	146.1	656	164	113	107	26	6	9	11	52	1	127	3	3	8	12	.400	0	0--	-	5.43	6.58
2010	Iowa	AAA	28	15	0	3	106.2	454	98	49	43	14	3	0	3	42	1	76	3	0	8	3	.727	0	1--	-	3.91	3.63
2009	ChC	NL	2	0	0	1	2.0	7	1	0	0	0	0	0	0	0	0	0	0	0	0	0	-	0	0-0	0	0.54	0.00
2010	ChC	NL	5	0	0	2	10.0	49	12	8	7	2	0	0	1	6	0	10	0	0	0	0	-	0	0-0	0	7.19	6.30
2 ML YEARS			7	0	0	3	12.0	56	13	8	7	2	0	0	1	6	0	10	0	0	0	0	-	0	0-0	0	5.69	5.25

Brad Ausmus

Bats: R **Throws:** R **Pos:** C-21   **Ht:** 5'11" **Wt:** 187 **Born:** 4/14/1969 **Age:** 42

Year	Team	Lg	G	AB	H	2B	3B	HR	(Hm	Rd)	TB	R	RBI	RC	TBB	IBB	SO	HBP	SH	SF	SB	CS	SB%	GDP	Avg	OBP	Slg
2010	InldEm*	A+	4	12	6	0	0	0	(-	-)	6	1	2	3	2	0	1	0	0	0	0	0	-	0	.500	.571	.500
2010	Albq*	AAA	4	8	1	0	0	0	(-	-)	1	0	0	0	0	0	2	0	0	0	0	0	-	0	.125	.125	.125
1993	SD	NL	49	160	41	8	1	5	(4	1)	66	18	12	19	6	0	28	0	0	0	2	0	1.00	0	.256	.283	.413
1994	SD	NL	101	327	82	12	1	7	(6	1)	117	45	24	36	30	12	63	1	6	2	5	1	.83	8	.251	.314	.358
1995	SD	NL	103	328	96	16	4	5	(2	3)	135	44	34	49	31	3	56	2	4	4	16	5	.76	6	.293	.353	.412
1996	2 Tms		125	375	83	16	0	5	(2	3)	114	46	35	32	39	1	72	5	6	2	4	8	.33	8	.221	.302	.304
1997	Hou	NL	130	425	113	25	1	4	(1	3)	152	45	44	51	38	4	78	3	6	6	14	6	.70	8	.266	.326	.358
1998	Hou	NL	128	412	111	10	4	6	(2	4)	147	62	45	51	53	11	50	6	3	3	10	3	.77	18	.269	.356	.357
1999	Det	AL	127	458	126	25	6	9	(5	4)	190	62	54	69	51	0	71	14	3	1	12	9	.57	11	.275	.365	.415
2000	Det	AL	150	523	139	25	3	7	(3	4)	191	75	51	68	69	0	79	6	4	2	11	5	.69	19	.266	.357	.365
2001	Hou	NL	128	422	98	23	4	5	(4	1)	144	45	34	38	30	6	64	1	6	2	4	1	.80	13	.232	.284	.341
2002	Hou	NL	130	447	115	19	3	6	(4	2)	158	57	50	44	38	3	71	6	2	3	2	3	.40	30	.257	.322	.353
2003	Hou	NL	143	450	103	12	2	4	(1	3)	131	43	47	34	46	1	66	4	4	5	5	3	.63	8	.229	.303	.291
2004	Hou	NL	129	403	100	14	1	5	(2	3)	131	38	31	34	33	11	56	2	7	3	2	2	.50	13	.248	.306	.325
2005	Hou	NL	134	387	100	19	0	3	(2	1)	128	35	47	42	51	8	48	5	7	1	5	3	.63	17	.258	.351	.331
2006	Hou	NL	139	439	101	16	1	2	(1	1)	125	37	39	36	45	2	71	6	9	3	3	1	.75	21	.230	.308	.285
2007	Hou	NL	117	349	82	16	3	3	(1	2)	113	38	25	28	37	3	74	6	4	1	6	1	.86	11	.235	.318	.324
2008	Hou	NL	81	216	47	8	0	3	(1	2)	64	15	24	25	25	3	41	2	6	1	0	2	.00	4	.218	.303	.296
2009	LAD	NL	36	95	28	4	0	1	(0	1)	35	9	9	13	5	0	21	2	5	0	1	0	1.00	1	.295	.343	.368
2010	LAD	NL	21	63	14	2	0	0	(0	0)	16	4	2	3	7	1	15	1	0	0	0	0	-	3	.222	.310	.254
96	SD	NL	50	149	27	4	0	1	(2	2)	34	16	13	6	13	0	27	3	1	0	1	4	.20	4	.181	.261	.228
96	Det	AL	75	226	56	12	0	4	(2	2)	80	30	22	26	26	1	45	2	5	2	3	4	.43	4	.248	.328	.354
Postseason			35	106	26	5	0	3	(2	1)	40	12	7	8	9	3	29	1	2	1	1	0	1.00	5	.245	.308	.377
18 ML YEARS			1971	6279	1579	270	34	80	(42	38)	2157	718	607	682	634	69	1034	69	82	37	102	53	.66	201	.251	.325	.344

Alex Avila

Bats: L **Throws:** R **Pos:** C-98; PH-9   ah-VEE-lah   **Ht:** 5'11" **Wt:** 210 **Born:** 1/29/1987 **Age:** 24

Year	Team	Lg	G	AB	H	2B	3B	HR	(Hm	Rd)	TB	R	RBI	RC	TBB	IBB	SO	HBP	SH	SF	SB	CS	SB%	GDP	Avg	OBP	Slg
2008	WMich	A	58	213	65	14	0	1	(-	-)	82	21	22	33	27	0	41	1	1	2	0	1	.00	8	.305	.383	.385
2009	Erie	AA	93	329	87	23	1	12	(-	-)	148	52	55	57	52	2	77	1	3	2	2	1	.67	6	.264	.365	.450
2009	Det	AL	29	61	17	4	0	5	(4	1)	36	9	14	12	10	0	18	0	0	1	0	0	-	0	.279	.375	.590
2010	Det	AL	104	294	67	12	0	7	(4	3)	100	28	31	26	36	0	71	2	2	0	2	2	.50	12	.228	.316	.340
2 ML YEARS			133	355	84	16	0	12	(8	4)	136	37	45	38	46	0	89	2	1	1	2	2	.50	12	.237	.327	.383

Mike Aviles

Bats: R **Throws:** R **Pos:** 2B-87; SS-13; 3B-5; PH-4; PR-3; DH-2 uh-VEE-less **Ht:** 5'10" **Wt:** 204 **Born:** 3/13/1981 **Age:** 30

								BATTING												BASERUNNING				AVERAGES		
Year Team	Lg	G	AB	H	2B	3B	HR	(Hm Rd)	TB	R	RBI	RC	TBB	IBB	SO	HBP	SH	SF	SB	CS	SB%	GDP	Avg	OBP	Slg
2010 Omha*	AAA	17	70	19	3	1	1	(- -)	27	8	8	8	4	0	10	1	0	0	0	0	-	1	.271	.320	.386
2008 KC	AL	102	419	136	27	4	10	(4 6)	201	68	51	62	18	4	58	2	0	2	8	3	.73	12	.325	.354	.480
2009 KC	AL	36	120	22	3	1	1	(1 0)	30	10	8	4	4	0	26	0	2	1	1	0	1.00	3	.183	.208	.250
2010 KC	AL	110	424	129	16	3	8	(4 4)	175	63	32	47	20	0	49	1	0	3	14	5	.74	13	.304	.335	.413
3 ML YEARS		248	963	287	46	8	19	(9 10)	406	141	91	113	42	4	133	3	2	6	23	8	.74	28	.298	.327	.422

John Axford

Pitches: R **Bats:** R **Pos:** RP-50 **Ht:** 6'5" **Wt:** 195 **Born:** 4/1/1983 **Age:** 28

				HOW MUCH HE PITCHED							WHAT HE GAVE UP											THE RESULTS					
Year Team	Lg	G	GS	CG	GF	IP	BFP	H	R	ER	HR	SH	SF	HB	TBB	IBB	SO	WP	Bk	W	L	Pct	Sh	Sv-Op	Hld	ERC	ERA
2007 Tampa	A+	5	0	0	2	11.1	45	6	5	3	2	1	0	0	7	0	15	3	0	0	0	-	0	2- -	-	3.00	2.38
2007 S-WB	A	1	0	0	1	0.2	5	2	1	1	0	0	0	0	1	0	1	1	0	0	0	-	0	0- -	-	22.07	13.50
2007 CtnSC	A	13	5	0	3	26.2	129	29	20	13	2	1	1	0	22	0	21	7	0	0	3	.000	0	0- -	-	6.06	4.39
2007 StlsInd	A-	8	0	0	5	24.1	102	13	8	6	0	1	0	0	15	1	30	3	0	1	1	.500	0	2- -	-	1.85	2.22
2008 BrvdCt	A+	26	14	0	1	95.0	433	86	58	48	5	2	3	5	73	0	89	12	0	5	10	.333	0	0- -	-	4.89	4.55
2009 BrvdCt	A+	19	0	0	4	27.2	110	14	5	5	0	1	0	0	16	1	43	1	0	4	1	.800	0	0- -	-	1.60	1.63
2009 Hntsvl	AA	4	0	0	1	7.2	33	7	3	3	1	1	0	0	3	0	9	0	0	0	0	-	0	1- -	-	4.33	3.52
2009 Nashv	AAA	22	0	0	11	33.0	138	23	13	13	2	1	1	0	19	1	37	2	0	5	0	1.000	0	0- -	-	2.81	3.55
2010 Nashv	AAA	12	0	0	3	13.1	58	14	7	3	0	0	0	0	5	0	19	0	0	3	2	.600	0	2- -	-	3.52	2.03
2009 Mil	NL	7	0	0	6	7.2	34	5	3	3	0	0	0	0	6	1	9	1	0	0	0	-	0	1-1	0	2.62	3.52
2010 Mil	NL	50	0	0	43	58.0	238	42	17	16	1	2	2	1	27	3	76	4	0	8	2	.800	0	24-27	3	2.33	2.48
2 ML YEARS		57	0	0	49	65.2	272	47	20	19	1	2	2	1	33	4	85	5	0	8	2	.800	0	25-28	3	2.37	2.60

Erick Aybar

Bats: B **Throws:** R **Pos:** SS-135; PH-4; DH-1; PR-1 EYE-barr **Ht:** 5'10" **Wt:** 170 **Born:** 1/14/1984 **Age:** 27

								BATTING												BASERUNNING				AVERAGES		
Year Team	Lg	G	AB	H	2B	3B	HR	(Hm Rd)	TB	R	RBI	RC	TBB	IBB	SO	HBP	SH	SF	SB	CS	SB%	GDP	Avg	OBP	Slg
2006 LAA	Al	34	40	10	1	1	0	(0 0)	13	5	2	4	0	0	8	0	0	0	1	0	1.00	0	.250	.250	.325
2007 LAA	AL	79	194	46	5	1	1	(0 1)	56	18	19	16	10	0	32	2	3	2	4	4	.50	8	.237	.279	.289
2008 LAA	AL	98	346	96	18	5	3	(2 1)	133	53	39	49	14	0	45	5	9	1	7	2	.78	2	.277	.314	.384
2009 LAA	AL	137	504	157	23	9	5	(2 3)	213	70	58	73	30	1	54	1	11	5	14	7	.67	9	.312	.353	.423
2010 LAA	AL	138	534	135	18	4	5	(3 2)	176	69	29	51	35	1	81	7	11	2	22	8	.73	7	.253	.306	.330
Postseason		14	50	11	2	1	0	(0 0)	15	4	4	4	1	0	4	0	2	0	3	0	1.00	2	.220	.235	.300
5 ML YEARS		486	1618	444	65	20	14	(7 7)	591	215	147	193	89	2	220	19	35	10	48	21	.70	27	.274	.318	.365

Willy Aybar

Bats: B **Throws:** R **Pos:** DH-69; PH-30; 2B-9; 3B-7; 1B-3 EYE-barr **Ht:** 5'11" **Wt:** 205 **Born:** 3/9/1983 **Age:** 28

								BATTING												BASERUNNING				AVERAGES		
Year Team	Lg	G	AB	H	2B	3B	HR	(Hm Rd)	TB	R	RBI	RC	TBB	IBB	SO	HBP	SH	SF	SB	CS	SB%	GDP	Avg	OBP	Slg
2005 LAD	NL	26	86	28	8	0	1	(0 1)	39	12	10	21	18	0	11	1	0	0	3	1	.75	0	.326	.448	.453
2006 2 Tms	NL	79	243	68	18	0	4	(3 1)	98	32	30	33	28	0	36	4	3	0	1	2	.33	7	.280	.364	.403
2008 TB	AL	95	324	82	17	2	10	(4 0)	100	35	39	52	32	3	44	1	1	1	2	2	.60	7	.253	.327	.410
2009 TB	Al	105	296	75	12	0	12	(8 4)	123	38	41	39	34	2	54	2	1	3	1	0	1.00	4	.253	.331	.416
2010 TB	AL	100	270	62	13	0	6	(4 2)	93	22	43	36	30	1	61	3	2	4	0	0	-	4	.230	.309	.344
06 LAD	NL	43	128	32	12	0	3	(2 1)	53	15	22	19	18	0	17	3	2	0	1	0	1.00	5	.250	.356	.414
06 Atl	NL	36	115	36	6	0	1	(1 0)	45	17	8	14	10	0	19	1	1	0	0	2	.00	2	.313	.373	.391
Postseason		14	34	12	2	0	2	(1 1)	20	5	7	9	1	0	6	0	1	1	0	0	-	0	.353	.361	.588
6 ML YEARS		405	1219	315	68	2	33	(19 14)	486	137	157	161	142	6	206	14	7	8	7	5	.58	22	.258	.341	.399

Burke Badenhop

Pitches: R **Bats:** R **Pos:** RP-53 BADE-en-hopp **Ht:** 6'5" **Wt:** 200 **Born:** 2/8/1983 **Age:** 28

				HOW MUCH HE PITCHED							WHAT HE GAVE UP											THE RESULTS					
Year Team	Lg	G	GS	CG	GF	IP	BFP	H	R	ER	HR	SH	SF	HB	TBB	IBB	SO	WP	Bk	W	L	Pct	Sh	Sv-Op	Hld	ERC	ERA
2010 NewOr*	AAA	12	1	0	0	16.0	72	16	6	5	0	1	1	3	7	0	9	2	0	0	1	.000	0	0- -	-	4.21	2.81
2008 Fla	NL	13	8	0	2	47.1	218	55	34	32	7	2	2	3	21	1	35	2	0	2	3	.400	0	0-0	0	5.74	6.08
2009 Fla	NL	35	2	0	7	72.0	303	71	32	30	5	3	2	1	24	4	57	1	0	7	4	.636	0	0-1	2	3.53	3.75
2010 Fla	NL	53	0	0	16	67.2	281	62	33	30	5	5	1	2	21	5	47	1	0	2	5	.286	0	1-3	8	3.12	3.99
3 ML YEARS		101	10	0	25	187.0	802	188	99	92	17	10	5	6	66	10	139	4	0	11	12	.478	0	1-4	10	3.91	4.43

Danys Baez

Pitches: R **Bats:** R **Pos:** RP-51 BYE-ezz **Ht:** 6'3" **Wt:** 225 **Born:** 9/10/1977 **Age:** 33

				HOW MUCH HE PITCHED							WHAT HE GAVE UP											THE RESULTS					
Year Team	Lg	G	GS	CG	GF	IP	BFP	H	R	ER	HR	SH	SF	HB	TBB	IBB	SO	WP	Bk	W	L	Pct	Sh	Sv-Op	Hld	ERC	ERA
2010 LV*	AAA	1	0	0	0	1.0	5	2	1	1	0	0	0	0	0	0	0	0	0	0	0	-	0	0- -	-	7.48	9.00
2001 Cle	AL	43	0	0	8	50.1	202	34	22	14	5	0	1	3	20	4	52	3	0	5	3	.625	0	0-1	14	2.51	2.50
2002 Cle	AL	39	26	1	9	165.1	726	160	84	81	14	2	8	9	82	5	130	6	1	10	11	.476	0	6-8	0	4.35	4.41
2003 Cle	AL	73	0	0	46	75.2	318	65	36	32	9	6	1	4	23	0	66	5	0	2	9	.182	0	25-35	5	3.22	3.81
2004 TB	AL	62	0	0	59	68.0	295	60	31	27	6	5	1	7	29	4	52	3	1	4	4	.500	0	30-33	1	3.73	3.57
2005 TB	AL	67	0	0	64	72.1	308	66	27	23	7	4	2	2	30	4	51	0	0	5	4	.556	0	41-49	3	3.74	2.86
2006 2 Tms	NL	57	0	0	28	59.2	257	60	35	30	3	4	5	7	17	3	39	3	0	5	6	.455	0	9-17	12	3.69	4.53
2007 Bal	AL	53	0	0	25	50.1	233	50	36	36	8	3	1	7	29	5	29	0	0	4	6	.000	0	3-5	14	5.56	6.44
2009 Bal	AL	59	0	0	9	71.2	295	59	36	32	7	1	2	5	22	3	40	2	1	4	6	.400	0	0-2	15	3.06	4.02

Year Team	Lg	HOW MUCH HE PITCHED					WHAT HE GAVE UP												THE RESULTS							
		G	GS	CG	GF	IP	BFP	H	R	ER	HR	SH	SF	HB	TBB	IBB	SO	WP	Bk	W	L	Pct	Sh	Sv-Op	Hld	ERC	ERA
2010 Phi		51	0	0	17	47.2	216	55	31	29	6	4	3	3	23	2	28	1	0	3	4	.429	0	0-2	6	5.78	5.48
06 LAD	NL	46	0	0	27	49.2	213	53	29	24	3	4	5	6	11	2	29	3	0	5	5	.500	0	9-16	6	3.90	4.35
06 Atl	NL	11	0	0	1	10.0	44	7	6	6	0	0	0	1	6	1	10	0	0	0	1	.000	0	0-1	6	2.64	5.40
Postseason		3	0	0	2	3.2	15	4	1	1	0	0	0	0	0	0	6	0	0	0	0	-	0	0-0	0	2.36	2.45
9 ML YEARS		504	26	1	265	661.2	2850	609	338	304	66	28	24	47	275	26	487	23	3	38	53	.418	0	114-152	67	3.92	4.14

Andrew Bailey

Pitches: R Bats: R Pos: RP-47 **Ht: 6'3" Wt: 243 Born: 5/31/1984 Age: 27**

Year Team	Lg	HOW MUCH HE PITCHED					WHAT HE GAVE UP												THE RESULTS							
		G	GS	CG	GF	IP	BFP	H	R	ER	HR	SH	SF	HB	TBB	IBB	SO	WP	Bk	W	L	Pct	Sh	Sv-Op	Hld	ERC	ERA
2006 Vancvr	A-	13	10	0	0	58.0	237	39	20	13	2	3	2	3	20	0	53	2	0	2	5	.286	0	0--	-	1.93	2.02
2007 Kane	A	11	10	1	1	51.0	218	42	25	19	6	1	0	3	22	1	74	2	0	1	4	.200	0	0--	-	3.51	3.35
2007 Stcktn	A+	11	11	0	0	66.0	280	56	31	28	8	1	4	9	31	0	72	0	0	3	4	.429	0	0--	-	4.33	3.82
2007 Scrmto	AAA	1	1	0	0	8.0	28	3	1	1	0	0	1	0	1	0	4	0	0	1	0	1.000	0	0--	-	0.47	1.13
2008 Mdland	AA	38	15	0	7	111.1	489	99	63	53	13	6	5	6	57	1	112	6	0	5	9	.357	0	0--	-	4.18	4.28
2010 Scrmto	AAA	1	1	0	0	0.2	5	3	2	2	0	0	1	0	0	0	1	2	0	0	0	-	0	0--	-	26.58	27.00
2009 Oak	AL	68	0	0	54	83.1	323	49	17	17	5	3	2	0	24	3	91	6	0	6	3	.667	0	26-30	2	1.44	1.84
2010 Oak	AL	47	0	0	42	49.0	189	34	8	8	3	2	3	0	13	1	42	0	0	1	3	.250	0	25-28	0	1.82	1.47
2 ML YEARS		115	0	0	96	132.1	512	83	25	25	8	5	5	0	37	4	133	6	0	7	6	.538	0	51-58	2	1.56	1.70

Homer Bailey

Pitches: R Bats: R Pos: SP-19 **Ht: 6'3" Wt: 210 Born: 5/3/1986 Age: 25**

Year Team	Lg	HOW MUCH HE PITCHED					WHAT HE GAVE UP												THE RESULTS							
		G	GS	CG	GF	IP	BFP	H	R	ER	HR	SH	SF	HB	TBB	IBB	SO	WP	Bk	W	L	Pct	Sh	Sv-Op	Hld	ERC	ERA
2010 Lsvlle*	AAA	4	3	0	0	19.0	74	15	5	5	0	0	0	1	5	0	15	1	0	2	0	1.000	0	0--	-	2.14	2.37
2010 Dayton*	A	1	1	0	0	4.0	17	4	3	3	0	0	0	0	1	0	5	0	0	1	0	1.000	0	0--	-	2.77	6.75
2007 Cin	NL	9	9	0	0	45.1	205	43	32	29	3	1	6	3	28	1	28	1	1	4	2	.667	0	0-0	0	4.61	5.76
2008 Cin	NL	8	8	0	0	36.1	180	59	36	32	8	5	2	0	17	1	18	4	1	0	6	.000	0	0-0	0	9.31	7.93
2009 Cin	NL	20	20	0	0	113.1	496	115	61	57	12	4	4	3	52	1	86	6	0	8	5	.615	0	0-0	0	4.56	4.53
2010 Cin	NL	19	19	1	0	109.0	465	109	55	54	11	2	1	3	40	6	100	3	1	4	3	.571	1	0-0	0	4.01	4.46
4 ML YEARS		56	56	1	0	304.0	1346	326	184	172	34	12	13	9	137	9	232	14	3	16	16	.500	1	0-0	0	4.88	5.09

Jeff Baker

Bats: R Throws: R Pos: 3B-33; 2B-26; PH-21; 1B-4; RF-4; PR-1 **Ht: 6'2" Wt: 210 Born: 6/21/1981 Age: 30**

Year Team	Lg	BATTING																	BASERUNNING				AVERAGES		
		G	AB	H	2B	3B	HR	(Hm	Rd)	TB	R	RBI	RC	TBB	IBB	SO	HBP	SH	SF	SB	CS	SB%	GDP	Avg	OBP	Slg
2005 Col	NL	12	38	8	4	0	1	(1	0)	15	6	4	4	5	0	12	0	0	0	0	0	-	1	.211	.302	.395
2006 Col	NL	18	57	21	7	2	5	(4	1)	47	13	21	17	1	0	14	0	0	0	2	0	1.00	0	.368	.379	.825
2007 Col	NL	85	144	32	2	2	4	(4	0)	50	17	12	8	13	1	40	2	0	0	0	0	-	7	.222	.296	.347
2008 Col	NL	104	299	80	22	1	12	(8	4)	140	55	48	40	26	2	85	1	1	6	4	0	1.00	5	.268	.322	.468
2009 2 Tms		81	226	65	15	2	4	(3	1)	96	27	24	28	18	0	53	2	0	2	1	0	1.00	8	.288	.343	.425
2010 ChC	NL	79	206	56	13	2	4	(3	1)	85	29	21	21	16	0	50	1	0	1	1	0	1.00	6	.272	.326	.413
09 Col	NL	12	23	3	0	1	0	(0	0)	5	0	3	0	1	0	7	0	0	0	1	0	1.00	3	.130	.167	.217
09 ChC	NL	69	203	62	15	1	4	(3	1)	91	27	21	28	17	0	46	2	0	2	0	0	-	5	.305	.362	.448
Postseason		4	4	2	0	0	0	(0	0)	2	0	1	1	0	0	1	0	0	0	0	0	-	0	.500	.500	.500
6 ML YEARS		379	970	262	63	9	30	(23	7)	433	147	130	118	79	3	254	6	1	9	8	0	1.00	27	.270	.326	.446

John Baker

Bats: L Throws: R Pos: C-21; PH-3 **Ht: 6'1" Wt: 220 Born: 1/20/1981 Age: 30**

Year Team	Lg	BATTING																	BASERUNNING				AVERAGES		
		G	AB	H	2B	3B	HR	(Hm	Rd)	TB	R	RBI	RC	TBB	IBB	SO	HBP	SH	SF	SB	CS	SB%	GDP	Avg	OBP	Slg
2010 Jupiter*	A+	3	6	2	0	0	0	(-	-)	2	2	0	1	2	0	1	0	0	0	0	0	-	0	.333	.500	.333
2008 Fla	NL	61	197	59	14	0	5	(3	2)	88	32	32	36	30	4	48	2	1	3	0	0	-	9	.299	.392	.447
2009 Fla	NL	112	373	101	25	1	9	(3	6)	153	59	50	54	41	5	89	5	2	2	0	0	-	10	.271	.349	.410
2010 Fla	NL	23	78	17	3	1	0	(0	0)	22	7	6	4	9	1	18	1	0	0	0	0	-	5	.218	.307	.282
3 ML YEARS		196	648	177	42	1	14	(6	8)	263	98	88	94	80	10	155	8	3	5	0	0	-	21	.273	.358	.406

Scott Baker

Pitches: R Bats: R Pos: SP-29 **Ht: 6'4" Wt: 220 Born: 9/19/1981 Age: 29**

Year Team	Lg	HOW MUCH HE PITCHED					WHAT HE GAVE UP												THE RESULTS							
		G	GS	CG	GF	IP	BFP	H	R	ER	HR	SH	SF	HB	TBB	IBB	SO	WP	Bk	W	L	Pct	Sh	Sv-Op	Hld	ERC	ERA
2005 Min	AL	10	9	0	0	53.2	217	48	21	20	5	2	2	0	14	0	32	0	0	3	3	.500	0	0-0	1	2.97	3.35
2006 Min	AL	16	16	0	0	83.1	377	114	63	59	17	2	4	3	16	1	62	0	0	5	8	.385	0	0-0	0	6.26	6.37
2007 Min	AL	24	23	2	0	143.2	606	162	70	68	15	6	2	5	29	4	102	0	0	9	9	.500	1	0-0	1	4.19	4.26
2008 Min	AL	28	28	0	0	172.1	703	161	66	66	20	2	3	3	42	2	141	6	0	11	4	.733	0	0-0	0	3.31	3.45
2009 Min	AL	33	33	1	0	200.0	828	199	99	97	28	1	6	4	48	1	162	4	0	15	9	.625	1	0-0	0	3.51	4.37
2010 Min	AL	29	29	0	0	170.1	725	186	87	85	23	1	4	6	43	0	148	7	0	12	9	.571	0	0-0	0	4.43	4.49
6 ML YEARS		140	138	3	0	823.1	3456	861	406	395	108	14	21	21	192	8	647	17	0	55	42	.567	2	0-0	2	3.99	4.32

Rocco Baldelli

Bats: R Throws: R Pos: DH-5; RF-4; PH-3   Ht: 6'4" Wt: 200 Born: 9/25/1981 Age: 29

Year	Team	Lg	G	AB	H	2B	3B	HR	(Hm	Rd)	TB	R	RBI	RC	TBB	IBB	SO	HBP	SH	SF	SB	CS	SB%	GDP	Avg	OBP	Slg
2010	Charltt*	A+	12	46	13	4	0	0	(-	-)	17	6	6	5	1	0	11	0	0	0	0	0	-	1	.283	.298	.370
2010	Drham*	AAA	11	44	12	3	0	2	(-	-)	21	7	8	6	1	0	11	1	0	2	0	0	-	2	.273	.292	.477
2003	TB	AL	156	637	184	32	8	11	(2	9)	265	89	78	77	30	4	128	8	3	6	27	10	.73	10	.289	.326	.416
2004	TB	AL	136	518	145	27	3	16	(6	10)	226	79	74	70	30	2	88	8	3	6	17	4	.81	12	.280	.326	.436
2006	TB	AL	92	364	110	24	6	16	(6	10)	194	59	57	65	14	1	70	7	0	2	10	1	.91	2	.302	.339	.533
2007	TB	AL	35	137	28	6	0	5	(4	1)	49	16	12	14	9	1	35	3	1	0	4	1	.80	1	.204	.268	.358
2008	TB	AL	28	80	21	5	0	4	(0	4)	38	12	13	11	7	0	25	3	0	0	0	0	-	1	.263	.344	.475
2009	Bos	AL	62	150	38	4	1	7	(2	5)	65	23	23	17	11	0	37	2	0	1	1	0	1.00	6	.253	.311	.433
2010	TB	AL	10	24	5	1	0	1	(0	1)	9	3	5	4	1	0	5	0	0	0	1	0	1.00	1	.208	.240	.375
	Postseason		8	20	4	0	0	2	(0	2)	10	4	6	5	3	0	5	0	0	0	0	0	-	0	.200	.304	.500
	7 ML YEARS		519	1910	531	99	18	60	(20	40)	846	281	262	258	102	8	388	31	7	15	60	16	.79	33	.278	.323	.443

Collin Balester

Pitches: R Bats: R Pos: RP-17   BAL-iss-ster   Ht: 6'5" Wt: 199 Born: 6/6/1986 Age: 25

Year	Team	Lg	G	GS	CG	GF	IP	BFP	H	R	ER	HR	SH	SF	HB	TBB	IBB	SO	WP	Bk	W	L	Pct	Sh	Sv-Op	Hld	ERC	ERA
2010	Syrcse*	AAA	35	5	0	5	69.0	309	74	47	45	8	2	4	3	32	4	52	7	0	3	3	.500	0	0- -	-	4.94	5.87
2008	Was	NL	15	15	0	0	80.0	358	92	53	49	12	2	3	6	28	1	50	4	0	3	7	.300	0	0-0	0	5.40	5.51
2009	Was	NL	7	7	0	0	30.1	135	34	24	23	10	0	0	0	14	0	20	0	0	1	4	.200	0	0-0	0	6.85	6.82
2010	Was	NL	17	0	0	8	21.0	89	15	6	6	2	2	0	2	11	1	28	4	0	0	1	.000	0	0-0	0	3.26	2.57
	3 ML YEARS		39	22	0	8	131.1	582	141	83	78	24	4	3	8	53	2	98	8	0	4	12	.250	0	0-0	0	5.37	5.35

Grant Balfour

Pitches: R Bats: R Pos: RP-57   BAL-fore   Ht: 6'2" Wt: 195 Born: 12/30/1977 Age: 33

Year	Team	Lg	G	GS	CG	GF	IP	BFP	H	R	ER	HR	SH	SF	HB	TBB	IBB	SO	WP	Bk	W	L	Pct	Sh	Sv-Op	Hld	ERC	ERA
2010	Charltt*	A+	2	2	0	0	1.2	10	2	3	2	0	0	0	0	3	0	2	0	0	0	1	.000	0	0- -	-	10.01	10.80
2001	Min	AL	2	0	0	1	2.2	14	3	4	4	2	1	1	0	3	0	2	0	0	0	0	-	0	0-0	0	13.78	13.50
2003	Min	AL	17	1	0	6	26.0	115	23	12	12	4	2	1	0	14	2	30	0	0	1	0	1.000	0	0-1	1	4.14	4.15
2004	Min	AL	36	0	0	14	39.1	172	35	19	19	4	2	0	2	21	1	42	3	0	4	1	.800	0	0-1	4	4.16	4.35
2007	2 Tms		25	0	0	8	24.2	121	30	21	21	2	2	3	1	20	0	30	0	0	1	2	.333	0	0-0	1	7.15	7.00
2008	TB	AL	51	0	0	12	58.1	224	28	10	10	3	1	3	0	24	1	82	2	0	6	2	.750	0	4-5	14	1.38	1.54
2009	TB	AL	73	0	0	15	67.1	289	59	38	36	6	1	2	2	33	0	69	1	0	5	4	.556	0	4-9	18	3.79	4.81
2010	TB	AL	57	0	0	8	55.1	222	43	16	14	3	2	4	0	17	2	56	4	1	2	1	.667	0	0-1	16	2.24	2.28
07	Mil	NL	3	0	0	2	2.2	18	4	6	6	1	1	0	1	4	0	3	0	0	0	2	.000	0	0-0	0	15.83	20.25
07	TB	NL	22	0	0	6	22.0	103	26	15	16	1	1	3	0	16	0	27	0	0	1	0	1.000	0	0-0	1	6.19	6.14
	Postseason		12	0	0	2	11.1	53	11	6	6	2	1	0	1	8	3	9	1	0	0	0	-	0	0-0	2	5.59	4.76
	7 ML YEARS		261	1	0	64	273.2	1157	221	120	116	24	11	14	5	132	6	311	10	1	19	10	.655	0	8-17	54	3.30	3.81

Josh Banks

Pitches: R Bats: R Pos: SP-1   Ht: 6'3" Wt: 215 Born: 7/18/1982 Age: 28

Year	Team	Lg	G	GS	CG	GF	IP	BFP	H	R	ER	HR	SH	SF	HB	TBB	IBB	SO	WP	Bk	W	L	Pct	Sh	Sv-Op	Hld	ERC	ERA
2010	RdRck*	AAA	27	27	3	0	171.2	716	177	88	77	25	16	4	3	37	0	72	7	1	9	12	.429	1	0- -	-	3.91	4.04
2007	Tor	AL	3	1	0	1	7.1	35	11	6	6	1	0	1	0	2	0	2	0	0	0	0	-	0	0-0	0	6.66	7.36
2008	SD	NL	17	14	1	1	86.1	372	94	47	45	12	8	4	3	32	5	43	0	0	3	6	.333	0	0-0	0	4.97	4.75
2009	SD	NL	6	3	0	0	22.2	100	30	18	18	6	2	2	1	4	1	9	1	0	1	1	.500	0	0-0	0	6.45	7.15
2010	Hou	NL	1	1	0	0	4.0	24	8	6	6	1	0	0	0	4	0	1	0	0	0	1	.000	0	0-0	0	14.76	13.50
	4 ML YEARS		27	19	1	2	119.1	531	143	77	75	20	10	7	4	42	6	55	1	0	4	8	.333	0	0-0	0	5.64	5.66

Brian Bannister

Pitches: R Bats: R Pos: SP-23; RP-1   Ht: 6'1" Wt: 216 Born: 2/28/1981 Age: 30

Year	Team	Lg	G	GS	CG	GF	IP	BFP	H	R	ER	HR	SH	SF	HB	TBB	IBB	SO	WP	Bk	W	L	Pct	Sh	Sv-Op	Hld	ERC	ERA
2010	Omha*	AAA	3	3	0	0	7.1	30	10	3	3	1	0	0	0	3	0	3	0	0	0	1	.000	0	0- -	-	5.01	3.68
2006	NYM	NL	8	6	0	0	38.0	171	34	18	18	4	1	4	2	22	2	19	2	0	2	1	.667	0	0-0	0	4.27	4.26
2007	KC	AL	27	27	1	0	165.0	683	156	76	71	15	2	4	6	44	1	77	4	0	12	9	.571	0	0-0	0	3.36	3.87
2008	KC	AL	32	32	1	0	182.2	811	215	127	117	29	3	10	7	58	1	113	7	1	9	16	.360	0	0-0	0	5.34	5.76
2009	KC	AL	26	26	0	0	154.0	668	161	94	81	15	3	10	4	50	4	98	12	2	7	12	.368	0	0-0	0	4.04	4.73
2010	KC	AL	24	23	0	1	127.2	581	158	92	90	23	2	2	3	50	0	77	10	0	7	12	.368	0	0-0	0	6.16	6.34
	5 ML YEARS		117	114	2	2	667.1	2914	724	407	377	86	11	30	22	224	8	384	35	3	37	50	.425	0	0-0	0	4.61	5.08

Rod Barajas

Bats: R Throws: R Pos: C-96; PH-3   bah-RAH-hahss   Ht: 6'1" Wt: 245 Born: 9/5/1975 Age: 35

Year	Team	Lg	G	AB	H	2B	3B	HR	(Hm	Rd)	TB	R	RBI	RC	TBB	IBB	SO	HBP	SH	SF	SB	CS	SB%	GDP	Avg	OBP	Slg
2010	Mets*	R	1	4	1	0	0	1	(-	-)	4	1	3	1	0	0	1	0	0	0	0	0	-	0	.250	.250	1.000
2010	StLuci*	A+	4	17	4	0	0	0	(-	-)	4	1	2	0	0	0	2	0	0	0	0	0	-	0	.235	.235	.235
1999	Ari	NL	5	16	4	1	0	1	(1	0)	8	3	3	2	1	0	1	0	1	0	0	0	-	0	.250	.294	.500
2000	Ari	NL	5	13	3	0	0	1	(1	0)	6	1	3	1	0	0	4	0	0	0	0	0	-	0	.231	.231	.462
2001	Ari	NL	51	106	17	3	0	3	(2	1)	29	9	9	4	4	0	26	0	0	0	0	0	-	0	.160	.191	.274
2002	Ari	NL	70	154	36	10	0	3	(1	2)	55	12	23	15	10	4	25	3	2	3	1	0	1.00	4	.234	.288	.357

Year	Team	Lg	G	AB	H	2B	3B	HR	(Hm	Rd)	TB	R	RBI	RC	TBB	IBB	SO	HBP	SH	SF	SB	CS	SB%	GDP	Avg	OBP	Slg
2003	Ari	NL	80	220	48	15	0	3	(3	0)	72	19	28	19	14	7	43	1	1	3	0	0	-	6	.218	.265	.327
2004	Tex	AL	108	358	89	26	1	15	(8	7)	162	50	58	43	13	0	63	3	8	7	0	1	.00	3	.249	.276	.453
2005	Tex	AL	120	410	104	24	0	21	(7	14)	191	53	60	56	26	0	70	6	4	3	0	0	-	6	.254	.306	.466
2006	Tex	AL	97	344	88	20	0	11	(6	5)	141	49	41	36	17	0	51	4	5	1	0	0	-	9	.256	.298	.410
2007	Phi	NL	48	122	28	8	0	4	(1	3)	48	16	10	12	21	3	24	2	1	0	0	1	.00	5	.230	.352	.393
2008	Tor	AL	104	349	87	23	0	11	(4	7)	143	44	49	37	17	0	61	7	0	4	0	0	-	6	.249	.294	.410
2009	Tor	AL	125	429	97	19	0	19	(8	11)	173	43	71	50	20	2	76	1	3	7	1	0	1.00	4	.226	.258	.403
2010	2 Tms	NL	99	313	75	14	0	17	(7	10)	140	39	47	42	13	6	54	8	1	4	0	0	-	6	.240	.284	.447
10	NYM	NL	74	249	56	11	0	12	(5	7)	103	30	34	27	8	3	39	6	1	3	0	0	-	4	.225	.263	.414
10	LAD	NL	25	64	19	3	0	5	(2	3)	37	9	13	15	5	3	15	2	0	1	0	0	-	2	.297	.361	.578
Postseason			5	9	3	0	0	2	(0	2)	9	2	2	2	0	0	1	0	0	0	0	0	-	0	.333	.333	1.000
12 ML YEARS			912	2834	676	163	1	109	(49	60)	1168	338	402	317	156	22	498	35	26	32	2	2	.50	52	.239	.284	.412

Daniel Bard

Pitches: R Bats: R Pos: RP-73 Ht: 6'4" Wt: 200 Born: 6/25/1985 Age: 26

	HOW MUCH HE PITCHED						WHAT HE GAVE UP											THE RESULTS							
Year	Team	Lg	G	GS	CG	GF	IP	BFP	H	R	ER	HR	SH	SF	HB	TBB	IBB	SO	WP	Bk	W	L	Pct	Sh	Sv-Op Hld	ERC	ERA
2007	Lancst	A+	5	5	0	0	13.1	86	21	23	15	2	2	1	1	22	0	9	5	0	0	2	.000	0	0- - -	13.68	10.13
2007	Grnville	A	17	17	0	0	61.2	289	55	49	44	3	1	5	7	56	0	38	22	1	3	5	.375	0	0- - -	5.64	6.42
2008	Grnville	A	15	0	0	3	28.0	100	12	2	2	1	0	0	3	4	0	43	0	0	1	0	1.000	0	0- - -	0.91	0.64
2008	Portlnd	AA	31	0	0	14	49.2	203	30	14	11	3	1	0	3	26	0	64	9	0	4	1	.800	0	7- - -	2.45	1.99
2009	Pwtckt	AAA	11	0	0	8	16.0	58	6	2	2	2	0	0	1	5	0	29	0	0	1	0	1.000	0	6- - -	1.30	1.13
2009	Bos	AL	49	0	0	12	49.1	212	41	24	20	5	4	3	3	22	3	63	1	1	2	2	.500	0	1-4 13	3.43	3.65
2010	Bos	AL	73	0	0	12	74.2	295	45	18	16	6	2	5	2	30	3	76	2	0	1	2	.333	0	3-10 32	1.99	1.93
Postseason			2	0	0	1	3.0	8	0	0	0	0	0	0	0	0	0	4	0	0	0	0	-	0	0-0 1	0.00	0.00
2 ML YEARS			122	0	0	24	124.0	507	86	42	36	11	6	8	5	52	6	139	3	1	3	4	.429	0	4-14 45	2.54	2.61

Josh Bard

Bats: B Throws: R Pos: C-39; PH-1 Ht: 6'3" Wt: 225 Born: 3/30/1978 Age: 33

Year	Team	Lg	G	AB	H	2B	3B	HR	(Hm	Rd)	TB	R	RBI	RC	TBB	IBB	SO	HBP	SH	SF	SB	CS	SB%	GDP	Avg	OBP	Slg
2010	Tacom*	AAA	24	85	20	6	0	3	(-	-)	35	7	15	10	7	0	18	0	0	3	0	0	-	4	.235	.284	.412
2002	Cle	AL	24	90	20	5	0	3	(2	1)	34	9	12	7	4	0	13	0	1	0	0	0	-	6	.222	.255	.378
2003	Cle	AL	91	303	74	13	1	8	(5	3)	113	25	36	34	22	1	53	0	1	3	0	2	.00	9	.244	.293	.373
2004	Cle	AL	7	19	8	2	0	1	(0	1)	13	5	4	9	3	0	0	0	0	1	0	0	-	2	.421	.478	.684
2005	Cle	AL	34	83	16	4	0	1	(0	1)	23	6	9	8	9	0	11	0	1	2	0	0	-	2	.193	.266	.277
2006	2 Tms		100	249	83	20	0	9	(5	4)	130	30	40	44	30	1	42	1	2	2	1	0	1.00	9	.333	.404	.522
2007	SD	NL	118	389	111	27	2	5	(4	1)	157	42	51	65	50	7	58	0	1	3	0	1	.00	16	.285	.364	.404
2008	SD	NL	57	178	36	9	0	1	(0	1)	48	11	16	13	18	2	25	1	1	0	0	0	-	5	.202	.279	.270
2009	Was	NL	90	274	63	18	0	6	(4	2)	99	20	31	27	24	1	50	1	1	1	0	1	.00	5	.230	.293	.361
2010	Sea	AL	39	112	24	7	0	3	(1	2)	40	9	10	8	10	0	27	0	3	1	0	0	-	4	.214	.276	.357
06	Bos	AL	7	18	5	1	0	0	(0	0)	6	2	0	2	3	0	3	0	0	0	0	0	-	0	.278	.381	.333
06	SD	NL	93	231	78	19	0	9	(5	4)	124	28	40	42	27	1	39	1	2	2	1	0	1.00	9	.338	.406	.537
Postseason			3	7	1	0	0	0	(0	0)	1	0	0	0	1	0	2	0	0	0	0	0	-	0	.143	.333	.143
9 ML YEARS			560	1697	435	105	3	37	(22	15)	657	157	209	212	170	12	279	3	11	13	1	4	.20	56	.256	.323	.387

Brian Barden

Bats: R Throws: R Pos: 3B-16; PR-9; SS-7; PH-7; 2B-2 Ht: 5'11" Wt: 200 Born: 4/2/1981 Age: 30

Year	Team	Lg	G	AB	H	2B	3B	HR	(Hm	Rd)	TB	R	RBI	RC	TBB	IBB	SO	HBP	SH	SF	SB	CS	SB%	GDP	Avg	OBP	Slg
2010	NewOr*	AAA	49	184	65	14	1	3	(-	-)	90	30	23	36	18	0	38	0	0	2	3	3	.50	2	.353	.407	.489
2007	2 Tms	NL	23	35	6	1	0	0	(0	0)	7	6	0	1	2	0	7	0	0	0	0	0	-	2	.171	.216	.200
2008	StL	NL	9	9	2	0	0	0	(0	0)	2	0	1	0	0	0	4	0	1	0	0	0	-	0	.222	.222	.222
2009	StL	NL	52	103	24	3	0	4	(1	3)	39	13	10	8	6	0	21	2	2	1	0	0	-	3	.233	.286	.379
2010	Fla	NL	35	28	5	0	0	0	(0	0)	5	2	3	1	3	0	12	1	0	0	0	2	.00	0	.179	.281	.179
07	Ari	NL	8	12	1	0	0	0	(0	0)	1	0	0	0	0	0	3	0	0	0	0	0	-	0	.083	.083	.083
07	StL	NL	15	23	5	1	0	0	(0	0)	6	6	0	1	2	0	4	0	0	0	0	0	-	2	.217	.280	.261
4 ML YEARS			119	175	37	4	0	4	(1	3)	53	21	14	10	11	0	44	3	3	1	0	2	.00	5	.211	.268	.303

Clint Barmes

Bats: R Throws: R Pos: 2B-88; SS-47; PH-4; PR-2; 3B-1 BAR-mess Ht: 6'1" Wt: 205 Born: 3/6/1979 Age: 32

Year	Team	Lg	G	AB	H	2B	3B	HR	(Hm	Rd)	TB	R	RBI	RC	TBB	IBB	SO	HBP	SH	SF	SB	CS	SB%	GDP	Avg	OBP	Slg
2003	Col	NL	12	25	8	2	0	0	(0	0)	10	2	2	3	0	0	10	2	0	1	0	0	-	0	.320	.357	.400
2004	Col	NL	20	71	20	3	1	2	(0	2)	31	14	10	12	3	0	10	1	2	0	0	1	.00	2	.282	.320	.437
2005	Col	NL	81	350	101	19	1	10	(7	3)	152	55	46	49	16	1	36	6	4	1	6	4	.60	4	.289	.330	.434
2006	Col	NL	131	478	105	26	4	7	(3	4)	160	57	56	47	22	6	72	9	19	7	5	4	.56	2	.220	.264	.335
2007	Col	NL	27	37	8	3	0	0	(0	0)	11	5	1	1	1	1	13	0	1	0	0	0	-	1	.216	.237	.297
2008	Col	NL	107	393	114	25	6	11	(8	3)	184	47	44	54	17	0	69	2	4	1	13	4	.76	9	.290	.322	.468
2009	Col	NL	154	550	135	32	3	23	(13	10)	242	69	76	63	31	2	121	10	6	7	12	10	.55	6	.245	.294	.440
2010	Col	NL	133	387	91	21	0	8	(4	4)	136	43	50	43	35	10	66	5	2	3	3	2	.60	5	.235	.305	.351
Postseason			4	14	0	0	0	0	(0	0)	0	0	0	0	0	0	2	0	1	0	0	0	-	0	.000	.000	.000
8 ML YEARS			665	2291	582	131	15	61	(35	26)	926	292	285	272	125	20	397	35	38	20	39	25	.61	29	.254	.300	.404

Darwin Barney

Bats: R **Throws:** R **Pos:** SS-11; 2B-10; 3B-6; PH-5; PR-2   **Ht:** 5'10" **Wt:** 179 **Born:** 11/8/1985 **Age:** 25

Year	Team	Lg	G	AB	H	2B	3B	HR	(Hm	Rd)	TB	R	RBI	RC	TBB	IBB	SO	HBP	SH	SF	SB	CS	SB%	GDP	Avg	OBP	Slg
2007	Cubs	R	5	18	8	3	0	0	(-	-)	11	6	2	5	4	1	0	0	0	0	0	0	-	0	.444	.545	.611
2007	Peoria	A	44	176	48	9	3	2	(-	-)	69	27	21	23	11	0	22	3	0	2	5	2	.71	5	.273	.323	.392
2008	Dytona	A+	123	409	107	22	4	3	(-	-)	146	46	51	51	38	2	58	3	4	5	8	3	.73	8	.262	.325	.357
2009	Tenn	AA	74	252	80	12	0	3	(-	-)	101	30	32	40	23	3	33	0	4	5	5	1	.83	5	.317	.368	.401
2009	Iowa	AAA	63	212	56	12	1	0	(-	-)	70	25	17	22	13	0	32	0	2	2	4	1	.80	7	.264	.304	.330
2010	Iowa	AAA	114	479	143	24	4	2	(-	-)	181	72	49	63	23	1	52	3	2	3	11	3	.79	12	.299	.333	.378
2010	ChC	NL	30	79	19	4	0	0	(0	0)	23	12	2	6	6	0	12	0	0	0	0	0	-	0	.241	.294	.291

Jason Bartlett

Bats: R **Throws:** R **Pos:** SS-131; PH-5; PR-5; DH-1   **Ht:** 6'0" **Wt:** 190 **Born:** 10/30/1979 **Age:** 31

Year	Team	Lg	G	AB	H	2B	3B	HR	(Hm	Rd)	TB	R	RBI	RC	TBB	IBB	SO	HBP	SH	SF	SB	CS	SB%	GDP	Avg	OBP	Slg
2010	Drham*	AAA	1	3	2	1	0	0	(-	-)	3	0	0	1	1	0	1	0	0	0	0	0	-	0	.667	.750	1.000
2004	Min	AL	8	12	1	0	0	0	(0	0)	1	2	1	1	1	0	1	0	1	0	2	0	1.00	0	.083	.154	.083
2005	Min	AL	74	224	54	10	1	3	(2	1)	75	33	16	22	21	0	37	4	2	1	4	0	1.00	6	.241	.316	.335
2006	Min	AL	99	333	103	18	2	2	(0	2)	131	44	32	50	22	1	46	11	1	5	10	5	.67	8	.309	.367	.393
2007	Min	AL	140	510	135	20	7	5	(2	3)	184	75	43	65	50	3	73	8	0	2	23	3	.88	8	.265	.339	.361
2008	TB	AL	128	454	130	25	3	1	(1	0)	164	48	37	56	22	1	69	9	5	4	20	6	.77	9	.286	.329	.361
2009	TB	AL	137	500	160	29	7	14	(3	11)	245	90	66	97	54	2	89	5	4	4	30	7	.81	5	.320	.389	.490
2010	TB	AL	135	468	119	27	3	4	(1	3)	164	71	47	62	45	1	83	5	11	3	11	6	.65	6	.254	.324	.350
	Postseason		19	62	15	2	1	1	(1	0)	22	8	3	5	4	0	12	2	1	0	2	0	1.00	2	.242	.309	.355
7 ML YEARS			721	2501	702	129	23	29	(9	20)	964	363	242	353	215	8	398	42	24	19	100	27	.79	42	.281	.345	.385

Daric Barton

Bats: L **Throws:** R **Pos:** 1B-157; PH-3   **Ht:** 6'0" **Wt:** 207 **Born:** 8/16/1985 **Age:** 25

Year	Team	Lg	G	AB	H	2B	3B	HR	(Hm	Rd)	TB	R	RBI	RC	TBB	IBB	SO	HBP	SH	SF	SB	CS	SB%	GDP	Avg	OBP	Slg
2007	Oak	AL	18	72	25	9	0	4	(2	2)	46	16	8	14	10	0	11	1	0	1	0	1	1.00	6	.347	.429	.639
2008	Oak	AL	140	446	101	17	5	9	(1	8)	155	59	47	56	65	5	99	3	6	3	2	1	.67	6	.226	.327	.348
2009	Oak	AL	54	160	43	12	1	3	(2	1)	66	31	24	28	26	0	25	2	1	3	0	2	.00	1	.269	.372	.413
2010	Oak	AL	159	556	152	33	5	10	(1	9)	225	79	57	92	110	2	102	3	12	5	7	3	.70	8	.273	.393	.405
4 ML YEARS			371	1234	321	71	11	26	(6	20)	492	185	136	190	211	7	237	9	19	12	10	6	.63	17	.260	.369	.399

Brian Bass

Pitches: R **Bats:** R **Pos:** RP-4   **Ht:** 6'2" **Wt:** 215 **Born:** 1/6/1982 **Age:** 29

			HOW MUCH HE PITCHED					WHAT HE GAVE UP										THE RESULTS						
Year	Team	Lg	G	GS	CG	GF	IP	BFP	H	R	ER	HR	SH	SF	HB	TBB	IBB	SO	WP	Bk	W	L	Pct	Sh	Sv-Op	Hld	ERC	ERA
2010	Indy*	AAA	41	1	0	15	69.0	298	74	26	25	3	3	2	6	23	1	53	1	0	4	4	.500	0	2--	-	4.20	3.26
2008	2 Tms	AL	49	4	0	14	89.1	388	98	55	48	12	1	1	5	31	4	45	6	0	4	4	.500	0	1-2	3	4.89	4.04
2009	Bal	AL	48	0	0	13	86.1	400	106	52	47	11	3	2	5	44	5	54	6	0	5	3	.625	0	0-0	1	6.30	4.90
2010	Pit	NL	4	0	0	0	7.1	42	9	11	10	0	1	1	1	10	2	5	1	0	0	0	-	0	0-0	-	8.20	12.27
08	Min	AL	44	0	0	14	68.1	303	84	42	37	11	0	1	3	22	0	32	4	0	3	4	.429	0	1-2	3	5.74	4.87
08	Bal	AL	5	4	0	0	21.0	85	14	13	11	1	1	0	2	9	1	13	2	0	1	0	1.000	0	0-0	0	2.42	4.71
3 ML YEARS			101	4	0	27	183.0	830	213	118	105	23	5	4	11	85	11	104	13	0	9	7	.563	0	1-2	4	5.70	5.16

Antonio Bastardo

Pitches: L **Bats:** R **Pos:** RP-25   **Ht:** 5'11" **Wt:** 193 **Born:** 9/21/1985 **Age:** 25

			HOW MUCH HE PITCHED					WHAT HE GAVE UP										THE RESULTS						
Year	Team	Lg	G	GS	CG	GF	IP	BFP	H	R	ER	HR	SH	SF	HB	TBB	IBB	SO	WP	Bk	W	L	Pct	Sh	Sv-Op	Hld	ERC	ERA
2006	Phillies	R	9	2	0	2	23.0	106	20	16	10	1	0	1	0	14	0	27	3	3	1	2	.333	0	0--	-	3.53	3.91
2007	Lakwd	A	15	15	0	0	91.2	382	63	23	19	3	1	2	4	42	0	98	12	3	9	0	1.000	0	0--	-	2.34	1.87
2007	Clrwtr	A+	1	1	0	0	5.0	24	5	4	4	0	0	1	0	3	0	12	1	0	1	0	1.000	0	0--	-	3.80	7.20
2008	Clrwtr	A+	5	5	0	0	30.2	120	20	4	4	2	0	0	1	10	0	47	0	1	2	0	1.000	0	0--	-	1.97	1.17
2008	Rdng	AA	14	14	0	0	67.0	291	56	35	28	13	1	1	1	37	0	62	3	2	1	5	.167	0	0--	-	4.46	3.76
2009	Rdng	AA	11	5	0	5	36.0	134	22	7	7	1	2	0	2	7	0	41	0	0	2	2	.500	0	3---	-	1.39	1.75
2009	LV	AAA	2	2	0	0	13.0	50	11	3	3	1	0	0	0	3	0	12	0	0	1	0	1.000	0	0--	-	2.62	2.08
2009	Phillies	R	3	2	0	0	4.1	19	2	1	0	0	0	0	0	2	0	3	1	0	0	0	-	0	0--	-	2.37	0.00
2009	Clrwtr	A+	1	0	0	0	1.0	6	4	3	3	0	0	1	0	0	0	0	0	0	0	0	-	0	0--	-	26.25	27.00
2010	LV	AAA	20	0	0	6	17.1	70	12	4	4	0	1	0	0	6	0	27	0	0	1	1	.500	0	3---	-	1.68	2.08
2010	Clrwtr	A+	3	0	0	0	3.0	12	3	0	0	0	0	0	0	1	0	6	0	0	0	0	-	0	0--	-	1.95	0.00
2009	Phi	NL	6	5	0	0	23.2	106	26	18	17	4	0	0	2	9	0	19	0	0	2	3	.400	0	0-0	-	5.41	6.46
2010	Phi	NL	25	0	0	2	18.2	86	19	9	9	1	0	0	2	9	0	26	0	0	2	0	1.000	0	0-1	2	4.46	4.34
	Postseason		2	0	0	0	0.1	2	1	0	0	0	0	0	0	0	0	1	0	0	0	0	-	0	0-0	0	14.52	0.00
2 ML YEARS			31	5	0	2	42.1	192	45	27	26	5	0	0	4	18	0	45	0	0	4	3	.571	0	0-1	2	4.99	5.53

Miguel Batista

Pitches: R Bats: R Pos: RP-57; SP-1   Ht: 6'1" Wt: 210 Born: 2/19/1971 Age: 40

			HOW MUCH HE PITCHED						WHAT HE GAVE UP												THE RESULTS							
Year	Team	Lg	G	GS	CG	GF	IP	BFP	H	R	ER	HR	SH	SF	HB	TBB	IBB	SO	WP	Bk	W	L	Pct	Sh	Sv-Op	Hld	ERC	ERA
1992	Pit	NL	1	0	0	1	2.0	13	4	2	2	1	0	0	0	3	0	1	0	0	0	0	-	0	0-0	0	20.26	9.00
1996	Fla	NL	9	0	0	4	11.1	49	9	8	7	0	3	0	0	7	2	6	1	0	0	0	-	0	0-0	0	2.77	5.56
1997	ChC	NL	11	6	0	2	36.1	168	36	24	23	4	4	4	1	24	2	27	2	0	0	5	.000	0	0-0	0	5.09	5.70
1998	Mon	NL	56	13	0	12	135.0	598	141	66	57	12	7	5	6	65	7	92	6	1	3	5	.375	0	0-0	3	4.70	3.80
1999	Mon	NL	39	17	2	3	134.2	606	146	88	73	10	8	11	7	58	2	95	6	0	8	7	.533	1	1-1	0	4.62	4.88
2000	2 Tms		18	9	0	2	65.1	310	85	68	62	19	1	2	2	37	2	37	4	0	2	7	.222	0	0-2	0	8.37	8.54
2001	Ari	NL	48	18	0	6	139.1	581	113	57	52	13	9	3	10	60	2	90	6	0	11	8	.579	0	0-0	4	3.43	3.36
2002	Ari	NL	36	29	1	2	184.2	790	172	99	88	12	5	8	6	70	3	112	9	2	8	9	.471	0	0-0	2	3.45	4.29
2003	Ari	NL	36	29	2	5	193.1	822	197	85	76	13	10	6	8	60	3	142	7	0	10	9	.526	1	0-0	0	3.77	3.54
2004	Tor	AL	38	31	2	7	198.2	867	206	115	106	22	7	6	3	96	1	104	12	0	10	13	.435	1	5-5	0	4.84	4.80
2005	Tor	AL	71	0	0	62	74.2	331	80	39	34	9	2	2	2	27	5	54	3	0	5	8	.385	0	31-39	0	4.39	4.10
2006	Ari	NL	34	33	3	0	206.1	910	231	116	105	18	12	5	6	84	5	110	14	1	11	8	.579	1	0-0	0	4.82	4.58
2007	Sea	AL	33	32	0	0	193.0	860	209	101	92	18	5	5	8	85	3	133	15	2	16	11	.593	0	0-0	0	4.81	4.29
2008	Sea	AL	44	20	0	9	115.0	556	135	89	80	19	3	11	6	79	6	73	5	0	4	14	.222	0	1-4	4	6.92	6.26
2009	Sea	AL	56	0	0	18	71.1	326	79	37	32	7	4	1	2	39	1	52	4	0	7	4	.636	0	1-5	14	5.37	4.04
2010	Was	NL	58	1	0	18	82.2	350	71	36	34	9	1	2	5	39	8	55	4	0	1	2	.333	0	2-2	1	3.78	3.70
00	Mon		4	0	0	0	8.1	49	19	14	13	2	1	1	2	3	0	7	0	0	0	1	.000	0	0-2	0	14.73	14.04
00	KC	AL	14	9	0	2	57.0	261	66	54	49	17	0	1	0	34	2	30	4	0	2	6	.250	0	0-0	0	7.50	7.74
	Postseason		7	4	0	1	25.1	104	18	10	10	3	3	0	1	11	0	14	1	0	1	2	.333	0	0-0	0	2.94	3.55
	16 ML YEARS		588	238	10	151	1843.2	8137	1914	1030	923	186	81	71	72	833	52	1183	98	6	96	110	.466	4	41-58	28	4.63	4.51

Denny Bautista

Pitches: R Bats: R Pos: RP-31   Ht: 6'5" Wt: 190 Born: 8/23/1980 Age: 30

			HOW MUCH HE PITCHED						WHAT HE GAVE UP												THE RESULTS							
Year	Team	Lg	G	GS	CG	GF	IP	BFP	H	R	ER	HR	SH	SF	HB	TBB	IBB	SO	WP	Bk	W	L	Pct	Sh	Sv-Op	Hld	ERC	ERA
2010	Fresno*	AAA	19	0	0	15	22.2	92	14	8	8	1	0	0	3	9	2	28	1	0	3	2	.600	0	9- --	-	2.10	3.18
2004	2 Tms	AL	7	5	0	0	29.2	142	44	28	28	3	0	1	3	13	1	19	3	2	0	4	.000	0	0-0	0	7.76	8.49
2005	KC	AL	7	7	0	0	35.2	160	36	23	23	2	1	1	2	17	0	23	3	0	2	2	.500	0	0-0	0	4.27	5.80
2006	2 Tms		12	8	0	3	41.2	194	47	34	26	5	1	2	4	21	0	27	5	0	0	3	.000	0	0-0	0	5.75	5.62
2007	Col	NL	9	1	0	2	8.2	48	18	12	12	0	1	0	1	4	0	8	0	0	2	1	.667	0	0-0	2	10.84	12.46
2008	2 Tms		51	0	0	8	60.1	271	61	35	35	6	2	4	2	42	2	44	4	0	4	4	.500	0	0-1	10	5.58	5.22
2009	Pit	NL	14	0	0	4	13.2	61	15	8	8	1	1	3	1	7	0	15	3	0	1	1	.500	0	0-1	1	5.32	5.27
2010	SF	NL	31	0	0	8	33.2	157	25	14	14	4	3	2	3	27	4	44	7	0	2	0	1.000	0	0-1	0	4.33	3.74
04	Bal	AL	2	0	0	0	2.0	15	6	8	8	1	0	1	1	2	0	1	1	0	0	-	-	0	0-0	0	28.67	36.00
04	KC	AL	5	5	0	0	27.2	127	38	20	20	2	0	0	2	11	1	18	2	2	0	4	.000	0	0-0	0	6.50	6.51
06	KC	AL	8	7	0	0	35.0	161	38	24	22	5	1	2	4	17	0	22	5	0	0	2	.000	0	0-0	0	5.70	5.66
06	Col	NL	4	1	0	3	6.2	33	9	10	4	0	0	0	0	4	0	5	0	0	0	1	.000	0	0-0	0	5.98	5.40
08	Det	AL	16	0	0	3	19.0	83	15	7	7	1	1	1	2	14	0	10	1	0	0	1	.000	0	0-0	3	4.42	3.32
08	Pit	NL	35	0	0	5	41.1	188	46	28	28	5	1	3	0	28	2	34	3	0	4	3	.571	0	0-1	7	6.14	6.10
	7 ML YEARS		131	21	0	25	223.1	1033	246	154	146	21	9	13	16	131	7	180	25	2	11	15	.423	0	0-3	13	5.64	5.88

Jose Bautista

Bats: R Throws: R Pos: RF-113; 3B-48; 1B-4; DH-2; CF-1   Ht: 6'0" Wt: 195 Born: 10/19/1980 Age: 30

			BATTING																		BASERUNNING				AVERAGES		
Year	Team	Lg	G	AB	H	2B	3B	HR	(Hm	Rd)	TB	R	RBI	RC	TBB	IBB	SO	HBP	SH	SF	SB	CS	SB%	GDP	Avg	OBP	Slg
2004	4 Tms		64	88	18	3	0	0	(0	0)	21	6	2	2	7	0	40	0	1	0	0	1	.00	1	.205	.263	.239
2005	Pit	NL	11	28	4	1	0	0	(0	0)	5	3	1	0	3	0	7	0	0	0	1	0	1.00	2	.143	.226	.179
2006	Pit	NL	117	400	94	20	3	16	(11	5)	168	58	51	55	46	2	110	16	3	4	2	4	.33	12	.235	.335	.420
2007	Pit	NL	142	532	135	36	2	15	(8	7)	220	75	63	71	68	1	101	4	4	6	6	3	.67	16	.254	.339	.414
2008	2 Tms		128	370	88	17	0	15	(5	10)	150	45	54	43	40	5	91	2	8	4	1	1	.50	12	.238	.313	.405
2009	Tor	AL	113	336	79	13	3	13	(5	8)	137	54	40	42	56	1	85	4	6	2	4	0	1.00	9	.235	.349	.408
2010	Tor	AL	161	569	148	35	3	54	(33	21)	351	109	124	132	100	2	116	10	0	4	9	2	.82	10	.260	.378	.617
04	Bal	AL	16	11	3	0	0	0	(0	0)	3	3	0	1	1	0	3	0	0	0	0	0	-	0	.273	.333	.273
04	TB	AL	12	12	2	0	0	0	(0	0)	2	1	1	0	3	0	7	0	0	0	0	1	.00	0	.167	.333	.167
04	KC	AL	13	25	5	1	0	0	(0	0)	6	1	1	0	1	0	12	0	0	0	0	0	-	0	.200	.231	.240
04	Pit	NL	23	40	8	2	0	0	(0	0)	10	1	0	1	2	0	18	0	1	0	0	0	-	1	.200	.238	.250
08	Pit	NL	107	314	76	15	0	12	(3	9)	127	38	44	39	38	4	77	2	6	3	1	1	.50	10	.242	.325	.404
08	Tor	AL	21	56	12	2	0	3	(2	1)	23	7	10	4	2	1	14	0	2	1	0	0	-	2	.214	.237	.411
	7 ML YEARS		736	2323	566	125	11	113	(62	51)	1052	350	335	345	320	11	550	36	22	20	23	11	.68	62	.244	.342	.453

Mike Baxter

Bats: L Throws: R Pos: PH-8; 1B-1   Ht: 6'0" Wt: 190 Born: 12/7/1984 Age: 26

			BATTING																		BASERUNNING				AVERAGES		
Year	Team	Lg	G	AB	H	2B	3B	HR	(Hm	Rd)	TB	R	RBI	RC	TBB	IBB	SO	HBP	SH	SF	SB	CS	SB%	GDP	Avg	OBP	Slg
2005	FtWyn	A	45	183	40	12	1	1	(-	-)	57	11	17	15	12	0	29	0	1	1	4	1	.80	4	.219	.267	.311
2006	FtWyn	A	117	476	122	28	7	3	(-	-)	173	67	40	55	31	2	66	4	1	5	13	5	.72	7	.256	.304	.363
2007	Lk Els	A+	111	417	115	21	6	7	(-	-)	169	74	44	62	44	2	75	3	2	4	12	6	.67	14	.276	.346	.405
2007	Portlnd	AAA	10	29	6	2	1	0	(-	-)	10	1	7	2	1	0	8	0	0	0	1	0	1.00	0	.207	.233	.345
2008	Lk Els	A+	24	92	22	4	1	1	(-	-)	31	13	17	11	10	0	12	2	0	0	3	0	1.00	1	.239	.324	.337
2008	SnAnt	AA	100	324	88	18	4	8	(-	-)	138	41	48	51	39	5	41	2	2	3	2	2	.50	9	.272	.351	.426
2009	SnAnt	AA	51	202	76	23	1	4	(-	-)	113	38	45	48	23	1	42	2	0	2	5	2	.71	3	.376	.441	.559
2009	Portlnd	AAA	82	303	84	17	4	5	(-	-)	124	38	34	47	38	1	53	3	0	1	9	5	.64	10	.277	.362	.409
2010	Portlnd	AAA	136	482	145	30	10	18	(-	-)	249	89	72	97	58	1	78	8	0	4	22	10	.69	11	.301	.382	.517
2010	SD	NL	9	8	1	0	0	0	(0	0)	1	0	1	0	0	0	2	0	0	1	0	0	-	1	.125	.111	.125

Jason Bay

Bats: R Throws: R Pos: LF-93; PH-2　　　　　　　　　　Ht: 6'2" Wt: 205 Born: 9/20/1978 Age: 32

Year	Team	Lg	G	AB	H	2B	3B	HR	(Hm	Rd)	TB	R	RBI	RC	TBB	IBB	SO	HBP	SH	SF	SB	CS	SB%	GDP	Avg	OBP	Slg
2003	2 Tms	NL	30	87	25	7	1	4	(2	2)	46	15	14	19	19	0	29	1	0	1	3	1	.75	0	.287	.421	.529
2004	Pit	NL	120	411	116	24	4	26	(15	11)	226	61	82	75	41	2	129	10	5	5	4	6	.40	9	.282	.358	.550
2005	Pit	NL	162	599	183	44	6	32	(9	23)	335	110	101	128	95	9	142	6	0	7	21	1	.95	12	.306	.402	.559
2006	Pit	NL	159	570	163	29	3	35	(13	22)	303	101	109	103	102	9	156	8	0	9	11	2	.85	15	.286	.396	.532
2007	Pit	NL	145	538	133	25	2	21	(7	14)	225	78	84	74	59	3	141	9	0	8	4	1	.80	8	.247	.327	.418
2008	2 Tms	NL	155	577	165	35	4	31	(18	13)	301	111	101	104	81	4	137	4	0	8	10	0	1.00	7	.286	.373	.522
2009	Bos	AL	151	531	142	29	3	36	(15	21)	285	103	119	122	94	4	162	9	0	4	13	3	.81	9	.267	.384	.537
2010	NYM	NL	95	348	90	20	6	6	(3	3)	140	48	47	50	44	3	91	5	0	4	10	0	1.00	7	.259	.347	.402
03	SD	NL	3	8	2	1	0	1	(0	1)	6	2	2	2	1	0	1	1	0	0	0	0	-	0	.250	.400	.750
03	Pit	NL	27	79	23	6	1	3	(2	1)	40	13	12	17	18	0	28	0	0	1	3	1	.75	0	.291	.423	.506
08	Pit	NL	106	393	111	23	2	22	(15	7)	204	72	64	73	59	2	86	2	0	5	7	0	1.00	3	.282	.375	.519
08	Bos	AL	49	184	54	12	2	9	(3	6)	97	39	37	31	22	2	51	2	0	3	3	0	1.00	4	.293	.370	.527
	Postseason		14	49	15	3	0	3	(0	3)	27	6	9	11	12	1	15	1	0	0	0	0	-	0	.306	.452	.551
	8 ML YEARS		1017	3661	1017	213	29	191	(82	109)	1861	627	657	675	535	34	987	52	5	45	76	14	.84	67	.278	.374	.508

Brandon Beachy

Pitches: R Bats: R Pos: SP-3　　　　　　　　　　Ht: 6'2" Wt: 210 Born: 9/3/1986 Age: 24

| | | | HOW MUCH HE PITCHED | | | | | | WHAT HE GAVE UP | | | | | | | | | | | THE RESULTS | | | | | | | |
Year	Team	Lg	G	GS	CG	GF	IP	BFP	H	R	ER	HR	SH	SF	HB	TBB	IBB	SO	WP	Bk	W	L	Pct	Sh	Sv-Op	Hld	ERC	ERA
2008	Danvle	R	6	0	0	0	12.0	51	12	5	3	1	1	1	1	2	0	16	2	0	2	0	1.000	0	0--	-	3.31	2.25
2009	Rome	A	12	0	0	5	17.2	75	20	11	11	0	0	0	2	4	0	17	0	0	0	0	-	0	0--	-	3.98	5.60
2009	Missi	AA	1	0	0	0	1.0	4	1	0	0	0	0	0	0	0	0	0	0	0	0	0	-	0	0--	-	1.95	0.00
2009	MrtlBh	A+	22	8	0	8	58.0	248	59	31	22	2	1	2	8	15	1	47	5	0	4	3	.571	0	1--	-	3.70	3.41
2010	Missi	AA	27	6	0	6	73.2	295	53	17	12	3	5	1	2	22	0	100	2	0	3	1	.750	0	1--	-	1.99	1.47
2010	Gwnntt	AAA	8	7	0	1	45.2	187	40	17	11	2	2	2	2	6	0	48	1	0	2	0	1.000	0	1--	-	2.17	2.17
2010	Atl	NL	3	3	0	0	15.0	67	16	9	5	0	0	0	0	7	3	15	1	0	0	2	.000	0	0-0	0	3.58	3.00

Josh Beckett

Pitches: R Bats: R Pos: SP-21　　　　　　　　　　Ht: 6'5" Wt: 225 Born: 5/15/1980 Age: 31

| | | | HOW MUCH HE PITCHED | | | | | | WHAT HE GAVE UP | | | | | | | | | | | THE RESULTS | | | | | | | |
Year	Team	Lg	G	GS	CG	GF	IP	BFP	H	R	ER	HR	SH	SF	HB	TBB	IBB	SO	WP	Bk	W	L	Pct	Sh	Sv-Op	Hld	ERC	ERA
2010	Pwtckt*	AAA	2	2	0	0	8.0	32	7	4	4	2	0	0	1	1	0	7	0	0	0	0	-	0	0--	-	3.17	4.50
2001	Fla	NL	4	4	0	0	24.0	99	14	9	4	3	0	0	1	11	0	24	1	0	2	2	.500	0	0-0	0	2.36	1.50
2002	Fla	NL	23	21	0	0	107.2	454	93	56	49	13	5	3	1	44	2	113	5	0	6	7	.462	0	0-0	0	3.50	4.10
2003	Fla	NL	24	23	0	1	142.0	601	132	54	48	9	5	1	2	56	4	152	6	1	9	8	.529	0	0-0	0	3.44	3.04
2004	Fla	NL	26	26	1	0	156.2	654	137	72	66	16	9	3	6	54	3	152	5	0	9	9	.500	1	0 0	0	3.32	3.79
2005	Fla	NL	29	29	2	0	178.2	729	153	75	67	14	8	2	7	58	2	166	5	0	15	8	.652	1	0-0	0	3.06	3.38
2006	Bos	AL	33	33	0	0	204.2	869	191	120	114	36	2	3	10	74	1	158	11	1	16	11	.593	0	0-0	0	4.28	5.01
2007	Bos	AL	30	30	1	0	200.2	822	189	76	73	17	3	2	5	40	0	194	3	0	20	7	.741	0	0-0	0	2.99	3.27
2008	Bos	AL	27	27	1	0	174.1	725	173	80	78	18	4	3	9	34	1	172	5	0	12	10	.545	0	0-0	0	3.45	4.03
2009	Bos	AL	32	32	4	0	212.1	883	198	99	91	25	5	5	7	55	1	199	3	1	17	6	.739	2	0-0	0	3.39	3.86
2010	Bos	AL	21	21	0	0	127.2	577	151	99	82	20	4	2	8	45	3	116	3	0	6	6	.500	0	0 0	0	5.56	5.78
	Postseason		14	13	3	0	93.2	366	67	32	32	11	2	1	4	21	1	99	3	0	7	3	.700	3	0-0	0	2.22	3.07
	10 ML YEARS		249	246	9	1	1528.2	6413	1431	730	672	171	45	24	56	471	17	1446	47	3	112	74	.602	4	0-0	0	3.58	3.96

Gordon Beckham

Bats: R Throws: R Pos: 2B-126; DH-4; PR-4　　　　　　　　　　Ht: 6'0" Wt: 185 Born: 9/16/1986 Age: 24

Year	Team	Lg	G	AB	H	2B	3B	HR	(Hm	Rd)	TB	R	RBI	RC	TBB	IBB	SO	HBP	SH	SF	SB	CS	SB%	GDP	Avg	OBP	Slg
2008	Knapol	A	14	58	18	2	0	3	(-	-)	29	11	8	10	5	0	7	0	0	0	0	1	.00	1	.310	.365	.500
2009	Brham	AA	38	147	44	17	0	4	(-	-)	73	23	22	27	14	1	24	2	2	1	1	0	1.00	4	.299	.300	.497
2009	Charltt	AAA	7	28	13	6	0	0	(-	-)	19	6	3	7	0	0	2	0	1	1	1	0	1.00	0	.464	.448	.679
2009	CWS	AL	103	378	102	28	1	14	(4	10)	174	58	63	60	41	0	65	6	1	4	7	4	.64	10	.270	.347	.460
2010	CWS	AL	131	444	112	25	2	9	(7	2)	100	50	49	52	37	0	92	7	6	4	4	6	.40	9	.252	.317	.378
	2 ML YEARS		234	822	214	53	3	23	(11	12)	342	116	112	112	78	0	157	13	7	8	11	10	.52	19	.260	.331	.416

Erik Bedard

Pitches: L Bats: L Pos: P　　　　　　　　　　Ht: 6'1" Wt: 200 Born: 3/5/1979 Age: 32

| | | | HOW MUCH HE PITCHED | | | | | | WHAT HE GAVE UP | | | | | | | | | | | THE RESULTS | | | | | | | |
Year	Team	Lg	G	GS	CG	GF	IP	BFP	H	R	ER	HR	SH	SF	HB	TBB	IBB	SO	WP	Bk	W	L	Pct	Sh	Sv-Op	Hld	ERC	ERA
2010	Tacom*	AAA	1	1	0	0	4.1	19	3	1	0	0	1	0	0	3	0	3	0	0	0	0	-	0	0--	-	2.74	0.00
2002	Bal	AL	2	0	0	0	0.2	4	2	1	1	0	0	0	0	1	0	1	0	0	0	0	-	0	0-0	0	14.52	13.50
2004	Bal	AL	27	26	0	0	137.1	633	149	83	70	13	0	4	7	71	1	121	7	2	6	10	.375	0	0-0	0	5.11	4.59
2005	Bal	AL	24	24	0	0	141.2	606	139	66	63	10	3	6	5	57	1	125	4	1	6	8	.429	0	0-0	0	3.95	4.00
2006	Bal	AL	33	33	0	0	196.1	844	196	92	82	16	4	5	5	69	0	171	6	0	15	11	.577	0	0-0	0	3.83	3.76
2007	Bal	AL	28	28	1	0	182.0	733	141	66	64	19	2	4	5	57	0	221	3	0	13	5	.722	1	0-0	0	2.71	3.16
2008	Sea	AL	15	15	0	0	81.0	347	70	38	33	9	1	2	4	37	0	72	3	0	6	4	.600	0	0-0	0	3.82	3.67
2009	Sea	AL	15	15	0	0	83.0	348	65	29	26	8	2	1	4	34	0	90	2	0	5	3	.625	0	0-0	0	3.08	2.82
	7 ML YEARS		144	141	1	0	822.0	3515	762	375	339	75	14	21	30	325	2	801	25	3	51	41	.554	1	0-0	0	3.73	3.71

Joe Beimel

Pitches: L Bats: L Pos: RP-71

BYE-mull

Ht: 6'3" Wt: 215 Born: 4/19/1977 Age: 34

Year	Team	Lg	G	GS	CG	GF	IP	BFP	H	R	ER	HR	SH	SF	HB	TBB	IBB	SO	WP	Bk	W	L	Pct	Sh	Sv-Op	Hld	ERC	ERA
2010	ColSpr*	AAA	2	0	0	0	2.2	10	2	0	0	0	0	0	0	0	0	2	0	0	0	0	-	0	0--	-	1.13	0.00
2001	Pit	NL	42	15	0	9	115.1	511	131	72	67	12	3	1	6	49	4	58	3	0	7	11	.389	0	0-0	0	5.24	5.23
2002	Pit	NL	53	8	0	8	85.1	389	88	49	44	9	7	3	4	45	12	53	2	0	2	5	.286	0	0-1	5	4.68	4.64
2003	Pit	NL	69	0	0	11	62.1	276	69	35	35	7	3	5	4	33	6	42	0	1	1	3	.250	0	0-5	12	5.62	5.05
2004	Min	AL	3	0	0	0	1.2	15	8	8	8	1	0	0	0	2	0	2	0	0	0	0	-	0	0-0	0	44.44	43.20
2005	TB	AL	7	0	0	3	11.0	51	15	4	4	1	0	0	0	4	1	3	1	0	0	0	-	0	0-0	0	5.80	3.27
2006	LAD	NL	62	0	0	10	70.0	295	70	26	23	7	4	3	0	21	3	30	6	1	2	1	.667	0	2-2	10	3.62	2.96
2007	LAD	NL	83	0	0	10	67.1	281	63	30	29	1	5	2	1	24	6	39	3	2	4	2	.667	0	1-1	16	2.93	3.88
2008	LAD	NL	71	0	0	10	49.0	214	50	11	11	0	1	4	3	21	4	32	1	1	5	1	.833	0	0-0	12	3.70	2.02
2009	2 Tms	NL	71	0	0	26	55.1	240	57	24	22	5	4	6	1	19	5	35	4	1	1	6	.143	0	1-6	13	3.84	3.58
2010	Col	NL	71	0	0	11	45.0	188	46	18	17	5	1	4	1	15	3	21	2	1	1	2	.333	0	0-1	20	4.00	3.40
09	Was	NL	45	0	0	19	39.2	172	38	17	15	3	2	4	1	15	4	24	2	1	1	5	.167	0	1-5	10	3.46	3.40
09	Col	NL	26	0	0	7	15.2	68	19	7	7	2	2	2	0	4	1	11	2	0	0	1	.000	0	0-1	3	4.84	4.02
	Postseason		6	0	0	1	1.1	7	1	0	0	0	0	0	0	2	0	0	0	0	0	0	-	0	0-0	0	5.91	0.00
10 ML YEARS			532	23	0	98	562.1	2460	597	277	260	48	28	25	19	233	44	315	22	7	23	31	.426	0	4-16	88	4.41	4.16

Ronald Belisario

Pitches: R Bats: R Pos: RP-59

bell-ih-SAR-ee-oh

Ht: 6'3" Wt: 237 Born: 12/31/1982 Age: 28

Year	Team	Lg	G	GS	CG	GF	IP	BFP	H	R	ER	HR	SH	SF	HB	TBB	IBB	SO	WP	Bk	W	L	Pct	Sh	Sv-Op	Hld	ERC	ERA
2001	Mrlns	R	13	13	1	0	73.0	309	62	29	19	4	4	3	11	20	0	54	8	1	4	6	.400	1	0--	-	3.02	2.34
2002	Kane	A	23	22	1	0	140.1	619	131	67	54	4	5	5	21	56	0	98	13	4	6	5	.545	4	0--	-	3.73	3.46
2003	Grnsbr	A	10	8	1	1	48.0	207	41	23	16	3	1	1	8	18	0	45	2	0	5	1	.833	0	0--	-	3.55	3.00
2003	Jupiter	A+	6	4	0	2	18.1	82	20	10	10	0	1	0	1	8	0	13	0	0	1	2	.333	0	0--	-	4.19	4.91
2004	Carlina	AA	15	15	0	0	73.0	331	75	52	45	10	9	4	6	43	3	58	7	2	3	5	.375	0	0--	-	5.63	5.55
2004	Mrlns	R	2	0	0	0	2.0	6	1	0	0	0	0	0	0	0	0	2	0	0	0	0	-	0	0--	-	0.63	0.00
2004	Jupiter	A+	6	0	0	1	8.2	34	2	1	0	0	0	0	1	6	0	7	0	0	1	1	.500	0	1--	-	1.27	0.00
2007	Lynbrg	A+	19	0	0	9	34.1	153	38	18	17	5	3	1	1	13	0	19	2	0	0	3	.000	0	4--	-	5.01	4.46
2007	Altna	AA	18	0	0	6	24.2	114	23	11	9	4	1	2	3	14	0	21	4	0	1	0	1.000	0	9--	-	5.20	3.28
2008	Altna	AA	38	0	0	21	57.0	254	63	31	30	4	4	1	4	25	3	36	2	0	4	4	.500	0	9--	-	4.90	4.74
2009	InldEm	A+	2	2	0	0	2.0	9	2	0	0	0	0	0	0	1	0	3	0	0	0	0	-	0	0--	-	3.63	0.00
2010	InldEm	A+	2	2	0	0	2.0	8	1	1	1	0	0	1	0	2	0	1	0	0	0	0	-	0	0--	-	3.21	4.50
2009	LAD	NL	69	0	0	13	70.2	299	52	21	16	4	3	2	6	29	7	64	4	0	4	3	.571	0	0-7	12	2.54	2.04
2010	LAD	NL	59	0	0	13	55.1	233	52	31	31	6	3	0	3	19	4	38	4	1	3	1	.750	0	2-4	15	3.72	5.04
	Postseason		6	0	0	2	4.2	20	5	4	4	1	0	0	0	1	0	1	0	1	0	0	-	0	0-0	2	4.41	7.71
2 ML YEARS			128	0	0	26	126.0	532	104	52	47	10	6	2	9	48	11	102	8	1	7	4	.636	0	2-11	28	3.04	3.36

Matt Belisle

Pitches: R Bats: R Pos: RP-76

bell-EYE-el

Ht: 6'4" Wt: 225 Born: 6/6/1980 Age: 31

Year	Team	Lg	G	GS	CG	GF	IP	BFP	H	R	ER	HR	SH	SF	HB	TBB	IBB	SO	WP	Bk	W	L	Pct	Sh	Sv-Op	Hld	ERC	ERA
2003	Cin	NL	6	0	0	2	8.2	39	10	5	5	1	2	1	1	2	0	6	0	0	1	1	.500	0	0-1	0	4.73	5.19
2005	Cin	NL	60	5	0	17	85.2	382	101	49	42	11	4	2	6	26	6	59	3	0	4	8	.333	0	1-4	8	5.08	4.41
2006	Cin	NL	30	2	0	5	40.0	180	43	18	16	5	1	4	2	19	1	26	3	0	2	0	1.000	0	0-1	0	5.29	3.60
2007	Cin	NL	30	30	1	0	177.2	771	212	111	105	26	7	9	7	43	4	125	6	1	8	9	.471	0	0-0	0	5.05	5.32
2008	Cin	NL	6	6	0	0	29.2	142	47	27	24	4	1	2	0	6	0	14	2	0	1	4	.200	0	0-0	0	6.87	7.28
2009	Col	NL	24	0	0	6	31.0	133	35	21	19	6	0	2	1	5	1	22	1	0	3	1	.750	0	0-0	1	4.50	5.52
2010	Col	NL	76	0	0	11	92.0	365	84	34	30	7	4	2	2	16	5	91	3	1	7	5	.583	0	1-2	21	2.67	2.93
	Postseason		2	0	0	0	2.0	7	0	0	0	0	0	0	0	1	0	2	0	0	0	0	-	0	0-0	1	0.27	0.00
7 ML YEARS			232	43	1	41	464.2	2012	532	265	241	60	19	20	20	117	17	343	18	2	26	28	.481	0	2-8	30	4.64	4.67

Heath Bell

Pitches: R Bats: R Pos: RP-67

Ht: 6'3" Wt: 250 Born: 9/29/1977 Age: 33

Year	Team	Lg	G	GS	CG	GF	IP	BFP	H	R	ER	HR	SH	SF	HB	TBB	IBB	SO	WP	Bk	W	L	Pct	Sh	Sv-Op	Hld	ERC	ERA
2004	NYM	NL	17	0	0	2	24.1	94	22	9	9	5	1	0	0	6	0	27	0	0	0	2	.000	0	0-1	1	3.86	3.33
2005	NYM	NL	42	0	0	12	46.2	206	56	30	29	3	4	0	1	13	3	43	0	1	1	3	.250	0	0-0	4	4.42	5.59
2006	NYM	NL	22	0	0	6	37.0	166	51	25	21	6	1	0	0	11	2	35	1	0	0	0	-	0	0-0	0	6.40	5.11
2007	SD	NL	81	0	0	16	93.2	363	60	21	21	3	4	1	2	30	1	102	0	0	6	4	.600	0	2-6	34	1.67	2.02
2008	SD	NL	74	0	0	8	78.0	324	66	31	31	5	3	2	3	28	4	71	2	0	6	6	.500	0	0-7	23	2.93	3.58
2009	SD	NL	68	0	0	59	69.2	278	54	21	21	3	0	0	0	24	1	79	4	0	6	4	.600	0	42-48	0	2.36	2.71
2010	SD	NL	67	0	0	57	70.0	287	56	17	15	1	4	1	1	28	3	86	1	0	6	1	.857	0	47-50	0	2.47	1.93
7 ML YEARS			371	0	0	160	419.1	1718	365	154	147	26	17	4	7	140	14	443	12	1	25	20	.556	0	91-112	62	2.93	3.16

Josh Bell

Bats: B Throws: R Pos: 3B-50; DH-2; PH-1; PR-1

Ht: 6'3" Wt: 220 Born: 11/13/1986 Age: 24

Year	Team	Lg	G	AB	H	2B	3B	HR	(Hm	Rd)	TB	R	RBI	RC	TBB	IBB	SO	HBP	SH	SF	SB	CS	SB%	GDP	Avg	OBP	Slg
2005	Ddgrs	R	45	157	50	7	1	1	(-	-)	62	26	21	26	20	1	33	1	0	1	5	2	.71	2	.318	.399	.395
2006	Ogden	R+	64	250	77	17	3	12	(-	-)	136	45	53	50	23	3	72	1	1	1	4	0	1.00	5	.308	.367	.544
2007	Gt Lks	A	108	398	115	21	3	15	(-	-)	187	65	62	67	39	2	109	1	0	0	5	1	.83	11	.289	.354	.470
2007	InldEm	A+	20	75	13	2	1	2	(-	-)	23	4	9	4	3	0	19	0	0	1	0	0	-	4	.173	.203	.307
2008	InldEm	A+	51	187	51	12	2	6	(-	-)	85	34	21	33	31	1	56	0	0	2	4	2	.67	3	.273	.373	.455

Year Team	Lg	G	AB	H	2B	3B	HR	(Hm	Rd)	TB	R	RBI	RC	TBB	IBB	SO	HBP	SH	SF	SB	CS	SB%	GDP	Avg	OBP	Slg
2009 Chatt	AA	94	334	99	30	2	11	(-	-)	166	47	52	65	50	2	70	2	0	5	3	5	.38	7	.296	.386	.497
2009 Bowie	AA	33	114	34	5	0	9	(-	-)	66	18	24	23	11	0	28	0	0	2	0	0	-	4	.298	.354	.579
2010 Norfolk	AAA	81	316	88	25	0	13	(-	-)	152	43	50	49	23	3	79	2	0	3	2	4	.33	3	.278	.328	.481
2010 Bal	AL	53	159	34	5	0	3	(2	1)	48	15	12	10	2	0	53	0	0	0	0	1	.00	4	.214	.224	.302

Trevor Bell

Pitches: R **Bats:** L **Pos:** RP-18; SP-7   **Ht:** 6'2" **Wt:** 185 **Born:** 10/12/1986 **Age:** 24

		HOW MUCH HE PITCHED						WHAT HE GAVE UP												THE RESULTS							
Year Team	Lg	G	GS	CG	GF	IP	BFP	H	R	ER	HR	SH	SF	HB	TBB	IBB	SO	WP	Bk	W	L	Pct	Sh	Sv-Op	Hld	ERC	ERA
2005 Angels	R	4	4	0	0	8.0	38	10	4	4	0	1	1	1	3	0	7	1	0	0			0	0- -		5.00	4.50
2006 Orem	R+	16	16	0	0	82.1	337	82	35	32	8	1	2	5	15	0	53	4	1	4	2	.667	0	0- -		3.49	3.50
2007 CRpds	A	21	21	0	0	115.1	499	136	64	53	8	1	7	3	23	0	90	6	1	8	4	.667	0	0- -		4.15	4.14
2008 RCuca	A+	36	12	2	11	100.1	441	106	60	47	8	9	2	4	39	2	80	5	2	4	3	.429	1	0- -		4.32	4.22
2008 CRpds	A	3	2	1	0	17.0	61	13	4	4	0	0	1	0	4	0	13	0	2	1	0	1.000	0	0- -		1.91	2.12
2009 Ark	AA	11	11	0	0	68.2	281	54	24	17	1	3	1	2	20	0	51	2	0	4	3	.571	0	0- -		2.10	2.23
2009 Salt Lk	AAA	11	11	2	0	71.1	286	67	27	25	5	0	1	2	15	1	38	0	0	3	4	.429	2	0- -		3.00	3.15
2010 Salt Lk	AAA	6	6	0	0	30.0	127	30	12	10	3	0	2	2	6	0	19	1	0	2	0	1.000	0	0- -		3.51	3.00
2009 LAA	AL	8	4	0	1	20.1	110	40	25	22	3	0	2	0	11	2	14	1	0	1	2	.333	0	0-0	0	11.15	9.74
2010 LAA	AL	25	7	0	8	61.0	273	77	35	32	2	3	1	1	21	2	45	5	0	2	5	.286	0	0-0	1	4.90	4.72
2 ML YEARS		33	11	0	9	81.1	383	117	60	54	5	3	3	1	32	4	59	6	0	3	7	.300	0	0-0	1	6.34	5.98

Ronnie Belliard

Bats: R **Throws:** R **Pos:** PH-45; 2B-20; 3B-16; 1B-10   **Ht:** 5'9" **Wt:** 211 **Born:** 4/7/1975 **Age:** 36

		BATTING																		BASERUNNING				AVERAGES		
Year Team	Lg	G	AB	H	2B	3B	HR	(Hm	Rd)	TB	R	RBI	RC	TBB	IBB	SO	HBP	SH	SF	SB	CS	SB%	GDP	Avg	OBP	Slg
1998 Mil	NL	8	5	1	0	0	0	(0	0)	1	1	0	0	0	0	0	0	0	0	0	0	-	0	.200	.200	.200
1999 Mil	NL	124	457	135	29	4	8	(5	3)	196	60	58	72	64	0	59	0	6	4	4	5	.44	16	.295	.379	.429
2000 Mil	NL	152	571	150	30	9	8	(4	4)	222	83	54	81	82	4	84	3	4	7	7	5	.58	12	.263	.354	.389
2001 Mil	NL	101	364	96	30	3	11	(7	4)	165	69	36	56	35	2	65	5	4	2	5	2	.71	5	.264	.335	.453
2002 Mil	NL	104	289	61	13	0	3	(0	3)	83	30	26	15	18	0	46	1	6	3	2	3	.40	9	.211	.257	.287
2003 Col	NL	116	447	124	31	2	8	(6	2)	183	73	50	71	49	0	71	2	6	1	7	2	.78	7	.277	.351	.409
2004 Cle	AL	152	599	169	48	1	12	(4	8)	255	78	70	87	60	5	98	2	0	2	3	2	.60	18	.282	.348	.426
2005 Cle	AL	115	536	152	36	1	17	(7	10)	241	71	78	71	35	0	72	1	8	7	2	2	.50	7	.284	.325	.450
2006 2 Tms		147	544	148	30	1	13	(5	8)	219	63	67	62	36	2	81	5	3	2	2	3	.40	17	.272	.322	.403
2007 Was	NL	147	511	148	35	1	11	(5	6)	218	57	58	64	34	1	72	1	6	5	3	0	1.00	12	.290	.332	.427
2008 Was	NL	96	296	85	22	0	11	(7	4)	140	37	46	53	37	1	58	3	1	0	3	2	.60	6	.287	.372	.473
2009 2 Tms		110	264	73	14	1	10	(5	5)	119	39	39	44	20	0	56	0	1	2	3	0	1.00	10	.277	.325	.451
2010 LAD	NL	82	162	35	10	1	2	(1	1)	53	24	19	17	18	1	35	1	2	2	2	2	.50	4	.216	.295	.327
06 Cle	AL	93	350	102	21	0	8	(3	5)	147	43	44	47	21	0	45	4	2	2	2	0	1.00	8	.291	.337	.420
06 StL	NL	54	194	46	9	1	5	(2	3)	72	20	23	15	15	2	36	1	1	0	0	3	.00	9	.237	.295	.371
09 Was	NL	86	187	46	7	1	5	(2	3)	70	26	22	18	14	0	40	0	1	2	2	0	1.00	7	.246	.296	.374
09 LAD	NL	24	77	27	7	0	5	(3	2)	49	13	17	16	6	0	16	0	0	0	1	0	1.00	3	.351	.398	.636
Postseason		22	80	21	1	0	0	(0	0)	22	6	5	8	7	1	12	1	1	0	3	0	1.00	1	.263	.330	.275
13 ML YEARS		1484	5045	1377	328	24	114	(56	58)	2095	685	601	683	488	16	797	24	47	37	43	28	.61	133	.273	.338	.415

Carlos Beltran

Bats: B **Throws:** R **Pos:** CF-61; PH-5   **Ht:** 6'1" **Wt:** 199 **Born:** 4/24/1977 **Age:** 34

		BATTING																		BASERUNNING				AVERAGES		
Year Team	Lg	G	AB	H	2B	3B	HR	(Hm	Rd)	TB	R	RBI	RC	TBB	IBB	SO	HBP	SH	SF	SB	CS	SB%	GDP	Avg	OBP	Slg
2010 StLuci*	A+	14	49	18	5	0	0	(-	-)	23	5	5	10	7	1	6	0	0	1	0	0	-	1	.367	.439	.469
1998 KC	AL	14	58	16	5	3	0	(0	0)	27	12	7	9	3	0	12	1	0	1	3	0	1.00	2	.276	.317	.466
1999 KC	AL	156	663	194	27	7	22	(12	10)	301	112	108	100	46	2	123	4	0	10	27	8	.77	17	.293	.337	.454
2000 KC	AL	98	372	92	15	4	7	(4	3)	136	49	44	43	35	2	69	0	2	4	13	0	1.00	12	.247	.309	.366
2001 KC	AL	155	617	189	32	12	24	(7	17)	317	106	101	118	52	2	120	5	1	5	31	1	.97	7	.306	.362	.514
2002 KC	AL	162	637	174	44	7	29	(19	10)	319	114	105	117	71	1	135	4	3	7	35	7	.83	12	.273	.346	.501
2003 KC	AL	141	521	160	14	10	26	(10	16)	272	102	100	117	72	4	81	2	0	7	41	4	.91	8	.307	.389	.522
2004 2 Tms		159	599	160	36	9	38	(15	23)	328	121	104	128	92	10	101	7	3	7	42	3	.93	6	.267	.367	.548
2005 NYM	NL	151	582	155	34	2	16	(6	10)	241	83	78	88	56	5	96	2	4	6	17	6	.74	9	.266	.330	.414
2006 NYM	NL	140	510	140	38	1	41	(15	26)	303	127	116	121	95	4	99	4	1	7	18	3	.86	6	.275	.388	.594
2007 NYM	NL	144	554	153	33	3	33	(11	22)	291	93	112	97	69	10	111	2	1	10	23	2	.92	8	.276	.353	.525
2008 NYM	NL	161	606	172	40	5	27	(14	13)	303	116	112	116	92	13	96	1	1	6	25	3	.89	11	.284	.376	.500
2009 NYM	NL	81	308	100	22	1	10	(3	7)	154	50	48	54	47	10	43	1	0	1	11	1	.92	9	.325	.415	.500
2010 NYM	NL	64	220	56	11	3	7	(3	4)	94	21	27	31	30	5	39	1	0	4	3	1	.75	4	.255	.341	.427
04 KC	AL	69	266	74	19	2	15	(8	7)	142	51	51	57	37	7	44	2	1	3	14	3	.82	4	.278	.367	.534
04 Hou	NL	90	333	86	17	7	23	(7	16)	186	70	53	67	55	3	57	5	2	4	28	0	1.00	2	.258	.368	.559
Postseason		22	82	30	4	0	11	(4	7)	67	31	19	26	18	1	13	1	0	0	6	0	1.00	1	.366	.485	.817
13 ML YEARS		1626	6247	1761	351	67	280	(119	161)	3086	1106	1062	1135	760	70	1125	34	16	75	289	39	.88	113	.282	.359	.494

Adrian Beltre

Bats: R **Throws:** R **Pos:** 3B-154; PR-1   **Ht:** 5'11" **Wt:** 220 **Born:** 4/7/1979 **Age:** 32

		BATTING																		BASERUNNING				AVERAGES		
Year Team	Lg	G	AB	H	2B	3B	HR	(Hm	Rd)	TB	R	RBI	RC	TBB	IBB	SO	HBP	SH	SF	SB	CS	SB%	GDP	Avg	OBP	Slg
1998 LAD	NL	77	195	42	9	0	7	(5	2)	72	18	22	20	14	0	37	3	2	0	3	1	.75	4	.215	.278	.369
1999 LAD	NL	152	538	148	27	5	15	(6	9)	230	84	67	84	61	12	105	6	4	5	18	7	.72	4	.275	.352	.428
2000 LAD	NL	138	510	148	30	2	20	(7	13)	242	71	85	85	56	2	80	2	3	4	12	5	.71	13	.290	.360	.411
2001 LAD	NL	126	475	126	22	4	13	(4	9)	195	59	60	60	28	1	82	5	2	5	13	4	.76	9	.265	.310	.411
2002 LAD	NL	159	587	151	26	5	21	(7	14)	250	70	75	74	37	4	96	4	1	6	7	5	.58	17	.257	.303	.426

Year Team	Lg	G	AB	H	2B	3B	HR	(Hm	Rd)	TB	R	RBI	RC	TBB	IBB	SO	HBP	SH	SF	SB	CS	SB%	GDP	Avg	OBP	Slg
2003 LAD	NL	158	559	134	30	2	23	(13	10)	237	50	80	66	37	4	103	5	1	6	2	2	.50	13	.240	.290	.424
2004 LAD	NL	156	598	200	32	0	**48**	(23	25)	376	104	121	120	53	9	87	2	0	4	7	2	.78	15	.334	.388	.629
2005 Sea	AL	156	603	154	36	1	19	(7	12)	249	69	87	75	38	6	108	5	0	4	3	1	.75	15	.255	.303	.413
2006 Sea	AL	156	620	166	39	4	25	(16	9)	288	88	89	85	47	4	118	10	1	3	11	5	.69	15	.268	.328	.465
2007 Sea	AL	149	595	164	41	2	26	(11	15)	287	87	99	79	38	2	104	2	0	4	14	2	.88	18	.276	.319	.482
2008 Sea	AL	143	556	148	29	1	25	(10	15)	254	74	77	71	50	10	90	2	0	4	8	2	.80	11	.266	.327	.457
2009 Sea	AL	111	449	119	27	0	8	(4	4)	170	54	44	48	19	1	74	1	0	2	13	2	.87	19	.265	.304	.379
2010 Bos	AL	154	589	189	**49**	2	28	(13	15)	326	84	102	103	40	10	82	5	0	7	2	1	.67	25	.321	.365	.553
Postseason		4	15	4	0	0	0	(0	0)	4	1	1	1	0	0	3	0	0	1	0	0	-	0	.267	.250	.267
13 ML YEARS		1835	6874	1889	397	28	278	(126	152)	3176	912	1008	970	518	65	1166	58	14	54	113	39	.74	178	.275	.328	.462

Omar Beltre

Pitches: R Bats: R Pos: SP-2

Ht: 6'3" Wt: 190 Born: 8/24/1981 Age: 29

Year Team	Lg	G	GS	CG	GF	IP	BFP	H	R	ER	HR	SH	SF	HB	TBB	IBB	SO	WP	Bk	W	L	Pct	Sh	Sv-Op	Hld	ERC	ERA
2000 Rngrs	R	13	13	0	0	61.0	251	54	30	24	2	1	2	6	15	0	44	2	2	5	4	.556	0	0--	-	2.83	3.54
2001 Pulaski	R+	13	12	0	0	69.1	290	56	28	26	4	3	3	9	23	0	83	12	1	6	3	.667	0	0--	-	2.99	3.38
2003 Clinton	A	16	5	0	7	49.0	198	46	19	13	4	1	1	1	11	0	27	5	1	3	3	.500	0	1--	-	3.09	2.39
2004 Stcktn	A+	46	0	0	22	58.2	262	60	32	16	1	0	0	3	24	1	47	6	1	4	5	.444	0	6--	-	3.72	2.45
2010 OKCity	AAA	24	14	0	6	85.0	348	69	35	25	2	3	4	2	38	1	85	9	0	3	9	.250	0	2--	-	2.88	2.65
2010 Tex	AL	2	2	0	0	7.0	38	9	7	7	3	1	0	2	7	0	9	0	0	0	1	.000	0	0-0	0	13.10	9.00

Joaquin Benoit

ben-WAH

Pitches: R Bats: R Pos: RP-63

Ht: 6'3" Wt: 220 Born: 7/26/1977 Age: 33

Year Team	Lg	G	GS	CG	GF	IP	BFP	H	R	ER	HR	SH	SF	HB	TBB	IBB	SO	WP	Bk	W	L	Pct	Sh	Sv-Op	Hld	ERC	ERA
2010 Drham*	AAA	8	0	0	4	9.2	40	8	3	3	2	0	1	0	3	0	17	0	0	0	1	.000	0	2--	-	3.41	2.79
2001 Tex	AL	1	1	0	0	5.0	26	8	6	6	3	0	1	0	3	0	4	0	0	0	0	-	0	0-0	0	13.11	10.80
2002 Tex	AL	17	13	0	2	84.2	405	91	51	50	6	4	3	5	58	2	59	7	0	4	5	.444	0	1-1	0	5.52	5.31
2003 Tex	AL	25	17	0	1	105.0	462	99	67	64	23	1	4	3	51	0	95	3	1	8	5	.615	0	0-0	0	5.03	5.49
2004 Tex	AL	28	15	0	2	103.0	456	113	67	65	19	2	10	8	31	0	95	3	0	3	5	.375	0	0-0	0	5.10	5.68
2005 Tex	AL	32	9	0	6	87.0	369	69	39	36	9	2	1	2	38	0	78	1	0	4	4	.500	0	0-0	5	3.15	3.72
2006 Tex	AL	56	0	0	7	79.2	347	68	49	43	5	0	3	3	38	4	85	3	0	1	1	.500	0	0-2	7	3.30	4.86
2007 Tex	AL	70	0	0	22	82.0	337	68	28	26	6	3	2	2	28	2	87	3	0	7	4	.636	0	6-13	19	2.83	2.85
2008 Tex	AL	44	0	0	8	45.0	209	40	28	25	6	2	0	0	35	2	43	3	0	3	2	.600	0	1-4	13	5.02	5.00
2010 TB	AL	63	0	0	16	60.1	217	30	10	9	6	0	2	0	11	1	75	1	0	1	2	.333	0	1-4	25	1.14	1.34
9 ML YEARS		336	55	0	64	651.2	2828	586	345	324	83	14	26	23	293	11	613	24	1	31	28	.525	0	9-24	69	3.97	4.47

Kris Benson

Pitches: R Bats: R Pos: SP-3

Ht: 6'4" Wt: 205 Born: 11/7/1974 Age: 36

Year Team	Lg	G	GS	CG	GF	IP	BFP	H	R	ER	HR	SH	SF	HB	TBB	IBB	SO	WP	Bk	W	L	Pct	Sh	Sv-Op	Hld	ERC	ERA
2010 Reno*	AAA	7	7	0	0	22.1	114	34	26	22	5	1	1	2	11	0	14	0	1	1	2	.333	0	0--	-	8.99	8.87
1999 Pit	NL	31	31	2	0	196.2	840	184	105	89	16	6	7	6	83	5	139	2	1	11	14	.440	0	0-0	0	3.78	4.07
2000 Pit	NL	32	32	2	0	217.2	936	206	104	93	24	7	6	10	86	5	184	5	0	10	12	.455	1	0-0	0	3.97	3.85
2002 Pit	NL	25	25	0	0	130.1	576	152	76	68	18	5	3	3	50	8	79	3	1	9	6	.600	0	0-0	0	5.31	4.70
2003 Pit	NL	18	18	0	0	105.0	475	127	67	58	14	3	4	1	36	4	68	7	0	5	9	.357	0	0-0	0	5.20	4.97
2004 2 Tms	NL	31	31	1	0	200.1	854	202	106	96	15	8	6	10	61	8	134	5	0	12	12	.500	1	0-0	0	3.71	4.31
2005 NYM	NL	28	28	0	0	174.1	737	171	86	80	24	5	3	4	49	5	95	4	0	10	8	.556	0	0-0	0	3.78	4.13
2006 Bal	AL	30	30	3	0	183.0	781	199	105	98	33	**9**	**13**	7	58	2	88	6	0	11	12	.478	0	0-0	0	5.06	4.82
2009 Tex	AL	8	2	0	2	22.1	114	33	23	21	6	0	2	3	12	0	11	0	0	1	1	.500	0	0-0	0	9.61	8.46
2010 Ari	NL	3	3	0	0	14.0	67	18	9	8	2	1	0	1	6	0	8	1	0	1	1	.500	0	0-0	0	6.37	5.14
04 Pit	NL	20	20	0	0	132.1	564	137	69	62	7	7	4	6	44	5	83	2	0	8	8	.500	0	0-0	0	3.84	4.22
04 NYM	NL	11	11	1	0	68.0	290	65	37	34	8	1	2	4	17	3	51	3	0	4	4	.500	1	0-0	0	3.45	4.50
9 ML YEARS		206	200	8	2	1243.2	5380	1292	681	611	152	44	44	45	441	37	806	33	2	70	75	.483	2	0-0	0	4.38	4.42

Justin Berg

Pitches: R Bats: R Pos: RP-41

Ht: 6'3" Wt: 230 Born: 6/7/1984 Age: 27

Year Team	Lg	G	GS	CG	GF	IP	BFP	H	R	ER	HR	SH	SF	HB	TBB	IBB	SO	WP	Bk	W	L	Pct	Sh	Sv-Op	Hld	ERC	ERA
2004 Yanks	R	15	1	0	4	30.2	147	40	22	20	3	0	3	3	15	0	29	3	0	3	2	.600	0	1--	-	6.63	5.87
2005 StIsInd	A-	15	9	0	2	58.2	238	48	26	23	3	2	0	4	20	0	52	0	2	6	2	.750	0	0--	-	2.89	3.53
2005 Peoria	A	2	1	0	0	6.2	32	9	7	7	0	0	1	0	6	0	3	2	0	0	0	-	0	0--	-	7.93	9.45
2006 Dytona	A+	24	24	0	0	115.0	525	126	67	56	4	4	4	10	53	0	82	19	0	7	7	.500	0	0--	-	4.67	4.38
2007 Tenn	AA	27	26	0	0	140.0	629	157	88	76	4	9	1	14	69	3	69	15	0	7	7	.500	0	0--	-	5.08	4.89
2008 Tenn	AA	5	5	0	0	28.1	127	29	14	11	1	1	4	1	11	0	10	1	0	3	0	1.000	0	0--	-	4.20	3.49
2008 Iowa	AAA	27	16	0	2	90.1	400	91	64	57	11	6	1	7	48	0	49	8	0	4	6	.400	0	0--	-	5.23	5.68
2009 Iowa	AAA	37	0	0	8	55.2	238	41	17	15	2	3	0	6	29	2	35	4	0	6	2	.750	0	0--	-	3.01	2.43
2010 Iowa	AAA	21	0	0	4	29.2	124	24	14	12	2	8	1	2	12	0	16	3	1	4	1	.800	0	0--	-	3.12	3.64
2009 ChC	NL	11	0	0	6	12.0	46	10	1	1	0	1	0	0	1	0	7	0	1	0	0	-	0	0-0	0	1.58	0.75
2010 ChC	NL	41	0	0	12	40.0	187	45	27	23	3	1	2	3	20	1	14	2	0	0	1	.000	0	0-0	5	5.16	5.18
2 ML YEARS		52	0	0	18	52.0	233	55	28	24	3	2	2	3	21	1	21	2	1	0	1	.000	0	0-0	5	4.23	4.15

Brad Bergesen

Pitches: R **Bats:** L **Pos:** SP-28; RP-2 — BURR-guess-inn — **Ht:** 6'3" **Wt:** 205 **Born:** 9/25/1985 **Age:** 25

Year	Team	Lg	G	GS	CG	GF	IP	BFP	H	R	ER	HR	SH	SF	HB	TBB	IBB	SO	WP	Bk	W	L	Pct	Sh	Sv-Op	Hld	ERC	ERA
2004	Bluefld	R+	5	0	0	0	5.2	27	7	5	5	1	0	0	0	3	1	6	0	0	0	0	-	0	0- -	-	6.14	7.94
2005	Abrdn	A-	15	15	0	0	71.0	311	89	45	38	5	2	5	1	14	0	54	3	0	1	3	.250	0	0- -	-	4.53	4.82
2006	Dlmrva	A	18	14	1	3	86.1	370	97	44	41	6	1	4	9	10	0	49	5	0	5	4	.556	0	0- -	-	3.81	4.27
2007	Dlmrva	A	15	15	1	0	94.1	377	75	30	23	3	2	0	7	17	0	73	2	1	7	3	.700	0	0- -	-	2.06	2.19
2007	Frdrck	A+	10	10	1	0	56.1	256	78	38	36	4	1	4	7	9	0	35	3	1	3	6	.333	0	0- -	-	5.65	5.75
2008	Frdrck	A+	4	3	0	0	17.1	73	15	6	4	2	0	0	1	6	0	15	0	0	1	1	.500	0	0- -	-	3.44	2.08
2008	Bowie	AA	24	23	3	0	148.0	603	143	59	53	11	3	4	3	27	0	72	5	0	15	6	.714	2	0- -	-	2.99	3.22
2009	Norfolk	AAA	2	2	0	0	11.0	45	6	4	3	0	1	0	2	3	0	9	0	0	1	1	.500	0	0- -	-	1.43	2.45
2010	Norfolk	AAA	3	3	0	0	14.2	65	17	7	7	2	0	0	0	3	0	10	0	0	1	0	1.000	0	0- -	-	4.26	4.30
2009	Bal	AL	19	19	1	0	123.1	519	126	52	47	11	3	4	5	32	4	65	2	0	7	5	.583	0	0-0	0	3.70	3.43
2010	Bal	AL	30	28	2	1	170.0	746	193	104	94	26	5	5	7	51	4	81	0	3	8	12	.400	0	0-0	0	4.95	4.98
	2 ML YEARS		49	47	3	1	293.1	1265	319	156	141	37	8	9	12	83	8	146	2	3	15	17	.469	0	0-0	0	4.41	4.33

Jason Bergmann

Pitches: R **Bats:** R **Pos:** RP-4 — **Ht:** 6'3" **Wt:** 222 **Born:** 9/25/1981 **Age:** 29

Year	Team	Lg	G	GS	CG	GF	IP	BFP	H	R	ER	HR	SH	SF	HB	TBB	IBB	SO	WP	Bk	W	L	Pct	Sh	Sv-Op	Hld	ERC	ERA
2010	Syrcse*	AAA	43	0	0	9	50.2	219	42	26	16	6	4	1	5	19	2	56	2	0	6	4	.600	0	0- -	-	3.40	2.84
2005	Was	NL	15	1	0	4	19.2	85	14	6	6	1	1	1	2	11	1	21	0	0	2	0	1.000	0	0-0	1	3.05	2.75
2006	Was	NL	29	6	0	7	64.2	303	81	49	48	12	6	1	6	27	6	54	3	0	0	2	.000	0	0-0	1	6.50	6.68
2007	Was	NL	21	21	0	0	115.1	480	99	59	57	18	6	1	2	42	1	86	4	0	6	6	.500	0	0-0	0	3.59	4.45
2008	Was	NL	30	22	1	1	139.2	614	153	94	79	25	9	8	1	47	2	96	2	0	2	11	.154	0	0-0	0	4.88	5.09
2009	Was	NL	56	0	0	6	48.0	213	50	28	24	7	5	0	3	25	7	40	3	0	2	4	.333	0	0-1	10	5.26	4.50
2010	Was	NL	4	0	0	0	2.1	11	3	4	4	2	0	0	1	0	2	0	0	0	1	.000	0	0-0	1	11.78	15.43
	6 ML YEARS		155	50	1	18	389.2	1706	400	240	218	65	27	14	14	153	17	299	12	0	12	24	.333	0	0-1	13	4.73	5.04

Jason Berken

Pitches: R **Bats:** R **Pos:** RP-41 — **Ht:** 6'0" **Wt:** 210 **Born:** 11/27/1983 **Age:** 27

Year	Team	Lg	G	GS	CG	GF	IP	BFP	H	R	ER	HR	SH	SF	HB	TBB	IBB	SO	WP	Bk	W	L	Pct	Sh	Sv-Op	Hld	ERC	ERA
2006	Abrdn	A-	9	8	0	0	45.0	178	39	20	14	4	1	3	2	5	0	46	1	0	1	4	.200	0	0- -	-	2.40	2.80
2007	Frdrck	A+	27	26	2	1	151.0	650	160	90	76	12	3	7	6	49	0	124	4	0	9	9	.500	1	0- -	-	4.15	4.53
2008	Bowie	AA	26	25	2	0	145.2	611	141	69	58	9	4	7	8	38	0	125	5	0	12	4	.750	1	0- -	-	3.32	3.58
2009	Bowie	AA	2	2	0	0	8.0	34	4	5	5	1	0	0	1	6	0	8	0	0	1	1	.500	0	0- -	-	3.38	5.63
2009	Norfolk	AAA	5	5	0	0	25.2	98	19	3	3	1	2	0	0	6	0	16	0	0	2	0	1.000	0	0- -	-	1.86	1.05
2009	Bal	AL	24	24	0	0	119.2	560	164	92	87	19	3	5	6	44	2	66	0	1	6	12	.333	0	0-0	0	6.81	6.54
2010	Bal	AL	41	0	0	8	62.1	262	64	24	21	5	4	1	0	19	3	45	3	0	3	3	.500	0	0-4	7	3.68	3.03
	2 ML YEARS		65	24	0	8	182.0	822	228	116	108	24	7	6	6	63	5	111	3	1	9	15	.375	0	0-4	7	5.68	5.34

Lance Berkman

Bats: B **Throws:** L **Pos:** 1B-93; DH-23; PH-9 — **Ht:** 6'1" **Wt:** 229 **Born:** 2/10/1976 **Age:** 35

Year	Team	Lg	G	AB	H	2B	3B	HR	(Hm	Rd)	TB	R	RBI	RC	TBB	IBB	SO	HBP	SH	SF	SB	CS	SB%	GDP	Avg	OBP	Slg
2010	RdRck*	AAA	2	6	3	2	0	1	(-	-)	8	3	3	2	0	0	2	0	0	1	0	0	-	0	.500	.429	1.333
2010	Trntn*	AA	2	8	2	0	0	0	(-	-)	2	1	0	0	1	0	3	0	0	0	0	0	-	0	.250	.333	.250
1999	Hou	NL	34	93	22	2	0	4	(2	2)	36	10	15	12	12	0	21	0	0	1	3	1	.65	2	.237	.321	.387
2000	Hou	NL	114	353	105	28	1	21	(10	11)	198	76	67	76	56	1	73	1	0	7	6	2	.75	6	.297	.388	.561
2001	Hou	NL	156	577	191	55	5	34	(13	21)	358	110	126	144	92	5	121	13	0	6	7	9	.44	8	.331	.430	.620
2002	Hou	NL	158	578	169	35	2	42	(20	22)	334	106	128	130	107	20	118	4	0	3	8	4	.67	10	.292	.405	.578
2003	Hou	NL	153	538	155	35	6	25	(11	14)	277	110	93	115	107	13	108	9	1	3	5	3	.63	10	.288	.412	.515
2004	Hou	NL	160	544	172	40	3	30	(8	22)	308	104	106	126	127	14	101	10	0	6	9	7	.56	10	.316	.450	.566
2005	Hou	NL	132	468	137	34	1	24	(13	11)	245	76	82	88	91	12	72	4	0	7	4	1	.80	18	.293	.411	.524
2006	Hou	NL	152	536	169	29	0	45	(24	21)	333	95	136	138	98	22	106	4	0	8	3	2	.60	11	.315	.420	.621
2007	Hou	NL	153	561	156	24	2	34	(13	21)	286	95	102	105	94	11	123	8	0	5	7	3	.70	11	.278	.386	.510
2008	Hou	NL	159	554	173	46	4	29	(16	13)	314	114	106	129	99	18	108	7	0	5	18	4	.82	13	.312	.420	.567
2009	Hou	NL	136	460	126	31	1	25	(14	11)	234	73	80	83	97	14	98	1	0	4	7	4	.64	13	.274	.399	.509
2010	2 Tms		122	404	100	23	1	14	(10	4)	167	48	58	61	77	7	85	0	0	0	3	2	.60	18	.248	.368	.413
10	Hou	NL	85	298	73	16	1	13	(9	4)	130	39	49	48	60	4	70	0	0	0	3	2	.60	12	.245	.372	.436
10	NYY	AL	37	106	27	7	0	1	(1	0)	37	9	9	13	17	3	15	0	0	0	0	0	-	6	.255	.358	.349
	Postseason		29	106	34	8	0	6	(4	2)	60	18	26	27	20	5	26	1	0	2	2	1	.67	4	.321	.426	.566
	12 ML YEARS		1629	5666	1675	382	26	327	(154	173)	3090	1017	1099	1207	1057	137	1136	61	1	50	82	42	.66	130	.296	.409	.545

Roger Bernadina

Bats: L **Throws:** L **Pos:** RF-77; LF-44; CF-26; PH-5; PR-4 — burn-ah-DEEN-ah — **Ht:** 6'2" **Wt:** 198 **Born:** 6/12/1984 **Age:** 27

Year	Team	Lg	G	AB	H	2B	3B	HR	(Hm	Rd)	TB	R	RBI	RC	TBB	IBB	SO	HBP	SH	SF	SB	CS	SB%	GDP	Avg	OBP	Slg
2010	Syrcse*	AAA	14	61	23	2	1	2	(-	-)	33	8	8	14	6	0	5	0	1	1	7	2	.78	2	.377	.426	.541
2008	Was	NL	26	76	16	1	1	0	(0	0)	19	10	2	4	9	0	21	0	1	0	4	3	.57	3	.211	.294	.250
2009	Was	NL	3	4	1	1	0	0	(0	0)	2	1	0	1	1	0	1	0	0	0	1	0	1.00	0	.250	.400	.500
2010	Was	NL	134	414	102	18	3	11	(3	8)	159	52	47	53	35	1	93	4	2	6	16	2	.89	3	.246	.307	.384
	3 ML YEARS		163	494	119	20	4	11	(3	8)	180	63	49	58	45	1	115	4	3	6	21	5	.81	6	.241	.306	.364

Rafael Betancourt

Pitches: R **Bats:** R **Pos:** RP-72 — BETT-an-court — **Ht:** 6'2" **Wt:** 215 **Born:** 4/29/1975 **Age:** 36

			HOW MUCH HE PITCHED						WHAT HE GAVE UP										THE RESULTS							
Year	Team	Lg	G	GS	CG	GF	IP	BFP	H	R	ER	HR	SH	SF	HB	TBB	IBB	SO	WP	Bk	W	L	Pct	Sh	Sv-Op	Hld	ERC	ERA
2003	Cle	AL	33	0	0	13	38.0	154	27	11	9	5	1	1	1	13	2	36	1	0	2	2	.500	0	1-3	4	2.54	2.13
2004	Cle	AL	68	0	0	21	66.2	286	71	32	29	7	1	2	0	18	6	76	5	1	5	6	.455	0	4-11	12	3.77	3.92
2005	Cle	AL	54	0	0	12	67.2	272	57	23	21	5	1	0	0	17	2	73	0	0	4	3	.571	0	1-3	10	2.49	2.79
2006	Cle	AL	50	0	0	17	56.2	231	52	25	24	7	2	2	0	11	5	48	0	0	3	4	.429	0	3-6	7	2.84	3.81
2007	Cle	AL	68	0	0	15	79.1	289	51	13	13	4	0	2	0	9	3	80	0	0	5	1	.833	0	3-6	31	1.24	1.47
2008	Cle	AL	69	0	0	20	71.0	309	76	41	40	11	4	5	0	25	5	64	2	0	3	4	.429	0	4-8	12	4.53	5.07
2009	2 Tms		61	0	0	10	56.0	227	42	20	17	4	2	4	0	20	5	61	0	0	4	3	.571	0	2-6	20	2.30	2.73
2010	Col	NL	72	0	0	18	62.1	248	52	25	25	9	3	1	0	8	2	89	7	0	5	1	.833	0	1-5	23	2.35	3.61
09	Cle	AL	29	0	0	7	30.2	129	25	15	12	3	1	2	0	15	4	32	0	0	1	2	.333	0	1-3	8	3.21	3.52
09	Col	NL	32	0	0	3	25.1	98	17	5	5	1	1	2	0	5	1	29	0	0	3	1	.750	0	1-3	12	1.42	1.78
	Postseason		10	0	0	2	12.1	49	9	8	7	2	1	0	2	2	1	12	0	0	0	0	-	0	0-0	3	1.98	5.11
	8 ML YEARS		475	0	0	126	497.2	2016	428	190	178	52	14	17	1	121	30	527	15	1	31	24	.564	0	19-48	119	2.68	3.22

Yuniesky Betancourt

Bats: R **Throws:** R **Pos:** SS-151 — yoon-ee-ESS-kee BETT-an-court — **Ht:** 5'11" **Wt:** 210 **Born:** 1/31/1982 **Age:** 29

						BATTING																BASERUNNING				AVERAGES		
Year	Team	Lg	G	AB	H	2B	3B	HR	(Hm	Rd)	TB	R	RBI	RC	TBB	IBB	SO	HBP	SH	SF		SB	CS	SB%	GDP	Avg	OBP	Slg
2005	Sea	AL	60	211	54	11	5	1	(1	0)	78	24	15	21	11	0	24	2	2	2		1	3	.25	2	.256	.296	.370
2006	Sea	AL	157	558	161	28	6	8	(2	6)	225	68	47	60	17	0	54	1	7	1		18	8	.58	10	.289	.310	.403
2007	Sea	AL	155	536	155	38	2	9	(6	3)	224	72	67	73	15	3	48	1	3	4		5	4	.56	10	.289	.308	.418
2008	Sea	AL	153	559	156	36	3	7	(3	4)	219	66	51	53	17	0	42	2	6	6		4	4	.50	23	.279	.300	.392
2009	2 Tms		134	470	115	20	6	6	(2	4)	165	40	49	41	21	0	44	0	11	6		3	3	.50	17	.245	.274	.351
2010	KC	AL	151	556	144	29	2	16	(8	8)	225	60	78	56	23	1	64	1	4	4		2	3	.40	13	.259	.288	.405
09	Sea	AL	63	224	56	10	1	2	(1	1)	74	15	22	19	10	0	18	0	8	3		3	1	.75	9	.250	.278	.330
09	KC	AL	71	246	59	10	5	4	(1	3)	91	25	27	22	11	0	26	0	3	3		0	2	.00	8	.240	.269	.370
	6 ML YEARS		810	2890	785	162	24	47	(22	25)	1136	330	307	304	104	4	276	7	33	23		26	25	.51	75	.272	.296	.393

Wilson Betemit

Bats: B **Throws:** R **Pos:** 3B-53; DH-14; PH-10; 1B-5; 2B-2; LF-2; PR-1 — BETT-uh-meet — **Ht:** 6'2" **Wt:** 222 **Born:** 11/2/1981 **Age:** 29

						BATTING																BASERUNNING				AVERAGES		
Year	Team	Lg	G	AB	H	2B	3B	HR	(Hm	Rd)	TB	R	RBI	RC	TBB	IBB	SO	HBP	SH	SF		SB	CS	SB%	GDP	Avg	OBP	Slg
2010	Omha*	AAA	29	113	30	6	2	2	(-	-)	46	9	17	18	17	0	23	1	1	3		1	1	.50	1	.265	.358	.407
2001	Atl	NL	8	3	0	0	0	0	(0	0)	0	1	0	0	2	0	3	0	0	0		1	0	1.00	0	.000	.400	.000
2004	Atl	NL	22	47	8	0	0	0	(0	0)	8	2	3	0	4	0	16	0	0	1		0	1	.00	0	.170	.231	.170
2005	Atl	NL	115	246	75	12	4	4	(0	4)	107	36	20	36	22	4	55	0	4	2		1	3	.25	5	.305	.359	.435
2006	2 Tms	NL	143	373	98	23	0	18	(7	11)	175	49	53	52	36	6	102	0	1	2		3	1	.75	11	.263	.326	.469
2007	2 Tms		121	240	55	12	0	14	(8	6)	109	33	50	42	38	0	82	1	2	3		0	0	-	2	.229	.333	.454
2008	NYY	AL	87	189	50	13	0	6	(5	1)	81	24	25	17	6	0	56	1	1	1		0	1	.00	2	.265	.289	.429
2009	CWS	AL	20	45	9	5	0	0	(0	0)	14	2	3	3	5	0	13	0	0	0		0	0	-	2	.200	.280	.311
2010	KC	AL	84	276	82	20	0	13	(7	6)	141	36	43	48	36	2	74	1	0	2		0	0	-	3	.297	.378	.511
06	Atl	NL	88	199	56	16	0	9	(7	6)	99	30	29	35	19	3	57	0	1	0		2	1	.67	4	.281	.344	.497
06	LAD	NL	55	174	42	7	0	9	(4	5)	76	19	24	17	17	3	45	0	0	2		1	0	1.00	7	.241	.306	.437
07	LAD	NL	84	156	36	8	0	10	(6	4)	74	22	26	26	32	0	49	1	0	3		0	0	-	1	.231	.359	.474
07	NYY	AL	37	84	19	4	0	4	(2	2)	35	11	24	16	6	0	33	0	2	0		0	0	-	1	.226	.278	.417
	Postseason		6	10	5	1	0	1	(0	1)	9	3	1	2	2	1	2	0	0	0		0	0	-	0	.500	.583	.900
	8 ML YEARS		600	1419	377	85	4	55	(27	28)	635	183	197	198	149	12	401	3	8	11		5	6	.45	30	.266	.334	.447

Chad Billingsley

Pitches: R **Bats:** R **Pos:** SP-31 — **Ht:** 6'1" **Wt:** 240 **Born:** 7/29/1984 **Age:** 26

			HOW MUCH HE PITCHED						WHAT HE GAVE UP										THE RESULTS							
Year	Team	Lg	G	GS	CG	GF	IP	BFP	H	R	ER	HR	SH	SF	HB	TBB	IBB	SO	WP	Bk	W	L	Pct	Sh	Sv-Op	Hld	ERC	ERA
2006	LAD	NL	18	16	0	0	90.0	403	92	43	38	7	4	0	3	58	3	59	5	0	7	4	.636	0	0-0	0	5.22	3.80
2007	LAD	NL	43	20	1	6	147.0	623	131	56	54	15	9	3	3	64	3	141	5	0	12	5	.706	0	0-1	3	3.70	3.31
2008	LAD	NL	35	32	1	1	200.2	859	188	76	70	14	8	5	8	80	6	201	10	0	16	10	.615	1	0-0	1	3.62	3.14
2009	LAD	NL	33	32	0	0	196.1	823	173	94	88	17	9	11	7	86	7	179	14	0	12	11	.522	0	0-0	0	3.63	4.03
2010	LAD	NL	31	31	1	0	191.2	817	176	82	76	8	7	11	10	69	7	171	4	0	12	11	.522	1	0-0	0	3.20	3.57
	Postseason		6	3	0	0	17.0	78	20	14	13	1	0	0	0	10	2	22	2	0	1	2	.333	0	0-0	0	5.40	6.88
	5 ML YEARS		160	131	3	7	825.2	3525	760	351	326	61	37	30	31	357	26	751	38	0	59	41	.590	2	0-1	4	3.70	3.55

Joe Bisenius

Pitches: R **Bats:** R **Pos:** RP-5 — biss-ENN-ee-us — **Ht:** 6'4" **Wt:** 205 **Born:** 9/18/1982 **Age:** 28

			HOW MUCH HE PITCHED						WHAT HE GAVE UP										THE RESULTS							
Year	Team	Lg	G	GS	CG	GF	IP	BFP	H	R	ER	HR	SH	SF	HB	TBB	IBB	SO	WP	Bk	W	L	Pct	Sh	Sv-Op	Hld	ERC	ERA
2004	Batvia	A-	11	11	0	0	50.1	199	39	12	8	5	3	3	1	14	0	38	4	1	0	1	.000	0	0- -	-	2.55	1.43
2005	Lakwd	A	40	4	1	14	64.1	300	66	45	42	5	3	4	6	37	0	56	10	3	6	4	.600	0	4- -	-	5.03	5.88
2006	Clrwtr	A+	35	0	0	9	60.2	250	48	17	13	4	4	1	2	22	0	62	2	0	4	1	.800	0	2- -	-	2.65	1.93
2006	Rdng	AA	16	0	0	9	23.1	87	14	9	8	2	1	1	0	8	0	33	0	0	1	2	.667	0	5- -	-	1.88	3.09
2007	Ottawa	AAA	35	0	0	11	46.0	212	52	29	28	5	3	5	0	31	2	41	7	1	3	4	.429	0	0- -	-	6.07	5.48
2008	LV	AAA	15	0	0	6	21.2	106	24	18	17	1	4	3	0	18	1	21	5	0	0	2	.000	0	0- -	-	5.82	7.06
2008	Rdng	AA	28	0	0	8	42.0	175	33	18	16	5	2	4	0	24	1	33	5	0	3	3	.500	0	0- -	-	3.76	3.43
2009	Rdng	AA	9	0	0	2	12.0	60	15	15	15	3	0	0	0	9	0	17	3	0	0	2	.000	0	0- -	-	8.18	11.25
2009	Phillies	R	1	0	0	1	1.0	4	1	0	0	0	0	0	0	0	0	3	0	0	0	0	-	0	0- -	-	1.95	0.00
2009	Clrwtr	A+	3	0	0	0	4.0	15	2	0	0	0	0	0	0	2	0	5	0	0	0	0	-	0	0- -	-	1.51	0.00
2009	LV	AAA	7	1	0	0	9.2	45	14	9	9	1	0	0	0	12	0	16	0	0	0	1	.000	0	0- -	-	7.01	8.38

Year Team	Lg	G	GS	CG	GF	IP	BFP	H	R	ER	HR	SH	SF	HB	TBB	IBB	SO	WP	Bk	W	L	Pct	Sh	Sv-Op	Hld	ERC	ERA
		HOW MUCH HE PITCHED						**WHAT HE GAVE UP**												**THE RESULTS**							
2010 Ptomc	A+	6	0	0	3	7.1	33	6	4	1	0	0	0	2	2	0	9	4	0	0	0	-	0	1--	-	2.77	1.23
2010 Hrsbrg	AA	14	0	0	4	14.1	61	10	7	7	0	0	0	1	8	0	17	4	0	3	0	1.000	0	0--	-	3.09	4.40
2010 Syrcse	AAA	14	0	0	4	16.2	73	14	6	5	1	1	2	2	6	0	20	1	0	1	0	1.000	0	0--	-	3.11	2.70
2007 Phi	NL	2	0	0	0	2.0	9	2	0	0	0	0	0	0	2	0	3	0	0	0	0	-	0	0-0	0	6.15	0.00
2010 Was	NL	5	0	0	2	4.2	26	6	6	5	1	0	0	0	6	0	5	0	0	0	0	-	0	0-0	0	10.57	9.64
2 ML YEARS		7	0	0	2	6.2	35	8	6	5	1	0	0	0	8	0	8	0	0	0	0	-	0	0-0	0	9.23	6.75

Nick Blackburn

Pitches: R Bats: R Pos: SP-26; RP-2   **Ht: 6'4" Wt: 225 Born: 2/24/1982 Age: 29**

Year Team	Lg	G	GS	CG	GF	IP	BFP	H	R	ER	HR	SH	SF	HB	TBB	IBB	SO	WP	Bk	W	L	Pct	Sh	Sv-Op	Hld	ERC	ERA
		HOW MUCH HE PITCHED						**WHAT HE GAVE UP**												**THE RESULTS**							
2010 Roch*	AAA	4	4	0	0	21.2	89	19	7	6	2	0	0	0	6	0	13	2	0	1	0	1.000	0	0--	-	2.88	2.49
2007 Min	AL	6	0	0	3	11.2	54	19	12	10	2	0	0	0	2	0	8	0	0	0	2	.000	0	0-1	1	7.61	7.71
2008 Min	AL	33	33	0	0	193.1	823	224	102	87	23	5	4	7	39	4	96	2	0	11	11	.500	0	0-0	0	4.48	4.05
2009 Min	AL	33	33	3	0	205.2	882	**240**	103	92	25	5	5	3	41	1	98	2	0	11	11	.500	0	0-0	0	4.42	4.03
2010 Min	AL	28	26	1	2	161.0	692	194	101	97	25	2	3	4	40	1	68	3	1	10	12	.455	0	0-0	0	5.24	5.42
Postseason		1	1	0	0	5.2	22	3	1	1	0	0	0	0	2	0	3	0	0	0	0	-	0	0-0	0	1.21	1.59
4 ML YEARS		100	92	4	5	571.2	2451	677	318	286	75	12	12	14	122	6	270	7	1	32	36	.471	0	0-1	1	4.73	4.50

Casey Blake

Bats: R Throws: R Pos: 3B-139; PH-8; 1B-1   **Ht: 6'2" Wt: 204 Born: 8/23/1973 Age: 37**

Year Team	Lg	G	AB	H	2B	3B	HR	(Hm	Rd)	TB	R	RBI	RC	TBB	IBB	SO	HBP	SH	SF	SB	CS	SB%	GDP	Avg	OBP	Slg
						BATTING															**BASERUNNING**			**AVERAGES**		
1999 Tor	AL	14	39	10	2	0	1	(0	1)	15	6	1	4	2	0	7	0	0	0	0	0	-	1	.256	.293	.385
2000 Min	AL	7	16	3	2	0	0	(0	0)	5	1	1	2	3	0	7	1	0	1	0	0	-	1	.188	.333	.313
2001 2 Tms	AL	19	37	9	1	0	1	(0	1)	13	3	4	5	4	1	12	0	0	0	3	0	1.00	0	.243	.317	.351
2002 Min	AL	9	20	4	1	0	0	(0	0)	5	2	1	1	2	0	7	0	0	0	0	0	-	0	.200	.273	.250
2003 Cle	AL	152	557	143	35	0	17	(2	15)	229	80	67	68	38	1	109	10	8	8	7	9	.44	11	.257	.312	.411
2004 Cle	AL	152	587	159	36	3	28	(13	15)	285	93	88	88	68	2	139	9	1	3	5	8	.38	19	.271	.354	.486
2005 Cle	AL	147	523	126	32	1	23	(7	16)	229	72	58	53	43	3	116	10	2	5	4	5	.44	9	.241	.308	.438
2006 Cle	AL	109	401	113	20	1	19	(9	10)	192	63	68	62	45	5	93	4	1	5	6	0	1.00	11	.282	.356	.479
2007 Cle	AL	156	588	159	36	4	18	(11	7)	257	81	78	69	54	2	123	10	5	5	4	5	.44	14	.270	.339	.437
2008 2 Tms		152	536	147	36	1	21	(6	15)	248	71	81	85	49	11	120	11	1	4	3	0	1.00	12	.274	.345	.463
2009 LAD	NL	139	485	136	25	6	18	(7	11)	227	84	79	76	63	8	116	6	1	10	3	4	.43	12	.280	.363	.468
2010 LAD	NL	146	509	126	28	1	17	(6	11)	207	56	64	60	48	3	138	8	3	3	0	4	.00	8	.248	.320	.407
01 Min	AL	13	22	7	1	0	0	(0	0)	8	1	2	4	3	1	8	0	0	0	1	0	1.00	1	.318	.400	.364
01 Bal	AL	6	15	2	0	0	1	(0	1)	5	2	2	1	1	0	4	0	0	0	2	0	1.00	0	.133	.188	.333
08 Cle	AL	94	325	94	24	0	11	(1	10)	151	46	58	64	33	6	68	7	1	2	2	0	1.00	3	.289	.365	.465
08 LAD	NL	58	211	53	12	1	10	(5	5)	97	25	23	21	16	5	52	4	0	2	1	0	1.00	9	.251	.313	.460
Postseason		27	103	24	3	0	2	(2	0)	33	10	10	9	5	1	23	1	1	0	1	0	1.00	2	.233	.275	.320
12 ML YEARS		1202	4298	1135	254	17	163	(61	102)	1912	612	590	573	419	36	987	69	22	44	35	35	.50	98	.264	.336	.445

Hank Blalock

Bats: L Throws: R Pos: DH-14; PH-11; 3B-2; RF-2; 1B-1   BLAY-lock   **Ht: 6'1" Wt: 200 Born: 11/21/1980 Age: 30**

Year Team	Lg	G	AB	H	2B	3B	HR	(Hm	Rd)	TB	R	RBI	RC	TBB	IBB	SO	HBP	SH	SF	SB	CS	SB%	GDP	Avg	OBP	Slg
						BATTING															**BASERUNNING**			**AVERAGES**		
2010 Drham*	AAA	26	109	38	5	0	4	(-	-)	55	18	24	22	10	1	19	1	0	1	2	0	1.00	1	.349	.405	.505
2002 Tex	AL	49	147	31	8	0	3	(2	1)	48	16	17	15	20	1	43	1	2	2	0	0	-	2	.211	.306	.327
2003 Tex	AL	143	567	170	33	3	29	(18	11)	296	89	90	90	44	1	97	1	0	3	2	3	.40	16	.300	.360	.522
2004 Tex	AL	159	624	172	38	3	32	(18	10)	312	107	110	119	75	7	149	6	0	8	2	2	.50	13	.276	.355	.500
2005 Tex	AL	161	647	170	34	0	25	(20	5)	279	80	92	86	51	1	132	3	0	4	1	0	1.00	16	.263	.318	.431
2006 Tex	AL	152	591	157	26	3	16	(8	8)	237	76	89	87	51	6	98	2	0	2	1	0	1.00	15	.266	.325	.401
2007 Tex	AL	58	208	61	16	3	10	(7	3)	113	32	33	30	21	1	38	1	0	2	4	1	.80	8	.293	.358	.543
2008 Tex	AL	65	258	74	19	1	12	(6	6)	131	37	38	36	19	3	40	2	0	2	1	0	1.00	10	.287	.338	.508
2009 Tex	AL	123	462	108	21	4	25	(13	12)	212	62	66	54	26	2	108	3	0	4	2	0	1.00	6	.234	.277	.459
2010 TB	AL	26	63	16	3	0	1	(0	1)	22	8	7	6	6	0	15	0	0	0	1	1	.50	1	.254	.319	.349
9 ML YEARS		936	3567	959	198	17	153	(90	63)	1650	507	542	531	313	22	720	19	2	27	14	7	.67	87	.269	.329	.463

Andres Blanco

Bats: B Throws: R Pos: 2B-40; SS-16; 3B-9; PH-4; PR-2; DH-1   **Ht: 5'10" Wt: 190 Born: 4/11/1984 Age: 27**

Year Team	Lg	G	AB	H	2B	3B	HR	(Hm	Rd)	TB	R	RBI	RC	TBB	IBB	SO	HBP	SH	SF	SB	CS	SB%	GDP	Avg	OBP	Slg
						BATTING															**BASERUNNING**			**AVERAGES**		
2004 KC	AL	19	60	19	2	2	0	(0	0)	25	9	5	12	5	0	6	1	1	0	1	2	.33	0	.317	.379	.417
2005 KC	AL	26	79	17	0	1	0	(0	0)	19	6	5	3	0	0	5	1	4	2	0	1	.00	3	.215	.220	.241
2006 KC	AL	33	87	21	4	1	0	(0	0)	27	9	9	9	5	0	14	1	3	0	0	1	.00	2	.241	.290	.310
2009 ChC	NL	53	123	31	8	0	1	(1	0)	42	15	12	9	8	3	14	1	6	0	0	2	.00	4	.252	.303	.341
2010 Tex	AL	68	166	46	10	1	0	(0	0)	58	17	13	19	11	1	24	3	3	2	0	2	.00	0	.277	.330	.349
5 ML YEARS		199	515	134	24	5	1	(1	0)	171	56	44	52	29	4	63	7	17	4	1	8	.11	9	.260	.306	.332

Gregor Blanco

Bats: L Throws: L Pos: CF-66; LF-8; PR-6; PH-5; RF-3   Ht: 5'11" Wt: 170 Born: 12/24/1983 Age: 27

Year	Team	Lg	G	AB	H	2B	3B	HR	(Hm	Rd)	TB	R	RBI	RC	TBB	IBB	SO	HBP	SH	SF	SB	CS	SB%	GDP	Avg	OBP	Slg
2010	Gwnntt*	AAA	44	154	44	8	0	1	(-	-)	55	26	11	25	23	0	28	1	9	0	9	1	.90	1	.286	.382	.357
2008	Atl	NL	144	430	108	14	4	1	(0	1)	133	52	38	60	74	2	99	6	6	3	13	5	.72	3	.251	.366	.309
2009	Atl	NL	24	43	8	0	1	0	(0	0)	10	5	1	2	4	0	9	0	1	0	2	0	1.00	1	.186	.255	.233
2010	2 Tms		85	237	67	9	4	1	(1	0)	87	31	14	30	29	1	50	0	2	1	11	4	.73	5	.283	.360	.367
10	Atl	NL	36	58	18	1	1	0	(0	0)	21	9	3	8	8	1	15	0	0	0	1	2	.33	2	.310	.394	.362
10	KC	AL	49	179	49	8	3	1	(1	0)	66	22	11	22	21	0	35	0	2	1	10	2	.83	3	.274	.348	.369
3 ML YEARS			253	710	183	23	9	2	(1	1)	230	88	53	92	107	3	158	6	9	4	26	9	.74	9	.258	.358	.324

Henry Blanco

Bats: R Throws: R Pos: C-46; PH-5; PR-1   Ht: 5'11" Wt: 220 Born: 8/29/1971 Age: 39

Year	Team	Lg	G	AB	H	2B	3B	HR	(Hm	Rd)	TB	R	RBI	RC	TBB	IBB	SO	HBP	SH	SF	SB	CS	SB%	GDP	Avg	OBP	Slg
1997	LAD	NL	3	5	2	0	0	1	(0	1)	5	1	1	2	0	0	1	0	0	0	0	0	-	0	.400	.400	1.000
1999	Col	NL	88	263	61	12	3	6	(3	3)	97	30	28	32	34	1	38	1	3	2	1	1	.50	4	.232	.320	.369
2000	Mil	NL	93	284	67	24	0	7	(3	4)	112	29	31	33	36	6	60	0	0	4	0	3	.00	9	.236	.318	.394
2001	Mil	NL	104	314	66	18	3	6	(4	2)	108	33	31	30	34	6	72	2	5	2	3	1	.75	10	.210	.290	.344
2002	Atl	NL	81	221	45	9	1	6	(4	2)	74	17	22	15	20	5	51	1	2	5	0	2	.00	5	.204	.267	.335
2003	Atl	NL	55	151	30	8	0	1	(0	1)	41	11	13	13	10	2	21	1	3	1	0	0	-	3	.199	.252	.272
2004	Min	AL	114	315	65	19	1	10	(4	6)	116	36	37	25	21	0	56	3	11	3	0	3	.00	8	.206	.260	.368
2005	ChC	NL	54	161	39	6	0	6	(2	4)	63	16	25	17	11	1	24	0	4	2	0	0	-	6	.242	.287	.391
2006	ChC	NL	74	241	64	15	2	6	(2	4)	101	23	37	26	14	1	38	0	4	2	0	0	-	8	.266	.304	.419
2007	ChC	NL	22	54	9	3	0	0	(0	0)	12	3	4	2	2	0	12	0	1	1	0	0	-	1	.167	.193	.222
2008	ChC	NL	58	120	35	3	0	3	(2	1)	47	15	12	11	6	1	22	0	2	0	0	0	-	4	.292	.325	.392
2009	SD	NL	67	204	48	12	0	6	(4	2)	78	21	16	20	26	2	50	0	1	1	0	0	-	5	.235	.320	.382
2010	NYM	NL	50	130	28	5	0	2	(2	0)	39	10	8	7	11	2	26	0	0	3	1	0	1.00	1	.215	.271	.300
Postseason			6	14	3	0	0	1	(1	0)	6	1	2	0	0	0	4	0	1	1	0	0	-	1	.214	.200	.429
13 ML YEARS			863	2463	559	134	10	60	(30	30)	893	245	265	233	225	27	471	8	36	26	5	10	.33	63	.227	.291	.363

Kyle Blanks

Bats: R Throws: R Pos: LF-30; 1B-4; PH-1   Ht: 6'6" Wt: 270 Born: 9/11/1986 Age: 24

Year	Team	Lg	G	AB	H	2B	3B	HR	(Hm	Rd)	TB	R	RBI	RC	TBB	IBB	SO	HBP	SH	SF	SB	CS	SB%	GDP	Avg	OBP	Slg
2005	Padres	R	48	164	49	10	1	7	(-	-)	82	33	30	36	25	3	49	10	0	1	3	1	.75	3	.299	.420	.500
2006	FtWyn	A	86	308	90	20	0	10	(-	-)	140	41	52	56	36	2	79	11	0	4	2	0	1.00	6	.292	.382	.455
2007	Lk Els	A+	119	465	140	31	4	24	(-	-)	251	94	100	97	44	1	98	18	0	4	11	2	.85	12	.301	.380	.540
2008	SnAnt	AA	132	492	160	23	5	20	(-	-)	253	75	107	102	51	0	90	17	0	5	5	4	.56	16	.325	.404	.514
2009	Portlnd	AAA	66	233	66	9	1	12	(-	-)	113	35	38	46	39	0	63	5	0	3	0	0	-	3	.283	.393	.485
2010	Lk Els	A+	10	37	10	3	0	0	(-	-)	13	3	4	5	6	1	12	1	0	0	0	0	-	0	.270	.386	.351
2010	Portlnd	AAA	1	3	1	0	0	0	(-	-)	1	0	0	0	1	0	1	0	0	0	0	0	-	0	.333	.500	.333
2009	SD	NL	54	148	37	9	0	10	(6	4)	76	24	22	21	18	1	55	6	0	0	1	1	.50	4	.250	.355	.514
2010	SD	NL	33	102	16	6	1	3	(2	1)	33	14	15	10	15	0	46	3	0	0	1	0	1.00	1	.157	.283	.324
2 ML YEARS			87	250	53	15	1	13	(8	5)	109	38	37	31	33	1	101	9	0	0	2	1	.67	5	.212	.325	.436

Joe Blanton

Pitches: R Bats: R Pos: SP-28; RP-1   Ht: 6'3" Wt: 244 Born: 12/11/1980 Age: 30

Year	Team	Lg	G	GS	CG	GF	IP	BFP	H	R	ER	HR	SH	SF	HB	TBB	IBB	SO	WP	Bk	W	L	Pct	Sh	Sv-Op	Hld	ERC	ERA
2010	Lakwd*	A	1	1	0	0	2.0	6	0	0	0	0	0	0	0	0	0	2	0	0	0	0	-	0	0--	-	0.00	0.00
2010	Rdng*	AA	2	2	0	0	8.0	35	9	5	5	2	0	0	0	2	0	5	0	0	0	1	.000	0	0--	-	5.12	5.63
2004	Oak	AL	3	0	0	1	8.0	30	6	5	5	1	0	0	0	2	0	6	0	0	0	0	-	0	0-0	0	2.52	5.63
2005	Oak	AL	33	33	2	0	201.1	835	178	86	79	23	2	7	5	67	3	116	4	2	12	12	.500	1	0-0	0	3.37	3.53
2006	Oak	AL	32	31	1	0	194.1	856	241	111	104	17	3	9	5	58	4	107	3	0	16	12	.571	1	0-0	0	5.09	4.82
2007	Oak	AL	34	34	3	0	230.0	950	240	106	101	16	3	7	6	40	4	140	3	1	14	10	.583	1	0-0	0	3.30	3.95
2008	2 Tms		33	33	0	0	197.2	855	211	110	103	22	2	4	4	66	3	111	2	0	9	12	.429	0	0-0	0	4.33	4.69
2009	Phi	NL	31	31	0	0	195.1	837	198	89	88	30	11	4	8	59	4	163	7	0	12	8	.600	0	0-0	0	4.25	4.05
2010	Phi	NL	29	28	0	0	175.2	765	206	104	94	27	5	7	3	43	6	134	2	0	9	6	.600	0	0-0	0	4.81	4.82
08	Oak	AL	20	20	0	0	127.0	550	145	74	70	12	1	2	1	35	3	62	1	0	5	12	.294	0	0-0	0	4.33	4.96
08	Phi	NL	13	13	0	0	70.2	305	66	36	33	10	1	2	3	31	0	49	1	0	4	0	1.000	0	0-0	0	4.33	4.20
Postseason			8	5	0	1	34.2	148	31	16	15	5	1	1	2	12	2	30	0	0	2	0	1.000	0	0-0	0	3.67	3.89
7 ML YEARS			195	190	6	1	1202.1	5128	1280	611	574	136	28	39	29	335	24	777	21	3	72	60	.545	2	0-0	0	4.13	4.30

Jerry Blevins

Pitches: L Bats: L Pos: RP-63   Ht: 6'6" Wt: 178 Born: 9/6/1983 Age: 27

Year	Team	Lg	G	GS	CG	GF	IP	BFP	H	R	ER	HR	SH	SF	HB	TBB	IBB	SO	WP	Bk	W	L	Pct	Sh	Sv-Op	Hld	ERC	ERA
2007	Oak	AL	6	0	0	1	4.2	25	8	6	5	1	0	2	0	2	0	3	0	0	0	1	.000	0	0-0	-	9.08	9.64
2008	Oak	AL	36	0	0	8	37.2	156	32	14	13	2	0	1	3	13	2	35	0	0	1	3	.250	0	0-1	5	3.00	3.11
2009	Oak	AL	20	0	0	5	22.1	90	19	12	12	2	0	1	0	6	1	23	0	0	0	0	-	0	0-0	0	2.68	4.84
2010	Oak	AL	63	0	0	9	48.2	220	54	20	20	7	3	1	1	18	1	46	0	0	2	1	.667	0	1-2	11	4.81	3.70
4 ML YEARS			125	0	0	23	113.1	491	113	52	50	12	3	3	4	39	4	107	0	0	3	5	.375	0	1-3	16	3.92	3.97

50

Willie Bloomquist

Bats: R **Throws:** R **Pos:** RF-27; PR-19; PH-12; 3B-11; LF-9; CF-8; DH-7; 2B-6; 1B-3; SS-1 **Ht:** 5'11" **Wt:** 194 **Born:** 11/27/1977 **Age:** 33

Year	Team	Lg	G	AB	H	2B	3B	HR	(Hm	Rd)	TB	R	RBI	RC	TBB	IBB	SO	HBP	SH	SF	SB	CS	SB%	GDP	Avg	OBP	Slg
2002	Sea	AL	12	33	15	4	0	0	(0	0)	19	11	7	10	5	0	2	0	0	0	3	1	.75	0	.455	.526	.576
2003	Sea	AL	89	196	49	7	2	1	(1	0)	63	30	14	18	19	1	39	1	2	2	4	1	.80	5	.250	.317	.321
2004	Sea	AL	93	188	46	10	0	2	(0	2)	62	27	18	18	10	0	48	0	3	0	13	2	.87	2	.245	.283	.330
2005	Sea	AL	82	249	64	15	2	0	(0	0)	83	27	22	26	11	0	38	1	4	2	14	1	.93	5	.257	.289	.333
2006	Sea	AL	102	251	62	6	2	1	(0	1)	75	36	15	27	24	0	40	4	2	2	16	3	.84	1	.247	.320	.299
2007	Sea	AL	91	173	48	3	0	2	(1	1)	57	28	13	16	10	0	35	1	4	0	7	5	.58	7	.277	.321	.329
2008	Sea	AL	71	165	46	1	0	0	(0	0)	47	32	9	24	25	1	29	1	1	0	14	3	.82	1	.279	.377	.285
2009	KC	AL	125	434	115	11	8	4	(0	4)	154	52	29	45	27	1	73	1	4	2	25	6	.81	7	.265	.308	.355
2010	2 Tms		83	187	50	10	1	3	(2	1)	71	31	17	19	9	0	28	0	2	1	8	5	.62	4	.267	.299	.380
10	KC	AL	72	170	45	10	1	3	(2	1)	66	31	17	18	8	0	25	0	2	1	8	5	.62	4	.265	.296	.388
10	Cin	NL	11	17	5	0	0	0	(0	0)	5	0	0	1	1	0	3	0	0	0	0	0	-	0	.294	.333	.294
9 ML YEARS			748	1876	495	67	15	13	(4	9)	631	274	144	203	140	3	332	9	22	9	104	27	.79	35	.264	.317	.336

Geoff Blum

Bats: B **Throws:** R **Pos:** PH-45; SS-18; 1B-14; 3B-14; 2B-8 **Ht:** 6'3" **Wt:** 221 **Born:** 4/26/1973 **Age:** 38

Year	Team	Lg	G	AB	H	2B	3B	HR	(Hm	Rd)	TB	R	RBI	RC	TBB	IBB	SO	HBP	SH	SF	SB	CS	SB%	GDP	Avg	OBP	Slg
2010	CpChr*	AA	3	9	2	2	0	0	(-	-)	4	0	1	1	1	0	0	0	0	0	0	0	-	0	.222	.300	.444
1999	Mon	NL	45	133	32	7	2	8	(0	8)	67	21	18	22	17	3	25	0	3	0	1	0	1.00	3	.241	.327	.504
2000	Mon	NL	124	343	97	20	2	11	(5	6)	154	40	45	50	26	2	60	3	3	4	1	4	.20	4	.283	.335	.449
2001	Mon	NL	148	453	107	25	0	9	(6	3)	159	57	50	49	43	8	94	10	3	5	9	5	.64	12	.236	.313	.351
2002	Hou	NL	130	368	104	20	4	10	(6	4)	162	45	52	62	49	5	70	1	1	2	2	0	1.00	4	.283	.367	.440
2003	Hou	NL	123	420	110	19	0	10	(8	4)	159	51	52	40	20	1	50	2	2	5	0	0	-	15	.262	.295	.379
2004	TB	AL	112	339	73	21	0	8	(2	6)	118	38	35	29	24	1	58	0	4	2	2	3	.40	4	.215	.266	.348
2005	2 Tms		109	319	73	15	2	6	(1	5)	110	32	25	27	28	0	43	3	0	1	3	3	.50	6	.229	.296	.345
2006	SD	NL	109	276	70	17	1	4	(0	4)	101	27	34	26	17	1	51	0	2	4	0	1	.00	5	.254	.293	.366
2007	SD	NL	122	330	83	21	1	5	(1	4)	121	34	33	38	32	4	52	2	3	3	0	0	-	10	.252	.319	.367
2008	Hou	NL	114	325	78	14	1	14	(6	8)	136	36	53	42	21	2	54	3	0	7	1	2	.33	5	.240	.287	.418
2009	Hou	NL	120	381	94	14	1	10	(4	6)	140	34	49	39	33	4	61	7	0	6	0	1	.00	9	.247	.314	.367
2010	Hou	NL	93	202	54	10	1	2	(1	1)	71	22	22	28	15	2	33	1	0	0	0	0	-	3	.267	.321	.356
05	SD	NL	78	224	54	13	1	5	(1	4)	84	26	22	23	24	0	28	3	0	1	3	2	.60	5	.241	.321	.375
05	CWS	AL	31	95	19	2	1	1	(0	1)	26	6	3	4	4	0	15	0	0	0	0	1	.00	1	.200	.232	.274
Postseason			6	10	2	1	0	1	(0	1)	6	1	2	1	4	1	1	0	0	1	0	0	-	1	.200	.400	.600
12 ML YEARS			1349	3889	975	203	15	97	(38	59)	1499	437	468	452	325	33	651	32	21	39	19	19	.50	84	.251	.311	.385

Brian Bocock

Bats: R **Throws:** R **Pos:** SS-6; PR-2 **Ht:** 5'11" **Wt:** 185 **Born:** 3/9/1985 **Age:** 26

Year	Team	Lg	G	AB	H	2B	3B	HR	(Hm	Rd)	TB	R	RBI	RC	TBB	IBB	SO	HBP	SH	SF	SB	CS	SB%	GDP	Avg	OBP	Slg
2006	SlmKzr	A-	39	103	23	6	0	0	(-	-)	29	12	7	10	12	0	29	1	3	2	6	1	.86	3	.223	.305	.282
2006	Augsta	A	2	1	0	0	0	0	(-	-)	0	1	1	0	0	0	0	0	0	1	0	0	-	0	.000	.000	.000
2007	Augsta	A	39	161	47	9	1	1	(-	-)	61	24	20	24	16	0	19	0	0	1	26	8	.76	4	.292	.354	.379
2007	SnJos	A+	87	345	76	19	3	4	(-	-)	113	42	37	35	35	0	105	3	9	6	15	10	.60	7	.220	.293	.328
2008	Fresno	AAA	35	123	20	3	0	0	(-	-)	23	14	3	5	14	0	39	1	3	0	7	3	.70	2	.163	.254	.187
2009	Conn	AA	25	70	12	1	0	0	(-	-)	13	9	3	4	12	0	20	1	4	1	2	3	.40	2	.171	.298	.186
2009	SnJos	A+	97	386	93	25	2	3	(-	-)	131	56	48	41	36	0	96	1	1	6	6	7	.46	10	.241	.303	.339
2010	LV	AAA	120	380	85	11	3	4	(-	-)	114	37	31	39	49	4	88	1	4	5	13	6	.68	14	.224	.310	.300
2008	SF	NL	32	77	11	1	0	0	(0	0)	12	4	2	3	12	0	20	0	4	0	4	2	.67	2	.143	.258	.156
2010	Phi	NL	6	5	0	0	0	0	(0	0)	0	2	0	0	0	0	3	0	0	0	0	0	-	0	.000	.000	.000
2 ML YEARS			38	82	11	1	0	0	(0	0)	12	6	2	3	12	0	32	0	4	0	4	2	.67	2	.134	.245	.146

Brennan Boesch

Bats: L **Throws:** L **Pos:** RF-79; LF-44; DH-14; PH-5; PR-2 BOSH **Ht:** 6'6" **Wt:** 210 **Born:** 4/12/1985 **Age:** 26

Year	Team	Lg	G	AB	H	2B	3B	HR	(Hm	Rd)	TB	R	RBI	RC	TBB	IBB	SO	HBP	SH	SF	SB	CS	SB%	GDP	Avg	OBP	Slg
2006	Oneont	A-	70	292	85	15	6	5	(-	-)	127	27	54	43	21	2	42	3	0	1	3	4	.43	4	.291	.344	.435
2007	WMich	A	126	513	137	19	4	10	(-	-)	194	52	86	60	23	2	81	1	0	5	15	4	.79	16	.267	.297	.378
2008	Lkland	A+	111	417	104	17	8	7	(-	-)	158	46	64	50	36	6	90	3	0	5	3	5	.38	9	.249	.310	.379
2009	Erie	AA	131	527	145	26	7	28	(-	-)	269	89	93	88	33	6	127	3	1	7	11	2	.85	10	.275	.318	.510
2010	Toledo	AAA	15	58	22	3	1	3	(-	-)	36	6	17	15	4	0	17	4	0	0	2	1	.67	1	.379	.455	.621
2010	Det	AL	133	464	119	26	3	14	(7	7)	193	49	67	61	40	5	99	5	0	3	7	1	.88	5	.256	.320	.416

Brandon Boggs

Bats: B **Throws:** R **Pos:** RF-3; LF-1; PH-1 **Ht:** 5'10" **Wt:** 212 **Born:** 1/9/1983 **Age:** 28

Year	Team	Lg	G	AB	H	2B	3B	HR	(Hm	Rd)	TB	R	RBI	RC	TBB	IBB	SO	HBP	SH	SF	SB	CS	SB%	GDP	Avg	OBP	Slg
2010	OKCity*	AAA	103	362	105	25	5	10	(-	-)	170	72	50	71	72	4	93	1	1	3	3	6	.33	5	.290	.406	.470
2008	Tex	AL	101	283	64	17	4	8	(6	2)	113	30	41	37	44	1	93	3	1	3	3	2	.60	3	.226	.333	.399
2009	Tex	AL	9	17	1	1	0	0	(0	0)	2	0	0	0	1	0	8	0	0	0	0	0	-	0	.059	.111	.118
2010	Tex	AL	4	7	0	0	0	0	(0	0)	0	0	0	0	1	0	4	0	0	0	0	0	-	0	.000	.125	.000
3 ML YEARS			114	307	65	18	4	8	(6	2)	115	30	41	37	46	1	105	3	1	3	3	2	.60	3	.212	.318	.375

Mitchell Boggs

Pitches: R Bats: R Pos: RP-61 Ht: 6'4" Wt: 215 Born: 2/15/1984 Age: 27

			HOW MUCH HE PITCHED						WHAT HE GAVE UP												THE RESULTS							
Year	Team	Lg	G	GS	CG	GF	IP	BFP	H	R	ER	HR	SH	SF	HB	TBB	IBB	SO	WP	Bk	W	L	Pct	Sh	Sv-Op	Hld	ERC	ERA
2008	StL	NL	8	6	0	1	34.0	164	42	29	28	5	1	1	2	22	0	13	2	0	3	2	.600	0	0-0	0	7.17	7.41
2009	StL	NL	16	9	0	2	58.0	268	71	28	27	3	1	2	4	33	0	46	4	1	2	3	.400	0	0-0	1	6.15	4.19
2010	StL	NL	61	0	0	22	67.1	285	60	29	27	5	4	3	4	27	2	52	5	0	2	3	.400	0	0-0	6	3.51	3.61
	Postseason		1	0	0	1	1.0	5	0	0	0	0	0	0	0	2	0	1	0	0	0	0	-	0	0-0	0	3.47	0.00
	3 ML YEARS		85	15	0	25	159.1	717	173	86	82	13	6	6	10	82	2	111	11	1	7	8	.467	0	0-0	7	5.19	4.63

Brian Bogusevic

Bats: L Throws: L Pos: PH-11; LF-7; CF-3; RF-2 boe-gah-SEVV-ick Ht: 6'3" Wt: 215 Born: 2/18/1984 Age: 27

						BATTING																BASERUNNING				AVERAGES		
Year	Team	Lg	G	AB	H	2B	3B	HR	(Hm	Rd)	TB	R	RBI	RC	TBB	IBB	SO	HBP	SH	SF		SB	CS	SB%	GDP		Avg	OBP	Slg
2006	Lxngtn	A	17	0	0	0	0	0	(-	-)	0	0	0	0	0	0	0	0	0	0		0	0	-	0		-	-	-
2006	TriCity	A-	3	0	0	0	0	0	(-	-)	0	0	0	0	0	0	0	0	0	0		0	0	-	0		-	-	-
2007	Salem	A+	21	0	0	0	0	0	(-	-)	0	0	0	0	0	0	0	0	0	0		0	0	-	0		-	-	-
2007	CpChr	AA	7	2	1	0	0	0	(-	-)	1	0	0	0	0	0	0	0	0	0		0	0	-	0		.500	.500	.500
2008	CpChr	AA	51	124	46	10	2	3	(-	-)	69	21	20	31	16	1	24	1	4	0		8	1	.89	3		.371	.447	.556
2008	Salem	A+	8	23	5	2	0	1	(-	-)	10	4	6	4	4	1	1	1	0	0		0	1	1.00	2		.217	.357	.435
2009	RdRck	AAA	138	520	141	25	3	6	(-	-)	190	68	53	72	53	3	118	3	5	0		22	3	.88	11		.271	.342	.365
2010	RdRck	AAA	131	502	139	26	2	13	(-	-)	208	91	57	84	67	2	108	3	1	2		23	1	.96	13		.277	.364	.414
2010	Hou	NL	19	28	5	3	0	0	(0	0)	8	5	3	2	3	0	12	0	0	0		1	1	.50	2		.179	.258	.286

Jeremy Bonderman

Pitches: R Bats: R Pos: SP-29; RP-1 Ht: 6'2" Wt: 220 Born: 10/28/1982 Age: 28

			HOW MUCH HE PITCHED						WHAT HE GAVE UP												THE RESULTS							
Year	Team	Lg	G	GS	CG	GF	IP	BFP	H	R	ER	HR	SH	SF	HB	TBB	IBB	SO	WP	Bk	W	L	Pct	Sh	Sv-Op	Hld	ERC	ERA
2003	Det	AL	33	28	0	0	162.0	727	193	100	100	23	3	6	4	58	2	108	12	2	6	19	.240	0	0-0	0	5.39	5.56
2004	Det	AL	33	32	2	0	184.0	793	168	101	100	24	10	5	10	73	5	168	7	0	11	13	.458	2	0-0	0	3.93	4.89
2005	Det	AL	29	29	4	0	189.0	801	199	101	96	21	3	3	4	57	0	145	5	1	14	13	.519	0	0-0	0	4.20	4.57
2006	Det	AL	34	34	0	0	214.0	903	214	104	97	18	3	6	3	64	7	202	3	1	14	8	.636	0	0-0	0	3.58	4.08
2007	Det	AL	28	28	0	0	174.1	753	193	105	97	23	2	4	4	48	6	145	12	1	11	9	.550	0	0-0	0	4.44	5.01
2008	Det	AL	12	12	0	0	71.1	319	75	39	34	9	2	3	3	36	2	44	1	0	3	4	.429	0	0-0	0	5.14	4.29
2009	Det	AL	8	1	0	1	10.1	53	16	10	10	4	0	0	1	8	0	5	0	0	1	0	1.000	0	0-0	0	12.87	8.71
2010	Det	AL	30	29	0	0	171.0	754	187	113	105	25	3	5	10	60	1	112	8	0	8	10	.444	0	0-0	1	4.98	5.53
	Postseason		3	3	0	0	20.1	84	17	7	7	1	1	0	0	7	1	11	1	0	1	0	1.000	0	0-0	0	2.58	3.10
	8 ML YEARS		207	193	6	1	1176.0	5103	1245	691	639	147	26	32	39	404	23	929	48	5	67	77	.465	2	0-0	1	4.46	4.89

Emilio Bonifacio

Bats: B Throws: R Pos: PH-23; CF-17; SS-9; LF-7; PR-7; 3B-6; RF-6; 2B-5 Ht: 5'11" Wt: 200 Born: 4/23/1985 Age: 26

						BATTING																BASERUNNING				AVERAGES		
Year	Team	Lg	G	AB	H	2B	3B	HR	(Hm	Rd)	TB	R	RBI	RC	TBB	IBB	SO	HBP	SH	SF		SB	CS	SB%	GDP		Avg	OBP	Slg
2010	NewOr*	AAA	40	164	45	8	3	0	(-	-)	59	19	11	21	16	0	33	0	2	0		8	4	.67	1		.274	.339	.360
2007	Ari	NL	11	23	5	1	0	0	(0	0)	6	2	2	4	4	0	3	0	0	0		0	1	.00	0		.217	.333	.261
2008	2 Tms	NL	49	169	41	6	5	0	(0	0)	57	29	14	16	14	0	46	0	0	3		7	4	.64	2		.243	.296	.337
2009	Fla	NL	127	461	116	11	6	1	(1	0)	142	72	27	41	34	0	95	2	8	4		21	9	.70	5		.252	.303	.308
2010	Fla	NL	73	180	47	6	3	0	(0	0)	59	30	10	24	17	0	42	0	1	3		12	0	1.00	1		.261	.320	.328
08	Ari	NL	8	12	2	1	0	0	(0	0)	3	3	2	1	0	0	5	0	0	0		1	0	1.00	0		.167	.167	.250
08	Was	NL	41	157	39	5	5	0	(0	0)	54	26	12	15	14	0	41	0	0	3		6	4	.60	2		.248	.305	.344
	4 ML YEARS		260	833	209	24	14	1	(1	0)	264	133	53	85	69	0	186	2	9	10		40	14	.74	8		.251	.306	.317

Eddie Bonine

Pitches: R Bats: R Pos: RP-46; SP-1 Ht: 6'5" Wt: 220 Born: 6/6/1981 Age: 30

			HOW MUCH HE PITCHED						WHAT HE GAVE UP												THE RESULTS							
Year	Team	Lg	G	GS	CG	GF	IP	BFP	H	R	ER	HR	SH	SF	HB	TBB	IBB	SO	WP	Bk	W	L	Pct	Sh	Sv-Op	Hld	ERC	ERA
2008	Det	AL	5	5	0	0	26.2	117	36	16	16	3	1	1	2	5	0	9	0	0	2	1	.667	0	0-0	0	5.82	5.40
2009	Det	AL	10	4	0	2	34.1	145	40	19	17	7	0	2	1	12	1	19	0	0	1	1	.500	0	0-0	0	6.00	4.46
2010	Det	AL	47	1	0	14	68.0	303	84	37	35	7	0	3	3	22	2	26	4	0	4	1	.800	0	0-0	2	5.33	4.63
	3 ML YEARS		62	10	0	16	129.0	565	160	75	68	17	1	6	6	39	3	54	4	0	7	3	.700	0	0-0	2	5.61	4.74

Boof Bonser

Pitches: R Bats: R Pos: RP-15 Ht: 6'4" Wt: 245 Born: 10/14/1981 Age: 29

			HOW MUCH HE PITCHED						WHAT HE GAVE UP												THE RESULTS							
Year	Team	Lg	G	GS	CG	GF	IP	BFP	H	R	ER	HR	SH	SF	HB	TBB	IBB	SO	WP	Bk	W	L	Pct	Sh	Sv-Op	Hld	ERC	ERA
2010	Pwtckt*	AAA	9	8	0	0	32.2	148	37	23	23	3	3	3	2	14	0	25	2	0	0	2	.000	0	0--	-	5.12	6.34
2010	Scrmto*	AAA	5	5	0	0	23.2	97	20	14	12	2	0	0	0	11	0	17	0	0	2	1	.667	0	0--	-	3.50	4.56
2006	Min	AL	18	18	0	0	100.1	419	104	50	47	18	2	2	1	24	0	84	2	0	7	6	.538	0	0-0	0	4.25	4.22
2007	Min	AL	31	30	0	0	173.0	772	199	108	98	27	4	3	5	65	4	136	3	1	8	12	.400	0	0-0	0	5.33	5.10
2008	Min	AL	47	12	0	9	118.1	532	139	87	78	16	3	4	1	36	1	97	6	1	3	7	.300	0	0-2	0	4.84	5.93
2010	2 Tms	AL	15	0	0	4	25.0	112	33	17	17	2	0	0	0	8	0	17	1	0	1	0	1.000	0	0-0	3	5.53	6.12
10	Bos	AL	2	0	0	1	2.0	13	6	4	4	0	0	0	0	2	0	0	0	0	0	0	-	0	0-0	0	21.10	18.00
10	Oak	AL	13	0	0	3	23.0	99	27	13	13	2	3	0	0	6	0	17	1	0	1	0	1.000	0	0-0	3	4.45	5.09
	Postseason		1	1	0	0	6.0	25	7	2	2	0	0	0	0	1	0	3	0	0	0	0	-	0	0-0	0	3.46	3.00
	4 ML YEARS		111	60	0	13	416.2	1835	475	262	240	63	12	9	7	133	5	334	12	2	19	25	.432	0	0-2	5	4.94	5.18

Julio Borbon

Bats: L **Throws:** L **Pos:** CF-133; PR-4; DH-2; LF-1; PH-1   bore-BONE   **Ht:** 6'0" **Wt:** 195 **Born:** 2/20/1986 **Age:** 25

						BATTING															BASERUNNING				AVERAGES		
Year	Team	Lg	G	AB	H	2B	3B	HR	(Hm	Rd)	TB	R	RBI	RC	TBB	IBB	SO	HBP	SH	SF	SB	CS	SB%	GDP	Avg	OBP	Slg
2007	Spkane	A-	7	29	5	0	0	0	(-	-)	5	1	2	0	2	0	3	0	0	0	3	1	.75	1	.172	.226	.172
2007	Rngrs	R	2	8	2	1	0	0	(-	-)	3	0	0	0	1	0	1	0	0	0	0	1	.00	0	.250	.333	.375
2008	Bkrsfld	A+	66	291	89	20	0	2	(-	-)	115	47	36	45	15	0	30	4	2	2	36	7	.84	4	.306	.346	.395
2008	Frisco	AA	60	255	86	12	2	5	(-	-)	117	40	22	43	14	0	32	4	6	1	17	11	.61	3	.337	.380	.459
2009	Okla	AAA	96	407	126	12	7	2	(-	-)	158	71	35	64	33	2	40	7	8	2	25	7	.78	7	.310	.370	.388
2009	Tex	AL	46	157	49	4	0	4	(2	2)	65	30	20	27	15	0	28	1	6	0	19	4	.83	3	.312	.376	.414
2010	Tex	AL	137	438	121	11	4	3	(2	1)	149	60	42	48	19	0	59	2	8	1	15	7	.68	5	.276	.309	.340
	2 ML YEARS		183	595	170	15	4	7	(4	3)	214	90	62	75	34	0	87	3	14	1	34	11	.76	8	.286	.327	.360

J.C. Boscan

Bats: R **Throws:** R **Pos:** C-1   BAHS-cann   **Ht:** 6'2" **Wt:** 215 **Born:** 12/26/1979 **Age:** 31

						BATTING															BASERUNNING				AVERAGES		
Year	Team	Lg	G	AB	H	2B	3B	HR	(Hm	Rd)	TB	R	RBI	RC	TBB	IBB	SO	HBP	SH	SF	SB	CS	SB%	GDP	Avg	OBP	Slg
1997	Braves	R	36	104	21	5	0	1	(-	-)	29	7	12	10	16	0	21	2	0	1	0	1	.00	2	.202	.317	.279
1998	Danvle	R+	51	170	37	3	0	4	(-	-)	52	35	24	22	37	0	44	2	1	1	2	3	.40	4	.218	.362	.306
1999	Macon	A	105	368	83	17	0	4	(-	-)	112	40	38	31	26	0	94	2	2	3	2	4	.33	10	.226	.278	.304
2000	Macon	A	93	302	62	12	0	9	(-	-)	101	31	35	34	42	1	74	5	2	1	1	1	.50	6	.205	.311	.334
2001	MrtlBh	A+	18	54	9	2	0	0	(-	-)	11	3	6	1	3	0	25	1	1	1	0	1	.00	1	.167	.220	.204
2001	Braves	R	8	30	10	4	0	0	(-	-)	14	5	6	4	0	0	3	0	0	1	0	1	.00	1	.333	.323	.467
2001	Macon	A	35	124	35	7	0	4	(-	-)	54	16	22	20	14	0	27	1	2	1	2	0	1.00	1	.282	.357	.435
2002	MrtlBh	A+	86	276	60	19	0	2	(-	-)	85	21	27	27	28	1	71	3	4	2	3	1	.75	8	.217	.294	.308
2002	Grnvlle	A	10	27	7	1	0	1	(-	-)	11	2	3	4	4	0	10	0	0	0	0	0	-	0	.259	.355	.407
2002	Rchmd	AAA	2	6	1	0	0	0	(	)	1	0	0	0	1	0	2	0	0	0	0	1	.00	1	.167	.286	.167
2003	MrtlBh	A+	28	87	18	4	0	1	(-	-)	25	9	11	8	11	0	33	0	2	0	2	0	1.00	1	.207	.296	.287
2003	Rchmd	AAA	3	12	3	2	0	0	(-	-)	5	0	1	1	1	0	4	0	0	0	0	0	-	1	.250	.308	.417
2003	Grnville	A	41	130	24	5	0	2	(	)	35	13	15	9	14	0	35	0	1	3	0	1	.00	2	.185	.259	.269
2004	Grnville	A	53	163	36	10	0	1	(-	-)	49	15	15	18	25	1	40	1	4	1	1	1	.50	3	.221	.326	.301
2004	Rchmd	AAA	21	61	19	2	0	0	(-	-)	21	4	6	9	9	0	14	1	0	1	0	1	.00	2	.311	.403	.344
2005	Rchmd	AAA	72	212	47	6	0	3	(-	-)	62	17	20	21	25	1	59	4	5	2	1	2	.33	8	.222	.313	.292
2006	Hntsvl	AA	43	124	24	7	0	0	(-	-)	31	7	14	7	11	1	38	1	1	3	0	1	.00	2	.194	.259	.250
2006	Nashv	AAA	2	8	2	1	0	0	(-	-)	3	0	1	0	0	0	3	0	0	0	0	0	-	0	.250	.250	.375
2007	Lsvlle	AAA	8	21	6	0	0	0	(-	-)	6	0	1	3	5	0	5	0	0	1	0	0	-	1	.286	.407	.286
2007	Chatt	AA	30	86	17	4	0	0	(-	-)	21	7	9	10	24	3	21	0	0	1	1	0	1.00	2	.198	.369	.244
2008	Missi	AA	79	255	60	13	0	2	(-	-)	79	26	29	29	34	3	49	4	4	0	0	0	-	5	.235	.334	.310
2009	Gwnntt	AAA	13	44	11	4	0	0	(-	-)	15	5	2	4	2	0	9	1	1	0	0	0	-	2	.250	.298	.341
2009	Missi	AA	73	250	65	12	0	0	(-	-)	77	20	30	30	33	0	50	2	2	2	1	1	.50	12	.260	.348	.308
2010	Gwnntt	AAA	66	220	55	11	0	5	(-	-)	81	20	21	28	22	0	51	2	4	0	1	0	1.00	7	.250	.324	.368
2010	Atl	NL	1	0	0	0	0	0	(0	0)	0	1	0	0	1	0	0	0	0	0	0	0	-	0	-	1.000	-

Jason Bourgeois

Bats: R **Throws:** R **Pos:** LF-25; CF-24; PH-23; PR-8; 2B-2; RF-1   boosh-WAH   **Ht:** 5'9" **Wt:** 190 **Born:** 1/4/1982 **Age:** 29

						BATTING															BASERUNNING				AVERAGES		
Year	Team	Lg	G	AB	H	2B	3B	HR	(Hm	Rd)	TB	R	RBI	RC	TBB	IBB	SO	HBP	SH	SF	SB	CS	SB%	GDP	Avg	OBP	Slg
2010	RdRck*	AAA	65	235	81	10	3	5	(-	-)	112	37	28	46	21	2	28	3	2	0	18	6	.75	3	.345	.405	.477
2008	CWS	AL	6	3	1	1	0	0	(0	0)	2	0	0	0	0	0	0	0	0	0	0	0	-	0	.333	.333	.667
2009	Mil	NL	24	37	7	0	0	1	(1	0)	10	6	3	1	3	0	7	0	0	0	3	0	1.00	2	.189	.250	.270
2010	Hou	NL	69	123	27	4	1	0	(0	0)	33	16	3	8	13	0	16	0	0	0	12	4	.75	5	.220	.294	.268
	3 ML YEARS		99	163	35	5	1	1	(1	0)	45	22	6	9	16	0	23	0	0	0	15	4	.79	7	.215	.285	.276

Peter Bourjos

Bats: R **Throws:** R **Pos:** CF-51   BORE-juss   **Ht:** 6'1" **Wt:** 180 **Born:** 3/31/1987 **Age:** 24

						BATTING															BASERUNNING				AVERAGES		
Year	Team	Lg	G	AB	H	2B	3B	HR	(Hm	Rd)	TB	R	RBI	RC	TBB	IBB	SO	HBP	SH	SF	SB	CS	SB%	GDP	Avg	OBP	Slg
2006	Orem	R+	65	250	73	16	7	5	(-	-)	118	42	28	42	22	1	67	2	5	0	13	5	.72	3	.292	.354	.472
2007	CRpds	A	63	237	65	9	6	5	(-	-)	101	37	29	36	20	0	53	4	4	5	19	9	.68	3	.274	.335	.426
2007	Angels	R	4	16	5	0	1	0	(-	-)	7	3	2	2	1	0	2	0	0	0	0	0	-	0	.313	.353	.438
2008	RCuca	A+	121	509	150	29	10	9	(-	-)	226	83	51	80	19	0	96	7	5	5	50	10	.83	5	.295	.326	.444
2009	Ark	AA	110	437	123	16	14	6	(-	-)	185	72	51	71	49	1	77	3	10	5	32	12	.73	8	.281	.354	.423
2010	Salt Lk	AAA	102	414	130	13	12	13	(-	-)	206	85	51	78	24	1	78	10	4	3	27	5	.84	5	.314	.364	.498
2010	LAA	AL	51	181	37	6	4	6	(1	5)	69	19	15	13	6	0	40	2	3	1	10	3	.77	2	.204	.237	.381

Michael Bourn

Bats: L **Throws:** R **Pos:** CF-138; PH-4; PR-2   BORN   **Ht:** 5'11" **Wt:** 180 **Born:** 12/27/1982 **Age:** 28

						BATTING															BASERUNNING				AVERAGES		
Year	Team	Lg	G	AB	H	2B	3B	HR	(Hm	Rd)	TB	R	RBI	RC	TBB	IBB	SO	HBP	SH	SF	SB	CS	SB%	GDP	Avg	OBP	Slg
2006	Phi	NL	17	8	1	0	0	0	(0	0)	1	2	0	0	1	0	3	0	0	0	1	2	.33	0	.125	.222	.125
2007	Phi	NL	105	119	33	3	3	1	(1	0)	45	29	6	19	13	2	21	0	1	0	18	1	.95	1	.277	.348	.378
2008	Hou	NL	138	467	107	10	4	5	(3	2)	140	57	29	43	37	0	111	2	7	1	41	10	.80	3	.229	.288	.300
2009	Hou	NL	157	606	173	27	12	3	(0	3)	233	97	35	94	63	1	140	2	5	2	61	12	.84	1	.285	.354	.384
2010	Hou	NL	141	535	142	25	6	2	(0	2)	185	84	38	74	59	5	109	3	6	2	52	12	.81	6	.265	.341	.346
	Postseason		2	1	0	0	0	0	(0	0)	0	0	0	0	0	0	0	0	0	0	0	0	-	0	.000	.000	.000
	5 ML YEARS		558	1735	456	65	25	11	(6	5)	604	269	108	230	173	8	384	7	21	5	173	37	.82	11	.263	.331	.348

Michael Bowden

Pitches: R Bats: R Pos: RP-14   BOE-din   Ht: 6'3" Wt: 215 Born: 9/9/1986 Age: 24

			HOW MUCH HE PITCHED					WHAT HE GAVE UP												THE RESULTS							
Year	Team	Lg	G	GS	CG	GF	IP	BFP	H	R	ER	HR	SH	SF	HB	TBB	IBB	SO	WP	Bk	W	L	Pct	Sh	Sv-Op	Hld	ERC	ERA
2010	Pwtckt*	AAA	31	16	0	4	105.2	427	84	43	43	13	1	8	2	37	1	77	4	1	6	4	.600	0	1- -	-	3.04	3.66
2008	Bos	AL	1	1	0	0	5.0	22	7	2	2	0	0	0	0	1	0	3	0	0	1	0	1.000	0	0-0	-	4.92	3.60
2009	Bos	AL	8	1	0	3	16.0	75	23	17	17	3	0	0	0	6	0	12	3	0	1	1	.500	0	0-0	1	7.35	9.56
2010	Bos	AL	14	0	0	7	15.1	66	20	8	8	2	0	0	0	4	0	13	2	0	0	1	.000	0	0-0	-	5.73	4.70
3 ML YEARS			23	2	0	10	36.1	163	50	27	27	5	0	0	0	11	0	28	5	0	2	2	.500	0	0-0	1	6.32	6.69

Cedrick Bowers

Pitches: L Bats: R Pos: RP-14   Ht: 6'2" Wt: 220 Born: 2/10/1978 Age: 33

			HOW MUCH HE PITCHED					WHAT HE GAVE UP												THE RESULTS							
Year	Team	Lg	G	GS	CG	GF	IP	BFP	H	R	ER	HR	SH	SF	HB	TBB	IBB	SO	WP	Bk	W	L	Pct	Sh	Sv-Op	Hld	ERC	ERA
1996	DRays	R	13	13	0	0	60.1	268	50	39	36	2	0	2	3	39	0	85	5	5	3	5	.375	0	0- -	-	3.75	5.37
1997	CtnSC	A	28	28	0	0	157.0	657	119	74	56	11	4	3	3	78	0	164	15	1	8	10	.444	0	0- -	-	3.02	3.21
1998	StPete	A+	28	26	0	1	150.0	655	144	89	73	14	6	4	1	80	1	156	6	2	5	9	.357	0	0- -	-	4.38	4.38
1999	Orlndo	AA	27	27	1	0	125.0	567	125	94	83	18	3	5	4	76	0	138	12	1	6	9	.400	0	0- -	-	5.39	5.98
2000	Orlndo	AA	20	19	1	0	106.2	443	85	45	33	8	4	2	3	44	0	92	3	1	5	8	.385	0	0- -	-	2.98	2.78
2000	Drham	AAA	4	4	0	0	19.2	92	21	13	12	2	0	0	0	13	0	20	1	0	3	1	.750	0	0- -	-	5.46	5.49
2001	Drham	AAA	42	11	0	14	94.0	412	83	38	32	10	4	4	3	56	1	67	3	0	6	5	.545	0	0- -	-	4.38	3.06
2002	Drham	AAA	47	0	0	12	69.1	326	75	36	24	9	3	2	3	43	1	79	11	1	4	3	.571	0	0- -	-	5.75	3.12
2003	Drham	AAA	32	8	0	5	83.2	364	75	46	41	6	4	8	6	39	0	80	12	0	4	3	.571	0	2- -	-	3.82	4.41
2008	ColSpr	AAA	35	2	0	8	65.0	282	50	28	27	5	2	0	2	43	1	74	4	0	6	1	.857	0	1- -	-	3.76	3.74
2009	LV	AAA	48	0	0	18	60.2	259	38	15	13	1	1	1	3	45	1	67	3	0	4	3	.571	0	5- -	-	2.95	1.93
2010	Scrmto	AAA	29	0	0	7	32.0	146	24	14	13	1	1	0	1	26	0	50	1	0	2	1	.667	0	0- -	-	3.80	3.66
2008	Col	NL	5	0	0	3	6.2	33	11	10	10	2	0	1	1	5	0	5	1	0	0	0	-	0	0-0	0	13.72	13.50
2010	Oak	AL	14	0	0	10	14.0	62	12	9	7	4	0	0	1	6	1	18	0	0	0	1	.000	0	0-0	0	4.67	4.50
2 ML YEARS			19	0	0	13	20.2	95	23	19	17	6	0	1	2	11	1	23	1	0	0	1	.000	0	0-0	0	7.21	7.40

John Bowker

Bats: L Throws: L Pos: PH-27; RF-24; LF-17; 1B-5   BAU-ker   Ht: 6'1" Wt: 203 Born: 7/8/1983 Age: 27

			BATTING																		BASERUNNING				AVERAGES		
Year	Team	Lg	G	AB	H	2B	3B	HR	(Hm	Rd)	TB	R	RBI	RC	TBB	IBB	SO	HBP	SH	SF	SB	CS	SB%	GDP	Avg	OBP	Slg
2010	Fresno*	AAA	51	197	61	12	1	14	(-	-)	117	36	36	43	23	3	37	3	0	1	1	2	.33	8	.310	.388	.594
2010	Indy*	AAA	25	91	29	7	2	4	(-	-)	52	10	10	18	6	2	20	1	0	0	0	0	-	0	.319	.367	.571
2008	SF	NL	111	326	83	14	3	10	(6	4)	133	31	43	41	19	1	74	3	0	2	1	1	.50	7	.255	.300	.408
2009	SF	NL	31	67	13	2	2	2	(2	0)	25	7	7	4	4	0	18	1	0	1	1	0	1.00	0	.194	.247	.373
2010	2 Tms	NL	67	151	33	8	0	5	(2	3)	56	16	21	12	14	2	33	0	0	2	0	1	.00	4	.219	.281	.371
10	SF	NL	41	82	17	3	0	3	(0	3)	29	9	8	5	6	1	23	0	0	2	0	0	-	1	.207	.256	.354
10	Pit	NL	26	69	16	5	0	2	(2	0)	27	7	13	7	8	1	10	0	0	0	0	1	.00	3	.232	.312	.391
3 ML YEARS			209	544	129	24	5	17	(10	7)	214	54	71	57	37	3	125	4	0	5	2	2	.50	11	.237	.288	.393

Blaine Boyer

Pitches: R Bats: R Pos: RP-54   Ht: 6'3" Wt: 215 Born: 7/11/1981 Age: 29

			HOW MUCH HE PITCHED					WHAT HE GAVE UP												THE RESULTS							
Year	Team	Lg	G	GS	CG	GF	IP	BFP	H	R	ER	HR	SH	SF	HB	TBB	IBB	SO	WP	Bk	W	L	Pct	Sh	Sv-Op	Hld	ERC	ERA
2010	Reno*	AAA	5	0	0	3	6.0	24	5	1	1	0	1	0	0	1	0	9	0	0	1	0	1.000	0	2- -	-	1.74	1.50
2005	Atl	NL	43	0	0	5	37.2	158	32	13	13	1	1	1	2	17	0	33	2	0	4	2	.667	0	0-2	9	3.21	3.11
2006	Atl	NL	2	0	0	0	0.2	7	4	3	3	0	0	0	0	1	0	0	0	0	0	0	-	0	0-0	1	47.92	40.50
2007	Atl	NL	5	0	0	2	5.1	26	10	3	2	0	1	0	0	1	1	3	2	0	0	0	-	0	0-0	1	7.41	3.38
2008	Atl	NL	76	0	0	18	72.0	313	73	51	47	10	3	4	2	25	4	67	2	0	2	6	.250	0	1-5	14	4.19	5.88
2009	3 Tms	NL	48	0	0	21	54.2	241	56	36	25	1	4	1	5	20	0	29	2	0	0	2	.000	0	0-0	4	3.81	4.12
2010	Ari	NL	54	0	0	11	57.0	251	59	32	27	3	3	2	1	29	1	29	2	0	3	2	.600	0	0-4	5	4.45	4.26
09	Atl	NL	3	0	0	1	1.1	11	3	6	6	0	0	0	0	3	0	2	0	0	0	1	.000	0	0-0	0	23.46	40.50
09	StL	NL	15	0	0	4	16.1	70	14	10	8	1	3	0	1	5	0	9	0	0	0	0	-	0	0-0	2	2.82	4.41
09	Ari	NL	30	0	0	16	37.0	160	39	20	11	0	1	1	3	12	0	18	2	0	0	1	.000	0	0-0	2	3.71	2.68
6 ML YEARS			228	0	0	57	227.1	996	234	138	117	15	12	8	10	93	6	161	10	0	9	12	.429	0	1-11	34	4.16	4.63

Zach Braddock

Pitches: L Bats: L Pos: RP-46   Ht: 6'2" Wt: 233 Born: 8/23/1987 Age: 23

			HOW MUCH HE PITCHED					WHAT HE GAVE UP												THE RESULTS							
Year	Team	Lg	G	GS	CG	GF	IP	BFP	H	R	ER	HR	SH	SF	HB	TBB	IBB	SO	WP	Bk	W	L	Pct	Sh	Sv-Op	Hld	ERC	ERA
2006	Helena	R+	14	8	0	0	39.1	175	32	26	24	3	2	0	1	31	0	30	3	0	2	2	.500	0	0- -	-	4.54	5.49
2007	WV	A	10	9	0	0	47.0	183	28	6	6	1	0	0	1	15	0	68	0	0	3	1	.750	0	0- -	-	1.47	1.15
2008	WV	A	2	2	0	0	6.0	24	2	1	0	0	0	0	0	3	0	13	0	0	0	0	-	0	0- -	-	0.92	0.00
2008	BrvdCt	A+	21	11	0	3	65.1	295	55	44	40	7	2	1	7	42	0	80	6	3	4	7	.364	0	0- -	-	4.59	5.51
2009	BrvdCt	A+	14	0	0	2	24.2	92	13	3	3	2	2	0	2	4	1	40	2	0	1	1	.500	0	0- -	-	1.13	1.09
2009	Hntsvl	AA	12	0	0	2	15.2	68	16	9	5	2	2	1	1	3	0	22	0	0	2	1	.667	0	0- -	-	3.66	2.87
2010	Nashv	AAA	11	0	0	4	16.0	69	10	8	8	1	1	2	2	9	0	28	2	0	0	0	-	0	1- -	-	2.82	4.50
2010	Mil	NL	46	0	0	4	33.2	151	29	11	11	1	1	2	2	19	0	41	2	0	1	2	.333	0	0-2	15	3.56	2.94

Dallas Braden

Pitches: L Bats: L Pos: SP-30   Ht: 6'1" Wt: 184 Born: 8/13/1983 Age: 27

		HOW MUCH HE PITCHED						WHAT HE GAVE UP													THE RESULTS							
Year	Team	Lg	G	GS	CG	GF	IP	BFP	H	R	ER	HR	SH	SF	HB	TBB	IBB	SO	WP	Bk	W	L	Pct	Sh	Sv-Op	Hld	ERC	ERA
2010	Stcktn*	A+	1	1	0	0	4.0	22	7	3	3	2	0	0	0	1	0	4	0	0	0	0	-	0	0--	-	10.29	6.75
2007	Oak	AL	20	14	0	1	72.1	332	91	59	54	9	4	0	2	26	1	55	6	1	1	8	.111	0	0-0	0	5.63	6.72
2008	Oak	AL	19	10	0	7	71.2	301	77	36	33	8	1	2	2	25	2	41	0	1	5	4	.556	0	0-0	0	4.63	4.14
2009	Oak	AL	22	22	0	0	136.2	589	144	63	59	9	4	4	2	42	2	81	1	0	8	9	.471	0	0-0	0	3.78	3.89
2010	Oak	AL	30	30	5	0	192.2	781	180	83	75	17	6	4	5	43	1	113	2	1	11	14	.440	2	0-0	0	3.11	3.50
4 ML YEARS			91	76	5	8	473.1	2003	492	241	221	43	15	10	11	136	5	290	9	3	25	35	.417	2	0-0	1	3.89	4.20

Milton Bradley

Bats: B Throws: R Pos: LF-39; DH-28; PH-6; RF-1   Ht: 6'0" Wt: 215 Born: 4/15/1978 Age: 33

			BATTING																BASERUNNING				AVERAGES		
Year	Team	Lg	G	AB	H	2B	3B	HR	(Hm | Rd)	TB	R	RBI	RC	TBB	IBB	SO	HBP	SH	SF	SB	CS	SB%	GDP	Avg	OBP	Slg
2000	Mon	NL	42	154	34	8	1	2	(1 | 1)	50	20	15	14	14	0	32	1	1	1	2	1	.67	3	.221	.288	.325
2001	2 Tms		77	238	53	17	3	1	(0 | 1)	79	22	19	21	21	0	65	1	2	0	8	5	.62	7	.223	.288	.332
2002	Cle	AL	98	325	81	18	3	9	(4 | 5)	132	48	38	40	32	2	58	0	1	0	6	3	.67	12	.249	.317	.406
2003	Cle	AL	101	377	121	34	2	10	(4 | 6)	189	61	56	77	64	8	73	5	0	5	17	7	.71	10	.321	.421	.501
2004	LAD	NL	141	516	138	24	0	19	(8 | 11)	219	72	67	70	71	3	123	6	3	1	15	11	.58	12	.267	.362	.424
2005	LAD	NL	75	283	82	14	1	13	(6 | 7)	137	49	38	40	25	1	47	2	4	1	6	1	.86	6	.290	.350	.484
2006	Oak	AL	96	351	97	14	2	14	(7 | 7)	157	53	52	52	51	1	65	2	0	1	10	2	.83	13	.276	.370	.447
2007	2 Tms		61	209	64	9	1	13	(7 | 6)	114	37	37	42	31	3	41	3	0	1	5	2	.71	5	.306	.402	.545
2008	Tex	AL	126	414	133	32	1	22	(16 | 6)	233	78	77	90	80	13	112	9	0	6	5	3	.63	10	.321	.436	.563
2009	ChC	NL	124	393	101	17	1	12	(9 | 3)	156	61	40	56	66	4	95	11	2	1	2	3	.40	10	.257	.378	.397
2010	Sea	AL	73	244	50	9	1	8	(2 | 6)	85	28	29	23	28	2	75	3	1	2	8	2	.80	2	.205	.292	.348
01	Mon	NL	67	220	49	16	3	1	(0 | 0)	74	19	19	20	19	0	62	1	2	0	7	4	.64	6	.223	.288	.336
01	Cle	AL	10	18	4	1	0	0	(0 | 0)	5	3	0	1	2	0	3	0	0	0	1	1	.50	1	.222	.300	.278
07	Oak	AL	19	65	19	4	0	2	(1 | 1)	29	6	7	10	8	1	14	1	0	1	2	1	.67	2	.292	.373	.446
07	SD	NL	42	144	45	5	1	11	(6 | 5)	85	31	30	32	23	2	27	2	0	0	3	1	.75	3	.313	.414	.590
Postseason			11	42	13	3	0	4	(3 | 1)	28	6	8	7	5	0	5	0	0	0	2	0	1.00	3	.310	.383	.667
11 ML YEARS			1014	3504	954	196	16	123	(64 | 59)	1551	529	468	533	483	37	786	43	14	19	84	40	.68	90	.272	.366	.443

Michael Brantley

Bats: L Throws: L Pos: CF-65, LF-7; PH-2   Ht: 6'2" Wt: 200 Born: 5/15/1987 Age: 24

			BATTING																BASERUNNING				AVERAGES		
Year	Team	Lg	G	AB	H	2B	3B	HR	(Hm | Rd)	TB	R	RBI	RC	TBB	IBB	SO	HBP	SH	SF	SB	CS	SB%	GDP	Avg	OBP	Slg
2005	Brewrs	R	44	173	60	3	1	0	(- | -)	65	34	19	31	22	0	13	2	4	0	14	5	.74	2	.347	.426	.376
2005	Helena	R+	10	34	11	2	0	0	(- | -)	13	8	3	6	6	0	4	0	0	0	2	0	1.00	0	.324	.425	.382
2006	WV	A	108	360	108	10	2	0	(- | -)	122	47	42	60	61	0	51	4	5	5	24	7	.77	5	.300	.402	.339
2007	WV	A	56	218	73	15	1	2	(- | -)	96	41	32	43	31	0	22	1	1	4	18	6	.75	3	.335	.413	.440
2007	Hntsvl	AA	59	187	47	6	1	0	(- | -)	55	28	21	24	20	1	25	1	5	1	16	3	.84	8	.251	.353	.294
2008	Hntsvl	AA	106	420	134	17	2	4	(- | -)	167	80	40	73	50	5	27	4	3	2	28	8	.78	6	.319	.395	.398
2009	Clmbs	AAA	116	457	122	21	2	6	(- | -)	165	80	37	70	59	1	48	1	8	3	46	5	.90	7	.267	.350	.361
2010	Clmbs	AAA	67	273	87	13	2	4	(- | -)	116	54	20	40	34	1	28	2	5	2	13	5	.72	7	.319	.395	.425
2009	Cle	AL	28	112	35	4	0	0	(0 | 0)	39	10	11	16	8	0	19	0	1	0	4	4	.50	3	.313	.358	.348
2010	Clo	AL	72	297	73	9	3	3	(2 | 1)	97	38	22	32	22	0	38	0	4	2	10	2	.83	8	.246	.298	.327
2 ML YEARS			100	409	108	13	3	3	(2 | 1)	136	48	33	48	30	0	57	0	5	2	14	6	.70	9	.264	.313	.333

Russell Branyan

Bats: L Throws: R Pos: DH-53; 1B-51; PH-9   BRAN-yenn   Ht: 6'3" Wt: 230 Born: 12/19/1975 Age: 35

			BATTING																BASERUNNING				AVERAGES		
Year	Team	Lg	G	AB	H	2B	3B	HR	(Hm | Rd)	TB	R	RBI	RC	TBB	IBB	SO	HBP	SH	SF	SB	CS	SB%	GDP	Avg	OBP	Slg
2010	Clmbs*	AAA	4	14	4	2	0	0	(- | -)	6	1	1	2	1	0	2	0	0	0	0	0	-	1	.286	.333	.429
2010	Akron*	AA	2	8	2	0	0	0	(- | -)	2	1	0	0	0	0	2	0	0	0	0	0	-	0	.250	.250	.250
1998	Cle	AL	1	4	0	0	0	0	(0 | 0)	0	0	0	0	0	0	2	0	0	0	0	0	-	0	.000	.000	.000
1999	Cle	AL	11	38	8	2	0	1	(0 | 1)	13	4	0	4	3	0	19	1	0	0	0	0	-	0	.211	.286	.342
2000	Cle	AL	67	193	46	7	2	16	(13 | 3)	105	32	38	34	22	1	76	4	0	1	0	0	-	2	.238	.327	.544
2001	Cle	AL	113	315	73	16	2	20	(11 | 9)	153	48	54	50	38	1	132	3	0	5	1	1	.50	2	.232	.316	.486
2002	2 Tms		134	378	86	13	1	24	(5 | 19)	173	50	56	49	51	3	151	2	0	4	4	3	.57	5	.228	.320	.458
2003	Cin	NL	74	176	38	12	0	9	(7 | 2)	77	22	26	23	27	0	69	1	0	1	0	0	-	3	.216	.322	.438
2004	Mil	NL	51	158	37	11	1	11	(8 | 3)	83	21	27	23	20	0	68	2	0	2	1	0	1.00	1	.234	.324	.525
2005	Mil	NL	85	202	52	11	0	12	(3 | 9)	99	23	31	38	39	10	80	0	1	0	1	0	1.00	3	.257	.378	.490
2006	2 Tms		91	241	55	11	0	18	(9 | 9)	120	37	36	34	34	1	89	3	1	3	2	0	1.00	2	.228	.327	.498
2007	3 Tms	NL	89	163	32	5	1	10	(6 | 4)	69	22	26	23	28	1	69	2	0	1	1	0	1.00	2	.196	.320	.423
2008	Mil	NL	50	132	33	8	0	12	(9 | 3)	77	24	20	22	19	4	42	0	0	1	1	0	1.00	0	.250	.342	.583
2009	Sea	AL	116	431	108	21	1	31	(16 | 15)	224	64	76	69	58	6	149	9	1	6	2	0	1.00	6	.251	.347	.520
2010	2 Tms	AL	109	376	89	19	0	25	(7 | 18)	183	47	57	45	46	3	131	3	1	2	1	0	1.00	6	.237	.323	.487
02	Cle	AL	50	161	33	4	0	8	(1 | 7)	61	16	17	14	17	0	65	0	0	2	1	2	.33	3	.205	.278	.379
02	Cin	NL	84	217	53	9	1	16	(4 | 12)	112	34	39	35	34	3	86	2	0	2	3	1	.75	2	.244	.349	.516
06	TB	AL	64	169	34	10	0	12	(7 | 5)	80	23	27	24	19	0	62	2	1	2	2	0	1.00	1	.201	.286	.473
06	SD	NL	27	72	21	1	0	6	(2 | 4)	40	14	9	12	15	1	27	1	0	1	0	0	-	1	.292	.416	.556
07	SD	NL	61	122	24	5	1	7	(5 | 2)	52	16	19	18	21	1	48	2	0	1	1	0	1.00	1	.197	.322	.426
07	Phi	NL	7	9	2	0	0	2	(0 | 2)	8	2	5	2	0	0	6	0	0	0	0	0	-	0	.222	.222	.889
07	StL	NL	21	32	6	0	0	1	(1 | 0)	9	4	2	3	7	0	15	0	0	0	0	0	-	1	.188	.333	.281
10	Cle	AL	52	171	45	9	0	10	(1 | 9)	84	24	24	23	16	1	49	1	1	0	0	0	-	2	.263	.328	.491
10	Sea	AL	57	205	44	10	0	15	(6 | 9)	99	23	33	22	30	2	82	2	0	1	1	0	1.00	4	.215	.319	.483
Postseason			6	16	4	1	0	0	(0 | 0)	7	2	3	1	1	0	6	0	0	0	0	0	-	0	.250	.294	.438
13 ML YEARS			991	2807	657	136	8	189	(94 | 95)	1376	394	453	414	385	30	1077	30	4	26	14	4	.78	29	.234	.330	.490

Ryan Braun

Bats: R Throws: R Pos: LF-153; PH-2; DH-1; PR-1   Ht: 6'1" Wt: 200 Born: 11/17/1983 Age: 27

Year	Team	Lg	G	AB	H	2B	3B	HR	(Hm	Rd)	TB	R	RBI	RC	TBB	IBB	SO	HBP	SH	SF	SB	CS	SB%	GDP	Avg	OBP	Slg
2007	Mil	NL	113	451	146	26	6	34	(17	17)	286	91	97	94	29	1	112	7	0	5	15	5	.75	13	.324	.370	**.634**
2008	Mil	NL	151	611	174	39	7	37	(23	14)	338	92	106	100	42	4	129	6	0	4	14	4	.78	13	.285	.335	.553
2009	Mil	NL	158	635	**203**	39	6	32	(15	17)	350	113	114	133	57	1	121	13	0	3	20	6	.77	7	.320	.386	.551
2010	Mil	NL	157	619	188	45	1	25	(12	13)	310	101	103	104	56	1	105	6	0	3	14	3	.82	17	.304	.365	.501
	Postseason		4	16	5	2	0	0	(0	0)	7	0	2	2	0	0	4	0	0	1	0	0	-	0	.313	.294	.438
	4 ML YEARS		579	2316	711	149	20	128	(68	60)	1284	397	420	431	184	7	467	32	0	15	63	18	.78	50	.307	.364	.554

Bill Bray

Pitches: L Bats: L Pos: RP-35   Ht: 6'3" Wt: 221 Born: 6/5/1983 Age: 28

			HOW MUCH HE PITCHED						WHAT HE GAVE UP										THE RESULTS						
Year	Team	Lg	G	GS	CG	GF	IP	BFP	H	R	ER	HR	SH	SF	HB	TBB	IBB	SO	WP	Bk	W	L	Pct	Sh	Sv-Op	Hld	ERC	ERA
2010	Lynbrg*	A+	4	0	0	1	4.2	18	1	0	0	0	0	0	0	2	0	9	0	0	0	0	-	0	0--	-	0.54	0.00
2010	Lsvlle*	AAA	6	0	0	2	5.2	20	2	0	0	0	0	0	0	1	0	7	0	0	0	0	-	0	1--	-	0.50	0.00
2006	2 Tms	NL	48	0	0	10	50.2	223	57	27	23	5	2	1	1	18	3	39	0	0	3	2	.600	0	2-3	3	4.58	4.09
2007	Cin	NL	19	0	0	5	14.1	63	16	10	10	1	0	1	0	5	1	14	0	0	3	3	.500	0	1-1	3	4.16	6.28
2008	Cin	NL	63	0	0	11	47.0	215	50	19	15	4	3	1	1	24	5	54	2	0	2	2	.500	0	0-4	9	4.57	2.87
2010	Cin	NL	35	0	0	4	28.1	117	21	13	13	4	1	0	0	10	1	30	2	0	0	2	.000	0	0-0	2	2.66	4.13
06	Was	NL	19	0	0	4	23.0	100	24	11	10	2	1	1	1	9	2	16	0	0	1	1	.500	0	0-0	1	4.25	3.91
06	Cin	NL	29	0	0	6	27.2	123	33	16	13	3	1	0	0	9	1	23	0	0	2	1	.667	0	2-3	2	4.85	4.23
	4 ML YEARS		165	0	0	30	140.1	618	144	69	61	14	6	3	2	57	10	137	4	0	8	9	.471	0	3-8	17	4.13	3.91

Craig Breslow

Pitches: L Bats: L Pos: RP-75   Ht: 6'1" Wt: 181 Born: 8/8/1980 Age: 30

			HOW MUCH HE PITCHED						WHAT HE GAVE UP										THE RESULTS						
Year	Team	Lg	G	GS	CG	GF	IP	BFP	H	R	ER	HR	SH	SF	HB	TBB	IBB	SO	WP	Bk	W	L	Pct	Sh	Sv-Op	Hld	ERC	ERA
2005	SD	NL	14	0	0	3	16.1	78	15	6	4	1	0	1	1	13	0	14	1	0	0	0	-	0	0-0	1	4.98	2.20
2006	Bos	AL	13	0	0	3	12.0	55	12	5	5	0	0	2	1	6	1	12	2	1	0	2	.000	0	0-0	3	3.78	3.75
2008	2 Tms	AL	49	0	0	13	47.0	189	34	12	10	1	2	0	0	19	2	39	4	1	0	2	.000	0	1-2	5	2.12	1.91
2009	2 Tms	AL	77	0	0	9	69.2	281	48	31	26	8	4	1	3	29	0	55	3	1	8	7	.533	0	0-2	15	2.79	3.36
2010	Oak	AL	75	0	0	23	74.2	304	53	26	25	9	2	0	0	29	4	71	0	1	4	4	.500	0	5-7	16	2.53	3.01
08	Cle	AL	7	0	0	3	8.1	40	10	3	3	1	0	0	0	5	0	7	0	0	0	0	-	0	0-0	0	6.09	3.24
08	Min	AL	42	0	0	10	38.2	149	24	9	7	0	2	0	0	14	2	32	4	1	0	2	.000	0	1-2	5	1.49	1.63
09	Min	AL	17	0	0	5	14.1	64	11	11	10	3	2	0	1	11	0	11	3	0	1	2	.333	0	0-0	2	5.38	6.28
09	Oak	AL	60	0	0	4	55.1	217	37	20	16	5	2	1	2	18	0	44	0	1	7	5	.583	0	0-2	13	2.21	2.60
	5 ML YEARS		228	0	0	51	219.2	907	162	80	70	19	8	4	5	96	7	191	10	4	12	15	.444	0	6-11	40	2.77	2.87

Reid Brignac

Bats: L Throws: R Pos: 2B-68; SS-50; PH-27; RF-2; PR-2; DH-1   BRINN-yak   Ht: 6'3" Wt: 195 Born: 1/16/1986 Age: 25

Year	Team	Lg	G	AB	H	2B	3B	HR	(Hm	Rd)	TB	R	RBI	RC	TBB	IBB	SO	HBP	SH	SF	SB	CS	SB%	GDP	Avg	OBP	Slg
2008	TB	AL	4	10	0	0	0	0	(0	0)	0	1	0	0	1	0	5	0	0	0	0	0	-	0	.000	.091	.000
2009	TB	AL	31	90	25	8	2	1	(0	1)	40	10	6	10	3	0	20	0	0	0	2	2	.50	1	.278	.301	.444
2010	TB	AL	113	301	77	13	1	8	(3	5)	116	39	45	38	20	3	77	3	0	2	3	3	.50	6	.256	.307	.385
	3 ML YEARS		148	401	102	21	3	9	(3	6)	156	50	51	48	24	3	102	3	0	2	5	5	.50	7	.254	.300	.389

Domonic Brown

Bats: L Throws: L Pos: PH-20; RF-15   Ht: 6'5" Wt: 200 Born: 9/3/1987 Age: 23

Year	Team	Lg	G	AB	H	2B	3B	HR	(Hm	Rd)	TB	R	RBI	RC	TBB	IBB	SO	HBP	SH	SF	SB	CS	SB%	GDP	Avg	OBP	Slg
2006	Phillies	R	34	117	25	3	0	1	(-	-)	31	13	7	10	12	0	30	1	1	0	13	3	.81	2	.214	.292	.265
2007	Clrwtr	A+	3	9	4	1	0	1	(-	-)	8	2	7	3	2	0	0	0	0	0	0	0	-	0	.444	.545	.889
2007	Wmspt	A-	74	285	84	11	5	3	(-	-)	114	43	32	43	27	0	49	2	0	3	14	7	.67	1	.295	.356	.400
2008	Lakwd	A	114	444	129	23	3	9	(-	-)	185	77	54	76	64	4	72	3	0	5	20	9	.69	11	.291	.380	.417
2009	Clrwtr	A+	66	238	72	12	3	11	(-	-)	123	41	44	48	34	3	48	2	0	6	15	8	.65	3	.303	.386	.517
2009	Phillies	R	3	10	5	0	2	0	(-	-)	9	4	0	3	1	0	1	1	0	0	1	0	1.00	0	.500	.583	.900
2009	Rdng	AA	37	147	41	9	4	3	(-	-)	67	20	20	24	14	3	37	1	0	0	8	1	.89	3	.279	.346	.456
2010	Rdng	AA	65	236	75	16	3	15	(-	-)	142	50	47	54	29	2	51	2	0	4	12	6	.67	2	.318	.391	.602
2010	LV	AAA	28	107	37	6	1	5	(-	-)	60	15	21	23	8	0	23	1	0	2	5	1	.83	6	.346	.390	.561
2010	Phi	NL	35	62	13	3	0	2	(2	0)	22	8	13	5	5	1	24	0	0	3	2	1	.67	1	.210	.257	.355

Dusty Brown

Bats: R Throws: R Pos: C-7   Ht: 6'0" Wt: 180 Born: 6/19/1982 Age: 29

Year	Team	Lg	G	AB	H	2B	3B	HR	(Hm	Rd)	TB	R	RBI	RC	TBB	IBB	SO	HBP	SH	SF	SB	CS	SB%	GDP	Avg	OBP	Slg
2001	RedSx	R	36	126	32	5	4	0	(-	-)	45	15	14	12	7	0	24	0	0	2	1	2	.33	3	.254	.289	.357
2002	RedSx	R	45	159	51	12	2	1	(-	-)	70	28	20	30	23	1	24	0	0	1	11	4	.73	1	.321	.404	.440
2002	Lowell	A-	21	78	22	3	1	0	(-	-)	27	12	12	11	8	0	20	3	1	0	1	0	1.00	0	.282	.371	.346
2003	Augsta	A	87	285	75	17	6	2	(-	-)	110	27	41	44	37	2	69	7	1	3	7	1	.88	4	.263	.358	.386
2004	Srsota	A+	38	118	27	3	0	1	(-	-)	33	11	8	12	15	1	28	1	0	0	2	0	1.00	0	.229	.321	.280
2005	Wilmg	A+	62	219	56	12	0	8	(-	-)	92	32	36	34	31	0	52	1	0	2	1	1	.50	7	.256	.348	.420
2005	RedSx	R	6	18	4	1	0	0	(-	-)	5	3	3	2	4	0	2	0	0	0	0	0	-	2	.222	.364	.278
2006	Portlnd	AA	85	295	66	17	0	5	(-	-)	98	32	40	29	24	0	65	3	4	5	2	1	.67	5	.224	.284	.332

Year	Team	Lg	G	AB	H	2B	3B	HR	(Hm	Rd)	TB	R	RBI	RC	TBB	IBB	SO	HBP	SH	SF	SB	CS	SB%	GDP	Avg	OBP	Slg
2007	Portlnd	AA	69	254	68	16	2	9	(-	-)	115	43	43	40	28	0	64	2	0	1	0	0	-	7	.268	.344	.453
2007	Pwtckt	AAA	8	27	5	2	0	0	(-	-)	7	1	3	1	2	0	10	0	0	0	0	0	-		.185	.241	.259
2008	Pwtckt	AAA	84	297	86	14	2	12	(-	-)	140	39	55	55	40	1	81	6	0	7	0	0	-	7	.290	.377	.471
2009	Pwtckt	AAA	86	295	78	13	0	2	(-	-)	97	22	23	36	37	0	74	0	0	1	0	0	-	4	.264	.345	.329
2010	Pwtckt	AAA	71	238	52	19	0	7	(-	-)	92	32	29	30	27	0	66	3	1	2	1	0	1.00	6	.218	.304	.387
2010	RedSx	R	1	2	1	0	0	0	(-	-)	1	0	0	0	0	0	1	0	0	0	0	0	-		.500	.500	.500
2010	Lowell	A-	2	8	4	1	0	1	(-	-)	8	1	1	3	0	0	1	0	1	0	0	0	-		.500	.500	1.000
2009	Bos	AL	7	3	1	0	0	1	(1	0)	4	1	1	1	1	0	0	0	0	0	0	0	-		.333	.500	1.333
2010	Bos	AL	7	12	3	1	0	0	(0	0)	4	0	2	1	0	0	2	0	0	0	0	0	-	1	.250	.250	.333
	2 ML YEARS		14	15	4	1	0	1	(1	0)	8	1	3	2	1	0	2	0	0	0	0	0	-	1	.267	.313	.533

Jordan Brown

Bats: L Throws: L Pos: 1B-10; LF-7; DH-7; PH-6   Ht: 6'0" Wt: 205 Born: 12/18/1983 Age: 27

Year	Team	Lg	G	AB	H	2B	3B	HR	(Hm	Rd)	TB	R	RBI	RC	TBB	IBB	SO	HBP	SH	SF	SB	CS	SB%	GDP	Avg	OBP	Slg
2005	MhVlly	A-	19	75	19	1	0	3	(-	-)	29	15	7	8	3	1	7	1	0	0	2	1	.67	3	.253	.291	.387
2006	Knstn	A+	125	473	137	26	7	15	(-	-)	222	71	87	83	51	3	59	5	2	4	5	2	.71	15	.290	.362	.469
2007	Akron	AA	127	483	161	36	2	11	(-	-)	234	85	76	102	63	8	56	11	0	1	11	2	.85	11	.333	.421	.484
2008	Buffalo	AAA	109	420	118	30	3	7	(-	-)	175	52	51	60	35	6	67	2	0	3	3	4	.43	8	.281	.337	.417
2009	Clmbs	AAA	111	417	140	35	1	15	(-	-)	222	65	67	81	30	3	64	2	3	3	2	4	.33	7	.336	.381	.532
2010	Clmbs	AAA	83	326	97	28	1	8	(-	-)	151	31	67	53	21	1	48	3	0	5	2	0	1.00	6	.298	.341	.463
2010	Cle	AL	26	87	20	7	0	0	(0	0)	27	9	2	1	4	0	10	1	0	0	0	0	-	3	.230	.272	.310

Jonathan Broxton

Pitches: R Bats: R Pos: RP-64   Ht: 6'4" Wt: 300 Born: 6/16/1984 Age: 27

| | | | HOW MUCH HE PITCHED | | | | | WHAT HE GAVE UP | | | | | | | | | | THE RESULTS | | | | | | | |
Year	Team	Lg	G	GS	CG	GF	IP	BFP	H	R	ER	HR	SH	SF	HB	TBB	IBB	SO	WP	Bk	W	L	Pct	Sh	Sv-Op	Hld	ERC	ERA
2005	LAD	NL	14	0	0	5	13.2	68	13	11	9	0	0	2	1	12	2	22	2	0	1	0	1.000	0	0-1	1	4.65	5.93
2006	LAD	NL	68	0	0	20	76.1	320	61	25	22	7	3	1	1	33	6	97	7	0	4	1	.800	0	3-7	12	2.97	2.59
2007	LAD	NL	83	0	0	18	82.0	334	69	30	26	6	0	1	1	25	3	99	4	0	4	4	.500	0	2-8	32	2.71	2.85
2008	LAD	NL	70	0	0	32	69.0	285	54	29	24	2	3	3	3	27	5	88	3	0	3	5	.375	0	14-22	13	2.48	3.13
2009	LAD	NL	73	0	0	58	76.0	300	44	24	22	4	0	3	1	29	1	114	2	0	7	2	.778	0	36-42	1	1.65	2.61
2010	LAD	NL	64	0	0	46	62.1	271	64	30	28	4	3	1	2	28	5	73	1	0	5	6	.455	0	22-29	3	4.21	4.04
	Postseason		13	0	0	10	14.1	64	14	7	7	1	0	0	1	6	0	15	0	0	0	2	.000	0	3-5	0	3.97	4.40
	6 ML YEARS		372	0	0	179	379.1	1578	305	149	131	23	9	11	9	154	22	493	19	0	24	18	.571	0	77-109	62	2.79	3.11

Jay Bruce

Bats: L Throws: L Pos: RF-146; PH-9   Ht: 6'3" Wt: 225 Born: 4/3/1987 Age: 24

Year	Team	Lg	G	AB	H	2B	3B	HR	(Hm	Rd)	TB	R	RBI	RC	TBB	IBB	SO	HBP	SH	SF	SB	CS	SB%	GDP	Avg	OBP	Slg
2008	Cin	NL	108	413	105	17	1	21	(13	8)	187	63	52	49	33	1	110	4	0	2	4	6	.40	8	.254	.314	.453
2009	Cin	NL	101	345	77	15	2	22	(13	9)	162	47	58	47	38	2	75	2	1	1	3	3	.50	5	.223	.303	.470
2010	Cin	NL	148	509	143	23	5	25	(19	6)	251	80	70	71	58	5	136	1	0	5	5	4	.56	12	.281	.353	.493
	3 ML YEARS		357	1267	325	55	8	68	(45	23)	600	190	180	167	129	8	321	7	1	8	12	13	.48	25	.257	.027	.474

Brian Bruney

Pitches: R Bats: R Pos: RP-19   BRUE-nee   Ht: 6'3" Wt: 235 Born: 2/17/1982 Age: 29

| | | | HOW MUCH HE PITCHED | | | | | WHAT HE GAVE UP | | | | | | | | | | THE RESULTS | | | | | | | |
Year	Team	Lg	G	GS	CG	GF	IP	BFP	H	R	ER	HR	SH	SF	HB	TBB	IBB	SO	WP	Bk	W	L	Pct	Sh	Sv-Op	Hld	ERC	ERA
2010	Nashv*	AAA	2	0	0	0	3.1	15	4	0	0	0	1	0	0	1	0	2	0	0	0	0	-	0	0- -	-	3.97	0.00
2010	Buffalo*	AAA	8	0	0	1	8.0	41	9	7	4	1	0	1	0	7	0	7	0	0	0	1	.000	0	0- -	-	5.57	4.50
2004	Ari	NL	30	0	0	14	31.1	135	20	16	15	2	1	0	1	27	5	34	2	0	3	4	.429	0	0-1	3	3.54	4.31
2005	Ari	NL	47	0	0	21	46.0	230	56	39	38	6	2	1	5	35	2	51	2	0	1	3	.250	0	12-16	4	7.48	7.43
2006	NYY	AL	19	0	0	2	20.2	90	14	2	2	1	0	0	1	15	0	25	2	0	1	1	.500	0	0-0	4	3.37	0.87
2007	NYY	AL	58	0	0	16	50.0	228	44	28	26	5	1	6	3	37	2	39	4	0	3	2	.600	0	0-2	6	4.92	4.68
2008	NYY	AL	32	1	0	5	34.1	137	18	7	7	2	0	2	1	16	0	33	1	0	3	0	1.000	0	1-2	12	1.75	1.83
2009	NYY	AL	44	0	0	6	39.0	175	36	17	17	6	2	1	1	23	3	36	2	0	5	0	1.000	0	0-1	14	4.71	3.92
2010	Was	NL	19	0	0	6	17.2	93	21	18	15	1	3	2	0	20	1	16	1	0	1	2	.333	0	0-0	3	7.65	7.64
	Postseason		4	0	0	1	3.0	13	4	3	3	1	0	1	0	0	0	4	0	0	0	0	-	0	0-0	1	5.82	9.00
	7 ML YEARS		249	1	0	70	239.0	1088	209	127	120	23	9	12	12	173	13	234	14	0	17	12	.586	0	13-22	46	4.70	4.52

Clay Buchholz

Pitches: R Bats: L Pos: SP-28   BUCK-holtz   Ht: 6'3" Wt: 190 Born: 8/14/1984 Age: 26

| | | | HOW MUCH HE PITCHED | | | | | WHAT HE GAVE UP | | | | | | | | | | THE RESULTS | | | | | | | |
Year	Team	Lg	G	GS	CG	GF	IP	BFP	H	R	ER	HR	SH	SF	HB	TBB	IBB	SO	WP	Bk	W	L	Pct	Sh	Sv-Op	Hld	ERC	ERA
2010	Pwtckt*	AAA	1	1	0	0	3.2	16	4	2	2	1	0	0	1	1	0	2	0	1	0	0	-	0	0- -	-	6.83	4.91
2007	Bos	AL	4	3	1	0	22.2	88	14	6	4	0	0	1	1	10	0	22	0	0	3	1	.750	1	0-0	0	1.90	1.59
2008	Bos	AL	16	15	1	0	76.0	357	93	63	57	11	0	3	2	41	1	72	2	1	2	9	.182	0	0-0	0	6.40	6.75
2009	Bos	AL	16	16	0	0	92.0	399	91	44	43	13	2	3	2	36	1	68	1	0	7	4	.636	0	0-0	0	4.31	4.21
2010	Bos	AL	28	28	1	0	173.2	711	142	55	45	9	5	5	5	67	1	120	7	1	17	7	.708	1	0-0	0	2.88	2.33
	Postseason		1	1	0	0	5.0	23	6	2	2	1	0	0	1	0	0	3	0	1	0	0	-	0	0-0	0	5.87	3.60
	4 ML YEARS		64	62	3	0	364.1	1555	340	168	149	33	7	12	10	154	3	282	10	2	29	21	.580	2	0-0	0	3.85	3.68

Taylor Buchholz

Pitches: R **Bats:** R **Pos:** RP-9   BUCK-holtz   **Ht:** 6'4" **Wt:** 220 **Born:** 10/13/1981 **Age:** 29

Year	Team	Lg	G	GS	CG	GF	IP	BFP	H	R	ER	HR	SH	SF	HB	TBB	IBB	SO	WP	Bk	W	L	Pct	Sh	Sv-Op	Hld	ERC	ERA
2010	Mdest*	A+	3	1	0	0	3.0	9	0	0	0	0	0	0	0	0	0	4	0	0	1	0	1.000	0	0- -	0	0.00	0.00
2010	ColSpr*	AAA	18	0	0	2	18.1	84	22	12	12	3	1	0	1	9	2	12	1	0	1	0	1.000	0	0- -	0	6.24	5.89
2006	Hou	NL	22	19	1	1	113.0	479	107	80	74	21	5	6	3	34	4	77	5	0	6	10	.375	1	0-0	0	3.97	5.89
2007	Col	NL	41	8	0	6	93.2	396	105	47	44	8	5	5	2	20	4	61	3	1	6	5	.545	0	0-0	1	3.97	4.23
2008	Col	NL	63	0	0	19	66.1	263	45	23	16	5	2	2	2	18	2	56	5	1	6	6	.500	0	1-3	21	1.87	2.17
2010	2 Tms		9	0	0	4	12.0	49	10	5	5	2	1	0	0	6	0	9	0	0	1	0	1.000	0	0-0	0	4.19	3.75
10	Col	NL	7	0	0	2	10.0	43	10	5	5	2	1	0	0	6	0	9	0	0	1	0	1.000	0	0-0	0	5.94	4.50
10	Tor	AL	2	0	0	2	2.0	6	0	0	0	0	0	0	0	0	0	0	0	0	0	0	-	0	0-0	0	0.00	0.00
	4 ML YEARS		135	27	1	30	285.0	1187	267	155	139	36	13	13	7	78	10	203	13	2	19	21	.475	1	1-3	22	3.45	4.39

John Buck

Bats: R **Throws:** R **Pos:** C-112; PH-5; DH-4   **Ht:** 6'3" **Wt:** 210 **Born:** 7/7/1980 **Age:** 30

							BATTING														BASERUNNING				AVERAGES		
Year	Team	Lg	G	AB	H	2B	3B	HR	(Hm Rd)	TB	R	RBI	RC	TBB	IBB	SO	HBP	SH	SF	SB	CS	SB%	GDP	Avg	OBP	Slg
2010	NHam*	AA	3	11	3	0	0	2	(- -)	9	2	6	2	1	0	3	0	0	0	0	0	-	0	.273	.333	.818
2004	KC	AL	71	238	56	9	0	12	(6 6)	101	36	30	26	15	0	79	0	4	1	1	1	.50	6	.235	.280	.424
2005	KC	AL	118	401	97	21	1	12	(3 9)	156	40	47	43	23	2	94	3	1	2	2	2	.50	9	.242	.287	.389
2006	KC	AL	114	371	91	21	1	11	(6 5)	147	37	50	43	26	2	84	7	4	1	0	2	.00	7	.245	.306	.396
2007	KC	AL	113	347	77	18	0	18	(6 12)	149	41	48	37	36	0	92	10	0	6	0	1	.00	11	.222	.308	.429
2008	KC	AL	109	370	83	23	1	9	(4 5)	135	48	48	42	38	2	96	6	0	4	0	3	.00	12	.224	.304	.365
2009	KC	AL	59	186	46	12	4	8	(3 5)	90	16	36	30	13	0	55	1	1	1	1	1	.50	2	.247	.299	.484
2010	Tor	AL	118	409	115	25	0	20	(9 11)	200	53	66	61	16	1	111	6	0	6	0	0	-	6	.281	.314	.489
	7 ML YEARS		702	2322	565	129	7	90	(37 53)	978	271	325	282	167	7	611	33	10	21	4	10	.29	53	.243	.301	.421

Travis Buck

Bats: L **Throws:** R **Pos:** LF-10; RF-3; DH-1; PR-1   **Ht:** 6'2" **Wt:** 232 **Born:** 11/18/1983 **Age:** 27

							BATTING														BASERUNNING				AVERAGES		
Year	Team	Lg	G	AB	H	2B	3B	HR	(Hm Rd)	TB	R	RBI	RC	TBB	IBB	SO	HBP	SH	SF	SB	CS	SB%	GDP	Avg	OBP	Slg
2010	As*	R	6	16	3	1	0	0	(- -)	4	3	4	2	5	0	4	0	0	0	0	0	-	0	.188	.381	.250
2010	Scrmto*	AAA	32	121	36	7	2	3	(- -)	56	22	17	21	11	0	28	4	1	4	3	2	.60	1	.298	.364	.463
2007	Oak	AL	82	285	82	22	5	7	(3 4)	135	41	34	48	39	2	66	4	2	4	4	1	.80	9	.288	.377	.474
2008	Oak	AL	38	155	35	9	1	7	(3 4)	67	16	25	22	11	0	38	4	0	2	1	0	1.00	2	.226	.291	.432
2009	Oak	AL	36	105	23	3	0	3	(2 1)	35	11	10	10	10	0	20	0	0	0	1	1	.50	0	.219	.287	.333
2010	Oak	AL	14	42	7	2	0	1	(1 0)	12	6	2	2	4	0	14	1	1	0	1	0	1.00	0	.167	.255	.286
	4 ML YEARS		170	587	147	36	6	18	(9 9)	249	74	71	82	64	2	138	9	3	6	7	2	.78	11	.250	.330	.424

Billy Buckner

Pitches: R **Bats:** R **Pos:** SP-3   **Ht:** 6'2" **Wt:** 205 **Born:** 8/27/1983 **Age:** 27

Year	Team	Lg	G	GS	CG	GF	IP	BFP	H	R	ER	HR	SH	SF	HB	TBB	IBB	SO	WP	Bk	W	L	Pct	Sh	Sv-Op	Hld	ERC	ERA
2010	Reno*	AAA	7	7	0	0	43.1	183	40	19	17	2	0	3	6	17	0	27	7	0	3	1	.750	0	0- -	0	3.90	3.53
2010	Toledo*	AAA	8	8	1	0	37.1	189	60	44	39	8	3	1	2	16	0	21	3	0	3	5	.375	0	0- -	0	9.05	9.40
2007	KC	AL	7	5	0	1	34.0	143	37	20	20	5	0	1	0	16	0	17	0	0	1	2	.333	0	0-0	0	5.57	5.29
2008	Ari	NL	10	0	0	5	14.0	59	16	5	5	3	0	0	1	4	1	11	2	0	1	0	1.000	0	0-0	0	5.72	3.21
2009	Ari	NL	16	13	0	0	77.1	342	94	57	55	12	2	1	3	29	0	64	6	0	4	6	.400	0	0-0	0	5.97	6.40
2010	Ari	NL	3	3	0	0	13.0	72	26	17	16	4	0	1	2	5	0	11	1	0	0	3	.000	0	0-0	0	13.00	11.08
	4 ML YEARS		36	21	0	6	138.1	616	173	99	96	24	2	3	6	54	1	103	9	0	6	11	.353	0	0-0	0	6.45	6.25

Ryan Budde

Bats: R **Throws:** R **Pos:** C-6   BUDD-ee   **Ht:** 5'11" **Wt:** 210 **Born:** 8/15/1979 **Age:** 31

							BATTING														BASERUNNING				AVERAGES		
Year	Team	Lg	G	AB	H	2B	3B	HR	(Hm Rd)	TB	R	RBI	RC	TBB	IBB	SO	HBP	SH	SF	SB	CS	SB%	GDP	Avg	OBP	Slg
2010	Salt Lk*	AAA	53	172	42	7	0	1	(- -)	52	24	13	18	21	0	58	1	2	3	1	1	.50	1	.244	.325	.302
2007	LAA	AL	12	18	3	1	0	0	(0 0)	4	0	1	0	0	0	6	0	0	0	0	0	-	1	.167	.167	.222
2008	LAA	AL	8	2	0	0	0	0	(0 0)	0	0	0	0	0	0	1	0	0	0	0	0	-	0	.000	.000	.000
2009	LAA	AL	3	3	0	0	0	0	(0 0)	0	0	0	0	0	0	2	0	0	0	0	0	-	0	.000	.000	.000
2010	LAA	AL	6	10	4	1	0	1	(0 1)	8	2	3	4	1	0	5	0	0	0	0	0	-	0	.400	.455	.800
	4 ML YEARS		29	33	7	2	0	1	(0 1)	12	2	4	4	1	0	13	0	0	0	0	0	-	2	.212	.235	.364

Mark Buehrle

Pitches: L **Bats:** L **Pos:** SP-33   BURR-lee   **Ht:** 6'2" **Wt:** 235 **Born:** 3/23/1979 **Age:** 32

Year	Team	Lg	G	GS	CG	GF	IP	BFP	H	R	ER	HR	SH	SF	HB	TBB	IBB	SO	WP	Bk	W	L	Pct	Sh	Sv-Op	Hld	ERC	ERA
2000	CWS	AL	28	3	0	6	51.1	225	55	27	24	5	1	0	3	19	1	37	0	0	4	1	.800	0	0-2	3	4.56	4.21
2001	CWS	AL	32	32	4	0	221.1	885	188	89	81	24	9	4	8	48	2	126	1	5	16	8	.667	2	0-0	0	2.79	3.29
2002	CWS	AL	34	34	5	0	239.0	984	236	102	95	25	9	3	3	61	7	134	6	1	19	12	.613	2	0-0	0	3.53	3.58
2003	CWS	AL	35	35	2	0	230.1	978	250	124	106	22	7	7	5	61	2	119	1	0	14	14	.500	0	0-0	0	4.10	4.14
2004	CWS	AL	35	35	4	0	245.1	1016	257	119	106	33	4	6	8	51	2	165	0	0	16	10	.615	1	0-0	0	4.00	3.89
2005	CWS	AL	33	33	3	0	236.2	971	240	99	82	20	7	4	4	40	4	149	2	2	16	8	.667	1	0-0	0	3.21	3.12
2006	CWS	AL	32	32	3	0	204.0	876	247	124	113	36	6	7	6	48	5	98	0	1	12	13	.480	1	0-0	0	5.37	4.99
2007	CWS	AL	30	30	3	0	201.0	835	208	86	81	22	7	5	5	45	5	115	1	0	10	9	.526	1	0-0	0	3.75	3.63
2008	CWS	AL	34	34	1	0	218.2	918	240	106	92	22	2	6	4	52	4	140	4	0	15	12	.556	0	0-0	0	4.12	3.79

Year	Team	Lg	G	GS	CG	GF	IP	BFP	H	R	ER	HR	SH	SF	HB	TBB	IBB	SO	WP	Bk	W	L	Pct	Sh	Sv-Op	Hld	ERC	ERA
2009	CWS	AL	33	33	1	0	213.1	874	222	97	91	27	11	7	5	45	3	105	2	1	13	10	.565	1	0-0	0	3.91	3.84
2010	CWS	AL	33	33	3	0	210.1	897	246	105	100	17	6	7	11	49	1	99	3	5	13	13	.500	0	0-0	0	4.29	4.28
	Postseason		6	4	1	2	30.2	124	32	14	14	3	2	1	1	1	1	16	0	0	2	1	.667	0	1-1	0	2.95	4.11
	11 ML YEARS		359	334	27	6	2271.1	9459	2389	1078	971	253	69	56	53	519	36	1287	20	15	148	110	.574	8	0-2	3	3.89	3.85

Jay Buente

Pitches: R **Bats:** R **Pos:** RP-8

BENN-tay

Ht: 6'2" **Wt:** 187 **Born:** 9/28/1983 **Age:** 27

Year	Team	Lg	G	GS	CG	GF	IP	BFP	H	R	ER	HR	SH	SF	HB	TBB	IBB	SO	WP	Bk	W	L	Pct	Sh	Sv-Op	Hld	ERC	ERA
2006	Jmstwn	A-	22	3	0	5	43.2	182	40	17	15	2	1	1	2	13	0	41	3	0	2	3	.400	0	1--	-	3.05	3.09
2007	Grnsbr	A	42	0	0	18	60.0	261	58	36	25	6	1	1	3	19	2	71	11	0	5	2	.714	0	2--	-	3.61	3.75
2008	Jupiter	A+	40	0	0	9	60.0	258	49	22	20	4	4	1	3	27	0	63	9	1	5	1	.833	0	1--	-	3.17	3.00
2009	Jaxnvl	AA	16	0	0	7	22.0	91	17	6	6	1	0	1	0	11	0	23	2	0	0	1	.000	0	1--	-	2.91	2.45
2009	NewOr	AAA	35	0	0	14	61.0	270	59	24	23	6	4	0	1	32	5	56	5	0	5	1	.833	0	1--	-	4.28	3.39
2010	NewOr	AAA	20	0	0	8	30.1	130	22	13	9	3	2	0	0	18	0	38	2	0	0	1	.000	0	0--	-	3.27	2.67
2010	Jaxnvl	AA	10	1	0	3	13.1	55	13	6	6	1	0	0	0	5	0	12	0	0	1	0	1.000	0	1--	-	3.81	4.05
2010	Mrlns	R	4	0	0	0	5.0	19	5	2	2	0	0	0	0	1	0	4	0	0	1	0	1.000	0	0--	-	2.93	3.60
2010	Fla	NL	8	0	0	2	11.0	59	16	8	8	0	1	0	0	11	2	9	1	0	0	0	-	0	0-0	0	8.02	6.55

Jason Bulger

Pitches: R **Bats:** R **Pos:** RP-25

BULL-jerr

Ht: 6'4" **Wt:** 210 **Born:** 12/6/1978 **Age:** 32

Year	Team	Lg	G	GS	CG	GF	IP	BFP	H	R	ER	HR	SH	SF	HB	TBB	IBB	SO	WP	Bk	W	L	Pct	Sh	Sv-Op	Hld	ERC	ERA
2010	RCuca*	A+	1	0	0	0	0.2	4	2	2	2	0	0	0	0	0	0	1	0	0	0	0	-	0	0--	-	14.52	27.00
2010	Salt Lk*	AAA	10	0	0	2	9.1	41	3	1	1	0	1	0	2	9	0	12	0	0	0	0	-	0	0--	-	2.57	0.96
2005	Ari	NL	9	0	0	5	10.0	48	14	6	6	1	1	0	0	5	1	9	0	0	1	0	1.000	0	0-0	0	6.68	5.40
2006	LAA	AL	2	0	0	1	1.2	9	1	3	3	0	0	0	0	3	0	1	1	0	0	0	-	0	0-0	0	6.15	16.20
2007	LAA	AL	6	0	0	4	6.1	25	5	2	2	0	0	0	0	3	0	8	1	0	0	0	-	0	0-0	0	2.74	2.84
2008	LAA	AL	14	0	0	7	16.0	73	15	13	13	3	0	0	2	9	0	20	0	0	0	0	-	0	0-0	0	5.50	7.31
2009	LAA	AL	64	0	0	20	65.2	262	46	26	26	7	5	4	1	30	1	68	5	0	6	1	.857	0	1-4	9	2.88	3.56
2010	LAA	AL	25	0	0	5	24.0	111	25	14	13	3	1	0	2	15	0	25	1	0	0	0	-	0	0-0	2	5.79	4.88
	Postseason		4	0	0	0	3.1	16	1	1	1	1	0	0	1	4	0	5	1	0	0	0	-	0	0-0	0	5.00	2.70
	6 ML YEARS		120	0	0	42	123.2	528	106	64	63	14	7	4	5	65	2	131	8	0	7	1	.875	0	1-4	11	4.07	4.50

Bryan Bullington

Pitches: R **Bats:** R **Pos:** RP-8; SP-5

Ht: 6'6" **Wt:** 209 **Born:** 9/30/1980 **Age:** 30

Year	Team	Lg	G	GS	CG	GF	IP	BFP	H	R	ER	HR	SH	SF	HB	TBB	IBB	SO	WP	Bk	W	L	Pct	Sh	Sv-Op	Hld	ERC	ERA
2010	Omha*	AAA	20	15	1	1	102.0	412	86	35	32	8	3	2	7	28	0	73	2	0	8	2	.800	0	0--	-	2.94	2.82
2005	Pit	NL	1	0	0	0	1.1	7	1	2	2	0	0	0	0	1	0	1	0	0	0	0	-	0	0-0	0	5.91	13.50
2007	Pit	NL	5	3	0	0	17.0	76	24	11	10	3	1	0	0	5	0	7	1	0	0	3	.000	0	0-0	0	6.90	5.29
2008	Cle	AL	3	2	0	0	14.2	60	15	9	8	4	0	1	1	2	0	12	1	0	0	2	.000	0	0-0	0	4.63	4.91
2009	Tor	AL	4	0	0	3	6.0	31	7	2	2	0	1	1	0	6	1	5	0	0	0	0	-	0	0-0	0	6.12	3.00
2010	KC	AL	13	5	0	2	42.2	196	51	29	29	6	1	2	4	17	2	29	1	0	1	4	.200	0	0-0	0	6.81	6.12
	5 ML YEARS		26	10	0	5	81.2	370	98	53	51	13	3	5	6	31	3	54	3	0	1	9	.100	0	0-0	0	5.88	5.62

Madison Bumgarner

Pitches: L **Bats:** R **Pos:** SP-18

Ht: 6'5" **Wt:** 227 **Born:** 8/1/1989 **Age:** 21

Year	Team	Lg	G	GS	CG	GF	IP	BFP	H	R	ER	HR	SH	SF	HB	TBB	IBB	SO	WP	Bk	W	L	Pct	Sh	Sv-Op	Hld	ERC	ERA
2008	Augsta	A	24	24	1	0	141.2	548	111	28	23	3	3	4	5	21	0	164	3	2	15	3	.833	1	0--	-	1.74	1.45
2009	SnJos	A+	5	5	0	0	24.1	100	20	10	4	0	0	2	4	4	0	23	0	0	3	1	.750	0	0--	-	1.91	1.48
2009	Conn	AA	20	19	1	0	107.0	421	80	28	23	6	2	3	3	30	1	69	4	0	9	1	.900	1	0--	-	2.19	1.93
2010	Fresno	AAA	14	14	1	0	82.2	348	88	32	29	5	3	1	2	22	0	59	1	1	7	1	.875	1	0--	-	3.78	3.16
2009	SF	NL	4	1	0	1	10.0	40	8	2	2	2	1	1	0	3	1	10	0	0	0	0	-	0	0-0	0	3.14	1.80
2010	SF	NL	18	18	0	0	111.0	472	119	40	37	11	0	4	5	26	2	86	1	1	7	6	.538	0	0-0	0	3.98	3.00
	2 ML YEARS		22	19	0	1	121.0	512	127	42	39	13	1	5	5	29	3	96	1	1	7	6	.538	0	0-0	0	3.91	2.90

Jamie Burke

Bats: R **Throws:** R **Pos:** C-1

Ht: 6'0" **Wt:** 225 **Born:** 9/24/1971 **Age:** 39

Year	Team	Lg	G	AB	H	2B	3B	HR	(Hm	Rd)	TB	R	RBI	RC	TBB	IBB	SO	HBP	SH	SF	SB	CS	SB%	GDP	Avg	OBP	Slg
2010	Syrcse*	AAA	47	128	30	8	0	1	(-	-)	41	12	9	14	13	1	25	3	0	1	1	0	1.00	2	.234	.317	.320
2001	LAA	AL	9	5	1	0	0	0	(0	0)	1	1	0	0	0	0	2	0	0	0	0	0	-	0	.200	.200	.200
2003	CWS	AL	6	8	3	0	0	0	(0	0)	3	0	2	2	0	0	0	0	0	0	0	0	-	0	.375	.375	.375
2004	CWS	AL	57	120	40	9	0	0	(0	0)	49	22	15	21	10	0	13	1	1	1	0	0	-	3	.333	.386	.408
2005	CWS	AL	1	1	0	0	0	0	(0	0)	0	0	0	0	0	0	0	0	0	0	0	0	-	0	.000	.000	.000
2007	Sea	AL	50	113	34	8	0	1	(1	0)	45	19	12	16	7	0	17	4	5	0	0	1	.00	2	.301	.363	.398
2008	Sea	AL	48	92	24	3	0	1	(0	1)	30	10	8	9	5	0	7	1	1	1	0	1	.00	3	.261	.303	.326
2009	2 Tms		19	51	6	0	0	1	(0	1)	9	1	2	3	0	0	18	0	1	1	0	0	-	2	.118	.164	.176
2010	Was	NL	1	0	0	0	0	0	(0	0)	0	0	0	0	0	0	0	0	0	0	0	0	-	0	-	-	-
09	Sea	AL	13	41	5	0	0	1	(1	0)	8	1	1	2	0	0	13	0	0	0	0	0	-	2	.122	.163	.195
09	Was	NL	6	10	1	0	0	0	(0	0)	1	0	1	1	0	0	5	0	1	1	0	0	-	0	.100	.167	.100
	8 ML YEARS		191	390	108	20	0	3	(2	2)	137	53	39	48	25	0	57	6	8	3	0	2	.00	10	.277	.328	.351

A.J. Burnett

Pitches: R Bats: R Pos: SP-33 · **Ht:** 6'4" **Wt:** 230 **Born:** 1/3/1977 **Age:** 34

Year	Team	Lg	G	GS	CG	GF	IP	BFP	H	R	ER	HR	SH	SF	HB	TBB	IBB	SO	WP	Bk	W	L	Pct	Sh	Sv-Op	Hld	ERC	ERA
							HOW MUCH HE PITCHED				**WHAT HE GAVE UP**												**THE RESULTS**					
1999	Fla	NL	7	7	0	0	41.1	182	37	23	16	3	1	3	0	25	2	33	0	0	4	2	.667	0	0-0	0	4.00	3.48
2000	Fla	NL	13	13	0	0	82.2	364	80	46	44	8	6	3	2	44	3	57	2	0	3	7	.300	0	0-0	0	4.45	4.79
2001	Fla	NL	27	27	2	0	173.1	733	145	82	78	20	6	8	7	83	3	128	7	1	11	12	.478	1	0-0	0	3.76	4.05
2002	Fla	NL	31	29	7	0	204.1	844	153	84	75	12	9	4	9	90	5	203	14	0	12	9	.571	5	0-1	0	2.77	3.30
2003	Fla	NL	4	4	0	0	23.0	106	18	13	12	2	2	1	2	18	2	21	2	0	1	2	.000	0	0-0	0	4.36	4.70
2004	Fla	NL	20	19	1	0	120.0	490	102	50	49	9	3	3	4	38	0	113	7	0	7	6	.538	0	0-0	0	2.95	3.68
2005	Fla	NL	32	32	4	0	209.0	873	184	97	80	12	7	5	7	79	1	198	12	0	12	12	.500	2	0-0	0	3.20	3.44
2006	Tor	AL	21	21	2	0	135.2	577	138	67	60	14	4	3	8	39	3	118	6	1	10	8	.556	1	0-0	0	3.97	3.98
2007	Tor	AL	25	25	2	0	165.2	691	131	74	69	23	0	2	12	66	2	176	5	0	10	8	.556	0	0-0	0	3.47	3.75
2008	Tor	AL	35	**34**	1	1	221.1	957	211	109	100	19	8	5	9	86	2	**231**	11	2	18	10	.643	0	0-0	0	3.78	4.07
2009	NYY	AL	33	33	1	0	207.0	896	193	99	93	25	2	5	10	**97**	0	195	**17**	1	13	9	.591	0	0-0	0	4.34	4.04
2010	NYY	AL	33	33	1	0	186.2	829	204	118	109	25	7	10	**19**	78	2	145	16	0	10	15	.400	0	0-0	0	5.43	5.26
	Postseason		5	5	0	0	27.1	122	22	16	16	1	0	0	6	16	1	24	2	0	1	1	.500	0	0-0	0	3.88	5.27
	12 ML YEARS		281	277	21	1	1770.0	7542	1596	862	785	172	55	52	89	743	25	1618	99	5	110	100	.524	9	0-1	0	3.79	3.99

Alex Burnett

Pitches: R Bats: R Pos: RP-41 · **Ht:** 6'0" **Wt:** 210 **Born:** 7/26/1987 **Age:** 23

Year	Team	Lg	G	GS	CG	GF	IP	BFP	H	R	ER	HR	SH	SF	HB	TBB	IBB	SO	WP	Bk	W	L	Pct	Sh	Sv-Op	Hld	ERC	ERA
							HOW MUCH HE PITCHED				**WHAT HE GAVE UP**												**THE RESULTS**					
2005	Twins	R	13	8	0	2	48.1	212	50	25	22	6	1	3	7	14	0	33	1	0	4	2	.667	0	0--	-	4.57	4.10
2006	Elizab	R+	13	13	1	0	71.1	294	66	41	32	6	0	2	6	13	0	71	1	1	4	3	.571	1	0--	-	3.05	4.04
2007	Beloit	A	27	27	1	0	155.0	640	140	60	52	9	3	4	10	38	1	117	6	1	9	8	.529	0	0--	-	2.93	3.02
2008	FtMyrs	A+	28	25	0	0	143.2	608	151	72	60	12	2	3	5	36	0	84	7	0	8	6	.571	0	0--	-	3.81	3.76
2009	FtMyrs	A+	18	0	0	16	22.2	91	14	6	5	0	2	1	1	7	0	26	0	0	2	1	.667	0	4--	-	1.45	1.99
2009	NwBrit	AA	40	0	0	19	55.1	217	37	14	14	2	1	1	3	19	4	52	1	0	1	2	.333	0	9--	-	1.93	2.28
2010	Roch	AAA	14	0	0	7	19.2	91	26	12	12	1	1	3	0	8	2	18	2	0	0	2	.000	0	2--	-	5.40	5.49
2010	Min	AL	41	0	0	11	47.2	211	52	28	28	6	4	1	2	23	3	37	2	2	2	2	.500	0	0-0	2	5.30	5.29

Sean Burnett

Pitches: L Bats: L Pos: RP-73 · **Ht:** 6'1" **Wt:** 200 **Born:** 9/17/1982 **Age:** 28

Year	Team	Lg	G	GS	CG	GF	IP	BFP	H	R	ER	HR	SH	SF	HB	TBB	IBB	SO	WP	Bk	W	L	Pct	Sh	Sv-Op	Hld	ERC	ERA
							HOW MUCH HE PITCHED				**WHAT HE GAVE UP**												**THE RESULTS**					
2004	Pit	NL	13	13	1	0	71.2	318	86	41	40	9	2	1	1	28	2	30	2	0	5	5	.500	1	0-0	0	5.49	5.02
2008	Pit	NL	58	0	0	16	56.2	253	57	31	30	7	4	3	2	34	3	42	4	0	1	1	.500	0	0-0	8	5.23	4.76
2009	2 Tms	NL	71	0	0	8	57.2	237	36	21	20	6	6	1	3	28	8	43	4	0	2	3	.400	0	1-3	11	2.43	3.12
2010	Was	NL	73	0	0	10	63.0	261	52	17	15	3	4	0	1	20	4	62	2	0	1	7	.125	0	3-4	20	2.43	2.14
09	Pit	NL	38	0	0	7	32.1	133	22	12	11	3	4	1	3	15	4	23	2	0	1	2	.333	0	1-2	6	2.77	3.06
09	Was	NL	33	0	0	1	25.1	104	14	9	9	3	2	0	0	13	4	20	2	0	1	1	.500	0	0-1	5	2.02	3.20
	4 ML YEARS		215	13	1	34	249.0	1069	231	110	105	25	16	5	7	110	17	177	12	0	9	16	.360	1	4-7	39	3.85	3.80

Pat Burrell

Bats: R Throws: R Pos: LF-87; DH-26; PH-8 · BURL · **Ht:** 6'4" **Wt:** 235 **Born:** 10/10/1976 **Age:** 34

Year	Team	Lg	G	AB	H	2B	3B	HR	(Hm	Rd)	TB	R	RBI	RC	TBB	IBB	SO	HBP	SH	SF	SB	CS	SB%	GDP	Avg	OBP	Slg
						BATTING															**BASERUNNING**				**AVERAGES**		
2010	Fresno*	AAA	5	16	5	1	0	1	(-	-)	9	4	6	4	3	0	4	1	0	2	0	0	-	0	.313	.409	.563
2000	Phi	NL	111	408	106	27	1	18	(7	11)	189	57	79	69	63	2	139	1	0	2	0	0	-	5	.260	.359	.463
2001	Phi	NL	155	539	139	29	2	27	(10	17)	253	70	89	86	70	7	162	5	0	4	2	1	.67	12	.258	.346	.469
2002	Phi	NL	157	586	165	39	2	37	(18	19)	319	96	116	104	89	9	153	3	0	6	1	0	1.00	16	.282	.376	.544
2003	Phi	NL	146	522	109	31	4	21	(9	12)	211	57	64	57	72	2	142	4	0	1	0	0	-	18	.209	.309	.404
2004	Phi	NL	127	448	115	17	0	24	(14	10)	204	66	84	72	78	7	130	2	0	6	2	0	1.00	10	.257	.365	.455
2005	Phi	NL	154	562	158	27	1	32	(20	12)	283	78	117	109	99	6	160	3	0	5	0	0	-	12	.281	.389	.504
2006	Phi	NL	144	462	119	24	1	29	(12	17)	232	80	95	81	98	5	131	3	0	4	0	0	-	11	.258	.388	.502
2007	Phi	NL	155	472	121	26	0	30	(16	14)	237	77	97	98	114	1	120	4	0	8	0	0	-	10	.256	.400	.502
2008	Phi	NL	157	536	134	33	3	33	(12	21)	272	74	86	93	102	8	136	1	0	6	0	0	-	10	.250	.367	.507
2009	TB	AL	122	412	91	16	1	14	(8	6)	151	45	64	52	57	2	119	2	0	5	2	0	1.00	6	.221	.315	.367
2010	2 Tms	NL	120	373	94	21	0	18	(10	10)	175	50	64	63	57	4	105	1	0	6	0	2	.00	7	.252	.348	.469
10	TB	AL	24	84	17	5	0	2	(1	1)	28	9	13	9	10	0	28	1	0	1	0	0	-	2	.202	.292	.333
10	SF	NL	96	289	77	16	0	18	(9	9)	147	41	51	54	47	4	77	0	0	5	0	2	.00	5	.266	.364	.509
	Postseason		17	55	12	1	0	4	(2	2)	25	4	9	6	10	0	16	0	0	0	0	0	-	2	.218	.338	.455
	11 ML YEARS		1548	5320	1351	290	15	285	(136	149)	2526	750	955	884	899	53	1497	29	0	53	7	3	.70	117	.254	.362	.475

Brian Burres

Pitches: L Bats: L Pos: SP-13; RP-7 · BURR-iss · **Ht:** 6'2" **Wt:** 188 **Born:** 4/8/1981 **Age:** 30

Year	Team	Lg	G	GS	CG	GF	IP	BFP	H	R	ER	HR	SH	SF	HB	TBB	IBB	SO	WP	Bk	W	L	Pct	Sh	Sv-Op	Hld	ERC	ERA
							HOW MUCH HE PITCHED				**WHAT HE GAVE UP**												**THE RESULTS**					
2010	Indy*	AAA	15	14	0	0	82.0	350	75	42	41	10	2	3	5	34	0	61	6	0	5	4	.556	0	0--	-	4.09	4.50
2006	Bal	AL	11	0	0	2	8.0	31	6	2	2	1	0	0	0	1	0	6	0	0	0	0	-	0	0-0	4	1.91	2.25
2007	Bal	AL	37	17	0	9	121.0	559	140	81	80	14	2	0	5	66	1	96	8	0	6	8	.429	0	0-0	0	5.89	5.95
2008	Bal	AL	31	22	0	1	129.2	596	165	90	87	17	1	8	6	50	2	63	3	1	7	10	.412	0	0-1	0	6.03	6.04
2009	Tor	AL	2	2	0	0	6.1	37	12	12	10	0	0	0	6	5	0	4	0	0	0	2	.000	0	0-0	0	10.02	14.21
2010	Pit	NL	20	13	0	1	79.1	362	87	48	44	9	3	3	6	34	4	45	3	0	4	5	.444	0	0-0	0	4.99	4.99
	5 ML YEARS		101	54	0	13	344.1	1585	410	233	223	41	6	11	17	156	7	214	14	1	17	25	.405	0	0-1	4	5.70	5.83

Emmanuel Burriss

Bats: B **Throws:** R **Pos:** 2B-5; PR-3   **Ht:** 6'0" **Wt:** 203 **Born:** 1/17/1985 **Age:** 26

Year	Team	Lg	G	AB	H	2B	3B	HR	(Hm	Rd)	TB	R	RBI	RC	TBB	IBB	SO	HBP	SH	SF	SB	CS	SB%	GDP	Avg	OBP	Slg
2010	SnJos*	A+	5	14	3	0	0	0	(-	-)	3	2	1	0	0	0	3	1	1	0	1	1	.50	0	.214	.267	.214
2010	Fresno*	AAA	67	273	77	11	2	0	(-	-)	92	32	22	33	19	0	29	3	9	1	11	5	.69	5	.282	.334	.337
2008	SF	NL	95	240	68	6	1	1	(0	1)	79	37	18	22	23	1	24	5	5	1	13	5	.72	7	.283	.357	.329
2009	SF	NL	61	202	48	6	0	0	(0	0)	54	18	13	15	14	1	34	2	1	1	11	4	.73	3	.238	.292	.267
2010	SF	NL	7	5	2	0	0	0	(0	0)	2	3	0	1	0	0	1	0	0	0	0	0	-	0	.400	.400	.400
	3 ML YEARS		163	447	118	12	1	1	(0	1)	135	58	31	38	37	2	59	7	6	2	24	9	.73	10	.264	.329	.302

Jared Burton

Pitches: R **Bats:** R **Pos:** RP-4   **Ht:** 6'5" **Wt:** 228 **Born:** 6/2/1981 **Age:** 30

Year	Team	Lg	G	GS	CG	GF	IP	BFP	H	R	ER	HR	SH	SF	HB	TBB	IBB	SO	WP	Bk	W	L	Pct	Sh	Sv-Op	Hld	ERC	ERA
2010	Lsvlle*	AAA	33	0	0	12	38.0	159	29	14	11	4	0	0	1	16	0	34	1	0	3	2	.600	0	4- -	-	2.98	2.61
2007	Cin	NL	47	0	0	12	43.0	176	28	15	12	2	1	1	2	22	4	36	3	1	4	2	.667	0	0-3	11	2.37	2.51
2008	Cin	NL	54	0	0	12	58.2	257	56	24	21	6	2	3	2	25	3	58	2	1	5	1	.833	0	0-2	11	3.93	3.22
2009	Cin	NL	53	0	0	13	59.1	265	61	30	29	5	3	1	4	23	6	45	2	0	1	0	1.000	0	0-0	7	4.08	4.40
2010	Cin	NL	4	0	0	2	3.1	10	0	0	0	0	0	0	0	0	0	1	0	0	0	0	-	0	0-0	1	0.00	0.00
	4 ML YEARS		158	0	0	39	164.1	708	145	69	62	13	6	5	8	70	13	140	7	2	10	3	.769	0	0-5	30	3.41	3.40

Dave Bush

Pitches: R **Bats:** R **Pos:** SP-31; RP-1   **Ht:** 6'2" **Wt:** 204 **Born:** 11/9/1979 **Age:** 31

Year	Team	Lg	G	GS	CG	GF	IP	BFP	H	R	ER	HR	SH	SF	HB	TBB	IBB	SO	WP	Bk	W	L	Pct	Sh	Sv-Op	Hld	ERC	ERA
2004	Tor	AL	16	16	1	0	97.2	412	95	47	40	11	4	4	6	25	2	64	3	0	5	4	.556	1	0-0	0	3.65	3.69
2005	Tor	AL	25	24	2	1	136.1	575	142	73	68	20	3	2	13	29	3	75	2	0	5	11	.313	0	0-0	0	4.28	4.49
2006	Mil	NL	34	32	3	0	210.0	869	201	111	103	26	9	6	18	38	2	166	6	0	12	11	.522	2	0-0	1	3.47	4.41
2007	Mil	NL	33	31	0	2	186.1	810	217	110	106	27	6	2	11	44	1	134	3	0	12	10	.545	0	0-0	0	4.93	5.12
2008	Mil	NL	31	29	0	0	185.0	763	163	92	86	29	4	3	10	48	3	109	2	1	9	10	.474	0	0-0	0	3.44	4.18
2009	Mil	NL	22	21	0	0	114.1	508	131	84	81	19	6	5	15	37	2	89	2	0	5	9	.357	0	0-0	0	5.70	6.38
2010	Mil	NL	32	31	0	0	174.1	781	198	108	88	28	9	10	4	65	6	107	1	1	8	13	.381	0	0-0	1	5.17	4.54
	Postseason		1	1	0	0	5.1	21	5	1	1	0	0	0	0	0	0	3	0	0	1	0	1.000	0	0-0	0	1.68	1.69
	7 ML YEARS		193	184	6	3	1104.0	4718	1147	625	572	160	41	32	77	286	19	744	19	2	56	68	.452	3	0-0	2	4.31	4.66

Drew Butera

Bats: R **Throws:** R **Pos:** C-47; PH-2; DH-1; PR-1   bue-TARE-ah   **Ht:** 6'1" **Wt:** 200 **Born:** 8/9/1983 **Age:** 27

Year	Team	Lg	G	AB	H	2B	3B	HR	(Hm	Rd)	TB	R	RBI	RC	TBB	IBB	SO	HBP	SH	SF	3B	CS	3D%	GDP	Avg	OBP	Slg
2005	Bklyn	A-	55	175	38	9	1	1	(-	-)	52	13	23	18	22	0	33	2	1	4	1	0	1.00	7	.217	.305	.297
2006	Hgrstn	A	95	295	55	13	0	5	(-	-)	83	24	38	28	42	1	72	7	5	6	1	0	1.00	5	.186	.297	.281
2007	StLuci	A+	52	182	47	14	0	5	(-	-)	76	22	22	28	24	0	28	2	0	2	0	0	-	5	.258	.348	.418
2007	Bnghtn	AA	30	117	22	2	0	1	(-	-)	27	7	4	4	2	0	22	1	1	0	0	0	-	4	.188	.208	.231
2007	NwBrit	AA	17	50	13	3	1	0	(-	-)	18	3	3	6	5	0	5	0	1	0	0	0	-	1	.260	.327	.360
2008	NwBrit	AA	96	302	66	18	1	7	(-	-)	107	39	39	36	35	0	55	6	4	4	0	1	.00	7	.219	.308	.354
2009	Roch	AAA	69	298	63	16	1	2	(-	-)	87	23	25	23	22	0	49	2	8	3	0	1	.00	9	.211	.268	.292
2010	Min	AL	49	142	28	6	1	2	(0	2)	42	12	13	7	4	0	25	4	3	2	0	0	-	5	.197	.237	.296

Billy Butler

Bats: R **Throws:** R **Pos:** 1B-127; DH-31; PH-1   **Ht:** 6'1" **Wt:** 240 **Born:** 4/18/1986 **Age:** 25

Year	Team	Lg	G	AB	H	2B	3B	HR	(Hm	Rd)	TB	R	RBI	RC	TBB	IBB	SO	HBP	SH	SF	SB	CS	SB%	GDP	Avg	OBP	Slg
2007	KC	AL	92	329	96	23	2	8	(5	3)	147	38	52	50	27	5	55	2	0	2	0	0	-	8	.292	.347	.447
2008	KC	AL	124	443	122	22	0	11	(4	7)	177	44	55	57	33	0	57	0	0	2	0	1	.00	23	.275	.324	.400
2009	KC	AL	159	608	183	51	1	21	(16	5)	299	78	93	99	58	3	103	2	0	4	1	0	1.00	20	.301	.362	.492
2010	KC	AL	158	595	189	45	0	15	(9	6)	279	77	78	91	69	8	78	5	0	9	0	0	-	32	.318	.388	.469
	4 ML YEARS		533	1975	590	141	3	55	(34	21)	902	237	278	297	187	16	293	9	0	17	1	1	.50	83	.299	.359	.457

Marlon Byrd

Bats: R **Throws:** R **Pos:** CF-151; PH-3; DH-1   **Ht:** 6'0" **Wt:** 245 **Born:** 8/30/1977 **Age:** 33

Year	Team	Lg	G	AB	H	2B	3B	HR	(Hm	Rd)	TB	R	RBI	RC	TBB	IBB	SO	HBP	SH	SF	SB	CS	SB%	GDP	Avg	OBP	Slg
2002	Phi	NL	10	35	8	2	0	1	(1	0)	13	2	1	0	1	0	8	0	0	0	0	2	.00	0	.229	.250	.371
2003	Phi	NL	135	495	150	28	4	7	(3	4)	207	86	45	72	44	3	94	7	4	3	11	1	.92	8	.303	.366	.418
2004	Phi	NL	106	346	79	13	2	5	(3	2)	111	48	33	35	22	1	68	7	2	1	2	2	.50	10	.228	.287	.321
2005	2 Tms	NL	79	229	61	15	2	2	(0	2)	86	20	26	30	19	1	50	2	5	4	5	1	.83	5	.266	.323	.376
2006	Was	NL	78	197	44	8	1	5	(1	4)	69	28	18	18	22	1	47	6	1	2	3	3	.50	6	.223	.317	.350
2007	Tex	AL	109	414	127	17	8	10	(4	6)	190	60	70	68	29	3	88	5	0	6	5	3	.63	9	.307	.355	.459
2008	Tex	AL	122	403	120	28	4	10	(7	3)	186	70	53	63	46	3	62	9	2	2	7	2	.78	10	.298	.380	.462
2009	Tex	AL	146	547	155	43	2	20	(14	6)	262	66	89	91	32	2	98	10	0	10	8	4	.67	11	.283	.329	.479
2010	ChC	NL	152	580	170	39	2	12	(6	6)	249	84	66	80	31	1	98	17	0	2	5	1	.83	12	.293	.346	.429
05	Phi	NL	5	13	4	0	0	0	(0	0)	4	0	0	2	1	0	3	1	0	0	0	0	-	0	.308	.400	.308
05	Was	NL	74	216	57	15	2	2	(0	2)	82	20	26	28	18	1	47	1	5	4	5	1	.83	5	.264	.318	.380
	9 ML YEARS		937	3246	914	193	25	72	(39	33)	1373	464	401	457	246	15	613	63	14	30	46	19	.71	71	.282	.341	.423

Tim Byrdak

Pitches: L **Bats:** L **Pos:** RP-64 | BURR-dack | **Ht:** 5'11" **Wt:** 196 **Born:** 10/31/1973 **Age:** 37

Year	Team	Lg	G	GS	CG	GF	IP	BFP	H	R	ER	HR	SH	SF	HB	TBB	IBB	SO	WP	Bk	W	L	Pct	Sh	Sv-Op	Hld	ERC	ERA
2010	RdRck*	AAA	2	1	0	0	2.0	9	1	1	1	0	0	1	0	2	0	1	0	0	0	0	-	0	0--	-	2.80	4.50
1998	KC	AL	3	0	0	0	1.2	9	5	1	1	1	0	0	0	0	0	1	0	0	0	0	-	0	0-0	0	23.52	5.40
1999	KC	AL	33	0	0	5	24.2	128	32	24	21	5	3	0	1	20	2	17	3	1	0	3	.000	0	1-4	10	8.29	7.66
2000	KC	AL	12	0	0	0	6.1	34	11	8	8	3	0	0	0	4	0	8	1	0	0	0	.000	0	0-2	3	13.14	11.37
2005	Bal	AL	41	0	0	3	26.2	131	27	14	12	1	2	1	1	21	1	31	5	0	0	1	.000	0	1-1	11	5.04	4.05
2006	Bal	AL	16	0	0	2	7.0	42	14	10	10	2	2	0	0	8	1	2	1	0	1	0	1.000	0	0-0	3	15.90	12.86
2007	Det	AL	39	0	0	0	45.0	199	38	23	16	3	2	5	1	26	4	49	3	0	3	0	1.000	0	1-2	8	3.53	3.20
2008	Hou	NL	59	0	0	9	55.1	237	45	24	24	10	2	1	2	29	2	47	0	0	2	1	.667	0	0-0	8	4.18	3.90
2009	Hou	NL	76	0	0	8	61.1	261	39	23	22	10	0	3	3	36	0	58	2	0	1	2	.333	0	0-2	9	3.38	3.23
2010	Hou	NL	64	0	0	9	38.2	170	40	15	15	4	0	3	0	20	0	29	2	0	2	2	.500	0	0-0	11	4.83	3.49
	9 ML YEARS		343	0	0	40	266.2	1211	251	142	129	39	11	13	8	164	10	242	17	1	9	10	.474	0	3-11	63	4.94	4.35

Eric Byrnes

Bats: R **Throws:** R **Pos:** LF-10; DH-4; PR-4; CF-1 | BURNS | **Ht:** 6'2" **Wt:** 205 **Born:** 2/16/1976 **Age:** 35

Year	Team	Lg	G	AB	H	2B	3B	HR	(Hm	Rd)	TB	R	RBI	RC	TBB	IBB	SO	HBP	SH	SF	SB	CS	SB%	GDP	Avg	OBP	Slg
2000	Oak	AL	10	10	3	0	0	0	(0	0)	3	5	0	1	0	0	1	1	0	0	2	1	.67	0	.300	.364	.300
2001	Oak	AL	19	38	9	1	0	0	(2	1)	19	9	5	7	4	0	6	1	0	0	1	0	1.00	0	.237	.326	.500
2002	Oak	AL	90	94	23	4	2	3	(2	1)	40	24	11	10	4	0	17	3	1	2	3	0	1.00	3	.245	.291	.426
2003	Oak	AL	121	414	109	27	9	12	(7	5)	190	64	51	68	42	4	71	2	0	2	10	2	.83	3	.263	.333	.459
2004	Oak	AL	143	569	161	39	3	20	(10	10)	266	91	73	87	46	0	111	12	0	5	17	1	.94	11	.283	.347	.467
2005	3 Tms		126	412	93	24	3	10	(5	5)	153	49	40	41	32	0	71	8	3	1	7	2	.78	7	.226	.294	.371
2006	Ari	NL	143	562	150	37	3	26	(12	14)	271	82	79	78	34	2	88	5	2	3	25	3	.89	12	.267	.313	.482
2007	Ari	NL	160	626	179	30	8	21	(11	10)	288	103	83	103	57	5	98	10	1	4	50	7	.88	12	.286	.353	.460
2008	Ari	NL	52	206	43	13	1	6	(3	3)	76	28	23	19	16	0	36	2	0	0	4	4	.50	5	.209	.272	.369
2009	Ari	NL	84	239	54	14	1	8	(4	4)	94	26	31	24	12	0	30	3	2	2	9	3	.75	4	.226	.270	.393
2010	Sea	AL	15	32	3	2	0	0	(0	0)	5	1	0	0	6	0	9	0	0	0	1	0	1.00	1	.094	.237	.156
05	Oak	AL	59	192	51	15	2	7	(3	4)	91	30	24	29	14	0	27	7	1	1	2	2	.50	1	.266	.336	.474
05	Col	NL	15	53	10	2	0	0	(0	0)	12	2	5	4	7	0	11	0	0	0	2	0	1.00	0	.189	.283	.226
05	Bal	AL	52	167	32	7	1	3	(2	1)	50	17	11	8	11	0	33	1	2	0	3	0	1.00	5	.192	.246	.299
	Postseason		16	45	12	2	1	1	(0	1)	19	3	7	3	2	0	14	0	0	0	2	0	1.00	0	.267	.298	.422
	11 ML YEARS		963	3202	827	191	30	109	(56	53)	1405	482	396	438	253	11	538	47	9	19	129	23	.85	58	.258	.320	.439

Asdrubal Cabrera

Bats: B **Throws:** R **Pos:** SS-95; PH-2; DH-1; PR-1 | azz-DRUE-bull | **Ht:** 6'0" **Wt:** 180 **Born:** 11/13/1985 **Age:** 25

Year	Team	Lg	G	AB	H	2B	3B	HR	(Hm	Rd)	TB	R	RBI	RC	TBB	IBB	SO	HBP	SH	SF	SB	CS	SB%	GDP	Avg	OBP	Slg
2010	MhVlly*	A-	2	6	2	1	0	0	(-	-)	3	0	2	1	1	0	1	0	0	0	0	0	-	0	.333	.429	.500
2010	Akron*	AA	4	14	5	2	0	1	(-	-)	10	4	1	4	3	0	3	0	0	0	2	0	1.00	-	.357	.471	.714
2007	Cle	AL	45	159	45	9	2	3	(1	2)	67	30	22	27	17	0	29	2	5	3	0	0	-	7	.283	.354	.421
2008	Cle	AL	114	352	91	20	0	6	(5	1)	129	48	47	48	46	2	77	4	11	5	4	4	.50	8	.259	.346	.366
2009	Cle	AL	131	523	161	42	4	6	(4	2)	229	81	68	81	44	1	89	1	10	3	17	4	.81	13	.308	.361	.438
2010	Cle	AL	97	381	105	16	1	3	(2	1)	132	39	29	46	25	0	60	5	11	3	6	4	.60	10	.276	.326	.346
	Postseason		11	46	10	0	0	1	(1	0)	13	5	6	5	2	0	12	0	3	1	0	0	-	2	.217	.245	.283
	4 ML YEARS		387	1415	402	87	7	18	(12	6)	557	198	166	202	132	3	255	12	37	14	27	12	.69	38	.284	.347	.394

Everth Cabrera

Bats: B **Throws:** R **Pos:** SS-61; PH-8; 2B-6; PR-5 | **Ht:** 5'10" **Wt:** 176 **Born:** 11/17/1986 **Age:** 24

Year	Team	Lg	G	AB	H	2B	3B	HR	(Hm	Rd)	TB	R	RBI	RC	TBB	IBB	SO	HBP	SH	SF	SB	CS	SB%	GDP	Avg	OBP	Slg
2006	Casper	R+	54	185	47	4	2	0	(-	-)	55	30	14	26	37	1	45	2	3	1	18	7	.72	0	.254	.382	.297
2007	Mdest	A+	4	15	4	0	1	0	(-	-)	6	3	2	3	2	0	7	2	1	0	1	0	1.00	1	.267	.421	.400
2007	TriCity	A-	42	150	45	8	3	1	(-	-)	62	29	23	30	27	2	24	8	1	0	12	5	.71	1	.300	.432	.413
2008	Ashvll	A	121	479	136	25	6	6	(-	-)	191	80	38	81	51	2	101	8	10	2	73	16	.82	6	.284	.361	.399
2009	Lk Els	A+	7	23	9	1	1	0	(-	-)	12	7	4	5	5	0	2	0	0	0	4	3	.57	0	.391	.500	.522
2009	Portlnd	AAA	7	27	9	2	0	0	(-	-)	11	5	0	4	1	0	6	1	0	0	1	0	1.00	0	.333	.379	.407
2010	Lk Els	A+	3	10	3	0	0	0	(-	-)	3	1	1	1	2	0	1	0	0	0	1	0	1.00	0	.300	.417	.300
2010	Portlnd	AAA	8	31	8	1	0	0	(-	-)	9	7	3	4	6	0	13	0	0	0	3	0	1.00	0	.258	.378	.290
2009	SD	NL	103	377	96	18	8	2	(1	1)	136	59	31	48	46	5	88	5	8	2	25	8	.76	3	.255	.342	.361
2010	SD	NL	76	212	44	6	3	1	(0	1)	59	22	22	15	19	3	54	2	8	0	10	6	.63	8	.208	.279	.278
	2 ML YEARS		179	589	140	24	11	3	(1	2)	195	81	53	63	65	8	142	7	16	2	35	14	.71	11	.238	.320	.331

Fernando Cabrera

Pitches: R **Bats:** R **Pos:** RP-1 | **Ht:** 6'4" **Wt:** 225 **Born:** 11/16/1981 **Age:** 29

Year	Team	Lg	G	GS	CG	GF	IP	BFP	H	R	ER	HR	SH	SF	HB	TBB	IBB	SO	WP	Bk	W	L	Pct	Sh	Sv-Op	Hld	ERC	ERA
2010	Pwtckt*	AAA	54	0	0	44	60.2	260	64	29	26	5	3	1	1	24	1	76	3	0	2	5	.286	0	22--	-	4.37	3.86
2004	Cle	AL	4	0	0	2	5.1	20	3	3	2	0	0	0	0	1	0	6	0	0	0	0	-	0	0-0	0	0.99	3.38
2005	Cle	AL	15	0	0	6	30.2	124	24	7	5	1	0	0	0	11	1	29	1	1	2	1	.667	0	0-0	1	2.33	1.47
2006	Cle	AL	51	0	0	20	60.2	256	53	36	35	12	1	4	1	32	2	71	5	0	3	3	.500	0	0-4	6	4.72	5.19
2007	2 Tms	AL	33	0	0	13	43.2	207	50	36	35	9	0	2	0	31	3	48	2	0	1	2	.333	0	1-1	1	6.98	7.21
2008	Bal	AL	22	0	0	8	28.1	132	32	18	17	9	0	0	0	17	2	31	3	0	2	1	.667	0	0-1	0	7.24	5.40
2009	Bos	AL	6	0	0	3	5.1	28	7	5	5	0	0	0	1	4	1	8	0	0	0	0	-	0	0-0	1	6.71	8.44

			HOW MUCH HE PITCHED				WHAT HE GAVE UP										THE RESULTS						
Year	Team	Lg	G	GS	CG	GF	IP	BFP	H	R	ER	HR	SH	SF	HB	TBB	IBB	SO	WP	Bk	W	L	Pct	Sh	Sv-Op	Hld	ERC	ERA
2010	Bos	AL	1	0	0	0	1.1	7	2	3	3	1	0	0	0	2	0	0	0	0	0	0	-	0	0-0	0	21.80	20.25
07	Cle	AL	24	0	0	9	33.2	157	38	22	21	7	0	2	0	23	3	39	1	0	1	2	.333	0	0-0	1	6.61	5.61
07	Bal	AL	9	0	0	4	10.0	50	12	14	14	2	0	0	0	9	0	9	1	0	0	0	-	0	1-1	0	8.26	12.60
7 ML YEARS			132	0	0	52	175.1	774	171	108	102	32	1	9	2	98	9	193	11	1	8	7	.533	0	1-6	9	5.19	5.24

Melky Cabrera

Bats: B **Throws:** L **Pos:** LF-84; CF-55; RF-25; PH-15 **Ht:** 6'0" **Wt:** 200 **Born:** 8/11/1984 **Age:** 26

			BATTING																			BASERUNNING				AVERAGES		
Year	Team	Lg	G	AB	H	2B	3B	HR	(Hm	Rd)	TB	R	RBI	RC	TBB	IBB	SO	HBP	SH	SF	SB	CS	SB%	GDP	Avg	OBP	Slg
2005	NYY	AL	6	19	4	0	0	0	(0	0)	4	1	0	0	0	0	2	0	0	0	0	0	-	0	.211	.211	.211
2006	NYY	AL	130	460	129	26	2	7	(3	4)	180	75	50	68	56	3	59	2	5	1	12	5	.71	9	.280	.360	.391
2007	NYY	AL	150	545	149	24	8	8	(4	4)	213	66	73	70	43	0	68	5	10	9	13	5	.72	14	.273	.327	.391
2008	NYY	AL	129	414	103	12	1	8	(4	4)	141	42	37	37	29	5	58	3	4	3	9	2	.82	11	.249	.301	.341
2009	NYY	AL	154	485	133	28	1	13	(9	4)	202	66	68	69	43	4	59	4	4	4	10	2	.83	15	.274	.336	.416
2010	Atl	NL	147	458	117	27	3	4	(1	3)	162	50	42	45	42	11	64	1	5	3	7	1	.88	8	.255	.317	.354
Postseason			19	67	16	2	0	1	(0	1)	21	7	6	5	3	0	15	0	2	0	0	0	-	0	.239	.271	.313
6 ML YEARS			716	2381	635	117	15	40	(21	19)	902	300	270	289	213	23	310	15	28	20	51	15	.77	57	.267	.328	.379

Miguel Cabrera

Bats: R **Throws:** R **Pos:** 1B-148; DH-2 **Ht:** 6'4" **Wt:** 240 **Born:** 4/18/1983 **Age:** 28

			BATTING																			BASERUNNING				AVERAGES		
Year	Team	Lg	G	AB	H	2B	3B	HR	(Hm	Rd)	TB	R	RBI	RC	TBB	IBB	SO	HBP	SH	SF	SB	CS	SB%	GDP	Avg	OBP	Slg
2003	Fla	NL	87	314	84	21	3	12	(7	5)	147	39	62	51	25	3	84	2	4	1	0	2	.00	12	.268	.325	.468
2004	Fla	NL	160	603	177	31	1	33	(14	19)	309	101	112	92	68	9	148	6	0	8	5	2	.71	20	.294	.366	.512
2005	Fla	NL	158	613	198	43	2	33	(11	22)	344	106	116	108	64	12	125	2	0	6	1	0	1.00	20	.323	.385	.561
2006	Fla	NL	158	576	195	50	2	26	(15	11)	327	112	114	132	86	27	108	10	0	4	9	6	.60	18	.339	.430	.568
2007	Fla	NL	157	588	188	38	2	34	(19	15)	332	91	119	122	79	23	127	5	1	7	2	1	.67	17	.320	.401	.565
2008	Det	AL	160	616	180	36	2	37	(19	18)	331	85	127	109	56	6	126	3	0	9	1	0	1.00	16	.292	.349	.537
2009	Det	AL	160	611	198	34	0	34	(19	15)	334	96	103	114	68	14	107	5	0	1	6	2	.75	22	.324	.396	.547
2010	Det	AL	150	548	180	45	1	38	(17	21)	341	111	126	122	89	32	95	3	0	8	3	3	.50	17	.328	.420	.622
Postseason			17	68	18	2	0	4	(1	3)	32	11	12	9	4	0	19	1	1	0	0	0	-	2	.265	.315	.471
8 ML YEARS			1190	4469	1400	298	13	247	(121	126)	2465	741	879	850	535	122	920	36	5	44	27	16	.63	142	.313	.388	.552

Orlando Cabrera

Bats: R **Throws:** R **Pos:** SS-121; PH-3 **Ht:** 5'10" **Wt:** 194 **Born:** 11/2/1974 **Age:** 36

			BATTING																			BASERUNNING				AVERAGES		
Year	Team	Lg	G	AB	H	2B	3B	HR	(Hm	Rd)	TB	R	RBI	RC	TBB	IBB	SO	HBP	SH	SF	SB	CS	SB%	GDP	Avg	OBP	Slg
2010	Dayton*	A	1	3	0	0	0	0	(-	-)	0	0	0	0	0	0	0	0	0	0	0	0	-	0	.000	.000	.000
1997	Mon	NL	16	18	4	0	0	0	(0	0)	4	4	2	0	1	0	3	0	1	0	1	2	.33	1	.222	.263	.222
1998	Mon	NL	79	261	73	16	5	3	(2	1)	108	44	22	34	18	1	27	0	5	1	6	2	.75	6	.280	.325	.414
1999	Mon	NL	104	382	97	23	5	8	(6	2)	154	48	39	42	18	4	38	3	4	0	2	2	.50	9	.254	.293	.403
2000	Mon	NL	125	422	100	25	1	13	(7	6)	166	47	55	43	25	3	28	1	3	3	4	4	.50	12	.237	.279	.393
2001	Mon	NL	162	626	173	41	6	14	(7	7)	268	64	96	85	43	5	54	4	4	7	19	7	.73	15	.270	.324	.428
2002	Mon	NL	153	563	148	43	1	7	(3	4)	214	64	58	61	40	4	53	2	0	4	25	7	.78	16	.263	.321	.380
2003	Mon	NL	162	626	186	47	2	17	(8	9)	288	95	80	92	52	3	64	1	3	9	24	2	.92	18	.297	.347	.460
2004	2 Tms		161	618	163	38	3	10	(2	8)	237	74	62	67	39	0	54	3	3	10	16	4	.80	16	.264	.306	.383
2005	LAA	AL	141	540	139	28	3	8	(2	6)	197	70	57	61	38	4	50	3	4	2	21	2	.91	10	.257	.309	.365
2006	LAA	AL	153	607	171	45	1	9	(3	6)	245	95	72	77	51	0	58	3	3	11	27	3	.90	12	.282	.335	.404
2007	LAA	AL	155	638	192	35	1	8	(3	5)	253	101	86	95	44	0	64	5	3	11	20	4	.83	12	.301	.345	.397
2008	CWS	AL	161	661	186	33	1	8	(5	3)	245	93	57	83	56	1	71	1	3	9	19	6	.76	16	.281	.334	.371
2009	2 Tms	AL	160	656	186	36	3	9	(6	3)	255	83	77	74	36	1	71	0	6	10	13	4	.76	22	.284	.316	.389
2010	Cin	NL	123	494	130	33	0	4	(3	1)	175	64	42	49	28	0	53	3	5	7	11	4	.73	11	.263	.303	.354
04	Mon	NL	103	390	96	19	2	4	(1	3)	131	41	31	37	28	0	31	2	2	3	12	3	.80	12	.246	.298	.336
04	Bos	AL	58	228	67	19	1	6	(1	5)	106	33	31	30	11	0	23	1	1	7	4	1	.80	4	.294	.320	.465
09	Oak	AL	101	414	116	23	0	4	(0	4)	151	41	41	48	25	1	39	0	5	4	11	4	.73	13	.280	.318	.365
09	Min	AL	59	242	70	13	3	5	(3	2)	104	42	36	26	11	0	32	0	1	6	2	0	1.00	9	.289	.313	.430
Postseason			34	141	33	8	0	1	(1	0)	44	15	18	15	11	0	18	2	0	1	2	0	1.00	1	.234	.297	.312
14 ML YEARS			1855	7112	1948	443	32	118	(54	64)	2809	946	803	863	497	26	688	29	56	84	208	53	.80	176	.274	.320	.395

Trevor Cahill

Pitches: R **Bats:** R **Pos:** SP-30 KAY-hill **Ht:** 6'4" **Wt:** 222 **Born:** 3/1/1988 **Age:** 23

			HOW MUCH HE PITCHED						WHAT HE GAVE UP												THE RESULTS						
Year	Team	Lg	G	GS	CG	GF	IP	BFP	H	R	ER	HR	SH	SF	HB	TBB	IBB	SO	WP	Bk	W	L	Pct	Sh	Sv-Op	Hld	ERC	ERA
2006	As	R	4	4	0	0	9.0	36	2	4	3	0	0	1	0	7	0	11	3	0	0	0	-	0	0- -	-	1.15	3.00
2007	Kane	A	20	19	0	0	105.1	437	85	38	32	3	1	1	9	40	1	117	8	0	11	4	.733	0	0- -	-	2.82	2.73
2008	Stcktn	A+	14	13	0	0	87.1	344	52	29	27	3	6	0	8	31	0	103	9	0	5	4	.556	0	0- -	-	1.82	2.78
2008	Mdland	AA	7	6	0	0	37.0	151	24	15	9	2	1	2	3	19	0	33	3	0	6	1	.857	0	0- -	-	2.70	2.19
2010	Scrmto	AAA	2	2	0	0	8.2	36	7	3	1	0	0	0	0	5	0	8	1	0	1	0	1.000	0	0- -	-	3.12	1.04
2009	Oak	AL	32	32	0	0	178.2	773	185	99	92	27	4	7	4	72	1	90	5	0	10	13	.435	0	0-0	0	4.79	4.63
2010	Oak	AL	30	30	1	0	196.2	783	155	73	66	19	3	6	6	63	1	118	2	2	18	8	.692	1	0-0	0	2.81	2.97
2 ML YEARS			62	62	1	0	375.1	1556	340	172	157	46	7	13	10	135	2	208	7	2	28	21	.571	1	0-0	0	3.72	3.76

Lorenzo Cain

Bats: R **Throws:** R **Pos:** CF-38; PH-4; LF-1; RF-1   **Ht:** 6'2" **Wt:** 192 **Born:** 4/13/1986 **Age:** 25

Year	Team	Lg	G	AB	H	2B	3B	HR	(Hm	Rd)	TB	R	RBI	RC	TBB	IBB	SO	HBP	SH	SF	SB	CS	SB%	GDP	Avg	OBP	Slg
2005	Brewrs	R	50	205	73	18	5	5	(-	-)	116	45	37	48	20	0	32	4	0	3	12	3	.80	7	.356	.418	.566
2005	Helena	R+	6	24	5	0	0	0	(-	-)	5	4	1	1	1	0	6	3	0	0	0	0	-	1	.208	.321	.208
2006	WV	A	132	527	162	36	4	6	(-	-)	224	91	60	93	58	1	104	11	2	5	34	11	.76	12	.307	.384	.425
2007	BrvdCt	A+	126	482	133	21	3	2	(-	-)	166	67	44	61	37	0	97	9	4	1	24	9	.73	9	.276	.338	.344
2008	BrvdCt	A+	80	317	91	22	4	7	(-	-)	142	50	41	54	29	1	68	7	1	2	19	4	.83	7	.287	.358	.448
2008	Nashv	AAA	6	19	3	0	0	0	(-	-)	3	0	2	0	3	1	6	0	0	0	0	0	-	1	.158	.273	.158
2008	Hntsvl	AA	40	148	41	9	5	4	(-	-)	72	21	17	27	19	1	41	2	1	2	6	2	.75	3	.277	.363	.486
2009	Hntsvl	AA	42	145	31	6	0	4	(-	-)	49	17	15	13	10	0	35	3	1	1	3	3	.50	1	.214	.277	.338
2009	Brewrs	R	3	9	4	1	0	0	(-	-)	5	1	1	2	1	0	0	0	0	1	0	0	-	0	.444	.455	.556
2009	Wisc	A	15	52	10	4	0	0	(-	-)	14	3	3	4	9	0	15	0	0	0	0	0	-	1	.192	.311	.269
2010	Hntsvl	AA	62	244	79	6	6	3	(-	-)	106	45	18	48	34	2	52	1	1	0	21	2	.91	4	.324	.409	.434
2010	Nashv	AAA	22	87	26	5	3	0	(-	-)	37	13	9	15	11	0	17	1	1	0	5	1	.83	5	.299	.384	.425
2010	Mil	NL	43	147	45	11	1	1	(1	0)	61	17	13	23	9	0	28	1	0	1	7	1	.88	1	.306	.348	.415

Matt Cain

Pitches: R **Bats:** R **Pos:** SP-33   **Ht:** 6'3" **Wt:** 225 **Born:** 10/1/1984 **Age:** 26

			HOW MUCH HE PITCHED					WHAT HE GAVE UP										THE RESULTS							
Year	Team	Lg	G	GS	CG	GF	IP	BFP	H	R	ER	HR	SH	SF	HB	TBB	IBB	SO	WP	Bk	W	L	Pct	Sh	Sv-Op	Hld	ERC	ERA
2005	SF	NL	7	7	1	0	46.1	181	24	12	12	4	2	1	0	19	1	30	1	0	2	1	.667	0	0-0	0	1.61	2.33
2006	SF	NL	32	31	1	1	190.2	818	157	93	88	18	11	6	6	87	1	179	9	2	13	12	.520	1	0-0	0	3.35	4.15
2007	SF	NL	32	32	1	0	200.0	832	173	84	81	14	8	5	5	79	3	163	12	0	7	16	.304	0	0-0	0	3.23	3.65
2008	SF	NL	34	34	1	0	217.2	933	206	95	91	19	7	7	7	91	9	186	7	2	8	14	.364	1	0-0	0	3.84	3.76
2009	SF	NL	33	33	4	0	217.2	886	184	73	70	22	10	6	3	73	6	171	9	0	14	8	.636	0	0-0	0	3.06	2.89
2010	SF	NL	33	33	4	0	223.1	896	181	84	78	22	6	7	4	61	4	177	8	0	13	11	.542	2	0-0	0	2.65	3.14
6 ML YEARS			171	170	12	1	1095.2	4546	925	441	420	99	44	32	25	410	24	906	46	4	57	62	.479	4	0-0	0	3.14	3.45

Miguel Cairo

Bats: R **Throws:** R **Pos:** PH-38; 3B-37; 1B-14; 2B-6; DH-2; SS-1; RF-1; PR-1   **Ht:** 6'1" **Wt:** 224 **Born:** 5/4/1974 **Age:** 37

Year	Team	Lg	G	AB	H	2B	3B	HR	(Hm	Rd)	TB	R	RBI	RC	TBB	IBB	SO	HBP	SH	SF	SB	CS	SB%	GDP	Avg	OBP	Slg
1996	Tor	AL	9	27	6	2	0	0	(0	0)	8	5	1	2	2	0	9	1	0	0	0	0	-	1	.222	.300	.296
1997	ChC	NL	16	29	7	1	0	0	(0	0)	8	7	1	3	2	0	3	1	0	0	0	0	-	0	.241	.313	.276
1998	TB	AL	150	515	138	26	5	5	(3	2)	189	49	46	58	24	0	44	6	11	2	19	8	.70	9	.268	.307	.367
1999	TB	AL	120	465	137	15	5	3	(1	2)	171	61	36	57	24	0	46	7	7	5	22	7	.76	13	.295	.335	.368
2000	TB	AL	119	375	98	18	2	1	(0	1)	123	49	34	42	29	0	34	2	6	5	28	7	.80	7	.261	.314	.328
2001	2 Tms	NL	93	156	46	8	1	3	(2	1)	65	25	16	23	18	1	23	0	7	1	2	1	.67	4	.295	.366	.417
2002	StL	NL	108	184	46	9	2	2	(1	1)	65	28	23	19	13	2	36	3	6	2	1	1	.50	5	.250	.307	.353
2003	StL	NL	92	261	64	15	2	5	(2	3)	98	41	32	25	13	1	30	6	3	7	4	1	.80	6	.245	.289	.375
2004	NYY	AL	122	360	105	17	5	6	(4	2)	150	48	42	50	18	1	49	14	12	4	11	3	.79	7	.292	.346	.417
2005	NYM	NL	100	327	82	18	0	2	(1	1)	106	31	19	29	19	2	31	4	12	5	13	3	.81	5	.251	.296	.324
2006	NYY	AL	81	222	53	12	3	0	(0	0)	71	28	30	26	13	0	31	1	5	3	13	1	.93	4	.239	.280	.320
2007	2 Tms	AL	82	174	44	9	2	0	(0	0)	57	20	15	21	11	1	24	2	5	1	10	2	.83	3	.253	.303	.328
2008	Sea	AL	108	221	55	14	2	0	(0	0)	73	34	23	20	18	0	32	4	6	1	5	2	.71	6	.249	.316	.330
2009	Phi	NL	27	45	12	2	1	1	(1	0)	19	6	2	2	0	0	4	1	1	0	0	0	-	1	.267	.283	.422
2010	Cin	NL	91	200	58	12	0	4	(4	0)	82	30	28	27	17	0	30	4	2	3	4	0	1.00	4	.290	.353	.410
01	ChC	NL	66	123	35	3	1	2	(1	1)	46	20	9	17	16	1	21	0	7	1	2	1	.67	3	.285	.364	.374
01	StL	NL	27	33	11	5	0	1	(1	0)	19	5	7	6	2	0	2	0	0	0	0	0	-	1	.333	.371	.576
07	NYY	AL	54	107	27	7	0	0	(0	0)	34	12	10	12	8	1	19	1	4	1	8	1	.89	3	.252	.308	.318
07	StL	NL	28	67	17	2	2	0	(0	0)	23	8	5	9	3	0	5	1	1	0	2	1	.67	0	.254	.296	.343
Postseason			23	66	20	5	0	1	(1	0)	28	11	6	9	4	0	13	5	2	0	2	1	.67	0	.303	.387	.424
15 ML YEARS			1318	3561	951	178	30	32	(19	13)	1285	462	348	410	221	8	426	56	83	39	132	36	.79	75	.267	.317	.361

Alberto Callaspo

Bats: B **Throws:** R **Pos:** 3B-130; 2B-12; PH-6; LF-1; DH-1   ky-AHS-po   **Ht:** 5'8" **Wt:** 202 **Born:** 4/19/1983 **Age:** 28

Year	Team	Lg	G	AB	H	2B	3B	HR	(Hm	Rd)	TB	R	RBI	RC	TBB	IBB	SO	HBP	SH	SF	SB	CS	SB%	GDP	Avg	OBP	Slg
2006	Ari	NL	23	42	10	1	1	0	(0	0)	13	2	6	5	4	0	6	0	1	0	0	1	.00	0	.238	.298	.310
2007	Ari	NL	56	144	31	8	0	0	(0	0)	39	10	7	7	9	0	14	1	1	1	1	1	.50	8	.215	.265	.271
2008	KC	AL	74	213	65	8	3	0	(0	0)	79	21	16	25	19	0	14	0	1	1	2	1	.67	6	.305	.361	.371
2009	KC	AL	155	576	173	41	8	11	(6	5)	263	79	73	90	52	4	51	1	0	5	2	1	.67	15	.300	.356	.457
2010	2 Tms	AL	146	562	149	27	2	10	(2	8)	210	61	56	54	31	3	42	1	1	6	5	3	.63	22	.265	.302	.374
10	KC	AL	88	349	96	19	2	8	(2	6)	143	40	43	38	19	2	29	0	0	5	3	1	.75	14	.275	.308	.410
10	LAA	AL	58	213	53	8	0	2	(0	2)	67	21	13	16	12	1	13	1	1	1	2	2	.50	8	.249	.291	.315
Postseason			2	2	0	0	0	0	(0	0)	0	0	0	0	0	0	0	0	0	0	0	0	-	0	.000	.000	.000
5 ML YEARS			454	1537	428	85	14	21	(8	13)	604	173	158	181	115	7	127	3	3	14	10	7	.59	51	.278	.327	.393

Mike Cameron

Bats: R **Throws:** R **Pos:** CF-46; PH-2; PR-2   **Ht:** 6'2" **Wt:** 205 **Born:** 1/8/1973 **Age:** 38

Year	Team	Lg	G	AB	H	2B	3B	HR	(Hm	Rd)	TB	R	RBI	RC	TBB	IBB	SO	HBP	SH	SF	SB	CS	SB%	GDP	Avg	OBP	Slg
2010	Pwtckt*	AAA	5	14	4	1	0	1	(-	-)	8	3	3	3	4	1	4	0	0	1	0	0	-	0	.286	.421	.571
2010	PortInd*	AA	3	13	5	2	0	2	(-	-)	13	4	3	4	0	0	4	0	0	0	0	0	-	0	.385	.385	1.000
1995	CWS	AL	28	38	7	2	0	1	(0	1)	12	4	2	3	3	0	15	0	3	0	0	0	-	0	.184	.244	.316
1996	CWS	AL	11	11	1	0	0	0	(0	0)	1	1	0	0	1	0	3	0	0	0	0	1	.00	0	.091	.167	.091

			BATTING																	BASERUNNING				AVERAGES		
Year	Team	Lg	G	AB	H	2B	3B	HR	(Hm	Rd)	TB	R	RBI	RC	TBB	IBB	SO	HBP	SH	SF	SB	CS	SB%	GDP	Avg	OBP	Slg
1997	CWS	AL	116	379	98	18	3	14	(10	4)	164	63	55	63	55	1	105	5	2	5	23	2	.92	8	.259	.356	.433
1998	CWS	AL	141	396	83	16	5	8	(5	3)	133	53	43	39	37	0	101	6	1	3	27	11	.71	6	.210	.285	.336
1999	Cin	NL	146	542	139	34	9	21	(12	9)	254	93	66	96	80	2	145	6	5	3	38	12	.76	4	.256	.357	.469
2000	Sea	AL	155	543	145	28	4	19	(5	14)	238	96	78	91	78	0	133	9	7	6	24	7	.77	10	.267	.365	.438
2001	Sea	AL	150	540	144	30	5	25	(7	18)	259	99	110	96	69	3	155	10	1	13	34	5	.87	13	.267	.353	.480
2002	Sea	AL	158	545	130	26	5	25	(7	18)	241	84	80	78	79	3	176	7	4	5	31	8	.79	8	.239	.340	.442
2003	Sea	AL	147	534	135	31	5	18	(11	7)	230	74	76	80	70	1	137	5	1	2	17	7	.71	13	.253	.344	.431
2004	NYM	NL	140	493	114	30	1	30	(11	19)	236	76	76	70	57	2	143	8	1	3	22	6	.79	5	.231	.319	.479
2005	NYM	NL	76	308	84	23	2	12	(7	5)	147	47	39	52	29	0	85	4	1	1	13	1	.93	5	.273	.342	.477
2006	SD	NL	141	552	148	34	9	22	(11	11)	266	88	83	98	71	2	142	6	0	5	25	9	.74	8	.268	.355	.482
2007	SD	NL	151	571	138	33	6	21	(10	11)	246	88	78	83	67	1	160	8	2	3	18	5	.78	9	.242	.328	.431
2008	Mil	NL	120	444	100	25	2	25	(18	7)	212	69	70	70	54	1	142	6	1	3	17	5	.77	4	.243	.331	.477
2009	Mil	NL	149	544	136	32	3	24	(14	10)	246	78	70	75	75	3	156	4	0	5	7	3	.70	12	.250	.342	.452
2010	Bos	AL	48	162	42	11	0	4	(1	3)	65	24	15	17	14	0	44	3	0	1	0	1	.00	3	.259	.328	.401
	Postseason		27	92	16	6	0	1	(1	0)	25	14	7	7	14	0	29	4	2	0	3	1	.75	2	.174	.309	.272
	16 ML YEARS		1877	6602	1652	373	59	269	(118	151)	2950	1037	941	1011	839	19	1842	87	29	58	296	83	.78	108	.250	.340	.447

Shawn Camp

Pitches: R **Bats:** R **Pos:** RP-70   **Ht:** 6'0" **Wt:** 204 **Born:** 11/18/1975 **Age:** 35

			HOW MUCH HE PITCHED					WHAT HE GAVE UP											THE RESULTS							
Year	Team	Lg	G	GS	CG	GF	IP	BFP	H	R	ER	HR	SH	SF	HB	TBB	IBB	SO	WP	Bk	W	L	Pct	Sh	Sv-Op	Hld	ERC	ERA
2004	KC	AL	42	0	0	12	66.2	286	74	37	29	14	2	3	5	16	1	51	2	1	2	2	.500	0	2-3	5	4.74	3.92
2005	KC	AL	29	0	0	7	49.0	228	69	40	35	4	0	3	4	13	3	28	3	0	1	4	.200	0	0-2	0	6.00	6.43
2006	TB	AL	75	0	0	15	75.0	328	93	43	39	9	2	3	7	19	3	53	4	0	7	4	.636	0	4-6	12	5.48	4.68
2007	TB	AL	50	0	0	8	40.0	198	63	33	32	7	5	1	3	18	6	36	2	0	0	3	.000	0	0-2	11	8.59	7.20
2008	Tor	AL	40	0	0	16	39.1	166	40	18	18	2	0	1	2	11	3	31	0	0	3	1	.750	0	0-0	7	3.47	4.12
2009	Tor	AL	59	0	0	17	79.2	333	73	36	31	7	1	1	4	29	4	58	0	0	2	6	.250	0	1-1	6	3.57	3.50
2010	Tor	AL	70	0	0	13	72.1	298	71	26	24	8	0	2	4	18	5	46	2	0	4	3	.571	0	2-4	13	3.65	2.99
	7 ML YEARS		365	0	0	88	422.0	1837	483	233	208	47	10	14	29	124	25	303	13	1	19	23	.452	0	9-18	54	4.80	4.44

Robinson Cano

Bats: L **Throws:** R **Pos:** 2B-158; DH-2; PH-1   kuh-NOE   **Ht:** 6'0" **Wt:** 205 **Born:** 10/22/1982 **Age:** 28

			BATTING																	BASERUNNING				AVERAGES		
Year	Team	Lg	G	AB	H	2B	3B	HR	(Hm	Rd)	TB	R	RBI	RC	TBB	IBB	SO	HBP	SH	SF	SB	CS	SB%	GDP	Avg	OBP	Slg
2005	NYY	AL	132	522	155	34	4	14	(5	9)	239	78	62	60	16	1	68	3	7	3	1	3	.25	16	.297	.320	.458
2006	NYY	AL	122	482	165	41	1	15	(9	6)	253	62	78	74	18	3	54	2	5	1	5	2	.71	19	.342	.365	.525
2007	NYY	AL	160	617	189	41	7	19	(10	9)	301	93	97	94	39	5	85	8	1	4	4	5	.44	19	.306	.353	.488
2008	NYY	AL	159	597	162	35	4	14	(7	7)	245	70	72	64	26	3	65	5	1	5	2	4	.33	18	.271	.305	.410
2009	NYY	AL	161	637	204	48	2	25	(14	11)	331	103	85	79	30	2	63	3	0	4	5	7	.42	22	.320	.352	.520
2010	NYY	AL	160	626	200	41	3	29	(16	13)	334	103	109	118	57	14	77	8	0	5	3	2	.60	19	.319	.381	.534
	Postseason		28	106	23	5	2	2	(1	1)	38	11	14	10	7	1	15	2	0	1	0	2	.00	4	.217	.276	.358
	6 ML YEARS		894	3481	1075	240	20	116	(61	55)	1703	509	503	488	186	28	412	29	10	26	20	23	.47	113	.309	.347	.489

Jorge Cantu

Bats: R **Throws:** R **Pos:** 3B-89; 1B-63; DH-9; PH-2; 2B-1; PR-1   **Ht:** 6'3" **Wt:** 210 **Born:** 1/30/1982 **Age:** 29

			BATTING																	BASERUNNING				AVERAGES		
Year	Team	Lg	G	AB	H	2B	3B	HR	(Hm	Rd)	TB	R	RBI	RC	TBB	IBB	SO	HBP	SH	SF	SB	CS	SB%	GDP	Avg	OBP	Slg
2004	TB	AL	50	173	52	20	1	2	(0	2)	80	25	17	22	9	0	44	2	0	1	0	0	-	5	.301	.341	.462
2005	TB	AL	150	598	171	40	1	28	(16	12)	297	73	117	88	19	1	83	6	0	7	1	0	1.00	24	.286	.311	.497
2006	TB	AL	107	413	103	18	2	14	(7	7)	167	40	62	42	26	2	91	3	0	6	1	1	.50	16	.249	.295	.404
2007	2 Tms		52	115	29	9	0	1	(0	1)	41	12	13	12	12	0	26	3	0	3	0	0	-	6	.252	.331	.357
2008	Fla	NL	155	628	174	41	0	29	(18	11)	302	92	95	89	40	6	111	10	0	7	6	2	.75	15	.277	.327	.481
2009	Fla	NL	149	585	169	42	0	16	(8	8)	259	67	100	85	47	4	81	6	0	5	3	1	.75	15	.289	.345	.443
2010	2 Tms		127	472	121	29	1	11	(4	7)	185	50	56	52	29	1	95	6	1	7	0	0	-	15	.256	.304	.392
07	TB	AL	25	58	12	1	0	0	(0	0)	13	4	4	3	5	0	16	1	0	1	0	0	-	3	.207	.277	.224
07	Cin	NL	27	57	17	8	0	1	(0	1)	28	8	9	9	7	0	10	2	0	2	0	0	-	3	.298	.382	.491
10	Fla	NL	97	374	98	25	0	10	(4	6)	153	41	54	47	23	1	76	6	0	7	0	0	-	11	.262	.310	.409
10	Tex	AL	30	98	23	4	1	1	(0	1)	32	9	2	5	6	0	19	0	1	0	0	0	-	4	.235	.279	.327
	7 ML YEARS		790	2984	819	199	5	101	(53	48)	1331	359	460	390	182	14	531	36	1	36	11	4	.73	96	.274	.320	.446

Matt Capps

Pitches: R **Bats:** R **Pos:** RP-74   **Ht:** 6'2" **Wt:** 245 **Born:** 9/3/1983 **Age:** 27

			HOW MUCH HE PITCHED					WHAT HE GAVE UP											THE RESULTS							
Year	Team	Lg	G	GS	CG	GF	IP	BFP	H	R	ER	HR	SH	SF	HB	TBB	IBB	SO	WP	Bk	W	L	Pct	Sh	Sv-Op	Hld	ERC	ERA
2005	Pit	NL	4	0	0	0	4.0	16	5	2	2	0	0	0	1	0	0	3	0	0	0	0	-	0	0-0	0	4.62	4.50
2006	Pit	NL	85	0	0	15	80.2	329	81	37	34	12	8	2	3	12	5	56	4	0	9	1	.900	0	1-10	13	3.52	3.79
2007	Pit	NL	76	0	0	47	79.0	315	64	22	20	5	3	2	3	16	10	64	1	0	4	7	.364	0	18-21	15	2.10	2.28
2008	Pit	NL	49	0	0	39	53.2	211	47	20	18	5	2	0	2	5	0	39	0	0	3	4	.400	0	21-26	0	2.39	3.02
2009	Pit	NL	57	0	0	50	54.1	251	73	36	35	10	2	4	3	17	3	46	0	0	4	8	.333	0	27-32	1	6.53	5.80
2010	2 Tms		74	0	0	66	73.0	305	75	27	20	6	5	0	0	17	4	59	1	0	5	3	.625	0	42-48	0	3.37	2.47
10	Was	NL	47	0	0	43	46.0	199	51	20	14	5	4	0	0	9	3	38	0	0	3	3	.500	0	26-30	0	3.72	2.74
10	Min	AL	27	0	0	23	27.0	106	24	7	6	1	1	0	0	8	1	21	1	0	2	0	1.000	0	16-18	0	2.78	2.00
	6 ML YEARS		345	0	0	217	344.2	1427	345	144	129	38	20	8	12	67	22	267	6	0	24	22	.522	0	109-137	29	3.40	3.37

Chris Capuano

Pitches: L Bats: L Pos: RP-15; SP-9   capp-ue-AHH-noe   Ht: 6'2" Wt: 224 Born: 8/19/1978 Age: 32

Year	Team	Lg	G	GS	CG	GF	IP	BFP	H	R	ER	HR	SH	SF	HB	TBB	IBB	SO	WP	Bk	W	L	Pct	Sh	Sv-Op	Hld	ERC	ERA
2010	BrvdCt*	A+	3	3	0	0	14.2	56	12	2	2	1	0	0	0	0	0	17	1	0	2	0	1.000	0	0--	1	1.56	1.23
2010	Nashv*	AAA	4	4	0	0	25.0	102	21	6	5	0	2	0	1	4	0	16	0	0	1	1	.500	0	0--	-	1.85	1.80
2003	Ari	NL	9	5	0	2	33.0	139	27	19	17	3	4	1	6	11	1	23	3	0	2	4	.333	0	0-0	1	3.45	4.64
2004	Mil	NL	17	17	0	0	88.1	385	91	55	49	18	4	1	5	37	1	80	3	1	6	8	.429	0	0-0	0	5.37	4.99
2005	Mil	NL	35	35	0	0	219.0	949	212	105	97	31	14	5	12	91	6	176	3	4	18	12	.600	0	0-0	0	4.44	3.99
2006	Mil	NL	34	34	3	0	221.1	936	229	108	99	29	9	8	9	47	4	174	7	0	11	12	.478	2	0-0	0	3.84	4.03
2007	Mil	NL	29	25	0	0	150.0	669	170	93	85	20	10	3	8	54	2	132	10	0	5	12	.294	0	0-0	0	5.11	5.10
2010	Mil	NL	24	9	0	5	66.0	278	65	29	29	9	3	2	1	21	1	54	5	0	4	4	.500	0	0-0	1	3.98	3.95
6 ML YEARS			148	125	3	7	777.2	3356	794	409	376	110	44	20	41	261	15	639	31	5	46	52	.469	2	0-0	2	4.42	4.35

Esmailin Caridad

Pitches: R Bats: R Pos: RP-8   ess-MY-linn CARR-ee-dahd   Ht: 5'10" Wt: 193 Born: 10/28/1983 Age: 27

Year	Team	Lg	G	GS	CG	GF	IP	BFP	H	R	ER	HR	SH	SF	HB	TBB	IBB	SO	WP	Bk	W	L	Pct	Sh	Sv-Op	Hld	ERC	ERA
2008	Dytona	A+	14	13	0	0	69.1	279	64	35	34	3	2	4	2	17	0	38	1	0	6	4	.600	0	0--	-	2.89	4.41
2008	Tenn	AA	14	14	0	0	82.2	337	67	31	29	15	6	1	2	21	0	50	1	1	7	3	.700	0	0--	-	3.06	3.16
2009	Iowa	AAA	25	25	0	0	131.2	578	139	71	61	17	11	5	3	46	4	114	2	1	5	10	.333	0	0--	-	4.38	4.17
2010	Iowa	AAA	2	0	0	1	3.0	12	2	1	1	1	0	0	0	1	0	2	0	0	0	1	.000	0	0--	-	3.37	3.00
2010	Cubs	R	1	1	0	0	0.2	5	3	1	1	0	0	0	0	0	0	1	0	0	0	0	-	0	0--	-	26.58	13.50
2010	Tenn	AA	7	0	0	2	8.2	40	12	5	5	1	0	0	0	3	0	8	0	0	0	1	.000	0	1--	-	6.27	5.19
2009	ChC	NL	14	0	0	2	19.1	74	15	4	3	0	0	0	3	3	0	17	0	0	1	0	1.000	0	0-0	2	2.10	1.40
2010	ChC	NL	8	0	0	3	4.0	23	4	7	5	1	0	1	0	5	0	4	0	0	0	1	.000	0	0-2	1	7.99	11.25
2 ML YEARS			22	0	0	5	23.1	97	19	11	8	1	0	1	3	8	0	21	0	0	1	1	.500	0	0-2	3	3.00	3.09

Luke Carlin

Bats: B Throws: R Pos: C-6   Ht: 5'11" Wt: 185 Born: 12/20/1980 Age: 30

Year	Team	Lg	G	AB	H	2B	3B	HR	(Hm	Rd)	TB	R	RBI	RC	TBB	IBB	SO	HBP	SH	SF	SB	CS	SB%	GDP	Avg	OBP	Slg
2010	Indy*	AAA	63	205	49	8	1	2	(-	-)	65	23	23	24	27	1	49	2	0	2	5	2	.71	6	.239	.331	.317
2010	Clmbs*	AAA	13	38	9	2	0	2	(-	-)	17	8	6	6	7	0	11	0	1	1	0	0	-	0	.237	.348	.447
2008	SD	NL	36	94	14	3	1	1	(0	1)	22	12	6	2	10	0	34	1	0	0	0	0	-	3	.149	.238	.234
2009	Ari	NL	10	18	3	0	0	0	(0	0)	3	3	1	2	3	0	3	0	0	0	0	0	-	0	.167	.286	.167
2010	Cle	AL	6	14	5	0	0	2	(1	1)	11	4	3	3	2	0	5	0	0	0	0	0	-	0	.357	.438	.786
3 ML YEARS			52	126	22	3	1	3	(1	2)	36	19	10	7	15	0	42	1	0	0	0	0	-	3	.175	.268	.286

Jesse Carlson

Pitches: L Bats: L Pos: RP-20   Ht: 6'1" Wt: 160 Born: 12/31/1980 Age: 30

Year	Team	Lg	G	GS	CG	GF	IP	BFP	H	R	ER	HR	SH	SF	HB	TBB	IBB	SO	WP	Bk	W	L	Pct	Sh	Sv-Op	Hld	ERC	ERA
2010	LsVgs*	AAA	45	0	0	18	51.0	220	56	32	24	6	0	1	4	11	0	43	6	2	3	1	.750	0	4--	-	4.32	4.24
2008	Tor	AL	69	0	0	10	60.0	237	41	16	15	6	1	3	4	21	7	55	2	1	7	2	.778	0	2-2	19	2.32	2.25
2009	Tor	AL	73	0	0	12	67.2	291	67	37	35	7	2	5	3	21	3	51	2	1	1	6	.143	0	0-3	12	3.75	4.66
2010	Tor	AL	20	0	0	5	13.2	59	13	7	7	3	1	0	1	5	2	8	0	0	0	0	-	0	1-1	2	4.55	4.61
3 ML YEARS			162	0	0	27	141.1	587	121	60	57	16	4	8	7	47	12	114	4	2	8	8	.500	0	3-6	33	3.19	3.63

Fausto Carmona

Pitches: R Bats: R Pos: SP-33   FAHW-sto   Ht: 6'4" Wt: 230 Born: 12/7/1983 Age: 27

Year	Team	Lg	G	GS	CG	GF	IP	BFP	H	R	ER	HR	SH	SF	HB	TBB	IBB	SO	WP	Bk	W	L	Pct	Sh	Sv-Op	Hld	ERC	ERA
2006	Cle	AL	38	7	0	12	74.2	340	88	46	45	9	2	4	7	31	3	58	3	1	1	10	.091	0	0-3	10	5.69	5.42
2007	Cle	AL	32	32	2	0	215.0	879	199	78	73	16	2	4	11	61	2	137	5	1	19	8	.704	1	0-0	0	3.32	3.06
2008	Cle	AL	22	22	1	0	120.2	549	126	80	73	7	1	4	9	70	0	58	8	1	8	7	.533	1	0-0	0	5.07	5.44
2009	Cle	AL	24	24	0	0	125.1	596	151	97	88	16	4	8	8	70	0	79	5	1	5	12	.294	0	0-0	0	6.38	6.32
2010	Cle	AL	33	33	4	0	210.1	880	203	98	88	17	2	10	9	72	0	124	3	0	13	14	.481	1	0-0	0	3.77	3.77
Postseason			3	3	0	0	15.0	66	13	12	12	2	0	0	0	11	0	12	0	0	0	1	.000	0	0-0	0	5.02	7.20
5 ML YEARS			149	118	7	12	746.0	3244	767	399	367	65	11	24	44	304	5	456	24	4	46	51	.474	3	0-3	10	4.45	4.43

Mike Carp

Bats: L Throws: R Pos: 1B-9; PH-3; LF-1; DH-1   Ht: 6'2" Wt: 215 Born: 6/30/1986 Age: 25

Year	Team	Lg	G	AB	H	2B	3B	HR	(Hm	Rd)	TB	R	RBI	RC	TBB	IBB	SO	HBP	SH	SF	SB	CS	SB%	GDP	Avg	OBP	Slg
2004	Mets	R	57	191	51	12	0	4	(-	-)	75	30	26	28	22	3	51	5	0	0	2	1	.67	1	.267	.358	.393
2005	Hgrstn	A	89	313	78	12	1	19	(-	-)	149	49	63	56	35	3	96	21	1	5	2	2	.50	2	.249	.358	.476
2006	StLuci	A+	137	491	141	27	1	17	(-	-)	221	69	88	88	51	5	107	25	0	6	2	1	.67	13	.287	.379	.450
2007	Bnghtn	AA	97	359	90	16	0	11	(-	-)	139	55	48	50	39	1	75	10	0	4	2	1	.67	13	.251	.337	.387
2007	StLuci	A+	1	4	1	0	0	0	(-	-)	1	0	0	0	0	0	0	0	0	0	0	0	-	0	.250	.250	.250
2008	Bnghtn	AA	134	478	143	29	1	17	(-	-)	225	67	72	94	79	5	88	6	0	3	1	2	.33	14	.299	.403	.471
2009	Tacom	AAA	110	413	112	25	1	15	(-	-)	184	66	64	73	58	1	99	12	1	6	0	1	.00	10	.271	.372	.446
2010	Tacom	AAA	110	409	105	17	1	29	(-	-)	211	67	76	71	41	1	93	6	0	7	1	2	.33	7	.257	.328	.516
2009	Sea	AL	21	54	17	3	1	1	(1	0)	25	7	5	8	8	0	10	2	0	1	0	0	-	1	.315	.415	.463
2010	Sea	AL	14	37	7	2	0	0	(0	0)	9	1	0	2	4	0	8	0	0	0	0	0	-	0	.189	.268	.243
2 ML YEARS			35	91	24	5	1	1	(1	0)	34	8	5	10	12	0	18	2	0	1	0	0	-	1	.264	.358	.374

Chris Carpenter

Pitches: R Bats: R Pos: SP-35 Ht: 6'6" Wt: 230 Born: 4/27/1975 Age: 36

		HOW MUCH HE PITCHED						WHAT HE GAVE UP											THE RESULTS						
Year	Team	Lg	G	GS	CG	GF	IP	BFP	H	R	ER	HR	SH	SF	HB	TBB	IBB	SO	WP	Bk	W	L	Pct	Sh	Sv-Op	Hld	ERC	ERA
1997	Tor	AL	14	13	1	1	81.1	374	108	55	46	7	1	2	2	37	0	55	7	1	3	7	.300	1	0-0	0	6.38	5.09
1998	Tor	AL	33	24	1	4	175.0	742	177	97	85	18	4	5	5	61	1	136	5	0	12	7	.632	1	0-0	0	4.12	4.37
1999	Tor	AL	24	24	4	0	150.0	663	177	81	73	16	4	6	3	48	1	106	9	1	9	8	.529	1	0-0	0	4.90	4.38
2000	Tor	AL	34	27	2	1	175.1	795	204	130	122	30	3	1	5	83	1	113	3	0	10	12	.455	0	0-0	0	6.04	6.26
2001	Tor	AL	34	34	3	0	215.2	930	229	112	98	29	3	1	16	75	5	157	5	0	11	11	.500	2	0-0	0	4.82	4.09
2002	Tor	AL	13	13	1	0	73.1	327	89	45	43	11	1	4	4	27	0	45	3	0	4	5	.444	0	0-0	0	5.91	5.28
2004	StL	NL	28	28	1	0	182.0	746	169	75	70	24	6	3	8	38	2	152	4	0	15	5	.750	0	0-0	0	3.32	3.46
2005	StL	NL	33	33	7	0	241.2	953	204	82	76	18	7	7	3	51	0	213	5	0	21	5	.808	4	0-0	0	2.49	2.83
2006	StL	NL	32	32	5	0	221.2	896	194	81	76	21	12	4	10	43	3	184	3	0	15	8	.652	3	0-0	0	2.75	3.09
2007	StL	NL	1	1	0	0	6.0	29	9	5	5	0	1	0	1	1	0	3	0	0	0	1	.000	0	0-0	0	5.80	7.50
2008	StL	NL	4	3	0	0	15.1	63	16	5	3	0	2	1	0	4	0	7	0	0	0	1	.000	0	0-0	0	3.19	1.76
2009	StL	NL	28	28	3	0	192.2	750	156	64	48	7	10	4	7	38	1	144	1	0	17	4	.810	1	0-0	0	2.14	2.24
2010	StL	NL	35	35	1	0	235.0	969	214	99	84	21	9	7	13	63	4	179	3	0	16	9	.640	0	0-0	0	3.23	3.22
	Postseason		9	9	0	0	58.1	244	54	20	19	6	7	2	3	19	0	38	1	0	5	2	.714	0	0-0	0	3.63	2.93
13 ML YEARS			313	295	29	6	1965.0	8237	1946	916	829	202	63	45	77	569	18	1494	48	2	133	83	.616	13	0-0	0	3.79	3.80

Drew Carpenter

Pitches: R Bats: R Pos: RP-1 Ht: 6'3" Wt: 238 Born: 5/18/1985 Age: 26

		HOW MUCH HE PITCHED						WHAT HE GAVE UP											THE RESULTS						
Year	Team	Lg	G	GS	CG	GF	IP	BFP	H	R	ER	HR	SH	SF	HB	TBB	IBB	SO	WP	Bk	W	L	Pct	Sh	Sv-Op	Hld	ERC	ERA
2010	LV*	AAA	27	27	0	0	151.0	649	152	75	68	18	6	2	7	54	2	116	4	0	8	11	.421	0	0- -	-	4.27	4.05
2008	Phi	NL	1	0	0	1	1.0	5	1	0	0	0	1	0	0	1	1	1	0	0	0	0	-	0	0-0	0	3.46	0.00
2009	Phi	NL	3	1	0	0	5.2	32	11	7	7	1	1	0	0	4	0	5	0	0	1	0	1.000	0	0-0	0	13.36	11.12
2010	Phi	NL	1	0	0	0	3.0	14	5	3	3	1	1	0	0	0	0	2	1	0	0	1	.000	0	0-0	0	8.04	9.00
3 ML YEARS			5	1	0	1	9.2	51	17	10	10	2	3	0	1	5	1	8	1	0	1	1	.500	0	0-0	0	10.64	9.31

Carlos Carrasco

Pitches: R Bats: R Pos: SP 7 Ht: 6'3" Wt: 215 Born: 3/21/1987 Age: 24

		HOW MUCH HE PITCHED						WHAT HE GAVE UP											THE RESULTS						
Year	Team	Lg	G	GS	CG	GF	IP	BFP	H	R	ER	HR	SH	SF	HB	TBB	IBB	SO	WP	Bk	W	L	Pct	Sh	Sv-Op	Hld	ERC	ERA
2004	Phillies	R	11	8	0	0	48.0	212	53	23	19	2	0	2	3	15	0	34	2	0	5	4	.556	0	0- -	-	4.10	3.56
2005	Lakwd	A	13	13	1	0	62.2	297	78	50	49	11	0	2	9	28	0	46	1	1	1	7	.125	0	0- -	-	6.93	7.04
2005	Batvia	A-	4	4	0	0	15.1	82	29	25	23	8	0	1	2	5	0	12	3	1	0	3	.000	0	0- -	-	13.83	13.50
2005	Phillies	R	2	2	0	0	5.0	20	3	1	1	0	0	0	2	1	0	2	0	1	0	0	-	0	0- -	-	2.16	1.80
2006	Lakwd	A	26	26	2	0	159.1	643	103	50	40	6	2	0	9	65	0	159	12	2	12	6	.667	0	0- -	-	2.10	2.26
2007	Clrwtr	A+	12	12	1	0	69.2	277	49	22	22	8	2	1	6	22	0	53	2	0	6	2	.750	1	0- -	-	2.67	2.84
2007	Rdng	AA	14	13	1	0	70.1	321	65	42	38	9	3	4	5	46	0	49	0	2	6	4	.600	1	0- -	-	5.13	4.86
2008	Rdng	AA	20	19	1	0	114.2	485	108	58	55	13	1	4	6	45	1	109	8	1	7	7	.500	0	0- -	-	4.08	4.32
2008	LV	AAA	6	6	0	0	36.2	163	36	15	7	1	0	1	1	13	0	46	2	1	2	2	.500	0	0- -	-	3.24	1.72
2009	LV	AAA	20	20	0	0	114.2	501	118	73	66	14	4	2	7	38	0	112	3	0	6	9	.400	0	0- -	-	4.32	5.18
2009	Clmbs	AAA	6	6	0	0	42.1	166	31	18	15	3	0	1	0	7	0	36	2	0	5	1	.833	0	0- -	-	1.67	3.19
2010	Clmbs	AAA	25	25	0	0	150.1	624	139	69	61	16	10	5	7	46	0	133	1	0	10	6	.625	0	0-0		3.57	3.65
2009	Cle	AL	5	5	0	0	22.1	112	40	23	22	6	0	1	0	11	1	11	0	0	0	4	.000	0	0-0	0	11.30	8.87
2010	Cle	AL	7	7	1	0	44.2	188	47	20	19	6	2	1	1	14	1	38	1	0	2	2	.500	0	0-0	0	4.42	3.83
2 ML YEARS			12	12	1	0	67.0	300	87	43	41	12	2	2	1	25	2	49	1	1	2	6	.250	0	0-0	0	6.52	5.51

D.J. Carrasco

Pitches: R Bats: R Pos: RP-63 Ht: 6'4" Wt: 220 Born: 4/12/1977 Age: 34

		HOW MUCH HE PITCHED						WHAT HE GAVE UP											THE RESULTS						
Year	Team	Lg	G	GS	CG	GF	IP	BFP	H	R	ER	HR	SH	SF	HB	TBB	IBB	SO	WP	Bk	W	L	Pct	Sh	Sv-Op	Hld	ERC	ERA
2003	KC	AL	50	2	0	21	80.1	355	82	44	43	8	1	4	7	40	4	57	6	0	6	5	.545	0	2-5	6	4.94	4.82
2004	KC	AL	30	0	0	11	35.1	163	41	22	19	5	1	1	3	15	3	22	2	0	2	2	.500	0	0-3	4	5.56	4.84
2005	KC	AL	21	20	1	0	114.2	511	129	67	61	11	3	5	6	51	2	49	7	3	6	8	.429	0	0-0	0	5.20	4.79
2008	CWS	AL	31	0	0	6	38.2	158	30	17	17	2	1	1	5	14	1	30	0	0	1	0	1.000	0	0-1	7	2.01	3.96
2009	CWS	AL	49	1	0	11	93.1	405	103	42	39	5	2	4	2	29	4	62	3	0	5	1	.833	0	0-1	0	3.98	3.76
2010	2 Tms	NL	63	0	0	8	78.1	330	68	39	32	5	3	3	5	34	3	65	6	0	3	2	.600	0	0-1	7	3.48	3.68
10	Pit	NL	45	0	0	6	55.2	232	50	24	24	4	3	1	4	22	1	45	4	0	2	2	.500	0	0-0	5	3.66	3.88
10	Ari	NL	18	0	0	2	22.2	98	18	15	8	1	0	2	1	12	2	20	2	0	1	0	1.000	0	0-1	2	3.05	3.18
6 ML YEARS			244	23	1	57	440.2	1922	453	231	211	36	11	18	28	183	17	285	24	3	23	18	.561	0	2-11	24	4.40	4.31

Brett Carroll

Bats: R Throws: R Pos: RF-20; PH-8; LF-7; PR-1 Ht: 6'0" Wt: 210 Born: 10/3/1982 Age: 28

			BATTING																		BASERUNNING				AVERAGES		
Year	Team	Lg	G	AB	H	2B	3B	HR	(Hm	Rd)	TB	R	RBI	RC	TBB	IBB	SO	HBP	SH	SF	SB	CS	SB%	GDP	Avg	OBP	Slg
2010	Jupiter*	A+	5	17	5	1	0	0	(-	-)	6	4	0	4	3	5	4	0	0	0	2	1	.67	0	.294	.500	.353
2010	NewOr*	AAA	70	244	54	16	0	8	(-	-)	94	32	30	30	22	0	54	6	3	2	4	2	.67	3	.221	.299	.385
2007	Fla	NL	23	49	9	1	0	0	(0	0)	10	10	2	0	3	0	15	0	1	0	0	0	-	1	.184	.231	.204
2008	Fla	NL	26	17	1	0	1	0	(0	0)	3	5	1	0	1	0	6	0	0	0	0	0	-	0	.059	.111	.176
2009	Fla	NL	92	141	33	8	2	3	(1	2)	54	18	18	20	11	1	33	4	1	1	0	0	-	0	.234	.306	.383
2010	Fla	NL	32	76	15	4	0	2	(1	1)	25	13	7	5	6	3	29	7	0	1	2	1	.67	2	.197	.311	.329
4 ML YEARS			173	283	58	13	3	5	(2	3)	92	46	28	25	21	4	83	11	2	2	2	1	.67	5	.205	.284	.325

Jamey Carroll

Bats: R Throws: R Pos: SS-69; 2B-48; PH-16; 3B-11; LF-5; PR-4   Ht: 5'9" Wt: 168 Born: 2/18/1974 Age: 37

							BATTING											BASERUNNING				AVERAGES		
Year	Team	Lg	G	AB	H	2B	3B	HR	(Hm | Rd)	TB	R	RBI	RC	TBB	IBB	SO	HBP	SH	SF	SB	CS	SB%	GDP	Avg	OBP	Slg
2002	Mon	NL	16	71	22	5	3	1	(1 | 0)	36	16	6	12	4	0	12	0	4	0	1	0	1.00	1	.310	.347	.507
2003	Mon	NL	105	227	59	10	1	1	(1 | 0)	74	31	10	18	19	0	39	3	9	2	5	2	.71	10	.260	.323	.326
2004	Mon	NL	102	218	63	14	2	0	(0 | 0)	81	36	16	28	32	1	21	1	2	3	5	1	.83	3	.289	.378	.372
2005	Was	NL	113	303	76	8	1	0	(0 | 0)	86	44	22	38	34	1	55	5	13	3	3	4	.43	2	.251	.333	.284
2006	Col	NL	136	463	139	23	5	5	(2 | 3)	187	84	36	65	56	1	66	3	9	3	10	12	.45	10	.300	.377	.404
2007	Col	NL	108	227	51	9	1	2	(1 | 1)	68	45	22	24	28	1	34	4	6	3	6	2	.75	2	.225	.317	.300
2008	Cle	AL	113	347	96	13	4	1	(0 | 1)	120	60	36	48	34	0	65	9	10	2	7	3	.70	2	.277	.355	.346
2009	Cle	AL	93	315	87	10	2	2	(0 | 2)	107	53	26	43	36	0	63	3	3	1	4	2	.67	8	.276	.355	.340
2010	LAD	NL	133	351	102	15	1	0	(0 | 0)	119	48	23	48	51	3	64	2	5	5	12	4	.75	8	.291	.379	.339
	Postseason		4	2	0	0	0	0	(0 | 0)	0	0	0	0	1	0	0	0	0	0	0	0	-	0	.000	.333	.000
	9 ML YEARS		919	2522	695	107	20	12	(5 | 7)	878	417	197	324	294	7	419	30	61	22	53	30	.64	46	.276	.355	.348

Matt Carson

Bats: R Throws: R Pos: RF-25; PH-11; LF-6; CF-3; DH-1; PR-1   Ht: 6'2" Wt: 200 Born: 7/1/1981 Age: 29

							BATTING											BASERUNNING				AVERAGES		
Year	Team	Lg	G	AB	H	2B	3B	HR	(Hm | Rd)	TB	R	RBI	RC	TBB	IBB	SO	HBP	SH	SF	SB	CS	SB%	GDP	Avg	OBP	Slg
2002	StIsInd	A-	48	177	36	8	4	1	(- | -)	55	19	11	15	11	1	48	4	0	1	4	1	.80	6	.203	.264	.311
2003	Btl Crk	A	119	432	112	20	1	11	(- | -)	167	61	52	57	37	3	100	6	0	7	1	1	.50	5	.259	.322	.387
2004	Tampa	A+	37	129	22	7	0	3	(- | -)	38	16	17	7	6	1	33	1	1	0	2	1	.67	2	.171	.213	.295
2004	Btl Crk	A	95	381	116	23	2	12	(- | -)	179	59	58	65	22	0	78	9	0	2	21	7	.75	4	.304	.355	.470
2005	Tampa	A+	84	321	81	14	3	8	(- | -)	125	43	39	45	31	0	68	8	0	4	10	2	.83	6	.252	.330	.389
2005	Trnton	AA	28	99	19	5	0	1	(- | -)	27	10	5	3	0	0	25	2	2	0	2	3	.40	2	.192	.208	.273
2006	Tampa	A+	40	136	33	4	1	8	(- | -)	63	15	21	23	21	1	31	2	3	3	5	3	.63	4	.243	.346	.463
2006	Trnton	AA	29	86	22	8	1	2	(- | -)	38	10	9	11	4	0	25	2	5	0	0	0	-	2	.256	.304	.442
2007	Trnton	AA	129	471	117	24	3	16	(- | -)	195	72	76	64	33	0	109	9	2	6	9	0	1.00	13	.248	.306	.414
2008	Trnton	AA	27	112	31	7	4	5	(- | -)	61	17	26	20	9	1	20	0	1	0	1	1	.50	2	.277	.331	.545
2008	S-WB	AAA	84	305	88	10	6	10	(- | -)	140	53	38	50	21	3	63	8	2	3	10	3	.77	8	.289	.347	.459
2009	Scrmto	AAA	118	440	116	29	3	25	(- | -)	226	68	77	77	38	1	94	6	4	5	15	4	.79	6	.264	.327	.514
2010	Scrmto	AAA	64	244	74	18	2	13	(- | -)	135	53	36	51	24	1	58	6	0	2	13	4	.76	7	.303	.377	.553
2009	Oak	AL	10	21	6	0	0	1	(1 | 0)	9	1	5	4	0	0	7	0	0	1	0	0	-	0	.286	.273	.429
2010	Oak	AL	36	79	14	2	0	4	(2 | 2)	28	7	9	3	2	0	23	0	0	2	4	0	1.00	0	.177	.193	.354
	2 ML YEARS		46	100	20	2	0	5	(3 | 2)	37	8	14	7	2	0	30	0	0	3	4	0	1.00	0	.200	.210	.370

Chris Carter

Bats: R Throws: R Pos: LF-22; DH-2; PH-1   Ht: 6'5" Wt: 231 Born: 12/18/1986 Age: 24

							BATTING											BASERUNNING				AVERAGES		
Year	Team	Lg	G	AB	H	2B	3B	HR	(Hm | Rd)	TB	R	RBI	RC	TBB	IBB	SO	HBP	SH	SF	SB	CS	SB%	GDP	Avg	OBP	Slg
2005	Bristol	R+	65	233	66	17	0	10	(- | -)	113	33	37	40	17	0	64	8	2	2	2	1	.67	4	.283	.350	.485
2006	Knapol	A	13	46	6	3	0	1	(- | -)	12	4	5	2	5	0	17	1	0	0	0	0	-	1	.130	.231	.261
2006	Gr Falls	R+	69	251	75	21	1	15	(- | -)	143	37	59	55	34	5	70	8	0	1	4	4	.50	3	.299	.398	.570
2007	Knapol	A	126	467	136	27	3	25	(- | -)	244	84	93	95	67	3	112	6	0	5	3	2	.60	6	.291	.383	.522
2008	Stcktn	A+	137	506	131	32	4	39	(- | -)	288	101	104	106	77	2	156	7	0	6	4	0	1.00	8	.259	.361	.569
2009	Mdland	AA	125	490	165	41	2	24	(- | -)	282	108	101	123	82	2	119	11	0	10	13	5	.72	11	.337	.435	.576
2009	Scrmto	AAA	13	54	14	2	0	4	(- | -)	28	7	14	8	3	0	14	0	0	1	1	0	1.00	1	.259	.293	.519
2010	Scrmto	AAA	125	465	120	29	2	31	(- | -)	246	92	94	92	73	1	138	8	0	5	1	1	.50	8	.258	.365	.529
2010	Oak	AL	24	70	13	1	0	3	(1 | 2)	23	8	7	5	7	0	21	0	0	1	1	0	1.00	3	.186	.256	.329

Chris Carter

Bats: L Throws: L Pos: PH-65; LF-17; RF-13; DH-7   Ht: 6'0" Wt: 230 Born: 9/16/1982 Age: 28

							BATTING											BASERUNNING				AVERAGES		
Year	Team	Lg	G	AB	H	2B	3B	HR	(Hm | Rd)	TB	R	RBI	RC	TBB	IBB	SO	HBP	SH	SF	SB	CS	SB%	GDP	Avg	OBP	Slg
2010	Buffalo*	AAA	29	113	38	9	2	6	(- | -)	69	17	22	25	8	0	8	2	0	0	0	0	-	0	.336	.390	.611
2008	Bos	AL	9	18	6	0	0	0	(0 | 0)	6	5	3	2	2	0	5	0	0	0	0	0	-	0	.333	.400	.333
2009	Bos	AL	4	5	0	0	0	0	(0 | 0)	0	0	1	0	0	0	4	0	0	1	0	0	-	0	.000	.000	.000
2010	NYM	NL	100	167	44	9	0	4	(1 | 3)	65	15	24	23	12	0	17	1	0	0	1	2	.33	2	.263	.317	.389
	3 ML YEARS		113	190	50	9	0	4	(1 | 3)	71	20	28	25	14	0	26	1	0	1	1	2	.33	2	.263	.316	.374

Kevin Cash

Bats: R Throws: R Pos: C-48   Ht: 6'0" Wt: 190 Born: 12/6/1977 Age: 33

							BATTING											BASERUNNING				AVERAGES		
Year	Team	Lg	G	AB	H	2B	3B	HR	(Hm | Rd)	TB	R	RBI	RC	TBB	IBB	SO	HBP	SH	SF	SB	CS	SB%	GDP	Avg	OBP	Slg
2010	RdRck*	AAA	10	34	8	0	0	0	(- | -)	8	3	4	2	3	0	10	0	0	0	0	0	-	1	.235	.297	.235
2010	Pwtckt*	AAA	1	4	1	0	0	0	(- | -)	1	1	1	0	0	0	1	0	0	0	0	0	-	0	.250	.250	.250
2010	Lowell*	A-	1	4	1	1	0	0	(- | -)	2	0	0	0	0	0	0	0	0	0	0	0	-	0	.250	.250	.500
2002	Tor	AL	7	14	2	0	0	0	(0 | 0)	2	1	0	0	1	0	4	0	0	0	0	0	-	1	.143	.200	.143
2003	Tor	AL	34	106	15	3	0	1	(1 | 0)	21	10	8	0	4	0	22	1	5	1	0	0	-	6	.142	.179	.198
2004	Tor	AL	60	181	35	9	0	4	(2 | 2)	56	18	21	11	10	0	59	4	0	2	0	0	-	3	.193	.249	.309
2005	TB	AL	13	31	5	1	0	2	(1 | 1)	12	4	2	0	1	0	13	1	0	0	0	0	-	0	.161	.212	.387
2007	Bos	AL	12	27	3	1	0	0	(0 | 0)	4	2	4	1	4	0	13	1	0	1	0	0	-	2	.111	.242	.148
2008	Bos	AL	61	142	32	7	0	3	(3 | 0)	48	11	15	11	18	1	50	0	0	0	0	0	-	6	.225	.309	.338
2009	NYY	AL	10	26	6	2	0	0	(0 | 0)	8	1	3	2	0	0	5	1	0	1	0	0	-	1	.231	.250	.308
2010	2 Tms	AL	49	114	19	2	0	2	(1 | 1)	27	4	5	5	11	0	29	1	3	0	0	0	-	4	.167	.246	.237

Year Team	Lg	G	AB	H	2B	3B	HR	(Hm	Rd)	TB	R	RBI	RC	TBB	IBB	SO	HBP	SH	SF	SB	CS	SB%	GDP	Avg	OBP	Slg
10 Hou	NL	20	54	11	1	0	2	(1	1)	18	3	4	5	5	0	13	0	2	0	0	0	-	2	.204	.271	.333
10 Bos	AL	29	60	8	1	0	0	(0	0)	9	1	1	0	6	0	16	1	1	0	0	0	-	2	.133	.224	.150
Postseason		4	3	1	0	0	1	(1	0)	4	1	1	0	0	0	1	0	0	0	0	0	-	0	.333	.333	1.333
8 ML YEARS		246	641	117	25	0	12	(8	4)	178	51	58	30	49	1	195	9	8	7	0	0	-	26	.183	.248	.278

Andrew Cashner

Pitches: R Bats: R Pos: RP-53 **Ht: 6'6" Wt: 210 Born: 9/11/1986 Age: 24**

		HOW MUCH HE PITCHED						WHAT HE GAVE UP											THE RESULTS						
Year Team	Lg	G	GS	CG	GF	IP	BFP	H	R	ER	HR	SH	SF	HB	TBB	IBB	SO	WP	Bk	W	L	Pct	Sh	Sv-Op Hld	ERC	ERA
2008 Cubs	R	1	1	0	0	1.0	4	1	1	0	0	0	1	0	0	0	2	0	0	0	0	-	0	0-- -	1.95	0.00
2008 Boise	A-	6	4	0	0	16.1	85	19	12	9	1	0	2	1	19	0	16	1	0	1	1	.500	0	0-- -	8.25	4.96
2008 Dytona	A+	1	1	0	0	2.2	16	4	4	4	0	1	0	0	4	0	1	0	1	0	1	.000	0	0-- -	10.76	13.50
2009 Dytona	A+	12	12	0	0	42.0	173	31	8	7	1	0	1	3	15	0	34	0	1	0	0	-	0	0-- -	2.30	1.50
2009 Tenn	AA	12	12	0	0	58.1	248	45	30	22	0	1	4	2	27	0	41	1	0	3	4	.429	0	0-- -	2.50	3.39
2010 Tenn	AA	6	6	1	0	36.0	139	22	12	11	1	1	0	0	13	0	42	1	0	3	1	.750	0	0-- -	1.62	2.75
2010 Iowa	AAA	5	3	0	0	21.0	80	17	3	2	0	0	0	1	2	0	17	1	0	3	0	1.000	0	0-- -	1.66	0.86
2010 ChC	NL	53	0	0	9	54.1	248	55	31	29	8	6	2	4	30	5	50	4	1	2	6	.250	0	0-1 16	5.22	4.80

Alexi Casilla

Bats: B Throws: R Pos: SS-30; 2B-24; PR-12; DH-7; 3B-6; PH-6; CF-1 **Ht: 5'9" Wt: 185 Born: 7/20/1984 Age: 26**

								BATTING												BASERUNNING			AVERAGES		
Year Team	Lg	G	AB	H	2B	3B	HR	(Hm	Rd)	TB	R	RBI	RC	TBB	IBB	SO	HBP	SH	SF	SB	CS	SB%	GDP	Avg	OBP	Slg
2010 Twins*	R	5	14	2	1	0	0	(-	-)	3	1	0	1	3	0	0	0	0	0	0	0	-	1	.143	.294	.214
2010 FtMyrs*	A+	3	12	2	0	0	0	(-	-)	2	0	1	0	2	0	2	0	0	0	1	1	.50	1	.167	.286	.167
2010 NwBrit*	AA	6	20	7	0	0	0	(-	-)	7	1	0	3	3	0	1	0	0	0	1	0	1.00	0	.350	.435	.350
2006 Min	AL	9	4	1	0	0	0	(0	0)	1	1	0	1	2	0	1	0	0	0	0	0	-	0	.250	.500	.250
2007 Min	AL	56	189	42	5	1	0	(0	0)	49	15	9	11	9	0	29	0	5	1	11	1	.92	5	.222	.256	.259
2008 Min	AL	98	385	108	15	0	7	(2	5)	144	58	50	50	31	0	45	2	13	6	7	2	.78	8	.281	.333	.374
2009 Min	AL	80	228	46	7	3	0	(0	0)	59	25	17	20	22	0	36	3	2	1	11	0	1.00	6	.202	.280	.259
2010 Min	AL	69	152	42	7	4	1	(1	0)	60	26	20	23	13	0	17	0	4	1	6	1	.86	5	.276	.331	.395
5 ML YEARS		312	958	239	34	8	8	(3	5)	313	125	96	105	77	0	128	5	24	9	35	4	.90	24	.249	.306	.327

Santiago Casilla

Pitches: R Bats: R Pos: RP-52 **Ht: 6'0" Wt: 202 Born: 7/25/1980 Age: 30**

		HOW MUCH HE PITCHED						WHAT HE GAVE UP											THE RESULTS						
Year Team	Lg	G	GS	CG	GF	IP	BFP	H	R	ER	HR	SH	SF	HB	TBB	IBB	SO	WP	Bk	W	L	Pct	Sh	Sv-Op Hld	ERC	ERA
2010 Fresno*	AAA	4	0	0	3	4.0	17	2	0	0	0	0	0	1	2	0	7	0	0	0	0	-	0	2-- -	2.03	0.00
2004 Oak	AL	4	0	0	2	5.2	32	5	8	8	3	0	0	1	9	0	5	0	0	0	0	0-0	0	0-0 0	13.22	12.71
2005 Oak	AL	3	0	0	2	3.0	12	2	1	1	0	0	0	0	1	0	1	1	0	0	0	-	0	0-0 0	1.57	3.00
2006 Oak	AL	2	0	0	1	2.1	10	2	3	3	0	0	0	0	2	0	2	0	0	0	0	-	0	0-0 0	4.61	11.57
2007 Oak	AL	46	0	0	10	50.2	219	43	25	25	6	0	3	1	23	6	52	5	0	3	1	.750	0	2-5 12	3.39	4.44
2008 Oak	AL	51	0	0	9	50.1	229	60	22	22	5	3	2	3	20	2	43	6	0	2	1	.667	0	2-3 7	5.34	3.93
2009 Oak	AL	46	0	0	15	48.1	233	61	36	32	6	1	3	3	25	3	35	5	0	1	2	.333	0	0-0 5	6.32	5.96
2010 SF	NL	52	0	0	13	55.1	225	40	14	12	2	2	1	4	26	4	56	10	0	7	2	.778	0	2-3 11	2.68	1.95
7 ML YEARS		204	0	0	53	215.2	960	213	109	103	22	6	9	12	106	15	194	27	0	13	6	.684	0	6-11 35	4.47	4.30

Bobby Cassevah

Pitches: R Bats: R Pos: RP-16 CASS-eh-vah **Ht: 6'3" Wt: 195 Born: 9/11/1985 Age: 25**

		HOW MUCH HE PITCHED						WHAT HE GAVE UP											THE RESULTS						
Year Team	Lg	G	GS	CG	GF	IP	BFP	H	R	ER	HR	SH	SF	HB	TBB	IBB	SO	WP	Bk	W	L	Pct	Sh	Sv-Op Hld	ERC	ERA
2005 Angels	R	15	4	0	2	45.0	204	57	28	27	2	3	1	7	14	0	27	2	0	2	5	.286	0	0-- -	5.58	5.40
2006 Orem	R+	16	10	0	0	41.0	214	57	40	31	1	3	2	2	38	0	32	0	0	2	5	.286	0	0-- -	8.25	6.80
2007 CRpds	A	18	0	0	10	31.0	132	25	9	8	0	3	1	5	13	1	25	1	0	2	1	.667	0	1-- -	2.98	2.32
2007 Orem	R+	6	0	0	3	8.1	40	9	6	4	0	0	0	4	5	1	9	3	0	0	0	-	0	0-- -	6.50	4.32
2008 RCuca	A+	44	0	0	10	71.1	318	67	33	30	1	2	2	5	40	2	52	7	0	2	3	.400	0	1-- -	3.94	3.79
2009 Ark	AA	57	0	0	27	73.2	315	64	40	31	2	1	3	4	37	6	45	3	0	3	7	.300	0	4-- -	3.35	3.79
2010 Salt Lk	AAA	45	0	0	21	59.0	269	69	32	28	7	2	0	4	25	3	38	2	0	3	4	.429	0	5-- -	5.48	4.27
2010 LAA	AL	16	0	0	9	20.0	94	23	11	7	0	1	1	1	8	2	8	1	0	1	2	.333	0	0-0 0	3.98	3.15

Alberto Castillo

Pitches: L Bats: L Pos: RP-14 **Ht: 6'3" Wt: 220 Born: 7/5/1975 Age: 35**

		HOW MUCH HE PITCHED						WHAT HE GAVE UP											THE RESULTS						
Year Team	Lg	G	GS	CG	GF	IP	BFP	H	R	ER	HR	SH	SF	HB	TBB	IBB	SO	WP	Bk	W	L	Pct	Sh	Sv-Op Hld	ERC	ERA
2010 Norfolk*	AAA	39	0	0	16	39.2	186	46	20	20	4	0	2	7	15	1	43	1	1	1	2	.333	0	4-- -	5.49	4.54
2008 Bal	AL	28	0	0	5	26.0	121	27	11	11	3	0	0	7	10	0	23	1	0	1	0	1.000	0	0-1 0	5.36	3.81
2009 Bal	AL	20	0	0	4	12.0	49	12	4	3	0	1	0	1	4	1	8	0	0	0	0	-	0	0-0 5	3.51	2.25
2010 Bal	AL	14	0	0	6	10.2	51	16	12	12	5	0	0	0	6	0	11	1	0	1	0	1.000	0	0-0 1	11.61	10.13
3 ML YEARS		62	0	0	15	48.2	221	55	27	26	8	1	0	8	20	1	42	2	0	2	0	1.000	0	0-1 6	6.11	4.81

Luis Castillo

Bats: B **Throws:** R **Pos:** 2B-74; PH-12; PR-3   **Ht:** 5'11" **Wt:** 197 **Born:** 9/12/1975 **Age:** 35

Year	Team	Lg	G	AB	H	2B	3B	HR	(Hm	Rd)	TB	R	RBI	RC	TBB	IBB	SO	HBP	SH	SF	SB	CS	SB%	GDP	Avg	OBP	Slg
2010	StLuci*	A+	4	13	2	1	0	0	(-	-)	3	3	0	1	3	0	2	0	0	0	0	0	-	0	.154	.313	.231
1996	Fla	NL	41	164	43	2	1	1	(0	1)	50	26	8	19	14	0	46	0	2	0	17	4	.81	0	.262	.320	.305
1997	Fla	NL	75	263	63	8	0	0	(0	0)	71	27	8	21	27	0	53	0	1	0	16	10	.62	6	.240	.310	.270
1998	Fla	NL	44	153	31	3	2	1	(0	1)	41	21	10	14	22	0	33	1	1	0	3	0	1.00	6	.203	.307	.268
1999	Fla	NL	128	487	147	23	4	0	(0	0)	178	76	28	78	67	0	85	0	6	3	50	17	.75	3	.302	.384	.366
2000	Fla	NL	136	539	180	17	3	2	(1	1)	209	101	17	95	78	0	86	0	9	0	62	22	.74	11	.334	.418	.388
2001	Fla	NL	134	537	141	16	10	2	(1	1)	183	76	45	67	67	0	90	1	4	3	33	16	.67	9	.263	.344	.341
2002	Fla	NL	146	606	185	18	5	2	(0	2)	219	86	39	84	55	4	76	2	4	1	48	15	.76	7	.305	.364	.361
2003	Fla	NL	152	595	187	19	6	6	(2	4)	236	99	39	87	63	0	60	1	2	15	21	19	.53	7	.314	.381	.397
2004	Fla	NL	150	564	164	12	7	2	(1	1)	196	91	47	84	75	2	68	1	5	4	21	4	.84	15	.291	.373	.348
2005	Fla	NL	122	439	132	12	4	4	(0	4)	164	72	30	61	65	1	32	1	18	1	10	7	.59	11	.301	.391	.374
2006	Min	AL	142	584	173	22	6	3	(3	0)	216	84	49	80	56	0	58	1	9	2	25	11	.69	14	.296	.358	.370
2007	2 Tms		135	548	165	19	5	1	(0	0)	197	91	38	76	53	0	45	0	12	2	19	6	.76	5	.301	.362	.359
2008	NYM	NL	87	298	73	7	1	3	(2	1)	91	46	28	40	50	2	35	2	7	2	17	2	.89	13	.245	.355	.305
2009	NYM	NL	142	486	147	12	3	1	(1	0)	168	77	40	70	69	3	58	1	19	5	20	6	.77	15	.302	.387	.346
2010	NYM	NL	86	247	58	4	2	0	(0	0)	66	28	17	25	39	1	25	0	11	2	8	3	.73	6	.235	.337	.267
07	Min	AL	85	349	106	11	3	0	(0	0)	123	54	18	45	29	0	28	0	5	1	9	4	.69	3	.304	.356	.352
07	NYM	NL	50	199	59	8	2	1	(0	0)	74	37	20	31	24	0	17	0	7	1	10	2	.83	2	.296	.371	.372
	Postseason		20	82	18	4	0	0	(0	0)	22	6	4	6	11	0	15	0	2	0	3	2	.60	0	.220	.312	.268
	15 ML YEARS		1720	6510	1889	194	59	28	(11	17)	2285	1001	443	901	800	13	850	12	123	26	370	142	.72	120	.290	.368	.351

Welington Castillo

Bats: R **Throws:** R **Pos:** C-5; PH-2   **Ht:** 5'10" **Wt:** 200 **Born:** 4/24/1987 **Age:** 24

Year	Team	Lg	G	AB	H	2B	3B	HR	(Hm	Rd)	TB	R	RBI	RC	TBB	IBB	SO	HBP	SH	SF	SB	CS	SB%	GDP	Avg	OBP	Slg
2006	Boise	A-	3	6	1	0	0	0	(-	-)	1	1	0	0	1	0	0	0	1	0	0	0	-	0	.167	.286	.167
2006	Cubs	R	7	26	5	0	0	0	(-	-)	5	4	0	1	1	0	6	1	0	0	0	0	-	2	.192	.250	.192
2007	Peoria	A	98	317	86	11	2	11	(-	-)	134	41	44	46	23	1	77	8	3	2	1	1	.50	9	.271	.334	.423
2008	Dytona	A+	33	121	33	8	0	0	(-	-)	41	15	12	13	4	0	23	1	0	1	1	0	1.00	3	.273	.299	.339
2008	Tenn	AA	57	198	59	11	0	4	(-	-)	82	25	24	30	14	2	50	6	2	0	0	0	-	11	.298	.362	.414
2008	Iowa	AAA	1	5	1	0	0	0	(-	-)	1	0	1	0	0	0	1	0	0	0	0	0	-	0	.200	.200	.200
2009	Tenn	AA	95	319	74	16	0	11	(-	-)	123	27	38	34	15	2	71	4	1	0	1	0	1.00	8	.232	.275	.386
2010	Iowa	AAA	69	239	61	17	1	13	(-	-)	119	35	59	39	19	1	58	6	1	7	0	2	.00	11	.255	.317	.498
2010	ChC	NL	7	20	6	4	0	1	(0	1)	13	3	5	3	1	0	7	0	0	0	0	0	-	0	.300	.333	.650

Jason Castro

Bats: L **Throws:** R **Pos:** C-67; PH-5; PR-2   **Ht:** 6'3" **Wt:** 200 **Born:** 6/18/1987 **Age:** 24

Year	Team	Lg	G	AB	H	2B	3B	HR	(Hm	Rd)	TB	R	RBI	RC	TBB	IBB	SO	HBP	SH	SF	SB	CS	SB%	GDP	Avg	OBP	Slg
2008	TriCity	A-	39	138	38	9	0	2	(-	-)	53	10	12	22	22	2	32	2	6	0	0	1	.00	1	.275	.383	.384
2009	Lancst	A+	56	207	64	20	1	7	(-	-)	107	27	44	43	30	2	41	3	3	3	0	0	-	5	.309	.399	.517
2009	CpChr	AA	63	239	70	11	1	3	(-	-)	92	38	29	35	25	0	35	2	0	2	2	1	.67	5	.293	.362	.385
2010	RdRck	AAA	57	211	56	7	0	4	(-	-)	75	31	26	30	32	0	34	1	0	0	1	1	.50	5	.265	.365	.355
2010	Hou	NL	67	195	40	8	1	2	(1	1)	56	26	8	12	22	2	41	0	0	0	0	0	-	4	.205	.286	.287

Juan Castro

Bats: R **Throws:** R **Pos:** SS-33; 3B-11; 2B-7; PH-7; PR-1   **Ht:** 5'11" **Wt:** 190 **Born:** 6/20/1972 **Age:** 39

Year	Team	Lg	G	AB	H	2B	3B	HR	(Hm	Rd)	TB	R	RBI	RC	TBB	IBB	SO	HBP	SH	SF	SB	CS	SB%	GDP	Avg	OBP	Slg
2010	Albq*	AAA	5	14	4	0	0	0	(-	-)	4	2	1	1	2	0	2	0	0	0	0	0	-	0	.286	.375	.286
1995	LAD	NL	11	4	1	0	0	0	(0	0)	1	0	0	1	1	0	1	0	0	0	0	0	-	0	.250	.400	.250
1996	LAD	NL	70	132	26	5	3	0	(0	0)	37	16	5	8	10	0	27	0	4	0	1	0	1.00	3	.197	.254	.280
1997	LAD	NL	40	75	11	3	1	0	(0	0)	16	3	4	2	7	1	20	0	2	0	0	0	-	0	.147	.220	.213
1998	LAD	NL	89	220	43	7	0	2	(0	2)	56	25	14	12	15	0	37	0	9	2	0	0	-	5	.195	.245	.255
1999	LAD	NL	2	1	0	0	0	0	(0	0)	0	0	0	0	0	0	1	0	0	0	0	0	-	0	.000	.000	.000
2000	Cin	NL	82	224	54	12	2	4	(1	3)	82	20	23	20	14	1	33	0	4	2	0	2	.00	9	.241	.283	.366
2001	Cin	NL	96	242	54	10	0	3	(0	3)	73	27	13	16	13	2	50	0	4	2	0	0	-	9	.223	.261	.302
2002	Cin	NL	54	82	18	3	0	2	(0	2)	27	5	11	11	7	0	18	0	1	1	0	0	-	0	.220	.278	.329
2003	Cin	NL	113	320	81	14	1	9	(4	5)	124	28	33	36	18	1	58	0	7	3	2	3	.40	7	.253	.290	.388
2004	Cin	NL	111	299	73	21	2	5	(3	2)	113	36	26	26	14	1	51	0	2	1	1	0	1.00	11	.244	.277	.378
2005	Min	AL	97	272	70	18	1	5	(2	3)	105	27	33	28	9	1	39	0	9	2	0	1	.00	8	.257	.279	.386
2006	2 Tms		104	251	63	10	3	3	(3	0)	88	18	28	26	11	0	36	0	1	1	1	2	.33	6	.251	.281	.351
2007	Cin	NL	54	89	16	5	0	2	(0	0)	21	5	5	2	4	0	21	0	3	2	0	0	-	2	.180	.211	.236
2008	2 Tms		61	161	31	6	0	2	(0	2)	43	16	16	7	11	0	26	1	2	2	0	0	-	9	.193	.246	.267
2009	LAD	NL	57	112	31	4	0	1	(0	1)	38	18	9	11	6	1	25	0	2	1	0	0	-	1	.277	.311	.339
2010	2 Tms	NL	55	129	25	5	0	0	(0	0)	30	7	13	9	8	0	25	0	1	2	0	1	.00	1	.194	.237	.233
06	Min	AL	50	156	36	5	2	1	(1	0)	48	10	14	11	6	0	23	0	1	1	1	1	.50	6	.231	.258	.308
06	Cin	NL	54	95	27	5	1	2	(2	0)	40	8	14	15	5	0	13	0	0	0	0	1	.00	0	.284	.320	.421
08	Cin	NL	7	10	0	0	0	0	(0	0)	0	1	0	0	1	0	0	0	0	0	0	0	-	0	.000	.091	.000
08	Bal	AL	54	151	31	6	0	2	(0	2)	43	15	16	7	10	0	26	1	2	2	0	0	-	9	.205	.256	.285
10	Phi	NL	54	126	25	5	0	0	(0	0)	30	7	13	9	7	0	23	0	1	2	0	1	.00	1	.198	.237	.238
10	LAD	NL	1	3	0	0	0	0	(0	0)	0	0	0	0	1	0	2	0	0	0	0	0	-	0	.000	.250	.000
	Postseason		3	5	1	1	0	0	(0	0)	2	0	1	1	1	0	1	0	0	0	0	0	-	0	.200	.333	.400
	16 ML YEARS		1096	2613	597	123	13	36	(13	23)	854	251	233	215	148	8	468	1	51	21	5	9	.36	73	.228	.268	.327

Ramon Castro

Bats: R Throws: R Pos: C-34; DH-3; PH-3; PR-1   Ht: 6'3" Wt: 240 Born: 3/1/1976 Age: 35

Year	Team	Lg	G	AB	H	2B	3B	HR	(Hm	Rd)	TB	R	RBI	RC	TBB	IBB	SO	HBP	SH	SF	SB	CS	SB%	GDP	Avg	OBP	Slg
2010	Charltt*	AAA	4	13	2	0	0	1	(-	-)	5	1	2	1	3	0	5	0	0	0	0	0	-	1	.154	.313	.385
1999	Fla	NL	24	67	12	4	0	2	(0	2)	22	4	4	6	10	3	14	0	0	1	0	0	-	1	.179	.282	.328
2000	Fla	NL	50	138	33	4	0	2	(0	2)	43	10	14	14	16	7	36	1	0	2	0	0	-	1	.239	.318	.312
2001	Fla	NL	7	11	2	0	0	0	(0	0)	2	0	1	0	1	0	1	0	0	0	0	0	-	0	.182	.250	.182
2002	Fla	NL	54	101	24	4	0	6	(4	2)	46	11	18	14	14	3	24	0	1	3	0	0	-	4	.238	.322	.455
2003	Fla	NL	40	53	15	2	0	5	(4	1)	32	6	8	8	4	0	11	0	0	0	0	0	-	0	.283	.333	.604
2004	Fla	NL	32	96	13	3	0	3	(0	3)	25	9	8	4	11	2	30	1	0	0	0	0	-	1	.135	.231	.260
2005	NYM	NL	99	209	51	16	0	8	(5	3)	91	26	41	30	25	2	58	0	3	3	1	0	1.00	7	.244	.321	.435
2006	NYM	NL	40	126	30	7	0	4	(1	3)	49	13	12	11	15	2	40	1	1	1	0	0	-	2	.238	.322	.389
2007	NYM	NL	52	144	41	6	0	11	(3	8)	80	24	31	23	10	0	39	1	0	2	0	0	-	1	.285	.331	.556
2008	NYM	NL	52	143	35	7	0	7	(5	2)	63	15	24	23	13	2	34	1	0	0	0	0	-	2	.245	.312	.441
2009	2 Tms		57	155	34	8	0	7	(2	5)	63	13	25	18	16	1	39	0	0	0	0	0	-	4	.219	.292	.406
2010	CWS	AL	37	115	32	2	0	8	(3	5)	58	18	21	20	9	0	26	0	3	1	1	0	1.00	3	.278	.328	.504
09	NYM	NL	26	79	20	5	0	3	(1	2)	34	5	13	9	8	1	16	0	0	0	0	0	-	3	.253	.322	.430
09	CWS	AL	31	76	14	3	0	4	(1	3)	29	8	12	9	8	0	23	0	0	0	0	0	-	1	.184	.262	.382
12 ML YEARS			544	1358	322	63	0	63	(27	36)	574	149	207	171	144	22	352	5	8	13	2	0	1.00	26	.237	.310	.423

Starlin Castro

Bats: R Throws: R Pos: SS-123; PH-2; PR-1   Ht: 6'0" Wt: 190 Born: 3/24/1990 Age: 21

Year	Team	Lg	G	AB	H	2B	3B	HR	(Hm	Rd)	TB	R	RBI	RC	TBB	IBB	SO	HBP	SH	SF	SB	CS	SB%	GDP	Avg	OBP	Slg
2008	Cubs	R	50	190	56	11	5	3	(-	-)	86	32	21	30	14	0	33	3	1	1	6	5	.55	4	.295	.351	.453
2009	Dytona	A+	96	358	108	17	3	3	(-	-)	140	45	35	49	19	1	41	3	5	2	22	11	.67	4	.302	.340	.391
2009	Tenn	AA	31	111	32	6	3	0	(-	-)	44	11	14	17	10	0	12	0	1	0	6	0	1.00	2	.288	.347	.396
2010	Tenn	AA	26	109	41	8	5	1	(-	-)	62	20	20	24	9	0	11	1	0	2	4	5	.44	3	.376	.421	.569
2010	ChC	NL	125	463	139	31	5	3	(1	2)	189	53	41	56	29	7	71	6	4	4	10	8	.56	14	.300	.347	.408

Frank Catalanotto

Bats: L Throws: R Pos: PH-24; 1B-1; LF-1   catt-ah-lah-NOTT-oh   Ht: 6'0" Wt: 195 Born: 4/27/1974 Age: 37

Year	Team	Lg	G	AB	H	2B	3B	HR	(Hm	Rd)	TB	R	RBI	RC	TBB	IBB	SO	HBP	SH	SF	SB	CS	SB%	GDP	Avg	OBP	Slg
1997	Det	AL	13	26	8	2	0	0	(0	0)	10	2	3	4	3	0	7	0	0	0	0	0	-	0	.308	.379	.385
1998	Det	AL	89	213	60	13	2	6	(3	3)	95	23	25	30	12	1	39	4	0	5	3	2	.60	4	.282	.325	.446
1999	Det	AL	100	286	79	19	0	11	(6	5)	131	35	42	42	15	1	49	9	0	5	3	4	.43	4	.276	.327	.458
2000	Tex	AL	103	282	82	13	2	10	(6	4)	129	55	42	49	33	0	36	4	0	0	6	2	.75	5	.291	.375	.457
2001	Tex	AL	133	463	153	31	5	11	(4	7)	227	77	54	88	39	3	55	8	1	1	15	5	.75	5	.330	.391	.490
2002	Tex	AI	68	212	57	16	6	3	(2	1)	94	42	23	39	25	0	27	8	3	2	9	5	.64	3	.269	.364	.443
2003	Tor	AL	133	489	146	34	6	13	(7	6)	231	83	59	84	35	1	62	6	2	3	2	2	.50	9	.299	.351	.472
2004	Tor	AL	75	249	73	19	1	1	(1	0)	97	27	26	34	17	1	33	4	1	3	1	0	1.00	7	.293	.344	.390
2005	Tor	AL	130	419	126	29	5	8	(3	5)	189	56	59	80	37	0	53	10	4	5	0	2	.00	9	.301	.367	.451
2006	Tor	AL	128	437	131	36	2	7	(2	5)	192	56	56	72	52	0	37	4	2	4	1	3	.25	11	.300	.376	.439
2007	Tex	AL	103	331	86	20	4	11	(9	2)	147	52	44	51	28	0	37	11	6	1	2	1	.67	6	.260	.337	.444
2008	Tex	AL	88	248	68	23	1	2	(0	2)	99	28	21	30	20	0	29	6	3	1	1	1	.50	6	.274	.342	.399
2009	Mil	NL	77	144	40	6	3	1	(1	0)	55	18	9	18	14	5	23	2	0	2	2	0	1.00	2	.278	.346	.382
2010	NYM	NL	25	25	4	1	0	0	(0	0)	5	2	1	1	1	0	5	0	0	0	0	0	-	0	.100	.192	.200
14 ML YEARS			1265	3824	1113	262	37	84	(44	40)	1701	562	457	622	331	12	492	78	25	34	45	27	.63	71	.291	.357	.445

Brett Cecil

Pitches: L Bats: R Pos: SP-28   Ht: 6'1" Wt: 235 Born: 7/2/1986 Age: 24

Year	Team	Lg	G	GS	CG	GF	IP	BFP	H	R	ER	HR	SH	SF	HB	TBB	IBB	SO	WP	Bk	W	L	Pct	Sh	Sv-Op	Hld	ERC	ERA
2007	Auburn	A-	14	13	0	0	49.2	197	36	10	7	1	0	0	3	11	0	56	0	0	1	0	1.000	0	0--	-	1.76	1.27
2008	Dnedin	A+	4	4	0	0	10.1	38	6	2	2	1	0	0	0	2	0	11	0	0	0	0	-	0	0--	-	1.41	1.74
2008	NHam	AA	18	18	0	0	77.2	324	66	24	22	4	3	2	5	23	0	87	2	0	6	2	.750	0	0--	-	2.77	2.55
2008	Syrcse	AAA	6	6	0	0	30.2	135	28	17	14	1	1	0	0	16	0	31	2	0	2	3	.400	0	0--	-	3.52	4.11
2009	LsVgs	AAA	9	9	1	0	49.0	219	53	37	31	2	2	1	3	19	0	32	1	0	1	5	.167	0	0--	-	4.25	5.69
2010	LsVgs	AAA	2	2	0	0	11.0	46	13	4	3	0	1	0	0	2	0	11	1	0	2	0	1.000	0	0--	-	3.61	2.45
2009	Tor	AL	18	17	0	1	93.1	422	116	59	55	17	0	2	5	38	0	69	0	0	7	4	.636	0	0-0	0	6.53	5.30
2010	Tor	AL	28	28	0	0	172.2	726	175	87	81	18	1	6	1	54	2	117	7	1	15	7	.682	0	0-0	0	3.88	4.22
2 ML YEARS			46	45	0	1	266.0	1148	291	146	136	35	1	8	6	92	2	186	7	1	22	11	.667	0	0-0	0	4.76	4.60

Jose Ceda

Pitches: R Bats: R Pos: RP-8   SAY-dah   Ht: 6'4" Wt: 275 Born: 1/28/1987 Age: 24

Year	Team	Lg	G	GS	CG	GF	IP	BFP	H	R	ER	HR	SH	SF	HB	TBB	IBB	SO	WP	Bk	W	L	Pct	Sh	Sv-Op	Hld	ERC	ERA
2006	Padres	R	8	4	0	0	23.0	100	20	14	13	1	0	1	1	13	0	31	0	0	2	0	1.000	0	0--	-	3.78	5.09
2006	Cubs	R	5	3	0	0	12.0	47	6	2	1	0	1	0	0	7	0	21	1	0	0	0	-	0	0--	-	1.65	0.75
2006	Boise	A-	3	3	0	0	11.0	41	5	4	4	1	0	0	2	2	0	11	2	0	1	0	1.000	0	0--	-	1.62	3.27
2007	Peoria	A	21	6	0	5	46.1	186	14	18	16	1	0	0	2	31	0	66	8	0	2	2	.500	0	0--	-	1.35	3.11
2007	Cubs	R	2	1	0	0	3.2	15	2	1	1	0	0	1	0	3	0	3	0	0	0	0	-	0	0--	-	2.64	2.45
2008	Dytona	A+	15	12	0	1	54.1	229	41	29	29	4	0	4	4	28	0	53	3	1	2	2	.500	0	0--	-	3.32	4.80

Year Team	Lg	G	GS	CG	GF	IP	BFP	H	R	ER	HR	SH	SF	HB	TBB	IBB	SO	WP	Bk	W	L	Pct	Sh	Sv-Op	Hld	ERC	ERA
2008 Tenn	AA	22	0	0	19	30.1	129	26	8	8	2	3	0	1	14	1	42	3	0	2	1	.667	0	9--	-	3.38	2.37
2010 Grnsbr	A	7	0	0	0	8.0	33	7	4	4	2	0	0	1	1	0	5	0	0	0	0	-	0	0--	-	3.68	4.50
2010 Jaxnvl	AA	27	0	0	18	32.1	134	18	5	5	2	3	1	3	20	2	45	0	0	4	1	.800	0	6--	-	2.57	1.39
2010 Fla	NL	8	0	0	1	8.2	45	8	5	5	1	0	0	1	11	1	9	0	1	0	0	-	0	0-0	0	7.53	5.19

Ronny Cedeno

Bats: R **Throws:** R **Pos:** SS-136; PH-4; PR-2   **Ht:** 6'0" **Wt:** 190 **Born:** 2/2/1983 **Age:** 28

Year Team	Lg	G	AB	H	2B	3B	HR	(Hm	Rd)	TB	R	RBI	RC	TBB	IBB	SO	HBP	SH	SF	SB	CS	SB%	GDP	Avg	OBP	Slg
2005 ChC	NL	41	80	24	3	0	1	(0	1)	30	13	6	11	5	1	11	2	2	0	1	0	1.00	4	.300	.356	.375
2006 ChC	NL	151	534	131	18	7	6	(4	2)	181	51	41	41	17	4	109	3	15	3	8	8	.50	10	.245	.271	.339
2007 ChC	NL	38	74	15	2	0	4	(2	2)	29	6	13	8	3	0	18	0	2	1	2	1	.67	0	.203	.231	.392
2008 ChC	NL	99	216	58	12	0	2	(2	0)	76	36	28	23	18	2	41	1	1	0	4	1	.80	6	.269	.328	.352
2009 2 Tms		105	341	71	8	3	10	(7	3)	115	32	38	29	19	3	79	3	13	0	5	2	.71	9	.208	.256	.337
2010 Pit	NL	139	468	120	29	3	8	(4	4)	179	42	38	46	23	4	106	2	7	2	12	3	.80	10	.256	.293	.382
09 Sea	AL	59	186	31	4	2	5	(2	3)	54	15	17	7	10	1	50	1	9	0	3	2	.60	6	.167	.213	.290
09 Pit	NL	46	155	40	4	1	5	(5	0)	61	17	21	22	9	2	29	2	4	0	2	0	1.00	3	.258	.307	.394
Postseason		3	0	0	0	0	0	(0	0)	0	0	0	0	0	0	0	0	0	0	1	0	1.00	0	-	-	-
6 ML YEARS		573	1713	419	72	13	31	(19	12)	610	180	164	158	85	14	364	11	40	6	32	15	.68	39	.245	.284	.356

Francisco Cervelli

Bats: R **Throws:** R **Pos:** C-90; PH-4; 3B-2; PR-1   serr-VELL-ee   **Ht:** 6'1" **Wt:** 210 **Born:** 3/6/1986 **Age:** 25

Year Team	Lg	G	AB	H	2B	3B	HR	(Hm	Rd)	TB	R	RBI	RC	TBB	IBB	SO	HBP	SH	SF	SB	CS	SB%	GDP	Avg	OBP	Slg
2008 NYY	AL	3	5	0	0	0	0	(0	0)	0	0	0	0	0	0	3	0	0	0	0	0	-	1	.000	.000	.000
2009 NYY	AL	42	94	28	4	0	1	(0	1)	35	13	11	11	2	0	11	0	4	1	0	3	.00	1	.298	.309	.372
2010 NYY	AL	93	266	72	11	3	0	(0	0)	89	27	38	40	33	1	42	6	8	4	1	1	.50	7	.271	.359	.335
Postseason		2	1	0	0	0	0	(0	0)	0	0	0	0	0	0	1	0	0	0	0	0	-	0	.000	.000	.000
3 ML YEARS		138	365	100	15	3	1	(0	1)	124	40	49	51	35	1	56	6	12	5	1	4	.20	9	.274	.343	.340

Gustavo Chacin

Pitches: L **Bats:** L **Pos:** RP-44   chah-SEEN   **Ht:** 5'11" **Wt:** 207 **Born:** 11/4/1980 **Age:** 30

Year Team	Lg	G	GS	CG	GF	IP	BFP	H	R	ER	HR	SH	SF	HB	TBB	IBB	SO	WP	Bk	W	L	Pct	Sh	Sv-Op	Hld	ERC	ERA
2010 RdRck*	AAA	6	5	0	0	25.0	101	24	10	10	5	1	0	0	6	0	14	0	0	1	1	.500	0	0--	-	3.97	3.60
2004 Tor	AL	2	2	0	0	14.0	52	8	4	4	0	0	0	1	3	0	6	0	0	1	1	.500	0	0-0	-	1.24	2.57
2005 Tor	AL	34	34	0	0	203.0	872	213	93	84	20	8	10	8	70	3	121	3	0	13	9	.591	0	0-0	0	4.30	3.72
2006 Tor	AL	17	17	0	0	87.1	384	90	51	49	19	2	0	6	38	2	47	0	0	9	4	.692	0	0-0	0	5.57	5.05
2007 Tor	AL	5	5	0	0	27.1	118	29	17	17	6	0	0	2	7	1	11	0	0	2	1	.667	0	0-0	0	4.90	5.60
2010 Hou	NL	44	0	0	12	38.1	186	51	22	20	3	3	1	0	20	3	31	2	0	2	2	.500	0	1-1	5	6.06	4.70
5 ML YEARS		102	58	0	12	370.0	1612	391	187	174	48	13	11	17	138	9	216	5	0	27	17	.614	0	1-1	5	4.68	4.23

Jhoulys Chacin

Pitches: R **Bats:** R **Pos:** SP-21; RP-7   yoe-LEASE chah-SEEN   **Ht:** 6'3" **Wt:** 215 **Born:** 1/7/1988 **Age:** 23

Year Team	Lg	G	GS	CG	GF	IP	BFP	H	R	ER	HR	SH	SF	HB	TBB	IBB	SO	WP	Bk	W	L	Pct	Sh	Sv-Op	Hld	ERC	ERA
2007 Casper	R+	16	16	0	0	92.0	380	85	45	32	5	5	4	2	26	0	77	6	0	6	5	.545	0	0--	-	3.01	3.13
2008 Ashvll	A	16	16	2	0	111.1	447	82	30	23	3	3	2	12	30	0	98	8	0	10	1	.909	0	0--	-	2.19	1.86
2008 Mdest	A+	12	12	0	0	59.2	264	61	20	17	3	1	0	4	12	0	62	4	0	8	2	.800	0	0--	-	3.15	2.56
2009 Tulsa	AA	18	18	1	0	103.1	431	87	45	36	10	4	1	7	35	0	86	5	0	8	6	.571	0	0--	-	3.22	3.14
2009 ColSpr	AAA	4	4	0	0	14.1	64	11	7	6	2	1	0	0	13	0	11	0	1	1	2	.333	0	0--	-	5.20	3.77
2010 ColSpr	AAA	7	7	0	0	35.2	146	27	10	6	1	1	0	2	17	1	34	0	1	3	2	.600	0	0--	-	2.83	1.51
2009 Col	NL	9	1	0	3	11.0	48	6	6	6	1	1	0	0	11	0	13	2	0	1	0	1.000	0	0-0	0	3.87	4.91
2010 Col	NL	28	21	0	2	137.1	583	114	64	50	10	6	5	9	61	5	138	4	0	9	11	.450	0	0-0	0	3.33	3.28
2 ML YEARS		37	22	0	5	148.1	631	120	70	56	11	7	5	9	72	5	151	6	0	9	12	.429	0	0-0	0	3.37	3.40

Joba Chamberlain

Pitches: R **Bats:** R **Pos:** RP-73   JOBB-ah CHAME-berr-linn   **Ht:** 6'2" **Wt:** 230 **Born:** 9/23/1985 **Age:** 25

Year Team	Lg	G	GS	CG	GF	IP	BFP	H	R	ER	HR	SH	SF	HB	TBB	IBB	SO	WP	Bk	W	L	Pct	Sh	Sv-Op	Hld	ERC	ERA
2007 NYY	AL	19	0	0	3	24.0	91	12	2	1	1	1	0	1	6	0	34	1	0	2	0	1.000	0	1-1	8	1.16	0.38
2008 NYY	AL	42	12	0	5	100.1	417	87	32	29	5	2	1	2	39	3	118	4	2	4	3	.571	0	0-1	19	3.04	2.60
2009 NYY	AL	32	31	0	0	157.1	709	167	94	83	21	6	5	12	76	2	133	5	2	9	6	.600	0	0-0	0	5.32	4.75
2010 NYY	AL	73	0	0	18	71.2	305	71	37	35	6	0	1	4	22	2	77	5	1	3	4	.429	0	3-7	26	3.53	4.40
Postseason		12	0	0	0	10.0	46	12	4	4	1	1	1	1	4	0	11	2	0	1	0	1.000	0	0-2	3	5.64	3.60
4 ML YEARS		166	43	0	26	353.1	1522	337	165	148	33	9	7	16	143	7	362	15	5	18	13	.581	0	4-9	53	3.94	3.77

Aroldis Chapman

Pitches: L **Bats:** L **Pos:** RP-15   ah-ROLL-diss   **Ht:** 6'4" **Wt:** 185 **Born:** 2/28/1988 **Age:** 23

Year Team	Lg	G	GS	CG	GF	IP	BFP	H	R	ER	HR	SH	SF	HB	TBB	IBB	SO	WP	Bk	W	L	Pct	Sh	Sv-Op	Hld	ERC	ERA
2010 Lsvlle	AAA	39	13	1	12	95.2	412	77	46	38	7	1	1	5	52	0	125	14	0	9	6	.600	0	8--	-	3.57	3.57
2010 Cin	NL	15	0	0	3	13.1	51	9	4	3	0	0	0	0	5	0	19	2	0	2	2	.500	0	0-1	4	1.82	2.03

Eric Chavez

Bats: L Throws: R Pos: DH-31; PH-3; 1B-1   shah-VEZZ   **Ht: 6'1" Wt: 215 Born: 12/7/1977 Age: 33**

Year	Team	Lg	G	AB	H	2B	3B	HR	(Hm	Rd)	TB	R	RBI	RC	TBB	IBB	SO	HBP	SH	SF	SB	CS	SB%	GDP	Avg	OBP	Slg
2010	As*	R	1	3	1	0	0	0	(-	-)	1	0	0	0	0	0	1	0	0	0	0	0	-	0	.333	.333	.333
1998	Oak	AL	16	45	14	4	1	0	(0	0)	20	6	6	7	3	1	5	0	0	0	1	1	.50	1	.311	.354	.444
1999	Oak	AL	115	356	88	21	2	13	(8	5)	152	47	50	50	46	4	56	0	0	0	1	1	.50	7	.247	.333	.427
2000	Oak	AL	153	501	139	23	4	26	(15	11)	248	89	86	86	62	8	94	1	0	5	2	2	.50	9	.277	.355	.495
2001	Oak	AL	151	552	159	43	0	32	(14	18)	298	91	114	99	41	9	99	4	0	7	8	2	.80	7	.288	.338	.540
2002	Oak	AL	153	585	161	31	3	34	(17	17)	300	87	109	103	65	13	119	1	0	2	8	3	.73	8	.275	.348	.513
2003	Oak	AL	156	588	166	39	5	29	(12	17)	302	94	101	97	62	10	89	1	0	3	8	3	.73	14	.282	.350	.514
2004	Oak	AL	125	475	131	20	0	29	(15	14)	238	87	77	84	95	10	99	3	0	4	6	3	.67	21	.276	.397	.501
2005	Oak	AL	160	625	168	40	1	27	(15	12)	291	92	101	95	58	4	129	2	0	9	6	0	1.00	9	.269	.329	.466
2006	Oak	AL	137	485	117	24	2	22	(8	14)	211	74	72	70	84	6	100	1	0	6	3	0	1.00	19	.241	.351	.435
2007	Oak	AL	90	341	82	21	2	15	(10	5)	152	43	46	38	34	2	76	0	0	4	4	2	.67	9	.240	.306	.446
2008	Oak	AL	23	89	22	7	0	2	(1	1)	35	10	14	14	6	0	18	0	0	0	0	0	-	2	.247	.295	.393
2009	Oak	AL	8	30	3	1	0	0	(0	0)	4	0	1	0	1	0	7	0	0	0	0	0	-	0	.100	.129	.133
2010	Oak	AL	33	111	26	8	0	1	(0	1)	37	10	10	7	8	0	31	0	0	4	0	0	-	3	.234	.276	.333
	Postseason		27	108	24	7	0	3	(3	0)	40	11	12	12	7	2	22	0	0	0	1	0	1.00	2	.222	.270	.370
	13 ML YEARS		1320	4783	1276	282	20	230	(115	115)	2288	730	787	750	565	67	922	13	0	44	47	17	.73	109	.267	.343	.478

Jesse Chavez

Pitches: R Bats: R Pos: RP-51   CHAH-vezz   **Ht: 6'2" Wt: 170 Born: 8/21/1983 Age: 27**

			HOW MUCH HE PITCHED					WHAT HE GAVE UP										THE RESULTS						
Year	Team	Lg	G	GS	CG	GF	IP	BFP	H	R	HR	SH	SF	HB	TBB	IBB	SO	WP	Bk	W	L	Pct	Sh	Sv-Op	Hld	ERC	ERA
2008	Pit	NL	15	0	0	6	15.0	74	20	11	11	2	3	1	0	9	2	16	2	0	0	1	.000	0	0-2	0	6.76	6.60
2009	Pit	NL	73	0	0	24	67.1	286	69	33	30	11	1	1	1	22	3	47	5	0	1	4	.200	0	0-4	15	4.39	4.01
2010	2 Tms		51	0	0	26	62.2	280	69	44	41	11	5	3	1	23	7	45	2	0	5	5	.500	0	0-1	6	4.85	5.89
10	Atl	NL	28	0	0	16	36.2	162	40	24	24	6	3	2	1	12	3	29	0	0	3	2	.600	0	0-0	0	4.65	5.89
10	KC	AL	23	0	0	10	26.0	118	29	20	17	5	2	1	0	11	4	16	2	0	2	3	.400	0	0-1	6	5.13	5.88
	3 ML YEARS		139	0	0	56	145.0	640	158	88	82	24	9	5	2	54	12	108	9	0	6	10	.375	0	0-7	21	4.83	5.09

Bruce Chen

Pitches: L Bats: L Pos: SP-23; RP-10   **Ht: 6'1" Wt: 215 Born: 6/19/1977 Age: 34**

			HOW MUCH HE PITCHED					WHAT HE GAVE UP										THE RESULTS						
Year	Team	Lg	G	GS	CG	GF	IP	BFP	H	R	ER	HR	SH	SF	HB	TBB	IBB	SO	WP	Bk	W	L	Pct	Sh	Sv-Op	Hld	ERC	ERA
2010	Omha*		3	3	0	0	20.2	76	13	3	3	1	0	0	0	5	1	20	0	0	0	1	.000	0	0- -	-	1.30	1.31
1998	Atl	NL	4	4	0	0	20.1	91	23	9	9	3	1	0	1	9	1	17	0	0	2	0	1.000	0	0-0	0	5.55	3.98
1999	Atl	NL	16	7	0	3	51.0	214	38	32	31	11	1	1	2	27	3	45	0	0	2	2	.500	0	0-0	0	4.07	5.47
2000	2 Tms	NL	37	15	0	4	134.0	559	116	54	49	18	8	3	2	46	4	112	4	1	7	4	.636	0	0-0	0	3.35	3.29
2001	2 Tms	NL	27	27	0	0	146.0	634	146	90	79	29	4	7	1	59	4	126	5	0	7	7	.500	0	0-0	0	4.75	4.87
2002	3 Tms	NL	55	6	0	9	77.2	360	85	53	48	16	2	3	2	43	5	80	4	0	2	5	.286	0	0-0	4	5.99	5.56
2003	2 Tms	NL	16	2	0	4	24.1	110	26	16	15	6	3	3	2	10	1	20	0	0	0	1	.000	0	0-0	1	5.81	5.55
2004	Bal	AL	8	7	1	0	47.2	196	39	19	16	7	2	1	0	16	0	32	0	0	2	1	.667	0	0-0	0	3.13	3.02
2005	Bal	AL	34	32	1	0	197.1	832	187	94	84	33	3	3	9	63	0	133	2	1	13	10	.565	0	0-0	0	4.12	3.83
2006	Bal	AL	40	12	0	16	98.2	453	137	81	76	28	3	5	0	35	3	70	1	0	0	7	.000	0	0-1	1	7.73	6.93
2007	Tex	AL	5	0	0	3	10.0	46	11	11	8	3	0	0	0	6	1	7	0	0	0	0	-	0	0-0	0	6.90	7.20
2009	KC	AL	17	9	0	4	62.1	279	74	42	40	12	2	2	4	25	3	45	4	0	1	6	.143	0	0-0	0	6.18	5.78
2010	KC	AL	33	23	1	0	140.1	608	136	68	65	17	0	7	0	57	4	98	3	0	12	7	.632	1	1-1	0	4.09	4.17
00	Atl	NL	22	0	0	4	39.2	170	35	16	11	4	3	2	1	19	2	32	0	0	4	0	1.000	0	0-0	0	3.62	2.50
00	Phi	NL	15	15	0	0	94.1	383	81	39	38	14	5	1	1	27	2	80	4	0	3	4	.429	0	0-0	0	3.22	3.63
01	Phi	NL	16	16	0	0	86.1	381	90	53	48	19	2	4	1	31	4	79	2	0	4	5	.444	0	0-0	0	4.87	5.00
01	NYM	NL	11	11	0	0	59.2	253	56	37	31	10	2	3	0	28	0	47	3	0	3	2	.600	0	0-0	0	4.58	4.68
02	NYM	NL	1	0	0	0	0.2	3	1	0	0	0	0	0	0	0	0	0	0	0	0	0	-	0	0-0	0	4.47	0.00
02	Mon	NL	15	5	0	4	37.1	179	47	29	29	9	0	0	1	23	3	43	3	0	2	3	.400	0	0-0	0	7.69	6.99
02	Cin	NL	39	1	0	5	39.2	178	37	24	19	7	2	3	1	20	2	37	1	0	0	2	.000	0	0-0	4	4.55	4.31
03	Hou	NL	11	0	0	2	12.0	60	14	8	8	2	3	2	2	8	1	8	0	0	0	0	-	0	0-0	1	7.11	6.00
03	Bos	AL	5	2	0	2	12.1	50	12	8	7	4	0	1	0	2	0	12	0	0	0	1	.000	0	0-0	0	4.40	5.11
	12 ML YEARS		292	144	3	47	1009.2	4382	1018	569	520	183	35	35	26	396	29	785	23	2	48	50	.490	1	1-1	6	4.72	4.64

Matt Chico

Pitches: L Bats: L Pos: SP-1   CHEEK-oh   **Ht: 5'11" Wt: 221 Born: 6/10/1983 Age: 28**

			HOW MUCH HE PITCHED					WHAT HE GAVE UP										THE RESULTS						
Year	Team	Lg	G	GS	CG	GF	IP	BFP	H	R	ER	HR	SH	SF	HB	TBB	IBB	SO	WP	Bk	W	L	Pct	Sh	Sv-Op	Hld	ERC	ERA
2010	Hrsbrg*	AA	5	5	0	0	26.0	109	26	14	9	2	0	1	0	7	0	17	5	1	1	2	.333	0	0- -	-	3.41	3.12
2010	Syrcse*	AAA	21	21	0	0	115.2	491	120	53	48	12	4	6	0	34	1	69	5	0	6	7	.462	0	0- -	-	3.88	3.73
2007	Was	NL	31	31	0	0	167.0	747	183	96	86	26	6	10	5	74	3	94	7	0	7	9	.438	0	0-0	0	5.31	4.63
2008	Was	NL	11	8	0	0	48.0	219	63	34	33	10	4	2	1	17	1	31	1	0	0	6	.000	0	0-0	0	6.67	6.19
2010	Was	NL	1	1	0	0	5.0	22	6	2	2	0	0	0	1	0	0	3	1	0	0	0	-	0	0-0	0	3.60	3.60
	3 ML YEARS		43	40	0	0	220.0	988	252	132	121	36	10	12	7	91	4	128	9	0	7	15	.318	0	0-0	0	5.56	4.95

Randy Choate

Pitches: L Bats: L Pos: RP-85

CHOTE

Ht: 6'1" **Wt:** 200 **Born:** 9/5/1975 **Age:** 35

		HOW MUCH HE PITCHED						WHAT HE GAVE UP												THE RESULTS						
Year Team	Lg	G	GS	CG	GF	IP	BFP	H	R	ER	HR	SH	SF	HB	TBB	IBB	SO	WP	Bk	W	L	Pct	Sh	Sv-Op	Hld	ERC	ERA
2000 NYY	AL	22	0	0	6	17.0	75	14	10	9	3	0	1	1	8	0	12	1	0	0	1	.000	0	0-0	2	3.99	4.76
2001 NYY	AL	37	0	0	13	48.1	207	34	21	18	0	2	1	9	27	2	35	3	0	3	1	.750	0	0-0	3	3.03	3.35
2002 NYY	AL	18	0	0	11	22.1	101	18	18	15	1	0	0	3	15	0	17	3	0	0	0	-	0	0-0	1	4.13	6.04
2003 NYY	AL	5	0	0	2	3.2	16	7	3	3	0	0	0	0	1	0	0	0	0	0	0	-	0	0-0	0	9.72	7.36
2004 Ari	NL	74	0	0	17	50.2	232	52	26	26	1	0	4	5	28	11	49	1	1	2	4	.333	0	0-2	11	4.18	4.62
2005 Ari	NL	8	0	0	1	7.0	35	8	7	7	0	0	0	1	5	1	4	1	0	0	0	-	0	0-0	5	5.48	9.00
2006 Ari	NL	30	0	0	3	16.0	75	21	9	7	0	0	0	3	3	0	12	0	0	0	1	.000	0	0-0	5	4.87	3.94
2007 Ari	NL	2	0	0	0	0.0	3	3	0	0	0	0	0	0	0	0	0	0	0	0	0	-	0	0-0	0	-	-
2009 TB	AL	61	0	0	13	36.1	142	28	15	14	4	0	0	0	11	3	28	0	0	1	0	1.000	0	5-5	9	2.54	3.47
2010 TB	AL	**85**	0	0	8	44.2	187	41	23	21	3	2	2	3	17	5	40	4	0	4	3	.571	0	0-2	18	3.48	4.23
Postseason		4	0	0	0	5.1	27	7	5	2	0	0	0	0	2	1	4	0	0	0	0	-	0	0-0	0	4.15	3.38
10 ML YEARS		342	0	0	73	246.0	1073	226	132	120	12	4	8	25	115	22	197	13	1	10	10	.500	0	5-9	50	3.78	4.39

Shin-Soo Choo

Bats: L Throws: L Pos: RF-142; DH-2

Ht: 5'11" **Wt:** 200 **Born:** 7/13/1982 **Age:** 28

							BATTING												BASERUNNING				AVERAGES		
Year Team	Lg	G	AB	H	2B	3B	HR	(Hm	Rd)	TB	R	RBI	RC	TBB	IBB	SO	HBP	SH	SF	SB	CS	SB%	GDP	Avg	OBP	Slg
2010 Akron*	AA	3	11	1	0	0	0	(-	-)	1	1	0	0	0	0	3	0	0	0	1	0	1.00	1	.091	.091	.091
2005 Sea	AL	10	18	1	0	0	0	(0	0)	1	1	1	0	3	0	4	0	0	0	0	0	-	0	.056	.190	.056
2006 2 Tms	AL	49	157	44	12	3	3	(2	1)	71	23	22	24	18	2	50	2	1	1	5	3	.63	3	.280	.360	.452
2007 Cle	AL	6	17	5	0	0	0	(0	0)	5	5	5	3	2	1	5	0	0	1	0	1	.00	0	.294	.350	.294
2008 Cle	AL	94	317	98	28	3	14	(10	4)	174	68	66	72	44	4	78	5	0	4	4	3	.57	5	.309	.397	.549
2009 Cle	AL	156	583	175	38	6	20	(11	9)	285	87	86	111	78	5	151	17	0	7	21	2	.91	9	.300	.394	.489
2010 Cle	AL	144	550	165	31	2	22	(8	14)	266	81	90	106	83	11	118	11	0	2	22	7	.76	11	.300	.401	.484
06 Sea	AL	4	11	1	1	0	0	(0	0)	2	0	0	0	0	0	4	1	0	0	0	0	-	1	.091	.167	.182
06 Cle	AL	45	146	43	11	3	3	(2	1)	69	23	22	24	18	2	46	1	1	1	5	3	.63	2	.295	.373	.473
6 ML YEARS		459	1642	488	109	14	59	(31	28)	802	265	270	316	228	23	406	35	1	15	52	16	.76	28	.297	.391	.488

Ryan Church

Bats: L Throws: L Pos: PH-51; RF-33; LF-22; CF-7; DH-3

Ht: 6'2" **Wt:** 215 **Born:** 10/14/1978 **Age:** 32

							BATTING												BASERUNNING				AVERAGES		
Year Team	Lg	G	AB	H	2B	3B	HR	(Hm	Rd)	TB	R	RBI	RC	TBB	IBB	SO	HBP	SH	SF	SB	CS	SB%	GDP	Avg	OBP	Slg
2004 Mon	NL	30	63	11	1	0	1	(0	1)	15	6	6	2	7	1	16	0	1	0	0	0	-	3	.175	.257	.238
2005 Was	NL	102	268	77	15	3	9	(5	4)	125	41	42	34	24	0	70	5	1	3	3	2	.60	6	.287	.353	.466
2006 Was	NL	71	196	54	17	1	10	(6	4)	103	22	35	36	26	0	60	3	3	2	6	1	.86	4	.276	.366	.526
2007 Was	NL	144	470	128	43	1	15	(5	10)	218	57	70	70	49	4	107	8	0	3	3	2	.60	12	.272	.349	.464
2008 NYM	NL	90	319	88	14	1	12	(6	6)	140	54	49	46	33	3	83	3	1	3	2	3	.40	9	.276	.346	.439
2009 2 Tms	NL	111	359	98	28	0	4	(2	2)	138	46	40	40	33	6	58	3	2	2	6	2	.75	11	.273	.338	.384
2010 2 Tms	NL	106	219	44	16	1	5	(3	2)	77	25	25	19	16	1	65	3	0	0	1	0	1.00	3	.201	.265	.352
09 NYM	NL	67	232	65	16	0	2	(1	1)	87	26	22	22	17	4	36	2	2	2	6	2	.75	7	.280	.332	.375
09 Atl	NL	44	127	33	12	0	2	(1	1)	51	20	18	18	16	2	22	1	0	0	0	0	-	4	.260	.347	.402
10 Pit	NL	69	170	31	11	1	3	(3	0)	53	16	18	10	12	0	46	1	0	0	1	0	1.00	3	.182	.240	.312
10 Ari	NL	37	49	13	5	0	2	(0	2)	24	9	7	9	4	1	19	2	0	0	0	0	-	0	.265	.345	.490
7 ML YEARS		654	1894	500	134	7	56	(27	29)	816	251	267	247	188	15	459	25	8	13	21	10	.68	48	.264	.336	.431

Pedro Ciriaco

Bats: R Throws: R Pos: PH-5; PR-2; SS-1

see-ree-AH-koe

Ht: 6'0" **Wt:** 160 **Born:** 9/27/1985 **Age:** 25

							BATTING												BASERUNNING				AVERAGES		
Year Team	Lg	G	AB	H	2B	3B	HR	(Hm	Rd)	TB	R	RBI	RC	TBB	IBB	SO	HBP	SH	SF	SB	CS	SB%	GDP	Avg	OBP	Slg
2005 Msoula	R+	69	254	61	9	4	2	(-	-)	84	28	31	22	7	0	50	2	3	2	7	2	.78	3	.240	.264	.331
2006 Sbend	A	128	550	145	15	5	2	(-	-)	176	77	32	57	32	0	96	5	10	3	19	8	.70	8	.264	.308	.320
2007 Visalia	A+	119	463	116	14	5	3	(-	-)	149	61	39	43	20	1	81	4	5	3	20	11	.65	12	.251	.286	.322
2008 Visalia	A+	124	520	161	26	5	5	(-	-)	212	85	61	77	18	0	89	6	7	11	39	9	.81	9	.310	.333	.408
2009 Mobile	AA	121	469	139	15	3	4	(-	-)	172	56	54	60	16	2	71	2	5	5	39	10	.80	10	.296	.319	.367
2010 Reno	AAA	87	355	92	15	7	6	(-	-)	139	44	51	41	10	1	53	1	6	4	14	3	.82	7	.259	.278	.392
2010 Indy	AAA	32	121	34	9	1	0	(-	-)	45	19	6	13	2	0	21	0	1	2	5	1	.83	1	.281	.288	.372
2010 Pit	NL	8	6	3	1	1	0	(0	0)	6	3	1	3	0	0	3	0	0	0	0	0	-	0	.500	.500	1.000

Steve Cishek

Pitches: R Bats: R Pos: RP-3

SEE-sheck

Ht: 6'6" **Wt:** 200 **Born:** 6/18/1986 **Age:** 25

		HOW MUCH HE PITCHED						WHAT HE GAVE UP												THE RESULTS						
Year Team	Lg	G	GS	CG	GF	IP	BFP	H	R	ER	HR	SH	SF	HB	TBB	IBB	SO	WP	Bk	W	L	Pct	Sh	Sv-Op	Hld	ERC	ERA
2007 Jmstwn	A-	25	0	0	19	32.1	137	20	13	7	1	2	0	2	19	0	30	3	0	1	2	.333	0	9- -	-	2.48	1.95
2008 Grnsbr	A	49	0	0	22	74.1	325	68	39	38	7	2	3	10	34	3	74	6	0	3	5	.375	0	2- -	-	4.28	4.60
2009 Jupiter	A+	37	0	0	11	57.0	230	36	23	18	2	6	1	9	16	1	45	5	2	3	4	.429	0	2- -	-	1.89	2.84
2010 Jupiter	A+	26	0	0	11	35.0	157	29	15	11	0	1	1	6	19	3	28	2	0	0	6	.000	0	4- -	-	3.39	2.83
2010 Jaxnvl	AA	22	0	0	5	31.1	135	30	16	15	0	0	0	5	10	2	34	6	0	3	1	.750	0	2- -	-	3.35	4.31
2010 Fla	NL	3	0	0	2	4.1	15	1	0	0	0	0	0	0	0	0	3	0	0	0	0	-	0	0-0	0	0.35	0.00

Jeff Clement

Bats: L **Throws:** R **Pos:** 1B-38; PH-18 CLEMM-ent **Ht:** 6'1" **Wt:** 224 **Born:** 8/21/1983 **Age:** 27

							BATTING													BASERUNNING				AVERAGES		
Year	Team	Lg	G	AB	H	2B	3B	HR	(Hm | Rd)	TB	R	RBI	RC	TBB	IBB	SO	HBP	SH	SF	SB	CS	SB%	GDP	Avg	OBP	Slg
2010	Indy*	AAA	42	168	51	15	1	8	(- | -)	92	23	33	29	9	0	48	0	0	1	1	4	.20	4	.304	.337	.548
2007	Sea	AL	9	16	6	1	0	2	(2 | 0)	13	4	3	6	3	0	3	0	0	0	0	0	-	0	.375	.474	.813
2008	Sea	AL	66	203	46	10	1	5	(2 | 3)	73	17	23	22	15	0	63	5	0	1	0	1	1.00	1	.227	.295	.360
2010	Pit	NL	54	144	29	3	0	7	(1 | 6)	53	11	12	6	6	3	37	1	1	1	0	0	-	2	.201	.237	.368
3 ML YEARS			129	363	81	14	1	14	(5 | 9)	139	32	38	34	24	3	103	6	1	2	0	1	.00	6	.223	.281	.383

Brent Clevlen

Bats: R **Throws:** R **Pos:** PR-3; LF-2 **Ht:** 6'1" **Wt:** 205 **Born:** 10/27/1983 **Age:** 27

							BATTING													BASERUNNING				AVERAGES		
Year	Team	Lg	G	AB	H	2B	3B	HR	(Hm | Rd)	TB	R	RBI	RC	TBB	IBB	SO	HBP	SH	SF	SB	CS	SB%	GDP	Avg	OBP	Slg
2010	Gwnntt*	AAA	53	191	49	8	0	3	(- | -)	66	19	29	24	22	2	62	0	0	1	3	0	1.00	4	.257	.332	.346
2010	Rome*	A	1	4	3	0	0	0	(- | -)	3	1	0	1	0	0	0	0	0	0	0	0	-	0	.750	.750	.750
2006	Det	AL	31	39	11	1	2	3	(0 | 3)	25	9	6	6	2	0	15	0	1	0	0	0	-	0	.282	.317	.641
2007	Det	AL	13	10	1	0	0	0	(0 | 0)	1	2	0	0	0	0	7	0	0	0	0	0	-	1	.100	.100	.100
2008	Det	AL	11	24	5	0	0	0	(0 | 0)	5	4	1	2	3	0	8	0	1	0	0	0	-	0	.208	.296	.208
2010	Atl	NL	4	4	1	1	0	0	(0 | 0)	2	2	0	0	0	0	1	0	0	0	0	0	-	1	.250	.250	.500
4 ML YEARS			59	77	18	2	2	3	(0 | 3)	33	17	7	8	5	0	31	0	2	0	0	0	-	2	.234	.280	.429

Tyler Clippard

Pitches: R **Bats:** R **Pos:** RP-78 **Ht:** 6'3" **Wt:** 200 **Born:** 2/14/1985 **Age:** 26

			HOW MUCH HE PITCHED						WHAT HE GAVE UP											THE RESULTS						
Year	Team	Lg	G	GS	CG	GF	IP	BFP	H	R	ER	HR	SH	SF	HB	TBB	IBB	SO	WP	Bk	W	L	Pct	Sh	Sv-Op	Hld	ERC	ERA
2007	NYY	AL	6	6	0	0	27.0	124	29	19	19	6	0	0	0	17	1	18	2	1	3	1	.750	0	0-0	0	6.37	6.33
2008	Was	NL	2	2	0	0	10.1	48	12	5	5	2	0	0	0	7	1	8	1	0	1	1	.500	0	0-0	0	6.90	4.35
2009	Was	NL	41	0	0	8	60.1	246	36	20	18	9	3	1	1	32	1	67	1	1	4	2	.667	0	0-1	3	2.79	2.69
2010	Was	NL	78	0	0	18	91.0	378	69	33	31	8	3	7	2	41	4	112	1	1	11	8	.579	0	1-11	23	2.91	3.07
4 ML YEARS			127	8	0	26	188.2	796	146	77	73	25	6	8	3	97	7	205	5	3	19	12	.613	0	1-12	26	3.51	3.48

Robert Coello

Pitches: R **Bats:** R **Pos:** RP-6 koe-AY-oh **Ht:** 6'4" **Wt:** 215 **Born:** 11/23/1984 **Age:** 26

			HOW MUCH HE PITCHED						WHAT HE GAVE UP											THE RESULTS						
Year	Team	Lg	G	GS	CG	GF	IP	BFP	H	R	ER	HR	SH	SF	HB	TBB	IBB	SO	WP	Bk	W	L	Pct	Sh	Sv-Op	Hld	ERC	ERA
2007	Angels	R	20	0	0	6	26.1	111	23	9	4	0	1	0	4	7	0	26	4	2	1	1	.500	0	0- -	-	2.77	1.37
2008	Calgary	IND	12	0	0	5	15.2	74	19	12	10	2	2	0	1	7	1	18	0	1	1	1	.500	0	0- -	-	5.73	5.74
2008	Edmtn	IND	20	0	0	9	25.1	114	18	6	5	2	0	1	2	17	1	29	3	0	2	0	1.000	0	0- -	-	3.48	1.78
2009	Pwtckt	AAA	1	0	0	1	1.1	5	1	0	0	0	0	0	0	0	0	1	0	0	0	0	-	0	0	-	1.13	0.00
2009	Salem	A+	33	0	0	13	66.0	274	38	22	15	4	3	2	7	34	0	82	2	1	5	3	.625	0	2- -	-	2.40	2.05
2010	Portlnd	AA	14	4	0	4	43.1	180	37	16	16	4	2	0	1	14	0	51	2	0	4	1	.800	0	1- -	-	3.01	3.32
2010	Pwtckt	AAA	18	9	0	1	64.0	269	44	33	30	10	1	3	6	30	0	79	1	2	3	5	.375	0	0- -	-	3.36	4.22
2010	Bos	AL	6	0	0	2	5.2	26	4	3	3	0	0	0	0	5	0	5	1	0	0	0	-	0	0-0	-	3.44	4.76

Todd Coffey

Pitches: R **Bats:** R **Pos:** RP-69 **Ht:** 6'4" **Wt:** 241 **Born:** 9/9/1980 **Age:** 30

			HOW MUCH HE PITCHED						WHAT HE GAVE UP											THE RESULTS						
Year	Team	Lg	G	GS	CG	GF	IP	BFP	H	R	ER	HR	SH	SF	HB	TBB	IBB	SO	WP	Bk	W	L	Pct	Sh	Sv-Op	Hld	ERC	ERA
2010	Nashv*	AAA	1	0	0	0	1.0	3	0	0	0	0	0	0	0	0	0	1	0	0	0	0	-	0	0- -	-	0.00	0.00
2005	Cin	NL	57	0	0	14	58.0	265	84	33	29	5	3	2	5	11	2	26	1	0	4	1	.800	0	1-2	3	6.11	4.50
2006	Cin	NL	81	0	0	28	78.0	340	85	34	31	7	0	1	2	27	5	60	4	0	6	7	.462	0	8-12	15	4.29	3.58
2007	Cin	NL	58	0	0	8	51.0	242	70	36	33	12	1	0	5	10	4	43	4	0	2	1	.667	0	0-3	7	7.58	5.82
2008	2 Tms	NL	26	0	0	9	26.2	116	31	13	13	4	2	1	1	8	0	15	0	0	1	0	1.000	0	0-0	1	5.19	4.39
2009	Mil	NL	78	0	0	17	83.2	336	76	28	27	8	2	2	3	21	3	65	1	0	4	4	.500	0	2-6	27	3.16	2.90
2010	Mil	NL	69	0	0	12	62.1	274	65	40	33	8	2	5	3	23	5	56	6	0	2	4	.333	0	0-2	13	4.42	4.76
08	Cin	NL	17	0	0	6	19.1	87	25	13	13	4	1	1	1	6	0	8	0	0	0	0	-	0	0-0	0	6.57	6.05
08	Mil	NL	9	0	0	3	7.1	29	6	0	0	0	1	0	0	2	0	7	0	0	1	0	1.000	0	0-0	1	2.09	0.00
6 ML YEARS			369	0	0	88	359.2	1573	411	184	166	44	10	11	19	109	19	265	16	0	19	17	.528	0	11-25	66	4.82	4.15

Chris Coghlan

Bats: L **Throws:** R **Pos:** LF-90; PH-2 COGG-lan **Ht:** 6'0" **Wt:** 204 **Born:** 6/18/1985 **Age:** 26

							BATTING													BASERUNNING				AVERAGES		
Year	Team	Lg	G	AB	H	2B	3B	HR	(Hm	Rd)	TB	R	RBI	RC	TBB	IBB	SO	HBP	SH	SF	SB	CS	SB%	GDP	Avg	OBP	Slg
2006	Mrlns	R	2	7	2	0	0	0	(-	-)	2	2	3	0	0	0	1	0	0	0	0	0	-	0	.286	.286	.286
2006	Jmstwn	A-	28	94	28	5	1	0	(-	-)	35	14	12	15	13	0	9	0	1	3	5	2	.71	1	.298	.373	.372
2007	Grnsbr	A	81	305	99	26	4	10	(-	-)	163	60	64	71	47	4	43	5	0	3	19	4	.83	1	.325	.419	.534
2007	Jupiter	A+	34	130	26	5	3	2	(-	-)	43	17	18	13	15	0	19	0	0	3	5	1	.83	4	.200	.277	.331
2008	Carlina	AA	132	483	144	32	5	7	(-	-)	207	83	74	90	67	1	65	12	2	1	34	10	.77	9	.298	.396	.429
2009	NewOr	AAA	25	96	33	9	1	3	(-	-)	53	21	22	23	12	0	10	1	0	1	9	1	.90	3	.344	.418	.552
2009	Fla	NL	128	504	162	31	6	9	(5	4)	232	84	47	91	53	2	77	4	3	1	8	5	.62	3	.321	.390	.460
2010	Fla	NL	91	358	96	20	3	5	(5	0)	137	60	28	43	33	1	84	4	3	2	10	3	.77	3	.268	.335	.383
2 ML YEARS			219	862	258	51	9	14	(10	4)	369	144	75	134	86	3	161	8	6	3	18	8	.69	6	.299	.367	.428

Phil Coke

Pitches: L **Bats:** L **Pos:** RP-73; SP-1   **Ht:** 6'1" **Wt:** 210 **Born:** 7/19/1982 **Age:** 28

			HOW MUCH HE PITCHED					WHAT HE GAVE UP											THE RESULTS						
Year	Team	Lg	G	GS	CG	GF	IP	BFP	H	R	ER	HR	SH	SF	HB	TBB	IBB	SO	WP	Bk	W	L	Pct	Sh	Sv-Op Hld	ERC	ERA
2008	NYY	AL	12	0	0	0	14.2	52	8	1	1	0	0	0	0	2	0	14	1	0	1	0	1.000	0	0-0 5	0.89	0.61
2009	NYY	AL	72	0	0	13	60.0	238	44	34	30	10	1	5	1	20	4	49	7	0	4	3	.571	0	2-7 21	2.84	4.50
2010	Det	AL	74	1	0	18	64.2	279	67	29	27	2	2	3	4	26	4	53	3	0	7	5	.583	0	2-4 17	4.00	3.76
	Postseason		6	0	0	1	2.2	11	4	2	2	2	0	0	0	1	0	3	0	0	-	-	-	0	0-0 0	14.65	6.75
3 ML YEARS			158	1	0	31	139.1	569	119	64	58	12	3	8	5	48	8	116	11	0	12	8	.600	0	4-11 43	3.10	3.75

Casey Coleman

Pitches: R **Bats:** L **Pos:** SP-8; RP-4   **Ht:** 6'0" **Wt:** 180 **Born:** 7/3/1987 **Age:** 23

			HOW MUCH HE PITCHED					WHAT HE GAVE UP											THE RESULTS						
Year	Team	Lg	G	GS	CG	GF	IP	BFP	H	R	ER	HR	SH	SF	HB	TBB	IBB	SO	WP	Bk	W	L	Pct	Sh	Sv-Op Hld	ERC	ERA
2008	Boise	A-	7	4	0	0	26.2	115	27	13	12	4	1	1	1	7	0	24	2	0	1	1	.500	0	0- - -	4.00	4.05
2008	Peoria	A	5	5	0	0	23.1	96	25	11	7	1	0	0	0	4	0	18	0	0	2	2	.500	0	0- - -	3.24	2.70
2008	Dytona	A+	1	1	0	0	5.0	21	4	1	0	0	1	0	0	2	0	2	0	0	1	0	1.000	0	0- - -	2.31	0.00
2009	Tenn	AA	27	27	1	0	149.0	633	142	63	61	8	10	4	5	58	0	84	2	1	14	6	.700	0	0- - -	3.62	3.68
2010	Iowa	AAA	21	21	2	0	117.1	481	106	58	53	10	3	5	2	35	0	59	4	0	10	7	.588	0	0- - -	3.17	4.07
2010	ChC	NL	12	8	0	0	57.0	248	56	27	26	3	2	4	2	25	2	27	3	0	4	2	.667	0	0-0 0	3.87	4.11

Jesus Colome

Pitches: R **Bats:** R **Pos:** RP-12   COLL-ah-may   **Ht:** 6'2" **Wt:** 240 **Born:** 12/23/1977 **Age:** 33

			HOW MUCH HE PITCHED					WHAT HE GAVE UP											THE RESULTS						
Year	Team	Lg	G	GS	CG	GF	IP	BFP	H	R	ER	HR	SH	SF	HB	TBB	IBB	SO	WP	Bk	W	L	Pct	Sh	Sv-Op Hld	ERC	ERA
2010	Albq*	AAA	3	0	0	0	1.1	10	4	5	5	0	0	0	0	2	0	1	1	0	0	0	-	0	0- - -	22.07	33.75
2010	OKCity*	AAA	4	0	0	1	3.1	16	3	5	3	0	0	1	0	2	0	2	1	0	0	0	-	0	0- - -	2.08	8.10
2001	TB	AL	30	0	0	9	48.2	209	37	22	18	8	2	2	2	25	4	31	2	0	2	3	.400	0	0-0 6	3.62	3.33
2002	TB	AL	32	0	0	15	41.1	204	56	41	38	6	4	1	2	33	5	33	5	0	2	7	.222	0	0-5 3	8.57	8.27
2003	TB	AL	54	0	0	24	74.0	334	69	37	37	9	2	4	3	46	5	69	7	0	3	7	.300	0	2-8 11	4.76	4.50
2004	TB	AL	33	0	0	9	41.1	169	28	16	15	4	5	0	1	18	1	40	1	1	2	2	.500	0	3-4 8	2.54	3.27
2005	TB	AL	36	0	0	18	45.1	212	54	29	23	7	1	0	2	18	3	28	5	0	2	3	.400	0	0-1 5	5.46	4.57
2006	TB	AL	1	0	0	0	0.1	2	0	1	1	0	0	0	0	1	0	0	0	0	-	-	-	0	0-0 0	7.00	27.00
2007	Was	NL	61	0	0	16	66.0	286	64	30	28	6	4	6	1	27	3	43	4	0	5	1	.833	0	1-4 12	3.83	3.82
2008	Was	NL	61	0	0	25	71.0	312	61	38	34	6	7	2	4	39	4	55	7	0	2	2	.500	0	0-2 1	3.86	4.31
2009	2 Tms	NL	21	0	0	8	21.1	103	34	18	18	2	1	1	1	6	1	15	3	2	1	1	.500	0	0-1 0	7.20	7.59
2010	Sea	AL	12	0	0	1	17.0	77	15	10	10	1	0	3	1	11	0	16	3	0	0	1	.000	0	0-0 0	4.25	5.29
	09 Was	NL	16	0	0	5	15.0	75	23	14	14	1	1	1	1	6	1	12	2	2	1	1	.500	0	0-1 0	7.00	8.40
	09 Mil	NL	5	0	0	3	6.1	28	11	4	4	1	0	0	0	0	0	3	1	0	0	0	-	0	0-0 0	7.66	5.68
10 ML YEARS			341	0	0	125	426.1	1908	418	242	222	49	26	19	17	224	26	330	37	3	19	27	.413	0	6-25 43	4.59	4.69

Roman Colon

Pitches: R **Bats:** R **Pos:** RP-5   row-MAHN ko-LONE   **Ht:** 6'5" **Wt:** 243 **Born:** 8/13/1979 **Age:** 31

			HOW MUCH HE PITCHED					WHAT HE GAVE UP											THE RESULTS						
Year	Team	Lg	G	GS	CG	GF	IP	BFP	H	R	ER	HR	SH	SF	HB	TBB	IBB	SO	WP	Bk	W	L	Pct	Sh	Sv-Op Hld	ERC	ERA
2010	Omha*	AAA	2	0	0	0	2.0	8	1	1	0	0	0	0	0	1	0	1	1	1	0	0	-	0	0- - -	1.41	0.00
2004	Atl	NL	18	0	0	7	19.0	82	18	9	7	0	1	2	0	8	1	15	0	0	2	1	.667	0	0-1 1	3.05	3.32
2005	2 Tms		35	7	0	7	69.1	306	82	45	43	17	2	3	0	21	1	47	4	1	2	6	.250	0	0-1 2	5.75	5.58
2006	Det	AL	20	1	0	4	38.2	170	46	21	21	6	1	2	1	14	2	25	6	0	2	0	1.000	0	1-1 3	5.56	4.89
2009	KC	AL	43	0	0	13	50.1	220	50	27	27	7	1	0	2	22	1	29	1	2	2	3	.400	0	0-3 6	4.60	4.83
2010	KC	AL	5	0	0	2	2.0	14	5	4	4	0	0	0	1	2	0	1	0	0	0	0	-	0	0-0 0	18.12	18.00
	05 Atl	NL	23	4	0	6	44.1	191	47	28	26	10	2	2	0	14	1	30	2	1	1	5	.167	0	0-0 2	4.90	5.28
	05 Det	AL	12	3	0	1	25.0	115	35	17	17	7	0	1	0	7	0	17	2	0	1	1	.500	0	0-1 0	7.34	6.12
5 ML YEARS			121	8	0	33	179.1	792	201	106	102	30	5	7	4	67	5	117	11	3	8	10	.444	0	1-6 12	5.21	5.12

Tyler Colvin

Bats: L **Throws:** L **Pos:** RF-59; LF-55; PH-24; CF-18; PR-5   **Ht:** 6'3" **Wt:** 210 **Born:** 9/5/1985 **Age:** 25

			BATTING																			BASERUNNING				AVERAGES		
Year	Team	Lg	G	AB	H	2B	3B	HR	(Hm	Rd)	TB	R	RBI	RC	TBB	IBB	SO	HBP	SH	SF	SB	CS	SB%	GDP	Avg	OBP	Slg
2006	Boise	A-	64	265	71	12	6	11	(-	-)	128	50	53	41	17	1	55	2	0	4	12	5	.71	3	.268	.313	.483
2007	Dytona	A+	63	245	75	24	3	7	(-	-)	126	38	50	42	10	2	47	3	0	4	10	4	.71	3	.306	.336	.514
2007	Tenn	AA	62	247	72	11	2	9	(-	-)	114	34	31	36	5	0	54	3	1	1	7	1	.88	5	.291	.313	.462
2008	Tenn	AA	137	540	138	27	11	14	(-	-)	229	68	80	75	44	0	101	4	5	9	7	4	.64	7	.256	.312	.424
2009	Dytona	A+	32	112	28	5	2	1	(-	-)	40	18	10	14	13	0	27	1	0	3	3	1	.75	8	.250	.326	.357
2009	Tenn	AA	84	307	92	13	7	14	(-	-)	161	51	50	54	16	2	57	1	4	2	5	1	.83	3	.300	.334	.524
2009	ChC	NL	6	17	3	0	0	0	(0	0)	3	2	1	2	2	0	5	0	0	0	0	0	-	0	.176	.250	.176
2010	ChC	NL	135	358	91	18	5	20	(9	11)	179	60	56	46	30	2	100	3	1	2	6	1	.86	6	.254	.316	.500
2 ML YEARS			141	375	94	18	5	20	(9	11)	182	61	58	47	32	2	105	3	1	3	6	1	.86	6	.251	.312	.485

Hank Conger

Bats: B Throws: R Pos: C-10; PH-4; DH-1 KONG-gerr **Ht: 6'0" Wt: 205 Born: 1/29/1988 Age: 23**

Year	Team	Lg	G	AB	H	2B	3B	HR	(Hm	Rd)	TB	R	RBI	RC	TBB	IBB	SO	HBP	SH	SF	SB	CS	SB%	GDP	Avg	OBP	Slg
2006	Angels	R	19	69	22	3	4	1	(-	-)	36	11	11	13	7	0	11	0	0	0	1	0	1.00	0	.319	.382	.522
2007	CRpds	A	84	290	84	20	0	11	(-	-)	137	33	48	47	21	0	48	2	2	5	9	4	.69	9	.290	.336	.472
2007	Angels	R	3	15	4	1	0	0	(-	-)	5	2	3	1	0	0	3	0	0	0	0	0	-	1	.267	.267	.333
2008	RCuca	A+	73	294	89	20	2	13	(-	-)	152	47	75	51	14	1	55	3	0	7	2	1	.67	3	.303	.333	.517
2009	Ark	AA	123	459	135	20	3	11	(-	-)	194	61	68	75	55	5	68	2	3	6	3	2	.60	19	.294	.368	.423
2010	Salt Lk	AAA	108	387	116	26	2	11	(-	-)	179	56	49	71	55	1	58	1	5	4	0	2	.00	5	.300	.385	.463
2010	LAA	AL	13	29	5	1	1	0	(0	0)	8	2	5	3	5	0	9	0	0	0	0	0	-	1	.172	.294	.276

Brooks Conrad

Bats: B Throws: R Pos: PH-63; 3B-37; 2B-9; PR-8 **Ht: 5'11" Wt: 190 Born: 1/16/1980 Age: 31**

Year	Team	Lg	G	AB	H	2B	3B	HR	(Hm	Rd)	TB	R	RBI	RC	TBB	IBB	SO	HBP	SH	SF	SB	CS	SB%	GDP	Avg	OBP	Slg
2008	Oak	AL	6	19	3	1	0	0	(0	0)	4	0	2	1	0	0	9	0	0	0	0	0	-	1	.158	.158	.211
2009	Atl	NL	30	54	11	1	2	2	(0	2)	22	7	8	6	3	1	14	1	0	0	0	0	-	1	.204	.259	.407
2010	Atl	NL	103	156	39	11	1	8	(4	4)	76	31	33	32	16	0	45	1	4	0	5	1	.83	0	.250	.324	.487
	3 ML YEARS		139	229	53	13	3	10	(4	6)	102	38	43	39	19	1	68	2	4	0	5	1	.83	2	.231	.296	.445

Jose Contreras

Pitches: R Bats: R Pos: RP-67 conn-TRAIR-us **Ht: 6'4" Wt: 255 Born: 12/6/1971 Age: 39**

			HOW MUCH HE PITCHED						WHAT HE GAVE UP											THE RESULTS						
Year	Team	Lg	G	GS	CG	GF	IP	BFP	H	R	ER	HR	SH	SF	HB	TBB	IBB	SO	WP	Bk	W	L	Pct	Sh	Sv-Op	Hld	ERC	ERA
2003	NYY	AL	18	9	0	2	71.0	293	52	27	26	4	0	1	5	30	1	72	2	0	7	2	.778	0	0-1	1	2.71	3.30
2004	2 Tms	AL	31	31	0	0	170.1	758	166	114	104	31	3	6	8	84	1	150	17	0	13	9	.591	0	0-0	0	5.05	5.50
2005	CWS	AL	32	32	1	0	204.2	857	177	91	82	23	7	2	9	75	2	154	20	2	15	7	.682	0	0-0	0	3.46	3.61
2006	CWS	AL	30	30	1	0	196.0	833	194	101	93	20	2	8	10	55	4	134	16	0	13	9	.591	1	0-0	0	3.72	4.27
2007	CWS	AL	32	30	2	2	189.0	858	232	134	117	21	8	10	11	62	1	113	3	0	10	17	.370	2	0-0	0	5.49	5.57
2008	CWS	AL	20	20	1	0	121.0	522	130	64	61	12	4	2	3	35	0	70	6	0	7	6	.538	0	0-0	0	4.13	4.54
2009	2 Tms	AL	28	23	0	0	131.2	589	141	86	72	13	10	2	6	53	4	100	0	0	6	13	.316	0	0 1	1	4.55	4.92
2010	Phi	NL	67	0	0	21	56.2	233	53	22	21	5	4	1	4	16	2	57	0	0	6	4	.600	0	4-5	13	3.50	3.34
04	NYY	AL	18	18	0	0	95.2	425	93	66	60	22	1	4	6	42	1	82	10	0	8	5	.615	0	0-0	0	5.18	5.64
04	CWS	AL	13	13	0	0	74.2	333	73	48	44	9	2	2	2	42	0	68	7	0	5	4	.556	0	0-0	0	4.87	5.30
09	CWS	AL	21	21	0	0	114.2	513	121	83	60	11	7	2	6	45	3	89	8	0	5	13	.278	0	0-0	0	4.41	5.42
09	Col	NL	7	2	0	0	17.0	76	20	3	3	2	3	0	0	8	1	17	0	0	1	0	1.000	0	0-1	1	5.51	1.59
	Postseason		14	4	1	3	45.0	186	40	19	19	2	5	1	3	11	0	34	3	0	3	3	.500	0	0-1	3	2.77	3.80
	8 ML YEARS		258	175	5	25	1140.1	4943	1145	639	576	129	38	32	60	410	15	856	72	2	77	67	.535	3	4-7	15	4.21	4.55

Aaron Cook

Pitches: R Bats: R Pos: SP-23 **Ht: 6'3" Wt: 215 Born: 2/8/1979 Age: 32**

			HOW MUCH HE PITCHED						WHAT HE GAVE UP											THE RESULTS						
Year	Team	Lg	G	GS	CG	GF	IP	BFP	H	R	ER	HR	SH	SF	HB	TBB	IBB	SO	WP	Bk	W	L	Pct	Sh	Sv-Op	Hld	ERC	ERA
2010	Tulsa*	AA	2	2	0	0	10.2	41	8	3	3	1	0	0	2	3	1	10	1	0	1	1	.500	0	0-	-	2.27	2.53
2002	Col	NL	9	5	0	1	35.2	154	41	18	18	4	0	0	2	13	0	14	0	0	2	1	.667	0	0-0	1	5.31	4.54
2003	Col	NL	43	16	1	4	124.0	579	160	89	83	8	4	6	8	57	7	43	10	0	4	6	.400	0	0 0	1	6.96	6.02
2004	Col	NL	16	16	1	0	96.2	433	112	47	46	7	5	1	7	39	6	40	6	1	6	4	.600	0	0-0	0	5.05	4.28
2005	Col	NL	13	13	2	0	83.1	357	101	38	34	8	1	3	2	16	2	24	3	0	7	2	.778	0	0-0	0	4.53	3.67
2006	Col	NL	32	32	0	0	212.2	915	242	107	100	17	8	5	7	55	11	92	2	0	9	15	.375	0	0-0	0	4.23	4.23
2007	Col	NL	25	25	2	0	166.0	698	178	87	76	15	6	3	6	44	6	61	0	0	8	7	.533	0	0-0	0	4.05	4.12
2008	Col	NL	32	32	2	0	211.1	886	236	102	93	13	9	4	4	48	2	96	6	0	16	9	.640	1	0-0	0	3.92	3.96
2009	Col	NL	27	27	1	0	158.0	675	175	76	73	19	3	6	2	47	2	78	2	0	11	6	.647	0	0-0	0	4.51	4.16
2010	Col	NL	23	23	2	0	127.2	572	147	77	72	11	3	6	4	52	4	62	3	1	6	8	.429	0	0-0	0	4.95	5.08
	Postseason		2	2	0	0	11.0	45	13	6	6	1	0	0	0	2	0	6	0	0	1	1	.500	0	0-0	0	4.37	4.91
	9 ML YEARS		220	189	11	5	1215.1	5269	1392	641	595	102	39	34	42	371	39	510	32	2	69	58	.543	2	0-0	2	4.55	4.41

Alex Cora

Bats: L Throws: R Pos: 2B-49; PH-13; SS-6; 1B-2; PR-2; 3B-1 **Ht: 6'0" Wt: 200 Born: 10/18/1975 Age: 35**

Year	Team	Lg	G	AB	H	2B	3B	HR	(Hm	Rd)	TB	R	RBI	RC	TBB	IBB	SO	HBP	SH	SF	SB	CS	SB%	GDP	Avg	OBP	Slg
2010	OKCity*	AAA	6	22	4	1	0	1	(-	-)	8	5	2	2	3	0	2	0	0	0	1	0	1.00	1	.182	.280	.364
1998	LAD	NL	29	33	4	0	1	0	(0	0)	6	1	0	1	2	0	8	1	2	0	0	0	-	0	.121	.194	.182
1999	LAD	NL	11	30	5	1	0	0	(0	0)	6	2	3	0	0	0	4	1	0	0	0	0	-	0	.167	.194	.200
2000	LAD	NL	109	353	84	18	6	4	(2	2)	126	39	32	38	26	4	53	7	6	2	4	1	.80	6	.238	.302	.357
2001	LAD	NL	134	405	88	18	3	4	(2	2)	124	38	29	30	31	6	58	8	3	2	0	2	.00	16	.217	.285	.306
2002	LAD	NL	115	258	75	14	4	5	(4	1)	112	37	28	46	24	4	38	7	2	0	7	2	.78	3	.291	.371	.434
2003	LAD	NL	148	477	119	24	3	4	(3	1)	161	39	34	49	16	3	59	10	9	2	4	2	.67	5	.249	.287	.338
2004	LAD	NL	138	405	107	9	4	10	(4	6)	154	47	47	63	47	10	41	18	12	2	3	4	.43	9	.264	.364	.380
2005	2 Tms	AL	96	250	58	8	4	3	(1	2)	83	25	24	21	11	0	30	5	4	3	7	2	.78	6	.232	.275	.332
2006	Bos	AL	96	235	56	7	2	1	(1	0)	70	31	18	24	19	1	29	6	4	0	6	2	.75	4	.238	.312	.298
2007	Bos	AL	83	207	51	10	5	3	(0	3)	80	30	18	19	7	2	23	9	7	2	1	1	.50	5	.246	.298	.386
2008	Bos	AL	75	152	41	8	2	0	(0	0)	53	14	9	19	16	1	13	9	1	1	1	1	.50	5	.270	.371	.349
2009	NYM	NL	82	271	68	11	1	1	(0	1)	84	31	18	26	25	1	28	3	8	1	8	3	.73	2	.251	.320	.310
2010	Bos	AL	66	176	37	6	3	0	(0	0)	49	14	20	17	10	1	16	4	2	2	4	1	.80	4	.210	.266	.278
05	Cle	AL	49	146	30	5	2	1	(1	0)	42	11	8	9	5	0	18	4	1	1	6	0	1.00	3	.205	.250	.288
05	Bos	AL	47	104	28	3	2	2	(0	2)	41	14	16	12	6	0	12	1	3	2	1	2	.33	3	.269	.310	.394

			BATTING																					BASERUNNING				AVERAGES		
Year	Team	Lg	G	AB	H	2B	3B	HR	(Hm	Rd)	TB	R	RBI	RC	TBB	IBB	SO	HBP	SH	SF		SB	CS	SB%	GDP	Avg	OBP	Slg
10	NYM	NL	62	169	35	6	3	0	(0	0)	47	14	20	16	10	1	16	4	2	2		4	1	.80	4	.207	.265	.278
10	Tex	AL	4	7	2	0	0	0	(0	0)	2	0	0	1	0	0	0	0	0	0		0	0	-	0	.286	.286	.286
	Postseason		13	26	4	1	1	0	(0	0)	7	2	1	1	1	0	5	1	1	0		0	0	-	2	.154	.214	.269
	13 ML YEARS		1182	3252	793	134	38	35	(17	18)	1108	348	280	350	236	33	400	88	60	17		45	21	.68	64	.244	.311	.341

Chad Cordero

Pitches: R **Bats:** R **Pos:** RP-9   **Ht:** 6'0" **Wt:** 220 **Born:** 3/18/1982 **Age:** 29

			HOW MUCH HE PITCHED					WHAT HE GAVE UP										THE RESULTS							
Year	Team	Lg	G	GS	CG	GF	IP	BFP	H	R	ER	HR	SH	SF	HB	TBB	IBB	SO	WP	Bk	W	L	Pct	Sh	Sv-Op	Hld	ERC	ERA
2010	Tacom*	AAA	17	0	0	14	19.2	83	19	11	9	2	0	3	0	4	0	22	1	0	0	1	.000	0	6--	-	3.03	4.12
2010	Buffalo*	AAA	17	0	0	3	16.0	65	15	4	3	0	1	0	0	5	1	14	1	0	1	1	.500	0	0--	-	2.73	1.69
2003	Mon	NL	12	0	0	4	11.0	40	4	2	2	1	1	0	0	3	1	12	1	0	1	0	1.000	0	1-1	1	0.86	1.64
2004	Was	NL	69	0	0	40	82.2	357	68	28	27	8	2	4	1	43	4	83	5	0	7	3	.700	0	14-18	8	3.47	2.94
2005	Was	NL	74	0	0	62	74.1	300	55	24	15	9	2	1	2	17	2	61	0	0	2	4	.333	0	47-54	0	2.22	1.82
2006	Was	NL	68	0	0	59	73.1	307	59	27	26	13	6	2	3	22	5	69	0	0	7	4	.636	0	29-33	0	3.10	3.19
2007	Was	NL	76	0	0	59	75.0	321	75	31	28	8	2	1	0	29	3	62	5	1	3	3	.500	0	37-46	1	4.02	3.36
2008	Was	NL	6	0	0	2	4.1	22	6	1	1	0	0	0	0	3	1	5	1	0	0	0	-	0	0-0	0	6.09	2.08
2010	Sea	AL	9	0	0	4	9.2	41	10	7	7	1	1	2	1	5	0	6	1	0	0	1	.000	0	0-0	0	5.61	6.52
	7 ML YEARS		314	0	0	230	330.1	1388	277	120	106	40	14	10	7	122	16	298	13	1	20	15	.571	0	128-152	11	3.19	2.89

Francisco Cordero

Pitches: R **Bats:** R **Pos:** RP-75   **Ht:** 6'3" **Wt:** 238 **Born:** 5/11/1975 **Age:** 36

			HOW MUCH HE PITCHED					WHAT HE GAVE UP										THE RESULTS							
Year	Team	Lg	G	GS	CG	GF	IP	BFP	H	R	ER	HR	SH	SF	HB	TBB	IBB	SO	WP	Bk	W	L	Pct	Sh	Sv-Op	Hld	ERC	ERA
1999	Det	AL	20	0	0	4	19.0	91	19	7	7	2	2	4	0	18	2	19	1	0	2	2	.500	0	0-0	6	6.19	3.32
2000	Tex	AL	56	0	0	13	77.1	365	87	51	46	11	2	6	4	48	3	49	7	0	1	2	.333	0	0-3	4	6.15	5.35
2001	Tex	AL	3	0	0	2	2.1	12	3	1	1	0	0	0	0	2	1	1	1	0	0	1	.000	0	0-0	1	5.73	3.86
2002	Tex	AL	39	0	0	25	45.1	177	33	12	9	2	0	0	2	13	1	41	1	0	2	0	1.000	0	10-12	1	2.11	1.79
2003	Tex	AL	73	0	0	36	82.2	352	70	33	27	4	3	4	2	38	6	90	1	0	5	8	.385	0	15-25	18	3.08	2.94
2004	Tex	AL	67	0	0	63	71.2	304	60	19	17	1	5	1	4	32	2	79	3	2	3	4	.429	0	49-54	0	2.78	2.13
2005	Tex	AL	69	0	0	60	69.0	302	61	28	26	5	4	3	4	30	2	79	0	0	3	1	.750	0	37-45	0	3.47	3.39
2006	2 Tms		77	0	0	47	75.1	322	69	32	31	7	3	5	3	32	2	84	4	0	10	5	.667	0	22-33	16	3.79	3.70
2007	Mil	NL	66	0	0	58	63.1	261	52	23	21	4	2	1	1	18	1	86	2	0	0	4	.000	0	44-51	0	2.45	2.98
2008	Cin	NL	72	0	0	63	70.1	307	61	28	26	6	3	3	3	38	3	78	3	0	5	4	.556	0	34-40	0	3.86	3.33
2009	Cin	NL	68	0	0	59	66.2	276	58	21	16	2	3	4	0	30	2	58	3	0	2	6	.250	0	39-43	0	3.11	2.16
2010	Cin	NL	75	0	0	64	72.2	316	68	32	31	5	1	1	2	36	1	59	2	0	6	5	.545	0	40-48	1	3.96	3.84
06	Tex	AL	49	0	0	21	48.2	210	49	27	26	5	1	5	3	16	1	54	3	0	7	4	.636	0	6-15	15	4.05	4.81
06	Mil	NL	28	0	0	26	26.2	112	20	5	5	2	2	0	0	16	1	30	1	0	3	1	.750	0	16-18	1	3.30	1.69
	12 ML YEARS		685	0	0	494	715.2	3085	641	287	258	49	28	32	22	335	26	723	28	2	39	42	.481	0	290-354	47	3.59	3.24

Lance Cormier

Pitches: R **Bats:** R **Pos:** RP-60   CORE-mee-ay   **Ht:** 6'1" **Wt:** 200 **Born:** 8/19/1980 **Age:** 30

			HOW MUCH HE PITCHED					WHAT HE GAVE UP										THE RESULTS							
Year	Team	Lg	G	GS	CG	GF	IP	BFP	H	R	ER	HR	SH	SF	HB	TBB	IBB	SO	WP	Bk	W	L	Pct	Sh	Sv-Op	Hld	ERC	ERA
2004	Ari	NL	17	5	0	3	45.1	218	62	42	41	13	2	3	2	25	2	24	2	1	1	4	.200	0	0-0	2	8.76	8.14
2005	Ari	NL	67	0	0	13	79.1	356	86	50	45	7	4	1	5	43	5	63	6	0	7	3	.700	0	0-1	13	5.30	5.11
2006	Atl	NL	29	9	0	5	73.2	333	90	44	40	8	1	4	2	39	7	43	2	0	4	5	.444	0	0-0	2	6.13	4.89
2007	Atl	NL	10	9	0	1	45.2	210	56	38	36	16	3	0	0	23	3	27	4	0	2	6	.250	0	0-0	0	7.66	7.09
2008	Bal	AL	45	1	0	10	71.2	319	78	36	32	4	1	3	1	34	3	46	2	1	3	3	.500	0	1-3	0	4.55	4.02
2009	TB	AL	53	0	0	11	77.1	331	75	31	28	6	2	2	1	25	2	36	3	1	3	3	.500	0	2-2	6	3.41	3.26
2010	TB	AL	60	0	0	17	62.0	279	68	28	27	7	2	1	0	34	3	30	3	1	4	3	.571	0	0-0	4	5.30	3.92
	7 ML YEARS		281	24	0	60	455.0	2046	515	269	249	61	15	14	11	222	25	269	22	4	24	27	.471	0	3-6	27	5.52	4.93

Manuel Corpas

Pitches: R **Bats:** R **Pos:** RP-56   mann-WELL   **Ht:** 6'3" **Wt:** 210 **Born:** 12/3/1982 **Age:** 28

			HOW MUCH HE PITCHED					WHAT HE GAVE UP										THE RESULTS							
Year	Team	Lg	G	GS	CG	GF	IP	BFP	H	R	ER	HR	SH	SF	HB	TBB	IBB	SO	WP	Bk	W	L	Pct	Sh	Sv-Op	Hld	ERC	ERA
2006	Col	NL	35	0	0	3	32.1	136	36	13	13	3	0	0	2	8	1	27	2	0	1	2	.333	0	0-2	7	4.39	3.62
2007	Col	NL	78	0	0	46	78.0	306	63	20	18	6	2	1	2	20	3	58	0	0	4	2	.667	0	19-22	16	2.51	2.08
2008	Col	NL	76	0	0	20	79.2	346	93	44	40	7	6	1	2	23	4	50	1	0	3	4	.429	0	4-13	19	4.55	4.52
2009	Col	NL	35	0	0	16	33.2	146	44	22	22	3	2	1	1	7	0	24	0	0	1	3	.250	0	1-3	7	5.24	5.88
2010	Col	NL	56	0	0	27	62.1	274	66	33	32	7	2	3	2	22	5	47	1	0	3	5	.375	0	10-14	2	4.25	4.62
	Postseason		9	0	0	8	10.1	37	6	1	1	0	0	0	1	0	0	7	0	0	1	0	1.000	0	5-6	0	0.90	0.87
	5 ML YEARS		280	0	0	112	286.0	1208	302	129	125	26	12	6	9	80	13	206	4	0	12	16	.429	0	34-54	51	3.96	3.93

Kevin Correia

Pitches: R **Bats:** R **Pos:** SP-26; RP-2   kore-AY-ah   **Ht:** 6'3" **Wt:** 200 **Born:** 8/24/1980 **Age:** 30

			HOW MUCH HE PITCHED					WHAT HE GAVE UP										THE RESULTS							
Year	Team	Lg	G	GS	CG	GF	IP	BFP	H	R	ER	HR	SH	SF	HB	TBB	IBB	SO	WP	Bk	W	L	Pct	Sh	Sv-Op	Hld	ERC	ERA
2003	SF	NL	10	7	0	1	39.1	173	41	16	16	4	0	1	4	18	1	28	2	0	3	1	.750	0	0-0	0	5.46	3.66
2004	SF	NL	12	1	0	5	19.0	92	25	20	17	3	3	3	1	10	0	14	0	0	0	1	.000	0	0-0	0	7.12	8.05
2005	SF	NL	16	11	0	1	58.1	264	61	31	30	12	5	1	4	31	2	44	2	0	2	5	.286	0	0-0	0	5.94	4.63
2006	SF	NL	48	0	0	9	69.2	295	64	27	27	5	1	4	3	22	0	57	0	0	2	0	1.000	0	0-1	10	3.25	3.49
2007	SF	NL	59	8	0	9	101.2	437	94	39	39	9	4	3	2	40	7	80	1	1	4	7	.364	0	0-3	12	3.48	3.45

Year	Team	Lg	HOW MUCH HE PITCHED							WHAT HE GAVE UP												THE RESULTS							
			G	GS	CG	GF	IP	BFP	H	R	ER	HR	SH	SF	HB	TBB	IBB	SO	WP	Bk	W	L	Pct	Sh	Sv-Op	Hld	ERC	ERA
2008	SF	NL	25	19	0	2	110.0	514	141	80	74	15	3	5	4	47	3	66	5	0	3	8	.273	0	0-0	0	6.19	6.05
2009	SD	NL	33	33	1	0	198.0	830	194	92	86	17	9	3	4	64	6	142	5	1	12	11	.522	1	0-0	0	3.64	3.91
2010	SD	NL	28	26	0	0	145.0	641	152	89	87	20	6	5	5	64	6	115	3	0	10	10	.500	0	0-0	0	4.87	5.40
8 ML YEARS			231	105	1	27	741.0	3246	772	394	376	87	32	25	27	296	25	546	18	2	36	43	.456	1	0-4	22	4.53	4.57

Dan Cortes

Pitches: R **Bats:** R **Pos:** RP-4

Ht: 6'5" **Wt:** 205 **Born:** 3/4/1987 **Age:** 24

Year	Team	Lg	HOW MUCH HE PITCHED						WHAT HE GAVE UP												THE RESULTS							
			G	GS	CG	GF	IP	BFP	H	R	ER	HR	SH	SF	HB	TBB	IBB	SO	WP	Bk	W	L	Pct	Sh	Sv-Op	Hld	ERC	ERA
2005	Bristol	R+	15	7	0	3	38.1	171	44	23	22	2	0	2	4	13	0	38	3	0	1	4	.200	0	0- -	-	4.76	5.17
2006	Knapol	A	20	19	0	0	107.2	470	109	61	48	6	5	2	5	38	0	96	12	0	3	9	.250	0	0- -	-	3.78	4.01
2006	Burlgtn	A	7	7	0	0	35.0	165	40	27	26	7	2	2	3	17	0	30	2	0	1	2	.333	0	0- -	-	6.26	6.69
2007	Wilmg	A+	24	24	0	0	123.0	513	102	50	42	7	4	5	8	45	0	120	11	0	8	8	.500	0	0- -	-	2.99	3.07
2008	NWArk	AA	23	23	0	0	116.2	497	103	51	49	13	4	3	8	55	0	109	3	0	10	4	.714	0	0- -	-	4.13	3.78
2009	NWArk	AA	16	15	0	0	80.1	360	77	43	35	3	2	5	4	50	0	57	6	0	6	6	.500	0	0- -	-	4.48	3.92
2009	WTenn	AA	10	10	0	0	54.2	244	51	33	30	4	0	2	1	35	1	55	6	0	1	5	.167	0	0- -	-	4.51	4.94
2010	WTenn	AA	25	16	0	7	83.2	383	77	54	49	4	2	2	4	53	1	85	19	0	6	4	.600	0	1- -	-	4.22	5.27
2010	Tacom	AAA	9	0	0	7	12.2	54	13	8	7	1	1	0	2	4	0	13	2	0	1	2	.333	0	1- -	-	4.52	4.97
2010	Sea	AL	4	0	0	2	5.1	23	3	3	2	0	0	1	0	3	0	6	2	0	0	1	.000	0	0-1	0	1.66	3.38

Craig Counsell

Bats: L **Throws:** R **Pos:** PH-46; SS-42; 3B-20; 2B-3

Ht: 6'0" **Wt:** 179 **Born:** 8/21/1970 **Age:** 40

Year	Team	Lg	BATTING																			BASERUNNING				AVERAGES		
			G	AB	H	2B	3B	HR	(Hm	Rd)	TB	R	RBI	RC	TBB	IBB	SO	HBP	SH	SF	SB	CS	SB%	GDP	Avg	OBP	Slg
1995	Col	NL	3	1	0	0	0	0	(0	0)	0	0	0	0	1	0	0	0	0	0	0	0	-	0	.000	.500	.000
1997	2 Tms	NL	52	164	49	9	2	1	(1	0)	65	20	16	24	18	2	17	3	3	1	1	1	.50	5	.299	.376	.396
1998	Fla	NL	107	335	84	19	5	4	(2	2)	125	43	40	48	51	7	47	4	8	1	3	0	1.00	5	.251	.355	.373
1999	2 Tms	NL	87	174	38	7	0	0	(0	0)	45	24	11	12	14	0	24	0	5	2	1	0	1.00	2	.218	.274	.259
2000	Ari	NL	67	152	48	8	1	2	(0	2)	64	23	11	25	20	0	18	2	1	1	3	3	.50	4	.316	.400	.421
2001	Ari	NL	141	458	126	22	3	4	(4	0)	166	76	38	61	61	3	76	2	6	6	6	8	.43	9	.275	.359	.362
2002	Ari	NL	112	436	123	22	1	2	(0	2)	153	63	51	65	45	3	52	1	4	3	7	5	.58	10	.282	.348	.351
2003	Ari	NL	89	303	71	6	3	3	(3	0)	92	40	21	29	41	0	32	2	3	2	11	4	.73	4	.234	.328	.304
2004	Mil	NL	140	473	114	10	5	2	(1	1)	149	59	23	48	59	9	88	5	5	3	17	4	.81	5	.241	.330	.315
2005	Ari	NL	150	578	148	34	4	9	(5	4)	217	85	42	80	78	4	69	8	2	4	26	7	.79	8	.256	.350	.375
2006	Ari	NL	105	372	95	14	4	4	(3	1)	129	56	30	45	31	0	47	9	2	1	15	8	.65	1	.255	.327	.347
2007	Mil	NL	122	282	62	12	2	3	(0	3)	87	31	24	29	41	4	47	3	6	2	4	2	.67	7	.220	.323	.309
2008	Mil	NL	110	248	56	14	1	1	(1	0)	75	31	14	26	46	1	42	5	1	2	3	1	.75	5	.226	.355	.302
2009	Mil	NL	130	404	115	22	8	4	(2	2)	165	61	39	57	42	0	54	6	3	4	3	4	.43	12	.285	.357	.408
2010	Mil	NL	102	204	51	8	0	2	(1	1)	65	16	21	27	21	0	29	1	3	1	1	1	.50	0	.250	.322	.319
97	Col	NL	1	0	0	0	0	0	(0	0)	0	0	0	0	0	0	0	0	0	0	0	0	-	0	-	-	-
97	Fla	NL	51	164	49	9	2	1	(1	0)	65	20	16	24	18	2	17	3	3	1	1	1	.50	5	.299	.376	.396
99	Fla	NL	37	66	10	1	0	0	(0	0)	11	4	2	1	5	0	10	0	2	0	0	0	-	1	.152	.211	.167
99	LAD	NL	50	108	28	6	0	0	(0	0)	34	20	9	11	9	0	14	0	3	2	1	0	1.00	1	.259	.311	.315
	Postseason		35	114	27	5	0	2	(1	1)	38	12	14	11	12	3	23	1	7	1	2	0	1.00	1	.237	.313	.333
15 ML YEARS			1517	4584	1180	216	39	41	(23	18)	1597	628	381	576	569	33	642	51	52	33	101	48	.68	77	.257	.344	.348

Scott Cousins

Bats: L **Throws:** L **Pos:** PH-17; CF-8; RF-3; PR-1

Ht: 6'2" **Wt:** 190 **Born:** 1/22/1985 **Age:** 26

Year	Team	Lg	BATTING																			BASERUNNING				AVERAGES		
			G	AB	H	2B	3B	HR	(Hm	Rd)	TB	R	RBI	RC	TBB	IBB	SO	HBP	SH	SF	SB	CS	SB%	GDP	Avg	OBP	Slg
2006	Jmstwn	A-	21	90	19	1	0	1	(-	-)	23	11	6	5	4	0	17	1	2	0	3	1	.75	2	.211	.253	.256
2007	Grnsbr	A	110	421	123	25	0	18	(-	-)	202	69	74	74	38	3	92	7	3	3	16	7	.70	8	.292	.358	.480
2008	Jupiter	A+	49	191	58	9	2	9	(-	-)	98	35	29	37	20	2	47	0	0	0	11	3	.79	4	.304	.372	.513
2008	Mrlns	R	2	6	0	0	0	0	(-	-)	0	0	0	0	0	0	5	0	0	0	0	0	-	0	.000	.000	.000
2008	Carlina	AA	27	91	24	7	1	1	(-	-)	36	15	9	13	10	1	28	2	0	0	4	1	.80	1	.264	.350	.396
2009	Jaxnvl	AA	130	482	127	31	11	12	(-	-)	216	60	74	74	42	1	107	3	1	5	27	9	.75	6	.263	.323	.448
2010	NewOr	AAA	118	410	117	20	5	14	(-	-)	189	74	49	66	32	3	78	2	1	6	12	4	.75	2	.285	.336	.461
2010	Fla	NL	27	37	11	2	2	0	(0	0)	17	2	2	4	1	0	13	0	0	0	0	0	-	0	.297	.316	.459

Allen Craig

Bats: R **Throws:** R **Pos:** RF-30; PH-8; 1B-5; LF-5; 3B-2; 2B-1; PR-1

Ht: 6'2" **Wt:** 210 **Born:** 7/18/1984 **Age:** 26

Year	Team	Lg	BATTING																			BASERUNNING				AVERAGES		
			G	AB	H	2B	3B	HR	(Hm	Rd)	TB	R	RBI	RC	TBB	IBB	SO	HBP	SH	SF	SB	CS	SB%	GDP	Avg	OBP	Slg
2006	StCol	A-	48	175	45	13	0	4	(-	-)	70	21	29	24	13	0	28	7	1	5	0	0	-	1	.257	.325	.400
2007	PlmBh	A+	112	423	132	25	2	21	(-	-)	224	77	77	83	35	4	79	6	0	4	8	3	.73	10	.312	.370	.530
2007	Sprgfld	AA	7	24	7	2	0	3	(-	-)	18	5	3	5	1	0	6	0	0	0	0	0	-	1	.292	.320	.750
2008	Sprgfld	AA	129	506	154	30	0	22	(-	-)	250	84	86	94	48	1	87	10	0	4	2	1	.67	16	.304	.373	.494
2009	Memp	AAA	126	472	152	26	1	26	(-	-)	258	78	83	96	37	1	95	6	0	6	3	0	1.00	12	.322	.374	.547
2010	Memp	AAA	83	306	98	24	2	14	(-	-)	168	57	81	65	34	0	59	4	0	6	1	0	1.00	6	.320	.389	.549
2010	StL	NL	44	114	28	7	0	4	(3	1)	47	12	18	14	9	1	26	0	0	1	0	1	.00	1	.246	.298	.412

Jesse Crain

Pitches: R Bats: R Pos: RP-71   **Ht: 6'1" Wt: 215 Born: 7/5/1981 Age: 29**

			HOW MUCH HE PITCHED						WHAT HE GAVE UP											THE RESULTS						
Year	Team	Lg	G	GS	CG	GF	IP	BFP	H	R	ER	HR	SH	SF	HB	TBB	IBB	SO	WP	Bk	W	L	Pct	Sh	Sv-Op	Hld	ERC	ERA
2004	Min	AL	22	0	0	3	27.0	109	17	6	6	2	1	0	1	12	1	14	1	0	3	0	1.000	0	0-1	2	2.25	2.00
2005	Min	AL	75	0	0	17	79.2	326	61	28	24	6	9	3	5	29	7	25	2	0	12	5	.706	0	1-4	11	2.66	2.71
2006	Min	AL	68	0	0	24	76.2	325	79	31	30	6	1	2	2	18	2	60	1	0	4	5	.444	0	1-4	10	3.48	3.52
2007	Min	AL	18	0	0	5	16.1	71	19	16	10	4	0	1	1	4	0	10	0	1	1	2	.333	0	0-0	6	5.73	5.51
2008	Min	AL	66	0	0	14	62.2	268	62	29	25	6	0	2	1	24	3	50	2	0	5	4	.556	0	0-3	17	3.93	3.59
2009	Min	AL	56	0	0	15	51.2	230	48	28	27	3	3	3	5	27	3	43	1	1	7	4	.636	0	0-0	7	4.12	4.70
2010	Min	AL	71	0	0	16	68.0	278	53	27	23	5	3	0	1	27	4	62	3	0	1	1	.500	0	1-4	21	2.71	3.04
	Postseason		3	0	0	0	1.1	10	4	3	1	1	0	0	0	1	0	1	0	0	0	0	—	0	0-0	0	24.65	6.75
	7 ML YEARS		376	0	0	94	382.0	1607	339	165	145	32	17	11	16	141	20	264	10	2	33	21	.611	0	3-16	71	3.32	3.42

Bobby Cramer

Pitches: L Bats: L Pos: SP-4   **Ht: 6'1" Wt: 193 Born: 10/28/1979 Age: 31**

			HOW MUCH HE PITCHED						WHAT HE GAVE UP											THE RESULTS						
Year	Team	Lg	G	GS	CG	GF	IP	BFP	H	R	ER	HR	SH	SF	HB	TBB	IBB	SO	WP	Bk	W	L	Pct	Sh	Sv-Op	Hld	ERC	ERA
2003	HudVal	A-	5	2	0	2	10.2	41	9	2	2	1	1	0	0	1	0	6	0	0	0	1	.000	0	1--	-	2.13	1.69
2003	Bkrsfld	A+	5	0	0	0	12.2	52	10	6	5	1	1	0	0	5	0	10	0	0	0	0	-	0	0--	-	2.80	3.55
2004	CtnSC	A	35	0	0	12	62.1	254	52	27	23	4	0	0	4	12	0	48	6	1	6	4	.600	0	4--	-	2.41	3.32
2007	Stcktn	A+	9	8	0	0	45.0	192	45	23	19	1	0	1	5	10	1	41	4	0	4	1	.800	0	0--	-	3.22	3.80
2007	Mdland	AA	12	7	0	0	52.1	213	45	17	11	3	2	0	1	10	0	50	5	0	5	1	.833	0	0--	-	2.32	1.89
2008	OgCty	IND	19	13	5	1	92.2	403	100	53	40	8	4	1	6	16	0	95	3	0	7	4	.636	0	0--	-	3.66	3.88
2009	Scrmto	AAA	6	1	0	2	14.0	73	24	11	10	0	1	2	0	8	2	14	0	0	1	1	.500	0	0--	-	7.94	6.43
2009	Stcktn	A+	2	0	0	1	5.2	24	4	1	1	1	0	0	1	2	0	6	0	0	1	0	1.000	0	0--	-	3.42	1.59
2009	Mdland	AA	12	8	0	0	43.0	194	48	29	16	1	3	1	2	13	0	39	3	0	3	4	.429	0	0--	-	3.82	3.35
2010	Scrmto	AAA	7	7	0	0	41.2	174	41	10	9	0	0	0	0	11	0	35	3	0	2	2	.500	0	0--	-	2.79	1.94
2010	Oak	AL	4	4	0	0	23.2	93	20	8	8	5	1	0	0	6	0	13	0	0	2	1	.667	0	0-0	0	3.47	3.04

Carl Crawford

Bats: L Throws: L Pos: LF-147; DH-3; PR-3; PH-2   **Ht: 6'2" Wt: 215 Born: 8/5/1981 Age: 29**

						BATTING														BASERUNNING				AVERAGES		
Year	Team	Lg	G	AB	H	2B	3B	HR	(Hm	Rd)	TB	R	RBI	RC	TBB	IBB	SO	HBP	SH	SF	SB	CS	SB%	GDP	Avg	OBP	Slg
2002	TB	AL	63	259	67	11	6	2	(1	1)	96	23	30	34	9	0	41	3	6	1	9	5	.64	0	.259	.290	.371
2003	TB	AL	151	630	177	18	9	5	(5	0)	228	80	54	80	26	4	102	1	1	3	55	10	.85	5	.281	.309	.362
2004	TB	AL	152	626	185	26	19	11	(6	5)	282	104	55	96	35	2	81	1	4	6	59	15	.80	2	.296	.331	.450
2005	TB	AL	156	644	194	33	15	15	(5	10)	302	101	81	102	27	1	84	5	5	6	46	8	.85	11	.301	.331	.469
2006	TB	AL	151	600	183	20	16	18	(7	11)	289	89	77	113	37	3	85	4	9	2	58	9	.87	8	.305	.348	.482
2007	TB	AL	143	584	184	37	9	11	(6	5)	272	93	80	97	32	5	112	5	1	2	50	10	.83	11	.315	.355	.466
2008	TB	AL	109	443	121	12	10	8	(3	5)	177	69	57	57	30	1	60	2	0	5	25	7	.78	10	.273	.319	.400
2009	TB	AL	156	606	185	28	8	15	(9	6)	274	96	68	91	51	1	99	8	2	5	60	16	.79	7	.305	.364	.452
2010	TB	AL	154	600	184	30	13	19	(11	8)	297	110	90	120	46	3	104	3	3	5	47	10	.82	2	.307	.356	.495
	Postseason		16	62	18	3	1	2	(1	1)	29	9	8	11	3	0	10	1	0	0	7	0	1.00	6	.290	.333	.468
	9 ML YEARS		1235	4992	1480	215	105	104	(53	51)	2217	765	592	790	293	20	768	32	31	35	409	90	.82	56	.296	.337	.444

Coco Crisp

Bats: B Throws: R Pos: CF-73; DH-1; PH-1   **Ht: 6'0" Wt: 180 Born: 11/1/1979 Age: 31**

						BATTING														BASERUNNING				AVERAGES		
Year	Team	Lg	G	AB	H	2B	3B	HR	(Hm	Rd)	TB	R	RBI	RC	TBB	IBB	SO	HBP	SH	SF	SB	CS	SB%	GDP	Avg	OBP	Slg
2010	Stcktn*	A+	2	6	5	0	1	1	(-	-)	10	2	3	5	1	0	0	0	0	0	0	0	-	0	.833	.857	1.667
2010	Scrmto*	AAA	6	22	13	2	1	0	(-	-)	17	7	5	8	2	1	3	0	0	0	2	1	.67	0	.591	.625	.773
2002	Cle	AL	32	127	33	9	2	1	(1	0)	49	16	9	19	1	0	19	0	3	2	4	1	.80	0	.260	.314	.386
2003	Cle	AL	99	414	110	15	6	3	(3	0)	146	55	27	48	23	1	51	0	7	3	15	9	.63	4	.266	.302	.353
2004	Cle	AL	139	491	146	24	2	15	(8	7)	219	78	71	72	36	4	69	0	9	2	20	13	.61	8	.297	.344	.446
2005	Cle	AL	145	594	178	42	4	16	(4	12)	276	86	69	92	44	1	81	0	13	5	15	6	.71	7	.300	.345	.465
2006	Bos	AL	105	413	109	22	2	8	(4	4)	159	58	36	51	31	1	67	1	7	0	22	4	.85	5	.264	.317	.385
2007	Bos	AL	145	526	141	28	7	6	(1	5)	201	85	60	68	50	1	84	1	9	5	28	6	.82	12	.268	.330	.382
2008	Bos	AL	118	361	102	18	3	7	(1	6)	147	55	41	49	35	0	59	1	8	4	20	7	.74	6	.283	.344	.407
2009	KC	AL	49	180	41	8	5	3	(0	3)	68	30	14	25	29	1	23	1	4	1	13	2	.87	4	.228	.336	.378
2010	Oak	AL	75	290	81	14	4	8	(6	2)	127	51	38	49	30	0	49	0	3	5	32	3	.91	6	.279	.342	.438
	Postseason		20	57	16	3	0	0	(0	0)	19	7	3	6	6	0	12	0	0	0	3	0	1.00	3	.281	.349	.333
	9 ML YEARS		907	3396	941	180	35	67	(28	39)	1392	514	365	473	289	9	502	4	63	27	169	51	.77	52	.277	.332	.410

Bobby Crosby

Bats: R Throws: R Pos: PH-23; SS-22; 2B-16; 3B-10; 1B-7; PR-2   **Ht: 6'3" Wt: 203 Born: 1/12/1980 Age: 31**

						BATTING														BASERUNNING				AVERAGES		
Year	Team	Lg	G	AB	H	2B	3B	HR	(Hm	Rd)	TB	R	RBI	RC	TBB	IBB	SO	HBP	SH	SF	SB	CS	SB%	GDP	Avg	OBP	Slg
2003	Oak	AL	11	12	0	0	0	0	(0	0)	0	1	0	0	1	0	5	1	0	0	0	0	-	0	.000	.143	.000
2004	Oak	AL	151	545	130	34	1	22	(11	11)	232	70	64	60	58	0	141	9	5	6	7	3	.70	20	.239	.319	.426
2005	Oak	AL	84	333	92	25	4	9	(3	6)	152	66	38	47	35	0	54	1	1	1	0	0	-	10	.276	.346	.456
2006	Oak	AL	96	358	82	12	0	9	(3	6)	121	42	40	38	36	1	76	0	2	2	8	1	.89	11	.229	.298	.338
2007	Oak	AL	93	349	79	16	0	8	(7	1)	119	40	31	26	23	1	62	2	0	0	10	2	.83	11	.226	.278	.341
2008	Oak	AL	145	556	132	39	1	7	(2	5)	194	66	61	52	47	0	96	0	0	2	7	3	.70	18	.237	.296	.349
2009	Oak	AL	97	238	53	10	2	6	(2	4)	85	35	29	21	24	0	44	2	4	4	2	1	.67	7	.223	.295	.357

Year Team	Lg	G	AB	H	2B	3B	HR	(Hm	Rd)	TB	R	RBI	RC	TBB	IBB	SO	HBP	SH	SF	SB	CS	SB%	GDP	Avg	OBP	Slg
2010 2 Tms	NL	70	168	37	10	0	1	(0	1)	50	9	13	15	17	2	38	1	2	1	0	3	.00	2	.220	.294	.298
10 Pit	NL	61	156	35	8	0	1	(0	1)	46	9	11	15	16	2	33	1	2	0	0	2	.00	1	.224	.301	.295
10 Ari	NL	9	12	2	2	0	0	(0	0)	4	0	2	0	1	0	5	0	0	1	0	1	.00	1	.167	.214	.333
8 ML YEARS		747	2559	605	146	8	62	(28	34)	953	329	276	259	241	4	516	16	14	16	34	13	.72	79	.236	.304	.372

Trevor Crowe

Bats: B Throws: R Pos: CF-68; LF-48; PH-7; RF-4; PR-1   Ht: 6'0" Wt: 190 Born: 11/17/1983 Age: 27

Year Team	Lg	G	AB	H	2B	3B	HR	(Hm	Rd)	TB	R	RBI	RC	TBB	IBB	SO	HBP	SH	SF	SB	CS	SB%	GDP	Avg	OBP	Slg
2005 MhVlly	A-	12	51	13	2	1	1	(-	-)	20	9	6	7	6	0	8	1	0	0	4	3	.57	0	.255	.345	.392
2005 Lk Cty	A	44	178	46	8	2	0	(-	-)	58	18	23	20	18	1	25	1	0	4	7	5	.58	6	.258	.327	.326
2005 Akron	AA	3	10	1	0	0	0	(-	-)	1	1	0	0	0	0	3	0	0	0	0	0	-	0	.100	.100	.100
2006 Knstn	A+	60	219	72	15	2	4	(-	-)	103	51	31	53	48	0	46	2	1	3	29	6	.83	6	.329	.449	.470
2006 Lk Cty	A	2	5	0	0	0	0	(-	-)	0	0	0	0	0	0	1	0	0	0	0	0	-	0	.000	.000	.000
2006 Akron	AA	39	154	36	7	2	1	(-	-)	50	20	13	24	20	1	24	0	0	2	16	6	.73	6	.234	.318	.325
2007 Akron	AA	133	518	134	26	4	5	(-	-)	183	87	50	70	62	3	71	4	2	3	28	9	.76	15	.259	.341	.353
2008 Akron	AA	49	198	64	16	2	4	(-	-)	96	45	28	40	27	1	29	1	1	2	13	5	.72	3	.323	.404	.485
2008 Buffalo	AAA	35	146	40	12	2	5	(-	-)	71	25	13	25	15	1	43	2	1	0	5	2	.71	0	.274	.350	.486
2009 Clmbs	AAA	49	185	55	11	1	2	(-	-)	74	27	20	32	30	2	31	2	2	0	14	7	.67	5	.297	.401	.400
2010 Clmbs	AAA	29	119	29	4	1	1	(-	-)	38	21	13	11	7	1	19	0	1	2	6	1	.86	2	.244	.281	.319
2009 Cle	AL	68	183	43	9	3	1	(0	1)	61	22	17	18	11	0	39	1	4	3	6	0	1.00	7	.235	.278	.333
2010 Cle	AL	122	442	111	24	3	2	(1	1)	147	48	36	43	29	1	73	3	5	0	20	7	.74	13	.251	.302	.333
2 ML YEARS		190	625	154	33	6	3	(1	2)	208	70	53	61	40	1	112	4	9	3	26	7	.79	20	.246	.295	.333

Juan Cruz

Pitches: R Bats: R Pos: RP-5   Ht: 6'1" Wt: 165 Born: 10/15/1978 Age: 32

Year Team	Lg	G	GS	CG	GF	IP	BFP	H	R	ER	HR	SH	SF	HB	TBB	IBB	SO	WP	Bk	W	L	Pct	Sh	Sv-Op	Hld	ERC	ERA
2001 ChC	NL	8	8	0	0	44.2	185	40	16	16	4	2	0	2	17	1	39	0	0	3	1	.750	0	0-0	0	3.59	3.22
2002 ChC	NL	45	9	0	14	97.1	431	84	56	43	11	7	8	8	59	4	81	1	0	3	11	.214	0	1-4	3	4.49	3.98
2003 ChC	NL	25	6	0	3	61.0	284	66	44	41	7	7	2	7	28	0	65	4	0	2	7	.222	0	0-1	1	5.23	6.05
2004 Atl	NL	50	0	0	22	72.0	300	59	24	22	7	4	1	2	30	1	70	1	0	6	2	.750	0	0-0	2	3.25	2.75
2005 Oak	AL	28	0	0	14	32.2	159	38	33	27	5	0	2	4	22	4	34	3	0	0	3	.000	0	0-0	0	6.87	7.44
2006 Ari	NL	31	15	0	5	94.2	413	80	45	44	7	5	2	11	47	2	88	2	0	5	6	.455	0	0-0	0	3.82	4.18
2007 Ari	NL	53	0	0	15	61.0	262	45	28	21	7	2	2	5	32	3	87	1	2	1	6	.857	0	0-0	4	3.43	3.10
2008 Ari	NL	57	0	0	10	51.2	215	34	17	15	5	2	2	3	31	0	71	1	0	4	0	1.000	0	0-2	8	3.25	2.61
2009 KC	AL	46	0	0	18	50.1	219	46	34	32	6	1	1	1	29	1	38	6	0	3	4	.429	0	2-6	7	4.55	5.72
2010 KC	AL	5	0	0	1	5.1	28	9	2	2	0	1	0	0	4	0	7	0	0	0	1	.000	0	0-1	0	9.07	3.38
Postseason		8	0	0	2	9.0	44	7	5	4	0	1	0	1	8	0	15	1	0	0	0	-	0	0-0	0	4.12	4.00
10 ML YEARS		340	30	0	102	570.2	2496	501	299	263	59	31	20	43	200	16	580	10	2	32	35	.478	0	3 14	25	4.16	4.15

Luis Cruz

Bats: R Throws: R Pos: SS-5; PH-2   Ht: 6'1" Wt: 213 Born: 2/10/1984 Age: 27

Year Team	Lg	G	AB	H	2B	3B	HR	(Hm	Rd)	TB	R	RBI	RC	TBB	IBB	SO	HBP	SH	SF	SB	CS	SB%	GDP	Avg	OBP	Slg
2010 Nashv*	AAA	129	488	137	29	3	10	(-	-)	202	54	68	64	15	0	56	7	4	4	0	0	-	20	.281	.309	.414
2008 Pit	NL	22	67	15	3	0	0	(0	0)	18	6	3	4	3	0	2	2	2	0	1	1	.50	3	.224	.278	.269
2009 Pit	NL	27	70	15	1	0	0	(0	0)	16	5	2	3	6	1	7	1	0	1	0	0	-	1	.214	.282	.229
2010 Mil	NL	7	17	4	0	1	0	(0	0)	6	2	1	2	0	0	2	0	0	0	0	0	-	1	.235	.235	.353
3 ML YEARS		56	154	34	4	1	0	(0	0)	40	13	6	9	9	1	11	3	2	1	1	1	.50	5	.221	.275	.260

Nelson Cruz

Bats: R Throws: R Pos: RF-94; LF-14; PH-5; DH-2   Ht: 6'2" Wt: 240 Born: 7/1/1980 Age: 30

Year Team	Lg	G	AB	H	2B	3B	HR	(Hm	Rd)	TB	R	RBI	RC	TBB	IBB	SO	HBP	SH	SF	SB	CS	SB%	GDP	Avg	OBP	Slg
2010 OKCity*	AAA	5	19	4	1	0	0	(-	-)	5	1	4	1	2	0	5	0	0	1	0	0	-	3	.211	.273	.263
2010 Frisco*	AA	3	11	4	1	0	0	(-	-)	5	1	1	2	1	0	0	0	0	1	1	0	1.00	2	.364	.385	.455
2005 Mil	NL	8	5	1	1	0	0	(0	0)	2	1	0	1	2	0	0	0	0	0	0	0	-	0	.200	.429	.400
2006 Tex	AL	41	130	29	3	0	6	(3	3)	50	15	22	18	7	0	32	0	0	1	1	0	1.00	1	.223	.261	.385
2007 Tex	AL	96	307	72	15	2	9	(4	5)	118	35	34	32	21	1	87	2	1	4	2	4	.33	5	.235	.287	.384
2008 Tex	AL	31	115	38	9	1	7	(4	3)	70	19	26	30	17	2	28	1	0	0	3	1	.75	1	.330	.421	.609
2009 Tex	AL	128	462	120	21	1	33	(18	15)	242	75	76	72	49	6	118	2	0	2	20	4	.83	9	.260	.332	.524
2010 Tex	AL	108	399	127	31	3	22	(13	9)	230	60	78	77	38	5	81	1	1	6	17	4	.81	12	.318	.374	.576
6 ML YEARS		412	1418	387	80	7	77	(42	35)	712	205	236	230	134	14	346	6	2	10	43	13	.77	28	.273	.336	.502

Michael Cuddyer

Bats: R Throws: R Pos: 1B-84; RF-66; 3B-14; CF-2; 2B-1; PH-1   cuh-DYE-err   Ht: 6'2" Wt: 225 Born: 3/27/1979 Age: 32

Year Team	Lg	G	AB	H	2B	3B	HR	(Hm	Rd)	TB	R	RBI	RC	TBB	IBB	SO	HBP	SH	SF	SB	CS	SB%	GDP	Avg	OBP	Slg
2001 Min	AL	8	18	4	2	0	0	(0	0)	6	1	1	2	2	0	6	0	0	0	1	0	1.00	1	.222	.300	.333
2002 Min	AL	41	112	29	7	0	4	(2	2)	48	12	13	14	8	0	30	1	1	1	2	0	1.00	3	.259	.311	.429
2003 Min	AL	35	102	25	1	3	4	(1	3)	44	14	8	10	12	0	19	0	0	0	1	1	.50	6	.245	.325	.431
2004 Min	AL	115	339	89	22	1	12	(8	4)	149	49	45	51	37	2	74	3	2	1	5	5	.50	8	.263	.339	.440
2005 Min	AL	126	422	111	25	3	12	(8	4)	178	57	42	43	41	5	93	3	1	3	3	4	.43	19	.263	.330	.422
2006 Min	AL	150	557	158	41	5	24	(15	9)	281	102	109	101	62	5	130	10	0	6	6	0	1.00	11	.284	.362	.504

Year Team	Lg	G	AB	H	2B	3B	HR	(Hm	Rd)	TB	R	RBI	RC	TBB	IBB	SO	HBP	SH	SF	SB	CS	SB%	GDP	Avg	OBP	Slg
2007 Min	AL	144	547	151	28	5	16	(8	8)	237	87	81	82	64	1	107	7	0	5	5	0	1.00	19	.276	.356	.433
2008 Min	AL	71	249	62	13	4	3	(1	2)	92	30	36	37	25	4	40	5	0	0	5	1	.83	7	.249	.330	.369
2009 Min	AL	153	588	162	34	7	32	(18	14)	306	93	94	89	54	3	118	6	0	2	6	1	.86	22	.276	.342	.520
2010 Min	AL	157	609	165	37	5	14	(7	7)	254	93	81	77	58	7	93	4	0	4	7	3	.70	26	.271	.336	.417
Postseason		19	63	23	1	1	1	(1	0)	29	4	6	3	4	1	14	0	0	0	0	2	.00	1	.365	.403	.460
10 ML YEARS		1000	3543	956	210	33	121	(68	53)	1595	536	510	506	363	27	710	39	4	22	41	15	.73	122	.270	.342	.450

Johnny Cueto

Pitches: R **Bats:** R **Pos:** SP-31   KWAY-toe   **Ht:** 5'10" **Wt:** 211 **Born:** 2/15/1986 **Age:** 25

Year Team	Lg	G	GS	CG	GF	IP	BFP	H	R	ER	HR	SH	SF	HB	TBB	IBB	SO	WP	Bk	W	L	Pct	Sh	Sv-Op	Hld	ERC	ERA
2008 Cin	NL	31	31	0	0	174.0	769	178	101	93	29	9	5	14	68	1	158	6	1	9	14	.391	0	0-0	0	4.95	4.81
2009 Cin	NL	30	30	0	0	171.1	740	172	90	84	24	5	3	14	61	0	132	4	0	11	11	.500	0	0-0	0	4.57	4.41
2010 Cin	NL	31	31	1	0	185.2	780	181	79	75	19	9	3	9	56	5	138	5	2	12	7	.632	1	0-0	0	3.75	3.64
3 ML YEARS		92	92	1	0	531.0	2289	531	270	252	72	23	11	37	185	6	428	15	3	32	32	.500	1	0-0	0	4.40	4.27

Aaron Cunningham

Bats: R **Throws:** R **Pos:** LF-23; RF-17; PH-17; CF-2   **Ht:** 5'11" **Wt:** 203 **Born:** 4/24/1986 **Age:** 25

Year Team	Lg	G	AB	H	2B	3B	HR	(Hm	Rd)	TB	R	RBI	RC	TBB	IBB	SO	HBP	SH	SF	SB	CS	SB%	GDP	Avg	OBP	Slg
2010 Portlnd*	AAA	80	271	68	17	3	7	(-	-)	112	30	45	37	28	0	68	6	2	1	2	7	.22	8	.251	.333	.413
2008 Oak	AL	22	80	20	7	1	1	(1	0)	32	7	14	12	6	1	24	1	0	0	2	0	1.00	1	.250	.310	.400
2009 Oak	AL	23	53	8	2	0	1	(0	1)	13	6	6	3	3	0	16	1	0	0	1	0	-	3	.151	.211	.245
2010 SD	NL	53	132	38	12	1	1	(1	0)	55	17	15	16	7	1	28	3	2	3	1	3	.25	3	.288	.331	.417
3 ML YEARS		98	265	66	21	2	3	(2	1)	100	30	35	31	16	2	68	5	2	3	3	3	.50	7	.249	.301	.377

Colin Curtis

Bats: L **Throws:** L **Pos:** RF-17; PH-12; LF-7; DH-2; PR-2   **Ht:** 6'1" **Wt:** 200 **Born:** 2/1/1985 **Age:** 26

Year Team	Lg	G	AB	H	2B	3B	HR	(Hm	Rd)	TB	R	RBI	RC	TBB	IBB	SO	HBP	SH	SF	SB	CS	SB%	GDP	Avg	OBP	Slg
2006 Yanks	R	3	8	4	2	0	1	(-	-)	9	3	4	4	1	0	0	1	0	0	1	0	1.00	0	.500	.600	1.125
2006 StIslnd	A-	44	159	48	9	2	1	(-	-)	64	25	18	23	12	1	19	4	0	2	4	5	.44	3	.302	.362	.403
2007 Tampa	A+	65	245	73	9	2	5	(-	-)	101	37	26	39	29	2	43	3	3	1	4	4	.50	5	.298	.378	.412
2007 Trntn	AA	61	240	58	11	1	3	(-	-)	80	32	15	24	17	1	47	3	0	2	1	1	.50	4	.242	.298	.333
2008 Trntn	AA	131	490	123	20	3	9	(-	-)	176	66	68	62	55	9	86	3	2	7	6	3	.67	11	.251	.326	.359
2009 Trntn	AA	56	213	57	14	4	1	(-	-)	82	28	19	31	20	1	37	5	1	1	7	0	1.00	4	.268	.343	.385
2009 S-WB	AAA	70	251	59	10	0	6	(-	-)	87	29	29	27	24	0	46	1	1	2	1	2	.33	4	.235	.302	.347
2010 S-WB	AAA	66	239	69	24	0	5	(-	-)	108	28	27	39	21	3	38	6	1	2	1	2	.33	5	.289	.358	.452
2010 NYY	AL	31	59	11	3	0	1	(1	0)	17	7	8	5	4	0	15	1	0	0	0	0	-	0	.186	.250	.288

Jack Cust

Bats: L **Throws:** R **Pos:** DH-90; LF-13; PH-9; RF-3   **Ht:** 6'1" **Wt:** 235 **Born:** 1/7/1979 **Age:** 32

Year Team	Lg	G	AB	H	2B	3B	HR	(Hm	Rd)	TB	R	RBI	RC	TBB	IBB	SO	HBP	SH	SF	SB	CS	SB%	GDP	Avg	OBP	Slg
2010 Scrmto*	AAA	33	110	30	6	0	4	(-	-)	48	21	19	24	33	2	33	1	0	0	0	0	-	2	.273	.444	.436
2001 Ari	NL	3	2	1	0	0	0	(0	0)	1	0	0	1	0	0	0	0	0	0	0	0	-	0	.500	.667	.500
2002 Col	NL	35	65	11	2	0	1	(0	1)	16	8	8	6	12	0	32	0	0	1	0	1	.00	3	.169	.295	.246
2003 Bal	AL	27	73	19	7	0	4	(2	2)	38	7	11	17	10	0	25	1	0	0	0	0	-	0	.260	.357	.521
2004 Bal	AL	1	1	0	0	0	0	(0	0)	0	0	0	0	0	0	1	0	0	0	0	0	-	0	.000	.000	.000
2006 SD	NL	4	3	1	0	0	0	(0	0)	1	1	0	0	0	0	1	0	0	0	0	0	-	0	.333	.333	.333
2007 Oak	AL	124	395	101	18	1	26	(14	12)	199	61	82	87	105	2	164	1	0	6	0	2	.00	6	.256	.408	.504
2008 Oak	AL	148	481	111	19	0	33	(20	13)	229	77	77	84	111	3	197	2	0	4	0	0	-	7	.231	.375	.476
2009 Oak	AL	149	513	123	16	0	25	(14	11)	214	88	70	83	93	5	185	2	0	4	4	1	.80	7	.240	.356	.417
2010 Oak	AL	112	349	95	19	0	13	(7	6)	153	50	52	58	68	0	127	5	0	3	2	2	.50	6	.272	.395	.438
9 ML YEARS		603	1882	462	81	1	102	(57	45)	851	292	300	336	400	10	732	11	0	18	6	6	.50	29	.245	.378	.452

Casey Daigle

Pitches: R **Bats:** R **Pos:** RP-13   DAY-gull   **Ht:** 6'5" **Wt:** 226 **Born:** 4/4/1981 **Age:** 30

Year Team	Lg	G	GS	CG	GF	IP	BFP	H	R	ER	HR	SH	SF	HB	TBB	IBB	SO	WP	Bk	W	L	Pct	Sh	Sv-Op	Hld	ERC	ERA
2010 RdRck*	AAA	35	0	0	29	44.0	196	54	27	24	6	0	0	1	13	2	35	2	0	2	3	.400	0	8--	-	5.24	4.91
2004 Ari	NL	10	10	0	0	49.0	230	63	41	39	9	3	1	2	27	3	17	1	1	2	3	.400	0	0-0	0	7.30	7.16
2006 Ari	NL	10	0	0	1	12.1	52	14	5	5	1	0	1	0	6	0	7	0	0	0	0	-	0	0-0	2	5.46	3.65
2010 Hou	NL	13	0	0	4	10.1	63	25	13	13	3	0	0	0	6	1	6	4	0	1	1	.500	0	0-0	3	15.75	11.32
3 ML YEARS		33	10	0	5	71.2	345	102	59	57	13	3	2	2	39	4	30	5	1	3	4	.429	0	0-0	5	8.10	7.16

Matt Daley

Pitches: R Bats: R Pos: RP-28   Ht: 6'2" Wt: 180 Born: 6/23/1982 Age: 29

Year	Team	Lg	G	GS	CG	GF	IP	BFP	H	R	ER	HR	SH	SF	HB	TBB	IBB	SO	WP	Bk	W	L	Pct	Sh	Sv-Op	Hld	ERC	ERA
2004	Casper	R+	21	0	0	7	30.1	131	31	19	16	3	0	0	4	5	1	30	1	0	2	1	.667	0	0--	-	3.65	4.75
2005	Ashvll	A	45	0	0	21	79.0	349	90	46	35	10	2	3	12	16	0	49	5	0	8	2	.800	0	1--	-	4.86	3.99
2006	Mdest	A+	51	0	0	27	68.2	298	70	27	24	3	0	3	4	20	0	79	3	0	4	3	.571	0	15--	-	3.53	3.15
2006	Tulsa	AA	3	0	0	0	6.1	24	4	1	1	0	0	1	0	3	0	2	0	0	0	0	-	0	0--	-	1.99	1.42
2007	Tulsa	AA	43	10	0	7	95.1	400	83	40	37	12	2	5	6	22	3	84	3	0	2	6	.250	0	0--	-	3.00	3.49
2008	Tulsa	AA	3	0	0	0	4.0	18	5	1	1	0	0	0	0	1	0	4	0	0	0	0	-	0	0--	-	4.05	2.25
2008	ColSpr	AAA	60	0	0	17	62.1	278	56	27	26	6	2	6	5	33	3	61	5	0	4	6	.400	0	1--	-	4.17	3.75
2009	ColSpr	AAA	7	0	0	1	10.0	38	8	1	1	0	0	0	0	1	0	19	0	0	0	0	-	0	0--	-	1.52	0.90
2010	ColSpr	AAA	6	0	0	2	5.1	28	10	8	8	2	1	0	0	3	0	7	0	0	0	0	-	0	0--	-	13.34	13.50
2010	Tulsa	AA	3	0	0	0	3.0	10	1	1	1	1	0	0	0	0	0	1	0	0	0	0	-	0	0--	-	0.80	3.00
2009	Col	NL	57	0	0	15	51.0	211	43	24	24	6	2	3	2	18	2	55	0	0	1	1	.500	0	0-3	12	3.27	4.24
2010	Col	NL	28	0	0	4	23.1	108	27	11	11	2	2	1	3	10	1	18	1	0	0	1	.000	0	0-0	6	5.41	4.24
	Postseason		1	0	0	0	1.0	5	1	0	0	0	1	0	0	1	0	0	1	0	0	0	-	0	0-0	0	5.48	0.00
	2 ML YEARS		85	0	0	19	74.1	319	70	35	35	8	4	4	5	28	3	73	1	0	1	2	.333	0	0-3	18	3.92	4.24

Johnny Damon

Bats: L Throws: L Pos: DH-98; LF-33; PH-13; CF-4   Ht: 6'2" Wt: 205 Born: 11/5/1973 Age: 37

Year	Team	Lg	G	AB	H	2B	3B	HR	(Hm	Rd)	TB	R	RBI	RC	TBB	IBB	SO	HBP	SH	SF	SB	CS	SB%	GDP	Avg	OBP	Slg
1995	KC	AL	47	188	53	11	5	3	(1	2)	83	32	23	29	12	0	22	1	2	3	7	0	1.00	2	.282	.324	.441
1996	KC	AL	145	517	140	22	5	6	(3	3)	190	61	50	64	31	3	64	3	10	5	25	5	.83	4	.271	.313	.368
1997	KC	AL	146	472	130	12	8	8	(3	5)	182	70	48	63	42	2	70	3	6	1	16	10	.62	3	.275	.338	.386
1998	KC	AL	161	642	178	30	10	18	(11	7)	282	104	66	98	58	4	84	4	3	3	26	12	.68	4	.277	.339	.439
1999	KC	AL	145	583	179	39	9	14	(5	9)	278	101	77	108	67	5	50	3	3	4	36	6	.86	13	.307	.379	.477
2000	KC	AL	159	655	214	42	10	16	(10	6)	324	136	88	129	65	4	60	1	8	12	46	9	.84	7	.327	.382	.495
2001	Oak	AL	155	644	165	34	4	9	(2	7)	234	108	49	79	61	1	70	5	5	4	27	12	.69	7	.256	.324	.363
2002	Bos	AL	154	623	178	34	11	14	(5	9)	276	118	63	101	65	3	70	6	3	5	31	6	.84	4	.286	.356	.443
2003	Bos	AL	145	608	166	32	6	12	(5	7)	246	103	67	92	68	4	74	2	6	6	30	6	.83	5	.273	.345	.405
2004	Bos	AL	150	621	189	35	6	20	(9	11)	296	123	94	115	76	2	71	2	0	3	19	8	.70	5	.304	.380	.477
2005	Bos	AL	148	624	197	35	6	10	(3	7)	274	117	75	105	53	3	69	2	0	9	18	1	.95	5	.316	.366	.439
2006	NYY	AL	149	593	169	35	5	24	(13	11)	286	115	80	99	67	1	85	4	2	5	25	10	.71	4	.285	.359	.482
2007	NYY	AL	141	533	144	27	2	12	(5	7)	211	93	63	84	66	1	79	2	1	3	27	3	.90	4	.270	.351	.396
2008	NYY	Al	143	555	168	27	5	17	(7	10)	256	95	71	109	64	0	82	1	2	1	29	8	.78	6	.303	.375	.461
2009	NYY	AL	143	550	155	36	3	24	(17	7)	269	107	82	97	71	1	98	2	2	1	12	0	1.00	9	.282	.365	.489
2010	Det	AL	145	539	146	36	5	8	(7	1)	216	81	51	73	69	2	90	2	2	1	11	1	.92	5	.271	.355	.401
	Postseason		55	244	68	12	2	9	(3	6)	111	36	30	36	17	0	36	1	0	0	13	1	.93	5	.279	.328	.455
	16 ML YEARS		2276	8947	2571	487	100	215	(106	109)	3903	1564	1047	1445	935	37	1138	43	55	66	385	97	.80	90	.287	.355	.436

John Danks

Pitches: L Bats: L Pos: SP-32   Ht: 6'2" Wt: 210 Born: 4/15/1985 Age: 26

Year	Team	Lg	G	GS	CG	GF	IP	BFP	H	R	ER	HR	SH	SF	HB	TBB	IBB	SO	WP	Bk	W	L	Pct	Sh	Sv-Op	Hld	ERC	ERA
2007	CWS	AL	26	26	0	0	139.0	622	160	92	85	28	7	4	4	54	4	109	3	0	6	13	.316	0	0-0	0	5.73	5.50
2008	CWS	AL	33	33	0	0	195.0	804	182	74	72	15	2	2	4	57	1	159	7	0	12	9	.571	0	0-0	0	3.26	3.32
2009	CWS	AL	32	32	1	0	200.1	839	184	89	84	28	5	6	5	73	1	149	1	0	13	11	.542	0	0-0	0	3.89	3.77
2010	CWS	AL	32	32	1	0	213.0	878	189	93	88	18	5	0	4	70	2	162	3	0	15	11	.577	1	0-0	0	3.18	3.72
	Postseason		1	1	0	0	6.2	30	7	3	3	1	0	0	0	3	0	7	0	0	1	0	1.000	0	0-0	0	4.81	4.05
	4 ML YEARS		123	123	2	0	747.1	3143	715	348	329	89	19	12	17	254	8	579	13	1	46	44	.511	1	0-0	0	3.84	3.96

Yu Darvish

Pitches: R Bats: R Pos: P   Ht: 6'5" Wt: 198 Born: 8/16/1986 Age: 24

Year	Team	Lg	G	GS	CG	GF	IP	BFP	H	R	ER	HR	SH	SF	HB	TBB	IBB	SO	WP	Bk	W	L	Pct	Sh	Sv-Op	Hld	ERC	ERA
2005	HNHF	Jap	14	-	2	-	94.1	410	97	37	37	7	-	-	3	48	-	52	2	0	5	5	.500	1	0--	-	4.74	3.53
2006	HNHF	Jap	25	-	3	-	149.2	627	128	55	48	12	-	-	6	64	-	115	5	1	12	5	.706	2	0--	-	3.46	2.89
2007	HNHF	Jap	26	-	12	-	207.2	790	123	48	42	9	-	-	13	49	-	210	4	0	15	5	.750	3	0--	-	1.48	1.82
2008	HNHF	Jap	25	-	10	-	200.2	764	136	44	42	11	-	-	9	44	-	208	4	1	16	4	.800	2	0--	-	1.75	1.88
2009	HNHF	Jap	23	-	8	-	182.0	701	118	36	35	9	-	-	6	45	-	167	5	0	15	5	.750	2	0--	-	1.63	1.73
2010	HNHF	Jap	26	-	10	-	202.0	805	158	48	40	5	-	-	7	47	-	222	6	0	12	8	.600	2	0--	-	2.01	1.78

Kyle Davies

Pitches: R Bats: R Pos: SP-32   DAY-vees   Ht: 6'1" Wt: 211 Born: 9/9/1983 Age: 27

Year	Team	Lg	G	GS	CG	GF	IP	BFP	H	R	ER	HR	SH	SF	HB	TBB	IBB	SO	WP	Bk	W	L	Pct	Sh	Sv-Op	Hld	ERC	ERA
2005	Atl	NL	21	14	0	2	87.2	403	98	54	48	8	3	0	1	49	5	62	4	0	7	6	.538	0	0-1	2	5.25	4.93
2006	Atl	NL	14	14	1	0	63.1	312	90	60	59	14	3	2	3	33	0	51	3	0	3	7	.300	0	0-0	0	8.33	8.38
2007	2 Tms		28	28	0	0	136.0	628	155	102	92	22	5	3	5	70	4	99	8	1	7	15	.318	0	0-0	0	5.90	6.09
2008	KC	AL	21	21	0	0	113.0	487	121	57	51	10	1	3	2	43	0	71	8	1	9	7	.563	0	0-0	0	4.46	4.06
2009	KC	AL	22	22	1	0	123.0	538	122	76	72	18	3	4	4	66	1	86	10	0	8	9	.471	0	0-0	0	5.16	5.27
2010	KC	AL	32	32	1	0	183.2	817	206	114	109	20	3	5	2	80	1	126	5	1	8	12	.400	0	0-0	0	5.04	5.34
07	Atl	NL	17	17	0	0	86.0	389	92	61	55	12	3	2	2	44	3	59	1	1	4	8	.333	0	0-0	0	5.24	5.76
07	KC	AL	11	11	0	0	50.0	239	63	41	37	10	2	1	3	26	1	40	7	0	3	7	.300	0	0-0	0	7.09	6.66
	6 ML YEARS		138	131	3	2	706.2	3185	792	460	431	92	18	17	17	341	11	495	38	3	42	56	.429	0	0-1	2	5.44	5.49

Brad Davis

Bats: R **Throws:** R **Pos:** C-32; PH-1   **Ht:** 6'1" **Wt:** 192 **Born:** 12/29/1982 **Age:** 28

Year	Team	Lg	G	AB	H	2B	3B	HR	(Hm	Rd)	TB	R	RBI	RC	TBB	IBB	SO	HBP	SH	SF	SB	CS	SB%	GDP	Avg	OBP	Slg
2004	Jmstwn	A-	42	149	44	12	1	0	(-	-)	58	23	14	20	10	1	18	2	2	2	2	3	.40	3	.295	.344	.389
2005	Grnsbr	A	64	228	52	13	1	5	(-	-)	82	26	24	23	17	0	62	2	3	2	0	2	.00	9	.228	.285	.360
2006	Jupiter	A+	106	347	91	21	1	4	(-	-)	126	43	46	44	34	0	62	5	7	1	5	5	.50	8	.262	.336	.363
2007	Carlina	AA	45	150	43	16	1	3	(-	-)	70	13	20	26	18	1	39	2	2	1	0	1	.00	4	.287	.368	.467
2007	Albq	AAA	1	2	1	1	0	0	(-	-)	2	0	1	1	1	1	0	0	0	0	0	0	-	0	.500	.667	1.000
2007	Jupiter	A+	14	43	7	2	0	0	(-	-)	9	0	3	3	9	0	11	0	0	1	0	0	-	0	.163	.302	.209
2008	Carlina	AA	81	249	51	15	1	6	(-	-)	86	30	28	28	35	1	57	3	5	4	0	2	.00	6	.205	.306	.345
2009	Jaxnvl	AA	88	280	66	23	0	10	(-	-)	119	36	43	38	28	0	62	3	2	1	0	0	-	10	.236	.311	.425
2009	NewOr	AAA	10	35	4	2	0	0	(-	-)	6	1	4	0	2	1	10	0	0	1	1	0	1.00	4	.114	.158	.171
2010	NewOr	AAA	73	244	70	14	0	9	(-	-)	111	35	34	39	24	0	53	2	1	1	1	2	.33	3	.287	.354	.455
2010	Fla	NL	33	109	23	7	1	3	(2	1)	41	8	16	11	9	2	37	1	1	3	2	0	1.00	1	.211	.270	.376

Chris Davis

Bats: L **Throws:** R **Pos:** 1B-41; PH-6; 3B-1; PR-1   **Ht:** 6'3" **Wt:** 232 **Born:** 3/17/1986 **Age:** 25

Year	Team	Lg	G	AB	H	2B	3B	HR	(Hm	Rd)	TB	R	RBI	RC	TBB	IBB	SO	HBP	SH	SF	SB	CS	SB%	GDP	Avg	OBP	Slg
2010	OKCity*	AAA	103	398	130	31	2	14	(-	-)	207	67	80	78	37	4	105	3	0	6	3	2	.60	7	.327	.383	.520
2008	Tex	AL	80	295	84	23	2	17	(8	9)	162	51	55	44	20	1	88	1	0	1	1	2	.33	5	.285	.331	.549
2009	Tex	AL	113	391	93	15	1	21	(11	10)	173	48	59	50	24	2	150	2	0	2	0	0	-	4	.238	.284	.442
2010	Tex	AL	45	120	23	9	0	1	(0	1)	35	7	4	5	15	3	40	0	0	1	3	0	1.00	3	.192	.279	.292
	3 ML YEARS		238	806	200	47	3	39	(19	20)	370	106	118	99	59	6	278	3	0	4	4	2	.67	14	.248	.300	.459

Doug Davis

Pitches: L **Bats:** R **Pos:** SP-8   **Ht:** 6'4" **Wt:** 213 **Born:** 9/21/1975 **Age:** 35

Year	Team	Lg	G	GS	CG	GF	IP	BFP	H	R	ER	HR	SH	SF	HB	TBB	IBB	SO	WP	Bk	W	L	Pct	Sh	Sv-Op	Hld	ERC	ERA
2010	Nashv*	AAA	2	2	0	0	8.0	32	5	1	1	0	0	1	0	2	0	12	0	0	1	0	1.000	0	0- -	-	1.24	1.13
2010	Wisc*	A	1	1	0	0	7.0	29	6	1	1	0	0	0	1	3	0	4	0	0	1	0	1.000	0	0- -	-	3.40	1.29
1999	Tex	AL	2	0	0	0	2.2	20	12	10	10	3	0	0	0	0	0	3	0	0	0	0	-	0	0-0	0	41.42	33.75
2000	Tex	AL	30	13	1	4	98.2	450	109	61	59	14	6	4	3	58	3	66	5	1	7	6	.538	0	0-3	2	5.93	5.38
2001	Tex	AL	30	30	1	0	186.0	828	220	103	92	14	4	6	3	69	1	115	7	2	11	10	.524	0	0-0	0	4.90	4.45
2002	Tex	AL	10	10	1	0	59.2	262	67	36	33	7	3	3	3	22	0	28	2	2	3	5	.375	1	0-0	0	5.05	4.98
2003	3 Tms		21	20	1	0	109.1	491	123	55	49	16	6	2	1	51	1	62	7	0	7	8	.467	0	0-0	0	5.46	4.03
2004	Mil	NL	34	34	0	0	207.1	880	192	84	78	14	11	5	7	79	3	166	4	1	12	12	.500	0	0-0	0	3.49	3.39
2005	Mil	NL	35	**35**	2	0	222.2	946	196	103	95	26	12	2	4	93	5	208	3	2	11	11	.500	1	0-0	0	3.62	3.84
2006	Mil	NL	34	34	1	0	203.1	904	206	118	111	19	16	8	5	102	1	159	3	0	11	11	.500	1	0-0	0	4.59	4.91
2007	Ari	NL	33	33	0	0	192.2	862	211	100	91	21	10	2	5	95	7	144	10	1	13	12	.520	0	0-0	0	5.15	4.25
2008	Ari	NL	26	26	0	0	146.0	650	160	76	70	13	10	4	4	64	4	112	7	0	6	8	.429	0	0-0	0	4.77	4.32
2009	Ari	NL	34	**34**	0	0	203.1	889	203	101	93	25	15	6	4	**103**	1	146	12	1	9	14	.391	0	0-0	0	4.80	4.12
2010	Mil	NL	8	8	0	0	38.1	191	55	36	32	6	2	0	3	21	1	34	3	0	1	4	.200	0	0-0	0	8.08	7.51
03	Tex	AL	1	1	0	0	3.0	17	4	4	4	2	0	0	0	4	0	2	0	0	0	0	-	0	0-0	0	15.81	12.00
03	Tor	AL	12	11	0	0	54.0	250	70	33	30	6	3	0	1	26	1	25	6	0	4	6	.400	0	0-0	0	6.39	5.00
03	Mil	AL	8	8	1	0	52.1	224	49	18	15	8	3	2	0	21	0	35	1	0	3	2	.600	0	0-0	0	4.06	2.58
	Postseason		2	2	0	0	10.2	50	10	6	5	1	1	1	0	8	0	13	0	0	1	0	1.000	0	0-0	0	4.94	4.22
	12 ML YEARS		297	277	7	4	1670.0	7373	1754	883	813	178	95	42	42	757	27	1243	63	10	91	101	.474	3	0-3	2	4.71	4.38

Ike Davis

Bats: L **Throws:** L **Pos:** 1B-146; PH-5   **Ht:** 6'4" **Wt:** 215 **Born:** 3/22/1987 **Age:** 24

Year	Team	Lg	G	AB	H	2B	3B	HR	(Hm	Rd)	TB	R	RBI	RC	TBB	IBB	SO	HBP	SH	SF	SB	CS	SB%	GDP	Avg	OBP	Slg
2008	Bklyn	A-	58	215	55	15	0	0	(-	-)	70	17	17	24	23	2	43	0	0	1	0	0	-	8	.256	.326	.326
2009	StLuci	A+	59	222	64	17	3	7	(-	-)	108	28	28	41	31	3	52	1	0	1	0	2	.00	2	.288	.376	.486
2009	Bnghtn	AA	55	207	64	14	0	13	(-	-)	117	30	43	44	26	0	60	0	0	0	0	0	-	1	.309	.386	.565
2010	Buffalo	AAA	10	33	12	3	0	2	(-	-)	21	8	4	10	9	0	5	0	0	0	0	0	-	0	.364	.500	.636
2010	NYM	NL	147	523	138	33	1	19	(8	11)	230	73	71	75	72	6	138	1	0	5	3	2	.60	13	.264	.351	.440

Rajai Davis

Bats: R **Throws:** R **Pos:** CF-83; LF-47; RF-27; PR-5; DH-2; PH-1   RAHJ-ay   **Ht:** 5'10" **Wt:** 195 **Born:** 10/19/1980 **Age:** 30

Year	Team	Lg	G	AB	H	2B	3B	HR	(Hm	Rd)	TB	R	RBI	RC	TBB	IBB	SO	HBP	SH	SF	SB	CS	SB%	GDP	Avg	OBP	Slg
2006	Pit	NL	20	14	2	1	0	0	(0	0)	3	1	0	0	2	0	3	0	1	0	1	3	.25	0	.143	.250	.214
2007	2 Tms	NL	75	190	53	11	2	1	(0	1)	71	32	9	26	21	1	28	4	3	1	22	6	.79	1	.279	.361	.374
2008	2 Tms		113	214	52	5	4	3	(0	3)	74	30	19	24	8	0	40	1	2	1	29	6	.83	1	.243	.272	.346
2009	Oak	AL	125	390	119	27	5	3	(1	2)	165	65	48	63	29	0	70	7	2	4	41	12	.77	12	.305	.360	.423
2010	Oak	AL	143	525	149	28	3	5	(5	0)	198	66	52	62	26	0	78	4	1	5	50	11	.82	10	.284	.320	.377
07	Pit	NL	24	48	13	2	1	0	(0	0)	17	6	2	6	7	0	3	0	1	0	5	2	.71	1	.271	.357	.354
07	SF	NL	51	142	40	9	1	1	(0	1)	54	26	7	20	14	1	25	4	2	0	17	4	.81	0	.282	.363	.380
08	SF	NL	12	18	1	0	0	0	(0	0)	1	2	0	0	1	0	6	0	0	0	4	0	1.00	0	.056	.105	.056
08	Oak	AL	101	196	51	5	4	3	(0	3)	73	28	19	24	7	0	34	1	2	1	25	6	.81	1	.260	.288	.372
	5 ML YEARS		476	1333	375	72	14	12	(6	6)	511	194	128	175	86	1	219	16	9	11	143	38	.79	24	.281	.330	.383

Wade Davis

Pitches: R **Bats:** R **Pos:** SP-29   **Ht:** 6'5" **Wt:** 220 **Born:** 9/7/1985 **Age:** 25

		HOW MUCH HE PITCHED					WHAT HE GAVE UP										THE RESULTS							
Year	Team	Lg	G	GS	CG	GF	IP	BFP	H	R	ER	HR	SH	SF	HB	TBB	IBB	SO	WP	Bk	W	L	Pct	Sh	Sv-Op Hld	ERC	ERA
2004	Princtn	R+	13	13	0	0	57.2	264	71	46	39	8	1	6	2	19	0	38	3	0	3	5	.375	0	0- - -	5.46	6.09
2005	HudVal	A-	15	15	0	0	86.0	353	75	35	26	5	4	0	5	23	0	97	3	0	7	4	.636	0	0- - -	2.85	2.72
2006	SWMch	A	27	27	1	0	146.0	608	124	61	49	5	0	5	8	64	0	165	4	1	7	12	.368	0	0- - -	3.24	3.02
2007	VeroB	A+	13	13	1	0	78.1	305	54	20	16	5	4	0	4	21	0	88	4	0	3	0	1.000	1	0- - -	2.02	1.84
2007	Mont	AA	14	14	0	0	80.0	340	74	37	28	3	4	5	4	30	0	81	5	0	7	3	.700	0	0- - -	3.34	3.15
2008	Mont	AA	19	19	0	0	107.2	455	104	49	46	7	3	2	9	42	1	81	4	0	9	6	.600	0	0- - -	4.03	3.85
2008	Drham	AAA	9	9	0	0	53.0	221	39	16	16	5	1	2	4	24	1	55	0	0	4	2	.667	0	0- - -	3.09	2.72
2009	Drham	AAA	28	28	0	0	158.2	673	139	71	60	14	2	4	6	60	1	140	7	0	10	8	.556	0	0- - -	3.34	3.40
2009	TB	AL	6	6	1	0	36.1	150	33	19	15	2	0	0	0	13	1	36	1	0	2	2	.500	1	0-0 0	3.12	3.72
2010	TB	AL	29	29	0	0	168.0	722	165	77	76	24	3	6	5	62	2	113	4	0	12	10	.545	0	0-0 0	4.25	4.07
	2 ML YEARS		35	35	1	0	204.1	872	198	96	91	26	3	6	5	75	3	149	5	0	14	12	.538	1	0-0 0	4.04	4.01

Alejandro De Aza

Bats: L **Throws:** L **Pos:** CF-9; PR-6; RF-5; PH-4; DH-3   day-AH-zah   **Ht:** 5'11" **Wt:** 189 **Born:** 4/11/1984 **Age:** 27

			BATTING																BASERUNNING				AVERAGES		
Year	Team	Lg	G	AB	H	2B	3B	HR	(Hm | Rd)	TB	R	RBI	RC	TBB	IBB	SO	HBP	SH	SF	SB	CS	SB%	GDP	Avg	OBP	Slg
2010	Charltt	AAA	79	318	96	21	4	5	(- | -)	140	53	49	55	29	0	60	5	3	3	16	3	.84	4	.302	.366	.440
2007	Fla	NL	45	144	33	8	2	0	(0 | 0)	45	14	8	11	6	1	37	1	5	2	2	0	1.00	2	.229	.261	.313
2009	Fla	NL	22	20	5	1	0	0	(0 | 0)	6	6	3	4	5	0	5	0	1	0	0	0	-	0	.250	.385	.300
2010	CWS	AL	19	30	9	3	0	0	(0 | 0)	12	7	2	4	1	0	4	0	1	0	2	1	.67	1	.300	.323	.400
	3 ML YEARS		86	194	47	12	2	0	(0 | 0)	63	27	13	19	12	1	46	1	7	3	4	1	.80	2	.242	.286	.325

Jorge de la Rosa

Pitches: L **Bats:** L **Pos:** SP-20   **Ht:** 6'1" **Wt:** 215 **Born:** 4/5/1981 **Age:** 30

			HOW MUCH HE PITCHED						WHAT HE GAVE UP												THE RESULTS					
Year	Team	Lg	G	GS	CG	GF	IP	BFP	H	R	ER	HR	SH	SF	HB	TBB	IBB	SO	WP	Bk	W	L	Pct	Sh	Sv-Op Hld	ERC	ERA
2010	ColSpr*	AAA	3	3	0	0	14.2	63	17	10	9	1	1	0	0	4	0	15	0	0	1	2	.333	0	0- - -	4.28	5.52
2004	Mil	NL	5	5	0	0	22.2	113	29	20	18	1	1	3	1	14	0	5	3	0	0	3	.000	0	0-0 0	6.12	6.35
2005	Mil	NL	38	0	0	13	42.1	208	48	23	21	1	2	2	0	38	4	42	6	0	2	2	.500	0	0-2 5	6.04	4.46
2006	2 Tms		28	13	0	4	79.0	367	81	59	57	14	2	4	2	54	1	67	6	1	5	6	.455	0	0-0 1	6.05	6.49
2007	KC	AL	26	23	0	1	130.0	589	160	84	84	20	2	4	3	53	6	82	4	1	8	12	.400	0	0-0 0	5.93	5.82
2008	Col	NL	28	23	0	0	130.0	571	128	77	71	13	6	7	7	62	3	128	14	1	10	8	.556	0	0-0 0	4.50	4.92
2009	Col	NL	33	32	0	0	185.0	799	172	95	90	20	11	6	9	83	3	193	12	1	16	9	.640	0	0-0 0	4.11	4.38
2010	Col	NL	20	20	0	0	121.2	512	105	62	57	15	3	3	5	55	4	113	9	1	8	7	.533	0	0-0 0	3.86	4.22
	06	Mil	NL	18	3	0	4	30.1	146	32	30	29	4	1	3	1	22	1	31	4	0	2	2	.500	0	0-0 1	5.90	8.60
	06	KC	AL	10	10	0	0	48.2	221	49	29	28	10	1	1	1	32	0	36	2	1	3	4	.429	0	0-0 0	6.14	5.18
	7 ML YEARS		178	116	0	18	710.2	3159	723	424	396	84	27	29	27	359	21	630	54	5	49	47	.510	0	0-2 6	4.85	5.02

Sam Deduno

Pitches: R **Bats:** R **Pos:** RP-4   deh-DUE-noh   **Ht:** 6'3" **Wt:** 190 **Born:** 7/2/1983 **Age:** 27

			HOW MUCH HE PITCHED						WHAT HE GAVE UP												THE RESULTS					
Year	Team	Lg	G	GS	CG	GF	IP	BFP	H	R	ER	HR	SH	SF	HB	TBB	IBB	SO	WP	Bk	W	L	Pct	Sh	Sv-Op Hld	ERC	ERA
2004	Casper	R+	15	15	0	0	76.1	331	62	40	27	3	4	3	10	32	0	118	14	0	8	4	.600	0	0- - -	3.15	3.18
2005	Ashvll	A	20	20	1	0	89.2	410	82	67	56	9	3	1	11	65	0	110	13	1	8	8	.500	0	0- - -	5.48	5.62
2006	Mdest	A+	27	26	0	0	146.1	670	121	88	78	3	4	7	22	92	0	167	34	1	5	8	.385	0	0- - -	3.89	4.80
2007	Mdest	A+	2	2	0	0	11.0	51	9	8	8	1	0	0	2	7	0	8	2	0	1	1	.500	0	0- - -	4.50	6.55
2007	Tulsa	AA	21	21	1	0	124.0	564	120	90	74	13	7	1	11	66	1	122	11	0	5	8	.385	0	0- - -	4.72	5.37
2009	Tulsa	AA	24	24	1	0	133.0	551	94	48	38	3	3	2	8	72	0	123	9	1	12	4	.750	1	0- - -	2.80	2.57
2009	ColSpr	AAA	1	1	0	0	5.2	25	5	4	4	0	0	1	0	4	0	8	1	0	0	1	.000	0	0- - -	3.91	6.35
2010	ColSpr	AAA	6	6	0	0	30.2	133	20	12	10	3	3	2	5	18	0	29	4	0	3	1	.750	0	0- - -	3.48	2.93
2010	TriCity	A-	4	4	0	0	16.1	70	18	11	10	0	1	1	1	5	0	20	0	0	0	2	.000	0	0- - -	3.87	5.51
2010	Col	NL	4	0	0	3	2.2	12	3	1	1	1	0	0	0	1	0	3	0	0	0	0	-	0	0-0 1	6.59	3.38

David DeJesus

Bats: L **Throws:** L **Pos:** RF-70; CF-19; LF-2; DH-2; PH-1; PR-1   **Ht:** 5'11" **Wt:** 192 **Born:** 12/20/1979 **Age:** 31

			BATTING																BASERUNNING				AVERAGES		
Year	Team	Lg	G	AB	H	2B	3B	HR	(Hm	Rd)	TB	R	RBI	RC	TBB	IBB	SO	HBP	SH	SF	SB	CS	SB%	GDP	Avg	OBP	Slg
2003	KC	AL	12	7	2	0	1	0	(0	0)	4	0	0	2	1	0	2	1	1	0	0	0	-	0	.286	.444	.571
2004	KC	AL	96	363	104	15	3	7	(2	5)	146	58	39	53	33	0	53	9	8	0	8	11	.42	6	.287	.360	.402
2005	KC	AL	122	461	135	31	6	9	(6	3)	205	69	56	77	42	1	76	9	5	6	5	5	.50	6	.293	.359	.445
2006	KC	AL	119	491	145	36	7	8	(4	4)	219	83	56	76	43	4	70	12	2	4	6	3	.67	10	.295	.364	.446
2007	KC	AL	157	605	157	29	9	9	(3	4)	225	101	58	87	64	7	83	23	7	4	10	4	.71	10	.260	.351	.372
2008	KC	AL	135	518	159	25	7	12	(6	6)	234	70	73	93	46	3	71	5	4	4	11	8	.58	10	.307	.366	.452
2009	KC	AL	144	558	157	28	9	13	(4	9)	242	74	71	83	51	0	87	8	5	5	4	9	.31	10	.281	.347	.434
2010	KC	AL	91	352	112	23	3	5	(2	3)	156	46	37	50	34	2	47	4	3	1	3	3	.50	10	.318	.384	.443
	8 ML YEARS		876	3355	971	187	45	61	(27	34)	1431	501	390	521	314	17	489	71	35	24	47	43	.52	62	.289	.360	.427

Enerio Del Rosario

Pitches: R Bats: R Pos: RP-11   en-AIR-ee-oh   Ht: 6'2" Wt: 165 Born: 10/16/1985 Age: 25

			HOW MUCH HE PITCHED						WHAT HE GAVE UP											THE RESULTS						
Year	Team	Lg	G	GS	CG	GF	IP	BFP	H	R	ER	HR	SH	SF	HB	TBB	IBB	SO	WP	Bk	W	L	Pct	Sh	Sv-Op Hld	ERC	ERA
2007	Billings	R+	15	15	0	0	70.1	305	77	40	31	6	4	3	1	30	0	40	6	2	5	4	.556	0	0-- -	4.79	3.97
2008	Dayton	A	19	9	1	8	70.0	269	52	19	9	3	5	1	0	11	0	49	0	1	5	2	.714	1	5-- -	1.62	1.16
2008	Srsota	A+	13	6	0	1	44.1	205	57	31	30	2	0	2	1	23	0	32	2	0	1	4	.200	0	0-- -	6.02	6.09
2009	Srsota	A+	31	0	0	17	50.0	200	40	14	11	2	2	1	5	6	0	33	1	0	2	1	.667	0	7-- -	2.00	1.98
2009	Carlina	AA	4	0	0	2	5.2	21	2	1	1	0	0	0	2	0	0	9	0	0	0	0	-	0	1-- -	0.76	1.59
2009	Lsvlle	AAA	15	0	0	7	24.2	99	24	6	3	1	0	0	0	6	0	12	2	0	1	0	1.000	0	4-- -	3.05	1.09
2010	Lsvlle	AAA	50	0	0	14	64.0	264	61	22	22	7	0	0	3	17	0	34	5	0	4	4	.500	0	4-- -	3.60	3.09
2010	2 Tms	NL	11	0	0	3	10.0	51	17	7	5	0	3	1	1	4	0	4	0	0	1	1	.500	0	0-2 0	7.90	4.50
10	Cin	NL	9	0	0	2	8.2	42	13	4	2	0	3	1	0	4	0	3	0	0	1	1	.500	0	0-2 0	6.48	2.08
10	Hou	NL	2	0	0	1	1.1	9	4	3	3	0	0	0	1	0	0	1	0	0	0	0	-	0	0-0 0	18.29	20.25

Rob Delaney

Pitches: R Bats: L Pos: RP-1   Ht: 6'3" Wt: 225 Born: 9/8/1984 Age: 26

			HOW MUCH HE PITCHED						WHAT HE GAVE UP											THE RESULTS						
Year	Team	Lg	G	GS	CG	GF	IP	BFP	H	R	ER	HR	SH	SF	HB	TBB	IBB	SO	WP	Bk	W	L	Pct	Sh	Sv-Op Hld	ERC	ERA
2006	Twins	R	17	0	0	7	33.0	142	37	23	17	4	3	1	4	1	0	27	1	0	1	3	.250	0	2-- -	3.79	4.64
2006	FtMyrs	A+	3	0	0	2	5.0	21	7	3	3	1	0	0	0	0	0	3	0	0	0	0	-	0	0-- -	5.60	5.40
2007	Beloit	A	36	0	0	32	46.2	172	25	8	4	1	0	0	2	6	1	56	1	0	1	0	1.000	0	28-- -	0.95	0.77
2007	FtMyrs	A+	17	0	0	15	23.1	98	19	4	4	1	1	1	0	10	2	27	2	0	2	0	1.000	0	7-- -	2.65	1.54
2008	FtMyrs	A+	23	0	0	18	31.2	121	24	6	5	1	1	0	0	4	1	34	2	0	1	2	.333	0	13-- -	1.53	1.42
2008	NwBrit	AA	24	0	0	16	34.1	126	20	4	4	2	0	0	0	7	0	38	1	0	2	1	.667	0	5-- -	1.46	1.05
2009	NwBrit	AA	26	0	0	4	36.0	143	33	12	9	1	2	1	1	6	0	40	2	0	1	1	.500	0	0-- -	2.46	2.25
2009	Roch	AAA	36	0	0	23	47.2	199	43	25	24	5	2	3	0	15	2	38	2	0	7	3	.700	0	7-- -	3.16	4.53
2010	Roch	AAA	61	0	0	31	80.0	343	82	48	42	12	5	2	1	23	5	92	4	1	7	9	.438	0	4-- -	4.01	4.73
2010	Min	AL	1	0	0	1	1.0	5	2	1	1	1	0	0	0	1	0	0	0	0	0	0	-	0	0-0 0	27.72	9.00

Manny Delcarmen

Pitches: R Bats: R Pos: RP-57   dell-CAR-men   Ht: 6'2" Wt: 205 Born: 2/16/1982 Age: 29

			HOW MUCH HE PITCHED						WHAT HE GAVE UP											THE RESULTS						
Year	Team	Lg	G	GS	CG	GF	IP	BFP	H	R	ER	HR	SH	SF	HB	TBB	IBB	SO	WP	Bk	W	L	Pct	Sh	Sv-Op Hld	ERC	ERA
2010	Portlnd*	AA	1	1	0	0	1.0	3	0	0	0	0	0	0	0	0	0	0	0	0	0	0	-	0	0-- -	0.00	0.00
2005	Bos	AL	10	0	0	2	9.0	41	8	3	3	0	0	0	1	7	0	9	0	0	0	0	-	0	0-0 0	4.68	3.00
2006	Bos	AL	50	0	0	11	53.1	243	68	32	30	2	3	1	2	17	2	45	0	0	2	0	1.000	0	0-4 14	4.90	5.06
2007	Bos	AL	44	0	0	5	44.0	176	28	11	10	4	2	2	2	17	1	41	0	0	0	0	-	0	1-2 11	2.23	2.05
2008	Bos	AL	73	0	0	16	74.1	307	55	28	27	5	4	4	3	28	1	72	0	0	1	2	.333	0	2-5 18	2.51	3.27
2009	Bos	AL	64	0	0	6	59.2	278	64	34	30	5	2	1	4	34	3	44	1	0	5	2	.714	0	0-3 6	5.16	4.53
2010	2 Tms		57	0	0	12	52.1	234	45	30	29	8	1	1	1	32	2	38	1	0	3	4	.429	0	0-3 8	4.44	4.99
10	Bos	AL	48	0	0	9	44.0	193	33	24	23	7	1	1	1	28	1	32	0	0	3	2	.600	0	0-2 8	4.02	4.70
10	Col	NL	9	0	0	3	8.1	41	12	6	6	1	0	0	0	4	1	6	1	0	0	2	.000	0	0-1 0	6.83	6.48
Postseason			11	0	0	2	8.2	46	11	11	11	2	0	0	2	8	0	8	0	0	1	0	1.000	0	0-0 1	10.24	11.42
6 ML YEARS			298	0	0	52	292.2	1279	268	138	129	24	12	9	13	135	9	249	2	0	11	8	.579	0	3-17 57	3.80	3.97

Sam Demel

Pitches: R Bats: R Pos: RP-37   DEMM-ell   Ht: 6'0" Wt: 215 Born: 10/23/1985 Age: 25

			HOW MUCH HE PITCHED						WHAT HE GAVE UP											THE RESULTS						
Year	Team	Lg	G	GS	CG	GF	IP	BFP	H	R	ER	HR	SH	SF	HB	TBB	IBB	SO	WP	Bk	W	L	Pct	Sh	Sv-Op Hld	ERC	ERA
2007	Stcktn	A+	11	0	0	2	14.0	72	16	16	11	2	1	1	2	15	1	13	4	0	0	0	-	0	0-- -	8.79	7.07
2007	Kane	A	9	0	0	8	9.1	34	3	2	1	0	2	0	0	4	1	10	2	0	0	1	.000	0	4-- -	0.75	0.96
2008	Stcktn	A+	54	0	0	35	67.0	307	61	31	25	5	1	2	3	32	1	90	10	0	5	2	.714	0	18-- -	3.61	3.36
2009	Mdland	AA	27	0	0	23	29.1	121	23	5	2	1	2	0	0	9	1	26	1	0	2	0	1.000	0	11-- -	2.09	0.61
2009	Scrmto	AAA	28	0	0	10	32.1	146	27	14	13	1	3	1	1	21	4	33	5	0	2	3	.400	0	3-- -	3.43	3.62
2010	Scrmto	AAA	22	0	0	11	28.2	116	22	6	4	1	0	2	1	9	0	28	1	0	2	0	1.000	0	6-- -	2.26	1.26
2010	Ari	NL	37	0	0	10	37.0	165	42	27	22	5	0	1	1	12	2	33	5	0	2	1	.667	0	2-2 4	4.73	5.35

Ryan Dempster

Pitches: R Bats: R Pos: SP-34   Ht: 6'2" Wt: 215 Born: 5/3/1977 Age: 34

			HOW MUCH HE PITCHED						WHAT HE GAVE UP											THE RESULTS						
Year	Team	Lg	G	GS	CG	GF	IP	BFP	H	R	ER	HR	SH	SF	HB	TBB	IBB	SO	WP	Bk	W	L	Pct	Sh	Sv-Op Hld	ERC	ERA
1998	Fla	NL	14	11	0	1	54.2	272	72	47	43	6	5	6	9	38	1	35	5	0	1	5	.167	0	0-1 0	8.14	7.08
1999	Fla	NL	25	25	0	0	147.0	666	146	81	77	21	3	6	6	93	2	126	8	0	7	8	.467	0	0-0 0	5.49	4.71
2000	Fla	NL	33	33	2	0	226.1	974	210	102	92	30	4	5	5	97	7	209	4	0	14	10	.583	1	0-0 0	4.04	3.66
2001	Fla	NL	34	34	2	0	211.1	954	218	123	116	21	15	7	10	112	5	171	5	0	15	12	.556	1	0-0 0	4.91	4.94
2002	2 Tms	NL	33	33	4	0	209.0	915	228	127	125	28	9	6	10	93	2	153	2	0	10	13	.435	0	0-0 0	5.35	5.38
2003	Cin	NL	22	20	0	1	115.2	545	134	89	84	14	9	4	5	70	4	84	3	0	3	7	.300	0	0-0 0	6.11	6.54
2004	ChC	NL	23	0	0	8	20.2	93	16	9	9	1	1	0	2	13	0	18	1	0	1	1	.500	0	2-2 3	3.61	3.92
2005	ChC	NL	63	6	0	53	92.0	401	83	35	32	4	5	0	4	49	7	89	4	0	5	3	.625	0	33-35 0	3.69	3.13
2006	ChC	NL	74	0	0	64	75.0	342	77	47	40	5	5	4	3	36	3	67	6	0	1	9	.100	0	24-33 2	4.26	4.80
2007	ChC	NL	66	0	0	58	66.2	282	59	36	35	8	3	2	1	30	4	55	2	1	2	7	.222	0	28-31 0	3.77	4.73
2008	ChC	NL	33	33	1	0	206.2	856	174	75	68	14	4	3	7	76	1	187	6	0	17	6	.739	0	0-0 0	3.03	2.96
2009	ChC	NL	31	31	1	0	200.0	842	196	94	81	22	10	8	4	65	4	172	11	0	11	9	.550	0	0-0 0	3.87	3.65
2010	ChC	NL	34	34	1	0	215.1	918	198	110	81	25	9	2	10	86	4	208	6	0	15	12	.556	0	0-0 0	3.91	3.85

			HOW MUCH HE PITCHED						WHAT HE GAVE UP												THE RESULTS							
Year	Team	Lg	G	GS	CG	GF	IP	BFP	H	R	ER	HR	SH	SF	HB	TBB	IBB	SO	WP	Bk	W	L	Pct	Sh	Sv-Op	Hld	ERC	ERA
02	Fla	NL	18	18	3	0	120.1	521	126	66	64	12	7	3	7	55	1	87	0	0	5	8	.385	0	0-0	0	4.95	4.79
02	Cin	NL	15	15	1	0	88.2	394	102	61	61	16	2	3	3	38	1	66	2	0	5	5	.500	0	0-0	0	5.90	6.19
	Postseason		2	1	0	1	5.2	27	4	4	4	1	0	0	0	7	0	4	0	0	0	1	.000	0	0-0	0	6.45	6.35
	13 ML YEARS		485	260	11	185	1840.1	8060	1811	971	894	199	82	53	78	858	44	1574	62	1	102	102	.500	3	87-102	5	4.45	4.37

Chris Denorfia

Bats: R **Throws:** R **Pos:** CF-50; LF-44; RF-18; PH-13; PR-3   denn-ORE-fee-ah   **Ht:** 6'0" **Wt:** 204 **Born:** 7/15/1980 **Age:** 30

			BATTING																	BASERUNNING				AVERAGES		
Year	Team	Lg	G	AB	H	2B	3B	HR	(Hm | Rd)	TB	R	RBI	RC	TBB	IBB	SO	HBP	SH	SF	SB	CS	SB%	GDP	Avg	OBP	Slg
2010	Portlnd*	AAA	34	121	37	10	4	2	(- | -)	61	17	12	23	12	0	18	0	1	0	7	1	.88	5	.306	.368	.504
2005	Cin	NL	18	38	10	3	0	1	(1 | 0)	16	8	2	3	6	0	9	0	0	0	1	0	1.00	1	.263	.364	.421
2006	Cin	NL	49	106	30	6	0	1	(0 | 1)	39	14	7	13	11	1	21	1	2	0	1	1	.50	1	.283	.356	.368
2008	Oak	AL	29	62	18	3	0	1	(0 | 1)	24	10	9	9	6	0	16	1	2	0	2	0	1.00	3	.290	.362	.387
2009	Oak	AL	4	2	0	0	0	0	(0 | 0)	0	1	1	0	0	0	0	0	0	0	0	0	-	0	.000	.000	.000
2010	SD	NL	99	284	77	15	2	9	(3 | 6)	123	41	36	37	27	3	51	2	1	3	8	4	.67	5	.271	.335	.433
	5 ML YEARS		199	492	135	27	2	12	(4 | 8)	202	74	55	62	50	4	97	4	5	3	12	5	.71	10	.274	.344	.411

Mark DeRosa

Bats: R **Throws:** R **Pos:** LF-21; 2B-7; PH-1   **Ht:** 6'0" **Wt:** 211 **Born:** 2/26/1975 **Age:** 36

			BATTING																	BASERUNNING				AVERAGES		
Year	Team	Lg	G	AB	H	2B	3B	HR	(Hm | Rd)	TB	R	RBI	RC	TBB	IBB	SO	HBP	SH	SF	SB	CS	SB%	GDP	Avg	OBP	Slg
2010	SnJos*	A+	1	4	0	0	0	0	(- | -)	0	0	0	0	1	0	1	0	0	0	0	0	-	2	.000	.200	.000
2010	Fresno*	AAA	3	11	4	1	0	0	(- | -)	5	1	1	2	1	0	2	0	0	0	0	0	-	0	.364	.417	.455
1998	Atl	NL	5	3	1	0	0	0	(0 | 0)	1	2	0	0	0	0	1	0	0	0	0	0	-	0	.333	.333	.333
1999	Atl	NL	7	8	0	0	0	0	(0 | 0)	0	0	0	0	0	0	2	0	0	0	0	0	-	0	.000	.000	.000
2000	Atl	NL	22	13	4	1	0	0	(0 | 0)	5	9	3	2	2	0	1	0	0	0	0	0	-	0	.308	.400	.385
2001	Atl	NL	66	164	47	8	0	3	(3 | 0)	64	27	20	22	12	6	19	5	1	2	2	1	.67	3	.287	.350	.390
2002	Atl	NL	72	212	63	9	2	5	(3 | 2)	91	24	23	27	12	3	24	3	2	3	2	3	.40	5	.297	.339	.429
2003	Atl	NL	103	266	70	14	0	6	(3 | 3)	102	40	22	28	16	0	49	5	0	1	1	0	1.00	6	.263	.316	.383
2004	Atl	NL	118	309	74	16	0	3	(0 | 3)	99	33	31	24	23	3	53	3	4	6	1	3	.25	6	.239	.293	.320
2005	Tex	AL	66	148	36	5	0	8	(7 | 1)	65	26	20	20	16	0	35	2	0	1	1	0	1.00	5	.243	.325	.439
2006	Tex	AL	136	520	154	40	2	13	(5 | 8)	237	78	74	78	44	1	102	6	0	2	4	4	.50	13	.296	.357	.456
2007	ChC	NL	149	502	147	28	3	10	(5 | 5)	211	64	72	76	58	2	93	7	3	4	1	2	.33	17	.293	.371	.420
2008	ChC	NL	149	505	144	30	3	21	(11 | 10)	243	103	87	95	69	0	106	9	2	8	6	0	1.00	9	.285	.376	.481
2009	2 Tms		139	515	129	23	1	23	(11 | 12)	223	70	70	68	47	1	121	7	2	5	3	2	.60	11	.250	.319	.433
2010	SF	NL	26	93	18	3	0	1	(0 | 1)	24	9	10	6	9	0	16	2	0	0	0	2	.00	6	.194	.279	.258
09	Cle	AL	71	278	75	13	0	13	(8 | 5)	127	47	50	45	29	1	63	3	1	3	1	1	.50	6	.270	.342	.457
09	StL	NL	68	237	54	10	1	10	(3 | 7)	96	31	28	23	18	0	58	4	1	2	2	1	.67	5	.228	.291	.405
	Postseason		22	53	19	6	1	1	(1 | 0)	30	8	10	7	4	0	8	1	0	0	0	0	-	2	.358	.414	.566
	13 ML YEARS		1058	3258	887	177	11	93	(48 | 45)	1365	493	440	446	308	16	622	49	14	31	21	17	.55	81	.272	.341	.419

Daniel Descalso

Bats: L **Throws:** R **Pos:** 3B-9; PH-2; SS-1   dess-CAL-so   **Ht:** 5'10" **Wt:** 190 **Born:** 10/19/1986 **Age:** 24

			BATTING																	BASERUNNING				AVERAGES		
Year	Team	Lg	G	AB	H	2B	3B	HR	(Hm | Rd)	TB	R	RBI	RC	TBB	IBB	SO	HBP	SH	SF	SB	CS	SB%	GDP	Avg	OBP	Slg
2007	Batvia	A-	66	250	67	7	5	0	(- | -)	84	29	31	33	26	0	37	5	0	2	12	3	.80	6	.268	.346	.336
2008	PlmBh	A+	115	403	98	24	2	8	(- | -)	150	57	50	49	33	3	53	10	5	5	7	7	.50	11	.243	.313	.372
2008	Sprgfld	AA	9	37	13	1	1	0	(- | -)	16	6	4	6	3	1	3	1	0	1	1	1	.50	1	.351	.405	.432
2009	Sprgfld	AA	73	288	93	26	5	8	(- | -)	153	46	51	59	31	1	41	4	1	0	0	1	.00	7	.323	.396	.531
2009	Memp	AAA	46	150	38	4	0	2	(- | -)	48	23	17	17	16	0	21	1	4	1	3	0	1.00	3	.253	.327	.320
2010	Memp	AAA	116	468	132	32	3	9	(- | -)	197	86	71	73	47	1	48	5	5	6	8	4	.67	13	.282	.350	.421
2010	StL	NL	11	34	9	2	0	0	(0 | 0)	11	6	4	5	2	0	6	1	0	0	1	0	1.00	0	.265	.324	.324

Ian Desmond

Bats: R **Throws:** R **Pos:** SS-149; PH-10; PR-2; RF-1   **Ht:** 6'2" **Wt:** 210 **Born:** 9/20/1985 **Age:** 25

			BATTING																	BASERUNNING				AVERAGES		
Year	Team	Lg	G	AB	H	2B	3B	HR	(Hm | Rd)	TB	R	RBI	RC	TBB	IBB	SO	HBP	SH	SF	SB	CS	SB%	GDP	Avg	OBP	Slg
2004	Expos	R	55	216	49	11	0	1	(- | -)	63	28	27	18	10	0	40	4	2	2	13	3	.81	6	.227	.272	.292
2004	Vrmnt	A-	4	12	3	0	0	1	(- | -)	6	2	1	1	0	0	2	1	0	0	0	1	.00	2	.250	.308	.500
2005	Savann	A	73	296	73	10	2	4	(- | -)	99	37	23	31	13	0	60	6	4	1	20	6	.77	5	.247	.291	.334
2005	Ptomc	A+	55	219	56	13	3	3	(- | -)	84	37	15	29	21	0	53	2	5	1	13	6	.68	6	.256	.325	.384
2006	Hrsbrg	AA	37	121	22	4	1	0	(- | -)	28	8	3	5	5	0	35	0	6	0	4	1	.80	1	.182	.214	.231
2006	Ptomc	A+	92	365	89	20	2	9	(- | -)	140	50	45	46	29	0	79	9	2	3	14	8	.64	7	.244	.313	.384
2007	Ptomc	A+	129	458	121	30	4	13	(- | -)	198	69	45	76	57	0	99	11	6	4	27	11	.71	8	.264	.357	.432
2008	Hrsbrg	AA	93	323	81	14	0	12	(- | -)	131	42	44	43	31	4	78	2	6	2	12	8	.60	7	.251	.318	.406
2008	Nats	R	3	13	5	1	0	0	(- | -)	6	1	2	2	0	0	2	0	0	0	3	0	1.00	0	.385	.385	.462
2009	Hrsbrg	AA	42	170	52	12	1	6	(- | -)	84	29	18	32	16	2	40	2	1	0	13	4	.76	2	.306	.372	.494
2009	Syrcse	AAA	55	178	63	12	2	1	(- | -)	82	25	14	37	20	1	31	3	4	0	8	1	.89	5	.354	.428	.461
2009	Was	NL	21	82	23	7	2	4	(2 | 2)	46	9	12	10	5	0	14	0	1	1	1	0	1.00	2	.280	.318	.561
2010	Was	NL	154	525	141	27	4	10	(8 | 2)	206	59	65	58	28	3	109	5	9	7	17	5	.77	9	.269	.308	.392
	2 ML YEARS		175	607	164	34	6	14	(10 | 4)	252	68	77	68	33	3	123	5	10	8	18	5	.78	11	.270	.309	.415

Elmer Dessens

Pitches: R **Bats:** R **Pos:** RP-53

dess-ENNS

Ht: 5'11" **Wt:** 200 **Born:** 1/13/1971 **Age:** 40

Year	Team	Lg		HOW MUCH HE PITCHED					WHAT HE GAVE UP												THE RESULTS					
			G	GS	CG	GF	IP	BFP	H	R	ER	HR	SH	SF	HB	TBB	IBB	SO	WP	Bk	W	L	Pct	Sh	Sv-Op	Hld	ERC	ERA
2010	Buffalo*	AAA	13	0	0	10	17.0	72	20	4	4	0	2	0	0	3	1	18	0	0	5	0	1.000	0	6--	5	3.41	2.12
1996	Pit	NL	15	3	0	1	25.0	112	40	23	23	2	3	1	4	4	0	13	0	0	0	2	.000	0	0-0	3	6.77	8.28
1997	Pit	NL	3	0	0	1	3.1	13	2	0	0	0	0	0	1	0	0	2	0	0	0	0	-	0	0-0	0	1.31	0.00
1998	Pit	NL	43	5	0	8	74.2	332	90	50	47	10	4	3	0	25	2	43	1	0	2	6	.250	0	0-1	6	5.19	5.67
2000	Cin	NL	40	16	1	6	147.1	640	170	73	70	10	12	7	3	43	7	85	4	0	11	5	.688	0	1-1	1	4.31	4.28
2001	Cin	NL	34	34	1	0	205.0	862	221	103	102	32	7	7	1	56	1	128	4	1	10	14	.417	1	0-0	0	4.49	4.48
2002	Cin	NL	30	30	0	0	178.0	737	173	70	60	24	7	1	7	49	8	93	3	1	7	8	.467	0	0-0	0	3.82	3.03
2003	Ari	NL	34	30	0	1	175.2	781	212	107	99	22	9	3	4	57	6	113	3	2	8	8	.500	0	0-0	0	5.19	5.07
2004	2 Tms	NL	50	10	0	9	105.0	468	123	61	52	15	4	3	1	31	4	73	2	0	2	6	.250	0	2-5	4	4.83	4.46
2005	LAD	NL	28	7	0	4	65.2	277	63	30	26	6	1	4	3	19	2	37	1	0	1	2	.333	0	0-0	1	3.35	3.56
2006	2 Tms	NL	62	0	0	12	77.0	334	86	43	39	8	5	1	1	22	8	52	3	0	5	8	.385	0	2-7	18	4.17	4.56
2007	2 Tms	NL	17	5	0	7	34.0	156	45	32	27	6	2	1	0	12	0	22	0	0	2	2	.500	0	0-0	6	6.37	7.15
2008	Atl	NL	4	0	0	1	4.0	26	10	10	10	1	0	2	0	4	0	2	0	0	0	1	.000	0	0-1	0	18.65	22.50
2009	NYM	NL	28	0	0	8	32.2	130	24	12	12	5	2	2	2	10	1	14	1	0	0	0	-	0	0-0	5	2.89	3.31
2010	NYM	NL	53	0	0	6	47.0	194	41	14	12	4	3	1	3	16	6	16	0	0	4	2	.667	0	0-1	11	3.16	2.30
04	Ari	NL	38	9	0	7	85.1	386	107	54	45	11	4	3	1	23	4	55	2	0	1	6	.143	0	2-4	4	5.08	4.75
04	LAD	NL	12	1	0	2	19.2	82	16	7	7	4	0	0	0	8	0	18	0	0	1	0	1.000	0	0-1	0	3.74	3.20
06	KC	AL	43	0	0	10	54.0	234	63	31	27	4	3	1	1	13	6	36	2	0	5	7	.417	0	2-7	12	4.08	4.50
06	LAD	NL	19	0	0	2	23.0	100	23	12	12	4	2	0	0	9	2	16	1	0	0	1	.000	0	0-0	6	4.37	4.70
07	Mil	NL	12	0	0	7	15.0	69	24	16	11	3	0	1	0	3	0	12	0	0	1	1	.500	0	0-0	1	7.85	6.60
07	Col	NL	5	5	0	0	19.0	87	21	16	16	3	2	0	0	9	0	10	0	0	1	1	.500	0	0-0	5	5.29	7.58
	Postseason		1	0	0	0	1.1	5	1	1	1	1	0	0	0	0	0	1	0	0	0	0	-	0	0-0	0	4.25	6.75
14 ML YEARS			441	140	2	64	1174.1	5062	1300	628	579	145	59	35	24	348	45	693	22	4	52	64	.448	1	5-16	44	4.48	4.44

Ross Detwiler

Pitches: L **Bats:** R **Pos:** SP-5; RP-3

DETT-wy-lerr

Ht: 6'5" **Wt:** 174 **Born:** 3/6/1986 **Age:** 25

Year	Team	Lg		HOW MUCH HE PITCHED					WHAT HE GAVE UP													THE RESULTS					
			G	GS	CG	GF	IP	BFP	H	R	ER	HR	SH	SF	HB	TBB	IBB	SO	WP	Bk	W	L	Pct	Sh	Sv-Op	Hld	ERC	ERA
2010	Ptomc*	A+	2	2	0	0	6.0	25	6	1	1	0	0	0	0	1	0	6	0	0	0	0	-	0	0--	-	3.52	1.50
2010	Hrsbrg*	AA	7	7	0	0	32.2	142	38	10	9	1	2	1	2	7	0	31	1	0	2	2	.500	0	0--	-	3.99	2.48
2010	Syrcse*	AAA	1	1	0	0	5.0	18	5	3	1	0	0	0	0	1	0	2	0	0	1	0	1.000	0	0--	-	3.13	1.80
2007	Was	NL	1	0	0	1	1.0	4	0	0	0	0	0	0	0	0	0	1	0	0	0	0	-	0	0-0	0	0.00	0.00
2009	Was	NL	15	14	1	0	75.2	341	87	43	42	3	4	1	2	33	3	43	4	0	1	6	.143	0	0-0	0	4.65	5.00
2010	Was	NL	8	5	0	1	29.2	135	34	22	14	5	2	0	1	14	1	17	1	0	1	3	.250	0	0-0	0	5.83	4.25
3 ML YEARS			24	19	1	2	106.1	480	121	65	56	8	6	1	3	47	4	61	5	0	2	9	.182	0	0-0	0	4.88	4.74

Blake DeWitt

Bats: L **Throws:** R **Pos:** 2B-126; PH-10; 3B-1; PR-1

Ht: 5'11" **Wt:** 199 **Born:** 8/20/1985 **Age:** 25

Year	Team	Lg						BATTING													BASERUNNING				AVERAGES		
			G	AB	H	2B	3B	HR	(Hm	Rd)	TB	R	RBI	RC	TBB	IBB	SO	HBP	SH	SF	SB	CS	SB%	GDP	Avg	OBP	Slg
2008	LAD	NL	117	368	97	13	2	9	(5	4)	141	45	52	51	45	9	68	3	0	5	3	0	1.00	6	.264	.344	.383
2009	LAD	NL	31	49	10	3	0	2	(1	1)	19	4	4	1	3	0	7	0	0	1	0	0	-	2	.204	.245	.388
2010	2 Tms	NL	135	440	115	24	5	5	(4	1)	164	47	52	62	47	8	86	4	2	3	3	2	.60	5	.261	.336	.373
10	LAD	NL	82	256	69	15	4	1	(1	0)	95	29	30	36	30	4	49	3	2	1	2	2	.50	4	.270	.352	.371
10	ChC	NL	53	184	46	9	1	4	(3	1)	69	18	22	26	17	4	37	1	0	2	1	0	1.00	1	.250	.314	.375
	Postseason		8	24	4	2	1	0	(0	0)	8	2	6	0	1	0	6	0	0	1	0	0	-	3	.167	.192	.333
3 ML YEARS			283	857	222	40	7	16	(10	6)	324	96	108	114	95	17	161	7	2	9	6	2	.75	13	.259	.335	.378

Thomas Diamond

Pitches: R **Bats:** R **Pos:** RP-13; SP-3

Ht: 6'3" **Wt:** 240 **Born:** 4/6/1983 **Age:** 28

Year	Team	Lg		HOW MUCH HE PITCHED					WHAT HE GAVE UP													THE RESULTS					
			G	GS	CG	GF	IP	BFP	H	R	ER	HR	SH	SF	HB	TBB	IBB	SO	WP	Bk	W	L	Pct	Sh	Sv-Op	Hld	ERC	ERA
2004	Spkane	A-	5	3	0	1	15.1	65	13	5	4	0	0	0	1	5	0	26	1	0	0	2	.000	0	1--	-	2.51	2.35
2004	Clinton	A	7	7	0	0	30.2	114	18	8	7	1	1	0	2	8	0	42	2	0	1	0	1.000	0	0--	-	1.52	2.05
2005	Bkrsfld	A+	14	14	1	0	81.1	322	53	20	18	3	3	2	9	31	0	101	5	0	8	0	1.000	1	0--	-	2.28	1.99
2005	Frisco	AA	14	14	0	0	69.0	311	66	44	41	8	0	4	4	38	0	68	10	0	5	4	.556	0	0--	-	4.73	5.35
2006	Frisco	AA	27	27	1	0	129.1	561	104	65	61	14	3	1	4	78	0	145	9	0	12	5	.706	1	0--	-	3.97	4.24
2008	Frisco	AA	12	11	0	0	53.2	251	54	39	37	3	1	5	6	37	0	47	2	0	3	3	.500	0	0--	-	5.38	6.20
2009	Okla	AAA	6	1	0	0	11.0	52	12	8	8	1	0	0	1	7	0	8	2	0	1	0	1.000	0	0--	-	5.84	6.55
2009	Frisco	AA	32	0	0	10	44.2	212	43	26	18	3	2	1	3	37	0	50	7	0	1	3	.250	0	1--	-	5.57	3.63
2010	Iowa	AAA	21	21	0	0	108.1	451	86	40	38	9	5	3	2	46	0	104	2	0	5	4	.556	0	0--	-	3.02	3.16
2010	ChC	NL	16	3	0	3	29.0	138	33	23	22	5	2	3	2	18	2	36	2	0	1	3	.250	0	0-0	0	6.49	6.83

Argenis Diaz

Bats: R **Throws:** R **Pos:** SS-15; PH-7; PR-2

ahr-HANE-iss

Ht: 6'0" **Wt:** 190 **Born:** 2/12/1987 **Age:** 24

Year	Team	Lg						BATTING													BASERUNNING				AVERAGES		
			G	AB	H	2B	3B	HR	(Hm	Rd)	TB	R	RBI	RC	TBB	IBB	SO	HBP	SH	SF	SB	CS	SB%	GDP	Avg	OBP	Slg
2006	RedSx	R	37	133	35	2	1	0	(-	-)	39	16	11	12	6	0	23	1	2	0	3	1	.75	2	.263	.300	.293
2007	Grnville	A	99	405	113	25	5	2	(-	-)	154	62	40	53	36	0	92	4	0	2	5	9	.36	11	.279	.342	.380
2008	Lancst	A+	71	256	72	9	6	0	(-	-)	93	31	29	32	20	0	60	1	0	5	3	2	.60	4	.281	.330	.363
2008	Portlnd	AA	39	139	40	8	2	2	(-	-)	58	20	23	19	10	0	30	1	1	2	0	1	.00	3	.288	.336	.417

Year	Team	Lg	BATTING																					BASERUNNING				AVERAGES		
			G	AB	H	2B	3B	HR	(Hm	Rd)	TB	R	RBI	RC	TBB	IBB	SO	HBP	SH	SF				SB	CS	SB%	GDP	Avg	OBP	Slg
2009	Portlnd	AA	76	277	70	14	1	0	(-	-)	86	21	24	28	21	1	60	2	6	1				7	4	.64	7	.253	.309	.310
2009	Indy	AAA	43	146	34	1	0	0	(-	-)	35	14	8	9	8	1	27	0	4	0				1	1	.50	5	.233	.273	.240
2010	Indy	AAA	80	274	68	8	1	0	(-	-)	78	28	22	25	19	0	61	2	9	0				5	1	.83	12	.248	.302	.285
2010	Pit	NL	22	33	8	1	0	0	(0	0)	9	0	2	2	3	1	10	0	0	0				0	1	.00	1	.242	.306	.273

Matt Diaz

Bats: R **Throws:** R **Pos:** LF-63; PH-26; PR-2 DYE-azz **Ht:** 6'1" **Wt:** 215 **Born:** 3/3/1978 **Age:** 33

Year	Team	Lg	BATTING																					BASERUNNING				AVERAGES		
			G	AB	H	2B	3B	HR	(Hm	Rd)	TB	R	RBI	RC	TBB	IBB	SO	HBP	SH	SF				SB	CS	SB%	GDP	Avg	OBP	Slg
2010	Gwnntt*	AAA	3	12	3	1	0	0	(-	-)	4	2	3	0	0	0	3	0	0	0				0	0	-	0	.250	.250	.333
2003	TB	AL	4	9	1	0	0	0	(0	0)	1	2	0	0	1	0	3	0	0	0				0	0	-	0	.111	.200	.111
2004	TB	AL	10	21	4	1	1	1	(1	0)	10	3	3	2	1	0	6	2	0	0				0	0	-	0	.190	.292	.476
2005	KC	AL	34	89	25	4	2	1	(0	1)	36	7	9	11	4	0	15	2	1	1				0	1	.00	3	.281	.323	.404
2006	Atl	NL	124	297	97	15	4	7	(3	4)	141	37	32	40	11	3	49	9	1	4				5	5	.50	9	.327	.364	.475
2007	Atl	NL	135	358	121	21	0	12	(5	7)	178	44	45	53	16	3	63	4	1	5				4	0	1.00	8	.338	.368	.497
2008	Atl	NL	43	135	33	2	0	2	(2	0)	41	9	14	10	3	0	32	1	0	1				4	2	.67	4	.244	.264	.304
2009	Atl	NL	125	371	116	18	4	13	(4	9)	181	56	58	67	35	2	90	13	5	1				12	5	.71	14	.313	.390	.488
2010	Atl	NL	84	224	56	17	2	7	(5	2)	98	27	31	30	13	3	44	4	2	1				3	1	.75	6	.250	.302	.438
8 ML YEARS			559	1504	453	78	13	43	(20	23)	686	185	192	213	84	11	302	35	10	13				28	14	.67	44	.301	.350	.456

Chris Dickerson

Bats: L **Throws:** L **Pos:** CF-20; PH-15; LF-8; RF-4; PR-2 **Ht:** 6'3" **Wt:** 228 **Born:** 4/10/1982 **Age:** 29

Year	Team	Lg	BATTING																					BASERUNNING				AVERAGES		
			G	AB	H	2B	3B	HR	(Hm	Rd)	TB	R	RBI	RC	TBB	IBB	SO	HBP	SH	SF				SB	CS	SB%	GDP	Avg	OBP	Slg
2010	Lsvlle*	AAA	13	43	19	5	0	3	(-	-)	33	12	7	16	9	0	13	0	2	1				6	1	.86	0	.442	.528	.767
2008	Cin	NL	31	102	31	9	2	6	(4	2)	62	20	15	22	17	0	35	2	1	0				5	3	.63	0	.304	.413	.608
2009	Cin	NL	97	255	70	13	3	2	(0	2)	95	31	15	34	39	1	66	1	2	2				11	3	.79	3	.275	.370	.373
2010	2 Tms	NL	45	97	20	2	2	0	(0	0)	26	11	5	6	6	0	34	0	2	1				4	0	1.00	1	.206	.250	.268
10	Cin	NL	20	44	9	1	1	0	(0	0)	12	9	0	3	1	0	19	0	0	0				3	0	1.00	1	.205	.222	.273
10	Mil	NL	25	53	11	1	1	0	(0	0)	14	2	5	3	5	0	15	0	2	1				1	0	1.00	0	.208	.271	.264
3 ML YEARS			173	454	121	24	7	8	(4	4)	183	62	35	62	62	1	135	3	5	3				20	6	.77	4	.267	.356	.403

R.A. Dickey

Pitches: R **Bats:** R **Pos:** SP-26; RP-1 **Ht:** 6'2" **Wt:** 216 **Born:** 10/29/1974 **Age:** 36

Year	Team	Lg	HOW MUCH HE PITCHED						WHAT HE GAVE UP												THE RESULTS						
			G	GS	CG	GF	IP	BFP	H	R	ER	HR	SH	SF	HB	TBB	IBB	SO	WP	Bk	W	L	Pct	Sh	Sv-Op	Hld	ERC	ERA
2010	Buffalo*	AAA	8	8	2	0	60.2	243	55	21	15	3	1	0	3	8	0	37	4	1	4	2	.667	1	0- -	-	2.46	2.23
2001	Tex	AL	4	0	0	1	12.0	53	13	9	9	3	0	0	0	7	1	4	1	0	0	1	.000	0	0-0	0	6.57	6.75
2003	Tex	AL	38	13	1	6	116.2	513	135	68	66	16	4	3	5	38	5	94	5	2	9	8	.529	1	1-1	3	5.09	5.09
2004	Tex	AL	25	15	0	2	104.1	480	136	77	65	17	3	3	4	33	1	57	5	1	6	7	.462	0	1-1	0	6.08	5.61
2005	Tex	AL	9	4	0	2	29.2	134	29	23	22	4	0	1	2	17	0	15	2	0	1	2	.333	0	0-0	0	5.18	6.67
2006	Tex	AL	1	1	0	0	3.1	18	8	7	7	6	0	0	0	1	0	1	0	0	0	1	.000	0	0-0	0	32.05	18.90
2008	Sea	AL	32	14	0	9	112.1	500	124	65	65	15	4	6	2	51	4	58	11	1	5	8	.385	0	0-0	0	5.19	5.21
2009	Min	AL	35	1	0	13	64.1	293	74	34	33	8	2	2	4	30	1	42	4	0	1	1	.500	0	0-0	1	5.66	4.62
2010	NYM	NL	27	26	2	0	174.1	713	165	62	55	13	7	3	4	42	3	104	11	0	11	9	.550	1	0-0	1	3.11	2.84
8 ML YEARS			171	74	3	33	617.0	2704	684	345	322	82	20	18	21	219	15	375	39	4	33	37	.471	2	2-2	5	4.87	4.70

Mark DiFelice

Pitches: R **Bats:** R **Pos:** P **Ht:** 6'2" **Wt:** 181 **Born:** 8/23/1976 **Age:** 34

Year	Team	Lg	HOW MUCH HE PITCHED						WHAT HE GAVE UP												THE RESULTS						
			G	GS	CG	GF	IP	BFP	H	R	ER	HR	SH	SF	HB	TBB	IBB	SO	WP	Bk	W	L	Pct	Sh	Sv-Op	Hld	ERC	ERA
1990	Portlnd	A-	15	13	0	2	81.2	343	83	45	30	6	1	2	3	11	0	62	3	1	4	6	.400	0	0- -	-	3.03	3.31
1999	Salem	A+	27	23	3	1	156.1	642	142	71	67	20	4	6	4	36	0	142	3	1	8	12	.400	0	0- -	-	3.19	3.86
2000	Carlina	AA	23	22	2	0	133.0	556	152	58	53	15	2	3	0	19	0	98	2	0	7	5	.583	0	0- -	-	3.96	3.59
2001	Carlina	AA	19	18	2	0	123.0	498	108	47	43	13	3	5	3	23	0	98	1	0	6	4	.600	1	0- -	-	2.73	3.15
2001	ColSpr	AAA	8	8	0	0	46.0	207	56	29	27	11	2	1	8	8	3	43	1	0	3	2	.600	0	0- -	-	6.02	5.28
2002	TriCity	A-	6	1	0	0	17.0	77	18	12	10	2	1	1	2	0	0	13	1	0	0	0	-	0	0- -	-	3.03	5.29
2002	Salem	A+	6	6	0	0	35.1	146	40	12	11	3	1	0	2	5	0	21	0	0	3	0	1.000	0	0- -	-	4.03	2.80
2003	Tulsa	AA	21	21	0	0	113.2	479	121	61	47	16	4	2	4	24	2	75	7	0	7	6	.538	0	0- -	-	4.09	3.72
2004	Ottawa	AAA	36	4	0	0	89.0	365	73	42	34	10	1	1	2	27	1	70	3	1	9	4	.692	0	1- -	-	2.88	3.44
2005	NewOr	AAA	14	2	0	4	31.0	148	39	35	28	10	3	3	1	13	1	21	1	0	2	2	.333	0	0- -	-	7.27	8.13
2005	Smrset	IND	14	11	1	1	75.2	297	72	26	26	11	1	1	1	8	0	53	1	1	7	4	.636	0	0- -	-	3.08	3.09
2006	Cam	IND	25	25	7	0	158.0	656	163	66	56	18	6	7	4	24	2	132	0	0	12	9	.571	2	0- -	-	3.19	3.19
2007	Hntsvl	AA	26	3	0	5	66.2	250	50	12	12	3	1	1	1	6	1	60	3	0	6	1	.857	0	0- -	-	1.54	1.62
2007	Nashv	AAA	10	10	0	0	58.0	229	45	21	20	6	2	3	3	9	0	63	1	0	4	2	.667	0	0- -	-	2.21	3.10
2008	Nashv	AAA	13	12	0	0	64.1	252	50	25	23	5	2	2	4	8	0	65	3	0	5	1	.833	0	0- -	-	2.01	3.22
2008	Mil	NL	15	0	0	5	19.0	78	17	7	6	4	0	0	0	4	0	20	1	0	1	0	1.000	0	0-0	1	3.39	2.84
2009	Mil	NL	59	0	0	9	51.2	219	49	21	21	6	3	0	1	15	6	48	1	0	4	1	.800	0	0-1	9	3.32	3.66
2 ML YEARS			74	0	0	14	70.2	297	66	28	27	10	3	0	1	19	6	68	2	0	5	1	.833	0	0-1	10	3.35	3.44

Greg Dobbs

Bats: L **Throws:** R **Pos:** PH-55; 3B-36; 1B-2; RF-1; DH-1   **Ht:** 6'1" **Wt:** 207 **Born:** 7/2/1978 **Age:** 32

Year	Team	Lg	G	AB	H	2B	3B	HR	(Hm	Rd)	TB	R	RBI	RC	TBB	IBB	SO	HBP	SH	SF	SB	CS	SB%	GDP	Avg	OBP	Slg
2010	LV*	AAA	16	62	13	3	1	2	(-	-)	24	10	9	7	7	0	12	0	0	1	2	0	1.00	0	.210	.286	.387
2004	Sea	AL	18	53	12	1	0	1	(1	0)	16	4	9	5	1	0	14	1	0	1	0	0	-	0	.226	.250	.302
2005	Sea	AL	59	142	35	7	1	1	(0	1)	47	8	20	16	9	3	25	0	1	2	1	0	1.00	4	.246	.288	.331
2006	Sea	AL	23	27	10	3	1	0	(0	0)	15	4	3	5	0	0	4	1	0	0	0	1	.00	0	.370	.393	.556
2007	Phi	NL	142	324	88	20	4	10	(5	5)	146	45	55	42	29	4	67	1	0	4	3	0	1.00	7	.272	.330	.451
2008	Phi	NL	128	226	68	14	1	9	(3	6)	111	30	40	38	11	1	40	1	0	2	3	1	.75	4	.301	.333	.491
2009	Phi	NL	97	154	38	6	0	5	(3	2)	59	15	20	15	11	1	29	1	0	3	1	0	1.00	2	.247	.296	.383
2010	Phi	NL	88	163	32	7	0	5	(2	3)	54	13	15	14	12	1	39	0	1	0	1	1	.50	2	.196	.251	.331
	Postseason		16	21	7	1	0	0	(0	0)	8	2	0	2	3	2	6	0	0	0	0	0	-	0	.333	.417	.381
	7 ML YEARS		555	1089	283	58	7	31	(14	17)	448	119	162	135	73	10	218	5	2	12	9	3	.75	19	.260	.306	.411

Jason Donald

Bats: R **Throws:** R **Pos:** SS-47; 2B-41; DH-1; PH-1; PR-1   **Ht:** 6'1" **Wt:** 190 **Born:** 9/4/1984 **Age:** 26

Year	Team	Lg	G	AB	H	2B	3B	HR	(Hm	Rd)	TB	R	RBI	RC	TBB	IBB	SO	HBP	SH	SF	SB	CS	SB%	GDP	Avg	OBP	Slg
2006	Batvia	A-	63	213	56	14	2	1	(-	-)	77	33	24	31	23	0	42	5	1	1	12	1	.92	5	.263	.347	.362
2007	Lakwd	A	51	197	61	9	3	4	(-	-)	88	41	30	37	29	0	39	6	3	3	2	5	.29	5	.310	.409	.447
2007	Clrwtr	A+	83	293	88	22	5	8	(-	-)	144	48	41	56	35	0	70	6	2	0	3	2	.60	8	.300	.386	.491
2008	Rdng	AA	92	362	111	19	4	14	(-	-)	180	57	54	72	47	1	86	4	0	1	11	2	.85	9	.307	.391	.497
2009	LV	AAA	51	208	49	15	1	1	(-	-)	69	26	16	22	14	1	53	5	1	2	6	0	1.00	4	.236	.297	.332
2009	Phillies	R	9	26	6	1	1	0	(-	-)	9	4	1	2	2	0	5	0	0	0	1	0	1.00	1	.231	.286	.346
2009	Clmbs	AAA	10	35	9	2	0	1	(-	-)	14	10	1	5	3	0	11	2	0	0	1	0	1.00	0	.257	.350	.400
2010	Clmbs	AAA	37	137	38	10	2	2	(-	-)	58	27	17	26	21	0	33	6	1	0	10	2	.83	3	.277	.396	.423
2010	Cle	AL	88	296	75	19	3	4	(2	2)	112	39	24	29	22	2	70	3	4	0	5	1	.83	3	.253	.312	.378

Josh Donaldson

Bats: R **Throws:** R **Pos:** C-7; PH-4; DH-3; 1B-2   **Ht:** 6'0" **Wt:** 214 **Born:** 12/8/1985 **Age:** 25

Year	Team	Lg	G	AB	H	2B	3B	HR	(Hm	Rd)	TB	R	RBI	RC	TBB	IBB	SO	HBP	SH	SF	SB	CS	SB%	GDP	Avg	OBP	Slg
2007	Cubs	R	4	11	2	2	0	0	(-	-)	4	1	0	0	2	0	4	0	0	0	0	1	.00	0	.182	.308	.364
2007	Boise	A-	49	162	56	11	2	9	(-	-)	98	37	35	45	37	1	34	2	0	1	6	2	.75	3	.346	.470	.605
2008	Peoria	A	63	235	51	13	0	6	(-	-)	82	27	23	23	17	1	41	2	6	0	0	1	.00	3	.217	.276	.349
2008	Stcktn	A+	47	188	62	13	2	9	(-	-)	106	37	39	40	17	0	29	2	12	0	0	2	.00	1	.330	.391	.564
2009	Mdland	AA	124	455	123	37	1	9	(-	-)	189	67	91	78	79	2	92	2	3	2	7	2	.78	17	.270	.379	.415
2010	Scrmto	AAA	86	294	70	14	1	18	(-	-)	140	52	67	50	45	2	79	2	0	7	3	1	.75	15	.238	.336	.476
2010	Oak	AL	14	32	5	1	0	1	(0	1)	9	1	4	3	2	0	12	0	0	0	0	0	-	0	.156	.206	.281

Brendan Donnelly

Pitches: R **Bats:** R **Pos:** RP-38   **Ht:** 6'3" **Wt:** 240 **Born:** 7/4/1971 **Age:** 39

Year	Team	Lg	G	GS	CG	GF	IP	BFP	H	R	ER	HR	SH	SF	HB	TBB	IBB	SO	WP	Bk	W	L	Pct	Sh	Sv-Op	Hld	ERC	ERA
2002	LAA	AL	46	0	0	11	49.2	199	32	13	12	2	3	1	2	19	3	54	1	0	1	1	.500	0	1-3	13	1.89	2.17
2003	LAA	AL	63	0	0	15	74.0	307	55	14	13	2	3	1	4	24	1	79	1	0	2	2	.500	0	3-5	29	2.12	1.58
2004	LAA	AL	40	0	0	10	42.0	172	34	14	14	5	2	2	1	15	0	56	0	0	5	2	.714	0	0-0	5	3.12	3.00
2005	LAA	AL	66	0	0	14	65.1	271	60	30	27	9	3	1	2	19	3	53	3	0	9	3	.750	0	0-5	16	3.52	3.72
2006	LAA	AL	62	0	0	17	64.0	278	58	32	28	8	2	2	4	28	3	53	6	0	6	0	1.000	0	0-1	11	4.02	3.94
2007	Bos	AL	27	0	0	4	20.2	90	19	8	7	0	0	0	4	5	0	15	2	0	1	1	.667	0	0-0	8	3.00	3.05
2008	Cle	AL	15	0	0	3	13.2	69	20	13	13	2	0	2	0	10	0	8	0	0	1	0	1.000	0	0-0	4	8.84	8.56
2009	Fla	NL	30	0	0	9	25.1	104	22	8	5	1	2	0	1	9	1	25	1	1	3	0	1.000	0	2-2	9	2.94	1.78
2010	Pit	NL	38	0	0	14	30.2	142	26	21	19	6	2	3	1	25	1	26	1	1	3	1	.750	0	0-0	9	5.64	5.58
	Postseason		17	0	0	3	20.0	83	14	12	11	2	0	0	1	9	2	23	2	0	1	0	1.000	0	0-0	4	2.69	4.95
	9 ML YEARS		387	0	0	97	385.1	1632	326	153	138	35	17	12	19	154	12	369	15	2	32	10	.762	0	6-16	104	3.29	3.22

Octavio Dotel

Pitches: R **Bats:** R **Pos:** RP-68   **Ht:** 6'0" **Wt:** 220 **Born:** 11/25/1973 **Age:** 37

Year	Team	Lg	G	GS	CG	GF	IP	BFP	H	R	ER	HR	SH	SF	HB	TBB	IBB	SO	WP	Bk	W	L	Pct	Sh	Sv-Op	Hld	ERC	ERA
1999	NYM	NL	19	14	0	1	85.1	368	69	52	51	12	3	6	6	49	1	85	3	2	8	3	.727	0	0-0	0	4.30	5.38
2000	Hou	NL	50	16	0	25	125.0	563	127	80	75	26	7	8	7	61	3	142	6	0	3	7	.300	0	16-23	0	5.47	5.40
2001	Hou	NL	61	4	0	20	105.0	438	79	35	31	5	2	2	2	47	2	145	4	0	7	5	.583	0	2-4	14	2.62	2.66
2002	Hou	NL	83	0	0	22	97.1	376	58	21	20	7	3	7	4	27	2	118	2	0	6	4	.600	0	6-10	31	1.61	1.85
2003	Hou	NL	76	0	0	13	87.0	346	53	25	24	9	2	1	3	31	2	97	2	0	6	4	.600	0	4-6	33	2.02	2.48
2004	2 Tms		77	0	0	70	85.1	356	68	38	35	13	4	3	4	33	7	122	4	1	6	6	.500	0	36-45	0	3.31	3.69
2005	Oak	AL	15	0	0	13	15.1	65	10	6	6	2	0	0	4	11	2	16	1	0	1	2	.333	0	7-11	0	3.44	3.52
2006	NYY	AL	14	0	0	7	10.0	59	18	13	12	2	0	1	0	11	1	7	3	0	0	0	-	0	0-0	1	12.97	10.80
2007	2 Tms		33	0	0	25	30.2	138	29	16	14	4	1	0	4	12	4	41	2	0	2	1	.667	0	11-15	1	4.12	4.11
2008	CWS	AL	72	0	0	10	67.0	288	52	34	28	12	4	0	5	29	3	92	4	0	4	4	.500	0	1-5	21	3.64	3.76
2009	CWS	AL	62	0	0	12	62.1	268	54	26	23	7	3	3	0	36	1	75	4	1	3	3	.500	0	0-3	16	4.14	3.32
2010	3 Tms		68	0	0	50	64.0	279	52	32	29	9	2	4	3	32	5	75	8	0	3	4	.429	0	22-28	4	3.69	4.08
04	Hou	NL	32	0	0	29	34.2	146	27	15	12	4	2	1	1	15	4	50	3	1	0	4	.000	0	14-17	0	3.01	3.12
04	Oak	AL	45	0	0	41	50.2	210	41	23	23	9	2	1	3	18	3	72	1	0	6	2	.750	0	22-28	0	3.52	4.09
07	KC	AL	24	0	0	22	23.0	108	24	11	10	3	1	0	4	11	4	29	2	0	1	1	.667	0	11-14	0	5.13	3.91
07	Atl	NL	9	0	0	3	7.2	30	5	5	4	1	0	0	0	1	0	12	0	0	0	0	-	0	0-1	1	1.51	4.70
10	Pit	NL	41	0	0	37	40.0	173	35	21	19	5	2	3	2	17	2	48	2	0	2	2	.500	0	21-26	0	3.83	4.28

			HOW MUCH HE PITCHED					WHAT HE GAVE UP												THE RESULTS						
Year	Team	Lg	G	GS	CG	GF	IP	BFP	H	R	ER	HR	SH	SF	HB	TBB	IBB	SO	WP	Bk	W	L	Pct	Sh	Sv-Op	Hld	ERC	ERA
10	LAD	NL	19	0	0	12	18.2	78	11	7	7	3	0	1	0	11	3	21	3	0	1	1	.500	0	1-2	3	2.72	3.38
10	Col	NL	8	0	0	1	5.1	28	6	4	3	1	0	0	0	4	0	6	3	0	0	1	.000	0	0-0	1	6.30	5.06
	Postseason		8	0	0	2	8.0	40	12	7	7	1	0	0	1	4	1	13	1	0	1	0	1.000	0	0-0	1	8.09	7.88
12 ML YEARS			630	34	0	268	834.1	3544	669	378	348	108	31	33	38	379	33	1015	43	4	49	43	.533	0	105-150	121	3.49	3.75

Felix Doubront

Pitches: L **Bats:** L **Pos:** RP-9; SP-3   due-BRAWNDT   **Ht:** 6'2" **Wt:** 165 **Born:** 10/23/1987 **Age:** 23

			HOW MUCH HE PITCHED					WHAT HE GAVE UP												THE RESULTS						
Year	Team	Lg	G	GS	CG	GF	IP	BFP	H	R	ER	HR	SH	SF	HB	TBB	IBB	SO	WP	Bk	W	L	Pct	Sh	Sv-Op	Hld	ERC	ERA
2006	RedSx	R	11	11	0	0	53.2	212	41	17	15	6	1	2	3	13	0	36	1	0	2	3	.400	0	0- -	-	2.57	2.52
2006	Lowell	A-	2	2	0	0	11.0	43	7	6	6	1	0	0	1	3	0	7	0	0	2	0	1.000	0	0- -	-	2.06	4.91
2007	Grnville	A	11	11	0	0	42.1	206	63	49	42	8	0	1	1	17	0	22	4	0	3	7	.300	0	0- -	-	7.80	8.93
2007	Lowell	A-	8	8	0	0	35.0	160	41	24	22	2	1	1	2	11	0	25	2	0	1	3	.250	0	0- -	-	4.47	5.66
2008	Grnville	A	23	23	0	0	115.1	475	115	53	47	9	3	2	4	24	0	118	5	0	12	8	.600	0	0- -	-	3.34	3.67
2008	Lancst	A+	3	3	0	0	14.0	59	15	6	6	1	0	1	0	4	0	20	0	0	1	1	.500	0	0- -	-	3.88	3.86
2009	Portlnd	AA	26	26	1	0	121.0	536	119	59	45	8	1	7	9	52	0	101	3	1	8	6	.571	1	0- -	-	4.10	3.35
2010	Portlnd	AA	8	8	0	0	43.0	177	39	13	12	0	1	1	2	17	0	38	1	2	4	0	1.000	0	0- -	-	3.16	2.51
2010	Pwtckt	AAA	9	8	0	0	37.0	158	36	13	13	1	0	0	4	16	0	34	2	1	4	3	.571	0	0- -	-	4.08	3.16
2010	Bos	AL	12	3	0	5	25.0	113	27	16	12	3	1	1	1	10	0	23	3	0	2	2	.500	0	2-3	1	4.72	4.32

Ryan Doumit

Bats: B **Throws:** R **Pos:** C-100; RF-18; PH-11; 1B-3; DH-1   DOE-mitt   **Ht:** 6'1" **Wt:** 210 **Born:** 4/3/1981 **Age:** 30

			BATTING																			BASERUNNING				AVERAGES		
Year	Team	Lg	G	AB	H	2B	3B	HR	(Hm	Rd)	TB	R	RBI	RC	TBB	IBB	SO	HBP	SH	SF	SB	CS	SB%	GDP	Avg	OBP	Slg
2010	Indy*	AAA	4	12	2	1	0	1	(-	-)	6	2	2	1	1	0	2	0	0	0	0	0	-	0	.167	.231	.500
2005	Pit	NL	75	231	59	13	1	6	(4	2)	92	25	35	32	11	1	48	13	1	1	2	1	.67	5	.255	.324	.398
2006	Pit	NL	61	149	31	9	0	6	(3	3)	58	15	17	17	15	1	42	11	1	2	0	0	-	3	.208	.322	.389
2007	Pit	NL	83	252	69	19	2	9	(7	2)	119	33	32	34	22	2	59	4	0	1	1	2	.33	5	.274	.341	.472
2008	Pit	NL	116	431	137	34	0	15	(8	7)	216	71	69	79	23	4	55	6	0	5	2	2	.50	10	.318	.357	.501
2009	Pit	NL	75	280	70	16	0	10	(6	4)	116	31	38	26	20	6	49	1	0	3	1	0	1.00	12	.250	.299	.414
2010	Pit	NL	124	406	102	22	1	13	(7	6)	165	42	45	47	41	4	87	8	0	1	1	0	1.00	18	.251	.331	.406
6 ML YEARS			534	1749	468	113	4	59	(35	24)	766	217	236	235	132	18	340	43	2	13	10	5	.67	53	.268	.332	.438

Matt Downs

Bats: R **Throws:** R **Pos:** 2B-21; PH-16; 3B-2; SS-2; DH-1   **Ht:** 6'1" **Wt:** 184 **Born:** 3/19/1984 **Age:** 27

			BATTING																			BASERUNNING				AVERAGES		
Year	Team	Lg	G	AB	H	2B	3B	HR	(Hm	Rd)	TB	R	RBI	RC	TBB	IBB	SO	HBP	SH	SF	SB	CS	SB%	GDP	Avg	OBP	Slg
2006	Giants	R	46	168	52	16	4	0	(-	-)	76	34	29	31	17	0	9	3	3	5	6	1	.06	5	.310	.373	.452
2007	SlmKzr	A-	73	287	97	33	0	8	(-	-)	154	68	48	65	28	0	34	10	7	4	16	2	.89	5	.338	.410	.537
2008	SnJos	A+	109	437	133	30	1	17	(-	-)	216	74	75	78	34	0	57	5	7	6	24	13	.65	9	.304	.357	.494
2008	Fresno	AAA	22	86	21	5	0	3	(-	-)	35	10	7	11	4	1	10	3	0	1	1	0	1.00	2	.244	.298	.407
2009	Fresno	AAA	109	424	127	33	3	14	(-	-)	208	68	74	73	25	0	58	7	4	7	8	2	.80	6	.300	.343	.491
2010	Fresno	AAA	56	197	50	9	1	7	(-	-)	82	37	28	29	25	0	35	4	1	1	3	4	.43	4	.254	.348	.416
2010	Giants	R	2	7	2	1	0	0	(-	-)	3	1	2	1	1	0	1	0	0	0	0	0	-	0	.286	.375	.429
2010	RdRck	AAA	8	19	2	1	0	0	(-	-)	3	0	2	1	1	0	2	1	0	0	1	1	.50	1	.105	.190	.158
2009	SF	NL	17	53	9	2	0	1	(0	1)	14	6	2	1	6	1	13	0	0	1	1	0	1.00	2	.170	.250	.264
2010	2 Tms	NL	40	97	21	7	0	1	(1	0)	31	8	7	9	9	0	20	2	0	0	0	0	-	1	.216	.294	.320
10	SF	NL	29	78	19	7	0	1	(1	0)	29	6	7	9	8	0	18	1	0	1	0	0	-	1	.244	.318	.372
10	Hou	NL	11	19	2	0	0	0	(0	0)	2	2	0	0	1	0	2	1	0	0	0	0	-	0	.105	.190	.105
2 ML YEARS			57	150	30	9	0	2	(1	1)	45	14	9	10	15	1	33	2	0	2	1	0	1.00	3	.200	.278	.300

Scott Downs

Pitches: L **Bats:** L **Pos:** RP-67   **Ht:** 6'2" **Wt:** 209 **Born:** 3/17/1976 **Age:** 35

			HOW MUCH HE PITCHED					WHAT HE GAVE UP												THE RESULTS						
Year	Team	Lg	G	GS	CG	GF	IP	BFP	H	R	ER	HR	SH	SF	HB	TBB	IBB	SO	WP	Bk	W	L	Pct	Sh	Sv-Op	Hld	ERC	ERA
2000	2 Tms	NL	19	19	0	0	97.0	442	122	62	57	13	2	4	5	40	1	63	1	0	4	3	.571	0	0-0	0	6.19	5.29
2003	Mon	NL	1	1	0	0	3.0	17	5	5	5	2	0	0	0	3	2	4	0	1	0	1	.000	0	0-0	0	15.01	15.00
2004	Mon	NL	12	12	1	0	63.0	284	79	47	36	9	2	1	3	23	2	38	2	0	3	6	.333	1	0-0	0	5.97	5.14
2005	Tor	AL	26	13	0	0	94.0	407	93	49	45	12	0	1	5	34	0	75	3	0	4	3	.571	0	0-0	0	4.25	4.31
2006	Tor	AL	59	5	0	13	77.0	327	73	38	35	9	1	1	2	30	6	61	7	0	6	2	.750	0	1-4	6	3.87	4.09
2007	Tor	AL	81	0	0	13	58.0	239	47	15	14	3	1	2	1	24	3	57	2	1	4	2	.667	0	1-4	24	2.81	2.17
2008	Tor	AL	66	0	0	14	70.2	290	54	15	14	3	5	0	4	27	7	57	3	0	0	3	.000	0	5-9	24	2.47	1.78
2009	Tor	AL	48	0	0	24	46.2	200	46	18	16	4	0	2	2	13	1	43	1	0	1	3	.250	0	9-13	10	3.50	3.09
2010	Tor	AL	67	0	0	14	61.1	241	47	19	18	3	0	0	4	14	3	48	1	0	5	5	.500	0	0-2	26	2.14	2.64
00	ChC	NL	18	18	0	0	94.0	426	117	59	54	13	2	4	5	37	1	63	1	0	4	3	.571	0	0-0	0	6.07	5.17
00	Mon	NL	1	1	0	0	3.0	16	5	3	3	0	0	0	0	3	0	0	0	0	0	0	-	0	0-0	0	10.34	9.00
9 ML YEARS			379	50	1	78	570.2	2447	566	268	240	58	11	11	26	208	25	446	20	2	27	28	.491	1	16-32	90	4.03	3.79

Kyle Drabek

Pitches: R **Bats:** R **Pos:** SP-3   **Ht:** 6'0" **Wt:** 185 **Born:** 12/8/1987 **Age:** 23

			HOW MUCH HE PITCHED						WHAT HE GAVE UP											THE RESULTS						
Year	Team	Lg	G	GS	CG	GF	IP	BFP	H	R	ER	HR	SH	SF	HB	TBB	IBB	SO	WP	Bk	W	L	Pct	Sh	Sv-Op	Hld	ERC	ERA
2006	Phillies	R	6	6	0	0	23.1	112	33	24	20	2	0	0	2	11	0	14	0	1	1	3	.250	0	0--	-	7.21	7.71
2007	Lakwd	A	11	10	0	0	54.0	236	50	29	26	9	1	1	2	23	0	46	1	0	5	1	.833	0	0--	-	4.30	4.33
2008	Phillies	R	4	4	0	0	12.0	47	6	3	3	0	0	0	1	6	0	6	2	0	0	1	.000	0	0--	-	1.65	2.25
2008	Wmspt	A-	4	4	0	0	20.1	78	11	6	5	1	1	1	1	6	0	10	3	0	1	2	.333	0	0--	-	1.43	2.21
2009	Clrwtr	A+	10	9	1	0	61.2	249	49	19	17	0	3	0	2	19	0	74	1	1	4	1	.800	1	0--	-	2.17	2.48
2009	Rdng	AA	15	14	0	0	96.1	405	92	40	39	9	5	3	1	31	2	76	2	3	8	2	.800	0	0--	-	3.49	3.64
2010	NHam	AA	27	27	1	0	162.0	663	126	67	53	12	2	2	4	68	0	132	5	2	14	9	.609	1	0--	-	2.93	2.94
2010	Tor	AL	3	3	0	0	17.0	69	18	9	9	2	1	2	0	5	0	12	2	0	0	3	.000	0	0-0	0	4.34	4.76

J.D. Drew

Bats: L **Throws:** R **Pos:** RF-133; PH-10; DH-1   **Ht:** 6'1" **Wt:** 200 **Born:** 11/20/1975 **Age:** 35

						BATTING															BASERUNNING				AVERAGES		
Year	Team	Lg	G	AB	H	2B	3B	HR	(Hm	Rd)	TB	R	RBI	RC	TBB	IBB	SO	HBP	SH	SF	SB	CS	SB%	GDP	Avg	OBP	Slg
1998	StL	NL	14	36	15	3	1	5	(4	1)	35	9	13	12	4	0	10	0	0	1	0	0	-	4	.417	.463	.972
1999	StL	NL	104	368	89	16	6	13	(5	8)	156	72	39	58	50	0	77	6	3	3	19	3	.86	4	.242	.340	.424
2000	StL	NL	135	407	120	17	2	18	(11	7)	195	73	57	80	67	4	99	6	5	1	17	9	.65	3	.295	.401	.479
2001	StL	NL	109	375	121	18	5	27	(15	12)	230	80	73	92	57	4	75	4	3	4	13	3	.81	6	.323	.414	.613
2002	StL	NL	135	424	107	19	1	18	(9	9)	182	61	56	65	57	4	104	8	3	4	8	2	.80	4	.252	.349	.429
2003	StL	NL	100	287	83	13	3	15	(7	8)	147	60	42	58	36	0	48	3	2	0	2	2	.50	6	.289	.374	.512
2004	Atl	NL	145	518	158	28	8	31	(14	17)	295	118	93	121	118	2	116	5	1	3	12	3	.80	7	.305	.436	.569
2005	LAD	NL	72	252	72	12	1	15	(10	5)	131	48	36	49	51	3	50	5	0	3	1	1	.50	3	.286	.412	.520
2006	LAD	NL	146	494	140	34	6	20	(12	8)	246	84	100	92	89	8	106	4	1	6	2	3	.40	4	.283	.393	.498
2007	Bos	AL	140	466	126	30	4	11	(4	7)	197	84	64	68	79	10	100	1	0	6	4	2	.67	12	.270	.373	.423
2008	Bos	AL	109	368	103	23	4	19	(10	9)	191	79	64	72	79	5	80	4	0	5	4	1	.80	11	.280	.408	.519
2009	Bos	AL	137	452	126	30	4	24	(11	13)	236	84	68	81	82	5	109	3	1	1	2	6	.25	6	.279	.392	.522
2010	Bos	AL	139	478	122	24	2	22	(9	13)	216	69	68	67	60	3	105	4	0	4	3	1	.75	12	.255	.341	.452
	Postseason		55	184	48	6	0	7	(4	3)	75	19	25	22	18	0	36	2	2	0	3	1	.75	4	.261	.333	.408
	13 ML YEARS		1485	4925	1382	267	47	238	(121	117)	2457	921	773	915	829	48	1079	53	19	41	87	36	.71	82	.281	.387	.499

Stephen Drew

Bats: L **Throws:** R **Pos:** SS-147; PH-6   **Ht:** 6'0" **Wt:** 185 **Born:** 3/16/1983 **Age:** 28

						BATTING															BASERUNNING				AVERAGES		
Year	Team	Lg	G	AB	H	2B	3B	HR	(Hm	Rd)	TB	R	RBI	RC	TBB	IBB	SO	HBP	SH	SF	SB	CS	SB%	GDP	Avg	OBP	Slg
2006	Ari	NL	59	209	66	13	7	5	(3	2)	108	27	23	31	14	4	50	0	2	1	2	0	1.00	1	.316	.357	.517
2007	Ari	NL	150	543	129	28	4	12	(6	6)	201	60	60	71	60	5	100	3	5	8	9	0	1.00	4	.238	.313	.370
2008	Ari	NL	152	611	178	44	11	21	(9	12)	307	91	67	97	41	6	109	1	3	7	3	3	.50	5	.291	.333	.502
2009	Ari	NL	135	533	139	29	12	12	(4	8)	228	71	65	76	49	7	87	1	5	7	5	1	.83	5	.261	.320	.428
2010	Ari	NL	151	565	157	33	12	15	(5	10)	259	83	61	84	62	2	108	3	2	1	10	5	.67	8	.278	.352	.458
	Postseason		7	31	12	1	1	2	(1	1)	21	6	4	5	1	0	7	0	0	0	1	0	1.00	1	.387	.406	.677
	5 ML YEARS		647	2461	669	147	46	65	(27	38)	1103	332	276	359	226	24	454	8	17	24	29	9	.76	23	.272	.332	.448

Justin Duchscherer

Pitches: R **Bats:** R **Pos:** SP-5   DUKE-sherr   **Ht:** 6'3" **Wt:** 199 **Born:** 11/19/1977 **Age:** 33

						HOW MUCH HE PITCHED						WHAT HE GAVE UP											THE RESULTS					
Year	Team	Lg	G	GS	CG	GF	IP	BFP	H	R	ER	HR	SH	SF	HB	TBB	IBB	SO	WP	Bk	W	L	Pct	Sh	Sv-Op	Hld	ERC	ERA
2001	Tex	AL	5	2	0	1	14.2	76	24	20	20	5	0	0	4	4	0	11	1	0	1	1	.500	0	0-0	0	10.68	12.27
2003	Oak	AL	4	3	0	0	16.1	71	17	7	6	1	1	0	2	3	0	15	0	0	1	1	.500	0	0-0	0	3.58	3.31
2004	Oak	AL	53	0	0	18	96.1	398	85	37	35	13	7	1	5	32	6	59	1	1	7	6	.538	0	0-2	6	3.57	3.27
2005	Oak	AL	65	0	0	24	85.2	338	67	25	21	7	4	2	2	19	3	85	2	0	7	4	.636	0	5-7	10	2.23	2.21
2006	Oak	AL	53	0	0	17	55.2	224	52	18	18	4	1	0	1	9	0	51	3	0	2	1	.667	0	9-11	17	2.73	2.91
2007	Oak	AL	17	0	0	7	16.1	75	18	9	9	3	1	2	0	8	3	13	0	0	3	3	.500	0	0-2	5	5.22	4.96
2008	Oak	AL	22	22	1	0	141.2	557	107	45	40	11	1	4	8	34	2	95	1	0	10	8	.556	1	0-0	0	2.31	2.54
2010	Oak	AL	5	5	0	0	28.0	116	26	11	9	3	0	1	1	12	0	18	2	0	2	1	.667	0	0-0	0	4.16	2.89
	Postseason		2	0	0	0	4.0	13	1	1	1	1	0	0	0	0	0	4	0	0	0	0	-	0	0-0	2	0.46	2.25
	8 ML YEARS		224	32	1	62	454.2	1855	396	172	158	47	15	10	23	121	14	347	10	1	33	25	.569	1	14-22	38	3.07	3.13

Lucas Duda

Bats: L **Throws:** R **Pos:** LF-24; PH-5   **Ht:** 6'4" **Wt:** 225 **Born:** 2/3/1986 **Age:** 25

						BATTING															BASERUNNING				AVERAGES		
Year	Team	Lg	G	AB	H	2B	3B	HR	(Hm	Rd)	TB	R	RBI	RC	TBB	IBB	SO	HBP	SH	SF	SB	CS	SB%	GDP	Avg	OBP	Slg
2007	Bklyn	A-	67	234	70	20	3	4	(-	-)	108	32	32	43	34	3	45	5	0	1	3	5	.38	2	.299	.398	.462
2008	StLuci	A+	133	483	127	26	3	11	(-	-)	192	58	66	71	66	3	129	7	0	3	2	7	.22	15	.263	.358	.398
2009	Bnghtn	AA	110	395	111	29	1	9	(-	-)	169	49	53	69	61	5	91	5	1	5	2	2	.50	10	.281	.380	.428
2010	Bnghtn	AA	45	161	46	17	0	6	(-	-)	81	30	34	35	29	1	27	6	0	1	1	0	1.00	2	.286	.411	.503
2010	Buffalo	AAA	70	264	83	23	2	17	(-	-)	161	44	53	60	31	3	57	2	0	1	0	0	-	4	.314	.389	.610
2010	NYM	NL	29	84	17	6	0	4	(3	1)	35	11	13	5	6	0	22	1	0	1	0	0	-	2	.202	.261	.417

Brian Duensing

Pitches: L Bats: L Pos: RP-40; SP-13   DUNN-sing   Ht: 5'11" Wt: 205 Born: 2/22/1983 Age: 28

		HOW MUCH HE PITCHED						WHAT HE GAVE UP											THE RESULTS						
Year	Team	Lg	G	GS	CG	GF	IP	BFP	H	R	ER	HR	SH	SF	HB	TBB	IBB	SO	WP	Bk	W	L	Pct	Sh	Sv-Op	Hld	ERC	ERA
2005	Elizab	R+	12	9	0	0	50.1	215	49	19	13	4	1	1	0	16	0	55	6	0	4	3	.571	0	0--	-	3.41	2.32
2006	Beloit	A	11	11	0	0	70.1	291	68	26	23	3	7	4	1	14	0	55	1	0	2	3	.400	0	0--	-	2.79	2.94
2006	FtMyrs	A+	7	7	0	0	40.1	170	47	25	19	4	0	3	0	8	0	33	1	0	2	5	.286	0	0--	-	4.26	4.24
2006	NwBrit	AA	10	9	0	0	49.1	211	51	29	20	6	3	5	1	18	0	30	0	0	1	2	.333	0	0--	-	4.42	3.65
2007	NwBrit	AA	9	9	0	0	50.2	206	47	19	15	2	1	1	1	7	0	38	0	0	4	1	.800	0	0--	-	2.37	2.66
2007	Roch	AAA	19	19	3	0	116.2	483	115	54	42	13	2	6	5	30	0	86	1	0	11	5	.688	1	0--	-	3.75	3.24
2008	Roch	AAA	25	24	0	0	138.2	590	150	75	66	16	7	4	6	34	2	77	4	0	5	11	.313	0	0--	-	4.20	4.28
2009	Roch	AAA	13	13	0	0	75.1	321	87	40	39	2	2	6	2	19	2	44	2	0	4	6	.400	0	0--	-	3.97	4.66
2009	Min	AL	24	9	0	3	84.0	359	84	37	34	7	3	2	3	31	1	53	1	0	5	2	.714	0	0-0	1	4.00	3.64
2010	Min	AL	53	13	1	11	130.2	535	122	42	38	11	4	0	3	35	5	78	1	0	10	3	.769	1	0-0	9	3.18	2.62
	Postseason		1	1	0	0	4.2	22	7	5	5	1	0	0	0	1	0	3	1	0	0	1	.000	0	0-0	0	7.03	9.64
	2 ML YEARS		77	22	1	14	214.2	894	206	79	72	18	7	2	6	66	6	131	2	0	15	5	.750	1	0-0	10	3.49	3.02

Zach Duke

Pitches: L Bats: L Pos: SP-29   Ht: 6'2" Wt: 205 Born: 4/19/1983 Age: 28

		HOW MUCH HE PITCHED						WHAT HE GAVE UP											THE RESULTS						
Year	Team	Lg	G	GS	CG	GF	IP	BFP	H	R	ER	HR	SH	SF	HB	TBB	IBB	SO	WP	Bk	W	L	Pct	Sh	Sv-Op	Hld	ERC	ERA
2010	Altna*	AA	2	2	0	0	7.0	24	5	2	2	1	0	0	0	1	0	1	0	0	0	0	-	0	0--	-	2.20	2.57
2005	Pit	NL	14	14	0	0	84.2	341	79	20	17	3	3	1	2	23	2	58	1	0	8	2	.800	0	0-0	0	2.96	1.81
2006	Pit	NL	34	34	2	0	215.1	935	255	116	107	17	13	4	7	68	6	117	8	1	10	15	.400	1	0-0	0	4.82	4.47
2007	Pit	NL	20	19	0	0	107.1	482	161	74	66	14	2	4	3	25	2	41	0	1	3	8	.273	0	0-0	0	6.96	5.53
2008	Pit	NL	31	31	1	0	185.0	829	230	111	99	19	14	4	7	47	1	87	2	2	5	14	.263	1	0-0	0	4.99	4.82
2009	Pit	NL	32	32	3	0	213.0	891	231	101	96	23	18	10	3	49	0	106	2	1	11	16	.407	1	0-0	0	4.05	4.06
2010	Pit	NL	29	29	0	0	159.0	730	212	115	101	25	9	6	4	51	2	96	4	3	8	15	.348	0	0-0	0	6.22	5.72
	6 ML YEARS		160	159	6	0	964.1	4208	1168	537	486	101	59	29	26	263	13	505	17	8	45	70	.391	3	0-0	0	4.95	4.54

Elijah Dukes

Bats: R Throws: R Pos: RF   Ht: 6'1" Wt: 248 Born: 6/26/1984 Age: 27

			BATTING																BASERUNNING				AVERAGES		
Year	Team	Lg	G	AB	H	2B	3B	HR	(Hm | Rd)	TB	R	RBI	RC	TBB	IBB	SO	HBP	SH	SF	SB	CS	SB%	GDP	Avg	OBP	Slg
2007	TB	AL	52	184	35	3	2	10	(4 | 6)	72	27	21	20	33	3	44	2	0	1	2	1	.33	6	.190	.318	.391
2008	Was	NL	81	276	73	16	2	13	(7 | 6)	132	48	44	40	50	1	70	6	0	1	13	4	.76	10	.264	.386	.478
2009	Was	NL	107	364	91	20	4	8	(6 | 2)	143	38	58	44	46	2	74	3	0	3	3	10	.23	8	.250	.337	.393
	3 ML YEARS		240	824	199	39	8	31	(17 | 14)	347	113	123	110	129	3	197	11	0	6	18	18	.50	24	.242	.349	.421

Shelley Duncan

Bats: R Throws: R Pos: LF-41; DH-22; DH 17; RF 8; 1B-4   Ht: 6'5" Wt: 225 Born: 9/29/1979 Age: 31

			BATTING																BASERUNNING				AVERAGES		
Year	Team	Lg	G	AB	H	2B	3B	HR	(Hm | Rd)	TB	R	RBI	RC	TBB	IBB	SO	HBP	SH	SF	SB	CS	SB%	GDP	Avg	OBP	Slg
2010	Clmbs*	AAA	38	146	44	11	0	6	(- | -)	73	21	34	28	17	0	28	2	0	1	0	0	-	5	.301	.380	.500
2007	NYY	AL	34	74	19	1	0	7	(6 | 1)	41	16	17	14	8	0	20	0	1	0	0	0	-	2	.257	.329	.554
2008	NYY	AL	23	57	10	3	0	1	(1 | 0)	16	7	6	4	7	0	13	0	0	0	0	0	-	1	.175	.262	.281
2009	NYY	AL	11	15	3	0	0	0	(0 | 0)	3	1	1	1	0	0	5	0	0	0	0	0	-	0	.200	.200	.200
2010	Cle	AL	85	229	53	10	0	11	(9 | 2)	96	29	36	30	20	2	70	3	0	1	1	0	1.00	4	.231	.317	.419
	Postseason		3	4	2	0	0	0	(0 | 0)	2	1	0	1	0	0	1	0	0	0	0	0	-	0	.500	.500	.500
	4 ML YEARS		153	375	85	14	0	19	(16 | 3)	156	53	60	49	41	2	114	3	1	2	1	0	1.00	8	.227	.306	.416

Adam Dunn

Bats: L Throws: R Pos: 1B-153, PH-5; DH-2   Ht: 6'6" Wt: 287 Born: 11/9/1979 Age: 31

			BATTING																BASERUNNING				AVERAGES		
Year	Team	Lg	G	AB	H	2B	3B	HR	(Hm | Rd)	TB	R	RBI	RC	TBB	IBB	SO	HBP	SH	SF	SB	CS	SB%	GDP	Avg	OBP	Slg
2001	Cin	NL	66	244	64	18	1	19	(8 | 11)	141	54	43	51	38	2	74	4	0	0	4	2	.67	4	.262	.371	.578
2002	Cin	NL	158	535	133	28	2	26	(13 | 13)	243	84	71	96	128	13	170	9	1	3	19	9	.68	8	.249	.400	.454
2003	Cin	NL	116	381	82	12	1	27	(16 | 11)	177	70	57	61	74	8	126	10	0	4	8	2	.80	4	.215	.354	.465
2004	Cin	NL	161	568	151	34	0	46	(25 | 21)	323	105	102	108	108	11	195	5	0	4	6	1	.86	8	.266	.388	.569
2005	Cin	NL	160	543	134	35	2	40	(26 | 14)	293	107	101	112	114	14	168	12	0	2	4	2	.67	6	.247	.387	.540
2006	Cin	NL	160	561	131	24	0	40	(22 | 18)	275	99	92	96	112	12	194	6	1	3	7	0	1.00	8	.234	.365	.490
2007	Cin	NL	152	522	138	27	2	40	(19 | 21)	289	101	106	103	101	8	165	5	0	4	9	2	.82	12	.264	.386	.554
2008	2 Tms	NL	158	517	122	23	0	40	(19 | 21)	265	79	100	101	122	13	164	7	0	5	2	1	.67	7	.236	.386	.513
2009	Was	NL	159	546	146	29	2	38	(19 | 19)	289	81	105	109	116	16	177	4	0	2	0	1	.00	8	.267	.398	.529
2010	Was	NL	158	558	145	36	2	38	(20 | 18)	299	85	103	88	77	10	199	9	0	4	0	1	.00	10	.260	.356	.536
08	Cin	NL	114	373	87	14	0	32	(16 | 16)	197	58	74	74	80	6	120	6	0	5	1	1	.50	4	.233	.373	.528
08	Ari	NL	44	144	35	9	0	8	(5 | 3)	68	21	26	27	42	7	44	1	0	0	1	0	1.00	3	.243	.417	.472
	10 ML YEARS		1448	4975	1246	266	10	354	(189 | 165)	2594	865	880	925	990	107	1632	71	2	27	59	21	.74	75	.250	.381	.521

Michael Dunn

Pitches: L Bats: L Pos: RP-25   Ht: 6'1" Wt: 195 Born: 5/23/1985 Age: 26

Year	Team	Lg	G	GS	CG	GF	IP	BFP	H	R	ER	HR	SH	SF	HB	TBB	IBB	SO	WP	Bk	W	L	Pct	Sh	Sv-Op	Hld	ERC	ERA
2006	Yanks	R	11	0	0	7	24.2	95	13	2	2	0	1	0	1	9	0	26	1	0	3	0	1.000	0	4--	-	1.33	0.73
2006	StIsInd	A-	3	0	0	0	6.1	31	3	6	4	0	0	0	0	7	0	7	2	0	0	0	-	0	0--	-	2.77	5.68
2007	CtnSC	A	27	27	0	0	144.2	597	136	69	55	14	3	8	3	45	0	138	10	0	12	5	.706	0	0--	-	3.52	3.42
2008	Tampa	A+	30	22	0	4	124.2	543	124	70	63	10	8	6	5	58	2	118	7	0	4	7	.364	0	1--	-	4.34	4.55
2008	Trntn	AA	1	0	0	0	1.2	7	1	0	0	0	0	0	0	1	0	2	0	0	1	0	1.000	0	0--	-	2.03	0.00
2009	Trntn	AA	26	0	0	6	53.1	230	41	23	22	3	2	0	2	32	2	76	0	0	3	3	.500	0	2--	-	3.35	3.71
2009	S-WB	AAA	12	0	0	2	20.0	90	17	5	5	1	0	1	1	14	0	23	1	0	1	0	1.000	0	0--	-	4.21	2.25
2010	Gwnntt	AAA	38	0	0	18	47.1	200	31	12	8	1	2	2	2	25	0	64	4	1	2	0	1.000	0	7--	-	2.32	1.52
2009	NYY	AL	4	0	0	3	4.0	20	3	3	3	1	0	0	0	5	0	5	1	0	0	0	-	0	0-0	0	7.17	6.75
2010	Atl	NL	25	0	0	1	19.0	88	15	4	4	1	0	0	0	17	2	27	2	0	2	0	1.000	0	0-0	1	4.19	1.89
	2 ML YEARS		29	0	0	8	23.0	108	18	7	7	2	0	0	0	22	2	32	3	0	2	0	1.000	0	0-0	1	4.69	2.74

Luis Durango

Bats: B Throws: R Pos: PH-17; CF-10; PR-2   Ht: 5'9" Wt: 158 Born: 4/23/1986 Age: 25

Year	Team	Lg	G	AB	H	2B	3B	HR	(Hm	Rd)	TB	R	RBI	RC	TBB	IBB	SO	HBP	SH	SF	SB	CS	SB%	GDP	Avg	OBP	Slg
2006	Padres	R	39	143	54	2	4	0	(-	-)	64	35	14	32	23	0	16	2	2	0	17	6	.74	2	.378	.470	.448
2007	Eugene	A-	69	300	110	6	8	2	(-	-)	138	60	32	58	29	2	32	1	3	2	17	10	.63	5	.367	.422	.460
2008	FtWyn	A	93	334	102	11	3	1	(-	-)	122	56	25	53	49	0	43	1	4	1	14	7	.67	9	.305	.395	.365
2008	Lk Els	A+	17	72	31	4	1	0	(-	-)	37	20	10	18	13	0	7	0	0	2	1	1	.50	1	.431	.506	.514
2009	SnAnt	AA	129	456	128	9	2	0	(-	-)	141	78	25	68	81	2	70	2	19	2	44	17	.72	7	.281	.390	.309
2010	Portlnd	AAA	106	363	109	5	2	0	(-	-)	118	42	24	51	45	1	59	1	13	1	35	16	.69	8	.300	.378	.325
2009	SD	NL	9	11	6	0	0	0	(0	0)	6	3	0	3	2	0	2	0	1	0	2	1	.67	0	.545	.615	.545
2010	SD	NL	28	48	12	0	0	0	(0	0)	12	8	4	3	4	0	7	0	1	0	5	0	1.00	3	.250	.308	.250
	2 ML YEARS		37	59	18	0	0	0	(0	0)	18	11	4	6	6	0	9	0	2	0	7	1	.88	3	.305	.369	.305

Chad Durbin

Pitches: R Bats: B Pos: RP-64   DURR-binn   Ht: 6'2" Wt: 224 Born: 12/3/1977 Age: 33

Year	Team	Lg	G	GS	CG	GF	IP	BFP	H	R	ER	HR	SH	SF	HB	TBB	IBB	SO	WP	Bk	W	L	Pct	Sh	Sv-Op	Hld	ERC	ERA
2010	Clrwtr*	A+	2	0	0	0	3.0	9	0	0	0	0	0	0	0	0	0	3	0	0	1	0	1.000	0	0--	-	0.00	0.00
1999	KC	AL	1	0	0	0	2.1	9	1	0	0	0	0	0	0	1	0	3	1	0	0	0	-	0	0-0	0	1.08	0.00
2000	KC	AL	16	16	0	0	72.1	349	91	71	66	14	1	3	0	43	1	37	7	0	2	5	.286	0	0-0	0	7.05	8.21
2001	KC	AL	29	29	2	0	179.0	777	201	109	98	26	2	7	11	58	0	95	6	0	9	16	.360	0	0-0	0	5.15	4.93
2002	KC	AL	2	2	0	0	8.1	43	13	11	11	3	0	0	1	4	0	5	0	0	0	1	.000	0	0-0	0	10.58	11.88
2003	Cle	AL	3	1	0	0	8.2	45	18	12	7	2	0	0	1	3	0	8	2	0	0	1	.000	0	0-0	0	12.37	7.27
2004	2 Tms		24	8	1	5	60.2	291	72	50	47	11	2	2	5	35	3	48	5	0	6	7	.462	0	0-0	1	6.75	6.97
2006	Det	AL	3	0	0	1	6.0	24	6	1	1	1	0	0	0	3	0	3	0	0	0	0	-	0	0-0	0	2.87	1.50
2007	Det	AL	36	19	0	7	127.2	561	133	71	67	21	1	7	8	49	4	66	2	0	8	7	.533	0	1-2	3	4.92	4.72
2008	Phi	NL	71	0	0	12	87.2	365	81	33	28	8	4	3	7	35	7	63	3	0	5	4	.556	0	1-7	17	3.51	2.87
2009	Phi	NL	59	0	0	15	69.2	314	56	38	34	8	3	3	7	47	2	62	2	0	2	2	.500	0	2-3	8	4.47	4.39
2010	Phi	NL	64	0	0	9	68.2	291	63	29	29	7	1	2	5	27	2	63	0	0	4	1	.800	0	0-1	15	3.90	3.80
04	Cle	AL	17	8	1	5	51.1	239	63	40	38	10	0	2	4	24	3	38	3	0	5	6	.455	0	0-0	0	6.70	6.66
04	Ari	NL	7	0	0	0	9.1	52	9	10	9	1	2	0	1	11	0	10	2	0	1	1	.500	0	0-0	1	6.92	8.68
	Postseason		13	0	0	2	8.2	43	10	6	5	1	1	0	2	5	0	6	0	0	2	0	1.000	0	0-0	3	6.64	5.19
	11 ML YEARS		308	75	3	49	691.0	3069	735	425	388	98	14	26	41	302	19	453	28	0	36	44	.450	0	4-13	44	5.12	5.05

Jermaine Dye

Bats: R Throws: R Pos: RF   Ht: 6'5" Wt: 245 Born: 1/28/1974 Age: 37

Year	Team	Lg	G	AB	H	2B	3B	HR	(Hm	Rd)	TB	R	RBI	RC	TBB	IBB	SO	HBP	SH	SF	SB	CS	SB%	GDP	Avg	OBP	Slg
1996	Atl	NL	98	292	82	16	0	12	(4	8)	134	32	37	36	8	0	67	3	0	3	1	4	.20	11	.281	.304	.459
1997	KC	AL	75	263	62	14	0	7	(3	4)	97	26	22	26	17	0	51	1	1	1	2	1	.67	6	.236	.284	.369
1998	KC	AL	60	214	50	5	1	5	(3	2)	72	24	23	17	11	2	46	1	0	4	2	2	.50	8	.234	.270	.336
1999	KC	AL	158	608	179	44	8	27	(15	12)	320	96	119	106	58	4	119	1	0	6	2	3	.40	17	.294	.354	.526
2000	KC	AL	157	601	193	41	2	33	(15	18)	337	107	118	125	69	6	99	3	0	6	0	1	.00	12	.321	.390	.561
2001	2 Tms		158	599	169	31	1	26	(16	10)	280	91	106	99	57	6	112	7	1	11	9	1	.90	8	.282	.346	.467
2002	Oak	AL	131	488	123	27	1	24	(13	11)	224	74	86	70	52	2	108	10	0	5	2	0	1.00	15	.252	.333	.459
2003	Oak	AL	65	221	38	6	0	4	(3	1)	56	28	20	10	25	2	42	3	0	4	1	0	1.00	11	.172	.261	.253
2004	Oak	AL	137	532	141	29	4	23	(12	11)	247	87	80	69	49	4	128	4	0	5	4	2	.67	16	.265	.329	.464
2005	CWS	AL	145	529	145	29	2	31	(15	16)	271	74	86	80	39	3	99	9	0	2	11	4	.73	15	.274	.333	.512
2006	CWS	AL	146	539	170	27	3	44	(21	23)	335	103	120	116	59	4	118	6	0	7	7	3	.70	15	.315	.385	.622
2007	CWS	AL	138	508	129	34	0	28	(14	14)	247	68	78	67	45	2	107	4	0	4	2	1	.67	17	.254	.317	.486
2008	CWS	AL	154	590	172	41	2	34	(18	16)	319	96	96	91	44	3	104	4	0	6	3	2	.60	18	.292	.344	.541
2009	CWS	AL	141	503	126	19	1	27	(15	12)	228	78	81	79	64	2	108	5	0	2	0	2	.00	15	.250	.340	.453
01	KC	AL	97	367	100	14	0	13	(8	5)	153	50	47	54	30	3	68	6	1	6	7	1	.88	2	.272	.333	.417
01	Oak	AL	61	232	69	17	1	13	(8	5)	127	41	59	45	27	3	44	1	0	5	2	0	1.00	6	.297	.366	.547
	Postseason		44	163	44	9	0	5	(2	3)	68	16	17	17	12	0	33	3	1	2	2	1	.67	2	.270	.328	.417
	14 ML YEARS		1763	6487	1779	363	25	325	(167	158)	3167	984	1072	991	597	40	1308	63	2	65	46	26	.64	184	.274	.338	.488

Jarrod Dyson

Bats: L **Throws:** R **Pos:** CF-15; PR-2; PH-1   **Ht:** 5'9" **Wt:** 161 **Born:** 8/15/1984 **Age:** 26

Year Team	Lg	G	AB	H	2B	3B	HR	(Hm	Rd)	TB	R	RBI	RC	TBB	IBB	SO	HBP	SH	SF	SB	CS	SB%	GDP	Avg	OBP	Slg
2006 Royals	R	51	161	44	4	6	0	(-	-)	60	40	19	26	18	1	30	5	2	3	19	4	.83	0	.273	.358	.373
2007 Burlgtn	A	10	37	10	1	0	0	(-	-)	11	6	0	3	2	0	12	0	0	0	3	1	.75	0	.270	.308	.297
2008 Wilmg	A+	93	288	75	8	0	0	(-	-)	83	40	24	35	32	0	60	2	8	1	39	9	.81	1	.260	.337	.288
2009 Burlgtn	A+	17	67	23	2	1	0	(-	-)	27	14	5	11	5	0	14	1	2	0	9	4	.69	0	.343	.397	.403
2009 NWArk	AA	63	248	64	7	4	0	(-	-)	79	38	14	33	27	0	54	0	8	0	37	6	.86	6	.258	.331	.319
2010 Royals	R	6	25	13	1	1	0	(-	-)	16	4	6	6	0	0	3	0	0	0	3	1	.75	0	.520	.520	.640
2010 Wilmg	A+	12	49	16	6	2	0	(-	-)	26	7	9	9	1	0	9	0	0	2	5	1	.83	0	.327	.327	.531
2010 NWArk	AA	7	25	6	0	0	0	(-	-)	6	6	6	2	5	0	2	1	0	1	3	3	.50	2	.240	.375	.240
2010 Omha	AAA	46	195	53	10	1	1	(-	-)	68	33	19	25	16	0	32	1	5	2	13	3	.81	6	.272	.327	.349
2010 KC	AL	18	57	12	4	2	1	(1	0)	23	11	5	9	6	0	16	0	2	0	9	1	.90	2	.211	.286	.404

David Eckstein

Bats: R **Throws:** R **Pos:** 2B-113; PH-7   **Ht:** 5'7" **Wt:** 177 **Born:** 1/20/1975 **Age:** 36

Year Team	Lg	G	AB	H	2B	3B	HR	(Hm	Rd)	TB	R	RBI	RC	TBB	IBB	SO	HBP	SH	SF	SB	CS	SB%	GDP	Avg	OBP	Slg
2010 FtWyn*	A	3	9	3	1	0	0	(-	-)	4	1	3	2	2	0	0	1	0	0	0	0	-		.333	.500	.444
2001 LAA	AL	153	582	166	26	2	4	(3	1)	208	82	41	80	43	0	60	21	16	2	29	4	.88	11	.285	.355	.357
2002 LAA	AL	152	608	178	22	6	8	(3	5)	236	107	63	93	45	0	44	27	14	8	21	13	.62	7	.293	.363	.388
2003 LAA	AL	120	452	114	22	1	3	(1	2)	147	59	31	53	36	0	45	15	10	4	16	5	.76	9	.252	.325	.325
2004 LAA	AL	142	566	156	24	1	2	(2	0)	188	92	35	60	42	1	49	13	14	2	16	5	.76	11	.276	.339	.332
2005 StL	NL	158	630	185	26	7	8	(3	5)	249	90	61	103	58	0	44	13	8	4	11	8	.58	13	.294	.363	.395
2006 StL	NL	123	500	146	18	1	2	(0	2)	172	68	23	60	31	0	41	15	3	3	7	6	.54	7	.292	.350	.344
2007 StL	NL	117	434	134	23	0	3	(1	2)	166	58	31	55	24	0	22	12	7	7	10	1	.91	9	.309	.356	.382
2008 2 Tms		94	324	86	21	0	2	(2	0)	113	32	27	42	31	1	32	9	9	3	2	1	.67	9	.265	.343	.349
2009 SD	NL	136	503	131	27	2	2	(2	0)	168	64	51	62	39	1	46	9	13	4	3	1	.75	8	.260	.323	.334
2010 SD	NL	116	442	118	23	0	1	(1	0)	144	49	29	49	27	0	35	9	12	2	8	1	.89	6	.267	.321	.326
08 Tor	AL	76	260	72	18	0	1	(1	0)	93	27	23	37	24	1	27	8	9	2	2	1	.67	6	.277	.354	.358
08 Ari	AL	18	64	14	3	0	1	(1	0)	20	5	4	5	7	0	5	1	0	1	0	0	-	1	.219	.301	.313
Postseason		44	170	49	4	0	2	(1	1)	59	26	18	25	12	0	9	7	3	2	7	1	.88	2	.278	.345	.335
10 ML YEARS		1311	5041	1414	232	20	35	(18	17)	1791	701	392	657	376	3	418	143	106	39	123	45	.73	88	.280	.345	.355

Jim Edmonds

Bats: L **Throws:** L **Pos:** CF-52; PH-26; RF-14; 1B-6; LF-1   **Ht:** 6'1" **Wt:** 212 **Born:** 6/27/1970 **Age:** 41

Year Team	Lg	G	AB	H	2B	3B	HR	(Hm	Rd)	TB	R	RBI	RC	TBB	IBB	SO	HBP	SH	SF	SB	CS	SB%	GDP	Avg	OBP	Slg
1993 LAA	AL	18	61	15	4	1	0	(0	0)	21	5	4	4	2	1	16	0	0	0	0	2	.00	1	.246	.270	.344
1994 LAA	AL	94	289	79	13	1	5	(3	2)	109	35	37	38	30	3	72	1	1	1	4	2	.67	3	.273	.343	.377
1995 LAA	AL	141	558	162	30	4	33	(16	17)	299	120	107	100	51	4	130	5	1	5	1	4	.20	10	.290	.352	.536
1996 LAA	AL	114	431	131	28	3	27	(17	10)	246	73	66	88	46	2	101	4	0	2	4	0	1.00	6	.304	.375	.571
1997 LAA	AL	133	502	146	27	0	26	(14	12)	251	82	80	90	60	5	80	4	0	5	5	7	.42	7	.291	.368	.500
1998 LAA	AL	154	599	184	42	1	25	(9	16)	303	115	91	104	57	7	114	1	1	1	7	5	.58	16	.307	.368	.506
1999 LAA	AL	55	204	51	17	2	5	(3	2)	87	34	23	30	28	0	45	0	0	1	5	4	.56	3	.250	.339	.426
2000 StL	NL	152	525	155	25	0	42	(22	20)	306	129	108	126	103	3	167	6	1	8	10	3	.77	5	.295	.411	.583
2001 StL	NL	150	500	150	38	1	30	(16	14)	282	95	110	113	93	12	138	4	1	10	5	5	.50	8	.304	.410	.664
2002 StL	NL	144	476	148	31	2	28	(17	11)	267	96	83	101	86	14	134	8	0	6	4	3	.57	9	.311	.420	.561
2003 StL	NL	137	447	123	32	2	39	(17	22)	276	89	89	87	77	6	127	4	1	2	1	3	.25	11	.275	.385	.617
2004 StL	NL	153	498	150	30	3	42	(24	18)	320	102	111	115	101	12	150	5	0	8	8	3	.73	4	.301	.385	.643
2005 StL	NL	142	467	123	37	1	29	(15	14)	249	88	89	95	91	10	139	4	1	4	5	5	.50	6	.263	.385	.533
2006 StL	NL	110	350	90	18	0	19	(11	8)	165	52	70	51	53	7	101	0	0	5	4	0	1.00	11	.257	.350	.471
2007 StL	NL	117	365	92	15	2	12	(5	7)	147	39	53	43	41	2	75	0	2	3	0	2	.00	9	.252	.325	.403
2008 2 Tms	NL	111	340	80	19	2	20	(11	9)	163	53	55	48	55	3	82	2	1	3	2	2	.50	4	.235	.343	.479
2010 2 Tms	NL	86	246	68	23	0	11	(4	7)	124	44	23	33	24	0	60	1	0	1	2	0	1.00	2	.276	.342	.504
08 SD	NL	26	90	16	2	0	1	(0	1)	21	6	6	5	10	1	24	1	1	1	2	1	.67	1	.178	.265	.233
08 ChC	NL	85	250	64	17	2	19	(11	8)	142	47	49	43	45	2	58	1	0	2	0	1	.00	7	.256	.369	.568
10 Mil	NL	73	217	62	21	0	8	(4	4)	107	30	20	61	21	0	53	1	0	1	2	0	1.00	2	.286	.350	.493
10 Cin	NL	13	29	6	2	0	3	(0	3)	17	6	3	2	3	0	7	0	0	0	0	0	-	0	.207	.281	.586
Postseason		64	230	63	16	0	13	(7	6)	118	33	42	38	30	3	72	2	0	1	2	2	.50	1	.274	.361	.513
17 ML YEARS		2011	6858	1949	437	25	393	(204	189)	3615	1251	1199	1266	998	91	1729	49	10	65	67	50	.57	122	.284	.376	.527

Mike Ekstrom

Pitches: R **Bats:** R **Pos:** RP-15   **Ht:** 5'11" **Wt:** 190 **Born:** 8/30/1983 **Age:** 27

Year Team	Lg	G	GS	CG	GF	IP	BFP	H	R	ER	HR	SH	SF	HB	TBB	IBB	SO	WP	Bk	W	L	Pct	Sh	Sv-Op	Hld	ERC	ERA
2010 Drham*	AAA	39	1	0	11	58.0	242	55	21	18	5	2	1	2	19	1	48	2	0	6	1	.857	0	1--	-	3.57	2.79
2008 SD	NL	8	0	0	1	9.2	47	14	8	8	2	0	0	0	7	1	6	0	0	0	2	.000	0	0-0	0	9.38	7.45
2009 SD	NL	12	0	0	5	18.1	83	21	14	13	3	0	2	1	8	0	19	2	0	0	0	-	0	0-0	0	5.80	6.38
2010 TB	AL	15	0	0	10	16.1	68	12	6	6	0	0	1	2	9	1	10	1	0	0	1	.000	0	0-0	0	2.98	3.31
3 ML YEARS		35	0	0	16	44.1	198	47	28	27	5	0	3	3	24	2	35	3	0	0	3	.000	0	0-0	0	5.41	5.48

Scott Elbert

Pitches: L Bats: L Pos: RP-1 Ht: 6'2" Wt: 213 Born: 8/13/1985 Age: 25

				HOW MUCH HE PITCHED					WHAT HE GAVE UP												THE RESULTS							
Year	Team	Lg	G	GS	CG	GF	IP	BFP	H	R	ER	HR	SH	SF	HB	TBB	IBB	SO	WP	Bk	W	L	Pct	Sh	Sv-Op	Hld	ERC	ERA
2010	Albq*	AAA	9	9	0	0	43.1	209	46	26	24	4	5	2	2	34	0	45	4	0	1	1	.500	0	0- -	-	6.07	4.98
2008	LAD	NL	10	0	0	1	6.0	31	9	8	8	2	0	0	1	4	0	8	0	0	0	1	.000	0	0-0	2	11.46	12.00
2009	LAD	NL	19	0	0	3	19.2	83	19	11	11	4	1	0	0	7	0	21	1	0	2	0	1.000	0	0-0	3	4.45	5.03
2010	LAD	NL	1	0	0	0	0.2	6	1	1	1	0	0	0	0	3	0	0	0	0	0	0	-	0	0-0	0	24.61	13.50
	Postseason		1	0	0	0	0.1	3	0	0	0	0	0	0	0	2	0	1	0	0	0	0	-	0	0-0	0	19.60	0.00
	3 ML YEARS		30	0	0	4	26.1	120	29	20	20	6	1	0	1	14	0	29	1	0	2	1	.667	0	0-0	5	6.39	6.84

Brad Eldred

Bats: R Throws: R Pos: 1B-6; PH-5 Ht: 6'5" Wt: 290 Born: 7/12/1980 Age: 30

									BATTING													BASERUNNING				AVERAGES		
Year	Team	Lg	G	AB	H	2B	3B	HR	(Hm	Rd)	TB	R	RBI	RC	TBB	IBB	SO	HBP	SH	SF			SB	CS	SB%	GDP	Avg	OBP	Slg
2010	ColSpr*	AAA	106	394	104	27	1	30	(-	-)	223	67	84	74	33	2	119	5	0	2			6	0	1.00	12	.264	.327	.566
2005	Pit	NL	55	190	42	9	0	12	(4	8)	87	23	27	14	13	0	77	3	0	2			1	1	.50	5	.221	.279	.458
2007	Pit	NL	19	46	5	1	0	2	(1	1)	12	3	3	0	1	1	16	0	0	0			0	0	-	0	.109	.128	.261
2010	Col	NL	11	24	6	1	0	1	(1	0)	10	4	3	3	2	0	10	1	0	0			0	0	-	0	.250	.333	.417
	3 ML YEARS		85	260	53	11	0	15	(6	9)	109	30	33	17	16	1	103	4	0	2			1	1	.50	6	.204	.259	.419

A.J. Ellis

Bats: R Throws: R Pos: C-43; PH-1 Ht: 6'2" Wt: 224 Born: 4/9/1981 Age: 30

									BATTING													BASERUNNING				AVERAGES		
Year	Team	Lg	G	AB	H	2B	3B	HR	(Hm	Rd)	TB	R	RBI	RC	TBB	IBB	SO	HBP	SH	SF			SB	CS	SB%	GDP	Avg	OBP	Slg
2010	Albq*	AAA	18	61	16	5	1	0	(-	-)	23	11	7	10	13	0	12	1	1	0			1	0	1.00	1	.262	.400	.377
2008	LAD	NL	4	3	0	0	0	0	(0	0)	0	1	0	0	0	0	2	0	0	0			0	0	-	0	.000	.000	.000
2009	LAD	NL	8	10	1	0	0	0	(0	0)	1	0	1	0	0	0	1	0	0	0			0	0	-	0	.100	.100	.100
2010	LAD	NL	44	108	30	5	0	0	(0	0)	35	6	16	16	14	1	18	1	4	1			0	0	-	5	.278	.363	.324
	3 ML YEARS		56	121	31	5	0	0	(0	0)	36	7	17	16	14	1	21	1	4	1			0	0	-	5	.256	.336	.298

Mark Ellis

Bats: R Throws: R Pos: 2B-116; DH-6; PH-4 Ht: 5'11" Wt: 193 Born: 6/6/1977 Age: 34

									BATTING													BASERUNNING				AVERAGES		
Year	Team	Lg	G	AB	H	2B	3B	HR	(Hm	Rd)	TB	R	RBI	RC	TBB	IBB	SO	HBP	SH	SF			SB	CS	SB%	GDP	Avg	OBP	Slg
2010	Stcktn*	A+	2	5	1	0	0	0	(-	-)	1	0	1	0	1	0	0	0	0	1			0	0	-	0	.200	.286	.200
2010	Scrmto*	AAA	1	4	1	0	0	0	(-	-)	1	0	0	0	0	0	1	0	0	0			0	0	-	0	.250	.250	.250
2002	Oak	AL	98	345	94	16	4	6	(6	0)	136	58	35	55	44	1	54	4	8	3			4	2	.67	3	.272	.359	.394
2003	Oak	AL	154	553	137	31	5	9	(7	2)	205	78	52	69	44	4	94	7	9	5			6	2	.75	7	.248	.313	.371
2005	Oak	AL	122	434	137	21	5	13	(5	8)	207	76	52	78	44	1	51	4	4	0			1	3	.25	10	.316	.384	.477
2006	Oak	AL	124	441	110	25	1	11	(7	4)	170	64	52	53	40	1	76	8	4	7			4	0	1.00	13	.249	.319	.385
2007	Oak	AL	150	583	161	33	3	19	(10	9)	257	84	76	76	44	1	94	10	2	3			9	4	.69	10	.276	.336	.441
2008	Oak	AL	117	442	103	20	3	12	(7	5)	165	55	41	54	53	2	65	5	5	2			14	2	.88	14	.233	.321	.373
2009	Oak	AL	105	377	99	23	0	10	(4	6)	152	52	61	54	23	1	54	2	3	5			10	3	.77	10	.263	.305	.403
2010	Oak	AL	124	436	127	24	0	5	(0	5)	166	45	49	66	40	4	56	8	3	5			7	6	.54	7	.291	.358	.381
	Postseason		12	43	11	2	0	1	(1	0)	16	3	4	6	5	0	11	1	0	0			0	0	-	0	.256	.347	.372
	8 ML YEARS		994	3611	968	193	21	85	(46	39)	1458	512	418	505	336	15	544	48	38	30			55	22	.71	71	.268	.336	.404

Jacoby Ellsbury

Bats: L Throws: L Pos: CF-13; LF-6 Ht: 6'1" Wt: 185 Born: 9/11/1983 Age: 27

									BATTING													BASERUNNING				AVERAGES		
Year	Team	Lg	G	AB	H	2B	3B	HR	(Hm	Rd)	TB	R	RBI	RC	TBB	IBB	SO	HBP	SH	SF			SB	CS	SB%	GDP	Avg	OBP	Slg
2010	Pwtckt*	AAA	4	17	8	1	0	0	(-	-)	9	5	2	4	1	0	0	0	0	0			0	0	-	0	.471	.500	.529
2010	Portlnd*	AA	2	7	3	1	0	0	(-	-)	4	2	0	2	1	0	0	0	0	0			1	0	1.00	0	.429	.500	.571
2010	RedSx*	R	3	8	2	0	0	0	(-	-)	2	3	0	1	2	0	0	1	0	0			1	0	1.00	1	.250	.455	.250
2007	Bos	AL	33	116	41	7	1	3	(3	0)	59	20	18	26	8	0	15	1	0	2			9	1	1.00	2	.353	.394	.509
2008	Bos	AL	145	554	155	22	7	9	(4	5)	218	98	47	71	41	2	80	7	4	3			50	11	.82	10	.280	.336	.394
2009	Bos	AL	153	624	188	27	10	8	(4	4)	259	94	60	97	49	3	74	6	6	6			70	12	.85	13	.301	.355	.415
2010	Bos	AL	18	78	15	4	0	0	(0	0)	19	10	5	4	4	0	9	1	0	0			7	1	.88	1	.192	.241	.244
	Postseason		22	69	18	7	1	0	(0	0)	27	12	11	11	6	1	10	0	0	1			5	1	.83	2	.261	.316	.391
	4 ML YEARS		349	1372	399	60	18	20	(11	9)	555	222	130	198	102	5	178	15	10	11			136	24	.85	25	.291	.344	.405

John Ely

Pitches: R Bats: R Pos: SP-18 Ht: 6'2" Wt: 200 Born: 5/13/1986 Age: 25

									WHAT HE GAVE UP												THE RESULTS							
Year	Team	Lg	G	GS	CG	GF	IP	BFP	H	R	ER	HR	SH	SF	HB	TBB	IBB	SO	WP	Bk	W	L	Pct	Sh	Sv-Op	Hld	ERC	ERA
2007	Gr Falls	R+	13	12	0	0	56.0	230	55	26	24	4	1	0	3	14	0	56	1	0	6	1	.857	0	0- -	-	3.75	3.86
2008	WinSa	A+	27	27	0	0	145.1	610	142	83	76	18	8	3	5	46	0	134	4	3	10	12	.455	0	0- -	-	3.97	4.71
2009	Brham	AA	27	27	1	0	156.1	638	140	63	49	9	5	2	1	50	0	125	6	0	14	2	.875	0	0- -	-	3.01	2.82
2010	Albq	AAA	13	13	1	0	68.0	299	70	48	47	10	6	1	3	29	0	56	3	1	5	4	.556	0	0- -	-	4.88	6.22
2010	LAD	NL	18	18	0	0	100.0	430	105	63	61	12	4	4	2	40	2	76	4	0	4	10	.286	0	0-0	0	4.64	5.49

Edwin Encarnacion

Bats: R Throws: R Pos: 3B-95; DH-1   Ht: 6'2" Wt: 231 Born: 1/7/1983 Age: 28

Year	Team	Lg	G	AB	H	2B	3B	HR	(Hm	Rd)	TB	R	RBI	RC	TBB	IBB	SO	HBP	SH	SF	SB	CS	SB%	GDP	Avg	OBP	Slg
2010	Dnedin*	A+	3	10	1	0	0	1	(-	-)	4	2	1	1	2	0	3	1	0	0	0	0	-	0	.100	.308	.400
2010	LsVgs*	AAA	7	32	14	2	0	3	(-	-)	25	9	13	10	2	0	2	1	0	0	0	0	-	1	.438	.486	.781
2005	Cin	NL	69	211	49	16	0	9	(3	6)	92	25	31	24	20	2	60	3	0	0	3	0	1.00	8	.232	.308	.436
2006	Cin	NL	117	406	112	33	1	15	(7	8)	192	60	72	66	41	3	78	13	0	3	6	3	.67	9	.276	.359	.473
2007	Cin	NL	139	502	145	25	1	16	(10	6)	220	66	76	86	39	4	86	14	0	1	8	1	.89	5	.289	.356	.438
2008	Cin	NL	146	506	127	29	1	26	(15	11)	236	75	68	72	61	1	102	10	0	5	4	0	1.00	13	.251	.340	.466
2009	2 Tms		85	293	66	11	2	13	(5	8)	120	35	39	37	37	0	67	5	0	3	2	1	.67	5	.225	.320	.410
2010	Tor	AL	96	332	81	16	0	21	(7	14)	160	47	51	41	29	1	60	2	0	4	1	0	1.00	9	.244	.305	.482
09	Cin	NL	43	139	29	6	1	5	(3	2)	52	10	16	19	24	0	38	2	0	1	1	1	.50	3	.209	.333	.374
09	Tor	AL	42	154	37	5	1	8	(2	6)	68	25	23	18	13	0	29	3	0	1	1	0	1.00	2	.240	.306	.442
6 ML YEARS			652	2250	580	130	5	100	(47	53)	1020	308	337	326	227	11	453	47	0	16	21	5	.81	49	.258	.336	.453

Jesse English

Pitches: L Bats: L Pos: RP-7   Ht: 6'3" Wt: 220 Born: 9/13/1984 Age: 26

Year	Team	Lg	G	GS	CG	GF	IP	BFP	H	R	ER	HR	SH	SF	HB	TBB	IBB	SO	WP	Bk	W	L	Pct	Sh	Sv-Op	Hld	ERC	ERA
2002	Giants	R	12	12	0	0	47.0	195	33	17	14	2	0	0	7	18	0	68	2	1	4	1	.800	0	0- -	-	2.62	2.68
2003	Giants	R	7	6	0	0	20.1	88	11	11	9	0	0	0	1	19	0	31	3	0	0	1	.000	0	0- -	-	3.10	3.98
2004	Hgrstn	A	17	4	0	3	43.1	209	39	37	36	4	0	0	5	40	0	46	6	0	0	1	.000	0	0- -	-	6.00	7.48
2006	SlmKzr	A-	17	0	0	2	28.1	122	21	21	20	6	1	0	2	18	0	40	0	0	3	0	1.000	0	0- -	-	4.70	6.35
2007	SlmKzr	A-	10	0	0	1	26.0	97	14	2	2	0	0	0	1	5	0	46	1	0	5	0	1.000	0	0- -	-	1.02	0.69
2007	SnJos	A+	5	2	0	0	8.1	38	8	3	3	0	0	0	1	6	0	11	0	0	0	1	.000	0	0- -	-	4.92	3.24
2008	SnJos	A+	26	26	0	0	135.1	566	121	57	48	12	1	4	6	51	1	135	9	0	13	7	.650	1	0- -	-	3.54	3.19
2009	Conn	AA	26	19	1	2	100.2	446	98	54	47	9	6	5	1	57	0	71	4	0	7	7	.500	1	0- -	-	4.57	4.20
2010	Nats	R	3	0	0	0	4.0	14	1	1	0	0	0	0	0	0	0	6	0	0	0	0	-	0	0- -	-	0.13	0.00
2010	Syrcsc	AAA	16	0	0	3	19.2	83	18	11	11	1	0	0	1	10	1	14	1	0	2	1	.667	0	0- -	-	3.94	5.03
2010	Was	NL	7	0	0	0	7.0	33	10	3	3	0	0	0	0	2	0	4	1	0	0	0	-	0	0-0	0	5.19	3.86

Barry Enright

Pitches: R Bats: R Pos: SP-17   Ht: 6'3" Wt: 220 Born: 3/30/1986 Age: 25

Year	Team	Lg	G	GS	CG	GF	IP	BFP	H	R	ER	HR	SH	SF	HB	TBB	IBB	SO	WP	Bk	W	L	Pct	Sh	Sv-Op	Hld	ERC	ERA
2007	Yakima	A-	5	0	0	2	8.0	30	4	0	0	0	0	0	0	3	0	12	0	0	0	0	-	0	0- -	-	1.21	0.00
2007	Sbend	A	1	0	0	1	2.0	6	1	0	0	0	0	0	0	0	0	1	0	0	0	0	-	0	1- -	-	0.63	0.00
2007	Visalia	A+	4	0	0	2	5.0	20	3	1	0	0	0	0	0	2	1	4	0	0	0	0	-	0	1- -	-	1.32	0.00
2008	Visalia	A+	29	29	0	0	164.1	705	185	88	81	17	2	5	4	35	1	143	7	2	12	8	.600	0	0- -	-	4.13	4.44
2009	Mobile	AA	27	27	0	0	156.0	661	171	73	69	16	10	8	4	37	1	103	1	0	10	9	.526	0	0- -	-	4.11	3.98
2010	Mobile	AA	14	14	1	0	93.2	368	81	34	30	9	5	3	5	15	0	83	7	0	4	1	.800	0	0- -	-	2.70	2.88
2010	Ari	NL	17	17	0	0	99.0	410	97	43	43	20	8	1	1	29	0	49	0	0	6	7	.462	0	0-0	0	4.34	3.91

Edgmer Escalona

Pitches: R Bats: R Pos: RP-5

EGG-merr

Ht: 6'4" Wt: 175 Born: 10/6/1986 Age: 24

Year	Team	Lg	G	GS	CG	GF	IP	BFP	H	R	ER	HR	SH	SF	HB	TBB	IBB	SO	WP	Bk	W	L	Pct	Sh	Sv-Op	Hld	ERC	ERA
2007	Casper	R+	18	0	0	8	26.2	118	22	17	12	1	0	0	1	13	1	20	3	0	1	1	.500	0	1- -	-	2.97	4.05
2008	Ashvll	A	44	0	0	17	70.1	320	71	32	28	9	2	1	6	18	0	79	4	1	6	2	.750	0	1- -	-	3.35	3.22
2009	Mdcst	A+	28	0	0	7	32.2	130	25	10	9	3	0	0	2	7	0	34	3	0	2	0	1.000	0	0- -	-	2.34	2.48
2009	Tulsa	AA	31	0	0	15	36.2	158	33	12	10	5	2	0	3	11	0	32	1	0	1	2	.333	0	4- -	-	3.00	2.45
2010	ColSpr	AAA	57	0	0	18	69.0	306	66	47	46	17	3	6	4	32	3	74	6	4	3	5	.375	0	1- -	-	5.25	6.00
2010	Col	NL	5	0	0	2	6.0	26	4	1	1	0	0	1	0	4	2	2	1	0	0	0	-	0	0-0	0	2.02	1.50

Alcides Escobar

Bats: R Throws: R Pos: SS-138; PH-6; LF-2; RF-2; CF-1; PR-1

al-SEE-dees

Ht: 6'1" Wt: 182 Born: 12/16/1986 Age: 24

Year	Team	Lg	G	AB	H	2B	3B	HR	(Hm	Rd)	TB	R	RBI	RC	TBB	IBB	SO	HBP	SH	SF	SB	CS	SB%	GDP	Avg	OBP	Slg
2008	Mil	NL	9	4	2	0	0	0	(0	0)	2	2	0	0	0	0	1	0	0	0	0	0	-	0	.500	.500	.500
2009	Mil	NL	38	125	38	3	1	1	(0	1)	46	20	11	16	4	0	18	2	2	1	4	2	.67	0	.304	.333	.368
2010	Mil	NL	145	506	119	14	10	4	(3	1)	165	57	41	51	36	7	70	3	4	3	10	4	.71	8	.235	.288	.326
3 ML YEARS			192	635	159	17	11	5	(3	2)	213	79	52	67	40	7	89	5	6	4	14	6	.70	8	.250	.298	.335

Kelvim Escobar

Pitches: R Bats: R Pos: P

kell-VEEM

Ht: 6'1" Wt: 230 Born: 4/11/1976 Age: 35

Year	Team	Lg	G	GS	CG	GF	IP	BFP	H	R	ER	HR	SH	SF	HB	TBB	IBB	SO	WP	Bk	W	L	Pct	Sh	Sv-Op	Hld	ERC	ERA
1997	Tor	AL	27	0	0	23	31.0	139	28	12	10	1	2	0	0	19	2	36	0	0	3	2	.600	0	14-17	1	3.68	2.90
1998	Tor	AL	22	10	0	2	79.2	342	72	37	33	5	0	3	0	35	0	72	0	0	7	3	.700	0	0-1	5	3.41	3.73
1999	Tor	AL	33	30	1	2	174.0	795	203	118	110	19	2	8	10	81	2	129	6	1	14	11	.560	0	0-0	0	5.62	5.69
2000	Tor	AL	43	24	3	8	180.0	794	186	108	107	26	5	4	3	85	3	142	4	0	10	15	.400	1	2-3	2	4.94	5.35
2001	Tor	AL	59	11	1	15	126.0	517	93	51	49	8	2	5	3	52	5	121	2	0	6	8	.429	1	0-0	13	2.54	3.50
2002	Tor	AL	76	0	0	68	78.0	355	75	39	37	10	1	0	5	44	6	85	4	0	5	7	.417	0	38-46	0	4.77	4.27
2003	Tor	AL	41	26	1	12	180.1	797	189	94	86	15	5	5	9	78	3	159	9	0	13	9	.591	1	4-5	0	4.53	4.29
2004	LAA	AL	33	33	0	0	208.1	878	192	91	91	24	6	7	7	76	2	191	9	0	11	12	.478	0	0-0	0	3.65	3.93

Year	Team	Lg	G	GS	CG	GF	IP	BFP	H	R	ER	HR	SH	SF	HB	TBB	IBB	SO	WP	Bk	W	L	Pct	Sh	Sv-Op	Hld	ERC	ERA
2005	LAA	AL	16	7	0	0	59.2	242	45	21	20	4	2	0	2	21	1	63	4	0	3	2	.600	0	1-1	2	2.51	3.02
2006	LAA	AL	30	30	1	0	189.1	789	192	93	76	17	6	3	4	50	2	147	7	0	11	14	.440	0	0-0	0	3.67	3.61
2007	LAA	AL	30	30	3	0	195.2	812	182	79	74	11	5	4	3	66	2	160	9	0	18	7	.720	1	0-0	0	3.25	3.40
2009	LAA	AL	1	1	0	0	5.0	23	4	2	2	0	0	1	1	4	0	5	0	0	1	0	1.000	0	0-0	0	4.56	3.60
Postseason			8	2	0	2	19.2	92	15	12	8	2	0	2	0	17	2	24	2	0	1	2	.333	0	0-1	2	4.22	3.66
12 ML YEARS			411	202	10	132	1507.0	6483	1461	755	695	137	33	39	47	611	28	1310	54	1	101	91	.526	4	59-73	23	3.97	4.15

Yunel Escobar

Bats: R Throws: R Pos: SS-134; PH-1 you-NELL **Ht: 6'2" Wt: 200 Born: 11/2/1982 Age: 28**

Year	Team	Lg	G	AB	H	2B	3B	HR	(Hm	Rd)	TB	R	RBI	RC	TBB	IBB	SO	HBP	SH	SF	SB	CS	SB%	GDP	Avg	OBP	Slg
2010	Gwnntt*	AAA	1	3	2	0	0	0	(-	-)	2	1	0	1	1	1	1	0	0	0	0	0	-	0	.667	.750	.667
2007	Atl	NL	94	319	104	25	0	5	(3	2)	144	54	28	52	27	1	44	5	2	2	5	3	.63	6	.326	.385	.451
2008	Atl	NL	136	514	148	24	2	10	(5	5)	206	71	60	70	59	4	62	5	7	2	2	5	.29	24	.288	.366	.401
2009	Atl	NL	141	528	158	26	2	14	(7	7)	230	89	76	90	57	3	62	10	7	2	5	4	.56	21	.299	.377	.436
2010	2 Tms		135	497	127	19	0	4	(2	2)	158	60	35	53	56	1	57	5	9	0	6	2	.75	18	.256	.337	.318
10	Atl	NL	75	261	62	12	0	0	(0	0)	74	28	19	25	37	1	31	1	2	0	5	1	.83	9	.238	.334	.284
10	Tor	AL	60	236	65	7	0	4	(2	2)	84	32	16	28	19	0	26	4	7	0	1	1	.50	9	.275	.340	.356
4 ML YEARS			506	1858	537	94	4	33	(17	16)	738	274	199	265	199	9	225	25	25	6	18	14	.56	69	.289	.364	.397

Danny Espinosa

Bats: B Throws: R Pos: 2B-25; SS-2; PH-1 **Ht: 6'0" Wt: 190 Born: 4/25/1987 Age: 24**

Year	Team	Lg	G	AB	H	2B	3B	HR	(Hm	Rd)	TB	R	RBI	RC	TBB	IBB	SO	HBP	SH	SF	SB	CS	SB%	GDP	Avg	OBP	Slg
2008	Vrmnt	A-	19	64	21	2	0	0	(-	-)	23	8	4	13	17	1	17	2	3	1	2	2	.50	1	.328	.476	.359
2009	Ptomc	A+	133	474	125	31	4	18	(-	-)	218	90	72	88	74	2	129	13	10	5	29	11	.73	8	.264	.375	.460
2010	Hrsbrg	AA	99	386	101	16	4	18	(-	-)	179	66	54	62	33	0	94	10	3	2	20	8	.71	9	.262	.334	.464
2010	Syrcse	AAA	24	95	28	2	1	4	(-	-)	44	14	15	15	8	2	22	1	2	2	5	3	.63	2	.295	.349	.463
2010	Was	NL	28	103	22	4	1	6	(4	2)	46	16	15	15	9	1	30	0	0	0	0	2	.00	0	.214	.277	.447

Brian Esposito

Bats: R Throws: R Pos: C-2; PH-2 **Ht: 6'1" Wt: 205 Born: 2/24/1979 Age: 32**

Year	Team	Lg	G	AB	H	2B	3B	HR	(Hm	Rd)	TB	R	RBI	RC	TBB	IBB	SO	HBP	SH	SF	SB	CS	SB%	GDP	Avg	OBP	Slg
2000	Lowell	A-	42	154	37	9	1	3	(-	-)	57	15	20	17	11	0	31	1	1	2	0	1	.00	2	.240	.292	.370
2001	Augsta	A	90	311	59	13	0	3	(-	-)	81	21	30	16	13	0	81	2	2	5	0	0	-	5	.190	.224	.260
2002	Augsta	A	40	154	39	5	0	5	(-	-)	59	20	15	18	7	0	32	5	2	0	0	0	-	4	.253	.307	.383
2002	Srsota	A+	31	99	16	5	0	2	(-	-)	27	8	7	4	5	0	20	1	1	1	0	0	-	1	.162	.208	.273
2003	Srsota	A+	2	7	0	0	0	0	(-	-)	0	0	0	0	0	0	0	0	0	0	0	0	-	0	.000	.000	.000
2003	Provo	R+	3	11	1	0	0	0	(-	-)	1	0	0	0	0	0	4	0	0	0	0	0	-	1	.091	.091	.091
2003	RCuca	A+	9	32	11	2	0	0	(-	-)	13	2	2	4	0	0	5	0	1	0	0	0	-	1	.344	.344	.406
2004	Stcktn	A+	22	78	20	2	1	5	(-	-)	39	10	14	12	6	1	17	0	0	0	1	0	1.00	0	.256	.310	.500
2004	OKC	AAA	1	4	0	0	0	0	(-	-)	0	0	1	0	0	0	1	0	0	0	0	0	-	0	.000	.000	.000
2004	Frisco	AA	31	92	19	4	0	1	(-	-)	26	11	11	5	4	0	27	0	2	3	0	1	.00	3	.207	.232	.283
2005	Frisco	AA	38	136	31	7	0	0	(-	-)	38	12	5	10	7	0	33	2	2	0	1	0	1.00	2	.228	.276	.279
2005	Okla	AAA	8	27	11	1	0	0	(-	-)	12	6	4	5	1	0	6	1	0	0	0	0	-	1	.407	.448	.444
2006	Memp	AAA	55	175	41	9	0	2	(-	-)	56	13	12	14	3	0	32	4	4	0	0	1	.00	8	.234	.264	.320
2007	Memp	AAA	77	242	43	6	0	4	(-	-)	61	11	16	10	11	0	52	1	0	0	0	2	.00	10	.178	.217	.252
2008	Tulsa	AA	68	247	51	2	1	5	(-	-)	70	27	26	16	8	0	46	4	5	2	4	1	.80	11	.206	.241	.283
2009	CpChr	AA	49	172	36	5	1	3	(-	-)	52	16	22	12	5	0	27	4	3	0	0	0	-	5	.209	.249	.302
2009	RdRck	AAA	31	88	28	4	0	2	(-	-)	38	7	16	13	4	2	14	2	0	1	0	0	-	3	.318	.358	.432
2010	CpChr	AA	14	46	6	2	1	0	(-	-)	10	2	0	0	0	0	9	0	2	0	0	0	-	2	.130	.130	.217
2010	RdRck	AAA	46	151	34	5	0	2	(-	-)	45	11	18	11	5	2	31	3	3	1	0	0	-	4	.225	.263	.298
2007	StL	NL	1	0	0	0	0	0	(0	0)	0	0	0	0	0	0	0	0	0	0	0	0	-	0	-	-	-
2010	Hou	NL	2	3	0	0	0	0	(0	0)	0	0	0	0	0	0	1	0	0	0	0	0	-	0	.000	.000	.000
2 ML YEARS			3	3	0	0	0	0	(0	0)	0	0	0	0	0	0	1	0	0	0	0	0	-	0	.000	.000	.000

Marco Estrada

Pitches: R Bats: R Pos: RP-6; SP-1 **Ht: 6'0" Wt: 180 Born: 7/5/1983 Age: 27**

Year	Team	Lg	G	GS	CG	GF	IP	BFP	H	R	ER	HR	SH	SF	HB	TBB	IBB	SO	WP	Bk	W	L	Pct	Sh	Sv-Op	Hld	ERC	ERA
2010	Nashv*	AAA	7	7	0	0	40.0	158	30	15	14	1	2	1	0	11	0	33	0	0	1	2	.333	0	0--	-	1.90	3.15
2008	Was	NL	11	0	0	3	12.2	63	17	13	11	4	0	0	2	5	1	10	0	0	0	0	-	0	0-1	3	8.13	7.82
2009	Was	NL	4	1	0	1	7.1	33	6	6	5	1	0	0	0	4	0	9	1	0	0	1	.000	0	0-0	0	3.67	6.14
2010	Mil	NL	7	1	0	0	11.1	58	14	13	12	3	1	0	1	6	0	13	2	0	0	0	-	0	0-0	0	7.17	9.53
3 ML YEARS			22	2	0	4	31.1	154	37	32	28	8	2	0	3	15	1	32	3	0	0	1	.000	0	0-1	3	6.66	8.04

Andre Ethier

Bats: L Throws: L Pos: RF-132; PH-8; 1B-1 **Ht: 6'2" Wt: 205 Born: 4/10/1982 Age: 29**

Year	Team	Lg	G	AB	H	2B	3B	HR	(Hm	Rd)	TB	R	RBI	RC	TBB	IBB	SO	HBP	SH	SF	SB	CS	SB%	GDP	Avg	OBP	Slg
2010	Albq*	AAA	2	5	3	0	0	0	(-	-)	3	4	2	2	2	0	0	1	0	1	0	0	-	0	.600	.667	.600
2006	LAD	NL	126	396	122	20	7	11	(9	2)	189	50	55	62	34	2	77	5	0	6	5	5	.50	11	.308	.365	.477
2007	LAD	NL	153	447	127	32	2	13	(8	5)	202	50	64	65	46	12	68	4	0	8	0	4	.00	10	.284	.350	.452
2008	LAD	NL	141	525	160	38	5	20	(10	10)	268	90	77	99	59	0	88	4	1	7	6	3	.67	6	.305	.375	.510

Year	Team	Lg	G	AB	H	2B	3B	HR	(Hm	Rd)	TB	R	RBI	RC	TBB	IBB	SO	HBP	SH	SF	SB	CS	SB%	GDP	Avg	OBP	Slg
2009	LAD	NL	160	596	162	42	3	31	(22	9)	303	92	106	94	72	10	116	13	0	4	6	4	.60	19	.272	.361	.508
2010	LAD	NL	139	517	151	33	1	23	(14	9)	255	71	82	89	59	11	102	3	0	6	2	1	.67	11	.292	.364	.493
Postseason			18	64	17	4	1	3	(1	2)	32	13	6	8	8	0	16	1	0	0	0	1	.00	1	.266	.356	.500
5 ML YEARS			719	2481	722	165	18	98	(63	35)	1217	353	384	409	270	35	451	29	1	31	19	17	.53	57	.291	.363	.491

Nick Evans

Bats: R **Throws:** R **Pos:** PH-14; LF-8; RF-3; CF-1; PR-1   **Ht:** 6'2" **Wt:** 219 **Born:** 1/30/1986 **Age:** 25

Year	Team	Lg	G	AB	H	2B	3B	HR	(Hm	Rd)	TB	R	RBI	RC	TBB	IBB	SO	HBP	SH	SF	SB	CS	SB%	GDP	Avg	OBP	Slg
2010	Bnghtn*	AA	88	347	102	30	0	17	(-	-)	183	62	55	67	40	3	65	1	0	3	0	1	.00	12	.294	.366	.527
2010	Buffalo*	AAA	37	140	44	14	1	6	(-	-)	78	26	25	29	15	0	23	1	1	0	0	0	-	3	.314	.385	.557
2008	NYM	NL	50	109	28	10	0	2	(0	2)	44	18	9	10	7	2	24	1	0	2	0	0	-	1	.257	.303	.404
2009	NYM	NL	30	65	15	5	1	1	(1	0)	25	5	7	8	4	0	20	0	0	0	0	0	-	4	.231	.275	.385
2010	NYM	NL	20	36	11	3	0	1	(1	0)	17	5	5	5	1	0	10	0	0	0	0	0	-	1	.306	.324	.472
3 ML YEARS			100	210	54	18	1	4	(2	2)	86	28	21	23	12	2	54	1	0	2	0	0	-	6	.257	.298	.410

Terry Evans

Bats: R **Throws:** R **Pos:** CF-1   **Ht:** 6'3" **Wt:** 205 **Born:** 1/19/1982 **Age:** 29

Year	Team	Lg	G	AB	H	2B	3B	HR	(Hm	Rd)	TB	R	RBI	RC	TBB	IBB	SO	HBP	SH	SF	SB	CS	SB%	GDP	Avg	OBP	Slg
2010	Salt Lk*	AAA	122	466	132	27	4	15	(-	-)	212	80	72	70	28	0	100	2	1	5	19	8	.70	8	.283	.323	.455
2007	LAA	AL	8	11	1	0	0	1	(1	0)	4	3	2	0	2	0	4	0	0	0	0	0	-	1	.091	.231	.364
2009	LAA	AL	11	7	2	0	0	0	(0	0)	2	2	1	1	0	0	2	0	0	0	0	0	-	0	.286	.286	.286
2010	LAA	AL	1	1	0	0	0	0	(0	0)	0	0	0	0	0	0	1	0	0	0	0	0	-	0	.000	.000	.000
3 ML YEARS			20	19	3	0	0	1	(1	0)	6	5	3	1	2	0	7	0	0	0	0	0	-	1	.158	.238	.316

Dana Eveland

Pitches: L **Bats:** L **Pos:** SP-10; RP-2   EVE-land   **Ht:** 6'1" **Wt:** 235 **Born:** 10/29/1983 **Age:** 27

Year	Team	Lg	G	GS	CG	GF	IP	BFP	H	R	ER	HR	SH	SF	HB	TBB	IBB	SO	WP	Bk	W	L	Pct	Sh	Sv-Op	Hld	ERC	ERA
2010	Indy*	AAA	11	5	0	2	26.0	124	41	25	23	5	1	1	0	6	0	26	1	0	0	2	.000	0	0- -	-	7.49	7.96
2005	Mil	NL	27	0	0	3	31.2	146	40	21	21	2	0	1	1	18	3	23	1	0	1	1	.500	0	1-2	7	6.16	5.97
2006	Mil	NL	9	5	0	1	27.2	141	39	25	25	4	1	1	5	16	2	32	2	0	3	0	.000	0	0-1	0	8.30	8.13
2007	Ari	NL	5	1	0	0	5.0	28	8	8	8	0	0	1	0	5	0	3	1	0	1	0	1.000	0	0-0	0	9.25	14.40
2008	Oak	AL	29	29	1	0	168.0	737	172	82	81	10	2	5	12	77	2	118	6	1	9	9	.500	0	0-0	0	4.47	4.34
2009	Oak	AL	13	9	0	1	44.0	221	70	39	35	4	1	1	1	26	1	22	2	0	2	4	.333	0	0-0	0	8.50	7.16
2010	2 Tms		12	10	0	1	54.1	262	72	44	41	4	0	4	4	32	2	24	4	0	3	5	.375	0	0-0	0	6.90	6.79
10	Tor	AL	9	9	0	0	44.2	213	57	35	32	4	0	2	2	27	1	21	3	0	3	4	.429	0	0-0	0	6.69	6.45
10	Pit	NL	3	1	0	1	9.2	49	15	9	9	0	0	2	2	5	1	3	1	0	0	1	.000	0	0-0	0	7.85	8.38
6 ML YEARS			95	54	1	7	330.2	1535	401	219	211	24	4	14	22	174	10	222	16	1	16	22	.421	0	1-3	7	5.90	5.74

Adam Everett

Bats: R **Throws:** R **Pos:** SS-31; PH-1   **Ht:** 6'0" **Wt:** 178 **Born:** 2/5/1977 **Age:** 34

Year	Team	Lg	G	AB	H	2B	3B	HR	(Hm	Rd)	TB	R	RBI	RC	TBB	IBB	SO	HBP	SH	SF	SB	CS	SB%	GDP	Avg	OBP	Slg
2001	Hou	NL	9	3	0	0	0	0	(0	0)	0	1	0	0	0	0	1	0	0	0	1	0	1.00	0	.000	.000	.000
2002	Hou	NL	40	88	17	3	0	0	(0	0)	20	11	4	6	12	1	19	1	2	0	3	0	1.00	1	.193	.297	.227
2003	Hou	NL	128	387	99	18	3	8	(5	3)	147	51	51	50	28	6	66	9	11	7	8	1	.89	7	.256	.320	.380
2004	Hou	NL	104	384	105	15	2	8	(5	3)	148	66	31	51	17	0	56	9	22	3	13	2	.87	4	.273	.317	.385
2005	Hou	NL	152	549	136	27	2	11	(7	4)	200	58	54	61	26	1	103	8	8	4	21	7	.75	5	.248	.290	.364
2006	Hou	NL	150	514	123	28	6	6	(2	4)	181	52	59	50	34	5	71	4	10	4	9	6	.60	5	.239	.290	.352
2007	Hou	NL	66	220	51	11	1	2	(1	1)	70	18	15	21	14	0	31	1	1	0	4	2	.67	3	.232	.281	.318
2008	Min	AL	48	127	27	6	1	2	(0	2)	41	19	20	15	12	1	15	1	6	4	0	0	-	4	.213	.278	.323
2009	Det	AL	118	345	82	21	0	3	(1	2)	112	43	44	34	22	0	61	4	15	4	5	2	.71	9	.238	.288	.325
2010	Det	AL	31	81	15	5	0	0	(0	0)	20	6	4	1	4	0	18	0	3	1	2	1	.67	1	.185	.221	.247
Postseason			19	53	11	1	1	0	(0	0)	14	5	3	1	2	0	9	0	2	1	0	1	.00	2	.208	.232	.264
10 ML YEARS			846	2698	655	134	15	40	(23	17)	939	325	282	289	169	14	441	37	78	21	66	21	.76	35	.243	.294	.348

Kyle Farnsworth

Pitches: R **Bats:** R **Pos:** RP-60   **Ht:** 6'4" **Wt:** 231 **Born:** 4/14/1976 **Age:** 35

Year	Team	Lg	G	GS	CG	GF	IP	BFP	H	R	ER	HR	SH	SF	HB	TBB	IBB	SO	WP	Bk	W	L	Pct	Sh	Sv-Op	Hld	ERC	ERA
1999	ChC	NL	27	21	1	1	130.0	579	140	80	73	28	6	2	3	52	1	70	7	1	5	9	.357	1	0-0	0	5.39	5.05
2000	ChC	NL	46	5	0	9	77.0	371	90	58	55	14	4	4	4	50	8	74	3	0	2	9	.182	0	1-6	6	6.72	6.43
2001	ChC	NL	76	0	0	24	82.0	339	65	26	25	8	2	2	1	29	2	107	2	2	4	6	.400	0	2-3	24	2.76	2.74
2002	ChC	NL	45	0	0	17	46.2	213	53	47	38	9	2	5	1	24	7	46	1	0	4	6	.400	0	1-7	6	5.89	7.33
2003	ChC	NL	77	0	0	13	76.1	312	53	31	28	6	4	1	0	36	1	92	6	0	3	2	.600	0	0-3	19	2.58	3.30
2004	ChC	NL	72	0	0	25	66.2	298	67	39	35	10	5	0	2	33	1	78	1	0	4	5	.444	0	0-4	18	4.91	4.73
2005	2 Tms		72	0	0	34	70.0	277	44	18	17	5	2	1	3	27	0	87	3	1	1	1	.500	0	16-18	19	2.12	2.19
2006	NYY	AL	72	0	0	44	66.0	289	62	34	32	8	3	2	1	28	3	75	5	1	3	6	.333	0	6-10	19	3.88	4.36
2007	NYY	AL	64	0	0	11	60.0	266	60	35	32	9	1	2	2	27	2	48	4	2	2	1	.667	0	0-3	15	4.67	4.80
2008	2 Tms		61	0	0	11	60.1	261	70	32	30	15	3	1	1	22	4	61	1	1	2	3	.400	0	1-4	14	6.11	4.48
2009	KC	AL	41	0	0	18	37.1	168	43	22	19	3	1	2	1	14	2	42	2	1	1	5	.167	0	0-2	5	4.65	4.58
2010	2 Tms		60	0	0	15	64.2	267	55	25	24	4	3	2	4	19	1	61	3	0	3	2	.600	0	0-3	9	2.84	3.34
05	Det	AL	46	0	0	16	42.2	174	29	12	11	1	1	1	1	20	0	55	2	0	1	1	.500	0	6-8	15	2.26	2.32

Year	Team	Lg	G	GS	CG	GF	IP	BFP	H	R	ER	HR	SH	SF	HB	TBB	IBB	SO	WP	Bk	W	L	Pct	Sh	Sv-Op	Hld	ERC	ERA
05	Atl	NL	26	0	0	18	27.1	103	15	6	4	1	0	2		7	0	32	1	1	0	0	-	0	10-10	4	1.86	1.98
08	NYY	AL	45	0	0	6	44.1	185	43	18	18	11	3	1	1	17	3	43	1	1	1	2	.333	0	1-1	11	5.02	3.65
08	Det	AL	16	0	0	5	16.0	76	27	14	12	4	0	0	0	5	1	18	0	0	1	1	.500	0	0-3	3	9.43	6.75
10	KC	AL	37	0	0	9	44.2	185	40	13	12	2	1	1	4	12	0	36	2	0	3	0	1.000	0	0-2	7	3.01	2.42
10	Atl	NL	23	0	0	6	20.0	82	15	12	12	2	2	1	0	7	1	25	1	0	0	2	.000	0	0-1	5	2.46	5.40
	Postseason		13	0	0	3	14.0	58	11	9	9	2	1	1	0	5	2	16	0	0	0	0	-	0	0-0	2	2.78	5.79
	12 ML YEARS		713	26	1	201	837.0	3640	802	447	408	119	36	24	23	361	32	841	38	9	34	55	.382	1	27-63	154	4.29	4.39

Scott Feldman

Pitches: R **Bats:** L **Pos:** SP-22; RP-7 | **Ht:** 6'7" **Wt:** 230 **Born:** 2/7/1983 **Age:** 28

Year	Team	Lg	G	GS	CG	GF	IP	BFP	H	R	ER	HR	SH	SF	HB	TBB	IBB	SO	WP	Bk	W	L	Pct	Sh	Sv-Op	Hld	ERC	ERA
2010	OKCity*	AAA	1	0	0	0	4.0	16	5	2	2	2	0	0	0	0	0	3	0	0	0	0	-	0	0--		6.80	4.50
2005	Tex	AL	8	0	0	3	9.1	37	9	1	1	0	0	0	0	2	1	4	0	0	0	1	.000	0	0-0	1	2.48	0.96
2006	Tex	AL	36	0	0	5	41.1	175	42	19	18	4	2	1	4	10	0	30	0	0	0	2	.000	0	0-1	7	3.94	3.92
2007	Tex	AL	29	0	0	10	39.0	192	44	26	25	3	0	2	3	32	5	19	2	2	1	2	.333	0	0-0	6	6.40	5.77
2008	Tex	AL	28	25	0	2	151.1	651	161	103	89	22	1	9	10	56	2	74	4	2	6	8	.429	0	0-0	0	5.03	5.29
2009	Tex	AL	34	31	0	0	189.2	791	178	87	86	18	1	3	9	65	0	113	5	2	17	8	.680	0	0-0	0	3.74	4.08
2010	Tex	AL	29	22	0	2	141.1	641	181	98	86	18	5	8	5	45	2	75	11	0	7	11	.389	0	0-0	0	5.71	5.48
	6 ML YEARS		164	78	0	22	572.0	2487	615	334	305	65	9	23	31	210	10	315	22	6	31	32	.492	0	0-1	8	4.72	4.80

Jesus Feliciano

Bats: L **Throws:** L **Pos:** PH-22; RF-14; LF-13; CF-12; PR-1 | **Ht:** 5'10" **Wt:** 190 **Born:** 6/6/1979 **Age:** 32

							BATTING															BASERUNNING				AVERAGES		
Year	Team	Lg	G	AB	H	2B	3B	HR	(Hm	Rd)	TB	R	RBI	RC	TBB	IBB	SO	HBP	SH	SF	SB	CS	SB%	GDP	Avg	OBP	Slg
1998	Yakima	A-	73	302	92	7	1	0	(-	-)	101	47	26	45	32	0	37	3	2	4	34	10	.77	4	.305	.372	.334
1999	VeroB	A+	98	370	94	13	0	0	(-	-)	107	44	21	36	29	1	38	4	2	2	20	10	.67	4	.254	.314	.289
2000	SnBrn	A+	114	405	117	13	3	0	(-	-)	136	56	43	51	32	0	41	1	8	3	31	11	.74	8	.289	.340	.336
2001	VeroB	A+	116	401	105	11	3	3	(-	-)	131	48	29	45	31	2	35	4	4	2	22	10	.69	15	.262	.320	.327
2002	Jaxnvl	AA	100	245	58	5	1	0	(-	-)	65	32	13	17	13	0	28	3	4	2	10	10	.50	2	.237	.281	.265
2003	Jaxnvl	AA	37	81	12	0	0	1	(-	-)	15	7	4	3	11	1	16	1	0	1	2	3	.40	3	.148	.255	.185
2003	Orlndo	AA	72	251	70	11	0	1	(-	-)	84	31	21	30	15	2	25	3	6	1	7	1	.88	7	.279	.326	.335
2004	Bkrsfld	A+	70	251	76	13	3	0	(-	-)	95	41	23	35	18	0	20	1	9	3	9	4	.69	7	.303	.348	.378
2004	Mont	AA	28	93	19	2	0	1	(-	-)	24	10	4	5	4	0	16	1	1	1	0	1	.00	3	.204	.242	.258
2005	Hrsbrg	AA	85	318	89	13	2	2	(-	-)	112	50	24	36	14	0	34	2	6	3	10	6	.63	7	.280	.312	.352
2006	Hrsbrg	AA	64	178	41	3	0	1	(-	-)	47	15	13	11	10	0	15	1	3	1	3	5	.38	3	.230	.274	.264
2007	NewOr	AAA	90	235	74	11	0	4	(-	-)	97	35	26	37	21	2	24	1	1	3	5	2	.71	8	.315	.369	.413
2008	NewOr	AAA	138	504	155	21	4	3	(-	-)	193	68	54	72	41	3	56	8	4	5	12	14	.46	17	.308	.366	.383
2009	Buffalo	AAA	130	495	154	30	1	1	(-	-)	189	57	42	69	25	5	44	5	4	4	13	5	.72	18	.311	.348	.382
2010	Buffalo	AAA	89	336	114	18	1	1	(-	-)	137	55	28	54	21	1	35	6	3	3	6	5	.55	9	.339	.385	.408
2010	NYM	NL	54	108	25	4	1	0	(0	0)	31	12	3	8	6	0	12	1	3	1	1	0	1.00	3	.231	.276	.287

Pedro Feliciano

Pitches: L **Bats:** L **Pos:** RP-92 | **Ht:** 5'10" **Wt:** 192 **Born:** 8/25/1976 **Age:** 34

Year	Team	Lg	G	GS	CG	GF	IP	BFP	H	R	ER	HR	SH	SF	HB	TBB	IBB	SO	WP	Bk	W	L	Pct	Sh	Sv-Op	Hld	ERC	ERA
2002	NYM	NL	6	0	0	3	6.0	26	9	5	5	0	0	0	0	1	0	4	0	0	0	0	-	0	0-0	0	5.56	7.50
2003	NYM	NL	23	0	0	8	48.1	218	52	21	18	5	0	1	3	21	3	43	3	1	0	0	-	0	0-0	4	4.77	3.35
2004	NYM	NL	22	0	0	3	18.1	82	14	12	11	2	1	1	1	12	0	14	1	0	1	1	.500	0	0-0	2	3.93	5.40
2006	NYM	NL	64	0	0	10	60.1	256	56	15	14	4	4	3	3	20	1	54	1	0	7	2	.778	0	0-3	10	3.34	2.09
2007	NYM	NL	78	0	0	12	64.0	275	47	26	22	3	2	2	5	31	4	61	1	1	2	2	.500	0	2-3	18	2.74	3.09
2008	NYM	NL	86	0	0	14	53.1	237	57	24	24	7	2	3	3	26	8	50	2	0	3	4	.429	0	2-4	21	5.11	4.05
2009	NYM	NL	88	0	0	11	59.1	242	51	25	20	7	2	1	0	18	4	59	2	1	6	4	.600	0	0-2	24	2.98	3.03
2010	NYM	NL	92	0	0	16	62.2	280	66	24	23	1	2	0	6	30	6	56	1	0	3	6	.333	0	0-1	23	4.30	3.30
	Postseason		6	0	0	0	4.2	18	2	1	1	1	0	0	0	2	0	3	1	0	1	0	1.000	0	0-0	1	1.92	1.93
	8 ML YEARS		459	0	0	77	372.1	1616	352	152	137	29	13	11	21	159	26	341	11	3	22	19	.537	0	4-13	98	3.82	3.31

Neftali Feliz

Pitches: R **Bats:** R **Pos:** RP-70 | **Ht:** 6'3" **Wt:** 215 **Born:** 5/2/1988 **Age:** 23

neff-TAH-lee

Year	Team	Lg	G	GS	CG	GF	IP	BFP	H	R	ER	HR	SH	SF	HB	TBB	IBB	SO	WP	Bk	W	L	Pct	Sh	Sv-Op	Hld	ERC	ERA
2006	Braves	R	11	5	0	2	29.0	118	20	13	13	0	0	0	0	14	0	42	4	1	0	2	.000	0	2--	-	2.14	4.03
2007	Danvle	R+	8	7	0	0	27.1	107	18	8	6	0	0	1	0	12	0	28	0	0	2	0	1.000	0	0--	-	1.92	1.98
2007	Spkane	A-	8	1	0	0	15.0	71	13	8	6	2	1	0	1	12	0	27	2	0	0	2	.000	0	0--	-	5.30	3.60
2008	Clinton	A	17	17	0	0	82.0	324	55	25	23	2	3	2	6	28	0	106	5	1	6	3	.667	0	0--	-	2.01	2.52
2008	Frisco	AA	10	10	0	0	45.1	185	34	16	15	1	1	2	2	23	0	47	2	0	4	3	.571	0	0--	-	2.89	2.98
2009	Okla	AAA	25	13	0	6	77.1	323	69	36	30	2	2	0	3	30	0	75	4	1	4	6	.400	0	0--	-	3.13	3.49
2009	Tex	AL	20	0	0	3	31.0	117	13	6	6	2	1	0	3	8	0	39	0	0	1	0	1.000	0	2-3	9	1.14	1.74
2010	Tex	AL	70	0	0	59	69.1	269	43	21	21	5	1	0	5	18	1	71	5	0	4	3	.571	0	40-43	3	1.75	2.73
	2 ML YEARS		90	0	0	62	100.1	386	56	27	27	7	2	0	8	26	1	110	5	0	5	3	.625	0	42-46	12	1.54	2.42

Pedro Feliz

Bats: R Throws: R Pos: 3B-102; PH-27; 1B-15   Ht: 6'1" Wt: 210 Born: 4/27/1975 Age: 36

Year	Team	Lg	G	AB	H	2B	3B	HR	(Hm	Rd)	TB	R	RBI	RC	TBB	IBB	SO	HBP	SH	SF	SB	CS	SB%	GDP	Avg	OBP	Slg
									BATTING												BASERUNNING				AVERAGES		
2000	SF	NL	8	7	2	0	0	0	(0	0)	2	1	0	1	0	0	1	0	0	0	0	0	-	0	.286	.286	.286
2001	SF	NL	94	220	50	9	1	7	(3	4)	82	23	22	20	10	2	50	2	3	3	2	1	.67	5	.227	.264	.373
2002	SF	NL	67	146	37	4	1	2	(1	1)	49	14	13	12	6	1	27	0	0	-	2	0	-	2	.253	.281	.336
2003	SF	NL	95	235	58	9	3	16	(6	10)	121	31	48	34	10	0	53	1	1	2	2	2	.50	7	.247	.278	.515
2004	SF	NL	144	503	139	33	3	22	(11	11)	244	72	84	56	23	1	85	0	0	5	5	2	.71	18	.276	.305	.485
2005	SF	NL	156	569	142	30	4	20	(10	10)	240	69	81	58	38	1	102	1	1	6	2	0	.00	20	.250	.295	.422
2006	SF	NL	160	603	147	35	5	22	(6	16)	258	75	98	71	33	4	112	1	1	6	1	1	.50	18	.244	.281	.428
2007	SF	NL	150	557	141	28	2	20	(8	12)	233	61	72	67	29	2	70	1	0	3	2	2	.50	15	.253	.290	.418
2008	Phi	NL	133	425	106	19	2	14	(8	6)	171	43	58	47	33	3	54	0	3	2	0	0	-	14	.249	.302	.402
2009	Phi	NL	158	580	154	30	2	12	(8	4)	224	62	82	77	35	3	68	3	2	5	0	1	.00	12	.266	.308	.386
2010	2 Tms	NL	137	409	89	12	2	5	(2	3)	120	36	40	23	13	1	41	1	0	6	1	1	.50	13	.218	.240	.293
10	Hou	NL	97	289	64	12	1	4	(2	2)	90	22	31	20	9	1	31	1	0	5	1	1	.50	9	.221	.243	.311
10	StL	NL	40	120	25	0	1	1	(0	1)	30	14	9	3	4	0	10	0	0	1	0	0	-	4	.208	.232	.250
	Postseason		37	108	22	3	2	2	(2	0)	35	7	9	5	4	0	21	0	0	0	0	0	-	4	.204	.232	.324
11 ML YEARS			1302	4254	1065	209	25	140	(63	77)	1744	487	598	466	230	18	663	10	11	39	13	12	.52	124	.250	.288	.410

Prince Fielder

Bats: L Throws: R Pos: 1B-160; DH-1   Ht: 5'11" Wt: 268 Born: 5/9/1984 Age: 27

Year	Team	Lg	G	AB	H	2B	3B	HR	(Hm	Rd)	TB	R	RBI	RC	TBB	IBB	SO	HBP	SH	SF	SB	CS	SB%	GDP	Avg	OBP	Slg
									BATTING												BASERUNNING				AVERAGES		
2005	Mil	NL	39	59	17	4	0	2	(2	0)	27	2	10	10	2	0	17	0	0	1	0	0	-	0	.288	.306	.458
2006	Mil	NL	157	569	154	35	1	28	(11	17)	275	82	81	84	59	5	125	12	0	8	7	2	.78	17	.271	.347	.483
2007	Mil	NL	158	573	165	35	2	50	(27	23)	354	109	119	125	90	21	121	14	0	4	2	2	.50	9	.288	.395	.618
2008	Mil	NL	159	588	162	30	2	34	(18	16)	298	86	102	105	84	19	134	12	0	10	3	2	.60	12	.276	.372	.507
2009	Mil	NL	162	591	177	35	3	46	(23	23)	356	103	141	134	110	21	138	9	0	9	2	3	.40	14	.299	.412	.602
2010	Mil	NL	161	578	151	25	0	32	(18	14)	272	94	83	94	114	17	138	21	0	1	1	0	1.00	12	.261	.401	.471
	Postseason		4	14	1	0	0	1	(1	0)	4	1	2	0	2	2	5	0	0	1	0	0	-	0	.071	.176	.286
6 ML YEARS			836	2958	826	164	8	192	(99	93)	1582	476	536	552	459	83	673	68	0	33	15	9	.63	64	.279	.385	.535

Josh Fields

Bats: R Throws: R Pos: 3B-12; PH-1   Ht: 6'2" Wt: 225 Born: 12/14/1982 Age: 28

Year	Team	Lg	G	AB	H	2B	3B	HR	(Hm	Rd)	TB	R	RBI	RC	TBB	IBB	SO	HBP	SH	SF	SB	CS	SB%	GDP	Avg	OBP	Slg
									BATTING												BASERUNNING				AVERAGES		
2010	Royals*	R	3	10	4	1	1	0	(-	-)	7	2	4	3	3	0	2	0	0	0	0	0	-	0	.400	.538	.700
2010	NWArk*	AA	11	39	17	8	0	0	(-	-)	25	10	9	10	1	0	4	0	0	1	1	0	1.00	0	.436	.439	.641
2006	CWS	AL	11	20	3	2	0	1	(1	0)	8	4	2	1	5	0	8	0	0	0	0	0	-	0	.150	.320	.400
2007	CWS	AL	100	373	91	17	1	23	(15	8)	179	54	67	56	35	0	125	1	6	3	1	1	.50	11	.244	.308	.480
2008	CWS	AL	14	32	5	1	0	0	(0	0)	6	3	2	1	3	0	17	0	0	0	0	0	-	0	.156	.229	.188
2009	CWS	AL	79	239	53	5	2	7	(4	3)	83	29	30	22	25	0	76	2	2	0	2	3	.40	5	.222	.301	.347
2010	KC	AL	13	49	15	0	0	3	(2	1)	24	5	6	6	1	0	9	0	0	0	0	0	-	1	.306	.320	.490
5 ML YEARS			217	713	167	25	3	34	(22	12)	300	95	107	86	69	0	235	3	8	3	3	4	.43	17	.234	.303	.421

Casey Flen
FEEN

Pitches: R Bats: R Pos: RP-2   Ht: 6'2" Wt: 195 Born: 10/21/1983 Age: 27

Year	Team	Lg	G	GS	CG	GF	IP	BFP	H	R	ER	HR	SH	SF	HB	TBB	IBB	SO	WP	Bk	W	L	Pct	Sh	Sv-Op	Hld	ERC	ERA
			HOW MUCH HE PITCHED						WHAT HE GAVE UP												THE RESULTS							
2006	Oneonta	A-	20	0	0	3	42.2	169	39	17	13	1	3	1	0	8	0	37	2	0	1	1	.500	0	1- -	-	2.40	2.74
2007	WMich	A	39	0	0	21	61.0	253	55	28	21	4	2	1	3	10	0	77	2	0	6	1	.857	0	6	-	2.55	3.10
2008	Erie	AA	40	0	0	33	45.2	193	38	16	15	5	2	1	0	12	3	42	2	0	3	3	.500	0	12- -	-	2.65	2.96
2008	Toledo	AAA	12	0	0	4	15.0	62	14	4	4	2	0	0	1	4	0	17	1	0	2	0	1.000	0	1- -	-	3.73	2.40
2009	Toledo	AAA	42	0	0	26	58.0	234	51	23	22	5	1	1	2	15	3	66	2	1	2	1	.667	0	14- -	-	2.91	3.41
2010	Toledo	AAA	44	0	0	29	62.1	246	54	21	18	8	1	1	1	13	1	44	0	0	3	3	.500	0	8- -	-	2.92	2.60
2009	Det	AL	9	0	0	5	11.1	53	13	11	10	2	0	2	0	6	0	9	0	0	0	1	.000	0	0-0	0	5.92	7.94
2010	Det	AL	2	0	0	2	2.2	12	4	3	3	2	1	0	0	0	0	0	0	0	0	0	-	0	0-0	0	9.96	10.13
2 ML YEARS			11	0	0	7	14.0	65	17	14	13	4	1	2	0	6	0	9	0	0	0	1	.000	0	0-0	0	6.75	8.36

Alfredo Figaro

Pitches: R Bats: R Pos: RP-7; SP-1   Ht: 6'0" Wt: 173 Born: 7/7/1984 Age: 26

Year	Team	Lg	G	GS	CG	GF	IP	BFP	H	R	ER	HR	SH	SF	HB	TBB	IBB	SO	WP	Bk	W	L	Pct	Sh	Sv-Op	Hld	ERC	ERA
			HOW MUCH HE PITCHED						WHAT HE GAVE UP												THE RESULTS							
2006	Tigers	R	14	4	0	5	38.1	152	29	7	3	0	1	0	1	12	0	31	0	1	3	1	.750	0	1- -	-	2.01	0.70
2007	Lkland	A+	5	4	0	0	22.2	99	26	15	12	0	0	1	3	6	0	6	3	0	0	2	.000	0	0- -	-	4.22	4.76
2007	Oneonta	A-	11	11	0	0	53.1	231	56	23	20	1	0	2	5	16	0	40	3	2	4	2	.667	0	0- -	-	3.76	3.38
2008	WMich	A	19	19	2	0	123.0	493	99	35	28	0	3	2	4	30	0	96	7	0	12	2	.857	2	0- -	-	2.00	2.05
2008	Lkland	A+	6	5	1	0	29.1	133	37	22	16	2	1	0	1	12	1	23	3	0	5	0	1.000	0	0- -	-	5.55	4.91
2009	Erie	AA	16	11	0	1	80.0	326	67	36	32	8	3	1	1	23	2	69	2	0	6	3	.667	0	0- -	-	2.79	3.60
2010	Toledo	AAA	23	23	0	0	124.0	542	142	60	57	11	6	2	5	39	0	112	3	0	10	6	.625	0	0- -	-	4.66	4.14
2009	Det	AL	5	3	0	0	17.0	83	23	13	12	3	1	0	1	10	0	16	0	0	2	2	.500	0	0-0	0	7.94	6.35
2010	Det	AL	8	1	0	5	14.2	69	18	12	11	1	2	1	0	8	2	5	2	0	0	2	.000	0	0-0	0	5.43	6.75
2 ML YEARS			13	4	0	5	31.2	152	41	25	23	4	3	1	1	18	2	21	2	0	2	4	.333	0	0-0	0	6.74	6.54

Chone Figgins

Bats: B Throws: R Pos: 2B-161   SHAWN   Ht: 5'8" Wt: 180 Born: 1/22/1978 Age: 33

Year	Team	Lg	G	AB	H	2B	3B	HR	(Hm	Rd)	TB	R	RBI	RC	TBB	IBB	SO	HBP	SH	SF	SB	CS	SB%	GDP	Avg	OBP	Slg
2002	LAA	AL	15	12	2	1	0	0	(0	0)	3	6	1	0	0	0	5	0	0	0	2	1	.67	1	.167	.167	.250
2003	LAA	AL	71	240	71	9	4	0	(0	0)	88	34	27	39	20	0	38	0	6	4	13	7	.65	1	.296	.345	.367
2004	LAA	AL	148	577	171	22	17	5	(3	2)	242	83	60	93	49	0	94	0	10	2	34	13	.72	6	.296	.350	.419
2005	LAA	AL	158	642	186	25	10	8	(2	6)	255	113	57	94	64	1	101	0	9	5	62	17	.78	9	.290	.352	.397
2006	LAA	AL	155	604	161	23	8	9	(2	7)	227	93	62	84	65	1	100	2	5	7	52	16	.76	6	.267	.336	.376
2007	LAA	AL	115	442	146	24	6	3	(1	2)	191	81	58	88	51	0	81	0	2	8	41	12	.77	7	.330	.393	.432
2008	LAA	AL	116	453	125	14	1	1	(0	1)	144	72	22	59	62	3	80	3	2	0	34	13	.72	7	.276	.367	.318
2009	LAA	AL	158	615	183	30	7	5	(2	3)	242	114	54	110	101	0	114	1	8	4	42	17	.71	8	.298	.395	.393
2010	Sea	AL	161	602	156	21	2	1	(0	1)	184	62	35	66	74	0	114	3	17	6	42	15	.74	20	.259	.340	.306
	Postseason		35	122	21	5	2	0	(0	0)	30	13	6	6	6	0	35	2	5	0	4	1	.80	1	.172	.223	.246
	9 ML YEARS		1097	4187	1201	169	55	32	(10	22)	1576	658	376	633	486	5	727	9	59	36	322	111	.74	65	.287	.359	.376

Nelson Figueroa

Pitches: R Bats: R Pos: RP-20; SP-11   figg-uh-ROE-ah   Ht: 6'1" Wt: 180 Born: 5/18/1974 Age: 37

Year	Team	Lg	G	GS	CG	GF	IP	BFP	H	R	ER	HR	SH	SF	HB	TBB	IBB	SO	WP	Bk	W	L	Pct	Sh	Sv-Op	Hld	ERC	ERA
2010	LV*	AAA	3	3	0	0	19.0	70	10	2	2	1	0	0	0	3	0	18	0	0	3	0	1.000	0	0- -	-	1.01	0.95
2000	Ari	NL	3	3	0	0	15.2	68	17	13	13	4	1	2	0	5	0	7	2	0	0	1	.000	0	0-0	0	5.31	7.47
2001	Phi	NL	19	13	0	1	89.0	393	95	40	39	8	4	0	7	37	3	61	2	0	4	5	.444	0	0-0	0	4.76	3.94
2002	Mil	NL	30	11	0	4	93.0	412	96	59	52	18	11	5	4	37	6	51	5	0	1	7	.125	0	0-0	1	4.94	5.03
2003	Pit	NL	12	3	0	1	35.1	146	28	13	13	8	2	2	2	13	2	23	2	0	2	1	.667	0	0-0	0	3.80	3.31
2004	Pit	NL	10	3	0	0	28.1	121	32	18	18	4	4	0	0	11	1	10	3	0	0	3	.000	0	0-0	0	5.21	5.72
2008	NYM	NL	16	6	0	2	45.1	211	48	26	23	3	2	1	2	26	1	36	0	0	3	3	.500	0	0-1	0	4.88	4.57
2009	NYM	NL	16	10	1	2	70.1	320	80	33	32	8	3	4	9	24	4	59	1	0	3	8	.273	1	0-0	0	5.09	4.09
2010	2 Tms	NL	31	11	0	6	93.0	390	84	38	34	10	5	3	2	34	4	73	6	0	7	4	.636	0	1-1	0	3.49	3.29
10	Phi	NL	13	1	0	5	26.0	104	20	10	10	1	4	0	0	9	2	15	2	0	2	1	.667	0	1-1	0	2.21	3.46
10	Hou	NL	18	10	0	1	67.0	286	64	28	24	9	1	3	2	25	2	58	4	0	5	3	.625	0	0-0	0	4.03	3.22
	8 ML YEARS		137	60	1	16	470.0	2061	480	240	224	63	32	17	26	187	21	320	21	0	20	32	.385	1	1-2	1	4.58	4.29

Carlos Fisher

Pitches: R Bats: R Pos: RP-18   Ht: 6'4" Wt: 225 Born: 2/22/1983 Age: 28

Year	Team	Lg	G	GS	CG	GF	IP	BFP	H	R	ER	HR	SH	SF	HB	TBB	IBB	SO	WP	Bk	W	L	Pct	Sh	Sv-Op	Hld	ERC	ERA
2005	Billings	R+	15	8	0	1	53.2	235	56	30	25	3	0	2	5	19	0	45	3	0	4	4	.500	0	1- -	-	4.20	4.19
2006	Dayton	A	27	27	0	0	150.0	609	133	53	46	5	4	1	5	38	0	122	6	0	12	5	.706	0	0- -	-	2.65	2.76
2007	Srsota	A+	7	7	0	0	41.0	164	34	12	10	1	0	2	1	7	0	41	0	0	4	1	.800	0	0- -	-	1.96	2.20
2007	Chatt	AA	21	21	0	0	113.1	502	127	61	54	11	7	7	10	42	0	94	9	0	5	9	.357	0	0- -	-	5.04	4.29
2008	Chatt	AA	36	0	0	21	50.2	226	52	28	21	3	4	0	1	20	4	46	6	0	1	5	.167	0	8- -	-	3.74	3.73
2008	Lsvlle	AAA	14	0	0	3	17.1	77	14	2	2	0	1	1	1	9	2	21	0	0	5	0	1.000	0	0- -	-	2.70	1.04
2009	Lsvlle	AAA	13	0	0	6	18.0	69	11	4	4	0	1	0	1	4	0	21	2	0	2	0	1.000	0	2- -	-	1.31	2.00
2009	Srsota	A+	2	0	0	1	2.0	9	1	0	0	0	0	0	0	2	0	2	0	0	0	0	-	0	0- -	-	2.80	0.00
2010	Lsvlle	AAA	30	0	0	11	36.1	139	23	10	9	4	1	0	1	8	0	38	1	1	1	1	.500	0	4- -	-	1.75	2.23
2009	Cin	NL	39	0	0	17	52.1	226	50	26	26	4	2	1	1	31	2	48	6	0	1	1	.500	0	0-1	2	4.58	4.47
2010	Cin	NL	18	0	0	5	22.1	100	22	14	14	1	0	0	1	13	2	21	2	0	1	1	.500	0	0-0	0	4.33	5.64
	2 ML YEARS		57	0	0	22	74.2	326	72	40	40	5	2	1	2	44	4	69	8	0	2	2	.500	0	0-1	2	4.51	4.82

Doug Fister

Pitches: R Bats: L Pos: SP-28   Ht: 6'8" Wt: 195 Born: 2/4/1984 Age: 27

Year	Team	Lg	G	GS	CG	GF	IP	BFP	H	R	ER	HR	SH	SF	HB	TBB	IBB	SO	WP	Bk	W	L	Pct	Sh	Sv-Op	Hld	ERC	ERA
2006	Everett	A-	20	4	0	13	40.0	167	35	18	10	2	2	0	1	11	0	35	2	1	3	5	.375	0	4- -	-	2.65	2.25
2007	WTenn	AA	24	24	1	0	131.0	560	156	78	67	14	5	4	3	32	0	85	3	0	7	8	.467	0	0- -	-	4.78	4.60
2008	WTenn	AA	31	23	0	5	134.1	602	155	95	81	12	2	8	11	45	0	104	4	2	6	14	.300	0	0- -	-	4.93	5.43
2009	WTenn	AA	2	0	0	0	5.2	19	2	0	0	0	0	0	0	1	0	5	0	0	1	0	1.000	0	0- -	-	0.53	0.00
2009	Tacom	AAA	22	17	0	1	106.1	458	132	51	46	10	5	4	5	11	0	79	4	1	6	4	.600	0	0- -	-	4.39	3.89
2010	Tacom	AAA	1	1	0	0	4.0	15	4	2	2	0	0	0	0	0	0	3	0	0	0	0	-	0	0- -	-	2.12	4.50
2009	Sea	AL	11	10	0	1	61.0	256	63	29	28	11	0	0	2	15	0	36	1	0	3	4	.429	0	0-0	0	4.36	4.13
2010	Sea	AL	28	28	0	0	171.0	720	187	85	78	13	2	4	6	32	2	93	8	3	6	14	.300	0	0-0	0	3.73	4.11
	2 ML YEARS		39	38	0	1	232.0	976	250	114	106	24	2	4	8	47	2	129	9	3	9	18	.333	0	0-0	0	3.90	4.11

Jesus Flores

Bats: R Throws: R Pos: C   Ht: 6'1" Wt: 229 Born: 10/26/1984 Age: 26

Year	Team	Lg	G	AB	H	2B	3B	HR	(Hm	Rd)	TB	R	RBI	RC	TBB	IBB	SO	HBP	SH	SF	SB	CS	SB%	GDP	Avg	OBP	Slg
2007	Was	NL	79	180	44	9	0	4	(1	3)	65	21	25	19	14	0	48	3	0	0	0	1	.00	5	.244	.310	.361
2008	Was	NL	90	301	77	18	1	8	(2	6)	121	23	59	45	15	1	78	4	0	4	0	1	.00	7	.256	.296	.402
2009	Was	NL	29	93	28	3	2	4	(0	4)	47	13	15	14	11	1	26	0	1	1	0	0	-	1	.301	.371	.505
	3 ML YEARS		198	574	149	30	3	16	(3	13)	233	57	99	78	40	2	152	7	1	5	0	2	.00	13	.260	.313	.406

Randy Flores

Pitches: L **Bats:** L **Pos:** RP-58   **Ht:** 6'0" **Wt:** 190 **Born:** 7/31/1975 **Age:** 35

			HOW MUCH HE PITCHED					WHAT HE GAVE UP											THE RESULTS							
Year	Team	Lg	G	GS	CG	GF	IP	BFP	H	R	ER	HR	SH	SF	HB	TBB	IBB	SO	WP	Bk	W	L	Pct	Sh	Sv-Op	Hld	ERC	ERA
2002	2 Tms		28	2	0	9	29.0	140	40	26	24	7	2	2	3	16	3	14	4	0	0	2	.000	0	1-2	2	8.69	7.45
2004	StL	NL	9	1	0	3	14.0	57	13	3	3	0	1	1	3	3	1	7	0	0	1	0	1.000	0	0-0	1	3.15	1.93
2005	StL	NL	50	0	0	6	41.2	174	37	22	16	5	1	3	3	13	0	43	2	0	3	1	.750	0	1-3	11	3.55	3.46
2006	StL	NL	65	0	0	10	41.2	196	49	29	26	5	3	1	1	22	3	40	1	0	1	1	.500	0	0-1	18	5.64	5.62
2007	StL	NL	70	0	0	11	55.0	253	71	31	26	2	4	2	3	15	0	47	3	0	3	0	1.000	0	1-2	14	4.87	4.25
2008	StL	NL	43	0	0	3	25.2	131	34	16	15	2	0	2	1	20	3	17	1	0	1	0	1.000	0	1-3	14	7.23	5.26
2009	Col	NL	27	0	0	3	12.0	52	14	7	7	2	0	0	0	2	0	14	0	0	0	1	.000	0	0-0	10	4.43	5.25
2010	2 Tms		58	0	0	11	31.0	138	32	12	11	6	3	1	1	15	1	20	0	0	2	0	1.000	0	0-1	7	5.38	3.19
02	Tex	AL	20	0	0	5	12.0	52	11	7	6	2	1	2	0	8	2	7	3	0	0	0	-	0	1-2	2	5.07	4.50
02	Col	NL	8	2	0	4	17.0	88	29	19	18	5	1	0	3	8	1	7	1	0	0	2	.000	0	0-0	0	11.52	9.53
10	Col	NL	47	0	0	10	27.1	115	22	10	9	4	3	0	1	13	1	18	0	0	2	0	1.000	0	0-1	4	3.73	2.96
10	Min	AL	11	0	0	1	3.2	23	10	2	2	2	0	1	0	2	0	2	0	0	0	0	-	0	0-0	3	21.44	4.91
	Postseason		12	0	0	0	9.0	34	7	1	1	1	0	0	0	2	0	7	0	0	1	0	1.000	0	0-0	3	2.45	1.00
	8 ML YEARS		350	3	0	55	250.0	1141	290	146	128	29	14	12	15	106	11	202	11	0	11	5	.688	0	4-12	76	5.36	4.61

Tyler Flowers

Bats: R **Throws:** R **Pos:** C-7; PH-2   **Ht:** 6'4" **Wt:** 245 **Born:** 1/24/1986 **Age:** 25

					BATTING														BASERUNNING				AVERAGES		
Year	Team	Lg	G	AB	H	2B	3B	HR	(Hm | Rd)	TB	R	RBI	RC	TBB	IBB	SO	HBP	SH	SF	SB	CS	SB%	GDP	Avg	OBP	Slg
2006	Danvle	R+	34	129	36	9	0	5	(- | -)	60	24	16	23	16	0	30	4	0	1	0	0	-	1	.279	.373	.465
2007	Rome	A	106	389	116	34	2	12	(- | -)	190	65	70	72	49	1	74	3	0	4	3	4	.43	8	.298	.378	.488
2008	MrtlBh	A+	122	413	119	32	1	17	(- | -)	204	72	88	92	98	2	102	5	0	4	8	7	.53	8	.288	.427	.494
2009	Brham	AA	77	248	75	18	2	13	(- | -)	136	54	43	63	57	5	76	9	0	3	3	0	1.00	6	.302	.445	.548
2009	Charltt	AAA	31	105	30	10	0	2	(- | -)	46	13	13	17	10	0	32	3	1	0	0	0	-	4	.286	.364	.438
2010	Charltt	AAA	100	346	76	22	2	16	(- | -)	150	43	53	54	55	1	121	6	2	3	2	1	.67	8	.220	.334	.434
2009	CWS	AL	10	16	3	1	0	0	(0 | 0)	4	3	0	2	3	0	8	1	0	0	0	0	-	1	.188	.350	.250
2010	CWS	AL	8	11	1	0	0	0	(0 | 0)	1	2	0	1	4	0	5	0	0	0	0	0	-	0	.091	.333	.091
	2 ML YEARS		18	27	4	1	0	0	(0 | 0)	5	5	0	3	7	0	13	1	0	0	0	0	-	1	.148	.343	.185

Gavin Floyd

Pitches: R **Bats:** R **Pos:** SP-31   **Ht:** 6'6" **Wt:** 235 **Born:** 1/27/1983 **Age:** 28

			HOW MUCH HE PITCHED					WHAT HE GAVE UP										THE RESULTS							
Year	Team	Lg	G	GS	CG	GF	IP	BFP	H	R	ER	HR	SH	SF	HB	TBB	IBB	SO	WP	Bk	W	L	Pct	Sh	Sv-Op	Hld	ERC	ERA
2004	Phi	NL	6	4	0	0	28.1	126	25	11	11	1	1	0	5	16	0	24	1	1	2	0	1.000	0	0-0	0	4.33	3.49
2005	Phi	NL	7	4	0	0	26.0	127	30	31	29	5	1	1	3	16	2	17	2	0	1	2	.333	0	0-0	0	6.82	10.04
2006	Phi	NL	11	11	1	0	54.1	264	70	48	44	14	2	5	3	32	3	34	2	0	4	3	.571	1	0-0	0	8.02	7.29
2007	CWS	AL	10	10	0	4	70.0	314	85	45	41	17	3	2	6	19	0	49	1	0	1	5	.167	0	0-0	0	6.22	5.27
2008	CWS	AL	33	33	1	0	206.1	878	190	107	88	30	7	5	9	70	4	145	9	0	17	8	.680	0	0-0	0	3.80	3.84
2009	CWS	AL	30	30	1	0	193.0	797	178	93	87	21	2	3	2	59	4	163	8	0	11	11	.500	0	0-0	0	3.38	4.06
2010	CWS	AL	31	31	0	0	187.1	798	199	92	85	14	3	4	6	58	4	151	9	1	10	13	.435	0	0-0	0	4.03	4.08
	Postseason		1	1	0	0	3.0	16	5	4	4	2	0	0	0	2	0	4	0	0	1	0	1.000	0	0-0	0	14.65	12.00
	7 ML YEARS		134	123	4	4	765.1	3304	777	427	385	102	19	20	34	270	19	583	32	2	46	42	.523	1	0-0	0	4.35	4.53

Mike Fontenot

Bats: L **Throws:** R **Pos:** 2B-49; PH-37; 3B-19; SS-9; PR-1   FONT-uh-no   **Ht:** 5'8" **Wt:** 170 **Born:** 6/9/1980 **Age:** 31

					BATTING														BASERUNNING				AVERAGES		
Year	Team	Lg	G	AB	H	2B	3B	HR	(Hm | Rd)	TB	R	RBI	RC	TBB	IBB	SO	HBP	SH	SF	SB	CS	SB%	GDP	Avg	OBP	Slg
2005	ChC	NL	7	2	0	0	0	0	(0 | 0)	0	4	0	1	2	0	0	1	0	0	0	0	-	0	.000	.600	.000
2007	ChC	NL	86	234	65	12	4	3	(2 | 1)	94	32	29	26	22	0	43	0	1	3	5	4	.56	5	.278	.336	.402
2008	ChC	NL	119	243	74	22	1	9	(4 | 5)	125	42	40	49	34	2	51	3	3	1	2	0	1.00	1	.305	.395	.514
2009	ChC	NL	135	377	89	22	2	9	(3 | 6)	142	38	43	37	35	4	83	2	0	5	4	1	.80	7	.236	.301	.377
2010	2 Tms	NL	103	240	68	13	3	1	(0 | 1)	90	24	25	32	15	0	41	3	1	2	1	4	.20	3	.283	.331	.375
10	ChC	NL	75	169	48	11	3	1	(0 | 1)	68	14	20	25	10	0	28	3	1	2	1	2	.33	3	.284	.332	.402
10	SF	NL	28	71	20	2	0	0	(0 | 0)	22	10	5	7	5	0	13	0	0	0	0	2	.00	0	.282	.329	.310
	Postseason		5	8	2	0	0	0	(0 | 0)	2	0	0	0	0	0	1	0	0	0	0	0	-	0	.250	.250	.250
	5 ML YEARS		450	1096	296	69	10	22	(9 | 13)	451	140	137	145	108	6	218	9	5	11	12	9	.57	16	.270	.337	.411

Darren Ford

Bats: R **Throws:** R **Pos:** PR-6; CF-1   **Ht:** 5'11" **Wt:** 195 **Born:** 10/1/1985 **Age:** 25

					BATTING														BASERUNNING				AVERAGES		
Year	Team	Lg	G	AB	H	2B	3B	HR	(Hm | Rd)	TB	R	RBI	RC	TBB	IBB	SO	HBP	SH	SF	SB	CS	SB%	GDP	Avg	OBP	Slg
2005	Helena	R+	61	236	64	4	3	1	(- | -)	77	57	24	33	33	0	70	3	3	2	18	4	.82	1	.271	.365	.326
2006	WV	A	125	491	139	24	3	7	(- | -)	190	93	54	79	56	1	133	4	14	1	65	15	.81	4	.283	.361	.387
2007	WV	A	51	224	75	15	4	5	(- | -)	113	48	33	46	23	1	56	1	5	1	31	10	.76	2	.335	.398	.504
2007	BrvdCt	A+	72	273	63	7	1	4	(- | -)	84	46	27	34	35	0	67	1	5	3	36	6	.86	1	.231	.317	.308
2008	BrvdCt	A+	91	343	79	13	3	2	(- | -)	104	57	27	42	46	1	88	2	7	3	48	11	.81	4	.230	.322	.303
2008	SnJos	A+	38	128	28	4	1	0	(- | -)	34	21	7	16	23	1	42	2	2	0	14	1	.93	1	.219	.346	.266
2009	SnJos	A+	101	380	114	17	9	9	(- | -)	176	81	50	72	49	1	97	6	3	3	35	12	.74	4	.300	.386	.463
2010	Rchmd	AA	113	463	116	20	9	5	(- | -)	169	64	40	57	39	0	106	5	8	1	37	15	.71	6	.251	.315	.365
2010	SF	NL	7	0	0	0	0	0	(0 | 0)	0	1	0	0	0	0	0	0	0	0	2	1	.67	0	-	-	-

Dexter Fowler

Bats: B Throws: R Pos: CF-120; PH-18; PR-5   Ht: 6'4" Wt: 190 Born: 3/22/1986 Age: 25

Year	Team	Lg	G	AB	H	2B	3B	HR	(Hm	Rd)	TB	R	RBI	RC	TBB	IBB	SO	HBP	SH	SF	SB	CS	SB%	GDP	Avg	OBP	Slg
2010	ColSpr*	AAA	27	106	36	10	4	2	(-	-)	60	23	13	25	17	1	27	1	0	1	1	0	1.00	4	.340	.435	.566
2008	Col	NL	13	26	4	0	0	0	(0	0)	4	3	0	0	0	0	5	1	0	0	0	1	.00	0	.154	.185	.154
2009	Col	NL	135	433	115	29	10	4	(2	2)	176	73	34	68	67	1	116	1	14	3	27	10	.73	4	.266	.363	.406
2010	Col	NL	132	439	114	20	14	6	(5	1)	180	73	36	68	57	0	104	2	7	0	13	8	.62	5	.260	.347	.410
	Postseason		4	14	3	0	0	0	(0	0)	3	1	2	1	1	0	3	0	1	2	0	0	-	1	.214	.235	.214
	3 ML YEARS		280	898	233	49	24	10	(7	3)	360	149	70	136	124	1	225	4	21	3	40	19	.68	9	.259	.351	.401

Jake Fox

Bats: R Throws: R Pos: DH-24; C-19; PH-18; LF-13; 1B-10; 3B-4; PR-3   Ht: 6'0" Wt: 220 Born: 7/20/1982 Age: 28

Year	Team	Lg	G	AB	H	2B	3B	HR	(Hm	Rd)	TB	R	RBI	RC	TBB	IBB	SO	HBP	SH	SF	SB	CS	SB%	GDP	Avg	OBP	Slg
2007	ChC	NL	7	14	2	2	0	0	(0	0)	4	3	1	1	1	0	2	0	0	0	0	0	-	1	.143	.200	.286
2009	ChC	NL	82	216	56	12	0	11	(4	7)	101	23	44	32	14	1	47	5	0	6	0	0	-	5	.259	.311	.468
2010	2 Tms	AL	77	198	43	10	1	7	(1	6)	76	21	22	15	8	0	49	4	0	1	0	0	-	7	.217	.261	.384
10	Oak	AL	39	98	21	5	0	2	(1	1)	32	11	12	7	5	0	26	2	0	1	0	0	-	6	.214	.264	.327
10	Bal	AL	38	100	22	5	1	5	(0	5)	44	10	10	8	3	0	23	2	0	0	0	0	-	1	.220	.257	.440
	3 ML YEARS		166	428	101	24	1	18	(5	13)	181	47	67	48	23	1	98	9	0	7	0	0	-	13	.236	.285	.423

Matt Fox

Pitches: R Bats: R Pos: RP-3; SP-1   Ht: 6'3" Wt: 192 Born: 12/4/1982 Age: 28

Year	Team	Lg	G	GS	CG	GF	IP	BFP	H	R	ER	HR	SH	SF	HB	TBB	IBB	SO	WP	Bk	W	L	Pct	Sh	Sv-Op	Hld	ERC	ERA
2004	Elizab	R+	8	5	0	0	26.2	111	27	18	16	6	1	0	0	8	0	32	4	0	2	1	.667	0	0- -	-	4.69	5.40
2006	Elizab	R+	20	1	0	8	40.1	166	32	18	17	1	0	2	3	13	0	46	7	0	4	0	1.000	0	2- -	-	2.48	3.79
2007	Beloit	A	22	13	0	2	82.1	338	75	35	32	7	1	2	4	23	0	66	1	0	7	2	.778	0	0- -	-	3.27	3.50
2008	FtMyrs	A+	32	14	0	6	117.2	487	120	47	44	9	3	1	2	33	0	99	5	0	7	7	.500	0	1- -	-	3.72	3.37
2009	NwBrit	AA	28	26	1	1	151.0	640	143	67	60	12	4	2	7	56	3	120	13	1	9	9	.500	0	0- -	-	3.71	3.58
2010	Roch	AAA	35	21	0	4	123.0	527	124	61	54	17	0	5	2	51	2	104	7	0	6	9	.400	0	0- -	-	4.57	3.95
2010	2 Tms	AL	4	1	0	1	7.1	31	8	4	4	0	0	2	0	2	0	1	0	0	0	0	-	0	0-0	0	3.42	4.91
10	Min	AL	1	1	0	0	5.2	21	4	2	2	0	0	1	0	1	0	1	0	0	0	0	-	0	0-0	0	1.43	3.18
10	Bos	AL	3	0	0	1	1.2	10	4	2	2	0	0	1	0	1	0	0	0	0	0	0	-	0	0-0	0	13.02	10.80

Jeff Francis

Pitches: L Bats: L Pos: SP-19; RP-1   Ht: 6'5" Wt: 220 Born: 1/8/1981 Age: 30

Year	Team	Lg	G	GS	CG	GF	IP	BFP	H	R	ER	HR	SH	SF	HB	TBB	IBB	SO	WP	Bk	W	L	Pct	Sh	Sv-Op	Hld	ERC	ERA
2010	Tulsa*	AA	2	2	0	0	11.2	46	11	2	2	1	0	0	1	2	0	5	0	0	0	0	-	0	0- -	-	3.29	1.54
2010	ColSpr*	AAA	1	1	0	0	3.0	10	1	0	0	0	0	0	0	1	0	3	0	0	0	0	-	0	0- -	-	0.75	0.00
2004	Col	NL	7	7	0	0	36.2	164	42	22	21	8	2	1	1	13	1	32	2	0	3	2	.600	0	0-0	0	5.62	5.15
2005	Col	NL	33	33	0	0	183.2	828	228	119	116	26	6	10	4	70	5	128	2	0	14	12	.538	0	0-0	0	5.94	5.68
2006	Col	NL	32	32	1	0	199.0	843	187	101	92	18	7	7	13	69	15	117	0	0	13	11	.542	1	0-0	0	3.63	4.16
2007	Col	NL	34	34	1	0	215.1	922	234	103	101	25	7	4	7	63	7	165	1	1	17	9	.654	1	0-0	0	4.37	4.22
2008	Col	NL	24	24	0	0	143.2	636	164	84	80	21	6	4	3	49	4	94	0	0	4	10	.286	0	0-0	0	5.00	5.01
2010	Col	NL	20	19	0	0	104.1	441	119	61	58	11	6	4	2	23	3	67	1	0	4	6	.400	0	0-0	0	4.29	5.00
	Postseason		3	3	0	0	16.2	75	21	9	9	3	0	0	2	6	2	15	0	0	2	1	.667	0	0-0	0	6.57	4.86
	6 ML YEARS		150	149	2	0	882.2	3834	974	490	468	109	34	30	34	287	35	603	6	1	55	50	.524	2	0-0	0	4.66	4.77

Ben Francisco

Bats: R Throws: R Pos: PH-46; LF-23; RF-20; DH-5; CF-2; PR-1   Ht: 6'1" Wt: 190 Born: 10/23/1981 Age: 29

Year	Team	Lg	G	AB	H	2B	3B	HR	(Hm	Rd)	TB	R	RBI	RC	TBB	IBB	SO	HBP	SH	SF	SB	CS	SB%	GDP	Avg	OBP	Slg
2007	Cle	AL	25	62	17	5	0	3	(2	1)	31	10	12	6	3	0	19	0	0	1	0	2	.00	2	.274	.303	.500
2008	Cle	AL	121	447	119	32	0	15	(7	8)	196	65	54	57	40	0	86	6	2	4	4	3	.57	10	.266	.332	.438
2009	2 Tms		126	405	104	30	1	15	(6	9)	181	58	46	56	38	0	83	9	4	3	14	7	.67	12	.257	.332	.447
2010	Phi	NL	88	179	48	13	0	6	(1	5)	79	24	28	26	14	1	35	2	1	1	8	0	1.00	6	.268	.327	.441
09	Cle	AL	89	308	77	21	1	10	(4	6)	130	48	33	43	33	0	59	8	4	2	13	3	.81	11	.250	.336	.422
09	Phi	NL	37	97	27	9	0	5	(2	3)	51	10	13	13	5	0	24	1	0	1	1	4	.20	1	.278	.317	.526
	Postseason		11	11	0	0	0	0	(0	0)	0	0	0	0	1	0	2	0	0	0	0	0	-	1	.000	.083	.000
	4 ML YEARS		360	1093	288	80	1	39	(16	23)	487	157	140	145	95	1	223	17	7	9	26	12	.68	30	.263	.329	.446

Frank Francisco

Pitches: R Bats: R Pos: RP-56   Ht: 6'2" Wt: 250 Born: 9/11/1979 Age: 31

Year	Team	Lg	G	GS	CG	GF	IP	BFP	H	R	ER	HR	SH	SF	HB	TBB	IBB	SO	WP	Bk	W	L	Pct	Sh	Sv-Op	Hld	ERC	ERA
2004	Tex	AL	45	0	0	7	51.1	216	36	19	19	4	2	1	3	28	2	60	4	1	5	1	.833	0	0-3	10	3.04	3.33
2006	Tex	AL	8	0	0	2	7.1	32	8	4	4	2	0	0	0	2	0	6	1	0	0	1	.000	0	0-0	2	5.17	4.91
2007	Tex	AL	59	0	0	16	59.1	268	57	33	30	3	6	1	2	38	4	49	8	0	1	1	.500	0	0-0	21	4.44	4.55
2008	Tex	AL	58	0	0	18	63.1	264	47	24	22	7	0	3	0	26	2	83	5	0	3	5	.375	0	5-11	12	2.70	3.13
2009	Tex	AL	51	0	0	42	49.1	203	40	21	21	6	0	0	1	15	1	57	3	0	2	3	.400	0	25-29	4	2.85	3.83
2010	Tex	AL	56	0	0	20	52.2	221	49	23	22	5	3	1	1	18	2	60	2	1	6	4	.600	0	2-6	15	3.46	3.76
	6 ML YEARS		277	0	0	105	283.1	1204	237	124	118	27	11	6	7	127	11	315	23	2	17	15	.531	0	32-49	64	3.35	3.75

Juan Francisco

Bats: L Throws: R Pos: PH-26; 3B-12   Ht: 6'2" Wt: 180 Born: 6/24/1987 Age: 24

								BATTING												BASERUNNING				AVERAGES		
Year	Team	Lg	G	AB	H	2B	3B	HR	(Hm | Rd)	TB	R	RBI	RC	TBB	IBB	SO	HBP	SH	SF	SB	CS	SB%	GDP	Avg	OBP	Slg
2006	Reds	R	45	182	51	14	0	3	(- | -)	74	24	30	23	6	1	35	1	0	1	2	0	1.00	6	.280	.305	.407
2006	Billings	R+	9	36	12	3	0	0	(- | -)	15	6	2	4	0	0	8	0	0	0	2	1	.67	2	.333	.333	.417
2007	Dayton	A	135	534	143	21	4	25	(- | -)	247	69	90	74	23	6	161	3	0	2	12	6	.67	14	.268	.301	.463
2008	Srsota	A+	127	516	143	34	5	23	(- | -)	256	71	92	77	19	5	123	2	0	4	1	2	.33	14	.277	.303	.496
2009	Carlina	AA	109	437	123	26	2	22	(- | -)	219	64	74	70	20	4	91	4	0	3	6	2	.75	7	.281	.317	.501
2009	Lsvlle	AAA	22	92	33	5	1	5	(- | -)	55	17	19	20	4	1	24	1	0	2	0	0	-	3	.359	.384	.598
2010	Lsvlle	AAA	77	308	88	24	4	18	(- | -)	174	46	59	56	16	1	81	3	0	2	1	0	1.00	1	.286	.325	.565
2009	Cin	NL	14	21	9	1	0	1	(1 | 0)	13	4	7	6	3	0	7	1	0	0	0	0	-	0	.429	.520	.619
2010	Cin	NL	36	55	15	3	0	1	(1 | 0)	21	3	7	3	4	0	20	0	0	0	0	1	.00	2	.273	.322	.382
	2 ML YEARS		50	76	24	4	0	2	(2 | 0)	34	7	14	9	7	0	27	1	0	0	0	1	.00	2	.316	.381	.447

Jeff Francoeur

Bats: R Throws: R Pos: RF-131; PH-9; LF-2; PR-2; DH-1   frann-COOR   Ht: 6'5" Wt: 220 Born: 1/8/1984 Age: 27

								BATTING												BASERUNNING				AVERAGES		
Year	Team	Lg	G	AB	H	2B	3B	HR	(Hm | Rd)	TB	R	RBI	RC	TBB	IBB	SO	HBP	SH	SF	SB	CS	SB%	GDP	Avg	OBP	Slg
2005	Atl	NL	70	257	77	20	1	14	(11 | 3)	141	41	45	50	11	3	58	4	0	2	3	2	.60	4	.300	.336	.549
2006	Atl	NL	162	651	169	24	6	29	(19 | 10)	292	83	103	91	23	6	132	9	0	3	1	6	.14	15	.260	.293	.449
2007	Atl	NL	162	642	188	40	0	19	(7 | 12)	285	84	105	97	42	5	129	5	0	7	5	2	.71	14	.293	.338	.444
2008	Atl	NL	155	599	143	33	3	11	(5 | 6)	215	70	71	49	39	5	111	10	0	4	0	1	.00	18	.239	.294	.359
2009	2 Tms	NL	157	593	166	32	4	15	(7 | 8)	251	72	76	59	23	5	92	6	1	9	6	4	.60	13	.280	.309	.423
2010	2 Tms	NL	139	454	113	18	2	13	(5 | 8)	174	52	65	46	30	8	81	8	0	11	8	3	.73	9	.249	.300	.383
09	Atl	NL	82	304	76	12	2	5	(3 | 2)	107	32	35	25	12	2	46	3	1	4	5	1	.83	10	.250	.282	.352
09	NYM	NL	75	289	90	20	2	10	(4 | 6)	144	40	41	34	11	3	46	3	0	5	1	3	.25	3	.311	.338	.498
10	NYM	NL	124	401	95	16	2	11	(5 | 6)	148	43	54	39	29	8	76	7	0	10	8	2	.80	7	.237	.293	.369
10	Tex	AL	15	53	18	2	0	2	(0 | 2)	26	9	11	7	1	0	5	1	0	1	0	1	.00	2	.340	.357	.491
	Postseason		4	17	4	1	1	0	(0 | 0)	7	2	1	2	2	1	4	1	1	0	0	0	-	1	.235	.350	.412
	6 ML YEARS		845	3196	856	167	16	101	(54 | 47)	1358	402	465	392	168	32	603	42	1	36	23	18	.56	73	.268	.310	.425

Kevin Frandsen

Bats: R Throws: R Pos: 3B-43; PR-5; 1B-4; 2B-4; DH-2; PH-2; LF-1   Ht: 6'0" Wt: 184 Born: 5/24/1982 Age: 29

								BATTING												BASERUNNING				AVERAGES		
Year	Team	Lg	G	AB	H	2B	3B	HR	(Hm | Rd)	TB	R	RBI	RC	TBB	IBB	SO	HBP	SH	SF	SB	CS	SB%	GDP	Avg	OBP	Slg
2010	Pwtckt*	AAA	17	62	16	3	0	2	(- | -)	25	9	4	9	5	0	3	3	1	0	2	0	1.00	2	.258	.343	.403
2010	Salt Lk*	AAA	36	137	38	9	1	1	(- | -)	52	25	12	19	7	0	19	9	2	0	1	1	.67	4	.277	.353	.380
2006	SF	NL	41	93	20	4	0	2	(0 | 2)	30	12	7	7	3	0	14	6	0	0	0	1	.00	3	.215	.284	.323
2007	SF	NL	109	264	71	12	1	5	(1 | 4)	100	26	31	29	21	3	24	5	3	3	4	3	.57	17	.269	.331	.379
2008	SF	NL	1	1	0	0	0	0	(0 | 0)	0	0	0	0	0	0	0	0	0	0	0	0	-	0	.000	.000	.000
2009	SF	NL	23	50	7	2	0	0	(0 | 0)	9	3	1	0	3	0	4	1	0	0	0	0	-	2	.140	.204	.180
2010	LAA	AL	54	160	40	11	0	0	(0 | 0)	51	24	14	16	9	0	10	1	3	0	2	0	1.00	5	.250	.294	.319
	5 ML YEARS		228	568	138	29	1	7	(1 | 6)	190	65	53	52	36	3	52	13	6	3	6	4	.60	27	.243	.302	.335

Ryan Franklin

Pitches: R Bats: R Pos: RP-59   Ht: 6'3" Wt: 190 Born: 3/5/1973 Age: 38

			HOW MUCH HE PITCHED						WHAT HE GAVE UP										THE RESULTS					
Year	Team	Lg	G	GS	CG	GF	IP	BFP	H	R	ER	HR	SH	SF	HB	TBB	IBB	SO	WP	Bk	W	L	Pct	Sh	Sv-Op Hld	ERC	ERA
1999	Sea	AL	6	0	0	2	11.1	51	10	0	0	0	0	0	1	8	1	6	0	0	0	0	-	0	0-0 1	5.52	4.76
2001	Sea	AL	38	0	0	14	78.1	335	76	32	31	13	1	2	4	24	4	60	2	0	5	1	.833	0	0-1 5	4.08	3.56
2002	Sea	AL	41	12	0	10	118.2	495	117	62	53	14	5	5	5	22	1	65	0	0	7	5	.583	0	0-1 3	3.40	4.02
2003	Sea	AL	32	32	2	0	212.0	877	199	93	84	34	8	5	9	61	3	99	1	2	11	13	.458	1	0-0 0	3.90	3.57
2004	Sea	AL	32	32	2	0	200.1	870	224	116	109	33	2	11	10	61	1	104	0	3	4	16	.200	1	0-0 0	5.08	4.90
2005	Sea	AL	32	30	2	0	190.2	832	212	110	108	28	3	3	7	62	4	93	3	1	8	15	.040	1	0-0 0	4.80	5.10
2006	2 Tms	NL	66	0	0	19	77.1	343	86	42	39	13	2	2	4	33	10	43	2	0	6	7	.462	0	0-3 8	5.41	4.54
2007	StL	NL	69	0	0	8	80.0	317	70	28	27	8	2	2	3	11	0	44	2	0	4	4	.500	0	1-6 25	2.59	3.04
2008	StL	NL	74	0	0	39	78.2	346	86	34	31	10	2	2	3	30	4	51	3	0	6	6	.500	0	17-25 13	4.82	3.55
2009	StL	NL	62	0	0	54	61.0	250	49	13	13	2	0	2	1	24	3	44	1	0	4	3	.571	0	38-43 1	2.58	1.92
2010	StL	NL	59	0	0	51	65.0	264	57	25	25	7	1	1	4	10	1	42	5	0	6	2	.750	0	27-29 0	2.72	3.46
06	Phi	NL	46	0	0	13	53.0	233	59	28	27	10	0	1	4	17	4	25	1	0	1	5	.167	0	0-1 8	5.26	4.58
06	Cin	NL	20	0	0	6	24.1	110	27	14	12	3	2	1	0	16	6	18	1	0	5	2	.714	0	0-2 0	5.67	4.44
	Postseason		2	0	0	2	1.1	10	3	2	0	0	0	0	0	2	0	1	0	0	0	1	.000	0	0-1 0	14.53	0.00
	11 ML YEARS		511	106	6	197	1173.1	4980	1186	561	526	164	26	35	51	346	32	651	19	6	61	72	.459	3	83-108 56	4.15	4.03

Jason Frasor

Pitches: R Bats: R Pos: RP-69   FRAY-zer   Ht: 5'10" Wt: 175 Born: 8/9/1977 Age: 33

			HOW MUCH HE PITCHED						WHAT HE GAVE UP										THE RESULTS					
Year	Team	Lg	G	GS	CG	GF	IP	BFP	H	R	ER	HR	SH	SF	HB	TBB	IBB	SO	WP	Bk	W	L	Pct	Sh	Sv-Op Hld	ERC	ERA
2004	Tor	AL	63	0	0	37	68.1	299	64	31	31	4	3	3	2	36	3	54	4	2	4	6	.400	0	17-19 8	3.97	4.08
2005	Tor	AL	67	0	0	12	74.2	305	67	31	27	8	2	1	3	28	2	62	1	0	3	5	.375	0	1-3 15	3.72	3.25
2006	Tor	AL	51	0	0	12	50.0	215	47	24	24	8	0	3	2	17	1	51	3	0	3	2	.600	0	0-1 12	3.98	4.32
2007	Tor	AL	51	0	0	18	57.0	242	47	29	29	3	1	2	2	23	1	59	2	1	1	5	.167	0	3-6 4	2.88	4.58
2008	Tor	AL	49	0	0	21	47.1	208	36	23	22	4	0	2	1	32	4	42	6	0	1	2	.333	0	0-1 4	3.62	4.18
2009	Tor	AL	61	0	0	36	57.2	227	43	17	16	4	1	2	2	16	3	56	2	0	7	3	.700	0	11-14 5	2.22	2.50
2010	Tor	AL	69	0	0	18	63.2	279	61	30	26	4	1	0	4	27	6	65	5	0	3	4	.429	0	4-8 14	3.72	3.68
	7 ML YEARS		411	0	0	154	418.2	1775	365	185	175	35	8	13	16	179	20	389	23	3	22	27	.449	0	36-52 61	3.45	3.76

Jeff Frazier

Bats: R Throws: R Pos: LF-3; DH-3; PH-3; RF-1 | Ht: 6'3" Wt: 195 Born: 8/10/1982 Age: 28

Year	Team	Lg	G	AB	H	2B	3B	HR	(Hm	Rd)	TB	R	RBI	RC	TBB	IBB	SO	HBP	SH	SF	SB	CS	SB%	GDP	Avg	OBP	Slg
2004	Oneont	A-	20	79	24	5	1	1	(-	-)	34	15	13	14	9	0	11	3	0	2	2	1	.67	0	.304	.387	.430
2005	WMich	A	137	537	154	45	4	12	(-	-)	243	79	81	90	46	3	86	10	1	8	16	3	.84	17	.287	.349	.453
2006	Lkland	A+	135	526	120	21	1	13	(-	-)	182	61	73	54	37	1	88	3	0	7	12	3	.80	25	.228	.279	.346
2007	WTenn	AA	78	302	74	12	1	4	(-	-)	100	29	30	30	21	0	54	2	1	2	0	2	.00	11	.245	.297	.331
2007	Hi Dsrt	A+	44	173	57	19	1	4	(-	-)	90	20	27	32	12	0	14	2	0	0	0	2	.00	5	.329	.380	.520
2008	Erie	AA	116	446	135	22	1	6	(-	-)	177	55	55	64	31	1	51	3	1	3	1	1	.50	15	.303	.350	.397
2008	Toledo	AAA	3	12	3	0	0	0	(-	-)	3	0	1	0	0	0	3	0	0	0	0	0	-	0	.250	.250	.250
2009	Erie	AA	23	87	28	10	0	1	(-	-)	41	11	13	15	7	0	13	1	0	1	0	1	.00	5	.322	.375	.471
2009	Toledo	AAA	105	399	123	24	1	11	(-	-)	182	52	54	62	20	0	49	1	0	9	1	2	.33	11	.308	.336	.456
2010	Toledo	AAA	123	477	122	34	2	25	(-	-)	235	72	73	74	32	1	89	4	0	3	7	1	.88	13	.256	.306	.493
2010	Det	AL	9	23	5	1	0	0	(0	0)	6	3	1	0	1	0	6	0	0	0	0	0	-	2	.217	.250	.261

Freddie Freeman

Bats: L Throws: R Pos: 1B-12; PH-11; PR-2 | Ht: 6'5" Wt: 220 Born: 9/12/1989 Age: 21

Year	Team	Lg	G	AB	H	2B	3B	HR	(Hm	Rd)	TB	R	RBI	RC	TBB	IBB	SO	HBP	SH	SF	SB	CS	SB%	GDP	Avg	OBP	Slg
2007	Braves	R	59	224	60	7	0	6	(-	-)	85	24	30	24	7	0	33	2	0	1	1	2	.33	3	.268	.295	.379
2008	Rome	A	129	487	154	33	7	18	(-	-)	255	69	94	94	46	1	84	3	0	0	5	5	.50	9	.316	.379	.524
2009	MrtlBh	A+	70	255	77	19	0	6	(-	-)	114	43	34	46	26	0	41	14	0	2	1	4	.20	8	.302	.394	.447
2009	Missi	AA	41	149	37	8	0	2	(-	-)	51	15	24	17	11	1	19	4	0	5	0	0	-	5	.248	.308	.342
2010	Gwnntt	AAA	124	461	147	35	2	18	(-	-)	240	73	87	92	43	3	84	6	0	9	6	2	.75	14	.319	.378	.521
2010	Atl	NL	20	24	4	1	0	0	(0	1)	8	3	1	0	0	0	8	0	0	0	0	0	-	1	.167	.167	.333

David Freese

Bats: R Throws: R Pos: 3B-66; PH-6; 1B-1 | FREEZE | Ht: 6'2" Wt: 220 Born: 4/28/1983 Age: 28

Year	Team	Lg	G	AB	H	2B	3B	HR	(Hm	Rd)	TB	R	RBI	RC	TBB	IBB	SO	HBP	SH	SF	SB	CS	SB%	GDP	Avg	OBP	Slg
2006	Eugene	A-	18	58	22	8	0	5	(-	-)	45	19	26	19	7	0	12	4	0	2	0	0	-	2	.379	.465	.776
2006	FtWyn	A	53	204	61	13	3	8	(-	-)	104	27	44	39	21	1	44	4	0	1	1	1	.50	2	.299	.374	.510
2007	Lk Els	A+	128	503	152	31	6	17	(-	-)	246	104	96	103	69	0	99	16	0	4	6	1	.86	11	.302	.400	.489
2008	Memp	AAA	131	464	142	29	3	26	(-	-)	255	83	91	91	39	0	111	3	0	4	5	2	.71	11	.306	.361	.550
2009	Memp	AAA	56	200	60	15	0	10	(-	-)	105	34	37	39	22	1	51	1	0	2	1	0	1.00	9	.300	.369	.525
2009	Cards	R	4	11	5	2	0	1	(-	-)	10	2	6	4	1	0	3	0	0	0	0	0	-	0	.455	.500	.909
2009	Sprgfld	AA	4	16	6	1	0	1	(-	-)	10	3	5	4	2	0	2	0	0	0	0	0	-	2	.375	.444	.625
2010	Sprgfld	AA	1	2	1	1	0	0	(-	-)	2	0	0	1	1	0	1	0	0	0	0	0	-	0	.500	.667	1.000
2009	StL	NL	17	31	10	2	0	1	(0	1)	15	3	7	4	2	0	7	0	0	1	0	0	-	1	.323	.353	.484
2010	StL	NL	70	240	71	12	1	4	(3	1)	97	28	36	36	21	0	59	4	4	1	1	1	.50	7	.296	.361	.404
	2 ML YEARS		87	271	81	14	1	5	(3	2)	112	31	43	40	23	0	66	4	4	2	1	1	.50	8	.299	.360	.413

Luke French

Pitches: L Bats: L Pos: SP-13; RP-3 | Ht: 6'4" Wt: 220 Born: 9/13/1985 Age: 25

Year	Team	Lg	G	GS	CG	GF	IP	BFP	H	R	ER	HR	SH	SF	HB	TBB	IBB	SO	WP	Bk	W	L	Pct	Sh	Sv-Op Hld	ERC	ERA
2004	Tigers	R	11	10	0	0	49.1	212	43	21	15	1	4	4	1	19	0	49	2	1	1	3	.250	0	0- - -	2.78	2.74
2005	Tigers	R	2	2	0	0	10.2	47	16	10	9	3	0	0	0	0	0	9	1	0	1	0	1.000	0	0- - -	6.68	7.59
2005	Lkland	A	4	4	0	0	22.1	103	29	14	11	3	0	0	0	9	0	17	1	1	3	1	.750	0	0- - -	6.09	4.43
2005	WMich	A	6	6	0	0	34.2	159	42	23	21	4	2	1	1	14	0	24	7	0	1	2	.333	0	0- - -	5.50	5.45
2006	WMich	A	26	26	1	0	157.1	668	156	75	65	10	9	3	7	44	0	94	8	0	11	8	.579	1	0- - -	3.47	3.72
2007	Lkland	A+	27	27	0	0	149.0	654	172	94	67	10	2	8	5	47	1	93	5	0	5	14	.263	0	0- - -	4.51	4.05
2008	Erie	AA	27	26	3	0	170.0	745	195	92	76	16	5	7	6	60	1	88	10	0	9	11	.450	0	0- - -	4.88	4.02
2009	Toledo	AAA	13	13	1	0	81.2	328	71	32	27	6	5	3	1	20	0	72	1	0	4	4	.500	0	0- - -	2.71	2.98
2010	Tacom	AAA	17	17	1	0	113.1	458	109	45	37	7	5	4	5	23	0	63	6	1	11	3	.786	0	0- - -	3.11	2.94
2009	2 Tms	AL	15	12	0	2	67.1	312	87	45	39	11	0	5	2	28	1	42	3	0	4	5	.444	0	0-0 -	6.47	5.21
2010	Sea	AL	16	13	0	2	87.2	371	88	47	47	13	0	2	4	29	2	37	4	0	5	7	.417	0	0-0 -	4.38	4.83
09	Det	AL	7	5	0	1	29.1	133	33	13	11	2	0	1	1	11	1	19	1	0	1	2	.333	0	0-0 -	4.41	3.38
09	Sea	AL	8	7	0	1	38.0	179	54	32	28	9	0	4	1	17	0	23	2	0	3	3	.500	0	0-0 -	8.24	6.63
	2 ML YEARS		31	25	0	4	155.0	683	175	92	86	24	0	7	6	57	3	79	7	0	9	12	.429	0	0-0 - 0	5.26	4.99

Ernesto Frieri

Pitches: R Bats: R Pos: RP-33 | free-AIR-ee | Ht: 6'2" Wt: 200 Born: 7/19/1985 Age: 25

Year	Team	Lg	G	GS	CG	GF	IP	BFP	H	R	ER	HR	SH	SF	HB	TBB	IBB	SO	WP	Bk	W	L	Pct	Sh	Sv-Op Hld	ERC	ERA
2005	Padres	R	17	5	0	5	46.1	187	21	7	6	0	1	0	4	29	0	59	2	1	7	1	.875	0	0- - -	1.79	1.17
2005	Lk Els	A+	2	0	0	0	3.1	14	3	1	1	1	0	0	0	3	0	3	0	0	0	0	-	0	0- - -	4.34	2.70
2006	FtWyn	A	1	0	0	0	1.0	8	1	4	1	0	0	0	0	5	0	1	0	0	0	0	-	0	0- - -	25.88	9.00
2006	Eugene	A-	27	1	0	10	37.2	158	31	18	16	3	2	3	4	15	0	38	2	0	3	3	.500	0	2- - -	3.42	3.82
2006	Lk Els	A+	2	0	0	0	6.0	28	8	4	4	0	2	0	0	3	0	4	0	0	0	0	-	0	0- - -	5.70	6.00
2007	FtWyn	A	40	0	0	4	64.2	262	48	19	19	4	2	5	2	23	1	65	1	0	1	2	.333	0	0- - -	2.42	2.64
2007	Lk Els	A+	13	1	0	6	21.2	78	11	3	3	1	0	1	0	6	0	27	1	0	1	0	1.000	0	1- - -	1.23	1.25
2008	Lk Els	A+	33	18	0	4	123.2	521	125	61	55	14	3	5	4	32	1	108	3	1	8	6	.571	0	0- - -	3.79	4.00
2008	Portlnd	AAA	1	1	0	0	6.0	23	2	1	1	0	0	0	0	2	0	7	1	0	0	1	.000	0	0- - -	0.66	1.50
2008	SnAnt	AA	2	2	0	0	11.0	41	7	5	5	3	0	0	1	2	0	10	1	0	1	0	1.000	0	0- - -	2.80	4.09
2009	SnAnt	AA	27	26	0	0	140.1	602	125	61	56	13	4	5	4	62	1	118	6	0	10	9	.526	0	0- - -	3.67	3.59

Year Team	Lg	G	GS	CG	GF	IP	BFP	H	R	ER	HR	SH	SF	HB	TBB	IBB	SO	WP	Bk	W	L	Pct	Sh	Sv-Op	Hld	ERC	ERA
2010 Portlnd	AAA	34	0	0	30	37.2	144	14	6	6	2	1	0	2	18	1	49	1	1	3	1	.750	0	17--	-	1.32	1.43
2009 SD	NL	2	0	0	2	2.0	7	0	0	0	0	0	0	0	1	0	2	0	0	0	0	-	0	0-0	0	0.27	0.00
2010 SD	NL	33	0	0	12	31.2	128	18	7	6	2	0	0	0	17	3	41	2	0	1	1	.500	0	0-0	7	1.99	1.71
2 ML YEARS		35	0	0	14	33.2	135	18	7	6	2	0	0	0	18	3	43	2	0	1	1	.500	0	0-0	7	1.82	1.60

Brian Fuentes

Pitches: L Bats: L Pos: RP-48 **Ht: 6'4" Wt: 230 Born: 8/9/1975 Age: 35**

		HOW MUCH HE PITCHED						WHAT HE GAVE UP												THE RESULTS							
Year Team	Lg	G	GS	CG	GF	IP	BFP	H	R	ER	HR	SH	SF	HB	TBB	IBB	SO	WP	Bk	W	L	Pct	Sh	Sv-Op	Hld	ERC	ERA
2010 RCuca*	A+	1	1	0	0	1.0	3	0	0	0	0	0	0	0	0	0	1	0	0	0	0	-	0	0--	-	0.00	0.00
2001 Sea	AL	10	0	0	3	11.2	47	6	6	6	2	0	1	3	8	0	10	1	0	1	1	.500	0	0-1	1	4.39	4.63
2002 Col	NL	31	0	0	9	26.2	118	25	14	14	4	0	2	3	13	0	38	1	0	2	0	1.000	0	0-0	0	4.91	4.73
2003 Col	NL	75	0	0	23	75.1	320	64	24	23	7	0	3	6	34	2	82	2	1	3	3	.500	0	4-6	19	3.71	2.75
2004 Col	NL	47	0	0	12	44.2	201	46	30	28	5	7	0	4	19	6	48	3	0	2	4	.333	0	0-1	13	4.50	5.64
2005 Col	NL	78	0	0	55	74.1	321	59	25	24	6	5	1	10	34	4	91	8	0	2	5	.286	0	31-34	6	3.44	2.91
2006 Col	NL	66	0	0	58	65.1	274	50	25	25	8	2	1	6	26	4	73	6	0	3	4	.429	0	30-36	0	3.19	3.44
2007 Col	NL	64	0	0	38	61.1	255	46	26	21	6	1	1	7	23	0	56	2	0	3	5	.375	0	20-27	8	3.06	3.08
2008 Col	NL	67	0	0	48	62.2	256	47	22	19	3	3	1	1	22	1	82	1	0	1	5	.167	0	30-34	6	2.27	2.73
2009 LAA	AL	65	0	0	57	55.0	242	53	24	24	6	2	2	5	24	2	46	1	0	1	5	.167	0	48-55	0	4.37	3.93
2010 2 Tms	AL	48	0	0	35	48.0	196	31	17	15	5	2	1	2	20	1	47	3	1	4	1	.800	0	24-28	5	2.41	2.81
10 LAA	AL	39	0	0	33	38.1	161	28	17	15	5	2	1	1	18	1	39	2	1	4	1	.800	0	23-27	0	3.11	3.52
10 Min	AL	9	0	0	2	9.2	35	3	0	0	0	0	0	1	2	0	8	1	0	0	0	-	0	1-1	3	0.60	0.00
Postseason		15	0	0	3	14.1	67	15	8	8	3	0	0	1	9	2	14	1	0	1	0	1.000	0	3-4	5	6.13	5.02
10 ML YEARS		551	0	0	338	525.0	2230	427	213	199	52	22	13	47	223	20	573	28	2	22	33	.400	0	187-222	56	3.43	3.41

Kosuke Fukudome

Bats: L Throws: R Pos: RF-110; PH-24   KOE-skay foo-koo-DOE-may   **Ht: 6'0" Wt: 200 Born: 4/26/1977 Age: 34**

		BATTING																BASERUNNING				AVERAGES		
Year Team	Lg	G	AB	H	2B	3B	HR	(Hm | Rd)	TB	R	RBI	RC	TBB	IBB	SO	HBP	SH	SF	SB	CS	SB%	GDP	Avg	OBP	Slg
2008 ChC	NL	150	501	129	25	3	10	(6 | 4)	190	79	58	77	81	9	104	1	2	5	12	4	.75	7	.257	.359	.379
2009 ChC	NL	146	499	129	38	5	11	(4 | 7)	210	79	54	76	93	3	112	3	3	5	6	10	.38	15	.259	.375	.421
2010 ChC	NL	130	358	94	20	2	13	(4 | 9)	157	45	44	59	64	1	67	0	3	4	7	8	.47	5	.263	.371	.439
Postseason		3	10	1				(0 | 0)	1	0	0	0	0	0	4	0	0	0	0	0	-	0	.100	.100	.100
3 ML YEARS		426	1358	352	83	10	34	(14 | 20)	557	203	156	212	238	13	283	4	8	14	25	22	.53	27	.259	.368	.410

Jeff Fulchino

Pitches: R Bats: R Pos: RP-50 **Ht: 6'5" Wt: 286 Born: 11/26/1979 Age: 31**

		HOW MUCH HE PITCHED						WHAT HE GAVE UP												THE RESULTS							
Year Team	Lg	G	GS	CG	GF	IP	BFP	H	R	ER	HR	SH	SF	HB	TBB	IBB	SO	WP	Bk	W	L	Pct	Sh	Sv-Op	Hld	ERC	ERA
2010 RdRck*	AAA	4	0	0	0	4.0	15	3	0	0	0	0	0	0	1	0	2	0	0	0	0	-	0	0--	-	1.79	0.00
2006 Fla	NL	1	0	0	0	0.1	2	0	0	0	0	0	0	0	1	0	0	0	0	0	0	-	0	0-0	0	7.00	0.00
2008 KC	AL	12	0	0	7	14.0	72	21	15	14	2	0	1	1	8	0	12	1	0	0	1	.000	0	0-0	0	8.38	9.00
2009 Hou	NL	61	0	0	18	82.0	336	70	33	31	7	4	1	3	27	3	71	2	1	6	4	.600	0	0-3	12	3.05	3.40
2010 Hou	NL	50	0	0	16	47.1	217	53	30	29	7	1	1	3	22	2	40	2	0	2	1	.667	0	0-1	5	5.54	5.51
4 ML YEARS		124	0	0	41	143.2	627	144	78	74	16	5	3	7	58	5	123	5	1	8	6	.571	0	0-4	17	4.32	4.64

Sam Fuld

Bats: L Throws: L Pos: LF-8; CF-7; PH-5 **Ht: 5'10" Wt: 175 Born: 11/20/1981 Age: 29**

		BATTING																BASERUNNING				AVERAGES		
Year Team	Lg	G	AB	H	2B	3B	HR	(Hm | Rd)	TB	R	RBI	RC	TBB	IBB	SO	HBP	SH	SF	SB	CS	SB%	GDP	Avg	OBP	Slg
2010 Iowa*	AAA	112	368	100	15	9	4	(- | -)	145	69	27	62	66	2	37	2	1	3	21	9	.70	4	.272	.383	.394
2007 ChC	NL	14	6	0	0	0	0	(0 | 0)	0	3	0	0	3	0	0	0	0	0	0	0	-	0	.000	.333	.000
2009 ChC	NL	65	97	29	6	1	1	(1 | 0)	40	17	2	15	17	1	10	1	0	0	2	1	.67	1	.299	.409	.412
2010 ChO	NL	10	28	4	1	0	0	(0 | 0)	5	3	3	1	3	0	5	0	0	0	0	0	-	2	.143	.226	.179
3 ML YEARS		98	131	33	7	1	1	(1 | 0)	45	23	5	16	23	1	18	1	0	0	2	1	.67	3	.252	.388	.344

Rafael Furcal

Bats: B Throws: R Pos: SS-93; PH-6   furr-CALL   **Ht: 5'8" Wt: 187 Born: 10/24/1977 Age: 33**

		BATTING																BASERUNNING				AVERAGES		
Year Team	Lg	G	AB	H	2B	3B	HR	(Hm | Rd)	TB	R	RBI	RC	TBB	IBB	SO	HBP	SH	SF	SB	CS	SB%	GDP	Avg	OBP	Slg
2010 InldEm*	A+	2	4	0	0	0	0	(- | -)	0	0	0	0	2	0	2	0	0	0	0	0	-	0	.000	.333	.000
2010 Albq*	AAA	2	5	3	1	1	1	(- | -)	9	3	4	3	1	0	0	0	0	0	0	0	-	0	.600	.667	1.800
2000 Atl	NL	131	455	134	20	4	4	(1 | 3)	174	87	37	78	73	0	80	3	9	2	40	14	.74	2	.295	.394	.382
2001 Atl	NL	79	324	89	19	0	4	(3 | 1)	120	39	30	41	24	1	56	1	4	6	22	6	.79	5	.275	.321	.370
2002 Atl	NL	154	636	175	31	8	8	(4 | 4)	246	95	47	80	43	0	114	3	9	2	27	15	.64	8	.275	.323	.387
2003 Atl	NL	156	664	194	35	10	15	(4 | 11)	294	130	61	107	60	2	76	3	3	4	25	2	.93	1	.292	.352	.443
2004 Atl	NL	143	563	157	24	5	14	(5 | 9)	233	103	59	82	58	4	71	1	5	5	29	6	.83	9	.279	.344	.414
2005 Atl	NL	154	616	175	31	11	12	(9 | 3)	264	100	58	98	62	3	78	1	5	5	46	10	.82	11	.284	.348	.429
2006 LAD	NL	159	654	196	32	9	15	(12 | 3)	291	113	63	110	73	3	98	1	5	3	37	13	.74	7	.300	.369	.445
2007 LAD	NL	138	581	157	23	4	6	(4 | 2)	206	87	47	65	55	3	68	1	2	3	25	6	.81	11	.270	.333	.355
2008 LAD	NL	36	143	51	12	2	5	(3 | 2)	82	34	16	33	20	0	17	1	0	0	8	3	.73	3	.357	.439	.573
2009 LAD	NL	150	613	165	28	5	9	(5 | 4)	230	92	47	73	61	2	89	1	3	2	12	6	.67	11	.269	.335	.375
2010 LAD	NL	97	383	115	23	7	8	(5 | 3)	176	66	43	66	40	5	60	1	2	2	22	4	.85	5	.300	.366	.460
Postseason		41	170	41	2	3	3	(3 | 0)	58	25	13	22	23	1	25	1	4	2	12	2	.86	1	.241	.332	.341
11 ML YEARS		1397	5632	1608	278	65	100	(55 | 45)	2316	946	508	833	569	23	807	17	47	34	293	85	.78	73	.286	.351	.411

Armando Gabino

Pitches: R Bats: R Pos: RP-5 gah-BEE-no **Ht: 6'3" Wt: 250 Born: 8/31/1983 Age: 27**

			HOW MUCH HE PITCHED						WHAT HE GAVE UP												THE RESULTS							
Year	Team	Lg	G	GS	CG	GF	IP	BFP	H	R	ER	HR	SH	SF	HB	TBB	IBB	SO	WP	Bk	W	L	Pct	Sh	Sv-Op	Hld	ERC	ERA
2004	Burlgtn	R+	5	4	0	0	19.0	85	20	13	9	1	1	2	3	5	0	12	0	0	0	1	.000	0	0--	-	4.01	4.26
2005	Elizab	R+	17	3	0	1	30.0	152	45	28	27	7	1	0	6	12	0	23	7	0	1	2	.333	0	0--	-	9.07	8.10
2006	Elizab	R+	5	1	0	0	10.1	39	5	1	1	0	0	0	1	2	0	8	0	0	1	0	1.000	0	0--	-	0.97	0.87
2006	Beloit	A	16	0	0	6	30.1	123	29	15	14	4	4	1	2	5	0	20	2	0	2	3	.400	0	1--	-	3.44	4.15
2007	Beloit	A	12	0	0	4	22.0	85	18	2	2	1	1	0	1	4	0	16	0	0	1	0	1.000	0	0--	-	2.25	0.82
2007	FtMyrs	A+	26	0	0	15	37.0	151	27	17	13	1	1	1	0	15	0	25	1	0	2	2	.500	0	4--	-	2.21	3.16
2007	NwBrit	AA	10	0	0	4	16.0	68	12	4	0	1	1	0	0	8	0	14	1	0	2	0	1.000	0	4--	-	2.40	0.00
2008	NwBrit	AA	49	0	0	23	81.1	349	84	28	28	6	1	2	6	31	0	61	3	1	6	5	.545	0	3--	-	4.40	3.10
2009	Roch	AAA	38	7	1	12	98.0	390	80	34	32	7	3	6	5	24	1	64	3	0	6	4	.600	0	1--	-	2.57	2.94
2010	Bowie	AA	2	0	0	1	4.1	22	6	4	2	0	0	0	0	2	0	2	0	0	0	0	-	0	1--	-	5.35	4.15
2010	Norfolk	AAA	30	8	0	9	83.2	334	62	29	22	7	1	4	2	23	1	75	0	0	7	0	1.000	0	2--	-	2.33	2.37
2009	Min	AL	2	1	0	0	3.2	25	9	7	7	1	0	0	0	5	0	2	0	0	0	0	-	0	0-0	0	20.46	17.18
2010	Bal	AL	5	0	0	3	4.2	26	9	7	7	3	0	0	0	3	0	2	0	0	0	0	-	0	0-0	0	16.41	13.50
	2 ML YEARS		7	1	0	3	8.1	51	18	14	14	4	0	0	0	8	0	4	0	0	0	0	-	0	0-0	0	18.36	15.12

Armando Galarraga

Pitches: R Bats: R Pos: SP-24; RP-1 **Ht: 6'4" Wt: 180 Born: 1/15/1982 Age: 29**

			HOW MUCH HE PITCHED						WHAT HE GAVE UP												THE RESULTS							
Year	Team	Lg	G	GS	CG	GF	IP	BFP	H	R	ER	HR	SH	SF	HB	TBB	IBB	SO	WP	Bk	W	L	Pct	Sh	Sv-Op	Hld	ERC	ERA
2010	Toledo*	AAA	8	7	0	0	44.1	187	40	18	18	4	0	1	2	14	1	40	1	0	4	2	.667	0	0--	-	3.26	3.65
2007	Tex	AL	3	1	0	2	8.2	40	8	6	6	2	0	1	0	7	0	6	0	0	0	0	-	0	0-0	0	6.35	6.23
2008	Det	AL	30	28	0	0	178.2	746	152	83	74	28	2	4	6	61	2	126	6	0	13	7	.650	0	0-1	0	3.50	3.73
2009	Det	AL	29	25	0	1	143.2	642	158	93	90	24	1	11	6	67	1	95	1	0	6	10	.375	0	0-0	0	5.65	5.64
2010	Det	AL	25	24	2	0	144.1	617	143	75	72	21	1	7	4	51	1	74	4	3	4	9	.308	1	0-0	0	4.27	4.49
	4 ML YEARS		87	78	2	3	475.1	2045	461	257	242	75	4	23	16	186	4	301	11	3	23	26	.469	1	0-1	0	4.41	4.58

Sean Gallagher

Pitches: R Bats: R Pos: RP-46 **Ht: 6'2" Wt: 235 Born: 12/30/1985 Age: 25**

			HOW MUCH HE PITCHED						WHAT HE GAVE UP												THE RESULTS							
Year	Team	Lg	G	GS	CG	GF	IP	BFP	H	R	ER	HR	SH	SF	HB	TBB	IBB	SO	WP	Bk	W	L	Pct	Sh	Sv-Op	Hld	ERC	ERA
2010	Portlnd*	AAA	3	3	0	0	11.0	52	14	6	6	0	0	0	1	4	0	12	1	0	0	2	.000	0	0--	-	4.95	4.91
2007	ChC	NL	8	0	0	3	14.2	74	19	15	14	3	0	1	1	12	0	5	0	0	0	0	-	0	1-1	0	8.95	8.59
2008	2 Tms		23	21	0	1	115.1	522	118	73	66	13	3	6	6	58	2	103	2	0	5	7	.417	0	0-0	0	4.83	5.15
2009	2 Tms		14	2	0	5	19.2	96	26	16	13	1	1	1	2	12	1	14	1	0	3	2	.600	0	0-0	0	6.83	5.95
2010	2 Tms	NL	46	0	0	12	57.2	273	62	40	37	7	5	0	3	41	2	43	0	2	2	1	.667	0	0-0	3	6.10	5.77
08	ChC	NL	12	10	0	1	58.2	256	58	31	29	6	2	1	4	22	1	49	2	0	3	4	.429	0	0-0	0	4.14	4.45
08	Oak	AL	11	11	0	0	56.2	266	60	42	37	7	1	5	2	36	1	54	0	0	2	3	.400	0	0-0	0	5.57	5.88
09	Oak	AL	6	2	0	3	14.1	71	21	16	13	1	1	1	2	7	0	10	1	0	1	2	.333	0	0-0	0	7.65	8.16
09	SD	NL	8	0	0	2	5.1	25	5	0	0	0	0	0	0	5	1	4	0	0	2	0	1.000	0	0-0	0	4.72	0.00
10	SD	NL	15	0	0	7	23.1	110	24	14	14	5	2	0	2	19	0	21	0	0	0	0	-	0	0-0	0	7.45	5.40
10	Pit	NL	31	0	0	5	34.1	163	38	26	23	2	3	0	1	22	2	22	0	2	2	1	.667	0	0-0	3	5.24	6.03
	4 ML YEARS		91	23	0	21	207.1	965	225	144	130	24	9	8	12	123	5	165	3	2	10	10	.500	0	1-1	3	5.64	5.64

Yovani Gallardo

Pitches: R Bats: R Pos: SP-31 guy-YARR-doe **Ht: 6'2" Wt: 222 Born: 2/27/1986 Age: 25**

			HOW MUCH HE PITCHED						WHAT HE GAVE UP												THE RESULTS							
Year	Team	Lg	G	GS	CG	GF	IP	BFP	H	R	ER	HR	SH	SF	HB	TBB	IBB	SO	WP	Bk	W	L	Pct	Sh	Sv-Op	Hld	ERC	ERA
2007	Mil	NL	20	17	0	1	110.1	466	103	48	45	8	4	3	2	37	2	101	3	0	9	5	.643	0	0-0	0	3.30	3.67
2008	Mil	NL	4	4	0	0	24.0	97	22	5	5	3	2	1	0	8	0	20	0	0	0	0	-	0	0-0	0	3.66	1.88
2009	Mil	NL	30	30	1	0	185.2	793	150	78	77	21	5	3	5	94	5	204	9	0	13	12	.520	0	0-0	0	3.57	3.73
2010	Mil	NL	31	31	2	0	185.0	803	178	89	79	12	11	4	3	75	5	200	7	1	14	7	.667	2	0-0	0	3.61	3.84
	Postseason		2	1	0	0	7.0	30	4	3	0	1	0	0	0	5	1	4	0	0	0	1	.000	0	0-0	0	2.03	0.00
	4 ML YEARS		85	82	3	1	505.0	2159	453	220	206	44	22	11	10	214	12	525	19	1	36	24	.600	2	0-0	0	3.53	3.67

Mat Gamel

Bats: L Throws: R Pos: PH-8; 3B-3; LF-1 GAMM-ell **Ht: 6'0" Wt: 200 Born: 7/26/1985 Age: 25**

			BATTING																			BASERUNNING				AVERAGES		
Year	Team	Lg	G	AB	H	2B	3B	HR	(Hm	Rd)	TB	R	RBI	RC	TBB	IBB	SO	HBP	SH	SF	SB	CS	SB%	GDP	Avg	OBP	Slg
2010	BrvdCt*	A+	6	20	2	1	0	0	(-	-)	3	3	2	1	6	0	8	0	0	0	0	0	-		.100	.308	.150
2010	Hntsvl*	AA	8	28	11	2	0	1	(-	-)	16	6	5	7	4	0	9	0	0	0	0	0	-		.393	.469	.571
2010	Nashv*	AAA	82	311	96	24	0	13	(-	-)	159	54	67	63	38	5	64	5	0	5	3	1	.75	7	.309	.387	.511
2008	Mil	NL	2	2	1	1	0	0	(0	0)	2	0	0	1	0	0	1	0	0	0	0	0	-		.500	.500	1.000
2009	Mil	NL	61	128	31	6	1	5	(4	1)	54	11	20	20	18	2	54	1	0	1	1	0	1.00		.242	.338	.422
2010	Mil	NL	12	15	3	1	0	0	(0	0)	4	1	1	1	1	0	8	1	0	0	0	0	-	1	.200	.294	.267
	3 ML YEARS		75	145	35	8	1	5	(4	1)	60	12	21	22	19	2	63	2	0	1	1	0	1.00	2	.241	.335	.414

Freddy Garcia

Pitches: R Bats: R Pos: SP-28   Ht: 6'4" Wt: 250 Born: 10/6/1976 Age: 34

Year	Team	Lg	G	GS	CG	GF	IP	BFP	H	R	ER	HR	SH	SF	HB	TBB	IBB	SO	WP	Bk	W	L	Pct	Sh	Sv-Op	Hld	ERC	ERA
1999	Sea	AL	33	33	3	0	201.1	888	205	96	91	18	3	6	10	90	4	170	12	3	17	8	.680	1	0-0	0	4.46	4.07
2000	Sea	AL	21	20	0	0	124.1	538	112	62	54	16	6	1	2	64	4	79	4	2	9	5	.643	0	0-0	0	4.20	3.91
2001	Sea	AL	34	34	4	0	238.2	971	199	88	81	16	8	5	5	69	6	163	3	1	18	6	.750	3	0-0	0	2.61	3.05
2002	Sea	AL	34	34	1	0	223.2	955	227	110	109	30	4	8	6	63	3	181	7	1	16	10	.615	0	0-0	0	3.98	4.39
2003	Sea	AL	33	33	1	0	201.1	862	196	109	101	31	2	8	11	71	2	144	11	0	12	14	.462	0	0-0	0	4.33	4.51
2004	2 Tms	AL	31	31	1	0	210.0	878	192	92	89	22	8	3	7	64	3	184	8	0	13	11	.542	0	0-0	0	3.37	3.81
2005	CWS	AL	33	33	2	0	228.0	943	225	102	98	26	5	5	3	60	2	146	20	1	14	8	.636	0	0-0	0	3.65	3.87
2006	CWS	AL	33	33	1	0	216.1	917	228	116	109	32	1	6	7	48	3	135	4	0	17	9	.654	0	0-0	0	4.09	4.53
2007	Phi	NL	11	11	0	0	58.0	264	74	39	38	12	4	3	5	19	3	50	5	0	1	5	.167	0	0-0	0	6.57	5.90
2008	Det	AL	3	3	0	0	15.0	61	11	8	7	3	0	0	1	6	0	12	0	0	1	1	.500	0	0-0	0	3.61	4.20
2009	CWS	AL	9	9	0	0	56.0	229	56	27	27	4	0	1	0	12	0	37	2	0	3	4	.429	0	0-0	0	3.21	4.34
2010	CWS	AL	28	28	0	0	157.0	671	171	85	81	23	5	4	3	45	5	89	4	0	12	6	.667	0	0-0	0	4.52	4.64
04	Sea	AL	15	15	1	0	107.0	446	96	39	38	8	4	1	2	32	1	82	5	0	4	7	.364	0	0-0	0	3.00	3.20
04	CWS	AL	16	16	0	0	103.0	432	96	53	51	14	4	2	5	32	2	102	3	0	9	4	.692	0	0-0	0	3.77	4.46
	Postseason		9	9	1	0	55.0	230	51	20	19	5	2	0	2	22	1	45	1	0	6	2	.750	0	0-0	0	3.82	3.11
	12 ML YEARS		303	302	12	0	1929.2	8177	1896	934	885	233	46	50	60	611	35	1390	80	8	133	87	.605	4	0-0	0	3.90	4.13

Jaime Garcia

Pitches: L Bats: L Pos: SP-28   HY-may   Ht: 6'2" Wt: 215 Born: 7/8/1986 Age: 24

Year	Team	Lg	G	GS	CG	GF	IP	BFP	H	R	ER	HR	SH	SF	HB	TBB	IBB	SO	WP	Bk	W	L	Pct	Sh	Sv-Op	Hld	ERC	ERA
2006	QuadC	A	13	13	1	0	77.2	317	67	28	25	1	5	0	2	18	0	80	7	4	5	4	.556	0	0--	-	2.25	2.90
2006	PlmBh	A+	12	12	0	0	77.1	319	84	33	33	3	2	1	1	16	0	51	5	5	5	4	.556	0	0--	-	3.52	3.84
2007	Sprgfld	AA	18	18	0	0	103.1	440	93	47	43	14	10	3	3	45	1	97	13	1	5	9	.357	0	0--	-	4.03	3.75
2008	Sprgfld	AA	6	6	1	0	35.0	145	26	10	8	0	1	0	2	16	0	41	1	0	3	2	.600	0	0--	-	2.49	2.06
2008	Memp	AAA	13	12	0	0	71.0	310	74	41	35	6	4	3	3	26	0	59	9	3	4	4	.500	0	0--	-	4.22	4.44
2009	Cards	R	2	2	0	0	4.0	17	4	2	2	0	0	0	0	1	0	3	1	0	0	1	.000	0	0--	-	2.77	4.50
2009	PlmBh	A+	3	2	0	0	12.2	42	4	1	1	0	0	0	0	4	0	16	0	0	0	1	.000	0	0--	-	0.68	0.71
2009	Memp	AAA	4	4	0	0	21.0	87	17	14	9	5	0	1	2	9	0	22	2	0	2	0	1.000	0	0--	-	4.59	3.86
2008	StL	NL	10	1	0	4	16.0	69	14	10	10	4	0	0	1	8	0	8	3	0	1	1	.500	0	0-0	3	5.15	5.63
2010	StL	NL	28	28	1	0	163.1	695	151	64	49	9	3	3	3	64	4	132	4	1	13	8	.619	1	0-0	0	3.34	2.70
	2 ML YEARS		38	29	1	4	179.1	764	165	74	59	13	3	3	4	72	4	140	7	1	14	9	.609	1	0-0	3	3.50	2.96

Brett Gardner

Bats: L Throws: L Pos: LF-123; CF-44; PR-5; PH-4; DH-2   Ht: 5'10" Wt: 183 Born: 8/24/1983 Age: 27

Year	Team	Lg	G	AB	H	2B	3B	HR	(Hm	Rd)	TB	R	RBI	RC	TBB	IBB	SO	HBP	SH	SF	SB	CS	SB%	GDP	Avg	OBP	Slg
2008	NYY	AL	42	127	29	5	2	0	(0	0)	38	18	16	17	8	0	30	2	3	1	13	1	.93	0	.228	.283	.299
2009	NYY	AL	108	248	67	6	6	3	(1	2)	94	48	23	38	26	0	40	3	6	1	26	5	.84	5	.270	.345	.379
2010	NYY	AL	150	477	132	20	7	5	(5	0)	181	97	47	77	79	1	101	5	5	3	47	9	.84	6	.277	.383	.379
	Postseason		14	13	2	0	0	0	(0	0)	2	3	0	0	4	0	1	0	1	2	.33	0	.154	.154	.154
	0 ML YEARS		300	852	228	31	15	8	(6	2)	313	163	86	132	113	1	171	10	14	5	86	15	.85	9	.268	.358	.367

Ryan Garko

Bats: R Throws: R Pos: 1B-6; DH-5; PH-5   Ht: 6'2" Wt: 225 Born: 1/2/1981 Age: 30

Year	Team	Lg	G	AB	H	2B	3B	HR	(Hm	Rd)	TB	R	RBI	RC	TBB	IBB	SO	HBP	SH	SF	SB	CS	SB%	GDP	Avg	OBP	Slg
2010	OKCity*	AAA	93	340	80	11	1	12	(-	-)	129	42	48	45	41	0	62	5	0	1	1	1	.50	14	.235	.326	.379
2005	Cle	AL	1	1	0	0	0	0	(0	0)	0	0	0	0	0	0	1	0	0	0	0	0	-	0	.000	.000	.000
2006	Cle	AL	50	185	54	12	0	7	(4	3)	87	28	45	32	14	0	37	7	0	3	0	0	-	5	.292	.359	.470
2007	Cle	AL	138	484	140	29	1	21	(12	9)	234	62	61	71	34	1	94	20	0	3	0	1	.00	12	.289	.359	.483
2008	Cle	AL	141	495	135	21	1	14	(8	6)	200	61	90	81	45	1	86	15	0	8	0	0	-	10	.273	.346	.404
2009	2 Tms		118	354	95	13	1	10	(6	7)	140	29	51	58	29	1	50	13	2	2	0	0	-	8	.268	.344	.421
2010	Tex	AL	15	33	3	0	0	0	(0	0)	3	0	3	0	3	1	4	0	2	0	0	0	-	0	.091	.167	.091
09	Cle	AL	78	239	68	10	0	11	(6	5)	111	29	39	43	20	1	40	10	2	2	0	0	-	6	.285	.362	.464
09	SF	NL	40	115	27	3	1	2	(0	2)	38	10	12	15	9	0	10	3	0	0	0	0	-	2	.235	.307	.330
	Postseason		9	35	11	2	1	1	(1	0)	18	7	5	6	1	0	6	3	0	0	0	0	-	1	.314	.385	.514
	6 ML YEARS		463	1552	427	75	3	55	(30	25)	673	190	250	242	125	4	272	55	4	16	0	1	.00	36	.275	.347	.434

Jon Garland

Pitches: R Bats: R Pos: SP-33   Ht: 6'6" Wt: 210 Born: 9/27/1979 Age: 31

Year	Team	Lg	G	GS	CG	GF	IP	BFP	H	R	ER	HR	SH	SF	HB	TBB	IBB	SO	WP	Bk	W	L	Pct	Sh	Sv-Op	Hld	ERC	ERA
2000	CWS	AL	15	13	0	1	69.2	324	82	55	50	10	0	2	1	40	0	42	4	0	4	8	.333	0	0-0	1	6.26	6.46
2001	CWS	AL	35	16	0	8	117.0	510	123	59	48	16	2	5	4	55	2	61	3	0	6	7	.462	0	1-1	2	5.16	3.69
2002	CWS	AL	33	33	1	0	192.2	827	188	109	98	23	3	4	6	83	2	112	5	0	12	12	.500	1	0-0	0	4.46	4.58
2003	CWS	AL	32	32	0	0	191.2	813	188	103	96	28	4	8	6	74	1	108	8	0	12	13	.480	0	0-0	0	4.38	4.51
2004	CWS	AL	34	34	1	0	217.0	923	223	125	118	34	9	5	4	76	2	113	3	0	12	11	.522	0	0-0	0	4.56	4.89
2005	CWS	AL	32	32	3	0	221.0	901	212	93	86	26	9	8	7	47	3	115	2	0	18	10	.643	3	0-0	0	3.39	3.50
2006	CWS	AL	33	32	1	0	211.1	900	247	112	106	26	5	8	6	41	4	112	4	0	18	7	.720	1	0-0	0	4.50	4.51
2007	CWS	AL	32	32	2	0	208.1	883	219	114	98	19	3	7	4	57	3	98	1	0	10	13	.435	1	0-0	0	3.87	4.23
2008	LAA	AL	32	32	1	0	196.2	864	237	116	107	23	8	4	5	59	4	90	4	0	14	8	.636	0	0-0	0	5.18	4.90
2009	2 Tms	NL	33	33	1	0	204.0	882	225	106	91	23	11	6	6	61	7	109	6	0	11	13	.458	0	0-0	0	4.42	4.01
2010	SD	NL	33	33	0	0	200.0	837	176	86	77	20	5	5	6	87	9	136	6	0	14	12	.538	0	0-0	0	3.67	3.47

		HOW MUCH HE PITCHED						WHAT HE GAVE UP													THE RESULTS							
Year	Team	Lg	G	GS	CG	GF	IP	BFP	H	R	ER	HR	SH	SF	HB	TBB	IBB	SO	WP	Bk	W	L	Pct	Sh	Sv-Op	Hld	ERC	ERA
09	Ari	NL	27	27	1	0	167.2	728	188	90	80	19	9	4	6	52	5	83	5	0	8	11	.421	0	0-0	0	4.63	4.29
09	LAD	NL	6	6	0	0	36.1	154	37	16	11	4	2	2	0	9	2	26	1	0	3	2	.600	0	0-0	0	3.51	2.72
	Postseason		2	2	1	0	16.0	58	11	6	4	2	2	0	0	3	0	11	0	0	1	0	1.000	0	0-0	0	2.00	2.25
	11 ML YEARS		344	321	10	9	2029.1	8664	2120	1078	975	248	59	66	59	680	36	1096	46	0	131	114	.535	6	1-1	3	4.37	4.32

Matt Garza

Pitches: R **Bats:** R **Pos:** SP-32; RP-1 **Ht:** 6'4" **Wt:** 215 **Born:** 11/26/1983 **Age:** 27

		HOW MUCH HE PITCHED						WHAT HE GAVE UP													THE RESULTS							
Year	Team	Lg	G	GS	CG	GF	IP	BFP	H	R	ER	HR	SH	SF	HB	TBB	IBB	SO	WP	Bk	W	L	Pct	Sh	Sv-Op	Hld	ERC	ERA
2006	Min	AL	10	9	0	0	50.0	232	62	33	32	6	0	3	0	23	0	38	1	0	3	6	.333	0	0-0	0	5.82	5.76
2007	Min	AL	16	15	0	1	83.0	367	96	44	34	8	1	4	4	32	4	67	4	0	5	7	.417	0	0-0	0	5.08	3.69
2008	TB	AL	30	30	3	0	184.2	772	170	83	76	19	3	9	6	59	2	128	3	2	11	9	.550	2	0-0	0	3.47	3.70
2009	TB	AL	32	32	0	0	203.0	861	177	93	89	25	2	8	11	79	0	189	3	0	8	12	.400	0	0-0	0	3.69	3.95
2010	TB	AL	33	32	3	1	204.2	855	193	94	89	28	1	6	7	63	2	150	12	2	15	10	.600	1	1-1	0	3.80	3.91
	Postseason		4	4	0	0	25.0	107	21	11	11	4	0	1	1	12	0	25	2	0	2	1	.667	0	0-0	0	4.07	3.96
	5 ML YEARS		121	118	6	2	725.1	3087	698	347	320	86	7	30	28	256	8	572	23	4	42	44	.488	3	1-1	0	3.96	3.97

Chad Gaudin

Pitches: R **Bats:** R **Pos:** RP-42 goe-DANN **Ht:** 5'10" **Wt:** 188 **Born:** 3/24/1983 **Age:** 28

		HOW MUCH HE PITCHED						WHAT HE GAVE UP													THE RESULTS							
Year	Team	Lg	G	GS	CG	GF	IP	BFP	H	R	ER	HR	SH	SF	HB	TBB	IBB	SO	WP	Bk	W	L	Pct	Sh	Sv-Op	Hld	ERC	ERA
2003	TB	AL	15	3	0	5	40.0	173	37	18	16	4	0	2	1	16	0	23	1	0	2	0	1.000	0	0-0	0	3.70	3.60
2004	TB	AL	26	4	0	5	42.2	201	59	27	23	4	2	4	4	16	4	30	0	0	1	2	.333	0	0-1	5	6.46	4.85
2005	Tor	AL	5	3	0	0	13.0	74	31	19	19	6	0	1	1	6	0	12	0	0	1	3	.250	0	0-0	0	18.35	13.15
2006	Oak	AL	55	0	0	13	64.0	276	51	24	22	3	0	3	6	42	2	36	2	2	4	2	.667	0	2-3	11	3.62	3.09
2007	Oak	AL	34	34	1	0	199.1	886	205	108	98	21	3	6	8	100	8	154	3	1	11	13	.458	0	0-0	0	4.80	4.42
2008	2 Tms		50	6	0	14	90.0	382	92	50	44	11	2	2	3	27	3	71	2	2	9	5	.643	0	0-1	4	4.06	4.40
2009	2 Tms		31	25	0	4	147.1	664	146	85	76	14	7	8	8	76	4	139	7	1	6	10	.375	0	0-0	0	4.56	4.64
2010	2 Tms	AL	42	0	0	23	65.1	295	73	45	41	16	4	2	8	25	0	53	3	0	1	4	.200	0	0-1	1	6.33	5.65
08	Oak	AL	26	6	0	9	62.2	263	63	29	25	6	2	1	3	17	1	44	2	1	5	3	.625	0	0-0	2	3.78	3.59
08	ChC	NL	24	0	0	5	27.1	119	29	21	19	5	0	1	0	10	2	27	0	1	4	2	.667	0	0-1	2	4.74	6.26
09	SD	NL	20	19	0	0	105.1	476	105	69	60	7	7	6	5	56	3	105	4	1	4	10	.286	0	0-0	0	4.41	5.13
09	NYY	AL	11	6	0	4	42.0	188	41	16	16	7	0	2	3	20	1	34	3	0	2	0	1.000	0	0-0	0	4.93	3.43
10	Oak	AL	12	0	0	6	17.1	86	27	18	17	5	2	1	3	5	0	20	0	0	0	2	.000	0	0-0	1	9.34	8.83
10	NYY	AL	30	0	0	17	48.0	209	46	27	24	11	2	1	5	20	0	33	3	0	1	2	.333	0	0-1	0	5.32	4.50
	Postseason		4	0	0	1	4.1	18	2	0	0	0	1	0	0	3	1	1	0	0	0	0	-	0	0-0	0	1.45	0.00
	8 ML YEARS		258	75	1	64	661.2	2951	694	376	339	79	18	28	34	308	21	518	18	6	35	39	.473	0	2-6	21	4.92	4.61

Dillon Gee

Pitches: R **Bats:** R **Pos:** SP-5 JEE **Ht:** 6'1" **Wt:** 195 **Born:** 4/28/1986 **Age:** 25

		HOW MUCH HE PITCHED						WHAT HE GAVE UP													THE RESULTS							
Year	Team	Lg	G	GS	CG	GF	IP	BFP	H	R	ER	HR	SH	SF	HB	TBB	IBB	SO	WP	Bk	W	L	Pct	Sh	Sv-Op	Hld	ERC	ERA
2007	Bklyn	A-	14	11	0	0	62.0	250	57	17	17	1	3	3	6	9	1	56	0	0	3	1	.750	0	0- -	-	2.53	2.47
2008	StLuci	A+	21	21	0	0	127.1	510	117	49	46	6	2	3	9	19	0	94	3	0	8	6	.571	0	0- -	-	2.68	3.25
2008	Bnghtn	AA	4	4	0	0	27.0	101	18	4	4	1	1	1	1	5	0	20	0	0	2	0	1.000	0	0- -	-	1.54	1.33
2009	Buffalo	AAA	9	9	1	0	48.1	209	47	22	22	5	0	2	5	16	0	42	1	0	1	3	.250	0	0- -	-	4.07	4.10
2010	Buffalo	AAA	28	28	0	0	161.1	697	174	96	89	23	3	7	13	41	1	165	3	0	13	8	.619	0	0- -	-	4.55	4.96
2010	NYM	NL	5	5	0	0	33.0	136	25	10	8	2	3	0	0	15	2	17	0	0	2	2	.500	0	0-0	0	2.66	2.18

Craig Gentry

Bats: R **Throws:** R **Pos:** CF-7; LF-6; RF-4; PR-4; PH-3 **Ht:** 6'2" **Wt:** 190 **Born:** 11/29/1983 **Age:** 27

		BATTING																		BASERUNNING				AVERAGES		
Year	Team	Lg	G	AB	H	2B	3B	HR	(Hm	Rd)	TB	R	RBI	RC	TBB	IBB	SO	HBP	SH	SF	SB	CS	SB%	GDP	Avg	OBP	Slg
2006	Spkane	A-	56	221	62	15	4	0	(-	-)	85	27	13	33	9	0	37	15	0	1	20	6	.77	2	.281	.350	.385
2007	Clinton	A	55	223	61	15	0	3	(-	-)	85	40	12	33	15	0	37	7	0	3	24	3	.89	5	.274	.335	.381
2007	Rngrs	R	3	11	3	0	0	0	(-	-)	3	4	1	1	1	0	3	1	0	0	2	0	1.00	0	.273	.385	.273
2007	Bkrsfld	A+	51	213	58	16	1	1	(-	-)	79	31	18	27	12	0	46	6	1	3	16	7	.70	4	.272	.325	.371
2008	Frisco	AA	76	301	83	17	0	4	(-	-)	112	43	33	39	17	2	55	11	3	4	15	8	.65	3	.276	.333	.372
2008	Okla	AAA	18	59	12	1	0	0	(-	-)	13	6	1	4	9	0	18	0	1	0	1	0	1.00	0	.203	.309	.220
2009	Frisco	AA	127	512	155	21	7	8	(-	-)	214	100	53	93	49	1	64	16	6	5	49	6	.89	4	.303	.378	.418
2010	OKCity	AAA	69	259	80	7	4	4	(-	-)	107	43	35	45	29	0	47	8	3	2	12	5	.71	5	.309	.393	.413
2009	Tex	AL	11	17	2	1	0	0	(0	0)	3	4	1	1	2	0	5	0	0	0	0	0	-	0	.118	.211	.176
2010	Tex	AL	20	33	7	0	0	0	(0	0)	7	4	3	1	1	0	11	0	0	1	1	0	1.00	1	.212	.229	.212
	2 ML YEARS		31	50	9	1	0	0	(0	0)	10	8	4	2	3	0	16	0	0	1	1	0	1.00	1	.180	.222	.200

Esteban German

Bats: R **Throws:** R **Pos:** PR-9; DH-5; 2B-3; SS-1; LF-1 **Ht:** 5'9" **Wt:** 195 **Born:** 1/26/1978 **Age:** 33

		BATTING																		BASERUNNING				AVERAGES		
Year	Team	Lg	G	AB	H	2B	3B	HR	(Hm	Rd)	TB	R	RBI	RC	TBB	IBB	SO	HBP	SH	SF	SB	CS	SB%	GDP	Avg	OBP	Slg
2010	OKCity*	AAA	126	485	136	27	5	5	(-	-)	188	79	55	83	64	1	77	9	4	5	50	7	.88	11	.280	.371	.388
2002	Oak	AL	9	35	7	0	0	0	(0	0)	7	4	0	2	4	0	11	1	0	0	1	0	1.00	0	.200	.300	.200
2003	Oak	AL	5	4	1	0	0	0	(0	0)	1	0	1	1	0	0	0	0	0	0	0	0	-	1	.250	.250	.250
2004	Oak	AL	31	60	15	1	1	0	(0	0)	18	9	7	8	4	0	13	0	1	0	0	1	.00	1	.250	.297	.300
2005	Tex	AL	5	4	3	1	0	0	(0	0)	4	3	1	2	0	0	1	0	0	0	2	0	1.00	0	.750	.750	1.000
2006	KC	AL	106	279	91	18	5	3	(2	1)	128	44	34	55	40	0	49	6	6	0	7	3	.70	8	.326	.422	.459

110

Year	Team	Lg	G	AB	H	2B	3B	HR	(Hm	Rd)	TB	R	RBI	RC	TBB	IBB	SO	HBP	SH	SF	SB	CS	SB%	GDP	Avg	OBP	Slg
2007	KC	AL	121	348	92	15	6	4	(3	1)	131	49	37	48	43	0	60	5	6	3	11	7	.61	11	.264	.351	.376
2008	KC	AL	89	216	53	14	3	0	(0	0)	73	30	22	26	18	1	42	1	4	3	7	3	.70	5	.245	.303	.338
2009	Tex	AL	19	46	14	4	0	0	(0	0)	18	9	4	7	4	0	7	0	0	0	1	0	1.00	0	.304	.360	.391
2010	Tex	AL	13	13	3	0	0	0	(0	0)	3	5	1	3	3	0	2	0	0	0	4	1	.80	0	.231	.375	.231
9 ML YEARS			398	1005	279	53	15	7	(5	2)	383	153	107	152	116	1	186	13	17	6	33	15	.69	26	.278	.358	.381

Justin Germano

Pitches: R **Bats:** R **Pos:** RP-22; SP-1   jerr-MAHN-oh   **Ht:** 6'3" **Wt:** 205 **Born:** 8/6/1982 **Age:** 28

Year	Team	Lg	G	GS	CG	GF	IP	BFP	H	R	ER	HR	SH	SF	HB	TBB	IBB	SO	WP	Bk	W	L	Pct	Sh	Sv-Op Hld	ERC	ERA
2010	Akron*	AA	7	1	0	0	19.1	77	17	6	6	0	1	0	0	4	1	16	0	0	2	1	.667	0	- - -	2.06	2.79
2010	Clmbs*	AAA	17	6	1	5	53.1	217	49	23	20	8	2	1	1	10	1	37	2	0	3	2	.600	1	1- - -	3.17	3.38
2004	SD	NL	7	5	0	0	21.1	109	31	24	21	2	3	1	0	14	0	16	0	0	1	2	.333	0	0-0	0	7.69	8.86
2006	Cin	NL	2	1	0	0	6.2	31	8	4	4	1	0	0	1	3	1	8	0	0	0	1	.000	0	0-0	0	6.26	5.40
2007	SD	NL	26	23	0	3	133.1	566	133	72	66	14	4	0	6	40	3	78	1	0	7	10	.412	0	0-0	0	3.93	4.46
2008	SD	NL	12	6	0	4	43.2	194	54	31	29	8	2	1	1	13	2	17	4	0	0	3	.000	0	0-0	0	5.69	5.98
2010	Cle	NL	23	1	0	4	35.1	146	27	15	13	6	1	0	6	8	1	29	0	0	0	3	.000	0	0-1	2	3.17	3.31
5 ML YEARS			70	36	0	11	240.1	1046	253	146	133	31	10	2	16	78	7	148	5	0	8	19	.296	0	0-1	2	4.50	4.98

Jody Gerut

Bats: L **Throws:** L **Pos:** PH-15; CF-10; LF-6; RF-4   GARE-utt   **Ht:** 6'0" **Wt:** 190 **Born:** 9/18/1977 **Age:** 33

Year	Team	Lg	G	AB	H	2B	3B	HR	(Hm	Rd)	TB	R	RBI	RC	TBB	IBB	SO	HBP	SH	SF	SB	CS	SB%	GDP	Avg	OBP	Slg
2010	Brewrs*	R	14	49	17	5	0	2	(-	-)	28	11	11	12	9	0	3	0	0	0	0	0	-	1	.347	.448	.571
2010	Portlnd*	AAA	14	53	16	4	0	1	(-	-)	23	7	11	9	7	0	5	1	0	0	0	0	-	2	.302	.393	.434
2003	Cle	AL	127	480	134	33	2	22	(13	9)	237	66	75	73	35	4	70	7	1	2	4	5	.44	13	.279	.336	.494
2004	Cle	AL	134	481	121	31	5	11	(3	8)	195	72	51	60	54	4	59	7	3	3	13	6	.68	9	.252	.334	.405
2005	3 Tms		59	170	43	11	1	1	(1	0)	59	15	14	18	20	1	20	0	0	1	1	1	.50	4	.253	.330	.347
2008	SD	NL	100	328	97	15	4	14	(4	10)	162	46	43	55	28	0	52	0	0	0	6	4	.60	1	.296	.351	.494
2009	2 Tms	NL	122	274	63	13	0	9	(3	6)	103	40	35	23	10	1	43	1	0	4	6	2	.75	8	.230	.279	.376
2010	Mil	NL	32	71	14	4	1	2	(0	2)	26	7	8	4	3	0	17	0	0	0	0	1	.00	1	.197	.230	.366
05	Cle	AL	44	138	30	9	1	1	(1	0)	52	12	12	17	18	1	14	0	0	1	1	1	.50	3	.275	.357	.377
05	ChC	NL	11	14	1	1	0	0	(0	0)	2	1	0	0	2	0	3	0	0	0	0	0	-	0	.071	.188	.143
05	Pit	NL	4	18	4	1	0	0	(0	0)	5	2	2	1	0	0	3	0	0	0	0	0	-	1	.222	.222	.278
09	SD	NL	37	113	25	6	0	4	(0	4)	43	17	14	9	5	1	22	0	0	3	2	0	1.00	2	.221	.248	.381
09	Mil	NL	85	161	38	7	0	5	(3	2)	60	23	21	14	14	0	21	1	0	1	4	2	.67	6	.236	.299	.373
6 ML YEARS			574	1804	472	107	13	59	(24	35)	782	246	226	233	159	10	261	15	4	10	30	19	.61	36	.262	.325	.433

Sammy Gervacio

Pitches: R **Bats:** R **Pos:** RP-6   jerr-VASS-ee-oh   **Ht:** 6'0" **Wt:** 175 **Born:** 1/10/1985 **Age:** 26

Year	Team	Lg	G	GS	CG	GF	IP	BFP	H	R	ER	HR	SH	SF	HB	TBB	IBB	SO	WP	Bk	W	L	Pct	Sh	Sv-Op Hld	ERC	ERA
2005	Grnsvle	R+	21	0	0	16	37.2	134	24	10	10	1	1	1	0	6	0	53	2	0	3	2	.600	0	8- -	-	1.46	2.87
2005	Lxngtn	A	5	0	0	2	9.1	33	4	1	1	0	0	0	0	1	0	11	1	2	1	0	1.000	0	0- -	-	0.66	0.96
2006	Lxngtn	A	47	0	0	28	83.2	340	58	28	24	8	5	4	0	28	0	89	2	0	7	5	.583	0	10- -	-	2.55	2.58
2007	Salem	A+	39	0	0	33	55.1	228	42	16	15	1	2	0	5	15	1	80	3	1	1	3	.250	0	18- -	-	2.09	2.44
2007	CpChr	AA	13	0	0	4	22.2	89	15	7	5	1	2	0	0	11	2	24	1	0	3	2	.600	0	0- -	-	2.25	1.99
2008	CpChr	AA	47	0	0	31	65.1	206	69	36	30	8	3	0	3	26	2	82	1	0	2	5	.286	0	5- -	-	4.71	4.13
2008	RdRck	AAA	3	0	0	0	8.0	34	6	2	2	0	0	1	1	3	0	14	0	0	1	0	1.000	0	0- -	-	2.40	2.25
2009	RdRck	AAA	39	0	0	11	52.1	216	43	30	28	5	4	3	3	21	4	58	3	3	2	2	.500	0	0- -	-	3.11	4.82
2010	RdRck	AAA	7	0	0	2	10.1	43	6	4	4	0	0	0	3	5	2	10	0	0	0	0	-	0	0- -	-	2.29	3.48
2009	Hou	NL	29	0	0	4	21.0	83	16	5	5	1	1	0	1	8	3	25	0	0	1	1	.500	0	0-1	8	2.50	2.14
2010	Hou	NL	6	0	0	1	3.2	21	4	6	5	1	1	0	0	5	0	3	1	1	0	1	.000	0	0-0	0	9.66	12.27
2 ML YEARS			35	0	0	5	24.2	104	20	11	10	2	2	0	1	13	3	28	1	1	1	2	.333	0	0-1	6	3.42	3.65

Chris Getz

Bats: L **Throws:** R **Pos:** 2B-64; PH-5; PR-3; 3B-2   **Ht:** 5'11" **Wt:** 181 **Born:** 8/30/1983 **Age:** 27

Year	Team	Lg	G	AB	H	2B	3B	HR	(Hm	Rd)	TB	R	RBI	RC	TBB	IBB	SO	HBP	SH	SF	SB	CS	SB%	GDP	Avg	OBP	Slg
2010	Omha*	AAA	2	6	2	0	0	0	(-	-)	2	3	0	1	2	0	1	0	0	0	0	0	-	0	.333	.500	.333
2008	CWS	AL	10	7	2	0	0	0	(0	0)	2	2	1	1	0	0	1	0	0	0	1	1	.50	0	.286	.286	.286
2009	CWS	AL	107	375	98	18	4	2	(1	1)	130	49	31	47	30	1	54	6	1	3	25	2	**.93**	4	.261	.324	.347
2010	KC	AL	72	224	53	9	0	0	(0	0)	62	23	18	21	19	1	28	2	3	0	15	2	.88	3	.237	.302	.277
3 ML YEARS			189	606	153	27	4	2	(1	1)	194	74	50	69	49	2	83	8	4	3	41	5	.89	7	.252	.315	.320

Jason Giambi

Bats: L **Throws:** R **Pos:** PH-44; 1B-37; DH-8   **Ht:** 6'3" **Wt:** 240 **Born:** 1/8/1971 **Age:** 40

Year	Team	Lg	G	AB	H	2B	3B	HR	(Hm	Rd)	TB	R	RBI	RC	TBB	IBB	SO	HBP	SH	SF	SB	CS	SB%	GDP	Avg	OBP	Slg
1995	Oak	AL	54	176	45	7	0	6	(3	3)	70	27	25	27	28	0	31	3	1	2	2	1	.67	4	.256	.364	.398
1996	Oak	AL	140	536	156	40	1	20	(6	14)	258	84	79	88	51	3	95	5	1	5	0	1	.00	15	.291	.355	.481
1997	Oak	AL	142	519	152	41	2	20	(14	6)	257	66	81	91	55	3	89	6	0	8	0	1	.00	11	.293	.362	.495
1998	Oak	AL	153	562	166	28	0	27	(12	15)	275	92	110	103	81	7	102	5	0	9	2	2	.50	16	.295	.384	.489
1999	Oak	AL	158	575	181	36	1	33	(17	16)	318	115	123	132	105	6	106	7	0	8	1	1	.50	11	.315	.422	.553
2000	Oak	AL	152	510	170	29	1	43	(23	20)	330	108	137	152	**137**	6	96	9	0	8	2	0	1.00	9	.333	**.476**	.647

Year	Team	Lg	G	AB	H	2B	3B	HR	(Hm	Rd)	TB	R	RBI	RC	TBB	IBB	SO	HBP	SH	SF	SB	CS	SB%	GDP	Avg	OBP	Slg
2001	Oak	AL	154	520	178	47	2	38	(27	11)	343	109	120	153	129	24	83	13	0	9	2	0	1.00	17	.342	.477	.660
2002	NYY	AL	155	560	176	34	1	41	(19	22)	335	120	122	139	109	4	112	15	0	5	2	2	.50	18	.314	.435	.598
2003	NYY	AL	156	535	134	25	0	41	(12	29)	282	97	107	120	129	9	140	21	0	5	2	1	.67	9	.250	.412	.527
2004	NYY	AL	80	264	55	9	0	12	(5	7)	100	33	40	42	47	1	62	8	0	3	0	1	.00	5	.208	.342	.379
2005	NYY	AL	139	417	113	14	0	32	(16	16)	223	74	87	102	108	5	109	19	0	1	0	0	-	7	.271	.440	.535
2006	NYY	AL	139	446	113	25	0	37	(20	17)	249	92	90	106	110	12	106	16	0	7	2	0	1.00	10	.253	.413	.558
2007	NYY	AL	83	254	60	8	0	14	(6	8)	110	31	39	41	40	2	66	8	0	1	1	0	1.00	1	.236	.356	.433
2008	NYY	AL	145	458	113	19	1	32	(16	16)	230	68	96	79	76	5	111	22	0	9	2	1	.67	6	.247	.373	.502
2009	2 Tms		102	293	59	14	0	13	(7	6)	112	43	51	44	57	1	80	7	0	2	0	0	-	6	.201	.343	.382
2010	Col	NL	87	176	43	9	0	6	(4	2)	70	17	35	35	35	5	47	6	0	5	2	0	1.00	5	.244	.378	.398
09	Oak	AL	83	269	52	13	0	11	(7	4)	98	39	40	36	50	1	72	7	0	2	0	0	-	6	.193	.332	.364
09	Col	NL	19	24	7	1	0	2	(0	2)	14	4	11	8	7	0	8	0	0	0	0	0	-	0	.292	.452	.583
	Postseason		45	138	40	6	0	7	(5	2)	67	19	19	25	30	2	30	4	0	2	2	0	1.00	3	.290	.425	.486
	16 ML YEARS		2039	6801	1914	385	9	415	(207	208)	3562	1176	1365	1454	1297	93	1435	170	2	87	20	11	.65	150	.281	.405	.524

Jay Gibbons

Bats: L **Throws:** L **Pos:** PH-21; LF-15; 1B-3; RF-1   **Ht:** 5'11" **Wt:** 190 **Born:** 3/2/1977 **Age:** 34

Year	Team	Lg	G	AB	H	2B	3B	HR	(Hm	Rd)	TB	R	RBI	RC	TBB	IBB	SO	HBP	SH	SF	SB	CS	SB%	GDP	Avg	OBP	Slg
2010	Albq*	AAA	95	352	122	28	1	19	(-	-)	209	60	83	75	19	2	30	0	0	5	0	0	-	5	.347	.375	.594
2001	Bal	AL	73	225	53	10	0	15	(9	6)	108	27	36	31	17	0	39	4	0	0	0	1	.00	7	.236	.301	.480
2002	Bal	AL	136	490	121	29	1	28	(17	11)	236	71	69	71	45	3	66	2	0	4	1	3	.25	9	.247	.311	.482
2003	Bal	AL	160	625	173	39	2	23	(12	11)	285	80	100	84	49	11	89	3	0	5	0	1	.00	12	.277	.330	.456
2004	Bal	AL	97	346	85	14	1	10	(4	6)	131	36	47	38	29	0	64	1	1	3	1	1	.50	11	.246	.303	.379
2005	Bal	AL	139	488	135	33	3	26	(13	13)	252	72	79	73	28	3	56	1	0	1	0	0	-	15	.277	.317	.516
2006	Bal	AL	90	343	95	23	0	13	(8	5)	157	34	46	50	32	2	48	2	0	1	0	0	-	12	.277	.341	.458
2007	Bal	AL	84	270	62	14	0	6	(1	5)	94	28	28	23	15	1	52	0	0	3	2	0	1.00	5	.230	.272	.348
2010	LAD	NL	37	75	21	2	0	5	(2	3)	38	11	17	13	4	0	14	0	0	1	0	1	.00	2	.280	.313	.507
	8 ML YEARS		816	2862	745	164	7	126	(66	60)	1301	359	422	393	219	20	428	15	1	18	2	7	.22	73	.260	.314	.455

Cole Gillespie

Bats: R **Throws:** R **Pos:** LF-24; PH-11; RF-9; CF-7; PR-1   **Ht:** 6'1" **Wt:** 205 **Born:** 6/20/1984 **Age:** 27

Year	Team	Lg	G	AB	H	2B	3B	HR	(Hm	Rd)	TB	R	RBI	RC	TBB	IBB	SO	HBP	SH	SF	SB	CS	SB%	GDP	Avg	OBP	Slg
2006	Helena	R+	51	186	64	12	1	8	(-	-)	102	49	31	50	40	1	34	4	0	3	18	4	.82	4	.344	.464	.548
2007	BrvdCt	A+	129	438	117	25	3	12	(-	-)	184	75	62	75	72	1	95	8	1	3	16	8	.67	9	.267	.378	.420
2008	Hntsvl	AA	131	462	130	38	4	14	(-	-)	218	73	79	91	74	1	102	7	3	4	17	1	.94	10	.281	.386	.472
2009	BrvdCt	A+	12	43	15	2	3	1	(-	-)	26	10	9	11	7	1	11	0	0	1	4	0	1.00	1	.349	.431	.605
2009	Nashv	AAA	75	236	57	12	5	7	(-	-)	100	29	27	35	31	1	56	3	3	4	6	5	.55	5	.242	.332	.424
2009	Reno	AAA	42	138	42	6	4	5	(-	-)	71	33	27	32	27	0	31	2	0	3	8	0	1.00	6	.304	.418	.514
2010	Reno	AAA	69	264	76	14	6	8	(-	-)	126	54	49	51	44	1	49	3	0	1	8	5	.62	11	.288	.394	.477
2010	Ari	NL	45	104	24	8	0	2	(2	0)	38	11	12	10	7	1	29	1	0	1	1	1	.50	2	.231	.283	.365

Chris Gimenez

Bats: R **Throws:** R **Pos:** C-24; PR-2; LF-1; RF-1; DH-1; PH-1   JIMM-inn-ezz   **Ht:** 6'2" **Wt:** 215 **Born:** 12/27/1982 **Age:** 28

Year	Team	Lg	G	AB	H	2B	3B	HR	(Hm	Rd)	TB	R	RBI	RC	TBB	IBB	SO	HBP	SH	SF	SB	CS	SB%	GDP	Avg	OBP	Slg
2004	MhVlly	A-	71	260	78	23	3	10	(-	-)	137	40	38	58	30	1	62	24	1	1	2	2	.50	4	.300	.419	.527
2005	Lk Cty	A	112	384	90	24	1	13	(-	-)	155	54	66	60	48	0	90	25	2	4	4	3	.57	4	.234	.354	.404
2006	Lk Cty	A	91	329	84	25	1	11	(-	-)	144	55	40	55	33	1	72	26	1	5	6	8	.43	8	.255	.364	.438
2007	Knstn	A+	83	269	76	14	1	20	(-	-)	152	56	54	63	50	0	55	8	2	3	3	2	.60	3	.283	.406	.565
2007	Akron	AA	30	113	25	6	0	6	(-	-)	49	20	12	14	9	0	31	1	0	0	1	0	1.00	1	.221	.285	.434
2008	Akron	AA	55	177	60	15	1	6	(-	-)	95	46	26	48	52	3	33	1	1	2	0	1	.00	7	.339	.487	.537
2008	Buffalo	AAA	54	195	53	9	1	3	(-	-)	73	23	19	28	23	1	60	4	3	4	2	1	.67	4	.272	.354	.374
2009	Clmbs	AAA	39	136	32	8	0	6	(-	-)	58	20	15	19	15	1	40	3	2	1	0	0	-	4	.235	.323	.426
2010	Clmbs	AAA	55	196	54	10	0	9	(-	-)	91	32	32	31	20	0	38	0	2	1	1	1	.50	5	.276	.341	.464
2009	Cle	AL	45	111	16	2	0	3	(0	3)	27	12	7	3	17	0	36	0	1	1	1	1	.50	3	.144	.256	.243
2010	Cle	AL	28	58	11	5	0	1	(1	0)	19	6	8	5	8	0	22	0	1	0	0	0	-	1	.190	.288	.328
	2 ML YEARS		73	169	27	7	0	4	(1	3)	46	18	15	8	25	0	58	0	2	1	1	1	.50	4	.160	.267	.272

Troy Glaus

Bats: R **Throws:** R **Pos:** 1B-114; PH-18; DH-2; 3B-1   GLOSS   **Ht:** 6'5" **Wt:** 240 **Born:** 8/3/1976 **Age:** 34

Year	Team	Lg	G	AB	H	2B	3B	HR	(Hm	Rd)	TB	R	RBI	RC	TBB	IBB	SO	HBP	SH	SF	SB	CS	SB%	GDP	Avg	OBP	Slg
2010	Gwnntt*	AAA	8	30	10	2	0	2	(-	-)	18	10	8	7	4	0	10	1	0	0	0	0	-	1	.333	.429	.600
1998	LAA	AL	48	165	36	9	0	1	(-	-)	48	19	23	13	15	0	51	0	0	2	1	0	1.00	3	.218	.280	.291
1999	LAA	AL	154	551	132	29	0	29	(12	17)	248	85	79	84	71	1	143	6	0	3	5	1	.83	9	.240	.331	.450
2000	LAA	AL	159	563	160	37	1	47	(24	23)	340	120	102	129	112	6	163	2	0	1	14	11	.56	14	.284	.404	.604
2001	LAA	AL	161	588	147	38	2	41	(22	19)	312	100	108	114	107	7	158	6	0	7	10	3	.77	16	.250	.367	.531
2002	LAA	AL	156	569	142	24	1	30	(13	17)	258	99	111	100	88	4	144	6	0	1	10	3	.77	12	.250	.352	.453
2003	LAA	AL	91	319	79	17	2	16	(9	7)	148	53	50	48	46	4	73	1	0	1	7	2	.78	8	.248	.343	.464
2004	LAA	AL	58	207	52	11	1	18	(9	9)	119	47	42	41	31	3	52	3	0	1	2	3	.40	6	.251	.355	.575
2005	Ari	NL	149	538	139	29	1	37	(20	17)	281	78	97	87	84	2	145	7	0	5	4	2	.67	7	.258	.363	.522
2006	Tor	AL	153	540	136	27	0	38	(25	13)	277	105	104	84	86	6	134	3	0	5	3	2	.60	25	.252	.355	.513
2007	Tor	AL	115	385	101	19	1	20	(7	13)	182	60	62	65	61	2	102	5	0	5	0	1	.00	7	.262	.366	.473
2008	StL	NL	151	544	147	33	1	27	(13	14)	263	69	99	88	87	3	104	3	0	3	0	0	-	14	.270	.372	.483

Year	Team	Lg		BATTING																		BASERUNNING				AVERAGES		
			G	AB	H	2B	3B	HR	(Hm	Rd)	TB	R	RBI	RC	TBB	IBB	SO	HBP	SH	SF		SB	CS	SB%	GDP	Avg	OBP	Slg
2009	StL	NL	14	29	5	2	0	0	(0	0)	7	2	2	2	3	0	8	0	0	0		0	0	-	1	.172	.250	.241
2010	Atl	NL	128	412	99	18	0	16	(8	8)	165	52	71	60	63	2	100	4	0	4		0	0	-	16	.240	.344	.400
Postseason			21	74	25	5	1	9	(4	5)	59	18	16	15	9	2	19	1	0	0		0	0	-	1	.338	.417	.797
13 ML YEARS			1537	5410	1375	293	10	320	(162	158)	2648	889	950	915	854	40	1377	46	0	45		56	29	.66	138	.254	.358	.489

Ross Gload

Bats: L **Throws:** L **Pos:** PH-72; 1B-18; RF-7; LF-1; DH-1   **Ht:** 6'1" **Wt:** 190 **Born:** 4/5/1976 **Age:** 35

Year	Team	Lg		BATTING																		BASERUNNING				AVERAGES		
			G	AB	H	2B	3B	HR	(Hm	Rd)	TB	R	RBI	RC	TBB	IBB	SO	HBP	SH	SF		SB	CS	SB%	GDP	Avg	OBP	Slg
2010	Clrwtr*	A+	2	8	1	0	0	1	(-	-)	4	1	1	0	0	0	1	0	0	0		0	0	-	1	.125	.125	.500
2000	ChC	NL	18	31	6	0	1	1	(0	1)	11	4	3	3	3	0	10	0	0	1		0	0	-	1	.194	.257	.355
2002	Col	NL	26	31	8	1	0	1	(1	0)	12	4	4	3	3	0	7	0	0	0		0	0	-	0	.258	.324	.387
2004	CWS	AL	110	234	75	16	0	7	(3	4)	112	28	44	41	20	1	37	2	1	3		0	3	.00	11	.321	.375	.479
2005	CWS	AL	28	42	7	2	0	0	(0	0)	9	2	5	2	2	0	9	0	0	0		0	0	-	1	.167	.205	.214
2006	CWS	AL	77	156	51	8	2	3	(1	2)	72	22	18	24	6	0	15	1	3	1		6	0	1.00	4	.327	.354	.462
2007	KC	AL	102	320	92	22	3	7	(2	5)	141	37	51	45	16	2	39	2	0	8		2	2	.50	13	.288	.318	.441
2008	KC	AL	122	388	106	18	1	3	(2	1)	135	46	37	41	23	4	39	3	1	3		3	4	.43	12	.273	.317	.348
2009	Fla	NL	125	230	60	10	2	6	(3	3)	92	33	30	26	23	4	30	2	1	3		0	0	-	3	.261	.329	.400
2010	Phi	NL	94	128	36	8	0	6	(5	1)	62	16	22	22	8	3	15	1	1	0		1	0	1.00	1	.281	.328	.484
9 ML YEARS			702	1560	441	85	9	34	(17	17)	646	192	214	207	104	14	201	11	7	19		12	9	.57	45	.283	.328	.414

Greg Golson

Bats: R **Throws:** R **Pos:** RF-17; CF-6; PR-3; LF-2   GOLE-sun   **Ht:** 6'0" **Wt:** 190 **Born:** 9/17/1985 **Age:** 25

Year	Team	Lg		BATTING																		BASERUNNING				AVERAGES		
			G	AB	H	2B	3B	HR	(Hm	Rd)	TB	R	RBI	RC	TBB	IBB	SO	HBP	SH	SF		SB	CS	SB%	GDP	Avg	OBP	Slg
2010	S-WB*	AAA	116	415	109	23	5	10	(-	-)	172	51	40	57	25	0	99	6	6	2		17	4	.81	7	.263	.313	.414
2008	Phi	NL	6	6	0	0	0	0	(0	0)	0	2	0	0	0	0	4	0	0	0		1	0	1.00	0	.000	.000	.000
2009	Tex	AL	1	1	0	0	0	0	(0	0)	0	0	0	0	0	0	1	0	0	0		0	0	-	0	.000	.000	.000
2010	NYY	Al	24	23	6	2	0	0	(0	0)	8	3	2	1	0	0	3	0	0	0		0	2	.00	0	.261	.261	.348
3 ML YEARS			31	30	6	2	0	0	(0	0)	8	5	2	1	0	0	8	0	0	0		1	2	.33	0	.200	.200	.267

Jonny Gomes

Bats: R **Throws:** R **Pos:** LF-129; PH-15; DH-7   GOHMS   **Ht:** 6'1" **Wt:** 225 **Born:** 11/22/1980 **Age:** 30

Year	Team	Lg		BATTING																		BASERUNNING				AVERAGES		
			G	AB	H	2B	3B	HR	(Hm	Rd)	TB	R	RBI	RC	TBB	IBB	SO	HBP	SH	SF		SB	CS	SB%	GDP	Avg	OBP	Slg
2003	TB	AL	8	15	2	1	0	0	(0	0)	3	1	0	0	0	0	6	1	0	0		0	0	-	0	.133	.188	.200
2004	TB	AL	5	14	1	0	0	0	(0	0)	1	0	1	0	1	0	6	0	0	0		0	0	-	0	.071	.133	.071
2005	TB	AL	101	348	98	13	6	21	(11	10)	186	61	54	62	39	1	113	14	1	5		9	5	.64	6	.282	.372	.534
2006	TB	AL	117	385	83	21	1	20	(7	13)	166	53	59	53	61	2	116	6	0	9		1	5	.17	10	.216	.325	.431
2007	TB	AL	107	348	85	20	2	17	(10	7)	160	48	49	47	35	1	126	7	0	4		12	4	.75	1	.244	.322	.460
2008	TB	AL	77	154	28	5	1	8	(2	6)	59	23	21	18	15	1	46	7	0	1		8	1	.89	1	.182	.282	.383
2009	Cin	NL	98	281	75	17	0	20	(11	9)	152	39	51	46	26	2	85	5	0	2		3	1	.75	8	.267	.338	.541
2010	Cin	NL	148	511	100	24	3	18	(11	7)	220	77	86	83	39	3	123	12	0	9		5	3	.63	4	.266	.327	.431
8 ML YEARS			661	2056	508	101	13	104	(52	52)	947	302	321	309	216	10	621	52	1	30		38	19	.67	30	.247	.330	.461

Carlos Gomez

Bats: R **Throws:** R **Pos:** CF-75; PH-18; LF-5; PR-5; RF-2   **Ht:** 6'4" **Wt:** 215 **Born:** 12/4/1985 **Age:** 25

Year	Team	Lg		BATTING																		BASERUNNING				AVERAGES		
			G	AB	H	2B	3B	HR	(Hm	Rd)	TB	R	RBI	RC	TBB	IBB	SO	HBP	SH	SF		SB	CS	SB%	GDP	Avg	OBP	Slg
2010	Wisc*	A	2	7	2	0	0	0	(-	-)	2	0	0	0	1	0	0	0	0	0		2	1	.67	0	.286	.375	.286
2010	Nashv*	AAA	8	28	8	0	0	0	(-	-)	8	7	2	4	5	0	9	1	0	0		2	1	.67	1	.286	.412	.286
2007	NYM	NL	58	125	29	3	0	2	(1	1)	38	14	12	11	8	2	27	3	0	3		12	3	.80	0	.232	.288	.304
2008	Min	AL	153	577	149	24	7	7	(3	4)	208	79	59	66	25	0	142	7	3	2		33	11	.75	7	.258	.296	.360
2009	Min	AL	137	315	72	15	5	3	(1	2)	106	51	28	33	22	0	72	4	7	1		14	7	.67	1	.229	.287	.337
2010	Mil	NL	97	291	72	11	3	5	(3	2)	104	38	24	28	17	1	72	4	6	0		18	3	.86	10	.247	.298	.357
Postseason			1	4	0	0	0	0	(0	0)	0	1	0	0	1	0	2	1	0	0		0	0	-	0	.000	.333	.000
4 ML YEARS			445	1308	322	53	15	17	(8	9)	456	182	123	138	72	3	313	18	16	6		77	24	.76	18	.246	.293	.349

Jeanmar Gomez

Pitches: R **Bats:** R **Pos:** SP-11   JENN-marr   **Ht:** 6'3" **Wt:** 170 **Born:** 2/10/1988 **Age:** 23

Year	Team	Lg		HOW MUCH HE PITCHED					WHAT HE GAVE UP												THE RESULTS						
			G	GS	CG	GF	IP	BFP	H	R	ER	HR	SH	SF	HB	TBB	IBB	SO	WP	Bk	W	L	Pct	Sh	Sv-Op	Hld	ERC	ERA
2006	Indns	R	11	9	0	0	54.1	231	50	24	15	2	1	2	6	12	0	34	2	1	4	3	.571	0	0- -	-	2.89	2.48
2007	Lk Cty	A	27	27	1	0	140.2	609	152	84	75	19	3	6	8	46	0	94	10	0	11	7	.611	0	0- -	-	4.77	4.80
2008	Knstn	A+	27	27	0	0	138.1	609	154	76	70	14	3	4	12	46	0	110	3	1	5	9	.357	0	0- -	-	4.85	4.55
2009	Knstn	A+	4	4	0	0	24.0	92	17	8	7	2	1	1	1	5	0	15	1	0	2	2	.500	0	0- -	-	1.99	2.63
2009	Akron	AA	22	22	1	0	123.1	521	117	56	47	11	4	5	3	40	0	109	3	0	10	4	.714	1	0- -	-	3.51	3.43
2010	Clmbs	AAA	20	20	1	0	116.0	504	129	74	67	16	1	5	1	42	0	78	8	1	8	8	.500	0	0- -	-	4.93	5.20
2010	Cle	AL	11	11	0	0	57.2	265	73	36	30	7	0	3	2	22	3	34	1	0	4	5	.444	0	0-0	0	5.75	4.68

Adrian Gonzalez

Bats: L **Throws:** L **Pos:** 1B-159; DH-1   **Ht:** 6'2" **Wt:** 225 **Born:** 5/8/1982 **Age:** 29

Year	Team	Lg	G	AB	H	2B	3B	HR	(Hm	Rd)	TB	R	RBI	RC	TBB	IBB	SO	HBP	SH	SF	SB	CS	SB%	GDP	Avg	OBP	Slg
2004	Tex	AL	16	42	10	3	0	1	(1	0)	16	7	7	7	2	0	6	0	0	0	0	0	-	0	.238	.273	.381
2005	Tex	AL	43	150	34	7	1	6	(3	3)	61	17	17	13	10	2	37	0	0	2	0	0	-	3	.227	.272	.407
2006	SD	NL	156	570	173	38	1	24	(10	14)	285	83	82	82	52	9	113	3	1	5	0	1	.00	24	.304	.362	.500
2007	SD	NL	161	646	182	46	3	30	(10	20)	324	101	100	108	65	9	140	3	0	6	0	0	-	6	.282	.347	.502
2008	SD	NL	**162**	616	172	32	1	36	(14	22)	314	103	119	107	74	18	142	7	0	3	0	0	-	24	.279	.361	.510
2009	SD	NL	160	552	153	27	2	40	(12	28)	304	90	99	109	**119**	22	109	5	1	4	1	1	.50	23	.277	.407	.551
2010	SD	NL	160	591	176	33	0	31	(11	20)	302	87	101	122	93	35	114	2	2	4	0	0	-	15	.298	.393	.511
	Postseason		4	14	5	0	0	0	(0	0)	5	2	0	1	3	0	3	0	0	0	0	0	-	0	.357	.471	.357
	7 ML YEARS		858	3167	900	186	8	168	(61	107)	1606	488	525	548	415	95	661	20	4	24	1	2	.33	95	.284	.368	.507

Alberto Gonzalez

Bats: R **Throws:** R **Pos:** PH-47; 2B-38; 3B-28; SS-16; 1B-3; RF-1; PR-1   **Ht:** 5'10" **Wt:** 194 **Born:** 4/18/1983 **Age:** 28

Year	Team	Lg	G	AB	H	2B	3B	HR	(Hm	Rd)	TB	R	RBI	RC	TBB	IBB	SO	HBP	SH	SF	SB	CS	SB%	GDP	Avg	OBP	Slg
2007	NYY	AL	12	14	1	0	0	0	(0	0)	1	3	1	0	1	0	1	0	0	0	0	1	.00	1	.071	.133	.071
2008	2 Tms		45	101	26	8	0	1	(0	1)	37	13	10	11	8	0	14	1	2	0	0	1	.00	6	.257	.318	.366
2009	Was	NL	105	291	77	16	3	1	(1	0)	102	31	33	30	14	1	27	3	2	6	1	1	.50	8	.265	.299	.351
2010	Was	NL	115	186	46	8	1	0	(0	0)	56	19	5	9	7	0	30	1	3	1	0	0	-	8	.247	.277	.301
08	NYY	AL	28	52	9	2	0	0	(0	0)	11	4	1	0	4	0	8	0	2	0	0	0	-	4	.173	.232	.212
08	Was	NL	17	49	17	6	0	1	(0	1)	26	9	9	11	4	0	6	1	0	0	0	1	.00	2	.347	.407	.531
	4 ML YEARS		277	592	150	32	4	2	(1	1)	196	66	49	50	30	1	72	5	7	7	1	3	.25	23	.253	.292	.331

Alex Gonzalez

Bats: R **Throws:** R **Pos:** SS-157   **Ht:** 5'11" **Wt:** 216 **Born:** 2/15/1977 **Age:** 34

Year	Team	Lg	G	AB	H	2B	3B	HR	(Hm	Rd)	TB	R	RBI	RC	TBB	IBB	SO	HBP	SH	SF	SB	CS	SB%	GDP	Avg	OBP	Slg
1998	Fla	NL	25	86	13	2	0	3	(1	2)	24	11	7	5	9	0	30	1	2	0	0	0	-	2	.151	.240	.279
1999	Fla	NL	136	560	155	28	8	14	(7	7)	241	81	59	69	15	0	113	12	1	3	3	5	.38	13	.277	.308	.430
2000	Fla	NL	109	385	77	17	4	7	(5	2)	123	35	42	26	13	0	77	2	5	2	7	1	.88	7	.200	.229	.319
2001	Fla	NL	145	515	129	36	1	9	(5	4)	194	57	48	56	30	6	107	10	3	3	2	2	.50	13	.250	.303	.377
2002	Fla	NL	42	151	34	7	1	2	(1	1)	49	15	18	14	12	1	32	4	3	2	3	1	.75	2	.225	.296	.325
2003	Fla	NL	150	528	135	33	6	18	(7	11)	234	52	77	67	33	13	106	13	3	5	4	4	.00	8	.256	.313	.443
2004	Fla	NL	159	561	130	30	3	23	(13	10)	235	67	79	58	27	9	126	4	3	4	3	1	.75	17	.232	.270	.419
2005	Fla	NL	130	435	115	30	0	5	(2	3)	160	45	45	47	31	10	81	5	4	3	5	3	.63	11	.264	.319	.368
2006	Bos	AL	111	388	99	24	2	9	(4	5)	154	48	50	40	22	1	67	5	7	7	1	0	1.00	6	.255	.299	.397
2007	Cin	NL	110	393	107	27	1	16	(8	8)	184	55	55	51	24	1	75	8	2	3	0	1	.00	13	.272	.325	.468
2009	2 Tms		112	391	93	22	0	8	(7	1)	139	42	41	40	20	4	65	4	10	4	2	1	.67	7	.238	.279	.355
2010	2 Tms		157	595	149	42	3	23	(11	12)	266	74	88	75	31	2	118	7	3	4	1	2	.33	16	.250	.294	.447
09	Cin	NL	68	243	51	12	0	3	(2	1)	72	16	26	25	15	4	36	2	6	4	0	1	.00	3	.210	.258	.296
09	Bos	AL	44	148	42	10	0	5	(5	0)	67	26	15	15	5	0	29	2	4	0	2	0	1.00	4	.284	.316	.453
10	Tor	AL	85	328	85	25	1	17	(8	9)	163	47	50	47	17	0	65	1	0	2	1	0	1.00	9	.259	.296	.497
10	Atl	NL	72	267	64	17	2	6	(3	3)	103	27	38	28	14	2	53	6	3	2	0	2	.00	7	.240	.291	.386
	Postseason		20	68	11	4	0	1	(1	0)	18	7	6	2	2	0	17	0	1	0	0	1	.00	2	.162	.186	.265
	12 ML YEARS		1386	4988	1236	298	29	137	(71	66)	2003	582	609	548	267	47	997	75	46	40	27	21	.56	115	.248	.294	.402

Carlos Gonzalez

Bats: L **Throws:** L **Pos:** LF-63; CF-58; RF-40; PH-2; PR-1   **Ht:** 6'1" **Wt:** 205 **Born:** 10/17/1985 **Age:** 25

Year	Team	Lg	G	AB	H	2B	3B	HR	(Hm	Rd)	TB	R	RBI	RC	TBB	IBB	SO	HBP	SH	SF	SB	CS	SB%	GDP	Avg	OBP	Slg
2008	Oak	AL	85	302	73	22	1	4	(3	1)	109	31	26	30	13	1	81	0	1	0	4	1	.80	7	.242	.273	.361
2009	Col	NL	89	278	79	14	7	13	(7	6)	146	53	29	42	28	3	70	3	5	3	16	4	.80	3	.284	.353	.525
2010	Col	NL	145	587	**197**	34	9	34	(26	8)	**351**	111	117	118	40	8	135	2	0	7	26	8	.76	9	**.336**	.376	.598
	Postseason		4	17	10	2	0	1	(1	0)	15	5	1	5	2	0	1	0	0	0	2	1	.67	0	.588	.632	.882
	3 ML YEARS		319	1167	349	70	17	51	(36	15)	606	195	172	190	81	12	286	5	6	10	46	13	.78	19	.299	.344	.519

Enrique Gonzalez

Pitches: R **Bats:** R **Pos:** RP-18   **Ht:** 5'10" **Wt:** 224 **Born:** 7/14/1982 **Age:** 28

			HOW MUCH HE PITCHED						WHAT HE GAVE UP											THE RESULTS						
Year	Team	Lg	G	GS	CG	GF	IP	BFP	H	R	ER	HR	SH	SF	HB	TBB	IBB	SO	WP	Bk	W	L	Pct	Sh	Sv-Op Hld	ERC	ERA
2010	Toledo*	AAA	12	11	1	0	66.0	282	69	29	25	9	2	0	2	16	1	54	3	0	4	5	.444	1	0- -	4.01	3.41
2006	Ari	NL	22	18	0	1	106.1	462	114	71	67	14	7	3	4	34	0	66	1	0	3	7	.300	0	0-0	4.53	5.67
2007	Ari	NL	1	0	0	1	2.0	11	4	4	3	0	0	0	0	1	0	0	0	0	0	0	-	0	0-0	9.72	13.50
2008	SD	NL	4	0	0	3	3.1	15	4	4	4	0	0	0	0	2	0	1	0	0	1	0	1.000	0	0-1	5.47	10.80
2009	Bos	AL	2	0	0	2	3.2	18	5	2	2	1	0	0	0	2	0	1	0	0	0	0	-	0	0-0	8.17	4.91
2010	Det	AL	18	0	0	13	26.0	107	21	11	11	4	0	1	0	17	0	13	1	0	0	1	.000	0	0-0	4.70	3.81
	5 ML YEARS		47	18	0	20	141.1	613	148	92	87	19	7	4	4	56	0	81	2	0	4	8	.333	0	0-1	4.74	5.54

Gio Gonzalez

Pitches: L Bats: R Pos: SP-33   Ht: 5'11" Wt: 205 Born: 9/19/1985 Age: 25

Year Team	Lg	G	GS	CG	GF	IP	BFP	H	R	ER	HR	SH	SF	HB	TBB	IBB	SO	WP	Bk	W	L	Pct	Sh	Sv-Op	Hld	ERC	ERA
2008 Oak	AL	10	7	0	3	34.0	163	32	34	29	9	2	1	3	25	1	34	1	0	1	4	.200	0	0-0	0	6.54	7.68
2009 Oak	AL	20	17	0	0	98.2	455	113	68	63	14	2	3	1	56	2	109	2	0	6	7	.462	0	0-0	0	5.96	5.75
2010 Oak	AL	33	33	1	0	200.2	851	171	75	72	15	5	2	4	92	1	171	4	1	15	9	.625	0	0-0	0	3.39	3.23
3 ML YEARS		63	57	1	3	333.1	1469	316	177	164	38	9	6	8	173	4	314	7	1	22	20	.524	0	0-0	0	4.42	4.43

Mike Gonzalez

Pitches: L Bats: R Pos: RP-29   Ht: 6'2" Wt: 215 Born: 5/23/1978 Age: 33

Year Team	Lg	G	GS	CG	GF	IP	BFP	H	R	ER	HR	SH	SF	HB	TBB	IBB	SO	WP	Bk	W	L	Pct	Sh	Sv-Op	Hld	ERC	ERA
2010 Orioles*	R	2	2	0	0	2.0	7	1	0	0	0	0	0	0	0	0	3	0	0	0	0	-	0	0- -	-	0.54	0.00
2010 Abrdn*	A-	4	1	0	0	5.0	21	7	3	3	2	0	0	0	0	0	5	0	0	0	1	.000	0	0- -	-	7.06	5.40
2010 Bowie*	AA	4	0	0	0	4.0	15	2	1	1	1	0	0	0	1	0	4	0	0	1	0	1.000	0	0- -	-	1.80	2.25
2010 Norfolk*	AAA	2	1	0	0	1.2	10	3	2	2	0	0	0	0	2	0	4	0	0	0	0	-	0	0- -	-	11.51	10.80
2003 Pit	NL	16	0	0	2	8.1	38	7	7	7	4	1	1	0	6	0	6	1	0	0	1	.000	0	0-0	3	7.18	7.56
2004 Pit	NL	47	0	0	12	43.1	169	32	7	6	2	3	0	1	6	0	55	4	0	3	1	.750	0	1-4	13	1.60	1.25
2005 Pit	NL	51	0	0	15	50.0	212	35	15	15	2	0	2	1	31	2	58	3	0	1	3	.250	0	3-3	15	2.90	2.70
2006 Pit	NL	54	0	0	54	54.0	234	42	13	13	1	3	1	2	31	2	64	0	0	3	4	.429	0	24-24	3	3.00	2.17
2007 Atl	NL	18	0	0	5	17.0	70	15	3	3	0	1	0	0	8	0	13	0	0	2	0	1.000	0	2-2	5	3.13	1.59
2008 Atl	NL	36	0	0	29	33.2	142	26	21	16	6	1	2	1	14	3	44	0	0	0	3	.000	0	14-16	0	3.43	4.28
2009 Atl	NL	80	0	0	29	74.1	315	56	28	20	7	6	1	7	33	8	90	5	0	5	4	.556	0	10-17	17	3.04	2.42
2010 Bal	AL	29	0	0	7	24.2	106	18	11	11	1	3	1	0	14	4	31	3	0	1	3	.250	0	1-3	10	2.54	4.01
8 ML YEARS		331	0	0	146	305.1	1286	231	105	91	23	17	9	12	143	19	361	16	0	15	19	.441	0	55-69	66	2.89	2.68

Alex Gordon

Bats: L Throws: R Pos: LF-55, 3B-10; RF-3; PH-3; PR-3; DH-2; 1B-1   Ht: 6'2" Wt: 220 Born: 2/10/1984 Age: 27

Year Team	Lg	G	AB	H	2B	3B	HR	(Hm	Rd)	TB	R	RBI	RC	TBB	IBB	SO	HBP	SH	SF	SB	CS	SB%	GDP	Avg	OBP	Slg
2010 Wilmg*	A+	7	17	4	3	0	0	(-	-)	7	7	2	5	9	2	3	4	0	1	1	0	1.00	0	.235	.548	.412
2010 Omha*	AAA	68	260	82	20	3	14	(-	-)	150	59	44	66	51	0	72	8	2	0	7	2	.78	5	.315	.442	.577
2007 KC	AL	151	543	134	36	4	15	(8	7)	223	60	60	69	41	4	137	13	1	2	14	4	.78	12	.247	.314	.411
2008 KC	AL	134	493	128	35	1	16	(9	7)	213	72	59	71	66	5	120	6	1	5	9	2	.82	8	.260	.351	.432
2009 KC	AL	49	164	38	6	0	6	(2	4)	62	28	22	16	21	0	43	2	1	1	5	0	1.00	6	.232	.324	.378
2010 KC	AL	74	242	52	10	0	8	(5	3)	86	34	20	23	34	1	62	2	2	1	1	5	.17	9	.215	.315	.355
4 ML YEARS		408	1442	352	87	5	45	(24	21)	584	194	161	179	162	10	362	23	5	9	29	11	.73	34	.244	.328	.405

Tom Gorzelanny

Pitches: L Bats: L Pos: SP-23; RP-6   gore-zah-LAWN-ee   Ht: 6'2" Wt: 205 Born: 7/12/1982 Age: 28

Year Team	Lg	G	GS	CG	GF	IP	BFP	H	R	ER	HR	SH	SF	HB	TBB	IBB	SO	WP	Bk	W	L	Pct	Sh	Sv-Op	Hld	ERC	ERA
2005 Pit	NL	3	1	0	0	6.0	32	10	8	8	1	1	0	0	3	0	3	0	0	0	1	.000	0	0-0	0	8.76	12.00
2006 Pit	NL	11	11	0	0	61.2	267	50	29	26	3	7	4	4	35	2	40	3	0	2	5	.286	0	0-0	0	3.23	3.79
2007 Pit	NL	32	32	1	0	201.2	874	214	90	87	18	3	9	11	68	3	135	5	1	14	10	.583	1	0-0	0	4.31	3.88
2008 Pit	NL	21	21	0	0	105.1	490	120	79	78	20	3	6	1	70	0	67	5	1	6	9	.400	0	0-0	0	6.86	6.66
2009 2 Tms	NL	22	7	0	2	47.0	204	45	30	29	6	3	3	1	17	0	47	1	0	3	7	.700	0	0-1	2	3.88	5.55
2010 ChC	NL	29	23	0	3	136.1	604	136	70	62	11	4	6	2	68	4	119	0	0	7	9	.438	0	1-1	1	4.30	4.09
09 Pit	NL	9	0	0	2	8.2	36	6	5	5	0	1	0	0	4	0	7	0	0	3	1	.750	0	0-1	1	2.02	5.19
09 ChC	NL	13	7	0	0	38.1	168	39	25	24	6	2	3	1	13	0	40	1	0	4	2	.667	0	0-0	1	4.33	5.63
6 ML YEARS		118	95	1	5	558.0	2471	575	306	290	59	21	28	19	257	9	411	14	2	36	37	.493	1	1-2	3	4.64	4.68

John Grabow

Pitches: L Bats: L Pos: RP-28   GRAE-boe   Ht: 6'2" Wt: 205 Born: 11/4/1978 Age: 32

Year Team	Lg	G	GS	CG	GF	IP	BFP	H	R	ER	HR	SH	SF	HB	TBB	IBB	SO	WP	Bk	W	L	Pct	Sh	Sv-Op	Hld	ERC	ERA
2010 Iowa*	AAA	4	0	0	1	4.0	17	6	3	3	0	0	0	0	1	0	2	1	0	0	0	-	0	0- -	-	6.17	6.75
2003 Pit	NL	5	0	0	1	5.0	22	6	3	2	0	0	0	0	0	0	9	0	0	0	0	-	0	0-0	0	2.73	3.60
2004 Pit	NL	68	0	0	10	61.2	286	81	39	35	8	6	1	0	28	7	64	5	0	2	5	.286	0	1-7	11	6.21	5.11
2005 Pit	NL	63	0	0	17	52.0	222	46	31	28	6	2	0	2	25	2	42	1	0	2	3	.400	0	0-1	14	4.00	4.85
2006 Pit	NL	72	0	0	17	69.2	303	68	34	32	7	5	3	3	30	3	66	0	0	4	2	.667	0	0-2	11	4.17	4.13
2007 Pit	NL	63	0	0	14	51.2	228	56	27	26	6	4	2	1	19	2	42	3	0	3	2	.600	0	1-2	8	4.51	4.53
2008 Pit	NL	74	0	0	18	76.0	322	60	25	24	9	3	2	1	37	2	62	4	2	3	3	.667	0	4-8	16	3.37	2.84
2009 2 Tms	NL	75	0	0	12	72.1	314	62	28	27	5	1	4	3	40	3	57	1	0	3	0	1.000	0	0-2	23	3.76	3.36
2010 ChC	NL	28	0	0	9	25.2	126	35	24	21	5	3	0	1	13	0	20	1	0	1	3	.250	0	0-1	7	7.51	7.36
09 Pit	NL	45	0	0	4	47.1	209	43	19	18	4	1	3	2	28	2	41	0	0	3	0	1.000	0	0-2	16	4.32	3.42
09 ChC	NL	30	0	0	8	25.0	105	19	9	9	1	0	1	1	12	1	16	1	0	0	0	-	0	0-0	7	2.77	3.24
8 ML YEARS		448	0	0	89	414.0	1823	414	211	195	46	24	12	11	192	19	362	15	2	21	18	.538	0	6-23	90	4.43	4.24

Curtis Granderson

Bats: L Throws: R Pos: CF-134; PH-8; PR-2   **Ht: 6'1" Wt: 185 Born: 3/16/1981 Age: 30**

									BATTING											BASERUNNING				AVERAGES		
Year Team	Lg	G	AB	H	2B	3B	HR	(Hm Rd)	TB	R	RBI	RC	TBB	IBB	SO	HBP	SH	SF	SB	CS	SB%	GDP	Avg	OBP	Slg		
2010 S-WB*	AAA	5	16	4	0	0	0	(- -)	4	0	2	1	2	1	2	0	0	0	0	0	-	0	.250	.333	.250		
2004 Det	AL	9	25	6	1	1	0	(0 0)	9	2	0	2	3	0	8	0	0	0	0	0	-	1	.240	.321	.360		
2005 Det	AL	47	162	44	6	3	8	(5 3)	80	18	20	26	10	0	43	0	2	0	1	1	.50	2	.272	.314	.494		
2006 Det	AL	159	596	155	31	9	19	(7 12)	261	90	68	89	66	0	174	4	7	6	8	5	.62	4	.260	.335	.438		
2007 Det	AL	158	612	185	38	23	23	(10 13)	338	122	74	106	52	3	141	5	5	2	26	1	.96	3	.302	.361	.552		
2008 Det	AL	141	553	155	26	13	22	(11 11)	273	112	66	100	71	1	111	3	1	1	12	4	.75	7	.280	.365	.494		
2009 Det	AL	160	631	157	23	8	30	(10 20)	286	91	71	92	72	4	141	2	2	4	20	6	.77	1	.249	.327	.453		
2010 NYY	AL	136	466	115	17	7	24	(14 10)	218	76	67	71	53	3	116	2	4	3	12	2	.86	3	.247	.324	.468		
Postseason		13	53	12	3	1	3	(1 2)	26	8	7	8	5	0	10	0	0	1	2	0	1.00	1	.226	.288	.491		
7 ML YEARS		810	3045	817	142	64	126	(57 69)	1465	511	366	486	327	11	734	16	22	14	79	19	.81	21	.268	.341	.481		

Jeff Gray

Pitches: R Bats: R Pos: RP-7   **Ht: 6'3" Wt: 196 Born: 11/19/1981 Age: 29**

		HOW MUCH HE PITCHED						WHAT HE GAVE UP											THE RESULTS							
Year Team	Lg	G	GS	CG	GF	IP	BFP	H	R	ER	HR	SH	SF	HB	TBB	IBB	SO	WP	Bk	W	L	Pct	Sh	Sv-Op	Hld	ERC	ERA
2010 Iowa*	AAA	25	0	0	11	35.0	165	45	27	22	2	3	0	4	15	1	25	0	0	3	1	.750	0	1--	-	5.95	5.66
2010 Cubs*	R	3	2	0	0	4.0	14	3	1	1	0	0	0	0	0	0	3	0	0	0	0	-	0	0--	-	1.21	2.25
2008 Oak	AL	5	0	0	2	4.2	24	8	4	4	1	0	0	1	1	0	4	0	0	0	0	-	0	0-0	0	9.48	7.71
2009 Oak	AL	24	0	0	11	26.1	116	30	12	11	3	2	0	2	4	1	19	0	0	0	1	.000	0	0-0	1	4.07	3.76
2010 ChC	NL	7	0	0	0	9.1	45	12	9	7	1	1	0	1	5	0	4	1	0	1	0	1.000	0	0-0	0	6.85	6.75
3 ML YEARS		36	0	0	13	40.1	185	50	25	22	5	3	0	4	10	1	27	1	0	1	1	.500	0	0-0	1	5.26	4.91

Nick Green

Bats: R Throws: R Pos: 2B-6; SS-4; PR-4; DH-1; PH-1   **Ht: 6'0" Wt: 180 Born: 9/10/1978 Age: 32**

									BATTING											BASERUNNING				AVERAGES		
Year Team	Lg	G	AB	H	2B	3B	HR	(Hm Rd)	TB	R	RBI	RC	TBB	IBB	SO	HBP	SH	SF	SB	CS	SB%	GDP	Avg	OBP	Slg		
2010 Albq*	AAA	29	98	20	9	2	2	(- -)	39	15	10	9	3	0	19	1	2	0	1	0	1.00	1	.204	.235	.398		
2010 PortInd*	AAA	40	144	38	9	1	2	(- -)	55	17	21	17	13	0	33	0	2	0	0	4	.00	6	.264	.325	.382		
2004 Atl	NL	95	264	72	15	3	3	(- -)	102	40	26	36	12	1	63	4	8	2	1	2	.33	0	.273	.312	.386		
2005 TB	AL	111	318	76	15	2	5	(2 3)	110	53	29	38	33	0	86	11	10	3	3	1	.75	5	.239	.329	.346		
2006 2 Tms	AL	63	114	21	5	0	2	(1 1)	32	12	4	10	11	0	40	1	1	0	1	4	.20	2	.184	.262	.281		
2007 Sea	AL	6	7	0	0	0	0	(0 0)	0	0	0	0	0	0	3	0	0	0	0	0	-	0	.000	.000	.000		
2009 Bos	AL	104	276	65	18	0	6	(4 2)	101	35	35	28	20	1	69	8	2	3	1	4	.20	10	.236	.303	.366		
2010 2 Tms	AL	14	21	3	0	0	0	(0 0)	3	2	2	1	1	0	5	1	0	0	0	0	-	0	.143	.217	.143		
06 TB	AL	17	39	3	0	0	0	(0 0)	3	4	0	0	6	0	11	0	0	0	0	3	.00	2	.077	.200	.077		
06 NYY	AL	46	75	18	5	0	2	(1 1)	29	8	4	10	5	0	29	1	1	0	1	1	.50	0	.240	.296	.387		
10 LAD	NL	5	8	1	0	0	0	(0 0)	1	0	1	0	0	0	2	1	0	0	0	0	-	0	.125	.222	.125		
10 Tor	AL	9	13	2	0	0	0	(0 0)	2	2	1	1	1	0	3	0	0	0	0	0	-	0	.154	.214	.154		
Postseason		2	0	0	0	0	0	(0 0)	0	0	0	0	0	0	0	0	0	0	0	0	-	0	-	-	-		
6 ML YEARS		393	1000	237	53	5	16	(10 6)	348	142	96	113	77	2	266	25	21	8	6	11	.35	17	.237	.305	.348		

Sean Green

Pitches: R Bats: R Pos: RP-11   **Ht: 6'6" Wt: 227 Born: 4/20/1979 Age: 32**

		HOW MUCH HE PITCHED						WHAT HE GAVE UP											THE RESULTS							
Year Team	Lg	G	GS	CG	GF	IP	BFP	H	R	ER	HR	SH	SF	HB	TBB	IBB	SO	WP	Bk	W	L	Pct	Sh	Sv-Op	Hld	ERC	ERA
2010 Mets*	R	3	0	0	0	3.0	12	1	1	1	0	0	0	0	2	0	5	0	0	1	0	1.000	0	0--	-	1.26	3.00
2010 StLuci*	A+	4	0	0	4	4.0	19	6	2	2	0	0	0	0	1	0	6	2	0	0	0	-	0	0--	-	5.46	4.50
2010 Buffalo*	AAA	17	0	0	3	21.1	91	23	11	11	1	1	0	2	8	1	20	0	0	1	1	.500	0	0--	-	4.52	4.64
2006 Sea	AL	24	0	0	11	32.0	139	34	16	16	2	1	1	2	13	1	15	2	0	0	0	-	0	0-1	3	4.47	4.50
2007 Sea	AL	64	0	0	10	68.0	304	77	31	29	2	4	5	3	34	6	53	2	0	5	2	.714	0	0-3	13	4.81	3.84
2008 Sea	AL	72	0	0	13	79.0	358	80	47	41	3	3	7	6	36	1	62	5	1	4	5	.444	0	1-4	17	4.09	4.67
2009 NYM	NL	79	0	0	19	69.2	316	64	37	35	5	4	0	9	36	5	54	8	1	1	4	.200	0	1-3	14	4.17	4.52
2010 NYM	NL	11	0	0	0	9.1	48	7	6	4	1	1	0	4	8	3	12	0	0	0	0	-	0	0-0	2	5.28	3.86
5 ML YEARS		250	0	0	53	258.0	1165	262	137	125	13	13	13	24	127	16	196	17	2	10	11	.476	0	2-11	49	4.39	4.36

Tyler Greene

Bats: R Throws: R Pos: SS-22; 2B-15; 3B-11; PH-8; PR-1   **Ht: 6'2" Wt: 190 Born: 8/17/1983 Age: 27**

									BATTING											BASERUNNING				AVERAGES		
Year Team	Lg	G	AB	H	2B	3B	HR	(Hm Rd)	TB	R	RBI	RC	TBB	IBB	SO	HBP	SH	SF	SB	CS	SB%	GDP	Avg	OBP	Slg		
2005 NewJrs	A-	35	138	36	12	0	1	(- -)	51	28	18	21	15	1	37	5	0	1	13	1	.93	7	.261	.352	.370		
2005 PlmBh	A+	20	85	23	4	0	2	(- -)	33	17	5	12	5	0	28	2	0	0	6	0	1.00	1	.271	.326	.388		
2006 PlmBh	A+	71	268	60	10	1	5	(- -)	87	38	19	31	29	0	90	4	1	1	22	3	.88	7	.224	.308	.325		
2006 QuadC	A	59	223	64	8	3	15	(- -)	123	42	47	48	12	0	65	12	0	1	11	0	1.00	6	.287	.375	.552		
2007 Sprgfld	AA	65	221	54	17	2	8	(- -)	99	41	25	32	16	2	62	5	4	1	10	2	.83	3	.244	.309	.448		
2008 Sprgfld	AA	97	374	97	15	4	16	(- -)	168	62	41	53	22	1	99	5	4	3	14	6	.70	5	.259	.307	.449		
2008 Memp	AAA	30	111	26	7	0	0	(- -)	33	17	7	13	11	0	35	4	2	0	5	0	1.00	1	.234	.325	.297		
2009 Memp	AAA	89	340	99	10	5	15	(- -)	164	70	42	66	38	1	86	5	3	2	31	3	.91	7	.291	.369	.482		
2010 Memp	AAA	82	338	96	21	5	9	(- -)	154	67	34	56	32	2	89	6	8	1	12	5	.71	4	.284	.355	.456		
2010 PlmBh	A+	2	7	0	0	0	0	(- -)	0	0	0	0	1	0	4	0	0	0	0	0	-	0	.000	.125	.000		
2009 StL	NL	48	108	24	5	0	2	(1 1)	35	9	7	6	4	0	32	3	1	0	3	0	1.00	2	.222	.270	.324		
2010 StL	NL	44	104	23	3	1	2	(2 0)	34	14	10	10	13	4	24	4	0	1	2	0	1.00	1	.221	.328	.327		
2 ML YEARS		92	212	47	8	1	4	(3 1)	69	23	17	16	17	4	56	7	1	1	5	0	1.00	3	.222	.300	.325		

Luke Gregerson

Pitches: R **Bats:** L **Pos:** RP-80   **Ht:** 6'3" **Wt:** 200 **Born:** 5/14/1984 **Age:** 27

Year	Team	Lg	G	GS	CG	GF	IP	BFP	H	R	ER	HR	SH	SF	HB	TBB	IBB	SO	WP	Bk	W	L	Pct	Sh	Sv-Op	Hld	ERC	ERA
2006	JhsCty	R+	15	0	0	7	16.1	70	14	10	7	0	0	0	1	6	0	24	4	2	0	1	.000	0	5--	-	2.67	3.86
2006	StCol	A-	12	0	0	10	15.2	66	9	5	3	0	1	1	0	9	0	22	5	0	6	1	.857	0	4--	-	1.80	1.72
2007	PlmBh	A+	53	0	0	43	64.0	251	42	14	14	0	5	2	1	20	3	69	5	1	3	4	.429	0	29--	-	1.51	1.97
2007	Sprgfld	AA	1	0	0	1	1.0	4	1	0	0	0	0	0	0	0	0	3	0	0	0	0	-	0	0--	-	1.95	0.00
2008	Sprgfld	AA	57	0	0	29	75.1	312	62	32	28	6	3	0	3	26	5	78	5	1	7	6	.538	0	10--	-	2.83	3.35
2009	SD	NL	72	0	0	7	75.0	318	62	29	27	3	3	1	3	31	9	93	4	0	2	4	.333	0	1-7	27	2.72	3.24
2010	SD	NL	80	0	0	9	78.1	297	47	30	28	8	1	1	1	18	2	89	0	0	4	7	.364	0	2-7	**40**	1.56	3.22
	2 ML YEARS		152	0	0	16	153.1	615	109	59	55	11	4	2	4	49	11	182	4	0	6	11	.353	0	3-14	67	2.10	3.23

Kevin Gregg

Pitches: R **Bats:** R **Pos:** RP-63   **Ht:** 6'6" **Wt:** 240 **Born:** 6/20/1978 **Age:** 33

Year	Team	Lg	G	GS	CG	GF	IP	BFP	H	R	ER	HR	SH	SF	HB	TBB	IBB	SO	WP	Bk	W	L	Pct	Sh	Sv-Op	Hld	ERC	ERA
2003	LAA	AL	5	3	0	0	24.2	97	18	9	9	3	0	0	1	8	0	14	0	0	2	0	1.000	0	0-0	0	2.74	3.28
2004	LAA	AL	55	0	0	23	87.2	377	86	43	41	6	4	5	3	28	3	84	13	1	5	2	.714	0	1-2	3	3.47	4.21
2005	LAA	AL	33	2	0	9	64.1	290	70	37	36	8	1	1	3	29	2	52	5	0	1	2	.333	0	0-1	1	5.08	5.04
2006	LAA	AL	32	3	0	12	78.1	341	88	41	36	10	0	3	2	21	0	71	6	0	3	4	.429	0	0-0	0	4.51	4.14
2007	Fla	NL	74	0	0	55	84.0	355	63	34	33	7	3	0	6	40	1	87	6	0	0	5	.000	0	32-36	6	3.15	3.54
2008	Fla	NL	72	0	0	59	68.2	296	51	30	26	3	3	1	4	37	4	58	7	0	7	8	.467	0	29-38	4	2.90	3.41
2009	ChC	NL	72	0	0	51	68.2	298	60	38	36	13	0	3	0	30	2	71	7	0	5	6	.455	0	23-30	1	4.19	4.72
2010	Tor	AL	63	0	0	56	59.0	254	52	24	23	4	1	3	1	30	1	58	3	0	2	6	.250	0	37-43	3	3.66	3.51
	Postseason		2	0	0	0	4.0	18	4	0	0	0	0	0	0	2	0	3	1	0	0	0	-	0	0-0	0	3.63	0.00
	8 ML YEARS		406	8	0	265	535.1	2308	488	256	240	54	12	16	23	223	13	495	47	1	25	33	.431	0	122-150	18	3.76	4.03

Zack Greinke

Pitches: R **Bats:** R **Pos:** SP-33   GRAIN-key   **Ht:** 6'2" **Wt:** 190 **Born:** 10/21/1983 **Age:** 27

Year	Team	Lg	G	GS	CG	GF	IP	BFP	H	R	ER	HR	SH	SF	HB	TBB	IBB	SO	WP	Bk	W	L	Pct	Sh	Sv-Op	Hld	ERC	ERA
2004	KC	AL	24	24	0	0	145.0	599	143	64	64	26	3	2	8	26	3	100	1	1	8	11	.421	0	0-0	0	3.85	3.97
2005	KC	AL	33	33	2	0	183.0	829	233	125	118	23	4	4	13	53	0	114	4	2	5	17	.227	0	0-0	0	5.71	5.80
2006	KC	AL	3	0	0	1	6.1	28	7	3	3	1	0	0	0	3	2	5	0	0	1	0	1.000	0	0-0	0	4.93	4.26
2007	KC	AL	52	14	0	7	122.0	507	122	52	50	12	4	3	3	36	5	106	3	1	7	7	.500	0	1-1	12	3.77	3.69
2008	KC	AL	32	32	1	0	202.1	851	202	87	78	21	2	4	4	56	1	183	8	1	13	10	.565	0	0-0	0	3.68	3.47
2009	KC	AL	33	33	6	0	229.1	915	195	64	55	11	8	3	4	51	0	242	5	0	16	8	.667	3	0-0	0	**2.39**	**2.16**
2010	KC	AL	33	33	3	0	220.0	919	219	114	102	18	6	7	7	55	1	181	4	0	10	14	.417	0	0-0	0	3.48	4.17
	7 ML YEARS		210	169	12	8	1108.0	4648	1121	509	470	112	26	24	39	280	12	931	25	5	60	67	.472	3	1-1	12	3.71	3.82

Ken Griffey Jr.

Bats: L **Throws:** L **Pos:** DH-25; PH-8   **Ht:** 6'2" **Wt:** 230 **Born:** 11/21/1969 **Age:** 41

Year	Team	Lg	G	AB	H	2B	3B	HR	(Hm	Rd)	TB	R	RBI	RC	TBB	IBB	SO	HBP	SH	SF	3B	CS	3D%	GDP	Avg	OBP	Slg
1989	Sea	AL	127	455	120	23	0	16	(10	6)	191	61	61	64	44	8	83	2	1	4	16	7	.70	4	.264	.329	.420
1990	Sea	AL	155	597	179	28	7	22	(8	14)	287	91	80	101	63	12	81	2	0	4	16	11	.59	12	.300	.366	.481
1991	Sea	AL	154	548	179	42	1	22	(16	6)	289	76	100	112	71	21	82	1	4	9	18	6	.75	10	.327	.399	.527
1992	Sea	AL	142	565	174	39	4	27	(16	11)	302	83	103	102	44	15	67	5	0	3	10	5	.67	15	.308	.361	.535
1993	Sea	AL	156	582	180	38	3	45	(21	24)	359	113	109	137	96	25	91	6	0	7	17	9	.65	14	.309	.408	.617
1994	Sea	AL	111	433	140	24	4	40	(18	22)	292	94	90	107	56	19	73	2	0	2	11	3	.79	9	.323	.402	.674
1995	Sea	AL	72	260	67	7	0	17	(13	4)	125	52	42	49	52	6	53	0	0	2	4	2	.67	4	.258	.379	.481
1996	Sea	AL	140	545	165	26	2	49	(26	23)	342	125	140	131	78	13	104	7	1	7	16	1	.94	7	.303	.392	.628
1997	Sea	AL	157	608	185	34	3	56	(27	**29**)	393	125	**147**	142	76	**23**	121	8	0	12	15	4	.79	12	.304	.382	**.646**
1998	Sea	AL	161	633	180	33	3	56	(30	26)	387	120	146	136	76	11	121	7	0	4	20	5	.80	14	.284	.365	.611
1999	Sea	AL	160	606	173	26	3	48	(27	21)	349	123	134	132	91	**17**	108	7	0	2	24	7	.77	6	.285	.384	.576
2000	Cin	NL	145	520	141	22	3	40	(22	18)	289	100	118	111	94	17	117	9	0	8	6	4	.60	7	.271	.387	.556
2001	Cin	NL	111	364	104	20	2	22	(12	10)	194	57	65	69	44	6	72	4	1	4	2	0	1.00	6	.286	.365	.533
2002	Cin	NL	70	197	52	8	0	8	(4	4)	84	17	23	27	28	6	39	3	0	4	1	2	.33	6	.264	.358	.426
2003	Cin	NL	53	166	41	12	1	13	(5	8)	94	34	26	26	27	5	44	6	1	1	1	0	1.00	3	.247	.370	.566
2004	Cin	NL	83	300	76	18	0	20	(11	9)	154	49	60	56	44	3	67	2	0	2	1	0	1.00	9	.253	.351	.513
2005	Cin	NL	128	491	148	30	0	35	(15	20)	283	85	92	89	54	3	93	3	0	7	0	1	.00	9	.301	.369	.576
2006	Cin	NL	109	428	108	19	0	27	(13	14)	208	62	72	55	39	6	78	2	0	3	0	0	-	13	.252	.316	.486
2007	Cin	NL	144	528	146	24	1	30	(17	13)	262	78	93	87	85	14	99	1	0	9	6	1	.86	14	.277	.372	.496
2008	2 Tms		143	490	122	30	1	18	(8	10)	208	67	71	79	78	14	89	3	0	4	0	1	.00	13	.249	.353	.424
2009	Sea	AL	117	387	83	19	0	19	(13	6)	159	44	57	50	63	2	80	1	0	3	0	0	-	6	.214	.324	.411
2010	Sea	AL	33	98	18	2	0	0	(0	0)	20	6	7	3	9	0	17	0	0	1	0	0	-	3	.184	.250	.204
	08 Cin	NL	102	359	88	20	1	15	(7	8)	155	51	53	59	61	13	64	2	0	3	0	1	.00	7	.245	.355	.432
	08 CWS	AL	41	131	34	10	0	3	(1	2)	53	16	18	20	17	1	25	1	0	1	0	0	-	6	.260	.347	.405
	Postseason		18	69	20	2	0	6	(3	3)	40	12	11	15	8	1	16	1	0	1	5	1	.83	0	.290	.367	.580
	22 ML YEARS		2671	9801	2781	524	38	630	(332	298)	5271	1662	1836	1865	1312	246	1779	81	8	102	184	69	.73	199	.284	.370	.538

Gabe Gross

Bats: L Throws: R Pos: RF-50; LF-44; PH-14; CF-10; PR-10; DH-3   Ht: 6'3" Wt: 220 Born: 10/21/1979 Age: 31

Year	Team	Lg	G	AB	H	2B	3B	HR	(Hm	Rd)	TB	R	RBI	RC	TBB	IBB	SO	HBP	SH	SF	SB	CS	SB%	GDP	Avg	OBP	Slg
2004	Tor	AL	44	129	27	4	0	3	(2	1)	40	18	16	15	19	0	31	0	0	0	2	2	.50	1	.209	.311	.310
2005	Tor	AL	40	92	23	4	1	1	(1	0)	32	11	7	11	10	0	21	0	0	0	1	1	.50	0	.250	.324	.348
2006	Mil	NL	117	208	57	15	0	9	(5	4)	99	42	38	42	36	3	60	2	3	3	1	0	1.00	3	.274	.382	.476
2007	Mil	NL	93	183	43	12	2	7	(4	3)	80	28	24	23	25	2	37	1	0	1	3	1	.75	1	.235	.329	.437
2008	2 Tms		143	345	82	16	3	13	(7	6)	143	46	40	46	50	0	82	2	0	2	4	2	.67	6	.238	.336	.414
2009	TB	AL	115	282	64	16	1	6	(2	4)	100	31	36	40	42	1	79	0	1	1	6	3	.67	2	.227	.326	.355
2010	Oak	AL	105	222	53	11	1	1	(0	1)	69	27	25	23	17	2	39	0	2	2	5	1	.83	5	.239	.290	.311
08	Mil	NL	16	43	9	3	0	0	(0	0)	12	6	2	6	10	0	7	0	0	1	2	0	1.00	0	.209	.352	.279
08	TB	AL	127	302	73	13	3	13	(7	6)	131	40	38	40	40	0	75	2	0	1	2	2	.50	6	.242	.333	.434
	Postseason		10	19	1	0	0	0	(0	0)	1	0	2	0	3	0	7	0	0	1	2	0	1.00	1	.053	.174	.053
7 ML YEARS			657	1461	349	78	8	40	(21	19)	563	203	186	200	199	8	349	5	6	9	22	10	.69	18	.239	.330	.385

Mark Grudzielanek

Bats: R Throws: R Pos: 2B-27; PH-2; DH-1   grudd-zuh-LAH-nick   Ht: 6'1" Wt: 190 Born: 6/30/1970 Age: 41

Year	Team	Lg	G	AB	H	2B	3B	HR	(Hm	Rd)	TB	R	RBI	RC	TBB	IBB	SO	HBP	SH	SF	SB	CS	SB%	GDP	Avg	OBP	Slg
1995	Mon	NL	78	269	66	12	2	1	(1	0)	85	27	20	24	14	4	47	7	3	0	8	3	.73	7	.245	.300	.316
1996	Mon	NL	153	657	201	34	4	6	(5	1)	261	99	49	90	26	3	83	9	1	3	33	7	.83	10	.306	.340	.397
1997	Mon	NL	156	649	177	54	3	4	(1	3)	249	76	51	75	23	0	76	10	3	3	25	9	.74	13	.273	.307	.384
1998	2 Tms		156	589	160	21	1	10	(5	5)	213	62	62	64	26	2	73	11	8	7	18	5	.78	18	.272	.311	.362
1999	LAD	NL	123	488	159	23	5	7	(4	3)	213	72	46	76	31	1	65	10	2	3	6	6	.50	13	.326	.376	.436
2000	LAD	NL	148	617	172	35	6	7	(4	3)	240	101	49	80	45	0	81	9	2	3	12	3	.80	16	.279	.335	.389
2001	LAD	NL	133	539	146	21	3	13	(8	5)	212	83	55	66	28	0	83	11	3	5	4	4	.50	9	.271	.317	.393
2002	LAD	NL	150	536	145	23	0	9	(5	4)	195	56	50	53	22	4	89	3	1	4	4	1	.80	17	.271	.301	.364
2003	ChC	NL	121	481	151	38	1	3	(2	1)	200	73	38	71	30	0	64	11	7	2	6	2	.75	12	.314	.366	.416
2004	ChC	NL	81	257	79	12	1	6	(3	3)	111	32	23	35	15	0	32	1	4	1	1	1	.50	7	.307	.347	.432
2005	StL	NL	137	528	155	30	3	8	(5	3)	215	64	59	68	23	3	81	7	0	2	8	6	.57	14	.294	.334	.407
2006	KC	AL	134	548	163	32	4	7	(5	2)	224	85	52	69	28	4	69	2	3	5	3	2	.60	12	.297	.331	.409
2007	KC	AL	116	453	137	32	3	6	(4	2)	193	70	51	64	23	2	60	8	0	2	1	2	.33	14	.302	.346	.426
2008	KC	AL	86	331	99	24	0	3	(2	1)	132	36	24	41	19	1	41	5	3	2	2	1	.67	8	.299	.345	.399
2010	Cle	AL	30	110	30	0	0	0	(0	0)	30	10	11	12	8	0	10	1	0	1	2	0	1.00	4	.273	.328	.273
98	Mon	NL	105	396	109	15	1	8	(3	5)	150	51	41	47	21	1	50	9	5	4	11	5	.69	11	.275	.323	.379
98	LAD	NL	51	193	51	6	0	2	(2	0)	63	11	21	17	5	1	23	2	3	3	7	0	1.00	7	.264	.286	.326
	Postseason		21	85	16	1	1	0	(0	0)	19	8	5	4	3	0	13	1	2	0	0	0	-	2	.188	.225	.224
15 ML YEARS			1802	7052	2040	391	36	90	(52	38)	2773	946	640	888	364	24	954	105	40	42	133	52	.72	174	.289	.332	.393

Vladimir Guerrero

Bats: R Throws: R Pos: DH-129; RF-17; PH-7; LF-1   Ht: 6'3" Wt: 235 Born: 2/9/1975 Age: 36

Year	Team	Lg	G	AB	H	2B	3B	HR	(Hm	Rd)	TB	R	RBI	RC	TBB	IBB	SO	HBP	SH	SF	SB	CS	SB%	GDP	Avg	OBP	Slg
1996	Mon	NL	9	27	5	0	0	1	(0	1)	8	2	1	1	0	0	3	0	0	0	0	0	-	0	.185	.185	.296
1997	Mon	NL	90	325	98	22	2	11	(5	6)	157	44	40	51	19	2	39	7	0	3	3	4	.43	11	.302	.350	.483
1998	Mon	NL	159	623	202	37	7	38	(19	19)	367	108	109	124	42	13	95	7	0	5	11	9	.55	15	.324	.371	.589
1999	Mon	NL	160	610	193	37	5	42	(23	19)	366	102	131	127	55	14	62	7	0	2	14	7	.67	18	.316	.378	.600
2000	Mon	NL	154	571	197	28	11	44	(25	19)	379	101	123	137	58	23	74	8	0	4	9	10	.47	15	.345	.410	.664
2001	Mon	NL	159	599	184	45	4	34	(21	13)	339	107	108	116	60	24	88	9	0	3	37	16	.70	24	.307	.377	.566
2002	Mon	NL	161	614	206	37	2	39	(20	19)	364	106	111	123	84	32	70	6	0	5	40	20	.67	20	.336	.417	.593
2003	Mon	NL	112	394	130	20	3	25	(15	10)	231	71	79	83	63	22	53	6	0	4	9	5	.64	18	.330	.426	.586
2004	LAA	AL	156	612	206	39	2	39	(19	20)	366	124	126	122	52	14	74	4	0	8	15	3	.83	19	.337	.391	.598
2005	LAA	AL	141	520	165	29	2	32	(19	13)	294	95	108	108	61	26	48	8	0	5	13	1	.93	16	.317	.394	.565
2006	LAA	AL	156	607	200	34	1	33	(14	19)	335	92	116	109	50	25	68	4	0	4	15	5	.75	16	.329	.382	.552
2007	LAA	AL	150	574	186	45	1	27	(13	14)	314	89	125	127	71	28	62	9	0	6	2	3	.40	19	.324	.403	.547
2008	LAA	AL	143	541	164	31	3	27	(13	14)	282	85	91	96	51	16	77	4	0	4	5	3	.63	27	.303	.365	.521
2009	LAA	AL	100	383	113	16	1	15	(7	8)	176	59	50	51	19	3	56	4	0	1	2	1	.67	16	.295	.334	.460
2010	Tex	AL	152	593	178	27	1	29	(16	13)	294	83	115	97	35	5	60	9	0	6	4	5	.44	19	.300	.345	.496
	Postseason		29	112	32	4	0	2	(1	1)	42	13	14	15	12	2	14	2	0	0	2	1	.67	2	.286	.365	.375
15 ML YEARS			2002	7593	2427	447	45	436	(229	207)	4272	1268	1433	1472	720	247	929	96	0	60	179	92	.66	254	.320	.383	.563

Matt Guerrier

Pitches: R Bats: R Pos: RP-74   gurr-REAR   Ht: 6'3" Wt: 195 Born: 8/2/1978 Age: 32

			HOW MUCH HE PITCHED					WHAT HE GAVE UP										THE RESULTS						
Year	Team	Lg	G	GS	CG	GF	IP	BFP	H	R	ER	HR	SH	SF	HB	TBB	IBB	SO	WP	Bk	W	L	Pct	Sh	Sv-Op	Hld	ERC	ERA
2004	Min	AL	9	2	0	5	19.0	84	22	13	12	5	2	0	1	6	0	11	0	0	0	1	.000	0	0-0	0	6.10	5.68
2005	Min	AL	43	0	0	14	71.2	306	71	29	27	6	4	1	3	24	5	46	3	0	0	3	.000	0	0-0	1	3.71	3.39
2006	Min	AL	39	1	0	13	69.2	300	78	29	26	9	3	4	0	21	0	37	6	0	1	0	1.000	0	1-1	2	4.59	3.36
2007	Min	AL	73	0	0	16	88.0	351	71	23	23	9	0	3	5	21	1	68	6	0	2	4	.333	0	1-4	14	2.70	2.35
2008	Min	AL	76	0	0	15	76.1	344	84	47	44	12	1	1	0	37	9	59	2	0	6	9	.400	0	1-5	20	5.20	5.19
2009	Min	AL	79	0	0	15	76.1	304	58	23	20	10	3	1	4	16	2	47	6	0	5	1	.833	0	1-4	33	2.44	2.36
2010	Min	AL	74	0	0	13	71.0	286	56	28	25	7	2	3	3	22	1	42	2	0	5	7	.417	0	1-7	23	2.78	3.17
	Postseason		3	0	0	1	3.0	9	0	0	0	0	0	0	0	0	0	2	0	0	0	0	-	0	0-0	1	0.00	0.00
7 ML YEARS			393	3	0	91	472.0	1975	440	192	177	58	15	13	16	147	18	310	25	0	19	25	.432	0	5-21	93	3.60	3.38

Carlos Guillen

Bats: B Throws: R Pos: 2B-47; DH-16; LF-4; PH-3   Ht: 6'1" Wt: 213 Born: 9/30/1975 Age: 35

Year	Team	Lg	G	AB	H	2B	3B	HR	(Hm	Rd)	TB	R	RBI	RC	TBB	IBB	SO	HBP	SH	SF	SB	CS	SB%	GDP	Avg	OBP	Slg
2010	Toledo*	AAA	5	18	6	3	0	1	(-	-)	12	5	2	4	2	1	4	0	0	0	0	0	-	0	.333	.400	.667
2010	WMich*	A	2	6	2	0	0	0	(-	-)	2	0	0	1	1	0	0	0	0	0	0	0	-	1	.333	.429	.333
1998	Sea	AL	10	39	13	1	1	0	(0	0)	16	9	5	7	3	0	9	0	0	0	2	0	1.00	0	.333	.381	.410
1999	Sea	AL	5	19	3	0	0	1	(1	0)	6	2	3	1	1	0	6	0	1	0	0	0	-	1	.158	.200	.316
2000	Sea	AL	90	288	74	15	2	7	(3	4)	114	45	42	36	28	0	53	2	7	3	1	3	.25	6	.257	.324	.396
2001	Sea	AL	140	456	118	21	4	5	(2	3)	162	72	53	56	53	0	89	1	7	6	4	1	.80	9	.259	.333	.355
2002	Sea	AL	134	475	124	24	6	9	(4	5)	187	73	56	58	46	4	91	1	3	3	4	5	.44	8	.261	.326	.394
2003	Sea	AL	109	388	107	19	3	7	(4	3)	153	63	52	53	52	2	64	1	5	5	4	4	.50	12	.276	.359	.394
2004	Det	AL	136	522	166	37	10	20	(7	13)	283	97	97	98	52	3	87	2	3	4	12	5	.71	12	.318	.379	.542
2005	Det	AL	87	334	107	15	4	5	(3	2)	145	48	23	39	24	3	45	2	0	1	2	3	.40	9	.320	.368	.434
2006	Det	AL	153	543	174	41	5	19	(10	9)	282	100	85	106	71	10	87	4	0	4	20	9	.69	16	.320	.400	.519
2007	Det	AL	151	564	167	35	9	21	(12	9)	283	86	102	94	55	10	93	3	0	8	13	8	.62	14	.296	.357	.502
2008	Det	AL	113	420	120	29	2	10	(8	2)	183	68	54	65	60	3	67	3	2	4	9	3	.75	11	.286	.376	.436
2009	Det	AL	81	277	67	10	3	11	(6	5)	116	36	41	38	39	2	56	3	0	3	1	3	.25	7	.242	.339	.419
2010	Det	AL	68	253	69	17	1	6	(4	2)	106	26	34	29	21	2	41	0	0	1	1	2	.33	10	.273	.327	.419
	Postseason		19	61	21	5	1	2	(0	2)	34	8	7	10	8	0	12	0	0	0	1	1	.50	2	.344	.420	.557
	13 ML YEARS		1277	4578	1309	264	50	121	(64	57)	2036	725	647	680	505	39	788	22	28	42	73	46	.61	115	.286	.357	.445

Jose Guillen

Bats: R Throws: R Pos: DH-84; RF-60; PH-5   Ht: 6'0" Wt: 216 Born: 5/17/1976 Age: 35

Year	Team	Lg	G	AB	H	2B	3B	HR	(Hm	Rd)	TB	R	RBI	RC	TBB	IBB	SO	HBP	SH	SF	SB	CS	SB%	GDP	Avg	OBP	Slg
1997	Pit	NL	143	498	133	20	5	14	(5	9)	205	58	70	56	17	0	88	8	0	3	1	2	.33	16	.267	.300	.412
1998	Pit	NL	153	573	153	38	2	14	(10	4)	237	60	84	68	21	0	100	6	1	4	3	5	.38	7	.267	.298	.414
1999	2 Tms		87	288	73	16	0	3	(1	2)	98	42	31	28	20	2	57	7	1	2	1	0	1.00	16	.253	.315	.340
2000	TB	AL	105	316	80	16	5	10	(5	5)	136	40	41	43	18	1	65	13	2	0	3	1	.75	6	.253	.320	.430
2001	TB	AL	41	135	37	5	0	3	(0	3)	51	14	11	15	6	2	26	3	0	1	2	3	.40	2	.274	.317	.378
2002	2 Tms	NL	85	240	57	7	0	8	(5	3)	88	25	31	16	14	1	43	3	1	1	4	5	.44	13	.238	.287	.367
2003	2 Tms		136	485	151	28	2	31	(14	17)	276	77	86	86	24	2	95	14	8	3	1	3	.25	16	.311	.359	.569
2004	LAA	AL	148	565	166	28	3	27	(13	14)	281	88	104	98	37	5	92	15	0	3	5	4	.56	14	.294	.352	.497
2005	Was	AL	148	551	156	32	2	24	(3	21)	264	81	76	72	31	6	102	19	1	9	1	1	.50	14	.283	.338	.479
2006	Was	NL	69	241	52	16	1	9	(4	5)	96	28	40	23	15	4	48	7	0	5	1	0	1.00	8	.216	.276	.398
2007	Sea	AL	153	593	172	28	2	23	(12	11)	273	84	99	90	41	2	118	19	0	5	5	1	.83	17	.290	.353	.460
2008	KC	AL	153	598	158	42	1	20	(8	12)	262	66	97	68	23	3	106	9	0	3	2	1	.67	23	.264	.300	.438
2009	KC	AL	81	281	68	8	0	9	(4	5)	103	30	40	33	22	1	50	8	0	1	1	0	1.00	13	.242	.314	.367
2010	2 Tms		148	524	135	22	2	19	(10	9)	218	55	77	67	32	1	113	14	0	6	1	0	1.00	17	.258	.314	.416
99	Pit	NL	40	120	32	6	0	1	(0	1)	41	18	18	12	10	1	21	0	1	1	1	0	1.00	7	.267	.321	.342
99	TB	AL	47	168	41	10	0	2	(1	1)	57	24	13	16	10	1	36	7	0	1	0	0	-	9	.244	.312	.339
02	Ari	NL	54	131	30	4	0	4	(3	1)	46	13	15	7	7	1	25	2	0	1	3	4	.43	7	.229	.277	.351
02	Cin	NL	31	109	27	3	0	4	(2	2)	42	12	16	9	7	0	18	1	1	0	1	1	.50	6	.248	.299	.385
03	Cin	NL	91	315	106	21	1	23	(10	13)	198	52	63	64	17	1	63	9	6	2	1	3	.25	8	.337	.385	.629
03	Oak	AL	45	170	45	7	1	8	(4	4)	78	25	23	22	7	1	32	5	2	1	0	0	-	8	.265	.311	.459
10	KC	AL	106	396	101	17	2	16	(8	8)	170	46	62	53	27	1	84	9	0	5	1	0	1.00	9	.255	.314	.429
10	SF	NL	42	128	34	5	0	3	(2	1)	48	9	15	14	5	0	29	5	0	1	0	0	-	8	.266	.317	.375
	Postseason		4	11	5	1	0	0	(0	0)	6	1	1	3	3	0	2	0	0	0	0	0	-	0	.455	.571	.545
	14 ML YEARS		1650	5888	1591	305	25	214	(94	120)	2588	748	887	763	321	30	1103	145	14	46	31	26	.54	182	.270	.321	.440

Jeremy Guthrie

Pitches: R Bats: R Pos: SP-32   Ht: 6'1" Wt: 205 Born: 4/8/1979 Age: 32

			HOW MUCH HE PITCHED					WHAT HE GAVE UP										THE RESULTS						
Year	Team	Lg	G	GS	CG	GF	IP	BFP	H	R	ER	HR	SH	SF	HB	TBB	IBB	SO	WP	Bk	W	L	Pct	Sh	Sv-Op	Hld	ERC	ERA
2004	Cle	AL	6	0	0	2	11.2	49	9	6	6	1	0	0	1	6	0	7	1	0	0	0	-	0	0-0	0	3.58	4.63
2005	Cle	AL	1	0	0	1	6.0	29	9	4	4	2	1	1	0	2	0	3	0	0	0	0	-	0	0-0	0	8.58	6.00
2006	Cle	AL	9	1	0	1	19.1	93	24	15	15	2	0	0	2	15	1	14	3	0	0	0	-	0	0-0	0	7.78	6.98
2007	Bal	AL	32	26	0	3	175.1	723	165	78	72	23	4	6	4	47	2	123	8	1	7	5	.583	0	0-1	0	3.55	3.70
2008	Bal	AL	30	30	1	0	190.2	796	176	82	77	24	2	2	7	58	2	120	3	0	10	12	.455	0	0-0	0	3.59	3.63
2009	Bal	AL	33	33	1	0	200.0	874	224	120	112	35	1	8	9	60	1	110	1	1	10	17	.370	0	0-0	0	5.08	5.04
2010	Bal	AL	32	32	0	0	209.1	872	193	93	89	25	3	9	16	50	1	119	1	1	11	14	.440	0	0-0	0	3.44	3.83
	7 ML YEARS		143	122	2	7	812.1	3436	800	398	375	112	11	26	39	238	7	496	17	3	38	48	.442	0	0-1	0	4.02	4.15

Franklin Gutierrez

Bats: R Throws: R Pos: CF-146; DH-5; PH-2   Ht: 6'2" Wt: 190 Born: 2/21/1983 Age: 28

Year	Team	Lg	G	AB	H	2B	3B	HR	(Hm	Rd)	TB	R	RBI	RC	TBB	IBB	SO	HBP	SH	SF	SB	CS	SB%	GDP	Avg	OBP	Slg
2005	Cle	AL	7	1	0	0	0	0	(0	0)	0	2	0	0	1	0	0	0	0	0	0	0	-	0	.000	.500	.000
2006	Cle	AL	43	136	37	9	0	1	(1	0)	49	21	8	12	3	0	28	1	0	2	0	0	-	4	.272	.288	.360
2007	Cle	AL	100	271	72	13	2	13	(10	3)	128	41	36	36	21	1	77	1	5	3	8	3	.73	7	.266	.318	.472
2008	Cle	AL	134	399	99	26	2	8	(6	2)	153	54	41	37	27	1	87	8	4	2	9	3	.75	10	.248	.307	.383
2009	Sea	AL	153	565	160	24	1	18	(7	11)	240	85	70	80	46	3	122	3	13	6	16	5	.76	14	.283	.339	.425
2010	Sea	AL	152	568	139	25	3	12	(6	6)	206	61	64	61	50	5	137	1	2	8	25	3	.89	10	.245	.303	.363
	Postseason		10	29	6	0	0	1	(0	1)	9	5	4	3	5	0	11	0	0	0	0	0	-	1	.207	.324	.310
	6 ML YEARS		589	1940	507	97	8	52	(30	22)	776	264	219	226	148	10	451	13	26	15	58	14	.81	45	.261	.316	.400

Juan Gutierrez

Pitches: R Bats: R Pos: RP-58 Ht: 6'3" Wt: 210 Born: 7/14/1983 Age: 27

			HOW MUCH HE PITCHED						WHAT HE GAVE UP											THE RESULTS							
Year	Team	Lg	G	GS	CG	GF	IP	BFP	H	R	ER	HR	SH	SF	HB	TBB	IBB	SO	WP	Bk	W	L	Pct	Sh	Sv-Op	Hld	ERC	ERA
2007	Hou	NL	7	3	0	1	21.1	93	25	14	14	3	0	3	0	6	2	16	1	0	1	1	.500	0	0-0	0	4.71	5.91
2009	Ari	NL	65	0	0	21	71.0	307	67	33	32	2	2	4	3	30	5	66	5	0	4	3	.571	0	9-10	7	3.38	4.06
2010	Ari	NL	58	0	0	35	56.2	247	55	33	32	13	1	1	4	23	5	47	1	0	0	6	.000	0	15-17	8	5.00	5.08
3 ML YEARS			130	3	0	57	149.0	647	147	80	78	18	3	8	7	59	12	129	7	0	5	10	.333	0	24-27	15	4.18	4.71

Angel Guzman

Pitches: R Bats: R Pos: P ANE-jell Ht: 6'3" Wt: 200 Born: 12/14/1981 Age: 29

			HOW MUCH HE PITCHED						WHAT HE GAVE UP											THE RESULTS							
Year	Team	Lg	G	GS	CG	GF	IP	BFP	H	R	ER	HR	SH	SF	HB	TBB	IBB	SO	WP	Bk	W	L	Pct	Sh	Sv-Op	Hld	ERC	ERA
2006	ChC	NL	15	10	0	1	56.0	272	68	48	46	9	5	3	6	37	1	60	8	1	0	6	.000	0	0-0	0	7.41	7.39
2007	ChC	NL	12	3	0	3	30.1	128	32	12	12	2	1	1	2	9	0	26	3	0	0	1	.000	0	0-1	0	4.10	3.56
2008	ChC	NL	6	1	0	1	9.2	44	10	6	6	1	0	0	1	4	0	10	1	0	0	0	-	0	0-0	0	4.65	5.59
2009	ChC	NL	55	0	0	14	61.0	245	41	20	20	8	5	2	1	23	4	47	1	0	3	3	.500	0	1-1	15	2.44	2.95
4 ML YEARS			88	14	0	19	157.0	689	151	86	84	20	11	6	10	73	5	143	13	1	3	10	.231	0	1-2	15	4.53	4.82

Cristian Guzman

Bats: B Throws: R Pos: 2B-72; SS-23; PH-12; RF-8; DH-4; PR-2 Ht: 6'0" Wt: 211 Born: 3/21/1978 Age: 33

			BATTING																	BASERUNNING				AVERAGES		
Year	Team	Lg	G	AB	H	2B	3B	HR	(Hm	Rd)	TB	R	RBI	RC	TBB	IBB	SO	HBP	SH	SF	SB	CS	SB%	GDP	Avg	OBP	Slg
2010	Frisco*	AA	4	13	4	0	0	0	(-	-)	4	1	3	2	3	0	1	0	0	0	1	0	1.00	6	.308	.438	.308
1999	Min	AL	131	420	95	12	3	1	(1	0)	116	47	26	29	22	0	90	3	7	4	9	7	.56	6	.226	.267	.276
2000	Min	AL	156	631	156	25	20	8	(3	5)	245	89	54	76	46	1	101	2	7	4	28	10	.74	5	.247	.299	.388
2001	Min	AL	118	493	149	28	14	10	(7	3)	235	80	51	79	21	0	78	5	8	0	25	8	.76	6	.302	.337	.477
2002	Min	AL	148	623	170	31	6	9	(6	3)	240	80	59	63	17	2	79	2	8	6	12	13	.48	12	.273	.292	.385
2003	Min	AL	143	534	143	15	14	3	(1	2)	195	78	53	62	30	0	79	5	12	4	18	9	.67	4	.268	.311	.365
2004	Min	AL	145	576	158	31	4	8	(5	3)	221	84	46	66	30	4	64	1	13	4	10	5	.67	15	.274	.309	.384
2005	Was	NL	142	456	100	19	6	4	(0	4)	143	39	31	26	25	6	76	1	8	2	7	4	.64	12	.219	.260	.314
2007	Was	NL	46	174	57	6	6	2	(1	1)	81	31	14	30	15	1	21	1	0	2	2	0	1.00	1	.328	.380	.466
2008	Was	NL	138	579	183	35	5	9	(4	5)	255	72	55	58	23	1	57	5	1	4	6	5	.55	10	.316	.345	.440
2009	Was	NL	135	531	151	24	7	6	(5	1)	207	74	52	58	16	0	75	1	6	1	4	5	.44	5	.284	.306	.390
2010	2 Tms		104	365	97	12	4	2	(1	1)	123	48	26	39	20	3	63	5	4	2	4	2	.67	9	.266	.311	.337
10	Was	NL	89	319	90	11	4	2	(1	1)	115	44	25	39	17	3	53	5	3	2	4	2	.67	7	.282	.327	.361
10	Tex	AL	15	46	7	1	0	0	(0	0)	8	4	1	0	3	0	10	0	1	0	0	0	-	2	.152	.204	.174
Postseason			18	67	16	3	0	1	(0	1)	22	9	2	5	5	0	12	1	2	0	3	0	1.00	0	.239	.301	.328
11 ML YEARS			1406	5382	1459	238	89	62	(34	28)	2061	727	467	612	265	18	783	31	74	33	125	68	.65	89	.271	.307	.383

Tony Gwynn

Bats: L Throws: R Pos: CF-105; PH-24; PR-1 Ht: 5'11" Wt: 193 Born: 10/4/1982 Age: 28

			BATTING																	BASERUNNING				AVERAGES		
Year	Team	Lg	G	AB	H	2B	3B	HR	(Hm	Rd)	TB	R	RBI	RC	TBB	IBB	SO	HBP	SH	SF	SB	CS	SB%	GDP	Avg	OBP	Slg
2006	Mil	NL	32	77	20	2	1	0	(0	0)	24	5	4	5	2	0	15	0	0	1	3	1	.75	2	.260	.275	.312
2007	Mil	NL	69	123	32	3	2	0	(0	0)	39	13	10	16	12	1	24	0	0	0	8	1	.89	6	.260	.326	.317
2008	Mil	NL	29	42	8	1	0	0	(0	0)	9	5	1	2	4	0	7	1	1	0	3	1	.75	1	.190	.271	.214
2009	SD	NL	119	393	106	11	6	2	(1	1)	135	59	21	48	48	2	65	2	5	3	11	7	.61	2	.270	.350	.344
2010	SD	NL	117	289	59	9	3	3	(2	1)	83	30	20	31	41	4	50	1	7	1	17	4	.81	3	.204	.304	.287
Postseason			3	3	1	0	0	0	(0	0)	1	0	0	0	0	0	1	0	0	0	0	0	-	0	.333	.333	.333
5 ML YEARS			366	924	225	26	12	5	(3	2)	290	112	56	102	107	7	161	4	13	6	42	14	.75	8	.244	.323	.314

Charlie Haeger

Pitches: R Bats: R Pos: SP-6; RP-3 HAY-gurr Ht: 6'1" Wt: 214 Born: 9/19/1983 Age: 27

			HOW MUCH HE PITCHED						WHAT HE GAVE UP											THE RESULTS							
Year	Team	Lg	G	GS	CG	GF	IP	BFP	H	R	ER	HR	SH	SF	HB	TBB	IBB	SO	WP	Bk	W	L	Pct	Sh	Sv-Op	Hld	ERC	ERA
2010	InldEm*	A+	5	5	0	0	21.0	93	21	14	12	2	0	1	0	12	0	17	0	0	2	3	.400	0	0- -	-	4.77	5.14
2010	Albq*	AAA	11	10	0	0	53.2	245	45	38	34	4	2	4	1	42	0	41	8	0	4	3	.571	0	0- -	-	4.51	5.70
2010	Ddgrs*	R	1	1	0	0	2.0	7	0	0	0	0	0	0	0	0	0	4	0	0	0	0	-	0	0-0	-	0.00	0.00
2006	CWS	AL	7	1	0	4	18.1	79	12	10	7	0	0	0	0	13	0	19	0	0	1	1	.500	0	1-1	0	2.65	3.44
2007	CWS	AL	8	0	0	5	11.1	59	17	11	9	3	1	1	1	8	2	1	0	0	0	1	.000	0	0-0	1	10.02	7.15
2008	SD	NL	4	0	0	1	4.1	28	8	10	8	2	0	0	2	5	0	4	0	0	0	0	-	0	0-0	0	19.18	16.62
2009	LAD	NL	6	3	0	2	19.0	79	13	7	7	4	1	0	2	7	0	15	0	0	1	1	.500	0	0-0	0	3.31	3.32
2010	LAD	NL	9	6	0	1	30.0	151	36	32	28	4	1	1	1	26	0	30	4	0	0	4	.000	0	0-0	0	7.59	8.40
5 ML YEARS			34	10	0	13	83.0	396	86	70	59	13	3	2	6	59	2	69	4	0	2	7	.222	0	1-1	1	6.18	6.40

Travis Hafner

Bats: L Throws: R Pos: DH-109; PH-10 HAFF-nerr Ht: 6'3" Wt: 240 Born: 6/3/1977 Age: 34

			BATTING																	BASERUNNING				AVERAGES		
Year	Team	Lg	G	AB	H	2B	3B	HR	(Hm	Rd)	TB	R	RBI	RC	TBB	IBB	SO	HBP	SH	SF	SB	CS	SB%	GDP	Avg	OBP	Slg
2002	Tex	AL	23	62	15	4	1	1	(0	1)	24	6	6	7	8	1	15	0	0	0	0	1	.00	0	.242	.329	.387
2003	Cle	AL	91	291	74	19	3	14	(7	7)	141	35	40	42	22	2	81	10	0	1	2	1	.67	7	.254	.327	.485
2004	Cle	AL	140	482	150	41	3	28	(7	21)	281	96	109	103	68	7	111	17	0	6	3	2	.60	11	.311	.410	.583
2005	Cle	AL	137	486	148	42	0	33	(14	19)	289	94	108	115	79	7	123	9	0	4	0	0	-	9	.305	.408	.595
2006	Cle	AL	129	454	140	31	1	42	(21	21)	299	100	117	118	100	16	111	7	0	2	0	0	-	10	.308	.439	.659
2007	Cle	AL	152	545	145	25	2	24	(12	12)	246	80	100	94	102	17	115	4	0	5	1	1	.50	15	.266	.385	.451

Year Team	Lg	G	AB	H	2B	3B	HR	(Hm	Rd)	TB	R	RBI	RC	TBB	IBB	SO	HBP	SH	SF	SB	CS	SB%	GDP	Avg	OBP	Slg
2008 Cle	AL	57	198	39	10	0	5	(2	3)	64	21	24	21	27	6	55	5	0	3	1	1	.50	4	.197	.305	.323
2009 Cle	AL	94	338	92	19	0	16	(9	7)	159	46	49	49	41	6	67	3	0	1	0	0	-	7	.272	.355	.470
2010 Cle	AL	118	396	110	29	0	13	(10	3)	178	46	50	57	51	10	94	12	0	3	2	1	.67	2	.278	.374	.449
Postseason		11	43	8	1	0	2	(1	1)	15	6	4	3	7	1	15	0	0	0	0	0	-	1	.186	.300	.349
9 ML YEARS		941	3252	913	220	10	176	(82	94)	1681	524	603	606	498	72	772	70	0	25	9	7	.56	65	.281	.385	.517

Jerry Hairston

Bats: R Throws: R Pos: SS-62; 2B-47; RF-8; PH-7; LF-4; 3B-3; PR-1   Ht: 5'10" Wt: 190 Born: 5/29/1976 Age: 35

Year Team	Lg	G	AB	H	2B	3B	HR	(Hm	Rd)	TB	R	RBI	RC	TBB	IBB	SO	HBP	SH	SF	SB	CS	SB%	GDP	Avg	OBP	Slg
1998 Bal	AL	6	7	0	0	0	0	(0	0)	0	2	0	0	0	0	1	0	0	0	0	0	-	0	.000	.000	.000
1999 Bal	AL	50	175	47	12	1	4	(1	3)	73	26	17	24	11	0	24	3	4	0	9	4	.69	2	.269	.323	.417
2000 Bal	AL	49	180	46	5	0	5	(2	3)	66	27	19	22	21	0	22	6	5	0	8	5	.62	8	.256	.353	.367
2001 Bal	AL	159	532	124	25	5	8	(5	3)	183	63	47	57	44	0	73	13	9	4	29	11	.73	12	.233	.305	.344
2002 Bal	AL	122	426	114	25	3	5	(2	3)	160	55	32	55	34	0	55	7	8	4	21	6	.78	5	.268	.329	.376
2003 Bal	AL	58	218	59	12	2	2	(1	1)	81	25	21	32	23	0	25	6	10	2	14	5	.74	8	.271	.353	.372
2004 Bal	AL	86	287	87	19	1	2	(0	2)	114	43	24	45	29	1	29	8	6	4	13	8	.62	3	.303	.378	.397
2005 ChC	NL	114	380	99	25	2	4	(3	1)	140	51	30	46	31	0	46	12	7	0	8	9	.47	5	.261	.336	.368
2006 2 Tms		101	170	35	6	1	0	(0	0)	43	25	10	9	13	2	34	2	7	0	5	2	.71	5	.206	.270	.253
2007 Tex	AL	73	159	30	7	0	3	(1	2)	46	26	16	12	11	0	24	3	7	4	5	1	.83	5	.189	.249	.289
2008 Cin	NL	80	261	85	20	2	6	(3	3)	127	47	36	52	23	0	36	3	8	2	15	3	.83	0	.326	.384	.487
2009 2 Tms		131	383	96	23	1	10	(8	2)	151	62	39	42	32	0	54	6	8	4	7	4	.64	3	.251	.315	.394
2010 SD	NL	119	430	105	13	2	10	(7	3)	152	53	50	47	31	2	54	5	4	6	9	6	.60	5	.244	.299	.353
06 ChC	NL	38	82	17	3	0	0	(0	0)	20	8	4	5	4	2	14	1	5	0	3	0	1.00	1	.207	.253	.244
06 Tex	AL	63	88	18	3	1	0	(0	0)	23	17	6	4	9	0	20	1	2	0	2	2	.50	4	.205	.286	.261
09 Cin	NL	86	307	78	18	1	8	(6	2)	122	47	27	30	21	0	46	3	6	3	7	3	.70	2	.254	.305	.397
09 NYY	AL	45	76	18	5	0	2	(2	0)	29	15	12	12	11	0	8	3	2	1	0	1	.00	1	.237	.352	.382
Postseason		6	8	2	0	0	0	(0	0)	2	1	0	0	0	0	2	0	1	0	0	0	-	0	.250	.250	.250
13 ML YEARS		1148	3608	927	192	20	59	(33	26)	1336	501	341	443	303	5	477	74	83	30	143	64	.69	61	.257	.325	.370

Scott Hairston

Bats: R Throws: R Pos: LF-71; PH-21; CF-19; RF-6; DH-1; PR-1   Ht: 6'0" Wt: 196 Born: 5/25/1980 Age: 31

Year Team	Lg	G	AB	H	2B	3B	HR	(Hm	Rd)	TB	R	RBI	RC	TBB	IBB	SO	HBP	SH	SF	SB	CS	SB%	GDP	Avg	OBP	Slg
2010 Lk Els*	A+	3	7	4	1	0	0	(-	-)	5	1	1	3	4	0	1	0	0	0	0	0	-	0	.571	.727	.714
2004	NL	101	339	84	15	6	13	(6	7)	150	39	29	32	21	0	88	1	2	1	3	3	.50	4	.248	.293	.442
2005 Ari	NL	15	20	2	1	0	0	(0	0)	3	0	0	0	1	0	6	0	0	0	0	0	-	1	.100	.100	.150
2006 Ari	NL	9	15	6	2	0	0	(0	0)	8	2	2	2	1	0	5	0	0	0	0	0	-	1	.400	.438	.533
2007 2 Tms		107	263	64	18	2	11	(6	5)	119	37	36	36	26	0	55	1	3	1	2	0	1.00	4	.243	.313	.452
2008 SD	NL	112	326	81	18	3	17	(9	8)	156	42	31	43	28	2	84	3	3	2	3	1	.75	2	.248	.312	.479
2009 2 Tms		116	430	114	27	2	17	(9	8)	196	50	64	60	25	0	83	3	1	5	11	3	.79	9	.265	.307	.456
2010 SD	NL	104	295	62	10	0	10	(5	5)	102	34	36	28	31	1	69	6	0	4	6	1	.86	3	.210	.295	.346
07 Ari	NL	76	176	39	13	1	3	(1	2)	63	21	16	19	19	0	37	1	3	0	2	0	1.00	4	.222	.301	.358
07 SD	NL	31	87	25	5	1	8	(5	3)	56	16	20	17	7	0	18	0	0	1	0	0	-	0	.287	.337	.644
09 SD	NL	56	197	59	14	1	10	(5	5)	105	20	29	35	17	0	45	1	1	0	8	1	.80	4	.290	.368	.533
09 Oak	AL	60	233	55	13	1	7	(4	3)	91	24	35	25	8	0	38	2	0	5	3	2	.60	5	.236	.262	.391
7 ML YEARS		564	1688	413	91	13	68	(35	33)	734	204	198	201	132	3	390	14	9	13	25	8	.76	24	.245	.303	.435

Bill Hall

Bats: R Throws: R Pos: LF-55; 2B-51; PH-13; RF-9; CF-7; SS-6; 3B-6; PR-4   Ht: 6'0" Wt: 210 Born: 12/28/1979 Age: 31

Year Team	Lg	G	AB	H	2B	3B	HR	(Hm	Rd)	TB	R	RBI	RC	TBB	IBB	SO	HBP	SH	SF	SB	CS	SB%	GDP	Avg	OBP	Slg
2002 Mil	NL	19	36	7	1	1	1	(0	1)	13	3	5	3	3	0	13	0	0	0	0	1	.00	1	.194	.256	.361
2003 Mil	NL	52	142	37	9	2	5	(2	3)	65	23	20	18	7	0	28	1	4	1	1	2	.33	5	.261	.298	.458
2004 Mil	NL	126	390	93	20	3	9	(5	4)	146	43	53	41	20	1	119	1	2	2	12	6	.67	4	.238	.276	.374
2005 Mil	NL	146	501	146	39	6	17	(12	5)	248	69	62	73	39	2	103	1	2	3	18	6	.75	11	.291	.342	.495
2006 Mil	NL	148	537	145	39	4	35	(18	17)	297	101	85	87	63	6	162	1	3	4	8	9	.47	12	.270	.345	.553
2007 Mil	NL	136	452	115	35	0	14	(10	4)	192	59	63	59	40	1	128	3	1	7	5	4	.44	9	.254	.315	.425
2008 Mil	NL	128	404	91	22	1	15	(10	5)	160	50	55	43	37	2	124	3	1	3	5	6	.45	9	.225	.293	.396
2009 2 Tms		110	334	67	20	1	8	(4	4)	113	32	36	23	27	0	120	0	0	4	2	2	.50	11	.201	.258	.338
2010 Bos	AL	120	344	85	16	1	18	(8	10)	157	44	46	51	34	0	104	1	2	1	9	1	.90	1	.247	.316	.456
09 Mil	NL	76	214	43	12	0	6	(3	3)	73	22	24	15	19	0	72	0	0	1	1	0	1.00	10	.201	.265	.341
09 Sea	AL	34	120	24	8	1	2	(1	1)	40	10	12	8	8	0	48	0	0	3	1	2	.33	1	.200	.244	.333
Postseason		3	8	2	0	0	0	(0	0)	2	1	0	1	1	0	3	0	0	0	0	0	-	0	.250	.333	.250
9 ML YEARS		985	3140	786	201	19	122	(69	53)	1391	424	425	398	270	12	901	11	15	25	59	38	.61	61	.250	.310	.443

Roy Halladay

Pitches: R Bats: R Pos: SP-33   Ht: 6'6" Wt: 230 Born: 5/14/1977 Age: 34

	HOW MUCH HE PITCHED						WHAT HE GAVE UP											THE RESULTS						
Year Team	Lg	G	GS	CG	GF	IP	BFP	H	R	ER	HR	SH	SF	HB	TBB	IBB	SO	WP	Bk	W	L	Pct	Sh	Sv-Op	Hld	ERC	ERA
1998 Tor	AL	2	2	1	0	14.0	53	9	4	3	2	0	0	2	2	0	13	0	0	1	0	1.000	1	0-0	0	1.61	1.93
1999 Tor	AL	36	18	1	2	149.1	668	156	76	65	19	3	4	4	79	1	82	6	0	8	7	.533	1	1-1	2	5.19	3.92
2000 Tor	AL	19	13	0	4	67.2	349	107	87	80	14	2	3	2	42	0	44	6	1	4	7	.364	0	0-0	0	9.70	10.64
2001 Tor	AL	17	16	1	0	105.1	432	97	41	37	3	3	1	1	25	0	96	4	1	5	3	.625	1	0-0	0	2.61	3.16
2002 Tor	AL	34	34	2	0	239.1	993	223	93	78	10	2	9	7	62	6	168	4	1	19	7	.731	1	0-0	0	2.85	2.93
2003 Tor	AL	36	36	9	0	266.0	1071	253	111	96	26	3	2	9	32	1	204	6	1	22	7	.759	2	0-0	0	2.86	3.25
2004 Tor	AL	21	21	1	0	133.0	561	140	66	62	13	4	3	1	39	1	95	2	2	8	8	.500	1	0-0	0	4.00	4.20

Year	Team	Lg	HOW MUCH HE PITCHED						WHAT HE GAVE UP													THE RESULTS							
			G	GS	CG	GF	IP	BFP	H	R	ER	HR	SH	SF	HB	TBB	IBB	SO	WP	Bk	W	L	Pct	Sh	Sv-Op	Hld	ERC	ERA
2005	Tor	AL	19	19	5	0	141.2	553	118	39	38	11	2	1	7	18	2	108	2	1	12	4	.750	2	0-0	0	2.26	2.41
2006	Tor	AL	32	32	4	0	220.0	876	208	82	78	19	3	5	5	34	5	132	3	1	16	5	.762	0	0-0	0	2.87	3.19
2007	Tor	AL	31	31	7	0	225.1	927	232	101	93	15	2	7	3	48	3	139	4	0	16	7	.696	1	0-0	0	3.37	3.71
2008	Tor	AL	34	33	9	0	246.0	987	220	88	76	18	5	4	12	39	3	206	4	0	20	11	.645	2	0-0	1	2.62	2.78
2009	Tor	AL	32	32	9	0	239.0	963	234	82	74	22	1	9	5	35	0	208	2	0	17	10	.630	4	0-0	0	3.06	2.79
2010	Phi	NL	33	33	9	0	250.2	993	231	74	68	24	9	5	6	30	1	219	5	1	21	10	.677	4	0-0	0	2.69	2.44
13 ML YEARS			346	320	58	6	2297.1	9426	2228	944	848	196	46	46	62	485	23	1714	48	8	169	86	.663	19	1-1	3	3.20	3.32

Greg Halman

Bats: R **Throws:** R **Pos:** LF-4; CF-4; PR-2; RF-1   HALL-min   **Ht:** 6'4" **Wt:** 192 **Born:** 8/26/1987 **Age:** 23

Year	Team	Lg	BATTING																			BASERUNNING				AVERAGES		
			G	AB	H	2B	3B	HR	(Hm	Rd)	TB	R	RBI	RC	TBB	IBB	SO	HBP	SH	SF	SB	CS	SB%	GDP	Avg	OBP	Slg
2005	Ms	R	26	89	23	2	3	3	(-	-)	40	17	11	13	10	0	19	3	0	1	1	3	.25	5	.258	.350	.449
2006	Everett	A-	28	116	30	6	4	5	(-	-)	59	19	15	17	3	1	32	3	1	0	10	4	.71	2	.259	.295	.509
2007	Wisc	A	52	187	34	5	0	4	(-	-)	51	26	15	11	8	0	77	5	1	1	15	7	.68	1	.182	.234	.273
2007	Everett	A-	62	238	73	19	1	16	(-	-)	142	37	37	51	21	4	85	4	1	1	16	8	.67	2	.307	.371	.597
2008	Hi Dsrt	A+	67	257	69	15	3	19	(-	-)	147	52	53	51	16	1	76	5	1	3	23	1	.96	6	.268	.320	.572
2008	WTenn	AA	62	236	65	14	2	10	(-	-)	113	43	30	37	16	2	67	4	0	1	8	6	.57	6	.275	.331	.479
2009	WTenn	AA	121	457	96	17	2	25	(-	-)	192	64	72	54	29	1	183	15	2	3	9	7	.56	9	.210	.278	.420
2009	Ms	R	3	11	2	0	1	0	(-	-)	4	1	2	1	2	0	8	0	0	0	0	0	-	0	.182	.308	.364
2010	Tacom	AAA	112	424	103	21	4	33	(-	-)	231	82	80	73	37	0	169	4	0	0	15	4	.79	8	.243	.310	.545
2010	Sea	AL	9	29	4	1	0	0	(0	0)	5	1	3	1	1	0	11	0	0	0	1	0	1.00	0	.138	.167	.172

Cole Hamels

Pitches: L **Bats:** L **Pos:** SP-33   **Ht:** 6'3" **Wt:** 192 **Born:** 12/27/1983 **Age:** 27

Year	Team	Lg	HOW MUCH HE PITCHED						WHAT HE GAVE UP													THE RESULTS							
			G	GS	CG	GF	IP	BFP	H	R	ER	HR	SH	SF	HB	TBB	IBB	SO	WP	Bk	W	L	Pct	Sh	Sv-Op	Hld	ERC	ERA
2006	Phi	NL	23	23	0	0	132.1	558	117	66	60	19	6	8	3	48	4	145	5	0	9	8	.529	0	0-0	0	3.61	4.08
2007	Phi	NL	28	28	2	0	183.1	743	163	72	69	25	5	5	3	43	4	177	5	0	15	5	.750	0	0-0	0	3.12	3.39
2008	Phi	NL	33	33	2	0	227.1	914	193	80	78	28	6	2	1	53	7	196	0	0	14	10	.583	2	0-0	0	2.76	3.09
2009	Phi	NL	32	32	2	0	193.2	814	206	95	93	24	7	5	5	43	4	168	1	0	10	11	.476	2	0-0	0	3.98	4.32
2010	Phi	NL	33	33	1	0	208.2	856	185	74	71	26	7	0	8	61	5	211	3	0	12	11	.522	0	0-0	0	3.36	3.06
Postseason			10	10	0	0	60.2	244	51	26	26	9	2	2	1	17	0	52	0	0	5	3	.625	0	0-0	0	3.18	3.86
5 ML YEARS			149	149	7	0	945.1	3885	864	396	371	122	31	20	20	248	24	897	14	0	60	45	.571	4	0-0	0	3.32	3.53

Josh Hamilton

Bats: L **Throws:** L **Pos:** LF-92; CF-40; DH-13; PH-4   **Ht:** 6'4" **Wt:** 240 **Born:** 5/21/1981 **Age:** 30

Year	Team	Lg	BATTING																			BASERUNNING				AVERAGES		
			G	AB	H	2B	3B	HR	(Hm	Rd)	TB	R	RBI	RC	TBB	IBB	SO	HBP	SH	SF	SB	CS	SB%	GDP	Avg	OBP	Slg
2007	Cin	NL	90	298	87	17	2	19	(11	8)	165	52	47	58	33	4	65	4	0	2	3	3	.50	6	.292	.368	.554
2008	Tex	AL	156	624	190	35	5	32	(19	13)	331	98	130	119	64	9	126	7	0	9	9	1	.90	8	.304	.371	.530
2009	Tex	AL	89	336	90	19	2	10	(6	4)	143	43	54	51	24	2	79	1	0	4	8	3	.73	5	.268	.315	.426
2010	Tex	AL	133	518	186	40	3	32	(22	10)	328	95	100	121	43	5	95	5	1	4	8	1	.89	11	.359	.411	.633
4 ML YEARS			468	1776	553	111	12	93	(58	35)	967	288	331	349	164	20	365	17	1	19	28	8	.78	30	.311	.371	.544

Mark Hamilton

Bats: L **Throws:** L **Pos:** PH-6; 1B-4   **Ht:** 6'3" **Wt:** 220 **Born:** 7/29/1984 **Age:** 26

Year	Team	Lg	BATTING																			BASERUNNING				AVERAGES		
			G	AB	H	2B	3B	HR	(Hm	Rd)	TB	R	RBI	RC	TBB	IBB	SO	HBP	SH	SF	SB	CS	SB%	GDP	Avg	OBP	Slg
2006	StCol	A-	30	106	28	3	1	8	(-	-)	57	18	24	20	13	2	24	1	0	1	1	1	.50	1	.264	.347	.538
2006	QuadC	A	38	142	36	8	0	3	(-	-)	53	16	25	16	10	0	32	1	0	0	0	0	-	5	.254	.307	.373
2007	PlmBh	A+	60	221	64	12	0	13	(-	-)	115	31	49	40	20	0	48	1	0	2	1	0	1.00	5	.290	.348	.520
2007	Sprgfld	AA	68	248	62	15	0	6	(-	-)	95	32	41	31	24	2	55	1	2	1	1	1	.50	4	.250	.318	.383
2008	Sprgfld	AA	70	245	59	11	0	8	(-	-)	94	27	29	34	35	2	67	1	0	0	0	0	-	7	.241	.338	.384
2009	Sprgfld	AA	48	163	50	11	0	8	(-	-)	85	26	28	36	28	3	44	4	0	0	1	1	.00	6	.307	.421	.521
2009	Memp	AAA	46	130	40	11	0	6	(-	-)	69	22	19	25	13	0	34	1	0	0	0	0	-	3	.308	.375	.531
2010	Memp	AAA	72	258	77	20	0	18	(-	-)	151	53	60	59	35	1	70	7	0	6	0	0	-	2	.298	.389	.585
2010	Cards	R	9	27	8	1	0	2	(-	-)	15	2	2	6	4	0	9	1	0	0	0	0	-	0	.296	.406	.556
2010	StL	NL	9	14	2	0	0	0	(0	0)	2	0	0	0	1	0	5	0	0	0	0	0	-	0	.143	.200	.143

Jason Hammel

Pitches: R **Bats:** R **Pos:** SP-30   **Ht:** 6'6" **Wt:** 215 **Born:** 9/2/1982 **Age:** 28

Year	Team	Lg	HOW MUCH HE PITCHED						WHAT HE GAVE UP													THE RESULTS							
			G	GS	CG	GF	IP	BFP	H	R	ER	HR	SH	SF	HB	TBB	IBB	SO	WP	Bk	W	L	Pct	Sh	Sv-Op	Hld	ERC	ERA
2010	ColSpr*	AAA	1	1	0	0	7.0	29	9	4	4	1	0	1	0	6	0	6	0	0	1	0	1.000	0	0--	-	5.23	5.14
2006	TB	AL	9	9	0	0	44.0	208	61	38	38	7	0	3	1	21	0	32	3	2	0	6	.000	0	0-0	0	7.40	7.77
2007	TB	AL	24	14	0	2	85.0	384	100	58	58	12	2	0	2	40	1	64	3	0	3	5	.375	0	0-0	0	5.86	6.14
2008	TB	AL	40	5	0	21	78.1	346	83	45	40	11	2	2	2	35	4	44	7	0	4	4	.500	0	2-2	1	4.94	4.60
2009	Col	NL	34	30	1	0	176.2	771	203	94	85	17	10	9	9	42	6	133	4	0	10	8	.556	0	0-0	0	4.37	4.33
2010	Col	NL	30	30	0	0	177.2	770	201	97	95	18	11	6	6	47	1	141	13	2	10	9	.526	0	0-0	0	4.41	4.81
Postseason			1	1	0	0	3.2	17	4	4	4	1	0	0	0	3	0	5	0	0	0	0	-	0	0-0	0	8.12	9.82
5 ML YEARS			137	88	1	23	561.2	2479	648	332	316	65	25	20	20	185	12	414	30	4	27	32	.458	0	2-2	1	4.90	5.06

Mike Hampton

Pitches: L **Bats:** R **Pos:** RP-10   **Ht:** 5'10" **Wt:** 195 **Born:** 9/9/1972 **Age:** 38

Year	Team	Lg	G	GS	CG	GF	IP	BFP	H	R	ER	HR	SH	SF	HB	TBB	IBB	SO	WP	Bk	W	L	Pct	Sh	Sv-Op	Hld	ERC	ERA
2010	Reno*	AAA	4	0	0	0	3.1	15	3	1	1	0	1	0	1	2	0	1	0	0	1	0	1.000	0	0-0	0	3.46	2.70
1993	Sea	AL	13	3	0	2	17.0	95	28	20	18	3	1	1	0	17	3	8	1	1	1	3	.250	0	1-1	2	11.09	9.53
1994	Hou	NL	44	0	0	7	41.1	181	46	19	17	4	0	0	2	16	1	24	5	1	2	1	.667	0	0-1	10	4.88	3.70
1995	Hou	NL	24	24	0	0	150.2	641	141	73	56	13	11	5	4	49	3	115	3	1	9	8	.529	0	0-0	0	3.37	3.35
1996	Hou	NL	27	27	2	0	160.1	691	175	79	64	12	10	3	3	49	1	101	7	2	10	10	.500	1	0-0	0	4.11	3.59
1997	Hou	NL	34	34	7	0	223.0	941	217	105	95	16	11	7	2	77	2	139	6	1	15	10	.600	2	0-0	0	3.56	3.83
1998	Hou	NL	32	32	1	0	211.2	917	227	92	79	18	7	7	5	81	1	137	4	2	11	7	.611	1	0-0	0	4.45	3.36
1999	Hou	NL	34	34	3	0	239.0	979	206	86	77	12	10	9	5	101	2	177	9	0	**22**	4	**.846**	2	0-0	0	3.25	2.90
2000	NYM	NL	33	33	3	0	217.2	929	194	89	76	10	11	5	8	99	5	151	10	0	15	10	.600	1	0-0	0	3.44	3.14
2001	Col	NL	32	32	2	0	203.0	904	236	138	122	31	8	6	8	85	7	122	6	0	14	13	.519	1	0-0	0	5.69	5.41
2002	Col	NL	30	30	0	0	178.2	838	228	**135**	122	24	2	9	7	91	4	74	9	2	7	15	.318	0	0-0	0	6.61	6.15
2003	Atl	NL	31	31	1	0	190.0	823	186	91	81	14	10	5	1	78	4	110	10	1	14	8	.636	0	0-0	0	3.77	3.84
2004	Atl	NL	29	29	1	0	172.1	760	198	86	82	15	8	3	1	65	3	87	3	2	13	9	.591	0	0-0	0	4.76	4.28
2005	Atl	NL	12	12	1	0	69.1	284	74	28	27	5	2	1	0	18	0	27	1	0	5	3	.625	1	0-0	0	3.85	3.50
2008	Atl	NL	13	13	0	0	78.0	331	83	45	42	10	5	2	1	28	6	38	0	0	3	4	.429	0	0-0	0	4.52	4.85
2009	Hou	NL	21	21	0	0	112.0	494	128	71	66	13	11	5	2	46	6	74	1	0	7	10	.412	0	0-0	0	5.12	5.30
2010	Ari	NL	10	0	0	3	4.1	16	3	0	0	0	0	1	0	1	1	3	0	0	0	0	-	0	0-0	1	1.30	0.00
	Postseason		11	10	1	0	65.0	271	48	27	27	8	2	0	1	32	2	53	4	0	2	4	.333	1	0-0	0	3.19	3.74
	16 ML YEARS		419	355	21	12	2268.1	9824	2370	1157	1024	200	107	69	49	901	49	1387	75	13	148	115	.563	9	1-2	13	4.32	4.06

Ryan Hanigan

Bats: R **Throws:** R **Pos:** C-68; PH-5   HANN-eh-gann   **Ht:** 6'0" **Wt:** 201 **Born:** 8/16/1980 **Age:** 30

											BATTING												BASERUNNING				AVERAGES		
Year	Team	Lg	G	AB	H	2B	3B	HR	(Hm	Rd)	TB	R	RBI	RC	TBB	IBB	SO	HBP	SH	SF	SB	CS	SB%	GDP	Avg	OBP	Slg
2010	Lsvlle*	AAA	13	46	11	3	0	0	(-	-)	14	6	2	5	4	0	6	2	0	0	0	0	-	1	.239	.327	.304
2007	Cin	NL	5	10	3	1	0	0	(0	0)	4	3	2	2	1	1	2	0	0	0	0	0	-	0	.300	.364	.400
2008	Cin	NL	31	85	23	2	0	2	(1	1)	31	9	9	12	10	1	9	3	0	0	0	0	-	2	.271	.367	.365
2009	Cin	NL	90	251	66	6	1	3	(3	0)	83	22	11	25	37	7	31	2	2	1	0	0	-	9	.263	.361	.331
2010	Cin	NL	70	203	61	11	0	5	(2	3)	87	25	40	41	33	4	21	4	1	2	0	0	-	6	.300	.405	.429
	4 ML YEARS		196	549	153	20	1	10	(6	4)	205	59	62	80	81	13	63	9	3	3	0	0	-	17	.279	.379	.373

Joel Hanrahan

Pitches: R **Bats:** R **Pos:** RP-72   **Ht:** 6'4" **Wt:** 245 **Born:** 10/6/1981 **Age:** 29

Year	Team	Lg	G	GS	CG	GF	IP	BFP	H	R	ER	HR	SH	SF	HB	TBB	IBB	SO	WP	Bk	W	L	Pct	Sh	Sv-Op	Hld	ERC	ERA
2010	Bradtn*	A+	2	0	0	0	2.0	6	0	0	0	0	0	0	0	0	0	3	0	0	0	0	-	0	0- -	-	0.00	0.00
2007	Was	NL	12	11	0	0	51.0	247	59	35	34	9	2	1	0	38	0	43	3	0	5	3	.625	0	0- -	0	7.01	6.00
2008	Was	NL	69	0	0	34	84.1	364	73	40	37	9	2	6	1	42	7	93	6	0	6	3	.667	0	9-13	3	3.65	3.95
2009	2 Tms	NL	67	0	0	30	64.0	297	73	40	34	3	0	1	3	34	1	72	11	1	1	4	.200	0	5-10	9	5.12	4.78
2010	Pit	NL	72	0	0	27	69.2	294	58	28	28	6	0	1	4	26	0	100	5	0	4	1	.800	0	6-10	18	3.16	3.62
09	Was	NL	34	0	0	23	32.2	163	50	28	28	3	0	1	2	14	0	35	6	1	1	3	.250	0	5-10	2	7.49	7.71
09	Pit	NL	33	0	0	7	31.1	134	23	12	6	0	0	0	1	20	1	37	5	0	0	1	.000	0	0-0	7	2.92	1.72
	4 ML YEARS		220	11	0	91	269.0	1202	263	143	133	27	4	9	8	140	8	308	25	1	16	11	.593	0	20-33	30	4.15	4.45

Tommy Hanson

Pitches: R **Bats:** R **Pos:** SP-34   **Ht:** 6'6" **Wt:** 220 **Born:** 8/28/1986 **Age:** 24

Year	Team	Lg	G	GS	CG	GF	IP	BFP	H	R	ER	HR	SH	SF	HB	TBB	IBB	SO	WP	Bk	W	L	Pct	Sh	Sv-Op	Hld	ERC	ERA
2006	Danvle	R+	13	8	0	0	51.2	208	42	15	12	2	3	2	1	9	0	56	3	0	4	1	.800	0	0- -	-	1.94	2.09
2007	Rome	A	15	14	0	0	73.0	296	51	28	21	6	1	0	6	26	0	90	5	0	2	6	.250	0	0- -	-	2.54	2.59
2007	MrtlBh	A+	11	11	0	0	60.0	260	53	33	28	10	2	3	4	32	0	64	0	1	3	3	.500	0	0- -	-	4.77	4.20
2008	MrtlBh	A+	7	7	0	0	40.0	148	15	6	4	0	1	2	5	11	0	49	5	0	3	1	.750	0	0- -	-	0.91	0.90
2008	Missi	AA	18	18	1	0	98.0	410	70	39	33	9	4	0	9	41	0	114	5	0	8	4	.667	1	0- -	-	2.89	3.03
2009	Gwnntt	AAA	11	11	0	0	66.1	257	40	16	11	5	0	0	4	17	0	90	4	0	3	3	.500	0	0- -	-	1.66	1.49
2009	Atl	NL	21	21	0	0	127.2	522	105	42	41	10	4	1	5	46	1	116	2	0	11	4	.733	0	0-0	0	3.02	2.89
2010	Atl	NL	34	34	1	0	202.2	845	182	86	75	14	9	5	**14**	56	3	173	3	0	10	11	.476	0	0-0	0	3.08	3.33
	2 ML YEARS		55	55	1	0	330.1	1367	287	128	116	24	8	6	19	102	4	289	5	0	21	15	.583	0	0-0	0	3.06	3.16

J.A. Happ

Pitches: L **Bats:** L **Pos:** SP-16   JAY   **Ht:** 6'6" **Wt:** 200 **Born:** 10/19/1982 **Age:** 28

Year	Team	Lg	G	GS	CG	GF	IP	BFP	H	R	ER	HR	SH	SF	HB	TBB	IBB	SO	WP	Bk	W	L	Pct	Sh	Sv-Op	Hld	ERC	ERA
2010	LV*	AAA	5	4	0	0	22.1	106	26	12	12	3	2	1	0	15	0	22	0	0	0	1	.000	0	0- -	-	6.42	4.84
2010	Clrwtr*	A+	1	1	0	0	3.0	13	3	2	2	0	0	0	0	0	0	2	0	0	0	1	.000	0	0- -	-	1.76	6.00
2010	Rdng*	AA	3	3	0	0	12.1	59	18	11	11	3	0	0	1	4	0	10	1	0	1	0	1.000	0	0- -	-	8.04	8.03
2007	Phi	NL	1	1	0	0	4.0	21	7	5	5	3	0	0	0	2	0	5	0	0	0	1	.000	0	0-0	0	15.13	11.25
2008	Phi	NL	8	4	0	1	31.2	138	28	13	13	3	2	1	1	14	1	26	1	0	1	0	1.000	0	0-0	1	3.55	3.69
2009	Phi	NL	35	23	3	4	166.0	685	149	55	54	20	7	6	5	56	2	119	2	0	12	4	.750	2	0-0	0	3.57	2.93
2010	2 Tms	NL	16	16	1	0	87.1	374	73	37	33	8	5	4	1	47	1	70	4	0	6	4	.600	1	0-0	0	3.69	3.40
10	Phi	NL	3	3	0	0	15.1	70	13	4	3	1	1	1	0	12	0	9	1	0	1	0	1.000	0	0-0	0	4.40	1.76
10	Hou	NL	13	13	1	0	72.0	304	60	33	30	7	4	3	1	35	1	61	3	0	5	4	.556	1	0-0	0	3.69	3.40
	Postseason		8	1	0	0	9.1	46	12	5	5	1	0	0	0	8	0	10	0	0	0	0	-	0	0-0	1	7.96	4.82
	4 ML YEARS		60	44	4	5	289.0	1218	257	110	105	34	14	11	7	119	4	220	7	0	19	9	.679	3	0-0	1	3.73	3.27

Aaron Harang

Pitches: R **Bats:** R **Pos:** SP-20; RP-2   huh-RANG   **Ht:** 6'7" **Wt:** 261 **Born:** 5/9/1978 **Age:** 33

Year	Team	Lg	G	GS	CG	GF	IP	BFP	H	R	ER	HR	SH	SF	HB	TBB	IBB	SO	WP	Bk	W	L	Pct	Sh	Sv-Op	Hld	ERC	ERA
2010	Lsvlle*	AAA	2	2	0	0	11.0	50	14	11	11	1	0	2	1	2	0	10	0	0	0	2	.000	0	0--	-	4.94	9.00
2002	Oak	AL	16	15	0	0	78.1	354	78	44	42	7	3	4	3	45	2	64	1	0	5	4	.556	0	0-0	0	4.76	4.83
2003	2 Tms		16	15	0	1	76.1	327	89	47	45	11	5	1	1	19	0	42	3	1	5	6	.455	0	0-0	0	4.84	5.31
2004	Cin	NL	28	28	1	0	161.0	711	177	90	87	26	13	6	5	53	5	125	7	0	10	9	.526	1	0-0	0	4.81	4.86
2005	Cin	NL	32	32	1	0	211.2	887	217	93	90	22	11	5	8	51	3	163	6	0	11	13	.458	0	0-0	0	3.77	3.83
2006	Cin	NL	36	35	6	0	234.1	993	242	109	98	28	21	8	8	56	8	216	6	1	16	11	.593	2	0-0	0	3.82	3.76
2007	Cin	NL	34	34	2	0	231.2	948	213	100	96	28	4	5	8	52	3	218	12	1	16	6	.727	1	0-0	0	3.22	3.73
2008	Cin	NL	30	29	1	0	184.1	793	205	104	98	35	11	7	2	50	5	153	2	0	6	17	.261	1	0-0	0	4.83	4.78
2009	Cin	NL	26	26	2	0	162.1	703	186	82	76	24	6	2	4	43	6	142	6	0	6	14	.300	1	0-0	0	4.76	4.21
2010	Cin	NL	22	20	0	1	111.2	504	139	71	66	16	4	3	4	38	0	82	9	0	6	7	.462	0	0-0	0	5.75	5.32
03	Oak	AL	7	6	0	1	30.1	136	41	19	18	5	2	1	0	9	0	16	0	1	1	3	.250	0	0-0	0	6.32	5.34
03	Cin	NL	9	9	0	0	46.0	191	48	28	27	6	3	0	1	10	0	26	3	0	4	3	.571	0	0-0	0	3.94	5.28
9 ML YEARS			240	234	13	2	1451.2	6220	1546	740	698	197	78	41	43	407	32	1205	52	3	81	87	.482	6	0-0	0	4.30	4.33

Rich Harden

Pitches: R **Bats:** L **Pos:** SP-18; RP-2   **Ht:** 6'1" **Wt:** 195 **Born:** 11/30/1981 **Age:** 29

Year	Team	Lg	G	GS	CG	GF	IP	BFP	H	R	ER	HR	SH	SF	HB	TBB	IBB	SO	WP	Bk	W	L	Pct	Sh	Sv-Op	Hld	ERC	ERA
2010	OKCity*	AAA	5	5	0	0	23.1	101	21	13	10	3	0	3	0	8	0	34	0	0	0	2	.000	0	0--	-	3.54	3.86
2003	Oak	AL	15	13	0	0	74.2	324	72	38	37	5	2	3	1	40	1	67	6	0	5	4	.556	0	0-0	0	4.28	4.46
2004	Oak	AL	31	31	0	0	189.2	803	171	90	84	16	5	6	3	81	6	167	4	1	11	7	.611	0	0-0	0	3.57	3.99
2005	Oak	AL	22	19	2	0	128.0	514	93	42	36	7	4	2	2	43	0	121	6	0	10	5	.667	1	0-1	0	2.20	2.53
2006	Oak	AL	9	9	0	0	46.2	191	31	22	22	5	0	2	1	26	0	49	0	0	4	0	1.000	0	0-0	0	3.07	4.24
2007	Oak	AL	7	4	0	2	25.2	100	18	7	7	3	0	0	0	11	1	27	0	0	1	2	.333	0	0-0	0	2.80	2.45
2008	2 Tms		25	25	0	0	148.0	595	96	38	34	11	2	3	3	61	2	181	3	0	10	2	.833	0	0-0	0	2.20	2.07
2009	ChC	NL	26	26	0	0	141.0	609	122	74	64	23	12	3	6	67	5	171	7	0	9	9	.500	0	0-0	0	4.15	4.09
2010	Tex	AL	20	18	0	0	92.0	430	91	61	57	18	0	4	9	62	0	75	4	0	5	5	.500	0	0-0	0	6.27	5.58
08	Oak	AL	13	13	0	0	77.0	311	57	21	20	5	0	2	1	31	1	92	1	0	5	1	.833	0	0-0	0	2.56	2.34
08	ChC	NL	12	12	0	0	71.0	284	39	17	14	6	2	1	2	30	1	89	2	0	5	1	.833	0	0-0	0	1.84	1.77
Postseason			4	2	0	2	11.1	55	12	8	8	2	0	0	0	10	3	9	1	0	1	3	.250	0	0-0	0	6.49	6.35
8 ML YEARS			155	145	2	2	845.2	3566	694	372	341	88	25	23	25	391	15	858	30	1	55	34	.618	1	0-0	1	3.46	3.63

J.J. Hardy

Bats: R **Throws:** R **Pos:** SS-100; PR-4   **Ht:** 6'2" **Wt:** 202 **Born:** 8/19/1982 **Age:** 28

Year	Team	Lg	G	AB	H	2B	3B	HR	(Hm	Rd)	TB	R	RBI	RC	TBB	IBB	SO	HBP	SH	SF	SB	CS	SB%	GDP	Avg	OBP	Slg
2010	Beloit*	A	3	10	2	0	0	0	(-	-)	2	0	0	0	1	0	2	1	0	0	0	0	-	0	.200	.333	.200
2005	Mil	NL	124	372	92	22	1	9	(6	3)	143	46	50	49	44	7	48	1	8	2	0	0	-	10	.247	.327	.384
2006	Mil	NL	35	128	31	5	0	5	(4	1)	51	13	14	13	10	0	23	0	0	1	1	1	.50	4	.242	.295	.398
2007	Mil	NL	151	592	164	30	1	26	(15	11)	274	89	80	84	40	1	73	1	4	1	2	3	.40	13	.277	.323	.463
2008	Mil	NL	146	569	161	31	4	24	(14	10)	272	78	74	78	52	3	98	1	5	2	2	1	.67	18	.283	.343	.478
2009	Mil	NL	115	414	95	16	2	11	(6	5)	148	53	47	32	43	0	85	2	1	5	0	1	.00	14	.229	.302	.357
2010	Min	AL	101	340	91	19	3	6	(1	5)	134	44	38	41	28	1	54	0	3	4	1	1	.50	8	.268	.320	.394
Postseason			4	14	6	1	0	0	(0	0)	7	2	2	3	2	0	0	0	0	0	0	0	-	0	.429	.500	.500
6 ML YEARS			672	2415	634	123	11	81	(46	35)	1022	323	303	297	217	12	381	5	21	15	6	7	.46	67	.263	.323	.423

Dan Haren

Pitches: R **Bats:** R **Pos:** SP-35   **Ht:** 6'5" **Wt:** 215 **Born:** 9/17/1980 **Age:** 30

Year	Team	Lg	G	GS	CG	GF	IP	BFP	H	R	ER	HR	SH	SF	HB	TBB	IBB	SO	WP	Bk	W	L	Pct	Sh	Sv-Op	Hld	ERC	ERA
2003	StL	NL	14	14	0	0	72.2	320	84	44	41	9	4	2	5	22	0	43	3	0	3	7	.300	0	0-0	0	5.07	5.08
2004	StL	NL	14	5	0	2	46.0	195	45	23	23	4	4	2	2	17	2	32	1	0	3	3	.500	0	0-0	0	3.91	4.50
2005	Oak	AL	34	34	3	0	217.0	897	212	101	90	26	3	5	6	53	5	163	6	0	14	12	.538	0	0-0	0	3.58	3.73
2006	Oak	AL	34	34	2	0	223.0	930	224	109	102	31	3	3	10	45	6	176	10	0	14	13	.519	0	0-0	0	3.72	4.12
2007	Oak	AL	34	34	0	0	222.2	935	214	91	76	24	2	8	3	55	1	192	10	0	15	9	.625	0	0-0	0	3.32	3.07
2008	Ari	NL	33	33	1	0	216.0	881	204	86	80	19	7	3	6	40	4	206	11	0	16	8	.667	1	0-0	0	2.96	3.33
2009	Ari	NL	33	33	3	0	229.1	909	192	83	80	27	8	3	4	38	2	223	13	0	14	10	.583	1	0-0	0	2.50	3.14
2010	2 Tms		35	35	2	0	235.0	994	245	110	102	31	6	10	5	54	6	216	12	2	12	12	.500	0	0-0	0	3.88	3.91
10	Ari	NL	21	21	1	0	141.0	607	161	79	72	23	6	4	3	29	4	141	8	1	7	8	.467	0	0-0	0	4.55	4.60
10	LAA	AL	14	14	1	0	94.0	387	84	31	30	8	0	6	2	25	2	75	4	1	5	4	.556	0	0-0	0	2.94	2.87
Postseason			7	2	0	0	19.1	86	24	7	7	3	1	0	0	7	0	16	2	0	2	0	1.000	0	0-0	0	5.83	3.26
8 ML YEARS			231	222	11	2	1461.2	6061	1420	647	594	171	37	36	41	324	26	1251	66	2	91	74	.552	2	0-0	0	3.42	3.66

Lucas Harrell

Pitches: R **Bats:** B **Pos:** RP-5; SP-3   HAH-rell   **Ht:** 6'2" **Wt:** 200 **Born:** 6/3/1985 **Age:** 26

Year	Team	Lg	G	GS	CG	GF	IP	BFP	H	R	ER	HR	SH	SF	HB	TBB	IBB	SO	WP	Bk	W	L	Pct	Sh	Sv-Op	Hld	ERC	ERA
2004	Bristol	R+	13	9	0	1	48.1	230	53	39	30	5	3	3	4	32	1	33	2	0	3	5	.375	0	0--	-	6.00	5.59
2005	Knapol	A-	26	26	0	0	133.1	607	128	86	54	8	2	7	11	71	0	85	13	4	7	11	.389	0	0--	-	4.31	3.65
2006	WinSa	A+	17	17	0	0	91.2	374	58	29	25	3	2	2	7	44	0	70	3	0	7	2	.778	0	0--	-	2.32	2.45
2006	Brham	AA	3	3	0	0	9.2	52	12	12	11	1	0	1	0	14	0	4	2	1	0	2	.000	0	0--	-	10.47	10.24
2008	Brham	AA	11	10	0	0	54.2	231	56	30	21	3	3	1	2	19	0	34	3	0	3	3	.500	0	0--	-	3.92	3.46
2008	Bristol	R+	1	1	0	0	3.0	12	3	1	1	0	0	0	0	1	0	5	0	0	0	0	-	0	0--	-	3.35	3.00
2008	Knapol	A	3	3	0	0	10.2	49	13	7	7	0	1	0	1	4	0	7	0	0	1	1	.500	0	0--	-	4.81	5.91

Year	Team	Lg	G	GS	CG	GF	IP	BFP	H	R	ER	HR	SH	SF	HB	TBB	IBB	SO	WP	Bk	W	L	Pct	Sh	Sv-Op	Hld	ERC	ERA
			HOW MUCH HE PITCHED						**WHAT HE GAVE UP**												**THE RESULTS**							
2009	Brham	AA	14	14	0	0	80.1	334	78	38	29	4	1	3	2	32	0	51	5	0	8	3	.727	0	0--	-	3.80	3.25
2009	Charltt	AAA	11	11	0	0	65.2	280	58	26	24	3	2	1		37	0	42	3	1	4	1	.800	0	0--	-	3.97	3.29
2010	Charltt	AAA	26	26	0	0	137.2	602	141	79	70	11	3	6	5	61	1	84	4	1	10	10	.500	0	0--	-	4.40	4.58
2010	CWS	AL	8	3	0	3	24.0	119	34	18	13	2	1	0	0	17	1	15	1	0	1	0	1.000	0	0-0	0	7.77	4.88

Brendan Harris

Bats: R **Throws:** R **Pos:** 3B-27; SS-11; PR-4; 1B-3; PH-2; 2B-1; DH-1   **Ht:** 6'1" **Wt:** 205 **Born:** 8/26/1980 **Age:** 30

Year	Team	Lg	G	AB	H	2B	3B	HR	(Hm	Rd)	TB	R	RBI	RC	TBB	IBB	SO	HBP	SH	SF	SB	CS	SB%	GDP	Avg	OBP	Slg
			BATTING																		**BASERUNNING**				**AVERAGES**		
2010	Roch*	AAA	62	232	54	14	1	4	(-	-)	82	31	29	25	14	0	41	7	1	4	1	0	1.00	11	.233	.292	.353
2004	2 Tms	NL	23	59	10	3	0	1	(0	1)	16	4	3	2	3	0	12	1	0	0	0	0	-	0	.169	.222	.271
2005	Was	NL	4	9	3	1	0	1	(0	1)	7	1	3	3	0	0	0	1	0	0	0	0	-	2	.333	.400	.778
2006	2 Tms	NL	25	42	10	2	0	1	(1	0)	15	5	3	4	4	0	7	1	0	0	0	0	-	2	.238	.319	.357
2007	TB	AL	137	521	149	35	3	12	(5	7)	226	72	59	70	42	1	96	4	8	1	4	1	.80	19	.286	.343	.434
2008	Min	AL	130	434	115	29	3	7	(3	4)	171	57	49	52	39	0	98	4	7	6	1	1	.50	13	.265	.327	.394
2009	Min	AL	123	414	108	22	1	6	(5	1)	150	44	37	43	29	0	78	3	1	6	0	2	.00	16	.261	.310	.362
2010	Min	AL	43	108	17	3	0	1	(0	1)	23	11	4	4	9	0	23	2	0	1	0	0	-	2	.157	.233	.213
04	ChC	NL	3	9	2	1	0	0	(0	0)	3	0	1	1	1	0	1	0	0	0	0	0	-	0	.222	.300	.333
04	Mon	NL	20	50	8	2	0	1	(0	1)	13	4	2	1	2	0	11	1	0	0	0	0	-	0	.160	.208	.260
06	Was	NL	17	32	8	2	0	0	(0	0)	10	3	2	3	3	0	3	1	0	0	0	0	-	1	.250	.333	.313
06	Cin	NL	8	10	2	0	0	1	(1	0)	5	2	1	1	1	0	4	0	0	0	0	0	-	1	.200	.273	.500
Postseason			3	12	3	0	1	0	(0	0)	5	1	1	1	0	0	3	0	0	0	0	0	-	0	.250	.250	.417
7 ML YEARS			485	1587	412	95	7	29	(14	15)	608	194	158	178	126	1	314	16	16	14	5	4	.56	54	.260	.318	.383

Willie Harris

Bats: L **Throws:** R **Pos:** PH-60; LF-46; RF-43; 3B-6; CF-2; DH-1; PR-1   **Ht:** 5'9" **Wt:** 191 **Born:** 6/22/1978 **Age:** 33

Year	Team	Lg	G	AB	H	2B	3B	HR	(Hm	Rd)	TB	R	RBI	RC	TBB	IBB	SO	HBP	SH	SF	SB	CS	SB%	GDP	Avg	OBP	Slg
			BATTING																		**BASERUNNING**				**AVERAGES**		
2001	Bal	AL	9	24	3	1	0	0	(0	0)	4	3	0	0	0	0	7	0	1	0	0	0	-	0	.125	.125	.167
2002	CWS	AL	49	163	38	4	0	2	(2	0)	48	14	12	15	9	0	21	0	3	2	8	0	1.00	3	.233	.270	.294
2003	CWS	AL	79	137	28	3	1	0	(0	0)	33	19	5	11	10	0	28	0	3	0	12	2	.86	1	.204	.259	.241
2004	CWS	AL	129	409	107	15	2	2	(2	0)	132	68	27	53	51	0	79	1	7	3	19	7	.73	4	.262	.343	.323
2005	CWS	AL	56	121	31	2	1	1	(1	0)	38	17	8	15	13	0	25	1	4	0	10	3	.77	1	.256	.333	.314
2006	Bos	AL	47	45	7	2	0	0	(0	0)	9	17	1	1	4	0	11	2	0	1	6	3	.67	0	.156	.250	.200
2007	Atl	NL	117	344	93	20	8	2	(1	1)	135	56	32	47	40	0	71	3	1	3	17	11	.61	3	.270	.349	.392
2008	Was	NL	140	367	92	14	4	13	(4	9)	153	58	43	50	50	2	66	3	3	1	13	3	.81	4	.251	.344	.417
2009	Was	NL	137	323	76	18	6	7	(6	1)	127	47	27	47	57	1	62	9	3	1	11	4	.73	4	.235	.364	.393
2010	Was	NL	132	224	41	6	2	10	(7	3)	81	25	32	25	33	0	60	2	1	2	5	2	.71	3	.183	.291	.362
Postseason			3	2	2	0	0	0	(0	0)	2	1	1	2	0	0	0	0	0	0	1	0	1.00	0	1.000	1.000	1.000
10 ML YEARS			895	2157	516	85	24	37	(23	14)	760	324	187	264	267	3	430	21	26	13	101	35	.74	27	.239	.327	.352

Matt Harrison

Pitches: L **Bats:** L **Pos:** RP-31; SP-6   **Ht:** 6'4" **Wt:** 240 **Born:** 9/16/1985 **Age:** 25

Year	Team	Lg	G	GS	CG	GF	IP	BFP	H	R	ER	HR	SH	SF	HB	TBB	IBB	SO	WP	Bk	W	L	Pct	Sh	Sv-Op	Hld	ERC	ERA
			HOW MUCH HE PITCHED						**WHAT HE GAVE UP**												**THE RESULTS**							
2010	Frisco*	AA	2	0	0	0	3.0	12	3	1	1	0	0	0	0	0	0	4	0	0	0	0	-	0	1--	-	1.95	3.00
2010	OKCity*	AAA	1	1	0	0	4.1	22	9	4	3	1	1	0	0	1	0	4	1	0	0	1	.000	0	0--	-	11.77	6.23
2008	Tex	AL	15	15	1	0	83.2	372	100	57	51	12	1	5	2	31	2	42	2	2	9	3	.750	1	0-0	0	5.53	5.49
2009	Tex	AL	11	11	2	0	63.1	283	81	43	43	9	1	1	2	23	0	34	0	0	4	5	.444	0	0-0	0	6.17	6.11
2010	Tex	AL	37	6	0	9	78.1	356	80	45	41	10	2	8	2	39	3	46	4	0	3	2	.600	0	2-3	3	4.71	4.71
3 ML YEARS			63	32	3	9	225.1	1011	261	145	135	31	4	14	6	93	5	122	6	2	16	10	.615	2	2-3	3	5.41	5.39

Corey Hart

Bats: R **Throws:** R **Pos:** RF-141; PH-6   **Ht:** 6'6" **Wt:** 229 **Born:** 3/24/1982 **Age:** 29

Year	Team	Lg	G	AB	H	2B	3B	HR	(Hm	Rd)	TB	R	RBI	RC	TBB	IBB	SO	HBP	SH	SF	SB	CS	SB%	GDP	Avg	OBP	Slg
			BATTING																		**BASERUNNING**				**AVERAGES**		
2004	Mil	NL	1	1	0	0	0	0	(0	0)	0	0	0	0	0	0	1	0	0	0	0	0	-	0	.000	.000	.000
2005	Mil	NL	21	57	11	2	1	2	(2	0)	21	9	7	4	6	0	11	0	0	0	2	0	1.00	6	.193	.270	.368
2006	Mil	NL	87	237	67	13	2	9	(6	3)	111	32	33	30	17	1	58	0	0	2	5	8	.38	7	.283	.328	.468
2007	Mil	NL	140	505	149	33	9	24	(15	9)	272	86	81	94	36	3	99	13	5	7	23	7	.77	6	.295	.353	.539
2008	Mil	NL	157	612	164	45	6	20	(7	13)	281	76	91	81	27	2	109	5	4	9	23	7	.77	17	.268	.300	.459
2009	Mil	NL	115	419	109	24	3	12	(9	3)	175	64	48	51	43	0	92	6	1	3	11	6	.65	9	.260	.335	.418
2010	Mil	NL	145	558	158	34	4	31	(16	15)	293	91	102	83	45	2	140	6	0	5	7	6	.54	14	.283	.340	.525
Postseason			4	13	3	0	0	0	(0	0)	3	0	0	0	1	0	3	1	1	0	0	0	-	0	.231	.333	.231
7 ML YEARS			666	2389	658	151	25	98	(55	43)	1153	358	362	343	174	8	510	30	10	26	71	34	.68	59	.275	.329	.483

Chris Hatcher

Bats: B **Throws:** R **Pos:** C-4; PH-1   **Ht:** 6'2" **Wt:** 190 **Born:** 1/12/1985 **Age:** 26

Year	Team	Lg	G	AB	H	2B	3B	HR	(Hm	Rd)	TB	R	RBI	RC	TBB	IBB	SO	HBP	SH	SF	SB	CS	SB%	GDP	Avg	OBP	Slg
			BATTING																		**BASERUNNING**				**AVERAGES**		
2006	Jmstwn	A-	36	127	23	4	2	2	(-	-)	37	19	17	10	11	1	40	5	7	0	0	0	-	3	.181	.273	.291
2007	Grnsbr	A	102	356	86	23	1	15	(-	-)	156	62	50	50	34	1	104	5	0	6	8	6	.57	6	.242	.312	.438
2008	Jupiter	A+	63	202	36	12	0	6	(-	-)	66	22	28	20	23	0	78	6	8	3	0	0	-	6	.178	.278	.327
2009	Jupiter	A+	6	18	6	1	0	0	(-	-)	7	4	2	2	1	0	8	1	0	0	0	0	-	0	.333	.400	.389

Year	Team	Lg	G	AB	H	2B	3B	HR	(Hm	Rd)	TB	R	RBI	RC	TBB	IBB	SO	HBP	SH	SF	SB	CS	SB%	GDP	Avg	OBP	Slg
																	BATTING						BASERUNNING			AVERAGES	
2009	Jaxnvl	AA	51	156	34	9	3	8	(-	-)	73	29	27	23	14	2	43	4	2	3	1	0	1.00	0	.218	.294	.468
2010	Jaxnvl	AA	84	267	54	9	1	3	(-	-)	74	23	26	18	20	0	92	2	2	2	1	2	.33	5	.202	.261	.277
2010	NewOr	AAA	17	48	8	1	0	2	(-	-)	15	10	10	5	9	1	19	3	1	0	1	2	.33	5	.167	.333	.313
2010	Fla	NL	5	6	0	0	0	0	(0	0)	0	0	0	0	2	1	5	0	0	0	0	0	-	0	.000	.250	.000

LaTroy Hawkins

Pitches: R Bats: R Pos: RP-18 **Ht: 6'5" Wt: 195 Born: 12/21/1972 Age: 38**

Year	Team	Lg	G	GS	CG	GF	IP	BFP	H	R	ER	HR	SH	SF	HB	TBB	IBB	SO	WP	Bk	W	L	Pct	Sh	Sv-Op	Hld	ERC	ERA
							HOW MUCH HE PITCHED						WHAT HE GAVE UP												THE RESULTS			
2010	Brewrs*	R	2	2	0	0	3.2	15	4	1	1	0	0	0	0	0	0	5	0	0	0	0	-	0	0--	-	2.36	2.45
2010	Nashv*	AAA	4	0	0	1	6.1	22	4	0	0	0	0	0	0	0	0	1	0	0	0	0	-	0	1--	-	0.87	0.00
1995	Min	AL	6	6	1	0	27.0	131	39	29	26	3	0	3	1	12	0	9	1	1	2	3	.400	0	0-0	0	7.14	8.67
1996	Min	AL	7	6	0	1	26.1	124	42	24	24	8	1	1	0	9	0	24	1	1	1	1	.500	0	0-0	0	9.49	8.20
1997	Min	AL	20	20	0	0	103.1	478	134	71	67	19	2	2	4	47	0	58	6	3	6	12	.333	0	0-0	0	7.01	5.84
1998	Min	AL	33	33	0	0	190.1	840	227	126	111	27	4	10	5	61	1	105	10	2	7	14	.333	0	0-0	0	5.31	5.25
1999	Min	AL	33	33	1	0	174.1	803	238	**136**	**129**	29	1	5	1	60	2	103	9	0	10	14	.417	0	0-0	0	6.55	6.66
2000	Min	AL	66	0	0	38	87.2	370	85	34	33	7	4	1	1	32	1	59	6	0	2	5	.286	0	14-14	7	3.70	3.39
2001	Min	AL	62	0	0	51	51.1	248	59	34	34	3	1	4	1	39	3	36	7	0	1	5	.167	0	28-37	1	6.02	5.96
2002	Min	AL	65	0	0	15	80.1	310	63	23	19	5	2	3	0	15	1	63	5	0	6	0	1.000	0	0-3	13	1.99	2.13
2003	Min	AL	74	0	0	12	77.1	310	69	20	16	4	4	1	1	15	1	75	5	0	9	3	.750	0	2-8	28	2.48	1.86
2004	ChC	NL	77	0	0	50	82.0	333	72	27	24	10	6	2	2	14	5	69	2	0	5	4	.556	0	25-34	4	2.66	2.63
2005	2 Tms	NL	66	0	0	21	56.1	247	58	27	24	7	3	1	0	24	3	43	1	0	2	8	.200	0	6-15	15	4.41	3.83
2006	Bal	AL	60	0	0	12	60.1	261	73	30	30	4	1	2	0	15	3	27	2	0	3	2	.600	0	0-4	16	4.37	4.48
2007	Col	NL	62	0	0	10	55.1	225	52	21	21	6	2	1	0	16	1	29	2	0	2	5	.286	0	0-5	18	3.43	3.42
2008	2 Tms		57	0	0	15	62.0	252	53	29	27	3	1	3	0	22	4	48	3	0	3	1	.750	0	1-2	13	2.75	3.92
2009	Hou	NL	65	0	0	34	63.1	259	60	16	15	7	2	2	2	16	2	45	2	0	1	4	.200	0	11-15	19	3.42	2.13
2010	Mil	NL	18	0	0	5	16.0	74	21	15	15	2	1	0	2	6	1	18	1	0	0	3	.000	0	0-2	6	6.55	8.44
05	ChC	NL	21	0	0	12	19.0	80	18	9	7	4	1	0	0	7	0	13	0	0	1	4	.200	0	4-8	0	4.44	3.32
05	SF	A	45	0	0	9	37.1	167	40	18	17	3	2	1	0	17	3	30	1	0	1	4	.200	0	2-7	15	4.36	4.10
08	NYY	AL	33	0	0	11	41.0	173	42	26	26	3	1	2	0	17	3	23	2	0	1	1	.500	0	0-1	1	4.09	5.71
08	Hou	NL	24	0	0	4	21.0	79	11	3	1	0	0	1	0	5	1	25	1	0	2	0	1.000	0	1-1	12	0.95	0.43
	Postseason		15	0	0	4	11.2	48	11	7	6	0	2	1	0	2	0	14	0	0	1	0	1.000	0	0-0	4	2.24	4.63
	16 ML YEARS		771	98	2	264	1213.1	5265	1345	662	615	144	35	41	20	403	28	811	63	7	60	84	.417	0	87-139	140	4.61	4.56

Blake Hawksworth

Pitches: R Bats: R Pos: RP-37; SP-8 **Ht: 6'3" Wt: 195 Born: 3/1/1983 Age: 28**

Year	Team	Lg	G	GS	CG	GF	IP	BFP	H	R	ER	HR	SH	SF	HB	TBB	IBB	SO	WP	Bk	W	L	Pct	Sh	Sv-Op	Hld	ERC	ERA
							HOW MUCH HE PITCHED						WHAT HE GAVE UP												THE RESULTS			
2002	JhsCty	R+	13	12	0	0	66.0	275	58	31	23	8	1	1	4	18	0	61	4	0	2	4	.333	0	0--	-	3.27	3.14
2002	NewJrs	A-	2	2	0	0	9.2	37	6	0	0	0	0	0	0	2	0	8	0	0	1	0	1.000	0	0--	-	1.18	0.00
2003	Peoria	A	10	10	0	0	54.2	213	37	16	14	0	1	1	1	12	0	57	1	1	5	1	.833	0	0--	-	1.41	2.30
2003	PlmBh	A+	6	6	0	0	32.0	132	28	14	14	2	0	1	1	11	0	32	2	0	1	3	.250	0	0--	-	3.09	3.94
2004	PlmBh	A+	2	2	0	0	10.2	45	10	7	7	2	1	1	0	3	0	11	3	1	1	0	1.000	0	0--	-	3.76	5.91
2005	NewJrs	A-	7	6	0	0	14.2	72	18	18	13	0	0	1	5	10	0	12	3	0	0	3	.000	0	0--	-	7.46	7.98
2006	PlmBh	A+	14	14	0	0	83.2	333	75	23	23	0	2	2	6	19	0	55	5	2	7	2	.778	0	0--	-	2.60	2.47
2006	Sprgfld	AA	13	13	0	0	79.2	329	72	34	30	8	3	3	2	31	1	66	2	0	4	2	.667	0	0--	-	3.69	3.39
2007	Memp	AAA	25	25	0	0	129.2	571	150	82	76	24	6	5	10	41	0	88	9	1	4	13	.235	0	0--	-	5.66	5.28
2008	Memp	AAA	18	16	0	0	88.2	413	111	71	60	12	3	3	8	38	1	83	7	1	5	7	.417	0	0--	-	6.33	6.09
2008	Cards	R	2	2	0	0	7.0	24	2	0	0	0	0	0	0	2	0	6	0	0	0	0	-	0	0--	-	0.54	0.00
2009	Memp	AAA	12	12	1	0	73.0	303	61	31	29	3	4	2	2	20	1	57	0	0	5	4	.556	0	0--	-	2.39	3.58
2009	StL	NL	30	0	0	10	40.0	160	29	10	9	2	4	1	1	15	3	20	0	0	4	0	1.000	0	0-0	2	2.26	2.03
2010	StL	NL	45	8	0	9	90.1	409	113	56	50	15	4	4	2	35	4	61	1	**3**	4	8	.333	0	0-0	4	6.15	4.98
	Postseason		1	0	0	0	1.0	4	1	0	0	0	0	0	0	1	0	1	0	0	0	0	-	0	0-0	0	6.99	0.00
	2 ML YEARS		75	8	0	19	130.1	569	142	66	59	17	8	5	3	50	3	81	1	3	8	8	.500	0	0-0	6	4.84	4.07

Brad Hawpe

Bats: L Throws: L Pos: RF-66; PH-24; 1B-9; DH-8 **Ht: 6'3" Wt: 210 Born: 6/22/1979 Age: 32**

Year	Team	Lg	G	AB	H	2B	3B	HR	(Hm	Rd)	TB	R	RBI	RC	TBB	IBB	SO	HBP	SH	SF	SB	CS	SB%	GDP	Avg	OBP	Slg
															BATTING						BASERUNNING			AVERAGES		
2010	Mdest*	A+	1	4	1	1	0	0	(-	-)	2	0	1	0	0	0	2	0	0	0	0	0	-	0	.250	.250	.500
2010	ColSpr*	AAA	2	9	2	1	0	0	(-	-)	3	2	0	0	1	0	3	0	0	0	0	0	-	0	.222	.300	.333
2010	Charltt*	A+	2	4	1	0	0	0	(-	-)	1	0	0	0	2	0	1	0	0	0	0	0	-	1	.250	.500	.250
2004	Col	NL	42	105	26	3	2	3	(1	2)	42	12	9	11	11	3	34	1	0	1	1	1	.50	4	.248	.322	.400
2005	Col	NL	101	305	80	10	3	9	(5	4)	123	38	47	44	43	3	70	0	0	3	2	2	.50	4	.262	.350	.403
2006	Col	NL	150	499	146	33	6	22	(6	16)	257	67	84	85	74	11	123	0	0	2	5	5	.50	8	.293	.383	.515
2007	Col	NL	152	516	150	33	4	29	(19	10)	278	80	116	103	81	11	137	3	1	5	0	2	.00	13	.291	.387	.539
2008	Col	NL	138	488	138	24	3	25	(14	11)	243	69	85	86	76	6	134	3	0	2	2	2	.50	7	.283	.381	.498
2009	Col	NL	145	501	143	42	3	23	(9	14)	260	82	86	91	79	7	145	4	0	4	1	3	.25	18	.285	.384	.519
2010	2 Tms	NL	103	298	73	21	2	9	(6	3)	125	31	44	35	42	4	85	2	0	4	2	1	.67	5	.245	.338	.419
10	Col	NL	88	259	66	21	2	7	(6	1)	112	24	37	30	36	4	68	1	0	4	2	1	.67	4	.255	.343	.432
10	TB	AL	15	39	7	0	0	2	(0	2)	13	7	7	5	6	0	17	1	0	1	0	0	-	1	.179	.304	.333
	Postseason		13	43	11	0	1	1	(1	0)	16	4	4	6	0	0	17	0	0	0	0	0	-	0	.256	.373	.372
	7 ML YEARS		831	2712	756	166	23	120	(60	60)	1328	379	471	455	406	45	728	13	1	21	13	16	.45	60	.279	.373	.490

Brett Hayes

Bats: R **Throws:** R **Pos:** C-24; PR-2; PH-1   **Ht:** 6'1" **Wt:** 205 **Born:** 2/13/1984 **Age:** 27

Year	Team	Lg	G	AB	H	2B	3B	HR	(Hm	Rd)	TB	R	RBI	RC	TBB	IBB	SO	HBP	SH	SF	SB	CS	SB%	GDP	Avg	OBP	Slg
2005	Mrlns	R	3	12	5	1	0	0	(-	-)	6	2	2	1	0	0	2	0	0	0	0	1	.00	0	.417	.417	.500
2005	Jmstwn	A-	36	117	28	6	1	1	(-	-)	39	11	12	12	12	0	21	1	0	1	3	3	.50	3	.239	.313	.333
2006	Grnsbr	A	82	278	68	13	1	9	(-	-)	110	39	38	37	29	0	61	4	1	4	4	3	.57	5	.245	.321	.396
2007	Jupiter	A+	17	65	22	3	1	1	(-	-)	30	10	11	12	9	1	10	0	0	1	2	3	.40	2	.338	.413	.462
2007	Carlina	AA	74	273	64	16	0	3	(-	-)	89	22	31	26	18	0	51	0	2	2	2	0	1.00	7	.234	.280	.326
2008	Albq	AAA	37	116	34	3	1	5	(-	-)	54	21	17	17	4	0	23	3	2	1	1	1	.50	3	.293	.331	.466
2008	Carlina	AA	54	181	42	8	0	6	(-	-)	68	19	18	17	10	0	43	1	1	1	1	4	.20	1	.232	.275	.376
2009	NewOr	AAA	90	321	77	15	0	4	(-	-)	104	27	37	31	20	2	66	1	4	7	2	0	1.00	10	.240	.281	.324
2010	NewOr	AAA	16	59	13	3	0	1	(-	-)	19	7	5	4	2	0	9	1	0	1	0	0	-	1	.220	.254	.322
2010	Jupiter	A+	7	23	5	1	0	2	(-	-)	12	6	7	4	4	1	7	0	0	0	0	0	-	0	.217	.333	.522
2009	Fla	NL	14	11	3	1	0	1	(0	1)	7	5	2	1	0	0	4	1	0	0	0	0	-	1	.273	.333	.636
2010	Fla	NL	26	77	16	6	1	2	(1	1)	30	6	6	7	6	1	26	0	0	0	0	0	-	1	.208	.265	.390
	2 ML YEARS		40	88	19	7	1	3	(1	2)	37	11	8	8	6	1	30	1	0	0	0	0	-	2	.216	.274	.420

Chase Headley

Bats: B **Throws:** R **Pos:** 3B-158; PH-3   HEDD-lee   **Ht:** 6'2" **Wt:** 211 **Born:** 5/9/1984 **Age:** 27

Year	Team	Lg	G	AB	H	2B	3B	HR	(Hm	Rd)	TB	R	RBI	RC	TBB	IBB	SO	HBP	SH	SF	SB	CS	SB%	GDP	Avg	OBP	Slg
2007	SD	NL	8	18	4	1	0	0	(0	0)	5	1	0	1	2	0	4	1	0	0	0	0	-	2	.222	.333	.278
2008	SD	NL	91	331	89	19	2	9	(4	5)	139	34	38	42	30	1	104	5	0	2	4	1	.80	5	.269	.337	.420
2009	SD	NL	156	543	142	31	2	12	(7	5)	213	62	64	68	62	3	133	5	0	2	10	2	.83	19	.262	.342	.392
2010	SD	NL	161	610	161	29	3	11	(3	8)	229	77	58	70	56	3	139	3	1	4	17	5	.77	11	.264	.327	.375
	4 ML YEARS		416	1502	396	80	7	32	(14	18)	586	174	160	181	150	7	380	14	1	8	31	8	.79	37	.264	.335	.390

Aaron Heilman

Pitches: R **Bats:** R **Pos:** RP-70   HYLE-man   **Ht:** 6'5" **Wt:** 225 **Born:** 11/11/1978 **Age:** 32

Year	Team	Lg	G	GS	CG	GF	IP	BFP	H	R	ER	HR	SH	SF	HB	TBB	IBB	SO	WP	Bk	W	L	Pct	Sh	Sv-Op	Hld	ERC	ERA
2003	NYM	NL	14	13	0	0	65.1	315	79	53	49	13	5	3	3	41	2	51	5	0	2	7	.222	0	0-0	0	7.16	6.75
2004	NYM	NL	5	5	0	0	20.0	110	27	17	17	4	1	0	0	13	0	22	0	0	1	3	.250	0	0-0	0	4.54	5.46
2005	NYM	NL	53	7	1	20	108.0	439	87	40	38	6	4	1	6	37	4	106	1	1	5	3	.625	1	5-6	5	2.74	3.17
2006	NYM	NL	74	0	0	14	87.0	356	73	37	35	5	7	2	3	28	2	73	5	0	4	5	.444	0	0-5	27	2.76	3.62
2007	NYM	NL	81	0	0	28	86.0	352	72	36	29	8	4	2	5	20	1	63	2	0	7	7	.500	0	1-6	22	2.71	3.03
2008	NYM	NL	78	0	0	23	76.0	356	75	48	44	10	8	2	9	46	8	80	2	0	3	8	.273	0	3-8	15	5.26	5.21
2009	ChC	NL	70	0	0	11	72.1	313	68	34	33	9	9	4	1	34	4	65	4	0	4	4	.500	0	1-7	10	4.16	4.11
2010	Ari	NL	70	0	0	26	72.0	316	73	37	36	9	2	2	5	26	4	55	8	0	5	8	.385	0	6-14	12	4.32	4.50
	Postseason		6	0	0	1	7.1	30	7	3	3	2	0	0	1	1	1	6	1	0	0	1	.000	0	0-0	1	3.60	3.68
	8 ML YEARS		445	25	1	122	594.2	2566	554	302	281	64	40	16	32	245	25	515	27	1	31	45	.408	1	16-46	91	3.93	4.25

Chris Heisey

Bats: R **Throws:** R **Pos:** LF-38; PH-29; RF-27; CF-22; PR-2   HY-zee   **Ht:** 6'0" **Wt:** 215 **Born:** 12/14/1984 **Age:** 26

Year	Team	Lg	G	AB	H	2B	3B	HR	(Hm	Rd)	TB	R	RBI	RC	TBB	IBB	SO	HBP	SH	SF	SB	CS	SB%	GDP	Avg	OBP	Slg
2006	Billings	R+	70	245	70	10	0	6	(-	-)	98	46	37	38	28	0	33	2	9	4	11	5	.69	4	.286	.362	.400
2007	Dayton	A	104	374	108	24	2	9	(-	-)	163	60	46	60	25	0	57	10	5	5	19	5	.79	5	.289	.350	.436
2007	Srsota	A+	12	43	15	1	0	1	(-	-)	19	6	5	8	4	0	6	0	1	1	3	1	.75	1	.349	.396	.442
2008	Srsota	A+	117	436	125	31	7	7	(-	-)	191	77	51	82	57	2	69	11	8	3	27	2	.93	2	.287	.381	.438
2008	Chatt	AA	19	79	25	6	1	2	(-	-)	39	11	10	14	3	0	15	0	0	0	5	0	1.00	1	.316	.341	.494
2009	Carlina	AA	71	271	94	18	2	13	(-	-)	155	54	40	66	34	1	34	5	2	2	13	1	.93	3	.347	.426	.572
2009	Lsvlle	AAA	63	245	68	17	1	9	(-	-)	114	37	37	39	14	0	43	5	2	5	8	2	.80	1	.278	.323	.465
2010	Lsvlle	AAA	20	79	19	3	0	4	(-	-)	34	6	13	11	7	0	23	1	1	1	2	0	1.00	1	.241	.307	.430
2010	Cin	NL	97	201	51	10	1	8	(2	6)	87	33	21	22	16	1	57	6	1	2	1	2	.33	3	.254	.324	.433

Jeremy Hellickson

Pitches: R **Bats:** R **Pos:** RP-6; SP-4   **Ht:** 6'1" **Wt:** 185 **Born:** 4/8/1987 **Age:** 24

Year	Team	Lg	G	GS	CG	GF	IP	BFP	H	R	ER	HR	SH	SF	HB	TBB	IBB	SO	WP	Bk	W	L	Pct	Sh	Sv-Op	Hld	ERC	ERA
2005	Princtn	R+	4	0	0	1	6.0	27	6	4	4	1	0	0	1	1	0	11	0	0	0	0	-	0	0--	-	4.00	6.00
2006	HudVal	A-	15	14	0	0	77.2	309	55	24	21	3	1	0	6	16	0	96	4	0	4	3	.571	0	0--	-	1.78	2.43
2007	Clmbs	A	21	21	1	0	111.1	446	87	36	33	7	1	2	3	34	0	106	4	0	13	3	.813	0	0--	-	2.47	2.67
2008	VeroB	A+	14	14	0	0	76.2	296	64	19	17	7	0	1	4	5	0	83	3	1	7	1	.875	0	0--	-	2.15	2.00
2008	Mont	AA	13	13	0	0	75.1	308	84	36	33	15	3	0	2	15	1	79	1	0	4	4	.500	0	0--	-	4.90	3.94
2009	Mont	AA	11	11	0	0	56.2	226	41	16	15	4	0	1	4	14	0	62	1	0	3	1	.750	0	0--	-	2.16	2.38
2009	Drham	AAA	9	9	0	0	57.1	220	31	19	16	4	2	2	4	15	0	70	2	0	6	1	.857	0	0--	-	1.47	2.51
2010	Drham	AAA	21	21	0	0	117.2	483	103	35	32	5	5	3	7	35	0	123	0	0	12	3	.800	0	0--	-	2.90	2.45
2010	Charltt	A+	1	0	0	0	1.2	11	4	4	4	0	0	0	0	2	0	4	0	0	0	0	-	0	0--	-	15.90	21.60
2010	TB	AL	10	4	0	0	36.1	149	32	14	14	5	0	1	2	8	2	33	2	0	4	0	1.000	0	0-1	0	3.10	3.47

Wes Helms

Bats: R **Throws:** R **Pos:** 3B-90; PH-48; 1B-2 **Ht:** 6'4" **Wt:** 227 **Born:** 5/12/1976 **Age:** 35

Year	Team	Lg	G	AB	H	2B	3B	HR	(Hm	Rd)	TB	R	RBI	RC	TBB	IBB	SO	HBP	SH	SF	SB	CS	SB%	GDP	Avg	OBP	Slg
1998	Atl	NL	7	13	4	1	0	1	(0	1)	8	2	2	2	0	0	4	0	0	0	0	0	-	0	.308	.308	.615
2000	Atl	NL	6	5	1	0	0	0	(0	0)	1	0	0	0	0	0	2	0	0	0	0	0	-	0	.200	.200	.200
2001	Atl	NL	100	216	48	10	3	10	(6	4)	94	28	36	27	21	2	56	1	0	1	1	1	.50	3	.222	.293	.435
2002	Atl	NL	85	210	51	16	0	6	(4	2)	85	20	22	15	11	2	57	3	1	6	1	1	.50	5	.243	.283	.405
2003	Mil	NL	134	476	124	21	0	23	(16	7)	214	56	67	66	43	3	131	10	0	7	0	1	.00	10	.261	.330	.450
2004	Mil	NL	92	274	72	13	1	4	(3	1)	99	24	28	28	24	1	60	5	1	2	0	1	.00	10	.263	.331	.361
2005	Mil	NL	95	168	50	13	1	4	(2	2)	77	18	24	26	14	0	30	3	0	3	0	1	.00	7	.298	.356	.458
2006	Fla	NL	140	240	79	19	5	10	(4	6)	138	30	47	45	21	1	55	6	6	5	0	4	.00	7	.329	.390	.575
2007	Phi	NL	112	280	69	19	0	5	(3	2)	103	21	39	24	19	2	62	3	2	4	0	0	-	10	.246	.297	.368
2008	Fla	NL	132	251	61	11	0	5	(1	4)	87	28	31	29	17	0	65	5	0	5	0	0	-	6	.243	.299	.347
2009	Fla	NL	113	214	58	11	0	3	(1	2)	78	18	33	26	13	1	54	3	1	3	1	1	.50	10	.271	.318	.364
2010	Fla	NL	127	254	56	12	4	4	(1	3)	88	25	39	35	26	1	76	4	0	3	0	2	.00	7	.220	.300	.346
	Postseason		3	2	0	0	0	0	(0	0)	0	1	0	0	1	0	0	0	0	0	0	0	-	0	.000	.333	.000
	12 ML YEARS		1143	2601	673	146	14	75	(41	34)	1072	270	368	323	209	13	652	43	11	39	3	12	.20	75	.259	.320	.412

Todd Helton

Bats: L **Throws:** L **Pos:** 1B-115; PH-3 **Ht:** 6'2" **Wt:** 215 **Born:** 8/20/1973 **Age:** 37

Year	Team	Lg	G	AB	H	2B	3B	HR	(Hm	Rd)	TB	R	RBI	RC	TBB	IBB	SO	HBP	SH	SF	SB	CS	SB%	GDP	Avg	OBP	Slg
2010	Casper*	R+	3	10	5	1	0	0	(-	-)	6	1	5	3	2	0	1	0	0	1	0	0	-	0	.500	.538	.600
1997	Col	NL	35	93	26	2	1	5	(3	2)	45	13	11	15	8	0	11	0	0	0	0	1	.00	1	.280	.337	.484
1998	Col	NL	152	530	167	37	1	25	(13	12)	281	78	97	101	53	5	54	6	1	5	3	3	.50	15	.315	.380	.530
1999	Col	NL	159	578	185	39	5	35	(23	12)	339	114	113	124	68	6	77	6	0	4	7	6	.54	14	.320	.395	.587
2000	Col	NL	160	580	216	59	2	42	(27	15)	405	138	147	169	103	22	61	4	0	10	5	3	.63	12	.372	.463	.698
2001	Col	NL	159	587	197	54	2	49	(27	22)	402	132	146	157	98	15	104	5	1	5	7	5	.58	14	.336	.432	.685
2002	Col	NL	156	553	182	39	4	30	(18	12)	319	107	109	127	99	21	91	5	0	10	5	1	.83	10	.329	.429	.577
2003	Col	NL	160	583	209	49	5	33	(23	10)	367	135	117	160	111	21	72	2	0	7	0	4	.00	19	.358	.458	.630
2004	Col	NL	154	547	190	49	2	32	(21	11)	339	115	96	143	127	19	72	3	0	6	3	0	1.00	12	.347	.469	.620
2005	Col	NL	144	509	163	45	2	20	(13	7)	272	92	79	114	106	22	80	9	1	1	3	0	1.00	14	.320	.445	.534
2006	Col	NL	145	546	165	40	5	15	(8	7)	260	94	81	118	91	15	64	6	0	6	3	2	.60	10	.302	.404	.476
2007	Col	NL	154	557	178	42	2	17	(9	8)	275	86	91	115	116	16	74	2	0	7	0	1	.00	15	.320	.434	.494
2008	Col	NL	83	299	79	16	0	7	(5	2)	116	39	29	45	61	8	50	1	0	0	0	0	-	9	.264	.391	.388
2009	Col	NL	151	544	177	38	3	15	(10	5)	266	79	86	108	89	5	73	2	0	10	0	1	.00	15	.325	.416	.489
2010	Col	NL	118	398	102	18	1	8	(4	4)	146	48	37	51	67	3	90	2	0	6	0	0	-	10	.256	.362	.367
	Postseason		15	57	12	2	1	0	(0	0)	16	11	4	2	8	0	11	0	0	1	0	0	-	0	.211	.303	.281
	14 ML YEARS		1930	6904	2236	527	35	333	(204	129)	3832	1270	1239	1547	1197	178	973	53	3	77	36	27	.57	170	.324	.424	.555

Mark Hendrickson

Pitches: L **Bats:** L **Pos:** RP-51; SP-1 **Ht:** 6'9" **Wt:** 240 **Born:** 6/23/1974 **Age:** 37

| | | | HOW MUCH HE PITCHED | | | | | | WHAT HE GAVE UP | | | | | | | | | | THE RESULTS | | | | | | |
Year	Team	Lg	G	GS	CG	GF	IP	BFP	H	R	ER	HR	SH	SF	HB	TBB	IBB	SO	WP	Bk	W	L	Pct	Sh	Sv-Op	Hld	ERC	ERA
2002	Tor	AL	16	4	0	0	36.2	142	25	11	10	1	2	2	2	12	3	21	0	0	3	0	1.000	0	0-1	1	1.90	2.45
2003	Tor	AL	30	30	1	0	158.1	703	207	111	97	24	1	8	4	40	3	76	4	0	9	9	.500	1	0-0	0	5.64	5.51
2004	TB	AL	32	30	2	1	183.1	803	211	113	98	21	4	5	7	46	5	87	5	2	10	15	.400	0	0-0	0	4.51	4.81
2005	TB	AL	31	31	1	0	178.1	796	227	126	117	24	8	7	2	49	1	89	4	1	11	8	.579	0	0-0	0	5.44	5.90
2006	2 Tms		31	25	1	0	164.2	719	173	87	77	17	5	4	4	62	0	99	6	1	6	15	.286	1	0-0	1	4.38	4.21
2007	LAD	NL	39	15	0	4	122.2	532	142	75	71	15	12	4	1	29	4	92	4	0	4	8	.333	0	0-1	2	4.42	5.21
2008	Fla	NL	36	19	0	4	133.2	590	148	87	81	17	9	5	5	48	7	81	4	0	7	8	.467	0	0-0	3	4.78	5.45
2009	Bal	AL	53	11	0	12	105.0	457	116	59	51	16	2	5	2	33	4	61	2	1	6	5	.545	0	1-3	2	4.71	4.37
2010	Bal	AL	52	1	0	6	75.1	339	97	47	44	9	3	3	3	20	4	55	2	0	1	6	.143	0	0-2	8	5.40	5.26
06	TB	AL	13	13	1	0	89.2	377	81	42	38	10	2	3	2	34	0	51	4	0	4	8	.333	1	0-0	0	3.65	3.81
06	LAD	NL	18	12	0	0	75.0	342	92	45	39	7	3	1	2	28	0	48	2	1	2	7	.222	0	0-0	1	5.29	4.68
	Postseason		3	0	0	0	2.2	10	1	0	0	0	0	0	0	1	0	1	0	0	0	0	-	0	0-0	0	1.70	0.00
	9 ML YEARS		320	166	5	27	1158.0	5081	1346	716	646	144	46	43	26	339	31	661	31	5	57	74	.435	2	1-7	17	4.78	5.02

Clay Hensley

Pitches: R **Bats:** R **Pos:** RP-68 **Ht:** 5'11" **Wt:** 188 **Born:** 8/31/1979 **Age:** 31

| | | | HOW MUCH HE PITCHED | | | | | | WHAT HE GAVE UP | | | | | | | | | | THE RESULTS | | | | | | |
Year	Team	Lg	G	GS	CG	GF	IP	BFP	H	R	ER	HR	SH	SF	HB	TBB	IBB	SO	WP	Bk	W	L	Pct	Sh	Sv-Op	Hld	ERC	ERA
2010	Jupiter*	A+	2	0	0	0	2.2	10	1	0	0	0	0	0	0	1	0	2	0	0	0	0	-	0	0- -	0	0.85	0.00
2005	SD	NL	24	1	0	5	47.2	189	33	12	9	0	1	2	0	17	2	28	2	0	1	1	.500	0	0-0	2	1.70	1.70
2006	SD	NL	37	29	1	2	187.0	787	174	82	77	15	10	3	3	76	7	122	3	0	11	12	.478	1	0-1	1	3.64	3.71
2007	SD	NL	13	9	0	1	50.0	238	62	40	38	5	2	1	1	32	2	30	4	1	2	3	.400	0	0-0	0	6.54	6.84
2008	SD	NL	32	1	0	8	39.0	173	36	27	23	2	1	3	1	25	3	26	1	0	1	2	.333	0	0-1	3	4.23	5.31
2010	Fla	NL	68	0	0	23	75.0	307	54	20	18	3	3	1	4	29	4	77	2	0	3	4	.429	0	7-10	22	2.29	2.16
	Postseason		5	0	0	1	7.1	32	6	2	2	0	1	0	0	4	0	1	0	0	0	0	-	0	0-0	0	2.87	2.45
	5 ML YEARS		174	40	1	39	398.2	1694	359	181	165	25	17	10	9	179	18	283	12	1	18	22	.450	1	7-12	28	3.50	3.72

Jeremy Hermida

Bats: L Throws: R Pos: LF-47; RF-24; PH-10; DH-1   her-MEE-dah   Ht: 6'3" Wt: 222 Born: 1/30/1984 Age: 27

									BATTING													BASERUNNING				AVERAGES		
Year	Team	Lg	G	AB	H	2B	3B	HR	(Hm	Rd)	TB	R	RBI	RC	TBB	IBB	SO	HBP	SH	SF	SB	CS	SB%	GDP	Avg	OBP	Slg
2010	Portlnd*	AA	3	11	3	2	0	0	(-	-)	5	1	3	1	1	0	0	0	0	0	0	0	-	0	.273	.333	.455
2010	Pwtckt*	AAA	19	66	19	1	0	2	(-	-)	26	7	12	9	4	0	16	1	0	2	0	0	-	0	.288	.329	.394
2010	Scrmto*	AAA	3	13	4	2	0	0	(-	-)	6	3	3	2	1	0	3	0	0	0	0	0	-	0	.308	.357	.462
2005	Fla	NL	23	41	12	2	0	4	(4	0)	26	9	11	10	6	1	12	0	0	0	2	0	1.00	1	.293	.383	.634
2006	Fla	NL	99	307	77	19	1	5	(3	2)	113	37	28	38	33	3	70	5	2	1	4	1	.80	6	.251	.332	.368
2007	Fla	NL	123	429	127	32	1	18	(8	10)	215	54	63	69	47	2	105	4	1	3	3	4	.43	10	.296	.369	.501
2008	Fla	NL	142	502	125	22	3	17	(4	13)	204	74	61	65	48	5	138	7	1	1	6	1	.86	12	.249	.323	.406
2009	Fla	NL	129	429	111	14	2	13	(4	9)	168	48	47	57	56	4	101	4	0	2	5	2	.71	6	.259	.348	.392
2010	2 Tms	AL	73	222	48	12	0	6	(4	2)	78	19	29	20	16	0	58	0	0	1	1	0	1.00	6	.216	.268	.351
10	Bos	AL	52	158	32	8	0	5	(4	1)	55	14	27	17	12	0	45	0	0	1	1	0	1.00	1	.203	.257	.348
10	Oak	AL	21	64	16	4	0	1	(0	1)	23	5	2	3	4	0	13	0	0	0	0	0	-	5	.250	.294	.359
6 ML YEARS			589	1930	500	101	7	63	(27	36)	804	241	239	259	206	15	484	20	4	8	21	8	.72	41	.259	.335	.417

Anderson Hernandez

Bats: B Throws: R Pos: PH-21; SS-18; 2B-11; PR-3; 3B-1; LF-1   Ht: 5'9" Wt: 186 Born: 10/30/1982 Age: 28

									BATTING													BASERUNNING				AVERAGES		
Year	Team	Lg	G	AB	H	2B	3B	HR	(Hm	Rd)	TB	R	RBI	RC	TBB	IBB	SO	HBP	SH	SF	SB	CS	SB%	GDP	Avg	OBP	Slg
2010	Clmbs*	AAA	47	171	40	4	0	1	(-	-)	47	13	17	12	12	0	23	0	1	3	2	4	.33	3	.234	.280	.275
2010	RdRck*	AAA	7	29	7	1	0	0	(-	-)	8	5	1	2	1	0	6	0	0	0	2	0	1.00	1	.241	.267	.276
2005	NYM	NL	6	18	1	0	0	0	(0	0)	1	1	0	0	1	0	4	0	0	0	0	1	.00	0	.056	.105	.056
2006	NYM	NL	25	66	10	1	1	1	(1	0)	16	4	3	0	1	0	12	0	0	0	0	0	-	3	.152	.164	.242
2007	NYM	NL	4	3	1	0	0	0	(0	0)	1	1	0	0	0	0	1	0	0	0	0	0	-	0	.333	.333	.333
2008	Was	NL	28	81	27	4	0	0	(0	0)	31	11	17	18	10	0	8	0	0	0	0	0	-	1	.333	.407	.383
2009	2 Tms	NL	123	366	92	15	4	3	(0	3)	124	39	37	38	33	2	63	0	3	2	7	5	.58	10	.251	.312	.339
2010	2 Tms	NL	54	109	24	5	0	0	(0	0)	29	13	3	6	10	0	19	0	0	0	3	0	1.00	3	.220	.286	.266
09	Was	NL	77	231	58	9	2	1	(0	1)	74	25	23	21	20	1	41	0	3	1	5	3	.63	6	.251	.310	.320
09	NYM	NL	46	135	34	6	2	2	(0	2)	50	14	14	17	13	1	22	0	0	1	2	2	.50	4	.252	.315	.370
10	Cle	AL	22	61	15	3	0	0	(0	0)	18	6	2	3	2	0	9	0	0	0	1	0	1.00	2	.246	.270	.295
10	Hou	NL	32	48	9	2	0	0	(0	0)	11	7	1	3	8	0	10	0	0	0	2	0	1.00	1	.188	.304	.229
Postseason			2	1	0	0	0	0	(0	0)	0	0	0	0	0	0	1	0	0	0	0	0	-	0	.000	.000	.000
6 ML YEARS			240	643	155	25	5	4	(1	3)	202	69	60	62	55	2	107	0	3	2	10	6	.63	17	.241	.300	.314

David Hernandez

Pitches: R Bats: R Pos: RP-33; SP-8   Ht: 6'2" Wt: 240 Born: 5/13/1985 Age: 26

			HOW MUCH HE PITCHED							WHAT HE GAVE UP											THE RESULTS						
Year	Team	Lg	G	GS	CG	GF	IP	BFP	H	R	ER	HR	SH	SF	HB	TBB	IBB	SO	WP	Bk	W	L	Pct	Sh	Sv-Op	Hld	CRC	ERA
2005	Abrdn	A-	12	8	0	0	41.2	188	41	21	18	2	1	2	7	17	0	47	3	1	1	2	.333	0	0- -	-	4.23	3.89
2006	Dlmrva	A	28	28	0	0	145.1	639	134	83	67	13	4	3	10	71	0	154	22	0	7	8	.467	0	0- -	-	4.17	4.15
2007	Frdrck	A+	28	27	0	0	145.1	622	139	86	80	16	1	4	11	47	0	168	12	1	7	11	.389	0	0- -	-	3.89	4.95
2008	Bowie	AA	27	27	0	0	141.0	599	112	53	42	10	4	2	7	71	0	166	6	1	10	4	.714	0	0- -	-	3.35	2.68
2009	Norfolk	AAA	11	11	0	0	67.1	232	42	26	21	5	1	0	2	18	1	79	3	0	3	2	.600	0	0- -	-	2.37	3.30
2009	Bowie	AA	1	1	0	0	4.0	15	2	1	1	0	0	0	0	1	0	4	0	0	0	0	-	0	0- -	-	0.94	2.25
2010	Bowie	AA	2	0	0	1	2.0	7	1	0	0	0	0	0	0	0	0	3	0	0	0	0	-	0	0- -	-	0.54	0.00
2009	Bal	AL	20	19	0	0	101.1	462	118	62	61	27	2	3	1	46	0	68	3	0	4	10	.286	0	0 0	0	6.55	5.42
2010	Bal	AL	41	8	0	16	79.1	348	72	40	38	9	1	3	4	42	4	72	9	0	8	8	.500	0	2-6	2	4.28	4.31
2 ML YEARS			61	27	0	16	180.2	810	190	102	99	36	3	6	5	88	4	140	12	0	12	18	.400	0	2-6	2	5.53	4.93

Diory Hernandez

Bats: R Throws: R Pos: PH-10; PR-8; SS-4; 2B-1   dee-OR-ee   Ht: 6'0" Wt: 185 Born: 4/8/1984 Age: 27

									BATTING													BASERUNNING				AVERAGES		
Year	Team	Lg	G	AB	H	2B	3B	HR	(Hm	Rd)	TB	R	RBI	RC	TBB	IBB	SO	HBP	SH	SF	SB	CS	SB%	GDP	Avg	OBP	Slg
2003	Braves	R	54	190	42	9	2	1	(-	-)	58	26	12	16	14	0	24	4	1	1	2	4	.33	3	.221	.287	.305
2004	Rome	A	90	306	83	20	1	3	(-	-)	114	40	38	39	26	1	67	1	2	5	7	4	.64	8	.271	.325	.373
2005	Braves	R	7	28	10	1	0	1	(-	-)	14	5	4	4	0	0	2	0	0	0	0	2	.00	0	.357	.357	.500
2005	MrtlBh	A+	73	265	67	15	1	5	(-	-)	99	30	30	32	18	0	53	8	4	5	5	5	.50	5	.253	.314	.374
2006	MrtlBh	A+	76	286	68	10	0	6	(-	-)	96	37	47	31	19	2	51	5	0	2	11	1	.92	8	.238	.295	.336
2006	Braves	R	8	30	8	1	0	1	(-	-)	12	6	2	4	3	0	5	2	0	0	0	0	-	0	.267	.371	.400
2007	MrtlBh	A+	17	64	20	8	2	0	(-	-)	32	9	9	10	2	0	11	1	0	0	2	2	.50	1	.313	.343	.500
2007	Missi	AA	115	433	133	25	1	7	(-	-)	181	50	59	65	29	1	68	14	5	0	22	21	.51	13	.307	.370	.418
2008	Missi	AA	22	77	22	3	1	2	(-	-)	33	8	8	10	6	0	8	1	0	1	1	4	.20	3	.286	.341	.429
2008	Rchmd	AAA	120	459	132	23	3	5	(-	-)	176	46	53	57	20	0	73	2	4	5	7	5	.58	16	.288	.317	.383
2009	Gwnntt	AAA	54	204	65	16	1	1	(-	-)	86	18	32	35	21	0	34	7	1	1	8	6	.57	5	.319	.399	.422
2010	Gwnntt	AAA	30	116	37	7	2	0	(-	-)	48	13	17	16	4	0	21	1	0	1	3	1	.75	1	.319	.344	.414
2009	Atl	NL	33	85	12	3	0	1	(1	0)	18	6	6	0	6	3	22	0	2	0	0	1	.00	4	.141	.198	.212
2010	Atl	NL	20	9	1	0	0	1	(1	0)	4	5	1	0	0	0	4	0	1	0	0	0	-	0	.111	.111	.444
2 ML YEARS			53	94	13	3	0	2	(2	0)	22	11	7	0	6	3	26	0	3	0	0	1	.00	4	.138	.190	.234

Felix Hernandez

Pitches: R Bats: R Pos: SP-34

Ht: 6'3" Wt: 225 Born: 4/8/1986 Age: 25

Year	Team	Lg	G	GS	CG	GF	IP	BFP	H	R	ER	HR	SH	SF	HB	TBB	IBB	SO	WP	Bk	W	L	Pct	Sh	Sv-Op	Hld	ERC	ERA
2005	Sea	AL	12	12	0	0	84.1	328	61	26	25	5	1	2	2	23	0	77	3	0	4	4	.500	0	0-0	0	2.08	2.67
2006	Sea	AL	31	31	2	0	191.0	816	195	105	96	23	2	3	6	60	2	176	11	0	12	14	.462	1	0-0	0	4.11	4.52
2007	Sea	AL	30	30	1	0	190.1	808	209	88	83	20	6	1	3	53	4	165	7	1	14	7	.667	1	0-0	0	4.27	3.92
2008	Sea	AL	31	31	2	0	200.2	857	198	85	77	17	4	6	8	80	7	175	8	1	9	11	.450	0	0-0	0	4.05	3.45
2009	Sea	AL	34	34	2	0	238.2	977	200	81	66	15	6	11	8	71	0	217	17	1	19	5	.792	1	0-0	0	2.72	2.49
2010	Sea	AL	34	34	6	0	249.2	1001	194	80	63	17	6	3	8	70	1	232	14	1	13	12	.520	1	0-0	0	2.39	2.27
6 ML YEARS			172	172	13	0	1154.2	4787	1057	465	410	97	25	26	35	357	14	1042	60	4	71	53	.573	4	0-0	0	3.28	3.20

Livan Hernandez

Pitches: R Bats: R Pos: SP-33

lee-VAHN

Ht: 6'2" Wt: 245 Born: 2/20/1975 Age: 36

Year	Team	Lg	G	GS	CG	GF	IP	BFP	H	R	ER	HR	SH	SF	HB	TBB	IBB	SO	WP	Bk	W	L	Pct	Sh	Sv-Op	Hld	ERC	ERA
1996	Fla	NL	1	0	0	0	3.0	13	3	0	0	0	0	0	0	2	0	2	0	0	0	0	-	0	0-0	0	4.60	0.00
1997	Fla	NL	17	17	0	0	96.1	405	81	39	34	5	4	7	3	38	1	72	0	0	9	3	.750	0	0-0	0	2.96	3.18
1998	Fla	NL	33	33	9	0	234.1	1040	265	133	123	37	8	5	6	104	8	162	4	3	10	12	.455	0	0-0	0	5.58	4.72
1999	2 Tms	NL	30	30	2	0	199.2	886	227	110	103	23	7	6	2	76	5	144	2	2	8	12	.400	0	0-0	0	4.88	4.64
2000	SF	NL	33	33	5	0	240.0	1030	254	114	100	22	12	9	4	73	3	165	3	0	17	11	.607	2	0-0	0	4.01	3.75
2001	SF	NL	34	34	2	0	226.2	1008	266	143	132	24	12	12	3	85	7	138	7	0	13	15	.464	0	0-0	0	5.03	5.24
2002	SF	NL	33	33	5	0	216.0	921	233	113	105	19	14	8	4	71	5	134	1	1	12	16	.429	3	0-0	0	4.26	4.38
2003	Mon	NL	33	33	8	0	233.1	967	225	92	83	27	6	4	10	57	3	178	6	1	15	10	.600	0	0-0	0	3.55	3.20
2004	Mon	NL	35	35	9	0	255.0	1053	234	105	102	26	11	4	10	83	9	186	1	0	11	15	.423	2	0-0	0	3.52	3.60
2005	Was	NL	35	35	2	0	246.1	1065	268	116	109	25	15	9	13	84	14	147	3	2	15	10	.600	0	0-0	0	4.54	3.98
2006	2 Tms	NL	34	34	0	0	216.0	959	246	125	116	29	16	8	4	78	6	128	1	0	13	13	.500	0	0-0	0	4.97	4.83
2007	Ari	NL	33	33	1	0	204.1	913	247	116	112	34	17	8	6	79	1	90	3	2	11	11	.500	0	0-0	0	5.94	4.93
2008	2 Tms		31	31	2	0	180.0	811	257	129	121	25	5	9	2	43	4	67	3	1	13	11	.542	0	0-0	0	6.35	6.05
2009	2 Tms	NL	31	31	2	0	183.2	806	220	112	111	19	13	10	1	67	5	102	1	0	9	12	.429	0	0-0	0	5.17	5.44
2010	Was	NL	33	33	2	0	211.2	896	216	93	86	16	17	10	4	64	5	114	1	1	10	12	.455	1	0-0	0	3.69	3.66
99	Fla	NL	20	20	2	0	136.0	612	161	78	72	17	3	4	2	55	3	97	2	1	5	9	.357	0	0-0	0	5.37	4.76
99	SF	NL	10	10	0	0	63.2	274	66	32	31	6	4	2	0	21	2	47	0	1	3	3	.500	0	0-0	0	3.88	4.38
06	Was	NL	24	24	0	0	146.2	661	176	94	87	22	10	7	2	52	4	89	0	0	9	8	.529	0	0-0	0	5.38	5.34
06	Ari	NL	10	10	0	0	69.1	298	70	31	29	7	6	1	2	26	2	39	1	0	4	5	.444	0	0-0	0	4.13	3.76
08	Min	AL	23	23	2	0	139.2	627	199	93	85	18	4	9	1	29	3	54	2	1	10	8	.556	0	0-0	0	6.06	5.48
08	Col	NL	8	8	0	0	40.1	184	58	36	36	7	1	0	1	14	1	13	1	0	3	3	.500	0	0-0	0	7.38	8.03
09	NYM	NL	23	23	1	0	135.0	593	164	83	82	16	8	8	1	51	3	75	1	0	7	8	.467	0	0-0	0	5.50	5.47
09	Was	NL	8	8	1	0	48.2	213	56	29	29	3	5	2	0	16	2	27	0	0	2	4	.333	0	0-0	0	4.30	5.36
	Postseason		12	10	1	0	68.0	305	67	32	30	6	5	2	4	36	3	47	1	0	7	3	.700	0	0-0	0	4.56	3.97
15 ML YEARS			446	445	49	0	2946.1	12773	3242	1540	1437	331	157	109	72	1004	76	1829	36	13	166	163	.505	8	0-0	0	4.59	4.39

Luis Hernandez

Bats: B Throws: R Pos: 2B-10; SS-4; PH-3; 3B-2

Ht: 5'10" Wt: 182 Born: 6/26/1984 Age: 27

Year	Team	Lg	G	AB	H	2B	3B	HR	(Hm	Rd)	TB	R	RBI	RC	TBB	IBB	SO	HBP	SH	SF	SB	CS	SB%	GDP	Avg	OBP	Slg
2010	Buffalo*	AAA	47	189	53	10	4	0	(-	-)	71	25	12	23	10	3	31	2	4	3	2	1	.67	2	.280	.319	.376
2010	Bnghtn*	AA	57	225	67	12	4	3	(-	-)	96	28	32	33	16	0	30	2	1	5	4	4	.50	8	.298	.343	.427
2007	Bal	AL	30	69	20	2	0	1	(1	0)	25	5	7	6	1	0	10	0	1	0	2	2	.50	1	.290	.300	.362
2008	Bal	AL	36	79	19	1	0	0	(0	0)	20	9	3	6	7	0	11	0	3	2	2	0	1.00	2	.241	.295	.253
2009	KC	AL	37	73	15	1	0	0	(0	0)	16	4	4	4	4	0	18	1	3	0	1	0	1.00	2	.205	.256	.219
2010	NYM	NL	17	44	11	1	0	2	(1	1)	18	4	6	6	2	0	7	1	0	0	1	0	1.00	1	.250	.298	.409
4 ML YEARS			120	265	65	5	0	3	(2	1)	79	22	20	22	14	0	46	2	7	2	6	2	.75	6	.245	.286	.298

Ramon Hernandez

Bats: R Throws: R Pos: C-91; PH-6; 1B-5

Ht: 6'0" Wt: 225 Born: 5/20/1976 Age: 35

Year	Team	Lg	G	AB	H	2B	3B	HR	(Hm	Rd)	TB	R	RBI	RC	TBB	IBB	SO	HBP	SH	SF	SB	CS	SB%	GDP	Avg	OBP	Slg
1999	Oak	AL	40	136	38	7	0	3	(1	2)	54	13	21	20	18	0	11	1	1	2	1	0	1.00	5	.279	.363	.397
2000	Oak	AL	143	419	101	19	0	14	(7	7)	162	52	62	49	38	1	64	7	10	5	1	0	1.00	14	.241	.311	.387
2001	Oak	AL	136	453	115	25	0	15	(5	10)	185	55	60	58	37	3	68	6	9	4	1	1	.50	10	.254	.316	.408
2002	Oak	AL	136	403	94	20	0	7	(3	4)	135	51	42	41	43	1	64	5	3	3	0	0	-	11	.233	.313	.335
2003	Oak	AL	140	483	132	24	1	21	(9	12)	221	70	78	69	33	2	79	12	2	6	0	0	-	14	.273	.331	.458
2004	SD	NL	111	384	106	23	0	18	(10	8)	183	45	63	50	35	0	45	5	4	4	1	0	1.00	16	.276	.341	.477
2005	SD	NL	99	369	107	19	2	12	(5	7)	166	36	58	44	18	0	40	1	1	3	1	0	1.00	14	.290	.322	.450
2006	Bal	AL	144	501	138	29	2	23	(17	6)	240	66	91	82	43	2	79	11	0	5	1	0	1.00	13	.275	.343	.479
2007	Bal	AL	106	364	94	18	0	9	(4	5)	139	40	62	56	36	1	59	6	0	3	1	3	.25	9	.258	.333	.382
2008	Bal	AL	133	463	119	22	1	15	(10	5)	188	49	65	59	32	3	62	5	1	6	0	0	-	9	.257	.308	.406
2009	Cin	NL	81	287	74	13	1	5	(3	2)	104	25	37	42	33	2	34	3	4	4	1	0	1.00	9	.258	.336	.362
2010	Cin	NL	97	313	93	18	1	7	(3	4)	134	30	48	49	29	1	49	5	3	2	0	0	-	8	.297	.364	.428
	Postseason		22	69	15	2	0	1	(1	0)	20	6	6	7	5	0	13	3	2	0	0	0	-	2	.217	.299	.290
12 ML YEARS			1366	4575	1211	237	8	149	(76	73)	1911	532	687	619	395	16	654	67	38	47	8	4	.67	130	.265	.329	.418

130

David Herndon

Pitches: R Bats: R Pos: RP-47   **Ht: 6'5" Wt: 230 Born: 9/4/1985 Age: 25**

			HOW MUCH HE PITCHED						WHAT HE GAVE UP											THE RESULTS						
Year	Team	Lg	G	GS	CG	GF	IP	BFP	H	R	ER	HR	SH	SF	HB	TBB	IBB	SO	WP	Bk	W	L	Pct	Sh	Sv-Op	Hld	ERC	ERA
2006	Orem	R+	14	14	0	0	69.1	283	65	25	17	6	2	0	2	10	0	36	2	0	5	2	.714	0	0- -	-	2.76	2.21
2007	CRpds	A	25	24	2	1	152.1	640	175	80	68	10	4	7	6	20	0	83	2	0	13	8	.619	0	0- -	-	3.79	4.02
2008	RCuca	A+	43	12	0	30	100.2	426	120	58	56	10	3	5	3	16	1	70	0	0	3	7	.300	0	17- -	-	4.36	5.01
2009	Ark	AA	50	0	0	30	65.1	271	70	25	22	9	7	0	2	14	3	35	0	0	5	6	.455	0	11- -	-	4.14	3.03
2010	Phi	NL	47	0	0	14	52.1	232	67	27	25	2	2	2	2	17	4	29	1	0	1	3	.250	0	0-1	1	5.06	4.30

Daniel Ray Herrera

Pitches: L Bats: L Pos: RP-36   **Ht: 5'6" Wt: 165 Born: 10/21/1984 Age: 26**

			HOW MUCH HE PITCHED						WHAT HE GAVE UP											THE RESULTS						
Year	Team	Lg	G	GS	CG	GF	IP	BFP	H	R	ER	HR	SH	SF	HB	TBB	IBB	SO	WP	Bk	W	L	Pct	Sh	Sv-Op	Hld	ERC	ERA
2010	Lsvlle*	AAA	26	1	0	12	37.2	150	31	18	18	2	1	2	5	5	0	34	1	0	2	2	.500	0	5- -	-	2.39	4.30
2008	Cin	NL	7	0	0	0	7.1	37	10	7	6	1	2	0	2	3	2	8	0	0	0	0	-	0	0-0	0	7.05	7.36
2009	Cin	NL	70	0	0	13	61.2	262	63	30	21	5	3	5	2	24	2	44	1	0	4	4	.500	0	0-0	9	4.20	3.06
2010	Cin	NL	36	0	0	3	23.0	104	31	10	10	2	0	2	0	6	0	14	0	0	1	3	.250	0	0-1	9	5.41	3.91
	3 ML YEARS		113	0	0	16	92.0	403	104	47	37	8	5	7	4	33	4	66	1	0	5	7	.417	0	0-1	18	4.72	3.62

Jonathan Herrera

Bats: B Throws: R Pos: 2B-57; 3B-16; PH-8; SS-7; PR-3   **Ht: 5'9" Wt: 150 Born: 11/3/1984 Age: 26**

			BATTING																	BASERUNNING				AVERAGES		
Year	Team	Lg	G	AB	H	2B	3B	HR	(Hm	Rd)	TB	R	RBI	RC	TBB	IBB	SO	HBP	SH	SF	SB	CS	SB%	GDP	Avg	OBP	Slg
2003	Casper	R+	39	159	49	7	1	1	(-	-)	61	27	25	23	10	0	25	2	4	1	12	3	.80	2	.308	.355	.384
2004	Ashvll	A	95	380	106	20	2	6	(-	-)	148	71	35	51	26	0	80	7	3	2	21	12	.64	5	.279	.335	.389
2005	Ashvll	A	19	87	27	2	0	0	(-	-)	29	17	5	11	8	0	11	3	0	1	6	6	.50	1	.310	.384	.333
2005	Mdest	A+	73	310	80	9	4	2	(-	-)	103	48	30	34	23	0	52	3	8	1	9	4	.69	9	.258	.315	.332
2006	Mdest	A+	127	487	151	20	8	7	(-	-)	208	87	77	85	58	0	67	3	13	7	34	15	.69	7	.310	.382	.427
2007	Tulsa	AA	131	509	131	24	4	3	(-	-)	172	65	40	57	36	0	69	8	17	3	18	12	.60	5	.257	.315	.338
2008	ColSpr	AAA	66	226	70	7	0	3	(-	-)	86	40	31	35	19	0	30	2	2	1	15	2	.88	6	.310	.367	.381
2009	ColSpr	AAA	119	381	102	11	5	2	(-	-)	129	63	33	52	49	2	51	3	14	3	16	5	.76	9	.268	.353	.339
2010	ColSpr	AAA	58	222	58	6	1	2	(-	-)	72	30	17	27	27	0	29	1	7	3	3	3	.50	3	.261	.340	.324
2008	Col	NL	28	61	14	1	1	0	(0	0)	17	5	3	6	4	0	10	0	1	0	1	1	.50	0	.230	.277	.279
2010	Col	NL	76	222	63	6	2	1	(0	1)	76	34	21	29	25	1	36	0	7	3	2	2	.50	2	.284	.352	.342
	2 ML YEARS		104	283	77	7	3	1	(0	1)	93	39	24	35	29	1	46	0	8	3	3	3	.50	2	.272	.337	.329

Frank Herrmann

Pitches: R Bats: L Pos: RP-40   **Ht: 6'4" Wt: 220 Born: 5/30/1984 Age: 27**

			HOW MUCH HE PITCHED						WHAT HE GAVE UP											THE RESULTS						
Year	Team	Lg	G	GS	CG	GF	IP	BFP	H	R	ER	HR	SH	SF	HB	TBB	IBB	SO	WP	Bk	W	L	Pct	Sh	Sv-Op	Hld	ERC	ERA
2006	Lk Cty	A	26	26	0	0	122.1	540	122	61	53	8	7	1	17	47	0	89	5	0	4	6	.400	0	0- -	-	4.30	3.90
2007	Knstn	A+	26	26	3	0	146.0	623	163	75	65	15	5	7	11	28	1	88	2	1	11	5	.688	0	0- -	-	4.24	4.01
2008	Akron	A+	23	23	0	0	131.2	563	142	70	60	9	1	7	3	36	0	86	6	0	11	6	.647	0	0- -	-	3.89	4.10
2008	Knstn	A+	1	1	0	0	5.1	25	8	7	7	1	0	0	0	1	0	4	1	0	0	0	-	0	0- -	-	6.69	11.81
2008	Buffalo	AAA	2	2	0	0	13.0	55	11	3	2	1	3	0	0	6	0	14	0	0	0	2	.000	0	0- -	-	3.31	1.38
2009	Akron	AA	5	5	0	0	30.2	119	27	11	10	4	1	2	0	5	0	12	2	0	2	1	.667	0	0- -	-	2.81	2.93
2009	Clmbs	AAA	44	0	0	9	76.0	319	83	33	25	3	4	2	2	13	3	50	4	0	2	3	.400	0	2- -	-	3.32	2.96
2010	Clmbs	AAA	19	0	0	4	28.2	105	15	1	1	0	1	0	0	8	1	22	1	0	3	0	1.000	0	2- -	-	1.07	0.31
2010	Cle	AL	40	0	0	8	44.2	189	48	22	20	6	1	2	2	9	0	24	2	0	0	1	.000	0	1-2	7	4.12	4.03

Mike Hessman

Bats: R Throws: R Pos: PH-19; 3B-8; 1B-6; PR-1   **Ht: 6'5" Wt: 215 Born: 3/5/1978 Age: 33**

			BATTING																	BASERUNNING				AVERAGES		
Year	Team	Lg	G	AB	H	2B	3B	HR	(Hm	Rd)	TB	R	RBI	RC	TBB	IBB	SO	HBP	SH	SF	SB	CS	SB%	GDP	Avg	OBP	Slg
2010	Buffalo*	AAA	94	240	66	20	0	16	(	)	142	43	58	50	27	4	60	4	0	3	0	0	-	2	.274	.351	.573
2010	Mets*	R	1	4	2	0	0	0	(-	-)	2	1	0	0	0	0	0	0	0	0	0	0	-	0	.500	.500	.500
2003	Atl	NL	19	21	6	2	0	2	(1	1)	14	2	3	5	5	1	6	0	0	0	0	0	-	2	.286	.423	.667
2004	Atl	NL	29	69	9	3	0	2	(2	0)	18	8	5	1	1	0	24	1	0	0	0	0	-	0	.130	.155	.261
2007	Det	AL	17	51	12	0	0	4	(3	1)	24	7	12	7	5	0	17	0	0	1	0	0	-	0	.235	.298	.471
2008	Det	AL	12	27	8	1	0	5	(4	1)	24	6	7	7	2	0	9	2	0	0	0	0	-	0	.296	.387	.889
2010	NYM	NL	32	55	7	2	1	1	(0	1)	14	6	6	4	8	1	23	2	0	0	0	0	-	2	.127	.262	.255
	5 ML YEARS		109	223	42	8	1	14	(10	4)	94	29	33	24	21	2	79	5	0	1	0	0	-	4	.188	.272	.422

John Hester

Bats: R Throws: R Pos: C-33; PH-5; PR-1   **Ht: 6'3" Wt: 220 Born: 9/14/1983 Age: 27**

			BATTING																	BASERUNNING				AVERAGES		
Year	Team	Lg	G	AB	H	2B	3B	HR	(Hm	Rd)	TB	R	RBI	RC	TBB	IBB	SO	HBP	SH	SF	SB	CS	SB%	GDP	Avg	OBP	Slg
2006	Msoula	R+	56	192	52	16	4	6	(-	-)	94	36	41	36	27	1	52	5	0	3	6	2	.75	5	.271	.370	.490
2007	Visalia	A+	79	297	78	16	1	10	(-	-)	126	38	43	40	22	0	64	1	0	0	4	2	.67	4	.263	.316	.424
2008	Moblle	AA	92	306	82	20	2	11	(-	-)	145	38	49	45	16	0	78	2	0	7	3	2	.60	10	.268	.302	.474
2009	Reno	AAA	92	329	108	31	5	9	(-	-)	176	61	66	65	22	1	65	3	0	1	13	3	.81	7	.328	.375	.535
2010	Reno	AAA	37	138	51	12	4	7	(-	-)	92	34	29	36	16	1	26	3	0	2	2	4	.33	5	.370	.440	.667
2009	Ari	NL	15	28	7	2	0	1	(1	0)	12	4	4	5	2	0	7	0	0	0	0	0	-	0	.250	.300	.429
2010	Ari	NL	38	95	20	7	0	2	(1	1)	33	9	7	9	11	1	32	0	0	0	1	0	1.00	2	.211	.292	.347
	2 ML YEARS		53	123	27	9	0	3	(2	1)	45	13	11	14	13	1	39	0	0	0	1	0	1.00	2	.220	.294	.366

Jason Heyward

Bats: L Throws: L Pos: RF-140; PH-4; PR-1 — Ht: 6'5" Wt: 240 Born: 8/9/1989 Age: 21

Year	Team	Lg	G	AB	H	2B	3B	HR	(Hm	Rd)	TB	R	RBI	RC	TBB	IBB	SO	HBP	SH	SF	SB	CS	SB%	GDP	Avg	OBP	Slg
2007	Braves	R	8	27	8	4	0	1	(-	-)	15	1	5	5	2	0	4	1	0	1	1	1	.50	1	.296	.355	.556
2007	Danvle	R+	4	16	5	1	0	0	(-	-)	6	3	1	2	1	0	5	0	0	0	0	0	-	1	.313	.353	.375
2008	Rome	A	120	449	145	27	6	11	(-	-)	217	88	52	87	49	3	74	3	0	7	15	3	.83	4	.323	.388	.483
2008	MrtlBh	A+	7	22	4	2	0	0	(-	-)	6	3	4	1	2	0	4	0	0	1	0	0	-	1	.182	.240	.273
2009	MrtlBh	A+	49	189	56	12	0	10	(-	-)	98	34	31	37	21	1	30	2	0	2	4	0	1.00	2	.296	.369	.519
2009	Missi	AA	47	162	57	13	4	7	(-	-)	99	32	30	43	28	4	19	2	0	3	5	1	.83	1	.352	.446	.611
2009	Gwnntt	AAA	3	11	4	0	0	0	(-	-)	4	3	2	2	2	0	2	0	0	0	1	0	1.00	0	.364	.462	.364
2010	Atl	NL	142	520	144	29	5	18	(9	9)	237	83	72	96	91	2	128	10	0	2	11	6	.65	13	.277	.393	.456

Brandon Hicks

Bats: R Throws: R Pos: PR-10; PH-5; 3B-3; SS-2; 2B-1 — Ht: 6'2" Wt: 200 Born: 9/14/1985 Age: 25

Year	Team	Lg	G	AB	H	2B	3B	HR	(Hm	Rd)	TB	R	RBI	RC	TBB	IBB	SO	HBP	SH	SF	SB	CS	SB%	GDP	Avg	OBP	Slg
2007	Danvle	R+	18	58	13	3	1	3	(-	-)	27	14	13	10	12	0	18	2	1	1	1	2	.33	1	.224	.370	.466
2007	Rome	A	37	128	40	11	0	4	(-	-)	63	26	15	28	27	2	26	1	0	1	5	3	.63	2	.313	.433	.492
2008	MrtlBh	A+	93	342	80	23	2	19	(-	-)	164	68	56	59	45	1	122	8	3	2	14	3	.82	9	.234	.335	.480
2008	Missi	AA	16	54	13	3	1	1	(-	-)	21	9	7	7	7	0	17	1	1	1	0	0	-	2	.241	.333	.389
2009	Missi	AA	128	464	110	25	4	10	(-	-)	173	63	48	62	53	1	131	5	8	4	17	1	.94	5	.237	.319	.373
2010	Gwnntt	AAA	77	261	55	9	1	7	(-	-)	87	27	22	24	20	1	74	5	1	0	10	6	.63	6	.211	.280	.333
2010	Atl	NL	16	5	0	0	0	0	(0	0)	0	7	0	0	1	0	2	0	0	0	0	0	-	0	.000	.167	.000

Aaron Hill

Bats: R Throws: R Pos: 2B-137; DH-1 — Ht: 5'11" Wt: 205 Born: 3/21/1982 Age: 29

Year	Team	Lg	G	AB	H	2B	3B	HR	(Hm	Rd)	TB	R	RBI	RC	TBB	IBB	SO	HBP	SH	SF	SB	CS	SB%	GDP	Avg	OBP	Slg
2005	Tor	AL	105	361	99	25	3	3	(3	0)	139	49	40	50	34	0	41	5	3	4	2	1	.67	5	.274	.342	.385
2006	Tor	AL	155	546	159	28	3	6	(4	2)	211	70	50	68	42	5	66	9	4	5	5	2	.71	15	.291	.349	.386
2007	Tor	AL	160	608	177	47	2	17	(8	9)	279	87	78	88	41	1	102	0	3	5	4	3	.57	21	.291	.333	.459
2008	Tor	AL	55	205	54	14	0	2	(1	1)	74	19	20	24	16	0	31	3	4	1	4	2	.67	4	.263	.324	.361
2009	Tor	AL	158	682	195	37	0	36	(21	15)	340	103	108	110	42	1	98	5	1	4	6	2	.75	17	.286	.330	.499
2010	Tor	AL	138	528	108	22	0	26	(15	11)	208	70	68	57	41	2	85	8	1	2	2	2	.50	8	.205	.271	.394
6 ML YEARS			771	2930	792	173	8	90	(52	38)	1251	398	364	397	216	9	423	30	16	21	23	12	.66	70	.270	.325	.427

Koyie Hill

Bats: B Throws: R Pos: C-72; PH-5; 3B-1 — KOY-ee — Ht: 6'1" Wt: 210 Born: 3/9/1979 Age: 32

Year	Team	Lg	G	AB	H	2B	3B	HR	(Hm	Rd)	TB	R	RBI	RC	TBB	IBB	SO	HBP	SH	SF	SB	CS	SB%	GDP	Avg	OBP	Slg
2003	LAD	NL	3	3	1	1	0	0	(0	0)	2	0	0	0	0	0	2	0	0	0	0	0	-	0	.333	.333	.667
2004	Ari	NL	13	36	9	1	0	1	(1	0)	13	3	6	5	2	1	6	0	0	0	1	0	1.00	1	.250	.289	.361
2005	Ari	NL	34	78	17	5	0	0	(0	0)	22	6	6	6	11	0	27	0	0	2	0	1	.00	0	.218	.308	.282
2007	ChC	NL	36	93	15	4	0	2	(1	1)	25	7	12	3	8	0	18	1	1	2	0	0	-	4	.161	.231	.269
2008	ChC	NL	10	21	2	1	0	0	(0	0)	3	0	1	0	0	0	12	1	0	1	0	0	-	0	.095	.095	.143
2009	ChC	NL	83	253	60	12	2	2	(1	1)	82	26	24	23	27	6	78	1	2	1	0	0	-	9	.237	.312	.324
2010	ChC	NL	77	215	46	13	1	1	(1	0)	64	18	17	17	12	3	61	0	3	1	1	0	1.00	0	.214	.254	.298
7 ML YEARS			256	699	150	37	3	6	(4	2)	211	60	66	54	60	10	204	2	7	6	2	1	.67	19	.215	.276	.302

Rich Hill

Pitches: L Bats: L Pos: RP-6 — Ht: 6'5" Wt: 205 Born: 3/11/1980 Age: 31

Year	Team	Lg	G	GS	CG	GF	IP	BFP	H	R	ER	HR	SH	SF	HB	TBB	IBB	SO	WP	Bk	W	L	Pct	Sh	Sv-Op	Hld	ERC	ERA
2010	Memp*	AAA	23	4	0	4	46.0	203	35	26	22	5	1	3	8	30	1	47	1	1	4	3	.571	0	0--	-	4.51	4.30
2010	Pwtckt*	AAA	19	6	0	4	53.0	233	45	22	22	3	1	1	9	29	0	55	1	2	3	1	.750	0	0--	-	4.21	3.74
2005	ChC	NL	10	4	0	1	23.2	115	25	24	24	3	1	0	1	17	1	21	0	0	0	2	.000	0	0-0	0	5.81	9.13
2006	ChC	NL	17	16	2	1	99.1	417	83	51	46	16	8	3	2	39	1	90	3	0	6	7	.462	1	0-0	0	3.59	4.17
2007	ChC	NL	32	32	0	0	195.0	812	170	89	85	27	9	4	12	63	3	183	1	1	11	8	.579	0	0-0	0	3.56	3.92
2008	ChC	NL	5	5	0	0	19.2	89	13	9	9	2	0	2	1	18	0	15	1	0	1	0	1.000	0	0-0	0	4.38	4.12
2009	Bal	AL	14	13	0	0	57.2	275	68	53	50	7	2	2	1	40	2	46	1	1	3	3	.500	0	0-0	0	6.55	7.80
2010	Bos	AL	6	0	0	0	4.0	18	5	0	0	0	0	0	0	1	0	3	0	0	1	0	1.000	0	0-0	1	4.05	0.00
Postseason			1	1	0	0	3.0	18	6	3	3	1	0	0	1	2	0	3	0	0	0	1	.000	0	0-0	0	15.68	9.00
6 ML YEARS			84	70	2	2	399.1	1726	364	226	214	55	20	11	17	178	7	358	6	2	22	20	.524	1	0-0	1	4.16	4.82

Shawn Hill

Pitches: R Bats: R Pos: SP-4 — Ht: 6'2" Wt: 225 Born: 4/28/1981 Age: 30

Year	Team	Lg	G	GS	CG	GF	IP	BFP	H	R	ER	HR	SH	SF	HB	TBB	IBB	SO	WP	Bk	W	L	Pct	Sh	Sv-Op	Hld	ERC	ERA
2010	B Jays*	R	4	4	0	0	22.0	85	18	1	1	0	0	0	0	1	0	21	0	0	3	0	1.000	0	0--	-	1.42	0.41
2010	Dnedin*	A+	1	1	0	0	6.0	25	7	2	2	0	1	1	0	0	0	5	0	0	0	0	-	0	0--	-	2.72	3.00
2010	NHam*	AA	1	1	0	0	7.0	26	3	0	0	0	0	0	0	2	0	4	0	0	1	0	1.000	0	0--	-	0.83	0.00
2010	LsVgs*	AAA	5	5	0	0	21.0	81	16	8	7	2	1	0	0	5	0	9	0	0	2	2	.500	0	0--	-	2.28	3.00
2004	Mon	NL	3	3	0	0	9.0	51	17	16	16	1	0	2	1	7	0	10	0	0	1	2	.333	0	0-0	0	12.14	16.00
2006	Was	NL	6	6	0	0	36.2	163	43	20	19	2	2	1	3	12	2	16	1	0	3	3	.250	0	0-0	0	4.70	4.66
2007	Was	NL	16	16	0	0	97.1	399	86	42	37	9	2	1	5	25	2	65	2	0	4	5	.444	0	0-0	0	3.03	3.42

Year	Team	Lg	G	GS	CG	GF	IP	BFP	H	R	ER	HR	SH	SF	HB	TBB	IBB	SO	WP	Bk	W	L	Pct	Sh	Sv-Op	Hld	ERC	ERA
2008	Was	NL	12	12	0	0	63.1	296	88	47	41	5	3	3	1	23	2	39	2	1	1	5	.167	0	0-0	0	6.04	5.83
2009	SD	NL	3	3	0	0	12.0	56	15	7	7	1	2	1	1	3	0	7	0	0	1	1	.500	0	0-0	0	4.90	5.25
2010	Tor	AL	4	4	0	0	20.2	91	24	8	6	1	0	1	1	4	0	14	1	0	1	2	.333	0	0-0	0	3.89	2.61
	6 ML YEARS		44	44	0	0	239.0	1056	273	140	126	19	9	9	12	74	6	151	6	1	9	18	.333	0	0-0	0	4.51	4.74

Steven Hill

Bats: R **Throws:** R **Pos:** C-1

Ht: 5'11" **Wt:** 200 **Born:** 3/14/1985 **Age:** 26

							BATTING													BASERUNNING				AVERAGES		
Year	Team	Lg	G	AB	H	2B	3B	HR	(Hm | Rd)	TB	R	RBI	RC	TBB	IBB	SO	HBP	SH	SF	SB	CS	SB%	GDP	Avg	OBP	Slg
2007	Batvia	A-	10	39	17	5	1	1	(- | -)	27	4	11	12	5	0	5	1	0	0	0	0	-	-	.436	.511	.692
2007	QuadC	A	62	261	79	15	0	11	(- | -)	127	38	44	41	9	0	58	2	0	1	1	1	.50	4	.303	.330	.487
2008	PlmBh	A+	46	172	49	11	2	9	(- | -)	91	28	34	31	15	0	42	0	0	2	0	0	-	5	.285	.339	.529
2008	Sprgfld	AA	26	99	30	3	1	5	(- | -)	50	13	9	16	3	0	31	1	0	0	0	0	-	3	.303	.330	.505
2008	Cards	R	4	16	5	1	0	3	(- | -)	15	4	5	4	0	0	7	0	0	0	0	0	-	1	.313	.313	.938
2009	Sprgfld	AA	120	464	131	26	2	19	(- | -)	218	62	64	73	36	6	106	2	0	6	1	2	.33	11	.282	.333	.470
2010	Sprgfld	AA	93	361	101	27	1	22	(- | -)	196	60	86	69	38	3	90	4	0	3	1	0	1.00	11	.280	.352	.543
2010	Memp	AAA	9	34	6	1	0	2	(- | -)	13	2	6	3	3	0	10	1	0	0	0	0	-	3	.176	.263	.382
2010	StL	NL	1	3	1	0	0	1	(1 | 0)	4	1	1	0	0	0	1	0	0	0	0	0	-	0	.333	.333	1.333

Eric Hinske

Bats: L **Throws:** R **Pos:** PH-56; LF-50; 1B-32; 3B-1; DH-1

Ht: 6'2" **Wt:** 235 **Born:** 8/5/1977 **Age:** 33

							BATTING													BASERUNNING				AVERAGES		
Year	Team	Lg	G	AB	H	2B	3B	HR	(Hm | Rd)	TB	R	RBI	RC	TBB	IBB	SO	HBP	SH	SF	SB	CS	SB%	GDP	Avg	OBP	Slg
2002	Tor	AL	151	566	158	38	2	24	(15 | 9)	272	99	84	103	77	5	138	2	0	5	13	1	.93	12	.279	.365	.481
2003	Tor	AL	124	449	109	45	3	12	(4 | 8)	196	74	63	66	59	1	104	1	0	5	12	2	.86	11	.243	.329	.437
2004	Tor	AL	155	570	140	23	3	15	(6 | 9)	214	66	69	60	54	2	109	4	0	6	12	8	.60	14	.246	.312	.375
2005	Tor	AL	147	477	125	31	2	15	(7 | 8)	205	79	68	71	46	4	121	8	0	6	8	4	.67	8	.262	.333	.430
2006	2 Tms	AL	109	277	75	17	2	13	(7 | 6)	135	43	34	39	35	2	79	0	0	0	2	2	.50	8	.271	.353	.487
2007	Bos	AL	84	186	38	12	3	6	(4 | 2)	74	25	21	22	28	2	54	3	0	1	3	0	1.00	7	.204	.317	.398
2008	TB	AL	133	381	94	21	1	20	(8 | 12)	177	59	60	53	47	4	88	3	0	1	10	3	.77	13	.247	.333	.465
2009	2 Tms	NL	93	190	46	12	0	8	(2 | 6)	82	31	25	27	27	1	52	5	0	2	1	0	1.00	2	.242	.348	.432
2010	Atl	NL	131	281	72	21	1	11	(7 | 4)	128	38	51	40	33	5	75	3	0	3	0	0	-	4	.256	.330	.456
06	Tor	AL	78	197	52	9	2	12	(6 | 6)	101	35	29	29	27	2	49	0	0	0	1	1	.50	6	.264	.353	.513
06	Bos	AL	31	80	23	8	0	1	(1 | 0)	34	8	5	10	8	0	30	0	0	0	1	1	.50	2	.288	.352	.425
09	Pit	NL	54	106	27	9	0	1	(0 | 1)	39	18	11	16	17	0	27	3	0	0	0	0	-	0	.255	.373	.368
09	NYY	NL	39	84	19	3	0	7	(2 | 5)	43	13	14	11	10	1	25	2	0	2	1	0	1.00	2	.226	.316	.512
	Postseason		6	4	1	0	0	1	(0 | 1)	4	3	1	0	1	0	3	0	0	0	0	0	-	0	.250	.400	1.000
	9 ML YEARS		1127	3377	857	220	17	124	(60 | 64)	1483	514	475	481	406	26	820	29	0	29	61	20	75	79	.254	.336	.439

Luke Hochevar

Pitches: R **Bats:** R **Pos:** SP-17; RP-1

HOE-chay-vur

Ht: 6'5" **Wt:** 218 **Born:** 9/15/1983 **Age:** 27

							HOW MUCH HE PITCHED							WHAT HE GAVE UP								THE RESULTS				
Year	Team	Lg	G	GS	CG	GF	IP	BFP	H	R	ER	HR	SH	SF	HB	TBB	IBB	SO	WP	Bk	W	L	Pct	Sh	Sv-Op	Hld	ERC	ERA
2010	Omha*	AAA	2	2	0	0	5.0	20	3	1	1	0	0	0	1	1	0	4	2	0	0	0	-	0	0- -	1	1.51	1.80
2007	KC	AL	4	1	0	1	12.2	54	11	4	3	1	1	0	3	4	0	5	1	0	0	1	.000	0	0-0	0	3.86	2.13
2008	KC	AL	22	22	0	0	129.0	566	143	84	79	12	1	2	5	47	1	72	7	0	6	12	.333	0	0-0	0	4.67	5.51
2009	KC	AL	25	25	2	0	143.0	631	167	109	104	23	2	0	8	46	0	106	9	0	7	13	.350	1	0-0	0	5.46	6.55
2010	KC	AL	18	17	1	0	103.0	450	110	61	55	9	2	2	4	37	1	76	2	1	6	6	.500	0	0-0	0	4.34	4.81
	4 ML YEARS		69	65	3	1	387.2	1701	431	258	241	45	6	4	20	134	2	259	19	1	19	32	.373	1	0-0	0	4.84	5.60

Trevor Hoffman

Pitches: R **Bats:** R **Pos:** RP-50

Ht: 6'0" **Wt:** 221 **Born:** 10/13/1967 **Age:** 43

							HOW MUCH HE PITCHED							WHAT HE GAVE UP								THE RESULTS				
Year	Team	Lg	G	CG	CG	GF	IP	BFP	H	R	ER	HR	SH	SF	HB	TBB	IBB	SO	WP	Bk	W	L	Pct	Sh	Sv-Op	Hld	ERC	ERA
1993	2 Tms	NL	67	0	0	26	90.0	391	80	43	39	10	4	5	1	39	13	79	5	0	4	6	.400	0	5-8	15	3.40	3.90
1994	SD	NL	47	0	0	41	56.0	225	39	16	16	4	1	2	0	20	6	68	3	0	4	4	.500	0	20-23	1	2.02	2.57
1995	SD	NL	55	0	0	51	53.1	218	48	25	23	10	0	0	0	14	3	52	1	0	7	4	.636	0	31-38	0	3.48	3.88
1996	SD	NL	70	0	0	62	88.0	348	50	23	22	6	2	2	2	31	5	111	2	0	9	5	.643	0	42-49	0	1.58	2.25
1997	SD	NL	70	0	0	59	81.1	322	59	25	24	9	2	1	0	24	4	111	7	0	6	4	.600	0	37-44	0	2.27	2.66
1998	SD	NL	66	0	0	61	73.0	274	41	12	12	2	3	0	1	21	2	86	8	0	4	2	.667	0	53-54	0	1.32	1.48
1999	SD	NL	64	0	0	54	67.1	263	48	23	16	5	1	3	0	15	2	73	4	0	2	3	.400	0	40-43	0	1.78	2.14
2000	SD	NL	70	0	0	59	72.1	291	61	29	24	7	4	4	1	11	4	85	4	0	4	7	.364	0	43-50	0	2.18	2.99
2001	SD	NL	62	0	0	55	60.1	248	48	25	23	10	2	2	1	21	2	63	3	0	3	4	.429	0	43-46	0	3.20	3.43
2002	SD	NL	61	0	0	52	59.1	245	52	20	18	2	2	2	1	18	2	69	3	0	2	5	.286	0	38-41	0	2.63	2.73
2003	SD	NL	9	0	0	7	9.0	36	7	2	2	1	0	0	0	3	0	11	0	0	0	0	-	0	0-0	0	2.76	2.00
2004	SD	NL	55	0	0	51	54.2	206	42	14	14	5	2	0	0	8	1	53	2	0	3	3	.500	0	41-45	0	1.92	2.30
2005	SD	NL	60	0	0	54	57.2	240	52	23	19	3	2	3	1	12	1	54	1	0	1	6	.143	0	43-46	0	2.49	2.97
2006	SD	NL	65	0	0	50	63.0	248	48	16	15	6	0	0	1	13	1	50	2	0	0	2	.000	0	46-51	0	2.14	2.14
2007	SD	NL	61	0	0	50	57.1	235	49	21	19	2	3	2	0	9	5	44	0	0	4	5	.444	0	42-49	0	2.23	2.98
2008	SD	NL	48	0	0	42	45.1	180	38	19	19	8	1	0	0	9	2	46	2	0	3	6	.333	0	30-34	0	2.86	3.77
2009	Mil	NL	55	0	0	46	54.0	210	35	11	11	2	2	1	0	14	2	48	2	0	3	2	.600	0	37-41	0	1.53	1.83
2010	Mil	NL	50	0	0	36	47.1	205	49	31	31	8	2	1	0	19	3	30	2	0	2	7	.222	0	10-15	2	4.69	5.89
93	Fla	NL	28	0	0	13	35.2	152	24	13	13	5	2	1	0	19	7	26	3	0	2	2	.500	0	2-3	8	2.71	3.28
93	SD	NL	39	0	0	13	54.1	239	56	30	26	5	2	4	1	20	6	53	2	0	2	4	.333	0	3-5	7	3.88	4.31
	Postseason		12	0	0	11	13.0	55	11	6	5	2	0	1	0	5	1	14	0	0	1	2	.333	0	4-6	0	3.35	3.46
	18 ML YEARS		1035	0	0	856	1089.1	4388	846	378	347	100	32	30	9	307	58	1133	49	0	61	75	.449	0	601-677	18	2.36	2.87

Jarrett Hoffpauir

Bats: R **Throws:** R **Pos:** 3B-11; 2B-2; PH-1   HOFF-pah-werr   **Ht:** 5'9" **Wt:** 190 **Born:** 6/18/1983 **Age:** 28

Year	Team	Lg	G	AB	H	2B	3B	HR	(Hm	Rd)	TB	R	RBI	RC	TBB	IBB	SO	HBP	SH	SF	SB	CS	SB%	GDP	Avg	OBP	Slg
2004	NewJrs	A-	9	36	13	3	0	3	(-	-)	25	8	6	9	3	0	2	0	0	0	1	0	1.00	1	.361	.410	.694
2004	Peoria	A	62	231	62	20	1	5	(-	-)	99	34	30	37	29	2	21	6	0	1	2	4	.33	4	.268	.363	.429
2005	QuadC	A	61	227	71	15	1	2	(-	-)	94	27	28	38	21	1	14	4	1	3	5	1	.83	3	.313	.376	.414
2005	PlmBh	A+	63	226	58	10	1	0	(-	-)	70	23	19	28	32	0	26	0	5	2	11	5	.69	2	.257	.346	.310
2006	Sprgfld	AA	120	393	98	20	1	7	(-	-)	141	55	46	53	54	4	41	5	5	3	9	6	.60	9	.249	.345	.359
2007	Sprgfld	AA	61	203	70	16	0	7	(-	-)	107	23	33	45	26	2	18	1	5	1	3	1	.75	9	.345	.420	.527
2007	Memp	AAA	55	190	57	10	0	4	(-	-)	79	27	24	33	29	0	21	1	4	1	2	3	.40	7	.300	.394	.416
2008	Memp	AAA	121	410	112	31	1	4	(-	-)	157	48	45	59	49	3	45	4	6	6	2	4	.33	12	.273	.352	.383
2009	Memp	AAA	108	358	104	22	3	14	(-	-)	174	53	53	64	35	1	28	3	4	2	4	1	.80	10	.291	.357	.486
2010	LsVgs	AAA	107	431	127	26	6	16	(-	-)	213	73	73	83	58	1	34	2	3	6	8	3	.73	8	.295	.376	.494
2009	StL	NL	8	12	3	2	0	0	(0	0)	5	1	2	3	4	0	2	0	0	0	0	0	-	1	.250	.438	.417
2010	Tor	AL	13	34	7	1	0	0	(0	0)	8	1	0	1	2	0	5	0	1	0	0	0	-	1	.206	.250	.235
	2 ML YEARS		21	46	10	3	0	0	(0	0)	13	2	2	4	6	0	7	0	1	0	0	0	-	2	.217	.308	.283

Micah Hoffpauir

Bats: L **Throws:** L **Pos:** 1B-12; PH-11; LF-3; RF-2   HOFF-pah-werr   **Ht:** 6'3" **Wt:** 215 **Born:** 3/1/1980 **Age:** 31

Year	Team	Lg	G	AB	H	2B	3B	HR	(Hm	Rd)	TB	R	RBI	RC	TBB	IBB	SO	HBP	SH	SF	SB	CS	SB%	GDP	Avg	OBP	Slg
2010	Iowa*	AAA	118	427	121	35	2	22			226	81	95	85	56	2	74	5	0	6	1	0	1.00	6	.283	.368	.529
2008	ChC	NL	33	73	25	8	0	2	(0	2)	39	14	8	14	6	0	24	1	0	1	1	0	1.00	6	.342	.400	.534
2009	ChC	NL	105	234	56	12	1	10	(4	6)	100	28	35	27	20	1	46	1	0	2	1	0	1.00	3	.239	.300	.427
2010	ChC	NL	24	52	9	3	0	0	(0	0)	12	5	5	2	5	0	15	0	0	0	0	0	-	3	.173	.246	.231
	3 ML YEARS		162	359	90	23	1	12	(4	8)	151	47	48	43	31	1	85	2	0	2	2	0	1.00	6	.251	.312	.421

Derek Holland

Pitches: L **Bats:** B **Pos:** SP-10; RP-4   **Ht:** 6'2" **Wt:** 193 **Born:** 10/9/1986 **Age:** 24

Year	Team	Lg	G	GS	CG	GF	IP	BFP	H	R	ER	HR	SH	SF	HB	TBB	IBB	SO	WP	Bk	W	L	Pct	Sh	Sv-Op	Hld	ERC	ERA
2007	Spkane	A-	16	14	0	0	67.0	284	57	33	24	7	1	1	6	21	0	83	7	0	4	5	.444	0	0--	-	3.25	3.22
2008	Clinton	A	17	17	0	0	93.2	376	77	30	25	2	4	3	2	29	0	91	3	0	7	0	1.000	0	0--	-	2.43	2.40
2008	Bkrsfld	A+	5	5	0	0	31.0	114	20	12	11	1	0	0	1	5	0	37	1	1	3	1	.750	0	0--	-	1.40	3.19
2008	Frisco	AA	4	4	0	0	26.0	94	14	4	2	0	2	0	0	6	0	29	0	0	3	0	1.000	0	0--	-	1.05	0.69
2009	Okla	AAA	1	1	0	0	4.0	17	5	4	4	1	0	0	0	3	0	5	0	0	0	1	.000	0	0--	-	9.72	9.00
2010	OKCity	AAA	11	11	0	0	62.2	254	50	17	13	5	2	1	2	18	0	51	2	0	6	2	.750	0	0--	-	2.58	1.87
2010	Rngrs	R	1	1	0	0	3.0	10	0	0	0	0	0	0	0	0	0	6	0	0	0	0	-	0	0--	-	0.00	0.00
2009	Tex	AL	33	21	1	0	138.1	611	160	98	94	26	2	3	4	47	0	107	3	3	8	13	.381	1	0-1	2	5.52	6.12
2010	Tex	AL	14	10	0	2	57.1	253	55	30	26	6	0	2	4	24	0	54	0	1	3	4	.429	0	0-0	1	4.17	4.08
	2 ML YEARS		47	31	1	2	195.2	864	215	128	120	32	2	5	8	71	0	161	3	4	11	17	.393	1	0-1	3	5.11	5.52

Greg Holland

Pitches: R **Bats:** R **Pos:** RP-15   **Ht:** 5'11" **Wt:** 189 **Born:** 11/20/1985 **Age:** 25

Year	Team	Lg	G	GS	CG	GF	IP	BFP	H	R	ER	HR	SH	SF	HB	TBB	IBB	SO	WP	Bk	W	L	Pct	Sh	Sv-Op	Hld	ERC	ERA
2007	Idaho	R+	22	0	0	18	33.2	143	28	16	13	1	1	0	1	15	0	37	3	1	6	1	.857	0	6--	-	2.95	3.48
2008	Wilmg	A+	32	7	0	8	84.1	355	70	37	32	4	3	6	1	35	2	96	8	0	4	5	.444	0	4--	-	2.85	3.42
2009	NWArk	AA	29	0	0	19	45.1	194	46	16	16	2	0	1	0	19	0	49	6	0	3	2	.600	0	8--	-	3.89	3.18
2009	Omha	AAA	6	0	0	3	9.0	42	12	7	7	2	0	1	1	5	0	10	1	0	1	1	.500	0	2--	-	8.72	7.00
2010	Omha	AAA	36	0	0	16	56.2	235	40	26	24	3	2	2	0	30	1	60	4	0	3	3	.500	0	3--	-	2.67	3.81
2010	KC	AL	15	0	0	10	18.2	87	23	15	14	3	1	0	0	8	0	23	2	0	0	1	.000	0	0-0	0	5.88	6.75

Matt Holliday

Bats: R **Throws:** R **Pos:** LF-155; PH-2; DH-1   **Ht:** 6'4" **Wt:** 235 **Born:** 1/15/1980 **Age:** 31

Year	Team	Lg	G	AB	H	2B	3B	HR	(Hm	Rd)	TB	R	RBI	RC	TBB	IBB	SO	HBP	SH	SF	SB	CS	SB%	GDP	Avg	OBP	Slg
2004	Col	NL	121	400	116	31	3	14	(10	4)	195	65	57	61	31	0	86	6	1	1	3	3	.50	9	.290	.349	.488
2005	Col	NL	125	479	147	24	7	19	(12	7)	242	68	87	88	36	7	79	7	0	4	14	3	.82	11	.307	.361	.505
2006	Col	NL	155	602	196	45	5	34	(22	12)	353	119	114	112	47	3	110	15	0	3	10	5	.67	22	.326	.387	.586
2007	Col	NL	158	636	216	50	6	36	(25	11)	386	120	137	134	63	7	126	10	0	3	11	4	.73	23	.340	.405	.607
2008	Col	NL	139	539	173	38	2	25	(15	10)	290	107	88	104	74	6	104	8	0	2	28	2	.93	9	.321	.409	.538
2009	2 Tms		156	581	182	39	3	24	(16	8)	299	94	109	112	72	8	101	10	0	1	14	7	.67	13	.313	.394	.515
2010	StL	NL	158	596	186	45	1	28	(13	15)	317	95	103	107	69	10	93	8	0	2	9	5	.64	13	.312	.390	.532
09	Oak	AL	93	346	99	23	1	11	(7	4)	157	52	54	62	46	3	58	6	0	2	12	3	.80	8	.286	.378	.454
09	StL	NL	63	235	83	16	2	13	(9	4)	142	42	55	50	26	5	43	4	0	5	2	4	.33	5	.353	.419	.604
	Postseason		14	57	15	0	0	6	(3	3)	33	7	11	7	1	0	14	2	0	0	0	0	-	1	.263	.300	.579
	7 ML YEARS		1012	3833	1216	272	27	180	(113	67)	2082	668	695	718	392	35	699	64	1	23	89	29	.75	100	.317	.388	.543

Paul Hoover

Bats: R **Throws:** R **Pos:** C-9; PR-1   **Ht:** 6'1" **Wt:** 218 **Born:** 4/14/1976 **Age:** 35

										BATTING											BASERUNNING				AVERAGES		
Year	Team	Lg	G	AB	H	2B	3B	HR	(Hm	Rd)	TB	R	RBI	RC	TBB	IBB	SO	HBP	SH	SF	SB	CS	SB%	GDP	Avg	OBP	Slg
2010	LV*	AAA	77	255	63	13	3	2	(-	-)	88	23	21	30	26	1	65	4	1	0	0	0	-	10	.247	.326	.345
2001	TB	AL	3	4	1	0	0	0	(0	0)	1	1	0	0	0	0	1	0	0	0	0	0	-	0	.250	.250	.250
2002	TB	AL	5	17	3	0	0	0	(0	0)	3	1	2	1	0	0	5	0	0	0	0	0	-	0	.176	.176	.176
2006	Fla	NL	4	5	2	0	0	0	(0	0)	2	0	1	1	0	0	0	0	0	0	0	0	-	0	.400	.400	.400
2007	Fla	NL	3	8	3	0	0	0	(0	0)	3	1	0	0	0	0	2	0	0	0	0	0	-	0	.375	.375	.375
2008	Fla	NL	13	40	8	1	0	0	(0	0)	9	1	2	0	2	1	17	0	0	0	0	0	-	2	.200	.238	.225
2009	Phi	NL	3	4	3	0	0	0	(0	0)	3	0	1	2	0	0	1	0	0	0	0	0	-	0	.750	.750	.750
2010	Phi	NL	9	22	5	2	0	0	(0	0)	7	6	2	1	3	2	5	0	0	0	0	0	-	3	.227	.320	.318
	7 ML YEARS		40	100	25	3	0	0	(0	0)	28	10	8	5	5	3	31	0	0	0	0	0	-	5	.250	.286	.280

James Houser

Pitches: L **Bats:** L **Pos:** RP-1   HOW-zer   **Ht:** 6'4" **Wt:** 205 **Born:** 12/15/1984 **Age:** 26

			HOW MUCH HE PITCHED						WHAT HE GAVE UP										THE RESULTS							
Year	Team	Lg	G	GS	CG	GF	IP	BFP	H	R	ER	HR	SH	SF	HB	TBB	IBB	SO	WP	Bk	W	L	Pct	Sh	Sv-Op	Hld	ERC	ERA
2003	Princtn	R+	10	10	0	0	41.0	182	43	23	17	1	1	2	2	13	0	44	5	0	0	4	.000	0	0--	-	3.56	3.73
2004	CtnSC	A	7	7	0	0	32.2	131	27	9	8	1	1	1	3	13	0	27	0	1	3	1	.750	0	0--	-	3.20	2.20
2005	SWMch	A	22	22	0	0	115.0	461	100	50	48	12	1	2	8	31	0	109	4	2	8	8	.500	0	0--	-	3.28	3.76
2006	Visalia	A+	28	27	0	0	151.0	630	140	80	74	20	3	3	10	46	0	137	1	3	12	4	.750	0	0--	-	3.83	4.41
2007	Mont	AA	20	20	0	0	103.2	438	88	51	42	10	8	3	5	39	3	91	2	2	5	4	.556	0	0--	-	3.25	3.65
2008	Mont	AA	20	20	0	0	94.1	392	69	38	30	9	3	2	10	40	1	77	6	3	3	3	.500	0	0--	-	3.10	2.86
2009	Drham	AAA	18	15	0	1	82.0	375	83	52	47	10	0	4	7	50	0	44	2	1	4	5	.444	0	0--	-	5.55	5.16
2010	NewOr	AAA	24	4	0	5	49.0	216	53	22	20	6	0	0	0	20	1	41	0	0	1	2	.333	0	1--	-	4.69	3.67
2010	Jaxnvl	AA	4	2	0	0	7.2	44	16	12	12	1	1	0	2	4	0	7	1	0	0	2	.000	0	0--	-	13.34	14.09
2010	Fla	NL	1	0	0	0	1.1	9	3	3	3	1	1	0	1	1	0	1	0	0	0	0	-	0	0-0	0	25.37	20.25

Ryan Howard

Bats: L **Throws:** L **Pos:** 1B-139; DH-2; PH-1   **Ht:** 6'4" **Wt:** 255 **Born:** 11/19/1979 **Age:** 31

										BATTING											BASERUNNING				AVERAGES		
Year	Team	Lg	G	AB	H	2B	3B	HR	(Hm	Rd)	TB	R	RBI	RC	TBB	IBB	SO	HBP	SH	SF	SB	CS	SB%	GDP	Avg	OBP	Slg
2010	Lakwd*	A	1	2	1	0	0	0	(-	-)	2	0	1	1	0	0	0	0	0	0	0	0	-	0	.500	.667	1.000
2004	Phi	NL	19	39	11	5	0	2	(1	1)	22	5	5	7	2	0	13	1	0	0	0	0	-	2	.282	.333	.564
2005	Phi	NL	88	312	90	17	2	22	(11	11)	177	52	63	50	33	8	100	1	0	2	0	1	.00	6	.288	.356	.567
2006	Phi	NL	159	581	182	25	1	58	(29	29)	383	104	149	130	108	37	181	9	0	6	0	0	-	7	.313	.425	.659
2007	Phi	NL	144	529	142	26	0	47	(23	24)	309	94	136	119	107	35	199	5	0	7	1	0	1.00	13	.268	.392	.584
2008	Phi	NL	162	610	153	26	4	48	(26	22)	331	105	146	117	81	17	199	3	0	6	1	1	.50	11	.251	.339	.543
2009	Phi	NL	160	616	172	37	4	45	(18	27)	352	105	141	117	75	8	186	6	0	6	8	1	.89	11	.279	.360	.571
2010	Phi	NL	143	550	152	23	5	31	(16	15)	278	87	108	94	59	11	157	8	0	3	1	1	.50	14	.276	.353	.505
	Postseason		32	118	32	9	1	7	(5	2)	64	20	27	22	20	5	44	1	0	1	1	1	.50	1	.271	.379	.542
	7 ML YEARS		875	3237	902	159	16	253	(124	129)	1852	552	748	642	465	116	1035	33	0	30	11	4	.73	64	.279	.372	.572

J.P. Howell

Pitches: L **Bats:** L **Pos:** P   **Ht:** 6'0" **Wt:** 180 **Born:** 4/25/1983 **Age:** 28

			HOW MUCH HE PITCHED						WHAT HE GAVE UP										THE RESULTS							
Year	Team	Lg	G	GS	CG	GF	IP	BFP	H	R	ER	HR	SH	SF	HB	TBB	IBB	SO	WP	Bk	W	L	Pct	Sh	Sv-Op	Hld	ERC	ERA
2005	KC	AL	15	15	0	0	72.2	328	73	55	50	9	3	3	6	39	0	54	7	0	3	5	.375	0	0-0	0	5.18	6.19
2006	TB	AL	8	8	0	0	42.1	187	52	25	24	4	0	2	3	14	0	33	1	0	1	3	.250	0	0-0	0	5.51	5.10
2007	TB	AL	10	10	0	0	51.0	244	69	45	43	8	2	1	3	21	0	49	3	0	1	6	.143	0	0-0	0	6.84	7.59
2008	TB	AL	64	0	0	9	89.1	370	62	29	22	6	6	1	4	39	1	92	5	0	6	1	.857	0	3-6	14	2.61	2.22
2009	TB	AL	69	0	0	41	66.2	278	47	22	21	7	2	1	3	33	3	79	3	1	7	5	.583	0	17-25	4	2.99	2.84
	Postseason		12	0	0	1	12.0	50	9	4	4	0	0	1	2	4	1	17	1	0	0	3	.000	0	0-0	4	2.33	3.00
	5 ML YEARS		166	33	0	50	322.0	1407	303	176	160	34	13	8	19	146	4	307	19	1	18	20	.474	0	20-30	18	4.20	4.47

Bob Howry

Pitches: R **Bats:** L **Pos:** RP-38   **Ht:** 6'5" **Wt:** 220 **Born:** 8/4/1973 **Age:** 37

			HOW MUCH HE PITCHED						WHAT HE GAVE UP										THE RESULTS							
Year	Team	Lg	G	GS	CG	GF	IP	BFP	H	R	ER	HR	SH	SF	HB	TBB	IBB	SO	WP	Bk	W	L	Pct	Sh	Sv-Op	Hld	ERC	ERA
1998	CWS	AL	44	0	0	15	54.1	217	37	20	19	7	2	3	2	19	2	51	2	0	0	3	.000	0	9-11	19	2.50	3.15
1999	CWS	AL	69	0	0	54	67.2	289	58	34	27	8	3	1	3	38	3	80	3	1	5	3	.625	0	28-34	1	4.11	3.59
2000	CWS	AL	65	0	0	29	71.0	289	54	26	25	6	2	4	4	29	2	60	2	0	2	4	.333	0	7-12	14	2.96	3.17
2001	CWS	AL	69	0	0	23	78.2	346	85	41	41	11	4	3	4	30	9	64	6	0	4	5	.444	0	5-11	21	4.78	4.69
2002	2 Tms	AL	67	0	0	26	68.2	292	67	37	32	9	4	6	5	21	4	45	2	0	3	5	.375	0	0-1	15	4.00	4.19
2003	Bos	AL	4	0	0	3	4.1	27	11	6	6	1	0	1	0	3	1	4	0	0	0	0	-	0	0-1	0	16.51	12.46
2004	Cle	AL	37	0	0	6	42.2	178	37	14	13	5	1	1	2	12	0	39	0	0	4	2	.667	0	0-2	8	3.15	2.74
2005	Cle	AL	79	0	0	24	73.0	277	49	23	20	4	3	1	3	16	1	48	0	0	7	4	.636	0	3-5	29	1.58	2.47
2006	ChC	NL	84	0	0	26	76.2	314	70	28	27	8	5	3	3	17	4	71	1	0	5-9	21						3.03	3.17
2007	ChC	NL	78	0	0	32	81.1	336	76	31	30	8	4	1	4	19	3	72	1	0	6	7	.462	0	8-12	22	3.10	3.32
2008	ChC	NL	72	0	0	27	70.2	311	90	44	42	13	1	4	2	13	5	59	0	0	7	5	.583	0	1-5	15	5.37	5.35
2009	SF	NL	63	0	0	26	63.2	268	50	26	24	5	3	6	2	23	6	46	4	0	2	6	.250	0	0-3	10	2.55	3.39
2010	2 Tms	NL	38	0	0	10	35.0	168	47	36	30	8	3	1	0	13	2	14	3	0	1	3	.250	0	0-1	3	6.62	7.71
02	CWS	AL	47	0	0	17	50.2	209	45	22	22	7	1	4	3	17	2	31	1	0	2	2	.500	0	0-0	10	3.72	3.91
02	Bos	AL	20	0	0	9	18.0	83	22	15	14	2	3	2	2	4	2	14	1	0	1	3	.250	0	0-1	5	4.79	5.00

Year Team	Lg	HOW MUCH HE PITCHED						WHAT HE GAVE UP							THE RESULTS								
		G	GS	CG	GF	IP	BFP	H	R	ER	HR	SH	SF	HB	TBB	IBB	SO	WP	Bk	W	L	Pct	Sh	Sv-Op	Hld	ERC	ERA
10 Ari	NL	14	0	0	4	14.1	67	18	17	17	6	0	1	0	6	1	6	1	0	1	0	1.000	0	0-1	1	7.89	10.67
10 ChC	NL	24	0	0	6	20.2	101	29	19	13	2	3	0	0	7	1	8	2	0	0	3	.000	0	0-0	2	5.75	5.66
Postseason		4	0	0	1	5.2	21	3	1	1	0	1	0	0	2	0	10	0	0	0	0	-	0	0-0	1	1.27	1.59
13 ML YEARS		769	0	0	295	787.2	3321	731	366	336	93	35	36	29	253	42	653	24	1	45	52	.464	0	66-107	178	3.55	3.84

Chin-lung Hu

Bats: R **Throws:** R **Pos:** SS-10; PR-5; PH-1   **Ht:** 5'11" **Wt:** 188 **Born:** 2/2/1984 **Age:** 27

Year Team	Lg	BATTING																		BASERUNNING				AVERAGES		
		G	AB	H	2B	3B	HR	(Hm	Rd)	TB	R	RBI	RC	TBB	IBB	SO	HBP	SH	SF	SB	CS	SB%	GDP	Avg	OBP	Slg
2010 Albq*	AAA	58	208	66	11	1	4	(-	-)	91	37	25	32	8	2	16	0	5	2	8	1	.89	5	.317	.339	.438
2007 LAD	NL	12	29	7	0	1	2	(2	0)	15	5	5	5	0	0	8	0	2	0	0	0	-	0	.241	.241	.517
2008 LAD	NL	65	116	21	2	2	0	(0	0)	27	16	9	5	11	4	23	0	2	0	2	0	1.00	5	.181	.252	.233
2009 LAD	NL	5	5	2	1	0	0	(0	0)	3	2	2	1	0	0	2	0	0	1	0	0	-	1	.400	.333	.600
2010 LAD	NL	14	23	3	1	0	0	(0	0)	4	2	1	0	0	0	5	1	0	1	1	0	1.00	1	.130	.160	.174
4 ML YEARS		96	173	33	4	3	2	(2	0)	49	25	17	11	11	4	38	1	4	2	3	0	1.00	7	.191	.241	.283

Daniel Hudson

Pitches: R **Bats:** R **Pos:** SP-14   **Ht:** 6'3" **Wt:** 225 **Born:** 3/9/1987 **Age:** 24

Year Team	Lg	HOW MUCH HE PITCHED						WHAT HE GAVE UP							THE RESULTS								
		G	GS	CG	GF	IP	BFP	H	R	ER	HR	SH	SF	HB	TBB	IBB	SO	WP	Bk	W	L	Pct	Sh	Sv-Op	Hld	ERC	ERA
2008 Gr Falls	R+	14	14	0	0	69.2	283	52	30	26	6	1	0	3	22	0	90	3	0	5	4	.556	0	0- --	-	2.49	3.36
2009 Knapol	A	4	4	0	0	22.0	85	15	5	3	0	1	0	3	2	0	30	0	0	1	2	.333	0	0- --	-	1.41	1.23
2009 WinSa	A+	8	8	1	0	45.0	178	31	19	17	3	2	2	2	13	0	49	1	0	4	3	.571	0	0- --	-	2.04	3.40
2009 Brham	AA	9	9	0	0	56.1	211	37	11	10	1	0	1	3	10	0	63	1	0	7	0	1.000	0	0- --	-	1.45	1.60
2009 Charltt	AAA	5	5	0	0	24.0	103	22	10	8	1	0	3	2	9	0	24	1	0	2	0	1.000	0	0- --	-	3.43	3.00
2010 Charltt	AAA	17	17	1	0	93.1	394	81	41	36	13	2	1	4	31	1	108	3	0	11	4	.733	0	0- --	-	3.45	3.47
2009 CWS	AL	6	2	0	1	18.2	82	16	9	7	3	0	1	1	9	0	14	1	0	1	1	.500	0	0-0	0	4.15	3.38
2010 2 Tms		14	14	0	0	95.1	372	68	26	26	8	2	2	4	27	1	84	5	0	8	2	.800	0	0-0	0	2.26	2.45
10 CWS	AL	3	3	0	0	15.2	71	17	11	11	1	1	1	0	11	0	14	2	0	1	1	.500	0	0-0	0	5.69	6.32
10 Ari	NL	11	11	0	0	79.2	301	51	15	15	7	1	1	4	16	1	70	3	0	7	1	.875	0	0-0	0	1.70	1.69
2 ML YEARS		20	16	0	1	114.0	454	84	35	33	11	2	3	5	36	1	98	6	0	9	3	.750	0	0-0	0	2.55	2.61

Orlando Hudson

Bats: B **Throws:** R **Pos:** 2B-123; DH-2   **Ht:** 6'0" **Wt:** 190 **Born:** 12/12/1977 **Age:** 33

Year Team	Lg	BATTING																		BASERUNNING				AVERAGES		
		G	AB	H	2B	3B	HR	(Hm	Rd)	TB	R	RBI	RC	TBB	IBB	SO	HBP	SH	SF	SB	CS	SB%	GDP	Avg	OBP	Slg
2002 Tor	AL	54	192	53	10	5	4	(2	2)	85	20	23	30	11	0	27	2	0	2	0	1	.00	6	.276	.319	.443
2003 Tor	AL	142	474	127	21	6	9	(5	4)	187	54	57	64	39	1	87	5	0	3	5	4	.56	13	.268	.328	.395
2004 Tor	AL	135	489	132	32	7	12	(5	7)	214	73	58	71	51	0	98	4	3	4	7	3	.70	12	.270	.341	.438
2005 Tor	AL	131	461	125	25	5	10	(4	6)	190	62	63	59	30	1	65	3	0	7	7	1	.88	10	.271	.315	.412
2006 Ari	NL	157	579	166	34	9	15	(7	8)	263	87	67	89	61	5	78	2	4	4	9	6	.60	17	.287	.354	.454
2007 Ari	NL	139	517	152	28	9	10	(7	3)	228	69	63	82	70	1	87	2	5	7	10	2	.83	21	.294	.376	.441
2008 Ari	NL	107	407	124	29	3	8	(6	2)	183	54	41	66	40	2	62	2	3	3	4	1	.80	18	.305	.367	.450
2009 LAD	NL	149	551	156	35	6	9	(4	5)	230	74	62	78	62	4	99	4	9	5	8	1	.89	16	.283	.357	.417
2010 Min	AL	126	497	133	24	5	6	(3	3)	185	80	37	56	50	0	87	4	5	3	10	3	.77	14	.268	.338	.372
Postseason		8	4	1	0	0	1	(0	1)	4	1	1	0	0	0	1	0	0	0	0	0	-	0	.250	.250	1.000
9 ML YEARS		1140	4167	1168	238	55	83	(43	40)	1765	573	471	595	414	14	690	28	29	38	60	22	.73	127	.280	.346	.424

Tim Hudson

Pitches: R **Bats:** R **Pos:** SP-34   **Ht:** 6'1" **Wt:** 174 **Born:** 7/14/1975 **Age:** 35

Year Team	Lg	HOW MUCH HE PITCHED						WHAT HE GAVE UP							THE RESULTS								
		G	GS	CG	GF	IP	BFP	H	R	ER	HR	SH	SF	HB	TBB	IBB	SO	WP	Bk	W	L	Pct	Sh	Sv-Op	Hld	ERC	ERA
1999 Oak	AL	21	21	1	0	136.1	580	121	56	49	8	1	1	4	62	2	132	6	0	11	2	.846	0	0-0	0	3.50	3.23
2000 Oak	AL	32	32	2	0	202.1	847	169	100	93	24	5	7	7	82	5	169	7	0	20	6	.769	2	0-0	0	3.43	4.14
2001 Oak	AL	35	35	3	0	235.0	980	216	100	88	20	12	8	6	71	5	181	9	1	18	9	.667	0	0-0	0	3.22	3.37
2002 Oak	AL	34	34	4	0	238.1	983	237	87	79	19	6	5	8	62	9	152	7	1	15	9	.625	2	0-0	0	3.51	2.98
2003 Oak	AL	34	34	3	0	240.0	967	197	84	72	15	11	2	10	61	9	162	6	0	16	7	.696	2	0-0	0	2.47	2.70
2004 Oak	AL	27	27	3	0	188.2	793	194	82	74	8	7	4	12	44	3	103	4	1	12	6	.667	2	0-0	0	3.44	3.53
2005 Atl	NL	29	29	2	0	192.0	817	194	79	75	20	9	1	9	65	5	115	4	0	14	9	.609	0	0-0	0	4.12	3.52
2006 Atl	NL	35	35	2	0	218.1	959	235	129	118	25	8	3	9	79	10	141	7	0	13	12	.520	1	0-0	0	4.54	4.86
2007 Atl	NL	34	34	1	0	224.1	925	221	87	83	10	11	6	8	53	8	132	5	2	16	10	.615	1	0-0	0	3.12	3.33
2008 Atl	NL	23	22	1	0	142.0	573	125	53	50	11	5	4	2	40	5	85	3	1	11	7	.611	0	0-0	0	2.90	3.17
2009 Atl	NL	7	7	0	0	42.1	180	49	17	17	4	1	0	0	13	0	30	0	0	2	1	.667	0	0-0	0	4.70	3.61
2010 Atl	NL	34	34	1	0	228.2	920	189	74	72	20	9	2	9	74	8	139	5	0	17	9	.654	1	0-0	0	2.95	2.83
Postseason		9	8	1	0	47.2	207	50	27	21	5	4	2	2	16	1	32	1	0	1	3	.250	0	0-0	0	4.25	3.97
12 ML YEARS		345	344	23	0	2288.1	9524	2147	948	870	184	85	44	84	706	69	1541	63	6	165	87	.655	11	0-0	0	3.38	3.42

Aubrey Huff

Bats: L **Throws:** R **Pos:** 1B-100; LF-46; RF-34; PH-3   **Ht:** 6'4" **Wt:** 217 **Born:** 12/20/1976 **Age:** 34

Year Team	Lg	BATTING																		BASERUNNING				AVERAGES		
		G	AB	H	2B	3B	HR	(Hm	Rd)	TB	R	RBI	RC	TBB	IBB	SO	HBP	SH	SF	SB	CS	SB%	GDP	Avg	OBP	Slg
2000 TB	AL	39	122	35	7	0	4	(3	1)	54	12	14	15	5	1	18	1	0	1	0	0	-	6	.287	.318	.443
2001 TB	AL	111	411	102	25	1	8	(5	3)	153	42	45	37	23	2	72	1	0	0	1	3	.25	18	.248	.288	.372
2002 TB	AL	113	454	142	25	0	23	(17	6)	236	67	59	66	37	7	55	1	0	2	4	1	.80	17	.313	.364	.520
2003 TB	AL	162	636	198	47	3	34	(15	19)	353	91	107	112	53	17	80	8	0	9	2	3	.40	19	.311	.367	.555

Year	Team	Lg	BATTING G	AB	H	2B	3B	HR	(Hm	Rd)	TB	R	RBI	RC	TBB	IBB	SO	HBP	SH	SF	BASERUNNING SB	CS	SB%	GDP	AVERAGES Avg	OBP	Slg
2004	TB	AL	157	600	178	27	2	29	(16	13)	296	92	104	96	56	6	74	6	0	5	5	1	.83	9	.297	.360	.493
2005	TB	AL	154	575	150	26	2	22	(9	13)	246	70	92	77	49	13	88	5	0	7	8	7	.53	12	.261	.321	.428
2006	2 Tms		131	454	121	25	2	21	(9	12)	213	57	66	55	50	6	64	7	0	6	0	0	-	11	.267	.344	.469
2007	Bal	AL	151	550	154	34	5	15	(8	7)	243	68	72	79	48	2	87	1	0	4	1	1	.50	13	.280	.337	.442
2008	Bal	AL	154	598	182	48	2	32	(18	14)	330	96	108	111	53	7	89	3	0	7	4	0	1.00	9	.304	.360	.552
2009	2 Tms		150	536	129	30	1	15	(11	4)	206	59	85	67	51	7	87	5	0	5	0	6	.00	15	.241	.310	.384
2010	SF	NL	157	569	165	35	5	26	(12	14)	288	100	86	108	83	5	91	9	0	7	7	0	1.00	17	.290	.385	.506
06	TB	AL	63	230	65	15	1	8	(4	4)	106	26	28	28	24	3	25	0	0	2	0	0	-	4	.283	.348	.461
06	Hou	NL	68	224	56	10	1	13	(5	8)	107	31	38	27	26	3	39	7	0	4	0	0	-	7	.250	.341	.478
09	Bal	AL	110	430	109	24	1	13	(10	3)	174	51	72	58	41	7	74	4	0	5	0	6	.00	12	.253	.321	.405
09	Det	AL	40	106	20	6	0	2	(1	1)	32	8	13	9	10	0	13	1	0	0	0	0	-	3	.189	.265	.302
11 ML YEARS			1479	5505	1556	329	23	229	(123	106)	2618	754	838	823	508	73	805	46	0	53	32	22	.59	146	.283	.345	.476

David Huff

Pitches: L Bats: B Pos: SP-15 Ht: 6'2" Wt: 215 Born: 8/22/1984 Age: 26

Year	Team	Lg	HOW MUCH HE PITCHED G	GS	CG	GF	IP	BFP	WHAT HE GAVE UP H	R	ER	HR	SH	SF	HB	TBB	IBB	SO	WP	Bk	THE RESULTS W	L	Pct	Sh	Sv-Op	Hld	ERC	ERA
2006	MhVlly	A-	4	4	0	0	7.2	38	9	5	5	0	0	0	1	7	0	8	1	0	0	1	.000	0	0- -		7.07	5.87
2007	Knstn	A+	11	11	0	0	59.2	249	57	23	18	4	4	2	1	15	0	46	2	0	4	2	.667	0	0- -		3.08	2.72
2008	Akron	AA	11	10	1	1	65.2	253	44	17	14	5	4	1	1	14	0	62	1	0	5	1	.833	1	0- -		1.67	1.92
2008	Buffalo	AAA	16	16	0	0	80.2	323	68	31	27	8	2	0	3	15	1	81	3	0	6	4	.600	0	0- -		2.56	3.01
2009	Clmbs	AAA	7	7	0	0	39.1	163	35	19	19	5	1	1	0	16	0	32	1	0	5	1	.833	0	0- -		3.75	4.35
2010	Clmbs	AAA	12	12	0	0	74.1	319	84	37	36	8	3	1	2	21	0	52	3	0	8	2	.800	0	0- -		4.57	4.36
2009	Cle	AL	23	23	0	0	128.1	574	159	82	80	16	2	2	1	41	1	65	1	0	11	8	.579	0	0-0	0	5.33	5.61
2010	Cle	AL	15	15	1	0	79.2	369	101	61	55	14	3	3	3	34	1	37	2	0	2	11	.154	0	0-0	0	6.50	6.21
2 ML YEARS			38	38	1	0	208.0	943	260	143	135	30	5	4	4	75	2	102	3	0	13	19	.406	0	0-0	0	5.77	5.84

Chad Huffman

Bats: R Throws: R Pos: LF-4; RF-3; PH-2; 1B-1 Ht: 6'1" Wt: 215 Born: 4/29/1985 Age: 26

Year	Team	Lg	BATTING G	AB	H	2B	3B	HR	(Hm	Rd)	TB	R	RBI	RC	TBB	IBB	SO	HBP	SH	SF	BASERUNNING SB	CS	SB%	GDP	AVERAGES Avg	OBP	Slg
2006	Eugene	A-	54	198	68	17	1	9	(-	-)	114	41	40	50	25	0	34	14	0	7	2	3	.40	3	.343	.439	.576
2006	FtWyn	A	5	14	3	0	1	0	(-	-)	5	2	0	1	2	0	2	0	0	0	0	1	.00	1	.214	.313	.357
2007	Lk Els	A+	84	316	97	19	2	15	(-	-)	165	63	76	67	42	0	56	10	0	3	0	1	.00	7	.307	.402	.522
2007	SnAnt	AA	49	167	45	4	1	7	(-	-)	72	28	28	28	22	0	44	4	1	3	0	0	-	1	.269	.362	.431
2008	SnAnt	AA	119	437	124	30	1	9	(-	-)	183	68	58	76	67	2	83	7	0	6	1	1	.50	12	.284	.383	.419
2009	Portlnd	AAA	135	469	126	30	2	20	(-	-)	220	65	68	82	57	0	115	12	0	2	8	5	.62	9	.269	.361	.469
2010	S-WB	AAA	104	368	101	20	0	10	(-	-)	151	48	45	55	40	0	81	5	1	1	0	2	.00	12	.274	.353	.410
2010	NYY	AL	9	18	3	0	0	0	(0	0)	3	1	2	0	2	0	5	1	0	0	0	0	-	1	.167	.286	.167

Dusty Hughes

Pitches: L Bats: L Pos: RP-57 Ht: 5'10" Wt: 186 Born: 6/29/1982 Age: 29

Year	Team	Lg	HOW MUCH HE PITCHED G	GS	CG	GF	IP	BFP	WHAT HE GAVE UP H	R	ER	HR	SH	SF	HB	TBB	IBB	SO	WP	Bk	THE RESULTS W	L	Pct	Sh	Sv-Op	Hld	ERC	ERA
2003	Royals	R	11	6	0	1	50.2	202	38	21	16	4	0	0	0	18	0	54	4	1	5	2	.714	0	0- -		2.51	2.84
2004	Burlgtn	A	8	8	0	0	52.0	203	39	12	9	2	3	1	1	15	0	36	1	0	4	2	.667	0	0- -		2.13	1.56
2004	Wilmg	A+	18	18	0	0	108.1	437	95	37	29	5	8	7	3	31	3	68	1	1	5	5	.500	0	0- -		2.77	2.41
2005	Hi Dsrt	A+	19	19	0	0	92.0	432	119	74	58	13	5	4	5	45	0	87	9	1	5	7	.417	0	0- -		6.81	5.67
2007	Wichta	AA	25	15	0	3	108.0	467	98	44	37	5	1	4	8	45	1	77	6	1	6	2	.750	0	1- -		3.60	3.08
2008	NWArk	AA	20	4	0	7	52.2	209	47	17	17	3	2	1	0	16	1	43	1	1	5	2	.714	0	3- -		2.95	2.91
2008	Omha	AAA	12	11	0	0	55.1	245	65	32	31	8	1	1	0	25	0	36	3	0	3	2	.600	0	0- -		5.78	5.04
2009	Omha	AAA	34	11	0	12	87.1	371	79	35	34	6	4	5	2	41	0	76	8	0	3	3	.500	0	1- -		3.74	3.50
2009	KC	AL	8	1	0	0	14.0	63	13	9	8	2	0	0	2	8	0	15	1	0	2	0	.000	0	0-0	2	5.31	5.14
2010	KC	AL	57	0	0	19	56.1	252	59	28	24	3	1	6	5	24	0	34	1	0	1	3	.250	0	0-0	7	4.43	3.83
2 ML YEARS			65	1	0	19	70.1	315	72	37	32	5	1	6	7	32	0	49	2	0	1	5	.167	0	0-0	9	4.60	4.09

Luke Hughes

Bats: R Throws: R Pos: 3B-2 Ht: 5'11" Wt: 205 Born: 8/2/1984 Age: 26

Year	Team	Lg	BATTING G	AB	H	2B	3B	HR	(Hm	Rd)	TB	R	RBI	RC	TBB	IBB	SO	HBP	SH	SF	BASERUNNING SB	CS	SB%	GDP	AVERAGES Avg	OBP	Slg
2003	Twins	R	54	190	58	9	4	2	(-	-)	81	22	25	29	15	1	22	2	4	1	5	5	.50	5	.305	.361	.426
2004	Elizab	R+	44	141	40	8	1	3	(-	-)	59	20	19	20	9	0	30	4	2	3	1	3	.25	1	.284	.338	.418
2005	Beloit	A	72	292	75	14	2	7	(-	-)	114	42	42	38	21	0	63	7	2	3	4	2	.67	6	.257	.319	.390
2005	FtMyrs	A+	23	84	17	3	1	0	(-	-)	22	9	7	4	2	0	15	1	2	3	0	0	-	3	.202	.222	.262
2006	FtMyrs	A+	95	333	77	15	0	4	(-	-)	104	31	37	32	23	1	72	5	2	5	6	2	.75	8	.231	.287	.312
2007	NwBrit	AA	92	315	89	18	2	9	(-	-)	138	56	43	52	34	2	68	4	5	4	4	1	.80	5	.283	.356	.438
2008	NwBrit	AA	70	285	91	15	3	15	(-	-)	157	53	40	59	28	0	70	3	2	1	4	1	.80	3	.319	.385	.551
2008	Roch	AAA	29	106	30	7	1	3	(-	-)	48	17	21	16	7	0	30	1	0	3	2	0	1.00	2	.283	.325	.453
2009	Roch	AAA	37	135	35	8	2	6	(-	-)	65	19	28	23	18	0	38	1	0	3	2	0	1.00	1	.259	.344	.481
2009	Twins	R	4	11	3	0	0	0	(-	-)	3	0	0	2	4	0	1	0	0	0	0	0	-	0	.273	.467	.273
2009	NwBrit	AA	56	200	50	15	3	6	(-	-)	89	22	36	30	19	2	38	4	1	5	1	1	.50	6	.250	.320	.445
2010	Roch	AAA	22	74	19	8	0	1	(-	-)	30	12	7	10	5	0	18	1	1	0	2	0	1.00	3	.257	.313	.405
2010	Min	AL	2	7	2	0	0	1	(0	1)	5	1	1	0	0	0	3	0	0	0	0	0	1.00	0	.286	.286	.714

Phil Hughes

Pitches: R Bats: R Pos: SP-29; RP-2 — Ht: 6'5" Wt: 240 Born: 6/24/1986 Age: 25

Year	Team	Lg	G	GS	CG	GF	IP	BFP	H	R	ER	HR	SH	SF	HB	TBB	IBB	SO	WP	Bk	W	L	Pct	Sh	Sv-Op	Hld	ERC	ERA
2007	NYY	AL	13	13	0	0	72.2	306	64	39	36	8	2	1	2	29	0	58	4	0	5	3	.625	0	0-0	0	3.61	4.46
2008	NYY	AL	8	8	0	0	34.0	157	43	26	25	3	1	3	1	15	0	23	2	0	0	4	.000	0	0-0	0	5.84	6.62
2009	NYY	AL	51	7	0	6	86.0	351	68	31	29	8	0	4	5	28	1	96	4	2	8	3	.727	0	3-6	18	2.86	3.03
2010	NYY	AL	31	29	0	0	176.1	730	162	83	82	25	2	5	0	58	1	146	9	1	18	8	.692	0	0-0	0	3.65	4.19
	Postseason		11	0	0	2	12.0	54	14	7	7	2	0	0	0	4	0	13	1	0	1	1	.500	0	0-1	2	5.13	5.25
4 ML YEARS			103	57	0	6	369.0	1544	337	179	172	44	5	13	8	130	2	323	19	3	31	18	.633	0	3-6	18	3.64	4.20

Rhyne Hughes

Bats: L Throws: L Pos: 1B-11; PH-2; DH-1 — Ht: 6'2" Wt: 215 Born: 9/9/1983 Age: 27

Year	Team	Lg	G	AB	H	2B	3B	HR	(Hm	Rd)	TB	R	RBI	RC	TBB	IBB	SO	HBP	SH	SF	SB	CS	SB%	GDP	Avg	OBP	Slg
2005	HudVal	A-	58	219	61	18	0	8	(-	-)	103	34	30	34	15	0	53	4	0	1	3	2	.60	6	.279	.335	.470
2006	SWMch	A	114	386	90	16	4	3	(-	-)	123	22	39	35	33	3	102	3	0	6	1	8	.11	6	.233	.294	.319
2007	VeroB	A+	94	334	110	24	1	12	(-	-)	172	65	57	67	35	2	62	1	1	2	1	1	.50	7	.329	.392	.515
2007	Mont	AA	21	78	23	4	1	2	(-	-)	35	12	15	13	9	0	23	2	1	1	0	1	.00	1	.295	.378	.449
2008	Mont	AA	107	395	106	27	1	14	(-	-)	177	57	52	65	46	1	112	8	0	1	2	1	.67	8	.268	.356	.448
2009	Mont	AA	58	226	57	11	0	15	(-	-)	113	31	46	40	25	2	80	6	0	2	3	0	1.00	5	.252	.340	.500
2009	Drhm	AAA	56	214	67	22	2	7	(-	-)	114	31	26	40	12	1	69	4	0	0	0	0	-	4	.313	.361	.533
2009	Norfolk	AAA	20	72	19	2	1	3	(-	-)	32	9	7	11	7	1	22	2	0	0	0	0	-	1	.264	.346	.444
2010	Norfolk	AAA	104	388	100	25	2	10	(-	-)	159	44	39	52	29	2	121	4	1	3	8	3	.73	7	.258	.314	.410
2010	Bal	AL	14	47	10	2	0	0	(0	0)	12	3	4	5	4	0	19	0	0	0	0	0	-	0	.213	.275	.255

Philip Humber

Pitches: R Bats: R Pos: RP-7; SP-1 — Ht: 6'3" Wt: 209 Born: 12/21/1982 Age: 28

Year	Team	Lg	G	GS	CG	GF	IP	BFP	H	R	ER	HR	SH	SF	HB	TBB	IBB	SO	WP	Bk	W	L	Pct	Sh	Sv-Op	Hld	ERC	ERA
2010	Omha*	AAA	21	20	1	0	118.2	508	131	68	59	17	5	4	6	20	1	80	2	0	5	6	.455	1	0--	-	4.17	4.47
2006	NYM	NL	2	0	0	1	2.0	7	0	0	0	0	0	0	0	1	0	2	0	0	0	0	-	0	0-0	0	0.27	0.00
2007	NYM	NL	3	1	0	2	7.0	32	9	6	6	1	0	0	0	2	0	2	0	0	0	0	-	0	0-0	0	5.46	7.71
2008	Min	AL	5	0	0	4	11.2	50	11	6	6	4	0	0	1	5	0	6	0	0	0	0	-	0	0-0	0	6.11	4.63
2009	Min	AL	8	0	0	1	9.0	50	17	8	8	1	0	0	0	9	2	9	1	0	0	0	-	0	0-0	0	12.62	8.00
2010	KC	AL	8	1	0	1	21.2	94	22	10	10	1	0	1	1	7	2	16	2	0	2	1	.667	0	0-0	1	3.47	4.15
5 ML YEARS			26	2	0	9	51.1	233	59	30	30	7	0	1	2	24	4	35	3	0	2	1	.667	0	0-0	1	5.54	5.26

Nick Hundley

Bats: R Throws: R Pos: C-76; PH-9; PR-1 — Ht: 6'1" Wt: 205 Born: 9/8/1983 Age: 27

Year	Team	Lg	G	AB	H	2B	3B	HR	(Hm	Rd)	TB	R	RBI	RC	TBB	IBB	SO	HBP	SH	SF	SB	CS	SB%	GDP	Avg	OBP	Slg
2008	SD	NL	60	198	47	7	1	5	(4	1)	71	21	24	17	11	0	52	2	0	5	0	0	-	1	.237	.278	.359
2009	SD	NL	78	256	61	15	2	8	(4	4)	104	23	30	33	28	1	76	1	1	3	5	1	.83	2	.238	.313	.406
2010	SD	NL	85	273	68	18	2	8	(7	1)	114	33	43	37	25	0	66	1	2	6	0	5	.00	8	.249	.308	.418
3 ML YEARS			223	727	176	40	5	21	(15	6)	289	77	97	87	64	1	194	4	3	14	5	6	.45	11	.242	.302	.398

Tommy Hunter

Pitches: R Bats: R Pos: SP-22; RP-1 — Ht: 6'3" Wt: 280 Born: 7/3/1986 Age: 24

Year	Team	Lg	G	GS	CG	GF	IP	BFP	H	R	ER	HR	SH	SF	HB	TBB	IBB	SO	WP	Bk	W	L	Pct	Sh	Sv-Op	Hld	ERC	ERA
2010	OKCity*	AAA	6	6	0	0	26.2	117	28	12	12	2	5	2	0	11	0	14	0	0	1	2	.333	0	0--	-	4.20	4.05
2008	Tex	AL	3	3	0	0	11.0	63	23	20	20	4	0	0	1	3	0	9	0	0	0	2	.000	0	0-0	0	12.66	16.36
2009	Tex	AL	19	19	1	0	112.0	475	113	55	51	13	2	1	2	33	2	64	6	1	9	6	.600	0	0-0	0	3.86	4.10
2010	Tex	AL	23	22	1	0	128.0	536	126	55	53	21	3	2	3	33	0	68	1	0	13	4	.765	0	0-0	0	3.95	3.73
3 ML YEARS			45	44	2	0	251.0	1074	262	130	124	38	5	3	6	69	2	141	7	1	22	12	.647	0	0-0	0	4.24	4.45

Torii Hunter

Bats: R Throws: R Pos: CF-98; RF-46; DH-9 — Ht: 6'2" Wt: 225 Born: 7/18/1975 Age: 35

Year	Team	Lg	G	AB	H	2B	3B	HR	(Hm	Rd)	TB	R	RBI	RC	TBB	IBB	SO	HBP	SH	SF	SB	CS	SB%	GDP	Avg	OBP	Slg
1997	Min	AL	1	0	0	0	0	0	(0	0)	0	0	0	0	0	0	0	0	0	0	0	0	-	0	-	-	-
1998	Min	AL	6	17	4	1	0	0	(0	0)	5	0	2	1	2	0	6	0	0	0	0	1	.00	1	.235	.316	.294
1999	Min	AL	135	384	98	17	2	9	(2	7)	146	52	35	44	26	1	72	6	1	5	10	6	.63	9	.255	.309	.380
2000	Min	AL	99	336	94	14	7	5	(4	1)	137	44	44	39	18	2	68	2	0	2	4	3	.57	13	.280	.318	.408
2001	Min	AL	148	564	147	32	5	27	(13	14)	270	82	92	79	29	0	125	8	1	1	9	6	.60	12	.261	.306	.479
2002	Min	AL	148	561	162	37	4	29	(13	16)	294	89	94	85	35	3	118	5	0	3	23	8	.74	17	.289	.334	.524
2003	Min	AL	154	581	145	31	4	26	(12	14)	262	83	102	76	50	7	106	5	0	6	6	7	.46	15	.250	.312	.451
2004	Min	AL	138	520	141	37	0	23	(9	14)	247	79	81	69	40	4	101	7	0	2	21	7	.75	23	.271	.330	.475
2005	Min	AL	98	372	100	24	1	14	(6	8)	168	63	56	53	34	4	65	4	0	4	23	7	.77	8	.269	.337	.452
2006	Min	AL	147	557	155	21	2	31	(15	16)	273	86	98	81	45	2	108	5	0	4	12	6	.67	19	.278	.336	.490
2007	Min	AL	160	600	172	45	1	28	(11	17)	303	94	107	99	40	10	101	5	0	5	18	9	.67	17	.287	.334	.505
2008	LAA	AL	146	551	153	37	2	21	(10	11)	257	85	78	80	50	6	108	6	0	1	19	5	.79	15	.278	.344	.466

Year	Team	Lg	G	AB	H	2B	3B	HR	(Hm	Rd)	TB	R	RBI	RC	TBB	IBB	SO	HBP	SH	SF	SB	CS	SB%	GDP	Avg	OBP	Slg
								BATTING														**BASERUNNING**				**AVERAGES**	
2009	LAA	AL	119	451	135	26	1	22	(15	7)	229	74	90	84	47	4	92	3	0	5	18	4	.82	9	.299	.366	.508
2010	LAA	AL	152	573	161	36	0	23	(8	15)	266	76	90	93	61	6	106	7	0	5	9	12	.43	22	.281	.354	.464
	Postseason		34	131	40	10	1	4	(1	3)	64	19	18	18	13	2	19	1	2	1	3	1	.75	4	.305	.370	.489
	14 ML YEARS		1651	6067	1667	358	29	258	(118	140)	2857	907	969	883	477	48	1176	65	2	43	172	81	.68	180	.275	.332	.471

Chris Iannetta

Bats: R **Throws:** R **Pos:** C-52; PH-5; 1B-3; 3B-1; DH-1   eye-ah-NETT-ah   **Ht:** 6'0" **Wt:** 230 **Born:** 4/8/1983 **Age:** 28

Year	Team	Lg	G	AB	H	2B	3B	HR	(Hm	Rd)	TB	R	RBI	RC	TBB	IBB	SO	HBP	SH	SF	SB	CS	SB%	GDP	Avg	OBP	Slg
								BATTING														**BASERUNNING**				**AVERAGES**	
2010	ColSpr*	AAA	17	63	22	7	0	5	(-	-)	44	17	21	18	10	0	10	2	0	1	0	0	-	3	.349	.447	.698
2006	Col	NL	21	77	20	4	0	2	(0	2)	30	12	10	9	13	2	17	1	1	1	0	1	.00	1	.260	.370	.390
2007	Col	NL	67	197	43	8	3	4	(1	3)	69	22	27	27	29	3	58	5	1	2	0	0	-	3	.218	.330	.350
2008	Col	NL	104	333	88	22	2	18	(11	7)	168	50	65	65	56	0	92	14	2	2	0	0	-	6	.264	.390	.505
2009	Col	NL	93	289	66	15	2	16	(8	8)	133	41	52	47	43	3	75	11	1	6	0	1	.00	4	.228	.344	.460
2010	Col	NL	61	188	37	6	1	9	(7	2)	72	20	27	21	30	2	48	4	0	1	1	0	1.00	4	.197	.318	.383
	5 ML YEARS		346	1084	254	55	8	49	(27	22)	472	145	181	169	171	10	290	35	5	12	1	2	.33	18	.234	.353	.435

Raul Ibanez

Bats: L **Throws:** R **Pos:** LF-145; PH-9; 1B-1; DH-1   ee-BAHN-yezz   **Ht:** 6'2" **Wt:** 227 **Born:** 6/2/1972 **Age:** 39

Year	Team	Lg	G	AB	H	2B	3B	HR	(Hm	Rd)	TB	R	RBI	RC	TBB	IBB	SO	HBP	SH	SF	SB	CS	SB%	GDP	Avg	OBP	Slg
								BATTING														**BASERUNNING**				**AVERAGES**	
1996	Sea	AL	4	5	0	0	0	0	(0	0)	0	0	0	0	0	0	1	1	0	0	0	0	-	0	.000	.167	.000
1997	Sea	AL	11	26	4	0	1	1	(1	0)	9	3	4	1	0	0	6	0	0	0	0	0	-	0	.154	.154	.346
1998	Sea	AL	37	98	25	7	1	2	(1	1)	40	12	12	10	5	0	22	0	0	0	0	0	-	4	.255	.291	.408
1999	Sea	AL	87	209	54	7	0	9	(3	6)	88	23	27	28	17	1	32	0	0	1	5	1	.83	4	.258	.313	.421
2000	Sea	AL	92	140	32	8	0	2	(2	0)	46	21	15	15	14	1	25	1	0	1	2	0	1.00	1	.229	.301	.329
2001	KC	AL	104	279	78	11	5	13	(5	8)	138	44	54	46	32	2	51	0	0	1	0	2	.00	6	.280	.353	.495
2002	KC	AL	137	497	146	37	6	24	(14	10)	267	70	103	89	40	5	76	2	1	4	5	3	.63	11	.294	.346	.537
2003	KC	AL	157	608	179	33	5	18	(8	10)	276	95	90	91	49	5	81	3	1	10	8	4	.67	10	.294	.345	.454
2004	Sea	AL	123	481	140	31	1	16	(9	7)	227	67	62	67	36	5	72	3	0	4	1	2	.33	10	.304	.353	.472
2005	Sea	AL	162	614	172	32	2	20	(9	11)	268	92	89	99	71	6	99	2	0	3	9	4	.69	12	.280	.355	.436
2006	Sea	AL	159	626	181	33	5	33	(17	16)	323	103	123	114	65	15	115	1	0	7	2	4	.33	13	.289	.353	.516
2007	Sea	AL	149	573	167	35	5	21	(7	14)	275	80	105	101	53	4	97	3	0	7	0	0	-	14	.291	.351	.480
2008	Sea	AL	162	635	186	43	3	23	(14	9)	304	85	110	107	64	11	110	3	0	6	2	1	.77	13	.293	.358	.479
2009	Phi	NL	134	500	136	32	3	34	(13	21)	276	93	93	80	56	8	119	4	0	5	4	0	1.00	16	.272	.347	.552
2010	Phi	NL	155	561	154	37	5	16	(9	7)	249	75	83	86	68	11	108	0	0	7	4	3	.57	15	.275	.349	.444
	Postseason		24	71	17	6	0	2	(1	1)	29	10	13	10	6	0	19	0	0	0	0	0	-	1	.239	.299	.408
	15 ML YEARS		1673	6852	1660	346	42	232	(112	120)	2786	863	970	934	570	74	1014	23	2	55	42	27	.61	129	.284	.347	.476

Ryota Igarashi

Pitches: R **Bats:** R **Pos:** RP-34   ree-OH-tah ig-ah-RAH-she   **Ht:** 5'11" **Wt:** 198 **Born:** 5/28/1979 **Age:** 32

Year	Team	Lg	G	GS	CG	GF	IP	BFP	H	R	ER	HR	SH	SF	HB	TBB	IBB	SO	WP	Bk	W	L	Pct	Sh	Sv-Op	Hld	ERC	ERA
			HOW MUCH HE PITCHED						**WHAT HE GAVE UP**												**THE RESULTS**							
1999	Yakult	Jap	36	0	0	-	47.2	206	34	27	26	4	-	-	1	29	-	59	3	1	6	4	.600	0	1--	-	3.23	4.91
2000	Yakult	Jap	56	0	0	-	75.1	301	42	28	26	11	-	-	1	33	-	90	6	0	11	4	.733	0	1--	-	2.24	3.11
2001	Yakult	Jap	41	-	-	-	41.2	178	25	13	12	2	-	-	2	20	-	51	1	0	2	3	.400	-	0--	-	2.75	2.59
2002	Yakult	Jap	64	0	0	-	78.0	301	49	19	18	8	-	-	3	18	-	97	8	0	8	2	.800	0	4--	-	1.75	2.08
2003	Yakult	Jap	66	0	0	-	74.0	315	60	33	32	0	-	-	1	33	-	83	7	1	5	5	.500	0	0--	-	3.30	3.09
2004	Yakult	Jap	66	0	0	-	74.1	316	57	24	22	9	-	-	1	36	-	86	4	0	5	3	.625	0	37-	-	3.27	2.66
2005	Yakult	Jap	49	0	0	-	56.2	249	52	24	22	6	-	-	1	27	-	60	6	0	3	2	.600	0	4--	-	3.95	3.49
2006	Yakult	Jap	29	0	0	-	25.0	119	33	20	17	3	-	-	2	11	-	18	4	0	1	2	.333	0	1--	-	6.60	6.12
2008	Yakult	Jap	44	0	0	-	43.2	171	35	13	12	3	-	-	2	6	0	42	3	0	3	2	.600	0	3--	-	2.08	2.47
2009	Yakult	Jap	56	0	0	-	53.2	221	42	19	19	3	-	-	3	20	1	44	1	0	3	2	.600	0	3--	-	2.72	3.19
2010	StLuci	A+	5	2	0	1	7.2	34	10	2	2	0	0	1	0	1	0	11	1	0	1	0	1.000	0	0--	-	3.89	2.35
2010	Buffalo	AAA	15	0	0	9	16.1	73	18	8	6	2	2	0	0	6	0	16	3	0	2	1	.667	0	2--	-	4.58	3.31
2010	NYM	NL	34	0	0	11	30.1	135	29	24	24	4	0	3	0	10	1	26	3	0	1	1	.600	0	0-0	?	4.78	7.12

Gregory Infante

Pitches: R **Bats:** R **Pos:** RP-5   **Ht:** 6'2" **Wt:** 185 **Born:** 7/10/1987 **Age:** 23

Year	Team	Lg	G	GS	CG	GF	IP	BFP	H	R	ER	HR	SH	SF	HB	TBB	IBB	SO	WP	Bk	W	L	Pct	Sh	Sv-Op	Hld	ERC	ERA
			HOW MUCH HE PITCHED						**WHAT HE GAVE UP**												**THE RESULTS**							
2007	Bristol	R	10	8	0	0	33.2	148	25	17	15	1	0	2	2	23	0	33	9	1	2	3	.400	0	0--	-	3.45	4.01
2008	Knapol	A	4	3	0	0	13.2	71	16	12	10	0	0	2	1	12	0	11	1	0	1	2	.333	0	0--	-	6.21	6.59
2008	Bristol	R	13	12	0	0	74.1	303	63	26	22	4	0	5	8	19	0	57	4	1	4	3	.571	0	0--	-	2.87	2.66
2009	Knapol	A	15	15	0	0	88.1	371	76	37	32	4	4	3	9	37	0	75	7	0	3	5	.375	0	0--	-	3.47	3.26
2009	WinSa	A+	5	5	0	0	20.2	104	18	20	18	3	1	1	5	23	0	10	5	0	1	2	.333	0	0--	-	7.74	7.84
2010	WinSa	A+	31	0	0	26	33.2	147	32	15	13	0	1	1	2	15	0	35	4	0	1	2	.333	0	9--	-	3.47	3.48
2010	Brham	AA	24	0	0	11	26.1	113	23	11	10	0	2	0	1	12	1	34	3	0	2	2	.500	0	3--	-	2.97	3.42
2010	CWS	AL	5	0	0	5	4.2	19	2	0	0	0	0	0	0	4	0	5	0	0	0	0	-	0	0-0	0	2.16	0.00

Omar Infante

Bats: R **Throws:** R **Pos:** 2B-65; 3B-29; SS-19; LF-15; PH-13; RF-6; PR-1   **Ht:** 6'0" **Wt:** 180 **Born:** 12/26/1981 **Age:** 29

Year	Team	Lg	G	AB	H	2B	3B	HR	(Hm	Rd)	TB	R	RBI	RC	TBB	IBB	SO	HBP	SH	SF	SB	CS	SB%	GDP	Avg	OBP	Slg
2002	Det	AL	18	72	24	3	0	1	(0	1)	30	4	6	12	3	0	10	0	0	0	0	1	.00	0	.333	.360	.417
2003	Det	AL	69	221	49	6	1	0	(0	0)	57	24	8	16	18	0	37	0	3	2	6	3	.67	1	.222	.278	.258
2004	Det	AL	142	503	133	27	9	16	(7	9)	226	69	55	69	40	3	112	1	7	5	13	7	.65	4	.264	.317	.449
2005	Det	AL	121	406	90	28	2	9	(3	6)	149	36	43	38	16	0	73	2	8	2	8	0	1.00	5	.222	.254	.367
2006	Det	AL	78	224	62	11	4	4	(0	4)	93	35	25	26	14	0	45	3	2	2	3	2	.60	5	.277	.325	.415
2007	Det	AL	66	166	45	6	1	2	(0	2)	59	24	17	23	9	0	29	0	2	1	4	1	.80	4	.271	.307	.355
2008	Atl	NL	96	317	93	24	3	3	(1	2)	132	45	40	45	22	2	44	2	2	5	0	1	.00	4	.293	.338	.416
2009	Atl	NL	70	203	62	9	1	2	(1	1)	79	24	27	29	19	0	28	1	2	4	2	0	1.00	5	.305	.361	.389
2010	Atl	NL	134	471	151	15	3	8	(1	7)	196	65	47	70	29	1	62	0	4	2	7	6	.54	14	.321	.359	.416
Postseason			2	3	1	0	0	0	(0	0)	1	0	0	1	1	0	1	0	0	0	1	0	1.00	0	.333	.500	.333
9 ML YEARS			794	2583	709	129	24	45	(13	32)	1021	326	268	328	170	6	440	9	30	23	43	21	.67	42	.274	.319	.395

Brandon Inge

Bats: R **Throws:** R **Pos:** 3B-144; PH-5   **Ht:** 5'11" **Wt:** 188 **Born:** 5/19/1977 **Age:** 34

Year	Team	Lg	G	AB	H	2B	3B	HR	(Hm	Rd)	TB	R	RBI	RC	TBB	IBB	SO	HBP	SH	SF	SB	CS	SB%	GDP	Avg	OBP	Slg
2010	WMich*	A	1	5	2	2	0	0	(-	-)	4	0	1	1	0	0	2	0	0	0	0	0	-	0	.400	.400	.800
2001	Det	AL	79	189	34	11	0	0	(0	0)	45	13	15	6	9	0	41	0	2	2	1	4	.20	2	.180	.215	.238
2002	Det	AL	95	321	65	15	3	7	(3	4)	107	27	24	24	24	0	101	4	1	1	1	3	.25	7	.202	.266	.333
2003	Det	AL	104	330	67	15	3	8	(4	4)	112	32	30	23	24	0	79	5	4	3	4	4	.50	8	.203	.265	.339
2004	Det	AL	131	408	117	15	7	13	(9	4)	185	43	64	63	32	0	72	4	8	6	5	4	.56	4	.287	.340	.453
2005	Det	AL	160	616	161	31	9	16	(10	6)	258	75	72	82	63	1	140	3	6	6	7	6	.54	14	.261	.330	.419
2006	Det	AL	159	542	137	29	2	27	(12	15)	251	83	83	79	43	2	128	7	4	5	7	4	.64	12	.253	.313	.463
2007	Det	AL	151	508	120	25	2	14	(9	5)	191	64	71	65	47	5	150	11	7	4	9	2	.82	8	.236	.312	.376
2008	Det	AL	113	347	71	16	4	11	(8	3)	128	41	51	44	43	2	94	8	5	4	4	3	.57	4	.205	.303	.369
2009	Det	AL	161	562	129	16	1	27	(14	13)	228	71	84	70	54	1	170	17	1	3	2	5	.29	12	.230	.314	.406
2010	Det	AL	144	514	127	28	5	13	(4	9)	204	47	70	64	54	4	134	5	0	7	4	3	.57	12	.247	.321	.397
Postseason			13	44	12	3	0	1	(0	1)	18	4	4	5	4	2	15	0	1	1	0	0	-	1	.273	.327	.409
10 ML YEARS			1297	4337	1028	201	36	136	(73	63)	1709	496	564	520	393	15	1109	64	38	41	44	38	.54	83	.237	.307	.394

Joe Inglett

Bats: L **Throws:** R **Pos:** PH-78; RF-14; LF-10; 2B-8   **Ht:** 5'9" **Wt:** 177 **Born:** 6/29/1978 **Age:** 33

Year	Team	Lg	G	AB	H	2B	3B	HR	(Hm	Rd)	TB	R	RBI	RC	TBB	IBB	SO	HBP	SH	SF	SB	CS	SB%	GDP	Avg	OBP	Slg
2006	Cle	AL	64	201	57	8	3	2	(1	1)	77	26	21	28	14	0	39	1	5	1	5	1	.83	1	.284	.332	.383
2007	Tor	AL	2	5	3	0	1	0	(0	0)	5	0	2	3	0	0	0	0	0	0	1	0	1.00	0	.600	.600	1.000
2008	Tor	AL	109	344	102	15	7	3	(2	1)	140	45	39	52	28	0	43	4	8	1	9	2	.82	5	.297	.355	.407
2009	Tor	AL	36	89	25	4	1	0	(0	0)	31	11	6	14	8	0	21	1	1	0	3	1	.75	0	.281	.347	.348
2010	Mil	NL	102	142	36	8	5	1	(1	0)	57	15	8	19	15	0	34	2	0	1	1	0	1.00	1	.254	.331	.401
5 ML YEARS			313	781	223	35	17	6	(4	2)	310	97	76	116	65	0	137	8	14	3	19	4	.83	7	.286	.345	.397

Travis Ishikawa

Bats: L **Throws:** L **Pos:** 1B-73; PH-55; PR-2   ee-shee-KAU-wuh   **Ht:** 6'3" **Wt:** 233 **Born:** 9/24/1983 **Age:** 27

Year	Team	Lg	G	AB	H	2B	3B	HR	(Hm	Rd)	TB	R	RBI	RC	TBB	IBB	SO	HBP	SH	SF	SB	CS	SB%	GDP	Avg	OBP	Slg
2006	SF	NL	12	24	7	3	1	0	(0	0)	12	1	4	4	1	0	6	0	0	0	0	0	-	1	.292	.320	.500
2008	SF	NL	33	95	26	6	0	3	(1	2)	41	12	15	17	9	1	27	0	0	0	1	0	1.00	1	.274	.337	.432
2009	SF	NL	120	326	85	10	2	9	(7	2)	126	49	39	44	30	3	89	4	1	2	2	2	.50	7	.261	.329	.387
2010	SF	NL	116	158	42	11	0	3	(0	3)	62	18	22	19	13	2	29	0	1	1	0	0	-	3	.266	.320	.392
4 ML YEARS			281	603	160	30	3	15	(8	7)	241	80	80	84	53	6	151	4	2	3	3	2	.60	12	.265	.327	.400

Hisashi Iwakuma

Pitches: R **Bats:** R **Pos:** P   hee-SAH-shee ee-wah-KOOM-ah   **Ht:** 6'3" **Wt:** 170 **Born:** 4/12/1981 **Age:** 30

| | | | HOW MUCH HE PITCHED | | | | | | WHAT HE GAVE UP | | | | | | | | | | | | THE RESULTS | | | | | | |
Year	Team	Lg	G	GS	CG	GF	IP	BFP	H	R	ER	HR	SH	SF	HB	TBB	IBB	SO	WP	Bk	W	L	Pct	Sh	Sv-Op	Hld	ERC	ERA
2001	Kintets	Jap	9	-	1	-	43.2	192	46	28	22	3	-	-	3	13	-	25	1	0	4	2	.667	1	0- -	-	3.94	4.53
2002	Kintets	Jap	23	-	2	-	141.1	594	132	62	58	10	-	-	8	42	-	131	4	1	8	7	.533	0	0- -	-	3.34	3.69
2003	Kintets	Jap	27	-	11	-	195.2	809	201	85	75	19	-	-	3	48	-	149	2	0	15	10	.600	0	0- -	-	3.73	3.45
2004	Kintets	Jap	21	-	7	-	158.2	647	149	57	53	13	-	-	8	30	-	123	0	0	15	2	.882	1	0- -	-	3.04	3.01
2005	Tohoku	Jap	27	-	9	-	182.1	796	218	113	101	19	-	-	6	40	-	124	7	0	9	15	.375	0	0- -	-	4.61	4.99
2006	Tohoku	Jap	6	-	2	-	38.2	169	43	18	16	4	-	-	1	12	-	16	0	0	1	2	.333	0	0- -	-	4.46	3.72
2007	Tohoku	Jap	16	-	0	-	90.0	388	95	47	34	6	-	-	2	23	-	84	0	0	5	5	.500	0	0- -	-	3.61	3.40
2008	Tohoku	Jap	28	-	5	-	201.2	787	161	48	42	3	-	-	4	36	-	159	4	0	21	4	.840	2	0- -	-	1.83	1.87
2009	Tohoku	Jap	24	-	5	-	169.0	710	179	62	61	15	-	-	6	43	-	121	3	0	13	6	.684	0	0- -	-	3.96	3.25
2010	Tohoku	Jap	28	-	4	-	201.0	821	184	68	63	11	-	-	12	36	-	153	1	1	10	9	.526	1	0- -	-	2.72	2.82

Akinori Iwamura

Bats: L **Throws:** R **Pos:** 2B-40; PH-14; 3B-10   ah-kin-OH-ree ee-wah-MOO-rah   **Ht:** 5'9" **Wt:** 200 **Born:** 2/9/1979 **Age:** 32

Year	Team	Lg	G	AB	H	2B	3B	HR	(Hm	Rd)	TB	R	RBI	RC	TBB	IBB	SO	HBP	SH	SF	SB	CS	SB%	GDP	Avg	OBP	Slg
2010	Indy*	AAA	50	163	43	10	1	3	(-	-)	64	26	16	28	38	1	32	1	0	1	0	2	.00	1	.264	.404	.393
2007	TB	AL	123	491	140	21	10	7	(4	3)	202	82	34	68	58	0	114	1	4	5	12	8	.60	2	.285	.359	.411
2008	TB	AL	152	627	172	30	9	6	(3	3)	238	91	48	85	70	3	131	4	3	3	8	6	.57	2	.274	.349	.380
2009	TB	AL	69	231	67	16	2	1	(0	1)	90	28	22	29	24	0	44	1	1	3	9	1	.90	1	.290	.355	.390
2010	2 Tms		64	196	34	7	1	2	(0	2)	49	21	13	16	31	0	41	0	1	1	3	1	.75	4	.173	.285	.250
10	Pit	NL	54	165	30	6	1	2	(0	2)	44	18	9	15	26	0	31	0	1	1	3	1	.75	4	.182	.292	.267
10	Oak	AL	10	31	4	1	0	0	(0	0)	5	3	4	1	5	0	10	0	0	0	0	0	-	0	.129	.250	.161
	Postseason		16	66	18	4	1	1	(1	0)	27	8	5	12	7	1	12	0	0	0	2	0	1.00	0	.273	.342	.409
	4 ML YEARS		408	1545	413	74	22	16	(7	9)	579	222	117	198	183	3	330	6	9	12	32	16	.67	9	.267	.345	.375

Cesar Izturis

Bats: B **Throws:** R **Pos:** SS-150; PR-3   izz-TOUR-iss   **Ht:** 5'9" **Wt:** 180 **Born:** 2/10/1980 **Age:** 31

Year	Team	Lg	G	AB	H	2B	3B	HR	(Hm	Rd)	TB	R	RBI	RC	TBB	IBB	SO	HBP	SH	SF	SB	CS	SB%	GDP	Avg	OBP	Slg
2001	Tor	AL	46	134	36	6	2	2	(1	1)	52	19	9	16	2	0	15	0	4	0	8	1	.89	0	.269	.279	.388
2002	LAD	NL	135	439	102	24	2	1	(0	1)	133	43	31	26	14	1	39	0	10	5	7	7	.50	12	.232	.253	.303
2003	LAD	NL	158	558	140	21	6	1	(0	1)	176	47	40	42	25	8	70	0	7	3	10	5	.67	8	.251	.282	.315
2004	LAD	NL	159	670	193	32	9	4	(1	3)	255	90	62	95	43	2	70	0	12	3	25	9	.74	6	.288	.330	.381
2005	LAD	NL	106	444	114	19	2	2	(1	1)	143	48	31	37	25	1	51	4	4	1	8	8	.50	11	.257	.302	.322
2006	2 Tms	NL	54	192	47	9	1	1	(1	0)	61	14	18	14	12	3	14	2	1	1	1	4	.20	4	.245	.295	.318
2007	2 Tms	NL	110	314	81	14	2	0	(0	0)	99	31	16	27	19	2	19	1	3	0	3	3	.50	7	.258	.302	.315
2008	StL	NL	135	414	109	10	3	1	(0	1)	128	50	24	39	29	1	26	6	3	2	24	6	.80	6	.263	.319	.309
2009	Bal	AL	114	387	99	14	4	2	(1	1)	127	34	30	37	18	0	38	3	4	0	12	4	.75	11	.256	.294	.328
2010	Bal	AL	150	473	109	13	1	1	(0	1)	127	42	28	32	25	1	53	6	7	2	11	5	.69	11	.230	.277	.268
06	LAD	NL	32	119	30	7	1	1	(1	0)	42	10	12	10	7	3	6	2	0	1	1	3	.25	1	.252	.302	.353
06	ChC	NL	22	73	17	2	0	0	(0	0)	19	4	6	4	5	0	8	0	1	0	0	1	.00	3	.233	.282	.260
07	ChC	NL	65	191	47	11	0	0	(0	0)	58	15	8	13	13	2	16	1	2	0	3	0	1.00	6	.246	.298	.304
07	Pit	NL	45	123	34	3	2	0	(0	0)	41	16	8	14	6	0	3	0	1	0	0	3	.00	1	.276	.310	.333
	Postseason		4	17	3	1	0	0	(0	0)	4	1	0	0	1	0	2	0	0	0	0	0	-	0	.176	.222	.235
	10 ML YEARS		1167	4025	1030	162	32	15	(5	10)	1301	418	289	365	212	19	395	22	55	17	109	52	.68	76	.256	.296	.323

Maicer Izturis

Bats: B **Throws:** R **Pos:** 3B-28; 2B-22; SS-7; PH-6; DH-3   MY-sare izz-TOUR-iss   **Ht:** 5'8" **Wt:** 170 **Born:** 9/12/1980 **Age:** 30

Year	Team	Lg	G	AB	H	2B	3B	HR	(Hm	Rd)	TB	R	RBI	RC	TBB	IBB	SO	HBP	SH	SF	SB	CS	SB%	GDP	Avg	OBP	Slg
2010	Salt Lk*	AAA	2	7	2	0	0	0	(-	-)	2	1	1	0	0	0	0	0	0	0	0	1	.00	0	.286	.286	.286
2004	Mon	NL	32	107	22	5	2	1	(1	0)	34	10	4	8	10	1	20	2	2	0	4	0	1.00	1	.206	.286	.318
2005	LAA	AL	77	191	47	8	4	1	(0	1)	66	18	15	25	17	2	21	0	1	1	9	3	.75	5	.246	.306	.346
2006	LAA	AL	104	352	103	21	3	5	(1	4)	145	64	44	56	38	1	35	3	5	1	14	6	.70	7	.293	.365	.412
2007	LAA	AL	102	336	97	17	2	6	(4	2)	136	47	51	65	33	2	39	0	1	4	7	1	.88	4	.289	.349	.405
2008	LAA	AL	79	290	78	14	2	3	(1	2)	105	44	37	39	26	0	27	1	2	2	11	2	.85	0	.269	.329	.362
2009	LAA	AL	114	387	116	22	3	8	(3	5)	168	74	65	66	35	2	41	5	3	7	13	5	.72	7	.300	.359	.434
2010	LAA	AL	81	212	53	11	3	0	(0	0)	77	27	27	30	21	0	27	2	1	2	7	3	.70	1	.250	.321	.363
	Postseason		10	29	6	3	0	0	(0	0)	9	3	2	2	1	1	5	0	0	1	3	0	1.00	0	.207	.226	.310
	7 ML YEARS		569	1875	516	100	17	27	(10	17)	731	284	243	289	180	8	210	13	15	17	65	20	.76	34	.275	.340	.390

Austin Jackson

Bats: R **Throws:** R **Pos:** CF-149; PH-6   **Ht:** 6'1" **Wt:** 185 **Born:** 2/1/1987 **Age:** 24

Year	Team	Lg	G	AB	H	2B	3B	HR	(Hm	Rd)	TB	R	RBI	RC	TBB	IBB	SO	HBP	SH	SF	SB	CS	SB%	GDP	Avg	OBP	Slg
2005	Yanks	R	40	148	45	11	2	0	(-	-)	60	32	14	25	18	0	26	1	0	4	11	2	.85	4	.304	.374	.405
2006	CtnSC	A	134	535	139	24	5	4	(-	-)	185	90	47	71	61	0	151	6	5	4	37	12	.76	7	.260	.340	.346
2007	CtnSC	A	60	235	61	16	1	3	(-	-)	88	33	25	33	24	0	59	4	1	2	19	6	.76	1	.260	.336	.374
2007	Tampa	A+	67	258	89	15	6	10	(-	-)	146	53	34	56	22	0	48	2	0	2	13	5	.72	9	.345	.398	.566
2007	S-WB	AAA	1	3	1	1	0	0	(-	-)	2	2	0	1	2	0	2	0	0	0	1	0	1.00	0	.333	.600	.667
2008	Trntn	AA	131	520	148	33	5	9	(-	-)	218	75	69	82	56	3	113	2	2	4	19	6	.76	9	.285	.354	.419
2009	S-WB	AAA	132	504	151	23	9	4	(-	-)	204	67	65	78	40	1	123	6	1	6	24	4	.86	10	.300	.354	.405
2010	Det	AL	151	618	181	34	10	4	(0	4)	247	103	41	84	47	1	**170**	4	3	3	27	6	.82	5	.293	.345	.400

Conor Jackson

Bats: R **Throws:** R **Pos:** LF-52; PH-6; 1B-3; DH-2   **Ht:** 6'2" **Wt:** 215 **Born:** 5/7/1982 **Age:** 29

Year	Team	Lg	G	AB	H	2B	3B	HR	(Hm	Rd)	TB	R	RBI	RC	TBB	IBB	SO	HBP	SH	SF	SB	CS	SB%	GDP	Avg	OBP	Slg
2010	Reno*	AAA	3	11	3	0	0	1	(-	-)	6	4	2	2	0	0	2	1	0	0	0	0	-	0	.273	.333	.545
2010	As*	R	3	7	0	0	0	0	(-	-)	0	0	1	0	0	0	0	0	0	1	0	0	-	0	.000	.000	.000
2010	Stcktn*	A+	2	7	2	1	0	0	(-	-)	3	1	2	0	0	0	1	0	0	0	0	0	-	0	.286	.250	.429
2010	Scrmto*	AAA	2	8	0	0	0	0	(-	-)	0	1	0	0	1	0	1	0	0	0	0	0	-	0	.000	.111	.000
2005	Ari	NL	40	85	17	3	0	2	(2	0)	26	8	8	6	12	0	11	1	0	1	0	0	-	0	.200	.303	.306
2006	Ari	NL	140	485	141	26	1	15	(8	7)	214	75	79	77	54	2	73	9	1	7	1	0	1.00	18	.291	.368	.441
2007	Ari	NL	130	415	118	29	1	15	(8	7)	194	56	60	67	53	2	50	4	2	3	2	2	.50	8	.284	.368	.467
2008	Ari	NL	144	540	162	31	6	12	(6	6)	241	87	75	88	59	3	61	9	1	3	10	2	.83	14	.300	.376	.446
2009	Ari	NL	30	99	18	4	0	1	(1	0)	25	8	14	10	11	0	16	0	0	0	5	0	1.00	1	.182	.264	.253
2010	2 Tms		60	208	49	13	0	2	(2	0)	68	25	16	24	31	1	27	1	0	1	6	1	.86	6	.236	.336	.327

			BATTING																		BASERUNNING			AVERAGES		
Year	Team	Lg	G	AB	H	2B	3B	HR	(Hm	Rd)	TB	R	RBI	RC	TBB	IBB	SO	HBP	SH	SF	SB	CS	SB%	GDP	Avg	OBP	Slg
10	Ari	NL	42	151	36	11	0	1	(1	0)	50	19	11	19	20	2	18	0	0	1	4	1	.80	4	.238	.326	.331
10	Oak	AL	18	57	13	2	0	1	(1	0)	18	6	5	5	11	1	9	1	0	0	2	0	1.00	2	.228	.362	.316
	Postseason		6	17	4	1	0	0	(0	0)	5	1	2	1	0	0	3	0	0	1	0	0	-	1	.235	.222	.294
	6 ML YEARS		544	1832	505	106	8	47	(27	20)	768	259	252	272	220	10	238	24	4	15	24	5	.83	53	.276	.358	.419

Edwin Jackson

Pitches: R **Bats:** R **Pos:** SP-32   **Ht:** 6'3" **Wt:** 210 **Born:** 9/9/1983 **Age:** 27

			HOW MUCH HE PITCHED						WHAT HE GAVE UP										THE RESULTS							
Year	Team	Lg	G	GS	CG	GF	IP	BFP	H	R	ER	HR	SH	SF	HB	TBB	IBB	SO	WP	Bk	W	L	Pct	Sh	Sv-Op	Hld	ERC	ERA
2003	LAD	NL	4	3	0	0	22.0	91	17	6	6	2	1	1	1	11	1	19	3	0	2	1	.667	0	0-0	0	3.36	2.45
2004	LAD	NL	8	5	0	1	24.2	113	31	20	20	7	1	0	0	11	1	16	0	0	2	1	.667	0	0-0	0	7.21	7.30
2005	LAD	NL	7	6	0	0	28.2	134	31	22	20	2	0	2	1	17	0	13	2	1	2	2	.500	0	0-0	0	5.13	6.28
2006	TB	AL	23	1	0	7	36.1	174	42	27	22	2	2	2	1	25	0	27	3	1	0	0	-	0	0-0	0	5.86	5.45
2007	TB	AL	32	31	1	0	161.0	755	195	116	103	19	5	6	4	88	3	128	7	1	5	15	.250	1	0-0	0	6.11	5.76
2008	TB	AL	32	31	0	0	183.1	792	199	91	90	23	3	3	2	77	1	108	7	1	14	11	.560	0	0-1	0	4.99	4.42
2009	Det	AL	33	33	1	0	214.0	890	200	93	86	27	4	2	5	70	3	161	6	0	13	9	.591	0	0-0	0	3.72	3.62
2010	2 Tms		32	32	1	0	209.1	902	214	111	104	21	6	4	6	78	4	181	20	0	10	12	.455	1	0-0	0	4.20	4.47
10	Ari	NL	21	21	1	0	134.1	587	141	80	77	13	6	2	5	60	2	104	13	0	6	10	.375	1	0-0	0	4.72	5.16
10	CWS	AL	11	11	0	0	75.0	315	73	31	27	8	0	2	1	18	2	77	7	0	4	2	.667	0	0-0	0	3.32	3.24
	Postseason		3	0	0	2	4.1	17	2	1	1	1	0	0	0	3	1	5	0	0	0	0	-	0	0-0	0	2.98	2.08
	8 ML YEARS		171	142	3	8	879.1	3851	929	486	451	103	22	20	20	377	13	653	48	4	48	51	.485	2	0-1	0	4.74	4.62

Steven Jackson

Pitches: R **Bats:** R **Pos:** RP-11   **Ht:** 6'5" **Wt:** 230 **Born:** 3/15/1982 **Age:** 29

			HOW MUCH HE PITCHED						WHAT HE GAVE UP										THE RESULTS							
Year	Team	Lg	G	GS	CG	GF	IP	BFP	H	R	ER	HR	SH	SF	HB	TBB	IBB	SO	WP	Bk	W	L	Pct	Sh	Sv-Op	Hld	ERC	ERA
2004	Msoula	R+	7	0	0	0	10.0	50	16	9	4	1	0	0	2	2	0	8	1	0	0	1	.000	0	0--	-	7.56	3.60
2004	Yakima	A-	9	2	0	1	23.2	102	24	12	12	4	1	1	0	6	0	18	3	0	1	0	1.000	0	0--	-	3.91	4.56
2005	Sbend	A	28	28	0	0	158.2	708	205	109	94	14	1	10	2	57	0	89	12	0	10	5	.667	0	0--	-	5.71	5.33
2006	Tenn	AA	24	24	1	0	149.2	605	131	52	44	6	3	8	1	45	2	125	3	0	8	11	.421	1	0--	-	2.71	2.65
2007	S-WB	AAA	18	11	0	0	69.0	327	93	57	45	11	1	1	3	29	1	50	3	0	4	8	.333	0	0--	-	6.82	5.87
2007	Trntn	AA	10	0	0	4	21.0	91	20	11	9	1	0	3	1	9	0	16	5	0	1	0	1.000	0	1--	-	3.73	3.86
2008	Trntn	AA	15	0	0	6	31.1	129	28	20	20	2	1	0	1	12	1	37	0	0	1	3	.250	0	2--	-	3.35	5.74
2008	S-WB	AAA	34	1	0	11	48.1	208	44	18	17	2	1	4	3	19	0	54	4	0	3	0	1.000	0	4--	-	3.36	3.17
2009	S-WB	AAA	7	1	0	3	14.1	61	16	3	3	1	0	0	0	3	0	8	0	0	0	0	-	0	1--	-	3.74	1.88
2009	Indy	AAA	12	0	0	1	18.0	81	23	14	13	1	2	2	0	5	0	17	2	0	1	0	1.000	0	0--	-	4.79	6.50
2010	Indy	AAA	41	0	0	8	56.1	247	59	24	22	6	1	1	5	19	3	37	2	0	4	0	1.000	0	0--	-	4.40	3.51
2009	Pit	NL	40	0	0	10	43.0	186	38	20	15	2	1	2	0	22	3	21	3	0	2	3	.400	0	0-1	4	3.35	3.14
2010	Pit	NL	11	0	0	3	11.1	55	17	11	11	4	1	1	0	6	0	7	0	0	0	1	.000	0	0-0	0	10.11	8.74
	2 ML YEARS		51	0	0	13	54.1	241	55	31	26	6	2	3	0	28	3	28	3	0	2	4	.333	0	0-1	4	4.58	4.31

Mike Jacobs

Bats: L **Throws:** R **Pos:** 1B-7   **Ht:** 6'3" **Wt:** 215 **Born:** 10/30/1980 **Age:** 30

			BATTING																		BASERUNNING			AVERAGES		
Year	Team	Lg	G	AB	H	2B	3B	HR	(Hm	Rd)	TB	R	RBI	RC	TBB	IBB	SO	HBP	SH	SF	SB	CS	SB%	GDP	Avg	OBP	Slg
2010	Buffalo*	AAA	86	339	88	23	3	15	(-	-)	162	53	57	52	28	4	65	0	0	4	1	0	1.00	8	.260	.313	.478
2010	LsVgs*	AAA	34	130	40	6	0	6	(-	-)	64	26	34	26	21	0	21	0	0	6	0	0	-	2	.308	.389	.492
2005	NYM	NL	30	100	31	7	0	11	(6	5)	71	19	23	21	10	0	22	1	0	1	0	0	-	5	.310	.375	.710
2006	Fla	NL	136	469	123	37	1	20	(12	8)	222	54	77	66	45	2	105	1	0	5	3	0	1.00	16	.262	.325	.473
2007	Fla	NL	114	426	113	27	2	17	(10	7)	195	57	54	51	31	3	101	2	0	1	1	2	.33	12	.265	.317	.458
2008	Fla	NL	141	477	118	27	2	32	(14	18)	245	67	93	69	36	10	119	1	0	5	1	0	1.00	9	.247	.299	.514
2009	KC	AL	128	434	99	16	1	19	(8	11)	174	46	61	50	41	2	132	2	0	1	0	0	-	9	.228	.297	.401
2010	NYM	NL	7	24	5	1	0	1	(1	0)	9	1	2	3	3	0	7	0	1	0	0	0	-	0	.208	.296	.375
	6 ML YEARS		556	1930	489	115	6	100	(51	49)	916	244	310	260	166	17	486	7	1	13	5	2	.71	49	.253	.313	.475

Chris Jakubauskas

Pitches: R **Bats:** L **Pos:** SP-1   jack-uh-BAU-skiss   **Ht:** 6'2" **Wt:** 215 **Born:** 12/22/1978 **Age:** 32

			HOW MUCH HE PITCHED						WHAT HE GAVE UP										THE RESULTS							
Year	Team	Lg	G	GS	CG	GF	IP	BFP	H	R	ER	HR	SH	SF	HB	TBB	IBB	SO	WP	Bk	W	L	Pct	Sh	Sv-Op	Hld	ERC	ERA
2007	WTenn	AA	16	3	1	3	51.0	219	53	30	28	3	1	2	1	21	0	39	2	0	0	4	.000	0	0--	-	4.21	4.94
2008	WTenn	AA	6	6	0	0	32.2	127	25	4	3	1	1	0	1	7	0	24	0	0	3	0	1.000	0	0--	-	1.93	0.83
2008	Tacom	AAA	12	9	0	0	55.2	231	52	22	16	5	1	1	1	14	0	48	4	2	5	1	.833	0	0--	-	3.13	2.59
2008	Everett	A-	1	1	0	0	2.2	9	1	0	0	0	0	0	0	0	0	7	1	0	0	0	-	0	0--	-	0.31	0.00
2009	Tacom	AAA	1	0	0	0	1.0	3	0	0	0	0	0	0	0	1	0	1	0	0	0	0	-	0	0--	-	1.26	0.00
2010	Indy	AAA	8	5	0	0	30.1	134	35	15	15	2	1	1	0	10	0	24	0	0	1	4	.200	0	0--	-	4.38	4.45
2010	Pirates	R	2	2	0	0	6.0	30	9	5	5	1	0	1	0	3	0	6	1	0	0	2	.000	0	0--	-	7.95	7.50
2010	Bradtn	A+	1	1	0	0	4.1	21	7	3	3	0	0	0	0	2	0	3	0	0	0	0	-	0	0--	-	7.40	6.23
2009	Sea	AL	35	8	1	6	93.0	390	91	60	55	15	0	3	2	27	3	47	8	1	6	7	.462	0	0-1	3	3.99	5.32
2010	Pit	NL	1	1	0	0	0.2	4	2	2	2	0	0	0	0	0	0	0	0	0	0	1	.000	0	0-0	0	14.52	27.00
	2 ML YEARS		36	9	1	6	93.2	394	93	62	57	15	0	3	2	27	3	47	8	1	6	8	.429	0	0-1	3	4.05	5.48

Justin James

Pitches: R Bats: R Pos: RP-5　　　　　　　　　　　　　　　　　　　　　**Ht: 6'3" Wt: 215 Born: 9/13/1981 Age: 29**

			HOW MUCH HE PITCHED					WHAT HE GAVE UP										THE RESULTS						
Year	Team	Lg	G	GS	CG	GF	IP	BFP	H	R	ER	HR	SH	SF	HB	TBB	IBB	SO	WP	Bk	W	L	Pct	Sh	Sv-Op Hld	ERC	ERA
2003	Auburn	A-	13	8	0	0	39.1	159	34	14	14	2	2	2	1	11	0	42	7	0	2	1	.667	0	0--	2.72	3.20
2004	CtnWV	A	14	14	0	0	78.0	319	67	31	26	2	3	2	6	24	1	83	6	0	5	4	.556	0	0--	2.81	3.00
2004	Dnedin	A+	11	11	0	0	50.0	224	59	32	30	2	4	2	3	19	0	41	7	0	3	6	.333	0	0--	4.85	5.40
2005	Dnedin	A+	44	5	0	8	94.0	403	107	44	30	6	2	2	4	21	0	56	3	1	4	7	.364	0	0--	4.09	2.87
2006	Dnedin	A+	24	0	0	7	43.2	188	39	21	20	2	0	3	3	15	0	34	5	1	2	2	.000	0	0--	3.10	4.12
2006	NHam	AA	24	0	0	8	41.2	172	42	11	11	2	1	0	2	10	0	38	3	0	2	0	1.000	0	0--	3.41	2.38
2007	NHam	AA	7	1	0	2	17.0	78	20	10	9	0	0	0	1	6	0	15	2	0	0	2	.000	0	0--	4.25	4.76
2007	Syrcse	AAA	36	4	0	9	71.0	298	66	35	29	7	2	1	3	20	2	43	6	0	3	3	.500	0	2--	3.32	3.68
2008	Chatt	AA	12	0	0	3	14.2	72	21	17	12	2	0	0	0	8	1	10	3	1	0	2	.000	0	0--	7.41	7.36
2008	Reds	R	3	1	0	0	5.0	19	4	2	1	0	1	0	1	0	0	5	0	0	0	0	-	0	0--	1.82	1.80
2008	Srsota	A+	7	3	0	2	17.1	63	6	3	3	1	0	0	0	5	0	11	1	0	1	1	.500	0	0--	0.81	1.56
2009	KC	IND	34	11	1	6	88.0	389	98	57	56	14	2	3	3	27	1	74	15	1	4	6	.400	1	0--	4.82	5.73
2010	Mdland	AA	12	0	0	5	19.2	77	11	5	5	1	0	0	0	7	2	21	0	0	1	0	1.000	0	1--	1.41	2.29
2010	Scrmto	AAA	16	0	0	10	19.2	83	14	3	3	0	1	0	1	9	3	28	1	0	1	1	.500	0	4--	2.03	1.37
2010	Oak	AL	5	0	0	3	4.0	23	7	2	2	0	0	0	1	4	0	5	0	0	0	0	-	0	0-1	11.91	4.50

Paul Janish

Bats: R Throws: R Pos: SS-62; 3B-11; 2B-7; PH-4; PR-3　　　YONN-ish　　　　　　　　　**Ht: 6'2" Wt: 193 Born: 10/12/1982 Age: 28**

			BATTING																BASERUNNING				AVERAGES		
Year	Team	Lg	G	AB	H	2B	3B	HR	(Hm | Rd)	TB	R	RBI	RC	TBB	IBB	SO	HBP	SH	SF	SB	CS	SB%	GDP	Avg	OBP	Slg
2008	Cin	NL	38	80	15	2	0	1	(1 | 0)	20	5	6	5	7	0	18	2	0	0	0	0	-	2	.188	.270	.250
2009	Cin	NL	90	256	54	21	0	1	(1 | 0)	78	36	16	18	26	1	40	5	5	0	2	0	1.00	8	.211	.296	.305
2010	Cin	NL	82	200	52	10	0	5	(0 | 5)	77	23	25	31	22	2	30	2	3	1	1	3	.25	4	.260	.338	.385
	3 ML YEARS		210	536	121	33	0	7	(2 | 5)	175	64	47	54	55	3	88	9	8	1	3	3	.50	14	.226	.308	.326

Kenley Jansen

Pitches: R Bats: B Pos: RP-25　　　　　　　　　　　　　　　　　　　　　**Ht: 6'5" Wt: 257 Born: 9/30/1987 Age: 23**

			HOW MUCH HE PITCHED					WHAT HE GAVE UP										THE RESULTS						
Year	Team	Lg	G	GS	CG	GF	IP	BFP	H	R	ER	HR	SH	SF	HB	TBB	IBB	SO	WP	Bk	W	L	Pct	Sh	Sv-Op Hld	ERC	FRA
2009	InldEm	A+	12	0	0	4	11.2	58	14	6	6	1	0	0	0	11	0	19	1	1	0	0	-	0	0--	7.50	4.63
2010	InldEm	A+	11	0	0	4	18.0	73	15	3	3	0	2	0	0	6	1	28	1	0	1	1	.500	0	0--	2.25	1.50
2010	Chatt	AA	22	0	0	13	27.0	111	14	6	5	0	1	0	0	17	0	50	3	0	4	0	1.000	0	8--	1.78	1.67
2010	LAD	NL	25	0	0	8	27.0	109	12	2	2	0	1	0	1	15	1	41	1	0	4	0	1.000	0	4-4	1.40	0.67

Casey Janssen

Pitches: R Bats: R Pos: RP-56　　　　　　　　JANN-sen　　　　　　　　　　**Ht: 6'4" Wt: 210 Born: 9/17/1981 Age: 29**

			HOW MUCH HE PITCHED					WHAT HE GAVE UP										THE RESULTS						
Year	Team	Lg	G	GS	CG	GF	IP	BFP	H	R	ER	HR	SH	SF	HB	TBB	IBB	SO	WP	Bk	W	L	Pct	Sh	Sv-Op Hld	ERC	ERA
2006	Tor	AL	19	17	0	1	94.0	407	103	58	53	12	2	2	7	21	3	44	3	2	6	10	.375	0	0-0 0	4.32	5.07
2007	Tor	AL	70	0	0	21	72.2	297	67	22	19	4	0	3	3	20	2	39	4	0	2	3	.400	0	0-11 24	3.06	2.35
2009	Tor	AL	21	5	0	5	40.0	192	59	29	26	5	1	2	2	14	1	24	1	0	2	4	.333	0	1-1 2	7.04	5.85
2010	Tor	AL	56	0	0	16	68.2	298	74	29	28	8	0	1	4	21	1	63	3	0	5	2	.714	0	0-0 2	4.48	3.67
	4 ML YEARS		166	22	0	43	275.1	1194	303	138	126	29	3	8	16	76	7	170	11	2	15	19	.441	0	7-12 28	4.38	4.12

Jason Jaramillo

Bats: B Throws: R Pos: C-31; PH-3　　　　　　hare-ah-MEE-yoh　　　　　　　**Ht: 6'0" Wt: 209 Born: 10/9/1982 Age: 28**

			BATTING																BASERUNNING				AVERAGES		
Year	Team	Lg	G	AB	H	2B	3B	HR	(Hm | Rd)	TB	R	RBI	RC	TBB	IBB	SO	HBP	SH	SF	SB	CS	SB%	GDP	Avg	OBP	Slg
2004	Phillies	R	1	3	2	0	0	0	(- | -)	2	1	1	1	0	0	0	0	0	0	0	0	-	0	.667	.667	.667
2004	Batvia	A-	31	112	25	5	0	1	(- | -)	33	11	14	10	12	0	27	1	0	2	0	1	.00	3	.223	.299	.295
2005	Lakwd	A	119	448	136	28	4	8	(- | -)	196	46	63	73	44	3	72	2	1	1	2	3	.40	15	.304	.368	.438
2006	Rdng	AA	93	322	80	25	1	6	(- | -)	125	35	39	42	32	2	55	4	1	5	0	1	.00	13	.248	.320	.388
2006	S-WB	AAA	2	6	1	0	0	0	(- | -)	1	0	1	0	0	0	1	0	0	1	0	0	-	0	.167	.143	.167
2007	Ottawa	AAA	118	435	118	14	4	6	(- | -)	158	52	56	60	50	3	79	5	2	4	0	1	.00	18	.271	.350	.363
2008	LV	AAA	115	421	112	20	0	8	(- | -)	156	48	39	56	42	4	82	6	2	2	1	1	.50	12	.266	.340	.371
2010	Indy	AAA	25	88	21	3	0	1	(- | -)	27	3	13	8	5	0	16	1	0	2	0	0	-	3	.239	.281	.307
2009	Pit	NL	63	206	52	14	0	3	(3 | 0)	75	20	26	18	17	2	33	0	1	0	1	0	1.00	11	.252	.309	.364
2010	Pit	NL	33	87	13	2	0	1	(0 | 1)	18	2	6	0	8	1	14	1	0	1	0	0	-	7	.149	.227	.207
	2 ML YEARS		96	293	65	16	0	4	(3 | 1)	93	22	32	18	25	3	47	1	1	1	1	0	1.00	18	.222	.284	.317

John Jaso

Bats: L Throws: R Pos: C-96; PH-17; DH-9; 1B-1　　　　　JAY-soe　　　　　　**Ht: 6'2" Wt: 205 Born: 9/19/1983 Age: 27**

			BATTING																BASERUNNING				AVERAGES		
Year	Team	Lg	G	AB	H	2B	3B	HR	(Hm | Rd)	TB	R	RBI	RC	TBB	IBB	SO	HBP	SH	SF	SB	CS	SB%	GDP	Avg	OBP	Slg
2003	HudVal	A-	47	154	35	7	0	2	(- | -)	48	20	20	20	25	3	26	4	2	3	2	0	1.00	2	.227	.344	.312
2004	HudVal	A-	57	199	60	17	2	2	(- | -)	87	34	35	34	22	2	32	3	0	1	1	0	1.00	10	.302	.378	.437
2005	SWMch	A	92	332	102	25	1	14	(- | -)	171	61	50	67	42	2	53	4	0	8	3	1	.75	10	.307	.383	.515
2006	Visalia	A+	95	366	113	22	0	10	(- | -)	165	58	55	61	31	1	48	3	0	6	1	2	.33	8	.309	.362	.451
2007	Mont	AA	109	380	120	24	2	12	(- | -)	184	62	71	78	59	1	49	4	2	5	2	2	.50	8	.316	.408	.484
2008	Mont	AA	85	284	77	13	2	7	(- | -)	115	51	43	54	62	1	33	6	1	3	1	0	1.00	12	.271	.408	.405
2008	Drham	AAA	31	108	30	7	0	5	(- | -)	52	14	24	17	10	0	14	0	0	0	1	1	.50	2	.278	.339	.481
2009	Drham	AAA	104	331	88	14	2	5	(- | -)	121	42	30	49	46	0	49	6	0	4	1	0	1.00	8	.266	.362	.366

Year Team	Lg	G	AB	H	2B	3B	HR	(Hm	Rd)	TB	R	RBI	RC	TBB	IBB	SO	HBP	SH	SF	SB	CS	SB%	GDP	Avg	OBP	Slg
2010 Drham	AAA	3	11	4	1	0	0	(-	-)	5	1	2	1	0	0	2	0	0	1	0	0	-	0	.364	.333	.455
2008 TB	AL	5	10	2	0	0	0	(0	0)	2	2	0	0	0	0	2	0	0	0	0	0	-	0	.200	.200	.200
2010 TB	AL	109	339	89	18	3	5	(1	4)	128	57	44	57	59	1	39	2	1	3	4	0	1.00	8	.263	.372	.378
2 ML YEARS		114	349	91	18	3	5	(1	4)	130	59	44	57	59	1	41	2	1	3	4	0	1.00	9	.261	.368	.372

Jon Jay

Bats: L **Throws:** L **Pos:** RF-61; CF-27; PH-27; LF-9; PR-2   **Ht:** 5'11" **Wt:** 200 **Born:** 3/15/1985 **Age:** 26

Year Team	Lg	G	AB	H	2B	3B	HR	(Hm	Rd)	TB	R	RBI	RC	TBB	IBB	SO	HBP	SH	SF	SB	CS	SB%	GDP	Avg	OBP	Slg
2006 QuadC	A	60	234	80	13	3	3	(-	-)	108	42	45	46	28	3	27	3	1	2	9	4	.69	3	.342	.416	.462
2007 Sprgfld	AA	26	102	24	4	2	2	(-	-)	38	17	11	14	11	0	19	4	0	0	4	1	.80	0	.235	.333	.373
2007 Cards	R	1	2	1	0	0	0	(-	-)	1	0	0	0	0	0	1	0	0	0	0	0	-	0	.500	.500	.500
2007 PlmBh	A+	32	126	36	8	0	2	(-	-)	50	19	10	16	5	0	25	2	0	1	5	2	.71	1	.286	.321	.397
2008 Sprgfld	AA	96	372	114	17	3	11	(-	-)	170	57	47	66	39	2	46	6	7	3	10	7	.59	5	.306	.379	.457
2008 Memp	AAA	16	58	20	4	1	1	(-	-)	29	8	10	11	6	0	10	0	0	1	0	1	.00	0	.345	.406	.500
2009 Memp	AAA	136	505	142	23	2	10	(-	-)	199	72	54	72	34	3	64	12	8	5	20	8	.71	6	.281	.338	.394
2010 Memp	AAA	42	165	53	16	0	4	(-	-)	81	31	32	35	17	0	22	4	3	2	13	0	1.00	0	.321	.394	.491
2010 StL	NL	105	287	86	19	2	4	(2	2)	121	47	27	40	24	0	50	3	8	1	2	4	.33	5	.300	.359	.422

Jeremy Jeffress

Pitches: R **Bats:** R **Pos:** RP-10   **Ht:** 6'0" **Wt:** 197 **Born:** 9/21/1987 **Age:** 23

Year Team	Lg	G	GS	CG	GF	IP	BFP	H	R	ER	HR	SH	SF	HB	TBB	IBB	SO	WP	Bk	W	L	Pct	Sh	Sv-Op	Hld	ERC	ERA
2006 Brewrs	R	13	4	0	2	33.2	168	30	26	22	0	2	3	6	25	0	37	13	0	2	5	.286	0	0- -	-	4.38	5.88
2007 WV	A	18	18	0	0	86.1	366	62	43	30	8	2	5	7	44	0	95	13	5	9	5	.643	0	0- -	-	3.22	3.13
2008 BrvdCt	A+	15	14	1	0	79.1	339	65	39	36	5	5	1	5	41	0	102	4	1	4	6	.400	1	0- -	-	3.55	4.08
2008 Hntsvl	AA	4	4	0	0	14.2	71	17	9	9	2	0	1	2	11	0	13	0	1	2	1	.667	0	0- -	-	7.52	5.52
2009 Hntsvl	AA	8	8	0	0	27.1	138	26	29	23	1	1	1	1	33	0	34	3	0	1	3	.250	0	0- -	-	6.67	7.57
2009 BrvdCt	A+	6	5	1	0	33.0	137	16	13	8	2	1	1	3	22	0	36	5	0	2	1	.667	0	0- -	-	2.44	2.18
2010 Wisc	A	5	0	0	0	8.0	28	0	0	0	0	0	0	0	3	0	14	0	0	0	0	-	0	0- -	-	0.27	0.00
2010 BrvdCt	A+	8	0	0	4	10.0	48	10	8	6	0	0	0	0	7	0	14	3	0	0	0	-	0	1- -	-	4.25	5.40
2010 Hntsvl	AA	11	0	0	9	14.1	53	8	3	2	0	0	0	1	2	0	15	1	0	1	1	.500	0	3- -	-	1.04	1.26
2010 Mil	NL	10	0	0	5	10.0	42	8	4	3	0	0	1	0	6	1	8	1	0	1	0	1.000	0	0-0	0	2.96	2.70

Bobby Jenks

Pitches: R **Bats:** R **Pos:** RP-55   **Ht:** 6'4" **Wt:** 275 **Born:** 3/14/1981 **Age:** 30

Year Team	Lg	G	GS	CG	GF	IP	BFP	H	R	ER	HR	SH	SF	HB	TBB	IBB	SO	WP	Bk	W	L	Pct	Sh	Sv-Op	Hld	ERC	ERA
2005 CWS	AL	32	0	0	18	39.1	168	34	15	12	5	1	0	1	15	3	50	4	0	1	1	.500	0	6-8	3	3.02	2.75
2006 CWS	AL	67	0	0	58	69.2	300	66	32	31	5	4	2	2	31	10	80	3	0	3	4	.429	0	41-45	0	3.65	4.00
2007 CWS	AL	66	0	0	62	65.0	249	45	20	20	2	5	3	1	13	4	56	4	0	3	5	.375	0	40-46	0	1.49	2.77
2008 CWS	AL	57	0	0	52	61.2	243	51	18	18	3	2	1	1	17	4	38	3	0	3	1	.750	0	30-34	0	2.43	2.63
2009 CWS	AL	52	0	0	46	53.1	228	52	24	22	9	0	2	2	16	1	49	0	0	3	4	.429	0	29-35	0	4.08	3.71
2010 CWS	AL	55	0	0	46	52.2	231	54	28	26	3	4	0	1	18	1	61	2	0	1	3	.250	0	27-31	0	3.64	4.44
Postseason		7	0	0	5	9.0	36	5	2	2	0	1	0	1	3	0	9	0	0	0	0	-	0	5-6	0	1.47	2.00
6 ML YEARS		329	0	0	282	341.2	1419	302	137	129	25	16	8	8	110	23	334	16	0	14	18	.438	0	173-199	3	2.96	3.40

Desmond Jennings

Bats: R **Throws:** R **Pos:** PR-8; RF-5; CF-4; LF-2; DH-2; PH-2   **Ht:** 6'2" **Wt:** 200 **Born:** 10/30/1986 **Age:** 24

Year Team	Lg	G	AB	H	2B	3B	HR	(Hm	Rd)	TB	R	RBI	RC	TBB	IBB	SO	HBP	SH	SF	SB	CS	SB%	GDP	Avg	OBP	Slg
2006 Princtn	R+	56	213	59	10	1	4	(-	-)	83	48	20	36	22	0	39	6	4	1	32	5	.86	3	.277	.360	.390
2007 Clmbs	A	99	387	122	21	5	9	(-	-)	180	75	37	78	45	1	53	12	2	2	45	15	.75	1	.315	.401	.465
2008 VeroB	A+	24	85	22	5	1	2	(-	-)	35	17	6	14	14	0	16	0	2	1	5	2	.71	0	.259	.360	.412
2009 Mont	AA	100	383	120	25	8	8	(-	-)	185	69	45	80	48	2	52	5	0	4	37	5	.88	4	.313	.393	.483
2009 Drham	AAA	32	114	37	6	2	3	(-	-)	56	23	17	26	19	0	15	1	1	2	15	2	.88	3	.325	.419	.491
2010 Drham	AAA	109	399	111	25	6	3	(-	-)	157	82	36	66	47	1	67	6	5	1	37	4	.90	8	.278	.362	.393
2010 TB	AL	17	21	4	1	1	0	(0	0)	7	5	2	2	2	0	4	1	0	0	2	2	.50	0	.190	.292	.333

Kevin Jepsen

Pitches: R **Bats:** R **Pos:** RP-68   **Ht:** 6'3" **Wt:** 215 **Born:** 7/26/1984 **Age:** 26

Year Team	Lg	G	GS	CG	GF	IP	BFP	H	R	ER	HR	SH	SF	HB	TBB	IBB	SO	WP	Bk	W	L	Pct	Sh	Sv-Op	Hld	ERC	ERA
2008 LAA	AL	9	0	0	0	8.1	36	8	5	4	0	0	0	0	4	0	7	1	0	0	1	.000	0	0-0	3	3.46	4.32
2009 LAA	AL	54	0	0	13	54.2	237	63	33	30	2	0	2	0	19	2	48	6	0	6	4	.600	0	1-2	17	4.27	4.94
2010 LAA	AL	68	0	0	4	59.0	253	54	26	26	2	4	2	2	29	5	61	8	0	2	4	.333	0	0-4	27	3.53	3.97
Postseason		5	0	0	0	5.0	24	8	2	2	1	0	0	0	2	0	3	0	0	1	0	1.000	0	0-0	1	8.81	3.60
3 ML YEARS		131	0	0	17	122.0	526	125	64	60	4	4	4	2	52	7	116	15	0	8	9	.471	0	1-6	47	3.85	4.43

Derek Jeter

Bats: R **Throws:** R **Pos:** SS-151; DH-5; PH-2   **Ht:** 6'3" **Wt:** 195 **Born:** 6/26/1974 **Age:** 37

Year	Team	Lg	G	AB	H	2B	3B	HR	(Hm	Rd)	TB	R	RBI	RC	TBB	IBB	SO	HBP	SH	SF	SB	CS	SB%	GDP	Avg	OBP	Slg
1995	NYY	AL	15	48	12	4	1	0	(0	0)	18	5	7	5	3	0	11	0	0	0	0	0	-	0	.250	.294	.375
1996	NYY	AL	157	582	183	25	6	10	(3	7)	250	104	78	92	48	1	102	9	6	9	14	7	.67	13	.314	.370	.430
1997	NYY	AL	159	654	190	31	7	10	(5	5)	265	116	70	99	74	0	125	10	8	2	23	12	.66	14	.291	.370	.405
1998	NYY	AL	149	626	203	25	8	19	(9	10)	301	127	84	115	57	1	119	5	3	3	30	6	.83	13	.324	.384	.481
1999	NYY	AL	158	627	219	37	9	24	(15	9)	346	134	102	146	91	5	116	12	3	6	19	8	.70	12	.349	.438	.552
2000	NYY	AL	148	593	201	31	4	15	(8	7)	285	119	73	118	68	4	99	12	3	3	22	4	.85	14	.339	.416	.481
2001	NYY	AL	150	614	191	35	3	21	(13	8)	295	110	74	112	56	3	99	10	5	1	27	3	.90	13	.311	.377	.480
2002	NYY	AL	157	644	191	26	0	18	(8	10)	271	124	75	108	73	2	114	7	3	3	32	3	.91	14	.297	.373	.421
2003	NYY	AL	119	482	156	25	3	10	(7	3)	217	87	52	86	43	2	88	13	3	1	11	5	.69	10	.324	.393	.450
2004	NYY	AL	154	643	188	44	1	23	(11	12)	303	111	78	100	46	1	99	14	16	2	23	4	.85	19	.292	.352	.471
2005	NYY	AL	159	654	202	25	5	19	(12	7)	294	122	70	105	77	3	117	11	7	3	14	5	.74	15	.309	.389	.450
2006	NYY	AL	154	623	214	39	3	14	(8	6)	301	118	97	132	69	4	102	12	7	4	34	5	.87	13	.343	.417	.483
2007	NYY	AL	156	639	206	39	4	12	(4	8)	289	102	73	112	56	3	100	14	3	2	15	8	.65	21	.322	.388	.452
2008	NYY	AL	150	596	179	25	3	11	(3	8)	243	88	69	88	52	0	85	9	7	4	11	5	.69	24	.300	.363	.408
2009	NYY	AL	153	634	212	27	1	18	(13	5)	295	107	66	109	72	4	90	5	4	1	30	5	.86	18	.334	.406	.465
2010	NYY	AL	157	663	179	30	3	10	(7	3)	245	111	67	86	63	4	106	9	1	3	18	5	.78	22	.270	.340	.370
	Postseason		138	559	175	27	3	20	(12	8)	268	99	55	90	61	3	107	5	8	4	16	5	.76	12	.313	.383	.479
	16 ML YEARS		2295	9322	2926	468	61	234	(126	108)	4218	1685	1135	1613	948	37	1572	152	79	47	323	85	.79	235	.314	.385	.452

Ubaldo Jimenez

Pitches: R **Bats:** R **Pos:** SP-33   ooh-BALL-doh hee-MENN-ez   **Ht:** 6'4" **Wt:** 210 **Born:** 1/22/1984 **Age:** 27

Year	Team	Lg	G	GS	CG	GF	IP	BFP	H	R	ER	HR	SH	SF	HB	TBB	IBB	SO	WP	Bk	W	L	Pct	Sh	Sv-Op	Hld	ERC	ERA
2006	Col	NL	2	1	0	0	7.2	30	5	4	3	1	0	0	0	3	0	3	0	0	0	0	-	0	0-0	0	2.48	3.52
2007	Col	NL	15	15	0	0	82.0	354	70	46	39	11	0	3	6	37	4	68	3	0	4	4	.500	0	0-0	0	3.80	4.28
2008	Col	NL	34	34	1	0	198.2	868	182	97	88	11	7	4	10	103	4	172	16	0	12	12	.500	0	0-0	0	3.92	3.99
2009	Col	NL	33	33	1	0	218.0	914	183	87	84	13	15	6	10	85	6	198	8	3	15	12	.556	0	0-0	0	3.03	3.47
2010	Col	NL	33	33	4	0	221.2	894	164	73	71	10	7	1	9	92	7	214	16	1	19	8	.704	2	0-0	0	2.57	2.88
	Postseason		5	5	0	0	28.0	123	26	11	11	3	0	1	1	16	2	24	1	0	0	2	.000	0	0-0	0	4.47	3.54
	5 ML YEARS		117	116	6	0	728.0	3060	604	307	285	45	32	12	35	320	21	655	43	4	50	36	.581	2	0-0	0	3.20	3.52

Waldis Joaquin

Pitches: R **Bats:** R **Pos:** RP-4   WALL-diss wah-KEEN   **Ht:** 6'0" **Wt:** 238 **Born:** 12/25/1986 **Age:** 24

Year	Team	Lg	G	GS	CG	GF	IP	BFP	H	R	ER	HR	SH	SF	HB	TBB	IBB	SO	WP	Bk	W	L	Pct	Sh	Sv-Op	Hld	ERC	ERA
2005	Giants	R	10	5	0	3	29.2	129	28	17	12	1	1	1	1	10	0	37	1	1	1	1	.500	0	1--	-	3.10	3.64
2007	SlmKzr	A-	15	5	0	4	38.0	155	24	13	12	2	0	1	2	16	0	30	2	0	3	0	1.000	0	0--	-	2.12	2.84
2008	Augsta	A	27	3	0	6	52.0	223	49	32	25	1	1	3	1	20	0	49	3	1	2	2	.333	0	2--	-	3.19	4.33
2008	SnJos	A+	9	4	0	2	19.1	85	20	13	10	2	0	1	0	11	1	23	0	0	0	1	.000	0	0--	-	5.01	4.66
2009	Conn	AA	36	0	0	9	54.0	222	36	17	16	0	4	1	0	28	3	40	3	0	4	5	.444	0	1--	-	2.04	2.67
2009	Fresno	AAA	8	0	0	1	10.0	37	5	0	0	0	0	0	0	2	0	16	0	0	1	0	1.000	0	1--	-	0.86	0.00
2010	Fresno	AAA	23	5	0	8	34.2	170	44	24	19	4	3	2	3	22	0	33	1	0	1	2	.333	0	2--	-	7.12	4.93
2010	Giants	R	4	4	0	0	6.0	25	3	1	1	0	0	0	1	3	0	7	1	0	0	0	-	0	0--	-	1.79	1.50
2009	SF	NL	10	0	0	4	10.2	51	10	5	5	1	0	0	2	7	0	12	3	0	0	0	-	0	0-0	0	5.30	4.22
2010	SF	NL	4	0	0	0	4.2	27	6	6	5	0	1	0	1	7	0	2	2	1	0	0	-	0	0-0	1	10.62	9.64
	2 ML YEARS		14	0	0	4	15.1	78	16	11	10	1	1	0	3	14	0	14	5	1	0	0	-	0	0-0	1	6.85	5.87

Chris Johnson

Bats: R **Throws:** R **Pos:** 3B-90; PH-4   **Ht:** 6'3" **Wt:** 220 **Born:** 10/1/1984 **Age:** 26

Year	Team	Lg	G	AB	H	2B	3B	HR	(Hm	Rd)	TB	R	RBI	RC	TBB	IBB	SO	HBP	SH	SF	SB	CS	SB%	GDP	Avg	OBP	Slg
2006	TriCity	A-	60	222	47	7	1	1	(-	-)	59	18	29	14	11	1	35	2	0	4	7	3	.70	13	.212	.251	.266
2007	Lxngtn	A	64	255	66	14	0	8	(-	-)	104	37	44	32	17	0	38	1	1	3	3	4	.43	8	.259	.304	.408
2007	Salem	A+	60	224	59	11	0	6	(-	-)	88	24	38	27	8	1	41	3	0	5	1	0	1.00	9	.263	.292	.393
2008	CpChr	AA	85	334	107	24	0	12	(-	-)	167	43	58	61	20	0	63	3	1	4	5	0	1.00	14	.320	.360	.500
2008	RdRck	AAA	30	101	22	2	1	1	(-	-)	29	10	9	7	5	0	25	0	0	1	0	0	-	1	.218	.252	.287
2009	RdRck	AAA	104	384	108	20	5	13	(-	-)	177	48	42	58	21	1	90	4	0	3	2	1	.67	16	.281	.323	.461
2009	Lancst	A+	4	16	7	5	0	0	(-	-)	12	5	6	4	1	0	3	0	0	1	0	0	-	1	.438	.471	.750
2010	RdRck	AAA	38	149	49	10	1	8	(-	-)	85	26	33	30	9	2	23	1	0	4	0	0	-	2	.329	.362	.570
2009	Hou	NL	11	22	2	0	0	0	(0	0)	2	1	1	0	1	0	6	0	0	0	0	0	-	0	.091	.130	.091
2010	Hou	NL	94	341	105	22	2	11	(6	5)	164	40	52	55	15	2	91	2	0	4	3	0	1.00	8	.308	.337	.481
	2 ML YEARS		105	363	107	22	2	11	(6	5)	166	41	53	55	16	2	97	2	0	4	3	0	1.00	8	.295	.325	.457

Dan Johnson

Bats: L **Throws:** R **Pos:** DH-18; 1B-13; PH-7; 3B-6; LF-3   **Ht:** 6'2" **Wt:** 216 **Born:** 8/10/1979 **Age:** 31

Year	Team	Lg	G	AB	H	2B	3B	HR	(Hm	Rd)	TB	R	RBI	RC	TBB	IBB	SO	HBP	SH	SF	SB	CS	SB%	GDP	Avg	OBP	Slg
2010	Drham*	AAA	98	340	103	19	0	30	(-	-)	212	66	95	91	75	6	71	5	0	6	0	0	-	6	.303	.430	.624
2005	Oak	AL	109	375	103	21	0	15	(2	13)	169	54	58	56	50	1	52	1	0	8	0	1	.00	11	.275	.355	.451
2006	Oak	AL	91	286	67	13	1	9	(4	5)	109	30	37	33	40	2	45	0	0	5	0	0	-	6	.234	.323	.381
2007	Oak	AL	117	416	98	20	1	18	(9	9)	174	53	62	58	72	4	77	3	0	4	0	0	-	12	.236	.349	.418
2008	2 Tms	AL	11	26	5	0	0	2	(1	1)	11	3	4	3	3	0	7	0	0	0	0	0	-	0	.192	.276	.423

BATTING																		BASERUNNING				AVERAGES		
Year Team	Lg	G	AB	H	2B	3B	HR	(Hm Rd)	TB	R	RBI	RC	TBB	IBB	SO	HBP	SH	SF	SB	CS	SB%	GDP	Avg	OBP	Slg
2010 TB	AL	40	111	22	3	0	7	(4 3)	46	15	23	20	25	0	27	1	0	3	1	0	1.00	1	.198	.343	.414
08 Oak	AL	1	1	0	0	0	0	(0 0)	0	0	0	0	0	0	0	0	0	0	0	0	-	0	.000	.000	.000
08 TB	AL	10	25	5	0	0	2	(1 1)	11	3	4	3	3	0	7	0	0	0	0	0	-	0	.200	.286	.440
5 ML YEARS		368	1214	295	57	2	51	(20 31)	509	155	184	170	190	7	208	5	0	20	1	1	.50	30	.243	.343	.419

Jim Johnson

Pitches: R **Bats:** R **Pos:** RP-26 **Ht:** 6'6" **Wt:** 230 **Born:** 6/27/1983 **Age:** 28

HOW MUCH HE PITCHED							WHAT HE GAVE UP												THE RESULTS								
Year Team	Lg	G	GS	CG	GF	IP	BFP	H	R	ER	HR	SH	SF	HB	TBB	IBB	SO	WP	Bk	W	L	Pct	Sh	Sv-Op	Hld	ERC	ERA
2010 Norfolk*	AAA	1	0	0	0	1.0	4	1	0	0	0	0	0	0	0	0	0	0	0	0	0	-	0	0--	-	1.95	0.00
2010 Orioles*	R	4	4	0	0	4.0	17	5	3	3	1	0	0	0	1	0	5	0	0	0	0	-	0	0--	-	6.26	6.75
2010 Bowie*	AA	4	1	0	0	5.0	17	2	1	1	1	0	0	0	0	0	6	0	0	0	0	-	0	0--	-	0.74	1.80
2010 Frdrck*	A+	2	0	0	0	3.0	14	6	1	1	0	0	0	0	0	0	1	0	0	0	0	-	0	0--	-	8.06	3.00
2006 Bal	AL	1	1	0	0	3.0	21	9	8	8	1	0	1	1	3	0	0	0	0	0	1	.000	0	0-0	0	26.81	24.00
2007 Bal	AL	1	0	0	1	2.0	11	3	2	2	0	0	1	0	2	0	1	0	0	0	0	-	0	0-0	0	8.58	9.00
2008 Bal	AL	54	0	0	18	68.2	281	54	18	17	0	2	1	3	28	3	38	1	1	2	4	.333	0	1-1	19	2.45	2.23
2009 Bal	AL	64	0	0	29	70.0	300	73	32	32	8	2	2	3	23	3	49	2	1	4	6	.400	0	10-16	14	4.28	4.11
2010 Bal	AL	26	0	0	6	26.1	117	32	11	10	2	3	0	1	5	1	22	4	0	1	1	.500	0	1-6	11	4.26	3.42
5 ML YEARS		146	1	0	54	170.0	730	171	71	69	11	7	5	8	61	7	110	7	2	7	12	.368	0	12-23	44	3.84	3.65

Josh Johnson

Pitches: R **Bats:** L **Pos:** SP-28 **Ht:** 6'7" **Wt:** 249 **Born:** 1/31/1984 **Age:** 27

HOW MUCH HE PITCHED							WHAT HE GAVE UP												THE RESULTS								
Year Team	Lg	G	GS	CG	GF	IP	BFP	H	R	ER	HR	SH	SF	HB	TBB	IBB	SO	WP	Bk	W	L	Pct	Sh	Sv-Op	Hld	ERC	ERA
2005 Fla	NL	4	1	0	0	12.1	55	5	5	5	0	1	0	1	10	0	10	0	0	0	0	-	0	0-0	0	4.82	3.65
2006 Fla	NL	31	24	0	1	157.0	659	136	63	54	14	11	0	4	68	6	133	3	1	12	7	.632	0	0-1	0	3.48	3.10
2007 Fla	NL	4	4	0	0	15.2	82	26	17	13	1	2	1	0	12	3	14	1	0	0	3	.000	0	0-0	0	9.16	7.47
2008 Fla	NL	14	14	1	0	87.1	365	91	36	35	7	5	1	1	27	1	77	4	0	7	1	.875	0	0-0	0	3.94	3.61
2009 Fla	NL	33	33	2	0	209.0	855	184	77	75	14	11	4	6	58	6	191	10	0	15	5	.750	0	0-0	0	2.84	3.23
2010 Fla	NL	28	28	1	0	183.2	744	155	51	47	7	5	8	5	48	2	186	4	0	11	6	.647	0	0-0	0	2.44	**2.30**
6 ML YEARS		114	104	4	1	665.0	2760	603	249	229	43	35	14	17	223	18	611	22	1	45	22	.672	0	0-1	0	3.17	3.10

Kelly Johnson

Bats: L **Throws:** R **Pos:** 2B-149; PH-5; DH-2 **Ht:** 6'1" **Wt:** 205 **Born:** 2/22/1982 **Age:** 29

BATTING																		BASERUNNING				AVERAGES		
Year Team	Lg	G	AB	H	2B	3B	HR	(Hm Rd)	TB	R	RBI	RC	TBB	IBB	SO	HBP	SH	SF	SB	CS	SB%	GDP	Avg	OBP	Slg
2005 Atl	NL	87	290	70	12	3	9	(2 7)	115	46	40	41	40	1	75	1	2	1	2	1	.67	11	.241	.334	.397
2007 Atl	NL	147	521	144	26	10	16	(5 11)	238	91	68	87	79	3	117	4	2	2	9	5	.64	8	.276	.375	.457
2008 Atl	NL	150	547	157	39	6	12	(5 7)	244	86	69	87	52	2	113	2	9	4	11	6	.65	3	.287	.349	.446
2009 Atl	NL	106	303	68	20	3	8	(4 4)	118	47	29	31	32	1	54	3	6	2	7	2	.78	4	.224	.303	.389
2010 Ari	NL	154	585	166	36	5	26	(16 10)	290	93	71	92	79	1	148	2	3	2	13	7	.65	12	.284	.370	.496
Postseason		4	2	0	0	0	0	(0 0)	0	0	0	0	1	0	0	0	0	0	0	0	-	0	.000	.333	.000
5 ML YEARS		644	2246	605	133	27	71	(32 39)	1005	363	277	338	282	8	507	12	22	11	42	21	.67	38	.269	.352	.447

Nick Johnson

Bats: L **Throws:** L **Pos:** DH-20; PH-3; 1B-2 **Ht:** 6'3" **Wt:** 235 **Born:** 9/19/1978 **Age:** 32

BATTING																		BASERUNNING				AVERAGES		
Year Team	Lg	G	AB	H	2B	3B	HR	(Hm Rd)	TB	R	RBI	RC	TBB	IBB	SO	HBP	SH	SF	SB	CS	SB%	GDP	Avg	OBP	Slg
2001 NYY	AL	23	67	13	2	0	2	(1 1)	21	6	8	6	7	0	15	4	0	0	0	0	-	3	.194	.308	.313
2002 NYY	AL	129	378	92	15	0	15	(7 8)	152	56	58	59	48	5	98	12	3	0	1	3	.25	11	.243	.347	.402
2003 NYY	AL	96	324	92	19	0	14	(8 6)	153	60	47	65	70	4	57	8	3	1	5	2	.71	9	.284	.422	.472
2004 Mon	NL	73	251	63	16	0	7	(4 3)	100	35	33	36	40	2	58	3	0	1	6	3	.67	5	.251	.359	.398
2005 Was	NL	131	453	131	35	3	15	(7 8)	217	66	74	83	80	8	87	6	0	2	3	8	.27	15	.289	.408	.479
2006 Was	NL	147	500	145	46	0	23	(10 13)	260	100	77	104	110	15	99	13	2	3	10	3	.77	12	.290	.428	.520
2008 Was	NL	38	109	24	8	0	5	(2 3)	47	15	20	21	33	4	25	4	0	1	0	0	-	2	.220	.415	.431
2009 2 Tms	NL	133	457	133	24	2	8	(2 6)	185	71	62	85	99	4	84	12	1	5	2	4	.33	15	.291	.426	.405
2010 NYY	AL	24	72	12	4	0	2	(2 0)	22	12	8	12	24	0	23	2	0	0	1	0	1.00	2	.167	.388	.306
09 Was	NL	98	353	104	16	2	6	(2 4)	142	47	44	60	63	3	66	6	0	2	2	2	.50	11	.295	.408	.402
09 Fla	NL	35	104	29	8	0	2	(0 2)	43	24	18	25	36	1	18	6	1	3	0	2	.00	4	.279	.477	.413
Postseason		20	67	14	3	0	1	(1 0)	20	10	6	6	8	1	14	1	0	0	0	0	-	2	.209	.303	.299
9 ML YEARS		794	2611	705	169	5	91	(43 48)	1157	421	387	471	511	42	546	70	9	13	27	24	.53	74	.270	.401	.443

Reed Johnson

Bats: R **Throws:** R **Pos:** LF-62; PH-25; RF-22; CF-7; PR-6 **Ht:** 5'10" **Wt:** 185 **Born:** 12/8/1976 **Age:** 34

BATTING																		BASERUNNING				AVERAGES		
Year Team	Lg	G	AB	H	2B	3B	HR	(Hm Rd)	TB	R	RBI	RC	TBB	IBB	SO	HBP	SH	SF	SB	CS	SB%	GDP	Avg	OBP	Slg
2010 InldEm*	A+	2	6	3	1	0	0	(- -)	4	2	0	1	0	0	0	0	0	0					.500	.500	.667
2003 Tor	AL	114	412	121	21	2	10	(6 4)	176	79	52	64	20	1	67	20	1	4	5	3	.63	10	.294	.353	.427
2004 Tor	AL	141	537	145	25	2	10	(8 2)	204	68	61	65	28	2	98	12	3	2	6	3	.67	17	.270	.320	.380
2005 Tor	AL	142	398	107	21	6	8	(4 4)	164	55	58	57	22	1	82	16	2	1	5	6	.45	9	.269	.332	.412
2006 Tor	AL	134	461	147	34	2	12	(4 8)	221	86	49	76	33	4	81	**21**	1	1	8	2	.80	9	.319	.390	.479
2007 Tor	AL	79	275	65	13	2	2	(1 1)	88	31	14	24	16	0	56	11	5	0	4	2	.67	7	.236	.305	.320

Year	Team	Lg	G	AB	H	2B	3B	HR	(Hm	Rd)	TB	R	RBI	RC	TBB	IBB	SO	HBP	SH	SF	SB	CS	SB%	GDP	Avg	OBP	Slg
2008	ChC	NL	109	333	101	21	0	6	(3	3)	140	52	50	57	19	1	68	12	5	5	5	6	.45	3	.303	.358	.420
2009	ChC	NL	65	165	42	10	2	4	(3	1)	68	23	22	19	13	0	27	6	1	1	2	1	.67	5	.255	.330	.412
2010	LAD	NL	102	202	53	11	2	2	(1	1)	74	24	15	18	5	0	50	4	2	2	2	2	.50	3	.262	.291	.366
8 ML YEARS			886	2783	781	156	18	54	(30	24)	1135	418	321	380	156	9	529	102	20	16	37	25	.60	62	.281	.340	.408

Rob Johnson

Bats: R **Throws:** R **Pos:** C-61; PR-2 **Ht:** 6'1" **Wt:** 215 **Born:** 7/22/1982 **Age:** 28

Year	Team	Lg	G	AB	H	2B	3B	HR	(Hm	Rd)	TB	R	RBI	RC	TBB	IBB	SO	HBP	SH	SF	SB	CS	SB%	GDP	Avg	OBP	Slg
2010	Tacom*	AAA	19	64	19	7	0	1	(-	-)	29	9	8	12	10	0	12	2	0	1	0	0	-	4	.297	.403	.453
2007	Sea	AL	6	3	1	0	0	0	(0	0)	1	1	0	0	0	0	0	0	0	0	1	0	1.00	0	.333	.333	.333
2008	Sea	AL	14	31	4	0	0	1	(1	0)	7	2	2	0	0	0	6	0	1	0	0	0	-	1	.129	.129	.226
2009	Sea	AL	80	258	55	19	2	2	(2	0)	84	21	27	22	26	1	60	2	3	1	1	1	.50	11	.213	.289	.326
2010	Sea	AL	61	178	34	10	0	2	(0	2)	50	24	13	12	25	2	46	2	1	3	1	1	.50	5	.191	.293	.281
4 ML YEARS			161	470	94	29	2	5	(3	2)	142	48	42	34	51	3	112	4	5	4	3	2	.60	17	.200	.282	.302

Adam Jones

Bats: R **Throws:** R **Pos:** CF-149 **Ht:** 6'2" **Wt:** 215 **Born:** 8/1/1985 **Age:** 25

Year	Team	Lg	G	AB	H	2B	3B	HR	(Hm	Rd)	TB	R	RBI	RC	TBB	IBB	SO	HBP	SH	SF	SB	CS	SB%	GDP	Avg	OBP	Slg
2006	Sea	AL	32	74	16	4	0	1	(0	1)	23	6	8	4	2	0	22	0	0	0	3	1	.75	3	.216	.237	.311
2007	Sea	AL	41	65	16	2	1	2	(1	1)	26	16	4	5	4	0	21	1	1	0	2	1	.67	0	.246	.300	.400
2008	Bal	AL	132	477	129	21	7	9	(4	5)	191	61	57	56	23	0	108	7	2	5	10	3	.77	12	.270	.311	.400
2009	Bal	AL	119	473	131	22	7	19	(11	8)	216	83	70	71	36	3	93	7	0	3	10	4	.71	13	.277	.335	.457
2010	Bal	AL	149	581	165	25	5	19	(9	10)	257	76	69	72	23	1	119	13	2	2	7	7	.50	17	.284	.325	.442
5 ML YEARS			473	1670	457	74	16	50	(25	25)	713	242	208	208	88	4	363	28	5	10	32	16	.67	45	.274	.319	.427

Andruw Jones

Bats: R **Throws:** R **Pos:** RF-62; CF-17; DH-14; LF-12; PH-10; PR-2 **Ht:** 6'1" **Wt:** 230 **Born:** 4/23/1977 **Age:** 34

Year	Team	Lg	G	AB	H	2B	3B	HR	(Hm	Rd)	TB	R	RBI	RC	TBB	IBB	SO	HBP	SH	SF	SB	CS	SB%	GDP	Avg	OBP	Slg
1996	Atl	NL	31	106	23	7	1	5	(3	2)	47	11	13	13	7	0	29	0	0	0	3	0	1.00	1	.217	.265	.443
1997	Atl	NL	153	399	92	18	1	18	(5	13)	166	60	70	54	56	2	107	4	5	3	20	11	.65	11	.231	.329	.416
1998	Atl	NL	159	582	158	33	8	31	(16	15)	300	89	90	97	40	8	129	4	1	4	27	4	.87	10	.271	.321	.515
1999	Atl	NL	162	592	163	35	5	26	(10	16)	286	97	84	103	76	11	103	9	0	2	24	12	.67	12	.275	.365	.483
2000	Atl	NL	161	656	199	36	6	36	(15	21)	355	122	104	127	59	0	100	9	0	5	21	6	.78	12	.303	.366	.541
2001	Atl	NL	161	625	157	25	2	34	(16	18)	288	104	104	90	56	3	142	3	0	9	11	4	.73	10	.251	.312	.461
2002	Atl	NL	154	560	148	34	0	35	(18	17)	287	91	94	94	83	4	135	10	0	6	8	3	.73	14	.264	.366	.513
2003	Atl	NL	156	595	165	28	2	36	(16	20)	305	101	116	92	53	2	125	5	0	6	4	3	.57	18	.277	.338	.513
2004	Atl	NL	154	570	149	34	4	29	(13	16)	278	85	91	75	71	9	147	3	0	2	6	6	.50	24	.261	.345	.488
2005	Atl	NL	160	586	154	24	3	51	(21	30)	337	95	128	91	64	13	112	15	0	7	5	3	.63	19	.263	.347	.575
2006	Atl	NL	156	566	148	29	0	41	(19	22)	300	107	129	108	82	9	127	13	0	9	4	1	.80	13	.262	.363	.531
2007	Atl	NL	154	572	127	27	2	26	(16	10)	236	83	94	71	70	4	138	8	0	9	5	2	.71	16	.222	.311	.413
2008	LAD	NL	75	209	33	8	1	3	(0	3)	52	21	14	6	27	0	76	1	0	1	0	1	.00	5	.158	.256	.249
2009	Tex	AL	82	281	60	18	0	17	(9	8)	129	43	43	42	45	3	72	2	0	3	5	1	.83	7	.214	.323	.459
2010	CWS	AL	107	278	64	12	1	19	(12	7)	135	41	48	45	45	0	73	3	0	2	9	2	.82	15	.230	.341	.486
Postseason			75	238	65	8	0	10	(5	5)	103	43	33	34	34	2	50	2	1	3	5	5	.50	5	.273	.365	.433
15 ML YEARS			2025	7176	1840	368	36	407	(189	218)	3501	1150	1222	1100	834	60	1615	89	6	68	152	50	.72	187	.256	.338	.488

Chipper Jones

Bats: B **Throws:** R **Pos:** 3B-89; PH-8; DH-1 **Ht:** 6'4" **Wt:** 210 **Born:** 4/24/1972 **Age:** 39

Year	Team	Lg	G	AB	H	2B	3B	HR	(Hm	Rd)	TB	R	RBI	RC	TBB	IBB	SO	HBP	SH	SF	SB	CS	SB%	GDP	Avg	OBP	Slg
1993	Atl	NL	0	3	2	1	0	0	(0	0)	3	2	0	2	1	0	1	0	0	0	0	0	-	0	.667	.750	1.000
1995	Atl	NL	140	524	139	22	3	23	(15	8)	236	87	86	84	73	1	99	0	1	4	8	4	.67	10	.265	.353	.450
1996	Atl	NL	157	598	185	32	5	30	(18	12)	317	114	110	123	87	0	88	0	1	7	14	1	.93	14	.309	.393	.530
1997	Atl	NL	157	597	176	41	3	21	(7	14)	286	100	111	104	76	8	88	0	0	6	20	5	.80	19	.295	.371	.479
1998	Atl	NL	160	601	188	29	5	34	(17	17)	329	123	107	129	96	1	93	1	1	8	16	6	.73	17	.313	.404	.547
1999	Atl	NL	157	567	181	41	1	45	(25	20)	359	116	110	150	126	18	94	2	0	6	25	3	.89	20	.319	.441	.633
2000	Atl	NL	156	579	180	38	1	36	(18	18)	328	118	111	128	95	10	64	2	0	10	14	7	.67	14	.311	.404	.566
2001	Atl	NL	159	572	189	33	5	38	(19	19)	346	113	102	136	98	20	82	2	0	5	9	10	.47	13	.330	.427	.605
2002	Atl	NL	158	548	179	35	1	26	(17	9)	294	90	100	119	107	23	89	2	0	5	8	2	.80	18	.327	.435	.536
2003	Atl	NL	153	555	169	33	2	27	(16	11)	287	103	106	110	94	13	83	1	0	6	2	2	.50	10	.305	.402	.517
2004	Atl	NL	137	472	117	20	1	30	(19	11)	229	69	96	82	84	8	96	4	0	7	2	0	1.00	14	.248	.362	.485
2005	Atl	NL	109	358	106	30	0	21	(9	12)	199	66	72	78	72	5	56	0	0	2	5	1	.83	9	.296	.412	.556
2006	Atl	NL	110	411	133	28	3	26	(12	14)	245	87	86	94	61	4	73	1	0	4	6	1	.86	12	.324	.409	.596
2007	Atl	NL	134	513	173	42	4	29	(14	15)	310	108	102	110	82	10	75	0	0	5	5	1	.83	21	.337	.425	.604
2008	Atl	NL	128	439	160	24	1	22	(12	10)	252	82	75	98	90	16	61	1	0	4	4	0	1.00	13	**.364**	**.470**	.574
2009	Atl	NL	143	488	129	23	2	18	(10	8)	210	80	71	85	101	18	89	1	0	6	4	1	.80	14	.264	.388	.430
2010	Atl	NL	95	317	84	21	0	10	(9	1)	135	47	46	53	61	6	47	0	0	3	5	0	1.00	10	.265	.381	.426
Postseason			92	333	96	18	0	13	(7	6)	153	58	47	60	72	11	60	1	1	5	8	3	.73	10	.288	.411	.459
17 ML YEARS			2261	8142	2490	493	37	436	(237	199)	4365	1505	1491	1685	1404	161	1278	17	3	88	147	44	.77	228	.306	.405	.536

Garrett Jones

Bats: L **Throws:** L **Pos:** 1B-112; RF-48; PH-4; LF-1; DH-1　　**Ht:** 6'4" **Wt:** 230 **Born:** 6/21/1981 **Age:** 30

								BATTING													BASERUNNING				AVERAGES		
Year	Team	Lg	G	AB	H	2B	3B	HR	(Hm	Rd)	TB	R	RBI	RC	TBB	IBB	SO	HBP	SH	SF	SB	CS	SB%	GDP	Avg	OBP	Slg
2007	Min	AL	31	77	16	2	1	2	(1	1)	26	7	5	3	6	0	20	0	0	1	1	1	.50	2	.208	.262	.338
2009	Pit	NL	82	314	92	21	1	21	(13	8)	178	45	44	47	40	8	76	1	0	3	10	2	.83	6	.293	.372	.567
2010	Pit	NL	158	592	146	34	1	21	(11	10)	245	64	86	69	53	2	123	1	0	8	7	3	.70	18	.247	.306	.414
	3 ML YEARS		271	983	254	57	3	44	(25	19)	449	116	135	119	99	10	219	2	0	12	18	6	.75	26	.258	.324	.457

Hunter Jones

Pitches: L **Bats:** L **Pos:** RP-3　　**Ht:** 6'4" **Wt:** 249 **Born:** 1/10/1984 **Age:** 27

				HOW MUCH HE PITCHED				WHAT HE GAVE UP												THE RESULTS						
Year	Team	Lg	G	GS	CG	GF	IP	BFP	H	R	ER	HR	SH	SF	HB	TBB	IBB	SO	WP	Bk	W	L	Pct	Sh	Sv-Op Hld	ERC	ERA
2005	Lowell	A-	12	1	0	1	28.0	118	29	12	10	2	0	0	0	5	0	30	2	0	1	1	.500	0	1-- -	3.15	3.21
2006	Grnville	A	35	5	0	18	94.1	385	87	41	35	8	1	5	5	20	0	100	7	0	4	5	.444	0	5-- -	3.07	3.34
2007	Lancst	A+	24	0	0	4	47.0	192	35	16	11	2	2	1	3	21	0	40	1	0	4	1	.800	0	0-- -	2.82	2.11
2007	Portlnd	AA	23	0	0	8	42.1	175	35	17	15	3	2	1	1	16	1	43	3	0	2	1	.667	0	2-- -	2.94	3.19
2008	Portlnd	AA	13	0	0	6	22.2	94	21	3	3	0	1	1	1	4	1	26	3	0	0	1	.000	0	4-- -	2.26	1.19
2008	Pwtckt	AAA	35	0	0	15	50.2	217	55	19	17	3	1	1	0	14	1	50	1	0	7	2	.778	0	8-- -	3.73	3.02
2009	Pwtckt	AAA	36	0	0	15	53.0	228	45	27	25	7	5	4	1	24	6	39	1	1	4	3	.571	0	2-- -	3.51	4.25
2010	NewOr	AAA	10	7	0	0	45.1	208	47	28	21	3	4	0	3	22	1	31	0	1	0	5	.000	0	0-- -	4.47	4.17
2009	Bos	AL	11	0	0	1	12.2	63	16	13	13	3	1	1	1	7	1	9	2	0	0	0	-	0	0-0 1	7.32	9.24
2010	Fla	NL	3	0	0	1	1.2	7	0	0	0	0	0	0	1	1	0	3	0	0	0	0	-	0	0-0 0	1.30	0.00
	2 ML YEARS		14	0	0	2	14.1	70	16	13	13	3	1	1	2	8	1	12	2	0	0	0	-	0	0-0 1	6.49	8.16

Matt Joyce

Bats: L **Throws:** R **Pos:** RF-52; LF-13; PH-13; DH-11; PR-1　　**Ht:** 6'2" **Wt:** 205 **Born:** 8/3/1984 **Age:** 26

								BATTING													BASERUNNING				AVERAGES		
Year	Team	Lg	G	AB	H	2B	3B	HR	(Hm	Rd)	TB	R	RBI	RC	TBB	IBB	SO	HBP	SH	SF	SB	CS	SB%	GDP	Avg	OBP	Slg
2010	Drham*	AAA	25	92	27	8	0	3	(-	-)	44	18	12	19	22	3	21	1	0	0	1	3	.25	0	.293	.435	.478
2010	Charltt*	A+	10	29	11	5	0	2	(-	-)	22	6	8	11	10	1	8	0	0	1	1	0	1.00	0	.379	.525	.759
2008	Det	AL	92	242	61	16	3	12	(6	6)	119	40	33	36	31	0	65	2	0	2	0	2	.00	3	.252	.339	.492
2009	TB	AL	11	32	6	1	0	3	(2	1)	16	3	7	5	3	0	7	1	0	1	1	0	1.00	0	.188	.270	.500
2010	TB	AL	77	216	52	15	3	10	(4	6)	103	30	40	41	40	2	55	2	0	3	2	2	.50	2	.241	.360	.477
	3 ML YEARS		180	490	119	32	6	25	(12	13)	238	73	80	82	74	2	127	5	0	6	3	4	.43	5	.243	.344	.486

Jair Jurrjens

Pitches: R **Bats:** R **Pos:** SP-20　　jye-AIR JURR-jens　　**Ht:** 6'1" **Wt:** 200 **Born:** 1/29/1986 **Age:** 25

				HOW MUCH HE PITCHED				WHAT HE GAVE UP												THE RESULTS						
Year	Team	Lg	G	GS	CG	GF	IP	BFP	H	R	ER	HR	SH	SF	HB	TBB	IBB	SO	WP	Bk	W	L	Pct	Sh	Sv-Op Hld	ERC	ERA
2010	Gwnntt*	AAA	3	3	0	0	13.0	63	20	8	8	2	1	0	0	6	0	9	1	0	1	1	.500	0	0-- -	8.18	5.54
2007	Det	AL	7	7	0	0	30.2	122	24	16	16	4	0	1	0	11	0	13	2	0	3	1	.750	0	0-0 0	3.19	4.70
2008	Atl	NL	31	31	0	0	188.1	813	188	87	77	11	12	5	4	70	9	139	3	0	13	10	.565	0	0-0 0	3.65	3.68
2009	Atl	NL	34	**34**	0	0	215.0	884	186	71	62	15	16	4	3	75	1	152	3	2	14	10	.583	0	0-0 0	3.03	2.60
2010	Atl	NL	20	20	0	0	116.1	500	120	63	60	13	7	4	2	42	5	86	2	0	7	6	.538	0	0-0 0	4.20	4.64
	4 ML YEARS		92	92	0	0	550.1	2319	518	237	215	43	35	14	10	198	15	390	10	2	37	27	.578	0	0-0 0	3.49	3.52

Kila Ka'aihue

Bats: L **Throws:** R **Pos:** 1B-34; DH-15; PH-3　　KEY-luh kuh-eye-HOO-ah　　**Ht:** 6'4" **Wt:** 235 **Born:** 3/29/1984 **Age:** 27

								BATTING													BASERUNNING				AVERAGES		
Year	Team	Lg	G	AB	H	2B	3B	HR	(Hm	Rd)	TB	R	RBI	RC	TBB	IBB	SO	HBP	SH	SF	SB	CS	SB%	GDP	Avg	OBP	Slg
2002	Royals	R	43	139	36	8	0	3	(-	-)	53	15	21	22	26	0	35	2	0	1	0	0	-	4	.259	.381	.381
2003	Burlgtn	A	114	395	94	21	1	11	(-	-)	150	53	63	59	67	1	87	8	6	6	1	3	.25	13	.238	.355	.380
2004	Burlgtn	A	125	390	96	23	2	15	(-	-)	168	57	62	66	64	4	98	9	3	5	1	0	1.00	6	.246	.361	.431
2005	Hi Dsrt	A+	132	493	150	31	2	20	(-	-)	245	84	90	110	97	2	97	12	0	3	2	1	.67	12	.304	.428	.497
2006	Wichta	AA	103	327	65	15	0	6	(-	-)	98	40	45	34	49	0	73	4	5	10	0	1	.00	5	.199	.303	.300
2007	Wilmg	A+	60	207	52	0	0	9	(-	-)	87	28	42	35	35	0	38	4	0	7	1	0	1.00	5	.251	.360	.420
2007	Wichta	AA	70	244	60	13	0	12	(-	-)	109	37	40	41	41	3	40	2	1	0	0	0	-	4	.246	.359	.447
2008	NWArk	AA	91	287	90	11	0	26	(-	-)	179	64	79	83	80	7	41	4	0	5	3	2	.60	3	.314	.463	.624
2008	Omha	AAA	33	114	36	4	0	11	(-	-)	73	27	21	27	24	0	26	1	0	0	0	0	-	1	.316	.439	.640
2009	Omha	AAA	131	441	111	27	1	17	(-	-)	191	83	57	84	102	7	85	4	1	7	0	1	.00	11	.252	.392	.433
2010	Omha	AAA	94	323	103	16	1	24	(-	-)	193	67	78	90	88	6	69	1	1	3	2	0	1.00	5	.319	.463	.598
2008	KC	AL	12	21	6	0	0	1	(1	0)	9	4	1	3	3	0	2	0	0	0	0	0	-	0	.286	.375	.429
2010	KC	AL	52	180	39	6	1	8	(5	3)	71	22	25	15	24	2	39	0	1	1	0	1	.00	5	.217	.307	.394
	2 ML YEARS		64	201	45	6	1	9	(6	3)	80	26	26	18	27	2	41	0	1	1	0	1	.00	5	.224	.314	.398

Ryan Kalish

Bats: L **Throws:** L **Pos:** CF-38; LF-12; PH-6; RF-2; PR-2　　KAY-lish　　**Ht:** 6'1" **Wt:** 205 **Born:** 3/28/1988 **Age:** 23

								BATTING													BASERUNNING				AVERAGES		
Year	Team	Lg	G	AB	H	2B	3B	HR	(Hm	Rd)	TB	R	RBI	RC	TBB	IBB	SO	HBP	SH	SF	SB	CS	SB%	GDP	Avg	OBP	Slg
2006	RedSx	R	6	20	6	2	0	1	(-	-)	11	6	2	3	1	0	2	0	0	0	0	0	-	0	.300	.333	.550
2006	Lowell	A-	11	35	7	0	1	0	(-	-)	9	8	4	3	2	0	14	2	0	1	2	0	1.00	0	.200	.275	.257
2007	Lowell	A-	23	87	32	4	1	3	(-	-)	47	27	13	24	16	1	12	1	0	0	18	3	.86	0	.368	.471	.540
2008	Grnville	A	96	360	101	16	1	3	(-	-)	128	51	32	56	53	1	76	4	0	3	18	4	.82	9	.281	.376	.356
2008	Lancst	A+	18	73	17	6	0	2	(-	-)	29	6	14	9	8	0	23	0	0	1	1	0	1.00	2	.233	.305	.397
2009	Salem	A+	32	115	35	5	2	5	(-	-)	59	21	21	27	26	1	20	1	0	1	7	3	.70	2	.304	.434	.513

			BATTING																		BASERUNNING				AVERAGES		
Year	Team	Lg	G	AB	H	2B	3B	HR	(Hm Rd)	TB	R	RBI	RC	TBB	IBB	SO	HBP	SH	SF	SB	CS	SB%	GDP	Avg	OBP	Slg
2009	Portlnd	AA	103	391	106	19	4	13	(- -)	172	63	56	62	42	0	87	1	0	3	14	3	.82	9	.271	.341	.440
2010	Portlnd	AA	41	150	44	9	1	8	(- -)	79	35	29	35	28	2	21	2	0	3	13	1	.93	1	.293	.404	.527
2010	Pwtckt	AAA	37	143	42	9	1	5	(- -)	68	22	18	26	14	0	32	1	0	2	12	2	.86	3	.294	.356	.476
2010	Bos	AL	53	163	41	11	1	4	(2 2)	66	26	24	23	12	0	38	1	2	1	10	1	.91	5	.252	.305	.405

Gabe Kapler

Bats: R **Throws:** R **Pos:** RF-39; PH-14; LF-12; DH-5; PR-4; CF-2   **Ht:** 6'2" **Wt:** 205 **Born:** 7/31/1975 **Age:** 35

			BATTING																		BASERUNNING				AVERAGES		
Year	Team	Lg	G	AB	H	2B	3B	HR	(Hm Rd)	TB	R	RBI	RC	TBB	IBB	SO	HBP	SH	SF	SB	CS	SB%	GDP	Avg	OBP	Slg
2010	Charltt*	A+	4	13	1	0	0	0	(- -)	1	0	1	0	1	0	3	0	0	0	0	0	-	0	.077	.143	.077
1998	Det	AL	7	25	5	0	1	0	(0 0)	7	3	0	2	1	0	4	0	0	0	2	0	1.00	0	.200	.231	.280
1999	Det	AL	130	416	102	22	4	18	(12 6)	186	60	49	59	42	0	74	0	0	4	11	5	.69	7	.245	.315	.447
2000	Tex	AL	116	444	134	32	1	14	(11 3)	210	59	66	72	42	2	57	0	2	3	8	4	.67	12	.302	.360	.473
2001	Tex	AL	134	483	129	29	1	17	(11 6)	211	77	72	77	61	2	70	3	2	7	23	6	.79	10	.267	.348	.437
2002	2 Tms		112	315	88	16	4	2	(1 1)	118	37	34	44	16	0	53	1	7	3	11	4	.73	5	.279	.313	.375
2003	2 Tms		107	225	61	13	1	4	(2 2)	88	39	27	28	22	1	41	0	0	0	6	2	.75	8	.271	.336	.391
2004	Bos	AL	136	290	79	14	1	6	(3 3)	113	51	33	32	15	0	49	2	1	2	5	4	.56	5	.272	.311	.390
2005	Bos	AL	36	97	24	7	0	1	(0 1)	34	15	9	7	3	0	15	2	1	1	1	0	1.00	1	.247	.282	.351
2006	Bos	AL	72	130	33	7	0	2	(1 1)	46	21	12	14	14	0	15	3	0	0	1	1	.50	1	.254	.340	.354
2008	Mil	NL	96	229	69	17	2	8	(4 4)	114	36	38	35	13	0	39	1	1	1	3	1	.75	3	.301	.340	.498
2009	TB	AL	99	205	49	15	1	8	(3 5)	90	26	32	26	29	1	39	0	1	3	5	2	.71	9	.239	.329	.439
2010	TB	AL	59	124	26	4	0	2	(1 1)	36	19	14	12	11	0	24	1	1	1	1	1	.50	3	.210	.288	.290
02	Tex	AL	72	196	51	12	1	0	(0 0)	65	25	17	20	8	0	30	0	7	3	5	2	.71	3	.260	.285	.332
02	Col	NL	40	119	37	4	3	2	(1 1)	53	12	17	24	8	0	23	1	0	0	6	2	.75	2	.311	.359	.445
03	Col	NL	39	67	15	2	0	0	(0 0)	17	10	4	5	8	1	18	0	0	0	2	0	1.00	3	.224	.307	.254
03	Bos	AL	68	158	46	11	1	4	(2 2)	71	29	23	23	14	0	23	0	0	0	4	2	.67	5	.291	.349	.449
	Postseason		15	27	3	0	0	0	(0 0)	3	2	0	1	0	0	7	0	0	0	0	1	.00	1	.111	.111	.111
	12 ML YEARS		1104	2983	799	176	16	82	(49 33)	1253	443	386	408	269	6	480	17	20	25	77	30	.72	68	.268	.329	.420

Jeff Karstens

Pitches: R **Bats:** R **Pos:** SP-19; RP-7   **Ht:** 6'3" **Wt:** 185 **Born:** 9/24/1982 **Age:** 28

			HOW MUCH HE PITCHED						WHAT HE GAVE UP											THE RESULTS						
Year	Team	Lg	G	GS	CG	GF	IP	BFP	H	R	ER	HR	SH	SF	HB	TBB	IBB	SO	WP	Bk	W	L	Pct	Sh	Sv-Op	Hld	ERC	ERA
2010	Indy*	AAA	5	1	0	1	16.0	71	21	14	13	3	0	0	0	2	0	12	0	0	1	2	.333	0	0--	-	5.25	7.31
2006	NYY	AL	8	6	0	2	42.2	179	40	20	18	6	0	2	1	11	2	16	3	1	2	1	.667	0	0-0	0	3.42	3.80
2007	NYY	AL	7	3	0	2	14.2	80	27	21	18	4	2	1	0	9	0	5	2	0	1	4	.200	0	0-0	0	11.86	11.05
2008	Pit	NL	9	9	1	0	51.1	220	56	32	23	7	2	4	0	13	0	23	1	0	2	6	.250	1	0-0	0	4.22	4.03
2009	Pit	NL	39	13	0	8	108.0	471	115	66	65	12	8	8	2	45	5	52	1	0	4	6	.400	0	0-0	1	4.64	5.42
2010	Pit	NL	26	19	0	1	122.2	525	146	72	67	21	2	9	1	27	5	72	0	1	3	10	.231	0	0-0	0	4.97	4.92
	5 ML YEARS		89	50	1	13	339.1	1475	384	211	191	50	12	22	4	105	12	168	7	2	12	27	.308	1	0-0	1	4.81	5.07

Kenshin Kawakami

Pitches: R **Bats:** R **Pos:** SP-16; RP-2   **Ht:** 5'11" **Wt:** 200 **Born:** 6/22/1975 **Age:** 36

			HOW MUCH HE PITCHED						WHAT HE GAVE UP											THE RESULTS						
Year	Team	Lg	G	GS	CG	GF	IP	BFP	H	R	ER	HR	SH	SF	HB	TBB	IBB	SO	WP	Bk	W	L	Pct	Sh	Sv-Op	Hld	ERC	ERA
1998	Chnchi	Jap	24	21	4	1	161.1	649	123	48	46	14	-	-	2	51	-	124	4	0	14	6	.700	3	0--	-	2.48	2.57
1999	Chnchi	Jap	29	22	3	1	162.0	695	173	84	80	20	-	-	2	43	-	102	3	0	8	9	.471	1	1--	-	4.10	4.44
2000	Chnchi	Jap	14	10	0	2	60.1	260	65	32	32	10	-	-	4	20	-	24	1	0	2	3	.400	0	0--	-	4.81	4.77
2001	Chnchi	Jap	26	22	3	1	145.0	608	153	61	60	12	-	-	4	36	-	127	4	0	6	10	.375	1	0--	-	3.83	3.72
2002	Chnchi	Jap	27	24	3	0	187.2	760	170	54	49	13	-	-	8	34	-	149	0	0	12	6	.667	3	0--	-	2.72	2.35
2003	Chnchi	Jap	8	7	1	0	53.2	234	60	22	18	2	-	-	1	14	0	37	3	0	4	3	.571	0	0--	-	3.76	3.02
2004	Chnchi	Jap	27	22	5	0	192.1	774	173	72	71	27	11	1	4	38	2	176	2	0	17	7	.708	2	0--	-	3.10	3.32
2005	Chnchi	Jap	25	22	3	0	180.1	738	186	75	75	20	9	3	4	28	4	138	1	0	11	8	.579	2	0--	-	3.45	3.74
2006	Chnchi	Jap	29	22	6	0	215.0	841	166	74	60	22	11	2	5	39	1	194	3	0	17	7	.708	3	0--	-	2.19	2.51
2007	Chnchi	Jap	26	26	0	0	167.1	696	175	72	66	18	-	-	6	23	2	145	1	0	12	8	.600	0	0--	-	3.45	3.55
2008	Chnchi	Jap	20	16	1	1	117.1	466	99	33	30	11	-	-	5	25	*	112	1	0	9	5	.640	0	0	-	2.72	2.30
2010	Gwnntt	AAA	5	5	0	0	21.0	92	26	12	10	5	0	0	1	5	0	22	2	0	1	0	1.000	0	0--	-	6.09	4.29
2009	Atl	NL	32	25	0	3	156.1	669	153	73	67	15	10	7	6	57	6	105	8	1	7	12	.368	0	1-1	0	3.89	3.86
2010	Atl	NL	18	16	0	1	87.1	391	98	57	50	10	6	7	1	32	10	59	4	0	1	10	.091	0	0-0	0	4.51	5.15
	2 ML YEARS		50	41	0	4	243.2	1060	251	130	117	25	16	14	7	89	16	164	12	1	8	22	.267	0	1-1	0	4.11	4.32

Scott Kazmir

Pitches: L **Bats:** L **Pos:** SP-28   **Ht:** 6'0" **Wt:** 175 **Born:** 1/24/1984 **Age:** 27

			HOW MUCH HE PITCHED						WHAT HE GAVE UP											THE RESULTS						
Year	Team	Lg	G	GS	CG	GF	IP	BFP	H	R	ER	HR	SH	SF	HB	TBB	IBB	SO	WP	Bk	W	L	Pct	Sh	Sv-Op	Hld	ERC	ERA
2010	RCuca*	A+	1	1	0	0	6.1	27	8	3	3	0	0	0	0	0	0	6	1	0	0	0	-	0	0--	-	3.20	4.26
2004	TB	AL	8	7	0	0	33.1	152	33	22	21	4	0	0	2	21	0	41	3	0	2	3	.400	0	0-0	0	5.36	5.67
2005	TB	AL	32	32	0	0	186.0	818	172	90	78	12	6	9	10	100	3	174	7	1	10	9	.526	0	0-0	0	4.13	3.77
2006	TB	AL	24	24	1	0	144.2	610	132	59	52	15	0	5	2	52	3	163	6	0	10	8	.556	1	0-0	0	3.47	3.24
2007	TB	AL	34	34	0	0	206.2	887	196	91	80	18	6	3	7	89	1	239	10	0	13	9	.591	0	0-0	0	3.97	3.48
2008	TB	AL	27	27	0	0	152.1	641	123	61	59	23	4	5	4	70	2	166	5	0	12	8	.600	0	0-0	0	3.69	3.49
2009	2 Tms		26	26	0	0	147.1	647	149	85	80	16	1	4	6	60	0	117	13	0	10	9	.526	0	0-0	0	4.36	4.89
2010	LAA	AL	28	28	0	0	150.0	682	158	103	99	25	3	6	12	79	2	93	6	0	9	15	.375	0	0-0	0	5.74	5.94
09	TB	AL	20	20	0	0	111.0	504	121	77	73	15	1	4	5	50	0	91	10	0	8	7	.533	0	0-0	0	5.18	5.92
09	LAA	AL	6	6	0	0	36.1	143	28	8	7	1	0	0	1	10	0	26	3	0	2	2	.500	0	0-0	0	2.13	1.73
	Postseason		8	7	0	0	36.1	176	37	22	21	5	3	2	3	26	0	26	2	0	1	2	.333	0	0-0	0	5.92	5.20
	7 ML YEARS		179	178	1	0	1020.1	4437	963	511	469	113	20	32	43	471	11	993	50	1	66	61	.520	1	0-0	0	4.24	4.14

Austin Kearns

Bats: R Throws: R Pos: LF-91; RF-32; PH-6; CF-5; DH-2; PR-1   Ht: 6'3" Wt: 240 Born: 5/20/1980 Age: 31

Year	Team	Lg	G	AB	H	2B	3B	HR	(Hm	Rd)	TB	R	RBI	RC	TBB	IBB	SO	HBP	SH	SF	SB	CS	SB%	GDP	Avg	OBP	Slg
2002	Cin	NL	107	372	117	24	3	13	(7	6)	186	66	56	70	54	3	81	6	0	3	6	3	.67	11	.315	.407	.500
2003	Cin	NL	82	292	77	11	0	15	(8	7)	133	39	58	52	41	1	68	5	0	0	5	2	.71	7	.264	.364	.455
2004	Cin	NL	64	217	50	10	2	9	(3	6)	91	28	32	26	28	0	71	1	0	0	2	1	.67	8	.230	.321	.419
2005	Cin	NL	112	387	93	26	1	18	(9	9)	175	62	67	55	48	2	107	8	0	5	0	0	-	8	.240	.333	.452
2006	2 Tms	NL	150	537	142	33	2	24	(12	12)	251	86	86	81	76	4	135	10	1	5	9	4	.69	18	.264	.363	.467
2007	Was	NL	161	587	156	35	1	16	(8	8)	241	84	74	87	71	5	106	12	0	4	2	2	.50	13	.266	.355	.411
2008	Was	NL	86	313	68	10	0	7	(1	6)	99	40	32	28	35	0	63	8	0	1	2	2	.50	11	.217	.311	.316
2009	Was	NL	80	174	34	6	2	3	(1	2)	53	20	17	17	32	1	51	5	0	0	1	1	.50	12	.195	.336	.305
2010	2 Tms	NL	120	403	106	21	1	10	(5	5)	159	55	49	51	46	2	116	10	0	2	4	1	.80	16	.263	.351	.395
06	Cin	NL	87	325	89	21	1	16	(8	8)	160	53	50	46	35	2	85	5	0	3	7	1	.88	14	.274	.351	.492
06	Was	NL	63	212	53	12	1	8	(4	4)	91	33	36	35	41	2	50	5	1	2	2	3	.40	4	.250	.381	.429
10	Cle	AL	84	301	82	18	1	8	(4	4)	126	42	42	43	34	2	78	5	0	2	4	1	.80	12	.272	.354	.419
10	NYY	AL	36	102	24	3	0	2	(1	1)	33	13	7	8	12	0	38	5	0	0	0	0	-	4	.235	.345	.324
9 ML YEARS			962	3282	843	176	12	115	(54	61)	1388	480	471	467	431	18	798	65	1	20	31	16	.66	104	.257	.353	.423

Shawn Kelley

Pitches: R Bats: R Pos: RP-22   Ht: 6'2" Wt: 215 Born: 4/26/1984 Age: 27

Year	Team	Lg	G	GS	CG	GF	IP	BFP	H	R	ER	HR	SH	SF	HB	TBB	IBB	SO	WP	Bk	W	L	Pct	Sh	Sv-Op	Hld	ERC	ERA
2007	Everett	A-	3	0	0	0	3.0	10	2	1	1	1	0	0	0	0	0	4	0	0	1	0	1.000	0	0- -	-	2.25	3.00
2007	Wisc	A	9	0	0	4	12.0	57	16	4	3	1	1	0	0	4	1	14	2	0	1	1	.500	0	0- -	-	5.23	2.25
2008	Wisc	A	8	0	0	8	7.2	33	10	3	3	0	0	0	0	2	0	12	0	0	0	0	-	0	3- -	-	4.69	3.52
2008	Hi Dsrt	A+	12	0	0	10	12.0	47	8	1	0	0	0	0	1	3	1	12	1	0	0	0	-	0	3- -	-	1.52	0.00
2008	WTenn	AA	29	0	0	24	42.2	172	31	12	10	2	3	0	1	17	4	44	2	1	3	1	.750	0	9- -	-	2.29	2.11
2009	Ms	R	2	2	0	0	2.0	6	0	0	0	0	0	0	0	0	0	3	0	0	0	0	-	0	0- -	-	0.00	0.00
2009	Tacom	AAA	1	0	0	0	1.0	3	0	0	0	0	0	0	0	0	0	0	0	0	0	0	-	0	0- -	-	0.00	0.00
2010	Tacom	AAA	3	0	0	1	3.2	15	1	2	2	0	1	0	0	3	0	6	0	0	0	0	-	0	1- -	-	1.37	4.91
2009	Sea	AL	41	0	0	12	46.0	191	45	23	23	9	2	2	3	9	1	41	2	1	5	4	.556	0	0-4	9	4.02	4.50
2010	Sea	AL	22	0	0	7	25.0	112	26	11	11	5	0	1	2	12	2	26	0	0	3	1	.750	0	0-0	3	5.38	3.96
2 ML YEARS			63	0	0	19	71.0	303	71	34	34	14	2	2	4	21	3	67	2	1	8	5	.615	0	0-4	12	4.49	4.31

Don Kelly

Bats: L Throws: R Pos: LF-65; 1B-28; 3B-15; PH-13; CF-12; PR-4; RF-2   Ht: 6'4" Wt: 190 Born: 2/15/1980 Age: 31

Year	Team	Lg	G	AB	H	2B	3B	HR	(Hm	Rd)	TB	R	RBI	RC	TBB	IBB	SO	HBP	SH	SF	SB	CS	SB%	GDP	Avg	OBP	Slg
2007	Pit	NL	25	27	4	0	0	0	(0	0)	4	2	0	1	3	0	3	2	0	0	0	0	-	1	.148	.281	.148
2009	Det	AL	31	56	14	3	1	0	(0	0)	19	8	3	7	4	0	10	1	1	0	1	0	1.00	0	.250	.311	.339
2010	Det	AL	119	238	58	4	0	9	(4	5)	89	30	27	26	8	0	42	2	1	2	4	0	1.00	2	.244	.272	.374
3 ML YEARS			175	321	76	7	1	9	(4	5)	112	40	30	34	15	0	55	5	2	2	4	0	1.00	2	.237	.280	.349

Matt Kemp

Bats: R Throws: R Pos: CF-158; PH-6; PR-1   Ht: 6'3" Wt: 220 Born: 9/23/1984 Age: 26

Year	Team	Lg	G	AB	H	2B	3B	HR	(Hm	Rd)	TB	R	RBI	RC	TBB	IBB	SO	HBP	SH	SF	SB	CS	SB%	GDP	Avg	OBP	Slg
2006	LAD	NL	52	154	39	7	1	7	(4	3)	69	30	23	20	9	1	53	0	0	3	6	0	1.00	1	.253	.289	.448
2007	LAD	NL	98	292	100	12	5	10	(9	1)	152	47	42	49	16	0	66	0	0	3	10	5	.67	6	.342	.373	.521
2008	LAD	NL	155	606	176	38	5	18	(14	4)	278	93	76	86	46	6	153	1	1	3	35	11	.76	11	.290	.340	.459
2009	LAD	NL	159	606	180	25	7	26	(13	13)	297	97	101	100	52	6	139	3	0	6	34	8	.81	14	.297	.352	.490
2010	LAD	NL	162	602	150	25	6	28	(15	13)	271	82	89	74	53	4	170	4	0	9	19	15	.56	14	.249	.310	.450
Postseason			16	62	14	3	0	2	(1	1)	23	5	5	1	5	0	25	0	0	0	0	2	.00	2	.226	.284	.371
5 ML YEARS			626	2260	645	107	24	89	(55	34)	1067	349	331	329	176	17	581	8	1	24	104	39	.73	46	.285	.336	.472

Jason Kendall

Bats: R Throws: R Pos: C-118   Ht: 6'0" Wt: 192 Born: 6/26/1974 Age: 37

Year	Team	Lg	G	AB	H	2B	3B	HR	(Hm	Rd)	TB	R	RBI	RC	TBB	IBB	SO	HBP	SH	SF	SB	CS	SB%	GDP	Avg	OBP	Slg
1996	Pit	NL	130	414	124	23	5	3	(2	1)	166	54	42	63	35	11	30	15	3	4	5	2	.71	7	.300	.372	.401
1997	Pit	NL	144	486	143	36	4	8	(5	3)	211	71	49	86	49	2	53	31	1	5	18	6	.75	11	.294	.391	.434
1998	Pit	NL	149	535	175	36	3	12	(6	6)	253	95	75	110	51	3	51	31	2	8	26	8	.76	6	.327	.411	.473
1999	Pit	NL	78	280	93	20	3	8	(5	3)	143	61	41	63	38	3	32	12	0	4	22	3	.88	8	.332	.428	.511
2000	Pit	NL	152	579	185	33	6	14	(7	7)	272	112	58	112	79	3	79	15	1	4	22	12	.65	13	.320	.412	.470
2001	Pit	NL	157	606	161	22	2	10	(3	7)	217	84	53	68	44	4	48	20	0	2	13	14	.48	18	.266	.335	.358
2002	Pit	NL	145	545	154	25	3	3	(1	2)	194	59	44	66	49	1	29	9	0	2	15	8	.65	11	.283	.350	.356
2003	Pit	NL	150	587	191	29	3	6	(3	3)	244	84	58	97	49	3	40	25	1	3	8	7	.53	9	.325	.399	.416
2004	Pit	NL	147	574	183	32	0	3	(2	1)	224	86	51	95	60	2	41	19	1	4	11	8	.58	12	.319	.399	.390
2005	Oak	AL	150	601	163	28	1	0	(0	0)	193	70	53	79	50	0	39	20	0	5	8	3	.73	26	.271	.345	.321
2006	Oak	AL	143	552	163	23	0	1	(1	0)	189	76	50	80	53	2	54	12	4	5	11	5	.69	19	.295	.367	.342
2007	2 Tms	NL	137	466	113	20	1	3	(1	2)	144	45	41	43	31	2	42	9	5	3	4	4	.43	8	.242	.301	.309
2008	Mil	NL	151	516	127	30	2	2	(1	1)	167	46	49	59	50	7	45	13	6	2	8	3	.73	5	.246	.327	.324
2009	Mil	NL	134	452	109	19	2	2	(0	0)	138	43	43	53	46	6	58	17	6	5	7	2	.78	11	.241	.331	.305
2010	KC	AL	118	434	111	18	0	0	(0	0)	129	39	37	38	37	2	45	6	6	7	12	7	.63	12	.256	.318	.297

Year	Team	Lg	G	AB	H	2B	3B	HR	(Hm	Rd)	TB	R	RBI	RC	TBB	IBB	SO	HBP	SH	SF	SB	CS	SB%	GDP	Avg	OBP	Slg
07	Oak	AL	80	292	66	10	0	2	(0	2)	82	24	22	18	12	0	27	3	2	3	3	1	.75	7	.226	.261	.281
07	ChC	NL	57	174	47	10	1	1	(1	0)	62	21	19	25	19	2	15	6	3	0	0	3	.00	1	.270	.362	.356
	Postseason		12	49	11	1	0	0	(0	0)	12	1	3	3	2	0	9	0	0	0	0	0	-	0	.224	.255	.245
	15 ML YEARS		2085	7627	2195	394	35	75	(37	38)	2884	1030	744	1107	721	51	686	254	36	63	189	89	.68	176	.288	.366	.378

Howie Kendrick

Bats: R **Throws:** R **Pos:** 2B-143; 1B-15; PH-6; CF-1   **Ht:** 5'10" **Wt:** 215 **Born:** 7/12/1983 **Age:** 27

Year	Team	Lg	G	AB	H	2B	3B	HR	(Hm	Rd)	TB	R	RBI	RC	TBB	IBB	SO	HBP	SH	SF	SB	CS	SB%	GDP	Avg	OBP	Slg
2006	LAA	AL	72	267	76	21	1	4	(2	2)	111	25	30	32	9	2	44	4	0	3	6	0	1.00	5	.285	.314	.416
2007	LAA	AL	88	338	109	24	2	5	(3	2)	152	55	39	41	9	2	61	4	1	1	5	4	.56	15	.322	.347	.450
2008	LAA	AL	92	340	104	26	2	3	(1	2)	143	43	37	50	12	3	58	4	1	4	11	4	.73	8	.306	.333	.421
2009	LAA	AL	105	374	109	21	3	10	(5	5)	166	61	61	58	20	1	71	4	2	0	11	4	.73	8	.291	.334	.444
2010	LAA	AL	158	616	172	41	4	10	(4	6)	251	67	75	81	28	2	94	5	4	5	14	4	.78	16	.279	.313	.407
	Postseason		13	46	9	0	1	1	(1	0)	14	4	2	3	1	0	11	0	2	1	3	0	1.00	1	.196	.208	.304
	5 ML YEARS		515	1935	570	133	12	32	(15	17)	823	251	242	262	78	10	328	21	8	13	47	16	.75	52	.295	.327	.425

Kyle Kendrick

Pitches: R **Bats:** R **Pos:** SP-31; RP-2   **Ht:** 6'3" **Wt:** 213 **Born:** 8/26/1984 **Age:** 26

Year	Team	Lg	G	GS	CG	GF	IP	BFP	H	R	ER	HR	SH	SF	HB	TBB	IBB	SO	WP	Bk	W	L	Pct	Sh	Sv-Op	Hld	ERC	ERA
2007	Phi	NL	20	20	0	0	121.0	499	129	53	52	16	4	2	7	25	3	49	0	0	10	4	.714	0	0-0	0	4.23	3.87
2008	Phi	NL	31	30	0	1	155.2	722	194	103	95	23	8	4	14	57	2	68	4	1	11	9	.550	0	0-0	0	6.05	5.49
2009	Phi	NL	9	2	0	2	26.1	112	27	11	10	1	1	2	1	9	0	15	0	1	3	1	.750	0	0-0	0	3.75	3.42
2010	Phi	NL	33	31	1	1	180.2	771	199	103	95	26	9	6	3	49	4	84	1	2	11	10	.524	0	0-0	0	4.51	4.73
	Postseason		1	1	0	0	3.2	18	5	5	5	2	0	0	0	2	1	2	0	0	0	1	.000	0	0-0	0	9.97	12.27
	4 ML YEARS		93	83	1	4	483.2	2104	549	270	252	66	22	14	25	140	9	216	5	4	35	24	.593	0	0-0	0	4.88	4.69

Adam Kennedy

Bats: L **Throws:** R **Pos:** 2B-86; 1B-51; PH-25; 3B-8; PR-6   **Ht:** 6'1" **Wt:** 195 **Born:** 1/10/1976 **Age:** 35

Year	Team	Lg	G	AB	H	2B	3B	HR	(Hm	Rd)	TB	R	RBI	RC	TBB	IBB	SO	HBP	SH	SF	SB	CS	SB%	GDP	Avg	OBP	Slg
1999	StL	NL	33	102	26	10	1	1	(1	0)	41	12	16	12	3	0	8	2	1	2	0	1	.00	1	.255	.284	.402
2000	LAA	AL	156	598	159	33	11	9	(7	2)	241	82	72	72	28	5	73	3	8	4	22	8	.73	10	.266	.300	.403
2001	LAA	AL	137	478	129	25	3	6	(4	2)	178	48	40	57	27	3	71	11	7	9	12	7	.63	7	.270	.318	.372
2002	LAA	AL	144	474	148	32	6	7	(6	1)	213	65	52	70	19	1	80	7	5	4	17	4	.81	5	.312	.345	.449
2003	LAA	AL	143	449	121	17	1	13	(8	5)	179	71	49	61	45	4	73	9	2	5	22	9	.71	7	.269	.344	.399
2004	LAA	AL	144	468	130	20	5	10	(5	5)	190	70	48	60	41	7	92	13	9	2	15	5	.75	10	.278	.351	.406
2005	LAA	AL	129	416	125	23	0	2	(1	1)	154	49	37	62	29	1	64	7	5	3	19	4	.83	9	.300	.354	.370
2006	LAA	AL	139	451	123	26	6	4	(3	1)	173	50	55	62	39	5	72	5	3	5	16	10	.62	15	.273	.334	.384
2007	StL	NL	87	279	61	9	1	3	(0	3)	81	27	18	19	22	6	33	3	1	1	6	2	.75	9	.219	.282	.290
2008	StL	NL	115	339	95	17	4	2	(1	1)	126	42	36	39	21	4	43	1	0	4	7	1	.88	13	.280	.321	.372
2009	Oak	AL	129	529	153	29	4	11	(4	7)	217	65	63	88	45	2	86	4	5	3	20	6	.77	8	.289	.348	.410
2010	Was	NL	135	342	85	16	1	3	(0	3)	112	43	31	37	37	1	44	5	1	4	14	2	.88	10	.249	.327	.327
	Postseason		25	78	24	3	1	4	(4	0)	41	13	13	11	1	0	15	1	3	2	1	2	.33	1	.308	.317	.526
	12 ML YEARS		1491	4925	1355	257	40	71	(40	31)	1905	624	517	639	356	39	739	70	47	46	170	59	.74	100	.275	.330	.387

Ian Kennedy

Pitches: R **Bats:** R **Pos:** SP-32   **Ht:** 6'0" **Wt:** 195 **Born:** 12/19/1984 **Age:** 26

Year	Team	Lg	G	GS	CG	GF	IP	BFP	H	R	ER	HR	SH	SF	HB	TBB	IBB	SO	WP	Bk	W	L	Pct	Sh	Sv-Op	Hld	ERC	ERA
2007	NYY	AL	3	3	0	0	19.0	77	13	6	4	1	0	0	0	9	0	15	0	0	1	0	1.000	0	0-0	0	2.42	1.89
2008	NYY	AL	10	9	0	1	39.2	194	50	37	36	5	1	4	1	26	0	27	3	0	0	4	.000	0	0-0	0	6.93	8.17
2009	NYY	AL	1	0	0	0	1.0	6	0	0	0	0	0	0	0	2	0	1	0	0	0	0	-	0	0-0	1	7.00	0.00
2010	Ari	NL	32	32	0	0	194.0	810	163	87	82	26	11	5	10	70	2	168	16	0	9	10	.474	0	0-0	0	3.47	3.80
	4 ML YEARS		46	44	0	1	253.2	1087	226	130	122	32	12	9	12	107	2	211	19	0	10	14	.417	0	0-0	1	3.90	4.33

Jeff Keppinger

Bats: R **Throws:** R **Pos:** 2B-126; SS-12; PH-5   **Ht:** 6'0" **Wt:** 187 **Born:** 4/21/1980 **Age:** 31

Year	Team	Lg	G	AB	H	2B	3B	HR	(Hm	Rd)	TB	R	RBI	RC	TBB	IBB	SO	HBP	SH	SF	SB	CS	SB%	GDP	Avg	OBP	Slg
2010	CpChr*	AA	2	5	2	0	0	0	(-	-)	2	0	1	1	1	0	0	0	0	0	0	0	-	0	.400	.500	.400
2004	NYM	NL	33	116	33	2	0	3	(3	0)	44	9	9	12	6	0	7	0	0	1	2	1	.67	6	.284	.317	.379
2006	KC	AL	22	60	16	2	0	2	(0	2)	24	11	8	8	5	1	6	0	2	0	0	0	-	2	.267	.323	.400
2007	Cin	NL	67	241	80	16	2	5	(2	3)	115	39	32	42	24	0	12	4	6	1	2	1	.67	11	.332	.400	.477
2008	Cin	NL	121	459	122	24	2	3	(3	0)	159	45	43	52	30	3	24	2	6	5	3	1	.75	14	.266	.310	.346
2009	Hou	NL	107	305	78	13	3	7	(1	6)	118	35	29	28	27	3	33	3	7	2	0	2	.00	13	.256	.320	.387
2010	Hou	NL	137	514	148	34	1	6	(4	2)	202	62	59	72	51	1	36	1	5	4	4	1	.80	15	.288	.351	.393
	6 ML YEARS		487	1695	477	91	8	26	(13	13)	662	201	180	214	143	8	118	10	26	13	11	6	.65	61	.281	.339	.391

Clayton Kershaw

Pitches: L **Bats:** L **Pos:** SP-32   **Ht:** 6'3" **Wt:** 217 **Born:** 3/19/1988 **Age:** 23

Year	Team	Lg	G	GS	CG	GF	IP	BFP	H	R	ER	HR	SH	SF	HB	TBB	IBB	SO	WP	Bk	W	L	Pct	Sh	Sv-Op	Hld	ERC	ERA
2008	LAD	NL	22	21	0	0	107.2	470	109	51	51	11	3	3	1	52	3	100	7	0	5	5	.500	0	0-0	1	4.53	4.26
2009	LAD	NL	31	30	0	1	171.0	701	119	55	53	7	11	2	1	91	4	185	11	2	8	8	.500	0	0-0	0	2.60	2.79
2010	LAD	NL	32	32	1	0	204.1	848	160	73	66	13	8	4	7	81	9	212	5	2	13	10	.565	1	0-0	0	2.72	2.91
	Postseason		5	2	0	0	15.1	68	15	10	10	3	3	0	1	9	1	11	4	0	0	1	.000	0	0-0	1	5.72	5.87
	3 ML YEARS		85	83	1	1	483.0	2019	388	179	170	31	22	9	9	224	16	497	23	4	26	23	.531	1	0-0	1	3.05	3.17

Brad Kilby

Pitches: L **Bats:** L **Pos:** RP-5   **Ht:** 6'2" **Wt:** 241 **Born:** 2/19/1983 **Age:** 28

Year	Team	Lg	G	GS	CG	GF	IP	BFP	H	R	ER	HR	SH	SF	HB	TBB	IBB	SO	WP	Bk	W	L	Pct	Sh	Sv-Op	Hld	ERC	ERA
2005	Vancvr	A-	23	0	0	18	27.2	115	20	7	6	2	0	1	0	11	0	38	1	0	2	0	1.000	0	14--	-	2.37	1.95
2006	Kane	A	49	0	0	26	60.2	243	38	13	11	0	3	1	4	23	0	73	2	0	5	1	.833	0	9--	-	1.72	1.63
2007	Stcktn	R	7	0	0	5	8.1	41	6	5	3	0	1	0	0	6	1	16	2	0	0	0	-	0	3--	-	2.44	3.24
2007	Mdland	AA	47	0	0	11	65.2	272	63	24	21	6	3	1	2	22	1	69	1	1	3	3	.500	0	0--	-	3.73	2.88
2008	Scrmto	AAA	51	0	0	14	70.0	287	51	33	27	9	4	1	3	26	1	66	3	0	7	2	.778	0	2--	-	2.83	3.47
2009	Scrmto	AAA	45	0	0	6	63.1	252	40	15	15	5	0	2	2	24	1	77	5	0	4	2	.667	0	2--	-	2.08	2.13
2010	Scrmto	AAA	12	0	0	3	13.0	63	18	8	8	0	1	0	1	6	0	18	0	0	0	0	-	0	0--	-	6.04	5.54
2009	Oak	AL	11	1	0	1	17.0	65	10	2	1	1	0	0	0	4	0	20	0	0	1	0	1.000	0	0-0	1	1.36	0.53
2010	Oak	AL	5	0	0	2	8.1	32	7	2	2	2	0	0	0	0	0	8	0	0	0	0	-	0	0-0	0	2.44	2.16
	2 ML YEARS		16	1	0	3	25.1	97	17	4	3	3	0	0	0	4	0	28	0	0	1	0	1.000	0	0-0	1	1.65	1.07

Craig Kimbrel

Pitches: R **Bats:** R **Pos:** RP-21   **Ht:** 5'11" **Wt:** 205 **Born:** 5/28/1988 **Age:** 23

Year	Team	Lg	G	GS	CG	GF	IP	BFP	H	R	ER	HR	SH	SF	HB	TBB	IBB	SO	WP	Bk	W	L	Pct	Sh	Sv-Op	Hld	ERC	ERA
2008	Danvle	R	12	0	0	11	19.0	81	5	4	1	0	1	1	3	10	1	27	4	0	1	2	.333	0	6--	-	0.97	0.47
2008	Rome	A	10	0	0	9	12.2	48	6	1	1	0	0	0	0	4	0	26	0	0	2	0	1.000	0	4--	-	0.99	0.71
2008	MrtlBh	A+	2	0	0	0	3.2	14	5	0	0	0	0	0	0	1	0	3	0	0	0	0	-	0	0--	-	5.90	0.00
2009	MrtlBh	A+	19	0	0	8	26.1	123	18	19	16	2	2	2	1	28	1	45	8	1	0	2	.000	0	2--	-	4.75	5.47
2009	Rome	A	16	0	0	14	20.0	76	9	2	2	0	1	0	1	6	0	38	0	0	0	0	-	0	10--	-	0.99	0.90
2009	Missi	AA	12	0	0	12	11.2	45	3	1	1	0	0	1	1	7	0	17	1	0	2	1	.667	0	6--	-	1.11	0.77
2009	Gwnntt	AAA	2	0	0	1	2.0	10	0	0	0	0	0	0	0	4	0	3	1	0	0	0	-	0	0--	-	3.47	0.00
2010	Gwnntt	AAA	48	0	0	43	55.2	230	28	13	10	3	2	0	4	35	0	83	8	1	3	2	.600	0	23--	-	2.29	1.62
2010	Atl	NL	21	0	0	7	20.2	88	9	2	1	0	0	0	0	16	1	40	4	0	4	0	1.000	0	1-1	2	1.72	0.44

Ian Kinsler

Bats: R **Throws:** R **Pos:** 2B-103; PH-1   **Ht:** 6'0" **Wt:** 200 **Born:** 6/22/1982 **Age:** 29

Year	Team	Lg	G	AB	H	2B	3B	HR	(Hm	Rd)	TB	R	RBI	RC	TBB	IBB	SO	HBP	SH	SF	SB	CS	SB%	GDP	Avg	OBP	Slg
2010	Frisco*	AA	6	19	5	0	1	0	(-	-)	7	3	6	3	2	0	3	1	0	1	2	0	1.00	2	.263	.348	.368
2006	Tex	AL	120	423	121	21	1	14	(10	4)	192	65	55	65	40	1	64	3	1	7	11	4	.73	12	.286	.347	.454
2007	Tex	AL	130	483	127	22	2	20	(12	8)	213	96	61	79	62	2	83	9	8	4	23	2	.92	14	.263	.355	.441
2008	Tex	AL	121	518	165	41	4	18	(4	14)	268	102	71	106	45	1	67	6	7	7	26	2	.93	12	.319	.375	.517
2009	Tex	AL	144	566	143	32	4	31	(20	11)	276	101	86	99	59	0	77	6	3	6	31	5	.86	9	.253	.327	.488
2010	Tex	AL	103	391	112	20	1	9	(4	5)	161	73	45	59	56	2	57	7	2	4	15	5	.75	11	.286	.382	.412
	5 ML YEARS		618	2381	668	142	12	92	(50	42)	1110	437	318	408	262	6	348	31	21	28	106	18	.85	58	.281	.356	.466

Brandon Kintzler

Pitches: R **Bats:** R **Pos:** RP-7   **Ht:** 6'1" **Wt:** 180 **Born:** 8/1/1984 **Age:** 26

Year	Team	Lg	G	GS	CG	GF	IP	BFP	H	R	ER	HR	SH	SF	HB	TBB	IBB	SO	WP	Bk	W	L	Pct	Sh	Sv-Op	Hld	ERC	ERA
2004	Padres	R	21	0	0	12	34.0	140	36	12	9	0	1	1	1	9	4	38	3	0	3	2	.600	0	6--	-	3.10	2.38
2004	Eugene	A-	3	0	0	3	3.0	12	3	0	0	0	0	0	0	0	0	4	0	0	0	0	-	0	3--	-	1.95	0.00
2005	Padres	R	8	0	0	6	11.0	54	15	5	5	2	1	0	0	4	0	17	1	0	2	0	1.000	0	1--	-	6.31	4.09
2005	Eugene	A-	3	0	0	3	3.1	12	3	0	0	0	1	0	0	0	0	1	0	0	0	0	-	0	0--	-	1.70	0.00
2005	FtWyn	A	19	0	0	9	23.1	97	20	12	8	2	1	0	2	7	0	19	0	0	1	2	.333	0	0--	-	3.16	3.09
2007	Winpg	IND	29	8	0	9	77.1	327	78	43	35	8	1	4	7	13	1	41	2	1	5	2	.714	0	1--	-	3.53	4.07
2008	Winpg	IND	20	19	0	0	112.1	497	139	68	58	8	1	2	1	36	2	73	8	0	7	6	.538	0	0--	-	4.96	4.65
2009	St. Paul	IND	14	11	1	0	80.2	348	89	28	25	3	2	0	1	24	0	46	1	0	8	3	.727	0	0--	-	3.85	2.79
2009	Hntsvl	AA	9	6	0	0	35.2	154	41	21	18	5	0	0	1	9	0	32	1	0	2	2	.333	0	0--	-	4.76	4.54
2010	Hntsvl	AA	20	0	0	19	22.1	80	11	2	1	0	0	0	1	1	0	23	0	0	1	0	1.000	0	10--	-	0.66	0.40
2010	Nashv	AAA	22	0	0	13	26.2	105	19	7	7	1	1	0	1	6	1	21	1	0	3	0	1.000	0	6--	-	1.70	2.36
2010	Mil	NL	7	0	0	2	7.1	33	10	6	6	2	1	0	0	4	1	9	1	0	0	1	.000	0	0-0	0	8.67	7.36

Michael Kirkman

Pitches: L **Bats:** L **Pos:** RP-14   **Ht:** 6'4" **Wt:** 195 **Born:** 9/18/1986 **Age:** 24

Year	Team	Lg	G	GS	CG	GF	IP	BFP	H	R	ER	HR	SH	SF	HB	TBB	IBB	SO	WP	Bk	W	L	Pct	Sh	Sv-Op	Hld	ERC	ERA
2005	Rngrs	R	14	9	0	1	52.1	227	51	28	20	0	1	1	1	19	0	58	3	0	3	1	.750	0	0--	-	3.11	3.44
2006	Clinton	A	6	6	0	0	19.1	103	23	17	15	0	2	0	1	24	0	22	5	0	0	3	.000	0	0--	-	8.05	6.98
2006	Rngrs	R	8	4	0	2	15.0	97	21	27	22	0	0	2	5	27	0	8	9	0	1	2	.333	0	0--	-	13.00	13.20
2007	Spkane	A-	9	6	0	0	27.0	140	33	30	21	2	2	3	2	25	0	24	7	0	1	4	.200	0	0--	-	7.56	7.00

Year	Team	Lg	G	GS	CG	GF	IP	BFP	H	R	ER	HR	SH	SF	HB	TBB	IBB	SO	WP	Bk	W	L	Pct	Sh	Sv-Op	Hld	ERC	ERA
2007	Clinton	A	5	2	0	1	13.1	69	17	12	11	1	1	0	0	12	0	12	1	0	0	1	.000	0	0--	-	7.43	7.43
2008	Clinton	A	15	14	0	0	74.1	321	78	43	36	8	2	3	3	23	0	58	6	1	4	3	.571	0	0--	-	4.20	4.36
2008	Spkane	A-	2	2	0	0	10.0	41	7	4	0	0	0	0	1	2	0	9	0	0	1	1	.500	0	0--	-	1.56	0.00
2009	Bkrsfld	A+	8	7	0	0	48.0	202	43	16	11	1	1	3	4	18	0	54	3	0	4	1	.800	0	0--	-	3.23	2.06
2009	Frisco	AA	18	18	0	0	96.2	418	93	54	45	9	3	2	4	43	0	64	5	0	5	7	.417	0	0--	-	4.19	4.19
2010	OKCity	AAA	24	22	0	0	131.0	571	115	52	45	8	4	7	3	68	0	130	9	0	13	3	.813	0	0--	-	3.64	3.09
2010	Tex	AL	14	0	0	2	16.1	68	9	3	3	0	0	2	0	10	1	16	0	0	0	0	-	0	0-1	2	1.76	1.65

Hiroyuki Kobayashi

Pitches: R **Bats:** R **Pos:** P   hee-roe-YOO-kee   **Ht:** 6'0" **Wt:** 176 **Born:** 6/4/1978 **Age:** 33

			HOW MUCH HE PITCHED						WHAT HE GAVE UP												THE RESULTS						
Year	Team	Lg	G	GS	CG	GF	IP	BFP	H	R	ER	HR	SH	SF	HB	TBB	IBB	SO	WP	Bk	W	L	Pct	Sh	Sv-Op	Hld	ERC	ERA
1998	Chiba	Jap	2	-	0	-	2.1	11	3	0	0	0	-	-	0	1	-	0	0	0	0	0	-	0	0--	-	4.93	0.00
2001	Chiba	Jap	22	-	0	-	56.0	238	49	24	23	11	-	-	1	23	-	45	3	0	1	4	.200	0	0--	-	4.13	3.70
2002	Chiba	Jap	58	-	0	-	81.2	333	67	25	23	12	-	-	1	27	-	84	9	1	7	4	.636	0	0--	-	3.21	2.53
2003	Chiba	Jap	50	-	3	-	145.1	592	135	66	62	17	-	-	3	36	-	117	7	1	10	10	.500	0	0--	-	3.34	3.84
2004	Chiba	Jap	24	-	2	-	154.1	666	162	77	73	22	-	-	4	57	-	137	7	0	9	7	.563	0	0--	-	4.69	4.26
2005	Chiba	Jap	23	-	4	-	160.2	666	157	60	59	14	-	-	6	28	-	129	6	0	12	6	.667	1	0--	-	3.11	3.30
2006	Chiba	Jap	20	-	3	-	142.2	578	129	51	44	14	-	-	4	27	-	120	5	0	10	7	.588	1	0--	-	2.86	2.78
2007	Chiba	Jap	25	-	5	-	170.2	699	157	56	51	9	-	-	4	38	-	163	7	0	13	3	.813	2	0--	-	2.76	2.69
2008	Chiba	Jap	23	-	1	-	138.0	618	155	85	77	15	-	-	2	45	-	112	5	0	5	12	.294	0	0--	-	4.47	5.02
2009	Chiba	Jap	24	-	4	-	134.1	582	142	70	64	16	-	-	7	35	-	120	7	0	4	13	.235	0	0--	-	4.13	4.29
2010	Chiba	Jap	57	-	0	-	61.0	249	51	17	15	2	-	-	3	14	-	53	6	0	3	3	.500	0	29--	-	2.32	2.21

Mike Kohn

Pitches: R **Bats:** R **Pos:** RP-24   KAHN   **Ht:** 6'0" **Wt:** 200 **Born:** 6/26/1986 **Age:** 25

			HOW MUCH HE PITCHED						WHAT HE GAVE UP												THE RESULTS						
Year	Team	Lg	G	GS	CG	GF	IP	BFP	H	R	ER	HR	SH	SF	HB	TBB	IBB	SO	WP	Bk	W	L	Pct	Sh	Sv-Op	Hld	ERC	ERA
2008	Orem	R+	16	0	0	4	23.1	93	11	5	5	1	0	0	0	11	0	44	3	0	2	0	1.000	0	0--	-	1.43	1.93
2009	CRpds	A	28	0	0	11	37.0	140	20	9	9	1	0	1	2	12	0	60	1	1	4	1	.800	0	6--	-	1.45	2.19
2009	RCuca	A+	22	0	0	14	28.2	108	13	3	3	0	1	1	0	14	0	43	2	0	2	0	1.000	0	3--	-	1.32	0.94
2010	Ark	AA	15	0	0	13	18.1	72	12	5	5	0	1	0	1	8	1	25	2	0	2	2	.500	0	3--	-	2.00	2.45
2010	Salt Lk	AAA	26	0	0	23	27.2	115	16	7	6	3	3	0	1	17	2	32	0	0	3	2	.600	0	8--	-	2.73	1.95
2010	LAA	AL	24	0	0	8	21.1	95	17	5	5	0	4	0	0	16	1	20	0	0	2	0	1.000	0	1-1	1	3.45	2.11

Paul Konerko

Bats: R **Throws:** R **Pos:** 1B-125; DH-23; PH-1   **Ht:** 6'2" **Wt:** 220 **Born:** 3/5/1976 **Age:** 35

						BATTING																BASERUNNING				AVERAGES		
Year	Team	Lg	G	AB	H	2B	3B	HR	(Hm	Rd)	TB	R	RBI	RC	TBB	IBB	SO	HBP	SH	SF	SB	CS	SB%	GDP	Avg	OBP	Slg
1997	LAD	NL	6	7	1	0	0	0	(0	0)	1	0	0	0	1	0	2	0	0	0	0	0	-	1	.143	.250	.143
1998	2 Tms	NL	75	217	47	4	0	7	(2	5)	72	21	29	17	16	0	40	3	0	3	0	1	.00	10	.217	.276	.332
1999	CWS	AL	142	513	151	31	4	24	(16	8)	262	71	81	86	45	0	68	2	1	3	1	0	1.00	19	.294	.352	.511
2000	CWS	AL	143	524	156	31	1	21	(10	11)	252	84	97	86	47	0	72	10	0	5	1	0	1.00	22	.298	.363	.481
2001	CWS	AL	156	582	164	35	0	32	(19	13)	295	92	99	99	54	6	89	9	0	5	1	0	1.00	17	.282	.349	.507
2002	CWS	AL	151	570	151	30	0	27	(13	14)	284	81	104	96	44	2	72	9	0	7	0	0	-	17	.304	.359	.498
2003	CWS	AL	137	444	104	19	0	18	(9	9)	177	49	65	42	43	7	50	4	0	4	0	0	-	20	.234	.305	.399
2004	CWS	AL	155	563	156	22	0	41	(29	12)	301	84	117	106	69	5	107	6	0	5	1	0	1.00	23	.277	.359	.535
2005	CWS	AL	150	575	163	24	0	40	(23	17)	307	98	100	106	81	10	100	6	0	3	0	0	-	9	.283	.375	.534
2006	CWS	AL	152	566	177	30	0	35	(21	14)	312	97	113	110	60	3	104	8	0	9	1	0	1.00	25	.313	.381	.551
2007	CWS	AL	151	549	142	34	0	31	(17	14)	269	71	90	88	78	9	102	3	0	6	0	1	.00	21	.259	.351	.490
2008	CWS	AL	122	438	105	19	1	22	(15	7)	192	59	62	60	65	4	80	7	0	4	2	0	1.00	17	.240	.344	.438
2009	CWS	AL	152	546	151	30	1	28	(18	10)	267	75	88	91	58	4	89	10	0	7	1	0	1.00	15	.277	.353	.489
2010	CWS	AL	149	548	171	30	1	39	(26	13)	320	89	111	118	72	7	110	5	0	6	0	1	.00	9	.312	.393	.584
98	LAD	NL	49	144	31	1	0	4	(2	2)	44	14	16	10	10	0	30	2	0	2	0	1	.00	5	.215	.272	.306
98	Cin	NL	26	73	16	3	0	3	(0	3)	28	7	13	7	6	0	10	1	0	1	0	0	-	5	.219	.284	.384
Postseason			19	74	18	2	0	7	(3	4)	41	10	17	12	5	2	10	1	0	0	0	0	-	4	.240	.000	.554
14 ML YEARS			1849	6642	1861	339	8	365	(218	147)	3311	971	1156	1105	733	57	1094	81	1	67	8	3	.73	233	.280	.356	.498

Casey Kotchman

Bats: L **Throws:** L **Pos:** 1B-116; PH-7; DH-3   **Ht:** 6'3" **Wt:** 215 **Born:** 2/22/1983 **Age:** 28

						BATTING																BASERUNNING				AVERAGES		
Year	Team	Lg	G	AB	H	2B	3B	HR	(Hm	Rd)	TB	R	RBI	RC	TBB	IBB	SO	HBP	SH	SF	SB	CS	SB%	GDP	Avg	OBP	Slg
2004	LAA	AL	38	116	26	6	0	0	(0	0)	32	7	15	14	7	3	11	4	0	1	3	0	1.00	3	.224	.289	.276
2005	LAA	AL	47	126	35	5	0	7	(5	2)	61	16	22	21	15	0	18	0	1	1	1	1	.50	3	.278	.352	.484
2006	LAA	AL	29	79	12	2	0	1	(0	1)	17	6	6	1	7	0	13	0	2	0	0	1	.00	2	.152	.221	.215
2007	LAA	AL	137	443	131	37	3	11	(5	6)	207	64	68	74	53	1	43	4	3	5	2	4	.33	17	.296	.372	.467
2008	2 Tms	AL	143	525	143	28	1	14	(3	11)	215	65	74	70	36	5	39	9	0	3	2	1	.67	21	.272	.328	.410
2009	2 Tms	AL	126	385	103	23	0	7	(1	6)	147	37	48	49	39	6	42	4	0	3	1	0	1.00	11	.268	.339	.382
2010	Sea	AL	125	414	90	20	1	9	(5	4)	139	37	51	40	35	6	52	3	0	5	0	0	-	15	.217	.280	.336
08	LAA	AL	100	373	107	24	1	12	(2	10)	167	47	54	53	18	3	23	5	0	2	2	1	.67	14	.287	.327	.448
08	Atl	NL	43	152	36	4	1	2	(1	1)	48	18	20	17	18	2	16	4	0	1	0	0	-	4	.237	.331	.316
09	Atl	NL	87	298	84	20	0	6	(1	5)	122	28	41	43	32	6	28	3	0	3	0	0	-	7	.282	.354	.409
09	Bos	AL	39	87	19	3	0	1	(0	1)	25	9	7	6	7	0	14	1	0	0	1	0	1.00	4	.218	.284	.287
Postseason			11	16	2	1	0	0	(0	0)	3	1	1	1	3	0	2	0	0	0	0	0	-	0	.125	.263	.188
7 ML YEARS			645	2088	540	121	5	49	(19	30)	818	232	284	269	192	21	223	24	6	18	9	7	.56	69	.259	.326	.392

Mark Kotsay

Bats: L **Throws:** L **Pos:** DH-47; 1B-38; PH-17; RF-8   **Ht:** 6'0" **Wt:** 210 **Born:** 12/2/1975 **Age:** 35

Year	Team	Lg	G	AB	H	2B	3B	HR	(Hm	Rd)	TB	R	RBI	RC	TBB	IBB	SO	HBP	SH	SF	SB	CS	SB%	GDP	Avg	OBP	Slg
1997	Fla	NL	14	52	10	1	1	0	(0	0)	13	5	4	3	4	0	7	0	1	0	3	0	1.00	1	.192	.250	.250
1998	Fla	NL	154	578	161	25	7	11	(5	6)	233	72	68	70	34	2	61	1	7	3	10	5	.67	17	.279	.318	.403
1999	Fla	NL	148	495	134	23	9	8	(5	3)	199	57	50	58	29	5	50	0	2	9	7	6	.54	11	.271	.306	.402
2000	Fla	NL	152	530	158	31	5	12	(5	7)	235	87	57	78	42	2	46	0	2	4	19	9	.68	17	.298	.347	.443
2001	SD	NL	119	406	118	29	1	10	(3	7)	179	67	58	65	48	1	58	2	1	3	13	5	.72	11	.291	.366	.441
2002	SD	NL	153	578	169	27	7	17	(11	6)	261	82	61	92	59	0	89	3	2	4	11	9	.55	10	.292	.359	.452
2003	SD	NL	128	482	128	28	4	7	(1	6)	185	64	38	59	56	3	82	1	1	1	6	3	.67	8	.266	.343	.384
2004	Oak	AL	148	606	190	37	3	15	(9	6)	278	78	63	94	55	5	70	2	5	5	8	5	.62	6	.314	.370	.459
2005	Oak	AL	139	582	163	35	1	15	(4	11)	245	75	82	86	40	3	51	1	2	4	5	5	.50	13	.280	.325	.421
2006	Oak	AL	129	502	138	29	3	7	(1	6)	194	57	59	63	44	1	55	2	4	6	6	3	.67	18	.275	.332	.386
2007	Oak	AL	56	206	44	14	0	1	(0	1)	61	20	20	19	19	3	20	0	0	1	1	1	.50	4	.214	.279	.296
2008	2 Tms		110	402	111	25	4	6	(4	2)	162	45	49	49	32	3	45	0	1	1	2	4	.33	14	.276	.329	.403
2009	2 Tms	AL	67	187	52	9	0	4	(4	0)	73	16	23	22	15	3	21	0	1	3	3	2	.60	6	.278	.327	.390
2010	CWS	AL	107	327	78	17	2	8	(4	4)	123	30	31	33	32	3	36	0	0	0	1	3	.25	9	.239	.306	.376
08	Atl	NL	88	318	92	17	3	6	(4	2)	133	39	37	37	25	2	34	0	1	1	2	3	.40	13	.289	.340	.418
08	Bos	AL	22	84	19	8	1	0	(0	0)	29	6	12	12	7	1	11	0	0	0	0	1	.00	1	.226	.286	.345
09	Bos	AL	27	74	19	2	0	1	(1	0)	24	4	5	6	4	1	12	0	0	1	2	1	.67	1	.257	.291	.324
09	CWS	AL	40	113	33	7	0	3	(3	0)	49	12	18	16	11	2	9	0	1	2	1	1	.50	5	.292	.349	.434
	Postseason		17	70	16	5	0	1	(0	1)	24	7	2	3	2	0	10	0	0	0	0	0	-	4	.229	.250	.343
14 ML YEARS			1624	5933	1654	330	47	121	(56	65)	2441	755	663	791	509	34	691	12	29	44	95	60	.61	145	.279	.335	.411

George Kottaras

Bats: L **Throws:** R **Pos:** C-61; PH-3; 1B-2; RF-1   kah-TARR-iss   **Ht:** 6'0" **Wt:** 185 **Born:** 5/10/1983 **Age:** 28

Year	Team	Lg	G	AB	H	2B	3B	HR	(Hm	Rd)	TB	R	RBI	RC	TBB	IBB	SO	HBP	SH	SF	SB	CS	SB%	GDP	Avg	OBP	Slg
2008	Bos	AL	3	5	1	1	0	0	(0	0)	2	1	0	0	0	0	2	0	0	0	0	0	-	0	.200	.200	.400
2009	Bos	AL	45	93	22	11	0	1	(1	0)	36	15	10	10	11	0	25	0	0	3	0	0	-	1	.237	.308	.387
2010	Mil	NL	67	212	43	12	1	9	(5	4)	84	24	26	22	33	1	44	0	1	4	2	0	1.00	5	.203	.305	.396
3 ML YEARS			115	310	66	24	1	10	(6	4)	122	40	36	32	44	1	71	0	1	7	2	0	1.00	6	.213	.305	.394

Kevin Kouzmanoff

Bats: R **Throws:** R **Pos:** 3B-142; PH-1   KOOZ-man-off   **Ht:** 6'1" **Wt:** 210 **Born:** 7/25/1981 **Age:** 29

Year	Team	Lg	G	AB	H	2B	3B	HR	(Hm	Rd)	TB	R	RBI	RC	TBB	IBB	SO	HBP	SH	SF	SB	CS	SB%	GDP	Avg	OBP	Slg
2006	Cle	AL	16	56	12	2	0	3	(0	3)	23	4	11	7	5	0	12	0	0	0	0	0	-	3	.214	.279	.411
2007	SD	NL	145	484	133	30	2	18	(5	13)	221	57	74	69	32	2	94	10	2	6	1	0	1.00	6	.275	.329	.457
2008	SD	NL	154	624	162	31	4	23	(11	12)	270	71	84	70	23	3	139	15	0	6	0	0	-	14	.260	.299	.433
2009	SD	NL	141	529	135	31	1	18	(9	9)	222	50	88	64	27	3	106	11	0	6	1	0	1.00	25	.255	.302	.420
2010	Oak	AL	143	551	136	32	1	16	(5	11)	218	59	71	49	24	2	96	6	0	5	2	1	.67	20	.247	.283	.396
5 ML YEARS			599	2244	578	126	8	78	(30	48)	954	241	328	259	111	10	447	42	2	23	4	1	.80	71	.258	.302	.425

Erik Kratz

Bats: R **Throws:** R **Pos:** C-9   **Ht:** 6'4" **Wt:** 255 **Born:** 6/15/1980 **Age:** 31

Year	Team	Lg	G	AB	H	2B	3B	HR	(Hm	Rd)	TB	R	RBI	RC	TBB	IBB	SO	HBP	SH	SF	SB	CS	SB%	GDP	Avg	OBP	Slg
2002	MdHat	R+	44	142	39	5	0	4	(-	-)	56	20	11	17	6	1	32	3	0	0	0	1	.00	4	.275	.318	.394
2003	CtnWV	A	8	19	6	3	0	0	(-	-)	9	0	2	3	1	0	7	2	0	0	0	0	-	1	.316	.409	.474
2003	Auburn	A-	49	157	49	15	0	5	(-	-)	79	25	26	33	21	0	31	6	0	1	0	1	.00	2	.312	.411	.503
2003	NwHav	AA	1	4	0	0	0	0	(-	-)	0	0	0	0	0	0	1	0	0	0	0	0	-	0	.000	.000	.000
2004	Dnedin	A+	15	49	14	4	0	1	(-	-)	21	6	6	6	2	0	16	1	0	0	0	0	-	2	.286	.327	.429
2004	NHam	AA	4	9	3	1	0	0	(-	-)	4	1	0	2	2	0	2	1	0	0	0	0	-	0	.333	.500	.444
2004	Auburn	A-	10	39	12	6	0	0	(-	-)	18	5	10	5	1	0	8	0	0	1	0	0	-	2	.308	.317	.462
2005	NHam	AA	91	293	60	10	0	11	(-	-)	103	27	33	31	27	1	86	6	3	3	2	0	1.00	7	.205	.283	.352
2006	NHam	AA	72	258	58	10	0	6	(-	-)	86	34	27	26	16	0	54	8	1	1	1	0	1.00	6	.225	.290	.333
2006	Syrcse	AAA	12	40	10	2	0	1	(-	-)	15	12	7	5	5	0	4	0	0	2	0	0	-	0	.250	.319	.375
2007	NHam	AA	49	160	40	15	1	8	(-	-)	81	22	30	26	12	1	33	5	2	3	0	0	-	3	.250	.317	.506
2007	Syrcse	AAA	35	112	24	2	0	5	(-	-)	41	10	19	11	8	0	28	1	3	0	0	1	.00	2	.214	.273	.366
2008	NHam	AA	33	102	25	5	0	7	(-	-)	51	15	19	19	13	2	26	4	0	2	2	0	1.00	4	.245	.347	.500
2008	Syrcse	AAA	40	145	34	11	1	9	(-	-)	74	20	24	22	9	0	33	2	1	1	1	0	1.00	4	.234	.287	.510
2009	Indy	AAA	93	319	87	30	0	11	(-	-)	150	45	43	53	31	2	72	1	0	2	7	0	1.00	7	.273	.337	.470
2010	Indy	AAA	70	230	63	22	1	9	(-	-)	114	30	41	44	32	0	54	9	0	3	1	2	.33	9	.274	.380	.496
2010	Pit	NL	9	34	4	0	0	0	(0	0)	4	2	1	0	2	0	9	0	0	0	0	0	-	0	.118	.167	.118

Zach Kroenke

Pitches: L **Bats:** R **Pos:** RP-2; SP-1   KRONN-neck-ee   **Ht:** 6'3" **Wt:** 210 **Born:** 4/21/1984 **Age:** 27

			HOW MUCH HE PITCHED						WHAT HE GAVE UP											THE RESULTS						
Year	Team	Lg	G	GS	CG	GF	IP	BFP	H	R	ER	HR	SH	SF	HB	TBB	IBB	SO	WP	Bk	W	L	Pct	Sh	Sv-Op	Hld	ERC	ERA
2005	Yanks	R	1	1	0	0	2.0	10	4	2	1	0	0	0	0	0	0	2	1	0	0	1	.000	0	0--	-	7.48	4.50
2005	StsIsnd	A-	11	5	0	3	39.0	159	30	14	11	2	1	3	3	15	0	28	2	0	1	1	.500	0	2--	-	2.82	2.54
2006	Tampa	A+	4	4	0	0	14.0	74	23	19	13	0	0	1	0	8	0	8	0	0	0	3	.000	0	0--	-	7.56	8.36
2006	CtnSC	A	25	20	0	5	113.0	502	124	65	45	9	5	3	5	41	0	86	11	0	8	6	.571	0	0--	-	4.46	3.58
2007	Tampa	A+	29	0	0	5	43.2	188	34	16	11	2	3	2	1	19	3	33	2	0	2	2	.500	0	2--	-	2.54	2.27
2007	Trntn	AA	15	0	0	5	14.1	73	21	16	15	5	0	0	0	12	0	12	2	0	0	1	.000	0	2--	-	11.47	9.42
2008	Trntn	AA	36	0	0	9	42.2	182	28	16	15	4	5	3	1	26	0	42	3	0	6	0	1.000	0	1--	-	3.02	3.16

			HOW MUCH HE PITCHED						WHAT HE GAVE UP											THE RESULTS							
Year	Team	Lg	G	GS	CG	GF	IP	BFP	H	R	ER	HR	SH	SF	HB	TBB	IBB	SO	WP	Bk	W	L	Pct	Sh	Sv-Op	Hld	ERC	ERA
2008	S-WB	AAA	4	0	0	0	10.0	38	7	3	2	0	1	0	1	2	0	10	1	0	1	0	1.000	0	0- -	-	1.69	1.80
2009	S-WB	AAA	36	2	0	8	72.1	292	54	24	16	4	4	4	0	30	1	55	3	0	7	1	.875	0	4- -	-	2.53	1.99
2010	Reno	AAA	40	9	0	12	97.1	416	94	41	38	5	6	2	1	39	2	69	11	1	7	3	.700	0	2- -	-	3.56	3.51
2010	Ari	NL	3	1	0	0	6.2	32	9	5	5	2	1	0	0	4	0	2	0	0	1	0	1.000	0	0-0	0	8.86	6.75

Jason Kubel

Bats: L **Throws:** R **Pos:** RF-83; DH-42; LF-16; PH-5   KOO-bull   **Ht:** 6'0" **Wt:** 210 **Born:** 5/25/1982 **Age:** 29

			BATTING																BASERUNNING				AVERAGES		
Year	Team	Lg	G	AB	H	2B	3B	HR	(Hm | Rd)	TB	R	RBI	RC	TBB	IBB	SO	HBP	SH	SF	SB	CS	SB%	GDP	Avg	OBP	Slg
2004	Min	AL	23	60	18	2	0	2	(0 | 2)	26	10	7	13	6	0	9	0	0	1	1	1	.50	0	.300	.358	.433
2006	Min	AL	73	220	53	8	0	8	(3 | 5)	85	23	26	20	12	0	45	0	2	1	2	0	1.00	13	.241	.279	.386
2007	Min	AL	128	418	114	31	2	13	(6 | 7)	188	49	65	64	41	2	79	1	1	5	5	0	1.00	9	.273	.335	.450
2008	Min	AL	141	463	126	22	5	20	(9 | 11)	218	74	78	66	47	2	91	0	0	7	0	1	.00	12	.272	.335	.471
2009	Min	AL	146	514	154	35	2	28	(15 | 13)	277	73	103	95	56	9	106	3	0	5	1	1	.50	13	.300	.369	.539
2010	Min	AL	143	518	129	23	3	21	(8 | 13)	221	68	92	65	56	5	116	3	0	5	0	1	.00	16	.249	.323	.427
	Postseason		5	21	2	1	0	0	(0 | 0)	3	0	0	0	0	0	11	0	0	0	0	0	-	0	.095	.095	.143
	6 ML YEARS		654	2193	594	121	12	92	(41 | 51)	1015	297	371	323	218	18	446	7	3	24	9	4	.69	63	.271	.335	.463

Hong-Chih Kuo

Pitches: L **Bats:** L **Pos:** RP-56   KWO   **Ht:** 6'2" **Wt:** 241 **Born:** 7/23/1981 **Age:** 29

			HOW MUCH HE PITCHED						WHAT HE GAVE UP											THE RESULTS							
Year	Team	Lg	G	GS	CG	GF	IP	BFP	H	R	ER	HR	SH	SF	HB	TBB	IBB	SO	WP	Bk	W	L	Pct	Sh	Sv-Op	Hld	ERC	ERA
2010	InldEm*	A+	2	1	0	0	2.0	6	0	0	0	0	0	0	0	0	0	3	0	0	0	0	-	0	0- -	-	0.00	0.00
2005	LAD	NL	9	0	0	0	5.1	26	5	4	4	1	0	0	0	5	1	10	0	1	0	1	.000	0	0-1	3	6.10	6.75
2006	LAD	NL	28	5	0	6	59.2	258	54	30	28	3	2	1	1	33	5	71	2	0	1	5	.167	0	0-0	2	3.76	4.22
2007	LAD	NL	8	6	0	1	30.1	140	35	26	25	3	1	1	1	14	0	27	1	0	1	4	.200	0	0-0	0	5.25	7.42
2008	LAD	NL	42	3	0	10	80.0	323	60	21	19	4	4	1	3	21	2	96	1	1	5	3	.625	0	1-3	12	2.05	2.14
2009	LAD	NL	35	0	0	2	30.0	124	21	10	10	2	3	0	2	13	2	32	5	0	2	0	1.000	0	0-1	14	2.54	3.00
2010	LAD	NL	56	0	0	16	60.0	229	29	8	8	1	1	1	1	18	0	73	3	1	3	2	.600	0	12-13	21	1.07	1.20
	Postseason		9	1	0	2	12.1	47	10	4	4	1	1	0	0	2	1	15	1	0	1	1	.500	0	0-0	3	2.08	2.92
	6 ML YEARS		178	14	0	35	265.1	1100	204	99	94	14	11	4	8	104	10	309	12	3	12	15	.444	0	13-18	52	2.55	3.19

Hiroki Kuroda

Pitches: R **Bats:** R **Pos:** SP-31   **Ht:** 6'1" **Wt:** 215 **Born:** 2/10/1975 **Age:** 36

			HOW MUCH HE PITCHED						WHAT HE GAVE UP											THE RESULTS							
Year	Team	Lg	C	GS	CG	GF	IP	BFP	H	R	ER	HR	SH	SF	HB	TBB	IBB	SO	WP	Bk	W	L	Pct	Sh	Sv-Op	Hld	ERC	ERA
2008	LAD	NL	31	31	2	0	183.1	776	181	85	76	13	7	5	7	42	8	116	5	0	9	10	.474	2	0-0	0	3.18	3.73
2009	LAD	NL	21	20	0	0	117.1	485	110	59	49	12	7	1	1	24	1	87	5	0	8	7	.533	0	0-0	0	2.98	3.76
2010	LAD	NL	31	31	0	0	196.1	810	180	87	74	15	9	7	5	48	13	159	12	0	11	13	.458	0	0-0	0	2.87	3.39
	Postseason		3	3	0	0	13.2	60	17	8	8	1	1	0	0	3	1	8	0	0	2	1	.667	0	0-0	0	4.39	5.27
	3 ML YEARS		83	82	2	0	497.0	2071	471	231	199	40	23	13	13	114	22	362	22	0	28	30	.483	2	0-0	0	3.01	3.60

John Lackey

Pitches: R **Bats:** R **Pos:** SP-33   **Ht:** 6'6" **Wt:** 245 **Born:** 10/23/1978 **Age:** 32

			HOW MUCH HE PITCHED						WHAT HE GAVE UP											THE RESULTS							
Year	Team	Lg	G	GS	CG	GF	IP	BFP	H	R	ER	HR	SH	SF	HB	TBB	IBB	SO	WP	Bk	W	L	Pct	Sh	Sv-Op	Hld	ERC	ERA
2002	LAA	AL	18	18	1	0	108.1	465	113	52	44	10	0	4	4	33	0	69	7	2	9	4	.692	0	0-0	0	4.03	3.66
2003	LAA	AL	33	33	2	0	204.0	885	223	117	105	31	2	6	10	66	4	151	11	1	10	16	.385	2	0-0	0	4.88	4.63
2004	LAA	AL	33	32	1	0	198.1	855	215	108	103	22	9	4	8	60	4	144	11	1	14	13	.519	1	0-0	0	4.39	4.67
2005	LAA	AL	33	33	1	0	209.0	892	208	85	80	13	1	2	11	71	3	199	18	0	14	5	.737	0	0-0	0	3.76	3.44
2006	LAA	AL	33	33	3	0	217.2	922	203	98	86	14	8	6	9	72	4	190	16	0	13	11	.542	2	0-0	0	3.31	3.56
2007	LAA	AL	33	33	2	0	224.0	929	219	87	75	18	1	1	12	52	2	179	9	1	19	9	.679	2	0-0	0	3.40	**3.01**
2008	LAA	AL	24	24	3	0	163.1	675	161	71	68	26	5	1	10	40	1	130	5	0	12	5	.706	0	0-0	0	4.10	3.75
2009	LAA	AL	27	27	1	0	176.1	748	177	84	75	17	0	10	0	47	1	139	6	0	11	8	.579	1	0-0	0	3.73	3.83
2010	Bos	AL	33	33	0	0	215.0	930	233	114	105	18	4	5	9	72	2	156	3	0	14	11	.560	0	0-0	0	4.37	4.40
	Postseason		14	12	0	0	78.0	328	75	29	27	4	2	3	1	29	4	53	4	0	3	4	.429	0	0-0	0	3.43	3.12
	9 ML YEARS		267	266	14	0	1716.0	7301	1752	816	741	169	39	39	82	513	21	1357	86	5	116	82	.586	8	0-0	0	3.98	3.89

Aaron Laffey

Pitches: L **Bats:** L **Pos:** RP-24; SP-5   LAFF-ee   **Ht:** 6'0" **Wt:** 200 **Born:** 4/15/1985 **Age:** 26

			HOW MUCH HE PITCHED						WHAT HE GAVE UP											THE RESULTS							
Year	Team	Lg	G	GS	CG	GF	IP	BFP	H	R	ER	HR	SH	SF	HB	TBB	IBB	SO	WP	Bk	W	L	Pct	Sh	Sv-Op	Hld	ERC	ERA
2010	Clmbs*	AAA	10	4	0	1	27.0	124	29	11	11	1	2	2	0	16	0	12	1	0	0	1	.000	0	0- -	-	4.74	3.67
2010	Lk Cty*	A	2	1	0	0	2.0	8	2	1	1	1	0	0	0	0	0	3	0	0	0	0	-	0	0- -	-	4.70	4.50
2010	Akron*	AA	1	0	0	0	1.0	3	1	0	0	0	0	0	0	0	0	0	0	0	0	0	-	0	0- -	-	2.79	0.00
2007	Cle	AL	9	9	0	0	49.1	207	54	26	25	2	1	2	4	12	0	25	2	1	4	2	.667	0	0-0	0	4.02	4.56
2008	Cle	AL	16	16	0	0	93.2	409	103	52	44	10	2	0	9	31	1	43	5	1	5	7	.417	0	0-0	0	4.86	4.23
2009	Cle	AL	25	19	0	3	121.2	539	140	69	60	9	0	4	2	57	1	59	1	1	7	9	.438	0	1-1	0	5.20	4.44
2010	Cle	AL	29	5	0	1	55.2	253	62	30	28	1	0	3	2	28	1	28	1	0	2	3	.400	0	0-0	5	4.61	4.53
	Postseason		1	0	0	0	4.2	16	1	0	0	0	0	0	0	1	0	3	0	0	0	0	-	0	0-0	0	0.30	0.00
	4 ML YEARS		79	49	0	4	320.1	1408	359	177	157	22	3	9	17	128	3	155	9	3	18	21	.462	0	1-1	5	4.81	4.41

Gerald Laird

Bats: R **Throws:** R **Pos:** C-87; PH-8; PR-2   **Ht:** 6'1" **Wt:** 225 **Born:** 11/13/1979 **Age:** 31

Year	Team	Lg	G	AB	H	2B	3B	HR	(Hm	Rd)	TB	R	RBI	RC	TBB	IBB	SO	HBP	SH	SF	SB	CS	SB%	GDP	Avg	OBP	Slg
2003	Tex	AL	19	44	12	2	1	1	(0	1)	19	9	4	5	5	0	11	1	0	0	0	0	-	2	.273	.360	.432
2004	Tex	AL	49	147	33	6	0	1	(1	0)	42	20	16	11	12	0	35	2	4	3	0	1	.00	5	.224	.287	.286
2005	Tex	AL	13	40	9	2	0	1	(0	1)	14	7	4	4	2	0	7	0	0	0	0	0	-	0	.225	.262	.350
2006	Tex	AL	78	243	72	20	1	7	(3	4)	115	46	22	24	12	0	54	2	1	2	3	1	.75	7	.296	.332	.473
2007	Tex	AL	120	407	91	18	3	9	(6	3)	142	48	47	45	30	1	103	2	5	4	6	2	.75	3	.224	.278	.349
2008	Tex	AL	95	344	95	24	0	6	(3	3)	137	54	41	46	23	2	63	6	4	4	2	4	.33	5	.276	.329	.398
2009	Det	AL	135	413	93	23	2	4	(1	3)	132	49	33	41	40	0	68	10	10	4	5	0	1.00	11	.225	.306	.320
2010	Det	AL	89	270	56	11	0	5	(2	3)	82	22	25	22	18	0	57	3	6	2	3	1	.75	7	.207	.263	.304
	8 ML YEARS		598	1908	461	106	7	34	(16	18)	683	255	192	198	142	3	398	26	30	19	19	9	.68	41	.242	.300	.358

Mike Lamb

Bats: L **Throws:** R **Pos:** PH-38; 1B-1   **Ht:** 6'1" **Wt:** 207 **Born:** 8/9/1975 **Age:** 35

Year	Team	Lg	G	AB	H	2B	3B	HR	(Hm	Rd)	TB	R	RBI	RC	TBB	IBB	SO	HBP	SH	SF	SB	CS	SB%	GDP	Avg	OBP	Slg
2010	NewOr*	AAA	60	213	68	7	0	7	(-	-)	96	36	42	38	21	1	17	3	0	2	0	0	-	9	.319	.385	.451
2000	Tex	AL	138	493	137	25	2	6	(4	2)	184	65	47	59	34	6	60	4	5	2	0	2	.00	10	.278	.328	.373
2001	Tex	AL	76	284	87	18	0	4	(1	3)	117	42	35	40	14	1	27	5	1	2	2	1	.67	6	.306	.348	.412
2002	Tex	AL	115	314	89	13	0	9	(7	2)	129	54	33	46	33	5	48	3	2	3	0	0	-	7	.283	.354	.411
2003	Tex	AL	28	38	5	0	0	0	(0	0)	5	3	2	0	2	0	7	1	0	1	1	0	1.00	1	.132	.190	.132
2004	Hou	NL	112	278	80	14	3	14	(8	6)	142	38	58	51	31	3	63	0	0	3	1	1	.50	4	.288	.356	.511
2005	Hou	NL	125	322	76	13	5	12	(4	8)	135	41	53	38	22	1	65	1	0	4	1	1	.50	10	.236	.284	.419
2006	Hou	NL	126	381	117	22	3	12	(5	7)	181	70	45	52	35	6	55	0	0	5	2	4	.33	10	.307	.361	.475
2007	Hou	NL	124	311	90	14	2	11	(5	6)	141	45	40	48	36	5	45	3	1	2	0	0	-	5	.289	.366	.453
2008	2 Tms		92	247	58	12	3	1	(0	1)	79	22	32	29	17	4	33	0	0	8	0	1	.00	3	.235	.276	.320
2010	Fla	NL	39	38	7	1	1	0	(0	0)	10	2	4	3	2	0	6	0	0	0	0	0	-	0	.184	.225	.263
08	Min	AL	81	236	55	12	3	1	(0	1)	76	20	32	28	17	4	32	0	0	8	0	1	.00	3	.233	.276	.322
08	Mil	NL	11	11	3	0	0	0	(0	0)	3	2	0	1	0	0	1	0	0	0	0	0	-	0	.273	.273	.273
	Postseason		16	40	10	2	0	5	(2	3)	27	7	7	5	5	3	7	0	0	1	0	0	-	1	.250	.326	.675
	10 ML YEARS		975	2706	746	132	19	69	(34	35)	1123	382	349	366	226	31	409	17	9	30	7	10	.41	56	.276	.332	.415

Ryan Langerhans

Bats: L **Throws:** L **Pos:** LF-30; PH-11; RF-8; PR-8; 1B-6; DH-3; CF-2   LANG-err-hans   **Ht:** 6'3" **Wt:** 220 **Born:** 2/20/1980 **Age:** 31

Year	Team	Lg	G	AB	H	2B	3B	HR	(Hm	Rd)	TB	R	RBI	RC	TBB	IBB	SO	HBP	SH	SF	SB	CS	SB%	GDP	Avg	OBP	Slg
2010	Tacom*	AAA	12	39	11	5	0	0	(-	-)	16	8	3	7	7	0	11	0	2	0	3	1	.75	0	.282	.391	.410
2002	Atl	NL	1	1	0	0	0	0	(0	0)	0	0	0	0	0	0	0	0	0	0	0	0	-	0	.000	.000	.000
2003	Atl	NL	16	15	4	0	0	0	(0	0)	4	2	0	1	0	0	6	0	0	0	0	0	-	1	.267	.267	.267
2005	Atl	NL	128	326	87	22	3	8	(3	5)	139	48	42	53	37	3	75	5	2	3	0	2	.00	2	.267	.348	.426
2006	Atl	NL	131	315	76	16	3	7	(3	4)	119	46	28	45	50	8	91	3	0	1	1	2	.33	9	.241	.350	.378
2007	3 Tms		125	210	35	7	2	6	(1	5)	64	27	23	22	29	2	81	2	1	2	3	1	.75	4	.167	.272	.305
2008	Was	NL	73	111	26	5	2	3	(1	2)	44	17	12	18	25	1	31	1	2	0	2	0	1.00	1	.234	.380	.396
2009	Sea	AL	38	101	22	6	1	3	(2	1)	39	12	10	11	14	1	28	1	3	3	0	1	.00	0	.218	.311	.386
2010	Sea	AL	60	107	21	2	1	3	(1	2)	34	16	4	11	24	1	51	0	1	0	4	1	.80	0	.196	.344	.318
07	Atl	NL	20	44	3	1	0	0	(0	0)	4	3	1	0	6	1	16	1	0	1	0	1	.00	3	.068	.192	.091
07	Oak	AL	2	4	0	0	0	0	(0	0)	0	0	0	0	1	0	2	0	0	0	0	0	-	0	.000	.200	.000
07	Was	NL	103	162	32	6	2	6	(1	5)	60	24	22	22	22	1	63	1	1	1	3	0	1.00	1	.198	.296	.370
	Postseason		4	12	4	1	0	0	(0	0)	5	1	0	2	3	1	3	1	0	0	1	0	1.00	0	.333	.500	.417
	8 ML YEARS		572	1186	271	58	12	30	(11	19)	443	168	119	161	179	16	363	12	9	9	10	7	.59	17	.228	.333	.374

John Lannan

Pitches: L **Bats:** L **Pos:** SP-25   **Ht:** 6'4" **Wt:** 215 **Born:** 9/27/1984 **Age:** 26

Year	Team	Lg	G	GS	CG	GF	IP	BFP	H	R	ER	HR	SH	SF	HB	TBB	IBB	SO	WP	Bk	W	L	Pct	Sh	Sv-Op	Hld	ERC	ERA
2010	Hrsbrg*	AA	7	7	0	0	40.2	178	49	25	19	2	4	4	0	10	0	28	0	0	1	4	.200	0	0	-	4.92	4.20
2007	Was	NL	6	6	0	0	34.2	153	36	17	16	3	2	0	2	17	1	10	1	0	2	2	.500	0	0-0	0	4.82	4.15
2008	Was	NL	31	31	0	0	182.0	779	172	89	79	23	13	5	7	72	1	117	6	2	9	15	.375	0	0-0	0	4.09	3.91
2009	Was	NL	33	33	2	0	206.1	875	210	100	89	22	12	1	6	68	5	89	3	0	9	13	.409	1	0-0	0	4.07	3.88
2010	Was	NL	25	25	0	0	143.1	643	175	82	74	14	5	5	4	49	3	71	1	0	8	8	.500	0	0-0	0	5.18	4.65
	4 ML YEARS		95	95	2	0	566.1	2450	593	288	258	62	32	11	19	206	10	287	11	2	28	38	.424	1	0-0	0	4.40	4.10

Matt LaPorta

Bats: R **Throws:** R **Pos:** 1B-93; DH-8; LF-7; PH-2   lah-POR-tah   **Ht:** 6'2" **Wt:** 210 **Born:** 1/8/1985 **Age:** 26

Year	Team	Lg	G	AB	H	2B	3B	HR	(Hm	Rd)	TB	R	RBI	RC	TBB	IBB	SO	HBP	SH	SF	SB	CS	SB%	GDP	Avg	OBP	Slg
2007	Helena	R+	7	27	7	1	0	2	(-	-)	14	4	4	4	1	0	8	0	0	0	0	0	-	2	.259	.286	.519
2007	WV	A	23	88	28	8	0	10	(-	-)	66	18	27	23	7	1	22	5	0	2	0	1	.00	2	.318	.392	.750
2008	Hntsvl	AA	84	302	87	23	2	20	(-	-)	174	56	66	71	45	3	63	15	0	4	2	1	.67	9	.288	.402	.576
2008	Akron	AA	17	60	14	1	0	2	(-	-)	21	6	8	6	4	1	12	2	0	1	0	0	-	1	.233	.299	.350
2009	Clmbs	AAA	93	338	101	23	2	17	(-	-)	179	63	60	69	42	1	57	9	1	3	1	3	.25	11	.299	.388	.530
2010	Clmbs	AAA	18	69	25	4	0	5	(-	-)	44	7	16	18	12	0	10	0	0	0	1	0	1.00	2	.362	.457	.638
2009	Cle	AL	52	181	46	13	0	7	(2	5)	80	29	21	24	12	0	37	3	0	2	2	0	1.00	6	.254	.308	.442
2010	Cle	AL	110	376	83	15	1	12	(9	3)	136	41	41	41	46	1	82	1	0	2	0	0	-	12	.221	.306	.362
	2 ML YEARS		162	557	129	28	1	19	(11	8)	216	70	62	66	58	1	119	4	0	4	2	0	1.00	18	.232	.307	.388

Jeff Larish

Bats: L Throws: R Pos: 1B-11; LF-7; 3B-5; DH-5; PH-4   Ht: 6'2" Wt: 200 Born: 10/11/1982 Age: 28

								BATTING													BASERUNNING				AVERAGES		
Year	Team	Lg	G	AB	H	2B	3B	HR	(Hm	Rd)	TB	R	RBI	RC	TBB	IBB	SO	HBP	SH	SF	SB	CS	SB%	GDP	Avg	OBP	Slg
2010	Toledo*	AAA	84	298	82	21	0	15	(-	-)	148	43	55	57	45	4	84	4	1	4	1	0	1.00	10	.275	.373	.497
2010	Scrmto*	AAA	8	36	13	2	0	5	(-	-)	30	8	19	10	3	0	9	0	0	0	0	1	.00	1	.361	.410	.833
2008	Det	AL	42	104	27	6	0	2	(1	1)	39	12	16	14	7	0	34	0	0	0	2	2	.50	2	.260	.306	.375
2009	Det	AL	32	74	16	3	1	4	(1	3)	33	13	7	5	15	0	25	0	0	1	1	0	.00	4	.216	.344	.446
2010	2 Tms	AL	27	67	12	3	0	2	(0	2)	21	5	9	5	7	0	24	1	0	0	1	0	1.00	1	.179	.267	.313
10	Det	AL	3	10	2	0	0	0	(0	0)	2	0	1	0	0	0	4	0	0	0	0	0	-	1	.200	.200	.200
10	Oak	AL	24	57	10	3	0	2	(0	2)	19	5	8	5	7	0	20	1	0	0	1	0	1.00	1	.175	.277	.333
	3 ML YEARS		101	245	55	12	1	8	(2	6)	93	30	32	24	29	0	83	1	0	1	3	3	.50	8	.224	.308	.380

Adam LaRoche

Bats: L Throws: L Pos: 1B-146; PH-6; DH-2   Ht: 6'3" Wt: 205 Born: 11/6/1979 Age: 31

								BATTING													BASERUNNING				AVERAGES		
Year	Team	Lg	G	AB	H	2B	3B	HR	(Hm	Rd)	TB	R	RBI	RC	TBB	IBB	SO	HBP	SH	SF	SB	CS	SB%	GDP	Avg	OBP	Slg
2004	Atl	NL	110	324	90	27	1	13	(7	6)	158	45	45	43	27	1	78	1	2	2	0	0	-	10	.278	.333	.488
2005	Atl	NL	141	451	117	28	0	20	(11	9)	205	53	78	63	39	7	87	4	2	6	0	2	.00	15	.259	.320	.455
2006	Atl	NL	149	492	140	38	1	32	(11	21)	276	89	90	83	55	5	128	2	1	7	0	2	.00	9	.285	.354	.561
2007	Pit	NL	152	563	153	42	0	21	(10	11)	258	71	88	84	62	5	131	3	0	4	1	1	.50	18	.272	.345	.458
2008	Pit	NL	136	492	133	32	3	25	(14	11)	246	66	85	76	54	7	122	2	0	6	1	1	.50	9	.270	.341	.500
2009	3 Tms	NL	150	555	154	38	2	25	(13	12)	271	78	83	84	69	12	142	0	0	5	2	2	.50	11	.277	.355	.488
2010	Ari	NL	151	560	146	37	2	25	(13	12)	262	75	100	84	48	4	172	3	0	4	0	1	.00	6	.261	.320	.468
09	Pit	NL	87	324	80	25	1	12	(7	5)	143	46	40	38	41	6	81	0	0	3	2	2	.50	9	.247	.329	.441
09	Bos	NL	6	19	5	2	0	1	(1	0)	10	2	3	3	0	0	2	0	0	0	0	0	-	1	.263	.263	.526
09	Atl	NL	57	212	69	11	1	12	(7	5)	118	30	40	43	28	6	59	0	0	2	0	0	-	1	.325	.401	.557
	Postseason		8	25	8	2	0	2	(0	2)	16	3	10	6	5	1	6	0	1	0	0	0	-	1	.320	.433	.640
	7 ML YEARS		989	3437	933	242	9	161	(81	80)	1676	477	569	517	354	41	860	15	5	34	4	9	.31	80	.271	.339	.488

Andy LaRoche

Bats: R Throws: R Pos: 3B-54; PH-41; 2B-6; 1B-2; DH-1   Ht: 6'1" Wt: 195 Born: 9/13/1983 Age: 27

								BATTING													BASERUNNING				AVERAGES		
Year	Team	Lg	G	AB	H	2B	3B	HR	(Hm	Rd)	TB	R	RBI	RC	TBB	IBB	SO	HBP	SH	SF	SB	CS	SB%	GDP	Avg	OBP	Slg
2007	LAD	NL	35	93	21	5	0	1	(0	1)	29	16	10	12	20	5	24	1	0	1	2	1	.67	1	.226	.365	.312
2008	2 Tms	NL	76	223	37	5	1	4	(1	4)	57	17	18	10	24	1	37	2	2	1	2	0	1.00	4	.166	.252	.256
2009	Pit	NL	150	524	135	29	5	12	(7	5)	210	64	64	64	50	1	84	8	6	2	3	1	.75	16	.258	.330	.401
2010	Pit	NL	102	247	51	8	0	4	(2	2)	71	26	16	17	19	0	43	2	2	1	1	1	.50	7	.206	.268	.287
08	LAD	NL	27	59	12	1	0	2	(0	2)	19	6	6	3	10	0	7	0	0	0	0	0	-	1	.203	.319	.322
08	Pit	NL	49	164	25	4	0	3	(1	2)	38	11	12	7	14	1	30	2	2	1	2	0	1.00	3	.152	.227	.232
	4 ML YEARS		363	1087	244	47	5	22	(10	12)	367	123	108	103	113	7	188	13	10	5	8	3	.73	32	.224	.304	.338

Jason LaRue

Bats: R Throws: R Pos: C-28; PH-2; 1B-1   loh RUE   Ht: 5'11" Wt: 205 Born: 3/19/1974 Age: 37

								BATTING													BASERUNNING				AVERAGES		
Year	Team	Lg	G	AB	H	2B	3B	HR	(Hm	Rd)	TB	R	RBI	RC	TBB	IBB	SO	HBP	SH	SF	SB	CS	SB%	GDP	Avg	OBP	Slg
1999	Cin	NL	36	90	19	7	0	3	(1	2)	35	12	10	10	11	1	32	2	0	0	4	1	.80	4	.211	.311	.389
2000	Cin	NL	31	98	23	3	0	5	(1	4)	41	12	12	12	5	2	19	4	0	0	0	0	-	1	.235	.299	.418
2001	Cin	NL	121	364	86	21	2	12	(3	9)	147	39	43	42	27	4	106	9	1	2	3	3	.50	11	.236	.303	.404
2002	Cin	NL	113	353	88	17	1	12	(5	7)	143	42	52	44	27	6	117	13	2	2	1	2	.33	13	.249	.324	.405
2003	Cin	NL	118	379	87	23	1	16	(12	4)	160	52	50	47	33	4	111	20	1	4	3	3	.50	9	.230	.321	.422
2004	Cin	NL	114	390	98	24	2	14	(3	11)	168	46	55	53	26	5	108	24	2	3	2	0	1.00	7	.251	.334	.431
2005	Cin	NL	110	361	94	27	0	14	(6	8)	163	38	60	63	41	7	101	13	5	2	0	0	-	8	.260	.355	.452
2006	Cin	NL	72	191	37	5	0	8	(5	3)	66	22	21	17	27	9	51	8	3	1	1	0	1.00	6	.194	.317	.346
2007	KC	AL	66	169	25	9	0	4	(2	2)	46	14	13	7	17	0	66	4	1	2	1	0	1.00	6	.148	.240	.272
2008	StL	NL	61	164	35	8	1	4	(1	3)	57	17	21	17	15	1	20	5	3	2	0	0	-	6	.213	.296	.348
2009	StL	NL	51	104	25	3	0	2	(1	1)	34	10	6	7	3	0	22	4	1	0	1	0	1.00	3	.240	.288	.327
2010	StL	NL	29	56	11	1	0	2	(1	1)	18	3	5	1	5	0	7	1	1	0	0	0	-	3	.196	.274	.321
	Postseason		1	1	0	0	0	0	(0	0)	0	0	0	0	0	0	0	0	0	0	0	0	-	0	.000	.000	.000
	12 ML YEARS		922	2719	628	148	7	96	(41	55)	1078	307	348	319	237	39	760	107	22	18	14	11	.56	74	.231	.315	.396

Mat Latos

Pitches: R Bats: R Pos: SP-31   LAY-tos   Ht: 6'6" Wt: 225 Born: 12/9/1987 Age: 23

				HOW MUCH HE PITCHED						WHAT HE GAVE UP												THE RESULTS						
Year	Team	Lg	G	GS	CG	GF	IP	BFP	H	R	ER	HR	SH	SF	HB	TBB	IBB	SO	WP	Bk	W	L	Pct	Sh	Sv-Op	Hld	ERC	ERA
2007	Eugene	A-	16	13	0	0	56.1	246	58	30	24	1	1	1	4	22	0	74	8	4	1	4	.200	0	0--	-	3.90	3.83
2008	FtWyn	A	7	5	0	0	24.2	106	24	12	9	3	1	0	1	8	0	23	0	0	0	3	.000	0	0--	-	3.89	3.28
2008	Padres	R	5	3	0	0	14.0	56	12	5	5	0	0	0	2	2	0	23	2	0	1	0	1.000	0	0--	-	2.31	3.21
2008	Eugene	A-	3	3	0	0	17.1	70	13	3	2	1	0	0	1	3	0	23	2	1	2	0	1.000	0	0--	-	1.86	1.04
2009	FtWyn	A	4	2	0	1	25.1	86	10	1	1	1	0	0	1	3	0	27	0	0	3	0	1.000	0	0--	-	0.62	0.36
2009	SnAnt	AA	9	9	0	0	47.0	181	32	11	10	0	0	4	1	9	0	46	1	0	5	1	.833	0	0--	-	1.38	1.91
2009	SD	NL	10	10	0	0	50.2	212	43	29	26	7	3	1	0	23	1	39	0	2	4	5	.444	0	0-0	0	3.72	4.62
2010	SD	NL	31	31	1	0	184.2	748	150	63	60	16	4	1	2	50	3	189	5	1	14	10	.583	1	0-0	0	2.52	2.92
	2 ML YEARS		41	41	1	0	235.1	960	193	92	86	23	7	2	2	73	4	228	5	3	18	15	.545	1	0-0	0	2.77	3.29

Brandon League

Pitches: R Bats: R Pos: RP-70   **Ht: 6'2" Wt: 205 Born: 3/16/1983 Age: 28**

Year	Team	Lg	G	GS	CG	GF	IP	BFP	H	R	ER	HR	SH	SF	HB	TBB	IBB	SO	WP	Bk	W	L	Pct	Sh	Sv-Op	Hld	ERC	ERA
2004	Tor	AL	3	0	0	0	4.2	18	3	0	0	0	0	0	0	1	0	2	0	0	1	0	1.000	0	0-0	1	1.26	0.00
2005	Tor	AL	20	0	0	4	35.2	162	42	27	26	8	0	1	2	20	1	17	5	0	1	0	1.000	0	0-0	1	7.24	6.56
2006	Tor	AL	33	0	0	8	42.2	173	34	17	12	3	2	0	3	9	2	29	0	0	1	2	.333	0	1-4	12	2.30	2.53
2007	Tor	AL	14	0	0	2	11.2	58	19	8	8	1	0	1	0	7	0	7	3	0	0	-	-	0	0-1	0	8.98	6.17
2008	Tor	AL	31	0	0	8	33.0	141	28	9	8	2	1	0	3	15	2	23	2	0	1	2	.333	0	1-1	5	3.45	2.18
2009	Tor	AL	67	0	0	18	74.2	313	72	40	38	8	5	0	7	21	2	76	9	0	3	6	.333	0	0-3	9	3.85	4.58
2010	Sea	AL	70	0	0	30	79.0	326	67	38	30	7	4	1	2	27	6	56	7	0	9	7	.563	0	6-12	13	2.96	3.42
	7 ML YEARS		238	0	0	70	281.1	1191	265	139	122	29	12	3	17	100	13	210	26	0	16	17	.485	0	8-21	41	3.80	3.90

Mike Leake

Pitches: R Bats: R Pos: SP-22; RP-2   LEEK   **Ht: 6'1" Wt: 190 Born: 11/12/1987 Age: 23**

Year	Team	Lg	G	GS	CG	GF	IP	BFP	H	R	ER	HR	SH	SF	HB	TBB	IBB	SO	WP	Bk	W	L	Pct	Sh	Sv-Op	Hld	ERC	ERA
2010	Cin	NL	24	22	0	0	138.1	604	158	77	65	19	7	3	3	49	2	91	2	0	8	4	.667	0	0-0	0	5.12	4.23

Wade LeBlanc

Pitches: L Bats: L Pos: SP-25; RP-1   lah-BLAHNK   **Ht: 6'3" Wt: 202 Born: 8/7/1984 Age: 26**

Year	Team	Lg	G	GS	CG	GF	IP	BFP	H	R	ER	HR	SH	SF	HB	TBB	IBB	SO	WP	Bk	W	L	Pct	Sh	Sv-Op	Hld	ERC	ERA
2010	Portlnd*	AAA	2	2	0	0	10.0	45	13	8	8	1	1	0	0	1	0	15	0	0	1	0	1.000	0	0- -	-	4.35	7.20
2008	SD	NL	5	4	0	0	21.1	104	29	19	19	7	1	0	0	15	2	14	0	0	1	3	.250	0	0-0	0	9.57	8.02
2009	SD	NL	9	9	0	0	46.1	194	35	19	19	6	3	1	4	19	1	30	0	0	3	1	.750	0	0-0	0	3.28	3.69
2010	SD	NL	26	25	0	0	146.0	625	157	69	69	24	7	2	2	51	5	110	2	0	8	12	.400	0	0-0	0	4.84	4.25
	3 ML YEARS		40	38	0	0	213.2	923	221	107	107	37	11	3	6	85	8	154	2	0	12	16	.429	0	0-0	0	4.90	4.51

Sam LeCure

Pitches: R Bats: R Pos: RP-9; SP-6   **Ht: 6'1" Wt: 205 Born: 5/4/1984 Age: 27**

Year	Team	Lg	G	GS	CG	GF	IP	BFP	H	R	ER	HR	SH	SF	HB	TBB	IBB	SO	WP	Bk	W	L	Pct	Sh	Sv-Op	Hld	ERC	ERA
2005	Billings	R+	13	6	0	0	41.1	176	43	18	15	2	1	0	2	15	0	44	2	1	5	1	.833	0	0- -	-	4.07	3.27
2006	Srsota	A+	27	27	0	0	141.2	592	130	63	54	12	2	4	6	46	0	115	7	0	7	12	.368	0	0- -	-	3.42	3.43
2007	Chatt	AA	21	21	0	0	110.0	482	119	55	51	12	3	5	4	46	0	104	1	0	7	5	.583	0	0- -	-	4.90	4.17
2007	Srsota	A+	1	1	0	0	5.0	17	2	1	1	0	0	1	0	0	0	8	0	0	1	0	1.000	0	0- -	-	0.35	1.80
2008	Chatt	AA	27	27	0	0	155.1	660	146	61	59	12	6	3	6	58	2	128	3	0	9	7	.563	0	0- -	-	3.69	3.42
2009	Lsvlle	AAA	25	25	0	0	143.1	605	143	76	71	17	6	6	7	44	0	125	4	0	10	8	.556	0	0- -	-	4.07	4.46
2010	Lsvlle	AAA	15	15	1	0	98.0	403	98	40	40	8	0	0	6	23	0	87	3	0	8	3	.727	1	0- -	-	3.64	3.67
2010	Cin	NL	15	6	0	4	48.0	217	50	24	24	6	1	2	5	25	3	37	1	0	2	5	.286	0	0-0	0	5.36	4.50

Wil Ledezma

Pitches: L Bats: L Pos: RP-27   **Ht: 6'4" Wt: 227 Born: 1/21/1981 Age: 30**

Year	Team	Lg	G	GS	CG	GF	IP	BFP	H	R	ER	HR	SH	SF	HB	TBB	IBB	SO	WP	Bk	W	L	Pct	Sh	Sv-Op	Hld	ERC	ERA
2010	Indy*	AAA	35	0	0	16	38.1	148	20	6	4	1	0	0	1	19	0	50	1	0	0	1	.000	0	8- -	-	1.72	0.94
2003	Det	AL	34	8	0	13	84.0	376	99	55	54	12	1	4	3	35	3	49	2	0	3	7	.300	0	0-1	1	5.67	5.79
2004	Det	AL	15	8	0	0	53.1	225	55	28	26	3	0	3	2	18	0	29	3	1	4	3	.571	0	0-1	0	3.94	4.39
2005	Det	AL	10	10	0	0	49.2	234	61	46	39	10	3	4	2	24	0	30	2	2	2	4	.333	0	0-0	0	6.66	7.07
2006	Det	AL	24	7	0	2	60.1	264	60	28	24	5	2	1	2	23	0	39	2	0	3	3	.500	0	0-1	2	3.92	3.58
2007	3 Tms		44	1	0	13	59.1	280	70	42	37	7	2	3	0	38	4	47	3	2	3	3	.500	0	0-2	4	6.13	5.61
2008	2 Tms	NL	28	6	0	8	58.1	266	51	29	27	4	4	4	3	41	2	53	4	0	0	2	.000	0	0-0	0	4.41	4.17
2009	Was	NL	5	0	0	2	5.2	30	8	7	6	1	0	2	0	4	0	8	1	0	0	0	-	0	0-0	0	8.09	9.53
2010	Pit	NL	27	0	0	4	19.2	92	25	16	15	2	0	0	1	6	0	22	1	0	0	3	.000	0	0-0	3	5.29	6.86
07	Det	AL	23	0	0	5	35.2	166	38	21	19	4	2	1	0	26	2	24	3	2	3	1	.750	0	0-2	2	5.83	4.79
07	Atl	NL	12	0	0	4	9.1	45	12	10	8	1	0	1	0	8	2	7	0	0	0	2	.000	0	0-0	2	5.64	7.71
07	SD	NL	9	1	0	4	14.1	69	20	11	10	2	0	1	0	4	0	16	0	0	0	0	-	0	0-0	0	7.23	6.28
08	SD	NL	25	6	0	6	54.1	249	49	29	27	4	4	4	3	38	2	49	4	0	0	2	.000	0	0-0	0	4.61	4.47
08	Ari	NL	3	0	0	2	4.0	17	2	0	0	0	0	0	0	3	0	4	0	0	0	0	-	0	0-0	0	2.03	0.00
	Postseason		4	0	0	1	4.0	17	4	1	1	1	0	0	0	1	0	2	0	0	1	0	1.000	0	0-0	1	4.38	2.25
	8 ML YEARS		187	40	0	43	390.1	1767	429	251	228	44	12	21	13	189	9	277	18	5	15	25	.375	0	0-5	10	5.16	5.26

Carlos Lee

Bats: R Throws: R Pos: LF-133; 1B-20; DH-7   **Ht: 6'2" Wt: 266 Born: 6/20/1976 Age: 35**

Year	Team	Lg	G	AB	H	2B	3B	HR	(Hm	Rd)	TB	R	RBI	RC	TBB	IBB	SO	HBP	SH	SF	SB	CS	SB%	GDP	Avg	OBP	Slg
1999	CWS	AL	127	492	144	32	2	16	(10	6)	228	66	84	68	13	0	72	4	1	7	4	2	.67	11	.293	.312	.463
2000	CWS	AL	152	572	172	29	2	24	(12	12)	277	107	92	91	38	1	94	3	1	5	13	4	.76	17	.301	.345	.484
2001	CWS	AL	150	558	150	33	3	24	(12	12)	261	75	84	81	38	2	85	6	1	2	17	7	.71	15	.269	.321	.468
2002	CWS	AL	140	492	130	26	2	26	(14	12)	238	82	80	86	75	4	73	2	0	7	1	4	.20	5	.264	.359	.484
2003	CWS	AL	158	623	181	35	1	31	(18	13)	311	100	113	105	37	2	91	4	0	7	18	4	.82	20	.291	.331	.499
2004	CWS	AL	153	591	180	37	0	31	(17	14)	310	103	99	112	54	3	86	7	0	6	11	5	.69	10	.305	.366	.525
2005	Mil	NL	162	618	164	41	4	32	(15	17)	301	85	114	98	57	7	87	2	0	11	13	4	.76	8	.265	.324	.487
2006	2 Tms		161	624	187	37	1	37	(15	22)	337	102	116	113	58	6	65	2	0	11	19	2	.90	22	.300	.355	.540
2007	Hou	NL	162	627	190	43	1	32	(17	15)	331	93	119	104	53	10	63	4	0	13	10	5	.67	27	.303	.354	.528

			BATTING																	BASERUNNING				AVERAGES		
Year Team	Lg	G	AB	H	2B	3B	HR	(Hm	Rd)	TB	R	RBI	RC	TBB	IBB	SO	HBP	SH	SF	SB	CS	SB%	GDP	Avg	OBP	Slg
2008 Hou	NL	115	436	137	27	0	28	(11	17)	248	61	100	85	37	7	49	3	0	5	4	1	.80	8	.314	.368	.569
2009 Hou	NL	160	610	183	35	1	26	(16	10)	298	65	102	85	41	5	51	3	0	8	5	3	.63	21	.300	.343	.489
2010 Hou	NL	157	605	149	29	1	24	(16	8)	252	67	89	75	37	1	59	3	0	4	3	3	.50	20	.246	.291	.417
06 Mil	NL	102	388	111	18	0	28	(10	18)	213	60	81	75	38	4	39	2	0	7	12	2	.86	13	.286	.347	.549
06 Tex	AL	59	236	76	19	1	9	(5	4)	124	42	35	38	20	2	26	0	0	4	7	0	1.00	9	.322	.369	.525
Postseason		3	11	1	1	0	0	(0	0)	2	0	1	0	0	0	2	0	0	1	0	0	-	0	.091	.083	.182
12 ML YEARS		1797	6848	1967	404	14	331	(173	158)	3392	1006	1192	1103	538	48	875	43	3	86	118	44	.73	184	.287	.339	.495

Cliff Lee

Pitches: L **Bats:** L **Pos:** SP-28   **Ht:** 6'3" **Wt:** 190 **Born:** 8/30/1978 **Age:** 32

		HOW MUCH HE PITCHED						WHAT HE GAVE UP											THE RESULTS						
Year Team	Lg	G	GS	CG	GF	IP	BFP	H	R	ER	HR	SH	SF	HB	TBB	IBB	SO	WP	Bk	W	L	Pct	Sh	Sv-Op	Hld	ERC	ERA
2010 Tacom*	AAA	1	1	0	0	6.0	20	3	0	0	0	1	0	0	0	0	4	0	0	0	0	-	0	0- -	-	0.57	0.00
2002 Cle	AL	2	2	0	0	10.1	44	6	2	2	0	1	0	0	8	1	6	0	1	0	1	.000	0	0-0	0	2.38	1.74
2003 Cle	AL	9	9	0	0	52.1	210	41	28	21	7	1	1	2	20	1	44	3	0	3	3	.500	0	0-0	0	3.29	3.61
2004 Cle	AL	33	33	0	0	179.0	802	188	113	108	30	2	6	11	81	1	161	6	0	14	8	.636	0	0-0	0	5.31	5.43
2005 Cle	AL	32	32	1	0	202.0	838	194	91	85	22	5	7	0	52	1	143	4	0	18	5	.783	0	0-0	0	3.35	3.79
2006 Cle	AL	33	33	1	0	200.2	882	224	114	98	29	3	6	8	58	3	129	3	0	14	11	.560	0	0-0	0	4.69	4.40
2007 Cle	AL	20	16	1	1	97.1	443	112	73	68	17	3	2	7	36	1	66	5	0	5	8	.385	0	0-0	0	5.59	6.29
2008 Cle	AL	31	31	4	0	223.1	891	214	68	63	12	2	3	5	34	1	170	4	0	22	3	.880	2	0-0	0	2.75	2.54
2009 2 Tms		34	34	6	0	231.2	969	245	88	83	17	11	9	5	43	1	181	7	0	14	13	.519	2	0-0	0	3.45	3.22
2010 2 Tms		28	28	7	0	212.1	843	195	84	75	16	4	6	1	18	2	185	3	1	12	9	.571	1	0-0	0	2.31	3.18
09 Cle	AL	22	22	3	0	152.0	641	165	53	53	10	6	5	3	33	1	107	6	0	7	9	.438	1	0-0	0	3.68	3.14
09 Phi	NL	12	12	3	0	79.2	328	80	35	30	7	5	4	2	10	0	74	1	0	7	4	.636	1	0-0	0	3.03	3.39
10 Sea	AL	13	13	5	0	103.2	408	92	31	27	5	0	3	0	6	0	89	2	1	8	3	.727	1	0-0	0	1.91	2.34
10 Tex	AL	15	15	2	0	108.2	435	103	53	48	11	4	3	1	12	2	96	1	0	4	6	.400	0	0-0	0	2.71	3.90
Postseason		5	5	2	0	40.1	151	27	10	7	0	0	0	0	6	0	33	2	0	4	0	1.000	0	0-0	0	1.23	1.56
9 ML YEARS		222	218	20	1	1409.0	5922	1419	661	603	150	32	40	39	350	12	1085	35	2	102	61	.626	5	0-0	0	3.66	3.85

Derrek Lee

Bats: R **Throws:** R **Pos:** 1B-144; DH-3; PH-3   **Ht:** 6'5" **Wt:** 245 **Born:** 9/6/1975 **Age:** 35

			BATTING																	BASERUNNING				AVERAGES		
Year Team	Lg	G	AB	H	2B	3B	HR	(Hm	Rd)	TB	R	RBI	RC	TBB	IBB	SO	HBP	SH	SF	SB	CS	SB%	GDP	Avg	OBP	Slg
1997 SD	NL	22	54	14	3	0	1	(0	1)	20	9	4	8	9	0	24	0	0	0	0	0	-	1	.259	.365	.370
1998 Fla	NL	141	454	106	29	1	17	(4	13)	188	62	74	59	47	1	120	10	0	2	5	2	.71	12	.233	.318	.414
1999 Fla	NL	70	218	45	9	1	5	(0	5)	71	21	20	18	17	1	70	0	0	1	2	1	.67	3	.206	.263	.326
2000 Fla	NL	158	477	134	18	3	28	(9	19)	242	70	70	84	63	6	123	4	0	2	0	3	.00	14	.281	.368	.507
2001 Fla	NL	158	561	158	37	4	21	(8	13)	266	83	75	88	50	1	126	8	0	6	4	2	.67	18	.282	.346	.474
2002 Fla	NL	162	581	157	35	7	27	(9	18)	287	95	86	96	98	8	164	5	0	4	19	9	.68	14	.270	.378	.494
2003 Fla	NL	155	539	146	31	2	31	(11	20)	274	91	92	99	88	7	131	10	0	6	21	8	.72	9	.271	.379	.508
2004 ChC	NL	161	605	168	39	1	32	(18	14)	305	90	98	101	68	4	128	8	2	5	12	5	.71	14	.278	.356	.504
2005 ChC	NL	158	594	199	50	3	46	(24	22)	393	120	107	135	85	23	109	5	0	7	15	3	.83	12	.335	.418	.662
2006 ChC	NL	50	175	50	9	0	8	(5	3)	83	30	30	27	25	1	41	0	0	4	8	4	.67	11	.286	.368	.474
2007 ChC	NL	150	567	160	43	1	22	(10	12)	291	91	82	108	71	8	114	9	0	3	6	5	.55	15	.317	.400	.513
2008 ChC	NL	155	623	181	41	3	20	(15	5)	288	93	90	93	71	3	119	0	0	4	8	2	.80	27	.291	.361	.462
2009 ChC	NL	141	532	163	36	2	35	(20	15)	308	91	111	112	76	6	109	3	0	4	1	0	1.00	12	.306	.393	.579
2010 2 Tms	NL	148	547	142	35	0	19	(9	10)	234	80	80	71	73	1	134	2	0	4	1	3	.25	23	.260	.347	.428
10 ChC	NL	109	418	105	21	0	16	(7	9)	174	63	56	49	52	1	101	2	0	3	1	3	.25	16	.251	.335	.416
10 Atl	NL	39	129	37	14	0	3	(2	1)	60	17	24	22	21	0	33	0	0	1	0	0	-	7	.287	.384	.465
Postseason		23	95	25	6	0	1	(0	1)	34	9	8	6	5	0	23	3	0	0	2	0	1.00	5	.263	.320	.358
14 ML YEARS		1829	6527	1843	415	28	312	(148	164)	3250	1026	1019	1099	841	70	1512	64	2	52	102	47	.68	185	.282	.367	.498

Anthony Lerew

Pitches: R **Bats:** L **Pos:** SP-6   **Ht:** 6'4" **Wt:** 225 **Born:** 10/28/1982 **Age:** 28

		HOW MUCH HE PITCHED						WHAT HE GAVE UP											THE RESULTS						
Year Team	Lg	G	GS	CG	GF	IP	BFP	H	R	ER	HR	SH	SF	HB	TBB	IBB	SO	WP	Bk	W	L	Pct	Sh	Sv-Op	Hld	ERC	ERA
2010 Omha*	AAA	22	19	1	0	123.2	526	121	43	35	4	5	2	5	44	1	74	1	0	9	4	.692	1	0- -	-	3.48	2.55
2005 Atl	NL	7	0	0	4	8.0	37	9	5	5	1	1	0	0	5	2	5	0	0	0	0	-	0	0-1	0	5.47	5.63
2006 Atl	NL	1	0	0	0	2.0	15	5	5	5	0	0	0	1	3	0	1	0	0	0	0	-	0	0-0	0	20.57	22.50
2007 Atl	NL	3	3	0	0	11.2	57	14	10	10	4	3	0	0	7	1	9	1	0	0	2	.000	0	0-0	0	7.62	7.71
2009 KC	AL	3	2	0	0	13.1	62	14	8	6	4	0	1	0	8	0	7	0	0	0	1	.000	0	0-0	0	6.60	4.05
2010 KC	AL	6	6	0	0	26.1	120	34	25	25	9	0	3	2	9	0	18	1	0	1	4	.200	0	0-0	0	7.91	8.54
5 ML YEARS		20	11	0	4	61.1	291	76	53	51	18	4	4	3	32	3	40	2	0	1	7	.125	0	0-1	0	7.66	7.48

Chris Leroux

Pitches: R **Bats:** L **Pos:** RP-23   leh-RUE   **Ht:** 6'6" **Wt:** 226 **Born:** 4/14/1984 **Age:** 27

		HOW MUCH HE PITCHED						WHAT HE GAVE UP											THE RESULTS						
Year Team	Lg	G	GS	CG	GF	IP	BFP	H	R	ER	HR	SH	SF	HB	TBB	IBB	SO	WP	Bk	W	L	Pct	Sh	Sv-Op	Hld	ERC	ERA
2006 Grnsbr	A	3	3	0	0	10.1	50	13	7	7	2	2	0	2	6	0	9	0	0	0	3	.000	0	0- -	-	8.18	6.10
2006 Mrlns	R	4	4	0	0	11.0	45	10	9	5	0	2	0	2	1	0	9	2	0	0	0	-	0	0- -	-	2.48	4.09
2006 Jmstwn	A-	4	4	0	0	11.1	61	13	13	10	0	0	1	2	12	0	4	2	0	0	1	.000	0	0- -	-	7.30	7.94
2007 Grnsbr	A	46	0	0	8	71.2	316	72	38	33	6	3	3	5	29	3	76	4	1	2	3	.400	0	0- -	-	4.18	4.14
2008 Jupiter	A+	57	0	0	19	74.0	305	60	37	30	6	4	2	6	26	2	78	0	0	6	7	.462	0	1- -	-	3.05	3.65
2009 Jaxnvl	AA	46	0	0	11	60.0	250	59	19	18	0	2	1	1	17	1	55	2	0	5	3	.625	0	2- -	-	2.92	2.70
2010 NewOr	AAA	21	0	0	10	22.0	98	26	17	17	2	1	0	2	9	1	20	1	0	0	3	.000	0	1- -	-	5.13	6.95
2010 Jupiter	A+	2	0	0	0	2.2	12	2	1	1	0	0	0	1	1	0	0	0	0	0	0	-	0	0- -	-	3.21	3.38
2010 Mrlns	R	3	0	0	0	4.0	16	4	2	2	0	1	0	0	0	0	3	0	0	1	0	1.000	0	0- -	-	1.95	4.50

Year	Team	Lg	G	GS	CG	GF	IP	BFP	H	R	ER	HR	SH	SF	HB	TBB	IBB	SO	WP	Bk	W	L	Pct	Sh	Sv-Op	Hld	ERC	ERA
2009	Fla	NL	5	0	0	3	6.2	35	11	8	8	0	0	0	0	4	0	2	0	0	0	0	-	0	0-0	0	7.84	10.80
2010	2 Tms	NL	23	0	0	7	22.2	105	28	18	17	1	0	3	0	14	2	22	1	0	0	1	.000	0	0-2	3	5.86	6.75
10	Fla	NL	17	0	0	5	18.0	84	24	15	14	1	0	3	0	11	2	18	0	0	0	0	-	0	0-1	3	6.58	7.00
10	Pit	NL	6	0	0	2	4.2	21	4	3	3	0	0	0	0	3	0	4	1	0	0	1	.000	0	0-1	0	3.39	5.79
2 ML YEARS			28	0	0	10	29.1	140	39	26	25	1	0	3	0	18	2	24	1	0	0	1	.000	0	0-2	3	6.31	7.67

Jon Lester

Pitches: L **Bats:** L **Pos:** SP-32   **Ht:** 6'4" **Wt:** 240 **Born:** 1/7/1984 **Age:** 27

Year	Team	Lg	G	GS	CG	GF	IP	BFP	H	R	ER	HR	SH	SF	HB	TBB	IBB	SO	WP	Bk	W	L	Pct	Sh	Sv-Op	Hld	ERC	ERA
2006	Bos	AL	15	15	0	0	81.1	367	91	43	43	7	2	8	5	43	1	60	5	0	7	2	.778	0	0-0	0	5.52	4.76
2007	Bos	AL	12	11	0	0	63.0	275	61	33	32	10	1	5	1	31	0	50	1	0	4	0	1.000	0	0-0	0	4.78	4.57
2008	Bos	AL	33	33	2	0	210.1	874	202	78	75	14	6	3	10	66	1	152	3	1	16	6	.727	2	0-0	0	3.55	3.21
2009	Bos	AL	32	32	2	0	203.1	843	186	80	77	20	2	6	3	64	0	225	6	0	15	8	.652	0	0-0	0	3.35	3.41
2010	Bos	AL	32	32	2	0	208.0	861	167	81	75	14	4	6	10	83	0	225	6	0	19	9	.679	0	0-0	0	3.00	3.25
Postseason			8	6	0	2	42.0	175	34	14	12	5	2	0	0	13	0	39	0	0	2	3	.400	0	0-0	0	2.75	2.57
5 ML YEARS			124	123	6	0	766.0	3220	707	315	302	65	15	28	29	287	2	712	21	1	61	25	.709	2	0-0	0	3.64	3.55

Colby Lewis

Pitches: R **Bats:** R **Pos:** SP-32   **Ht:** 6'4" **Wt:** 230 **Born:** 8/2/1979 **Age:** 31

Year	Team	Lg	G	GS	CG	GF	IP	BFP	H	R	ER	HR	SH	SF	HB	TBB	IBB	SO	WP	Bk	W	L	Pct	Sh	Sv-Op	Hld	ERC	ERA
2002	Tex	AL	15	4	0	4	34.1	168	42	26	24	4	2	0	2	26	2	28	3	1	1	3	.250	0	0-2	1	7.22	6.29
2003	Tex	AL	26	26	0	0	127.0	594	163	104	103	23	2	2	5	70	1	88	5	0	10	9	.526	0	0-0	0	7.38	7.30
2004	Tex	AL	3	3	0	0	15.1	71	13	7	7	1	0	0	1	13	0	11	0	0	1	1	.500	0	0-0	0	4.98	4.11
2006	Det	AL	2	0	0	1	3.0	18	8	1	1	1	0	0	0	1	0	5	0	0	0	0	-	0	0-0	0	17.35	3.00
2007	Oak	AL	26	1	0	8	37.2	170	44	28	27	7	1	2	3	14	3	23	1	1	0	2	.000	0	0-1	3	5.79	6.45
2010	Tex	AL	32	32	1	0	201.0	844	174	90	83	21	4	4	6	65	0	196	9	0	12	13	.480	0	0-0	0	3.15	3.72
6 ML YEARS			104	66	1	13	418.1	1865	444	256	245	57	9	8	17	189	6	351	18	2	24	28	.462	0	0-3	4	5.04	5.27

Fred Lewis

Bats: L **Throws:** R **Pos:** LF-84; RF-10; DH-8; CF-7; PH-5   **Ht:** 6'2" **Wt:** 205 **Born:** 12/9/1980 **Age:** 30

Year	Team	Lg	G	AB	H	2B	3B	HR	(Hm	Rd)	TB	R	RBI	RC	TBB	IBB	SO	HBP	SH	SF	SB	CS	SB%	GDP	Avg	OBP	Slg
2010	Fresno*	AAA	7	22	9	3	1	1	(-	-)	17	6	6	8	6	0	2	0	0	0	2	1	.67	1	.409	.536	.773
2006	SF	NL	13	11	5	1	0	0	(0	0)	6	5	2	4	0	0	3	0	0	0	0	0	-	0	.455	.455	.545
2007	SF	NL	58	157	45	6	2	3	(0	3)	64	34	19	27	19	0	32	3	1	0	5	1	.83	4	.287	.374	.408
2008	SF	NL	133	468	132	25	11	9	(4	5)	206	81	40	67	51	3	124	0	0	2	21	7	.75	5	.282	.351	.440
2009	SF	NL	122	295	76	21	3	4	(2	2)	115	49	20	37	36	3	84	5	0	0	8	4	.67	4	.258	.348	.390
2010	Tor	AL	110	428	112	31	5	8	(4	4)	177	70	36	56	38	1	104	9	1	4	17	6	.74	9	.262	.332	.414
5 ML YEARS			436	1359	370	84	21	24	(10	14)	568	239	117	191	144	7	347	17	2	6	51	18	.74	22	.272	.348	.418

Jensen Lewis

Pitches: R **Bats:** R **Pos:** RP-37   **Ht:** 6'3" **Wt:** 220 **Born:** 5/16/1984 **Age:** 27

Year	Team	Lg	G	GS	CG	GF	IP	BFP	H	R	ER	HR	SH	SF	HB	TBB	IBB	SO	WP	Bk	W	L	Pct	Sh	Sv-Op	Hld	ERC	ERA
2010	Clmbs*	AAA	24	0	0	8	30.1	126	29	9	9	2	0	1	1	8	0	30	0	0	2	1	.667	0	2--	-	3.23	2.67
2007	Cle	AL	26	0	0	5	29.1	125	26	8	7	1	2	1	1	10	1	34	1	0	1	1	.500	0	0-0	5	2.81	2.15
2008	Cle	AL	51	0	0	28	66.0	292	68	29	28	8	2	2	5	27	3	52	0	0	0	4	.000	0	13-14	3	4.66	3.82
2009	Cle	AL	47	0	0	15	66.1	285	62	37	34	13	3	2	2	29	3	62	2	1	2	4	.333	0	1-5	4	4.61	4.61
2010	Cle	AL	37	0	0	11	36.1	153	28	12	12	1	2	2	0	19	1	29	0	0	4	2	.667	0	0-0	1	2.77	2.97
Postseason			7	0	0	1	7.2	27	6	4	4	2	0	0	0	0	0	7	0	0	0	0	-	0	0-0	1	2.46	4.70
4 ML YEARS			161	0	0	59	198.0	855	184	86	81	23	9	7	8	85	8	177	3	1	7	11	.389	0	14-19	14	3.99	3.68

Rommie Lewis

Pitches: L **Bats:** L **Pos:** RP-14   **Ht:** 6'6" **Wt:** 203 **Born:** 9/2/1982 **Age:** 28

Year	Team	Lg	G	GS	CG	GF	IP	BFP	H	R	ER	HR	SH	SF	HB	TBB	IBB	SO	WP	Bk	W	L	Pct	Sh	Sv-Op	Hld	ERC	ERA
2001	Orioles	R	10	7	0	1	33.2	144	37	16	8	3	1	1	2	6	0	27	2	1	1	1	.500	0	0--	-	3.88	2.14
2001	Frdrck	A+	1	0	0	0	4.0	22	8	7	4	1	1	0	1	1	0	2	0	0	0	1	.000	0	0--	-	10.43	9.00
2002	Dlmrva	A	53	0	0	36	71.0	282	50	19	17	1	4	1	4	20	1	77	5	0	1	2	.333	0	25--	-	1.81	2.15
2003	Frdrck	A+	26	20	1	2	113.1	503	108	54	42	9	2	4	6	60	1	69	6	0	4	9	.308	0	0--	-	4.36	3.34
2004	Frdrck	A+	47	4	0	14	86.2	395	92	64	54	4	4	1	7	41	3	52	5	0	1	7	.125	0	0--	-	4.51	5.61
2006	Frdrck	A+	31	0	0	15	51.2	213	46	16	12	3	1	0	4	11	2	36	6	0	5	3	.625	0	6--	-	2.73	2.09
2007	Bowie	AA	47	1	0	12	69.0	312	80	44	41	10	6	3	2	29	2	64	2	1	5	5	.500	0	1--	-	5.47	5.35
2008	Bowie	AA	38	5	0	12	66.0	295	81	29	25	4	3	0	3	26	3	63	3	0	1	6	.143	0	0--	-	5.28	3.41
2009	NHam	AA	26	0	0	5	42.0	179	35	12	12	2	2	0	2	22	0	45	0	0	2	4	.333	0	1--	-	3.50	2.57
2009	LsVgs	AAA	19	0	0	3	24.0	105	23	10	9	1	1	2	2	9	1	20	1	0	2	3	.400	0	0--	-	3.54	3.38
2010	LsVgs	AAA	24	8	0	9	53.1	249	72	51	45	7	1	2	1	22	0	41	5	0	1	5	.167	0	5--	-	6.55	7.59
2010	Tor	AL	14	0	0	4	18.2	82	20	14	14	4	0	0	0	8	0	15	0	0	0	0	-	0	0-0	0	5.46	6.75

Brad Lidge

Pitches: R Bats: R Pos: RP-50   **Ht: 6'5" Wt: 210 Born: 12/23/1976 Age: 34**

Year	Team	Lg	G	GS	CG	GF	IP	BFP	H	R	ER	HR	SH	SF	HB	TBB	IBB	SO	WP	Bk	W	L	Pct	Sh	Sv-Op	Hld	ERC	ERA
2010	Clrwtr*	A+	6	3	0	0	5.2	22	5	5	5	0	0	0	0	2	0	5	0	0	0	1	.000	0	0--	-	2.83	7.94
2010	LV*	AAA	1	0	0	0	1.0	4	0	0	0	0	0	0	0	1	0	1	0	0	0	0	-	0	0--	-	0.95	0.00
2010	Rdng*	AA	2	0	0	1	3.0	12	1	0	0	0	0	0	0	1	0	4	0	0	0	0	-	0	0--	-	0.63	0.00
2002	Hou	NL	6	1	0	2	8.2	48	12	6	6	0	1	0	2	9	1	12	0	0	1	0	1.000	0	0-0	0	8.90	6.23
2003	Hou	NL	78	0	0	9	85.0	349	60	36	34	6	2	3	5	42	7	97	4	1	6	3	.667	0	1-6	28	2.82	3.60
2004	Hou	NL	80	0	0	44	94.2	369	57	21	20	8	3	2	6	30	5	157	3	1	6	5	.545	0	29-33	17	1.85	1.90
2005	Hou	NL	70	0	0	65	70.2	291	58	21	18	5	4	1	3	23	1	103	8	0	4	4	.500	0	42-46	5	2.79	2.29
2006	Hou	NL	78	0	0	52	75.0	340	69	47	44	10	6	2	6	36	4	104	11	0	1	5	.167	0	32-38	6	4.25	5.28
2007	Hou	NL	66	0	0	34	67.0	287	54	29	25	9	5	1	4	30	4	88	6	0	5	3	.625	0	19-27	7	3.52	3.36
2008	Phi	NL	72	0	0	61	69.1	292	50	17	15	2	2	1	1	35	4	92	5	0	2	0	1.000	0	41-41	0	2.45	1.95
2009	Phi	NL	67	0	0	55	58.2	283	72	51	47	11	4	1	5	34	3	61	4	0	0	8	.000	0	31-42	1	7.11	7.21
2010	Phi	NL	50	0	0	38	45.2	193	32	16	15	5	3	0	1	24	4	52	3	1	1	1	.500	0	27-32	0	2.92	2.96
	Postseason		32	0	0	27	39.1	158	27	11	11	2	2	0	2	15	0	56	3	0	2	4	.333	0	16-18	0	2.28	2.52
	9 ML YEARS		567	1	0	360	574.2	2452	464	244	224	56	30	11	33	263	33	766	44	3	26	29	.473	0	222-265	59	3.33	3.51

Brent Lillibridge

Bats: R Throws: R Pos: 2B-25; PR-22; DH-15; PH-8; CF-6; SS-4; 3B-3; LF-1; RF-1   **Ht: 5'11" Wt: 185 Born: 9/18/1983 Age: 27**

							BATTING																BASERUNNING				AVERAGES		
Year	Team	Lg	G	AB	H	2B	3B	HR	(Hm	Rd)	TB	R	RBI	RC	TBB	IBB	SO	HBP	SH	SF	SB	CS	SB%	GDP	Avg	OBP	Slg
2010	Charltt*	AAA	48	185	50	8	0	4	(-	-)	70	26	16	27	17	0	46	1	0	3	19	3	.86	0	.270	.330	.378
2008	Atl	NL	29	80	16	6	1	1	(0	1)	27	9	8	6	3	0	23	1	1	0	2	0	1.00	0	.200	.238	.338
2009	CWS	AL	46	95	15	2	0	0	(0	0)	17	9	3	5	14	0	26	1	2	0	6	3	.67	2	.158	.273	.179
2010	CWS	AL	64	98	22	5	2	2	(1	1)	37	19	16	11	3	0	36	0	0	0	5	3	.63	2	.224	.248	.378
	3 ML YEARS		139	273	53	13	3	3	(1	2)	81	37	27	22	20	0	85	2	3	0	13	6	.68	4	.194	.254	.297

Ted Lilly

Pitches: L Bats: L Pos: SP-30   **Ht: 6'1" Wt: 195 Born: 1/4/1976 Age: 35**

Year	Team	Lg	G	GS	CG	GF	IP	BFP	H	R	ER	HR	SH	SF	HB	TBB	IBB	SO	WP	Bk	W	L	Pct	Sh	Sv-Op	Hld	ERC	ERA
2010	Iowa*	AAA	1	1	0	0	4.0	14	1	1	1	1	0	0	0	1	0	4	0	0	0	0	-	0	0--	-	0.99	2.25
2010	Peoria*	A	1	1	0	0	7.0	25	3	1	1	0	0	0	0	1	0	9	0	0	1	0	1.000	0	0--	-	0.60	1.29
1999	Mon	NL	9	3	0	1	23.2	110	30	20	20	7	0	1	3	9	0	28	1	0	0	1	.000	0	0-0	0	7.76	7.61
2000	NYY	AL	7	0	0	1	8.0	39	8	6	5	1	0	0	0	5	0	11	1	1	0	0	-	0	0-0	0	4.76	5.63
2001	NYY	AL	26	21	0	2	120.2	537	126	81	72	20	2	5	7	51	1	112	9	2	5	6	.455	0	0-0	0	5.10	5.37
2002	2 Tms	AL	22	16	2	1	100.0	413	80	43	41	15	0	3	6	31	3	77	6	1	5	7	.417	1	0-0	0	3.14	3.69
2003	Oak	AL	32	31	0	0	178.1	773	179	92	86	24	3	4	5	58	3	147	5	4	12	10	.545	0	0-0	0	4.06	4.34
2004	Tor	AL	32	32	2	0	197.1	845	171	92	89	26	3	3	6	89	2	168	6	4	12	10	.545	1	0-0	0	3.84	4.06
2005	Tor	AL	25	25	0	0	126.1	566	135	79	78	23	3	5	3	58	1	96	2	2	10	11	.476	0	0-0	0	5.38	5.56
2006	Tor	AL	32	32	0	0	181.2	797	179	98	87	28	4	2	4	81	6	160	7	4	15	13	.536	0	0-0	0	4.57	4.31
2007	ChC	NL	34	34	0	0	207.0	847	181	91	88	28	11	3	3	55	2	174	7	0	15	8	.652	0	0-0	0	3.14	3.83
2008	ChC	NL	34	34	0	0	204.2	861	187	96	93	32	5	3	7	64	2	184	4	4	17	9	.654	0	0-0	0	3.73	4.09
2009	ChC	NL	27	27	0	0	177.0	706	151	66	61	22	9	3	2	36	2	151	3	3	12	9	.571	0	0-0	0	2.74	3.10
2010	2 Tms	NL	30	30	1	0	193.2	785	165	83	78	32	14	2	5	44	4	166	2	2	10	12	.455	1	0-0	0	3.08	3.62
02	NYY	AL	16	11	2	1	76.2	314	57	31	29	10	0	3	5	24	3	59	6	0	3	6	.333	1	0-0	0	2.74	3.40
02	Oak	AL	6	5	0	0	23.1	99	23	12	12	5	0	0	1	7	0	18	0	1	2	1	.667	0	0-0	0	4.56	4.63
10	ChC	NL	18	18	0	0	117.0	480	104	53	48	19	8	1	2	29	3	89	2	2	3	8	.273	0	0-0	0	3.30	3.69
10	LAD	NL	12	12	1	0	76.2	305	61	30	30	13	6	1	3	15	1	77	0	0	7	4	.636	1	0-0	0	2.77	3.52
	Postseason		5	2	0	0	16.1	76	19	13	12	2	1	0	1	7	0	14	1	0	0	2	.000	0	0-1	0	5.43	6.61
	12 ML YEARS		310	285	5	5	1718.1	7279	1592	847	790	258	54	40	51	581	26	1474	53	27	113	96	.541	3	0-0	0	3.84	4.18

Chang-Yong Lim

Pitches: R Bats: R Pos: P   **Ht: 5'11" Wt: 176 Born: 6/4/1976 Age: 35**

Year	Team	Lg	G	GS	CG	GF	IP	BFP	H	R	ER	HR	SH	SF	HB	TBB	IBB	SO	WP	Bk	W	L	Pct	Sh	Sv-Op	Hld	ERC	ERA
2008	Yakult	Jap	54	-	-	-	51.0	214	55	18	17	6	-	-	2	9	-	50	1	0	1	5	.167	-	33--	-	3.92	3.00
2009	Yakult	Jap	57	-	-	-	57.0	229	40	15	13	4	-	-	2	19	-	52	2	0	5	4	.556	-	28--	-	2.22	2.05
2010	Yakult	Jap	53	-	-	-	55.2	214	32	9	9	3	-	-	2	16	-	53	1	0	1	2	.333	-	35--	-	1.51	1.46

Tim Lincecum

Pitches: R Bats: L Pos: SP-33   **Ht: 5'11" Wt: 163 Born: 6/15/1984 Age: 27**

Year	Team	Lg	G	GS	CG	GF	IP	BFP	H	R	ER	HR	SH	SF	HB	TBB	IBB	SO	WP	Bk	W	L	Pct	Sh	Sv-Op	Hld	ERC	ERA
2007	SF	NL	24	24	0	0	146.1	618	122	70	65	12	5	7	2	65	5	150	10	0	7	5	.583	0	0-0	0	3.21	4.00
2008	SF	NL	34	33	2	0	227.0	928	182	72	66	11	11	3	6	84	1	265	17	2	18	5	.783	1	0-0	0	2.69	2.62
2009	SF	NL	32	32	4	0	225.1	905	168	69	62	10	12	5	6	68	2	261	11	0	15	7	.682	2	0-0	0	2.14	2.48
2010	SF	NL	33	33	1	0	212.1	897	194	84	81	18	9	5	5	76	7	231	9	0	16	10	.615	2	0-0	0	3.37	3.43
	4 ML YEARS		123	122	7	0	811.0	3348	666	295	274	51	37	20	19	293	15	907	47	2	56	27	.675	4	0-0	0	2.79	3.04

Brad Lincoln

Pitches: R Bats: L Pos: SP-9; RP-2   Ht: 6'0" Wt: 210 Born: 5/25/1985 Age: 26

Year	Team	Lg	G	GS	CG	GF	IP	BFP	H	R	ER	HR	SH	SF	HB	TBB	IBB	SO	WP	Bk	W	L	Pct	Sh	Sv-Op	Hld	ERC	ERA
2006	Pirates	R	2	2	0	0	7.2	29	6	1	0	0	1	0	0	1	0	9	0	0	0	0	—	0	0–	–	1.54	0.00
2006	Hkry	A	4	4	0	0	16.0	76	25	15	12	2	1	0	1	6	0	10	1	0	1	2	.333	0	0–	–	8.14	6.75
2008	Hkry	A	11	11	0	0	62.0	260	72	34	32	8	2	0	2	6	0	46	1	2	5	5	.500	0	0–	–	4.11	4.65
2008	Lynbrg	A+	8	8	1	0	41.2	176	42	24	22	5	1	1	1	11	0	29	0	0	1	5	.167	0	0–	–	3.80	4.75
2009	Altna	AA	13	13	1	0	75.0	298	63	22	19	4	1	1	2	18	0	65	3	0	1	5	.167	1	0–	–	2.49	2.28
2009	Indy	AAA	12	12	0	0	61.1	257	72	37	32	7	1	5	1	10	1	42	2	1	6	2	.750	0	0–	–	4.33	4.70
2010	Indy	AAA	17	17	0	0	94.0	388	83	47	43	9	2	2	7	24	0	84	4	0	7	5	.583	0	0–	–	3.15	4.12
2010	Pit	NL	11	9	0	0	52.2	240	66	42	39	9	3	4	5	15	0	25	1	0	1	4	.200	0	0-0	0	5.99	6.66

Mike Lincoln

Pitches: R Bats: R Pos: RP-19   Ht: 6'2" Wt: 208 Born: 4/10/1975 Age: 36

Year	Team	Lg	G	GS	CG	GF	IP	BFP	H	R	ER	HR	SH	SF	HB	TBB	IBB	SO	WP	Bk	W	L	Pct	Sh	Sv-Op	Hld	ERC	ERA
1999	Min	AL	18	15	0	0	76.1	353	102	59	58	11	2	6	1	26	0	27	4	0	3	10	.231	0	0-0	1	6.16	6.84
2000	Min	AL	8	4	0	1	20.2	109	36	25	25	10	0	0	2	13	0	15	1	0	0	3	.000	0	0-0	0	14.32	10.89
2001	Pit	NL	31	0	0	5	40.1	168	34	16	12	3	1	1	4	11	0	24	2	0	2	1	.667	0	0-2	7	2.94	2.68
2002	Pit	NL	55	0	0	9	72.1	309	80	28	25	7	2	4	0	27	8	50	2	0	2	4	.333	0	0-3	11	4.49	3.11
2003	Pit	NL	36	0	0	14	36.1	153	38	22	21	5	1	1	1	13	0	28	1	0	3	4	.429	0	5-8	5	4.70	5.20
2004	StL	NL	13	0	0	1	17.1	71	10	12	10	1	1	2	1	6	0	14	0	0	3	2	.600	0	0-2	1	1.63	5.19
2008	Cin	NL	64	0	0	12	70.1	297	66	37	35	10	3	3	3	24	1	57	3	0	2	5	.286	0	0-1	10	3.96	4.48
2009	Cin	NL	19	0	0	8	23.0	115	29	21	21	7	3	0	4	19	2	9	1	0	1	1	.500	0	0-0	1	10.28	8.22
2010	Cin	NL	19	0	0	5	19.2	94	25	16	16	1	0	1	2	10	0	12	1	0	1	0	1.000	0	0-0	3	6.12	7.32
9 ML YEARS			263	19	0	55	376.1	1669	420	236	223	55	13	18	18	149	11	236	15	0	17	30	.362	0	5-16	39	5.25	5.33

Adam Lind

Bats: L Throws: L Pos: DH-122; LF-16; 1B-11; PH-5   Ht: 6'1" Wt: 215 Born: 7/17/1983 Age: 27

Year	Team	Lg	G	AB	H	2B	3B	HR	(Hm	Rd)	TB	R	RBI	RC	TBB	IBB	SO	HBP	SH	SF	SB	CS	SB%	GDP	Avg	OBP	Slg
2006	Tor	AL	18	60	22	8	0	2	(0	2)	36	8	8	13	5	0	12	0	0	0	0	0	–	0	.367	.415	.600
2007	Tor	AL	89	290	69	14	0	11	(10	1)	116	34	46	38	16	0	65	1	2	2	1	2	.33	7	.238	.278	.400
2008	Tor	AL	88	326	92	16	4	9	(2	7)	143	48	40	39	16	3	59	2	1	4	2	0	1.00	6	.282	.316	.439
2009	Tor	AL	151	587	179	46	0	35	(14	21)	330	93	114	114	58	7	110	5	0	4	1	1	.50	15	.305	.370	.562
2010	Tor	AL	150	569	135	32	3	23	(15	8)	242	57	72	65	38	3	144	3	0	3	0	0	–	10	.237	.287	.425
5 ML YEARS			496	1832	497	116	7	80	(41	39)	867	240	280	269	133	13	390	11	3	13	4	3	.57	40	.271	.322	.473

John Lindsey

Bats: R Throws: R Pos: PH-9; 1B-2   Ht: 6'2" Wt: 255 Born: 1/30/1977 Age: 34

Year	Team	Lg	G	AB	H	2B	3B	HR	(Hm	Rd)	TB	R	RBI	RC	TBB	IBB	SO	HBP	SH	SF	SB	CS	SB%	GDP	Avg	OBP	Slg
1995	Rckies	R	48	179	42	10	0	2	(-	-)	58	23	22	17	11	0	48	7	0	1	0	2	.00	4	.235	.303	.324
1996	Portlnd	A-	57	208	53	11	1	2	(-	-)	72	32	22	27	26	0	63	4	0	0	1	1	.50	3	.255	.349	.346
1997	Ashvll	A	110	399	94	20	2	12	(-	-)	154	54	67	48	29	1	110	11	1	3	3	2	.60	14	.236	.303	.386
1998	Ashvll	A	126	472	130	21	3	14	(-	-)	199	59	73	66	24	2	114	15	3	2	2	4	.33	11	.275	.329	.422
1999	Salem	A+	75	260	54	15	1	4	(-	-)	83	32	35	24	20	1	69	7	3	1	2	1	.67	3	.208	.281	.319
2000	Salem	A+	104	343	96	23	1	9	(-	-)	148	43	56	58	37	0	76	15	0	3	5	3	.63	6	.280	.372	.431
2001	Salem	A+	51	168	47	13	0	7	(-	-)	81	19	32	28	13	2	51	5	0	0	1	1	.50	2	.280	.349	.482
2002	SnBrn	A+	127	472	140	30	6	22	(-	-)	248	75	93	97	48	1	109	25	0	6	0	1	.00	17	.297	.387	.525
2003	SnAnt	AA	88	307	91	22	1	8	(-	-)	139	40	43	53	22	1	81	11	2	2	9	1	.90	5	.296	.363	.453
2004	SnAnt	AA	123	457	129	31	2	19	(-	-)	221	68	72	81	48	0	98	14	2	4	1	7	.13	9	.282	.365	.484
2005	NewJrs	IND	56	209	67	15	6	9	(-	-)	121	35	62	50	24	1	34	13	0	1	0	0	–	3	.321	.421	.579
2005	Jupiter	A+	30	96	21	8	0	1	(-	-)	32	13	16	11	11	0	22	4	0	0	0	0	–	5	.219	.324	.333
2006	NewJrs	IND	69	238	74	20	0	10	(-	-)	124	37	41	48	24	0	51	9	0	1	0	2	.00	7	.311	.393	.521
2007	Jaxnvl	AA	56	154	44	6	0	11	(-	-)	83	28	33	30	14	4	38	6	0	0	0	0	–	1	.286	.368	.539
2007	LsVgs	AAA	77	300	100	26	1	19	(-	-)	185	51	88	69	21	1	56	10	0	2	0	0	–	6	.333	.393	.617
2008	LsVgs	AAA	133	481	152	36	1	26	(-	-)	268	85	100	109	63	2	82	14	0	5	0	0	–	20	.316	.407	.557
2009	NewOr	AAA	133	443	111	22	1	19	(-	-)	192	53	83	66	38	2	112	17	0	4	1	2	.33	20	.251	.331	.433
2010	Albq	AAA	107	408	144	41	4	25	(-	-)	268	74	97	100	19	0	78	16	0	4	0	0	–	16	.353	.400	.657
2010	Ddgrs	R	1	3	0	0	0	0	(-	-)	0	0	0	0	0	0	1	0	0	0	0	0	–	0	.000	.000	.000
2010	LAD	NL	11	12	1	0	0	0	(0	0)	1	0	0	0	0	0	3	1	0	0	0	0	–	1	.083	.154	.083

Matt Lindstrom

Pitches: R Bats: R Pos: RP-58   Ht: 6'3" Wt: 218 Born: 2/11/1980 Age: 31

Year	Team	Lg	G	GS	CG	GF	IP	BFP	H	R	ER	HR	SH	SF	HB	TBB	IBB	SO	WP	Bk	W	L	Pct	Sh	Sv-Op	Hld	ERC	ERA
2010	CpChr*	AA	1	1	0	0	1.0	4	0	0	0	0	0	0	0	1	0	1	0	0	0	0	—	0	0–	–	0.95	0.00
2007	Fla	NL	71	0	0	11	67.0	284	66	27	23	2	3	1	3	21	4	62	5	0	3	4	.429	0	0-2	19	3.26	3.09
2008	Fla	NL	66	0	0	27	57.1	245	57	21	20	1	6	1	4	26	4	43	4	0	3	3	.500	0	5-6	14	3.69	3.14
2009	Fla	NL	54	0	0	32	47.1	219	54	35	31	5	1	0	2	24	2	39	0	1	2	1	.667	0	15-17	8	5.41	5.89
2010	Hou	NL	58	0	0	41	53.1	244	68	26	26	5	2	0	0	20	1	43	8	0	2	5	.286	0	23-29	5	5.45	4.39
4 ML YEARS			249	0	0	111	225.0	992	245	109	100	13	12	2	6	91	11	187	17	1	10	13	.435	0	43-54	45	4.32	4.00

Scott Linebrink

Pitches: R **Bats:** R **Pos:** RP-52   LYNE-brink   **Ht:** 6'3" **Wt:** 220 **Born:** 8/4/1976 **Age:** 34

Year	Team	Lg	G	GS	CG	GF	IP	BFP	H	R	ER	HR	SH	SF	HB	TBB	IBB	SO	WP	Bk	W	L	Pct	Sh	Sv-Op	Hld	ERC	ERA
2000	2 Tms	NL	11	0	0	4	12.0	63	18	8	8	4	0	0	3	8	0	6	0	0	0	0	-	0	0-0	0	11.88	6.00
2001	Hou	NL	9	0	0	2	10.1	44	6	4	3	0	1	1	2	6	0	9	1	0	0	0	-	0	0-0	1	2.54	2.61
2002	Hou	NL	22	0	0	4	24.1	120	31	21	19	2	0	2	1	13	4	24	0	0	0	0	-	0	0-0	1	5.70	7.03
2003	2 Tms	NL	52	6	0	8	92.1	397	93	37	34	9	4	6	6	36	4	68	11	0	3	2	.600	0	0-0	6	4.32	3.31
2004	SD	NL	73	0	0	7	84.0	326	61	22	20	8	2	3	3	26	2	83	3	0	7	3	.700	0	0-5	28	2.48	2.14
2005	SD	NL	73	0	0	17	73.2	288	55	17	15	4	2	0	0	23	4	70	3	0	8	1	.889	0	1-6	26	2.15	1.83
2006	SD	NL	73	0	0	11	75.2	314	70	31	30	9	1	2	1	22	3	68	2	0	7	4	.636	0	2-11	36	3.36	3.57
2007	2 Tms	NL	71	0	0	11	70.1	295	68	33	29	12	0	0	1	25	3	50	6	0	5	6	.455	0	1-8	21	4.26	3.71
2008	CWS	AL	50	0	0	13	46.1	186	41	20	19	8	2	0	0	9	1	40	3	0	2	2	.500	0	1-4	19	3.09	3.69
2009	CWS	AL	57	0	0	24	56.0	259	70	34	29	9	0	3	3	23	6	55	5	0	3	7	.300	0	2-4	7	6.07	4.66
2010	CWS	AL	52	0	0	28	57.1	249	59	31	28	11	4	0	3	17	0	52	7	0	3	2	.600	0	0-1	4	4.62	4.40
00	SF	NL	3	0	0	1	2.1	16	7	3	3	1	0	0	0	2	0	0	0	0	0	0	-	0	0-0	0	24.13	11.57
00	Hou	NL	8	0	0	3	9.2	47	11	5	5	3	0	0	3	6	0	6	0	0	0	0	-	0	0-0	0	9.21	4.66
03	Hou	NL	9	6	0	2	31.2	140	38	15	15	4	2	1	3	14	1	17	5	0	1	1	.500	0	0-0	0	6.27	4.26
03	SD	NL	43	0	0	6	60.2	257	55	22	19	5	2	5	3	22	3	51	6	0	2	1	.667	0	0-0	6	3.41	2.82
07	SD	NL	44	0	0	7	45.0	186	41	19	19	9	0	0	1	14	1	25	4	0	3	3	.500	0	1-7	15	3.99	3.80
07	Mil	NL	27	0	0	4	25.1	109	27	14	10	3	0	0	0	11	2	25	2	0	2	3	.400	0	0-1	6	4.71	3.55
	Postseason		4	0	0	3	3.1	15	4	1	1	1	0	0	0	2	1	2	0	0	0	0	-	0	0-0	1	7.51	2.70
	11 ML YEARS		543	6	0	129	602.1	2541	572	258	234	76	16	17	23	208	27	525	41	0	38	27	.585	0	7-39	148	3.87	3.50

Jon Link

Pitches: R **Bats:** R **Pos:** RP-9   **Ht:** 6'0" **Wt:** 207 **Born:** 3/23/1984 **Age:** 27

Year	Team	Lg	G	GS	CG	GF	IP	BFP	H	R	ER	HR	SH	SF	HB	TBB	IBB	SO	WP	Bk	W	L	Pct	Sh	Sv-Op	Hld	ERC	ERA
2005	Eugene	A-	25	7	0	1	59.0	248	67	33	29	7	1	2	2	18	0	44	5	0	3	3	.500	0	0--	-	3.83	4.42
2006	FtWyn	A	53	0	0	24	62.1	205	72	45	34	3	1	5	1	24	0	57	5	0	5	5	.500	0	3--	-	4.44	4.91
2007	Lk Els	A+	41	0	0	33	41.0	164	32	16	14	5	0	0	0	11	1	45	1	0	2	1	.667	0	13--	-	2.52	3.07
2007	WinSa	A+	14	0	0	13	17.2	69	16	5	5	1	0	0	0	4	1	19	0	0	1	0	1.000	0	3--	-	2.69	2.55
2008	Brham	AA	56	0	0	49	56.2	240	48	21	19	3	4	1	2	27	3	66	1	1	5	4	.556	0	35--	-	3.15	3.02
2009	Charltt	AAA	48	0	0	43	56.1	247	55	26	25	5	1	2	2	27	4	66	2	0	1	2	.333	0	13--	-	4.20	3.99
2010	Albq	AAA	45	1	0	16	60.2	267	65	33	25	5	7	1	1	21	6	55	3	0	3	2	.600	0	4--	-	3.97	3.71
2010	LAD	NL	0	0	0	6	8.2	40	12	7	4	0	0	0	0	4	1	4	1	0	0	0	-	0	0-0	0	5.71	4.15

Francisco Liriano

Pitches: L **Bats:** L **Pos:** SP-31   **Ht:** 6'2" **Wt:** 215 **Born:** 10/26/1983 **Age:** 27

Year	Team	Lg	G	GS	CG	GF	IP	BFP	H	R	ER	HR	SH	SF	HB	TBB	IBB	SO	WP	Bk	W	L	Pct	Sh	Sv-Op	Hld	ERC	ERA
2005	Min	AL	6	4	0	2	23.2	93	19	15	15	4	0	0	0	7	0	33	0	0	1	2	.333	0	0-0	0	3.15	5.70
2006	Min	AL	28	16	0	2	121.0	473	89	31	29	9	4	2	1	32	0	144	9	1	12	3	.800	0	1-1	1	2.12	2.16
2008	Min	AL	14	14	0	0	76.0	329	74	40	33	7	2	3	1	32	1	67	3	0	6	4	.600	0	0-0	0	3.97	3.91
2009	Min	AL	29	24	0	2	136.2	609	147	93	88	21	5	6	6	65	0	122	5	1	5	13	.278	0	0-0	0	5.46	5.80
2010	Min	AL	31	31	0	0	191.2	806	184	77	77	9	6	2	10	58	0	201	10	1	14	10	.583	0	0-0	0	3.34	3.62
	Postseason		1	0	0	0	2.0	8	1	2	1	0	0	0	0	1	0	1	0	0	0	0	-	0	0-0	0	4.08	4.50
	5 ML YEARS		108	89	0	6	549.0	2310	513	256	242	50	17	13	18	194	1	567	27	3	38	32	.543	0	1-1	1	3.62	3.97

Jesse Litsch

Pitches: R **Bats:** R **Pos:** SP-9   **Ht:** 6'1" **Wt:** 215 **Born:** 3/9/1985 **Age:** 26

Year	Team	Lg	G	GS	CG	GF	IP	BFP	H	R	ER	HR	SH	SF	HB	TBB	IBB	SO	WP	Bk	W	L	Pct	Sh	Sv-Op	Hld	ERC	ERA
2010	Dnedin*	A+	2	2	0	0	15.0	68	9	3	3	1	0	0	1	4	0	10	0	0	1	1	.500	0	0--	-	1.66	1.80
2010	LsVgs*	AAA	4	4	0	0	22.0	105	34	26	20	4	0	1	3	3	0	13	3	0	0	3	.000	0	0--	-	7.40	8.18
2007	Tor	AL	20	20	0	0	111.0	478	116	56	47	14	3	3	7	36	2	50	2	0	7	9	.438	0	0-0	0	4.48	3.81
2008	Tor	AL	20	28	2	0	176.0	735	178	79	70	20	1	4	8	39	2	99	4	0	13	9	.591	2	0-0	0	3.71	3.58
2009	Tor	AL	2	2	0	0	9.0	42	14	9	9	4	0	0	1	1	0	8	0	0	0	1	.000	0	0-0	0	9.55	9.00
2010	Tor	AL	9	9	0	0	46.2	202	53	30	30	7	0	0	2	15	0	16	1	0	1	5	.167	0	0-0	0	5.18	5.79
	4 ML YEARS		60	59	2	0	342.2	1457	361	174	156	45	4	7	18	91	4	173	7	0	21	24	.467	2	0-0	0	4.29	4.10

Kameron Loe

Pitches: R **Bats:** R **Pos:** RP-53   **Ht:** 6'8" **Wt:** 228 **Born:** 9/10/1981 **Age:** 29

Year	Team	Lg	G	GS	CG	GF	IP	BFP	H	R	ER	HR	SH	SF	HB	TBB	IBB	SO	WP	Bk	W	L	Pct	Sh	Sv-Op	Hld	ERC	ERA
2010	Nashv*	AAA	10	10	0	0	62.2	262	57	28	22	6	2	1	4	19	0	39	3	0	4	3	.571	0	0--	-	3.44	3.16
2004	Tex	AL	2	1	0	0	6.2	29	6	5	4	0	0	0	1	6	0	3	0	0	0	0	-	0	0-0	0	5.87	5.40
2005	Tex	AL	48	8	0	13	92.0	392	89	43	35	7	5	1	2	31	6	45	2	0	9	6	.600	0	1-4	4	3.45	3.42
2006	Tex	AL	15	15	1	0	78.1	358	105	54	51	10	1	3	1	22	0	34	3	0	3	6	.333	1	0-0	0	5.79	5.86
2007	Tex	AL	28	23	0	0	136.0	615	162	96	81	13	1	5	1	56	6	78	6	0	6	11	.353	0	0-0	0	5.24	5.36
2008	Tex	AL	14	0	0	4	30.2	134	36	18	11	3	0	1	0	8	1	20	0	0	1	0	1.000	0	0-1	2	4.40	3.23
2010	Mil	NL	53	0	0	9	58.1	240	54	23	18	6	1	2	2	15	1	46	4	0	3	5	.375	0	0-2	22	3.27	2.78
	6 ML YEARS		160	47	1	26	402.0	1768	452	239	200	39	8	12	10	138	14	226	15	0	22	28	.440	1	1-7	28	4.57	4.48

Boone Logan

Pitches: L Bats: R Pos: RP-51　　　　　　　　　　　　　　Ht: 6'5" Wt: 215 Born: 8/13/1984 Age: 26

Year	Team	Lg	G	GS	CG	GF	IP	BFP	H	R	ER	HR	SH	SF	HB	TBB	IBB	SO	WP	Bk	W	L	Pct	Sh	Sv-Op	Hld	ERC	ERA
2010	S-WB*	AAA	14	0	0	4	21.1	86	18	5	5	1	0	1	2	4	0	23	1	0	0	1	.000	0	0--	-	2.49	2.11
2006	CWS	AL	21	0	0	4	17.1	93	21	18	16	2	1	1	3	15	2	15	1	0	0	0	-	0	1-2	2	7.56	8.31
2007	CWS	AL	68	0	0	13	50.2	226	59	30	28	7	2	6	0	20	3	35	2	0	2	1	.667	0	0-2	11	5.18	4.97
2008	CWS	AL	55	0	0	12	42.1	197	57	31	28	7	2	0	1	14	3	42	1	0	2	3	.400	0	0-1	3	6.24	5.95
2009	Atl	NL	20	0	0	7	17.1	82	21	12	10	1	0	0	1	9	3	10	0	0	1	1	.500	0	0-0	1	5.29	5.19
2010	NYY	AL	51	0	0	8	40.0	169	34	13	13	3	0	1	1	20	3	38	1	0	2	0	1.000	0	0-0	13	3.50	2.93
5 ML YEARS			215	0	0	44	167.2	767	192	104	95	20	5	8	6	78	14	140	5	0	7	5	.583	0	1-5	30	5.28	5.10

Kyle Lohse

Pitches: R Bats: R Pos: SP-18　　　　　　LOESH　　　　　　Ht: 6'2" Wt: 210 Born: 10/4/1978 Age: 32

Year	Team	Lg	G	GS	CG	GF	IP	BFP	H	R	ER	HR	SH	SF	HB	TBB	IBB	SO	WP	Bk	W	L	Pct	Sh	Sv-Op	Hld	ERC	ERA
2010	Memp*	AAA	3	3	0	0	14.0	55	9	6	6	3	0	0	0	2	0	14	0	0	1	0	1.000	0	0--	-	1.82	3.21
2010	Sprgfld*	AA	1	1	0	0	5.0	26	12	5	5	0	1	1	0	0	0	4	0	0	0	1	.000	0	0--	-	10.58	9.00
2001	Min	AL	19	16	0	2	90.1	402	120	60	57	16	1	5	8	29	0	64	5	0	4	7	.364	0	0-0	0	5.43	5.68
2002	Min	AL	32	31	1	0	180.2	783	181	92	85	26	3	3	9	70	2	124	8	0	13	8	.619	1	0-1	0	4.55	4.23
2003	Min	AL	33	33	2	0	201.0	850	211	107	103	28	8	5	5	45	1	130	10	1	14	11	.560	1	0-0	0	4.00	4.61
2004	Min	AL	35	34	1	1	194.0	883	240	128	115	28	5	7	7	76	5	111	6	0	9	13	.409	1	0-0	0	5.89	5.34
2005	Min	AL	31	30	0	1	178.2	769	211	85	83	22	3	7	9	44	5	86	4	1	9	13	.409	0	0-0	0	4.91	4.18
2006	2 Tms		34	19	0	6	126.2	567	150	83	82	15	8	5	6	44	4	97	3	1	5	10	.333	0	0-0	0	5.20	5.83
2007	2 Tms	NL	34	32	2	0	192.2	829	207	109	99	22	14	4	12	57	3	122	3	0	9	12	.429	1	0-0	0	4.45	4.62
2008	StL	NL	33	33	0	0	200.0	839	211	88	84	18	6	4	3	49	3	119	5	0	15	6	.714	0	0-0	0	3.77	3.78
2009	StL	NL	23	22	1	0	117.2	512	125	69	62	16	3	5	3	36	2	77	3	1	6	10	.375	1	0-0	0	4.33	4.74
2010	StL	NL	18	18	0	0	92.0	431	129	75	67	9	5	4	3	35	2	54	1	0	4	8	.333	0	0-0	0	6.50	6.55
06	Min	AL	22	8	0	5	63.2	295	80	50	50	8	1	3	6	25	2	46	1	1	2	5	.286	0	0-0	0	6.10	7.07
06	Cin	NL	12	11	0	1	63.0	272	70	33	32	7	7	2	0	19	2	51	2	0	3	5	.375	0	0-0	0	4.34	4.57
07	Cin	NL	21	21	2	0	131.2	561	143	76	67	16	8	4	6	33	1	80	3	0	6	12	.333	1	0-0	0	4.32	4.58
07	Phi	NL	13	11	0	0	61.0	268	64	33	32	6	6	0	6	24	2	42	0	0	3	0	1.000	0	0-0	0	4.71	4.72
Postseason			6	1	0	3	13.1	52	10	5	5	2	0	0	0	2	0	15	1	0	0	2	.000	0	0-0	0	2.12	3.38
10 ML YEARS			292	268	7	10	1573.2	6865	1767	896	837	200	56	49	65	485	27	984	48	4	88	98	.473	5	0-1	0	4.76	4.79

James Loney

Bats: L Throws: L Pos: 1B-160; PH-4　　　　　　　　　　Ht: 6'2" Wt: 204 Born: 5/7/1984 Age: 27

Year	Team	Lg	G	AB	H	2B	3B	HR	(Hm	Rd)	TB	R	RBI	RC	TBB	IBB	SO	HBP	SH	SF	SB	CS	SB%	GDP	Avg	OBP	Slg
2006	LAD	NL	48	102	29	6	5	4	(1	3)	57	20	18	17	8	1	10	1	0	0	1	0	1.00	8	.284	.342	.559
2007	LAD	NL	96	344	114	18	4	15	(5	10)	185	41	67	71	28	5	48	1	0	2	0	1	.00	6	.331	.381	.538
2008	LAD	NL	161	595	172	35	6	13	(5	8)	258	66	90	79	45	6	85	3	1	7	7	4	.64	25	.289	.338	.434
2009	LAD	NL	158	576	162	25	2	13	(1	12)	230	73	90	84	70	10	68	0	1	4	7	3	.70	16	.281	.357	.399
2010	LAD	NL	161	588	157	41	2	10	(6	4)	232	67	88	81	52	9	95	4	0	4	10	5	.67	14	.267	.329	.395
Postseason			17	63	22	3	0	3	(1	2)	34	5	14	13	7	1	10	0	0	0	0	0	-	2	.349	.414	.540
5 ML YEARS			624	2205	634	125	19	55	(18	37)	962	267	353	332	203	31	306	9	2	17	25	13	.66	69	.288	.348	.436

Evan Longoria

Bats: R Throws: R Pos: 3B-151　　　　　　　　　　　　　　Ht: 6'2" Wt: 210 Born: 10/7/1985 Age: 25

Year	Team	Lg	G	AB	H	2B	3B	HR	(Hm	Rd)	TB	R	RBI	RC	TBB	IBB	SO	HBP	SH	SF	SB	CS	SB%	GDP	Avg	OBP	Slg
2008	TB	AL	122	448	122	31	2	27	(18	9)	238	67	85	72	46	4	122	6	0	8	7	0	1.00	8	.272	.343	.531
2009	TB	AL	157	584	164	44	0	33	(16	17)	307	100	113	102	72	11	140	8	0	7	9	0	1.00	27	.281	.364	.526
2010	TB	AL	151	574	169	46	5	22	(10	12)	291	96	104	99	72	12	124	5	0	10	15	5	.75	15	.294	.372	.507
Postseason			16	62	12	3	0	6	(3	3)	33	10	13	6	5	0	20	0	0	0	1	0	1.00	3	.194	.254	.532
3 ML YEARS			430	1606	455	121	7	82	(44	38)	836	263	302	273	190	27	386	19	0	25	31	5	.86	50	.283	.361	.521

Felipe Lopez

Bats: B Throws: R Pos: 3B-60; 2B-27; SS-25; PH-18; 1B-2; RF-1　　Ht: 6'0" Wt: 203 Born: 5/12/1980 Age: 31

Year	Team	Lg	G	AB	H	2B	3B	HR	(Hm	Rd)	TB	R	RBI	RC	TBB	IBB	SO	HBP	SH	SF	SB	CS	SB%	GDP	Avg	OBP	Slg
2001	Tor	AL	49	177	46	5	4	5	(3	2)	74	21	23	22	12	1	39	0	1	2	4	3	.57	2	.260	.304	.418
2002	Tor	AL	85	282	64	15	3	8	(5	3)	109	35	34	32	23	1	90	1	2	1	5	4	.56	4	.227	.287	.387
2003	Cin	NL	59	197	42	7	2	2	(0	2)	59	28	13	21	28	1	59	1	2	1	8	5	.62	2	.213	.313	.299
2004	Cin	NL	79	264	64	18	2	7	(3	4)	107	35	31	34	25	0	81	3	2	1	1	1	.50	1	.242	.314	.405
2005	Cin	NL	148	580	169	34	5	23	(16	7)	282	97	85	95	57	2	111	1	3	7	15	7	.68	8	.291	.352	.486
2006	2 Tms	NL	156	617	169	27	3	11	(5	6)	235	98	52	84	81	1	126	2	11	3	44	12	.79	9	.274	.358	.381
2007	Was	NL	154	603	148	25	6	9	(2	7)	212	70	50	63	53	1	109	4	5	6	24	9	.73	11	.245	.308	.352
2008	2 Tms	NL	143	481	136	28	2	6	(4	2)	186	64	46	56	43	2	82	3	2	3	8	8	.50	13	.283	.343	.387
2009	2 Tms	NL	151	604	187	38	3	9	(8	1)	258	88	57	98	71	4	100	2	1	2	6	6	.50	5	.310	.383	.427
2010	2 Tms	NL	113	391	91	18	1	8	(4	4)	135	52	37	46	44	1	81	1	3	2	8	2	.80	7	.233	.311	.345
06	Cin	NL	85	343	92	14	1	9	(5	4)	135	55	30	48	47	1	66	0	3	1	23	6	.79	6	.268	.355	.394
06	Was	NL	71	274	77	13	2	2	(0	2)	100	43	22	36	34	0	60	2	8	2	21	6	.78	3	.281	.362	.365
08	Was	NL	100	325	76	20	0	2	(1	1)	102	34	25	25	32	1	54	2	2	2	4	5	.44	13	.234	.305	.314
08	StL	NL	43	156	60	8	2	4	(1	3)	84	30	21	31	11	1	28	1	0	1	4	3	.57	0	.385	.426	.538
09	Ari	NL	85	345	104	18	1	6	(5	1)	142	44	25	49	34	3	59	1	1	2	6	3	.67	2	.301	.364	.412

Year Team	Lg	BATTING																				BASERUNNING				AVERAGES		
		G	AB	H	2B	3B	HR	(Hm	Rd)	TB	R	RBI	RC	TBB	IBB	SO	HBP	SH	SF	SB	CS	SB%	GDP	Avg	OBP	Slg
09 Mil	NL	66	259	83	20	2	3	(3	0)	116	44	32	49	37	1	41	1	0	0	0	3	.00	3	.320	.407	.448
10 StL	NL	109	376	87	18	1	7	(3	4)	128	50	36	45	43	1	77	1	3	2	8	2	.80	7	.231	.310	.340
10 Bos	AL	4	15	4	0	0	1	(1	0)	7	2	1	1	1	0	4	0	0	0	0	0	-	0	.267	.313	.467
10 ML YEARS		1137	4196	1116	215	31	88	(48	40)	1657	588	428	551	437	14	878	18	32	28	123	57	.68	62	.266	.336	.395

Javier Lopez

Pitches: L **Bats:** L **Pos:** RP-77   **Ht:** 6'4" **Wt:** 230 **Born:** 7/11/1977 **Age:** 33

Year Team	Lg	HOW MUCH HE PITCHED						WHAT HE GAVE UP												THE RESULTS						
		G	GS	CG	GF	IP	BFP	H	R	ER	HR	SH	SF	HB	TBB	IBB	SO	WP	Bk	W	L	Pct	Sh	Sv-Op Hld	ERC	ERA
2003 Col	NL	75	0	0	11	58.1	242	58	25	24	5	1	0	4	12	2	40	1	3	4	1	.800	0	1-2 15	3.44	3.70
2004 Col	NL	64	0	0	10	40.2	187	45	34	34	1	1	0	3	26	4	20	3	0	1	2	.333	0	0-1 12	5.28	7.52
2005 2 Tms	NL	32	0	0	6	16.1	87	26	20	20	2	1	0	1	11	3	12	0	0	1	1	.500	0	2-4 6	8.82	11.02
2006 Bos	AL	27	0	0	8	16.2	69	13	10	5	1	0	1	2	10	1	11	0	0	1	0	1.000	0	1-1 6	3.96	2.70
2007 Bos	AL	61	0	0	11	40.2	174	36	16	14	2	1	1	4	18	2	26	1	0	2	1	.667	0	0-2 13	3.59	3.10
2008 Bos	AL	70	0	0	10	59.1	247	53	18	16	4	1	1	2	27	0	38	1	0	2	0	1.000	0	0-1 10	3.73	2.43
2009 Bos	AL	14	0	0	5	11.2	64	20	13	12	1	1	1	2	9	0	5	1	0	0	2	.000	0	0-0 0	11.00	9.26
2010 2 Tms	NL	77	0	0	18	57.2	235	50	17	15	2	1	2	2	20	3	38	3	0	4	2	.667	0	0-0 11	2.85	2.34
05 Col	NL	3	0	0	1	2.0	13	7	5	5	0	0	0	0	0	0	1	0	0	0	0	-	0	0-1 0	18.39	22.50
05 Ari	NL	29	0	0	5	14.1	74	19	15	15	2	1	0	1	11	3	11	0	0	1	1	.500	0	2-3 6	7.63	9.42
10 Pit	NL	50	0	0	14	38.2	166	39	14	12	2	1	2	2	18	3	22	3	0	2	2	.500	0	0-0 6	4.24	2.79
10 SF	NL	27	0	0	4	19.0	69	11	3	3	0	0	0	0	2	0	16	0	0	2	0	1.000	0	0-0 5	0.90	1.42
Postseason		8	0	0	1	5.0	28	11	5	5	0	1	1	0	2	1	1	1	0	0	1	.000	0	0-0 0	10.18	9.00
8 ML YEARS		420	0	0	79	301.1	1305	301	153	140	18	7	6	20	133	15	190	10	3	15	9	.625	0	4-11 73	4.19	4.18

Jose Lopez

Bats: R **Throws:** R **Pos:** 3B-142; DH-8; PH-1   **Ht:** 6'0" **Wt:** 205 **Born:** 11/24/1983 **Age:** 27

Year Team	Lg	BATTING																				BASERUNNING				AVERAGES		
		G	AB	H	2B	3B	HR	(Hm	Rd)	TB	R	RBI	RC	TBB	IBB	SO	HBP	SH	SF	SB	CS	SB%	GDP	Avg	OBP	Slg
2004 Sea	AL	57	207	48	13	0	5	(4	1)	76	28	22	20	8	0	31	1	1	1	0	1	.00	1	.232	.263	.367
2005 Sea	AL	54	190	47	19	0	2	(1	1)	72	18	25	24	6	0	25	4	1	2	4	2	.67	5	.247	.282	.379
2006 Sea	AL	151	603	170	28	8	10	(4	6)	244	78	79	84	26	1	80	9	12	5	5	2	.71	17	.282	.319	.405
2007 Sea	AL	149	524	132	17	2	11	(5	6)	186	58	62	52	20	0	64	5	9	3	2	3	.40	16	.252	.284	.355
2008 Sea	AL	159	644	191	41	1	17	(13	4)	285	80	89	83	27	5	67	1	6	9	6	3	.67	14	.297	.322	.443
2009 Sea	AL	153	613	167	42	0	25	(6	17)	284	69	96	71	24	5	69	6	3	7	3	3	.50	25	.272	.303	.463
2010 Sea	AL	150	593	142	29	0	10	(3	7)	201	49	58	42	23	1	66	3	0	3	3	2	.60	20	.239	.270	.339
7 ML YEARS		873	3374	897	189	11	80	(38	42)	1348	380	431	376	134	12	402	29	32	30	23	16	.59	98	.266	.297	.400

Rodrigo Lopez

Pitches: R **Bats:** R **Pos:** SP-33   **Ht:** 6'1" **Wt:** 185 **Born:** 12/14/1975 **Age:** 35

Year Team	Lg	HOW MUCH HE PITCHED						WHAT HE GAVE UP												THE RESULTS						
		G	GS	CG	GF	IP	BFP	H	R	ER	HR	SH	SF	HB	TBB	IBB	SO	WP	Bk	W	L	Pct	Sh	Sv-Op Hld	ERC	ERA
2000 SD	NL	6	6	0	0	24.2	120	40	24	24	5	0	1	0	13	0	17	0	0	0	3	.000	0	0-0 0	9.78	8.76
2002 Bal	AL	33	28	1	0	196.2	809	172	83	78	23	2	4	5	62	4	136	2	1	15	9	.625	0	0-0 0	3.27	3.57
2003 Bal	AL	26	26	3	0	147.0	663	188	101	93	24	3	7	10	40	0	103	2	1	7	10	.412	1	0-0 0	6.00	5.82
2004 Bal	AL	37	23	1	3	170.2	714	164	71	68	21	5	2	2	54	2	121	4	1	14	9	.609	1	0-1 0	3.74	3.59
2005 Bal	AL	35	35	0	0	209.1	918	232	126	114	28	3	5	7	63	1	118	5	1	15	12	.556	0	0-0 0	4.62	4.90
2006 Bal	AL	36	29	0	2	189.0	847	234	129	124	32	5	5	4	59	2	136	6	1	9	18	.333	0	0-0 0	5.68	5.90
2007 Col	NL	14	14	0	0	79.1	333	83	43	39	11	3	5	0	21	6	43	0	0	5	4	.556	0	0-0 0	3.97	4.42
2009 Phi	NL	7	5	0	0	30.0	137	42	24	19	3	0	2	0	11	1	19	0	0	3	1	.750	0	0-0 0	6.39	5.70
2010 Ari	NL	33	33	0	0	200.0	874	227	126	111	37	14	7	3	56	1	116	2	0	7	16	.304	0	0-0 0	4.98	5.00
9 ML YEARS		227	199	5	5	1246.2	5415	1382	727	672	184	35	38	31	382	23	809	21	5	75	82	.478	2	0-1 4	4.73	4.85

Wilton Lopez

Pitches: R **Bats:** R **Pos:** RP-68   **Ht:** 6'0" **Wt:** 188 **Born:** 7/19/1983 **Age:** 27

Year Team	Lg	HOW MUCH HE PITCHED						WHAT HE GAVE UP												THE RESULTS						
		G	GS	CG	GF	IP	BFP	H	R	ER	HR	SH	SF	HB	TBB	IBB	SO	WP	Bk	W	L	Pct	Sh	Sv-Op Hld	ERC	ERA
2004 Tampa	A+	1	0	0	0	2.0	9	2	1	1	0	0	0	0	1	0	2	0	0	0	0	-	0	0-- -	3.63	4.50
2004 Btl Crk	A	2	0	0	1	1.2	10	4	5	0	0	0	0	0	1	0	2	0	0	0	1	.000	0	0-- -	13.02	0.00
2004 StIsInd	A-	2	0	0	1	3.0	16	5	5	4	2	0	0	1	1	0	2	0	0	0	0	-	0	0-- -	14.65	12.00
2004 Yanks	R	4	0	0	3	5.2	22	2	0	0	0	0	0	0	0	0	6	2	0	1	0	1.000	0	1-- -	0.45	0.00
2007 FtWyn	A	22	0	0	7	30.0	121	34	11	11	2	0	1	0	2	0	17	1	0	1	0	1.000	0	0-- -	3.53	3.30
2007 Lk Els	A+	22	0	0	15	20.2	95	35	16	14	3	0	0	0	1	0	19	3	0	2	1	.667	0	3-- -	7.19	6.10
2008 SnAnt	AA	27	0	0	4	38.1	162	41	21	21	2	1	0	1	9	2	24	0	0	0	2	.000	0	0-- -	3.52	4.93
2008 Portlnd	AAA	1	0	0	0	1.0	6	1	1	1	0	0	0	0	2	0	1	1	0	0	0	-	0	0-- -	9.51	9.00
2008 Lk Els	A+	30	0	0	29	30.2	126	34	10	9	0	0	1	1	4	1	26	2	0	2	1	.667	0	12-- -	3.09	2.64
2009 CpChr	AA	29	15	1	4	110.1	469	133	62	58	8	2	4	1	13	1	69	2	0	4	5	.444	1	0-- -	3.92	4.73
2010 RdRck	AAA	3	0	0	1	5.0	22	8	3	3	0	0	0	0	0	0	2	0	0	2	1	.667	0	0-- -	5.29	5.40
2009 Hou	NL	8	2	0	0	19.1	97	32	21	18	4	3	2	1	8	0	9	1	0	0	2	.000	0	0-1 0	9.39	8.38
2010 Hou	NL	68	0	0	14	67.0	262	66	23	22	4	2	2	0	5	1	50	2	2	5	2	.714	0	1-3 14	2.56	2.96
2 ML YEARS		76	2	0	14	86.1	359	98	44	40	8	5	4	1	13	1	59	3	2	5	4	.556	0	1-4 14	3.87	4.17

Derek Lowe

Pitches: R **Bats:** R **Pos:** SP-33 **Ht:** 6'6" **Wt:** 230 **Born:** 6/1/1973 **Age:** 38

Year	Team	Lg	G	GS	CG	GF	IP	BFP	H	R	ER	HR	SH	SF	HB	TBB	IBB	SO	WP	Bk	W	L	Pct	Sh	Sv-Op	Hld	ERC	ERA
1997	2 Tms	AL	20	9	0	1	69.0	298	74	49	47	11	4	2	4	23	3	52	2	0	2	6	.250	0	0-2	1	4.88	6.13
1998	Bos	AL	63	10	0	8	123.0	527	126	65	55	5	4	5	4	42	5	77	8	0	3	9	.250	0	4-9	12	3.64	4.02
1999	Bos	AL	74	0	0	32	109.1	436	84	35	32	7	1	2	4	25	1	80	1	0	6	3	.667	0	15-20	22	2.14	2.63
2000	Bos	AL	74	0	0	64	91.1	379	90	27	26	6	4	1	2	22	5	79	2	1	4	4	.500	0	42-47	0	3.17	2.56
2001	Bos	AL	67	3	0	50	91.2	404	103	39	36	7	5	1	5	29	9	82	4	0	5	10	.333	0	24-30	4	4.31	3.53
2002	Bos	AL	32	32	1	0	219.2	854	166	65	63	12	5	2	14	48	0	127	5	0	21	8	.724	1	0-0	0	2.13	2.58
2003	Bos	AL	33	33	0	0	203.1	886	216	113	101	17	3	5	11	72	4	110	3	0	17	7	.708	0	0-0	0	4.32	4.47
2004	Bos	AL	33	33	0	0	182.2	839	224	138	110	15	8	4	8	71	2	105	3	0	14	12	.538	0	0-0	0	5.31	5.42
2005	LAD	NL	35	35	2	0	222.0	934	223	113	89	28	12	5	5	55	1	146	3	2	12	15	.444	2	0-0	0	3.75	3.61
2006	LAD	NL	35	34	1	1	218.0	913	221	97	88	14	7	2	5	55	2	123	3	2	16	8	.667	0	0-0	0	3.42	3.63
2007	LAD	NL	33	32	3	0	199.1	831	194	100	86	20	6	2	1	59	2	147	3	1	12	14	.462	0	0-0	1	3.55	3.88
2008	LAD	NL	34	34	1	0	211.0	851	194	84	76	14	8	7	1	45	7	147	2	0	14	11	.560	0	0-0	0	2.72	3.24
2009	Atl	NL	34	34	0	0	194.2	855	232	109	101	16	11	6	4	63	7	111	4	2	15	10	.600	0	0-0	0	4.80	4.67
2010	Atl	NL	33	33	0	0	193.2	824	204	88	86	18	10	2	4	61	10	136	4	2	16	12	.571	0	0-0	0	4.03	4.00
97	Sea	AL	12	9	0	1	53.0	234	59	43	41	11	2	1	2	20	2	39	2	0	2	4	.333	0	0-0	1	5.55	6.96
97	Bos	AL	8	0	0	0	16.0	64	15	6	6	0	2	1	2	3	1	13	0	0	0	2	.000	0	0-2	1	2.78	3.38
	Postseason		21	10	0	3	83.2	352	72	38	31	9	5	0	4	26	5	55	1	0	5	5	.500	0	1-2	1	3.07	3.33
	14 ML YEARS		600	322	9	156	2328.2	9831	2351	1122	996	190	88	46	70	670	58	1522	47	10	157	129	.549	3	85-108	40	3.66	3.85

Mark Lowe

Pitches: R **Bats:** L **Pos:** RP-14 **Ht:** 6'3" **Wt:** 210 **Born:** 6/7/1983 **Age:** 28

Year	Team	Lg	G	GS	CG	GF	IP	BFP	H	R	ER	HR	SH	SF	HB	TBB	IBB	SO	WP	Bk	W	L	Pct	Sh	Sv-Op	Hld	ERC	ERA
2006	Sea	AL	15	0	0	3	18.2	75	12	4	4	1	1	0	2	9	1	20	1	0	1	0	1.000	0	0-0	6	2.61	1.93
2007	Sea	AL	4	0	0	1	2.2	13	2	2	2	1	0	0	0	3	0	3	0	0	0	0	-	0	0-0	2	7.69	6.75
2008	Sea	AL	57	0	0	19	63.2	303	78	44	38	6	3	3	4	34	0	55	2	0	1	5	.167	0	1-5	1	6.10	5.37
2009	Sea	AL	75	0	0	18	80.0	339	71	39	29	7	0	4	0	29	1	69	4	0	2	7	.222	0	3-13	26	3.16	3.26
2010	2 Tms	AL	14	0	0	5	13.1	61	18	9	8	2	0	1	0	6	1	12	1	0	1	3	.250	0	0-0	4	6.82	5.40
10	Sea	AL	11	0	0	4	10.1	45	11	5	4	1	0	1	0	5	1	7	1	0	1	3	.250	0	0-0	4	4.70	3.48
10	Tex	AL	3	0	0	1	3.0	16	7	4	4	1	0	0	0	1	0	5	0	0	0	0	-	0	0-0	0	15.67	12.00
	5 ML YEARS		165	0	0	46	178.1	791	181	98	81	17	4	8	6	81	3	159	8	0	5	15	.250	0	4-18	39	4.41	4.09

Mike Lowell

Bats: R **Throws:** R **Pos:** 1B-43; DH-16; PH-15; 3B-4 LOW-ull **Ht:** 6'3" **Wt:** 210 **Born:** 2/24/1974 **Age:** 37

Year	Team	Lg	G	AB	H	2B	3B	HR	(Hm	Rd)	TB	R	RBI	RC	TBB	IBB	SO	HBP	SH	SF	SB	CS	SB%	GDP	Avg	OBP	Slg
2010 Pwtckt*	AAA		5	22	11	4	0	4	(-	-)	27	5	10	10	0	0	3	0	0	0	0	0	-	0	.500	.500	1.227
1998	NYY	AL	8	15	4	0	0	0	(0	0)	4	1	0	1	0	0	1	0	0	0	0	0	-	0	.267	.267	.267
1999	Fla	NL	97	308	78	15	0	12	(7	5)	129	32	47	40	26	1	69	5	0	5	0	0	-	8	.253	.317	.419
2000	Fla	NL	140	508	137	38	0	22	(11	11)	241	73	91	86	54	4	75	9	0	11	4	0	1.00	4	.270	.344	.474
2001	Fla	NL	146	551	156	37	0	18	(12	6)	247	65	100	84	43	3	79	10	0	10	1	2	.33	9	.283	.340	.448
2002	Fla	NL	160	597	165	44	0	24	(13	11)	281	88	92	84	65	5	92	4	0	11	4	3	.57	16	.276	.346	.471
2003	Fla	NL	130	492	136	27	1	32	(14	18)	261	76	105	88	56	6	78	3	0	6	1	1	.75	14	.276	.350	.530
2004	Fla	NL	158	598	175	44	1	27	(14	13)	302	87	85	96	64	8	77	6	0	3	5	1	.83	17	.293	.365	.505
2005	Fla	NL	150	500	118	36	1	8	(5	3)	180	56	58	46	46	1	58	2	1	9	4	0	1.00	14	.236	.298	.360
2006	Bos	AL	153	573	163	47	1	20	(9	11)	272	79	80	77	47	5	61	4	0	7	2	2	.50	22	.284	.339	.475
2007	Bos	AL	154	589	191	37	2	21	(14	7)	295	79	120	106	53	4	71	3	0	8	3	2	.60	19	.324	.378	.501
2008	Bos	AL	113	419	115	27	0	17	(6	11)	193	58	73	59	38	2	61	5	0	6	2	2	.50	14	.274	.338	.461
2009	Bos	AL	119	445	129	29	1	17	(12	5)	211	54	75	66	33	5	61	1	0	5	2	1	.67	24	.290	.337	.474
2010	Bos	AL	73	218	52	13	0	5	(3	2)	80	23	26	19	23	1	34	0	0	3	0	0	-	9	.239	.307	.367
	Postseason		34	115	29	8	0	4	(2	2)	49	17	21	17	13	2	15	1	0	3	1	0	1.00	3	.252	.326	.426
	13 ML YEARS		1601	5813	1619	394	7	223	(120	103)	2696	771	952	852	548	45	817	52	1	84	30	14	.68	170	.279	.342	.464

Jed Lowrie

Bats: B **Throws:** R **Pos:** 2B-28; SS-23; PH-9; 1B-7; 3B-1 LAU-ree **Ht:** 6'0" **Wt:** 180 **Born:** 4/17/1984 **Age:** 27

Year	Team	Lg	G	AB	H	2B	3B	HR	(Hm	Rd)	TB	R	RBI	RC	TBB	IBB	SO	HBP	SH	SF	SB	CS	SB%	GDP	Avg	OBP	Slg
2010 Lowell*	A-		6	15	6	1	0	0	(-	-)	7	2	5	4	5	0	1	0	0	1	0	0	-	0	.400	.524	.467
2010 Pwtckt*	AAA		4	15	5	3	0	1	(-	-)	11	3	4	4	1	0	4	0	0	1	1	0	1.00	0	.333	.353	.733
2008	Bos	AL	81	260	67	25	3	2	(0	2)	104	34	46	35	35	0	68	1	2	8	1	0	1.00	8	.258	.339	.400
2009	Bos	AL	32	68	10	2	0	2	(1	1)	18	5	11	5	6	0	20	0	0	2	0	0	-	0	.147	.211	.265
2010	Bos	AL	55	171	49	14	0	9	(3	6)	90	31	24	32	25	0	25	1	0	0	1	1	.50	2	.287	.381	.526
	Postseason		12	31	6	1	0	0	(0	0)	7	4	2	2	5	0	8	1	0	1	0	0	-	0	.194	.316	.226
	3 ML YEARS		168	499	126	41	3	13	(4	9)	212	70	81	72	66	0	113	2	2	10	2	1	.67	10	.253	.336	.425

Jonathan Lucroy

Bats: R **Throws:** R **Pos:** C-75; PH-1 LOO-croy **Ht:** 6'0" **Wt:** 185 **Born:** 6/13/1986 **Age:** 25

Year	Team	Lg	G	AB	H	2B	3B	HR	(Hm	Rd)	TB	R	RBI	RC	TBB	IBB	SO	HBP	SH	SF	SB	CS	SB%	GDP	Avg	OBP	Slg
2007	Helena	R+	61	234	80	18	2	4	(-	-)	114	35	39	42	16	0	37	1	0	2	0	3	.00	8	.342	.383	.487
2008	WV	A	65	239	74	16	1	10	(-	-)	122	45	33	48	30	1	39	3	0	2	8	1	.89	2	.310	.391	.510
2008	BrvdCt	A+	64	236	69	12	1	10	(-	-)	113	31	44	43	28	0	45	2	0	6	1	2	.33	5	.292	.364	.479

Year	Team	Lg	G	AB	H	2B	3B	HR	(Hm	Rd)	TB	R	RBI	RC	TBB	IBB	SO	HBP	SH	SF	SB	CS	SB%	GDP	Avg	OBP	Slg
																BATTING					BASERUNNING				AVERAGES		
2009	Hntsvl	AA	125	419	112	32	2	9	(-	-)	175	61	66	73	78	1	66	2	1	6	1	1	.50	14	.267	.380	.418
2010	Hntsvl	AA	10	42	19	3	0	0	(-	-)	22	8	5	10	4	0	3	0	1	0	0	0	-	0	.452	.500	.524
2010	Nashv	AAA	21	80	19	4	0	2	(-	-)	29	8	11	7	3	0	14	0	0	0	0	0	-	4	.238	.265	.363
2010	Mil	NL	75	277	70	9	0	4	(4	0)	91	24	26	23	18	1	44	1	0	1	4	2	.67	9	.253	.300	.329

Donny Lucy

Bats: R **Throws:** R **Pos:** C-7; PH-1   **Ht:** 6'2" **Wt:** 205 **Born:** 8/8/1982 **Age:** 28

Year	Team	Lg	G	AB	H	2B	3B	HR	(Hm	Rd)	TB	R	RBI	RC	TBB	IBB	SO	HBP	SH	SF	SB	CS	SB%	GDP	Avg	OBP	Slg
																BATTING					BASERUNNING				AVERAGES		
2004	Gr Falls	R+	50	176	42	7	1	1	(-	-)	54	19	26	20	17	0	36	3	5	3	13	1	.93	4	.239	.312	.307
2005	Knapol	A-	54	178	47	5	0	1	(-	-)	55	25	22	22	21	0	41	5	4	3	6	3	.67	4	.264	.353	.309
2006	WinSa	A+	97	332	87	17	1	7	(-	-)	127	48	32	47	33	0	67	8	6	2	12	3	.80	8	.262	.341	.383
2006	Brham	AA	18	60	17	1	0	0	(-	-)	18	2	3	7	4	1	15	3	2	0	1	0	1.00	5	.283	.358	.300
2007	Brham	AA	87	290	78	17	0	6	(-	-)	113	42	27	43	30	0	59	3	2	1	14	1	.93	7	.269	.343	.390
2007	Charltt	AAA	19	75	15	3	0	0	(-	-)	18	5	3	3	3	0	25	0	0	0	0	0	-	3	.200	.231	.240
2008	Charltt	AAA	12	43	12	2	0	2	(-	-)	20	6	6	6	2	0	12	1	0	0	1	0	1.00	0	.279	.326	.465
2009	Charltt	AAA	45	153	33	8	0	2	(-	-)	47	14	10	12	10	0	38	0	2	3	2	2	.50	5	.216	.259	.307
2009	Brham	AA	20	69	15	1	0	0	(-	-)	16	6	2	3	2	0	23	1	1	0	0	0	-	2	.217	.250	.232
2010	Charltt	AAA	59	204	46	10	2	2	(-	-)	66	24	11	18	10	0	52	3	7	1	3	2	.60	3	.225	.271	.324
2007	CWS	AL	8	15	3	0	0	0	(0	0)	3	0	0	0	0	0	6	0	0	0	0	0	-	0	.200	.200	.200
2010	CWS	AL	7	15	5	3	0	1	(0	1)	11	2	2	4	2	0	3	1	0	0	1	0	1.00	0	.333	.444	.733
	2 ML YEARS		15	30	8	3	0	1	(0	1)	14	2	2	4	2	0	9	1	0	0	1	0	1.00	0	.267	.333	.467

Ryan Ludwick

Bats: R **Throws:** L **Pos:** RF-125; PH-11; CF-5; LF-1; DH-1   **Ht:** 6'3" **Wt:** 218 **Born:** 7/13/1978 **Age:** 32

Year	Team	Lg	G	AB	H	2B	3B	HR	(Hm	Rd)	TB	R	RBI	RC	TBB	IBB	SO	HBP	SH	SF	SB	CS	SB%	GDP	Avg	OBP	Slg
																BATTING					BASERUNNING				AVERAGES		
2010	Memp*	AAA	3	9	3	1	0	2	(-	-)	10	2	5	3	0	0	3	0	0	2	0	0	-	1	.333	.273	1.111
2002	Tex	AL	23	81	19	6	0	1	(1	0)	28	10	9	6	7	0	24	0	0	0	2	1	.67	4	.235	.295	.346
2003	2 Tms	AL	47	162	40	8	1	7	(2	5)	71	17	26	28	12	1	48	0	1	0	2	0	1.00	1	.247	.299	.438
2004	Cle	AL	15	50	11	2	0	2	(0	2)	19	3	4	4	2	0	14	2	0	0	0	0	-	0	.220	.278	.380
2005	Cle	AL	19	41	9	0	0	4	(3	1)	21	8	5	3	7	0	13	0	0	1	0	1	.00	1	.220	.333	.512
2007	StL	NL	120	303	81	22	0	14	(7	7)	145	42	52	45	26	1	72	7	3	0	4	4	.50	1	.267	.339	.479
2008	StL	NL	152	538	161	40	3	37	(18	19)	318	104	113	100	62	3	146	8	1	8	4	4	.50	9	.299	.375	.591
2009	StL	NL	139	486	129	20	1	22	(4	18)	217	63	97	82	41	3	106	7	1	4	4	2	.67	6	.265	.329	.447
2010	2 Tms	NL	136	490	123	27	2	17	(8	9)	205	63	69	76	48	0	121	8	0	5	0	4	.00	13	.251	.325	.418
03	Tex	AL	8	26	4	1	0	0	(0	0)	5	3	0	1	4	0	9	0	0	0	0	0	-	0	.154	.267	.192
03	Cle	AL	39	136	36	7	1	7	(2	5)	66	14	26	27	8	1	39	0	1	0	2	0	1.00	1	.265	.306	.485
10	StL	NL	77	281	79	20	2	11	(4	7)	136	44	43	55	24	0	64	4	0	3	0	3	.00	4	.281	.343	.484
10	SD	NL	59	209	44	7	0	6	(4	2)	69	19	26	21	24	0	57	4	0	2	0	1	.00	9	.211	.301	.330
	Postseason		3	12	4	0	0	0	(0	0)	4	1	1	1	1	0	0	0	0	0	0	0	-	0	.333	.385	.333
	8 ML YEARS		651	2151	573	125	7	104	(43	61)	1024	310	375	344	205	8	544	32	6	17	16	16	.50	35	.266	.337	.476

Cory Luebke

Pitches: L **Bats:** R **Pos:** SP-3; RP-1   LUBE-key   **Ht:** 6'4" **Wt:** 200 **Born:** 3/4/1985 **Age:** 26

Year	Team	Lg	G	GS	CG	GF	IP	BFP	H	R	ER	HR	SH	SF	HB	TBB	IBB	SO	WP	Bk	W	L	Pct	Sh	Sv-Op	Hld	ERC	ERA
			HOW MUCH HE PITCHED						WHAT HE GAVE UP												THE RESULTS						
2007	Eugene	A-	8	3	0	0	24.2	95	18	6	4	2	0	0	2	0	26	0	0	3	0	1.000	0	0--	-	1.50	1.46
2007	FtWyn	A	5	5	0	0	27.0	118	29	13	10	2	1	2	2	5	0	30	0	0	1	2	.333	0	0--	-	3.63	3.33
2007	Lk Els	A+	2	1	0	0	7.0	31	10	6	6	1	0	1	1	1	0	5	0	0	1	1	.500	0	0--	-	6.77	7.71
2008	Lk Els	A+	17	15	0	0	72.1	329	97	61	55	8	2	4	0	23	0	60	2	0	3	6	.333	0	0	-	5.83	6.84
2008	FtWyn	A	10	10	0	0	56.0	216	52	19	18	6	6	2	3	9	0	40	2	0	3	3	.500	0	0--	-	3.22	2.89
2009	Lk Els	A+	14	14	1	0	88.1	347	73	24	23	3	2	1	5	17	1	80	1	1	8	2	.800	0	0--	-	2.25	2.34
2009	SnAnt	AA	9	9	0	0	41.1	179	38	21	17	3	3	1	2	15	0	32	2	0	3	2	.600	0	0--	-	3.41	3.70
2010	SnAnt	AA	10	8	1	0	56.1	227	41	18	15	2	6	2	2	12	0	44	2	1	5	1	.833	0	0--	-	1.71	2.40
2010	Portlnd	AAA	9	9	0	0	57.2	227	42	22	19	0	0	1	0	17	0	44	0	0	5	0	1.000	0	0--	-	2.32	2.97
2010	SD	NL	4	3	0	1	17.2	76	17	8	8	3	0	0	1	6	0	18	0	0	1	1	.500	0	0-0	0	4.30	4.08

Julio Lugo

Bats: R **Throws:** R **Pos:** 2B-59; SS-26; PR-12; 3B-7; DH-2; PH-2; LF-1   **Ht:** 6'1" **Wt:** 175 **Born:** 11/16/1975 **Age:** 35

Year	Team	Lg	G	AB	H	2B	3B	HR	(Hm	Rd)	TB	R	RBI	RC	TBB	IBB	SO	HBP	SH	SF	SB	CS	SB%	GDP	Avg	OBP	Slg
																BATTING					BASERUNNING				AVERAGES		
2000	Hou	NL	116	420	119	22	5	10	(6	4)	181	78	40	62	37	0	93	4	3	1	22	9	.71	9	.283	.346	.431
2001	Hou	NL	140	513	135	20	3	10	(6	4)	191	93	37	63	46	0	116	5	15	1	12	11	.52	7	.263	.326	.372
2002	Hou	NL	88	322	84	15	1	8	(6	2)	125	45	35	43	28	3	74	2	4	2	9	3	.75	6	.261	.322	.388
2003	2 Tms		139	498	135	16	4	15	(5	10)	204	64	55	68	44	1	100	4	7	5	12	4	.75	7	.271	.333	.410
2004	TB	AL	157	581	160	41	4	7	(3	4)	230	83	75	86	54	0	106	4	3	8	21	5	.81	5	.275	.338	.396
2005	TB	AL	158	616	182	36	6	6	(0	6)	248	89	57	94	61	0	72	6	3	4	39	11	.78	5	.295	.362	.403
2006	2 Tms		122	435	121	22	2	12	(7	5)	183	69	37	61	39	0	76	4	5	3	24	9	.73	9	.278	.341	.421
2007	Bos	AL	147	570	135	36	2	8	(2	6)	199	71	73	65	48	0	82	4	2	4	33	6	.85	9	.237	.294	.349
2008	Bos	AL	82	261	70	13	0	1	(1	0)	86	27	22	20	34	0	51	4	3	5	12	4	.75	13	.268	.355	.330
2009	2 Tms		88	257	72	13	5	3	(2	1)	104	40	21	37	29	0	45	1	3	3	9	0	1.00	3	.280	.352	.405
2010	Bal	AL	93	241	60	4	2	0	(0	0)	68	26	20	20	15	0	50	2	6	0	5	7	.42	6	.249	.298	.282
03	Hou	NL	22	65	16	3	0	0	(0	0)	19	6	7	9	1	0	12	0	0	0	2	1	.67	2	.246	.338	.292
03	TB	AL	117	433	119	13	4	15	(5	10)	185	58	53	61	35	0	88	4	7	5	10	3	.77	5	.275	.333	.427
06	TB	AL	73	289	89	17	1	12	(7	5)	144	53	27	52	27	0	47	3	3	0	18	4	.82	7	.308	.373	.498
06	LAD	NL	49	146	32	5	1	0	(0	0)	39	16	10	9	12	0	29	1	2	3	6	5	.55	2	.219	.278	.267

Year	Team	Lg	G	AB	H	2B	3B	HR	(Hm	Rd)	TB	R	RBI	RC	TBB	IBB	SO	HBP	SH	SF	SB	CS	SB%	GDP	Avg	OBP	Slg
09	Bos	AL	37	109	31	4	1	1	(1	0)	40	16	8	15	12	0	18	0	1	1	3	0	1.00		.284	.352	.367
09	StL	NL	51	148	41	9	4	2	(1	1)	64	24	13	22	17	0	27	1	2	2	6	0	1.00	3	.277	.351	.432
	Postseason		22	65	16	5	0	0	(0	0)	21	9	3	4	7	0	13	0	2	0	3	1	.75	6	.246	.319	.323
	11 ML YEARS		1330	4714	1273	238	34	80	(38	42)	1819	685	472	619	435	4	865	37	64	40	198	69	.74	82	.270	.334	.386

Hector Luna

Bats: R **Throws:** R **Pos:** PH-22; 3B-4; PR-2; 2B-1   LUE-na   **Ht:** 6'1" **Wt:** 223 **Born:** 2/1/1980 **Age:** 31

								BATTING													BASERUNNING				AVERAGES		
Year	Team	Lg	G	AB	H	2B	3B	HR	(Hm	Rd)	TB	R	RBI	RC	TBB	IBB	SO	HBP	SH	SF	SB	CS	SB%	GDP	Avg	OBP	Slg
2010	NewOr*	AAA	97	354	104	17	0	16	(-	-)	169	55	71	66	42	0	64	5	0	10	7	1	.88	15	.294	.367	.477
2004	StL	NL	83	173	43	7	2	3	(1	2)	63	25	22	20	13	0	37	2	1	3	6	3	.67	2	.249	.304	.364
2005	StL	NL	64	137	39	10	2	1	(0	1)	56	26	18	19	9	0	25	4	2	1	10	2	.83	4	.285	.344	.409
2006	2 Tms		113	350	100	21	2	6	(1	5)	143	41	38	46	27	1	60	1	0	1	5	4	.56	7	.286	.338	.409
2007	Tor	AL	22	42	7	0	0	1	(1	0)	10	5	4	1	2	0	10	1	0	1	2	0	1.00	1	.167	.217	.238
2008	Tor	AL	2	1	1	0	0	0	(0	0)	1	0	0	0	0	0	0	0	0	0	0	1	.00	0	1.000	1.000	1.000
2010	Fla	NL	27	29	4	1	0	2	(0	0)	11	2	4	0	0	0	13	0	0	1	0	1	.00	0	.138	.133	.379
06	StL	NL	76	223	65	14	1	4	(1	3)	93	27	21	32	21	1	34	1	0	0	5	3	.63	3	.291	.355	.417
06	Cle	AL	37	127	35	7	1	2	(0	2)	50	14	17	14	6	0	26	0	0	1	0	1	.00	4	.276	.306	.394
	Postseason		5	9	0	0	0	0	(0	0)	0	0	0	0	0	0	5	0	0	0	0	0	-	0	.000	.000	.000
	6 ML YEARS		311	732	194	39	6	13	(5	8)	284	99	86	86	51	1	145	8	3	7	23	11	.68	13	.265	.317	.388

Brandon Lyon

Pitches: R **Bats:** R **Pos:** RP-79   **Ht:** 6'1" **Wt:** 195 **Born:** 8/10/1979 **Age:** 31

			HOW MUCH HE PITCHED						WHAT HE GAVE UP												THE RESULTS							
Year	Team	Lg	G	GS	CG	GF	IP	BFP	H	R	ER	HR	SH	SF	HB	TBB	IBB	SO	WP	Bk	W	L	Pct	Sh	Sv-Op	Hld	ERC	ERA
2001	Tor	AL	11	11	0	0	63.0	261	63	31	31	6	2	6	1	15	0	35	0	1	5	4	.556	0	0-0	0	3.50	4.29
2002	Tor	AL	15	10	0	0	62.0	279	78	47	45	14	3	2	2	19	2	30	2	0	1	4	.200	0	0-1	0	6.24	6.53
2003	Bos	AL	49	0	0	31	59.0	273	73	33	27	6	1	4	2	19	5	50	0	0	4	6	.400	0	9-12	2	4.96	4.12
2005	Ari	NL	32	0	0	22	29.1	144	44	25	21	6	2	1	2	10	2	17	1	1	0	2	.000	0	14-15	1	7.72	6.44
2006	Ari	NL	68	0	0	22	69.1	293	68	32	30	7	3	4	0	22	7	46	1	0	2	4	.333	0	0-7	23	3.49	3.89
2007	Ari	NL	73	0	0	20	74.0	307	70	25	22	2	3	2	1	22	2	40	3	1	6	4	.600	0	2-5	35	2.93	2.68
2008	Ari	NL	61	0	0	50	59.1	265	75	34	31	7	2	1	0	21	4	44	1	0	3	5	.375	0	26-31	3	4.86	4.70
2009	Det	NL	65	0	0	27	78.2	314	56	25	25	7	5	3	2	31	9	57	3	0	6	5	.545	0	3-6	15	2.46	2.86
2010	Hou	NL	79	0	0	28	78.0	333	68	28	27	2	4	0	3	31	12	54	3	0	6	6	.500	0	20-22	19	2.73	3.12
	Postseason		5	0	0	1	6.0	20	1	0	0	0	0	0	0	1	0	5	0	0	0	0	-	0	0-0	2	0.19	0.00
	9 ML YEARS		453	21	0	200	572.2	2469	595	280	258	57	25	23	13	182	40	373	14	3	33	40	.452	0	74-99	98	3.92	4.05

Mike MacDougal

Pitches: R **Bats:** B **Pos:** RP-17   **Ht:** 6'4" **Wt:** 175 **Born:** 3/5/1977 **Age:** 34

			HOW MUCH HE PITCHED						WHAT HE GAVE UP												THE RESULTS							
Year	Team	Lg	G	GS	CG	GF	IP	BFP	H	R	ER	HR	SH	SF	HB	TBB	IBB	SO	WP	Bk	W	L	Pct	Sh	Sv-Op	Hld	ERC	ERA
2010	Hrsbrg*	AA	8	0	0	2	7.1	37	11	6	6	0	0	1	0	5	0	4	2	0	2	1	.667	0	1--	-	7.45	7.36
2010	Syrcse*	AAA	10	0	0	2	13.2	57	13	5	5	2	1	1	0	6	1	9	1	0	2	0	1.000	0	1--	-	4.31	3.29
2010	Memp*	AAA	8	0	0	2	9.1	37	8	4	4	1	1	1	0	3	0	6	0	0	2	0	1.000	0	1--	-	3.18	3.86
2001	KC	AL	3	3	0	0	15.1	67	18	10	8	2	0	0	1	4	0	7	3	0	1	1	.500	0	0-0	0	5.04	4.70
2002	KC	AL	6	0	0	1	9.0	38	5	5	5	0	0	0	0	7	1	10	1	0	0	1	.000	0	0-0	0	2.26	5.00
2003	KC	AL	68	0	0	61	64.0	285	64	36	29	4	3	2	8	32	0	57	6	0	3	5	.375	0	27-35	1	4.76	4.08
2004	KC	AL	13	0	0	8	11.1	61	16	8	7	2	0	0	1	9	0	14	2	0	1	1	.500	0	1-3	0	9.04	5.56
2005	KC	AL	68	0	0	53	70.1	298	69	32	26	6	1	1	3	24	2	72	6	1	5	6	.455	0	21-25	0	3.80	3.33
2006	2 Tms		29	0	0	7	29.0	110	21	5	5	1	1	0	1	6	0	21	1	0	1	1	.500	0	1-2	11	1.80	1.55
2007	CWS	AL	54	0	0	8	42.1	208	50	37	32	3	0	1	2	33	3	39	8	0	2	5	.286	0	0-3	19	6.49	6.80
2008	CWS	AL	16	0	0	8	17.0	78	16	4	4	0	0	0	2	12	2	12	4	1	0	0	-	0	0-0	0	4.45	2.12
2009	2 Tms		57	0	0	41	54.1	246	52	31	26	3	2	3	3	38	3	34	10	0	1	1	.500	0	20-21	0	4.87	4.33
2010	StL	NL	17	0	0	7	18.2	92	23	15	15	1	0	0	1	12	2	14	1	0	1	1	.500	0	0-1	0	5.91	7.23
06	KC	AL	4	0	0	3	4.0	13	2	0	0	0	0	0	0	0	0	2	0	0	0	0	-	0	1-1	0	0.58	0.00
06	CWS	AL	25	0	0	4	25.0	97	19	5	5	1	1	0	1	6	0	19	1	0	1	1	.500	0	0-1	11	2.10	1.80
09	CWS	AL	5	0	0	1	4.1	25	7	6	6	0	0	0	0	7	0	3	3	0	0	0	-	0	0-0	0	13.09	12.46
09	Was	NL	52	0	0	40	50.0	221	45	25	20	3	2	3	3	31	3	31	7	0	1	1	.500	0	20-21	0	4.26	3.60
	10 ML YEARS		331	3	0	194	331.1	1483	334	183	157	22	8	7	22	177	13	280	42	2	15	22	.405	0	70-90	31	4.62	4.26

Evan MacLane

Pitches: L **Bats:** L **Pos:** RP-2   **Ht:** 6'2" **Wt:** 185 **Born:** 11/4/1982 **Age:** 28

			HOW MUCH HE PITCHED						WHAT HE GAVE UP												THE RESULTS							
Year	Team	Lg	G	GS	CG	GF	IP	BFP	H	R	ER	HR	SH	SF	HB	TBB	IBB	SO	WP	Bk	W	L	Pct	Sh	Sv-Op	Hld	ERC	ERA
2003	Kngspt	R+	14	6	0	4	56.1	231	59	20	18	4	2	2	1	8	0	57	5	1	4	1	.800	0	0--	-	3.24	2.88
2003	Bklyn	A-	1	1	0	0	6.0	23	3	0	0	0	0	0	0	1	0	5	0	0	1	0	1.000	0	0--	-	0.77	0.00
2004	CptCty	A	14	10	0	2	67.2	268	57	21	18	9	3	3	3	10	1	66	2	0	5	2	.714	0	0--	-	2.65	2.39
2004	Bklyn	A-	12	12	0	0	69.0	272	61	27	19	5	3	2	2	10	2	68	2	0	5	2	.714	0	0--	-	2.25	2.48
2005	StLuci	A+	19	19	1	0	112.1	451	96	51	40	14	2	3	2	15	0	92	6	1	8	5	.615	0	0--	-	2.47	3.20
2005	Bnghtn	AA	9	9	1	0	58.2	249	63	31	27	7	1	1	1	9	0	48	0	0	3	2	.600	1	0--	-	3.63	4.14
2006	Bnghtn	AA	6	6	0	0	33.0	134	34	17	17	4	1	1	2	2	0	25	0	0	3	1	.750	1	0--	-	3.31	4.64
2006	Norfolk	AAA	20	20	1	0	121.1	521	136	61	52	11	5	1	3	35	0	67	1	0	9	8	.529	1	0--	-	4.40	3.86
2006	Tucsn	AAA	2	1	0	0	8.0	33	10	3	3	1	0	1	0	1	0	4	0	0	1	0	1.000	0	0--	-	4.75	3.38
2007	Tucsn	AAA	32	19	0	1	115.2	566	190	117	99	21	11	5	4	37	1	53	6	1	7	7	.500	0	0--	-	8.52	7.70
2008	Tucsn	AAA	30	25	0	2	152.1	655	184	91	84	21	8	6	3	31	0	83	4	0	7	8	.467	0	0--	-	4.86	4.96

Year Team	Lg	HOW MUCH HE PITCHED						WHAT HE GAVE UP												THE RESULTS							
		G	GS	CG	GF	IP	BFP	H	R	ER	HR	SH	SF	HB	TBB	IBB	SO	WP	Bk	W	L	Pct	Sh	Sv-Op	Hld	ERC	ERA
2009 Reno	AAA	3	2	0	0	14.2	74	23	11	11	0	3	0	4	4	0	3	0	0	0	2	.000	0	0--	-	7.20	6.75
2009 Memp	AAA	24	24	0	0	151.0	642	171	73	63	23	9	2	7	20	1	92	1	0	8	9	.471	0	0--	-	4.25	3.75
2010 Memp	AAA	24	23	1	0	147.2	612	163	78	73	21	7	7	6	21	2	82	3	0	8	7	.533	0	0--	-	4.12	4.45
2010 StL	NL	2	0	0	1	1.0	4	1	1	1	1	0	0	0	1	0	0	0	0	0	1	.000	0	0-0	0	17.98	9.00

Ryan Madson

Pitches: R Bats: L Pos: RP-55 **Ht: 6'6" Wt: 202 Born: 8/28/1980 Age: 30**

Year Team	Lg	HOW MUCH HE PITCHED						WHAT HE GAVE UP												THE RESULTS							
		G	GS	CG	GF	IP	BFP	H	R	ER	HR	SH	SF	HB	TBB	IBB	SO	WP	Bk	W	L	Pct	Sh	Sv-Op	Hld	ERC	ERA
2010 Clrwtr*	A+	2	0	0	0	2.0	8	1	1	1	1	0	0	0	0	0	3	0	0	0	1	.000	0	0--	-	1.50	4.50
2010 Rdng*	AA	1	0	0	0	2.0	8	2	0	0	0	0	0	1	0	0	1	0	0	0	0	-	0	0--	-	4.15	0.00
2010 LV*	AAA	2	0	0	0	1.2	8	1	1	1	0	0	1	0	2	0	2	0	0	0	0	-	0	0--	-	3.97	5.40
2003 Phi	NL	1	0	0	0	2.0	6	0	0	0	0	0	0	0	0	0	0	0	0	0	0	-	0	0-0	0	0.00	0.00
2004 Phi	NL	52	1	0	14	77.0	312	68	23	20	6	1	1	5	19	4	55	7	0	9	3	.750	0	1-2	7	2.95	2.34
2005 Phi	NL	78	0	0	10	87.0	365	84	44	40	11	5	5	6	25	6	79	6	1	6	5	.545	0	0-7	32	3.83	4.14
2006 Phi	NL	50	17	0	8	134.1	620	176	92	85	20	9	3	10	50	4	99	12	0	11	9	.550	0	2-4	6	6.50	5.69
2007 Phi	NL	38	0	0	9	56.0	237	48	19	19	5	2	2	2	23	4	43	2	2	2	2	.500	0	1-2	7	3.28	3.05
2008 Phi	NL	76	0	0	14	82.2	340	79	29	28	6	3	2	1	23	4	67	2	1	4	2	.667	0	1-3	17	3.20	3.05
2009 Phi	NL	79	0	0	28	77.1	320	73	29	28	7	3	1	3	22	3	78	1	0	5	5	.500	0	10-16	26	3.39	3.26
2010 Phi	NL	55	0	0	21	53.0	217	42	16	15	4	2	0	4	13	3	64	2	0	6	2	.750	0	5-10	15	2.42	2.55
Postseason		23	0	0	6	23.0	100	24	7	7	1	2	2	1	7	1	26	1	0	2	0	1.000	0	1-5	5	3.59	2.74
8 ML YEARS		429	18	0	104	569.1	2417	570	252	235	59	25	14	31	175	28	485	32	4	43	28	.606	0	20-44	110	3.91	3.71

Ron Mahay

Pitches: L Bats: L Pos: RP-41 MAY-hay **Ht: 6'2" Wt: 195 Born: 6/28/1971 Age: 40**

Year Team	Lg	HOW MUCH HE PITCHED						WHAT HE GAVE UP												THE RESULTS							
		G	GS	CG	GF	IP	BFP	H	R	ER	HR	SH	SF	HB	TBB	IBB	SO	WP	Bk	W	L	Pct	Sh	Sv-Op	Hld	ERC	ERA
2010 FtMyrs*	A+	4	0	0	1	4.2	19	5	1	1	0	0	0	0	1	0	4	0	0	0	1	.000	0	0--	-	3.18	1.93
1997 Bos	AL	28	0	0	7	25.0	105	19	7	7	3	1	0	0	11	0	22	3	0	3	0	1.000	0	0-1	5	3.01	2.52
1998 Bos	AL	29	0	0	6	26.0	120	26	16	10	2	0	4	2	15	1	14	3	0	1	1	.500	0	1-2	7	4.76	3.46
1999 Oak	AL	6	1	0	2	19.1	68	8	4	4	2	0	0	0	3	0	15	0	0	2	0	1.000	0	1-1	0	0.88	1.86
2000 2 Tms		23	2	0	7	41.1	199	57	35	33	10	1	2	0	25	1	32	4	0	1	1	.500	0	0-0	2	8.55	7.19
2001 ChC	NL	17	0	0	4	20.2	86	14	6	6	4	0	0	0	15	1	24	1	0	0	0	-	0	0-0	2	4.32	2.61
2002 ChC	NL	11	0	0	1	14.2	65	13	14	14	6	0	0	0	8	0	14	0	0	2	0	1.000	0	0-0	0	6.11	8.59
2003 Tex	AL	35	0	0	5	45.1	189	33	19	16	3	0	0	0	20	7	38	6	0	4	3	.500	0	0-3	9	2.31	3.18
2004 Tex	AL	60	0	0	12	67.0	290	60	23	19	5	4	0	2	29	5	54	2	0	3	0	1.000	0	0-2	14	3.39	2.55
2005 Tex	AL	30	0	0	9	35.2	167	47	28	27	8	0	1	0	16	1	30	2	0	0	2	.000	0	1-1	6	7.10	6.81
2006 Tex	AL	62	0	0	14	57.0	246	54	30	25	7	1	1	0	28	2	56	1	0	1	3	.250	0	0-1	9	4.28	3.95
2007 2 Tms		58	0	0	8	67.0	281	52	20	19	4	3	2	1	37	2	55	1	1	3	0	1.000	0	1-2	7	3.23	2.55
2008 KC	AL	57	0	0	3	64.2	278	61	27	25	6	0	6	1	29	0	49	1	0	5	0	1.000	0	0-1	21	3.98	3.48
2009 2 Tms		57	0	0	11	50.1	239	62	29	24	10	1	2	4	22	2	42	5	0	2	1	.667	0	0-0	6	6.49	4.29
2010 Min	AL	41	0	0	11	34.0	141	33	15	13	5	1	1	0	8	0	25	1	0	1	1	.500	0	0-1	2	3.56	3.44
00 Oak	AL	5	2	0	1	16.0	82	26	18	16	4	1	1	0	9	0	5	2	0	0	1	.000	0	0-0	0	9.97	9.00
00 Fla	AL	18	0	0	6	25.1	117	31	17	17	6	0	1	0	16	1	27	2	0	1	0	1.000	0	0-0	2	7.67	6.04
07 Tex	AL	28	0	0	8	39.0	164	33	12	12	3	1	1	1	21	0	32	0	1	2	0	1.000	0	1-1	1	3.81	2.77
07 Atl	NL	30	0	0	0	28.0	117	19	8	7	1	2	1	0	16	2	23	1	0	1	0	1.000	0	0-1	6	2.47	2.25
09 KC	AL	41	0	0	11	41.1	200	55	26	22	9	1	2	2	19	1	34	4	0	1	1	.500	0	0-0	4	7.27	4.79
09 Min	AL	16	0	0	0	9.0	39	7	3	2	1	0	0	2	3	1	8	1	0	1	0	1.000	0	0-0	2	3.29	2.00
Postseason		3	0	0	1	1.2	6	0	1	1	0	0	0	0	1	0	2	0	0	0	0	-	0	0-0	0	0.38	5.40
14 ML YEARS		514	3	0	100	568.0	2474	539	273	242	75	12	19	10	266	22	470	28	1	27	12	.692	0	4-15	90	4.28	3.83

Paul Maholm

Pitches: L Bats: L Pos: SP-32 mah-HALL-uhm **Ht: 6'2" Wt: 224 Born: 6/25/1982 Age: 29**

Year Team	Lg	HOW MUCH HE PITCHED						WHAT HE GAVE UP												THE RESULTS							
		G	GS	CG	GF	IP	BFP	H	R	ER	HR	SH	SF	HB	TBB	IBB	SO	WP	Bk	W	L	Pct	Sh	Sv-Op	Hld	ERC	ERA
2005 Pit	NL	6	6	0	0	41.1	168	31	10	10	2	0	0	3	17	0	26	0	0	3	1	.750	0	0-0	0	2.79	2.18
2006 Pit	NL	30	30	0	0	176.0	788	202	98	93	19	7	4	12	81	6	117	3	1	8	10	.444	0	0-0	0	5.58	4.76
2007 Pit	NL	29	29	2	0	177.2	765	204	110	99	22	13	6	6	49	3	105	5	0	10	15	.400	1	0-0	0	4.77	5.02
2008 Pit	NL	31	31	1	0	206.1	853	201	89	85	21	8	8	9	63	2	139	2	1	9	9	.500	0	0-0	0	3.84	3.71
2009 Pit	NL	31	31	0	0	194.2	836	221	102	96	14	7	1	6	60	4	119	11	1	9	9	.471	0	0-0	0	4.45	4.44
2010 Pit	NL	32	32	1	0	185.1	840	228	119	105	15	10	6	9	62	2	102	2	0	9	15	.375	1	0-0	0	5.14	5.10
6 ML YEARS		159	159	4	0	981.1	4250	1087	528	488	93	45	25	45	332	17	608	23	3	47	59	.443	2	0-0	0	4.63	4.48

Mitch Maier

Bats: L Throws: R Pos: CF-65; RF-43; LF-8; PH-4; PR-2; 1B-1; DH-1 MY-err **Ht: 6'2" Wt: 213 Born: 6/30/1982 Age: 29**

Year Team	Lg	BATTING																		BASERUNNING				AVERAGES		
		G	AB	H	2B	3B	HR	(Hm	Rd)	TB	R	RBI	RC	TBB	IBB	SO	HBP	SH	SF	SB	CS	SB%	GDP	Avg	OBP	Slg
2006 KC	AL	5	13	2	0	0	0	(0	0)	2	3	0	0	2	0	4	0	0	1	0	0	-	1	.154	.267	.154
2008 KC	AL	34	91	26	1	1	0	(0	0)	29	9	9	7	2	0	18	2	2	0	0	2	.00	3	.286	.316	.319
2009 KC	AL	127	341	83	15	3	3	(1	2)	113	42	31	42	43	2	76	4	7	2	9	2	.82	6	.243	.333	.331
2010 KC	AL	117	373	98	15	6	5	(1	4)	140	41	39	49	41	2	68	0	4	3	3	2	.60	3	.263	.333	.375
4 ML YEARS		283	818	209	31	10	8	(2	6)	284	95	79	98	88	4	166	6	13	5	12	6	.67	13	.256	.330	.347

John Maine

Pitches: R **Bats:** R **Pos:** SP-9　　　　　　　　　　　　　　　**Ht:** 6'4" **Wt:** 200 **Born:** 5/8/1981 **Age:** 30

			HOW MUCH HE PITCHED						WHAT HE GAVE UP										THE RESULTS							
Year	Team	Lg	G	GS	CG	GF	IP	BFP	H	R	ER	HR	SH	SF	HB	TBB	IBB	SO	WP	Bk	W	L	Pct	Sh	Sv-Op	Hld	ERC	ERA
2010	Bnghtn*	AA	1	1	0	0	4.0	15	1	0	0	0	0	0	0	2	0	5	0	0	0	0	-	0	0- -	-	0.75	0.00
2010	Buffalo*	AAA	1	1	0	0	4.1	18	1	1	0	0	0	0	0	3	0	4	0	0	0	0	-	0	0- -	-	0.97	0.00
2004	Bal	AL	1	1	0	0	3.2	19	7	4	4	1	0	0	0	3	0	1	1	0	0	1	.000	0	0-0	0	14.87	9.82
2005	Bal	AL	10	8	0	1	40.0	184	39	30	28	8	0	2	1	24	0	24	0	1	2	3	.400	0	0-0	0	5.47	6.30
2006	NYM	NL	16	15	1	1	90.0	365	69	40	36	15	3	1	2	33	1	71	3	0	6	5	.545	1	0-0	0	3.22	3.60
2007	NYM	NL	32	32	1	0	191.0	810	168	90	83	23	11	4	5	75	3	180	2	0	15	10	.600	1	0-0	0	3.58	3.91
2008	NYM	NL	25	25	0	0	140.0	608	122	70	65	16	10	5	4	67	2	122	10	0	10	8	.556	0	0-0	0	3.81	4.18
2009	NYM	NL	15	15	0	0	81.1	349	67	42	40	8	6	2	4	38	2	55	5	0	7	6	.538	0	0-0	0	3.48	4.43
2010	NYM	NL	9	9	0	0	39.2	190	47	29	27	8	4	1	2	25	1	39	3	0	1	3	.250	. 0	0-0	0	7.09	6.13
	Postseason		3	3	0	0	13.2	62	10	5	4	1	1	0	1	11	2	13	0	0	1	0	1.000	0	0-0	0	3.93	2.63
	7 ML YEARS		108	105	2	2	585.2	2525	519	305	283	79	34	15	18	265	9	492	24	1	41	36	.532	2	0-0	0	3.96	4.35

Scott Maine

Pitches: L **Bats:** L **Pos:** RP-13　　　　　　　　　　　　　　**Ht:** 6'3" **Wt:** 210 **Born:** 2/2/1985 **Age:** 26

			HOW MUCH HE PITCHED						WHAT HE GAVE UP										THE RESULTS							
Year	Team	Lg	G	GS	CG	GF	IP	BFP	H	R	ER	HR	SH	SF	HB	TBB	IBB	SO	WP	Bk	W	L	Pct	Sh	Sv-Op	Hld	ERC	ERA
2007	Yakima	A-	8	0	0	3	10.1	52	6	9	7	0	0	0	1	12	0	20	3	0	1	0	1.000	0	1- -	-	3.89	6.10
2008	Visalia	A+	32	0	0	16	48.0	211	48	20	17	4	2	1	4	21	1	53	10	0	3	2	.600	0	5- -	-	4.42	3.19
2009	Mobile	AA	36	0	0	22	47.1	206	56	16	14	2	1	0	2	15	2	46	5	0	3	3	.500	0	5- -	-	4.55	2.66
2009	Reno	AAA	12	0	0	4	14.2	65	13	7	6	0	0	1	0	7	0	15	0	0	1	2	.333	0	2- -	-	2.92	3.68
2010	Iowa	AAA	33	0	0	12	41.0	180	33	17	16	4	2	0	2	21	3	47	1	0	3	1	.750	0	5- -	-	3.39	3.51
2010	Tenn	AA	12	0	0	8	16.1	66	12	8	4	1	1	0	1	4	1	15	0	0	1	1	.500	0	5- -	-	2.01	2.20
2010	ChC	NL	13	0	0	4	13.0	54	9	4	3	1	0	1	0	5	1	11	0	0	0	0	-	0	0-0	2	2.08	2.08

Gary Majewski

Pitches: R **Bats:** R **Pos:** RP-2　　　　　　　muh-JESS-kee　　　　　　**Ht:** 6'2" **Wt:** 217 **Born:** 2/26/1980 **Age:** 31

			HOW MUCH HE PITCHED						WHAT HE GAVE UP										THE RESULTS							
Year	Team	Lg	G	GS	CG	GF	IP	BFP	H	R	ER	HR	SH	SF	HB	TBB	IBB	SO	WP	Bk	W	L	Pct	Sh	Sv-Op	Hld	ERC	ERA
2010	RdRck*	AAA	40	0	0	18	53.1	244	69	42	37	7	2	4	4	18	2	40	2	0	4	5	.444	0	2- -	-	6.07	6.24
2004	Mon	NL	16	0	0	7	21.0	95	28	15	9	2	1	1	2	5	1	12	0	0	0	1	.000	0	1-2	0	5.68	3.86
2005	Was	NL	79	0	0	24	86.0	376	80	32	28	2	5	4	7	37	6	50	1	0	4	4	.500	0	1-5	24	3.43	2.93
2006	2 Tms	NL	65	0	0	21	70.1	316	79	38	36	5	1	3	4	29	3	43	6	0	4	4	.500	0	0-7	8	4.76	4.61
2007	Cin	NL	32	0	0	3	23.0	113	43	22	21	3	0	0	2	3	1	10	0	0	0	4	.000	0	0-3	6	9.01	8.22
2008	Cin	NL	37	0	0	8	40.0	192	61	31	29	6	2	4	3	15	0	27	1	0	1	0	1.000	0	0-1	2	8.04	6.53
2010	Hou	NL	2	0	0	2	2.0	13	5	5	5	1	0	0	0	1	0	1	0	0	0	0	-	0	0-0	0	17.28	22.50
06	Was	NL	46	0	0	14	55.1	237	49	24	22	4	1	0	1	25	1	34	6	0	3	2	.600	0	0-5	6	3.48	3.58
06	Cin	NL	19	0	0	7	15.0	79	30	14	14	1	0	3	3	4	2	9	0	0	1	2	.333	0	0-2	2	10.33	8.40
	6 ML YEARS		231	0	0	65	242.1	1105	296	143	128	19	9	12	18	90	11	143	8	0	9	13	.409	0	2-18	40	5.30	4.75

Carlos Maldonado

Bats: R **Throws:** R **Pos:** C-4　　　　　　　　　　　　　　　　**Ht:** 6'1" **Wt:** 249 **Born:** 1/3/1979 **Age:** 32

			BATTING																	BASERUNNING				AVERAGES		
Year	Team	Lg	G	AB	H	2B	3B	HR	(Hm	Rd)	TB	R	RBI	RC	TBB	IBB	SO	HBP	SH	SF	SB	CS	SB%	GDP	Avg	OBP	Slg
2010	Syrcse*	AAA	63	188	42	8	0	3	(-	-)	59	16	27	19	19	0	45	2	3	6	2	1	.67	5	.223	.293	.314
2010	Nats*	R	3	9	2	0	0	0	(-	-)	2	1	2	0	1	0	2	0	0	0	0	0	-	0	.222	.300	.222
2006	Pit	NL	8	19	2	0	0	0	(0	0)	2	0	0	0	1	1	10	0	0	0	1	0	1.00	0	.105	.150	.105
2007	Pit	NL	13	24	5	1	0	2	(0	2)	12	2	4	2	5	2	8	0	0	1	0	0	-	2	.208	.333	.500
2010	Was	NL	4	11	3	0	0	1	(0	1)	6	1	3	3	1	0	2	0	0	0	0	0	-	0	.273	.333	.545
	3 ML YEARS		25	54	10	1	0	3	(0	3)	20	3	7	5	7	3	20	0	0	1	1	0	1.00	2	.185	.274	.370

Matt Maloney

Pitches: L **Bats:** L **Pos:** RP-5; SP-2　　　　　　　　　　　　　**Ht:** 6'4" **Wt:** 220 **Born:** 1/16/1984 **Age:** 27

			HOW MUCH HE PITCHED						WHAT HE GAVE UP										THE RESULTS							
Year	Team	Lg	G	GS	CG	GF	IP	BFP	H	R	ER	HR	SH	SF	HB	TBB	IBB	SO	WP	Bk	W	L	Pct	Sh	Sv-Op	Hld	ERC	ERA
2005	Batvia	A-	8	8	0	0	37.0	156	38	20	16	2	1	2	1	15	0	36	3	0	2	1	.667	0	0- -	-	4.18	3.89
2006	Lakwd	A	27	27	2	0	168.2	709	120	54	38	5	7	1	8	73	0	180	10	1	16	9	.640	1	0- -	-	2.34	2.03
2007	Rdng	AA	21	21	1	0	125.2	541	117	70	55	13	9	8	4	45	0	115	5	1	9	7	.563	0	0- -	-	3.61	3.94
2007	Chatt	AA	4	4	0	0	28.0	104	17	9	8	4	2	1	1	3	0	39	2	0	2	2	.500	0	0- -	-	1.51	2.57
2007	Lsvlle	AAA	3	3	0	0	17.0	66	10	6	6	2	1	0	0	6	1	23	2	0	2	1	.667	0	0- -	-	1.86	3.18
2008	Lsvlle	AAA	25	25	2	0	140.1	601	143	75	73	18	10	3	7	39	2	132	4	0	11	5	.688	1	0- -	-	4.05	4.68
2008	Reds	R	1	0	0	0	5.2	18	1	0	0	0	0	0	0	0	0	9	0	0	1	0	1.000	0	0- -	-	0.07	0.00
2009	Lsvlle	AAA	22	22	3	0	143.0	591	143	56	49	11	10	5	7	24	0	125	4	0	9	9	.500	1	0- -	-	3.22	3.08
2009	Carlina	AA	1	1	0	0	7.0	24	3	1	1	1	0	0	2	0	5	1	0	0	0	-	0	0- -	-	1.39	1.29
2010	Lsvlle	AAA	24	23	0	1	134.2	561	132	65	50	9	9	4	10	28	0	104	4	1	10	7	.588	0	0- -	-	3.30	3.34
2009	Cin	NL	7	7	0	0	40.2	170	43	22	22	9	2	4	3	8	1	28	0	0	2	4	.333	0	0-0	0	4.76	4.87
2010	Cin	NL	7	2	0	0	20.2	86	20	7	7	2	2	0	1	5	1	13	0	0	2	2	.500	0	0-0	0	3.39	3.05
	2 ML YEARS		14	9	0	0	61.1	256	63	29	29	11	4	4	4	13	2	41	0	0	4	6	.400	0	0-0	0	4.28	4.26

Matt Mangini

Bats: L **Throws:** R **Pos:** 3B-7; DH-3; PH-1   **Ht:** 6'4" **Wt:** 220 **Born:** 12/21/1985 **Age:** 25

								BATTING													BASERUNNING				AVERAGES		
Year	Team	Lg	G	AB	H	2B	3B	HR	(Hm	Rd)	TB	R	RBI	RC	TBB	IBB	SO	HBP	SH	SF	SB	CS	SB%	GDP	Avg	OBP	Slg
2007	Everett	A-	22	79	23	4	0	2	(-	-)	33	12	9	14	13	1	18	1	0	0	3	0	1.00	0	.291	.398	.418
2007	Ms	R	2	6	0	0	0	0	(-	-)	0	0	0	0	2	0	1	0	0	0	0	0	-	0	.000	.250	.000
2007	Hi Dsrt	A+	17	62	14	1	2	2	(-	-)	25	7	8	8	6	0	21	1	0	0	1	0	1.00	0	.226	.304	.403
2008	Hi Dsrt	A+	52	181	48	12	0	6	(-	-)	78	27	25	31	23	0	52	9	1	0	3	1	.75	2	.265	.376	.431
2008	WTenn	AA	68	237	48	5	0	2	(-	-)	59	22	25	13	12	1	64	3	2	2	0	1	.00	5	.203	.248	.249
2009	WTenn	AA	124	422	115	18	5	12	(-	-)	179	48	67	64	38	1	92	6	0	3	10	2	.83	13	.273	.339	.424
2010	Tacom	AAA	117	447	140	31	4	18	(-	-)	233	73	63	81	26	3	96	2	0	2	3	0	1.00	14	.313	.352	.521
2010	Sea	AL	11	38	8	0	0	0	(0	0)	8	2	1	0	2	0	13	0	1	0	0	0	-	1	.211	.250	.211

Jeff Manship

Pitches: R **Bats:** R **Pos:** RP-12; SP-1   **Ht:** 6'2" **Wt:** 210 **Born:** 1/16/1985 **Age:** 26

			HOW MUCH HE PITCHED						WHAT HE GAVE UP										THE RESULTS							
Year	Team	Lg	G	GS	CG	GF	IP	BFP	H	R	ER	HR	SH	SF	HB	TBB	IBB	SO	WP	Bk	W	L	Pct	Sh	Sv-Op	Hld	ERC	ERA
2006	Twins	R	2	0	0	0	5.2	21	3	0	0	0	0	0	0	1	0	10	0	1	0	0	-	0	0--		0.89	0.00
2006	FtMyrs	A+	4	3	0	0	8.2	36	7	3	2	0	1	0	0	2	0	12	0	0	0	0	-	0	0--		1.76	2.08
2007	Beloit	A	13	13	0	0	77.2	288	51	15	13	4	1	1	1	9	0	77	7	0	7	1	.875	0	0--		1.33	1.51
2007	FtMyrs	A+	13	13	0	0	71.1	314	77	38	25	5	1	1	2	25	0	59	1	0	8	5	.615	0	0--		4.18	3.15
2008	FtMyrs	A+	13	13	1	0	78.2	320	68	31	25	0	0	2	4	20	0	63	4	0	7	3	.700	1	0--		2.38	2.86
2008	NwBrit	AA	14	14	0	0	76.2	340	90	47	38	8	2	3	3	24	0	62	6	1	3	6	.333	0	0--		4.90	4.46
2009	NwBrit	AA	13	13	0	0	75.2	314	72	37	36	2	1	2	2	20	0	45	0	0	6	4	.600	0	0--		2.92	4.28
2009	Roch	AAA	8	8	0	0	50.1	212	53	23	18	1	2	1	1	17	0	30	1	1	4	2	.667	0	0--		3.73	3.22
2010	Roch	AAA	19	18	1	1	98.1	437	134	60	56	13	2	4	2	22	2	83	1	0	3	8	.273	1	0--		5.85	5.13
2009	Min	AL	11	5	0	1	31.2	146	39	21	20	4	1	3	1	15	0	21	2	0	1	1	.500	0	0-0	0	6.11	5.68
2010	Min	AL	13	1	0	1	29.0	124	34	20	17	3	1	1	0	6	0	21	0	0	2	1	.667	0	0-0	0	4.31	5.28
	2 ML YEARS		24	6	0	2	60.2	270	73	41	37	7	2	4	1	21	0	42	2	0	3	2	.600	0	0-0	0	5.23	5.49

Robert Manuel

Pitches: R **Bats:** R **Pos:** RP-10   MAN-you-el   **Ht:** 6'3" **Wt:** 205 **Born:** 7/9/1983 **Age:** 27

			HOW MUCH HE PITCHED						WHAT HE GAVE UP										THE RESULTS							
Year	Team	Lg	G	GS	CG	GF	IP	BFP	H	R	ER	HR	SH	SF	HB	TBB	IBB	SO	WP	Bk	W	L	Pct	Sh	Sv-Op	Hld	ERC	ERA
2005	Mets	R	12	5	0	4	56.2	228	55	19	13	2	2	1	1	4	0	49	1	0	8	1	.889	0	0--		2.33	2.06
2005	Bklyn	A-	2	0	0	0	5.0	20	5	1	1	1	0	0	0	0	0	5	0	0	0	0	-	0	0--		3.05	1.00
2006	Dayton	A	13	7	0	1	48.0	208	58	27	23	5	3	2	2	4	1	36	1	0	0	3	.000	0	1--		4.04	4.31
2006	Srsota	A+	6	0	0	1	8.0	36	10	7	4	3	1	1	0	2	0	4	0	0	0	0	-	0	0--		6.80	4.50
2007	Srsota	A+	33	11	0	3	98.1	411	100	47	44	3	4	4	3	22	0	93	1	0	6	5	.545	0	1--		3.14	4.03
2008	Srsota	A+	4	0	0	0	7.2	32	5	1	0	0	0	0	0	3	0	11	0	0	1	0	1.000	0	0--		1.60	0.00
2008	Chatt	AA	47	0	0	13	77.0	300	47	16	12	2	6	2	3	15	6	92	0	0	5	3	.625	0	3--		1.22	1.40
2008	Lsvlle	AAA	1	0	0	0	2.0	8	2	0	0	0	0	0	0	0	0	0	0	0	0	0	-	0	0--		1.95	0.00
2009	Lsvlle	AAA	36	0	0	17	46.2	188	37	17	14	2	4	0	2	10	0	38	0	0	3	4	.429	0	10--		2.10	2.70
2009	Tacom	AAA	15	0	0	11	19.0	75	13	8	7	4	0	0	0	6	0	11	1	0	1	1	.500	0	4--		2.76	3.32
2010	Pwtckt	AAA	45	0	0	32	64.1	248	46	14	12	4	3	1	1	13	0	48	0	0	8	2	.800	0	13--		1.78	1.68
2009	Cin	NL	3	0	0	1	4.1	18	5	0	0	0	0	0	0	1	0	2	0	0	0	0	-	0	0-0	0	3.69	0.00
2010	Bos	AL	10	0	0	6	12.2	54	10	6	6	5	0	0	0	7	1	5	0	0	1	0	1.000	0	0-0	0	5.42	4.20
	2 ML YEARS		13	0	0	7	17.0	72	15	6	6	5	0	0	0	8	1	7	0	0	1	0	1.000	0	0-0	0	5.00	3.18

Tommy Manzella

Bats: R **Throws:** R **Pos:** SS-82; PH-2   **Ht:** 6'2" **Wt:** 200 **Born:** 4/16/1983 **Age:** 28

								BATTING													BASERUNNING				AVERAGES		
Year	Team	Lg	G	AB	H	2B	3B	HR	(Hm	Rd)	TB	R	RBI	RC	TBB	IBB	SO	HBP	SH	SF	SB	CS	SB%	GDP	Avg	OBP	Slg
2005	TriCity	A-	53	220	51	6	4	0	(-	-)	65	24	18	16	9	0	39	0	2	2	5	3	.63	7	.232	.260	.295
2006	Lxngtn	A	99	338	93	22	1	7	(-	-)	138	50	43	50	33	1	80	3	8	5	16	8	.67	12	.275	.340	.408
2007	Salem	A+	57	223	53	13	0	0	(-	-)	66	28	24	22	19	0	30	3	5	1	5	2	.71	3	.238	.305	.296
2007	CpChr	AA	64	228	66	12	3	1	(-	-)	87	35	15	32	19	0	40	0	6	1	10	2	.83	4	.289	.343	.382
2008	CpChr	AA	54	224	67	11	5	4	(-	-)	100	27	34	35	17	0	35	1	3	4	4	4	.50	7	.299	.346	.446
2008	RdRck	AAA	61	228	50	15	1	0	(-	-)	67	19	15	17	17	0	39	0	2	0	0	4	.00	7	.219	.273	.294
2009	RdRck	AAA	133	530	153	31	5	9	(-	-)	221	68	56	78	40	2	99	1	7	2	12	3	.80	18	.289	.339	.417
2010	CpChr	AA	5	14	6	1	0	0	(-	-)	7	4	1	2	0	0	2	0	0	1	0	2	.00	1	.429	.429	.500
2010	RdRck	AAA	6	27	9	2	0	1	(-	-)	14	4	4	5	2	0	6	0	0	0	0	0	-	2	.333	.379	.519
2009	Hou	NL	7	5	1	0	0	0	(0	0)	1	0	0	0	0	0	4	0	0	0	0	0	-	0	.200	.200	.200
2010	Hou	NL	83	258	58	7	0	1	(1	0)	68	17	21	18	13	1	71	3	5	3	0	1	.00	6	.225	.267	.264
	2 ML YEARS		90	263	59	7	0	1	(1	0)	69	17	21	18	13	1	75	3	5	3	0	1	.00	6	.224	.266	.262

Shaun Marcum

Pitches: R **Bats:** R **Pos:** SP-31   **Ht:** 6'0" **Wt:** 197 **Born:** 12/14/1981 **Age:** 29

			HOW MUCH HE PITCHED						WHAT HE GAVE UP										THE RESULTS							
Year	Team	Lg	G	GS	CG	GF	IP	BFP	H	R	ER	HR	SH	SF	HB	TBB	IBB	SO	WP	Bk	W	L	Pct	Sh	Sv-Op	Hld	ERC	ERA
2005	Tor	AL	5	0	0	3	8.0	32	6	0	0	0	0	0	0	4	0	4	0	0	0	0	-	0	0-0	0	2.58	0.00
2006	Tor	AL	21	14	0	3	78.1	357	87	44	44	14	1	2	4	38	0	65	1	0	3	4	.429	0	0-0	0	5.80	5.06
2007	Tor	AL	38	25	0	3	159.0	660	149	76	73	27	3	3	5	49	1	122	1	0	12	6	.667	0	1-2	1	4.00	4.13
2008	Tor	AL	25	25	0	0	151.1	630	126	60	57	21	1	3	3	50	2	123	3	0	9	7	.563	0	0-0	0	3.32	3.39
2010	Tor	AL	31	31	1	0	195.1	800	181	84	79	24	1	3	6	43	3	165	3	0	13	8	.619	0	0-0	0	3.24	3.64
	5 ML YEARS		120	95	1	12	592.0	2479	549	264	253	86	6	11	23	184	9	479	8	0	37	25	.597	0	1-2	1	3.77	3.85

Jhan Marinez

Pitches: R Bats: R Pos: RP-4   YAN mah-REE-nyez   Ht: 6'1" Wt: 165 Born: 8/12/1988 Age: 22

			HOW MUCH HE PITCHED						WHAT HE GAVE UP										THE RESULTS						
Year	Team	Lg	G	GS	CG	GF	IP	BFP	H	R	ER	HR	SH	SF	HB	TBB	IBB	SO	WP	Bk	W	L	Pct	Sh	Sv-Op Hld	ERC	ERA
2007	Mrlns	R	3	0	0	0	3.1	19	5	5	4	0	0	0	1	4	0	4	1	0	0	0	—	0	0- -	11.36	10.80
2008	Mrlns	R	11	1	0	1	16.2	82	18	13	11	0	0	0	2	14	0	18	1	1	1	1	.500	0	0- -	5.95	5.94
2009	Jupiter	A+	29	0	0	10	43.0	179	28	17	15	4	1	3	4	20	0	42	3	0	1	1	.500	0	1- -	2.75	3.14
2010	Jupiter	A+	21	1	0	14	25.1	99	12	4	4	1	3	0	1	14	1	44	6	0	0	0	.000	0	4- -	1.73	1.42
2010	Jaxnvl	AA	15	0	0	11	16.2	63	9	5	4	1	0	1	0	7	0	20	2	0	1	0	1.000	0	6- -	1.69	2.16
2010	Fla	NL	4	0	0	2	2.2	14	3	3	2	1	0	0	0	3	0	3	0	0	1	1	.500	0	0-2	0 10.25	6.75

Nick Markakis

Bats: L Throws: L Pos: RF-159; DH-1   mar-KAY-kiss   Ht: 6'1" Wt: 200 Born: 11/17/1983 Age: 27

							BATTING														BASERUNNING				AVERAGES		
Year	Team	Lg	G	AB	H	2B	3B	HR	(Hm	Rd)	TB	R	RBI	RC	TBB	IBB	SO	HBP	SH	SF	SB	CS	SB%	GDP	Avg	OBP	Slg
2006	Bal	AL	147	491	143	25	2	16	(9	7)	220	72	62	67	43	3	72	3	3	2	2	0	1.00	15	.291	.351	.448
2007	Bal	AL	161	637	191	43	3	23	(15	8)	309	97	112	103	61	5	112	5	1	6	18	6	.75	22	.300	.362	.485
2008	Bal	AL	157	595	182	48	1	20	(11	9)	292	106	87	113	99	7	113	2	0	1	10	7	.59	10	.306	.406	.491
2009	Bal	AL	161	642	188	45	2	18	(8	10)	291	94	101	97	56	0	98	3	0	10	6	2	.75	12	.293	.347	.453
2010	Bal	AL	160	629	187	45	3	12	(8	4)	274	79	60	99	73	9	93	2	0	5	7	2	.78	18	.297	.370	.436
	5 ML YEARS		786	2994	891	206	11	89	(51	38)	1386	448	422	479	332	24	488	15	4	24	43	17	.72	77	.298	.368	.463

Carlos Marmol

Pitches: R Bats: R Pos: RP-77   Ht: 6'2" Wt: 215 Born: 10/14/1982 Age: 28

			HOW MUCH HE PITCHED						WHAT HE GAVE UP										THE RESULTS						
Year	Team	Lg	G	GS	CG	GF	IP	BFP	H	R	ER	HR	SH	SF	HB	TBB	IBB	SO	WP	Bk	W	L	Pct	Sh	Sv-Op Hld	ERC	ERA
2006	ChC	NL	19	13	0	1	77.0	356	71	54	52	14	6	2	5	59	2	59	3	1	5	7	.417	0	0-0	6.01	6.08
2007	ChC	NL	59	0	0	6	69.1	285	41	11	11	3	1	2	4	35	3	96	5	1	5	1	.833	0	1-2 16	2.11	1.43
2008	ChC	NL	82	0	0	22	87.1	348	40	30	26	10	2	3	6	41	3	114	6	1	2	4	.333	0	7-9 30	1.86	2.68
2009	ChC	NL	79	0	0	29	74.0	335	43	29	28	2	4	1	12	65	3	93	6	1	2	4	.333	0	15-19 27	3.55	3.41
2010	ChC	NL	77	0	0	70	77.2	332	40	23	22	1	0	0	8	52	4	138	2	2	2	3	.400	0	38-43 0	2.18	2.55
	Postseason		4	0	0	0	5.2	26	6	5	5	2	1	1	0	3	0	9	0	0	0	1	.000	0	0-0	6.73	7.94
	5 ML YEARS		316	13	0	128	385.1	1656	235	147	139	30	13	8	35	252	15	500	22	6	16	19	.457	0	61-73 73	3.03	3.25

Jeff Marquez

Pitches: R Bats: R Pos: RP-1   marr-KEZZ   Ht: 6'2" Wt: 190 Born: 8/10/1984 Age: 26

			HOW MUCH HE PITCHED						WHAT HE GAVE UP										THE RESULTS						
Year	Team	Lg	G	GS	CG	GF	IP	BFP	H	R	ER	HR	SH	SF	HB	TBB	IBB	SO	WP	Bk	W	L	Pct	Sh	Sv-Op Hld	ERC	ERA
2004	Yanks	R	4	2	0	0	14.1	58	10	1	1	0	0	0	1	4	0	18	0	1	2	0	1.000	0	0- -	1.71	0.63
2004	StsInd	A-	11	11	0	0	50.2	222	51	26	17	2	3	3	5	20	0	36	2	1	2	4	.333	0	0- -	4.05	3.02
2005	CtnSC	A	27	27	1	0	139.2	604	138	64	53	4	1	3	3	61	0	107	10	0	9	13	.409	0	0- -	3.74	3.42
2006	Tampa	A+	18	17	0	0	92.1	401	102	56	37	4	2	2	3	29	0	82	2	0	7	5	.583	0	0- -	4.05	3.61
2006	Yanks	R	2	2	0	0	5.2	24	7	2	2	1	0	0	0	1	0	8	0	0	1	0	1.000	0	0- -	5.17	3.18
2007	Trntn	AA	27	27	2	0	155.1	673	166	80	63	11	1	5	8	44	0	94	9	1	15	9	.625	0	0- -	3.97	3.65
2008	S-WB	AAA	14	14	1	0	80.2	349	93	51	42	12	7	4	4	24	1	33	1	0	6	7	.462	0	0- -	5.18	4.69
2008	Yanks	R	2	1	0	0	6.2	33	10	4	4	0	0	1	1	1	0	6	1	0	1	0	1.000	0	0- -	5.47	5.40
2008	Trntn	AA	3	3	0	0	15.1	63	12	5	5	0	0	0	2	7	0	12	0	0	1	1	.500	0	0- -	2.77	2.93
2009	Charltt	AAA	11	11	0	0	45.2	227	72	51	50	12	1	3	2	22	0	27	5	0	2	8	.200	0	0- -	9.71	9.85
2010	Charltt	AAA	27	26	0	0	144.2	623	160	79	72	14	2	1	3	49	1	89	4	1	8	9	.471	0	0- -	4.55	4.48
2010	CWS	AL	1	0	0	1	1.0	5	2	2	2	1	0	0	0	0	0	0	0	0	0	0	—	0	0-0	0 16.28	18.00

Jason Marquis

Pitches: R Bats: L Pos: SP-13   marr-KEE   Ht: 6'1" Wt: 210 Born: 8/21/1978 Age: 32

			HOW MUCH HE PITCHED						WHAT HE GAVE UP										THE RESULTS						
Year	Team	Lg	G	GS	CG	GF	IP	BFP	H	R	ER	HR	SH	SF	HB	TBB	IBB	SO	WP	Bk	W	L	Pct	Sh	Sv-Op Hld	ERC	ERA
2010	Ptomc*	A+	1	1	0	0	3.2	18	6	3	3	0	0	0	1	1	0	3	0	0	0	0	—	0	0- -	7.97	7.36
2010	Nats*	R	1	1	0	0	3.0	10	2	0	0	0	0	0	0	0	4	0	0	0	0	0	—	0	0- -	1.01	0.00
2010	Hrsbrg*	AA	1	1	0	0	3.1	16	5	3	3	0	1	0	0	1	0	3	1	0	0	0	—	0	0- -	5.66	8.10
2010	Syrcse*	AAA	2	2	0	0	11.0	42	7	6	5	2	1	0	1	3	0	11	0	0	0	0	—	0	0- -	2.64	4.09
2000	Atl	NL	15	0	0	7	23.1	103	23	16	13	4	1	1	1	12	1	17	1	0	1	0	1.000	0	0-1	5.13	5.01
2001	Atl	NL	38	16	0	9	129.1	556	113	62	50	14	6	5	4	59	4	98	1	2	5	6	.455	0	0-2 2	3.70	3.48
2002	Atl	NL	22	22	0	0	114.1	507	127	66	64	19	4	3	3	49	3	84	4	0	8	9	.471	0	0-0	5.43	5.04
2003	Atl	NL	21	2	0	10	40.2	182	43	27	25	3	0	3	2	16	2	29	2	0	0	1-1	0	4.45	5.53			
2004	StL	NL	32	32	0	0	201.1	874	215	90	83	26	5	6	10	70	1	138	6	0	15	7	.682	0	0-0	4.69	3.71
2005	StL	NL	33	32	3	0	207.0	868	206	110	95	29	4	3	5	69	2	100	10	3	13	14	.481	1	0-0	4.23	4.13
2006	StL	NL	33	33	0	0	194.1	870	221	136	130	35	12	3	16	75	2	96	2	1	14	16	.467	0	0-0	5.79	6.02
2007	ChC	NL	34	33	1	0	191.2	846	190	111	98	22	13	1	13	76	6	109	3	0	12	9	.571	1	0-0	4.28	4.60
2008	ChC	NL	29	28	0	0	167.0	738	172	87	84	15	10	7	8	70	6	91	8	1	11	9	.550	0	0-0 1	4.35	4.53
2009	Col	NL	33	33	2	0	216.0	921	218	104	97	15	10	10	4	80	6	115	6	1	15	13	.536	1	0-0	3.86	4.04
2010	Was	NL	13	13	0	0	58.2	276	76	47	43	9	3	0	4	24	0	31	1	1	2	9	.182	0	0-0	6.93	6.60
	Postseason		11	3	0	6	23.2	115	25	17	12	6	4	1	0	18	1	14	0	0	0	2	.000	0	0-0	6.85	4.56
	11 ML YEARS		303	244	6	26	1543.2	6741	1604	856	782	191	68	42	74	602	33	898	44	9	96	92	.511	3	1-4 4	4.60	4.56

Sean Marshall

Pitches: L Bats: L Pos: RP-80 **Ht: 6'7" Wt: 220 Born: 8/30/1982 Age: 28**

Year	Team	Lg	G	GS	CG	GF	IP	BFP	H	R	ER	HR	SH	SF	HB	TBB	IBB	SO	WP	Bk	W	L	Pct	Sh	Sv-Op	Hld	ERC	ERA
2006	ChC	NL	24	24	0	0	125.2	563	132	85	78	20	7	1	7	59	3	77	6	0	6	9	.400	0	0-0	0	5.27	5.59
2007	ChC	NL	21	19	0	0	103.1	446	107	52	45	13	7	2	1	35	3	67	4	0	7	8	.467	0	0-0	0	4.18	3.92
2008	ChC	NL	34	7	0	6	65.1	279	60	28	28	9	4	3	4	23	4	58	3	0	3	5	.375	0	1-2	3	3.82	3.86
2009	ChC	NL	55	9	1	10	85.1	373	91	43	41	10	7	1	1	32	4	68	2	0	3	7	.300	0	0-0	7	4.43	4.32
2010	ChC	NL	80	0	0	16	74.2	307	58	25	22	3	2	2	2	25	5	90	1	0	7	5	.583	0	1-3	22	2.26	2.65
	Postseason		2	0	0	0	3.1	13	2	1	1	1	0	0	0	1	0	5	0	0	0	0	-	0	0-0	0	2.70	2.70
	5 ML YEARS		214	59	1	32	454.1	1968	448	233	214	55	27	9	15	174	19	360	16	0	26	34	.433	0	2-5	32	4.12	4.24

Lou Marson

Bats: R Throws: R Pos: C-87 MARR-son **Ht: 6'1" Wt: 200 Born: 6/26/1986 Age: 25**

Year	Team	Lg	G	AB	H	2B	3B	HR	(Hm	Rd)	TB	R	RBI	RC	TBB	IBB	SO	HBP	SH	SF	SB	CS	SB%	GDP	Avg	OBP	Slg
2010 Clmbs*	AAA		37	124	25	7	1	4	(-	-)	46	19	14	17	22	0	24	1	0	0	5	0	1.00	1	.202	.327	.371
2008 Phi	NL		1	4	2	0	0	1	(1	0)	5	2	2	2	0	0	2	0	0	0	0	0	-	0	.500	.500	1.250
2009 2 Tms			21	61	15	7	0	0	(0	0)	22	9	4	7	10	0	21	0	0	1	0	0	-	3	.246	.347	.361
2010 Cle	AL		87	262	51	15	0	3	(0	3)	75	29	22	17	26	0	55	3	2	1	8	1	.89	7	.195	.274	.286
09 Phi	NL		7	17	4	1	0	0	(0	0)	5	3	0	1	3	0	7	0	0	0	0	0	-	1	.235	.350	.294
09 Cle	AL		14	44	11	6	0	0	(0	0)	17	6	4	6	7	0	14	0	0	1	0	0	-	2	.250	.346	.386
3 ML YEARS			109	327	68	22	0	4	(1	3)	102	40	28	26	36	0	78	3	2	2	8	1	.89	10	.208	.291	.312

Andy Marte

Bats: R Throws: R Pos: 3B-45; 1B-32; PH-9; DH-2; PR-1 MARR-tay **Ht: 6'1" Wt: 205 Born: 10/21/1983 Age: 27**

Year	Team	Lg	G	AB	H	2B	3B	HR	(Hm	Rd)	TB	R	RBI	RC	TBB	IBB	SO	HBP	SH	SF	SB	CS	SB%	GDP	Avg	OBP	Slg
2010 Lk Cty*	A		1	4	2	0	0	0	(-	-)	2	2	0	1	1	0	0	0	0	0	0	0	-	0	.500	.600	.500
2005 Atl	NL		24	57	8	2	1	0	(0	0)	12	3	4	1	7	0	13	0	0	2	0	1	.00	3	.140	.227	.211
2006 Cle	AL		50	164	37	15	1	5	(3	2)	69	20	23	21	13	0	38	1	0	0	0	0	-	3	.226	.287	.421
2007 Cle	AL		20	57	11	4	0	1	(0	1)	18	3	8	4	2	0	9	1	0	0	0	0	-	0	.193	.233	.316
2008 Cle	AL		80	235	52	11	1	3	(2	1)	74	21	17	17	14	0	52	1	7	0	1	2	.33	5	.221	.268	.315
2009 Cle	AL		47	155	36	6	1	6	(2	4)	62	20	25	20	14	1	30	1	1	4	0	0	-	5	.232	.293	.400
2010 Cle	AL		81	170	39	7	2	5	(1	4)	65	18	19	19	17	0	35	0	0	1	0	3	.00	2	.229	.298	.382
6 ML YEARS			302	838	183	45	6	20	(8	12)	300	85	96	82	67	1	177	4	8	7	1	6	.14	17	.218	.277	.358

Damaso Marte

Pitches: L Bats: L Pos: RP-30 duh-MAH-soe marr-TAY **Ht: 6'2" Wt: 213 Born: 2/14/1975 Age: 36**

Year	Team	Lg	G	GS	CG	GF	IP	BFP	H	R	ER	HR	SH	SF	HB	TBB	IBB	SO	WP	Bk	W	L	Pct	Sh	Sv-Op	Hld	ERC	ERA
1999 Sea	AL	5	0	0	2	8.2	47	16	9	9	3	0	0	0	6	0	3	0	0	0	1	.000	0	0-0	0	13.32	9.35
2001 Pit	NL	23	0	0	4	36.1	154	34	21	19	5	1	2	3	12	3	39	1	0	0	1	.000	0	0-0	0	3.93	4.71
2002 CWS	AL	68	0	0	22	60.1	240	44	19	19	5	1	1	4	18	2	72	3	1	1	1	.500	0	10-12	14	2.42	2.83
2003 CWS	AL	71	0	0	25	79.2	314	50	16	14	3	3	3	3	34	6	87	1	0	4	2	.667	0	11-18	14	1.96	1.58
2004 CWS	AL	74	0	0	24	73.2	303	56	28	28	10	2	6	3	34	4	68	3	0	6	5	.545	0	6-12	21	3.39	3.42
2005 CWS	AL	66	0	0	15	45.1	213	45	21	19	5	1	0	3	33	4	54	1	1	3	4	.429	0	4-8	22	5.51	3.77
2006 Pit	NL	75	0	0	15	58.1	255	51	30	24	5	8	3	4	31	6	63	3	1	7	.125	0	0-4	13	3.88	3.70
2007 Pit	NL	65	0	0	11	45.1	182	32	14	12	2	0	2	2	18	1	51	0	1	2	0	1.000	0	0-0	15	2.35	2.38
2008 2 Tms		72	0	0	10	65.0	272	52	29	29	6	1	0	2	26	2	71	1	0	5	3	.625	0	5-7	25	2.90	4.02
2009 NYY	AL	21	0	0	6	13.1	62	15	14	14	3	1	0	1	6	1	13	0	0	1	3	.250	0	0-1	5	6.01	9.45
2010 NYY	AL	30	0	0	3	17.2	76	10	8	8	2	0	2	1	11	1	12	2	1	0	0	-	0	0-2	9	2.72	4.08
08 Pit	NL	47	0	0	8	46.2	192	38	18	18	4	0	0	1	16	1	47	1	0	4	0	1.000	0	5-7	15	2.82	3.47
08 NYY	AL	25	0	0	2	18.1	80	14	11	11	1	1	0	1	10	1	24	0	0	1	3	.250	0	0-0	10	3.07	5.40
	Postseason		10	0	0	0	5.2	25	3	0	0	0	1	0	0	4	0	8	0	0	1	0	1.000	0	0-0	3	1.93	0.00
	11 ML YEARS		570	0	0	137	503.2	2118	405	209	195	48	18	19	26	229	30	533	15	5	23	27	.460	0	36-64	138	3.31	3.48

Victor Marte

Pitches: R Bats: R Pos: RP-22 marr-TAY **Ht: 6'2" Wt: 254 Born: 11/8/1980 Age: 30**

Year	Team	Lg	G	GS	CG	GF	IP	BFP	H	R	ER	HR	SH	SF	HB	TBB	IBB	SO	WP	Bk	W	L	Pct	Sh	Sv-Op	Hld	ERC	ERA
2006 Hshma	Jap	12	0	0	-	11.1	45	5	7	2	1	-	-	1	6	-	5	3	0	0	1	.000	0	0- -		1.97	1.59
2007 Hshma	Jap	17	0	0	-	17.1	90	28	16	16	2	-	-	2	10	-	13	1	0	0	1	.000	0	0- -		9.34	8.31
2008 Hshma	Jap	1	0	0	-	2.0	11	4	3	3	0	-	-	0	1	-	2	1	0	0	0	-	0	0- -		9.72	13.50
2009 NWArk	AA	13	0	0	8	22.0	86	15	7	6	1	0	1	1	5	0	17	1	0	2	1	.667	0	4- -		1.69	2.45
2009 Omha	AAA	26	0	0	17	42.1	182	35	14	10	0	3	2	1	20	2	36	4	0	1	4	.200	0	4- -		2.69	2.13
2010 Omha	AAA	25	0	0	12	40.2	175	40	17	15	3	3	2	0	15	3	29	6	0	4	1	.800	0	3- -		3.52	3.32
2009 KC	AL	8	0	0	4	12.0	58	13	12	11	2	0	0	0	12	1	7	1	0	0	0	-	0	0-0	0	7.71	8.25
2010 KC	AL	22	0	0	4	27.2	137	38	30	30	8	1	0	2	15	1	19	1	0	3	0	1.000	0	0-0	1	8.71	9.76
2 ML YEARS		30	0	0	8	39.2	195	51	42	41	10	1	0	2	27	2	26	2	0	3	0	1.000	0	0-0	1	8.42	9.30

J.D. Martin

Pitches: R Bats: R Pos: SP-9   Ht: 6'4" Wt: 200 Born: 1/2/1983 Age: 28

Year	Team	Lg	G	GS	CG	GF	IP	BFP	H	R	ER	HR	SH	SF	HB	TBB	IBB	SO	WP	Bk	W	L	Pct	Sh	Sv-Op	Hld	ERC	ERA
2001	Burlgtn	R+	10	10	0	0	45.2	174	26	9	7	3	0	0	4	11	0	72	3	1	5	1	.833	0	0--		1.56	1.38
2002	Clmbs	A	27	26	0	0	138.1	594	141	76	60	12	2	3	13	46	0	131	2	1	14	5	.737	0	0--		4.26	3.90
2003	Knstn	A+	16	16	0	0	86.1	375	95	50	41	7	3	1	3	30	0	57	3	0	5	3	.625	0	0--		4.48	4.27
2004	Knstn	A+	25	25	2	0	147.2	605	139	75	72	15	6	8	12	41	0	98	6	0	11	10	.524	0	0--		3.73	4.39
2004	Buffalo	AAA	1	1	0	0	5.0	26	9	6	6	1	0	0	0	2	0	2	0	1	0	0	-	0	0--		9.81	10.80
2005	Akron	AA	10	10	0	0	56.2	223	43	17	15	3	1	1	3	8	0	63	1	0	3	1	.750	0	0--		1.81	2.38
2006	MhVlly	A-	6	6	0	0	18.0	67	11	3	3	1	0	0	1	1	0	13	0	0	0	1	.000	0	0--		1.15	1.50
2006	Lk Cty	A	5	5	0	0	15.0	60	13	7	7	2	0	2	1	3	0	16	0	0	0	1	.000	0	0--		3.12	4.20
2006	Knstn	A+	3	2	0	0	11.1	40	6	0	0	0	0	0	0	1	0	11	0	0	1	0	1.000	0	0--		0.76	0.00
2007	Akron	AA	9	9	0	0	42.1	185	42	22	20	4	4	0	3	16	0	23	1	0	2	3	.400	0	0--		4.16	4.25
2008	Akron	AA	31	8	0	4	79.2	323	73	25	22	5	3	4	4	19	0	71	2	2	11	3	.786	0	0--		3.02	2.49
2008	Buffalo	AAA	4	1	0	1	10.0	37	6	2	2	2	0	0	0	2	0	8	0	0	1	0	1.000	0	0--		1.91	1.80
2009	Syrcse	AAA	16	15	0	0	88.0	338	75	33	26	4	2	7	2	10	1	63	2	1	8	3	.727	0	0--		2.06	2.66
2010	Syrcse	AAA	7	7	0	0	41.0	170	40	18	16	3	2	5	1	8	0	25	2	1	2	2	.500	0	0--		3.05	3.51
2009	Was	NL	15	15	0	0	77.0	341	85	40	38	14	4	2	6	24	4	37	0	0	5	4	.556	0	0-0		5.10	4.44
2010	Was	NL	9	9	0	0	48.0	212	56	30	22	9	1	4	1	11	1	31	1	0	1	5	.167	0	0-0		4.89	4.13
2 ML YEARS			24	24	0	0	125.0	553	141	70	60	23	5	6	7	35	5	68	1	0	6	9	.400	0	0-0	0	5.02	4.32

Russell Martin

Bats: R Throws: R Pos: C-93; PH-7   Ht: 5'10" Wt: 231 Born: 2/15/1983 Age: 28

Year	Team	Lg	G	AB	H	2B	3B	HR	(Hm	Rd)	TB	R	RBI	RC	TBB	IBB	SO	HBP	SH	SF	SB	CS	SB%	GDP	Avg	OBP	Slg
2006	LAD	NL	121	415	117	26	4	10	(8	2)	181	65	65	58	45	8	57	4	1	3	10	5	.67	17	.282	.355	.436
2007	LAD	NL	151	540	158	32	3	19	(8	11)	253	87	87	84	67	1	89	7	0	6	21	9	.70	16	.293	.374	.469
2008	LAD	NL	155	553	155	25	0	13	(6	7)	219	87	69	89	90	8	83	5	0	2	18	6	.75	16	.280	.385	.396
2009	LAD	NL	143	505	126	19	0	7	(3	4)	166	63	53	62	69	9	80	11	2	1	11	6	.65	18	.250	.352	.329
2010	LAD	NL	97	331	82	13	0	5	(2	3)	110	45	26	40	48	7	61	4	1	3	6	2	.75	7	.248	.347	.332
Postseason			19	67	15	4	0	1	(0	1)	22	9	9	6	9	0	16	4	0	0	1	0	1.00	1	.224	.350	.328
5 ML YEARS			667	2344	638	115	7	54	(27	27)	929	347	300	333	319	33	370	31	4	15	66	28	.70	74	.272	.365	.396

Cristhian Martinez

Pitches: R Bats: R Pos: RP-18   KRISS-jen   Ht: 6'1" Wt: 185 Born: 3/6/1982 Age: 29

Year	Team	Lg	G	GS	CG	GF	IP	BFP	H	R	ER	HR	SH	SF	HB	TBB	IBB	SO	WP	Bk	W	L	Pct	Sh	Sv-Op	Hld	ERC	ERA
2003	Tigers	R	9	5	0	2	35.1	155	34	25	23	9	0	1	3	11	0	39	1	0	3	2	.600	0	0--		4.79	5.86
2004	Oneont	A-	2	2	0	0	13.0	47	9	3	3	1	0	0	1	1	0	12	0	0	1	0	1.000	0	0--		1.65	2.08
2004	WMich	A	12	12	1	0	73.2	296	59	27	20	6	4	1	7	20	0	45	3	0	5	2	.714	1	0--		2.84	2.44
2005	Lkland	A+	3	2	0	0	11.0	49	11	6	6	0	0	0	2	4	0	9	0	0	2	0	1.000	0	0--		3.88	4.91
2006	Lkland	A+	5	5	0	0	21.2	93	27	14	12	3	0	1	1	5	0	15	1	0	1	1	.500	0	0--		5.46	4.98
2006	Tigers	R	7	6	0	0	35.0	135	30	11	6	1	1	0	1	4	0	27	2	1	3	2	.600	0	0--		2.02	1.54
2006	Oneont	A-	7	7	0	0	41.2	167	38	15	10	4	0	1	3	5	0	30	1	0	1	2	.333	0	0--		2.81	2.16
2007	Grnsbr	A	18	18	0	0	97.0	404	97	55	44	16	3	3	6	18	0	74	4	0	9	5	.643	0	0--		3.91	4.08
2008	Grnsbr	A	8	8	0	0	44.1	180	44	24	23	2	1	2	3	9	0	14	2	0	4	1	.800	0	0--		3.13	4.67
2008	Jupiter	A+	20	19	1	1	109.1	462	117	56	46	7	8	4	4	16	0	78	0	0	2	7	.222	0	0--		3.32	3.79
2009	Jaxnvl	AA	17	16	0	0	104.0	417	96	39	34	7	3	4	4	22	0	62	1	0	9	3	.750	0	0--		2.96	2.94
2010	Gwnntt	AAA	23	2	0	7	52.2	209	45	22	18	3	0	1	0	8	0	49	0	1	5	1	.833	0	0--		2.13	3.08
2009	Fla	NL	15	0	0	4	26.1	112	27	16	15	2	1	0	0	8	1	18	1	0	1	1	.500	0	0-1	0	3.60	5.13
2010	Atl	NL	18	0	0	8	26.0	110	28	14	14	3	0	1	0	6	1	22	1	0	0	0	-	0	0-0	0	3.87	4.85
2 ML YEARS			33	0	0	12	52.1	222	55	30	29	5	1	1	0	14	2	40	2	0	1	1	.500	0	0-1	0	3.74	4.99

Fernando Martinez

Bats: L Throws: R Pos: LF-6; RF-2; PH-1   Ht: 6'1" Wt: 200 Born: 10/10/1988 Age: 22

Year	Team	Lg	G	AB	H	2B	3B	HR	(Hm	Rd)	TB	R	RBI	RC	TBB	IBB	SO	HBP	SH	SF	SB	CS	SB%	GDP	Avg	OBP	Slg
2006	Hgrstn	A	45	192	64	14	2	5	(-	-)	97	24	28	37	15	0	36	3	0	1	7	4	.64	5	.333	.389	.505
2006	Mets	R	1	4	1	0	0	0	(-	-)	1	1	0	0	0	0	1	0	0	0	0	0	-	0	.250	.250	.250
2006	StLuci	A+	30	119	23	4	2	5	(-	-)	46	18	11	12	6	0	24	4	0	1	1	1	.50	1	.193	.254	.387
2007	Mets	R	3	9	1	0	1	0	(-	-)	3	1	1	0	1	0	6	0	0	0	0	0	-	0	.111	.200	.333
2007	Bnghtn	AA	60	236	64	11	1	4	(-	-)	89	32	21	30	20	2	51	3	0	3	3	4	.43	5	.271	.336	.377
2008	Bnghtn	AA	86	352	101	19	4	8	(-	-)	152	48	43	53	27	2	73	3	0	3	6	2	.75	9	.287	.340	.432
2008	Mets	R	4	14	6	1	1	0	(-	-)	9	2	0	3	0	0	2	1	0	0	0	0	-	0	.429	.467	.643
2009	Buffalo	AAA	45	176	51	16	2	8	(-	-)	95	24	28	32	11	0	33	2	0	1	2	1	.67	4	.290	.337	.540
2010	Buffalo	AAA	71	257	65	16	0	12	(-	-)	117	39	33	38	17	0	65	8	3	2	1	1	1.00	4	.253	.317	.455
2010	StLuci	A+	4	15	4	1	0	0	(-	-)	5	1	0	1	1	1	2	0	0	0	0	0	-	0	.267	.313	.333
2009	NYM	NL	29	91	16	6	0	1	(0	1)	25	11	8	5	5	0	14	3	1	0	2	0	1.00	0	.176	.242	.275
2010	NYM	NL	7	18	3	0	0	0	(0	0)	3	1	2	1	1	0	5	2	0	1	0	1	.00	0	.167	.273	.167
2 ML YEARS			36	109	19	6	0	1	(0	1)	28	12	10	6	6	0	19	5	1	1	2	1	.67	0	.174	.248	.257

Joe Martinez

Pitches: R **Bats:** L **Pos:** RP-8; SP-1 **Ht:** 6'2" **Wt:** 184 **Born:** 2/26/1983 **Age:** 28

Year	Team	Lg	G	GS	CG	GF	IP	BFP	H	R	ER	HR	SH	SF	HB	TBB	IBB	SO	WP	Bk	W	L	Pct	Sh	Sv-Op	Hld	ERC	ERA
2005	SlmKzr	A-	15	13	0	1	69.0	285	69	33	33	9	4	0	5	15	0	59	4	1	4	3	.571	0	0--	0	3.93	4.30
2006	Augsta	A	27	27	1	0	167.2	682	156	66	56	9	6	5	11	26	0	135	7	3	15	5	.750	1	0--	0	2.74	3.01
2007	SnJos	A+	28	28	0	0	162.2	678	172	85	77	11	4	8	5	36	0	151	7	2	10	10	.500	0	0--	0	3.65	4.26
2008	Conn	AA	27	27	0	0	148.0	611	131	58	41	6	7	8	4	37	0	112	3	0	10	10	.500	0	0--	0	2.59	2.49
2009	Giants	R	1	1	0	0	2.2	13	4	3	3	0	0	1	1	0	0	1	0	0	0	0	-	0	0--	0	5.97	10.13
2009	SnJos	A+	2	2	0	0	7.1	26	3	2	2	1	0	0	0	2	0	7	0	0	0	0	-	0	0--	0	1.22	2.45
2009	Fresno	AAA	7	5	0	0	35.0	150	39	21	19	1	1	1	1	8	0	22	1	1	0	2	.000	0	0--	0	3.64	4.89
2010	Fresno	AAA	14	13	1	0	81.1	339	78	35	30	6	3	1	2	26	0	65	6	0	5	3	.625	0	0--	0	3.50	3.32
2010	Indy	AAA	7	4	0	1	28.1	137	46	22	18	6	2	0	2	7	1	18	1	0	1	2	.333	0	1--	0	8.43	5.72
2009	SF	NL	9	5	0	1	30.0	148	46	27	25	4	2	2	1	12	2	19	0	0	3	2	.600	0	0-0	0	7.49	7.50
2010	2 Tms	NL	9	1	0	0	19.2	94	26	11	9	1	0	1	2	9	2	9	1	1	0	1	.000	0	0-0	0	6.02	4.12
10	SF	NL	4	1	0	0	11.0	53	15	6	6	1	0	1	0	6	2	3	0	0	0	1	.000	0	0-0	0	6.91	4.91
10	Pit	NL	5	0	0	0	8.2	41	11	5	3	0	0	0	1	3	0	6	1	1	0	0	-	0	0-0	0	4.96	3.12
2 ML YEARS			18	6	0	1	49.2	242	72	38	34	5	2	3	3	21	4	28	1	1	3	3	.500	0	0-0	0	6.90	6.16

Osvaldo Martinez

Bats: R **Throws:** R **Pos:** SS-11; PH-4 **Ht:** 5'10" **Wt:** 170 **Born:** 5/7/1988 **Age:** 23

Year	Team	Lg	G	AB	H	2B	3B	HR	(Hm	Rd)	TB	R	RBI	RC	TBB	IBB	SO	HBP	SH	SF	SB	CS	SB%	GDP	Avg	OBP	Slg
2006	Mrlns	R	49	171	45	4	1	1	(-	-)	54	21	21	19	19	0	21	0	3	1	7	4	.64	4	.263	.335	.316
2007	Jupiter	A+	1	0	0	0	0	0	(-	-)	0	0	0	0	1	0	0	0	0	0	0	0	-	0	-	1.000	-
2007	Jmstwn	A-	38	114	21	5	0	0	(-	-)	26	8	6	7	11	0	25	1	4	0	7	2	.78	3	.184	.262	.228
2008	Grnsbr	A	85	304	90	11	3	6	(-	-)	125	44	29	41	13	0	46	4	8	2	5	5	.50	12	.296	.331	.411
2009	Jupiter	A+	130	433	110	16	5	1	(-	-)	139	54	45	50	41	0	51	4	5	2	16	4	.80	15	.254	.323	.321
2010	Jaxnvl	AA	130	516	156	28	4	5	(-	-)	207	90	54	80	49	0	64	9	11	2	13	9	.59	10	.302	.372	.401
2010	Fla	NL	14	43	14	4	1	0	(0	0)	20	8	2	7	4	0	6	0	1	0	1	0	1.00	0	.326	.383	.465

Victor Martinez

Bats: B **Throws:** R **Pos:** C-110; 1B-14; DH-4; PH-4 **Ht:** 6'2" **Wt:** 210 **Born:** 12/23/1978 **Age:** 32

Year	Team	Lg	G	AB	H	2B	3B	HR	(Hm	Rd)	TB	R	RBI	RC	TBB	IBB	SO	HBP	SH	SF	SB	CS	SB%	GDP	Avg	OBP	Slg
2002	Cle	AL	12	32	9	1	0	1	(1	0)	13	2	5	5	3	0	2	0	0	1	0	0	-	1	.281	.333	.406
2003	Cle	AL	49	159	46	4	0	1	(0	1)	53	13	10	17	10	0	21	1	0	1	1	1	.50	8	.289	.345	.333
2004	Cle	AL	141	520	147	38	1	23	(8	15)	256	77	108	90	60	11	69	5	0	6	0	1	.00	16	.283	.359	.492
2005	Cle	AL	147	547	167	33	0	20	(10	10)	260	73	80	90	63	9	78	5	0	7	0	1	.00	16	.305	.378	.475
2006	Cle	AL	153	572	181	37	0	16	(4	12)	266	82	93	96	71	8	78	3	0	6	0	0	-	27	.316	.391	.465
2007	Cle	AL	147	562	169	40	0	25	(12	13)	284	78	114	108	62	12	76	10	0	11	0	0	-	19	.301	.374	.505
2008	Cle	AL	73	266	74	17	0	2	(2	0)	97	30	35	36	24	4	32	1	0	3	0	0	-	12	.278	.337	.365
2009	2 Tms	AL	155	588	178	33	1	23	(7	16)	282	88	108	101	75	3	74	3	0	6	1	0	1.00	17	.303	.381	.480
2010	Bos	AL	127	493	149	32	1	20	(10	10)	243	64	79	74	40	5	52	0	0	5	1	0	1.00	17	.302	.351	.493
09	Cle	AL	99	377	107	21	1	15	(6	9)	175	56	67	64	51	3	51	2	0	5	0	0	-	11	.284	.368	.464
09	Bos	AL	56	211	71	12	0	8	(1	7)	107	32	41	37	24	0	23	1	0	1	1	0	1.00	6	.336	.405	.507
Postseason			14	55	16	2	0	1	(1	1)	24	6	9	10	3	3	10	1	0	0	0	0	-	0	.291	.361	.436
9 ML YEARS			1004	3739	1120	235	3	131	(54	77)	1754	509	630	617	411	62	482	28	0	46	3	3	.50	133	.300	.369	.469

Nick Masset

Pitches: R **Bats:** R **Pos:** RP-82 MASS-it **Ht:** 6'4" **Wt:** 235 **Born:** 5/17/1982 **Age:** 29

Year	Team	Lg	G	GS	CG	GF	IP	BFP	H	R	ER	HR	SH	SF	HB	TBB	IBB	SO	WP	Bk	W	L	Pct	Sh	Sv-Op	Hld	ERC	ERA
2006	Tex	AL	8	1	0	7	8.2	36	9	4	4	0	0	2	2	2	0	4	0	0	0	0	-	0	0-0	0	4.05	4.15
2007	CWS	AL	27	1	0	4	39.1	193	52	33	31	2	1	3	2	26	5	21	4	0	2	3	.400	0	0-1	2	6.63	7.09
2008	2 Tms	AL	42	1	0	12	62.0	271	71	32	27	7	3	1	2	26	4	43	3	1	2	0	1.000	0	1-3	2	5.27	3.92
2009	Cin	NL	74	0	0	15	70.0	202	51	23	20	6	1	1	0	24	1	70	6	0	5	1	.833	0	0-2	20	2.24	2.37
2010	Cin	NL	82	0	0	22	76.2	322	64	31	29	7	3	2	1	33	3	85	8	0	4	4	.500	0	2-5	20	3.23	3.40
08	CWS	AL	32	1	0	11	44.2	203	55	26	23	4	3	1	2	21	4	32	2	1	1	0	1.000	0	1-1	1	5.78	4.63
08	Cin	NL	10	0	0	1	17.1	68	16	6	4	3	0	0	0	5	0	11	1	0	1	0	1.000	0	0-2	1	3.93	2.08
5 ML YEARS			233	2	0	60	262.2	1114	250	122	111	22	8	9	7	111	12	223	21	1	13	8	.619	0	3-11	44	3.88	3.80

Justin Masterson

Pitches: R **Bats:** R **Pos:** SP-29; RP-5 **Ht:** 6'6" **Wt:** 250 **Born:** 3/22/1985 **Age:** 26

Year	Team	Lg	G	GS	CG	GF	IP	BFP	H	R	ER	HR	SH	SF	HB	TBB	IBB	SO	WP	Bk	W	L	Pct	Sh	Sv-Op	Hld	ERC	ERA
2008	Bos	AL	36	9	0	6	88.1	365	68	31	31	10	1	1	8	40	3	68	1	0	6	5	.545	0	0-1	3	3.51	3.16
2009	2 Tms	AL	42	16	1	4	129.1	568	128	73	65	12	10	7	8	60	3	119	5	0	4	10	.286	0	0-1	6	4.45	4.52
2010	Cle	AL	34	29	1	0	180.0	802	197	107	94	14	5	4	11	73	4	140	12	0	6	13	.316	1	0-0	2	4.68	4.70
09	Bos	AL	31	6	0	4	72.0	312	72	38	36	7	9	6	7	25	2	67	3	0	3	3	.500	0	0-1	6	4.13	4.50
09	Cle	AL	11	10	1	0	57.1	256	56	35	29	5	1	1	2	35	1	52	2	0	1	7	.125	0	0-0	0	4.85	4.55
Postseason			9	0	0	1	9.2	40	10	3	2	0	1	0	1	5	0	9	0	0	1	0	1.000	0	0-1	4	4.85	1.86
3 ML YEARS			112	54	2	10	397.2	1735	393	211	190	36	16	12	27	173	10	327	18	0	16	28	.364	1	0-2	11	4.34	4.30

Frank Mata

Pitches: R **Bats:** R **Pos:** RP-15   **Ht:** 6'1" **Wt:** 250 **Born:** 3/11/1984 **Age:** 27

			HOW MUCH HE PITCHED					WHAT HE GAVE UP									THE RESULTS							
Year	Team	Lg	G	GS	CG	GF	IP	BFP	H	R	ER	HR	SH	SF	HB	TBB	IBB	SO	WP	Bk	W	L	Pct	Sh	Sv-Op	Hld	ERC	ERA
2004	Elizab	R+	26	1	0	23	31.1	124	22	15	13	1	0	0	4	6	0	39	3	2	2	2	.500	0	13--	-	1.64	3.73
2006	Beloit	A	41	0	0	24	53.1	232	58	30	25	4	2	2	4	18	0	30	10	1	5	3	.625	0	5--	-	4.50	4.22
2007	FtMyrs	A+	13	0	0	5	20.1	84	19	4	3	0	0	1	0	7	0	14	1	0	2	0	1.000	0	1--	-	2.88	1.33
2007	NwBrit	AA	32	0	0	13	48.2	232	66	29	28	4	2	1	5	22	2	28	1	0	0	4	.000	0	3--	-	6.67	5.18
2008	FtMyrs	A+	11	0	0	2	14.0	57	10	4	3	0	0	0	0	4	0	15	2	0	1	0	1.000	0	0--	-	1.59	1.93
2008	NwBrit	AA	23	0	0	11	30.0	144	36	26	24	7	1	0	5	18	0	22	2	1	1	1	.500	0	1--	-	8.07	7.20
2009	NwBrit	AA	53	5	0	15	78.2	358	83	49	33	3	4	3	7	34	2	60	5	2	2	5	.286	0	3--	-	4.27	3.78
2010	Norfolk	AAA	36	0	0	23	42.2	180	34	17	15	2	3	0	2	20	1	30	7	0	5	3	.625	0	8--	-	3.02	3.16
2010	Bal	AL	15	0	0	6	17.1	85	24	16	15	2	0	1	2	8	3	9	1	0	0	0	-	0	0-0	1	6.84	7.79

Marcos Mateo

Pitches: R **Bats:** R **Pos:** RP-21   **Ht:** 6'1" **Wt:** 160 **Born:** 4/18/1984 **Age:** 27

			HOW MUCH HE PITCHED					WHAT HE GAVE UP									THE RESULTS							
Year	Team	Lg	G	GS	CG	GF	IP	BFP	H	R	ER	HR	SH	SF	HB	TBB	IBB	SO	WP	Bk	W	L	Pct	Sh	Sv-Op	Hld	ERC	ERA
2005	Reds	R	13	4	0	6	44.0	192	54	26	21	2	3	1	3	10	0	23	7	0	2	3	.400	0	0--	-	4.61	4.30
2006	Billings	R+	18	0	0	1	45.0	191	43	17	16	2	1	3	3	20	0	30	5	0	5	1	.833	0	1--	-	3.99	3.20
2007	Dayton	A	41	0	0	22	72.0	300	68	29	28	2	7	4	3	24	3	63	8	0	2	4	.333	0	6--	-	3.17	3.50
2008	Peoria	A	8	0	0	6	15.0	54	4	3	2	1	0	0	0	7	0	20	0	0	1	0	1.000	0	1--	-	0.99	1.20
2008	Dytona	A+	25	16	0	3	88.1	380	87	42	35	6	2	3	7	29	0	65	10	2	4	3	.571	0	0--	-	3.79	3.57
2009	Dytona	A+	3	3	0	0	9.0	32	4	0	0	0	1	0	1	2	0	7	0	0	0	0	-	0	0--	-	1.01	0.00
2009	Tenn	AA	34	14	0	0	97.1	435	97	47	44	9	6	0	10	43	0	70	1	1	3	6	.333	0	0--	-	4.54	4.07
2010	Tenn	AA	17	1	0	9	20.2	92	23	8	5	2	0	0	0	3	0	29	0	0	0	0	-	0	4--	-	3.41	2.18
2010	Iowa	AAA	8	0	0	6	12.2	55	12	8	7	0	0	0	0	4	0	15	0	0	0	1	.000	0	0--	-	2.67	4.97
2010	Cubs	R	1	0	0	0	1.0	3	0	0	0	0	0	0	0	0	0	1	0	0	0	0	-	0	0--	-	0.00	0.00
2010	ChC	NL	21	0	0	5	21.2	93	20	15	14	6	0	2	1	9	1	26	1	0	0	1	.000	0	0-0	-	5.07	5.82

Joe Mather

Bats: R **Throws:** R **Pos:** PH-15; CF-14; RF-8; LF-7; PR-4; 1B-3; 3B-1   **Ht:** 6'4" **Wt:** 215 **Born:** 7/23/1982 **Age:** 28

			BATTING																		BASERUNNING				AVERAGES		
Year	Team	Lg	G	AB	H	2B	3B	HR	(Hm	Rd)	TB	R	RBI	RC	TBB	IBB	SO	HBP	SH	SF	SB	CS	SB%	GDP	Avg	OBP	Slg
2001	JhsCty	R+	45	165	41	3	0	5	(-	-)	59	25	21	17	7	0	60	3	1	2	2	2	.50	5	.248	.288	.358
2002	JhsCty	R+	62	224	52	15	2	8	(-	-)	95	29	39	33	27	0	57	3	0	2	9	1	.90	5	.232	.320	.424
2003	NewJrs	A-	65	196	45	12	1	2	(-	-)	65	23	22	21	18	0	38	6	3	0	4	4	.50	4	.230	.314	.332
2004	NewJrs	A-	3	8	1	0	0	0	(-	-)	1	0	0	0	0	0	2	0	0	0	2	0	1.00	0	.125	.125	.125
2004	Peoria	A	65	241	61	18	2	7	(-	-)	104	34	31	35	24	0	70	5	0	0	3	3	.50	2	.253	.333	.432
2005	QuadC	A	54	209	46	15	2	9	(-	-)	92	30	33	28	20	3	49	3	0	2	0	0	-	8	.220	.295	.440
2005	PlmBh	A+	57	200	55	12	2	8	(-	-)	95	37	27	34	12	1	39	9	3	1	4	0	1.00	5	.275	.342	.475
2006	PlmBh	A+	124	443	119	33	1	16	(-	-)	202	64	74	71	36	3	91	8	3	4	9	0	1.00	8	.269	.332	.456
2007	Sprgfld	AA	64	234	71	17	0	18	(-	-)	142	48	46	55	29	6	32	5	1	3	4	0	1.00	2	.303	.387	.607
2007	Memp	AAA	70	253	61	10	1	13	(-	-)	112	32	31	39	23	0	51	10	2	0	6	0	1.00	12	.241	.329	.443
2008	Memp	AAA	59	211	64	14	2	17	(-	-)	133	45	41	54	32	0	36	8	1	2	7	2	.78	5	.303	.411	.630
2009	Memp	AAA	39	136	24	6	2	1	(-	-)	37	12	14	9	9	1	27	2	0	3	7	1	.88	2	.176	.233	.272
2009	Sprgfld	AA	17	58	12	3	0	3	(-	-)	24	8	11	6	5	0	11	1	0	1	0	2	.00	1	.207	.277	.414
2009	Cards	R	3	8	2	1	0	0	(-	-)	3	1	3	1	3	0	1	0	0	0	0	0	-	0	.250	.455	.375
2010	Memp	AAA	91	335	92	18	4	10	(-	-)	148	55	46	53	37	1	74	2	0	2	6	4	.60	5	.275	.348	.442
2008	StL	NL	54	133	32	7	0	8	(2	6)	63	20	18	18	12	1	32	1	0	1	1	0	1.00	2	.241	.306	.474
2010	StL	NL	36	60	13	4	0	0	(0	0)	17	7	3	1	2	0	11	0	0	2	1	1	.50	2	.217	.242	.283
	2 ML YEARS		90	193	45	11	0	8	(2	6)	80	27	21	19	14	1	43	1	0	2	2	1	.67	4	.233	.287	.415

Scott Mathieson

Pitches: R **Bats:** R **Pos:** RP-2   MATH-ih-sun   **Ht:** 6'3" **Wt:** 190 **Born:** 2/27/1984 **Age:** 27

			HOW MUCH HE PITCHED					WHAT HE GAVE UP									THE RESULTS							
Year	Team	Lg	G	GS	CG	GF	IP	BFP	H	R	ER	HR	SH	SF	HB	TBB	IBB	SO	WP	Bk	W	L	Pct	Sh	Sv-Op	Hld	ERC	ERA
2002	Phillies	R	7	2	0	1	16.2	81	24	11	10	0	1	1	2	6	0	14	0	1	0	2	.000	0	0--	-	6.11	5.40
2003	Phillies	R	11	11	0	0	58.2	257	59	42	36	5	1	3	1	13	0	51	4	0	2	7	.222	0	0--	-	3.19	5.52
2003	Batvia	A-	2	0	0	1	6.0	18	0	0	0	0	0	0	0	0	0	7	0	0	0	0	-	0	1--	-	0.00	0.00
2004	Lakwd	A	25	25	1	0	131.1	572	130	73	63	7	6	7	9	50	0	112	9	0	8	9	.471	0	0--	-	3.86	4.32
2005	Clrwtr	A+	23	23	1	0	121.2	508	111	62	56	17	4	5	5	34	0	118	7	0	3	8	.273	0	0--	-	3.53	4.14
2006	Rdng	AA	14	14	0	0	92.2	375	73	35	33	8	3	5	7	29	1	99	1	0	7	2	.778	0	0--	-	2.85	3.21
2006	S-WB	AAA	5	5	0	0	34.1	138	26	16	15	2	1	1	1	10	0	36	3	0	3	1	.750	0	0--	-	2.26	3.93
2007	Phillies	R	2	2	0	0	2.0	6	0	0	0	0	0	0	0	1	0	3	0	0	0	0	-	0	0--	-	0.32	0.00
2007	Clrwtr	A+	3	2	0	1	4.0	17	3	3	2	0	0	0	0	3	0	5	1	0	0	0	-	0	0--	-	3.44	4.50
2007	Rdng	AA	2	0	0	0	2.0	11	3	3	2	1	0	0	0	2	0	1	0	0	0	0	-	0	0--	-	13.58	9.00
2009	Phillies	R	4	0	0	0	6.0	25	3	1	0	0	0	0	0	2	0	8	0	0	2	0	1.000	0	0--	-	1.01	0.00
2009	Clrwtr	A+	5	0	0	3	7.0	27	4	0	0	0	0	0	0	3	0	9	1	0	0	0	-	0	1--	-	1.54	0.00
2009	Rdng	AA	13	0	0	9	19.1	75	10	6	3	1	0	1	0	7	0	17	2	0	2	0	1.000	0	1--	-	1.39	1.40
2010	LV	AAA	54	0	0	49	64.1	262	49	21	20	8	3	1	0	24	0	83	1	0	3	6	.333	0	26--	-	3.07	2.80
2006	Phi	NL	9	8	0	0	37.1	177	48	36	31	8	5	1	1	16	1	28	2	1	1	4	.200	0	0-0	-	6.71	7.47
2010	Phi	NL	2	0	0	0	1.2	12	5	3	2	0	1	0	0	2	0	1	1	0	0	0	-	0	0-0	0	20.56	10.80
	2 ML YEARS		11	8	0	0	39.0	189	53	39	33	8	6	1	1	18	1	29	3	1	1	4	.200	0	0-0	0	7.25	7.62

Doug Mathis

Pitches: R Bats: R Pos: RP-13 **Ht: 6'3" Wt: 220 Born: 6/7/1983 Age: 28**

Year Team	Lg	G	GS	CG	GF	IP	BFP	H	R	ER	HR	SH	SF	HB	TBB	IBB	SO	WP	Bk	W	L	Pct	Sh	Sv-Op	Hld	ERC	ERA
2010 OKCity*	AAA	18	15	1	0	89.0	406	116	61	56	7	2	2	5	31	0	54	4	0	5	7	.417	0	0--	-	5.76	5.66
2008 Tex	AL	8	4	0	3	22.1	112	37	20	17	3	1	0	0	14	2	9	1	0	2	1	.667	0	0-0	0	9.60	6.85
2009 Tex	AL	24	2	0	13	42.2	172	39	17	15	4	0	0	2	10	0	25	0	0	0	1	.000	0	1-1	1	3.20	3.16
2010 Tex	AL	13	0	0	7	22.1	100	30	15	15	7	0	0	0	11	0	10	0	0	1	1	.500	0	0-0	0	8.82	6.04
3 ML YEARS		45	6	0	23	87.1	384	106	52	47	14	1	0	2	35	2	44	1	0	3	3	.500	0	1-1	1	6.05	4.84

Jeff Mathis

Bats: R Throws: R Pos: C-67; PH-1 **Ht: 6'0" Wt: 200 Born: 3/31/1983 Age: 28**

Year Team	Lg	G	AB	H	2B	3B	HR	(Hm	Rd)	TB	R	RBI	RC	TBB	IBB	SO	HBP	SH	SF	SB	CS	SB%	GDP	Avg	OBP	Slg
2010 Salt Lk*	AAA	9	33	8	1	1	1	(-	-)	14	6	5	4	4	0	10	0	0	0	0	0	-	1	.242	.324	.424
2005 LAA	AL	5	3	1	0	0	0	(0	0)	1	1	0	0	0	0	1	0	0	0	0	0	-	0	.333	.333	.333
2006 LAA	AL	23	55	8	2	0	2	(1	1)	16	9	6	4	7	1	14	0	0	1	0	0	-	0	.145	.238	.291
2007 LAA	AL	59	171	36	12	0	4	(3	1)	60	24	23	13	15	0	49	2	3	4	0	1	.00	3	.211	.276	.351
2008 LAA	AL	94	283	55	8	0	9	(4	5)	90	35	42	33	30	4	90	3	8	4	2	2	.50	1	.194	.275	.318
2009 LAA	AL	84	237	50	8	0	5	(3	2)	73	26	28	24	22	0	73	4	3	1	2	3	.40	2	.211	.288	.308
2010 LAA	AL	68	205	40	6	1	3	(2	1)	57	19	18	10	6	0	59	1	3	3	3	0	1.00	3	.195	.219	.278
Postseason		10	20	9	5	0	0	(0	0)	14	2	2	3	0	0	5	0	1	0	0	0	-	0	.450	.450	.700
6 ML YEARS		333	954	190	36	1	23	(13	10)	297	114	117	84	80	5	286	10	22	13	7	6	.54	9	.199	.265	.311

Hideki Matsui

Bats: L Throws: R Pos: DH-120; LF-18; PH-9 **Ht: 6'2" Wt: 210 Born: 6/12/1974 Age: 37**

Year Team	Lg	G	AB	H	2B	3B	HR	(Hm	Rd)	TB	R	RBI	RC	TBB	IBB	SO	HBP	SH	SF	SB	CS	SB%	GDP	Avg	OBP	Slg
2003 NYY	AL	163	623	179	42	1	16	(9	7)	271	82	106	96	63	5	86	3	0	6	2	2	.50	25	.287	.353	.435
2004 NYY	AL	162	584	174	34	2	31	(18	13)	305	109	108	117	88	2	103	3	0	5	3	0	1.00	11	.298	.390	.522
2005 NYY	AL	162	629	192	45	3	23	(15	8)	312	108	116	109	63	7	78	3	0	8	2	2	.50	16	.305	.367	.496
2006 NYY	AL	51	172	52	9	0	8	(1	7)	85	32	29	30	27	2	23	0	0	2	1	0	1.00	6	.302	.393	.494
2007 NYY	AL	143	547	156	28	4	25	(16	9)	267	100	103	91	73	2	73	3	0	10	4	2	.67	9	.285	.367	.488
2008 NYY	AL	93	337	99	17	0	9	(3	6)	143	43	45	56	38	6	47	3	0	0	0	0	-	10	.294	.370	.424
2009 NYY	AL	142	456	125	21	1	28	(13	15)	232	62	90	88	64	1	75	4	0	2	0	1	.00	4	.274	.367	.509
2010 LAA	AL	145	482	132	24	1	21	(10	11)	221	55	84	89	67	6	98	1	0	4	0	1	.00	10	.274	.361	.459
Postseason		56	205	64	15	1	10	(5	5)	111	32	39	40	27	2	33	1	0	2	0	0	-	5	.312	.391	.541
8 ML YEARS		1061	3830	1109	220	12	161	(85	76)	1836	591	681	676	483	31	583	20	0	37	12	8	.60	91	.290	.369	.479

Kaz Matsui

Bats: B Throws: R Pos: 2B-21; PH-6, PR-1 **Ht: 5'10" Wt: 183 Born: 10/23/1975 Age: 35**

Year Team	Lg	G	AB	H	2B	3B	HR	(Hm	Rd)	TB	R	RBI	RC	TBB	IBB	SO	HBP	SH	SF	SB	CS	SB%	GDP	Avg	OBP	Slg
2010 ColSpr*	AAA	82	301	79	12	4	2	(-	-)	105	54	29	38	31	0	50	1	3	2	7	0	1.00	3	.262	.331	.349
2004 NYM	NL	114	460	125	32	2	7	(4	3)	102	65	44	63	40	4	97	2	5	2	14	3	.82	3	.272	.331	.396
2005 NYM	NL	87	267	68	9	4	3	(1	2)	94	31	24	27	14	1	43	5	5	4	6	1	.86	2	.255	.300	.352
2006 2 Tms	NL	70	243	65	12	3	3	(0	3)	92	32	26	28	16	1	46	0	4	2	10	1	.91	1	.267	.310	.379
2007 Col	NL	104	410	118	24	6	4	(4	0)	166	84	37	61	34	1	69	0	8	1	32	4	.89	1	.288	.342	.405
2008 Hou	NL	96	375	110	26	3	6	(4	2)	160	58	33	53	37	0	53	0	7	3	20	5	.80	3	.293	.354	.427
2009 Hou	NL	132	476	119	20	2	9	(5	4)	170	56	46	59	34	2	85	1	3	4	19	3	.86	4	.250	.302	.357
2010 Hou	NL	27	71	10	1	0	0	(0	0)	11	4	1	0	4	0	10	1	2	0	1	1	.50	0	.141	.197	.155
06 NYM	NL	38	130	26	6	0	1	(0	1)	35	10	7	5	6	1	19	0	3	0	2	0	1.00	1	.200	.235	.269
06 Col	NL	32	113	39	6	3	2	(0	2)	57	22	19	23	10	0	27	0	1	2	8	1	.89	0	.345	.392	.504
Postseason		11	40	14	2	2	1	(0	1)	23	5	8	9	3	1	12	0	1	0	2	0	1.00	0	.304	.347	.500
7 ML YEARS		630	2302	615	124	20	32	(18	14)	875	330	211	291	179	9	403	11	47	16	102	18	.85	14	.267	.321	.380

Daisuke Matsuzaka

Pitches: R Bats: R Pos: SP-25 DICE-kay maht-soo-ZAH-kah **Ht: 6'0" Wt: 185 Born: 9/13/1980 Age: 30**

Year Team	Lg	G	GS	CG	GF	IP	BFP	H	R	ER	HR	SH	SF	HB	TBB	IBB	SO	WP	Bk	W	L	Pct	Sh	Sv-Op	Hld	ERC	ERA
2010 Pwtckt*	AAA	3	3	0	0	16.2	64	11	4	3	1	1	0	3	1	0	13	1	0	2	0	1.000	0	0--	-	1.61	1.62
2007 Bos	AL	32	32	1	0	204.2	874	191	100	100	25	3	2	13	80	1	201	5	0	15	12	.556	0	0-0	0	4.10	4.40
2008 Bos	AL	29	29	0	0	167.2	716	128	58	54	12	3	4	7	94	1	154	5	0	18	3	.857	0	0-0	0	3.36	2.90
2009 Bos	AL	12	12	0	0	59.1	283	81	38	38	10	1	1	2	30	1	54	8	0	4	6	.400	0	0-0	0	7.45	5.76
2010 Bos	AL	25	25	0	0	153.2	664	137	84	80	13	3	8	8	74	1	133	4	0	9	6	.600	0	0-0	0	3.89	4.69
Postseason		7	7	0	0	35.2	163	39	19	19	4	0	1	1	17	0	33	4	0	3	1	.750	0	0-0	0	5.04	4.79
4 ML YEARS		98	98	1	0	585.1	2537	537	280	272	60	10	15	30	278	4	542	22	0	46	27	.630	0	0-0	0	4.13	4.18

Gary Matthews Jr.

Bats: B Throws: R Pos: PH-21; CF-10; RF-7; LF-3 **Ht: 6'3" Wt: 225 Born: 8/25/1974 Age: 36**

Year Team	Lg	G	AB	H	2B	3B	HR	(Hm	Rd)	TB	R	RBI	RC	TBB	IBB	SO	HBP	SH	SF	SB	CS	SB%	GDP	Avg	OBP	Slg
2010 Lsvlle*	AAA	23	101	32	7	1	3	(-	-)	50	16	6	17	7	0	26	0	0	0	3	2	.60	1	.317	.361	.495
1999 SD	NL	23	36	8	0	0	0	(0	0)	8	4	7	4	9	0	9	0	0	0	2	0	1.00	1	.222	.378	.222
2000 ChC	NL	80	158	30	1	2	4	(2	2)	47	24	14	13	15	1	28	1	1	0	3	0	1.00	2	.190	.264	.297
2001 2 Tms	NL	152	405	92	15	2	14	(4	10)	153	63	44	51	60	2	100	1	5	1	8	5	.62	8	.227	.328	.378

Year	Team	Lg	G	AB	H	2B	3B	HR	(Hm	Rd)	TB	R	RBI	RC	TBB	IBB	SO	HBP	SH	SF	SB	CS	SB%	GDP	Avg	OBP	Slg
2002	2 Tms		111	345	95	25	3	7	(6	1)	147	54	38	55	43	1	69	1	5	4	15	5	.75	4	.275	.354	.426
2003	2 Tms		144	468	116	31	2	6	(3	3)	169	71	42	51	43	0	95	2	0	4	12	8	.60	8	.248	.314	.361
2004	Tex	AL	87	280	77	17	1	11	(7	4)	129	37	36	48	33	5	64	1	0	3	5	1	.83	1	.275	.350	.461
2005	Tex	AL	131	475	121	25	5	17	(8	9)	207	72	55	63	47	1	90	0	1	3	9	2	.82	11	.255	.320	.436
2006	Tex	AL	147	620	194	44	6	19	(11	8)	307	102	79	109	58	5	99	4	0	8	10	7	.59	8	.313	.371	.495
2007	LAA	AL	140	516	130	26	3	18	(7	11)	216	79	72	66	55	6	102	2	0	6	18	4	.82	12	.252	.323	.419
2008	LAA	AL	127	426	103	19	3	8	(2	6)	152	53	46	47	45	2	95	4	0	2	8	3	.73	12	.242	.319	.357
2009	LAA	AL	103	316	79	19	2	4	(2	2)	114	44	50	50	40	2	74	2	0	2	4	1	.80	4	.250	.336	.361
2010	NYM	NL	36	58	11	3	0	0	(0	0)	14	9	1	3	6	1	24	0	1	0	1	0	1.00	1	.190	.266	.241
01	ChC	NL	106	258	56	9	1	9	(2	7)	94	41	30	31	38	2	55	1	5	0	5	3	.63	4	.217	.320	.364
01	Pit	NL	46	147	36	6	1	5	(2	3)	59	22	14	20	22	0	45	0	0	1	3	2	.60	4	.245	.341	.401
02	NYM	NL	2	1	0	0	0	0	(0	0)	0	0	0	0	0	0	0	0	0	0	0	0	-	0	.000	.000	.000
02	Bal	AL	109	344	95	25	3	7	(6	1)	147	54	38	55	43	1	69	1	5	4	15	5	.75	4	.276	.355	.427
03	Bal	AL	41	162	33	12	1	2	(2	0)	53	21	20	15	9	0	29	1	0	0	0	3	.00	4	.204	.250	.327
03	SD	NL	103	306	83	19	1	4	(1	3)	116	50	22	36	34	0	66	1	0	0	12	5	.71	4	.271	.346	.379
Postseason			7	10	0	0	0	0	(0	0)	0	1	0	0	1	0	5	0	0	0	0	0	-	0	.000	.091	.000
12 ML YEARS			1281	4103	1056	225	29	108	(52	56)	1663	612	484	560	454	26	849	18	13	29	95	36	.73	72	.257	.332	.405

Brian Matusz

Pitches: L **Bats:** L **Pos:** SP-32

MATT-uss

Ht: 6'4" **Wt:** 190 **Born:** 2/11/1987 **Age:** 24

			HOW MUCH HE PITCHED					WHAT HE GAVE UP										THE RESULTS						
Year	Team	Lg	G	GS	CG	GF	IP	BFP	H	R	ER	HR	SH	SF	HB	TBB	IBB	SO	WP	Bk	W	L	Pct	Sh	Sv-Op Hld	ERC	ERA
2009	Frdrck	A+	11	11	0	0	66.2	276	56	22	16	5	4	1	1	21	0	75	5	0	4	2	.667	0	0- - -	2.76	2.16
2009	Bowie	AA	8	8	1	0	46.1	176	31	9	8	2	0	0	1	11	0	46	0	0	7	0	1.000	1	0- - -	1.65	1.55
2009	Bal	AL	8	8	0	0	44.2	196	52	24	23	6	2	2	0	14	0	38	0	0	5	2	.714	0	0-0 0	4.91	4.63
2010	Bal	AL	32	32	0	0	175.2	760	173	88	84	19	6	6	7	63	3	143	1	0	10	12	.455	0	0-0 0	3.98	4.30
2 ML YEARS			40	40	0	0	220.1	956	225	112	107	25	8	8	7	77	3	181	1	0	15	14	.517	0	0-0 0	4.16	4.37

Joe Mauer

Bats: L **Throws:** R **Pos:** C-112; DH-22; PH-8

Ht: 6'5" **Wt:** 230 **Born:** 4/19/1983 **Age:** 28

Year	Team	Lg	G	AB	H	2B	3B	HR	(Hm	Rd)	TB	R	RBI	RC	TBB	IBB	SO	HBP	SH	SF	SB	CS	SB%	GDP	Avg	OBP	Slg
2004	Min	AL	35	107	33	8	1	6	(4	2)	61	18	17	21	11	0	14	1	0	3	1	0	1.00	1	.308	.369	.570
2005	Min	AL	131	489	144	26	2	9	(4	5)	201	61	55	78	61	12	64	1	0	3	13	1	.93	9	.294	.372	.411
2006	Min	AL	140	521	181	36	4	13	(3	10)	264	86	84	103	79	21	54	1	0	7	8	3	.73	24	.347	.429	.507
2007	Min	AL	109	406	119	27	3	7	(2	5)	173	62	60	69	57	10	51	3	2	3	7	1	.88	11	.293	.382	.426
2008	Min	AL	146	536	176	31	4	9	(7	2)	242	98	85	103	84	8	50	1	1	11	1	1	.50	21	.328	.413	.451
2009	Min	AL	138	523	191	30	1	28	(16	12)	307	94	96	123	76	14	63	2	0	5	4	1	.80	13	.365	.444	.587
2010	Min	AL	137	510	167	43	1	9	(1	8)	239	88	75	91	65	14	53	3	0	6	1	4	.20	19	.327	.402	.469
Postseason			6	23	7	1	0	0	(0	0)	8	1	1	1	3	0	4	0	0	0	0	0	-	0	.304	.385	.348
7 ML YEARS			836	3092	1011	201	16	81	(37	44)	1487	507	472	588	433	79	349	12	3	38	35	11	.76	98	.327	.407	.481

Justin Maxwell

Bats: R **Throws:** R **Pos:** RF-29; CF-20; PH-18; PR-8; LF-5

Ht: 6'5" **Wt:** 235 **Born:** 11/6/1983 **Age:** 27

Year	Team	Lg	G	AB	H	2B	3B	HR	(Hm	Rd)	TB	R	RBI	RC	TBB	IBB	SO	HBP	SH	SF	SB	CS	SB%	GDP	Avg	OBP	Slg
2010	Syrcse*	AAA	66	230	66	17	0	6	(-	-)	101	34	21	42	35	1	75	4	3	0	16	7	.70	5	.287	.390	.439
2007	Was	NL	15	26	7	0	0	2	(0	2)	13	5	5	4	1	0	8	0	0	0	0	0	-	0	.269	.296	.500
2009	Was	NL	40	89	22	4	1	4	(1	3)	40	13	9	15	12	0	32	1	0	0	6	1	.86	1	.247	.343	.449
2010	Was	NL	67	104	15	6	0	3	(1	2)	30	16	12	11	25	2	43	0	0	2	5	1	.83	3	.144	.305	.288
3 ML YEARS			122	219	44	10	1	9	(2	7)	83	34	26	30	38	2	83	1	0	2	11	2	.85	4	.201	.319	.379

Lucas May

Bats: R **Throws:** R **Pos:** C-10; PH-2; DH-1

Ht: 6'0" **Wt:** 190 **Born:** 10/24/1984 **Age:** 26

Year	Team	Lg	G	AB	H	2B	3B	HR	(Hm	Rd)	TB	R	RBI	RC	TBB	IBB	SO	HBP	SH	SF	SB	CS	SB%	GDP	Avg	OBP	Slg
2003	Ddgrs	R	48	159	40	8	0	0	(-	-)	48	19	10	20	19	0	38	5	1	0	11	1	.92	5	.252	.350	.302
2004	Ogden	R+	34	147	42	5	2	5	(-	-)	66	25	30	21	8	0	37	2	0	1	4	3	.57	4	.286	.329	.449
2005	Clmbs	A	99	385	88	14	2	9	(-	-)	133	46	53	36	16	1	92	7	1	7	5	2	.71	7	.229	.267	.345
2006	Clmbs	A	119	450	123	27	9	18	(-	-)	222	76	82	77	35	1	130	7	0	5	14	2	.88	10	.273	.332	.493
2007	InldEm	A+	128	507	130	25	3	25	(-	-)	236	81	89	74	36	1	107	7	1	3	5	7	.42	8	.256	.313	.465
2008	Jaxnvl	AA	107	392	90	27	1	13	(-	-)	158	54	54	50	32	1	112	7	2	8	6	1	.86	5	.230	.294	.403
2009	Chatt	AA	68	235	72	18	1	6	(-	-)	110	32	32	45	31	2	58	5	0	6	2	1	.67	6	.306	.390	.468
2010	Chatt	AA	7	24	4	1	0	0	(-	-)	5	2	1	1	2	0	7	1	0	0	0	0	-	0	.167	.259	.208
2010	Albq	AAA	73	260	77	13	3	11	(-	-)	129	47	45	45	22	0	60	1	1	1	4	2	.67	5	.296	.352	.496
2010	Omha	AAA	24	91	25	7	0	5	(-	-)	47	14	13	17	12	0	19	1	0	1	0	0	-	1	.275	.362	.516
2010	KC	AL	12	37	7	1	0	0	(0	0)	8	3	6	1	0	0	10	1	0	1	0	1	.00	1	.189	.205	.216

Yunesky Maya

Pitches: R **Bats:** R **Pos:** SP-5
Ht: 5'11" **Wt:** 170 **Born:** 8/28/1981 **Age:** 29

Year	Team	Lg	G	GS	CG	GF	IP	BFP	H	R	ER	HR	SH	SF	HB	TBB	IBB	SO	WP	Bk	W	L	Pct	Sh	Sv-Op	Hld	ERC	ERA
2010	Nats	R	2	2	0	0	7.0	27	3	2	1	0	0	0	1	2	0	5	0	0	0	0	-	0	0--	-	1.08	1.29
2010	Ptomc	A+	1	1	0	0	4.0	23	7	6	6	1	0	1	1	3	0	4	1	0	0	1	.000	0	0--	-	12.89	13.50
2010	Syrcse	AAA	2	2	0	0	10.1	44	8	2	1	0	1	0	0	5	0	9	2	1	1	1	.500	0	0--	-	2.46	0.87
2010	Was	NL	5	5	0	0	26.0	118	30	18	17	3	2	1	2	11	1	12	2	3	0	3	.000	0	0-0	-	5.44	5.88

John Mayberry

Bats: R **Throws:** R **Pos:** PH-6; RF-3; PR-3; CF-2
Ht: 6'6" **Wt:** 234 **Born:** 12/21/1983 **Age:** 27

Year	Team	Lg	G	AB	H	2B	3B	HR	(Hm	Rd)	TB	R	RBI	RC	TBB	IBB	SO	HBP	SH	SF	SB	CS	SB%	GDP	Avg	OBP	Slg
2005	Spkane	A-	71	265	67	16	0	11	(-	-)	116	51	26	41	26	1	71	10	0	1	7	3	.70	1	.253	.341	.438
2006	Clinton	A	126	459	123	26	4	21	(-	-)	220	77	77	83	59	2	117	9	0	6	9	3	.75	7	.268	.358	.479
2007	Bkrsfld	A+	63	244	56	15	1	16	(-	-)	121	47	45	41	28	2	64	3	0	2	9	1	.90	7	.230	.314	.496
2007	Frisco	AA	69	245	59	10	0	14	(-	-)	111	35	38	36	20	0	62	4	1	1	7	1	.88	6	.241	.307	.453
2008	Frisco	AA	21	82	22	8	0	4	(-	-)	42	16	13	14	4	0	21	3	0	1	4	1	.80	3	.268	.322	.512
2008	Okla	AAA	114	437	115	30	7	16	(-	-)	207	49	58	67	30	2	85	5	1	2	6	2	.75	9	.263	.316	.474
2009	LV	AAA	89	316	81	20	2	13	(-	-)	144	44	43	50	34	0	94	4	4	4	6	2	.75	6	.256	.332	.456
2010	LV	AAA	128	495	132	25	1	15	(-	-)	204	75	65	72	39	4	111	8	1	4	21	3	.88	14	.267	.328	.412
2009	Phi	NL	39	57	12	3	0	4	(1	3)	27	9	8	5	2	0	23	1	0	0	0	0	-	2	.211	.250	.474
2010	Phi	NL	11	12	4	0	0	2	(0	2)	10	4	6	4	1	0	4	0	0	0	0	1	.00	0	.333	.385	.833
	2 ML YEARS		50	69	16	3	0	6	(1	5)	37	12	14	9	3	0	27	1	0	0	0	1	.00	2	.232	.274	.536

Cameron Maybin

Bats: R **Throws:** R **Pos:** CF-77; PH-8
Ht: 6'3" **Wt:** 210 **Born:** 4/4/1987 **Age:** 24

Year	Team	Lg	G	AB	H	2B	3B	HR	(Hm	Rd)	TB	R	RBI	RC	TBB	IBB	SO	HBP	SH	SF	SB	CS	SB%	GDP	Avg	OBP	Slg
2010	NewOr*	AAA	33	130	44	6	2	4	(-	-)	66	21	23	27	13	1	24	2	2	0	5	1	.83	4	.338	.407	.508
2010	MrlInc*	R	3	11	4	1	0	1	(-	-)	8	4	5	3	2	0	1	1	0	0	0	0	-	0	.364	.500	.727
2007	Det	AL	24	49	7	3	0	1	(0	1)	13	8	2	2	3	0	21	1	0	0	5	0	1.00	0	.143	.208	.265
2008	Fla	NL	8	32	16	2	0	0	(0	0)	18	9	2	8	3	0	8	0	1	0	4	0	1.00	0	.500	.543	.563
2009	Fla	NL	54	176	44	12	2	4	(1	3)	72	30	13	15	17	1	51	1	4	1	1	3	.25	2	.250	.318	.409
2010	Fla	NL	82	291	68	7	3	8	(5	3)	105	46	28	37	24	1	92	5	1	1	9	2	.82	4	.234	.302	.361
	4 ML YEARS		168	548	135	24	5	13	(6	7)	208	93	45	62	47	2	172	7	6	2	19	5	.79	6	.246	.313	.380

Vin Mazzaro

Pitches: R **Bats:** R **Pos:** SP-18; RP-6
mah-ZARR-oh
Ht: 6'2" **Wt:** 210 **Born:** 9/27/1986 **Age:** 24

Year	Team	Lg	G	GS	CG	GF	IP	BFP	H	R	ER	HR	SH	SF	HB	TBB	IBB	SO	WP	Bk	W	L	Pct	Sh	Sv-Op	Hld	ERC	ERA
2006	Kane	A	24	24	0	0	119.1	530	146	81	67	7	2	4	11	42	0	81	10	3	9	9	.500	0	0--	-	5.38	5.05
2007	Stckton	A+	28	28	0	0	153.2	678	159	97	91	13	2	6	13	71	0	115	13	1	9	12	.429	0	0--	-	4.82	5.33
2008	Mdland	AA	23	23	0	0	145.1	585	119	40	29	3	6	2	11	36	0	114	6	0	13	3	.813	0	0--	-	2.37	1.80
2008	Scrmto	AAA	6	5	0	0	33.2	161	49	26	23	3	1	2	5	9	0	27	2	0	3	3	.600	0	0--	-	6.75	6.15
2009	Scrmto	AAA	10	9	0	1	56.2	230	42	17	15	2	1	1	6	17	1	44	5	0	2	2	.500	0	0--	-	2.32	2.38
2010	Scrmto	AAA	7	6	0	0	37.1	164	35	16	13	2	1	0	3	17	0	38	2	0	3	1	.750	0	0--	-	3.90	3.13
2009	Oak	AL	17	17	0	0	91.1	423	120	61	54	17	4	5	4	39	3	59	5	0	4	9	.308	0	0-0	-	6.49	5.32
2010	Oak	AL	24	18	0	4	122.1	537	127	70	58	19	4	4	4	50	0	79	5	0	6	8	.429	0	0-0	-	4.86	4.27
	2 ML YEARS		41	35	0	4	213.2	960	247	131	112	31	5	7	8	89	3	138	10	0	10	17	.370	0	0-0	-	5.54	4.72

Paul McAnulty

Bats: L **Throws:** R **Pos:** 1B-5; PH-3; DH-1
MACK-uh-null-lee
Ht: 5'10" **Wt:** 220 **Born:** 2/24/1981 **Age:** 30

Year	Team	Lg	G	AB	H	2B	3B	HR	(Hm	Rd)	TB	R	RBI	RC	TBB	IBB	SO	HBP	SH	SF	SB	CS	SB%	GDP	Avg	OBP	Slg
2010	Ark*	AA	44	148	49	3	1	14	(-	-)	96	31	27	38	24	2	36	2	0	2	1	2	.33	2	.331	.426	.649
2010	Salt Lk*	AAA	73	275	83	18	1	10	(-	-)	133	43	54	48	27	2	39	0	0	3	0	1	.00	6	.302	.361	.484
2005	SD	NL	22	24	5	0	0	0	(0	0)	5	2	3	1	3	1	7	1	1	0	1	0	1.00	0	.208	.321	.208
2006	SD	NL	16	13	3	1	0	1	(1	0)	7	3	3	3	2	0	4	0	0	0	0	0	-	0	.231	.333	.538
2007	SD	NL	20	40	8	1	0	1	(0	1)	12	5	5	3	3	1	10	0	0	0	0	0	-	0	.200	.256	.300
2008	SD	NL	66	135	28	7	1	3	(1	2)	46	9	13	19	26	2	41	2	0	1	0	0	-	0	.207	.341	.341
2010	LAA	AL	9	22	3	0	0	1	(1	0)	6	2	2	2	2	0	11	0	0	0	0	0	-	0	.136	.208	.273
	5 ML YEARS		133	234	47	9	1	6	(3	3)	76	23	23	28	36	4	73	3	1	1	1	0	1.00	0	.201	.314	.325

Brian McCann

Bats: L **Throws:** R **Pos:** C-136; PH-12; DH-2
Ht: 6'3" **Wt:** 230 **Born:** 2/20/1984 **Age:** 27

Year	Team	Lg	G	AB	H	2B	3B	HR	(Hm	Rd)	TB	R	RBI	RC	TBB	IBB	SO	HBP	SH	SF	SB	CS	SB%	GDP	Avg	OBP	Slg
2005	Atl	NL	59	180	50	7	0	5	(2	3)	72	20	23	25	18	5	26	1	4	1	1	1	.50	5	.278	.345	.400
2006	Atl	NL	130	442	147	34	0	24	(10	14)	253	61	93	94	41	8	54	3	0	6	2	0	1.00	12	.333	.388	.572
2007	Atl	NL	139	504	136	38	0	18	(6	12)	228	51	92	68	35	7	74	5	2	6	0	1	.00	19	.270	.320	.452
2008	Atl	NL	145	509	153	42	1	23	(10	13)	266	68	87	84	57	4	64	4	0	3	5	0	1.00	17	.301	.373	.523
2009	Atl	NL	138	488	137	35	1	21	(12	9)	237	63	94	83	49	3	83	5	3	6	4	1	.80	17	.281	.349	.486
2010	Atl	NL	143	479	129	25	0	21	(13	8)	217	63	77	76	74	10	98	9	0	4	5	2	.71	12	.269	.375	.453
	Postseason		3	16	3	0	0	2	(1	1)	9	2	5	2	0	0	6	0	0	0	0	0	-	0	.188	.188	.563
	6 ML YEARS		754	2602	752	181	2	112	(53	59)	1273	326	466	430	274	37	399	27	9	26	17	5	.77	82	.289	.360	.489

Brandon McCarthy

Pitches: R **Bats:** R **Pos:** P **Ht:** 6'7" **Wt:** 200 **Born:** 7/7/1983 **Age:** 27

Year	Team	Lg	G	GS	CG	GF	IP	BFP	H	R	ER	HR	SH	SF	HB	TBB	IBB	SO	WP	Bk	W	L	Pct	Sh	Sv-Op	Hld	ERC	ERA
2010	OKCity*	AAA	11	9	0	1	56.1	233	51	22	21	8	1	0	3	11	0	44	0	0	4	2	.667	0	0- -		3.20	3.36
2005	CWS	AL	12	10	0	0	67.0	277	62	30	30	13	1	1	2	17	0	48	1	1	3	2	.600	0	0-0		3.83	4.03
2006	CWS	AL	53	2	0	13	84.2	354	77	44	44	17	3	1	0	33	9	69	5	0	4	7	.364	0	0-1	11	4.10	4.68
2007	Tex	AL	23	22	0	0	101.2	459	111	62	55	9	3	5	3	48	0	59	4	1	5	10	.333	0	0-0		4.89	4.87
2008	Tex	AL	5	5	0	0	22.0	93	20	11	10	3	0	2	1	8	0	10	0	0	1	1	.500	0	0-0		3.87	4.09
2009	Tex	AL	17	17	1	0	97.1	420	96	55	50	13	0	5	3	36	0	65	0	0	7	4	.636	1	0-0		4.22	4.62
	5 ML YEARS		110	56	1	13	372.2	1603	366	202	189	55	7	14	9	142	9	251	10	2	20	24	.455	1	0-1	11	4.29	4.56

Kyle McClellan

Pitches: R **Bats:** R **Pos:** RP-68 **Ht:** 6'2" **Wt:** 215 **Born:** 6/12/1984 **Age:** 27

Year	Team	Lg	G	GS	CG	GF	IP	BFP	H	R	ER	HR	SH	SF	HB	TBB	IBB	SO	WP	Bk	W	L	Pct	Sh	Sv-Op	Hld	ERC	ERA
2008	StL	NL	68	0	0	7	75.2	233	79	37	34	7	2	1	4	26	2	59	6	0	2	7	.222	0	1-6	30	4.24	4.04
2009	StL	NL	66	0	0	14	66.2	288	56	27	25	4	5	2	2	34	4	51	4	0	4	4	.500	0	3-6	15	3.38	3.38
2010	StL	NL	68	0	0	18	75.1	307	58	20	19	9	4	1	3	23	3	60	2	0	1	4	.200	0	2-3	19	2.70	2.27
	Postseason		1	0	0	0	0.2	5	1	0	0	0	0	0	1	1	0	0	0	0	0	0	-	0	0-0	0	17.56	0.00
	3 ML YEARS		202	0	0	39	217.2	922	193	84	78	20	11	4	9	83	7	170	12	0	7	15	.318	0	6-15	64	3.43	3.23

Mike McClendon

Pitches: R **Bats:** R **Pos:** RP-17 **Ht:** 6'5" **Wt:** 215 **Born:** 4/3/1985 **Age:** 26

Year	Team	Lg	G	GS	CG	GF	IP	BFP	H	R	ER	HR	SH	SF	HB	TBB	IBB	SO	WP	Bk	W	L	Pct	Sh	Sv-Op	Hld	ERC	ERA
2006	Helena	R+	18	4	0	6	44.2	191	54	23	21	4	0	1	0	8	0	34	3	0	3	2	.600	0	0- -		4.32	4.23
2007	WV	A	11	11	0	0	62.2	246	46	22	20	6	1	0	1	12	0	47	1	0	5	2	.714	0	0- -		1.97	2.87
2007	BrvdCt	A+	16	14	2	1	89.1	398	108	52	42	6	3	3	4	19	0	46	5	1	5	6	.455	1	1- -		4.35	4.23
2007	WV	A-	11	11	0	0	62.2	246	46	22	20	6	1	0	1	12	0	47	1	0	5	2	.714	0	0- -		1.97	2.87
2008	BrvdCt	A+	46	5	0	30	88.0	386	103	50	41	6	6	1	5	15	4	61	4	0	7	6	.538	0	10- -		3.96	4.19
2009	Hntsvl	AA	41	2	0	8	84.2	354	86	40	31	4	5	4	3	20	0	57	3	0	4	3	.571	0	3- -		3.25	3.30
2010	Nashv	AAA	25	3	0	9	55.1	225	53	16	15	1	2	1	3	14	0	44	2	1	4	3	.571	0	2- -		3.04	2.44
2010	Hntsvl	AA	7	0	0	2	14.2	52	7	1	1	0	0	1	1	1	0	15	0	0	1	1	.500	0	0- -		0.71	0.61
2010	Mil	NL	17	0	0	3	21.0	84	15	7	7	2	0	0	0	7	0	21	1	0	2	0	1.000	0	0-1	3	2.31	3.00

Mike McCoy

Bats: R **Throws:** R **Pos:** 2B-14; PR-9; LF-8; SS-7; RF-6; 3B-4; PH-4; CF-2 **Ht:** 5'9" **Wt:** 175 **Born:** 4/2/1981 **Age:** 30

Year	Team	Lg	G	AB	H	2B	3B	HR	(Hm	Rd)	TB	R	RBI	RC	TBB	IBB	SO	HBP	SH	SF	SB	CS	SB%	GDP	Avg	OBP	Slg
2002	JhsCty	R+	50	154	48	9	1	4	(-	-)	71	46	22	37	42	0	23	3	2	1	18	7	.72	0	.312	.465	.461
2003	Peoria	A	131	464	117	16	5	5	(-	-)	158	67	46	61	51	0	77	16	10	3	24	10	.71	2	.252	.345	.341
2004	Peoria	A	55	194	42	8	3	2	(-	-)	62	26	17	22	24	1	35	3	8	2	9	3	.75	4	.216	.309	.320
2004	PlmBh	A+	61	176	53	12	1	2	(-	-)	73	34	23	33	31	2	32	5	2	1	7	4	.64	1	.301	.418	.415
2004	Tenn	AA	3	6	0	0	0	0	(-	-)	0	0	0	0	0	0	3	0	0	0	0	0	-	0	.000	.000	.000
2005	PlmBh	A+	86	282	76	13	2	1	(-	-)	96	47	27	40	36	1	56	3	8	3	18	3	.86	2	.270	.355	.340
2005	Sprgfld	AA	5	14	2	0	0	0	(-	-)	2	1	1	0	0	0	5	1	0	1	0	0	-	0	.143	.188	.143
2006	Sprgfld	AA	130	474	118	14	2	3	(-	-)	145	64	37	59	62	0	98	7	16	0	30	9	.77	7	.249	.344	.306
2007	Sprgfld	AA	24	68	15	3	1	0	(-	-)	20	5	10	7	14	1	14	0	2	1	1	3	.25	0	.221	.349	.294
2007	Memp	AAA	89	238	59	8	0	3	(-	-)	76	31	16	34	45	0	42	1	11	0	12	4	.75	3	.248	.370	.319
2008	Norfolk	AAA	53	152	42	6	1	2	(-	-)	56	25	16	21	19	0	27	0	4	1	6	3	.67	3	.276	.355	.368
2008	Frdrck	A+	1	5	3	0	0	0	(-	-)	3	1	1	1	0	0	1	0	0	0	0	1	.00	0	.600	.600	.600
2008	ColSpr	AAA	39	140	48	7	2	4	(-	-)	71	32	27	29	15	0	20	0	1	6	7	1	.88	3	.343	.391	.507
2009	ColSpr	AAA	132	462	142	27	5	2	(-	-)	185	102	52	90	80	1	70	3	16	11	40	6	.87	7	.307	.405	.400
2010	LsVgs	AAA	53	213	66	14	1	6	(-	-)	100	48	26	46	37	0	31	1	6	2	17	2	.89	4	.310	.411	.469
2009	Col	NL	12	5	0	0	0	0	(0	0)	0	1	0	0	0	0	2	0	1	0	2	0	1.00	0	.000	.000	.000
2010	Tor	AL	46	82	16	4	0	0	(0	0)	20	9	3	5	8	0	20	0	0	0	5	1	.83	0	.195	.267	.244
	2 ML YEARS		58	87	16	4	0	0	(0	0)	20	10	3	5	8	0	22	0	1	0	7	1	.88	0	.184	.253	.230

Andrew McCutchen

Bats: R **Throws:** R **Pos:** CF-152; PH-2 **Ht:** 5'10" **Wt:** 175 **Born:** 10/10/1986 **Age:** 24

Year	Team	Lg	G	AB	H	2B	3B	HR	(Hm	Rd)	TB	R	RBI	RC	TBB	IBB	SO	HBP	SH	SF	SB	CS	SB%	GDP	Avg	OBP	Slg
2005	Pirates	R	45	158	47	9	3	2	(-	-)	68	36	30	32	29	0	24	3	0	2	13	1	.93	3	.297	.411	.430
2005	Wmspt	A-	13	52	18	3	1	0	(-	-)	23	12	5	11	8	0	6	1	1	0	4	1	.80	0	.346	.443	.442
2006	Hkry	A	114	453	132	20	4	14	(-	-)	202	77	62	75	42	3	91	5	0	3	22	7	.76	8	.291	.356	.446
2006	Altna	AA	20	78	24	4	0	3	(-	-)	37	12	12	14	8	0	20	1	0	0	1	1	.50	2	.308	.379	.474
2007	Altna	AA	118	446	115	20	3	10	(-	-)	171	70	48	62	44	1	83	3	2	3	17	1	.94	9	.258	.327	.383
2007	Indy	AAA	17	67	21	4	0	1	(-	-)	28	7	5	9	4	0	11	0	0	1	4	3	.57	1	.313	.347	.418
2008	Indy	AAA	135	512	145	26	3	9	(-	-)	204	75	50	81	68	1	87	6	1	3	34	19	.64	8	.283	.372	.398
2009	Indy	AAA	49	201	61	10	8	4	(-	-)	99	41	20	37	17	0	24	1	0	0	10	2	.83	0	.303	.361	.493
2009	Pit	NL	108	433	124	26	9	12	(8	4)	204	74	54	78	54	2	83	2	0	4	22	5	.81	3	.286	.365	.471
2010	Pit	NL	154	570	163	35	5	16	(8	8)	256	94	56	86	70	1	89	5	1	7	33	10	.77	6	.286	.365	.449
	2 ML YEARS		262	1003	287	61	14	28	(16	12)	460	168	110	164	124	3	172	7	1	11	55	15	.79	9	.286	.365	.459

Daniel McCutchen

Pitches: R **Bats:** R **Pos:** RP-19; SP-9   **Ht:** 6'2" **Wt:** 214 **Born:** 9/26/1982 **Age:** 28

Year	Team	Lg	G	GS	CG	GF	IP	BFP	H	R	ER	HR	SH	SF	HB	TBB	IBB	SO	WP	Bk	W	L	Pct	Sh	Sv-Op	Hld	ERC	ERA
2006	StIsInd	A-	2	2	0	0	8.0	28	4	1	1	0	0	0	1	0	11	0	0	1	0	1.000	0	0--	-	1.13	1.13
2006	CtnSC	A	7	0	0	4	21.0	76	13	5	5	2	1	0	0	5	0	18	0	0	1	0	1.000	0	1--	-	1.69	2.14
2007	Tampa	A+	17	16	0	1	101.0	391	86	29	28	7	2	0	4	21	1	67	1	0	11	2	.846	0	0--	-	2.64	2.50
2007	Trntn	AA	7	7	0	0	41.0	162	30	11	11	2	2	1	1	12	0	36	2	0	3	2	.600	0	0--	-	2.10	2.41
2008	Trntn	AA	9	9	0	0	53.0	215	43	16	15	4	0	1	1	18	0	52	3	0	4	3	.571	0	0--	-	2.79	2.55
2008	S-WB	AAA	11	11	2	0	70.1	288	73	32	28	10	0	1	1	11	0	58	0	0	4	6	.400	2	0--	-	3.70	3.58
2008	Indy	AAA	8	8	0	0	48.0	198	49	25	25	12	1	0	2	7	0	41	0	0	3	3	.500	0	0--	-	4.33	4.69
2009	Indy	AAA	24	24	0	0	142.2	594	145	63	55	10	7	5	3	29	1	110	5	0	13	6	.684	0	0--	-	3.27	3.47
2010	Indy	AAA	13	13	0	0	79.0	320	71	35	35	12	1	2	6	19	1	39	0	1	4	8	.333	0	0--	-	3.61	3.99
2009	Pit	NL	6	6	0	0	36.1	155	38	17	17	6	3	0	1	11	2	19	0	0	1	2	.333	0	0-0	0	4.45	4.21
2010	Pit	NL	28	9	0	4	67.2	316	83	48	46	13	4	4	2	28	0	38	2	0	2	5	.286	0	0-0	0	6.16	6.12
	2 ML YEARS		34	15	0	4	104.0	471	121	65	63	19	7	4	3	39	2	57	2	0	3	7	.300	0	0-0	0	5.55	5.45

Darnell McDonald

Bats: R **Throws:** R **Pos:** CF-69; RF-34; LF-30; PH-16; PR-7   **Ht:** 5'11" **Wt:** 205 **Born:** 11/17/1978 **Age:** 32

Year	Team	Lg	G	AB	H	2B	3B	HR	(Hm	Rd)	TB	R	RBI	RC	TBB	IBB	SO	HBP	SH	SF	SB	CS	SB%	GDP	Avg	OBP	Slg
2010	Pwtckt*	AAA	10	41	14	6	1	2	(-	-)	28	6	8	9	2	0	7	0	0	0	1	0	1.00	0	.341	.372	.683
2004	Bal	AL	17	32	5	1	0	0	(0	0)	6	3	1	2	2	0	6	0	0	0	1	0	1.00	0	.156	.206	.188
2007	Min	AL	4	10	1	0	0	0	(0	0)	1	0	0	0	1	0	3	0	0	0	0	0	-	0	.100	.182	.100
2009	Cin	NL	47	105	28	6	1	2	(2	0)	42	12	10	10	5	0	31	1	0	0	1	0	1.00	4	.267	.306	.400
2010	Bos	AL	117	319	86	18	3	9	(5	4)	137	40	34	46	30	1	85	2	12	0	9	1	.90	5	.270	.336	.429
	4 ML YEARS		185	466	120	25	4	11	(7	4)	186	55	45	58	38	1	125	3	12	0	11	1	.92	9	.258	.318	.399

James McDonald

Pitches: R **Bats:** L **Pos:** SP-12; RP-3   **Ht:** 6'4" **Wt:** 203 **Born:** 10/19/1984 **Age:** 26

Year	Team	Lg	G	GS	CG	GF	IP	BFP	H	R	ER	HR	SH	SF	HB	TBB	IBB	SO	WP	Bk	W	L	Pct	Sh	Sv-Op	Hld	ERC	ERA
2010	Albq*	AAA	12	12	0	0	63.1	278	64	31	31	4	3	2	5	24	0	57	2	0	6	1	.857	0	0--	-	4.07	4.41
2010	Ddgrs*	R	2	2	0	0	5.2	23	3	3	1	0	0	1	0	3	0	8	2	0	0	0	-	0	0--	-	1.56	1.59
2008	LAD	NL	4	0	0	1	6.0	24	5	0	0	0	1	0	1	1	0	2	0	0	0	0	-	0	0-0	0	1.74	0.00
2009	LAD	NL	45	4	0	10	63.0	200	60	34	28	6	2	3	5	34	5	54	4	0	5	5	.500	0	0-0	5	4.53	4.00
2010	2 Tms	NL	15	12	0	0	71.2	306	70	32	32	4	5	3	0	29	5	68	5	0	4	6	.400	0	0-0	1	3.56	4.02
10	LAD	NL	4	1	0	0	7.2	38	11	7	7	1	0	1	0	5	1	7	0	0	0	1	.000	0	0-0	1	7.83	8.22
10	Pit	NL	11	11	0	0	64.0	268	59	25	25	3	5	2	0	24	4	61	5	0	4	5	.444	0	0-0	0	3.12	3.52
	Postseason		2	0	0	0	5.1	21	3	0	0	0	0	0	0	2	0	7	0	0	0	0	-	0	0-0	0	1.35	0.00
	3 ML YEARS		64	16	0	11	140.2	610	135	66	60	10	8	6	5	64	10	124	9	0	9	11	.450	0	0-0	6	3.90	3.84

John McDonald

Bats: R **Throws:** R **Pos:** 2B-23; 3B-19; SS-19; PR-12; LF-2; PH-1   **Ht:** 5'10" **Wt:** 177 **Born:** 9/24/1974 **Age:** 36

Year	Team	Lg	G	AB	H	2B	3B	HR	(Hm	Rd)	TB	R	RBI	RC	TBB	IBB	SO	HBP	SH	SF	SB	CS	SB%	GDP	Avg	OBP	Slg
1999	Cle	AL	18	21	7	0	0	0	(0	0)	7	2	0	1	0	0	3	0	0	0	0	1	.00	2	.333	.333	.333
2000	Cle	AL	9	9	4	0	0	0	(0	0)	4	0	0	2	0	0	1	0	0	0	0	0	-	0	.444	.444	.444
2001	Cle	AL	17	22	2	1	0	0	(0	0)	3	1	0	0	1	0	7	1	1	0	0	0	-	0	.091	.167	.136
2002	Cle	AL	93	264	66	11	3	1	(0	1)	86	35	12	24	10	0	50	5	7	2	3	0	1.00	4	.250	.288	.326
2003	Cle	AL	82	214	46	9	1	1	(0	1)	60	21	14	18	11	0	31	2	4	2	3	3	.50	4	.215	.258	.280
2004	Cle	AL	66	93	19	5	1	2	(0	2)	32	17	7	6	4	0	11	0	3	0	0	0	-	4	.204	.237	.344
2005	2 Tms	AL	68	166	46	6	1	0	(0	0)	54	18	16	19	11	0	24	2	3	2	6	1	.86	6	.277	.326	.325
2006	Tor	AL	104	260	58	7	3	3	(1	2)	80	35	23	20	16	0	41	2	6	2	7	2	.78	8	.223	.271	.308
2007	Tor	AL	123	327	82	20	2	1	(1	0)	109	32	31	35	11	0	48	2	12	1	7	2	.78	4	.251	.279	.333
2008	Tor	AL	84	186	39	8	0	1	(1	0)	50	21	18	11	10	0	25	2	7	2	3	1	.75	3	.210	.255	.269
2009	Tor	AL	73	151	39	7	0	4	(2	2)	58	18	13	16	1	0	18	2	1	1	2	0	1.00	1	.258	.271	.384
2010	Tor	AL	63	152	38	9	2	6	(3	3)	69	27	23	20	6	0	26	0	2	3	2	1	.67	3	.250	.273	.454
05	Tor	AL	37	93	27	3	0	0	(0	0)	30	8	12	13	6	0	12	2	3	2	5	0	1.00	3	.290	.340	.323
05	Det	AL	31	73	19	3	1	0	(0	0)	24	10	4	6	5	0	12	0	0	0	1	1	.50	3	.260	.308	.329
	12 ML YEARS		800	1865	446	83	13	19	(8	11)	612	227	157	172	81	0	285	18	46	15	31	13	.70	39	.239	.275	.328

Jake McGee

Pitches: L **Bats:** L **Pos:** RP-8   **Ht:** 6'3" **Wt:** 190 **Born:** 8/6/1986 **Age:** 24

Year	Team	Lg	G	GS	CG	GF	IP	BFP	H	R	ER	HR	SH	SF	HB	TBB	IBB	SO	WP	Bk	W	L	Pct	Sh	Sv-Op	Hld	ERC	ERA
2004	Princtn	R+	12	12	0	0	56.2	233	49	30	25	5	3	4	6	25	1	53	5	0	4	1	.800	0	0--	-	3.49	3.97
2005	HudVal	A-	15	14	0	0	76.2	309	64	32	31	4	1	1	1	23	0	89	5	0	5	4	.556	0	0--	-	2.61	3.64
2006	SWMch	A	26	26	0	0	134.0	561	103	54	44	7	3	2	3	65	0	171	13	0	7	9	.438	0	0--	-	2.92	2.96
2007	VeroB	A+	21	21	0	0	116.2	470	86	45	38	8	2	3	3	39	0	145	9	0	4	4	.556	0	0--	-	2.36	2.93
2007	Mont	AA	5	5	0	0	23.1	99	19	11	11	2	1	0	0	13	0	30	1	0	3	2	.600	0	0--	-	3.60	4.24
2008	Mont	AA	15	15	0	0	77.2	325	65	38	34	6	2	1	1	37	0	65	3	0	6	4	.600	0	0--	-	3.43	3.94
2009	Rays	R	5	5	0	0	7.2	32	5	4	3	0	0	0	0	3	0	14	2	0	0	2	.000	0	0--	-	1.60	3.52
2009	Charltt	A+	11	11	0	0	22.1	97	26	16	16	2	1	0	0	9	0	26	4	0	0	2	.000	0	0--	-	5.11	6.45
2010	Mont	AA	19	19	0	0	88.1	375	81	42	35	3	7	4	1	33	0	100	7	0	3	7	.300	0	0--	-	3.09	3.57
2010	Drham	AAA	11	1	0	1	17.1	64	9	1	1	0	0	0	0	3	0	27	2	0	1	1	.500	0	1--	-	0.86	0.52
2010	TB	AL	8	0	0	3	5.0	20	2	1	1	0	0	0	0	3	0	6	0	0	0	0	-	0	0-0	0	1.32	1.80

Casey McGehee

Bats: R **Throws:** R **Pos:** 3B-153; 1B-3; DH-3   mah-GEE   **Ht:** 6'1" **Wt:** 195 **Born:** 10/12/1982 **Age:** 28

								BATTING													BASERUNNING				AVERAGES		
Year	Team	Lg	G	AB	H	2B	3B	HR	(Hm	Rd)	TB	R	RBI	RC	TBB	IBB	SO	HBP	SH	SF	SB	CS	SB%	GDP	Avg	OBP	Slg
2008	ChC	NL	9	24	4	1	0	0	(0	0)	5	1	5	0	0	0	8	0	0	1	0	0	-	1	.167	.160	.208
2009	Mil	NL	116	355	107	20	1	16	(6	10)	177	58	66	65	34	2	67	1	0	4	0	2	.00	13	.301	.360	.499
2010	Mil	NL	157	610	174	38	1	23	(13	10)	283	70	104	93	50	5	102	2	0	8	1	1	.50	18	.285	.337	.464
	3 ML YEARS		282	989	285	59	2	39	(19	20)	465	129	175	158	84	7	177	3	0	13	1	3	.25	32	.288	.342	.470

Michael McKenry

Bats: R **Throws:** R **Pos:** PH-5; C-2   **Ht:** 5'10" **Wt:** 200 **Born:** 3/4/1985 **Age:** 26

								BATTING													BASERUNNING				AVERAGES		
Year	Team	Lg	G	AB	H	2B	3B	HR	(Hm	Rd)	TB	R	RBI	RC	TBB	IBB	SO	HBP	SH	SF	SB	CS	SB%	GDP	Avg	OBP	Slg
2006	TriCity	A-	66	245	53	16	1	4	(-	-)	83	28	23	27	22	0	49	11	6	6	3	3	.50	1	.216	.303	.339
2007	Ashvll	A	113	408	117	35	1	22	(-	-)	220	79	90	86	66	0	84	6	3	2	8	9	.47	4	.287	.392	.539
2008	Mdest	A+	111	400	103	28	1	18	(-	-)	187	59	75	71	55	0	101	10	5	2	2	4	.33	8	.258	.360	.468
2009	Tulsa	AA	102	358	100	25	1	12	(-	-)	163	52	50	64	54	2	69	2	2	1	2	2	.50	12	.279	.376	.455
2010	ColSpr	AAA	99	347	92	25	1	10	(-	-)	147	44	49	50	32	1	77	2	0	3	1	1	.50	8	.265	.328	.424
2010	Col	NL	6	8	0	0	0	0	(0	0)	0	0	0	0	1	0	5	0	0	0	0	0	-	0	.000	.111	.000

Nate McLouth

Bats: L **Throws:** R **Pos:** CF-71; LF-8; PH-8; PR-5   mc-CLOWTH   **Ht:** 5'11" **Wt:** 180 **Born:** 10/28/1981 **Age:** 29

								BATTING													BASERUNNING				AVERAGES		
Year	Team	Lg	G	AB	H	2B	3B	HR	(Hm	Rd)	TB	R	RBI	RC	TBB	IBB	SO	HBP	SH	SF	SB	CS	SB%	GDP	Avg	OBP	Slg
2010	Gwnntt	AAA	34	128	30	1	0	6	(-	-)	49	18	18	19	19	0	21	2	0	2	7	0	1.00	1	.234	.338	.383
2005	Pit	NL	41	109	28	6	0	5	(2	3)	49	20	12	9	3	0	20	5	2	1	2	0	1.00	3	.257	.305	.450
2006	Pit	NL	106	270	63	16	2	7	(3	4)	104	50	16	25	18	0	59	5	3	1	10	1	.91	7	.233	.293	.385
2007	Pit	NL	137	329	85	21	3	13	(5	8)	151	62	38	52	39	2	77	9	3	2	22	1	**.96**	2	.258	.351	.459
2008	Pit	NL	152	597	165	**46**	4	26	(15	11)	297	113	94	105	65	11	93	12	5	6	23	3	.88	5	.276	.356	.497
2009	2 Tms	NL	129	507	130	27	2	20	(9	11)	221	86	70	85	68	1	99	9	3	4	19	6	.76	8	.256	.352	.436
2010	Atl	NL	85	242	46	12	1	6	(5	1)	78	30	24	23	33	2	57	5	6	2	7	2	.78	3	.190	.298	.322
09	Pit	NL	45	168	43	7	1	9	(5	4)	79	27	34	33	21	0	29	4	0	2	7	0	1.00	2	.256	.349	.470
09	Atl	NL	84	339	87	20	1	11	(4	7)	142	59	36	52	47	1	70	5	3	2	12	6	.67	6	.257	.354	.419
	6 ML YEARS		650	2054	517	128	12	77	(39	38)	900	361	254	299	226	16	405	45	22	16	83	13	.86	28	.252	.337	.438

Gil Meche

Pitches: R **Bats:** R **Pos:** RP-11; SP-9   MESH   **Ht:** 6'3" **Wt:** 218 **Born:** 9/8/1978 **Age:** 32

			HOW MUCH HE PITCHED						WHAT HE GAVE UP											THE RESULTS						
Year	Team	Lg	G	GS	CG	GF	IP	BFP	H	R	ER	HR	SH	SF	HB	TBB	IBB	SO	WP	Bk	W	L	Pct	Sh	Sv-Op	Hld	ERC	ERA
2010	NWArk*	AA	1	1	0	0	4.0	16	2	0	0	0	0	0	0	3	0	3	0	0	0	0	-	0	0--	-	2.19	0.00
2010	Omha*	AAA	4	1	0	0	8.2	39	10	8	8	1	0	1	0	4	0	6	0	0	0	1	.000	0	0--	-	5.35	8.31
1999	Sea	AL	16	15	0	0	85.2	375	73	48	45	9	5	3	2	57	1	47	1	0	8	4	.667	0	0-0	0	4.47	4.73
2000	Sea	AL	15	15	1	0	85.2	363	75	37	36	7	5	4	1	40	0	60	2	0	4	4	.500	1	0-0	0	3.60	3.78
2003	Sea	AL	32	32	1	0	186.1	785	187	97	95	30	3	5	3	63	2	130	7	0	15	13	.536	0	0-0	0	4.39	4.59
2004	Sea	AL	23	23	1	0	127.2	565	139	73	71	21	1	3	5	47	0	99	4	0	7	7	.500	1	0-0	0	5.06	5.01
2005	Sea	AL	29	26	0	0	143.1	638	153	92	81	18	1	5	2	72	1	83	4	0	10	8	.556	0	0-0	0	5.15	5.09
2006	Sea	AL	32	32	1	0	186.2	811	183	106	93	24	3	2	8	84	2	156	4	2	11	8	.579	0	0-0	0	4.56	4.48
2007	KC	AL	34	**34**	1	0	216.0	906	218	98	88	22	5	7	3	62	2	156	3	0	9	13	.409	0	0-0	0	3.77	3.67
2008	KC	AL	34	**34**	0	0	210.1	886	204	98	93	19	4	10	0	73	2	183	5	0	14	11	.560	0	0-0	0	3.64	3.98
2009	KC	AL	23	23	1	0	129.0	581	144	81	73	17	1	6	3	58	0	95	7	0	6	10	.375	1	0-0	0	5.26	5.09
2010	KC	AL	20	9	1	3	61.2	281	65	42	39	9	2	1	2	38	3	41	1	0	0	5	.000	0	0-0	6	5.73	5.69
	10 ML YEARS		258	243	7	3	1432.1	6191	1441	772	714	176	30	46	29	594	13	1050	38	2	84	83	.503	3	0-0	6	4.43	4.49

Brandon Medders

Pitches: R **Bats:** R **Pos:** RP-14   MEDD-urrs   **Ht:** 6'2" **Wt:** 199 **Born:** 1/26/1980 **Age:** 31

			HOW MUCH HE PITCHED						WHAT HE GAVE UP											THE RESULTS						
Year	Team	Lg	G	GS	CG	GF	IP	BFP	H	R	ER	HR	SH	SF	HB	TBB	IBB	SO	WP	Bk	W	L	Pct	Sh	Sv-Op	Hld	ERC	ERA
2010	Fresno*	AAA	22	0	0	6	28.0	121	28	17	17	5	2	1	0	10	2	26	2	0	2	1	.667	0	1--	-	4.47	5.46
2005	Ari	NL	27	0	0	10	30.1	122	21	6	6	2	0	2	1	11	0	31	1	0	4	1	.800	0	0-0	2	2.25	1.78
2006	Ari	NL	60	0	0	13	71.2	316	76	37	29	5	3	2	2	28	3	47	2	0	5	3	.625	0	0-1	10	4.17	3.64
2007	Ari	NL	30	0	0	7	29.1	128	30	16	14	9	1	0	1	16	0	23	1	0	1	2	.333	0	0-1	1	6.76	4.30
2008	Ari	NL	18	0	0	3	19.2	88	17	11	10	2	1	2	2	11	2	8	1	0	1	0	1.000	0	0-1	1	4.13	4.58
2009	SF	NL	61	0	0	11	68.2	300	63	26	23	6	5	6	3	32	5	58	2	0	5	1	.833	0	1-4	8	3.80	3.01
2010	SF	NL	14	0	0	7	15.0	73	26	12	12	3	0	0	0	6	1	8	0	0	0	0	-	0	0-0	0	9.74	7.20
	6 ML YEARS		210	0	0	51	234.2	1027	233	108	94	27	10	12	9	104	11	175	7	0	16	7	.696	0	1-7	21	4.39	3.61

Kris Medlen

Pitches: R **Bats:** B **Pos:** RP-17; SP-14   **Ht:** 5'10" **Wt:** 190 **Born:** 10/7/1985 **Age:** 25

			HOW MUCH HE PITCHED						WHAT HE GAVE UP											THE RESULTS						
Year	Team	Lg	G	GS	CG	GF	IP	BFP	H	R	ER	HR	SH	SF	HB	TBB	IBB	SO	WP	Bk	W	L	Pct	Sh	Sv-Op	Hld	ERC	ERA
2006	Danvle	R+	20	0	0	19	22.0	83	14	2	1	0	0	0	1	2	0	36	2	0	1	0	1.000	0	10--	-	1.09	0.41
2007	Rome	A	17	0	0	15	20.2	80	13	4	2	1	0	0	0	3	0	33	0	0	0	1	.000	0	8--	-	1.22	0.87
2007	MrtlBh	A+	18	0	0	8	24.0	101	22	7	3	1	1	1	0	7	2	28	0	0	2	0	1.000	0	2--	-	2.65	1.13
2007	Missi	AA	3	0	0	1	2.1	11	4	3	3	0	0	0	0	2	0	2	0	0	0	0	-	0	1--	-	11.20	11.57
2008	Missi	AA	36	17	0	8	120.1	491	121	47	47	8	4	4	5	27	2	120	3	0	7	8	.467	0	1--	-	3.44	3.52

Year	Team	Lg	G	GS	CG	GF	IP	BFP	H	R	ER	HR	SH	SF	HB	TBB	IBB	SO	WP	Bk	W	L	Pct	Sh	Sv-Op	Hld	ERC	ERA
2009	Gwnntt	AAA	8	6	0	1	37.2	138	20	5	5	0	1	0	0	10	0	44	0	1	5	0	1.000	0	0--	-	1.09	1.19
2009	Atl	NL	37	4	0	10	67.2	294	65	34	32	5	6	2	2	30	2	72	3	1	3	5	.375	0	0-2	1	3.90	4.26
2010	Atl	NL	31	14	0	5	107.2	438	108	48	44	13	7	3	3	21	1	83	1	1	6	2	.750	0	0-0	1	3.60	3.68
	2 ML YEARS		68	18	0	15	175.1	732	173	82	76	18	13	5	5	51	3	155	4	2	9	7	.563	0	0-2	2	3.73	3.90

Evan Meek

Pitches: R **Bats:** R **Pos:** RP-70

Ht: 6'0" **Wt:** 225 **Born:** 5/12/1983 **Age:** 28

Year	Team	Lg	G	GS	CG	GF	IP	BFP	H	R	ER	HR	SH	SF	HB	TBB	IBB	SO	WP	Bk	W	L	Pct	Sh	Sv-Op	Hld	ERC	ERA
2008	Pit	NL	9	0	0	7	13.0	61	11	11	10	3	1	1	1	12	2	7	3	0	0	1	.000	0	0-0	6	6.46	6.92
2009	Pit	NL	41	0	0	14	47.0	195	34	18	18	2	2	1	0	29	2	42	5	0	1	1	.500	0	0-1	4	3.03	3.45
2010	Pit	NL	70	0	0	16	80.0	324	53	25	19	5	2	1	4	31	4	70	2	0	5	4	.556	0	4-10	15	2.15	2.14
	3 ML YEARS		120	0	0	37	140.0	580	98	54	47	10	5	3	5	72	8	119	10	0	6	6	.500	0	4-11	19	2.79	3.02

Jenrry Mejia

HENN-ree mah-HEE-ah

Pitches: R **Bats:** R **Pos:** RP-30; SP-3

Ht: 6'0" **Wt:** 162 **Born:** 10/11/1989 **Age:** 21

Year	Team	Lg	G	GS	CG	GF	IP	BFP	H	R	ER	HR	SH	SF	HB	TBB	IBB	SO	WP	Bk	W	L	Pct	Sh	Sv-Op	Hld	ERC	ERA
2008	Mets	R	3	3	1	0	15.0	58	9	1	1	0	0	0	0	3	0	15	0	0	2	0	1.000	1	0--	-	1.09	0.60
2008	Bklyn	A-	11	11	0	0	56.2	228	42	22	22	4	2	1	1	23	0	52	3	0	3	2	.600	0	0--	-	2.66	3.49
2009	StLuci	A+	9	9	0	0	50.1	209	41	18	11	0	2	0	2	16	0	44	2	1	4	1	.800	0	0--	-	2.26	1.97
2009	Bnghtn	AA	10	10	0	0	44.1	202	44	28	22	2	5	1	4	23	1	47	2	0	0	5	.000	0	0--	-	4.33	4.47
2010	Bnghtn	AA	6	6	1	0	27.1	111	19	5	4	0	2	0	0	14	0	26	1	0	2	0	1.000	1	0--	-	2.28	1.32
2010	Mets	R	1	1	0	0	3.0	13	4	1	1	0	0	0	0	1	0	3	0	0	0	0	-	0	0--	-	5.24	3.00
2010	StLuci	A+	1	1	0	0	4.0	13	1	0	0	0	0	0	0	0	0	7	1	0	0	0	-	0	0--	-	0.14	0.00
2010	Buffalo	AAA	1	1	0	0	8.0	28	5	1	1	1	1	0	1	1	0	9	0	0	0	0	-	0	0--	-	2.01	1.13
2010	NYM	NL	33	3	0	8	39.0	183	46	21	20	3	0	1	3	20	2	22	7	0	0	4	.000	0	0-1	2	5.57	4.62

Mark Melancon

muh-LANN-sun

Pitches: R **Bats:** R **Pos:** RP-22

Ht: 6'2" **Wt:** 215 **Born:** 3/28/1985 **Age:** 26

Year	Team	Lg	G	GS	CG	GF	IP	BFP	H	R	ER	HR	SH	SF	HB	TBB	IBB	SO	WP	Bk	W	L	Pct	Sh	Sv-Op	Hld	ERC	ERA
2006	StIslnd	A-	7	0	0	3	7.2	36	9	7	3	0	2	0	0	2	0	8	1	0	0	1	.000	0	2--	-	3.45	3.52
2008	Tampa	A+	13	0	0	2	25.1	107	26	9	8	2	1	1	1	6	1	20	0	1	1	0	1.000	0	2--	-	3.53	2.84
2008	Trntn	AA	19	0	0	13	49.2	190	32	14	10	3	3	0	0	12	0	47	1	0	6	0	1.000	0	2--	-	1.57	1.81
2008	S WB	AAA	12	0	0	4	20.0	75	11	7	6	1	1	1	1	4	0	22	1	0	1	1	.500	0	1--	-	1.26	2.70
2009	S-WB	AAA	32	0	0	20	53.0	208	37	22	17	3	0	2	6	11	0	54	5	0	4	0	1.000	0	3--	-	2.00	2.89
2010	S-WB	AAA	40	0	0	17	56.1	258	63	24	23	5	2	1	3	31	0	58	7	0	6	1	.857	0	6--	-	5.54	3.67
2010	RdRck	AAA	3	0	0	2	4.1	19	5	0	0	0	0	0	0	1	0	2	0	0	1	0	1.000	0	1--	-	3.47	0.00
2009	NYY	AL	13	0	0	4	16.1	74	13	8	7	0	0	0	4	10	0	10	3	0	0	1	.000	0	0-1	0	3.94	3.86
2010	2 Tms		22	0	0	4	21.1	90	19	13	10	2	0	1	1	8	0	22	2	0	2	0	1.000	0	0-1	8	3.53	4.22
10	NYY	AL	2	0	0	2	4.0	19	7	5	4	1	0	1	0	0	0	3	0	0	0	0	-	0	0-0	0	7.95	9.00
10	Hou	NL	20	0	0	2	17.1	71	12	8	6	1	0	0	1	8	0	19	2	0	2	0	1.000	0	0-1	8	2.65	3.12
	2 ML YEARS		35	0	0	8	37.2	164	32	21	17	2	0	1	5	18	0	32	5	0	2	1	.667	0	0-2	8	3.73	4.06

Kevin Mench

Bats: R **Throws:** R **Pos:** PH-26; LF-1

Ht: 6'0" **Wt:** 215 **Born:** 1/7/1978 **Age:** 33

Year	Team	Lg	G	AB	H	2B	3B	HR	(Hm	Rd)	TB	R	RBI	RC	TBB	IBB	SO	HBP	SH	SF	SB	CS	SB%	GDP	Avg	OBP	Slg
2010	Syrcse*	AAA	86	281	70	16	0	3	(-	-)	95	27	40	35	35	4	30	3	0	7	3	1	.75	11	.249	.331	.338
2002	Tex	AL	110	366	95	20	2	15	(8	7)	164	52	60	60	31	0	83	8	2	5	1	1	.50	4	.260	.327	.448
2003	Tex	AL	38	125	40	12	0	2	(1	1)	58	15	11	23	10	0	17	3	0	1	1	1	.50	2	.320	.381	.464
2004	Tex	AL	125	438	122	30	3	26	(14	12)	236	69	71	72	33	2	63	6	0	4	0	0	-	6	.279	.335	.539
2005	Tex	AL	160	557	147	22	3	25	(13	12)	251	71	73	75	50	4	68	5	0	3	4	3	.57	6	.264	.328	.469
2006	2 Tms		127	446	120	24	2	13	(9	4)	187	45	68	57	27	5	59	4	0	5	1	0	1.00	8	.269	.313	.419
2007	Mil	NL	101	288	77	20	3	8	(3	5)	127	39	37	42	16	2	21	1	0	3	3	1	.75	3	.267	.305	.441
2008	Tor	NL	51	115	28	11	1	0	(0	0)	41	18	10	13	14	2	18	0	0	2	2	0	1.00	3	.243	.321	.357
2010	Was	NL	27	27	3	0	0	0	(0	0)	3	2	1	0	2	0	6	0	0	0	0	0	-	0	.111	.172	.111
06	Tex	AL	87	320	91	18	1	12	(8	4)	147	36	50	48	23	5	42	4	0	2	1	0	1.00	4	.284	.338	.459
06	Mil	NL	40	126	29	6	1	1	(1	0)	40	9	18	9	4	0	17	0	0	3	0	0	-	4	.230	.248	.317
	8 ML YEARS		729	2362	632	150	14	89	(48	41)	1077	311	331	341	183	15	335	27	2	23	12	6	.67	32	.268	.324	.456

Adalberto Mendez

add-ell-BURR-toe

Pitches: R **Bats:** R **Pos:** SP-5

Ht: 6'2" **Wt:** 160 **Born:** 2/22/1982 **Age:** 29

Year	Team	Lg	G	GS	CG	GF	IP	BFP	H	R	ER	HR	SH	SF	HB	TBB	IBB	SO	WP	Bk	W	L	Pct	Sh	Sv-Op	Hld	ERC	ERA
2003	Lansng	A	9	1	0	3	12.1	59	15	9	6	1	0	1	0	6	0	11	0	0	0	0	-	0	0--	-	5.30	4.38
2003	Boise	A-	15	5	0	9	33.0	143	29	18	15	4	2	1	3	15	1	33	3	2	0	4	.000	0	7--	-	4.07	4.09
2004	Lansng	A	56	0	0	41	64.1	291	63	37	33	7	1	1	5	28	2	55	5	0	5	7	.417	0	20--	-	4.28	4.62
2005	Dytona	A+	23	0	10	28.1	147	37	24	21	2	1	2	0	25	0	32	2	0	1	1	.500	0	3--	-	7.51	6.67
2005	Peoria	A	22	0	0	14	29.0	122	26	10	10	1	0	2	1	10	0	24	2	0	2	1	.667	0	6--	-	3.13	3.10
2005	Iowa	AAA	3	0	0	3	3.0	11	1	0	0	0	0	0	0	1	0	3	0	0	0	0	-	0	0--	-	0.69	0.00
2006	Dytona	A+	43	0	0	29	59.0	241	48	20	14	4	1	1	1	17	0	64	6	0	4	2	.667	0	14--	-	2.51	2.14
2006	Iowa	AAA	2	0	0	1	2.1	9	2	2	2	0	0	0	0	1	0	3	1	0	0	0	-	0	0--	-	3.03	7.71
2006	WTenn	AA	8	0	0	5	9.2	36	4	0	0	0	0	0	1	3	0	11	0	0	0	0	-	0	2--	-	1.04	0.00

Year	Team	Lg	G	GS	CG	GF	IP	BFP	H	R	ER	HR	SH	SF	HB	TBB	IBB	SO	WP	Bk	W	L	Pct	Sh	Sv-Op	Hld	ERC	ERA

HOW MUCH HE PITCHED / WHAT HE GAVE UP / THE RESULTS

Year	Team	Lg	G	GS	CG	GF	IP	BFP	H	R	ER	HR	SH	SF	HB	TBB	IBB	SO	WP	Bk	W	L	Pct	Sh	Sv-Op	Hld	ERC	ERA
2007	Tenn	AA	40	0	0	9	59.2	264	52	36	32	10	3	2	3	33	2	50	13	1	3	4	.429	0	1--	-	4.55	4.83
2007	Dytona	A+	5	5	0	0	27.0	126	30	19	17	6	1	2	1	16	0	16	4	0	0	2	.000	0	0--	-	6.61	5.67
2008	Jupiter	A+	57	0	0	53	57.0	244	46	25	22	3	2	2	2	24	0	59	4	1	3	7	.300	0	29--	-	2.85	3.47
2009	Jaxnvl	AA	27	0	0	6	36.0	148	29	15	14	2	0	0	0	16	0	32	5	0	2	4	.333	0	0--	-	2.95	3.50
2010	Jaxnvl	AA	12	0	0	5	14.1	71	15	8	5	1	1	0	0	12	0	15	5	0	0	1	.000	0	0--	-	5.63	3.14
2010	NewOr	AAA	28	9	0	8	71.2	307	64	35	33	7	3	3	3	29	1	73	2	0	5	4	.556	0	1--	-	3.60	4.14
2010	Fla	NL	5	5	0	0	24.2	109	28	14	14	7	0	0	2	12	0	11	0	0	1	3	.250	0	0-0	0	7.34	5.11

Luis Mendoza

Pitches: R **Bats:** R **Pos:** RP-4
Ht: 6'3" **Wt:** 235 **Born:** 10/31/1983 **Age:** 27

Year	Team	Lg	G	GS	CG	GF	IP	BFP	H	R	ER	HR	SH	SF	HB	TBB	IBB	SO	WP	Bk	W	L	Pct	Sh	Sv-Op	Hld	ERC	ERA
2010	Omha*	AAA	24	22	0	0	131.2	558	145	66	60	13	1	3	7	32	0	59	1	0	10	9	.526	0	0--	-	4.30	4.10
2007	Tex	AL	6	3	0	2	16.0	64	13	4	4	1	0	2	2	4	0	7	0	0	1	0	1.000	0	0-0	0	2.83	2.25
2008	Tex	AL	25	11	0	6	63.1	316	97	74	61	7	0	2	6	25	4	35	5	0	3	8	.273	0	1-2	0	7.53	8.67
2009	Tex	AL	1	0	0	0	1.0	7	2	4	4	1	0	0	1	1	0	0	0	0	0	0	-	0	0-0	0	29.25	36.00
2010	KC	AL	4	0	0	1	4.0	25	10	10	10	4	0	0	0	3	0	1	0	0	0	1	.000	0	0-1	0	25.91	22.50
4 ML YEARS			36	14	0	9	84.1	412	122	92	79	13	0	4	9	33	4	43	5	0	4	9	.308	0	1-3	0	7.48	8.43

Cla Meredith

Pitches: R **Bats:** R **Pos:** RP-21
CLAY
Ht: 6'0" **Wt:** 195 **Born:** 6/4/1983 **Age:** 28

Year	Team	Lg	G	GS	CG	GF	IP	BFP	H	R	ER	HR	SH	SF	HB	TBB	IBB	SO	WP	Bk	W	L	Pct	Sh	Sv-Op	Hld	ERC	ERA
2010	Norfolk*	AAA	20	0	0	7	27.0	128	32	21	18	2	2	2	2	12	0	17	1	0	1	2	.333	0	0--	-	5.25	6.00
2005	Bos	AL	3	0	0	0	2.1	18	6	7	7	1	0	0	1	4	0	1	0	0	0	0	-	0	0-0	0	27.60	27.00
2006	SD	NL	45	0	0	11	50.2	185	30	6	6	3	1	0	2	6	3	37	0	2	5	1	.833	0	0-2	16	1.19	1.07
2007	SD	NL	80	0	0	18	79.2	342	94	38	31	6	1	3	0	17	4	59	3	1	5	6	.455	0	0-5	10	4.28	3.50
2008	SD	NL	73	0	0	19	70.1	302	79	34	32	6	2	3	1	24	3	49	2	0	0	3	.000	0	0-6	11	4.52	4.09
2009	2 Tms		64	0	0	25	65.1	283	73	31	29	4	3	3	4	25	8	37	3	0	4	2	.667	0	0-3	4	4.56	3.99
2010	Bal	AL	21	0	0	10	15.0	67	18	9	9	4	1	1	2	4	1	7	0	0	0	2	.000	0	1-2	3	6.06	5.40
09	SD	NL	35	0	0	13	36.2	165	47	19	17	1	2	3	2	13	4	20	3	0	4	2	.667	0	0-3	1	5.08	4.17
09	Bal	AL	29	0	0	12	28.2	118	26	12	12	3	1	0	2	12	4	17	0	0	0	0	-	0	0-0	3	3.91	3.77
Postseason			2	0	0	0	3.2	15	3	2	0	0	1	0	1	0	0	3	0	0	0	0	-	0	0-0	0	2.00	0.00
6 ML YEARS			286	0	0	83	283.1	1197	300	125	114	24	8	10	12	80	19	189	9	3	14	14	.500	0	1-18	44	3.96	3.62

Dan Meyer

Pitches: L **Bats:** R **Pos:** RP-13
Ht: 6'2" **Wt:** 222 **Born:** 7/3/1981 **Age:** 29

Year	Team	Lg	G	GS	CG	GF	IP	BFP	H	R	ER	HR	SH	SF	HB	TBB	IBB	SO	WP	Bk	W	L	Pct	Sh	Sv-Op	Hld	ERC	ERA
2010	Jupiter*	A+	3	0	0	1	4.0	16	1	1	0	0	0	0	0	1	0	8	1	0	0	0	-	0	0--	-	0.35	0.00
2010	Jaxnvl*	AA	1	0	0	0	2.0	9	1	0	0	0	0	0	0	2	0	1	0	0	0	0	-	0	0--	-	2.80	0.00
2010	NewOr*	AAA	32	0	0	11	40.0	169	32	17	15	4	4	6	2	16	1	27	5	1	1	2	.333	0	2--	-	3.10	3.38
2004	Atl	NL	2	0	0	1	2.0	8	2	0	0	0	0	0	0	1	1	1	0	0	0	0	-	0	0-0	0	3.21	0.00
2007	Oak	AL	6	3	0	2	16.1	79	20	19	16	2	1	1	0	9	0	11	3	0	0	2	.000	0	0-0	0	5.97	8.82
2008	Oak	AL	11	4	0	5	27.2	132	35	28	23	6	0	2	1	14	0	20	0	0	0	4	.000	0	0-0	0	7.10	7.48
2009	Fla	NL	71	0	0	8	58.1	242	47	24	20	7	3	2	1	21	2	56	2	0	3	2	.600	0	2-2	20	2.99	3.09
2010	Fla	NL	13	0	0	3	9.1	55	15	10	10	1	1	0	1	12	0	4	0	0	0	1	.000	0	0-1	1	12.44	9.64
5 ML YEARS			103	7	0	19	113.2	516	119	81	69	16	5	5	3	57	3	92	5	0	3	9	.250	0	2-3	21	5.04	5.46

Jason Michaels

Bats: R **Throws:** R **Pos:** PH-58; LF-41; CF-11; RF-5; DH-2; PR-1
Ht: 6'0" **Wt:** 212 **Born:** 5/4/1976 **Age:** 35

Year	Team	Lg	G	AB	H	2B	3B	HR	(Hm	Rd)	TB	R	RBI	RC	TBB	IBB	SO	HBP	SH	SF	SB	CS	SB%	GDP	Avg	OBP	Slg
2001	Phi	NL	6	6	1	0	0	0	(0	0)	1	0	1	0	0	0	2	0	0	0	0	0	-	0	.167	.167	.167
2002	Phi	NL	81	105	28	10	3	2	(0	2)	50	16	11	14	13	1	33	1	0	2	1	1	.50	1	.267	.347	.476
2003	Phi	NL	76	109	36	11	0	5	(1	4)	62	20	17	19	15	1	22	1	0	0	0	0	-	3	.330	.416	.569
2004	Phi	NL	115	299	82	12	0	10	(5	5)	124	44	40	47	42	1	80	2	0	3	2	2	.50	3	.274	.364	.415
2005	Phi	NL	105	289	88	16	2	4	(1	3)	120	54	31	47	44	1	45	4	2	4	3	3	.50	3	.304	.399	.415
2006	Cle	AL	123	494	132	32	1	9	(4	5)	193	77	55	62	43	0	101	3	2	6	9	5	.64	6	.267	.326	.391
2007	Cle	AL	105	267	72	11	1	7	(5	2)	106	43	39	37	20	1	50	3	2	3	3	4	.43	3	.270	.324	.397
2008	2 Tms		123	286	64	13	1	8	(4	4)	103	28	53	37	27	0	65	2	2	4	2	1	.67	9	.224	.292	.360
2009	Hou	NL	102	135	32	12	1	4	(3	1)	58	17	16	15	16	0	38	1	0	0	1	2	.33	2	.237	.322	.430
2010	Hou	NL	106	186	47	14	1	8	(4	4)	87	23	26	28	12	1	29	4	0	1	0	0	-	3	.253	.310	.468
08	Cle	AL	21	58	12	4	0	0	(0	0)	16	3	9	5	4	0	13	1	1	3	1	1	.50	0	.207	.258	.276
08	Pit	NL	102	228	52	9	1	8	(4	4)	87	25	44	32	23	0	52	1	1	1	1	0	1.00	9	.228	.300	.382
Postseason			2	1	1	1	0	0	(0	0)	2	1	0	1	0	0	0	0	1	0	0	0	-	0	1.000	1.000	2.000
10 ML YEARS			942	2176	582	131	10	57	(27	30)	904	322	289	306	232	6	465	21	8	23	21	18	.54	33	.267	.341	.415

Kam Mickolio

Pitches: R **Bats:** R **Pos:** RP-3   mick-oh-LYE-oh   **Ht:** 6'9" **Wt:** 240 **Born:** 5/10/1984 **Age:** 27

Year	Team	Lg	G	GS	CG	GF	IP	BFP	H	R	ER	HR	SH	SF	HB	TBB	IBB	SO	WP	Bk	W	L	Pct	Sh	Sv-Op	Hld	ERC	ERA
2010	Norfolk*	AAA	30	0	0	8	35.1	169	44	25	25	4	4	0	0	17	0	48	0	0	4	3	.571	0	0- -		5.73	6.37
2010	Abrdn*	A-	4	0	0	4	5.0	17	1	1	1	1	0	0	0	1	0	7	1	0	1	0	1.000	0	0- -		0.65	1.80
2008	Bal	AL	9	0	0	5	7.2	36	8	5	5	0	1	1	0	4	0	8	2	0	0	1	.000	0	0-1	0	3.81	5.87
2009	Bal	AL	11	0	0	7	13.2	59	11	4	4	0	0	2	0	7	1	14	0	0	0	2	.000	0	0-0	2	2.58	2.63
2010	Bal	AL	3	0	0	2	3.2	19	5	3	3	1	0	0	0	3	0	4	0	0	0	0	-	0	0-0	0	9.47	7.36
	3 ML YEARS		23	0	0	14	25.0	114	24	12	12	1	1	3	0	14	1	26	2	0	0	3	.000	0	0-1	2	3.82	4.32

Jose Mijares

Pitches: L **Bats:** L **Pos:** RP-47   mee-HAHR-ess   **Ht:** 6'0" **Wt:** 230 **Born:** 10/29/1984 **Age:** 26

Year	Team	Lg	G	GS	CG	GF	IP	BFP	H	R	ER	HR	SH	SF	HB	TBB	IBB	SO	WP	Bk	W	L	Pct	Sh	Sv-Op	Hld	ERC	ERA
2010	Roch*	AAA	2	0	0	0	1.2	12	6	5	5	1	0	0	0	1	0	2	0	0	0	0	-	0	0- -		30.01	27.00
2008	Min	AL	10	0	0	3	10.1	34	3	1	1	0	0	0	0	0	0	5	1	0	0	1	.000	0	0-0	2	0.19	0.87
2009	Min	AL	71	0	0	12	61.2	253	50	17	16	7	2	3	2	23	1	55	0	0	2	2	.500	0	0-1	27	3.18	2.34
2010	Min	AL	47	0	0	10	32.2	139	34	14	12	4	1	1	1	9	1	28	1	0	1	1	.500	0	0-0	9	4.04	3.31
	Postseason		2	0	0	1	0.2	3	1	1	1	0	0	0	0	1	0	0	0	0	0	1	.000	0	0-0	0	36.52	13.50
	3 ML YEARS		128	0	0	25	104.2	426	87	32	29	11	3	4	3	32	2	88	2	0	3	4	.429	0	0-1	38	2.95	2.49

Aaron Miles

Bats: B **Throws:** R **Pos:** 2B-50; PH-32; SS-6; 3B-5; DH-1   **Ht:** 5'8" **Wt:** 180 **Born:** 12/15/1976 **Age:** 34

Year	Team	Lg	G	AB	H	2B	3B	HR	(Hm	Rd)	TB	R	RBI	RC	TBB	IBB	SO	HBP	SH	SF	SB	CS	SB%	GDP	Avg	OBP	Slg
2010	Sprgfld*	AA	16	61	17	4	0	0	(-	-)	21	11	13	8	7	0	8	1	2	0	0	1	.00	1	.279	.362	.344
2003	CWS	AL	8	12	4	3	0	0	(0	0)	7	3	2	3	0	0	0	0	0	0	0	0	-	0	.333	.333	.583
2004	Col	NL	134	522	153	15	3	6	(4	2)	192	75	47	70	29	0	53	2	7	6	12	7	.63	12	.293	.329	.368
2005	Col	NL	99	324	91	12	3	2	(0	2)	115	37	28	42	8	1	38	4	10	1	4	2	.67	6	.281	.306	.355
2006	StL	NL	135	426	112	20	5	2	(1	1)	148	48	30	49	38	9	42	2	2	3	2	1	.67	11	.263	.324	.347
2007	StL	NL	133	414	120	16	1	2	(0	2)	144	55	32	49	25	1	40	1	4	5	2	1	.67	11	.290	.328	.348
2008	StL	NL	134	379	120	15	2	4	(1	3)	151	44	37	44	23	2	37	0	5	1	3	3	.50	13	.317	.355	.398
2009	ChC	NL	74	157	29	7	1	0	(0	0)	38	17	5	3	8	1	21	0	5	0	3	0	1.00	4	.185	.224	.242
2010	StL	NL	79	139	39	5	0	0	(0	0)	44	14	9	13	6	1	14	1	3	2	0	1	.00	4	.281	.311	.317
	Postseason		7	11	4	0	1	0	(0	0)	6	2	0	2	1	1	2	0	0	0	1	0	1.00	0	.364	.417	.545
	8 ML YEARS		796	2373	668	93	15	16	(6	10)	839	298	184	273	137	15	245	10	36	18	26	15	.63	55	.282	.321	.354

Lastings Milledge

Bats: R **Throws:** R **Pos:** LF-63; RF-45; PH-13   **Ht:** 5'11" **Wt:** 200 **Born:** 4/5/1985 **Age:** 26

Year	Team	Lg	G	AB	H	2B	3B	HR	(Hm	Rd)	TB	R	RBI	RC	TBB	IBB	SO	HBP	SH	SF	SB	CS	SB%	GDP	Avg	OBP	Slg
2006	NYM	NL	56	166	40	7	2	4	(2	2)	63	14	22	21	12	4	39	5	1	1	1	2	.33	4	.241	.310	.380
2007	NYM	NL	59	184	50	9	1	7	(6	1)	82	27	29	27	13	2	42	7	1	1	3	2	.60	5	.272	.341	.446
2008	Was	NL	138	523	140	24	7	7	(7	7)	210	65	61	60	38	1	96	14	5	7	24	9	.73	19	.268	.330	.402
2009	2 Tms	NL	65	244	68	11	0	4	(3	1)	91	21	21	24	13	0	47	4	2	2	7	4	.64	5	.279	.323	.373
2010	Pit	NL	113	379	105	21	3	4	(1	3)	144	38	34	48	28	3	62	3	2	0	5	3	.63	7	.277	.332	.380
09	Was	NL	7	24	4	0	0	0	(0	0)	4	1	1	1	1	0	10	1	0	0	1	0	1.00	1	.167	.231	.167
09	Pit	NL	58	220	64	11	0	4	(3	1)	87	20	20	23	12	0	37	3	2	2	6	4	.60	4	.291	.333	.395
	5 ML YEARS		431	1496	403	72	8	33	(19	14)	590	165	167	180	104	10	286	33	11	11	40	20	.67	40	.269	.328	.394

Andrew Miller

Pitches: L **Bats:** L **Pos:** SP-7; RP-2   **Ht:** 6'7" **Wt:** 210 **Born:** 5/21/1985 **Age:** 20

Year	Team	Lg	G	GS	CG	GF	IP	BFP	H	R	ER	HR	SH	SF	HB	TBB	IBB	SO	WP	Bk	W	L	Pct	Sh	Sv-Op	Hld	ERC	ERA
2010	Jupiter*	A+	3	3	0	0	15.2	71	8	8	3	0	0	0	1	15	0	23	1	0	1	1	.500	0	0- -		2.92	1.72
2010	Jaxnvl*	AA	18	18	0	0	85.1	410	98	63	57	6	7	4	5	61	1	66	10	0	1	8	.111	0	0- -		6.21	6.01
2006	Det	AL	8	0	0	3	10.1	51	8	9	7	0	0	0	2	10	0	6	1	0	0	0	1.000	0	0-0	1	4.79	6.10
2007	Det	AL	13	13	0	0	64.0	309	73	43	40	8	3	1	7	39	0	56	4	1	5	5	.500	0	0-0	0	6.31	5.63
2008	Fla	NL	29	20	0	1	107.1	492	120	78	70	7	10	7	4	56	4	89	4	0	6	10	.375	0	0-0	2	5.04	5.87
2009	Fla	NL	20	14	0	1	80.0	366	85	52	43	7	6	4	2	43	1	59	10	0	3	5	.375	0	0-0	1	4.90	4.84
2010	Fla	NL	9	7	0	1	32.2	171	51	34	31	6	5	2	1	26	2	28	5	0	1	5	.167	0	0-0	0	10.20	8.54
	5 ML YEARS		79	54	0	6	294.1	1389	337	216	191	28	24	14	16	174	7	238	24	1	15	26	.366	0	0-0	4	5.79	5.84

Corky Miller

Bats: R **Throws:** R **Pos:** C-32; PH-5   **Ht:** 6'1" **Wt:** 245 **Born:** 3/18/1976 **Age:** 35

Year	Team	Lg	G	AB	H	2B	3B	HR	(Hm	Rd)	TB	R	RBI	RC	TBB	IBB	SO	HBP	SH	SF	SB	CS	SB%	GDP	Avg	OBP	Slg
2010	Lsvlle*	AAA	54	181	50	13	0	6	(-	-)	81	29	35	30	19	0	31	5	3	1	0	1	.00	5	.276	.359	.448
2001	Cin	NL	17	49	9	2	0	3	(1	2)	20	5	7	6	4	0	16	2	0	2	1	0	1.00	1	.184	.263	.408
2002	Cin	NL	39	114	29	10	0	3	(2	1)	48	9	15	15	9	2	20	4	1	1	0	0	-	1	.254	.328	.421
2003	Cin	NL	14	30	8	0	0	0	(0	0)	8	4	1	5	5	0	7	2	0	1	0	0	-	1	.267	.395	.267
2004	Cin	NL	13	39	1	0	0	0	(0	0)	1	2	3	0	6	0	12	3	0	1	0	0	-	3	.026	.204	.026
2005	Min	AL	5	12	0	0	0	0	(0	0)	0	0	0	0	0	0	2	0	0	0	0	0	-	0	.000	.000	.000
2006	Bos	AL	1	4	0	0	0	0	(0	0)	0	0	0	0	0	0	1	0	0	0	0	0	-	0	.000	.000	.000
2007	Atl	NL	12	27	7	2	0	1	(0	1)	12	3	4	4	1	0	5	1	0	0	0	0	-	1	.259	.310	.444

Year Team	Lg	G	AB	H	2B	3B	HR	(Hm	Rd)	TB	R	RBI	RC	TBB	IBB	SO	HBP	SH	SF	SB	CS	SB%	GDP	Avg	OBP	Slg
2008 Atl	NL	31	60	5	0	0	1	(0	1)	8	4	5	0	5	0	15	0	1	1	0	0	-	2	.083	.152	.133
2009 2 Tms		35	95	18	4	0	1	(1	0)	25	9	15	11	12	0	23	1	2	1	0	0	-	2	.189	.284	.263
2010 Cin	NL	32	74	18	5	0	2	(1	1)	29	5	9	9	2	0	16	2	1	0	0	0	-	2	.243	.282	.392
09 CWS	AL	14	39	8	3	0	0	(0	0)	11	5	5	3	3	0	9	0	0	0	0	0	-	1	.205	.262	.282
09 Cin	NL	21	56	10	1	0	1	(1	0)	14	4	10	8	9	0	14	1	2	1	0	0	-	1	.179	.299	.250
10 ML YEARS		199	504	95	23	0	11	(5	6)	151	41	59	50	44	2	117	15	5	7	1	0	1.00	19	.188	.270	.300

Jai Miller

Bats: R **Throws:** R **Pos:** RF-16; LF-3; PH-2; DH-1; PR-1   JAY   **Ht:** 6'3" **Wt:** 205 **Born:** 1/17/1985 **Age:** 26

Year Team	Lg	G	AB	H	2B	3B	HR	(Hm	Rd)	TB	R	RBI	RC	TBB	IBB	SO	HBP	SH	SF	SB	CS	SB%	GDP	Avg	OBP	Slg
2003 Mrlns	R	46	146	29	4	1	1	(-	-)	38	17	15	11	15	0	45	2	1	2	9	3	.75	4	.199	.279	.260
2003 Jmstwn	A-	11	43	10	3	0	0	(-	-)	13	5	6	3	3	0	15	1	0	1	1	1	.50	0	.233	.292	.302
2004 Grnsbr	A	113	390	80	15	3	12	(-	-)	137	51	49	38	32	0	163	5	5	1	11	4	.73	10	.205	.273	.351
2005 Grnsbr	A	115	415	86	14	2	13	(-	-)	143	69	34	46	57	1	139	3	1	3	16	11	.59	5	.207	.305	.345
2006 Jupiter	A+	111	344	72	16	2	0	(-	-)	92	40	24	32	45	1	115	5	5	2	24	10	.71	5	.209	.308	.267
2007 Carlina	AA	129	406	106	26	2	14	(-	-)	178	54	58	67	55	5	127	5	4	3	12	5	.71	10	.261	.354	.438
2008 Albq	AAA	117	434	116	22	5	19	(-	-)	205	67	56	75	52	3	133	5	2	5	19	6	.76	5	.267	.349	.472
2009 NewOr	AAA	102	343	99	24	2	16	(-	-)	175	55	52	64	38	2	106	3	1	5	6	3	.67	4	.289	.360	.510
2010 Scrmto	AAA	10	34	4	0	0	0	(-	-)	4	2	1	0	3	0	19	0	0	0	3	0	1.00	0	.118	.189	.118
2010 Omha	AAA	84	311	83	24	2	18	(-	-)	165	45	56	56	35	0	113	1	0	3	2	3	.40	7	.267	.340	.531
2008 Fla	NL	1	1	0	0	0	0	(0	0)	0	0	0	0	0	0	1	0	0	0	0	0	-	0	.000	.000	.000
2010 KC	AL	20	55	13	3	0	1	(1	0)	19	5	4	4	4	0	23	1	0	0	1	0	1.00	0	.236	.300	.345
2 ML YEARS		21	56	13	3	0	1	(1	0)	19	5	4	4	4	0	24	1	0	0	1	0	1.00	0	.232	.295	.339

Justin Miller

Pitches: R **Bats:** R **Pos:** RP-19   **Ht:** 6'2" **Wt:** 217 **Born:** 8/27/1977 **Age:** 33

		HOW MUCH HE PITCHED						WHAT HE GAVE UP										THE RESULTS						
Year Team	Lg	G	GS	CG	GF	IP	BFP	H	R	ER	HR	SH	SF	HB	TBB	IBB	SO	WP	Bk	W	L	Pct	Sh	Sv-Op	Hld	ERC	ERA
2010 Albq*	AAA	32	0	0	8	37.0	154	29	9	8	2	2	0	0	16	0	37	2	0	1	0	.000	0	0- -	-	2.73	1.95
2002 Tor	AL	25	18	0	2	102.1	469	103	70	63	12	1	6	11	66	2	68	6	0	9	5	.643	0	0-0	1	5.73	5.54
2004 Tor	AL	19	15	0	0	81.2	375	101	58	55	14	2	6	5	42	3	47	3	1	3	4	.429	0	0-0	0	6.91	6.06
2005 Tor	AL	1	0	0	0	2.1	12	5	4	4	3	0	0	0	0	0	2	0	0	0	0	-	0	0-0	0	20.19	15.43
2007 Fla	NL	62	0	0	10	61.2	259	53	27	25	5	3	0	0	24	6	74	4	1	5	0	1.000	0	0-3	17	2.98	3.65
2008 Fla	NL	46	0	0	8	46.2	202	46	26	22	4	0	1	3	20	3	43	1	1	4	2	.667	0	0-1	7	4.21	4.24
2009 SF	NL	44	0	0	6	56.2	236	47	20	20	7	4	5	1	27	2	36	3	0	3	3	.500	0	0-0	1	3.69	3.18
2010 LAD	NL	19	0	0	7	24.1	103	22	12	12	4	0	2	3	8	2	30	2	1	0	0	-	0	0-0	1	4.11	4.44
7 ML YEARS		216	33	0	33	375.2	1656	377	217	201	49	10	20	23	187	18	300	19	4	24	14	.632	0	0-4	27	4.95	4.82

Trever Miller

Pitches: L **Bats:** R **Pos:** RP-57   **Ht:** 6'3" **Wt:** 185 **Born:** 5/29/1973 **Age:** 38

		HOW MUCH HE PITCHED						WHAT HE GAVE UP										THE RESULTS						
Year Team	Lg	G	GS	CG	GF	IP	BFP	H	R	ER	HR	SH	SF	HB	TBB	IBB	SO	WP	Bk	W	L	Pct	Sh	Sv-Op	Hld	ERC	ERA
1996 Det	AL	5	4	0	0	16.2	88	28	17	17	3	2	2	2	9	0	8	0	0	0	4	.000	0	0-0	0	10.15	9.18
1998 Hou	NL	37	1	0	15	53.1	235	57	21	18	4	0	0	1	20	1	30	1	0	2	0	1.000	0	1-2	1	4.18	3.04
1999 Hou	NL	47	0	0	11	49.2	232	58	29	28	6	2	2	5	29	1	37	4	0	3	2	.600	0	1-1	4	6.48	5.07
2000 2 Tms	NL	16	0	0	2	16.1	90	27	22	19	3	1	1	2	12	1	11	1	0	0	0	-	0	0-0	0	10.68	10.47
2003 Tor	AL	79	0	0	18	52.2	233	46	30	27	7	1	0	5	28	3	44	2	0	2	2	.500	0	3-4	16	4.38	4.61
2004 TB	AL	60	0	0	15	49.0	208	48	21	17	3	3	0	3	15	4	43	2	0	1	1	.500	0	1-3	9	3.45	3.12
2005 TB	AL	61	0	0	13	44.1	206	45	23	20	4	3	5	7	29	6	35	2	0	2	2	.500	0	0-3	11	5.57	4.06
2006 Hou	NL	70	0	0	14	50.2	207	42	17	17	7	1	2	4	13	2	56	1	0	2	3	.400	0	1-3	12	3.11	3.02
2007 Hou	NL	76	0	0	12	46.1	211	45	26	25	6	3	0	4	23	6	46	1	0	1	3	.250	0	1-3	12	4.52	4.86
2008 TB	AL	68	0	0	16	43.1	187	39	21	20	2	1	1	4	20	1	44	1	0	2	0	1.000	0	2-3	11	3.73	4.15
2009 StL	NL	70	0	0	9	43.2	173	31	11	10	5	2	1	2	11	1	46	1	0	4	1	.800	0	0-1	13	2.25	2.06
2010 StL	NL	57	0	0	3	36.0	151	30	17	16	2	2	2	2	16	0	22	4	0	1	0	1.000	0	0-1	11	3.29	4.00
00 Phi	NL	14	0	0	2	14.0	72	19	16	13	3	1	1	2	9	1	10	1	0	0	0	-	0	0-0	0	8.14	8.36
00 LAD	NL	2	0	0	0	2.1	18	8	6	6	0	0	0	1	3	0	1	0	0	0	0	-	0	0-0	0	28.18	23.14
Postseason		11	0	0	2	3.2	18	3	2	2	1	0	0	0	4	0	5	1	0	0	0	-	0	0-0	2	7.11	4.91
12 ML YEARS		646	5	0	128	502.0	2221	496	255	234	52	21	16	41	225	26	422	20	0	18	16	.529	0	10-24	100	4.46	4.20

Brad Mills

Pitches: L **Bats:** L **Pos:** RP-4; SP-3   **Ht:** 5'11" **Wt:** 185 **Born:** 3/5/1985 **Age:** 26

		HOW MUCH HE PITCHED						WHAT HE GAVE UP										THE RESULTS						
Year Team	Lg	G	GS	CG	GF	IP	BFP	H	R	ER	HR	SH	SF	HB	TBB	IBB	SO	WP	Bk	W	L	Pct	Sh	Sv-Op	Hld	ERC	ERA
2007 Auburn	A-	6	2	0	0	18.0	70	9	4	4	0	0	0	0	6	0	21	0	0	2	0	1.000	0	0- -	-	1.20	2.00
2008 Lansng	A	15	15	0	0	81.1	341	71	30	23	3	2	1	5	28	1	92	2	0	6	3	.667	0	0- -	-	2.97	2.55
2008 Dnedin	A+	6	6	0	0	33.1	133	25	5	5	2	1	1	0	12	0	35	1	0	4	0	1.000	0	0- -	-	2.41	1.35
2008 NHam	AA	6	6	0	0	32.2	131	24	11	4	2	0	1	1	12	0	32	2	0	3	2	.600	0	0- -	-	2.47	1.10
2009 LsVgs	AAA	14	14	1	0	84.1	362	83	43	38	6	4	2	4	35	0	72	4	1	2	8	.200	0	0- -	-	4.09	4.06
2010 LsVgs	AAA	20	20	0	0	112.1	492	118	66	62	15	4	3	2	43	0	100	4	1	8	6	.571	0	0- -	-	4.58	4.97
2009 Tor	AL	2	2	0	0	7.2	42	14	12	12	4	0	1	0	6	0	9	0	0	0	1	.000	0	0-0	0	15.52	14.09
2010 Tor	AL	7	3	0	0	22.1	98	20	14	14	2	0	1	1	13	1	18	1	0	1	0	1.000	0	0-0	1	4.26	5.64
2 ML YEARS		9	5	0	0	30.0	140	34	26	26	6	0	2	1	19	1	27	1	0	1	1	.500	0	0-0	1	6.76	7.80

Kevin Millwood

Pitches: R **Bats:** R **Pos:** SP-31   **Ht:** 6'4" **Wt:** 235 **Born:** 12/24/1974 **Age:** 36

Year	Team	Lg	G	GS	CG	GF	IP	BFP	H	R	ER	HR	SH	SF	HB	TBB	IBB	SO	WP	Bk	W	L	Pct	Sh	Sv-Op	Hld	ERC	ERA
1997	Atl	NL	12	8	0	2	51.1	227	55	26	23	1	3	5	2	21	1	42	1	0	5	3	.625	0	0-0	0	4.03	4.03
1998	Atl	NL	31	29	3	1	174.1	748	175	86	79	18	8	3	3	56	3	163	6	1	17	8	.680	1	0-0	1	3.81	4.08
1999	Atl	NL	33	33	2	0	228.0	906	168	80	68	24	9	3	4	59	2	205	5	0	18	7	.720	0	0-0	0	**2.26**	2.68
2000	Atl	NL	36	35	0	0	212.2	903	213	115	110	26	8	5	3	62	2	168	4	0	10	13	.435	0	0-0	0	3.83	4.66
2001	Atl	NL	21	21	0	0	121.0	515	121	66	58	20	7	2	1	40	6	84	5	1	7	7	.500	0	0-0	0	4.20	4.31
2002	Atl	NL	35	34	1	0	217.0	895	186	83	78	16	9	4	8	65	7	178	4	0	18	8	.692	1	0-0	0	2.85	3.24
2003	Phi	NL	35	35	5	0	222.0	930	210	103	99	19	12	5	4	68	6	169	2	0	14	12	.538	3	0-0	0	3.35	4.01
2004	Phi	NL	25	25	0	0	141.0	628	155	81	76	14	11	2	7	51	5	125	4	0	9	6	.600	0	0-0	0	4.57	4.85
2005	Cle	AL	30	30	1	0	192.0	799	182	72	61	20	6	4	4	52	0	146	2	0	9	11	.450	0	0-0	0	3.40	**2.86**
2006	Tex	AL	34	34	2	0	215.0	907	228	114	108	23	8	3	4	53	4	157	6	0	16	12	.571	0	0-0	0	3.92	4.52
2007	Tex	AL	31	31	0	0	172.2	788	213	111	99	19	1	4	8	67	2	123	4	0	10	14	.417	0	0-0	0	5.64	5.16
2008	Tex	AL	29	29	3	0	168.2	767	220	104	95	18	5	2	6	49	3	125	2	1	9	10	.474	0	0-0	0	5.54	5.07
2009	Tex	AL	31	31	3	0	198.2	850	195	88	81	26	4	5	11	71	0	123	8	0	13	10	.565	0	0-0	0	4.27	3.67
2010	Bal	AL	31	31	0	0	190.2	842	223	116	108	30	6	2	6	65	2	132	7	1	4	**16**	.200	0	0-0	0	5.39	5.10
	Postseason		9	7	1	1	41.1	164	33	20	18	7	1	1	0	6	0	38	1	1	3	3	.500	0	1-1	0	2.41	3.92
	14 ML YEARS		414	406	21	3	2505.0	10705	2544	1245	1143	274	97	49	71	779	43	1940	60	4	159	137	.537	5	0-0	1	3.95	4.11

Zach Miner

Pitches: R **Bats:** R **Pos:** P   **Ht:** 6'3" **Wt:** 200 **Born:** 3/12/1982 **Age:** 29

Year	Team	Lg	G	GS	CG	GF	IP	BFP	H	R	ER	HR	SH	SF	HB	TBB	IBB	SO	WP	Bk	W	L	Pct	Sh	Sv-Op	Hld	ERC	ERA
2006	Det	AL	27	16	1	4	93.0	398	100	53	50	11	2	2	0	32	1	59	1	0	7	6	.538	0	0-0	1	4.44	4.84
2007	Det	AL	34	1	0	8	53.2	232	56	22	18	3	4	1	0	22	4	34	1	0	3	4	.429	0	0-2	9	3.95	3.02
2008	Det	AL	45	13	0	3	118.0	509	118	60	56	10	4	3	6	46	3	62	4	0	8	5	.615	0	0-3	6	4.12	4.27
2009	Det	AL	51	5	0	9	92.1	409	101	49	44	11	2	1	2	45	1	62	2	0	7	5	.583	0	1-5	8	5.28	4.29
	Postseason		1	0	0	1	0.2	2	0	0	0	0	0	1	0	0	0	0	1	0	0	0	-	0	0-0	0	3.22	0.00
	4 ML YEARS		157	35	1	24	357.0	1548	375	184	168	35	12	7	8	145	9	217	8	0	25	20	.556	0	1-10	24	4.47	4.24

Mike Minor

Pitches: L **Bats:** R **Pos:** SP-8; RP-1   **Ht:** 6'4" **Wt:** 205 **Born:** 12/26/1987 **Age:** 23

Year	Team	Lg	G	GS	CG	GF	IP	BFP	H	R	ER	HR	SH	SF	HB	TBB	IBB	SO	WP	Bk	W	L	Pct	Sh	Sv-Op	Hld	ERC	ERA
2009	Rome	A	4	4	0	0	14.0	48	10	1	1	0	0	0	0	4	0	17	0	0	0	1	.000	0	0- -	-	1.12	0.64
2010	Missi	AA	15	15	0	0	87.0	360	74	48	39	8	5	3	1	34	1	109	2	1	2	6	.250	0	0- -	-	3.24	4.03
2010	Gwnntt	AAA	6	6	0	0	33.1	127	19	7	7	1	1	3	0	12	0	37	0	0	4	1	.000	0	0- -	-	1.60	1.89
2010	Atl	NL	9	8	0	1	40.2	185	53	28	27	6	1	3	1	11	0	43	0	0	3	2	.600	0	0-0	0	5.71	5.98

Juan Miranda

Bats: L **Throws:** L **Pos:** DH-14; 1B-13; PH-11; PR-2   **Ht:** 6'0" **Wt:** 220 **Born:** 4/25/1983 **Age:** 28

Year	Team	Lg	G	AB	H	2B	3B	HR	(Hm	Rd)	TB	R	RBI	RC	TBB	IBB	SO	HBP	SH	SF	SB	CS	SB%	GDP	Avg	OBP	Slg
2010	S-WB*	AAA	80	295	84	15	1	15	(-	-)	146	52	43	56	33	4	71	9	0	3	1	0	1.00	6	.285	.371	.495
2008	NYY	AL	5	10	4	1	0	0	(0	0)	5	2	1	3	2	0	4	1	0	1	0	0	-	0	.400	.500	.500
2009	NYY	AL	8	9	3	0	0	1	(0	1)	6	2	3	2	0	0	4	0	0	0	0	0	-	0	.333	.333	.667
2010	NYY	AL	33	64	14	2	1	3	(3	0)	27	7	10	8	7	0	12	0	0	0	0	0	-	1	.219	.296	.422
	3 ML YEARS		46	83	21	3	1	4	(3	1)	38	11	14	13	9	0	20	1	0	1	0	0	-	1	.253	.330	.458

Pat Misch

Pitches: L **Bats:** R **Pos:** SP-6; RP-6   MISHH   **Ht:** 6'2" **Wt:** 196 **Born:** 8/18/1981 **Age:** 29

Year	Team	Lg	G	GS	CG	GF	IP	BFP	H	R	ER	HR	SH	SF	HB	TBB	IBB	SO	WP	Bk	W	L	Pct	Sh	Sv-Op	Hld	ERC	ERA
2010	Buffalo*	AAA	23	23	2	0	150.2	619	150	61	54	11	5	4	6	24	0	99	4	0	11	4	.733	1	0- -		3.11	3.23
2006	SF	NL	1	0	0	0	1.0	5	2	0	0	0	0	0	0	0	0	1	0	0	0	0	-	0	0-0	0	7.48	0.00
2007	SF	NL	18	4	0	2	40.1	176	47	21	19	3	1	2	2	12	2	26	0	0	0	4	.000	0	0-0	2	4.59	4.24
2008	SF	NL	15	7	0	6	52.1	230	56	34	33	11	3	4	3	15	2	38	1	1	0	3	.000	0	0-0	0	4.88	5.68
2009	2 Tms	NL	26	7	1	2	62.1	270	68	31	31	9	6	1	2	22	2	23	1	0	3	4	.429	1	0-1	0	4.86	4.48
2010	NYM	NL	12	6	0	2	37.2	159	43	20	16	4	0	2	1	4	1	23	0	0	0	4	.000	0	0-0	0	3.77	3.82
09	SF	NL	4	0	0	2	3.1	19	6	4	4	0	0	0	0	3	0	0	0	0	0	0	-	0	0-0	0	10.16	10.80
09	NYM	NL	22	7	1	0	59.0	251	62	27	27	9	6	1	2	19	2	23	1	0	3	4	.429	1	0-1	0	4.58	4.12
	5 ML YEARS		72	24	1	12	193.2	840	216	106	99	27	10	9	8	53	7	111	2	1	3	15	.167	1	0-1	2	4.61	4.60

Russ Mitchell

Bats: R **Throws:** R **Pos:** 3B-6; PH-4; 1B-3; LF-3   **Ht:** 6'1" **Wt:** 182 **Born:** 2/15/1985 **Age:** 26

Year	Team	Lg	G	AB	H	2B	3B	HR	(Hm	Rd)	TB	R	RBI	RC	TBB	IBB	SO	HBP	SH	SF	SB	CS	SB%	GDP	Avg	OBP	Slg
2003	Ddgrs	R	26	77	26	8	1	1	(-	-)	39	13	9	17	12	0	5	3	1	1	2	1	.67	1	.338	.441	.506
2004	VeroB	A+	46	169	42	8	1	0	(-	-)	52	12	17	14	4	0	32	3	5	0	1	1	.50	7	.249	.278	.308
2004	Clmbs	AAA	63	209	42	12	1	0	(-	-)	56	24	14	13	10	0	49	6	5	1	2	4	.33	6	.201	.257	.268
2005	VeroB	A+	13	33	10	1	0	1	(-	-)	14	5	4	4	2	0	6	0	1	1	0	0	-	2	.303	.333	.424
2005	Jaxnvl	AA	3	5	1	1	0	0	(-	-)	2	1	3	0	0	0	4	0	0	0	0	0	-	0	.200	.200	.400
2005	Ogden	R+	69	270	78	19	1	13	(-	-)	138	54	54	56	26	1	52	4	1	2	3	3	.50	14	.289	.358	.511
2006	Clmbs	A	105	435	104	32	2	15	(-	-)	185	71	75	56	29	2	83	3	1	5	3	0	1.00	13	.239	.288	.425

Year	Team	Lg	G	AB	H	2B	3B	HR	(Hm	Rd)	TB	R	RBI	RC	TBB	IBB	SO	HBP	SH	SF	SB	CS	SB%	GDP	Avg	OBP	Slg
2006	VeroB	A+	22	83	23	8	0	4	(-	-)	43	12	16	13	4	0	14	1	2	1	1	1	.50	1	.277	.315	.518
2007	InldEm	A+	126	488	132	32	4	22	(-	-)	238	81	82	78	31	0	126	10	3	5	5	5	.50	9	.270	.324	.488
2008	Jaxnvl	AA	133	485	128	22	4	16	(-	-)	206	65	75	70	43	4	95	3	3	8	8	4	.67	16	.264	.323	.425
2009	Chatt	AA	131	456	110	30	3	13	(-	-)	185	63	63	58	36	2	84	2	4	3	4	1	.80	11	.241	.298	.406
2010	Albq	AAA	127	505	159	38	2	23	(-	-)	270	97	87	97	38	2	78	4	4	6	1	3	.25	7	.315	.363	.535
2010	LAD	NL	15	42	6	0	0	2	(1	1)	12	3	4	0	0	0	8	0	0	1	0	0	-	1	.143	.140	.286

Sergio Mitre

Pitches: R Bats: R Pos: RP-24; SP-3 　　MEE-tray 　　Ht: 6'3" Wt: 225 Born: 2/16/1981 Age: 30

Year	Team	Lg	G	GS	CG	GF	IP	BFP	H	R	ER	HR	SH	SF	HB	TBB	IBB	SO	WP	Bk	W	L	Pct	Sh	Sv-Op	Hld	ERC	ERA
2010	Tampa*	A+	1	0	0	0	1.0	3	0	0	0	0	0	0	0	0	0	1	0	0	0	0	-	0	0- -	-	0.00	0.00
2010	Yanks*	R	2	2	0	0	5.0	17	2	1	1	0	0	0	0	0	0	8	0	0	0	1	.000	0	0- -	-	0.35	1.80
2010	S-WB*	AAA	2	2	0	0	7.2	34	9	6	6	1	0	1	1	2	0	7	1	0	0	1	.000	0	0- -	-	5.31	7.04
2003	ChC	NL	3	2	0	1	8.2	43	15	8	8	1	0	1	0	4	1	3	0	0	0	1	.000	0	0-0	0	9.02	8.31
2004	ChC	NL	12	9	0	2	51.2	244	71	38	38	6	3	0	4	20	1	37	5	1	2	4	.333	0	0-0	0	6.69	6.62
2005	ChC	NL	21	7	1	7	60.1	268	62	37	36	11	1	3	3	23	2	37	5	0	2	5	.286	1	0-0	0	4.81	5.37
2006	Fla	NL	15	7	0	3	41.0	189	44	28	26	7	2	1	6	20	3	31	1	0	1	5	.167	0	0-1	2	5.87	5.71
2007	Fla	NL	27	27	0	0	149.0	662	180	88	77	9	6	10	10	41	3	80	6	0	5	8	.385	0	0-0	0	4.71	4.65
2009	NYY	AL	12	9	0	2	51.2	241	71	45	39	10	0	4	3	13	0	32	3	0	3	3	.500	0	0-0	0	6.53	6.79
2010	NYY	AL	27	3	0	13	54.0	213	43	23	20	7	1	1	2	16	0	29	1	0	0	3	.000	0	1-1	1	3.03	3.33
	7 ML YEARS		117	64	1	28	416.1	1860	486	267	244	51	13	20	28	137	10	249	21	1	13	29	.310	1	1-2	3	5.15	5.27

Garrett Mock

Pitches: R Bats: R Pos: SP-1 　　　　Ht: 6'4" Wt: 228 Born: 4/25/1983 Age: 28

Year	Team	Lg	G	GS	CG	GF	IP	BFP	H	R	ER	HR	SH	SF	HB	TBB	IBB	SO	WP	Bk	W	L	Pct	Sh	Sv-Op	Hld	ERC	ERA
2010	Hgrstn*	A	1	1	0	0	3.0	11	1	0	0	0	0	0	0	1	0	3	0	0	0	0	-	0	0- -	-	0.69	0.00
2010	Ptomc*	A+	2	2	0	0	8.0	36	12	4	4	1	0	0	3	0	0	9	1	0	0	1	.000	0	0- -	-	7.66	4.50
2010	Hrsbrg*	AA	1	1	0	0	5.0	21	6	4	4	1	1	0	1	2	0	0	0	0	0	1	.000	0	0- -	-	7.79	7.20
2010	Syrcse*	AAA	2	2	0	0	11.0	46	11	5	5	0	0	0	0	3	0	6	2	0	1	1	.500	0	0- -	-	2.92	4.09
2008	Was	NL	26	3	0	5	41.0	180	37	20	19	4	1	1	0	23	3	46	3	1	1	3	.250	0	0-0	0	4.00	4.17
2009	Was	NL	28	15	0	1	91.1	422	114	65	57	9	4	3	1	44	3	72	10	0	3	10	.231	0	0-2	4	5.86	5.62
2010	Was	NL	1	1	0	0	3.1	19	4	2	2	2	0	0	0	5	0	3	0	0	0	0	-	0	0-0	0	14.98	5.40
	3 ML YEARS		55	19	0	6	135.2	621	155	87	78	15	5	4	1	72	6	121	13	1	4	13	.235	0	0-2	4	5.46	5.17

Brian Moehler

Pitches: R Bats: R Pos: RP-12; SP-8 　　MOE-lerr 　　Ht: 6'3" Wt: 222 Born: 12/31/1971 Age: 39

Year	Team	Lg	G	GS	CG	GF	IP	BFP	H	R	ER	HR	SH	SF	HB	TBB	IBB	SO	WP	Bk	W	L	Pct	Sh	Sv-Op	Hld	ERC	ERA
2010	RdRck*	AAA	1	1	0	0	3.0	11	1	0	0	0	0	0	0	0	0	1	0	0	0	0	-	0	0- -	-	0.23	0.00
1996	Det	AL	2	2	0	0	10.1	51	11	10	5	1	1	0	0	8	1	2	1	0	0	1	.000	0	0-0	0	5.49	4.35
1997	Det	AL	31	31	2	0	175.1	770	198	97	91	22	1	8	5	61	1	97	3	0	11	12	.478	1	0-0	0	4.92	4.67
1998	Det	AL	33	33	4	0	221.1	912	220	103	96	30	3	3	2	56	1	123	4	0	14	13	.519	3	0-0	0	3.79	3.90
1999	Det	AL	32	32	2	0	196.1	859	229	116	110	22	8	5	7	59	5	106	4	0	10	16	.385	2	0-0	0	4.85	5.04
2000	Det	AL	29	29	2	0	178.0	776	222	99	89	20	3	4	2	40	0	103	2	1	12	9	.571	0	0-0	0	4.95	4.50
2001	Det	AL	1	1	0	0	8.0	30	6	3	3	0	0	1	0	1	0	2	0	0	0	0	-	0	0-0	0	1.43	3.38
2002	2 Tms		13	12	0	0	63.0	278	78	39	34	11	4	2	1	13	0	31	0	0	3	5	.375	0	0-0	0	5.20	4.86
2003	Hou	NL	3	3	0	0	13.2	66	22	12	12	4	1	1	0	6	0	5	0	0	0	0	-	0	0-0	0	9.97	7.90
2005	Fla	NL	37	25	0	4	158.1	696	198	82	80	16	13	4	1	42	9	95	1	0	6	12	.333	0	0-0	1	5.07	4.55
2006	Fla	NL	29	21	0	2	122.0	556	164	95	89	19	7	2	5	38	3	58	2	1	7	11	.389	0	0-1	0	6.36	6.57
2007	Hou	NL	42	0	0	29	59.2	257	67	29	27	8	1	1	0	17	3	36	1	0	1	4	.200	0	1-1	1	4.48	4.07
2008	Hou	NL	31	26	0	0	150.0	650	166	79	76	20	7	8	4	36	1	82	3	0	11	8	.579	0	0-0	0	4.31	4.56
2009	Hou	NL	29	29	1	0	154.2	694	187	101	94	21	9	3	4	51	12	91	4	0	8	12	.400	0	0-0	0	5.21	5.47
2010	Hou	NL	20	8	0	5	56.2	249	66	32	31	5	0	1	1	26	1	28	0	1	1	4	.200	0	0-0	0	5.40	4.92
02	Det	AL	3	3	0	0	19.2	77	17	5	5	3	1	1	0	2	0	13	0	0	1	1	.500	0	0-0	0	2.54	2.29
02	Cin	NL	10	9	0	0	43.1	201	61	34	29	8	3	1	1	11	0	18	0	0	2	4	.333	0	0-0	0	6.56	6.02
	14 ML YEARS		332	252	11	40	1567.1	6844	1834	897	837	199	58	42	36	454	37	859	25	3	84	107	.440	6	1-2	2	4.88	4.81

Chad Moeller

Bats: R Throws: R Pos: C-9 　　MOE-lerr 　　Ht: 6'3" Wt: 210 Born: 2/18/1975 Age: 36

Year	Team	Lg	G	AB	H	2B	3B	HR	(Hm	Rd)	TB	R	RBI	RC	TBB	IBB	SO	HBP	SH	SF	SB	CS	SB%	GDP	Avg	OBP	Slg
2010	S-WB*	AAA	28	87	20	6	0	1	(-	-)	29	8	9	9	6	0	15	3	0	0	0	0	-	3	.230	.302	.333
2000	Min	AL	48	128	27	3	1	1	(1	0)	35	13	9	8	9	0	33	0	1	1	1	0	1.00	3	.211	.261	.273
2001	Ari	NL	25	56	13	0	1	1	(1	0)	18	8	2	5	6	1	12	1	0	1	0	0	-	2	.232	.306	.321
2002	Ari	NL	37	105	30	11	1	2	(2	0)	49	10	16	17	17	3	23	0	1	0	0	1	.00	6	.286	.385	.467
2003	Ari	NL	78	239	64	17	1	7	(2	5)	104	29	29	28	23	11	59	2	3	2	1	2	.33	7	.268	.335	.435
2004	Mil	NL	101	317	66	13	1	5	(3	2)	96	25	27	14	21	1	74	4	6	1	0	1	.00	12	.208	.265	.303
2005	Mil	NL	66	199	41	9	1	7	(5	2)	73	23	23	14	13	1	48	1	2	1	0	0	-	9	.206	.257	.367
2006	Mil	NL	29	98	18	3	0	2	(2	0)	27	9	5	3	4	0	26	2	0	0	0	0	-	3	.184	.231	.276
2007	2 Tms	NL	37	56	9	1	0	1	(1	0)	13	8	2	0	0	0	18	1	1	0	0	0	-	3	.161	.175	.232
2008	NYY	NL	41	91	21	6	0	1	(0	1)	30	9	9	7	7	1	18	4	0	1	0	0	-	2	.231	.311	.330
2009	Bal	AL	30	89	23	8	1	2	(1	1)	39	6	10	8	7	0	16	1	1	2	0	0	-	3	.258	.313	.438
2010	NYY	AL	9	14	3	3	0	0	(0	0)	6	2	0	1	1	0	4	0	0	0	0	0	-	0	.214	.267	.429

Year Team	Lg	G	AB	H	2B	3B	HR	(Hm	Rd)	TB	R	RBI	RC	TBB	IBB	SO	HBP	SH	SF	SB	CS	SB%	GDP	Avg	OBP	Slg
07 Cin	NL	30	48	8	1	0	1	(1	0)	12	6	2	0	0	0	17	0	1	0	0	0	-	2	.167	.167	.250
07 LAD	NL	7	8	1	0	0	0	(0	0)	1	2	0	0	0	0	1	1	0	0	0	0	-	1	.125	.222	.125
Postseason		3	5	2	0	0	0	(0	0)	2	0	0	1	0	0	1	0	0	0	0	0	-		.400	.400	.400
11 ML YEARS		501	1392	315	74	7	29	(18	11)	490	146	132	107	108	18	331	15	16	8	2	4	.33	50	.226	.288	.352

Bengie Molina

Bats: R Throws: R Pos: C-113; PH-6; DH-2   Ht: 5'10" Wt: 233 Born: 7/20/1974 Age: 36

Year Team	Lg	G	AB	H	2B	3B	HR	(Hm	Rd)	TB	R	RBI	RC	TBB	IBB	SO	HBP	SH	SF	SB	CS	SB%	GDP	Avg	OBP	Slg
1998 LAA	AL	2	1	0	0	0	0	(0	0)	0	0	0	0	0	0	0	0	0	0	0	0	-	0	.000	.000	.000
1999 LAA	AL	31	101	26	5	0	1	(0	1)	34	8	10	9	6	0	6	2	0	0	0	1	.00	5	.257	.312	.337
2000 LAA	AL	130	473	133	20	2	14	(11	3)	199	59	71	60	23	0	33	6	4	7	1	0	1.00	17	.281	.318	.421
2001 LAA	AL	96	325	85	11	0	6	(6	0)	114	31	40	34	16	3	51	8	2	4	0	1	.00	8	.262	.309	.351
2002 LAA	AL	122	428	105	18	0	5	(2	3)	138	34	47	33	15	3	34	4	6	6	0	0	-	15	.245	.274	.322
2003 LAA	AL	119	409	115	24	0	14	(7	7)	181	37	71	57	13	2	31	2	2	4	1	1	.50	17	.281	.304	.443
2004 LAA	AL	97	337	93	13	0	10	(5	5)	136	36	54	44	18	1	35	2	2	4	0	1	.00	18	.276	.313	.404
2005 LAA	AL	119	410	121	17	0	15	(8	7)	183	45	69	53	27	2	41	1	5	6	0	2	.00	14	.295	.336	.446
2006 Tor	AL	117	433	123	20	1	19	(12	7)	202	44	57	58	19	1	47	4	0	2	1	1	.50	15	.284	.319	.467
2007 SF	NL	134	497	137	19	1	19	(9	10)	215	38	81	64	15	2	53	2	1	2	0	0	-	13	.276	.298	.433
2008 SF	NL	145	530	155	33	0	16	(9	7)	236	46	95	70	19	5	38	9	0	11	0	0	-	23	.292	.322	.445
2009 SF	NL	132	491	130	25	1	20	(12	8)	217	52	80	56	13	3	68	5	0	11	0	0	-	14	.265	.285	.442
2010 2 Tms		118	377	94	12	1	5	(3	2)	123	27	36	34	24	4	34	4	5	6	0	0	-	14	.249	.297	.326
10 SF	NL	61	202	52	6	0	3	(3	0)	67	17	17	20	14	4	19	3	0	2	0	0	-	7	.257	.312	.332
10 Tex	AL	57	175	42	6	1	2	(0	2)	56	10	19	14	10	0	15	1	5	4	0	0	-	7	.240	.279	.320
Postseason		29	91	24	4	1	3	(2	1)	39	7	12	14	4	2	8	3	2	0	0	0	-	3	.264	.316	.429
13 ML YEARS		1362	4812	1317	217	6	144	(84	60)	1978	457	711	572	208	26	471	49	27	63	3	7	.30	173	.274	.307	.411

Gustavo Molina

Bats: R Throws: R Pos: C-4   Ht: 6'1" Wt: 245 Born: 2/24/1982 Age: 29

Year Team	Lg	G	AB	H	2B	3B	HR	(Hm	Rd)	TB	R	RBI	RC	TBB	IBB	SO	HBP	SH	SF	SB	CS	SB%	GDP	Avg	OBP	Slg
2010 Pwtckt*	AAA	35	112	27	5	0	8	(-	-)	56	12	18	16	7	0	23	0	0	0	0	0	-	1	.241	.286	.500
2007 2 Tms	NL	17	27	3	1	0	0	(0	0)	4	1	1	1	1	0	7	0	1	1	0	0	-	0	.111	.138	.148
2008 NYM	NL	2	7	1	0	0	0	(0	0)	1	0	0	0	1	0	1	0	0	0	0	0	-	0	.143	.250	.143
2010 Bos	AL	4	7	1	0	0	0	(0	0)	1	1	0	0	0	0	2	0	0	0	0	0	-	0	.143	.143	.143
07 CWS	AL	10	18	1	0	0	0	(0	0)	1	0	1	0	1	0	4	0	1	1	0	0	-	0	.056	.100	.056
07 Bal	AL	7	9	2	1	0	0	(0	0)	3	1	0	1	0	0	3	0	0	0	0	0	-	0	.222	.222	.333
3 ML YEARS		23	41	5	1	0	0	(0	0)	6	2	1	1	2	0	10	0	1	1	0	0	-	0	.122	.159	.146

Jose Molina

Bats: R Throws: R Pos: C-56; DH-1   Ht: 6'2" Wt: 235 Born: 6/3/1975 Age: 36

Year Team	Lg	G	AB	H	2B	3B	HR	(Hm	Rd)	TB	R	RBI	RC	TBB	IBB	SO	HBP	SH	SF	SB	CS	SB%	GDP	Avg	OBP	Slg
1999 ChC	NL	10	19	5	1	0	0	(0	0)	6	3	1	2	2	1	4	0	0	0	0	0	-	0	.263	.333	.316
2001 LAA	AL	15	37	10	3	0	2	(0	2)	19	8	4	6	3	0	8	0	2	0	0	0	-	2	.270	.325	.514
2002 LAA	AL	29	70	19	3	0	0	(0	0)	22	5	5	4	5	0	15	0	4	2	0	2	.00	1	.271	.312	.314
2003 LAA	AL	53	114	21	4	0	0	(0	0)	25	12	6	5	1	0	26	3	4	1	0	0	-	1	.184	.210	.219
2004 LAA	AL	73	203	53	10	2	3	(1	2)	76	26	25	19	10	0	52	0	5	0	4	1	.80	6	.261	.296	.374
2005 LAA	AL	75	184	42	4	0	6	(2	4)	64	14	25	19	13	0	41	2	4	0	2	0	1.00	6	.228	.286	.348
2006 LAA	AL	78	225	54	17	0	4	(0	4)	83	18	22	21	9	0	49	2	7	2	1	0	1.00	6	.240	.273	.369
2007 2 Tms	AL	69	191	49	13	0	1	(1	0)	65	18	19	20	5	0	43	0	5	1	2	1	.67	1	.257	.274	.340
2008 NYY	AL	100	268	58	17	0	3	(2	1)	84	32	18	15	12	0	52	6	8	3	0	0	-	9	.216	.263	.313
2009 NYY	AL	52	138	30	4	0	1	(0	1)	37	15	11	12	14	0	28	1	1	1	0	0	-	6	.217	.292	.268
2010 Tor	AL	57	167	41	4	0	6	(4	2)	63	13	12	12	9	1	36	5	2	0	1	0	1.00	7	.246	.304	.377
07 LAA	AL	40	125	28	8	0	0	(0	0)	36	9	10	9	3	0	30	0	3	0	2	1	.67	0	.224	.242	.288
07 NYY	AL	29	66	21	5	0	1	(1	0)	29	9	9	11	2	0	13	0	2	1	0	0	-	1	.318	.333	.439
Postseason		15	14	4	0	0	0	(0	0)	4	3	1	2	3	0	1	0	1	0	0	0	-	0	.286	.412	.286
11 ML YEARS		611	1616	382	80	2	26	(10	16)	544	164	148	135	83	2	354	19	42	10	10	4	.71	48	.236	.280	.337

Yadier Molina

Bats: R Throws: R Pos: C-135; 1B-7   Ht: 5'11" Wt: 230 Born: 7/13/1982 Age: 28

Year Team	Lg	G	AB	H	2B	3B	HR	(Hm	Rd)	TB	R	RBI	RC	TBB	IBB	SO	HBP	SH	SF	SB	CS	SB%	GDP	Avg	OBP	Slg
2004 StL	NL	51	135	36	6	0	2	(1	1)	48	12	15	15	13	3	20	0	2	1	0	1	.00	4	.267	.329	.356
2005 StL	NL	114	385	97	15	1	8	(6	2)	138	36	49	46	23	3	30	2	8	3	2	3	.40	10	.252	.295	.358
2006 StL	NL	129	417	90	26	0	6	(2	4)	134	29	49	35	26	2	41	8	8	2	1	2	.33	15	.216	.274	.321
2007 StL	NL	111	353	97	15	0	6	(4	2)	130	30	40	38	34	5	43	3	2	4	1	1	.50	18	.275	.340	.368
2008 StL	NL	124	444	135	18	0	7	(2	5)	174	37	56	57	32	4	29	1	3	5	0	2	.00	21	.304	.349	.392
2009 StL	NL	140	481	141	23	1	6	(5	1)	184	45	54	64	50	2	39	6	6	1	9	3	.75	27	.293	.366	.383
2010 StL	NL	136	465	122	19	0	6	(1	5)	159	34	62	55	42	6	51	7	2	5	8	4	.67	19	.262	.329	.342
Postseason		32	108	34	8	0	2	(1	1)	48	7	11	12	6	1	10	0	0	0	0	1	.00	4	.315	.351	.444
7 ML YEARS		805	2680	718	122	2	41	(21	20)	967	223	325	310	220	25	253	27	31	21	21	16	.57	114	.268	.327	.361

Carlos Monasterios

Pitches: R Bats: R Pos: RP-19; SP-13   mahn-uh-STAIR-ee-ohse   **Ht:** 6'1" **Wt:** 203 **Born:** 3/21/1986 **Age:** 25

Year	Team	Lg	G	GS	CG	GF	IP	BFP	H	R	ER	HR	SH	SF	HB	TBB	IBB	SO	WP	Bk	W	L	Pct	Sh	Sv-Op	Hld	ERC	ERA
2006	Yanks	R	7	3	0	1	30.1	119	23	12	10	2	1	0	3	3	0	24	1	0	1	2	.333	0	0--	-	1.89	2.97
2006	Phillies	R	4	3	0	1	14.2	65	18	7	6	1	0	1	0	3	0	11	0	1	1	2	.000	0	0--	-	4.24	3.68
2007	Lakwd	A	26	26	1	0	156.0	669	155	93	80	13	3	7	9	55	2	114	11	2	11	11	.500	0	0--	-	3.97	4.62
2008	Clrwtr	A+	17	15	1	0	94.1	415	109	64	59	19	2	4	3	33	1	66	2	0	5	8	.385	0	0--	-	5.70	5.63
2009	Clrwtr	A+	35	7	1	10	82.0	341	71	39	34	4	6	4	5	27	2	71	4	0	5	6	.455	1	2--	-	2.95	3.73
2009	Rdng	AA	2	1	0	1	7.1	28	8	3	3	0	0	0	0	2	0	4	0	0	0	0	-	0	0--	-	3.85	3.68
2010	Albq	AAA	2	2	0	0	6.2	32	7	5	4	1	1	0	2	3	0	5	1	0	0	0	-	0	0--	-	6.05	5.40
2010	LAD	NL	32	13	0	5	88.1	399	99	48	43	15	5	4	8	29	3	52	7	1	3	5	.375	0	0-0	0	5.21	4.38

Lou Montanez

Bats: R Throws: R Pos: LF-17; PH-4; PR-4; RF-2; DH-2; CF-1   MONN-tah-nezz   **Ht:** 6'1" **Wt:** 195 **Born:** 12/15/1981 **Age:** 29

Year	Team	Lg	G	AB	H	2B	3B	HR	(Hm	Rd)	TB	R	RBI	RC	TBB	IBB	SO	HBP	SH	SF	SB	CS	SB%	GDP	Avg	OBP	Slg
2010	Norfolk*	AAA	24	97	28	5	2	2	(-	-)	43	14	20	13	4	0	12	0	0	0	2	1	.67	0	.289	.317	.443
2010	Orioles*	R	4	15	3	0	0	0	(-	-)	3	1	1	0	0	0	2	0	0	0	0	0	-	0	.200	.200	.200
2010	Bowie*	AA	2	9	4	1	0	0	(-	-)	5	2	0	2	0	0	1	0	0	0	0	0	-	0	.444	.444	.556
2008	Bal	AL	38	112	33	6	1	3	(2	1)	50	18	14	17	4	0	20	0	0	1	0	0	-	0	.295	.316	.446
2009	Bal	AL	29	82	15	5	0	1	(1	0)	23	5	6	8	5	0	16	2	1	1	0	1	.00	0	.183	.244	.280
2010	Bal	AL	26	57	8	0	0	0	(0	0)	8	2	3	0	1	0	9	0	0	0	1	0	1.00	3	.140	.155	.140
	3 ML YEARS		93	251	56	11	1	4	(3	1)	81	25	23	25	10	0	45	2	1	2	1	1	.50	3	.223	.257	.323

Miguel Montero

Bats: L Throws: R Pos: C-79; PH-7; DH-2   **Ht:** 5'11" **Wt:** 190 **Born:** 7/9/1983 **Age:** 27

Year	Team	Lg	G	AB	H	2B	3B	HR	(Hm	Rd)	TB	R	RBI	RC	TBB	IBB	SO	HBP	SH	SF	SB	CS	SB%	GDP	Avg	OBP	Slg
2010	Reno*	AAA	4	15	5	0	0	0	(-	-)	5	1	2	2	1	0	1	0	0	0	0	0	-	2	.333	.412	.333
2006	Ari	NL	6	16	4	1	0	0	(0	0)	5	0	3	2	1	0	3	0	0	0	0	0	-	0	.250	.294	.313
2007	Ari	NL	84	214	48	7	0	10	(7	3)	85	30	37	19	20	2	35	3	1	6	0	0	-	7	.224	.292	.397
2008	Ari	NL	70	184	47	16	1	5	(1	4)	80	24	18	21	19	3	44	2	1	1	0	0	-	1	.255	.330	.435
2009	Ari	NL	128	425	125	30	0	16	(5	11)	203	61	59	65	38	5	78	3	2	2	1	2	.33	6	.294	.355	.478
2010	Ari	NL	85	297	79	20	2	9	(0	9)	130	36	43	38	29	3	71	2	0	3	0	1	.00	10	.266	.332	.438
	Postseason		4	7	2	0	0	0	(0	0)	2	1	0	0	1	0	0	0	0	0	0	0	-	0	.286	.375	.286
	5 ML YEARS		373	1136	303	74	3	40	(13	27)	503	151	160	145	107	13	236	10	4	12	1	3	.25	24	.267	.332	.443

Adam Moore

Bats: R Throws: R Pos: C-59; PR-1   **Ht:** 6'3" **Wt:** 220 **Born:** 5/8/1984 **Age:** 27

Year	Team	Lg	G	AB	H	2B	3B	HR	(Hm	Rd)	TB	R	RBI	RC	TBB	IBB	SO	HBP	SH	SF	SB	CS	SB%	GDP	Avg	OBP	Slg
2006	Everett	A-	16	63	20	9	0	0	(-	-)	29	8	9	10	2	0	10	1	0	0	0	0	-	3	.317	.348	.460
2006	Wisc	A	44	165	44	6	0	7	(-	-)	71	21	24	25	14	1	38	6	0	2	0	0	-	7	.267	.342	.430
2007	Hi Dsrt	A+	115	433	133	30	3	22	(-	-)	235	74	102	88	41	1	84	8	0	9	1	0	1.00	18	.307	.371	.543
2008	WTenn	AA	119	428	137	35	2	14	(-	-)	218	60	71	87	41	0	77	16	3	2	0	1	.00	16	.320	.398	.509
2009	WTenn	AA	27	95	25	5	0	3	(-	-)	39	14	13	16	16	2	21	2	0	3	0	0	-	2	.263	.371	.411
2009	Tacom	AAA	91	340	100	19	0	9	(-	-)	146	41	43	51	26	0	51	1	1	0	1	1	.50	6	.294	.346	.429
2010	Tacom	AAA	36	134	43	8	1	3	(-	-)	62	18	15	22	7	1	24	1	0	0	1	0	1.00	5	.321	.359	.463
2009	Sea	AL	6	23	5	1	0	1	(1	0)	9	4	2	2	0	0	7	1	0	0	1	0	1.00	1	.217	.250	.391
2010	Sea	AL	60	205	40	6	0	4	(1	3)	58	12	15	9	8	1	63	2	1	2	0	1	.00	3	.195	.230	.283
	2 ML YEARS		66	228	45	7	0	5	(2	3)	67	16	17	11	8	1	70	3	1	2	1	1	.50	4	.197	.232	.294

Scott Moore

Bats: L Throws: R Pos: 2B-22; PH-12; 1B-10; PR-6; 3B-4; DH-1   **Ht:** 6'2" **Wt:** 195 **Born:** 11/17/1983 **Age:** 27

Year	Team	Lg	G	AB	H	2B	3B	HR	(Hm	Rd)	TB	R	RBI	RC	TBB	IBB	SO	HBP	SH	SF	SB	CS	SB%	GDP	Avg	OBP	Slg
2010	Norfolk*	AAA	61	225	63	9	1	11	(-	-)	107	34	45	37	21	1	47	3	1	3	2	3	.40	6	.280	.345	.476
2006	ChC	NL	16	38	10	2	0	2	(1	1)	18	6	5	5	2	0	10	1	1	0	0	0	-	1	.263	.317	.474
2007	2 Tms		19	52	12	2	0	1	(1	0)	17	2	11	6	1	0	17	0	0	2	0	1	.00	1	.231	.236	.327
2008	Bal	AL	4	8	1	0	0	1	(0	1)	4	1	1	1	1	0	3	0	0	0	0	0	-	0	.125	.222	.500
2010	Bal	AL	41	86	18	2	0	3	(2	1)	29	8	10	8	8	1	19	0	1	1	3	0	1.00	1	.209	.274	.337
	07 ChC	NL	2	5	0	0	0	0	(0	0)	0	0	0	0	0	0	2	0	0	0	0	0	-	0	.000	.000	.000
	07 Bal	AL	17	47	12	2	0	1	(1	0)	17	2	11	6	1	0	15	0	0	2	0	1	.00	1	.255	.260	.362
	4 ML YEARS		80	184	41	6	0	7	(4	3)	68	17	27	20	12	1	49	1	2	3	3	1	.75	2	.223	.270	.370

Melvin Mora

Bats: R Throws: R Pos: 3B-63; 1B-25; PH-20; 2B-19; LF-4; PR-1   **Ht:** 5'11" **Wt:** 200 **Born:** 2/7/1972 **Age:** 39

Year	Team	Lg	G	AB	H	2B	3B	HR	(Hm	Rd)	TB	R	RBI	RC	TBB	IBB	SO	HBP	SH	SF	SB	CS	SB%	GDP	Avg	OBP	Slg
1999	NYM	NL	66	31	5	0	0	0	(0	0)	5	6	1	2	4	0	7	1	3	0	2	1	.67	0	.161	.278	.161
2000	2 Tms		132	414	114	22	5	8	(5	3)	170	60	47	56	35	3	80	6	4	5	12	11	.52	5	.275	.337	.411
2001	Bal	AL	128	436	109	28	0	7	(6	1)	158	49	48	55	41	2	91	14	5	7	11	4	.73	6	.250	.329	.362
2002	Bal	AL	149	557	130	30	4	19	(8	11)	225	86	64	78	70	2	108	20	1	4	16	10	.62	7	.233	.338	.404
2003	Bal	AL	96	344	109	17	1	15	(8	7)	173	68	48	67	49	0	71	12	6	2	6	3	.67	3	.317	.418	.503
2004	Bal	AL	140	550	187	41	0	27	(15	12)	309	111	104	115	66	0	95	11	6	3	11	6	.65	10	.340	**.419**	.562

Year Team	Lg	G	AB	H	2B	3B	HR	(Hm	Rd)	TB	R	RBI	RC	TBB	IBB	SO	HBP	SH	SF	SB	CS	SB%	GDP	Avg	OBP	Slg
2005 Bal	AL	149	593	168	30	1	27	(13	14)	281	86	88	88	50	0	112	10	8	3	7	4	.64	9	.283	.348	.474
2006 Bal	AL	155	624	171	25	0	16	(8	8)	244	96	83	93	54	1	99	14	6	7	11	1	.92	9	.274	.342	.391
2007 Bal	AL	126	467	128	23	1	14	(7	7)	195	67	58	61	47	3	83	3	5	5	9	3	.75	22	.274	.341	.418
2008 Bal	AL	135	513	146	29	2	23	(15	8)	248	77	104	88	37	3	70	11	3	6	3	7	.30	14	.285	.342	.483
2009 Bal	AL	125	450	117	20	0	8	(8	0)	161	44	48	48	34	1	60	8	1	3	3	3	.50	13	.260	.321	.358
2010 Col	NL	113	316	90	12	5	7	(2	5)	133	39	45	49	31	2	53	5	2	0	2	1	.67	9	.285	.358	.421
00 NYM	NL	79	215	56	13	2	6	(4	2)	91	35	30	29	18	3	48	2	2	5	7	3	.70	3	.260	.317	.423
00 Bal	AL	53	199	58	9	3	2	(1	1)	79	25	17	27	17	0	32	4	2	0	5	8	.38	2	.291	.359	.397
Postseason		9	15	6	0	0	1	(0	1)	9	4	2	4	3	0	2	0	1	0	2	0	1.00	0	.400	.500	.600
12 ML YEARS		1514	5295	1474	277	19	171	(95	76)	2302	789	738	800	518	17	929	115	50	45	93	54	.63	107	.278	.353	.435

Franklin Morales

Pitches: L **Bats:** L **Pos:** RP-35
Ht: 6'0" **Wt:** 210 **Born:** 1/24/1986 **Age:** 25

Year Team	Lg	G	GS	CG	GF	IP	BFP	H	R	ER	HR	SH	SF	HB	TBB	IBB	SO	WP	Bk	W	L	Pct	Sh	Sv-Op	Hld	ERC	ERA
2010 ColSpr*	AAA	24	0	0	8	30.1	129	20	9	9	3	3	1	2	19	1	34	3	0	3	0	1.000	0	1- -	-	3.29	2.67
2007 Col	NL	8	8	0	0	39.1	163	34	15	15	2	4	2	1	14	1	26	0	0	3	2	.600	0	0-0	0	3.04	3.43
2008 Col	NL	5	5	0	0	25.1	120	28	18	18	2	2	2	1	17	2	9	1	3	1	2	.333	0	0-0	0	5.58	6.39
2009 Col	NL	40	2	0	14	40.0	179	38	22	20	4	3	0	1	23	4	41	2	0	3	2	.600	0	7-8	7	4.38	4.50
2010 Col	NL	35	0	0	15	28.2	140	28	22	20	5	1	2	3	24	2	27	3	2	0	4	.000	0	3-6	1	6.53	6.28
Postseason		8	2	0	0	12.2	59	15	11	11	1	0	0	2	7	1	7	0	1	0	0	-	0	0-0	1	6.28	7.82
4 ML YEARS		88	15	0	29	133.1	602	128	77	73	13	10	6	7	78	9	103	6	5	7	10	.412	0	10-14	8	4.63	4.93

Jose Morales

Bats: B **Throws:** R **Pos:** C-11; PH-6; DH-5; 1B-2; PR-1
Ht: 5'11" **Wt:** 202 **Born:** 2/20/1983 **Age:** 28

Year Team	Lg	G	AB	H	2B	3B	HR	(Hm	Rd)	TB	R	RBI	RC	TBB	IBB	SO	HBP	SH	SF	SB	CS	SB%	GDP	Avg	OBP	Slg
2010 Roch*	AAA	73	258	68	19	1	3	(-	-)	98	30	25	37	34	1	63	1	1	1	0	0	-	9	.264	.350	.380
2007 Min	AL	1	3	3	1	0	0	(0	0)	4	1	0	2	0	0	0	0	0	0	0	0	-	0	1.000	1.000	1.333
2009 Min	AL	54	119	37	6	0	0	(0	0)	43	14	7	19	14	1	22	0	0	1	0	0	-	4	.311	.381	.361
2010 Min	AL	19	36	7	2	0	0	(0	0)	9	4	7	4	6	0	14	0	0	2	0	0	-	2	.194	.295	.250
Postseason		1	3	0	0	0	0	(0	0)	0	0	0	0	0	0	2	0	0	0	0	0	-	0	.000	.000	.000
3 ML YEARS		74	158	47	9	0	0	(0	0)	56	19	14	25	20	1	36	0	0	3	0	0	-	6	.297	.370	.354

Kendry Morales

Bats: B **Throws:** R **Pos:** 1B-51
Ht: 6'1" **Wt:** 225 **Born:** 6/20/1983 **Age:** 28

Year Team	Lg	G	AB	H	2B	3B	HR	(Hm	Rd)	TB	R	RBI	RC	TBB	IBB	SO	HBP	SH	SF	SB	CS	SB%	GDP	Avg	OBP	Slg
2006 LAA	AL	57	197	46	10	1	5	(1	4)	73	21	22	19	17	1	28	0	0	1	1	1	.50	11	.234	.293	.371
2007 LAA	AL	43	119	35	10	4	0	(2	2)	57	12	15	15	6	2	21	1	0	0	0	1	.00	5	.294	.333	.479
2008 LAA	AL	27	61	13	2	0	3	(0	3)	24	7	8	3	4	0	7	1	0	0	0	1	.00	3	.213	.273	.393
2009 LAA	AL	152	566	173	43	2	34	(21	13)	322	86	108	105	40	10	117	2	0	8	3	7	.30	15	.306	.355	.569
2010 LAA	AL	51	193	56	5	0	11	(7	4)	94	29	39	34	12	3	31	5	0	1	0	1	.00	5	.290	.346	.487
Postseason		16	47	9	1	0	2	(1	1)	16	3	7	3	2	0	8	1	0	1	0	0	-	1	.191	.235	.340
5 ML YEARS		330	1136	323	70	3	57	(31	26)	570	155	192	176	85	16	204	9	0	10	4	11	.27	39	.284	.336	.502

Brent Morel

Bats: R **Throws:** R **Pos:** 3B-20; PH-2
moe-RELL
Ht: 6'2" **Wt:** 220 **Born:** 4/21/1987 **Age:** 24

Year Team	Lg	G	AB	H	2B	3B	HR	(Hm	Rd)	TB	R	RBI	RC	TBB	IBB	SO	HBP	SH	SF	SB	CS	SB%	GDP	Avg	OBP	Slg
2008 Gr Falls	R+	15	64	24	6	2	0	(-	-)	28	11	3	13	6	0	7	1	0	0	7	0	1.00	0	.375	.437	.438
2008 Knapol	A	46	173	51	6	2	6	(-	-)	79	26	24	29	16	0	28	2	0	2	5	2	.71	2	.295	.358	.457
2009 WinSa	A+	128	481	135	33	1	16	(-	-)	218	82	79	76	38	2	66	3	1	3	25	9	.74	14	.281	.335	.453
2010 Brham	AA	49	184	60	13	1	2	(-	-)	81	25	30	30	14	0	38	2	1	2	5	5	.50	2	.326	.376	.440
2010 Charltt	AAA	81	306	98	24	4	8	(-	-)	154	40	34	53	13	0	50	0	5	0	3	0	1.00	6	.320	.348	.503
2010 CWS	AL	21	65	15	3	0	3	(3	0)	27	9	7	4	4	0	17	0	0	1	2	0	1.00	2	.231	.271	.415

Mitch Moreland

Bats: L **Throws:** L **Pos:** 1B-40; RF-7; PH-4; PR-1
Ht: 6'2" **Wt:** 230 **Born:** 9/6/1985 **Age:** 25

Year Team	Lg	G	AB	H	2B	3B	HR	(Hm	Rd)	TB	R	RBI	RC	TBB	IBB	SO	HBP	SH	SF	SB	CS	SB%	GDP	Avg	OBP	Slg
2007 Spkane	A-	27	108	28	7	1	2	(-	-)	43	10	15	13	8	0	25	0	1	1	1	0	1.00	2	.259	.308	.398
2008 Clinton	A	123	466	151	37	4	18	(-	-)	250	64	99	99	60	3	67	2	0	5	2	4	.33	15	.324	.400	.536
2009 Bkrsfld	A+	43	170	58	19	0	8	(-	-)	101	34	26	41	21	1	26	4	0	2	1	0	1.00	4	.341	.421	.594
2009 Frisco	AA	73	301	98	19	3	8	(-	-)	147	51	59	54	23	1	42	1	0	2	1	1	.50	17	.326	.373	.488
2010 OKCity	AAA	95	353	102	29	2	12	(-	-)	171	52	65	66	47	2	63	3	2	7	2	1	.67	15	.289	.371	.484
2010 Tex	AL	47	145	37	4	0	9	(3	6)	68	20	25	27	25	5	36	1	0	2	3	1	.75	3	.255	.364	.469

Nyjer Morgan

Bats: L **Throws:** L **Pos:** CF-134; PH-6   NYE-jerr   **Ht:** 6'0" **Wt:** 175 **Born:** 7/2/1980 **Age:** 30

Year	Team	Lg	G	AB	H	2B	3B	HR	(Hm	Rd)	TB	R	RBI	RC	TBB	IBB	SO	HBP	SH	SF	SB	CS	SB%	GDP	Avg	OBP	Slg
2010	Ptomc*	A+	1	3	0	0	0	0	(-	-)	0	0	0	0	0	0	0	0	0	0	0	0	-	0	.000	.000	.000
2010	Hgrstn*	A	1	3	0	0	0	0	(-	-)	0	0	0	0	1	0	1	0	0	0	0	0	-	0	.000	.250	.000
2007	Pit	NL	28	107	32	3	4	1	(1	0)	46	15	7	18	9	0	19	1	1	0	7	3	.70	0	.299	.359	.430
2008	Pit	NL	58	160	47	13	0	0	(0	0)	60	26	7	18	10	0	32	3	1	1	9	5	.64	0	.294	.345	.375
2009	2 Tms	NL	120	469	144	15	7	3	(1	2)	182	74	39	69	40	2	74	9	10	5	42	17	.71	9	.307	.369	.388
2010	Was	NL	136	509	129	17	7	0	(0	0)	160	60	24	53	40	1	88	10	15	3	34	17	.67	2	.253	.319	.314
09	Pit	NL	71	278	77	6	5	2	(1	1)	99	39	27	37	29	2	49	5	5	4	18	10	.64	6	.277	.351	.356
09	Was	NL	49	191	67	9	2	1	(0	1)	83	35	12	32	11	0	25	4	5	1	24	7	.77	3	.351	.396	.435
	4 ML YEARS		342	1245	352	48	18	4	(2	2)	448	175	77	158	99	3	213	23	27	9	92	42	.69	11	.283	.344	.360

Justin Morneau

Bats: L **Throws:** R **Pos:** 1B-77; DH-2; PH-2   MORE-no   **Ht:** 6'4" **Wt:** 233 **Born:** 5/15/1981 **Age:** 30

Year	Team	Lg	G	AB	H	2B	3B	HR	(Hm	Rd)	TB	R	RBI	RC	TBB	IBB	SO	HBP	SH	SF	SB	CS	SB%	GDP	Avg	OBP	Slg
2003	Min	AL	40	106	24	4	0	4	(1	3)	40	14	16	11	9	1	30	0	0	0	0	0	-	4	.226	.287	.377
2004	Min	AL	74	280	76	17	0	19	(9	10)	150	39	58	48	28	8	54	2	0	2	0	0	-	4	.271	.340	.536
2005	Min	AL	141	490	117	23	4	22	(9	13)	214	62	79	58	44	8	94	4	0	5	0	2	.00	12	.239	.304	.437
2006	Min	AL	157	592	190	37	1	34	(17	17)	331	97	130	118	53	9	93	5	0	11	3	3	.50	10	.321	.375	.559
2007	Min	AL	157	590	160	31	3	31	(15	16)	290	84	111	95	64	11	91	5	0	9	1	1	.50	7	.271	.343	.492
2008	Min	AL	163	623	187	47	4	23	(12	11)	311	97	129	122	76	16	85	3	0	10	0	1	.00	20	.300	.374	.499
2009	Min	AL	135	508	139	31	1	30	(14	16)	262	85	100	91	72	12	86	3	0	7	0	0	-	12	.274	.363	.516
2010	Min	AL	81	296	102	25	1	18	(4	14)	183	53	56	65	50	7	62	0	0	2	0	0	-	6	.345	.437	.618
	Postseason		7	29	9	3	0	2	(1	1)	18	4	4	3	0	0	3	0	0	0	0	0	-	0	.310	.310	.621
	8 ML YEARS		948	3485	995	215	14	181	(81	100)	1781	531	679	608	396	72	595	22	0	46	4	7	.36	85	.286	.358	.511

Logan Morrison

Bats: L **Throws:** L **Pos:** LF-62   **Ht:** 6'3" **Wt:** 237 **Born:** 8/25/1987 **Age:** 23

Year	Team	Lg	G	AB	H	2B	3B	HR	(Hm	Rd)	TB	R	RBI	RC	TBB	IBB	SO	HBP	SH	SF	SB	CS	SB%	GDP	Avg	OBP	Slg
2006	Mrlns	R	26	89	24	4	0	1	(-	-)	31	10	7	11	10	0	12	0	0	0	1	0	1.00	3	.270	.343	.348
2006	Jmstwn	A-	23	74	15	3	0	1	(-	-)	21	6	11	7	11	0	17	0	0	3	0	0	-	1	.203	.295	.284
2007	Grnsbr	A	128	453	121	22	2	24	(-	-)	219	71	86	77	48	5	96	7	0	5	2	2	.50	8	.267	.343	.483
2008	Jupiter	A+	130	488	162	38	1	13	(-	-)	241	71	74	99	57	6	80	4	0	6	9	3	.75	11	.332	.402	.494
2009	Jaxnvl	AA	79	278	77	18	2	8	(-	-)	123	48	47	55	63	5	46	1	0	1	9	4	.69	3	.277	.411	.442
2009	Jupiter	A+	3	11	3	1	0	0	(-	-)	4	0	2	1	1	0	2	0	0	0	0	1	.00	2	.273	.333	.364
2010	NewOr	AAA	68	238	73	17	4	6	(-	-)	116	36	45	52	48	4	35	4	0	3	1	2	.33	5	.307	.427	.487
2010	Jupiter	A+	5	21	8	2	2	0	(-	-)	14	3	2	4	0	0	3	0	0	0	0	0	-	1	.381	.381	.667
2010	Fla	NL	62	244	69	20	7	2	(1	1)	109	43	18	41	41	0	51	2	0	0	0	1	.00	4	.283	.390	.447

Brandon Morrow

Pitches: R **Bats:** R **Pos:** SP-26   **Ht:** 6'3" **Wt:** 195 **Born:** 7/26/1984 **Age:** 26

			HOW MUCH HE PITCHED					WHAT HE GAVE UP										THE RESULTS						
Year	Team	Lg	G	GS	CG	GF	IP	BFP	H	R	ER	HR	SH	SF	HB	TBB	IBB	SO	WP	Bk	W	L	Pct	Sh	Sv-Op	Hld	ERC	ERA
2007	Sea	AL	60	0	0	18	63.1	289	56	29	29	3	4	4	1	50	5	66	4	0	3	4	.429	0	0-2	18	4.47	4.12
2008	Sea	AL	45	5	0	24	64.2	265	40	26	24	10	1	0	0	34	1	75	5	0	3	4	.429	0	10-12	3	2.84	3.34
2009	Sea	AL	26	10	0	9	69.2	313	66	38	34	10	1	2	0	44	1	63	3	0	2	4	.333	0	6-8	1	4.99	4.39
2010	Tor	AL	26	26	1	0	146.1	629	136	76	73	11	2	4	9	66	0	178	8	0	10	7	.588	1	0-0	0	3.99	4.49
	4 ML YEARS		157	41	1	51	344.0	1496	298	169	160	34	8	10	10	194	7	382	20	0	18	19	.486	1	16-22	22	4.06	4.19

Mike Morse

Bats: R **Throws:** R **Pos:** RF-72; 1B-19; PH-19; DH-1; PR-1   **Ht:** 6'5" **Wt:** 230 **Born:** 3/22/1982 **Age:** 29

Year	Team	Lg	G	AB	H	2B	3B	HR	(Hm	Rd)	TB	R	RBI	RC	TBB	IBB	SO	HBP	SH	SF	SB	CS	SB%	GDP	Avg	OBP	Slg
2010	Syrcse*	AAA	15	51	13	2	0	3	(-	-)	24	12	8	9	8	0	11	1	0	0	0	0	-	5	.255	.367	.471
2005	Sea	AL	72	230	64	10	1	3	(3	0)	85	27	23	28	18	0	50	8	0	2	3	1	.75	9	.278	.349	.370
2006	Sea	AL	21	43	16	5	0	0	(0	0)	21	5	11	9	3	0	7	0	0	2	1	0	1.00	2	.372	.396	.488
2007	Sea	AL	9	18	8	2	0	0	(0	0)	10	1	3	6	1	0	4	1	0	0	0	0	-	0	.444	.500	.556
2008	Sea	AL	5	9	2	1	0	0	(0	0)	3	0	0	1	1	0	4	1	0	0	0	0	-	0	.222	.364	.333
2009	Was	NL	32	52	13	3	0	3	(3	0)	25	4	10	8	3	0	16	0	0	0	0	0	-	1	.250	.291	.481
2010	Was	NL	98	266	77	12	2	15	(6	9)	138	36	41	42	22	1	64	4	0	1	0	1	.00	6	.289	.352	.519
	6 ML YEARS		237	618	180	33	3	21	(12	9)	282	73	88	94	48	1	145	14	0	5	4	2	.67	18	.291	.353	.456

Clay Mortensen

Pitches: R **Bats:** R **Pos:** SP-1   **Ht:** 6'4" **Wt:** 180 **Born:** 4/10/1985 **Age:** 26

			HOW MUCH HE PITCHED					WHAT HE GAVE UP										THE RESULTS						
Year	Team	Lg	G	GS	CG	GF	IP	BFP	H	R	ER	HR	SH	SF	HB	TBB	IBB	SO	WP	Bk	W	L	Pct	Sh	Sv-Op	Hld	ERC	ERA
2007	Batvia	A-	6	4	0	0	20.1	83	13	4	4	0	1	0	2	11	0	23	1	0	1	1	.500	0	0-	-	2.46	1.77
2007	QuadC	A	10	10	0	0	40.1	172	44	17	14	2	0	0	4	8	0	45	2	0	0	2	.000	0	0-	-	3.85	3.12
2008	Sprgfld	AA	11	11	0	0	59.2	258	59	31	28	6	0	1	4	22	0	48	4	0	3	4	.429	0	0-	-	4.17	4.22
2008	Memp	AAA	15	14	0	0	80.0	361	87	50	49	12	1	2	6	42	1	57	14	1	5	6	.455	0	0-	-	5.87	5.51
2009	Memp	AAA	17	17	1	0	105.0	443	103	58	51	11	4	2	4	34	0	82	3	0	7	6	.538	0	0-	-	3.89	4.37
2009	Scrmto	AAA	6	6	0	0	32.1	145	40	20	16	2	0	2	0	14	0	18	2	0	2	2	.500	0	0-	-	5.39	4.45

Year Team	Lg	G	GS	CG	GF	IP	BFP	H	R	ER	HR	SH	SF	HB	TBB	IBB	SO	WP	Bk	W	L	Pct	Sh	Sv-Op	Hld	ERC	ERA
2010 Scrmto	AAA	26	26	0	0	165.1	688	161	91	78	20	5	5	2	53	3	112	14	0	13	6	.684	0	0--	-	3.85	4.25
2009 2 Tms		7	6	0	1	30.2	149	42	34	26	6	1	4	3	13	0	13	1	0	2	4	.333	0	0-0	0	7.50	7.63
2010 Oak	AL	1	1	0	0	6.0	26	6	4	3	1	0	0	0	2	0	7	0	0	0	0	-	0	0-0	0	4.18	4.50
09 StL	NL	1	0	0	1	3.0	16	5	6	2	1	1	1	1	1	0	2	0	0	0	0	-	0	0-0	0	11.45	6.00
09 Oak	AL	6	6	0	0	27.2	133	37	28	24	5	0	3	2	12	0	11	1	0	2	4	.333	0	0-0	0	7.10	7.81
2 ML YEARS		8	7	0	1	36.2	175	48	38	29	7	1	4	3	15	0	20	1	0	2	4	.333	0	0-0	0	6.92	7.12

Charlie Morton

Pitches: R **Bats:** R **Pos:** SP-17 **Ht:** 6'5" **Wt:** 230 **Born:** 11/12/1983 **Age:** 27

Year Team	Lg	G	GS	CG	GF	IP	BFP	H	R	ER	HR	SH	SF	HB	TBB	IBB	SO	WP	Bk	W	L	Pct	Sh	Sv-Op	Hld	ERC	ERA
2010 Indy*	AAA	14	14	1	0	80.0	351	83	46	34	6	1	1	6	30	0	53	3	1	4	4	.500	0	0--	-	4.30	3.83
2008 Atl	NL	16	15	0	0	74.2	345	80	56	51	9	5	4	2	41	2	48	2	0	4	8	.333	0	0-0	0	5.21	6.15
2009 Pit	NL	18	18	1	0	97.0	416	102	49	49	7	1	1	5	40	0	62	4	0	5	9	.357	1	0-0	0	4.56	4.55
2010 Pit	NL	17	17	0	0	79.2	382	112	79	67	15	6	6	7	26	3	59	5	1	2	12	.143	0	0-0	0	7.10	7.57
3 ML YEARS		51	50	1	0	251.1	1143	294	184	167	31	12	11	14	107	5	169	11	1	11	29	.275	1	0-0	0	5.54	5.98

Guillermo Moscoso

Pitches: R **Bats:** R **Pos:** RP-1 mahs-KOE-soe **Ht:** 6'1" **Wt:** 200 **Born:** 11/14/1983 **Age:** 27

Year Team	Lg	G	GS	CG	GF	IP	BFP	H	R	ER	HR	SH	SF	HB	TBB	IBB	SO	WP	Bk	W	L	Pct	Sh	Sv-Op	Hld	ERC	ERA
2005 Oneont	A-	11	10	0	0	47.1	202	49	27	23	4	0	2	1	11	0	44	4	0	2	2	.500	0	0--	-	3.53	4.37
2006 Tigers	R	13	3	0	2	36.0	151	37	14	10	3	0	2	0	8	0	33	2	1	3	2	.600	0	0--	-	3.40	2.50
2007 Lkland	A+	1	1	0	0	3.0	12	2	0	0	0	0	0	0	1	0	4	0	0	0	0	-	0	0--	-	1.57	0.00
2007 Oneont	A-	14	14	2	0	79.2	320	75	25	21	3	2	0	1	15	0	68	1	1	8	2	.800	1	0--	-	2.65	2.37
2007 WMich	A	1	1	0	0	8.0	28	5	1	1	1	1	0	0	0	0	7	0	0	0	0	-	0	0--	-	1.21	1.13
2008 Lkland	A+	15	6	0	3	52.0	205	36	16	14	4	2	4	2	13	0	72	2	0	2	3	.400	0	1--	-	1.95	2.42
2008 Erie	AA	6	6	0	0	34.2	135	24	17	12	4	0	1	0	8	0	50	1	0	3	1	.750	0	0--	-	1.97	3.12
2009 Frisco	AA	9	7	0	0	42.1	182	41	23	21	1	0	1	0	14	0	36	3	0	3	1	.750	0	0--	-	3.04	4.46
2009 Okla	AAA	12	11	0	0	70.0	277	56	20	18	2	0	2	3	15	0	60	1	0	5	4	.556	0	0--	-	2.10	2.31
2010 OKCity	AAA	23	22	1	0	123.1	563	142	82	71	17	7	2	4	49	0	107	4	4	7	7	.500	0	0--	-	5.25	5.18
2009 Tex	AL	10	0	0	6	14.0	64	15	7	5	1	0	1	1	6	0	12	4	0	0	0	-	0	0-0	0	4.55	3.21
2010 Tex	AL	1	0	0	0	0.2	7	2	2	2	0	0	0	1	2	0	2	0	0	0	0	-	0	0-0	0	37.18	27.00
2 ML YEARS		11	0	0	6	14.2	71	17	9	7	1	0	1	2	8	0	14	4	0	0	0	-	0	0-0	0	5.75	4.30

Dustin Moseley

Pitches: R **Bats:** R **Pos:** SP-9; RP-7 MOZE-lee **Ht:** 6'4" **Wt:** 215 **Born:** 12/26/1981 **Age:** 29

Year Team	Lg	G	GS	CG	GF	IP	BFP	H	R	ER	HR	SH	SF	HB	TBB	IBB	SO	WP	Bk	W	L	Pct	Sh	Sv-Op	Hld	ERC	ERA
2010 S-WB*	AAA	12	12	0	0	72.2	314	83	40	34	6	0	1	4	18	0	55	4	1	4	4	.500	0	0--	-	4.40	4.21
2006 LAA	AL	3	2	0	1	11.0	54	22	11	11	3	0	1	0	2	0	3	0	0	1	0	1.000	0	0-0	0	11.45	9.00
2007 LAA	AL	46	8	0	13	92.0	383	97	45	45	7	1	2	3	27	3	50	6	1	4	3	.571	0	0-0	4	4.00	4.40
2008 LAA	AL	12	10	0	0	50.1	237	70	38	38	6	1	3	2	20	0	37	3	1	2	4	.333	0	0-0	0	6.74	6.79
2009 LAA	AL	3	3	0	0	14.2	65	20	8	7	3	0	0	0	3	1	8	0	0	1	0	1.000	0	0-0	0	6.13	4.30
2010 NYY	AL	16	9	0	2	65.1	278	66	36	36	13	0	4	2	27	0	33	0	0	4	4	.500	0	0-0	0	5.17	4.96
Postseason		1	0	0	0	1.0	3	1	0	0	0	0	0	0	0	0	1	0	0	0	0	-	0	0-0	0	2.79	0.00
5 ML YEARS		80	32	0	17	233.1	1017	275	138	137	32	2	10	7	79	4	131	9	2	12	11	.522	0	0-0	4	5.34	5.28

Brandon Moss

Bats: L **Throws:** R **Pos:** PH-12; RF-5; LF-2 **Ht:** 6'0" **Wt:** 205 **Born:** 9/16/1983 **Age:** 27

Year Team	Lg	G	AB	H	2B	3B	HR	(Hm	Rd)	TB	R	RBI	RC	TBB	IBB	SO	HBP	SH	SF	SB	CS	SB%	GDP	Avg	OBP	Slg
2010 Indy*	AAA	136	500	133	32	2	22	(-	-)	235	73	96	79	42	1	118	7	4	3	12	7	.63	11	.266	.330	.470
2007 Bos	AL	15	25	7	2	1	0	(0	0)	11	6	1	3	4	0	0	0	0	0	0	0	-	1	.280	.379	.440
2008 2 Tms		79	236	58	15	3	8	(4	4)	103	19	34	30	21	1	70	1	0	5	1	2	.33	2	.246	.304	.436
2009 Pit	NL	133	385	91	20	4	7	(4	3)	140	47	41	37	34	3	84	4	0	1	1	5	.17	7	.236	.304	.364
2010 Pit	NL	17	26	4	1	0	0	(0	0)	5	2	2	2	1	0	6	0	0	0	0	0	-	1	.154	.185	.192
08 Bos	AL	34	78	23	5	1	2	(1	1)	36	7	11	11	6	0	25	0	0	2	1	1	.50	0	.295	.337	.462
08 Pit	NL	45	158	35	10	2	6	(3	3)	67	12	23	19	15	1	45	1	0	3	0	1	.00	2	.222	.288	.424
4 ML YEARS		244	672	160	38	8	15	(8	7)	259	74	78	72	60	4	166	5	0	6	2	7	.22	11	.238	.303	.385

Guillermo Mota

Pitches: R **Bats:** R **Pos:** RP-56 **Ht:** 6'6" **Wt:** 210 **Born:** 7/25/1973 **Age:** 37

Year Team	Lg	G	GS	CG	GF	IP	BFP	H	R	ER	HR	SH	SF	HB	TBB	IBB	SO	WP	Bk	W	L	Pct	Sh	Sv-Op	Hld	ERC	ERA
1999 Mon	NL	51	0	0	18	55.1	243	54	24	18	5	3	3	2	25	3	27	1	1	2	4	.333	0	0-1	3	4.10	2.93
2000 Mon	NL	29	0	0	7	30.0	126	27	21	20	3	1	1	2	12	0	24	1	1	1	1	.500	0	0-0	5	3.86	6.00
2001 Mon	NL	53	0	0	12	49.2	212	51	30	29	9	3	2	1	18	1	31	1	0	1	3	.250	0	0-3	12	4.77	5.26
2002 LAD	NL	43	0	0	11	60.2	256	45	30	28	4	3	1	2	27	6	49	3	0	1	3	.250	0	0-1	4	2.57	4.15
2003 LAD	NL	76	0	0	18	105.0	410	78	23	23	7	3	1	1	26	4	99	0	0	6	3	.667	0	1-3	13	2.01	1.97
2004 2 Tms	NL	78	0	0	18	96.2	393	75	33	33	8	5	3	4	37	6	85	5	0	9	8	.529	0	4-8	30	2.82	3.07
2005 Fla	NL	56	0	0	24	67.0	293	65	38	35	5	1	3	1	32	7	60	4	0	2	2	.500	0	2-4	14	3.90	4.70
2006 2 Tms	NL	52	0	0	17	55.2	241	55	29	29	1	0	3	0	24	4	46	2	0	4	3	.571	0	0-0	9	4.71	4.53
2007 NYM	NL	52	0	0	10	59.1	261	63	39	38	8	2	0	2	18	2	47	2	0	2	2	.500	0	0-3	8	4.26	5.76
2008 Mil	NL	58	0	0	18	57.0	244	52	28	26	7	1	3	0	28	0	50	4	1	5	6	.455	0	1-4	11	4.14	4.11

Year	Team	Lg	G	GS	CG	GF	IP	BFP	H	R	ER	HR	SH	SF	HB	TBB	IBB	SO	WP	Bk	W	L	Pct	Sh	Sv-Op	Hld	ERC	ERA
2009	LAD	NL	61	0	0	27	65.1	273	53	25	25	6	3	4	5	24	8	39	3	0	3	4	.429	0	0-2	2	2.98	3.44
2010	SF	NL	56	0	0	17	54.0	228	49	29	26	4	0	4	0	22	5	38	5	0	1	3	.250	0	1-3	8	3.28	4.33
04	LAD	NL	52	0	0	11	63.0	259	51	15	15	4	2	2	2	27	5	52	5	0	8	4	.667	0	1-1	17	2.98	2.14
04	Fla	NL	26	0	0	7	33.2	134	24	18	18	4	1	1	2	10	1	33	0	0	1	4	.200	0	3-7	13	2.51	4.81
06	Cle	AL	34	0	0	13	37.2	173	45	27	26	9	0	3	0	19	3	27	2	0	1	3	.250	0	0-0	5	6.62	6.21
06	NYM	NL	18	0	0	4	18.0	68	10	2	2	2	0	0	0	5	1	19	0	0	3	0	1.000	0	0-0	4	1.51	1.00
	Postseason		9	0	0	4	10.0	42	12	6	6	1	0	0	0	2	0	7	0	0	1	0	1.000	0	0-2	3	4.53	5.40
12 ML YEARS			665	0	0	197	755.2	3180	667	349	329	77	25	28	20	293	46	595	31	3	37	42	.468	0	9-32	117	3.41	3.92

Jason Motte

Pitches: R **Bats:** R **Pos:** RP-56

MOTT

Ht: 6'0" **Wt:** 200 **Born:** 6/22/1982 **Age:** 29

Year	Team	Lg	G	GS	CG	GF	IP	BFP	H	R	ER	HR	SH	SF	HB	TBB	IBB	SO	WP	Bk	W	L	Pct	Sh	Sv-Op	Hld	ERC	ERA
2010	Memp*	AAA	2	0	0	0	2.2	11	2	1	1	0	0	0	0	1	0	2	0	0	0	0	-	0	0- -	-	2.01	3.38
2008	StL	NL	12	0	0	4	11.0	40	5	2	1	0	1	0	0	3	0	16	0	0	0	0	-	0	1-1	4	0.89	0.82
2009	StL	NL	69	0	0	14	56.2	244	57	32	30	10	0	3	2	23	1	54	2	1	4	4	.500	0	0-3	15	4.86	4.76
2010	StL	NL	56	0	0	13	52.1	208	41	13	13	5	1	3	0	18	3	54	1	0	4	2	.667	0	2-3	12	2.68	2.24
	Postseason		1	0	0	0	1.0	3	0	0	0	0	0	0	0	0	0	0	0	0	0	0	-	0	0-0	0	0.00	0.00
3 ML YEARS			137	0	0	31	120.0	492	103	47	44	15	2	6	2	44	4	124	3	1	8	6	.571	0	3-7	31	3.42	3.30

Jamie Moyer

Pitches: L **Bats:** L **Pos:** SP-19

Ht: 6'0" **Wt:** 185 **Born:** 11/18/1962 **Age:** 48

Year	Team	Lg	G	GS	CG	GF	IP	BFP	H	R	ER	HR	SH	SF	HB	TBB	IBB	SO	WP	Bk	W	L	Pct	Sh	Sv-Op	Hld	ERC	ERA
1986	ChC	NL	16	16	1	0	87.1	395	107	52	49	10	3	3	3	42	1	45	3	3	7	4	.636	1	0-0	0	6.13	5.05
1987	ChC	NL	35	33	1	1	201.0	899	210	127	114	28	14	7	5	97	9	147	11	2	12	15	.444	0	0-0	0	4.96	5.10
1988	ChC	NL	34	30	3	1	202.0	855	212	84	78	20	14	4	4	55	7	121	4	0	9	15	.375	1	0-2	0	3.89	3.48
1989	Tex	AL	15	15	1	0	76.0	337	84	51	41	10	1	4	2	33	0	44	1	0	4	9	.308	0	0-0	0	5.20	4.86
1990	Tex	AL	33	10	1	6	102.1	447	115	59	53	6	1	7	4	39	4	58	1	0	2	6	.250	0	0-0	1	4.57	4.66
1991	StL	NL	8	7	0	1	31.1	142	38	21	20	5	4	2	1	16	0	20	2	1	0	5	.000	0	0-0	0	6.58	5.74
1993	Bal	AL	25	25	3	0	152.0	630	154	63	58	11	3	1	6	38	2	90	1	1	12	9	.571	1	0-0	0	3.58	3.43
1994	Bal	AL	23	23	0	0	149.0	631	158	81	79	23	5	2	2	38	3	87	1	0	5	7	.417	0	0-0	0	4.24	4.77
1995	Bal	AL	27	18	0	3	115.2	483	117	70	67	18	5	3	3	30	0	65	0	0	8	6	.571	0	0-0	0	4.11	5.21
1996	2 Tms	AL	34	21	0	1	160.2	703	177	86	71	23	7	6	2	46	5	79	3	1	13	3	.813	0	0-0	1	4.42	3.98
1997	Sea	AL	30	30	2	0	188.2	787	187	82	81	21	6	1	7	43	2	113	3	0	17	5	.773	0	0-0	0	3.56	3.86
1998	Sea	AL	34	34	4	0	234.1	974	234	99	92	23	4	3	10	42	2	158	3	1	15	9	.625	3	0-0	0	3.34	3.53
1999	Sea	AL	32	32	4	0	228.0	945	235	108	98	23	6	2	9	48	1	137	3	0	14	8	.636	0	0-0	0	3.71	3.87
2000	Sea	AL	26	26	0	0	154.0	678	173	103	94	22	3	3	3	53	2	98	4	1	13	10	.565	0	0-0	0	4.91	5.49
2001	Sea	AL	33	33	1	0	209.2	851	187	84	80	24	5	11	10	44	4	119	1	0	20	6	.769	0	0-0	0	3.03	3.43
2002	Sea	AL	34	34	4	0	230.2	931	198	89	85	28	5	7	9	50	2	147	3	0	13	8	.619	2	0-0	0	2.89	3.32
2003	Sea	AL	33	33	1	0	215.0	897	199	83	78	19	7	6	8	66	3	129	0	0	21	7	.750	0	0-0	0	3.37	3.27
2004	Sea	AL	34	33	1	0	202.0	888	217	127	117	44	9	6	11	63	3	125	1	0	7	13	.350	0	0-0	0	5.13	5.21
2005	Sea	AL	32	32	1	0	200.0	868	225	99	95	23	6	6	8	52	2	102	3	0	13	7	.650	0	0-0	0	4.46	4.28
2006	2 Tms		33	33	2	0	211.1	894	228	110	101	33	5	9	5	51	5	108	3	1	11	14	.440	1	0-0	0	4.36	4.30
2007	Phi	NL	33	33	1	0	199.1	867	222	118	111	30	11	5	5	66	3	133	2	0	14	12	.538	0	0-0	0	4.92	5.01
2008	Phi	NL	33	33	0	0	196.1	841	199	85	84	20	7	2	11	62	4	123	3	0	16	7	.696	0	0-0	0	4.03	3.71
2009	Phi	NL	30	25	0	1	162.0	699	177	91	89	27	8	4	10	43	1	94	1	1	12	10	.545	0	0-0	1	4.79	4.94
2010	Phi	NL	19	19	2	0	111.2	460	103	64	60	20	3	1	6	20	0	63	0	0	9	9	.500	1	0-0	0	3.47	4.84
96	Bos	AL	23	10	0	0	90.0	405	111	50	45	14	4	3	1	27	2	50	2	1	7	1	.875	0	0-0	1	5.37	4.50
96	Sea	AL	11	11	0	0	70.2	298	66	36	26	9	3	3	1	19	3	29	1	0	6	2	.750	0	0-0	0	3.31	3.31
06	Sea	AL	25	25	2	0	160.0	685	179	85	78	25	3	7	3	44	3	82	3	1	6	12	.333	1	0-0	0	4.74	4.39
06	Phi	NL	8	8	0	0	51.1	209	49	25	23	8	2	2	2	7	2	26	0	0	5	2	.714	0	0-0	0	3.24	4.03
	Postseason		8	8	0	0	41.1	168	37	19	19	3	2	2	2	10	0	29	1	0	3	3	.500	0	0-0	0	2.96	4.14
24 ML YEARS			686	628	33	15	4020.1	17102	4156	2036	1892	511	142	105	144	1137	67	2405	57	12	267	204	.567	10	0-2	3	4.12	4.24

Peter Moylan

Pitches: R **Bats:** R **Pos:** RP-85

Ht: 6'2" **Wt:** 200 **Born:** 12/2/1978 **Age:** 32

Year	Team	Lg	G	GS	CG	GF	IP	BFP	H	R	ER	HR	SH	SF	HB	TBB	IBB	SO	WP	Bk	W	L	Pct	Sh	Sv-Op	Hld	ERC	ERA
2006	Atl	NL	15	0	0	5	15.0	68	18	8	8	1	1	0	0	5	1	14	0	0	0	0	-	0	0-0	0	4.47	4.80
2007	Atl	NL	80	0	0	16	90.0	359	65	27	18	6	4	4	7	31	12	63	2	0	5	3	.625	0	1-2	8	2.36	1.80
2008	Atl	NL	7	0	0	2	5.2	25	5	1	1	1	0	0	1	3	0	5	0	0	0	1	.000	0	1-2	4	3.51	1.59
2009	Atl	NL	87	0	0	6	73.0	309	65	29	23	0	4	3	2	35	8	61	1	0	6	2	.750	0	0-5	25	3.06	2.84
2010	Atl	NL	85	0	0	7	63.2	271	53	24	21	5	5	2	2	37	6	52	3	0	6	2	.750	0	1-4	21	3.75	2.97
5 ML YEARS			274	0	0	36	247.1	1032	206	89	71	13	14	9	12	109	27	195	6	0	17	8	.680	0	3-13	58	3.07	2.58

Edward Mujica

Pitches: R **Bats:** R **Pos:** RP-59

moo-HEE-kah

Ht: 6'2" **Wt:** 215 **Born:** 5/10/1984 **Age:** 27

Year	Team	Lg	G	GS	CG	GF	IP	BFP	H	R	ER	HR	SH	SF	HB	TBB	IBB	SO	WP	Bk	W	L	Pct	Sh	Sv-Op	Hld	ERC	ERA
2006	Cle	AL	10	0	0	2	18.1	78	25	6	6	1	0	2	1	0	0	12	0	0	0	1	.000	0	0-0	0	4.50	2.95
2007	Cle	AL	10	0	0	5	13.0	60	19	12	12	3	0	1	0	2	0	7	0	0	0	0	-	0	0-0	0	6.63	8.31
2008	Cle	AL	33	0	0	13	38.2	168	46	29	29	5	0	4	1	10	3	27	1	0	3	2	.600	0	0-2	1	4.82	6.75
2009	SD	NL	67	4	0	15	93.2	393	101	47	41	14	1	3	0	19	4	76	3	1	3	5	.375	0	2-3	11	4.00	3.94
2010	SD	NL	59	0	0	24	69.2	268	59	29	28	14	1	0	0	6	0	72	1	0	2	1	.667	0	0-1	4	2.68	3.62
5 ML YEARS			179	4	0	59	233.1	967	250	123	116	37	2	10	2	37	7	194	5	1	8	9	.471	0	2-6	16	3.91	4.47

Kevin Mulvey

Pitches: R **Bats:** R **Pos:** RP-2   **Ht:** 6'2" **Wt:** 195 **Born:** 5/26/1985 **Age:** 26

			HOW MUCH HE PITCHED						WHAT HE GAVE UP											THE RESULTS						
Year	Team	Lg	G	GS	CG	GF	IP	BFP	H	R	ER	HR	SH	SF	HB	TBB	IBB	SO	WP	Bk	W	L	Pct	Sh	Sv-Op	Hld	ERC	ERA
2006	Mets	R	1	1	0	0	2.0	7	1	0	0	0	0	0	0	0	0	1	0	0	0	0	-	0	0- -	-	0.54	0.00
2006	Bnghtn	AA	3	3	1	0	13.1	51	10	4	2	1	0	0	0	5	0	10	1	0	0	1	.000	0	0- -	-	2.70	1.35
2007	Bnghtn	AA	26	26	0	0	151.2	639	145	74	56	4	7	6	7	43	0	110	12	1	11	10	.524	0	0- -	-	3.06	3.32
2007	NewOr	AAA	1	1	0	0	6.0	21	2	0	0	0	0	0	0	0	0	3	0	0	1	0	1.000	0	0- -	-	0.24	0.00
2008	Roch	AAA	27	27	1	0	148.0	640	152	80	62	16	7	6	6	48	0	121	7	2	7	9	.438	0	0- -	-	4.12	3.77
2009	Roch	AAA	24	24	2	0	149.0	644	153	84	65	12	4	8	7	54	1	113	8	0	5	8	.385	1	0- -	-	4.13	3.93
2010	Reno	AAA	27	27	0	0	156.2	682	161	85	81	11	8	5	10	60	2	109	10	0	7	8	.467	0	0- -	-	4.20	4.65
2009	2 Tms		8	4	0	1	24.1	114	29	22	22	5	1	2	2	12	0	18	1	0	0	3	.000	0	0-0	0	6.76	8.14
2010	Ari	NL	2	0	0	1	3.0	17	5	2	2	2	0	0	1	2	0	1	0	0	0	0	-	0	0-0	0	16.59	6.00
09	Min	AL	2	0	0	1	1.1	10	6	4	4	0	0	0	0	0	0	0	1	0	0	0	-	0	0-0	0	26.58	27.00
09	Ari	NL	6	4	0	0	23.0	104	23	18	18	5	1	2	2	12	0	18	0	0	0	3	.000	0	0-0	0	5.81	7.04
	2 ML YEARS		10	4	0	2	27.1	131	34	24	24	7	1	2	3	14	0	19	1	0	0	3	.000	0	0-0	0	7.72	7.90

Daniel Murphy

Bats: L **Throws:** R **Pos:** 1B   **Ht:** 6'2" **Wt:** 215 **Born:** 4/1/1985 **Age:** 26

			BATTING																		BASERUNNING				AVERAGES		
Year	Team	Lg	G	AB	H	2B	3B	HR	(Hm	Rd)	TB	R	RBI	RC	TBB	IBB	SO	HBP	SH	SF	SB	CS	SB%	GDP	Avg	OBP	Slg
2006	Mets	R	8	18	1	0	0	0	(-	-)	1	2	0	0	4	0	3	0	0	0	0	0	-	0	.056	.227	.056
2006	Kngspt	R+	9	33	9	0	0	2	(-	-)	15	2	7	5	4	0	1	0	0	0	0	0	-	4	.273	.351	.455
2006	Bklyn	A-	8	29	7	1	0	0	(-	-)	8	2	3	3	4	1	3	0	0	0	0	0	-	0	.241	.324	.276
2007	StLuci	A+	135	502	143	34	3	11	(-	-)	216	68	78	77	42	5	61	4	0	11	6	3	.67	8	.285	.338	.430
2008	Bnghtn	AA	95	357	110	26	1	13	(-	-)	177	56	67	69	39	7	46	3	1	7	14	5	.74	10	.308	.374	.496
2008	Bklyn	A-	3	14	7	0	0	0	(-	-)	7	1	2	3	0	0	2	0	0	0	0	0	-	0	.500	.500	.500
2008	NewOr	AAA	1	4	1	0	0	0	(-	-)	1	2	0	0	1	0	0	0	0	0	0	0	-	1	.250	.400	.250
2010	StLuci	A+	3	11	8	1	0	1	(-	-)	12	2	6	6	2	0	0	0	0	0	0	0	-	0	.727	.769	1.091
2010	Buffalo	AAA	8	34	10	3	0	1	(-	-)	16	4	8	5	1	0	2	0	0	0	1	0	1.00	2	.294	.314	.471
2008	NYM	NL	49	131	41	9	3	2	(1	1)	62	24	17	26	18	1	28	1	0	1	0	2	.00	4	.313	.397	.473
2009	NYM	NL	155	508	135	38	4	12	(7	5)	217	60	63	60	38	4	69	0	4	6	4	2	.67	13	.266	.313	.427
	2 ML YEARS		204	639	176	47	7	14	(8	6)	279	84	80	86	56	5	97	1	4	7	4	4	.50	17	.275	.331	.437

David Murphy

Bats: L **Throws:** L **Pos:** LF-74; RF-51; PH-19; CF-10; PR-2; DH-1   **Ht:** 6'4" **Wt:** 205 **Born:** 10/10/1981 **Age:** 29

			BATTING																		BASERUNNING				AVERAGES		
Year	Team	Lg	G	AB	H	2B	3B	HR	(Hm	Rd)	TB	R	RBI	RC	TBB	IBB	SO	HBP	SH	SF	SB	CS	SB%	GDP	Avg	OBP	Slg
2006	Bos	AL	20	22	5	1	0	0	(0	1)	9	4	2	2	4	0	4	0	0	0	0	0	-	1	.227	.346	.409
2007	2 Tms	AL	46	105	36	12	2	2	(1	1)	58	17	14	23	7	0	20	0	0	0	0	0	-	1	.343	.384	.552
2008	Tex	AL	108	415	114	28	3	15	(8	7)	193	64	74	62	31	3	70	0	2	6	7	2	.78	7	.275	.321	.465
2009	Tex	AL	128	432	116	24	1	17	(8	9)	193	61	57	60	49	3	106	1	2	9	9	4	.69	5	.269	.338	.447
2010	Tex	AL	138	419	122	26	2	12	(7	5)	188	54	65	68	45	2	71	0	0	6	14	2	.88	6	.291	.358	.449
07	Bos	AL	3	2	1	0	1	0	(0	0)	3	1	0	1	0	0	1	0	0	0	0	0	-	0	.500	.500	1.500
07	Tex	AL	43	103	35	12	1	2	(1	1)	55	16	14	22	7	0	19	0	0	0	0	0	-	1	.340	.382	.534
	5 ML YEARS		440	1393	393	91	8	47	(24	23)	641	200	212	216	136	8	271	1	4	18	30	8	.79	20	.282	.342	.460

Donnie Murphy

Bats: R **Throws:** R **Pos:** PH-21; 3B-4; SS-4; 2B-1; PR-1   **Ht:** 5'10" **Wt:** 195 **Born:** 3/10/1983 **Age:** 28

			BATTING																		BASERUNNING				AVERAGES		
Year	Team	Lg	G	AB	H	2B	3B	HR	(Hm	Rd)	TB	R	RBI	RC	TBB	IBB	SO	HBP	SH	SF	SB	CS	SB%	GDP	Avg	OBP	Slg
2010	NewOr*	AAA	57	206	57	12	1	12	(	)	107	31	35	38	16	0	41	2	0	0	0	0	-	3	.277	.335	.519
2004	KC	AL	7	27	5	3	0	0	(0	0)	8	1	3	2	0	0	7	0	0	0	1	0	1.00	1	.185	.185	.296
2005	KC	AL	32	77	12	5	0	1	(0	1)	20	4	8	1	9	0	23	0	1	1	0	1	.00	3	.156	.241	.260
2007	Oak	AL	42	118	26	8	0	6	(2	4)	52	21	21	16	10	0	35	2	1	1	1	0	1.00	3	.220	.290	.441
2008	Oak	AL	46	103	19	3	0	3	(2	1)	31	10	13	6	11	0	38	2	0	1	2	1	.67	1	.184	.274	.301
2010	Fla	NL	29	44	14	6	1	3	(2	1)	31	9	16	12	2	0	19	0	1	0	0	0	-	0	.318	.318	.705
	5 ML YEARS		156	369	76	25	1	13	(6	7)	142	45	61	37	32	0	122	4	3	3	4	2	.67	8	.206	.275	.385

Brett Myers

Pitches: R **Bats:** R **Pos:** SP-33   **Ht:** 6'4" **Wt:** 238 **Born:** 8/17/1980 **Age:** 30

			HOW MUCH HE PITCHED						WHAT HE GAVE UP											THE RESULTS						
Year	Team	Lg	G	GS	CG	GF	IP	BFP	H	R	ER	HR	SH	SF	HB	TBB	IBB	SO	WP	Bk	W	L	Pct	Sh	Sv-Op	Hld	ERC	ERA
2002	Phi	NL	12	12	1	0	72.0	307	73	38	34	11	6	2	6	29	1	34	2	1	4	5	.444	0	0-0	0	5.04	4.25
2003	Phi	NL	32	32	1	0	193.0	848	205	99	95	20	6	3	9	76	8	143	9	0	14	9	.609	0	0-0	0	4.56	4.43
2004	Phi	NL	32	31	1	1	176.0	778	196	113	108	31	9	3	6	62	4	116	5	0	11	11	.500	1	0-0	0	5.17	5.52
2005	Phi	NL	34	34	2	0	215.1	905	193	94	89	31	9	3	11	60	2	208	4	4	13	8	.619	0	0-0	0	3.64	3.72
2006	Phi	NL	31	31	1	0	198.0	833	194	93	86	29	7	4	3	63	3	189	3	0	12	7	.632	0	0-0	0	4.02	3.91
2007	Phi	NL	51	3	0	37	68.2	293	61	33	33	9	3	1	1	27	1	83	5	0	5	7	.417	0	21-24	3	3.63	4.33
2008	Phi	NL	30	30	2	0	190.0	817	197	103	96	29	4	3	6	65	6	163	2	0	10	13	.435	1	0-0	0	4.53	4.55
2009	Phi	NL	18	10	0	1	70.2	304	74	38	38	18	3	2	4	23	1	50	1	0	4	3	.571	0	0-0	3	5.41	4.84
2010	Hou	NL	33	33	2	0	223.2	936	212	88	78	20	9	4	3	66	3	180	2	0	14	8	.636	0	0-0	0	3.34	3.14
	Postseason		7	3	0	2	22.0	96	18	12	11	2	2	0	2	12	3	17	1	0	2	1	.667	0	0-0	0	3.69	4.50
	9 ML YEARS		273	216	10	39	1407.1	6021	1405	699	657	198	56	25	49	479	29	1166	33	5	87	71	.551	3	21-24	6	4.23	4.20

Xavier Nady

Bats: R Throws: R Pos: 1B-52; PH-40; RF-23; LF-6; DH-2   Ht: 6'2" Wt: 215 Born: 11/14/1978 Age: 32

Year	Team	Lg	G	AB	H	2B	3B	HR	(Hm	Rd)	TB	R	RBI	RC	TBB	IBB	SO	HBP	SH	SF	SB	CS	SB%	GDP	Avg	OBP	Slg
2000	SD	NL	1	1	1	0	0	0	(0	0)	1	1	0	1	0	0	0	0	0	0	0	0	-	0	1.000	1.000	1.000
2003	SD	NL	110	371	99	17	1	9	(5	4)	145	50	39	39	24	0	74	6	2	1	6	2	.75	14	.267	.321	.391
2004	SD	NL	34	77	19	4	0	3	(1	2)	32	7	9	8	5	0	13	1	1	0	0	0	-	4	.247	.301	.416
2005	SD	NL	124	326	85	15	2	13	(5	8)	143	40	43	37	22	1	67	7	1	0	2	1	.67	5	.261	.321	.439
2006	2 Tms	NL	130	468	131	28	1	17	(10	7)	212	57	63	62	30	7	85	11	2	1	3	3	.50	12	.280	.337	.453
2007	Pit	NL	125	431	120	23	1	20	(7	13)	205	55	72	60	23	2	101	12	0	4	3	1	.75	16	.278	.330	.476
2008	2 Tms	NL	148	555	169	37	1	25	(11	14)	283	76	97	93	39	2	103	9	0	4	2	1	.67	14	.305	.357	.510
2009	NYY	AL	7	28	8	4	0	0	(0	0)	12	4	2	2	1	0	6	0	0	0	0	0	-	2	.286	.310	.429
2010	ChC	NL	119	317	81	13	0	6	(2	4)	112	33	33	33	17	0	85	8	1	4	0	0	-	12	.256	.306	.353
06	NYM	NL	75	265	70	15	1	14	(10	4)	129	37	40	35	19	4	51	6	1	1	2	1	.67	7	.264	.326	.487
06	Pit	NL	55	203	61	13	0	3	(0	3)	83	20	23	27	11	3	34	5	1	0	1	2	.33	5	.300	.352	.409
08	Pit	NL	89	327	108	26	1	13	(6	7)	175	50	57	59	25	1	55	5	0	3	1	0	1.00	9	.330	.383	.535
08	NYY	NL	59	228	61	11	0	12	(5	7)	108	26	40	34	14	1	48	4	0	1	1	1	.50	5	.268	.320	.474
	Postseason		2	3	1	0	0	0	(0	0)	1	0	2	1	0	0	1	2	0	0	0	0	-	0	.333	.600	.333
	9 ML YEARS		798	2574	713	141	6	93	(41	52)	1145	323	358	335	161	12	534	54	7	14	16	8	.67	79	.277	.331	.445

Hiroyuki Nakajima

Bats: R Throws: R Pos: SS   hee-roe-YOO-kee nah-kah-JEE-mah   Ht: 5'11" Wt: 183 Born: 7/31/1982 Age: 28

Year	Team	Lg	G	AB	H	2B	3B	HR	(Hm	Rd)	TB	R	RBI	RC	TBB	IBB	SO	HBP	SH	SF	SB	CS	SB%	GDP	Avg	OBP	Slg
2002	Seibu	Jap	4	7	1	0	0	0	(-	-)	1	0	0	0	0	0	2	0	0	0	0	0	-	1	.143	.143	.143
2003	Seibu	Jap	44	89	23	3	1	4	(-	-)	40	12	11	12	5	-	22	4	0	0	1	2	.33	0	.258	.327	.449
2004	Seibu	Jap	133	502	144	22	3	27	(-	-)	253	70	90	92	39	-	108	11	3	4	18	2	.90	7	.287	.349	.504
2005	Seibu	Jap	116	405	111	21	2	11	(-	-)	169	56	60	58	22	-	67	11	3	3	11	3	.79	17	.274	.327	.417
2006	Seibu	Jap	105	412	126	22	1	16	(-	-)	198	76	63	75	30	-	66	13	0	4	14	4	.78	12	.306	.368	.481
2007	Seibu	Jap	143	533	160	28	5	12	(-	-)	234	68	74	87	41	-	134	13	1	5	9	4	.69	15	.300	.361	.439
2008	Seibu	Jap	124	486	161	32	0	21	(-	-)	256	75	81	107	55	-	96	12	0	3	25	5	.83	15	.331	.410	.527
2009	Seibu	Jap	144	560	173	31	3	22	(-	-)	276	100	92	111	75	-	113	10	0	3	20	12	.63	17	.309	.398	.493
2010	Seibu	Jap	130	503	158	33	3	20	(-	-)	257	80	93	102	52	-	97	13	0	11	15	5	.75	20	.314	.385	.511

Mike Napoli

Bats: R Throws: R Pos: 1B-70; C-66; PH-8; DH-2; PR-1   NAPP-uh-lee   Ht: 6'0" Wt: 215 Born: 10/31/1981 Age: 29

Year	Team	Lg	G	AB	H	2B	3B	HR	(Hm	Rd)	TB	R	RBI	RC	TBB	IBB	SO	HBP	SH	SF	SB	CS	SB%	GDP	Avg	OBP	Slg
2006	LAA	AL	99	268	61	13	0	16	(10	6)	122	47	42	40	51	0	90	5	0	1	2	3	.40	2	.228	.360	.455
2007	LAA	AL	75	219	54	11	1	10	(5	5)	97	40	34	35	33	2	63	5	1	5	2	2	.71	5	.247	.351	.443
2008	LAA	AL	78	227	62	9	1	20	(10	10)	133	39	49	46	35	5	70	5	1	6	7	3	.70	3	.273	.374	.586
2009	LAA	AL	114	382	104	22	1	20	(10	10)	188	60	56	52	40	1	103	7	0	3	3	3	.50	6	.272	.350	.492
2010	LAA	AL	140	453	108	24	1	26	(13	13)	212	60	68	60	42	2	137	11	0	4	4	2	.67	15	.238	.316	.468
	Postseason		14	31	6	1	0	2	(0	2)	13	4	4	4	2	0	10	3	0	0	0	0	-	0	.194	.306	.419
	5 ML YEARS		506	1549	389	79	4	92	(48	44)	752	246	249	233	201	10	463	33	2	19	21	13	.62	31	.251	.346	.485

Chris Narveson

Pitches: L Bats: L Pos: SP-28; RP-9   NARR-vih-son   Ht: 6'3" Wt: 205 Born: 12/20/1981 Age: 29

Year	Team	Lg	G	GS	CG	GF	IP	BFP	H	R	ER	HR	SH	SF	HB	TBB	IBB	SO	WP	Bk	W	L	Pct	Sh	Sv-Op	Hld	ERC	ERA
2006	StL	NL	5	1	0	1	9.1	40	6	5	5	1	0	0	1	5	0	12	1	1	0	0	-	0	0-0	0	3.06	4.82
2009	Mil	NL	21	4	0	5	47.0	205	45	22	20	7	2	3	2	16	1	46	4	0	2	0	1.000	0	0-0	0	3.96	3.83
2010	Mil	NL	37	28	0	2	167.2	724	172	96	93	21	8	5	5	59	3	137	6	0	12	9	.571	0	0-1	3	4.30	4.99
	3 ML YEARS		63	33	0	8	224.0	969	223	123	118	29	10	8	8	80	4	195	11	1	14	9	.609	0	0-1	3	4.17	4.74

Joe Nathan

Pitches: R Bats: R Pos: P   Ht: 6'4" Wt: 225 Born: 11/22/1974 Age: 36

Year	Team	Lg	G	GS	CG	GF	IP	BFP	H	R	ER	HR	SH	SF	HB	TBB	IBB	SO	WP	Bk	W	L	Pct	Sh	Sv-Op	Hld	ERC	ERA
1999	SF	NL	19	14	0	2	90.1	395	84	45	42	17	2	0	1	46	0	54	2	0	7	4	.636	0	1-1	0	4.78	4.18
2000	SF	NL	20	15	0	0	93.1	426	89	63	54	12	5	5	4	63	4	61	5	0	5	2	.714	0	0-1	0	5.23	5.21
2002	SF	NL	4	0	0	3	3.2	12	1	0	0	0	0	0	0	0	0	2	0	0	0	0	-	0	0-0	0	0.17	0.00
2003	SF	NL	78	0	0	9	79.0	316	51	26	26	7	2	4	3	33	3	83	4	1	12	4	.750	0	0-3	20	2.34	2.96
2004	Min	AL	73	0	0	63	72.1	284	48	14	13	3	2	0	2	23	3	89	5	0	1	2	.333	0	44-47	0	1.78	1.62
2005	Min	AL	69	0	0	58	70.0	276	46	22	21	5	1	2	0	22	1	94	2	0	7	4	.636	0	43-48	0	1.83	2.70
2006	Min	AL	64	0	0	61	68.1	262	38	12	12	3	3	2	1	16	4	95	3	0	7	0	1.000	0	36-38	0	1.18	1.58
2007	Min	AL	68	0	0	60	71.2	282	54	15	15	4	2	2	1	19	2	77	3	0	4	2	.667	0	37-41	0	2.08	1.88
2008	Min	AL	68	0	0	57	67.2	261	43	13	10	5	1	0	2	18	4	74	2	0	1	2	.333	0	39-45	0	1.67	1.33
2009	Min	AL	70	0	0	62	68.2	271	42	16	16	7	1	0	2	22	1	89	4	0	2	2	.500	0	47-52	0	1.89	2.10
	Postseason		8	0	0	3	8.0	43	12	7	7	2	0	0	0	7	3	10	1	0	0	2	.000	0	1-3	0	9.65	7.88
	10 ML YEARS		533	29	0	375	685.0	2785	496	226	209	63	19	15	16	262	22	718	30	1	46	22	.676	0	247-276	20	2.55	2.75

Daniel Nava

Bats: B **Throws:** L **Pos:** LF-54; PH-13; DH-1; PR-1   NAH-vah   **Ht:** 5'10" **Wt:** 200 **Born:** 2/22/1983 **Age:** 28

Year	Team	Lg	G	AB	H	2B	3B	HR	(Hm	Rd)	TB	R	RBI	RC	TBB	IBB	SO	HBP	SH	SF	SB	CS	SB%	GDP	Avg	OBP	Slg
2007	Chico	IND	72	256	95	23	3	12	(-	-)	160	70	59	76	48	3	42	6	0	4	18	2	.90	8	.371	.475	.625
2008	Lancst	A+	86	323	110	27	1	10	(-	-)	169	54	59	72	43	1	70	7	2	4	4	3	.57	8	.341	.424	.523
2009	Salem	A+	29	109	37	12	1	1	(-	-)	54	18	13	24	18	0	21	1	1	1	0	2	.00	5	.339	.434	.495
2009	Portlnd	AA	32	118	43	10	1	4	(-	-)	67	25	23	31	25	1	12	1	0	0	0	0	-	0	.364	.479	.568
2010	Pwtckt	AAA	77	284	82	16	1	10	(-	-)	130	41	48	50	28	0	64	11	0	2	4	2	.67	4	.289	.372	.458
2010	Bos	AL	60	161	39	14	1	1	(1	0)	58	23	26	26	19	1	46	8	0	0	1	1	.50	5	.242	.351	.360

Dioner Navarro

Bats: B **Throws:** R **Pos:** C-46; PH-4   dee-AHN-err   **Ht:** 5'9" **Wt:** 205 **Born:** 2/9/1984 **Age:** 27

Year	Team	Lg	G	AB	H	2B	3B	HR	(Hm	Rd)	TB	R	RBI	RC	TBB	IBB	SO	HBP	SH	SF	SB	CS	SB%	GDP	Avg	OBP	Slg
2010	Drham*	AAA	43	141	40	9	0	2	(-	-)	55	19	21	24	23	1	25	2	1	2	3	0	1.00	3	.284	.387	.390
2004	NYY	AL	5	7	3	0	0	0	(0	0)	3	2	1	1	0	0	0	0	0	0	0	0	-	1	.429	.429	.429
2005	LAD	NL	50	176	48	9	0	3	(3	0)	66	21	14	18	20	1	21	2	1	0	0	0	-	3	.273	.354	.375
2006	2 Tms		81	268	68	9	0	6	(4	2)	95	28	28	27	31	6	51	1	1	1	2	1	.67	7	.254	.332	.354
2007	TB	AL	119	388	88	19	2	9	(5	4)	138	46	44	35	33	3	67	1	7	5	3	1	.75	11	.227	.286	.356
2008	TB	AL	120	427	126	27	0	7	(4	3)	174	43	54	59	34	1	49	3	3	3	0	4	.00	16	.295	.349	.407
2009	TB	AL	115	376	82	15	0	8	(4	4)	121	38	32	22	18	1	51	5	8	3	5	2	.71	14	.218	.261	.322
2010	TB	AL	48	124	24	5	0	1	(1	0)	32	11	7	4	12	0	20	1	5	0	0	1	.00	3	.194	.270	.258
06	LAD	NL	25	75	21	2	0	2	(1	1)	29	5	8	8	11	4	18	0	0	0	1	0	1.00	1	.280	.372	.387
06	TB	AL	56	193	47	7	0	4	(3	1)	66	23	20	19	20	2	33	1	1	1	1	1	.50	6	.244	.316	.342
	Postseason		16	58	17	4	0	0	(0	0)	21	4	5	6	4	0	11	0	0	0	0	1	.00	2	.293	.339	.362
	7 ML YEARS		538	1766	439	84	2	34	(21	13)	629	189	180	166	148	12	259	13	25	12	10	9	.53	55	.249	.309	.356

Oswaldo Navarro

Bats: R **Throws:** R **Pos:** SS-10; PH-4; PR-2   ohz-WALL-doh   **Ht:** 6'0" **Wt:** 155 **Born:** 10/2/1984 **Age:** 26

Year	Team	Lg	G	AB	H	2B	3B	HR	(Hm	Rd)	TB	R	RBI	RC	TBB	IBB	SO	HBP	SH	SF	SB	CS	SB%	GDP	Avg	OBP	Slg
2003	Everett	A-	61	233	60	12	1	0	(-	-)	74	42	23	25	10	0	39	5	0	0	16	3	.84	4	.258	.302	.318
2004	Wisc	A	40	109	23	4	0	0	(-	-)	27	13	7	9	11	0	19	2	1	0	4	1	.80	4	.211	.295	.248
2004	Everett	A-	68	267	73	27	1	1	(-	-)	105	38	30	38	21	0	59	3	3	2	17	4	.81	3	.273	.331	.393
2005	Wisc	A	120	450	121	29	0	9	(-	-)	177	57	69	62	39	0	60	6	4	10	11	7	.61	9	.269	.329	.393
2006	SnAnt	AA	79	266	71	13	1	1	(-	-)	89	27	24	36	39	1	57	5	3	0	7	6	.54	5	.267	.371	.335
2006	Tacom	AAA	55	183	45	9	0	2	(-	-)	60	15	21	20	19	0	33	1	2	4	1	2	.33	6	.246	.314	.328
2007	Tacom	AAA	128	446	111	21	0	4	(-	-)	144	51	45	47	33	0	86	7	5	2	4	3	.57	12	.249	.309	.323
2008	Tacom	AAA	104	357	93	21	1	1	(-	-)	119	47	31	40	31	0	71	4	2	1	2	3	.40	16	.261	.326	.333
2009	WTenn	AA	63	190	49	6	1	1	(-	-)	60	23	13	26	33	1	44	3	4	0	4	2	.67	3	.258	.376	.316
2009	Tacom	AAA	48	159	40	7	0	0	(-	-)	47	13	12	15	8	0	34	3	4	1	4	1	.80	4	.252	.298	.296
2010	RdRck	AAA	81	288	78	24	1	6	(-	-)	122	41	37	46	34	0	67	8	1	2	3	3	.50	3	.271	.361	.424
2006	Sea	AL	4	3	2	0	0	0	(0	0)	2	0	0	1	0	0	1	0	1	0	0	0	-	0	.667	.667	.667
2010	Hou	NL	14	20	1	0	0	0	(0	0)	1	2	0	0	5	0	4	0	0	0	0	0	-	0	.050	.240	.050
	2 ML YEARS		18	23	3	0	0	0	(0	0)	3	2	0	1	5	0	5	0	1	0	0	0	-	0	.130	.286	.130

Yamaico Navarro

Bats: R **Throws:** R **Pos:** SS-15; 3B-4; PR-4; 2B-3; PH-1   yah-MY-koe   **Ht:** 5'11" **Wt:** 170 **Born:** 10/31/1987 **Age:** 23

Year	Team	Lg	G	AB	H	2B	3B	HR	(Hm	Rd)	TB	R	RBI	RC	TBB	IBB	SO	HBP	SH	SF	SB	CS	SB%	GDP	Avg	OBP	Slg
2007	Lowell	A-	62	225	65	10	1	5	(-	-)	92	36	37	34	22	0	52	3	1	2	12	6	.67	9	.289	.357	.409
2008	Grnville	A	83	325	91	14	4	7	(-	-)	134	46	54	47	29	0	73	3	0	4	3	2	.60	16	.280	.341	.412
2008	Lancst	A+	42	181	63	13	2	4	(-	-)	92	33	23	34	12	0	30	2	0	1	3	2	.60	2	.348	.393	.508
2009	Salem	A+	23	94	30	9	0	4	(-	-)	51	10	17	17	6	0	12	2	0	0	2	2	.50	6	.319	.373	.543
2009	Lowell	A-	5	21	5	1	0	0	(-	-)	6	1	2	1	2	0	3	0	0	0	0	2	.00	0	.238	.304	.286
2009	Portlnd	AA	39	135	25	6	2	2	(-	-)	41	10	11	12	14	0	20	2	0	1	6	1	.87	7	.185	.270	.304
2010	Portlnd	AA	88	329	90	19	3	8	(-	-)	139	49	55	54	42	0	53	3	1	3	16	5	.76	9	.274	.358	.422
2010	Pwtckt	AAA	16	53	15	4	0	3	(-	-)	28	8	6	9	5	0	6	0	0	1	2	1	.67	2	.283	.339	.528
2010	Bos	AL	20	42	6	0	0	0	(0	0)	6	4	5	1	2	1	17	0	0	2	0	0	-	0	.143	.174	.143

Chris Nelson

Bats: R **Throws:** R **Pos:** PH-9; 2B-4; 3B-4; PR-2   **Ht:** 5'11" **Wt:** 175 **Born:** 9/3/1985 **Age:** 25

Year	Team	Lg	G	AB	H	2B	3B	HR	(Hm	Rd)	TB	R	RBI	RC	TBB	IBB	SO	HBP	SH	SF	SB	CS	SB%	GDP	Avg	OBP	Slg
2004	Casper	R+	38	147	51	6	3	4	(-	-)	75	36	20	31	20	0	42	2	0	0	6	5	.55	2	.347	.432	.510
2005	Ashvll	A	79	315	76	13	3	3	(-	-)	104	51	38	33	25	0	88	5	0	4	7	4	.64	2	.241	.304	.330
2006	Ashvll	A	118	466	121	38	1	11	(-	-)	194	69	76	65	32	0	101	7	5	7	14	2	.88	9	.260	.313	.416
2007	Mdest	A+	133	529	153	42	7	19	(-	-)	266	97	99	101	55	2	92	7	0	9	27	5	.84	11	.289	.358	.503
2008	Tulsa	AA	73	283	67	18	2	3	(-	-)	98	38	42	36	35	1	69	4	2	5	6	1	.86	10	.237	.324	.346
2008	Mdest	A+	8	30	5	1	0	1	(-	-)	9	2	5	1	2	0	8	0	0	0	0	2	.00	0	.167	.219	.300
2009	Tulsa	AA	29	107	30	5	2	4	(-	-)	51	21	17	18	12	1	21	1	1	1	5	2	.71	1	.280	.355	.477
2010	ColSpr	AAA	85	319	100	15	3	12	(-	-)	157	60	55	59	29	1	53	4	2	2	7	3	.70	8	.313	.376	.492
2010	Col	NL	17	25	7	1	0	0	(0	0)	8	7	0	1	1	0	4	0	1	0	1	0	1.00	1	.280	.308	.320

Joe Nelson

Pitches: R Bats: R Pos: RP-8

Ht: 6'1" Wt: 205 Born: 10/25/1974 Age: 36

Year	Team	Lg	G	GS	CG	GF	IP	BFP	H	R	ER	HR	SH	SF	HB	TBB	IBB	SO	WP	Bk	W	L	Pct	Sh	Sv-Op	Hld	ERC	ERA
2010	Pwtckt*	AAA	16	0	0	3	21.2	93	18	7	6	1	1	0	1	14	1	21	1	0	3	2	.600	0	1--	-	3.92	2.49
2010	Tacom*	AAA	8	0	0	1	8.0	41	10	6	6	0	0	0	0	7	0	8	1	0	0	0	-	0	0--	-	6.48	6.75
2001	Atl	NL	2	0	0	0	2.0	16	7	9	8	1	0	1	1	2	0	0	0	0	0	0	-	0	0-0	0	33.03	36.00
2004	Bos	AL	3	0	0	1	2.2	17	4	5	5	0	1	0	2	3	0	5	0	0	0	0	-	0	0-0	0	12.43	16.88
2006	KC	AL	43	0	0	20	44.2	193	37	22	22	5	3	1	1	24	4	44	1	0	1	1	.500	0	9-10	5	3.67	4.43
2008	Fla	NL	59	0	0	20	54.0	230	42	16	12	5	2	0	2	22	4	60	3	0	3	1	.750	0	1-5	11	2.80	2.00
2009	TB	AL	42	0	0	13	40.1	182	32	22	18	7	2	2	1	27	1	36	3	1	3	0	1.000	0	3-4	7	4.44	4.02
2010	Bos	AL	8	0	0	4	8.1	45	14	9	9	2	0	0	0	6	0	6	0	0	0	0	-	0	0-0	0	10.90	9.72
	6 ML YEARS		157	0	0	58	152.0	683	136	83	74	20	8	4	7	84	9	154	7	1	7	2	.778	0	13-19	23	4.29	4.38

Pat Neshek

Pitches: R Bats: B Pos: RP-11

NEE-sheck

Ht: 6'3" Wt: 210 Born: 9/4/1980 Age: 30

Year	Team	Lg	G	GS	CG	GF	IP	BFP	H	R	ER	HR	SH	SF	HB	TBB	IBB	SO	WP	Bk	W	L	Pct	Sh	Sv-Op	Hld	ERC	ERA
2010	FtMyrs*	A+	2	0	0	0	2.0	11	3	3	3	0	0	0	0	2	0	2	0	0	0	0	-	0	0--	-	8.58	13.50
2010	Roch*	AAA	30	0	0	9	39.1	170	40	21	17	4	2	4	3	13	6	25	0	0	5	1	.833	0	1--	-	3.97	3.89
2006	Min	AL	32	0	0	3	37.0	138	23	9	9	6	0	1	0	6	0	53	0	0	4	2	.667	0	0-2	10	1.68	2.19
2007	Min	AL	74	0	0	20	70.1	278	44	25	23	7	4	5	2	27	5	74	2	0	7	2	.778	0	0-3	15	2.12	2.94
2008	Min	AL	15	0	0	3	13.1	56	12	7	7	2	1	1	0	4	1	15	0	0	0	1	.000	0	0-2	6	3.29	4.73
2010	Min	AL	11	0	0	3	9.0	43	7	5	5	1	0	0	1	8	0	9	0	0	0	1	.000	0	0-1	1	5.13	5.00
	Postseason		2	0	0	1	1.0	4	1	1	1	0	0	0	0	0	0	1	0	0	0	1	.000	0	0-0	0	1.95	9.00
	4 ML YEARS		132	0	0	29	129.2	515	86	46	44	16	5	7	3	45	6	151	2	0	11	6	.647	0	0-8	32	2.31	3.05

Fu-Te Ni

Pitches: L Bats: L Pos: RP-22

FOO TAY NEE

Ht: 6'0" Wt: 172 Born: 11/14/1982 Age: 28

Year	Team	Lg	G	GS	CG	GF	IP	BFP	H	R	ER	HR	SH	SF	HB	TBB	IBB	SO	WP	Bk	W	L	Pct	Sh	Sv-Op	Hld	ERC	ERA
2009	Toledo	AAA	24	0	0	10	34.2	139	31	10	10	4	0	1	0	9	0	32	2	0	3	0	1.000	0	0--	-	3.13	2.60
2010	Toledo	AAA	12	0	0	5	12.0	60	18	10	10	3	0	0	0	8	0	16	1	1	0	0	-	0	0--	-	9.81	7.50
2009	Det	AL	36	0	0	9	31.0	121	20	9	9	3	1	1	1	11	2	21	2	0	0	0	-	0	0-2	3	2.15	2.61
2010	Det	AL	22	0	0	5	23.0	116	27	19	17	2	1	1	2	19	4	22	2	1	0	1	.000	0	0-0	1	6.66	6.65
	2 ML YEARS		58	0	0	14	54.0	237	47	28	26	5	2	2	3	30	6	43	4	1	0	1	.000	0	0-2	4	3.93	4.33

Mike Nickeas

Bats: R Throws: R Pos: C-4; PH-1

NICK-ee-us

Ht: 6'0" Wt: 220 Born: 2/13/1983 Age: 28

Year	Team	Lg	G	AB	H	2B	3B	HR	(Hm	Rd)	TB	R	RBI	RC	TBB	IBB	SO	HBP	SH	SF	SB	CS	SB%	GDP	Avg	OBP	Slg
2004	Spkane	A-	62	233	67	18	0	10	(-	-)	115	42	55	46	33	0	53	4	2	1	2	0	1.00	4	.288	.384	.494
2005	Frisco	AA	68	242	49	7	1	5	(-	-)	73	22	24	19	20	0	43	1	2	3	1	1	.50	6	.202	.263	.302
2005	Rngrs	R	6	21	6	1	0	1	(-	-)	10	2	6	4	3	0	4	1	0	0	0	0	-	1	.286	.400	.476
2006	Bkrsfld	A+	17	64	19	4	0	0	(-	-)	23	6	6	10	6	0	17	5	0	1	0	0	-	1	.297	.395	.359
2006	Frisco	AA	39	113	28	7	0	2	(-	-)	41	15	15	18	21	0	22	6	3	4	1	1	.50	3	.248	.382	.363
2006	Bnghtn	AA	4	12	2	0	0	0	(-	-)	2	1	3	0	1	0	4	1	0	1	0	0	-	0	.167	.267	.167
2007	Bnghtn	AA	65	212	46	10	0	1	(-	-)	59	26	15	16	18	0	37	2	2	3	2	3	.40	12	.217	.281	.278
2007	StLuci	A+	26	77	16	7	0	0	(-	-)	23	6	4	11	17	1	20	4	0	0	0	0	-	0	.208	.378	.299
2008	NewOr	AAA	54	163	35	9	0	2	(-	-)	50	16	17	14	14	1	42	1	2	4	0	1	.00	7	.215	.275	.307
2008	Bnghtn	AA	17	51	10	1	0	1	(-	-)	14	2	4	7	7	1	7	0	0	1	0	0	-	3	.196	.288	.275
2009	Bnghtn	AA	18	55	10	1	0	0	(-	-)	11	3	7	3	9	0	9	0	2	1	0	0	-	3	.182	.292	.200
2009	Buffalo	AAA	2	6	0	0	0	0	(-	-)	0	0	0	0	1	0	3	0	0	0	0	0	-	0	.000	.143	.000
2010	Bnghtn	AA	82	265	75	15	0	5	(-	-)	105	27	33	46	49	0	43	4	0	0	1	1	.50	8	.283	.403	.396
2010	Buffalo	AAA	7	28	6	1	0	0	(-	-)	7	1	0	1	1	0	7	0	0	0	0	0	-	0	.214	.241	.250
2010	NYM	NL	5	10	2	0	0	0	(0	0)	2	0	0	0	0	0	5	0	0	0	0	0	-	1	.200	.200	.200

Jeff Niemann

Pitches: R Bats: R Pos: SP-29; RP-1

NEE-min

Ht: 6'9" Wt: 260 Born: 2/28/1983 Age: 28

Year	Team	Lg	G	GS	CG	GF	IP	BFP	H	R	ER	HR	SH	SF	HB	TBB	IBB	SO	WP	Bk	W	L	Pct	Sh	Sv-Op	Hld	ERC	ERA
2008	TB	AL	5	2	0	2	16.0	76	18	12	9	3	2	0	1	8	0	14	0	0	2	2	.500	0	0-0	0	5.93	5.06
2009	TB	AL	31	30	2	1	180.2	769	185	84	79	17	2	4	9	59	1	125	6	0	13	6	.684	2	0-0	0	4.12	3.94
2010	TB	AL	30	29	1	0	174.1	733	159	86	85	25	5	2	7	61	6	131	4	0	12	8	.600	1	0-0	0	3.81	4.39
	3 ML YEARS		66	61	3	3	371.0	1578	362	182	173	45	9	6	17	128	7	270	10	0	27	16	.628	3	0-0	0	4.05	4.20

Jonathon Niese

Pitches: L Bats: L Pos: SP-30

NEESS

Ht: 6'4" Wt: 215 Born: 10/27/1986 Age: 24

Year	Team	Lg	G	GS	CG	GF	IP	BFP	H	R	ER	HR	SH	SF	HB	TBB	IBB	SO	WP	Bk	W	L	Pct	Sh	Sv-Op	Hld	ERC	ERA
2010	Buffalo*	AAA	1	1	0	0	6.0	25	8	2	2	1	1	0	0	0	0	3	0	0	0	0	-	0	0--	-	4.90	3.00
2008	NYM	NL	3	3	0	0	14.0	69	20	11	11	2	1	0	0	8	0	11	0	0	1	1	.500	0	0-0	0	7.71	7.07
2009	NYM	NL	5	5	0	0	25.2	110	27	12	12	1	2	1	0	9	0	18	1	0	1	1	.500	0	0-0	0	3.76	4.21
2010	NYM	NL	30	30	2	0	173.2	770	192	97	81	20	9	4	9	62	3	148	5	0	9	10	.474	1	0-0	0	4.77	4.20
	3 ML YEARS		38	38	2	0	213.1	949	239	120	104	23	12	5	9	79	3	177	6	0	11	12	.478	1	0-0	0	4.83	4.39

Fernando Nieve

Pitches: R **Bats:** R **Pos:** RP-39; SP-1   **Ht:** 6'0" **Wt:** 214 **Born:** 7/15/1982 **Age:** 28

			HOW MUCH HE PITCHED						WHAT HE GAVE UP									THE RESULTS						
Year	Team	Lg	G	GS	CG	GF	IP	BFP	H	R	ER	HR	SH	SF	HB	TBB	IBB	SO	WP	Bk	W	L	Pct	Sh	Sv-Op	Hld	ERC	ERA
2010	Buffalo*	AAA	8	8	0	0	40.0	177	49	25	25	3	1	1		13	0	31	1	0	2	1	.667	0	0- -		5.04	5.63
2006	Hou	NL	40	11	0	11	96.1	411	87	46	45	18	5	3	2	41	5	70	1	0	3	3	.500	0	0-0	0	4.24	4.20
2008	Hou	NL	11	0	0	1	10.2	49	17	10	10	2	0	0	0	2	0	12	0	0	0	1	.000	0	0-1	0	7.62	8.44
2009	NYM	NL	8	7	0	1	36.2	161	36	13	12	4	3	1	1	19	1	23	2	0	3	3	.500	0	0-0	0	4.62	2.95
2010	NYM	NL	40	1	0	9	42.0	185	37	28	28	10	1	1	2	22	2	38	2	0	2	4	.333	0	0-2	6	4.96	6.00
	4 ML YEARS		99	19	0	22	185.2	806	177	97	95	34	9	5	5	84	8	143	5	0	8	11	.421	0	0-3	6	4.66	4.61

Wil Nieves

Bats: R **Throws:** R **Pos:** C-51; PH-9   **Ht:** 5'10" **Wt:** 182 **Born:** 9/25/1977 **Age:** 33

						BATTING															BASERUNNING				AVERAGES		
Year	Team	Lg	G	AB	H	2B	3B	HR	(Hm	Rd)	TB	R	RBI	RC	TBB	IBB	SO	HBP	SH	SF	SB	CS	SB%	GDP	Avg	OBP	Slg
2002	SD	NL	28	72	13	3	1	0	(0	0)	18	2	3	4	4	4	15	0	0	0	1	0	1.00	1	.181	.224	.250
2005	NYY	AL	3	4	0	0	0	0	(0	0)	0	0	0	0	0	0	1	0	0	0	0	0	-	0	.000	.000	.000
2006	NYY	AL	6	6	0	0	0	0	(0	0)	0	0	0	0	0	0	1	0	0	0	0	0	-	0	.000	.000	.000
2007	NYY	AL	26	61	10	4	0	0	(0	0)	14	6	8	4	2	0	9	0	3	0	0	0	-	3	.164	.190	.230
2008	Was	NL	68	176	46	9	1	1	(1	0)	60	15	20	20	13	1	29	0	5	2	0	1	.00	7	.261	.309	.341
2009	Was	NL	72	224	58	6	0	1	(0	1)	67	20	26	21	17	1	45	3	0	5	1	0	1.00	7	.259	.313	.299
2010	Was	NL	59	158	32	8	0	3	(1	2)	49	10	16	9	8	2	29	1	4	1	0	0	-	6	.203	.244	.310
	7 ML YEARS		262	701	159	30	2	5	(2	3)	208	53	73	58	44	8	129	4	12	8	2	1	.67	24	.227	.273	.297

Dustin Nippert

Pitches: R **Bats:** R **Pos:** RP-36; SP-2   **Ht:** 6'8" **Wt:** 225 **Born:** 5/6/1981 **Age:** 30

			HOW MUCH HE PITCHED						WHAT HE GAVE UP									THE RESULTS						
Year	Team	Lg	G	GS	CG	GF	IP	BFP	H	R	ER	HR	SH	SF	HB	TBB	IBB	SO	WP	Bk	W	L	Pct	Sh	Sv-Op	Hld	ERC	ERA
2010	Frisco*	AA	2	2	0	0	3.1	12	1	0	0	0	0	0	1	1	0	7	0	0	0	0	-	0	0- -		0.57	0.00
2010	OKCity*	AAA	1	1	0	0	3.0	9	1	0	0	0	0	0	0	0	0	3	0	0	0	0	-	0	0- -		0.28	0.00
2005	Ari	NL	3	3	0	0	14.2	68	10	9	9	1	0	0	1	13	0	11	1	0	1	0	1.000	0	0-0	0	4.09	5.52
2006	Ari	NL	2	2	0	0	10.0	51	15	13	13	5	1	0	0	7	0	9	0	0	0	2	.000	0	0-0	0	12.21	11.70
2007	Ari	NL	20	6	0	6	45.1	196	48	30	28	5	0	0	0	16	1	38	4	0	1	1	.500	0	0-0	0	4.25	5.56
2008	Tex	AL	20	6	0	6	71.2	341	92	52	51	10	3	1	1	37	3	55	1	1	3	5	.375	0	0-0	0	6.47	6.40
2009	Tex	AL	20	10	0	3	69.2	300	64	31	30	7	1	5	4	29	0	54	2	0	5	3	.625	0	0-0	1	3.91	3.88
2010	Tex	AL	38	2	0	7	56.2	262	61	28	27	7	2	1	5	34	3	47	3	0	4	5	.444	0	0-1	5	5.83	4.29
	Postseason		2	0	0	1	2.1		1	0	0	0	0	0	0	0	0	2	0	0	0	0	-	0	0-0	0	0.40	0.00
	6 ML YEARS		119	23	0	24	268.0	1218	290	163	158	35	7	7	11	136	7	214	11	1	14	16	.467	0	0-1	8	5.32	5.31

Jayson Nix

Bats: R **Throws:** R **Pos:** 3B-56; 2B-28; DH-9; PH-7; PR-3; SS-2; LF-2; RF-1   **Ht:** 5'11" **Wt:** 195 **Born:** 8/26/1982 **Age:** 28

						BATTING															BASERUNNING				AVERAGES		
Year	Team	Lg	G	AB	H	2B	3B	HR	(Hm	Rd)	TB	R	RBI	RC	TBB	IBB	SO	HBP	SH	SF	SB	CS	SB%	GDP	Avg	OBP	Slg
2008	Col	NL	22	56	7	2	0	0	(0	0)	9	2	2	0	7	2	17	1	1	0	1	0	1.00	1	.125	.234	.161
2009	CWS	AL	94	255	57	11	0	12	(4	8)	104	36	32	31	28	1	64	4	1	2	10	2	.83	5	.224	.308	.408
2010	2 Tms	AL	102	331	74	15	0	14	(7	7)	131	32	34	35	20	2	87	7	3	2	1	2	.33	6	.224	.281	.396
10	CWS	AL	24	49	8	1	0	1	(0	1)	12	3	5	4	7	2	12	0	1	0	0	0	-	1	.163	.268	.245
10	Cle	AL	78	282	66	14	0	13	(7	6)	119	29	29	31	13	0	75	7	2	2	1	2	.33	5	.234	.283	.422
	3 ML YEARS		218	642	138	28	0	26	(11	15)	244	70	68	66	55	5	168	12	5	4	12	4	.75	12	.215	.288	.380

Laynce Nix

Bats: L **Throws:** L **Pos:** LF-50; PH-49; CF-5; RF-4   LANCE   **Ht:** 6'1" **Wt:** 220 **Born:** 10/30/1980 **Age:** 30

						BATTING															BASERUNNING				AVERAGES		
Year	Team	Lg	G	AB	H	2B	3B	HR	(Hm	Rd)	TB	R	RBI	RC	TBB	IBB	SO	HBP	SH	SF	SB	CS	SB%	GDP	Avg	OBP	Slg
2003	Tex	AL	53	184	47	10	4	8	(7	1)	81	25	30	25	9	0	53	0	1	1	3	0	1.00	1	.255	.289	.440
2004	Tex	AL	115	371	92	20	4	14	(9	5)	162	58	46	44	23	4	113	2	1	3	1	1	.50	6	.248	.293	.437
2005	Tex	AL	63	229	55	12	3	6	(3	3)	91	28	32	26	9	3	45	0	0	2	2	0	1.00	3	.240	.267	.397
2006	2 Tms		19	67	11	2	0	1	(1	0)	16	3	10	3	0	0	28	2	0	1	0	0	-	1	.164	.186	.239
2007	Mil	NL	10	12	0	0	0	0	(0	0)	0	0	0	0	0	0	4	0	0	0	0	0	-	0	.000	.000	.000
2008	Mil	NL	10	12	1	0	0	0	(0	0)	1	1	0	1	0	0	3	0	0	0	0	0	-	0	.083	.154	.083
2009	Cin	NL	116	309	74	26	1	15	(5	10)	147	42	46	35	22	3	81	2	0	4	0	1	.00	5	.239	.291	.476
2010	Cin	NL	97	165	48	11	2	4	(1	3)	75	16	18	21	15	4	39	0	2	0	0	1	.00	5	.291	.350	.455
06	Tex	AL	9	32	3	1	0	0	(0	0)	4	1	4	0	0	0	17	1	0	1	0	0	-	0	.094	.118	.125
06	Mil	NL	10	35	8	1	0	1	(1	0)	12	2	6	3	0	0	11	1	0	0	0	0	-	1	.229	.250	.343
	8 ML YEARS		483	1349	328	81	10	48	(26	22)	573	173	182	154	79	14	366	6	4	11	6	3	.67	21	.243	.286	.425

Ricky Nolasco

Pitches: R **Bats:** R **Pos:** SP-26   **Ht:** 6'2" **Wt:** 230 **Born:** 12/13/1982 **Age:** 28

			HOW MUCH HE PITCHED						WHAT HE GAVE UP									THE RESULTS						
Year	Team	Lg	G	GS	CG	GF	IP	BFP	H	R	ER	HR	SH	SF	HB	TBB	IBB	SO	WP	Bk	W	L	Pct	Sh	Sv-Op	Hld	ERC	ERA
2006	Fla	NL	35	22	0	0	140.0	613	157	86	75	20	8	6	10	41	5	99	7	0	11	11	.500	0	0-0	2	4.89	4.82
2007	Fla	NL	5	4	0	0	21.1	99	26	16	13	3	3	5	1	9	2	11	1	0	1	2	.333	0	0-0	0	5.71	5.48
2008	Fla	NL	34	32	1	0	212.1	868	192	88	83	28	6	9	6	42	6	186	1	3	15	8	.652	1	0-0	0	3.03	3.52
2009	Fla	NL	31	31	2	0	185.0	785	188	111	104	23	8	5	2	44	7	195	2	0	13	9	.591	0	0-0	0	3.62	5.06
2010	Fla	NL	26	26	1	0	157.2	665	169	82	79	24	5	5	2	33	1	147	5	0	14	9	.609	0	0-0	0	4.11	4.51
	5 ML YEARS		131	115	4	0	716.1	3030	732	383	354	98	30	30	21	169	21	638	16	3	54	39	.581	1	0-0	2	3.84	4.45

Jordan Norberto

Pitches: L **Bats:** L **Pos:** RP-33   **Ht:** 6'0" **Wt:** 195 **Born:** 12/8/1986 **Age:** 24

			HOW MUCH HE PITCHED						WHAT HE GAVE UP											THE RESULTS							
Year	Team	Lg	G	GS	CG	GF	IP	BFP	H	R	ER	HR	SH	SF	HB	TBB	IBB	SO	WP	Bk	W	L	Pct	Sh	Sv-Op Hld	ERC	ERA
2006	Msoula	R+	16	16	0	0	75.2	326	59	30	26	4	8	1	4	40	0	64	6	3	3	2	.600	0	0- - -	3.21	3.09
2007	Sbend	A	21	21	0	0	102.1	443	102	67	60	10	2	9	2	46	0	111	6	0	6	7	.462	0	0- - -	4.36	5.28
2008	Sbend	A	31	18	0	3	101.2	460	108	72	60	15	2	6	5	56	1	109	4	6	5	7	.417	0	0- - -	5.65	5.31
2009	Visalia	A+	29	0	0	8	44.2	185	36	9	8	1	2	1	0	22	1	59	4	0	4	1	.800	0	2- - -	2.88	1.61
2009	Mobile	AA	19	0	0	11	23.2	119	29	23	21	4	0	3	2	18	0	30	8	0	0	2	.000	0	2- - -	7.80	7.99
2010	Reno	AAA	21	0	0	7	29.1	131	25	12	10	2	2	0	0	19	1	38	5	1	3	0	1.000	0	4- - -	3.86	3.07
2010	Ari	NL	33	0	0	5	20.0	94	16	13	13	3	1	0	0	22	1	15	2	0	0	2	.000	0	0-1 3	6.16	5.85

Bud Norris

Pitches: R **Bats:** R **Pos:** SP-27   **Ht:** 6'0" **Wt:** 228 **Born:** 3/2/1985 **Age:** 26

			HOW MUCH HE PITCHED						WHAT HE GAVE UP											THE RESULTS							
Year	Team	Lg	G	GS	CG	GF	IP	BFP	H	R	ER	HR	SH	SF	HB	TBB	IBB	SO	WP	Bk	W	L	Pct	Sh	Sv-Op Hld	ERC	ERA
2006	TriCity	A-	15	3	0	6	38.0	161	28	20	16	1	3	1	4	13	0	46	1	0	2	0	1.000	0	2- - -	2.30	3.79
2007	Lxngtn	A	22	22	0	0	96.2	416	85	58	51	8	2	2	6	41	0	117	6	0	2	8	.200	0	0- - -	3.60	4.75
2007	Salem	A+	1	1	0	0	6.0	22	4	1	1	0	0	0	0	1	0	2	0	0	1	0	1.000	0	0- - -	1.29	1.50
2008	CpChr	AA	19	19	0	0	80.0	352	89	42	36	8	2	1	7	31	0	84	1	3	3	8	.273	0	0- - -	5.13	4.05
2009	RdRck	AAA	19	19	0	0	120.0	509	104	42	35	6	11	3	4	53	4	112	4	0	4	9	.308	0	0- - -	3.25	2.63
2010	RdRck	AAA	3	3	0	0	14.2	64	16	5	5	1	0	1	0	6	0	14	1	0	1	0	1.000	0	0- - -	4.43	3.07
2009	Hou	NL	11	10	0	0	55.2	249	59	29	28	9	1	3	3	25	1	54	3	0	6	3	.667	0	0-0	5.26	4.53
2010	Hou	NL	27	27	0	0	153.2	683	151	94	84	18	6	4	6	77	3	158	5	2	9	10	.474	0	0-0	4.61	4.92
	2 ML YEARS		38	37	0	0	209.1	932	210	123	112	27	7	7	9	102	4	212	8	2	15	13	.536	0	0-0	4.78	4.82

Ivan Nova

Pitches: R **Bats:** R **Pos:** SP-7; RP-3   **Ht:** 6'4" **Wt:** 210 **Born:** 1/12/1987 **Age:** 24

			HOW MUCH HE PITCHED						WHAT HE GAVE UP											THE RESULTS							
Year	Team	Lg	G	GS	CG	GF	IP	BFP	H	R	ER	HR	SH	SF	HB	TBB	IBB	SO	WP	Bk	W	L	Pct	Sh	Sv-Op Hld	ERC	ERA
2006	Yanks	R	10	5	0	2	43.0	167	36	13	13	5	0	0	3	7	0	36	3	0	3	0	1.000	0	1- - -	2.79	2.72
2007	CtnSC	A	21	21	0	0	99.1	440	121	64	55	8	4	3	6	31	0	54	4	0	6	8	.429	0	0- - -	5.15	4.98
2008	Tampa	A+	26	24	0	1	148.2	637	168	81	72	6	6	4	9	46	2	109	12	1	8	13	.381	0	0- - -	4.36	4.36
2009	Trntn	AA	12	12	0	0	72.1	305	65	27	19	3	3	3	2	31	0	47	5	3	5	4	.556	0	0- - -	3.37	2.36
2009	S-WB	AAA	12	12	1	0	67.0	292	72	39	38	4	2	6	3	28	0	43	4	0	1	4	.200	0	0- - -	4.54	5.10
2010	S-WB	AAA	23	23	0	0	145.0	595	135	50	46	10	3	3	2	48	1	115	4	1	12	3	.800	0	0- - -	3.35	2.86
2010	NYY	AL	10	7	0	3	42.0	185	44	22	21	4	1	1	1	17	2	26	2	0	1	2	.333	0	0-1	4.31	4.50

Eduardo Nunez

Bats: R **Throws:** R **Pos:** 3B-15; SS-11; PR-8; DH-4; 2B-1   **Ht:** 6'0" **Wt:** 155 **Born:** 6/15/1987 **Age:** 24

			BATTING																	BASERUNNING				AVERAGES		
Year	Team	Lg	G	AB	H	2B	3B	HR	(Hm	Rd)	TB	R	RBI	RC	TBB	IBB	SO	HBP	SH	SF	SB	CS	SB%	GDP	Avg	OBP	Slg
2005	StIsInd	A-	73	281	88	11	6	3	(-	-)	120	37	46	44	20	1	43	3	6	0	6	3	.67	2	.313	.365	.427
2006	Tampa	A+	37	147	27	5	3	4	(-	-)	50	17	26	12	8	0	28	0	4	2	6	1	.86	3	.184	.223	.340
2006	CtnSC	A	90	344	78	11	3	2	(-	-)	101	36	40	30	23	1	48	2	0	2	16	5	.76	6	.227	.278	.294
2007	CtnSC	A	91	328	78	10	2	1	(-	-)	95	36	28	30	25	0	42	2	2	3	20	8	.71	16	.238	.293	.290
2007	Tampa	A+	30	123	35	5	0	1	(-	-)	43	16	13	17	7	0	18	3	0	1	9	0	1.00	1	.285	.336	.350
2008	Tampa	A+	94	373	101	18	3	6	(-	-)	143	45	42	44	19	1	48	1	5	4	14	10	.58	9	.271	.305	.383
2009	Trntn	AA	123	497	160	26	1	9	(-	-)	215	70	55	77	22	3	63	1	4	4	19	7	.73	19	.322	.349	.433
2010	S-WB	AAA	118	464	134	25	3	4	(-	-)	177	55	50	65	32	1	60	5	3	2	23	5	.82	10	.289	.340	.381
2010	NYY	AL	30	50	14	1	0	1	(0	1)	18	12	7	8	3	0	2	0	0	0	5	0	1.00	4	.280	.321	.360

Leo Nunez

Pitches: R **Bats:** R **Pos:** RP-68   **Ht:** 6'2" **Wt:** 190 **Born:** 8/14/1983 **Age:** 27

			HOW MUCH HE PITCHED						WHAT HE GAVE UP											THE RESULTS							
Year	Team	Lg	G	GS	CG	GF	IP	BFP	H	R	ER	HR	SH	SF	HB	TBB	IBB	SO	WP	Bk	W	L	Pct	Sh	Sv-Op Hld	ERC	ERA
2005	KC	AL	41	0	0	10	53.2	246	73	45	45	9	1	2	3	18	2	32	1	0	3	2	.600	0	0-1 2	6.76	7.55
2006	KC	AL	7	0	0	5	13.1	58	15	7	7	2	0	1	2	5	0	7	0	0	0	0	-	0	0-0 0	5.98	4.73
2007	KC	AL	13	6	0	2	43.2	182	44	21	19	8	0	2	0	10	0	37	1	0	2	4	.333	0	0-0 1	3.98	3.92
2008	KC	AL	45	0	0	12	48.1	205	45	19	16	2	3	2	4	15	2	26	3	0	4	1	.800	0	0-3 7	3.20	2.98
2009	Fla	NL	75	0	0	41	68.2	293	59	33	31	13	4	2	4	27	5	60	1	1	4	6	.400	0	26-33 14	3.96	4.06
2010	Fla	NL	68	0	0	50	65.0	270	62	27	25	5	1	0	0	21	2	71	1	1	4	3	.571	0	30-38 5	3.36	3.46
	6 ML YEARS		249	6	0	120	292.2	1254	298	152	143	39	9	9	13	96	11	233	7	2	17	16	.515	0	56-75 29	4.26	4.40

Darren O'Day

Pitches: R **Bats:** R **Pos:** RP-72   **Ht:** 6'4" **Wt:** 220 **Born:** 10/22/1982 **Age:** 28

			HOW MUCH HE PITCHED						WHAT HE GAVE UP											THE RESULTS							
Year	Team	Lg	G	GS	CG	GF	IP	BFP	H	R	ER	HR	SH	SF	HB	TBB	IBB	SO	WP	Bk	W	L	Pct	Sh	Sv-Op Hld	ERC	ERA
2008	LAA	AL	30	0	0	17	43.1	194	49	24	22	2	2	1	4	14	6	29	1	0	0	1	.000	0	0-0 1	4.20	4.57
2009	2 Tms		68	0	0	15	58.2	233	41	14	12	3	1	3	5	18	1	56	1	0	2	1	.667	0	2-2 20	2.20	1.84
2010	Tex	AL	72	0	0	14	62.0	240	43	15	14	5	1	3	5	12	2	45	0	0	6	2	.750	0	0-2 22	1.93	2.03
	09 NYM	NL	4	0	0	1	3.0	17	5	2	0	0	0	1	1	1	0	2	0	0	0	0	-	0	0-0 0	7.72	0.00
	09 Tex	AL	64	0	0	14	55.2	216	36	12	12	3	1	2	4	17	1	54	1	0	2	1	.667	0	2-2 20	1.95	1.94
	3 ML YEARS		170	0	0	46	164.0	667	133	53	48	10	4	7	14	44	9	130	2	0	8	4	.667	0	2-4 43	2.59	2.63

Trent Oeltjen

Bats: L **Throws:** L **Pos:** PH-6; LF-5; CF-4; PR-1   OLT-jenn   **Ht:** 6'1" **Wt:** 190 **Born:** 2/28/1983 **Age:** 28

								BATTING (Hm Rd)												BASERUNNING				AVERAGES		
Year Team	Lg	G	AB	H	2B	3B	HR	Hm	Rd	TB	R	RBI	RC	TBB	IBB	SO	HBP	SH	SF	SB	CS	SB%	GDP	Avg	OBP	Slg
2001 Twins	R	45	134	43	7	3	0	-	-	56	21	18	24	14	0	16	3	2	4	10	3	.77	2	.321	.387	.418
2001 Elizab	R+	9	30	7	1	0	0	-	-	8	4	4	2	0	0	6	0	1	1	2	0	1.00	0	.233	.226	.267
2002 Elizab	R+	54	215	64	7	2	3	-	-	84	36	18	32	16	0	34	7	3	2	7	5	.58	0	.298	.363	.391
2002 QuadC	A	10	25	6	1	0	0	-	-	7	4	1	2	3	0	2	0	1	0	1	0	1.00	1	.240	.321	.280
2003 QuadC	A	123	466	139	12	8	4	-	-	179	73	44	72	37	1	57	20	4	5	29	14	.67	3	.298	.371	.384
2004 FtMyrs	A+	90	324	90	8	5	2	-	-	114	45	28	42	18	2	61	12	4	2	25	8	.76	6	.278	.337	.352
2005 FtMyrs	A+	98	341	98	17	4	4	-	-	135	44	43	54	26	0	77	20	5	3	21	9	.70	3	.287	.369	.396
2006 NwBrit	AA	113	401	120	16	10	3	-	-	165	61	44	67	36	1	58	16	9	2	24	11	.69	3	.299	.378	.411
2007 Roch	AAA	97	244	58	9	5	2	-	-	83	33	23	26	10	1	44	13	4	0	14	7	.67	4	.238	.303	.340
2008 Tucsn	AAA	127	442	140	28	10	6	-	-	206	75	60	76	24	1	68	10	4	11	15	7	.68	6	.317	.357	.466
2009 Reno	AAA	114	442	134	29	14	10	-	-	221	78	64	81	31	3	101	10	4	1	22	8	.73	6	.303	.362	.500
2010 Nashv	AAA	70	266	79	23	2	8	-	-	130	47	38	48	21	2	59	3	4	3	13	2	.87	5	.297	.352	.489
2010 Albq	AAA	49	199	69	18	5	5	-	-	112	40	33	46	23	2	43	2	0	2	14	5	.74	1	.347	.416	.563
2009 Ari	NL	24	70	17	4	1	3	1	2	32	11	4	4	1	0	13	0	1	1	3	1	.75	0	.243	.250	.457
2010 LAD	NL	15	23	5	1	1	0	0	0	8	5	1	2	4	0	8	1	2	0	0	0	-	1	.217	.357	.348
2 ML YEARS		39	93	22	5	2	3	1	2	40	16	5	6	5	0	21	1	3	1	3	1	.75	1	.237	.280	.430

Eric O'Flaherty

Pitches: L **Bats:** L **Pos:** RP-56   **Ht:** 6'2" **Wt:** 220 **Born:** 2/5/1985 **Age:** 26

					HOW MUCH HE PITCHED			WHAT HE GAVE UP											THE RESULTS						
Year Team	Lg	G	GS	CG	GF	IP	BFP	H	R	ER	HR	SH	SF	HB	TBB	IBB	SO	WP	Bk	W	L	Pct	Sh	Sv-Op	Hld	ERC	ERA
2010 Gwnntt*	AAA	3	0	0	0	4.0	14	1	0	0	0	0	0	0	1	0	5	0	0	0	0	-	0	0--		0.40	0.00
2006 Sea	AL	15	0	0	5	11.0	57	18	9	5	2	1	0	0	6	3	6	2	0	0	0	-	0	0-0	1	8.63	4.09
2007 Sea	AL	56	0	0	9	52.1	221	45	26	26	1	0	2	5	20	1	36	4	1	7	1	.875	0	0-1	4	3.04	4.47
2008 Sea	AL	7	0	0	1	6.2	42	16	15	15	2	0	1	2	4	2	4	0	0	0	0	1.000	0	0-0	2	17.12	20.25
2009 Atl	NL	78	0	0	8	56.1	236	52	23	19	2	1	1	6	18	4	39	2	0	2	1	.667	0	0-2	15	3.26	3.04
2010 Atl	NL	56	0	0	7	44.0	181	37	14	12	2	1	0	1	18	2	36	3	0	3	2	.600	0	0-1	9	2.97	2.45
5 ML YEARS		212	0	0	30	170.1	737	168	87	77	9	3	4	14	66	12	121	11	1	12	5	.706	0	0-4	31	3.84	4.07

Alexi Ogando

Pitches: R **Bats:** R **Pos:** RP-44   oh-GONE-doh   **Ht:** 6'4" **Wt:** 185 **Born:** 10/5/1983 **Age:** 27

					HOW MUCH HE PITCHED			WHAT HE GAVE UP											THE RESULTS						
Year Team	Lg	G	GS	CG	GF	IP	BFP	H	R	ER	HR	SH	SF	HB	TBB	IBB	SO	WP	Bk	W	L	Pct	Sh	Sv-Op	Hld	ERC	ERA
2010 Frisco	AA	7	3	0	1	15.2	56	4	2	2	1	0	0	0	5	0	21	0	0	0	0	-	0	0--		0.67	1.15
2010 OKCity	AAA	11	0	0	4	15.0	63	10	7	5	0	0	0	0	6	1	21	0	0	0	0	-	0	1--		1.60	3.00
2010 Tex	AL	44	0	0	12	41.2	171	31	6	6	2	3	2	1	16	2	39	3	0	4	1	.800	0	0-2	7	2.34	1.30

Ross Ohlendorf

Pitches: R **Bats:** R **Pos:** SP-21   OH-lenn-dorf   **Ht:** 6'4" **Wt:** 245 **Born:** 8/8/1982 **Age:** 28

					HOW MUCH HE PITCHED			WHAT HE GAVE UP											THE RESULTS						
Year Team	Lg	G	GS	CG	GF	IP	BFP	H	R	ER	HR	SH	SF	HB	TBB	IBB	SO	WP	Bk	W	L	Pct	Sh	Sv-Op	Hld	ERC	ERA
2010 Altna*	AA	1	1	0	0	4.0	16	3	0	0	0	0	0	0	6	0	0	0	0	0	0	-	0	0--		1.65	0.00
2007 NYY	AL	6	0	0	3	6.1	26	5	2	2	1	0	0	0	2	0	9	0	0	0	0	-	0	0-0	1	2.94	2.84
2008 2 Tms		30	5	0	3	62.2	300	86	49	45	10	1	1	1	33	3	49	10	1	1	4	.200	0	0-0	4	7.16	6.46
2009 Pit	NL	29	29	0	0	176.2	725	165	80	77	25	11	8	7	53	1	109	2	1	11	10	.524	0	0-0	0	3.84	3.92
2010 Pit	NL	21	21	0	0	108.1	475	106	54	49	12	9	8	6	44	2	79	5	0	1	11	.083	0	0-0	0	4.20	4.07
08 NYY	AL	25	0	0	3	40.0	187	50	31	29	7	0	1	0	19	3	36	6	0	1	1	.500	0	0-0	4	6.39	6.53
08 Pit	NL	5	5	0	0	22.2	113	36	18	16	3	1	1	0	12	0	13	4	1	0	3	.000	0	0-0	0	8.59	6.35
Postseason		1	0	0	0	1.0	9	4	3	3	1	0	0	1	1	0	0	0	0	0	0	-	0	0-0	0	47.63	27.00
4 ML YEARS		86	55	0	6	354.0	1526	362	185	173	48	21	17	14	130	6	246	17	2	13	25	.342	0	0-0	5	4.49	4.40

Will Ohman

Pitches: L **Bats:** L **Pos:** RP-68   OH-min   **Ht:** 6'2" **Wt:** 240 **Born:** 8/13/1977 **Age:** 33

					HOW MUCH HE PITCHED			WHAT HE GAVE UP											THE RESULTS						
Year Team	Lg	G	GS	CG	GF	IP	BFP	H	R	ER	HR	SH	SF	HB	TBB	IBB	SO	WP	Bk	W	L	Pct	Sh	Sv-Op	Hld	ERC	ERA
2000 ChC	NL	6	0	0	2	3.1	17	4	3	3	0	0	0	0	4	1	2	1	0	1	0	1.000	0	0-0	1	7.25	8.10
2001 ChC	NL	11	0	0	0	11.2	54	14	10	10	2	0	0	0	6	0	12	2	0	1	0	1.000	0	0-0		6.26	7.71
2005 ChC	NL	69	0	0	13	43.1	187	32	14	14	6	1	0	3	24	3	45	6	1	2	2	.500	0	0-3	13	3.62	2.91
2006 ChC	NL	78	0	0	14	58.2	248	51	30	30	6	2	5	2	34	2	74	4	0	1	1	.500	0	0-0	9	4.13	4.13
2007 ChC	NL	56	0	0	11	36.1	168	42	20	20	3	2	0	1	16	4	33	2	0	2	4	.333	0	1-1	12	4.79	4.95
2008 Atl	NL	83	0	0	16	58.2	248	51	27	24	3	3	0	1	22	4	53	2	0	4	1	.800	0	1-4	23	2.87	3.68
2009 LAD	NL	21	0	0	5	12.1	54	12	8	8	4	0	0	0	8	1	7	0	0	1	0	1.000	0	1-2	4	6.76	5.84
2010 2 Tms		68	0	0	12	42.0	186	40	18	15	4	2	4	1	23	5	43	3	0	0	2	.000	0	0-1	18	4.24	3.21
10 Bal	AL	51	0	0	9	30.0	135	30	12	11	3	2	3	1	18	4	29	2	0	0	0	-	0	0-1	15	4.80	3.30
10 Fla	NL	17	0	0	3	12.0	51	10	6	4	1	0	1	0	5	1	14	1	0	0	2	.000	0	0-0	3	2.94	3.00
8 ML YEARS		392	0	0	73	273.0	1200	246	130	124	28	8	6	11	137	20	269	20	1	11	11	.500	0	3-11	81	3.93	4.09

Augie Ojeda

Bats: B Throws: R Pos: PH-28; 2B-15; 3B-12; SS-9; PR-5   oh-HAY-duh   Ht: 5'9" Wt: 174 Born: 12/20/1974 Age: 36

											BATTING											BASERUNNING				AVERAGES		
Year	Team	Lg	G	AB	H	2B	3B	HR	(Hm	Rd)	TB	R	RBI	RC	TBB	IBB	SO	HBP	SH	SF	SB	CS	SB%	GDP	Avg	OBP	Slg
2000	ChC	NL	28	77	17	3	1	2	(1	1)	28	10	8	9	10	1	9	0	1	1	1	0	.00	1	.221	.307	.364
2001	ChC	NL	78	144	29	5	1	1	(1	0)	39	16	12	10	12	1	20	2	2	2	1	0	1.00	2	.201	.269	.271
2002	ChC	NL	30	70	13	4	0	0	(0	0)	17	4	4	4	5	0	5	1	4	1	1	0	1.00	2	.186	.247	.243
2003	ChC	NL	12	25	3	0	0	0	(0	0)	3	2	0	0	1	1	5	1	0	0	0	0	-	1	.120	.185	.120
2004	Min	AL	30	59	20	1	0	2	(0	2)	27	16	7	11	10	0	3	0	2	1	1	1	.50	1	.339	.429	.458
2007	Ari	NL	57	113	31	2	2	1	(0	1)	40	16	12	16	15	3	13	0	2	2	1	0	1.00	1	.274	.354	.354
2008	Ari	NL	105	231	56	9	2	0	(0	0)	69	27	17	27	26	2	24	10	4	1	0	0	-	6	.242	.343	.299
2009	Ari	NL	103	264	65	17	3	1	(1	0)	91	38	16	29	32	3	28	6	6	1	3	1	.75	4	.246	.340	.345
2010	Ari	NL	59	79	15	3	0	0	(0	0)	18	6	5	3	8	0	8	0	3	2	0	1	.00	3	.190	.258	.228
	Postseason		7	21	6	1	0	0	(0	0)	7	1	1	2	1	0	3	1	0	0	0	0	-	3	.286	.348	.333
	9 ML YEARS		502	1062	249	44	9	7	(3	4)	332	135	81	109	119	11	115	20	24	11	7	4	.64	20	.234	.320	.313

Hideki Okajima

Pitches: L Bats: L Pos: RP-56   oh-kuh-JEE-muh   Ht: 6'1" Wt: 195 Born: 12/25/1975 Age: 35

			HOW MUCH HE PITCHED						WHAT HE GAVE UP										THE RESULTS						
Year	Team	Lg	G	GS	CG	GF	IP	BFP	H	R	ER	HR	SH	SF	HB	TBB	IBB	SO	WP	Bk	W	L	Pct	Sh	Sv-Op Hld	ERC	ERA
2010 Pwtckt*	AAA		3	0	0	1	2.1	12	6	5	5	1	0	0	0	0	0	0	0	0	0	0	-	0	0- -	17.08	19.29
2007	Bos	AL	66	0	0	13	69.0	272	50	17	17	6	5	1	1	17	2	63	0	0	3	2	.600	0	5-7 27	2.03	2.22
2008	Bos	AL	64	0	0	11	62.0	258	49	18	18	6	0	3	1	23	1	60	2	0	3	2	.600	0	1-9 23	2.82	2.61
2009	Bos	AL	68	0	0	6	61.0	258	56	23	23	8	3	1	2	21	3	53	0	0	6	0	1.000	0	0-2 23	3.65	3.39
2010	Bos	AL	56	0	0	12	46.0	213	59	24	23	6	4	1	0	20	5	33	2	0	4	4	.500	0	0-4 11	5.90	4.50
	Postseason		17	0	0	2	21.1	82	13	5	5	2	0	0	0	5	1	16	0	0	0	0	-	0	0-0 8	1.50	2.11
	4 ML YEARS		254	0	0	42	238.0	1001	214	82	81	26	12	6	4	81	11	209	4	0	16	8	.667	0	6-22 84	3.33	3.06

Andrew Oliver

Pitches: L Bats: L Pos: SP-5   Ht: 6'3" Wt: 210 Born: 12/3/1987 Age: 23

			HOW MUCH HE PITCHED						WHAT HE GAVE UP										THE RESULTS						
Year	Team	Lg	G	GS	CG	GF	IP	BFP	H	R	ER	HR	SH	SF	HB	TBB	IBB	SO	WP	Bk	W	L	Pct	Sh	Sv-Op Hld	ERC	ERA
2010 Erie	AA		14	14	0	0	77.1	322	74	35	31	7	2	1	1	25	0	70	7	0	6	4	.600	0	0- -	3.57	3.61
2010 Toledo	AAA		9	9	0	0	53.0	220	43	23	19	6	2	2	1	25	0	49	1	0	3	4	.429	0	0- -	3.55	3.23
2010 Det	AL		5	5	0	0	22.0	102	26	22	18	3	2	1	2	13	2	18	3	0	0	4	.000	0	0-0 0	6.62	7.36

Darren Oliver

Pitches: L Bats: R Pos: RP-64   Ht: 6'2" Wt: 200 Born: 10/6/1970 Age: 40

			HOW MUCH HE PITCHED						WHAT HE GAVE UP										THE RESULTS						
Year	Team	Lg	G	GS	CG	GF	IP	BFP	H	R	ER	HR	SH	SF	HB	TBB	IBB	SO	WP	Bk	W	L	Pct	Sh	Sv-Op Hld	ERC	ERA
1993	Tex	AL	2	0	0	0	3.1	14	2	1	1	1	0	0	0	1	1	4	0	0	0	0	-	0	0-0 0	2.15	2.70
1994	Tex	AL	43	0	0	10	50.0	226	40	24	19	4	6	0	6	35	4	50	2	2	4	0	1.000	0	2-3 9	4.29	3.42
1995	Tex	AL	17	7	0	2	49.0	222	47	25	23	3	5	1	1	32	1	39	4	0	4	2	.667	0	0-0 0	4.59	4.22
1996	Tex	AL	30	30	1	0	173.2	777	190	97	90	20	2	7	10	76	3	112	5	1	14	6	.700	1	0-0 0	5.10	4.66
1997	Tex	AL	32	32	3	0	201.1	887	213	111	94	29	2	5	11	82	3	104	7	0	13	12	.520	1	0-0 0	4.98	4.20
1998	2 Tms		29	29	2	0	160.1	749	204	115	102	18	8	8	10	66	2	87	7	4	10	11	.476	1	0-0 0	6.01	5.73
1999	StL	NL	30	30	2	0	196.1	842	197	96	93	11	4	11	74	4	119	6	2	9	9	.500	1	0-0 0	4.11	4.26
2000	Tex	AL	21	21	0	0	108.0	501	151	95	89	16	5	4	4	42	3	49	4	1	2	9	.182	0	0-0 0	7.04	7.42
2001	Tex	AL	28	28	1	0	154.0	696	189	109	103	23	1	5	6	65	0	104	8	2	11	11	.500	0	0-0 0	6.14	6.02
2002	Bos	AL	14	9	1	0	58.0	258	70	30	30	7	1	3	6	27	0	32	1	0	4	5	.444	1	0-0 0	6.49	4.66
2003	Col	NL	33	32	1	0	180.1	786	201	108	101	21	4	5	8	61	3	88	0	0	13	11	.542	0	0-0 0	4.80	5.04
2004	2 Tms		27	10	0	5	72.2	314	87	50	48	14	4	3	1	21	1	46	1	0	3	3	.500	0	0-0 0	5.59	5.94
2006	NYM	NL	45	0	0	10	81.0	333	70	33	31	13	2	4	3	21	2	60	1	0	4	1	.800	0	0-0 3	3.27	3.44
2007	LAA	AL	61	0	0	20	64.1	273	58	31	27	5	2	4	1	23	2	51	1	1	3	1	.750	0	0-0 8	3.19	3.78
2008	LAA	AL	54	0	0	9	72.0	291	67	24	23	5	4	3	4	16	2	48	3	0	7	1	.875	0	0-2 12	3.07	2.88
2009	LAA	AL	63	1	0	9	73.0	293	61	22	22	5	4	5	6	22	8	65	7	0	5	1	.833	0	0-1 20	2.81	2.71
2010	Tex	AL	64	0	0	7	61.2	244	53	20	17	4	5	3	2	15	4	65	0	0	1	2	.333	0	1-4 14	2.63	2.48
98	Tex	AL	19	19	2	0	103.1	493	140	84	75	11	3	6	10	43	1	58	6	1	6	7	.462	0	0-0 0	6.68	6.53
98	StL	NL	10	10	0	0	57.0	256	64	31	27	7	5	2	0	23	1	29	1	3	4	4	.500	0	0-0 0	4.85	4.26
04	Fla	NL	18	8	0	3	58.2	260	75	44	42	13	4	3	1	17	1	33	1	0	2	3	.400	0	0-0 0	6.30	6.44
04	Hou	NL	9	2	0	2	14.0	54	12	6	6	1	0	0	0	4	0	13	0	0	1	0	1.000	0	0-0 0	2.89	3.86
	Postseason		14	1	0	1	26.0	101	21	11	11	2	2	0	1	8	2	15	1	0	1	1	.500	0	0-1 1	2.76	3.81
	17 ML YEARS		593	229	11	72	1759.0	7706	1900	991	913	204	66	64	89	679	43	1123	57	13	107	85	.557	4	3-10 66	4.80	4.67

Miguel Olivo

Bats: R Throws: R Pos: C-111; PH-1; PR-1   oh-LEEV-oh   Ht: 6'0" Wt: 229 Born: 7/15/1978 Age: 32

											BATTING											BASERUNNING				AVERAGES		
Year	Team	Lg	G	AB	H	2B	3B	HR	(Hm	Rd)	TB	R	RBI	RC	TBB	IBB	SO	HBP	SH	SF	SB	CS	SB%	GDP	Avg	OBP	Slg
2002	CWS	AL	6	19	4	1	0	1	(0	1)	8	2	5	4	2	0	5	0	0	0	0	0	-	1	.211	.286	.421
2003	CWS	AL	114	317	75	19	1	6	(4	2)	114	37	27	32	19	0	80	4	4	2	6	4	.60	3	.237	.286	.360
2004	2 Tms	AL	96	301	70	15	4	13	(8	5)	132	46	40	33	20	2	84	3	4	1	7	6	.54	4	.233	.286	.439
2005	2 Tms		91	267	58	11	1	9	(5	4)	98	30	34	23	8	2	80	3	1	2	7	2	.78	7	.217	.246	.367
2006	Fla	NL	127	430	113	22	3	16	(7	9)	189	52	58	49	9	4	103	7	3	3	2	3	.40	8	.263	.287	.440
2007	Fla	NL	122	452	107	20	4	16	(11	5)	183	43	60	43	14	2	123	2	0	1	3	2	.60	13	.237	.262	.405
2008	KC	AL	84	306	78	22	0	12	(3	9)	136	29	41	35	7	2	82	3	0	1	7	0	1.00	6	.255	.278	.444
2009	KC	AL	114	390	97	15	5	23	(10	13)	191	51	65	47	19	0	126	5	1	1	5	2	.71	10	.249	.292	.490
2010	Col	NL	112	394	106	17	6	14	(10	4)	177	55	58	49	27	5	117	1	2	3	7	4	.64	6	.269	.315	.449
04	CWS	AL	46	141	38	7	2	7	(4	3)	70	21	26	21	10	1	29	0	4	1	5	4	.56	2	.270	.316	.496

			BATTING																			BASERUNNING				AVERAGES		
Year	Team	Lg	G	AB	H	2B	3B	HR	(Hm	Rd)	TB	R	RBI	RC	TBB	IBB	SO	HBP	SH	SF	SB	CS	SB%	GDP	Avg	OBP	Slg
04	Sea	AL	50	160	32	8	2	6	(4	2)	62	25	14	12	10	1	55	3	0	0	2	2	.50	2	.200	.260	.388
05	Sea	AL	54	152	23	4	0	5	(4	1)	42	14	18	6	4	0	49	0	0	1	1	1	.50	3	.151	.172	.276
05	SD	NL	37	115	35	7	1	4	(1	3)	56	16	16	17	4	2	31	3	1	1	6	1	.86	4	.304	.341	.487
	Postseason		1	1	0	0	0	0	(0	0)	0	0	0	0	0	0	0	0	0	0	0	0	-	1	.000	.000	.000
	9 ML YEARS		866	2876	708	142	24	110	(58	52)	1228	345	388	315	125	17	800	28	15	14	44	23	.66	59	.246	.283	.427

Scott Olsen

Pitches: L **Bats:** L **Pos:** SP-15; RP-2 **Ht:** 6'4" **Wt:** 211 **Born:** 1/12/1984 **Age:** 27

			HOW MUCH HE PITCHED						WHAT HE GAVE UP											THE RESULTS							
Year	Team	Lg	G	GS	CG	GF	IP	BFP	H	R	ER	HR	SH	SF	HB	TBB	IBB	SO	WP	Bk	W	L	Pct	Sh	Sv-Op	Hld	ERC	ERA
2010	Syrcse*	AAA	1	1	0	0	6.1	28	8	4	4	0	1	0	0	1	0	4	0	0	0	0	-	0	0--	-	3.78	5.68
2010	Nats*	R	2	2	0	0	5.0	20	3	1	1	0	1	1	0	1	0	3	1	0	0	0	-	0	0--	-	1.06	1.80
2010	Hgrstn*	A	1	1	0	0	4.0	15	2	1	1	0	1	0	1	0	0	4	1	0	0	0	-	0	0--	-	0.94	2.25
2010	Ptomc*	A+	1	1	0	0	5.0	21	6	4	3	1	0	0	0	0	0	4	0	0	0	0	-	0	0--	-	4.14	5.40
2005	Fla	NL	5	4	0	0	20.1	91	21	13	9	5	0	0	0	10	0	21	1	0	1	1	.500	0	0-0	0	5.66	3.98
2006	Fla	NL	31	31	0	0	180.2	761	160	94	81	23	7	2	7	75	1	166	8	0	12	10	.545	0	0-0	0	3.88	4.04
2007	Fla	NL	33	33	0	0	176.2	826	226	134	114	29	14	8	1	85	4	133	8	0	10	15	.400	0	0-0	0	6.54	5.81
2008	Fla	NL	33	33	0	0	201.2	855	195	106	94	30	7	4	3	69	13	113	5	0	8	11	.421	0	0-0	0	3.96	4.20
2009	Was	NL	11	11	0	0	62.2	289	83	45	42	11	4	1	0	25	2	42	2	0	2	4	.333	0	0-0	0	6.55	6.03
2010	Was	NL	17	15	0	0	81.0	357	93	54	50	10	3	3	2	27	4	53	0	0	4	8	.333	0	0-0	0	4.84	5.56
	6 ML YEARS		130	127	0	0	723.0	3179	778	446	390	108	35	18	13	291	24	528	24	0	37	49	.430	0	0-0	0	4.90	4.85

Garrett Olson

Pitches: L **Bats:** R **Pos:** RP-35 **Ht:** 6'1" **Wt:** 205 **Born:** 10/18/1983 **Age:** 27

			HOW MUCH HE PITCHED						WHAT HE GAVE UP											THE RESULTS							
Year	Team	Lg	G	GS	CG	GF	IP	BFP	H	R	ER	HR	SH	SF	HB	TBB	IBB	SO	WP	Bk	W	L	Pct	Sh	Sv-Op	Hld	ERC	ERA
2010	Tacom*	AAA	12	6	0	2	46.2	189	36	22	19	4	3	2	2	15	0	50	1	0	2	5	.286	0	0--	-	2.66	3.66
2007	Bal	AL	7	7	0	0	32.1	162	42	28	28	4	0	3	2	28	1	28	1	1	1	3	.250	0	0-0	0	8.46	7.79
2008	Bal	AL	26	26	0	0	132.2	621	168	100	98	17	4	4	8	62	1	83	6	0	9	10	.474	0	0-0	0	6.40	6.65
2009	Sea	AL	31	11	0	5	80.1	347	79	52	50	19	1	2	4	34	0	47	2	0	3	5	.375	0	0-0	5	5.33	5.60
2010	Sea	AL	35	0	0	11	37.2	172	42	20	19	6	1	1	0	15	1	31	4	0	0	3	.000	0	1-1	6	4.94	4.54
	4 ML YEARS		99	44	0	16	283.0	1302	331	200	195	46	6	10	14	139	3	189	13	1	13	21	.382	0	1-1	6	6.13	6.20

Logan Ondrusek

Pitches: R **Bats:** R **Pos:** RP-60
ahn-DREW-seck
Ht: 6'8" **Wt:** 225 **Born:** 2/13/1985 **Age:** 26

			HOW MUCH HE PITCHED						WHAT HE GAVE UP											THE RESULTS							
Year	Team	Lg	G	GS	CG	GF	IP	BFP	H	R	ER	HR	SH	SF	HB	TBB	IBB	SO	WP	Bk	W	L	Pct	Sh	Sv-Op	Hld	ERC	ERA
2005	Billings	R+	15	9	0	1	55.1	257	72	49	37	9	2	1	6	19	0	46	10	0	1	6	.143	0	0--	-	6.59	6.02
2006	Dayton	A	27	0	0	6	52.2	226	48	24	20	2	3	1	3	19	0	47	4	0	4	5	.444	0	0--	-	3.19	3.42
2006	Billings	R+	1	0	0	1	1.0	8	4	3	3	0	0	0	0	1	0	3	1	0	0	1	.000	0	0--	-	27.72	27.00
2006	Chatt	AA	1	0	0	0	4.0	13	0	0	0	0	1	0	0	3	0	7	0	0	0	0	-	0	0--	-	0.65	0.00
2007	Srsota	A+	31	22	0	3	124.0	538	131	72	61	4	3	7	8	48	0	88	6	0	7	10	.412	0	1--	-	4.17	4.43
2008	Srsota	A+	40	3	0	6	79.2	367	93	47	44	5	1	1	6	32	2	58	3	0	1	7	.125	0	1--	-	4.93	4.97
2008	Lsvlle	AAA	1	0	0	0	1.1	6	1	0	0	0	0	0	0	2	0	1	0	0	0	0	-	0	0--	-	6.99	0.00
2009	Srsota	A+	13	0	0	7	18.2	71	7	4	2	0	2	0	2	7	0	12	0	0	2	0	1.000	0	0--	-	1.05	0.96
2009	Carolina	AA	24	0	0	15	32.2	128	21	7	6	0	2	0	0	12	2	24	3	0	2	1	.667	0	7--	-	1.55	1.65
2009	Lsvlle	AAA	19	0	0	17	20.2	77	16	4	4	1	1	0	1	2	0	11	1	0	0	0	-	0	12--	-	1.80	1.74
2010	Lsvlle	AAA	14	0	0	2	19.2	79	21	9	9	0	1	0	2	3	0	14	2	0	0	1	.000	0	1--	-	3.39	4.12
2010	Cin	NL	60	0	0	11	58.2	240	49	25	24	7	1	1	0	20	1	39	2	0	5	0	1.000	0	0-2	6	3.08	3.68

Magglio Ordonez

Bats: R **Throws:** R **Pos:** RF-71; DH-13 **Ht:** 6'0" **Wt:** 215 **Born:** 1/28/1974 **Age:** 37

			BATTING																			BASERUNNING				AVERAGES		
Year	Team	Lg	G	AB	H	2B	3B	HR	(Hm	Rd)	TB	R	RBI	RC	TBB	IBB	SO	HBP	SH	SF	SB	CS	SB%	GDP	Avg	OBP	Slg
1997	CWS	AL	21	69	22	6	0	4	(2	2)	40	12	11	12	2	0	8	0	1	0	1	2	.33	1	.319	.338	.580
1998	CWS	AL	145	535	151	25	2	14	(8	6)	222	70	65	67	28	1	53	9	2	4	9	7	.56	19	.282	.326	.415
1999	CWS	AL	157	624	188	34	3	30	(16	14)	318	100	117	102	47	4	64	1	0	5	13	6	.68	24	.301	.349	.510
2000	CWS	AL	153	588	185	34	3	32	(21	11)	321	102	126	112	60	3	64	2	0	15	18	4	.82	28	.315	.371	.546
2001	CWS	AL	160	593	181	40	1	31	(17	14)	316	97	113	117	70	7	70	5	0	3	25	7	.78	14	.305	.382	.533
2002	CWS	AL	153	590	189	47	1	38	(24	14)	352	116	135	119	53	2	77	4	0	3	7	5	.58	21	.320	.381	.597
2003	CWS	AL	160	606	192	46	3	29	(17	12)	331	95	99	109	57	1	73	7	0	4	9	5	.64	20	.317	.380	.546
2004	CWS	AL	52	202	59	8	2	9	(4	5)	98	32	37	39	16	2	22	3	0	1	0	2	.00	4	.292	.351	.485
2005	Det	AL	82	305	92	17	0	8	(2	6)	133	38	46	51	30	1	35	1	0	7	0	0	-	8	.302	.359	.436
2006	Det	AL	155	593	177	32	1	24	(8	16)	283	82	104	97	45	3	87	4	0	4	1	4	.20	13	.298	.350	.477
2007	Det	AL	157	595	216	54	0	28	(17	11)	354	117	139	146	76	8	79	2	0	5	4	1	.80	20	.363	.434	.595
2008	Det	AL	146	561	178	32	2	21	(13	8)	277	72	103	92	53	2	76	3	0	6	1	5	.17	27	.317	.376	.494
2009	Det	AL	131	465	144	24	2	9	(6	3)	199	54	50	69	51	2	65	0	0	2	3	1	.75	19	.310	.376	.428
2010	Det	AL	84	323	98	17	1	12	(7	5)	153	56	59	53	40	0	38	0	0	2	1	0	1.00	14	.303	.378	.474
	Postseason		16	62	12	1	1	3	(3	0)	24	8	9	4	6	0	10	0	0	0	1	1	.50	3	.194	.265	.387
	14 ML YEARS		1756	6649	2072	416	21	289	(162	127)	3397	1043	1204	1185	628	36	811	44	3	61	92	49	.65	232	.312	.372	.511

David Ortiz

Bats: L Throws: L Pos: DH-135; PH-7; 1B-4

Ht: 6'4" Wt: 230 Born: 11/18/1975 Age: 35

										BATTING													BASERUNNING				AVERAGES		
Year	Team	Lg	G	AB	H	2B	3B	HR	(Hm	Rd)	TB	R	RBI	RC	TBB	IBB	SO	HBP	SH	SF		SB	CS	SB%	GDP	Avg	OBP	Slg
1997	Min	AL	15	49	16	3	0	1	(0	1)	22	10	6	7	2	0	19	0	0	0		0	0	-	1	.327	.353	.449
1998	Min	AL	86	278	77	20	0	9	(2	7)	124	47	46	46	39	3	72	5	0	4		1	0	1.00	8	.277	.371	.446
1999	Min	AL	10	20	0	0	0	0	(0	0)	0	1	0	0	5	0	12	0	0	0		0	0	-	2	.000	.200	.000
2000	Min	AL	130	415	117	36	1	10	(7	3)	185	59	63	66	57	2	81	0	0	6		1	0	1.00	13	.282	.364	.446
2001	Min	AL	89	303	71	17	1	18	(6	12)	144	46	48	46	40	8	68	1	1	2		1	0	1.00	6	.234	.324	.475
2002	Min	AL	125	412	112	32	1	20	(5	15)	206	52	75	62	43	0	87	3	0	8		1	2	.33	5	.272	.339	.500
2003	Bos	AL	128	448	129	39	2	31	(17	14)	265	79	101	80	58	8	83	1	0	2		0	0	-	9	.288	.369	.592
2004	Bos	AL	150	582	175	47	3	41	(17	24)	351	94	139	127	75	8	133	4	0	8		0	0	-	12	.301	.380	.603
2005	Bos	AL	159	601	180	40	1	47	(20	27)	363	119	148	137	102	9	124	1	0	9		1	0	1.00	13	.300	.397	.604
2006	Bos	AL	151	558	160	29	2	54	(22	32)	355	115	137	137	119	23	117	4	0	5		1	0	1.00	12	.287	.413	.636
2007	Bos	AL	149	549	182	52	1	35	(16	19)	341	116	117	138	111	12	103	4	0	3		3	1	.75	16	.332	.445	.621
2008	Bos	AL	109	416	110	30	1	23	(12	11)	211	74	89	82	70	12	74	1	1	3		1	0	1.00	11	.264	.369	.507
2009	Bos	AL	150	541	129	35	1	28	(18	10)	250	77	99	79	74	5	134	5	0	7		0	2	.00	9	.238	.332	.462
2010	Bos	AL	145	518	140	36	1	32	(15	17)	274	86	102	94	82	14	145	2	0	6		0	0	-	12	.270	.370	.529
	Postseason		66	244	69	18	2	12	(7	5)	127	39	47	51	41	7	64	2	0	2		0	1	.00	3	.283	.388	.520
	14 ML YEARS		1596	5690	1598	416	15	349	(157	192)	3091	975	1170	1093	877	104	1252	31	2	61		10	6	.63	129	.281	.376	.543

Ramon Ortiz

Pitches: R Bats: R Pos: RP-14; SP-2

Ht: 5'11" Wt: 168 Born: 5/23/1973 Age: 38

			HOW MUCH HE PITCHED						WHAT HE GAVE UP											THE RESULTS						
Year	Team	Lg	G	GS	CG	GF	IP	BFP	H	R	ER	HR	SH	SF	HB	TBB	IBB	SO	WP	Bk	W	L	Pct	Sh	Sv-Op	Hld	ERC	ERA
2010	Buffalo*	AAA	8	8	1	0	48.0	193	43	22	21	1	3	0	2	8	0	32	1	1	2	3	.400	0	0- -		2.33	3.94
2010	Drham*	AAA	4	4	0	0	17.0	80	23	13	12	2	0	1	0	6	0	12	0	0	0	1	.000	0	0- -		5.95	6.35
1999	LAA	AL	9	9	0	0	48.1	218	50	35	35	7	0	2	2	25	0	44	2	2	3	4	.400	0	0-0		5.23	6.52
2000	LAA	AL	18	18	2	0	111.1	472	96	69	63	18	4	4	2	55	0	73	7	4	8	6	.571	0	0-0		4.24	5.09
2001	LAA	AL	32	32	2	0	208.2	916	223	114	101	25	9	6	12	76	6	135	7	0	13	11	.542	0	0-0		4.65	4.36
2002	LAA	AL	32	32	4	0	217.1	896	188	97	91	40	2	5	5	68	0	162	7	3	15	9	.625	1	0-0		3.64	3.77
2003	LAA	AL	32	32	1	0	180.0	814	209	121	104	28	3	7	12	63	0	94	4	0	16	13	.552	0	0-0		5.44	5.20
2004	LAA	AL	34	14	0	13	128.0	543	139	64	63	18	2	3	4	38	4	82	5	3	5	7	.417	0	0-0		4.61	4.43
2005	Cin	NL	30	30	1	0	171.1	755	206	110	102	34	7	8	7	51	1	96	4	1	9	11	.450	0	0-0		5.78	5.36
2006	Was	NL	33	33	0	0	190.2	871	230	127	118	31	10	4	18	64	14	104	4	3	11	16	.407	0	0-0		5.71	5.57
2007	2 Tms		38	10	0	15	104.0	459	127	65	63	16	1	5	6	22	1	51	2	1	5	4	.556	0	0-0		5.17	5.45
2010	LAD	NL	16	2	0	3	30.0	135	33	22	21	5	3	1	0	16	2	21	1	1	1	2	.333	0	0-0	1	5.64	6.30
07	Min	AL	28	10	0	11	91.0	400	112	54	52	12	0	4	5	15	1	44	2	1	4	4	.500	0	0-0		4.83	5.14
07	Col	NL	10	0	0	4	13.0	59	15	11	11	4	1	1	1	7	0	7	0	0	1	0	1.000	0	0-0		7.81	7.62
	Postseason		4	3	0	1	15.0	73	20	14	14	2	1	2	1	10	2	7	1	0	2	0	1.000	0	0-0		7.66	8.40
	10 ML YEARS		274	212	10	31	1389.2	6079	1501	824	761	222	41	45	68	478	28	862	43	18	85	82	.509	1	0-0		4.91	4.93

Russ Ortiz

Pitches: R Bats: R Pos: RP-6

Ht: 6'0" Wt: 177 Born: 6/5/1974 Age: 37

			HOW MUCH HE PITCHED						WHAT HE GAVE UP											THE RESULTS						
Year	Team	Lg	G	GS	CG	GF	IP	BFP	H	R	ER	HR	SH	SF	HB	TBB	IBB	SO	WP	Bk	W	L	Pct	Sh	Sv-Op	Hld	ERC	ERA
1998	SF	NL	22	13	0	3	88.1	394	90	51	49	11	5	4	4	46	1	75	3	0	4	4	.500	0	0-0	1	5.05	4.99
1999	SF	NL	33	33	3	0	207.2	922	189	109	88	24	11	6	6	125	1	164	13	0	18	9	.667	0	0-0	0	4.56	3.81
2000	SF	NL	33	32	0	0	195.2	871	192	117	109	28	10	6	7	112	1	167	8	0	14	12	.538	0	0-0	0	5.17	5.01
2001	SF	NL	33	33	1	0	218.2	911	187	90	80	13	10	4	0	91	3	169	8	1	17	9	.654	1	0-0	0	3.08	3.29
2002	SF	NL	33	33	2	0	214.1	911	191	89	86	15	15	6	4	94	5	137	5	0	14	10	.583	0	0-0	0	3.46	3.61
2003	Atl	NL	34	34	1	0	212.1	912	177	101	90	17	6	7	4	102	7	149	5	0	21	7	.750	1	0-0	0	3.32	3.81
2004	Atl	NL	34	34	2	0	204.2	896	197	98	94	23	10	7	3	112	7	143	4	1	15	9	.625	0	0-0	0	4.60	4.13
2005	Ari	NL	22	22	0	0	115.0	551	147	92	88	18	5	8	4	65	3	46	5	0	5	11	.313	0	0-0	0	6.96	6.89
2006	2 Tms		26	11	0	5	63.0	303	86	60	57	18	1	1	3	40	1	44	2	0	0	8	.000	0	0-0	0	9.39	8.14
2007	SF	NL	12	8	0	1	49.0	223	57	32	30	4	3	1	6	20	1	27	0	0	2	3	.400	0	0-0	0	5.42	5.51
2009	Hou	NL	23	13	0	3	85.2	387	95	56	53	8	2	4	4	48	2	65	3	0	3	6	.333	0	0-0	1	5.57	5.57
2010	LAD	NL	6	0	0	1	7.0	35	10	8	8	0	0	1	0	5	1	6	1	0	0	1	.000	0	0-0	0	6.83	10.29
06	Ari	NL	6	6	0	0	22.2	113	27	21	19	3	1	0	1	22	1	21	0	0	0	5	.000	0	0-0	0	8.19	7.54
06	Bal	AL	20	5	0	5	40.1	190	59	39	38	15	0	1	2	18	0	23	2	0	0	3	.000	0	0-0	0	9.99	8.48
	Postseason		9	9	0	0	44.0	204	51	28	28	5	0	2	0	25	3	27	3	0	3	1	.750	0	0-0	0	5.65	5.73
	12 ML YEARS		311	266	9	13	1661.1	7316	1618	903	832	179	78	55	45	860	37	1192	57	2	113	89	.559	3	0-0	2	4.54	4.51

Sean O'Sullivan

Pitches: R Bats: R Pos: SP-14; RP-5

Ht: 6'2" Wt: 230 Born: 9/1/1987 Age: 23

			HOW MUCH HE PITCHED						WHAT HE GAVE UP											THE RESULTS						
Year	Team	Lg	G	GS	CG	GF	IP	BFP	H	R	ER	HR	SH	SF	HB	TBB	IBB	SO	WP	Bk	W	L	Pct	Sh	Sv-Op	Hld	ERC	ERA
2006	Orem	R+	14	14	0	0	71.1	291	65	23	17	2	2	5	5	7	0	55	2	0	4	0	1.000	0	0- -		2.25	2.14
2007	CRpds	A	25	25	0	0	158.1	656	136	58	39	6	2	5	9	40	0	125	9	0	10	7	.588	0	0- -		2.55	2.22
2008	RCuca	A+	28	25	1	1	158.0	692	167	94	83	8	2	6	11	50	0	111	12	0	16	8	.667	0	0- -		3.95	4.73
2009	Ark	AA	3	3	0	0	18.2	76	21	11	11	1	2	1	0	4	0	14	0	0	1	2	.333	0	0- -		2.89	5.30
2009	Salt Lk	AAA	14	13	1	0	69.0	301	74	42	42	9	1	3	6	20	0	48	3	0	6	4	.600	1	0- -		4.38	5.48
2010	Salt Lk	AAA	15	15	1	0	85.0	368	95	50	45	8	2	2	3	31	1	58	3	1	5	5	.500	0	0- -		4.79	4.76
2009	LAA	AL	12	10	0	0	51.2	227	60	34	34	12	2	4	1	16	1	29	1	0	4	2	.667	0	0-0	0	5.66	5.92
2010	2 Tms	AL	19	14	0	3	83.2	368	90	53	51	15	0	3	1	31	2	43	4	2	4	6	.400	0	0-0	0	4.93	5.49
10	LAA	AL	5	1	0	2	13.0	49	7	3	3	1	0	0	0	4	2	6	0	0	1	0	1.000	0	0-0	0	1.33	2.08
10	KC	AL	14	13	0	1	70.2	319	83	50	48	14	0	3	1	27	0	37	4	2	3	6	.333	0	0-0	0	5.76	6.11
	2 ML YEARS		31	24	0	4	135.1	595	150	87	85	27	2	7	2	47	3	72	5	2	8	8	.500	0	0-0	0	5.21	5.65

Roy Oswalt

Pitches: R Bats: R Pos: SP-32; RP-1   OWES-walt   Ht: 6'0" Wt: 192 Born: 8/29/1977 Age: 33

Year	Team	Lg	G	GS	CG	GF	IP	BFP	H	R	ER	HR	SH	SF	HB	TBB	IBB	SO	WP	Bk	W	L	Pct	Sh	Sv-Op	Hld	ERC	ERA
2001	Hou	NL	28	20	3	4	141.2	575	126	48	43	13	4	4	6	24	2	144	0	0	14	3	.824	1	0-0	0	2.68	2.73
2002	Hou	NL	35	34	0	0	233.0	956	215	86	78	17	12	7	5	62	4	208	3	0	19	9	.679	0	0-0	0	3.05	3.01
2003	Hou	NL	21	21	0	0	127.1	514	116	48	42	15	7	1	5	29	0	108	1	0	10	5	.667	0	0-0	0	3.26	2.97
2004	Hou	NL	36	35	2	0	237.0	983	233	100	92	17	11	4	11	62	5	206	5	1	20	10	.667	2	0-0	0	3.46	3.49
2005	Hou	NL	35	35	4	0	241.2	1002	243	85	79	18	12	7	8	48	3	184	5	1	20	12	.625	1	0-0	0	3.27	2.94
2006	Hou	NL	33	32	2	1	220.2	896	220	76	73	18	12	4	6	38	4	166	1	1	15	8	.652	0	0-0	0	3.19	2.98
2007	Hou	NL	33	32	1	0	212.0	910	221	80	75	14	6	4	7	60	6	154	1	1	14	7	.667	0	0-0	1	3.68	3.18
2008	Hou	NL	32	32	3	0	208.2	862	199	89	82	23	8	9	10	47	2	165	1	0	17	10	.630	2	0-0	0	3.40	3.54
2009	Hou	NL	30	30	3	0	181.1	757	183	83	83	19	12	5	8	42	4	138	4	0	8	6	.571	0	0-0	0	3.67	4.12
2010	2 Tms	NL	33	32	2	0	211.2	837	162	70	65	19	10	6	5	55	2	193	2	1	13	13	.500	2	0-0	0	2.37	2.76
10	Hou	NL	20	20	1	0	129.0	521	109	52	49	13	4	5	2	34	2	120	2	1	6	12	.333	1	0-0	0	2.79	3.42
10	Phi	NL	13	12	1	0	82.2	316	53	18	16	6	6	1	3	21	0	73	0	0	7	1	.875	1	0-0	0	1.76	1.74
	Postseason		8	7	0	1	46.2	206	48	19	19	5	2	2	4	19	0	32	0	0	4	0	1.000	0	0-0	0	4.67	3.66
10 ML YEARS			316	303	20	5	2015.0	8292	1918	765	712	173	94	51	71	467	32	1666	23	5	150	83	.644	8	0-0	1	3.21	3.18

Adam Ottavino

Pitches: R Bats: B Pos: SP-3; RP-2   ott-tah-VEE-no   Ht: 6'5" Wt: 230 Born: 11/22/1985 Age: 25

Year	Team	Lg	G	GS	CG	GF	IP	BFP	H	R	ER	HR	SH	SF	HB	TBB	IBB	SO	WP	Bk	W	L	Pct	Sh	Sv-Op	Hld	ERC	ERA
2006	StCol	A-	6	6	0	0	28.2	125	23	12	10	1	1	0	1	13	0	26	0	0	2	2	.500	0	0--	0	2.78	3.14
2006	QuadC	A	8	8	0	0	36.2	157	28	21	14	3	0	1	4	19	0	38	3	0	2	3	.400	0	0--	0	3.54	3.44
2007	PlmBh	A+	27	27	1	0	143.1	620	130	63	49	10	1	5	8	63	0	128	6	0	12	8	.600	0	0--	0	3.70	3.08
2008	Sprgfld	AA	24	24	1	0	115.1	530	133	75	67	16	5	6	10	52	0	96	6	0	3	7	.300	0	0--	0	5.82	5.23
2009	Memp	AAA	27	27	0	0	144.0	642	141	80	76	12	3	7	10	82	1	119	13	1	7	12	.368	0	0--	0	4.83	4.75
2010	Memp	AAA	9	9	0	0	47.2	196	43	23	21	5	1	0	3	12	0	43	3	0	5	3	.625	0	0--	0	3.28	3.97
2010	StL	NL	5	3	0	0	22.1	110	37	21	21	5	1	0	0	9	1	12	1	0	0	2	.000	0	0-0	0	9.22	8.46

Josh Outman

Pitches: L Bats: L Pos: P   Ht: 6'1" Wt: 186 Born: 9/14/1984 Age: 26

Year	Team	Lg	G	GS	CG	GF	IP	BFP	H	R	ER	HR	SH	SF	HB	TBB	IBB	SO	WP	Bk	W	L	Pct	Sh	Sv-Op	Hld	ERC	ERA
2005	Batvia	A-	11	4	0	0	29.1	128	23	14	9	1	1	0	2	14	0	31	3	0	2	1	.667	0	0--	0	2.91	2.76
2006	Lakwd	A	27	27	1	0	155.1	652	119	61	51	5	5	5	8	75	0	161	12	1	14	6	.700	1	0--	0	2.88	2.95
2007	Clrwtr	A+	20	18	0	0	117.1	504	104	35	32	7	2	2	5	54	0	117	4	0	10	4	.714	0	0--	0	3.57	2.45
2007	Rdng	AA	7	7	1	0	42.0	184	38	25	21	5	1	2	1	23	1	34	2	0	2	3	.400	1	0--	0	4.32	4.50
2008	Rdng	AA	33	5	0	7	70.1	310	68	27	25	3	3	3	2	37	0	66	3	0	4	5	.556	0	1--	0	4.08	3.20
2008	Mdland	AA	4	4	0	0	12.2	54	13	7	6	1	1	0	0	3	0	5	1	0	1	0	1.000	0	0--	0	3.36	4.26
2008	Scrmto	AAA	5	2	0	1	15.1	59	9	3	3	1	0	0	0	5	1	15	2	0	1	0	1.000	0	0--	0	1.54	1.70
2008	Oak	AL	6	4	0	0	25.2	116	34	14	13	1	0	2	2	8	1	19	1	0	1	2	.333	0	0-0	0	5.49	4.56
2009	Oak	AL	14	12	0	1	67.1	276	53	30	26	9	1	0	0	25	0	53	1	0	4	1	.800	0	0-0	0	3.04	3.48
2 ML YEARS			20	16	0	1	93.0	392	87	44	39	10	1	2	2	33	1	72	2	0	5	3	.625	0	0-0	0	3.60	3.77

Lyle Overbay

Bats: L Throws: L Pos: 1B-153; PH-3   Ht: 6'2" Wt: 235 Born: 1/28/1977 Age: 34

Year	Team	Lg	G	AB	H	2B	3B	HR	(Hm	Rd)	TB	R	RBI	RC	TBB	IBB	SO	HBP	SH	SF	SB	CS	SB%	GDP	Avg	OBP	Slg
2001	Ari	NL	2	2	1	0	0	0	(0	0)	1	0	0	0	0	0	1	0	0	0	0	0	-	0	.500	.500	.500
2002	Ari	NL	10	10	1	0	0	0	(0	0)	1	0	1	0	0	0	5	0	0	0	0	0	-	0	.100	.100	.100
2003	Ari	NL	86	254	70	20	0	4	(2	2)	102	23	28	34	35	7	67	2	0	2	1	0	1.00	8	.276	.365	.402
2004	Mil	NL	159	579	174	53	1	16	(6	10)	277	83	87	94	81	9	128	2	0	6	2	1	.67	11	.301	.385	.478
2005	Mil	NL	158	537	148	34	1	19	(10	9)	241	80	72	84	78	8	98	2	1	4	1	0	1.00	17	.276	.367	.449
2006	Tor	AL	157	581	181	46	1	22	(17	5)	295	82	92	89	55	7	96	2	0	5	5	3	.63	19	.312	.372	.508
2007	Tor	AL	122	425	102	30	2	10	(6	4)	166	49	44	48	47	4	75	1	0	3	2	1	1.00	12	.240	.315	.391
2008	Tor	AL	158	544	147	32	2	15	(7	8)	228	74	69	73	74	3	116	3	1	5	1	2	.33	24	.270	.358	.419
2009	Tor	AL	132	423	112	35	1	16	(6	10)	197	57	64	64	74	6	95	0	0	3	0	0	-	8	.265	.372	.466
2010	Tor	AL	154	534	130	37	2	20	(13	7)	231	75	67	75	67	7	131	3	0	3	1	0	1.00	9	.243	.329	.433
10 ML YEARS			1138	3889	1066	287	10	122	(67	55)	1739	523	524	558	511	51	815	15	2	28	13	6	.68	108	.274	.358	.447

Micah Owings

Pitches: R Bats: R Pos: RP-22   Ht: 6'5" Wt: 230 Born: 9/28/1982 Age: 28

Year	Team	Lg	G	GS	CG	GF	IP	BFP	H	R	ER	HR	SH	SF	HB	TBB	IBB	SO	WP	Bk	W	L	Pct	Sh	Sv-Op	Hld	ERC	ERA
2010	Lsvlle*	AAA	8	5	0	0	20.1	94	20	5	5	1	2	2	6	10	0	13	0	0	0	0	-	0	0--	-	5.16	2.21
2007	Ari	NL	29	27	2	0	152.2	651	146	81	73	20	7	3	14	50	2	106	5	0	8	8	.500	0	0-0	0	4.13	4.30
2008	2 Tms	NL	22	18	0	2	104.2	466	104	73	69	14	2	4	12	41	0	87	4	0	6	9	.400	0	0-0	1	4.66	5.93
2009	Cin	NL	26	19	0	0	119.2	542	126	75	71	18	3	5	6	64	3	68	1	0	7	12	.368	0	1-1	0	5.48	5.34
2010	Cin	NL	22	0	0	9	33.1	153	28	20	20	3	2	1	3	25	0	35	1	1	3	2	.600	0	0-0	0	4.80	5.40
	Postseason		1	1	0	0	3.2	21	6	6	2	1	0	0	1	2	0	2	0	0	0	1	.000	0	0-0	0	10.83	4.91
4 ML YEARS			99	64	2	15	410.1	1812	404	249	233	55	14	13	35	180	5	296	11	1	24	31	.436	1	1-1	1	4.71	5.11

Vicente Padilla

Pitches: R Bats: R Pos: SP-16 pah-DEE-ah **Ht:** 6'0" **Wt:** 232 **Born:** 9/27/1977 **Age:** 33

Year	Team	Lg	G	GS	CG	GF	IP	BFP	H	R	ER	HR	SH	SF	HB	TBB	IBB	SO	WP	Bk	W	L	Pct	Sh	Sv-Op	Hld	ERC	ERA
2010	InldEm*	A+	3	3	0	0	10.2	38	6	1	1	0	0	0	0	1	0	10	0	0	0	0	-	0	0--	-	0.85	0.84
2010	Albq*	AAA	1	1	0	0	5.2	26	8	6	4	2	0	1	0	0	0	5	1	0	0	1	.000	0	0--	-	6.19	6.35
1999	Ari	NL	5	0	0	2	2.2	19	7	5	5	1	1	0	0	3	0	0	0	0	0	1	.000	0	0-1	1	20.65	16.88
2000	2 Tms	NL	55	0	0	16	65.1	291	72	33	27	3	5	3	1	28	7	51	1	0	4	7	.364	0	2-7	15	4.22	3.72
2001	Phi	NL	23	0	0	5	34.0	144	36	18	16	1	0	0	0	12	0	29	1	0	3	1	.750	0	0-3	1	3.80	4.24
2002	Phi	NL	32	32	1	0	206.0	862	198	83	75	16	10	3	15	53	5	128	6	2	14	11	.560	1	0-0	0	3.42	3.28
2003	Phi	NL	32	32	1	0	208.2	876	196	94	84	22	11	7	16	62	4	133	3	2	14	12	.538	1	0-0	0	3.68	3.62
2004	Phi	NL	20	20	0	0	115.1	503	119	63	58	16	7	5	10	36	6	82	2	0	7	7	.500	0	0-0	0	4.42	4.53
2005	Phi	NL	27	27	0	0	147.0	654	146	79	77	22	7	3	8	74	9	103	1	0	9	12	.429	0	0-0	0	4.94	4.71
2006	Tex	AL	33	33	0	0	200.0	872	206	108	100	21	6	6	17	70	2	156	4	2	15	10	.600	0	0-0	0	4.41	4.53
2007	Tex	AL	23	23	0	0	120.1	553	146	88	77	16	3	2	9	50	1	71	2	0	6	10	.375	0	0-0	0	5.95	5.76
2008	Tex	AL	29	29	1	0	171.0	757	185	100	90	26	1	3	15	65	4	127	12	3	14	8	.636	1	0-0	0	5.20	4.74
2009	2 Tms	NL	26	25	0	0	147.1	634	156	76	73	16	6	3	8	54	0	97	5	2	12	6	.667	0	0-0	0	4.65	4.46
2010	LAD	NL	16	16	1	0	95.0	389	79	46	43	14	5	3	7	24	4	84	0	1	6	5	.545	1	0-0	0	3.13	4.07
00	Ari	NL	27	0	0	12	35.0	143	32	10	9	0	0	1	0	10	2	30	0	0	2	1	.667	0	0-1	7	2.48	2.31
00	Phi	NL	28	0	0	4	30.1	148	40	23	18	3	5	2	1	18	5	21	1	0	2	6	.250	0	2-6	8	6.52	5.34
09	Tex	AL	18	18	0	0	108.0	475	120	61	59	12	3	2	8	42	0	59	4	2	8	6	.571	0	0-0	0	5.15	4.92
09	LAD	NL	8	7	0	0	39.1	159	36	15	14	4	3	1	0	12	0	38	1	0	4	0	1.000	0	0-0	0	3.36	3.20
	Postseason		3	3	0	0	17.1	67	12	7	7	3	0	0	0	4	0	13	0	0	1	1	.500	0	0-0	0	2.29	3.63
	12 ML YEARS		321	237	4	23	1512.2	6554	1546	793	725	174	62	38	106	531	42	1061	37	12	104	90	.536	4	2-11	17	4.36	4.31

Angel Pagan

Bats: B Throws: R Pos: CF-94; RF-33; LF-27; PH-6; PR-3 ANE-gell pah-GONN **Ht:** 6'2" **Wt:** 195 **Born:** 7/2/1981 **Age:** 29

Year	Team	Lg	G	AB	H	2B	3B	HR	Hm	Rd	TB	R	RBI	RC	TBB	IBB	SO	HBP	SH	SF	SB	CS	SB%	GDP	Avg	OBP	Slg
2006	ChC	NL	77	170	42	6	2	5	(4	1)	67	28	18	21	15	0	28	0	1	1	4	2	.67	3	.247	.306	.394
2007	ChC	NL	71	148	39	10	2	4	(3	1)	65	21	21	23	10	0	32	0	1	2	4	1	.80	5	.264	.306	.439
2008	NYM	NL	31	91	25	7	1	0	(0	0)	34	12	13	15	11	0	18	0	1	2	4	0	1.00	0	.275	.346	.374
2009	NYM	NL	88	343	105	22	6	4	(5	1)	167	54	32	53	25	2	56	0	5	3	14	7	.67	3	.306	.350	.487
2010	NYM	NL	151	579	168	31	7	11	(6	5)	246	80	69	90	44	5	97	1	6	3	37	9	.80	9	.290	.340	.425
	5 ML YEARS		418	1331	379	76	23	26	(18	8)	579	195	153	202	105	7	231	1	14	11	63	19	.77	15	.285	.335	.435

Matt Pagnozzi

Bats: R Throws: R Pos: C-15 **Ht:** 6'2" **Wt:** 195 **Born:** 11/10/1982 **Age:** 28

Year	Team	Lg	G	AB	H	2B	3B	HR	Hm	Rd	TB	R	RBI	RC	TBB	IBB	SO	HBP	SH	SF	SB	CS	SB%	GDP	Avg	OBP	Slg
2003	NewJrs	A-	59	152	27	4	1	1	(-	-)	36	13	19	12	23	0	42	5	3	2	3	2	.60	1	.178	.302	.237
2004	Peoria	A	74	215	45	10	1	0	(-	-)	57	29	14	16	15	1	54	5	4	0	4	1	.80	4	.209	.277	.265
2005	PlmBh	A+	61	187	36	11	0	1	(-	-)	50	14	18	14	20	1	49	2	2	0	3	2	.60	6	.193	.278	.267
2005	Sprgfld	AA	15	37	6	2	0	0	(-	-)	8	3	1	1	3	0	8	1	0	0	0	0	-	2	.162	.244	.216
2006	PlmBh	A+	77	268	58	15	3	3	(-	-)	88	25	27	25	20	0	67	5	2	0	0	1	.00	4	.216	.283	.328
2007	Sprgfld	AA	13	43	9	3	0	0	(-	-)	12	5	3	3	2	0	11	1	1	0	0	0	-	4	.209	.261	.279
2007	Memp	AAA	47	139	31	6	0	2	(-	-)	43	10	9	12	6	0	36	4	2	1	1	0	1.00	4	.223	.273	.309
2008	Memp	AAA	3	5	1	1	0	0	(-	-)	2	0	1	1	2	1	1	0	0	0	0	0	-	0	.200	.429	.400
2008	Sprgfld	AA	68	216	51	10	0	3	(-	-)	70	24	19	22	16	1	47	3	6	3	2	1	.67	10	.236	.294	.324
2009	Memp	AAA	86	253	56	7	0	5	(-	-)	78	21	32	24	26	0	78	3	7	2	0	1	.00	11	.221	.299	.308
2010	Memp	AAA	68	207	50	11	0	1	(-	-)	64	20	21	24	27	1	49	3	5	0	0	0	-	10	.242	.338	.309
2009	StL	NL	6	3	0	0	0	0	(0	0)	0	1	0	0	1	0	0	0	0	0	0	0	-	0	.000	.250	.000
2010	StL	NL	15	39	14	2	0	1	(1	0)	19	4	10	7	2	0	8	1	2	0	0	0	-	1	.359	.405	.487
	2 ML YEARS		21	42	14	2	0	1	(1	0)	19	5	10	7	3	0	8	1	3	0	0	0	-	1	.333	.391	.452

Matt Palmer

Pitches: R Bats: R Pos: RP-13; SP-1 **Ht:** 6'2" **Wt:** 225 **Born:** 3/21/1979 **Age:** 32

Year	Team	Lg	G	GS	CG	GF	IP	BFP	H	R	ER	HR	SH	SF	HB	TBB	IBB	SO	WP	Bk	W	L	Pct	Sh	Sv-Op	Hld	ERC	ERA
2010	Angels*	R	2	1	0	0	4.0	12	2	0	0	0	0	0	0	1	0	2	0	0	0	0	-	0	0--	-	1.18	0.00
2010	Salt Lk*	AAA	13	7	0	3	46.1	184	32	17	14	4	1	0	2	19	1	36	3	0	2	3	.400	0	2--	-	2.61	2.72
2008	SF	NL	3	3	0	0	12.2	67	17	13	12	1	1	0	2	13	1	3	0	0	0	2	.000	0	0-0	0	9.37	8.53
2009	LAA	AL	40	13	1	10	121.1	505	105	55	53	12	6	3	4	55	2	69	5	0	11	2	.846	0	0-0	0	3.74	3.93
2010	LAA	AL	14	1	0	3	33.2	157	38	20	17	1	0	1	1	20	1	17	2	0	1	2	.333	0	0-0	0	5.07	4.44
	Postseason		2	0	0	2	2.2	14	5	4	4	1	0	0	1	1	0	2	0	0	0	0	-	0	0-0	0	11.86	13.50
	3 ML YEARS		57	17	1	13	167.2	729	160	88	82	14	8	3	7	88	4	89	7	0	12	6	.667	0	0-0	1	4.39	4.40

Jonathan Papelbon

Pitches: R Bats: R Pos: RP-65 PAHP-ill-bonn **Ht:** 6'4" **Wt:** 225 **Born:** 11/23/1980 **Age:** 30

Year	Team	Lg	G	GS	CG	GF	IP	BFP	H	R	ER	HR	SH	SF	HB	TBB	IBB	SO	WP	Bk	W	L	Pct	Sh	Sv-Op	Hld	ERC	ERA
2005	Bos	AL	17	3	0	4	34.0	148	33	11	10	4	1	0	3	17	2	34	1	0	3	1	.750	0	0-1	4	4.82	2.65
2006	Bos	AL	59	0	0	49	68.1	257	40	8	7	3	1	2	1	13	2	75	2	0	4	2	.667	0	35-41	1	1.22	0.92
2007	Bos	AL	59	0	0	53	58.1	224	30	12	12	5	0	0	4	15	0	84	0	0	1	3	.250	0	37-40	2	1.43	1.85
2008	Bos	AL	67	0	0	62	69.1	273	58	24	18	4	4	1	0	8	0	77	2	0	5	4	.556	0	41-46	0	1.92	2.34

Year Team	Lg	G	GS	CG	GF	IP	BFP	H	R	ER	HR	SH	SF	HB	TBB	IBB	SO	WP	Bk	W	L	Pct	Sh	Sv-Op	Hld	ERC	ERA
		HOW MUCH HE PITCHED						**WHAT HE GAVE UP**												**THE RESULTS**							
2009 Bos	AL	66	0	0	59	68.0	285	54	15	14	5	1	2	4	24	1	76	0	0	1	1	.500	0	38-41	0	2.78	1.85
2010 Bos	AL	65	0	0	53	67.0	287	57	34	29	7	5	0	2	28	4	76	4	0	5	7	.417	0	37-45	0	3.32	3.90
Postseason		18	0	0	12	27.0	100	14	3	3	0	0	1	0	8	3	23	0	0	2	1	.667	0	7-9	0	1.01	1.00
6 ML YEARS		333	3	0	280	365.0	1474	272	104	90	28	12	5	14	105	9	422	9	0	19	18	.514	0	188-214	7	2.28	2.22

Chan Ho Park

Pitches: R Bats: R Pos: RP-53 **Ht: 6'2" Wt: 210 Born: 6/30/1973 Age: 38**

Year Team	Lg	G	GS	CG	GF	IP	BFP	H	R	ER	HR	SH	SF	HB	TBB	IBB	SO	WP	Bk	W	L	Pct	Sh	Sv-Op	Hld	ERC	ERA
		HOW MUCH HE PITCHED						**WHAT HE GAVE UP**												**THE RESULTS**							
2010 S-WB*	AAA	1	1	0	0	1.0	4	1	0	0	0	0	0	0	0	0	2	1	0	0	0	-	0	0- -	-	1.95	0.00
1994 LAD	NL	2	0	0	1	4.0	23	5	5	5	1	0	0	1	5	0	6	0	0	0	0	-	0	0-0	0	11.69	11.25
1995 LAD	NL	2	1	0	0	4.0	16	2	2	2	1	0	0	0	2	0	7	0	1	0	0	-	0	0-0	0	2.70	4.50
1996 LAD	NL	48	10	0	7	108.2	477	82	48	44	7	8	1	4	71	3	119	4	3	5	5	.500	0	0-0	0	3.50	3.64
1997 LAD	NL	32	29	2	1	192.0	792	149	80	72	24	9	5	8	70	1	166	4	1	14	8	.636	0	0-0	0	3.04	3.38
1998 LAD	NL	34	34	2	0	220.2	946	199	101	91	16	11	10	11	97	1	191	6	2	15	9	.625	0	0-0	0	3.69	3.71
1999 LAD	NL	33	33	0	0	194.1	883	208	120	113	31	10	5	14	100	4	174	11	1	13	11	.542	0	0-0	0	5.68	5.23
2000 LAD	NL	34	34	3	0	226.0	963	173	92	82	21	12	5	12	124	4	217	13	0	18	10	.643	1	0-0	0	3.51	3.27
2001 LAD	NL	36	35	2	0	234.0	981	183	98	91	23	16	7	20	91	1	218	3	3	15	11	.577	1	0-0	0	3.15	3.50
2002 Tex	AL	25	25	0	0	145.2	666	154	95	93	20	4	3	17	78	2	121	9	0	9	8	.529	0	0-0	0	5.75	5.75
2003 Tex	AL	7	7	0	0	29.2	146	34	26	25	5	1	3	6	25	0	16	1	1	1	3	.250	0	0-0	0	8.56	7.58
2004 Tex	AL	16	16	0	0	95.2	428	105	63	58	22	4	4	13	33	0	63	1	1	4	7	.364	0	0-0	0	5.97	5.46
2005 2 Tms		30	29	0	0	155.1	715	180	103	99	11	7	3	10	80	1	113	6	0	12	8	.600	1	0-0	0	5.52	5.74
2006 SD	NL	24	21	1	0	136.2	606	146	81	73	20	10	4	10	44	7	96	5	0	7	7	.500	1	0-0	0	4.62	4.81
2007 NYM	NL	1	1	0	0	4.0	20	6	7	7	2	0	0	0	2	0	4	1	0	0	1	.000	0	0-0	0	10.88	15.75
2008 LAD	NL	54	5	0	11	95.1	412	97	43	36	12	4	0	4	36	7	79	2	1	4	4	.500	0	2 5	5	4.34	3.40
2009 Phi	NL	45	7	0	6	83.1	362	84	43	41	5	1	5	5	33	3	73	2	0	3	3	.500	0	0-1	13	4.01	4.43
2010 2 Tms		53	0	0	26	63.2	278	65	39	33	9	2	1	3	19	1	52	7	0	4	3	.571	0	0-3	1	4.14	4.66
05 Tex	AL	20	20	0	0	109.2	502	130	70	69	8	5	2	6	54	1	80	3	0	8	5	.615	0	0-0	0	5.58	5.66
05 SD	NL	10	9	0	0	45.2	213	50	33	30	3	2	1	4	26	0	33	3	0	4	3	.571	0	0-0	0	5.36	5.91
10 NYY	AL	27	0	0	15	35.1	157	40	25	22	7	1	0	1	12	0	29	2	0	2	1	.667	0	0-2	0	5.38	5.60
10 Pit	NL	26	0	0	11	28.1	121	25	14	11	2	1	1	2	7	1	23	5	0	2	2	.500	0	0-1	1	2.77	3.49
Postseason		13	0	0	1	10.1	40	8	3	3	0	0	1	1	3	0	7	1	0	0	1	.000	0	0-2	1	2.36	2.61
17 ML YEARS		476	287	10	52	1993.0	8714	1872	1046	965	230	99	56	138	910	35	1715	75	14	124	98	.559	3	2-9	23	4.31	4.36

Bobby Parnell

Pitches: R Bats: R Pos: RP-41 **Ht: 6'4" Wt: 200 Born: 9/8/1984 Age: 26**

Year Team	Lg	G	GS	CG	GF	IP	BFP	H	R	ER	HR	SH	SF	HB	TBB	IBB	SO	WP	Bk	W	L	Pct	Sh	Sv-Op	Hld	ERC	ERA
		HOW MUCH HE PITCHED						**WHAT HE GAVE UP**												**THE RESULTS**							
2010 Buffalo*	AAA	24	0	0	10	41.1	177	36	22	19	3	0	3	1	17	0	42	1	0	1	1	.500	0	4- -	-	3.27	4.14
2008 NYM	NL	6	0	0	3	5.0	19	3	3	3	0	0	0	0	2	0	3	1	0	0	0	-	0	0-0	0	1.59	5.40
2009 NYM	NL	68	8	0	14	88.1	413	101	56	52	8	3	1	4	46	2	74	6	1	4	8	.333	0	1-5	16	5.37	5.30
2010 NYM	NL	41	0	0	10	35.0	149	41	13	11	1	2	0	0	8	2	33	0	0	0	1	.000	0	0-2	9	3.80	2.83
3 ML YEARS		115	8	0	27	128.1	581	145	72	66	9	5	1	4	56	4	110	7	1	4	9	.308	0	1-7	25	4.77	4.63

Gerardo Parra

Bats: L Throws: L Pos: LF-76; RF-36; PH-30; CF-7 **Ht: 5'11" Wt: 195 Born: 5/6/1987 Age: 24**

Year Team	Lg	G	AB	H	2B	3B	HR	(Hm	Rd)	TB	R	RBI	RC	TBB	IBB	SO	HBP	SH	SF	SB	CS	SB%	GDP	Avg	OBP	Slg
		BATTING																		**BASERUNNING**				**AVERAGES**		
2006 Msoula	R+	69	271	89	18	4	4	(-	-)	127	46	43	52	25	3	30	3	0	4	23	7	.77	4	.328	.386	.469
2007 Sbend	A	110	444	142	25	4	6	(-	-)	193	64	57	75	30	2	51	8	1	5	24	8	.75	12	.320	.370	.435
2007 Visalia	A+	24	102	29	2	1	2	(-	-)	39	11	14	11	4	1	17	0	0	3	2	3	.40	1	.284	.303	.382
2008 Visalia	A+	50	196	59	8	4	2	(-	-)	81	26	19	33	23	1	31	3	1	1	12	4	.75	7	.301	.381	.413
2008 Mobile	AA	73	265	73	14	6	4	(-	-)	111	35	33	40	23	2	34	6	3	5	17	9	.65	11	.275	.341	.419
2009 Mobile	AA	29	108	39	3	1	3	(-	-)	53	23	12	25	22	4	13	0	0	0	7	4	.64	3	.361	.469	.491
2010 Reno	AAA	9	36	15	4	0	1	(-	-)	22	8	7	9	2	0	5	1	0	1	3	1	.75	1	.417	.462	.611
2009 Ari	NL	120	455	132	21	8	5	(4	1)	184	59	60	58	25	1	89	1	4	6	5	7	.42	18	.290	.324	.404
2010 Ari	NL	133	364	95	19	6	3	(1	2)	135	31	30	38	23	10	76	2	3	1	1	0	1.00	8	.261	.308	.371
2 ML YEARS		253	819	227	40	14	8	(5	3)	319	90	90	96	48	11	165	3	7	7	6	7	.46	26	.277	.317	.389

Manny Parra

Pitches: L Bats: L Pos: RP-26; SP-16 **Ht: 6'3" Wt: 216 Born: 10/30/1982 Age: 28**

Year Team	Lg	G	GS	CG	GF	IP	BFP	H	R	ER	HR	SH	SF	HB	TBB	IBB	SO	WP	Bk	W	L	Pct	Sh	Sv-Op	Hld	ERC	ERA
		HOW MUCH HE PITCHED						**WHAT HE GAVE UP**												**THE RESULTS**							
2007 Mil	NL	9	2	0	3	26.1	116	25	13	11	1	1	3	2	12	0	26	1	0	0	1	.000	0	0-0	0	3.83	3.76
2008 Mil	NL	32	29	0	0	166.0	741	181	91	81	18	10	2	2	75	1	147	17	2	10	8	.556	0	0-0	0	4.89	4.39
2009 Mil	NL	27	27	0	0	140.0	671	179	108	99	19	5	3	1	77	5	116	4	1	11	11	.500	0	0-0	0	6.51	6.36
2010 Mil	NL	42	16	0	9	122.0	560	135	76	68	18	6	7	3	63	3	129	14	1	3	10	.231	0	0-0	0	5.53	5.02
Postseason		2	0	0	0	2.1	9	2	0	0	0	0	0	0	1	0	3	0	0	0	0	-	0	0-0	0	3.03	0.00
4 ML YEARS		110	74	0	12	454.1	2088	520	288	259	56	22	15	8	227	9	418	36	4	24	30	.444	0	0-0	1	5.49	5.13

John Parrish

Pitches: L Bats: L Pos: RP-9   Ht: 5'11" Wt: 198 Born: 11/26/1977 Age: 33

			HOW MUCH HE PITCHED						WHAT HE GAVE UP											THE RESULTS							
Year	Team	Lg	G	GS	CG	GF	IP	BFP	H	R	ER	HR	SH	SF	HB	TBB	IBB	SO	WP	Bk	W	L	Pct	Sh	Sv-Op	Hld	ERC	ERA
2010	Omha*	AAA	3	2	0	0	2.0	9	1	2	2	0	0	0	0	2	0	2	0	0	0	1	.000	0	0- -	-	2.80	9.00
2000	Bal	AL	8	8	0	0	36.1	180	40	32	29	6	1	4	1	35	0	28	1	0	2	4	.333	0	0-0	0	7.75	7.18
2001	Bal	AL	16	1	0	7	22.0	107	22	17	15	5	1	0	3	17	1	20	1	0	1	2	.333	0	0-0	0	7.06	6.14
2003	Bal	AL	14	0	0	2	23.2	93	17	7	5	2	0	1	1	8	2	15	2	0	0	1	.000	0	0-2	1	2.39	1.90
2004	Bal	AL	56	1	0	17	78.0	353	68	39	30	4	3	6	3	55	6	71	6	0	6	3	.667	0	1-1	2	4.17	3.46
2005	Bal	AL	14	0	0	2	17.1	86	19	6	6	1	1	0	0	17	1	25	6	0	1	0	1.000	0	0-0	1	6.53	3.12
2007	2 Tms	AL	53	0	0	14	52.0	254	63	34	33	2	1	1	2	37	4	41	3	0	2	2	.500	0	0-2	10	6.03	5.71
2008	Tor	AL	13	6	0	1	42.1	179	47	19	19	5	0	1	0	15	0	21	4	0	1	1	.500	0	0-0	0	4.82	4.04
2010	KC	AL	9	0	0	1	6.0	26	4	2	2	2	0	0	0	5	0	4	0	0	1	1	.500	0	0-2	2	5.75	3.00
07	Bal	AL	45	0	0	9	41.2	199	41	26	25	2	0	1	2	33	4	36	2	0	2	2	.500	0	0-2	9	5.05	5.40
07	Sea	AL	8	0	0	5	10.1	55	22	8	8	0	1	0	0	4	0	5	1	0	0	0	-	0	0-0	1	10.48	6.97
	8 ML YEARS		183	16	0	44	277.2	1278	280	156	139	27	7	13	10	189	14	225	23	0	14	14	.500	0	1-7	16	5.30	4.51

Corey Patterson

Bats: L Throws: R Pos: LF-56; DH-17; CF-10; PH-8; PR-6; RF-1   Ht: 5'10" Wt: 180 Born: 8/13/1979 Age: 31

						BATTING															BASERUNNING				AVERAGES		
Year	Team	Lg	G	AB	H	2B	3B	HR	(Hm	Rd)	TB	R	RBI	RC	TBB	IBB	SO	HBP	SH	SF	SB	CS	SB%	GDP	Avg	OBP	Slg
2010	Norfolk*	AAA	14	57	21	5	1	0	(-	-)	28	6	2	10	5	0	8	0	0	0	3	3	.50	1	.368	.419	.491
2000	ChC	NL	11	42	7	1	0	2	(1	1)	14	9	2	3	3	0	14	1	1	0	1	1	.50	0	.167	.239	.333
2001	ChC	NL	59	131	29	3	0	4	(1	3)	44	26	14	13	6	0	33	3	2	3	4	0	1.00	1	.221	.266	.336
2002	ChC	NL	153	592	150	30	5	14	(7	7)	232	71	54	61	19	1	142	8	4	5	18	3	.86	8	.253	.284	.392
2003	ChC	NL	83	329	98	17	7	13	(7	6)	168	49	55	55	15	2	77	1	0	2	16	5	.76	5	.298	.329	.511
2004	ChC	NL	157	631	168	33	6	24	(14	10)	285	91	72	87	45	7	168	5	5	1	32	9	.78	7	.266	.320	.452
2005	ChC	NL	126	451	97	15	3	13	(9	4)	157	47	34	32	23	3	118	1	5	1	15	5	.75	5	.215	.254	.348
2006	Bal	AL	135	463	128	19	5	16	(9	7)	205	75	53	66	21	5	94	5	8	1	45	9	.83	0	.276	.314	.443
2007	Bal	AL	132	461	124	26	2	8	(5	3)	178	65	45	51	21	1	65	4	13	4	37	9	.80	3	.269	.304	.386
2008	Cin	NL	135	366	75	17	2	10	(2	8)	126	46	34	23	16	0	57	1	5	4	14	9	.61	3	.205	.238	.344
2009	2 Tms		16	29	3	0	0	0	(0	0)	3	0	0	0	0	0	13	0	1	0	2	1	.67	1	.103	.103	.103
2010	Bal	AL	90	308	83	16	1	8	(4	4)	125	43	32	41	20	2	75	1	10	1	21	4	.84	3	.269	.315	.406
09	Was	NL	5	15	2	0	0	0	(0	0)	2	0	0	0	0	0	6	0	0	0	2	0	1.00	0	.133	.133	.133
09	Mil	NL	11	14	1	0	0	0	(0	0)	1	0	0	0	0	0	7	0	1	0	0	1	.00	1	.071	.071	.071
	11 ML YEARS		1097	3803	962	177	31	112	(59	53)	1537	522	395	432	189	21	856	30	54	22	205	55	.79	36	.253	.292	.404

Eric Patterson

Bats: L Throws: R Pos: LF-47; PR-21; CF-20; 2B-14; PH-13; DH-3   Ht: 6'0" Wt: 168 Born: 4/8/1983 Age: 28

						BATTING															BASERUNNING				AVERAGES		
Year	Team	Lg	G	AB	H	2B	3B	HR	(Hm	Rd)	TB	R	RBI	RC	TBB	IBB	SO	HBP	SH	SF	SB	CS	SB%	GDP	Avg	OBP	Slg
2010	Pwtckt*	AAA	4	17	4	2	1	0	(-	-)	8	4	0	2	1	0	7	0	0	0	3	0	1.00	0	.235	.278	.471
2007	ChC	NL	7	8	2	1	0	0	(0	0)	3	0	0	0	0	0	3	0	1	0	0	0	-	0	.250	.250	.375
2008	2 Tms		43	130	25	4	0	1	(1	0)	32	16	15	11	17	0	36	0	0	1	10	1	.91	1	.192	.284	.246
2009	Oak	AL	39	94	27	5	1	1	(1	0)	37	15	14	14	14	0	25	0	0	2	6	1	.86	0	.287	.373	.394
2010	2 Tms		90	187	40	8	5	6	(2	4)	76	26	16	20	14	0	62	1	2	0	11	1	.92	2	.214	.272	.406
08	ChC	NL	13	38	9	1	0	1	(1	0)	13	5	7	5	5	0	12	0	0	1	2	1	.67	1	.237	.318	.342
08	Oak	AL	30	92	16	3	0	0	(0	0)	19	11	8	6	12	0	24	0	0	0	8	0	1.00	0	.174	.269	.207
10	Oak	AL	45	103	21	5	2	4	(2	2)	42	13	9	9	7	0	31	0	1	0	6	0	1.00	1	.204	.255	.408
10	Bos	AL	45	84	19	3	3	2	(0	2)	34	13	7	11	7	0	31	1	1	0	5	1	.83	1	.226	.293	.405
	4 ML YEARS		179	419	94	18	6	8	(4	4)	148	57	42	45	45	0	126	1	3	3	27	3	.90	3	.224	.299	.353

Troy Patton

Pitches: L Bats: B Pos: RP-1   Ht: 6'1" Wt: 185 Born: 9/3/1985 Age: 25

			HOW MUCH HE PITCHED						WHAT HE GAVE UP											THE RESULTS							
Year	Team	Lg	G	GS	CG	GF	IP	BFP	H	R	ER	HR	SH	SF	HB	TBB	IBB	SO	WP	Bk	W	L	Pct	Sh	Sv-Op	Hld	ERC	ERA
2004	Grnsvle	R	6	6	0	0	28.0	111	23	8	6	1	0	3	1	5	0	32	0	0	2	2	.500	0	0- -	-	2.08	1.93
2005	Lxngtn	A	15	15	0	0	78.2	310	60	24	17	3	4	0	5	20	0	94	0	0	5	2	.714	0	0- -	-	2.14	1.94
2005	Salem	A+	10	9	0	0	41.0	162	34	12	12	2	0	2	2	8	0	38	1	0	1	4	.200	0	0- -	-	2.33	2.63
2006	Salem	A+	19	19	1	0	101.1	435	92	49	33	4	6	4	5	37	0	102	3	0	7	7	.500	0	0- -	-	3.16	2.93
2006	CpChr	AA	8	8	0	0	45.1	195	48	26	22	6	2	1	2	13	0	37	3	0	2	5	.286	0	0- -	-	4.36	4.37
2007	CpChr	AA	16	16	0	0	102.1	437	96	38	34	10	5	1	9	33	1	69	2	0	6	6	.500	0	0- -	-	3.73	2.99
2007	RdRck	AAA	8	8	0	0	49.0	200	44	26	25	5	4	3	3	11	0	25	0	0	4	2	.667	0	0- -	-	3.13	4.59
2009	Bowie	AA	11	11	0	0	63.1	260	50	18	14	4	1	1	3	18	0	47	0	0	6	2	.750	0	0- -	-	2.44	1.99
2009	Norfolk	AAA	9	9	0	0	44.2	207	62	35	32	12	1	3	5	14	0	26	0	0	1	3	.250	0	0- -	-	8.05	6.45
2010	Norfolk	AAA	25	25	0	0	136.0	593	144	79	67	15	5	5	8	43	0	89	1	0	8	11	.421	0	0- -	-	4.36	4.43
2007	Hou	NL	3	2	0	1	12.2	54	10	6	5	3	1	0	2	4	0	8	0	0	0	2	.000	0	0-0	4	4.04	3.55
2010	Bal	AL	1	0	0	0	0.2	4	1	0	0	0	0	0	0	1	0	1	0	0	0	0	-	0	0-0	0	10.76	0.00
	2 ML YEARS		4	2	0	1	13.1	58	11	6	5	3	1	0	2	5	0	9	0	0	0	2	.000	0	0-0	4	4.37	3.38

Xavier Paul

Bats: L Throws: R Pos: LF-23; RF-15; PH-9   Ht: 5'9" Wt: 206 Born: 2/25/1985 Age: 26

						BATTING															BASERUNNING				AVERAGES		
Year	Team	Lg	G	AB	H	2B	3B	HR	(Hm	Rd)	TB	R	RBI	RC	TBB	IBB	SO	HBP	SH	SF	SB	CS	SB%	GDP	Avg	OBP	Slg
2003	Ogden	R+	69	264	81	15	6	7	(-	-)	129	60	47	51	34	1	58	2	3	5	11	4	.73	2	.307	.384	.489
2004	Clmbs	A	128	465	122	26	6	9	(-	-)	187	69	72	67	56	4	127	3	5	7	10	7	.59	4	.262	.341	.402
2005	VeroB	A+	85	288	71	15	3	7	(-	-)	113	42	41	37	32	2	81	4	4	2	1	5	.17	3	.247	.328	.392
2006	VeroB	A+	120	470	134	23	3	13	(-	-)	202	62	69	69	38	4	114	4	7	1	22	15	.59	10	.285	.343	.430

Year	Team	Lg	G	AB	H	2B	3B	HR	(Hm	Rd)	TB	R	RBI	RC	TBB	IBB	SO	HBP	SH	SF	SB	CS	SB%	GDP	Avg	OBP	Slg
2007	Jaxnvl	AA	118	422	123	21	2	11	(-	-)	181	64	50	69	48	2	112	3	7	2	18	9	.67	6	.291	.366	.429
2008	LsVgs	AAA	115	443	140	28	5	9	(-	-)	205	82	68	80	43	2	96	5	9	6	17	7	.71	9	.316	.378	.463
2009	Albq	AAA	31	116	38	10	2	2	(-	-)	58	13	16	22	10	1	22	0	2	1	8	2	.80	2	.328	.378	.500
2010	Albq	AAA	57	228	74	20	1	12	(-	-)	132	46	38	49	18	4	41	4	0	4	7	3	.70	6	.325	.384	.579
2009	LAD	NL	11	14	3	1	0	1	(0	1)	7	3	1	0	2	0	4	0	0	0	0	1	1.00	1	.214	.313	.500
2010	LAD	NL	44	121	28	8	1	0	(0	0)	38	16	11	8	8	0	24	0	3	1	3	1	.75	3	.231	.277	.314
2 ML YEARS			55	135	31	9	1	1	(0	1)	45	19	12	8	10	0	28	0	3	1	3	2	.60	4	.230	.281	.333

David Pauley

Pitches: R **Bats:** R **Pos:** SP-15; RP-4   **Ht:** 6'2" **Wt:** 210 **Born:** 6/17/1983 **Age:** 28

	HOW MUCH HE PITCHED						WHAT HE GAVE UP											THE RESULTS						
Year	Team	Lg	G	GS	CG	GF	IP	BFP	H	R	ER	HR	SH	SF	HB	TBB	IBB	SO	WP	Bk	W	L	Pct	Sh	Sv-Op Hld	ERC	ERA
2010	Tacom*	AAA	15	14	1	0	85.2	360	82	38	35	6	3	3	5	26	1	56	3	0	1	6	.143	0	0- -	3.50	3.68
2006	Bos	AL	3	3	0	0	16.0	82	31	14	14	1	0	0	2	6	1	10	0	0	0	2	.000	0	0-0 0	10.41	7.88
2008	Bos	AL	6	2	0	3	12.1	67	23	17	16	2	0	1	1	5	0	11	0	0	0	1	.000	0	0-0 0	10.16	11.68
2010	Sea	AL	19	15	0	2	90.2	390	89	44	41	13	2	3	4	30	2	51	4	0	4	9	.308	0	0-0 0	4.11	4.07
3 ML YEARS			28	20	0	5	119.0	539	143	75	71	16	2	4	7	41	3	72	4	0	4	12	.250	0	0-0 0	5.44	5.37

Felipe Paulino

Pitches: R **Bats:** R **Pos:** SP-14; RP-5   **Ht:** 6'2" **Wt:** 180 **Born:** 10/5/1983 **Age:** 27

	HOW MUCH HE PITCHED						WHAT HE GAVE UP											THE RESULTS						
Year	Team	Lg	G	GS	CG	GF	IP	BFP	H	R	ER	HR	SH	SF	HB	TBB	IBB	SO	WP	Bk	W	L	Pct	Sh	Sv-Op Hld	ERC	ERA
2010	CpChr*	AA	1	1	0	0	4.0	14	2	0	0	0	0	0	0	1	0	3	0	0	0	0	-	0	0- -	1.01	0.00
2007	Hou	NL	5	3	0	0	19.0	85	22	15	15	5	2	0	0	7	1	11	1	0	2	1	.667	0	0-0 1	5.93	7.11
2009	Hou	NL	23	17	0	0	97.2	448	126	73	68	20	8	1	4	37	2	93	5	0	3	11	.214	0	0-1 0	6.70	6.27
2010	Hou	NL	19	14	0	0	91.2	411	95	63	52	4	6	3	3	46	4	83	6	1	1	9	.100	0	0-1 1	4.29	5.11
3 ML YEARS			47	34	0	0	208.1	944	243	151	135	29	16	4	7	90	7	187	12	1	6	21	.222	0	0-2 2	5.55	5.83

Ronny Paulino

Bats: R **Throws:** R **Pos:** C-85; PH-7   **Ht:** 6'3" **Wt:** 250 **Born:** 4/21/1981 **Age:** 30

	BATTING															BASERUNNING				AVERAGES		
Year	Team	Lg	G	AB	H	2B	3B	HR	(Hm | Rd)	TB	R	RBI	RC	TBB	IBB	SO	HBP	SH	SF	SB	CS	SB%	GDP	Avg	OBP	Slg
2005	Pit	NL	2	4	2	0	0	0	(0 | 0)	2	1	0	1	1	0	0	0	0	0	0	0	-	0	.500	.600	.500
2006	Pit	NL	129	442	137	19	0	6	(2 | 4)	174	37	55	60	34	5	79	2	1	2	0	0	-	17	.310	.360	.394
2007	Pit	NL	133	457	120	25	0	11	(7 | 4)	178	56	55	49	33	0	79	2	0	2	2	2	.50	14	.263	.314	.389
2008	Pit	NL	40	118	25	5	0	2	(0 | 2)	36	8	18	14	11	1	24	0	0	1	0	0	-	4	.212	.277	.305
2009	Fla	NL	80	239	65	10	1	8	(4 | 4)	101	24	27	31	25	2	48	0	1	1	1	0	1.00	8	.272	.340	.423
2010	Fla	NL	91	316	82	18	0	4	(0 | 4)	112	31	37	32	25	4	51	0	0	3	1	0	1.00	11	.259	.311	.354
6 ML YEARS			475	1576	431	77	1	31	(13 | 18)	603	157	192	187	129	12	281	4	2	9	4	2	.67	54	.273	.328	.383

Carl Pavano

Pitches: R **Bats:** R **Pos:** SP-32   pah-VAH-no   **Ht:** 6'5" **Wt:** 250 **Born:** 1/8/1976 **Age:** 35

	HOW MUCH HE PITCHED						WHAT HE GAVE UP											THE RESULTS						
Year	Team	Lg	G	GS	CG	GF	IP	BFP	H	R	ER	HR	SH	SF	HB	TBB	IBB	SO	WP	Bk	W	L	Pct	Sh	Sv-Op Hld	ERC	ERA
1998	Mon	NL	24	23	0	0	134.2	580	130	70	63	18	5	6	8	43	1	83	1	0	6	9	.400	0	0-0 0	3.97	4.21
1999	Mon	NL	19	18	1	0	104.0	457	117	66	65	8	5	2	4	36	1	70	1	3	6	8	.429	1	0-0 0	4.51	5.63
2000	Mon	NL	15	15	0	0	97.0	400	99	40	33	0	4	3	0	34	1	64	1	1	8	4	.667	0	0-0 0	3.67	3.06
2001	Mon	NL	8	8	0	0	42.2	199	59	33	30	7	2	1	2	16	1	36	0	1	1	6	.143	0	0-0 0	6.99	6.33
2002	2 Tms	NL	37	22	0	2	136.0	619	174	88	78	19	4	4	10	45	8	92	3	2	6	10	.375	0	0-0 3	5.98	5.16
2003	Fla	NL	33	32	2	1	201.0	846	204	99	96	19	9	10	7	49	10	133	3	2	12	13	.480	0	0-0 0	3.57	4.30
2004	Fla	NL	31	31	2	0	222.1	909	212	80	74	16	7	4	11	49	13	139	2	3	18	8	.692	2	0-0 0	3.10	3.00
2005	NYY	AL	17	17	1	0	100.0	442	129	66	53	17	4	3	8	18	1	56	2	1	4	6	.400	1	0-0 0	5.74	4.77
2007	NYY	AL	2	2	0	0	11.1	46	12	7	6	1	0	0	0	2	0	4	0	0	1	0	1.000	0	0-0 0	3.54	4.76
2008	NYY	AL	7	7	0	0	34.1	154	41	23	22	5	3	3	4	10	0	15	0	1	4	2	.667	0	0-0 0	5.60	5.77
2009	2 Tms	AL	33	33	1	0	199.1	854	235	119	113	26	2	7	6	39	1	147	5	0	14	12	.538	1	0-0 0	4.63	5.10
2010	Min	AL	32	32	7	0	221.0	906	227	99	92	24	5	5	6	37	2	117	4	0	17	11	.607	2	0-0 0	3.51	3.75
02	Mon	NL	15	14	0	0	74.1	350	98	55	52	14	2	2	7	31	5	51	2	1	3	8	.273	0	0-0 0	7.07	6.30
02	Fla	NL	22	8	0	2	61.2	269	76	33	26	5	2	2	3	14	3	41	1	1	3	2	.600	0	0-0 3	4.74	3.79
09	Cle	AL	21	21	1	0	125.2	534	150	80	75	19	1	6	3	23	0	88	4	0	9	8	.529	1	0-0 0	4.83	5.37
09	Min	AL	12	12	0	0	73.2	320	85	39	38	7	1	1	3	16	1	59	1	0	5	4	.556	0	0-0 0	4.29	4.64
Postseason			9	3	0	1	26.1	100	22	5	5	2	1	1	1	3	1	24	0	0	2	1	.667	0	0-0 0	2.21	1.71
12 ML YEARS			258	240	14	3	1503.2	6420	1629	786	725	168	50	48	74	377	39	956	22	14	97	89	.522	7	0-0 3	4.21	4.34

Jay Payton

Bats: R **Throws:** R **Pos:** PH-10; LF-9; PR-2; CF-1   **Ht:** 5'10" **Wt:** 207 **Born:** 11/22/1972 **Age:** 38

	BATTING															BASERUNNING				AVERAGES		
Year	Team	Lg	G	AB	H	2B	3B	HR	(Hm | Rd)	TB	R	RBI	RC	TBB	IBB	SO	HBP	SH	SF	SB	CS	SB%	GDP	Avg	OBP	Slg
2010	ColSpr*	AAA	116	439	142	36	5	6	(- | -)	206	62	74	76	25	1	47	4	1	1	13	3	.81	13	.323	.365	.469
1998	NYM	NL	15	22	7	1	0	0	(0 | 0)	8	2	0	3	1	0	4	0	0	0	0	0	-	0	.318	.348	.364
1999	NYM	NL	13	8	2	1	0	0	(0 | 0)	3	1	1	0	0	0	2	1	0	0	1	2	.33	0	.250	.333	.375
2000	NYM	NL	149	488	142	23	1	17	(9 | 8)	218	63	62	68	30	0	60	3	0	8	5	11	.31	9	.291	.331	.447
2001	NYM	NL	104	361	92	16	1	8	(6 | 2)	134	44	34	37	18	1	52	5	0	2	4	3	.57	11	.255	.298	.371
2002	2 Tms	NL	134	445	135	20	7	16	(9 | 7)	217	69	59	71	29	0	54	4	2	1	7	4	.64	11	.303	.351	.488
2003	Col	NL	157	600	181	32	5	28	(13 | 15)	307	93	89	95	43	3	77	7	5	3	6	4	.60	27	.302	.354	.512
2004	SD	NL	143	458	119	17	4	8	(0 | 8)	168	57	55	61	43	2	56	4	2	4	2	0	1.00	12	.260	.326	.367

			BATTING																		BASERUNNING				AVERAGES		
Year	Team	Lg	G	AB	H	2B	3B	HR	(Hm	Rd)	TB	R	RBI	RC	TBB	IBB	SO	HBP	SH	SF	SB	CS	SB%	GDP	Avg	OBP	Slg
2005	2 Tms	AL	124	408	109	16	1	18	(11	7)	181	62	63	56	24	2	47	0	0	3	0	1	.00	8	.267	.306	.444
2006	Oak	AL	142	557	165	32	3	10	(5	5)	233	78	59	76	22	1	52	4	0	5	8	4	.67	12	.296	.325	.418
2007	Bal	AL	131	434	111	21	5	7	(6	1)	163	48	58	49	22	0	42	3	5	6	5	2	.71	9	.256	.292	.376
2008	Bal	AL	127	338	82	10	2	7	(2	5)	117	41	41	37	22	1	53	1	2	0	8	1	.89	7	.243	.291	.346
2010	Col	AL	20	35	12	4	1	0	(0	0)	18	3	1	4	1	0	4	0	0	0	1	0	1.00	2	.343	.361	.514
02	NYM	NL	87	275	78	6	3	8	(4	4)	114	33	31	38	21	0	34	1	2	1	4	1	.80	8	.284	.336	.415
02	Col	NL	47	170	57	14	4	8	(5	3)	103	36	28	33	8	0	20	3	0	0	3	3	.50	3	.335	.376	.606
05	Bos	AL	55	133	35	7	0	5	(2	3)	57	24	21	16	10	0	14	0	0	1	0	0	-	4	.263	.313	.429
05	Oak	AL	69	275	74	9	1	13	(9	4)	124	38	42	40	14	2	33	0	0	2	0	1	.00	4	.269	.302	.451
	Postseason		21	83	21	2	0	3	(0	3)	32	9	10	5	3	0	17	1	0	1	1	1	.50	2	.253	.284	.386
	12 ML YEARS		1259	4154	1157	193	30	119	(61	58)	1767	561	522	557	255	10	503	32	16	32	47	32	.59	108	.279	.323	.425

Steve Pearce

Bats: R **Throws:** R **Pos:** 1B-11; PH-4   **Ht:** 5'11" **Wt:** 192 **Born:** 4/13/1983 **Age:** 28

			BATTING																		BASERUNNING				AVERAGES		
Year	Team	Lg	G	AB	H	2B	3B	HR	(Hm	Rd)	TB	R	RBI	RC	TBB	IBB	SO	HBP	SH	SF	SB	CS	SB%	GDP	Avg	OBP	Slg
2010	Indy*	AAA	35	129	42	14	2	3	(-	-)	69	25	15	31	24	3	27	1	0	4	7	2	.78	2	.326	.424	.535
2010	Bradtn*	A+	2	7	3	2	0	0	(-	-)	5	2	2	2	1	0	1	0	0	0	0	0	-	1	.429	.500	.714
2007	Pit	NL	23	68	20	5	1	0	(0	0)	27	13	6	9	5	0	12	0	0	0	2	1	.67	2	.294	.342	.397
2008	Pit	NL	37	109	27	7	0	4	(0	4)	46	6	15	13	5	0	22	3	0	2	2	0	1.00	1	.248	.294	.422
2009	Pit	NL	60	165	34	13	1	4	(3	1)	61	19	16	17	21	0	43	0	0	0	1	0	1.00	5	.206	.296	.370
2010	Pit	NL	15	29	8	2	1	0	(0	0)	12	4	5	5	7	0	6	0	0	2	0	0	-	0	.276	.395	.414
	4 ML YEARS		135	371	89	27	3	8	(3	5)	146	42	42	44	38	0	83	3	0	4	5	1	.83	5	.240	.313	.394

Jake Peavy

Pitches: R **Bats:** R **Pos:** SP-17   **Ht:** 6'1" **Wt:** 195 **Born:** 5/31/1981 **Age:** 30

			HOW MUCH HE PITCHED						WHAT HE GAVE UP											THE RESULTS							
Year	Team	Lg	G	GS	CG	GF	IP	BFP	H	R	ER	HR	SH	SF	HB	TBB	IBB	SO	WP	Bk	W	L	Pct	Sh	Sv-Op	Hld	ERC	ERA
2002	SD	NL	17	17	0	0	97.2	430	106	54	49	11	5	2	3	33	4	90	4	1	6	7	.462	0	0-0	0	4.41	4.52
2003	SD	NL	32	32	0	0	194.2	827	173	94	89	33	7	5	6	82	3	156	2	0	12	11	.522	0	0-0	0	4.13	4.11
2004	SD	NL	27	27	0	0	166.1	694	146	49	42	13	5	6	11	53	4	173	1	1	15	6	.714	0	0-0	0	3.18	2.27
2005	SD	NL	30	30	3	0	203.0	812	162	70	65	18	4	5	7	50	3	216	3	1	13	7	.650	3	0-0	0	2.49	2.88
2006	SD	NL	32	32	2	0	202.1	846	187	93	92	23	5	1	6	62	11	215	4	0	11	14	.440	0	0-0	0	3.42	4.09
2007	SD	NL	34	34	0	0	223.1	898	169	67	63	13	5	7	6	68	5	240	4	0	19	6	.760	0	0-0	0	2.27	2.54
2008	SD	NL	27	27	1	0	173.2	709	146	57	55	17	7	1	5	59	1	166	6	0	10	11	.476	0	0-0	0	3.12	2.85
2009	2 Tms		16	16	1	0	101.2	410	80	41	39	8	3	2	1	34	0	110	2	2	9	6	.600	0	0-0	0	2.63	3.45
2010	CWS	AL	17	17	1	0	107.0	450	98	55	55	13	1	5	5	34	2	93	2	1	7	6	.538	1	0-0	0	3.59	4.63
09	SD	NL	13	13	1	0	81.2	335	69	38	36	7	2	2	1	28	0	92	2	1	6	6	.500	0	0-0	0	3.00	3.97
09	CWS	AL	3	3	0	0	20.0	75	11	3	3	1	1	0	0	6	0	18	0	1	3	0	1.000	0	0-0	0	1.38	1.35
	Postseason		2	2	0	0	9.2	49	19	13	13	3	1	1	0	4	3	5	1	0	0	2	.000	0	0-0	0	12.16	12.10
	9 ML YEARS		232	232	8	0	1469.2	6076	1267	580	549	149	42	34	50	475	33	1459	28	6	102	74	.580	4	0-0	0	3.15	3.36

Dustin Pedroia

Bats: R **Throws:** R **Pos:** 2B-75   peh-DROY-uh   **Ht:** 5'9" **Wt:** 180 **Born:** 8/17/1983 **Age:** 27

			BATTING																		BASERUNNING				AVERAGES		
Year	Team	Lg	G	AB	H	2B	3B	HR	(Hm	Rd)	TB	R	RBI	RC	TBB	IBB	SO	HBP	SH	SF	SB	CS	SB%	GDP	Avg	OBP	Slg
2010	Pwtckt*	AAA	2	6	1	0	0	0	(-	-)	1	1	0	0	1	0	0	0	0	0	0	0	-	1	.167	.286	.167
2006	Bos	AL	31	89	17	4	0	2	(1	1)	27	5	7	3	7	0	7	1	1	0	0	1	.00	1	.191	.258	.303
2007	Bos	AL	139	520	165	39	1	8	(5	3)	230	86	50	79	47	1	42	7	5	2	7	1	.88	8	.317	.380	.442
2008	Bos	AL	157	653	213	54	2	17	(7	10)	322	118	83	107	50	1	52	7	7	9	20	1	.95	17	.326	.376	.493
2009	Bos	AL	154	626	185	48	1	15	(10	5)	280	115	72	104	74	3	45	5	3	6	20	8	.71	19	.296	.371	.447
2010	Bos	AL	75	302	87	24	1	12	(4	8)	149	53	41	52	37	1	38	4	0	9	9	1	.90	7	.288	.367	.493
	Postseason		28	115	29	9	0	5	(2	3)	53	22	18	18	14	0	12	2	1	0	2	1	.67	3	.252	.344	.461
	5 ML YEARS		556	2190	667	169	5	54	(27	27)	1008	377	253	345	215	6	184	24	18	23	56	12	.82	52	.305	.369	.460

Mike Pelfrey

Pitches: R **Bats:** R **Pos:** SP-33; RP-1   PELL-free   **Ht:** 6'7" **Wt:** 230 **Born:** 1/14/1984 **Age:** 27

			HOW MUCH HE PITCHED						WHAT HE GAVE UP											THE RESULTS							
Year	Team	Lg	G	GS	CG	GF	IP	BFP	H	R	ER	HR	SH	SF	HB	TBB	IBB	SO	WP	Bk	W	L	Pct	Sh	Sv-Op	Hld	ERC	ERA
2006	NYM	NL	4	4	0	0	21.1	99	25	14	13	1	1	1	3	12	0	13	2	0	2	1	.667	0	0-0	0	6.05	5.48
2007	NYM	NL	15	13	0	0	72.2	342	85	47	45	6	6	3	9	39	1	45	3	0	3	8	.273	0	0-0	0	5.99	5.57
2008	NYM	NL	32	32	2	0	200.2	851	209	86	83	12	11	5	13	64	1	110	2	0	13	11	.542	0	0-0	0	4.04	3.72
2009	NYM	NL	31	31	0	0	184.1	824	213	112	103	18	8	5	7	66	8	107	1	6	10	12	.455	0	0-0	0	4.83	5.03
2010	NYM	NL	34	33	0	1	204.0	870	213	88	83	12	17	4	6	68	5	113	1	1	15	9	.625	0	1-1	0	3.89	3.66
	5 ML YEARS		116	113	2	1	683.0	2986	745	347	327	49	43	18	38	249	15	388	9	7	43	41	.512	0	1-1	0	4.47	4.31

Brayan Pena

Bats: B **Throws:** R **Pos:** C-47; PH-16; DH-4; PR-2   BRIAN   **Ht:** 5'11" **Wt:** 234 **Born:** 1/7/1982 **Age:** 29

			BATTING																		BASERUNNING				AVERAGES		
Year	Team	Lg	G	AB	H	2B	3B	HR	(Hm	Rd)	TB	R	RBI	RC	TBB	IBB	SO	HBP	SH	SF	SB	CS	SB%	GDP	Avg	OBP	Slg
2005	Atl	NL	18	39	7	2	0	0	(0	0)	9	2	4	0	1	1	7	0	0	0	0	0	-	1	.179	.200	.231
2006	Atl	NL	23	41	11	2	0	1	(0	1)	16	9	5	4	2	0	5	0	0	0	0	0	-	2	.268	.302	.390
2007	Atl	NL	16	33	7	0	0	1	(1	0)	10	2	3	0	0	0	3	0	0	0	0	1	.00	2	.212	.212	.303

Year Team	Lg	G	AB	H	2B	3B	HR	(Hm	Rd)	TB	R	RBI	RC	TBB	IBB	SO	HBP	SH	SF	SB	CS	SB%	GDP	Avg	OBP	Slg
2008 Atl	NL	14	14	4	1	0	0	(0	0)	5	3	0	0	1	0	2	0	0	0	0	0	-	0	.286	.333	.357
2009 KC	AL	64	165	45	10	0	6	(3	3)	73	17	18	18	12	2	18	0	4	2	0	0	-	5	.273	.318	.442
2010 KC	AL	60	158	40	10	0	1	(0	1)	53	11	19	16	12	0	27	1	1	2	2	0	1.00	8	.253	.306	.335
6 ML YEARS		195	450	114	25	0	9	(4	5)	166	44	49	38	28	3	62	1	5	4	2	1	.67	18	.253	.296	.369

Carlos Pena

Bats: L Throws: L Pos: 1B-142; DH-2   Ht: 6'2" Wt: 225 Born: 5/17/1978 Age: 33

Year Team	Lg	G	AB	H	2B	3B	HR	(Hm	Rd)	TB	R	RBI	RC	TBB	IBB	SO	HBP	SH	SF	SB	CS	SB%	GDP	Avg	OBP	Slg
2010 Charltt*	A+	1	3	2	0	0	0	(-	-)	2	1	1	1	0	0	0	0	0	0	0	0	-	0	.667	.667	.667
2001 Tex	AL	22	62	16	4	1	3	(2	1)	31	6	12	11	10	0	17	0	0	0	0	0	-	1	.258	.361	.500
2002 2 Tms	AL	115	397	96	17	4	19	(10	9)	178	43	52	56	41	0	111	3	0	2	2	2	.50	2	.242	.316	.448
2003 Det	AL	131	452	112	21	6	18	(8	10)	199	51	50	61	53	1	123	6	1	4	4	5	.44	6	.248	.332	.440
2004 Det	AL	142	481	116	22	4	27	(10	17)	227	89	82	73	70	2	146	3	2	5	7	1	.88	11	.241	.338	.472
2005 Det	AL	79	260	61	9	0	18	(14	4)	124	37	44	40	31	2	95	4	0	0	0	1	.00	3	.235	.325	.477
2006 Bos	AL	18	33	9	2	0	1	(1	0)	14	3	3	3	4	0	10	0	0	0	0	0	-	1	.273	.351	.424
2007 TB	AL	148	490	138	29	1	46	(23	23)	307	99	121	114	103	10	142	10	1	8	1	0	1.00	7	.282	.411	.627
2008 TB	AL	139	490	121	24	2	31	(14	17)	242	76	102	92	96	7	166	12	0	9	1	1	.50	9	.247	.377	.494
2009 TB	AL	135	471	107	25	2	39	(19	20)	253	91	100	88	87	11	163	9	0	3	3	3	.50	5	.227	.356	.537
2010 TB	AL	144	484	95	18	0	28	(18	10)	197	64	84	73	87	4	158	7	0	4	5	1	.83	2	.196	.325	.407
02 Oak	AL	40	124	27	4	0	7	(5	2)	52	12	16	17	15	0	38	1	0	1	0	0	-	2	.218	.305	.419
02 Det	AL	75	273	69	13	4	12	(5	7)	126	31	36	39	26	0	73	2	0	1	2	2	.50	0	.253	.321	.462
Postseason		15	53	14	2	0	3	(0	3)	25	9	10	11	10	2	17	0	0	0	3	2	.60	1	.264	.381	.472
10 ML YEARS		1073	3620	871	171	20	230	(119	111)	1772	559	650	611	582	37	1131	54	4	35	23	14	.62	49	.241	.351	.490

Ramiro Pena

Bats: B Throws: R Pos: 3B-48; SS-23; PR-14; 2B-8; PH-5; RF-2; DH-2   Ht: 5'11" Wt: 165 Born: 7/18/1985 Age: 25

Year Team	Lg	G	AB	H	2B	3B	HR	(Hm	Rd)	TB	R	RBI	RC	TBB	IBB	SO	HBP	SH	SF	SB	CS	SB%	GDP	Avg	OBP	Slg
2005 Tampa	A+	23	73	18	4	1	1	(-	-)	27	11	6	9	9	0	12	0	2	2	1	0	1.00	4	.247	.321	.370
2005 Trntn	AA	68	236	59	5	2	0	(-	-)	68	28	11	19	10	0	48	0	8	1	4	1	.80	5	.250	.279	.288
2006 Trntn	AA	26	86	17	2	0	0	(-	-)	19	6	6	4	5	0	19	1	5	1	0	1	.00	0	.198	.247	.221
2006 Tampa	A+	54	218	61	4	2	0	(-	-)	69	31	23	25	16	0	26	4	4	4	8	4	.67	2	.280	.335	.317
2007 Trntn	AA	52	203	51	7	1	0	(	-)	60	23	10	22	22	1	33	2	6	0	7	3	.70	7	.251	.330	.296
2008 Trntn	AA	110	439	115	20	7	2	(-	-)	155	56	45	54	40	1	85	4	12	6	8	5	.62	7	.262	.325	.353
2009 S-WB	AAA	43	156	36	9	0	2	(-	-)	51	18	9	17	18	0	28	0	6	0	5	1	.83	6	.231	.310	.327
2009 NYY	AL	69	115	33	6	1	1	(1	0)	44	17	10	15	5	0	20	0	1	0	4	1	.80	2	.287	.317	.383
2010 NYY	AL	85	154	35	1	1	0	(0	0)	38	18	18	10	6	0	27	1	4	2	7	1	.88	4	.227	.258	.247
2 ML YEARS		154	269	68	7	2	1	(1	0)	82	35	28	25	11	0	47	1	5	2	11	2	.85	6	.253	.283	.305

Tony Pena

Pitches: R Bats: R Pos: RP-49, 3P-3   Ht: 6'2" Wt: 230 Born: 1/9/1982 Age: 29

Year Team	Lg	G	GS	CG	GF	IP	BFP	H	R	ER	HR	SH	SF	HB	TBB	IBB	SO	WP	Bk	W	L	Pct	Sh	Sv-Op	Hld	ERC	ERA
2006 Ari	NL	25	0	0	6	30.2	135	36	21	19	6	2	1	0	8	0	21	1	0	3	4	.429	0	1-1	2	5.12	5.58
2007 Ari	NL	75	0	0	13	85.1	344	63	36	31	8	1	3	5	31	4	63	3	1	5	4	.556	0	2-5	30	2.71	3.27
2008 Ari	NL	72	0	0	20	72.2	313	80	38	35	5	4	4	3	17	5	52	4	0	3	2	.600	0	3-8	23	3.79	4.33
2009 2 Tms		72	0	0	28	70.0	312	81	37	31	7	2	2	2	20	3	55	3	0	6	5	.545	0	2-4	13	4.46	3.99
2010 CWS	AL	52	3	0	19	100.2	444	108	63	57	10	4	6	1	45	6	56	6	1	5	3	.625	0	0-0	1	4.63	5.10
09 Ari	NL	37	0	0	13	34.0	153	41	20	16	3	1	1	1	11	0	26	2	0	5	3	.625	0	1-2	8	4.93	4.24
09 CWS	AL	35	0	0	15	36.0	159	40	17	15	4	1	1	1	9	3	29	1	0	1	2	.333	0	1-2	5	4.03	3.75
Postseason		5	0	0	1	5.1	17	3	0	0	0	0	0	0	0	0	7	0	0	0	0	-	0	0-0	1	0.75	0.00
5 ML YEARS		296	3	0	86	359.1	1548	368	195	173	36	13	16	11	121	18	247	17	2	22	18	.550	0	8-18	69	3.99	4.33

Hunter Pence

Bats: R Throws: R Pos: RF-155; PH-1   Ht: 6'4" Wt: 218 Born: 4/13/1983 Age: 28

Year Team	Lg	G	AB	H	2B	3B	HR	(Hm	Rd)	TB	R	RBI	RC	TBB	IBB	SO	HBP	SH	SF	SB	CS	SB%	GDP	Avg	OBP	Slg
2007 Hou	NL	108	456	147	30	9	17	(7	10)	246	57	69	77	26	0	95	1	0	1	11	5	.69	10	.322	.360	.539
2008 Hou	NL	157	595	160	34	4	25	(14	11)	277	78	83	82	40	2	124	4	0	3	11	10	.52	14	.269	.318	.466
2009 Hou	NL	159	585	165	26	5	25	(14	11)	276	76	72	80	58	1	109	1	0	3	14	11	.56	25	.282	.346	.472
2010 Hou	NL	156	614	173	29	3	25	(14	11)	283	93	91	89	41	2	105	0	0	3	18	9	.67	11	.282	.325	.461
4 ML YEARS		580	2250	645	119	21	92	(49	43)	1082	304	315	328	165	5	433	6	0	10	54	35	.61	60	.287	.336	.481

Hayden Penn

Pitches: R Bats: R Pos: RP-3   Ht: 6'3" Wt: 200 Born: 10/13/1984 Age: 26

Year Team	Lg	G	GS	CG	GF	IP	BFP	H	R	ER	HR	SH	SF	HB	TBB	IBB	SO	WP	Bk	W	L	Pct	Sh	Sv-Op	Hld	ERC	ERA
2010 Indy*	AAA	12	12	0	0	65.1	288	76	37	34	3	6	1	4	23	0	56	4	0	4	4	.500	0	0--	-	4.73	4.68
2005 Bal	AL	8	8	0	0	38.1	178	46	30	27	6	1	0	0	21	3	18	3	1	3	2	.600	0	0-0	0	6.17	6.34
2006 Bal	AL	6	6	0	0	19.2	112	38	33	33	8	0	0	2	13	0	8	0	0	1	4	.200	0	0-0	0	14.68	15.10
2009 Fla	NL	16	1	0	5	22.0	120	30	27	19	3	4	0	2	20	2	27	1	0	1	0	1.000	0	0-0	1	8.66	7.77
2010 Pit	NL	3	0	0	1	2.1	16	8	8	8	0	0	0	0	3	0	0	1	0	0	0	-	0	0-0	0	27.59	30.86
4 ML YEARS		33	15	0	6	82.1	426	122	98	87	17	5	0	4	57	5	53	5	1	4	6	.400	0	0-0	1	9.26	9.51

Cliff Pennington

Bats: B Throws: R Pos: SS-156; PH-3   Ht: 5'11" Wt: 198 Born: 6/15/1984 Age: 27

Year	Team	Lg	G	AB	H	2B	3B	HR	(Hm	Rd)	TB	R	RBI	RC	TBB	IBB	SO	HBP	SH	SF	SB	CS	SB%	GDP	Avg	OBP	Slg
2008	Oak	AL	36	99	24	5	0	0	(0	0)	29	14	9	12	13	0	18	2	2	1	4	1	.80	1	.242	.339	.293
2009	Oak	AL	60	208	58	11	3	4	(3	1)	87	27	21	29	19	0	46	1	1	0	7	5	.58	5	.279	.342	.418
2010	Oak	AL	156	508	127	26	8	6	(2	4)	187	64	46	66	50	0	96	3	12	3	29	5	.85	7	.250	.319	.368
	3 ML YEARS		252	815	209	42	11	10	(5	5)	303	105	76	107	82	0	160	6	15	4	40	11	.78	13	.256	.327	.372

Brad Penny

Pitches: R Bats: R Pos: SP-9   Ht: 6'4" Wt: 230 Born: 5/24/1978 Age: 33

Year	Team	Lg	G	GS	CG	GF	IP	BFP	H	R	ER	HR	SH	SF	HB	TBB	IBB	SO	WP	Bk	W	L	Pct	Sh	Sv-Op	Hld	ERC	ERA
2000	Fla	NL	23	22	0	0	119.2	529	120	70	64	13	6	2	5	60	4	80	4	1	8	7	.533	0	0-0	0	4.70	4.81
2001	Fla	NL	31	31	1	0	205.0	833	183	92	84	15	8	2	7	54	3	154	2	0	10	10	.500	1	0-0	0	2.96	3.69
2002	Fla	NL	24	24	1	0	129.1	574	148	76	67	18	6	4	1	50	7	93	4	0	8	7	.533	1	0-0	0	5.08	4.66
2003	Fla	NL	32	32	0	0	196.1	811	195	96	90	21	7	5	3	56	6	138	3	4	14	10	.583	0	0-0	0	3.73	4.13
2004	2 Tms	NL	24	24	0	0	143.0	590	130	55	50	12	3	3	3	45	6	111	5	0	9	10	.474	0	0-0	0	3.20	3.15
2005	LAD	NL	29	29	1	0	175.1	738	185	78	76	17	7	1	3	41	2	122	3	0	7	9	.438	0	0-0	0	3.77	3.90
2006	LAD	NL	34	33	0	0	189.0	813	206	94	91	19	8	3	9	54	4	148	6	0	**16**	9	.640	0	0-0	1	4.32	4.33
2007	LAD	NL	33	33	0	0	208.0	865	199	75	70	9	13	9	5	73	2	135	6	0	16	4	**.800**	0	0-0	0	3.41	3.03
2008	LAD	NL	19	17	0	1	94.2	426	112	68	66	13	10	2	4	42	0	51	1	1	6	9	.400	0	0-0	0	5.82	6.27
2009	2 Tms	NL	30	30	1	0	173.1	751	191	102	94	22	0	7	5	51	0	109	6	0	11	9	.550	0	0-0	0	4.54	4.88
2010	StL	NL	9	9	0	0	55.2	232	63	25	20	4	2	3	3	9	1	35	1	0	3	4	.429	0	0-0	0	3.95	3.23
04	Fla	NL	21	21	0	0	131.1	545	124	50	46	10	3	3	3	39	6	105	5	0	8	8	.500	0	0-0	0	3.26	3.15
04	LAD	NL	3	3	0	0	11.2	45	6	5	4	2	0	0	0	6	0	6	0	0	1	2	.333	0	0-0	0	2.51	3.09
09	Bos	AL	24	24	0	0	131.2	590	160	89	82	17	0	7	5	42	0	89	4	0	7	8	.467	0	0-0	0	5.35	5.61
09	SF	NL	6	6	1	0	41.2	161	31	13	12	5	0	0	0	9	0	20	2	0	4	1	.800	0	0-0	0	2.22	2.59
	Postseason		8	4	0	0	23.0	106	31	17	16	3	2	1	0	11	1	14	0	0	3	2	.600	0	0-1	0	6.81	6.26
	11 ML YEARS		288	284	4	1	1689.1	7162	1732	831	772	163	70	41	47	535	35	1176	41	6	108	88	.551	2	0-0	1	3.98	4.11

Jhonny Peralta

Bats: R Throws: R Pos: 3B-100; SS-46; DH-4; 1B-2; PH-2   pah-RALL-tah   Ht: 6'2" Wt: 215 Born: 5/28/1982 Age: 29

Year	Team	Lg	G	AB	H	2B	3B	HR	(Hm	Rd)	TB	R	RBI	RC	TBB	IBB	SO	HBP	SH	SF	SB	CS	SB%	GDP	Avg	OBP	Slg
2003	Cle	AL	77	242	55	10	1	4	(3	1)	79	24	21	24	20	0	65	4	2	2	1	3	.25	5	.227	.295	.326
2004	Cle	AL	8	25	6	1	0	0	(0	0)	7	2	2	2	3	0	6	0	0	0	0	1	.00	0	.240	.321	.280
2005	Cle	AL	141	504	147	35	4	24	(14	10)	262	82	78	87	58	3	128	3	1	4	0	2	.00	12	.292	.366	.520
2006	Cle	AL	149	569	146	28	3	13	(7	6)	219	84	68	66	56	0	152	1	3	3	0	1	.00	19	.257	.323	.385
2007	Cle	AL	152	574	155	27	1	21	(16	5)	247	87	72	85	61	2	146	4	1	7	4	4	.50	12	.270	.341	.430
2008	Cle	AL	154	605	167	42	4	23	(11	12)	286	104	89	84	48	2	126	4	2	5	3	1	.75	26	.276	.331	.473
2009	Cle	AL	151	582	148	35	1	11	(2	9)	218	57	83	63	51	0	134	4	2	6	0	2	.00	20	.254	.316	.375
2010	2 Tms	AL	148	551	137	30	2	15	(4	11)	216	60	81	71	53	2	103	1	0	10	1	0	1.00	11	.249	.311	.392
10	Cle	AL	91	334	82	23	2	7	(3	4)	130	37	43	41	32	1	69	1	0	6	1	0	1.00	7	.246	.308	.389
10	Det	AL	57	217	55	7	0	8	(1	7)	86	23	38	30	21	1	34	0	0	4	0	0	-	4	.253	.314	.396
	Postseason		11	42	14	5	0	2	(1	1)	25	6	10	9	5	0	11	0	0	1	1	0	1.00	2	.333	.396	.595
	8 ML YEARS		980	3652	961	208	16	111	(57	54)	1534	500	494	482	350	9	860	21	11	37	9	14	.39	105	.263	.328	.420

Joel Peralta

Pitches: R Bats: R Pos: RP-39   joe-ELL pah-RALL-tah   Ht: 5'11" Wt: 195 Born: 3/23/1976 Age: 35

Year	Team	Lg	G	GS	CG	GF	IP	BFP	H	R	ER	HR	SH	SF	HB	TBB	IBB	SO	WP	Bk	W	L	Pct	Sh	Sv-Op	Hld	ERC	ERA
2010	Syrcse*	AAA	28	0	0	27	33.1	130	24	5	4	1	2	0	1	7	1	38	1	0	2	0	1.000	0	20--	-	1.65	1.08
2005	LAA	AL	28	0	0	10	34.2	145	28	15	15	6	2	1	0	14	2	30	2	0	1	0	1.000	0	0-0	0	3.40	3.89
2006	KC	AL	64	0	0	21	73.2	304	74	37	36	10	1	3	2	17	2	57	5	0	1	3	.250	0	1-3	17	3.80	4.40
2007	KC	AL	62	0	0	18	87.2	366	93	39	37	9	2	4	2	19	5	66	2	0	1	3	.250	0	1-5	7	3.75	3.80
2008	KC	AL	40	0	0	12	52.2	224	56	37	35	15	1	3	2	14	0	38	1	0	1	2	.333	0	0-1	1	5.38	5.98
2009	Col	NL	27	0	0	6	24.2	113	27	17	17	3	0	1	3	12	2	22	0	0	3	0	.000	0	0-1	6	5.51	6.20
2010	Was	NL	39	0	0	10	49.0	189	30	12	11	5	2	1	1	9	4	49	0	0	1	0	1.000	0	0-2	9	1.43	2.02
	6 ML YEARS		260	0	0	77	322.1	1341	308	157	151	48	8	13	10	85	15	262	10	0	5	11	.313	0	2-12	40	3.69	4.22

Luis Perdomo

Pitches: R Bats: L Pos: RP-1   Ht: 6'0" Wt: 170 Born: 4/27/1984 Age: 27

Year	Team	Lg	G	GS	CG	GF	IP	BFP	H	R	ER	HR	SH	SF	HB	TBB	IBB	SO	WP	Bk	W	L	Pct	Sh	Sv-Op	Hld	ERC	ERA
2006	Indns	R	19	0	0	17	20.0	79	11	9	8	1	0	1	2	5	0	29	3	0	0	2	.000	0	9--	-	1.43	3.60
2007	Lk Cty	A	56	0	0	40	66.0	270	43	28	24	6	1	1	4	26	1	81	3	1	4	6	.400	0	10--	-	2.35	3.27
2008	Knstn	A+	31	0	0	25	39.0	153	19	6	4	0	2	2	2	17	0	43	5	0	3	1	.750	0	18--	-	1.37	0.92
2008	Akron	AA	9	0	0	5	15.1	63	12	6	6	1	0	1	0	7	0	17	0	0	2	0	1.000	0	1--	-	2.94	3.52
2008	Sprgfld	AA	15	0	0	5	18.0	80	18	12	9	2	0	0	1	6	0	22	2	0	2	2	.500	0	1--	-	3.96	4.50
2009	Portlnd	AAA	1	0	0	1	1.0	7	3	2	2	0	0	0	0	1	0	0	0	0	0	0	-	0	0--	-	19.55	18.00
2010	Portlnd	AAA	58	3	0	17	82.0	350	76	40	31	7	5	1	3	34	3	49	10	0	4	6	.400	0	1--	-	3.73	3.40
2009	SD	NL	35	0	0	10	60.0	268	57	36	32	11	1	1	0	34	3	55	8	0	1	0	1.000	0	0-1	0	4.94	4.80
2010	SD	NL	1	0	0	1	1.0	4	1	1	1	1	0	0	0	0	0	0	0	0	0	0	-	0	0-0	0	7.45	9.00
	2 ML YEARS		36	0	0	11	61.0	272	58	37	33	12	1	1	0	34	3	55	8	0	1	0	1.000	0	0-1	0	5.00	4.87

Chris Perez

Pitches: R Bats: R Pos: RP-63
Ht: 6'4" Wt: 230 Born: 7/1/1985 Age: 25

Year	Team	Lg	G	GS	CG	GF	IP	BFP	H	R	ER	HR	SH	SF	HB	TBB	IBB	SO	WP	Bk	W	L	Pct	Sh	Sv-Op	Hld	ERC	ERA
2008	StL	NL	41	0	0	23	41.2	177	34	18	16	5	1	3	1	22	0	42	2	0	3	3	.500	0	7-11	6	3.83	3.46
2009	2 Tms	NL	61	0	0	16	57.0	239	41	28	27	8	0	2	6	27	0	68	8	0	1	2	.333	0	2-5	7	3.54	4.26
2010	Cle	AL	63	0	0	37	63.0	260	40	15	12	4	6	1	5	28	3	61	4	0	2	2	.500	0	23-27	9	2.30	1.71
09	StL	NL	29	0	0	8	23.2	106	17	12	11	3	0	1	3	15	0	30	4	0	1	1	.500	0	1-2	3	4.01	4.18
09	Cle	AL	32	0	0	8	33.1	133	24	16	16	5	0	1	3	12	0	38	4	0	0	1	.000	0	1-3	4	3.19	4.32
3 ML YEARS			165	0	0	76	161.2	676	115	61	55	17	7	6	12	77	3	171	14	0	6	7	.462	0	32-43	22	3.10	3.06

Oliver Perez

Pitches: L Bats: L Pos: RP-10; SP-7
Ht: 6'3" Wt: 205 Born: 8/15/1981 Age: 29

Year	Team	Lg	G	GS	CG	GF	IP	BFP	H	R	ER	HR	SH	SF	HB	TBB	IBB	SO	WP	Bk	W	L	Pct	Sh	Sv-Op	Hld	ERC	ERA
2010	StLuci*	A+	2	2	0	0	11.2	47	7	6	6	2	0	0	1	4	0	14	1	0	1	1	.500	0	0- -		2.49	4.63
2010	Buffalo*	AAA	2	2	0	0	11.2	53	10	4	3	2	1	0	2	7	0	10	2	0	0	0		0	0- -		5.27	2.31
2002	SD	NL	16	15	0	0	90.0	387	71	37	35	13	5	3	5	48	1	94	3	0	4	5	.444	0	0-0	0	3.93	3.50
2003	2 Tms	NL	24	24	0	0	126.2	579	129	80	77	22	5	2	4	77	3	141	7	1	4	10	.286	0	0-0	0	5.66	5.47
2004	Pit	NL	30	30	2	0	196.0	805	145	71	65	22	9	5	9	81	2	239	2	1	12	10	.545	1	0-0	0	2.99	2.98
2005	Pit	NL	20	20	0	0	103.0	471	102	68	67	23	5	4	6	70	1	97	3	0	7	5	.583	0	0-0	0	6.44	5.85
2006	2 Tms	NL	22	22	1	0	112.2	529	129	90	82	20	5	10	6	68	0	102	5	1	1	13	.188	1	0-0	0	6.62	6.55
2007	NYM	NL	29	29	0	0	177.0	765	153	90	70	22	4	7	7	79	1	174	6	0	15	10	.600	0	0-0	0	3.76	3.56
2008	NYM	NL	34	34	0	0	194.0	847	167	100	91	24	9	7	11	105	4	180	9	1	10	7	.588	0	0-0	0	4.21	4.22
2009	NYM	NL	14	14	0	0	66.0	324	69	51	50	12	5	4	4	58	2	62	2	0	3	4	.429	0	0-0	0	7.16	6.82
2010	NYM	NL	17	7	0	4	46.1	234	54	37	35	9	1	3	4	42	3	37	4	0	0	5	.000	0	0-0	0	8.27	6.80
03	SD	NL	19	19	0	0	103.2	473	103	65	62	20	4	2	3	65	2	117	6	1	4	7	.364	0	0-0	0	5.74	5.38
03	Pit	NL	5	5	0	0	23.0	106	26	15	15	2	1	0	1	12	1	24	1	0	0	3	.000	0	0-0	0	5.29	5.87
06	Pit	NL	15	15	0	0	76.0	364	88	64	56	13	5	8	3	51	0	61	4	1	2	10	.167	0	0-0	0	6.85	6.63
06	NYM	NL	7	7	1	0	36.2	165	41	26	26	7	0	2	3	17	0	41	1	0	1	3	.250	1	0-0	0	6.16	6.38
Postseason			2	2	0	0	11.2	50	13	6	6	3	2	0	1	3	1	7	0	0	1	0	1.000	0	0-0	0	5.61	4.63
9 ML YEARS			206	195	3	4	1111.2	4941	1019	624	572	167	48	45	56	628	17	1126	41	4	58	69	.457	2	0-0	0	4.80	4.63

Rafael Perez

Pitches: L Bats: L Pos: RP-70
Ht: 6'3" Wt: 195 Born: 5/15/1982 Age: 29

Year	Team	Lg	G	GS	CG	GF	IP	BFP	H	R	ER	HR	SH	SF	HB	TBB	IBB	SO	WP	Bk	W	L	Pct	Sh	Sv-Op	Hld	ERC	ERA
2006	Cle	AL	18	0	0	5	12.1	56	10	6	6	2	1	0	0	6	1	15	4	1	0	0	-	0	0-1	1	3.37	4.38
2007	Cle	AL	44	0	0	11	60.2	236	41	15	12	5	1	1	0	15	2	62	4	0	1	2	.333	0	1-2	12	1.74	1.78
2008	Cle	AL	73	0	0	14	76.1	313	67	32	30	8	2	0	2	23	3	86	3	0	4	4	.500	0	2-7	25	3.14	3.54
2009	Cle	AL	54	0	0	12	48.0	230	66	41	39	5	4	2	2	25	6	32	1	2	4	3	.571	0	0-1	6	6.85	7.31
2010	Cle	AL	70	0	0	13	61.0	272	72	23	22	3	6	1	0	25	4	36	6	0	6	1	.857	0	0-4	13	4.68	3.25
Postseason			6	0	0	1	7.0	34	10	9	6	3	0	0	0	3	0	6	0	0	1	0	1.000	0	0-0	0	9.36	7.71
5 ML YEARS			259	0	0	55	258.1	1107	256	117	109	23	14	4	4	94	16	231	18	3	15	10	.600	0	3-15	57	3.76	3.80

Glen Perkins

Pitches: L Bats: L Pos: RP-12; SP-1
Ht: 6'0" Wt: 205 Born: 3/2/1983 Age: 28

Year	Team	Lg	G	GS	CG	GF	IP	BFP	H	R	ER	HR	SH	SF	HB	TBB	IBB	SO	WP	Bk	W	L	Pct	Sh	Sv-Op	Hld	ERC	ERA
2010	Roch*	AAA	26	24	0	1	124.0	568	160	91	80	14	6	4	5	36	2	98	1	1	4	9	.308	0	0- -		5.47	5.81
2006	Min	AL	4	0	0	1	5.2	20	3	1	1	0	0	0	0	0	0	6	0	0	0	0	-	0	0-0	1	0.60	1.59
2007	Min	AL	19	0	0	3	20.2	115	23	10	10	2	1	1	2	12	0	20	2	0	0	0	-	0	0-0	3	3.32	3.14
2008	Min	AL	26	26	0	0	151.0	661	183	81	74	25	7	4	3	39	0	74	2	1	12	4	.750	0	0-0	0	5.30	4.41
2009	Min	AL	18	17	0	1	96.1	423	120	64	63	13	1	3	1	23	0	45	2	1	6	7	.462	0	0-0	0	5.14	5.89
2010	Min	AL	13	1	0	5	21.2	98	29	16	14	3	1	2	4	5	1	14	0	0	1	1	.500	0	0-0	0	6.56	5.82
Postseason			1	0	0	0	0.1	3	2	0	0	0	0	0	0	0	0	0	0	0	0	0	-	0	0-0	0	39.65	0.00
5 ML YEARS			80	44	0	10	303.1	1317	358	172	162	43	10	10	10	79	1	159	6	2	19	12	.613	0	0-0	4	5.02	4.81

Ryan Perry

Pitches: R Bats: R Pos: RP-60
Ht: 6'4" Wt: 200 Born: 2/13/1987 Age: 24

Year	Team	Lg	G	GS	CG	GF	IP	BFP	H	R	ER	HR	SH	SF	HB	TBB	IBB	SO	WP	Bk	W	L	Pct	Sh	Sv-Op	Hld	ERC	ERA
2008	Tigers	R	2	0	0	0	2.0	6	0	0	0	0	0	0	0	0	0	4	0	0	0	0	-	0	0- -	-	0.00	0.00
2008	Lkland	A+	12	0	0	9	11.2	59	15	6	5	0	0	1	1	7	0	12	2	0	1	2	.333	0	4- -	-	5.83	3.86
2009	Toledo	AAA	8	0	0	5	13.2	58	13	4	4	1	1	0	0	4	0	12	1	0	0	1	.000	0	3- -	-	3.15	2.63
2010	Toledo	AAA	3	0	0	0	3.2	17	1	1	0	0	0	0	0	4	0	4	0	0	0	0	1.000	0	0- -	-	1.86	0.00
2009	Det	AL	53	0	0	12	61.2	273	56	30	26	7	3	3	1	38	5	60	6	1	0	1	.000	0	0-3	6	4.45	3.79
2010	Det	AL	60	0	0	21	62.2	261	55	26	25	6	4	3	5	23	1	45	3	0	3	5	.375	0	2-5	19	3.61	3.59
2 ML YEARS			113	0	0	33	124.1	534	111	56	51	13	7	6	6	61	6	105	9	1	3	6	.333	0	2-8	25	4.02	3.69

Vinnie Pestano

Pitches: R Bats: R Pos: RP-5   Ht: 6'0" Wt: 205 Born: 2/20/1985 Age: 26

				HOW MUCH HE PITCHED					WHAT HE GAVE UP											THE RESULTS						
Year	Team	Lg	G	GS	CG	GF	IP	BFP	H	R	ER	HR	SH	SF	HB	TBB	IBB	SO	WP	Bk	W	L	Pct	Sh	Sv-Op	Hld	ERC	ERA
2007	MhVlly	A-	21	0	0	17	22.2	95	17	9	9	5	0	0	2	7	0	27	1	0	1	1	.500	0	6--	-	3.38	3.57
2008	Lk Cty	A	29	0	0	25	29.0	125	25	10	5	1	2	0	2	13	0	23	2	1	1	1	.500	0	15--	-	3.29	1.55
2008	Knstn	A+	25	0	0	20	27.0	120	23	13	12	1	2	0	2	11	1	27	2	0	1	2	.333	0	9--	-	2.93	4.00
2009	Akron	AA	34	0	0	31	34.2	147	30	11	11	2	4	0	2	13	3	31	0	0	2	3	.400	0	24--	-	3.03	2.86
2010	Akron	AA	14	0	0	12	13.1	54	12	6	4	1	0	1	0	2	0	18	1	0	1	1	.500	0	3--	-	2.41	2.70
2010	Clmbs	AAA	43	0	0	30	46.1	188	35	10	8	1	0	0	1	14	0	59	1	0	1	2	.333	0	14--	-	2.02	1.55
2010	Cle	AL	5	0	0	5	5.0	23	4	2	2	0	0	0	0	5	0	8	0	0	0	0	-	0	1-1	0	4.56	3.60

Bryan Petersen

Bats: L Throws: R Pos: PH-19; LF-5; RF-1; DH-1   Ht: 6'0" Wt: 205 Born: 4/9/1986 Age: 25

									BATTING												BASERUNNING				AVERAGES		
Year	Team	Lg	G	AB	H	2B	3B	HR	(Hm	Rd)	TB	R	RBI	RC	TBB	IBB	SO	HBP	SH	SF	SB	CS	SB%	GDP	Avg	OBP	Slg
2007	Jmstwn	A-	57	216	54	13	1	5	(-	-)	84	27	24	29	18	0	53	4	1	1	11	2	.85	3	.250	.318	.389
2008	Grnsbr	A	79	296	89	10	2	19	(-	-)	160	60	58	62	38	0	74	4	1	6	15	6	.71	5	.301	.381	.541
2008	Jupiter	A+	40	155	41	5	0	3	(-	-)	55	23	12	21	15	1	29	3	1	1	7	1	.88	1	.265	.339	.355
2008	Carlina	AA	12	37	13	2	0	1	(-	-)	18	5	10	7	5	1	6	0	0	2	1	2	.33	0	.351	.409	.486
2009	Jaxnvl	AA	121	431	128	15	7	7	(-	-)	178	64	49	68	50	3	66	4	0	9	13	12	.52	4	.297	.368	.413
2010	NewOr	AAA	91	322	82	13	2	5	(-	-)	114	47	27	40	34	5	63	5	4	3	5	4	.56	4	.255	.332	.354
2010	Fla	NL	23	24	2	0	0	0	(0	0)	2	1	2	0	1	0	6	0	0	0	0	0	-	0	.083	.120	.083

Andy Pettitte

Pitches: L Bats: L Pos: SP-21   Ht: 6'5" Wt: 225 Born: 6/15/1972 Age: 39
PETT-it

				HOW MUCH HE PITCHED					WHAT HE GAVE UP											THE RESULTS						
Year	Team	Lg	G	GS	CG	GF	IP	BFP	H	R	ER	HR	SH	SF	HB	TBB	IBB	SO	WP	Bk	W	L	Pct	Sh	Sv-Op	Hld	ERC	ERA
1995	NYY	AL	31	26	3	1	175.0	745	183	86	81	15	4	5	1	63	3	114	8	1	12	9	.571	0	0-0	0	4.13	4.17
1996	NYY	AL	35	34	2	1	221.0	929	229	105	95	23	7	3	3	72	2	162	6	1	21	8	.724	0	0-0	0	4.14	3.87
1997	NYY	AL	35	35	4	0	240.1	986	233	86	77	7	6	2	3	65	0	166	7	0	18	7	.720	1	0-0	0	3.05	2.88
1998	NYY	AL	33	32	5	0	216.1	932	226	110	102	20	6	7	6	87	1	146	5	0	16	11	.593	0	0-0	0	4.46	4.24
1999	NYY	AL	31	31	0	0	191.2	851	216	105	100	20	6	6	3	89	3	121	3	1	14	11	.560	0	0-0	0	5.22	4.70
2000	NYY	AL	32	32	3	0	204.2	903	219	111	99	17	7	4	4	80	4	125	2	3	19	9	.679	1	0-0	0	4.32	4.35
2001	NYY	AL	31	31	2	0	200.2	858	224	103	89	14	8	7	6	41	3	164	2	2	15	10	.600	1	0-0	0	3.82	3.99
2002	NYY	AL	22	22	3	0	134.2	570	144	58	49	6	3	2	4	32	2	97	2	1	13	5	.722	1	0-0	0	3.55	3.27
2003	NYY	AL	33	33	1	0	208.1	896	227	109	93	21	5	5	1	50	3	180	5	0	21	8	.724	0	0-0	0	3.89	4.02
2004	Hou	NL	15	15	0	0	83.0	346	71	37	36	8	1	0	0	31	2	79	4	0	6	4	.600	0	0-0	0	3.12	3.90
2005	Hou	NL	33	33	0	0	222.1	875	188	66	59	17	10	4	3	41	0	171	2	0	17	9	.654	0	0-0	0	2.40	2.39
2006	Hou	NL	36	35	2	1	214.1	929	238	114	100	27	14	5	2	70	9	178	2	1	14	13	.519	1	0-0	0	4.58	4.20
2007	NYY	AL	36	34	0	0	215.1	916	238	106	97	16	5	9	4	69	1	141	3	0	15	9	.625	0	0-0	1	4.27	4.05
2008	NYY	AL	33	33	0	0	204.0	881	233	112	103	19	8	7	7	55	4	158	6	1	14	14	.500	0	0-0	0	4.45	4.54
2009	NYY	AL	32	32	0	0	194.2	834	193	101	90	20	4	4	4	76	4	148	3	0	14	8	.636	0	0-0	0	4.11	4.16
2010	NYY	AL	21	21	0	0	129.0	536	123	52	47	13	8	5	3	41	3	101	2	0	11	3	.786	0	0-0	0	3.62	3.28
Postseason			40	40	0	0	249.0	1046	261	112	108	29	12	8	3	71	3	164	4	1	18	9	.667	0	0-0	0	4.10	3.90
16 ML YEARS			489	479	25	3	3055.1	12987	3185	1461	1317	263	102	75	51	962	41	2251	62	11	240	138	.635	4	0-0	1	3.96	3.88

Brandon Phillips

Bats: R Throws: R Pos: 2B-152; PR-3; PH-1   Ht: 6'0" Wt: 200 Born: 6/28/1981 Age: 30

									BATTING												BASERUNNING				AVERAGES		
Year	Team	Lg	G	AB	H	2B	3B	HR	(Hm	Rd)	TB	R	RBI	RC	TBB	IBB	SO	HBP	SH	SF	SB	CS	SB%	GDP	Avg	OBP	Slg
2002	Cle	AL	11	31	8	3	1	0	(0	0)	13	5	4	5	3	0	6	1	1	0	0	0	-	0	.258	.343	.419
2003	Cle	AL	112	370	77	18	1	6	(3	3)	115	36	33	22	14	0	77	3	5	1	4	5	.44	12	.208	.242	.311
2004	Cle	AL	6	22	4	2	0	0	(0	0)	6	1	1	0	2	0	5	0	0	0	0	2	.00	1	.182	.250	.273
2005	Cle	AL	6	11	0	0	0	0	(0	0)	0	1	0	0	0	0	4	0	0	0	0	0	-	0	.000	.000	.000
2006	Cin	NL	149	536	148	28	1	17	(9	8)	229	65	75	74	35	3	88	6	4	6	25	2	.93	19	.276	.324	.427
2007	Cin	NL	158	650	187	26	6	30	(17	13)	315	107	94	88	33	4	109	12	2	5	32	8	.80	26	.288	.331	.485
2008	Cin	NL	141	559	146	24	7	21	(13	8)	247	80	78	74	39	6	93	5	0	6	23	10	.70	13	.261	.312	.442
2009	Cin	NL	153	584	161	30	5	20	(10	10)	261	78	98	80	44	3	75	6	2	8	25	9	.74	21	.276	.329	.447
2010	Cin	NL	155	626	172	33	5	18	(10	8)	269	100	59	77	46	1	83	8	6	1	16	12	.57	14	.275	.332	.430
9 ML YEARS			891	3387	903	164	26	112	(62	50)	1455	473	442	420	216	17	540	41	20	27	125	48	.72	106	.267	.316	.430

Paul Phillips

Bats: R Throws: R Pos: C-10; 1B-1; PH-1; PR-1   Ht: 5'11" Wt: 200 Born: 4/15/1977 Age: 34

									BATTING												BASERUNNING				AVERAGES		
Year	Team	Lg	G	AB	H	2B	3B	HR	(Hm	Rd)	TB	R	RBI	RC	TBB	IBB	SO	HBP	SH	SF	SB	CS	SB%	GDP	Avg	OBP	Slg
2010	ColSpr*	AAA	34	122	29	8	1	0	(-	-)	39	15	10	13	13	1	12	1	0	0	1	1	.50	4	.238	.316	.320
2004	KC	AL	4	5	1	0	0	0	(0	0)	1	2	0	0	0	0	1	1	0	0	0	0	-	0	.200	.333	.200
2005	KC	AL	23	67	18	4	1	1	(0	1)	27	6	9	8	0	0	5	0	0	0	0	0	-	4	.269	.269	.403
2006	KC	AL	23	65	18	3	0	1	(0	1)	24	8	5	8	1	0	8	0	2	1	0	0	-	0	.277	.284	.369
2007	KC	AL	8	14	2	1	0	0	(0	0)	3	2	2	1	0	0	1	0	0	0	0	0	-	1	.143	.200	.214
2008	CWS	AL	4	2	0	0	0	0	(0	0)	0	0	0	0	0	0	1	0	0	0	0	0	-	0	.000	.000	.000
2009	Col	NL	17	45	14	2	0	1	(0	1)	19	5	9	11	7	1	3	0	1	0	0	0	-	0	.311	.396	.422
2010	Col	NL	12	23	5	0	0	0	(0	0)	5	4	1	1	2	0	7	0	0	0	0	0	-	0	.217	.280	.217
7 ML YEARS			91	221	58	10	1	3	(0	3)	79	27	26	29	11	1	26	1	3	2	0	0	-	5	.262	.298	.357

Felix Pie

Bats: L Throws: L Pos: LF-70; CF-9; PH-4; RF-2; PR-2   pee-AY   Ht: 6'2" Wt: 190 Born: 2/8/1985 Age: 26

Year	Team	Lg	G	AB	H	2B	3B	HR	(Hm	Rd)	TB	R	RBI	RC	TBB	IBB	SO	HBP	SH	SF	SB	CS	SB%	GDP	Avg	OBP	Slg
2010	Orioles*	R	2	8	1	0	0	0	(-	-)	1	1	0	0	0	0	2	0	0	0	0	0	-	0	.125	.125	.125
2010	Frdrck*	A+	3	12	5	0	0	0	(-	-)	5	3	2	2	2	0	2	0	0	0	0	0	-	0	.417	.500	.417
2010	Bowie*	AA	6	23	8	2	1	0	(-	-)	12	2	1	5	3	0	4	1	0	0	1	0	1.00	0	.348	.444	.522
2007	ChC	NL	87	177	38	9	3	2	(0	2)	59	26	20	21	14	0	43	0	2	1	8	1	.89	0	.215	.271	.333
2008	ChC	NL	43	83	20	2	1	1	(0	1)	27	9	10	9	7	0	29	2	0	1	3	0	1.00	3	.241	.312	.325
2009	Bal	AL	101	252	67	10	3	9	(6	3)	110	38	29	30	24	1	58	0	2	3	1	3	.25	6	.266	.326	.437
2010	Bal	AL	82	288	79	15	5	5	(3	2)	119	39	31	34	13	0	52	1	3	3	5	2	.71	10	.274	.305	.413
	Postseason		2	1	0	0	0	0	(0	0)	0	0	0	0	1	0	1	0	0	0	0	0	-	0	.000	.500	.000
	4 ML YEARS		313	800	204	36	12	17	(10	7)	315	112	90	94	58	1	182	3	7	8	17	6	.74	19	.255	.305	.394

Juan Pierre

Bats: L Throws: L Pos: LF-149; DH-10; PH-1   Ht: 5'11" Wt: 185 Born: 8/14/1977 Age: 33

Year	Team	Lg	G	AB	H	2B	3B	HR	(Hm	Rd)	TB	R	RBI	RC	TBB	IBB	SO	HBP	SH	SF	SB	CS	SB%	GDP	Avg	OBP	Slg
2000	Col	NL	51	200	62	2	0	0	(0	0)	64	26	20	23	13	0	15	1	4	1	7	6	.54	2	.310	.353	.320
2001	Col	NL	156	617	202	26	11	2	(0	2)	256	108	55	101	41	1	29	10	14	1	46	17	.73	6	.327	.378	.415
2002	Col	NL	152	592	170	20	5	1	(0	1)	203	90	35	79	31	0	52	9	8	0	47	12	.80	7	.287	.332	.343
2003	Fla	NL	162	668	204	28	7	1	(1	0)	249	100	41	92	55	1	35	5	15	3	65	20	.76	9	.305	.361	.373
2004	Fla	NL	162	678	221	22	12	3	(1	2)	276	100	49	101	45	1	35	8	15	2	45	24	.65	9	.326	.374	.407
2005	Fla	NL	162	656	181	19	13	2	(1	1)	232	96	47	76	41	1	45	9	10	2	57	17	.77	10	.276	.326	.354
2006	ChC	NL	162	699	204	32	13	3	(1	2)	271	87	40	84	32	0	38	8	10	1	58	20	.74	6	.292	.330	.388
2007	LAD	NL	162	668	196	24	8	0	(0	0)	236	96	41	75	33	0	37	6	20	2	64	15	.81	10	.293	.331	.353
2008	LAD	NL	119	375	106	10	2	1	(0	1)	123	44	28	48	22	1	24	3	5	1	40	12	.77	3	.283	.327	.328
2009	LAD	NL	145	380	117	16	8	0	(0	0)	149	57	31	58	27	3	27	8	9	1	30	12	.71	7	.308	.365	.392
2010	CWS	AL	160	651	179	18	3	1	(0	1)	206	96	47	84	45	0	47	21	15	2	68	18	.79	8	.275	.341	.316
	Postseason		26	79	24	5	2	0	(0	0)	33	16	7	14	8	2	4	1	2	0	3	5	.38	0	.304	.375	.418
	11 ML YEARS		1593	6184	1842	217	82	14	(4	10)	2265	900	434	821	385	8	384	88	125	16	527	173	.75	77	.298	.347	.366

A.J. Pierzynski

Bats: L Throws: R Pos: C-127; PH-5   perr-ZINN-ski   Ht: 6'3" Wt: 230 Born: 12/30/1976 Age: 34

Year	Team	Lg	G	AB	H	2B	3B	HR	(Hm	Rd)	TB	R	RBI	RC	TBB	IBB	SO	HBP	SH	SF	SB	CS	SB%	GDP	Avg	OBP	Slg
1998	Min	AL	7	10	3	0	0	0	(0	0)	3	1	1	2	1	0	2	1	0	1	0	0	-	0	.300	.385	.300
1999	Min	AL	9	22	6	2	0	0	(0	0)	8	3	3	3	1	0	4	1	0	0	0	0	-	0	.273	.333	.364
2000	Min	AL	33	88	27	5	1	2	(1	1)	40	12	11	14	5	0	14	2	0	1	1	0	1.00	6	.307	.354	.455
2001	Min	AL	114	381	110	33	2	7	(3	4)	168	51	55	50	16	4	57	4	1	3	1	7	.13	7	.289	.322	.441
2002	Min	AL	130	440	132	31	6	6	(2	4)	193	54	49	60	13	1	61	11	2	3	1	2	.33	14	.300	.334	.439
2003	Min	AL	137	487	152	35	3	11	(6	5)	226	63	74	80	24	12	55	15	2	5	3	1	.75	13	.312	.360	.464
2004	SF	NL	131	471	128	28	2	11	(3	8)	193	45	77	58	19	4	27	15	2	3	0	1	.00	27	.272	.319	.410
2005	CWS	AL	128	460	118	21	0	18	(12	6)	193	61	56	55	23	5	68	12	1	1	0	2	.00	13	.257	.308	.420
2006	CWS	AL	140	509	150	24	0	16	(9	7)	222	65	64	68	22	6	72	8	3	1	1	0	1.00	10	.295	.333	.436
2007	CWS	AL	136	472	131	34	0	14	(8	6)	190	54	50	49	25	5	66	8	1	3	1	1	.50	21	.263	.309	.403
2008	CWS	AL	134	534	150	31	1	13	(7	6)	222	66	60	64	19	5	71	8	3	6	1	0	1.00	14	.281	.312	.416
2009	CWS	AL	138	504	151	22	1	13	(8	5)	214	57	49	59	24	6	52	1	3	3	1	1	.50	18	.300	.331	.425
2010	CWS	AL	128	474	128	29	0	9	(7	2)	184	43	56	51	15	2	39	6	6	2	3	4	.43	17	.270	.300	.388
	Postseason		30	100	30	5	1	5	(3	2)	52	16	17	19	10	1	13	2	1	1	2	3	.40	2	.300	.372	.520
	13 ML YEARS		1365	4852	1379	285	16	120	(66	54)	2056	575	605	613	207	50	588	92	24	32	13	19	.41	155	.284	.324	.424

Joel Pineiro

Pitches: R Bats: R Pos: SP-23   pinn-YAIR-oh   Ht: 6'1" Wt: 200 Born: 9/25/1978 Age: 32

			HOW MUCH HE PITCHED						WHAT HE GAVE UP											THE RESULTS						
Year	Team	Lg	G	GS	CG	GF	IP	BFP	H	R	ER	HR	SH	SF	HB	TBB	IBB	SO	WP	Bk	W	L	Pct	Sho	Sv-Op	Hld	ERC	ERA
2000	Sea	AL	8	1	0	5	19.1	94	25	13	12	3	0	2	0	13	0	10	0	0	1	0	1.000	0	0-0	0	7.44	5.60
2001	Sea	AL	17	11	0	1	75.1	289	50	24	17	2	1	2	3	21	0	56	2	0	6	2	.750	0	0-0	1	1.71	2.03
2002	Sea	AL	37	28	2	4	194.1	812	189	75	70	24	5	7	7	54	1	136	8	0	14	7	.667	1	0-0	3	3.77	3.24
2003	Sea	AL	32	32	3	0	211.2	890	192	94	89	19	3	9	6	76	3	151	5	0	16	11	.593	2	0-0	0	3.43	3.78
2004	Sea	AL	21	21	1	0	140.2	596	144	77	73	21	1	5	4	43	1	111	4	0	6	11	.353	0	0-0	0	4.32	4.67
2005	Sea	AL	30	30	2	0	189.0	822	224	118	118	23	5	7	6	56	4	107	7	1	7	11	.389	0	0-0	0	5.05	5.62
2006	Sea	AL	40	25	1	6	165.2	753	209	123	117	23	1	6	10	64	13	87	4	1	8	13	.381	0	1-2	4	6.05	6.36
2007	2 Tms		42	11	0	15	97.2	419	110	49	47	14	3	1	2	26	0	60	3	0	7	5	.583	0	0-0	1	4.68	4.33
2008	StL	NL	26	25	0	1	148.2	645	180	89	85	22	7	3	2	35	0	81	1	0	7	7	.500	0	1-1	0	5.05	5.15
2009	StL	NL	32	32	3	0	214.0	865	218	94	83	11	12	6	8	27	1	105	4	0	15	12	.556	2	0-0	0	3.00	3.49
2010	LAA	AL	23	23	3	0	152.1	634	155	66	65	15	2	3	1	34	6	92	4	0	10	7	.588	1	0-0	0	3.44	3.84
07	Bos	AL	31	0	0	15	34.0	157	41	20	19	3	1	1	1	14	0	20	3	0	1	1	.500	0	0-0	1	5.25	5.03
07	StL	NL	11	11	0	0	63.2	262	69	29	28	11	2	0	1	12	0	40	0	0	6	4	.600	0	0-0	0	4.36	3.96
	Postseason		2	1	0	0	6.0	32	11	5	5	1	0	0	0	2	0	8	1	0	0	1	.000	0	0-0	0	9.10	7.50
	11 ML YEARS		308	239	15	32	1608.2	6819	1696	822	776	177	40	51	49	449	29	996	42	2	97	86	.530	6	2-3	9	4.10	4.34

Renyel Pinto

Pitches: L **Bats:** L **Pos:** RP-20   ray-NYELL   **Ht:** 6'4" **Wt:** 280 **Born:** 7/8/1982 **Age:** 28

		HOW MUCH HE PITCHED						WHAT HE GAVE UP												THE RESULTS							
Year	Team	Lg	G	GS	CG	GF	IP	BFP	H	R	ER	HR	SH	SF	HB	TBB	IBB	SO	WP	Bk	W	L	Pct	Sh	Sv-Op Hld	ERC	ERA
2010	Jupiter*	A+	3	3	0	0	5.0	22	2	1	1	0	0	0	0	6	0	9	1	0	0	1	.000	0	0- - -	3.10	1.80
2010	Memp*	AAA	18	0	0	3	26.1	128	24	17	14	1	0	2	5	22	0	31	3	0	0	0	-	0	0- - -	5.48	4.78
2006	Fla	NL	27	0	0	7	29.2	135	20	12	10	3	0	1	1	27	0	36	4	0	0	0	-	0	1-1 3	4.33	3.03
2007	Fla	NL	57	0	0	4	58.2	242	45	25	24	7	1	3	3	32	2	56	2	0	2	4	.333	0	1-6 16	3.79	3.68
2008	Fla	NL	67	0	0	11	64.2	284	52	33	32	9	6	5	4	39	2	56	8	0	2	5	.286	0	0-2 17	4.24	4.45
2009	Fla	NL	73	0	0	11	61.1	275	53	25	22	4	1	3	2	45	2	58	4	0	4	1	.800	0	0-4 13	4.46	3.23
2010	Fla	NL	20	0	0	6	16.2	77	16	5	5	1	0	0	4	9	0	16	2	0	0	0	-	0	0-0 4	5.05	2.70
5 ML YEARS			244	0	0	39	231.0	1013	186	100	93	24	8	12	14	152	6	222	20	0	8	10	.444	0	2-13 53	4.26	3.62

Trevor Plouffe

Bats: R **Throws:** R **Pos:** SS-9; DH-9; PR-8; PH-3; 2B-2   PLOOF   **Ht:** 6'2" **Wt:** 200 **Born:** 6/15/1986 **Age:** 25

			BATTING																	BASERUNNING				AVERAGES		
Year	Team	Lg	G	AB	H	2B	3B	HR	(Hm	Rd)	TB	R	RBI	RC	TBB	IBB	SO	HBP	SH	SF	SB	CS	SB%	GDP	Avg	OBP	Slg
2004	Elizab	R+	60	237	67	7	2	4	(-	-)	90	29	28	32	19	1	34	3	2	3	2	1	.67	4	.283	.340	.380
2005	Beloit	A	127	466	104	18	0	13	(-	-)	161	58	60	52	50	0	78	4	5	7	8	4	.67	7	.223	.300	.345
2006	FtMyrs	A+	125	455	112	26	4	4	(-	-)	158	60	45	57	58	1	93	4	2	5	8	5	.62	10	.246	.333	.347
2007	NwBrit	AA	126	497	136	37	2	9	(-	-)	204	75	50	69	38	0	89	2	15	3	12	7	.63	11	.274	.326	.410
2008	NwBrit	AA	58	227	61	17	3	3	(-	-)	93	32	21	31	16	2	43	3	3	0	4	2	.67	4	.269	.325	.410
2008	Roch	AAA	66	250	64	17	3	6	(-	-)	105	34	39	31	14	0	47	0	5	3	1	1	.50	2	.256	.292	.420
2009	Roch	AAA	118	430	112	23	5	10	(-	-)	175	53	60	56	34	1	68	2	4	7	3	6	.33	11	.260	.313	.407
2010	Roch	AAA	102	402	98	22	4	15	(-	-)	173	53	49	53	27	0	90	6	8	2	5	5	.50	8	.244	.300	.430
2010	Min	AL	22	41	6	1	0	2	(1	1)	13	7	6	2	0	0	14	0	2	1	0	0	-	0	.146	.143	.317

Scott Podsednik

Bats: L **Throws:** L **Pos:** LF-129; CF-6; PH-4; DH-2   puh-SEDD-nik   **Ht:** 6'0" **Wt:** 187 **Born:** 3/18/1976 **Age:** 35

			BATTING																	BASERUNNING				AVERAGES		
Year	Team	Lg	G	AB	H	2B	3B	HR	(Hm	Rd)	TB	R	RBI	RC	TBB	IBB	SO	HBP	SH	SF	SB	CS	SB%	GDP	Avg	OBP	Slg
2001	Sea	AL	5	6	1	0	1	0	(0	0)	3	1	3	0	0	0	1	0	0	0	0	0	-	1	.167	.167	.500
2002	Sea	AL	14	20	4	0	0	1	(0	1)	7	2	5	3	4	0	6	0	0	1	0	0	-	1	.200	.320	.350
2003	Mil	NL	154	558	175	29	8	9	(7	2)	247	100	58	101	56	2	91	4	8	2	43	10	.81	11	.314	.379	.443
2004	Mil	NL	154	640	156	27	7	12	(3	9)	233	85	39	76	58	2	105	7	6	1	70	13	.84	7	.244	.313	.364
2005	CWS	AL	129	507	147	28	1	0	(0	0)	177	80	25	64	47	0	75	3	6	5	59	23	.72	7	.290	.351	.349
2006	CWS	AL	139	524	137	27	6	3	(2	1)	185	86	45	65	54	1	96	2	8	4	40	19	.68	7	.261	.330	.353
2007	CWS	AL	62	214	52	13	4	2	(1	1)	79	30	11	17	13	0	36	4	4	0	12	5	.71	9	.243	.299	.369
2008	Col	NL	93	162	41	8	1	1	(0	1)	54	22	15	19	16	0	28	1	1	1	12	4	.75	3	.253	.322	.333
2009	CWS	AL	132	537	161	25	6	7	(3	4)	221	75	48	78	39	1	74	3	6	2	30	13	.70	8	.304	.353	.412
2010	2 Tms		134	539	160	14	7	6	(1	5)	206	63	51	73	40	1	83	0	10	6	35	15	.70	10	.297	.342	.382
10	KC	AL	95	390	121	8	6	5	(1	4)	156	46	44	59	29	1	57	0	10	6	30	12	.71	5	.310	.353	.400
10	LAD	NL	39	149	39	6	1	1	(0	1)	50	17	7	14	11	0	26	0	0	0	5	3	.63	5	.262	.313	.336
Postseason			12	49	14	1	3	2	(2	0)	27	9	6	10	7	0	10	2	1	0	6	3	.67	1	.286	.397	.551
10 ML YEARS			1016	3707	1036	171	41	41	(17	24)	1412	544	300	496	327	7	595	24	49	22	301	102	.75	64	.279	.340	.381

Placido Polanco

Bats: R **Throws:** R **Pos:** 3B-123; 2B-12; PH-2   PLAH-si-doh puh-LAHN-ko   **Ht:** 5'10" **Wt:** 189 **Born:** 10/10/1975 **Age:** 35

			BATTING																	BASERUNNING				AVERAGES		
Year	Team	Lg	G	AB	H	2B	3B	HR	(Hm	Rd)	TB	R	RBI	RC	TBB	IBB	SO	HBP	SH	SF	SB	CS	SB%	GDP	Avg	OBP	Slg
2010	Clrwtr*	A+	1	4	1	0	0	0	(-	-)	1	1	0	0	0	0	0	0	0	0	0	0	-	0	.250	.250	.250
2010	Phillies*	A	1	3	3	1	0	0	(-	-)	4	1	2	2	0	0	0	0	0	0	0	0	-	0	1.000	1.000	1.333
1998	StL	NL	45	114	29	3	2	1	(1	0)	39	10	11	12	5	0	9	1	2	0	2	0	1.00	1	.254	.292	.342
1999	StL	NL	88	220	61	9	3	1	(0	1)	79	24	19	23	15	1	24	0	3	2	1	3	.25	7	.277	.321	.359
2000	StL	NL	118	323	102	12	3	5	(2	3)	135	50	39	44	16	0	26	1	7	3	4	4	.50	8	.316	.347	.418
2001	StL	NL	144	564	173	26	4	3	(1	2)	216	87	38	70	25	0	43	6	14	1	12	3	.80	22	.307	.342	.383
2002	2 Tms	NL	147	548	158	32	2	9	(8	1)	221	75	49	64	26	1	41	8	13	0	5	3	.63	15	.288	.330	.403
2003	Phi	NL	122	492	142	30	3	14	(7	7)	220	87	63	74	42	1	38	8	8	4	14	2	.88	13	.289	.352	.447
2004	Phi	NL	126	503	150	21	0	17	(10	7)	222	74	55	71	27	0	39	12	7	6	7	4	.64	13	.298	.345	.441
2005	2 Tms		129	501	166	27	2	9	(6	3)	224	84	56	86	33	0	25	11	2	4	4	3	.57	12	.331	.383	.447
2006	Det	AL	110	461	136	18	1	4	(2	2)	168	58	52	65	17	0	27	7	8	2	1	2	.33	18	.295	.329	.364
2007	Det	AL	142	587	200	36	3	9	(7	2)	269	105	67	100	37	3	30	11	2	4	7	3	.70	9	.341	.388	.458
2008	Det	AL	141	580	178	34	3	8	(2	6)	242	90	58	81	35	2	43	6	4	4	7	1	.88	14	.307	.350	.417
2009	Det	AL	153	618	176	31	4	10	(5	5)	245	82	72	84	36	2	46	9	7	5	7	2	.78	15	.285	.331	.396
2010	Phi	NL	132	554	165	27	2	6	(4	2)	214	76	52	68	32	1	47	7	1	8	5	0	1.00	14	.298	.339	.386
02	StL	NL	94	342	97	19	1	5	(5	0)	133	47	27	38	12	1	27	4	9	0	3	1	.75	12	.284	.316	.389
02	Phi	NL	53	206	61	13	1	4	(3	1)	88	28	22	26	14	0	14	4	4	0	2	2	.50	3	.296	.353	.427
05	Phi	NL	43	158	50	7	0	3	(2	1)	66	26	20	26	12	0	9	3	0	0	0	0	-	3	.316	.376	.418
05	Det	AL	86	343	116	20	2	6	(4	2)	158	58	36	60	21	0	16	8	2	4	4	3	.57	9	.338	.386	.461
Postseason			25	81	24	2	0	0	(0	0)	26	7	8	8	8	2	5	1	3	1	2	1	.67	3	.296	.363	.321
13 ML YEARS			1597	6065	1836	306	32	96	(55	41)	2494	902	631	842	346	11	438	87	78	43	76	30	.72	164	.303	.347	.411

Rick Porcello

Pitches: R **Bats:** R **Pos:** SP-27 — pore-SELL-oh — **Ht:** 6'5" **Wt:** 200 **Born:** 12/27/1988 **Age:** 22

			HOW MUCH HE PITCHED							WHAT HE GAVE UP													THE RESULTS							
Year	Team	Lg	G	GS	CG	GF	IP	BFP	H	R	ER	HR	SH	SF	HB	TBB	IBB	SO	WP	Bk	W	L	Pct	Sh	Sv-Op	Hld	ERC	ERA
2008	Lkland	A+	24	24	0	0	125.0	527	116	51	37	7	4	3	11	33	0	72	3	0	8	6	.571	0	0- -	-	3.18	2.66
2010	Toledo	AAA	4	4	0	0	28.0	111	24	11	10	0	1	1	1	10	0	19	0	1	1	2	.333	0	0- -	-	2.78	3.21
2009	Det	AL	31	31	0	0	170.2	720	176	81	75	23	4	2	3	52	0	89	6	1	14	9	.609	0	0-0	0	4.24	3.96
2010	Det	AL	27	27	0	0	162.2	700	188	96	89	18	1	2	7	38	2	84	11	3	10	12	.455	0	0-0	0	4.56	4.92
	2 ML YEARS		58	58	0	0	333.1	1420	364	177	164	41	5	4	10	90	2	173	17	4	24	21	.533	0	0-0	0	4.39	4.43

Jorge Posada

Bats: B **Throws:** R **Pos:** C-83; DH-30; PH-14; 1B-1 — HORE-hay poe-SAH-dah — **Ht:** 6'2" **Wt:** 215 **Born:** 8/17/1971 **Age:** 39

									BATTING													BASERUNNING				AVERAGES		
Year	Team	Lg	G	AB	H	2B	3B	HR	(Hm	Rd)	TB	R	RBI	RC	TBB	IBB	SO	HBP	SH	SF	SB	CS	SB%	GDP	Avg	OBP	Slg
1995	NYY	AL	1	0	0	0	0	0	(0	0)	0	0	0	0	0	0	0	0	0	0	0	0	-	0			
1996	NYY	AL	8	14	1	0	0	0	(0	0)	1	1	0	0	1	0	6	0	0	0	0	0	-	1	.071	.133	.071
1997	NYY	AL	60	188	47	12	0	6	(2	4)	77	29	25	29	30	2	33	3	1	2	1	2	.33	2	.250	.359	.410
1998	NYY	AL	111	358	96	23	0	17	(6	11)	170	56	63	56	47	7	92	0	0	4	0	1	.00	14	.268	.350	.475
1999	NYY	AL	112	379	93	19	2	12	(4	8)	152	50	57	52	53	2	91	3	0	2	1	0	1.00	9	.245	.341	.401
2000	NYY	AL	151	505	145	35	1	28	(18	10)	266	92	86	110	107	10	151	8	0	4	2	2	.50	11	.287	.417	.527
2001	NYY	AL	138	484	134	28	1	22	(14	8)	230	59	95	80	62	10	132	6	0	5	2	6	.25	10	.277	.363	.475
2002	NYY	AL	143	511	137	40	1	20	(12	8)	239	79	99	92	81	9	143	3	0	3	1	0	1.00	23	.268	.370	.468
2003	NYY	AL	142	481	135	24	0	30	(15	15)	249	83	101	98	93	6	110	10	0	4	2	4	.33	13	.281	.405	.518
2004	NYY	AL	137	449	122	31	0	21	(11	10)	216	72	81	78	88	5	92	9	0	1	1	3	.25	24	.272	.400	.481
2005	NYY	AL	142	474	124	23	0	19	(11	8)	204	67	71	71	66	5	94	2	0	4	1	0	1.00	8	.262	.352	.430
2006	NYY	AL	143	465	129	27	2	23	(11	12)	229	65	93	89	64	1	97	11	0	5	3	0	1.00	10	.277	.374	.492
2007	NYY	AL	144	506	171	42	1	20	(11	9)	275	91	90	99	74	7	98	6	0	3	2	0	1.00	18	.338	.426	.543
2008	NYY	AL	51	168	45	13	1	3	(1	2)	69	18	22	23	24	3	38	2	0	1	0	0	-	7	.268	.364	.411
2009	NYY	AL	111	383	109	25	0	22	(14	8)	200	55	81	73	48	4	101	2	0	5	1	0	1.00	13	.285	.363	.522
2010	NYY	AL	120	383	95	23	1	18	(11	7)	174	49	57	57	59	3	99	7	0	2	3	1	.75	6	.248	.357	.454
	Postseason		111	372	89	21	0	11	(4	7)	143	46	39	42	64	9	91	2	0	3	3	3	.50	15	.239	.351	.384
	16 ML YEARS		1714	5748	1583	365	10	261	(141	120)	2751	866	1021	1007	897	74	1377	72	1	45	20	19	.51	169	.275	.377	.479

Buster Posey

Bats: R **Throws:** R **Pos:** C-76; 1B-30; PH-3 — **Ht:** 6'1" **Wt:** 219 **Born:** 3/27/1987 **Age:** 24

									BATTING													BASERUNNING				AVERAGES		
Year	Team	Lg	G	AB	H	2B	3B	HR	(Hm	Rd)	TB	R	RBI	RC	TBB	IBB	SO	HBP	SH	SF	SB	CS	SB%	GDP	Avg	OBP	Slg
2008	Giants	R	7	26	10	3	1	1	(-	-)	18	8	4	8	5	1	4	0	0	0	0	0	-	0	.385	.484	.692
2008	SlmKzr	A-	3	11	3	2	0	0	(-	-)	5	2	2	2	3	0	0	0	0	0	0	0	-	0	.273	.429	.455
2009	SnJos	A+	80	291	95	23	0	13	(-	-)	157	63	58	69	45	0	45	8	0	2	6	0	1.00	6	.326	.428	.540
2009	Fresno	AAA	35	131	42	8	1	5	(-	-)	67	21	22	26	17	0	23	0	0	3	0	1	.00	5	.321	.391	.511
2010	Fresno	AAA	47	172	60	13	2	6	(-	-)	95	31	32	42	28	2	30	4	0	4	1	1	.50	7	.349	.442	.552
2009	SF	NL	7	17	2	0	0	0	(0	0)	2	1	0	0	0	0	4	0	0	0	0	0	-	0	.118	.118	.118
2010	SF	NL	108	406	124	23	2	18	(6	12)	205	58	67	70	30	5	55	4	0	3	0	2	.00	12	.305	.357	.505
	2 ML YEARS		115	423	126	23	2	18	(6	12)	207	59	67	70	30	5	59	4	0	3	0	2	.00	12	.290	.340	.480

Landon Powell

Bats: B **Throws:** R **Pos:** C-38; PH-3; DH-2; 1B-1; PR-1 — **Ht:** 6'3" **Wt:** 253 **Born:** 3/19/1982 **Age:** 29

									BATTING													BASERUNNING				AVERAGES		
Year	Team	Lg	G	AB	H	2B	3B	HR	(Hm	Rd)	TB	R	RBI	RC	TBB	IBB	SO	HBP	SH	SF	SB	CS	SB%	GDP	Avg	OBP	Slg
2004	Vancvr	A-	38	135	32	6	1	3	(-	-)	49	24	19	20	26	1	22	1	0	1	0	0	-	4	.237	.362	.363
2006	Stcktn	A+	90	326	86	12	0	15	(-	-)	143	44	47	53	43	0	77	2	1	3	0	0	-	6	.264	.350	.439
2006	Mdland	AA	12	41	11	0	0	1	(-	-)	14	4	4	4	3	0	12	1	0	0	0	0	-	1	.268	.333	.341
2007	Mdland	AA	60	219	64	9	2	11	(-	-)	110	46	39	44	36	2	40	0	0	1	1	0	1.00	7	.292	.391	.502
2007	Scrmto	AAA	4	17	5	0	0	3	(-	-)	14	3	3	4	0	0	4	0	0	0	0	0	-	0	.294	.294	.824
2008	Scrmto	AAA	88	300	68	11	0	15	(-	-)	124	42	52	49	63	1	85	0	0	4	0	1	.00	5	.227	.357	.413
2010	Scrmto	AAA	14	45	9	2	0	1	(-	-)	14	6	2	5	10	0	9	0	0	0	0	0	-	2	.200	.345	.311
2009	Oak	AL	46	140	32	7	0	7	(4	3)	60	19	30	22	14	0	36	0	0	1	0	0	-	3	.229	.297	.429
2010	Oak	AL	41	112	24	4	0	2	(0	2)	34	13	11	12	15	0	29	0	1	1	1	0	1.00	2	.214	.305	.304
	2 ML YEARS		87	252	56	11	0	9	(4	5)	94	32	41	34	29	0	65	0	1	2	1	0	1.00	5	.222	.300	.373

Martin Prado

Bats: R **Throws:** R **Pos:** 2B-98; 3B-43; 1B-5 — mar-TEEN PRAH-doe — **Ht:** 6'1" **Wt:** 190 **Born:** 10/27/1983 **Age:** 27

									BATTING													BASERUNNING				AVERAGES		
Year	Team	Lg	G	AB	H	2B	3B	HR	(Hm	Rd)	TB	R	RBI	RC	TBB	IBB	SO	HBP	SH	SF	SB	CS	SB%	GDP	Avg	OBP	Slg
2010	Gwnntt*	AAA	1	4	1	0	0	0	(-	-)	1	0	0	0	0	0	0	0	0	0	0	0	-	0	.250	.250	.250
2006	Atl	NL	24	42	11	1	1	1	(1	0)	17	3	9	9	5	0	7	0	2	0	0	0	-	2	.262	.340	.405
2007	Atl	NL	28	59	17	3	0	0	(0	0)	20	5	2	6	3	0	6	0	0	0	0	0	-	0	.288	.323	.339
2008	Atl	NL	78	228	73	18	4	2	(1	1)	105	36	33	39	21	0	29	1	2	2	3	1	.75	3	.320	.377	.461
2009	Atl	NL	128	450	138	38	0	11	(4	7)	209	64	49	57	36	1	59	2	11	4	1	3	.25	17	.307	.358	.464
2010	Atl	NL	140	599	184	40	3	15	(4	11)	275	100	66	86	40	2	86	3	3	6	5	3	.63	13	.307	.350	.459
	5 ML YEARS		398	1378	423	100	8	29	(10	19)	626	208	159	197	105	3	187	6	18	12	9	7	.56	35	.307	.356	.454

Alex Presley

Bats: L **Throws:** L **Pos:** RF-8; PH-6; CF-4; PR-3; LF-2   **Ht:** 5'9" **Wt:** 180 **Born:** 7/25/1985 **Age:** 25

								BATTING															BASERUNNING				AVERAGES		
Year	Team	Lg	G	AB	H	2B	3B	HR	(Hm | Rd)	TB	R	RBI	RC	TBB	IBB	SO	HBP	SH	SF				SB	CS	SB%	GDP	Avg	OBP	Slg
2006	Wmspt	A-	61	223	58	7	8	3	(- | -)	90	26	23	28	17	2	55	1	1	2				3	3	.50	1	.260	.313	.404
2007	Hkry	A	121	495	145	22	8	11	(- | -)	216	79	63	77	45	2	108	0	7	6				18	10	.64	2	.293	.348	.436
2008	Lynbrg	A+	82	287	74	15	1	6	(- | -)	109	39	35	38	29	0	50	1	5	3				13	6	.68	1	.258	.325	.380
2009	Lynbrg	A+	115	417	107	17	11	4	(- | -)	158	51	37	49	30	0	87	0	7	2				9	5	.64	1	.257	.305	.379
2010	Altna	AA	67	246	86	13	7	6	(- | -)	131	42	47	51	19	2	33	2	1	1				5	1	.83	6	.350	.399	.533
2010	Indy	AAA	69	272	80	15	6	6	(- | -)	125	44	38	43	22	1	42	1	1	0				8	7	.53	4	.294	.349	.460
2010	Pit	NL	19	23	6	1	0	0	(0 | 0)	7	2	0	1	1	0	8	0	1	0				1	1	.50	0	.261	.292	.304

David Price

Pitches: L **Bats:** L **Pos:** SP-31; RP-1   **Ht:** 6'6" **Wt:** 225 **Born:** 8/26/1985 **Age:** 25

				HOW MUCH HE PITCHED					WHAT HE GAVE UP										THE RESULTS							
Year	Team	Lg	G	GS	CG	GF	IP	BFP	H	R	ER	HR	SH	SF	HB	TBB	IBB	SO	WP	Bk	W	L	Pct	Sh	Sv-Op	Hld	ERC	ERA
2008	TB	AL	5	1	0	0	14.0	57	9	4	3	1	0	1	1	4	0	12	0	0	0	0		0	0-0	1	1.86	1.93
2009	TB	AL	23	23	0	0	128.1	557	119	72	63	17	3	2	4	54	0	102	2	0	10	7	.588	0	0-0	0	4.05	4.42
2010	TB	AL	32	31	2	0	208.2	861	170	71	63	15	4	3	5	79	1	188	5	3	19	6	.760	1	0-0	0	2.91	2.72
	Postseason		5	0	0	5	5.2	24	2	2	1	1	0	0	0	4	0	8	0	0	1	0	1.000	0	1-1	0	2.19	1.59
	3 ML YEARS		60	55	2	0	351.0	1475	298	147	129	33	7	6	10	137	1	302	7	3	29	13	.690	1	0-0	1	3.27	3.31

Scott Proctor

Pitches: R **Bats:** R **Pos:** RP-6   **Ht:** 6'1" **Wt:** 195 **Born:** 1/2/1977 **Age:** 34

				HOW MUCH HE PITCHED					WHAT HE GAVE UP										THE RESULTS							
Year	Team	Lg	G	GS	CG	GF	IP	BFP	H	R	ER	HR	SH	SF	HB	TBB	IBB	SO	WP	Bk	W	L	Pct	Sh	Sv-Op	Hld	ERC	ERA
2010	Gwnntt*	AAA	31	0	0	4	34.1	162	45	29	27	6	1	5	1	15	2	29	4	1	4	3	.571	0	0- --	-	6.62	7.08
2010	MrtlBh*	A	6	0	0	0	7.1	34	8	5	5	0	0	0	2	2	0	5	0	0	1	0	1.000	0	0- --	-	4.28	6.14
2004	NYY	AL	26	0	0	12	25.0	118	29	18	15	5	0	2	0	14	0	21	1	1	2	1	.667	0	0--	2	6.32	5.40
2005	NYY	AL	29	1	0	11	44.2	199	46	32	30	10	0	1	2	17	4	36	4	1	1	0	1.000	0	0-0	0	4.98	6.04
2006	NYY	AL	83	0	0	12	102.1	426	89	41	40	12	2	6	2	33	6	89	2	0	6	4	.600	0	1-8	26	3.15	3.52
2007	2 Tms		83	0	0	14	86.1	382	78	41	35	12	3	7	6	44	4	64	5	1	5	5	.500	0	0-6	18	4.41	3.65
2008	LAD	NL	41	0	0	11	38.2	184	41	30	26	7	1	2	0	24	1	46	6	0	2	0	1.000	0	0-1	2	5.67	6.05
2010	Atl	NL	6	0	0	2	5.2	24	4	4	4	1	0	0	0	4	1	6	0	0	0	0	-	0	0-0	0	3.99	6.35
07	NYY	AL	52	0	0	10	54.1	245	53	27	23	8	1	6	3	29	3	37	3	0	2	5	.286	0	0-4	11	4.90	3.81
07	LAD	NL	31	0	0	4	32.0	137	25	14	12	4	2	1	3	15	1	27	2	1	3	0	1.000	0	0-2	7	3.61	3.38
	Postseason		5	0	0	2	6.0	26	8	1	1	0	0	0	0	2	1	2	1	0	0	0	-	0	0-0	0	4.37	1.50
	6 ML YEARS		268	1	0	62	302.2	1333	287	166	150	47	6	18	10	136	16	262	18	3	16	10	.615	0	1-15	48	4.35	4.46

Albert Pujols

Bats: R **Throws:** R **Pos:** 1B-157; PH-2   **Ht:** 6'3" **Wt:** 230 **Born:** 1/16/1980 **Age:** 31

								BATTING															BASERUNNING				AVERAGES		
Year	Team	Lg	G	AB	H	2B	3B	HR	(Hm	Rd)	TB	R	RBI	RC	TBB	IBB	SO	HBP	SH	SF				SB	CS	SB%	GDP	Avg	OBP	Slg
2001	StL	NL	161	590	194	47	4	37	(18	19)	360	112	130	132	69	6	93	9	1	7				1	3	.25	21	.329	.403	.610
2002	StL	NL	157	590	185	40	2	34	(14	20)	331	118	127	121	72	13	69	9	0	4				2	4	.33	20	.314	.394	.561
2003	StL	NL	157	591	212	51	1	43	(21	22)	394	137	124	160	79	12	65	10	0	5				5	1	.83	13	.359	.439	.667
2004	StL	NL	154	592	196	51	2	46	(18	28)	389	133	123	143	84	12	52	7	0	9				5	5	.50	21	.331	.415	.657
2005	StL	NL	161	591	195	38	2	41	(23	18)	360	129	117	139	97	27	65	9	0	3				16	2	.89	19	.330	.430	.609
2006	StL	NL	143	535	177	33	1	49	(24	25)	359	119	137	146	92	28	50	4	0	3				7	2	.78	20	.331	.431	.671
2007	StL	NL	158	565	185	38	1	32	(12	20)	321	99	103	118	99	22	58	7	0	8				2	6	.25	27	.327	.429	.568
2008	StL	NL	148	524	187	44	0	37	(19	18)	342	100	116	130	104	34	54	5	0	8				7	3	.70	16	.357	.462	.653
2009	StL	NL	160	568	186	45	1	47	(22	25)	374	124	135	145	115	44	64	9	0	8				16	4	.80	23	.327	.443	.658
2010	StL	NL	159	587	183	39	1	42	(17	25)	350	115	118	131	103	38	76	4	0	6				14	4	.78	23	.312	.414	.596
	Postseason		56	199	64	10	1	13	(7	6)	115	39	36	44	36	12	28	3	0	1				0	1	.00	5	.322	.431	.578
	10 ML YEARS		1558	5733	1900	426	15	408	(188	220)	3580	1186	1230	1365	914	236	646	73	1	61				75	34	.69	203	.331	.426	.624

Nick Punto

Bats: B **Throws:** R **Pos:** 3B-48; SS-31; 2B-12; PR-4; DH-1; PH-1   POON-toh   **Ht:** 5'9" **Wt:** 190 **Born:** 11/8/1977 **Age:** 33

								BATTING															BASERUNNING				AVERAGES		
Year	Team	Lg	G	AB	H	2B	3B	HR	(Hm	Rd)	TB	R	RBI	RC	TBB	IBB	SO	HBP	SH	SF				SB	CS	SB%	GDP	Avg	OBP	Slg
2001	Phi	NL	4	5	2	0	0	0	(0	0)	2	0	0	1	0	0	0	0	0	0				0	0	-	0	.400	.400	.400
2002	Phi	NL	9	6	1	0	0	0	(0	0)	1	0	0	0	0	0	3	0	1	0				0	0	-	0	.167	.167	.167
2003	Phi	NL	64	92	20	2	0	1	(0	1)	25	14	4	7	7	1	22	0	0	0				2	1	.67	0	.217	.273	.272
2004	Min	AL	38	91	23	0	0	2	(2	0)	29	17	12	15	12	0	19	0	0	0				6	0	1.00	2	.253	.340	.319
2005	Min	AL	112	394	94	18	4	4	(3	1)	132	45	26	35	36	0	86	0	7	2				13	8	.62	9	.239	.301	.335
2006	Min	AL	135	459	133	21	7	1	(0	1)	171	73	45	59	47	1	68	1	10	7				17	5	.77	8	.290	.352	.373
2007	Min	AL	150	472	99	18	4	1	(0	1)	128	53	25	37	55	1	90	0	6	3				16	6	.73	7	.210	.291	.271
2008	Min	AL	99	338	96	19	4	2	(1	1)	129	43	28	42	32	1	57	0	5	2				15	6	.71	10	.284	.344	.382
2009	Min	AL	125	359	82	15	1	1	(0	1)	102	56	38	46	61	1	70	1	13	6				16	3	.84	6	.228	.337	.284
2010	Min	AL	88	252	60	11	1	1	(0	1)	76	24	20	25	28	2	50	1	4	3				6	2	.75	3	.238	.313	.302
	Postseason		6	21	6	1	0	0	(0	0)	7	0	1	1	3	0	2	0	1	0				0	0	-	0	.286	.375	.333
	10 ML YEARS		824	2468	610	104	21	13	(6	7)	795	325	198	267	278	6	465	3	46	23				91	31	.75	46	.247	.321	.322

David Purcey

Pitches: L **Bats:** L **Pos:** RP-33 **Ht:** 6'5" **Wt:** 235 **Born:** 4/22/1982 **Age:** 29

Year	Team	Lg	G	GS	CG	GF	IP	BFP	H	R	ER	HR	SH	SF	HB	TBB	IBB	SO	WP	Bk	W	L	Pct	Sh	Sv-Op	Hld	ERC	ERA
2010	LsVgs*	AAA	17	0	0	3	18.2	85	14	9	7	2	2	1	0	15	0	23	2	0	2	1	.667	0	0--	-	4.20	3.38
2010	NHam*	AA	3	0	0	0	2.2	12	3	4	4	1	0	0	0	1	0	5	1	0	0	1	.000	0	0--	-	6.59	13.50
2008	Tor	AL	12	12	1	0	65.0	289	67	41	40	9	2	3	4	29	0	58	3	0	3	6	.333	0	0-0	0	4.96	5.54
2009	Tor	AL	9	9	0	0	48.0	223	54	35	33	6	3	1	1	30	1	39	3	0	1	3	.250	0	0-0	0	6.00	6.19
2010	Tor	AL	33	0	0	18	34.0	143	26	16	14	3	2	2	0	15	1	32	3	0	1	1	.500	0	1-1	3	2.80	3.71
	3 ML YEARS		54	21	1	18	147.0	655	147	92	87	18	7	6	5	74	2	129	9	0	5	10	.333	0	1-1	3	4.75	5.33

J.J. Putz

Pitches: R **Bats:** R **Pos:** RP-60 **PUTS** **Ht:** 6'5" **Wt:** 250 **Born:** 2/22/1977 **Age:** 34

Year	Team	Lg	G	GS	CG	GF	IP	BFP	H	R	ER	HR	SH	SF	HB	TBB	IBB	SO	WP	Bk	W	L	Pct	Sh	Sv-Op	Hld	ERC	ERA
2003	Sea	AL	3	0	0	0	3.2	18	4	2	2	0	0	0	0	3	0	3	0	0	0	0	-	0	0-0	0	5.31	4.91
2004	Sea	AL	54	0	0	30	63.0	275	66	35	33	10	3	2	5	24	4	47	1	0	0	3	.000	0	9-13	5	4.97	4.71
2005	Sea	AL	64	0	0	20	60.0	259	58	27	24	8	3	3	2	23	2	45	2	0	6	5	.545	0	1-4	21	4.11	3.60
2006	Sea	AL	72	0	0	57	78.1	303	59	20	20	4	1	2	2	13	1	104	1	0	4	1	.800	0	36-43	5	1.78	2.30
2007	Sea	AL	68	0	0	65	71.2	260	37	11	11	6	2	1	2	13	0	82	3	0	6	1	.857	0	40-42	0	1.21	1.38
2008	Sea	AL	47	0	0	35	46.1	211	46	20	20	4	0	1	2	28	2	56	2	0	6	5	.545	0	15-23	0	4.82	3.88
2009	NYM	NL	29	0	0	6	29.1	135	29	18	17	1	1	2	0	19	4	19	1	0	1	4	.200	0	2-4	10	4.16	5.22
2010	CWS	AL	60	0	0	16	54.0	219	41	18	17	4	1	1	1	15	2	65	4	0	7	5	.583	0	3-7	14	2.19	2.83
	8 ML YEARS		397	0	0	229	406.1	1680	340	151	144	37	11	12	14	138	15	421	14	0	30	24	.556	0	106-136	53	2.99	3.19

Chad Qualls

Pitches: R **Bats:** R **Pos:** RP-70 **Ht:** 6'5" **Wt:** 220 **Born:** 8/17/1978 **Age:** 32

Year	Team	Lg	G	GS	CG	GF	IP	BFP	H	R	ER	HR	SH	SF	HB	TBB	IBB	SO	WP	Bk	W	L	Pct	Sh	Sv-Op	Hld	ERC	ERA
2004	Hou	NL	25	0	0	4	33.0	141	34	14	13	3	0	1	4	8	1	24	0	0	4	0	1.000	0	1-2	9	4.02	3.55
2005	Hou	NL	77	0	0	19	79.2	329	73	33	29	7	4	3	6	23	2	60	1	0	6	4	.600	0	0-0	22	3.42	3.28
2006	Hou	NL	81	0	0	13	88.2	356	76	38	37	10	4	4	6	28	6	56	0	0	7	3	.700	0	0-6	23	3.36	3.76
2007	Hou	NL	79	0	0	16	82.2	345	84	29	28	10	6	2	3	25	5	78	2	0	6	5	.545	0	5-10	21	4.07	3.05
2008	Ari	NL	77	0	0	21	73.2	300	61	29	23	4	4	3	3	18	2	71	6	0	4	8	.333	0	9-17	22	2.40	2.81
2009	Ari	NL	51	0	0	44	52.0	217	53	23	21	5	1	0	2	7	2	45	2	0	2	2	.500	0	24-29	0	3.17	3.63
2010	2 Tms		70	0	0	29	59.0	281	85	56	48	7	4	4	2	21	4	49	4	0	3	4	.429	0	12-19	11	6.63	7.32
10	Ari	NL	43	0	0	28	38.0	190	61	41	35	5	4	2	1	15	4	34	3	0	1	4	.200	0	12-16	3	7.80	8.29
10	TB	AL	27	0	0	1	21.0	91	24	15	13	2	0	2	1	6	0	15	1	0	2	0	1.000	0	0-3	8	4.64	5.57
	Postseason		15	0	0	0	21.0	85	20	11	11	2	1	0	0	7	3	17	0	0	1	1	.500	0	0-2	2	3.45	4.71
	7 ML YEARS		460	0	0	146	468.2	1969	466	221	199	46	23	17	26	130	22	383	15	0	32	26	.552	0	51-83	108	3.73	3.82

Carlos Quentin

Bats: R **Throws:** R **Pos:** RF-104; DH-23; PH-5 **Ht:** 6'2" **Wt:** 235 **Born:** 8/28/1982 **Age:** 28

Year	Team	Lg	G	AB	H	2B	3B	HR	(Hm	Rd)	TB	R	RBI	RC	TBB	IBB	SO	HBP	SH	SF	SB	CS	SB%	GDP	Avg	OBP	Slg
2006	Ari	NL	57	166	42	13	3	9	(3	6)	88	23	32	29	15	2	34	8	1	1	0	1.00	6	.253	.342	.530
2007	Ari	NL	81	229	49	16	0	5	(5	0)	80	29	31	27	18	1	54	11	1	4	2	2	.50	5	.214	.298	.349
2008	CWS	AL	130	480	138	26	1	36	(21	15)	274	96	100	104	66	0	80	20	0	3	7	3	.70	16	.288	.394	.571
2009	CWS	AL	99	351	83	14	0	21	(12	9)	160	47	56	47	31	2	52	15	0	2	3	0	1.00	16	.236	.323	.456
2010	CWS	AL	131	453	110	25	2	26	(19	7)	217	73	87	78	50	3	83	20	0	4	2	2	.50	16	.243	.342	.479
	5 ML YEARS		498	1679	422	94	6	97	(60	37)	819	268	306	285	180	8	303	74	2	14	15	7	.68	54	.251	.347	.488

Robb Quinlan

Bats: R **Throws:** R **Pos:** 1B-13; RF-3; PH-3; PR-3; DH-2; 3B-1; LF-1 **Ht:** 6'1" **Wt:** 215 **Born:** 3/17/1977 **Age:** 34

Year	Team	Lg	G	AB	H	2B	3B	HR	(Hm	Rd)	TB	R	RBI	RC	TBB	IBB	SO	HBP	SH	SF	SB	CS	SB%	GDP	Avg	OBP	Slg
2010	Salt Lk*	AAA	34	128	33	6	0	0	(-	-)	39	13	8	14	15	0	23	0	1	0	1	0	1.00	9	.258	.336	.305
2003	LAA	AL	38	94	27	4	2	0	(0	0)	35	13	4	8	6	0	16	0	1	0	1	2	.33	3	.287	.330	.372
2004	LAA	AL	56	160	55	14	0	5	(3	2)	84	23	23	33	14	0	26	2	0	1	3	1	.75	1	.344	.401	.525
2005	LAA	AL	54	134	31	8	0	5	(3	2)	54	17	14	11	7	0	26	1	0	1	0	1	.00	4	.231	.273	.403
2006	LAA	AL	86	234	75	11	1	9	(3	6)	115	28	32	36	7	1	28	2	0	1	2	1	.67	6	.321	.344	.491
2007	LAA	AL	79	178	44	9	0	3	(1	2)	62	21	21	15	14	1	27	1	0	1	3	2	.60	6	.247	.304	.348
2008	LAA	AL	68	164	43	1	2	1	(1	0)	51	15	11	17	14	0	28	1	0	1	4	2	.67	5	.262	.326	.311
2009	LAA	AL	54	115	28	5	0	2	(1	1)	39	13	14	12	5	0	30	0	0	0	1	1	.50	3	.243	.275	.339
2010	LAA	AL	23	33	4	2	0	0	(0	0)	6	4	2	1	2	0	6	0	1	0	2	0	1.00	0	.121	.171	.182
	Postseason		4	6	2	0	0	1	(0	1)	5	1	1	2	0	0	2	0	0	0	0	0	-	0	.333	.333	.833
	8 ML YEARS		458	1112	307	54	5	25	(12	13)	446	134	121	133	69	2	187	8	2	5	16	10	.62	28	.276	.322	.401

Humberto Quintero

Bats: R **Throws:** R **Pos:** C-87; PH-5 **oom-BARE-toe keen-TARE-oh** **Ht:** 5'9" **Wt:** 221 **Born:** 8/2/1979 **Age:** 31

Year	Team	Lg	G	AB	H	2B	3B	HR	(Hm	Rd)	TB	R	RBI	RC	TBB	IBB	SO	HBP	SH	SF	SB	CS	SB%	GDP	Avg	OBP	Slg
2003	SD	NL	12	23	5	0	0	0	(0	0)	5	1	2	2	1	1	6	0	0	0	0	0	-	0	.217	.250	.217
2004	SD	NL	23	72	18	3	0	2	(1	1)	27	7	10	6	5	0	16	0	0	1	0	2	.00	3	.250	.295	.375
2005	Hou	NL	18	54	10	1	0	1	(1	0)	14	6	8	2	1	1	10	0	2	0	0	0	-	3	.185	.200	.259
2006	Hou	NL	11	21	7	2	0	0	(0	0)	9	2	2	1	1	0	3	0	0	0	0	0	-	2	.333	.364	.429

Year	Team	Lg	G	AB	H	2B	3B	HR	(Hm	Rd)	TB	R	RBI	RC	TBB	IBB	SO	HBP	SH	SF	SB	CS	SB%	GDP	Avg	OBP	Slg
2007	Hou	NL	29	53	12	2	0	0	(0	0)	14	2	1	3	2	1	13	2	0	0	0	0	-	2	.226	.281	.264
2008	Hou	NL	59	168	38	6	0	2	(1	1)	50	16	12	10	6	0	34	4	5	0	0	0	-	5	.226	.270	.298
2009	Hou	NL	60	157	37	8	1	4	(3	1)	59	11	14	13	7	1	41	4	0	0	0	0	-	8	.236	.286	.376
2010	Hou	NL	88	265	62	10	0	4	(2	2)	84	13	20	20	8	2	59	2	1	0	0	0	-	5	.234	.262	.317
8 ML YEARS			300	813	189	32	1	13	(8	5)	262	58	69	57	31	6	182	12	8	1	0	2	.00	30	.232	.271	.322

Guillermo Quiroz

Bats: R **Throws:** R **Pos:** C-2   key-ROSE   **Ht:** 6'1" **Wt:** 215 **Born:** 11/29/1981 **Age:** 29

Year	Team	Lg	G	AB	H	2B	3B	HR	(Hm	Rd)	TB	R	RBI	RC	TBB	IBB	SO	HBP	SH	SF	SB	CS	SB%	GDP	Avg	OBP	Slg
2010	WTenn*	AA	68	234	66	17	1	5	(-	-)	100	24	35	35	21	1	59	4	1	3	0	2	.00	6	.282	.347	.427
2010	Tacom*	AAA	28	91	27	5	1	2	(-	-)	40	13	11	14	6	0	16	1	0	0	0	0	-	3	.297	.347	.440
2004	Tor	AL	17	52	11	2	0	0	(0	0)	13	2	6	4	2	0	8	2	0	1	1	0	1.00	1	.212	.263	.250
2005	Tor	AL	12	36	7	2	0	0	(0	0)	9	3	4	3	2	0	13	1	0	0	0	0	-	0	.194	.256	.250
2006	Sea	AL	1	2	0	0	0	0	(0	0)	0	0	0	0	0	0	2	0	0	0	0	0	-	0	.000	.000	.000
2007	Tex	AL	9	10	4	1	0	0	(0	0)	5	1	2	3	1	0	2	0	0	0	0	0	-	0	.400	.455	.500
2008	Bal	AL	56	134	25	5	0	2	(1	1)	36	12	14	10	12	0	34	1	1	0	0	0	-	3	.187	.259	.269
2009	Sea	AL	4	14	4	0	0	0	(0	0)	4	0	2	1	0	0	3	0	1	0	0	0	-	0	.286	.286	.286
2010	Sea	AL	2	7	2	1	0	0	(0	0)	3	1	0	0	0	0	1	0	0	0	0	0	-	0	.286	.286	.429
7 ML YEARS			101	255	53	11	0	2	(1	1)	70	19	28	21	17	0	63	4	2	1	1	0	1.00	4	.208	.267	.275

Ryan Raburn

Bats: R **Throws:** R **Pos:** LF-73; RF-20; 2B-18; PH-18; CF-7; DH-3; 3B-2; 1B-1   RAYE-burn   **Ht:** 6'0" **Wt:** 185 **Born:** 4/17/1981 **Age:** 30

Year	Team	Lg	G	AB	H	2B	3B	HR	(Hm	Rd)	TB	R	RBI	RC	TBB	IBB	SO	HBP	SH	SF	SB	CS	SB%	GDP	Avg	OBP	Slg
2010	Toledo*	AAA	7	27	12	6	0	0	(-	-)	18	5	2	7	2	1	3	0	0	0	1	1	.50	2	.444	.483	.667
2004	Det	AL	12	29	4	1	0	0	(0	0)	5	4	1	1	2	0	15	0	0	0	1	0	1.00	0	.138	.194	.172
2007	Det	AL	49	138	42	12	2	4	(2	2)	70	28	27	21	8	1	33	0	0	1	3	0	1.00	7	.304	.340	.507
2008	Det	AL	92	182	43	10	1	4	(2	2)	67	26	20	20	16	1	49	0	1	0	3	1	.75	2	.236	.298	.368
2009	Det	AL	113	261	76	11	2	16	(9	7)	139	44	45	42	26	2	60	2	1	1	5	4	.56	5	.291	.359	.533
2010	Det	AL	113	371	104	25	1	15	(5	10)	176	54	62	54	27	0	92	8	1	3	2	2	.50	8	.280	.340	.474
5 ML YEARS			379	981	269	59	6	39	(18	21)	457	156	155	138	79	4	249	10	4	5	14	7	.67	23	.274	.333	.466

Alexei Ramirez

Bats: R **Throws:** R **Pos:** SS-156; PH-1; PR-1   ah-lexx-AY   **Ht:** 6'2" **Wt:** 170 **Born:** 9/22/1981 **Age:** 29

Year	Team	Lg	G	AB	H	2B	3B	HR	(Hm	Rd)	TB	R	RBI	RC	TBB	IBB	SO	HBP	SH	SF	SB	CS	SB%	GDP	Avg	OBP	Slg
2008	CWS	AL	136	480	139	22	2	21	(13	8)	228	65	77	78	18	3	61	3	4	4	13	9	.59	14	.290	.317	.475
2009	CWS	AL	148	542	150	14	1	15	(9	6)	211	71	68	74	49	3	66	1	6	8	14	5	.74	15	.277	.333	.389
2010	CWS	AL	156	585	165	29	2	18	(11	7)	252	83	70	72	27	2	82	2	7	5	13	8	.62	12	.282	.313	.431
Postseason			4	12	3	0	0	0	(0	0)	3	1	2	1	1	0	1	0	0	2	0	0	-	0	.250	.267	.250
3 ML YEARS			440	1607	454	65	5	54	(33	21)	691	219	215	224	94	8	209	6	17	17	40	22	.65	41	.283	.321	.430

Aramis Ramirez

Bats: R **Throws:** R **Pos:** 3B-118; PH-6; DH-1   ah-RAH-miss   **Ht:** 6'1" **Wt:** 205 **Born:** 6/25/1978 **Age:** 33

Year	Team	Lg	G	AB	H	2B	3B	HR	(Hm	Rd)	TB	R	RBI	RC	TBB	IBB	SO	HBP	SH	SF	SB	CS	SB%	GDP	Avg	OBP	Slg
2010	Peoria*	A	2	6	1	0	0	0	(-	-)	1	1	1	0	2	1	2	0	0	0	0	0	-	0	.167	.375	.167
1998	Pit	NL	72	251	59	9	1	6	(3	3)	88	23	24	26	18	0	72	4	1	1	0	1	.00	3	.235	.296	.351
1999	Pit	NL	18	56	10	2	1	0	(0	0)	14	2	7	4	6	0	9	1	1	1	0	0	-	0	.179	.254	.250
2000	Pit	NL	73	254	65	15	2	6	(4	2)	102	19	35	28	10	0	36	5	1	4	0	0	-	9	.256	.293	.402
2001	Pit	NL	158	603	181	40	0	34	(16	18)	323	83	112	108	40	4	100	8	0	4	5	4	.56	9	.300	.350	.536
2002	Pit	NL	142	522	122	26	2	18	(7	11)	202	51	71	49	29	3	95	8	0	11	2	0	1.00	17	.234	.279	.387
2003	2 Tms	NL	159	607	165	32	2	27	(10	17)	282	75	106	88	42	3	99	10	0	11	2	2	.50	21	.272	.324	.465
2004	ChC	NL	145	547	174	32	1	36	(22	14)	316	99	103	100	49	6	62	3	0	7	0	2	.00	25	.318	.373	.578
2005	ChC	NL	123	463	140	30	0	31	(11	20)	263	72	92	79	35	4	60	6	0	2	0	1	.00	15	.302	.358	.568
2006	ChC	NL	157	594	173	38	4	38	(14	24)	333	93	119	109	50	4	63	9	0	7	2	1	.67	15	.291	.352	.561
2007	ChC	NL	132	506	157	35	4	26	(17	9)	278	72	101	95	43	8	66	4	0	5	0	0	-	13	.310	.366	.549
2008	ChC	NL	149	554	160	44	1	27	(17	10)	287	97	111	108	74	7	94	11	0	6	2	2	.50	13	.289	.380	.518
2009	ChC	NL	82	306	97	14	1	15	(7	8)	158	46	65	66	28	3	43	8	0	0	2	1	.67	8	.317	.389	.516
2010	ChC	NL	124	465	112	21	1	25	(14	11)	210	61	83	64	34	3	90	3	0	5	0	0	-	10	.241	.294	.452
03	Pit	NL	96	375	105	25	1	12	(6	6)	168	44	67	49	25	3	68	7	0	8	1	1	.50	17	.280	.330	.448
03	ChC	NL	63	232	60	7	1	15	(4	11)	114	31	39	39	17	0	31	3	0	3	1	1	.50	4	.259	.314	.491
Postseason			18	67	13	2	1	4	(1	3)	29	7	10	8	9	0	15	1	0	0	0	0	-	5	.194	.299	.433
13 ML YEARS			1534	5728	1615	338	18	289	(142	147)	2856	793	1029	924	458	45	889	79	3	64	15	14	.52	158	.282	.340	.499

Edwar Ramirez

Pitches: R **Bats:** R **Pos:** RP-7   **Ht:** 6'3" **Wt:** 167 **Born:** 3/28/1981 **Age:** 30

Year	Team	Lg	G	GS	CG	GF	IP	BFP	H	R	ER	HR	SH	SF	HB	TBB	IBB	SO	WP	Bk	W	L	Pct	Sh	Sv-Op	Hld	ERC	ERA
2010	Scrmto*	AAA	36	0	0	8	49.2	218	48	24	20	5	4	3	1	23	3	35	5	0	3	4	.429	0	0- -	-	4.08	3.62
2007	NYY	AL	21	0	0	5	21.0	103	24	19	19	6	1	1	3	14	2	31	4	0	1	1	.500	0	1-3	3	7.95	8.14

			HOW MUCH HE PITCHED						WHAT HE GAVE UP										THE RESULTS						
Year	Team	Lg	G	GS	CG	GF	IP	BFP	H	R	ER	HR	SH	SF	HB	TBB	IBB	SO	WP	Bk	W	L	Pct	Sh	Sv-Op	Hld	ERC	ERA
2008	NYY	AL	55	0	0	16	55.1	233	44	25	24	7	0	1	3	24	2	63	3	0	5	1	.833	0	1-4	5	3.42	3.90
2009	NYY	AL	20	0	0	2	22.0	110	25	15	14	6	0	2	0	18	0	22	1	0	0	0	—	0	0-0	1	7.86	5.73
2010	Oak	AL	7	0	0	3	11.0	54	9	7	6	1	2	1	0	10	1	10	1	0	1	0	1.000	0	0-0	0	4.49	4.91
4 ML YEARS			103	0	0	26	109.1	500	102	66	63	20	3	5	6	66	5	126	9	0	7	2	.778	0	2-7	9	5.18	5.19

Hanley Ramirez

Bats: R **Throws:** R **Pos:** SS-140; PH-1; PR-1   **Ht:** 6'3" **Wt:** 229 **Born:** 12/23/1983 **Age:** 27

							BATTING													BASERUNNING				AVERAGES		
Year	Team	Lg	G	AB	H	2B	3B	HR	(Hm	Rd)	TB	R	RBI	RC	TBB	IBB	SO	HBP	SH	SF	SB	CS	SB%	GDP	Avg	OBP	Slg
2005	Bos	AL	2	2	0	0	0	0	(0	0)	0	0	0	0	0	0	2	0	0	0	0	0	—	0	.000	.000	.000
2006	Fla	NL	158	633	185	46	11	17	(9	8)	304	119	59	101	56	0	128	4	5	2	51	15	.77	7	.292	.353	.480
2007	Fla	NL	154	639	212	48	6	29	(15	14)	359	125	81	115	52	3	95	7	4	4	51	14	.78	10	.332	.386	.562
2008	Fla	NL	153	589	177	34	4	33	(17	16)	318	**125**	67	116	92	9	122	8	0	4	35	12	.74	5	.301	.400	.540
2009	Fla	NL	151	576	197	42	1	24	(17	7)	313	101	106	122	61	14	101	9	1	5	27	8	.77	9	**.342**	.410	.543
2010	Fla	NL	142	543	163	28	2	21	(12	9)	258	92	76	90	64	12	93	7	0	5	32	10	.76	14	.300	.378	.475
6 ML YEARS			760	2982	934	198	24	124	(70	54)	1552	562	389	544	325	38	541	35	10	20	196	59	.77	45	.313	.385	.520

Manny Ramirez

Bats: R **Throws:** R **Pos:** LF-46; DH-29; PH-15   **Ht:** 6'0" **Wt:** 236 **Born:** 5/30/1972 **Age:** 39

							BATTING													BASERUNNING				AVERAGES		
Year	Team	Lg	G	AB	H	2B	3B	HR	(Hm	Rd)	TB	R	RBI	RC	TBB	IBB	SO	HBP	SH	SF	SB	CS	SB%	GDP	Avg	OBP	Slg
2010 InldEm*	A+		8	19	2	0	0	0	(-	-)	2	1	1	0	3	0	11	0	0	0	0	0	—	1	.105	.227	.105
1993	Cle	AL	22	53	9	1	0	2	(0	2)	16	5	5	2	2	0	8	0	0	0	0	0	—	3	.170	.200	.302
1994	Cle	AL	91	290	78	22	0	17	(9	8)	151	51	60	53	42	4	72	0	0	4	4	2	.67	6	.269	.357	.521
1995	Cle	AL	137	484	149	26	1	31	(12	19)	270	85	107	103	75	6	112	5	2	5	6	6	.50	13	.308	.402	.558
1996	Cle	AL	152	550	170	45	3	33	(19	14)	320	94	112	120	85	8	104	3	0	9	8	5	.62	18	.309	.399	.582
1997	Cle	AL	150	561	184	40	0	26	(14	12)	302	99	88	117	79	5	115	7	0	4	2	3	.40	19	.328	.415	.538
1998	Cle	AL	150	571	168	35	2	45	(25	20)	342	108	145	121	76	6	121	6	0	10	5	3	.63	18	.294	.377	.599
1999	Cle	AL	147	522	174	34	3	44	(21	23)	346	131	**165**	141	96	9	131	13	0	9	2	4	.33	11	.333	.442	**.663**
2000	Cle	AL	118	439	154	34	2	38	(22	16)	306	92	122	127	86	9	117	3	0	4	1	1	.50	9	.351	.457	**.697**
2001	Bos	AL	142	529	162	33	2	41	(21	20)	322	93	125	122	81	**25**	147	8	0	2	0	1	.00	9	.306	.405	.609
2002	Bos	AL	120	436	152	31	0	33	(18	15)	282	84	107	125	73	14	85	8	0	1	0	0	—	13	**.349**	**.450**	.647
2003	Bos	AL	154	569	185	36	1	37	(18	19)	334	117	104	128	97	28	94	8	0	5	3	1	.75	22	**.325**	**.427**	.587
2004	Bos	AL	152	568	175	44	0	**43**	(23	20)	348	108	130	124	82	15	124	6	0	7	2	4	.33	17	.308	.397	**.613**
2005	Bos	AL	152	554	162	30	1	45	(22	23)	329	112	144	134	80	9	119	10	0	6	1	0	1.00	20	.292	.388	.594
2006	Bos	AL	130	449	144	27	1	35	(16	19)	278	79	102	114	100	16	102	1	0	8	0	1	.00	13	**.321**	**.439**	.619
2007	Bos	AL	133	483	143	33	1	20	(10	10)	238	84	88	78	71	13	92	7	0	8	0	0	—	21	.296	.388	.493
2008	2 Tms		153	552	183	36	1	37	(17	20)	332	102	121	133	87	24	124	11	0	4	3	0	1.00	17	.332	.430	.601
2009	LAD	NL	104	352	102	24	2	19	(10	9)	187	62	63	73	71	21	81	7	0	1	0	1	.00	7	.290	.418	.531
2010	2 Tms		90	265	79	16	0	9	(5	4)	122	38	42	50	46	4	61	6	0	3	1	1	.50	6	.298	.409	.460
08	Bos	AL	100	365	109	22	1	20	(8	12)	193	66	68	69	52	8	86	8	0	0	1	0	1.00	12	.299	.398	.529
08	LAD	NL	53	187	74	14	0	17	(9	8)	139	36	53	64	35	16	38	3	0	4	2	0	1.00	5	.396	.489	.743
10	LAD	NL	66	196	61	15	0	8	(4	4)	100	32	40	41	32	4	38	1	0	3	1	1	.50	4	.311	.405	.510
10	CWS	AL	24	69	18	1	0	1	(1	0)	22	6	2	9	14	0	23	5	0	0	0	0	—	2	.261	.420	.319
Postseason			111	410	117	19	0	29	(12	17)	223	67	78	84	72	12	91	5	0	8	1	1	.50	17	.285	.394	.544
18 ML YEARS			2297	8227	2573	547	20	555	(282	273)	4825	1544	1830	1865	1329	216	1809	109	2	90	38	33	.54	243	.313	.411	.586

Max Ramirez

Bats: R **Throws:** R **Pos:** C-26; PH-2; DH-1   **Ht:** 5'11" **Wt:** 175 **Born:** 10/11/1984 **Age:** 26

							BATTING													BASERUNNING				AVERAGES		
Year	Team	Lg	G	AB	H	2B	3B	HR	(Hm	Rd)	TB	R	RBI	RC	TBB	IBB	SO	HDP	SH	SF	SB	CS	SB%	GDP	Avg	OBP	Slg
2004	Braves	R	57	204	56	16	1	8	(-	-)	98	20	36	34	19	0	50	3	0	4	1	0	1.00	4	.275	.339	.480
2005	Danvle	R+	63	239	83	19	0	8	(-	-)	126	45	47	53	31	2	41	4	0	4	1	2	.33	5	.347	.424	.527
2006	Rome	A	80	267	76	17	0	9	(-	-)	120	50	37	53	54	0	72	3	0	2	2	0	1.00	5	.285	.408	.449
2006	Lk Cty	A-	37	127	39	6	1	4	(-	-)	59	19	26	28	30	0	27	1	0	3	0	0	—	3	.307	.435	.465
2007	Knstn	A+	77	277	84	20	0	12	(-	-)	140	48	62	62	53	2	63	6	0	6	1	0	1.00	9	.303	.418	.505
2007	Bkrsfld	A+	32	114	35	10	0	4	(-	-)	57	16	20	25	21	1	39	2	0	1	1	0	1.00	2	.307	.420	.500
2008	Frisco	AA	69	243	86	16	2	17	(-	-)	157	49	50	66	37	0	56	7	0	2	2	2	.50	4	.354	.450	.646
2008	Okla	AAA	10	37	9	1	0	2	(-	-)	16	5	6	4	3	0	13	0	0	1	0	0	—	0	.243	.293	.432
2008	Rngrs	R	2	5	4	2	0	0	(-	-)	6	4	1	3	2	0	0	0	0	0	0	0	—	0	.800	.857	1.200
2009	Okla	AAA	76	274	64	13	0	5	(-	-)	92	29	43	33	35	1	85	4	1	6	1	0	1.00	8	.234	.323	.336
2009	Rngrs	R	4	13	2	2	0	0	(-	-)	4	1	2	0	1	0	8	0	0	0	0	0	—	0	.154	.214	.308
2010	OKCity	AAA	56	189	54	9	0	3	(-	-)	72	24	29	30	27	0	51	3	1	6	0	0	—	6	.286	.373	.381
2008	Tex	AL	17	46	10	1	0	2	(1	1)	17	7	8	8	6	0	15	3	0	0	0	0	—	0	.217	.345	.370
2010	Tex	AL	28	69	15	3	0	2	(1	1)	24	8	8	6	12	0	22	2	0	2	0	0	—	3	.217	.341	.348
2 ML YEARS			45	115	25	4	0	4	(2	2)	41	16	17	14	18	0	37	5	0	2	0	0	—	3	.217	.343	.357

Ramon Ramirez

Pitches: R **Bats:** R **Pos:** RP-69   **Ht:** 5'11" **Wt:** 190 **Born:** 8/31/1981 **Age:** 29

			HOW MUCH HE PITCHED						WHAT HE GAVE UP												THE RESULTS						
Year	Team	Lg	G	GS	CG	GF	IP	BFP	H	R	ER	HR	SH	SF	HB	TBB	IBB	SO	WP	Bk	W	L	Pct	Sh	Sv-Op	Hld	ERC	ERA
2006	Col	NL	61	0	0	14	67.2	285	58	28	26	5	2	3	1	27	3	61	2	0	4	3	.571	0	0-2	10	3.09	3.46
2007	Col	NL	22	0	0	5	17.1	78	21	16	16	2	2	2	1	6	2	15	2	0	2	2	.500	0	0-0	3	5.24	8.31
2008	KC	AL	71	0	0	15	71.2	295	57	23	21	2	4	3	0	31	6	70	6	1	3	2	.600	0	1-5	21	2.53	2.64
2009	Bos	AL	70	0	0	16	69.2	301	61	26	22	7	3	0	4	32	4	52	2	2	7	4	.636	0	0-4	12	3.73	2.84
2010	2 Tms		69	0	0	23	69.1	284	52	24	23	7	2	4	0	27	3	46	5	2	1	3	.250	0	3-3	6	2.64	2.99

	HOW MUCH HE PITCHED						WHAT HE GAVE UP												THE RESULTS						
Year Team Lg	G	GS	CG	GF	IP	BFP	H	R	ER	HR	SH	SF	HB	TBB	IBB	SO	WP	Bk	W	L	Pct	Sh	Sv-Op	Hld	ERC	ERA
10 Bos AL	44	0	0	17	42.1	178	39	21	21	6	2	4	0	16	2	31	4	1	0	3	.000	0	2-2	2	3.78	4.46
10 SF NL	25	0	0	6	27.0	106	13	13	2	1	0	0	0	11	1	15	1	1	1	0	1.000	0	1-1	4	1.28	0.67
Postseason	1	0	0	0	0.0	3	1	2	2	0	0	0	1	1	0	0	0	0	0		-	0	0-0	-		
5 ML YEARS	293	0	0	73	295.2	1243	249	117	108	23	13	12	6	123	18	244	17	5	17	14	.548	0	4-14	52	3.11	3.29

Cesar Ramos

Pitches: L **Bats:** L **Pos:** RP-14   **Ht:** 6'2" **Wt:** 203 **Born:** 6/22/1984 **Age:** 27

	HOW MUCH HE PITCHED						WHAT HE GAVE UP												THE RESULTS						
Year Team Lg	G	GS	CG	GF	IP	BFP	H	R	ER	HR	SH	SF	HB	TBB	IBB	SO	WP	Bk	W	L	Pct	Sh	Sv-Op	Hld	ERC	ERA
2005 Eugene A-	6	4	0	0	20.2	101	27	21	15	3	0	2	3	7	0	13	2	0	0	1	.000	0	0- -	-	6.31	6.53
2005 FtWyn A	7	7	1	0	38.2	160	42	19	18	0	0	3	1	7	0	32	2	0	3	2	.600	0	0- -	-	3.18	4.19
2006 Lk Els A+	26	24	0	1	141.0	608	161	72	58	9	3	1	8	44	0	70	4	0	7	8	.467	0	0- -	-	4.60	3.70
2007 SnAnt AA	27	27	2	0	163.2	670	153	69	62	15	3	2	6	43	0	90	5	0	13	9	.591	2	0- -	-	3.34	3.41
2008 Portlnd AAA	28	27	0	1	149.2	671	183	108	88	17	4	7	5	57	0	105	2	0	9	11	.450	0	0- -	-	5.60	5.29
2009 Portlnd AAA	15	15	1	0	76.2	344	84	42	34	7	5	1	0	31	2	45	5	0	5	6	.455	0	0- -	-	4.43	3.99
2009 Padres R	4	2	0	0	8.0	32	8	3	2	0	0	0	0	0	0	8	0	0	0	1	.000	0	0- -	-	1.95	2.25
2009 Lk Els A+	2	1	0	0	9.0	41	9	1	1	0	0	0	0	5	0	6	0	0	1	0	1.000	0	0- -	-	3.83	1.00
2010 Portlnd AAA	30	15	1	5	96.0	402	90	37	35	7	7	4	2	43	1	63	3	0	6	7	.462	0	0- -	-	3.92	3.28
2009 SD NL	5	2	0	0	14.2	62	19	5	5	0	0	0	0	4	0	10	0	0	0	1	.000	0	0-0	0	4.78	3.07
2010 SD NL	14	0	0	4	8.1	47	18	11	11	1	0	0	0	4	0	9	1	1	0	1	.000	0	0-0	2	11.97	11.88
2 ML YEARS	19	2	0	4	23.0	109	37	16	16	1	0	0	0	8	0	19	1	1	0	2	.000	0	0-0	2	7.23	6.26

Wilson Ramos

Bats: R **Throws:** R **Pos:** C-22   **Ht:** 6'0" **Wt:** 221 **Born:** 8/10/1987 **Age:** 23

	BATTING																			BASERUNNING				AVERAGES		
Year Team Lg	G	AB	H	2B	3B	HR	(Hm	Rd)	TB	R	RBI	RC	TBB	IBB	SO	HBP	SH	SF	SB	CS	SB%	GDP	Avg	OBP	Slg
2006 Twins R	46	154	44	12	1	3	(-	-)	67	18	26	24	12	0	14	2	1	3	4	2	.67	5	.286	.339	.435
2007 Beloit A	73	292	85	17	1	8	(-	-)	128	40	42	44	19	2	61	5	0	0	1	1	.50	9	.291	.345	.438
2008 FtMyrs A+	126	452	130	23	2	13	(-	-)	196	50	78	70	37	0	103	6	5	5	1	1	.50	23	.288	.346	.434
2009 NwBrit AA	54	205	65	16	0	4	(-	-)	93	31	29	31	6	0	23	2	0	1	0	0	-	1	.317	.341	.454
2009 Twins R	5	19	6	1	1	3	(-	-)	18	4	6	5	0	0	0	0	0	0	0	0	-	0	.316	.316	.947
2010 Roch AAA	71	278	67	14	0	5	(-	-)	96	25	30	26	12	0	49	3	2	0	1	2	.33	8	.241	.280	.345
2010 Syrcse AAA	20	79	25	3	1	3	(-	-)	39	14	8	13	3	2	12	0	0	0	0	0	-	2	.316	.341	.494
2010 2 Tms	22	79	22	7	0	1	(1	0)	32	5	5	10	2	0	12	1	0	0	0	0	-	0	.278	.305	.405
10 Min AL	7	27	8	3	0	0	(0	0)	11	2	1	3	0	0	3	1	0	0	0	0	-	1	.296	.321	.407
10 Was NL	15	52	14	4	0	1	(1	0)	21	3	4	7	2	0	9	0	0	0	0	0	-	1	.269	.296	.404

Cody Ransom

Bats: R **Throws:** R **Pos:** 3B-9; PH-7; 2B-6; 1B-3; PR-1   **Ht:** 6'2" **Wt:** 190 **Born:** 2/17/1976 **Age:** 35

	BATTING																			BASERUNNING				AVERAGES		
Year Team Lg	G	AB	H	2B	3B	HR	(Hm	Rd)	TB	R	RBI	RC	TBB	IBB	SO	HBP	SH	SF	SB	CS	SB%	GDP	Avg	OBP	Slg
2010 LV* AAA	110	394	103	25	1	18	(-	-)	184	58	63	63	40	0	108	4	1	4	5	2	.71	10	.261	.333	.467
2001 SF NL	9	7	0	0	0	0	(0	0)	0	1	0	0	0	0	5	0	0	0	0	0	-	0	.000	.000	.000
2002 SF NL	7	3	2	0	0	0	(0	0)	2	2	1	1	1	1	1	0	0	0	0	0	-	0	.667	.750	.667
2003 SF NL	20	27	6	1	0	1	(1	0)	10	7	1	1	1	0	11	0	0	0	0	0	-	0	.222	.250	.370
2004 SF NL	78	68	17	6	0	1	(0	1)	26	13	11	9	6	0	20	1	3	0	2	2	.50	2	.250	.320	.382
2007 Hou NL	19	35	8	2	0	1	(1	0)	13	9	3	6	9	1	9	2	0	0	0	0	-	0	.229	.413	.371
2008 NYY AL	33	43	13	3	0	4	(1	3)	28	9	8	10	6	0	12	1	1	0	0	0	-	0	.302	.400	.651
2009 NYY AL	31	79	15	9	1	0	(0	0)	26	11	10	5	7	0	25	0	0	0	2	0	1.00	3	.190	.256	.329
2010 Phi NL	22	42	8	0	0	2	(2	0)	14	6	5	5	3	0	11	0	1	0	1	0	1.00	1	.190	.244	.333
8 ML YEARS	219	304	69	21	1	9	(5	4)	119	58	39	37	33	2	94	4	5	0	5	2	.71	6	.227	.311	.391

Clay Rapada

Pitches: L **Bats:** R **Pos:** RP-13   **Ht:** 6'5" **Wt:** 200 **Born:** 3/9/1981 **Age:** 30

	HOW MUCH HE PITCHED						WHAT HE GAVE UP												THE RESULTS						
Year Team Lg	G	GS	CG	GF	IP	BFP	H	R	ER	HR	SH	SF	HB	TBB	IBB	SO	WP	Bk	W	L	Pct	Sh	Sv-Op	Hld	ERC	ERA
2010 OKCity* AAA	50	0	0	16	59.1	231	32	16	12	1	3	1	4	21	2	61	0	0	1	2	.333	0	2- -	-	1.43	1.82
2007 2 Tms	5	0	0	2	2.2	13	3	3	3	2	0	0	0	2	0	4	2	0	0	0		0	0-0	0	11.59	10.13
2008 Det AL	25	0	0	3	21.1	94	19	11	10	0	1	0	1	14	1	15	1	0	3	0	1.000	0	0-0	2	3.87	4.22
2009 Det AL	3	0	0	1	3.1	16	4	2	2	1	0	0	0	2	1	2	0	0	0	0		-	0	0-0	0	7.00	5.40
2010 Tex AL	13	0	0	2	9.0	39	6	4	4	2	0	0	0	7	1	5	0	0	0	0		-	0	0-1	3	4.42	4.00
07 ChC NL	1	0	0	0	0.1	1	0	0	0	0	0	0	0	0	0	0	0	0	0	0		-	0	0-0	0	0.00	0.00
07 Det AL	4	0	0	2	2.1	12	3	3	3	2	0	0	0	2	0	4	2	0	0	0		-	0	0-0	0	14.48	11.57
4 ML YEARS	46	0	0	8	36.1	162	32	20	19	5	1	0	1	25	3	26	3	0	3	0	1.000	0	0-1	5	4.84	4.71

Colby Rasmus

Bats: L **Throws:** L **Pos:** CF-134; PH-16; PR-1   **Ht:** 6'2" **Wt:** 200 **Born:** 8/11/1986 **Age:** 24

	BATTING																			BASERUNNING				AVERAGES		
Year Team Lg	G	AB	H	2B	3B	HR	(Hm	Rd)	TB	R	RBI	RC	TBB	IBB	SO	HBP	SH	SF	SB	CS	SB%	GDP	Avg	OBP	Slg
2005 JhsCty R+	62	216	64	16	5	7	(-	-)	111	47	27	41	21	2	73	3	1	3	13	3	.81	0	.296	.362	.514
2006 QuadC A	78	303	94	22	3	11	(-	-)	155	49	50	59	29	2	55	3	3	3	17	5	.77	2	.310	.373	.512
2006 PlmBh A+	53	193	49	4	5	5	(-	-)	78	22	35	30	27	3	35	3	0	2	11	3	.79	3	.254	.351	.404
2007 Sprgfld AA	128	472	130	37	3	29	(-	-)	260	93	72	103	70	0	108	12	0	2	18	3	.86	2	.275	.381	.551
2008 Memp AAA	90	331	83	15	0	11	(-	-)	131	56	36	51	49	3	72	1	3	3	15	3	.83	7	.251	.346	.396
2008 PlmBh A+	3	9	0	0	0	0	(-	-)	0	1	0	0	1	0	3	1	0	0	0	0	-	0	.000	.182	.000

Year Team	Lg	G	AB	H	2B	3B	HR	(Hm Rd)	TB	R	RBI	RC	TBB	IBB	SO	HBP	SH	SF	SB	CS	SB%	GDP	Avg	OBP	Slg
								BATTING											BASERUNNING				AVERAGES		
2008 Cards	R	3	9	5	1	0	1	(- -)	9	1	2	4	3	0	2	0	0	0	0	0	-	0	.556	.667	1.000
2009 StL	NL	147	474	119	22	2	16	(7 9)	193	72	52	60	36	3	95	3	5	2	3	1	.75	5	.251	.307	.407
2010 StL	NL	144	464	128	28	3	23	(11 12)	231	85	66	76	63	9	148	1	2	4	12	8	.60	5	.276	.361	.498
Postseason		3	9	4	3	0	0	(0 0)	7	1	1	1	2	0	1	0	0	0	0	0	-	1	.444	.545	.778
2 ML YEARS		291	938	247	50	5	39	(18 21)	424	157	118	136	99	12	243	4	7	6	15	9	.63	10	.263	.334	.452

Jon Rauch

Pitches: R **Bats:** R **Pos:** RP-59   RAUSH   **Ht:** 6'11" **Wt:** 290 **Born:** 9/27/1978 **Age:** 32

Year Team	Lg	G	GS	CG	GF	IP	BFP	H	R	ER	HR	SH	SF	HB	TBB	IBB	SO	WP	Bk	W	L	Pct	Sh	Sv-Op	Hld	ERC	ERA
		HOW MUCH HE PITCHED						WHAT HE GAVE UP												THE RESULTS							
2002 CWS	AL	8	6	0	1	28.2	130	28	26	21	7	0	1	2	14	2	19	1	1	2	1	.667	0	0-0	0	5.41	6.59
2004 2 Tms		11	4	0	1	32.0	131	30	10	10	1	2	1	0	11	2	22	2	0	4	1	.800	0	0-0	0	3.05	2.81
2005 Was	NL	15	1	0	4	30.0	124	24	12	12	3	1	1	1	11	2	23	2	0	2	4	.333	0	0-0	0	2.90	3.60
2006 Was	NL	85	0	0	19	91.1	383	78	37	34	13	1	6	2	36	6	86	4	1	4	5	.444	0	2-5	18	3.52	3.35
2007 Was	NL	88	0	0	26	87.1	354	75	37	35	7	2	5	0	21	4	71	2	0	8	4	.667	0	4-10	23	2.53	3.61
2008 2 Tms	NL	74	0	0	51	71.2	295	69	36	33	11	6	3	0	16	2	66	1	0	4	8	.333	0	18-24	6	3.48	4.14
2009 2 Tms		75	0	0	15	70.0	299	70	30	28	6	3	4	2	23	1	49	6	0	7	3	.700	0	2-5	17	3.78	3.60
2010 Min	AL	59	0	0	41	57.2	245	61	20	20	3	1	1	1	14	0	46	1	0	3	1	.750	0	21-25	2	3.50	3.12
04 CWS	AL	2	2	0	0	8.2	43	16	6	6	0	1	1	0	4	0	4	1	0	1	1	.500	0	0-0	0	9.15	6.23
04 Mon	AL	9	2	0	1	23.1	88	14	4	4	1	1	0	0	7	2	18	1	0	3	0	1.000	0	0-0	0	1.44	1.54
08 Was	NL	48	0	0	41	48.1	192	42	18	16	5	3	1	0	7	1	44	0	0	4	2	.667	0	17-22	6	2.41	2.98
08 Ari	NL	26	0	0	10	23.1	103	27	18	17	6	3	2	0	9	1	22	1	0	0	6	.000	0	1-2	6	6.09	6.56
09 Ari	AL	58	0	0	13	54.1	235	57	27	25	5	1	2	1	17	0	35	6	0	2	2	.500	0	2-3	12	3.98	4.14
09 Min	AL	17	0	0	2	15.2	64	13	3	3	1	2	2	1	6	1	14	0	0	5	1	.833	0	0-2	5	3.09	1.72
Postseason		3	0	0	0	1.1	7	1	1	1	0	0	0	0	2	0	0	0	0	0	0	-	0	0-0	0	5.91	6.75
8 ML YEARS		415	11	0	158	468.2	1961	435	208	193	51	16	22	8	146	19	382	19	2	34	27	.557	0	47-69	76	3.40	3.71

Chris Ray

Pitches: R **Bats:** R **Pos:** RP-63   **Ht:** 6'3" **Wt:** 210 **Born:** 1/12/1982 **Age:** 29

Year Team	Lg	G	GS	CG	GF	IP	BFP	H	R	ER	HR	SH	SF	HB	TBB	IBB	SO	WP	Bk	W	L	Pct	Sh	Sv-Op	Hld	ERC	ERA
		HOW MUCH HE PITCHED						WHAT HE GAVE UP												THE RESULTS							
2010 SnJos*	A+	1	1	0	0	1.2	10	7	4	2	0	0	1	0	0	0	1	0	0	0	1	.000	0	0--	-	28.99	10.80
2005 Bal	AL	41	0	0	8	40.2	174	34	15	12	5	1	1	1	18	3	43	0	1	1	3	.250	0	0-4	8	3.13	2.66
2006 Bal	AL	61	0	0	56	66.0	267	45	22	20	10	2	4	1	27	2	51	2	0	4	4	.500	0	33-38	0	2.77	2.73
2007 Bal	AL	43	0	0	37	42.2	179	35	22	21	5	0	1	2	18	2	44	1	0	5	6	.455	0	16-20	0	3.42	4.43
2009 Bal	AL	46	0	0	12	43.1	214	64	36	35	8	4	4	1	23	7	39	0	0	0	4	.000	0	0-3	6	8.03	7.27
2010 2 Tms		63	0	0	13	55.2	234	48	23	23	5	5	0	0	25	2	31	1	0	5	0	1.000	0	2-4	9	3.41	3.72
10 Tex	AL	35	0	0	6	31.2	133	24	12	12	4	0	0	0	16	1	16	1	0	2	0	1.000	0	1-3	7	3.28	3.41
10 SF	NL	28	0	0	7	24.0	101	24	11	11	1	5	0	0	9	1	15	0	0	3	0	1.000	0	1-1	2	3.57	4.13
5 ML YEARS		254	0	0	126	248.1	1068	226	118	111	33	12	10	5	111	16	208	4	1	15	17	.469	0	51-69	23	3.96	4.02

Robert Ray

Pitches: R **Bats:** R **Pos:** RP-3   **Ht:** 6'5" **Wt:** 190 **Born:** 1/21/1984 **Age:** 27

Year Team	Lg	G	GS	CG	GF	IP	BFP	H	R	ER	HR	SH	SF	HB	TBB	IBB	SO	WP	Bk	W	L	Pct	Sh	Sv-Op	Hld	ERC	ERA
		HOW MUCH HE PITCHED						WHAT HE GAVE UP												THE RESULTS							
2005 Auburn	A-	15	13	0	0	61.2	253	46	22	19	2	0	3	4	20	0	58	3	1	4	3	.571	0	0--	-	2.25	2.77
2006 Dnedin	A+	14	9	0	1	48.2	216	59	34	27	2	2	2	6	13	0	37	2	0	2	4	.333	0	0--	-	4.88	4.99
2007 Dnedin	A+	18	15	1	2	66.2	304	83	40	36	3	1	0	6	24	0	57	4	0	3	3	.500	0	1--	-	5.30	4.86
2008 Dnedin	A+	13	13	1	0	70.2	299	71	37	33	6	0	0	5	18	0	60	5	0	5	3	.625	0	0--	-	3.72	4.20
2008 NHam	AA	16	16	2	0	96.1	421	108	43	34	6	3	1	7	27	2	72	7	0	8	6	.571	1	0--	-	4.27	3.18
2008 Dnedin	A+	2	2	0	0	6.2	28	8	3	2	0	0	0	0	0	0	4	0	0	0	1	.000	0	0--	-	2.89	2.70
2009 LsVgs	AAA	1	1	0	0	4.1	18	2	0	0	0	0	0	0	3	0	3	0	0	0	0	-	0	0--	-	1.70	0.00
2009 B Jays	R	2	2	0	0	2.0	10	4	1	1	0	0	0	0	0	0	2	1	0	0	1	.000	0	0--	-	7.48	4.50
2010 LsVgs	AAA	18	18	1	0	96.1	435	118	66	59	14	2	5	4	45	0	75	7	0	6	6	.500	1	0--	-	6.35	5.51
2000 Tor	AL	4	4	0	0	24.1	101	23	15	12	4	1	1	2	6	0	13	0	0	1	2	.333	0	0-0	0	3.97	4.44
2010 Tor	AL	3	0	0	0	3.2	18	2	1	1	0	0	0	0	5	2	3	0	0	0	0	-	0	0-0	0	3.18	2.46
2 ML YEARS		7	4	0	0	28.0	119	25	16	13	4	1	1	2	11	2	16	0	0	1	2	.333	0	0-0	0	3.94	4.18

John Raynor

Bats: R **Throws:** R **Pos:** PH-8; RF-2; CF-1   **Ht:** 6'1" **Wt:** 205 **Born:** 1/4/1984 **Age:** 27

Year Team	Lg	G	AB	H	2B	3B	HR	(Hm Rd)	TB	R	RBI	RC	TBB	IBB	SO	HBP	SH	SF	SB	CS	SB%	GDP	Avg	OBP	Slg
								BATTING											BASERUNNING				AVERAGES		
2006 Jmstwn	A-	54	199	57	8	4	4	(- -)	85	36	21	34	17	0	51	5	1	1	21	2	.91	1	.286	.356	.427
2007 Grnsbr	A	116	445	148	28	8	13	(- -)	231	110	57	107	66	0	98	11	2	2	54	8	.87	2	.333	.429	.519
2008 Carlina	AA	126	452	141	29	6	13	(- -)	221	104	51	97	62	2	122	11	1	8	48	11	.81	2	.312	.402	.489
2009 NewOr	AAA	123	447	115	24	2	6	(- -)	161	63	36	56	42	1	121	6	5	3	19	8	.70	5	.257	.327	.360
2010 NewOr	AAA	41	134	38	6	0	2	(- -)	50	21	13	19	13	1	27	1	2	1	3	0	1.00	4	.284	.349	.373
2010 Mrlns	R	2	3	0	0	0	0	(- -)	0	0	1	0	2	0	1	0	0	1	0	0	-	0	.000	.333	.000
2010 Pit	NL	11	10	2	0	0	0	(0 0)	2	1	0	1	1	0	3	0	0	0	0	0	-	0	.200	.273	.200

Josh Reddick

Bats: L Throws: R Pos: RF-15; LF-6; CF-6; PR-4; PH-3; DH-1 REDD-ik   Ht: 6'2" Wt: 180 Born: 2/19/1987 Age: 24

					BATTING														BASERUNNING				AVERAGES		
Year	Team	Lg	G	AB	H	2B	3B	HR	(Hm | Rd)	TB	R	RBI	RC	TBB	IBB	SO	HBP	SH	SF	SB	CS	SB%	GDP	Avg	OBP	Slg
2007	Grnville	A	94	369	113	17	6	18	(- | -)	196	60	72	68	26	2	51	3	0	5	8	5	.62	7	.306	.352	.531
2007	Portlnd	AA	1	1	0	0	0	0	(- | -)	0	0	0	0	0	0	0	0	0	0	0	0	-	0	.000	.000	.000
2008	Grnville	A	14	53	18	4	2	0	(- | -)	26	7	9	10	5	0	8	0	0	0	2	1	.67	0	.340	.397	.491
2008	Lancst	A+	76	312	107	11	8	17	(- | -)	185	60	57	67	17	0	49	0	0	0	9	1	.90	4	.343	.375	.593
2008	Portlnd	AA	34	117	25	4	2	6	(- | -)	51	22	25	15	12	1	25	1	1	1	3	1	.75	1	.214	.290	.436
2009	Portlnd	AA	63	256	71	17	3	13	(- | -)	133	47	29	46	30	3	62	0	0	1	5	5	.50	2	.277	.352	.520
2009	Pwtckt	AAA	18	71	9	0	2	0	(- | -)	13	1	6	1	6	0	13	0	0	2	0	1	.00	1	.127	.190	.183
2010	Pwtckt	AAA	114	451	120	28	4	18	(- | -)	210	59	65	63	25	1	73	0	0	5	4	7	.36	5	.266	.301	.466
2009	Bos	AL	27	59	10	4	0	2	(0 | 2)	20	5	4	4	2	0	17	1	0	0	0	0	-	0	.169	.210	.339
2010	Bos	AL	29	62	12	3	1	1	(1 | 0)	20	5	5	1	1	0	15	0	0	0	1	0	1.00	1	.194	.206	.323
	2 ML YEARS		56	121	22	7	1	3	(1 | 2)	40	10	9	5	3	0	32	1	0	0	1	0	1.00	1	.182	.208	.331

Mike Redmond

Bats: R Throws: R Pos: C-22   Ht: 5'11" Wt: 200 Born: 5/5/1971 Age: 40

					BATTING														BASERUNNING				AVERAGES		
Year	Team	Lg	G	AB	H	2B	3B	HR	(Hm | Rd)	TB	R	RBI	RC	TBB	IBB	SO	HBP	SH	SF	SB	CS	SB%	GDP	Avg	OBP	Slg
1998	Fla	NL	37	118	39	9	0	2	(1 | 1)	54	10	12	18	5	2	16	2	4	0	0	0	-	6	.331	.368	.458
1999	Fla	NL	84	242	73	9	0	1	(0 | 1)	85	22	27	33	26	2	34	5	5	0	0	0	-	8	.302	.381	.351
2000	Fla	NL	87	210	53	8	1	0	(0 | 0)	63	17	15	20	13	3	19	8	1	3	0	0	-	5	.252	.316	.300
2001	Fla	NL	48	141	44	4	0	4	(3 | 1)	60	19	14	21	13	4	13	2	1	1	0	0	-	6	.312	.376	.426
2002	Fla	NL	89	256	78	15	0	2	(1 | 1)	99	19	28	37	21	8	34	8	2	3	0	2	.00	4	.305	.372	.387
2003	Fla	NL	59	125	30	7	1	0	(0 | 0)	39	12	11	10	7	0	16	5	2	2	0	0	-	2	.240	.302	.312
2004	Fla	NL	81	246	63	15	0	2	(0 | 2)	84	19	25	27	14	0	28	8	3	2	1	0	1.00	10	.256	.315	.341
2005	Min	AL	45	148	46	9	0	1	(0 | 1)	58	17	26	23	6	0	14	3	2	0	0	0	-	9	.311	.350	.392
2006	Min	AL	47	179	61	13	0	0	(0 | 0)	74	20	23	22	4	0	18	4	1	2	0	0	-	9	.341	.365	.413
2007	Min	AL	82	272	80	13	0	1	(1 | 0)	96	23	38	38	18	3	23	5	0	3	0	0	-	9	.294	.346	.353
2008	Min	AL	38	129	37	6	0	0	(0 | 0)	43	14	12	12	5	0	11	2	0	1	0	0	-	6	.287	.321	.333
2009	Min	AL	45	135	32	5	1	0	(0 | 0)	39	9	7	8	11	0	19	1	0	0	0	0	-	8	.237	.299	.289
2010	Cle	AL	22	63	13	4	0	0	(0 | 0)	17	7	5	4	2	0	10	1	2	0	0	0	-	0	.206	.242	.270
	Postseason		2	1	0	0	0	0	(0 | 0)	0	1	0	0	1	0	0	0	0	0	0	0	-	0	.000	.500	.000
	13 ML YEARS		764	2264	649	117	3	13	(6 | 7)	811	208	243	273	145	22	255	54	23	17	1	2	.33	84	.287	.342	.358

Jeremy Reed

Bats: L Throws: L Pos: LF-6; PH-4; RF-3; 1B-2; PR-2   Ht: 6'0" Wt: 180 Born: 6/15/1981 Age: 30

					BATTING														BASERUNNING				AVERAGES		
Year	Team	Lg	G	AB	H	2B	3B	HR	(Hm | Rd)	TB	R	RBI	RC	TBB	IBB	SO	HBP	SH	SF	SB	CS	SB%	GDP	Avg	OBP	Slg
2010	LsVgs*	AAA	41	155	42	7	0	2	(- | -)	55	25	14	21	21	2	21	0	0	1	3	3	.50	8	.271	.356	.355
2010	Charltt*	AAA	44	168	48	8	2	6	(- | -)	78	24	22	25	10	0	28	1	1	1	0	1	.00	3	.286	.328	.464
2004	Sea	AL	18	58	23	4	0	0	(0 | 0)	27	11	5	11	7	1	4	1	0	0	3	1	.75	2	.397	.470	.466
2005	Sea	AL	141	488	124	33	3	3	(0 | 3)	172	61	45	49	48	1	74	2	4	2	12	11	.52	10	.254	.322	.352
2006	Sea	AL	67	212	46	6	5	6	(1 | 5)	80	27	17	13	11	1	31	2	2	2	2	3	.40	5	.217	.260	.377
2007	Sea	AL	13	17	3	0	1	0	(0 | 0)	5	2	0	0	0	0	3	0	0	0	0	0	-	0	.176	.176	.294
2008	Sea	AL	97	286	77	18	1	2	(1 | 1)	103	30	31	31	18	0	38	2	3	3	2	3	.40	5	.269	.314	.360
2009	NYM	NL	126	161	39	6	2	0	(0 | 0)	49	9	9	12	14	1	36	0	1	1	3	0	1.00	4	.242	.301	.304
2010	Tor	AL	14	21	3	0	0	1	(0 | 1)	6	1	3	1	2	0	8	0	0	0	1	0	1.00	0	.143	.217	.286
	7 ML YEARS		476	1243	315	67	12	12	(2 | 10)	442	141	110	117	100	4	194	7	10	8	20	21	.49	26	.253	.311	.356

Nolan Reimold

Bats: R Throws: R Pos: LF-22; DH-12; PH-4; RF-2   RYE-mold   Ht: 6'4" Wt: 205 Born: 10/12/1983 Age: 27

					BATTING														BASERUNNING				AVERAGES		
Year	Team	Lg	G	AB	H	2B	3B	HR	(Hm | Rd)	TB	R	RBI	RC	TBB	IBB	SO	HBP	SH	SF	SB	CS	SB%	GDP	Avg	OBP	Slg
2005	Abrdn	A-	50	180	53	15	2	9	(- | -)	99	33	30	39	29	1	44	1	0	2	2	0	1.00	2	.294	.392	.550
2005	Frdrck	A+	23	83	22	6	0	6	(- | -)	46	17	11	17	12	0	27	2	0	0	3	0	1.00	0	.265	.371	.554
2006	Frdrck	A+	119	415	106	26	0	19	(- | -)	189	73	75	77	76	4	107	9	0	4	14	8	.64	4	.255	.379	.455
2007	Bowie	AA	50	186	57	15	0	11	(- | -)	105	30	34	36	17	1	47	0	0	0	2	3	.40	5	.306	.365	.565
2007	Orioles	R	9	30	7	4	1	0	(- | -)	13	4	8	6	6	0	4	3	0	0	0	0	-	0	.233	.410	.433
2008	Bowie	AA	139	507	144	30	3	25	(- | -)	255	87	84	97	63	1	82	8	0	8	7	3	.70	9	.284	.367	.503
2009	Norfolk	AAA	31	109	43	11	0	9	(- | -)	81	21	27	36	18	2	25	2	0	1	6	1	.86	2	.394	.485	.743
2010	Norfolk	AAA	94	337	84	12	0	10	(- | -)	126	52	37	52	54	0	61	8	0	2	9	2	.82	8	.249	.364	.374
2009	Bal	AL	104	358	100	18	2	15	(8 | 7)	167	49	45	57	47	1	77	3	0	3	8	2	.80	8	.279	.365	.466
2010	Bal	AL	39	116	24	5	0	3	(0 | 3)	38	9	14	6	12	0	26	1	0	2	0	0	-	6	.207	.282	.328
	2 ML YEARS		143	474	124	23	2	18	(8 | 10)	205	58	59	63	59	1	103	4	0	5	8	2	.80	14	.262	.345	.432

Edgar Renteria

Bats: R Throws: R Pos: SS-68; PH-4; PR-1   Ht: 6'0" Wt: 216 Born: 8/7/1975 Age: 35

					BATTING														BASERUNNING				AVERAGES		
Year	Team	Lg	G	AB	H	2B	3B	HR	(Hm | Rd)	TB	R	RBI	RC	TBB	IBB	SO	HBP	SH	SF	SB	CS	SB%	GDP	Avg	OBP	Slg
2010	Fresno*	AAA	2	4	3	0	0	0	(- | -)	3	2	3	2	2	0	0	0	0	0	0	0	-	0	.750	.833	.750
1996	Fla	NL	106	431	133	18	3	5	(2 | 3)	172	68	31	62	33	0	68	2	2	3	16	2	.89	12	.309	.358	.399
1997	Fla	NL	154	617	171	21	3	4	(3 | 1)	210	90	52	68	45	1	108	4	19	6	32	15	.68	17	.277	.327	.340
1998	Fla	NL	133	517	146	18	2	3	(2 | 1)	177	79	31	61	48	1	78	4	9	2	41	22	.65	13	.282	.347	.342
1999	StL	NL	154	585	161	36	2	11	(6 | 5)	234	92	63	81	53	0	82	2	6	7	37	8	.82	16	.275	.334	.400
2000	StL	NL	150	562	156	32	1	16	(4 | 12)	238	94	76	80	63	4	77	1	8	9	21	13	.62	19	.278	.346	.423
2001	StL	NL	141	493	128	19	3	10	(3 | 7)	183	54	57	57	39	4	73	3	8	6	17	4	.81	15	.260	.314	.371

BATTING

Year	Team	Lg	G	AB	H	2B	3B	HR	(Hm	Rd)	TB	R	RBI	RC	TBB	IBB	SO	HBP	SH	SF	SB	CS	SB%	GDP	Avg	OBP	Slg
2002	StL	NL	152	544	166	36	2	11	(4	7)	239	77	83	94	49	7	57	4	7	5	22	7	.76	17	.305	.364	.439
2003	StL	NL	157	587	194	47	1	13	(4	9)	282	96	100	103	65	12	54	1	3	7	34	7	.83	21	.330	.394	.480
2004	StL	NL	149	586	168	37	0	10	(7	3)	235	84	72	74	39	5	78	1	6	10	17	11	.61	14	.287	.327	.401
2005	Bos	AL	153	623	172	36	4	8	(3	5)	240	100	70	82	55	0	100	3	6	5	9	4	.69	15	.276	.335	.385
2006	Atl	NL	149	598	175	40	2	14	(4	10)	261	100	70	89	62	0	89	3	8	2	17	6	.74	17	.293	.361	.436
2007	Atl	NL	124	494	164	30	1	12	(5	7)	232	87	57	82	46	0	77	1	2	0	11	2	.85	19	.332	.390	.470
2008	Det	AL	138	503	136	22	2	10	(5	5)	192	69	55	61	37	1	64	0	2	5	6	3	.67	19	.270	.317	.382
2009	SF	NL	124	460	115	19	1	3	(3	2)	151	50	48	50	39	5	69	1	5	5	7	2	.78	17	.250	.307	.328
2010	SF	NL	72	243	67	11	2	3	(2	1)	91	26	22	27	21	3	43	0	2	1	3	0	1.00	8	.276	.332	.374
	Postseason		55	207	51	12	0	1	(1	0)	66	30	17	23	23	1	34	3	6	2	9	1	.90	6	.246	.328	.319
	15 ML YEARS		2056	7843	2252	422	29	135	(57	78)	3137	1166	887	1071	694	42	1117	30	93	73	290	106	.73	234	.287	.344	.400

Jason Repko

Bats: R **Throws:** R **Pos:** RF-39; PR-8; PH-7; LF-6; CF-6; DH-3   **Ht:** 5'11" **Wt:** 190 **Born:** 12/27/1980 **Age:** 30

BATTING

Year	Team	Lg	G	AB	H	2B	3B	HR	(Hm	Rd)	TB	R	RBI	RC	TBB	IBB	SO	HBP	SH	SF	SB	CS	SB%	GDP	Avg	OBP	Slg
2010	Roch*	AAA	60	228	64	8	2	6	(-	-)	94	38	28	37	30	1	49	2	2	1	10	3	.77	5	.281	.368	.412
2005	LAD	NL	129	276	61	15	3	8	(4	4)	106	43	30	28	16	1	80	7	2	0	5	0	1.00	7	.221	.281	.384
2006	LAD	NL	69	130	33	5	1	3	(1	2)	49	21	16	21	15	1	24	3	2	0	10	4	.71	2	.254	.345	.377
2008	LAD	NL	22	18	3	1	0	0	(0	0)	4	0	0	0	2	0	9	0	0	0	1	0	1.00	0	.167	.250	.222
2009	LAD	NL	10	5	0	0	0	0	(0	0)	0	1	1	0	0	0	2	1	0	1	1	0	1.00	0	.000	.143	.000
2010	Min	AL	58	127	29	6	0	3	(0	3)	44	19	9	12	13	0	38	5	1	0	3	2	.60	2	.228	.324	.346
	Postseason		1	0	0	0	0	0	(0	0)	0	0	0	0	0	0	0	0	0	0	0	0	-	0	-	-	-
	5 ML YEARS		288	556	126	27	4	14	(5	9)	203	84	56	61	46	2	153	16	5	1	20	6	.77	11	.227	.304	.365

Chris Resop

Pitches: R **Bats:** R **Pos:** RP-23   **Ht:** 6'3" **Wt:** 222 **Born:** 11/4/1982 **Age:** 28

Year	Team	Lg	G	GS	CG	GF	IP	BFP	H	R	ER	HR	SH	SF	HB	TBB	IBB	SO	WP	Bk	W	L	Pct	Sh	Sv-Op	Hld	ERC	ERA
2010	Gwnntt*	AAA	15	15	1	0	82.0	319	53	20	19	4	1	0	2	32	1	91	4	0	6	3	.667	1	0--	1	2.06	2.09
2010	Missi*	AA	2	2	0	0	4.1	19	5	2	2	0	1	0	0	1	0	2	0	0	0	0	-	0	0--	1	3.47	4.15
2005	Fla	NL	15	0	0	6	17.0	80	22	16	16	1	0	2	1	9	0	15	3	0	2	0	1.000	0	0-0	0	6.35	8.47
2006	Fla	NL	22	0	0	10	24.1	101	26	9	8	1	0	0	1	10	5	10	0	0	1	2	.333	0	0-1	2	6.30	3.38
2007	LAA	AL	4	0	0	3	4.1	17	4	2	2	1	2	1	0	1	0	2	0	0	0	0	-	0	0-0	0	4.00	4.15
2008	Atl	NL	16	0	0	9	18.1	82	16	12	12	2	2	1	2	10	2	13	0	0	0	1	.000	0	0-0	2	4.19	5.89
2010	2 Tms	NL	23	0	0	5	21.0	91	15	9	9	1	1	2	0	13	0	26	0	1	0	0	-	0	0-0	5	2.93	3.86
10	Atl	NL	1	0	0	0	2.0	14	5	5	5	0	0	0	0	3	0	2	0	0	0	0	-	0	0-0	0	18.12	22.50
10	Pit	NL	22	0	0	5	19.0	77	10	4	4	1	1	2	0	10	0	24	0	1	0	0	-	0	0-0	5	1.80	1.89
	5 ML YEARS		80	0	0	33	82.0	371	83	48	47	5	5	6	4	49	7	66	3	1	3	3	.500	0	0-1	9	4.80	5.16

Ben Revere

Bats: L **Throws:** R **Pos:** CF-6; LF-3; RF-2; PR-2; DH-1; PH-1   **Ht:** 5'9" **Wt:** 175 **Born:** 5/3/1988 **Age:** 23

BATTING

Year	Team	Lg	G	AB	H	2B	3B	HR	(Hm	Rd)	TB	R	RBI	RC	TBB	IBB	SO	HBP	SH	SF	SB	CS	SB%	GDP	Avg	OBP	Slg
2007	Twins	R	50	191	66	9	1	0	(-	-)	88	46	29	35	13	0	20	8	2	2	21	9	.70	1	.325	.388	.461
2008	Beloit	A	83	340	129	17	10	1	(-	-)	169	51	43	75	27	2	31	5	2	0	44	13	.77	1	.379	.433	.497
2009	FtMyrs	A+	121	466	145	13	4	2	(-	-)	172	75	48	70	40	0	34	7	1	3	45	17	.73	6	.311	.372	.369
2010	NwBrit	AA	94	361	110	10	4	1	(-	-)	131	44	23	55	32	1	41	8	2	3	36	13	.73	2	.305	.371	.363
2010	Min	AL	13	28	5	0	0	0	(0	0)	5	1	2	0	2	0	5	0	0	0	0	1	.00	1	.179	.233	.179

Anthony Reyes

Pitches: R **Bats:** R **Pos:** P   **Ht:** 6'2" **Wt:** 230 **Born:** 10/16/1981 **Age:** 29

Year	Team	Lg	G	GS	CG	GF	IP	BFP	H	R	ER	HR	SH	SF	HB	TBB	IBB	SO	WP	Bk	W	L	Pct	Sh	Sv-Op	Hld	ERC	ERA
2010	Akron*	AA	3	3	0	0	5.2	36	8	16	16	0	2	0	0	11	0	3	5	0	0	2	.000	0	0--	1	12.09	25.41
2005	StL	NL	4	1	0	0	13.1	51	6	4	4	2	1	0	1	4	1	12	2	0	1	1	.500	0	0-0	0	1.32	2.70
2006	StL	NL	17	17	1	0	85.1	370	84	48	48	17	5	3	7	34	0	72	2	0	5	8	.385	0	0-0	0	5.08	5.06
2007	StL	NL	22	20	1	1	107.1	474	108	77	72	16	1	7	9	43	0	74	1	2	2	14	.125	0	0-0	0	4.78	6.04
2008	2 Tms	NL	16	6	0	6	49.0	203	47	15	15	4	1	0	1	15	0	25	0	0	4	2	.667	0	1-1	2	3.50	2.76
2009	Cle	AL	8	8	0	0	38.1	176	40	30	28	5	2	3	2	23	0	22	2	0	1	1	.500	0	0-0	0	5.59	6.57
08	StL	NL	10	0	0	6	14.2	61	16	8	8	2	0	0	0	3	0	10	0	0	2	1	.667	0	1-1	2	4.11	4.91
08	Cle	AL	6	6	0	0	34.1	142	31	7	7	2	1	0	1	12	0	15	0	0	2	1	.667	0	0-0	0	3.24	1.83
	Postseason		2	2	0	0	12.0	48	7	4	4	3	0	0	0	5	0	8	0	0	1	0	1.000	0	0-0	0	2.81	3.00
	5 ML YEARS		67	52	2	7	293.1	1274	285	174	167	44	10	14	19	119	1	205	7	2	13	26	.333	0	1-1	2	4.56	5.12

Dennys Reyes

Pitches: L **Bats:** R **Pos:** RP-59   DENN-eese   **Ht:** 6'3" **Wt:** 250 **Born:** 4/19/1977 **Age:** 34

Year	Team	Lg	G	GS	CG	GF	IP	BFP	H	R	ER	HR	SH	SF	TIB	TBB	IBB	SO	WP	Bk	W	L	Pct	Sh	Sv-Op	Hld	ERC	ERA
1997	LAD	NL	14	5	0	0	47.0	207	51	21	20	4	5	1	5	18	3	36	2	1	2	3	.400	0	0-0	0	4.34	3.83
1998	2 Tms	NL	19	10	0	4	67.1	300	62	36	34	3	7	2	1	47	5	77	6	1	3	5	.375	0	0-0	0	4.37	4.54
1999	Cin	NL	65	1	0	12	61.2	277	53	30	26	5	4	3	3	39	1	72	5	1	2	2	.500	0	2-3	14	4.16	3.79
2000	Cin	NL	62	0	0	15	43.2	200	43	31	22	5	3	3	1	29	0	36	5	0	2	1	.667	0	0-1	10	5.24	4.53
2001	Cin	NL	35	6	0	2	53.0	246	51	29	29	5	2	2	1	35	1	52	5	0	2	6	.250	0	0-0	6	4.77	4.92
2002	2 Tms		58	5	0	15	82.2	378	98	52	49	10	3	2	0	45	4	59	10	1	4	4	.500	0	0-0	4	5.90	5.33

(continued)

Year	Team	Lg	G	GS	CG	GF	IP	BFP	H	R	ER	HR	SH	SF	HB	TBB	IBB	SO	WP	Bk	W	L	Pct	Sh	Sv-Op	Hld	ERC	ERA
2003	2 Tms	NL	15	0	0	4	12.2	63	15	16	15	2	1	2	0	10	1	16	5	0	0	0	–	0	0-0	2	6.96	10.66
2004	KC	AL	40	12	0	5	108.0	483	114	64	57	12	7	5	4	50	3	91	6	2	4	8	.333	0	0-1	5	4.81	4.75
2005	SD	NL	36	1	0	9	43.2	215	57	30	25	3	1	0	1	32	2	35	3	1	3	2	.600	0	0-1	0	7.06	5.15
2006	Min	AL	66	0	0	8	50.2	194	35	8	5	3	1	0	0	15	2	49	4	0	5	0	1.000	0	0-1	16	1.90	0.89
2007	Min	AL	50	0	0	7	29.1	139	34	14	13	1	3	3	2	21	1	21	4	0	2	1	.667	0	0-0	8	6.08	3.99
2008	Min	AL	75	0	0	16	46.1	188	40	12	12	4	1	0	2	15	2	39	5	0	3	0	1.000	0	0-3	17	3.14	2.33
2009	StL	NL	75	0	0	10	41.0	180	35	17	15	2	5	1	3	21	1	33	5	1	0	2	.000	0	1-1	18	3.53	3.29
2010	StL	NL	59	0	0	13	38.0	163	34	15	15	2	2	1	2	21	3	25	4	0	3	1	.750	0	1-4	6	3.92	3.55
98	LAD	NL	11	3	0	4	28.2	130	27	17	15	1	3	1	0	20	4	33	1	1	0	4	.000	0	0-0	5	4.16	4.71
98	Cin	NL	8	7	0	0	38.2	170	35	19	19	2	4	1	1	27	1	44	5	0	3	1	.750	0	0-0	0	4.54	4.42
02	Col	NL	43	0	0	13	40.1	182	43	19	19	1	2	2	0	24	3	30	4	0	1	0	1.000	0	0-0	4	4.55	4.24
02	Tex	AL	15	5	0	2	42.1	196	55	33	30	9	1	0	0	21	1	29	6	1	4	3	.571	0	0-0	0	7.24	6.38
03	Pit	NL	12	0	0	4	10.1	50	10	13	12	1	1	2	0	9	1	11	5	0	0	0	–	0	0-0	2	5.43	10.45
03	Ari	NL	3	0	0	0	2.1	13	5	3	3	1	0	0	0	1	0	5	0	0	0	0	–	0	0-0	0	14.73	11.57
Postseason			4	0	0	0	2.0	10	2	4	2	1	0	0	0	2	1	2	0	0	0	0	–	0	0-0	0	8.87	9.00
14 ML YEARS			669	40	0	120	725.0	3233	722	381	337	61	45	25	21	398	29	641	69	8	35	35	.500	0	4-15	106	4.58	4.18

Jo-Jo Reyes

Pitches: L **Bats:** L **Pos:** RP-1 **Ht:** 6'2" **Wt:** 230 **Born:** 11/20/1984 **Age:** 26

Year	Team	Lg	G	GS	CG	GF	IP	BFP	H	R	ER	HR	SH	SF	HB	TBB	IBB	SO	WP	Bk	W	L	Pct	Sh	Sv-Op	Hld	ERC	ERA
2010	Gwnntt*	AAA	12	10	0	1	47.1	210	57	33	30	8	1	1	0	15	0	50	2	1	1	5	.167	0	0--	–	5.41	5.70
2010	NHam*	AA	2	2	0	0	14.0	54	7	4	4	0	0	1	0	4	0	10	0	0	1	1	.500	0	0--	–	1.14	2.57
2007	Atl	NL	11	10	0	0	50.2	230	55	39	35	9	5	2	1	30	2	27	1	0	2	2	.500	0	0-0	0	6.06	6.22
2008	Atl	NL	23	22	0	0	113.0	512	134	77	73	18	9	3	3	52	4	78	2	0	3	11	.214	0	0-0	0	5.97	5.81
2009	Atl	NL	6	5	0	0	27.0	119	27	25	21	4	1	1	1	13	3	21	0	0	0	2	.000	0	0-0	0	4.73	7.00
2010	Atl	NL	1	0	0	0	3.1	23	10	9	9	2	0	0	0	3	0	2	0	0	0	0	–	0	0-0	0	26.51	24.30
4 ML YEARS			41	37	0	0	194.0	884	226	150	138	33	15	6	5	98	9	128	3	0	5	15	.250	0	0-0	0	6.10	6.40

Jose Reyes

Bats: B **Throws:** R **Pos:** SS-133; PH-1 **Ht:** 6'1" **Wt:** 200 **Born:** 6/11/1983 **Age:** 28

Year	Team	Lg	G	AB	H	2B	3B	HR	(Hm	Rd)	TB	R	RBI	RC	TBB	IBB	SO	HBP	SH	SF	SB	CS	SB%	GDP	Avg	OBP	Slg
2010	StLuci*	A+	1	4	0	0	0	0	(-	-)	0	0	1	0	0	0	0	0	0	0	0			0	.000	.000	.000
2003	NYM	NL	69	274	84	12	4	5	(1	4)	119	47	32	46	13	0	36	0	2	3	13	3	.81	1	.307	.334	.434
2004	NYM	NL	53	220	56	16	2	2	(1	1)	82	33	14	25	5	0	31	0	4	0	19	2	.90	1	.255	.271	.373
2005	NYM	NL	161	696	190	24	17	7	(2	5)	269	99	58	84	27	0	78	2	4	4	60	15	.80	7	.273	.300	.386
2006	NYM	NL	153	647	194	30	17	19	(9	10)	315	122	81	121	53	6	81	1	2	0	64	17	.79	6	.300	.354	.487
2007	NYM	NL	160	681	191	36	12	12	(5	7)	287	119	57	99	77	13	78	1	5	1	78	21	.79	6	.280	.354	.421
2008	NYM	NL	159	688	204	37	19	16	(9	7)	327	113	68	117	66	8	82	1	5	3	56	15	.79	6	.297	.358	.475
2009	NYM	NL	36	147	41	7	2	2	(1	1)	58	18	15	20	18	1	19	0	0	1	11	2	.85	2	.279	.355	.395
2010	NYM	NL	133	563	159	29	10	11	(8	3)	241	83	54	76	31	4	63	2	4	3	30	10	.75	8	.282	.321	.428
Postseason			10	44	11	1	1	1	(1	0)	17	7	5	6	3	1	5	0	0	0	3	1	.75	0	.250	.298	.386
8 ML YEARS			924	3916	1119	191	83	74	(38	36)	1698	634	379	588	290	32	468	7	26	15	331	85	.80	40	.286	.335	.434

Mark Reynolds

Bats: R **Throws:** R **Pos:** 3B-142; 1B-5; PH-4 **Ht:** 6'2" **Wt:** 220 **Born:** 8/3/1983 **Age:** 27

Year	Team	Lg	G	AB	H	2B	3B	HR	(Hm	Rd)	TB	R	RBI	RC	TBB	IBB	SO	HBP	SH	SF	SB	CS	SB%	GDP	Avg	OBP	Slg
2007	Ari	NL	111	366	102	20	4	17	(7	10)	181	62	62	62	37	4	129	5	1	5	0	1	.00	5	.279	.349	.495
2008	Ari	NL	152	539	129	28	3	28	(13	15)	247	87	97	82	64	0	204	3	1	6	11	2	.85	10	.239	.320	.458
2009	Ari	NL	155	578	150	30	1	44	(19	25)	314	98	102	94	76	3	223	5	0	3	24	9	.73	8	.260	.349	.543
2010	Ari	NL	145	499	99	17	2	32	(21	11)	216	79	85	77	83	7	211	9	0	5	7	4	.64	8	.198	.320	.433
Postseason			7	26	4	0	0	2	(1	1)	10	3	2	1	2	0	9	1	0	0	0	0	–	0	.154	.241	.385
4 ML YEARS			563	1982	480	95	10	121	(60	61)	958	326	346	315	260	14	767	22	2	19	42	16	.72	31	.242	.334	.483

Matt Reynolds

Pitches: L **Bats:** L **Pos:** RP-21 **Ht:** 6'5" **Wt:** 240 **Born:** 10/2/1984 **Age:** 26

Year	Team	Lg	G	GS	CG	GF	IP	BFP	H	R	ER	HR	SH	SF	HB	TBB	IBB	SO	WP	Bk	W	L	Pct	Sh	Sv-Op	Hld	ERC	ERA
2007	TriCity	A-	20	0	0	5	35.0	148	37	21	14	4	2	1	1	4	0	27	0	0	1	4	.200	0	0--	–	3.37	3.60
2008	Ashvll	A	42	0	0	14	57.0	237	49	19	16	4	3	2	1	14	0	53	7	0	6	2	.750	0	2--	–	2.55	2.53
2009	Mdest	A+	39	0	0	14	49.0	178	32	8	7	2	2	0	0	8	0	58	1	0	5	3	.625	0	3--	–	1.40	1.29
2009	Tulsa	AA	21	0	0	9	25.2	108	23	12	12	3	1	0	1	9	0	29	2	0	1	2	.333	0	1--	–	3.58	4.21
2010	ColSpr	AAA	50	0	0	31	55.0	227	49	18	16	2	2	0	1	16	0	67	2	0	1	3	.250	0	7--	–	2.73	2.62
2010	Col	NL	21	0	0	2	18.0	70	10	4	4	2	1	1	2	5	0	17	1	0	1	0	1.000	0	0-0	2	1.87	2.00

Arthur Rhodes

Pitches: L **Bats:** L **Pos:** RP-70 **Ht:** 6'2" **Wt:** 220 **Born:** 10/24/1969 **Age:** 41

Year	Team	Lg	G	GS	CG	GF	IP	BFP	H	R	ER	HR	SH	SF	HB	TBB	IBB	SO	WP	Bk	W	L	Pct	Sh	Sv-Op	Hld	ERC	ERA
1991	Bal	AL	8	8	0	0	36.0	174	47	35	32	4	1	3	0	23	0	23	2	0	0	3	.000	0	0-0	0	7.00	8.00
1992	Bal	AL	15	15	2	0	94.1	394	87	39	38	6	5	1	1	38	2	77	2	1	7	5	.583	1	0-0	0	3.48	3.63
1993	Bal	AL	17	17	0	0	85.2	387	91	62	62	16	2	3	1	49	1	49	2	0	5	6	.455	0	0-0	0	5.88	6.51
1994	Bal	AL	10	10	3	0	52.2	238	51	34	34	8	2	3	2	30	1	47	3	0	3	5	.375	2	0-0	0	5.03	5.81

Year	Team	Lg	G	GS	CG	GF	IP	BFP	H	R	ER	HR	SH	SF	HB	TBB	IBB	SO	WP	Bk	W	L	Pct	Sh	Sv-Op	Hld	ERC	ERA
			HOW MUCH HE PITCHED						**WHAT HE GAVE UP**												**THE RESULTS**							
1995	Bal	AL	19	9	0	3	75.1	336	68	53	52	13	4	0	0	48	1	77	3	1	2	5	.286	0	0-1	0	4.97	6.21
1996	Bal	AL	28	2	0	5	53.0	224	48	28	24	6	1	1	0	23	3	62	0	0	9	1	.900	0	1-1	2	3.72	4.08
1997	Bal	AL	53	0	0	6	95.1	378	75	32	32	9	0	4	4	26	5	102	2	0	10	3	.769	0	1-2	9	2.58	3.02
1998	Bal	AL	45	0	0	10	77.0	321	65	30	30	8	2	5	1	34	2	83	1	1	4	4	.500	0	4-8	10	3.47	3.51
1999	Bal	AL	43	0	0	11	53.0	244	43	37	32	9	2	2	0	45	6	59	4	0	3	4	.429	0	3-5	5	5.07	5.43
2000	Sea	AL	72	0	0	9	69.1	281	51	34	33	6	1	2	0	29	3	77	4	0	5	8	.385	0	0-7	24	2.62	4.28
2001	Sea	AL	71	0	0	16	68.0	258	46	14	13	5	1	0	1	12	0	83	3	0	8	0	1.000	0	3-7	31	1.61	1.72
2002	Sea	AL	66	0	0	9	69.2	257	45	18	18	4	2	1	0	13	1	81	2	0	10	4	.714	0	2-7	27	1.46	2.33
2003	Sea	AL	67	0	0	14	54.0	228	53	25	25	4	2	0	1	18	2	48	2	0	3	3	.500	0	3-6	18	3.57	4.17
2004	Oak	AL	37	0	0	25	38.2	182	46	23	22	9	3	1	0	21	4	34	2	0	3	3	.500	0	9-14	3	6.54	5.12
2005	Cle	AL	47	0	0	8	43.1	175	33	13	10	2	0	2	1	12	2	43	0	0	3	1	.750	0	0-3	16	2.06	2.08
2006	Phi	NL	55	0	0	10	45.2	214	47	27	27	2	1	0	2	30	7	48	7	0	0	5	.000	0	4-7	23	4.63	5.32
2008	2 Tms		61	0	0	6	35.1	146	28	9	8	0	4	1	0	16	4	40	1	0	4	1	.800	0	2-3	24	2.36	2.04
2009	Cin	NL	66	0	0	10	53.1	215	37	16	15	3	5	2	1	20	3	48	1	0	1	1	.500	0	0-2	25	2.11	2.53
2010	Cin	NL	70	0	0	8	55.0	217	38	14	14	4	2	2	1	18	0	50	1	0	4	4	.500	0	0-2	26	2.14	2.29
08	Sea	AL	36	0	0	4	22.0	92	17	8	7	0	3	1	0	13	2	26	1	0	2	1	.667	0	1-2	13	2.79	2.86
08	Fla	NL	25	0	0	2	13.1	54	11	1	1	0	1	0	0	3	2	14	0	0	2	0	1.000	0	1-1	11	1.69	0.68
	Postseason		20	0	0	0	17.0	75	16	9	9	2	2	1	0	10	2	19	4	0	0	1	.000	0	0-3	4	4.44	4.76
	19 ML YEARS		850	61	5	150	1154.2	4869	999	543	521	118	40	33	16	505	47	1131	42	3	84	66	.560	3	32-75	243	3.50	4.06

Will Rhymes

Bats: L **Throws:** R **Pos:** 2B-53; PH-6   **Ht:** 5'9" **Wt:** 155 **Born:** 4/1/1983 **Age:** 28

Year	Team	Lg	G	AB	H	2B	3B	HR	(Hm	Rd)	TB	R	RBI	RC	TBB	IBB	SO	HBP	SH	SF	SB	CS	SB%	GDP	Avg	OBP	Slg
			BATTING																		**BASERUNNING**				**AVERAGES**		
2005	Oneont	A-	61	250	82	11	3	2	(-	-)	105	49	27	44	25	0	15	1	3	0	14	3	.82	1	.328	.391	.420
2006	WMich	A	126	506	132	19	2	3	(-	-)	164	80	39	62	53	0	53	3	12	4	23	6	.79	4	.261	.332	.324
2007	Lkland	A+	88	326	99	12	2	4	(-	-)	127	43	35	57	44	0	38	2	12	1	24	3	.89	2	.304	.389	.390
2007	Erie	AA	39	155	41	6	0	1	(-	-)	50	21	21	16	6	0	20	2	6	2	5	1	.83	2	.265	.297	.323
2008	Erie	AA	131	516	158	21	7	3	(-	-)	202	76	60	78	44	2	66	3	10	3	17	6	.74	5	.306	.362	.391
2008	Toledo	AAA	6	25	8	0	1	0	(-	-)	10	5	2	3	2	0	4	0	0	0	0	0	-	0	.320	.370	.400
2009	Toledo	AAA	109	404	105	17	6	3	(-	-)	143	48	41	50	36	0	58	3	10	2	20	8	.71	5	.260	.324	.354
2010	Toledo	AAA	95	364	111	20	7	2	(-	-)	151	59	36	62	36	1	35	4	13	4	22	5	.81	2	.305	.370	.416
2010	Det	AL	54	191	58	12	3	1	(1	0)	79	30	19	27	14	0	16	0	7	1	0	3	.00	1	.304	.350	.414

Clayton Richard

Pitches: L **Bats:** L **Pos:** SP-33   **Ht:** 6'5" **Wt:** 240 **Born:** 9/12/1983 **Age:** 27

Year	Team	Lg	G	GS	CG	GF	IP	BFP	H	R	ER	HR	SH	SF	HB	TBB	IBB	SO	WP	Bk	W	L	Pct	Sh	Sv-Op	Hld	ERC	ERA
			HOW MUCH HE PITCHED						**WHAT HE GAVE UP**												**THE RESULTS**							
2008	CWS	AL	13	8	0	3	47.2	215	61	37	32	5	0	1	4	13	2	29	1	1	2	5	.286	0	0-0	0	5.06	6.04
2009	2 Tms		38	26	1	3	153.0	663	154	81	75	17	8	5	3	71	0	114	7	3	9	5	.643	0	0-0	0	4.60	4.41
2010	SD	NL	33	33	1	0	201.2	861	206	89	84	16	6	2	4	78	6	153	4	2	14	9	.609	1	0-0	0	4.09	3.75
09	CWS	AL	26	14	1	3	89.0	387	94	50	46	10	3	4	3	37	0	66	5	2	4	3	.571	0	0-0	0	4.76	4.65
09	SD	NL	12	12	0	0	64.0	276	60	31	29	7	5	1	0	34	0	48	2	1	5	2	.714	0	0-0	0	4.38	4.08
	Postseason		2	0	0	0	6.1	25	5	1	1	0	0	0	0	3	0	0	0	0	0	0	-	0	0-0	0	2.74	1.42
	3 ML YEARS		84	67	2	6	402.1	1739	421	207	191	38	14	8	7	162	8	296	12	6	25	19	.568	1	0-0	0	4.40	4.27

Dustin Richardson

Pitches: L **Bats:** L **Pos:** RP-26   **Ht:** 6'6" **Wt:** 220 **Born:** 1/9/1984 **Age:** 27

Year	Team	Lg	G	GS	CG	GF	IP	BFP	H	R	ER	HR	SH	SF	HB	TBB	IBB	SO	WP	Bk	W	L	Pct	Sh	Sv-Op	Hld	ERC	ERA
			HOW MUCH HE PITCHED						**WHAT HE GAVE UP**												**THE RESULTS**							
2006	Lowell	A-	16	1	0	4	39.2	162	28	16	14	2	1	4	3	13	0	44	2	0	4	1	.800	0	2- -	-	2.22	3.18
2007	Grnville	A	21	21	0	0	99.2	423	86	46	37	4	1	3	6	47	0	98	4	1	5	7	.417	0	0- -	-	3.46	3.34
2007	Lancst	A+	4	4	0	0	23.0	89	14	8	7	1	1	1	1	5	0	25	0	0	4	0	1.000	0	0- -	-	1.41	2.74
2008	Portlnd	AA	22	22	0	0	106.2	469	108	76	75	17	3	5	5	51	0	114	0	0	7	10	.412	0	0- -	-	5.15	6.33
2009	Lowell	A-	2	2	0	0	5.0	27	8	5	5	2	0	0	1	2	0	4	2	0	0	1	.000	0	0- -	-	10.81	9.00
2009	Portlnd	AA	30	0	0	11	63.1	271	42	22	19	2	1	1	3	40	2	80	3	0	2	2	.500	0	4	-	2.77	2.70
2009	Pwtckt	AAA	7	0	0	2	10.2	40	8	2	2	1	0	0	0	2	0	16	0	0	0	0	-	0	0- -	-	2.08	1.09
2010	Pwtckt	AAA	32	0	0	8	44.0	180	26	14	13	4	0	0	0	31	0	56	6	0	3	0	1.000	0	2- -	-	3.08	2.66
2009	Bos	AL	3	0	0	1	3.1	14	3	0	0	0	0	1	0	1	0	1	1	1	0	0	-	0	0-0	0	2.46	0.00
2010	Bos	AL	26	0	0	4	13.0	67	15	6	6	2	1	1	1	14	1	12	0	0	0	0	-	0	0-0	2	8.58	4.15
	2 ML YEARS		29	0	0	5	16.1	81	18	6	6	2	1	2	1	15	1	12	1	1	0	0	-	0	0-0	2	7.16	3.31

Juan Rincon

Pitches: R **Bats:** R **Pos:** RP-2   **Ht:** 5'11" **Wt:** 210 **Born:** 1/23/1979 **Age:** 32

Year	Team	Lg	G	GS	CG	GF	IP	BFP	H	R	ER	HR	SH	SF	HB	TBB	IBB	SO	WP	Bk	W	L	Pct	Sh	Sv-Op	Hld	ERC	ERA
			HOW MUCH HE PITCHED						**WHAT HE GAVE UP**												**THE RESULTS**							
2010	ColSpr*	AAA	47	0	0	29	45.2	227	58	43	40	2	3	2	0	37	4	42	5	0	4	4	.500	0	8- -	-	7.11	7.88
2001	Min	AL	4	0	0	1	5.2	28	7	5	4	1	1	0	0	5	0	4	0	0	0	0	-	0	0-0	0	8.33	6.35
2002	Min	AL	10	3	0	0	28.2	135	44	23	20	5	0	1	0	9	0	21	2	0	0	2	.000	0	0-1	0	7.62	6.28
2003	Min	AL	58	0	0	20	85.2	370	74	38	35	5	2	5	4	38	7	63	7	0	5	6	.455	0	0-1	5	3.21	3.68
2004	Min	AL	77	0	0	18	82.0	327	52	27	24	5	3	3	2	32	1	106	2	0	11	6	.647	0	2	16	2.00	2.63
2005	Min	AL	75	0	0	18	77.0	319	63	26	21	2	4	1	3	30	3	84	5	1	6	6	.500	0	0-5	25	2.48	2.45
2006	Min	AL	75	0	0	22	74.1	315	76	30	24	2	5	1	3	24	3	65	2	0	3	1	.750	0	1-3	26	3.53	2.91
2007	Min	AL	63	0	0	16	59.2	272	65	38	34	9	2	1	3	28	3	49	4	0	3	3	.500	0	0-2	14	5.31	5.13
2008	2 Tms	AL	47	0	0	15	55.1	254	67	39	36	8	2	0	3	24	2	39	5	0	3	3	.500	0	0	3	5.96	5.86
2009	2 Tms		33	0	0	0	36.2	165	30	29	28	4	2	1	1	26	4	35	2	0	4	2	.667	0	0-0	1	4.20	6.87
2010	Col	NL	2	0	0	1	2.0	11	3	1	1	0	0	0	0	2	0	3	0	0	0	0	-	0	0-0	0	8.58	4.50

Year	Team	Lg	G	GS	CG	GF	IP	BFP	H	R	ER	HR	SH	SF	HB	TBB	IBB	SO	WP	Bk	W	L	Pct	Sh	Sv-Op	Hld	ERC	ERA
							HOW MUCH HE PITCHED				WHAT HE GAVE UP												THE RESULTS					
08	Min	AL	24	0	0	6	28.0	133	33	21	19	5	2	0	2	16	2	20	3	0	2	2	.500	0	0-0	1	6.59	6.11
08	Cle	AL	23	0	0	9	27.1	121	34	18	17	3	0	0	1	8	0	19	2	0	1	1	.500	0	0-0	2	5.33	5.60
09	Det	AL	7	0	0	6	10.1	49	12	6	6	2	1	1	0	6	0	10	1	0	1	0	1.000	0	0-0	1	6.37	5.23
09	Col	NL	26	0	0	1	26.1	116	18	23	22	2	1	0	1	20	4	25	1	0	3	2	.600	0	0-0	1	3.41	7.52
	Postseason		8	0	0	2	8.2	36	6	5	5	1	0	0	0	6	0	9	1	0	0	0	-	0	0-0	1	3.77	5.19
	10 ML YEARS		444	3	0	118	507.0	2196	481	256	227	41	21	13	19	218	23	469	29	1	35	29	.547	0	3-18	90	3.84	4.03

Royce Ring

Pitches: L **Bats:** L **Pos:** RP-5   **Ht:** 6'0" **Wt:** 220 **Born:** 12/21/1980 **Age:** 30

Year	Team	Lg	G	GS	CG	GF	IP	BFP	H	R	ER	HR	SH	SF	HB	TBB	IBB	SO	WP	Bk	W	L	Pct	Sh	Sv-Op	Hld	ERC	ERA
2010	S-WB*	AAA	52	0	0	14	42.0	175	35	12	9	2	0	1	5	11	0	39	2	0	2	1	.667	0	2- -	-	2.75	1.93
2005	NYM	NL	15	0	0	2	10.2	51	10	6	6	0	1	0	0	10	1	8	0	0	0	2	.000	0	0-0	3	4.80	5.06
2006	NYM	NL	11	0	0	2	12.2	48	7	3	3	2	0	0	0	3	0	8	0	0	0	0	-	0	0-0	2	1.60	2.13
2007	2 Tms	NL	26	0	0	7	20.0	88	13	8	6	1	0	1	0	17	2	21	2	0	1	0	1.000	0	0-0	0	3.33	2.70
2008	Atl	NL	42	0	0	8	22.1	113	32	25	21	2	3	2	2	10	3	16	0	1	2	1	.667	0	0-0	4	6.61	8.46
2010	NYY	NL	5	0	0	0	2.1	12	3	4	4	0	0	0	0	2	0	2	0	0	0	0	-	0	0-0	1	6.63	15.43
07	SD	NL	15	0	0	4	15.0	69	11	8	6	1	0	0	0	14	2	17	2	0	1	0	1.000	0	0-0	0	4.10	3.60
07	Atl	NL	11	0	0	3	5.0	19	2	0	0	0	0	1	0	3	0	4	0	0	0	0	-	0	0-0	0	1.39	0.00
	5 ML YEARS		99	0	0	19	68.0	312	65	46	40	5	4	3	2	42	6	55	2	1	3	3	.500	0	0-0	10	4.35	5.29

Alex Rios

Bats: R **Throws:** R **Pos:** CF-143; DH-2; PH-2; LF-1; PR-1   **Ht:** 6'5" **Wt:** 205 **Born:** 2/18/1981 **Age:** 30

Year	Team	Lg	G	AB	H	2B	3B	HR	(Hm	Rd)	TB	R	RBI	RC	TBB	IBB	SO	HBP	SH	SF	SB	CS	SB%	GDP	Avg	OBP	Slg
2004	Tor	AL	111	426	122	24	7	1	(0	1)	163	55	28	49	31	0	84	2	1	0	15	3	.83	14	.286	.338	.383
2005	Tor	AL	146	481	126	23	6	10	(5	5)	191	71	59	56	28	1	101	5	0	5	14	9	.61	14	.262	.306	.397
2006	Tor	AL	128	450	136	33	6	17	(12	5)	232	68	82	83	35	1	89	3	0	10	15	6	.71	10	.302	.349	.516
2007	Tor	AL	161	643	191	43	7	24	(13	11)	320	114	85	105	53	3	103	6	0	7	17	4	.81	9	.297	.354	.498
2008	Tor	AL	155	635	185	47	8	15	(9	6)	293	91	79	92	44	2	112	2	0	5	32	8	.80	20	.291	.337	.461
2009	2 Tms	AL	149	582	144	31	2	17	(15	2)	230	63	71	64	37	1	107	6	1	7	24	5	.83	21	.247	.296	.395
2010	CWS	AL	147	567	161	29	3	21	(10	11)	259	89	88	84	38	4	93	7	0	5	34	14	.71	21	.284	.334	.457
09	Tor	AL	108	436	115	25	2	14	(12	2)	186	52	62	60	31	1	78	6	0	6	19	3	.86	14	.264	.317	.427
09	CWS	AL	41	146	29	6	0	3	(3	0)	44	11	9	4	6	0	29	0	1	1	5	2	.71	7	.199	.229	.301
	7 ML YEARS		997	3784	1065	230	39	105	(64	41)	1688	551	492	533	268	12	689	31	2	39	151	49	.76	109	.281	.331	.446

David Riske

Pitches: R **Bats:** R **Pos:** RP-23   RISS-kee   **Ht:** 6'2" **Wt:** 189 **Born:** 10/23/1976 **Age:** 34

Year	Team	Lg	G	GS	CG	GF	IP	BFP	H	R	ER	HR	SH	SF	HB	TBB	IBB	SO	WP	Bk	W	L	Pct	Sh	Sv-Op	Hld	ERC	ERA
2010	BrvdCt*	A+	3	3	0	0	4.0	20	7	5	4	0	0	0	0	2	0	3	0	0	0	1	.000	0	0- -	-	8.49	9.00
2010	Nashv*	AAA	8	0	0	2	9.0	37	8	6	4	1	0	2	0	4	1	8	0	0	2	0	1.000	0	0- -	-	3.68	4.00
1999	Cle	AL	12	0	0	3	14.0	68	20	15	13	2	1	1	0	6	0	16	0	0	1	1	.500	0	0-1	0	6.96	8.36
2001	Cle	AL	26	0	0	6	27.1	118	20	7	6	3	0	1	2	18	3	29	1	0	2	0	1.000	0	1-1	3	3.81	1.98
2002	Cle	AL	51	0	0	17	51.1	237	49	32	30	8	4	3	4	35	4	55	1	0	2	2	.500	0	1-1	5	5.55	5.26
2003	Cle	AL	68	0	0	24	74.2	293	52	21	19	9	4	1	3	20	3	82	1	0	2	2	.500	0	8-13	17	2.26	2.29
2004	Cle	AL	72	0	0	27	77.1	336	69	32	32	11	3	2	2	41	4	78	3	0	7	3	.700	0	5-12	9	4.32	3.72
2005	Cle	AL	58	0	0	33	72.2	288	55	28	25	11	3	1	4	15	0	48	0	0	3	4	.429	0	1-1	0	2.59	3.10
2006	2 Tms	AL	41	0	0	12	44.0	189	40	20	19	6	1	2	3	17	1	28	0	0	1	2	.333	0	0-1	2	3.98	3.89
2007	KC	AL	65	0	0	27	69.2	289	61	19	19	8	4	3	1	27	4	52	0	0	1	4	.200	0	4-8	16	3.46	2.45
2008	Mil	NL	45	0	0	6	42.1	193	47	25	25	6	0	4	0	25	0	27	1	0	1	2	.333	0	2-7	11	5.88	5.31
2009	Mil	NL	1	0	0	0	1.0	6	4	2	2	0	0	0	0	1	0	0	0	0	0	0	-	0	0-0	0	26.25	18.00
2010	Mil	NL	23	0	0	5	23.1	104	25	14	13	2	0	1	2	8	0	16	1	0	0	0	-	0	0-0	0	4.43	5.01
06	Bos	AL	8	0	0	2	9.2	42	8	4	4	2	1	0	2	3	0	5	0	0	0	1	.000	0	0-0	0	4.23	3.72
06	CWS	AL	33	0	0	10	34.1	147	32	16	15	4	0	2	1	14	1	23	0	0	1	1	.500	0	0-1	2	3.91	3.93
	Postseason		3	0	0	0	3.2	14	2	0	0	0	0	0	0	1	0	5	0	0	0	0	-	0	0-0	0	1.10	0.00
	11 ML YEARS		462	0	0	160	497.2	2121	442	215	203	66	20	20	21	212	19	441	8	0	20	20	.500	0	22-45	63	3.90	3.67

Juan Rivera

Bats: R **Throws:** R **Pos:** LF-83; RF-25; 1B-13; PH-11; DH-3; CF-1   **Ht:** 6'2" **Wt:** 230 **Born:** 7/3/1978 **Age:** 32

Year	Team	Lg	G	AB	H	2B	3B	HR	(Hm	Rd)	TB	R	RBI	RC	TBB	IBB	SO	HBP	SH	SF	SB	CS	SB%	GDP	Avg	OBP	Slg
2001	NYY	AL	3	4	0	0	0	0	(0	0)	0	0	0	0	0	0	0	0	0	0	0	0	-	0	.000	.000	.000
2002	NYY	AL	28	83	22	5	0	1	(0	1)	30	9	6	8	6	0	10	0	1	1	1	1	.50	4	.265	.311	.361
2003	NYY	AL	57	173	46	14	0	7	(4	3)	81	22	26	23	10	1	27	0	1	1	0	0	-	8	.266	.304	.468
2004	Mon	NL	134	391	120	24	1	12	(6	6)	182	48	49	60	34	7	45	1	0	6	6	2	.75	11	.307	.364	.465
2005	LAA	AL	106	350	95	17	1	15	(8	7)	159	46	59	49	23	0	44	0	2	1	1	9	.10	15	.271	.316	.454
2006	LAA	AL	124	448	139	27	0	23	(12	11)	235	65	85	80	33	0	59	7	0	6	4	4	.00	14	.310	.362	.525
2007	LAA	AL	14	43	12	1	0	2	(1	1)	19	3	8	5	1	0	4	0	0	0	0	0	-	5	.279	.295	.442
2008	LAA	AL	89	256	63	13	0	12	(5	7)	112	31	45	28	16	0	33	0	0	8	1	1	.50	10	.246	.282	.438
2009	LAA	AL	138	529	152	24	1	25	(11	14)	253	72	88	82	36	1	57	2	0	5	0	1	.00	19	.287	.332	.478
2010	LAA	AL	124	416	105	20	0	15	(4	11)	170	53	52	50	33	4	58	4	0	2	2	2	.50	10	.252	.312	.409
	Postseason		36	105	25	5	0	1	(1	0)	33	10	8	5	8	2	14	0	1	0	1	0	1.00	6	.238	.292	.314
	10 ML YEARS		817	2693	754	145	3	112	(51	61)	1241	349	418	385	192	13	337	14	4	24	11	20	.35	96	.280	.328	.461

Mariano Rivera

Pitches: R **Bats:** R **Pos:** RP-61 **Ht:** 6'2" **Wt:** 185 **Born:** 11/29/1969 **Age:** 41

			HOW MUCH HE PITCHED						WHAT HE GAVE UP												THE RESULTS							
Year	Team	Lg	G	GS	CG	GF	IP	BFP	H	R	ER	HR	SH	SF	HB	TBB	IBB	SO	WP	Bk	W	L	Pct	Sh	Sv-Op	Hld	ERC	ERA
1995	NYY	AL	19	10	0	2	67.0	301	71	43	41	11	0	2	2	30	0	51	0	1	5	3	.625	0	0-1	0	5.14	5.51
1996	NYY	AL	61	0	0	14	107.2	425	73	25	25	1	2	1	2	34	3	130	1	0	8	3	.727	0	5-8	27	1.65	2.09
1997	NYY	AL	66	0	0	56	71.2	301	65	17	15	5	3	4	0	20	6	68	2	0	6	4	.600	0	43-52	0	2.73	1.88
1998	NYY	AL	54	0	0	49	61.1	246	48	13	13	3	2	3	1	17	1	36	0	0	3	0	1.000	0	36-41	0	2.21	1.91
1999	NYY	AL	66	0	0	63	69.0	268	43	15	14	2	0	2	3	18	3	52	2	1	4	3	.571	0	45-49	0	1.47	1.83
2000	NYY	AL	66	0	0	61	75.2	311	58	26	24	4	5	2	0	25	3	58	2	0	7	4	.636	0	36-41	0	2.20	2.85
2001	NYY	AL	71	0	0	66	80.2	310	61	24	21	5	4	1	1	12	2	83	1	0	4	6	.400	0	50-57	0	1.74	2.34
2002	NYY	AL	45	0	0	36	46.0	187	35	16	14	3	2	0	2	11	2	41	1	1	1	4	.200	0	28-32	2	2.08	2.74
2003	NYY	AL	64	0	0	57	70.2	277	61	15	13	3	1	2	4	10	1	63	0	0	5	2	.714	0	40-46	0	2.29	1.66
2004	NYY	AL	74	0	0	69	78.2	316	65	17	17	3	2	0	5	20	3	66	0	0	4	2	.667	0	53-57	0	2.45	1.94
2005	NYY	AL	71	0	0	67	78.1	306	50	18	12	2	0	1	4	18	0	80	0	0	7	4	.636	0	43-47	0	1.48	1.38
2006	NYY	AL	63	0	0	59	75.0	293	61	16	15	3	1	2	5	11	4	55	0	0	5	5	.500	0	34-37	0	2.03	1.80
2007	NYY	AL	67	0	0	59	71.1	295	68	25	25	4	1	1	6	12	2	74	1	0	3	4	.429	0	30-34	0	2.92	3.15
2008	NYY	AL	64	0	0	60	70.2	259	41	11	11	4	1	1	2	6	0	77	1	0	6	5	.545	0	39-40	0	1.09	1.40
2009	NYY	AL	66	0	0	55	66.1	257	48	14	13	7	0	0	1	12	1	72	1	0	3	3	.500	0	44-46	0	1.93	1.76
2010	NYY	AL	61	0	0	55	60.0	230	39	14	12	2	0	1	5	11	3	45	0	0	3	3	.500	0	33-38	0	1.50	1.80
	Postseason		88	0	0	70	133.1	501	82	13	11	2	6	3	3	21	4	107	3	0	8	1	.889	0	39-44	4	1.15	0.74
	16 ML YEARS		978	10	0	828	1150.0	4582	887	309	285	62	24	23	43	267	34	1051	12	3	74	55	.574	0	559-626	29	2.09	2.23

Mike Rivera

Bats: R **Throws:** R **Pos:** C-5; PH-3 **Ht:** 6'1" **Wt:** 236 **Born:** 9/8/1976 **Age:** 34

						BATTING															BASERUNNING				AVERAGES		
Year	Team	Lg	G	AB	H	2B	3B	HR	(Hm	Rd)	TB	R	RBI	RC	TBB	IBB	SO	HBP	SH	SF	SB	CS	SB%	GDP	Avg	OBP	Slg
2010	Chatt*	AA	58	183	47	16	0	2	(-	-)	69	20	22	30	35	0	48	4	0	2	2	2	.50	5	.257	.384	.377
2010	Albq*	AAA	14	48	6	2	0	2	(-	-)	14	4	2	1	2	0	19	1	1	0	0	0	-	3	.125	.176	.292
2010	NewOr*	AAA	3	9	1	0	0	0	(-	-)	1	1	0	0	0	0	1	1	0	0	0	0	-	0	.111	.200	.111
2001	Det	AL	4	12	4	2	0	0	(0	0)	6	2	1	2	0	0	2	0	0	0	0	0	-	0	.333	.333	.500
2002	Det	AL	39	132	30	8	1	1	(0	1)	43	11	11	8	4	0	35	1	0	1	0	0	-	5	.227	.254	.326
2003	SD	NL	19	53	9	1	0	1	(0	1)	13	2	2	0	5	0	11	0	0	0	0	0	-	4	.170	.241	.245
2006	Mil	NL	46	142	38	9	0	6	(3	3)	65	16	24	19	10	5	21	3	1	2	0	0	-	3	.268	.325	.458
2007	Mil	NL	11	13	3	0	0	2	(1	1)	9	2	3	2	1	0	3	0	0	0	0	0	-	0	.231	.286	.692
2008	Mil	NL	21	62	19	5	0	1	(0	1)	27	8	14	10	6	0	10	1	0	0	2	0	1.00	2	.306	.377	.435
2009	Mil	NL	41	114	26	7	0	2	(2	0)	39	10	14	15	15	3	32	2	0	1	1	0	1.00	6	.228	.326	.342
2010	Fla	NL	7	14	0	0	0	0	(0	0)	0	0	0	0	2	0	3	1	0	0	0	0	-	0	.000	.176	.000
	8 ML YEARS		188	542	129	32	1	13	(6	7)	202	51	69	59	43	8	117	8	2	4	3	0	1.00	20	.238	.302	.373

Saul Rivera

Pitches: R **Bats:** B **Pos:** RP-4 **Ht:** 5'10" **Wt:** 180 **Born:** 12/7/1977 **Age:** 33

						HOW MUCH HE PITCHED						WHAT HE GAVE UP											THE RESULTS						
Year	Team	Lg	G	GS	CG	GF	IP	BFP	H	R	ER	HR	SH	SF	HB	TBB	IBB	SO	WP	Bk	W	L	Pct	Sh	Sv-Op	Hld	ERC	ERA
2010	Clmbs*	AAA	21	0	0	20	24.0	96	13	5	4	0	1	2	0	12	0	14	3	0	2	1	.667	0	5--	-	1.56	1.50
2010	Reno*	AAA	11	0	0	5	14.0	68	22	11	11	1	0	0	1	6	0	6	2	0	0	1	.000	0	0--	-	7.92	7.07
2006	Was	NL	54	0	0	16	60.1	277	59	28	23	4	4	1	4	32	6	41	3	0	3	0	1.000	0	1-3	9	4.17	3.43
2007	Was	NL	85	0	0	17	93.0	398	88	39	38	1	5	4	2	42	4	64	4	0	6	4	.600	0	3-5	19	3.39	3.68
2008	Was	NL	76	0	0	14	84.0	371	90	41	37	3	3	6	2	35	2	65	4	1	5	6	.455	0	0-6	17	4.11	3.96
2009	Was	NL	30	0	0	9	38.1	176	48	28	26	7	3	1	3	14	4	21	1	0	1	3	.250	0	0-1	2	6.20	6.10
2010	Ari	NL	4	0	0	1	3.2	25	11	9	9	2	1	1	0	3	0	1	0	0	0	0	-	0	0-0	0	25.35	22.09
	5 ML YEARS		249	0	0	57	279.1	1247	296	145	133	17	16	13	11	126	16	192	12	1	13	15	.464	0	4-15	47	4.36	4.29

Brian Roberts

Bats: B **Throws:** R **Pos:** 2B-59, PH-1 **Ht:** 5'9" **Wt:** 175 **Born:** 10/9/1977 **Age:** 33

						BATTING															BASERUNNING				AVERAGES		
Year	Team	Lg	G	AB	H	2B	3B	HR	(Hm	Rd)	TB	R	RBI	RC	TBB	IBB	SO	HBP	SH	SF	SB	CS	SB%	GDP	Avg	OBP	Slg
2010	Orioles*	R	5	15	8	1	0	0	(-	-)	9	1	0	4	2	0	3	0	0	0	0	0	-	1	.533	.588	.600
2010	Bowie*	AA	3	14	6	2	0	0	(-	-)	8	3	3	3	0	0	2	0	0	0	0	0	-	0	.429	.429	.571
2001	Bal	AL	75	273	69	12	3	2	(0	2)	93	42	17	27	13	0	36	0	3	3	12	3	.80	3	.253	.284	.341
2002	Bal	AL	38	128	29	6	0	1	(1	0)	38	18	11	12	15	0	21	1	3	2	9	2	.82	3	.227	.308	.297
2003	Bal	AL	112	460	124	22	4	5	(3	2)	169	65	41	62	46	1	58	1	4	1	23	6	.79	9	.270	.337	.367
2004	Bal	AL	159	641	175	50	2	4	(0	4)	241	107	53	97	71	1	95	1	15	6	29	12	.71	3	.273	.344	.376
2005	Bal	AL	143	561	176	45	7	18	(9	9)	289	92	73	106	67	5	83	3	5	4	27	10	.73	6	.314	.387	.515
2006	Bal	AL	138	563	161	34	3	10	(6	4)	231	85	55	74	55	4	66	0	6	5	36	7	.84	16	.286	.347	.410
2007	Bal	AL	156	621	180	42	5	12	(6	6)	268	103	57	105	89	6	99	0	2	4	50	7	.88	8	.290	.377	.432
2008	Bal	AL	155	611	181	51	8	9	(6	3)	275	107	57	101	82	3	104	2	3	6	40	10	.80	8	.296	.378	.450
2009	Bal	AL	159	632	179	56	1	16	(4	12)	285	110	79	106	74	3	112	2	1	8	30	7	.81	9	.283	.356	.451
2010	Bal	AL	59	230	64	14	0	4	(2	2)	90	28	15	31	26	1	40	2	1	2	12	2	.86	2	.278	.354	.391
	10 ML YEARS		1194	4720	1338	332	33	81	(37	44)	1979	757	458	715	538	24	714	12	43	41	268	66	.80	65	.283	.355	.419

Ryan Roberts

Bats: R **Throws:** R **Pos:** PH-24; LF-14; 2B-1; 3B-1; RF-1   **Ht:** 5'11" **Wt:** 195 **Born:** 9/19/1980 **Age:** 30

										BATTING													BASERUNNING				AVERAGES		
Year	Team	Lg	G	AB	H	2B	3B	HR	(Hm	Rd)	TB	R	RBI	RC	TBB	IBB	SO	HBP	SH	SF			SB	CS	SB%	GDP	Avg	OBP	Slg
2010	Reno*	AAA	94	347	92	25	2	11	(-	-)	154	62	55	61	56	3	73	2	1	6			16	6	.73	14	.265	.365	.444
2006	Tor	AL	9	13	1	0	0	1	(0	1)	4	1	1	0	1	0	4	0	0	0			0	0	-	1	.077	.143	.308
2007	Tor	AL	8	13	1	0	0	0	(0	0)	1	2	0	0	2	0	7	1	0	0			0	0	-	0	.077	.250	.077
2008	Tex	AL	1	1	0	0	0	0	(0	0)	0	0	0	0	0	0	1	0	0	0			0	0	-	0	.000	.000	.000
2009	Ari	NL	110	305	85	17	2	7	(3	4)	127	41	25	41	40	1	55	3	2	1			7	3	.70	2	.279	.367	.416
2010	Ari	NL	36	66	13	4	0	2	(1	1)	23	8	9	7	3	1	17	0	1	1			0	0	-	0	.197	.229	.348
	5 ML YEARS		164	398	100	21	2	10	(4	6)	155	52	35	48	46	2	84	4	3	2			7	3	.70	3	.251	.333	.389

David Robertson

Pitches: R **Bats:** R **Pos:** RP-64   **Ht:** 5'11" **Wt:** 190 **Born:** 4/9/1985 **Age:** 26

			HOW MUCH HE PITCHED						WHAT HE GAVE UP											THE RESULTS							
Year	Team	Lg	G	GS	CG	GF	IP	BFP	H	R	ER	HR	SH	SF	HB	TBB	IBB	SO	WP	Bk	W	L	Pct	Sh	Sv-Op	Hld	ERC	ERA
2008	NYY	AL	25	0	0	8	30.1	131	29	18	18	3	0	3	0	15	2	36	6	0	4	0	1.000	0	0-0	0	4.12	5.34
2009	NYY	AL	45	0	0	20	43.2	191	36	19	16	4	0	0	1	23	1	63	6	0	2	1	.667	0	1-1	5	3.51	3.30
2010	NYY	AL	64	0	0	10	61.1	273	59	26	26	5	5	3	3	33	6	71	7	2	4	5	.444	0	1-3	14	4.29	3.82
	Postseason		5	0	0	2	5.1	24	4	0	0	0	1	0	0	3	2	3	0	0	2	0	1.000	0	0-0	0	1.91	0.00
	3 ML YEARS		134	0	0	38	135.1	595	124	63	60	12	5	6	4	71	9	170	19	2	10	6	.625	0	2-4	19	3.99	3.99

Nate Robertson

Pitches: L **Bats:** R **Pos:** SP-18; RP-3   **Ht:** 6'2" **Wt:** 225 **Born:** 9/3/1977 **Age:** 33

			HOW MUCH HE PITCHED						WHAT HE GAVE UP											THE RESULTS							
Year	Team	Lg	G	GS	CG	GF	IP	BFP	H	R	ER	HR	SH	SF	HB	TBB	IBB	SO	WP	Bk	W	L	Pct	Sh	Sv-Op	Hld	ERC	ERA
2010	Memp*	AAA	6	3	0	0	20.0	97	32	22	21	5	1	1	0	6	0	12	1	0	2	1	.667	0	0- -	-	8.49	9.45
2010	LV*	AAA	2	2	0	0	10.2	44	10	5	4	0	1	0	0	2	1	6	0	0	1	1	.500	0	0- -	-	2.14	3.38
2002	Fla	NL	6	1	0	1	8.1	46	15	11	11	3	0	0	2	4	1	3	0	0	0	1	.000	0	0-0	0	12.69	11.88
2003	Det	AL	8	8	0	0	44.2	203	55	27	27	6	0	0	0	23	2	33	3	0	1	2	.333	0	0-0	0	6.24	5.44
2004	Det	AL	34	32	1	1	196.2	852	210	116	107	30	12	4	4	66	1	155	5	1	12	10	.545	0	1-1	0	4.65	4.90
2005	Det	AL	32	32	2	0	196.2	846	202	113	98	28	3	11	7	65	2	122	6	1	7	16	.304	0	0-0	0	4.38	4.48
2006	Det	AL	32	32	1	0	208.2	881	206	98	89	29	4	7	8	67	2	137	6	0	13	13	.500	0	0-0	0	4.14	3.84
2007	Det	AL	30	30	0	0	177.2	781	199	98	94	27	3	5	5	63	2	119	5	1	9	13	.409	0	0-0	0	4.80	4.76
2008	Det	AL	32	28	0	1	168.2	761	218	124	119	26	4	0	2	62	7	108	5	1	7	11	.389	0	0-0	0	6.14	6.35
2009	Det	AL	28	6	0	3	49.2	234	59	33	30	4	2	2	2	28	3	35	2	0	2	3	.400	0	0-0	0	5.70	5.44
2010	2 Tms	NL	21	18	0	2	101.1	460	115	76	67	12	9	6	6	42	1	63	2	1	6	8	.429	0	0-0	0	5.23	5.95
10	Fla	NL	19	18	0	1	100.1	450	110	70	61	11	9	6	6	40	1	61	1	1	6	8	.429	0	0-0	0	4.88	5.47
10	Phi	NL	2	0	0	1	1.0	10	5	6	6	1	0	0	0	2	0	2	1	0	0	0	-	0	0-0	0	57.07	54.00
	Postseason		3	3	0	0	15.2	74	23	9	9	1	0	0	2	6	1	8	0	0	1	2	.333	0	0-0	0	7.15	5.17
	9 ML YEARS		223	187	4	8	1152.1	5064	1279	696	642	160	39	36	34	420	21	775	34	4	57	77	.425	0	1-1	0	4.95	5.01

Fernando Rodney

Pitches: R **Bats:** R **Pos:** RP-72   **Ht:** 5'11" **Wt:** 215 **Born:** 3/18/1977 **Age:** 34

			HOW MUCH HE PITCHED						WHAT HE GAVE UP											THE RESULTS							
Year	Team	Lg	G	GS	CG	GF	IP	BFP	H	R	ER	HR	SH	SF	HB	TBB	IBB	SO	WP	Bk	W	L	Pct	Sh	Sv-Op	Hld	ERC	ERA
2002	Det	AL	20	0	0	10	18.0	89	25	15	12	2	2	1	0	10	2	10	0	1	1	3	.250	0	0-4	0	6.77	6.00
2003	Det	AL	27	0	0	11	29.2	143	35	20	20	2	3	3	1	17	1	33	0	0	1	3	.250	0	0-3	3	5.46	6.07
2005	Det	AL	39	0	0	26	44.0	185	39	14	14	5	2	0	2	17	3	42	2	0	2	3	.400	0	9-15	3	3.59	2.86
2006	Det	AL	63	0	0	30	71.2	304	51	36	28	6	2	0	8	34	4	65	3	0	7	4	.636	0	7-11	18	3.01	3.52
2007	Det	AL	48	0	0	12	50.2	223	46	27	24	5	4	2	3	21	0	54	4	0	2	6	.250	0	1-3	12	3.74	4.26
2008	Det	AL	38	0	0	25	40.1	188	34	22	22	3	1	2	3	30	5	49	3	0	0	6	.000	0	13-19	5	4.29	4.91
2009	Det	AL	73	0	0	65	75.2	330	70	38	37	8	4	2	2	41	4	61	5	0	2	5	.286	0	37-38	0	4.31	4.40
2010	LAA	AL	72	0	0	30	68.0	308	70	33	32	4	1	0	5	35	1	53	4	0	4	3	.571	0	14-21	21	4.63	4.24
	Postseason		7	0	0	0	7.2	33	6	4	2	0	2	0	0	5	1	9	0	0	0	0	-	0	0-1	2	2.94	2.35
	8 ML YEARS		380	0	0	209	398.0	1770	370	205	189	35	19	10	24	205	20	367	21	1	19	33	.365	0	84-117	62	4.15	4.27

Alex Rodriguez

Bats: R **Throws:** R **Pos:** 3B-124; DH-12; PH-3   **Ht:** 6'3" **Wt:** 228 **Born:** 7/27/1975 **Age:** 35

									BATTING													BASERUNNING				AVERAGES		
Year	Team	Lg	G	AB	H	2B	3B	HR	(Hm	Rd)	TB	R	RBI	RC	TBB	IBB	SO	HBP	SH	SF			SB	CS	SB%	GDP	Avg	OBP	Slg
1994	Sea	AL	17	54	11	0	0	0	(0	0)	11	4	2	3	3	0	20	0	1	1			3	0	1.00	0	.204	.241	.204
1995	Sea	AL	48	142	33	6	2	5	(1	4)	58	15	19	15	6	0	42	0	1	0			4	2	.67	0	.232	.264	.408
1996	Sea	AL	146	601	215	54	1	36	(18	18)	379	141	123	144	59	1	104	4	6	7			15	4	.79	15	.358	.414	.631
1997	Sea	AL	141	587	176	40	3	23	(16	7)	291	100	84	100	41	1	99	5	4	1			29	6	.83	14	.300	.350	.496
1998	Sea	AL	161	686	213	35	5	42	(18	24)	384	123	124	135	45	0	121	10	3	4			46	13	.78	12	.310	.360	.560
1999	Sea	AL	129	502	143	25	0	42	(20	22)	294	110	111	102	56	2	109	5	1	8			21	7	.75	12	.285	.357	.586
2000	Sea	AL	148	554	175	34	2	41	(13	28)	336	134	132	134	100	5	121	7	0	11			15	4	.79	10	.316	.420	.606
2001	Tex	AL	162	632	201	34	1	52	(26	26)	393	133	135	148	75	6	131	16	0	9			18	3	.86	17	.318	.399	.622
2002	Tex	AL	162	624	187	27	2	57	(34	23)	389	125	142	152	87	12	122	10	0	4			9	4	.69	14	.300	.392	.623
2003	Tex	AL	161	607	181	30	6	47	(26	21)	364	124	118	131	87	10	126	15	0	6			17	3	.85	16	.298	.396	.600
2004	NYY	AL	155	601	172	24	2	36	(17	19)	308	112	106	112	80	6	131	10	0	7			28	4	.88	18	.286	.375	.512
2005	NYY	AL	162	605	194	29	1	48	(26	22)	369	124	130	137	91	8	139	16	0	3			21	6	.78	6	.321	.421	.610
2006	NYY	AL	154	572	166	26	1	35	(20	15)	299	113	121	112	90	8	139	8	0	4			15	4	.79	22	.290	.392	.523
2007	NYY	AL	158	583	183	31	0	54	(26	28)	376	143	156	159	95	11	120	21	0	9			24	4	.86	15	.314	.422	.645
2008	NYY	AL	138	510	154	33	0	35	(21	14)	292	104	103	97	65	9	117	14	0	5			18	3	.86	16	.302	.392	.573

Year	Team	Lg	G	AB	H	2B	3B	HR	(Hm	Rd)	TB	R	RBI	RC	TBB	IBB	SO	HBP	SH	SF	SB	CS	SB%	GDP	Avg	OBP	Slg
									BATTING												**BASERUNNING**				**AVERAGES**		
2009	NYY	AL	124	444	127	17	1	30	(18	12)	236	78	100	89	80	7	97	8	0	3	14	2	.88	13	.286	.402	.532
2010	NYY	AL	137	522	141	29	2	30	(15	15)	264	74	125	93	59	1	98	3	0	11	4	3	.57	7	.270	.341	.506
Postseason			54	199	60	14	0	13	(5	8)	113	36	35	40	29	4	51	8	1	1	6	3	.67	4	.302	.409	.568
17 ML YEARS			2303	8826	2672	474	29	613	(315	298)	5043	1757	1831	1867	1119	87	1836	152	16	93	301	72	.81	209	.303	.387	.571

Francisco Rodriguez

Pitches: R **Bats:** R **Pos:** RP-53   **Ht:** 6'0" **Wt:** 195 **Born:** 1/7/1982 **Age:** 29

Year	Team	Lg	G	GS	CG	GF	IP	BFP	H	R	ER	HR	SH	SF	HB	TBB	IBB	SO	WP	Bk	W	L	Pct	Sh	Sv-Op	Hld	ERC	ERA
				HOW MUCH HE PITCHED							**WHAT HE GAVE UP**												**THE RESULTS**				
2002	LAA	AL	5	0	0	4	5.2	21	3	0	0	0	0	0	1	2	1	13	0	0	0	0	-	0	0-0	0	1.52	0.00
2003	LAA	AL	59	0	0	23	86.0	334	50	30	29	12	2	4	2	35	5	95	7	0	8	3	.727	0	2-6	7	2.25	3.03
2004	LAA	AL	69	0	0	29	84.0	335	51	21	17	2	2	1	1	33	1	123	5	0	4	1	.800	0	12-19	27	1.64	1.82
2005	LAA	AL	66	0	0	58	67.1	279	45	20	20	7	1	1	0	32	3	91	8	0	2	5	.286	0	**45-50**	0	2.52	2.67
2006	LAA	AL	69	0	0	58	73.0	296	52	16	14	6	3	0	1	28	5	98	10	0	2	3	.400	0	**47-51**	0	2.35	1.73
2007	LAA	AL	64	0	0	56	67.1	285	50	22	21	3	1	1	0	34	0	90	7	1	5	2	.714	0	40-46	0	2.74	2.81
2008	LAA	AL	**76**	0	0	69	68.1	288	54	21	17	4	1	1	2	34	4	77	6	0	2	3	.400	0	**62-69**	0	3.06	2.24
2009	NYM	NL	70	0	0	66	68.0	295	51	34	28	7	4	1	1	38	6	73	0	0	3	6	.333	0	35-42	0	3.18	3.71
2010	NYM	NL	53	0	0	46	57.1	236	45	14	14	3	1	1	2	21	4	67	3	1	4	2	.667	0	25-30	0	2.53	2.20
Postseason			21	0	0	8	31.2	134	27	14	11	5	0	3	1	14	2	41	5	0	5	4	.556	0	3-5	3	3.86	3.13
9 ML YEARS			531	0	0	409	577.0	2369	401	178	160	44	15	13	11	257	29	727	47	2	30	25	.545	0	268-313	34	2.48	2.50

Francisco Rodriguez

Pitches: R **Bats:** R **Pos:** RP-43   **Ht:** 6'1" **Wt:** 195 **Born:** 2/26/1983 **Age:** 28

Year	Team	Lg	G	GS	CG	GF	IP	BFP	H	R	ER	HR	SH	SF	HB	TBB	IBB	SO	WP	Bk	W	L	Pct	Sh	Sv-Op	Hld	ERC	ERA
				HOW MUCH HE PITCHED							**WHAT HE GAVE UP**												**THE RESULTS**				
2006	RCuca	A+	26	25	1	0	133.1	617	158	95	81	11	6	4	13	68	0	83	10	0	5	13	.278	1	0--	-	5.94	5.47
2007	RCuca	A+	39	8	0	9	105.2	476	117	76	70	11	2	5	6	53	0	70	12	0	4	8	.333	0	2--	-	5.44	5.96
2008	Ark	AA	50	0	0	17	75.1	339	76	41	32	9	4	7	5	33	1	69	7	0	5	5	.500	0	2--	-	4.57	3.82
2009	Salt Lk	AAA	44	1	0	6	77.1	331	67	35	34	8	8	6	2	40	1	60	4	1	5	4	.556	0	0--	-	3.94	3.96
2010	Salt Lk	AAA	13	0	0	4	22.1	90	19	9	9	0	0	1	0	6	0	19	0	0	2	1	.667	0	0--	-	2.19	3.63
2010	LAA	AL	43	0	0	14	47.1	209	46	23	23	5	1	0	1	26	3	36	8	1	1	3	.250	0	0-1	2	4.56	4.37

Henry Rodriguez

Pitches: R **Bats:** R **Pos:** RP-29   **Ht:** 6'0" **Wt:** 219 **Born:** 2/25/1987 **Age:** 24

Year	Team	Lg	G	GS	CG	GF	IP	BFP	H	R	ER	HR	SH	SF	HB	TBB	IBB	SO	WP	Bk	W	L	Pct	Sh	Sv-Op	Hld	ERC	ERA
				HOW MUCH HE PITCHED							**WHAT HE GAVE UP**												**THE RESULTS**				
2006	Aa	R	15	4	0	3	43.2	222	46	39	36	1	2	2	6	50	0	59	10	1	5	2	.714	0	1--	-	7.51	7.42
2007	Kane	A	20	18	1	1	99.2	419	75	38	34	2	3	3	4	58	0	106	13	0	6	8	.429	0	0--	-	3.08	3.07
2008	Stcktn	A+	20	13	0	6	75.0	319	57	38	33	5	2	1	2	40	0	104	9	0	2	3	.400	0	0--	-	3.14	3.96
2008	Mdland	AA	14	9	0	2	41.0	215	51	39	34	1	1	0	1	44	0	43	16	0	2	7	.222	0	0--	-	7.73	7.46
2009	Stcktn	A+	3	0	0	0	5.0	20	3	0	0	0	0	0	1	1	0	11	1	0	0	0	-	0	0--	-	1.51	0.00
2009	Scrmto	AAA	37	0	0	18	43.2	207	38	28	20	4	1	1	0	38	2	71	8	0	2	1	.667	0	4--	-	4.92	5.77
2010	Scrmto	AAA	20	0	0	17	21.1	96	10	8	4	1	1	1	0	9	1	31	5	0	0	2	.000	0	11--	-	1.26	1.69
2009	Oak	AL	3	0	0	1	4.0	20	4	2	1	0	0	0	1	2	0	4	3	0	0	0	-	0	0-0	0	4.28	2.25
2010	Oak	AL	29	0	0	8	27.2	121	25	16	14	2	2	1	1	13	0	33	7	0	1	0	1.000	0	0-1	3	3.70	4.55
2 ML YEARS			32	0	0	9	31.2	141	29	18	15	2	2	1	2	15	0	37	10	0	1	0	1.000	0	0-1	3	3.78	4.26

Ivan Rodriguez

Bats: R **Throws:** R **Pos:** C-102; PH-8   ee-VAHN   **Ht:** 5'11" **Wt:** 190 **Born:** 11/30/1971 **Age:** 39

Year	Team	Lg	G	AB	H	2B	3B	HR	(Hm	Rd)	TB	R	RBI	RC	TBB	IBB	SO	HBP	SH	SF	SB	CS	SB%	GDP	Avg	OBP	Slg
									BATTING												**BASERUNNING**				**AVERAGES**		
2010 Ptomc*		A+	1	3	0	0	0	0	(-	-)	0	0	0	0	0	0	1	0	0	0	0	0	-	0	.000	.000	.000
1991	Tex	AL	88	280	74	16	0	3	(3	0)	99	24	27	23	5	0	42	0	2	1	0	1	.00	10	.264	.276	.354
1992	Tex	AL	123	420	109	16	1	8	(4	4)	151	39	37	41	24	2	73	1	7	2	0	0	-	15	.260	.300	.360
1993	Tex	AL	137	473	129	28	4	10	(7	3)	195	56	66	57	29	3	70	4	5	8	8	7	.53	16	.273	.315	.412
1994	Tex	AL	99	363	108	19	1	16	(7	9)	177	56	57	61	31	5	42	7	0	4	6	3	.67	10	.298	.360	.488
1995	Tex	AL	130	492	149	32	2	12	(5	7)	221	56	67	68	16	2	48	4	0	5	0	2	.00	11	.303	.327	.449
1996	Tex	AL	153	639	192	47	3	19	(10	9)	302	116	86	99	38	7	55	4	0	4	5	0	1.00	15	.300	.342	.473
1997	Tex	AL	150	597	187	34	4	20	(12	8)	289	98	77	98	38	7	89	8	1	4	7	3	.70	18	.313	.360	.484
1998	Tex	AL	145	579	186	40	4	21	(12	9)	297	88	91	100	32	4	88	3	0	3	9	0	1.00	18	.321	.358	.513
1999	Tex	AL	144	600	199	29	1	35	(12	23)	335	116	113	104	24	2	64	1	0	5	25	12	.68	31	.332	.356	.558
2000	Tex	AL	91	363	126	27	4	27	(16	11)	242	66	83	78	19	5	48	1	0	6	5	5	.50	17	.347	.375	.667
2001	Tex	AL	111	442	136	24	2	25	(16	9)	239	70	65	77	23	3	73	4	0	1	10	3	.77	13	.308	.347	.541
2002	Tex	AL	108	408	128	32	2	19	(15	4)	221	67	60	63	25	2	71	2	1	4	5	4	.56	13	.314	.353	.542
2003	Fla	NL	144	511	152	36	3	16	(8	8)	242	90	85	91	55	6	92	6	1	5	10	6	.63	18	.297	.369	.474
2004	Det	AL	135	527	176	32	2	19	(12	7)	269	72	86	98	41	6	91	3	0	4	7	4	.64	15	.334	.383	.510
2005	Det	AL	129	504	139	33	5	14	(8	6)	224	71	50	44	11	2	93	2	1	7	7	3	.70	19	.276	.290	.444
2006	Det	AL	136	547	164	28	4	13	(5	8)	239	74	69	82	26	4	86	1	4	2	8	3	.73	16	.300	.332	.437
2007	Det	AL	129	502	141	31	3	11	(4	7)	211	50	63	55	9	1	96	1	1	2	2	2	.50	16	.281	.294	.420
2008	2 Tms		115	398	110	20	2	7	(5	2)	157	44	35	40	23	2	67	3	3	2	10	1	.91	15	.276	.319	.394
2009	2 Tms		121	425	106	23	2	10	(3	7)	163	55	47	39	18	0	92	1	1	3	1	2	.33	20	.249	.280	.384
2010	Was	NL	111	398	106	18	1	4	(2	2)	138	32	49	37	16	2	66	1	2	2	2	3	.40	25	.266	.294	.347
08	Det	AL	82	302	89	16	3	5	(3	2)	126	33	32	36	19	1	52	2	3	2	6	1	.86	9	.295	.338	.417
08	NYY	AL	33	96	21	4	0	2	(2	0)	31	11	3	4	4	1	15	1	0	0	4	0	1.00	6	.219	.257	.323

Year	Team	Lg	G	AB	H	2B	3B	HR	(Hm	Rd)	TB	R	RBI	RC	TBB	IBB	SO	HBP	SH	SF	SB	CS	SB%	GDP	Avg	OBP	Slg
									BATTING												BASERUNNING				AVERAGES		
09	Hou	NL	93	327	82	15	2	8	(3	5)	125	41	34	21	13	0	74	1	1	2	0	2	.00	13	.251	.280	.382
09	Tex	AL	28	98	24	8	0	2	(0	2)	38	14	13	9	5	0	18	0	0	1	1	0	1.00	7	.245	.279	.388
	Postseason		40	153	39	9	0	4	(2	2)	60	17	25	22	14	3	32	0	1	2	1	0	1.00	3	.255	.314	.392
20 ML YEARS			2499	9468	2817	565	51	309	(161	148)	4411	1340	1313	1346	503	65	1446	57	29	76	127	64	.66	331	.298	.334	.466

Rafael Rodriguez

Pitches: R **Bats:** R **Pos:** RP-3
Ht: 6'1" **Wt:** 175 **Born:** 9/24/1984 **Age:** 26

Year	Team	Lg	G	GS	CG	GF	IP	BFP	H	R	ER	HR	SH	SF	HB	TBB	IBB	SO	WP	Bk	W	L	Pct	Sh	Sv-Op	Hld	ERC	ERA
				HOW MUCH HE PITCHED								WHAT HE GAVE UP												THE RESULTS				
2002	Angels	R	8	8	0	0	38.1	172	37	19	17	4	2	0	5	20	0	50	3	0	2	1	.667	0	0--	-	4.95	3.99
2002	Provo	R+	6	6	0	0	25.2	116	26	17	17	3	0	2	3	14	0	25	3	0	1	1	.500	0	0--	-	5.40	5.96
2003	CRpds	A	26	26	1	0	144.0	623	129	85	69	7	4	6	7	59	2	100	19	1	10	11	.476	1	0--	-	3.29	4.31
2004	CRpds	A	7	7	0	0	33.1	158	36	27	24	5	2	0	5	19	0	35	4	0	1	5	.167	0	0--	-	6.19	6.48
2004	Angels	R	4	4	0	0	15.1	68	18	12	11	1	0	0	2	5	0	13	2	0	0	2	.000	0	0--	-	5.15	6.46
2005	CRpds	A	13	13	0	0	74.1	311	61	24	23	5	1	1	4	27	0	74	2	1	5	2	.714	0	0--	-	2.94	2.78
2005	RCuca	A+	14	14	0	0	72.0	328	84	58	54	11	2	4	1	33	0	44	11	0	4	4	.500	0	0--	-	5.72	6.75
2006	RCuca	A+	3	3	0	0	17.0	67	15	1	1	0	0	0	1	2	0	20	0	0	3	0	1.000	0	0--	-	2.06	0.53
2006	Ark	AA	24	24	0	0	133.0	615	174	111	98	28	3	5	7	56	0	83	12	1	5	10	.333	0	0--	-	7.21	6.63
2007	Ark	AA	46	1	0	10	71.1	315	79	36	33	6	1	6	3	30	3	42	8	0	0	6	.000	0	0--	-	4.81	4.16
2008	Salt Lk	AAA	9	0	0	2	14.1	65	20	12	10	2	2	0	0	6	0	8	1	0	2	0	1.000	0	0--	-	7.12	6.28
2008	Ark	AA	42	0	0	26	53.1	212	46	11	11	3	3	1	2	11	0	48	4	0	2	4	.333	0	11--	-	2.54	1.86
2009	Salt Lk	AAA	22	0	0	9	34.0	131	27	7	7	3	0	0	1	10	1	23	1	0	1	0	1.000	0	0--	-	2.75	1.85
2010	Salt Lk	AAA	37	0	0	27	50.1	205	41	19	17	5	3	0	0	15	1	30	2	0	5	3	.625	0	10--	-	2.66	3.04
2010	Reno	AAA	10	0	0	3	13.0	62	16	15	13	3	0	0	0	6	1	7	4	0	0	2	.000	0	1--	-	6.32	9.00
2009	LAA	AL	18	0	0	6	30.2	145	47	22	19	4	1	2	1	9	1	10	1	0	0	1	.000	0	0-2	2	7.21	5.58
2010	2 Tms		3	0	0	2	4.2	24	5	3	3	1	0	0	2	3	0	3	0	0	0	0	-	0	0-0	0	8.14	5.79
10	LAA	AL	1	0	0	1	2.0	10	1	1	1	0	0	0	1	2	0	1	0	0	0	0	-	0	0-0	0	4.47	4.50
10	Ari	NL	2	0	0	1	2.2	14	4	2	2	1	0	0	1	1	0	2	0	0	0	0	-	0	0-0	0	11.06	6.75
2 ML YEARS			21	0	0	8	35.1	169	52	25	22	5	1	2	3	12	1	13	1	0	0	1	.000	0	0-2	2	7.33	5.60

Sean Rodriguez

Bats: R **Throws:** R **Pos:** 2B-92; PH-15; CF-9; RF-8; 3B-7; PR-6; SS-5; LF-5; 1B-3; DH-3
Ht: 6'1" **Wt:** 215 **Born:** 4/26/1985 **Age:** 26

Year	Team	Lg	G	AB	H	2B	3B	HR	(Hm	Rd)	TB	R	RBI	RC	TBB	IBB	SO	HBP	SH	SF	SB	CS	SB%	GDP	Avg	OBP	Slg
									BATTING												BASERUNNING				AVERAGES		
2008	LAA	AL	59	167	34	8	1	3	(2	1)	53	18	10	12	14	0	55	3	2	1	3	1	.75	3	.204	.276	.317
2009	LAA	AL	12	25	5	0	0	2	(0	2)	11	4	4	2	3	0	7	0	0	1	0	0	-	2	.200	.276	.440
2010	TB	AL	118	343	86	19	2	9	(5	4)	136	53	40	38	21	1	97	8	5	1	13	3	.81	10	.251	.308	.397
3 ML YEARS			189	535	125	27	3	14	(7	7)	200	75	54	52	38	1	159	11	7	3	16	4	.80	15	.234	.296	.374

Wandy Rodriguez

Pitches: L **Bats:** B **Pos:** SP-32
WONN-dee
Ht: 5'11" **Wt:** 193 **Born:** 1/18/1979 **Age:** 32

Year	Team	Lg	G	GS	CG	GF	IP	BFP	H	R	ER	HR	SH	SF	HB	TBB	IBB	SO	WP	Bk	W	L	Pct	Sh	Sv-Op	Hld	ERC	ERA
				HOW MUCH HE PITCHED								WHAT HE GAVE UP												THE RESULTS				
2005	Hou	NL	25	22	0	0	128.2	560	135	82	79	19	3	3	8	53	2	80	3	3	10	10	.500	0	0-0	0	5.08	5.53
2006	Hou	NL	30	24	0	1	135.2	611	154	96	85	17	7	4	6	63	7	98	6	0	9	10	.474	0	0-0	0	5.45	5.64
2007	Hou	NL	31	31	1	0	182.2	782	179	102	93	22	6	4	5	62	2	158	3	0	9	13	.409	1	0-0	0	3.94	4.58
2008	Hou	NL	25	25	0	0	137.1	587	136	65	54	14	2	5	5	44	3	131	2	3	9	7	.563	0	0-0	0	3.82	3.54
2009	Hou	NL	33	33	1	0	205.2	849	192	77	69	21	8	4	5	63	5	193	2	1	14	12	.538	1	0-0	0	3.47	3.02
2010	Hou	NL	32	32	0	0	195.0	822	183	95	78	16	6	5	9	68	3	178	8	0	11	12	.478	0	0-0	0	3.60	3.60
	Postseason		3	0	0	1	4.2	22	5	2	2	2	1	0	0	5	1	4	0	0	0	1	.000	0	0-0	0	10.58	3.86
6 ML YEARS			176	167	2	1	985.0	4211	979	517	458	109	32	25	38	353	22	838	24	7	62	64	.492	2	0-0	0	4.10	4.18

Josh Roenicke

Pitches: R **Bats:** R **Pos:** RP-16
RENN-ick-kee
Ht: 6'3" **Wt:** 195 **Born:** 8/4/1982 **Age:** 28

Year	Team	Lg	G	GS	CG	GF	IP	BFP	H	R	ER	HR	SH	SF	HB	TBB	IBB	SO	WP	Bk	W	L	Pct	Sh	Sv-Op	Hld	ERC	ERA
				HOW MUCH HE PITCHED								WHAT HE GAVE UP												THE RESULTS				
2010	LsVgs*	AAA	36	0	0	7	59.1	260	61	29	24	7	1	5	2	25	1	54	5	0	9	1	.900	0	1--	-	4.56	3.64
2008	Cin	NL	5	0	0	0	3.0	18	6	3	3	0	0	0	1	2	0	6	0	0	0	0	-	0	0-0	0	12.01	9.00
2009	2 Tms		24	0	0	5	31.0	138	32	19	18	2	0	1	1	16	1	33	2	0	0	0	-	0	0-0	1	4.55	5.23
2010	Tor	AL	16	0	0	3	19.0	91	18	15	12	1	0	0	2	13	0	18	1	0	1	0	1.000	0	0-0	2	4.76	5.68
09	Cin	NL	11	0	0	2	13.1	54	13	4	4	0	0	0	0	4	0	14	1	0	0	0	-	0	0-0	0	3.00	2.70
09	Tor	AL	13	0	0	3	17.2	84	19	15	14	2	0	1	1	12	1	19	1	0	0	0	-	0	0-0	1	5.81	7.13
3 ML YEARS			45	0	0	8	53.0	247	56	37	33	3	0	1	4	31	1	57	3	0	1	0	1.000	0	0-0	3	5.00	5.60

Esmil Rogers

Pitches: R **Bats:** R **Pos:** RP-20; SP-8
ESS-mill
Ht: 6'1" **Wt:** 190 **Born:** 8/14/1985 **Age:** 25

Year	Team	Lg	G	GS	CG	GF	IP	BFP	H	R	ER	HR	SH	SF	HB	TBB	IBB	SO	WP	Bk	W	L	Pct	Sh	Sv-Op	Hld	ERC	ERA
				HOW MUCH HE PITCHED								WHAT HE GAVE UP												THE RESULTS				
2006	Casper	R+	15	15	1	0	63.1	297	78	53	49	8	2	3	13	24	0	40	8	1	3	6	.333	0	0--	-	6.45	6.96
2007	Ashvll	A	19	18	1	0	117.2	517	125	60	49	6	3	4	7	42	0	90	10	4	7	4	.636	0	0--	-	4.12	3.75
2008	Mdest	A+	25	25	0	0	143.2	609	146	73	63	9	2	6	4	45	0	116	6	3	9	7	.563	0	0--	-	3.70	3.95
2009	Tulsa	AA	15	15	0	0	94.1	384	87	30	27	2	0	1	6	19	0	83	3	1	8	2	.800	0	0--	-	2.67	2.58
2009	ColSpr	AAA	12	11	0	0	60.2	287	77	50	50	9	2	4	3	35	2	46	7	3	3	5	.375	0	0--	-	7.06	7.42

Year	Team	Lg	G	GS	CG	GF	IP	BFP	H	R	ER	HR	SH	SF	HB	TBB	IBB	SO	WP	Bk	W	L	Pct	Sh	Sv-Op	Hld	ERC	ERA
2010	ColSpr	AAA	12	11	0	0	61.0	264	62	41	39	6	3	0	4	19	0	53	3	2	3	3	.500	0	0--		4.04	5.75
2009	Col	NL	1	1	0	0	4.0	16	3	2	2	0	0	1	0	2	0	3	0	0				0	0-0	0	2.58	4.50
2010	Col	NL	28	8	0	5	72.0	333	94	59	49	5	3	3	5	26	2	66	5	2	2	3	.400	0	0-1	1	5.70	6.13
2 ML YEARS			29	9	0	5	76.0	349	97	61	51	5	3	4	5	28	2	69	5	2	2	3	.400	0	0-1	1	5.52	6.04

Mark Rogers

Pitches: R **Bats:** R **Pos:** SP-2; RP-2   **Ht:** 6'3" **Wt:** 220 **Born:** 1/30/1986 **Age:** 25

Year	Team	Lg	G	GS	CG	GF	IP	BFP	H	R	ER	HR	SH	SF	HB	TBB	IBB	SO	WP	Bk	W	L	Pct	Sh	Sv-Op	Hld	ERC	ERA
2004	Brewrs	R	9	6	0	0	26.2	120	30	21	14	0	0	1	3	14	0	35	5	1	0	3	.000	0	0--		5.13	4.73
2005	WV	A	25	20	0	2	98.2	451	87	65	56	11	1	2	12	70	0	109	11	0	2	9	.182	0	1--		5.25	5.11
2006	BrvdCt	A+	16	16	0	0	71.0	329	68	46	40	6	2	2	3	53	0	96	12	0	1	2	.333	0	0--		5.27	5.07
2006	Brewrs	R	3	3	0	0	4.0	19	5	1	1	0	0	0	0	2	0	5	2	0	0	0	-	0	0--		5.00	2.25
2009	BrvdCt	A+	23	22	0	0	64.2	260	46	16	12	2	0	0	2	29	0	67	7	0	1	3	.250	0	0--		2.47	1.67
2010	Hntsvl	AA	24	24	0	0	111.2	490	86	60	46	3	3	3	6	69	0	111	12	1	6	8	.429	0	0--		3.29	3.71
2010	Nashv	AAA	1	1	0	0	4.1	19	3	1	1	0	0	0	0	3	0	3	0	0	0	0	-	0	0--		2.74	2.08
2010	Mil	NL	4	2	0	1	10.0	36	2	2	2	0	1	1	1	3	0	11	0	0	0	0	-	0	0-0	0	0.50	1.80

Ryan Rohlinger

Bats: R **Throws:** R **Pos:** PH-6; SS-4; 3B-3; PR-1   ROE-ling-er   **Ht:** 6'0" **Wt:** 193 **Born:** 10/7/1983 **Age:** 27

Year	Team	Lg	G	AB	H	2B	3B	HR	(Hm	Rd)	TB	R	RBI	RC	TBB	IBB	SO	HBP	SH	SF	SB	CS	SB%	GDP	Avg	OBP	Slg
2010	Fresno*	AAA	77	283	88	23	0	8	(-	-)	135	46	48	55	29	1	59	10	1	2	3	0	1.00	13	.311	.392	.477
2010	Giants*	R	3	9	4	0	0	3	(-	-)	13	5	3	4	0	0	2	0	0	0	1	0	1.00		.444	.444	1.444
2008	SF	NL	21	32	3	1	1	0	(0	0)	6	2	2	0	1	0	8	0	0	0	0	1	.00	2	.094	.121	.188
2009	SF	NL	12	19	3	1	0	0	(0	0)	4	0	4	1	1	0	6	0	0	0	0	0	-	1	.158	.200	.211
2010	SF	NL	12	15	3	0	0	0	(0	0)	3	1	1	0	2	0	5	0	1	0	0	0	-	1	.200	.294	.200
3 ML YEARS			45	66	9	2	1	0	(0	0)	13	3	7	1	4	0	19	0	1	0	0	1	.00	4	.136	.186	.197

Scott Rolen

Bats: R **Throws:** R **Pos:** 3B-130; PH-7   **Ht:** 6'4" **Wt:** 250 **Born:** 4/4/1975 **Age:** 36

Year	Team	Lg	G	AB	H	2B	3B	HR	(Hm	Rd)	TB	R	RBI	RC	TBB	IBB	SO	HBP	SH	SF	SB	CS	SB%	GDP	Avg	OBP	Slg
1996	Phi	NL	37	130	33	7	0	4	(2	2)	52	10	18	16	13	0	27	1	0	2	0	2	.00	4	.254	.322	.400
1997	Phi	NL	156	561	159	35	3	21	(11	10)	263	93	92	103	76	4	138	13	0	7	16	6	.73	6	.283	.377	.469
1998	Phi	NL	160	601	174	45	4	31	(19	12)	320	120	110	124	93	6	141	11	0	7	14	7	.67	10	.290	.391	.532
1999	Phi	NL	112	421	113	28	1	26	(9	17)	221	74	77	83	67	2	114	3	0	6	12	2	.86	8	.268	.368	.525
2000	Phi	NL	128	483	144	32	6	26	(12	14)	266	88	89	97	51	9	99	5	0	7	8	1	.89	4	.298	.370	.551
2001	Phi	NL	151	554	160	39	1	25	(12	13)	276	96	107	108	74	6	127	13	0	12	16	5	.76	6	.289	.378	.498
2002	2 Tms		155	580	154	29	8	31	(14	17)	292	89	110	98	72	4	102	12	0	3	8	4	.67	22	.266	.357	.503
2003	StL	NL	154	559	160	49	1	28	(12	16)	295	98	104	104	82	5	104	9	0	7	13	3	.81	19	.286	.382	.528
2004	StL	NL	142	500	157	32	4	34	(10	24)	299	109	124	124	72	5	92	13	1	7	4	3	.57	8	.314	.409	.598
2005	StL	NL	56	196	46	12	1	5	(2	3)	75	20	28	22	25	1	28	1	0	1	1	2	.33	3	.235	.323	.383
2006	StL	NL	142	521	154	48	1	22	(12	10)	270	94	95	89	56	7	69	9	0	8	7	4	.64	10	.296	.369	.518
2007	StL	NL	112	392	104	24	2	8	(4	4)	156	55	58	57	37	2	66	5	0	7	5	3	.63	13	.265	.331	.398
2008	Tor	AL	115	408	107	30	0	11	(6	5)	176	58	50	57	46	2	71	10	0	3	5	0	1.00	12	.262	.349	.431
2009	2 Tms		128	475	145	36	1	11	(8	3)	216	76	67	82	45	1	62	7	0	8	5	4	.56	4	.305	.368	.455
2010	Cin	NL	133	471	134	34	3	20	(10	10)	234	66	83	70	50	3	82	8	0	8	1	2	.33	12	.285	.358	.497
02	Phi	NL	100	375	97	21	4	17	(8	9)	177	52	66	60	52	2	68	8	0	3	5	2	.71	12	.259	.358	.472
02	StL	NL	55	205	57	8	4	14	(6	8)	115	37	44	38	20	2	34	4	0	0	3	2	.60	10	.278	.354	.561
09	Tor	AL	88	338	108	29	0	8	(6	2)	161	52	43	60	26	1	42	4	0	5	4	2	.67	2	.320	.370	.476
09	Cin	NL	40	137	37	7	1	3	(2	1)	55	24	24	22	19	0	20	3	0	3	1	2	.33	2	.270	.364	.401
Postseason			32	114	26	7	0	5	(3	2)	48	17	11	14	14	0	22	2	0	1	0	1	.00	5	.228	.321	.421
15 ML YEARS			1881	6852	1944	480	39	303	(143	160)	3411	1154	1212	1227	859	57	1312	120	1	87	115	48	.71	141	.284	.369	.498

Jimmy Rollins

Bats: B **Throws:** R **Pos:** SS-88; PH-2   **Ht:** 5'8" **Wt:** 170 **Born:** 11/27/1978 **Age:** 32

Year	Team	Lg	G	AB	H	2B	3B	HR	(Hm	Rd)	TB	R	RBI	RC	TBB	IBB	SO	HBP	SH	SF	SB	CS	SB%	GDP	Avg	OBP	Slg
2010	Clrwtr*	A+	5	14	2	0	0	0	(-	-)	2	2	2	0	1	0	1	0	0	2	0	0	-	0	.143	.176	.143
2000	Phi	NL	14	53	17	1	1	0	(0	0)	20	5	5	8	2	0	7	0	0	0	3	0	1.00	1	.321	.345	.377
2001	Phi	NL	158	656	180	29	12	14	(8	6)	275	97	54	96	48	2	108	2	9	5	46	8	.85	5	.274	.323	.419
2002	Phi	NL	154	637	156	33	10	11	(3	8)	242	82	60	72	54	3	103	4	6	4	31	13	.70	14	.245	.306	.380
2003	Phi	NL	156	628	165	42	6	8	(5	3)	243	85	62	76	54	4	113	0	5	2	20	12	.63	9	.263	.320	.387
2004	Phi	NL	154	657	190	43	12	14	(8	6)	299	119	73	108	57	3	73	3	6	2	30	9	.77	4	.289	.348	.455
2005	Phi	NL	158	677	196	38	11	12	(5	7)	292	115	54	100	47	8	71	4	2	2	41	6	.87	9	.290	.338	.431
2006	Phi	NL	158	689	191	45	9	25	(15	10)	329	127	83	114	57	2	80	5	0	7	36	4	.90	12	.277	.334	.478
2007	Phi	NL	162	716	212	38	20	30	(18	12)	380	139	94	124	49	5	85	7	0	6	41	6	.87	11	.296	.344	.531
2008	Phi	NL	137	556	154	38	9	11	(6	5)	243	76	59	95	58	7	55	5	3	3	47	3	.94	11	.277	.349	.437
2009	Phi	NL	155	672	168	43	5	21	(10	11)	284	100	77	88	44	1	70	2	2	5	31	8	.79	7	.250	.296	.423
2010	Phi	NL	88	350	85	16	3	8	(4	4)	131	48	41	54	40	2	32	1	0	3	17	1	.94	4	.243	.320	.374
Postseason			32	134	31	7	1	3	(1	2)	49	20	11	10	11	0	26	2	1	1	7	2	.78	4	.231	.297	.366
11 ML YEARS			1494	6291	1714	366	98	154	(81	73)	2738	993	662	935	510	37	797	33	33	39	343	70	.83	86	.272	.328	.435

J.C. Romero

Pitches: L **Bats:** B **Pos:** RP-60

Ht: 5'11" **Wt:** 215 **Born:** 6/4/1976 **Age:** 35

Year	Team	Lg	G	GS	CG	GF	IP	BFP	H	R	ER	HR	SH	SF	HB	TBB	IBB	SO	WP	Bk	W	L	Pct	Sh	Sv-Op	Hld	ERC	ERA
2010	Clrwtr*	A+	3	3	0	0	4.0	16	3	1	1	1	1	0	0	1	0	5	0	0	0	0	-	0	0- -	-	3.01	2.25
2010	LV*	AAA	3	1	0	0	2.1	13	2	1	0	0	0	0	0	4	1	4	1	0	0	1	.000	0	0- -	-	6.41	0.00
1999	Min	AL	5	0	0	3	9.2	39	13	4	4	0	0	0	0	0	0	4	0	0	0	0	-	0	0-0	0	3.95	3.72
2000	Min	AL	12	11	0	0	57.2	268	72	51	45	8	4	2	1	30	0	50	2	1	2	7	.222	0	0-0	0	6.48	7.02
2001	Min	AL	14	11	0	1	65.0	286	71	48	45	10	3	2	1	24	1	39	1	0	1	4	.200	0	0-0	0	4.89	6.23
2002	Min	AL	81	0	0	15	81.0	332	62	17	17	3	1	0	4	36	4	76	9	0	9	2	.818	0	1-5	33	2.74	1.89
2003	Min	AL	73	0	0	17	63.0	295	66	37	35	7	4	0	6	42	7	50	9	2	2	0	1.000	0	0-4	22	5.72	5.00
2004	Min	AL	74	0	0	12	74.1	319	61	32	29	4	3	1	5	38	6	69	5	0	7	4	.636	0	1-8	16	3.33	3.51
2005	Min	AL	68	0	0	11	57.0	264	50	26	22	6	5	1	6	39	8	48	1	1	4	3	.571	0	0-1	11	4.62	3.47
2006	LAA	AL	65	0	0	16	48.1	226	57	40	36	3	1	5	1	28	2	31	1	0	1	2	.333	0	0-1	7	5.54	6.70
2007	2 Tms		74	0	0	10	56.1	237	39	12	12	3	1	1	2	40	5	42	4	0	2	2	.500	0	1-2	24	3.35	1.92
2008	Phi	NL	81	0	0	14	59.0	255	41	18	18	5	4	0	5	38	5	52	2	1	4	4	.500	0	1-5	24	3.42	2.75
2009	Phi	NL	21	0	0	5	16.2	73	13	6	5	2	0	0	2	13	0	12	0	0	0	0	-	0	0-1	6	5.20	2.70
2010	Phi	NL	60	0	0	14	36.2	171	30	17	15	3	2	0	5	29	7	28	0	1	1	0	1.000	0	3-6	9	4.58	3.68
07	Bos	AL	23	0	0	5	20.0	94	24	7	7	2	0	1	0	15	3	11	0	0	1	0	1.000	0	1-1	2	6.61	3.15
07	Phi	NL	51	0	0	5	36.1	143	15	5	5	1	1	0	2	25	2	31	4	0	1	2	.333	0	0-1	22	1.86	1.24
	Postseason		23	0	0	7	19.0	79	15	7	7	1	2	1	0	9	1	15	1	0	2	2	.500	0	0-0	5	2.85	3.32
12 ML YEARS			628	22	0	118	624.2	2765	575	308	283	54	28	12	38	357	45	501	34	6	33	28	.541	0	7-33	152	4.34	4.08

Niuman Romero

Bats: B **Throws:** R **Pos:** 1B-1; 2B-1; PH-1; PR-1   NEW-min

Ht: 6'1" **Wt:** 190 **Born:** 1/24/1985 **Age:** 26

Year	Team	Lg	G	AB	H	2B	3B	HR	(Hm	Rd)	TB	R	RBI	RC	TBB	IBB	SO	HBP	SH	SF	SB	CS	SB%	GDP	Avg	OBP	Slg
2005	Burlgtn	R+	63	218	60	12	2	2	(-	-)	82	33	29	32	31	1	45	4	3	1	6	6	.50	5	.275	.374	.376
2006	Lk Cty	A	114	412	94	11	1	2	(-	-)	113	45	36	40	55	0	83	1	9	3	10	8	.56	13	.228	.318	.274
2007	Knstn	A+	12	40	14	2	0	0	(-	-)	16	5	6	7	4	0	9	0	0	1	1	0	1.00	0	.350	.400	.400
2007	Lk Cty	A	69	215	45	10	2	1	(-	-)	62	31	24	27	44	0	45	5	2	3	3	1	.75	6	.209	.352	.288
2008	Knstn	A+	108	395	117	22	1	6	(-	-)	159	64	53	59	34	1	55	2	4	5	10	4	.71	8	.296	.351	.403
2009	Akron	AA	38	115	24	4	0	0	(-	-)	28	13	8	9	12	0	19	2	4	1	3	1	.75	7	.209	.292	.243
2009	Clmbs	AAA	81	252	64	10	1	1	(-	-)	79	34	27	27	21	0	27	2	6	3	10	4	.71	6	.254	.313	.313
2010	Pwtckt	AAA	99	350	86	14	0	3	(-	-)	109	42	20	37	32	0	57	3	8	0	14	6	.70	8	.246	.314	.311
2009	Cle	AL	10	14	2	0	0	0	(0	0)	2	2	0	0	1	0	5	0	0	0	0	0	-	0	.143	.200	.143
2010	Bos	AL	2	4	0	0	0	0	(0	0)	0	1	0	0	0	0	0	0	0	0	0	0	-	0	.000	.000	.000
2 ML YEARS			12	18	2	0	0	0	(0	0)	2	3	0	0	1	0	5	0	0	0	0	0	-	0	.111	.158	.111

Ricky Romero

Pitches: L **Bats:** R **Pos:** SP-32

Ht: 6'0" **Wt:** 210 **Born:** 11/6/1984 **Age:** 26

Year	Team	Lg	G	GS	CG	GF	IP	BFP	H	R	ER	HR	SH	SF	HB	TBB	IBB	SO	WP	Bk	W	L	Pct	Sh	Sv-Op	Hld	ERC	ERA
2005	Dnedin	A+	8	8	0	0	30.2	134	36	13	13	2	0	0	0	7	0	22	5	1	1	0	1.000	0	0- -	-	4.06	3.82
2005	Auburn	A-	1	1	0	0	2.0	9	2	0	0	0	0	0	0	1	0	2	1	0	0	0	-	0	0- -	-	3.63	0.00
2006	Dnedin	A+	10	10	1	0	58.1	234	48	17	16	5	2	3	1	14	0	61	0	0	2	1	.667	1	0- -	-	2.52	2.47
2006	NHam	AA	12	12	0	0	67.1	288	65	43	38	7	5	2	1	26	0	41	6	0	2	7	.222	0	0- -	-	3.92	5.08
2007	NHam	AA	18	18	1	0	88.1	409	98	57	48	9	1	2	4	51	0	80	9	0	3	6	.333	0	0- -	-	5.62	4.89
2007	Dnedin	A+	1	1	0	0	4.2	17	4	2	2	0	0	0	0	1	0	2	0	0	0	0	-	0	0- -	-	2.29	3.86
2008	NHam	AA	21	21	0	0	121.2	540	139	70	67	9	2	4	6	55	0	78	11	1	5	5	.500	0	0- -	-	5.23	4.96
2008	Syrcse	AAA	7	7	1	0	42.2	184	42	17	16	3	1	1	2	20	0	38	2	0	3	3	.500	0	0- -	-	4.32	3.38
2009	Dnedin	A+	1	1	0	0	4.0	19	6	6	6	2	0	0	0	1	0	5	1	0	0	1	.000	0	0- -	-	9.51	13.50
2009	NHam	AA	1	1	0	0	5.1	22	3	2	1	0	1	0	0	5	0	4	0	0	0	0	-	0	0- -	-	3.21	1.69
2009	LsVgs	AAA	1	1	0	0	5.0	24	8	4	4	0	0	0	1	2	0	3	0	0	0	0	-	0	0- -	-	8.20	7.20
2009	Tor	AL	29	29	0	0	178.0	771	192	88	85	18	3	3	10	79	0	141	6	1	13	9	.591	0	0-0	0	5.12	4.30
2010	Tor	AL	32	32	3	0	210.0	882	189	98	87	15	9	3	8	82	3	174	18	1	14	9	.609	1	0-0	0	3.46	3.73
2 ML YEARS			61	61	3	0	388.0	1653	381	186	172	33	12	6	18	161	3	315	24	2	27	18	.600	1	0-0	0	4.19	3.99

Andrew Romine

Bats: B **Throws:** R **Pos:** SS-4; PH-1

Ht: 6'1" **Wt:** 190 **Born:** 12/24/1985 **Age:** 25

Year	Team	Lg	G	AB	H	2B	3B	HR	(Hm	Rd)	TB	R	RBI	RC	TBB	IBB	SO	HBP	SH	SF	SB	CS	SB%	GDP	Avg	OBP	Slg
2007	Orem	R+	56	231	66	6	6	5	(-	-)	99	38	35	34	16	0	38	2	0	0	12	4	.75	3	.286	.337	.429
2008	CRpds	A	126	461	120	21	4	2	(-	-)	155	79	34	65	55	2	76	9	12	6	62	18	.78	5	.260	.347	.336
2009	RCuca	A+	131	479	133	13	9	1	(-	-)	167	68	36	65	51	1	83	5	16	4	26	11	.70	7	.278	.351	.349
2010	Ark	AA	106	383	108	15	4	3	(-	-)	140	55	34	58	50	1	66	5	13	2	21	9	.70	4	.282	.370	.366
2010	LAA	AL	5	11	1	0	0	0	(0	0)	1	0	0	0	0	0	4	0	1	0	0	0	-	0	.091	.091	.091

Sergio Romo

Pitches: R **Bats:** R **Pos:** RP-68

Ht: 5'10" **Wt:** 185 **Born:** 3/4/1983 **Age:** 28

Year	Team	Lg	G	GS	CG	GF	IP	BFP	H	R	ER	HR	SH	SF	HB	TBB	IBB	SO	WP	Bk	W	L	Pct	Sh	Sv-Op	Hld	ERC	ERA
2008	SF	NL	29	0	0	8	34.0	130	16	13	8	3	2	1	3	8	1	33	0	0	3	1	.750	0	0-0	5	1.27	2.12
2009	SF	NL	45	0	0	8	34.0	143	30	15	15	1	2	0	1	11	0	41	2	0	5	2	.714	0	2-2	10	2.76	3.97
2010	SF	NL	68	0	0	13	62.0	247	46	16	15	6	2	2	4	14	2	70	0	0	5	3	.625	0	0-4	21	2.26	2.18
3 ML YEARS			142	0	0	30	130.0	520	92	44	38	10	6	3	8	33	3	144	2	0	13	6	.684	0	2-6	36	2.07	2.63

Carlos Rosa

Pitches: R Bats: R Pos: RP-22   Ht: 6'1" Wt: 210 Born: 9/21/1984 Age: 26

Year	Team	Lg	G	GS	CG	GF	IP	BFP	H	R	ER	HR	SH	SF	HB	TBB	IBB	SO	WP	Bk	W	L	Pct	Sh	Sv-Op	Hld	ERC	ERA
2010	Omha*	AAA	6	0	0	3	12.1	56	13	5	5	2	1	2	1	7	0	10	1	0	2	1	.667	0	0--	-	5.98	3.65
2010	Reno*	AAA	25	0	0	20	27.2	110	20	5	5	2	0	0	0	14	0	31	5	0	0	0	-	0	13--	-	2.97	1.63
2008	KC	AL	2	0	0	1	3.1	12	3	1	1	0	0	0	0	0	0	3	0	0	0	0	-	0	0-0	0	1.70	2.70
2009	KC	AL	7	0	0	5	10.2	43	10	4	4	1	0	1	0	3	0	4	0	0	0	0	-	0	1-1	0	3.34	3.38
2010	Ari	NL	22	0	0	9	20.0	89	20	10	10	1	1	6	0	12	2	9	0	0	0	2	.000	0	0-1	1	4.36	4.50
	3 ML YEARS		31	0	0	15	34.0	144	33	15	15	2	1	7	0	15	2	16	0	0	0	2	.000	0	1-2	1	3.77	3.97

Adam Rosales

Bats: R Throws: R Pos: 2B-47; SS-14; PH-10; 1B-7; 3B-5; LF-5; DH-4; PR-1   Ht: 6'2" Wt: 195 Born: 5/20/1983 Age: 28

Year	Team	Lg	G	AB	H	2B	3B	HR	(Hm	Rd)	TB	R	RBI	RC	TBB	IBB	SO	HBP	SH	SF	SB	CS	SB%	GDP	Avg	OBP	Slg
2008	Cin	NL	18	29	6	1	0	0	(0	0)	7	0	2	2	1	0	4	0	0	0	1	0	1.00	0	.207	.233	.241
2009	Cin	NL	87	230	49	10	1	4	(2	2)	73	23	19	22	26	0	46	5	2	3	1	2	.33	2	.213	.303	.317
2010	Oak	AL	80	255	69	8	2	7	(1	6)	102	31	31	31	19	0	65	1	2	2	2	2	.50	1	.271	.321	.400
	3 ML YEARS		185	514	124	19	3	11	(3	8)	182	54	52	55	46	0	115	6	4	5	4	4	.50	3	.241	.308	.354

Leo Rosales

Pitches: R Bats: R Pos: RP-16   Ht: 6'1" Wt: 205 Born: 5/28/1981 Age: 30

Year	Team	Lg	G	GS	CG	GF	IP	BFP	H	R	ER	HR	SH	SF	HB	TBB	IBB	SO	WP	Bk	W	L	Pct	Sh	Sv-Op	Hld	ERC	ERA
2010	Reno*	AAA	6	0	0	0	5.1	24	5	3	3	0	0	0	0	3	0	4	1	0	0	0	-	0	0--	-	3.53	5.06
2008	Ari	NL	27	0	0	6	30.0	136	32	15	14	2	1	1	1	15	3	18	2	0	1	1	.500	0	0-1	1	4.51	4.20
2009	Ari	NL	33	0	0	8	45.1	186	40	24	24	5	1	4	0	12	2	31	3	0	2	1	.667	0	0-0	2	2.91	4.76
2010	Ari	NL	16	0	0	3	16.1	80	25	13	13	2	0	2	0	9	0	12	1	0	2	0	1.000	0	0-0	2	8.30	7.16
	3 ML YEARS		76	0	0	17	91.2	402	97	52	51	9	2	7	1	36	5	61	6	0	5	2	.714	0	0-1	5	4.29	5.01

Sandy Rosario

Pitches: R Bats: R Pos: RP-2   Ht: 6'1" Wt: 170 Born: 8/22/1985 Age: 25

Year	Team	Lg	G	GS	CG	GF	IP	BFP	H	R	ER	HR	SH	SF	HB	TBB	IBB	SO	WP	Bk	W	L	Pct	Sh	Sv-Op	Hld	ERC	ERA
2006	Mrlns	R	10	6	0	0	40.0	176	41	20	10	0	6	0	0	10	0	27	3	1	3	2	.600	0	0--	-	2.79	2.25
2007	Grnsbr	A	2	2	0	0	7.1	38	11	8	8	1	0	0	0	2	0	7	2	0	0	1	.000	0	0--	-	7.10	9.82
2008	Grnsbr	A	1	1	0	0	2.0	12	3	4	3	0	0	1	0	3	0	4	1	0	0	0	-	0	0--	-	10.76	13.50
2009	Jmstwn	A-	9	9	0	0	42.1	186	48	12	8	1	0	0	5	8	0	41	1	0	4	2	.667	0	0--	-	3.86	1.70
2009	Grnsbr	A	7	7	0	0	40.1	185	57	28	23	4	1	0	1	6	0	36	1	0	3	2	.600	0	0--	-	5.41	5.13
2010	Grnsbr	A	43	0	0	16	90.0	377	92	47	36	9	5	2	3	17	1	122	4	0	7	2	.778	0	3--	-	3.46	3.60
2010	Jaxnvl	AA	1	0	0	0	2.0	6	0	0	0	0	0	0	0	0	0	3	0	0	1	0	1.000	0	0--	-	0.00	0.00
2010	Fla	NL	2	0	0	0	1.0	12	9	6	6	2	0	0	0	1	0	0	0	0	0	0	-	0	0-0	0	115.7	54.00

Cody Ross

Bats: R Throws: L Pos: CF-09; RF-54; LF-23; PH-3; PR-3   Ht: 6'10" Wt: 104 Born: 12/20/1980 Age: 30

Year	Team	Lg	G	AB	H	2B	3B	HR	(Hm	Rd)	TB	R	RBI	RC	TBB	IBB	SO	HBP	SH	SF	SB	CS	SB%	GDP	Avg	OBP	Slg
2003	Det	AL	6	19	4	1	0	1	(1	0)	8	1	5	4	1	0	3	1	1	0	0	0	-	0	.211	.286	.421
2005	LAD	NL	14	25	4	1	0	0	(0	0)	5	1	1	0	1	0	10	0	0	0	0	0	-	1	.160	.192	.200
2006	3 Tms	NL	101	269	61	12	2	13	(6	7)	116	34	46	36	22	0	65	4	1	2	1	1	.50	2	.227	.293	.431
2007	Fla	NL	66	173	58	19	0	12	(8	4)	113	35	39	42	20	3	38	3	0	1	2	0	1.00	2	.335	.411	.653
2008	Fla	NL	145	461	120	29	5	22	(7	15)	225	59	73	68	33	2	116	7	0	5	6	1	.86	5	.260	.316	.488
2009	Fla	NL	151	559	151	37	1	24	(13	11)	262	73	90	75	34	1	122	9	0	2	5	2	.71	18	.270	.321	.469
2010	2 Tms	NL	153	525	141	28	3	14	(5	9)	217	71	65	68	37	4	121	5	0	2	9	2	.82	9	.269	.322	.413
06	LAD	NL	8	14	7	1	1	2	(0	2)	16	4	9	6	0	0	2	0	0	0	1	0	1.00	0	.500	.500	1.143
06	Cin	NL	2	5	1	0	0	0	(0	0)	1	0	0	1	0	0	2	0	0	0	0	0	-	0	.200	.200	.200
06	Fla	NL	91	250	53	11	1	11	(6	5)	99	30	37	29	22	0	61	4	1	2	0	1	.00	8	.212	.284	.396
10	Fla	NL	120	452	120	24	3	11	(5	6)	183	60	58	58	30	4	100	4	0	1	9	1	.90	7	.265	.316	.405
10	SF	NL	33	73	21	4	0	3	(0	3)	34	11	7	10	7	0	21	1	0	1	0	1	.00	2	.288	.354	.466
	7 ML YEARS		636	2031	539	127	11	86	(40	46)	946	274	319	293	148	10	475	29	2	12	23	6	.79	43	.265	.323	.466

David Ross

Bats: R Throws: R Pos: C-57; PH-4; PR-2   Ht: 6'2" Wt: 205 Born: 3/19/1977 Age: 34

Year	Team	Lg	G	AB	H	2B	3B	HR	(Hm	Rd)	TB	R	RBI	RC	TBB	IBB	SO	HBP	SH	SF	SB	CS	SB%	GDP	Avg	OBP	Slg
2002	LAD	NL	8	10	2	1	0	1	(0	1)	6	2	2	2	2	0	4	1	0	0	0	0	-	0	.200	.385	.600
2003	LAD	NL	40	124	32	7	0	10	(5	5)	69	19	18	18	13	0	42	2	0	1	0	0	-	4	.258	.336	.556
2004	LAD	NL	70	165	28	3	1	5	(2	3)	48	13	15	11	15	1	62	5	0	5	0	0	-	3	.170	.253	.291
2005	2 Tms	NL	51	125	30	8	1	3	(2	1)	49	11	15	13	6	0	28	2	2	3	0	0	-	3	.240	.279	.392
2006	Cin	NL	90	247	63	15	1	21	(13	8)	143	37	52	43	37	7	75	3	4	5	0	0	-	4	.255	.353	.579
2007	Cin	NL	112	311	63	10	0	17	(12	5)	124	32	39	27	30	4	92	0	5	2	0	0	-	9	.203	.271	.399
2008	2 Tms	NL	60	142	32	9	0	3	(1	2)	50	18	13	19	32	4	39	1	6	1	0	1	.00	3	.225	.369	.352
2009	Atl	NL	54	128	35	9	0	7	(2	5)	65	18	20	20	21	0	39	1	1	0	0	0	-	1	.273	.368	.508
2010	Atl	NL	59	121	35	13	2	2	(2	0)	58	15	28	22	20	0	28	1	2	1	0	1	.00	2	.289	.392	.479
05	Pit	NL	40	108	24	8	0	3	(2	1)	41	9	15	9	6	0	24	1	1	3	0	0	-	3	.222	.263	.380
05	SD	NL	11	17	6	0	1	0	(0	0)	8	2	0	4	0	0	4	1	1	0	0	0	-	0	.353	.389	.471

Year Team	Lg	G	AB	H	2B	3B	HR	(Hm	Rd)	TB	R	RBI	RC	TBB	IBB	SO	HBP	SH	SF	SB	CS	SB%	GDP	Avg	OBP	Slg
08 Cin	NL	52	134	31	9	0	3	(1	2)	49	17	13	19	32	4	36	1	5	1	0	1	.00	3	.231	.381	.366
08 Bos	AL	8	8	1	0	0	0	(0	0)	1	1	0	0	0	0	3	0	1	0	0	0	-	0	.125	.125	.125
Postseason		3	3	0	0	0	0	(0	0)	0	0	0	0	1	0	0	0	0	0	0	0	-	0	.000	.250	.000
9 ML YEARS		544	1373	320	75	5	69	(39	30)	612	165	202	175	176	16	409	16	20	18	0	2	.00	32	.233	.323	.446

Tyson Ross

Pitches: R Bats: R Pos: RP-24; SP-2   Ht: 6'6" Wt: 225 Born: 4/22/1987 Age: 24

Year Team	Lg	G	GS	CG	GF	IP	BFP	H	R	ER	HR	SH	SF	HB	TBB	IBB	SO	WP	Bk	W	L	Pct	Sh	Sv-Op	Hld	ERC	ERA
2008 Kane	A	6	4	0	0	19.1	80	16	11	10	1	0	0	2	5	0	16	1	0	0	1	.000	0	0- -	-	2.68	4.66
2009 Stcktn	A+	18	18	0	0	86.1	378	78	49	40	10	4	4	8	33	1	82	5	0	5	6	.455	0	0- -	-	3.84	4.17
2009 Mdland	AA	9	9	1	0	50.0	203	40	22	22	3	1	3	1	20	0	31	4	0	5	4	.556	0	0- -	-	2.89	3.96
2010 Scrmto	AAA	6	6	0	0	25.1	106	22	10	10	1	2	0	4	13	0	30	1	0	2	1	.667	0	0- -	-	4.22	3.55
2010 Oak	AL	26	2	0	9	39.1	169	39	24	24	4	1	4	0	20	0	32	5	0	1	4	.200	0	1-2	2	4.60	5.49

Aaron Rowand

Bats: R Throws: R Pos: CF-85; PH-25; PR-1   ROW-and   Ht: 6'0" Wt: 213 Born: 8/29/1977 Age: 33

Year Team	Lg	G	AB	H	2B	3B	HR	(Hm	Rd)	TB	R	RBI	RC	TBB	IBB	SO	HBP	SH	SF	SB	CS	SB%	GDP	Avg	OBP	Slg
2001 CWS	AL	63	123	36	5	0	4	(3	1)	53	21	20	22	15	0	28	4	5	1	5	1	.83	2	.293	.385	.431
2002 CWS	AL	126	302	78	16	2	7	(5	2)	119	41	29	37	12	1	54	6	9	2	0	1	.00	8	.258	.298	.394
2003 CWS	AL	93	157	45	8	0	6	(5	1)	71	22	24	28	7	0	21	3	2	1	0	0	-	1	.287	.327	.452
2004 CWS	AL	140	487	151	38	2	24	(12	12)	265	94	69	92	30	1	91	10	5	2	17	5	.77	5	.310	.361	.544
2005 CWS	AL	157	578	156	30	5	13	(6	7)	235	77	69	78	32	3	116	21	5	4	16	5	.76	17	.270	.329	.407
2006 Phi	NL	109	405	106	24	3	12	(6	6)	172	59	47	47	18	2	76	18	2	2	10	4	.71	13	.262	.321	.425
2007 Phi	NL	161	612	189	45	0	27	(17	10)	315	105	89	100	47	3	119	19	2	4	6	3	.67	18	.309	.374	.515
2008 SF	NL	152	549	149	37	0	13	(6	7)	225	57	70	67	44	7	126	14	0	4	2	4	.33	21	.271	.339	.410
2009 SF	NL	144	499	130	30	2	15	(5	10)	209	61	64	63	30	2	125	14	0	3	4	1	.80	12	.261	.319	.419
2010 SF	NL	105	331	76	12	2	11	(6	5)	125	42	34	33	16	3	74	8	1	1	5	3	.63	11	.230	.281	.378
Postseason		15	57	13	6	0	1	(1	0)	22	9	4	3	4	1	13	1	0	1	1	0	1.00	3	.228	.286	.386
10 ML YEARS		1250	4043	1116	245	16	132	(73	59)	1789	579	515	567	251	22	830	117	31	24	65	27	.71	108	.276	.335	.442

Ryan Rowland-Smith

Pitches: L Bats: L Pos: SP-20; RP-7   Ht: 6'3" Wt: 240 Born: 1/26/1983 Age: 28

Year Team	Lg	G	GS	CG	GF	IP	BFP	H	R	ER	HR	SH	SF	HB	TBB	IBB	SO	WP	Bk	W	L	Pct	Sh	Sv-Op	Hld	ERC	ERA
2010 Tacom*	AAA	6	6	0	0	37.0	161	45	22	21	4	1	4	2	5	0	24	1	0	2	4	.333	0	0- -	-	4.19	5.11
2007 Sea	AL	26	0	0	6	38.2	168	39	19	17	4	1	4	2	15	1	42	0	0	1	0	1.000	0	0- -	3	4.27	3.96
2008 Sea	AL	47	12	0	9	118.1	506	114	49	45	13	2	3	2	48	0	77	2	1	5	3	.625	0	2-3	1	4.05	3.42
2009 Sea	AL	15	15	0	0	96.1	401	87	43	40	9	1	5	4	27	0	52	2	1	5	4	.556	0	0-0	0	3.19	3.74
2010 Sea	AL	27	20	0	2	109.1	510	141	94	82	25	4	6	7	44	2	49	7	0	1	10	.091	0	0-0	0	7.06	6.75
4 ML YEARS		115	47	0	17	362.2	1585	381	205	184	51	8	18	15	134	3	220	11	2	12	17	.414	0	2-3	4	4.68	4.57

Carlos Ruiz

Bats: R Throws: R Pos: C-118; PH-7   Ht: 5'10" Wt: 216 Born: 1/22/1979 Age: 32

Year Team	Lg	G	AB	H	2B	3B	HR	(Hm	Rd)	TB	R	RBI	RC	TBB	IBB	SO	HBP	SH	SF	SB	CS	SB%	GDP	Avg	OBP	Slg
2010 LV*	AAA	1	2	0	0	0	0	(-	-)	0	0	0	0	1	0	1	0	0	0	0	0	-	0	.000	.333	.000
2010 Lakwd*	A	2	8	4	2	0	0	(-	-)	6	1	1	2	0	0	2	0	0	0	0	0	-	0	.500	.500	.750
2006 Phi	NL	27	69	18	1	1	3	(2	1)	30	5	10	10	5	2	8	1	2	1	0	0	-	3	.261	.316	.435
2007 Phi	NL	115	374	97	29	2	6	(4	2)	148	42	54	49	42	10	49	5	5	3	6	1	.86	17	.259	.340	.396
2008 Phi	NL	117	320	70	14	0	4	(2	2)	96	47	31	28	44	6	38	4	4	1	2	3	.33	14	.219	.320	.300
2009 Phi	NL	107	322	82	26	1	9	(5	4)	137	32	43	49	47	8	39	4	4	2	3	2	.60	8	.255	.355	.425
2010 Phi	NL	121	371	112	28	1	8	(3	5)	166	43	53	62	55	13	54	6	0	1	0	1	.00	8	.302	.400	.447
Postseason		32	99	30	7	1	3	(2	1)	48	15	13	21	19	1	6	1	0	0	3	0	1.00	2	.303	.420	.485
5 ML YEARS		487	1456	379	98	5	30	(16	14)	577	169	191	198	193	39	188	20	15	8	10	6	.63	50	.260	.353	.396

Randy Ruiz

Bats: R Throws: R Pos: DH-8; 1B-3; PH-2   Ht: 6'3" Wt: 250 Born: 10/19/1977 Age: 33

Year Team	Lg	G	AB	H	2B	3B	HR	(Hm	Rd)	TB	R	RBI	RC	TBB	IBB	SO	HBP	SH	SF	SB	CS	SB%	GDP	Avg	OBP	Slg
2008 Min	AL	22	62	17	2	0	1	(1	0)	22	13	7	11	6	1	21	0	0	0	0	0	-	1	.274	.338	.355
2009 Tor	AL	33	115	36	7	0	10	(3	7)	73	25	17	18	10	0	35	4	0	1	1	1	.50	6	.313	.385	.635
2010 Tor	AL	13	40	6	2	0	1	(1	0)	11	3	1	0	0	0	11	0	0	0	1	0	1.00	0	.150	.150	.275
3 ML YEARS		68	217	59	11	0	12	(4	8)	106	41	25	29	16	1	67	4	0	1	2	1	.67	7	.272	.332	.488

Dan Runzler

Pitches: L **Bats:** L **Pos:** RP-41   **Ht:** 6'4" **Wt:** 233 **Born:** 3/30/1985 **Age:** 26

		HOW MUCH HE PITCHED						WHAT HE GAVE UP													THE RESULTS						
Year	Team	Lg	G	GS	CG	GF	IP	BFP	H	R	ER	HR	SH	SF	HB	TBB	IBB	SO	WP	Bk	W	L	Pct	Sh	Sv-Op Hld	ERC	ERA
2007	Giants	R	15	0	0	9	18.1	77	15	8	7	1	4	1	4	6	0	24	4	0	1	2	.333	0	4- - -	3.39	3.44
2007	SlmKzr	A-	1	0	0	0	1.0	7	2	1	1	0	0	0	0	2	0	1	0	0	0		-	0	0- - -	16.69	9.00
2008	Augsta	A	20	0	0	10	24.2	117	25	18	15	2	2	1	2	19	1	26	3	2	0	1	.000	0	0- - -	5.75	5.47
2008	SlmKzr	A-	27	0	0	2	30.0	127	19	8	7	1	2	0	1	21	0	43	4	0	0	1	.000	0	0- - -	2.93	2.10
2009	Augsta	A	19	0	0	17	26.1	103	8	2	2	0	0	0	4	13	0	45	5	0	1	1	.500	0	11- - -	1.15	0.68
2009	SnJos	A+	19	0	0	12	21.1	81	8	3	2	1	0	0	0	4	0	26	0	0	1	0	1.000	0	5- - -	0.64	0.84
2009	Conn	AA	7	0	0	3	9.1	40	5	1	1	1	2	1	1	7	1	11	0	0	3	0	1.000	0	1- - -	3.18	0.96
2009	Fresno	AAA	2	0	0	0	2.0	7	2	0	0	0	0	0	0	0	0	1	0	0	0	0	-	0	0- - -	2.31	0.00
2010	Giants	R	1	1	0	0	2.0	6	0	0	0	0	0	0	0	0	0	4	0	0	0	0	-	0	0- - -	0.00	0.00
2010	SnJos	A+	1	1	0	0	1.0	3	0	0	0	0	0	0	0	0	0	2	0	0	0	0	-	0	0- - -	0.00	0.00
2010	Fresno	AAA	6	0	0	1	7.0	31	8	4	3	0	0	0	0	4	1	5	0	0	0	1	.000	0	0- - -	4.72	3.86
2009	SF	NL	11	0	0	0	8.2	38	6	1	1	1	0	0	1	5	0	11	0	0	0	0	-	0	0-0 2	3.54	1.04
2010	SF	NL	41	0	0	7	32.2	144	29	12	11	1	4	0	1	20	3	37	2	0	3	0	1.000	0	0-0 5	3.74	3.03
	2 ML YEARS		52	0	0	7	41.1	182	35	13	12	2	4	0	2	25	3	48	2	0	3	0	1.000	0	0-0 7	3.70	2.61

Josh Rupe

Pitches: R **Bats:** R **Pos:** RP-11   **Ht:** 6'2" **Wt:** 215 **Born:** 8/18/1982 **Age:** 28

		HOW MUCH HE PITCHED						WHAT HE GAVE UP													THE RESULTS						
Year	Team	Lg	G	GS	CG	GF	IP	BFP	H	R	ER	HR	SH	SF	HB	TBB	IBB	SO	WP	Bk	W	L	Pct	Sh	Sv-Op Hld	ERC	ERA
2010	Omha*	AAA	40	0	0	32	52.1	230	49	19	17	5	2	0	5	22	5	49	11	1	2	4	.333	0	10- - -	4.04	2.92
2005	Tex	AL	4	1	0	1	9.2	39	7	4	3	0	1	0	2	4	0	6	1	0	1	0	1.000	0	0-0 -	2.91	2.79
2006	Tex	AL	16	0	0	3	29.0	126	33	11	11	2	1	0	1	9	0	14	2	0	0	1	.000	0	0-1 1	4.45	3.41
2008	Tex	AL	46	0	0	10	89.1	392	93	52	51	8	2	7	10	46	3	53	3	0	3	1	.750	0	0 2 2	5.30	5.14
2009	Tex	AL	4	0	0	2	4.2	31	12	8	8	2	0	0	0	5	0	2	0	0	0	0	-	0	0-0 0	21.74	15.43
2010	KC	AL	11	0	0	1	9.2	49	14	6	6	1	1	0	0	7	0	8	1	0	1	1	.500	0	0-0 5	8.22	5.59
	5 ML YEARS		81	1	0	17	142.1	637	159	81	79	13	5	7	13	71	3	83	7	0	5	3	.625	0	0-3 8	5.58	5.00

Adam Russell

Pitches: R **Bats:** R **Pos:** RP-12   **Ht:** 6'8" **Wt:** 255 **Born:** 4/14/1983 **Age:** 28

		HOW MUCH HE PITCHED						WHAT HE GAVE UP													THE RESULTS						
Year	Team	Lg	G	GS	CG	GF	IP	BFP	H	R	ER	HR	SH	SF	HB	TBB	IBB	SO	WP	Bk	W	L	Pct	Sh	Sv-Op Hld	ERC	ERA
2010	Portlnd*	AAA	50	0	0	31	51.2	244	50	30	28	4	2	0	3	32	3	51	4	0	4	9	.308	0	14- - -	5.58	4.88
2008	CWS	AL	22	0	0	16	26.0	118	30	15	15	1	2	1	2	10	1	22	3	0	0	1	1.000	0	0-0 0	4.63	5.19
2009	SD	NL	15	0	0	1	12.1	61	13	6	5	0	0	0	0	11	0	14	0	0	3	1	.750	0	0-0 4	5.38	3.65
2010	SD	NL	12	0	0	3	15.2	63	14	8	7	0	2	1	0	5	0	18	1	0	0	0	-	0	0-0 0	2.63	4.02
	3 ML YEARS		49	0	0	20	54.0	242	57	29	27	1	4	2	2	26	1	54	4	0	7	1	.875	0	0-0 4	4.20	4.50

James Russell

Pitches: L **Bats:** L **Pos:** RP-57   **Ht:** 6'4" **Wt:** 200 **Born:** 1/8/1986 **Age:** 25

		HOW MUCH HE PITCHED						WHAT HE GAVE UP													THE RESULTS						
Year	Team	Lg	G	GS	CG	GF	IP	BFP	H	R	ER	HR	SH	SF	HB	TBB	IBB	SO	WP	Bk	W	L	Pct	Sh	Sv-Op Hld	ERC	ERA
2007	Cubs	R	1	1	0	0	2.0	6	0	0	0	0	0	0	0	0	0	2	0	0	0	0	-	0	0- - -	0.00	0.00
2007	Peorla	A	2	2	0	0	7.0	26	3	0	0	0	0	0	0	4	0	9	0	0	0	0	-	0	0- - -	1.45	0.00
2008	Dytona	A+	8	8	0	0	41.0	163	36	18	16	4	1	1	0	13	0	24	0	0	2	2	.500	0	0- - -	3.22	3.51
2008	Tenn	AA	10	7	0	0	86.1	390	111	64	61	18	2	5	6	25	0	62	4	0	4	8	.333	0	0- - -	6.47	6.36
2009	Tenn	AA	11	5	0	0	37.0	161	45	24	21	5	1	0	1	9	0	26	3	0	2	3	.400	0	0- - -	5.10	5.11
2009	Iowa	AAA	26	7	0	3	65.2	287	71	25	25	6	3	1	0	19	1	46	2	0	3	3	.500	0	0- - -	3.91	3.43
2010	Iowa	AAA	5	0	0	0	11.0	47	11	7	7	5	0	0	1	4	0	10	0	0	0	0	-	0	0- - -	7.04	5.73
2010	ChC	NL	57	0	0	11	49.0	219	55	37	27	11	3	4	4	11	0	42	2	0	1	1	.500	0	0-2 8	5.12	4.96

Kevin Russo

Bats: R **Throws:** R **Pos:** 3B-16; LF-11; PR-5; 2B-2   RUE-soe   **Ht:** 5'11" **Wt:** 190 **Born:** 7/8/1984 **Age:** 26

					BATTING															BASERUNNING				AVERAGES		
Year	Team	Lg	G	AB	H	2B	3B	HR	(Hm Rd)	TB	R	RBI	RC	TBB	IBB	SO	HBP	SH	SF	SB	CS	SB%	GDP	Avg	OBP	Slg
2006	Yanks	R	45	150	41	10	0	3	(- -)	60	23	23	26	20	1	18	8	1	2	6	2	.75	1	.273	.383	.400
2007	Tampa	A+	109	385	108	22	3	2	(- -)	142	47	45	47	15	0	66	5	3	6	19	6	.76	6	.281	.311	.369
2008	Trntn	AA	70	263	82	17	3	2	(- -)	111	45	33	42	22	1	41	2	3	3	8	3	.73	4	.312	.366	.422
2009	S-WB	AAA	90	353	115	18	2	5	(- -)	152	51	31	63	42	2	55	3	3	5	13	7	.65	5	.326	.397	.431
2010	S-WB	AAA	81	332	86	16	2	1	(- -)	109	41	24	39	28	0	65	9	1	0	9	4	.69	1	.259	.333	.328
2010	NYY	AL	31	49	9	2	0	0	(0 0)	11	5	4	1	3	0	9	1	1	0	1	0	1.00	0	.184	.245	.224

Rusty Ryal

Bats: R **Throws:** R **Pos:** PH-55; LF-36; 1B-24; 3B-8; DH-1; PR-1   **Ht:** 6'2" **Wt:** 200 **Born:** 3/16/1983 **Age:** 28

					BATTING															BASERUNNING				AVERAGES		
Year	Team	Lg	G	AB	H	2B	3B	HR	(Hm Rd)	TB	R	RBI	RC	TBB	IBB	SO	HBP	SH	SF	SB	CS	SB%	GDP	Avg	OBP	Slg
2006	Mcoula	R+	72	294	98	22	4	6	(- -)	146	59	46	58	14	1	47	15	1	2	11	3	.79	7	.333	.391	.497
2006	Lancst	A+	97	350	97	17	6	11	(- -)	159	53	42	54	23	1	78	12	1	1	8	8	.50	15	.277	.342	.454
2007	Visalia	A+	70	276	83	15	3	11	(- -)	137	46	46	47	16	0	47	8	0	2	2	4	.33	8	.301	.354	.496
2007	Mobile	AA	47	168	40	6	2	6	(- -)	68	18	21	22	8	1	42	5	5	1	4	3	.57	4	.238	.291	.405
2008	Mobile	AA	128	460	126	22	4	16	(- -)	204	65	66	70	35	2	96	9	0	5	4	4	.50	8	.274	.334	.443

						BATTING																BASERUNNING					AVERAGES		
Year	Team	Lg	G	AB	H	2B	3B	HR	(Hm	Rd)	TB	R	RBI	RC	TBB	IBB	SO	HBP	SH	SF		SB	CS	SB%	GDP		Avg	OBP	Slg
2009	Reno	AAA	103	404	117	33	6	17	(-	-)	213	65	70	74	33	0	94	4	2	3		5	3	.63	13		.290	.347	.527
2009	Ari	NL	30	59	16	6	2	3	(2	1)	35	11	9	10	6	1	21	2	0	1		0	0	-	0		.271	.353	.593
2010	Ari	NL	104	207	54	7	1	3	(1	2)	72	19	11	16	8	0	67	6	1	0		0	3	.00	3		.261	.308	.348
	2 ML YEARS		134	266	70	13	3	6	(3	3)	107	30	20	26	14	1	88	8	1	1		0	3	.00	3		.263	.318	.402

Brendan Ryan

Bats: R **Throws:** R **Pos:** SS-139; PH-4; PR-2   **Ht:** 6'2" **Wt:** 195 **Born:** 3/26/1982 **Age:** 29

						BATTING																BASERUNNING					AVERAGES		
Year	Team	Lg	G	AB	H	2B	3B	HR	(Hm	Rd)	TB	R	RBI	RC	TBB	IBB	SO	HBP	SH	SF		SB	CS	SB%	GDP		Avg	OBP	Slg
2007	StL	NL	67	180	52	9	0	4	(2	2)	73	30	12	21	15	0	19	1	3	0		7	0	1.00	3		.289	.347	.406
2008	StL	NL	80	197	48	9	0	0	(0	0)	57	30	10	12	16	0	31	2	3	0		7	2	.78	4		.244	.307	.289
2009	StL	NL	129	390	114	19	7	3	(1	2)	156	55	37	48	24	3	56	6	6	3		14	7	.67	9		.292	.340	.400
2010	StL	NL	139	439	98	19	3	2	(0	2)	129	50	36	37	33	5	60	2	9	3		11	4	.73	6		.223	.279	.294
	Postseason		3	12	1	1	0	0	(0	0)	2	0	0	0	0	0	2	0	0	0		0	0	-	0		.083	.083	.167
	4 ML YEARS		415	1206	312	56	10	9	(3	6)	415	165	95	118	88	8	166	11	21	6		39	13	.75	22		.259	.314	.344

Michael Ryan

Bats: L **Throws:** R **Pos:** LF-11; PH-9; 1B-4   **Ht:** 5'11" **Wt:** 220 **Born:** 7/6/1977 **Age:** 33

						BATTING																BASERUNNING					AVERAGES		
Year	Team	Lg	G	AB	H	2B	3B	HR	(Hm	Rd)	TB	R	RBI	RC	TBB	IBB	SO	HBP	SH	SF		SB	CS	SB%	GDP		Avg	OBP	Slg
2010	Salt Lk*	AAA	81	307	85	22	4	4	(-	-)	127	48	37	43	24	0	46	0	2	5		2	0	1.00	8		.277	.324	.414
2002	Min	AL	7	11	1	0	0	0	(0	0)	1	3	0	0	0	0	2	0	0	0		0	0	-	0		.091	.091	.091
2003	Min	AL	27	61	24	7	0	5	(4	1)	46	13	13	15	6	0	12	0	0	1		2	1	.67	4		.393	.441	.754
2004	Min	AL	36	71	17	2	1	0	(0	0)	21	9	7	5	4	1	16	0	0	0		1	1	.50	2		.239	.280	.296
2005	Min	AL	57	117	27	5	0	2	(1	1)	38	7	13	10	9	1	22	0	4	1		1	2	.33	5		.231	.283	.325
2010	LAA	AL	22	39	8	4	0	0	(0	0)	12	3	2	2	1	0	5	0	0	1		0	0	-	0		.205	.220	.308
	Postseason		1	1	0	0	0	0	(0	0)	0	0	0	0	0	0	1	0	0	0		0	0	-	0		.000	.000	.000
	5 ML YEARS		149	299	77	18	1	7	(5	2)	118	35	35	32	20	2	57	0	4	3		4	4	.50	11		.258	.301	.395

Marc Rzepczynski

Pitches: L **Bats:** L **Pos:** SP-12; RP-2   zepp-CHINN-ski   **Ht:** 6'3" **Wt:** 205 **Born:** 8/29/1985 **Age:** 25

			HOW MUCH HE PITCHED						WHAT HE GAVE UP											THE RESULTS							
Year	Team	Lg	G	GS	CG	GF	IP	BFP	H	R	ER	HR	SH	SF	HB	TBB	IBB	SO	WP	Bk	W	L	Pct	Sh	Sv-Op	Hld	ERC	ERA
2007	Auburn	A-	11	7	0	0	45.2	183	33	21	14	2	1	4	1	17	0	49	0	0	5	0	1.000	0	0- -	-	2.29	2.76
2008	Lansng	A	22	22	0	0	121.0	491	100	41	38	2	6	1	8	42	1	124	11	0	7	6	.538	0	0- -	-	2.71	2.83
2009	NHam	AA	14	14	0	0	76.2	344	80	38	25	1	2	1	4	36	1	88	1	0	7	5	.583	0	0- -	-	4.09	2.93
2009	LsVgs	AAA	2	2	0	0	11.1	45	7	1	1	0	0	0	0	4	0	16	1	0	2	0	1.000	0	0- -	-	1.46	0.79
2010	LsVgs	AAA	12	12	0	0	67.0	304	81	49	45	10	4	0	4	27	0	61	3	1	5	5	.500	0	0- -	-	5.99	6.04
2009	Tor	AL	11	11	0	0	61.1	261	51	27	25	7	2	1	1	30	0	60	4	1	2	4	.333	0	0-0	-	3.65	3.67
2010	Tor	AL	14	12	0	0	63.2	287	72	37	35	8	1	2	5	30	1	57	4	1	4	4	.500	0	0-0	2	5.71	4.95
	2 ML YEARS		25	23	0	0	125.0	548	123	64	60	15	3	3	6	60	1	117	8	2	6	8	.429	0	0-0	2	4.67	4.32

CC Sabathia

Pitches: L **Bats:** L **Pos:** SP-34   **Ht:** 6'7" **Wt:** 290 **Born:** 7/21/1980 **Age:** 30

			HOW MUCH HE PITCHED						WHAT HE GAVE UP											THE RESULTS							
Year	Team	Lg	G	GS	CG	GF	IP	BFP	H	R	ER	HR	SH	SF	HB	TBB	IBB	SO	WP	Bk	W	L	Pct	Sh	Sv-Op	Hld	ERC	ERA
2001	Cle	AL	33	33	0	0	180.1	763	149	93	88	19	3	5	7	95	1	171	7	3	17	5	.773	0	0-0	0	3.86	4.39
2002	Cle	AL	33	33	2	0	210.0	891	198	109	102	17	5	10	1	88	2	149	6	3	13	11	.542	0	0-0	0	3.74	4.37
2003	Cle	AL	30	30	2	0	197.2	832	190	85	79	19	10	4	6	66	3	141	4	2	13	9	.591	1	0-0	0	3.70	3.60
2004	Cle	AL	30	30	1	0	188.0	787	176	90	86	20	3	6	7	72	3	139	1	1	11	10	.524	1	0-0	0	3.91	4.12
2005	Cle	AL	31	31	1	0	196.2	823	185	92	88	19	6	3	7	62	1	161	7	0	15	10	.600	0	0-0	0	3.55	4.03
2006	Cle	AL	28	28	6	0	192.2	802	182	83	69	17	8	5	7	44	3	172	3	0	12	11	.522	2	0-0	0	3.13	3.22
2007	Cle	AL	34	34	4	0	241.0	975	238	94	86	20	6	6	8	37	1	209	1	0	19	7	.731	1	0-0	0	3.12	3.21
2008	2 Tms		35	35	10	0	253.0	1023	223	85	76	19	9	6	7	59	1	251	2	2	17	10	.630	5	0-0	0	2.78	2.70
2009	NYY	AL	34	34	2	0	230.0	938	197	96	86	18	4	9	9	67	7	197	5	0	19	8	.704	1	0-0	0	2.89	3.37
2010	NYY	AL	34	34	2	0	237.2	970	209	92	84	20	5	8	7	74	6	197	8	1	21	7	.750	0	0-0	0	3.11	3.18
08	Cle	AL	18	18	3	0	122.1	507	117	54	52	13	3	3	3	34	1	123	1	2	6	8	.429	2	0-0	0	3.52	3.83
08	Mil	NL	17	17	7	0	130.2	516	106	31	24	6	6	3	4	25	0	128	1	0	11	2	.846	3	0-0	0	2.13	1.65
	Postseason		10	10	0	0	61.1	270	61	31	30	8	1	0	4	31	6	56	2	0	5	4	.556	0	0-0	0	4.86	4.40
	10 ML YEARS		322	322	30	0	2127.0	8804	1947	919	844	188	59	62	66	664	28	1787	44	12	157	88	.641	11	0-0	0	3.33	3.57

Takashi Saito

Pitches: R **Bats:** R **Pos:** RP-56   SYE-toe   **Ht:** 6'2" **Wt:** 200 **Born:** 2/14/1970 **Age:** 41

			HOW MUCH HE PITCHED						WHAT HE GAVE UP											THE RESULTS							
Year	Team	Lg	G	GS	CG	GF	IP	BFP	H	R	ER	HR	SH	SF	HB	TBB	IBB	SO	WP	Bk	W	L	Pct	Sh	Sv-Op	Hld	ERC	ERA
2010	Gwnntt*	AAA	1	1	0	0	1.0	3	1	0	0	0	0	0	0	0	0	1	0	0	0	0	-	0	0- -	-	2.79	0.00
2006	LAD	NL	72	0	0	48	78.1	303	48	19	18	3	3	4	2	23	3	107	2	0	6	2	.750	0	24-26	7	1.52	2.07
2007	LAD	NL	63	0	0	55	64.1	234	33	10	10	5	0	0	3	13	0	78	0	0	2	1	.667	0	39-43	1	1.28	1.40
2008	LAD	NL	45	0	0	35	47.0	197	40	14	13	1	0	2	2	16	3	60	1	0	4	4	.500	0	18-22	0	2.57	2.49
2009	Bos	AL	56	0	0	30	55.2	240	50	16	15	6	1	4	5	25	2	52	1	0	3	3	.500	0	2-4	3	4.08	2.43
2010	Atl	NL	56	0	0	14	54.0	221	41	20	17	4	2	0	0	17	2	69	2	0	2	3	.400	0	1-2	17	2.24	2.83
	Postseason		4	0	0	2	3.2	15	5	2	2	0	0	0	0	0	0	4	0	0	0	0	-	0	0-0	0	4.01	4.91
	5 ML YEARS		292	0	0	182	299.1	1195	212	79	73	19	6	10	12	94	10	366	6	0	17	13	.567	0	84-97	28	2.14	2.19

Fernando Salas

Pitches: R **Bats:** R **Pos:** RP-27   **Ht:** 6'2" **Wt:** 200 **Born:** 5/30/1985 **Age:** 26

Year	Team	Lg	G	GS	CG	GF	IP	BFP	H	R	ER	HR	SH	SF	HB	TBB	IBB	SO	WP	Bk	W	L	Pct	Sh	Sv-Op	Hld	ERC	ERA
2007	PlmBh	A+	16	4	0	2	39.1	166	39	25	23	12	1	2	3	10	1	25	2	0	2	3	.400	0	0- -		5.15	5.26
2008	Sprgfld	AA	60	0	0	37	74.0	300	65	31	30	12	4	2	2	16	2	100	2	2	7	3	.700	0	25- -		3.17	3.65
2009	Memp	AAA	24	0	0	10	27.0	113	22	12	11	4	1	1	1	10	0	24	3	0	3	2	.600	0	0- -		3.38	3.67
2009	Sprgfld	AA	10	0	0	1	11.1	45	10	5	4	0	0	2	0	2	0	7	1	0	1	0	1.000	0	0- -		2.04	3.18
2009	Cards	R	1	0	0	1	1.0	3	0	0	0	0	0	0	0	0	0	1	0	0	0	0	-	0	0- -		0.00	0.00
2010	Memp	AAA	34	0	0	24	35.2	137	26	15	15	2	1	1	1	9	0	44	2	0	1	0	1.000	0	19- -		2.06	3.79
2010	StL	NL	27	0	0	11	30.2	133	28	13	12	4	1	1	0	15	2	29	2	0	0	0	-	0	0-1		4.03	3.52

Oscar Salazar

Bats: R **Throws:** R **Pos:** PH-52; LF-17; 1B-7; RF-7; 2B-6; DH-2; 3B-1   **Ht:** 6'0" **Wt:** 195 **Born:** 6/27/1978 **Age:** 33

								BATTING												BASERUNNING				AVERAGES		
Year	Team	Lg	G	AB	H	2B	3B	HR	(Hm | Rd)	TB	R	RBI	RC	TBB	IBB	SO	HBP	SH	SF	SB	CS	SB%	GDP	Avg	OBP	Slg
2010	Lk Els*		7	25	7	1	0	1	(- | -)	11	3	4	3	1	0	5	0	0	1	0	0	-	1	.280	.296	.440
2002	Det	AL	8	21	4	1	0	1	(0 | 1)	8	2	3	3	1	0	2	0	1	0	0	0	-	0	.190	.227	.381
2008	Bal	AL	34	81	23	3	0	5	(4 | 1)	41	13	15	14	12	0	13	0	0	1	0	1	.00	1	.284	.372	.506
2009	2 Tms		72	139	42	8	2	5	(3 | 2)	69	16	25	26	14	1	20	0	0	1	0	0	-	8	.302	.364	.496
2010	SD	NL	85	131	31	4	0	3	(1 | 2)	44	19	19	17	16	1	23	0	0	1	1	2	.33	4	.237	.318	.336
09	Bal	AL	17	31	13	0	0	2	(2 | 0)	19	4	6	9	2	0	4	0	0	0	0	0	-	2	.419	.455	.613
09	SD	AL	55	108	29	8	2	3	(1 | 2)	50	12	19	17	12	1	16	0	0	1	0	0	-	6	.269	.339	.463
	4 ML YEARS		199	372	100	16	2	14	(8 | 6)	162	50	62	60	43	2	58	0	1	3	1	3	.25	13	.269	.342	.435

Chris Sale

Pitches: L **Bats:** L **Pos:** RP-21   SAIL   **Ht:** 6'5" **Wt:** 170 **Born:** 3/30/1989 **Age:** 22

Year	Team	Lg	G	GS	CG	GF	IP	BFP	H	R	ER	HR	SH	SF	HB	TBB	IBB	SO	WP	Bk	W	L	Pct	Sh	Sv-Op	Hld	ERC	ERA
2010	WinSa	A+	4	0	0	0	4.0	17	3	2	1	0	0	0	0	2	0	4	0	0	0	0	-	0	0- -		2.40	2.25
2010	Charltt	AAA	7	0	0	1	6.1	26	3	2	2	2	0	0	0	4	0	15	0	0	0	0	-	0	0- -		3.45	2.84
2010	CWS	AL	21	0	0	8	23.1	92	15	5	5	2	1	0	0	10	0	32	1	0	2	1	.667	0	4-4	2	2.30	1.93

Jarrod Saltalamacchia

Bats: B **Throws:** R **Pos:** C-7; PH-5; DH-2; 1B-1   salt-ah-luh-MOCK-ee-ah   **Ht:** 6'4" **Wt:** 235 **Born:** 5/2/1985 **Age:** 26

								BATTING												BASERUNNING				AVERAGES		
Year	Team	Lg	G	AB	H	2B	3B	HR	(Hm | Rd)	TB	R	RBI	RC	TBB	IBB	SO	HBP	SH	SF	SB	CS	SB%	GDP	Avg	OBP	Slg
2010	OKCity*	AAA	63	238	58	11	2	11	(- | -)	106	37	33	36	25	2	60	5	0	2	1	0	1.00	5	.244	.326	.445
2010	Pwtckt*	AAA	9	36	10	5	0	1	(- | -)	18	5	6	6	4	1	9	0	0	0	0	0	-	0	.278	.350	.500
2007	2 Tms		93	308	82	13	1	11	(6 | 5)	130	39	33	32	19	1	75	1	0	1	0	0	-	8	.266	.310	.422
2008	Tex	AL	61	198	50	13	0	3	(2 | 1)	72	27	26	29	31	1	74	0	0	1	0	2	.00	1	.253	.352	.364
2009	Tex	AL	84	283	66	12	0	9	(6 | 3)	105	34	34	30	22	1	97	1	3	1	0	2	.00	3	.233	.290	.371
2010	2 Tms	AL	12	24	4	3	0	0	(0 | 0)	7	2	2	3	6	0	5	0	0	0	0	0	-	0	.167	.333	.292
07	Atl	NL	47	141	40	6	0	4	(4 | 0)	58	11	12	13	10	1	28	1	0	1	0	0	-	4	.284	.333	.411
07	Tex	NL	46	167	42	7	1	7	(2 | 5)	72	28	21	19	9	0	47	0	0	0	0	0	-	4	.251	.290	.431
10	Tex	AL	2	5	1	0	0	0	(0 | 0)	1	0	1	1	0	0	1	0	0	0	0	0	-	0	.200	.200	.200
10	Bos	AL	10	19	3	3	0	0	(0 | 0)	6	2	1	2	6	0	4	0	0	0	0	0	-	0	.158	.360	.316
	4 ML YEARS		250	813	202	41	1	23	(14 | 9)	314	102	95	94	78	3	251	2	3	3	0	4	.00	12	.248	.315	.386

Jeff Samardzija

Pitches: R **Bats:** R **Pos:** RP-4; SP-3   suh-MAHR-jah   **Ht:** 6'5" **Wt:** 225 **Born:** 1/23/1985 **Age:** 26

Year	Team	Lg	G	GS	CG	GF	IP	BFP	H	R	ER	HR	SH	SF	HB	TBB	IBB	SO	WP	Bk	W	L	Pct	Sh	Sv-Op	Hld	ERC	ERA
2010	Iowa*	AAA	35	14	0	5	111.1	482	86	62	54	9	6	2	2	67	3	102	5	1	11	3	.786	0	0- -		3.47	4.37
2008	ChC	NL	26	0	0	6	27.2	124	24	12	7	0	1	1	1	15	2	25	2	0	1	0	1.000	0	1-4	3	3.08	2.28
2009	ChC	NL	20	2	0	7	34.2	161	46	29	29	7	4	1	1	15	1	21	2	0	1	3	.250	0	0-0	0	7.13	7.53
2010	ChC	NL	7	3	0	0	19.1	100	21	22	18	4	0	0	2	20	1	9	1	0	2	2	.500	0	0-0	0	8.45	8.38
	Postseason		1	0	0	0	1.0	4	2	1	1	0	0	0	0	0	0	0	0	0	0	0	-	0	0-0	0	9.49	9.00
	3 ML YEARS		53	5	0	13	81.2	385	91	63	54	11	5	2	4	50	4	55	5	0	4	5	.444	0	1-4	3	5.94	5.95

Chris Sampson

Pitches: R **Bats:** R **Pos:** RP-35   **Ht:** 6'1" **Wt:** 195 **Born:** 5/23/1978 **Age:** 33

Year	Team	Lg	G	GS	CG	GF	IP	BFP	H	R	ER	HR	SH	SF	HB	TBB	IBB	SO	WP	Bk	W	L	Pct	Sh	Sv-Op	Hld	ERC	ERA
2010	CpChr*	AA	1	1	0	0	1.0	4	0	0	0	0	0	0	0	1	0	1	0	0	0	0	-	0	0- -		0.95	0.00
2010	RdRck*	AAA	13	0	0	6	15.1	63	17	5	4	1	2	0	0	4	0	11	0	0	1	2	.333	0	0- -		4.07	2.35
2006	Hou	NL	12	3	0	0	34.0	130	25	10	8	1	1	1	1	5	1	15	0	0	2	1	.667	0	0-0	0	1.84	2.12
2007	Hou	NL	24	19	0	2	121.2	522	138	64	62	20	6	6	7	30	2	51	3	0	7	8	.467	0	0-0	0	4.96	4.59
2008	Hou	NL	54	11	0	6	117.1	478	118	60	55	8	3	5	3	23	5	61	0	0	6	4	.600	0	0-2	11	3.21	4.22
2009	Hou	NL	49	0	0	9	55.1	248	66	34	31	2	1	1	0	21	6	33	2	1	4	2	.667	0	3-6	15	4.40	5.04
2010	Hou	NL	35	0	0	9	30.1	139	43	22	20	7	2	0	1	8	0	16	1	0	1	0	1.000	0	0-2	5	7.23	5.93
	5 ML YEARS		174	33	0	26	358.2	1517	390	190	176	40	13	13	12	87	14	176	6	1	20	15	.571	0	3-10	31	4.14	4.42

Alex Sanabia

Pitches: R **Bats:** R **Pos:** SP-12; RP-3   suh-NAH-bee-ah   **Ht:** 6'2" **Wt:** 165 **Born:** 9/8/1988 **Age:** 22

				HOW MUCH HE PITCHED				WHAT HE GAVE UP											THE RESULTS					
Year	Team	Lg	G	GS	CG	GF	IP	BFP	H	R	ER	HR	SH	SF	HB	TBB	IBB	SO	WP	Bk	W	L	Pct	Sh	Sv-Op	Hld	ERC	ERA
2006	Mrlns	R	11	0	0	1	16.2	70	10	7	6	0	3	0	1	7	0	16	4	0	3	1	.750	0	0--	-	1.63	3.24
2007	Jmstwn	A-	15	15	1	0	66.2	296	73	45	38	5	2	1	7	17	0	69	13	2	2	6	.250	0	0--	-	4.18	5.13
2008	Grnsbr	A	19	19	0	0	96.2	420	106	60	53	11	1	3	2	25	0	75	6	1	5	5	.500	0	0--	-	4.17	4.93
2009	Jupiter	A+	19	18	0	0	104.1	434	89	45	40	6	2	3	7	36	0	68	7	0	9	5	.643	0	0--	-	3.06	3.45
2010	Jaxnvl	AA	14	14	0	0	84.1	325	59	22	19	2	1	1	3	16	0	65	2	0	5	1	.833	0	0--	-	1.56	2.03
2010	NewOr	AAA	2	2	0	0	14.0	52	9	2	2	0	0	0	0	3	0	5	0	0	1	0	1.000	0	0--	-	1.31	1.29
2010	Fla	NL	15	12	0	0	72.1	307	74	32	30	6	3	1	3	16	2	47	0	0	5	3	.625	0	0-0	0	3.47	3.73

Brian Sanches

Pitches: R **Bats:** R **Pos:** RP-61   **Ht:** 6'0" **Wt:** 189 **Born:** 8/8/1978 **Age:** 32

				HOW MUCH HE PITCHED				WHAT HE GAVE UP											THE RESULTS					
Year	Team	Lg	G	GS	CG	GF	IP	BFP	H	R	ER	HR	SH	SF	HB	TBB	IBB	SO	WP	Bk	W	L	Pct	Sh	Sv-Op	Hld	ERC	ERA
2010	Jupiter*	A+	3	1	0	0	4.0	15	2	1	1	0	0	0	1	0	0	6	1	0	0	1	.000	0	0--	-	0.94	2.25
2006	Phi	NL	18	0	0	5	21.1	98	23	14	14	5	0	0	1	13	3	22	0	1	0	0	-	0	0-0	0	6.18	5.91
2007	Phi	NL	12	0	0	4	14.2	68	13	11	9	6	1	0	1	12	2	9	1	0	1	1	.500	0	0-0	1	7.73	5.52
2008	Was	NL	12	0	0	2	11.0	54	16	10	9	2	0	1	1	5	0	10	0	0	2	0	1.000	0	0-1	0	8.15	7.36
2009	Fla	NL	47	0	0	7	56.1	248	50	18	16	5	3	0	6	26	8	51	5	0	4	2	.667	0	0-3	9	3.75	2.56
2010	Fla	NL	61	0	0	14	63.2	254	43	20	16	7	1	3	1	27	0	54	5	0	2	2	.500	0	0-1	12	2.63	2.26
	5 ML YEARS		150	0	0	32	167.0	722	145	73	64	25	5	4	9	83	13	146	11	1	9	5	.643	0	0-5	22	4.17	3.45

Angel Sanchez

Bats: R **Throws:** R **Pos:** SS-58; 2B-8; PH-2   ahn-HELL   **Ht:** 6'2" **Wt:** 190 **Born:** 9/20/1983 **Age:** 27

									BATTING													BASERUNNING				AVERAGES		
Year	Team	Lg	G	AB	H	2B	3B	HR	(Hm	Rd)	TB	R	RBI	RC	TBB	IBB	SO	HBP	SH	SF	SB	CS	SB%	GDP	Avg	OBP	Slg
2001	Royals	R	30	95	23	4	0	0	(-	-)	27	10	6	8	6	0	28	0	2	0	3	1	.75	2	.242	.287	.284
2002	Royals	R	49	175	44	4	0	0	(-	-)	48	21	12	16	10	0	24	4	5	3	9	2	.82	1	.251	.302	.274
2003	Burlgtn	A	106	408	110	8	1	2	(-	-)	126	54	35	44	28	0	52	4	6	3	14	5	.74	10	.270	.321	.309
2004	Burlgtn	A	90	337	85	12	1	2	(-	-)	105	34	24	33	15	0	47	9	9	2	16	7	.70	5	.252	.300	.312
2005	Hi Dsrt	A+	133	585	183	33	4	5	(-	-)	239	102	70	88	39	0	54	3	7	5	10	5	.67	11	.313	.356	.409
2006	Wichta	AA	133	542	153	24	1	4	(-	-)	191	105	57	68	44	0	63	7	11	8	8	9	.47	12	.282	.339	.352
2008	NWArk	AA	63	241	63	7	2	1	(-	-)	77	28	23	28	28	0	40	1	5	2	4	5	.44	5	.261	.338	.320
2008	Omha	AAA	38	131	29	7	1	1	(-	-)	41	13	13	11	9	0	20	0	5	0	1	1	.50	6	.221	.271	.313
2009	LsVgs	AAA	126	449	138	29	4	6	(-	-)	193	67	60	72	39	2	67	4	10	4	1	2	.33	12	.307	.365	.430
2010	Pwtckt	AAA	62	223	61	10	1	0	(-	-)	73	26	17	28	24	0	30	2	2	1	6	1	.86	9	.274	.348	.327
2006	KC	AL	8	27	6	0	0	0	(0	0)	6	2	1	0	0	0	4	0	0	1	0	0	-	0	.222	.214	.222
2010	2 Tms		66	253	70	9	4	0	(0	0)	87	30	25	29	11	0	45	2	6	0	0	1	.00	8	.277	.312	.344
10	Bos	AL	1	3	0	0	0	0	(0	0)	0	0	0	0	0	0	0	0	0	0	0	0	-	0	.000	.000	.000
10	Hou	NL	65	250	70	9	4	0	(0	0)	87	30	25	29	11	0	45	2	6	0	0	1	.00	8	.280	.316	.348
	2 ML YEARS		74	280	76	9	4	0	(0	0)	93	32	26	29	11	0	49	2	6	1	0	1	.00	8	.271	.303	.332

Anibal Sanchez

Pitches: R **Bats:** R **Pos:** SP-32   ah-NEE-bahl   **Ht:** 6'0" **Wt:** 207 **Born:** 2/27/1984 **Age:** 27

				HOW MUCH HE PITCHED				WHAT HE GAVE UP											THE RESULTS					
Year	Team	Lg	G	GS	CG	GF	IP	BFP	H	R	ER	HR	SH	SF	HB	TBB	IBB	SO	WP	Bk	W	L	Pct	Sh	Sv-Op	Hld	ERC	ERA
2006	Fla	NL	18	17	2	0	114.1	469	90	39	36	9	3	4	4	46	1	72	4	1	10	3	.769	0	0-0	0	2.96	2.83
2007	Fla	NL	6	6	0	0	30.0	151	43	17	16	3	2	2	2	19	1	14	3	0	2	1	.667	0	0-0	0	7.90	4.80
2008	Fla	NL	10	10	0	0	51.2	241	54	35	32	7	4	2	6	27	2	50	1	0	2	5	.286	0	0-0	0	5.40	5.57
2009	Fla	NL	16	16	0	0	86.0	383	84	39	37	10	2	2	1	46	5	71	0	1	4	8	.333	0	0-0	0	4.51	3.87
2010	Fla	NL	32	32	1	0	195.0	841	192	89	77	10	13	3	7	70	5	157	7	0	13	12	.520	1	0-0	0	3.56	3.55
	5 ML YEARS		82	81	3	0	477.0	2085	463	219	198	39	24	10	20	208	14	364	15	2	31	29	.517	2	0-0	0	4.02	3.74

Freddy Sanchez

Bats: R **Throws:** R **Pos:** 2B-109; PH-3   **Ht:** 6'0" **Wt:** 200 **Born:** 12/21/1977 **Age:** 33

									BATTING													BASERUNNING				AVERAGES		
Year	Team	Lg	G	AB	H	2B	3B	HR	(Hm	Rd)	TB	R	RBI	RC	TBB	IBB	SO	HBP	SH	SF	SB	CS	SB%	GDP	Avg	OBP	Slg
2010	SnJos*	A+	3	9	6	5	0	0	(-	-)	11	6	4	6	3	0	0	1	0	0	0	0	-	0	.667	.769	1.222
2010	Fresno*	AAA	4	11	3	0	0	0	(-	-)	3	1	0	1	2	0	3	0	0	0	0	1	.00	1	.273	.385	.273
2002	Bos	AL	12	16	3	0	0	0	(0	0)	3	3	2	1	2	0	3	0	0	0	0	0	-	0	.188	.278	.188
2003	Bos	AL	20	34	8	2	0	0	(0	0)	10	6	2	1	0	0	8	0	0	0	0	0	-	0	.235	.235	.294
2004	Pit	NL	9	19	3	0	0	0	(0	0)	3	2	2	2	0	0	3	0	1	0	0	0	-	0	.158	.158	.158
2005	Pit	NL	132	453	132	26	4	5	(3	2)	181	54	35	57	27	1	36	5	4	3	2	2	.50	6	.291	.336	.400
2006	Pit	NL	157	582	200	**53**	2	6	(2	4)	275	85	85	101	31	6	52	7	3	9	3	2	.60	12	**.344**	.378	.473
2007	Pit	NL	147	602	183	42	4	11	(5	6)	266	77	81	94	32	2	76	8	2	9	0	1	.00	13	.304	.343	.442
2008	Pit	NL	145	569	154	26	2	9	(1	8)	211	75	52	61	21	1	63	4	8	6	0	1	.00	13	.271	.298	.371
2009	2 Tms	NL	111	457	134	29	3	7	(3	4)	190	56	41	59	22	4	76	2	4	4	5	1	.83	12	.293	.326	.416
2010	SF	NL	111	431	126	22	1	7	(1	6)	171	55	47	59	32	1	68	3	8	5	3	1	.75	9	.292	.342	.397
09	Pit	NL	86	355	105	28	3	6	(3	3)	157	45	34	49	20	4	60	2	2	3	5	1	.83	9	.296	.334	.442
09	SF	NL	25	102	29	1	0	1	(0	1)	33	11	7	10	2	0	16	0	2	1	0	0	-	3	.284	.295	.324
	9 ML YEARS		844	3163	943	200	16	45	(15	30)	1310	413	347	435	167	15	385	29	30	36	13	8	.62	65	.298	.335	.414

Gaby Sanchez

Bats: R **Throws:** R **Pos:** 1B-149; PH-2   GABB-ee   **Ht:** 6'1" **Wt:** 216 **Born:** 9/2/1983 **Age:** 27

								BATTING													BASERUNNING				AVERAGES		
Year	Team	Lg	G	AB	H	2B	3B	HR	(Hm	Rd)	TB	R	RBI	RC	TBB	IBB	SO	HBP	SH	SF	SB	CS	SB%	GDP	Avg	OBP	Slg
2008	Fla	NL	5	8	3	2	0	0	(0	0)	5	0	1	2	0	0	2	0	0	0	0	0	-	0	.375	.375	.625
2009	Fla	NL	21	21	5	0	0	2	(2	0)	11	2	3	3	2	0	3	0	0	0	0	0	-	1	.238	.304	.524
2010	Fla	NL	151	572	156	37	3	19	(7	12)	256	72	85	88	57	2	101	5	3	6	5	0	1.00	14	.273	.341	.448
	3 ML YEARS		177	601	164	39	3	21	(9	12)	272	74	89	93	59	2	106	5	3	6	5	0	1.00	15	.273	.340	.453

Jonathan Sanchez

Pitches: L **Bats:** L **Pos:** SP-33; RP-1   **Ht:** 6'0" **Wt:** 194 **Born:** 11/19/1982 **Age:** 28

				HOW MUCH HE PITCHED						WHAT HE GAVE UP										THE RESULTS						
Year	Team	Lg	G	GS	CG	GF	IP	BFP	H	R	ER	HR	SH	SF	HB	TBB	IBB	SO	WP	Bk	W	L	Pct	Sh	Sv-Op	Hld	ERC	ERA
2006	SF	NL	27	4	0	4	40.0	185	39	26	22	2	0	2	4	23	0	33	2	0	3	1	.750	0	0-0	5	4.54	4.95
2007	SF	NL	33	4	0	8	52.0	238	57	34	34	8	2	2	5	28	1	62	4	0	1	5	.167	0	0-0	2	6.06	5.88
2008	SF	NL	29	29	0	0	158.0	695	154	90	88	14	9	5	7	75	1	157	7	0	9	12	.429	0	0-0	0	4.31	5.01
2009	SF	NL	32	29	1	2	163.1	710	135	82	77	19	3	1	6	88	5	177	11	0	8	12	.400	1	0-0	1	3.83	4.24
2010	SF	NL	34	33	0	0	193.1	812	142	74	66	21	7	4	9	96	4	205	15	1	13	9	.591	0	0-0	1	3.21	3.07
	5 ML YEARS		155	99	1	14	606.2	2640	527	306	287	64	21	14	31	310	11	634	39	1	34	39	.466	1	0-0	9	3.98	4.26

Romulo Sanchez

Pitches: R **Bats:** R **Pos:** RP-2   **Ht:** 6'5" **Wt:** 260 **Born:** 4/28/1984 **Age:** 27

				HOW MUCH HE PITCHED						WHAT HE GAVE UP										THE RESULTS						
Year	Team	Lg	G	GS	CG	GF	IP	BFP	H	R	ER	HR	SH	SF	HB	TBB	IBB	SO	WP	Bk	W	L	Pct	Sh	Sv-Op	Hld	ERC	ERA
2010	S-WB*	AAA	31	14	0	6	104.1	444	88	50	46	8	2	2	1	59	0	96	6	1	10	8	.556	0	0--	-	3.79	3.97
2007	Pit	NL	16	0	0	7	18.0	73	16	10	10	2	0	1	1	8	0	11	1	0	1	0	1.000	0	0-0	2	4.20	5.00
2008	Pit	NL	10	0	0	5	13.1	57	14	6	6	0	0	2	1	6	0	3	4	0	0	0	-	0	1-1	0	4.30	4.05
2010	NYY	AL	2	0	0	1	4.1	17	1	0	0	0	0	0	0	3	0	5	0	0	0	0	-	0	0-0	0	1.03	0.00
	3 ML YEARS		28	0	0	13	35.2	147	31	16	16	2	0	3	2	17	0	19	5	0	1	0	1.000	0	1-1	2	3.74	4.04

Pablo Sandoval

Bats: R **Throws:** R **Pos:** 3B-143, 1B-11; PH-4   **Ht:** 5'11" **Wt:** 262 **Born:** 8/11/1986 **Age:** 24

								BATTING													BASERUNNING				AVERAGES		
Year	Team	Lg	G	AB	H	2B	3B	HR	(Hm	Rd)	TB	R	RBI	RC	TBB	IBB	SO	HBP	SH	SF	SB	CS	SB%	GDP	Avg	OBP	Slg
2008	SF	NL	41	145	50	10	1	3	(1	2)	71	24	24	24	4	1	14	1	0	4	0	0	-	6	.345	.357	.490
2009	SF	NL	153	572	189	44	5	25	(13	12)	318	79	90	113	52	13	83	4	0	5	5	5	.50	10	.330	.387	.556
2010	SF	NL	152	563	151	34	3	13	(9	4)	230	61	63	55	47	12	81	1	0	5	3	2	.60	26	.268	.323	.409
	3 ML YEARS		346	1280	390	88	9	41	(23	18)	619	164	177	192	103	26	178	6	0	14	8	7	.53	42	.305	.356	.484

Carlos Santana

Bats: B **Throws:** R **Pos:** C-40; DH-5; PH-1   **Ht:** 5'11" **Wt:** 190 **Born:** 4/8/1986 **Age:** 25

								BATTING													BASERUNNING				AVERAGES		
Year	Team	Lg	G	AB	H	2B	3B	HR	(Hm	Rd)	TB	R	RBI	RC	TBB	IBB	SO	HBP	SH	SF	SB	CS	SB%	GDP	Avg	OBP	Slg
2005	Ddgrs	R	32	78	23	4	1	1	(-	-)	32	14	14	14	16	1	8	1	0	2	0	2	.00	2	.295	.412	.410
2006	VeroB	A+	54	198	53	10	2	3	(-	-)	76	16	18	26	23	0	43	1	0	1	0	3	.00	6	.268	.345	.384
2006	Ogden	R+	37	132	40	5	1	7	(-	-)	68	31	27	31	30	0	19	1	0	5	4	0	1.00	5	.303	.423	.515
2007	Gt Lks	A	86	292	65	20	1	7	(-	-)	108	32	36	37	40	0	45	1	1	0	5	3	.63	9	.223	.318	.370
2008	InldEm	A+	99	350	113	34	4	14	(-	-)	197	88	96	86	69	4	59	4	2	9	7	4	.64	7	.323	.431	.503
2008	Knstn	A+	29	105	37	5	1	6	(-	-)	62	34	19	28	20	0	24	0	0	1	3	0	1.00	1	.352	.452	.590
2008	Akron	AA	2	8	1	0	0	1	(-	-)	4	3	2	0	0	0	2	0	0	0	0	0	-	0	.125	.125	.500
2009	Akron	AA	131	429	124	30	2	23	(-	-)	227	97	97	98	90	7	84	7	0	10	2	2	.50	10	.289	.412	.529
2010	Clmbs	AAA	57	196	62	14	1	13	(-	-)	117	39	51	53	45	4	39	3	0	2	6	0	1.00	5	.316	.447	.597
2010	Cle	AL	46	150	39	13	0	6	(2	4)	70	23	22	25	37	2	29	1	0	4	3	0	1.00	3	.260	.401	.467

Ervin Santana

Pitches: R **Bats:** R **Pos:** SP-33   **Ht:** 6'2" **Wt:** 185 **Born:** 12/12/1982 **Age:** 28

				HOW MUCH HE PITCHED						WHAT HE GAVE UP										THE RESULTS						
Year	Team	Lg	G	GS	CG	GF	IP	BFP	H	R	ER	HR	SH	SF	HB	TBB	IBB	SO	WP	Bk	W	L	Pct	Sh	Sv-Op	Hld	ERC	ERA
2005	LAA	AL	23	23	1	0	133.2	583	139	73	69	17	1	4	8	47	2	99	4	0	12	8	.600	0	0-0	0	4.51	4.65
2006	LAA	AL	33	33	0	0	204.0	846	181	106	97	21	4	10	11	70	2	141	10	2	16	8	.667	0	0-0	0	3.51	4.28
2007	LAA	AL	28	26	0	1	150.0	675	174	103	96	26	3	2	8	58	3	126	7	0	7	14	.333	0	0-0	0	5.69	5.76
2008	LAA	AL	32	32	2	0	219.0	897	198	89	85	23	3	5	8	47	2	214	5	1	16	7	.696	1	0-0	0	3.00	3.49
2009	LAA	AL	24	23	2	0	139.2	614	159	83	78	24	2	1	10	47	4	107	4	0	8	8	.500	2	0-0	1	5.47	5.03
2010	LAA	AL	33	33	4	0	222.2	954	221	104	97	27	8	8	12	73	2	169	11	1	17	10	.630	1	0-0	0	4.10	3.92
	Postseason		8	2	0	3	22.2	101	21	17	14	4	1	1	3	9	1	14	0	0	2	2	.500	0	0-0	0	4.55	5.56
	6 ML YEARS		173	170	9	1	1069.0	4569	1072	558	522	138	21	30	57	342	15	856	41	4	76	55	.580	5	0-0	1	4.18	4.39

Johan Santana

Pitches: L **Bats:** L **Pos:** SP-29   YOE-hahn   **Ht:** 6'0" **Wt:** 208 **Born:** 3/13/1979 **Age:** 32

				HOW MUCH HE PITCHED						WHAT HE GAVE UP										THE RESULTS						
Year	Team	Lg	G	GS	CG	GF	IP	BFP	H	R	ER	HR	SH	SF	HB	TBB	IBB	SO	WP	Bk	W	L	Pct	Sh	Sv-Op	Hld	ERC	ERA
2000	Min	AL	30	5	0	9	86.0	398	102	64	62	11	1	3	2	54	0	64	5	2	2	3	.400	0	0-0	0	6.59	6.49
2001	Min	AL	15	4	0	3	43.2	195	50	25	23	6	2	3	3	16	0	28	3	0	1	0	1.000	0	0-0	0	5.36	4.74
2002	Min	AL	27	14	0	2	108.1	452	84	41	36	7	3	3	4	49	0	137	15	2	8	6	.571	0	1-1	3	2.86	2.99
2003	Min	AL	45	18	0	7	158.1	644	127	56	54	17	2	4	3	47	1	169	6	2	12	3	.800	0	0-0	5	2.73	3.07

			HOW MUCH HE PITCHED						WHAT HE GAVE UP										THE RESULTS							
Year	Team	Lg	G	GS	CG	GF	IP	BFP	H	R	ER	HR	SH	SF	HB	TBB	IBB	SO	WP	Bk	W	L	Pct	Sh	Sv-Op	Hld	ERC	ERA
2004	Min	AL	34	34	1	0	228.0	881	156	70	66	24	3	3	9	54	0	265	7	0	20	6	.769	1	0-0	0	2.07	2.61
2005	Min	AL	33	33	3	0	231.2	910	180	77	74	22	6	2	1	45	1	238	8	0	16	7	.696	2	0-0	0	2.14	2.87
2006	Min	AL	34	34	1	0	233.2	923	186	79	72	24	6	4	4	47	0	245	4	1	19	6	.760	1	0-0	0	2.36	2.77
2007	Min	AL	33	33	1	0	219.0	878	183	88	81	33	4	4	4	52	0	235	7	1	15	13	.536	1	0-0	0	2.98	3.33
2008	NYM	NL	34	34	3	0	234.1	964	206	74	66	23	9	1	4	63	5	206	9	2	16	7	.696	2	0-0	0	2.93	2.53
2009	NYM	NL	25	25	0	0	166.2	701	156	67	58	20	8	3	3	46	1	146	1	0	13	9	.591	0	0-0	0	3.37	3.13
2010	NYM	NL	29	29	4	0	199.0	817	179	67	66	16	10	5	2	55	2	144	2	2	11	9	.550	2	0-0	0	2.96	2.98
	Postseason		11	5	0	0	34.0	143	35	15	15	2	0	0	1	10	1	32	2	0	1	3	.250	0	0-0	1	3.66	3.97
	11 ML YEARS		339	263	13	23	1908.2	7763	1609	708	658	203	54	35	36	528	12	1877	67	12	133	69	.658	8	1-1	8	2.87	3.10

Ramon Santiago

Bats: B Throws: R Pos: SS-85; 2B-25; PH-23; DH-2

Ht: 5'11" Wt: 175 Born: 8/31/1979 Age: 31

			BATTING																		BASERUNNING				AVERAGES		
Year	Team	Lg	G	AB	H	2B	3B	HR	(Hm	Rd)	TB	R	RBI	RC	TBB	IBB	SO	HBP	SH	SF		SB	CS	SB%	GDP	Avg	OBP	Slg
2002	Det	AL	65	222	54	5	5	4	(3	1)	81	33	20	23	13	0	48	8	4	2		8	5	.62	2	.243	.306	.365
2003	Det	AL	141	444	100	18	1	2	(1	1)	126	41	29	38	33	0	66	10	18	2		10	4	.71	9	.225	.292	.284
2004	Sea	AL	19	39	7	1	0	0	(0	0)	8	8	2	1	3	0	3	1	2	0		0	0	-	1	.179	.256	.205
2005	Sea	AL	8	8	1	0	0	0	(0	0)	1	2	0	1	1	0	2	3	1	0		0	0	-	0	.125	.417	.125
2006	Det	AL	43	80	18	1	1	0	(0	0)	21	9	3	3	1	0	14	1	4	0		2	0	1.00	1	.225	.244	.263
2007	Det	AL	32	67	19	5	1	0	(0	0)	26	10	7	11	1	0	10	3	3	0		3	0	1.00	0	.284	.324	.388
2008	Det	AL	58	124	35	6	2	4	(4	0)	57	30	18	26	22	0	17	5	5	0		1	0	1.00	1	.282	.411	.460
2009	Det	AL	93	262	70	6	2	7	(4	3)	101	29	35	33	17	1	57	4	10	3		1	2	.33	3	.267	.318	.385
2010	Det	AL	112	320	84	9	1	3	(3	0)	104	38	22	37	30	0	56	7	8	2		2	2	.50	6	.263	.337	.325
	Postseason		6	12	1	0	0	0	(0	0)	1	0	0	0	1	0	2	0	1	0		0	0	-	0	.083	.154	.083
	9 ML YEARS		571	1566	388	51	13	20	(15	5)	525	200	136	173	121	1	273	42	55	9		27	13	.68	23	.248	.317	.335

Sergio Santos

Pitches: R Bats: R Pos: RP-56

Ht: 6'3" Wt: 210 Born: 7/4/1983 Age: 27

			HOW MUCH HE PITCHED						WHAT HE GAVE UP											THE RESULTS						
Year	Team	Lg	G	GS	CG	GF	IP	BFP	H	R	ER	HR	SH	SF	HB	TBB	IBB	SO	WP	Bk	W	L	Pct	Sh	Sv-Op	Hld	ERC	ERA
2009	Knapol	A	8	0	0	3	7.1	31	8	6	6	0	0	0	0	3	0	10	2	0	0	1	.000	0	0--	-	4.06	7.36
2009	WinSa	A+	8	0	0	0	7.2	35	9	5	5	2	0	0	1	3	0	7	1	0	0	0	-	0	0--	-	6.93	5.87
2009	Brham	AA	7	0	0	0	8.2	51	15	10	10	0	0	1	3	7	0	6	1	0	0	1	.000	0	0--	-	10.82	10.38
2009	Charltt	AAA	3	0	0	0	5.0	27	5	5	5	0	1	0	0	7	0	7	1	0	0	1	.000	0	0--	-	7.04	9.00
2010	CWS	AL	56	0	0	13	51.2	235	53	18	17	2	2	1	3	26	3	56	8	0	2	2	.500	0	1-3	14	4.22	2.96

Dane Sardinha

Bats: R Throws: R Pos: C-12; PH-4

sar-DEEN-yah

Ht: 6'0" Wt: 215 Born: 4/8/1979 Age: 32

			BATTING																		BASERUNNING				AVERAGES		
Year	Team	Lg	G	AB	H	2B	3B	HR	(Hm	Rd)	TB	R	RBI	RC	TBB	IBB	SO	HBP	SH	SF		SB	CS	SB%	GDP	Avg	OBP	Slg
2010	LV*	AAA	67	222	46	8	0	5	(-	-)	69	24	24	18	13	0	68	4	1	2		0	0	-	3	.207	.261	.311
2003	Cin	NL	1	2	0	0	0	0	(0	0)	0	0	0	0	0	0	1	0	0	0		0	0	-	0	.000	.000	.000
2005	Cin	NL	1	3	0	0	0	0	(0	0)	0	0	0	0	0	0	1	0	0	0		0	0	-	0	.000	.000	.000
2008	Det	AL	17	44	7	0	1	0	(0	0)	9	2	3	3	4	0	11	0	1	0		0	0	-	1	.159	.229	.205
2009	Det	AL	12	31	3	1	0	0	(0	0)	4	1	3	0	0	0	16	0	1	2		0	0	-	1	.097	.091	.129
2010	Phi	NL	13	39	8	2	0	3	(1	2)	19	5	8	3	1	0	13	0	0	0		0	0	-	1	.205	.225	.487
	5 ML YEARS		44	119	18	3	1	3	(1	2)	32	8	14	6	5	0	42	0	2	2		0	0	-	3	.151	.183	.269

Joe Saunders

Pitches: L Bats: L Pos: SP-33

Ht: 6'3" Wt: 210 Born: 6/16/1981 Age: 30

			HOW MUCH HE PITCHED						WHAT HE GAVE UP											THE RESULTS						
Year	Team	Lg	G	GS	CG	GF	IP	BFP	H	R	ER	HR	SH	SF	HB	TBB	IBB	SO	WP	Bk	W	L	Pct	Sh	Sv-Op	Hld	ERC	ERA
2005	LAA	AL	2	2	0	0	9.1	41	10	8	8	3	0	0	0	4	0	4	1	0	0	0	-	0	0-0	0	6.27	7.71
2006	LAA	AL	13	13	0	0	70.2	302	71	42	37	6	1	2	1	29	1	51	2	1	7	3	.700	0	0-0	0	4.13	4.71
2007	LAA	AL	18	18	0	0	107.1	473	129	56	53	11	0	5	1	34	1	69	3	0	8	5	.615	0	0-0	0	4.96	4.44
2008	LAA	AL	31	31	1	0	198.0	807	187	82	75	21	5	2	6	53	2	103	3	0	17	7	.708	1	0-0	0	3.49	3.41
2009	LAA	AL	31	31	1	0	186.0	805	202	102	95	29	6	4	6	64	2	101	5	1	16	7	.696	1	0-0	0	4.91	4.60
2010	2 Tms		33	33	3	0	203.1	880	232	120	101	25	6	8	5	64	1	114	6	0	9	17	.346	1	0-0	0	4.86	4.47
10	LAA	AL	20	20	2	0	120.2	522	135	70	62	14	5	5	1	45	1	64	3	0	6	10	.375	1	0-0	0	4.88	4.62
10	Ari	NL	13	13	1	0	82.2	358	97	50	39	11	1	3	4	19	0	50	3	0	3	7	.300	0	0-0	0	4.84	4.25
	Postseason		3	3	0	0	15.0	71	18	9	9	1	1	0	1	10	0	7	0	0	0	1	.000	0	0-0	0	6.48	5.40
	6 ML YEARS		128	128	5	0	774.2	3308	831	410	369	95	18	21	19	248	7	442	20	2	57	39	.594	2	0-0	0	4.48	4.29

Michael Saunders

Bats: L Throws: R Pos: LF-77; CF-14; PR-7; DH-4; PH-4

Ht: 6'4" Wt: 212 Born: 11/19/1986 Age: 24

			BATTING																		BASERUNNING				AVERAGES		
Year	Team	Lg	G	AB	H	2B	3B	HR	(Hm	Rd)	TB	R	RBI	RC	TBB	IBB	SO	HBP	SH	SF		SB	CS	SB%	GDP	Avg	OBP	Slg
2005	Everett	A-	56	196	53	13	3	7	(-	-)	93	24	39	32	27	1	74	2	1	2		2	7	.22	1	.270	.361	.474
2006	Wisc	A	104	359	86	10	8	4	(-	-)	124	48	39	46	48	2	103	2	2	5		22	7	.76	2	.240	.329	.345
2007	Hi Dsrt	A+	108	431	129	25	4	14	(-	-)	204	91	77	84	60	2	116	8	5	3		27	10	.73	7	.299	.392	.473
2007	WTenn	AA	15	52	15	1	2	1	(-	-)	23	8	7	8	7	0	20	0	1	0		1	0	1.00	1	.288	.373	.442
2008	WTenn	AA	67	248	72	18	3	8	(-	-)	120	46	30	46	30	2	66	4	6	1		12	6	.67	3	.290	.375	.484
2008	Tacom	AAA	24	95	23	4	1	3	(-	-)	38	12	16	11	9	0	30	0	1	0		1	2	.33	0	.242	.308	.400
2009	Tacom	AAA	64	248	77	15	2	13	(-	-)	135	58	32	50	25	0	48	3	4	2		6	3	.67	2	.310	.378	.544

Year	Team	Lg	G	AB	H	2B	3B	HR	(Hm	Rd)	TB	R	RBI	RC	TBB	IBB	SO	HBP	SH	SF	SB	CS	SB%	GDP	Avg	OBP	Slg
									BATTING												**BASERUNNING**				**AVERAGES**		
2010	Tacom	AAA	21	80	16	1	0	0	(-	-)	17	6	5	6	11	0	17	0	1	1	4	0	1.00	2	.200	.293	.213
2009	Sea	AL	46	122	27	1	3	0	(0	0)	34	13	4	8	6	0	40	0	1	0	4	1	.80	1	.221	.258	.279
2010	Sea	AL	100	289	61	11	2	10	(5	5)	106	29	33	31	35	0	84	0	2	1	6	3	.67	1	.211	.295	.367
	2 ML YEARS		146	411	88	12	5	10	(5	5)	140	42	37	39	41	0	124	0	3	1	10	4	.71	2	.214	.285	.341

Jay Sborz

Pitches: R Bats: R Pos: RP-1
SBORES
Ht: 6'4" **Wt:** 210 **Born:** 1/24/1985 **Age:** 26

				HOW MUCH HE PITCHED							**WHAT HE GAVE UP**										**THE RESULTS**					
Year	Team	Lg	G	GS	CG	GF	IP	BFP	H	R	ER	HR	SH	SF	HB	TBB	IBB	SO	WP	Bk	W	L	Pct	Sh	Sv-Op Hld	ERC	ERA
2003	Tigers	R	8	7	0	0	26.0	117	20	18	14	2	0	1	4	14	0	35	6	0	0	2	.000	0	0-- -	3.63	4.85
2004	Tigers	R	12	12	0	0	60.1	275	52	32	30	9	1	1	3	44	0	62	8	1	1	4	.200	0	0-- -	5.15	4.48
2005	WMich	A	21	0	0	10	27.1	147	36	27	24	1	2	9	23	0	31	8	0	1	1	.500	0	0-- -	9.04	7.90
2005	Oneont	A-	9	7	0	0	29.0	139	24	15	14	1	3	0	2	27	0	25	9	0	1	3	.250	0	0-- -	4.82	4.34
2006	WMich	A	3	0	0	1	5.0	27	8	3	3	0	0	1	0	4	0	4	2	0	1	0	1.000	0	0-- -	8.38	5.40
2007	Tigers	R	5	2	0	0	10.1	41	9	4	3	0	0	0	1	2	0	8	0	0	1	1	.500	0	0-- -	2.43	2.61
2007	Oneont	A-	5	1	0	0	10.0	46	10	10	6	1	1	1	0	6	0	9	1	0	0	0	-	0	0-- -	4.75	5.40
2008	Lkland	A+	40	0	0	19	53.1	231	44	22	17	3	2	2	5	25	0	48	3	0	3	2	.600	0	7-- -	3.40	2.87
2009	Erie	AA	14	1	0	5	25.0	102	16	9	7	3	0	1	1	13	0	29	4	0	1	2	.333	0	0-- -	2.94	2.52
2009	Lkland	A+	1	0	0	0	2.2	10	1	0	0	1	0	1	0	1	0	1	0	0	0	0	-	0	0-- -	0.85	0.00
2009	Toledo	AAA	2	0	0	1	4.0	14	1	1	1	1	0	0	0	1	0	5	0	0	1	0	1.000	0	0-- -	0.99	2.25
2010	Toledo	AAA	43	0	0	38	43.2	196	38	24	23	8	2	1	5	24	2	42	3	0	1	6	.143	0	19-- -	4.87	4.74
2010	Det	AL	1	0	0	0	0.2	7	3	5	5	0	0	0	2	0	0	1	0	0	0	0	-	0	0-0 0	42.55	67.50

Bobby Scales

Bats: B Throws: R Pos: 3B-7; PH-3
Ht: 6'0" **Wt:** 185 **Born:** 10/4/1977 **Age:** 33

									BATTING												**BASERUNNING**				**AVERAGES**		
Year	Team	Lg	G	AB	H	2B	3B	HR	(Hm	Rd)	TB	R	RBI	RC	TBB	IBB	SO	HBP	SH	SF	SB	CS	SB%	GDP	Avg	OBP	Slg
1999	Idaho	R+	44	169	49	14	6	1	(-	-)	78	47	30	33	29	0	31	2	2	1	7	2	.78	6	.290	.398	.462
2000	FtWyn	A	81	269	76	14	3	1	(-	-)	99	42	27	41	39	5	52	3	3	0	14	7	.67	9	.283	.379	.368
2001	Lk Els	A+	98	362	98	24	4	5	(-	-)	145	46	42	58	44	1	70	10	1	0	20	7	.74	7	.271	.365	.401
2002	Mobile	AA	97	250	69	13	3	4	(-	-)	100	40	27	37	27	1	56	4	1	0	6	3	.67	3	.276	.356	.400
2003	Mobile	AA	100	301	85	22	3	3	(-	-)	122	41	37	41	36	2	63	2	1	2	8	2	.80	4	.282	.361	.405
2003	Portlnd	AAA	11	43	16	7	0	0	(-	-)	23	8	2	11	7	0	6	0	0	0	3	0	1.00	0	.372	.460	.535
2004	Portlnd	AAA	73	213	50	13	2	1	(-	-)	70	26	24	20	27	2	56	5	0	0	3	1	.75	8	.235	.335	.329
2004	Mobile	AA	20	68	18	6	0	0	(-	-)	24	12	5	11	13	2	15	3	0	0	2	0	1.00	0	.265	.405	.353
2005	Portlnd	AAA	120	376	104	19	2	14	(-	-)	169	50	61	66	53	0	98	6	0	1	9	4	.69	9	.277	.374	.449
2006	S-WB	AAA	105	356	104	22	7	7	(-	-)	161	46	44	62	44	3	99	3	6	5	3	3	.50	3	.292	.370	.452
2007	Pwtckt	AAA	122	432	127	28	8	11	(-	-)	204	64	57	80	50	4	94	8	3	6	14	3	.82	5	.294	.373	.472
2008	Iowa	AAA	121	387	124	20	2	15	(-	-)	193	94	59	81	59	1	90	5	4	2	7	5	.58	8	.320	.415	.499
2000	Iowa	AAA	91	306	85	15	1	5	(-	-)	117	41	39	47	46	0	61	5	1	2	8	8	.50	6	.278	.379	.382
2010	Iowa	AAA	119	373	100	33	3	10	(-	-)	169	68	53	73	72	4	77	10	3	4	7	3	.70	9	.268	.397	.453
2009	ChC	NL	51	124	30	8	2	3	(2	1)	51	15	15	14	11	1	32	2	0	1	0	0	-	5	.242	.312	.411
2010	ChC	NL	10	13	4	0	0	0	(0	0)	4	4	2	3	7	0	5	0	0	0	1	0	1.00	0	.308	.550	.308
	2 ML YEARS		61	137	34	8	2	3	(2	1)	55	19	17	17	18	1	37	2	0	1	1	0	1.00	5	.248	.342	.401

Max Scherzer

Pitches: R Bats: R Pos: SP-31
SHERR-zer
Ht: 6'3" **Wt:** 220 **Born:** 7/27/1984 **Age:** 26

							HOW MUCH HE PITCHED					**WHAT HE GAVE UP**									**THE RESULTS**					
Year	Team	Lg	G	GS	CG	GF	IP	BFP	H	R	ER	HR	SH	SF	HB	TBB	IBB	SO	WP	Bk	W	L	Pct	Sh	Sv-Op Hld	ERC	ERA
2010	Toledo*	AAA	2	2	0	0	15.0	52	4	1	1	0	1	1	0	2	0	17	0	0	2	0	1.000	0	0-- -	0.29	0.60
2008	Ari	NL	16	7	0	2	56.0	237	48	24	19	5	4	2	5	21	1	66	2	0	0	4	.000	0	0-0 0	3.45	3.05
2009	Ari	NL	30	30	0	0	170.1	741	166	94	78	20	5	6	10	63	1	174	5	1	9	11	.450	0	0-0 0	4.12	4.12
2010	Det	AL	31	31	0	0	195.2	800	174	84	76	20	5	5	7	70	1	184	8	0	12	11	.522	0	0-0 0	3.56	3.50
	3 ML YEARS		77	68	0	2	422.0	1778	388	202	173	45	14	13	22	154	3	424	15	1	21	26	.447	0	0-0 0	3.77	3.69

Nate Schierholtz

Bats: L Throws: R Pos: RF-109; PH-37; PR-15
SHEER-holtz
Ht: 6'1" **Wt:** 205 **Born:** 2/15/1984 **Age:** 27

									BATTING												**BASERUNNING**				**AVERAGES**		
Year	Team	Lg	G	AB	H	2B	3B	HR	(Hm	Rd)	TB	R	RBI	RC	TBB	IBB	SO	HBP	SH	SF	SB	CS	SB%	GDP	Avg	OBP	Slg
2007	SF	NL	39	112	34	5	3	0	(0	0)	45	9	10	14	2	0	19	1	0	2	3	1	.75	0	.304	.316	.402
2008	SF	NL	19	75	24	8	1	1	(1	0)	37	12	5	12	3	0	8	3	0	0	0	1	.00	1	.320	.370	.493
2009	SF	NL	116	285	76	19	2	5	(1	4)	114	33	29	35	16	3	58	1	0	6	3	1	.75	5	.267	.302	.400
2010	SF	NL	137	227	55	13	3	3	(0	3)	83	34	17	26	20	5	38	3	1	1	4	5	.44	3	.242	.311	.366
	4 ML YEARS		311	699	189	45	9	9	(2	7)	279	88	61	87	41	8	123	8	1	9	10	8	.56	9	.270	.314	.399

Daniel Schlereth

Pitches: L Bats: L Pos: RP-18
SHLARE-ith
Ht: 6'0" **Wt:** 198 **Born:** 5/9/1986 **Age:** 25

							HOW MUCH HE PITCHED					**WHAT HE GAVE UP**									**THE RESULTS**					
Year	Team	Lg	G	GS	CG	GF	IP	BFP	H	R	ER	HR	SH	SF	HB	TBB	IBB	SO	WP	Bk	W	L	Pct	Sh	Sv-Op Hld	ERC	ERA
2008	Msoula	R+	3	0	0	1	3.0	15	3	1	0	0	1	0	0	2	0	6	1	0	0	0	-	0	0-- -	3.91	0.00
2008	Sbend	A	7	0	0	0	9.0	33	3	2	2	0	0	0	0	4	0	14	1	0	1	0	1.000	0	0-- -	0.89	2.00
2009	Mobile	AA	21	0	0	11	26.2	109	14	3	3	1	3	2	1	16	0	39	3	0	0	0	-	0	4-- -	2.09	1.01
2009	Reno	AAA	1	0	0	0	1.0	6	1	0	0	0	0	0	0	1	0	1	0	0	0	0	-	0	0-- -	9.51	0.00

Year Team	Lg	G	GS	CG	GF	IP	BFP	H	R	ER	HR	SH	SF	HB	TBB	IBB	SO	WP	Bk	W	L	Pct	Sh	Sv-Op	Hld	ERC	ERA
2010 Toledo	AAA	38	0	0	7	49.1	220	40	17	13	0	1	0	2	34	2	60	4	0	1	3	.250	0	0--	-	3.46	2.37
2009 Ari	NL	21	0	0	4	18.1	86	15	13	12	1	2	0	1	15	1	22	4	0	1	4	.200	0	0-3	0	4.32	5.89
2010 Det	AL	18	0	0	6	18.2	87	20	7	6	2	1	1	1	10	3	19	1	0	2	0	1.000	0	1-2	1	4.89	2.89
2 ML YEARS		39	0	0	10	37.0	173	35	20	18	3	3	1	2	25	4	41	5	0	3	4	.429	0	1-5	1	4.61	4.38

Travis Schlichting

Pitches: R **Bats:** R **Pos:** RP-14   SHLICK-ting   **Ht:** 6'4" **Wt:** 186 **Born:** 10/19/1984 **Age:** 26

		HOW MUCH HE PITCHED						WHAT HE GAVE UP												THE RESULTS							
Year Team	Lg	G	GS	CG	GF	IP	BFP	H	R	ER	HR	SH	SF	HB	TBB	IBB	SO	WP	Bk	W	L	Pct	Sh	Sv-Op	Hld	ERC	ERA
2006 Angels	R	5	0	0	3	7.2	30	4	0	0	0	0	0	1	2	0	13	0	0	0	0	-	0	0--	-	1.26	0.00
2007 KC	IND	41	0	0	9	51.0	256	72	33	30	4	4	4	6	29	1	47	11	0	1	2	.333	0	0--	-	7.50	5.29
2008 Jaxnvl	AA	33	0	0	11	59.2	254	58	31	25	4	6	1	6	18	3	49	1	0	6	4	.600	0	0--	-	3.64	3.77
2009 Chatt	AA	9	0	0	1	13.2	56	7	5	1	1	0	1	0	7	0	12	1	0	1	0	1.000	0	1--	-	1.77	0.66
2009 Albq	AAA	13	0	0	3	12.2	54	8	3	2	0	2	0	1	8	0	7	1	0	1	0	1.000	0	0--	-	2.57	1.42
2009 Ddgrs	R	3	3	0	0	3.0	11	2	0	0	0	0	0	0	0	0	4	0	0	0	0	-	0	0--	-	0.91	0.00
2010 Albq	AAA	27	0	0	3	47.1	208	55	27	25	5	2	3	3	13	0	29	1	2	3	0	1.000	0	1--	-	4.80	4.75
2009 LAD	NL	2	0	0	1	2.2	15	1	2	1	1	0	1	0	5	0	2	1	0	0	0	-	0	0-0	0	8.03	3.38
2010 LAD	NL	14	0	0	6	22.2	98	20	9	9	0	1	1	0	10	2	14	1	0	1	0	1.000	0	0-0	0	2.70	3.57
2 ML YEARS		16	0	0	7	25.1	113	21	11	10	1	1	2	0	15	2	16	2	0	1	0	1.000	0	0-0	0	3.20	3.55

Brian Schlitter

Pitches: R **Bats:** R **Pos:** RP-7   **Ht:** 6'5" **Wt:** 235 **Born:** 12/21/1985 **Age:** 25

		HOW MUCH HE PITCHED						WHAT HE GAVE UP												THE RESULTS							
Year Team	Lg	G	GS	CG	GF	IP	BFP	H	R	ER	HR	SH	SF	HB	TBB	IBB	SO	WP	Bk	W	L	Pct	Sh	Sv-Op	Hld	ERC	ERA
2007 Wmspt	A-	1	0	0	1	2.0	10	2	0	0	0	0	0	0	0	0	1	0	0	0	0	-	0	1--	-	3.21	0.00
2007 Lakwd	A	16	0	0	8	23.2	100	27	13	10	2	0	0	0	6	0	21	1	0	0	1	.000	0	3--	-	4.26	3.80
2008 Clrwtr	A+	34	0	0	24	48.2	205	39	13	12	1	0	0	1	21	4	58	1	0	4	3	.571	0	6--	-	2.53	2.22
2008 Dytona	A+	7	0	0	5	8.1	35	9	2	2	0	0	0	0	3	0	9	1	0	1	0	1.000	0	3--	-	3.78	2.16
2009 Tenn	AA	59	0	0	47	61.2	267	62	36	30	8	3	1	1	24	3	51	2	0	1	7	.125	0	22--	-	4.25	4.38
2010 Iowa	AAA	37	0	0	23	45.2	200	44	18	16	3	1	1	1	21	0	42	2	0	2	1	.667	0	13--	-	3.91	3.15
2010 ChC	NL	7	0	0	3	8.0	48	18	11	11	2	0	0	1	5	1	7	0	0	0	1	.000	0	0-0	0	15.07	12.38

Konrad Schmidt

Bats: R **Throws:** R **Pos:** C-2; PH-2   **Ht:** 6'0" **Wt:** 225 **Born:** 8/2/1984 **Age:** 26

		BATTING														BASERUNNING				AVERAGES		
Year Team	Lg	G	AB	H	2B	3B	HR	(Hm | Rd)	TB	R	RBI	RC	TBB	IBB	SO	HBP	SH	SF	SB	CS	SB%	GDP	Avg	OBP	Slg
2007 Yakima	A-	45	164	41	10	0	6	(- | -)	69	19	24	20	4	0	38	6	0	1	1	0	1.00	6	.250	.291	.421
2008 Sbend	A	62	216	56	10	0	2	(- | -)	72	21	18	25	20	1	41	4	1	3	3	3	.50	11	.259	.329	.333
2008 Visalia	A+	40	152	50	10	1	1	(- | -)	65	21	19	23	3	1	26	4	0	1	0	0	-	2	.329	.356	.428
2009 Visalia	A+	106	411	125	28	1	9	(- | -)	182	54	50	67	30	1	75	7	0	3	0	3	.00	14	.304	.359	.443
2009 Reno	AAA	5	16	7	2	0	0	(- | -)	9	1	4	3	0	0	1	0	0	0	0	0	-	0	.438	.438	.563
2010 Mobile	AA	107	394	124	30	3	11	(- | -)	193	48	65	73	32	10	63	8	0	6	7	3	.70	10	.315	.373	.490
2010 Ari	NL	4	8	1	0	0	0	(0 | 0)	1	0	0	0	1	0	0	0	0	0	0	0	-	0	.125	.222	.125

Brian Schneider

Bats: L **Throws:** R **Pos:** C-46; PH-3   SHNY-derr   **Ht:** 6'1" **Wt:** 210 **Born:** 11/26/1976 **Age:** 34

		BATTING														BASERUNNING				AVERAGES		
Year Team	Lg	G	AB	H	2B	3B	HR	(Hm | Rd)	TB	R	RBI	RC	TBB	IBB	SO	HBP	SH	SF	SB	CS	SB%	GDP	Avg	OBP	Slg
2010 LV*	AAA	3	8	0	0	0	0	(- | -)	0	0	0	0	1	0	0	0	0	0	0	0	-	0	.000	.111	.000
2000 Mon	NL	45	115	27	6	0	0	(0 | 0)	33	6	11	8	7	2	24	0	0	1	0	1	.00	1	.235	.276	.287
2001 Mon	NL	27	41	13	3	0	1	(1 | 0)	19	4	6	8	6	1	3	0	0	1	0	0	-	0	.317	.396	.463
2002 Mon	NL	73	207	57	19	2	5	(3 | 2)	95	21	29	29	21	8	41	0	2	2	1	2	.33	7	.275	.339	.459
2003 Mon	NL	108	335	77	26	1	9	(9 | 0)	132	34	46	36	37	8	75	2	1	2	0	2	.00	12	.230	.309	.394
2004 Mon	NL	135	436	112	20	3	12	(5 | 7)	174	40	49	52	42	10	63	3	5	2	0	1	.00	8	.257	.325	.399
2005 Was	NL	116	369	99	20	1	10	(5 | 5)	151	38	44	48	29	7	48	6	2	2	1	0	1.00	10	.268	.330	.409
2006 Was	NL	124	410	105	18	0	4	(3 | 1)	135	30	55	45	38	10	67	2	2	3	2	2	.50	14	.256	.320	.329
2007 Was	NL	129	408	96	21	1	6	(2 | 4)	137	33	54	41	56	7	56	2	4	7	0	0	-	15	.235	.326	.336
2008 NYM	NL	110	335	86	10	0	9	(4 | 5)	123	30	38	36	42	9	53	1	4	2	0	0	-	11	.257	.339	.367
2009 NYM	NL	59	170	37	11	0	3	(3 | 0)	57	11	24	16	18	1	21	1	2	3	0	0	-	5	.218	.292	.335
2010 Phi	NL	47	125	30	4	1	4	(2 | 2)	48	17	15	24	19	2	25	1	2	0	0	0	-	3	.240	.345	.384
11 ML YEARS		973	2951	739	158	9	63	(37 | 26)	1104	264	371	336	315	65	476	18	24	25	4	8	.33	86	.250	.324	.374

Scott Schoeneweis

Pitches: L **Bats:** L **Pos:** RP-15   SHOWN-wise   **Ht:** 6'0" **Wt:** 190 **Born:** 10/2/1973 **Age:** 37

		HOW MUCH HE PITCHED						WHAT HE GAVE UP												THE RESULTS							
Year Team	Lg	G	GS	CG	GF	IP	BFP	H	R	ER	HR	SH	SF	HB	TBB	IBB	SO	WP	Bk	W	L	Pct	Sh	Sv-Op	Hld	ERC	ERA
1999 LAA	AL	31	0	0	6	39.1	175	47	27	24	4	0	1	0	14	1	22	1	0	1	1	.500	0	0-0	3	4.99	5.49
2000 LAA	AL	27	27	1	0	170.0	742	183	112	103	21	2	5	6	67	2	78	4	3	7	10	.412	1	0-0	0	4.84	5.45
2001 LAA	AL	32	32	1	0	205.1	910	227	122	116	21	3	8	14	77	2	104	4	1	10	11	.476	0	0-0	0	4.87	5.08
2002 LAA	AL	54	15	0	4	118.0	510	119	68	64	17	1	5	5	49	4	65	1	1	9	8	.529	0	1-4	11	4.68	4.88
2003 2 Tms	AL	59	0	0	19	64.2	276	63	35	30	2	3	2	1	19	5	56	3	0	3	2	.600	0	0-2	9	3.25	4.18
2004 CWS	AL	20	19	0	0	112.2	500	129	74	70	17	3	2	3	49	0	69	3	0	6	9	.400	0	0-0	0	5.65	5.59
2005 Tor	AL	80	0	0	15	57.0	250	54	23	21	4	2	1	0	46	5	43	2	0	3	4	.429	0	1-4	21	3.56	3.32
2006 2 Tms	AL	71	0	0	16	51.2	221	48	28	28	4	1	2	1	24	6	29	3	0	4	2	.667	0	4-6	19	3.79	4.88
2007 NYM	NL	70	0	0	17	59.0	265	62	36	33	8	4	1	3	28	5	41	3	1	0	2	.000	0	2-3	11	4.97	5.03

Year	Team	Lg	G	GS	CG	GF	IP	BFP	H	R	ER	HR	SH	SF	HB	TBB	IBB	SO	WP	Bk	W	L	Pct	Sh	Sv-Op	Hld	ERC	ERA
2008	NYM	NL	73	0	0	12	56.2	243	55	23	21	7	2	2	4	23	6	34	3	0	2	6	.250	0	1-5	15	4.28	3.34
2009	Ari	NL	45	0	0	9	24.0	117	29	20	19	6	1	0	2	13	1	14	0	0	1	2	.333	0	0-3	6	7.18	7.13
2010	Bos	AL	15	0	0	6	13.2	68	19	12	12	2	0	1	0	10	1	13	1	0	1	0	1.000	0	0-0	1	8.19	7.90
03	LAA	AL	39	0	0	12	38.2	163	37	19	17	2	1	1	3	10	3	29	1	0	1	1	.500	0	0-1	4	3.14	3.96
03	CWS	AL	20	0	0	7	26.0	113	26	16	13	1	1	0	1	9	2	27	2	0	2	1	.667	0	0-1	0	3.41	4.50
06	Tor	AL	55	0	0	8	37.1	161	39	27	27	3	1	0	1	16	5	18	2	0	2	2	.500	0	1-3	18	4.27	6.51
06	Cin	NL	16	0	0	8	14.1	60	9	1	1	1	0	0	1	8	1	11	1	0	2	0	1.000	0	3-3	1	2.64	0.63
Postseason			6	0	0	1	3.0	12	3	1	1	0	0	0	0	1	0	2	0	0	–	0	–	0	0-1	0	3.35	3.00
12 ML YEARS			577	93	2	104	972.0	4277	1035	580	541	112	20	26	47	398	38	568	28	6	47	57	.452	1	9-27	91	4.75	5.01

Skip Schumaker

Bats: L **Throws:** R **Pos:** 2B-123; RF-12; PH-12; LF-4; CF-1; DH-1 **Ht:** 5'10" **Wt:** 195 **Born:** 2/3/1980 **Age:** 31

Year	Team	Lg	G	AB	H	2B	3B	HR	(Hm	Rd)	TB	R	RBI	RC	TBB	IBB	SO	HBP	SH	SF	SB	CS	SB%	GDP	Avg	OBP	Slg
2005	StL	NL	27	24	6	1	0	0	(0	0)	7	9	1	2	2	0	2	0	0	0	1	0	1.00	0	.250	.308	.292
2006	StL	NL	28	54	10	1	0	1	(0	1)	14	3	2	2	5	1	6	0	1	0	2	1	.67	1	.185	.254	.259
2007	StL	NL	88	177	59	12	2	2	(1	1)	81	19	19	30	8	0	20	0	1	2	1	1	.50	5	.333	.358	.458
2008	StL	NL	153	540	163	22	5	8	(4	4)	219	87	46	74	47	2	60	2	4	1	8	2	.80	19	.302	.359	.406
2009	StL	NL	153	532	161	34	1	4	(2	2)	209	85	35	74	52	2	69	0	1	1	2	2	.50	4	.303	.364	.393
2010	StL	NL	137	476	126	18	1	5	(1	4)	161	66	42	61	43	2	64	4	2	4	5	3	.63	7	.265	.328	.338
Postseason			2	6	2	1	0	0	(0	0)	3	1	1	1	1	0	1	0	0	0	0	0	–	0	.333	.500	.500
6 ML YEARS			586	1803	525	88	9	20	(8	12)	691	269	145	243	157	7	221	6	9	8	19	9	.68	36	.291	.349	.383

Luke Scott

Bats: L **Throws:** R **Pos:** DH-93; 1B-19; LF-14; PH-10 **Ht:** 6'0" **Wt:** 205 **Born:** 6/25/1978 **Age:** 33

Year	Team	Lg	G	AB	H	2B	3B	HR	(Hm	Rd)	TB	R	RBI	RC	TBB	IBB	SO	HBP	SH	SF	SB	CS	SB%	GDP	Avg	OBP	Slg
2010	Orioles*	R	3	9	2	0	0	0	(-	-)	2	1	2	0	2	0	1	0	0	0	0	0	–	0	.222	.364	.222
2005	Hou	NL	34	80	15	4	2	0	(0	0)	23	6	4	6	9	1	23	0	0	0	1	1	.50	0	.188	.270	.288
2006	Hou	NL	65	214	72	19	6	10	(8	2)	133	31	37	48	30	4	43	4	0	1	2	1	.67	2	.336	.426	.621
2007	Hou	NL	132	369	94	28	5	18	(8	10)	186	49	64	55	53	4	95	2	0	1	3	1	.75	6	.255	.351	.504
2008	Bal	AL	148	475	122	29	2	23	(11	12)	224	67	65	68	53	10	102	5	0	3	2	2	.50	7	.257	.336	.472
2009	Bal	AL	128	449	116	26	1	25	(18	7)	219	61	77	69	55	5	104	1	0	1	0	0	–	4	.258	.340	.488
2010	Bal	AL	131	447	127	29	1	27	(19	8)	239	70	72	71	59	4	98	4	0	7	2	0	1.00	9	.284	.368	.535
Postseason			2	2	0	0	0	0	(0	0)	0	1	0	0	1	0	1	0	0	0	0	0	–	0	.000	.333	.000
6 ML YEARS			638	2034	546	135	17	103	(64	39)	1024	284	319	317	259	28	465	16	0	13	10	5	.67	30	.268	.354	.503

Marco Scutaro

Bats: R **Throws:** R **Pos:** SS-132; 2B-16; PH-3 SKOO-tah-row **Ht:** 5'10" **Wt:** 185 **Born:** 10/30/1975 **Age:** 35

Year	Team	Lg	G	AB	H	2B	3B	HR	(Hm	Rd)	TB	R	RBI	RC	TBB	IBB	SO	HBP	SH	SF	SB	CS	SB%	GDP	Avg	OBP	Slg
2002	NYM	NL	27	36	8	0	1	1	(1	0)	13	2	6	2	0	0	11	0	1	1	0	1	.00	1	.222	.216	.361
2003	NYM	NL	48	75	16	4	0	2	(0	2)	26	10	6	10	13	2	14	1	1	1	2	0	1.00	1	.213	.333	.347
2004	Oak	AL	137	455	124	32	1	7	(6	1)	179	50	43	48	16	1	58	0	5	1	0	0	–	9	.273	.297	.393
2005	Oak	AL	110	301	94	22	3	9	(5	4)	149	40	37	45	36	1	40	0	4	2	5	2	.71	6	.247	.310	.391
2006	Oak	AL	117	365	97	21	6	5	(1	4)	145	52	41	47	50	0	66	0	3	5	5	1	.83	16	.266	.350	.397
2007	Oak	AL	104	338	88	13	0	7	(2	5)	122	49	41	42	35	1	40	2	2	2	2	1	.67	13	.260	.332	.361
2008	Tor	AL	145	517	138	23	1	7	(5	2)	104	70	60	72	57	0	65	5	0	7	7	2	.78	8	.267	.341	.350
2009	Tor	AL	144	574	162	35	1	12	(7	5)	235	100	60	97	90	0	75	4	5	7	14	5	.74	12	.282	.379	.409
2010	Bos	AL	150	632	174	38	0	11	(6	5)	245	92	56	81	53	1	71	3	4	3	5	4	.56	13	.275	.333	.388
Postseason			7	27	5	4	0	0	(0	0)	9	1	6	3	0	0	4	0	0	0	0	0	–	1	.185	.185	.333
9 ML YEARS			990	3373	901	188	13	61	(33	28)	1298	479	350	444	350	6	448	15	31	29	40	16	.71	79	.267	.336	.385

Bobby Seay

Pitches: L **Bats:** L **Pos:** P SEE **Ht:** 6'2" **Wt:** 235 **Born:** 6/20/1978 **Age:** 33

Year	Team	Lg	G	GS	CG	GF	IP	BFP	H	R	ER	HR	SH	SF	HB	TBB	IBB	SO	WP	Bk	W	L	Pct	Sh	Sv-Op	Hld	ERC	ERA
2001	TB	AL	12	0	0	4	13.0	58	13	11	9	3	2	0	1	5	1	12	1	0	1	1	.500	0	0-0	0	5.03	6.23
2003	TB	AL	12	0	0	2	9.0	39	7	3	3	0	0	2	0	6	0	5	0	0	0	0	–	0	0-1	0	3.17	3.00
2004	TB	AL	21	0	0	6	22.2	95	21	6	6	2	0	0	2	5	1	17	1	0	0	0	–	0	0-0	0	3.15	2.38
2005	Col	NL	17	0	0	5	11.2	58	18	11	11	3	1	0	0	8	1	11	0	1	0	0	–	0	0-1	1	10.28	8.49
2006	Det	AL	14	0	0	6	15.1	71	14	11	11	1	1	1	3	9	1	12	0	0	0	0	–	0	0-0	0	4.65	6.46
2007	Det	AL	58	0	0	19	46.1	189	38	12	12	1	2	2	2	15	4	38	1	1	3	0	1.000	0	1-2	10	2.39	2.33
2008	Det	AL	60	0	0	14	56.1	246	59	28	28	4	3	4	2	25	7	58	3	0	1	1	.333	0	0-1	13	4.29	4.47
2009	Det	AL	67	0	0	7	48.2	208	46	23	23	3	3	3	3	17	3	37	3	0	6	3	.667	0	0-4	28	3.44	4.25
8 ML YEARS			261	0	0	63	223.0	964	216	105	103	17	12	12	13	90	18	190	9	2	11	6	.647	0	1-9	52	3.85	4.16

Chris Seddon

Pitches: L **Bats:** L **Pos:** RP-14 SEDD-un **Ht:** 6'3" **Wt:** 220 **Born:** 10/13/1983 **Age:** 27

Year	Team	Lg	G	GS	CG	GF	IP	BFP	H	R	ER	HR	SH	SF	HB	TBB	IBB	SO	WP	Bk	W	L	Pct	Sh	Sv-Op	Hld	ERC	ERA
2001	Princtn	R	4	2	0	1	12.1	56	15	7	7	2	0	0	0	6	0	18	0	0	1	2	.333	0	0--	–	6.28	5.11
2002	CtnSC	A	26	20	2	2	117.0	507	93	63	47	7	2	3	6	68	0	88	10	0	6	8	.429	0	1--	–	3.56	3.62
2003	Bkrsfld	A+	26	26	0	0	133.1	595	147	93	74	12	2	6	7	54	0	95	7	1	9	11	.450	0	0--	–	4.81	5.00
2004	Bkrsfld	A+	7	7	0	0	41.1	156	30	4	3	0	1	0	2	8	0	41	2	1	5	0	1.000	0	0--	–	1.64	0.65

Year	Team	Lg	G	GS	CG	GF	IP	BFP	H	R	ER	HR	SH	SF	HB	TBB	IBB	SO	WP	Bk	W	L	Pct	Sh	Sv-Op	Hld	ERC	ERA
2004	Mont	AA	21	21	1	0	119.0	516	129	67	58	19	5	6	6	44	0	102	5	0	9	10	.474	0	0--	-	5.17	4.39
2005	Mont	AA	10	10	0	0	52.1	231	58	31	28	4	5	1	1	20	0	46	4	0	6	1	.857	0	0--	-	4.52	4.82
2005	Drham	AAA	19	19	0	0	95.2	453	114	74	58	11	1	9	13	43	0	70	7	5	4	9	.308	0	0--	-	5.99	5.46
2006	Drham	AAA	28	28	1	0	154.1	668	168	92	81	20	5	5	5	46	2	108	2	0	9	9	.500	0	0--	-	4.49	4.72
2007	Mont	AAA	12	12	0	0	71.0	292	71	40	39	7	2	4	4	23	1	40	4	0	3	4	.429	0	0--	-	4.16	4.94
2007	Carlina	AA	14	14	0	0	68.2	289	65	37	33	6	5	0	1	25	1	58	2	0	3	6	.333	0	0--	-	3.62	4.33
2008	Albq	AAA	28	27	2	0	152.0	679	170	95	86	23	10	5	10	69	1	126	10	1	10	9	.526	0	0--	-	5.73	5.09
2009	Tacom	AAA	25	24	0	0	131.2	578	140	74	66	17	3	5	5	54	0	80	8	4	9	8	.529	0	0--	-	4.88	4.51
2010	Tacom	AAA	18	15	2	2	101.0	420	94	45	37	7	1	3	3	29	0	65	3	0	10	4	.714	2	0--	-	3.18	3.30
2007	Fla	NL	7	4	0	1	17.1	91	29	19	17	2	1	1	1	5	0	10	0	0	0	2	.000	0	0-0	0	7.56	8.83
2010	Sea	AL	14	0	0	5	22.1	95	21	14	14	4	0	1	0	10	0	16	2	0	1	0	1.000	0	0-0	0	4.55	5.64
2 ML YEARS			21	4	0	6	39.2	186	50	33	31	6	1	2	1	15	0	26	2	0	1	2	.333	0	0-0	0	5.84	7.03

Ryan Shealy

Bats: R Throws: R Pos: PH-4; 1B-1 SHEE-lee **Ht: 6'5" Wt: 240 Born: 8/29/1979 Age: 31**

Year	Team	Lg	G	AB	H	2B	3B	HR	(Hm	Rd)	TB	R	RBI	RC	TBB	IBB	SO	HBP	SH	SF	SB	CS	SB%	GDP	Avg	OBP	Slg
2010	Drham*	AAA	48	172	41	15	1	10	(-	-)	88	27	38	32	29	0	48	3	0	2	0	0	-	3	.238	.354	.512
2010	Pwtckt*	AAA	32	114	25	7	0	5	(-	-)	47	14	17	16	17	0	34	2	0	0	0	0	-	1	.219	.331	.412
2005	Col	NL	36	91	30	7	0	2	(0	2)	43	14	16	14	13	0	22	0	0	0	1	0	1.00	6	.330	.413	.473
2006	2 Tms		56	202	56	12	1	7	(5	2)	91	31	37	32	15	1	54	2	0	0	1	1	.50	5	.277	.333	.450
2007	KC	AL	52	172	38	6	0	3	(0	3)	53	18	21	15	13	0	53	3	0	1	0	0	-	4	.221	.286	.308
2008	KC	AL	20	73	22	1	0	7	(3	4)	44	12	20	15	5	0	19	1	0	0	0	0	-	2	.301	.354	.603
2010	Bos	AL	5	7	0	0	0	0	(0	0)	0	0	0	0	0	0	2	0	0	0	0	0	-	0	.000	.000	.000
06	Col	NL	5	9	2	2	0	0	(0	0)	4	2	1	0	0	0	4	0	0	0	0	0	-	0	.222	.222	.444
06	KC	AL	51	193	54	10	1	7	(5	2)	87	29	36	32	15	1	50	2	0	1	1	1	.50	5	.280	.338	.451
5 ML YEARS			169	545	146	26	1	19	(8	11)	231	75	94	76	46	1	150	6	0	1	2	1	.67	17	.268	.331	.424

Ben Sheets

Pitches: R Bats: R Pos: SP-20 **Ht: 6'1" Wt: 222 Born: 7/18/1978 Age: 32**

Year	Team	Lg	G	GS	CG	GF	IP	BFP	H	R	ER	HR	SH	SF	HB	TBB	IBB	SO	WP	Bk	W	L	Pct	Sh	Sv-Op	Hld	ERC	ERA
2001	Mil	NL	25	25	1	0	151.1	653	166	89	80	23	8	5	5	48	6	94	3	0	11	10	.524	1	0-0	0	4.78	4.76
2002	Mil	NL	34	34	1	0	216.2	934	237	105	100	21	10	0	10	70	10	170	9	0	11	**16**	.407	0	0-0	0	4.45	4.15
2003	Mil	NL	34	34	1	0	220.2	931	232	122	109	29	11	6	6	43	2	157	7	0	11	13	.458	0	0-0	0	3.83	4.45
2004	Mil	NL	34	34	5	0	237.0	937	201	85	71	25	6	4	4	32	1	264	8	1	12	14	.462	0	0-0	0	2.37	2.70
2005	Mil	NL	22	22	3	0	156.2	633	142	66	58	19	6	2	2	25	1	141	7	0	10	9	.526	0	0-0	0	2.81	3.33
2006	Mil	NL	17	17	0	0	106.0	430	105	47	45	9	6	5	2	11	1	116	3	0	6	7	.462	0	0-0	0	2.84	3.82
2007	Mil	NL	24	24	2	0	141.1	592	138	62	60	17	4	5	1	37	2	106	4	0	12	5	.706	0	0-0	0	3.53	3.82
2008	Mil	NL	31	31	5	0	198.1	812	181	74	68	17	6	7	1	47	2	158	8	0	13	9	.591	3	0-0	0	2.89	3.09
2010	Oak	AL	20	20	0	0	119.1	511	123	65	60	18	3	3	0	43	2	84	3	0	4	9	.308	0	0-0	0	4.45	4.53
9 ML YEARS			241	241	18	0	1547.1	6433	1525	715	651	178	60	37	31	356	27	1290	52	1	90	92	.495	4	0-0	0	3.48	3.79

George Sherrill

Pitches: L Bats: L Pos: RP-65 **Ht: 5'11" Wt: 237 Born: 4/19/1977 Age: 34**

Year	Team	Lg	G	GS	CG	GF	IP	BFP	H	R	ER	HR	SH	SF	HB	TBB	IBB	SO	WP	Bk	W	L	Pct	Sh	Sv-Op	Hld	ERC	ERA
2010	InldEm*	A+	2	1	0	0	2.0	7	3	1	1	0	0	0	0	0	0	2	0	0	0	0	-	0	0--	-	5.90	4.50
2010	Albq*	AAA	2	1	0	0	1.2	7	2	0	0	0	0	0	0	0	0	3	0	0	0	0	-	0	0--	-	2.89	0.00
2004	Sea	AL	21	0	0	4	23.2	104	24	12	10	3	0	1	1	9	1	16	4	1	2	1	.667	0	0-0	3	4.31	3.80
2005	Sea	AL	29	0	0	2	19.0	77	13	12	11	3	1	1	1	7	2	24	0	0	4	3	.571	0	0-0	9	2.70	5.21
2006	Sea	AL	72	0	0	6	40.0	174	30	19	19	4	0	2	0	27	4	42	0	0	2	4	.333	0	1-1	17	2.86	4.28
2007	Sea	AL	73	0	0	16	45.2	182	28	12	12	4	4	4	1	17	1	56	1	1	2	0	1.000	0	3-7	22	1.96	2.36
2008	Bal	AL	57	0	0	49	53.1	239	47	28	28	6	1	3	1	33	6	58	1	0	3	5	.375	0	31-37	0	4.18	4.73
2009	2 Tms		72	0	0	39	69.0	282	53	13	13	4	1	1	2	24	4	61	1	0	1	1	.500	0	21-26	11	2.41	1.70
2010	LAD	NL	65	0	0	12	36.1	180	46	28	27	4	5	2	1	24	4	25	1	0	2	2	.500	0	0-4	7	6.56	6.69
09	Bal	AL	42	0	0	38	41.1	171	34	11	11	3	0	1	2	13	2	39	0	0	0	1	.000	0	20-23	0	2.72	2.40
09	LAD	NL	30	0	0	1	27.2	111	19	2	2	1	1	0	0	11	2	22	1	0	1	0	1.000	0	1-3	11	1.96	0.65
Postseason			6	0	0	1	4.1	22	3	4	4	1	0	0	3	4	0	2	1	0	1	0	1.000	0	0-0	2	8.61	8.31
7 ML YEARS			389	0	0	128	287.0	1238	241	124	120	24	16	14	7	141	22	282	8	2	16	16	.500	0	56-75	69	3.37	3.76

James Shields

Pitches: R Bats: R Pos: SP-33; RP-1 **Ht: 6'4" Wt: 220 Born: 12/20/1981 Age: 29**

Year	Team	Lg	G	GS	CG	GF	IP	BFP	H	R	ER	HR	SH	SF	HB	TBB	IBB	SO	WP	Bk	W	L	Pct	Sh	Sv-Op	Hld	ERC	ERA
2006	TB	AL	21	21	1	0	124.2	540	141	69	67	18	4	3	5	38	5	104	9	0	6	8	.429	0	0-0	0	4.92	4.84
2007	TB	AL	31	31	1	0	215.0	874	202	99	92	28	4	5	10	36	0	184	9	0	12	8	.600	0	0-0	0	3.24	3.85
2008	TB	AL	33	33	3	0	215.0	877	208	94	85	24	6	0	12	40	0	160	6	0	14	8	.636	2	0-0	0	3.41	3.56
2009	TB	AL	33	33	0	0	219.2	930	239	113	101	29	6	3	1	52	1	167	3	1	11	12	.478	0	0-0	0	4.16	4.14
2010	TB	AL	34	33	0	0	203.1	899	**246**	**128**	**117**	**34**	5	2	5	51	2	187	13	2	13	15	.464	0	0-0	0	5.21	5.18
Postseason			4	4	0	0	25.0	108	28	9	8	3	1	1	2	8	0	17	1	0	2	2	.500	0	0-0	0	4.82	2.88
5 ML YEARS			152	151	5	0	977.2	4120	1036	502	462	133	25	13	33	217	8	802	40	3	56	51	.523	2	0-0	0	4.09	4.25

Scot Shields

Pitches: R **Bats:** R **Pos:** RP-42; SP-1 **Ht:** 6'1" **Wt:** 180 **Born:** 7/22/1975 **Age:** 35

Year	Team	Lg	G	GS	CG	GF	IP	BFP	H	R	ER	HR	SH	SF	HB	TBB	IBB	SO	WP	Bk	W	L	Pct	Sh	Sv-Op	Hld	ERC	ERA
2001	LAA	AL	8	0	0	6	11.0	48	8	1	0	0	0	0	1	7	0	7	2	0	0	0	-	0	0-0	0	3.10	0.00
2002	LAA	AL	29	1	0	13	49.0	188	31	13	12	4	1	0	1	21	1	30	3	0	5	3	.625	0	0-0	3	2.35	2.20
2003	LAA	AL	44	13	0	5	148.1	609	138	56	47	12	3	4	5	38	6	111	4	0	5	6	.455	0	1-1	3	3.12	2.85
2004	LAA	AL	60	0	0	12	105.1	454	97	42	39	6	2	2	3	40	5	109	4	0	8	2	.800	0	4-7	17	3.24	3.33
2005	LAA	AL	78	0	0	21	91.2	375	66	33	28	5	4	3	2	37	2	98	12	0	10	11	.476	0	7-13	33	2.37	2.75
2006	LAA	AL	74	0	0	13	87.2	351	70	30	28	8	3	1	1	24	4	84	8	0	7	7	.500	0	2-8	31	2.48	2.87
2007	LAA	AL	71	0	0	13	77.0	320	62	36	33	7	0	1	4	33	0	77	6	0	4	5	.444	0	2-8	31	3.31	3.86
2008	LAA	AL	64	0	0	12	63.1	270	56	29	19	6	1	1	2	29	2	64	2	0	6	4	.600	0	4-9	31	3.72	2.70
2009	LAA	AL	20	0	0	2	17.2	83	16	14	13	1	1	0	0	15	0	12	1	0	1	3	.250	0	1-4	6	4.90	6.62
2010	LAA	AL	43	1	0	17	46.0	218	45	31	27	6	2	3	2	34	1	39	7	0	0	3	.000	0	0-1	1	5.58	5.28
Postseason			17	0	0	3	25.1	109	24	13	9	1	1	0	1	11	2	25	0	0	1	2	.333	0	0-1	1	3.91	3.20
10 ML YEARS			491	15	0	114	697.0	2916	589	285	246	55	17	15	21	278	21	631	49	0	46	44	.511	0	21-51	156	3.17	3.18

Kelly Shoppach

Bats: R **Throws:** R **Pos:** C-56; PH-12; DH-3 **Ht:** 6'0" **Wt:** 220 **Born:** 4/29/1980 **Age:** 31

Year	Team	Lg	G	AB	H	2B	3B	HR	(Hm	Rd)	TB	R	RBI	RC	TBB	IBB	SO	HBP	SH	SF	SB	CS	SB%	GDP	Avg	OBP	Slg
2010	Drham*	AAA	4	13	4	0	0	0	(-	-)	4	0	2	1	0	0	3	0	0	0	0	0	-	0	.308	.308	.308
2005	Bos	AL	9	15	0	0	0	0	(0	0)	0	1	0	0	0	0	7	1	0	0	0	0	-	0	.000	.063	.000
2006	Cle	AL	41	110	27	6	0	3	(2	1)	42	7	16	13	8	0	45	0	2	0	0	0	-	2	.245	.297	.382
2007	Cle	AL	59	161	42	13	0	7	(4	3)	76	26	30	24	11	0	56	1	3	1	0	0	-	2	.261	.310	.472
2008	Cle	AL	112	352	92	27	0	21	(9	12)	182	67	55	58	36	3	133	11	3	1	0	0	-	7	.261	.348	.517
2009	Cle	AL	89	271	58	14	0	12	(5	7)	108	33	40	32	33	0	98	18	2	3	0	0	-	8	.214	.335	.399
2010	TB	AL	63	158	31	8	0	5	(4	1)	54	17	17	18	20	0	71	6	2	1	0	0	-	2	.196	.308	.342
Postseason			2	6	3	2	0	0	(0	0)	5	1	0	2	0	0	2	2	0	0	0	0	-	0	.500	.625	.833
6 ML YEARS			373	1067	250	68	0	48	(24	24)	462	151	158	145	108	3	410	37	12	6	0	0	-	21	.234	.324	.433

Carlos Silva

Pitches: R **Bats:** R **Pos:** SP-21 **Ht:** 6'4" **Wt:** 250 **Born:** 4/23/1979 **Age:** 32

Year	Team	Lg	G	GS	CG	GF	IP	BFP	H	R	ER	HR	SH	SF	HB	TBB	IBB	SO	WP	Bk	W	L	Pct	Sh	Sv-Op	Hld	ERC	ERA
2010	Peoria*	A	2	2	0	0	7.1	31	8	5	5	1	0	0	0	2	0	5	0	0	0	1	.000	0	0- -	-	4.39	6.14
2002	Phi	NL	68	0	0	21	84.0	350	88	34	30	4	9	3	4	22	6	41	3	0	5	0	1.000	0	1-5	8	3.60	3.21
2003	Phi	NL	62	1	0	15	87.1	381	92	43	43	7	6	1	8	37	5	48	12	1	3	1	.750	0	1-3	4	4.71	4.43
2004	Min	AL	33	33	1	0	203.0	869	255	100	95	23	6	0	5	35	2	76	5	1	14	8	.636	1	0-0	0	4.89	4.21
2005	Min	AL	27	27	3	0	188.1	749	212	83	72	25	2	5	3	9	2	71	0	0	9	8	.529	0	0-0	0	3.78	3.44
2006	Min	AL	36	31	0	2	180.1	811	246	130	119	38	6	7	7	32	4	70	1	0	11	15	.423	0	0-0	2	6.23	5.94
2007	Min	AL	33	33	2	0	202.0	848	229	99	94	20	6	4	6	36	2	89	4	1	13	14	.481	1	0-0	0	4.05	4.19
2008	Sea	AL	28	28	1	0	153.1	689	213	114	110	20	3	7	4	32	2	69	1	0	4	15	.211	0	0-0	0	5.93	6.46
2009	Sea	AL	8	6	0	1	30.1	142	41	29	29	5	1	0	3	11	0	10	2	1	1	3	.250	0	0-0	0	7.01	8.60
2010	ChC	NL	21	21	0	0	113.0	400	120	55	53	11	4	0	7	24	2	80	4	0	10	6	.625	0	0-0	0	3.00	4.22
Postseason			1	1	0	0	5.0	24	10	6	6	1	0	0	0	1	0	1	0	0	0	1	.000	0	0-0	0	9.65	10.80
9 ML YEARS			316	180	6	39	1241.2	5319	1496	687	645	153	43	34	45	238	25	554	32	4	70	70	.500	2	2-8	14	4.75	4.68

Alfredo Simon

Pitches: R **Bats:** R **Pos:** RP-49 si-MOHN **Ht:** 6'5" **Wt:** 260 **Born:** 5/8/1981 **Age:** 30

Year	Team	Lg	G	GS	CG	GF	IP	BFP	H	R	ER	HR	SH	SF	HB	TBB	IBB	SO	WP	Bk	W	L	Pct	Sh	Sv-Op	Hld	ERC	ERA
2010	Norfolk*	AAA	4	3	0	0	17.0	71	15	4	3	1	2	0	1	5	0	14	1	0	1	1	.500	0	0- -	-	2.97	1.59
2008	Bal	AL	4	1	0	0	13.0	59	16	10	9	4	0	1	2	2	0	8	2	0	0	0	-	0	0-0	0	6.45	6.23
2009	Bal	AL	2	2	0	0	6.1	28	8	7	7	5	0	0	0	2	0	3	0	0	1	0	1.000	0	0-0	0	10.74	9.95
2010	Bal	AL	49	0	0	35	49.1	222	54	30	27	10	1	2	2	22	2	37	1	0	4	2	.667	0	17-21	1	5.66	4.93
3 ML YEARS			55	3	0	35	68.2	309	78	47	43	19	1	3	4	26	2	48	3	0	5	2	.714	0	17-21	1	6.28	5.04

Brett Sinkbeil

Pitches: R **Bats:** R **Pos:** RP-3 SINK-bill **Ht:** 6'3" **Wt:** 190 **Born:** 12/26/1984 **Age:** 26

Year	Team	Lg	G	GS	CG	GF	IP	BFP	H	R	ER	HR	SH	SF	HB	TBB	IBB	SO	WP	Bk	W	L	Pct	Sh	Sv-Op	Hld	ERC	ERA
2006	Jmstwn	A-	5	5	0	0	22.0	86	14	4	3	1	1	1	3	8	0	22	2	0	2	0	1.000	0	0- -	-	2.32	1.23
2006	Grnsbr	A	8	8	0	0	39.2	172	45	22	22	5	1	1	1	14	0	32	1	0	1	1	.500	0	0- -	-	5.05	4.99
2007	Jupiter	A+	14	14	1	0	79.0	330	82	41	30	8	4	1	5	14	0	49	5	0	6	4	.600	1	0- -	-	3.69	3.42
2008	Carlina	AA	26	26	1	0	143.1	633	172	84	80	12	7	6	6	51	1	66	11	1	5	9	.357	0	0- -	-	5.18	5.02
2009	NewOr	AAA	47	8	0	11	83.0	394	106	65	56	9	5	3	5	44	1	52	14	2	2	8	.200	0	0- -	-	6.58	6.07
2010	NewOr	AAA	58	0	0	17	63.0	299	76	44	40	4	4	2	5	31	3	56	3	0	3	3	.500	0	0- -	-	5.49	5.71
2010	Fla	NL	3	0	0	1	2.0	13	2	3	3	0	0	0	0	5	0	1	1	0	0	0	-	0	0-0	0	11.64	13.50

Tony Sipp

Pitches: L **Bats:** L **Pos:** RP-70   **Ht:** 6'0" **Wt:** 190 **Born:** 7/12/1983 **Age:** 27

			HOW MUCH HE PITCHED						WHAT HE GAVE UP												THE RESULTS							
Year	Team	Lg	G	GS	CG	GF	IP	BFP	H	R	ER	HR	SH	SF	HB	TBB	IBB	SO	WP	Bk	W	L	Pct	Sh	Sv-Op	Hld	ERC	ERA
2004	MhVlly	A-	10	10	0	0	42.2	174	33	23	15	5	3	1	1	13	0	74	3	3	3	1	.750	0	0--	-	2.68	3.16
2005	Lk Cty	A	13	12	0	1	69.0	263	47	19	17	5	3	1	0	19	0	71	5	0	4	1	.800	0	0--	-	1.91	2.22
2005	Knstn	A+	22	5	0	8	47.1	196	34	19	14	4	4	1	2	23	0	59	3	0	2	2	.500	0	2--	-	2.97	2.66
2006	Akron	AA	29	4	0	13	60.1	245	44	23	21	2	3	3	0	21	0	80	3	0	4	2	.667	0	3--	-	2.04	3.13
2008	Indns	R	3	1	0	0	4.0	12	0	0	0	0	0	0	0	1	0	4	0	0	0	0	-	0	0--	-	0.08	0.00
2008	Knstn	A+	5	0	0	1	8.0	31	4	2	1	0	0	1	0	3	0	10	0	0	0	0	-	0	0--	-	1.17	1.13
2008	Akron	AA	16	0	0	2	21.2	90	19	12	9	4	2	0	0	7	1	32	0	0	0	3	.000	0	1--	-	3.56	3.74
2009	Clmbs	AAA	12	0	0	3	17.0	74	17	8	7	1	0	1	0	6	0	22	5	0	0	1	.000	0	1--	-	3.52	3.71
2009	Cle	AL	46	0	0	8	40.0	168	27	16	13	5	3	1	0	25	2	48	3	0	2	0	1.000	0	0-0	9	3.29	2.93
2010	Cle	AL	70	0	0	16	63.0	266	48	30	29	12	3	2	2	39	3	69	4	0	2	2	.500	0	1-3	15	4.42	4.14
	2 ML YEARS		116	0	0	24	103.0	434	75	46	42	17	6	3	2	64	5	117	7	0	4	2	.667	0	1-3	24	3.97	3.67

Grady Sizemore

Bats: L **Throws:** L **Pos:** CF-32; PH-1; PR-1   **Ht:** 6'2" **Wt:** 200 **Born:** 8/2/1982 **Age:** 28

									BATTING												BASERUNNING				AVERAGES		
Year	Team	Lg	G	AB	H	2B	3B	HR	(Hm	Rd)	TB	R	RBI	RC	TBB	IBB	SO	HBP	SH	SF		SB	CS	SB%	GDP	Avg	OBP	Slg
2004	Cle	AL	43	138	34	6	2	4	(2	2)	56	15	24	21	14	0	34	5	0	2		2	0	1.00	0	.246	.333	.406
2005	Cle	AL	158	640	185	37	11	22	(10	12)	310	111	81	101	52	1	132	7	5	2		22	10	.69	17	.289	.348	.484
2006	Cle	AL	162	655	190	53	11	28	(14	14)	349	134	76	121	78	8	153	13	1	4		22	6	.79	2	.290	.375	.533
2007	Cle	AL	162	628	174	34	5	24	(11	13)	290	118	78	123	101	9	155	17	0	2		33	10	.77	3	.277	.390	.462
2008	Cle	AL	157	634	170	39	5	33	(21	12)	318	101	90	121	98	14	130	11	0	2		38	5	.88	5	.268	.374	.502
2009	Cle	AL	106	436	108	20	6	18	(5	13)	194	73	64	68	60	1	92	4	2	1		13	8	.62	4	.248	.343	.445
2010	Cle	AL	33	128	27	6	2	0	(0	0)	37	15	13	11	9	0	35	2	0	1		4	2	.67	1	.211	.271	.289
	Postseason		11	43	12	2	1	2	(0	2)	22	9	3	5	8	3	9	1	0	1		2	1	.67	2	.279	.396	.512
	7 ML YEARS		821	3259	888	195	42	129	(63	66)	1554	567	426	566	412	33	731	59	8	14		134	41	.77	32	.272	.363	.477

Scott Sizemore

Bats: R **Throws:** R **Pos:** 2B-40; 3B-6; PH-4; DH-2; PR-1   **Ht:** 6'0" **Wt:** 185 **Born:** 1/4/1985 **Age:** 26

									BATTING												BASERUNNING				AVERAGES		
Year	Team	Lg	G	AB	H	2B	3B	HR	(Hm	Rd)	TB	R	RBI	RC	TBB	IBB	SO	HBP	SH	SF		SB	CS	SB%	GDP	Avg	OBP	Slg
2006	Oneont	A-	70	294	96	15	4	3	(-	-)	128	49	37	52	32	2	47	2	3	2		7	5	.58	4	.327	.394	.435
2007	WMich	A	125	438	116	33	5	4	(-	-)	171	78	48	72	73	1	60	9	4	6		16	10	.62	11	.265	.376	.390
2008	Lkland	A+	53	203	58	11	1	4	(-	-)	83	32	20	34	24	1	44	3	1	3		14	3	.82	2	.286	.365	.409
2009	Erie	AA	59	228	70	17	4	9	(-	-)	122	39	33	49	35	0	46	2	3	1		7	3	.70	5	.307	.402	.535
2009	Toledo	AAA	71	292	90	22	1	8	(-	-)	138	49	33	55	29	0	49	4	5	0		14	1	.93	6	.308	.378	.473
2010	Toledo	AAA	76	299	89	23	1	9	(-	-)	141	49	37	54	31	0	77	9	1	2		2	2	.50	3	.298	.378	.472
2010	Det	AL	48	143	32	7	0	3	(1	2)	48	19	14	13	15	0	40	0	4	1		0	0	-	4	.224	.296	.336

Anthony Slama

Pitches: R **Bats:** R **Pos:** RP-5   SLAMM-ah   **Ht:** 6'3" **Wt:** 204 **Born:** 1/6/1984 **Age:** 27

			HOW MUCH HE PITCHED						WHAT HE GAVE UP												THE RESULTS							
Year	Team	Lg	G	GS	CG	GF	IP	BFP	H	R	ER	HR	SH	SF	HB	TBB	IBB	SO	WP	Bk	W	L	Pct	Sh	Sv-Op	Hld	ERC	ERA
2007	Elizab	R+	6	0	0	4	7.1	24	2	2	2	0	1	0	0	1	0	10	2	0	0	0	-	0	4--	-	0.32	2.45
2007	Beloit	A	21	0	0	19	24.1	98	15	4	4	0	1	0	1	9	0	39	3	0	1	1	.500	0	10--	-	1.58	1.48
2008	FtMyrs	A+	51	0	0	39	71.0	280	43	12	8	0	2	2	3	24	1	110	3	0	4	1	.800	0	25--	-	1.49	1.01
2009	NwBrit	AA	51	0	0	43	65.1	270	46	18	18	5	3	4	2	32	6	93	3	1	4	2	.667	0	25--	-	2.68	2.48
2009	Roch	AAA	11	0	0	10	15.2	63	11	6	6	0	2	1	0	8	3	19	2	0	0	2	.000	0	4--	-	2.05	3.45
2010	Roch	AAA	54	0	0	41	65.1	265	41	16	16	5	2	0	1	32	3	74	2	0	2	2	.500	0	17--	-	2.32	2.20
2010	Min	AL	5	0	0	2	4.2	25	6	4	4	1	0	0	0	5	0	5	1	0	0	1	.000	0	0-1	0	9.58	7.71

Doug Slaten

Pitches: L **Bats:** L **Pos:** RP-49   **Ht:** 6'5" **Wt:** 215 **Born:** 2/4/1980 **Age:** 31

			HOW MUCH HE PITCHED						WHAT HE GAVE UP												THE RESULTS							
Year	Team	Lg	G	GS	CG	GF	IP	BFP	H	R	ER	HR	SH	SF	HB	TBB	IBB	SO	WP	Bk	W	L	Pct	Sh	Sv-Op	Hld	ERC	ERA
2010	Syrcse*	AAA	11	0	0	2	17.0	61	12	0	0	0	0	0	0	1	0	17	0	0	1	0	1.000	0	0--	-	1.18	0.00
2006	Ari	NL	9	0	0	0	5.2	21	3	0	0	0	1	0	0	2	1	3	0	0	0	0	-	0	0-0	2	1.11	0.00
2007	Ari	NL	61	0	0	13	36.1	163	41	15	11	4	0	0	0	14	0	28	3	0	3	2	.600	0	0-1	7	4.74	2.72
2008	Ari	NL	45	0	0	13	32.1	147	33	20	17	4	1	1	4	14	1	20	0	0	0	3	.000	0	0-0	4	4.86	4.73
2009	Ari	NL	11	0	0	0	6.1	30	10	5	5	1	0	0	0	1	0	4	0	0	0	0	-	0	0-0	0	6.82	7.11
2010	Was	NL	49	0	0	13	40.2	174	34	18	14	2	0	0	0	19	2	36	2	0	4	1	.800	0	0-0	4	3.40	3.10
	Postseason		3	0	0	1	1.1	7	1	0	0	0	0	0	0	2	1	1	1	0	0	0	-	0	0-0	0	4.29	0.00
	5 ML YEARS		175	0	0	40	121.1	535	121	58	47	11	2	1	8	50	4	91	5	0	7	6	.538	0	0-1	17	4.21	3.49

Kevin Slowey

Pitches: R **Bats:** R **Pos:** SP-28; RP-2   **Ht:** 6'3" **Wt:** 205 **Born:** 5/4/1984 **Age:** 27

			HOW MUCH HE PITCHED						WHAT HE GAVE UP												THE RESULTS							
Year	Team	Lg	G	GS	CG	GF	IP	BFP	H	R	ER	HR	SH	SF	HB	TBB	IBB	SO	WP	Bk	W	L	Pct	Sh	Sv-Op	Hld	ERC	ERA
2007	Min	AL	13	11	0	0	66.2	297	82	39	35	16	0	1	0	11	0	47	3	0	4	1	.800	0			5.22	4.73
2008	Min	AL	27	27	3	0	160.1	653	161	74	71	22	1	5	4	24	1	123	1	0	12	11	.522	2	0-0	-	3.48	3.99
2009	Min	AL	16	16	0	0	90.2	394	113	50	49	15	3	5	1	15	1	75	3	0	10	3	.769	0	0-0	-	5.25	4.86
2010	Min	AL	30	28	0	0	155.2	662	172	80	77	21	2	11	4	29	0	116	3	0	13	6	.684	0	0-0	-	4.13	4.45
	4 ML YEARS		86	82	3	0	473.1	2006	528	243	232	74	6	22	13	79	2	361	10	0	39	21	.650	2	0-0	-	4.26	4.41

Chris Smith

Pitches: R **Bats:** R **Pos:** RP-3 **Ht:** 6'0" **Wt:** 190 **Born:** 4/9/1981 **Age:** 30

Year	Team	Lg	G	GS	CG	GF	IP	BFP	H	R	ER	HR	SH	SF	HB	TBB	IBB	SO	WP	Bk	W	L	Pct	Sh	Sv-Op	Hld	ERC	ERA
2010	Nashv*	AAA	47	0	0	43	48.0	207	47	23	19	7	3	0	0	21	1	62	3	0	4	3	.571	0	26--	-	4.42	3.56
2008	Bos	AL	12	0	0	3	18.1	78	18	16	16	6	1	1	0	7	0	13	0	0	1	0	1.000	0	0-0	0	5.53	7.85
2009	Mil	NL	35	0	0	12	46.0	200	41	21	21	11	1	0	3	19	0	35	1	0	0	0	-	0	0-1	0	4.68	4.11
2010	Mil	NL	3	0	0	1	3.1	14	4	2	2	0	0	0	0	1	0	4	0	0	0	0	-	0	0-0	0	4.29	5.40
	3 ML YEARS		50	0	0	16	67.2	292	63	39	39	17	2	1	3	27	0	52	1	0	1	0	1.000	0	0-1	0	4.89	5.19

Greg Smith

Pitches: L **Bats:** L **Pos:** SP-8 **Ht:** 6'2" **Wt:** 189 **Born:** 12/22/1983 **Age:** 27

Year	Team	Lg	G	GS	CG	GF	IP	BFP	H	R	ER	HR	SH	SF	HB	TBB	IBB	SO	WP	Bk	W	L	Pct	Sh	Sv-Op	Hld	ERC	ERA
2005	Msoula	R+	16	14	0	0	82.1	326	69	40	38	8	2	2	5	18	0	100	6	0	8	5	.615	0	0--	-	2.82	4.15
2006	Lancst	A+	13	13	2	0	88.1	339	57	21	16	3	3	1	4	31	0	71	2	1	9	0	1.000	2	0--	-	1.95	1.63
2006	Tenn	AA	11	11	0	0	60.0	261	65	32	26	4	3	2	4	23	0	38	2	4	5	4	.556	0	0--	-	4.59	3.90
2007	Mobile	AA	12	12	2	0	69.2	278	64	30	26	7	5	2	2	14	0	62	2	1	5	3	.625	0	0--	-	3.07	3.36
2007	Tucsn	AAA	10	10	1	0	52.1	224	61	27	22	4	0	0	0	18	0	34	3	1	4	2	.667	0	0--	-	4.78	3.78
2008	Scrmto	AAA	1	1	0	0	6.0	25	6	2	2	0	0	1	0	1	0	4	0	0	0	1	.000	0	0--	-	2.49	3.00
2009	Mdest	AA	2	2	0	0	11.2	48	11	6	5	1	0	0	0	4	0	7	1	0	1	0	1.000	0	0--	-	3.53	3.86
2009	ColSpr	AAA	7	7	0	0	29.2	129	34	24	24	5	3	4	1	11	0	15	2	0	1	2	.333	0	0--	-	5.60	7.28
2009	Tulsa	AA	2	2	0	0	8.0	35	12	7	7	3	0	0	0	1	0	5	0	0	0	1	.000	0	0--	-	8.34	7.88
2010	ColSpr	AAA	15	15	0	0	75.0	337	88	59	51	14	0	0	1	30	1	49	5	1	2	5	.286	0	0--	-	5.77	6.12
2008	Oak	AL	32	32	2	0	190.1	800	169	92	88	21	5	10	3	87	5	111	5	1	7	16	.304	0	0-0	0	3.84	4.16
2010	Col	NL	8	8	0	0	39.0	182	49	28	27	8	2	3	1	24	2	31	1	0	1	2	.333	0	0-0	0	7.62	6.23
	2 ML YEARS		40	40	2	0	229.1	982	218	120	115	29	7	13	4	111	7	142	6	1	8	18	.308	0	0-0	0	4.43	4.51

Joe Smith

Pitches: R **Bats:** R **Pos:** RP-53 **Ht:** 6'2" **Wt:** 205 **Born:** 3/22/1984 **Age:** 27

Year	Team	Lg	G	GS	CG	GF	IP	BFP	H	R	ER	HR	SH	SF	HB	TBB	IBB	SO	WP	Bk	W	L	Pct	Sh	Sv-Op	Hld	ERC	ERA
2010	Clmbs*	AAA	20	0	0	4	23.0	93	17	5	5	0	1	0	0	10	1	19	2	0	2	1	.667	0	2--	-	2.17	1.96
2007	NYM	NL	54	0	0	14	44.1	205	48	18	17	3	2	0	7	21	4	45	2	0	3	2	.600	0	0-0	10	5.04	3.45
2008	NYM	NL	82	0	0	12	63.1	271	51	28	25	4	4	0	4	31	4	52	1	0	6	3	.667	0	0-3	18	3.23	3.55
2009	Cle	AL	37	0	0	5	34.0	142	30	16	13	4	1	1	0	13	0	30	2	0	0	0	-	0	0-1	10	3.49	3.44
2010	Cle	AL	53	0	0	7	40.0	170	30	18	17	4	1	0	1	24	2	32	0	1	2	2	.500	0	0-1	17	3.53	3.83
	4 ML YEARS		226	0	0	38	181.2	788	159	80	72	15	8	1	12	89	10	159	5	1	11	7	.611	0	0-5	55	3.78	3.57

Jordan Smith

Pitches: R **Bats:** R **Pos:** RP-37 **Ht:** 6'4" **Wt:** 220 **Born:** 2/4/1986 **Age:** 25

Year	Team	Lg	G	GS	CG	GF	IP	BFP	H	R	ER	HR	SH	SF	HB	TBB	IBB	SO	WP	Bk	W	L	Pct	Sh	Sv-Op	Hld	ERC	ERA
2006	Billings	R+	14	14	0	0	68.2	284	58	29	23	3	2	1	6	20	0	49	3	0	6	3	.667	0	0--	-	2.80	3.01
2007	Dayton	A	26	26	0	0	133.2	574	133	74	57	8	1	6	11	40	0	96	8	1	10	8	.556	0	0--	-	3.68	3.84
2008	Srsota	A+	10	10	0	0	67.0	268	61	23	10	2	2	3	3	7	0	44	0	0	7	2	.778	0	0--	-	2.24	2.55
2008	Chatt	AA	11	11	0	0	55.0	255	72	42	33	6	2	4	4	17	1	42	6	1	2	6	.250	0	0--	-	5.78	5.40
2009	Carlina	AA	13	13	0	0	73.1	310	77	37	28	4	5	4	2	21	0	39	1	0	5	3	.625	0	0--	-	3.74	3.44
2010	Carlina	AA	27	0	0	23	28.1	120	30	20	16	3	0	0	1	8	1	14	1	0	1	3	.250	0	9--	-	5.77	5.08
2010	Lsvlle	AAA	3	0	0	1	3.1	16	5	3	3	1	0	0	0	1	0	0	0	1	0	0	-	0	0--	-	8.14	8.10
2010	Cin	NL	37	0	0	15	42.0	179	45	18	18	7	1	0	2	11	1	26	1	0	3	2	.600	0	1-2	2	4.58	3.86

Seth Smith

Bats: L **Throws:** L **Pos:** LF-71; PH-44; RF-33 **Ht:** 6'3" **Wt:** 210 **Born:** 9/30/1982 **Age:** 28

Year	Team	Lg	G	AB	H	2B	3B	HR	(Hm	Rd)	TB	R	RBI	RC	TBB	IBB	SO	HBP	SH	SF	SB	CS	SB%	GDP	Avg	OBP	Slg
2007	Col	NL	7	8	5	0	1	0	(0	0)	7	4	0	3	0	0	1	0	0	0	0	0	-	0	.625	.625	.875
2008	Col	NL	67	108	28	7	0	4	(2	2)	47	13	15	18	15	0	23	0	0	0	1	0	1.00	6	.259	.350	.435
2009	Col	NL	133	335	98	20	4	15	(8	7)	171	61	55	63	46	3	67	2	1	3	4	1	.80	5	.293	.378	.510
2010	Col	NL	133	358	88	19	5	17	(12	5)	168	55	52	51	35	1	67	2	0	3	2	1	.67	5	.246	.314	.469
	Postseason		9	11	4	1	0	0	(0	0)	5	2	2	3	1	1	2	0	0	0	0	0	-	0	.364	.417	.455
	4 ML YEARS		340	809	219	46	10	36	(22	14)	393	133	122	135	96	4	158	4	1	6	7	2	.78	10	.271	.349	.486

Justin Smoak

Bats: B **Throws:** L **Pos:** 1B-94; DH-5; PH-3 SMOKE **Ht:** 6'4" **Wt:** 220 **Born:** 12/5/1986 **Age:** 24

Year	Team	Lg	G	AB	H	2B	3B	HR	(Hm	Rd)	TB	R	RBI	RC	TBB	IBB	SO	HBP	SH	SF	SB	CS	SB%	GDP	Avg	OBP	Slg
2008	Clinton	A	14	56	17	3	0	3	(-	-)	29	9	6	10	5	0	10	0	0	1	0	0	-	3	.304	.355	.518
2009	Frisco	AA	50	183	60	10	0	6	(-	-)	88	30	29	42	39	2	35	3	0	2	0	0	-	8	.328	.449	.481
2009	Rngrs	R	2	6	4	0	1	2	(-	-)	12	3	5	5	1	0	1	0	0	0	0	0	-	0	.667	.714	2.000
2009	Okla	AAA	54	197	48	11	0	4	(-	-)	71	25	23	29	35	0	45	3	0	2	0	0	-	8	.244	.363	.360
2010	OKCity	AAA	15	50	15	6	0	2	(-	-)	27	10	5	13	16	0	8	0	0	0	0	0	-	0	.300	.470	.540
2010	Tacom	AAA	35	133	36	7	0	7	(-	-)	64	23	25	25	23	0	32	1	0	2	0	0	-	6	.271	.377	.481
2010	2 Tms		100	348	76	14	0	13	(4	9)	129	40	48	42	46	4	91	0	0	3	1	0	1.00	9	.218	.307	.371
10	Tex	AL	70	235	49	10	0	8	(4	4)	83	29	34	30	38	4	57	0	0	2	1	0	1.00	6	.209	.316	.353
10	Sea	AL	30	113	27	4	0	5	(0	5)	46	11	14	12	8	0	34	0	0	1	0	0	-	3	.239	.287	.407

Ian Snell

Pitches: R **Bats:** R **Pos:** SP-8; RP-4   **Ht:** 5'11" **Wt:** 200 **Born:** 10/30/1981 **Age:** 29

			HOW MUCH HE PITCHED						WHAT HE GAVE UP												THE RESULTS							
Year	Team	Lg	G	GS	CG	GF	IP	BFP	H	R	ER	HR	SH	SF	HB	TBB	IBB	SO	WP	Bk	W	L	Pct	Sh	Sv-Op	Hld	ERC	ERA
2010	Tacom*	AAA	9	9	0	0	48.2	221	58	37	36	6	2	4	2	22	0	39	4	0	3	4	.429	0	0- -	-	5.81	6.66
2004	Pit	NL	3	1	0	1	12.0	56	14	10	10	2	0	0	0	9	0	9	0	0	0	1	.000	0	0-0	0	7.31	7.50
2005	Pit	NL	15	5	0	2	42.0	189	43	25	24	5	2	1	1	24	3	34	4	0	1	2	.333	0	0-0	1	5.03	5.14
2006	Pit	NL	32	32	0	0	186.0	813	198	104	98	29	16	6	2	74	4	169	8	0	14	11	.560	0	0-0	0	4.86	4.74
2007	Pit	NL	32	32	1	0	208.0	882	209	94	87	22	6	7	8	68	4	177	12	0	9	12	.429	0	0-0	0	4.02	3.76
2008	Pit	NL	31	31	0	0	164.1	766	201	107	99	18	7	6	2	89	0	135	8	1	7	12	.368	0	0-0	0	6.11	5.42
2009	2 Tms		27	27	1	0	145.0	649	148	82	78	14	7	1	2	83	3	89	6	0	7	10	.412	0	0-0	0	4.91	4.84
2010	Sea	AL	12	8	0	0	46.1	227	60	36	33	10	1	3	1	25	0	26	3	0	0	5	.000	0	0-0	0	7.24	6.41
09	Pit	NL	15	15	1	0	80.2	360	87	50	48	7	5	1	1	44	3	52	3	0	2	8	.200	0	0-0	0	5.08	5.36
09	Sea	AL	12	12	0	0	64.1	289	61	32	30	7	2	0	1	39	0	37	3	0	5	2	.714	0	0-0	0	4.70	4.20
7 ML YEARS			152	136	2	3	803.2	3582	873	458	429	100	39	24	16	372	14	639	41	1	38	53	.418	0	0-0	1	5.07	4.80

Travis Snider

Bats: L **Throws:** L **Pos:** LF-53; RF-29; PH-4; PR-2   **Ht:** 6'0" **Wt:** 235 **Born:** 2/2/1988 **Age:** 23

						BATTING																BASERUNNING				AVERAGES		
Year	Team	Lg	G	AB	H	2B	3B	HR	(Hm	Rd)	TB	R	RBI	RC	TBB	IBB	SO	HBP	SH	SF		SB	CS	SB%	GDP		Avg	OBP	Slg
2010	B Jays*	R	4	14	4	0	0	0	(-	-)	4	2	1	0	0	0	1	0	0	1		1	1	.50	0		.286	.267	.286
2010	Dnedin*	A+	1	4	0	0	0	0	(-	-)	0	0	0	0	0	0	2	0	0	0		0	0	-	0		.000	.000	.000
2010	NHam*	AA	20	81	24	5	0	5	(-	-)	44	14	17	13	2	0	21	0	0	2		3	1	.75	3		.296	.306	.543
2008	Tor	AL	24	73	22	6	0	2	(1	1)	34	9	13	13	5	0	23	0	0	2		0	0	-	0		.301	.338	.466
2009	Tor	AL	77	241	58	14	1	9	(5	4)	101	34	29	30	29	1	78	3	2	1		1	1	.50	5		.241	.328	.419
2010	Tor	AL	82	298	76	20	0	14	(9	5)	138	36	32	40	21	2	79	0	0	0		6	3	.67	3		.255	.304	.463
3 ML YEARS			183	612	156	40	1	25	(15	10)	273	79	74	83	55	3	180	3	2	3		7	4	.64	8		.255	.318	.446

Brad Snyder

Bats: L **Throws:** L **Pos:** RF-6; PH-6; LF-3   **Ht:** 6'3" **Wt:** 200 **Born:** 5/25/1982 **Age:** 29

						BATTING																BASERUNNING				AVERAGES		
Year	Team	Lg	G	AB	H	2B	3B	HR	(Hm	Rd)	TB	R	RBI	RC	TBB	IBB	SO	HBP	SH	SF		SB	CS	SB%	GDP		Avg	OBP	Slg
2003	MhVlly	A-	62	225	64	11	6	6	(-	-)	105	52	31	44	41	1	82	1	1	3		14	5	.74	2		.284	.393	.467
2004	Lk Cty	A	79	304	85	15	5	10	(-	-)	140	52	54	57	48	1	78	5	0	4		11	4	.73	5		.280	.382	.461
2004	Knstn	A+	29	110	39	7	1	6	(-	-)	66	20	21	26	13	1	28	1	0	1		4	2	.67	1		.355	.424	.600
2005	Knstn	A+	58	209	58	10	2	6	(-	-)	90	36	28	36	24	1	64	6	0	2		12	1	.92	2		.278	.365	.431
2005	Akron	AA	75	304	85	21	5	16	(-	-)	164	56	54	56	25	3	94	6	1	1		5	3	.63	3		.280	.345	.539
2006	Akron	AA	135	523	141	28	5	18	(-	-)	233	86	72	88	62	1	158	5	1	3		20	2	.91	12		.270	.351	.446
2007	Buffalo	AAA	86	259	68	12	3	10	(-	-)	116	41	35	45	36	1	91	2	4	2		12	0	1.00	4		.263	.355	.448
2008	Buffalo	AAA	115	411	101	28	5	12	(-	-)	175	52	61	53	27	2	123	4	1	3		7	3	.70	3		.246	.297	.426
2009	Iowa	AAA	69	237	66	16	3	14	(-	-)	130	39	44	44	20	3	68	1	0	2		10	4	.71	5		.278	.335	.549
2009	Cubs	R	5	18	5	1	1	1	(-	-)	11	1	3	3	1	0	7	0	0	0		0	0	-	0		.278	.316	.611
2010	Iowa	AAA	132	477	147	37	6	25	(-	-)	271	97	106	104	56	3	125	4	0	6		19	4	.83	9		.308	.381	.568
2010	ChC	NL	12	27	5	1	0	0	(0	0)	6	1	5	2	1	0	12	0	0	0		0	0	-	0		.185	.214	.222

Brandon Snyder

Bats: R **Throws:** R **Pos:** 1B-10; PH-1   **Ht:** 6'2" **Wt:** 210 **Born:** 11/23/1986 **Age:** 24

						BATTING																BASERUNNING				AVERAGES		
Year	Team	Lg	G	AB	H	2B	3B	HR	(Hm	Rd)	TB	R	RBI	RC	TBB	IBB	SO	HBP	SH	SF		SB	CS	SB%	GDP		Avg	OBP	Slg
2005	Bluefld	R+	44	144	39	8	0	8	(-	-)	71	26	35	30	28	2	36	1	1	6		7	2	.78	2		.271	.380	.493
2005	Abrdn	A-	8	28	11	2	0	0	(-	-)	13	4	6	5	2	0	7	0	0	1		0	0	-	0		.393	.419	.464
2006	Dlmrva	A	38	144	28	12	0	3	(-	-)	49	12	20	11	9	0	55	0	3	3		0	0	-	3		.194	.237	.340
2006	Abrdn	A-	34	124	29	8	1	1	(-	-)	42	14	11	11	5	0	43	1	0	1		2	1	.67	2		.234	.267	.339
2007	Dlmrva	A	118	448	127	23	3	11	(-	-)	189	63	58	69	44	1	107	6	1	2		0	2	.00	11		.283	.354	.422
2008	Frdrck	A+	116	435	137	33	2	13	(-	-)	213	70	80	77	29	1	83	4	1	7		3	2	.60	14		.315	.358	.490
2009	Bowie	AA	58	201	69	19	1	10	(-	-)	120	24	45	48	27	4	45	2	0	3		0	1	.00	3		.343	.421	.597
2009	Norfolk	AAA	73	262	65	18	2	2	(-	-)	93	36	43	32	24	1	64	5	0	6		3	1	.75	5		.248	.316	.355
2010	Norfolk	AAA	98	339	87	22	1	9	(-	-)	138	36	43	47	28	0	101	7	0	2		4	1	.80	7		.257	.324	.407
2010	Abrdn	A-	3	13	3	1	0	1	(-	-)	7	2	4	1	0	0	2	0	0	0		0	0	-	2		.231	.231	.538
2010	Bal	AL	10	20	6	2	0	0	(0	0)	8	1	3	3	0	0	3	0	0	0		0	1	.00	0		.300	.300	.400

Chris Snyder

Bats: R **Throws:** R **Pos:** C-101; PH-4   **Ht:** 6'4" **Wt:** 245 **Born:** 2/12/1981 **Age:** 30

						BATTING																BASERUNNING				AVERAGES		
Year	Team	Lg	G	AB	H	2B	3B	HR	(Hm	Rd)	TB	R	RBI	RC	TBB	IBB	SO	HBP	SH	SF		SB	CS	SB%	GDP		Avg	OBP	Slg
2004	Ari	NL	29	96	23	6	0	5	(1	4)	44	10	15	11	13	1	25	0	0	1		0	0	-	0		.240	.327	.458
2005	Ari	NL	115	326	66	14	0	6	(2	4)	98	24	28	25	40	5	87	4	3	0		0	1	.00	6		.202	.297	.301
2006	Ari	NL	61	184	51	9	0	6	(4	2)	78	19	32	27	22	4	39	1	1	5		0	0	-	5		.277	.349	.424
2007	Ari	NL	110	326	82	20	0	13	(4	9)	141	37	47	48	40	3	67	7	3	4		0	1	.00	9		.252	.342	.433
2008	Ari	NL	115	334	79	22	1	16	(6	10)	151	47	64	53	56	5	101	4	5	5		0	0	-	7		.237	.348	.452
2009	Ari	NL	61	165	33	7	0	6	(3	3)	58	20	22	17	32	4	47	2	1	2		0	0	-	5		.200	.333	.352
2010	2 Tms	NL	105	319	66	9	0	15	(6	9)	120	34	48	38	52	10	94	2	1	2		0	0	-	11		.207	.320	.376
10	Ari	NL	65	195	45	8	0	10	(5	5)	83	22	32	30	36	6	61	1	1	1		0	0	-	5		.231	.352	.426
10	Pit	NL	40	124	21	1	0	5	(1	4)	37	12	16	8	16	4	33	1	0	1		0	0	-	6		.169	.268	.298
Postseason			6	19	5	2	0	1	(0	1)	10	3	3	2	2	0	6	0	0	0		0	0	-	3		.263	.333	.526
7 ML YEARS			596	1750	400	87	1	67	(26	41)	690	191	256	219	255	32	460	20	14	19		0	2	.00	43		.229	.330	.394

Eric Sogard

Bats: L Throws: R Pos: 2B-3; PH-2 | SO-guard | Ht: 5'10" Wt: 180 Born: 5/22/1986 Age: 25

Year	Team	Lg	G	AB	H	2B	3B	HR	(Hm	Rd)	TB	R	RBI	RC	TBB	IBB	SO	HBP	SH	SF	SB	CS	SB%	GDP	Avg	OBP	Slg
2007	FtWyn	A	22	83	21	2	0	2	(-	-)	29	7	15	9	6	0	13	1	1	1	2	2	.50	5	.253	.308	.349
2007	Eugene	A-	31	125	32	9	0	2	(-	-)	47	20	18	18	19	1	16	0	1	0	4	2	.67	1	.256	.354	.376
2007	PortInd	AAA	1	3	0	0	0	0	(-	-)	0	0	0	0	0	0	3	1	0	0	0	0	-	0	.000	.250	.000
2008	Lk Els	A+	133	536	165	42	3	10	(-	-)	243	97	87	101	79	3	62	1	0	6	16	7	.70	9	.308	.394	.453
2009	SnAnt	AA	117	458	134	25	3	6	(-	-)	183	79	51	73	58	2	48	2	6	7	10	6	.63	12	.293	.370	.400
2010	Scrmto	AAA	137	514	154	28	6	5	(-	-)	209	82	65	87	75	2	68	4	1	3	14	9	.61	7	.300	.391	.407
2010	Oak	AL	4	7	3	0	0	0	(0	0)	3	0	0	1	2	0	1	0	0	0	0	1	.00	0	.429	.556	.429

Andy Sonnanstine

Pitches: R Bats: L Pos: RP-37; SP-4 | SAHN-un-styne | Ht: 6'3" Wt: 190 Born: 3/18/1983 Age: 28

Year	Team	Lg	G	GS	CG	GF	IP	BFP	H	R	ER	HR	SH	SF	HB	TBB	IBB	SO	WP	Bk	W	L	Pct	Sh	Sv-Op	Hld	ERC	ERA
2010	Charltt*	A+	1	1	0	0	1.1	7	2	1	1	0	0	0	0	1	0	4	0	0	0	0	-	0	0--	0	7.52	6.75
2007	TB	AL	22	22	0	0	130.2	554	151	87	85	18	3	5	5	26	2	97	2	0	6	10	.375	0	0-0	0	4.62	5.85
2008	TB	AL	32	32	1	0	193.1	819	212	105	94	21	4	9	5	37	2	124	6	0	13	9	.591	1	0-0	0	3.92	4.38
2009	TB	AL	22	18	0	2	99.2	459	131	85	75	19	0	2	6	34	3	60	3	0	6	9	.400	0	0-0	0	6.38	6.77
2010	TB	AL	41	4	0	23	81.0	355	83	40	40	11	0	1	7	27	3	50	3	0	3	1	.750	0	1-1	0	4.45	4.44
	Postseason		3	3	0	0	17.0	74	15	11	8	4	0	0	0	5	0	8	0	0	2	1	.667	0	0-0	0	3.64	4.24
	4 ML YEARS		117	76	1	25	504.2	2187	577	317	294	69	7	17	19	124	10	331	14	0	28	29	.491	1	1-1	0	4.65	5.24

Joakim Soria

Pitches: R Bats: R Pos: RP-66 | WAH-keem SORE-ee-uh | Ht: 6'3" Wt: 199 Born: 5/18/1984 Age: 27

Year	Team	Lg	G	GS	CG	GF	IP	BFP	H	R	ER	HR	SH	SF	HB	TBB	IBB	SO	WP	Bk	W	L	Pct	Sh	Sv-Op	Hld	ERC	ERA
2007	KC	AL	62	0	0	38	69.0	270	46	20	19	3	1	3	1	19	3	75	2	0	2	3	.400	0	17-21	9	1.63	2.48
2008	KC	AL	63	0	0	57	67.1	260	39	13	12	5	2	2	6	19	1	66	1	1	2	3	.400	0	42-45	0	1.72	1.60
2009	KC	AL	47	0	0	41	53.0	222	44	14	13	5	1	2	2	16	1	60	3	0	3	2	.600	0	30-33	0	2.80	2.21
2010	KC	AL	66	0	0	56	65.2	270	53	13	13	4	3	4	2	16	1	71	3	1	1	2	.333	0	43-46	0	2.27	1.78
	4 ML YEARS		238	0	0	192	255.0	1022	182	60	57	17	7	11	11	70	6	281	9	2	8	10	.444	0	132-145	9	2.05	2.01

Alfonso Soriano

Bats: R Throws: R Pos: LF-134; PH-13; DH-1 | Ht: 6'1" Wt: 195 Born: 1/7/1976 Age: 35

Year	Team	Lg	G	AB	H	2B	3B	HR	(Hm	Rd)	TB	R	RBI	RC	TBB	IBB	SO	HBP	SH	SF	SB	CS	SB%	GDP	Avg	OBP	Slg
1999	NYY	AL	9	8	1	0	0	1	(1	0)	4	2	1	0	0	0	3	0	0	0	0	1	.00	0	.125	.125	.500
2000	NYY	AL	22	50	9	3	0	2	(0	2)	18	5	3	4	1	0	15	0	2	0	2	0	1.00	0	.180	.196	.360
2001	NYY	AL	158	574	154	34	3	18	(8	10)	248	77	73	77	29	0	125	3	3	5	43	14	.75	7	.268	.304	.432
2002	NYY	AL	156	696	209	51	2	39	(17	22)	381	128	102	121	23	1	157	14	1	7	41	13	.76	8	.300	.332	.547
2003	NYY	AL	156	682	198	36	5	38	(15	23)	358	114	91	110	38	7	130	12	0	2	35	8	.81	8	.290	.338	.525
2004	Tex	AL	145	608	170	32	4	28	(12	16)	294	77	91	90	33	4	121	10	0	7	18	5	.78	7	.280	.324	.484
2005	Tex	AL	156	637	171	43	2	36	(25	11)	326	102	104	93	33	3	125	7	0	5	30	2	.94	0	.268	.309	.512
2006	Was	NL	159	647	179	41	2	46	(24	22)	362	119	95	114	67	16	160	9	2	3	41	17	.71	3	.277	.351	.560
2007	ChC	NL	135	579	173	42	5	33	(13	20)	324	97	70	91	31	4	130	4	0	0	19	6	.76	9	.299	.337	.560
2008	ChC	NL	109	453	127	27	0	29	(17	12)	241	76	75	77	43	11	103	3	0	4	19	3	.86	9	.280	.344	.532
2009	ChC	NL	117	477	115	25	1	20	(7	13)	202	64	55	61	40	0	110	3	0	2	9	2	.82	7	.241	.303	.423
2010	ChC	NL	147	496	128	40	3	24	(11	13)	246	67	79	75	45	3	123	3	1	3	5	1	.83	12	.258	.322	.496
	Postseason		44	174	37	3	0	4	(3	1)	52	14	18	14	9	0	53	3	0	0	10	3	.77	3	.213	.263	.299
	12 ML YEARS		1469	5907	1634	374	27	314	(150	104)	3004	928	839	913	383	55	1310	68	9	41	262	72	.78	76	.277	.326	.509

Rafael Soriano

Pitches: R Bats: R Pos: RP-64 | Ht: 6'1" Wt: 220 Born: 12/19/1979 Age: 31

Year	Team	Lg	G	GS	CG	GF	IP	BFP	H	R	ER	HR	SH	SF	HB	TBB	IBB	SO	WP	Bk	W	L	Pct	Sh	Sv-Op	Hld	ERC	ERA
2002	Sea	AL	10	8	0	1	47.1	202	45	25	24	8	1	0	0	16	1	32	2	0	0	3	.000	0	1-1	0	3.93	4.56
2003	Sea	AL	40	0	0	12	53.0	201	30	9	9	2	0	1	3	12	1	68	0	0	3	0	1.000	0	1-2	5	1.32	1.53
2004	Sea	AL	6	0	0	0	3.1	23	9	6	5	0	0	0	0	3	0	3	0	0	0	3	.000	0	0-1	0	15.97	13.50
2005	Sea	AL	7	0	0	4	7.1	30	6	2	2	0	0	1	1	1	0	9	0	0	0	0	-	0	0-0	1	2.00	2.45
2006	Sea	AL	53	0	0	14	60.0	241	44	15	15	6	1	1	2	21	0	65	2	0	1	2	.333	0	2-6	18	2.64	2.25
2007	Atl	NL	71	0	0	28	72.0	276	47	26	24	12	0	0	2	15	2	70	0	0	3	3	.500	0	9-12	19	2.05	3.00
2008	Atl	NL	14	0	0	5	14.0	57	7	5	4	1	0	0	1	9	2	16	1	0	1	0	1.000	0	3-4	0	2.27	2.57
2009	Atl	NL	77	0	0	52	75.2	307	53	25	25	6	4	2	1	27	4	102	0	0	1	6	.143	0	27-31	6	2.18	2.97
2010	TB	AL	64	0	0	56	62.1	237	36	14	12	4	0	1	1	14	2	57	0	0	3	2	.600	0	45-48	0	1.33	1.73
	9 ML YEARS		342	8	0	172	395.0	1574	277	127	120	39	6	6	11	118	12	422	5	0	11	20	.355	0	88-105	49	2.20	2.73

Jorge Sosa

Pitches: R Bats: R Pos: RP-20; SP-2 | Ht: 6'2" Wt: 220 Born: 4/28/1977 Age: 34

Year	Team	Lg	G	GS	CG	GF	IP	BFP	H	R	ER	HR	SH	SF	HB	TBB	IBB	SO	WP	Bk	W	L	Pct	Sh	Sv-Op	Hld	ERC	ERA
2010	NewOr*	AAA	23	9	0	2	59.0	258	74	34	31	5	5	1	1	15	1	45	1	0	5	4	.556	0	1--	-	4.94	4.73
2002	TB	AL	31	14	0	10	99.1	434	88	63	61	16	0	5	2	54	0	48	5	0	2	7	.222	0	0-0	1	4.51	5.53
2003	TB	AL	29	19	1	4	128.2	566	137	71	66	14	4	5	4	60	4	72	8	1	5	12	.294	1	0-0	0	4.93	4.62
2004	TB	AL	43	8	0	6	99.1	447	100	67	61	17	2	4	1	54	3	94	2	0	4	7	.364	0	1-1	6	5.17	5.53

Year	Team	Lg	G	GS	CG	GF	IP	BFP	H	R	ER	HR	SH	SF	HB	TBB	IBB	SO	WP	Bk	W	L	Pct	Sh	Sv-Op	Hld	ERC	ERA
2005	Atl	NL	44	20	0	5	134.0	577	122	42	38	12	5	2	0	64	8	85	3	0	13	3	.813	0	0-0	4	3.70	2.55
2006	2 Tms	NL	45	13	0	12	118.0	524	138	79	71	30	7	4	1	40	6	75	2	0	3	11	.214	0	4-7	0	5.88	5.42
2007	NYM	NL	42	14	0	2	112.2	481	109	58	56	10	10	3	0	41	2	69	0	0	9	8	.529	0	0-2	9	3.63	4.47
2008	NYM	NL	20	0	0	8	21.2	107	30	23	17	4	3	0	0	11	4	12	2	0	4	1	.800	0	0-0	1	6.95	7.06
2009	Was	NL	18	0	0	4	22.1	103	28	16	16	5	0	1	0	12	2	17	2	0	2	1	.667	0	2-2	3	7.12	6.45
2010	Fla	NL	22	2	0	4	36.2	165	39	22	19	4	1	2	0	18	4	19	2	0	2	3	.400	0	0-0	0	4.63	4.66
06	Atl	NL	26	13	0	8	87.1	394	105	61	53	20	5	4	1	32	5	58	2	0	3	10	.231	0	3-6	0	6.00	5.46
06	StL	NL	19	0	0	4	30.2	130	33	18	18	10	2	0	0	8	1	17	0	0	0	1	.000	0	1-1	0	5.48	5.28
	Postseason		1	1	0	0	6.0	27	7	3	3	1	0	1	1	2	2	3	0	0	0	1	.000	0	0-0	0	5.45	4.50
	9 ML YEARS		294	90	1	55	772.2	3404	791	441	405	112	32	26	8	354	33	491	26	1	44	53	.454	1	7-12	24	4.73	4.72

Geovany Soto

Bats: R **Throws:** R **Pos:** C-104; DH-1; PH-1   **Ht:** 6'1" **Wt:** 218 **Born:** 1/20/1983 **Age:** 28

Year	Team	Lg	G	AB	H	2B	3B	HR	(Hm	Rd)	TB	R	RBI	RC	TBB	IBB	SO	HBP	SH	SF	SB	CS	SB%	GDP	Avg	OBP	Slg
2005	ChC	NL	1	1	0	0	0	0	(0	0)	0	0	0	0	0	0	0	0	0	0	0	0	-	0	.000	.000	.000
2006	ChC	NL	11	25	5	1	0	0	(0	0)	6	1	2	0	0	0	5	1	0	0	0	0	-	0	.200	.231	.240
2007	ChC	NL	18	54	21	6	0	3	(2	1)	36	12	8	13	5	0	14	0	0	1	0	0	-	1	.389	.433	.667
2008	ChC	NL	141	494	141	35	2	23	(11	12)	249	66	86	81	62	6	121	2	0	5	0	1	.00	11	.285	.364	.504
2009	ChC	NL	102	331	72	19	1	11	(6	5)	126	27	47	34	50	3	77	3	0	5	1	0	1.00	19	.218	.321	.381
2010	ChC	NL	105	322	90	19	0	17	(12	5)	160	47	53	59	62	4	83	0	0	3	0	1	.00	5	.280	.393	.497
	Postseason		5	17	3	1	0	1	(0	1)	7	1	2	1	3	0	4	0	0	0	0	0	-	0	.176	.300	.412
	6 ML YEARS		378	1227	329	80	3	54	(31	23)	577	153	196	187	179	13	300	6	0	14	1	2	.33	36	.268	.360	.470

Denard Span

Bats: L **Throws:** L **Pos:** CF-153   **Ht:** 6'0" **Wt:** 205 **Born:** 2/27/1984 **Age:** 27

Year	Team	Lg	G	AB	H	2B	3B	HR	(Hm	Rd)	TB	R	RBI	RC	TBB	IBB	SO	HBP	SH	SF	SB	CS	SB%	GDP	Avg	OBP	Slg
2008	Min	AL	93	347	102	16	7	6	(2	4)	150	70	47	68	50	3	60	4	8	2	18	7	.72	3	.294	.387	.432
2009	Min	AL	145	578	180	16	10	8	(5	3)	240	97	68	100	70	3	89	10	12	6	23	10	.70	7	.311	.392	.415
2010	Min	AL	153	629	166	24	10	3	(0	3)	219	85	58	85	60	0	74	4	10	2	26	4	.87	12	.264	.331	.348
	Postseason		3	15	6	1	0	0	(0	0)	7	1	1	1	0	0	2	0	0	0	1	0	1.00	1	.400	.400	.467
	3 ML YEARS		391	1554	448	56	27	17	(7	10)	609	252	173	253	180	6	223	18	30	10	67	21	.76	22	.288	.367	.392

Ryan Spilborghs

Bats: R **Throws:** R **Pos:** RF-62; LF-46; PH-41; CF-6; PR-1   SPILL-borgs   **Ht:** 6'1" **Wt:** 200 **Born:** 9/5/1979 **Age:** 31

Year	Team	Lg	G	AB	H	2B	3B	HR	(Hm	Rd)	TB	R	RBI	RC	TBB	IBB	SO	HBP	SH	SF	SB	CS	SB%	GDP	Avg	OBP	Slg
2005	Col	NL	1	4	2	0	0	0	(0	0)	2	0	1	1	0	0	1	0	0	0	0	0	-	0	.500	.500	.500
2006	Col	NL	67	167	48	6	3	4	(3	1)	72	26	21	22	14	0	30	0	2	3	5	2	.71	7	.287	.337	.431
2007	Col	NL	97	264	79	14	1	11	(5	6)	128	40	51	48	28	1	45	2	0	6	4	1	.80	5	.299	.363	.485
2008	Col	NL	89	233	73	14	2	6	(3	3)	109	38	36	42	38	0	41	1	0	3	7	4	.64	8	.313	.407	.468
2009	Col	NL	133	352	85	24	3	8	(4	4)	139	55	48	44	34	0	79	2	3	2	9	5	.64	9	.241	.310	.395
2010	Col	NL	134	341	95	20	2	10	(6	4)	149	41	39	53	39	0	83	5	2	1	4	5	.44	7	.279	.360	.437
	Postseason		13	29	5	1	0	0	(0	0)	6	4	0	1	6	1	9	0	0	0	0	0	-	0	.172	.314	.207
	6 ML YEARS		521	1361	382	78	11	39	(21	18)	599	200	196	210	153	1	279	10	7	15	29	17	.63	36	.281	.354	.440

Russ Springer

Pitches: R **Bats:** R **Pos:** RP-2   **Ht:** 6'4" **Wt:** 225 **Born:** 11/7/1968 **Age:** 42

Year	Team	Lg	G	GS	CG	GF	IP	BFP	H	R	ER	HR	SH	SF	HB	TBB	IBB	SO	WP	Bk	W	L	Pct	Sh	Sv-Op	Hld	ERC	ERA
2010	Lsvlle*	AAA	7	0	0	2	6.1	22	2	0	0	0	0	0	0	2	0	5	0	0	0	0	-	0	0--	0	0.65	0.00
1992	NYY	AL	14	0	0	5	16.0	75	18	11	11	0	0	0	1	10	0	12	0	0	0	0	-	0	0-0	2	5.15	6.19
1993	LAA	AL	14	9	1	3	60.0	278	73	48	48	11	1	1	3	32	1	31	6	0	1	6	.143	0	0-0	0	6.87	7.20
1994	LAA	AL	18	5	0	6	45.2	198	53	28	28	9	1	1	0	14	0	28	2	0	2	2	.500	0	2-3	1	5.38	5.52
1995	2 Tms		33	6	0	6	78.1	350	82	48	46	16	2	2	7	35	4	70	2	0	1	2	.333	0	1-2	0	5.63	5.29
1996	Phi	NL	51	7	0	12	96.2	437	106	60	50	12	5	3	1	38	6	94	5	0	3	10	.231	0	0-3	6	4.57	4.66
1997	Hou	NL	54	0	0	13	55.1	241	48	28	26	4	1	2	4	27	2	74	4	0	3	3	.500	0	3-7	9	3.69	4.23
1998	2 Tms	NL	48	0	0	14	52.2	232	51	26	24	4	2	1	1	30	4	56	5	0	5	4	.556	0	0-4	7	4.38	4.10
1999	Atl	NL	49	0	0	8	47.1	194	31	20	18	5	0	2	2	22	2	49	0	0	2	1	.667	0	1-1	8	2.63	3.42
2000	Ari	NL	52	0	0	10	62.0	282	63	36	35	11	2	3	2	34	6	59	3	0	2	4	.333	0	0-2	3	5.25	5.08
2001	Ari	NL	18	0	0	9	17.2	79	20	16	14	5	1	1	0	4	0	12	2	0	0	0	-	0	1-1	2	5.13	7.13
2003	StL	NL	17	0	0	4	17.1	77	19	16	16	8	0	0	1	6	0	11	1	0	1	1	.500	0	0-1	5	7.27	8.31
2004	Hou	NL	16	0	0	3	13.2	62	15	4	4	1	0	1	1	6	0	9	2	0	1	0	1.000	0	0-0	5	4.84	2.63
2005	Hou	NL	62	0	0	11	59.0	246	49	34	31	9	1	0	3	21	3	54	2	0	4	4	.500	0	0-3	10	3.45	4.73
2006	Hou	NL	72	0	0	17	59.2	240	46	23	23	10	2	0	4	16	1	46	2	0	1	1	.500	0	0-0	9	3.03	3.47
2007	StL	NL	76	0	0	18	66.0	257	41	18	16	3	3	6	3	19	1	66	1	0	8	1	.889	0	0-2	11	1.63	2.18
2008	StL	NL	70	0	0	9	50.1	205	39	14	13	4	2	0	1	18	0	45	2	0	2	1	.667	0	0-2	15	2.68	2.32
2009	2 Tms	AL	74	0	0	20	57.0	256	68	27	26	9	0	6	1	17	3	58	0	0	1	4	.200	0	1-3	14	5.08	4.11
2010	Cin	NL	2	0	0	0	1.2	7	2	1	1	0	0	0	0	0	0	1	0	0	0	0	-	0	0-0	0	2.89	5.40
95	LAA	AL	19	6	0	3	51.2	238	60	37	35	11	1	0	5	25	1	38	1	0	1	2	.333	0	1-2	0	6.69	6.10
95	Phi	NL	14	0	0	3	26.2	112	22	11	11	5	1	2	2	10	3	32	1	0	0	0	-	0	0-0	0	3.73	3.71
98	Ari	NL	26	0	0	13	32.2	140	29	16	15	4	0	0	1	14	1	37	3	0	4	3	.571	0	0-3	1	3.77	4.13
98	Atl	NL	22	0	0	1	20.0	92	22	10	9	0	2	1	0	16	3	19	2	0	1	1	.500	0	0-1	6	5.36	4.05

			HOW MUCH HE PITCHED						WHAT HE GAVE UP											THE RESULTS							
Year	Team	Lg	G	GS	CG	GF	IP	BFP	H	R	ER	HR	SH	SF	HB	TBB	IBB	SO	WP	Bk	W	L	Pct	Sh	Sv-Op	Hld	ERC	ERA
09	Oak	AL	48	0	0	11	41.2	191	52	20	19	5	0	3	0	14	2	47	0	0	0	1	.000	0	0-1	7	5.19	4.10
09	TB	AL	26	0	0	9	15.1	65	16	7	7	4	0	3	1	3	1	11	0	0	1	3	.250	0	1-2	7	4.74	4.11
	Postseason		14	0	0	4	14.1	63	15	7	7	1	1	0	1	6	0	14	0	0	1	1	.500	0	0-0	1	4.51	4.40
	18 ML YEARS		740	27	1	168	856.1	3716	824	458	430	121	23	29	35	349	33	775	39	0	36	45	.444	0	9-34	107	4.27	4.52

Max St. Pierre

Bats: R Throws: R Pos: C-4; PH-2   Ht: 6'0" Wt: 175 Born: 4/17/1980 Age: 31

						BATTING															BASERUNNING				AVERAGES		
Year	Team	Lg	G	AB	H	2B	3B	HR	(Hm	Rd)	TB	R	RBI	RC	TBB	IBB	SO	HBP	SH	SF	SB	CS	SB%	GDP	Avg	OBP	Slg
1997	Tigers	R	20	41	10	1	0	0	(-	-)	11	3	3	4	3	0	8	3	0	0	2	0	1.00	3	.244	.340	.268
1998	Tigers	R	31	104	40	3	0	2	(-	-)	49	18	15	23	15	0	12	1	0	0	6	2	.75	1	.385	.467	.471
1999	Oneont	A-	51	175	44	7	0	1	(-	-)	54	12	22	19	11	0	29	3	0	1	9	0	1.00	6	.251	.305	.309
2000	WMich	A	73	229	57	10	1	2	(-	-)	75	41	28	33	42	1	37	5	2	3	2	2	.50	10	.249	.373	.328
2001	Lkland	A+	99	330	82	15	0	4	(-	-)	109	42	43	40	43	1	50	4	0	5	2	5	.29	11	.248	.338	.330
2002	Lkland	A+	55	195	50	12	0	4	(-	-)	74	20	27	24	13	0	30	7	0	1	2	4	.33	4	.256	.324	.379
2002	Erie	AA	60	207	55	9	0	3	(-	-)	73	24	28	24	17	1	31	1	1	3	0	1	.00	10	.266	.320	.353
2002	Toledo	AAA	1	2	0	0	0	0	(-	-)	0	0	0	1	0	0	0	0	0	0	0	0	-	0	.000	.000	.000
2003	Erie	AA	115	399	94	16	0	11	(-	-)	143	50	54	46	33	1	66	5	5	5	2	0	1.00	9	.236	.299	.358
2004	Erie	AA	84	290	72	15	0	8	(-	-)	111	31	33	37	25	0	41	4	1	2	2	1	.67	7	.248	.315	.383
2005	Erie	AA	95	360	100	18	0	5	(-	-)	133	46	46	44	23	0	55	1	1	3	1	1	.50	14	.278	.320	.369
2006	Toledo	AAA	78	247	50	14	1	3	(-	-)	75	25	31	20	16	1	36	3	9	5	0	0	-	7	.202	.255	.304
2007	Hntsvl	AA	10	32	5	0	0	0	(-	-)	5	3	3	1	4	0	3	0	1	0	0	0	-	1	.156	.243	.156
2008	Erie	AA	44	156	39	9	0	6	(-	-)	66	22	31	22	16	2	23	3	0	0	1	0	1.00	1	.250	.331	.423
2008	Toledo	AAA	42	150	32	4	0	2	(-	-)	42	10	16	9	4	0	21	0	4	1	0	0	-	3	.213	.232	.280
2009	Erie	AA	16	58	13	4	0	2	(-	-)	23	8	6	7	3	0	11	3	1	0	0	0	-	1	.224	.297	.397
2009	Toledo	AAA	45	149	37	8	0	6	(-	-)	63	16	18	19	10	0	15	1	2	0	0	0	-	1	.248	.300	.423
2010	Erie	AA	20	60	13	0	1	5	(-	-)	30	13	14	11	11	0	5	1	2	0	2	0	1.00	2	.217	.347	.500
2010	Toledo	AAA	39	130	39	7	0	5	(-	-)	61	16	22	22	11	1	21	2	1	3	1	1	.50	4	.300	.356	.469
2010	Det	AL	6	9	2	1	0	0	(0	0)	3	1	0	1	0	0	2	0	0	0	0	0	-	0	.222	.222	.333

Matt Stairs

Bats: L Throws: R Pos: PH 61; LF-13; 1B-3; DH-2; RF-1   Ht: 5'9" Wt: 215 Born: 2/27/1968 Age: 43

						BATTING															BASERUNNING				AVERAGES		
Year	Team	Lg	G	AB	H	2B	3B	HR	(Hm	Rd)	TB	R	RBI	RC	TBB	IBB	SO	IDP	SH	SF	SB	CS	SB%	GDP	Avg	OBP	Slg
1992	Mon	NL	13	30	5	2	0	0	(0	0)	7	2	5	3	7	0	7	0	0	1	0	0	-	0	.167	.316	.233
1993	Mon	NL	6	8	3	1	0	0	(0	0)	4	1	2	1	0	0	1	0	0	0	0	0	-	1	.375	.375	.500
1995	Bos	AL	39	88	23	7	1	1	(0	1)	35	8	17	9	4	0	14	1	1	1	0	1	.00	1	.261	.298	.398
1996	Oak	AL	61	137	38	5	1	10	(5	5)	75	21	23	27	19	2	23	1	0	1	1	1	.50	2	.277	.367	.547
1997	Oak	AL	133	352	105	19	0	27	(20	7)	205	62	73	77	50	1	60	3	1	4	3	2	.60	6	.298	.386	.582
1998	Oak	AL	149	523	154	33	1	26	(16	10)	267	88	106	96	59	4	93	6	1	4	8	3	.73	13	.294	.370	.511
1999	Oak	AL	146	531	137	26	3	38	(15	23)	283	94	102	101	89	6	124	2	0	1	2	7	.22	8	.258	.366	.533
2000	Oak	AL	143	476	108	26	0	21	(9	12)	197	74	81	69	78	4	122	1	1	6	5	2	.71	7	.227	.333	.414
2001	ChC	NL	120	340	86	21	0	17	(5	12)	157	48	61	57	52	7	76	7	1	3	2	3	.40	4	.253	.358	.462
2002	Mil	NL	107	270	66	15	0	16	(6	10)	129	41	41	38	36	4	50	8	0	1	2	0	1.00	7	.244	.349	.478
2003	Pit	NL	121	305	89	20	1	20	(13	7)	171	49	57	58	45	3	64	5	0	2	0	1	.00	7	.292	.389	.561
2004	KC	AL	126	439	117	21	3	18	(6	12)	198	48	66	65	49	2	92	5	0	3	1	0	1.00	15	.267	.345	.451
2005	KC	AL	127	396	109	26	1	13	(5	8)	176	55	66	70	60	4	69	5	0	5	1	2	.33	9	.275	.373	.444
2006	3 Tms	AL	117	348	86	21	0	13	(6	7)	146	42	51	51	40	3	86	3	0	2	0	0	-	7	.247	.328	.420
2007	Tor	AL	125	357	103	28	1	21	(7	14)	196	58	64	65	44	5	66	2	0	2	2	1	.67	7	.289	.368	.549
2008	2 Tms	AL	121	337	85	12	1	13	(7	6)	138	46	49	44	42	9	90	5	0	3	1	1	.50	10	.252	.341	.409
2009	Phi	NL	99	103	20	4	0	5	(3	2)	39	15	17	15	23	3	30	3	0	0	0	0	-	0	.194	.357	.379
2010	SD	NL	78	99	23	6	0	6	(0	6)	47	14	16	13	11	2	32	0	0	1	2	0	1.00	1	.232	.306	.475
2006	KC	AL	77	226	59	14	0	8	(3	5)	97	31	32	35	31	2	52	2	0	2	0	0	-	5	.261	.352	.429
2006	Tex	AL	26	81	17	4	0	3	(2	1)	30	6	11	10	6	1	22	1	0	0	0	0	-	1	.210	.273	.370
2006	Det	AL	14	41	10	3	0	2	(1	1)	19	5	8	6	3	0	12	0	0	0	0	0	-	1	.244	.295	.463
2008	Tor	AL	105	320	80	11	1	11	(6	5)	126	42	44	41	41	9	87	5	0	2	1	1	.50	10	.250	.342	.394
2008	Phi	NL	16	17	5	1	0	2	(1	1)	12	4	5	3	1	0	3	0	0	1	0	0	-	0	.294	.316	.706
	Postseason		17	24	3	1	0	1	(0	1)	7	1	3	2	2	0	6	0	0	0	0	0	-	2	.125	.192	.292
	18 ML YEARS		1839	5139	1356	293	13	265	(123	142)	2470	766	897	859	708	59	1099	57	5	40	30	24	.56	108	.264	.357	.481

Craig Stammen

Pitches: R Bats: R Pos: SP-19; RP-16   STAMM-enn   Ht: 6'3" Wt: 200 Born: 3/9/1984 Age: 27

			HOW MUCH HE PITCHED						WHAT HE GAVE UP											THE RESULTS							
Year	Team	Lg	G	GS	CG	GF	IP	BFP	H	R	ER	HR	SH	SF	HB	TBB	IBB	SO	WP	Bk	W	L	Pct	Sh	Sv-Op	Hld	ERC	ERA
2005	Vrmnt	A-	13	7	0	0	51.0	225	62	36	23	2	0	2	2	12	0	32	3	1	4	5	.444	0	0- -	-	4.33	4.06
2006	Savann	A	21	21	0	0	113.0	479	110	55	45	10	3	6	2	29	0	93	8	0	6	9	.400	0	0- -	-	3.30	3.58
2006	Ptomc	A+	7	6	0	0	29.2	128	34	20	19	5	2	0	1	7	0	16	4	0	2	2	.000	0	0- -	-	4.88	5.76
2007	Ptomc	A+	28	22	0	0	125.0	566	156	79	58	9	1	6	4	54	0	96	16	0	8	6	.571	0	0- -	-	5.67	4.18
2007	Clmbs	AAA	1	1	0	0	3.2	18	4	5	5	1	0	0	0	3	0	2	0	0	0	1	.000	0	0- -	-	7.64	12.27
2008	Ptomc	A+	15	9	0	1	69.1	279	59	24	17	6	1	1	0	17	0	62	2	0	4	2	.667	0	1- -	-	2.69	2.21
2008	Clmbs	AAA	9	8	0	0	43.0	198	62	35	35	3	2	3	2	16	3	35	4	0	1	4	.200	0	0- -	-	6.63	7.33
2008	Hrsbrg	AA	6	6	0	0	38.1	144	22	8	7	1	2	2	0	11	1	31	0	0	3	1	.750	0	0- -	-	1.32	1.64
2009	Syrcse	AAA	7	7	0	0	40.0	162	33	10	8	4	5	1	0	8	0	14	0	0	4	2	.667	0	0- -	-	2.35	1.80
2010	Syrcse	AAA	3	3	1	0	20.0	81	18	5	5	2	1	0	1	3	0	10	0	0	2	0	1.000	1	0- -	-	2.77	2.25
2009	Was	NL	19	19	1	0	105.2	448	112	67	60	14	4	3	3	24	1	48	7	0	4	7	.364	0	0-0	0	4.03	5.11
2010	Was	NL	35	19	0	3	128.0	562	151	78	73	13	5	6	1	41	4	85	3	0	4	4	.500	0	0-0	1	4.79	5.13
	2 ML YEARS		54	38	1	3	233.2	1010	263	145	133	27	9	9	4	65	5	133	10	0	8	11	.421	0	0-0	1	4.45	5.12

Daniel Stange

Pitches: R **Bats:** R **Pos:** RP-4   STANG   **Ht:** 6'3" **Wt:** 185 **Born:** 12/22/1985 **Age:** 25

Year	Team	Lg	G	GS	CG	GF	IP	BFP	H	R	ER	HR	SH	SF	HB	TBB	IBB	SO	WP	Bk	W	L	Pct	Sh	Sv-Op	Hld	ERC	ERA
2006	Msoula	R+	27	0	0	24	36.0	167	39	19	17	2	2	2	0	17	0	48	2	1	5	2	.714	0	13--	-	4.30	4.25
2007	Visalia	A+	38	0	0	33	42.1	188	37	26	15	3	4	1	4	18	2	53	2	0	4	5	.444	0	16--	3	3.43	3.19
2007	Mobile	AA	5	0	0	4	6.2	30	8	4	4	1	0	0	0	2	0	5	0	0	1	0	1.000	0	1--	-	5.06	5.40
2008	Sbend	A	11	0	0	4	17.0	64	11	3	3	0	1	0	2	1	0	17	1	0	1	0	1.000	0	1--	-	1.21	1.59
2008	Visalia	A+	11	0	0	5	13.2	58	10	6	6	2	0	1	2	6	0	14	0	1	1	2	.333	0	0--	-	3.64	3.95
2009	Mobile	AA	39	0	0	21	51.2	235	66	35	29	4	5	4	1	15	1	44	3	1	0	4	.000	0	10--	5	5.03	5.05
2010	Reno	AAA	19	0	0	14	23.1	106	29	17	16	3	1	1	0	10	2	16	4	0	4	3	.571	0	2--	5	5.71	6.17
2010	Mobile	AA	30	0	0	23	32.0	116	14	6	6	1	1	2	2	11	0	18	3	2	4	1	.800	0	13--	5	1.25	1.69
2010	Ari	NL	4	0	0	1	4.0	22	4	6	6	1	0	0	0	6	0	2	0	0	0	0	-	0	0-0	0	9.94	13.50

Mike Stanton

Bats: R **Throws:** R **Pos:** RF-98; PH-3   **Ht:** 6'5" **Wt:** 233 **Born:** 11/8/1989 **Age:** 21

Year	Team	Lg	G	AB	H	2B	3B	HR	(Hm	Rd)	TB	R	RBI	RC	TBB	IBB	SO	HBP	SH	SF	SB	CS	SB%	GDP	Avg	OBP	Slg
2007	Mrlns	R	8	26	7	2	0	0	(-	-)	9	6	1	3	1	0	6	1	0	0	0	0	-	0	.269	.321	.346
2007	Jmstwn	A-	9	30	2	1	0	1	(-	-)	6	2	2	0	3	0	15	0	1	1	0	0	-	0	.067	.147	.200
2008	Grnsbr	A	125	468	137	26	3	39	(-	-)	286	89	97	107	58	7	153	11	0	3	4	2	.67	8	.293	.381	.611
2009	Jupiter	A+	50	180	53	9	3	12	(-	-)	104	27	39	40	28	0	45	1	0	1	2	2	.50	4	.294	.390	.578
2009	Jaxnvl	AA	79	299	69	15	2	16	(-	-)	136	49	53	44	31	1	99	6	0	5	1	1	.50	4	.231	.311	.455
2010	Jaxnvl	AA	53	192	60	13	2	21	(-	-)	140	42	52	59	44	11	53	2	0	2	1	0	1.00	7	.313	.442	.729
2010	Fla	NL	100	359	93	21	1	22	(7	15)	182	45	59	56	34	6	123	2	0	1	5	2	.71	7	.259	.326	.507

Tim Stauffer

Pitches: R **Bats:** R **Pos:** RP-25; SP-7   **Ht:** 6'1" **Wt:** 205 **Born:** 6/2/1982 **Age:** 29

Year	Team	Lg	G	GS	CG	GF	IP	BFP	H	R	ER	HR	SH	SF	HB	TBB	IBB	SO	WP	Bk	W	L	Pct	Sh	Sv-Op	Hld	ERC	ERA
2010	Portlnd*	AAA	6	5	0	0	17.2	85	24	13	9	0	0	0	0	7	0	8	2	0	0	0	-	0	0--	-	5.15	4.58
2005	SD	NL	15	14	0	0	81.0	355	92	50	48	10	2	0	2	29	0	49	0	0	3	6	.333	0	0-0	0	5.00	5.33
2006	SD	NL	1	1	0	0	6.0	21	3	2	1	0	0	0	0	1	0	2	0	0	1	0	1.000	0	0-0	0	0.84	1.50
2007	SD	NL	2	2	0	0	7.2	45	15	18	18	5	0	0	1	6	0	6	0	0	0	1	.000	0	0-0	0	18.32	21.13
2009	SD	NL	14	14	0	0	73.0	316	71	31	29	8	2	1	5	34	1	53	1	0	4	7	.364	0	0-0	0	4.60	3.58
2010	SD	NL	32	7	0	12	82.2	326	65	18	17	3	3	0	2	24	5	61	0	0	6	5	.545	0	0-0	0	2.23	1.85
	5 ML YEARS		64	38	0	12	250.1	1063	246	119	113	26	7	1	10	94	6	171	1	0	14	19	.424	0	0-0	0	4.09	4.06

Nick Stavinoha

Bats: R **Throws:** R **Pos:** PH-56; RF-22; LF-5; 1B-3; DH-2; C-1   stavv-in-OH-ah   **Ht:** 6'2" **Wt:** 240 **Born:** 5/3/1982 **Age:** 29

Year	Team	Lg	G	AB	H	2B	3B	HR	(Hm	Rd)	TB	R	RBI	RC	TBB	IBB	SO	HBP	SH	SF	SB	CS	SB%	GDP	Avg	OBP	Slg
2010	Memp*	AAA	23	100	39	9	1	6	(-	-)	68	19	28	25	5	0	16	0	0	2	0	0	-	6	.390	.411	.680
2008	StL	NL	29	57	11	1	0	0	(0	0)	12	4	4	0	2	1	11	0	1	1	0	0	-	0	.193	.217	.211
2009	StL	NL	39	87	20	7	0	2	(1	1)	33	6	17	9	2	0	15	0	0	2	1	0	1.00	2	.230	.242	.379
2010	StL	NL	79	121	31	4	0	2	(0	2)	41	11	9	10	4	0	28	1	0	0	0	0	-	5	.256	.286	.339
	3 ML YEARS		147	265	62	12	0	4	(1	3)	86	21	30	19	8	1	54	1	1	3	1	0	1.00	9	.234	.256	.325

Adam Stern

Bats: L **Throws:** R **Pos:** PH-4; CF-1; RF-1   **Ht:** 5'11" **Wt:** 190 **Born:** 2/12/1980 **Age:** 31

Year	Team	Lg	G	AB	H	2B	3B	HR	(Hm	Rd)	TB	R	RBI	RC	TBB	IBB	SO	HBP	SH	SF	SB	CS	SB%	GDP	Avg	OBP	Slg
2010	Nashv*	AAA	86	286	93	18	3	5	(-	-)	132	48	29	53	35	0	47	1	0	1	7	4	.64	7	.325	.399	.462
2005	Bos	AL	36	15	2	0	0	1	(0	1)	5	4	2	1	0	0	4	1	0	0	1	1	.50	0	.133	.188	.333
2006	Bos	AL	10	20	3	1	0	0	(0	0)	4	3	4	2	0	0	4	1	0	0	1	0	1.00	0	.150	.190	.200
2007	Bal	AL	2	0	0	0	0	0	(0	0)	0	0	0	0	0	0	0	0	0	0	0	0	-	0			
2010	Mil	NL	6	8	0	0	0	0	(0	0)	0	0	1	0	0	0	2	0	0	0	0	0	-	1	.000	.000	.000
	4 ML YEARS		54	43	5	1	0	1	(0	1)	9	7	7	3	0	0	10	2	0	0	2	1	.67	1	.116	.156	.209

Mitch Stetter

Pitches: L **Bats:** L **Pos:** RP-9   **Ht:** 6'4" **Wt:** 212 **Born:** 1/16/1981 **Age:** 30

Year	Team	Lg	G	GS	CG	GF	IP	BFP	H	R	ER	HR	SH	SF	HB	TBB	IBB	SO	WP	Bk	W	L	Pct	Sh	Sv-Op	Hld	ERC	ERA
2010	Nashv*	AAA	41	0	0	14	42.0	194	46	32	32	9	3	0	4	18	0	52	3	0	3	2	.600	0	0--	-	5.88	6.86
2007	Mil	NL	6	0	0	2	5.0	20	2	2	2	0	0	1	2	2	0	4	3	0	1	0	1.000	0	0-0	0	1.86	3.60
2008	Mil	NL	30	0	0	7	25.1	109	14	9	9	2	1	0	4	19	1	31	1	0	3	1	.750	0	0-1	4	3.40	3.20
2009	Mil	NL	71	0	0	13	45.0	203	37	19	18	4	0	0	5	27	6	44	2	0	4	1	.800	0	1-2	20	3.90	3.60
2010	Mil	NL	9	0	0	0	3.2	22	7	6	6	1	0	0	1	3	0	3	0	0	0	0	-	0	0-0	3	14.78	14.73
	Postseason		3	0	0	0	1.1	4	0	0	0	0	0	0	0	0	0	2	0	0	0	0	-	0	0-0	1	0.00	0.00
	4 ML YEARS		116	0	0	22	79.0	354	60	36	35	7	1	1	12	51	7	82	6	0	8	2	.800	0	1-3	27	4.01	3.99

Jeff Stevens

Pitches: R Bats: R Pos: RP-18   Ht: 6'2" Wt: 205 Born: 9/5/1983 Age: 27

			HOW MUCH HE PITCHED						WHAT HE GAVE UP												THE RESULTS							
Year	Team	Lg	G	GS	CG	GF	IP	BFP	H	R	ER	HR	SH	SF	HB	TBB	IBB	SO	WP	Bk	W	L	Pct	Sh	Sv-Op	Hld	ERC	ERA
2005	Billings	R+	13	8	0	1	54.1	222	44	20	18	4	0	2	5	15	0	58	1	0	4	4	.500	0	0--	-	2.79	2.98
2006	Dayton	A	14	6	0	1	42.2	179	42	22	21	6	1	0	1	16	0	43	3	0	2	4	.333	0	0--	-	4.38	4.43
2006	Lk Cty	A	16	15	0	0	73.1	319	65	40	36	4	2	2	12	23	0	60	5	0	7	3	.700	0	0--	-	3.36	4.42
2007	Knstn	A+	15	0	0	2	35.0	134	18	13	9	1	1	1	3	9	0	37	2	0	3	2	.600	0	0--	-	1.37	2.31
2007	Akron	AA	34	0	0	6	48.1	202	40	17	17	4	2	3	2	16	1	65	4	0	3	1	.750	0	2--	-	2.86	3.17
2008	Akron	AA	17	0	0	3	28.2	114	19	8	8	2	1	0	1	11	0	37	1	0	5	1	.833	0	1--	-	2.24	2.51
2008	Buffalo	AAA	19	0	0	11	29.2	123	19	14	13	3	0	1	1	16	0	44	0	0	0	3	.000	0	5--	-	2.82	3.94
2009	Iowa	AAA	42	0	0	10	57.2	232	35	15	13	1	3	2	2	25	4	61	5	0	1	3	.250	0	1--	-	1.71	2.03
2010	Iowa	AAA	36	0	0	21	42.2	186	31	16	15	3	2	4	0	26	0	43	3	0	0	2	.000	0	10--	-	3.09	3.16
2009	ChC	NL	11	0	0	2	12.2	59	14	10	10	2	1	0	1	8	1	9	0	0	1	0	1.000	0	0-0	0	6.37	7.11
2010	ChC	NL	18	0	0	3	17.2	84	21	15	12	4	0	1	0	10	0	15	3	0	0	0	-	0	0-1	1	6.74	6.11
	2 ML YEARS		29	0	0	5	30.1	143	35	25	22	6	1	1	1	18	1	24	3	0	1	0	1.000	0	0-1	1	6.59	6.53

Chris Stewart

Bats: R Throws: R Pos: C-1; 1B-1   Ht: 6'4" Wt: 210 Born: 2/19/1982 Age: 29

			BATTING																		BASERUNNING				AVERAGES		
Year	Team	Lg	G	AB	H	2B	3B	HR	(Hm	Rd)	TB	R	RBI	RC	TBB	IBB	SO	HBP	SH	SF	SB	CS	SB%	GDP	Avg	OBP	Slg
2010	Portlnd*	AAA	85	266	66	14	2	7	(-	-)	105	31	39	38	30	0	38	7	3	3	1	0	1.00	7	.248	.337	.395
2006	CWS	AL	6	8	0	0	0	0	(0	0)	0	0	0	0	0	0	2	0	0	0	0	0	-	0	.000	.000	.000
2007	Tex	AL	17	37	9	2	0	0	(0	0)	11	4	3	3	3	0	6	0	0	2	0	0	-	2	.243	.300	.297
2008	NYY	AL	1	3	0	0	0	0	(0	0)	0	0	0	0	0	0	1	0	0	0	0	0	-	0	.000	.000	.000
2010	SD	NL	2	0	0	0	0	0	(0	0)	0	0	0	0	0	0	0	0	0	0	0	0	-	0	-	-	-
	4 ML YEARS		26	48	9	2	0	0	(0	0)	11	4	3	3	3	0	9	0	0	2	0	0	-	2	.188	.235	.229

Ian Stewart

Bats: L Throws: R Pos: 3B-115; PH-9; PR-1   Ht: 6'3" Wt: 215 Born: 4/5/1985 Age: 26

			BATTING																		BASERUNNING				AVERAGES		
Year	Team	Lg	G	AB	H	2B	3B	HR	(Hm	Rd)	TB	R	RBI	RC	TBB	IBB	SO	HBP	SH	SF	SB	CS	SB%	GDP	Avg	OBP	Slg
2007	Col	NL	35	43	9	4	0	1	(1	0)	16	3	9	5	4	0	17	2	0	0	0	0	-	0	.209	.261	.372
2008	Col	NL	81	266	69	18	2	10	(5	5)	121	33	41	44	30	4	94	7	0	1	1	1	.50	3	.259	.349	.455
2009	Col	NL	147	425	97	19	3	25	(13	12)	197	74	70	59	56	3	138	5	0	5	7	4	.64	7	.228	.322	.464
2010	Col	NL	121	386	99	14	2	18	(6	12)	171	54	61	51	45	8	110	5	0	5	5	2	.256	8	.256	.338	.443
	Postseason		2	1	0	0	0	0	(0	0)	0	0	0	0	1	0	1	0	0	0	0	0	-	0	.000	.500	.000
	4 ML YEARS		384	1120	274	55	7	54	(25	29)	505	164	181	159	132	15	359	19	0	11	13	7	.65	18	.245	.332	.451

Brian Stokes

Pitches: R Bats: R Pos: RP-16   Ht: 6'1" Wt: 210 Born: 8/7/1979 Age: 31

			HOW MUCH HE PITCHED						WHAT HE GAVE UP												THE RESULTS							
Year	Team	Lg	G	GS	CG	GF	IP	BFP	H	R	ER	HR	SH	SF	HB	TBB	IBB	SO	WP	Bk	W	L	Pct	Sh	Sv-Op	Hld	ERC	ERA
2010	Salt Lk*	AAA	13	0	0	3	16.2	75	21	9	7	1	0	2	1	6	1	13	2	0	1	1	.500	0	0--	-	5.34	3.78
2010	RCuca*	A+	1	0	0	0	1.0	5	2	1	1	0	0	0	0	0	0	1	0	0	0	0	-	0	0	-	7.48	9.00
2006	TB	AL	5	4	0	0	24.0	110	31	13	13	2	0	3	1	9	0	15	0	0	1	0	1.000	0	0-0	0	5.75	4.88
2007	TB	AL	59	0	0	22	62.1	294	90	49	49	11	1	3	3	25	1	35	1	0	2	7	.222	0	0-2	8	7.70	7.07
2008	NYM	NL	24	1	0	5	33.1	138	35	13	13	5	2	3	0	8	3	26	1	0	1	0	1.000	0	1-3	4	3.99	3.51
2009	NYM	NL	69	0	0	19	70.1	316	72	33	31	6	2	3	2	38	7	45	1	0	2	4	.333	0	0-2	10	4.59	3.97
2010	LAA	AL	16	0	0	6	16.2	90	26	18	15	4	0	1	1	16	1	16	2	0	0	0	-	0	0-0	0	11.77	8.10
	5 ML YEARS		173	5	0	52	206.2	948	254	126	121	28	5	13	7	96	12	137	5	0	6	11	.353	0	1-7	22	6.05	5.27

Tobi Stoner

Pitches: R Bats: B Pos: RP-1   Ht: 6'2" Wt: 215 Born: 12/3/1984 Age: 26

			HOW MUCH HE PITCHED						WHAT HE GAVE UP												THE RESULTS							
Year	Team	Lg	G	GS	CG	GF	IP	BFP	H	R	ER	HR	SH	SF	HB	TBB	IBB	SO	WP	Bk	W	L	Pct	Sh	Sv-Op	Hld	ERC	ERA
2006	Bklyn	A-	14	14	1	0	83.2	329	66	25	20	1	4	3	4	17	0	62	2	1	6	2	.750	0	0--	-	1.94	2.15
2007	Savann	A	11	11	0	0	57.1	247	59	32	23	1	0	1	1	17	0	50	3	0	3	5	.375	0	0--	-	3.28	3.61
2007	StLuci	A+	16	16	0	0	82.2	356	90	57	45	9	2	5	2	25	0	57	3	1	4	5	.444	0	0--	-	4.36	4.90
2008	StLuci	A+	9	9	0	0	52.0	208	46	17	15	3	4	0	1	9	1	48	1	0	1	5	.167	0	0--	-	2.49	2.60
2008	Bnghtn	AA	15	15	0	0	79.0	338	79	39	38	7	1	5	3	29	1	59	4	0	4	6	.400	0	0--	-	4.03	4.33
2009	Bnghtn	AA	7	7	1	0	47.0	182	28	15	14	5	2	1	1	13	0	28	0	0	2	2	.500	1	0--	-	1.71	2.68
2009	Buffalo	AAA	16	16	1	0	97.2	414	92	45	43	9	3	5	2	34	0	64	3	0	7	7	.500	0	0--	-	3.57	3.96
2010	Buffalo	AAA	23	22	0	0	120.2	557	158	88	80	18	7	3	5	43	0	83	1	2	6	10	.375	0	0--	-	6.26	5.97
2009	NYM	NL	4	0	0	1	9.0	36	9	4	4	2	1	0	0	3	0	5	0	0	0	0	-	0	0-0	0	4.98	4.00
2010	NYM	NL	1	0	0	0	2.1	11	3	1	1	0	0	0	0	1	0	0	0	0	0	1	.000	0	0-0	0	4.93	3.86
	2 ML YEARS		5	0	0	1	11.1	47	12	5	5	2	1	0	0	4	0	5	0	0	0	1	.000	0	0-0	0	4.99	3.97

Drew Storen

Pitches: R Bats: B Pos: RP-54   Ht: 6'2" Wt: 180 Born: 8/11/1987 Age: 23

			HOW MUCH HE PITCHED						WHAT HE GAVE UP												THE RESULTS							
Year	Team	Lg	G	GS	CG	GF	IP	BFP	H	R	ER	HR	SH	SF	HB	TBB	IBB	SO	WP	Bk	W	L	Pct	Sh	Sv-Op	Hld	ERC	ERA
2009	Hgrstn	A	11	0	0	4	14.2	59	11	6	6	2	0	0	2	0	0	26	5	0	0	1	.000	0	0--	-	1.91	3.68
2009	Ptomc	A+	7	0	0	7	10.0	37	7	2	2	0	1	0	0	2	0	11	2	0	1	0	1.000	0	2--	-	1.47	1.80

Year	Team	Lg	G	GS	CG	GF	IP	BFP	H	R	ER	HR	SH	SF	HB	TBB	IBB	SO	WP	Bk	W	L	Pct	Sh	Sv-Op	Hld	ERC	ERA
2009	Hrsbrg	AA	10	0	0	10	12.1	45	3	0	0	0	0	0	0	6	0	12	0	0	1	0	1.000	0	9--	-	0.73	0.00
2010	Hrsbrg	AA	7	0	0	6	9.1	32	5	1	1	1	0	0	0	1	0	11	0	0	0	0	-	0	4--	-	1.16	0.96
2010	Syrcse	AAA	6	0	0	1	7.1	29	7	1	1	0	0	0	0	2	0	4	0	0	0	0	-	0	0--	-	2.84	1.23
2010	Was	NL	54	0	0	22	55.1	232	48	24	22	3	6	2	3	22	3	52	3	0	4	4	.500	0	5-7	10	3.19	3.58

Stephen Strasburg

Pitches: R **Bats:** R **Pos:** SP-12   **Ht:** 6'4" **Wt:** 220 **Born:** 7/20/1988 **Age:** 22

Year	Team	Lg	G	GS	CG	GF	IP	BFP	H	R	ER	HR	SH	SF	HB	TBB	IBB	SO	WP	Bk	W	L	Pct	Sh	Sv-Op	Hld	ERC	ERA
2010	Hrsbrg	AA	5	5	0	0	22.0	86	13	9	4	0	0	0	1	6	0	27	0	0	3	1	.750	0	0--	-	1.32	1.64
2010	Syrcse	AAA	6	6	0	0	33.1	124	18	5	4	1	0	0	0	7	0	38	1	1	4	1	.800	0	0--	-	1.08	1.08
2010	Was	NL	12	12	0	0	68.0	274	56	25	22	5	2	2	0	17	0	92	2	0	5	3	.625	0	0-0	0	2.41	2.91

Huston Street

Pitches: R **Bats:** R **Pos:** RP-44   **Ht:** 6'0" **Wt:** 190 **Born:** 8/2/1983 **Age:** 27

Year	Team	Lg	G	GS	CG	GF	IP	BFP	H	R	ER	HR	SH	SF	HB	TBB	IBB	SO	WP	Bk	W	L	Pct	Sh	Sv-Op	Hld	ERC	ERA
2010	Tulsa*	AA	2	1	0	0	1.1	6	1	0	0	0	0	0	0	1	0	2	0	0	0	0	-	0	0--	-	3.21	0.00
2010	ColSpr*	AAA	7	1	0	1	7.0	34	11	8	8	1	0	0	0	2	0	9	0	0	1	1	.500	0	0--	-	7.23	10.29
2005	Oak	AL	67	0	0	47	78.1	306	53	17	15	3	3	2	2	26	4	72	1	0	5	1	.833	0	23-27	0	1.87	1.72
2006	Oak	AL	69	0	0	55	70.2	290	64	28	26	4	3	3	2	13	3	67	4	0	4	4	.500	0	37-48	1	2.49	3.31
2007	Oak	AL	48	0	0	35	50.0	199	35	20	16	5	2	1	0	12	3	63	0	0	5	2	.714	0	16-21	5	1.84	2.88
2008	Oak	AL	63	0	0	37	70.0	287	58	29	29	6	3	3	1	27	6	69	2	0	7	5	.583	0	18-25	6	2.98	3.73
2009	Col	NL	64	0	0	52	61.2	240	43	22	21	7	3	2	0	13	4	70	0	0	4	1	.800	0	35-37	2	1.83	3.06
2010	Col	NL	44	0	0	39	47.1	187	39	21	19	5	0	1	2	11	4	45	2	1	4	4	.500	0	20-25	0	2.66	3.61
	Postseason		8	0	0	7	9.0	43	14	9	9	2	1	1	0	4	0	5	0	0	0	3	.000	0	3-4	0	8.97	9.00
6 ML YEARS			355	0	0	265	378.0	1509	292	137	126	30	14	12	7	102	24	386	9	1	29	17	.630	0	149-183	14	2.27	3.00

Scott Strickland

Pitches: R **Bats:** R **Pos:** RP-3   **Ht:** 5'11" **Wt:** 223 **Born:** 4/26/1976 **Age:** 35

Year	Team	Lg	G	GS	CG	GF	IP	BFP	H	R	ER	HR	SH	SF	HB	TBB	IBB	SO	WP	Bk	W	L	Pct	Sh	Sv-Op	Hld	ERC	ERA
2010	NewOr*	AAA	31	0	0	28	32.1	150	39	17	16	3	1	1	2	16	1	22	0	0	4	3	.571	0	14--	-	5.83	4.45
1999	Mon	NL	17	0	0	5	18.0	78	15	10	9	3	2	0	0	11	0	23	0	0	1	0	1.000	0	0-0	2	4.48	4.50
2000	Mon	NL	49	0	0	20	48.0	200	38	18	16	3	3	3	1	16	2	48	2	0	4	3	.571	0	9-13	6	2.44	3.00
2001	Mon	NL	77	0	0	31	81.1	351	67	36	29	9	3	1	4	41	5	85	4	0	2	6	.250	0	9-12	12	3.65	3.21
2002	2 Tms	NL	69	0	0	21	68.2	299	61	29	27	7	1	2	2	33	9	69	3	0	6	9	.400	0	2-6	15	3.64	3.54
2003	NYM	NL	19	0	0	3	20.0	84	16	6	5	1	0	0	1	10	1	16	1	0	0	2	.000	0	0-1	4	3.19	2.25
2005	Hou	NL	5	0	0	0	4.0	16	4	3	3	2	0	0	0	0	0	2	0	0	0	0	-	0	0-0	0	4.70	6.75
2010	Fla	NL	3	0	0	2	2.0	11	5	2	2	0	0	0	0	1	0	0	0	0	0	0	-	0	0-0	0	14.52	9.00
02	Mon	NL	1	0	0	0	1.0	3	0	0	0	0	0	0	0	0	0	2	0	0	0	0	-	0	0-0	0	0.00	0.00
02	NYM	NL	68	0	0	21	67.2	296	61	29	27	7	1	2	2	33	9	67	3	0	6	9	.400	0	2-6	15	3.74	3.59
7 ML YEARS			239	0	0	82	242.0	1039	206	104	91	25	9	6	8	112	17	243	10	0	12	21	.364	0	20-32	39	3.51	3.38

Pedro Strop

Pitches: R **Bats:** R **Pos:** RP-15   STROPE   **Ht:** 6'0" **Wt:** 175 **Born:** 6/13/1985 **Age:** 26

Year	Team	Lg	G	GS	CG	GF	IP	BFP	H	R	ER	HR	SH	SF	HB	TBB	IBB	SO	WP	Bk	W	L	Pct	Sh	Sv-Op	Hld	ERC	ERA
2006	Casper	R+	11	0	0	10	13.0	51	9	3	3	1	0	0	1	2	0	22	3	1	1	0	1.000	0	0--	-	1.75	2.08
2006	Ashvll	A	11	0	0	2	13.1	53	10	7	7	3	1	0	0	5	0	13	0	0	2	1	.667	0	0--	-	3.51	4.73
2007	Mdest	A+	48	0	0	25	54.2	237	43	28	26	4	2	3	3	29	1	75	11	0	5	2	.714	0	7--	-	3.36	4.28
2008	Tulsa	AA	7	0	0	5	7.0	31	6	2	2	0	0	0	1	4	0	7	0	0	0	0	-	0	3--	-	3.77	2.57
2009	Okla	AAA	11	0	0	6	12.2	54	13	11	11	2	0	1	1	4	0	13	2	0	1	1	.500	0	1--	-	4.70	7.82
2009	Frisco	AA	36	0	0	11	51.1	229	48	28	25	1	0	2	2	29	1	48	7	2	5	5	.500	0	4--	-	3.85	4.38
2010	OKCity	AAA	39	0	0	32	42.1	173	32	9	9	1	1	1	0	14	2	57	4	2	1	2	.333	0	13--	-	1.98	1.91
2009	Tex	AL	7	0	0	3	7.0	30	6	6	6	0	1	0	0	4	0	9	0	0	0	0	-	0	0-0	0	3.27	7.71
2010	Tex	AL	15	0	0	5	10.2	60	17	12	12	2	1	0	1	11	0	11	5	1	0	0	-	0	0-0	1	11.92	10.13
2 ML YEARS			22	0	0	8	17.2	90	23	18	18	2	1	0	1	15	0	20	5	1	0	0	-	0	0-0	1	8.17	9.17

Drew Stubbs

Bats: R **Throws:** R **Pos:** CF-147; PH-6; PR-2   **Ht:** 6'4" **Wt:** 205 **Born:** 10/4/1984 **Age:** 26

Year	Team	Lg	G	AB	H	2B	3B	HR	(Hm	Rd)	TB	R	RBI	RC	TBB	IBB	SO	HBP	SH	SF	SB	CS	SB%	GDP	Avg	OBP	Slg
2006	Billings	R+	56	210	53	7	3	6	(-	-)	84	39	24	36	32	0	64	7	2	1	19	4	.83	0	.252	.368	.400
2007	Dayton	A	129	497	134	29	5	12	(-	-)	209	93	43	79	69	1	142	6	1	2	23	15	.61	7	.270	.364	.421
2008	Srsota	A+	86	303	79	21	4	5	(-	-)	123	49	38	51	50	1	82	2	0	3	27	8	.77	1	.261	.366	.406
2008	Chatt	AA	26	92	29	8	0	0	(-	-)	37	12	9	16	11	0	21	2	1	0	3	1	.75	1	.315	.400	.402
2008	Lsvlle	AAA	19	75	22	4	2	2	(-	-)	36	14	10	13	6	0	20	1	2	0	3	0	1.00	0	.293	.354	.480
2009	Lsvlle	AAA	107	411	110	25	2	3	(-	-)	148	57	39	62	51	0	104	4	4	2	46	8	.85	4	.268	.353	.360
2009	Cin	NL	42	180	48	5	1	8	(7	1)	79	27	17	22	15	0	49	0	1	0	10	4	.71	1	.267	.323	.439
2010	Cin	NL	150	514	131	19	6	22	(13	9)	228	91	77	74	55	2	168	5	3	6	30	6	.83	6	.255	.329	.444
2 ML YEARS			192	694	179	24	7	30	(20	10)	307	118	94	96	70	2	217	5	4	6	40	10	.80	7	.258	.328	.442

Cory Sullivan

Bats: L **Throws:** L **Pos:** PH-44; LF-13; RF-3; CF-1 **Ht:** 6'0" **Wt:** 198 **Born:** 8/20/1979 **Age:** 31

Year	Team	Lg	G	AB	H	2B	3B	HR	(Hm	Rd)	TB	R	RBI	RC	TBB	IBB	SO	HBP	SH	SF	SB	CS	SB%	GDP	Avg	OBP	Slg
2005	Col	NL	139	378	111	15	4	4	(1	3)	146	64	30	54	28	0	83	3	10	5	12	3	.80	6	.294	.343	.386
2006	Col	NL	126	386	103	26	10	2	(0	2)	155	47	30	47	32	3	100	1	19	5	10	6	.63	5	.267	.321	.402
2007	Col	NL	72	140	40	6	1	2	(0	2)	54	19	14	20	9	1	25	2	1	1	2	0	1.00	5	.286	.336	.386
2008	Col	NL	18	23	5	0	1	0	(0	0)	7	3	4	3	0	0	5	1	0	0	1	0	1.00	0	.217	.250	.304
2009	NYM	NL	64	136	34	5	2	2	(2	0)	52	17	15	18	19	1	22	0	0	2	7	1	.88	5	.250	.338	.382
2010	Hou	NL	57	64	12	1	1	0	(0	0)	15	6	4	5	6	0	18	0	1	0	0	0	-	2	.188	.257	.234
	Postseason		6	6	2	0	0	0	(0	0)	2	0	0	0	0	0	1	0	0	0	0	0	-	0	.333	.333	.333
	6 ML YEARS		476	1127	305	50	22	10	(3	7)	429	156	97	147	94	5	253	7	31	13	32	10	.76	23	.271	.327	.381

Jeff Suppan

Pitches: R **Bats:** R **Pos:** SP-15; RP-15 **Ht:** 6'2" **Wt:** 230 **Born:** 1/2/1975 **Age:** 36

			HOW MUCH HE PITCHED						WHAT HE GAVE UP												THE RESULTS						
Year	Team	Lg	G	GS	CG	GF	IP	BFP	H	R	ER	HR	SH	SF	HB	TBB	IBB	SO	WP	Bk	W	L	Pct	Sh	Sv-Op	Hld	ERC	ERA
2010	Wisc*	A	1	1	0	0	4.1	21	7	1	1	0	0	0	0	3	0	4	0	0	0	0	-	0	0--	-	8.83	2.08
1995	Bos	AL	8	3	0	1	22.2	100	29	15	15	4	1	1	0	5	1	19	0	0	1	2	.333	0	0-0	0	5.43	5.96
1996	Bos	AL	8	4	0	2	22.2	107	29	19	19	3	1	4	1	13	0	13	3	0	1	1	.500	0	0-0	0	7.03	7.54
1997	Bos	AL	23	22	0	1	112.1	503	140	75	71	12	0	4	4	36	1	67	5	0	7	3	.700	0	0-0	0	5.39	5.69
1998	2 Tms		17	14	1	2	78.2	345	91	56	50	13	3	2	1	22	1	51	2	0	1	7	.125	0	0-0	0	4.95	5.72
1999	KC	AL	32	32	4	0	208.2	887	222	113	105	28	7	5	3	62	4	103	5	1	10	12	.455	1	0-0	0	4.33	4.53
2000	KC	AL	35	33	3	0	217.0	948	240	121	119	36	5	6	7	84	3	128	7	1	10	9	.526	1	0-0	0	5.31	4.94
2001	KC	AL	34	34	1	0	218.1	946	227	120	106	26	5	6	12	74	3	120	6	0	10	14	.417	0	0-0	0	4.40	4.37
2002	KC	AL	33	33	3	0	208.0	912	229	134	123	32	4	11	7	68	3	109	10	1	9	16	.360	1	0-0	0	4.84	5.32
2003	2 Tms		32	31	3	0	204.0	873	217	98	95	23	11	6	8	51	5	110	7	0	13	11	.542	2	0-0	0	4.03	4.19
2004	StL	NL	31	31	0	0	188.0	811	192	98	87	25	8	5	8	65	1	110	4	1	16	9	.640	0	0-0	0	4.38	4.16
2005	StL	NL	32	32	0	0	194.1	834	206	93	77	24	11	5	7	63	1	114	6	1	16	10	.615	0	0-0	0	4.46	3.57
2006	StL	NL	32	32	0	0	190.0	837	207	100	87	21	9	3	8	69	6	104	8	0	12	7	.632	0	0-0	0	4.62	4.12
2007	Mil	NL	34	34	1	0	206.2	919	243	113	106	18	18	11	11	68	10	114	7	0	12	12	.500	0	0-0	0	4.84	4.62
2008	Mil	NL	31	31	0	0	177.2	780	207	110	98	30	10	4	4	67	7	90	3	1	10	10	.500	0	0-0	0	5.58	4.96
2009	Mil	NL	30	30	0	0	161.2	748	200	106	95	25	11	4	11	74	8	80	12	0	7	12	.360	0	0-0	0	6.39	5.29
2010	2 Tms	NL	30	15	0	10	101.1	452	130	61	57	13	9	3	2	37	1	51	4	0	3	8	.273	0	0-0	0	6.02	5.06
98	Ari	NL	13	13	1	0	66.0	299	82	55	49	12	3	2	1	21	1	39	2	0	1	7	.125	0	0-0	0	5.73	6.68
98	KC		4	1	0	2	12.2	46	9	1	1	1	0	0	0	1	0	12	0	0	0	0	-	0	0-0	0	1.51	0.71
03	Pit	NL	21	21	3	0	141.0	597	147	57	56	11	10	2	6	31	5	78	3	0	10	7	.588	2	0-0	0	3.55	3.57
03	Bos	AL	11	10	0	0	63.0	276	70	41	39	12	1	4	2	20	0	32	4	0	3	4	.429	0	0-0	0	5.15	5.57
10	Mil	NL	15	2	0	9	31.0	148	50	29	27	4	4	2	1	12	1	18	1	0	0	2	.000	0	0-0	0	8.38	7.84
10	StL	NL	15	13	0	1	70.1	304	80	32	30	9	5	1	1	25	0	33	3	0	3	6	.333	0	0-0	0	5.06	3.84
	Postseason		10	10	0	0	57.0	241	46	24	23	9	1	2	3	24	4	36	1	0	3	4	.429	0	0-0	0	3.56	3.63
	16 ML YEARS		442	411	16	16	2512.0	11002	2809	1432	1310	333	109	80	94	858	55	1383	89	6	138	143	.491	5	0-0	1	4.89	4.69

Drew Sutton

Bats: B **Throws:** R **Pos:** SS-8; 2B-5; 3B-1; DH-1; PH-1; PR-1 **Ht:** 6'3" **Wt:** 200 **Born:** 6/30/1983 **Age:** 28

Year	Team	Lg	G	AB	H	2B	3B	HR	(Hm	Rd)	TB	R	RBI	RC	TBB	IBB	SO	HBP	SH	SF	SB	CS	SB%	GDP	Avg	OBP	Slg
2004	TriCity	A-	63	250	70	10	0	1	(-	-)	83	43	16	35	39	2	50	2	2	2	2	4	.33	5	.280	.379	.332
2005	Salem	A+	43	148	38	5	1	3	(-	-)	54	22	12	23	29	1	34	1	0	0	4	3	.57	3	.257	.382	.365
2005	Lxngtn	A	62	231	66	19	2	13	(-	-)	128	46	42	51	36	1	51	6	1	1	4	2	.67	5	.286	.394	.554
2006	Salem	A+	125	456	120	27	2	15	(-	-)	196	65	48	74	69	6	84	3	17	6	20	15	.57	7	.263	.360	.430
2007	CpChr	AA	128	480	129	28	1	9	(-	-)	186	81	53	73	57	3	86	7	8	6	24	5	.83	11	.269	.351	.388
2008	CpChr	AA	134	524	166	39	4	20	(-	-)	273	102	69	113	76	3	99	6	1	3	20	7	.74	8	.317	.407	.521
2009	RdRck	AAA	5	15	4	0	0	0	(-	-)	4	1	0	1	2	0	2	1	0	0	0	0	-	0	.267	.389	.267
2009	Lsvlle	AAA	44	157	40	13	2	5	(-	-)	72	32	22	28	26	1	39	5	1	1	1	2	.33	2	.255	.376	.459
2010	Lsvlle	AAA	84	263	69	16	1	3	(-	-)	96	35	27	39	43	2	71	3	5	5	5	3	.63	2	.262	.366	.365
2010	Clmbs	AAA	29	96	29	8	0	2	(-	-)	43	10	15	20	18	0	21	1	3	1	4	0	1.00	1	.302	.414	.448
2009	Cin	NL	42	66	14	4	1	1	(1	0)	23	10	9	12	7	0	20	1	2	0	0	2	.00	1	.212	.297	.348
2010	2 Tms		13	39	10	1	0	2	(1	1)	17	5	8	7	3	0	13	0	0	0	0	0	-	1	.250	.310	.436
10	Cin	NL	2	3	2	0	0	1	(1	0)	5	1	4	3	0	0	1	0	0	0	0	0	-	0	.667	.667	1.667
10	Cle	NL	11	36	8	1	0	1	(0	1)	12	4	4	4	3	0	12	0	0	0	0	0	-	1	.222	.282	.333
	2 ML YEARS		55	105	24	5	1	3	(2	1)	40	15	17	19	10	0	33	1	2	0	0	2	.00	2	.229	.302	.381

Ichiro Suzuki

Bats: L **Throws:** R **Pos:** RF-160; DH-2 **Ht:** 5'11" **Wt:** 172 **Born:** 10/22/1973 **Age:** 37

Year	Team	Lg	G	AB	H	2B	3B	HR	(Hm	Rd)	TB	R	RBI	RC	TBB	IBB	SO	HBP	SH	SF	SB	CS	SB%	GDP	Avg	OBP	Slg
2001	Sea	AL	157	692	242	34	8	8	(5	3)	316	127	69	124	30	10	53	8	4	4	56	14	.80	3	.350	.381	.457
2002	Sea	AL	157	647	208	27	8	8	(4	4)	275	111	51	110	68	27	62	5	3	5	31	15	.67	8	.321	.388	.425
2003	Sea	AL	159	679	212	29	8	13	(8	5)	296	111	62	107	36	7	69	6	3	1	34	8	.81	3	.312	.352	.436
2004	Sea	AL	161	704	262	24	5	8	(4	4)	320	101	60	125	49	19	63	4	2	3	36	11	.77	6	.372	.414	.455
2005	Sea	AL	162	679	206	21	12	15	(8	7)	296	111	68	109	48	23	66	4	2	6	33	8	.80	5	.303	.350	.436
2006	Sea	AL	161	695	224	20	9	9	(6	3)	289	110	49	107	49	16	71	5	1	2	45	2	.96	2	.322	.370	.416
2007	Sea	AL	161	678	238	22	7	6	(3	3)	292	111	68	128	49	13	77	3	4	2	37	8	.82	7	.351	.396	.431
2008	Sea	AL	162	686	213	20	7	6	(3	3)	265	103	42	100	51	12	65	5	3	4	43	4	.91	6	.310	.361	.386
2009	Sea	AL	146	639	225	31	4	11	(6	5)	297	88	46	111	32	15	71	4	2	1	26	9	.74	1	.352	.386	.465
2010	Sea	AL	162	680	214	30	3	6	(1	5)	268	74	43	96	45	13	86	3	3	1	42	9	.82	9	.315	.359	.394
	Postseason		10	38	16	2	0	0	(0	0)	18	7	3	8	5	2	4	0	0	0	3	2	.60	0	.421	.488	.474
	10 ML YEARS		1588	6779	2244	258	71	90	(48	42)	2914	1047	558	1117	457	155	683	47	27	29	383	88	.81	46	.331	.376	.430

Kurt Suzuki

Bats: R **Throws:** R **Pos:** C-123; DH-7; PH-1; PR-1 **Ht:** 5'11" **Wt:** 208 **Born:** 10/4/1983 **Age:** 27

Year	Team	Lg	G	AB	H	2B	3B	HR	(Hm	Rd)	TB	R	RBI	RC	TBB	IBB	SO	HBP	SH	SF	SB	CS	SB%	GDP	Avg	OBP	Slg
2010	Scrmto*	AAA	3	8	3	2	0	1	(-	-)	8	4	5	3	2	0	1	0	0	0	0	0	-	1	.375	.500	1.000
2007	Oak	AL	68	213	53	13	0	7	(4	3)	87	27	39	33	24	0	39	3	3	5	0	0	-	4	.249	.327	.408
2008	Oak	AL	148	530	148	25	1	7	(5	2)	196	54	42	66	44	2	69	11	2	1	2	3	.40	20	.279	.346	.370
2009	Oak	AL	147	570	156	37	1	15	(8	7)	240	74	88	77	28	0	59	8	1	7	8	2	.80	14	.274	.313	.421
2010	Oak	AL	131	495	120	18	2	13	(8	5)	181	55	71	54	33	3	49	12	0	4	3	2	.60	22	.242	.303	.366
	4 ML YEARS		494	1808	477	93	4	42	(25	17)	704	210	240	230	129	5	216	34	6	17	13	7	.65	60	.264	.322	.389

Brian Sweeney

Pitches: R **Bats:** R **Pos:** RP-24 **Ht:** 6'2" **Wt:** 200 **Born:** 6/13/1974 **Age:** 37

Year	Team	Lg	G	GS	CG	GF	IP	BFP	H	R	ER	HR	SH	SF	HB	TBB	IBB	SO	WP	Bk	W	L	Pct	Sh	Sv-Op	Hld	ERC	ERA
2010	Tacom*	AAA	15	0	0	3	28.2	115	20	11	8	1	0	0	3	8	0	32	2	0	2	1	.667	0	1--	-	2.06	2.51
2003	Sea	AL	5	0	0	2	9.1	35	7	2	2	0	0	0	1	1	0	7	0	0	0	0	-	0	0-0	0	1.66	1.93
2004	SD	NL	7	2	0	1	14.1	63	20	9	9	1	0	0	0	2	0	10	1	0	1	0	1.000	0	0-0	0	5.12	5.65
2006	SD	NL	37	0	0	15	56.1	237	53	22	20	6	5	2	1	16	5	23	2	0	2	0	1.000	0	2-3	0	3.24	3.20
2010	Sea	AL	24	0	0	8	37.0	148	33	16	13	5	2	2	0	6	1	14	2	0	1	2	.333	0	0-1	1	2.77	3.16
	4 ML YEARS		73	2	0	26	117.0	483	113	49	44	12	7	4	2	25	6	54	5	0	4	2	.667	0	2-4	1	3.17	3.38

Mike Sweeney

Bats: R **Throws:** R **Pos:** DH-22; PH-20; 1B-17; PR-1 **Ht:** 6'3" **Wt:** 225 **Born:** 7/22/1973 **Age:** 37

Year	Team	Lg	G	AB	H	2B	3B	HR	(Hm	Rd)	TB	R	RBI	RC	TBB	IBB	SO	HBP	SH	SF	SB	CS	SB%	GDP	Avg	OBP	Slg
2010	Tacom*	AAA	12	41	15	3	0	2	(-	-)	24	7	9	11	8	0	3	0	0	1	1	0	1.00	1	.366	.460	.585
1995	KC	AL	4	4	1	0	0	0	(0	0)	1	1	0	0	0	0	0	0	0	0	0	0	-	0	.250	.250	.250
1996	KC	AL	50	165	46	10	0	4	(1	3)	68	23	24	23	18	0	21	4	0	3	1	2	.33	7	.279	.358	.412
1997	KC	AL	84	240	58	8	0	7	(5	2)	87	30	31	25	17	0	33	6	1	2	3	2	.60	8	.242	.306	.363
1998	KC	AL	92	282	73	18	0	8	(6	2)	115	32	35	35	24	1	38	2	2	1	2	3	.40	7	.259	.320	.408
1999	KC	AL	150	575	185	44	2	22	(10	12)	299	101	102	109	54	0	48	10	0	4	6	1	.86	21	.322	.387	.520
2000	KC	AL	159	618	206	30	0	29	(17	12)	323	105	144	128	71	5	67	15	0	13	8	3	.73	15	.333	.407	.523
2001	KC	AL	147	559	170	46	0	29	(14	15)	303	97	99	109	64	13	64	2	1	6	10	3	.77	13	.304	.374	.542
2002	KC	AL	126	471	160	31	1	24	(14	10)	265	81	86	112	61	10	46	6	0	7	9	7	.56	9	.340	.417	.563
2003	KC	AL	108	392	115	18	1	16	(7	9)	183	62	83	83	64	5	56	2	0	5	3	2	.60	13	.293	.391	.467
2004	KC	AL	106	411	118	23	0	22	(8	14)	207	56	79	75	33	9	44	6	0	2	3	2	.60	7	.287	.347	.504
2005	KC	AL	122	470	141	39	0	21	(7	14)	243	63	83	80	33	7	61	4	1	6	3	0	1.00	16	.300	.347	.517
2006	KC	AL	60	217	56	15	0	8	(4	4)	95	23	33	33	28	5	48	4	0	3	2	0	1.00	5	.258	.349	.438
2007	KC	AL	74	265	69	15	1	7	(6	1)	107	26	38	39	17	4	29	5	0	2	0	0	-	5	.260	.315	.404
2008	Oak	AL	42	126	36	8	0	2	(1	1)	50	13	12	16	7	0	6	2	0	1	0	0	-	3	.286	.331	.397
2009	Sea	AL	74	242	68	15	0	8	(2	6)	107	25	34	34	17	2	31	4	0	3	0	0	-	4	.281	.335	.442
2010	2 Tms		56	151	38	5	0	8	(3	5)	67	21	26	21	14	0	21	2	0	1	3	0	1.00	5	.252	.321	.444
10	Sea	AL	30	99	26	3	0	6	(3	3)	47	11	18	16	9	0	14	1	0	1	2	0	1.00	3	.263	.327	.475
10	Phi	NL	26	52	12	2	0	2	(0	2)	20	10	8	5	5	0	7	1	0	0	1	0	1.00	2	.231	.310	.385
	16 ML YEARS		1454	5188	1540	325	5	215	(105	110)	2520	759	909	922	522	61	613	74	5	59	53	25	.68	142	.297	.366	.486

Ryan Sweeney

Bats: L **Throws:** L **Pos:** RF-80; PH-4; CF-1 **Ht:** 6'4" **Wt:** 223 **Born:** 2/20/1985 **Age:** 26

Year	Team	Lg	G	AB	H	2B	3B	HR	(Hm	Rd)	TB	R	RBI	RC	TBB	IBB	SO	HBP	SH	SF	SB	CS	SB%	GDP	Avg	OBP	Slg
2006	CWS	AL	18	35	8	0	0	0	(0	0)	8	1	5	1	0	0	7	0	0	0	0	0	-	4	.229	.229	.229
2007	CWS	AL	15	45	9	3	0	1	(1	0)	15	5	5	2	4	0	5	0	0	0	0	1	.00	2	.200	.265	.333
2008	Oak	AL	115	384	110	18	2	5	(1	4)	147	53	45	56	38	3	67	3	2	6	9	1	.90	9	.286	.350	.383
2009	Oak	AL	134	484	142	31	3	6	(2	4)	197	68	53	63	40	1	67	3	2	5	6	5	.55	14	.293	.348	.407
2010	Oak	AL	82	303	89	20	2	1	(1	0)	116	41	36	38	24	0	41	0	1	3	1	1	.50	14	.294	.342	.383
	5 ML YEARS		364	1251	358	72	7	13	(5	8)	483	168	144	160	106	6	187	6	5	14	16	8	.67	40	.286	.341	.386

Nick Swisher

Bats: B **Throws:** L **Pos:** RF-134; DH-11; PH-7; 1B-6; CF-1 **Ht:** 5'11" **Wt:** 210 **Born:** 11/25/1980 **Age:** 30

Year	Team	Lg	G	AB	H	2B	3B	HR	(Hm	Rd)	TB	R	RBI	RC	TBB	IBB	SO	HBP	SH	SF	SB	CS	SB%	GDP	Avg	OBP	Slg
2004	Oak	AL	20	60	15	4	0	2	(1	1)	25	11	8	8	8	0	11	2	0	1	0	0	-	2	.250	.352	.417
2005	Oak	AL	131	462	109	32	1	21	(11	10)	206	66	74	62	55	3	110	4	0	1	0	1	.00	9	.236	.322	.446
2006	Oak	AL	157	556	141	24	2	35	(17	18)	274	106	95	95	97	7	152	11	2	6	1	2	.33	13	.254	.372	.493
2007	Oak	AL	150	539	141	36	1	22	(8	14)	245	84	78	89	100	12	131	10	1	9	3	2	.60	13	.262	.381	.455
2008	CWS	AL	153	497	109	21	1	24	(19	5)	204	86	69	69	82	6	135	4	1	4	3	3	.50	14	.219	.332	.410
2009	NYY	AL	150	498	124	35	1	29	(8	21)	248	84	82	84	97	2	126	3	3	6	0	0	-	13	.249	.371	.498
2010	NYY	AL	150	566	163	33	3	29	(15	14)	289	91	89	100	58	0	139	6	3	2	1	2	.33	13	.288	.359	.511
	Postseason		24	71	11	4	0	1	(0	1)	18	9	3	6	16	0	23	1	1	0	0	0	-	0	.155	.318	.254
	7 ML YEARS		911	3178	802	185	9	162	(79	83)	1491	528	495	507	497	30	804	40	10	29	8	10	.44	77	.252	.358	.469

Jose Tabata

Bats: R Throws: R Pos: LF-93; CF-13; PH-1   TAH-bah-tah   Ht: 5'11" Wt: 210 Born: 8/12/1988 Age: 22

Year	Team	Lg	G	AB	H	2B	3B	HR	(Hm	Rd)	TB	R	RBI	RC	TBB	IBB	SO	HBP	SH	SF	SB	CS	SB%	GDP	Avg	OBP	Slg
2005	Yanks	R	44	156	49	5	1	3	(-	-)	65	30	25	27	15	1	14	2	0	0	22	6	.79	3	.314	.382	.417
2006	CtnSC	A	86	319	95	22	1	5	(-	-)	134	50	51	54	30	1	66	12	0	2	15	5	.75	10	.298	.377	.420
2007	Tampa	A+	103	411	126	16	2	5	(-	-)	161	56	54	63	33	4	70	10	1	1	15	7	.68	15	.307	.371	.392
2008	Trntn	AA	78	290	71	9	0	3	(-	-)	89	40	35	32	26	0	48	7	1	4	10	2	.83	15	.245	.318	.307
2008	Pirates	R	4	11	5	1	0	2	(-	-)	12	4	7	5	2	0	0	0	0	0	0	0	-	0	.455	.538	1.091
2008	Altna	AA	22	89	31	6	2	3	(-	-)	50	16	13	20	8	0	18	0	0	0	8	0	1.00	3	.348	.402	.562
2009	Altna	AA	61	228	69	15	1	2	(-	-)	92	31	25	35	20	2	25	5	0	1	7	6	.54	9	.303	.370	.404
2009	Indy	AAA	32	134	37	7	1	3	(-	-)	55	21	10	19	10	1	18	2	1	1	4	2	.67	2	.276	.333	.410
2010	Indy	AAA	53	224	69	13	2	3	(-	-)	95	42	19	39	23	1	35	2	0	3	25	6	.81	5	.308	.373	.424
2010	Pit	NL	102	405	121	21	4	4	(3	1)	162	61	35	59	28	0	57	2	5	1	19	7	.73	7	.299	.346	.400

Hisanori Takahashi

Pitches: L Bats: L Pos: RP-41; SP-12   EES-ah-nore-ee   Ht: 5'10" Wt: 170 Born: 4/2/1975 Age: 36

Year	Team	Lg	G	GS	CG	GF	IP	BFP	H	R	ER	HR	SH	SF	HB	TBB	IBB	SO	WP	Bk	W	L	Pct	Sh	Sv-Op	Hld	ERC	ERA
2000	Yomiuri	Jap	24	23	3	0	135.2	563	133	59	48	10	-	-	2	36	-	102	1	0	9	6	.600	2	0- -	-	3.35	3.18
2001	Yomiuri	Jap	30	23	3	0	134.2	584	126	65	59	20	17	4	3	52	2	99	4	0	9	9	.500	1	0- -	-	3.98	3.94
2002	Yomiuri	Jap	24	23	2	0	163.1	669	143	58	56	16	-	-	6	39	-	145	4	1	10	4	.714	0	0- -	-	2.91	3.09
2003	Yomiuri	Jap	13	13	3	0	86.2	364	79	42	37	14	-	-	4	27	1	78	1	1	4	4	.500	0	0- -	-	3.81	3.84
2004	Yomiuri	Jap	16	16	3	0	91.0	402	107	59	55	18	6	2	3	26	0	61	3	0	5	10	.333	1	0- -	-	5.45	5.44
2005	Yomiuri	Jap	27	26	4	0	163.0	695	171	88	81	18	14	7	4	48	1	135	1	0	8	12	.400	2	0- -	-	4.11	4.47
2006	Yomiuri	Jap	35	4	0	0	62.0	266	70	36	34	10	5	0	1	15	2	51	1	0	2	6	.250	0	15- -	-	4.62	4.94
2007	Yomiuri	Jap	28	27	2	0	186.2	764	168	63	57	21	-	-	2	50	4	141	1	0	14	4	.778	2	0- -	-	3.13	2.75
2008	Yomiuri	Jap	23	22	0	0	122.0	518	127	63	56	16	7	5	5	30	4	94	2	0	8	5	.615	0	0- -	-	4.07	4.13
2009	Yomiuri	Jap	25	25	1	0	144.0	610	147	58	47	16	-	-	6	36	1	126	0	2	10	6	.625	0	0- -	-	3.82	2.94
2010	NYM	NL	53	12	0	21	122.0	516	116	51	49	13	10	3	0	43	7	114	1	1	10	6	.625	0	8-8	3	3.57	3.61

Mitch Talbot

Pitches: R Bats: R Pos: SP-28   Ht: 6'2" Wt: 200 Born: 10/17/1983 Age: 27

Year	Team	Lg	G	GS	CG	GF	IP	BFP	H	R	ER	HR	SH	SF	IID	TBB	IBB	SO	WP	Bk	W	L	Pct	Sh	Sv-Op	Hld	ERC	ERA
2003	Mrtnsvl	R+	12	12	0	0	54.0	223	45	26	17	1	4	1	6	11	0	46	1	0	4	4	.500	0	0- -	-	2.32	2.83
2004	Lxngtn	A	27	27	1	0	152.2	647	145	78	65	16	7	3	11	49	1	115	6	1	10	10	.500	0	0- -	-	3.81	3.83
2005	Salem	A+	27	27	1	0	151.1	667	169	90	73	15	8	2	8	46	0	100	9	1	8	11	.421	1	0- -	-	4.52	4.34
2006	CpChr	AA	18	17	0	1	90.1	390	94	49	34	4	3	2	6	29	0	96	2	2	6	4	.600	0	1- -	-	3.87	3.39
2006	Mont	AA	10	10	0	0	66.1	264	51	16	14	2	2	1	4	18	0	59	5	0	4	3	.571	0	0- -	-	2.22	1.90
2007	Drham	AAA	29	29	1	0	161.0	695	169	89	81	13	5	5	10	59	0	124	4	3	13	9	.591	1	0- -	-	4.40	4.53
2008	Drham	AAA	28	28	1	0	161.0	683	165	79	69	9	3	6	11	35	0	141	7	0	13	9	.591	0	0- -	-	3.45	3.86
2009	Drham	AAA	10	10	0	0	54.1	240	67	29	27	3	0	2	2	18	0	40	1	1	4	4	.500	0	0- -	-	5.05	4.47
2009	Rays	R	4	4	0	0	11.0	38	5	1	1	0	0	0	0	0	0	21	1	0	0	0	-	0	0- -	-	0.45	0.82
2009	Charltt	A+	1	1	0	0	3.0	10	1	0	0	0	0	0	0	0	0	6	0	0	0	0	-	0	0- -	-	0.75	0.00
2010	MhVlly	A-	1	1	0	0	3.0	11	2	1	1	0	1	0	0	1	0	0	0	0	0	0	-	0	0- -	-	1.73	3.00
2008	TB	AL	3	1	0	0	9.2	54	16	12	12	3	0	0	1	11	0	5	1	0	0	0	-	0	0-0	0	14.85	11.17
2010	Cle	AL	28	28	1	0	159.1	696	169	88	78	15	2	5	8	69	2	88	3	1	10	13	.435	0	0-0	0	4.68	4.41
	2 ML YEARS		31	29	1	0	169.0	750	185	100	90	16	2	5	9	80	2	93	4	1	10	13	.435	0	0-0	0	5.17	4.79

Brian Tallet

Pitches: L Bats: L Pos: RP-29; SP-5   TAL-ett   Ht: 6'6" Wt: 220 Born: 9/21/1977 Age: 33

Year	Team	Lg	G	GS	CG	GF	IP	BFP	H	R	ER	HR	SH	SF	HB	TBB	IBB	SO	WP	Bk	W	L	Pct	Sh	Sv-Op	Hld	ERC	ERA
2010	Dnedin*	A+	1	1	0	0	4.0	14	2	0	0	0	0	0	0	3	0	0	0	0	0	0	-	0	0- -	-	1.01	0.00
2010	LsVgs*	AAA	1	1	0	0	1.1	14	9	8	8	2	0	0	0	1	0	1	0	0	0	1	.000	0	0- -	-	74.17	54.00
2002	Cle	AL	2	2	0	0	12.0	47	9	3	2	0	0	0	1	4	0	5	0	0	1	0	1.000	0	0-0	0	2.31	1.50
2003	Cle	AL	5	3	0	1	19.0	87	23	14	10	2	2	0	1	8	0	9	0	0	0	2	.000	0	0-0	0	5.65	4.74
2005	Cle	AL	2	0	0	0	4.2	24	6	4	4	2	0	0	1	3	0	2	0	0	0	0	-	0	0-0	0	10.55	7.71
2006	Tor	AL	44	1	0	8	54.1	229	45	24	23	5	1	5	3	31	4	37	2	1	3	0	1.000	0	0-0	5	3.97	3.81
2007	Tor	AL	48	0	0	11	62.1	267	49	26	24	1	2	3	6	28	7	54	1	0	4	.333		0	0-3	5	2.68	3.47
2008	Tor	AL	51	0	0	15	56.1	240	52	19	18	4	1	2	1	22	3	47	0	0	1	2	.333	0	0-0	4	3.39	2.88
2009	Tor	AL	37	25	0	3	160.2	717	169	99	95	20	1	7	6	72	2	120	2	0	7	9	.438	0	0-0	4	4.85	5.32
2010	Tor	AL	34	5	0	5	77.1	356	84	60	55	20	1	5	4	38	3	53	1	0	2	6	.250	0	0-2	1	6.22	6.40
	8 ML YEARS		223	36	0	43	446.2	1967	437	249	231	54	8	22	23	206	19	327	6	1	16	23	.410	0	0-5	11	4.47	4.65

Hitoshi Tamura

Bats: R Throws: R Pos: OF   Ht: 5'11" Wt: 181 Born: 3/28/1977 Age: 34

Year	Team	Lg	G	AB	H	2B	3B	HR	(Hm	Rd)	TB	R	RBI	RC	TBB	IBB	SO	HBP	SH	SF	SB	CS	SB%	GDP	Avg	OBP	Slg
1997	Yokha	Jap	18	26	7	1	0	1	(-	-)	11	2	4	2	0	-	9	0	0	1	0	0	-	0	.269	.259	.423
2000	Yokha	Jap	84	226	58	6	1	7	(-	-)	87	21	29	27	13	-	64	4	0	2	2	0	1.00	3	.257	.306	.385
2001	Yokha	Jap	33	43	7	2	0	1	(-	-)	12	8	2	4	8	-	15	2	0	0	0	0	-	1	.163	.321	.279
2002	Yokha	Jap	81	183	43	8	0	5	(-	-)	66	23	16	18	9	-	54	2	2	0	3	1	.75	1	.235	.278	.361
2003	Yokha	Jap	91	242	71	12	0	18	(-	-)	137	29	46	45	12	-	65	5	1	0	14	7	.67	7	.293	.340	.566
2004	Yokha	Jap	123	449	137	19	2	40	(-	-)	280	80	100	97	39	-	126	2	1	1	10	7	.59	8	.305	.364	.624
2005	Yokha	Jap	117	450	137	26	2	31	(-	-)	260	71	79	92	43	-	108	4	0	1	2	4	.33	6	.304	.369	.578
2006	Yokha	Jap	39	127	35	3	0	8	(-	-)	62	24	20	23	14	-	29	3	0	1	5	1	.83	5	.276	.359	.488

Year Team	Lg	G	AB	H	2B	3B	HR	(Hm	Rd)	TB	R	RBI	RC	TBB	IBB	SO	HBP	SH	SF	SB	CS	SB%	GDP	Avg	OBP	Slg
2007 Sbank	Jap	132	509	138	28	3	13	(-	-)	211	61	68	70	38	-	117	3	2	1	3	2	.60	8	.271	.325	.415
2008 Sbank	Jap	39	149	45	6	1	3	(-	-)	62	17	15	20	6	-	29	2	0	1	0	1	.00	6	.302	.335	.416
2009 Sbank	Jap	93	308	87	17	1	17	(-	-)	157	39	57	53	22	-	66	4	0	4	0	1	.00	11	.282	.334	.510
2010 Sbank	Jap	140	513	166	33	1	27	(-	-)	282	74	89	103	33	-	93	10	0	3	2	2	.50	11	.324	.374	.550

Taylor Tankersley

Pitches: L **Bats:** L **Pos:** RP-27   TANK-ers-lee   **Ht:** 6'0" **Wt:** 215 **Born:** 3/7/1983 **Age:** 28

Year Team	Lg	G	GS	CG	GF	IP	BFP	H	R	ER	HR	SH	SF	HB	TBB	IBB	SO	WP	Bk	W	L	Pct	Sh	Sv-Op	Hld	ERC	ERA
2010 NewOr*	AAA	27	0	0	3	26.1	106	20	12	10	3	1	0	0	8	1	22	2	0	4	2	.667	0	1--	-	2.47	3.42
2006 Fla	NL	49	0	0	10	41.0	178	33	14	13	4	3	3	1	26	5	46	3	0	2	1	.667	0	3-7	22	3.80	2.85
2007 Fla	NL	67	0	0	12	47.1	205	42	22	21	4	0	2	3	29	3	49	2	0	6	1	.857	0	1-3	16	4.45	3.99
2008 Fla	NL	25	0	0	3	17.2	84	22	16	16	6	1	0	1	8	0	13	3	0	0	1	.000	0	0-2	4	7.76	8.15
2010 Fla	NL	27	0	0	1	12.0	57	12	11	10	4	0	1	1	7	1	7	1	0	0	0	-	0	0-3	6	6.57	7.50
4 ML YEARS		168	0	0	26	118.0	524	109	63	60	18	4	6	6	70	9	115	9	0	8	3	.727	0	4-15	48	4.91	4.58

Jack Taschner

Pitches: L **Bats:** L **Pos:** RP-20   **Ht:** 6'3" **Wt:** 207 **Born:** 4/21/1978 **Age:** 33

Year Team	Lg	G	GS	CG	GF	IP	BFP	H	R	ER	HR	SH	SF	HB	TBB	IBB	SO	WP	Bk	W	L	Pct	Sh	Sv-Op	Hld	ERC	ERA
2010 Altna*	AA	2	0	0	0	2.0	9	2	1	1	0	0	0	0	1	0	2	0	0	0	0	-	0	0--	-	3.63	4.50
2010 Albq*	AAA	10	0	0	4	10.0	38	7	4	4	4	0	0	0	0	0	4	0	0	0	0	-	0	2--	-	2.36	3.60
2005 SF	NL	24	0	0	7	22.2	95	15	5	4	0	0	1	0	13	0	19	0	0	2	0	1.000	0	0-1	3	2.25	1.59
2006 SF	NL	24	0	0	6	19.1	101	31	23	18	4	0	2	2	7	0	15	3	0	0	1	.000	0	0-1	3	8.55	8.38
2007 SF	NL	63	0	0	16	50.0	222	44	31	30	4	2	3	1	29	2	51	2	0	3	1	.750	0	0-2	13	3.92	5.40
2008 SF	NL	67	0	0	7	48.0	227	57	27	26	5	3	3	2	24	2	39	5	0	3	2	.600	0	0-4	14	5.56	4.88
2009 Phi	NL	24	0	0	8	29.1	143	38	18	16	3	1	0	2	20	2	19	1	0	1	1	.500	0	0-1	0	7.29	4.91
2010 2 Tms	NL	20	0	0	3	19.2	94	23	14	14	3	0	0	0	11	0	17	2	0	1	0	1.000	0	0-1	2	5.93	6.41
10 Pit	NL	17	0	0	3	19.1	88	22	13	13	3	0	0	0	8	0	17	1	0	1	0	1.000	0	0-0	2	5.21	6.05
10 LAD	NL	3	0	0	0	0.1	6	1	1	1	0	0	0	0	3	0	0	1	0	0	0	-	0	0-1	0	49.79	27.00
6 ML YEARS		222	0	0	47	189.0	882	208	118	108	19	6	9	7	104	6	160	13	0	10	5	.667	0	0-10	35	5.25	5.14

Yoshinori Tateyama

Pitches: R **Bats:** R **Pos:** P   yoh-shinn-OH-ree taht-ay-YAHM-ah   **Ht:** 5'10" **Wt:** 165 **Born:** 12/26/1975 **Age:** 35

Year Team	Lg	G	GS	CG	GF	IP	BFP	H	R	ER	HR	SH	SF	HB	TBB	IBB	SO	WP	Bk	W	L	Pct	Sh	Sv-Op	Hld	ERC	ERA
1999 HNHF	Jap	22	-	1	-	106.0	442	101	43	34	11	-	-	1	29	-	62	0	0	6	5	.545	0	0--	-	3.38	2.89
2000 HNHF	Jap	28	-	2	-	89.1	396	106	57	55	15	-	-	2	29	-	55	1	0	6	8	.429	0	0--	-	5.45	5.54
2001 HNHF	Jap	10	-	0	-	14.1	72	22	17	17	5	-	-	2	9	-	9	0	0	1	0	1.000	0	0--	-	11.80	10.67
2002 HNHF	Jap	45	-	0	-	59.0	231	40	16	15	7	-	-	4	13	-	41	1	0	3	2	.600	0	4--	-	2.12	2.29
2003 HNHF	Jap	32	-	0	-	37.1	138	24	9	9	5	-	-	0	4	-	31	2	0	2	1	.667	0	15--	-	1.51	2.17
2004 HNHF	Jap	41	-	0	-	46.1	190	39	17	12	4	-	-	2	7	-	39	1	0	1	3	.250	0	0--	-	2.30	2.33
2005 HNHF	Jap	45	-	0	-	51.1	211	50	22	21	10	-	-	2	8	-	35	1	0	4	6	.400	0	2--	-	3.72	3.68
2006 HNHF	Jap	46	-	0	-	47.0	193	42	18	16	6	-	-	2	10	-	30	1	1	3	3	.500	0	0--	-	3.10	3.06
2007 HNHF	Jap	7	-	1	-	41.0	167	33	20	19	7	-	-	5	9	-	31	0	0	2	4	.333	0	0--	-	3.26	4.17
2008 HNHF	Jap	58	-	0	-	67.1	276	61	23	23	3	-	-	4	12	-	53	1	0	1	2	.333	0	2--	-	2.59	3.07
2009 HNHF	Jap	46	-	0	-	47.2	209	53	24	20	3	-	-	1	15	-	43	1	0	5	7	.417	0	0--	-	4.15	3.78
2010 HNHF	Jap	58	-	0	-	55.0	218	43	11	11	3	-	-	2	11	-	59	0	0	1	2	.333	0	4--	-	2.07	1.80

Fernando Tatis

Bats: R **Throws:** R **Pos:** PH-26; 1B-14; 3B-4; 2B-3; DH-3; PR-1   tah-TEESS   **Ht:** 5'11" **Wt:** 187 **Born:** 1/1/1975 **Age:** 36

Year Team	Lg	G	AB	H	2B	3B	HR	(Hm	Rd)	TB	R	RBI	RC	TBB	IBB	SO	HBP	SH	SF	SB	CS	SB%	GDP	Avg	OBP	Slg
1997 Tex	AL	60	223	57	9	0	8	(6	2)	90	29	29	26	14	0	42	0	2	2	3	0	1.00	6	.256	.297	.404
1998 2 Tms		150	532	147	33	4	11	(6	5)	221	69	58	69	36	4	123	6	4	1	13	5	.72	16	.276	.329	.415
1999 StL	NL	149	537	160	31	2	34	(16	18)	297	104	107	117	82	4	128	16	0	4	21	9	.70	11	.298	.404	.553
2000 StL	NL	96	324	82	21	1	18	(11	7)	159	59	64	58	57	1	94	10	1	2	2	3	.40	13	.253	.379	.491
2001 Mon	NL	41	145	37	9	0	2	(2	0)	52	20	11	18	16	0	43	4	0	3	0	0	-	5	.255	.339	.359
2002 Mon	NL	114	381	87	18	1	15	(5	10)	152	43	55	39	35	1	90	8	1	5	2	2	.50	15	.228	.303	.399
2003 Mon	NL	53	175	34	6	0	2	(1	1)	46	15	15	15	18	0	40	3	0	0	2	1	.67	7	.194	.281	.263
2006 Bal	AL	28	56	14	6	1	2	(1	1)	28	7	8	9	6	1	17	0	0	2	0	0	-	2	.250	.313	.500
2008 NYM	NL	92	273	81	16	1	11	(6	5)	132	33	47	55	29	3	59	3	0	1	3	0	1.00	7	.297	.369	.484
2009 NYM	NL	125	340	96	21	4	8	(5	3)	149	42	48	42	22	3	54	9	4	4	4	1	.80	13	.282	.339	.438
2010 NYM	NL	41	65	12	4	0	2	(1	1)	22	6	6	5	6	0	19	0	1	0	0	0	-	1	.185	.254	.338
98 Tex	AL	95	330	89	17	2	3	(1	2)	119	41	32	33	12	2	66	4	4	0	6	2	.75	10	.270	.303	.361
98 StL	NL	55	202	58	16	2	8	(5	3)	102	28	26	36	24	1	57	2	0	1	7	3	.70	6	.287	.367	.505
Postseason		5	13	3	2	0	0	(0	0)	5	1	2	1	1	0	5	0	0	1	0	0	-	0	.231	.267	.385
11 ML YEARS		949	3051	807	174	14	113	(58	55)	1348	427	448	453	321	16	709	59	13	24	50	21	.70	96	.265	.344	.442

Craig Tatum

Bats: R **Throws:** R **Pos:** C-42; PH-1; PR-1   **Ht:** 6'1" **Wt:** 230 **Born:** 3/18/1983 **Age:** 28

Year	Team	Lg	G	AB	H	2B	3B	HR	(Hm	Rd)	TB	R	RBI	RC	TBB	IBB	SO	HBP	SH	SF	SB	CS	SB%	GDP	Avg	OBP	Slg
2004	Billings	R+	42	149	33	8	3	2	(-	-)	53	19	21	19	21	0	36	2	0	2	2	0	1.00	9	.221	.322	.356
2005	Dayton	A	37	128	24	7	1	1	(-	-)	36	16	12	12	21	0	30	2	0	0	0	2	.00	2	.188	.311	.281
2006	Dayton	A	98	343	95	21	0	8	(-	-)	140	41	37	50	32	2	70	4	0	2	3	1	.75	7	.277	.344	.408
2007	Srsota	A+	58	219	70	15	0	10	(-	-)	115	29	39	38	9	0	41	1	1	1	0	1	.00	5	.320	.348	.525
2007	Chatt	AA	46	173	40	10	1	2	(-	-)	58	21	22	18	17	0	49	1	0	3	0	1	.00	3	.231	.299	.335
2008	Chatt	AA	86	293	74	18	1	8	(-	-)	118	31	57	39	26	2	58	2	1	6	1	1	.50	7	.253	.312	.403
2008	Lsvlle	AAA	10	39	7	0	0	0	(-	-)	7	1	4	0	0	0	16	0	0	1	0	0	-	1	.179	.175	.179
2009	Lsvlle	AAA	64	213	51	12	0	3	(-	-)	72	22	21	22	17	0	55	2	0	1	0	0	-	4	.239	.300	.338
2010	Norfolk	AAA	6	21	2	0	1	0	(-	-)	4	1	3	0	3	0	5	0	1	0	0	1	.00	1	.095	.208	.190
2009	Cin	NL	26	68	11	1	0	1	(1	0)	15	3	6	4	7	1	10	1	1	0	0	0	-	0	.162	.250	.221
2010	Bal	AL	43	114	32	4	0	0	(0	0)	36	11	9	12	12	0	21	0	0	0	1	0	1.00	5	.281	.349	.316
	2 ML YEARS		69	182	43	5	0	1	(1	0)	51	14	15	16	19	1	31	1	1	0	1	0	1.00	5	.236	.312	.280

Willy Taveras

Bats: R **Throws:** R **Pos:** RF-14; PR-8; LF-6; PH-4; CF-3   tahv-AIR-iss   **Ht:** 6'0" **Wt:** 182 **Born:** 12/25/1981 **Age:** 29

Year	Team	Lg	G	AB	H	2B	3B	HR	(Hm	Rd)	TB	R	RBI	RC	TBB	IBB	SO	HBP	SH	SF	SB	CS	SB%	GDP	Avg	OBP	Slg
2010	LV*	AAA	23	96	20	4	1	0	(-	-)	26	10	3	8	4	0	18	2	2	0	9	0	1.00	2	.208	.255	.271
2010	Gwnntt*	AAA	17	42	5	1	0	0	(-	-)	6	6	1	1	4	0	6	1	0	0	4	1	.80	2	.119	.213	.143
2010	OKCity*	AAA	23	91	25	3	1	2	(-	-)	36	12	10	11	6	0	9	1	1	1	2	2	.50	4	.275	.323	.396
2004	Hou	NL	10	1	0	0	0	0	(0	0)	0	2	0	0	0	0	1	0	1	0	1	0	1.00	0	.000	.000	.000
2005	Hou	NL	152	592	172	13	4	3	(2	1)	202	82	29	61	25	1	103	7	7	4	34	11	.76	4	.291	.325	.341
2006	Hou	NL	149	529	147	19	5	1	(0	1)	179	83	30	64	34	0	88	11	11	2	33	9	.79	6	.278	.333	.338
2007	Col	NL	97	372	119	13	2	2	(2	0)	142	64	24	56	21	0	55	7	7	1	33	9	.79	1	.320	.367	.382
2008	Col	NL	133	479	120	15	2	1	(0	1)	142	64	26	49	36	0	79	5	15	3	68	7	.91	4	.251	.308	.296
2009	Cin	NL	102	404	97	11	2	1	(1	0)	115	56	15	33	18	0	58	2	11	2	25	6	.81	2	.240	.275	.285
2010	Was	NL	27	35	7	0	1	0	(0	0)	9	7	4	4	2	0	6	0	0	0	1	2	.33	2	.200	.243	.257
	Postseason		21	69	18	4	1	0	(0	0)	24	9	1	8	4	0	13	3	4	0	2	1	.67	0	.261	.329	.348
	7 ML YEARS		670	2412	662	71	16	8	(5	3)	789	358	128	267	136	1	390	32	52	12	195	44	.82	17	.274	.320	.327

Taylor Teagarden

Bats: R **Throws:** R **Pos:** C-28; PR-2   **Ht:** 6'1" **Wt:** 200 **Born:** 12/21/1983 **Age:** 27

Year	Team	Lg	G	AB	H	2B	3B	HR	(Hm	Rd)	TB	R	RBI	RC	TBB	IBB	SO	HBP	SH	SF	SB	CS	SB%	GDP	Avg	OBP	Slg
2010	OKCity*	AAA	11	36	6	0	0	2	(-	-)	12	6	2	2	2	0	15	0	1	0	0	0	-	2	.167	.211	.333
2010	Frisco*	AA	52	190	46	10	1	3	(-	-)	67	24	32	24	25	0	75	3	0	2	0	0	-	2	.242	.338	.353
2008	Tex	AL	16	47	15	5	0	6	(3	3)	38	10	17	15	5	0	19	1	0	0	0	0	-	0	.319	.396	.809
2009	Tex	AL	60	198	43	13	0	6	(2	4)	74	26	24	16	14	0	76	1	3	2	0	0	-	6	.217	.270	.374
2010	Tex	AL	28	71	11	1	0	4	(1	3)	24	10	6	5	8	0	34	2	4	0	0	0	-	0	.155	.259	.338
	3 ML YEARS		104	316	69	19	0	16	(6	10)	136	46	47	36	27	0	129	4	7	2	0	0	-	6	.218	.287	.430

Mark Teahen

Bats: L **Throws:** R **Pos:** 3B-52; RF-10; DH-10; PH-6; 1B-3; PR-2   TEE-en   **Ht:** 6'3" **Wt:** 210 **Born:** 9/6/1981 **Age:** 29

Year	Team	Lg	G	AB	H	2B	3B	HR	(Hm	Rd)	TB	R	RBI	RC	TBB	IBB	SO	HBP	SH	SF	SB	CS	SB%	GDP	Avg	OBP	Slg
2010	Charltt*	AAA	11	33	12	2	0	0	(-	-)	14	7	4	8	10	0	7	1	0	2	0	0	-	2	.364	.500	.424
2005	KC	AL	130	447	110	29	4	7	(3	4)	168	60	55	52	40	2	107	1	2	1	7	2	.78	13	.246	.309	.376
2006	KC	AL	109	393	114	21	7	18	(9	9)	203	70	69	79	40	2	85	2	2	2	10	0	1.00	5	.290	.357	.517
2007	KC	AL	144	544	155	31	8	7	(6	1)	223	78	60	82	55	8	127	3	4	2	13	5	.72	23	.285	.353	.410
2008	KC	AL	149	572	146	31	4	15	(4	11)	230	66	59	66	46	4	131	3	0	2	4	3	.57	6	.255	.313	.402
2009	KC	AL	144	524	142	34	1	12	(6	6)	214	69	50	60	37	4	123	6	2	2	8	1	.89	12	.271	.325	.408
2010	CWS	AL	77	233	60	13	2	4	(2	2)	89	31	25	23	25	0	61	0	2	2	3	5	.38	8	.258	.327	.382
	6 ML YEARS		753	2713	727	159	26	63	(30	33)	1127	374	310	362	243	20	634	15	12	11	45	16	.74	67	.268	.330	.415

Mark Teixeira

Bats: B **Throws:** R **Pos:** 1B-149; DH-9; PH-1   tuh-SHARE-uh   **Ht:** 6'3" **Wt:** 220 **Born:** 4/11/1980 **Age:** 31

Year	Team	Lg	G	AB	H	2B	3B	HR	(Hm	Rd)	TB	R	RBI	RC	TBB	IBB	SO	HBP	SH	SF	SB	CS	SB%	GDP	Avg	OBP	Slg
2003	Tex	AL	146	529	137	29	5	26	(19	7)	254	66	84	78	44	5	120	14	0	2	1	2	.33	14	.259	.331	.480
2004	Tex	AL	145	545	153	34	2	38	(18	20)	305	101	112	120	68	12	117	10	0	4	4	1	.80	6	.281	.370	.560
2005	Tex	AL	162	644	194	41	3	43	(30	13)	370	112	144	148	72	5	124	11	0	3	4	0	1.00	18	.301	.379	.575
2006	Tex	AL	162	628	177	45	1	33	(12	21)	323	99	110	114	89	12	128	4	0	6	2	0	1.00	17	.282	.371	.514
2007	2 Tms		132	494	151	33	2	30	(14	16)	278	86	105	116	72	13	112	7	0	2	0	0	-	7	.306	.400	.563
2008	2 Tms		157	574	177	41	0	33	(19	14)	317	102	121	119	97	13	93	7	0	7	2	0	1.00	17	.308	.410	.552
2009	NYY	AL	156	609	178	43	3	39	(24	15)	344	103	122	112	81	9	114	12	0	5	2	0	1.00	13	.292	.383	.565
2010	NYY	AL	158	601	154	36	0	33	(19	14)	289	113	108	110	93	6	122	13	0	5	0	1	.00	15	.256	.365	.481
07	Tex	AL	78	286	85	24	1	13	(5	8)	150	48	49	58	45	10	66	3	0	1	0	0	-	5	.297	.397	.524
07	Atl	NL	54	208	66	9	1	17	(9	8)	128	38	56	58	27	3	46	4	0	1	0	0	-	2	.317	.404	.615
08	Atl	NL	103	381	108	27	0	20	(11	9)	195	63	78	69	65	9	70	3	0	2	0	0	-	13	.283	.390	.512
08	LAA	NL	54	193	69	14	0	13	(8	5)	122	39	43	50	32	4	23	4	0	5	2	0	1.00	4	.358	.449	.632
	Postseason		19	76	18	2	0	2	(2	0)	26	14	9	6	10	0	20	3	0	2	0	0	-	2	.237	.341	.342
	8 ML YEARS		1218	4624	1321	302	16	275	(155	120)	2480	782	906	917	616	75	930	78	0	32	15	4	.79	107	.286	.377	.536

Miguel Tejada

Bats: R **Throws:** R **Pos:** 3B-97; SS-58; DH-4 **Ht:** 5'9" **Wt:** 210 **Born:** 5/25/1974 **Age:** 37

Year	Team	Lg	G	AB	H	2B	3B	HR	(Hm	Rd)	TB	R	RBI	RC	TBB	IBB	SO	HBP	SH	SF	SB	CS	SB%	GDP	Avg	OBP	Slg
1997	Oak	AL	26	99	20	3	2	2	(1	1)	33	10	10	7	2	0	22	3	0	0	2	0	1.00	3	.202	.240	.333
1998	Oak	AL	105	365	85	20	1	11	(5	6)	140	53	45	40	28	0	86	7	4	3	5	6	.45	8	.233	.298	.384
1999	Oak	AL	159	593	149	33	4	21	(12	9)	253	93	84	82	57	3	94	10	9	5	8	7	.53	11	.251	.325	.427
2000	Oak	AL	160	607	167	32	1	30	(16	14)	291	105	115	99	66	6	102	4	2	2	6	0	1.00	15	.275	.349	.479
2001	Oak	AL	**162**	622	166	31	3	31	(17	14)	296	107	113	94	43	5	89	13	1	4	11	5	.69	14	.267	.326	.476
2002	Oak	AL	**162**	662	204	30	0	34	(17	17)	336	108	131	123	38	3	84	11	0	4	7	2	.78	21	.308	.354	.508
2003	Oak	AL	**162**	636	177	42	0	27	(15	12)	300	98	106	103	53	7	65	6	0	8	10	0	1.00	12	.278	.336	.472
2004	Bal	AL	**162**	653	203	40	2	34	(17	17)	349	107	**150**	124	48	6	73	10	0	**14**	4	1	.80	**24**	.311	.360	.534
2005	Bal	AL	**162**	654	199	**50**	5	26	(16	10)	337	89	98	102	40	9	83	7	0	3	5	1	.83	**26**	.304	.349	.515
2006	Bal	AL	**162**	648	214	37	0	24	(17	7)	323	99	100	99	46	10	79	9	0	6	6	2	.75	**28**	.330	.379	.498
2007	Bal	AL	133	514	152	19	1	18	(12	6)	227	72	81	76	41	9	55	10	0	3	2	1	.67	22	.296	.357	.442
2008	Hou	NL	158	632	179	38	3	13	(8	5)	262	92	66	61	24	4	72	6	1	3	7	7	.50	**32**	.283	.314	.415
2009	Hou	NL	158	635	199	**46**	1	14	(10	4)	289	83	86	84	19	2	48	11	0	8	5	2	.71	**29**	.313	.340	.455
2010	2 Tms		156	636	171	26	0	15	(7	8)	242	71	71	73	30	3	67	11	1	3	2	0	1.00	16	.269	.312	.381
10	Bal	AL	97	401	108	16	0	7	(5	2)	145	40	39	38	15	3	39	9	0	3	0	0	-	13	.269	.308	.362
10	SD		59	235	63	10	0	8	(2	6)	97	31	32	35	15	0	28	2	1	0	2	0	1.00	3	.268	.317	.413
	Postseason		20	85	18	7	0	1	(0	1)	28	9	8	6	3	0	16	1	0	2	1	0	1.00	0	.212	.242	.329
	14 ML YEARS		2027	7956	2285	447	23	300	(170	130)	3678	1187	1256	1167	535	67	1019	118	18	66	80	34	.70	261	.287	.339	.462

Ruben Tejada

Bats: R **Throws:** R **Pos:** 2B-50; SS-28; PR-2; PH-1 **Ht:** 5'11" **Wt:** 162 **Born:** 10/27/1989 **Age:** 21

Year	Team	Lg	G	AB	H	2B	3B	HR	(Hm	Rd)	TB	R	RBI	RC	TBB	IBB	SO	HBP	SH	SF	SB	CS	SB%	GDP	Avg	OBP	Slg
2007	Mets	R	35	120	34	4	3	0	(-	-)	44	13	16	17	19	0	16	6	2	2	2	1	.67	4	.283	.401	.367
2008	StLuci	A+	131	497	114	19	4	2	(-	-)	147	55	37	45	41	0	77	5	8	4	8	5	.62	11	.229	.293	.296
2009	Bnghtn	AA	134	488	141	24	3	5	(-	-)	186	59	46	72	37	1	59	11	15	2	19	3	.86	11	.289	.351	.381
2010	Buffalo	AAA	65	218	61	11	0	1	(-	-)	75	25	16	25	14	2	36	3	7	2	1	3	.25	9	.280	.329	.344
2010	NYM	NL	78	216	46	12	0	1	(0	1)	61	28	15	16	22	3	38	8	6	3	2	2	.50	2	.213	.305	.282

Robinson Tejeda

Pitches: R **Bats:** R **Pos:** RP-54 tuh-HAY-duh **Ht:** 6'2" **Wt:** 243 **Born:** 3/24/1982 **Age:** 29

			HOW MUCH HE PITCHED					WHAT HE GAVE UP											THE RESULTS						
Year	Team	Lg	G	GS	CG	GF	IP	BFP	H	R	ER	HR	SH	SF	HB	TBB	IBB	SO	WP	Bk	W	L	Pct	Sh	Sv-Op	Hld	ERC	ERA
2005	Phi	NL	26	13	0	5	85.2	371	67	36	34	5	3	2	8	51	4	72	3	1	4	3	.571	0	0-0	1	3.64	3.57
2006	Tex	AL	14	14	0	0	73.2	329	83	40	35	10	1	5	3	32	1	40	1	1	5	5	.500	0	0-0	0	5.41	4.28
2007	Tex	AL	19	19	0	0	95.1	454	110	78	70	17	3	6	6	60	2	69	10	0	5	9	.357	0	0-0	0	6.77	6.61
2008	2 Tms	AL	29	1	0	15	45.1	186	27	23	20	4	0	3	1	24	0	45	5	0	2	2	.500	0	0-1	1	2.43	3.97
2009	KC	AL	35	6	0	5	73.2	313	43	30	29	4	2	1	3	50	2	87	6	1	4	2	.667	0	0-0	2	2.68	3.54
2010	KC	AL	54	0	0	12	61.0	258	55	28	24	5	2	3	0	26	1	56	4	1	3	5	.375	0	0-6	12	3.50	3.54
08	Tex	AL	4	0	0	1	6.0	29	5	6	6	1	0	1	0	5	0	4	0	0	0	0	-	0	0-1	0	5.04	9.00
08	KC	AL	25	1	0	14	39.1	157	22	17	14	3	0	2	1	19	0	41	5	0	2	2	.500	0	0-0	1	2.08	3.20
	6 ML YEARS		177	53	0	37	434.2	1911	385	235	212	45	11	20	21	243	10	369	29	4	23	26	.469	0	0-7	16	4.24	4.39

Kanekoa Texeira

Pitches: R **Bats:** R **Pos:** RP-43 kan-ih-KOE-ah tuh-SHARE-uh **Ht:** 6'2" **Wt:** 190 **Born:** 2/6/1986 **Age:** 25

			HOW MUCH HE PITCHED					WHAT HE GAVE UP											THE RESULTS						
Year	Team	Lg	G	GS	CG	GF	IP	BFP	H	R	ER	HR	SH	SF	HB	TBB	IBB	SO	WP	Bk	W	L	Pct	Sh	Sv-Op	Hld	ERC	ERA
2006	Bristol	R+	19	0	0	11	23.2	92	15	3	2	0	2	0	1	5	0	29	4	0	1	2	.333	0	3--	-	1.31	0.76
2006	Knapol	A	4	0	0	3	6.0	26	8	3	3	1	0	0	1	1	0	2	2	0	0	0	-	0	0--	-	6.65	4.50
2007	Knapol	A	39	0	0	32	53.2	231	49	24	22	0	1	1	2	22	1	58	4	0	5	2	.714	0	16--	-	3.02	3.69
2008	WinSa	A+	36	0	0	33	38.2	160	28	10	4	0	0	1	1	14	1	36	2	0	3	1	.750	0	20--	-	1.80	0.93
2008	Brham	AA	15	0	0	7	22.1	90	18	5	5	2	1	0	2	7	0	24	2	0	3	2	.600	0	1--	-	3.07	2.01
2009	Trntn	AA	41	6	0	9	101.1	432	90	39	32	7	5	1	2	43	2	88	7	0	9	6	.600	0	2--	-	3.37	2.84
2010	2 Tms	AL	43	0	0	10	61.1	277	73	36	33	3	3	6	3	25	1	33	3	1	1	1	.500	0	0-0	2	5.00	4.84
10	Sea	AL	16	0	0	7	18.2	87	22	12	11	0	0	1	1	10	0	14	2	0	0	1	.000	0	0-0	1	5.06	5.30
10	KC	AL	27	0	0	3	42.2	190	51	24	22	3	3	5	2	15	1	19	1	1	1	0	1.000	0	0-0	1	4.97	4.64

Marcus Thames

Bats: R **Throws:** R **Pos:** DH-38; LF-25; PH-24; RF-8; 3B-1 TIMMS **Ht:** 6'2" **Wt:** 220 **Born:** 3/6/1977 **Age:** 34

Year	Team	Lg	G	AB	H	2B	3B	HR	(Hm	Rd)	TB	R	RBI	RC	TBB	IBB	SO	HBP	SH	SF	SB	CS	SB%	GDP	Avg	OBP	Slg
2010	S-WB*	AAA	4	15	3	0	0	0	(-	-)	3	0	1	0	0	0	1	0	0	0	0	0	-	1	.200	.200	.200
2002	NYY	AL	7	13	3	1	0	1	(0	1)	7	2	2	2	0	0	4	0	0	0	0	0	-	0	.231	.231	.538
2003	Tex	AL	30	73	15	2	0	1	(0	1)	20	12	4	5	8	0	18	2	0	1	0	1	.00	2	.205	.298	.274
2004	Det	AL	61	165	42	12	0	10	(5	5)	84	24	33	30	16	0	42	2	0	1	0	1	.00	3	.255	.326	.509
2005	Det	AL	38	107	21	2	0	7	(3	4)	44	11	16	10	9	1	38	1	0	1	0	0	-	1	.196	.263	.411
2006	Det	AL	110	348	89	20	2	26	(11	15)	191	61	60	60	37	0	92	4	0	1	1	1	.50	6	.256	.333	.549
2007	Det	AL	86	269	65	15	0	18	(14	4)	134	37	54	39	13	1	72	1	0	1	2	1	.67	6	.242	.278	.498
2008	Det	AL	103	316	76	12	0	25	(10	15)	163	50	56	44	24	0	95	0	0	2	0	3	.00	6	.241	.292	.516
2009	Det	AL	87	258	65	11	0	13	(6	7)	117	33	36	31	29	2	72	1	0	6	2	2	.00	5	.252	.323	.453
2010	NYY	AL	82	212	61	7	0	12	(4	8)	104	22	33	35	19	0	61	3	0	3	0	0	-	3	.288	.350	.491
	Postseason		8	21	5	2	0	0	(0	0)	7	3	1	3	1	0	6	0	0	0	0	0	-	0	.238	.273	.333
	9 ML YEARS		604	1761	437	82	3	113	(54	59)	864	252	294	256	155	4	494	14	0	16	3	9	.25	26	.248	.311	.491

Joe Thatcher

Pitches: L **Bats:** L **Pos:** RP-65   **Ht:** 6'2" **Wt:** 229 **Born:** 10/4/1981 **Age:** 29

			HOW MUCH HE PITCHED						WHAT HE GAVE UP											THE RESULTS							
Year	Team	Lg	G	GS	CG	GF	IP	BFP	H	R	ER	HR	SH	SF	HB	TBB	IBB	SO	WP	Bk	W	L	Pct	Sh	Sv-Op	Hld	ERC	ERA
2010	Portlnd*	AAA	6	0	0	1	5.0	24	6	2	2	0	1	0	1	3	0	3	0	0	0	1	.000	0	0- -		6.15	3.60
2007	SD	NL	22	0	0	5	21.0	85	13	6	3	1	0	0	1	6	2	16	0	0	2	2	.500	0	0-0	2	1.49	1.29
2008	SD	NL	25	0	0	7	25.2	128	42	25	24	4	2	3	0	13	2	17	0	0	0	4	.000	0	0-3	5	8.91	8.42
2009	SD	NL	52	0	0	7	45.0	188	37	14	14	2	1	2	4	18	7	55	2	1	1	0	1.000	0	0-1	9	2.87	2.80
2010	SD	NL	65	0	0	12	35.0	137	23	5	5	1	3	2	1	7	2	45	0	0	1	0	1.000	0	0-0	11	1.37	1.29
	4 ML YEARS		164	0	0	31	126.2	538	115	50	46	8	6	7	6	44	13	133	2	1	4	6	.400	0	0-4	27	3.12	3.27

Dale Thayer

Pitches: R **Bats:** R **Pos:** RP-1   **Ht:** 6'0" **Wt:** 195 **Born:** 12/17/1980 **Age:** 30

			HOW MUCH HE PITCHED						WHAT HE GAVE UP											THE RESULTS							
Year	Team	Lg	G	GS	CG	GF	IP	BFP	H	R	ER	HR	SH	SF	HB	TBB	IBB	SO	WP	Bk	W	L	Pct	Sh	Sv-Op	Hld	ERC	ERA
2003	FtWyn	A	45	0	0	35	48.0	194	31	15	11	2	5	2	2	15	1	72	1	0	1	3	.250	0	25- -	-	1.69	2.06
2004	Lk Els	A+	50	0	0	42	55.1	214	36	12	10	1	0	0	0	11	0	54	0	0	2	1	.667	0	23- -	-	1.31	1.63
2004	Mobile	AA	8	0	0	4	7.1	31	8	3	3	1	0	0	0	1	0	7	0	0	1	1	.500	0	0- -	-	3.69	3.68
2005	Mobile	AA	56	0	0	50	57.2	249	60	16	15	5	5	2	1	26	2	59	1	0	3	5	.375	0	28- -	-	4.52	2.34
2006	Mobile	AA	57	0	0	51	65.1	274	59	18	18	3	6	0	3	22	5	57	0	0	7	4	.636	0	27- -	-	3.01	2.48
2006	Portlnd	AAA	2	0	0	2	3.0	11	2	1	1	1	0	0	0	1	0	4	1	0	0	0	-	0	0- -	-	3.72	3.00
2007	Mont	AA	47	0	0	43	59.2	239	40	16	15	4	2	2	1	19	2	54	1	0	9	0	1.000	0	21- -	-	1.95	2.26
2007	Drham	AAA	8	0	0	4	9.1	35	5	3	3	0	1	0	0	4	0	9	2	0	0	0	-	0	0- -	-	1.46	2.89
2008	Drham	AAA	52	0	0	24	68.1	301	73	26	21	2	2	2	0	24	1	76	4	0	3	1	.750	0	9- -	-	3.65	2.77
2009	Drham	AAA	51	0	0	40	63.1	264	59	24	16	3	4	1	3	15	1	44	2	0	2	5	.286	0	17- -	-	2.87	2.27
2010	Drham	AAA	46	0	0	17	60.0	273	68	28	23	3	3	1	4	25	2	55	6	0	4	1	.800	0	3- -	-	4.68	3.45
2009	TB	AL	11	0	0	3	13.2	59	18	9	7	3	0	0	0	1	0	8	1	0	0	0	-	0	1-1	0	5.38	4.61
2010	TB	AL	1	0	0	0	2.0	13	7	6	6	1	0	0	0	0	0	2	0	0	0	0	-	0	0-0	0	24.30	27.00
	2 ML YEARS		12	0	0	3	15.2	72	25	15	13	4	0	0	0	1	0	10	1	0	0	0	-	0	1-1	0	7.38	7.47

Ryan Theriot

Bats: R **Throws:** R **Pos:** 2B-119; SS-29; PH-5; PR-1   TARE-ee-oh   **Ht:** 5'11" **Wt:** 100 **Born:** 12/7/1979 **Age:** 31

			BATTING																			BASERUNNING				AVERAGES		
Year	Team	Lg	G	AB	H	2B	3B	HR	(Hm	Rd)	TB	R	RBI	RC	TBB	IBB	SO	HBP	SH	SF	SB	CS	SB%	GDP	Avg	OBP	Slg
2005	ChC	NL	9	13	2	1	0	0	(0	0)	3	3	0	0	1	0	2	0	0	0	0	0	-	0	.154	.214	.231
2006	ChC	NL	53	134	44	11	3	3	(3	0)	70	34	16	31	17	0	18	2	6	0	13	2	.87	5	.328	.412	.522
2007	ChC	NL	148	537	143	30	2	3	(3	0)	186	80	45	64	49	1	50	0	8	3	28	4	.88	12	.266	.326	.346
2008	ChC	NL	149	580	178	19	4	1	(1	0)	208	85	38	78	73	1	58	3	4	1	22	13	.63	19	.307	.387	.359
2009	ChC	NL	154	602	171	20	5	7	(5	2)	222	81	54	79	51	1	93	6	13	5	21	10	.68	13	.284	.343	.369
2010	2 Tms	NL	150	586	158	15	2	2	(1	1)	183	72	29	58	41	3	74	4	7	2	20	9	.69	13	.270	.321	.312
10	ChC	NL	96	388	110	10	2	1	(0	1)	127	45	21	43	19	3	46	2	2	1	16	6	.73	8	.284	.320	.327
10	LAD	NL	54	198	48	5	0	1	(1	0)	56	27	8	15	22	0	28	2	5	1	4	3	.57	5	.242	.323	.283
	Postseason		6	23	6	0	0	0	(0	0)	6	0	1	2	2	1	4	0	0	0	1	0	1.00	1	.261	.320	.261
	6 ML YEARS		663	2452	696	96	16	16	(13	3)	872	355	182	310	232	6	295	15	38	11	104	38	.73	62	.284	.348	.356

Josh Thole

Bats: L **Throws:** R **Pos:** C-61; PH-18   TOE-lee   **Ht:** 6'1" **Wt:** 205 **Born:** 10/28/1986 **Age:** 24

			BATTING																			BASERUNNING				AVERAGES		
Year	Team	Lg	G	AB	H	2B	3B	HR	(Hm	Rd)	TB	R	RBI	RC	TBB	IBB	SO	HBP	SH	SF	SB	CS	SB%	GDP	Avg	OBP	Slg
2005	Mets	R	35	104	28	2	1	1	(-	-)	35	14	12	17	20	0	11	4	2	0	1	1	.50	2	.269	.406	.337
2006	Kngspt	R+	36	98	23	4	0	1	(-	-)	30	13	12	9	7	1	25	3	0	2	1	1	.50	1	.235	.300	.306
2007	Savann	A	117	389	104	17	0	0	(-	-)	121	46	36	51	61	1	57	4	4	0	4	4	.50	10	.267	.372	.311
2008	StLuci	A+	111	347	104	25	2	5	(-	-)	148	49	56	60	45	2	38	4	1	5	2	1	.67	8	.300	.382	.427
2009	Bnghtn	AA	103	384	126	29	2	1	(-	-)	162	48	46	68	43	4	34	5	1	9	8	4	.67	14	.328	.395	.422
2010	Buffalo	AAA	48	165	44	19	1	2	(-	-)	71	20	17	26	22	0	25	1	1	2	0	0	-	3	.267	.353	.430
2009	NYM	NL	17	53	17	2	1	0	(0	0)	21	2	9	4	0	5	0	0	0	2	1	0	1.00	1	.321	.356	.396
2010	NYM	NL	73	202	56	7	1	3	(2	1)	74	17	17	28	24	1	25	1	0	0	1	0	1.00	8	.277	.357	.366
	2 ML YEARS		90	255	73	9	2	3	(2	1)	95	19	26	37	28	1	30	1	0	2	2	0	1.00	9	.286	.357	.373

Brad Thomas

Pitches: L **Bats:** L **Pos:** RP-47; SP-2   **Ht:** 6'4" **Wt:** 234 **Born:** 10/12/1977 **Age:** 33

			HOW MUCH HE PITCHED						WHAT HE GAVE UP											THE RESULTS							
Year	Team	Lg	G	GS	CG	GF	IP	BFP	H	R	ER	HR	SH	SF	HB	TBB	IBB	SO	WP	Bk	W	L	Pct	Sh	Sv-Op	Hld	ERC	ERA
2001	Min	AL	5	5	0	0	16.1	82	20	17	17	6	1	0	1	14	0	6	2	0	0	2	.000	0	0-0	0	10.12	9.37
2003	Min	AL	3	0	0	1	4.2	22	6	4	4	1	0	0	0	3	1	2	0	0	0	1	.000	0	0-0	0	7.54	7.71
2004	Min	AL	3	0	0	0	2.2	16	7	5	5	0	1	0	0	1	0	0	1	0	0	0	-	0	0-0	0	13.58	16.88
2010	Det	AL	49	2	0	7	69.1	307	77	31	30	4	4	6	4	29	3	30	4	0	6	2	.750	0	0-0	3	4.68	3.89
	4 ML YEARS		60	7	0	8	93.0	427	110	57	56	11	6	6	5	47	4	38	7	0	6	5	.545	0	0-0	3	5.92	5.42

Justin Thomas

Pitches: L Bats: L Pos: RP-12   Ht: 6'3" Wt: 220 Born: 1/18/1984 Age: 27

				HOW	MUCH	HE	PITCHED				WHAT	HE	GAVE	UP								THE	RESULTS						
Year	Team	Lg	G	GS	CG	GF	IP	BFP	H	R	ER	HR	SH	SF	HB	TBB	IBB	SO	WP	Bk	W	L	Pct	Sh	Sv-Op	Hld	ERC	ERA
2005	Everett	A-	18	6	0	2	59.0	256	63	31	25	2	0	0	4	20	0	48	5	0	3	3	.500	0	0--	-	4.04	3.81
2006	Wisc	A	11	11	0	0	61.0	268	69	29	21	4	5	2	3	17	0	51	2	0	5	5	.500	0	0--	-	4.24	3.10
2006	InldEm	A+	17	17	1	0	105.1	454	108	58	48	10	2	3	3	45	0	111	6	0	9	4	.692	1	0--	-	4.49	4.10
2007	WTenn	AA	24	24	0	0	119.1	559	147	82	73	11	10	6	5	61	0	100	12	0	4	9	.308	0	0--	-	5.99	5.51
2008	WTenn	AA	25	17	1	1	118.2	525	116	66	57	11	6	1	10	57	1	106	6	3	7	7	.500	1	0--	-	4.55	4.32
2008	Tacom	AAA	7	1	0	4	17.0	71	15	7	7	2	0	0	0	9	0	21	2	0	2	1	.667	0	1--	-	4.21	3.71
2009	Tacom	AAA	53	0	0	23	60.1	291	67	33	30	5	3	1	4	40	4	53	7	0	2	4	.333	0	6--	-	5.67	4.48
2010	Indy	AAA	40	0	0	11	54.1	210	33	16	15	4	1	3	9	10	0	51	2	0	5	0	1.000	0	4--	-	1.79	2.48
2008	Sea	AL	8	0	0	2	4.0	22	9	3	3	0	1	0	0	2	0	2	1	0	0	1	.000	0	0-1	1	12.01	6.75
2010	Pit	NL	12	0	0	6	13.0	62	21	9	9	3	0	1	0	5	1	5	0	0	0	1	.000	0	0-0	0	9.03	6.23
	2 ML YEARS		20	0	0	8	17.0	84	30	12	12	3	1	1	0	7	1	7	1	0	0	2	.000	0	0-1	1	9.75	6.35

Jim Thome

Bats: L Throws: R Pos: DH-78; PH-30   TOE-mee   Ht: 6'3" Wt: 250 Born: 8/27/1970 Age: 40

						BATTING															BASERUNNING				AVERAGES		
Year	Team	Lg	G	AB	H	2B	3B	HR	(Hm	Rd)	TB	R	RBI	RC	TBB	IBB	SO	HBP	SH	SF	SB	CS	SB%	GDP	Avg	OBP	Slg
1991	Cle	AL	27	98	25	4	2	1	(0	1)	36	7	9	9	5	1	16	1	0	0	1	1	.50	4	.255	.298	.367
1992	Cle	AL	40	117	24	3	1	2	(1	1)	35	8	12	9	10	2	34	2	0	2	2	0	1.00	3	.205	.275	.299
1993	Cle	AL	47	154	41	11	0	7	(5	2)	73	28	22	30	29	1	36	4	0	5	2	1	.67	3	.266	.385	.474
1994	Cle	AL	98	321	86	20	1	20	(10	10)	168	58	52	56	46	5	84	0	1	1	3	3	.50	11	.268	.359	.523
1995	Cle	AL	137	452	142	29	3	25	(13	12)	252	92	73	109	97	3	113	5	0	3	4	3	.57	8	.314	.438	.558
1996	Cle	AL	151	505	157	28	5	38	(18	20)	309	122	116	132	123	8	141	6	0	2	2	2	.50	13	.311	.450	.612
1997	Cle	AL	147	496	142	25	0	40	(17	23)	287	104	102	120	120	9	146	3	0	8	1	1	.50	9	.286	.423	.579
1998	Cle	AL	123	440	129	34	2	30	(18	12)	257	89	85	104	89	8	141	4	0	4	1	0	1.00	7	.293	.413	.584
1999	Cle	AL	146	494	137	27	2	33	(19	14)	267	101	108	116	127	13	171	4	0	4	0	0	-	6	.277	.426	.540
2000	Cle	AL	158	557	150	33	1	37	(18	19)	296	106	106	119	118	4	171	4	0	5	1	0	1.00	8	.269	.398	.531
2001	Cle	AL	156	526	153	26	1	49	(30	19)	328	101	124	130	111	14	185	4	0	3	0	1	.00	9	.291	.416	.624
2002	Cle	AL	147	480	146	19	2	52	(30	22)	325	101	118	139	122	18	139	5	0	6	1	2	.33	5	.304	.445	.677
2003	Phi	NL	159	578	154	30	3	47	(28	19)	331	111	131	125	111	11	182	4	0	5	0	3	.00	5	.266	.385	.573
2004	Phi	NL	143	508	139	28	1	42	(19	23)	295	97	105	97	104	26	144	2	0	4	0	2	.00	10	.274	.396	.581
2005	Phi	NL	59	193	40	7	0	7	(6	1)	68	26	30	25	45	4	59	2	0	2	0	0	-	5	.207	.360	.352
2006	CWS	AL	143	490	141	26	0	42	(16	26)	293	108	109	120	107	12	147	6	0	7	0	0	-	4	.288	.416	.598
2007	CWS	AL	130	432	119	19	0	35	(21	14)	243	79	96	104	95	11	134	6	0	1	0	1	.00	10	.275	.410	.563
2008	CWS	AL	149	503	123	28	0	34	(19	15)	253	93	90	96	91	9	147	4	0	4	1	0	1.00	18	.245	.362	.503
2009	2 Tms		124	362	90	15	0	23	(9	14)	174	55	77	65	69	3	123	0	0	3	0	0	-	8	.249	.366	.481
2010	Min	AL	108	276	78	16	2	25	(15	10)	173	48	59	61	60	4	82	2	0	2	0	0	-	8	.283	.412	.627
09	CWS	AL	107	345	86	15	0	23	(14	9)	170	55	74	65	69	3	116	0	0	3	0	0	-	8	.249	.372	.493
09	LAD	AL	17	17	4	0	0	0	(0	0)	4	0	3	0	0	0	7	0	0	0	0	0	-	0	.235	.235	.235
	Postseason		64	207	46	2	1	17	(13	4)	101	33	37	31	27	1	65	3	1	0	0	0	-	3	.222	.321	.488
	20 ML YEARS		2392	7982	2216	428	26	589	(329	260)	4463	1534	1624	1766	1679	166	2395	68	1	73	19	20	.49	154	.278	.404	.559

Brad Thompson

Pitches: R Bats: R Pos: RP-16   Ht: 6'1" Wt: 188 Born: 1/31/1982 Age: 29

				HOW	MUCH	HE	PITCHED				WHAT	HE	GAVE	UP								THE	RESULTS						
Year	Team	Lg	G	GS	CG	GF	IP	BFP	H	R	ER	HR	SH	SF	HB	TBB	IBB	SO	WP	Bk	W	L	Pct	Sh	Sv-Op	Hld	ERC	ERA
2010	Omha*	AAA	3	3	0	0	11.2	52	16	8	7	1	1	1	1	1	0	3	0	0	0	1	.000	0	0--	-	5.16	5.40
2010	RdRck*	AAA	15	0	0	7	23.1	115	41	27	23	3	1	0	0	4	1	12	2	0	1	1	.500	0	0--	-	7.71	8.87
2005	StL	NL	40	0	0	8	55.0	225	46	22	18	5	3	0	4	15	2	29	0	0	4	0	1.000	0	1-1	7	2.90	2.95
2006	StL	NL	43	1	0	16	56.2	245	58	23	21	4	3	0	5	20	3	32	1	0	1	2	.333	0	0-0	3	4.11	3.34
2007	StL	NL	44	17	0	10	129.1	580	157	76	68	24	4	2	13	40	2	53	4	0	8	6	.571	0	0-0	0	5.99	4.73
2008	StL	NL	26	6	0	10	64.2	273	72	38	37	5	2	3	3	19	1	32	3	0	6	3	.667	0	0-1	1	4.44	5.15
2009	StL	NL	32	8	0	17	80.0	345	85	45	43	8	2	2	7	23	2	34	5	1	2	6	.250	0	0-0	0	4.32	4.84
2010	KC	AL	16	0	0	3	19.2	89	25	16	14	4	1	1	1	4	1	10	2	0	0	4	.000	0	0-1	1	5.60	6.41
	Postseason		8	0	0	1	4.1	23	8	5	4	2	0	1	0	1	0	4	0	0	0	1	.000	0	0-0	0	11.13	8.31
	6 ML YEARS		201	32	0	64	405.1	1757	443	220	201	49	15	8	33	121	11	190	14	1	21	21	.500	0	1-3	12	4.68	4.46

Rich Thompson

Pitches: R Bats: R Pos: RP-13   Ht: 6'1" Wt: 180 Born: 7/1/1984 Age: 26

				HOW	MUCH	HE	PITCHED				WHAT	HE	GAVE	UP								THE	RESULTS						
Year	Team	Lg	G	GS	CG	GF	IP	BFP	H	R	ER	HR	SH	SF	HB	TBB	IBB	SO	WP	Bk	W	L	Pct	Sh	Sv-Op	Hld	ERC	ERA
2010	Salt Lk*	AAA	19	0	0	6	29.2	109	17	2	2	0	0	3	0	10	0	30	1	0	1	1	.500	0	2--	-	1.39	0.61
2007	LAA	AL	7	0	0	2	6.2	32	10	8	8	4	0	0	0	3	0	9	2	0	0	0	-	0	0-0	0	11.85	10.80
2008	LAA	AL	2	0	0	1	2.0	12	4	5	5	0	0	0	0	2	0	1	1	0	0	0	-	0	0-0	0	12.01	22.50
2009	LAA	AL	13	0	0	2	19.1	92	27	11	11	6	1	1	1	7	0	21	5	0	0	0	-	0	0-0	0	8.17	5.12
2010	LAA	AL	13	0	0	7	19.2	75	12	4	3	2	1	0	0	4	0	15	4	0	2	0	1.000	0	0-0	1	1.50	1.37
	4 ML YEARS		35	0	0	12	47.2	211	53	28	27	12	2	1	1	16	0	46	12	0	2	0	1.000	0	0-0	1	5.58	5.10

Matt Thornton

Pitches: L **Bats:** L **Pos:** RP-61 **Ht:** 6'6" **Wt:** 235 **Born:** 9/15/1976 **Age:** 34

			HOW MUCH HE PITCHED						WHAT HE GAVE UP											THE RESULTS							
Year	Team	Lg	G	GS	CG	GF	IP	BFP	H	R	ER	HR	SH	SF	HB	TBB	IBB	SO	WP	Bk	W	L	Pct	Sh	Sv-Op	Hld	ERC	ERA
2004	Sea	AL	19	1	0	8	32.2	148	30	15	15	2	2	1	0	25	1	30	2	0	1	2	.333	0	0-0	0	4.75	4.13
2005	Sea	AL	55	0	0	15	57.0	262	54	33	33	13	1	1	0	42	2	57	7	0	0	4	.000	0	0-1	5	6.06	5.21
2006	CWS	AL	63	0	0	20	54.0	227	46	20	20	5	1	3	1	21	4	49	1	0	5	3	.625	0	2-5	18	3.12	3.33
2007	CWS	AL	68	0	0	13	56.1	249	59	31	30	4	0	2	2	26	6	55	3	0	4	4	.500	0	2-7	17	4.35	4.79
2008	CWS	AL	74	0	0	12	67.1	268	48	20	20	5	1	4	2	19	2	77	3	0	5	3	.625	0	1-6	20	2.07	2.67
2009	CWS	AL	70	0	0	17	72.1	291	58	22	22	5	2	1	1	20	2	87	4	0	6	3	.667	0	4-9	24	2.40	2.74
2010	CWS	AL	61	0	0	13	60.2	239	41	18	18	3	0	2	2	20	5	81	1	0	5	4	.556	0	8-10	21	1.89	2.67
	Postseason		3	0	0	1	3.1	14	2	0	0	0	0	0	0	2	1	2	0	0	0	0	-	0	0-0	1	1.62	0.00
	7 ML YEARS		410	1	0	98	400.1	1684	336	159	158	37	7	11	8	173	22	436	21	0	26	23	.531	0	17-38	105	3.27	3.55

Erick Threets

Pitches: L **Bats:** L **Pos:** RP-11 **Ht:** 6'5" **Wt:** 240 **Born:** 11/4/1981 **Age:** 29

			HOW MUCH HE PITCHED						WHAT HE GAVE UP											THE RESULTS							
Year	Team	Lg	G	GS	CG	GF	IP	BFP	H	R	ER	HR	SH	SF	HB	TBB	IBB	SO	WP	Bk	W	L	Pct	Sh	Sv-Op	Hld	ERC	ERA
2010	Charltt*	AAA	17	0	0	7	21.0	78	12	2	2	0	1	1	0	5	1	10	1	0	1	0	1.000	0	2- -	-	1.10	0.86
2007	SF	NL	3	0	0	1	2.1	15	5	5	5	0	0	0	0	3	0	1	1	0	0	0	-	0	0-0	0	14.38	19.29
2008	SF	NL	7	0	0	6	10.0	50	11	4	4	1	1	0	3	9	2	6	1	0	0	1	.000	0	0-0	0	7.86	3.60
2010	CWS	AL	11	0	0	1	12.1	45	9	1	0	0	0	1	0	3	0	6	0	0	0	0	-	0	0-0	0	1.72	0.00
	3 ML YEARS		21	0	0	8	24.2	110	25	10	9	1	1	1	3	15	2	13	2	0	0	1	.000	0	0-0	0	5.05	3.28

Chris Tillman

Pitches: R **Bats:** R **Pos:** SP-11 **Ht:** 6'6" **Wt:** 210 **Born:** 4/15/1988 **Age:** 23

			HOW MUCH HE PITCHED						WHAT HE GAVE UP											THE RESULTS							
Year	Team	Lg	G	GS	CG	GF	IP	BFP	H	R	ER	HR	SH	SF	HB	TBB	IBB	SO	WP	Bk	W	L	Pct	Sh	Sv-Op	Hld	ERC	ERA
2006	Ms	R	5	0	0	2	11.0	48	9	4	1	0	0	0	1	5	0	16	1	0	2	0	1.000	0	1- -	-	2.87	0.82
2006	Everett	A-	5	5	0	0	19.2	97	25	17	17	4	2	0	3	15	0	29	3	0	1	3	.250	0	0- -	-	9.13	7.78
2007	Wisc	A	8	8	0	0	33.0	145	31	21	13	1	1	0	1	13	0	34	3	1	1	4	.200	0	0- -	-	3.24	3.55
2007	Hi Dsrt	A+	20	20	0	0	102.2	472	107	79	60	12	4	5	12	48	0	105	13	0	6	7	.462	0	0- -	-	5.10	5.26
2008	Bowie	AA	28	28	0	0	135.2	580	115	53	48	10	3	1	4	65	1	154	10	0	11	4	.733	0	0- -	-	3.46	3.18
2009	Norfolk	AAA	18	18	0	0	96.2	399	85	36	29	5	2	1	4	26	1	99	6	2	8	6	.571	0	0- -	-	2.75	2.70
2010	Norfolk	AAA	21	21	2	0	121.1	501	120	50	45	10	1	3	2	30	0	94	8	1	11	7	.611	2	0- -	-	3.41	3.34
2009	Bal	AL	12	12	0	0	65.0	285	77	40	39	15	0	0	2	24	1	39	4	0	2	5	.286	0	0-0	0	6.28	5.40
2010	Bal	AL	11	11	0	0	53.2	236	51	37	35	9	1	3	1	31	1	31	2	0	2	5	.286	0	0-0	0	5.12	5.87
	2 ML YEARS		23	23	0	0	118.2	521	128	77	74	24	1	3	3	55	2	70	6	0	4	10	.286	0	0-0	0	5.75	5.61

Jess Todd

Pitches: R **Bats:** R **Pos:** RP-5 **Ht:** 5'11" **Wt:** 195 **Born:** 4/20/1986 **Age:** 25

			HOW MUCH HE PITCHED						WHAT HE GAVE UP											THE RESULTS							
Year	Team	Lg	G	GS	CG	GF	IP	BFP	H	R	ER	HR	SH	SF	HB	TBB	IBB	SO	WP	Bk	W	L	Pct	Sh	Sv-Op	Hld	ERC	ERA
2007	Batvia	A-	16	7	0	2	58.1	231	48	23	18	2	0	0	1	14	1	69	2	0	4	1	.800	0	0- -	-	2.23	2.78
2008	PlmBh	A+	7	4	0	1	27.1	108	18	7	5	0	2	0	1	7	0	35	0	1	3	0	1.000	0	1- -	-	1.46	1.65
2008	Sprgfld	AA	17	16	0	0	103.0	405	79	37	34	12	3	0	13	24	1	81	1	0	5	4	.444	0	0- -	-	2.89	2.97
2008	Memp	AAA	4	4	0	0	22.2	96	19	10	10	4	0	2	1	11	0	20	2	0	1	1	.500	0	0- -	-	4.28	3.97
2009	Memp	AAA	41	0	0	34	49.0	199	39	13	12	3	3	1	0	13	1	59	7	0	4	2	.667	0	24	-	2.21	2.20
2009	Clmbs	AAA	3	0	0	2	4.0	13	1	0	0	0	0	0	0	0	0	7	0	0	0	0	-	0	1- -	-	0.14	0.00
2010	Clmbs	AAA	44	0	0	18	49.0	213	46	20	18	6	1	0	3	18	3	53	1	0	4	2	.667	0	4- -	-	3.84	3.31
2009	2 Tms		20	0	0	6	22.1	109	34	19	19	4	1	4	0	9	1	20	1	0	0	1	.000	0	0-0	1	7.74	7.66
2010	Cle	AL	5	0	0	2	6.0	30	9	5	5	0	0	0	0	3	0	9	1	0	0	0	-	0	0-0	0	6.48	7.50
09	StL	NL	1	0	0	0	1.2	10	3	2	2	1	0	0	0	2	0	2	0	0	0	0	-	0	0-0	0	18.11	10.80
09	Cle	AL	19	0	0	6	20.2	99	31	17	17	3	1	4	0	7	1	18	1	0	0	1	.000	0	0-0	1	7.01	7.40
	2 ML YEARS		25	0	0	8	28.1	139	43	24	24	4	1	4	0	12	1	29	2	0	0	1	.000	0	0-0	1	7.48	7.62

Matt Tolbert

Bats: B **Throws:** R **Pos:** 2B-20; 3B-14; PR-8; PH-5; 1B-4; SS-3; DH-2; RF-1 **Ht:** 6'0" **Wt:** 185 **Born:** 5/4/1982 **Age:** 29

			BATTING																	BASERUNNING				AVERAGES		
Year	Team	Lg	G	AB	H	2B	3B	HR	(Hm	Rd)	TB	R	RBI	RC	TBB	IBB	SO	HBP	SH	SF	SB	CS	SB%	GDP	Avg	OBP	Slg
2010	Roch*	AAA	42	173	49	8	1	2	(-	-)	67	19	11	23	13	1	30	0	1	1	6	1	.86	2	.283	.332	.387
2010	Twins*	R	4	12	4	2	0	0	(-	-)	6	4	0	2	3	0	3	0	0	0	1	1	.50	0	.333	.467	.500
2008	Min	AL	41	113	32	6	3	0	(0	0)	44	18	6	13	7	0	19	0	2	1	7	1	.88	5	.283	.322	.389
2009	Min	AL	71	198	46	7	1	2	(0	2)	61	28	19	22	21	1	37	0	10	2	6	2	.75	1	.232	.303	.308
2010	Min	AL	48	87	20	4	3	1	(1	0)	33	8	18	12	9	0	18	0	1	2	1	1	.50	2	.230	.293	.379
	Postseason		2	5	1	0	0	0	(0	0)	1	0	0	0	0	0	1	1	0	0	0	0	-	0	.200	.333	.200
	3 ML YEARS		160	398	98	17	7	3	(1	2)	138	54	43	47	37	1	74	0	13	6	14	4	.78	8	.246	.306	.347

Steve Tolleson

Bats: R **Throws:** R **Pos:** SS-11; 3B-6; 2B-4; PH-3; LF-1; RF-1; PR-1 **Ht:** 5'11" **Wt:** 185 **Born:** 11/1/1983 **Age:** 27

			BATTING																	BASERUNNING				AVERAGES		
Year	Team	Lg	G	AB	H	2B	3B	HR	(Hm	Rd)	TB	R	RBI	RC	TBB	IBB	SO	HBP	SH	SF	SB	CS	SB%	GDP	Avg	OBP	Slg
2005	Elizab	R+	16	56	18	6	1	2	(-	-)	32	18	8	14	11	0	4	3	3	0	2	1	.67	2	.321	.457	.571
2005	Beloit	A	31	102	18	2	0	3	(-	-)	29	16	10	11	17	0	23	3	3	0	3	0	1.00	5	.176	.311	.284
2006	Beloit	A	47	171	49	8	2	2	(-	-)	67	23	16	26	27	0	34	2	4	0	7	9	.44	3	.287	.390	.392
2006	Twins	R	2	8	2	0	0	0	(-	-)	2	1	1	0	0	0	0	0	0	1	0	0	-	0	.250	.222	.250

Year	Team	Lg	G	AB	H	2B	3B	HR	(Hm	Rd)	TB	R	RBI	RC	TBB	IBB	SO	HBP	SH	SF	SB	CS	SB%	GDP	Avg	OBP	Slg
2006	FtMyrs	A+	49	157	42	8	1	4	(-	-)	64	23	23	25	22	0	24	1	2	4	3	1	.75	4	.268	.353	.408
2007	FtMyrs	A+	132	487	139	24	4	5	(-	-)	186	75	35	81	79	1	97	3	1	1	27	10	.73	10	.285	.388	.382
2008	NwBrit	AA	93	343	102	28	1	9	(-	-)	159	54	50	62	44	1	74	3	4	3	12	6	.67	6	.297	.379	.464
2009	NwBrit	AA	38	151	39	10	2	2	(-	-)	59	21	13	22	16	0	20	4	1	1	6	2	.75	5	.258	.343	.391
2009	Roch	AAA	92	352	95	17	1	6	(-	-)	132	57	27	47	36	1	52	2	1	3	7	6	.54	7	.270	.338	.375
2010	Scrmto	AAA	80	292	97	17	3	9	(-	-)	147	52	43	62	37	0	50	4	4	2	8	2	.80	6	.332	.412	.503
2010	Oak	AL	25	49	14	3	0	1	(1	0)	20	5	4	7	4	0	9	0	0	0	0	0	-	0	.286	.340	.408

Josh Tomlin

Pitches: R **Bats:** R **Pos:** SP-12   **Ht:** 6'1" **Wt:** 175 **Born:** 10/19/1984 **Age:** 26

				HOW MUCH HE PITCHED							WHAT HE GAVE UP										THE RESULTS						
Year	Team	Lg	G	GS	CG	GF	IP	BFP	H	R	ER	HR	SH	SF	HB	TBB	IBB	SO	WP	Bk	W	L	Pct	Sh	Sv-Op	Hld	ERC	ERA
2006	MhVlly	A-	15	15	0	0	77.1	307	56	24	18	5	0	3	4	15	0	69	3	0	8	2	.800	0	0--	-	1.87	2.09
2007	Lk Cty	A+	26	15	0	4	103.2	434	103	44	38	10	2	1	7	19	0	89	5	0	10	3	.769	0	0--	-	3.41	3.30
2007	Knstn	A+	6	5	0	0	27.2	119	24	13	11	0	0	3	0	12	0	20	2	0	1	1	.500	0	0--	-	2.74	3.58
2008	Knstn	A+	40	9	1	10	102.2	399	82	40	34	10	2	4	7	16	0	109	9	0	9	5	.643	1	3--	-	2.41	2.98
2008	Buffalo	AAA	1	1	0	0	7.0	25	6	3	3	2	0	0	0	1	0	3	0	0	1	0	1.000	0	0--	-	3.81	3.86
2009	Akron	AA	26	25	0	0	145.0	601	149	81	67	21	4	3	7	27	1	125	3	0	14	9	.609	0	0--	-	3.90	4.16
2010	Clmbs	AAA	20	17	1	0	107.1	429	83	34	32	11	1	2	2	33	0	80	4	0	8	4	.667	0	0--	-	2.65	2.68
2010	Cle	AL	12	12	1	0	73.0	301	72	38	37	10	3	3	3	19	3	43	1	0	6	4	.600	0	0-0	0	3.89	4.56

Yorvit Torrealba

Bats: R **Throws:** R **Pos:** C-92; PH-3   yorr-VEET   **Ht:** 5'11" **Wt:** 200 **Born:** 7/19/1978 **Age:** 32

Year	Team	Lg	G	AB	H	2B	3B	HR	(Hm	Rd)	TB	R	RBI	RC	TBB	IBB	SO	HBP	SH	SF	SB	CS	SB%	GDP	Avg	OBP	Slg
2001	SF	NL	3	4	2	0	1	0	(0	0)	4	0	2	2	0	0	0	0	0	0	0	0	-	0	.500	.500	1.000
2002	SF	NL	53	136	38	10	0	2	(0	2)	54	17	14	16	14	2	20	2	3	0	0	0	-	11	.279	.355	.397
2003	SF	NL	66	200	52	10	2	4	(3	1)	78	22	29	25	14	1	39	2	3	2	1	0	1.00	3	.260	.312	.390
2004	SF	NL	64	172	39	7	3	6	(3	3)	70	19	23	18	17	3	31	2	4	1	2	0	1.00	7	.227	.302	.407
2005	2 Tms		76	201	47	12	0	3	(2	1)	68	32	15	14	16	1	50	2	5	0	1	0	1.00	8	.234	.297	.338
2006	Col	NL	65	223	55	16	3	5	(3	4)	98	23	43	30	11	1	49	4	2	1	4	3	.57	7	.247	.293	.439
2007	Col	NL	113	396	101	22	1	8	(6	2)	149	47	47	34	34	1	73	6	6	1	2	1	.67	19	.255	.323	.376
2008	Col	NL	70	236	58	17	0	6	(5	1)	93	19	31	23	12	0	44	5	5	3	0	4	.00	10	.246	.293	.394
2009	Col	NL	64	213	62	11	1	2	(1	1)	81	27	31	37	21	5	42	1	3	4	1	1	.50	4	.291	.351	.380
2010	SD	NL	95	325	88	14	0	7	(4	3)	123	31	37	41	33	2	67	3	1	1	7	5	.58	12	.271	.343	.378
05	SF	NL	34	93	21	8	0	1	(1	0)	32	18	7	7	9	1	25	1	2	0	1	0	1.00	3	.226	.301	.344
05	Sea	AL	42	108	26	4	0	2	(1	1)	36	14	8	7	7	0	25	1	3	0	0	0	-	5	.241	.293	.333
	Postseason		17	56	15	4	0	2	(1	1)	25	6	13	9	4	1	11	0	3	1	0	0	-	2	.268	.311	.446
	10 ML YEARS		669	2106	542	119	11	45	(27	18)	818	237	272	240	172	16	415	27	32	13	18	14	.56	81	.257	.320	.388

Andres Torres

Bats: B **Throws:** R **Pos:** CF-84; RF-43; LF-37; PH-8; PR-2   **Ht:** 5'9" **Wt:** 191 **Born:** 1/26/1978 **Age:** 33

Year	Team	Lg	G	AB	H	2B	3B	HR	(Hm	Rd)	TB	R	RBI	RC	TBB	IBB	SO	HBP	SH	SF	SB	CS	SB%	GDP	Avg	OBP	Slg
2002	Det	AL	19	70	14	1	1	0	(0	0)	17	7	3	2	6	0	16	1	0	2	2	2	.50	2	.200	.266	.243
2003	Det	AL	59	168	37	4	3	1	(1	0)	50	23	9	9	10	0	35	0	6	1	5	5	.50	5	.220	.263	.298
2004	Det	AL	3	0	0	0	0	0	(0	0)	0	1	0	0	0	0	0	0	0	0	1	0	1.00	0	-	-	-
2005	Tex	AL	8	19	3	1	0	0	(0	0)	4	2	1	1	1	0	6	0	0	1	1	0	1.00	0	.158	.190	.211
2009	SF	NL	75	152	41	6	8	6	(4	2)	81	30	23	31	16	0	45	1	1	0	6	1	.86	0	.270	.343	.533
2010	SF	NL	139	507	136	43	8	16	(7	9)	243	84	63	87	56	2	128	2	5	0	26	7	.79	10	.268	.343	.479
	6 ML YEARS		303	916	231	55	20	23	(12	11)	395	147	99	130	89	2	230	4	12	4	41	15	.73	17	.252	.320	.431

Carlos Torres

Pitches: R **Bats:** R **Pos:** RP-4; SP-1   **Ht:** 6'1" **Wt:** 190 **Born:** 10/22/1982 **Age:** 28

				HOW MUCH HE PITCHED							WHAT HE GAVE UP										THE RESULTS						
Year	Team	Lg	G	GS	CG	GF	IP	BFP	H	R	ER	HR	SH	SF	HB	TBB	IBB	SO	WP	Bk	W	L	Pct	Sh	Sv-Op	Hld	ERC	ERA
2004	Bristol	R+	19	0	0	9	38.0	166	43	30	20	2	1	0	0	12	2	28	6	0	2	2	.500	0	1--	-	4.03	4.74
2005	Gr Falls	R+	5	5	0	0	25.0	97	18	8	8	1	1	0	0	8	0	26	0	0	1	1	.500	0	0--	-	2.05	2.88
2005	Knapol	A	8	8	0	0	43.1	182	28	20	17	4	0	2	1	23	0	54	3	0	1	3	.250	0	0--	-	2.67	3.53
2006	WinSa	A+	25	20	0	3	94.0	446	116	66	49	7	3	5	1	55	0	76	7	0	3	8	.273	0	1--	-	6.01	4.69
2007	WinSa	A+	19	0	0	7	36.1	147	33	16	15	0	2	0	2	10	0	41	4	0	0	2	.000	0	3--	-	2.74	3.72
2007	Brham	AA	36	0	0	6	56.0	240	57	26	23	3	4	1	1	22	1	59	5	0	2	2	.500	0	1--	-	3.90	3.70
2008	Brham	AA	21	17	0	0	101.1	407	86	40	36	4	3	2	1	29	0	93	4	0	9	5	.643	0	0--	-	2.71	3.20
2008	Charltt	AAA	8	1	0	4	19.2	91	23	10	10	2	2	0	0	11	1	19	0	0	0	0	-	0	0--	-	5.63	4.58
2009	Charltt	AAA	23	20	2	2	128.0	528	96	38	34	4	1	3	4	56	0	130	2	0	10	4	.714	1	1--	-	2.57	2.39
2010	Charltt	AAA	27	25	0	1	160.1	664	125	65	61	13	7	6	3	71	0	140	10	1	9	9	.500	0	0--	-	3.01	3.42
2009	CWS	AL	8	5	0	2	28.1	130	30	20	19	5	3	3	2	17	2	22	0	0	1	2	.333	0	0-0	0	6.05	6.05
2010	CWS	AL	5	1	0	1	13.2	71	23	13	13	2	0	1	0	9	1	13	0	0	0	1	.000	0	0-0	0	9.84	8.56
	2 ML YEARS		13	6	0	3	42.0	201	53	33	32	7	3	4	2	26	3	35	0	0	1	3	.250	0	0-0	0	7.24	6.86

J.R. Towles

Bats: R Throws: R Pos: C-15; PH-3   TOLLS   Ht: 6'2" Wt: 192 Born: 2/11/1984 Age: 27

Year	Team	Lg	G	AB	H	2B	3B	HR	(Hm	Rd)	TB	R	RBI	RC	TBB	IBB	SO	HBP	SH	SF	SB	CS	SB%	GDP	Avg	OBP	Slg
2010	CpChr*	AA	5	14	2	1	0	0	(-	-)	3	3	3	2	4	0	4	2	0	0	2	0	1.00	1	.143	.400	.214
2007	Hou	NL	14	40	15	5	0	1	(0	1)	23	9	12	11	3	1	1	1	0	0	0	1	.00	1	.375	.432	.575
2008	Hou	NL	54	146	20	5	0	4	(3	1)	37	10	16	10	16	1	40	6	3	0	0	0	-	3	.137	.250	.253
2009	Hou	NL	16	48	9	2	0	2	(0	2)	17	7	3	2	3	1	16	1	1	0	0	0	-	1	.188	.250	.354
2010	Hou	NL	17	47	9	3	0	1	(0	1)	15	3	8	6	2	0	12	1	0	1	0	0	-	2	.191	.235	.319
	4 ML YEARS		101	281	53	15	0	8	(3	5)	92	29	39	29	24	3	69	9	4	1	0	1	.00	7	.189	.273	.327

Chad Tracy

Bats: L Throws: R Pos: 3B-34; PH-31; 1B-7   Ht: 6'2" Wt: 215 Born: 5/22/1980 Age: 31

Year	Team	Lg	G	AB	H	2B	3B	HR	(Hm	Rd)	TB	R	RBI	RC	TBB	IBB	SO	HBP	SH	SF	SB	CS	SB%	GDP	Avg	OBP	Slg
2010	Iowa*	AAA	26	91	36	8	0	5	(-	-)	59	21	18	22	5	0	9	0	0	0	0	1	.00	1	.396	.427	.648
2010	S-WB*	AAA	18	68	22	5	0	6	(-	-)	45	14	18	15	4	1	6	0	0	1	0	0	-	1	.324	.356	.662
2004	Ari	NL	143	481	137	29	3	8	(6	2)	196	45	53	63	45	3	60	0	1	5	2	3	.40	11	.285	.343	.407
2005	Ari	NL	145	503	155	34	4	27	(9	18)	278	73	72	82	35	4	78	8	1	6	3	1	.75	10	.308	.359	.553
2006	Ari	NL	154	597	168	41	0	20	(14	6)	269	91	80	85	54	5	129	5	1	5	5	1	.83	11	.281	.343	.451
2007	Ari	NL	76	227	60	18	2	7	(3	4)	103	30	35	33	29	4	43	1	0	3	0	0	-	8	.264	.346	.454
2008	Ari	NL	88	273	73	16	0	8	(3	5)	113	25	29	32	16	2	49	1	0	2	0	0	-	5	.267	.308	.414
2009	Ari	NL	98	257	61	15	0	8	(7	1)	100	29	39	28	26	7	38	1	0	4	1	0	1.00	3	.237	.306	.389
2010	2 Tms		69	146	36	8	0	1	(0	1)	47	11	15	14	11	0	36	2	0	1	0	0	-	2	.247	.306	.322
10	ChC	NL	28	44	11	2	0	0	(0	0)	13	6	5	6	5	0	15	0	0	0	0	0	-	0	.250	.327	.295
10	Fla	NL	41	102	25	6	0	1	(0	1)	34	5	10	8	6	0	21	2	0	1	0	0	-	2	.245	.297	.333
	7 ML YEARS		773	2484	690	161	9	79	(42	37)	1106	304	333	337	216	25	433	18	3	26	11	5	.69	50	.278	.337	.445

Matt Treanor

Bats: R Throws: R Pos: C-81; PH-2; DH-1   TRAY-ner   Ht: 6'0" Wt: 205 Born: 3/3/1976 Age: 35

Year	Team	Lg	G	AB	H	2B	3B	HR	(Hm	Rd)	TB	R	RBI	RC	TBB	IBB	SO	HBP	SH	SF	SB	CS	SB%	GDP	Avg	OBP	Slg
2010	OKCity*	AAA	5	15	3	0	0	0	(-	-)	3	2	2	0	1	0	3	1	0	0	0	0	-	1	.200	.294	.200
2004	Fla	NL	29	55	13	2	0	0	(0	0)	15	7	1	4	4	0	13	2	0	0	0	0	-	3	.236	.311	.273
2005	Fla	NL	58	134	27	8	0	0	(0	0)	35	10	10	12	16	1	28	3	1	0	0	0	-	5	.201	.301	.261
2006	Fla	NL	67	157	36	6	1	2	(0	2)	50	12	14	16	19	4	34	5	2	2	0	1	.00	4	.229	.328	.318
2007	Fla	NL	55	171	46	7	1	4	(2	2)	67	16	19	26	19	1	29	5	2	1	0	0	-	2	.269	.357	.392
2008	Fla	NL	65	206	49	7	0	2	(1	1)	62	18	23	25	18	1	53	3	5	2	1	0	1.00	2	.238	.306	.301
2009	Det	NL	4	13	0	0	0	0	(0	0)	0	0	0	0	1	0	4	0	0	0	0	0	-	3	.000	.071	.000
2010	Tex	AL	82	237	50	6	1	5	(4	1)	73	22	27	19	22	0	43	5	4	4	1	2	.33	4	.211	.287	.308
	7 ML YEARS		360	973	221	36	3	13	(7	6)	302	85	97	103	99	7	204	23	14	9	2	3	.40	23	.227	.311	.310

Ramon Troncoso

Pitches: R Bats: R Pos: RP-52   tronn-KOE-soe   Ht: 6'1" Wt: 209 Born: 2/16/1983 Age: 28

			HOW MUCH HE PITCHED						WHAT HE GAVE UP										THE RESULTS						
Year	Team	Lg	G	GS	CG	GF	IP	BFP	H	R	ER	HR	SH	SF	HB	TBB	IBB	SO	WP	Bk	W	L	Pct	Sh	Sv-Op	Hld	ERC	ERA
2010	Albq*	AAA	15	0	0	6	22.0	94	23	14	14	5	0	0	0	11	1	19	0	0	0	2	.000	0	1--	-	5.88	5.73
2008	LAD	NL	32	0	0	12	38.0	160	37	19	18	2	4	3	2	11	1	38	2	0	1	1	.500	0	0-0	2	3.60	4.26
2009	LAD	NL	73	0	0	20	82.2	357	63	30	25	3	7	3	3	34	9	55	4	0	5	4	.556	0	6-7	14	3.67	2.72
2010	LAD	NL	52	0	0	13	54.0	234	55	28	26	7	1	2	3	18	5	34	2	0	2	3	.400	0	0-1	8	4.18	4.33
	Postseason		3	0	0	0	3.0	12	0	0	0	0	1	0	1	3	0	3	0	0	0	0	-	0	0-0	0	1.68	0.00
	3 ML YEARS		157	0	0	45	174.2	751	175	77	69	12	12	8	9	64	15	127	8	0	8	8	.500	0	6-8	24	3.82	3.56

Mark Trumbo

Bats: R Throws: R Pos: 1B-6; PR-2; RF-1; DH-1; PH-1   Ht: 6'4" Wt: 220 Born: 1/16/1986 Age: 25

Year	Team	Lg	G	AB	H	2B	3B	HR	(Hm	Rd)	TB	R	RBI	RC	TBB	IBB	SO	HBP	SH	SF	SB	CS	SB%	GDP	Avg	OBP	Slg
2005	Orem	R+	71	299	82	23	1	10	(-	-)	137	45	45	44	21	4	67	1	0	2	2	2	.50	2	.274	.322	.458
2006	CRpds	A	118	428	94	19	0	13	(-	-)	152	43	59	46	44	4	99	3	0	7	5	5	.50	8	.220	.293	.355
2007	CRpds	A	128	471	128	27	2	14	(-	-)	201	57	76	66	34	1	98	6	0	5	10	8	.56	15	.272	.326	.427
2008	RCuca	A+	103	407	115	28	2	26	(-	-)	225	70	68	74	26	4	67	3	0	2	7	3	.70	12	.283	.329	.553
2008	Ark	AA	32	123	34	7	1	6	(-	-)	61	13	25	18	7	0	29	0	2	2	1	2	.33	5	.276	.311	.496
2009	Ark	AA	137	533	155	35	3	15	(-	-)	241	54	88	82	37	2	100	1	2	8	6	3	.67	22	.291	.333	.452
2010	Salt Lk	AAA	139	532	160	29	5	36	(-	-)	307	103	122	110	58	8	126	1	0	4	3	4	.43	12	.301	.368	.577
2010	LAA	AL	8	15	1	0	0	0	(0	0)	1	2	2	0	1	0	8	0	0	0	0	0	-	0	.067	.125	.067

Matt Tuiasosopo

Bats: R Throws: R Pos: LF-14; 3B-12; 1B-9; SS-6; PR-6; PH-4; 2B-2; DH-2   Ht: 6'2" Wt: 225 Born: 5/10/1986 Age: 25

Year	Team	Lg	G	AB	H	2B	3B	HR	(Hm	Rd)	TB	R	RBI	RC	TBB	IBB	SO	HBP	SH	SF	SB	CS	SB%	GDP	Avg	OBP	Slg
2010	Tacom*	AAA	38	143	36	6	0	5	(-	-)	57	26	21	24	32	1	35	1	0	0	2	2	.50	4	.252	.392	.399
2008	Sea	AL	14	44	7	2	1	0	(0	0)	11	1	2	1	2	0	16	1	0	0	0	0	-	0	.159	.213	.250
2009	Sea	AL	7	22	5	1	0	1	(0	1)	9	2	2	2	2	0	5	0	0	1	0	0	-	0	.227	.280	.409
2010	Sea	AL	50	127	22	5	0	4	(0	4)	39	12	11	8	9	0	49	1	1	0	0	0	-	3	.173	.234	.307
	3 ML YEARS		71	193	34	8	1	5	(0	5)	59	15	15	11	13	0	70	2	1	1	0	0	-	3	.176	.234	.306

Troy Tulowitzki

Bats: R **Throws:** R **Pos:** SS-122   **Ht:** 6'3" **Wt:** 215 **Born:** 10/10/1984 **Age:** 26

Year	Team	Lg	G	AB	H	2B	3B	HR	(Hm	Rd)	TB	R	RBI	RC	TBB	IBB	SO	HBP	SH	SF	SB	CS	SB%	GDP	Avg	OBP	Slg
2010	ColSpr*	AAA	2	4	1	0	0	0	(-	-)	1	1	0	0	1	0	0	0	0	0	0	0	-	2	.250	.400	.250
2010	Tulsa*	AA	2	7	1	1	0	0	(-	-)	2	1	1	0	0	0	2	0	0	1	0	0	-	0	.143	.125	.286
2006	Col	NL	25	96	23	2	0	1	(0	1)	28	15	6	10	10	3	25	1	1	0	3	0	1.00	1	.240	.318	.292
2007	Col	NL	155	609	177	33	5	24	(15	9)	292	104	99	95	57	3	130	9	5	2	7	6	.54	14	.291	.359	.479
2008	Col	NL	101	377	99	24	2	8	(4	4)	151	48	46	42	38	5	56	2	2	2	1	6	.14	16	.263	.332	.401
2009	Col	NL	151	543	161	25	9	32	(17	15)	300	101	92	96	73	4	112	3	0	9	20	11	.65	20	.297	.377	.552
2010	Col	NL	122	470	148	32	3	27	(15	12)	267	89	95	88	48	4	78	5	1	5	11	2	.85	17	.315	.381	.568
	Postseason		15	57	12	5	0	1	(0	1)	20	3	6	3	4	0	17	1	0	1	0	1	.00	3	.211	.270	.351
	5 ML YEARS		554	2095	608	116	19	92	(51	41)	1038	357	338	331	226	19	401	20	9	18	42	25	.63	68	.290	.362	.495

Justin Turner

Bats: R **Throws:** R **Pos:** 2B-6; PH-2; 3B-1; SS-1; PR-1   **Ht:** 5'11" **Wt:** 200 **Born:** 11/23/1984 **Age:** 26

Year	Team	Lg	G	AB	H	2B	3B	HR	(Hm	Rd)	TB	R	RBI	RC	TBB	IBB	SO	HBP	SH	SF	SB	CS	SB%	GDP	Avg	OBP	Slg
2006	Billings	R+	60	231	78	16	3	6	(-	-)	118	53	41	50	23	1	38	7	0	2	12	2	.86	7	.338	.411	.511
2007	Dayton	A	117	466	145	25	4	10	(-	-)	208	70	59	79	39	0	72	9	0	2	12	8	.60	7	.311	.374	.446
2007	Srsota	A+	6	20	4	0	0	0	(-	-)	4	2	0	0	1	0	2	0	0	0	0	0	-	0	.200	.238	.200
2008	Srsota	A+	33	136	43	8	1	0	(-	-)	53	23	11	21	12	0	19	3	0	0	3	1	.75	3	.316	.384	.390
2008	Chatt	AA	78	280	81	14	1	8	(-	-)	121	45	42	46	33	0	54	1	3	6	2	1	.67	4	.289	.359	.432
2009	Norfolk	AAA	108	387	116	28	0	2	(-	-)	150	54	43	59	34	0	37	8	4	8	9	4	.69	12	.300	.362	.388
2010	Norfolk	AAA	23	84	21	8	0	1	(-	-)	32	11	8	11	9	0	13	0	1	1	2	0	1.00	1	.250	.319	.381
2010	Buffalo	AAA	78	312	104	22	1	11	(-	-)	161	58	35	62	24	0	38	6	4	2	5	3	.63	9	.333	.390	.516
2009	Bal	AL	12	18	3	0	0	0	(0	0)	3	2	3	1	4	0	3	0	0	0	0	0	-	1	.167	.318	.167
2010	2 Tms		9	17	1	1	0	0	(0	0)	2	1	0	0	1	0	3	0	0	0	0	0	-	0	.059	.111	.118
10	Bal	AL	5	9	0	0	0	0	(0	0)	0	0	0	0	0	0	3	0	0	0	0	0	-	0	.000	.000	.000
10	NYM	NL	4	8	1	1	0	0	(0	0)	2	1	0	0	1	0	0	0	0	0	0	0	-	0	.125	.222	.250
	2 ML YEARS		21	35	4	1	0	0	(0	0)	5	3	3	1	5	0	6	0	0	0	0	0	-	1	.114	.225	.143

Koji Uehara

Pitches: R **Bats:** R **Pos:** RP-43   you-ee-HAHR-ah   **Ht:** 6'2" **Wt:** 195 **Born:** 4/3/1975 **Age:** 36

Year	Team	Lg	G	GS	CG	GF	IP	BFP	H	R	ER	HR	SH	SF	HB	TBB	IBB	SO	WP	Bk	W	L	Pct	Sh	Sv-Op Hld	ERC	ERA
1999	Yomiuri	Jap	25	25	12	0	197.2	769	153	49	46	12	-	-	4	24	0	179	3	0	20	4	.833	1	0-- -	1.75	2.09
2000	Yomiuri	Jap	20	20	6	0	131.0	519	112	53	52	20	-	-	1	22	0	126	1	0	9	7	.563	1	0-- -	2.78	3.57
2001	Yomiuri	Jap	24	22	4	0	138.2	573	133	66	62	18	15	3	5	28	3	108	2	0	10	7	.588	1	0-- -	3.38	4.02
2002	Yomiuri	Jap	26	26	8	0	204.0	808	173	65	59	18	-	-	6	23	0	182	2	0	17	5	.773	3	0-- -	2.24	2.60
2003	Yomiuri	Jap	27	27	11	0	207.1	821	190	76	73	28	-	-	5	23	3	194	0	0	16	5	.762	1	0-- -	2.84	3.17
2004	Yomiuri	Jap	22	22	2	0	163.0	637	135	54	47	24	6	3	5	23	0	153	1	0	13	5	.722	0	0-- -	2.62	2.60
2005	Yomiuri	Jap	27	27	6	0	187.1	747	164	73	69	24	19	3	0	22	0	145	0	1	9	12	.429	2	0-- -	2.48	3.31
2006	Yomiuri	Jap	24	24	5	0	168.1	673	157	67	60	24	15	5	1	21	3	151	0	1	8	9	.471	0	0-- -	2.92	3.21
2007	Yomiuri	Jap	55	0	0	-	62.0	237	47	12	12	4	-	-	1	4	1	66	1	0	4	3	.571	0	32-- -	1.54	1.74
2008	Yomiuri	Jap	26	14	2	3	89.2	345	90	43	38	11	-	-	0	16	1	72	0	0	6	5	.545	0	1-- -	3.63	3.81
2010	Bowie	AA	2	2	0	0	2.0	7	1	0	0	0	0	0	0	1	0	1	0	0	0	0	-	0	0-- -	1.62	0.00
2010	Norfolk	AAA	2	0	0	0	2.0	8	2	0	0	0	0	0	0	0	1	1	0	0	0	0	-	0	0-- -	1.95	0.00
2009	Bal	AL	12	12	0	0	66.2	279	71	33	30	7	1	3	0	12	1	48	0	0	2	4	.333	0	0-0 0	3.56	4.05
2010	Bal	AL	43	0	0	22	44.0	174	37	15	14	5	1	0	0	5	0	55	1	0	1	2	.333	0	13-15 6	2.22	2.86
	2 ML YEARS		55	12	0	22	110.2	453	108	48	44	12	2	3	0	17	1	103	1	0	3	6	.333	0	13-15 6	3.01	3.58

Dan Uggla

Bats: R **Throws:** R **Pos:** 2B-158; PH-1   **Ht:** 5'11" **Wt:** 207 **Born:** 3/11/1980 **Age:** 31

Year	Team	Lg	G	AB	H	2B	3B	HR	(Hm	Rd)	TB	R	RBI	RC	TBB	IBB	SO	HBP	SH	SF	SB	CS	SB%	GDP	Avg	OBP	Slg
2006	Fla	NL	154	611	172	26	7	27	(10	17)	293	105	90	97	48	1	123	9	7	8	6	6	.50	5	.282	.339	.480
2007	Fla	NL	159	632	155	49	3	31	(18	13)	303	113	88	81	68	4	167	13	4	11	2	1	.67	10	.245	.326	.479
2008	Fla	NL	146	531	138	37	1	32	(15	17)	273	97	92	93	77	6	171	0	0	3	5	5	.50	10	.260	.360	.514
2009	Fla	NL	158	564	137	27	1	31	(21	10)	259	84	90	81	92	4	150	7	1	4	2	1	.67	10	.243	.354	.459
2010	Fla	NL	159	589	169	31	0	33	(14	19)	299	100	105	101	78	2	149	2	0	5	4	1	.80	10	.287	.369	.508
	5 ML YEARS		776	2927	771	170	12	154	(78	76)	1427	499	465	453	363	13	760	39	12	31	19	14	.58	45	.263	.349	.488

B.J. Upton

Bats: R **Throws:** R **Pos:** CF-154; PR-2; PH-1   **Ht:** 6'3" **Wt:** 185 **Born:** 8/21/1984 **Age:** 26

Year	Team	Lg	G	AB	H	2B	3B	HR	(Hm	Rd)	TB	R	RBI	RC	TBB	IBB	SO	HBP	SH	SF	SB	CS	SB%	GDP	Avg	OBP	Slg
2004	TB	AL	45	159	41	8	2	4	(2	2)	65	19	12	22	15	0	46	1	1	1	4	1	.80	1	.258	.324	.409
2006	TB	AL	50	175	43	5	0	1	(1	0)	51	20	10	17	13	0	40	1	0	0	11	3	.79	1	.246	.302	.291
2007	TB	AL	129	474	142	25	1	24	(13	11)	241	86	82	93	65	4	154	4	1	4	22	8	.73	14	.300	.386	.508
2008	TB	AL	145	531	145	37	2	9	(4	5)	213	85	67	87	97	4	134	2	3	7	44	16	.73	13	.273	.383	.401
2009	TB	AL	144	560	135	33	4	11	(7	4)	209	79	55	68	57	0	152	3	3	3	42	14	.75	7	.241	.313	.373
2010	TB	AL	154	536	127	38	4	18	(11	7)	227	89	62	74	67	1	164	2	1	4	42	9	.82	13	.237	.322	.424
	Postseason		16	66	19	1	1	7	(2	5)	43	16	16	13	5	1	16	0	0	1	6	0	1.00	4	.288	.333	.652
	6 ML YEARS		667	2435	633	146	13	67	(34	33)	1006	378	288	361	314	9	690	13	9	19	165	51	.76	49	.260	.345	.413

Justin Upton

Bats: R **Throws:** R **Pos:** RF-128; PR-3; DH-1; PH-1   **Ht:** 6'2" **Wt:** 205 **Born:** 8/25/1987 **Age:** 23

									BATTING										BASERUNNING				AVERAGES		
Year	Team	Lg	G	AB	H	2B	3B	HR	(Hm | Rd)	TB	R	RBI	RC	TBB	IBB	SO	HBP	SH	SF	SB	CS	SB%	GDP	Avg	OBP	Slg
2007	Ari	NL	43	140	31	8	3	2	(2 | 0)	51	17	11	13	11	4	37	1	0	0	2	0	1.00	3	.221	.283	.364
2008	Ari	NL	108	356	89	19	6	15	(12 | 3)	165	52	42	47	54	6	121	4	0	3	1	4	.20	3	.250	.353	.463
2009	Ari	NL	138	526	158	30	7	26	(14 | 12)	280	84	86	94	55	3	137	2	1	4	20	5	.80	10	.300	.366	.532
2010	Ari	NL	133	495	135	27	3	17	(8 | 9)	219	73	69	73	64	5	152	4	1	7	18	8	.69	20	.273	.356	.442
Postseason			6	14	5	1	1	0	(0 | 0)	8	2	1	4	3	0	3	2	0	0	1	0	1.00	0	.357	.526	.571
4 ML YEARS			422	1517	413	84	19	60	(36 | 24)	715	226	208	227	184	18	447	11	2	14	41	17	.71	36	.272	.352	.471

Juan Uribe

Bats: R **Throws:** R **Pos:** SS-103; 3B-26; 2B-24; PH-4; DH-2   **Ht:** 5'11" **Wt:** 230 **Born:** 3/22/1979 **Age:** 32

									BATTING										BASERUNNING				AVERAGES		
Year	Team	Lg	G	AB	H	2B	3B	HR	(Hm | Rd)	TB	R	RBI	RC	TBB	IBB	SO	HBP	SH	SF	SB	CS	SB%	GDP	Avg	OBP	Slg
2001	Col	NL	72	273	82	15	11	8	(3 | 5)	143	32	53	44	8	1	55	2	0	0	3	0	1.00	6	.300	.325	.524
2002	Col	NL	155	566	136	25	7	6	(4 | 2)	193	69	49	53	34	1	120	5	7	6	9	2	.82	17	.240	.286	.341
2003	Col	NL	87	316	80	19	3	10	(6 | 4)	135	45	33	45	17	0	60	3	6	1	7	2	.78	3	.253	.297	.427
2004	CWS	AL	134	502	142	31	6	23	(16 | 7)	254	82	74	81	32	1	96	3	11	5	9	11	.45	10	.283	.327	.506
2005	CWS	AL	146	481	121	23	3	16	(10 | 6)	198	58	71	59	34	0	77	4	11	10	4	6	.40	7	.252	.301	.412
2006	CWS	AL	132	463	109	28	2	21	(13 | 8)	204	53	71	52	13	1	82	3	9	7	1	1	.50	10	.235	.257	.441
2007	CWS	AL	150	513	120	18	2	20	(15 | 5)	202	55	68	52	34	2	112	4	7	5	1	9	.10	6	.234	.284	.394
2008	CWS	AL	110	324	80	22	1	7	(5 | 2)	125	38	40	43	22	0	64	1	5	1	1	3	.25	5	.247	.296	.386
2009	SF	NL	122	398	115	26	4	16	(9 | 7)	197	50	55	55	25	2	82	1	3	5	3	1	.75	7	.289	.329	.495
2010	SF	NL	148	521	129	24	2	24	(13 | 11)	229	64	85	68	45	6	92	4	0	5	1	2	.33	20	.248	.310	.440
Postseason			16	54	14	5	0	1	(1 | 0)	22	7	7	7	5	0	13	0	2	0	2	0	1.00	1	.259	.322	.407
10 ML YEARS			1256	4357	1114	231	41	151	(94 | 57)	1880	546	599	552	264	14	840	30	59	45	39	37	.51	91	.256	.300	.431

Chase Utley

Bats: L **Throws:** R **Pos:** 2B-114; PH-1   UTT-lee   **Ht:** 6'1" **Wt:** 192 **Born:** 12/17/1978 **Age:** 32

									BATTING										BASERUNNING				AVERAGES		
Year	Team	Lg	G	AB	H	2B	3B	HR	(Hm | Rd)	TB	R	RBI	RC	TBB	IBB	SO	HBP	SH	SF	SB	CS	SB%	GDP	Avg	OBP	Slg
2010	Clrwtr*	A+	4	12	3	0	2	0	(- | -)	7	1	1	2	1	0	2	0	0	1	0	0	-	1	.250	.308	.583
2003	Phi	NL	43	134	32	10	1	2	(1 | 1)	50	13	21	19	11	0	22	6	0	1	2	0	1.00	3	.239	.322	.373
2004	Phi	NL	94	267	71	11	2	13	(8 | 5)	125	36	57	37	15	1	40	2	1	2	4	1	.80	6	.266	.308	.468
2005	Phi	NL	147	543	158	39	6	28	(12 | 16)	293	93	105	102	69	5	109	9	0	7	16	3	.84	10	.291	.376	.540
2006	Phi	NL	160	658	203	40	4	32	(16 | 16)	347	131	102	122	63	1	132	14	0	4	15	4	.79	5	.309	.379	.527
2007	Phi	NL	132	530	176	48	5	22	(14 | 8)	300	104	103	111	50	1	89	25	1	7	9	1	.90	7	.332	.410	.566
2008	Phi	NL	159	607	177	41	4	33	(20 | 13)	325	113	104	104	64	14	104	27	1	8	14	2	.88	9	.292	.380	.535
2009	Phi	NL	156	571	161	28	4	31	(16 | 15)	290	112	93	115	88	3	110	24	0	5	23	0	1.00	5	.282	.397	.508
2010	Phi	NL	115	425	117	20	2	16	(10 | 6)	189	75	65	83	63	3	63	18	0	5	13	2	.87	4	.275	.387	.445
Postseason			32	115	29	4	0	9	(5 | 4)	60	25	19	23	27	2	31	1	0	0	6	1	.86	3	.252	.399	.522
8 ML YEARS			1006	3735	1095	237	28	177	(97 | 80)	1919	677	650	702	423	28	669	125	3	38	96	13	.88	53	.293	.380	.514

Chris Valalka

Bats: R **Throws:** R **Pos:** 2B-13; PH-6; PR-3; SS-1   vuh-LAKE-uh   **Ht:** 6'0" **Wt:** 215 **Born:** 8/14/1985 **Age:** 25

									BATTING										BASERUNNING				AVERAGES		
Year	Team	Lg	G	AB	H	2B	3B	HR	(Hm | Rd)	TB	R	RBI	RC	TBB	IBB	SO	HBP	SH	SF	SB	CS	SB%	GDP	Avg	OBP	Slg
2006	Billings	R+	70	276	80	22	4	8	(- | -)	143	58	60	55	24	0	61	8	2	6	2	2	.50	8	.324	.387	.520
2007	Dayton	A	79	300	92	20	3	10	(- | -)	148	38	56	51	17	0	72	8	0	6	1	4	.20	9	.307	.353	.493
2007	Srsota	A+	57	217	55	9	1	2	(- | -)	72	26	23	22	13	0	42	6	2	3	0	3	.00	7	.253	.310	.332
2008	Srsota	A+	32	135	49	9	0	7	(- | -)	79	20	31	30	7	0	28	1	0	2	2	0	1.00	4	.363	.393	.585
2008	Chatt	AA	97	379	114	19	1	11	(- | -)	168	58	50	60	28	0	74	3	5	2	7	4	.64	8	.301	.352	.443
2009	Lsvlle	AAA	95	366	86	20	1	6	(- | -)	126	32	36	35	16	1	76	4	1	5	1	0	1.00	7	.235	.271	.344
2010	Lsvlle	AAA	118	424	129	28	2	4	(- | -)	173	49	53	58	19	0	72	2	4	10	3	3	.50	14	.304	.330	.408
2010	Cin	NL	19	38	10	1	0	1	(1 | 0)	14	3	2	2	1	0	9	0	1	0	0	0	-	2	.263	.282	.368

Luis Valbuena

Bats: L **Throws:** R **Pos:** 2B-71; 3B-9; PR-8; SS-5; DH-3; PH-2; LF-1   val-BWAY-nah   **Ht:** 5'10" **Wt:** 195 **Born:** 11/30/1985 **Age:** 25

									BATTING										BASERUNNING				AVERAGES		
Year	Team	Lg	G	AB	H	2B	3B	HR	(Hm | Rd)	TB	R	RBI	RC	TBB	IBB	SO	HBP	SH	SF	SB	CS	SB%	GDP	Avg	OBP	Slg
2010	Clmbs*	AAA	25	96	30	8	1	6	(- | -)	58	23	20	25	19	0	21	1	2	1	2	0	1.00	2	.313	.427	.604
2008	Sea	AL	18	49	12	5	0	0	(0 | 0)	17	6	1	5	4	0	11	1	0	0	0	0	-	0	.245	.315	.347
2009	Cle	AL	103	368	92	25	3	10	(2 | 8)	153	52	31	35	26	0	83	0	2	2	2	3	.40	8	.250	.298	.416
2010	Cle	AL	91	275	53	12	0	2	(1 | 1)	71	22	24	21	28	1	61	3	2	2	1	2	.33	5	.193	.273	.258
3 ML YEARS			212	692	157	42	3	12	(3 | 9)	241	80	56	61	58	1	155	4	4	4	3	5	.38	13	.227	.289	.348

Raul Valdes

Pitches: L **Bats:** L **Pos:** RP-37; SP-1   **Ht:** 5'11" **Wt:** 190 **Born:** 11/27/1977 **Age:** 33

			HOW MUCH HE PITCHED						WHAT HE GAVE UP												THE RESULTS					
Year	Team	Lg	G	GS	CG	GF	IP	BFP	H	R	ER	HR	SH	SF	HB	TBB	IBB	SO	WP	Bk	W	L	Pct	Sh	Sv-Op Hld	ERC	ERA
2005	WTenn	AA	5	5	0	0	23.0	93	28	13	13	1	1	1	1	3	0	18	2	0	2	0	1.000	0	0- - -	4.28	5.09
2005	Iowa	AAA	25	17	0	3	98.2	461	135	71	65	7	8	1	4	39	1	73	5	2	6	7	.462	0	0- - -	6.18	5.93
2006	Iowa	AAA	7	7	0	0	32.0	148	44	27	27	5	4	2	2	11	0	20	1	0	1	3	.250	0	0- - -	6.88	7.59

Year	Team	Lg	G	GS	CG	GF	IP	BFP	H	R	ER	HR	SH	SF	HB	TBB	IBB	SO	WP	Bk	W	L	Pct	Sh	Sv-Op	Hld	ERC	ERA
2007	StLuci	A+	3	1	0	1	7.1	39	8	5	5	0	1	1	2	6	0	5	0	0	0	1	.000	0	0- -	-	6.19	6.14
2007	Bnghtn	AA	20	0	0	8	29.1	131	35	15	12	3	1	2	2	9	2	27	1	0	0	1	.000	0	1- -	-	4.98	3.68
2010	Buffalo	AAA	9	7	0	1	36.0	148	34	12	12	3	1	1	1	9	0	36	0	0	2	1	.667	0	0- -	-	3.22	3.00
2010	NYM	NL	38	1	0	8	58.2	262	59	33	32	7	2	2	4	27	1	56	2	0	3	3	.500	0	1-3	1	4.70	4.91

Cesar Valdez

Pitches: R Bats: R Pos: RP-7; SP-2   Ht: 6'2" Wt: 200 Born: 3/17/1985 Age: 26

			HOW MUCH HE PITCHED						WHAT HE GAVE UP											THE RESULTS							
Year	Team	Lg	G	GS	CG	GF	IP	BFP	H	R	ER	HR	SH	SF	HB	TBB	IBB	SO	WP	Bk	W	L	Pct	Sh	Sv-Op	Hld	ERC	ERA
2006	Yakima	A-	16	16	2	0	97.0	406	97	43	34	5	3	3	3	20	0	81	5	0	7	5	.583	0	0- -	-	3.10	3.15
2007	Sbend	A	25	25	2	0	148.0	602	130	63	56	11	2	3	12	32	0	106	12	0	7	10	.412	1	0- -	-	2.90	3.41
2008	Visalia	A+	15	15	1	0	96.0	390	88	36	27	5	2	0	3	16	0	80	5	1	10	3	.769	0	0- -	-	2.56	2.53
2008	Mobile	AA	12	12	0	0	64.1	272	63	30	29	2	4	0	4	23	1	60	0	0	3	5	.375	0	0- -	-	3.60	4.06
2009	Reno	AAA	19	18	0	1	96.0	419	103	58	51	16	3	3	4	30	1	60	6	1	7	6	.538	0	0- -	-	4.73	4.78
2010	Reno	AAA	20	18	0	0	97.2	446	110	68	64	12	3	1	5	49	0	92	14	0	6	10	.375	0	0- -	-	5.62	5.90
2010	Ari	NL	9	2	0	3	20.0	97	29	19	17	2	0	0	1	10	2	13	3	0	1	2	.333	0	0-0	0	7.29	7.65

Merkin Valdez

Pitches: R Bats: R Pos: RP-2   Ht: 6'5" Wt: 232 Born: 11/10/1981 Age: 29

			HOW MUCH HE PITCHED						WHAT HE GAVE UP											THE RESULTS							
Year	Team	Lg	G	GS	CG	GF	IP	BFP	H	R	ER	HR	SH	SF	HB	TBB	IBB	SO	WP	Bk	W	L	Pct	Sh	Sv-Op	Hld	ERC	ERA
2010	LsVgs*	AAA	39	1	0	16	58.0	289	92	59	51	5	1	2	3	26	0	35	7	3	3	5	.375	0	0- -	-	7.96	7.91
2004	SF	NL	2	0	0	0	1.2	12	4	5	5	1	0	0	0	3	0	2	0	0	0	0	-	0	0-0	0	26.50	27.00
2008	SF	NL	17	1	0	3	16.0	69	14	5	3	1	1	0	2	7	2	13	2	1	1	0	1.000	0	0-0	0	3.57	1.69
2009	SF	NL	48	0	0	20	49.1	225	57	33	31	5	1	1	0	28	2	38	5	0	2	1	.667	0	0-3	4	5.67	5.66
2010	Tor	AL	2	0	0	1	1.1	9	2	3	3	0	0	0	0	3	0	0	0	0	0	0	-	0	0-0	0	14.12	20.25
	4 ML YEARS		69	1	0	24	68.1	315	77	46	42	7	2	1	2	41	4	53	7	1	3	1	.750	0	0-3	6	5.71	5.53

Wilson Valdez

Bats: R Throws: R Pos: SS-59; 2B-42; PH-10; 3B-7; PR-7   Ht: 5'11" Wt: 170 Born: 5/20/1978 Age: 33

							BATTING														BASERUNNING				AVERAGES		
Year	Team	Lg	G	AB	H	2B	3B	HR	(Hm	Rd)	TB	R	RBI	RC	TBB	IBB	SO	HBP	SH	SF	SB	CS	SB%	GDP	Avg	OBP	Slg
2010	LV*	AAA	5	22	10	0	0	0	(-	-)	10	2	4	4	3	0	3	0	1	0	2	2	.50	1	.455	.520	.455
2004	CWS	AL	19	43	10	1	0	1	(1	0)	14	8	4	2	2	0	5	0	1	0	1	2	.33	1	.233	.267	.326
2005	2 Tms		51	139	28	7	1	0	(0	0)	37	9	9	8	8	0	26	0	1	0	2	2	.50	2	.201	.245	.266
2007	LAD	NL	41	74	16	2	1	0	(0	0)	20	12	7	7	4	0	12	1	0	1	1	0	1.00	0	.216	.263	.270
2009	NYM	NL	41	86	22	3	2	0	(0	0)	29	11	7	6	8	0	10	1	0	0	0	1	.00	6	.256	.326	.337
2010	Phi	NL	111	333	86	16	3	4	(2	2)	120	37	35	34	21	7	43	2	7	0	7	0	1.00	20	.258	.306	.360
05	Sea	AL	42	126	25	5	1	0	(0	0)	32	9	8	6	6	0	25	0	1	0	2	2	.50	1	.198	.235	.254
05	SD	NL	9	13	3	2	0	0	(0	0)	5	0	1	2	2	0	1	0	0	0	0	0	-	1	.231	.333	.385
	5 ML YEARS		263	675	162	29	7	5	(3	2)	220	77	62	57	43	7	96	4	9	1	11	5	.69	29	.240	.289	.326

Danny Valencia

Bats: R Throws: R Pos: 3B-81; PH-3; DH-1; PR-1   vuh-LENN-see-yah   Ht: 6'2" Wt: 210 Born: 9/19/1984 Age: 26

							BATTING														BASERUNNING				AVERAGES		
Year	Team	Lg	G	AB	H	2B	3B	HR	(Hm	Rd)	TB	R	RBI	RC	TBB	IBB	SO	HBP	SH	SF	SB	CS	SB%	GDP	Avg	OBP	Slg
2006	Elizab	R+	48	190	59	13	0	8	(-	-)	96	30	29	34	15	2	34	3	0	3	0	2	.00	9	.311	.365	.505
2007	Beloit	A	66	242	73	15	0	11	(-	-)	121	44	35	44	28	0	54	0	1	0	3	3	.50	1	.302	.374	.500
2007	FtMyrs	A+	61	230	67	8	2	6	(-	-)	97	28	31	33	16	0	48	0	0	4	1	0	1.00	10	.291	.332	.422
2008	FtMyrs	A+	60	220	74	19	3	5	(-	-)	114	35	44	45	27	2	43	0	0	4	2	2	.50	6	.336	.402	.518
2008	NwBrit	AA	69	266	77	18	2	10	(-	-)	129	40	32	43	18	1	70	1	0	2	2	1	.67	6	.289	.334	.485
2009	NwBrit	AA	57	218	62	14	4	7	(-	-)	105	44	29	40	31	3	40	1	0	2	0	2	.00	8	.284	.373	.482
2009	Roch	AAA	71	269	77	24	0	7	(-	-)	122	35	41	37	8	2	37	1	0	4	0	2	.00	7	.286	.305	.454
2010	Roch	AAA	49	185	54	15	0	0	(-	-)	69	22	24	25	14	0	34	2	0	1	2	0	1.00	6	.292	.347	.373
2010	Min	AL	85	299	93	18	1	7	(4	3)	134	30	40	50	20	0	46	0	0	3	2	0	1.00	11	.311	.351	.448

Jose Valverde

Pitches: R Bats: R Pos: RP-60   val-VARE-day   Ht: 6'4" Wt: 254 Born: 3/24/1978 Age: 33

			HOW MUCH HE PITCHED						WHAT HE GAVE UP											THE RESULTS							
Year	Team	Lg	G	GS	CG	GF	IP	BFP	H	R	ER	HR	SH	SF	HB	TBB	IBB	SO	WP	Bk	W	L	Pct	Sh	Sv-Op	Hld	ERC	ERA
2003	Ari	NL	54	0	0	33	50.1	204	24	16	12	4	0	1	2	26	2	71	2	0	2	1	.667	0	10-11	8	1.77	2.15
2004	Ari	NL	29	0	0	20	29.2	131	23	17	14	7	3	2	1	17	4	38	4	0	1	2	.333	0	8-10	5	4.25	4.25
2005	Ari	NL	61	0	0	34	66.1	268	51	19	18	5	3	1	2	20	1	75	3	0	3	4	.429	0	15-17	7	2.43	2.44
2006	Ari	NL	44	0	0	35	49.1	223	50	32	32	6	1	3	2	22	3	69	2	0	2	3	.400	0	18-22	1	4.42	5.84
2007	Ari	NL	65	0	0	59	64.1	265	46	21	19	7	0	1	3	26	1	78	1	0	1	4	.200	0	**47-54**	0	2.77	2.66
2008	Hou	NL	74	0	0	71	72.0	303	62	28	27	10	0	2	2	23	6	83	3	2	6	3	.667	0	**44-51**	0	3.18	3.38
2009	Hou	NL	52	0	0	45	54.0	219	40	15	14	5	1	2	2	21	1	56	1	0	4	2	.667	0	25-29	1	2.76	2.33
2010	Det	AL	60	0	0	55	63.0	259	41	24	21	5	0	1	3	32	1	63	3	0	2	4	.333	0	26-29	0	2.67	3.00
	Postseason		4	0	0	3	4.2	21	2	1	1	0	0	0	0	4	0	8	0	0	0	1	.000	0	1-1	0	1.91	1.93
	8 ML YEARS		439	0	0	352	449.0	1872	337	172	157	49	8	13	17	187	19	533	19	2	21	23	.477	0	193-223	22	2.91	3.15

Jonathan Van Every

Bats: L **Throws:** L **Pos:** CF-12; RF-6; PR-5; LF-3; PH-1   **Ht:** 6'1" **Wt:** 200 **Born:** 11/27/1979 **Age:** 31

							BATTING											BASERUNNING				AVERAGES		
Year	Team	Lg	G	AB	H	2B	3B	HR	(Hm | Rd)	TB	R	RBI	RC	TBB	IBB	SO	HBP	SH	SF	SB	CS	SB%	GDP	Avg	OBP	Slg
2010	Indy*	AAA	74	210	45	9	0	10	(- | -)	84	32	29	29	37	1	85	2	1	2	3	4	.43	2	.214	.335	.400
2008	Bos	AL	11	17	4	0	1	0	(0 | 0)	6	0	5	3	1	0	6	0	0	0	0	0	-	0	.235	.278	.353
2009	Bos	AL	7	11	4	0	0	1	(0 | 1)	7	1	3	4	2	0	5	0	0	0	0	0	-	0	.364	.462	.636
2010	Bos	AL	22	19	4	1	0	1	(0 | 1)	8	6	1	2	2	0	9	0	0	0	0	0	-	0	.211	.286	.421
	3 ML YEARS		40	47	12	1	1	2	(0 | 2)	21	7	9	9	5	0	20	0	0	0	0	0	-	0	.255	.327	.447

Rick VandenHurk

Pitches: R **Bats:** R **Pos:** RP-8; SP-1   VANN-denn-herk   **Ht:** 6'5" **Wt:** 219 **Born:** 5/22/1985 **Age:** 26

			HOW MUCH HE PITCHED					WHAT HE GAVE UP										THE RESULTS						
Year	Team	Lg	G	GS	CG	GF	IP	BFP	H	R	ER	HR	SH	SF	HB	TBB	IBB	SO	WP	Bk	W	L	Pct	Sh	Sv-Op	Hld	ERC	ERA
2010	NewOr*	AAA	19	19	2	0	98.0	435	100	54	51	11	4	0	6	40	1	87	1	0	8	4	.667	0	0- -	-	4.49	4.68
2010	Norfolk*	AAA	3	3	0	0	20.2	80	15	7	5	0	1	1	1	4	0	7	0	0	1	1	.500	0	0- -	-	1.60	2.18
2007	Fla	NL	18	17	0	0	81.2	379	94	63	62	15	5	3	3	48	5	82	4	4	4	6	.400	0	0-0	-	6.50	6.83
2008	Fla	NL	4	4	0	0	14.0	74	20	12	12	1	2	0	2	10	0	20	0	0	1	1	.500	0	0-0	-	8.20	7.71
2009	Fla	NL	11	11	0	0	58.2	256	57	29	28	11	3	2	4	21	3	49	2	0	3	2	.600	0	0-0	-	4.49	4.30
2010	2 Tms		9	1	0	2	17.2	76	16	14	10	2	0	1	2	8	0	18	0	0	0	1	.000	0	0-0	-	4.38	5.09
10	Fla	NL	2	0	0	0	1.1	9	3	4	1	0	0	0	0	1	0	1	0	0	0	0	-	0	0-0	-	11.17	6.75
10	Bal	AL	7	1	0	2	16.1	67	13	10	9	2	0	1	2	7	0	17	0	0	0	1	.000	0	0-0	-	3.86	4.96
	4 ML YEARS		42	33	0	2	172.0	785	187	118	112	29	10	6	11	87	8	169	6	4	8	10	.444	0	0-0	-	5.71	5.86

Claudio Vargas

Pitches: R **Bats:** R **Pos:** RP-17   **Ht:** 6'4" **Wt:** 234 **Born:** 6/19/1978 **Age:** 33

			HOW MUCH HE PITCHED					WHAT HE GAVE UP										THE RESULTS						
Year	Team	Lg	G	GS	CG	GF	IP	BFP	H	R	ER	HR	SH	SF	HB	TBB	IBB	SO	WP	Bk	W	L	Pct	Sh	Sv-Op	Hld	ERC	ERA
2010	Albq*	AAA	10	10	0	0	47.1	209	52	34	31	6	1	0	0	20	1	45	3	0	2	6	.250	0	0- -	-	4.90	5.89
2003	Mon	NL	23	20	0	0	114.0	491	111	59	55	16	4	4	7	41	5	62	2	0	6	8	.429	0	0-0	0	4.22	4.34
2004	Mon	NL	45	14	0	6	118.1	530	120	75	69	26	4	4	4	64	7	89	6	0	5	5	.500	0	0-0	0	5.84	5.25
2005	2 Tms		25	23	0	0	132.1	586	146	81	77	25	6	1	7	47	5	95	6	0	9	9	.500	0	0-0	0	5.20	5.24
2006	Ari	NL	31	30	0	1	167.2	747	185	101	90	27	8	3	8	52	2	123	9	1	12	10	.545	0	0-0	0	4.81	4.83
2007	Mil	NL	29	23	0	1	134.1	605	153	80	76	23	5	7	2	54	3	107	4	0	11	6	.647	0	1-2	0	5.38	5.09
2008	NYM	NL	11	4	0	1	37.0	150	33	20	19	4	1	1	2	11	0	20	1	0	3	2	.600	0	0-1	1	3.46	4.62
2009	2 Tms		36	0	0	6	41.1	159	25	8	8	3	0	1	2	15	1	30	0	0	1	0	1.000	0	0-2	11	1.98	1.74
2010	Mil	NL	17	0	0	2	19.2	84	20	10	10	3	1	0	0	10	0	18	2	0	1	0	1.000	0	0-0	0	7.62	7.32
05	Was	NL	4	4	0	0	12.2	66	22	15	13	4	0	0	0	7	2	5	0	0	0	3	.000	0	0-0	0	11.04	9.24
05	Arl	NL	21	19	0	0	119.2	520	124	66	64	21	6	1	7	40	3	90	6	0	9	6	.600	0	0-0	0	4.74	4.81
09	LAD	NL	8	0	0	4	11.0	43	7	2	2	1	0	0	1	4	0	10	0	0	0	0	-	0	0-0	0	2.42	1.64
09	Mil	NL	28	0	0	2	30.1	116	18	6	6	2	0	1	1	11	1	20	0	0	1	0	1.000	0	0-2	11	1.83	1.78
	8 ML YEARS		217	114	0	18	764.2	3362	801	440	410	127	29	21	35	294	23	544	32	1	48	40	.545	0	1-5	15	4.88	4.83

Jason Vargas

Pitches: L **Bats:** L **Pos:** SP-31   **Ht:** 6'0" **Wt:** 215 **Born:** 2/2/1983 **Age:** 28

			HOW MUCH HE PITCHED					WHAT HE GAVE UP										THE RESULTS						
Year	Team	Lg	G	GS	CG	GF	IP	BFP	H	R	ER	HR	SH	SF	HB	TBB	IBB	SO	WP	Bk	W	L	Pct	Sh	Sv-Op	Hld	ERC	ERA
2005	Fla	NL	17	13	1	0	73.2	325	71	34	33	4	4	1	4	31	4	59	0	0	5	5	.500	0	0-0	0	3.68	4.03
2006	Fla	NL	12	6	0	3	43.0	213	50	39	35	9	4	4	4	30	3	25	2	0	1	2	.333	0	0-0	0	7.30	7.33
2007	NYM	NL	2	2	0	0	10.1	51	17	14	14	4	0	0	0	2	1	4	1	1	0	1	.000	0	0-0	0	8.95	12.19
2009	Sea	AL	23	14	0	4	91.2	385	98	53	50	16	3	6	3	24	1	54	1	0	3	6	.333	0	0-0	0	4.64	4.91
2010	Sea	AL	31	31	0	0	192.2	811	187	86	81	18	4	7	1	54	3	116	1	4	9	12	.429	0	0-0	0	3.37	3.78
	5 ML YEARS		85	65	1	7	411.1	1785	423	226	213	51	15	18	12	141	12	258	5	5	18	26	.409	0	0-0	0	4.21	4.66

Jason Varitek

Bats: B **Throws:** R **Pos:** C-39, PR-1   VAIR uh teck   **Ht:** 6'2" **Wt:** 230 **Born:** 4/11/1972 **Age:** 39

							BATTING											BASERUNNING				AVERAGES		
Year	Team	Lg	G	AB	H	2B	3B	HR	(Hm | Rd)	TB	R	RBI	RC	TBB	IBB	SO	HBP	SH	SF	SB	CS	SB%	GDP	Avg	OBP	Slg
2010	Pwtckt*	AAA	2	5	2	0	0	0	(- | -)	2	0	1	0	0	0	1	0	0	1	0	0	-	0	.400	.333	.400
1997	Bos	AL	1	1	1	0	0	0	(0 | 0)	1	0	0	1	0	0	0	0	0	0	0	0	-	0	1.000	1.000	1.000
1998	Bos	AL	86	221	56	13	0	7	(1 | 6)	90	31	33	26	17	1	45	2	4	3	2	2	.50	8	.253	.309	.407
1999	Bos	AL	144	483	130	39	2	20	(12 | 8)	233	70	76	75	46	2	85	2	5	8	1	2	.33	13	.269	.330	.482
2000	Bos	AL	139	448	111	31	1	10	(2 | 8)	174	55	65	59	60	3	84	6	1	4	1	1	.50	16	.248	.342	.388
2001	Bos	AL	51	174	51	11	1	7	(2 | 5)	85	19	25	30	21	3	35	1	1	1	0	0	-	6	.293	.371	.489
2002	Bos	AL	132	467	124	27	1	10	(6 | 4)	183	58	61	52	41	3	95	7	1	3	4	3	.57	13	.266	.332	.392
2003	Bos	AL	142	451	123	31	1	25	(13 | 12)	231	63	85	79	51	8	106	7	5	7	3	2	.60	10	.273	.351	.512
2004	Bos	AL	137	463	137	30	1	18	(8 | 10)	223	67	73	79	62	9	126	10	0	1	10	3	.77	11	.296	.390	.482
2005	Bos	AL	133	470	132	30	1	22	(7 | 15)	230	70	70	78	62	3	117	3	1	3	2	0	1.00	10	.281	.366	.489
2006	Bos	AL	103	365	87	19	2	12	(2 | 10)	146	46	55	45	46	7	87	2	1	2	1	2	.33	10	.238	.325	.400
2007	Bos	AL	131	435	111	15	3	17	(9 | 8)	183	57	68	61	71	9	122	8	0	4	1	1	.50	9	.255	.367	.421
2008	Bos	AL	131	423	93	20	0	13	(4 | 9)	152	37	43	36	52	3	122	6	0	2	0	1	.00	13	.220	.313	.359
2009	Bos	AL	109	364	76	24	0	14	(10 | 4)	142	41	51	43	54	6	90	3	0	4	0	0	-	6	.209	.313	.390
2010	Bos	AL	39	112	26	6	0	7	(4 | 3)	53	18	16	11	10	2	35	0	0	1	0	0	-	1	.232	.293	.473
	Postseason		63	228	54	12	2	11	(3 | 8)	103	37	33	27	14	4	56	5	2	3	0	0	-	6	.237	.292	.452
	14 ML YEARS		1478	4877	1258	296	13	182	(80 | 102)	2126	632	721	675	593	59	1149	57	19	43	25	18	.58	126	.258	.343	.436

Anthony Varvaro

Pitches: R **Bats:** R **Pos:** RP-4   **Ht:** 6'0" **Wt:** 180 **Born:** 10/31/1984 **Age:** 26

Year	Team	Lg	G	GS	CG	GF	IP	BFP	H	R	ER	HR	SH	SF	HB	TBB	IBB	SO	WP	Bk	W	L	Pct	Sh	Sv-Op	Hld	ERC	ERA
2006	Ms	R	5	3	0	0	11.0	45	7	3	2	0	0	0	2	5	0	15	1	0	0	2	.000	0	0--	-	2.43	1.64
2007	Wisc	A	22	21	0	1	103.2	464	94	67	54	7	0	0	9	51	0	112	16	0	4	11	.267	0	1--	-	3.93	4.69
2008	Hi Dsrt	A+	30	24	0	0	122.2	595	154	105	97	22	5	3	13	82	0	113	10	0	3	9	.250	0	0--	-	8.01	7.12
2009	Hi Dsrt	A+	8	0	0	6	7.2	39	9	6	6	0	0	0	1	6	0	10	1	0	0	0	-	0	4--	-	5.50	7.04
2009	WTenn	AA	36	0	0	20	54.1	240	30	23	17	1	1	4	6	44	5	63	3	1	4	3	.571	0	8--	-	2.82	2.82
2010	WTenn	AA	31	0	0	23	39.1	165	27	15	14	2	2	3	0	21	4	46	2	0	1	3	.250	0	9--	-	2.41	3.20
2010	Tacom	AAA	19	0	0	2	25.2	119	24	17	15	1	0	2	4	14	0	26	3	0	0	0	-	0	0--	-	4.31	5.26
2010	Sea	AL	4	0	0	2	4.0	24	6	5	5	2	0	0	0	6	0	5	1	0	0	1	.000	0	0-0	0	16.26	11.25

Esmerling Vasquez

Pitches: R **Bats:** R **Pos:** RP-57   **Ht:** 6'1" **Wt:** 173 **Born:** 11/7/1983 **Age:** 27

Year	Team	Lg	G	GS	CG	GF	IP	BFP	H	R	ER	HR	SH	SF	HB	TBB	IBB	SO	WP	Bk	W	L	Pct	Sh	Sv-Op	Hld	ERC	ERA
2004	Msoula	R+	19	0	0	12	30.2	141	22	15	12	1	0	0	6	21	2	33	11	0	3	2	.600	0	5--	-	3.62	3.52
2004	Yakima	A-	5	0	0	4	5.2	27	10	6	4	1	0	0	0	0	0	7	1	0	0	0	-	0	1--	-	7.45	6.35
2005	Sbend	A	53	0	0	17	51.2	327	63	33	29	2	4	6	5	47	0	79	13	1	4	6	.600	0	3--	-	4.05	3.64
2006	Lancst	A+	34	18	0	6	117.2	547	129	89	77	9	6	2	12	51	0	115	6	1	4	9	.308	0	0--	-	4.85	5.89
2007	Mobile	AA	29	29	0	0	165.1	663	125	61	55	11	7	6	13	60	0	151	6	0	10	6	.625	0	0--	-	2.81	2.99
2008	Tucsn	AAA	24	15	0	2	83.0	398	79	68	62	11	8	4	12	73	2	57	2	0	3	6	.333	0	0--	-	6.66	6.72
2009	Reno	AAA	6	0	0	1	9.2	38	7	2	1	0	0	0	0	3	0	9	0	0	0	0	-	0	1--	-	1.77	0.93
2010	Reno	AAA	1	0	0	1	1.0	4	1	0	0	0	0	0	0	0	0	1	0	0	0	0	-	0	0--	-	1.95	0.00
2009	Ari	NL	53	0	0	10	53.0	238	52	27	26	4	1	1	3	29	2	45	4	0	3	3	.500	0	0-4	4	4.51	4.42
2010	Ari	NL	57	0	0	16	53.2	240	46	32	31	6	0	1	6	38	3	55	3	1	1	6	.143	0	0-2	5	5.04	5.20
	2 ML YEARS		110	0	0	26	106.2	478	98	59	57	10	1	2	9	67	5	100	7	1	4	9	.308	0	0-6	10	4.77	4.81

Javier Vazquez

Pitches: R **Bats:** R **Pos:** SP-26; RP-5   hah-vee-AIR VAZZ-kezz   **Ht:** 6'2" **Wt:** 210 **Born:** 7/25/1976 **Age:** 34

Year	Team	Lg	G	GS	CG	GF	IP	BFP	H	R	ER	HR	SH	SF	HB	TBB	IBB	SO	WP	Bk	W	L	Pct	Sh	Sv-Op	Hld	ERC	ERA
1998	Mon	NL	33	32	0	1	172.1	764	196	121	116	31	9	4	11	68	2	139	2	0	5	15	.250	0	0-0	0	5.79	6.06
1999	Mon	NL	26	26	3	0	154.2	667	154	98	86	20	3	3	4	52	4	113	2	0	9	8	.529	1	0-0	0	4.02	5.00
2000	Mon	NL	33	33	2	0	217.2	945	247	104	98	24	11	3	5	61	10	196	3	0	11	9	.550	1	0-0	0	4.45	4.05
2001	Mon	NL	32	32	5	0	223.2	898	197	92	85	24	9	2	3	44	4	208	3	1	16	11	.593	3	0-0	0	2.75	3.42
2002	Mon	NL	34	34	2	0	230.1	971	**243**	111	100	28	15	7	4	49	6	179	3	0	10	13	.435	0	0-0	0	3.80	3.91
2003	Mon	NL	34	34	4	0	230.2	938	198	93	83	28	6	6	4	57	5	241	11	1	13	12	.520	1	0-0	0	2.90	3.24
2004	NYY	AL	32	32	0	0	198.0	849	195	114	108	33	4	8	11	60	3	150	12	2	14	10	.583	0	0-0	0	4.23	4.91
2005	Ari	NL	33	33	3	0	215.2	904	223	112	106	35	13	3	5	46	4	192	7	0	11	15	.423	1	0-0	0	4.00	4.42
2006	CWS	AL	33	32	1	0	202.2	872	206	116	109	23	2	4	15	56	2	184	7	0	11	12	.478	0	0-0	0	4.02	4.84
2007	CWS	AL	32	32	2	0	216.2	882	197	95	90	29	5	7	7	50	2	213	5	0	15	8	.652	0	0-0	0	3.29	3.74
2008	CWS	AL	33	33	1	0	208.1	890	214	113	108	25	4	4	6	61	2	200	2	0	12	16	.429	0	0-0	0	4.03	4.67
2009	Atl	NL	32	32	3	0	219.1	874	181	75	70	20	12	2	4	44	2	238	6	0	15	10	.600	0	0-0	0	2.42	2.87
2010	NYY	AL	31	26	0	0	157.1	683	155	96	93	32	2	7	7	65	4	121	8	0	10	10	.500	0	0-0	1	4.94	5.32
	Postseason		4	2	0	0	15.2	80	24	18	18	6	0	3	2	10	0	18	0	0	1	1	.500	0	0-0	0	11.90	10.34
	13 ML YEARS		418	411	26	5	2647.1	11137	2606	1340	1252	352	95	60	86	713	50	2374	71	4	152	149	.505	7	0-0	1	3.80	4.26

Eugenio Velez

Bats: B **Throws:** R **Pos:** LF-13; PH-12; CF-5; PR-2; 2B-1; RF-1   aye-you-HEEN-ee-oh   **Ht:** 6'1" **Wt:** 169 **Born:** 5/16/1982 **Age:** 29

Year	Team	Lg	G	AB	H	2B	3B	HR	(Hm	Rd)	TB	R	RBI	RC	TBB	IBB	SO	HBP	SH	SF	SB	CS	SB%	GDP	Avg	OBP	Slg
2010	Fresno*	AAA	82	321	97	13	5	7	(-	-)	141	50	35	50	24	0	55	1	6	0	31	16	.66	8	.302	.353	.439
2007	SF	NL	14	11	3	0	2	0	(0	0)	7	5	2	4	2	0	3	0	0	0	4	0	1.00	0	.273	.385	.636
2008	SF	NL	98	275	72	16	7	1	(0	1)	105	32	30	29	14	2	40	1	1	1	15	6	.71	11	.262	.299	.382
2009	SF	NL	84	285	76	13	5	5	(3	2)	114	40	31	33	16	1	55	2	2	2	11	5	.69	6	.267	.308	.400
2010	SF	NL	29	55	9	2	0	2	(1	1)	17	7	8	6	6	0	9	0	5	0	0	0	-	0	.164	.246	.309
	4 ML YEARS		225	626	160	31	14	8	(4	4)	243	84	71	72	38	3	107	3	8	3	30	11	.73	17	.256	.300	.388

Will Venable

Bats: L **Throws:** L **Pos:** RF-89; CF-25; LF-23; PH-22; 1B-1   **Ht:** 6'2" **Wt:** 210 **Born:** 10/29/1982 **Age:** 28

Year	Team	Lg	G	AB	H	2B	3B	HR	(Hm	Rd)	TB	R	RBI	RC	TBB	IBB	SO	HBP	SH	SF	SB	CS	SB%	GDP	Avg	OBP	Slg
2010	Lk Els*	A+	5	14	1	1	0	0	(-	-)	2	0	0	0	4	1	8	0	0	0	1	0	1.00	0	.071	.278	.143
2010	SnAnt*	AA	2	6	2	0	0	0	(-	-)	2	2	1	1	2	0	2	0	0	0	2	0	1.00	0	.333	.500	.333
2008	SD	NL	28	110	29	4	2	2	(0	2)	43	16	10	15	13	1	21	0	0	1	1	1	.50	1	.264	.339	.391
2009	SD	NL	95	293	75	14	2	12	(5	7)	129	38	38	34	25	2	89	4	2	0	6	1	.86	6	.256	.323	.440
2010	SD	NL	131	392	96	11	7	13	(6	7)	160	60	51	57	45	8	128	3	0	5	29	7	.81	3	.245	.324	.408
	3 ML YEARS		254	795	200	29	11	27	(11	16)	332	114	99	106	83	11	238	7	2	6	36	9	.80	10	.252	.325	.418

Jonny Venters

Pitches: L Bats: L Pos: RP-79   Ht: 6'3" Wt: 195 Born: 3/20/1985 Age: 26

			HOW MUCH HE PITCHED						WHAT HE GAVE UP										THE RESULTS						
Year	Team	Lg	G	GS	CG	GF	IP	BFP	H	R	ER	HR	SH	SF	HB	TBB	IBB	SO	WP	Bk	W	L	Pct	Sh	Sv-Op	Hld	ERC	ERA
2004	Braves	R	11	8	0	0	42.1	198	53	31	27	3	0	0	7	12	0	54	4	0	1	6	.143	0	0- -	-	5.41	5.74
2005	Rome	A	23	12	0	8	103.0	454	100	51	45	4	3	3	8	52	0	66	12	0	8	6	.571	0	3- -	-	4.22	3.93
2007	MrtlBh	A+	17	12	0	2	79.2	333	60	39	30	4	3	1	5	38	0	64	10	0	3	3	.500	0	1- -	-	2.96	3.39
2008	Braves	R	4	4	0	0	7.2	35	10	6	4	1	0	0	1	2	0	10	0	0	0	0	-	0	0- -	-	6.11	4.70
2008	MrtlBh	A+	5	3	0	1	17.2	80	21	12	8	0	0	2	1	7	0	7	2	0	1	2	.333	0	1- -	-	4.60	4.08
2008	Missi	AA	3	2	0	1	9.0	42	10	2	1	0	0	0	0	5	0	7	0	0	1	0	1.000	0	0- -	-	4.43	1.00
2009	Missi	AA	12	12	1	0	65.1	280	60	24	20	2	2	1	3	35	0	40	3	0	4	4	.500	0	0- -	-	3.93	2.76
2009	Gwnntt	AAA	17	17	0	0	91.1	408	103	64	57	7	0	2	3	42	2	58	8	0	4	7	.364	0	0- -	-	5.02	5.62
2010	Gwnntt	AAA	2	1	0	0	6.2	25	4	1	1	0	0	0	0	1	0	6	0	0	1	0	1.000	0	0- -	-	1.02	1.35
2010	Atl	NL	79	0	0	17	83.0	350	61	30	18	1	2	1	8	39	2	93	4	0	4	4	.500	0	1-5	24	2.64	1.95

Jose Veras

Pitches: R Bats: R Pos: RP-48   Ht: 6'6" Wt: 235 Born: 10/20/1980 Age: 30

			HOW MUCH HE PITCHED						WHAT HE GAVE UP										THE RESULTS						
Year	Team	Lg	G	GS	CG	GF	IP	BFP	H	R	ER	HR	SH	SF	HB	TBB	IBB	SO	WP	Bk	W	L	Pct	Sh	Sv-Op	Hld	ERC	ERA
2010	NewOr*	AAA	24	0	0	8	29.1	135	34	15	15	2	0	0	0	15	2	37	4	0	1	1	.500	0	2- -	-	5.02	4.60
2006	NYY	AL	12	0	0	4	11.0	43	8	5	5	2	0	0	0	5	0	6	1	1	0	0	-	0	1-1	1	3.55	4.09
2007	NYY	AL	9	0	0	3	9.1	41	6	6	6	0	0	0	0	7	1	7	1	0	0	0	-	0	2-2	1	2.52	5.79
2008	NYY	AL	60	0	0	15	57.2	253	52	23	23	7	2	1	3	29	6	63	4	0	5	3	.625	0	0-2	10	4.09	3.59
2009	2 Tms	AL	47	0	0	19	50.1	225	42	33	29	8	4	0	6	28	0	40	0	1	4	3	.571	0	0-0	6	4.60	5.19
2010	Fla	NL	48	0	0	11	48.0	201	32	20	20	5	1	0	1	29	0	54	2	0	3	3	.500	0	0-2	19	3.19	3.75
09	NYY	AL	25	0	0	10	25.2	118	23	17	17	5	2	0	4	14	0	18	0	0	3	1	.750	0	0-0	3	5.29	5.96
09	Cle	AL	22	0	0	9	24.2	107	19	16	12	3	2	0	2	14	0	22	0	1	1	2	.333	0	0-0	3	3.92	4.38
	Postseason		2	0	0	0	0.2	4	1	0	0	0	0	0	0	1	1	1	0	0	0	0	-	0	0-0	-	6.98	0.00
	5 ML YEARS		176	0	0	52	176.1	763	140	87	83	22	7	1	10	98	7	170	8	2	12	9	.571	0	3-7	37	3.86	4.24

Justin Verlander

Pitches: R Bats: R Pos: SP-33   Ht: 6'5" Wt: 225 Born: 2/20/1983 Age: 28

			HOW MUCH HE PITCHED						WHAT HE GAVE UP										THE RESULTS						
Year	Team	Lg	G	GS	CG	GF	IP	BFP	H	R	ER	HR	SH	SF	HB	TBB	IBB	SO	WP	Bk	W	L	Pct	Sh	Sv-Op	Hld	ERC	ERA
2005	Det	AL	2	2	0	0	11.1	54	15	9	9	1	0	0	1	5	0	7	1	0	0	2	.000	0	0-0	0	6.41	7.15
2006	Det	AL	30	30	1	0	186.0	778	187	78	75	21	2	4	6	60	4	124	5	1	17	9	.654	1	0-0	0	4.12	3.63
2007	Det	AL	32	32	1	0	201.2	866	181	88	82	20	3	1	19	67	3	183	17	2	18	6	.750	1	0-0	0	3.53	3.66
2008	Det	AL	33	33	1	0	201.0	880	195	119	108	18	4	6	14	87	8	163	6	3	11	17	.393	0	0-0	0	4.17	4.84
2009	Det	AL	35	35	3	0	240.0	982	219	99	92	20	6	4	6	63	5	269	8	4	19	9	.679	1	0-0	0	3.06	3.45
2010	Det	AL	33	33	4	0	224.1	925	190	89	84	14	6	8	6	71	0	219	11	2	18	9	.667	0	0-0	0	2.79	3.37
	Postseason		4	4	0	0	21.2	100	26	17	14	5	1	0	0	10	0	23	3	1	1	2	.333	0	0-0	0	6.45	5.82
	6 ML YEARS		165	165	10	0	1064.1	4483	987	482	450	94	21	23	52	353	17	965	48	12	83	52	.615	3	0-0	0	3.51	3.81

Dayan Viciedo

Bats: R Throws: R Pos: 3B-23; PH-8; 1B-7; DH-4; PR-1   DYE-yahn vee-see-AYE-doe   Ht: 5'11" Wt: 240 Born: 3/10/1989 Age: 22

			BATTING																BASERUNNING				AVERAGES		
Year	Team	Lg	G	AB	H	2B	3B	HR	(Hm | Rd)	TB	R	RBI	RC	TBB	IBB	SO	HBP	SH	SF	SB	CS	SB%	GDP	Avg	OBP	Slg
2009	Brham	AA	130	504	141	20	0	12	(- | -)	197	72	78	64	23	4	89	7	0	6	5	2	.71	12	.280	.317	.391
2010	Charltt	AAA	86	343	94	15	0	20	(- | -)	169	42	47	52	11	1	78	6	3	0	1	1	.50	16	.274	.308	.493
2010	CWS	AL	38	104	32	7	0	5	(4 | 1)	54	17	13	15	2	0	25	0	0	0	1	0	1.00	5	.308	.321	.519

Shane Victorino

Bats: B Throws: R Pos: CF-143; PH-4   Ht: 5'9" Wt: 190 Born: 11/30/1980 Age: 30

			BATTING																BASERUNNING				AVERAGES		
Year	Team	Lg	G	AB	H	2B	3B	HR	(Hm | Rd)	TB	R	RBI	RC	TBB	IBB	SO	HBP	SH	SF	SB	CS	SB%	GDP	Avg	OBP	Slg
2010	LV*	AAA	2	6	4	0	1	1	(- | -)	9	1	3	3	0	0	0	0	0	0	0	0	-	0	.667	.667	1.500
2003	SD	NL	36	73	11	2	0	0	(0 | 0)	13	8	4	1	7	0	17	1	1	1	7	2	.78	5	.151	.232	.178
2005	Phi	NL	21	17	5	0	0	2	(1 | 1)	11	5	8	4	0	0	3	0	0	2	0	0	-	0	.294	.263	.647
2006	Phi	NL	153	415	119	19	8	6	(3 | 3)	172	70	46	58	24	0	54	14	8	1	4	3	.57	5	.287	.346	.414
2007	Phi	NL	131	456	128	23	3	12	(6 | 6)	193	78	46	65	37	1	62	10	5	2	37	4	.90	10	.281	.347	.423
2008	Phi	NL	146	570	167	30	8	14	(6 | 8)	255	102	58	86	45	2	69	7	5	0	36	11	.77	8	.293	.352	.447
2009	Phi	NL	156	620	181	39	13	10	(4 | 6)	276	102	62	99	60	1	71	6	4	4	25	8	.76	5	.292	.358	.445
2010	Phi	NL	147	587	152	26	10	18	(13 | 5)	252	84	69	89	53	5	79	7	0	1	34	6	.85	7	.259	.327	.429
	Postseason		32	119	33	6	2	6	(3 | 3)	61	18	23	22	12	4	9	3	2	1	6	1	.86	2	.277	.356	.513
	7 ML YEARS		790	2738	763	139	42	62	(33 | 29)	1172	449	293	402	226	9	355	45	23	11	143	34	.81	40	.279	.342	.428

Carlos Villanueva

Pitches: R Bats: R Pos: RP-50   vee-ah-nue-AY-vah   Ht: 6'2" Wt: 228 Born: 11/28/1983 Age: 27

			HOW MUCH HE PITCHED						WHAT HE GAVE UP										THE RESULTS						
Year	Team	Lg	G	GS	CG	GF	IP	BFP	H	R	ER	HR	SH	SF	HB	TBB	IBB	SO	WP	Bk	W	L	Pct	Sh	Sv-Op	Hld	ERC	ERA
2010	Nashv*	AAA	11	0	0	4	14.1	64	13	6	6	2	0	0	6	7	0	14	0	0	0	0	-	0	1- -	-	4.02	3.77
2006	Mil	NL	10	6	0	2	53.2	215	43	22	22	8	1	0	4	11	1	39	0	0	2	2	.500	0	0-0	1	2.85	3.69
2007	Mil	NL	59	6	0	8	114.1	489	101	52	50	16	4	1	3	53	3	99	3	0	8	5	.615	0	1-3	16	4.03	3.94
2008	Mil	NL	47	9	0	9	108.1	464	112	53	49	18	9	1	3	30	1	93	4	0	4	7	.364	0	1-1	11	4.29	4.07

	HOW MUCH HE PITCHED					WHAT HE GAVE UP											THE RESULTS							
Year Team Lg	G	GS	CG	GF	IP	BFP	H	R	ER	HR	SH	SF	HB	TBB	IBB	SO	WP	Bk	W	L	Pct	Sh	Sv-Op	Hld	ERC	ERA
2009 Mil NL	64	6	0	23	96.0	422	102	58	57	13	4	0	2	35	8	83	6	4 0	4	10	.286	0	3-8	9	4.44	5.34
2010 Mil NL	50	0	0	5	52.2	231	48	27	27	7	0	3	4	22	1	67	5	0	2	0	1.000	0	1-4	14	4.08	4.61
Postseason	2	0	0	0	3.2	11	0	0	0	0	0	0	0	0	0	3	0	0	0	0	-	0	0-0	1	0.00	0.00
5 ML YEARS	230	27	0	47	425.0	1821	406	212	205	62	18	5	16	151	14	381	16	0	20	24	.455	0	6-16	50	4.04	4.34

Henry Villar

Pitches: R Bats: R Pos: RP-8   vee-AHR   **Ht:** 5'11" **Wt:** 170 **Born:** 5/24/1987 **Age:** 24

	HOW MUCH HE PITCHED					WHAT HE GAVE UP											THE RESULTS							
Year Team Lg	G	GS	CG	GF	IP	BFP	H	R	ER	HR	SH	SF	HB	TBB	IBB	SO	WP	Bk	W	L	Pct	Sh	Sv-Op	Hld	ERC	ERA
2008 Grnville R	13	13	0	0	65.1	272	69	32	32	6	0	0	6	12	0	65	6	1	3	6	.333	0	0- -	-	3.93	4.41
2009 Lxngtn A	43	3	0	12	90.0	368	80	36	26	6	3	3	3	18	1	109	9	0	3	4	.429	0	5- -	-	2.60	2.60
2010 CpChr AA	36	11	0	9	102.0	445	95	49	47	11	5	3	2	42	3	68	2	1	4	7	.364	0	5- -	-	3.74	4.15
2010 Hou NL	8	0	0	3	6.0	27	5	3	3	0	0	1	1	3	0	3	0	1	0	0	-	0	0-0	1	3.35	4.50

Pedro Viola

Pitches: L Bats: R Pos: RP-2   **Ht:** 6'1" **Wt:** 185 **Born:** 6/29/1983 **Age:** 28

	HOW MUCH HE PITCHED					WHAT HE GAVE UP											THE RESULTS							
Year Team Lg	G	GS	CG	GF	IP	BFP	H	R	ER	HR	SH	SF	HB	TBB	IBB	SO	WP	Bk	W	L	Pct	Sh	Sv-Op	Hld	ERC	ERA
2007 Dayton A	22	0	0	8	43.1	174	29	14	9	3	1	2	1	17	1	49	2	0	3	1	.750	0	2- -	-	2.20	1.87
2007 Srsota A+	10	0	0	5	20.0	82	14	2	2	0	0	0	0	7	2	28	1	0	0	1	.000	0	2- -	-	1.59	0.90
2007 Chatt AA	14	0	0	4	19.0	76	12	3	2	2	2	0	0	6	0	17	0	0	0	0	-	0	2- -	-	1.87	0.95
2008 Chatt AA	52	7	0	17	82.1	369	88	50	41	6	8	3	4	36	4	84	6	0	4	7	.364	0	2- -	-	4.49	4.48
2009 Lsvlle AAA	54	0	0	16	49.1	230	48	30	30	7	5	1	0	33	1	57	4	0	2	2	.500	0	8- -	-	5.13	5.47
2010 Lsvlle AAA	1	0	0	0	1.0	3	0	0	0	0	0	0	0	0	0	1	0	0	0	0	-	0	0- -	-	0.00	0.00
2010 Norfolk AAA	11	0	0	3	8.2	55	19	18	17	1	0	0	1	10	0	8	2	0	0	2	.000	0	0- -	-	16.33	17.65
2010 Bowie AA	23	10	0	3	62.2	264	61	26	25	2	2	2	3	19	2	64	7	0	3	4	.429	0	0- -	-	3.24	3.59
2009 Cin NL	9	0	0	1	7.0	30	7	4	4	2	1	0	0	3	0	5	0	0	0	0	-	0	0-0	0	5.60	5.14
2010 Bal AL	2	0	0	1	1.1	6	1	2	2	1	0	0	0	1	0	3	0	0	0	0	-	0	0-0	0	8.71	13.50
2 ML YEARS	11	0	0	2	8.1	36	8	6	6	3	1	0	0	4	0	8	0	0	0	0	-	0	0-0	0	6.10	6.48

Omar Vizquel

Bats: B Throws: R Pos: 3B-83; 2B-19; SS-9; PR-4; PH-2; DH-1   vizz-KELL   **Ht:** 5'9" **Wt:** 175 **Born:** 4/24/1967 **Age:** 44

	BATTING																			BASERUNNING				AVERAGES		
Year Team Lg	G	AB	H	2B	3B	HR	(Hm	Rd)	TB	R	RBI	RC	TBB	IBB	SO	HBP	SH	SF		SB	CS	SB%	GDP	Avg	OBP	Slg
1989 Sea AL	143	387	85	7	3	1	(1	0)	101	45	20	25	28	0	40	1	13	2		1	4	.20	6	.220	.273	.261
1990 Sea AL	81	255	63	3	2	2	(1	2)	76	19	18	22	18	0	22	0	10	2		4	1	.80	7	.247	.295	.298
1991 Sea AL	142	426	98	16	4	1	(1	0)	125	42	41	39	45	0	37	0	8	3		7	2	.78	8	.230	.302	.293
1992 Sea AL	136	483	142	20	4	0	(0	0)	170	49	21	54	32	0	38	2	9	1		15	13	.54	14	.294	.340	.352
1993 Sea AL	158	560	143	14	2	2	(1	1)	167	68	31	53	50	2	71	4	13	3		12	14	.46	7	.255	.319	.298
1994 Cle AL	69	286	78	10	1	1	(0	1)	93	39	33	32	23	0	23	0	11	2		13	4	.76	4	.273	.325	.325
1995 Cle AL	136	542	144	28	0	6	(3	3)	190	87	56	70	59	0	59	1	10	10		29	11	.73	4	.266	.333	.351
1996 Cle AL	151	542	161	36	1	9	(2	7)	226	98	64	87	56	0	42	4	12	9		35	9	.80	10	.297	.362	.417
1997 Cle AL	153	565	158	23	6	5	(3	2)	208	89	49	75	57	1	58	2	**16**	2		43	12	.78	16	.280	.347	.368
1998 Cle AL	151	576	166	30	6	2	(0	2)	214	86	50	82	62	1	64	4	12	6		37	12	.76	10	.288	.358	.372
1999 Cle AL	144	574	191	36	4	5	(3	2)	250	112	66	106	65	0	50	1	**17**	7		42	9	.82	8	.333	.397	.436
2000 Cle AL	156	613	176	27	3	7	(1	6)	230	101	66	92	87	0	72	5	7	5		22	10	.69	13	.287	.377	.375
2001 Cle AL	155	611	156	26	8	2	(2	0)	204	84	50	66	61	0	72	2	15	4		13	9	.59	14	.255	.323	.334
2002 Cle AL	151	582	160	31	5	14	(9	5)	243	85	72	91	56	3	64	8	7	10		18	10	.64	7	.275	.341	.418
2003 Cle AL	64	250	61	13	2	2	(0	2)	84	43	19	25	29	0	20	0	5	1		8	3	.73	11	.244	.321	.336
2004 Cle AL	148	567	165	28	3	7	(2	5)	220	82	59	86	57	0	62	1	**20**	6		19	6	.76	12	.291	.353	.388
2005 SF NL	152	568	154	28	4	3	(0	3)	199	66	45	76	56	0	58	5	**20**	2		24	10	.71	10	.271	.341	.350
2006 SF NL	153	579	171	22	10	4	(2	2)	225	88	58	90	56	3	51	6	13	5		24	7	.77	13	.295	.361	.389
2007 SF NL	145	513	126	18	3	4	(2	2)	162	54	51	53	44	9	48	1	14	3		14	6	.70	14	.246	.305	.316
2008 SF NL	92	266	59	10	1	0	(0	0)	71	24	23	24	24	9	29	0	7	3		5	4	.56	4	.222	.283	.267
2009 Tex AL	62	177	47	7	2	1	(0	1)	61	17	14	24	13	0	27	0	5	0		4	0	1.00	6	.266	.316	.345
2010 CWS AL	108	344	95	11	1	2	(1	1)	114	36	30	41	34	0	45	2	7	4		11	7	.61	8	.276	.341	.331
Postseason	57	228	57	7	4	0	(0	0)	72	28	20	27	25	0	36	2	7	2		23	3	.88	0	.250	.327	.316
22 ML YEARS	2850	10266	2799	444	75	80	(35	45)	3633	1414	936	1313	1012	25	1052	49	251	90		400	163	.71	200	.273	.338	.354

Edinson Volquez

Pitches: R Bats: R Pos: SP-12   VOLE-kezz   **Ht:** 6'0" **Wt:** 210 **Born:** 7/3/1983 **Age:** 27

	HOW MUCH HE PITCHED					WHAT HE GAVE UP											THE RESULTS							
Year Team Lg	G	GS	CG	GF	IP	BFP	H	R	ER	HR	SH	SF	HB	TBB	IBB	SO	WP	Bk	W	L	Pct	Sh	Sv-Op	Hld	ERC	ERA
2010 Lynbrg* A+	2	2	0	0	8.0	28	3	0	0	0	0	0	1	0	0	7	0	0	1	0	1.000	0	0- -	-	0.47	0.00
2010 Lsvlle* AAA	4	4	0	0	23.0	88	11	5	5	1	0	2	1	8	0	21	2	0	3	0	1.000	0	0- -	-	1.32	1.96
2010 Dayton* A	2	2	0	0	13.0	54	11	4	2	2	0	0	1	4	0	19	0	0	0	0	-	0	0- -	-	3.54	1.38
2005 Tex AL	6	3	0	0	12.2	75	25	22	20	3	0	1	2	10	0	11	0	0	0	4	.000	0	0-0	0	14.15	14.21
2006 Tex AL	8	8	0	0	33.1	164	52	28	27	7	0	1	1	17	0	15	0	0	1	6	.143	0	0-0	0	9.27	7.29
2007 Tex AL	6	6	0	0	34.0	149	34	18	17	4	0	2	2	15	0	29	0	0	2	1	.667	0	0-0	0	4.63	4.50
2008 Cin NL	33	32	0	1	196.0	838	167	82	70	14	6	5	**14**	93	5	206	10	1	17	6	.739	0	0-0	0	3.61	3.21
2009 Cin NL	9	9	0	0	49.2	218	34	25	24	6	2	1	5	32	0	47	2	1	4	2	.667	0	0-0	0	3.77	4.35
2010 Cin NL	12	12	0	0	62.2	275	59	30	30	6	3	1	3	35	0	67	5	0	4	3	.571	0	0-0	0	4.60	4.31
6 ML YEARS	74	70	0	1	388.1	1719	371	205	188	40	11	11	27	202	5	375	17	2	28	22	.560	0	0-0	0	4.60	4.36

Chris Volstad

Pitches: R Bats: R Pos: SP-30 **Ht: 6'8" Wt: 232 Born: 9/23/1986 Age: 24**

Year Team	Lg	G	GS	CG	GF	IP	BFP	H	R	ER	HR	SH	SF	HB	TBB	IBB	SO	WP	Bk	W	L	Pct	Sh	Sv-Op	Hld	ERC	ERA
2010 NewOr*	AAA	3	3	0	0	17.0	71	13	6	6	1	2	0	0	9	0	13	0	0	1	0	1.000	0	0--	-	3.05	3.18
2008 Fla	NL	15	14	0	0	84.1	365	76	30	27	3	6	1	5	36	4	52	0	0	6	4	.600	0	0-0	0	3.30	2.88
2009 Fla	NL	29	29	1	0	159.0	682	169	100	92	29	8	3	3	59	3	107	8	0	9	13	.409	1	0-0	0	5.05	5.21
2010 Fla	NL	30	30	2	0	175.0	758	187	94	89	17	8	7	8	60	5	102	8	1	12	9	.571	1	0-0	0	4.38	4.58
3 ML YEARS		74	73	3	0	418.1	1805	432	224	208	49	22	11	16	155	12	261	16	1	27	26	.509	2	0-0	0	4.41	4.47

Joey Votto

Bats: L Throws: R Pos: 1B-148; PH-3 VAH-toe **Ht: 6'3" Wt: 229 Born: 9/10/1983 Age: 27**

Year Team	Lg	G	AB	H	2B	3B	HR	(Hm	Rd)	TB	R	RBI	RC	TBB	IBB	SO	HBP	SH	SF	SB	CS	SB%	GDP	Avg	OBP	Slg
2007 Cin	NL	24	84	27	7	0	4	(4	0)	46	11	17	17	5	1	15	0	0	0	1	0	1.00	0	.321	.360	.548
2008 Cin	NL	151	526	156	32	3	24	(14	10)	266	69	84	91	59	9	102	2	0	2	7	5	.58	7	.297	.368	.506
2009 Cin	NL	131	469	151	38	1	25	(14	11)	266	82	84	99	70	10	106	4	0	1	4	1	.80	8	.322	.414	.567
2010 Cin	NL	150	547	177	36	2	37	(18	19)	328	106	113	**132**	91	8	125	7	0	3	16	5	.76	11	.324	**.424**	**.600**
4 ML YEARS		456	1626	511	113	6	90	(50	40)	906	268	298	339	225	28	348	13	0	6	28	11	.72	26	.314	.401	.557

Billy Wagner

Pitches: L Bats: L Pos: RP-71 **Ht: 5'10" Wt: 180 Born: 7/25/1971 Age: 39**

Year Team	Lg	G	GS	CG	GF	IP	BFP	H	R	ER	HR	SH	SF	HB	TBB	IBB	SO	WP	Bk	W	L	Pct	Sh	Sv-Op	Hld	ERC	ERA
1995 Hou	NL	1	0	0	0	0.1	1	0	0	0	0	0	0	0	0	0	0	0	0	0	0	-	0	0-0	0	0.00	0.00
1996 Hou	NL	37	0	0	20	51.2	212	28	16	14	6	7	2	3	30	2	67	1	0	2	2	.500	0	9-13	3	2.61	2.44
1997 Hou	NL	62	0	0	49	66.1	277	49	23	21	5	3	1	3	30	1	106	3	0	7	8	.467	0	23-29	1	2.85	2.85
1998 Hou	NL	58	0	0	50	60.0	247	46	19	18	6	4	0	0	25	1	97	1	0	4	3	.571	0	30-35	1	2.87	2.70
1999 Hou	NL	66	0	0	55	74.2	286	35	14	13	5	2	1	1	23	1	124	2	0	4	1	.800	0	39-42	1	1.20	1.57
2000 Hou	NL	28	0	0	19	27.2	120	28	19	19	6	0	0	1	18	0	28	7	0	2	4	.333	0	6-15	0	6.15	6.18
2001 Hou	NL	64	0	0	58	62.2	251	44	19	19	6	3	1	5	20	0	79	3	0	2	5	.286	0	39-41	0	2.42	2.73
2002 Hou	NL	70	0	0	61	75.0	289	51	21	21	7	2	3	2	22	5	88	6	0	4	2	.667	0	35-41	0	2.08	2.52
2003 Hou	NL	78	0	0	67	86.0	335	52	18	17	0	1	0	3	23	5	105	4	0	1	4	.200	0	44-47	0	1.63	1.78
2004 Phi	NL	45	0	0	38	48.1	182	31	16	13	5	3	0	2	6	1	59	1	0	4	0	1.000	0	21-25	1	1.52	2.42
2005 Phi	NL	75	0	0	70	77.2	297	45	17	13	6	0	2	3	20	2	87	3	1	4	3	.571	0	38-41	1	1.53	1.51
2006 NYM	NL	70	0	0	59	72.1	297	59	22	18	7	2	0	4	21	1	94	2	0	3	2	.600	0	40-45	0	2.83	2.24
2007 NYM	NL	66	0	0	57	68.1	282	55	22	20	6	1	2	2	22	4	80	4	0	2	2	.500	0	34-39	1	2.66	2.63
2008 NYM	NL	45	0	0	34	47.0	184	32	17	12	4	0	1	0	10	0	52	2	0	0	1	.000	0	27-34	1	1.68	2.30
2009 2 Tms		17	0	0	2	15.2	63	8	5	3	1	2	0	1	8	0	26	1	0	1	1	.500	0	0-0	6	1.99	1.72
2010 Atl	NL	71	0	0	64	69.1	268	38	14	11	5	3	1	3	22	3	104	2	0	7	2	.778	0	37-44	1	1.53	1.43
09 NYM	NL	2	0	0	0	2.0	7	0	0	0	0	0	0	0	1	0	4	0	0	0	0	-	0	0-0	0	0.27	0.00
09 Bos	AL	15	0	0	2	13.2	56	8	5	3	1	2	0	1	7	0	22	1	0	1	1	.500	0	0-0	6	2.42	1.98
Postseason		13	0	0	9	11.1	57	20	13	13	3	0	0	1	2	0	13	1	0	1	1	.500	0	3-4	1	9.48	10.32
16 ML YEARS		853	0	0	703	903.0	3000	601	262	232	82	33	14	33	300	26	1196	43	1	47	40	.540	0	422-491	13	2.14	2.31

Adam Wainwright

Pitches: R Bats: R Pos: SP-33 **Ht: 6'7" Wt: 228 Born: 8/30/1981 Age: 29**

Year Team	Lg	G	GS	CG	GF	IP	BFP	H	R	ER	HR	SH	SF	HB	TBB	IBB	SO	WP	Bk	W	L	Pct	Sh	Sv-Op	Hld	ERC	ERA
2005 StL	NL	2	0	0	1	2.0	9	2	3	3	1	0	0	0	1	0	0	0	0	0	0	-	0	0-0	0	7.30	13.50
2006 StL	NL	61	0	0	10	75.0	309	64	26	26	6	4	1	4	22	2	72	0	0	2	1	.667	0	3-5	17	2.92	3.12
2007 StL	NL	32	32	1	0	202.0	882	212	93	83	13	9	5	9	70	4	136	6	0	14	12	.538	0	0-0	0	4.01	3.70
2008 StL	NL	20	20	1	0	132.0	544	122	51	47	12	6	4	3	34	1	91	3	0	11	3	.786	0	0-0	0	3.14	3.20
2009 StL	NL	34	34	1	0	233.0	970	216	75	68	17	10	5	3	66	1	212	7	0	**19**	8	.704	0	0-0	0	3.08	2.63
2010 StL	NL	33	33	5	0	230.1	910	186	68	62	15	13	6	4	56	2	213	2	0	20	11	.645	0	0-0	0	**2.36**	2.42
Postseason		10	1	0	9	17.2	67	10	1	1	1	0	0	1	3	0	22	1	0	1	0	1.000	0	4-5	0	1.27	0.51
6 ML YEARS		182	119	8	11	874.1	3624	802	316	289	64	42	21	23	249	10	724	21	0	66	35	.653	2	3-5	17	3.10	2.97

Tim Wakefield

Pitches: R Bats: R Pos: SP-19; RP-13 **Ht: 6'2" Wt: 210 Born: 8/2/1966 Age: 44**

Year Team	Lg	G	GS	CG	GF	IP	BFP	H	R	ER	HR	SH	SF	HB	TBB	IBB	SO	WP	Bk	W	L	Pct	Sh	Sv-Op	Hld	ERC	ERA
1992 Pit	NL	13	13	4	0	92.0	373	76	26	22	3	6	4	1	35	1	51	3	1	8	1	.889	1	0-0	0	2.72	2.15
1993 Pit	NL	24	20	3	1	128.1	595	145	83	80	14	7	5	9	75	2	59	6	0	6	11	.353	2	0-0	0	5.97	5.61
1995 Bos	AL	27	27	6	0	195.1	804	163	76	64	22	3	7	9	68	0	119	11	0	16	8	.667	1	0-0	0	3.28	2.95
1996 Bos	AL	32	32	6	0	211.2	963	238	**151**	121	38	1	9	14	90	0	140	4	1	14	13	.519	0	0-0	0	5.68	5.14
1997 Bos	AL	35	29	4	2	201.1	866	193	109	95	24	3	7	**16**	87	5	151	6	0	12	**15**	.444	2	0-0	1	4.47	4.25
1998 Bos	AL	36	33	2	1	216.0	939	211	123	110	30	4	8	14	79	1	146	6	1	17	8	.680	0	0-0	0	4.30	4.58
1999 Bos	AL	49	17	0	28	140.0	635	146	93	79	19	1	8	5	72	2	104	1	0	6	11	.353	0	15-18	1	5.12	5.08
2000 Bos	AL	51	17	0	13	159.1	706	170	107	97	31	4	8	4	65	3	102	4	0	6	10	.375	0	0-1	3	5.23	5.48
2001 Bos	AL	45	17	0	10	168.2	732	156	84	73	13	3	9	**18**	73	5	148	5	1	9	12	.429	0	3-5	3	4.02	3.90
2002 Bos	AL	45	15	0	10	163.1	657	121	57	51	15	1	4	9	51	2	134	5	2	11	5	.688	0	3-5	5	2.54	2.81
2003 Bos	AL	35	33	0	2	202.1	872	193	106	92	23	2	4	12	71	0	169	8	0	11	7	.611	0	1-1	0	3.92	4.09
2004 Bos	AL	32	30	0	0	188.1	831	197	121	102	29	2	4	16	63	3	116	9	0	12	10	.545	0	0-0	1	4.73	4.87
2005 Bos	AL	33	33	3	0	225.1	943	210	113	104	**35**	1	6	11	68	4	151	8	0	16	12	.571	0	0-0	0	3.87	4.15
2006 Bos	AL	23	23	1	0	140.0	610	135	80	72	19	1	3	10	51	0	90	6	0	7	11	.389	0	0-0	0	4.22	4.63
2007 Bos	AL	31	31	0	0	189.0	800	191	104	100	22	2	6	4	64	1	110	10	0	17	12	.586	0	0-0	0	4.14	4.76
2008 Bos	AL	30	30	1	0	181.0	754	154	89	83	25	2	4	13	60	0	117	12	0	10	11	.476	0	0-0	0	3.54	4.13

Year	Team	Lg	G	GS	CG	GF	IP	BFP	H	R	ER	HR	SH	SF	HB	TBB	IBB	SO	WP	Bk	W	L	Pct	Sh	Sv-Op	Hld	ERC	ERA
2009	Bos	AL	21	21	2	0	129.2	572	137	67	66	12	4	1	10	50	0	72	4	0	11	5	.688	0	0-0	0	4.60	4.58
2010	Bos	AL	32	19	0	10	140.0	610	153	92	83	19	3	4	5	36	3	84	11	1	4	10	.286	0	0-0	0	4.32	5.34
	Postseason		18	11	2	2	72.0	329	68	56	54	13	1	3	9	38	2	54	1	0	5	7	.417	0	0-0	0	5.25	6.75
	18 ML YEARS		594	440	32	72	3071.2	13262	2989	1681	1494	393	47	101	178	1158	32	2063	119	7	193	172	.529	6	22-30	13	4.25	4.38

Jordan Walden

Pitches: R **Bats:** R **Pos:** RP-16   **Ht:** 6'5" **Wt:** 220 **Born:** 11/16/1987 **Age:** 23

			HOW MUCH HE PITCHED						WHAT HE GAVE UP												THE RESULTS							
Year	Team	Lg	G	GS	CG	GF	IP	BFP	H	R	ER	HR	SH	SF	HB	TBB	IBB	SO	WP	Bk	W	L	Pct	Sh	Sv-Op	Hld	ERC	ERA
2007	Orem	R+	15	15	0	0	64.1	256	49	27	22	3	1	0	3	17	0	63	3	0	1	1	.500	0	0- -	-	2.20	3.08
2008	CRpds	A	18	18	1	0	107.1	426	80	32	26	3	3	1	3	32	0	91	5	1	4	6	.400	0	0- -	-	2.07	2.18
2008	RCuca	A+	9	9	0	0	49.0	214	42	30	22	4	1	1	2	24	0	50	2	0	5	2	.714	0	0- -	-	3.60	4.04
2009	Ark	AA	13	13	0	0	60.0	274	72	39	35	4	2	1	3	29	1	57	7	1	1	5	.167	0	0- -	-	5.56	5.25
2010	Ark	AA	38	0	0	30	43.0	186	44	18	16	2	3	2	0	22	2	38	5	0	1	1	.500	0	8- -	-	4.28	3.35
2010	Salt Lk	AAA	6	0	0	0	6.2	29	8	3	3	0	0	0	0	2	0	3	0	0	0	0	-	0	0- -	-	4.12	4.05
2010	LAA	AL	16	0	0	5	15.1	65	13	4	4	1	0	0	0	7	0	23	1	1	0	1	.000	0	1-1	6	3.21	2.35

Neil Walker

Bats: B **Throws:** R **Pos:** 2B-105; 3B-6; PH-1   **Ht:** 6'3" **Wt:** 208 **Born:** 9/10/1985 **Age:** 25

			BATTING																BASERUNNING				AVERAGES		
Year	Team	Lg	G	AB	H	2B	3B	HR	(Hm | Rd)	TB	R	RBI	RC	TBB	IBB	SO	HBP	SH	SF	SB	CS	SB%	GDP	Avg	OBP	Slg
2004	Pirates	R	52	192	52	12	3	4	(- | -)	82	28	20	26	10	2	33	3	0	3	3	1	.75	2	.271	.313	.427
2004	Wmspt	A-	8	32	10	3	0	0	(- | -)	13	2	7	4	2	0	1	0	0	1	1	2	.33	0	.313	.343	.406
2005	Hkry	A	120	485	146	33	2	12	(- | -)	219	78	68	74	20	2	71	6	0	7	7	4	.64	10	.301	.332	.452
2005	Lynbrg	A+	9	42	11	2	1	0	(- | -)	15	4	12	3	0	0	12	0	0	3	0	0	-	0	.262	.244	.357
2006	Lynbrg	A+	72	264	75	22	1	3	(- | -)	108	32	35	37	19	1	41	6	4	1	3	5	.38	6	.284	.345	.409
2006	Altna	AA	10	31	5	0	0	2	(- | -)	11	5	3	1	1	0	4	0	0	0	0	0	-	1	.161	.188	.355
2007	Altna	AA	117	431	124	30	3	13	(- | -)	199	77	66	75	53	3	73	0	1	5	9	4	.69	6	.288	.362	.462
2007	Indy	AAA	19	64	13	3	0	0	(- | -)	16	7	0	3	2	0	13	3	0	0	1	1	.50	2	.203	.261	.250
2008	Indy	AAA	133	505	122	25	7	16	(- | -)	209	69	80	61	29	0	102	2	4	10	10	6	.63	11	.242	.280	.414
2009	Indy	AAA	95	356	94	31	2	14	(- | -)	171	38	69	55	26	1	60	1	1	6	5	2	.71	13	.264	.311	.480
2009	Pirates	R	8	30	5	2	0	1	(- | -)	10	2	1	1	1	0	5	1	0	0	0	1	.00	1	.167	.219	.333
2010	Indy	AAA	43	168	54	18	2	6	(- | -)	94	25	26	37	19	0	31	1	0	1	10	1	.91	2	.321	.392	.560
2009	Pit	NL	17	36	7	1	0	0	(0 | 0)	8	5	0	2	4	0	11	0	0	0	1	0	1.00	1	.194	.275	.222
2010	Pit	NL	110	426	126	29	3	12	(5 | 7)	197	57	66	66	34	1	83	3	2	4	2	3	.40	4	.296	.349	.462
	2 ML YEARS		127	462	133	30	3	12	(5 | 7)	205	62	66	68	38	1	94	3	2	4	3	3	.50	5	.288	.343	.444

Tyler Walker

Pitches: R **Bats:** R **Pos:** RP-24   **Ht:** 6'3" **Wt:** 262 **Born:** 5/15/1976 **Age:** 35

			HOW MUCH HE PITCHED						WHAT HE GAVE UP												THE RESULTS							
Year	Team	Lg	G	GS	CG	GF	IP	BFP	H	R	ER	HR	SH	SF	HB	TBB	IBB	SO	WP	Bk	W	L	Pct	Sh	Sv-Op	Hld	ERC	ERA
2010	Ptomc*	A+	1	1	0	0	0.2	7	1	3	3	0	0	0	0	4	0	2	0	0	0	0	-	0	0- -	-	31.81	40.50
2010	Hrsbrg*	AA	1	0	0	0	2.0	6	0	0	0	0	0	0	0	0	0	2	0	0	0	0	-	0	0- -	-	0.00	0.00
2010	Syrcse*	AAA	2	0	0	0	1.2	10	2	3	3	2	0	0	1	2	0	1	0	0	0	0	-	0	0- -	-	23.20	16.20
2002	NYM	NL	5	1	0	3	10.2	49	11	7	7	3	0	0	0	5	1	7	0	0	1	0	1.000	0	0-0	0	5.46	5.91
2004	SF	NL	52	0	0	13	63.2	275	69	31	30	8	3	1	1	24	1	48	1	0	5	1	.833	0	1-1	5	4.76	4.24
2005	SF	NL	67	0	0	39	61.2	279	68	31	29	9	5	1	3	27	6	54	4	0	6	4	.600	0	23-28	2	5.15	4.23
2006	2 Tms		26	0	0	17	25.1	111	27	20	20	1	1	0	0	12	0	19	1	0	1	4	.200	0	10-14	1	4.35	7.11
2007	SF	NL	15	0	0	1	14.1	53	12	2	2	0	0	1	0	4	1	9	0	0	2	0	1.000	0	0-1	7	2.30	1.26
2008	SF	NL	65	0	0	19	53.1	226	47	29	27	7	2	1	1	21	3	49	5	0	5	8	.385	0	0-4	19	3.57	4.56
2009	Phi	NL	32	0	0	10	35.1	150	31	12	12	4	1	2	3	9	1	27	2	0	2	1	.667	0	0-0	1	3.13	3.06
2010	Was	NL	24	0	0	6	35.1	145	35	16	14	5	3	2	0	8	2	30	1	0	1	0	1.000	0	0-1	1	3.57	3.57
06	SF	NL	6	0	0	1	5.1	28	9	9	9	1	0	0	0	5	0	3	1	0	0	1	.000	0	0-2	1	12.35	15.19
06	TB	AL	20	0	0	16	20.0	83	18	11	11	0	1	0	0	7	0	16	0	0	1	3	.250	0	10-12	0	2.70	4.95
	8 ML YEARS		286	1	0	108	299.2	1288	300	148	141	37	15	14	8	110	15	243	14	0	23	18	.561	0	34-49	36	4.15	4.23

Brett Wallace

Bats: L **Throws:** R **Pos:** 1B-48; PH-3   **Ht:** 6'2" **Wt:** 205 **Born:** 8/26/1986 **Age:** 24

			BATTING																BASERUNNING				AVERAGES		
Year	Team	Lg	G	AB	H	2B	3B	HR	(Hm	Rd)	TB	R	RBI	RC	TBB	IBB	SO	HBP	SH	SF	SB	CS	SB%	GDP	Avg	OBP	Slg
2008	QuadC	A	41	153	50	8	1	5	(-	-)	75	28	25	31	17	1	32	7	0	0	0	0	-	2	.327	.418	.490
2008	Sprgfld	AA	13	49	18	5	0	3	(-	-)	32	13	11	13	2	0	7	6	0	0	0	0	-	3	.367	.456	.653
2009	Sprgfld	AA	32	128	36	5	0	5	(-	-)	56	22	16	24	18	2	34	8	0	0	0	0	-	7	.281	.403	.438
2009	Memp	AAA	62	222	65	11	0	6	(-	-)	94	22	19	33	15	1	42	4	0	2	0	1	.00	7	.293	.346	.423
2009	Scrmto	AAA	44	182	55	10	0	9	(-	-)	92	32	28	33	14	4	40	5	0	2	1	1	.50	5	.302	.365	.505
2010	LsVgs	AAA	95	385	116	24	1	18	(-	-)	196	64	61	70	27	1	83	9	0	2	1	1	.50	9	.301	.359	.509
2010	Hou	NL	51	144	32	6	1	2	(1	1)	46	14	13	10	8	3	50	7	0	0	0	0	-	3	.222	.296	.319

P.J. Walters

Pitches: R **Bats:** R **Pos:** RP-4; SP-3   **Ht:** 6'4" **Wt:** 200 **Born:** 3/12/1985 **Age:** 26

			HOW MUCH HE PITCHED					WHAT HE GAVE UP										THE RESULTS						
Year	Team	Lg	G	GS	CG	GF	IP	BFP	H	R	ER	HR	SH	SF	HB	TBB	IBB	SO	WP	Bk	W	L	Pct	Sh	Sv-Op	Hld	ERC	ERA
2006	StCol	A-	26	0	0	19	30.1	131	29	15	12	1	0	0	2	9	0	31	2	0	2	1	.667	0	8--	-	3.15	3.56
2007	QuadC	A	17	10	0	4	68.2	282	59	25	20	2	1	2	9	12	0	73	4	0	6	1	.857	0	1--	-	2.51	2.62
2007	PlmBh	A+	5	5	0	0	33.2	138	29	10	10	2	2	0	1	6	0	37	1	0	3	1	.750	0	0--	-	2.31	2.67
2007	Sprgfld	AA	8	8	1	0	49.1	206	42	13	13	4	3	0	4	15	0	37	3	0	4	3	.429	0	0--	-	3.08	2.37
2008	Sprgfld	AA	6	6	0	0	36.0	150	35	17	13	5	0	0	3	8	0	34	2	0	1	2	.333	0	0--	-	3.85	3.25
2008	Memp	AAA	23	23	0	0	122.0	547	123	71	66	17	7	7	8	62	2	122	11	1	9	4	.692	0	0--	-	5.09	4.87
2009	Memp	AAA	21	20	2	0	121.0	539	128	73	61	6	9	2	10	44	1	113	10	0	8	10	.444	0	0--	-	4.14	4.54
2010	Memp	AAA	19	18	0	0	108.2	461	106	51	46	12	5	1	8	30	1	106	3	1	8	5	.615	0	0--	-	3.80	3.81
2009	StL	NL	8	1	0	4	16.0	80	21	19	17	6	1	1	0	9	1	14	0	0	0	0	-	0	0-0	0	8.42	9.56
2010	StL	NL	7	3	0	3	30.0	129	32	20	20	5	1	2	0	10	0	22	0	0	2	0	1.000	0	0-0	0	4.67	6.00
	2 ML YEARS		15	4	0	7	46.0	209	53	39	37	11	2	3	0	19	1	36	0	0	2	0	1.000	0	0-0	0	5.92	7.24

Chien-Ming Wang

Pitches: R **Bats:** R **Pos:** P   CHENN-MING WONG   **Ht:** 6'3" **Wt:** 230 **Born:** 3/31/1980 **Age:** 31

			HOW MUCH HE PITCHED					WHAT HE GAVE UP										THE RESULTS						
Year	Team	Lg	G	GS	CG	GF	IP	BFP	H	R	ER	HR	SH	SF	HB	TBB	IBB	SO	WP	Bk	W	L	Pct	Sh	Sv-Op	Hld	ERC	ERA
2005	NYY	AL	18	17	0	0	116.1	486	113	58	52	9	3	4	6	32	3	47	3	0	8	5	.615	0	0-0	0	3.47	4.02
2006	NYY	AL	34	33	2	1	218.0	900	233	92	88	12	3	2	2	52	4	76	6	1	19	6	.760	1	1-1	0	3.62	3.63
2007	NYY	AL	30	30	1	0	199.1	823	199	84	82	9	2	3	8	59	1	104	9	1	19	7	.731	0	0-0	0	3.54	3.70
2008	NYY	AL	15	15	1	0	95.0	402	90	44	43	4	0	3	3	35	1	54	0	0	8	2	.800	0	0-0	0	3.39	4.07
2009	NYY	AL	12	9	0	2	42.0	206	66	46	45	7	3	1	2	19	1	29	3	0	1	6	.143	0	0-0	0	8.67	9.64
	Postseason		4	4	0	0	19.0	90	28	19	16	5	2	0	3	5	0	7	0	0	1	3	.250	0	0-0	0	8.53	7.58
	5 ML YEARS		109	104	4	3	670.2	2817	701	324	310	41	11	13	21	197	10	310	21	2	55	26	.679	1	1-1	0	3.82	4.16

Matt Watson

Bats: L **Throws:** R **Pos:** LF-12; PH-2   **Ht:** 5'11" **Wt:** 200 **Born:** 9/5/1978 **Age:** 32

			BATTING																	BASERUNNING				AVERAGES		
Year	Team	Lg	G	AB	H	2B	3B	HR	(Hm | Rd)	TB	R	RBI	RC	TBB	IBB	SO	HBP	SH	SF	SB	CS	SB%	GDP	Avg	OBP	Slg
2010	Scrmto*	AAA	37	153	44	11	2	0	9	(- -)	83	25	26	28	11	0	24	1	0	0	0	0	-	4	.288	.339	.542
2003	NYM	NL	15	23	4	2	0	0	(0 | 0)	6	0	2	0	1	0	5	0	1	0	0	0	-	1	.174	.208	.261
2005	Oak	AL	19	48	9	3	0	0	(0 | 0)	12	4	5	3	2	0	4	0	0	0	0	0	-	1	.188	.220	.250
2010	Oak	AL	12	30	6	2	0	1	(1 | 0)	11	2	4	3	3	0	5	0	0	0	0	0	-	0	.200	.273	.367
	3 ML YEARS		46	101	19	7	0	1	(1 | 0)	29	6	11	6	6	0	14	0	1	0	0	0	-	2	.188	.234	.287

Jeff Weaver

Pitches: R **Bats:** R **Pos:** RP-44   **Ht:** 6'5" **Wt:** 202 **Born:** 8/22/1976 **Age:** 34

			HOW MUCH HE PITCHED					WHAT HE GAVE UP										THE RESULTS						
Year	Team	Lg	G	GS	CG	GF	IP	BFP	H	R	ER	HR	SH	SF	HB	TBB	IBB	SO	WP	Bk	W	L	Pct	Sh	Sv-Op	Hld	ERC	ERA
2010	InldEm	A+	1	1	0	0	3.0	12	2	2	0	0	0	1	0	1	0	3	0	0	0	0	-	0	0--	-	1.57	0.00
1999	Det	AL	30	29	0	1	163.2	717	176	104	101	27	5	5	17	56	2	114	0	0	9	12	.429	0	0-0	0	5.21	5.55
2000	Det	AL	31	30	2	0	200.0	849	205	102	96	26	3	9	15	52	2	130	3	2	11	15	.423	0	0-0	0	4.18	4.32
2001	Det	AL	33	33	5	0	229.1	985	235	116	104	19	12	7	14	68	4	152	3	0	13	16	.448	0	0-0	0	3.89	4.08
2002	2 Tms	AL	32	25	0	3	199.2	840	193	88	78	16	6	3	11	48	4	132	8	0	11	11	.500	3	2-2	0	3.30	3.52
2003	NYY	AL	32	24	0	0	159.1	735	211	113	106	16	9	9	11	47	2	93	2	0	7	9	.438	0	0-0	1	6.77	5.99
2004	LAD	NL	34	34	0	0	220.0	935	219	103	98	19	5	7	14	67	9	153	9	0	13	13	.500	0	0-0	0	3.79	4.01
2005	LAD	NL	34	34	3	0	224.0	930	220	111	105	35	8	3	18	43	1	157	2	0	14	11	.560	2	0-0	0	3.87	4.22
2006	2 Tms	AL	31	31	0	0	172.0	770	213	114	110	34	7	4	10	47	1	107	5	0	8	14	.364	0	0-0	0	6.06	5.76
2007	Sea	AL	27	27	3	0	146.2	657	190	105	101	23	4	7	8	35	5	80	3	1	7	13	.350	2	0-0	0	5.74	6.20
2009	LAD	NL	28	7	0	5	79.0	355	87	34	32	7	5	2	5	33	9	64	4	0	6	4	.600	0	0-0	0	4.68	3.65
2010	LAD	NL	44	0	0	9	44.1	197	48	30	30	5	6	5	1	20	5	26	0	0	5	1	.833	0	0-1	5	4.76	6.09
02	Det	AL	17	17	3	0	121.2	509	112	50	43	9	4	5	2	33	1	75	4	0	6	8	.429	3	0-0	0	2.94	3.18
02	NYY	AL	15	8	0	3	78.0	331	81	38	35	12	1	1	3	15	3	57	2	0	5	3	.625	0	2-2	0	3.86	4.04
06	LAA	AL	16	16	0	0	88.2	397	114	68	62	18	2	1	4	21	0	62	4	0	3	10	.231	0	0-0	0	6.03	6.29
06	StL	NL	15	15	0	0	83.1	373	99	49	48	16	5	3	6	26	1	45	1	0	5	4	.556	0	0-0	0	5.78	5.18
	Postseason		10	6	0	2	39.1	174	39	18	17	4	3	1	4	14	2	25	1	0	4	4	.500	0	0-0	0	4.11	3.89
	11 ML YEARS		356	274	16	21	1838.0	7970	1997	1023	961	227	70	61	124	516	44	1214	37	3	104	119	.466	7	2-3	6	4.49	4.71

Jered Weaver

Pitches: R **Bats:** R **Pos:** SP-34   **Ht:** 6'7" **Wt:** 205 **Born:** 10/4/1982 **Age:** 28

			HOW MUCH HE PITCHED					WHAT HE GAVE UP										THE RESULTS						
Year	Team	Lg	G	GS	CG	GF	IP	BFP	H	R	ER	HR	SH	SF	HB	TBB	IBB	SO	WP	Bk	W	L	Pct	Sh	Sv-Op	Hld	ERC	ERA
2006	LAA	AL	19	19	0	0	123.0	490	94	36	35	15	2	2	3	33	1	105	2	0	11	2	.846	0	0-0	0	2.57	2.56
2007	LAA	AL	28	28	0	0	161.0	695	178	77	70	17	5	5	2	45	3	115	4	0	13	7	.650	0	0-0	0	4.24	3.91
2008	LAA	AL	30	30	0	0	176.2	745	173	88	85	20	1	4	6	54	4	152	3	0	11	10	.524	0	0-0	0	3.80	4.33
2009	LAA	AL	33	33	4	0	211.0	882	196	91	88	26	6	8	4	66	3	174	3	0	16	8	.667	2	0-0	0	3.56	3.75
2010	LAA	AL	34	34	0	0	224.1	905	187	83	75	23	2	5	0	54	0	233	7	1	13	12	.520	0	0-0	0	2.59	3.01
	Postseason		6	3	0	2	20.2	83	12	6	6	5	0	0	0	10	0	22	0	0	2	1	.667	0	0-0	1	3.04	2.61
	5 ML YEARS		144	144	4	0	896.0	3717	828	375	353	101	16	24	15	252	11	779	19	1	64	39	.621	2	0-0	0	3.33	3.55

Brandon Webb

Pitches: R **Bats:** R **Pos:** P **Ht:** 6'3" **Wt:** 228 **Born:** 5/9/1979 **Age:** 32

Year	Team	Lg	G	GS	CG	GF	IP	BFP	H	R	ER	HR	SH	SF	HB	TBB	IBB	SO	WP	Bk	W	L	Pct	Sh	Sv-Op	Hld	ERC	ERA
2003	Ari	NL	29	28	1	1	180.2	750	140	65	57	12	9	1	13	68	4	172	9	1	10	9	.526	1	0-0	0	2.80	2.84
2004	Ari	NL	35	35	1	0	208.0	933	194	111	83	17	14	6	11	119	11	164	17	1	7	16	.304	0	0-0	0	4.32	3.59
2005	Ari	NL	33	33	1	0	229.0	943	229	98	90	21	10	7	2	59	4	172	14	1	14	12	.538	0	0-0	0	3.54	3.54
2006	Ari	NL	33	33	5	0	235.0	950	216	91	81	15	10	6	6	50	4	178	5	2	16	8	.667	3	0-0	0	2.81	3.10
2007	Ari	NL	34	34	4	0	236.1	975	209	91	79	12	9	6	5	72	6	194	3	0	18	10	.643	3	0-0	0	2.82	3.01
2008	Ari	NL	34	34	3	0	226.2	944	206	95	83	13	8	9	12	65	5	183	8	1	22	7	.759	1	0-0	0	3.04	3.30
2009	Ari	NL	1	1	0	0	4.0	20	6	6	6	2	0	0	1	2	0	2	0	0	0	-	-	0	0-0	0	12.87	13.50
	Postseason		2	2	0	0	13.0	55	11	5	5	0	0	0	1	5	0	13	2	0	1	1	.500	0	0-0	0	2.79	3.46
	7 ML YEARS		199	198	15	1	1319.2	5515	1200	557	479	92	60	35	50	435	34	1065	56	6	87	62	.584	8	0-0	0	3.23	3.27

Ryan Webb

Pitches: R **Bats:** R **Pos:** RP-54 **Ht:** 6'6" **Wt:** 214 **Born:** 2/5/1986 **Age:** 25

Year	Team	Lg	G	GS	CG	GF	IP	BFP	H	R	ER	HR	SH	SF	HB	TBB	IBB	SO	WP	Bk	W	L	Pct	Sh	Sv-Op	Hld	ERC	ERA
2004	As	R	8	7	0	0	20.1	83	18	11	11	2	0	0	3	1	0	23	1	0	1	1	.500	0	0--	-	2.63	4.87
2005	Kane	A	24	23	0	0	128.2	561	139	82	68	16	5	10	9	41	0	84	7	1	5	11	.313	0	0--	-	4.68	4.76
2006	Stcktn	A+	23	23	0	0	117.2	529	160	75	69	9	1	5	4	37	0	96	5	1	8	9	.471	0	0--	-	5.94	5.28
2007	Stcktn	A+	15	15	0	0	83.0	356	83	59	53	13	1	3	5	22	0	71	6	1	4	7	.364	0	0--	-	4.12	5.75
2007	Mdland	AA	5	5	0	0	25.2	118	34	27	26	10	1	2	0	10	0	16	1	0	0	4	.000	0	0--	-	8.33	9.12
2008	Mdland	AA	25	22	0	0	130.0	590	165	86	75	12	3	8	2	44	0	94	3	1	9	8	.529	0	0--	-	5.37	5.19
2009	Scrmto	AAA	32	2	0	8	46.2	206	57	22	22	3	4	0	2	15	2	41	0	1	7	1	.875	0	2--	-	4.94	4.24
2009	Portlnd	AAA	3	0	0	1	3.0	12	3	1	1	0	1	0	0	1	0	0	0	0	0	0	-	0	0--	-	3.35	3.00
2010	Portlnd	AAA	17	0	0	3	20.2	77	12	2	2	1	1	0	0	5	0	23	1	0	1	0	1.000	0	1--	-	1.34	0.87
2009	SD	NL	28	0	0	9	25.2	117	27	14	11	3	2	1	1	11	1	19	4	0	2	1	.667	0	0-0	6	4.54	3.86
2010	SD	NL	54	0	0	15	59.0	253	64	21	19	1	1	1	1	19	5	44	2	1	3	1	.750	0	0-2	9	3.61	2.90
	2 ML YEARS		82	0	0	24	84.2	370	91	35	30	4	3	2	2	30	6	63	6	1	5	2	.714	0	0-2	15	3.89	3.19

Rickie Weeks

Bats: R **Throws:** R **Pos:** 2B-159; DH-1 **Ht:** 5'10" **Wt:** 213 **Born:** 9/13/1982 **Age:** 28

Year	Team	Lg	G	AB	H	2B	3B	HR	(Hm	Rd)	TB	R	RBI	RC	TBB	IBB	SO	HBP	SH	SF	SB	CS	SB%	GDP	Avg	OBP	Slg
2003	Mil	NL	7	12	2	1	0	0	(0	0)	3	1	0	0	1	0	6	1	0	0	0	0	-	0	.167	.286	.250
2005	Mil	NL	96	360	86	13	2	13	(8	5)	142	56	42	49	40	2	96	11	2	1	15	2	.88	11	.239	.333	.394
2006	Mil	NL	95	359	100	15	3	8	(6	2)	145	73	34	53	30	1	92	19	2	3	19	5	.79	6	.279	.363	.404
2007	Mil	NL	118	409	96	21	6	16	(5	11)	177	87	36	65	78	5	116	14	3	2	25	2	.93	3	.235	.374	.433
2008	Mil	NL	129	475	111	22	7	14	(3	11)	189	89	46	67	66	0	115	14	1	4	19	5	.79	5	.234	.342	.398
2009	Mil	NL	37	147	40	5	2	9	(7	2)	76	28	24	27	12	0	39	3	0	0	2	2	.50	1	.272	.340	.517
2010	Mil	NL	160	651	175	32	4	29	(16	13)	302	112	83	110	76	0	184	25	0	2	11	4	.73	5	.269	.366	.464
	Postseason		3	4	0	0	0	0	(0	0)	0	0	0	0	0	0	2	0	0	0	0	0	-	0	.000	.000	.000
	7 ML YEARS		642	2413	610	109	24	89	(45	44)	1034	446	265	371	303	8	648	87	8	12	91	20	.82	31	.253	.355	.429

Robbie Weinhardt

Pitches: R **Bats:** R **Pos:** RP-28 **Ht:** 6'2" **Wt:** 205 **Born:** 12/8/1985 **Age:** 25

Year	Team	Lg	G	GS	CG	GF	IP	BFP	H	R	ER	HR	SH	SF	HB	TBB	IBB	SO	WP	Bk	W	L	Pct	Sh	Sv-Op	Hld	ERC	ERA
2008	Tigers	R	3	0	0	0	5.2	26	6	3	0	0	0	1	0	2	0	4	0	0	0	0	-	0	0--	-	3.26	0.00
2008	Lkland	A+	21	0	0	10	35.1	139	19	11	8	1	6	3	2	11	2	44	3	0	3	1	.750	0	4--	-	1.31	2.04
2009	Lkland	A+	22	0	0	12	31.2	131	24	5	3	2	0	0	1	10	0	40	2	0	1	1	.500	0	3--	-	2.31	0.85
2009	Erie	AA	20	0	0	9	31.1	141	28	9	8	0	1	0	4	16	1	32	2	0	1	0	.000	0	2--	-	3.54	2.30
2010	Toledo	AAA	24	0	0	12	34.1	131	26	7	6	0	0	0	1	7	0	25	0	0	1	1	.500	0	1--	-	1.72	1.57
2010	Conn	A-	3	0	0	1	4.0	18	2	1	1	0	0	0	1	2	0	5	0	0	1	0	1.000	0	0--	-	1.89	2.25
2010	Det	AL	28	0	0	4	29.1	135	40	23	20	2	1	1	3	8	2	21	1	0	2	2	.500	0	0-2	5	5.77	6.14

Todd Wellemeyer

Pitches: R **Bats:** R **Pos:** SP-11; RP-2 **Ht:** 6'3" **Wt:** 216 **Born:** 8/30/1978 **Age:** 32

Year	Team	Lg	G	GS	CG	GF	IP	BFP	H	R	ER	HR	SH	SF	HB	TBB	IBB	SO	WP	Bk	W	L	Pct	Sh	Sv-Op	Hld	ERC	ERA
2010	Giants*	R	1	1	0	0	2.2	12	3	2	2	1	0	0	1	1	0	3	1	0	0	0	-	0	0--	-	6.59	6.75
2010	Fresno*	AAA	3	3	0	0	16.0	65	9	5	4	1	1	2	1	12	0	12	0	0	1	0	1.000	0	0--	-	3.20	2.25
2003	ChC	NL	15	0	0	8	27.2	122	25	22	20	5	1	0	0	19	1	30	0	0	1	1	.500	0	1-1	1	5.33	6.51
2004	ChC	NL	20	0	0	7	24.1	119	27	16	16	1	3	2	0	20	2	30	0	1	2	1	.667	0	0-0	0	5.67	5.92
2005	ChC	NL	22	0	0	6	32.1	146	32	23	22	7	2	1	0	22	1	32	3	0	2	1	.667	0	1-1	3	6.09	6.12
2006	2 Tms		46	0	0	10	78.1	345	68	38	36	6	3	6	4	50	3	54	9	0	1	4	.200	0	1-1	3	4.28	4.14
2007	2 Tms		32	11	0	7	79.1	353	77	50	40	11	3	4	3	40	2	60	4	0	3	3	.500	0	0-0	2	4.68	4.54
2008	StL	NL	32	32	0	0	191.2	807	178	84	79	25	6	6	7	62	1	134	7	1	13	9	.591	0	0-0	0	3.72	3.71
2009	StL	NL	28	21	0	4	122.1	561	160	88	80	19	9	4	3	57	2	78	2	0	7	10	.412	0	0-0	0	6.87	5.89
2010	SF	NL	13	11	0	0	58.2	265	57	37	37	12	4	3	3	35	1	41	3	0	3	5	.375	0	0-0	0	5.69	5.68
06	Fla	NL	18	0	0	6	21.1	97	20	13	13	1	1	3	2	13	1	17	2	0	0	2	.000	0	0-0	0	4.41	5.48
06	KC	AL	28	0	0	4	57.0	248	48	25	23	5	2	3	2	37	2	37	7	0	1	2	.333	0	1-1	3	4.23	3.63
07	KC	AL	12	0	0	5	15.2	84	25	19	18	4	1	0	1	11	2	9	2	0	0	1	.000	0	0-0	1	10.40	10.34
07	StL	NL	20	11	0	2	63.2	269	52	31	22	7	2	4	2	29	0	51	2	0	3	2	.600	0	0-0	1	3.48	3.11
	8 ML YEARS		208	75	0	42	614.2	2718	624	358	330	86	31	26	20	305	13	459	28	2	32	34	.485	0	3-3	9	4.97	4.83

Casper Wells

Bats: R **Throws:** R **Pos:** RF-29; LF-8; PH-7; CF-4   **Ht:** 6'2" **Wt:** 210 **Born:** 11/23/1984 **Age:** 26

Year	Team	Lg	G	AB	H	2B	3B	HR	(Hm	Rd)	TB	R	RBI	RC	TBB	IBB	SO	HBP	SH	SF	SB	CS	SB%	GDP	Avg	OBP	Slg
2005	Tigers	R	45	141	31	9	5	5	(-	-)	65	25	20	24	18	0	59	8	0	0	6	0	1.00	3	.220	.341	.461
2006	Lkland	A+	11	33	5	1	0	1	(-	-)	9	4	4	3	4	0	9	3	1	0	1	0	1.00	1	.152	.300	.273
2006	Oneont	A-	35	105	24	8	0	1	(-	-)	35	19	14	11	9	0	27	3	1	1	1	1	.50	1	.229	.305	.333
2007	Lkland	A+	2	2	1	1	0	0	(-	-)	2	0	0	0	0	0	1	0	0	0	0	0	-	0	.500	.500	1.000
2007	Oneont	A-	67	260	69	18	11	9	(-	-)	136	46	47	43	18	0	64	6	0	4	8	7	.53	3	.265	.323	.523
2008	WMich	A	50	179	43	7	0	10	(-	-)	80	30	26	31	22	0	39	9	0	1	17	5	.77	2	.240	.351	.447
2008	Erie	AA	75	270	78	18	6	17	(-	-)	159	60	53	59	30	0	66	9	2	2	8	3	.73	8	.289	.376	.589
2009	Erie	AA	86	311	81	18	4	15	(-	-)	152	52	41	56	43	3	103	11	1	1	8	8	.50	1	.260	.369	.489
2010	Toledo	AAA	103	387	90	22	6	21	(-	-)	187	56	46	57	34	0	111	9	0	0	7	8	.47	3	.233	.309	.483
2010	Det	AL	36	93	30	6	1	4	(1	3)	50	14	17	16	6	0	19	0	0	0	0	1	.00	2	.323	.364	.538

Randy Wells

Pitches: R **Bats:** R **Pos:** SP-32   **Ht:** 6'5" **Wt:** 230 **Born:** 8/28/1982 **Age:** 28

			HOW MUCH HE PITCHED					WHAT HE GAVE UP											THE RESULTS						
Year	Team	Lg	G	GS	CG	GF	IP	BFP	H	R	ER	HR	SH	SF	HB	TBB	IBB	SO	WP	Bk	W	L	Pct	Sh	Sv-Op	Hld	ERC	ERA
2008	2 Tms		4	0	0	2	5.1	18	0	0	0	0	0	0	0	3	0	1	0	0	0	0	-	0	0-0	0	0.35	0.00
2009	ChC	NL	27	27	0	0	165.1	694	165	67	56	14	7	4	6	46	4	104	3	1	12	10	.545	0	0-0	0	3.62	3.05
2010	ChC	NL	32	32	0	0	194.1	843	209	97	92	19	8	6	6	63	5	144	2	0	8	14	.364	0	0-0	0	4.26	4.26
08	Tor	AL	1	0	0	1	1.0	4	0	0	0	0	0	0	0	1	0	0	0	0	0	0	-	0	0-0	0	0.95	0.00
08	ChC	NL	3	0	0	1	4.1	14	0	0	0	0	0	0	0	2	0	1	0	0	0	0	-	0	0-0	0	0.25	0.00
	3 ML YEARS		63	59	0	2	365.0	1555	374	164	148	33	15	4	12	112	9	249	5	1	20	24	.455	0	0-0	0	3.88	3.65

Vernon Wells

Bats: R **Throws:** R **Pos:** CF-151; DH-4; PH-2   **Ht:** 6'1" **Wt:** 230 **Born:** 12/8/1978 **Age:** 32

Year	Team	Lg	G	AB	H	2B	3B	HR	(Hm	Rd)	TB	R	RBI	RC	TBB	IBB	SO	HBP	SH	SF	SB	CS	SB%	GDP	Avg	OBP	Slg
1999	Tor	AL	24	88	23	5	0	1	(1	0)	31	8	8	7	4	0	18	0	0	0	1	1	.50	6	.261	.293	.352
2000	Tor	AL	3	2	0	0	0	0	(0	0)	0	0	0	0	0	0	0	0	0	0	0	0	-	0	.000	.000	.000
2001	Tor	AL	30	96	30	8	0	1	(0	1)	41	14	6	16	5	0	15	1	0	1	5	0	1.00	6	.313	.350	.427
2002	Tor	AL	159	608	167	34	4	23	(10	13)	278	87	100	88	27	0	85	3	2	8	9	4	.69	15	.275	.305	.457
2003	Tor	AL	161	678	215	49	5	33	(13	20)	373	110	117	124	42	2	80	7	0	8	4	1	.80	21	.317	.359	.550
2004	Tor	AL	134	536	146	34	2	23	(14	9)	253	82	67	72	51	2	83	2	0	1	9	2	.82	17	.272	.337	.472
2005	Tor	AL	156	620	167	30	5	28	(14	14)	287	78	97	96	47	3	86	3	0	8	8	3	.73	13	.269	.320	.463
2006	Tor	AL	154	611	185	40	5	32	(24	8)	331	91	106	107	54	0	90	3	0	9	17	4	.81	13	.303	.357	.542
2007	Tor	AL	149	584	143	36	4	16	(8	8)	235	85	80	74	49	4	89	3	0	6	10	4	.71	9	.245	.304	.402
2008	Tor	AL	108	427	128	22	1	20	(11	9)	212	63	78	68	29	5	46	3	0	7	4	2	.67	16	.300	.343	.496
2009	Tor	AL	158	630	164	37	3	15	(8	7)	252	84	66	65	48	2	86	1	0	5	17	4	.81	18	.260	.311	.400
2010	Tor	AL	157	590	161	44	3	31	(20	11)	304	79	88	92	50	5	84	3	0	3	6	4	.60	18	.273	.331	.515
	12 ML YEARS		1393	5470	1529	339	30	223	(124	99)	2597	789	813	809	406	23	762	29	2	56	90	29	.76	146	.280	.329	.475

Jayson Werth

Bats: R **Throws:** R **Pos:** RF-135; CF-21; PH-4   **Ht:** 6'5" **Wt:** 218 **Born:** 5/20/1979 **Age:** 32

Year	Team	Lg	G	AB	H	2B	3B	HR	(Hm	Rd)	TB	R	RBI	RC	TBB	IBB	SO	HBP	SH	SF	SB	CS	SB%	GDP	Avg	OBP	Slg
2002	Tor	AL	15	46	12	2	1	0	(0	0)	16	4	6	5	6	0	11	0	0	1	1	0	1.00	4	.261	.340	.348
2003	Tor	AL	26	48	10	4	0	2	(0	2)	20	7	10	6	3	0	22	0	0	0	1	0	1.00	1	.208	.255	.417
2004	LAD	NL	89	290	76	11	3	16	(11	5)	141	56	47	47	30	0	85	4	1	1	4	1	.80	1	.262	.338	.486
2005	LAD	NL	102	337	79	22	2	7	(1	6)	126	46	43	44	48	2	114	6	1	3	11	2	.85	10	.234	.338	.374
2007	Phi	NL	94	255	76	11	3	8	(1	7)	117	43	49	57	44	1	73	2	2	1	7	1	.88	5	.298	.404	.459
2008	Phi	NL	134	418	114	16	3	24	(11	13)	208	73	67	74	57	1	119	4	0	3	20	1	.95	2	.273	.363	.498
2009	Phi	NL	159	571	153	26	1	36	(21	15)	289	98	99	107	91	8	156	8	0	6	20	3	.87	11	.268	.373	.506
2010	Phi	NL	156	554	164	46	3	27	(18	9)	295	106	85	91	82	6	147	7	0	9	13	3	.81	11	.296	.388	.532
	Postseason		35	123	35	8	2	11	(8	3)	80	25	20	24	22	2	40	0	0	0	4	0	1.00	3	.285	.393	.650
	8 ML YEARS		775	2519	684	138	15	120	(63	57)	1212	433	406	431	361	18	727	31	4	24	77	11	.88	39	.272	.367	.481

Sean West

Pitches: L **Bats:** R **Pos:** SP-2   **Ht:** 6'8" **Wt:** 258 **Born:** 6/15/1986 **Age:** 25

			HOW MUCH HE PITCHED					WHAT HE GAVE UP											THE RESULTS						
Year	Team	Lg	G	GS	CG	GF	IP	BFP	H	R	ER	HR	SH	SF	HB	TBB	IBB	SO	WP	Bk	W	L	Pct	Sh	Sv-Op	Hld	ERC	ERA
2005	Mrlns	R	9	8	0	1	38.1	157	33	12	10	2	0	3	3	7	0	40	2	1	2	3	.400	0	0- -	-	2.48	2.35
2005	Jmstwn	A-	3	3	0	0	11.0	52	17	7	7	1	0	0	0	5	0	14	1	0	0	2	.000	0	0- -	-	7.83	5.73
2006	Grnsbr	A	21	21	0	0	120.1	509	115	55	50	13	4	2	12	40	0	102	0	0	8	5	.615	0	0- -	-	4.09	3.74
2008	Jupiter	A+	21	20	0	1	100.2	426	79	33	27	3	4	3	6	60	1	92	13	0	6	5	.545	0	0- -	-	3.46	2.41
2009	Jaxnvl	AA	12	11	0	0	64.0	287	68	37	34	12	0	2	2	28	2	65	1	0	7	3	.700	0	0- -	-	5.25	4.78
2010	NewOr	AAA	11	11	2	0	57.2	249	60	28	20	4	4	5	0	19	1	46	1	0	4	3	.571	1	0- -	-	3.74	3.12
2009	Fla	NL	20	20	0	0	103.1	467	115	62	55	11	5	4	3	44	0	70	3	0	8	6	.571	0	0-0	0	4.93	4.79
2010	Fla	NL	2	2	0	0	9.1	47	15	9	8	2	3	0	0	4	1	8	0	0	0	2	.000	0	0-0	0	8.53	7.71
	2 ML YEARS		22	22	0	0	112.2	514	130	71	63	13	8	4	3	48	1	78	3	0	8	8	.500	0	0-0	0	5.21	5.03

Jake Westbrook

Pitches: R Bats: R Pos: SP-33   Ht: 6'3" Wt: 215 Born: 9/29/1977 Age: 33

Year	Team	Lg	G	GS	CG	GF	IP	BFP	H	R	ER	HR	SH	SF	HB	TBB	IBB	SO	WP	Bk	W	L	Pct	Sh	Sv-Op	Hld	ERC	ERA
2000	NYY	AL	3	2	0	1	6.2	38	15	10	10	1	0	2	0	4	1	1	0	0	0	2	.000	0	0-0	0	13.53	13.50
2001	Cle	AL	23	6	0	3	64.2	290	79	43	42	6	1	5	4	22	4	48	4	0	4	4	.500	0	0-0	5	5.25	5.85
2002	Cle	AL	11	4	0	1	41.2	185	50	30	27	6	2	1	1	12	1	20	1	0	1	3	.250	0	0-2	1	5.12	5.83
2003	Cle	AL	34	22	1	4	133.0	580	142	70	64	9	4	3	12	56	1	58	3	0	7	10	.412	0	0-0	1	4.78	4.33
2004	Cle	AL	33	30	5	2	215.2	895	208	95	81	19	6	6	5	61	3	116	4	1	14	9	.609	1	0-0	0	3.45	3.38
2005	Cle	AL	34	34	2	0	210.2	895	218	121	105	19	4	5	7	56	3	119	3	0	15	15	.500	0	0-0	0	3.78	4.49
2006	Cle	AL	32	32	3	0	211.1	904	247	106	98	15	5	4	4	55	4	109	5	0	15	10	.600	2	0-0	0	4.39	4.17
2007	Cle	AL	25	25	0	0	152.0	648	159	78	73	13	6	4	6	55	5	93	3	0	6	9	.400	0	0-0	0	4.28	4.32
2008	Cle	AL	5	5	1	0	34.2	139	33	13	12	5	0	2	1	7	0	19	1	0	1	2	.333	0	0-0	0	3.54	3.12
2010	2 Tms		33	33	1	0	202.2	860	203	99	95	20	5	3	8	68	4	128	8	0	10	11	.476	0	0-0	0	3.99	4.22
10	Cle	AL	21	21	1	0	127.2	543	133	68	66	15	3	3	6	44	4	73	6	0	6	7	.462	0	0-0	0	4.45	4.65
10	StL	NL	12	12	0	0	75.0	317	70	31	29	5	2	0	2	24	0	55	2	0	4	4	.500	0	0-0	0	3.25	3.48
	Postseason		3	3	0	0	17.2	74	25	11	11	2	0	1	0	4	1	8	0	0	1	2	.333	0	0-0	0	6.33	5.60
10 ML YEARS			233	193	13	11	1273.0	5434	1354	665	607	113	34	34	48	396	26	711	32	1	73	75	.493	3	0-2	7	4.17	4.29

Dan Wheeler

Pitches: R Bats: R Pos: RP-64   Ht: 6'3" Wt: 220 Born: 12/10/1977 Age: 33

Year	Team	Lg	G	GS	CG	GF	IP	BFP	H	R	ER	HR	SH	SF	HB	TBB	IBB	SO	WP	Bk	W	L	Pct	Sh	Sv-Op	Hld	ERC	ERA
1999	TB	AL	6	6	0	0	30.2	136	35	20	20	7	1	0	0	13	1	32	1	0	1	4	.000	0	0-0	0	5.96	5.87
2000	TB	AL	11	2	0	6	23.0	111	29	14	14	2	1	1	2	11	2	17	2	0	1	1	.500	0	0-1	1	5.87	5.48
2001	TB	AL	13	0	0	3	17.2	87	30	17	17	3	0	2	0	5	0	12	1	1	1	0	1.000	0	0-0	0	8.38	8.66
2003	NYM	NL	35	0	0	10	51.0	215	49	23	21	6	0	3	1	17	4	35	1	0	1	3	.250	0	2-3	0	3.69	3.71
2004	2 Tms	NL	46	1	0	11	65.0	287	76	33	31	10	2	1	1	20	2	55	4	1	3	1	.750	0	0-0	5	5.05	4.29
2005	Hou	NL	71	0	0	20	73.1	288	53	18	18	7	5	1	3	19	3	69	0	0	2	3	.400	0	3-5	17	2.22	2.21
2006	Hou	NL	75	0	0	25	71.1	295	58	22	20	5	3	3	2	24	8	68	0	0	3	5	.375	0	9-12	24	2.57	2.52
2007	2 Tms		70	0	0	29	74.2	321	74	48	44	11	3	3	3	23	3	82	2	0	1	9	.100	0	11-18	18	4.04	5.30
2008	TB	AL	70	0	0	26	66.1	264	44	25	23	10	0	2	0	22	4	53	1	0	5	6	.455	0	13-18	26	2.28	3.12
2009	TB	AL	69	0	0	20	57.2	219	41	22	21	11	3	1	0	9	2	45	3	0	4	5	.444	0	2-6	16	2.17	3.28
2010	TB	AL	64	0	0	13	48.1	195	36	20	18	7	1	3	1	16	2	46	3	0	2	4	.333	0	3-6	9	2.77	3.35
04	NYM	NL	32	1	0	7	50.2	232	65	29	27	9	2	1	0	17	2	46	4	1	3	1	.750	0	0-0	3	5.91	4.80
04	Hou	NL	14	0	0	4	14.1	55	11	4	4	1	0	0	1	3	0	9	0	0	0	0	-	0	0-0	2	2.35	2.51
07	Hou	NL	45	0	0	25	49.2	205	46	28	28	8	1	1	2	13	1	56	1	0	1	4	.200	0	11-15	6	3.69	5.07
07	TB	AL	25	0	0	4	25.0	116	28	20	16	3	2	2	1	10	2	26	1	0	0	5	.000	0	0-3	12	4.72	5.76
	Postseason		20	0	0	5	25.2	108	21	10	10	3	1	0	3	8	1	26	1	0	1	0	1.000	0	1-3	5	3.22	3.51
11 ML YEARS			530	9	0	163	579.0	2418	525	262	247	79	19	20	13	179	31	514	18	2	23	41	.359	0	43-69	116	3.45	3.84

Sean White

Pitches: R Bats: R Pos: RP-38   Ht: 6'4" Wt: 215 Born: 4/25/1981 Age: 30

Year	Team	Lg	G	GS	CG	GF	IP	BFP	H	R	ER	HR	SH	SF	HB	TBB	IBB	SO	WP	Bk	W	L	Pct	Sh	Sv-Op	Hld	ERC	ERA
2010	Tacom*	AAA	10	0	0	4	13.0	54	7	1	0	0	0	0	2	8	0	10	1	1	1	0	1.000	0	0--	-	2.36	0.00
2007	Sea	AL	15	0	0	4	35.1	165	35	24	22	2	0	3	8	20	0	16	5	1	1	1	.500	0	0-0	0	5.24	5.60
2009	Sea	AL	52	0	0	15	64.1	261	50	23	20	3	2	4	2	20	1	28	3	0	3	2	.600	0	1-3	15	2.33	2.80
2010	Sea	AL	38	0	0	13	34.1	150	45	20	20	4	1	4	0	11	4	15	0	1	0	1	.000	0	0-3	5	5.70	5.24
3 ML YEARS			105	0	0	32	134.0	576	130	67	62	9	3	11	10	51	5	59	8	2	4	4	.500	0	1-6	20	3.86	4.16

Eli Whiteside

Bats: R Throws: R Pos: C-55; PR-9   Ht: 6'2" Wt: 205 Born: 10/22/1979 Age: 31

Year	Team	Lg	G	AB	H	2B	3B	HR	(Hm	Rd)	TB	R	RBI	RC	TBB	IBB	SO	HBP	SH	SF	SB	CS	SB%	GDP	Avg	OBP	Slg
2005	Bal	AL	9	12	3	0	0	0	(0	0)	3	1	1	0	0	0	2	0	0	0	0	0	-	1	.250	.250	.250
2009	SF	NL	49	127	29	6	1	2	(1	1)	43	15	13	11	4	1	30	3	0	0	0	0	-	4	.228	.269	.339
2010	SF	NL	56	126	30	6	1	4	(3	1)	50	19	10	9	8	0	35	3	3	0	1	2	.33	4	.238	.299	.397
3 ML YEARS			114	265	62	12	2	6	(4	2)	96	35	24	20	12	1	67	6	3	0	1	2	.33	9	.234	.283	.362

Matt Wieters

Bats: B Throws: R Pos: C-126; PH-7; DH-2   WEE-ters   Ht: 6'5" Wt: 230 Born: 5/21/1986 Age: 25

Year	Team	Lg	G	AB	H	2B	3B	HR	(Hm	Rd)	TB	R	RBI	RC	TBB	IBB	SO	HBP	SH	SF	SB	CS	SB%	GDP	Avg	OBP	Slg
2008	Frdrck	A+	69	229	79	8	0	15	(-	-)	132	48	40	58	44	5	47	2	1	4	1	2	.33	6	.345	.448	.576
2008	Bowie	AA	61	208	76	14	2	12	(-	-)	130	41	51	58	38	3	29	1	0	3	1	0	1.00	9	.365	.460	.625
2009	Norfolk	AAA	39	141	43	9	2	5	(-	-)	71	25	30	28	20	1	30	0	0	2	0	0	-	6	.305	.387	.504
2009	Bal	AL	96	354	102	15	1	9	(5	4)	146	35	43	43	28	2	86	1	0	2	0	0	-	11	.288	.340	.412
2010	Bal	AL	130	446	111	22	1	11	(3	8)	168	37	55	47	47	7	94	2	0	7	0	1	.00	13	.249	.319	.377
2 ML YEARS			226	800	213	37	2	20	(8	12)	314	72	98	90	75	9	180	3	0	9	0	1	.00	24	.266	.328	.393

Ty Wigginton

Bats: R **Throws:** R **Pos:** 1B-99; 2B-40; 3B-22; DH-7; PH-3 **Ht:** 6'0" **Wt:** 230 **Born:** 10/11/1977 **Age:** 33

										BATTING											BASERUNNING				AVERAGES		
Year	Team	Lg	G	AB	H	2B	3B	HR	(Hm	Rd)	TB	R	RBI	RC	TBB	IBB	SO	HBP	SH	SF	SB	CS	SB%	GDP	Avg	OBP	Slg
2002	NYM	NL	46	116	35	8	0	6	(4	2)	61	18	18	15	8	0	19	2	0	1	2	1	.67	4	.302	.354	.526
2003	NYM	NL	156	573	146	36	6	11	(4	7)	227	73	71	76	46	2	124	9	1	4	12	2	.86	15	.255	.318	.396
2004	2 Tms	NL	144	494	129	30	2	17	(6	11)	214	63	66	59	45	6	82	2	1	3	7	1	.88	15	.261	.324	.433
2005	Pit	NL	57	155	40	9	1	7	(1	6)	72	20	25	22	14	0	30	1	1	0	0	1	.00	3	.258	.324	.465
2006	TB	AL	122	444	122	25	1	24	(18	6)	221	55	79	69	32	3	97	6	1	3	4	3	.57	11	.275	.330	.498
2007	2 Tms		148	547	152	33	0	22	(15	7)	251	71	67	64	41	0	113	8	0	8	3	4	.43	16	.278	.333	.459
2008	Hou	NL	111	386	110	22	1	23	(15	8)	203	50	58	57	32	1	69	8	0	3	4	6	.40	9	.285	.350	.526
2009	Bal	AL	122	410	112	19	0	11	(9	2)	164	44	41	41	23	1	57	2	0	1	1	2	.33	16	.273	.314	.400
2010	Bal	AL	154	581	144	29	1	22	(12	10)	241	63	76	62	50	3	116	8	1	9	0	1	.00	23	.248	.312	.415
04	NYM	NL	86	312	89	23	2	12	(5	7)	152	46	42	38	23	4	48	1	1	2	6	1	.86	11	.285	.334	.487
04	Pit	NL	58	182	40	7	0	5	(1	4)	62	17	24	21	22	2	34	1	0	1	1	0	1.00	4	.220	.306	.341
07	TB	AL	98	378	104	21	0	16	(9	7)	173	47	49	42	28	0	73	5	0	6	1	4	.20	8	.275	.329	.458
07	Hou	NL	50	169	48	12	0	6	(6	0)	78	24	18	22	13	0	40	3	0	2	2	0	1.00	8	.284	.342	.462
9 ML YEARS			1060	3706	990	211	12	143	(84	59)	1654	457	501	465	291	16	707	46	5	32	33	21	.61	112	.267	.326	.446

Randy Williams

Pitches: L **Bats:** L **Pos:** RP-27 **Ht:** 6'4" **Wt:** 200 **Born:** 9/18/1975 **Age:** 35

			HOW MUCH HE PITCHED						WHAT HE GAVE UP										THE RESULTS						
Year	Team	Lg	G	GS	CG	GF	IP	BFP	H	R	ER	HR	SH	SF	HB	TBB	IBB	SO	WP	Bk	W	L	Pct	Sh	Sv-Op	Hld	ERC	ERA
2010	Charltt*	AAA	21	1	0	8	32.0	128	26	10	9	1	0	0	0	9	0	22	2	0	1	0	1.000	0	2--	1	2.25	2.53
2004	Sea	AL	6	0	0	1	4.2	22	3	3	3	0	0	0	0	6	0	4	0	0	0	0	-	0	0-0	1	4.73	5.79
2005	2 Tms	NL	32	0	0	6	26.1	125	33	21	20	5	0	1	1	13	3	21	0	0	3	1	.750	0	0-2	4	6.54	6.84
2009	CWS	AL	25	0	0	6	17.2	80	13	9	9	2	1	1	3	12	4	22	0	0	0	1	.000	0	0-0	3	4.00	4.58
2010	CWS	AL	27	0	0	2	25.0	132	37	17	15	2	0	1	3	21	6	22	0	0	0	1	.000	0	0-1	1	8.81	5.40
05	SD	NL	2	0	0	0	4.1	25	7	6	6	1	0	0	1	4	0	2	0	0	1	0	1.000	0	0-0	0	12.46	12.46
05	Col	NL	30	0	0	6	22.0	100	26	15	14	4	0	1	0	9	3	19	0	0	2	1	.667	0	0-2	4	5.48	5.73
4 ML YEARS			90	0	0	15	73.2	359	86	50	47	9	1	3	7	52	13	69	0	0	3	3	.500	0	0-3	9	6.54	5.74

Josh Willingham

Bats: R **Throws:** R **Pos:** LF-108; PH-7, DH-2 **Ht:** 6'2" **Wt:** 215 **Born:** 2/17/1979 **Age:** 32

										BATTING											BASERUNNING				AVERAGES		
Year	Team	Lg	G	AB	H	2B	3B	HR	(Hm	Rd)	TB	R	RBI	RC	TBB	IBB	SO	HBP	SH	SF	SB	CS	SB%	GDP	Avg	OBP	Slg
2004	Fla	NL	12	25	5	0	0	1	(0	1)	8	2	1	1	4	0	8	0	0	0	0	0	-	1	.200	.310	.320
2005	Fla	NL	16	23	7	1	0	0	(0	0)	8	3	4	3	2	0	5	2	1	0	0	0	-	0	.304	.407	.348
2006	Fla	NL	142	502	139	28	2	26	(11	15)	249	62	74	74	54	2	109	11	0	6	2	0	1.00	13	.277	.356	.496
2007	Fla	NL	144	521	138	32	4	21	(10	11)	241	75	89	94	66	1	122	16	0	1	8	1	.89	11	.265	.364	.463
2008	Fla	NL	102	351	89	21	5	15	(6	9)	165	54	51	56	48	2	82	14	1	2	3	2	.60	7	.254	.364	.470
2009	Was	NL	133	427	111	29	0	24	(7	17)	212	70	61	61	61	2	104	12	0	2	4	3	.57	11	.260	.367	.496
2010	Was	NL	114	370	99	19	2	16	(11	5)	170	54	56	65	67	3	85	9	0	4	8	0	1.00	8	.268	.389	.459
7 ML YEARS			663	2219	588	130	13	103	(45	58)	1053	320	336	354	302	10	515	64	2	15	25	6	.81	52	.265	.367	.475

Dontrelle Willis

Pitches: L **Bats:** L **Pos:** SP-13; RP-2 **Ht:** 6'4" **Wt:** 225 **Born:** 1/12/1982 **Age:** 29

			HOW MUCH HE PITCHED						WHAT HE GAVE UP										THE RESULTS						
Year	Team	Lg	G	GS	CG	GF	IP	BFP	H	R	ER	HR	SH	SF	HB	TBB	IBB	SO	WP	Bk	W	L	Pct	Sh	Sv-Op	Hld	ERC	FRA
2010	Giants*	R	3	0	0	0	2.0	12	4	2	2	1	0	0	1	1	0	1	0	0	0	1	.000	0	0--	-	17.51	9.00
2010	Fresno*	AAA	5	0	0	1	5.1	25	2	3	3	1	0	0	3	4	0	6	1	0	0	0	-	0	0--	-	4.66	5.06
2003	Fla	NL	27	27	2	0	160.2	668	148	61	59	13	3	1	3	58	0	142	7	1	14	6	.700	2	0-0	0	3.49	3.30
2004	Fla	NL	32	32	2	0	197.0	848	210	99	88	20	8	2	8	61	8	139	2	0	10	11	.476	0	0-0	0	4.21	4.02
2005	Fla	NL	34	34	7	0	236.1	960	213	79	69	11	14	5	8	55	3	170	2	1	22	10	.688	5	0-0	0	2.71	2.63
2006	Fla	NL	34	34	4	0	223.1	975	234	106	96	21	11	6	19	83	6	160	6	1	12	12	.500	1	0-0	0	4.53	3.87
2007	Fla	NL	35	35	0	0	205.1	942	241	131	118	29	15	7	14	87	4	146	9	1	10	15	.400	0	0-0	0	5.72	5.17
2008	Det	AL	8	7	0	0	24.0	122	18	25	25	4	0	0	1	35	1	18	5	1	0	2	.000	0	0-0	0	7.65	9.38
2009	Det	AL	7	7	0	0	33.2	160	37	28	28	4	2	3	1	28	0	17	1	0	1	4	.200	0	0-0	0	6.87	7.49
2010	2 Tms		15	13	0	0	65.2	316	72	41	41	6	2	4	5	56	0	47	8	2	2	3	.400	0	0-0	0	6.90	5.62
10	Det	AL	9	8	0	0	43.1	202	48	24	24	3	1	0	2	29	0	33	4	0	1	2	.333	0	0-0	0	5.80	4.98
10	Ari	NL	6	5	0	0	22.1	114	24	17	17	3	1	4	3	27	0	14	4	2	1	1	.500	0	0-0	0	9.16	6.85
Postseason			7	2	0	0	12.2	63	15	12	12	1	1	2	0	10	0	10	1	0	0	1	.000	0	0-0	1	6.43	8.53
8 ML YEARS			192	189	15	0	1146.0	4991	1173	570	524	108	55	28	59	463	22	839	40	7	71	63	.530	8	0-0	0	4.38	4.12

Reggie Willits

Bats: B **Throws:** R **Pos:** LF-44; CF-29; PR-17; PH-14; DH-9; RF-8 **Ht:** 5'11" **Wt:** 185 **Born:** 5/30/1981 **Age:** 30

										BATTING											BASERUNNING				AVERAGES		
Year	Team	Lg	G	AB	H	2B	3B	HR	(Hm	Rd)	TB	R	RBI	RC	TBB	IBB	SO	HBP	SH	SF	SB	CS	SB%	GDP	Avg	OBP	Slg
2010	RCuca*	A+	5	15	4	1	0	0	(-	-)	5	3	1	3	4	0	2	1	0	1	2	0	1.00	0	.267	.429	.333
2006	LAA	AL	28	45	12	1	0	0	(0	0)	13	12	2	6	11	0	10	0	2	0	4	3	.57	0	.267	.411	.289
2007	LAA	AL	136	430	126	20	1	0	(0	0)	148	74	34	68	69	2	83	3	11	5	27	8	.77	7	.293	.391	.344
2008	LAA	AL	82	108	21	4	0	0	(0	0)	25	21	7	10	21	0	26	0	5	2	2	1	.67	4	.194	.321	.231
2009	LAA	AL	49	80	17	2	0	0	(0	0)	19	16	6	3	5	0	17	0	6	1	5	1	.83	0	.213	.256	.238
2010	LAA	AL	97	159	41	7	0	0	(0	0)	48	23	8	19	19	0	26	1	3	0	2	4	.33	1	.258	.341	.302
Postseason			10	4	0	0	0	0	(0	0)	0	0	0	0	1	0	2	0	0	0	1	1	.50	0	.000	.200	.000
5 ML YEARS			392	822	217	34	1	0	(0	0)	253	146	57	106	125	2	162	4	27	8	40	17	.70	9	.264	.361	.308

Bobby Wilson

Bats: R Throws: R Pos: C-38; 1B-1; DH-1; PH-1

Ht: 6'0" Wt: 220 Born: 4/8/1983 Age: 28

Year	Team	Lg		G	AB	H	2B	3B	HR	(Hm	Rd)	TB	R	RBI	RC	TBB	IBB	SO	HBP	SH	SF	SB	CS	SB%	GDP	Avg	OBP	Slg
			BATTING																			BASERUNNING				AVERAGES		
2010	RCuca*	A+		2	6	2	0	0	0	(-	-)	2	0	0	0	0	0	2	0	0	0	0	0	-	0	.333	.333	.333
2010	Salt Lk*	AAA		3	6	3	0	0	1	(-	-)	6	2	3	3	4	0	1	0	1	1	0	0	-	1	.500	.636	1.000
2008	LAA	AL		7	6	1	0	0	0	(0	0)	1	0	1	0	1	0	3	0	0	0	0	0	-	1	.167	.286	.167
2009	LAA	AL		12	5	1	1	0	0	(0	0)	2	0	0	0	0	0	1	0	1	0	0	0	-	1	.200	.200	.400
2010	LAA	AL		40	96	22	6	0	4	(3	1)	40	12	15	12	8	0	23	0	2	0	0	0	-	3	.229	.288	.417
	3 ML YEARS			59	107	24	7	0	4	(3	1)	43	12	16	12	9	0	27	0	3	0	0	0	-	4	.224	.284	.402

Brian Wilson

Pitches: R Bats: R Pos: RP-70

Ht: 6'2" Wt: 199 Born: 3/16/1982 Age: 29

Year	Team	Lg		G	GS	CG	GF	IP	BFP	H	R	ER	HR	SH	SF	HB	TBB	IBB	SO	WP	Bk	W	L	Pct	Sh	Sv-Op	Hld	ERC	ERA
			HOW MUCH HE PITCHED							WHAT HE GAVE UP												THE RESULTS						
2006	SF	NL		31	0	0	9	30.0	141	32	19	18	1	1	4	1	21	2	23	0	0	2	3	.400	0	1-2	4	5.11	5.40
2007	SF	NL		24	0	0	9	23.2	93	16	6	6	1	0	0	1	7	0	18	0	0	1	2	.333	0	6-7	9	1.87	2.28
2008	SF	NL		63	0	0	54	62.1	274	62	32	32	7	2	5	3	28	4	67	2	0	3	2	.600	0	41-47	0	4.41	4.62
2009	SF	NL		68	0	0	60	72.1	303	60	27	22	3	4	2	1	27	4	83	4	0	5	6	.455	0	38-45	1	2.61	2.74
2010	SF	NL		70	0	0	59	74.2	311	62	16	15	3	1	0	1	26	5	93	0	0	3	3	.500	0	48-53	2	2.51	1.81
	5 ML YEARS			256	0	0	191	263.0	1122	232	100	93	15	8	11	7	109	15	284	6	0	14	16	.467	0	134-154	14	3.18	3.18

C.J. Wilson

Pitches: L Bats: L Pos: SP-33

Ht: 6'1" Wt: 210 Born: 11/18/1980 Age: 30

Year	Team	Lg		G	GS	CG	GF	IP	BFP	H	R	ER	HR	SH	SF	HB	TBB	IBB	SO	WP	Bk	W	L	Pct	Sh	Sv-Op	Hld	ERC	ERA
			HOW MUCH HE PITCHED							WHAT HE GAVE UP												THE RESULTS						
2005	Tex	AL		24	6	0	4	48.0	220	63	39	37	5	1	2	2	18	1	30	4	1	1	7	.125	0	1-1	4	6.03	6.94
2006	Tex	AL		44	0	0	12	44.1	191	39	23	20	7	1	0	5	18	1	43	0	0	2	4	.333	0	1-2	7	4.25	4.06
2007	Tex	AL		66	0	0	22	68.1	285	50	25	23	4	2	4	6	33	1	63	5	0	2	1	.667	0	12-14	15	3.01	3.03
2008	Tex	AL		50	0	0	41	46.1	214	49	35	31	8	1	1	2	27	2	41	3	0	2	2	.500	0	24-28	1	5.77	6.02
2009	Tex	AL		74	0	0	30	73.2	323	66	29	23	3	3	0	6	32	3	84	3	0	5	6	.455	0	14-18	19	3.40	2.81
2010	Tex	AL		33	33	3	0	204.0	850	161	83	76	10	1	3	10	93	0	170	7	1	15	8	.652	0	0-0	0	3.03	3.35
	6 ML YEARS			291	39	3	110	484.2	2083	428	234	210	37	9	10	31	221	8	431	22	2	27	28	.491	0	52-63	46	3.71	3.90

Jack Wilson

Bats: R Throws: R Pos: SS-60; DH-1; PR-1

Ht: 6'0" Wt: 200 Born: 12/29/1977 Age: 33

Year	Team	Lg		G	AB	H	2B	3B	HR	(Hm	Rd)	TB	R	RBI	RC	TBB	IBB	SO	HBP	SH	SF	SB	CS	SB%	GDP	Avg	OBP	Slg
			BATTING																			BASERUNNING				AVERAGES		
2010	WTenn*	AA		1	2	1	0	0	0	(-	-)	1	1	0	0	0	0	0	0	0	0	0	0	-	0	.500	.500	.500
2010	Tacom*	AAA		9	33	10	2	0	1	(-	-)	15	3	4	4	1	0	2	0	0	0	2	1	.67	0	.303	.324	.455
2001	Pit	NL		108	390	87	17	1	3	(0	3)	115	44	25	27	16	2	70	1	17	1	1	3	.25	4	.223	.255	.295
2002	Pit	NL		147	527	133	22	4	4	(2	2)	175	77	47	60	37	2	74	4	17	1	5	2	.71	7	.252	.306	.332
2003	Pit	NL		150	558	143	21	3	9	(2	7)	197	58	62	62	36	3	74	4	11	6	5	5	.50	11	.256	.303	.353
2004	Pit	NL		157	652	201	41	12	11	(7	4)	299	82	59	84	26	0	71	3	7	5	8	4	.67	15	.308	.335	.459
2005	Pit	NL		158	587	151	24	7	8	(3	5)	213	60	52	60	31	6	58	6	11	4	7	3	.70	11	.257	.299	.363
2006	Pit	NL		142	543	148	27	1	8	(5	3)	201	70	35	58	33	0	65	4	9	5	4	3	.57	15	.273	.316	.370
2007	Pit	NL		135	477	141	29	2	12	(3	9)	210	67	56	70	38	9	46	6	7	7	2	5	.29	15	.296	.350	.440
2008	Pit	NL		87	305	83	18	1	1	(1	0)	106	24	22	32	13	0	27	5	6	1	2	2	.50	6	.272	.312	.348
2009	2 Tms			106	373	95	23	1	5	(2	3)	135	37	39	40	21	2	48	0	5	3	3	1	.75	6	.255	.292	.362
2010	Sea	AL		61	193	48	11	1	0	(0	0)	61	17	14	16	7	0	35	3	5	3	1	2	.33	2	.249	.282	.316
	09 Pit	NL		75	266	71	18	1	4	(1	3)	103	26	31	31	15	2	31	0	3	2	2	1	.67	4	.267	.304	.387
	09 Sea	AL		31	107	24	5	0	1	(1	0)	32	11	8	9	6	0	17	0	2	1	1	0	1.00	2	.224	.263	.299
	10 ML YEARS			1251	4605	1230	233	33	61	(25	36)	1712	536	411	509	258	24	568	36	95	36	38	30	.56	85	.267	.309	.372

Josh Wilson

Bats: R Throws: R Pos: SS-98; 3B-4; 1B-3; 2B-2; PR-2; PH-1

Ht: 6'0" Wt: 175 Born: 3/26/1981 Age: 30

Year	Team	Lg		G	AB	H	2B	3B	HR	(Hm	Rd)	TB	R	RBI	RC	TBB	IBB	SO	HBP	SH	SF	SB	CS	SB%	GDP	Avg	OBP	Slg
			BATTING																			BASERUNNING				AVERAGES		
2010	Tacom*	AAA		20	81	27	11	1	0	(-	-)	40	7	11	13	0	0	15	2	1	2	0	1	.00	1	.333	.341	.494
2005	Fla	NL		11	10	1	1	0	0	(0	0)	2	2	0	0	0	0	4	1	0	0	0	0	-	0	.100	.182	.200
2007	2 Tms			105	282	67	15	3	2	(0	2)	94	28	24	24	17	0	57	5	3	3	6	2	.75	5	.238	.290	.333
2009	3 Tms			72	192	42	11	1	3	(1	2)	64	19	13	14	12	1	44	4	3	0	1	2	.33	4	.219	.279	.333
2010	Sea	AL		108	361	82	14	2	2	(1	1)	106	22	25	31	14	0	74	12	0	1	5	0	1.00	6	.227	.278	.294
	07 Was	NL		15	19	1	0	0	0	(0	0)	1	3	0	0	5	0	6	1	0	0	0	0	-	0	.053	.280	.053
	07 TB	AL		90	263	66	15	3	2	(0	2)	93	25	24	24	12	0	51	4	3	3	6	2	.75	5	.251	.291	.354
	09 Ari	NL		11	26	6	1	0	0	(0	0)	7	1	2	4	3	0	3	1	0	0	0	0	-	0	.231	.333	.269
	09 SD	NL		16	38	4	2	0	0	(0	0)	6	2	1	1	3	1	9	1	1	0	0	0	-	0	.105	.190	.158
	09 Sea	AL		45	128	32	8	1	3	(1	2)	51	16	10	9	6	0	32	2	2	0	1	2	.33	4	.250	.294	.398
	4 ML YEARS			296	845	192	41	6	7	(2	5)	266	71	62	69	43	1	179	22	6	4	12	4	.75	15	.227	.281	.315

Randy Winn

Bats: B **Throws:** R **Pos:** PH-51; RF-46; LF-25; CF-9; PR-3; DH-1   **Ht:** 6'2" **Wt:** 193 **Born:** 6/9/1974 **Age:** 37

Year	Team	Lg	G	AB	H	2B	3B	HR	(Hm	Rd)	TB	R	RBI	RC	TBB	IBB	SO	HBP	SH	SF	SB	CS	SB%	GDP	Avg	OBP	Slg
1998	TB	AL	109	338	94	9	9	1	(0	1)	124	51	17	44	29	0	69	1	11	0	26	12	.68	2	.278	.337	.367
1999	TB	AL	79	303	81	16	4	2	(2	0)	111	44	24	32	17	0	63	1	1	2	9	9	.50	3	.267	.307	.366
2000	TB	AL	51	159	40	5	0	1	(1	0)	48	28	16	18	26	0	25	2	2	1	6	7	.46	2	.252	.362	.302
2001	TB	AL	128	429	117	25	6	6	(3	3)	172	54	50	56	38	0	81	6	5	2	12	10	.55	10	.273	.339	.401
2002	TB	AL	152	607	181	39	9	14	(9	5)	280	87	75	104	55	3	109	6	1	5	27	8	.77	9	.298	.360	.461
2003	Sea	AL	157	600	177	37	4	11	(6	5)	255	103	75	96	41	0	108	8	6	5	23	5	.82	9	.295	.346	.425
2004	Sea	AL	157	626	179	34	6	14	(6	8)	267	84	81	91	53	1	98	8	9	7	21	7	.75	16	.286	.346	.427
2005	2 Tms		160	617	189	47	6	20	(9	11)	308	85	63	95	48	4	91	5	10	3	19	11	.63	11	.306	.360	.499
2006	SF	NL	149	573	150	34	5	11	(5	6)	227	82	56	69	48	3	63	7	3	4	10	8	.56	7	.262	.324	.396
2007	SF	NL	155	593	178	42	1	14	(4	10)	264	73	65	86	44	3	85	7	4	5	15	3	.83	12	.300	.353	.445
2008	SF	NL	155	598	183	38	2	10	(4	6)	255	84	64	90	59	6	88	0	1	9	25	2	.93	6	.306	.363	.426
2009	SF	NL	149	538	141	33	5	2	(1	1)	190	65	51	73	47	2	93	1	3	8	16	2	.89	6	.262	.318	.353
2010	2 Tms		116	205	49	8	2	4	(4	0)	73	23	25	20	21	1	37	1	1	2	6	0	1.00	5	.239	.307	.356
05	Sea	AL	102	386	106	25	1	6	(2	4)	151	46	37	52	37	3	53	4	6	3	12	6	.67	7	.275	.342	.391
05	SF	NL	58	231	83	22	5	14	(7	7)	157	39	26	43	11	1	38	1	4	0	7	5	.58	4	.359	.391	.680
10	NYY	AL	29	61	13	0	1	1	(1	0)	18	7	8	4	8	0	15	0	1	1	1	0	1.00	1	.213	.300	.295
10	StL	NL	87	144	36	8	1	3	(3	0)	55	16	17	16	13	1	22	1	1	3	5	0	1.00	4	.250	.311	.382
13 ML YEARS			1717	6186	1759	367	59	110	(54	56)	2574	863	662	874	526	23	1010	53	58	55	215	84	.72	98	.284	.343	.416

DeWayne Wise

Bats: L **Throws:** L **Pos:** CF-18; RF-17; PR-11; LF-10; DH-4; PH-4   **Ht:** 5'11" **Wt:** 195 **Born:** 2/24/1978 **Age:** 33

Year	Team	Lg	G	AB	H	2B	3B	HR	(Hm	Rd)	TB	R	RBI	RC	TBB	IBB	SO	HBP	SH	SF	SB	CS	SB%	GDP	Avg	OBP	Slg
2010	LV*	AAA	37	137	37	11	5	4	(-	-)	70	17	13	21	8	0	27	1	0	0	2	2	.50	5	.270	.315	.511
2000	Tor	AL	28	22	3	0	0	0	(0	0)	3	3	0	0	1	0	5	1	0	0	1	0	1.00	0	.136	.208	.136
2002	Tor	AL	42	112	20	4	1	3	(2	1)	35	14	13	8	4	0	15	0	0	0	5	0	1.00	0	.179	.207	.313
2004	Atl	NL	77	162	37	9	4	6	(3	3)	72	24	17	20	9	1	28	1	2	1	6	1	.86	1	.228	.272	.444
2006	Cin	NL	31	38	7	2	0	0	(0	0)	9	3	1	0	0	0	6	0	2	0	0	0	-	2	.184	.184	.237
2007	Cin	NL	5	5	1	0	1	0	(0	0)	3	1	1	1	1	1	1	0	0	0	0	0	-	0	.200	.333	.600
2008	CWS	AL	57	129	32	4	2	6	(2	4)	58	20	18	14	8	0	32	1	3	2	9	0	1.00	1	.248	.293	.450
2009	CWS	AL	84	142	32	8	3	2	(2	0)	52	17	11	10	3	0	27	4	4	0	4	5	.44	1	.225	.262	.366
2010	Tor	AL	52	112	28	3	2	3	(1	2)	44	20	14	17	4	0	29	1	1	0	4	0	1.00	1	.250	.282	.393
Postseason			8	12	3	2	0	1	(0	1)	8	3	5	3	1	0	4	0	0	0	1	0	1.00	0	.250	.308	.667
8 ML YEARS			376	722	160	30	13	20	(10	10)	276	102	75	70	30	2	143	8	12	3	29	6	.83	10	.222	.260	.382

Randy Wolf

Pitches: L **Bats:** L **Pos:** SP-34   **Ht:** 6'0" **Wt:** 198 **Born:** 8/22/1976 **Age:** 34

	HOW MUCH HE PITCHED						WHAT HE GAVE UP												THE RESULTS						
Year	Team	Lg	G	GS	CG	GF	IP	BFP	H	R	ER	HR	SH	SF	HB	TBB	IBB	SO	WP	Bk	W	L	Pct	Sh	Sv-Op Hld	ERC	ERA
1999	Phi	NL	22	21	0	0	121.2	552	126	78	75	20	5	1	5	67	0	116	4	0	6	9	.400	0	0-0 0	5.54	5.55
2000	Phi	NL	32	32	1	0	206.1	889	210	107	100	28	10	8	8	83	2	160	1	0	11	9	.550	0	0-0 0	4.54	4.36
2001	Phi	NL	28	25	4	1	160.0	681	160	74	67	15	11	7	10	51	4	152	1	0	10	11	.476	2	0-0 0	3.46	3.70
2002	Phi	NL	31	31	3	0	210.2	855	172	77	75	23	7	6	7	63	5	172	4	0	11	9	.550	2	0-0 0	2.88	3.20
2003	Phi	NL	33	33	2	0	200.0	850	176	101	94	27	8	4	6	78	4	177	6	0	16	10	.615	2	0-0 0	3.67	4.23
2004	Phi	NL	23	23	1	0	136.2	585	145	73	65	20	6	3	5	36	4	89	2	0	5	8	.385	1	0-0 0	4.29	4.28
2005	Phi	NL	13	13	0	0	80.0	346	87	40	39	14	4	1	6	26	2	61	1	0	6	4	.600	0	0-0 0	5.17	4.39
2006	Phi	NL	12	12	0	0	56.2	261	63	37	35	13	2	3	2	33	2	44	2	0	4	0	1.000	0	0-0 0	6.63	5.56
2007	LAD	NL	18	18	0	0	102.2	458	110	55	54	10	5	5	6	39	2	94	4	0	9	6	.600	0	0-0 0	4.52	4.73
2008	2 Tms	NL	33	33	1	0	190.1	823	191	100	91	21	10	4	12	71	4	162	3	0	12	12	.500	1	0-0 0	4.30	4.30
2009	LAD	NL	34	34	0	0	214.1	882	178	81	77	24	12	2	6	58	1	160	4	0	11	7	.611	0	0-0 0	2.89	3.23
2010	Mil	NL	34	34	1	0	215.2	936	213	107	100	29	9	6	9	87	6	142	2	0	13	12	.520	1	0-0 0	4.39	4.17
08	SD	NL	21	21	0	0	119.2	522	123	69	63	14	6	2	8	47	0	105	2	0	6	10	.375	1	0-0 0	4.63	4.74
08	Hou	NL	12	12	1	0	70.2	301	68	31	28	7	4	2	4	24	4	57	1	0	6	2	.750	1	0-0 0	3.77	3.57
Postseason			2	2	0	0	9.0	44	10	5	5	1	1	0	1	7	2	4	0	0	0	0	-	0	0-0 0	6.38	5.00
12 ML YEARS			313	309	13	1	1898.0	8101	1821	930	872	241	89	50	82	692	36	1529	34	0	114	97	.540	9	0-0 0	4.06	4.13

Ross Wolf

Pitches: R **Bats:** R **Pos:** RP-11   **Ht:** 6'0" **Wt:** 180 **Born:** 10/18/1982 **Age:** 28

	HOW MUCH HE PITCHED						WHAT HE GAVE UP												THE RESULTS						
Year	Team	Lg	G	GS	CG	GF	IP	BFP	H	R	ER	HR	SH	SF	HB	TBB	IBB	SO	WP	Bk	W	L	Pct	Sh	Sv-Op Hld	ERC	ERA
2002	Jmstwn	A-	11	11	0	0	46.1	209	56	30	24	4	1	3	3	12	0	18	2	1	2	4	.333	0	0- - -	4.77	4.66
2003	Grnsbr	A	27	0	0	6	50.1	192	32	10	9	2	4	1	2	10	2	26	0	0	6	1	.857	0	2- - -	1.42	1.61
2004	Jupiter	A+	43	0	0	22	90.0	386	87	33	26	2	1	1	4	28	6	58	3	0	11	7	.611	0	5- - -	3.04	2.60
2005	Carlina	AA	54	1	0	15	78.0	373	106	54	43	6	4	5	1	31	4	59	3	0	5	4	.556	0	1- - -	5.79	4.96
2006	Carlina	AA	12	0	0	3	18.0	66	12	3	2	0	1	0	0	2	1	12	1	0	1	2	.333	0	0- - -	1.11	1.00
2006	Albq	AAA	48	0	0	8	48.2	217	65	28	28	1	4	1	3	15	1	29	2	0	4	1	.800	0	1- - -	5.42	5.18
2007	Albq	AAA	46	0	0	10	47.1	206	54	24	18	5	2	3	0	17	1	23	0	1	4	3	.571	0	2- - -	4.78	3.42
2008	Jupiter	A+	3	0	0	1	4.0	15	3	1	0	0	0	0	0	1	0	7	0	0	0	0	-	0	1- - -	1.79	2.25
2008	Albq	AAA	38	0	0	14	39.0	175	47	19	17	4	2	4	2	15	0	20	1	0	5	2	.714	0	1- - -	5.50	3.92
2009	Norfolk	AAA	47	0	0	8	82.0	345	70	38	36	5	2	0	3	33	0	73	5	1	4	2	.667	0	1- - -	3.17	3.95
2010	Norfolk	AAA	25	0	0	5	38.1	157	29	12	9	1	0	2	0	15	2	26	1	0	0	2	.000	0	0- - -	2.21	2.11
2010	Scrmto	AAA	10	0	0	4	9.2	49	13	8	6	1	0	0	1	6	0	11	0	0	0	1	.000	0	3- - -	5.64	5.59
2007	Fla	NL	14	0	0	2	12.1	66	24	16	16	4	1	0	1	3	0	6	1	0	0	1	.000	0	0-0 0	11.46	11.68
2010	Oak	AL	11	0	0	7	12.2	56	12	6	6	1	1	0	1	6	1	9	0	0	0	0	-	0	0-0 0	4.07	4.26
2 ML YEARS			25	0	0	9	25.0	122	36	22	22	5	2	0	2	9	1	15	1	0	0	1	.000	0	0-0 0	7.49	7.92

Blake Wood

Pitches: R Bats: R Pos: RP-51   Ht: 6'5" Wt: 228 Born: 8/8/1985 Age: 25

		HOW MUCH HE PITCHED						WHAT HE GAVE UP											THE RESULTS							
Year	Team	Lg	G	GS	CG	GF	IP	BFP	H	R	ER	HR	SH	SF	HB	TBB	IBB	SO	WP	Bk	W	L	Pct	Sh	Sv-Op	Hld	ERC	ERA
2006	Idaho	R+	12	12	0	0	52.0	224	50	28	26	1	2	3	10	15	0	46	2	0	3	1	.750	0	0--	-	3.63	4.50
2007	Royals	R	4	4	0	0	9.2	36	9	2	0	0	0	0	0	0	0	15	0	0	0	0	-	0	0--	-	1.78	0.00
2007	Burlgtn	A	7	7	0	0	35.2	152	32	12	12	3	1	0	3	14	0	26	0	0	2	1	.667	0	0--	-	3.72	3.03
2007	Wilmg	A+	2	2	0	0	9.2	41	9	5	5	1	0	0	3	3	0	11	0	0	1	0	1.000	0	0--	-	4.84	4.66
2008	Wilmg	A+	10	10	0	0	57.1	212	32	17	17	3	1	3	2	15	0	63	6	0	3	2	.600	0	0--	-	1.43	2.67
2008	NWArk	AA	18	18	2	0	86.2	383	96	55	51	7	3	2	7	32	0	76	11	0	5	7	.417	2	0--	-	4.79	5.30
2009	NWArk	AA	17	13	1	3	78.2	338	92	52	51	8	6	1	5	27	1	49	7	0	2	8	.200	0	0--	-	5.30	5.83
2009	Royals	R	3	2	0	0	4.0	18	4	1	0	0	0	1	0	1	0	4	2	0	1	0	1.000	0	0--	-	2.58	0.00
2010	Omha	AAA	12	0	0	10	16.2	67	12	5	4	0	1	1	0	7	0	12	1	0	2	1	.667	0	5--	-	2.09	2.16
2010	KC	AL	51	0	0	13	49.2	220	54	29	28	6	2	6	1	22	5	31	3	0	1	3	.250	0	0-4	15	4.83	5.07

Brandon Wood

Bats: R Throws: R Pos: 3B-56; SS-22; PH-4; 1B-2; PR-2; DH-1   Ht: 6'3" Wt: 210 Born: 3/2/1985 Age: 26

					BATTING																	BASERUNNING				AVERAGES		
Year	Team	Lg	G	AB	H	2B	3B	HR	(Hm	Rd)	TB	R	RBI	RC	TBB	IBB	SO	HBP	SH	SF	SB	CS	SB%	GDP	Avg	OBP	Slg
2010	Salt Lk*	AAA	13	51	10	0	0	1	(-	-)	13	4	2	2	3	0	17	0	0	0	0	0	-	1	.196	.241	.255
2007	LAA	AL	13	33	5	1	0	1	(0	1)	9	2	3	1	0	0	12	0	0	0	0	0	-	0	.152	.152	.273
2008	LAA	AL	55	150	30	4	0	5	(2	3)	49	12	13	7	4	0	43	1	1	1	4	0	1.00	0	.200	.224	.327
2009	LAA	AL	18	41	8	1	0	1	(1	0)	12	5	3	0	3	0	19	1	1	0	0	0	-	3	.195	.267	.293
2010	LAA	AL	81	226	33	2	0	4	(2	2)	47	20	14	4	6	0	71	2	8	1	1	0	1.00	3	.146	.174	.208
	4 ML YEARS		167	450	76	8	0	11	(5	6)	117	39	33	12	13	0	145	4	10	2	5	0	1.00	9	.169	.198	.260

Kerry Wood

Pitches: R Bats: R Pos: RP-47   Ht: 6'5" Wt: 211 Born: 6/16/1977 Age: 34

					HOW MUCH HE PITCHED					WHAT HE GAVE UP											THE RESULTS							
Year	Team	Lg	G	GS	CG	GF	IP	BFP	H	R	ER	HR	SH	SF	HB	TBB	IBB	SO	WP	Bk	W	L	Pct	Sh	Sv-Op	Hld	ERC	ERA
2010	Akron*	AA	3	1	0	0	2.2	15	4	6	6	0	1	0	0	3	0	2	1	0	0	1	.000	0	0--	-	9.12	20.25
1998	ChC	NL	26	26	1	0	166.2	699	117	69	63	14	2	4	11	85	1	233	6	3	13	6	.684	1	0-0	0	3.03	3.40
2000	ChC	NL	23	23	1	0	137.0	603	112	77	73	17	7	5	9	87	0	132	5	1	8	7	.533	0	0-0	0	4.43	4.80
2001	ChC	NL	28	28	1	0	174.1	740	127	70	65	16	4	5	10	92	3	217	9	0	12	6	.667	1	0-0	0	3.22	3.36
2002	ChC	NL	33	33	4	0	213.2	895	169	92	87	22	13	5	16	97	5	217	8	1	12	11	.522	1	0-0	0	3.46	3.66
2003	ChC	NL	32	32	4	0	211.0	887	152	77	75	24	11	6	21	100	2	266	10	0	14	11	.560	2	0-0	0	3.31	3.20
2004	ChC	NL	22	22	0	0	140.1	595	127	62	58	16	6	6	11	51	0	144	7	0	8	9	.471	0	0-0	0	3.83	3.72
2005	ChC	NL	21	10	0	4	66.0	273	52	32	31	14	2	1	2	26	0	77	0	0	3	4	.429	0	0-0	4	3.75	4.23
2006	ChC	NL	4	4	0	0	19.2	86	19	13	9	5	0	2	1	8	0	13	1	0	1	2	.333	0	0-0	0	5.17	4.12
2007	ChC	NL	22	0	0	2	24.1	101	18	9	9	0	1	0	0	13	1	24	1	0	1	1	.500	0	0-0	0	2.49	3.33
2008	ChC	NL	65	0	0	56	66.1	276	54	24	24	3	2	2	7	18	4	84	1	0	5	4	.556	0	34-40	2	2.52	3.26
2009	Cle	AL	58	0	0	50	55.0	241	48	26	26	7	1	3	3	28	0	63	5	0	3	3	.500	0	20-26	0	4.16	4.25
2010	2 Tms	AL	47	0	0	19	46.0	201	35	17	16	4	2	0	3	29	4	49	5	1	3	4	.429	0	8-12	11	3.65	3.13
10	Cle	AL	23	0	0	18	20.0	93	21	15	14	3	0	0	2	11	2	18	2	1	1	4	.200	0	8-11	1	5.52	6.30
10	NYY	AL	24	0	0	1	26.0	108	14	2	2	1	2	0	1	18	2	31	3	0	2	0	1.000	0	0-1	10	2.36	0.69
	Postseason		8	5	0	2	36.2	157	29	16	15	3	1	0	0	18	1	38	1	0	2	2	.500	0	0-0	0	3.06	3.68
	12 ML YEARS		381	178	11	131	1320.1	5597	1030	568	536	142	51	39	94	634	20	1519	58	6	83	68	.550	5	62-78	15	3.49	3.65

Tim Wood

Pitches: R Bats: R Pos: RP-26   Ht: 6'0" Wt: 180 Born: 11/16/1982 Age: 28

					HOW MUCH HE PITCHED					WHAT HE GAVE UP											THE RESULTS							
Year	Team	Lg	G	GS	CG	GF	IP	BFP	H	R	ER	HR	SH	SF	HB	TBB	IBB	SO	WP	Bk	W	L	Pct	Sh	Sv-Op	Hld	ERC	ERA
2003	Jmstwn	A-	16	4	0	5	38.2	185	44	33	23	2	1	3	1	28	0	32	6	0	0	2	.000	0	2--	-	5.89	5.35
2004	Grnsbr	A	24	8	0	7	70.1	305	73	47	33	12	2	2	1	22	0	70	6	0	2	3	.400	0	1--	-	4.42	4.22
2005	Grnsbr	A	5	5	0	0	21.1	109	29	23	22	2	0	1	0	15	0	10	5	0	1	2	.333	0	0--	-	7.22	9.28
2006	Jupiter	A+	16	16	0	0	63.1	275	65	43	41	4	3	4	5	25	0	52	4	0	2	7	.222	0	0--	-	4.31	5.83
2007	Jupiter	A+	17	0	0	5	26.0	109	24	14	11	1	3	0	0	8	1	26	0	0	0	2	.000	0	0--	-	2.81	3.81
2008	Jupiter	A+	27	1	0	9	40.0	158	25	10	8	1	1	1	4	15	1	22	2	0	5	2	.714	0	1--	-	1.97	1.80
2008	Carlina	AA	12	0	0	1	20.1	88	20	14	13	2	0	0	2	6	0	15	1	0	2	1	.667	0	0--	-	3.91	5.75
2009	NewOr	AAA	31	0	0	9	39.2	176	42	16	14	1	2	1	0	17	2	37	3	0	1	2	.333	0	0--	-	3.83	3.18
2010	NewOr	AAA	14	0	0	5	14.0	66	19	12	10	4	1	0	0	4	2	12	4	0	0	0	-	0	0--	-	6.63	6.43
2009	Fla	NL	18	0	0	8	22.1	97	22	8	7	2	2	3	1	10	1	16	2	0	1	0	1.000	0	0-0	1	4.25	2.82
2010	Fla	NL	26	0	0	8	27.2	129	33	19	17	2	4	2	0	15	1	10	0	0	0	1	.000	0	1-3	3	5.44	5.53
	2 ML YEARS		44	0	0	16	50.0	226	55	27	24	4	6	5	1	25	2	26	2	0	1	1	.500	0	1-3	4	4.90	4.32

Travis Wood

Pitches: L Bats: R Pos: SP-17   Ht: 5'11" Wt: 163 Born: 2/6/1987 Age: 24

					HOW MUCH HE PITCHED					WHAT HE GAVE UP											THE RESULTS							
Year	Team	Lg	G	GS	CG	GF	IP	BFP	H	R	ER	HR	SH	SF	HB	TBB	IBB	SO	WP	Bk	W	L	Pct	Sh	Sv-Op	Hld	ERC	ERA
2005	Reds	R	8	7	0	0	24.0	93	13	3	2	0	2	0	1	7	0	45	0	0	0	0	-	0	0--	-	1.21	0.75
2005	Billings	R+	6	4	0	0	24.2	104	15	6	5	0	1	0	4	13	0	22	2	0	2	0	1.000	0	0--	-	2.39	1.82
2006	Dayton	A	27	27	0	0	140.0	582	108	65	57	14	12	2	10	56	0	133	10	0	10	5	.667	0	0--	-	3.13	3.66
2007	Srsota	A+	12	12	0	0	46.1	214	49	33	25	6	1	2	1	27	0	54	0	0	3	2	.600	0	0--	-	5.39	4.86
2008	Srsota	A+	9	9	0	0	46.2	199	39	18	14	2	0	0	2	21	0	41	1	1	3	4	.429	0	0--	-	3.12	2.70
2008	Chatt	AA	17	17	0	0	80.0	380	91	67	63	9	4	2	11	48	3	57	5	1	4	9	.308	0	0--	-	6.32	7.09

Year	Team	Lg	G	GS	CG	GF	IP	BFP	H	R	ER	HR	SH	SF	HB	TBB	IBB	SO	WP	Bk	W	L	Pct	Sh	Sv-Op	Hld	ERC	ERA
2009	Carlina	AA	19	19	1	0	119.0	460	78	23	16	2	3	1	5	37	0	103	0	0	9	3	.750	1	0- -	-	1.72	1.21
2009	Lsvlle	AAA	8	8	0	0	48.2	198	43	17	17	4	1	1	1	16	0	32	0	0	4	2	.667	0	0- -	-	3.21	3.14
2010	Lsvlle	AAA	16	16	0	0	100.0	404	86	40	34	9	6	1	4	24	0	99	6	0	5	6	.455	0	0- -	-	2.84	3.06
2010	Cin	NL	17	17	0	0	102.2	419	85	45	40	9	3	3	4	26	1	86	0	1	5	4	.556	0	0-0	0	2.64	3.51

Chris Woodward

Bats: R Throws: R Pos: SS-7; PH-1 Ht: 6'0" **Wt:** 190 **Born:** 6/27/1976 **Age:** 35

Year	Team	Lg	G	AB	H	2B	3B	HR	(Hm	Rd)	TB	R	RBI	RC	TBB	IBB	SO	HBP	SH	SF	SB	CS	SB%	GDP	Avg	OBP	Slg
2010	Tacom*	AAA	103	401	93	17	2	6	(-	-)	132	49	35	43	40	1	73	2	7	3	4	1	.80	9	.232	.303	.329
1999	Tor	AL	14	26	6	1	0	0	(0	0)	7	1	2	2	2	0	6	0	0	1	0	0	-	1	.231	.276	.269
2000	Tor	AL	37	104	19	7	0	3	(1	2)	35	16	14	9	10	3	28	0	1	0	1	0	1.00	1	.183	.254	.337
2001	Tor	AL	37	63	12	3	2	2	(2	0)	25	9	5	4	1	0	14	0	2	0	0	1	1.00	1	.190	.203	.397
2002	Tor	AL	90	312	86	13	4	13	(9	4)	146	48	45	45	26	0	72	3	1	8	3	0	1.00	8	.276	.330	.468
2003	Tor	AL	104	349	91	22	2	7	(4	3)	138	49	45	42	28	0	72	3	0	6	1	2	.33	6	.261	.316	.395
2004	Tor	AL	69	213	50	13	4	1	(0	1)	74	21	24	24	14	0	46	1	2	2	1	2	.33	3	.235	.283	.347
2005	NYM	NL	81	173	49	10	0	3	(2	1)	68	16	18	20	13	0	46	2	2	2	0	0	-	2	.283	.337	.393
2006	NYM	NL	83	222	48	10	1	3	(2	1)	69	25	25	18	23	2	55	1	4	3	1	1	.50	2	.216	.289	.311
2007	Atl	NL	92	136	27	6	1	1	(1	0)	38	16	8	9	10	1	29	0	4	1	1	0	1.00	0	.199	.252	.279
2009	2 Tms	AL	33	79	17	1	0	0	(0	0)	18	7	5	5	7	0	19	2	1	1	0	1	1.00	1	.215	.292	.228
2010	Sea	AL	8	19	3	1	0	0	(0	0)	4	0	0	1	3	0	9	0	0	0	0	0	-	0	.158	.273	.211
09	Sea	AL	20	67	16	1	0	0	(0	0)	17	7	5	5	5	0	15	0	1	1	0	1	1.00	1	.239	.288	.254
09	Bos	AL	13	12	1	0	0	0	(0	0)	1	0	0	0	2	0	4	2	0	0	0	0	-	0	.083	.313	.083
	Postseason		1	1	1	1	0	0	(0	0)	2	1	0	1	0	0	0	0	0	0	0	0	-	0	1.000	1.000	2.000
	11 ML YEARS		648	1696	408	87	14	33	(21	12)	622	208	191	179	137	6	396	12	17	24	9	6	.60	28	.241	.298	.367

Vance Worley

Pitches: R Bats: R Pos: RP-3; SP-2 Ht: 6'2" **Wt:** 230 **Born:** 9/25/1987 **Age:** 23

Year	Team	Lg	G	GS	CG	GF	IP	BFP	H	R	ER	HR	SH	SF	HB	TBB	IBB	SO	WP	Bk	W	L	Pct	Sh	Sv-Op	Hld	ERC	ERA
2008	Wmspt	A-	2	2	0	0	8.0	26	3	1	1	0	0	0	1	0	0	8	0	0	0	0	-	0	0- -	-	0.51	1.13
2008	Lakwd	A	11	11	0	0	61.0	249	58	25	18	4	2	2	3	7	0	53	3	0	3	2	.600	0	0- -	-	2.67	2.66
2009	Rdng	AA	27	27	0	0	153.1	660	163	102	91	17	9	4	5	48	0	100	2	1	7	12	.368	0	0- -	-	4.74	5.34
2010	Rdng	AA	19	19	1	0	112.2	478	114	48	40	9	4	3	3	36	0	83	1	0	9	4	.692	1	0- -	-	3.82	3.20
2010	LV	AAA	8	8	1	0	45.1	187	46	19	19	3	1	1	2	10	1	36	1	0	1	3	.250	0	0- -	-	3.33	3.77
2010	Phi	NL	5	2	0	2	13.0	51	8	2	2	1	2	0	0	4	0	12	1	0	1	1	.500	0	0-0	0	1.66	1.38

Danny Worth

Bats: R Throws: R Pos: SS-24; 2B-12; 3B 3; PR 2; PH-1 Ht: 6'1" **Wt:** 185 **Born:** 9/30/1985 **Age:** 25

Year	Team	Lg	G	AB	H	2B	3B	HR	(Hm	Rd)	TB	R	RBI	RC	TBB	IBB	SO	HBP	SH	SF	SB	CS	SB%	GDP	Avg	OBP	Slg
2007	Lkland	A+	51	171	43	9	2	2	(-	-)	62	22	21	22	18	0	39	1	1	1	6	0	1.00	4	.251	.325	.363
2007	Erie	AA	5	14	0	2	1	0	(	)	10	4	4	4	1	0	1	0	0	1	1	0	1.00	0	.429	.438	.714
2008	Erie	AA	79	295	75	18	3	5	(-	-)	114	44	33	42	32	0	59	3	4	2	8	0	1.00	7	.254	.331	.386
2008	Toledo	AAA	1	2	1	0	0	0	(-	-)	1	0	0	0	0	0	0	0	0	0	0	0	-	0	.500	.500	.500
2009	Toledo	AAA	41	151	32	4	1	0	(-	-)	38	9	4	10	11	0	40	0	0	0	3	1	.75	2	.212	.265	.252
2009	Erie	AA	75	285	68	17	3	0	(	)	91	33	24	28	26	0	74	3	3	1	4	5	.44	2	.239	.308	.319
2010	Toledo	AAA	45	164	47	5	0	2	(-	-)	58	18	18	21	10	0	29	2	0	1	12	2	.86	1	.287	.333	.354
2010	Det	AL	39	106	27	5	0	2	(2	0)	38	10	8	11	6	0	13	0	3	0	1	2	.33	0	.255	.295	.358

David Wright

Bats: R Throws: R Pos: 3B-155; DH-1; PH-1 Ht: 6'0" **Wt:** 208 **Born:** 12/20/1982 **Age:** 28

Year	Team	Lg	G	AB	H	2B	3B	HR	(Hm	Rd)	TB	R	RBI	RC	TBB	IBB	SO	HBP	SH	SF	SB	CS	SB%	GDP	Avg	OBP	Slg
2004	NYM	NL	69	263	77	17	1	14	(8	6)	138	41	40	42	14	0	40	3	0	3	6	1	1.00	7	.293	.332	.525
2005	NYM	NL	160	575	176	42	1	27	(12	15)	301	99	102	105	72	2	113	7	0	3	17	7	.71	16	.306	.388	.523
2006	NYM	NL	154	582	181	40	5	26	(13	13)	309	96	116	119	66	13	113	5	0	8	20	5	.80	15	.311	.381	.531
2007	NYM	NL	160	604	196	42	1	30	(16	14)	330	113	107	127	94	6	115	6	0	7	34	5	.87	14	.325	.416	.546
2008	NYM	NL	160	626	189	42	2	33	(21	12)	334	115	124	116	94	5	118	4	0	11	15	5	.75	15	.302	.390	.534
2009	NYM	NL	144	535	164	39	3	10	(5	5)	239	88	72	86	74	8	140	3	0	6	27	9	.75	16	.307	.390	.447
2010	NYM	NL	157	587	166	36	3	29	(12	17)	295	87	103	97	69	9	161	2	0	12	19	11	.63	12	.283	.354	.503
	Postseason		10	37	8	3	0	1	(0	1)	14	3	6	5	5	1	8	0	0	0	0	0	-	0	.216	.310	.378
	7 ML YEARS		1004	3772	1149	258	16	169	(87	82)	1946	639	664	692	483	43	800	30	0	50	138	42	.77	95	.305	.383	.516

Jamey Wright

Pitches: R Bats: R Pos: RP-46 Ht: 6'6" **Wt:** 230 **Born:** 12/24/1974 **Age:** 36

Year	Team	Lg	G	GS	CG	GF	IP	BFP	H	R	ER	HR	SH	SF	HB	TBB	IBB	SO	WP	Bk	W	L	Pct	Sh	Sv-Op	Hld	ERC	ERA
2010	Scrmto*	AAA	10	0	0	3	14.0	71	23	14	14	2	0	0	5	9	1	16	1	0	1	0	1.000	0	1- -	-	9.60	9.00
1996	Col	NL	16	15	0	0	91.1	406	105	60	50	8	4	2	7	41	1	45	1	2	4	4	.500	0	0-0	1	5.50	4.93
1997	Col	NL	26	26	1	0	149.2	698	198	113	104	19	8	3	11	71	3	59	6	2	8	12	.400	0	0-0	0	6.96	6.25
1998	Col	NL	34	34	1	0	206.1	919	235	143	130	24	8	6	11	95	3	86	6	3	9	14	.391	0	0-0	0	5.57	5.67
1999	Col	NL	16	16	0	0	94.1	423	110	52	51	10	3	4	4	54	3	49	3	0	4	3	.571	0	0-0	0	6.19	4.87
2000	Mil	NL	26	25	0	0	164.2	718	157	81	75	12	4	6	18	88	5	96	9	2	7	9	.438	0	0-0	0	4.67	4.10
2001	Mil	NL	33	33	1	0	194.2	868	201	115	106	26	7	5	20	98	10	129	6	1	11	12	.478	1	0-0	0	5.36	4.90

HOW MUCH HE PITCHED								WHAT HE GAVE UP												THE RESULTS							
Year Team	Lg	G	GS	CG	GF	IP	BFP	H	R	ER	HR	SH	SF	HB	TBB	IBB	SO	WP	Bk	W	L	Pct	Sh	Sv-Op	Hld	ERC	ERA
2002 2 Tms	NL	23	22	1	0	129.1	585	130	80	76	17	9	6	11	75	9	77	9	0	7	13	.350	1	0-0	0	5.35	5.29
2003 KC	AL	4	4	2	0	25.1	106	23	14	12	1	0	1	0	11	0	19	0	0	1	2	.333	1	0-0	0	3.53	4.26
2004 Col	NL	14	14	0	0	78.2	361	82	39	36	8	1	1	6	45	3	41	3	0	2	3	.400	0	0-0	0	5.26	4.12
2005 Col	NL	34	27	0	1	171.1	782	201	119	104	22	4	3	15	81	4	101	2	2	8	16	.333	0	0-0	1	6.02	5.46
2006 SF	NL	34	21	0	2	156.0	676	167	95	90	16	5	4	10	64	4	79	6	0	6	10	.375	0	0-0	0	4.89	5.19
2007 Tex	AL	20	9	0	3	77.0	330	72	35	31	6	3	2	5	41	2	39	4	0	4	5	.444	0	0-0	1	4.44	3.62
2008 Tex	AL	75	0	0	17	84.1	379	93	57	48	5	3	4	8	35	3	60	5	0	8	7	.533	0	0-6	17	4.74	5.12
2009 KC	AL	65	0	0	14	79.0	350	73	51	38	8	4	0	7	44	5	60	7	0	5	3	.375	0	0-3	12	4.56	4.33
2010 2 Tms	AL	46	0	0	17	58.1	249	55	33	27	3	3	3	3	25	1	28	4	1	1	3	.250	0	0-1	9	3.75	4.17
02 Mil	NL	19	19	1	0	114.1	515	115	72	68	15	9	6	11	63	8	69	8	0	5	13	.278	1	0-0	0	5.28	5.35
02 StL	NL	4	3	0	0	15.0	70	15	8	8	2	0	0	0	12	1	8	1	0	2	0	1.000	0	0-0	0	5.87	4.80
10 Cle	AL	18	0	0	9	21.1	98	25	18	13	1	1	1	2	9	0	9	1	0	1	2	.333	0	0-0	1	5.10	5.48
10 Sea	AL	28	0	0	8	37.0	151	30	15	14	2	2	2	1	16	1	19	3	1	0	1	.000	0	0-1	8	3.03	3.41
15 ML YEARS		466	246	6	55	1760.1	7850	1902	1087	978	185	66	49	137	868	56	968	71	13	83	118	.413	3	0-10	41	5.32	5.00

Wesley Wright

Pitches: L **Bats:** R **Pos:** RP-10; SP-4

Ht: 5'11" **Wt:** 175 **Born:** 1/28/1985 **Age:** 26

HOW MUCH HE PITCHED								WHAT HE GAVE UP												THE RESULTS							
Year Team	Lg	G	GS	CG	GF	IP	BFP	H	R	ER	HR	SH	SF	HB	TBB	IBB	SO	WP	Bk	W	L	Pct	Sh	Sv-Op	Hld	ERC	ERA
2010 RdRck*	AAA	15	14	0	0	69.2	312	76	39	36	8	2	3	4	33	0	41	4	0	4	1	.800	0	0- -	-	5.30	4.65
2008 Hou	NL	71	0	0	15	55.2	250	45	34	31	8	1	1	4	34	4	57	2	1	4	3	.571	0	1-1	13	4.21	5.01
2009 Hou	NL	49	0	0	5	44.2	204	53	27	27	9	0	2	0	25	3	47	2	0	3	4	.429	0	0-2	6	6.64	5.44
2010 Hou	NL	14	4	0	3	33.0	148	37	27	21	6	2	1	3	13	0	29	0	0	1	2	.333	0	0-0	0	5.78	5.73
3 ML YEARS		134	4	0	23	133.1	602	135	88	79	23	3	4	7	72	7	133	4	1	8	9	.471	0	1-3	19	5.37	5.33

Michael Wuertz

Pitches: R **Bats:** R **Pos:** RP-48

WURTZ

Ht: 6'3" **Wt:** 223 **Born:** 12/15/1978 **Age:** 32

HOW MUCH HE PITCHED								WHAT HE GAVE UP												THE RESULTS							
Year Team	Lg	G	GS	CG	GF	IP	BFP	H	R	ER	HR	SH	SF	HB	TBB	IBB	SO	WP	Bk	W	L	Pct	Sh	Sv-Op	Hld	ERC	ERA
2010 Scrmto*	AAA	4	3	0	0	4.2	21	4	0	0	0	0	0	1	3	0	3	0	0	0	0	-	0	0- -	-	4.37	0.00
2010 Stcktn*	A+	2	2	0	0	3.0	12	3	0	0	0	0	0	0	0	0	3	0	0	0	0	-	0	0- -	-	1.95	0.00
2004 ChC	NL	31	0	0	11	29.0	124	22	14	14	4	4	2	0	17	1	30	2	1	1	0	1.000	0	1-1	1	3.67	4.34
2005 ChC	NL	75	0	0	12	75.2	319	60	36	32	6	3	2	0	40	7	89	7	0	6	2	.750	0	0-3	18	3.17	3.81
2006 ChC	NL	41	0	0	4	40.2	175	35	14	12	5	3	0	1	16	2	42	1	0	3	1	.750	0	0-1	6	3.37	2.66
2007 ChC	NL	73	0	0	19	72.1	312	64	30	28	8	3	1	0	35	6	79	6	0	2	3	.400	0	0-0	8	3.68	3.48
2008 ChC	NL	45	0	0	13	44.2	189	44	23	18	4	1	3	0	20	2	30	2	0	1	1	.500	0	0-3	3	4.15	3.63
2009 Oak	AL	74	0	0	9	78.2	304	52	25	23	6	2	3	0	23	1	102	6	0	6	1	.857	0	4-6	23	1.84	2.63
2010 Oak	AL	48	0	0	14	39.2	171	35	21	19	6	4	0	0	21	5	40	6	0	2	3	.400	0	6-6	11	4.10	4.31
Postseason		2	0	0	0	1.2	7	0	0	0	0	1	0	0	1	0	2	1	0	0	0	-	0	0-0	0	0.32	0.00
7 ML YEARS		387	0	0	82	380.2	1594	312	163	146	39	20	11	1	172	24	412	30	1	21	11	.656	0	11-20	70	3.23	3.45

Kevin Youkilis

Bats: R **Throws:** R **Pos:** 1B-101; 3B-2

YOU-kih-liss

Ht: 6'1" **Wt:** 220 **Born:** 3/15/1979 **Age:** 32

BATTING																BASERUNNING				AVERAGES		
Year Team	Lg	G	AB	H	2B	3B	HR	(Hm | Rd)	TB	R	RBI	RC	TBB	IBB	SO	HBP	SH	SF	SB	CS	SB%	GDP	Avg	OBP	Slg
2004 Bos	AL	72	208	54	11	0	7	(2 | 5)	86	38	35	36	33	0	45	4	0	3	0	1	.00	1	.260	.367	.413
2005 Bos	AL	44	79	22	7	0	1	(0 | 1)	32	11	9	13	14	0	19	2	0	0	0	1	.00	0	.278	.400	.405
2006 Bos	AL	147	569	159	42	2	13	(6 | 7)	244	100	72	104	91	0	120	9	0	11	5	2	.71	12	.279	.381	.429
2007 Bos	AL	145	528	152	35	2	16	(8 | 8)	239	85	83	101	77	0	105	15	0	5	4	2	.67	9	.288	.390	.453
2008 Bos	AL	145	538	168	43	4	29	(17 | 12)	306	91	115	120	62	7	108	12	0	9	3	5	.38	11	.312	.390	.569
2009 Bos	AL	136	491	150	36	1	27	(14 | 13)	269	99	94	114	77	6	125	16	0	4	7	2	.78	9	.305	.413	.548
2010 Bos	AL	102	362	111	26	5	19	(8 | 11)	204	77	62	77	58	3	67	10	0	5	4	1	.80	4	.307	.411	.564
Postseason		29	111	34	9	1	6	(2 | 4)	63	22	17	20	13	0	18	0	0	1	0	0	-	4	.306	.376	.568
7 ML YEARS		791	2775	816	200	14	112	(55 | 57)	1380	501	470	565	412	16	589	68	0	37	23	14	.62	46	.294	.394	.497

Chris Young

Pitches: R **Bats:** R **Pos:** SP-4

Ht: 6'10" **Wt:** 278 **Born:** 5/25/1979 **Age:** 32

HOW MUCH HE PITCHED								WHAT HE GAVE UP												THE RESULTS							
Year Team	Lg	G	GS	CG	GF	IP	BFP	H	R	ER	HR	SH	SF	HB	TBB	IBB	SO	WP	Bk	W	L	Pct	Sh	Sv-Op	Hld	ERC	ERA
2010 SnAnt*	AA	1	1	0	0	0.2	7	2	5	5	0	0	0	0	4	0	1	0	0	0	1	.000	0	0- -	-	51.21	67.50
2010 Portlnd*	AAA	2	2	0	0	6.1	23	2	1	1	0	0	0	0	2	0	4	0	0	0	0	-	0	0- -	-	1.07	1.42
2004 Tex	AL	7	7	0	0	36.1	158	36	21	19	7	1	0	2	10	0	27	1	0	3	2	.600	0	0-0	0	4.26	4.71
2005 Tex	AL	31	31	0	0	164.2	700	162	84	78	19	2	4	7	45	2	137	3	0	12	7	.632	0	0-0	0	3.71	4.26
2006 SD	NL	31	31	0	0	179.1	735	134	72	69	28	8	3	6	69	4	164	6	1	11	5	.688	0	0-0	0	3.12	3.46
2007 SD	NL	30	30	0	0	173.0	705	118	66	60	10	3	6	7	72	0	167	7	4	9	8	.529	0	0-0	0	2.35	3.12
2008 SD	NL	18	18	1	0	102.1	434	84	46	45	13	4	1	1	48	4	93	3	1	7	6	.538	0	0-0	0	3.50	3.96
2009 SD	NL	14	14	0	0	76.0	336	70	47	44	12	4	5	2	40	3	50	1	0	4	6	.400	0	0-0	0	4.55	5.21
2010 SD	NL	4	4	0	0	20.0	82	10	2	2	1	1	0	0	11	0	15	1	0	2	0	1.000	0	0-0	0	1.72	0.90
Postseason		1	1	0	0	6.2	25	4	0	0	0	0	0	0	2	1	9	0	0	1	0	1.000	0	0-0	0	1.22	0.00
7 ML YEARS		135	135	1	0	751.2	3150	614	338	317	90	23	19	25	295	13	653	22	6	48	34	.585	0	0-0	0	3.27	3.80

Chris Young

Bats: R **Throws:** R **Pos:** CF-156; PH-1 **Ht:** 6'2" **Wt:** 200 **Born:** 9/5/1983 **Age:** 27

Year	Team	Lg	G	AB	H	2B	3B	HR	(Hm	Rd)	TB	R	RBI	RC	TBB	IBB	SO	HBP	SH	SF	SB	CS	SB%	GDP	Avg	OBP	Slg
2006	Ari	NL	30	126	17	4	0	2	(1	1)	27	16	10	15	6	0	12	1	0	1	2	1	.67	0	.243	.308	.386
2007	Ari	NL	148	569	135	29	3	32	(14	18)	266	85	68	68	43	1	141	6	1	5	27	6	.82	5	.237	.295	.467
2008	Ari	NL	160	625	155	42	7	22	(9	13)	277	85	85	84	62	2	165	1	6	5	14	5	.74	10	.248	.315	.443
2009	Ari	NL	134	433	92	28	4	15	(7	8)	173	54	42	47	59	2	133	4	3	2	11	4	.73	3	.212	.311	.400
2010	Ari	NL	156	584	150	33	0	27	(20	7)	264	94	91	86	74	0	145	2	1	3	28	7	.80	10	.257	.341	.452
Postseason			7	25	7	1	0	2	(1	1)	14	4	5	7	7	0	13	1	0	0	1	2	.33	0	.280	.455	.560
5 ML YEARS			628	2281	549	136	14	98	(51	47)	1007	328	296	296	244	5	596	14	11	16	82	23	.78	28	.241	.316	.441

Delmon Young

Bats: R **Throws:** R **Pos:** LF-149; PH-4; DH-2; PR-1 **Ht:** 6'3" **Wt:** 200 **Born:** 9/14/1985 **Age:** 25

Year	Team	Lg	G	AB	H	2B	3B	HR	(Hm	Rd)	TB	R	RBI	RC	TBB	IBB	SO	HBP	SH	SF	SB	CS	SB%	GDP	Avg	OBP	Slg
2006	TB	AL	30	126	40	9	1	3	(1	2)	60	16	10	15	1	0	24	3	0	1	2	2	.50	0	.317	.336	.476
2007	TB	AL	162	645	186	38	0	13	(9	4)	263	65	93	90	26	2	127	3	0	7	10	3	.77	23	.288	.316	.408
2008	Min	AL	152	575	167	28	4	10	(7	3)	233	80	69	74	35	7	105	7	1	5	14	5	.74	19	.290	.336	.405
2009	Min	AL	108	395	112	16	2	12	(5	7)	168	50	60	46	12	1	92	4	0	5	2	5	.29	17	.284	.308	.425
2010	Min	AL	153	570	170	46	1	21	(6	15)	281	77	112	94	28	5	81	6	0	9	5	4	.56	16	.298	.333	.493
Postseason			3	12	1	1	0	0	(0	0)	2	1	0	0	1	0	5	1	0	0	1	0	1.00	0	.083	.214	.167
5 ML YEARS			605	2311	675	137	8	59	(30	29)	1005	288	344	319	102	15	429	23	1	27	33	19	.63	75	.292	.325	.435

Delwyn Young

Bats: B **Throws:** R **Pos:** PH-72; RF-21; 2B-10; 3B-8; DH-4; PR-1 **Ht:** 5'10" **Wt:** 190 **Born:** 6/30/1982 **Age:** 29

Year	Team	Lg	G	AB	H	2B	3B	HR	(Hm	Rd)	TB	R	RBI	RC	TBB	IBB	SO	HBP	SH	SF	SB	CS	SB%	GDP	Avg	OBP	Slg
2006	LAD	NL	8	5	0	0	0	0	(0	0)	0	0	0	0	0	0	1	0	0	0	0	0	-	0	.000	.000	.000
2007	LAD	NL	19	34	13	1	1	2	(2	0)	22	4	3	8	2	0	5	0	0	0	1	0	1.00	0	.382	.417	.647
2008	LAD	NL	83	126	31	9	0	1	(1	0)	43	10	7	11	14	0	34	0	3	0	0	0	-	2	.246	.321	.341
2009	Pit	NL	124	354	94	16	2	7	(4	3)	135	40	43	43	29	0	90	3	1	1	2	0	1.00	13	.266	.320	.381
2010	Pit	NL	110	191	45	11	1	7	(4	3)	79	22	28	20	13	0	52	1	1	1	1	0	1.00	5	.236	.286	.414
5 ML YEARS			344	710	183	37	4	17	(11	6)	279	76	81	82	50	0	182	4	5	2	4	0	1.00	20	.258	.317	.393

Michael Young

Bats: R **Throws:** R **Pos:** 3B-155; DH-2 **Ht:** 6'1" **Wt:** 200 **Born:** 10/19/1976 **Age:** 34

Year	Team	Lg	G	AB	H	2B	3B	HR	(Hm	Rd)	TB	R	RBI	RC	TBB	IBB	SO	HBP	SH	SF	SB	CS	SB%	GDP	Avg	OBP	Slg
2000	Tex	AL	2	2	0	0	0	0	(0	0)	0	0	0	0	0	0	1	0	0	0	0	0	-	0	.000	.000	.000
2001	Tex	AL	106	386	96	18	4	11	(7	4)	155	57	49	45	26	0	91	3	9	5	3	1	.75	9	.249	.298	.402
2002	Tex	AL	156	573	150	26	8	9	(3	6)	219	77	62	64	41	1	112	0	13	6	6	7	.46	14	.262	.308	.382
2003	Tex	AL	160	666	204	33	9	14	(9	5)	297	106	72	106	36	1	103	1	3	7	13	2	.87	14	.306	.339	.446
2004	Tex	AL	160	690	216	33	9	22	(9	13)	333	114	99	124	44	1	89	1	0	4	12	3	.80	11	.313	.353	.483
2005	Tex	AL	159	668	221	40	5	24	(12	12)	343	114	91	131	58	0	91	5	3	3	5	2	.71	20	.331	.385	.513
2006	Tex	AL	162	691	217	52	3	14	(8	6)	317	93	103	120	48	0	96	1	0	8	7	3	.70	27	.314	.356	.459
2007	Tex	AL	156	639	201	37	1	9	(8	1)	267	80	94	107	47	5	107	5	0	1	13	3	.81	21	.315	.366	.418
2008	Tex	AL	155	645	183	36	2	12	(8	4)	259	102	82	86	55	0	109	2	0	6	10	0	1.00	16	.284	.339	.402
2009	Tex	AL	135	541	174	36	2	22	(10	12)	280	76	68	87	47	2	90	1	0	4	8	3	.73	16	.322	.374	.518
2010	Tex	AL	157	656	186	36	3	21	(16	5)	291	99	91	85	50	4	115	1	0	11	4	2	.67	21	.284	.330	.444
11 ML YEARS			1508	6157	1848	347	46	158	(90	68)	2761	918	811	955	452	14	1004	18	25	55	81	26	.76	172	.300	.347	.448

Eric Young Jr.

Bats: B **Throws:** R **Pos:** 2B-35; LF-10; PH-7 **Ht:** 5'10" **Wt:** 180 **Born:** 5/25/1985 **Age:** 26

Year	Team	Lg	G	AB	H	2B	3B	HR	(Hm	Rd)	TB	R	RBI	RC	TBB	IBB	SO	HBP	SH	SF	SB	CS	SB%	GDP	Avg	OBP	Slg
2004	Casper	R+	23	87	23	5	1	0	(-	-)	30	20	7	17	20	0	13	1	2	0	14	1	.93	0	.264	.407	.345
2005	Casper	R+	63	219	66	7	7	3	(-	-)	96	48	25	42	35	0	52	4	4	2	25	10	.71	4	.301	.404	.438
2006	Ashvll	A	128	482	142	28	6	5	(-	-)	197	92	49	88	67	0	75	10	9	1	87	31	.74	1	.295	.391	.409
2007	Mdest	A+	130	540	157	29	11	8	(-	-)	232	113	63	94	46	1	105	13	12	2	73	18	.80	5	.291	.359	.430
2008	Tulsa	AA	105	403	117	23	4	3	(-	-)	157	74	33	70	61	1	77	6	6	0	46	16	.74	6	.290	.391	.390
2009	ColSpr	AAA	119	472	141	21	10	7	(-	-)	203	118	43	88	56	1	79	12	12	0	57	14	.80	2	.299	.387	.430
2010	ColSpr	AAA	33	123	31	5	1	1	(-	-)	41	20	9	17	15	0	32	2	1	1	10	0	1.00	1	.252	.340	.333
2010	Tulsa	AA	4	13	3	0	0	0	(-	-)	3	2	0	0	1	0	2	0	0	0	0	0	-	0	.231	.286	.231
2009	Col	NL	30	57	14	1	0	1	(1	0)	18	7	1	2	4	0	12	0	0	0	4	4	.50	1	.246	.295	.316
2010	Col	NL	51	172	42	5	1	0	(0	0)	49	26	8	16	17	0	32	0	0	0	17	6	.74	2	.244	.312	.285
Postseason			2	1	0	0	0	0	(0	0)	0	0	0	0	0	0	0	0	0	0	0	0	-	0	.000	.000	.000
2 ML YEARS			81	229	56	6	1	1	(1	0)	67	33	9	18	21	0	44	0	0	0	21	10	.68	3	.245	.308	.293

Mike Zagurski

Pitches: L Bats: L Pos: RP-8 • zah-GURR-skee • Ht: 6'0" Wt: 221 Born: 1/27/1983 Age: 28

Year	Team	Lg	G	GS	CG	GF	IP	BFP	H	R	ER	HR	SH	SF	HB	TBB	IBB	SO	WP	Bk	W	L	Pct	Sh	Sv-Op	Hld	ERC	ERA
2005	Batvia	A-	15	8	0	3	45.0	197	47	29	23	2	1	1	3	15	0	43	1	1	3	4	.429	0	0--	-	3.89	4.60
2006	Lakwd	A	42	0	0	13	56.1	231	46	22	22	0	3	0	0	22	0	75	4	0	4	4	.500	0	1--	-	2.44	3.51
2007	Clrwtr	A+	12	0	0	8	16.1	60	6	2	2	0	2	0	1	4	0	30	0	0	0	0	-	0	5--	-	0.72	1.10
2007	Rdng	AA	6	0	0	3	7.0	26	2	1	1	0	0	0	0	2	0	8	0	0	0	0	-	0	0--	-	0.50	1.29
2007	Ottawa	AAA	7	0	0	1	9.0	39	7	2	2	0	0	0	0	6	0	11	1	0	0	0	-	0	0--	-	3.17	2.00
2009	Clrwtr	A+	3	2	0	0	3.0	12	2	0	0	0	0	0	0	0	0	1	0	0	0	0	-	0	0--	-	0.84	0.00
2009	Rdng	AA	45	0	0	19	53.0	232	42	24	21	7	8	1	4	27	1	63	4	1	3	4	.429	0	8--	-	3.76	3.57
2010	LV	AAA	52	0	0	16	52.1	228	44	26	19	3	3	3	2	27	3	71	3	0	2	3	.400	0	3--	-	3.35	3.27
2007	Phi	NL	25	0	0	4	21.1	101	25	14	14	3	1	1	1	11	2	21	2	0	1	0	1.000	0	0-2	5	5.75	5.91
2010	Phi	NL	8	0	0	3	7.0	34	8	8	8	1	1	1	2	5	0	11	1	0	0	0	-	0	0-0	0	8.12	10.29
2 ML YEARS			33	0	0	7	28.1	135	33	22	22	4	2	2	3	16	2	32	3	0	1	0	1.000	0	0-2	5	6.31	6.99

Carlos Zambrano

Pitches: R Bats: B Pos: SP-20; RP-16 • Ht: 6'5" Wt: 260 Born: 6/1/1981 Age: 30

Year	Team	Lg	G	GS	CG	GF	IP	BFP	H	R	ER	HR	SH	SF	HB	TBB	IBB	SO	WP	Bk	W	L	Pct	Sh	Sv-Op	Hld	ERC	ERA
2010	Cubs*	R	1	0	0	0	1.0	3	0	0	0	0	0	0	0	0	0	1	0	0	0	0	-	0	0--	-	0.00	0.00
2010	Iowa*	AAA	3	0	0	0	4.0	20	6	3	3	0	0	0	1	1	0	4	0	0	0	0	-	0	0--	-	6.48	6.75
2001	ChC	NL	6	1	0	1	7.2	42	11	13	13	2	1	1	0	8	0	4	1	0	1	2	.333	0	0-1	0	11.86	15.26
2002	ChC	NL	32	16	0	3	108.1	477	94	53	44	9	9	1	4	63	2	93	6	0	4	8	.333	0	0-0	0	4.02	3.66
2003	ChC	NL	32	32	3	0	214.0	907	188	88	74	9	11	6	10	94	12	168	6	1	13	11	.542	1	0-0	0	3.28	3.11
2004	ChC	NL	31	31	1	0	209.2	887	174	73	64	14	10	3	20	81	4	188	6	2	16	8	.667	1	0-0	0	3.20	2.75
2005	ChC	NL	33	33	2	0	223.1	909	170	88	81	21	9	5	8	86	3	202	7	0	14	6	.700	0	0-0	0	2.86	3.26
2006	ChC	NL	33	33	0	0	214.0	917	162	91	81	20	11	4	9	115	4	210	9	1	16	7	.696	0	0-0	0	3.34	3.41
2007	ChC	NL	34	34	1	0	216.1	925	187	100	95	23	6	3	14	101	4	177	3	0	18	13	.581	0	0-0	0	3.88	3.95
2008	ChC	NL	30	30	1	0	188.2	796	172	85	82	18	5	0	6	72	1	130	4	0	14	6	.700	1	0-0	0	3.62	3.91
2009	ChC	NL	28	28	1	0	169.1	733	155	78	71	10	10	5	9	78	6	152	7	0	9	7	.563	1	0-0	0	3.70	3.77
2010	ChC	NL	36	20	0	2	129.2	571	119	55	48	7	9	3	6	69	0	117	7	1	11	6	.647	0	0-0	4	3.97	3.33
Postseason			5	5	0	0	29.0	132	35	19	14	6	1	1	2	8	0	27	1	0	0	2	.000	0	0-0	0	5.72	4.34
10 ML YEARS			295	258	9	6	1681.0	7164	1432	724	653	133	81	31	87	767	36	1441	56	5	116	74	.611	4	0-1	4	3.51	3.50

Gregg Zaun

Bats: B Throws: R Pos: C-28 • Ht: 5'10" Wt: 170 Born: 4/14/1971 Age: 40

Year	Team	Lg	G	AB	H	2B	3B	HR	(Hm	Rd)	TB	R	RBI	RC	TBB	IBB	SO	HBP	SH	SF	SB	CS	SB%	GDP	Avg	OBP	Slg
1995	Bal	AL	40	104	27	5	0	3	(1	2)	41	18	14	15	16	0	14	0	2	0	1	1	.50	2	.260	.358	.394
1996	2 Tms		60	139	34	9	1	2	(1	1)	51	20	15	16	14	3	20	2	1	2	1	0	1.00	5	.245	.318	.367
1997	Fla	NL	58	143	43	10	2	2	(1	2)	63	21	20	27	26	4	18	2	1	0	1	0	1.00	3	.301	.415	.441
1998	Fla	NL	106	298	56	12	2	5	(2	3)	87	19	29	23	35	2	52	1	2	2	5	2	.71	7	.188	.274	.292
1999	Tex	AL	43	93	23	2	1	1	(0	1)	30	12	12	10	10	0	7	0	1	2	1	0	1.00	2	.247	.314	.323
2000	KC	AL	83	234	64	11	0	7	(2	5)	96	36	33	40	43	3	34	3	0	2	7	3	.70	4	.274	.390	.410
2001	KC	AL	39	125	40	9	0	6	(1	5)	67	15	18	24	12	0	16	0	0	1	1	2	.33	2	.320	.377	.536
2002	Hou	NL	76	185	41	7	1	3	(3	0)	59	18	24	17	12	1	36	2	2	1	1	0	1.00	4	.222	.275	.319
2003	2 Tms		74	166	38	8	0	4	(1	3)	58	15	21	20	19	0	21	1	1	2	1	1	.50	5	.229	.309	.349
2004	Tor	AL	107	338	91	24	0	6	(2	4)	133	46	36	50	47	3	61	6	0	1	0	2	.00	7	.269	.367	.393
2005	Tor	AL	133	434	109	18	1	11	(7	4)	162	61	61	65	73	2	70	0	0	5	2	3	.40	11	.251	.355	.373
2006	Tor	AL	99	290	79	19	0	12	(7	5)	134	39	40	41	41	3	42	3	0	5	0	2	.00	10	.272	.363	.462
2007	Tor	AL	110	331	80	24	1	10	(6	4)	136	43	52	48	51	8	55	2	1	6	0	0	-	9	.242	.341	.411
2008	Tor	AL	86	245	58	12	0	6	(5	1)	88	29	30	32	38	1	38	1	3	1	2	1	.67	6	.237	.340	.359
2009	2 Tms		90	262	68	17	0	8	(3	5)	109	34	27	35	31	0	48	3	0	0	0	2	.00	4	.260	.345	.416
2010	Mil	NL	28	102	27	7	0	2	(2	0)	40	11	14	10	11	0	12	3	0	1	0	0	-	6	.265	.350	.392
96	Bal	AL	50	108	25	8	1	1	(1	0)	38	16	13	12	11	2	15	2	0	2	0	0	-	3	.231	.309	.352
96	Fla	AL	10	31	9	1	0	1	(0	1)	13	4	2	4	3	1	5	0	1	0	1	0	1.00	2	.290	.353	.419
03	Hou	NL	59	120	26	7	0	1	(1	0)	36	9	13	12	14	0	14	1	1	2	1	0	1.00	5	.217	.299	.300
03	Col	NL	15	46	12	1	0	3	(0	3)	22	6	8	8	5	0	7	0	0	0	0	1	.00	0	.261	.333	.478
09	Bal	AL	56	168	41	10	0	4	(1	3)	63	23	13	23	27	0	30	2	0	0	0	0	-	2	.244	.355	.375
09	TB	AL	34	94	27	7	0	4	(2	2)	46	11	14	12	4	0	18	1	0	0	0	2	.00	2	.287	.323	.489
Postseason			3	2	0	0	0	0	(0	0)	0	0	0	0	0	0	0	0	0	0	0	0	-	0	.000	.000	.000
16 ML YEARS			1232	3489	878	194	9	88	(41	47)	1354	437	446	473	479	30	544	29	14	31	23	19	.55	87	.252	.344	.388

Clay Zavada

Pitches: L Bats: L Pos: P • zuh-VAH-da • Ht: 6'1" Wt: 195 Born: 6/28/1984 Age: 27

Year	Team	Lg	G	GS	CG	GF	IP	BFP	H	R	ER	HR	SH	SF	HB	TBB	IBB	SO	WP	Bk	W	L	Pct	Sh	Sv-Op	Hld	ERC	ERA
2006	Msoula	R+	22	0	0	5	49.1	208	41	29	17	3	6	2	2	15	0	51	2	2	2	3	.400	0	2--	-	2.63	3.10
2008	So Ill	IND	12	0	0	7	15.2	58	7	3	3	0	1	1	1	4	0	22	1	0	2	1	.667	0	4--	-	0.95	1.72
2008	Sbend	A	24	0	0	15	35.1	115	6	2	2	1	1	0	1	5	0	54	0	0	3	1	.750	0	8--	-	0.25	0.51
2009	Mobile	AA	11	0	0	2	17.1	69	10	5	5	2	1	1	0	7	0	18	0	0	1	0	1.000	0	0--	-	2.00	2.60
2010	Reno	AAA	5	0	0	0	3.0	25	6	10	10	0	0	0	0	10	0	2	3	0	0	1	.000	0	0--	-	23.06	30.00
2009	Ari	NL	49	0	0	9	51.0	221	45	26	19	5	2	1	3	24	2	52	1	0	3	3	.500	0	0-0	4	3.84	3.35

Lance Zawadzki

Bats: B **Throws:** R **Pos:** PH-9; 2B-7; SS-3; 3B-1; PR-1   zah-WAHT-skee   **Ht:** 5'11" **Wt:** 194 **Born:** 5/26/1985 **Age:** 26

										BATTING												BASERUNNING				AVERAGES		
Year	Team	Lg	G	AB	H	2B	3B	HR	(Hm	Rd)	TB	R	RBI	RC	TBB	IBB	SO	HBP	SH	SF	SB	CS	SB%	GDP	Avg	OBP	Slg
2007	Eugene	A-	25	101	27	4	1	2	(-	-)	39	13	14	14	10	0	24	1	0	0	1	0	1.00	1	.267	.339	.386
2007	Padres	R	10	30	13	3	0	1	(-	-)	19	8	5	8	3	0	8	0	0	0	0	0	-	1	.433	.485	.633
2008	FtWyn	A	119	454	124	26	5	7	(-	-)	181	66	58	72	54	0	101	4	1	5	28	3	.90	15	.273	.352	.399
2008	SnAnt	AA	2	3	1	0	0	0	(-	-)	1	1	0	0	0	0	2	0	0	0	0	0	-	0	.333	.333	.333
2009	Lk Els	A+	36	145	40	6	2	10	(-	-)	80	19	34	29	18	2	29	1	0	0	3	1	.75	0	.276	.360	.552
2009	SnAnt	AA	92	346	100	19	5	5	(-	-)	144	59	43	58	44	4	74	2	0	0	14	1	.93	9	.289	.372	.416
2010	Portlnd	AAA	61	225	52	10	1	1	(-	-)	67	34	16	20	21	0	57	1	0	1	5	5	.50	5	.231	.298	.298
2010	SnAnt	AA	35	148	33	5	1	4	(-	-)	52	21	17	16	13	1	34	0	0	0	7	1	.88	3	.223	.286	.351
2010	SD	NL	20	35	7	2	0	0	(0	0)	9	4	1	3	5	2	7	0	2	0	1	0	1.00	1	.200	.300	.257

Brad Ziegler

Pitches: R **Bats:** R **Pos:** RP-64   ZIGG-lerr   **Ht:** 6'4" **Wt:** 212 **Born:** 10/10/1979 **Age:** 31

			HOW MUCH HE PITCHED						WHAT HE GAVE UP											THE RESULTS						
Year	Team	Lg	G	GS	CG	GF	IP	BFP	H	R	ER	HR	SH	SF	HB	TBB	IBB	SO	WP	Bk	W	L	Pct	Sh	Sv-Op	Hld	ERC	ERA
2008	Oak	AL	47	0	0	21	59.2	229	47	8	7	2	4	3	1	22	3	30	0	0	3	0	1.000	0	11-13	9	2.60	1.06
2009	Oak	AL	69	0	0	23	73.1	313	82	27	25	2	1	3	1	28	4	54	0	0	2	4	.333	0	7-10	14	4.25	3.07
2010	Oak	AL	64	0	0	12	60.2	257	54	24	22	4	1	3	3	28	9	41	0	1	3	7	.300	0	0-4	18	3.48	3.26
3 ML YEARS			180	0	0	56	193.2	799	183	59	54	8	6	7	5	78	16	125	0	1	8	11	.421	0	18-27	41	3.49	2.51

Ryan Zimmerman

Bats: R **Throws:** R **Pos:** 3B-137; PH-4; DH-1   **Ht:** 6'3" **Wt:** 228 **Born:** 9/28/1984 **Age:** 26

										BATTING												BASERUNNING				AVERAGES		
Year	Team	Lg	G	AB	H	2B	3B	HR	(Hm	Rd)	TB	R	RBI	RC	TBB	IBB	SO	HBP	SH	SF	SB	CS	SB%	GDP	Avg	OBP	Slg
2005	Was	NL	20	58	23	10	0	0	(0	0)	33	6	6	9	3	0	12	0	0	1	0	0	-	1	.397	.419	.569
2006	Was	NL	157	614	176	47	3	20	(10	10)	289	84	110	101	61	7	120	2	1	4	11	8	.58	15	.287	.351	.471
2007	Was	NL	162	653	174	43	5	24	(11	13)	299	99	91	83	61	3	125	3	0	5	4	1	.80	26	.266	.330	.458
2008	Was	NL	106	428	121	24	1	14	(7	7)	189	51	51	48	31	1	71	3	0	4	1	1	.50	12	.283	.333	.442
2009	Was	NL	157	610	178	37	3	33	(17	16)	320	110	106	96	72	9	119	2	0	9	2	0	1.00	22	.292	.364	.525
2010	Was	NL	142	525	161	32	0	25	(9	16)	268	85	85	97	69	6	98	4	0	5	4	1	.80	16	.307	.388	.510
6 ML YEARS			744	2888	833	193	12	116	(54	62)	1398	435	449	434	297	26	545	14	1	28	22	11	.67	92	.288	.355	.484

Jordan Zimmermann

Pitches: R **Bats:** R **Pos:** SP-7   **Ht:** 6'2" **Wt:** 218 **Born:** 5/23/1986 **Age:** 25

			HOW MUCH HE PITCHED						WHAT HE GAVE UP											THE RESULTS						
Year	Team	Lg	G	GS	CG	GF	IP	BFP	H	R	ER	HR	SH	SF	HB	TBB	IBB	SO	WP	Bk	W	L	Pct	Sh	Sv-Op	Hld	ERC	ERA
2007	Vrmnt	A-	13	11	0	0	53.0	216	45	14	14	2	0	1	0	18	0	71	2	2	5	2	.714	0	0--	-	2.67	2.38
2008	Ptomc	A+	5	4	0	1	27.1	99	15	6	5	1	1	0	0	8	0	31	0	0	3	1	.750	0	1--	-	1.30	1.05
2008	Hrsbrg	AA	20	20	0	0	106.2	439	89	42	38	9	2	1	3	39	2	103	2	1	7	2	.778	0	0--	-	3.06	3.21
2009	Syrcse	AAA	1	1	0	0	5.1	21	4	3	3	2	0	0	0	1	0	4	0	0	0	0	-	0	0--	-	3.42	5.06
2009	Ptomc	A+	1	1	0	0	3.1	14	2	2	1	1	1	0	0	1	0	6	0	0	0	0	-	0	0--	-	2.47	2.70
2010	Ptomc	A+	4	4	0	0	13.0	47	11	1	0	0	1	0	1	0	0	13	0	0	0	1	.000	0	0--	-	1.71	0.00
2010	Hgrstn	A	1	1	0	0	5.0	25	7	7	6	2	0	0	1	1	0	3	0	0	0	1	.000	0	0--	-	7.08	10.80
2010	Hrsbrg	AA	1	1	0	0	4.2	17	1	0	0	0	0	0	1	2	0	3	1	0	0	0	-	0	0--	-	0.95	0.00
2010	Syrcse	AAA	4	4	0	0	17.0	60	8	1	1	0	0	0	0	3	0	12	0	0	1	0	1.000	0	0--	-	0.77	0.63
2009	Was	NL	16	16	0	0	91.1	301	95	51	47	10	5	3	4	29	0	92	0	0	3	5	.375	0	0-0	0	4.25	4.63
2010	Was	NL	7	7	0	0	31.0	135	31	20	17	8	1	1	2	10	1	27	0	0	1	2	.333	0	0-0	0	5.02	4.94
2 ML YEARS			23	23	0	0	122.1	526	126	71	64	18	6	4	6	39	1	119	0	0	4	7	.364	0	0-0	0	4.45	4.71

Barry Zito

Pitches: L **Bats:** L **Pos:** SP-33; RP-1   **Ht:** 6'2" **Wt:** 204 **Born:** 5/13/1978 **Age:** 33

			HOW MUCH HE PITCHED						WHAT HE GAVE UP											THE RESULTS						
Year	Team	Lg	G	GS	CG	GF	IP	BFP	H	R	ER	HR	SH	SF	HB	TBB	IBB	SO	WP	Bk	W	L	Pct	Sh	Sv-Op	Hld	ERC	ERA
2000	Oak	AL	14	14	1	0	92.2	376	64	30	28	6	1	0	2	45	2	78	2	0	7	4	.636	1	0-0	0	2.63	2.72
2001	Oak	AL	35	35	3	0	214.1	902	184	92	83	18	5	4	13	80	0	205	6	1	17	8	.680	2	0-0	0	3.33	3.49
2002	Oak	AL	35	35	1	0	229.1	939	182	79	70	24	9	7	9	78	2	182	2	1	23	5	.821	0	0-0	0	2.92	2.75
2003	Oak	AL	35	35	4	0	231.2	957	186	98	85	19	7	7	6	88	3	146	4	0	14	12	.538	1	0-0	0	2.91	3.30
2004	Oak	AL	34	34	0	0	213.0	926	216	116	106	28	7	9	9	81	2	163	4	1	11	11	.500	0	0-0	0	4.45	4.48
2005	Oak	AL	35	35	0	0	228.1	953	185	106	98	26	8	7	13	89	0	171	4	0	14	13	.519	0	0-0	0	3.32	3.86
2006	Oak	AL	34	34	0	0	221.0	945	211	99	94	27	7	6	13	99	5	151	4	2	16	10	.615	0	0-0	0	4.47	3.83
2007	SF	NL	34	33	0	0	196.2	850	182	105	99	24	12	4	4	83	4	131	5	0	11	13	.458	0	0-0	0	3.91	4.53
2008	SF	NL	32	32	0	0	180.0	818	186	115	103	16	8	14	4	102	10	120	3	0	10	17	.370	0	0-0	0	4.81	5.15
2009	SF	NL	33	33	1	0	192.0	818	179	89	86	21	11	1	8	81	8	154	2	2	10	13	.435	0	0-0	0	4.00	4.03
2010	SF	NL	34	33	1	1	199.1	848	184	97	92	20	13	7	7	84	7	150	7	0	9	14	.391	0	0-0	0	3.85	4.15
Postseason			7	7	0	0	44.1	184	34	16	16	6	1	0	3	17	0	33	1	0	4	3	.571	0	0-0	0	3.24	3.25
11 ML YEARS			355	353	11	1	2198.1	9332	1959	1026	944	229	88	66	88	910	43	1651	43	7	142	120	.542	4	0-0	0	3.70	3.86

Ben Zobrist

Bats: B **Throws:** R **Pos:** RF-103; 2B-55; 1B-14; CF-14; PH-6; 3B-2; LF-1   ZOH-brist   **Ht:** 6'3" **Wt:** 200 **Born:** 5/26/1981 **Age:** 30

Year	Team	Lg	G	AB	H	2B	3B	HR	(Hm	Rd)	TB	R	RBI	RC	TBB	IBB	SO	HBP	SH	SF	SB	CS	SB%	GDP	Avg	OBP	Slg
2006	TB	AL	52	183	41	6	2	2	(2	0)	57	10	18	13	10	1	26	0	2	3	2	3	.40	2	.224	.260	.311
2007	TB	AL	31	97	15	2	0	1	(0	1)	20	8	9	0	3	0	21	1	2	2	2	0	1.00	1	.155	.184	.206
2008	TB	AL	62	198	50	10	2	12	(4	8)	100	32	30	31	25	1	37	2	0	2	3	0	1.00	4	.253	.339	.505
2009	TB	AL	152	501	149	28	7	27	(18	9)	272	91	91	109	91	4	104	2	1	4	17	6	.74	7	.297	.405	.543
2010	TB	AL	151	541	129	28	2	10	(3	7)	191	77	75	84	92	1	107	3	7	**12**	24	3	.89	10	.238	.346	.353
Postseason			7	11	1	0	0	0	(0	0)	1	0	0	0	2	0	0	0	0	0	0	0	-	0	.091	.231	.091
5 ML YEARS			448	1520	384	74	13	52	(27	25)	640	218	223	237	221	7	295	8	12	23	48	12	.80	24	.253	.346	.421

Joel Zumaya

Pitches: R **Bats:** R **Pos:** RP-31   zoo-MY-ah   **Ht:** 6'3" **Wt:** 210 **Born:** 11/9/1984 **Age:** 26

Year	Team	Lg	G	GS	CG	GF	IP	BFP	H	R	ER	HR	SH	SF	HB	TBB	IBB	SO	WP	Bk	W	L	Pct	Sh	Sv-Op	Hld	ERC	ERA
2006	Det	AL	62	0	0	12	83.1	350	56	20	18	6	2	4	2	42	2	97	4	0	6	3	.667	0	1-6	30	2.55	1.94
2007	Det	AL	28	0	0	7	33.2	142	23	16	16	3	1	1	1	17	2	27	3	0	2	3	.400	0	1-5	8	2.68	4.28
2008	Det	AL	21	0	0	5	23.1	114	24	13	9	3	0	1	0	22	4	22	6	0	0	2	.000	0	1-5	5	6.32	3.47
2009	Det	AL	29	0	0	5	31.0	149	34	18	17	5	1	1	1	22	3	30	1	0	3	3	.500	0	1-7	7	6.26	4.94
2010	Det	AL	31	0	0	6	38.1	156	32	13	11	1	2	3	0	11	0	34	2	0	2	1	.667	0	1-3	11	2.31	2.58
Postseason			6	0	0	2	6.0	24	2	4	2	0	0	0	0	3	0	6	1	0	0	1	.000	0	0-0	1	0.92	3.00
5 ML YEARS			171	0	0	35	209.2	911	169	80	71	18	6	10	4	114	11	210	16	0	13	12	.520	0	5-26	61	3.40	3.05

2010 Fielding Statistics

With the increased focus on defense over the last several years, it's only appropriate that the Fielding section gets an upgrade this year to reflect some of the new metrics.

Traditional defensive statistics such as putouts, assists, errors, double plays, and fielding percentage are still a part of the new charts. In this year's redesign, the most noticeable enhancement is the addition of Plus/Minus (PM) and Defensive Runs Saved (Runs Saved for short) numbers for each player. For regular players, we list players by position in order of best-to-worst Runs Saved. The Runs Saved numbers are broken down by component. Eight of the nine positions on the diamond are evaluated on range with Plus/Minus Runs Saved (Runs Saved +/-). Catchers are the exception and they are evaluated on pitcher handling and controlling the running game. Corner infielders are rated on their ability to handle bunts, middle infielders on their double play skills, and outfielders on their throwing arm. A bonus for outfielders is Runs Saved for home run robberies. For a more detailed explanation of Runs Saved, see the glossary.

In addition to adding the new metrics to the charts, the layout has been updated this year. The regulars at each of the non-pitcher positions are presented at the beginning of the section, followed by a record for every other fielder, except pitchers and catchers, followed by non-regular catchers. Pitcher fielding is in the next section.

First Basemen - Regulars

Player	Tm	G	GS	Inn	PO	A	E	DP	Pct.	PM	Runs Saved Bunts	+/-	Total
Barton,Daric	Oak	157	155	1333.2	1404	78	10	121	.993	+27	0	20	20
Davis,Ike	NYM	146	141	1263.0	1239	105	9	133	.993	+14	3	10	13
Overbay,Lyle	Tor	153	150	1320.2	1309	101	6	150	.996	+12	0	9	9
Youkilis,Kevin	Bos	101	97	862.0	809	72	3	66	.997	+7	-1	5	4
Helton,Todd	Col	115	105	947.2	932	77	8	116	.992	-1	4	-1	3
Lee,Derrek	TOT	144	141	1207.1	1067	116	7	99	.994	+3	0	2	2
LaRoche,Adam	Ari	146	143	1239.2	1139	122	11	117	.991	+2	1	1	2
Pena,Carlos	TB	142	135	1213.2	1074	83	6	95	.995	+2	0	1	1
Votto,Joey	Cin	148	145	1283.0	1132	128	5	101	.996	-1	2	-1	1
Pujols,Albert	StL	157	157	1380.2	1458	157	4	146	.998	+6	-4	4	0
Kotchman,Casey	Sea	116	108	966.2	946	74	1	92	.999	0	0	0	0
Gonzalez,Adrian	SD	159	157	1397.1	1324	127	8	125	.995	-2	1	-1	0
Loney,James	LAD	160	149	1338.2	1286	78	4	103	.997	-2	1	-1	0
Teixeira,Mark	NYY	149	148	1291.2	1227	80	3	137	.998	-1	0	-1	-1
Sanchez,Gaby	Fla	149	148	1253.1	1115	70	11	97	.991	-3	-1	-2	-3
Butler,Billy	KC	127	126	1102.1	1002	96	6	101	.995	-6	-1	-4	-5
Glaus,Troy	Atl	114	107	936.1	977	46	9	110	.991	-9	-1	-7	-8
Cabrera,Miguel	Det	148	148	1285.1	1218	96	13	133	.990	-10	-1	-7	-8
Dunn,Adam	Was	153	151	1246.0	1203	93	13	119	.990	-15	3	-11	-8
Jones,Garrett	Pit	112	106	924.2	893	88	9	70	.991	-10	-3	-7	-10
Fielder,Prince	Mil	160	160	1411.0	1251	86	4	116	.997	-19	1	-14	-13
Howard,Ryan	Phi	139	139	1229.0	1266	59	14	117	.990	-18	-1	-13	-14
Konerko,Paul	CWS	125	125	1102.1	1069	83	7	124	.994	-24	1	-18	-17

Second Basemen - Regulars

Player	Tm	G	GS	Inn	PO	A	E	DP	Pct.	Range	PM	Runs Saved GDP	+/-	Total
Hudson,Orlando	Min	123	123	1067.0	255	374	8	78	.987	5.31	+23	0	17	17
Utley,Chase	Phi	114	114	1007.0	228	347	11	86	.981	5.14	+16	2	12	14
Hill,Aaron	Tor	137	137	1188.0	236	383	10	89	.984	4.69	+8	3	6	9
Kinsler,Ian	Tex	103	102	905.1	190	278	7	64	.985	4.65	+10	0	8	8
Ellis,Mark	Oak	116	113	986.1	218	328	3	77	.995	4.98	+8	2	6	8
Cano,Robinson	NYY	158	157	1393.1	341	432	3	114	.996	4.99	+7	2	5	7
Eckstein,David	SD	113	107	967.1	191	284	0	71	1.000	4.42	+4	0	3	3
Prado,Martin	Atl	98	97	852.0	184	285	6	66	.987	4.95	+4	-1	3	2
Johnson,Kelly	Ari	149	146	1270.2	267	402	8	106	.988	4.74	0	2	0	2
Theriot,Ryan	TOT	119	112	992.1	220	275	7	56	.986	4.49	+5	-4	4	0
Phillips,Brandon	Cin	152	151	1311.0	281	419	3	95	.996	4.81	+3	-2	2	0
Sanchez,Freddy	SF	109	108	943.0	198	256	4	52	.991	4.33	0	-1	0	-1
DeWitt,Blake	TOT	126	122	1039.0	257	301	12	71	.979	4.83	-1	-2	-1	-3
Beckham,Gordon	CWS	126	125	1111.1	245	375	12	100	.981	5.02	-12	5	-9	-4
Keppinger,Jeff	Hou	126	122	1070.2	217	351	6	66	.990	4.77	-9	0	-7	-7
Schumaker,Skip	StL	123	118	1014.1	210	359	16	76	.973	5.05	-12	2	-9	-7
Walker,Neil	Pit	105	104	894.2	222	234	7	62	.985	4.59	-14	2	-11	-9
Uggla,Dan	Fla	158	158	1392.1	312	415	18	84	.976	4.70	-11	-3	-8	-11
Kendrick,Howie	LAA	143	140	1251.0	259	366	9	74	.986	4.50	-15	0	-11	-11
Weeks,Rickie	Mil	159	159	1389.1	332	389	15	102	.980	4.67	-14	0	-11	-11
Figgins,Chone	Sea	161	161	1417.0	274	414	19	110	.973	4.37	-19	3	-14	-11

Third Basemen - Regulars

Player	Tm	G	GS	Inn	PO	A	E	DP	Pct.	Range	PM	Runs Saved Bunts	+/-	Total
Headley,Chase	SD	158	156	1407.2	82	293	13	21	.966	2.40	+25	2	19	21
Zimmerman,Ryan	Was	137	137	1189.1	85	242	17	23	.951	2.47	+24	2	18	20
Lopez,Jose	Sea	142	142	1252.2	107	322	18	29	.960	3.08	+25	-4	19	15
Kouzmanoff,Kevin	Oak	142	140	1231.2	90	278	12	29	.968	2.69	+20	-2	15	13
Longoria,Evan	TB	151	151	1330.2	127	276	14	46	.966	2.73	+17	0	13	13
Blake,Casey	LAD	139	134	1204.0	80	257	15	17	.957	2.52	+13	0	10	10
Beltre,Adrian	Bos	154	151	1342.2	138	285	19	31	.957	2.84	+11	2	8	10
Rolen,Scott	Cin	130	125	1074.0	83	259	8	28	.977	2.87	+3	0	2	2
Sandoval,Pablo	SF	143	136	1224.2	93	228	13	23	.961	2.36	+3	0	2	2
Inge,Brandon	Det	144	138	1226.2	119	267	9	24	.977	2.83	+1	1	1	2
Polanco,Placido	Phi	123	121	1075.1	88	258	5	32	.986	2.90	+1	0	1	1
Callaspo,Alberto	TOT	130	128	1134.0	83	240	10	25	.970	2.56	-1	2	-1	1
Stewart,Ian	Col	115	103	925.1	59	212	10	17	.964	2.64	0	0	0	0
Reynolds,Mark	Ari	142	141	1214.0	101	250	18	24	.951	2.60	-5	1	-4	-3
Rodriguez,Alex	NYY	124	122	1046.1	61	224	7	25	.976	2.45	-5	-1	-4	-5
McGehee,Casey	Mil	153	152	1326.0	81	268	17	31	.954	2.37	-16	4	-12	-8
Ramirez,Aramis	ChC	118	116	1003.1	56	190	16	9	.939	2.21	-12	-1	-9	-10
Wright,David	NYM	155	155	1373.0	110	321	20	34	.956	2.83	-13	0	-10	-10
Young,Michael	Tex	155	155	1370.1	95	265	19	26	.950	2.36	-10	-5	-8	-13

Shortstops - Regulars

Player	Tm	G	GS	Inn	PO	A	E	DP	Pct.	Range	PM	Runs Saved GDP	+/-	Total
Ryan,Brendan	StL	139	124	1127.1	197	430	17	102	.974	5.01	+31	3	24	27
Escobar,Yunel	TOT	134	133	1179.1	204	423	18	110	.972	4.78	+22	2	17	19
Ramirez,Alexei	CWS	156	154	1376.2	249	499	20	109	.974	4.89	+20	1	15	16
Tulowitzki,Troy	Col	122	122	1065.0	211	389	10	103	.984	5.07	+16	4	12	16
Gonzalez,Alex	TOT	157	156	1368.2	195	486	19	117	.973	4.48	+15	4	12	16
Pennington,Cliff	Oak	156	147	1304.2	218	496	25	100	.966	4.93	+10	1	8	9
Hardy,J.J.	Min	100	95	858.1	150	289	11	62	.976	4.60	+6	-1	5	4
Izturis,Cesar	Bal	150	142	1250.0	212	382	9	78	.985	4.28	+2	1	2	3
Bartlett,Jason	TB	131	125	1104.0	152	309	11	58	.977	3.76	+6	-3	5	2
Castro,Starlin	ChC	123	121	1073.2	183	334	27	74	.950	4.33	+2	-1	2	1
Andrus,Elvis	Tex	148	144	1291.1	242	401	16	89	.976	4.48	+1	0	1	1
Aybar,Erick	LAA	135	133	1179.2	198	344	21	59	.963	4.14	+3	-2	2	0
Uribe,Juan	SF	103	96	864.0	134	233	6	38	.984	3.82	+1	-1	1	0
Reyes,Jose	NYM	133	132	1171.1	179	362	15	77	.973	4.16	-1	1	-1	0
Escobar,Alcides	Mil	138	134	1151.1	174	368	20	71	.964	4.16	-1	0	-1	-1
Drew,Stephen	Ari	147	143	1259.1	206	391	10	86	.984	4.27	-2	1	-2	-1
Cabrera,Orlando	Cin	121	119	1030.2	165	300	11	60	.977	4.06	-2	0	-2	-2
Scutaro,Marco	Bos	132	131	1160.0	152	344	18	57	.965	3.83	-6	-2	-5	-7
Desmond,Ian	Was	149	136	1208.0	221	382	34	87	.947	4.49	-9	0	-7	-7
Jeter,Derek	NYY	151	150	1303.2	102	365	6	94	.989	3.78	-17	0	-13	-13
Cedeno,Ronny	Pit	136	132	1149.0	183	382	18	68	.969	4.43	-18	-1	-14	-15
Ramirez,Hanley	Fla	140	140	1217.0	200	342	16	78	.971	4.01	-22	1	-17	-16
Betancourt,Yuniesky	KC	151	151	1331.2	256	418	18	84	.974	4.56	-20	-6	-15	-21

Left Fielders - Regulars

Player	Tm	G	GS	Inn	PO	A	E	DP	Pct.	Range	PM	Runs Saved Throws	HR-Save	+/-	Total
Crawford,Carl	TB	147	144	1260.1	306	7	2	0	.994	2.24	+22	2		12	14
Gardner,Brett	NYY	123	96	906.0	200	9	1	1	.995	2.08	+9	8		5	13
Holliday,Matt	StL	155	155	1341.2	261	8	3	0	.989	1.80	+14	0		8	8
Braun,Ryan	Mil	153	153	1326.0	279	6	3	1	.990	1.93	+8	-3	2	4	3
Pierre,Juan	CWS	149	149	1330.1	307	4	1	1	.997	2.10	0	-1	3	0	2
Willingham,Josh	Was	108	105	880.1	164	7	1	2	.994	1.75	-6	0		-3	-3
Soriano,Alfonso	ChC	134	133	1111.1	204	6	7	0	.968	1.70	-4	-2		-2	-4
Ibanez,Raul	Phi	145	145	1294.0	212	4	2	1	.991	1.50	-5	-3		-3	-6
Young,Delmon	Min	149	142	1277.2	239	12	4	2	.984	1.77	-20	3		-11	-8
Podsednik,Scott	TOT	129	122	1078.2	264	0	4	0	.985	2.20	-8	-5		-5	-10
Gomes,Jonny	Cin	129	126	1037.0	197	6	4	1	.981	1.76	-18	0		-10	-10
Lee,Carlos	Hou	133	133	1096.1	183	6	6	1	.969	1.55	-17	-5		-10	-15

Center Fielders - Regulars

Player	Tm	G	GS	Inn	PO	A	E	DP	Pct.	Range	PM	Runs Saved Throws	HR-Save	+/-	Total
Jackson,Austin	Det	149	140	1256.1	383	9	6	2	.985	2.81	+33	3		18	21
Bourn,Michael	Hou	138	133	1189.1	359	8	3	2	.992	2.78	+24	3		13	16
Gutierrez,Franklin	Sea	146	145	1277.1	413	2	0	0	1.000	2.92	+20	-2	5	11	14
Rios,Alex	CWS	143	141	1246.2	384	6	5	3	.987	2.82	+17	0	2	10	12
Byrd,Marlon	ChC	151	144	1261.2	371	6	3	2	.992	2.69	+9	6		5	11
Victorino,Shane	Phi	143	142	1265.1	360	11	2	4	.995	2.64	+3	7	2	2	11
Young,Chris	Ari	156	153	1350.0	418	10	7	6	.984	2.85	+9	5		5	10
Span,Denard	Min	153	151	1349.2	407	5	4	3	.990	2.75	+14	-1	2	8	9
Stubbs,Drew	Cin	147	135	1229.2	380	7	5	2	.987	2.83	+5	3	2	3	8
Borbon,Julio	Tex	133	121	1095.2	335	2	4	0	.988	2.77	+13	-2	2	7	7
Morgan,Nyjer	Was	134	128	1124.1	339	2	5	0	.986	2.73	+11	-3	2	6	5
Granderson,Curtis	NYY	134	123	1120.1	316	5	2	2	.994	2.58	+3	2		2	4
Fowler,Dexter	Col	120	103	948.1	239	2	1	0	.996	2.29	-2	-1	3	-1	1
Rasmus,Colby	StL	134	124	1105.1	260	1	5	0	.981	2.13	-7	2	3	-4	1
Jones,Adam	Bal	149	148	1298.1	422	12	7	6	.984	3.01	-12	8		-7	1
Wells,Vernon	Tor	151	151	1309.2	354	5	0	2	1.000	2.47	-10	0	2	-6	-4
Upton,B.J.	TB	154	147	1301.2	397	3	5	0	.988	2.77	-18	1		-10	-9
McCutchen,Andrew	Pit	152	152	1290.1	373	8	5	2	.987	2.66	-21	2		-12	-10
Kemp,Matt	LAD	158	150	1346.0	330	3	5	2	.985	2.23	-23	-2		-13	-15

Right Fielders - Regulars

Player	Tm	G	GS	Inn	PO	A	E	DP	Pct.	Range	PM	Runs Saved Throws	HR-Save	+/-	Total
Bruce,Jay	Cin	146	133	1199.1	343	7	3	1	.992	2.63	+24	1	2	14	17
Stanton,Mike	Fla	98	97	854.2	219	10	4	1	.983	2.41	+20	5		12	17
Suzuki,Ichiro	Sea	160	160	1412.0	354	7	4	1	.989	2.30	+16	-2	5	9	12
Choo,Shin-Soo	Cle	142	142	1249.2	267	14	4	3	.986	2.02	-5	12	2	-3	11
Heyward,Jason	Atl	140	136	1196.1	235	5	6	1	.976	1.81	+23	-3		13	10
Pence,Hunter	Hou	155	154	1370.1	340	9	6	2	.983	2.29	+9	2	2	5	9
Werth,Jayson	Phi	135	131	1171.0	249	8	4	2	.985	1.98	+2	8		1	9
Upton,Justin	Ari	128	128	1117.0	265	1	4	0	.985	2.14	+14	-1		8	7
Swisher,Nick	NYY	134	131	1102.0	265	10	4	1	.986	2.25	+8	2		5	7
Francoeur,Jeff	TOT	131	119	1070.0	240	11	3	5	.988	2.11	-6	10		-3	7
Ludwick,Ryan	TOT	125	120	1050.0	249	4	2	0	.992	2.17	+13	-2		8	6
Bautista,Jose	Tor	113	113	982.2	179	12	3	5	.985	1.75	-5	7		-3	4
Markakis,Nick	Bal	159	159	1402.1	332	7	3	1	.991	2.18	-9	3		-5	-2
Drew,J.D.	Bos	133	127	1102.2	234	1	1	1	.996	1.92	-9	2		-5	-3
Hart,Corey	Mil	141	138	1199.0	272	7	2	1	.993	2.09	-15	1		-9	-8
Ethier,Andre	LAD	132	131	1151.1	223	6	1	2	.996	1.79	-21	-2		-12	-14
Quentin,Carlos	CWS	104	103	897.0	183	4	8	1	.959	1.88	-25	-5		-14	-19

Catchers - Regulars

Player	Tm	G	GS	Inn	PO	A	E	DP	PB	Pct.	SBA	CS	PCS	CS%	ER	CERA	Runs Saved SB	Adj-ER	Total
Olivo,Miguel	Col	111	107	935.0	821	62	9	9	10	.990	78	30	3	.38	405	3.90	11	3	14
Molina,Yadier	StL	135	130	1138.0	895	79	5	10	7	.995	68	28	5	.41	409	3.23	6	6	12
Ruiz,Carlos	Phi	118	109	974.1	814	60	6	7	4	.993	70	18	2	.26	360	3.33	2	5	7
Torrealba,Yorvit	SD	92	89	795.2	681	45	3	5	7	.996	60	13	9	.22	278	3.14	1	6	7
Pierzynski,A.J.	CWS	127	123	1092.2	865	61	5	5	3	.995	102	16	11	.16	479	3.95	2	4	6
Wieters,Matt	Bal	126	121	1060.1	775	51	5	10	2	.994	77	21	3	.27	537	4.56	5	0	5
Suzuki,Kurt	Oak	123	121	1058.1	825	35	8	5	7	.991	85	10	9	.12	387	3.29	-2	6	4
Martin,Russell	LAD	93	89	791.1	681	59	10	2	5	.987	70	19	8	.27	354	4.03	4	0	4
Mauer,Joe	Min	112	107	951.2	696	34	3	3	4	.996	72	15	4	.21	404	3.82	-1	4	3
Barajas,Rod	TOT	96	87	776.0	681	27	3	5	3	.996	40	5	1	.13	334	3.87	-4	2	-2
Molina,Bengie	TOT	113	105	897.2	751	60	6	5	4	.993	103	22	2	.21	370	3.71	-1	-1	-2
McCann,Brian	Atl	136	129	1109.2	972	64	14	12	5	.987	120	31	5	.26	456	3.70	4	-6	-2
Rodriguez,Ivan	Was	102	102	884.0	709	55	4	5	2	.995	64	19	3	.30	417	4.25	2	-4	-2
Snyder,Chris	TOT	101	96	839.1	679	58	4	2	6	.995	82	14	5	.17	481	5.16	-3	0	-3
Soto,Geovany	ChC	104	97	847.1	762	45	4	7	2	.995	95	18	3	.19	404	4.29	-4	1	-3
Avila,Alex	Det	98	84	756.2	556	34	4	5	6	.993	63	20	0	.32	376	4.47	-2	-2	-4
Kendall,Jason	KC	118	118	1018.1	721	68	13	11	6	.984	142	32	9	.23	580	5.13	-1	-3	-4
Martinez,Victor	Bos	110	106	904.0	778	44	6	2	4	.993	126	17	10	.13	430	4.28	-2	-5	-7
Doumit,Ryan	Pit	100	91	790.1	533	55	6	3	9	.990	90	6	5	.07	435	4.95	-8	1	-7
Buck,John	Tor	112	104	933.0	733	40	5	6	4	.994	65	15	3	.23	462	4.46	-3	-5	-8

All Others (except catchers)

Player	Tm	Pos	G	GS	Inn	PO	A	E	DP	Pct.	Rng	+/-	RS
Abreu, B	LAA	LF	41	41	349	71	1	0	1	1.000	1.86	-3	-1
	LAA	RF	93	93	805	171	6	6	1	.967	1.98	-13	-6
Abreu, T	Ari	2B	12	11	88	16	18	3	3	.919	3.46	-2	-1
	Ari	3B	20	14	129	11	33	1	1	.978	3.07	+5	4
	Ari	SS	15	13	112	16	33	6	12	.891	3.94	-3	-2
Aldridge, C	LAA	LF	1	1	7	2	0	0	0	1.000	2.57	0	0
	LAA	RF	4	2	22	3	0	0	0	1.000	1.23	-1	-1
Allen, B	Ari	1B	4	2	17	14	0	0	2	1.000	-	0	0
	Ari	LF	14	14	103	27	0	0	0	1.000	2.34	+2	0
Alonso, Y	Cin	1B	6	3	30	24	4	2	5	.933	-	+1	1
Alvarez, P	Pit	3B	94	94	814	61	198	17	17	.938	2.86	-14	-11
Anderson, G	LAD	LF	27	20	189	27	1	2	0	.933	1.33	0	1
	LAD	RF	8	5	45	11	1	0	0	1.000	2.38	+2	2
Anderson, L	Bos	1B	18	11	111	96	9	0	9	1.000	-	+1	1
Andino, R	Bal	2B	8	5	50	6	10	0	1	1.000	2.88	+1	1
	Bal	3B	6	6	50	6	4	0	1	1.000	1.80	+1	1
	Bal	SS	7	5	42	5	14	1	3	.950	4.07	-1	-1
Ankiel, R	KC	CF	25	23	209	68	1	2	1	.972	2.97	-1	-3
	Atl	CF	45	34	325	73	4	2	1	.975	2.13	+1	3
Arias, J	Tex	1B	5	5	35	34	2	1	4	.973	-	-2	-1
	Tex	2B	25	16	149	27	45	1	13	.986	4.33	-1	-1
	NYM	2B	13	4	52	19	13	1	4	.970	5.47	-1	-1
	Tex	SS	3	1	12	5	6	0	2	1.000	8.25	0	0
	NYM	SS	2	1	8	1	0	1	0	.500	1.08	-1	-1
	NYM	LF	1	0	1	0	0	0	0	-	.00		
Atkins, G	Bal	1B	30	30	259	242	16	1	24	.996	-	-9	-7
Aviles, M	KC	2B	87	86	755	183	258	11	40	.976	5.25	-3	-6
	KC	3B	5	4	35	2	1	1	0	.750	.77	-1	-1
	KC	SS	13	11	104	18	29	2	5	.959	4.07	+1	1
Aybar, W	TB	1B	3	2	16	13	1	0	1	1.000	-	0	0
	TB	2B	9	0	15	2	5	0	0	1.000	4.20	+2	2
	TB	3B	7	1	25	0	6	1	0	.857	2.16	-3	-2
Baker, J	ChC	1B	4	1	20	19	1	0	0	1.000	-	0	0
	ChC	2B	26	20	174	52	54	0	13	1.000	5.47	-1	-1
	ChC	3B	33	23	210	9	56	7	2	.903	2.79	+6	4
	ChC	RF	4	4	27	5	0	0	0	1.000	1.67	+1	1
Baldelli, R	TB	RF	4	3	22	6	0	0	0	1.000	2.45	-2	0
Barden, B	Fla	2B	2	1	12	1	8	1	0	.900	6.75	-1	-1
	Fla	3B	16	0	27	3	10	0	3	1.000	4.28	+1	1
	Fla	SS	7	3	42	6	7	0	1	1.000	2.79	0	0
Barmes, C	Col	2B	80	60	633	163	197	5	59	.986	5.12	-2	-1
	Col	3B	1	0	1	0	0	0	0	-	.00		
	Col	SS	47	39	361	50	141	5	33	.974	4.76	+14	13
Barney, D	ChC	2B	10	5	54	13	17	2	4	.938	4.97	-1	-1
	ChC	3B	8	4	34	1	11	0	1	1.000	3.18	+4	3
	ChC	SS	11	9	85	10	30	0	9	1.000	4.24	+3	3
Bautista, J	Tor	1B	4	1	18	26	0	0	0	1.000	-	+1	1
	Tor	3B	48	45	393	26	100	4	7	.969	2.89	+2	0
	Tor	CF	1	0	3	1	0	0	0	1.000	3.00	-1	-1
	Tor	RF	113	113	982	179	12	3	5	.985	1.75	-5	4
Baxter, M	SD	1B	1	0	1	1	0	0	0	1.000	-		
Bay, J	NYM	LF	93	92	820	141	6	1	0	.993	1.61	-1	0
Bell, J	Bal	3B	50	40	369	27	77	4	8	.963	2.53	+1	1
Belliard, R	LAD	1B	10	7	63	46	6	1	6	.981	-	0	0
	LAD	2B	20	15	127	38	37	1	5	.987	5.29	-1	-2
	LAD	3B	16	14	115	10	23	3	3	.917	2.58	+1	1
Beltran, C	NYM	CF	61	58	517	146	4	0	1	1.000	2.61	-6	0
Berkman, L	NYY	1B	8	7	60	54	2	1	8	.982	-	-3	-2
	Hou	1B	85	84	739	696	72	1	60	.999	-	+4	5
Bernadina, R	Was	LF	44	34	318	58	2	1	1	.984	1.70	+5	7
	Was	CF	26	20	177	45	2	1	1	.979	2.38	-7	-4
	Was	RF	77	57	492	104	5	2	2	.982	1.99	-3	1
Betemit, W	KC	1B	5	4	35	33	0	1	1	.971	-	-1	-1
	KC	2B	2	2	16	1	4	1	0	.833	2.81	-3	-2
	KC	3B	53	51	455	30	75	8	9	.929	2.08	-15	-13
	KC	LF	2	2	18	3	0	0	0	1.000	1.50	0	0
Blake, C	LAD	1B	1	0	1	1	0	0	0	1.000	-		
Blalock, H	TB	1B	1	1	8	6	0	0	1	1.000	-		
	TB	3B	2	1	10	1	3	1	0	.800	3.60	+1	1
	TB	RF	2	0	5	1	0	0	0	1.000	1.80	+1	1
Blanco, A	Tex	2B	40	31	283	48	92	4	19	.972	4.45	-2	-1
	Tex	3B	9	2	33	1	5	1	0	.857	1.64	-1	-1

Player	Tm	Pos	G	GS	Inn	PO	A	E	DP	Pct.	Rng	+/-	RS
	Tex	SS	16	15	128	16	37	2	8	.964	3.73	-1	-1
Blanco, G	KC	LF	1	1	8	0	0	0	0	-	.00	-3	-2
	Atl	LF	7	0	13	2	0	0	0	1.000	1.35	0	0
	KC	CF	40	40	347	95	3	0	1	1.000	2.54	-4	-2
	Atl	CF	26	16	168	40	1	1	1	.976	2.20	+6	4
	KC	RF	3	3	27	4	0	0	0	1.000	1.33	-2	-1
Blanks, K	SD	1B	4	1	12	15	1	0	0	1.000	-	+1	1
	SD	LF	30	28	253	45	3	0	0	1.000	1.71	+1	2
Bloomquist, W	KC	1B	3	0	4	4	1	0	0	1.000	-	+1	1
	KC	2B	4	4	31	9	9	1	2	.947	5.23	0	0
	Cin	2B	2	0	3	0	0	0	0	-	.00	0	0
	KC	3B	11	9	79	5	18	4	4	.852	2.62	-3	-2
	KC	SS	1	0	1	0	0	0	0	-	.00	0	0
	KC	LF	4	4	39	8	0	0	0	1.000	1.85	-2	-1
	Cin	LF	3	0	8	0	0	0	0	-	.00	0	0
	KC	CF	8	8	69	20	1	0	0	1.000	2.74	-6	-3
	KC	RF	22	15	147	30	2	0	0	1.000	1.95	-4	-2
	Cin	RF	5	3	27	6	0	0	0	1.000	1.98	0	0
Blum, G	Hou	1B	14	10	90	90	4	1	16	.989	-	-1	-1
	Hou	2B	8	6	60	9	21	0	1	1.000	4.50	-1	-1
	Hou	3B	14	12	108	8	32	1	1	.976	3.31	+2	2
	Hou	SS	18	14	112	23	36	4	5	.937	4.73	-3	-3
Bocock, B	Phi	SS	6	0	15	3	2	0	0	1.000	3.00	0	0
Boesch, B	Det	LF	44	44	350	86	3	4	1	.957	2.29	+6	4
	Det	RF	79	67	587	130	6	6	1	.958	2.08	-13	-5
Boggs, B	Tex	LF	1	0	1	0	0	0	0	-	.00		
	Tex	RF	3	2	17	5	0	0	0	1.000	2.65	-2	-1
Bogusevic, B	Hou	LF	7	3	29	11	0	0	0	1.000	3.41	+2	1
	Hou	CF	3	2	17	4	0	0	0	1.000	2.12	+1	1
	Hou	RF	2	1	9	3	0	0	0	1.000	3.00	+1	1
Bonifacio, E	Fla	2B	5	2	27	2	14	1	3	.941	5.27	0	0
	Fla	3B	6	4	37	3	10	0	1	1.000	3.16	+1	1
	Fla	SS	9	8	71	11	11	0	1	1.000	2.76	0	0
	Fla	LF	7	5	48	8	1	0	0	1.000	1.68	0	0
	Fla	CF	17	14	130	40	2	1	0	.977	2.91	0	3
	Fla	RF	6	4	40	7	0	0	0	1.000	1.55	0	0
Borbon, J	Tex	LF	1	1	6	2	0	0	0	1.000	3.00	1	1
Bourgeois, J	Hou	2B	2	0	3	2	2	0	1	1.000	12.00	0	0
	Hou	LF	25	4	65	14	0	0	0	1.000	1.94	+2	2
	Hou	CF	24	10	162	50	0	0	0	1.000	2.78	-2	-3
	Hou	RF	1	0	1	1	0	0	0	1.000	9.00	0	0
Bourjos, P	LAA	CF	51	49	449	149	10	1	1	.994	3.18	+16	15
Bowker, J	Pit	1B	5	4	37	29	3	1	1	.970	-	0	0
	Pit	LF	1	0	1	0	0	0	0	-	.00	0	-1
	SF	LF	16	11	103	25	1	0	0	1.000	2.26	+1	1
	Pit	RF	16	15	113	30	0	0	0	1.000	2.39	+1	1
	SF	RF	8	7	59	8	0	0	0	1.000	1.21	+1	1
Bradley, M	Sea	LF	39	38	323	87	3	1	0	.989	2.51	11	2
	Sea	RF	1	1	7	1	0	1	0	.500	1.29	0	0
Brantley, M	Cle	LF	7	7	63	5	0	0	0	1.000	.71	-1	0
	Cle	CF	65	62	562	156	0	2	0	.987	2.50	-6	-4
Branyan, R	Cle	1B	47	44	383	426	44	5	64	.989	-	+10	7
	Sea	1B	4	4	33	32	1	0	2	1.000	-		
Brignac, R	TB	2B	68	39	389	77	129	5	19	.976	4.76	+5	2
	TB	SS	50	36	340	56	108	4	20	.976	4.33	+8	6
	TB	RF	2	0	2	1	0	0	0	1.000	4.50	-1	-1
Brown, D	Phi	RF	15	13	112	20	1	1	0	.967	2.33	-5	-2
Brown, J	Cle	1B	10	8	73	70	2	0	5	1.000	-	+1	1
	Cle	LF	7	7	57	17	1	0	0	1.000	2.84	-1	0
Buck, T	Oak	LF	10	10	87	12	0	0	0	1.000	1.24	-3	-2
	Oak	RF	4	3	22	7	0	0	0	1.000	1.33	+2	1
Burrell, P	SF	LF	87	86	632	121	4	2	0	.984	1.78	+2	6
Burriss, E	SF	2B	5	0	12	3	1	0	0	1.000	3.00	+1	1
Byrnes, E	Sea	LF	10	8	83	28	0	0	0	1.000	3.04	0	1
	Sea	CF	1	0	2	0	0	0	0	-	.00	0	0
Cabrera, A	Cle	SS	95	94	825	148	271	12	73	.972	4.57	-7	-3
Cabrera, E	SD	2B	6	5	44	7	15	0	3	1.000	4.50	+2	2
	SD	SS	61	50	456	63	137	7	30	.966	3.95	-3	-2
Cabrera, M	Atl	LF	84	45	481	82	3	1	1	.988	1.59	-12	-5
	Atl	CF	55	49	385	95	4	3	1	.971	2.31	-9	-4
	Atl	RF	25	21	197	36	1	0	0	1.000	1.68	-2	0
Cain, L	Mil	LF	1	1	8	3	0	0	0	1.000	3.38	0	0
	Mil	CF	38	34	306	96	2	2	2	.980	2.88	+8	6
	Mil	RF	1	1	9	2	1	0	0	1.000	3.00	0	1

Player	Tm	Pos	G	GS	Inn	PO	A	E	DP	Pct.	Rng	+/-	RS
Cairo, M	Cin	1B	14	10	100	97	4	1	14	.990	-	-2	-1
	Cin	2B	6	2	26	3	8	0	1	1.000	3.81	+1	1
	Cin	3B	37	25	241	17	29	2	4	.958	1.71	-5	-4
	Cin	SS	1	0	1	0	0	0	0	-	.00	0	0
	Cin	RF	1	1	7	1	0	0	0	1.000	1.29	0	0
Callaspo, A	LAA	2B	1	0	2	0	0	0	0	-	.00	0	0
	KC	2B	11	11	99	19	30	1	9	.980	4.45	-1	-1
	LAA	3B	54	52	465	38	101	4	12	.972	2.69	+3	3
	KC	3B	76	76	668	45	139	6	13	.968	2.48	-4	-2
	LAA	LF	1	0	1	0	0	0	0	-	.00		
Cameron, M	Bos	CF	46	43	392	111	3	2	1	.983	2.62	-13	-6
Cantu, J	Tex	1B	23	21	177	158	11	0	20	1.000	-	+2	1
	Fla	1B	40	7	125	109	10	0	15	1.000	-	-1	-1
	Tex	2B	1	0	2	0	0	0	0	-	.00	0	0
	Tex	3B	8	5	48	2	6	0	0	1.000	1.50	-3	-2
	Fla	3B	81	81	632	42	118	16	11	.909	2.28	-10	-7
Carp, M	Sea	1B	9	9	66	65	4	0	3	1.000	-	0	0
	Sea	LF	1	1	4	0	0	0	0	-	.00	0	0
Carroll, B	Fla	LF	7	6	54	11	0	1	0	.917	1.83	-1	-1
	Fla	RF	20	14	132	22	2	0	0	1.000	1.63	+3	4
Carroll, J	LAD	2B	48	19	219	48	78	0	12	1.000	5.18	-3	-3
	LAD	3B	11	8	73	5	14	2	1	.905	2.33	0	0
	LAD	SS	69	64	573	80	195	4	32	.986	4.32	+1	-1
	LAD	LF	5	5	38	13	0	0	0	1.000	3.08	+1	0
Carson, M	Oak	LF	6	1	19	6	0	0	0	1.000	2.84	+1	1
	Oak	CF	3	2	21	6	0	0	0	1.000	2.57	-1	-1
	Oak	RF	25	18	154	33	2	0	0	1.000	2.05	+3	3
Carter, C	Oak	LF	22	22	156	25	0	2	0	.926	1.44	-3	-2
Carter, C	NYM	LF	17	15	108	16	0	0	0	1.000	1.33	-2	-1
	NYM	RF	13	11	68	14	0	0	0	1.000	1.85	-1	-2
Casilla, A	Min	2B	24	16	159	34	51	1	11	.988	4.81	+3	1
	Min	3B	6	1	19	1	2	0	0	1.000	1.42	-3	-2
	Min	SS	30	20	189	30	69	4	15	.961	4.71	+2	3
	Min	CF	1	0	3	1	0	0	0	1.000	3.00	0	0
Castillo, L	NYM	2B	74	64	576	122	176	2	38	.993	4.65	+4	1
Castro, J	Phi	2B	7	3	36	12	13	2	5	.926	6.25	-3	-2
	Phi	3B	11	4	49	1	10	1	1	.917	2.02	-1	-1
	LAD	SS	1	1	8	1	1	0	1	1.000	2.25	0	0
	Phi	SS	32	27	239	31	78	3	15	.973	4.10	-4	-4
Catalanotto, F	NYM	1B	1	1	5	0	0	0	0	-	-	0	0
	NYM	LF	1	0	2	0	0	0	0	-	.00	0	0
Cervelli, F	NYY	3B	2	0	3	1	0	0	0	1.000	3.00		
Chavez, E	Oak	1B	1	0	5	7	0	0	0	1.000	-	0	0
Church, R	Ari	LF	9	4	46	11	0	0	0	1.000	2.15	+2	0
	Pit	LF	13	12	95	25	2	0	0	1.000	2.56	0	0
	Ari	CF	3	2	16	9	0	0	0	1.000	5.06	+2	1
	Pit	CF	4	1	18	6	0	0	0	1.000	3.00	0	0
	Pit	RF	33	23	205	45	3	0	1	1.000	2.10	-12	-2
Ciriaco, P	Pit	SS	1	0	2	1	2	0	1	1.000	13.50	0	0
Clement, J	Pit	1B	38	33	293	295	18	2	20	.994	-	+3	3
Clevlen, B	Atl	LF	2	1	12	5	0	0	0	1.000	3.75	0	0
Coghlan, C	Fla	LF	90	87	770	160	7	1	0	.994	1.95	-6	4
Colvin, T	ChC	LF	55	23	262	47	0	0	0	1.000	1.61	+5	0
	ChC	CF	18	14	128	31	1	1	0	.970	2.25	-10	-5
	ChC	RF	59	44	388	96	3	5	0	.952	2.29	0	3
Conrad, B	Atl	2B	9	2	29	2	13	1	0	.938	4.55	+1	1
	Atl	3B	37	22	227	17	48	7	5	.903	2.58	-4	-2
Cora, A	NYM	1B	2	0	1	1	0	0	0	1.000	-		
	Tex	2B	2	2	18	2	3	0	2	1.000	2.50	-1	-1
	NYM	2B	47	38	344	86	81	1	29	.994	4.36	-7	-6
	Tex	3B	1	0	2	1	1	0	0	1.000	9.00	0	0
	NYM	SS	6	3	32	7	11	1	4	.947	5.06	-1	-1
Counsell, C	Mil	2B	3	1	14	3	7	1	2	.909	6.14	+1	1
	Mil	3B	20	9	99	7	20	3	5	.900	2.45	-1	-1
	Mil	SS	42	25	253	30	79	2	17	.982	3.87	+1	2
Cousins, S	Fla	CF	8	3	34	15	0	0	0	1.000	3.97	+3	2
	Fla	RF	3	1	11	3	0	0	0	1.000	2.45	0	1
Craig, A	StL	1B	5	1	17	16	1	0	2	1.000	-	+1	1
	StL	2B	1	0	1	0	0	0	0	-	.00	0	0
	StL	3B	2	1	10	0	0	1	0	.000	.00	0	0
	StL	LF	5	2	28	7	0	0	0	1.000	2.25	0	0
	StL	RF	30	23	175	32	1	0	0	1.000	1.69	-4	0
Crisp, C	Oak	CF	73	73	625	182	2	2	0	.989	2.65	+12	9
Crosby, B	Pit	1B	7	5	43	47	3	0	6	1.000	-	+2	1

Player	Tm	Pos	G	GS	Inn	PO	A	E	DP	Pct.	Rng	+/-	RS
	Ari	2B	1	0	2	0	1	0	0	1.000	4.50	0	0
	Pit	2B	15	10	88	18	21	0	2	1.000	3.99	+1	1
	Ari	3B	2	2	13	1	5	1	1	.857	4.15	0	0
	Pit	3B	8	4	51	1	11	0	0	1.000	2.12	+2	2
	Pit	SS	22	22	178	33	62	8	9	.922	4.79	-11	-9
Crowe, T	Cle	LF	48	38	374	92	6	1	1	.990	2.36	+9	9
	Cle	CF	68	65	567	176	3	4	0	.978	2.84	-5	-2
	Cle	RF	4	3	27	6	0	0	0	1.000	2.00	-1	-1
Cruz, L	Mil	SS	5	3	34	7	7	0	1	1.000	3.71	-1	-1
Cruz, N	Tex	LF	14	10	88	22	0	0	0	1.000	2.23	+2	0
	Tex	RF	94	91	799	228	3	5	1	.979	2.60	+12	11
Cuddyer, M	Min	1B	84	81	721	760	39	3	70	.996	-	-8	-6
	Min	2B	1	1	8	3	3	0	0	1.000	6.75	-1	-1
	Min	3B	14	13	107	3	21	1	1	.960	2.02	0	-1
	Min	CF	2	1	11	1	0	0	0	1.000	.82	0	0
	Min	RF	66	60	539	117	5	2	0	.984	2.04	-17	-6
Cunningham, A	SD	LF	23	14	141	25	0	0	0	1.000	1.59	+2	0
	SD	CF	2	2	13	3	0	0	0	1.000	2.08	0	0
	SD	RF	17	14	126	29	0	0	0	1.000	2.07	+3	2
Curtis, C	NYY	LF	7	2	26	5	0	0	0	1.000	1.73	+1	0
	NYY	RF	17	9	88	17	0	0	0	1.000	1.73	-2	-1
Cust, J	Oak	LF	13	12	90	19	2	1	0	.955	2.10	0	0
	Oak	RF	3	2	15	10	1	0	0	1.000	6.46	0	0
Damon, J	Det	LF	33	31	239	51	2	2	1	.964	1.99	-4	-1
	Det	CF	4	4	29	6	0	0	0	1.000	1.86	+1	1
Davis, C	Tex	1B	41	30	298	269	22	2	27	.993	-	+1	1
	Tex	3B	1	0	2	0	1	0	0	1.000	4.50	0	0
Davis, R	Oak	LF	47	33	320	57	1	1	0	.983	1.63	+8	3
	Oak	CF	83	74	677	190	2	2	1	.990	2.55	-3	-5
	Oak	RF	27	26	186	47	2	1	1	.980	2.37	+7	5
De Aza, A	CWS	CF	9	7	52	11	0	0	0	1.000	1.90	-1	-2
	CWS	RF	5	1	19	6	0	0	0	1.000	2.84	+1	1
DeJesus, D	KC	LF	2	1	10	2	0	0	0	1.000	1.80	0	-1
	KC	CF	19	19	155	48	1	0	1	1.000	2.85	-2	0
	KC	RF	70	67	597	133	4	0	0	1.000	2.06	-3	-4
Denorfia, C	SD	LF	44	15	208	41	2	0	0	1.000	1.86	+5	5
	SD	CF	50	44	360	107	5	2	2	.982	2.79	-10	-7
	SD	RF	18	13	116	23	1	0	1	1.000	1.86	0	1
DeRosa, M	SF	2B	7	4	51	13	14	2	3	.931	4.76	0	0
	SF	LF	21	21	163	31	0	0	0	1.000	1.71	+6	3
Descalso, D	StL	3B	9	9	73	2	15	0	4	1.000	2.10	+2	2
	StL	SS	1	0	1	0	1	0	0	1.000	9.00	0	0
Desmond, I	Was	RF	1	0	0	0	0	0	0	-	.00		
DeWitt, B	ChC	2B	48	46	411	88	119	5	30	.976	4.53	-2	-2
	LAD	2B	78	76	628	169	182	7	41	.980	5.03	+1	-1
	ChC	3B	1	1	8	0	2	2	0	.500	2.25	-1	-1
Diaz, A	Pit	SS	15	8	82	5	19	2	3	.923	2.63	-3	-2
Diaz, M	Atl	LF	63	53	448	93	1	2	0	.979	1.89	+11	5
Dickerson, C	Cin	LF	8	3	33	7	0	0	0	1.000	1.89	+1	1
	Cin	CF	6	6	37	10	0	0	0	1.000	2.41	+3	2
	Mil	CF	14	11	95	25	0	0	0	1.000	2.35	-2	-1
	Cin	RF	1	1	7	3	0	0	0	1.000	3.86	+2	1
	Mil	RF	3	2	18	3	0	0	0	1.000	1.47	+1	1
Dobbs, G	Phi	1B	2	1	12	14	1	0	0	1.000	-	0	0
	Phi	3B	36	28	230	16	37	6	3	.898	2.07	-9	-7
	Phi	RF	1	1	6	0	0	0	0	-	.00	-1	-1
Donald, J	Cle	2B	41	40	356	61	128	3	18	.984	4.77	+5	3
	Cle	SS	47	44	388	58	138	9	34	.956	4.54	-13	-10
Donaldson, J	Oak	1B	2	1	6	2	0	1	1	.667	-	-1	-2
Doumit, R	Pit	1B	3	3	23	23	2	1	1	.962	-	-2	-1
	Pit	RF	18	17	146	38	1	3	0	.929	2.40	0	-1
Downs, M	Hou	2B	2	1	11	2	0	0	0	1.000	1.54	0	0
	SF	2B	19	18	174	30	47	1	12	.987	3.98	+2	2
	Hou	3B	2	1	11	0	3	0	1	1.000	2.45	+1	1
	Hou	SS	2	1	10	2	2	0	1	1.000	3.60	0	0
Duda, L	NYM	LF	24	23	192	32	1	0	1	1.000	1.55	0	1
Duncan, S	Cle	1B	4	2	17	15	0	0	1	1.000	-	-2	-1
	Cle	LF	41	38	309	66	6	0	1	1.000	2.10	+1	6
	Cle	RF	8	5	50	9	1	0	0	1.000	1.80	+1	1
Durango, L	SD	CF	10	8	76	17	2	1	0	.950	2.23	-4	0
Dyson, J	KC	CF	15	14	129	48	2	2	2	.962	3.49	+6	4
Edmonds, J	Cin	1B	3	2	18	17	0	0	2	1.000	-	0	0
	Mil	1B	3	1	13	12	1	0	3	1.000	-	+1	1
	Cin	LF	1	1	9	0	0	0	0	-	.00	0	0

Player	Tm	Pos	G	GS	Inn	PO	A	E	DP	Pct.	Rng	+/-	RS
	Cin	CF	5	4	26	7	0	0	0	1.000	2.42	-3	-2
	Mil	CF	47	43	360	128	5	1	3	.993	3.32	+6	4
	Cin	RF	1	0	3	1	0	0	0	1.000	3.00	0	0
	Mil	RF	13	7	77	18	1	0	0	1.000	2.20	-2	-1
Eldred, B	Col	1B	6	5	46	52	3	0	5	1.000	-	0	0
Ellsbury, J	Bos	LF	6	5	46	11	0	0	0	1.000	2.14	+1	1
	Bos	CF	13	13	104	33	0	0	0	1.000	2.84	+2	0
Encarnacion, E	Tor	3B	95	95	841	71	174	18	16	.932	2.62	+4	3
Escobar, A	Mil	LF	2	0	4	2	0	0	0	1.000	4.50	0	0
	Mil	CF	1	0	2	4	0	0	0	1.000	18.00	+1	1
	Mil	RF	2	1	11	2	0	0	0	1.000	1.64	0	0
Escobar, Y	Tor	SS	60	60	532	105	173	9	48	.969	4.70	0	2
	Atl	SS	74	73	646	99	250	9	62	.975	4.86	+22	17
Espinosa, D	Was	2B	25	23	211	57	74	0	20	1.000	5.58	0	1
	Was	SS	2	2	18	2	9	1	1	.917	5.50	0	0
Ethier, A	LAD	1B	1	0	1	0	0	0	0	-	-	0	0
Evans, N	NYM	LF	8	4	40	8	0	0	0	1.000	1.80	0	0
	NYM	CF	1	0	1	1	0	0	0	1.000	9.00	+1	1
	NYM	RF	3	1	12	4	0	0	0	1.000	3.00	-1	-1
Evans, T	LAA	CF	1	0	2	1	0	0	0	1.000	4.50	0	0
Everett, A	Det	SS	31	28	229	48	74	1	24	.992	4.79	-2	-1
Feliciano, J	NYM	LF	13	2	46	7	0	0	0	1.000	1.37	0	0
	NYM	CF	12	8	72	17	0	0	0	1.000	2.11	-3	0
	NYM	RF	14	9	99	28	1	0	0	1.000	2.62	+2	2
Feliz, P	Hou	1B	15	10	91	83	9	3	11	.968	-	-4	-3
	Hou	3B	63	60	529	28	103	8	13	.942	2.23	-11	-7
	StL	3B	39	30	275	18	70	2	4	.978	2.88	+4	4
Fields, J	KC	3B	12	12	106	9	19	5	0	.848	2.38	+1	1
Fontenot, M	ChC	2B	33	29	251	62	64	4	16	.969	4.51	-2	-3
	SF	2B	16	9	97	23	32	2	5	.965	5.10	-3	-3
	ChC	3B	13	7	68	3	17	2	1	.909	2.65	-4	-3
	SF	3B	6	3	26	1	5	0	1	1.000	2.03	0	0
	ChC	SS	9	4	32	7	9	0	2	1.000	4.50	-2	-2
	SF	SS	5	3	29	4	7	1	0	.917	3.41	-3	-2
Ford, D	SF	CF	1	0	2	0	0	0	0	-	.00	0	0
Fox, J	Bal	1B	10	7	66	58	4	1	5	.984	-	-1	-2
	Bal	3B	1	1	7	0	0	0	0	-	.00	-1	-1
	Oak	3B	3	0	3	0	1	0	0	1.000	3.00	0	0
	Bal	LF	4	1	13	4	0	0	0	1.000	2.77	0	0
	Oak	LF	9	6	56	12	1	0	0	1.000	2.08	0	0
Francisco, B	Phi	LF	23	17	160	30	3	0	0	1.000	1.86	+2	-1
	Phi	CF	2	1	13	2	0	0	0	1.000	1.38	0	0
	Phi	RF	20	10	113	28	0	0	0	1.000	2.22	-1	-2
Francisco, J	Cin	3B	12	6	74	3	8	1	3	.917	1.33	0	0
Francoeur, J	Tex	LF	2	0	12	1	0	1	0	.500	.75	0	0
	Tex	RF	13	10	88	19	0	0	0	1.000	1.94	0	0
	NYM	RF	118	109	982	221	11	3	5	.987	2.13	-6	7
Frandsen, K	LAA	1B	4	4	32	35	3	0	4	1.000	-	+1	1
	LAA	2B	4	2	20	3	6	1	2	.900	4.05	-2	-2
	LAA	3B	43	38	346	20	73	5	3	.953	2.62	0	-1
	LAA	LF	1	0	1	0	0	0	0	-	.00	-1	-1
Frazier, J	Det	LF	3	3	24	11	1	0	1	1.000	4.50	+1	2
	Det	RF	1	1	0	0	0	0	0	-	.00		
Freeman, F	Atl	1B	12	2	39	36	5	0	1	1.000	-	0	0
Freese, D	StL	1B	1	0	3	3	0	0	0	1.000	-	0	0
	StL	3B	66	64	557	31	139	9	22	.950	2.75	-5	-2
Fukudome, K	ChC	RF	110	87	816	190	4	1	1	.995	2.14	-6	-3
Fuld, S	ChC	LF	8	1	10	1	0	0	0	1.000	.90	-1	-1
	ChC	CF	7	4	47	22	0	0	0	1.000	4.21	+2	1
Furcal, R	LAD	SS	93	91	800	127	275	19	47	.955	4.52	+3	2
Gamel, M	Mil	3B	3	1	14	0	0	0	0	-	.00	0	0
	Mil	LF	1	1	6	1	0	0	0	1.000	1.50	-1	-1
Gardner, B	NYY	LF	123	96	906	200	9	1	1	.995	2.08	+9	13
	NYY	CF	44	38	305	87	3	0	1	1.000	2.66	+6	3
Garko, R	Tex	1B	6	3	33	17	6	0	3	1.000	-	0	0
Gentry, C	Tex	LF	6	3	28	7	1	0	0	1.000	2.57	0	1
	Tex	CF	7	6	44	9	0	0	0	1.000	1.84	+3	2
	Tex	RF	4	0	6	0	0	0	0	-	.00	0	0
German, E	Tex	2B	3	2	20	5	6	0	2	1.000	4.95	0	0
	Tex	SS	1	0	2	0	0	0	0	-	.00	0	0
	Tex	LF	1	1	7	0	0	0	0	-	.00	0	0
Gerut, J	Mil	LF	6	2	30	0	0	0	0	1.000	2.64	-2	-1
	Mil	CF	10	7	70	20	3	0	1	1.000	2.93	0	1
	Mil	RF	4	2	16	3	0	0	0	1.000	1.65	0	0

Player	Tm	Pos	G	GS	Inn	PO	A	E	DP	Pct.	Rng	+/-	RS
Getz, C	KC	2B	64	59	535	113	164	3	43	.989	4.66	-6	-3
	KC	3B	2	1	9	0	0	1	0	1.000	.00	-1	-1
Giambi, J	Col	1B	37	35	270	267	8	4	25	.986	-	-3	-2
Gibbons, J	LAD	1B	3	2	15	16	2	0	1	1.000	-	0	0
	LAD	LF	15	13	106	23	1	1	0	.960	2.04	-5	-3
	LAD	RF	1	0	3	2	0	0	0	1.000	6.00	-1	-1
Gillespie, C	Ari	LF	24	15	134	30	1	1	0	.969	2.07	-3	-4
	Ari	CF	7	4	41	7	0	0	0	1.000	1.52	-3	-2
	Ari	RF	9	7	59	10	0	0	0	1.000	1.53	+2	1
Gimenez, C	Cle	LF	1	0	2	1	0	0	0	1.000	4.50	0	0
	Cle	RF	1	0	1	0	0	0	0	-	.00		
Glaus, T	Atl	1B	114	107	936	977	46	9	110	.991	-	-9	-8
	Atl	3B	1	0	2	0	1	0	0	1.000	4.50	0	0
Gload, R	Phi	1B	18	8	92	92	6	0	9	1.000	-	-4	-3
	Phi	LF	1	0	0	0	0	0	0	-	.00		
	Phi	RF	7	6	43	10	0	1	0	.909	2.06	+2	1
Golson, G	NYY	LF	2	1	7	0	0	0	0	-	.00	0	0
	NYY	CF	6	1	16	6	0	0	0	1.000	3.38	+1	1
	NYY	RF	17	4	52	19	1	0	1	1.000	3.46	+3	3
Gomez, C	Mil	LF	5	0	12	2	0	0	0	1.000	1.42	-1	-1
	Mil	CF	75	66	594	152	2	5	0	.969	2.33	-4	2
	Mil	RF	2	1	11	3	0	0	0	1.000	2.45	+1	1
Gonzalez, A	Was	1B	3	2	16	15	0	0	3	1.000	-	0	0
	Was	2B	38	10	120	35	42	1	16	.987	5.76	-3	0
	Was	3B	28	17	178	16	47	3	3	.955	3.18	+11	8
	Was	SS	16	8	78	9	26	1	6	.972	4.00	-1	-1
	Was	RF	1	0	2	0	0	0	0	-	.00		
Gonzalez, A	Tor	SS	85	85	740	104	272	11	67	.972	4.57	+9	9
	Atl	SS	72	71	628	91	214	8	50	.974	4.37	+6	7
Gonzalez, C	Col	LF	63	51	472	77	5	1	0	.988	1.56	+4	4
	Col	CF	58	55	452	120	1	0	0	1.000	2.53	-8	5
	Col	RF	40	34	299	56	2	0	1	1.000	1.74	-1	-1
Gordon, A	KC	1B	1	0	3	1	0	0	0	1.000	-		
	KC	3B	10	9	84	3	10	4	0	.765	1.39	-6	-6
	KC	LF	55	55	486	132	2	2	1	.985	2.48	+5	6
	KC	RF	3	3	25	5	0	1	0	.833	1.80	-1	-2
Green, N	Tor	2B	3	2	18	3	8	0	1	1.000	5.30	0	0
	LAD	2B	3	2	20	4	9	0	2	1.000	5.85	+1	1
	Tor	SS	3	1	10	3	2	0	0	1.000	4.50	-1	-1
	LAD	SS	1	0	2	0	0	0	0	-	.00	0	0
Greene, T	StL	2B	15	9	76	7	22	2	6	.935	3.43	+1	2
	StL	3B	11	5	40	1	12	1	0	.929	2.93	0	0
	StL	SS	22	17	145	22	40	5	12	.934	4.40	+1	1
Gross, G	Oak	LF	44	21	229	42	1	1	0	.977	1.69	-7	-3
	Oak	CF	10	10	76	16	0	0	0	1.000	1.89	-3	-2
	Oak	RF	50	21	245	54	5	0	0	1.000	2.16	+3	4
Grudzielanek, M	Cle	2B	27	26	228	54	86	2	22	.986	5.52	+1	2
Guerrero, V	Tex	LF	1	1	7	1	0	0	0	1.000	1.29	0	0
	Tex	RF	17	15	118	27	1	2	0	.933	2.12	-1	-2
Guillen, C	Det	2B	47	45	393	86	138	3	32	.987	5.13	-7	-5
	Det	LF	4	4	28	6	0	1	0	.857	1.93	0	-1
Guillen, J	KC	RF	22	21	169	41	1	1	0	.977	2.24	+4	1
	SF	RF	38	38	269	57	2	2	0	.967	1.97	+1	0
Guzman, C	Tex	2B	9	9	77	12	21	1	3	.971	3.86	0	-1
	Was	2B	63	54	475	122	105	0	29	1.000	5.44	6	0
	Tex	SS	3	2	22	4	4	1	0	.889	3.27	0	0
	Was	SS	20	16	130	23	52	2	5	.974	5.18	+2	-1
	Was	RF	8	3	32	8	0	1	0	.889	2.23	-1	-1
Gwynn, T	SD	CF	105	72	701	160	5	0	0	1.000	2.12	+19	11
Hairston, J	SD	2B	47	44	381	77	112	1	26	.995	4.46	+2	2
	SD	3B	3	2	19	1	3	0	0	1.000	1.86	0	0
	SD	SS	62	53	489	87	162	6	27	.976	4.58	+3	1
	SD	LF	4	4	28	4	0	0	0	1.000	2.00	-1	-1
	SD	RF	8	4	51	12	0	0	0	1.000	2.12	+2	0
Hairston, S	SD	LF	71	56	487	94	0	3	0	.969	1.73	0	-4
	SD	CF	19	18	140	42	3	1	1	.978	2.89	+7	5
	SD	RF	6	3	27	5	0	0	0	1.000	1.67	0	0
Hall, B	Bos	2B	51	38	353	72	100	6	19	.966	4.38	-3	-3
	Bos	3B	5	2	27	4	6	1	1	.909	3.33	+1	1
	Bos	SS	3	3	36	3	8	1	1	.917	2.75	+1	1
	Bos	LF	55	42	341	78	3	1	0	.988	2.14	-16	-4
	Bos	CF	7	6	48	18	0	1	0	.947	3.38	+2	2
	Bos	RF	9	5	40	8	0	2	0	.800	1.79	0	0
Halman, G	Sea	LF	4	3	31	7	0	0	0	1.000	2.03	+2	1

Player	Tm	Pos	G	GS	Inn	PO	A	E	DP	Pct.	Rng	+/-	RS
	Sea	CF	4	4	34	13	0	0	0	1.000	3.38	+2	2
	Sea	RF	1	0	1	0	0	0	0		.00		
Hamilton, J	Tex	LF	92	87	772	179	7	4	1	.979	2.17	+3	3
	Tex	CF	40	29	262	75	2	0	1	1.000	2.65	+2	4
Hamilton, M	StL	1B	4	2	21	23	1	0	3	1.000	-	+1	1
Harris, B	Min	1B	3	2	18	14	0	0	1	1.000	-	-1	-1
	Min	2B	1	0	1	0	0	0	0		.00	0	0
	Min	3B	27	21	183	11	40	0	3	1.000	2.50	-1	-1
	Min	SS	11	9	75	9	21	0	5	1.000	3.60	-4	-3
Harris, W	Was	3B	6	2	22	1	8	1	0	.900	3.68	+2	2
	Was	LF	46	19	200	38	0	1	0	.974	1.71	-1	-1
	Was	CF	2	0	4	2	0	0	0	1.000	4.50	0	0
	Was	RF	43	23	220	58	0	1	0	.983	2.37	-4	-1
Hawpe, B	TB	1B	3	2	20	12	0	0	1	1.000	-	0	0
	Col	1B	6	6	52	42	4	0	6	1.000	-	+2	1
	TB	RF	3	0	5	1	0	0	0	1.000	1.80	0	0
	Col	RF	63	63	517	97	1	1	0	.990	1.71	-9	-6
Heisey, C	Cin	LF	38	4	96	24	1	0	0	1.000	2.33	+5	4
	Cin	CF	22	16	143	38	0	0	0	1.000	2.39	+2	1
	Cin	RF	27	22	189	44	1	2	0	.957	2.14	+6	4
Helms, W	Fla	1B	2	2	18	17	2	0	0	1.000	-	0	0
	Fla	3B	90	50	510	39	101	7	8	.952	2.47	-7	-5
Hermida, J	Bos	LF	46	41	348	84	3	4	0	.956	2.25	-12	-5
	Oak	LF	1	0	2	0	0	0	0		.00		
	Bos	RF	3	2	18	2	0	0	0	1.000	1.00	0	0
	Oak	RF	21	16	144	31	1	0	0	1.000	2.00	+1	1
Hernandez, A	Cle	2B	3	2	18	3	6	1	2	.900	4.50	+1	1
	Hou	2B	8	7	61	14	15	1	5	.967	4.28	0	0
	Cle	3B	1	0	1	0	2	0	0	1.000	18.00	0	0
	Cle	SS	16	14	127	25	43	0	12	1.000	4.81	0	0
	Hou	SS	2	2	17	2	10	0	3	1.000	6.35	+2	2
	Cle	LF	1	0	2	0	0	0	0	-	.00	0	0
Hernandez, D	Atl	2B	1	0	1	0	0	0	0	-	.00	0	0
	Atl	SS	4	0	6	3	1	0	1	1.000	6.00	0	0
Hernandez, L	NYM	2B	10	9	75	17	32	0	7	1.000	5.88	+4	3
	NYM	3B	2	0	3	0	0	0	0	-	.00		
	NYM	SS	4	2	19	4	8	0	2	1.000	5.49	-1	-1
Hernandez, R	Cin	1B	5	2	22	19	0	0	2	1.000	-	-1	-1
Herrera, J	Col	2B	57	47	425	91	149	4	32	.984	5.08	+4	3
	Col	3B	16	5	59	3	10	0	3	1.000	1.96	0	0
	Col	SS	7	1	16	1	1	0	0	1.000	1.13	-1	-1
Hessman, M	NYM	1B	6	6	53	50	1	0	4	1.000	-	0	0
	NYM	3B	8	5	57	4	13	0	3	1.000	2.68	+4	3
Hicks, B	Atl	2B	1	0	1	0	0	0	0	-	.00	0	0
	Atl	3B	3	0	4	0	3	0	0	1.000	6.75	+1	1
	Atl	SS	2	0	2	0	0	0	0	-	.00	0	0
Hill, K	ChC	3B	1	0	1	0	0	0	0	-	.00		
Hinske, E	Atl	1B	32	17	167	179	10	1	15	.995	-	-2	0
	Atl	3B	1	0	2	0	2	0	0	1.000	18.00	+1	1
	Atl	LF	50	50	360	65	0	1	0	.985	1.63	-2	-4
Hoffpauir, J	Tor	2B	2	1	10	1	5	0	0	1.000	5.40	+1	1
	Tor	3B	11	10	87	6	25	0	3	1.000	3.21	+1	1
Hoffpauir, M	ChC	1B	12	8	71	61	6	1	9	.985	-	-1	-1
	ChC	LF	3	0	13	3	0	0	0	1.000	1.98	0	0
	ChC	RF	2	1	10	2	0	0	0	1.000	1.80	0	0
Hu, C	LAD	SS	10	6	58	13	10	1	4	.958	3.57	-1	-1
Huff, A	SF	1B	100	97	821	756	54	3	54	.996	-	+6	6
	SF	LF	46	24	258	72	0	0	0	1.000	2.51	+6	3
	SF	RF	34	33	243	53	6	0	2	1.000	2.18	+2	2
Huffman, C	NYY	1B	1	0	1	0	0	0	0	-	-		
	NYY	LF	4	2	24	9	0	0	0	1.000	3.38	+2	1
	NYY	RF	3	2	20	5	0	0	0	1.000	2.25	0	0
Hughes, L	Min	3B	2	2	16	0	4	0	1	1.000	2.25	+1	1
Hughes, R	Bal	1B	11	11	98	98	3	1	6	.990	-	+1	1
Hunter, T	LAA	CF	98	97	828	252	2	1	0	.996	2.76	+2	-1
	LAA	RF	46	46	410	106	2	2	0	.982	2.37	-3	0
Iannetta, C	Col	1B	3	1	12	10	1	0	2	1.000	-	-1	-1
	Col	3B	1	0	2	0	0	0	0	-	.00		
Ibanez, R	Phi	1B	1	0	2	3	0	0	0	1.000	-	0	0
Infante, O	Atl	2B	65	63	555	110	195	7	43	.978	4.94	+3	4
	Atl	3B	29	12	139	7	30	3	1	.925	2.40	-1	0
	Atl	SS	19	18	156	29	69	5	13	.951	5.65	+2	2
	Atl	LF	15	8	72	11	1	1	0	.923	1.49	+1	2
	Atl	RF	6	5	45	12	0	0	0	1.000	2.38	-1	-1

Player	Tm	Pos	G	GS	Inn	PO	A	E	DP	Pct.	Rng	+/-	RS
Inglett, J	Mil	2B	8	2	35	6	10	1	4	.941	4.11	0	0
	Mil	LF	10	5	51	12	0	1	0	.923	2.09	-1	-2
	Mil	RF	14	10	94	18	2	0	0	1.000	1.90	+4	1
Ishikawa, T	SF	1B	73	25	305	263	22	0	22	1.000	-	+1	2
Iwamura, A	Pit	2B	40	40	341	75	94	3	26	.983	4.46	-12	-10
	Oak	3B	10	9	81	11	11	1	1	.957	2.44	-4	-4
Izturis, M	LAA	2B	22	20	176	30	52	1	6	.988	4.19	-1	-1
	LAA	3B	28	26	223	14	47	1	7	.984	2.45	+4	3
	LAA	SS	7	6	55	5	24	0	3	1.000	4.72	+1	1
Jackson, C	Ari	1B	3	3	26	27	2	0	4	1.000	-	0	0
	Oak	LF	16	15	133	24	1	0	0	1.000	1.69	+1	1
	Ari	LF	36	34	299	71	4	1	1	.986	2.19	+2	1
Jacobs, M	NYM	1B	7	6	58	50	1	1	3	.981	-	+1	1
Janish, P	Cin	2B	7	3	34	7	7	0	1	1.000	3.71	-2	-2
	Cin	3B	6	1	61	5	16	0	2	1.000	3.06	+2	2
	Cin	SS	62	43	416	88	119	4	33	.981	4.47	-1	0
Jaso, J	TB	1B	1	0	4	4	0	0	0	1.000	-	0	0
Jay, J	StL	LF	9	2	25	4	0	0	0	1.000	1.44	0	0
	StL	CF	27	21	195	63	2	0	0	1.000	3.00	-3	-1
	StL	RF	61	43	381	70	3	1	1	.986	1.72	0	0
Jennings, D	TB	LF	2	2	15	5	0	0	0	1.000	3.00	+1	1
	TB	CF	4	1	16	10	0	0	0	1.000	5.63	+3	2
	TB	RF	5	2	23	3	0	0	0	1.000	1.17	-2	-1
Johnson, C	Hou	3B	90	89	790	42	135	18	13	.908	2.02	-18	-13
Johnson, D	TB	1B	13	11	92	82	3	0	11	1.000	-	-4	-3
	TB	3B	6	5	40	5	6	2	0	.846	2.48	0	0
	TB	LF	3	0	8	1	0	0	0	1.000	1.13	0	0
Johnson, N	NYY	1B	2	2	17	18	0	0	1	1.000	-	-1	-1
Johnson, R	LAD	LF	62	24	264	65	0	0	0	1.000	2.21	+6	2
	LAD	CF	7	3	33	7	0	0	0	1.000	1.87	+2	1
	LAD	RF	22	15	141	28	0	0	0	1.000	1.79	-4	-1
Jones, A	CWS	LF	12	12	101	21	2	0	0	1.000	2.05	+2	2
	CWS	CF	17	13	125	33	0	1	0	.971	2.38	-3	-3
	CWS	RF	62	41	397	82	6	2	2	.978	1.99	+3	5
Jones, C	Atl	3B	89	86	696	40	159	10	10	.952	2.57	+9	6
Jones, G	Pit	1B	112	106	924	893	88	9	70	.991	-	-10	-10
	Pit	LF	1	1	8	3	0	0	0	1.000	3.38	-2	-1
	Pit	RF	48	46	397	98	4	3	0	.971	2.31	+3	4
Joyce, M	TB	LF	13	8	75	16	0	0	0	1.000	1.92	-2	-2
	TB	RF	52	45	397	94	3	0	0	.972	2.34	0	3
Kaaihue,K'	KC	1B	34	32	290	277	21	2	18	.993	-	+2	1
Kalish, R	Bos	LF	12	11	96	21	1	1	0	.957	2.06	-2	1
	Bos	CF	38	32	293	83	2	1	1	.988	2.61	-2	1
	Bos	RF	2	1	12	1	0	0	0	1.000	.75	+1	1
Kapler, G	TB	LF	12	7	72	12	1	0	0	1.000	1.62	-3	-1
	TB	CF	2	1	10	0	0	0	0	-	.00	-1	-1
	TB	RF	39	29	231	46	0	0	0	1.000	1.79	+3	1
Kearns, A	Cle	LF	69	63	558	134	1	4	0	.971	2.18	0	1
	NYY	LF	22	20	144	36	1	0	1	1.000	2.31	-3	-2
	Cle	CF	5	4	33	13	0	0	0	1.000	3.55	0	0
	Cle	RF	14	12	105	26	0	0	0	1.000	2.22	+1	2
	NYY	RF	18	8	92	19	0	0	0	1.000	1.86	-1	-1
Kelly, D	Det	1B	28	12	135	146	10	2	24	.987	-	+5	4
	Det	3B	15	12	105	5	33	3	5	.927	3.26	+5	3
	Det	LF	65	21	255	57	2	0	0	1.000	2.08	+3	5
	Det	CF	12	10	90	33	2	0	0	1.000	3.50	+4	2
	Det	RF	2	0	2	0	0	0	0	-	.00	0	0
Kendrick, H	LAA	1B	15	11	104	98	4	1	5	.990	-	-1	0
	LAA	CF	1	0	0	0	0	0	0	-	.00		
Kennedy, A	Was	1B	51	4	113	105	7	1	11	.991	-	-1	0
	Was	2B	86	75	628	143	207	7	44	.980	5.01	+3	0
	Was	3B	8	6	45	2	6	1	0	.889	1.59	+1	1
Keppinger, J	Hou	SS	12	10	87	14	19	1	9	.971	3.41	-6	-5
Kotsay, M	CWS	1B	38	34	307	298	20	1	23	.997	-	-2	-1
	CWS	RF	8	6	48	9	2	0	0	1.000	2.06	-4	-1
Kottaras, G	Mil	1B	2	0	2	1	0	0	0	1.000			
	Mil	RF	1	0	1	0	0	0	0	-	.00		
Kubel, J	Min	LF	16	16	131	27	1	1	1	.966	1.92	+2	1
	Min	RF	83	79	670	142	6	4	2	.974	1.99	-2	-1
Lamb, M	Fla	1B	1	1	6	11	0	0	1	1.000	-	-1	-1
Langerhans, R	Sea	1B	6	3	34	28	2	0	4	1.000	-	+1	1
	Sea	LF	30	24	227	56	4	1	0	.984	2.38	+3	2
	Sea	CF	2	2	16	5	1	0	0	1.000	3.38	-2	0
	Sea	RF	8	1	18	6	0	0	0	1.000	3.00	0	-1

Player	Tm	Pos	G	GS	Inn	PO	A	E	DP	Pct.	Rng	+/-	RS
LaPorta, M	Cle	1B	93	93	791	815	58	3	80	.997	-	+2	0
	Cle	LF	7	7	53	5	0	0	0	1.000	.85	-4	-2
Larish, J	Det	1B	1	1	9	5	0	0	0	1.000	-	0	0
	Oak	1B	10	3	45	41	5	0	8	1.000	-	0	0
	Oak	3B	5	3	28	3	5	2	0	.800	2.57	-1	-1
	Oak	LF	7	7	44	3	0	0	0	1.000	.61	0	-1
LaRoche, A	Pit	1B	2	2	15	15	0	0	2	1.000	-	0	0
	Pit	2B	6	4	36	8	11	1	1	.950	4.75	+2	2
	Pit	3B	54	52	448	33	119	10	8	.938	3.05	-5	-3
LaRue, J	StL	1B	1	0	1	1	0	0	0	1.000	-		
Lee, C	Hou	1B	20	17	143	115	12	1	6	.992	-	+2	1
Lee, D	Atl	1B	39	36	290	283	24	1	26	.997	-	-1	-1
	ChC	1B	105	105	916	784	92	6	73	.993	-	+4	3
Lewis, F	Tor	LF	84	81	726	134	1	3	0	.978	1.67	-2	0
	Tor	CF	7	5	49	15	0	0	0	1.000	2.74	-2	0
	Tor	RF	10	8	67	20	0	0	0	1.000	2.69	-5	-3
Lillibridge, B	CWS	2B	25	18	171	34	56	4	12	.957	4.74	-1	-1
	CWS	3B	3	1	14	1	1	0	0	1.000	1.29	0	0
	CWS	SS	4	0	4	1	0	0	0	1.000	1.93	0	0
	CWS	LF	1	0	4	1	0	0	0	1.000	2.25	0	0
	CWS	CF	6	1	22	6	0	0	0	1.000	2.38	+1	1
	CWS	RF	1	0	1	1	0	0	0	1.000	9.00	0	0
Lind, A	Tor	1B	11	8	76	70	9	0	7	1.000	-	+2	1
	Tor	LF	16	16	123	22	0	0	0	1.000	1.61	-1	-3
Lindsey, J	LAD	1B	2	2	12	8	1	0	2	1.000	-	0	0
Lohse, K	StL	LF	1	0	3	2	0	0	0	1.000	6.00	+1	1
Lopez, F	StL	1B	2	1	10	11	0	0	0	1.000	-	-1	-1
	Bos	2B	3	2	19	4	6	0	0	1.000	4.58	+1	1
	StL	2B	24	17	147	35	51	0	14	1.000	5.24	+1	2
	Bos	3B	2	1	10	1	0	1	0	.500	.90	-1	-1
	StL	3B	58	51	472	24	102	10	9	.926	2.40	-1	-1
	Bos	SS	1	0	2	2	0	0	0	1.000	9.00	0	0
	StL	SS	34	10	161	20	13	2	5	.969	3.52	-3	-4
	StL	RF	1	0	0	0	0	0	0	-	.00		
Lowell, M	Bos	1B	43	38	324	310	24	2	35	.994	-	+3	1
	Bos	3B	4	4	32	2	6	0	1	1.000	2.25	+1	1
Lowrie, J	Bos	1B	7	0	16	10	2	1	2	.923	-	0	0
	Bos	2B	28	24	209	44	77	3	14	.976	5.21	+3	2
	Bos	3B	1	0	3	0	1	0	0	1.000	3.00	+1	1
	Bos	SS	23	21	176	26	46	1	17	.986	3.67	-7	-4
Ludwick, R	StL	LF	1	1	5	2	0	0	0	1.000	3.60	+2	1
	StL	CF	5	3	24	9	0	0	0	1.000	3.38	0	0
	StL	RF	67	63	562	132	2	0	0	1.000	2.15	+13	9
	SD	RF	58	57	488	117	2	2	0	.983	2.19	0	-3
Lugo, J	Bal	2B	59	42	395	93	131	1	20	.990	5.10	-2	-1
	Bal	3B	7	2	10	0	1	0	0	1.000	.60	1	1
	Bal	SS	26	15	142	25	48	1	11	.986	4.62	-1	-1
	Bal	LF	1	1	9	1	0	0	0	1.000	1.00	-2	-1
Luna, H	Fla	2B	1	0	3	1	1	0	0	1.000	6.00	0	0
	Fla	3B	4	2	18	2	5	0	1	1.000	3.38	-2	-2
Maier, M	KC	1B	1	0	2	1	1	0	0	1.000	-	0	0
	KC	LF	8	5	46	5	0	0	0	1.000	.98	-2	-1
	KC	CF	65	58	525	173	3	1	1	.994	3.01	-5	0
	KC	RF	43	40	355	81	1	4	0	.953	2.08	-5	-4
Mangini, M	Sea	3B	7	7	62	4	14	0	3	1.000	2.59	-1	-1
Manzella, T	Hou	SS	82	75	674	121	207	9	41	.973	4.38	-5	-4
Marte, A	Cle	1B	32	15	168	186	11	2	17	.990	-	-3	-2
	Cle	3B	45	28	264	21	55	9	6	.894	2.59	+7	5
Martinez, F	NYM	LF	6	4	33	14	0	0	0	1.000	1.87	0	-1
	NYM	RF	2	1	9	0	0	0	0	-	.00	0	0
Martinez, O	Fla	SS	11	10	86	10	22	0	3	1.000	3.35	-3	-2
Martinez, V	Bos	1B	14	12	106	95	14	2	10	.982	-	+1	1
Mather, J	StL	1B	3	1	11	14	0	0	3	1.000	-	0	0
	StL	3B	1	0	1	1	0	0	0	1.000	9.00	-1	-1
	StL	LF	7	0	12	1	0	0	0	1.000	.75	0	0
	StL	CF	14	7	72	13	0	0	0	1.000	1.62	-3	-1
	StL	RF	8	0	16	2	0	0	0	1.000	1.13	0	0
Matsui, H	LAA	LF	18	17	123	16	1	0	0	1.000	1.24	-4	-2
Matsui, K	Hou	2B	21	19	162	42	56	1	12	.990	5.44	-2	-2
Matthews Jr., G	NYM	LF	3	3	9	0	0	0	0	-	.00	0	0
	NYM	CF	10	8	69	28	0	0	0	1.000	3.63	-2	-1
	NYM	RF	7	2	22	3	1	0	0	1.000	1.59	+1	2
Maxwell, J	Was	LF	5	3	26	5	1	2	0	.750	2.08	-1	-1
	Was	CF	20	13	115	36	2	0	1	1.000	2.97	+3	4

Player	Tm	Pos	G	GS	Inn	PO	A	E	DP	Pct.	Rng	+/-	RS
	Was	RF	29	10	120	32	1	0	0	1.000	2.48	+1	1
Mayberry, J	Phi	CF	2	0	7	2	0	0	0	1.000	2.57	0	0
	Phi	RF	3	1	10	0	0	0	0	-	.00	-1	0
McAnulty, P	LAA	1B	5	5	37	45	0	1	3	.978	-	+1	1
McCoy, M	Tor	2B	14	7	74	10	31	0	7	1.000	4.99	+6	6
	Tor	3B	4	0	5	0	2	0	0	1.000	3.60	+1	1
	Tor	SS	7	5	43	10	10	1	1	.952	4.19	0	0
	Tor	LF	8	6	53	16	0	1	0	.941	2.68	-2	-1
	Tor	CF	2	0	4	2	0	0	0	1.000	4.50	0	0
	Tor	RF	6	2	25	7	0	0	0	1.000	2.52	+2	0
McDonald, D	Bos	LF	30	10	125	31	1	0	0	1.000	2.30	-3	0
	Bos	CF	69	50	450	112	7	1	1	.992	2.38	-14	-5
	Bos	RF	34	20	201	44	1	1	0	.978	2.01	-8	-7
McDonald, J	Tor	2B	23	15	150	32	50	1	20	.988	4.92	-2	0
	Tor	3B	19	12	114	11	26	3	3	.925	2.92	-1	-1
	Tor	SS	19	11	115	24	42	1	13	.985	5.17	+4	3
	Tor	LF	2	2	15	2	0	0	0	1.000	1.20	-1	-1
McGehee, C	Mil	1B	3	1	13	12	0	0	3	1.000	-	0	0
McLouth, N	Atl	LF	8	5	52	8	0	0	0	1.000	1.38	-1	0
	Atl	CF	71	63	561	137	1	2	1	.986	2.21	-14	-10
Mench, K	Was	LF	1	1	5	0	0	0	0	-	.00		
Michaels, J	Hou	LF	41	18	204	35	1	0	0	1.000	1.59	+4	0
	Hou	CF	11	8	69	14	0	0	0	1.000	1.83	+3	2
	Hou	RF	5	4	36	7	0	0	0	1.000	1.75	-1	1
Miles, A	StL	2B	50	18	214	38	83	2	12	.984	5.07	0	-1
	StL	3B	5	2	25	3	4	2	0	.778	2.52	-3	-2
	StL	SS	6	2	19	9	5	0	3	1.000	6.63	0	0
Milledge, L	Pit	LF	63	56	515	110	5	0	1	1.000	2.01	-3	0
	Pit	RF	45	41	341	80	1	1	1	.988	2.14	-6	-1
Miller, J	KC	LF	3	2	23	7	0	1	0	.875	2.74	+1	1
	KC	RF	16	13	116	27	0	0	0	1.000	2.09	0	-1
Miranda, J	NYY	1B	13	4	50	53	5	0	5	1.000	-	+1	1
Mitchell, R	LAD	1B	0	0	20	22	1	1	1	.958	-	0	0
	LAD	3B	6	6	49	4	13	2	3	.895	3.12	+2	1
	LAD	LF	3	3	19	2	0	0	0	1.000	.92	0	0
Molina, Y	StL	1B	7	0	7	7	0	0	0	1.000	-	0	0
Montanez, L	Bal	LF	17	8	89	23	1	1	0	.960	2.42	+1	2
	Bal	CF	1	1	8	4	1	0	0	1.000	5.63	0	1
	Bal	RF	2	1	10	1	0	0	0	1.000	.90	+1	1
Moore, S	Bal	1B	10	1	17	19	3	0	0	1.000	-	+2	1
	Bal	2B	22	19	168	36	52	2	9	.978	4.71	+1	1
	Bal	3B	4	1	18	0	1	1	0	.500	.50	-3	-2
Mora, M	Col	1B	25	10	112	100	0	2	10	.983	-	1	1
	Col	2B	19	10	100	26	38	2	6	.970	5.76	-2	-3
	Col	3B	63	53	440	20	94	5	7	.957	2.26	6	6
	Col	LF	4	4	30	4	1	0	0	1.000	1.47	0	0
Morales, J	Min	1B	2	2	17	19	2	0	2	1.000	-	+1	1
Morales, K	LAA	1B	51	51	448	435	25	2	35	.996	-	+3	1
Morel, B	CWS	3B	20	19	164	5	32	1	2	.974	2.03	-5	-4
Moreland, M	Tex	1B	40	37	320	289	16	2	18	.993	-	+3	3
	Tex	RF	7	4	45	10	0	1	0	.909	2.00	+1	1
Morneau, J	Min	1B	77	77	688	674	59	1	64	.999	-	+12	9
Morrison, L	Fla	LF	62	62	544	116	4	3	0	.976	1.99	-14	-4
Morse, M	Was	1B	19	5	60	58	5	0	4	1.000	-	0	0
	Was	RF	72	64	510	123	2	0	1	1.000	2.20	0	2
Moss, B	Pit	LF	2	0	5	1	0	0	0	1.000	1.80	0	0
	Pit	RF	3	3	27	4	0	0	0	1.000	1.33	0	0
Murphy, D	Tex	LF	74	59	533	113	6	1	0	.992	2.01	+2	0
	Tex	CF	10	6	53	13	0	0	0	1.000	2.18	-2	0
	Tex	RF	51	40	381	80	3	0	0	1.000	1.96	+2	0
Murphy, D	Fla	2B	1	1	3	2	1	0	0	1.000	7.36	0	0
	Fla	3B	4	3	31	1	7	0	0	1.000	2.30	+1	1
	Fla	SS	4	1	21	1	6	0	1	1.000	2.91	0	1
Nady, X	ChC	1B	52	48	423	389	36	1	47	.998	-	+5	4
	ChC	LF	4	4	33	6	0	0	0	1.000	1.64	+1	1
	ChC	RF	23	22	153	24	2	1	0	.963	1.53	-2	-2
Napoli, M	LAA	1B	70	67	586	502	44	6	33	.989	-	+7	4
Nava, D	Bos	LF	54	44	380	65	2	0	0	1.000	1.59	-17	-7
Navarro, O	Hou	SS	10	6	55	8	21	1	3	.967	4.75	0	0
Navarro, Y	Bos	2B	3	2	18	4	5	0	1	1.000	4.50	-1	-1
	Bos	3B	4	2	27	3	7	1	0	.909	3.33	+1	1
	Bos	SS	15	6	67	14	17	1	4	.969	4.16	-4	-3
Nelson, C	Col	2B	4	3	26	8	7	2	0	.882	5.19	-4	-3

299

Player	Tm	Pos	G	GS	Inn	PO	A	E	DP	Pct.	Rng	+/-	RS
	Col	3B	4	1	14	2	2	0	0	1.000	2.57	0	0
Nix, J	CWS	2B	3	1	13	5	2	0	0	1.000	4.85	0	0
	Cle	2B	25	24	213	53	80	0	21	1.000	5.61	+4	4
	CWS	3B	16	12	113	8	17	5	2	.833	1.99	-3	-3
	Cle	3B	40	39	321	34	64	11	4	.899	2.75	-1	-1
	CWS	SS	2	0	4	2	1	0	0	1.000	6.75	-1	-1
	Cle	LF	2	2	14	2	1	0	0	1.000	1.93	-1	0
	CWS	RF	1	1	7	3	0	0	0	1.000	3.86	+1	1
Nix, L	Cin	LF	50	28	269	52	2	0	1	1.000	1.81	+10	10
	Cin	CF	5	1	17	4	1	0	1	1.000	2.65	0	1
	Cin	RF	4	2	20	5	0	0	0	1.000	2.21	+1	1
Nunez, E	NYY	2B	1	0	1	0	0	0	0	-	.00	0	0
	NYY	3B	15	10	83	3	14	1	1	.944	1.84	-2	-2
	NYY	SS	11	3	39	7	16	0	4	1.000	5.26	+2	2
Oeltjen, T	LAD	LF	5	2	22	1	0	0	0	1.000	.40	-2	-1
	LAD	CF	4	4	28	8	0	0	0	1.000	2.57	-3	-2
Ojeda, A	Ari	2B	15	4	63	10	19	0	2	1.000	4.14	+1	1
	Ari	3B	12	1	32	7	1	0	1	1.000	2.23	-1	-1
	Ari	SS	9	6	60	8	15	0	3	1.000	3.41	+1	1
Ordonez, M	Det	RF	71	71	608	135	7	3	3	.979	2.10	-3	-1
Ortiz, D	Bos	1B	4	4	26	23	1	0	1	1.000	-	0	0
Oswalt, R	Phi	LF	1	0	2	1	0	0	0	1.000	4.50	0	0
Pagan, A	NYM	LF	27	22	204	51	1	1	0	.981	2.29	+1	3
	NYM	CF	94	88	792	259	7	4	2	.985	3.02	+8	7
	NYM	RF	33	29	259	58	2	0	0	1.000	2.08	+5	4
Parra, G	Ari	LF	76	63	569	146	6	3	1	.981	2.40	+19	14
	Ari	CF	7	3	24	9	1	0	1	1.000	3.65	-1	0
	Ari	RF	36	27	255	65	2	1	1	.985	2.36	+5	6
Patterson, C	Bal	LF	56	53	466	116	4	5	1	.960	2.31	+1	3
	Bal	CF	10	6	66	21	0	0	0	1.000	2.86	+2	1
	Bal	RF	1	1	9	1	0	0	0	1.000	1.00	0	0
Patterson, E	Bos	2B	9	5	56	16	15	1	3	.969	4.98	0	0
	Oak	2B	5	1	16	6	4	0	0	1.000	5.63	+1	1
	Bos	LF	22	5	77	20	2	0	0	1.000	2.56	+2	2
	Oak	LF	25	22	191	45	1	1	0	.979	2.17	-3	-3
	Bos	CF	13	8	78	13	1	1	0	.933	1.60	-10	-5
	Oak	CF	7	2	24	9	0	0	0	1.000	3.33	0	0
Paul, X	LAD	LF	23	19	169	29	3	1	1	.970	1.70	-1	0
	LAD	RF	15	11	101	20	0	1	0	.952	1.78	+2	2
Payton, J	Col	LF	9	7	64	11	0	0	0	1.000	1.55	+1	1
	Col	CF	1	0	2	1	0	0	0	1.000	4.50	0	0
Pearce, S	Pit	1B	11	9	75	78	7	1	8	.988	-	+2	1
Pedroia, D	Bos	2B	75	75	667	137	212	3	50	.991	4.71	+2	4
Pena, R	NYY	2B	8	5	44	12	17	1	6	.967	5.93	-1	0
	NYY	3B	48	27	262	17	67	3	5	.966	2.89	+8	6
	NYY	SS	23	9	99	22	24	1	7	.979	4.17	+1	1
	NYY	RF	2	0	4	1	0	0	0	1.000	2.25	0	0
Peralta, J	Det	1B	2	0	7	7	1	0	0	1.000	-	+1	1
	Cle	3B	91	89	780	61	194	5	24	.981	2.94	+5	3
	Det	3B	9	7	60	7	9	0	3	1.000	2.39	-4	-3
	Det	SS	46	44	392	70	118	3	26	.984	4.31	-3	-2
Petersen, B	Fla	LF	5	0	9	1	0	0	0	1.000	1.00	-1	-1
	Fla	RF	1	1	8	1	0	0	0	1.000	1.13	-1	-1
Phillips, P	Col	1B	1	0	2	0	1	0	0	1.000	-	0	0
Pie, F	Bal	LF	70	65	580	147	7	1	3	.994	2.39	0	6
	Bal	CF	9	7	64	15	1	0	0	1.000	2.25	0	0
	Bal	RF	2	1	12	5	1	0	1	1.000	4.50	0	0
Plouffe, T	Min	2B	2	0	9	2	4	0	1	1.000	6.00	-1	-1
	Min	SS	9	7	68	13	20	1	5	.971	4.37	0	0
Podsednik, S	KC	LF	92	92	806	203	0	3	0	.985	2.27	-10	-10
	LAD	LF	37	30	272	61	0	1	0	.984	2.02	+2	0
	KC	CF	1	0	2	2	0	0	0	1.000	9.00	0	0
	LAD	CF	5	5	34	9	0	1	0	.900	2.38	-5	-3
Polanco, P	Phi	2B	12	9	82	15	37	0	7	1.000	5.71	+6	5
Posada, J	NYY	1B	1	0	1	0	0	0	0	-	-		
Posey, B	SF	1B	30	30	248	196	17	1	14	.995	-	-2	0
Powell, L	Oak	1B	1	0	4	4	0	0	1	1.000	-	+1	1
Prado, M	Atl	1B	5	0	7	7	0	0	0	1.000	-	0	0
	Atl	2B	98	97	852	184	285	6	66	.987	4.95	+4	2
	Atl	3B	43	42	369	29	84	5	12	.958	2.75	+2	2
Presley, A	Pit	LF	2	1	11	0	0	0	0	-	.00	0	0
	Pit	CF	4	0	10	1	0	0	0	1.000	.90	-2	-1
	Pit	RF	8	1	24	2	0	0	0	1.000	.75	+1	1
Punto, N	Min	2B	12	8	77	15	29	3	5	.936	5.14	+1	1
	Min	3B	48	38	344	29	93	0	6	1.000	3.19	+10	8
	Min	SS	31	31	258	48	80	5	16	.962	4.47	+8	7
Quinlan, R	LAA	1B	13	5	65	71	1	1	7	.986	-	-1	-1
	LAA	3B	1	0	1	0	0	0	0	-	.00	0	0
	LAA	LF	1	0	1	0	0	0	0	-	.00		
	LAA	RF	3	0	5	1	0	0	0	1.000	1.80	0	0
Raburn, R	Det	1B	1	1	8	6	1	0	1	1.000	-	+2	1
	Det	2B	18	15	120	27	43	1	11	.986	5.25	-3	-2
	Det	3B	2	0	3	1	1	0	0	1.000	5.40	0	0
	Det	LF	73	55	508	117	3	4	0	.968	2.12	+5	6
	Det	CF	7	5	44	11	0	0	0	1.000	2.25	+2	1
	Det	RF	20	10	94	22	1	1	0	.958	2.20	-5	-3
Ramirez, M	LAD	LF	46	46	359	68	2	3	0	.959	1.75	-5	-5
Ransom, C	Phi	1B	3	3	18	15	1	0	2	1.000	-	0	0
	Phi	2B	6	1	17	5	6	0	3	1.000	5.82	0	0
	Phi	3B	9	6	63	6	9	1	2	.938	2.14	0	0
Raynor, J	Pit	CF	1	0	2	1	0	0	0	1.000	4.50	-1	-1
	Pit	RF	2	0	3	1	0	0	0	1.000	2.70	0	0
Reddick, J	Bos	LF	6	4	37	9	0	0	0	1.000	2.19	-3	-2
	Bos	CF	6	5	44	16	0	0	0	1.000	3.27	-1	0
	Bos	RF	15	6	66	12	1	0	0	1.000	1.76	0	0
Reed, J	Tor	1B	2	0	3	2	0	0	0	1.000	-	0	0
	Tor	LF	6	2	24	3	0	0	0	1.000	1.13	0	1
	Tor	RF	3	2	21	8	0	0	0	1.000	3.43	+1	1
Reimold, N	Bal	LF	22	21	175	42	1	1	0	.977	2.21	0	1
	Bal	RF	2	0	3	0	0	0	0	-	.00	0	0
Renteria, E	SF	SS	68	62	553	80	149	4	27	.983	3.73	-2	-2
Repko, J	Min	LF	6	3	29	5	0	0	0	1.000	1.55	+2	2
	Min	CF	6	6	51	20	0	0	0	1.000	3.53	0	0
	Min	RF	39	22	226	62	5	0	1	1.000	2.67	+3	6
Revere, B	Min	LF	3	1	15	5	0	0	0	1.000	3.00	+1	1
	Min	CF	6	4	38	9	0	1	0	.900	2.13	+1	1
	Min	RF	2	1	16	4	0	0	0	1.000	2.25	0	0
Reynolds, M	Ari	1B	5	0	9	7	1	0	1	1.000	-	-2	-1
Rhymes, W	Det	2B	53	46	412	89	150	4	37	.984	5.21	+8	7
Rios, A	CWS	LF	1	1	11	4	0	0	0	1.000	3.27	+1	1
Rivera, J	LAA	1B	13	11	107	98	12	1	8	.991	-	+4	3
	LAA	LF	83	80	692	167	5	5	0	.972	2.23	-16	-8
	LAA	CF	1	0	1	0	0	0	0	-	.00	0	0
	LAA	RF	25	18	173	47	3	0	1	1.000	2.59	-2	0
Roberts, B	Bal	2B	59	58	498	86	146	3	38	.987	4.19	-2	0
Roberts, R	Ari	1B	1	1	8	3	4	0	2	1.000	7.88	0	0
	Ari	3B	1	1	8	1	1	0	0	1.000	2.25	0	0
	Ari	LF	14	9	85	16	1	0	0	1.000	1.79	+2	2
	Ari	RF	1	0	1	0	0	0	0	-	.00	-1	-1
Rodriguez, S	TB	1B	3	2	21	23	1	0	2	1.000	-	0	0
	TB	2B	92	78	678	138	222	6	56	.984	4.78	+20	17
	TB	3B	7	3	38	7	5	0	2	1.000	2.84	-1	-1
	TB	SS	5	1	9	0	3	0	0	1.000	3.00	-1	-1
	TB	LF	5	1	21	8	0	0	0	1.000	3.43	-1	-1
	TB	CF	9	4	42	8	0	0	0	1.000	1.69	-1	-1
	TB	RF	8	3	19	6	0	0	0	1.000	2.84	0	0
Rohlinger, R	SF	3B	3	2	17	0	2	0	0	1.000	1.06	0	0
	SF	SS	1	1	15	4	3	0	1	1.000	4.20	0	0
Rollins, J	Phi	SS	88	85	744	102	227	6	53	.982	3.98	+6	7
Romero, N	Bos	1B	1	0	5	4	1	0	0	1.000	-	0	0
	Bos	2B	1	0	1	0	0	0	0	-	.00	0	0
Romine, A	LAA	SS	4	3	29	9	8	2	3	.895	5.28	-1	-1
Rosales, A	Oak	1B	7	3	38	34	1	0	4	1.000	-	0	0
	Oak	2B	47	45	393	72	126	0	30	1.000	4.53	+1	3
	Oak	3B	5	5	44	4	12	0	1	1.000	3.27	+3	2
	Oak	SS	14	10	82	7	26	2	3	.943	3.62	-4	-3
	Oak	LF	5	3	27	4	0	0	0	1.000	1.30	0	0
Ross, C	Fla	LF	2	2	13	2	1	1	1	.750	2.08	+1	1
	SF	LF	21	3	77	9	1	0	0	1.000	1.16	0	0
	Fla	CF	77	71	640	165	4	1	1	.994	2.38	-4	-2
	SF	CF	12	9	77	15	0	0	0	1.000	1.75	+2	1
	Fla	RF	46	45	391	101	1	2	0	.981	2.35	+14	8
	SF	RF	8	5	41	9	1	0	0	1.000	2.18	-2	0
Rowand, A	SF	CF	85	76	695	192	4	0	2	1.000	2.54	+3	3
Ruiz, R	Tor	1B	3	3	23	25	2	0	2	1.000	-	0	0
Russo, K	NYY	2B	2	0	4	2	1	0	0	1.000	6.75	0	0
	NYY	3B	16	3	47	4	6	0	1	1.000	1.91	+1	1
	NYY	LF	11	10	85	14	0	1	0	.933	1.48	+6	2

Ryal, R	Ari	1B	24	14	140	127	9	4	16	.971	-	+2	1
	Ari	3B	8	3	35	2	5	1	2	.875	1.77	+1	0
	Ari	LF	36	23	193	44	2	2	1	.958	2.15	+4	3
Ryan, M	LAA	1B	4	4	24	28	2	0	3	1.000	-	0	0
	LAA	LF	11	5	48	11	0	0	0	1.000	2.06	0	0
Salazar, O	SD	1B	7	3	35	33	1	0	4	1.000	-	0	0
	SD	2B	6	0	9	1	4	0	0	1.000	4.66	0	0
	SD	3B	1	1	5	0	1	0	0	1.000	1.80	0	0
	SD	LF	17	15	101	15	0	0	0	1.000	1.34	-2	-1
	SD	RF	7	6	43	2	0	0	0	1.000	.42	-2	-1
Saltalamacchia	Bos	1B	1	0	1	0	0	0	0	-	-		
Sanchez, A	Hou	2B	8	7	71	14	19	0	5	1.000	4.18	+1	1
	Bos	SS	1	1	9	0	4	0	2	1.000	4.00	-1	-1
	Hou	SS	57	54	484	79	128	5	29	.976	3.85	-11	-8
Sandoval, P	SF	1B	11	10	86	79	0	0	6	1.000	-	-2	-1
Santiago, R	Det	2B	25	12	127	24	44	1	11	.986	4.82	+5	5
	Det	SS	85	66	617	106	227	7	53	.979	4.86	+11	8
Saunders, M	Sea	LF	77	74	647	165	8	4	4	.977	2.40	+4	4
	Sea	CF	14	11	108	32	0	0	0	1.000	2.67	+2	1
Scales, B	ChC	3B	7	3	39	7	6	3	1	.813	3.00	-2	-2
Schierholtz, N	SF	RF	109	41	542	118	7	1	1	.992	2.07	-1	4
Schumaker, S	StL	LF	4	0	6	2	0	0	0	1.000	3.00	0	0
	StL	CF	1	0	1	0	0	0	0	-	.00		
	StL	RF	12	3	39	16	4	0	1	1.000	4.62	+2	2
Scott, L	Bal	1B	19	19	158	153	11	3	17	.982	-	-1	-1
	Bal	LF	14	13	103	22	0	0	0	1.000	1.92	0	0
Scutaro, M	Bos	2B	16	16	132	17	46	2	8	.969	4.28	-2	-2
Shealy, R	Bos	1B	1	0	5	5	0	0	1	1.000	-	0	0
Sizemore, G	Cle	CF	32	31	269	64	0	1	0	.985	2.14	-2	-2
Sizemore, S	Det	2B	40	36	314	59	90	7	24	.955	4.27	-8	-6
	Det	3B	6	4	38	7	7	1	1	.933	3.32	0	-1
Smith, S	Col	LF	71	59	512	107	3	2	1	.982	1.93	+7	4
	Col	RF	33	23	225	40	1	1	1	.980	1.07	+1	-1
Smoak, J	Sea	1B	25	25	216	233	15	1	18	.996	-	0	-1
	Tex	1B	69	66	591	545	35	4	53	.993	-	+2	1
Snider, T	Tor	LF	53	48	433	88	2	3	0	.968	1.87	+10	4
	Tor	RF	29	27	245	47	1	0	0	1.000	1.76	+6	2
Snyder, B	ChC	LF	3	1	6	1	0	0	0	1.000	1.35	0	0
	ChC	RF	6	4	41	11	0	0	0	1.000	2.38	+2	1
Snyder, B	Bal	1B	10	5	51	44	2	2	2	.958	-	+3	2
Sogard, E	Oak	2B	3	1	15	4	5	0	4	1.000	5.40	-1	-1
Spilborghs, R	Col	LF	46	32	297	46	2	1	1	.980	1.45	-6	-1
	Col	CF	6	4	39	4	0	0	0	1.000	.92	+1	0
	Col	RF	62	42	401	81	0	4	0	.953	1.81	-8	-7
Stairs, M	SD	1B	3	1	8	12	1	0	1	1.000	-	0	0
	SD	LF	13	13	75	13	0	0	0	1.000	1.56	-3	-2
	Hou	RF	1	1	5	0	0	0	0	-	.00	0	0
Stavinoha, N	StL	1B	3	0	3	3	1	0	1	1.000	-	-1	-1
	StL	LF	5	1	13	1	0	0	0	1.000	.69	0	0
	StL	RF	22	16	116	25	1	0	0	1.000	2.01	+4	1
Stern, A	Mil	CF	1	1	9	3	0	0	0	1.000	3.00	-1	-1
	Mil	RF	1	0	1	0	0	0	0	-	.00	0	0
Stewart, C	SD	1B	1	0	1	2	0	0	0	1.000	-	-1	-1
Sullivan, C	Hou	LF	13	4	45	9	0	0	0	1.000	1.80	-1	-1
	Hou	CF	1	0	2	0	0	0	0	-	.00	-1	-1
	Hou	RF	3	3	23	5	0	0	0	1.000	1.96	0	1
Sutton, D	Cle	2B	4	4	35	5	17	0	4	1.000	5.66	-1	-1
	Cin	2B	1	0	2	0	1	0	0	1.000	4.50	0	0
	Cin	3B	1	0	1	0	0	0	0	-	.00		
	Cle	SS	7	6	50	11	16	0	2	1.000	4.86	+4	3
	Cin	SS	1	0	2	0	1	0	0	1.000	4.50	0	0
Sweeney, M	Sea	1B	3	3	25	28	1	0	1	1.000	-	0	0
	Phi	1B	14	11	103	104	6	2	8	.982	-	0	0
Sweeney, R	Oak	CF	1	1	8	2	0	0	0	1.000	2.25	0	0
	Oak	RF	80	76	659	147	4	0	1	1.000	2.06	+4	2
Swisher, N	NYY	1B	6	1	21	19	2	0	2	1.000	-	-1	-1
	NYY	CF	1	0	1	0	0	0	0	-	.00		
Tabata, J	Pit	LF	93	92	771	189	5	1	1	.995	2.26	+12	6
	Pit	CF	13	9	91	22	0	0	0	1.000	2.17	-12	-8
Tatis, F	NYM	1B	14	8	72	67	5	0	6	1.000	-	+2	2
	NYM	2B	3	0	4	0	0	0	0	-	.00	0	0
	NYM	3B	4	2	18	2	1	0	1	1.000	1.50	+1	1
Taveras, W	Was	LF	6	0	5	1	0	0	0	1.000	1.69	0	0
	Was	CF	3	1	14	4	0	0	0	1.000	2.57	-1	-1

Player	Tm	Pos	G	GS	Inn	PO	A	E	DP	Pct.	Rng	+/-	RS
	Was	RF	14	5	57	12	1	0	1	1.000	2.03	0	1
Teahen, M	CWS	1B	3	0	8	5	0	0	0	1.000	-	0	0
	CWS	3B	52	49	411	32	82	10	6	.919	2.50	-16	-13
	CWS	RF	10	10	77	12	0	0	0	1.000	1.40	-1	-2
Tejada, M	Bal	3B	93	93	808	68	197	15	22	.946	2.95	-8	-6
	SD	3B	4	2	15	1	3	0	0	1.000	2.35	0	0
	SD	SS	58	57	496	68	162	3	40	.987	4.17	+2	1
Tejada, R	NYM	2B	50	46	388	79	126	6	31	.972	4.76	-1	0
	NYM	SS	28	24	221	33	75	2	15	.982	4.38	+1	1
Thames, M	NYY	3B	1	0	1	0	0	1	0	.000	.00	-1	-1
	NYY	LF	25	17	123	22	2	1	1	.960	1.76	-1	-2
	NYY	RF	8	6	48	12	0	1	0	.923	2.25	-1	-2
Theriot, R	ChC	2B	66	62	545	117	150	6	31	.978	4.41	-1	-3
	LAD	2B	53	50	447	103	125	1	25	.996	4.59	+6	3
	ChC	SS	29	28	246	38	74	3	13	.974	4.10	-7	-5
Tolbert, M	Min	1B	4	0	8	5	0	0	0	1.000	-	0	0
	Min	2B	20	14	131	21	41	1	7	.984	4.24	-1	-1
	Min	3B	14	7	73	8	21	1	1	.967	3.58	+3	3
	Min	SS	3	0	4	2	2	0	1	1.000	9.00	0	0
	Min	RF	1	0	1	0	0	0	0	-	.00	0	0
Tolleson, S	Oak	2B	4	2	21	5	4	1	2	.900	3.86	-1	-1
	Oak	3B	6	5	44	3	7	0	0	1.000	2.05	0	0
	Oak	SS	11	5	45	9	9	0	4	1.000	3.60	-2	-2
	Oak	LF	1	0	1	1	0	0	0	1.000	9.00	0	0
	Oak	RF	1	0	0	0	0	0	0	-	.00		
Torres, A	SF	LF	37	13	162	47	2	0	1	1.000	2.71	+6	4
	SF	CF	84	73	655	193	1	1	1	.995	2.66	+6	1
	SF	RF	43	38	302	74	4	0	0	1.000	2.32	+8	7
Tracy, C	ChC	1B	2	0	5	4	0	0	0	1.000	-	0	0
	Fla	1B	5	4	36	46	3	0	4	1.000	-	+1	1
	ChC	3B	10	8	73	6	12	1	2	.947	2.21	-2	-2
	Fla	3B	24	22	181	13	42	3	5	.948	2.73	+1	0
Trumbo, M	LAA	1B	6	3	33	38	4	0	5	1.000	-	+2	1
	LAA	RF	1	1	7	1	1	1	0	.667	2.57	0	1
Tuiasosopo, M	Sea	1B	9	7	66	65	2	1	8	.985	-	+2	1
	Sea	2B	2	0	8	0	1	1	0	.500	1.13	-1	-1
	Sea	3B	12	10	91	8	24	2	0	.941	3.14	0	0
	Sea	SS	6	2	28	6	11	2	2	.895	6.46	+1	1
	Sea	LF	14	14	122	21	1	1	0	.957	1.62	-11	-7
Turner, J	Bal	2B	3	2	19	4	4	0	1	1.000	3.79	-2	-2
	NYM	2B	3	1	12	4	3	0	2	1.000	5.25	0	0
	NYM	3B	1	0	2	0	2	0	1	1.000	9.00	-1	-1
	Bal	SS	1	0	2	1	0	0	0	1.000	4.50	0	0
Uribe, J	SF	2B	24	22	174	44	54	0	12	1.000	5.05	+1	1
	SF	3B	26	21	192	20	46	3	2	.957	3.08	+2	3
	SF	SS	103	90	864	134	233	6	38	.984	3.82	+1	0
Valaika, C	Cin	2B	13	6	77	19	24	0	7	1.000	5.03	+2	2
	Cin	SS	1	0	3	0	2	0	1	1.000	6.00	0	0
Valbuena, L	Cle	2B	71	66	581	127	232	4	59	.989	5.55	+2	4
	Cle	3B	9	6	66	3	12	2	0	.882	2.03	+1	1
	Cle	SS	5	4	42	8	17	4	5	.862	5.36	-3	-2
	Cle	LF	1	0	1	0	0	0	0	-	.00	0	0
Valdez, W	Phi	2B	42	35	314	57	91	1	20	.993	4.24	-2	-1
	Phi	3B	7	3	39	3	12	0	0	1.000	3.46	-1	-1
	Phi	SS	59	50	458	83	148	2	35	.991	4.54	+7	0
Valencia, D	Min	3B	81	80	709	46	171	6	14	.973	2.75	+3	2
Van Every, J	Bos	LF	3	0	4	2	0	0	0	1.000	3.86	0	0
	Bos	CF	12	5	45	10	0	0	0	1.000	1.99	-1	-1
	Bos	RF	6	1	16	3	0	0	0	1.000	1.69	0	0
Velez, E	SF	2B	1	1	9	3	4	0	0	1.000	7.00	+2	2
	SF	LF	13	4	63	16	0	1	0	.941	2.26	+3	2
	SF	CF	5	4	31	9	0	0	0	1.000	2.61	+1	1
	SF	RF	1	0	3	0	0	0	0	-	.00	0	0
Venable, W	SD	1B	1	0	1	1	0	0	0	1.000	-		
	SD	LF	23	19	171	41	0	0	0	1.000	2.15	+1	0
	SD	CF	25	18	164	56	0	1	0	.982	3.07	+6	5
	SD	RF	89	64	600	144	4	3	1	.980	2.17	-1	2
Viciedo, D	CWS	1B	7	3	28	30	0	0	2	1.000	-	-2	-1
	CWS	3B	23	19	162	8	27	4	5	.897	1.94	-4	-3
Vizquel, O	CWS	2B	19	18	151	22	41	0	9	1.000	3.75	0	0
	CWS	3B	83	62	582	31	110	3	15	.979	2.18	-11	-9
	CWS	SS	9	8	61	13	15	0	6	1.000	4.13	+2	2
Walker, N	Pit	2B	105	104	894	222	234	7	62	.985	4.59	-14	-9
	Pit	3B	6	5	40	4	10	1	0	.933	3.15	+2	2

Player	Tm	Pos	G	GS	Inn	PO	A	E	DP	Pct.	Rng	+/-	RS
Wallace, B	Hou	1B	48	41	375	327	32	3	31	.992	-	+4	4
Watson, M	Oak	LF	12	10	74	6	0	0	0	1.000	.73	+1	1
Wells, C	Det	LF	8	4	39	5	1	0	0	1.000	1.38	-2	0
	Det	CF	4	3	25	6	1	0	0	1.000	2.52	0	2
	Det	RF	29	14	151	24	2	0	0	1.000	1.55	+3	3
Werth, J	Phi	CF	21	19	171	44	0	0	0	1.000	2.32	-6	-4
Wigginton, T	Bal	1B	99	89	787	748	73	10	75	.988	-	+4	3
	Bal	2B	40	36	306	66	97	6	13	.964	4.79	-6	-7
	Bal	3B	22	19	166	13	33	5	3	.902	2.49	-2	-1
Willits, R	LAA	LF	44	18	226	53	0	0	0	1.000	2.10	+9	5
	LAA	CF	29	16	167	50	4	0	0	1.000	2.90	-4	0
	LAA	RF	8	2	26	6	1	1	0	.875	2.42	0	1
Wilson, B	LAA	1B	1	0	2	4	0	0	0	1.000	-		
Wilson, J	Sea	SS	60	59	518	88	191	8	36	.972	4.84	+10	8
Wilson, J	Sea	1B	3	3	30	30	2	1	4	.970	-	-3	-2
	Sea	2B	2	1	13	6	5	0	4	1.000	7.62	0	0
	Sea	3B	4	3	31	2	8	1	1	.909	2.90	-2	-2
	Sea	SS	98	95	839	124	304	20	53	.955	4.59	+1	0
Winn, R	NYY	LF	18	14	126	22	1	0	0	1.000	1.63	-3	-3
	StL	LF	7	1	20	4	0	0	0	1.000	1.80	0	0
	StL	CF	9	7	56	12	0	0	0	1.000	1.93	-2	0
	NYY	RF	11	2	36	9	0	0	0	1.000	2.25	0	0
	StL	RF	35	14	162	42	0	1	0	.977	2.33	-2	-2
Wise, D	Tor	LF	10	7	65	13	0	0	0	1.000	1.80	-2	0
	Tor	CF	18	6	74	27	2	0	1	1.000	3.50	-4	-2
	Tor	RF	17	10	100	20	1	0	0	1.000	1.89	-1	-1
Wood, B	LAA	1B	2	1	9	11	0	0	1	1.000	-	0	0
	LAA	3B	56	46	412	33	76	5	6	.956	2.38	+7	6
	LAA	SS	22	20	185	22	56	5	7	.940	3.79	-8	-6
Woodward, C	Sea	SS	7	6	52	5	10	1	1	.938	2.56	-1	-1
Worth, D	Det	2B	12	8	77	14	31	0	9	1.000	5.26	+5	4
	Det	3B	3	1	11	0	2	0	0	1.000	1.64	0	0
	Det	SS	24	24	205	41	56	0	14	1.000	4.24	-4	-3
Youkilis, K	Bos	1B	101	97	862	809	72	3	66	.997	-	+7	4
	Bos	3B	2	2	15	3	5	0	0	1.000	4.80	-1	-1
Young, D	Pit	2B	10	4	52	5	11	0	2	1.000	2.77	-1	-1
	Pit	3B	8	7	58	6	10	3	1	.842	2.48	-3	-3
	Pit	RF	21	16	153	29	2	1	0	.969	1.82	-5	-3
Young Jr., E	Col	2B	35	33	257	44	94	6	23	.958	4.83	+3	3
	Col	LF	10	9	65	11	0	1	0	.917	1.52	+1	0
Zawadzki, L	SD	2B	7	6	54	9	18	2	2	.931	4.50	-1	-2
	SD	3B	1	1	9	1	4	0	1	1.000	5.00	0	0
	SD	SS	3	2	14	2	5	0	1	1.000	4.50	+1	1
Zobrist, B	TB	1B	14	9	79	77	8	0	6	1.000	-	+3	2
	TB	2B	55	45	371	74	116	3	27	.984	4.61	+10	8
	TB	3B	2	1	10	1	0	1	0	.500	.90	-1	-1
	TB	LF	1	0	2	0	0	0	0	-	.00	0	0
	TB	CF	14	9	83	22	0	0	0	1.000	2.38	+1	2
	TB	RF	103	80	749	182	6	0	3	1.000	2.26	+6	7

All Other Catchers

Player	Tm	G	GS	Inn	PO	A	E	DP	PB	Pct.	SBA	CS	PCS	CS%	ER	CERA	Runs Saved SB	Adj-ER	Total
Alfonzo,Eliezer	Sea	12	10	91.0	54	2	2	0	0	.966	4	1	1	.25	47	4.65	0	0	0
Anderson,Bryan	StL	8	6	55.0	40	4	1	0	0	.978	6	0	1	.00	39	6.38	-1	0	-1
Arencibia,JP	Tor	8	7	63.0	48	3	0	0	1	1.000	5	2	0	.40	31	4.43	0	0	0
Ausmus,Brad	LAD	21	19	167.2	168	5	1	0	0	.994	17	0	0	.00	79	4.24	-2	0	-2
Baker,John	Fla	21	20	178.0	152	9	2	1	1	.988	28	5	1	.18	80	4.04	-2	0	-2
Barajas,Rod	LAD	23	20	174.0	165	6	0	0	0	1.000	13	2	0	.15	68	3.52	0	0	0
Barajas,Rod	NYM	73	67	602.0	516	21	3	5	3	.994	27	3	1	.11	266	3.98	-4	2	-2
Bard,Josh	Sea	39	35	304.0	202	12	2	0	0	.991	18	3	3	.17	145	4.29	-1	0	-1
Blanco,Henry	NYM	46	41	361.0	284	27	1	4	3	.997	22	11	0	.50	136	3.39	3	0	3
Boscan,J.C.	Atl	1	0	1.0	2	0	0	0	0	1.000	0	0	0	-	0	0.00	0	0	0
Brown,Dusty	Bos	7	3	35.2	26	4	0	2	2	1.000	7	1	1	.14	16	4.04	0	0	0
Budde,Ryan	LAA	6	3	30.0	35	2	0	1	2	1.000	6	1	0	.17	4	1.20	0	0	0
Burke,Jamie	Was	1	0	1.0	1	0	0	0	0	1.000	0	0	0	-	1	9.00	0	0	0
Butera,Drew	Min	47	44	394.2	301	26	5	3	4	.985	37	14	2	.38	180	4.10	4	-1	3
Carlin,Luke	Cle	6	4	37.0	34	4	0	1	0	1.000	6	2	0	.33	11	2.68	0	0	0
Cash,Kevin	Bos	29	19	181.0	148	14	1	0	6	.994	26	2	1	.08	75	3.73	-2	1	-1
Cash,Kevin	Hou	19	18	156.2	131	9	0	2	1	1.000	19	3	1	.16	81	4.65	-1	-1	-2
Castillo,Welington	ChC	5	5	44.0	33	3	0	0	1	1.000	5	2	0	.40	21	4.30	1	0	1
Castro,Jason	Hou	67	57	509.1	449	34	2	6	7	.996	49	17	1	.35	222	3.92	2	0	2
Castro,Ramon	CWS	34	31	279.0	214	14	1	0	1	.996	32	6	3	.19	139	4.48	1	0	1
Cervelli,Francisco	NYY	90	80	724.0	579	45	13	2	2	.980	64	8	1	.13	325	4.04	-4	3	-1
Conger,Hank	LAA	10	9	80.0	63	3	3	0	0	.957	9	1	1	.11	17	1.91	-1	0	-1
Davis,Brad	Fla	32	32	278.0	215	16	4	0	1	.983	26	7	0	.27	121	3.92	0	1	1
Donaldson,Josh	Oak	7	5	47.1	44	3	1	0	1	.979	6	2	0	.33	21	3.99	0	0	0
Ellis,A.J.	LAD	43	34	308.2	263	22	1	4	1	.997	36	8	2	.22	142	4.14	0	0	0
Esposito,Brian	Hou	2	0	3.0	2	0	0	0	0	1.000	0	0	0	-	3	9.00	0	0	0
Flowers,Tyler	CWS	7	3	31.2	30	1	0	0	0	1.000	3	1	0	.33	15	4.26	0	0	0
Fox,Jake	Bal	11	7	65.1	49	6	0	0	0	1.000	6	1	0	.17	39	5.37	-1	0	-1
Fox,Jake	Oak	8	7	59.0	37	2	1	0	0	.975	3	1	1	.33	30	4.58	0	0	0
Gimenez,Chris	Cle	24	19	168.2	109	14	1	2	1	.992	34	9	2	.26	85	4.54	-1	0	-1
Hanigan,Ryan	Cin	68	58	525.2	436	21	4	4	2	.991	41	12	1	.29	196	3.36	0	5	5
Hatcher,Chris	Fla	4	2	22.2	20	2	0	0	0	1.000	1	1	0	1.00	14	5.56	1	0	1
Hayes,Brett	Fla	24	21	190.2	142	13	0	2	1	1.000	19	5	1	.26	85	4.01	0	0	0
Hernandez,Ramon	Cin	91	85	732.0	594	49	4	4	2	.994	53	14	4	.26	390	4.80	0	-10	-10
Hester,John	Ari	32	27	239.1	189	10	0	2	4	1.000	24	3	0	.13	134	5.04	-2	-1	-3
Hill,Koyle	ChC	72	60	545.1	493	29	4	4	4	.992	45	6	3	.11	252	4.16	-0	0	0
Hill,Steven	StL	1	0	4.0	2	0	0	0	0	1.000	0	0	0	-	1	2.25	0	0	0
Hoover,Paul	Phi	9	6	62.0	42	2	2	0	0	.957	2	1	0	.50	31	4.50	0	0	0
Hundley,Nick	SD	76	73	659.2	632	28	4	6	6	.994	58	11	6	.19	273	3.72	-1	-5	-6
Iannetta,Chris	Col	52	49	443.0	373	32	6	2	5	.985	45	6	4	.13	228	4.63	-2	-1	-3
Jaramillo,Jason	Pit	31	25	222.0	170	12	3	2	1	.984	28	6	4	.21	140	5.68	0	-1	-1
Jaso,John	TB	96	94	719.0	611	30	5	5	7	.992	53	9	3	.17	309	3.87	-2	-1	-3
Johnson,Rob	Sea	61	57	510.2	347	35	4	5	9	.990	34	12	0	.35	227	4.00	2	-2	0
Kottaras,George	Mil	61	60	541.2	434	20	4	4	4	.991	52	4	4	.08	268	4.45	-5	1	-4
Kratz,Erik	Pit	9	8	77.1	56	9	0	0	0	1.000	7	4	0	.57	38	4.42	2	0	2
Laird,Gerald	Det	87	76	670.2	516	52	5	5	5	.991	88	24	6	.27	306	4.11	-2	2	0
LaRue,Jason	StL	28	14	150.1	96	6	0	2	2	1.000	0	2	1	.33	91	5.45	1	0	1
Lucroy,Jonathan	Mil	75	74	655.0	614	44	5	6	1	.992	54	15	2	.28	320	4.40	2	-1	1
Lucy,Donny	CWS	7	5	43.0	43	0	0	0	0	1.000	7	0	2	.00	26	5.23	-1	0	-1
Maldonado,Carlos	Was	4	3	25.2	10	2	0	0	1	1.000	2	2	0	1.00	9	3.16	1	0	1
Marson,Lou	Cle	87	81	725.0	504	44	4	1	5	.993	82	26	5	.32	349	4.33	1	-1	0
Mathis,Jeff	LAA	67	62	553.2	433	36	7	2	6	.985	54	7	4	.13	226	3.67	-1	2	1
May,Lucas	KC	10	9	81.0	60	3	0	0	4	1.000	9	1	1	.11	36	4.00	0	0	0
McKenry,Michael	Col	2	1	9.0	5	1	0	0	0	1.000	0	0	0	-	6	6.00	0	0	0
Miller,Corky	Cin	32	19	195.1	126	10	0	1	0	1.000	11	3	0	.27	63	2.90	0	1	1
Moeller,Chad	NYY	9	4	40.0	33	6	0	0	2	1.000	6	0	1	.00	15	3.38	-1	0	-1
Molina,Bengie	SF	58	55	458.1	396	36	1	4	3	.998	61	12	2	.20	178	3.50	-1	2	1
Molina,Bengie	Tex	55	50	439.1	355	24	5	1	1	.987	42	10	2	.24	192	3.93	0	-3	-3
Molina,Gustavo	Bos	4	2	17.0	15	1	0	0	1	1.000	3	0	0	.00	13	6.88	-1	0	-1
Molina,Jose	Tor	56	51	444.2	417	37	2	3	5	.996	34	13	2	.38	184	3.72	3	3	6
Montero,Miguel	Ari	79	75	658.1	484	36	2	1	6	.996	68	16	5	.24	314	4.29	1	1	2
Moore,Adam	Sea	59	58	514.2	372	24	4	1	7	.990	43	7	1	.16	208	3.64	-1	3	2
Morales,Jose	Min	11	4	43.1	43	1	0	0	0	1.000	6	1	0	.17	31	6.44	0	0	0
Napoli,Mike	LAA	66	59	525.0	405	32	6	4	5	.986	71	13	6	.18	299	5.13	0	-7	-7
Navarro,Dioner	TB	46	36	331.0	272	20	4	2	0	.986	31	7	5	.23	107	2.91	0	3	3
Nickeas,Mike	NYM	4	3	22.2	14	1	1	0	0	.938	3	0	0	.00	15	5.96	-1	0	-1
Nieves,Wil	Was	51	43	395.0	290	20	5	4	1	.984	41	7	3	.17	176	4.01	-1	1	0
Pagnozzi,Matt	StL	15	12	106.0	77	4	1	1	1	.988	11	0	1	.00	36	3.06	-1	0	-1
Paulino,Ronny	Fla	85	84	740.1	644	47	6	4	6	.991	77	21	3	.27	331	4.02	1	0	0
Pena,Brayan	KC	47	35	337.1	269	24	3	3	1	.990	41	11	1	.27	178	4.75	0	1	0
Phillips,Paul	Col	10	5	55.0	43	2	1	0	0	.978	1	0	0	.00	24	3.93	0	0	0
Posada,Jorge	NYY	83	78	678.1	562	22	8	2	8	.986	85	10	3	.12	311	4.13	-6	-2	-8
Posey,Buster	SF	76	75	662.0	615	41	6	4	1	.991	62	18	5	.29	234	3.18	4	1	5
Powell,Landon	Oak	38	29	267.0	198	8	6	1	0	.972	26	4	5	.15	132	4.45	0	-1	-1
Quintero,Humberto	Hou	87	74	653.2	561	49	5	5	4	.992	54	17	2	.31	290	3.99	4	1	5
Quiroz,Guillermo	Sea	2	2	17.2	8	1	1	0	0	.900	3	1	0	.33	4	2.04	0	0	0
Ramirez,Max	Tex	26	22	187.1	154	7	2	0	2	.988	29	4	1	.14	74	3.56	-2	0	-2
Ramos,Wilson	Min	7	7	63.0	41	1	0	0	0	1.000	4	0	0	.00	23	3.29	0	0	0
Ramos,Wilson	Was	15	14	129.1	96	9	0	0	1	1.000	7	1	0	.14	56	3.90	0	0	0
Redmond,Mike	Cle	21	18	162.1	91	11	1	1	1	.990	27	2	0	.07	72	3.99	-2	0	-2
Rivera,Mike	Fla	5	3	28.2	28	2	1	0	2	.968	4	0	0	.00	23	7.22	0	0	0
Ross,David	Atl	57	33	328.2	276	22	4	1	1	.987	26	7	1	.27	115	3.15	1	1	2

Player	Tm	G	GS	Inn	PO	A	E	DP	PB	Pct.	SBA	CS	PCS	CS%	ER	CERA	Runs Saved		
																	SB	Adj-ER	Total
Saltalamacchia,J	Bos	6	5	43.2	38	2	1	0	0	.976	6	1	0	.17	21	4.33	0	0	0
Saltalamacchia,J	Tex	1	1	9.0	8	0	0	0	0	1.000	1	0	0	.00	4	4.00	0	0	0
Santana,Carlos	Cle	40	40	340.0	245	22	3	2	4	.989	34	9	3	.26	167	4.42	1	-1	0
Sardinha,Dane	Phi	12	9	87.0	84	4	0	0	1	1.000	5	1	1	.20	36	3.72	0	0	0
Schmidt,Konrad	Ari	2	2	17.0	12	0	0	0	0	1.000	0	0	0	-	8	4.24	0	0	0
Schneider,Brian	Phi	46	38	333.0	257	17	2	4	1	.993	38	8	0	.21	169	4.57	-1	-1	-2
Shoppach,Kelly	TB	56	46	403.2	324	18	2	1	2	.994	35	6	0	.17	195	4.35	-2	-3	-5
St. Pierre,Max	Det	4	2	17.0	12	1	0	0	0	1.000	0	0	0	-	8	4.24	0	0	0
Stavinoha,Nick	StL	1	0	0.1	1	0	0	0	0	1.000	0	0	0	-	1	27.00	0	0	0
Stewart,Chris	SD	1	0	1.0	1	0	0	0	0	1.000	0	0	0	-	0	0.00		0	0
Tatum,Craig	Bal	42	34	310.2	222	17	3	1	1	.988	27	2	0	.07	157	4.55	-2	0	-2
Teagarden,Taylor	Tex	28	22	205.0	171	9	2	2	3	.989	18	3	0	.17	98	4.30	-1	0	-1
Thole,Josh	NYM	61	51	467.1	341	29	3	2	4	.992	25	8	3	.32	185	3.56	0	-1	-1
Towles,J.R.	Hou	15	13	116.2	92	7	1	0	0	.990	11	3	0	.27	58	4.47	0	0	0
Treanor,Matt	Tex	81	67	614.2	512	21	3	1	2	.994	61	11	6	.18	268	3.92	-1	1	0
Varitek,Jason	Bos	39	27	275.1	242	13	0	2	1	1.000	43	8	1	.19	124	4.05	0	1	1
Whiteside,Eli	SF	55	32	340.2	334	26	2	3	2	.994	41	9	3	.22	134	3.54	1	0	1
Wilson,Bobby	LAA	38	29	260.2	217	12	1	2	3	.996	34	6	2	.18	105	3.63	-1	1	0
Zaun,Gregg	Mil	28	28	242.1	221	13	2	4	0	.992	25	4	2	.16	146	5.42	-1	-1	-2

38 Facts about Major League Baserunning in 2010

Bill James

1) An average major league player went from first to third on a single 28% of the time.

2) A very good baserunner will go from first to third on a single about 38% of the time.

3) A very slow runner will do it about 18% of the time.

4) An average major league player scored from second on a single 58% of the time.

5) A very good baserunner will score from second on a single about 70% of the time.

6) A very slow runner will score from second only about 41% of the time.

7) An average major league player will score from first on a double 44% of the time.

8) A very good baserunner will score from first on a double 62% of the time.

9) A very poor baserunner will score from first on a double about 27% of the time.

10) Elvis Andrus went first-to-third on a single 20 times in 2010, the most of any major league player.

11) Juan Pierre was second in this category, with 18. This is perhaps surprising, as Pierre's 68 stolen bases reduced sharply the number of times he was ON first base.

12) Brayan Pena of the Royals was 0-for-17 going first to third, the largest "oh-fer" of any player.

13) Prince Fielder was 3-for-64, the lowest percentage for any regular player.

14) The 64 times that Fielder was ON first when a single was hit was by far the largest in the majors. It appears, frankly, that Fielder is SO slow that he almost certainly stopped at second on a significant number of hits that would have been doubles had he been able to go to third. This is extremely unusual.

15) Alex Rios scored from second on a single 24 times, the most of any major league player.

16) Chone Figgins was 15-for-16 at scoring from second on a single, the highest percentage of any player with 10 or more opportunities.

17) Ivan Rodriguez was 1-for-12 at scoring from second on a single, the lowest percentage of any player with ten or more opportunities.

18) Carl Crawford and Jose Bautista both scored from first on a double 11 times in 2010. Bautista, however, was 11-for-16; Crawford was 11-for-19.

19) Jim Thome was on first base when a double was hit 8 times, and did not score on any of those plays.

20) We credit a player with a "Base Taken" whenever he moves up a base on a Passed Ball, a Wild Pitch, a Balk, a Sacrifice Fly, or Defensive Indifference. (We single out these five events because these events are already identified in the records; they're merely ignored from the standpoint of the offensive player. All we are doing is deciding not to ignore who the baserunner is, but to count it.)

21) Derek Jeter moved up a base on these five events 38 times in 2010, easily the most of any major league player, and the most in several years. (Grady Sizemore led in 2007, with 34, Jose Reyes in 2008, with 36, and Denard Span in 2009, with 31.) Jeter, who was under 20 all three of those seasons, suddenly spiked up to 38 last year—either because of a cluster of random events or because he decided to become aggressive on the bases.

22) Vladimir Guerrero was thrown out advancing ten times in 2010, the most of any major league player.

23) Numerous major league regulars were not thrown out at all advancing in 2010, including Elvis Andrus, Joe Mauer, Carlos Quentin, Austin Jackson, Alexei Ramirez and Derrek Lee.

24) Shin-Soo Choo, Matt Holliday, Aramis Ramirez, Chone Figgins and Brandon Inge tied for the major league lead in being doubled off base, with 5 each.   In past seasons we have seen higher totals.

25) The major league leader in baserunning outs, combining "Out Advancing" and "Doubled Off", was Vladimir Guerrero, with 12.   During the playoffs Ron Washington told reporters that Vladimir was perhaps the best baserunner on his team, which. . .you know, it's nice of him to say that.   But Guerrero is a terrible baserunner at this point, regardless of what his manager may tell you and gullible TV announcers may repeat.

26) Billy Butler led the majors in Grounding into Double Plays, with 32.

27) An average player grounds into a double play in 11% of those situations in which he bats with a runner on first and less than two out.

28) Butler's 32 GIDP have little to do with his having a large number of opportunities to do this. His 135 GIDP opportunities was the 25th highest total in the majors. Had he grounded into twin killings at a normal pace, that would have been 15 double plays. He more than doubled that.

29) Carl Crawford was the toughest player in the majors to double up, grounding into only 2 double plays in 132 double play situations.

30) Not counting stolen base attempts, the best baserunner in the major leagues in 2010, by far, by a mile, by a mile and a half, was Elvis Andrus of Texas.   Andrus was +44 bases compared to an average baserunner—basically, +11 runs.   Austin Jackson was second at +27 bases.

31) Including stolen base attempts, the best baserunner in the majors was Juan Pierre—+54 bases.   The top five were Juan Pierre, Carl Crawford, Brett Gardner, Elvis Andrus, and Michael Bourn.

32) The worst baserunner in the majors, not counting stolen base attempts, was Jason Kubel of Minnesota.

33) The worst baserunner if you do count stolen base attempts was still Jason Kubel.

34) The best baserunning *team* in the majors, by far, was Mad Joe Maddon's Runnin' Rays. The Rays were +196 bases, or something near 50 runs.

35) The worst baserunning team was the Kansas City Royals.

36) Of the eight teams that made the playoffs, five were above-average baserunning teams, and three were below-average. However, that's a little misleading because two of those (the Twins and the Reds) were just a little below average.

37) The Twins, normally a very good baserunning team, had a bad year running the bases in 2010. It is fair to ask whether this could be a park effect, but. . .not really. The Twins had 17 runners doubled off base, one away from the major-league leading 18 by the Mets. A park doesn't do that to you.

38) The three best baserunners in the major leagues—Juan Pierre, Carl Crawford and Brett Gardner—were all left fielders.

Historically, left field is interesting because that is where the greatest baserunners have played (Brock, Henderson, Raines, Coleman), but there have also been many left fielders who were absolutely terrible baserunners.

This is an All-Star team of the best baserunners in the major leagues in 2010:

C—John Jaso
1B—Kevin Youkilis
2B—Chase Utley
3B—Evan Longoria
SS—Elvis Andrus
LF—Juan Pierre
CF—Michael Bourn
RF—Ben Zobrist

2010 Baserunning

Player	1st to 3rd Moved	Chances	2nd to Home Moved	Chances	1st to Home Moved	Chances	Bases Taken	Out Adv	Doubled Off	BR Outs	GDP	GDP Opps	BR Gain	SB Gain	Net Gain
Abreu,Bobby	10	31	15	28	4	7	17	2	2	4	13	114	+1	+4	+5
Abreu,Tony	0	3	3	5	0	3	3	2	0	2	8	38	-10	0	-10
Alvarez,Pedro	4	22	4	7	1	6	5	1	1	2	8	59	-9	0	-9
Andrus,Elvis	20	44	18	26	7	12	32	0	0	0	6	95	+44	+2	+46
Ankiel,Rick	4	9	6	8	1	1	2	3	2	5	3	36	-10	+1	-9
Arias,Joaquin	2	8	4	8	1	2	5	0	0	0	2	23	+4	+1	+5
Avila,Alex	5	18	4	8	0	4	7	2	1	3	12	70	-11	-2	-13
Aviles,Mike	9	28	10	17	6	12	19	2	2	4	13	92	+3	+4	+7
Aybar,Erick	9	24	15	21	6	11	17	6	0	6	7	96	+5	+6	+11
Aybar,Willy	2	8	2	4	0	2	12	0	3	3	4	45	+1	0	+1
Baker,Jeff	0	11	6	8	0	3	6	1	0	1	6	46	-3	+1	-2
Barajas,Rod	2	15	3	11	2	3	4	2	1	3	6	60	-11	0	-11
Barmes,Clint	11	23	8	13	5	6	9	0	0	0	5	89	+18	-1	+17
Bartlett,Jason	12	25	13	23	2	7	26	2	0	2	6	82	+22	-1	+21
Barton,Daric	10	39	21	29	7	13	17	5	0	5	8	114	+6	+1	+7
Bautista,Jose	6	22	6	15	11	16	12	4	2	6	10	105	-8	+5	-3
Bay,Jason	4	16	7	12	2	5	13	1	0	1	7	82	+8	+10	+18
Beckham,Gordon	6	20	10	14	2	6	15	1	4	5	9	95	0	-8	-8
Belliard,Ronnie	4	11	4	7	1	3	5	1	0	1	4	45	+2	-2	0
Beltran,Carlos	4	10	0	1	0	2	7	1	0	1	4	37	+2	+1	+3
Beltre,Adrian	5	16	11	16	4	10	17	2	0	2	25	127	-3	0	-3
Berkman,Lance	4	29	8	14	4	4	9	2	0	2	18	108	-9	-1	-10
Bernadina,Roger	4	23	10	14	3	4	10	2	1	3	3	106	+7	+12	+19
Betancourt,Yuniesky	9	24	11	10	6	9	18	1	4	5	13	119	+3	-4	-1
Betemit,Wilson	7	23	4	11	1	4	5	4	0	4	3	49	-9	0	-9
Blake,Casey	11	17	14	16	3	6	11	1	2	4	8	100	+10	-8	+2
Blanco,Andres	9	22	1	7	0	0	8	2	1	3	0	24	0	-4	-4
Blanco,Gregor	10	20	6	10	1	2	8	2	0	2	5	38	+4	+3	+7
Bloomquist,Willie	4	12	3	6	2	3	9	1	1	2	4	40	+3	-2	+1
Blum,Geoff	2	12	6	9	2	3	4	1	1	2	3	32	-3	0	-3
Boesch,Brennan	6	21	9	19	4	9	5	3	2	5	5	111	-8	+5	-3
Bonifacio,Emilio	7	10	6	6	2	2	7	0	0	0	1	21	+15	+12	+27
Borbon,Julio	11	22	11	19	1	2	16	3	1	4	5	90	+10	+1	+11
Bourgeois,Jason	2	4	4	5	1	1	4	0	0	0	5	13	+2	+4	+6
Bourn,Michael	16	35	16	20	6	7	15	3	0	3	6	66	+16	+28	+44
Bradley,Milton	4	16	4	7	0	1	8	1	3	4	2	47	-4	+4	0
Brantley,Michael	7	26	8	11	3	6	12	1	1	2	6	46	+5	+6	+11
Branyan,Russell	2	16	4	11	0	6	11	1	1	2	6	91	-1	+1	0
Braun,Ryan	11	38	22	28	5	9	25	2	0	2	17	152	+21	+8	+29
Brignac,Reid	5	9	7	9	2	5	12	0	2	2	6	62	+9	-3	+6
Bruce,Jay	11	25	15	18	6	7	11	2	2	4	12	127	+9	-3	+6
Buck,John	4	12	6	9	0	2	11	1	0	1	6	67	+7	0	+7
Burrell,Pat	5	21	6	9	1	1	9	1	1	2	7	64	+1	-4	-3
Butler,Billy	5	38	9	26	1	10	21	4	0	4	32	135	-29	0	-29
Byrd,Marlon	7	28	12	23	6	15	23	3	1	4	12	122	+5	+3	+8
Cabrera,Asdrubal	6	22	7	9	6	9	16	4	3	7	10	79	-6	-2	-8
Cabrera,Everth	2	7	6	9	1	1	5	1	0	1	8	47	-1	-2	-3
Cabrera,Melky	3	27	2	11	5	5	17	4	0	4	8	81	-4	+5	+1
Cabrera,Miguel	13	50	13	20	3	14	15	2	1	3	17	144	-3	-3	-6
Cabrera,Orlando	12	31	8	18	2	5	13	2	3	5	11	65	-9	+3	-6
Cain,Lorenzo	2	7	3	5	0	0	9	0	1	1	1	35	+8	+5	+13
Cairo,Miguel	2	9	5	9	1	2	3	1	0	1	4	33	-3	+4	+1
Callaspo,Alberto	9	30	11	17	1	8	16	4	1	6	22	127	-15	-1	-16
Cameron,Mike	1	7	8	9	2	5	8	1	2	3	3	28	-1	-2	-3
Cano,Robinson	9	29	16	24	7	11	24	2	1	3	19	124	+10	-1	+9
Cantu,Jorge	4	25	12	16	2	4	13	1	0	1	15	105	+3	0	+3
Carroll,Jamey	10	28	12	14	1	5	16	2	2	4	8	60	+4	+4	+8
Carter,Chris (NYM)	2	8	1	6	0	0	2	1	0	1	2	31	-4	-3	-7
Casilla,Alexi	5	11	4	5	1	2	6	0	0	0	5	30	+6	+4	+10
Castillo,Luis	4	8	4	7	3	5	10	1	1	2	6	45	+3	+2	+5
Castro,Jason	1	11	0	4	2	5	5	2	0	2	4	46	-6	0	-6
Castro,Starlin	5	18	12	19	6	11	11	3	0	3	14	85	-5	-6	-11

2010 Baserunning

Player	1st to 3rd Moved	1st to 3rd Chances	2nd to Home Moved	2nd to Home Chances	1st to Home Moved	1st to Home Chances	Bases Taken	Out Adv	Doubled Off	BR Outs	GDP	GDP Opps	BR Gain	SB Gain	Net Gain
Cedeno,Ronny	8	15	3	7	2	2	10	3	2	5	10	88	-5	+6	+1
Cervelli,Francisco	6	18	1	3	2	4	6	1	2	3	7	78	-3	-1	-4
Choo,Shin-Soo	7	29	11	18	6	12	24	6	5	11	11	123	-11	+8	-3
Church,Ryan	1	8	2	6	1	4	8	0	0	0	3	40	+5	+1	+6
Coghlan,Chris	11	27	8	13	6	9	11	2	0	2	3	48	+10	+4	+14
Colvin,Tyler	11	22	6	10	1	4	11	0	1	1	6	72	+12	+4	+16
Conrad,Brooks	3	6	9	11	1	2	3	0	0	0	0	32	+9	+3	+12
Cora,Alex	1	12	3	3	0	0	3	1	2	3	4	38	-8	+2	-6
Counsell,Craig	2	13	2	10	1	1	7	3	1	4	0	39	-7	-1	-8
Crawford,Carl	7	32	15	23	11	19	27	2	2	4	2	132	+25	+27	+52
Crisp,Coco	5	14	6	9	3	4	15	3	0	3	6	41	+5	+26	+31
Crosby,Bobby	2	8	1	6	2	2	6	0	1	1	2	31	+1	-6	-5
Crowe,Trevor	6	19	11	18	1	6	14	1	0	1	13	91	+4	+6	+10
Cruz,Nelson	4	16	7	11	1	4	20	2	0	2	12	85	+7	+9	+16
Cuddyer,Michael	13	33	17	25	7	11	27	3	2	5	26	146	+5	+1	+6
Cunningham,Aaron	1	4	5	6	0	2	3	1	1	2	3	31	-3	-5	-8
Cust,Jack	4	24	7	12	0	5	19	2	2	4	6	83	+2	-2	0
Damon,Johnny	12	39	17	24	5	10	19	0	1	1	5	120	+24	+9	+33
Davis,Ike	5	30	11	19	6	10	16	1	1	2	13	116	+4	-1	+3
Davis,Rajai	8	22	11	17	8	9	28	5	2	7	10	92	+10	+28	+38
DeJesus,David	8	32	8	14	2	5	9	1	0	1	10	74	0	-3	-3
Denorfia,Chris	5	16	2	4	2	4	7	1	1	2	5	50	0	0	0
Desmond,Ian	6	21	10	14	4	5	16	4	2	7	9	103	-3	+7	+4
DeWitt,Blake	12	27	9	13	1	3	15	3	1	4	5	82	+9	-1	+8
Diaz,Matt	0	9	6	9	1	2	5	1	1	2	6	60	-4	+1	-3
Donald,Jason	3	12	10	13	2	6	16	0	0	0	3	49	+18	+3	+21
Doumit,Ryan	4	21	4	12	2	7	9	4	1	5	18	97	-22	+1	-21
Drew,J.D.	6	31	10	15	5	10	13	2	0	2	12	106	+2	+1	+3
Drew,Stephen	7	32	13	21	3	8	17	3	1	4	8	114	+3	0	+3
Duncan,Shelley	1	5	2	7	0	3	8	1	0	1	4	46	+1	+1	+2
Dunn,Adam	3	29	9	22	2	9	12	1	0	1	10	137	-1	-2	-3
Eckstein,David	5	20	8	13	4	6	11	3	0	4	6	76	-1	+6	+5
Edmonds,Jim	2	13	8	16	1	3	9	2	1	3	2	48	-2	+2	0
Ellis,A.J.	0	5	1	4	0	2	3	0	1	1	5	29	-6	0	-6
Ellis,Mark	6	22	15	23	3	5	11	1	1	3	7	88	+3	-5	-2
Encarnacion,Edwin	3	12	6	7	1	2	4	4	1	5	9	64	-13	+1	-12
Escobar,Alcides	7	19	11	12	6	7	13	1	2	3	8	98	+12	+2	+14
Escobar,Yunel	14	39	7	13	5	11	9	3	2	5	18	107	-14	+2	-12
Ethier,Andre	9	42	14	17	3	10	20	2	1	3	11	133	+10	0	+10
Feliz,Pedro	6	23	4	10	3	5	8	0	1	1	13	87	-2	-1	-3
Fielder,Prince	3	64	10	26	1	10	13	2	3	5	12	138	-28	+1	-27
Figgins,Chone	14	32	15	16	5	7	27	1	5	6	20	148	+13	+12	+25
Fontenot,Mike	6	21	5	11	1	3	6	1	1	2	3	39	-2	-7	-9
Fowler,Dexter	11	26	9	13	4	11	23	6	0	6	5	71	+9	-1	+8
Fox,Jake	1	9	1	8	1	2	4	3	0	3	7	46	-13	0	-13
Francisco,Ben	1	11	6	9	2	4	2	0	0	0	6	39	-2	+8	+6
Francoeur,Jeff	9	27	8	10	0	6	14	2	3	5	9	102	-1	+2	+1
Frandsen,Kevin	4	11	8	11	0	3	2	2	0	2	5	36	-5	+2	-3
Freese,David	5	17	3	4	0	1	5	0	0	0	7	48	+2	-1	+1
Fukudome,Kosuke	7	21	5	14	1	4	12	1	1	3	5	64	-1	-9	-10
Furcal,Rafael	9	18	9	16	2	4	20	2	1	3	5	58	+13	+14	+27
Gardner,Brett	9	27	17	26	6	9	24	2	1	3	6	103	+21	+29	+50
Getz,Chris	4	16	6	10	0	1	7	0	2	2	3	46	0	+11	+11
Giambi,Jason	4	11	2	3	0	3	4	0	0	0	5	48	+3	+2	+5
Glaus,Troy	4	22	4	11	8	14	11	0	1	1	16	112	-2	0	-2
Gomes,Jonny	14	39	8	21	5	9	15	2	3	5	4	132	+7	-1	+6
Gomez,Carlos	3	13	6	10	2	2	7	4	2	6	10	66	-15	+12	-3
Gonzalez,Adrian	6	43	9	26	2	7	22	2	0	2	15	137	-2	0	-2
Gonzalez,Alberto	0	8	3	11	0	1	4	1	0	1	8	45	-9	0	-9
Gonzalez,Alex	8	18	7	12	1	5	12	4	1	5	16	128	-7	-3	-10
Gonzalez,Carlos	8	28	20	25	6	9	24	2	0	2	9	124	+26	+10	+36
Gordon,Alex	5	17	4	7	0	5	2	1	1	2	9	56	-11	-9	-20
Granderson,Curtis	7	22	9	16	1	5	10	2	0	2	3	141	+12	+8	+20
Gross,Gabe	8	15	6	9	3	4	10	0	0	0	5	49	+14	+3	+17

2010 Baserunning

Player	1st to 3rd Moved	Chances	2nd to Home Moved	Chances	1st to Home Moved	Chances	Bases Taken	Out Adv	Doubled Off	BR Outs	GDP	GDP Opps	BR Gain	SB Gain	Net Gain
Guerrero,Vladimir	13	36	7	14	2	13	19	10	2	12	19	116	-30	-6	-36
Guillen,Carlos	4	13	3	9	3	7	10	2	1	4	10	57	-10	-3	-13
Guillen,Jose	5	31	8	16	1	5	8	4	2	6	17	98	-26	+1	-25
Gutierrez,Franklin	15	29	9	16	1	3	16	5	0	5	10	122	+7	+19	+26
Guzman,Cristian	8	26	9	13	3	6	9	0	0	0	9	65	+7	0	+7
Gwynn,Tony	5	14	7	8	2	2	10	1	0	1	3	55	+12	+9	+21
Hafner,Travis	5	28	5	12	1	9	11	2	1	3	2	78	-3	0	-3
Hairston,Jerry	2	18	11	13	3	7	6	4	1	5	5	74	-8	-3	-11
Hairston,Scott	2	16	8	16	2	2	11	2	0	2	3	52	+3	+4	+7
Hall,Bill	6	17	2	3	1	6	10	3	0	3	4	72	+2	+7	+9
Hamilton,Josh	13	38	14	23	8	10	21	1	1	2	11	126	+20	+6	+26
Hanigan,Ryan	3	12	5	10	1	2	5	1	0	1	6	36	-3	0	-3
Hardy,J.J.	10	21	7	12	1	10	11	1	0	1	8	60	+5	-1	+4
Harris,Willie	3	10	2	3	1	3	3	1	0	1	3	51	+1	+1	+2
Hart,Corey	8	24	12	17	6	10	11	2	0	2	14	134	+7	-5	+2
Hawpe,Brad	3	16	5	6	1	1	8	0	1	1	5	66	+6	0	+6
Headley,Chase	7	27	9	18	4	9	18	3	0	3	11	133	+6	+7	+13
Heisey,Chris	7	13	6	8	3	3	5	0	0	0	3	42	+12	-3	+9
Helms,Wes	0	14	5	8	3	6	4	2	1	3	7	58	-11	-4	-15
Helton,Todd	5	35	9	15	0	5	7	3	1	4	10	79	-16	0	-16
Hermida,Jeremy	1	6	0	5	2	5	6	0	1	1	6	47	-3	+1	-2
Hernandez,Ramon	2	14	3	9	2	5	3	4	2	6	8	65	-23	0	-23
Herrera,Jonathan	5	20	8	14	2	5	9	2	1	3	2	48	0	-2	-2
Heyward,Jason	14	42	13	19	6	10	19	3	2	5	13	122	+5	-1	+4
Hill,Aaron	8	22	6	10	2	8	8	2	0	2	8	98	+2	-2	0
Hill,Koyie	2	4	0	3	1	2	6	2	0	2	5	51	-2	+1	-1
Hinske,Eric	5	19	5	9	1	6	4	0	0	0	4	64	+3	0	+3
Holliday,Matt	10	46	21	31	2	3	17	5	5	10	13	127	-17	-1	-18
Howard,Ryan	5	28	9	20	6	17	9	4	0	4	14	125	-14	-1	-15
Hudson,Orlando	11	34	18	24	6	14	16	0	4	5	14	108	0	+4	+4
Huff,Aubrey	8	31	18	26	4	13	22	3	2	5	17	141	+1	+7	+8
Hundley,Nick	0	8	4	12	2	3	8	4	1	5	8	55	-15	-10	-25
Hunter,Torii	13	32	7	15	6	11	15	4	3	7	22	127	-15	-15	-30
Iannetta,Chris	0	7	3	6	1	4	6	0	0	0	4	34	+1	+1	+2
Ibanez,Raul	9	40	7	22	1	6	18	2	2	4	15	134	-8	-2	-10
Infante,Omar	15	30	10	17	3	9	13	2	0	2	14	91	+5	-5	0
Inge,Brandon	9	27	6	13	4	7	11	1	5	6	12	120	-10	-2	-12
Inglett,Joe	0	4	3	3	1	4	1	2	0	2	1	32	-4	+1	-3
Ishikawa,Travis	1	5	5	9	0	3	5	2	0	2	3	34	-3	0	-3
Iwamura,Akinori	0	8	4	8	2	3	3	1	2	3	4	32	-10	+1	-9
Izturis,Cesar	9	29	15	21	0	5	11	1	1	2	11	85	+1	+1	+2
Izturis,Maicer	4	5	2	7	3	6	4	1	0	1	1	38	+3	+1	+4
Jackson,Austin	12	37	23	35	5	9	21	0	0	0	5	93	+27	+15	+42
Jackson,Conor	5	10	6	10	0	0	11	1	0	1	6	51	+8	+4	+12
Janish,Paul	2	11	3	4	0	1	4	0	0	0	4	45	+2	-5	-3
Jaso,John	6	21	13	10	0	6	28	1	1	5	8	63	+13	+4	+17
Jay,Jon	6	25	11	13	2	5	7	2	0	2	5	61	+2	-6	-4
Jeter,Derek	14	44	12	21	3	15	38	0	0	0	22	120	+22	+8	+30
Johnson,Chris	4	16	10	15	4	5	8	2	0	2	8	71	+2	+3	+5
Johnson,Kelly	8	33	7	19	6	11	20	3	3	6	12	105	-7	-1	-8
Johnson,Reed	1	7	4	7	1	4	6	2	0	2	3	39	-2	-2	-4
Johnson,Rob	1	8	4	7	1	3	6	1	0	1	5	33	-1	-1	-2
Jones,Adam	6	30	11	13	6	8	19	1	1	2	17	116	+8	-7	+1
Jones,Andruw	3	12	4	9	2	3	6	1	1	2	15	67	-11	+5	-6
Jones,Chipper	7	22	7	9	5	9	9	0	0	0	10	83	+9	+5	+14
Jones,Garrett	7	22	10	15	3	5	5	2	0	2	18	136	-5	+1	-4
Joyce,Matt	4	15	3	9	1	2	6	1	3	4	2	41	-8	-2	-10
Ka'aihue,Kila	5	17	2	5	0	0	6	1	0	1	5	53	+2	-2	0
Kalish,Ryan	2	5	2	8	2	2	8	2	0	2	5	36	-1	+8	+7
Kapler,Gabe	0	5	3	7	3	3	3	2	0	2	3	33	-4	-1	-5
Kearns,Austin	6	23	11	16	3	6	11	3	1	4	16	105	-7	+2	-5
Kelly,Don	0	11	8	12	2	2	4	2	0	2	1	54	+1	+3	+4
Kemp,Matt	12	33	10	20	5	6	19	3	4	7	14	123	-3	-11	-14
Kendall,Jason	10	40	10	16	2	4	9	4	1	5	12	75	-13	-2	-15

311

2010 Baserunning

	1st to 3rd		2nd to Home		1st to Home		Bases Taken	Out Adv	Doubled Off	BR Outs	GDP	GDP Opps	BR Gain	SB Gain	Net Gain
Player	Moved	Chances	Moved	Chances	Moved	Chances									
Kendrick,Howie	14	29	13	20	4	6	14	2	1	3	16	120	+6	+6	+12
Kennedy,Adam	2	23	10	15	0	3	12	3	1	4	10	69	-10	+10	0
Keppinger,Jeff	3	40	9	16	4	8	12	3	0	3	15	91	-14	+2	-12
Kinsler,Ian	12	27	11	16	3	4	17	1	3	4	11	85	+7	+5	+12
Konerko,Paul	8	36	4	17	2	6	14	2	1	3	9	83	-8	-2	-10
Kotchman,Casey	3	17	6	17	1	4	6	7	0	7	15	81	-30	0	-30
Kotsay,Mark	5	16	1	6	1	3	11	6	1	7	9	72	-16	-5	-21
Kottaras,George	1	11	3	8	1	2	4	1	3	4	5	45	-13	+2	-11
Kouzmanoff,Kevin	7	24	4	11	1	3	19	1	0	1	20	134	+5	0	+5
Kubel,Jason	5	35	8	19	6	13	7	8	1	9	16	115	-35	-2	-37
Laird,Gerald	3	13	5	11	0	2	7	1	0	1	7	64	-1	+1	0
Langerhans,Ryan	2	7	2	3	0	0	7	1	0	1	0	21	+6	+2	+8
LaPorta,Matt	3	24	7	12	1	6	8	1	2	3	12	67	-14	0	-14
LaRoche,Adam	3	22	2	13	0	7	13	5	1	6	8	116	-16	-2	-18
LaRoche,Andy	5	17	6	10	0	1	3	1	0	1	7	50	-3	-1	-4
Lee,Carlos	10	25	6	13	2	12	8	2	1	3	20	121	-13	-3	-16
Lee,Derrek	6	25	8	18	5	13	19	0	1	1	23	141	0	-5	-5
Lewis,Fred	5	18	9	18	1	4	14	3	1	4	9	73	-5	+5	0
Lind,Adam	3	16	5	15	2	7	4	3	0	3	10	122	-11	0	-11
Loney,James	13	32	14	21	3	6	18	3	0	3	14	118	+10	0	+10
Longoria,Evan	6	21	18	21	5	8	20	1	0	1	15	125	+18	+5	+23
Lopez,Felipe	6	18	2	7	4	7	11	1	0	1	7	58	+4	+4	+8
Lopez,Jose	5	30	7	15	1	7	11	2	1	3	20	116	-16	-1	-17
Lowell,Mike	2	6	1	5	0	2	4	1	0	1	9	46	-7	0	-7
Lowrie,Jed	2	11	6	6	2	4	3	0	0	0	2	38	+5	-1	+4
Lucroy,Jonathan	4	13	8	12	0	2	7	1	1	3	9	61	-6	0	-6
Ludwick,Ryan	7	25	6	14	6	11	12	3	1	4	13	110	-6	-8	-14
Lugo,Julio	5	14	5	12	1	1	6	0	0	0	6	47	+3	-9	-6
Maier,Mitch	6	24	3	13	6	12	12	3	1	4	3	82	-2	-1	-3
Manzella,Tommy	4	11	3	5	1	4	2	0	1	1	6	50	-3	-2	-5
Markakis,Nick	9	36	12	23	3	8	26	3	0	4	18	139	+3	+3	+6
Marson,Lou	5	13	3	6	1	2	9	1	0	1	7	48	+3	+6	+9
Marte,Andy	2	12	3	3	1	1	4	0	0	0	2	33	+5	-6	-1
Martin,Russell	7	27	10	12	2	5	14	3	2	5	7	67	-1	+2	+1
Martinez,Victor	6	20	5	10	2	12	13	2	0	2	17	134	-3	+1	-2
Mathis,Jeff	2	10	3	4	0	0	4	2	0	2	3	37	-2	+3	+1
Matsui,Hideki	3	27	2	7	1	4	8	3	0	3	10	108	-10	-2	-12
Mauer,Joe	10	37	16	20	6	9	24	0	1	1	19	129	+17	-7	+10
Maybin,Cameron	7	14	7	8	7	7	7	0	2	2	4	41	+9	+5	+14
McCann,Brian	2	30	5	13	3	15	13	5	1	7	12	137	-22	+1	-21
McCutchen,Andrew	8	44	13	18	6	7	13	0	2	2	6	83	+6	+13	+19
McDonald,Darnell	7	23	5	15	2	4	8	1	0	1	5	66	+2	+7	+9
McDonald,John	1	6	2	3	0	1	9	2	0	2	5	29	-1	0	-1
McGehee,Casey	4	28	12	25	1	6	17	3	0	3	18	161	-5	-1	-6
McLouth,Nate	2	8	4	6	0	1	6	0	0	0	3	61	+8	+3	+11
Michaels,Jason	2	9	2	4	1	3	2	1	1	2	3	29	-6	0	-6
Miles,Aaron	1	7	1	1	0	1	4	0	0	0	1	25	+4	-2	+2
Milledge,Lastings	2	15	13	19	0	4	8	4	1	6	7	85	-13	-1	-14
Molina,Bengie	2	23	4	12	0	5	8	1	0	1	14	77	-13	0	-13
Molina,Jose	0	6	1	3	1	5	4	2	0	2	7	36	-10	+1	-9
Molina,Yadier	8	32	6	16	2	6	7	2	3	5	19	103	-24	0	-24
Montero,Miguel	4	20	4	6	1	4	4	3	0	3	10	56	-13	-2	-15
Moore,Adam	1	7	2	4	1	2	3	2	0	2	3	34	-5	-2	-7
Mora,Melvin	6	22	5	7	2	7	9	1	2	4	9	57	-9	0	-9
Morales,Kendry	3	12	5	5	2	3	10	0	0	0	5	38	+10	-2	+8
Moreland,Mitch	4	10	2	3	0	0	7	0	1	1	3	31	+5	+1	+6
Morgan,Nyjer	9	24	11	14	1	5	16	3	1	4	2	73	+10	0	+10
Morneau,Justin	4	23	4	12	1	8	10	2	0	2	6	76	-4	0	-4
Morrison,Logan	7	18	6	9	2	5	16	1	1	2	4	58	+13	-2	+11
Morse,Mike	2	16	6	12	1	3	6	1	3	6	8	48	-10	-2	-12
Murphy,David	11	23	10	19	1	2	18	1	1	2	6	79	+15	+10	+25
Nady,Xavier	1	15	7	7	3	6	8	0	2	2	12	66	-5	0	-5
Napoli,Mike	7	22	5	7	4	7	13	2	1	4	15	102	-3	0	-3
Nava,Daniel	3	12	5	7	1	3	8	0	1	1	5	44	+4	-1	+3

2010 Baserunning

Player	1st to 3rd Moved	Chances	2nd to Home Moved	Chances	1st to Home Moved	Chances	Bases Taken	Out Adv	Doubled Off	BR Outs	GDP	GDP Opps	BR Gain	SB Gain	Net Gain
Nix,Jayson	1	9	5	5	0	1	6	1	1	2	6	62	-1	-3	-4
Nix,Laynce	2	9	5	6	1	1	2	1	0	2	5	34	-5	-2	-7
Olivo,Miguel	7	17	9	9	5	6	10	3	0	3	6	105	+12	-1	+11
Ordonez,Magglio	9	32	4	6	5	10	8	1	0	1	14	83	-2	+1	-1
Ortiz,David	2	24	4	9	2	14	18	4	3	7	12	123	-16	-2	-18
Overbay,Lyle	6	33	4	11	2	8	14	1	0	1	9	96	+1	+1	+2
Pagan,Angel	14	25	10	15	4	10	22	2	2	4	9	106	+16	+19	+35
Parra,Gerardo	3	14	8	10	1	3	6	2	0	2	8	71	-2	+1	-1
Patterson,Corey	7	15	6	11	2	2	12	2	1	3	3	47	+6	+13	+19
Patterson,Eric	0	6	2	2	2	4	12	1	0	1	2	44	+10	+9	+19
Paulino,Ronny	2	9	7	12	1	3	6	1	0	1	11	65	-4	+1	-3
Pedroia,Dustin	2	10	6	8	3	10	7	1	1	2	7	78	-1	+7	+6
Pena,Brayan	0	17	1	2	1	3	8	2	0	2	8	42	-8	+2	-6
Pena,Carlos	12	33	1	6	4	11	14	3	0	3	2	112	+11	+3	+14
Pena,Ramiro	2	8	5	9	1	1	8	0	1	1	4	36	+4	+5	+9
Pence,Hunter	7	25	17	22	7	8	22	4	1	5	11	127	+13	0	+13
Pennington,Cliff	8	22	13	19	6	6	14	3	2	5	7	89	+5	+19	+24
Peralta,Jhonny	5	36	6	17	3	9	16	2	2	4	11	123	-7	+1	-6
Phillips,Brandon	12	33	17	25	8	10	28	5	1	6	14	101	+11	-8	+3
Pie,Felix	7	14	4	11	3	3	11	3	0	3	10	75	+1	+1	+2
Pierre,Juan	18	40	21	28	4	8	21	1	2	3	8	108	+22	+32	+54
Pierzynski,A.J.	3	26	7	14	0	4	10	2	0	3	17	102	-15	-5	-20
Podsednik,Scott	16	37	9	17	2	6	19	0	2	2	10	79	+12	+5	+17
Polanco,Placido	13	42	14	20	3	9	22	1	3	4	14	113	+7	+5	+12
Posada,Jorge	2	19	5	11	2	9	5	2	1	3	6	83	-11	+1	-10
Posey,Buster	3	21	8	15	5	5	17	2	0	2	12	95	+5	-4	+1
Prado,Martin	17	38	21	28	4	9	29	4	2	6	13	110	+17	-1	+16
Pujols,Albert	11	35	14	19	2	12	27	5	0	5	23	155	+1	+6	+7
Punto,Nick	5	18	2	8	1	4	9	1	1	2	3	51	0	+2	+2
Quentin,Carlos	8	23	5	13	6	8	23	0	1	1	16	101	+13	-2	+11
Quintero,Humberto	2	10	2	6	0	1	3	0	0	0	5	48	-1	0	-1
Raburn,Ryan	3	17	4	5	7	10	10	1	2	3	8	93	+2	-2	0
Ramirez,Alexei	12	34	13	18	5	8	20	0	1	1	12	125	+21	-3	+18
Ramirez,Aramis	4	21	5	12	0	6	8	4	5	9	10	93	-28	0	-28
Ramirez,Hanley	14	40	18	29	4	10	22	4	1	5	14	125	+5	+12	+17
Ramirez,Manny	7	22	5	7	1	9	6	2	0	2	6	55	-4	-1	-5
Rasmus,Colby	14	32	15	19	6	6	17	1	3	4	5	107	+20	-4	+16
Renteria,Edgar	5	17	6	9	2	5	5	0	1	1	8	44	-2	+3	+1
Repko,Jason	2	8	4	5	2	2	5	0	2	2	2	37	+2	-1	+1
Reyes,Jose	7	17	15	21	2	5	19	3	1	4	8	81	+9	+10	+19
Reynolds,Mark	3	29	10	19	2	8	7	2	1	3	8	103	-10	-1	-11
Rhymes,Will	6	14	2	6	2	4	5	0	1	1	1	39	+4	-6	-2
Rios,Alex	6	19	24	28	7	10	11	2	2	4	21	122	-2	+6	+4
Rivera,Juan	8	25	6	9	2	6	8	3	0	3	10	86	-3	-2	-5
Roberts,Brian	2	12	4	11	1	3	10	3	1	4	2	30	-7	+8	+1
Rodriguez,Alex	0	33	6	13	3	6	14	1	1	2	7	109	+3	-2	+1
Rodriguez,Ivan	4	26	1	12	0	2	11	3	2	5	25	88	-32	-4	-36
Rodriguez,Sean	4	14	11	17	3	5	14	3	1	4	10	72	-1	+7	+6
Rolen,Scott	5	24	10	16	3	9	10	4	3	7	12	113	-16	-3	-19
Rollins,Jimmy	9	27	9	11	2	3	10	1	0	1	4	49	+10	+15	+25
Rosales,Adam	4	11	4	5	1	5	8	1	2	3	1	58	+3	-2	+1
Ross,Cody	6	25	12	18	3	10	8	4	0	4	9	123	-4	+5	+1
Ross,David	0	10	2	7	1	2	6	0	0	0	5	34	-1	-2	-3
Rowand,Aaron	1	13	5	9	0	3	6	1	1	2	11	53	-12	-1	-13
Ruiz,Carlos	6	20	8	15	0	5	6	2	0	2	8	81	-5	-2	-7
Ryal,Rusty	1	5	4	6	2	2	8	0	0	0	3	43	+9	-6	+3
Ryan,Brendan	15	24	5	13	4	7	12	1	1	2	6	84	+13	+3	+16
Sanchez,Angel	5	19	6	9	1	2	8	2	0	2	8	41	-3	-2	-5
Sanchez,Freddy	10	27	4	7	5	10	14	1	3	4	9	78	+1	+1	+2
Sanchez,Gaby	8	36	14	20	2	8	15	4	1	5	14	139	-5	+5	0
Sandoval,Pablo	6	31	13	17	3	9	14	7	1	8	26	137	-26	-1	-27
Santana,Carlos	2	7	3	6	2	4	8	2	0	2	3	30	+1	+3	+4
Santiago,Ramon	10	26	7	9	2	5	11	2	1	3	6	65	+5	-2	+3
Saunders,Michael	5	18	4	10	2	3	5	1	0	1	1	50	+3	0	+3

2010 Baserunning

Player	1st to 3rd Moved	Chances	2nd to Home Moved	Chances	1st to Home Moved	Chances	Bases Taken	Out Adv	Doubled Off	BR Outs	GDP	GDP Opps	BR Gain	SB Gain	Net Gain
Schierholtz,Nate	7	14	5	9	3	4	15	0	0	0	3	42	+19	-6	+13
Schumaker,Skip	10	41	14	18	4	7	16	5	1	7	7	75	-4	-1	-5
Scott,Luke	6	35	9	19	1	6	19	4	0	4	9	91	-3	+2	-1
Scutaro,Marco	8	34	14	20	7	15	26	2	0	2	13	99	+14	-3	+11
Shoppach,Kelly	2	6	2	4	0	1	5	0	0	0	2	37	+5	0	+5
Smith,Seth	8	16	8	10	5	7	13	3	2	5	5	74	+6	0	+6
Smoak,Justin	6	17	6	10	2	7	7	1	0	1	9	77	+1	+1	+2
Snider,Travis	0	14	3	8	3	7	7	1	3	4	3	44	-11	0	-11
Snyder,Chris	2	15	3	7	3	6	5	0	0	0	11	74	-3	0	-3
Soriano,Alfonso	12	26	9	14	2	3	14	3	1	4	12	113	+5	+3	+8
Soto,Geovany	6	25	5	13	2	4	13	6	0	6	5	69	-9	-2	-11
Span,Denard	12	27	16	26	3	7	27	4	4	8	12	95	+1	+18	+19
Spilborghs,Ryan	6	19	6	13	3	5	9	4	2	6	7	71	-11	-6	-17
Stanton,Mike	2	14	3	8	2	4	6	0	0	0	7	79	+2	+1	+3
Stewart,Ian	12	23	6	10	3	6	11	1	0	1	8	85	+13	+1	+14
Stubbs,Drew	13	31	17	21	8	10	13	2	1	3	6	93	+17	+18	+35
Suzuki,Ichiro	15	42	13	31	1	8	27	3	2	5	3	87	+8	+24	+32
Suzuki,Kurt	13	39	10	17	5	10	9	1	0	1	22	131	-2	-1	-3
Sweeney,Mike	3	10	2	4	0	2	3	0	0	0	5	30	-1	+3	+2
Sweeney,Ryan	9	18	10	16	3	5	15	1	0	1	14	79	+9	-1	+8
Swisher,Nick	8	36	11	21	1	6	17	3	4	7	13	139	-11	-3	-14
Tabata,Jose	7	21	10	16	7	12	10	1	3	4	7	55	-3	+5	+2
Teahen,Mark	1	15	7	13	4	5	10	2	0	2	8	49	-2	-7	-9
Teixeira,Mark	9	39	12	20	9	18	13	6	1	7	15	160	-11	-2	-13
Tejada,Miguel	11	40	9	20	5	14	28	7	1	8	16	124	-7	+2	-5
Tejada,Ruben	8	11	8	12	1	3	4	0	0	0	2	40	+10	-2	+8
Thames,Marcus	4	13	2	3	1	1	5	0	1	1	3	43	+3	0	+3
Theriot,Ryan	6	33	15	22	3	8	28	5	1	6	13	96	+1	+2	+3
Thole,Josh	4	12	4	5	2	3	5	0	0	0	8	51	+3	+1	+4
Thome,Jim	1	12	7	9	0	8	5	2	0	2	8	68	-8	0	-8
Torrealba,Yorvit	4	19	7	15	1	3	6	1	3	4	12	70	-16	-3	-19
Torres,Andres	11	19	14	23	2	5	27	1	2	4	10	77	+16	+12	+28
Tracy,Chad	1	6	2	3	1	2	3	0	1	1	2	29	0	0	0
Treanor,Matt	3	20	5	12	0	1	12	0	0	0	4	50	+7	-3	+4
Tulowitzki,Troy	16	37	15	22	4	5	17	4	2	6	17	102	-1	+7	+6
Uggla,Dan	17	47	9	16	5	11	21	3	2	5	10	132	+9	+2	+11
Upton,B.J.	13	25	14	24	3	7	18	2	0	2	13	118	+14	+24	+38
Upton,Justin	10	26	12	19	5	10	11	3	2	5	20	137	-9	+2	-7
Uribe,Juan	9	28	7	14	1	6	12	2	2	4	20	125	-11	-3	-14
Utley,Chase	10	24	13	17	4	5	17	2	1	3	4	106	+20	+9	+29
Valbuena,Luis	4	13	5	7	0	3	7	0	1	1	5	49	+2	-3	-1
Valdez,Wilson	4	15	3	6	3	3	11	1	1	2	20	83	-8	+7	-1
Valencia,Danny	2	19	4	9	3	8	7	0	0	1	11	58	-8	+2	-6
Venable,Will	3	15	7	13	2	2	15	0	0	0	3	79	+17	+15	+32
Victorino,Shane	9	32	16	24	3	6	22	1	1	2	7	85	+17	+22	+39
Vizquel,Omar	6	19	7	15	2	3	8	3	1	5	8	67	-11	-3	-14
Votto,Joey	13	45	19	25	6	13	18	7	2	9	11	142	-4	+6	+2
Walker,Neil	7	17	5	12	4	9	14	2	2	4	4	88	+5	-4	+1
Wallace,Brett	0	7	4	7	0	2	2	0	0	0	3	32	-1	0	-1
Weeks,Rickie	14	45	16	21	10	14	15	3	2	5	5	112	+11	+3	+14
Wells,Vernon	8	22	6	8	5	7	16	2	1	3	18	114	+2	-2	0
Werth,Jayson	13	36	15	21	5	13	16	3	1	4	11	135	+8	+7	+15
Whiteside,Eli	6	11	0	2	2	3	2	0	0	0	4	29	+3	-3	0
Wieters,Matt	4	25	6	12	3	7	9	1	1	2	13	87	-8	-2	-10
Wigginton,Ty	7	27	11	18	1	7	14	4	2	6	23	131	-19	-2	-21
Willingham,Josh	9	33	11	15	3	7	11	3	1	4	8	92	0	+8	+8
Willits,Reggie	11	14	1	3	0	1	10	0	2	2	1	31	+11	-6	+5
Wilson,Jack	2	10	1	7	2	2	7	2	2	4	2	26	-8	-3	-11
Wilson,Josh	7	27	4	7	2	3	9	2	1	3	6	58	-2	+5	+3
Winn,Randy	3	14	6	12	0	0	5	2	0	2	5	47	-4	+6	+2
Wood,Brandon	4	9	2	4	1	1	7	0	0	0	3	39	+9	+1	+10
Wright,David	10	35	14	23	3	11	16	5	1	7	12	122	-9	-3	-12
Youkilis,Kevin	13	26	12	16	8	15	16	3	1	4	4	80	+15	+2	+17
Young Jr.,Eric	4	11	4	6	1	2	5	0	0	0	2	24	+6	+5	+11

2010 Baserunning

Player	1st to 3rd		2nd to Home		1st to Home		Bases Taken	Out Adv	Doubled Off	BR Outs	GDP	GDP Opps	BR Gain	SB Gain	Net Gain
	Moved	Chances	Moved	Chances	Moved	Chances									
Young,Chris	5	19	10	15	9	12	19	2	1	3	10	128	+14	+14	+28
Young,Delmon	7	28	15	24	2	4	22	4	1	5	16	145	+3	-3	0
Young,Delwyn	1	6	1	3	3	4	7	0	1	1	5	40	+2	+1	+3
Young,Michael	12	47	15	24	4	8	17	3	1	4	21	139	-5	0	-5
Zimmerman,Ryan	5	31	11	24	7	13	12	0	1	1	16	127	-3	+2	-1
Zobrist,Ben	15	37	6	14	7	10	29	2	1	3	10	120	+24	+18	+42

2010 Team Baserunning

Team	1st to 3rd Moved	1st to 3rd Chances	2nd to Home Moved	2nd to Home Chances	1st to Home Moved	1st to Home Chances	Bases Taken	Out Adv	Doubled Off	BR Outs	GDP	GDP Opps	BR Gain	SB Gain	Net Gain
Tampa Bay Rays	95	277	116	193	49	96	226	26	15	41	92	1122	+118	+78	+196
Oakland Athletics	92	298	120	201	45	82	199	26	10	37	129	1162	+64	+80	+144
Texas Rangers	126	369	119	215	30	71	214	28	11	39	129	1159	+66	+27	+93
Florida Marlins	92	318	111	183	42	86	149	23	8	31	108	1164	+46	+40	+86
Philadelphia Phillies	92	328	117	201	32	87	149	21	11	32	121	1190	+13	+66	+79
New York Yankees	86	328	110	194	39	91	187	25	13	38	124	1298	+35	+43	+78
Colorado Rockies	108	333	124	184	42	84	167	29	11	41	103	1138	+60	+17	+77
New York Mets	84	263	98	166	30	73	150	21	18	40	101	1105	+19	+42	+61
Boston Red Sox	69	272	99	164	47	124	177	27	9	37	131	1208	+12	+34	+46
Detroit Tigers	100	356	118	197	45	101	147	18	16	35	117	1250	+23	+9	+32
Los Angeles Dodgers	104	320	125	185	28	71	180	27	16	44	122	1154	+39	-8	+31
Cleveland Indians	64	291	110	185	33	94	183	25	17	42	118	1105	-5	+25	+20
San Diego Padres	59	276	109	194	32	65	148	26	9	36	106	1112	-4	+24	+20
Seattle Mariners	87	296	81	162	19	53	154	34	16	50	111	1026	-47	+64	+17
Atlanta Braves	92	339	109	193	46	102	165	25	10	36	136	1255	+9	+5	+14
Los Angeles Angels	100	278	92	155	38	75	146	30	10	41	125	1091	+7	0	+7
St Louis Cardinals	105	351	113	181	31	68	159	26	16	43	124	1157	+5	-3	+2
Chicago White Sox	85	294	118	201	37	69	160	21	15	38	148	1115	-11	+12	+1
Cincinnati Reds	104	327	128	204	49	81	143	35	17	53	113	1163	-10	+7	-3
Minnesota Twins	92	329	135	213	41	105	185	27	17	46	159	1211	-19	+12	-7
Houston Astros	68	279	100	164	37	71	113	23	8	31	130	1028	-36	+28	-8
Washington Nationals	63	292	105	186	26	66	135	24	10	36	124	1144	-37	+28	-9
Milwaukee Brewers	63	323	120	206	37	77	145	28	17	46	115	1246	-39	+29	-10
Chicago Cubs	73	276	101	178	31	82	165	27	13	41	124	1109	-13	-7	-20
Toronto Blue Jays	54	216	67	129	33	76	130	30	9	39	114	997	-44	+18	-26
Arizona D-Backs	54	254	86	162	33	82	138	28	9	37	115	1153	-30	+4	-26
Baltimore Orioles	75	298	100	190	27	67	175	30	9	40	154	1116	-39	+8	-31
Pittsburgh Pirates	60	260	84	153	37	75	105	19	17	37	119	1051	-62	+15	-47
San Francisco Giants	82	297	100	170	31	84	167	25	17	43	157	1135	-42	-9	-51
Kansas City Royals	100	380	101	197	29	84	166	31	17	49	152	1158	-78	+15	-63
MLB Totals	2528	9118	3216	5506	1076	2442	4827	785	391	1199	3721	34322			

The Bullpens of 2010

Bill James

In 1970, the term "reliever" was adequate to describe the job assignment of any pitcher who was not a starter. In modern baseball "reliever" is like "infielder"; it includes players whose jobs are quite different.

A modern bullpen consists of a Closer (CL), a Set Up Man or two set-up men (SU), some left-handers whose job is to get out left-handed hitters (LT), a Long Man (LM), and some auditioning relievers who pitch as they are needed and try to work their way into a better role. We call these latter pitchers Utility Relievers (UR). Many teams during the course of the season will face emergency situations in which they have to call on a starting pitcher to pitch relief, or have to have an outfielder pitch. We call these Emergency Relievers, or ER.

This chart documents the bullpen performance of each major league team and every major league reliever, giving the role that each pitcher was assigned, and his performance in twenty-some bullpen-specific performance categories. These are:

Games in Relief (Rel G)

Early Entry (Number of times the pitcher entered the game before the seventh inning.) D. J. Carrasco in 2010 was called into the game 30 times before the seventh inning. Closers virtually never come into the game that early, and set up men very rarely do.

Pitching on Consecutive Days (Cons Days). Just a count of how many times the pitcher pitched after having pitched the previous day. Pedro Feliciano pitched on consecutive days 43 times in 2010. This was the third consecutive year that he had led the majors in that category, but his total in 2010 was 9 higher than in 2008 or 2009.

Long Outings. (LO) Anything more than 25 pitches is considered a long outing for a reliever. Chad Gaudin had 22 Long Outings in 2010, the most in the majors.

Leverage Index (Lev Ind). We use the Leverage Index calculated by Tom Tango. An average Leverage Index is 1.000. If a pitcher pitches frequently with

the game on the line, his Leverage index will be high.   If he pitches generally in the 6th inning of 7-2 ballgames, his leverage index will be very low.

David Aardsma had the highest Leverage Index in the majors in 2010, 2.43.   Fourteen major league pitchers had Indexes over 2.00—all of them closers except Jim Johnson of Baltimore, who was over 2.00 as a setup man.   The lowest Leverage Index for any pitcher with 20 or more appearances was 0.18, by David Riske of Milwaukee.   His managers thought that to use him in critical situations was Too Riske.

Inherited Runners (#, Scored, And Percentage).

Wilton Lopez of Houston entered the game with 33 runners on base, of whom only 1 came in to score.   Ramon Troncoso entered the game with 37 runners on base, of whom 22 came in to score.

Easy, Regular and Tough Saves

An "Easy" Save opportunity is one in which the tying run is not on base or at the plate when the reliever enters, and three outs or less are needed to end the game.

A "Tough" Save is one in which the reliever enters with the tying run on base.

A "Regular" Save is a Save Opportunity which is neither easy nor tough. A "Regular" Save Opportunity is a "Middlin'" Save Opportunity.

In 2010 relievers converted successfully 88% of Easy Save Opportunities, 64% of Regular Opportunities, and 30% of Tough Opportunities.   In 2009 the percentages were 89, 61, and 24.

Among pitchers with 20 or more Save Opportunities in 2010, the ones who had the easiest Save Opportunities were 1. Fernando Rodney, 2. Billy Wagner, and 3. Leo Nunez.   Neither Rodney nor Wagner had ANY Tough Save Opportunities, and Nunez had only one.   The three who had the most difficult Save Opportunties were 1. Chris Perez, 2. Carlos Marmol, and 3. John Axford. These three had 16 Tough Save assignments among them.

Perhaps more interesting, however, is the guy with the grody Mohawk and the funky beard.   Brian Wilson had NINE Tough Save assignments, and converted seven of them.   He led the majors in Saves with 48—and his save chances were among the most difficult of any relief ace.

Clean Outings.

A Clean Outing is any appearance in which a reliever does not allow a run to score and does not allow an inherited run to score.   Brandon Lyon led the majors in Clean Outings, with 66.   Joaquin Benoit led in the percentage of Clean

Outings, 85%, while Kanekoa Texeira had only 15 Clean Outings in 43 games (35%).

BS Wins.

Tyler Clippard entered the Nationals/Marlins game on May 8th with his team (the Nationals) leading 3-2. Clippard gave up a 2-run homer, putting the Marlins ahead, then was credited with "winning" the game when the Nationals rallied for a 5-4 victory. That's a BS Win—A Blown Save/Win.

There were, in 2010, only 74 BS Wins in the major leagues, or two and a half per team. Clippard was the only pitcher to have more than three of them. He had five.

Saves.
Y'all probably know what Saves are.

Holds

A Hold is credited to any pitcher who enters the game with a Save Opportunity, records at least one out, does not surrender the lead, and passes the ball to another reliever. Holds were invented by John Dewan, a principle in this book.

Save/Hold Percentage.

We used to figure the "Save" percentage for each reliever, but the Save percentages for Set Up men were always very low, because the Set Up reliever does not have a legitimate opportunity to earn a Save. If the Set Up man blows the lead, he is charged with a Blown Save; if he does not blow the lead, the Closer will come in to finish off, so that was a non-event for the save percentage. Set Up men generally have "Save Percentages" around 70%, even if they pitch great, while Lefties almost always have Save Percentages less than 50%, even if they pitch great.

We decided it was more representative to figure the Save/Hold Percentage, which is Saves plus Holds, divided by Saves plus Holds plus Blown Saves. Boone Logan in 2010 was 13-for-13. . .13 holds, no Blown Saves.

Among pitchers with 20 or more chances, the pitchers with the highest Save/Hold Percentages were Hong-Chih Kuo of the Dodgers (34 of 35, 97%), Sean Burnett of the Nationals (96%), Matt Belisle of Colorado (96%), Kyle McClellan of St. Louis (95%) and Joe Beimel of Colorado (95%). The lowest percentage was 69%, by Aaron Heilman of whoever the hell Aaron Heilman is pitching for these days. Arizona. Sorry.

OPS Allowed.

Hong-Chih Kuo of the Dodgers in 2010 allowed hitters a collective OPS of .403 (are you kidding me? Is this a misprint? .403?). He was followed by Joaquin Benoit (.454), Joe Thatcher (.465), and a couple of old guys who tied at .493, Billy Wagner and Mariano Rivera. Anything less than .600 is fantastic.

George Sherrill allowed an OPS of .906, Chad Qualls .894, and Chad Gaudin .892.

ERA.
Closely tracks OPS allowed.

Just for the heck of it, and because I love ratings, I ranked all major league relief pitchers 1 through 492 in eight categories, which were Games Pitched, Leverage Index, the Percentage of Inherited Runners who Scored, Clean Outing Percentage, the Save/Hold Percentage, Opposition OPS, ERA and Saves vs. Expected Saves (expected Saves assuming that 88% of Easy Saves would be converted, 64% of Regular Save chances, and 30% of Tough Chances.) Then I ranked the relievers of each group based on the sum of the eight rankings. This is what I got:

Closers	1. Heath Bell	2. Neftali Feliz	3. Brian Wilson
Set Up Men	1. Matt Thornton	2. Hong-Chih Kuo	3. Sean Burnett
Lefties	1. Joe Thatcher	2. Chris Sale	3. Javier Lopez
Long Men	1. Nelson Figueroa	2. Sergio Mitre	3. Gustavo Chacin
Utility Guys	1. Mike Kohn	2. Santiago Casilla	3. Kenley Jansen
Emergency	1. David Bush	2. David Pauley	3. Kevin Slowey

Between you and me, those ratings may not be perfect, but most listings of quality relievers start and end with the Closers. I thought it would be fun to make a list that included some of the other guys.

Relief Pitching

Pitcher	Pos	T	Rel G	Early Entry	Cons Days	Long	Lev Ind	#	Scrd	Pct	Easy	Reg	Tough	Clean	BS Win	Saves	Opps	Holds	Sv/Hld Pct	Opp OPS	Rel ERA
Arizona Diamondbacks																					
Gutierrez, Juan, Ari	CL	R	58	1	11	9	1.5	17	5	.29	10 - 10	4 - 6	1 - 1	39	0	15	17	8	.92	.806	5.08
Heilman, Aaron, Ari	SU	R	70	0	20	14	1.5	29	13	.45	3 - 7	3 - 5	0 - 2	45	1	6	14	12	.69	.755	4.50
Norberto, Jordan, Ari	LT	L	33	8	6	2	0.8	26	5	.19	0 - 0	0 - 0	0 - 1	22	0	0	1	3	.75	.789	5.85
Hampton, Mike, Ari	LT	L	10	1	1	0	1.1	10	3	.30	0 - 0	0 - 0	0 - 0	7	0	0	0	1	1.00	.464	0.00
Kroenke, Zach, Ari	LT	L	2	2	0	1	0.4	2	2	1.00	0 - 0	0 - 0	0 - 0	0	0	0	0	0		1.692	21.60
Carrasco, D.J., Pit-Ari	LM	R	63	30	13	20	0.8	39	16	.41	0 - 1	0 - 0	0 - 0	36	0	0	1	7	.88	.678	3.68
Vasquez, Esmerling, Ari	UR	R	57	11	8	12	0.9	26	8	.31	0 - 0	0 - 1	0 - 1	36	1	0	2	6	.75	.754	5.20
Boyer, Blaine, Ari	UR	R	54	17	9	8	0.8	23	10	.43	0 - 1	0 - 3	0 - 0	31	0	0	4	5	.56	.734	4.26
Demel, Sam, Ari	UR	R	37	6	5	6	0.8	9	6	.67	0 - 0	1 - 1	1 - 1	22	0	2	2	4	1.00	.817	5.35
Rosa, Carlos, Ari	UR	R	22	5	4	2	0.8	12	6	.50	0 - 0	0 - 0	0 - 1	12	0	0	1	1	.50	.721	4.50
Rosales, Leo, Ari	UR	R	16	6	2	3	1.1	5	4	.80	0 - 0	0 - 0	0 - 0	10	0	0	0	2	1.00	.976	7.16
Valdez, Cesar, Ari	UR	R	7	4	0	4	1.1	4	2	.50	0 - 0	0 - 0	0 - 0	2	0	0	0	0		.844	8.10
Stange, Daniel, Ari	UR	R	4	1	0	3	0.1	1	1	1.00	0 - 0	0 - 0	0 - 0	1	0	0	0	0		.955	13.50
Rivera, Saul, Ari	UR	R	4	1	0	1	0.2	0	0		0 - 0	0 - 0	0 - 0	1	0	0	0	0		1.433	22.09
Rodriguez, Rafael, LAA-Ari	UR	R	3	0	0	2	0.0	0	0		0 - 0	0 - 0	0 - 0	1	0	0	0	0		.890	5.79
Mulvey, Kevin, Ari	UR	R	2	1	0	2	0.0	0	0		0 - 0	0 - 0	0 - 0	1	0	0	0	0		1.256	6.00
Willis, Dontrelle, Det-Ari	UR	L	2	2	0	1	1.1	0	0		0 - 0	0 - 0	0 - 0	0	0	0	0	0		1.016	22.50
Atlanta Braves																					
Wagner, Billy, Atl	CL	L	71	0	22	6	1.6	9	2	.22	27 - 29	10 - 15	0 - 0	60	2	37	44	0	.84	.493	1.43
Venters, Jonny, Atl	SU	L	79	7	29	12	1.1	25	7	.28	0 - 1	1 - 3	0 - 1	58	1	1	5	24	.86	.552	1.95
Saito, Takashi, Atl	SU	R	56	0	13	6	1.1	3	0	.00	1 - 2	0 - 0	0 - 0	44	0	1	2	17	.95	.577	2.83
O'Flaherty, Eric, Atl	LT	L	56	17	17	1	1.0	38	10	.26	0 - 0	0 - 0	0 - 0	36	0	0	1	9	.90	.647	2.45
Dunn, Michael, Atl	LT	L	25	8	6	2	0.4	16	6	.38	0 - 0	0 - 0	0 - 0	20	0	0	0	1	1.00	.659	1.89
Reyes, Jo-Jo, Atl	LT	L	1	1	0	1	0.0	2	2	1.00	0 - 0	0 - 0	0 - 0	0	0	0	0	0		1.465	24.30
Moylan, Peter, Atl	UR	R	85	22	35	5	1.3	68	21	.31	0 - 0	0 - 1	1 - 3	58	0	1	4	21	.88	.693	2.97
Farnsworth, Kyle, KC-Atl	UR	R	60	14	10	6	0.9	17	6	.35	0 - 0	0 - 3	0 - 0	40	0	0	3	9	.75	.634	3.34
Kimbrel, Craig, Atl	UR	R	21	1	5	3	0.7	3	1	.33	1 - 1	0 - 0	0 - 0	18	0	1	1	2	1.00	.437	0.44
Martinez, Cristhian, Atl	UR	R	18	8	2	7	0.4	9	3	.33	0 - 0	0 - 0	0 - 0	10	0	0	0	0		.746	4.85
Medlen, Kris, Atl	UR	R	17	6	2	8	1.0	2	0	.00	0 - 0	0 - 0	0 - 0	10	0	0	0	1	1.00	.594	3.04
Proctor, Scott, Atl	UR	R	6	3	1	1	0.1	6	0	.00	0 - 0	0 - 0	0 - 0	3	0	0	0	0		.783	6.35
Minor, Mike, Atl	UR	L	1	0	0	1	1.0	3	3	1.00	0 - 0	0 - 0	0 - 0	0	0	0	0	0		.929	.00
Kawakami, Kenshin, Atl	ER	R	2	0	0	0	1.0	0	0		0 - 0	0 - 0	0 - 0	0	0	0	0	0		1.455	18.00
Baltimore Orioles																					
Simon, Alfredo, Bal	CL	R	49	1	12	7	1.7	11	4	.36	11 - 12	6 - 8	0 - 1	29	0	17	21	1	.82	.825	4.93
Uehara, Koji, Bal	CL	R	43	1	8	0	1.2	13	0	.00	8 - 9	3 - 4	2 - 2	33	0	13	15	6	.90	.594	2.86
González, Mike, Bal	SU	L	29	2	6	1	2.0	10	1	.05	0 - 0	1 - 3	0 - 0	22	0	1	3	10	.85	.629	4.01
Johnson, Jim, Bal	SU	R	26	1	5	2	2.1	12	5	.42	0 - 0	1 - 4	0 - 2	17	0	1	6	11	.71	.722	3.42
Castillo, Alberto, Bal	LT	L	14	1	3	2	0.4	8	2	.25	0 - 0	0 - 0	0 - 0	7	0	0	0	1	1.00	1.107	10.13
Viola, Pedro, Bal	LT	L	2	0	0	0	0.0	1	1	1.00	0 - 0	0 - 0	0 - 0	1	0	0	0	0		1.133	13.50
Patton, Troy, Bal	LT	L	1	0	0	0	0.1	0	0		0 - 0	0 - 0	0 - 0	1	0	0	0	0		1.167	0.00
Hendrickson, Mark, Bal	LM	L	51	26	6	18	0.7	44	15	.34	0 - 0	0 - 1	0 - 1	27	0	0	2	8	.80	.812	5.25
Albers, Matt, Bal	UR	R	62	17	12	18	0.8	45	14	.31	0 - 0	0 - 1	0 - 1	34	0	0	2	7	.78	.726	4.52
Berken, Jason, Bal	UR	R	41	13	8	13	0.9	36	13	.36	0 - 0	0 - 3	0 - 1	19	1	0	4	7	.64	.728	3.03
Hernandez, David, Bal	UR	R	33	3	7	8	1.2	20	10	.50	1 - 1	1 - 4	0 - 1	20	1	2	6	2	.50	.686	3.16
Meredith, Cla, Bal	UR	R	21	1	5	0	0.9	15	4	.27	0 - 0	0 - 0	1 - 2	13	0	1	2	3	.80	.932	5.40
Mata, Frank, Bal	UR	R	15	2	2	6	0.2	12	4	.33	0 - 0	0 - 0	0 - 0	6	0	0	0	1	1.00	.900	7.79
VandenHurk, Rick, Fla-Bal	UR	R	8	3	0	3	0.7	1	0	.00	0 - 0	0 - 0	0 - 0	3	0	0	0	0		.733	4.61
Gabino, Armando, Bal	UR	R	5	0	1	0	0.4	2	0	.00	0 - 0	0 - 0	0 - 0	2	0	0	0	0		1.288	13.50
Mickolio, Kam, Bal	UR	R	3	0	0	2	0.1	2	2	1.00	0 - 0	0 - 0	0 - 0	0	0	0	0	0		1.046	7.36
Bergesen, Brad, Bal	ER	R	2	0	0	0	1.0	1	0	.00	0 - 0	0 - 0	0 - 0	1	0	0	0	0		.762	2.70
Boston Red Sox																					
Papelbon, Jonathan, Bos	CL	R	65	0	16	9	2.1	15	5	.33	27 - 29	9 - 14	1 - 2	46	2	37	45	0	.82	.674	3.90
Bard, Daniel, Bos	SU	R	73	1	18	8	1.9	46	14	.30	1 - 1	2 - 6	0 - 3	51	0	3	10	32	.83	.540	1.93
Okajima, Hideki, Bos	LT	L	56	4	11	3	1.4	34	10	.29	0 - 1	0 - 2	0 - 1	36	0	0	4	11	.73	.841	4.50
Richardson, Dustin, Bos	LT	L	26	9	7	1	0.8	26	7	.27	0 - 0	0 - 0	0 - 0	17	0	0	0	2	1.00	.915	4.15
Schoeneweis, Scott, Bos	LT	L	15	3	4	2	0.4	11	4	.36	0 - 0	0 - 0	0 - 0	9	0	0	0	1	1.00	.935	7.90
Doubront, Felix, Bos	LT	L	9	1	1	1	1.0	5	0	.00	0 - 0	2 - 2	0 - 1	6	1	2	3	1	.75	.806	4.66
Hill, Rich, Bos	LT	L	6	2	1	1	1.1	5	2	.40	0 - 0	0 - 0	0 - 0	4	0	0	1	0	1.00	.627	0.00
Atchison, Scott, Bos	LM	R	42	20	7	16	0.8	32	7	.22	0 - 0	0 - 0	0 - 0	19	0	0	0	7	1.00	.740	4.42
Bowden, Michael, Bos	UR	R	14	3	1	5	0.5	9	6	.67	0 - 0	0 - 0	0 - 0	8	0	0	0	0		.912	4.70
Wakefield, Tim, Bos	UR	R	13	3	1	8	0.9	4	0	.00	0 - 0	0 - 0	0 - 0	7	0	0	0	0		.677	3.60
Manuel, Robert, Bos	UR	R	10	3	1	3	0.8	10	4	.40	0 - 0	0 - 0	0 - 0	6	0	0	0	0		.911	4.26
Nelson, Joe, Bos	UR	R	8	2	2	3	0.2	8	3	.38	0 - 0	0 - 0	0 - 0	3	0	0	0	0		1.060	9.72
Coello, Robert, Bos	UR	R	6	2	1	1	0.2	3	0	.00	0 - 0	0 - 0	0 - 0	5	0	0	0	0		.537	4.76

Relief Pitching

Pitcher	Pos	T	Rel G	Early Entry	Cons Days	Long	Lev Ind	#	Scrd	Pct	Easy	Reg	Tough	Clean	BS Win	Saves	Opps	Holds	Sv/Hld Pct	Opp OPS	Rel ERA
			Usage					**Inherited Runners**			**Saves**			**Relief Results**							
Fox, Matt, Min-Bos	UR	R	3	0	0	0	1.1	2	1	.50	0 - 0	0 - 0	0 - 0	0	0	0	0	0		1.125	10.80
Cabrera, Fernando, Bos	UR	R	1	1	0	1	1.6	2	2	1.00	0 - 0	0 - 0	0 - 0	0	0	0	0	0		1.571	20.25
Van Every, Jonathan, Bos	ER	L	1	0	0	0	0.0	0	0		0 - 0	0 - 0	0 - 0	0	0	0	0	0		1.600	18.00
Cash, Kevin, Hou-Bos	ER	R	1	0	0	0	0.0	0	0		0 - 0	0 - 0	0 - 0	0	0	0	0	0		1.167	9.00
Hall, Bill, Bos	ER	R	1	0	0	0	0.0	0	0		0 - 0	0 - 0	0 - 0	1	0	0	0	0		.000	0.00
Lopez, Felipe, StL-Bos	ER	R	1	0	0	0	1.9	0	0		0 - 0	0 - 0	0 - 0	1	0	0	0	0		.833	0.00
Chicago Cubs																					
Marmol, Carlos, ChC	CL	R	77	0	24	13	2.0	40	9	.23	15 - 15	18 - 21	5 - 7	59	0	38	43	0	.88	.500	2.55
Marshall, Sean, ChC	SU	L	80	4	25	8	1.3	42	8	.19	0 - 0	1 - 2	0 - 1	61	0	1	3	22	.92	.569	2.65
Cashner, Andrew, ChC	SU	R	53	6	11	10	1.2	27	6	.22	0 - 0	0 - 1	0 - 0	33	0	0	1	16	.94	.795	4.80
Russell, James, ChC	LT	L	57	16	12	9	0.6	49	14	.29	0 - 0	0 - 1	0 - 1	31	0	0	2	6	.75	.822	4.96
Grabow, John, ChC	LT	L	28	1	8	4	1.0	9	1	.11	0 - 0	0 - 1	0 - 0	13	0	0	1	7	.88	.930	7.36
Maine, Scott, ChC	LT	L	13	6	0	3	0.5	7	0	.00	0 - 0	0 - 0	0 - 0	9	0	0	0	2	1.00	.572	2.08
Berg, Justin, ChC	UR	R	41	11	8	0	0.4	26	12	.46	0 - 0	0 - 0	0 - 0	22	0	0	0	5	1.00	.738	5.18
Howry, Bob, Ari-ChC	UR	R	38	6	10	9	0.6	19	9	.47	0 - 1	0 - 0	0 - 0	15	0	0	1	3	.75	.953	7.71
Mateo, Marcos, ChC	UR	R	21	4	5	2	0.5	5	1	.20	0 - 0	0 - 0	0 - 0	12	0	0	0	1	1.00	.829	5.82
Stevens, Jeff, ChC	UR	R	18	7	4	3	0.5	16	4	.25	0 - 0	0 - 0	0 - 1	9	0	0	1	1	.50	.931	6.11
Zambrano, Carlos, ChC	UR	R	16	1	3	4	1.0	12	3	.25	0 - 0	0 - 0	0 - 0	12	0	0	0	4	1.00	.795	4.32
Diamond, Thomas, ChC	UR	R	13	5	1	6	0.7	9	3	.33	0 - 0	0 - 0	0 - 0	8	0	0	0	0		.823	5.63
Caridad, Esmailin, ChC	UR	R	8	1	2	1	1.6	3	2	.67	0 - 1	0 - 1	0 - 0	4	0	0	2	1	.33	.862	11.25
Schlitter, Brian, ChC	UR	R	7	1	0	3	0.9	8	7	.88	0 - 0	0 - 0	0 - 0	2	0	0	0	0		1.167	12.38
Gray, Jeff, ChC	UR	R	7	4	0	2	0.4	0	0		0 - 0	0 - 0	0 - 0	3	0	0	0	0		.935	6.75
Gorzelanny, Tom, ChC	UR	L	6	3	2	1	0.9	2	1	.50	0 - 0	0 - 0	1 - 1	3	0	1	1	1	1.00	.658	1.42
Atkins, Mitch, ChC	UR	R	5	3	0	3	0.2	5	1	.20	0 - 0	0 - 0	0 - 0	1	0	0	0	0		.864	6.30
Samardzija, Jeff, ChC	UR	R	4	0	0	1	0.7	0	0		0 - 0	0 - 0	0 - 0	1	0	0	0	0		1.184	18.90
Coleman, Casey, ChC	UR	R	4	3	1	3	0.8	0	0		0 - 0	0 - 0	0 - 0	2	0	0	0	0		.724	8.64
Chicago White Sox																					
Jenks, Bobby, CWS	CL	R	55	0	18	6	1.8	16	2	.13	14 - 16	10 - 12	3 - 3	40	0	27	31	0	.87	.668	4.44
Thornton, Matt, CWS	SU	L	61	2	12	7	1.7	31	4	.13	3 - 3	2 - 4	3 - 3	49	0	8	10	21	.94	.547	2.67
Putz, J.J., CWS	SU	R	60	1	7	6	1.3	27	10	.37	2 - 2	0 - 3	1 - 2	47	1	3	7	14	.81	.575	2.83
Santos, Sergio, CWS	SU	R	56	10	4	6	1.3	31	10	.32	0 - 0	1 - 2	0 - 1	43	0	1	3	14	.88	.692	2.96
Williams, Randy, CWS	LT	L	27	10	7	7	0.5	22	13	.59	0 - 0	0 - 0	0 - 1	11	0	0	1	1	.50	.995	5.40
Sale, Chris, CWS	LT	L	21	3	2	3	1.3	13	3	.23	1 - 1	2 - 2	1 - 1	17	0	4	4	2	1.00	.546	1.93
Threets, Erick, CWS	LT	L	11	3	2	1	0.4	8	3	.38	0 - 0	0 - 0	0 - 0	8	0	0	0	0		.486	0.00
Linebrink, Scott, CWS	UR	R	52	5	8	13	0.6	29	6	.21	0 - 0	0 - 1	0 - 0	30	1	0	1	4	.80	.780	4.40
Pena, Tony, CWS	UR	R	49	17	3	21	0.7	43	12	.28	0 - 0	0 - 0	0 - 0	21	0	0	0	1	1.00	.773	4.85
Infante, Gregory, CWS	UR	R	5	0	0	0	0.1	0	0		0 - 0	0 - 0	0 - 0	5	0	0	0	0		.449	0.00
Harrell, Lucas, CWS	UR	R	5	1	0	4	0.7	3	0	.00	0 - 0	0 - 0	0 - 0	1	0	0	0	0		.845	2.79
Torres, Carlos, CWS	UR	R	4	1	0	4	0.3	0	0		0 - 0	0 - 0	0 - 0	1	0	0	0	0		1.167	9.39
Marquez, Jeff, CWS	UR	R	1	0	0	0	0.0	0	0		0 - 0	0 - 0	0 - 0	0	0	0	0	0		1.400	18.00
Cincinnati Reds																					
Cordero, Francisco, Cin	CL	R	75	0	30	9	2.1	4	3	.75	28 - 31	12 - 16	0 - 0	55	2	40	48	1	.84	.681	3.84
Masset, Nick, Cin	SU	R	82	3	28	7	1.3	32	9	.28	0 - 0	1 - 2	1 - 3	61	0	2	5	20	.88	.643	3.40
Rhodes, Arthur, Cin	SU	L	70	0	16	1	1.4	36	5	.14	0 - 2	0 - 0	0 - 0	59	0	0	2	26	.93	.574	2.29
Herrera, Daniel Ray, Cin	LT	L	36	11	12	2	1.1	39	11	.28	0 - 0	0 - 0	0 - 1	21	0	0	1	9	.90	.793	3.91
Bray, Bill, Cin	LT	L	35	11	4	5	0.7	24	7	.29	0 - 0	0 - 0	0 - 0	26	0	0	0	2	1.00	.626	4.13
Chapman, Aroldis, Cin	LT	L	15	1	4	0	1.6	8	5	.63	0 - 0	0 - 0	0 - 1	10	0	0	1	4	.80	.492	2.03
Maloney, Matt, Cin	LT	L	5	4	0	3	0.9	0	0		0 - 0	0 - 0	0 - 0	3	0	0	0	0		.727	3.00
Owings, Micah, Cin	LM	R	22	10	3	10	0.7	13	8	.62	0 - 0	0 - 0	0 - 0	12	0	0	0	0		.748	5.40
Ondrusek, Logan, Cin	UR	R	60	7	17	5	0.9	26	7	.27	0 - 1	0 - 0	0 - 1	47	0	0	2	6	.75	.669	3.68
Smith, Jordan, Cin	UR	R	37	10	8	5	0.7	17	6	.35	0 - 0	1 - 2	0 - 0	24	0	1	2	2	.75	.768	3.86
Lincoln, Mike, Cin	UR	R	19	4	5	5	0.5	9	4	.44	0 - 0	0 - 0	0 - 0	10	0	0	0	3	1.00	.813	7.32
Fisher, Carlos, Cin	UR	R	18	3	3	6	0.3	8	3	.38	0 - 0	0 - 0	0 - 0	11	0	0	0	0		.720	5.64
LeCure, Sam, Cin	UR	R	9	5	0	4	0.9	3	3	1.00	0 - 0	0 - 0	0 - 0	5	0	0	0	0		.674	3.68
Burton, Jared, Cin	UR	R	4	1	0	0	0.5	1	0	.00	0 - 0	0 - 0	0 - 0	4	0	0	0	1	1.00	.000	0.00
Springer, Russ, Cin	UR	R	2	0	0	0	0.2	0	0		0 - 0	0 - 0	0 - 0	1	0	0	0	0		.571	5.40
Leake, Mike, Cin	ER	R	2	2	0	2	0.9	0	0		0 - 0	0 - 0	0 - 0	0	0	0	0	0		1.672	27.00
Harang, Aaron, Cin	ER	R	2	1	0	1	0.9	0	0		0 - 0	0 - 0	0 - 0	1	0	0	0	0		1.214	9.00
Cleveland Indians																					
Perez, Chris, Cle	CL	R	63	0	13	9	2.1	31	7	.23	10 - 11	9 - 10	4 - 6	52	1	23	27	9	.89	.583	1.71
Smith, Joe, Cle	SU	R	53	6	13	4	1.1	36	7	.19	0 - 0	0 - 0	0 - 1	40	0	0	1	17	.94	.659	3.83
Sipp, Tony, Cle	LT	L	70	16	10	7	1.1	45	9	.20	0 - 0	1 - 1	0 - 2	50	0	1	3	15	.89	.770	4.14
Perez, Rafael, Cle	LT	L	70	8	14	9	1.1	42	10	.24	0 - 0	0 - 2	0 - 2	50	1	0	4	13	.76	.748	3.25
Laffey, Aaron, Cle	LM	R	24	13	1	8	0.9	21	7	.33	0 - 0	0 - 0	0 - 0	11	0	0	0	5	1.00	.740	5.28
Germano, Justin, Cle	LM	R	22	13	1	8	0.8	10	2	.20	0 - 0	0 - 1	0 - 0	16	0	0	1	2	.67	.588	2.16
Herrmann, Frank, Cle	UR	R	40	12	10	7	0.7	31	10	.32	1 - 1	0 - 1	0 - 0	19	0	1	2	7	.89	.775	4.03
Lewis, Jensen, Cle	UR	R	37	9	6	5	0.8	10	2	.20	0 - 0	0 - 0	0 - 0	27	0	0	0	1	1.00	.611	2.97

Relief Pitching

Pitcher	Pos	T	Usage					Inherited Runners			Saves			Relief Results							
			Rel G	Early Entry	Cons Days	Long	Lev Ind	#	Scrd	Pct	Easy	Reg	Tough	Clean	BS Win	Saves	Opps	Holds	Sv/Hld Pct	Opp OPS	Rel ERA
Ambriz, Hector, Cle	UR	R	34	8	3	13	0.4	19	12	.63	0 - 0	0 - 0	0 - 0	16	0	0	0	0		.960	5.59
Masterson, Justin, Cle	UR	R	5	1	0	1	1.0	4	2	.50	0 - 0	0 - 0	0 - 0	3	0	0	0	2	1.00	.513	3.38
Pestano, Vinnie, Cle	UR	R	5	0	0	1	0.5	0	0		1 - 1	0 - 0	0 - 0	3	0	1	1	0	1.00	.614	3.60
Todd, Jess, Cle	UR	R	5	1	1	3	0.1	0	0		0 - 0	0 - 0	0 - 0	2	0	0	0	0		.844	7.50
Marte, Andy, Cle	ER	R	1	0	0	0	0.0	0	0		0 - 0	0 - 0	0 - 0	1	0	0	0	0		.000	0.00
Colorado Rockies																					
Dotel, Octavio, Pit-LAD-Col	CL	R	68	4	13	9	1.4	10	8	.80	14 - 14	8 - 12	0 - 2	44	1	22	28	4	.81	.743	4.08
Street, Huston, Col	CL	R	44	1	18	5	1.9	1	0	.00	10 - 13	10 - 12	0 - 0	32	0	20	25	0	.80	.648	3.61
Belisle, Matt, Col	SU	R	76	13	21	16	1.2	29	10	.34	1 - 1	0 - 0	0 - 1	52	0	1	2	21	.96	.646	2.93
Betancourt, Rafael, Col	SU	R	72	1	22	1	1.4	37	11	.30	0 - 1	0 - 2	1 - 2	50	1	1	5	23	.86	.626	3.61
Beimel, Joe, Col	SU	L	71	8	19	1	1.2	41	11	.27	0 - 0	0 - 1	0 - 0	52	0	0	1	20	.95	.747	3.40
Morales, Franklin, Col	LT	L	35	4	5	6	1.3	14	3	.21	3 - 3	0 - 2	0 - 1	21	0	3	6	1	.57	.823	6.28
Reynolds, Matt, Col	LT	L	21	3	4	2	0.8	15	3	.20	0 - 0	0 - 0	0 - 0	17	0	0	0	2	1.00	.541	2.00
Rogers, Esmil, Col	LM	R	20	10	1	12	0.9	9	1	.11	0 - 1	0 - 0	0 - 0	9	0	0	1	1	.50	.822	5.88
Delcarmen, M., Bos-Col	UR	R	57	16	7	10	1.0	24	9	.38	0 - 0	0 - 1	0 - 2	37	1	0	3	8	.73	.717	4.99
Corpas, Manuel, Col	UR	R	56	14	13	9	1.2	29	12	.41	3 - 3	6 - 9	1 - 2	38	0	10	14	2	.75	.772	4.62
Daley, Matt, Col	UR	R	28	8	10	3	1.0	13	3	.23	0 - 0	0 - 0	0 - 0	19	0	0	0	6	1.00	.845	4.24
Chacin, Jhoulys, Col	UR	R	7	4	1	3	0.9	0	0		0 - 0	0 - 0	0 - 0	3	0	0	0	0		.748	6.75
Escalona, Edgmer, Col	UR	R	5	1	1	2	0.3	0	0		0 - 0	0 - 0	0 - 0	4	0	0	0	0		.546	1.50
Deduno, Sam, Col	UR	R	4	0	0	0	0.5	3	2	.67	0 - 0	0 - 0	0 - 0	2	0	0	0	1	1.00	.879	3.38
Rincon, Juan, Col	UR	R	2	0	0	1	0.0	1	1	1.00	0 - 0	0 - 0	0 - 0	0	0	0	0	0		.899	4.50
Francis, Jeff, Col	ER	L	1	1	0	1	1.0	0	0		0 - 0	0 - 0	0 - 0	0	0	0	0	0		1.000	9.00
Detroit Tigers																					
Valverde, Jose, Det	CL	R	60	0	14	6	1.4	9	2	.22	17 - 17	8 - 11	1 - 1	44	1	26	29	0	.90	.585	3.00
Perry, Ryan, Det	SU	R	60	4	12	7	1.5	35	7	.20	1 - 2	0 - 0	1 - 3	40	0	2	5	19	.88	.686	3.59
Zumaya, Joel, Det	SU	R	31	7	1	9	1.3	26	6	.23	0 - 0	1 - 2	0 - 1	18	0	1	3	11	.86	.586	2.58
Coke, Phil, Det	LT	L	73	2	21	4	1.3	40	13	.33	1 - 1	1 - 2	0 - 1	49	1	2	4	17	.90	.680	3.57
Schlereth, Daniel, Det	LT	L	18	5	3	5	1.2	12	3	.25	0 - 0	0 - 1	1 - 1	11	0	1	2	1	.67	.752	2.89
Thomas, Brad, Det	LM	L	47	26	7	14	0.7	35	17	.49	0 - 0	0 - 0	0 - 0	24	0	0	0	3	1.00	.736	3.41
Ni, Fu-Te, Det	LM	L	22	10	0	6	0.7	17	7	.41	0 - 0	0 - 0	0 - 0	10	0	0	0	1	1.00	.869	6.65
Bonine, Eddie, Det	UR	R	46	18	7	12	0.6	28	17	.61	0 - 0	0 - 0	0 - 0	23	0	0	0	2	1.00	.807	4.18
Weinhardt, Robbie, Det	UR	R	28	8	5	5	1.3	22	10	.45	0 - 0	0 - 1	0 - 1	13	1	0	2	5	.71	.831	6.14
Gonzalez, Enrique, Det	UR	R	18	4	3	6	0.3	14	5	.36	0 - 0	0 - 0	0 - 0	8	0	0	0	0		.771	3.81
Figaro, Alfredo, Det	UR	R	7	1	0	4	0.9	5	4	.80	0 - 0	0 - 0	0 - 0	2	0	0	0	0		.789	5.59
Fien, Casey, Det	UR	R	2	0	0	1	0.1	1	1	1.00	0 - 0	0 - 0	0 - 0	1	0	0	0	0		1.364	10.13
Sborz, Jay, Det	UR	R	1	1	0	0	0.4	2	2	1.00	0 - 0	0 - 0	0 - 0	0	0	0	0	0		1.314	67.50
Bonderman, Jeremy, Det	ER	R	1	1	0	0	0.9	2	0	.00	0 - 0	0 - 0	0 - 0	1	0	0	0	1	1.00	.000	0.00
Galarraga, Armando, Det	ER	R	1	1	0	0	1.0	2	0	.00	0 - 0	0 - 0	0 - 0	1	0	0	0	0		.400	0.00
Florida Marlins																					
Nunez, Leo, Fla	CL	R	68	0	18	5	1.9	8	3	.38	22 - 25	8 - 12	0 - 1	48	2	30	38	5	.81	.688	3.46
Hensley, Clay, Fla	SU	R	68	4	19	12	1.4	23	6	.26	5 - 5	1 - 3	1 - 2	51	0	7	10	22	.91	.568	2.16
Veras, Jose, Fla	SU	R	48	2	16	9	1.3	26	1	.04	0 - 0	0 - 2	0 - 0	35	2	0	2	19	.90	.622	3.75
Tankersley, Taylor, Fla	SU	L	27	6	4	0	1.4	32	11	.34	0 - 1	0 - 0	0 - 2	16	0	0	3	6	.67	.913	7.50
Ohman, Will, Bal-Fla	LT	L	68	5	22	1	1.2	40	12	.30	0 - 0	0 - 1	0 - 0	51	0	0	1	18	.95	.732	3.21
Pinto, Renyel, Fla	LT	L	20	2	5	4	0.6	12	5	.42	0 - 0	0 - 0	0 - 0	13	0	0	0	4	1.00	.736	2.70
Meyer, Dan, Fla	LT	L	13	2	3	3	0.8	7	3	.43	0 - 0	0 - 0	0 - 1	6	0	0	1	1	.50	1.031	9.64
Jones, Hunter, Fla	LT	L	3	0	0	0	0.3	4	1	.25	0 - 0	0 - 0	0 - 0	2	0	0	0	0		.286	0.00
Houser, James, Fla	LT	L	1	1	0	1	0.4	1	1	1.00	0 - 0	0 - 0	0 - 0	0	0	0	0	0		1.792	20.25
Sosa, Jorge, Fla	LM	R	20	10	3	11	0.9	10	2	.20	0 - 0	0 - 0	0 - 0	11	0	0	0	0		.698	4.45
Sanches, Brian, Fla	UR	R	61	18	14	7	0.9	26	7	.27	0 - 0	0 - 0	0 - 1	46	0	0	1	12	.92	.609	2.26
Badenhop, Burke, Fla	UR	R	53	17	10	12	0.9	24	7	.29	0 - 0	1 - 3	0 - 0	32	0	1	3	8	.82	.681	3.99
Wood, Tim, Fla	UR	R	26	3	3	5	1.0	9	4	.44	0 - 0	1 - 3	0 - 0	15	0	1	3	3	.67	.819	5.53
Buente, Jay, Fla	UR	R	8	3	0	7	0.5	2	0	.00	0 - 0	0 - 0	0 - 0	3	0	0	0	0		.848	6.55
Ceda, Jose, Fla	UR	R	8	5	0	3	0.2	3	1	.33	0 - 0	0 - 0	0 - 0	4	0	0	0	0		.808	5.19
Marinez, Jhan, Fla	UR	R	4	0	1	0	1.2	6	5	.83	0 - 0	0 - 0	0 - 2	2	1	0	2	0	.00	.974	6.75
Sinkbeil, Brett, Fla	UR	R	3	2	0	1	0.6	6	4	.67	0 - 0	0 - 0	0 - 0	1	0	0	0	0		.913	13.50
Strickland, Scott, Fla	UR	R	3	0	1	0	0.6	3	2	.67	0 - 0	0 - 0	0 - 0	0	0	0	0	0		1.245	9.00
Sanabia, Alex, Fla	UR	R	3	3	0	3	0.0	3	0	.00	0 - 0	0 - 0	0 - 0	0	0	0	0	0		.740	4.32
Cishek, Steve, Fla	UR	R	3	1	0	1	0.1	3	1	.33	0 - 0	0 - 0	0 - 0	2	0	0	0	0		.276	0.00
Miller, Andrew, Fla	UR	L	2	1	0	1	0.8	0	0		0 - 0	0 - 0	0 - 0	0	0	0	0	0		.996	7.20
Rosario, Sandy, Fla	UR	R	2	0	0	1	0.3	0	0		0 - 0	0 - 0	0 - 0	0	0	0	0	0		2.288	54.00
Houston Astros																					
Lyon, Brandon, Hou	CL	R	79	0	26	8	1.9	7	0	.00	10 - 10	10 - 12	0 - 0	66	0	20	22	19	.95	.622	3.12
Lindstrom, Matt, Hou	CL	R	58	0	15	4	1.7	8	4	.50	16 - 17	7 - 12	0 - 0	43	1	23	29	4	.82	.792	4.39
Melancon, Mark, NYY-Hou	SU	R	22	1	4	4	1.2	8	1	.13	0 - 0	0 - 1	0 - 0	15	1	0	1	8	.89	.674	4.22
Byrdak, Tim, Hou	LT	L	64	8	21	0	0.8	42	15	.36	0 - 0	0 - 0	0 - 0	47	0	0	0	11	1.00	.795	3.49
Abad, Fernando, Hou	LT	L	22	0	4	1	0.9	5	2	.40	0 - 0	0 - 0	0 - 0	18	0	0	0	6	1.00	.636	2.84

Relief Pitching

Pitcher	Pos	T	Rel G	Early Entry	Cons Days	Long	Lev Ind	#	Scrd	Pct	Easy	Reg	Tough	Clean	BS Win	Saves	Opps	Holds	Sv/Hld Pct	Opp OPS	Rel ERA
Wright, Wesley, Hou	LT	L	10	4	1	2	0.6	3	0	.00	0-0	0-0	0-0	6	0	0	0	0		.878	4.50
Chacin, Gustavo, Hou	LM	L	44	18	6	10	0.8	30	8	.27	1-1	0-0	0-0	27	0	1	1	5	1.00	.814	4.70
Figueroa, Nelson, Phi-Hou	LM	R	20	7	4	9	1.0	11	4	.36	1-1	0-0	0-0	10	0	1	1	0	1.00	.628	3.34
Lopez, Wilton, Hou	UR	R	68	10	20	4	0.9	33	1	.03	0-1	1-1	0-1	49	0	1	3	14	.88	.653	2.96
Fulchino, Jeff, Hou	UR	R	50	14	7	9	0.5	23	11	.48	0-0	0-0	0-1	33	0	0	1	5	.83	.793	5.51
Sampson, Chris, Hou	UR	R	35	9	8	3	0.6	15	5	.33	0-0	0-2	0-0	22	0	0	2	5	.71	.950	5.93
Daigle, Casey, Hou	UR	R	13	5	4	2	0.8	9	6	.67	0-0	0-0	0-0	3	0	0	0	3	1.00	1.246	11.32
Moehler, Brian, Hou	UR	R	12	5	1	3	0.8	5	3	.60	0-0	0-0	0-0	7	0	0	0	0		.744	4.42
Del Rosario, E., Cin-Hou	UR	R	11	2	2	1	0.9	10	7	.70	0-0	0-0	0-2	4	1	0	2	0	.00	.982	4.50
Villar, Henry, Hou	UR	R	8	3	0	0	0.4	7	1	.14	0-0	0-0	0-0	5	0	0	0	1	1.00	.561	4.50
Gervacio, Sammy, Hou	UR	R	6	0	1	0	0.4	3	2	.67	0-0	0-0	0-0	2	0	0	0	0		.983	12.27
Paulino, Felipe, Hou	UR	R	5	1	0	1	1.1	1	1	1.00	0-0	0-1	0-0	2	0	0	1	1	.50	.918	15.88
Majewski, Gary, Hou	UR	R	2	0	1	1	0.2	0	0		0-0	0-0	0-0	1	0	0	0	0		1.212	22.50
Kansas City Royals																					
Soria, Joakim, KC	CL	R	66	0	17	5	2.2	9	3	.33	22-23	21-22	0-1	54	0	43	46	0	.93	.568	1.78
Tejeda, Robinson, KC	SU	R	54	4	9	12	1.3	28	9	.32	0-2	0-1	0-3	36	0	0	6	12	.67	.691	3.54
Wood, Blake, KC	SU	R	51	2	13	6	1.4	22	13	.59	0-0	0-2	0-2	32	0	0	4	15	.79	.798	5.07
Rupe, Josh, KC	SU	R	11	1	3	1	1.7	10	4	.40	0-0	0-0	0-0	6	0	0	0	5	1.00	.925	5.59
Meche, Gil, KC	SU	R	11	2	0	2	1.0	0	0		0-0	0-0	0-0	8	0	0	0	6	1.00	.599	2.08
Hughes, Dusty, KC	LT	L	57	13	17	14	0.7	43	11	.26	0-0	0-0	0-0	32	0	0	0	7	1.00	.730	3.83
Parrish, John, KC	LT	L	9	1	1	1	1.6	9	2	.22	0-0	0-1	0-1	6	0	0	2	2	.50	.822	3.00
Texeira, Kanekoa, Sea-KC	LM	R	43	23	6	16	0.7	31	16	.52	0-0	0-0	0-0	15	0	0	0	2	1.00	.777	4.84
Marte, Victor, KC	LM	R	22	8	5	8	0.4	16	7	.44	0-0	0-0	0-0	8	0	0	0	1	1.00	1.001	9.76
Chavez, Jesse, Atl-KC	UR	R	51	11	6	16	0.8	17	2	.12	0-1	0-0	0-0	31	0	0	1	6	.86	.834	5.89
Thompson, Brad, KC	UR	R	16	6	3	6	0.9	13	3	.23	0-0	0-0	0-1	7	0	0	1	1	.50	.877	6.41
Holland, Greg, KC	UR	R	15	3	1	6	0.4	3	2	.67	0-0	0-0	0-0	6	0	0	0	0		.835	6.75
Chen, Bruce, KC	UR	L	10	3	3	4	1.0	13	4	.31	0-0	0-0	1-1	4	0	1	1	0	1.00	.569	2.89
Bullington, Bryan, KC	UR	R	8	5	1	4	0.8	6	2	.33	0-0	0-0	0-0	4	0	0	0	0		.843	5.65
Humber, Philip, KC	UR	R	7	4	0	6	1.5	11	6	.55	0-0	0-0	0-0	4	0	0	0	1	1.00	.624	2.81
Cruz, Juan, KC	UR	R	5	0	0	1	0.8	6	6	1.00	0-0	0-0	0-1	2	0	0	1	0	.00	.960	3.38
O'Sullivan, Sean, LAA-KC	UR	R	5	2	1	2	1.0	5	0	.00	0-0	0-0	0-0	4	0	0	0	0		.467	1.13
Colon, Roman, KC	UR	R	5	0	1	0	0.7	3	3	1.00	0-0	0-0	0-0	2	0	0	0	0		1.208	18.00
Mendoza, Luis, KC	UR	R	4	1	0	2	0.7	5	1	.20	0-0	0-0	0-1	1	0	0	1	0	.00	1.656	22.50
Bannister, Brian, KC	ER	R	1	0	0	1	0.9	0	0		0-0	0-0	0-0	0	0	0	0	0		.533	9.00
Hochevar, Luke, KC	ER	R	1	1	0	1	1.0	0	0		0-0	0-0	0-0	0	0	0	0	0		1.080	9.00
Los Angeles Angels																					
Rodney, Fernando, LAA	SU	R	72	0	18	11	1.9	10	4	.40	10-14	4-7	0-0	49	0	14	21	21	.83	.739	4.24
Jepsen, Kevin, LAA	SU	R	68	0	17	5	1.8	31	10	.32	0-0	0-3	0-1	45	1	0	4	27	.87	.665	3.97
Walden, Jordan, LAA	SU	R	16	0	2	0	1.3	1	0	.00	1-1	0-0	0-0	12	0	1	1	6	1.00	.670	2.35
Bell, Trevor, LAA	LM	R	18	8	1	7	0.9	14	5	.36	0-0	0-0	0-0	11	0	0	0	1	1.00	.771	4.81
Palmer, Matt, LAA	LM	R	13	9	0	10	0.8	9	6	.67	0-0	0-0	0-0	7	0	0	0	1	1.00	.762	3.77
Rodriguez, Francisco, LAA	UR	R	43	11	6	7	0.8	18	5	.28	0-0	0-0	0-1	27	0	0	1	2	.67	.732	4.37
Shields, Scot, LAA	UR	R	42	5	7	11	0.6	9	4	.44	0-0	0-1	0-0	22	0	0	1	1	.50	.711	5.08
Bulger, Jason, LAA	UR	R	25	6	5	4	0.8	16	8	.50	0-0	0-0	0-0	18	0	0	0	2	1.00	.823	4.88
Kohn, Mike, LAA	UR	R	24	5	4	3	1.2	13	2	.15	0-0	0-0	1-1	18	0	1	1	1	1.00	.616	2.11
Cassevah, Bobby, LAA	UR	R	16	2	2	4	1.2	7	2	.29	0-0	0-0	0-0	9	0	0	0	0		.730	3.15
Stokes, Brian, LAA	UR	R	16	3	3	3	0.4	11	8	.73	0-0	0-0	0-0	8	0	0	0	0		1.131	8.10
Thompson, Rich, LAA	UR	R	13	3	0	4	0.7	4	1	.25	0-0	0-0	0-0	10	0	0	0	1	1.00	.516	1.37
Los Angeles Dodgers																					
Broxton, Jonathan, LAD	CL	R	64	0	19	9	1.8	20	10	.50	11-13	11-13	0-3	43	1	22	29	3	.78	.718	4.04
Belisario, Ronald, LAD	SU	R	59	12	18	8	1.1	31	7	.23	1-1	1-2	0-1	41	1	2	4	16	.90	.702	5.04
Kuo, Hong-Chih, LAD	SU	L	56	1	4	4	1.5	28	8	.29	8-8	4-4	0-1	47	1	12	13	21	.97	.403	1.20
Sherrill, George, LAD	LT	L	65	9	18	1	0.9	59	24	.41	0-0	0-1	0-3	37	0	0	4	7	.64	.906	6.69
Taschner, Jack, Pit-LAD	LT	L	20	5	5	6	0.4	14	6	.43	0-0	0-0	0-1	10	0	0	1	2	.67	.844	6.41
Elbert, Scott, LAD	LT	L	1	1	0	0	0.3	2	2	1.00	0-0	0-0	0-0	0	0	0	0	0		1.000	13.50
Miller, Justin, LAD	LM	R	19	5	4	6	0.3	14	7	.50	0-0	0-0	0-0	9	0	0	0	1	1.00	.754	4.44
Monasterios, Carlos, LAD	LM	R	19	10	0	12	0.8	2	2	1.00	0-0	0-0	0-0	11	0	0	0	0		.620	2.06
Schlichting, Travis, LAD	LM	R	14	6	2	8	0.6	15	8	.53	0-0	0-0	0-0	5	0	0	0	0		.588	3.57
Troncoso, Ramon, LAD	UR	R	52	18	12	10	0.8	37	22	.59	0-0	0-0	0-1	29	0	0	1	8	.89	.726	4.33
Weaver, Jeff, LAD	UR	R	44	17	5	9	0.8	29	6	.21	0-0	0-1	0-0	28	0	0	1	5	.83	.822	6.09
Jansen, Kenley, LAD	UR	R	25	3	5	5	1.1	6	3	.50	0-0	3-3	1-1	20	0	4	4	4	1.00	.422	0.67
Ortiz, Ramon, LAD	UR	R	14	8	2	6	0.7	11	4	.36	0-0	0-0	0-0	6	0	0	0	1	1.00	.776	5.16
Link, Jon, LAD	UR	R	9	2	2	1	0.1	0	0	.00	0-0	0-0	0-0	6	0	0	0	0		.789	4.15
Ortiz, Russ, LAD	UR	R	6	1	1	2	0.9	0	0		0-0	0-0	0-0	3	0	0	0	0		.808	10.29
Haeger, Charlie, LAD	UR	R	3	1	0	2	0.9	0	0		0-0	0-0	0-0	1	0	0	0	0		.808	3.86
Milwaukee Brewers																					
Axford, John, Mil	CL	R	50	0	13	11	2.0	14	3	.21	10-10	12-14	2-3	33	1	24	27	3	.90	.588	2.48

Relief Pitching

Pitcher	Pos	T	Rel G	Early Entry	Cons Days	Long	Lev Ind	#	Scrd	Pct	Easy	Reg	Tough	Clean	BS Win	Saves	Opps	Holds	Sv/Hld Pct	Opp OPS	Rel ERA
Loe, Kameron, Mil	SU	R	53	6	15	7	1.2	36	12	.33	0 - 0	0 - 0	0 - 2	34	0	0	2	22	.92	.661	2.78
Villanueva, Carlos, Mil	SU	R	50	11	9	11	1.1	16	6	.38	0 - 1	1 - 2	0 - 1	32	0	1	4	14	.83	.702	4.61
Braddock, Zach, Mil	SU	L	46	4	12	2	1.1	37	13	.35	0 - 0	0 - 0	0 - 2	34	0	0	2	15	.88	.656	2.94
Hawkins, LaTroy, Mil	SU	R	18	0	2	1	1.3	1	0	.00	0 - 1	0 - 1	0 - 0	13	0	0	2	6	.75	.890	8.44
Parra, Manny, Mil	LT	L	26	7	4	11	0.9	7	7	1.00	0 - 0	0 - 0	0 - 0	17	0	0	0	0		.680	2.39
Capuano, Chris, Mil	LT	L	15	4	0	5	0.8	10	5	.50	0 - 0	0 - 0	0 - 0	10	0	0	0	1	1.00	.696	3.54
Stetter, Mitch, Mil	LT	L	9	1	4	1	0.9	9	0	.00	0 - 0	0 - 0	0 - 0	6	0	0	0	3	1.00	1.056	14.73
Vargas, Claudio, Mil	LM	R	17	9	2	5	0.4	10	2	.20	0 - 0	0 - 0	0 - 0	7	0	0	0	0		.903	7.32
Coffey, Todd, Mil	UR	R	69	21	18	5	0.9	60	21	.35	0 - 0	0 - 0	0 - 2	41	0	0	2	13	.87	.783	4.76
Hoffman, Trevor, Mil	UR	R	50	0	8	4	1.1	5	0	.00	6 - 8	3 - 6	1 - 1	35	1	10	15	2	.71	.832	5.89
Riske, David, Mil	UR	R	23	4	5	5	0.2	5	2	.40	0 - 0	0 - 0	0 - 0	15	0	0	0	0		.745	5.01
McClendon, Mike, Mil	UR	R	17	6	4	4	1.1	8	3	.38	0 - 0	0 - 1	0 - 0	9	0	0	1	3	.75	.587	3.00
Jeffress, Jeremy, Mil	UR	R	10	2	0	2	0.6	1	1	1.00	0 - 0	0 - 0	0 - 0	8	0	0	0	0		.676	2.70
Narveson, Chris, Mil	UR	L	9	3	1	2	0.9	0	0		0 - 0	0 - 1	0 - 0	2	1	0	1	3	.75	1.075	7.20
Kintzler, Brandon, Mil	UR	R	7	2	0	1	0.7	5	1	.20	0 - 0	0 - 0	0 - 0	4	0	0	0	0		1.045	7.36
Estrada, Marco, Mil	UR	R	6	3	2	4	1.1	2	0	.00	0 - 0	0 - 0	0 - 0	1	0	0	0	0		.952	10.80
Smith, Chris, Mil	UR	R	3	1	1	1	0.2	0	0		0 - 0	0 - 0	0 - 0	2	0	0	0	0		.819	5.40
Rogers, Mark, Mil	UR	R	2	0	0	0	0.9	0	0		0 - 0	0 - 0	0 - 0	2	0	0	0	0		.000	0.00
Bush, Dave, Mil	ER	R	1	1	0	0	0.9	3	0	.00	0 - 0	0 - 0	0 - 0	1	0	0	0	1	1.00	.000	0.00
Inglett, Joe, Mil	ER	R	1	0	0	0	0.0	0	0		0 - 0	0 - 0	0 - 0	1	0	0	0	0		.000	0.00
Minnesota Twins																					
Capps, Matt, Was-Min	CL	R	74	0	24	2	2.1	16	4	.25	27 - 28	14 - 19	1 - 1	53	0	42	48	0	.88	.688	2.47
Rauch, Jon, Min	CL	R	59	2	12	5	1.4	10	3	.30	10 - 10	11 - 15	0 - 0	44	2	21	25	2	.85	.671	3.12
Fuentes, Brian, LAA-Min	CL	L	48	0	10	6	1.9	3	1	.33	14 - 15	9 - 11	1 - 2	38	1	24	28	3	.87	.607	2.81
Guerrier, Matt, Min	SU	R	74	5	20	6	1.5	45	10	.22	1 - 3	0 - 0	0 - 4	53	0	1	7	23	.80	.625	3.17
Crain, Jesse, Min	SU	R	71	12	19	4	1.2	39	9	.23	0 - 1	0 - 2	1 - 1	54	0	1	4	21	.88	.627	3.04
Flores, Randy, Col-Min	LT	L	58	15	13	1	0.9	59	13	.22	0 - 0	0 - 0	0 - 1	42	0	0	1	7	.88	.847	3.19
Mijares, Jose, Min	LT	L	47	4	13	3	0.8	29	8	.28	0 - 0	0 - 0	0 - 0	31	0	0	0	9	1.00	.768	3.31
Mahay, Ron, Min	LT	L	41	13	8	5	0.4	40	10	.25	0 - 0	0 - 1	0 - 0	27	0	0	1	2	.67	.675	3.44
Duensing, Brian, Min	LT	L	40	9	11	6	0.9	21	3	.14	0 - 0	0 - 0	0 - 0	30	0	0	0	9	1.00	.617	1.80
Perkins, Glen, Min	LT	L	12	4	1	4	0.5	8	2	.25	0 - 0	0 - 0	0 - 0	8	0	0	0	0		.931	5.29
Burnett, Alex, Min	UR	R	41	14	6	11	0.7	23	5	.22	0 - 0	0 - 0	0 - 0	23	0	0	0	2	1.00	.847	5.29
Manship, Jeff, Min	UR	R	12	9	0	7	0.7	3	0	.00	0 - 0	0 - 0	0 - 0	2	0	0	0	0		.800	5.87
Neshek, Pat, Min	UR	R	11	4	2	1	0.9	7	4	.57	0 - 0	0 - 0	0 - 1	7	0	0	1	1	.50	.696	5.00
Slama, Anthony, Min	UR	R	5	2	0	1	0.5	3	0	.00	0 - 0	0 - 1	0 - 0	2	0	0	1	0	.00	.990	7.71
Delaney, Rob, Min	UR	R	1	0	0	0	0.0	0	0		0 - 0	0 - 0	0 - 0	0	0	0	0	0		1.850	9.00
Blackburn, Nick, Min	ER	R	2	0	0	1	0.9	0	0		0 - 0	0 - 0	0 - 0	0	0	0	0	0		1.067	12.00
Slowey, Kevin, Min	ER	R	2	2	0	0	0.9	0	0		0 - 0	0 - 0	0 - 0	2	0	0	0	0		.200	0.00
New York Mets																					
Rodriguez, F., NYM	CL	R	53	0	15	9	1.9	21	6	.29	15 - 16	6 - 9	4 - 5	40	3	25	30	0	.83	.597	2.20
Feliciano, Pedro, NYM	LT	L	92	3	44	4	1.2	50	9	.18	0 - 0	0 - 0	0 - 1	68	0	0	1	23	.96	.702	3.30
Takahashi, Hisanori, NYM	LT	L	41	9	9	13	1.1	17	6	.35	5 - 5	2 - 2	1 - 1	28	0	8	8	3	1.00	.582	2.04
Perez, Oliver, NYM	LT	L	10	2	0	7	1.1	5	1	.20	0 - 0	0 - 0	0 - 0	3	0	0	0	0		1.147	9.00
Valdes, Raul, NYM	LM	L	37	20	6	17	0.8	24	11	.46	0 - 0	1 - 1	0 - 2	20	0	1	3	1	.50	.791	5.23
Dessens, Elmer, NYM	UR	R	53	14	15	4	1.0	33	11	.33	0 - 0	0 - 0	0 - 1	41	0	0	1	11	.92	.694	2.30
Acosta, Manny, NYM	UR	R	41	10	13	4	0.8	31	13	.42	0 - 0	0 - 1	0 - 0	30	0	1	3	2	.60	.636	2.95
Parnell, Bobby, NYM	UR	R	41	0	13	2	1.0	11	2	.18	0 - 0	0 - 2	0 - 0	31	0	0	2	9	.82	.686	2.83
Nieve, Fernando, NYM	UR	R	39	6	12	9	1.1	20	4	.16	0 - 1	0 - 0	0 - 1	25	1	0	2	6	.75	.771	5.18
Igarashi, Ryota, NYM	UR	R	34	6	8	5	0.7	17	3	.18	0 - 0	0 - 0	0 - 0	22	0	0	0	2	1.00	.796	7.12
Mejia, Jenrry, NYM	UR	R	30	5	8	3	0.8	10	3	.30	0 - 0	0 - 1	0 - 0	21	0	0	1	2	.67	.728	3.25
Green, Sean, NYM	UR	R	11	5	3	2	0.6	7	4	.57	0 - 0	0 - 0	0 - 0	6	0	0	0	2	1.00	.719	3.86
Misch, Pat, NYM	UR	L	6	3	0	0	1.0	8	0	.00	0 - 0	0 - 0	0 - 0	6	0	0	0	0		.600	3.86
Stoner, Tobi, NYM	UR	R	1	1	0	1	2.0	0	0		0 - 0	0 - 0	0 - 0	0	0	0	0	0		.864	3.86
Pelfrey, Mike, NYM	ER	R	1	0	0	0	1.1	0	0		0 - 0	1 - 1	0 - 0	1	0	1	1	0	1.00	.650	0.00
Dickey, R.A., NYM	ER	R	1	0	0	0	1.1	0	0		0 - 0	0 - 0	0 - 0	1	0	0	0	1	1.00	.250	0.00
New York Yankees																					
Rivera, Mariano, NYY	CL	R	61	0	14	7	2.1	16	3	.19	19 - 19	14 - 17	0 - 2	51	0	33	38	0	.87	.493	1.80
Chamberlain, Joba, NYY	SU	R	73	3	15	8	1.2	37	9	.24	0 - 0	1 - 4	0 - 0	48	0	3	7	26	.88	.693	4.40
Wood, Kerry, Cle-NYY	SU	R	47	1	9	10	1.6	10	1	.10	4 - 4	4 - 8	0 - 0	36	1	8	12	11	.83	.654	3.13
Marte, Damaso, NYY	SU	L	30	3	6	4	1.0	22	6	.27	0 - 0	0 - 0	0 - 2	23	0	0	2	9	.82	.580	4.08
Logan, Boone, NYY	LT	L	51	21	12	6	0.8	33	8	.24	0 - 0	0 - 0	0 - 0	37	0	0	0	13	1.00	.659	2.93
Ring, Royce, NYY	LT	L	5	4	1	1	1.0	2	1	.50	0 - 0	0 - 0	0 - 0	1	0	0	0	1	1.00	.717	15.43
Gaudin, Chad, Oak-NYY	LM	R	42	14	5	22	0.5	20	5	.25	0 - 0	0 - 0	0 - 0	19	1	0	1	1	.50	.892	5.65
Mitre, Sergio, NYY	LM	R	24	9	4	10	0.4	9	4	.44	0 - 0	1 - 1	0 - 0	15	0	1	1	1	1.00	.598	2.45
Robertson, David, NYY	UR	R	64	16	11	11	1.3	32	10	.31	0 - 0	1 - 1	0 - 2	45	0	1	3	14	.88	.721	3.82
Albaladejo, Jonathan, NYY	UR	R	10	3	2	3	0.2	10	3	.30	0 - 0	0 - 0	0 - 0	5	0	0	0	0		.713	3.97
Aceves, Alfredo, NYY	UR	R	10	4	2	3	0.9	6	1	.17	0 - 0	0 - 0	1 - 1	7	0	1	1	1	1.00	.575	3.00

Relief Pitching

Pitcher	Pos	T	Rel G	Early Entry	Cons Days	Long	Lev Ind	#	Scrd	Pct	Easy	Reg	Tough	Clean	BS Win	Saves	Opps	Holds	Sv/Hld Pct	Opp OPS	Rel ERA
												Usage				**Inherited Runners**		**Saves**		**Relief Results**	
Moseley, Dustin, NYY	UR	R	7	5	0	4	0.9	4	3	.75	0 - 0	0 - 0	0 - 0	3	0	0	0	0		.798	3.77
Vazquez, Javier, NYY	UR	R	5	2	0	3	0.9	8	1	.13	0 - 0	0 - 0	0 - 0	1	0	0	0	1	1.00	.528	2.70
Nova, Ivan, NYY	UR	R	3	0	0	2	1.1	2	2	1.00	0 - 0	0 - 0	0 - 1	2	0	0	1	0	.00	.849	1.69
Sanchez, Romulo, NYY	UR	R	2	1	0	2	0.1	1	0	.00	0 - 0	0 - 0	0 - 0	2	0	0	0	0		.307	0.00
Hughes, Phil, NYY	ER	R	2	0	0	0	1.0	0	0		0 - 0	0 - 0	0 - 0	2	0	0	0	0		.000	0.00
Oakland Athletics																					
Bailey, Andrew, Oak	CL	R	47	0	9	7	1.9	16	6	.38	16 - 16	7 - 8	2 - 4	34	0	25	28	0	.89	.544	1.47
Breslow, Craig, Oak	SU	L	75	7	18	12	1.3	33	7	.21	2 - 3	3 - 3	0 - 1	50	0	5	7	16	.91	.620	3.01
Ziegler, Brad, Oak	SU	R	64	10	17	2	1.3	31	7	.23	0 - 1	0 - 1	0 - 2	43	0	0	4	18	.82	.694	3.26
Wuertz, Michael, Oak	SU	R	48	4	11	1	1.2	26	3	.12	2 - 2	4 - 4	0 - 0	34	0	6	6	11	1.00	.746	4.31
Blevins, Jerry, Oak	LT	L	63	12	13	3	0.9	34	12	.35	0 - 0	1 - 1	0 - 1	41	0	1	2	11	.92	.758	3.70
Bowers, Cedrick, Oak	LT	L	14	0	1	1	0.3	9	3	.33	0 - 0	0 - 0	0 - 0	9	0	0	0	0		.779	4.50
Kilby, Brad, Oak	LT	L	5	2	2	2	0.0	5	0	.00	0 - 0	0 - 0	0 - 0	4	0	0	0	0		.688	2.16
Ross, Tyson, Oak	LM	R	24	6	1	11	0.9	10	4	.40	0 - 0	0 - 1	0 - 2	11	1	1	2	2	.75	.748	5.12
Rodriguez, Henry, Oak	UR	R	29	3	3	7	0.5	7	3	.43	0 - 0	0 - 0	0 - 1	20	0	0	1	3	.75	.664	4.55
Bonser, Boof, Bos-Oak	UR	R	15	5	2	4	0.4	6	2	.33	0 - 0	0 - 0	0 - 0	9	0	0	0	3	1.00	.792	6.12
Wolf, Ross, Oak	UR	R	11	2	1	2	0.3	11	3	.27	0 - 0	0 - 0	0 - 0	8	0	0	0	0		.741	4.26
Ramirez, Edwar, Oak	UR	R	7	1	0	6	0.3	1	0	.00	0 - 0	0 - 0	0 - 0	3	0	0	0	0		.658	4.91
Mazzaro, Vin, Oak	UR	R	6	3	0	5	0.9	0	0		0 - 0	0 - 0	0 - 0	1	0	0	0	0		.996	4.15
James, Justin, Oak	UR	R	5	0	0	1	0.6	2	2	1.00	0 - 0	0 - 0	0 - 1	3	0	0	1	0	.00	.911	4.50
Philadelphia Phillies																					
Lidge, Brad, Phi	CL	R	50	0	14	5	2.2	6	2	.33	16 - 18	10 - 13	1 - 1	39	1	27	32	0	.84	.627	2.96
Madson, Ryan, Phi	SU	R	55	0	20	8	1.6	12	3	.25	1 - 2	4 - 7	0 - 1	41	2	5	10	15	.80	.582	2.55
Romero, J.C., Phi	LT	L	60	3	18	1	0.9	27	10	.37	3 - 3	0 - 1	0 - 2	44	0	3	6	9	.80	.690	3.68
Bastardo, Antonio, Phi	LT	L	25	9	8	0	0.5	12	3	.25	0 - 0	0 - 1	0 - 0	17	0	0	1	2	.67	.669	4.34
Zagurski, Mike, Phi	LT	L	8	2	0	2	0.4	5	3	.60	0 - 0	0 - 0	0 - 0	3	0	0	0	0		1.015	10.29
Contreras, Jose, Phi	UR	R	67	3	19	3	1.2	27	8	.30	2 - 2	2 - 2	0 - 1	53	0	4	5	13	.94	.699	3.34
Durbin, Chad, Phi	UR	R	64	17	18	15	0.8	31	8	.26	0 - 0	0 - 0	0 - 1	43	0	0	1	15	.94	.738	3.80
Baez, Danys, Phi	UR	R	51	6	8	7	0.8	6	0	.00	0 - 1	0 - 1	0 - 0	34	0	0	2	6	.75	.863	5.48
Herndon, David, Phi	UR	R	47	16	7	10	0.6	23	11	.48	0 - 0	0 - 1	0 - 0	30	1	0	1	1	.50	.814	4.30
Worley, Vance, Phi	UR	R	3	1	0	0	0.8	0	0		0 - 0	0 - 0	0 - 0	3	0	0	0	0		.282	0.00
Mathieson, Scott, Phi	UR	R	2	0	0	1	0.3	0	0		0 - 0	0 - 0	0 - 0	0	0	0	0	0		1.192	10.80
Carpenter, Drew, Phi	UR	R	1	1	0	1	0.8	0	0		0 - 0	0 - 0	0 - 0	0	0	0	0	0		1.077	9.00
Robertson, Nate, Fla-Phi	ER	L	3	1	0	2	0.9	5	1	.20	0 - 0	0 - 0	0 - 0	0	0	0	0	0		.858	9.45
Kendrick, Kyle, Phi	ER	R	2	1	0	1	0.9	0	0		0 - 0	0 - 0	0 - 0	2	0	0	0	0		.724	0.00
Oswalt, Roy, Hou-Phi	ER	R	1	1	0	0	0.9	0	0		0 - 0	0 - 0	0 - 0	0	0	0	0	0		1.500	9.00
Blanton, Joe, Phi	ER	R	1	1	0	0	0.9	0	0		0 - 0	0 - 0	0 - 0	0	0	0	0	0		1.881	18.00
Pittsburgh Pirates																					
Hanrahan, Joel, Pit	SU	R	72	1	19	9	1.2	9	3	.33	4 - 5	2 - 5	0 - 0	53	1	6	10	18	.86	.649	3.62
Meek, Evan, Pit	SU	R	70	8	16	13	1.3	21	7	.33	3 - 4	1 - 5	0 - 1	49	1	4	10	15	.76	.546	2.14
Ledezma, Wil, Pit	LT	L	27	4	5	1	0.6	8	2	.25	0 - 0	0 - 0	0 - 0	18	0	0	0	3	1.00	.807	6.86
Thomas, Justin, Pit	LT	L	12	3	3	2	0.1	5	3	.60	0 - 0	0 - 0	0 - 0	5	0	0	0	0		1.026	6.23
Gallagher, Sean, SD-Pit	LM	R	46	20	10	17	0.5	35	16	.46	0 - 0	0 - 0	0 - 0	21	0	0	0	3	1.00	.829	5.77
McCutchen, Daniel, Pit	LM	R	19	11	2	7	0.7	8	2	.25	0 - 0	0 - 0	0 - 0	10	0	0	0	0		.877	5.47
Park, Chan Ho, NYY-Pit	UR	R	53	9	10	14	0.6	15	9	.60	0 - 1	0 - 2	0 - 0	25	0	0	3	1	.25	.734	4.66
Donnelly, Brendan, Pit	UR	R	38	3	8	4	1.0	8	2	.25	0 - 0	0 - 0	0 - 0	23	0	0	0	9	1.00	.804	5.58
Leroux, Chris, Fla-Pit	UR	R	23	6	6	5	0.9	13	4	.31	0 - 0	0 - 1	0 - 1	13	0	0	2	3	.60	.866	6.75
Resop, Chris, Atl-Pit	UR	R	23	2	6	5	0.7	9	4	.44	0 - 0	0 - 0	0 - 0	16	0	0	0	5	1.00	.631	3.86
Jackson, Steven, Pit	UR	R	11	5	1	2	0.4	9	2	.22	0 - 0	0 - 0	0 - 0	5	0	0	0	0		1.043	8.74
Martinez, Joe, SF-Pit	UR	R	8	4	1	6	0.5	2	1	.50	0 - 0	0 - 0	0 - 0	3	0	0	0	0		.846	3.38
Burres, Brian, Pit	UR	L	7	3	2	3	0.9	4	2	.50	0 - 0	0 - 0	0 - 0	3	0	0	0	0		1.104	8.44
Karstens, Jeff, Pit	UR	R	7	4	1	5	0.9	4	1	.25	0 - 0	0 - 0	0 - 0	1	0	0	0	0		.915	5.87
Bass, Brian, Pit	UR	R	4	4	0	3	0.2	1	1	1.00	0 - 0	0 - 0	0 - 0	0	0	0	0	0		.902	12.27
McDonald, James, LAD-Pit	UR	R	3	2	1	1	1.1	2	1	.50	0 - 0	0 - 0	0 - 0	1	0	0	0	1	1.00	.792	10.13
Penn, Hayden, Pit	UR	R	3	1	1	1	0.3	1	1	1.00	0 - 0	0 - 0	0 - 0	1	0	0	0	0		1.534	30.86
Eveland, Dana, Tor-Pit	UR	L	2	1	0	2	0.9	3	1	.33	0 - 0	0 - 0	0 - 0	1	0	0	0	0		.981	11.57
Lincoln, Brad, Pit	UR	R	2	0	0	1	1.0	0	0		0 - 0	0 - 0	0 - 0	1	0	0	0	0		.762	9.00
San Diego Padres																					
Bell, Heath, SD	CL	R	67	0	27	8	2.1	9	0	.00	28 - 28	14 - 17	5 - 5	52	0	47	50	0	.94	.585	1.93
Gregerson, Luke, SD	SU	R	80	9	23	4	1.3	38	7	.18	1 - 1	1 - 5	0 - 1	59	1	2	7	40	.89	.524	3.22
Adams, Mike, SD	SU	R	70	0	24	6	1.6	7	4	.57	0 - 1	0 - 2	0 - 1	57	1	0	4	38	.90	.526	1.76
Thatcher, Joe, SD	LT	L	65	17	22	1	0.9	67	13	.19	0 - 0	0 - 0	0 - 0	53	0	0	0	11	1.00	.465	1.29
Ramos, Cesar, SD	LT	L	14	3	4	2	0.5	7	2	.29	0 - 0	0 - 0	0 - 0	9	0	0	0	2	1.00	1.049	11.88
Mujica, Edward, SD	UR	R	59	17	10	13	0.5	17	5	.29	0 - 1	0 - 0	0 - 0	40	0	0	1	4	.80	.684	3.62
Webb, Ryan, SD	UR	R	54	18	8	11	0.9	21	8	.38	0 - 0	0 - 1	0 - 1	38	1	0	2	9	.82	.680	2.90
Frieri, Ernesto, SD	UR	R	33	6	9	5	0.6	12	4	.33	0 - 0	0 - 0	0 - 0	26	0	0	0	7	1.00	.553	1.71
Stauffer, Tim, SD	UR	R	25	6	1	12	0.8	10	3	.30	0 - 0	0 - 0	0 - 0	19	0	0	0	0		.622	1.87

Relief Pitching

Pitcher	Pos	T	Rel G	Early Entry	Cons Days	Long	Lev Ind	#	Scrd	Pct	Easy	Reg	Tough	Clean	BS Win	Saves	Opps	Holds	Sv/Hld Pct	Opp OPS	Rel ERA
Russell, Adam, SD	UR	R	12	3	3	4	0.1	7	3	.43	0 - 0	0 - 0	0 - 0	9	0	0	0	0		.602	4.02
Perdomo, Luis, SD	UR	R	1	0	0	0	0.0	0	0		0 - 0	0 - 0	0 - 0	0	0	0	0	0		1.250	9.00
Luebke, Cory, SD	UR	L	1	0	0	1	0.8	2	1	.50	0 - 0	0 - 0	0 - 0	0	0	0	0	0		.222	0.00
Correia, Kevin, SD	ER	R	2	2	0	1	0.9	2	1	.50	0 - 0	0 - 0	0 - 0	0	0	0	0	0		.744	1.93
LeBlanc, Wade, SD	ER	L	1	1	0	1	0.9	0	0		0 - 0	0 - 0	0 - 0	0	0	0	0	0		1.126	9.00
San Francisco Giants																					
Wilson, Brian, SF	CL	R	70	0	23	12	2.1	30	4	.13	26 - 28	15 - 16	7 - 9	58	1	48	53	0	.91	.597	1.81
Romo, Sergio, SF	SU	R	68	6	16	2	1.2	46	14	.30	0 - 1	0 - 0	0 - 3	50	1	0	4	21	.84	.599	2.18
Lopez, Javier, Pit-SF	LT	L	77	14	26	3	0.8	57	9	.16	0 - 0	0 - 0	0 - 0	58	0	0	0	11	1.00	.636	2.34
Affeldt, Jeremy, SF	LT	L	53	2	11	5	1.2	22	8	.36	3 - 3	1 - 2	0 - 2	30	3	4	7	7	.79	.795	4.14
Runzler, Dan, SF	LT	L	41	11	8	5	0.8	31	9	.29	0 - 0	0 - 0	0 - 0	26	0	0	0	5	1.00	.685	3.03
Bautista, Denny, SF	LM	R	31	12	7	10	0.8	15	4	.27	0 - 0	0 - 0	0 - 1	22	1	0	1	0	.00	.685	3.74
Ramirez, Ramon, Bos-SF	UR	R	69	12	16	11	0.7	36	7	.19	2 - 2	1 - 1	0 - 0	49	0	3	3	6	.63	.631	2.99
Ray, Chris, Tex-SF	UR	R	63	12	15	4	0.9	35	12	.34	0 - 1	0 - 1	2 - 2	42	0	2	4	9	.85	.701	3.72
Mota, Guillermo, SF	UR	R	56	10	11	5	0.8	27	7	.26	1 - 2	0 - 0	0 - 1	33	0	1	3	8	.82	.727	4.33
Casilla, Santiago, SF	UR	R	52	18	10	15	1.3	47	6	.13	0 - 1	0 - 0	2 - 2	40	0	2	3	11	.93	.600	1.95
Medders, Brandon, SF	UR	R	14	3	4	3	0.4	8	4	.50	0 - 0	0 - 0	0 - 0	7	0	0	0	0		1.080	7.20
Joaquin, Waldis, SF	UR	R	4	1	1	2	0.4	0	0		0 - 0	0 - 0	0 - 0	1	0	0	0	1	1.00	.927	9.64
Wellemeyer, Todd, SF	UR	R	2	2	0	1	0.9	0	0		0 - 0	0 - 0	0 - 0	1	0	0	0	0		.838	3.00
Zito, Barry, SF	ER	L	1	0	0	1	1.1	0	0		0 - 0	0 - 0	0 - 0	0	0	0	0	0		1.238	9.00
Sanchez, Jonathan, SF	ER	L	1	0	0	0	1.0	2	1	.50	0 - 0	0 - 0	0 - 0	0	0	0	0	1	1.00	.500	0.00
Seattle Mariners																					
Aardsma, David, Sea	CL	R	53	0	9	5	2.4	4	0	.00	14 - 15	16 - 20	1 - 1	43	0	31	36	0	.86	.631	3.44
League, Brandon, Sea	SU	R	70	3	14	9	1.5	26	9	.35	2 - 3	2 - 5	2 - 4	46	1	6	12	13	.76	.630	3.42
Olson, Garrett, Sea	LT	L	35	5	5	5	0.8	14	3	.21	0 - 0	0 - 0	1 - 1	23	0	1	1	1	1.00	.785	4.54
Seddon, Chris, Sea	LT	L	14	7	2	6	0.3	8	2	.25	0 - 0	0 - 0	0 - 0	5	0	0	0	0		.826	5.64
Wright, Jamey, Clo Sea	UR	R	46	11	9	14	0.9	35	9	.26	0 - 0	0 - 0	0 - 1	23	0	0	1	9	.90	.705	4.17
White, Sean, Sea	UR	R	38	4	5	2	0.8	26	10	.38	0 - 0	0 - 0	0 - 3	21	0	0	3	5	.63	.891	5.24
Sweeney, Brian, Sea	UR	R	24	9	4	7	0.6	12	5	.42	0 - 0	0 - 0	0 - 1	10	0	0	1	1	.50	.644	3.16
Kelley, Shawn, Sea	UR	R	22	5	4	6	0.9	14	5	.36	0 - 0	0 - 0	0 - 0	15	0	0	0	3	1.00	.841	3.96
Colome, Jesus, Sea	UR	R	12	6	0	6	0.5	8	4	.50	0 - 0	0 - 0	0 - 0	3	0	0	0	0		.722	5.29
Cordero, Chad, Sea	UR	R	9	3	1	1	0.7	7	4	.57	0 - 0	0 - 0	0 - 0	4	0	0	0	0		.994	6.52
Rowland-Smith, Ryan, Sea	UR	L	7	2	0	2	0.9	3	1	.33	0 - 0	0 - 0	0 - 0	3	0	0	0	0		.968	4.50
Cortes, Dan, Sea	UR	R	4	0	0	2	1.6	2	2	1.00	0 - 0	0 - 1	0 - 0	2	0	0	1	0	.00	.471	3.38
Snell, Ian, Sea	UR	R	4	4	0	4	0.8	2	1	.50	0 - 0	0 - 0	0 - 0	0	0	0	0	0		.903	7.36
Varvaro, Anthony, Sea	UR	R	4	1	0	2	0.7	0	0		0 - 0	0 - 0	0 - 0	1	0	0	0	0		1.167	11.25
French, Luke, Sea	UR	L	3	1	0	2	0.0	1	1	1.00	0 - 0	0 - 0	0 - 0	0	0	0	0	0		.946	5.19
Pauley, David, Sea	ER	R	4	2	0	1	1.0	0	0		0 - 0	0 - 0	0 - 0	4	0	0	0	0		.594	0.00
St Louis Cardinals																					
Franklin, Ryan, StL	CL	R	59	0	11	8	1.6	16	4	.25	15 - 15	11 - 12	1 - 2	44	1	27	29	0	.93	.661	3.46
McClellan, Kyle, StL	SU	R	68	8	13	12	1.2	18	6	.33	2 - 2	0 - 0	0 - 1	49	0	2	3	19	.95	.621	2.27
Reyes, Dennys, StL	LT	L	59	6	12	0	0.9	41	12	.29	0 - 0	0 - 1	1 - 3	43	0	1	4	6	.70	.690	3.55
Miller, Trever, StL	LT	L	57	10	14	1	1.1	41	7	.17	0 - 0	0 - 1	0 - 0	39	0	0	1	11	.92	.640	4.00
MacLane, Evan, StL	LT	L	2	0	0	0	0.7	0	0		0 - 0	0 - 0	0 - 0	1	0	0	0	0		1.833	9.00
Boggs, Mitchell, StL	UR	R	61	17	11	13	0.8	33	10	.30	0 - 0	0 - 0	0 - 0	40	0	0	0	6	1.00	.696	3.61
Motte, Jason, StL	UR	R	56	6	11	4	1.3	34	9	.26	0 - 0	1 - 2	1 - 1	41	0	2	3	12	.93	.618	2.24
Hawksworth, Blake, StL	UR	R	37	11	4	12	0.8	11	5	.45	0 - 0	0 - 0	0 - 0	18	0	0	0	4	1.00	.822	4.25
Salas, Fernando, StL	UR	R	27	7	2	7	0.5	8	4	.50	0 - 0	0 - 1	0 - 0	16	0	0	1	1	.50	.748	3.52
MacDougal, Mike, StL	UR	R	17	2	2	5	0.4	8	6	.75	0 - 0	0 - 0	0 - 1	10	0	0	1	0	.00	.844	7.23
Suppan, Jeff, Mil-StL	UR	R	15	3	2	6	0.8	9	5	.56	0 - 0	0 - 0	0 - 0	5	0	0	0	0		.943	7.40
Walters, P.J., StL	UR	R	4	3	0	3	0.6	0	0		0 - 0	0 - 0	0 - 0	1	0	0	0	0		.838	8.36
Ottavino, Adam, StL	UR	R	2	2	0	2	0.5	0	0		0 - 0	0 - 0	0 - 0	0	0	0	0	0		1.088	10.13
Miles, Aaron, StL	ER	R	2	0	0	0	0.0	0	0		0 - 0	0 - 0	0 - 0	2	0	0	0	0		.625	0.00
Mather, Joe, StL	ER	R	1	0	0	1	2.7	0	0		0 - 0	0 - 0	0 - 0	0	0	0	0	0		.945	9.00
Tampa Bay Rays																					
Qualls, Chad, Ari-TB	CL	R	70	7	17	6	1.3	32	12	.38	7 - 9	4 - 7	1 - 3	39	1	12	19	11	.77	.894	7.32
Soriano, Rafael, TB	CL	R	64	0	24	4	1.9	11	6	.55	28 - 29	17 - 18	0 - 1	48	0	45	48	0	.94	.509	1.73
Benoit, Joaquin, TB	SU	R	63	1	19	4	1.2	23	2	.09	1 - 1	0 - 2	0 - 1	54	1	1	4	25	.90	.454	1.34
Balfour, Grant, TB	SU	R	57	9	13	6	1.2	31	8	.26	0 - 0	0 - 0	0 - 0	41	0	0	1	16	.94	.619	2.28
Choate, Randy, TB	LT	L	85	14	30	2	1.0	66	15	.23	0 - 0	0 - 1	0 - 1	60	0	0	2	18	.90	.686	4.23
McGee, Jake, TB	LT	L	8	3	1	0	0.5	5	1	.20	0 - 0	0 - 0	0 - 0	7	0	0	0	0		.426	1.80
Wheeler, Dan, TB	UR	R	64	10	16	0	1.1	33	6	.18	0 - 1	3 - 3	0 - 2	46	0	3	6	9	.80	.681	3.35
Cormier, Lance, TB	UR	R	60	10	17	10	0.8	34	8	.24	0 - 0	0 - 0	0 - 0	41	0	0	0	4	1.00	.810	3.92
Sonnanstine, Andy, TB	UR	R	37	11	7	15	0.5	17	10	.59	0 - 0	0 - 0	0 - 1	19	0	1	1	0	1.00	.792	4.71
Ekstrom, Mike, TB	UR	R	15	2	2	3	0.2	4	0	.00	0 - 0	0 - 0	0 - 0	12	0	0	0	0		.570	3.31
Hellickson, Jeremy, TB	UR	R	6	5	0	3	1.0	3	2	.67	0 - 0	0 - 0	0 - 1	1	0	0	1	0	.00	1.064	7.20
Thayer, Dale, TB	UR	R	1	1	0	1	0.4	0	0		0 - 0	0 - 0	0 - 0	0	0	0	0	0		1.385	27.00

Relief Pitching

Pitcher	Pos	T	Usage					Inherited Runners			Saves			Relief Results							
			Rel G	Early Entry	Cons Days	Long	Lev Ind	#	Scrd	Pct	Easy	Reg	Tough	Clean	BS Win	Saves	Opps	Holds	Sv/Hld Pct	Opp OPS	Rel ERA
Price, David, TB	ER	L	1	1	0	0	1.0	0	0		0-0	0-0	0-0	1	0	0	0	0		.000	0.00
Garza, Matt, TB	ER	R	1	0	0	0	0.9	1	1	1.00	1-1	0-0	0-0	0	0	1	1	0	1.00	1.167	0.00
Niemann, Jeff, TB	ER	R	1	0	0	0	1.0	0	0		0-0	0-0	0-0	1	0	0	0	0		.000	0.00
Shields, James, TB	ER	R	1	0	0	0	1.0	0	0		0-0	0-0	0-0	1	0	0	0	0		.250	0.00
Texas Rangers																					
Feliz, Neftali, Tex	CL	R	70	0	17	2	1.7	16	1	.06	19-20	20-21	1-2	58	1	40	43	3	.93	.516	2.73
O'Day, Darren, Tex	SU	R	72	15	28	1	1.1	50	13	.26	0-0	0-1	0-1	52	2	0	2	22	.92	.548	2.03
Francisco, Frank, Tex	SU	R	56	0	14	4	1.5	13	2	.15	2-3	0-2	0-1	40	0	2	6	15	.81	.681	3.76
Oliver, Darren, Tex	LT	L	64	6	11	7	1.3	41	9	.22	0-0	1-3	0-1	44	0	1	4	14	.83	.654	2.48
Harrison, Matt, Tex	LT	L	31	10	2	12	1.0	21	10	.48	0-0	2-3	0-0	15	0	2	3	3	.83	.764	4.26
Kirkman, Michael, Tex	LT	L	14	7	4	2	0.8	11	1	.09	0-0	0-1	0-0	11	0	0	1	2	.67	.458	1.65
Rapada, Clay, Tex	LT	L	13	3	6	1	0.8	12	1	.08	0-1	0-0	0-0	11	0	0	1	3	.75	.708	4.00
Nippert, Dustin, Tex	LM	R	36	19	4	13	1.1	21	6	.29	0-0	0-0	0-1	19	0	0	1	5	.83	.797	3.91
Ogando, Alexi, Tex	UR	R	44	6	11	5	1.0	32	12	.38	0-0	0-0	0-2	29	0	0	2	7	.78	.554	1.30
Strop, Pedro, Tex	UR	R	15	4	5	2	0.9	12	6	.50	0-0	0-0	0-0	7	0	0	0	1	1.00	1.109	10.13
Lowe, Mark, Sea-Tex	UR	R	14	0	3	1	1.4	2	0	.00	0-0	0-0	0-0	8	0	0	0	4	1.00	.893	5.40
Mathis, Doug, Tex	UR	R	13	5	1	6	0.4	4	3	.75	0-0	0-0	0-0	7	0	0	0	0		1.017	6.04
Feldman, Scott, Tex	UR	R	7	5	0	5	0.9	4	1	.25	0-0	0-0	0-0	1	0	0	0	0		.742	4.61
Holland, Derek, Tex	UR	L	4	3	0	3	1.0	3	0	.00	0-0	0-0	0-0	1	0	0	0	1	1.00	.661	2.53
Moscoso, Guillermo, Tex	UR	R	1	0	0	1	0.1	0	0		0-0	0-0	0-0	0	0	0	0	0		1.464	27.00
Harden, Rich, Tex	ER	R	2	2	0	1	1.0	2	0	.00	0-0	0-0	0-0	0	0	0	0	0		.967	13.50
Hunter, Tommy, Tex	ER	R	1	1	0	0	0.9	1	0	.00	0-0	0-0	0-0	1	0	0	0	0		.000	0.00
Toronto Blue Jays																					
Gregg, Kevin, Tor	CL	R	63	0	16	6	2.1	18	5	.28	20-22	16-20	1-1	43	0	37	43	3	.87	.712	3.51
Frasor, Jason, Tor	SU	R	69	6	10	8	1.2	31	6	.19	3-3	1-3	0-2	49	0	4	8	14	.82	.691	3.68
Downs, Scott, Tor	SU	L	67	1	15	3	1.5	24	9	.38	0-0	0-1	0-1	51	0	0	2	26	.93	.584	2.64
Purcey, David, Tor	LT	L	33	5	6	7	0.5	19	3	.16	0-0	1-1	0-0	25	0	1	1	3	1.00	.629	3.71
Carlson, Jesse, Tor	LT	L	20	4	6	2	0.8	19	2	.11	0-0	0-0	0-1	15	0	1	1	2	1.00	.808	4.61
Lewis, Rommie, Tor	LT	L	14	5	1	6	0.4	13	4	.31	0-0	0-0	0-0	7	0	0	0	0		.841	6.75
Mills, Brad, Tor	LT	L	4	3	0	2	0.8	2	0	.00	0-0	0-0	0-0	2	0	0	0	1	1.00	.693	6.43
Tallet, Brian, Tor	LM	L	29	21	2	19	0.8	22	11	.50	0-0	0-1	0-1	8	0	0	2	1	.33	.927	6.84
Camp, Shawn, Tor	UR	R	70	14	14	8	1.2	38	10	.26	0-0	1-2	1-2	48	0	2	4	13	.88	.728	2.99
Janssen, Casey, Tor	UR	R	56	14	6	17	0.4	31	15	.48	0-0	0-0	0-0	31	0	0	0	2	1.00	.748	3.67
Roenicke, Josh, Tor	UR	R	16	6	1	6	0.5	11	3	.27	0-0	0-0	0-0	7	0	0	0	2	1.00	.718	5.68
Buchholz, Taylor, Col-Tor	UR	R	9	3	0	2	0.2	0	0		0-0	0-0	0-0	6	0	0	0	0		.810	3.75
Accardo, Jeremy, Tor	UR	R	5	2	0	4	0.9	6	6	1.00	0-0	0-0	0-0	0	0	0	0	0		1.004	8.10
Ray, Robert, Tor	UR	R	3	3	0	2	0.6	1	0	.00	0-0	0-0	0-0	2	0	0	0	0		.774	2.45
Valdez, Merkin, Tor	UR	R	2	1	0	1	0.1	2	0	.00	0-0	0-0	0-0	1	0	0	0	0		.889	20.25
Rzepczynski, Marc, Tor	UR	L	2	0	0	0	1.0	0	0		0-0	0-0	0-0	2	0	0	0	2	1.00	.650	0.00
Washington Nationals																					
Clippard, Tyler, Was	SU	R	78	10	25	18	1.4	46	18	.39	1-3	0-3	0-5	53	5	1	11	23	.71	.646	3.07
Burnett, Sean, Was	SU	L	73	10	18	8	1.3	49	13	.27	0-0	2-2	1-2	51	0	3	4	20	.96	.581	2.14
Storen, Drew, Was	SU	R	54	9	7	9	1.3	27	4	.15	4-5	1-2	0-0	34	0	5	7	10	.88	.655	3.58
Slaten, Doug, Was	LT	L	49	14	11	3	0.7	26	4	.15	0-0	0-0	0-0	34	0	0	0	4	1.00	.626	3.10
English, Jesse, Was	LT	L	7	4	0	2	0.6	4	1	.25	0-0	0-0	0-0	4	0	0	0	0		.783	3.86
Batista, Miguel, Was	LM	R	57	25	12	15	0.7	48	19	.40	1-1	1-1	0-0	25	0	2	2	1	1.00	.707	3.94
Walker, Tyler, Was	LM	R	24	12	2	8	0.4	20	13	.65	0-0	0-0	0-1	15	0	0	1	1	.50	.742	3.57
Stammen, Craig, Was	LM	R	16	9	1	7	0.9	11	5	.45	0-0	0-0	0-0	8	0	0	0	1	1.00	.842	5.48
Peralta, Joel, Was	UR	R	39	13	8	9	0.7	12	3	.25	0-0	0-0	0-2	29	0	0	2	9	.82	.521	2.02
Bruney, Brian, Was	UR	R	19	1	1	3	1.2	3	0	.00	0-0	0-0	0-0	10	0	0	0	3	1.00	.867	7.64
Balester, Collin, Was	UR	R	17	4	2	3	0.5	6	2	.33	0-0	0-0	0-0	12	0	0	0	0		.633	2.57
Bisenius, Joe, Was	UR	R	5	0	0	2	0.1	0	0		0-0	0-0	0-0	3	0	0	0	0		1.012	9.64
Bergmann, Jason, Was	UR	R	4	1	0	1	0.8	4	3	.75	0-0	0-0	0-0	1	0	0	0	1	1.00	1.364	15.43
Detwiler, Ross, Was	UR	L	3	2	0	2	0.9	0	0		0-0	0-0	0-0	3	0	0	0	0		.396	0.00
Olsen, Scott, Was	ER	L	2	2	0	2	1.0	0	0		0-0	0-0	0-0	1	0	0	0	0		.554	1.50

Pitchers Hitting, Fielding & Holding Runners, and Hitters Pitching

Pitchers are notoriously poor hitters and this section displays the carnage. Many pitchers have batting averages well below their weight (and sometimes below their IQ), especially American League pitchers who get the opportunity to hit through interleague play. 2010 and career hitting statistics for each pitcher are printed in this section.

This section also includes 2010 fielding statistics for pitchers and data on how well they held runners last season. Like the Fielding section, we added the number of runs each pitcher saved based on their defense alone. A pitcher's Runs Saved (RS) is the sum of Plus/Minus Runs Saved to evaluate range and Stolen Base Runs Saved, which measures the ability to control the running game.

The final piece of this section is Hitters Pitching. There are several instances each season when a position player toes the rubber and the results are reported here. Hitters didn't pitch too badly this year with a respectable 4.50 ERA in 10 innings. Career statistics are listed for all active position players who have pitched, as well as any 2010 pitching statistics that they may have accrued.

Pitchers Hitting, Fielding and Holding Runners

Pitcher	T	2010 Hitting						Career Hitting										2010 Fielding and Holding Runners											
		Avg	AB	H	HR	RBI	SH	Avg	AB	H	2B	3B	HR	RBI	BB	SO	SH	Inn	PO	A	E	DP	Pct	SBA	CS	PCS	PPO	CS%	RS
Aardsma,David, Sea	R	-	0	0	0	0	0	.000	3	0	0	0	0	0	0	1	1	49.2	2	3	1	0	.833	3	1	0	0	.33	0
Abad,Fernando, Hou	L	.000	1	0	0	0	0	.000	1	0	0	0	0	0	0	1	0	19.0	0	3	0	0	1.000	0	0	0	0	-	0
Accardo,Jeremy, Tor	R	-	0	0	0	0	0	.143	7	1	0	0	0	0	0	1	0	6.2	0	1	0	0	1.000	1	0	0	0	.00	-1
Aceves,Alfredo, NYY	R	-	0	0	0	0	0	.000	2	0	0	0	0	0	0	1	0	12.0	0	2	0	0	1.000	3	0	0	0	.00	1
Acosta,Manny, NYM	R	-	0	0	0	0	0	.000	6	0	0	0	0	0	1	4	0	39.2	2	3	0	1	1.000	5	3	0	0	.60	0
Adams,Mike, SD	R	-	0	0	0	0	0	.000	2	0	0	0	0	0	0	0	0	66.2	4	6	0		1.000	7	1	0	0	.14	-2
Affeldt,Jeremy, SF	L	.000	1	0	0	0	0	.231	13	3	0	0	0	2	1	3	0	50.0	3	15	3	0	.857	4	2	0	0	.50	0
Albaladejo,J, NYY	R	-	0	0	0	0	0	-	0	0	0	0	0	0	0	0	0	11.1	0	2	0	0	1.000	3	1	0	0	.33	1
Albers,Matt, Bal	R	-	0	0	0	0	0	.059	34	2	0	0	0	0		21	3	75.2	6	15	1	3	.955	10	2	0	0	.20	-2
Ambriz,Hector, Cle	R	-	0	0	0	0	0	.000	0	0	0	0	0	0	0	0	0	48.1	1	7	0	0	1.000	4	0	0	1	.00	-1
Anderson,Brett, Oak	L	-	0	0	0	0	0	.000	3	0	0	0	0	0	0	2	0	112.1	4	31	1	1	.972	13	5	4	0	.38	2
Arrieta,Jake, Bal	R	.000	3	0	0	0	0	.000	3	0	0	0	0	0	1	1	0	100.1	8	13	2	1	.913	12	1	0	2	.08	1
Arroyo,Bronson, Cin	R	.147	68	10	1	8	6	.131	397	52	13	0	5	24	12	173	48	215.2	18	31	0	5	1.000	8	2	0	0	.25	6
Atchison,Scott, Bos	R	-	0	0	0	0	0	.000	2	0	0	0	0	0	0	1	0	60.0	7	6	0	1	1.000	8	2	0	0	.25	-1
Atilano,Luis, Was	R	.040	25	1	0	0	2	.040	25	1	0	0	0	0	0	10	2	85.2	10	14	2	2	.923	4	3	0	0	.75	2
Atkins,Mitch, ChC	R	.000	2	0	0	0	0	.000	2	0	0	0	0	0	0	1	0	10.0	0	2	0	0	1.000	1	1	0	0	1.00	0
Axford,John, Mil	R	-	0	0	0	0	0	-	0	0	0	0	0	0	0	0	0	58.0	4	5	0	2	1.000	2	0	0	0	.00	-1
Badenhop,Burke, Fla	R	.000	1	0	0	0	0	.043	23	1	0	0	0	1	0	12	5	67.2	1	21	1	2	.957	3	2	0	0	.67	3
Baez,Danys, Phi	R	-	0	0	0	0	0	.250	4	1	0	0	0	0	0	0	0	47.2	0	17	0	0	1.000	6	1	0	0	.17	4
Bailey,Andrew, Oak	R	-	0	0	0	0	0	-	0	0	0	0	0	0	0	0	0	49.0	4	5	0	0	1.000	4	1	0	0	.25	1
Bailey,Homer, Cin	R	.212	33	7	0	2	4	.152	92	14	2	0	0	6	2	42	12	109.0	15	6	1	1	.955	16	6	0	1	.38	-2
Baker,Scott, Min	R	.000	3	0	0	0	1	.050	20	1	0	0	0	0	0	8	4	170.1	15	13	1	1	.966	9	6	0	1	.67	3
Balester,Collin, Was	R	-	0	0	0	0	0	.174	23	4	0	0	0	1	2	10	10	21.0	0	2	0	0	1.000	1	1	0	0	1.00	0
Balfour,Grant, TB	R	-	0	0	0	0	0	.000	1	0	0	0	0	0	0	1	0	55.1	2	2	0		1.000	4	2	0	0	.50	0
Banks,Josh, Hou	R	-	0	0	0	0	0	.111	27	3	0	0	0	0	4	6	2	4.0	0	1	0	0	1.000	1	0	0	0	.00	0
Bannister,Brian, KC	R	.200	5	1	0	1	1	.276	29	8	4	0	0	4	0	9	3	127.2	16	19	1	1	.972	22	7	0	1	.32	1
Bard,Daniel, Bos	R	-	0	0	0	0	0	-	0	0	0	0	0	0	0	0	0	74.2	7	7	2	1	.875	9	1	0	0	.11	-2
Bass,Brian, Pit	R	.000	1	0	0	0	0	.000	2	0	0	0	0	0	0	1	0	7.1	0	1	0	0	1.000	2	0	0	0	.00	0
Bastardo,Antonio, Phi	L	-	0	0	0	0	0	.000	6	0	0	0	0	0	0	3	1	18.2	0	2	0	0	1.000	0	0	0	0	-	0
Batista,Miguel, Was	R	.125	8	1	0	0	1	.094	299	28	5	0	2	9	11	167	25	82.2	5	9	0	1	1.000	11	3	0	0	.27	0
Bautista,Denny, SF	R	1.000	1	1	0	1	0	.250	8	2	0	0	0	2	0	4	0	33.2	1	4	0		1.000	5	0	0	0	.00	-1
Beachy,Brandon, Atl	R	.200	5	1	0	0	0	.200	5	1	0	0	0	0	0	4	0	15.0	4	0	0		1.000	2	1	0	0	.50	0
Beckett,Josh, Bos	R	-	0	0	0	0	0	.148	216	32	9	0	3	16	10	80	26	127.2	9	20	1	0	.967	19	1	0	0	.05	0
Beimel,Joe, Col	L	.000	1	0	0	0	0	.227	44	10	1	0	0	1	2	18	6	45.0	7	9	0		1.000	3	0	0	3	.00	-1
Belisario,Ronald, LAD	R	-	0	0	0	0	0	.000	4	0	0	0	0	0	0	3	0	55.1	4	9	0	0	1.000	2	0	0	0	.00	1
Belisle,Matt, Col	R	.250	4	1	0	2	2	.077	78	6	2	0	0	3	3	45	17	92.0	4	10	2	2	.875	3	1	0	0	.33	1
Bell,Heath, SD	R	.000	1	0	0	0	0	.000	6	0	0	0	0	0	0	2	1	70.0	3	4	0		1.000	6	3	0	0	.50	0
Bell,Trevor, LAA	R	.000	1	0	0	0	0	.000	1	0	0	0	0	0	0	1	0	61.0	7	5	1	1	.923	12	2	0	0	.17	0
Beltre,Omar, Tex	R	-	0	0	0	0	0	-	0	0	0	0	0	0	0	0	0	7.0	0	3	0	0	1.000	3	0	0	1	.00	-1
Benoit,Joaquin, TB	R	-	0	0	0	0	0	.000	9	0	0	0	0	0	0	4	0	60.1	4	0	0		1.000	4	2	1	0	.50	1
Benson,Kris, Ari	R	.200	5	1	0	0	1	.131	321	42	7	0	1	22	15	127	47	14.0	1	1	0	0	1.000	4	0	0	0	.00	-1
Berg,Justin, ChC	R	-	0	0	0	0	0	-	0	0	0	0	0	0	0	0	0	40.0	4	4	0	0	1.000	1	1	0	1	1.00	-1
Bergesen,Brad, Bal	R	.333	3	1	0	0	0	.250	8	2	0	0	0	0	0	0	2	170.0	11	22	0	3	1.000	12	3	0	0	.25	5
Bergmann,Jason, Was	R	-	0	0	0	0	0	.067	90	6	0	0	0		3	39	11	2.1	0	0	0	0	-	0	0	0	0	-	0
Berken,Jason, Bal	R	-	0	0	0	0	0	.000	1	0	0	0	0	0	0	1	0	62.1	3	4	0		1.000	4	2	0	1	.50	-1
Betancourt,Rafael, Col	R	-	0	0	0	0	0	.000	1	0	0	0	0	0	0	1	0	62.1	3	4	0	0	1.000	10	2	0	0	.20	-1
Billingsley,Chad, LAD	R	.145	62	9	0	3	6	.129	241	31	4	0	1	14	15	121	23	191.2	12	20	1	1	.970	15	5	1	0	.33	0
Bisenius,Joe, Was	R	-	0	0	0	0	0	-	0	0	0	0	0	0	0	0	0	4.2	0	0	1	0	.000	2	0	0	0	.00	0
Blackburn,Nick, Min	R	.000	1	0	0	0	0	.125	8	1	0	0	0	0			2	161.0	11	25	2	4	.947	9	4	0	1	.44	3
Blanton,Joe, Phi	R	.119	59	7	0	1	5	.114	140	16	0	0	0	3	5	60	23	175.2	6	25	2	0	.939	13	2	0	2	.15	-1
Blevins,Jerry, Oak	L	-	0	0	0	0	0	-	0	0	0	0	0	0	0	0	0	48.2	2	5	2	0	.778	2	1	1	0	.50	-2
Boggs,Mitchell, StL	R	.000	3	0	0	0	0	.040	25	1	1	0	0	0	0	12	3	67.1	4	7	1	0	.917	4	2	0	0	.50	1
Bonderman,Jeremy, Det	R	.000	2	0	0	0	0	.036	28	1	0	0	0	0	0	16	1	171.0	12	10	3	4	.880	19	7	0	0	.37	-5
Bonine,Eddie, Det	R	-	0	0	0	0	0	.000	2	0	0	0	0	0	0	0	0	68.0	4	6	0	3	1.000	4	2	0	0	.50	-1
Bonser,Boof, Bos-Oak	R	-	0	0	0	0	0	.000	6	0	0	0	0	0	0	1	3	25.0	3	6	0	0	1.000	5	1	0	0	.20	0
Bowden,Michael, Bos	R	-	0	0	0	0	0	-	0	0	0	0	0	0	0	0	0	15.1	0	1	1	0	.500	5	0	0	0	.00	-1
Bowers,Cedrick, Oak	L	-	0	0	0	0	0	-	0	0	0	0	0	1	0	0	0	14.0	1	0	0	0	1.000	1	1	0	1	1.00	0
Boyer,Blaine, Ari	R	.000	2	0	0	0	0	.000	8	0	0	0	0	0	0	6	1	57.0	4	13	1	1	.944	4	0	0	0	.00	0
Braddock,Zach, Mil	L	-	0	0	0	0	0	-	0	0	0	0	0	0	0	0	0	33.2	0	2	0	0	1.000	3	0	0	0	.00	0
Braden,Dallas, Oak	L	.000	1	0	0	0	1	.000	4	0	0	0	0	0	0	2	2	192.2	12	32	2	4	.957	3	2	0	8	.67	7
Bray,Bill, Cin	L	-	0	0	0	0	0	.000	1	0	0	0	0	0	0	1	0	28.1	2	2	1	0	.800	3	0	0	0	.00	0
Breslow,Craig, Oak	L	-	0	0	0	0	0	.000	1	0	0	0	0	0	0	0	0	74.2	2	2	1	0	.800	5	1	1	0	.20	-2
Broxton,Jonathan, LAD	R	-	0	0	0	0	0	.000	5	0	0	0	0	0	2	2	1	62.1	3	7	0	0	1.000	10	4	1	0	.40	0
Bruney,Brian, Was	R	-	0	0	0	0	0	.000	1	0	0	0	0	0	0	0	0	17.2	1	2	1	0	.750	1	0	0	0	.00	1
Buchholz,Clay, Bos	R	1.000	1	1	0	0	0	1.000	1	1	0	0	0	0	0	0	0	173.2	21	24	2	1	.957	14	6	2	1	.43	3
Buchholz,Taylor, Col-Tor	R	1.000	1	1	0	0	0	.093	54	5	0	0	0	2	4	22	5	12.0	1	0	0	0	1.000	3	3	0	0	1.00	0
Buckner,Billy, Ari	R	.250	4	1	0	0	0	.231	26	6	2	0	0	6	1	8	2	13.0	3	1	0	0	1.000	2	1	0	0	.50	-2
Buehrle,Mark, CWS	L	.000	5	0	0	0	1	.089	45	4	0	0	1	2	1	24	8	210.1	4	46	0	4	1.000	12	6	5	6	.50	8

Pitchers Hitting, Fielding and Holding Runners

Pitcher	T	2010 Hitting						Career Hitting										2010 Fielding and Holding Runners											
		Avg	AB	H	HR	RBI	SH	Avg	AB	H	2B	3B	HR	RBI	BB	SO	SH	Inn	PO	A	E	DP	Pct	SBA	CS	PCS	PPO	CS%	RS
Buente,Jay, Fla	R	-	0	0	0	0	0	-	0	0	0	0	0	0	0	0	0	11.0	2	1	0	0	1.000	1	0	0	0	.00	0
Bulger,Jason, LAA	R	-	0	0	0	0	0	-	0	0	0	0	0	0	0	0	0	24.0	3	1	0	0	1.000	4	2	0	0	.50	0
Bullington,Bryan, KC	R	-	0	0	0	0	0	.333	3	1	0	0	0	0	0	1	0	42.2	6	2	2	1	.800	11	4	0	0	.36	-1
Bumgarner,Madison, SF	L	.179	39	7	0	3	3	.171	41	7	1	0	0	3	2	12	3	111.0	3	10	1	0	.929	10	2	1	0	.20	-1
Burnett,A.J., NYY	R	.000	1	0	0	0	2	.131	267	35	6	3	3	9	12	127	36	186.2	9	16	4	1	.862	42	5	2	2	.12	-4
Burnett,Alex, Min	R	-	0	0	0	0	0	-	0	0	0	0	0	0	0	0	0	47.2	1	5	1	0	.857	2	0	0	0	.00	-1
Burnett,Sean, Was	L	-	0	0	0	0	0	.036	28	1	1	0	0	0	2	9	2	63.0	5	12	0	1	1.000	4	0	0	0	.00	0
Burres,Brian, Pit	L	.120	25	3	0	3	2	.148	27	4	0	1	0	4	0	15	3	79.1	0	13	0	1	1.000	5	1	1	0	.20	2
Burton,Jared, Cin	R	-	0	0	0	0	0	.000	2	0	0	0	0	0	0	2	0	3.1	1	0	0	0	1.000	1	0	0	0	.00	0
Bush,Dave, Mil	R	.132	53	7	0	2	5	.129	263	34	7	0	0	13	9	96	27	174.1	7	14	1	1	.955	28	6	0	0	.21	-3
Byrdak,Tim, Hou	L	.000	2	0	0	0	0	.154	13	2	1	0	0	0	0	4	0	38.2	0	3	0	0	1.000	1	1	0	1	1.00	1
Cabrera,Fernando, Bos	R	-	0	0	0	0	0	-	0	0	0	0	0	0	0	0	0	1.1	0	0	0	0	-	0	0	0	0	-	0
Cahill,Trevor, Oak	R	.000	3	0	0	0	2	.200	5	1	0	0	0	0	0	1	2	196.2	6	54	1	2	.984	20	5	3	2	.25	9
Cain,Matt, SF	R	.106	66	7	0	1	10	.114	317	36	7	1	4	12	12	164	41	223.1	9	24	2	0	.943	29	10	3	0	.34	2
Camp,Shawn, Tor	R	1.000	1	1	0	0	0	1.000	1	1	0	0	0	0	0	0	1	72.1	4	4	0	1	1.000	8	1	0	0	.13	-1
Capps,Matt, Was-Min	R	.000	1	0	0	0	0	.200	5	1	0	0	0	0	1	3	0	73.0	3	8	0	1	1.000	5	2	0	0	.40	-1
Capuano,Chris, Mil	L	.056	18	1	0	0	0	.153	236	36	6	0	1	17	7	108	15	66.0	2	10	0	0	1.000	1	0	0	0	.00	0
Caridad,Esmailin, ChC	R	-	0	0	0	0	0	.000	2	0	0	0	0	0	0	0	0	4.0	0	1	0	0	1.000	2	0	0	0	.00	0
Carlson,Jesse, Tor	L	-	0	0	0	0	0	-	0	0	0	0	0	0	0	0	0	13.2	2	2	0	1	1.000	1	0	0	0	.00	0
Carmona,Fausto, Cle	R	.000	4	0	0	0	1	.000	11	0	0	0	0	0	0	6	2	210.1	22	39	2	6	.968	39	6	0	0	.15	3
Carpenter,Chris, StL	R	.111	72	8	1	4	10	.110	362	40	5	0	2	16	10	117	38	235.0	35	29	1	4	.985	12	9	0	0	.75	5
Carpenter,Drew, Phi	R	.000	1	0	0	0	0	.000	4	0	0	0	0	0	0	1	0	3.0	0	3	0	0	1.000	0	0	0	0	-	0
Carrasco,Carlos, Clo	R	-	0	0	0	0	0	-	0	0	0	0	0	0	0	0	0	44.2	3	5	0	0	1.000	11	6	0	0	.55	2
Carrasco,D.J., Pit-Ari	R	.000	6	0	0	0	0	.000	15	0	0	0	0	0	0	5	1	78.1	7	9	2	1	.889	14	3	0	0	.21	-2
Cashner,Andrew, ChC	R	.000	2	0	0	0	1	.000	2	0	0	0	0	0	0	2	1	54.1	3	13	0	2	1.000	7	2	0	0	.29	2
Casilla,Santiago, SF	R	-	0	0	0	0	0	-	0	0	0	0	0	0	0	0	0	55.1	0	12	1	0	.923	5	3	0	0	.60	3
Cassevah,Bobby, LAA	R	-	0	0	0	0	0	-	0	0	0	0	0	0	0	0	0	20.0	2	3	0	0	1.000	0	0	0	0	-	0
Castillo,Alberto, Bal	L	-	0	0	0	0	0	-	0	0	0	0	0	0	0	0	0	10.2	1	2	0	1	1.000	0	0	0	0	-	0
Cecil,Brett, Tor	L	.000	2	0	0	0	0	.000	4	0	0	0	0	0	0	4	0	172.2	3	21	1	2	.960	6	2	1	0	.33	1
Ceda,Jose, Fla	R	.000	2	0	0	0	0	.000	2	0	0	0	0	0	0	2	0	8.2	0	0	0	0	-	0	0	0	0	-	0
Chacin,Gustavo, Hou	L	1.000	1	1	1	1	0	.125	8	1	0	0	1	1	0	2	1	38.1	1	3	1	0	.800	4	0	0	0	.00	-2
Chacin,Jhoulys, Col	R	.075	40	3	0	1	4	.075	40	3	0	0	0	1	1	9	4	137.1	8	13	1	2	.955	10	3	0	0	.30	0
Chamberlain,Joba, NYY	R	-	0	0	0	0	0	.000	5	0	0	0	0	0	1	1	2	71.2	2	6	0	1	1.000	11	1	0	0	.09	-2
Chapman,Aroldis, Cin	L	-	0	0	0	0	0	-	0	0	0	0	0	0	0	0	0	13.1	2	1	0	0	1.000	4	2	1	0	.50	0
Chavez,Jesse, Atl-KC	R	.000	1	0	0	0	0	.000	2	0	0	0	0	0	0	2	0	62.2	3	6	0	0	1.000	2	1	0	0	.50	-2
Chen,Bruce, KC	L	1.000	1	1	0	0	1	.145	117	17	1	0	0	3	3	63	18	140.1	4	24	1	0	.966	12	7	7	1	.58	4
Chico,Matt, Was	L	.000	2	0	0	0	0	.159	63	10	0	0	0	3	0	15	11	5.0	0	0	0	0	-	0	0	0	0	-	0
Choate,Randy, TB	L	-	0	0	0	0	0	.000	5	0	0	0	0	0	0	3	0	44.2	4	8	1	1	.923	2	1	0	0	.50	0
Cishek,Steve, Fla	R	-	0	0	0	0	0	-	0	0	0	0	0	0	0	0	0	4.1	2	0	0	0	1.000	0	0	0	0	-	0
Clippard,Tyler, Was	R	.500	2	1	0	0	1	.250	12	3	1	0	0	0	0	8	2	91.0	2	3	0	1	1.000	6	1	0	1	.17	-1
Coello,Robert, Bos	R	-	0	0	0	0	0	-	0	0	0	0	0	0	0	0	0	5.2	0	0	0	0	-	1	0	0	0	.00	0
Coffey,Todd, Mil	R	.000	1	0	0	0	0	.000	7	0	0	0	0	0	0	5	3	62.1	2	8	2	1	.833	4	1	0	0	.25	1
Coke,Phil, Det	L	-	0	0	0	0	0	.000	1	0	0	0	0	0	0	1	0	64.2	2	6	1	1	.889	1	0	0	0	.00	-2
Coleman,Casey, ChC	R	.100	20	2	0	2	2	.100	20	2	1	0	0	2	1	11	2	57.0	3	9	0	4	1.000	3	2	0	0	.67	3
Colome,Jesus, Sea	R	-	0	0	0	0	0	.000	2	0	0	0	0	0	0	2	1	17.0	0	3	0	0	1.000	2	0	0	0	.00	0
Colon,Roman, KC	R	-	0	0	0	0	0	.000	7	0	0	0	0	0	0	5	1	2.0	0	0	0	0	-	0	0	0	0	-	0
Contreras,Jose, Phi	R	-	0	0	0	0	0	.000	29	0	0	0	0	0	3	18	1	56.2	1	7	0	0	1.000	6	1	0	0	.17	1
Cook,Aaron, Col	R	.150	40	6	0	1	5	.152	348	53	7	1	0	17	21	119	66	127.2	6	18	1	2	.960	4	0	0	2	.00	0
Cordero,Chad, Sea	R	-	0	0	0	0	0	.000	5	0	0	0	0	0	0	4	2	9.2	0	0	0	0	-	3	3	0	0	1.00	0
Cordero,Francisco, Cin	R	.000	1	0	0	0	0	.000	3	0	0	0	0	0	0	1	0	72.2	1	10	1	0	.917	13	1	0	0	.08	-3
Cormier,Lance, TB	R	-	0	0	0	0	0	.109	46	5	1	0	0	2	2	17	4	62.0	11	6	0	3	1.000	5	2	0	0	.40	0
Corpas,Manuel, Col	R	.000	5	0	0	0	0	.000	6	0	0	0	0	0	0	2	3	62.1	4	5	0	0	1.000	2	0	0	0	.00	-1
Correia,Kevin, SD	R	.136	44	6	0	5	6	.126	183	23	3	0	0	9	10	76	25	145.0	13	13	2	0	.929	16	5	0	0	.31	-1
Cortes,Dan, Sea	R	-	0	0	0	0	0	-	0	0	0	0	0	0	0	0	0	5.1	1	0	0	0	1.000	2	0	0	0	.00	0
Crain,Jesse, Min	R	.000	1	0	0	0	0	.000	1	0	0	0	0	0	0	0	1	68.0	3	14	1	3	.944	8	1	0	1	.13	0
Cramer,Bobby, Oak	L	-	0	0	0	0	0	-	0	0	0	0	0	0	0	0	0	23.2	0	4	0	0	1.000	1	1	1	0	1.00	2
Cruz,Juan, KC	R	-	0	0	0	0	0	.114	70	8	1	1	0	2	4	28	7	5.1	0	1	0	0	1.000	0	0	0	0	-	0
Cueto,Johnny, Cin	R	.111	54	6	0	2	8	.097	145	14	0	0	0	4	6	54	26	185.2	12	28	2	2	.952	7	4	2	1	.57	1
Daigle,Casey, Hou	R	-	0	0	0	0	0	.111	18	2	2	0	0	0	0	8	1	10.1	1	0	0	0	1.000	4	0	0	0	.00	-1
Daley,Matt, Col	R	-	0	0	0	0	0	-	0	0	0	0	0	0	0	0	0	23.1	2	3	1	0	.833	3	2	0	0	.67	0
Danks,John, CWS	L	.000	3	0	0	0	0	.077	13	1	0	0	0	1	6	1	0	213.0	5	35	0	4	1.000	12	6	4	0	.50	5
Davies,Kyle, KC	R	.000	1	0	0	0	1	.132	68	9	1	0	2	9	4	24	16	183.2	13	23	2	2	.947	20	3	0	0	.15	-1
Davis,Doug, Mil	L	.000	13	0	0	1	1	.085	402	34	4	2	0	13	4	171	45	38.1	1	6	0	1	1.000	5	2	1	0	.40	-1
Davis,Wade, TB	R	.000	1	0	0	0	0	.000	1	0	0	0	0	0	0	0	0	168.0	16	19	2	4	.946	18	5	1	1	.28	-1
de la Rosa,Jorge, Col	L	.171	41	7	0	4	3	.130	154	20	4	0	0	13	1	70	13	121.2	7	15	0	2	1.000	9	3	1	0	.33	3
Deduno,Sam, Col	R	-	0	0	0	0	0	-	0	0	0	0	0	0	0	0	0	2.2	0	0	0	0	-	0	0	0	0	-	0
Del Rosario,E., Cin-Hou	R	-	0	0	0	0	0	-	0	0	0	0	0	0	0	0	0	10.0	1	7	0	1	1.000	1	0	0	0	.00	0
Delaney,Rob, Min	R	-	0	0	0	0	0	-	0	0	0	0	0	0	0	0	0	1.0	0	0	0	0	-	0	0	0	0	-	0
Delcarmen,M., Bos-Col	R	.000	1	0	0	0	0	.000	1	0	0	0	0	0	0	1	0	52.1	4	6	0	0	1.000	1	0	0	0	.00	0
Demel,Sam, Ari	R	-	0	0	0	0	0	-	0	0	0	0	0	0	0	0	0	37.0	3	5	0	1	1.000	1	0	0	0	.00	2

Pitchers Hitting, Fielding and Holding Runners

Pitcher	T	2010 Hitting						Career Hitting										2010 Fielding and Holding Runners										
		Avg	AB	H	HR	RBI	SH	Avg	AB	H	2B	3B	HR	RBI	BB	SO	SH	Inn	PO	A	E	DP	Pct	SBA	CS	PCS	PPO	CS%	RS
Dempster,Ryan, ChC	R	.136	59	8	0	2	16	.100	498	50	9	1	0	16	12	193	74	215.1	23	23	1	2	.979	22	6	0	0	.27	1
Dessens,Elmer, NYM	R	-	0	0	0	0	0	.163	240	39	4	1	0	16	22	65	38	47.0	4	12	1	0	.941	4	3	1	0	.75	2
Detwiler,Ross, Was	L	.000	7	0	0	0	0	.038	26	1	0	0	0	1	0	15	0	29.2	3	5	0	0	1.000	6	2	1	0	.33	-1
Diamond,Thomas, ChC	R	.000	7	0	0	0	0	.000	7	0	0	0	0	0	1	6	0	29.0	1	4	0	1	1.000	1	0	0	0	.00	1
Dickey,R.A., NYM	R	.255	51	13	0	5	7	.268	56	15	2	0	0	5	3	8	7	174.1	17	44	0	4	1.000	12	3	1	0	.25	5
Donnelly,Brendan, Pit	R	-	0	0	0	0	0	.000	1	0	0	0	0	0	0	0	0	30.2	2	3	0	0	1.000	7	0	0	0	.00	-1
Dotel,O., Pit-LAD-Col	R	.000	1	0	0	0	0	.067	75	5	0	0	0	1	5	43	9	64.0	5	4	1	0	.900	10	1	0	0	.10	0
Doubront,Felix, Bos	L	-	0	0	0	0	0	-	0	0	0	0	0	0	0	0	0	25.0	2	1	3	0	.500	2	1	0	0	.50	-1
Downs,Scott, Tor	L	-	0	0	0	0	0	.067	45	3	0	0	0	1	3	17	10	61.1	5	12	2	3	.895	3	0	0	1	.00	3
Drabek,Kyle, Tor	R	-	0	0	0	0	0	-	0	0	0	0	0	0	0	0	0	17.0	3	3	1	2	.857	3	1	0	0	.33	-2
Duchscherer,Justin, Oak	R	-	0	0	0	0	0	.000	6	0	0	0	0	0	0	6	0	28.0	0	4	0	1	1.000	1	0	0	1	.00	0
Duensing,Brian, Min	L	.000	1	0	0	0	0	.000	1	0	0	0	0	0	0	1	0	130.2	5	25	0	1	1.000	4	1	0	1	.25	3
Duke,Zach, Pit	L	.063	48	3	0	0	8	.167	293	49	7	0	0	17	11	109	40	159.0	11	23	0	0	1.000	13	3	2	0	.23	2
Dunn,Michael, Atl	L	.000	2	0	0	0	0	.000	2	0	0	0	0	0	0	1	0	19.0	0	1	0	0	1.000	1	0	0	0	.00	0
Durbin,Chad, Phi	R	.000	2	0	0	0	0	.083	24	2	0	0	0	1	0	8	1	68.2	4	15	0	1	1.000	4	1	0	2	.25	1
Ekstrom,Mike, TB	R	-	0	0	0	0	0	.000	2	0	0	0	0	0	0	1	1	16.1	0	0	0	0	-	1	0	0	0	.00	1
Elbert,Scott, LAD	L	-	0	0	0	0	0	.167	6	1	1	0	0	1	0	2	0	0.2	0	0	0	0	-	0	0	0	0	-	0
Ely,John, LAD	R	.074	27	2	0	1	4	.074	27	2	0	0	0	1	1	13	4	100.0	3	5	0	0	1.000	7	3	0	1	.43	-1
English,Jesse, Was	R	-	0	0	0	0	1	-	0	0	0	0	0	0	0	0	1	7.0	0	0	0	0	-	0	0	0	0	-	0
Enright,Barry, Ari	R	.242	33	8	0	6	3	.242	33	8	1	0	0	6	0	9	3	99.0	7	12	0	2	1.000	9	3	1	0	.33	0
Escalona,Edgmer, Col	R	-	0	0	0	0	0	-	0	0	0	0	0	0	0	0	0	6.0	0	0	0	0	-	0	0	0	0	-	
Estrada,Marco, Mil	R	.000	1	0	0	0	0	.000	1	0	0	0	0	0	0	1	0	11.1	1	2	0	0	1.000	3	0	0	0	.00	0
Eveland,Dana, Tor-Pit	L	.000	1	0	0	0	0	.077	13	1	0	0	0	1	6	4	1	54.1	7	13	0	1	1.000	8	4	2	0	.50	1
Farnsworth,Kyle, KC-Atl	R	-	0	0	0	0	0	.074	54	4	1	0	0	3	2	18	8	64.2	6	6	2	0	.857	10	5	1	0	.50	1
Feldman,Scott, Tex	R	.167	6	1	0	0	0	.143	14	2	1	0	0	0	0	5	3	141.1	13	26	0	3	1.000	24	8	1	0	.33	1
Feliciano,Pedro, NYM	L	-	0	0	0	0	0	.000	6	0	0	0	0	0	2	2	1	62.2	6	17	1	2	.958	0	0	0	0	-	2
Feliz,Neftali, Tex	R	-	0	0	0	0	0	-	0	0	0	0	0	0	0	0	0	69.1	3	2	0	0	1.000	0	0	0	0	-	0
Fien,Casey, Det	R	-	0	0	0	0	0	-	0	0	0	0	0	0	0	0	0	2.2	1	1	0	0	1.000	0	0	0	0	-	0
Figaro,Alfredo, Det	R	-	0	0	0	0	0	.000	2	0	0	0	0	0	0	2	0	14.2	0	3	2	0	.600	1	0	0	0	.00	0
Figueroa,N., Phi-Hou	R	.235	17	4	0	0	5	.168	107	18	2	1	0	8	5	41	14	93.0	6	12	1	0	.947	14	5	0	0	.36	-2
Fisher,Carlos, Cin	R	.000	4	0	0	0	0	.000	5	0	0	0	0	0	0	5	0	22.1	1	2	0	0	1.000	5	0	0	0	.00	-1
Fister,Doug, Sea	R	.000	2	0	0	0	0	.000	2	0	0	0	0	0	0	2	0	171.0	17	19	1	3	.973	5	3	1	1	.60	1
Flores,Randy, Col-Min	L	-	0	0	0	0	0	.000	8	0	0	0	0	0	0	5	0	31.0	1	5	1	1	.857	2	2	0	1	1.00	0
Floyd,Gavin, CWS	R	.250	4	1	0	0	0	.060	50	3	0	0	0	1	1	28	3	187.1	9	24	2	2	.943	11	4	1	0	.36	2
Fox,Matt, Min-Bos	R	-	0	0	0	0	0	-	0	0	0	0	0	0	0	0	0	7.1	1	0	0	0	1.000	1	0	0	0	.00	
Francis,Jeff, Col	L	.091	22	2	0	1	3	.126	254	32	6	0	0	15	21	88	45	104.1	2	17	0	3	1.000	9	3	2	0	.33	2
Francisco,Frank, Tex	R	-	0	0	0	0	0	-	0	0	0	0	0	0	0	0	0	52.2	4	1	0	0	1.000	10	1	0	0	.10	-2
Franklin,Ryan, StL	R	.000	3	0	0	0	0	.100	20	2	0	0	0	1	2	11	2	65.0	9	5	0	1	1.000	3	1	0	0	.33	0
Frasor,Jason, Tor	R	-	0	0	0	0	0	-	0	0	0	0	0	0	0	0	0	63.2	6	5	1	1	.917	7	1	0	0	.14	-3
French,Luke, Sea	L	.000	1	0	0	0	0	.000	1	0	0	0	0	0	0	1	0	87.2	10	6	0	1	1.000	5	3	2	1	.60	1
Frieri,Ernesto, SD	R	.000	1	0	0	0	0	.000	1	0	0	0	0	0	0	1	0	31.2	1	1	0	0	1.000	3	1	0	0	.33	0
Fuentes,Brian, LAA-Min	L	-	0	0	0	0	0	.000	1	0	0	0	0	0	0	0	0	48.0	0	5	0	0	1.000	4	1	1	1	.25	2
Fulchino,Jeff, Hou	R	.000	1	0	0	0	0	.250	4	1	1	0	0	0	0	1	0	47.1	1	2	0	0	1.000	3	1	0	0	.33	-2
Gabino,Armando, Bal	R	-	0	0	0	0	0	-	0	0	0	0	0	0	0	0	0	4.2	1	0	0	0	1.000	0	0	0	0	-	0
Galarraga,Armando, Det	R	.000	5	0	0	0	0	.000	8	0	0	0	0	0	3	6	1	144.1	6	11	3	0	.850	9	3	0	0	.33	-2
Gallagher,Sean, SD-Pit	R	.000	7	0	0	0	0	.000	18	0	0	0	0	0	1	11	3	57.2	3	10	0	0	1.000	3	1	0	2	.33	2
Gallardo,Yovani, Mil	R	.254	63	16	4	10	2	.218	170	37	10	0	8	24	8	51	8	185.0	12	24	1	2	.973	17	6	1	0	.35	0
Garcia,Freddy, CWS	R	.000	5	0	0	0	1	.190	63	12	2	0	0	4	2	20	14	157.0	14	16	2	2	.938	25	5	0	1	.20	-5
Garcia,Jaime, StL	L	.185	54	10	0	2	4	.182	55	10	1	0	0	2	4	14	4	163.1	5	23	0	0	1.000	9	3	1	1	.33	2
Garland,Jon, SD	R	.214	56	12	0	2	6	.145	145	21	1	0	1	7	9	57	16	200.0	21	36	1	4	.983	14	8	1	0	.57	6
Garza,Matt, TB	R	.000	3	0	0	0	1	.000	11	0	0	0	0	0	1	9	3	204.2	10	13	1	0	.958	13	4	1	0	.31	-2
Gaudin,Chad, Oak-NYY	R	-	0	0	0	0	0	.031	32	1	0	0	0	0	2	16	3	65.1	2	6	1	0	.889	3	0	0	0	.00	-2
Gee,Dillon, NYM	R	.167	12	2	0	1	0	.167	12	2	1	0	0	1	0	8	0	33.0	2	3	0	0	1.000	0	0	0	0	-	0
Germano,Justin, Cle	R	-	0	0	0	0	0	.180	50	9	2	0	0	3	3	21	11	35.1	1	6	0	0	1.000	4	2	0	0	.50	1
Gervacio,Sammy, Hou	R	-	0	0	0	0	0	-	0	0	0	0	0	0	0	0	0	3.2	0	1	1	0	.500	1	0	0	0	.00	1
Gomez,Jeanmar, Cle	R	-	0	0	0	0	0	-	0	0	0	0	0	0	0	0	0	57.2	7	6	0	0	1.000	11	4	1	1	.36	-2
Gonzalez,Enrique, Det	R	-	0	0	0	0	0	.281	32	9	1	0	0	3	0	8	3	26.0	3	2	0	0	1.000	1	1	0	0	1.00	0
Gonzalez,Gio, Oak	L	.000	4	0	0	0	0	.000	4	0	0	0	0	0	0	3	0	200.2	7	33	1	0	.976	15	3	2	0	.20	0
Gonzalez,Mike, Bal	L	-	0	0	0	0	0	.333	3	1	1	0	0	2	0	0	0	24.2	0	0	1	0	.000	2	0	0	0	.00	0
Gorzelanny,Tom, ChC	L	.125	40	5	0	2	5	.085	165	14	0	0	0	11	6	78	20	136.1	5	16	1	0	.955	23	5	3	0	.22	-2
Grabow,John, ChC	L	-	0	0	0	0	0	.000	5	0	0	0	0	0	0	1	1	25.2	1	3	2	0	.667	6	0	0	0	.00	0
Gray,Jeff, ChC	R	-	0	0	0	0	0	-	0	0	0	0	0	0	0	0	0	9.1	0	2	0	1	1.000	0	0	0	0	-	0
Green,Sean, NYM	R	-	0	0	0	0	0	.000	2	0	0	0	0	0	0	2	0	9.1	1	1	0	0	1.000	2	0	0	0	.00	0
Gregerson,Luke, SD	R	-	0	0	0	0	0	.000	1	0	0	0	0	0	0	0	1	78.1	8	14	0	1	1.000	7	0	0	0	.00	2
Gregg,Kevin, Tor	R	-	0	0	0	0	0	.000	6	0	0	0	0	0	0	5	0	59.0	3	3	1	0	.857	2	0	0	0	.00	-1
Greinke,Zack, KC	R	.000	6	0	0	0	1	.167	24	4	2	0	1	1	0	6	2	220.0	14	34	1	1	.980	23	11	1	2	.48	7
Guerrier,Matt, Min	R	-	0	0	0	0	0	.000	2	0	0	0	0	0	0	1	0	71.0	8	11	0	0	1.000	3	2	0	1	.67	1
Guthrie,Jeremy, Bal	R	.000	3	0	0	0	0	.059	17	1	1	0	0	0	0	11	0	209.1	14	30	4	0	.917	7	2	0	0	.29	3
Gutierrez,Juan, Ari	R	-	0	0	0	0	0	.000	6	0	0	0	0	0	0	4	1	56.2	3	10	1	1	.929	8	0	0	0	.00	-1
Haeger,Charlie, LAD	R	.000	6	0	0	1	0	.091	11	1	0	0	0	1	1	9	2	30.0	1	7	0	0	1.000	5	2	0	0	.40	1

Pitchers Hitting, Fielding and Holding Runners

Pitcher	T	2010 Hitting						Career Hitting										2010 Fielding and Holding Runners											
		Avg	AB	H	HR	RBI	SH	Avg	AB	H	2B	3B	HR	RBI	BB	SO	SH	Inn	PO	A	E	DP	Pct	SBA	CS	PCS	PPO	CS%	RS
Halladay,Roy, Phi	R	.141	92	13	0	5	2	.123	130	16	0	0	0	6	1	59	5	250.2	16	40	1	0	.982	15	5	0	0	.33	1
Hamels,Cole, Phi	L	.149	67	10	0	2	5	.160	312	50	9	0	0	15	9	128	27	208.2	10	26	1	2	.973	16	6	1	0	.38	3
Hammel,Jason, Col	R	.105	57	6	0	2	5	.115	113	13	3	0	0	3	3	54	8	177.2	11	23	1	3	.971	23	5	1	1	.22	-2
Hampton,Mike, Ari	L	-	0	0	0	0	0	.246	725	178	22	5	16	79	47	195	63	4.1	0	0	0	0	-	0	0	0	0	-	0
Hanrahan,Joel, Pit	R	-	0	0	0	0	0	.235	17	4	2	1	0	3	0	5	4	69.2	5	5	0	0	1.000	8	1	0	0	.13	-2
Hanson,Tommy, Atl	R	.097	62	6	0	4	8	.081	99	8	0	0	0	5	3	47	16	202.2	15	25	3	3	.930	37	4	1	1	.11	-5
Happ,J.A., Phi-Hou	L	.000	26	0	0	0	3	.052	77	4	1	0	0	1	2	29	12	87.1	4	9	0	0	1.000	4	3	2	0	.75	1
Harang,Aaron, Cin	R	.135	37	5	0	2	3	.094	438	41	5	0	1	17	3	195	38	111.2	8	11	1	0	.950	7	4	0	1	.57	0
Harden,Rich, Tex	R	.000	11	0	0	0	0	.145	76	11	1	0	0	1	1	31	9	92.0	5	5	1	1	.909	2	1	0	0	.50	1
Haren,Dan, Ari-LAA	R	.364	55	20	1	7	1	.226	257	58	21	0	2	26	8	65	18	235.0	12	24	1	1	.973	28	9	1	1	.32	-5
Harrell,Lucas, CWS	R	-	0	0	0	0	0	-	0	0	0	0	0	0	0	0	0	24.0	4	4	0	0	1.000	7	1	0	0	.14	-1
Harrison,Matt, Tex	L	.000	1	0	0	0	0	.000	2	0	0	0	0	0	1	2	0	78.1	4	6	1	0	.909	6	1	0	0	.17	-1
Hawkins,LaTroy, Mil	R	-	0	0	0	0	0	.000	6	0	0	0	0	0	0	5	1	16.0	1	2	0	0	1.000	4	2	0	0	.50	0
Hawksworth,Blake, StL	R	.000	16	0	0	0	2	.000	16	0	0	0	0	0	0	9	2	90.1	8	16	1	1	.960	6	2	0	1	.33	0
Heilman,Aaron, Ari	R	.000	1	0	0	0	0	.022	46	1	0	0	0	1	2	24	5	72.0	8	9	2	0	.895	5	1	0	0	.20	1
Hellickson,Jeremy, TB	R	-	0	0	0	0	0	-	0	0	0	0	0	0	0	0	0	36.1	1	3	0	0	1.000	2	0	0	0	.00	-2
Hendrickson,Mark, Bal	L	-	0	0	0	0	0	.134	97	13	3	1	1	3	6	53	4	75.1	6	9	1	1	.938	2	1	0	0	.50	-1
Hensley,Clay, Fla	R	.000	2	0	0	0	0	.111	72	8	2	0	0	4	3	41	8	75.0	2	11	1	0	.929	6	1	0	0	.17	2
Hernandez,David, Bal	R	.000	3	0	0	0	0	.000	3	0	0	0	0	0	0	1	0	79.1	3	4	0	1	.000	7	3	0	0	.43	0
Hernandez,Felix, Sea	R	.000	2	0	0	0	2	.118	17	2	0	0	1	5	1	10	4	249.2	15	37	2	2	.963	20	5	0	0	.25	4
Hernandez,Livan, Was	R	.148	61	9	1	3	9	.222	923	205	37	2	10	78	9	127	108	211.2	6	39	0	3	1.000	13	9	2	1	.69	3
Herndon,David, Phi	R	.000	2	0	0	0	0	.000	2	0	0	0	0	0	0	2	0	52.1	2	3	1	0	.833	4	1	0	0	.25	-1
Herrora,Daniel Ray, Cin	L	.000	1	0	0	0	0	.000	3	0	0	0	0	0	1	2	1	23.0	5	1	0	1	1.000	0	0	0	0	-	0
Herrmann,Frank, Cle	R	-	0	0	0	0	0	-	0	0	0	0	0	0	0	0	0	44.2	0	4	0	0	1.000	5	2	0	0	.40	-1
Hill,Rich, Bos	L	-	0	0	0	0	0	.123	114	14	3	0	0	6	2	51	6	4.0	0	0	0	0	-	2	0	0	0	.00	0
Hill,Shawn, Tor	R	-	0	0	0	0	0	.067	45	3	0	0	0	0	6	19	15	20.2	1	2	0	0	1.000	1	0	0	0	.00	0
Hochevar,Luke, KC	R	.000	1	0	0	0	0	.000	9	0	0	0	0	0	0	8	1	103.0	5	12	1	1	.944	18	2	1	0	.11	-4
Hoffman,Trevor, Mil	R	.000	1	0	0	0	0	.118	34	4	2	0	0	5	0	11	2	47.1	2	3	0	0	1.000	1	0	0	0	.00	1
Holland,Derek, Tex	L	-	0	0	0	0	0	.000	5	0	0	0	0	0	0	2	1	57.1	3	9	1	0	.923	7	1	1	2	.14	0
Holland,Greg, KC	R	-	0	0	0	0	0	-	0	0	0	0	0	0	0	0	0	18.2	5	1	0	0	1.000	1	0	0	0	.00	0
Houser,James, Fla	L	-	0	0	0	0	0	-	0	0	0	0	0	0	0	0	0	1.1	0	0	0	0	-	0	0	0	0	-	0
Howry,Bob, Ari-ChC	R	-	0	0	0	0	0	.200	5	1	0	0	0	0	0	2	1	35.0	4	5	0	0	1.000	1	0	0	0	.00	0
Hudson,Daniel, CWS-Ari	R	.148	27	4	0	6	3	.148	27	4	2	0	0	6	0	7	3	95.1	8	7	0	1	1.000	4	1	0	0	.25	0
Hudson,Tim, Atl	R	.195	77	15	0	4	8	.175	360	63	12	1	1	27	13	107	38	228.2	17	57	3	2	.961	22	11	0	3	.50	6
Huff,David, Cle	R	.000	2	0	0	0	0	.000	4	0	0	0	0	0	0	2	2	79.2	4	7	0	0	1.000	2	1	0	0	.50	2
Hughes,Dusty, KC	L	-	0	0	0	0	0	-	0	0	0	0	0	0	0	0	0	56.1	5	8	0	2	1.000	4	1	0	0	.25	-1
Hughes,Phil, NYY	R	.000	1	0	0	0	1	.000	1	0	0	0	0	0	0	0	0	176.1	7	13	0	1	1.000	15	5	0	0	.33	0
Humber,Philip, KC	R	-	0	0	0	0	0	.000	1	0	0	0	0	0	0	0	0	21.2	1	0	0	0	1.000	2	0	0	0	.00	0
Hunter,Tommy, Tex	R	.000	1	0	0	0	0	.000	1	0	0	0	0	0	0	0	1	128.0	9	16	1	1	.962	7	2	1	0	.29	0
Igarashi,Ryota, NYM	R	-	0	0	0	0	0	-	0	0	0	0	0	0	0	0	0	30.1	1	2	2	0	.600	1	0	0	0	.00	0
Infante,Gregory, CWS	R	-	0	0	0	0	0	-	0	0	0	0	0	0	0	0	0	4.2	0	1	0	0	1.000	0	0	0	0	-	0
Jackson,Edwin, Ari-CWS	R	.158	38	6	1	3	3	.147	68	10	0	0	1	5	5	32	6	209.1	17	15	5	0	.865	25	8	0	0	.24	3
Jackson,Steven, Pit	R	-	0	0	0	0	0	.000	1	0	0	0	0	0	0	0	0	11.1	1	1	0	0	1.000	0	0	0	0	-	0
Jakubauskas,Chris, Pit	R	-	0	0	0	0	0	.000	2	0	0	0	0	0	0	1	0	0.2	0	0	0	0	-	0	0	0	0	-	0
James,Justin, Oak	R	-	0	0	0	0	0	-	0	0	0	0	0	0	0	0	0	4.0	0	0	0	0	-	0	0	0	0	-	0
Jansen,Kenley, LAD	R	1.000	1	1	0	0	0	1.000	1	1	0	0	0	1	0	0	0	27.0	1	1	0	0	1.000	5	0	0	0	.00	-1
Janssen,Casey, Tor	R	.000	1	0	0	0	0	.000	3	0	0	0	0	0	0	2	1	68.2	12	4	0	0	1.000	5	1	0	0	.20	-1
Jeffress,Jeremy, Mil	R	-	0	0	0	0	0	-	0	0	0	0	0	0	0	0	0	10.0	1	1	0	0	1.000	0	0	0	0	-	0
Jenks,Bobby, CWS	R	-	0	0	0	0	0	-	0	0	0	0	0	0	0	0	0	52.2	4	12	1	1	.941	11	0	0	0	.00	-2
Jepsen,Kevin, LAA	R	-	0	0	0	0	0	-	0	0	0	0	0	0	0	0	0	59.0	2	9	0	0	1.000	7	2	0	0	.29	-1
Jimenez,Ubaldo, Col	R	.104	77	8	0	4	4	.117	230	27	0	0	0	6	14	68	27	221.2	10	26	1	3	.973	25	13	0	2	.52	4
Joaquin,Waldis, SF	R	-	0	0	0	0	0	-	0	0	0	0	0	0	0	0	0	4.2	0	1	0	0	1.000	2	1	0	0	.50	0
Johnson,Jim, Bal	R	-	0	0	0	0	0	-	0	0	0	0	0	0	0	0	0	26.1	2	3	0	0	1.000	1	1	0	0	1.00	-1
Johnson,Josh, Fla	R	.085	59	5	0	4	6	.131	199	26	5	0	3	19	9	101	25	183.2	19	17	3	2	.923	23	8	2	0	.35	-2
Jones,Hunter, Fla	L	-	0	0	0	0	0	-	0	0	0	0	0	0	0	0	0	1.2	0	0	0	0	-	0	0	0	0	-	0
Jurrjens,Jair, Atl	R	.128	39	5	0	2	4	.117	162	19	3	1	0	6	16	56	18	116.1	5	12	1	0	.964	9	3	1	0	.33	-1
Karstens,Jeff, Pit	R	.061	33	2	0	0	4	.072	69	5	0	0	0	0	5	36	7	122.2	12	15	0	1	1.000	14	6	1	0	.43	1
Kawakami,Kenshin, Atl	R	.125	24	3	0	1	4	.108	65	7	1	0	0	1	6	22	9	87.1	2	11	3	0	.813	9	2	0	0	.22	0
Kazmir,Scott, LAA	L	.000	6	0	0	0	1	.071	14	1	0	0	0	1	0	6	1	150.0	6	25	2	0	.939	17	5	3	1	.29	2
Kelley,Shawn, Sea	R	-	0	0	0	0	0	-	0	0	0	0	0	0	0	0	0	25.0	2	1	0	0	1.000	0	0	0	0	-	0
Kendrick,Kyle, Phi	R	.098	51	5	0	0	6	.122	148	18	3	0	0	4	8	62	18	180.2	9	33	3	3	.933	8	4	0	1	.50	5
Kennedy,Ian, Ari	R	.204	54	11	0	2	5	.204	54	11	1	0	0	2	7	24	5	194.0	18	19	1	2	.974	18	6	1	0	.33	2
Kershaw,Clayton, LAD	L	.055	55	3	0	1	18	.076	132	10	0	0	3	4	46	35	-	204.1	5	30	1	0	.972	16	8	7	1	.50	2
Kilby,Brad, Oak	L	-	0	0	0	0	0	-	0	0	0	0	0	0	0	0	0	8.1	0	0	0	0	-	0	0	0	0	-	0
Kimbrel,Craig, Atl	R	-	0	0	0	0	0	-	0	0	0	0	0	0	0	0	0	20.2	0	1	0	0	.000	3	0	0	0	.00	-1
Kintzler,Brandon, Mil	R	-	0	0	0	0	0	-	0	0	0	0	0	0	0	0	0	7.1	0	1	0	0	1.000	0	0	0	0	-	0
Kirkman,Michael, Tex	L	-	0	0	0	0	0	-	0	0	0	0	0	0	0	0	0	16.1	1	3	0	0	1.000	0	0	0	0	-	0
Kohn,Mike, LAA	R	-	0	0	0	0	0	-	0	0	0	0	0	0	0	0	0	21.1	2	5	1	0	.875	4	2	1	0	.50	1
Kroenke,Zach, Ari	L	.000	2	0	0	0	0	.000	2	0	0	0	0	0	0	1	0	6.2	0	0	0	0	-	0	0	0	0	-	0
Kuo,Hong-Chih, LAD	L	.000	1	0	0	0	0	.185	27	5	2	0	1	1	1	14	8	60.0	2	4	1	1	.857	2	0	0	0	.00	-1

Pitchers Hitting, Fielding and Holding Runners

Pitcher	T	2010 Hitting						Career Hitting										2010 Fielding and Holding Runners											
		Avg	AB	H	HR	RBI	SH	Avg	AB	H	2B	3B	HR	RBI	BB	SO	SH	Inn	PO	A	E	DP	Pct	SBA	CS	PCS	PPO	CS%	RS
Kuroda,Hiroki, LAD	R	.036	55	2	0	0	11	.102	137	14	1	0	0	2	9	48	26	196.1	8	25	3	0	.917	21	7	0	1	.33	1
Lackey,John, Bos	R	.400	5	2	0	0	1	.086	35	3	1	0	0	1	0	10	2	215.0	22	21	3	1	.935	36	10	2	0	.28	-6
Laffey,Aaron, Cle	L	.000	1	0	0	0	0	.333	3	1	0	0	0	0	0	0	0	55.2	4	7	1	1	.917	1	0	0	0	.00	-2
Lannan,John, Was	L	.091	44	4	0	4	2	.100	160	16	4	0	0	5	10	72	13	143.1	12	26	0	2	1.000	21	3	1	0	.14	-2
Latos,Mat, SD	R	.111	54	6	1	3	9	.096	73	7	2	0	1	3	0	38	11	184.2	5	24	1	0	.967	7	0	0	1	.00	-2
League,Brandon, Sea	R	-	0	0	0	0	0	-	0	0	0	0	0	0	0	0	0	79.0	7	10	0	0	1.000	10	5	0	0	.50	0
Leake,Mike, Cin	R	.333	48	16	0	3	6	.333	48	16	1	0	0	3	5	15	6	138.1	18	23	3	3	.930	8	3	0	1	.38	-1
LeBlanc,Wade, SD	L	.295	44	13	0	1	4	.262	65	17	0	0	0	1	2	18	8	146.0	4	28	0	2	1.000	18	9	7	1	.50	5
LeCure,Sam, Cin	R	.091	11	1	0	0	1	.091	11	1	1	0	0	0	0	2	1	48.0	3	9	0	0	1.000	8	1	1	0	.13	-1
Ledezma,Wil, Pit	L	-	0	0	0	0	0	.000	12	0	0	0	0	0	1	6	2	19.2	0	3	0	0	1.000	1	1	1	1	1.00	0
Lee,Cliff, Sea-Tex	L	.000	3	0	0	0	0	.132	68	9	2	0	0	1	1	27	4	212.1	10	14	4	1	.857	7	3	0	0	.43	-3
Lerew,Anthony, KC	R	.000	1	0	0	0	1	.000	4	0	0	0	0	0	0	1	1	26.1	3	5	0	0	1.000	2	1	0	0	.50	0
Leroux,Chris, Fla-Pit	R	-	0	0	0	0	0	-	0	0	0	0	0	0	0	0	0	22.2	0	3	0	0	1.000	3	1	0	0	.33	1
Lester,Jon, Bos	L	.000	3	0	0	1	1	.000	15	0	0	0	0	1	1	9	3	208.0	5	35	3	2	.930	29	7	6	0	.24	2
Lewis,Colby, Tex	R	.286	7	2	0	2	1	.250	8	2	0	0	0	2	0	3	1	201.0	8	12	5	0	.800	17	4	0	0	.24	-4
Lewis,Jensen, Cle	R	-	0	0	0	0	0	.000	1	0	0	0	0	0	0	1	0	36.1	1	5	0	0	1.000	0	0	0	0	-	1
Lewis,Rommie, Tor	L	.000	1	0	0	0	0	.000	1	0	0	0	0	0	0	1	0	18.2	1	3	0	0	1.000	0	0	0	0	-	1
Lidge,Brad, Phi	R	-	0	0	0	0	0	.286	7	2	1	0	0	2	0	4	0	45.2	1	8	0	0	1.000	7	0	0	0	.00	0
Lilly,Ted, ChC-LAD	L	.037	54	2	0	1	4	.108	269	29	4	1	0	13	7	124	28	193.2	10	21	2	2	.939	21	1	1	0	.05	1
Lincecum,Tim, SF	R	.104	67	7	0	5	13	.130	246	32	3	1	0	13	16	118	38	212.1	7	18	2	1	.926	30	3	0	0	.10	-4
Lincoln,Brad, Pit	R	.400	15	6	0	3	3	.400	15	6	0	0	0	3	0	3	3	52.2	6	7	0	0	1.000	4	1	0	0	.25	-2
Lincoln,Mike, Cin	R	.000	1	0	0	0	0	.067	15	1	0	0	0	0	0	7	1	19.2	2	2	0	0	1.000	0	0	0	0	-	0
Lindstrom,Matt, Hou	R	-	0	0	0	0	0	.000	1	0	0	0	0	0	0	1	0	53.1	6	6	0	3	1.000	7	1	0	0	.14	-1
Linebrink,Scott, CWS	R	-	0	0	0	0	0	.222	18	4	1	0	0	0	0	10	2	57.1	2	6	1	0	.889	9	1	0	0	.11	-1
Link,Jon, LAD	R	-	0	0	0	0	0	-	0	0	0	0	0	0	0	0	0	8.2	0	1	0	0	1.000	2	1	0	0	.50	1
Liriano,Francisco, Min	L	.000	2	0	0	0	0	.083	12	1	0	0	0	1	1	7	2	191.2	4	24	1	1	.966	15	3	2	0	.20	-1
Litsch,Jesse, Tor	R	.000	1	0	0	0	0	.000	5	0	0	0	0	0	0	0	0	46.2	7	9	0	1	1.000	2	0	0	0	.00	0
Loe,Kameron, Mil	R	.000	2	0	0	0	0	.250	4	1	0	0	0	1	2	0	0	58.1	6	9	2	1	.882	2	0	0	0	.00	-2
Logan,Boone, NYY	L	-	0	0	0	0	0	-	0	0	0	0	0	0	0	0	0	40.0	1	3	0	0	1.000	4	0	0	0	.00	-1
Lohse,Kyle, StL	R	.171	35	6	0	3	2	.163	227	37	5	0	0	16	3	65	33	92.0	9	17	1	4	.963	4	3	1	0	.75	-1
Lopez,Javier, Pit-SF	L	.000	1	0	0	0	0	.111	9	1	0	0	0	0	0	4	1	57.2	4	22	2	1	.929	2	1	1	0	.50	2
Lopez,Rodrigo, Ari	R	.078	64	5	0	1	5	.061	115	7	0	0	0	1	2	64	7	200.0	10	25	4	2	.897	24	2	0	3	.08	-2
Lopez,Wilton, Hou	R	-	0	0	0	0	0	.000	5	0	0	0	0	0	0	2	0	67.0	7	15	0	1	1.000	4	3	0	0	.75	3
Lowe,Derek, Atl	R	.151	53	8	0	3	11	.142	380	54	9	0	0	18	25	111	58	193.2	14	30	0	2	1.000	21	11	1	0	.52	2
Lowe,Mark, Sea-Tex	R	-	0	0	0	0	0	.000	1	0	0	0	0	0	0	1	0	13.1	0	1	0	0	1.000	0	0	0	0	-	0
Luebke,Cory, SD	L	.000	5	0	0	0	0	.000	5	0	0	0	0	0	0	5	0	17.2	1	5	2	0	.750	1	1	1	1	1.00	0
Lyon,Brandon, Hou	R	-	0	0	0	0	0	-	0	0	0	0	0	0	1	0	0	78.0	12	12	2	0	.923	6	0	0	0	.00	-2
MacDougal,Mike, StL	R	-	0	0	0	0	0	-	0	0	0	0	0	0	0	0	0	18.2	1	2	1	0	.750	1	0	0	0	.00	0
MacLane,Evan, StL	L	-	0	0	0	0	0	-	0	0	0	0	0	0	0	0	0	1.0	0	0	0	-		0	0	0	0	-	
Madson,Ryan, Phi	R	.000	1	0	0	0	0	.125	48	6	1	0	0	2	2	20	7	53.0	2	3	0	1	1.000	4	0	0	0	.00	1
Mahay,Ron, Min	L	-	0	0	0	0	0	.214	28	6	3	0	1	3	1	8	1	34.0	2	1	0	0	1.000	4	1	0	0	.25	-1
Maholm,Paul, Pit	L	.089	56	5	0	0	7	.117	308	36	2	0	1	12	16	161	19	185.1	12	33	3	2	.938	10	2	1	1	.20	1
Maine,John, NYM	R	.000	10	0	0	0	4	.096	166	16	1	0	1	8	11	84	28	39.2	1	6	1	0	.875	5	0	0	0	.00	-2
Maine,Scott, ChC	L	-	0	0	0	0	0	-	0	0	0	0	0	0	0	0	0	13.0	0	2	0	0	1.000	0	0	0	0	-	1
Majewski,Gary, Hou	R	-	0	0	0	0	0	.000	14	0	0	0	0	0	0	8	2	2.0	1	1	0	0	1.000	0	0	0	0	-	0
Maloney,Matt, Cin	L	.333	3	1	0	0	2	.267	15	4	0	0	0	0	1	6	4	20.2	1	2	0	0	1.000	1	1	0	0	1.00	-1
Manship,Jeff, Min	R	.000	1	0	0	0	0	.000	1	0	0	0	0	0	0	1	0	29.0	1	4	0	0	1.000	2	1	0	0	.50	0
Manuel,Robert, Bos	R	-	0	0	0	0	0	-	0	0	0	0	0	0	0	0	0	12.2	1	1	0	0	1.000	0	0	0	0	-	0
Marcum,Shaun, Tor	R	.250	4	1	0	1	1	.100	10	1	1	0	0	1	2	4	1	195.1	18	24	0	1	1.000	15	8	0	0	.53	4
Marinez,Jhan, Fla	R	-	0	0	0	0	0	-	0	0	0	0	0	0	0	0	0	2.2	1	0	0	0	1.000	1	0	0	0	.00	
Marmol,Carlos, ChC	R	-	0	0	0	0	0	.200	30	6	1	0	1	1	0	11	3	77.2	4	1	0	0	1.000	11	1	0	0	.09	-3
Marquez,Jeff, CWS	R	-	0	0	0	0	0	-	0	0	0	0	0	0	0	0	0	1.0	0	0	0	0	-	0	0	0	0	-	0
Marquis,Jason, Was	R	.136	22	3	0	2	2	.199	527	105	29	2	5	50	13	125	34	58.2	5	4	2	0	.818	11	2	0	0	.18	-2
Marshall,Sean, ChC	L	.000	4	0	0	0	0	.158	101	16	1	0	1	5	2	48	8	74.2	8	6	0	1	1.000	3	0	0	0	.00	1
Marte,Damaso, NYY	L	-	0	0	0	0	0	.000	8	0	0	0	0	0	0	2	0	17.2	0	1	1	0	.500	3	0	0	0	.00	-1
Marte,Victor, KC	R	-	0	0	0	0	0	-	0	0	0	0	0	0	0	0	0	27.2	0	6	1	1	.857	1	0	0	0	.00	-1
Martin,J.D., Was	R	.167	12	2	0	0	2	.162	37	6	1	0	0	1	1	17	4	48.0	2	5	0	0	1.000	1	1	0	1	1.00	2
Martinez,Cristhian, Atl	R	.000	4	0	0	0	0	.000	6	0	0	0	0	0	0	3	0	26.0	2	4	0	0	1.000	2	1	0	0	.50	-1
Martinez,Joe, SF-Pit	R	.000	3	0	0	0	0	.182	11	2	1	0	0	0	0	2	1	19.2	1	5	0	0	1.000	4	1	0	1	.25	0
Masset,Nick, Cin	R	-	0	0	0	0	0	.000	5	0	0	0	0	0	0	5	0	76.2	9	4	0	0	1.000	9	3	1	0	.33	-1
Masterson,Justin, Cle	R	.250	4	1	0	0	1	.111	9	1	0	0	0	0	0	5	1	180.0	22	34	5	1	.918	21	8	2	0	.38	4
Mata,Frank, Bal	R	-	0	0	0	0	0	-	0	0	0	0	0	0	0	0	0	17.1	1	5	1	1	.857	3	0	0	0	.00	0
Mateo,Marcos, ChC	R	.000	2	0	0	0	0	.000	2	0	0	0	0	0	0	1	0	21.2	1	2	0	0	1.000	1	0	0	0	.00	0
Mathieson,Scott, Phi	R	-	0	0	0	0	0	.143	7	1	0	0	0	0	0	4	2	1.2	0	0	0	0	-	0	0	0	0	-	0
Mathis,Doug, Tex	R	-	0	0	0	0	0	-	0	0	0	0	0	0	0	0	0	22.1	0	3	0	1	1.000	3	2	0	0	.67	-2
Matsuzaka,Daisuke, Bos	R	.500	4	2	0	1	1	.167	12	2	0	0	0	1	0	4	1	153.2	8	12	2	2	.909	32	7	0	0	.18	-1
Matusz,Brian, Bal	L	.000	2	0	0	0	0	.000	2	0	0	0	0	0	0	0	0	175.2	8	21	1	1	.967	20	3	3	1	.15	1
Maya,Yunesky, Was	R	.143	7	1	0	0	2	.143	7	1	0	0	0	0	0	4	2	26.0	1	4	0	0	1.000	1	0	0	0	.00	0
Mazzaro,Vin, Oak	R	.000	4	0	0	0	0	.000	4	0	0	0	0	0	0	2	4	122.1	5	11	2	3	.889	10	1	1	0	.10	-1
McClellan,Kyle, StL	R	.500	2	1	0	0	0	.100	10	1	0	0	0	0	0	5	1	75.1	4	8	0	0	1.000	10	2	1	0	.20	-1

Pitchers Hitting, Fielding and Holding Runners

Pitcher	T	2010 Hitting						Career Hitting										2010 Fielding and Holding Runners											
		Avg	AB	H	HR	RBI	SH	Avg	AB	H	2B	3B	HR	RBI	BB	SO	SH	Inn	PO	A	E	DP	Pct	SBA	CS	PCS	PPO	CS%	RS
McClendon,Mike, Mil	R	.500	2	1	0	0	0	.500	2	1	0	0	0	0	0	0	0	21.0	1	3	0	0	1.000	0	0	0	0	-	0
McCutchen,Daniel, Pit	R	.071	14	1	0	0	2	.080	25	2	0	0	0	1	1	8	2	67.2	9	12	1	2	.955	9	1	0	2	.11	0
McDonald,J., LAD-Pit	R	.048	21	1	0	0	1	.033	30	1	1	0	0	0	1	18	2	71.2	6	8	1	1	.933	5	3	1	1	.60	1
McGee,Jake, TB	L	-	0	0	0	0	0	-	0	0	0	0	0	0	0	0	0	5.0	0	1	0	0	1.000	0	0	0	0	-	0
Meche,Gil, KC	R	-	0	0	0	0	0	.130	23	3	0	0	0	2	0	9	0	61.2	7	4	1	0	.917	21	4	0	1	.19	-2
Medders,Brandon, SF	R	-	0	0	0	0	0	.000	5	0	0	0	0	0	0	2	0	15.0	0	2	0	0	1.000	3	2	0	0	.67	0
Medlen,Kris, Atl	R	.185	27	5	0	2	2	.125	40	5	1	0	0	2	3	21	2	107.2	4	17	0	2	1.000	5	1	0	2	.20	1
Meek,Evan, Pit	R	1.000	1	1	0	0	1	1.000	1	1	0	0	0	0	0	0	1	80.0	19	14	0	1	1.000	12	2	0	0	.17	1
Mejia,Jenrry, NYM	R	.333	3	1	0	0	0	.333	3	1	0	0	0	0	0	1	0	39.0	6	6	0	0	1.000	4	1	0	0	.25	0
Melancon,M., NYY-Hou	R	-	0	0	0	0	0	-	0	0	0	0	0	0	0	0	0	21.1	3	3	0	1	1.000	0	0	0	0	-	1
Mendez,Adalberto, Fla	R	.286	7	2	0	0	3	.286	7	2	0	0	0	0	0	1	3	24.2	2	2	0	1	1.000	5	2	0	0	.40	0
Mendoza,Luis, KC	R	-	0	0	0	0	0	.000	1	0	0	0	0	0	0	1	1	4.0	0	1	0	0	1.000	0	0	0	0	-	0
Meredith,Cla, Bal	R	-	0	0	0	0	0	.000	2	0	0	0	0	0	0	1	1	15.0	0	5	0	0	1.000	2	0	0	0	.00	1
Meyer,Dan, Fla	L	-	0	0	0	0	0	.000	2	0	0	0	0	0	0	2	0	9.1	0	2	1	0	.667	2	0	0	0	.00	-1
Mickolio,Kam, Bal	R	-	0	0	0	0	0	-	0	0	0	0	0	0	0	0	0	3.2	0	0	0	0	-	1	0	0	0	.00	0
Mijares,Jose, Min	L	-	0	0	0	0	0	-	0	0	0	0	0	0	0	0	0	32.2	0	2	0	0	1.000	2	1	1	0	.50	-1
Miller,Andrew, Fla	L	.000	9	0	0	0	0	.059	68	4	0	0	0	3	0	32	4	32.2	1	4	0	0	1.000	4	0	0	0	.00	-1
Miller,Justin, LAD	R	-	0	0	0	0	0	.000	8	0	0	0	0	0	0	4	0	24.1	0	0	0	0	-	6	2	0	0	.33	0
Miller,Trever, StL	L	-	0	0	0	0	0	.167	6	1	1	0	0	0	0	1	2	36.0	9	13	0	2	1.000	4	3	2	0	.75	3
Mills,Brad, Tor	L	-	0	0	0	0	0	.000	1	0	0	0	0	0	0	0	0	22.1	3	0	0	0	1.000	4	0	0	0	.00	-1
Millwood,Kevin, Bal	R	.000	5	0	0	0	0	.121	448	54	15	0	2	24	20	207	52	190.2	17	14	0	0	1.000	11	5	0	0	.45	-1
Minor,Mike, Atl	L	.000	10	0	0	0	0	.000	10	0	0	0	0	0	1	7	0	40.2	0	4	0	0	1.000	5	2	2	0	.40	1
Misch,Pat, NYM	L	.125	8	1	0	0	1	.077	39	3	0	0	0	1	3	14	8	37.2	1	3	1	0	.800	1	0	0	0	.00	0
Mitre,Sergio, NYY	R	-	0	0	0	0	0	.141	78	11	4	0	0	2	3	33	13	54.0	5	7	0	0	1.000	9	0	0	0	.00	-2
Mock,Garrett, Was	R	.000	2	0	0	0	0	.069	29	2	0	0	0	0	0	17	4	3.1	0	0	0	0	-	0	0	0	0	-	0
Moehler,Brian, Hou	R	.100	10	1	0	0	0	.045	202	9	2	0	0	5	9	93	18	56.2	6	3	0	1	1.000	4	2	0	0	.50	0
Monasterios,Carlos, LAD	R	.071	14	1	0	0	4	.071	14	1	0	0	0	0	0	7	4	88.1	4	11	1	0	.938	11	1	0	0	.09	-1
Morales,Franklin, Col	L	-	0	0	0	0	0	.250	28	7	0	0	0	2	1	9	2	28.2	1	0	0	0	1.000	1	0	0	0	.00	0
Morrow,Brandon, Tor	R	.000	3	0	0	0	0	.000	6	0	0	0	0	0	0	2	0	146.1	4	12	0	2	1.000	17	9	1	0	.53	0
Mortensen,Clay, Oak	R	-	0	0	0	0	0	.000	1	0	0	0	0	0	0	0	0	6.0	0	1	0	0	1.000	0	0	0	0	-	0
Morton,Charlie, Pit	R	.038	26	1	0	0	2	.081	74	6	1	0	0	1	0	42	7	79.2	6	12	3	0	.857	14	2	1	1	.14	-3
Moscoso,Guillermo, Tex	R	-	0	0	0	0	0	-	0	0	0	0	0	0	0	0	0	0.2	0	0	0	0	-	0	0	0	0	-	0
Moseley,Dustin, NYY	R	-	0	0	0	0	0	-	0	0	0	0	0	0	0	0	0	65.1	7	10	0	1	1.000	11	2	0	0	.18	1
Mota,Guillermo, SF	R	.000	1	0	0	0	1	.211	38	8	1	0	2	7	0	19	2	54.0	0	7	1	0	.875	8	1	0	0	.13	-1
Motte,Jason, StL	R	.000	2	0	0	0	0	.000	3	0	0	0	0	0	0	3	0	52.1	4	4	1	0	.889	4	1	1	0	.25	0
Moyer,Jamie, Phi	L	.077	26	2	0	1	6	.127	387	49	5	0	0	13	34	142	61	111.2	2	16	1	0	.947	13	1	0	0	.08	-3
Moylan,Peter, Atl	R	-	0	0	0	0	0	.000	7	0	0	0	0	0	1	6	0	63.2	6	18	1	0	.960	14	4	0	0	.29	1
Mujica,Edward, SD	R	-	0	0	0	0	0	.250	8	2	0	0	0	0	0	2	2	69.2	3	7	0	0	1.000	3	1	1	0	.33	-1
Mulvey,Kevin, Ari	R	-	0	0	0	0	0	.143	7	1	0	0	0	0	0	3	0	3.0	0	1	0	0	1.000	0	0	0	0	-	0
Myers,Brett, Hou	R	.177	62	11	0	2	11	.130	408	53	10	0	0	12	21	139	56	223.2	25	30	2	1	.965	17	7	1	1	.41	0
Narveson,Chris, Mil	L	.327	49	16	0	7	7	.293	58	17	1	0	0	7	2	21	8	167.2	7	25	2	1	.941	18	8	3	0	.44	3
Nelson,Joe, Bos	R	-	0	0	0	0	0	.000	1	0	0	0	0	0	0	0	0	8.1	0	0	0	0	-	0	0	0	0	-	0
Neshek,Pat, Min	R	-	0	0	0	0	0	-	0	0	0	0	0	0	0	0	0	9.0	0	2	0	0	1.000	2	1	1	0	.50	1
Ni,Fu-Te, Det	L	-	0	0	0	0	0	-	0	0	0	0	0	0	0	0	0	23.0	1	5	0	0	1.000	3	2	2	0	.67	1
Niemann,Jeff, TB	R	.000	5	0	0	0	0	.000	10	0	0	0	0	0	0	7	0	174.1	8	14	1	1	.957	23	2	2	0	.09	-4
Niese,Jonathon, NYM	L	.189	53	10	0	4	5	.179	67	12	2	0	0	4	8	34	6	173.2	7	26	1	0	.971	4	4	1	0	1.00	3
Nieve,Fernando, NYM	R	.000	2	0	0	0	0	.179	28	5	0	0	0	2	2	11	5	42.0	3	3	0	0	1.000	1	0	0	0	.00	-1
Nippert,Dustin, Tex	R	.000	1	0	0	0	0	.111	9	1	0	0	0	0	1	6	0	56.2	3	4	0	1	1.000	13	1	0	0	.08	-3
Nolasco,Ricky, Fla	R	.170	47	8	0	3	6	.150	207	31	5	0	1	16	8	98	33	157.2	9	18	3	1	.900	11	6	2	0	.55	0
Norberto,Jordan, Ari	L	-	0	0	0	0	0	-	0	0	0	0	0	0	0	0	0	20.0	1	1	1	0	.667	2	1	0	0	.50	-1
Norris,Bud, Hou	R	.159	44	7	0	2	10	.167	60	10	2	0	0	2	2	17	11	153.2	12	21	3	3	.917	17	6	0	1	.29	1
Nova,Ivan, NYY	R	-	0	0	0	0	0	-	0	0	0	0	0	0	0	0	0	42.0	5	5	1	0	.909	3	0	0	0	.00	0
Nunez,Leo, Fla	R	-	0	0	0	0	0	-	0	0	0	0	0	0	0	0	0	65.0	9	5	0	0	1.000	6	4	1	0	.67	-1
O'Day,Darren, Tex	R	-	0	0	0	0	0	-	0	0	0	0	0	0	0	0	0	62.0	4	5	1	0	.900	4	1	0	0	.25	0
O'Flaherty,Eric, Atl	L	-	0	0	0	0	0	.000	2	0	0	0	0	0	0	2	0	44.0	1	5	0	0	1.000	3	0	0	0	.00	1
Ogando,Alexi, Tex	R	1.000	1	1	0	0	0	1.000	1	1	0	0	0	0	0	0	0	41.2	3	3	1	0	.857	7	1	0	0	.14	-1
Ohlendorf,Ross, Pit	R	.077	26	2	0	0	2	.065	92	6	0	0	0	0	3	41	6	108.1	6	8	4	0	.778	17	1	1	0	.06	-2
Ohman,Will, Bal-Fla	L	-	0	0	0	0	0	.400	5	2	0	0	0	1	1	2	1	42.0	1	4	0	0	1.000	3	1	0	0	.33	-1
Okajima,Hideki, Bos	L	-	0	0	0	0	0	-	0	0	0	0	0	0	0	0	0	46.0	4	8	0	1	1.000	2	1	1	0	.50	3
Oliver,Andy, Det	L	.000	2	0	0	0	0	.000	2	0	0	0	0	0	0	1	0	22.0	0	2	1	0	.667	5	3	1	0	.60	0
Oliver,Darren, Tex	L	-	0	0	0	0	0	.221	217	48	11	0	1	20	8	74	15	61.2	2	9	0	0	1.000	11	3	3	0	.27	0
Olsen,Scott, Was	L	.083	24	2	0	0	4	.150	213	32	5	0	0	15	7	89	32	81.0	1	7	0	1	1.000	5	2	0	0	.40	0
Olson,Garrett, Sea	L	-	0	0	0	0	0	.167	6	1	0	0	0	1	0	2	2	37.2	2	0	0	0	1.000	2	0	0	0	.00	-1
Ondrusek,Logan, Cin	R	.000	4	0	0	0	0	.000	4	0	0	0	0	0	0	4	0	58.2	11	8	1	1	.950	2	2	0	0	1.00	1
Ortiz,Ramon, Col	R	.000	5	0	0	0	0	.078	141	11	2	0	1	4	5	59	14	30.0	1	13	0	0	1.000	3	1	0	0	.33	2
Ortiz,Russ, LAD	R	-	0	0	0	0	0	.205	507	104	23	0	7	49	35	135	60	7.0	0	2	0	0	1.000	1	0	0	0	-	1
O'Sullivan,Sean, LAA-KC	R	.000	1	0	0	0	0	.250	4	1	0	0	0	0	0	1	0	83.2	8	7	1	1	.938	16	1	0	0	.06	-2
Oswalt,Roy, Hou-Phi	R	.140	57	8	0	1	11	.157	613	96	7	0	1	34	23	165	98	211.2	11	33	2	2	.957	21	6	1	0	.29	-1
Ottavino,Adam, StL	R	.000	6	0	0	0	0	.000	6	0	0	0	0	0	0	1	5	0	22.1	3	1	0	0	1.000	3	1	0	0	.33	-2
Owings,Micah, Cin	R	.214	14	3	1	3	0	.293	184	54	14	2	9	34	8	62	3	33.1	5	2	0	0	1.000	3	1	0	0	.33	0

Pitchers Hitting, Fielding and Holding Runners

Pitcher	T	2010 Hitting Avg	AB	H	HR	RBI	SH	Career Hitting Avg	AB	H	2B	3B	HR	RBI	BB	SO	SH	2010 Fielding and Holding Runners Inn	PO	A	E	DP	Pct	SBA	CS	PCS	PPO	CS%	RS
Padilla,Vicente, LAD	R	.154	26	4	0	2	6	.108	250	27	4	1	0	17	16	130	30	95.0	8	10	1	1	.947	5	3	0	0	.60	0
Palmer,Matt, LAA	R	-	0	0	0	0	0	.200	10	2	0	0	0	0	1	5	1	33.2	4	1	2	0	.714	2	1	0	0	.50	0
Papelbon,Jonathan, Bos	R	-	0	0	0	0	0	-	0	0	0	0	0	0	0	0	0	67.0	4	5	1	0	.900	11	0	0	0	.00	-2
Park,Chan Ho, NYY-Pit	R	.000	1	0	0	0	0	.179	430	77	15	1	3	31	20	155	54	63.2	3	14	0	0	1.000	2	0	0	0	.00	1
Parnell,Bobby, NYM	R	.000	1	0	0	0	0	.111	9	1	0	0	0	0	0	3	4	35.0	1	7	0	0	1.000	1	1	1	0	1.00	1
Parra,Manny, Mil	L	.176	34	6	0	1	0	.184	141	26	11	1	0	13	6	57	10	122.0	6	17	5	0	.821	13	2	1	0	.15	-4
Parrish,John, KC	L	-	0	0	0	0	0	.000	1	0	0	0	0	0	0	0	0	6.0	2	1	0	0	1.000	1	0	0	0	.00	0
Patton,Troy, Bal	L	-	0	0	0	0	0	.333	3	1	0	0	0	0	0	1	0	0.2	0	0	0	0	-	0	0	0	0	-	0
Pauley,David, Sea	R	-	0	0	0	0	0	-	0	0	0	0	0	0	0	0	0	90.2	6	8	0	0	1.000	8	0	0	0	.00	-2
Paulino,Felipe, Hou	R	.292	24	7	0	0	3	.145	55	8	1	0	0	0	1	28	6	91.2	6	10	2	1	.889	11	4	0	0	.36	-2
Pavano,Carl, Min	R	.500	6	3	0	0	2	.145	303	44	8	2	2	14	4	118	36	221.0	19	26	0	3	1.000	39	8	2	0	.21	-5
Peavy,Jake, CWS	R	.143	7	1	0	0	0	.180	412	74	14	1	2	26	18	119	45	107.0	8	16	0	0	1.000	15	3	2	1	.20	0
Pelfrey,Mike, NYM	R	.113	62	7	0	3	6	.094	203	19	2	0	0	9	9	56	19	204.0	11	35	2	4	.958	17	5	0	2	.29	-2
Pena,Tony, CWS	R	-	0	0	0	0	0	.143	7	1	0	0	0	1	0	2	0	100.2	5	14	3	1	.864	9	4	0	0	.44	2
Penn,Hayden, Pit	R	-	0	0	0	0	0	.000	1	0	0	0	0	0	2	0	2	2.1	0	0	0	0	-	0	0	0	0	-	0
Penny,Brad, StL	R	.158	19	3	1	4	1	.156	518	81	16	2	3	34	3	167	41	55.2	2	9	0	0	1.000	2	1	0	0	.50	-1
Peralta,Joel, Was	R	.000	3	0	0	0	0	.250	4	1	1	0	0	2	0	2	0	49.0	1	4	0	0	1.000	3	0	0	1	.00	0
Perdomo,Luis, SD	R	-	0	0	0	0	0	.000	6	0	0	0	0	0	0	5	0	1.0	0	0	0	0	-	0	0	0	0	-	0
Perez,Chris, Cle	R	-	0	0	0	0	0	.000	1	0	0	0	0	0	0	1	0	63.0	3	1	1	0	.800	9	0	0	0	.00	-2
Perez,Oliver, NYM	L	.111	9	1	0	1	1	.158	341	54	1	0	0	15	14	116	39	46.1	1	4	0	1	1.000	1	0	0	0	.00	-1
Perez,Rafael, Cle	L	-	0	0	0	0	0	.000	1	0	0	0	0	0	0	1	0	61.0	3	10	1	0	.929	6	1	0	0	.17	0
Perkins,Glen, Min	L	-	0	0	0	0	0	.000	4	0	0	0	0	0	0	4	3	21.2	1	9	0	1	1.000	3	1	1	0	.33	1
Perry,Ryan, Det	R	-	0	0	0	0	0	-	0	0	0	0	0	0	0	0	0	62.2	3	8	0	0	1.000	9	1	0	0	.11	-2
Pestano,Vinnie, Cle	R	-	0	0	0	0	0	-	0	0	0	0	0	0	0	0	0	5.0	1	0	0	0	1.000	1	0	0	0	.00	0
Pettitte,Andy, NYY	L	.250	4	1	0	0	1	.137	190	26	6	0	1	13	6	63	33	129.0	3	15	3	1	.857	3	1	1	1	.33	2
Pineiro,Joel, LAA	R	.000	3	0	0	0	0	.105	162	17	6	0	0	10	11	93	20	152.1	11	26	1	3	.974	4	1	0	0	.25	2
Pinto,Renyel, Fla	L	-	0	0	0	0	0	.000	6	0	0	0	0	0	1	4	2	16.2	1	0	0	0	1.000	4	1	0	0	.25	-1
Porcello,Rick, Det	R	.000	1	0	0	0	1	.333	6	2	0	0	0	2	0	2	1	162.2	9	15	1	3	.960	15	5	0	0	.33	-4
Price,David, TB	L	.143	7	1	0	0	0	.200	10	2	0	0	0	0	0	5	0	208.2	8	22	0	2	1.000	20	7	3	0	.35	0
Proctor,Scott, Atl	R	-	0	0	0	0	0	.000	3	0	0	0	0	0	0	3	0	5.2	0	0	0	0	-	1	0	0	0	.00	0
Purcey,David, Tor	L	-	0	0	0	0	0	.000	1	0	0	0	0	0	0	1	0	34.0	2	1	0	0	1.000	1	1	0	0	1.00	0
Putz,J.J., CWS	R	-	0	0	0	0	0	-	0	0	0	0	0	0	0	0	0	54.0	1	4	0	0	1.000	5	1	0	0	.20	0
Qualls,Chad, Ari-TB	R	-	0	0	0	0	0	.000	6	0	0	0	0	0	0	5	0	59.0	5	5	2	1	.833	6	1	0	0	.17	-5
Ramirez,Edwar, Oak	R	-	0	0	0	0	0	-	0	0	0	0	0	0	0	0	0	11.0	0	1	1	0	.500	0	0	0	0	-	-1
Ramirez,Ramon, Bos-SF	R	-	0	0	0	0	0	.400	5	2	0	0	0	0	0	3	1	69.1	3	8	2	0	.846	6	1	0	0	.17	-1
Ramos,Cesar, SD	L	-	0	0	0	0	0	.000	4	0	0	0	0	0	0	2	0	8.1	1	0	0	0	1.000	1	0	0	0	.00	0
Rapada,Clay, Tex	L	-	0	0	0	0	0	-	0	0	0	0	0	0	0	0	0	9.0	2	1	0	0	1.000	0	0	0	0	-	1
Rauch,Jon, Min	R	-	0	0	0	0	1	.095	21	2	0	0	1	3	0	15	2	57.2	3	2	0	1	1.000	1	1	0	0	1.00	-1
Ray,Chris, Tex-SF	R	-	0	0	0	0	0	-	0	0	0	0	0	0	0	0	0	55.2	2	15	0	1	1.000	7	2	0	0	.29	3
Ray,Robert, Tor	R	-	0	0	0	0	0	-	0	0	0	0	0	0	0	0	0	3.2	0	0	0	0	-	2	0	0	0	.00	0
Resop,Chris, Atl-Pit	R	-	0	0	0	0	0	.000	1	0	0	0	0	0	0	1	0	21.0	2	2	0	0	1.000	2	0	0	0	.00	0
Reyes,Dennys, StL	L	.000	2	0	0	0	0	.071	56	4	1	0	0	0	2	25	2	38.0	1	8	0	0	1.000	2	1	1	1	.50	1
Reyes,Jo-Jo, Atl	L	.000	1	0	0	0	0	.136	59	8	2	0	0	2	4	22	7	3.1	0	0	0	0	-	0	0	0	0	-	-1
Reynolds,Matt, Col	L	-	0	0	0	0	0	-	0	0	0	0	0	0	1	0	0	18.0	2	3	0	0	1.000	1	1	1	0	1.00	2
Rhodes,Arthur, Cin	L	-	0	0	0	0	0	.200	5	1	0	0	0	0	4	0	0	55.0	3	6	0	0	1.000	5	2	0	0	.40	0
Richard,Clayton, SD	L	.148	61	9	0	5	8	.131	84	11	3	0	0	7	1	31	11	201.2	6	33	4	3	.907	15	7	5	1	.47	4
Richardson,Dustin, Bos	L	-	0	0	0	0	0	-	0	0	0	0	0	0	0	0	0	13.0	0	1	0	0	.000	4	0	0	0	.00	-2
Rincon,Juan, Col	R	.000	1	0	0	0	0	.250	4	1	0	0	0	0	0	1	0	2.0	0	0	0	0	-	0	0	0	0	-	0
Ring,Royce, NYY	L	-	0	0	0	0	0	-	0	0	0	0	0	0	0	0	0	2.1	0	0	0	0	-	0	0	0	0	-	-1
Riske,David, Mil	R	-	0	0	0	0	0	.000	1	0	0	0	0	0	0	0	0	23.1	1	2	0	0	1.000	2	0	0	0	.00	-1
Rivera,Mariano, NYY	R	.000	1	0	0	0	0	.000	3	0	0	0	0	1	1	1	0	60.0	2	16	0	0	1.000	8	0	0	1	.00	2
Rivera,Saul, Ari	R	-	0	0	0	0	0	.111	9	1	0	0	0	0	2	2	1	3.2	0	0	0	0	-	0	0	0	0	-	-1
Robertson,David, NYY	R	-	0	0	0	0	0	-	0	0	0	0	0	0	0	0	0	61.1	0	5	0	0	1.000	7	1	0	0	.14	-2
Robertson,Nate, Fla-Phi	L	.192	26	5	0	1	7	.136	44	6	1	0	0	2	2	15	8	101.1	3	9	3	0	.800	8	3	0	1	.38	0
Rodney,Fernando, LAA	R	-	0	0	0	0	0	.000	1	0	0	0	0	0	0	0	0	68.0	7	10	0	0	1.000	14	1	1	0	.07	-2
Rodriguez,F., NYM	R	-	0	0	0	0	0	-	0	0	0	0	0	0	0	0	0	57.1	5	4	0	0	1.000	5	1	0	1	.20	-1
Rodriguez,F., LAA	R	-	0	0	0	0	0	-	0	0	0	0	0	0	0	0	0	47.1	1	7	0	2	1.000	1	0	0	0	.00	0
Rodriguez,Henry, Oak	R	-	0	0	0	0	0	-	0	0	0	0	0	0	0	0	0	27.2	2	1	0	0	1.000	8	0	0	0	.00	-1
Rodriguez,R., LAA-Ari	R	-	0	0	0	0	0	-	0	0	0	0	0	0	0	0	0	4.2	0	0	0	0	-	0	0	0	0	-	-1
Rodriguez,Wandy, Hou	L	.190	63	12	0	4	9	.137	293	40	7	0	0	13	7	94	37	195.0	9	31	1	2	.976	24	11	2	0	.46	4
Roenicke,Josh, Tor	R	-	0	0	0	0	0	-	0	0	0	0	0	0	0	0	0	19.0	2	1	2	0	.600	0	0	0	0	-	-2
Rogers,Esmil, Col	R	.167	18	3	0	1	3	.158	19	3	2	0	0	1	0	7	3	72.0	9	6	2	2	.882	10	4	1	0	.40	-1
Rogers,Mark, Mil	R	.500	2	1	0	0	0	.500	2	1	0	0	0	0	0	0	0	10.0	2	6	2	0	1.000	3	0	0	0	.00	0
Romero,J.C., Phi	L	-	0	0	0	0	0	.250	4	1	0	0	0	0	0	1	0	36.2	3	6	0	1	1.000	2	0	0	0	.00	-2
Romero,Ricky, Tor	L	.000	4	0	0	0	0	.000	10	0	0	0	0	0	0	7	0	210.0	7	47	3	2	.947	9	5	2	1	.56	10
Romo,Sergio, SF	R	.000	2	0	0	0	0	.000	4	0	0	0	0	0	0	3	0	62.0	1	5	0	0	1.000	1	1	0	1	1.00	1
Rosa,Carlos, Ari	R	-	0	0	0	0	0	-	0	0	0	0	0	0	0	0	0	20.0	1	3	0	0	1.000	1	0	0	0	.00	0
Rosales,Leo, Ari	R	.000	2	0	0	0	0	.000	5	0	0	0	0	0	0	2	0	16.1	2	0	0	0	1.000	3	1	0	0	.33	0
Rosario,Sandy, Fla	R	-	0	0	0	0	0	-	0	0	0	0	0	0	0	0	0	1.0	0	0	0	0	-	0	0	0	0	-	-1
Ross,Tyson, Oak	R	.000	1	0	0	0	0	.000	1	0	0	0	0	0	0	1	0	39.1	2	8	0	0	1.000	2	0	0	0	.00	0

Pitchers Hitting, Fielding and Holding Runners

Pitcher	T	2010 Hitting Avg	AB	H	HR	RBI	SH	Career Hitting Avg	AB	H	2B	3B	HR	RBI	BB	SO	SH	2010 Fielding and Holding Runners Inn	PO	A	E	DP	Pct	SBA	CS	PCS	PPO	CS%	RS
Rowland-Smith,R., Sea	L	.000	4	0	0	0	0	.000	4	0	0	0	0	0	0	3	0	109.1	3	9	2	0	.857	15	4	2	0	.27	-2
Runzler,Dan, SF	L	.000	1	0	0	0	0	.000	1	0	0	0	0	0	0	1	0	32.1	1	6	3	1	.700	4	2	1	0	.50	0
Rupe,Josh, KC	R	-	0	0	0	0	0	-	0	0	0	0	0	0	0	0	0	9.2	1	1	0	0	1.000	0	0	0	0	-	0
Russell,Adam, SD	R	-	0	0	0	0	0	.000	1	0	0	0	0	0	0	0	0	15.2	0	0	1	0	.000	0	0	0	0	-	0
Russell,James, ChC	L	.000	4	0	0	0	0	.000	4	0	0	0	0	0	0	0	2	0	49.0	2	6	0	0	1.000	4	1	1	0	.25	0
Rzepczynski,Marc, Tor	L	-	0	0	0	0	0	-	0	0	0	0	0	0	0	0	0	63.2	1	4	0	0	1.000	8	3	0	0	.38	-2
Sabathia,CC, NYY	L	.200	5	1	0	0	0	.258	97	25	3	0	3	14	1	26	3	237.2	4	30	1	3	.971	18	3	2	0	.17	0
Saito,Takashi, Atl	R	.000	1	0	0	0	0	.000	2	0	0	0	0	0	0	0	2	0	54.0	4	2	0	0	1.000	1	0	0	0	.00	-1
Salas,Fernando, StL	R	-	0	0	0	0	0	-	0	0	0	0	0	0	0	0	0	30.2	4	4	0	0	1.000	2	0	0	0	.00	0
Sale,Chris, CWS	L	-	0	0	0	0	0	-	0	0	0	0	0	0	0	0	0	23.1	0	1	0	0	1.000	0	0	0	0	-	0
Samardzija,Jeff, ChC	R	.250	4	1	0	1	1	.200	10	2	0	0	1	2	2	4	2	19.1	2	1	0	0	1.000	5	1	0	0	.20	1
Sampson,Chris, Hou	R	-	0	0	0	0	0	.127	55	7	0	0	0	1	22	13	30.1	0	3	0	0	1.000	2	1	0	0	.50	0
Sanabia,Alex, Fla	R	.045	22	1	0	0	3	.045	22	1	0	0	0	0	0	11	3	72.1	2	10	0	0	1.000	8	4	0	0	.50	1
Sanches,Brian, Fla	R	.000	1	0	0	0	0	.000	5	0	0	0	0	1	0	1	0	63.2	3	8	0	1	1.000	6	1	0	0	.17	1
Sanchez,Anibal, Fla	R	.102	59	6	0	1	6	.076	145	11	0	0	0	3	10	64	16	195.0	14	25	5	2	.886	14	3	0	0	.21	-5
Sanchez,Jonathan, SF	L	.138	58	8	0	3	7	.106	161	17	2	1	0	8	6	82	21	193.1	7	20	1	1	.964	26	9	4	1	.35	-1
Sanchez,Romulo, NYY	R	-	0	0	0	0	0	.000	1	0	0	0	0	0	0	1	0	4.1	0	0	0	0	-	0	0	0	0	-	0
Santana,Ervin, LAA	R	-	0	0	0	0	0	.133	15	2	1	0	0	2	0	8	0	222.2	15	17	0	2	1.000	44	8	0	1	.18	-6
Santana,Johan, NYM	L	.177	62	11	1	1	5	.174	213	37	12	1	1	9	9	64	17	199.0	12	18	1	1	.968	5	0	0	0	.00	2
Santos,Sergio, CWS	R	-	0	0	0	0	0	-	0	0	0	0	0	0	0	0	0	51.2	2	6	0	0	1.000	5	1	1	0	.20	-2
Saunders,Joe, LAA-Ari	L	.083	24	2	0	1	3	.074	27	2	0	0	0	1	1	10	3	203.1	6	46	1	1	.981	19	10	7	1	.53	4
Sborz,Jay, Det	R	-	0	0	0	0	0	-	0	0	0	0	0	0	0	0	0	0.2	0	0	0	0	-	1	0	0	0	.00	
Scherzer,Max, Det	R	.000	2	0	0	0	0	.176	68	12	2	0	0	3	4	21	6	195.2	14	14	2	0	.933	30	13	1	0	.43	0
Schlereth,Daniel, Det	L	-	0	0	0	0	0	-	0	0	0	0	0	0	0	0	0	18.2	0	0	0	0	-	5	0	0	0	.00	-2
Schlichting,Travis, LAD	R	.000	1	0	0	0	0	.000	1	0	0	0	0	0	0	0	0	22.2	1	1	0	0	1.000	0	0	0	0	-	-1
Schlitter,Brian, ChC	R	-	0	0	0	0	0	-	0	0	0	0	0	0	0	0	0	8.0	0	2	0	0	1.000	1	0	0	0	.00	-1
Schoeneweis,Scott, Bos	L	-	0	0	0	0	0	.250	8	2	1	0	0	1	2	2	0	13.2	2	1	0	0	1.000	3	0	0	0	.00	-1
Seddon,Chris, Sea	L	-	0	0	0	0	0	.000	3	0	0	0	0	0	0	2	2	22.1	1	1	0	0	1.000	0	0	0	0	-	0
Sheets,Ben, Oak	R	.333	3	1	0	0	1	.078	436	34	3	0	0	12	18	206	42	119.1	5	11	3	1	.842	22	9	2	0	.41	-2
Sherrill,George, LAD	L	-	0	0	0	0	0	-	0	0	0	0	0	0	1	0	0	36.1	0	4	0	0	1.000	0	0	0	0	-	-1
Shields,James, TB	R	.500	2	1	0	0	0	.250	24	6	0	0	0	1	2	5	1	203.1	18	17	4	2	.897	13	3	0	2	.23	-1
Shields,Scot, LAA	R	.000	1	0	0	0	0	.000	4	0	0	0	0	0	0	3	0	46.0	2	7	1	0	.900	7	3	1	0	.43	1
Silva,Carlos, ChC	R	.065	31	2	0	2	6	.086	58	5	2	0	0	3	4	22	9	113.0	3	13	0	0	1.000	10	3	0	0	.30	-2
Simon,Alfredo, Bal	R	-	0	0	0	0	0	-	0	0	0	0	0	0	0	0	0	49.1	6	3	0	0	1.000	7	2	0	0	.29	-2
Sinkbeil,Brett, Fla	R	-	0	0	0	0	0	-	0	0	0	0	0	0	0	0	0	2.0	0	0	0	0	-	0	0	0	0	-	
Sipp,Tony, Cle	L	-	0	0	0	0	0	-	0	0	0	0	0	0	0	0	0	63.0	1	10	0	0	1.000	14	6	6	0	.43	1
Slama,Anthony, Min	R	-	0	0	0	0	0	-	0	0	0	0	0	0	0	0	0	4.2	0	0	0	0	-	1	0	0	0	.00	0
Slaton,Doug, Was	L	-	0	0	0	0	0	-	0	0	0	0	0	0	0	0	0	40.2	0	4	1	0	.800	4	1	1	0	.25	-1
Slowey,Kevin, Min	R	.000	2	0	0	0	1	.154	13	2	1	0	0	2	0	3	2	155.2	11	12	2	0	.920	10	4	0	0	.40	1
Smith,Chris, Mil	R	-	0	0	0	0	0	.000	2	0	0	0	0	0	1	1	0	3.1	0	0	0	0	-	0	0	0	0	-	0
Smith,Greg, Col	L	.308	13	4	0	2	3	.333	15	5	2	0	0	2	0	2	4	39.0	1	5	0	0	1.000	2	1	0	1	.50	1
Smith,Joe, Cle	R	-	0	0	0	0	0	.000	2	0	0	0	0	0	0	2	0	40.0	1	8	0	2	1.000	7	1	1	0	.14	2
Smith,Jordan, Cin	R	.000	3	0	0	0	0	.000	3	0	0	0	0	0	0	1	0	42.0	1	1	0	0	1.000	2	1	0	0	.50	-2
Snell,Ian, Sea	R	-	0	0	0	0	0	.094	192	18	2	0	0	7	84	33	46.1	6	6	0	1	1.000	3	1	0	0	.33	-1
Sonnanstine,Andy, TB	R	.000	1	0	0	0	0	.318	22	7	1	0	0	2	3	12	2	81.0	9	7	0	0	1.000	6	0	0	0	.00	-2
Soria,Joakim, KC	R	-	0	0	0	0	0	-	0	0	0	0	0	0	0	0	0	65.2	9	10	0	1	1.000	2	1	0	0	.50	1
Soriano,Rafael, TB	R	-	0	0	0	0	0	.000	4	0	0	0	0	0	0	1	0	62.1	3	0	1	0	.750	3	0	0	0	.00	-1
Sosa,Jorge, Fla	R	.500	2	1	0	0	0	.145	83	12	2	0	3	4	7	37	12	36.2	0	2	0	0	1.000	4	1	0	0	.25	-1
Springer,Russ, Cin	R	-	0	0	0	0	0	.074	27	2	0	0	0	0	17	4	1.2	0	0	0	0	-	0	0	0	0	-	0
Stammen,Craig, Was	R	.237	38	9	0	6	3	.217	69	15	6	0	0	10	3	25	7	128.0	9	19	4	4	.875	5	1	0	0	.20	0
Stange,Daniel, Ari	R	-	0	0	0	0	0	-	0	0	0	0	0	0	0	0	0	4.0	0	1	0	0	1.000	0	0	0	0	-	0
Stauffer,Tim, SD	R	.176	17	3	0	2	2	.171	70	12	3	0	0	5	3	38	8	82.2	2	10	0	0	1.000	3	2	0	0	.67	1
Stetter,Mitch, Mil	L	-	0	0	0	0	0	.000	1	0	0	0	0	0	0	1	0	3.2	0	0	0	0	-	0	0	0	0	-	0
Stevens,Jeff, ChC	R	-	0	0	0	0	0	-	0	0	0	0	0	0	0	0	0	17.2	1	0	0	0	1.000	1	0	0	0	.00	0
Stokes,Brian, LAA	R	-	0	0	0	0	0	.667	3	2	0	0	0	0	0	1	1	16.2	1	3	1	1	.800	4	1	1	0	.25	0
Stoner,Tobi, NYM	R	-	0	0	0	0	0	-	0	0	0	0	0	0	0	0	0	2.1	0	0	0	0	-	0	0	0	0	-	0
Storen,Drew, Was	R	.500	2	1	0	0	0	.500	2	1	0	0	0	0	0	1	0	55.1	2	6	0	1	1.000	3	1	0	0	.33	-1
Strasburg,Stephen, Was	R	.050	20	1	0	1	2	.050	20	1	0	0	0	1	0	7	2	68.0	4	3	1	0	.875	3	1	0	0	.33	-3
Street,Huston, Col	R	.000	1	0	0	0	0	.000	1	0	0	0	0	0	0	1	0	47.1	2	4	0	1	1.000	3	1	1	0	.33	0
Strickland,Scott, Fla	R	-	0	0	0	0	0	.000	6	0	0	0	0	0	0	4	1	2.0	0	0	0	0	-	2	1	0	0	.50	0
Strop,Pedro, Tex	R	-	0	0	0	0	0	-	0	0	0	0	0	0	0	0	0	10.2	1	1	0	0	1.000	1	0	0	0	.00	0
Suppan,Jeff, Mil-StL	R	.192	26	5	0	1	1	.175	429	75	7	0	1	24	23	100	67	101.1	5	10	2	1	.882	7	4	2	0	.57	0
Sweeney,Brian, Sea	R	-	0	0	0	0	1	.000	5	0	0	0	0	0	0	3	1	37.0	1	6	0	0	1.000	2	1	0	0	.50	0
Takahashi,Hisanori, NYM	L	.063	16	1	0	0	4	.063	16	1	0	0	0	0	0	3	4	122.0	5	15	1	0	.952	7	4	0	0	.57	2
Talbot,Mitch, Cle	R	.000	5	0	0	0	0	.000	5	0	0	0	0	0	0	4	0	159.1	11	19	1	4	.968	15	11	0	1	.73	4
Tallet,Brian, Tor	L	.000	1	0	0	0	0	.000	5	0	0	0	0	0	0	2	0	77.1	2	6	0	0	1.000	3	0	0	0	.00	-1
Tankersley,Taylor, Fla	L	-	0	0	0	0	0	.000	2	0	0	0	0	0	0	2	0	12.0	0	0	0	0	-	2	0	0	0	.00	-1
Taschner,Jack, Pit-LAD	L	-	0	0	0	0	1	.000	2	0	0	0	0	0	1	0	3	19.2	1	6	0	0	1.000	1	0	0	0	.00	0
Tejeda,Robinson, KC	R	-	0	0	0	0	0	.080	25	2	0	1	0	0	0	13	7	61.0	2	5	2	0	.778	5	1	0	0	.20	-1
Texeira,K., Sea-KC	R	.000	1	0	0	0	0	.000	1	0	0	0	0	0	0	1	0	61.1	2	7	0	0	1.000	7	3	0	0	.43	-2

Pitchers Hitting, Fielding and Holding Runners

Pitcher	T	2010 Hitting Avg	AB	H	HR	RBI	SH	Career Hitting Avg	AB	H	2B	3B	HR	RBI	BB	SO	SH	2010 Fielding and Holding Runners Inn	PO	A	E	DP	Pct	SBA	CS	PCS	PPO	CS%	RS
Thatcher,Joe, SD	L	-	0	0	0	0	0	.000	1	0	0	0	0	0	0	1	0	35.0	1	0	0	0	1.000	3	0	0	0	.00	-2
Thayer,Dale, TB	R	-	0	0	0	0	0	.000	1	0	0	0	0	0	0	0	0	2.0	0	0	0	0	-	0	0	0	0	-	0
Thomas,Brad, Det	L	-	0	0	0	0	0	-	0	0	0	0	0	0	0	0	0	69.1	2	11	0	0	1.000	2	2	2	0	1.00	0
Thomas,Justin, Pit	L	.000	1	0	0	0	0	.000	1	0	0	0	0	0	0	1	0	13.0	0	2	0	0	1.000	1	1	0	0	1.00	0
Thompson,Brad, KC	R	-	0	0	0	0	0	.179	56	10	0	0	0	2	2	27	13	19.2	1	1	0	0	1.000	2	1	0	0	.50	0
Thompson,Rich, LAA	R	-	0	0	0	0	0	-	0	0	0	0	0	0	0	0	0	19.2	2	1	1	0	.750	1	0	0	0	.00	0
Thornton,Matt, CWS	L	-	0	0	0	0	0	.000	1	0	0	0	0	0	0	1	0	60.2	0	6	0	0	1.000	3	0	0	0	.00	1
Threets,Erick, CWS	L	-	0	0	0	0	0	-	0	0	0	0	0	0	0	0	0	12.1	0	3	1	0	.750	1	0	0	0	.00	0
Tillman,Chris, Bal	R	.000	1	0	0	0	0	.000	1	0	0	0	0	0	0	0	0	53.2	7	6	1	1	.929	4	1	0	0	.25	0
Todd,Jess, Cle	R	-	0	0	0	0	0	-	0	0	0	0	0	0	0	0	0	6.0	1	0	0	0	1.000	2	0	0	0	.00	0
Tomlin,Josh, Cle	R	-	0	0	0	0	0	-	0	0	0	0	0	0	0	0	0	73.0	4	9	0	3	1.000	5	3	0	0	.60	3
Torres,Carlos, CWS	R	-	0	0	0	0	0	.000	3	0	0	0	0	0	0	3	0	13.2	1	1	1	0	.667	1	1	1	0	1.00	1
Troncoso,Ramon, LAD	R	.000	2	0	0	1	0	.000	7	0	0	0	0	1	1	6	1	54.0	1	6	0	0	1.000	5	0	0	0	.00	0
Uehara,Koji, Bal	R	-	0	0	0	0	0	.000	2	0	0	0	0	0	1	1	0	44.0	2	3	0	0	1.000	1	0	0	0	.00	0
Valdes,Raul, NYM	L	.400	10	4	0	1	4	.400	10	4	1	0	0	1	0	3	4	58.2	3	8	0	0	1.000	2	1	0	0	.50	0
Valdez,Cesar, Ari	R	.000	4	0	0	0	0	.000	4	0	0	0	0	0	0	3	0	20.0	5	1	0	1	1.000	1	0	0	0	.00	-1
Valdez,Merkin, Tor	R	-	0	0	0	0	0	-	0	0	0	0	0	0	0	0	1	1.1	1	1	0	0	1.000	0	0	0	0	-	0
Valverde,Jose, Det	R	-	0	0	0	0	0	.500	2	1	1	0	0	0	0	1	0	63.0	4	4	0	2	1.000	4	1	0	0	.25	0
VandenHurk,R., Fla-Bal	R	-	0	0	0	0	0	.021	47	1	0	0	0	0	1	31	6	17.2	0	1	1	0	.500	1	0	0	1	.00	0
Vargas,Claudio, Mil	R	.000	3	0	0	0	0	.080	188	15	4	0	0	7	3	60	33	19.2	1	1	0	0	1.000	2	0	0	0	.00	0
Vargas,Jason, Sea	L	.000	6	0	0	0	1	.259	54	14	3	0	0	3	2	14	2	192.2	9	17	0	0	1.000	10	1	0	1	.10	0
Varvaro,Anthony, Sea	R	-	0	0	0	0	0	-	0	0	0	0	0	0	0	0	0	4.0	0	1	0	0	1.000	0	0	0	0	-	0
Vasquez,Esmerling, Ari	R	.000	2	0	0	0	0	.000	2	0	0	0	0	0	0	1	0	53.2	5	2	1	0	.875	7	4	1	0	.57	0
Vazquez,Javier, NYY	R	.000	1	0	0	0	2	.206	504	104	13	2	1	27	22	85	96	157.1	14	23	0	2	1.000	8	4	0	0	.50	4
Venters,Jonny, Atl	L	.000	1	0	0	0	0	.000	1	0	0	0	0	0	0	1	0	83.0	2	15	2	0	.895	5	2	0	0	.40	3
Veras,Jose, Fla	R	-	0	0	0	0	0	-	0	0	0	0	0	0	0	0	0	48.0	5	4	1	0	.900	5	1	0	0	.20	1
Verlander,Justin, Det	R	.000	4	0	0	0	1	.000	16	0	0	0	0	0	0	10	5	224.1	15	34	2	3	.961	31	7	0	3	.23	1
Villanueva,Carlos, Mil	R	.000	4	0	0	0	0	.083	60	5	0	0	0	3	2	29	10	52.2	3	3	0	1	1.000	9	1	0	0	.11	-1
Villar,Henry, Hou	R	-	0	0	0	0	0	-	0	0	0	0	0	0	0	0	0	6.0	1	0	1	0	.500	0	0	0	0	-	-1
Viola,Pedro, Bal	L	-	0	0	0	0	0	-	0	0	0	0	0	0	0	0	0	1.1	0	0	0	0	-	0	0	0	0	-	0
Volquez,Edinson, Cin	R	.118	17	2	0	0	3	.096	94	9	0	0	0	1	1	46	14	62.2	0	12	0	0	1.000	5	1	0	0	.20	2
Volstad,Chris, Fla	R	.093	54	5	0	2	9	.110	127	14	4	0	0	5	1	65	17	175.0	5	27	0	1	1.000	33	4	0	1	.12	-4
Wagner,Billy, Atl	L	-	0	0	0	0	0	.100	20	2	0	0	0	1	1	12	0	69.1	3	7	1	0	.909	4	1	1	0	.25	1
Wainwright,Adam, StL	R	.167	84	14	0	6	5	.223	301	67	16	1	5	23	13	87	22	230.1	21	36	1	5	.983	13	5	0	1	.38	1
Wakefield,Tim, Bos	R	.000	4	0	0	0	2	.121	107	13	2	0	1	4	3	43	15	140.0	9	15	2	0	.923	29	5	2	1	.17	-4
Walden,Jordan, LAA	R	-	0	0	0	0	0	-	0	0	0	0	0	0	0	0	0	15.1	2	4	0	0	1.000	2	0	0	0	.00	-1
Walker,Tyler, Was	R	.000	2	0	0	0	0	.000	12	0	0	0	0	0	1	7	1	35.1	2	6	1	0	.889	3	2	1	0	.67	1
Walters,P.J., StL	R	.000	7	0	0	0	1	.000	10	0	0	0	0	0	1	6	3	30.0	2	1	0	1	1.000	1	0	0	0	.00	-2
Weaver,Jeff, LAD	R	.200	5	1	0	0	0	.207	208	43	6	1	0	13	6	73	24	44.1	0	9	1	0	.900	8	2	1	0	.25	1
Weaver,Jered, LAA	R	.200	10	2	0	0	0	.136	22	3	0	0	0	1	1	7	0	224.1	10	18	0	0	1.000	31	4	1	2	.13	-2
Webb,Ryan, SD	R	.000	1	0	0	0	0	.000	1	0	0	0	0	0	0	1	0	59.0	7	13	1	4	.952	10	0	0	0	.00	-3
Weinhardt,Robbie, Det	R	-	0	0	0	0	0	-	0	0	0	0	0	0	0	0	0	29.1	4	2	3	1	.667	3	2	0	0	.67	-2
Wellemeyer,Todd, SF	R	.100	20	2	0	0	1	.136	140	19	0	0	0	6	2	68	23	58.2	1	2	0	0	1.000	6	1	0	0	.17	-1
Wells,Randy, ChC	R	.173	52	9	0	3	9	.182	99	18	5	0	0	5	4	22	21	194.1	18	25	5	1	.896	18	4	1	1	.22	-2
West,Sean, Fla	L	.000	3	0	0	0	0	.059	34	2	1	0	0	0	0	21	4	9.1	0	1	1	0	.500	1	0	0	0	.00	0
Westbrook,Jake, Cle-StL	R	.111	27	3	0	1	1	.128	39	5	2	0	0	2	2	20	4	202.2	16	47	2	3	.969	23	8	0	0	.35	9
Wheeler,Dan, TB	R	-	0	0	0	0	0	.143	7	1	0	0	0	0	0	1	1	48.1	1	8	0	1	1.000	3	1	0	0	.33	1
White,Sean, Sea	R	-	0	0	0	0	0	-	0	0	0	0	0	0	0	0	0	34.1	2	4	0	0	1.000	0	0	0	0	-	-2
Williams,Randy, CWS	L	-	0	0	0	0	0	.000	1	0	0	0	0	0	0	0	0	25.0	1	2	0	0	1.000	5	3	2	0	.60	-1
Willis,Dontrelle, Det-Ari	L	.167	6	1	0	0	0	.232	358	83	10	5	8	35	22	65	30	65.2	3	7	0	1	1.000	12	3	1	0	.25	-1
Wilson,Brian, SF	R	.000	5	0	0	0	0	.000	9	0	0	0	0	0	0	2	1	74.2	3	2	0	0	1.000	1	1	0	0	1.00	0
Wilson,C.J., Tex	L	.000	4	0	0	0	0	.000	4	0	0	0	0	0	0	1	1	204.0	8	25	2	0	.943	29	8	1	0	.28	1
Wolf,Randy, Mil	L	.247	77	19	0	5	4	.189	586	111	30	0	5	54	32	194	70	215.2	13	40	0	4	1.000	13	2	1	0	.15	4
Wolf,Ross, Oak	R	-	0	0	0	0	0	.000	1	0	0	0	0	0	0	1	0	12.2	0	4	0	0	1.000	0	0	0	0	-	0
Wood,Blake, KC	R	-	0	0	0	0	0	-	0	0	0	0	0	0	0	0	0	49.2	5	6	0	0	1.000	13	3	1	0	.23	0
Wood,Kerry, Cle-NYY	R	-	0	0	0	0	0	.171	345	59	6	0	7	32	11	113	46	46.0	3	6	0	0	1.000	9	0	0	0	.00	-1
Wood,Tim, Fla	R	-	0	0	0	0	0	.500	2	1	0	0	0	0	0	1	0	27.2	1	1	0	0	1.000	3	1	0	0	.33	0
Wood,Travis, Cin	L	.189	37	7	1	3	5	.189	37	7	2	1	1	3	0	15	5	102.2	2	8	3	1	.769	0	0	0	0	-	2
Worley,Vance, Phi	R	.000	3	0	0	0	0	.000	3	0	0	0	0	0	0	3	0	13.0	0	4	0	0	1.000	1	1	0	0	1.00	1
Wright,Jamey, Cle-Sea	R	-	0	0	0	0	0	.147	436	64	15	1	1	17	12	175	51	58.1	5	16	0	2	1.000	13	0	0	1	.00	0
Wright,Wesley, Hou	L	.000	8	0	0	0	0	.083	12	1	0	0	0	0	0	4	0	33.0	4	3	0	0	1.000	2	1	0	0	.50	0
Wuertz,Michael, Oak	R	-	0	0	0	0	0	.000	6	0	0	0	0	0	0	5	1	39.2	4	5	0	0	1.000	4	0	0	0	.00	0
Young,Chris, SD	R	.000	5	0	0	0	0	.137	161	22	4	1	1	10	9	66	21	20.0	2	1	0	0	1.000	2	0	0	0	.00	1
Zagurski,Mike, Phi	L	-	0	0	0	0	0	-	0	0	0	0	0	0	0	0	0	7.0	0	0	0	0	-	1	1	0	0	1.00	0
Zambrano,Carlos, ChC	R	.231	52	12	1	6	2	.236	615	145	24	3	21	64	8	218	33	129.2	10	19	3	1	.906	12	3	0	1	.25	-1
Ziegler,Brad, Oak	R	-	0	0	0	0	0	-	0	0	0	0	0	0	0	0	0	60.2	2	13	1	2	.938	3	1	0	0	.33	3
Zimmermann,J., Was	R	.200	10	2	0	0	0	.162	37	6	0	0	0	2	1	13	6	31.0	1	2	2	0	.600	4	1	0	0	.25	0
Zito,Barry, SF	L	.118	51	6	0	2	14	.107	244	26	0	0	0	7	11	74	37	199.1	5	22	1	1	.964	21	9	1	0	.43	0
Zumaya,Joel, Det	R	-	0	0	0	0	0	-	0	0	0	0	0	0	0	0	0	38.1	0	6	0	0	1.000	4	0	0	0	.00	0

Hitters Pitching

Player	2010 Pitching											Career Pitching										
	G	W	L	Sv	IP	H	R	ER	BB	SO	ERA	G	W	L	Sv	IP	H	R	ER	BB	SO	ERA
Ankiel,Rick, KC-Atl	0	0	0	0	0.0	0	0	0	0	0	-	51	13	10	1	242.0	198	119	105	130	269	3.90
Brown,Dusty, Bos	0	0	0	0	0.0	0	0	0	0	0	-	1	0	0	0	1.0	2	1	1	0	1	9.00
Burke,Jamie, Was	0	0	0	0	0.0	0	0	0	0	0	-	1	0	1	0	1.0	1	1	1	0	0	9.00
Cash,Kevin, Hou-Bos	1	0	0	0	1.0	3	1	1	0	0	9.00	1	0	0	0	1.0	3	1	1	0	0	9.00
Gload,Ross, Phi	0	0	0	0	0.0	0	0	0	0	0	-	1	0	0	0	1.0	0	0	0	2	0	0.00
Green,Nick, LAD-Tor	0	0	0	0	0.0	0	0	0	0	0	-	1	0	0	0	2.0	0	0	0	3	0	0.00
Hall,Bill, Bos	1	0	0	0	1.0	0	0	0	0	0	0.00	1	0	0	0	1.0	0	0	0	0	0	0.00
Inglett,Joe, Mil	1	0	0	0	1.0	0	0	0	0	0	0.00	1	0	0	0	1.0	0	0	0	0	0	0.00
Janish,Paul, Cin	0	0	0	0	0.0	0	0	0	0	0	-	2	0	0	0	2.0	9	11	11	2	3	49.50
Lopez,Felipe, StL-Bos	1	0	0	0	1.0	1	0	0	1	0	0.00	1	0	0	0	1.0	1	0	0	1	0	0.00
Marte,Andy, Cle	1	0	0	0	1.0	0	0	0	0	1	0.00	1	0	0	0	1.0	0	0	0	0	1	0.00
Mather,Joe, StL	1	0	1	0	2.0	2	2	2	3	0	9.00	1	0	1	0	2.0	2	2	2	3	0	9.00
Miles,Aaron, StL	2	0	0	0	2.0	2	0	0	0	0	0.00	5	0	0	0	5.0	5	2	2	0	0	3.60
Ojeda,Augie, Ari	0	0	0	0	0.0	0	0	0	0	0	-	1	0	0	0	1.0	0	0	0	0	0	0.00
Ross,Cody, Fla-SF	0	0	0	0	0.0	0	0	0	0	0	-	1	0	0	0	1.0	1	0	0	0	0	0.00
Swisher,Nick, NYY	0	0	0	0	0.0	0	0	0	0	0	-	1	0	0	0	1.0	1	0	0	1	1	0.00
Van Every,Jonathan, Bos	1	0	0	0	1.0	2	2	2	0	1	18.00	2	0	0	0	1.2	3	2	2	1	1	10.80
Wilson,Josh, Sea	0	0	0	0	0.0	0	0	0	0	0	-	3	0	1	0	3.0	4	3	3	3	0	9.00

2010 Pinch Hitting

One of the most difficult things for a hitter to do is enter the game late, after sitting on the bench for six to seven innings, and deliver a crucial base hit. Matt Stairs is one of the best in recent memory and has 23 career pinch hit home runs, including four in 2010.

For the second year, pinch hitting statistics are included in the *Handbook*. This section contains 2010 and career pinch hitting data for any player who had a plate appearance as a pinch hitter in 2010.

Some names will surely stand out as odd, such as Cubs pitcher Carlos Zambrano, who had seven pinch hit at-bats this season. Others, like Stairs and Ross Gload, have extended their careers by being able to enter a game late and get a hit.

Pinch Hitting

Batter	B	| 2010 Pinch Hitting													| Career Pinch Hitting												
		AB	H	2B	3B	HR	RBI	TBB	IBB	SO	GDP	Avg	OBP	Slg	AB	H	2B	3B	HR	RBI	TBB	IBB	SO	GDP	Avg	OBP	Slg
Bobby Abreu	L	2	0	0	0	0	0	1	0	1	0	.000	.333	.000	46	9	0	1	0	6	10	3	15	0	.196	.339	.239
Tony Abreu	B	36	11	1	0	0	1	0	0	12	2	.306	.297	.333	49	14	1	0	1	2	1	0	15	2	.286	.294	.367
Eliezer Alfonzo	R	1	0	0	0	0	0	0	0	0	0	.000	.000	.000	24	4	1	0	0	4	0	0	12	0	.167	.167	.208
Brandon Allen	L	3	1	1	0	0	0	1	0	2	0	.333	.500	.667	4	1	1	0	0	0	1	0	3	0	.250	.400	.500
Yonder Alonso	L	16	3	1	0	0	0	0	0	5	0	.188	.188	.250	16	3	1	0	0	0	0	0	5	0	.188	.188	.250
Pedro Alvarez	L	0	0	0	0	0	0	1	0	0	0	-	1.000	-	0	0	0	0	0	0	1	0	0	0	-	1.000	-
Bryan Anderson	L	8	3	2	0	0	2	0	0	2	0	.375	.375	.625	8	3	2	0	0	2	0	0	2	0	.375	.375	.625
Garret Anderson	L	50	12	3	0	1	5	2	0	10	2	.240	.269	.360	87	23	4	0	2	13	4	1	15	2	.264	.301	.379
Elvis Andrus	R	3	1	0	0	0	0	0	0	0	0	.333	.333	.333	3	1	0	0	0	0	1	0	0	0	.333	.500	.333
Rick Ankiel	L	5	1	1	0	0	0	0	0	3	0	.200	.200	.400	49	11	2	0	3	6	7	1	20	0	.224	.333	.449
Joaquin Arias	R	16	3	0	0	0	2	1	0	3	0	.188	.235	.188	19	5	1	0	0	3	2	0	3	0	.263	.333	.316
Garrett Atkins	R	4	0	0	0	0	0	0	0	0	0	.000	.000	.000	46	8	2	0	1	8	6	0	13	0	.174	.264	.283
Alex Avila	L	9	1	0	0	0	0	0	0	6	0	.111	.111	.111	13	3	0	0	0	3	2	0	7	0	.231	.313	.231
Mike Aviles	R	3	1	0	0	0	0	1	0	0	0	.333	.500	.333	4	2	0	0	0	1	1	0	0	0	.500	.600	.500
Erick Aybar	B	3	0	0	0	0	0	1	0	1	0	.000	.250	.000	31	5	1	2	0	5	5	0	9	1	.161	.289	.323
Willy Aybar	B	26	7	0	0	2	10	3	0	5	0	.269	.333	.500	73	18	1	0	3	16	7	0	15	1	.247	.305	.384
Jeff Baker	R	18	6	0	1	1	4	3	0	6	1	.333	.429	.611	109	22	3	1	3	9	12	1	43	3	.202	.285	.330
John Baker	L	3	1	0	0	0	0	0	0	2	0	.333	.333	.333	15	2	0	0	1	3	2	0	7	0	.133	.235	.333
Rocco Baldelli	R	3	2	0	0	1	2	0	0	0	0	.667	.667	1.667	32	10	2	0	2	8	5	1	9	1	.313	.405	.563
Rod Barajas	R	2	0	0	0	0	1	0	0	1	0	.000	.000	.000	26	10	1	0	2	5	3	1	7	0	.385	.433	.654
Josh Bard	B	1	0	0	0	0	0	0	0	1	0	.000	.000	.000	59	16	3	0	0	7	15	1	11	4	.271	.416	.322
Brian Barden	R	6	2	0	0	0	1	1	0	2	0	.333	.429	.333	33	7	1	0	0	4	2	0	6	1	.212	.250	.242
Clint Barmes	R	3	0	0	0	0	0	1	0	0	0	.000	.250	.000	31	8	2	0	1	6	1	0	6	0	.258	.303	.419
Darwin Barney	R	5	1	0	0	0	0	0	0	2	0	.200	.200	.200	5	1	0	0	0	0	0	0	2	0	.200	.200	.200
Jason Bartlett	R	5	1	0	0	1	4	0	0	3	0	.200	.200	.800	10	2	0	0	1	5	0	0	3	1	.200	.200	.500
Daric Barton	L	3	0	0	0	0	0	0	0	2	0	.000	.000	.000	13	1	0	0	0	2	0	0	8	0	.077	.077	.077
Mike Baxter	L	7	0	0	0	0	1	0	0	2	1	.000	.000	.000	7	0	0	0	0	1	0	0	2	1	.000	.000	.000
Jason Bay	R	2	1	0	0	0	0	0	0	0	0	.500	.500	.500	14	3	0	0	1	3	1	0	1	0	.214	.267	.429
Josh Bell	B	1	0	0	0	0	0	0	0	1	0	.000	.000	.000	1	0	0	0	0	0	0	0	1	0	.000	.000	.000
Ronnie Belliard	R	41	7	2	0	0	4	3	1	18	1	.171	.222	.220	156	36	8	0	3	27	16	1	44	4	.231	.297	.340
Carlos Beltran	B	4	1	0	0	0	0	1	1	0	0	.250	.400	.250	23	4	0	0	1	1	3	1	6	0	.174	.269	.304
Lance Berkman	B	7	2	1	0	0	0	2	0	2	0	.286	.444	.429	52	7	2	0	1	4	8	2	21	1	.135	.250	.231
Roger Bernadina	L	5	1	0	0	0	1	0	0	1	0	.200	.200	.200	9	3	1	0	0	1	1	0	3	0	.333	.400	.444
Wilson Betemit	B	7	4	2	0	0	1	3	0	3	0	.571	.700	.857	138	35	9	0	4	16	26	0	49	2	.254	.372	.406
Casey Blake	R	6	1	0	0	0	0	1	0	3	0	.167	.375	.167	26	5	2	0	0	3	4	0	11	0	.192	.314	.269
Hank Blalock	L	10	3	1	0	0	1	1	0	1	1	.300	.364	.400	36	9	3	0	2	13	3	1	7	2	.250	.308	.500
Andres Blanco	B	4	0	0	0	0	0	0	0	0	0	.000	.000	.000	10	2	1	0	0	0	0	0	0	0	.200	.200	.300
Gregor Blanco	L	5	4	1	0	0	0	0	0	0	0	.800	.800	1.000	19	6	2	0	0	0	1	0	6	0	.316	.350	.421
Henry Blanco	R	3	1	0	0	0	0	0	0	1	0	.333	.333	.333	47	11	1	0	0	6	5	0	13	2	.234	.308	.255
Kyle Blanks	R	1	0	0	0	0	0	0	0	0	0	.000	.000	.000	8	1	1	0	0	0	1	0	3	0	.125	.222	.250
Willie Bloomquist	R	12	3	0	0	1	2	0	0	2	0	.250	.250	.500	58	16	1	0	1	5	3	0	12	1	.276	.306	.345
Geoff Blum	B	42	14	1	1	0	11	2	0	5	1	.333	.364	.405	236	59	11	1	1	32	31	6	47	6	.250	.338	.318
Brennan Boesch	L	5	1	0	0	0	0	0	0	0	0	.200	.200	.200	5	1	0	0	0	0	0	0	0	0	.200	.200	.200
Brandon Boggs	B	1	0	0	0	0	0	0	0	1	0	.000	.000	.000	16	4	1	0	0	2	3	0	8	0	.250	.400	.313
Brian Bogusevic	L	9	3	2	0	0	3	1	0	3	0	.333	.400	.556	9	3	2	0	0	3	1	0	3	0	.333	.400	.556
Emilio Bonifacio	B	21	5	1	1	0	0	2	0	6	0	.238	.304	.381	37	9	2	1	0	2	3	0	11	0	.243	.300	.351
Julio Borbon	L	1	1	0	0	0	0	0	0	0	0	1.000	1.000	1.000	4	3	0	0	0	1	1	0	0	0	.750	.800	.750
Jason Bourgeois	R	20	5	0	0	0	1	3	0	2	1	.250	.348	.250	35	7	0	0	0	1	5	0	7	1	.200	.300	.200
Michael Bourn	L	4	2	1	0	0	0	0	0	1	0	.500	.500	.750	29	4	1	0	0	0	1	0	7	0	.138	.167	.172
John Bowker	L	24	7	2	0	1	6	3	0	7	0	.292	.370	.500	57	18	3	2	1	10	7	0	15	0	.316	.391	.491
Milton Bradley	B	5	1	0	0	0	1	1	0	2	0	.200	.333	.200	36	6	0	0	1	2	9	1	12	1	.167	.333	.250
Michael Brantley	L	2	1	1	0	0	2	0	0	1	0	.500	.500	1.000	3	2	1	0	0	3	1	0	1	0	.667	.750	1.000
Russell Branyan	L	7	0	0	0	0	0	2	0	5	0	.000	.222	.000	140	22	4	0	4	14	31	2	72	1	.157	.322	.271
Ryan Braun	R	2	0	0	0	0	0	0	0	1	0	.000	.000	.000	6	2	2	0	0	2	0	0	2	0	.333	.429	.667
Reid Brignac	L	25	7	1	0	0	6	2	0	7	0	.280	.333	.320	30	7	1	0	0	6	2	0	8	0	.233	.281	.267
Domonic Brown	L	16	3	1	0	1	2	1	0	9	0	.188	.235	.438	16	3	1	0	1	2	1	0	9	0	.188	.235	.438
Jordan Brown	L	6	1	0	0	0	0	0	1	1	1	.167	.167	.167	6	1	0	0	0	0	0	1	1	1	.167	.167	.167
Jay Bruce	L	9	2	0	0	0	1	0	0	4	0	.222	.222	.222	17	7	2	0	0	3	0	0	4	0	.412	.412	.529
John Buck	R	4	1	0	0	0	0	1	0	2	0	.250	.400	.250	19	3	0	0	0	0	2	0	9	2	.158	.238	.158
M. Bumgarner	R	1	0	0	0	0	0	0	0	1	0	.000	.000	.000	1	0	0	0	0	0	0	0	1	0	.000	.000	.000
Pat Burrell	R	7	1	0	0	1	3	0	0	3	0	.143	.125	.571	51	11	1	0	3	9	13	1	19	1	.216	.369	.412
Dave Bush	R	1	0	0	0	0	0	0	0	1	0	.000	.000	.000	3	0	0	0	0	0	0	0	1	0	.000	.000	.000
Drew Butera	R	2	1	0	0	1	1	0	0	0	0	.500	.500	2.000	2	1	0	0	1	1	0	0	0	0	.500	.500	2.000
Billy Butler	R	1	0	0	0	0	0	0	0	0	0	.000	.000	.000	18	5	1	0	0	3	0	0	4	0	.278	.381	.333
Marlon Byrd	R	3	1	0	0	0	0	0	0	1	0	.333	.333	.333	48	14	6	0	1	5	5	0	11	1	.292	.375	.479
Asdrubal Cabrera	B	2	1	0	0	0	0	0	0	0	0	.500	.500	.500	8	3	1	0	0	0	3	0	1	0	.375	.545	.500
Everth Cabrera	B	7	1	0	0	0	1	1	0	2	0	.143	.250	.143	8	1	0	0	0	1	1	0	2	0	.125	.222	.125
Melky Cabrera	B	12	4	0	0	0	0	1	1	2	1	.333	.385	.333	29	5	0	0	0	1	5	1	8	1	.172	.286	.172

Pinch Hitting

		2010 Pinch Hitting													Career Pinch Hitting												
Batter	B	AB	H	2B	3B	HR	RBI	TBB	IBB	SO	GDP	Avg	OBP	Slg	AB	H	2B	3B	HR	RBI	TBB	IBB	SO	GDP	Avg	OBP	Slg
Orlando Cabrera	R	3	0	0	0	0	1	0	0	0	0	.000	.000	.000	12	1	0	0	0	3	1	0	2	0	.083	.143	.083
Lorenzo Cain	R	4	2	2	0	0	0	0	0	1	0	.500	.500	1.000	4	2	2	0	0	0	0	0	1	0	.500	.500	1.000
Matt Cain	R	1	0	0	0	0	0	0	0	1	0	.000	.000	.000	1	0	0	0	0	0	0	0	1	0	.000	.000	.000
Miguel Cairo	R	36	7	1	0	0	6	1	0	5	1	.194	.211	.222	223	57	12	2	1	33	18	3	31	4	.256	.312	.341
Alberto Callaspo	B	5	0	0	0	0	0	1	0	1	1	.000	.167	.000	55	10	2	0	0	3	4	0	9	3	.182	.233	.218
Mike Cameron	R	2	0	0	0	0	0	0	0	0	0	.000	.000	.000	20	3	2	0	1	6	4	0	6	0	.150	.320	.400
Robinson Cano	L	1	0	0	0	0	0	0	0	0	0	.000	.000	.000	13	6	0	0	2	4	0	0	2	0	.462	.462	.923
Jorge Cantu	R	2	0	0	0	0	0	0	0	0	0	.000	.000	.000	33	10	4	0	0	4	3	0	7	0	.303	.378	.424
Mike Carp	L	2	1	0	0	0	0	1	0	1	0	.500	.667	.500	6	1	0	0	0	1	2	0	4	0	.167	.333	.167
Brett Carroll	R	8	1	0	0	0	0	0	0	7	0	.125	.125	.125	38	6	2	0	1	7	4	0	17	2	.158	.238	.289
Jamey Carroll	R	13	6	2	0	0	1	3	0	1	0	.462	.563	.615	106	38	3	0	1	13	17	0	22	4	.358	.444	.415
Matt Carson	R	8	1	0	0	0	3	1	0	2	0	.125	.182	.125	9	2	0	0	0	4	1	0	2	0	.222	.250	.222
Chris Carter	L	58	19	5	0	1	10	3	0	8	0	.328	.361	.466	65	20	5	0	1	11	3	0	10	0	.308	.338	.431
Chris Carter	R	1	0	0	0	0	0	0	0	0	0	.000	.000	.000	1	0	0	0	0	0	0	0	0	0	.000	.000	.000
Alexi Casilla	B	6	1	0	1	0	1	0	0	0	1	.167	.167	.500	9	1	0	1	0	1	2	0	0	1	.111	.273	.333
Luis Castillo	B	11	1	0	0	0	1	0	0	4	0	.091	.091	.091	37	7	1	0	0	4	1	0	9	0	.189	.200	.216
Welington Castillo	R	2	1	0	0	0	0	0	0	1	0	.500	.500	.500	2	1	0	0	0	0	0	0	1	0	.500	.500	.500
Jason Castro	L	3	0	0	0	0	0	2	1	1	0	.000	.400	.000	3	0	0	0	0	0	2	1	1	0	.000	.400	.000
Juan Castro	R	6	0	0	0	0	0	1	0	2	0	.000	.143	.000	108	20	1	1	3	10	6	0	28	2	.185	.228	.296
Ramon Castro	R	3	0	0	0	0	0	0	0	0	0	.000	.000	.000	76	19	3	0	3	10	5	0	18	0	.250	.296	.408
Starlin Castro	R	2	0	0	0	0	0	0	0	2	0	.000	.000	.000	2	0	0	0	0	0	0	0	2	0	.000	.000	.000
Frank Catalanotto	L	22	3	1	0	0	1	0	0	5	0	.136	.136	.182	249	65	15	4	2	36	29	3	43	7	.261	.340	.378
Ronny Cedeno	R	4	1	1	0	0	1	0	0	2	0	.250	.250	.500	57	15	5	0	1	5	6	0	13	0	.263	.354	.404
Francisco Cervelli	R	4	0	0	0	0	0	0	0	2	0	.000	.000	.000	5	0	0	0	0	0	0	0	2	0	.000	.000	.000
Eric Chavez	L	3	0	0	0	0	0	0	0	2	0	.000	.000	.000	40	10	4	0	0	7	1	0	9	1	.250	.268	.350
Ryan Church	L	46	7	1	0	0	5	3	0	25	0	.152	.235	.174	118	24	4	0	3	18	16	2	49	2	.203	.312	.314
Pedro Ciriaco	R	5	3	1	1	0	1	0	0	2	0	.600	.600	1.200	5	3	1	1	0	1	0	0	2	0	.000	.600	1.200
Jeff Clement	L	16	4	0	0	2	5	1	0	2	0	.250	.278	.625	30	10	2	0	3	8	1	0	4	1	.333	.344	.700
Chris Coghlan	L	2	1	0	0	1	3	0	0	0	0	.500	.500	2.000	7	2	0	0	2	4	0	0	1	0	.286	.286	1.143
Tyler Colvin	L	21	5	2	0	1	4	2	0	8	0	.230	.292	.470	21	5	2	0	1	4	2	0	8	0	.238	.292	.476
Hank Conger	B	2	0	0	0	0	1	2	0	1	0	.000	.500	.000	2	0	0	0	0	1	2	0	1	0	.000	.500	.000
Brooks Conrad	B	58	13	4	0	3	12	3	0	20	0	.224	.262	.448	76	14	4	0	4	15	4	0	24	1	.184	.225	.395
Aaron Cook	R	1	0	0	0	0	0	0	0	0	0	.000	.000	.000	6	2	0	0	0	0	0	0	2	0	.333	.333	.333
Alex Cora	L	11	1	0	0	0	1	1	0	3	0	.091	.167	.091	99	26	4	1	1	10	5	1	11	1	.263	.305	.354
Craig Counsell	L	39	13	1	0	0	5	6	0	4	0	.333	.422	.359	223	52	7	1	1	12	37	1	27	4	.233	.351	.287
Scott Cousins	L	17	5	2	2	0	2	0	0	7	0	.294	.294	.647	17	5	2	2	0	2	0	0	7	0	.294	.294	.647
Allen Craig	R	7	1	0	0	0	0	1	0	3	0	.143	.250	.143	7	1	0	0	0	0	1	0	3	0	.143	.250	.143
Carl Crawford	L	2	0	0	0	0	0	0	0	0	0	.000	.000	.000	17	1	0	0	0	1	4	1	3	0	.059	.238	.059
Coco Crisp	B	1	1	0	0	0	2	0	0	0	0	1.000	1.000	1.000	10	2	1	0	0	2	1	0	1	0	.200	.273	.300
Bobby Crosby	R	20	4	1	0	0	1	3	0	8	0	.200	.304	.250	27	4	1	0	0	1	3	0	12	0	.148	.233	.185
Trevor Crowe	B	5	0	0	0	0	0	2	0	2	0	.000	.286	.000	7	0	0	0	0	0	2	0	2	0	.000	.222	.000
Luis Cruz	R	2	0	0	0	0	0	0	0	1	0	.000	.000	.000	7	1	0	0	0	0	0	0	1	0	.143	.143	.143
Nelson Cruz	R	4	0	0	0	0	0	1	0	3	0	.000	.200	.000	16	0	0	0	0	1	1	0	8	0	.000	.059	.000
Michael Cuddyer	R	1	0	0	0	0	0	0	0	0	0	.000	.000	.000	36	14	4	1	2	12	4	1	4	1	.389	.450	.722
A. Cunningham	R	16	5	2	0	0	0	0	0	3	1	.313	.313	.438	19	6	3	0	0	2	0	0	4	1	.316	.316	.474
Colin Curtis	L	11	4	1	0	1	7	1	0	3	0	.364	.417	.727	11	4	1	0	1	7	1	0	3	0	.364	.417	.727
Jack Cust	L	8	2	1	0	0	1	1	0	2	0	.250	.333	.375	44	8	1	0	0	4	14	0	19	1	.182	.379	.205
Johnny Damon	L	11	5	2	1	0	2	1	0	3	0	.455	.500	.818	64	14	3	1	1	6	9	1	17	1	.219	.316	.344
Brad Davis	R	1	1	0	0	0	0	0	0	0	0	1.000	1.000	1.000	1	1	0	0	0	1	0	0	0	0	1.000	1.000	1.000
Chris Davis	L	5	2	0	0	1	1	1	0	2	0	.400	.500	1.000	8	4	0	0	1	2	1	0	3	0	.500	.556	.875
Ike Davis	L	3	1	0	0	0	2	2	1	1	0	.333	.600	.333	3	1	0	0	0	2	2	1	1	0	.333	.600	.333
Rajai Davis	R	1	0	0	0	0	0	0	0	0	0	.000	.000	.000	40	8	2	1	0	2	4	0	11	0	.200	.273	.300
Alejandro De Aza	L	4	0	0	0	0	0	0	0	0	0	.000	.000	.000	22	3	0	0	0	2	3	0	5	0	.136	.231	.136
David DeJesus	L	1	0	0	0	0	0	0	0	0	0	.000	.000	.000	6	0	0	0	0	0	0	0	2	0	.000	.143	.000
Ryan Dempster	R	1	0	0	0	0	0	0	0	0	0	.000	.000	.000	1	0	0	0	0	0	0	0	0	0	.000	.000	.000
Chris Denorfia	R	12	2	0	0	1	3	0	0	2	0	.167	.154	.417	32	8	2	0	2	5	2	0	7	0	.250	.286	.500
Mark DeRosa	R	1	0	0	0	0	0	1	0	0	0	.000	.000	.000	104	27	4	0	2	15	10	0	18	0	.260	.333	.356
Daniel Descalso	L	1	0	0	0	0	0	0	0	0	0	.000	.000	.000	1	0	0	0	0	0	0	0	0	0	.000	.000	.000
Ian Desmond	R	9	1	1	0	0	3	0	0	3	0	.111	.100	.222	10	1	1	0	0	3	0	0	3	0	.100	.091	.200
Blake DeWitt	L	9	1	0	0	0	1	0	0	3	0	.111	.200	.111	34	9	2	0	2	6	2	0	7	1	.265	.324	.500
Argenis Diaz	R	7	1	0	0	0	0	0	0	2	0	.143	.143	.143	7	1	0	0	0	0	0	0	2	0	.143	.143	.143
Matt Diaz	R	23	5	2	0	1	3	1	0	5	0	.217	.280	.435	150	40	7	2	1	14	4	0	30	5	.267	.298	.360
Chris Dickerson	L	13	2	0	1	0	0	1	0	4	0	.154	.214	.308	36	7	1	1	0	2	10	1	15	0	.194	.370	.278
Greg Dobbs	L	49	6	2	0	2	4	5	1	13	0	.122	.204	.286	259	64	17	2	8	52	23	3	60	4	.247	.308	.421
Jason Donald	R	1	0	0	0	0	0	0	0	0	0	.000	.000	.000	1	0	0	0	0	0	0	0	0	0	.000	.000	.000
Josh Donaldson	R	4	1	0	0	0	1	0	0	2	0	.250	.250	.250	4	1	0	0	0	1	0	0	2	0	.250	.250	.250
Ryan Doumit	B	10	4	1	0	1	3	0	0	1	2	.400	.455	.800	71	20	4	0	3	17	5	1	17	5	.282	.346	.465
Matt Downs	R	14	2	0	0	0	2	1	0	4	0	.143	.188	.143	14	2	0	0	0	2	1	0	4	0	.143	.188	.143
J.D. Drew	L	7	2	1	0	0	0	3	2	1	0	.286	.500	.429	96	24	4	1	4	16	19	3	29	2	.250	.371	.438
Stephen Drew	L	6	2	2	0	0	0	0	0	1	0	.333	.333	.667	19	7	2	0	1	1	3	0	3	0	.368	.455	.632

Pinch Hitting

Batter	B	AB	H	2B	3B	HR	RBI	TBB	IBB	SO	GDP	Avg	OBP	Slg	AB	H	2B	3B	HR	RBI	TBB	IBB	SO	GDP	Avg	OBP	Slg
						2010 Pinch Hitting													Career Pinch Hitting									
Lucas Duda	L	4	1	1	0	0	3	0	0	0	0	.250	.250	.500	4	1	1	0	0	3	0	0	0	0	.250	.250	.500
Zach Duke	L	2	0	0	0	0	0	0	0	2	0	.000	.000	.000	4	0	0	0	0	0	0	0	4	0	.000	.000	.000
Shelley Duncan	R	21	6	0	0	1	5	1	0	3	0	.286	.318	.429	33	6	0	0	1	5	1	0	8	0	.182	.206	.273
Adam Dunn	L	3	0	0	0	0	1	1	0	2	0	.000	.200	.000	32	8	1	0	3	10	6	0	12	0	.250	.359	.563
Luis Durango	B	15	3	0	0	0	1	1	0	1	2	.200	.250	.200	19	5	0	0	0	0	3	0	2	2	.263	.364	.263
Jarrod Dyson	L	0	0	0	0	0	0	1	0	0	0	-	1.000	-	0	0	0	0	0	0	1	0	0	0	-	1.000	-
David Eckstein	R	6	1	0	0	0	0	0	0	0	0	.167	.167	.333	28	7	2	0	1	4	3	0	2	0	.250	.323	.429
Jim Edmonds	L	22	6	2	0	1	1	4	0	4	0	.273	.385	.500	102	26	8	0	4	20	19	3	30	0	.255	.366	.451
Brad Eldred	R	5	0	0	0	0	0	0	0	3	0	.000	.000	.000	17	1	1	0	0	0	1	1	10	1	.059	.111	.118
A.J. Ellis	R	1	0	0	0	0	0	1	0	0	0	.000	.000	.000	2	0	0	0	0	0	1	0	1	0	.000	.000	.000
Mark Ellis	R	2	0	0	0	0	1	1	0	0	0	.000	.250	.000	9	0	0	0	0	1	2	0	3	0	.000	.167	.000
Barry Enright	R	1	0	0	0	0	0	0	0	1	0	.000	.000	.000	1	0	0	0	0	0	0	0	1	0	.000	.000	.000
Alcides Escobar	R	5	3	0	0	1	1	0	0	0	0	.600	.600	1.200	8	4	0	0	1	1	0	0	1	0	.500	.500	.875
Yunel Escobar	R	0	0	0	0	0	0	1	0	0	0	-	1.000	-	14	4	0	0	0	1	6	0	1	0	.286	.500	.286
Danny Espinosa	B	1	0	0	0	0	0	0	0	0	0	.000	.000	.000	1	0	0	0	0	0	0	0	0	0	.000	.000	.000
Brian Esposito	R	2	0	0	0	0	0	0	0	1	0	.000	.000	.000	2	0	0	0	0	0	0	0	1	0	.000	.000	.000
Andre Ethier	L	8	2	0	0	0	4	0	0	1	2	.250	.250	.250	48	13	2	0	2	13	8	0	14	3	.271	.375	.438
Nick Evans	R	14	5	2	0	0	2	0	0	6	0	.357	.357	.500	45	10	3	1	0	4	1	0	20	2	.222	.239	.333
Adam Everett	R	0	0	0	0	0	1	0	0	0	0	-	-	-	13	2	1	0	0	2	2	0	5	0	.154	.353	.231
Jesus Feliciano	L	21	3	1	0	0	1	0	0	6	0	.143	.182	.190	21	3	1	0	0	1	0	0	6	0	.143	.182	.190
Pedro Feliz	R	25	3	2	0	1	3	2	0	6	0	.120	.185	.320	149	37	12	2	3	23	8	0	41	2	.248	.287	.416
Josh Fields	R	1	0	0	0	0	0	0	0	1	0	.000	.000	.000	12	1	0	0	1	2	4	0	5	1	.083	.313	.333
Tyler Flowers	R	2	0	0	0	0	0	0	0	1	0	.000	.000	.000	4	0	0	0	0	0	0	0	2	0	.000	.000	.000
Mike Fontenot	L	34	10	2	0	1	8	2	0	13	0	.294	.333	.441	111	26	10	0	2	18	13	0	31	1	.234	.315	.378
Dexter Fowler	B	12	2	1	0	0	0	4	0	3	0	.167	.375	.250	25	6	2	0	0	1	6	0	6	0	.240	.387	.320
Jake Fox	R	15	4	0	0	0	2	2	0	5	1	.267	.389	.267	42	9	2	0	0	5	4	0	15	2	.214	.314	.262
Ben Francisco	R	39	11	3	0	0	7	5	0	7	1	.282	.378	.359	69	17	6	0	1	12	9	0	18	2	.246	.342	.377
Juan Francisco	L	22	5	1	0	1	3	3	0	6	1	.227	.320	.409	30	9	2	0	2	7	6	0	8	1	.300	.417	.567
Jeff Francoeur	R	7	0	0	0	0	1	1	0	0	0	.000	.111	.000	15	2	0	0	0	1	2	0	2	0	.133	.222	.133
Kevin Frandsen	R	2	1	0	0	0	0	0	0	0	0	.500	.500	.500	42	11	0	0	0	6	2	0	8	1	.262	.295	.262
Jeff Frazier	R	3	0	0	0	0	0	0	0	3	0	.000	.000	.000	3	0	0	0	0	0	0	0	3	0	.000	.000	.000
Freddie Freeman	L	11	2	0	0	1	1	0	0	4	0	.182	.182	.455	11	2	0	0	1	1	0	0	4	0	.182	.182	.455
David Freese	R	4	1	0	0	0	0	1	0	1	0	.250	.400	.250	11	3	1	0	0	1	2	0	2	0	.273	.385	.364
K. Fukudome	L	20	7	0	0	1	2	2	0	4	0	.350	.409	.500	42	14	1	0	2	6	5	0	7	0	.333	.404	.500
Sam Fuld	L	5	0	0	0	0	0	0	0	1	1	.000	.000	.000	21	3	0	0	0	0	2	0	3	1	.143	.217	.143
Rafael Furcal	B	6	0	0	0	0	0	2	0	0	0	.000	.000	.000	31	8	0	0	1	2	3	1	6	1	.258	.324	.355
Yovani Gallardo	R	2	0	0	0	0	0	0	0	1	0	.000	.000	.000	9	0	0	0	0	0	0	0	1	0	.000	.000	.000
Mat Gamel	L	7	1	0	0	0	0	1	0	3	1	.143	.250	.143	29	5	2	0	0	2	8	1	17	1	.172	.351	.241
Brett Gardner	L	3	0	0	0	0	0	0	0	0	0	.000	.000	.000	10	2	1	0	0	0	0	0	1	0	.200	.200	.300
Ryan Garko	R	4	1	0	0	0	1	1	1	1	0	.250	.400	.250	42	9	1	0	2	8	3	1	12	0	.214	.261	.381
Jon Garland	R	1	0	0	0	0	0	0	0	0	0	.000	.000	.000	2	0	0	0	0	0	0	0	1	0	.000	.000	.000
Craig Gentry	R	3	0	0	0	0	0	0	0	1	0	.000	.000	.000	3	0	0	0	0	0	0	0	1	0	.000	.000	.000
Jody Gerut	L	14	3	1	0	1	3	1	0	3	0	.214	.267	.500	105	23	3	0	1	17	10	0	17	2	.219	.291	.276
Chris Getz	L	5	0	0	0	0	0	0	0	0	0	.000	.000	.000	8	1	0	0	0	1	0	0	0	0	.125	.125	.125
Jason Giambi	L	34	8	0	0	2	8	8	2	11	0	.235	.386	.412	97	27	3	0	6	24	17	4	32	1	.278	.393	.495
Jay Gibbons	L	17	4	0	0	0	3	3	0	2	1	.235	.350	.235	56	8	1	0	1	6	7	0	14	2	.143	.238	.214
Cole Gillespie	R	11	3	2	0	0	1	0	0	2	0	.273	.273	.455	11	3	2	0	0	1	0	0	2	0	.273	.273	.455
Chris Gimenez	R	1	0	0	0	0	0	0	0	1	0	.000	.000	.000	2	0	0	0	0	0	0	0	1	0	.000	.000	.000
Troy Glaus	R	15	2	0	0	0	0	2	0	4	1	.133	.235	.133	33	4	0	0	1	4	9	2	13	1	.121	.310	.212
Ross Gload	L	66	15	3	0	3	9	4	1	6	1	.227	.271	.409	226	63	6	1	8	38	18	4	32	4	.279	.333	.420
Jonny Gomes	R	14	4	1	0	0	2	0	0	5	0	.286	.333	.357	73	14	5	0	2	12	6	0	27	1	.192	.280	.342
Carlos Gomez	R	15	3	0	0	0	2	0	0	3	0	.200	.294	.200	23	3	0	0	0	2	2	0	7	0	.130	.200	.130
Alberto Gonzalez	R	37	7	2	0	0	1	4	0	6	1	.189	.268	.243	57	14	3	0	0	7	5	0	9	2	.246	.306	.298
Carlos Gonzalez	L	1	0	0	0	0	0	1	0	1	0	.000	.500	.000	16	2	0	0	0	2	2	0	10	0	.125	.222	.125
Alex Gordon	L	2	1	0	0	1	1	1	0	0	0	.500	.667	2.000	4	1	0	0	1	1	2	0	0	0	.250	.500	1.000
Curtis Granderson	L	7	0	0	0	0	0	1	0	4	0	.000	.125	.000	25	5	0	0	0	1	2	0	12	0	.200	.250	.200
Nick Green	R	1	0	0	0	0	0	0	0	1	0	.000	.000	.000	19	3	1	0	0	1	2	0	7	1	.158	.273	.211
Tyler Greene	R	4	0	0	0	0	0	3	0	2	0	.000	.500	.000	10	3	0	0	1	1	3	0	4	0	.300	.533	.600
Ken Griffey Jr.	L	6	2	0	0	0	3	1	0	0	0	.333	.375	.333	92	24	3	0	6	23	20	6	30	2	.261	.388	.489
Gabe Gross	L	11	4	0	0	0	4	2	1	2	1	.364	.462	.364	140	25	4	0	3	23	26	1	51	2	.179	.311	.271
M. Grudzielanek	R	2	0	0	0	0	0	1	0	0	0	.000	.000	.000	29	5	0	0	1	1	2	0	10	1	.172	.226	.276
Vladimir Guerrero	R	6	3	0	0	0	1	1	1	0	0	.500	.571	.500	21	7	0	1	0	3	2	2	0	0	.333	.375	.429
Carlos Guillen	B	3	1	0	0	0	0	0	0	0	1	.333	.333	.333	28	6	1	0	0	2	7	1	11	1	.214	.361	.250
Jose Guillen	R	5	0	0	0	0	0	0	0	1	0	.000	.000	.000	88	21	0	1	2	11	3	1	23	6	.239	.287	.330
Franklin Gutierrez	R	2	0	0	0	0	0	0	0	0	0	.000	.000	.000	32	6	0	0	0	2	2	0	5	2	.188	.235	.188
Cristian Guzman	B	11	4	2	0	0	4	1	1	0	0	.364	.417	.545	47	9	3	0	0	6	4	2	9	3	.191	.255	.255
Tony Gwynn	L	21	5	0	0	0	1	0	6	1	.238	.273	.333	87	24	5	1	0	5	11	0	17	2	.276	.357	.356
Travis Hafner	L	7	1	1	0	0	1	2	0	1	1	.143	.400	.286	41	10	2	0	1	11	13	2	8	3	.244	.439	.439
Jerry Hairston	R	6	0	0	0	0	0	0	0	2	0	.000	.000	.000	58	8	2	1	0	2	3	0	11	2	.138	.177	.207
Scott Hairston	R	19	3	0	0	1	1	1	0	8	0	.158	.200	.316	100	17	3	0	3	9	13	0	38	2	.170	.265	.290

Pinch Hitting

Batter	B	AB	H	2B	3B	HR	RBI	TBB	IBB	SO	GDP	Avg	OBP	Slg	AB	H	2B	3B	HR	RBI	TBB	IBB	SO	GDP	Avg	OBP	Slg
								2010 Pinch Hitting													**Career Pinch Hitting**							
Bill Hall	R	11	4	2	0	1	1	2	0	2	0	.364	.462	.818	111	22	5	0	5	18	8	0	44	0	.198	.250	.378
Cole Hamels	L	1	0	0	0	0	0	0	0	0	0	.000	.000	.000	5	1	0	0	0	0	1	0	1	0	.200	.333	.200
Josh Hamilton	L	2	2	0	0	0	1	2	0	0	0	1.000	1.000	1.000	16	5	0	0	2	6	3	0	3	0	.313	.421	.688
Mark Hamilton	L	6	0	0	0	0	0	0	0	2	0	.000	.000	.000	6	0	0	0	0	0	0	0	2	0	.000	.000	.000
Ryan Hanigan	R	4	2	0	0	1	3	1	0	0	0	.500	.600	1.250	13	5	1	0	1	5	3	0	1	0	.385	.500	.692
Dan Haren	R	1	1	0	0	0	0	1	0	0	0	1.000	1.000	1.000	2	1	0	0	0	1	2	0	1	0	.500	.600	.500
Brendan Harris	R	2	0	0	0	0	0	0	0	1	0	.000	.000	.000	39	8	2	0	2	5	5	0	12	1	.205	.311	.410
Willie Harris	L	47	11	2	0	1	9	8	0	15	1	.234	.351	.340	146	33	4	0	4	16	20	0	32	2	.226	.325	.336
Corey Hart	R	5	1	1	0	0	0	1	0	0	0	.200	.333	.400	59	20	3	1	3	12	6	1	12	4	.339	.403	.576
Chris Hatcher	B	1	0	0	0	0	0	0	0	0	0	.000	.000	.000	1	0	0	0	0	0	0	0	1	0	.000	.000	.000
Brad Hawpe	L	18	4	2	0	1	4	5	0	5	0	.222	.391	.500	69	15	4	0	3	13	11	0	29	1	.217	.321	.406
Brett Hayes	R	1	0	0	0	0	0	0	0	0	0	.000	.000	.000	10	2	1	0	1	2	0	0	3	1	.200	.273	.600
Chase Headley	B	3	0	0	0	0	0	0	0	2	0	.000	.000	.000	20	6	1	0	2	2	4	0	8	0	.300	.440	.650
Chris Heisey	R	23	8	0	1	4	7	4	0	6	1	.348	.448	.957	23	8	0	1	4	7	4	0	6	1	.348	.448	.957
Wes Helms	R	44	5	1	1	0	3	3	0	17	1	.114	.188	.182	310	82	20	4	7	52	28	0	93	12	.265	.338	.423
Todd Helton	L	3	0	0	0	0	0	0	0	1	0	.000	.000	.000	44	7	1	0	1	7	6	2	15	1	.159	.260	.250
Jeremy Hermida	L	10	3	0	0	0	2	0	0	5	0	.300	.300	.300	51	13	1	0	2	10	6	0	16	1	.255	.345	.392
And. Hernandez	B	16	3	1	0	0	0	5	0	4	0	.188	.381	.250	48	9	2	1	0	1	6	0	14	0	.188	.278	.271
Diory Hernandez	R	8	1	0	0	1	1	0	0	3	0	.125	.125	.500	13	1	0	0	1	1	0	0	6	0	.077	.077	.308
Livan Hernandez	R	2	0	0	0	0	0	0	0	1	0	.000	.000	.000	14	1	0	0	0	0	0	0	6	1	.071	.071	.071
Luis Hernandez	B	3	0	0	0	0	0	0	0	0	0	.000	.000	.000	13	0	0	0	0	0	0	0	5	0	.000	.000	.000
Ram. Hernandez	R	5	0	0	0	0	0	0	0	1	1	.000	.000	.000	59	8	0	0	2	8	3	0	16	3	.136	.177	.237
Jonathan Herrera	B	6	0	0	0	0	2	1	0	1	0	.000	.125	.000	12	1	0	0	0	2	3	0	1	0	.083	.250	.083
Mike Hessman	R	18	3	0	0	1	4	0	0	9	0	.167	.167	.333	36	7	1	0	2	7	1	0	14	1	.194	.216	.389
John Hester	R	5	0	0	0	0	0	0	0	3	1	.000	.000	.000	11	2	0	0	1	3	0	0	6	1	.182	.182	.455
Jason Heyward	L	3	2	0	0	0	2	1	0	0	0	.667	.750	.667	3	2	0	0	0	2	1	0	0	0	.667	.750	.667
Brandon Hicks	R	4	0	0	0	0	0	1	0	1	0	.000	.200	.000	4	0	0	0	0	0	1	0	1	0	.000	.200	.000
Koyie Hill	B	3	0	0	0	0	0	1	1	0	0	.000	.250	.000	23	4	2	0	0	0	3	1	7	1	.174	.269	.261
Eric Hinske	L	47	14	3	1	3	12	5	1	7	1	.298	.389	.596	149	40	9	1	5	26	24	1	35	3	.268	.376	.443
Jarrett Hoffpauir	R	1	1	0	0	0	0	0	0	0	0	1.000	1.000	1.000	3	2	1	0	0	0	3	0	1	0	.667	.833	1.000
Micah Hoffpauir	L	10	3	2	0	0	3	0	0	4	0	.300	.300	.500	64	15	6	0	1	14	6	1	21	0	.234	.300	.375
Matt Holliday	R	1	1	0	0	0	0	0	0	0	0	1.000	1.000	1.000	15	4	1	0	0	0	2	0	4	0	.267	.353	.333
Ryan Howard	L	1	1	0	0	0	0	0	0	0	0	1.000	1.000	1.000	29	12	3	0	5	12	3	0	12	1	.414	.469	1.034
Chin-lung Hu	R	1	1	0	0	0	0	0	0	0	0	1.000	1.000	1.000	4	2	0	0	1	1	0	0	1	0	.500	.500	1.250
Tim Hudson	R	0	0	0	0	0	0	0	0	0	0	-	-	-	0	0	0	0	0	0	0	0	0	0	-	-	-
Aubrey Huff	L	2	0	0	0	0	0	1	1	0	0	.000	.333	.000	41	8	1	1	1	11	4	2	10	0	.195	.277	.341
Chad Huffman	R	2	0	0	0	0	0	0	0	0	0	.000	.000	.000	2	0	0	0	0	0	0	0	0	0	.000	.000	.000
Rhyne Hughes	L	1	0	0	0	0	0	1	0	1	0	.000	.500	.000	1	0	0	0	0	0	1	0	1	0	.000	.500	.000
Nick Hundley	R	8	3	1	0	1	5	1	0	1	0	.375	.444	.875	12	4	1	0	1	7	2	0	1	0	.333	.429	.667
Chris Iannetta	R	4	0	0	0	0	1	0	0	2	0	.000	.200	.000	20	7	0	0	2	6	3	0	6	0	.350	.458	.650
Raul Ibanez	L	8	1	1	0	0	0	1	0	1	0	.125	.222	.250	97	14	3	0	1	11	12	1	18	2	.144	.236	.206
Omar Infante	R	12	3	0	0	0	1	1	0	4	0	.250	.308	.250	58	14	2	2	0	12	4	0	17	2	.241	.281	.345
Brandon Inge	R	5	1	1	0	0	0	0	0	1	0	.200	.200	.400	8	3	2	0	0	1	1	0	1	0	.375	.545	.625
Joe Inglett	L	68	20	2	4	1	6	7	0	18	0	.294	.377	.485	92	26	3	4	1	8	8	0	21	0	.272	.343	.424
Travis Ishikawa	L	47	15	5	0	1	6	5	0	4	0	.319	.385	.489	69	20	6	0	1	6	6	0	14	1	.290	.347	.420
Akinori Iwamura	L	12	4	2	0	0	1	2	0	2	0	.333	.429	.500	15	4	2	0	0	1	3	0	4	0	.267	.389	.400
Maicer Izturis	B	6	2	0	0	0	0	0	0	1	0	.333	.333	.333	26	7	1	0	0	2	8	2	5	1	.269	.441	.308
Austin Jackson	R	4	2	0	0	0	1	1	0	1	0	.500	.667	.500	4	2	0	0	0	1	1	0	1	0	.500	.667	.500
Conor Jackson	R	6	1	0	0	0	0	0	0	1	0	.167	.167	.167	49	7	0	0	3	12	12	0	6	0	.143	.306	.327
Paul Janish	R	3	0	0	0	0	0	0	0	1	0	.000	.250	.000	10	2	0	0	0	2	2	0	4	0	.200	.385	.200
Kenley Jansen	B	1	1	0	0	0	0	0	0	0	0	1.000	1.000	1.000	1	1	0	0	0	0	0	0	0	0	1.000	1.000	1.000
Jason Jaramillo	B	3	0	0	0	0	0	0	0	0	0	.000	.000	.000	5	0	0	0	0	0	0	0	1	1	.000	.000	.000
John Jaso	L	12	1	0	0	0	1	5	0	4	1	.083	.353	.083	15	1	0	0	0	1	5	0	4	2	.067	.300	.067
Jon Jay	L	22	7	1	0	0	3	2	0	6	0	.318	.375	.364	22	7	1	0	0	3	2	0	6	0	.318	.375	.364
D.Jennings	R	1	1	1	0	0	1	1	0	0	0	1.000	1.000	2.000	1	1	1	0	0	1	1	0	0	0	1.000	1.000	2.000
Derek Jeter	R	2	1	0	0	0	0	0	0	0	0	.500	.500	.500	6	1	0	0	0	0	1	0	2	0	.167	.286	.167
Chris Johnson	R	4	1	0	0	0	0	0	0	1	0	.250	.250	.250	9	1	0	0	0	0	0	0	3	0	.111	.111	.111
Dan Johnson	L	5	2	0	0	0	1	1	0	0	0	.400	.429	.400	22	3	0	0	1	4	3	0	5	0	.136	.214	.273
Kelly Johnson	L	5	0	0	0	0	0	0	0	2	0	.000	.000	.000	49	14	2	1	1	8	14	1	10	0	.286	.444	.429
Nick Johnson	L	1	0	0	0	0	0	2	0	0	0	.000	.667	.000	24	5	0	0	0	3	7	0	3	1	.208	.406	.208
Reed Johnson	R	24	7	2	0	0	2	0	0	3	1	.292	.292	.375	104	26	7	0	2	14	6	1	21	3	.250	.301	.375
Andruw Jones	R	7	2	0	0	1	5	3	0	1	0	.286	.500	.714	56	11	3	0	3	13	13	0	16	1	.196	.348	.411
Chipper Jones	B	7	3	2	0	0	3	1	1	0	0	.429	.500	.714	57	15	4	0	2	18	12	4	16	0	.263	.386	.439
Garrett Jones	L	4	1	0	0	0	0	0	0	2	0	.250	.250	.250	9	1	0	0	0	0	0	0	3	1	.111	.111	.111
Matt Joyce	L	8	3	1	0	1	7	5	0	3	0	.375	.615	.875	19	4	1	1	1	8	6	0	6	0	.211	.400	.526
Kila Ka'aihue	L	2	1	0	0	1	1	1	0	0	1	.500	.667	.500	8	3	0	0	1	2	2	0	1	1	.500	.625	.500
Ryan Kalish	L	5	2	0	0	0	2	1	0	2	0	.400	.500	.400	5	2	0	0	0	2	1	0	2	0	.400	.500	.400
Gabe Kapler	R	13	2	2	0	0	2	0	0	5	0	.154	.154	.308	115	33	7	1	4	16	12	0	24	1	.287	.354	.470
Austin Kearns	R	5	0	0	0	0	0	0	0	4	0	.000	.167	.000	57	14	2	1	2	13	10	0	21	1	.246	.377	.421
Don Kelly	L	11	2	0	0	0	0	0	0	4	0	.182	.250	.182	31	5	0	0	0	2	2	0	7	1	.161	.257	.161

Pinch Hitting

		2010 Pinch Hitting												Career Pinch Hitting												
Batter	B	AB	H	2B	3B	HR	RBI	TBB	IBB	SO	GDP	Avg	OBP	Slg	AB	H	2B	3B	HR	RBI	TBB	IBB	SO	GDP	Avg	OBP	Slg
Matt Kemp	R	6	1	0	0	0	2	0	0	2	0	.167	.167	.167	32	6	0	0	1	3	2	0	15	0	.188	.235	.281
Howie Kendrick	R	6	2	0	0	0	0	0	0	1	1	.333	.333	.333	14	4	0	0	0	1	0	0	2	1	.286	.286	.286
Adam Kennedy	L	22	5	1	0	0	2	2	0	5	0	.227	.280	.273	101	21	5	0	1	11	7	1	22	4	.208	.259	.287
Jeff Keppinger	R	4	1	0	0	0	0	1	0	0	0	.250	.400	.250	35	10	1	0	0	4	2	0	3	1	.286	.316	.314
Ian Kinsler	R	0	0	0	0	0	0	1	0	0	0	-	1.000	-	2	0	0	0	0	0	2	1	1	0	.000	.500	.000
Paul Konerko	R	1	0	0	0	0	0	0	0	0	0	.000	.000	.000	53	14	0	0	2	12	7	3	7	2	.264	.344	.377
Casey Kotchman	L	6	0	0	0	0	0	1	0	2	2	.000	.143	.000	47	10	6	0	0	9	12	0	17	2	.213	.373	.340
Mark Kotsay	L	16	3	0	0	0	1	1	0	1	1	.188	.235	.188	92	29	5	0	3	13	6	2	18	1	.315	.357	.467
George Kottaras	L	2	0	0	0	0	0	1	0	1	0	.000	.333	.000	4	0	0	0	0	0	1	0	3	0	.000	.200	.000
Kevin Kouzmanoff	R	1	1	0	0	1	1	0	0	0	0	1.000	1.000	4.000	12	4	1	0	1	7	2	0	2	0	.333	.375	.667
Jason Kubel	L	4	0	0	0	0	0	1	0	3	0	.000	.200	.000	59	13	3	0	4	8	11	1	20	2	.220	.343	.475
John Lackey	R	1	0	0	0	0	0	0	0	0	0	.000	.000	.000	1	0	0	0	0	0	0	0	0	0	.000	.000	.000
Gerald Laird	R	5	0	0	0	0	1	2	0	5	0	.000	.286	.000	15	2	0	0	0	2	4	0	6	0	.133	.316	.133
Mike Lamb	L	35	7	1	1	0	4	2	0	6	0	.200	.243	.286	242	59	5	3	6	45	28	9	58	5	.244	.320	.364
Ryan Langerhans	L	10	2	0	0	1	1	1	0	6	0	.200	.273	.500	92	22	4	1	4	8	13	0	34	1	.239	.333	.435
Matt LaPorta	R	2	1	0	0	0	0	0	0	0	0	.500	.500	.500	3	1	0	0	0	0	0	0	1	0	.333	.333	.333
Jeff Larish	L	2	1	0	0	0	0	2	0	0	0	.500	.750	.500	18	6	2	0	0	2	5	0	6	0	.333	.478	.444
Adam LaRoche	L	5	1	0	0	0	0	1	0	3	0	.200	.333	.200	61	13	2	0	1	8	3	1	17	2	.213	.246	.295
Andy LaRoche	R	38	5	2	0	1	3	2	0	11	1	.132	.175	.263	59	9	2	0	1	4	4	0	16	1	.153	.206	.237
Jason LaRue	R	1	0	0	0	0	0	1	0	0	0	.000	.500	.000	41	10	3	0	4	12	3	0	10	2	.244	.326	.610
Mike Leake	R	3	0	0	0	0	0	1	0	2	0	.000	.250	.000	3	0	0	0	0	0	1	0	2	0	.000	.250	.000
Derrek Lee	R	3	0	0	0	0	0	2	0	0	0	.000	.000	.000	47	8	1	0	3	8	7	0	17	4	.170	.286	.383
Fred Lewis	L	5	0	0	0	0	0	0	0	4	0	.000	.000	.000	67	17	7	1	0	11	10	1	25	0	.254	.359	.388
Brent Lillibridge	R	8	5	3	1	1	7	0	0	1	0	.625	.625	1.625	14	5	3	1	1	7	0	0	3	0	.357	.357	.929
Adam Lind	L	5	1	0	0	1	1	0	0	3	0	.200	.200	.800	24	8	0	0	2	7	0	0	11	0	.333	.320	.583
John Lindsey	R	7	1	0	0	0	0	0	0	1	1	.143	.143	.143	7	1	0	0	0	0	0	0	1	1	.143	.143	.143
Kyle Lohse	R	1	0	0	0	0	0	0	0	0	0	.000	.000	.000	1	0	0	0	0	0	0	0	0	0	.000	.000	.000
James Loney	L	3	2	1	0	0	1	1	0	0	0	.667	.750	1.000	29	4	1	1	0	3	2	0	5	1	.138	.194	.241
Felipe Lopez	B	16	3	0	0	0	2	2	1	6	0	.188	.278	.188	54	9	1	0	0	5	5	1	18	1	.167	.250	.185
Jose Lopez	R	1	0	0	0	0	0	0	0	0	0	.000	.000	.000	7	0	0	0	0	0	0	0	1	0	.000	.000	.000
Derek Lowe	R	0	0	0	0	0	0	0	0	0	0	-	-	-	0	0	0	0	0	0	0	0	0	0	-	-	-
Mike Lowell	R	11	5	2	0	0	5	3	0	2	0	.455	.533	.636	52	15	4	0	1	13	5	1	8	1	.288	.333	.423
Jed Lowrie	B	7	2	1	0	0	0	2	0	2	0	.286	.444	.429	10	3	1	0	0	0	2	0	3	0	.300	.417	.400
Jonathan Lucroy	R	1	1	0	0	0	0	0	0	0	0	1.000	1.000	1.000	1	1	0	0	0	0	0	0	0	0	1.000	1.000	1.000
Donny Lucy	R	1	1	1	0	0	0	0	0	0	0	1.000	1.000	2.000	5	2	1	0	0	0	0	0	1	0	.400	.400	.600
Ryan Ludwick	R	11	2	1	0	0	0	0	0	6	0	.182	.182	.273	76	20	5	0	4	11	9	1	20	1	.263	.349	.487
Julio Lugo	R	1	0	0	0	0	0	0	0	0	0	.000	.000	.000	42	9	1	0	0	2	6	0	9	1	.214	.333	.238
Hector Luna	R	21	2	1	0	1	3	0	0	11	0	.095	.091	.286	74	16	4	1	1	7	4	0	26	2	.216	.263	.338
Mitch Maier	L	4	1	0	0	0	0	0	0	1	0	.250	.250	.250	10	2	1	0	0	0	1	0	3	0	.200	.273	.300
Matt Mangini	L	1	0	0	0	0	0	0	0	0	0	.000	.000	.000	1	0	0	0	0	0	0	0	0	0	.000	.000	.000
Tommy Manzella	R	2	1	0	0	0	0	0	0	1	0	.500	.500	.500	4	2	0	0	0	0	0	0	2	0	.500	.500	.500
Jason Marquis	L	3	0	0	0	0	0	0	0	0	0	.000	.000	.000	29	6	1	1	0	4	1	0	8	0	.207	.233	.310
Andy Marte	R	9	0	0	0	0	0	0	0	5	0	.000	.000	.000	24	1	0	0	0	0	2	0	12	1	.042	.115	.042
J.D. Martin	R	1	0	0	0	0	0	0	0	0	0	.000	.000	.000	1	0	0	0	0	0	0	0	0	0	.000	.000	.000
Russell Martin	R	5	1	0	0	0	0	2	0	0	0	.200	.429	.200	23	3	0	0	1	2	2	0	2	1	.136	.240	.273
F. Martinez	L	1	0	0	0	0	0	0	0	0	0	.000	.000	.000	5	1	0	0	0	0	0	0	0	0	.200	.200	.200
Osvaldo Martinez	R	3	0	0	0	0	0	1	0	1	0	.000	.250	.000	3	0	0	0	0	0	1	0	1	0	.000	.250	.000
Victor Martinez	B	4	0	0	0	0	0	0	0	0	0	.000	.000	.000	32	11	2	0	1	9	10	1	1	1	.344	.488	.500
Joe Mather	R	14	5	2	0	0	1	0	0	5	0	.357	.357	.500	32	11	4	0	2	4	1	0	10	0	.344	.364	.656
Jeff Mathis	R	1	0	0	0	0	0	0	0	1	0	.000	.000	.000	11	1	0	0	0	1	0	0	4	0	.091	.091	.091
Hideki Matsui	L	6	2	0	0	0	2	2	2	1	1	.333	.500	.333	36	12	2	0	1	7	7	3	10	2	.333	.432	.472
Kaz Matsui	B	6	2	0	0	0	0	0	0	1	0	.333	.333	.333	47	12	0	1	0	1	0	0	10	0	.255	.255	.298
Gary Matthews Jr.	B	19	4	1	0	0	0	1	0	10	0	.211	.250	.263	120	28	4	1	4	21	15	1	37	3	.233	.319	.383
Joe Mauer	L	7	0	0	0	0	0	1	0	2	0	.000	.125	.000	32	6	0	0	1	6	5	1	7	1	.188	.289	.281
Justin Maxwell	R	14	2	1	0	0	0	4	1	5	0	.143	.333	.214	23	5	2	0	1	4	5	1	8	0	.217	.379	.435
Lucas May	R	2	0	0	0	0	0	0	0	0	0	.000	.000	.000	2	0	0	0	0	0	0	0	0	0	.000	.000	.000
John Mayberry	R	5	2	0	0	1	3	1	0	2	0	.400	.500	1.000	16	5	1	0	2	4	2	0	6	1	.313	.389	.750
Cameron Maybin	B	7	1	0	0	0	0	0	0	4	0	.143	.250	.143	12	2	0	0	0	0	0	0	7	0	.167	.231	.167
Paul McAnulty	L	2	0	0	0	0	0	1	0	2	0	.000	.333	.000	58	7	2	0	1	5	9	1	23	0	.121	.239	.207
Brian McCann	L	11	3	0	0	1	5	0	0	3	0	.273	.333	.545	49	13	5	0	1	7	8	4	9	1	.265	.368	.429
Mike McCoy	R	4	0	0	0	0	0	0	0	1	0	.000	.000	.000	8	0	0	0	0	0	0	0	2	0	.000	.000	.000
A. McCutchen	R	0	0	0	0	0	0	2	0	0	0	-	1.000	-	2	0	0	0	0	0	2	0	0	0	-	1.000	-
Darnell McDonald	R	14	6	1	0	1	4	1	0	4	0	.429	.467	.714	31	10	2	1	1	5	2	0	8	2	.323	.364	.548
John McDonald	R	1	0	0	0	0	0	0	0	0	1	.000	.000	.000	38	8	0	0	0	2	2	0	8	1	.211	.250	.211
Michael McKenry	R	4	0	0	0	0	1	0	0	1	0	.000	.200	.000	4	0	0	0	0	1	0	0	1	0	.000	.200	.000
Nate McLouth	L	7	3	1	0	0	0	0	0	0	0	.429	.500	.571	96	21	4	1	1	10	5	0	23	0	.219	.269	.313
Kevin Mench	R	24	3	0	0	0	1	2	0	6	0	.125	.192	.125	84	12	3	1	1	6	5	1	15	0	.143	.209	.238
Jason Michaels	R	54	11	3	0	2	10	2	0	11	0	.204	.259	.370	327	75	17	2	7	44	44	1	93	4	.229	.323	.358
Aaron Miles	B	29	4	0	0	0	0	1	0	4	0	.138	.167	.138	163	34	5	1	0	13	5	0	22	4	.209	.234	.252
Lastings Milledge	R	13	2	0	0	0	0	0	0	3	0	.154	.154	.154	34	8	1	1	0	4	1	0	9	0	.235	.297	.324

Pinch Hitting

Batter	B	AB	H	2B	3B	HR	RBI	TBB	IBB	SO	GDP	Avg	OBP	Slg	AB	H	2B	3B	HR	RBI	TBB	IBB	SO	GDP	Avg	OBP	Slg
		\	\	\	\	2010 Pinch Hitting									\	\	\	\	Career Pinch Hitting								
Corky Miller	R	5	0	0	0	0	0	0	0	1	1	.000	.000	.000	19	2	0	0	1	2	1	0	6	1	.105	.150	.263
Jai Miller	R	2	0	0	0	0	0	0	0	0	0	.000	.000	.000	2	0	0	0	0	0	0	0	0	0	.000	.000	.000
Juan Miranda	L	9	2	0	0	0	2	2	0	4	1	.222	.364	.222	10	3	0	0	0	2	2	0	4	1	.300	.417	.300
Russ Mitchell	R	4	0	0	0	0	0	0	0	2	0	.000	.000	.000	4	0	0	0	0	0	0	0	2	0	.000	.000	.000
Bengie Molina	R	6	1	0	0	0	0	0	0	2	0	.167	.167	.167	60	12	2	0	3	18	4	2	15	3	.200	.257	.383
Lou Montanez	R	4	0	0	0	0	0	0	0	1	0	.000	.000	.000	16	1	0	0	0	0	0	0	4	1	.063	.063	.063
Miguel Montero	L	6	0	0	0	0	0	1	0	3	0	.000	.143	.000	61	13	2	0	3	12	10	1	19	2	.213	.347	.393
Scott Moore	L	11	2	0	0	1	2	0	0	4	0	.182	.182	.455	20	2	0	0	1	2	1	0	10	0	.100	.182	.250
Melvin Mora	R	17	3	0	0	1	2	3	1	5	0	.176	.300	.353	51	9	2	0	2	5	7	1	14	1	.176	.295	.333
Jose Morales	B	4	0	0	0	0	1	1	0	1	0	.000	.167	.000	19	6	1	0	0	4	3	1	5	0	.316	.391	.368
Brent Morel	R	2	0	0	0	0	0	0	0	1	0	.000	.000	.000	2	0	0	0	0	0	0	0	1	0	.000	.000	.000
Mitch Moreland	L	3	0	0	0	0	0	1	1	2	1	.000	.250	.000	3	0	0	0	0	0	1	1	2	1	.000	.250	.000
Nyjer Morgan	L	6	3	1	0	0	0	0	0	0	0	.500	.500	.667	22	6	2	0	0	0	2	0	5	0	.273	.360	.364
Justin Morneau	L	1	0	0	0	0	0	1	1	1	0	.000	.500	.000	21	8	1	0	3	9	4	1	5	2	.381	.480	.857
Mike Morse	R	17	5	1	1	0	6	0	0	6	1	.294	.278	.471	45	16	3	1	1	14	3	0	16	1	.356	.388	.533
Brandon Moss	L	12	1	0	0	0	0	0	0	3	1	.083	.083	.083	57	12	3	1	1	7	1	0	20	1	.211	.237	.351
David Murphy	L	16	3	0	0	0	1	2	0	4	0	.188	.278	.188	23	3	0	0	0	1	4	0	5	0	.130	.259	.130
Donnie Murphy	R	19	7	3	0	2	8	1	0	7	0	.368	.400	.842	30	8	4	0	2	9	2	0	15	0	.267	.313	.600
Xavier Nady	R	33	7	0	0	1	6	5	0	10	1	.212	.333	.303	80	19	2	0	3	10	13	0	20	5	.238	.371	.375
Mike Napoli	R	6	0	0	0	0	0	2	0	4	0	.000	.250	.000	23	2	0	0	0	3	6	0	15	1	.087	.300	.087
Daniel Nava	B	10	2	0	0	0	2	1	0	5	0	.200	.333	.200	10	2	0	0	0	2	1	0	5	0	.200	.333	.200
Dioner Navarro	B	3	1	1	0	0	2	0	0	0	0	.333	.333	.667	25	5	1	0	0	6	1	0	6	2	.200	.259	.240
Oswaldo Navarro	R	4	0	0	0	0	0	0	0	1	0	.000	.000	.000	6	1	0	0	0	0	0	0	2	0	.167	.167	.167
Yamalco Navarro	R	1	1	0	0	0	0	0	0	0	0	1.000	1.000	1.000	1	1	0	0	0	0	0	0	0	0	1.000	1.000	1.000
Chris Nelson	R	8	4	0	0	0	0	0	0	1	0	.500	.500	.500	8	4	0	0	0	0	0	0	1	0	.500	.500	.500
Mike Nickeas	R	1	0	0	0	0	0	0	0	1	0	.000	.000	.000	1	0	0	0	0	0	0	0	1	0	.000	.000	.000
Jonathon Niese	L	1	0	0	0	0	0	0	0	1	0	.000	.000	.000	1	0	0	0	0	0	0	0	1	0	.000	.000	.000
Wil Nieves	R	7	0	0	0	0	0	2	0	4	0	.000	.222	.000	20	0	0	0	0	0	2	0	10	0	.000	.091	.000
Jayson Nix	R	7	2	0	0	0	1	0	0	2	0	.286	.286	.286	20	3	0	0	0	1	4	0	6	0	.150	.292	.150
Laynce Nix	L	45	12	1	0	1	3	4	2	12	2	.267	.327	.356	105	21	5	0	2	8	13	3	34	3	.200	.288	.305
Trent Oeltjen	L	5	1	0	0	0	0	1	0	0	1	.200	.333	.200	7	1	0	0	0	0	1	0	1	1	.143	.250	.143
Augie Ojeda	B	20	7	2	0	0	2	4	0	2	0	.350	.440	.450	86	20	6	1	0	10	9	0	16	1	.233	.299	.326
Miguel Olivo	R	1	0	0	0	0	0	0	0	0	0	.000	.000	.000	34	6	1	0	2	7	0	0	10	0	.176	.194	.382
David Ortiz	L	4	0	0	0	0	0	3	0	2	0	.000	.429	.000	75	14	3	1	3	16	19	1	20	1	.187	.347	.373
Roy Oswalt	R	0	0	0	0	0	0	0	0	0	0	-	-	-	2	0	0	0	0	0	0	0	1	0	.000	.000	.000
Adam Ottavino	B	1	0	0	0	0	0	0	0	0	0	.000	.000	.000	1	0	0	0	0	0	0	0	1	0	.000	.000	.000
Lyle Overbay	L	2	1	1	0	0	1	1	1	0	0	.500	.667	1.000	45	12	4	0	2	14	6	1	15	2	.267	.340	.489
Micah Owings	R	7	1	0	0	0	0	0	0	5	0	.143	.143	.143	44	11	3	0	2	8	3	0	19	1	.250	.298	.455
Angel Pagan	B	6	1	0	0	0	1	0	0	2	0	.167	.167	.167	58	10	0	1	0	1	1	0	19	1	.172	.186	.207
Gerardo Parra	L	20	4	0	0	0	0	3	1	7	0	.154	.241	.154	35	4	0	0	0	0	3	1	10	1	.114	.179	.114
Corey Patterson	L	7	1	1	0	0	0	0	0	4	0	.143	.143	.286	76	15	4	0	1	5	1	0	28	1	.197	.205	.289
Eric Patterson	L	11	1	0	0	1	1	2	0	6	0	.091	.231	.364	20	2	1	0	1	1	2	0	9	0	.100	.182	.300
Xavier Paul	L	9	0	0	0	0	0	0	0	3	0	.000	.000	.000	16	3	1	0	1	1	0	0	4	1	.188	.188	.438
Ronny Paulino	R	7	4	1	0	0	0	0	0	0	0	.571	.571	.714	37	9	2	0	1	10	2	0	7	2	.243	.282	.378
Jay Payton	R	10	1	2	0	0	1	0	0	0	0	.400	.400	.600	96	27	7	0	1	12	7	0	14	4	.281	.343	.385
Steve Pearce	R	2	0	0	0	0	0	2	0	2	0	.000	.500	.000	29	4	3	1	0	1	5	0	10	0	.138	.265	.310
Brayan Pena	B	12	0	0	0	0	1	3	0	4	1	.000	.188	.000	67	15	3	0	1	8	6	0	16	2	.224	.284	.313
Ramiro Pena	B	4	1	0	0	0	1	0	0	1	0	.250	.250	.250	7	1	0	0	0	1	0	0	2	0	.143	.143	.143
Hunter Pence	R	0	0	0	0	0	0	1	0	0	0	-	1.000	-	4	1	0	0	0	0	1	0	1	0	.250	.400	.250
Cliff Pennington	B	2	0	0	0	0	0	2	0	0	0	.000	.333	.000	2	0	0	0	0	0	1	0	2	0	.000	.333	.000
Jhonny Peralta	R	1	0	0	0	0	0	1	0	0	0	.000	.500	.000	11	3	0	0	0	2	3	0	3	0	.273	.429	.273
Bryan Petersen	L	18	2	0	0	0	2	1	0	5	0	.111	.158	.111	18	2	0	0	0	2	1	0	5	0	.111	.158	.111
Brandon Phillips	R	1	0	0	0	0	0	0	0	0	0	.000	.000	.000	13	4	2	0	1	1	3	1	1	0	.308	.438	.692
Paul Phillips	R	1	0	0	0	0	0	0	0	1	0	.000	.000	.000	9	3	1	0	0	1	0	0	2	0	.333	.333	.444
Felix Pie	L	4	1	0	0	0	1	0	0	3	0	.250	.250	.250	22	5	1	0	0	1	0	0	12	0	.227	.227	.273
Juan Pierre	L	1	1	0	0	0	0	0	0	0	0	1.000	1.000	1.000	90	28	1	2	0	4	9	1	6	0	.311	.380	.367
A.J. Pierzynski	L	5	0	0	0	0	0	0	0	0	0	.000	.000	.000	85	18	4	0	2	15	9	4	14	5	.212	.289	.329
Trevor Plouffe	R	3	0	0	0	0	0	0	0	2	0	.000	.000	.000	3	0	0	0	0	0	0	0	2	0	.000	.000	.000
Scott Podsednik	L	3	1	0	0	0	0	1	0	0	0	.333	.500	.333	91	20	1	2	1	10	12	0	18	2	.220	.324	.308
Placido Polanco	R	2	0	0	0	0	0	0	0	0	0	.000	.000	.000	75	19	3	0	1	16	5	0	7	2	.253	.296	.333
Jorge Posada	B	13	1	0	0	1	1	1	0	5	1	.077	.143	.308	126	28	3	1	5	26	21	3	44	6	.222	.331	.381
Buster Posey	R	3	0	0	0	0	0	0	0	1	0	.000	.000	.000	4	0	0	0	0	0	0	0	1	0	.000	.000	.000
Landon Powell	B	3	0	0	0	0	0	0	0	1	0	.000	.000	.000	5	0	0	0	0	0	0	0	2	0	.000	.000	.000
Alex Presley	L	6	2	0	0	0	0	3	0	0	0	.333	.333	.333	6	2	0	0	0	0	0	0	3	0	.333	.333	.333
Albert Pujols	R	1	0	0	0	0	0	1	0	0	0	.000	.500	.000	22	8	0	0	2	9	7	2	6	0	.364	.500	.636
Nick Punto	B	1	0	0	0	0	0	0	0	1	0	.000	.000	.000	40	8	1	0	0	4	4	0	11	0	.200	.273	.225
Carlos Quentin	R	5	1	0	0	1	1	0	0	1	0	.200	.200	.800	25	7	4	0	2	10	0	0	6	0	.280	.333	.680
Robb Quinlan	R	1	0	0	0	0	0	0	0	1	0	.000	.000	.000	43	10	2	0	2	5	3	0	7	0	.233	.292	.419
H. Quintero	R	5	1	0	0	0	1	0	0	0	0	.200	.200	.200	19	4	0	0	0	1	0	0	4	3	.211	.211	.211
Ryan Raburn	R	15	2	0	0	1	2	1	0	4	0	.133	.222	.333	51	9	1	0	3	8	7	1	18	1	.176	.295	.373

Pinch Hitting

Batter	B	| 2010 Pinch Hitting													| Career Pinch Hitting												
		AB	H	2B	3B	HR	RBI	TBB	IBB	SO	GDP	Avg	OBP	Slg	AB	H	2B	3B	HR	RBI	TBB	IBB	SO	GDP	Avg	OBP	Slg
Alexei Ramirez	R	1	1	0	0	0	1	0	0	0	0	1.000	1.000	1.000	3	1	0	0	0	1	0	0	0	0	.333	.333	.333
Aramis Ramirez	R	6	1	0	0	1	3	0	0	2	0	.167	.167	.667	36	10	1	0	2	14	1	0	8	1	.278	.308	.472
Hanley Ramirez	R	1	0	0	0	0	0	0	0	0	0	.000	.000	.000	11	4	0	0	1	4	2	0	2	0	.364	.462	.636
Manny Ramirez	R	12	1	0	0	1	2	1	0	6	0	.083	.214	.333	42	5	0	0	2	9	9	3	16	0	.119	.283	.262
Max Ramirez	R	2	0	0	0	0	0	0	0	1	1	.000	.000	.000	3	0	0	0	0	0	0	0	2	1	.000	.000	.000
Cody Ransom	R	5	1	0	0	1	2	1	0	1	0	.200	.333	.800	28	5	1	0	2	4	5	0	10	1	.179	.303	.429
Colby Rasmus	L	13	6	1	0	1	4	3	1	4	0	.462	.563	.769	32	9	2	0	1	5	4	1	10	1	.281	.361	.438
John Raynor	R	7	2	0	0	0	0	1	0	1	0	.286	.375	.286	7	2	0	0	0	0	1	0	1	0	.286	.375	.286
Josh Reddick	L	3	0	0	0	0	0	0	0	2	0	.000	.000	.000	11	1	0	0	0	0	0	0	4	0	.091	.091	.091
Jeremy Reed	L	4	0	0	0	0	0	0	0	3	0	.000	.000	.000	98	24	4	1	0	9	5	0	26	0	.245	.279	.306
Nolan Reimold	R	3	0	0	0	0	0	0	0	3	0	.000	.000	.000	9	0	0	0	0	0	2	0	6	0	.000	.182	.000
Edgar Renteria	R	4	0	0	0	0	0	0	0	1	0	.000	.000	.000	33	7	1	0	0	6	1	0	13	1	.212	.243	.242
Jason Repko	R	6	1	0	0	0	0	1	0	3	0	.167	.286	.167	31	5	1	0	0	1	3	0	12	0	.161	.229	.194
Ben Revere	L	1	0	0	0	0	0	0	0	1	0	.000	.000	.000	1	0	0	0	0	0	0	0	1	0	.000	.000	.000
Jose Reyes	B	0	0	0	0	0	0	0	0	0	0	-	1.000	-	7	1	1	0	0	0	2	0	1	0	.143	.400	.286
Mark Reynolds	R	2	0	0	0	0	0	2	0	1	0	.000	.500	.000	15	2	0	0	2	5	2	0	8	2	.133	.222	.533
Will Rhymes	L	5	1	1	0	0	2	1	0	2	0	.200	.333	.400	5	1	1	0	0	2	1	0	2	0	.200	.333	.400
Alex Rios	R	2	1	0	0	0	0	0	0	0	0	.500	.500	.500	22	8	0	1	2	8	3	0	3	0	.364	.440	.727
Juan Rivera	R	8	2	0	0	0	1	1	1	1	2	.250	.400	.250	62	13	6	0	1	10	6	2	12	5	.210	.300	.355
Mike Rivera	R	2	0	0	0	0	0	1	0	0	0	.000	.333	.000	17	2	0	0	0	2	0	0	5	1	.118	.250	.118
Brian Roberts	B	1	0	0	0	0	0	0	0	1	0	.000	.000	.000	34	7	2	0	0	1	3	0	10	0	.206	.270	.265
Ryan Roberts	R	22	5	1	0	0	4	0	0	6	0	.227	.217	.273	51	11	2	0	0	5	5	0	17	1	.216	.305	.255
Alex Rodriguez	R	2	0	0	0	0	0	1	0	1	0	.000	.333	.000	11	0	0	0	0	0	2	0	4	0	.000	.154	.000
Ivan Rodriguez	R	7	1	0	0	0	1	0	0	3	1	.143	.125	.143	79	20	1	0	2	16	6	3	23	4	.253	.307	.342
Sean Rodriguez	R	15	1	1	0	0	1	0	0	8	0	.067	.067	.133	17	2	1	0	0	1	0	0	8	0	.118	.118	.176
Wandy Rodriguez	B	2	0	0	0	0	0	0	0	0	0	.000	.000	.000	2	0	0	0	0	0	0	0	0	0	.000	.000	.000
Esmil Rogers	R	1	0	0	0	0	0	0	0	0	0	.000	.000	.000	1	0	0	0	0	0	0	0	0	0	.000	.000	.000
Ryan Rohlinger	R	4	1	0	0	0	0	1	0	1	0	.250	.400	.250	9	2	0	0	0	2	1	0	2	1	.222	.300	.222
Scott Rolen	R	7	3	0	0	2	4	0	0	1	0	.429	.429	1.286	14	5	0	0	3	5	0	0	4	0	.357	.357	1.000
Jimmy Rollins	B	2	0	0	0	0	0	0	0	0	0	.000	.000	.000	18	2	0	0	1	1	1	0	2	0	.111	.158	.278
Niuman Romero	B	1	0	0	0	0	0	0	0	0	0	.000	.000	.000	3	1	0	0	0	0	0	0	1	0	.333	.333	.333
Andrew Romine	B	0	0	0	0	0	0	0	0	0	0	-	-	-	0	0	0	0	0	0	0	0	0	0	-	-	-
Adam Rosales	R	10	3	0	1	1	2	0	0	3	0	.300	.300	.800	37	7	1	1	2	7	1	0	12	0	.189	.211	.432
Cody Ross	R	1	1	0	0	0	0	2	0	0	0	1.000	1.000	1.000	50	14	4	0	4	10	7	0	16	0	.280	.390	.600
David Ross	R	3	0	0	0	0	2	1	0	0	0	.000	.250	.000	43	9	1	1	3	9	11	0	11	1	.209	.370	.488
Aaron Rowand	R	22	5	0	0	2	4	2	0	4	1	.227	.320	.500	67	14	4	0	2	7	5	0	22	2	.209	.274	.358
Carlos Ruiz	R	6	1	0	0	0	0	1	1	1	0	.167	.286	.167	26	7	2	0	0	6	2	1	3	1	.269	.321	.346
Randy Ruiz	R	2	0	0	0	0	0	0	0	0	0	.000	.000	.000	8	1	0	0	0	0	1	0	3	1	.125	.222	.125
Rusty Ryal	R	50	11	2	0	0	1	3	0	19	0	.220	.278	.260	63	14	3	0	0	2	4	0	23	0	.222	.279	.270
Brendan Ryan	R	4	1	0	0	0	0	0	0	0	0	.250	.250	.250	36	9	3	0	0	1	6	0	6	0	.250	.386	.333
Michael Ryan	L	8	1	0	0	0	1	0	0	2	0	.125	.111	.125	51	10	3	0	0	8	4	1	10	1	.196	.246	.255
Oscar Salazar	R	45	10	2	0	2	11	5	0	9	1	.222	.294	.400	92	27	5	0	6	25	11	1	17	2	.293	.362	.543
J. Saltalamacchia	B	3	0	0	0	0	0	2	0	3	0	.000	.400	.000	16	2	0	0	0	1	4	0	9	0	.125	.300	.125
Angel Sanchez	R	2	2	0	0	0	0	0	0	0	0	1.000	1.000	1.000	2	2	0	0	0	0	0	0	0	0	1.000	1.000	1.000
Anibal Sanchez	R	1	0	0	0	0	0	0	0	1	0	.000	.000	.000	1	0	0	0	0	0	0	0	1	0	.000	.000	.000
Freddy Sanchez	R	1	1	1	0	0	0	2	0	0	0	1.000	1.000	2.000	56	17	4	2	0	6	9	0	6	1	.304	.400	.446
Gaby Sanchez	R	2	0	0	0	0	0	0	0	0	0	.000	.000	.000	23	5	0	0	2	3	2	0	4	0	.217	.280	.478
Pablo Sandoval	B	4	1	0	0	0	1	0	0	0	0	.250	.250	.250	12	5	2	0	0	7	2	1	1	1	.417	.467	.583
Carlos Santana	B	0	0	0	0	0	0	1	0	0	0	-	1.000	-	0	0	0	0	0	0	1	0	0	0	-	1.000	-
Ramon Santiago	B	18	5	0	0	0	0	2	0	4	0	.278	.409	.278	37	11	1	0	0	3	3	0	9	0	.297	.409	.324
Dane Sardinha	R	4	0	0	0	0	0	0	0	2	0	.000	.000	.000	5	0	0	0	0	0	0	0	3	0	.000	.000	.000
Michael Saunders	L	4	1	0	0	0	0	0	0	2	0	.250	.250	.250	5	1	0	0	0	0	0	0	3	0	.200	.200	.200
Bobby Scales	R	3	0	0	0	0	0	2	0	0	0	.000	.400	.000	17	7	2	1	2	5	1	0	3	0	.412	.444	1.000
Nate Schierholtz	L	29	9	2	0	1	3	6	0	5	1	.310	.429	.483	75	25	6	0	1	9	7	0	17	1	.333	.381	.453
Konrad Schmidt	R	0	0	0	0	0	0	1	0	0	0	-	1.000	-	0	0	0	0	0	0	1	0	0	0	-	1.000	-
Brian Schneider	L	2	0	0	0	0	0	1	0	1	0	.000	.333	.000	54	12	2	0	1	10	7	2	9	4	.222	.323	.315
Skip Schumaker	L	10	3	0	0	1	1	0	0	3	0	.300	.417	.300	96	23	4	0	1	8	2	0	17	2	.240	.267	.313
Luke Scott	L	9	1	0	0	1	3	1	1	2	0	.111	.200	.444	73	16	8	0	1	8	8	1	23	0	.219	.296	.370
Marco Scutaro	R	3	0	0	0	0	0	0	0	1	0	.000	.000	.000	45	7	0	1	0	4	3	0	10	2	.156	.208	.200
Ryan Shealy	R	4	0	0	0	0	0	0	0	0	0	.000	.000	.000	20	3	0	0	0	2	2	0	7	0	.150	.227	.150
Kelly Shoppach	R	9	3	1	0	0	0	3	0	3	0	.333	.500	.444	21	6	1	0	1	5	6	0	8	0	.286	.429	.476
Grady Sizemore	L	1	0	0	0	0	0	0	0	1	0	.000	.000	.000	11	4	0	0	0	0	0	0	2	0	.364	.364	.364
Scott Sizemore	R	4	1	0	0	1	3	0	0	0	0	.250	.250	1.000	4	1	0	0	1	3	0	0	0	0	.250	.250	1.000
Seth Smith	L	37	7	2	1	2	12	6	0	11	0	.189	.295	.459	115	38	10	5	5	32	23	2	27	1	.330	.436	.635
Justin Smoak	B	3	1	0	0	0	0	0	0	0	1	.333	.333	.333	3	1	0	0	0	0	0	0	0	1	.333	.333	.333
Travis Snider	L	4	0	0	0	0	0	0	0	3	0	.000	.000	.000	8	1	0	0	0	0	0	0	5	0	.125	.125	.250
Brad Snyder	L	6	2	1	0	0	2	0	0	3	0	.333	.333	.500	6	2	1	0	0	2	0	0	3	0	.333	.333	.500
Brandon Snyder	R	1	0	0	0	0	0	0	0	0	0	.000	.000	.000	1	0	0	0	0	0	0	0	0	0	.000	.000	.000
Chris Snyder	R	3	1	0	0	0	1	0	0	1	0	.333	.500	.333	18	2	0	0	1	4	2	1	3	0	.111	.190	.278
Eric Sogard	L	1	0	0	0	0	0	1	0	0	0	.000	.500	.000	1	0	0	0	0	0	1	0	0	0	.000	.500	.000

Pinch Hitting

Batter	B	2010 Pinch Hitting AB	H	2B	3B	HR	RBI	TBB	IBB	SO	GDP	Avg	OBP	Slg	Career Pinch Hitting AB	H	2B	3B	HR	RBI	TBB	IBB	SO	GDP	Avg	OBP	Slg
Alfonso Soriano	R	11	1	0	0	1	3	2	0	4	0	.091	.231	.364	17	3	1	0	1	3	4	1	4	0	.176	.333	.412
Geovany Soto	R	1	0	0	0	0	0	0	0	0	0	.000	.000	.000	18	5	1	0	0	2	4	2	6	0	.278	.409	.333
Ryan Spilborghs	R	35	13	4	0	0	8	5	0	8	2	.371	.463	.486	141	46	13	1	1	33	25	0	33	6	.326	.426	.454
Max St. Pierre	R	2	0	0	0	0	0	0	0	0	0	.000	.000	.000	2	0	0	0	0	0	0	0	0	0	.000	.000	.000
Matt Stairs	L	52	12	3	0	4	9	4	1	21	1	.231	.281	.519	377	99	20	2	23	86	57	10	99	5	.263	.365	.509
Mike Stanton	R	2	0	0	0	0	0	0	0	1	0	.000	.000	.000	2	0	0	0	0	0	0	0	1	0	.000	.000	.000
Nick Stavinoha	R	53	15	2	0	2	4	3	0	12	3	.283	.321	.434	81	22	5	0	3	9	4	0	17	3	.272	.302	.444
Adam Stern	L	4	0	0	0	0	0	0	0	1	0	.000	.000	.000	5	0	0	0	0	0	0	0	1	0	.000	.000	.000
Ian Stewart	L	6	1	0	0	0	2	3	0	4	0	.167	.444	.167	60	15	7	0	2	10	5	0	24	1	.250	.328	.467
Drew Stubbs	R	4	2	1	0	0	0	2	0	1	0	.500	.667	.750	4	2	1	0	0	0	2	0	1	0	.500	.667	.750
Cory Sullivan	L	40	6	1	1	0	4	2	0	9	0	.150	.190	.225	143	30	2	2	1	17	9	1	43	1	.210	.266	.273
Drew Sutton	B	1	1	0	0	1	4	0	0	0	0	1.000	1.000	4.000	23	5	1	0	1	7	1	0	8	0	.217	.280	.391
Kurt Suzuki	R	1	0	0	0	0	0	0	0	0	0	.000	.000	.000	15	7	1	0	2	6	2	0	0	0	.467	.556	.933
Mike Sweeney	R	17	4	1	0	0	4	1	0	3	1	.235	.300	.294	69	18	4	0	0	8	5	0	11	4	.261	.325	.319
Ryan Sweeney	L	2	2	0	0	0	0	2	1	0	0	1.000	1.000	1.000	16	2	0	0	0	3	3	1	7	1	.125	.263	.125
Nick Swisher	B	6	0	0	0	0	0	0	0	1	0	.000	.000	.000	21	2	2	0	0	3	2	0	5	2	.095	.174	.190
Jose Tabata	R	1	0	0	0	0	0	0	0	0	0	.000	.000	.000	1	0	0	0	0	0	0	0	0	0	.000	.000	.000
Fernando Tatis	R	22	7	1	0	1	3	3	0	4	0	.318	.400	.500	101	24	3	0	3	15	10	1	21	5	.238	.307	.356
Craig Tatum	R	1	1	0	0	0	0	0	0	0	0	1.000	1.000	1.000	3	1	0	0	0	0	0	0	0	0	.333	.500	.333
Willy Taveras	R	4	0	0	0	0	0	0	0	1	0	.000	.000	.000	45	12	2	1	0	4	0	0	7	0	.267	.283	.356
Mark Teahen	L	5	2	1	0	0	2	1	0	1	0	.400	.500	.600	16	4	1	0	0	2	3	0	4	0	.250	.368	.313
Mark Teixeira	B	0	0	0	0	0	0	1	1	0	0	-	1.000	-	4	0	0	0	0	0	2	1	0	0	.000	.333	.000
Ruben Tejada	R	1	0	0	0	0	0	0	0	0	0	.000	.000	.000	1	0	0	0	0	0	0	0	0	0	.000	.000	.000
Marcus Thames	R	19	4	0	0	0	1	3	0	6	0	.211	.318	.211	74	22	2	0	5	15	13	2	26	1	.297	.402	.527
Ryan Theriot	R	5	0	0	0	0	0	0	0	1	0	.000	.000	.000	37	7	2	0	1	6	5	0	9	0	.189	.302	.324
Josh Thole	L	14	5	0	0	0	3	2	0	2	0	.357	.438	.357	15	5	0	0	0	3	2	0	2	0	.333	.412	.333
Jim Thome	L	25	7	4	0	1	2	4	1	10	0	.280	.400	.560	107	25	8	0	4	13	19	1	43	2	.234	.357	.421
Matt Tolbert	B	4	0	0	0	0	0	0	0	2	0	.000	.000	.000	9	2	0	0	0	0	2	0	3	0	.222	.364	.222
Steve Tolleson	R	2	0	0	0	0	0	0	0	2	0	.000	.000	.000	3	0	0	0	0	0	0	0	2	0	.000	.000	.000
Yorvit Torrealba	R	2	0	0	0	0	0	1	0	1	0	.000	.333	.000	22	1	0	0	0	1	2	0	11	0	.045	.130	.045
Andres Torres	B	6	3	0	0	0	3	0	0	1	0	.500	.500	.500	26	8	0	0	1	8	2	0	10	0	.308	.357	.423
J.R. Towles	R	3	0	0	0	0	0	0	0	2	0	.000	.000	.000	5	0	0	0	0	0	0	0	3	0	.000	.000	.000
Chad Tracy	L	24	1	0	0	0	0	4	0	11	0	.042	.179	.042	110	27	9	0	5	24	15	0	28	2	.245	.339	.464
Matt Treanor	R	2	1	0	1	0	2	0	0	0	0	.500	.500	1.500	19	4	0	1	0	3	0	0	2	0	.211	.211	.316
Mark Trumbo	R	1	0	0	0	0	0	0	0	1	0	.000	.000	.000	1	0	0	0	0	0	0	0	1	0	.000	.000	.000
Matt Tuiasosopo	R	4	0	0	0	0	0	0	0	2	0	.000	.000	.000	5	0	0	0	0	0	0	0	2	0	.000	.000	.000
Justin Turner	R	1	0	0	0	0	0	1	0	0	0	.000	.500	.000	6	1	0	0	0	0	2	0	1	0	.167	.286	.167
B.J. Upton	R	1	1	0	1	0	0	0	0	0	0	1.000	1.000	3.000	10	5	0	1	1	2	0	0	2	1	.500	.500	1.000
Justin Upton	R	1	0	0	0	0	0	0	0	0	1	.000	.000	.000	12	4	2	0	0	0	0	0	6	1	.333	.333	.500
Juan Uribe	R	4	2	0	0	0	1	0	0	1	0	.500	.600	.500	35	12	4	0	1	8	2	0	9	1	.343	.378	.543
Chase Utley	L	1	0	0	0	0	0	0	0	1	0	.000	.000	.000	44	13	2	0	4	15	5	1	16	0	.295	.373	.614
Chris Valaika	R	5	1	0	0	0	0	1	0	1	0	.200	.333	.200	5	1	0	0	0	0	1	0	1	0	.200	.333	.200
Luis Valbuena	L	2	0	0	0	0	0	0	0	0	0	.000	.000	.000	6	2	0	1	0	0	0	0	0	0	.333	.333	.667
Wilson Valdez	R	9	1	1	0	0	1	1	0	1	0	.111	.200	.222	22	3	1	0	0	2	0	0	3	0	.136	.240	.182
Danny Valencia	R	3	1	0	0	0	0	0	0	0	0	.333	.333	.333	3	1	0	0	0	0	0	0	0	0	.333	.333	.333
J. Van Every	L	0	0	0	0	0	0	1	0	0	0	-	1.000	-	1	0	0	0	0	0	1	0	1	0	.000	.500	.000
Eugenio Velez	B	9	1	0	0	0	1	1	0	3	0	.111	.200	.111	54	13	2	2	0	6	2	0	12	2	.241	.268	.352
Will Venable	L	21	5	1	1	0	3	0	0	9	0	.238	.227	.301	36	8	2	1	0	5	2	0	15	0	.222	.256	.333
Dayan Viciedo	R	7	2	0	0	0	1	1	0	3	0	.286	.375	.286	7	2	0	0	0	1	1	0	3	0	.286	.375	.286
Shane Victorino	B	3	0	0	0	0	0	1	0	2	0	.000	.250	.000	83	22	1	1	3	22	7	0	16	1	.265	.323	.410
Omar Vizquel	B	1	0	0	0	0	0	1	0	0	0	.000	.500	.000	55	6	3	0	0	3	4	0	11	1	.109	.169	.164
Joey Votto	L	1	0	0	0	0	0	2	1	1	0	.000	.667	.000	13	3	0	0	1	4	2	2	5	0	.231	.412	.462
Adam Wainwright	R	3	0	0	0	0	0	0	0	0	0	.000	.000	.000	16	3	0	0	0	1	0	0	7	0	.188	.176	.188
Neil Walker	B	1	0	0	0	0	0	0	0	0	0	.000	.000	.000	9	2	1	0	0	0	0	0	0	1	.222	.222	.333
Brett Wallace	L	3	1	0	0	0	1	0	0	0	0	.333	.333	.333	3	1	0	0	0	1	0	0	0	0	.333	.333	.333
Matt Watson	L	2	0	0	0	0	0	0	0	1	0	.000	.000	.000	18	1	1	0	0	0	0	0	5	1	.056	.056	.111
Casper Wells	R	7	2	0	0	0	0	0	0	3	0	.286	.286	.286	7	2	0	0	0	0	0	0	3	0	.286	.286	.286
Vernon Wells	R	2	0	0	0	0	0	1	0	0	0	.000	.000	.000	10	2	0	0	0	4	0	0	1	0	.200	.200	.200
Jayson Werth	R	3	0	0	0	0	0	1	0	0	0	.000	.250	.000	53	12	1	0	3	11	8	0	21	0	.226	.328	.415
Matt Wieters	B	6	1	1	0	0	1	1	0	3	1	.167	.286	.333	7	2	1	0	0	1	1	0	3	1	.286	.375	.429
Ty Wigginton	R	2	1	0	0	0	1	1	1	0	0	.500	.667	.500	57	17	2	0	3	21	7	1	9	2	.298	.388	.491
Josh Willingham	R	5	2	1	0	0	2	1	0	0	0	.400	.571	.400	46	11	0	0	2	10	5	0	15	0	.239	.327	.413
Reggie Willits	B	13	2	0	0	0	0	1	0	5	0	.154	.214	.154	38	7	0	0	0	0	5	0	11	0	.184	.279	.184
Bobby Wilson	R	1	1	0	0	0	0	0	0	0	0	1.000	1.000	1.000	1	1	0	0	0	0	0	0	0	0	1.000	1.000	1.000
Josh Wilson	R	1	1	0	0	0	0	0	0	0	0	1.000	1.000	2.000	19	5	1	0	0	3	1	0	6	1	.263	.300	.316
Randy Winn	B	44	7	1	3	1	4	5	0	6	2	.159	.255	.250	104	27	3	0	4	21	12	0	13	3	.260	.342	.404
DeWayne Wise	L	4	0	0	0	0	0	1	0	0	0	.000	.000	.000	65	20	2	1	3	12	0	0	15	1	.308	.303	.508
Randy Wolf	L	2	0	0	0	0	0	0	0	2	0	.000	.000	.000	8	1	0	0	0	0	0	0	4	0	.125	.125	.125
Brandon Wood	R	3	0	0	0	0	0	0	0	0	0	.000	.250	.000	7	2	1	0	1	3	0	0	0	0	.286	.375	.857

Pinch Hitting

Batter	B	2010 Pinch Hitting													Career Pinch Hitting											
		AB	H	2B	3B	HR	RBI	TBB	IBB	SO	GDP	Avg	OBP	Slg	AB	H	2B	3B	HR	RBI	TBB	IBB	SO	GDP	Avg	OBP	Slg
Chris Woodward	R	1	1	1	0	0	0	0	0	0	0	1.000	1.000	2.000	71	16	2	0	2	11	8	0	18	0	.225	.309	.338
Danny Worth	R	0	0	0	0	0	0	1	0	0	0	-	1.000	-	2	0	0	0	0	0	1	0	0	0	.000	.333	.000
David Wright	R	1	0	0	0	0	0	0	0	0	0	.000	.000	.000	4	1	0	0	0	1	0	0	1	0	.250	.250	.250
Chris Young	R	1	1	1	0	0	1	0	0	0	0	1.000	1.000	2.000	15	4	3	0	0	6	4	1	4	0	.267	.421	.467
Delmon Young	R	4	1	0	0	0	1	0	0	0	0	.250	.250	.250	6	3	1	0	0	1	0	0	0	0	.500	.500	.667
Delwyn Young	B	69	16	1	0	2	7	3	0	24	2	.232	.264	.333	170	46	7	0	3	17	14	0	49	5	.271	.330	.365
Eric Young Jr.	B	5	3	1	1	0	0	2	0	1	1	.600	.714	1.200	20	6	1	1	0	0	4	0	3	1	.300	.417	.450
Carlos Zambrano	B	7	0	0	0	0	0	0	0	3	0	.000	.000	.000	28	2	0	0	0	0	0	0	14	1	.071	.071	.071
Lance Zawadzki	B	8	1	1	0	0	0	1	0	2	1	.125	.222	.250	8	1	1	0	0	0	1	0	2	1	.125	.222	.250
Ryan Zimmerman	R	4	1	0	0	1	2	0	0	0	1	.250	.250	1.000	13	4	2	0	1	5	0	0	1	1	.308	.286	.692
Ben Zobrist	B	5	1	0	0	0	0	1	0	2	0	.200	.333	.200	30	5	0	0	3	9	3	1	8	0	.167	.242	.467

Manufactured Run Contributions

Bill James

The term "Manufactured Run" entered the baseball vocabulary about 1980, and we began documenting Manufactured Runs in 2006.   A manufactured run is essentially. . .general definition. . .any run on which at least two of the four bases are accounted for by doing something other than playing station-to-station baseball.   I'll give a fuller definition at the end of the article. The best major league team at Manufacturing Runs in 2010 was the Texas Rangers, a point very well illustrated in the fifth and deciding game of the American League Division Series. The Rangers won the game, 5-1, manufacturing the first three runs. In the first inning Elvis Andrus singled, stole second, and then scored from second base on a ground ball to first.   In the fourth inning Nelson Cruz doubled, stole third, and came home on a bad throw to third on the stolen base attempt.   In the sixth inning Vladimir Guerrero singled, moved to second on an infield single, and then (again) scored from second base on a ground ball to first.

No team manufactures three runs a game, but the Rangers manufacture almost one and a half a game, which is more than anybody else.   The Rangers manufactured 230 runs in 2010; the Toronto Blue Jays, 113. Here is the All-Guys-Who-Can-Manufacture-a-Run All Star team:

C	Joe Mauer	17
1B	Daric Barton	23
2B	Chone Figgins	28
3B	Chase Headley	20
SS	Elvis Andrus	40
LF	Juan Pierre	51
CF	Michael Bourn	44
RF	Ichiro Suzuki	34

Honorable Mention
Austin Jackson   42

Juan Pierre in 2010 contributed to 51 manufactured runs, easily the most of any major league player.   Single, stolen base, single. . .that's a manufactured run.   Two singles is just two bases.   The stolen base makes it a run.

There were 4,842 manufactured runs in the majors in 2010, which was up from 2009 (4,621) but down from 2007 (5,056). A little more than 20% of runs are manufactured runs.

This is the technical definition of a manufactured run:

1) A run that is created with no hits is always scored as a manufactured run.

2) A run that scores on a home run is never scored as a manufactured run.

3) A run which is driven in by a double or a triple is scored as a manufactured run only if two of the four bases result from advancing on one of four deliberate acts: A sacrifice bunt, a stolen base, a hit and run, or a bunt single.

Clarifying. . .suppose there is a walk, hit and run, runner goes to third, double. . .would that be a manufactured run, since the runner advanced two bases on the hit and run?

No, it would not. If there was a hit and run single, the runner advanced one base on the single and the second base because he was off with the pitch. You've got a walk, a single, and a double there; it doesn't require Lou Brock to work a walk, a single and a double into a run scored.

If there was a *bunt* hit, then a hit and run single, then a double, that would still be a manufactured run, because there are, in the run, two deliberate efforts to force the action—the bunt, and the hit and run. But generally, a run that scores as a result of an extra base hit is very rarely scored as a manufactured run.

4) Otherwise, a run is considered a Manufactured run if two of the four bases do not result from the runner being forced along by a walk, a hit batsmen, or a safe hit reaching the outfield.

A fielder's choice which does not improve the position of the baserunners does not count as contributing a base to the manufacturing of a run, and a double play never counts as contributing a base to a manufactured run.

Manufactured runs are created with speed, aggressiveness, and, to a lesser extent, by well-placed outs. For the first three years that we presented Manufactured Run Data, we presented it in two forms, MR-1 and MR-2. After three years we decided that was just confusing the audience, and we consolidated on MR-1. The two teams which have traditionally dominated the Manufactured Run counts, the Angels and Twins, were both way off in this area in 2010.

2010 Manufactured Runs

American League

Team	MR
Texas Rangers	230
Tampa Bay Rays	202
Oakland Athletics	202
Chicago White Sox	182
Kansas City Royals	177
Minnesota Twins	170
Detroit Tigers	166
Los Angeles Angels	163
New York Yankees	161
Seattle Mariners	155
Baltimore Orioles	150
Cleveland Indians	141
Boston Red Sox	133
Toronto Blue Jays	113

American League Opponents

Team	MR
Cleveland Indians	205
Boston Red Sox	202
Kansas City Royals	198
Detroit Tigers	194
Seattle Mariners	180
Texas Rangers	170
Los Angeles Angels	163
New York Yankees	162
Chicago White Sox	153
Oakland Athletics	147
Baltimore Orioles	147
Minnesota Twins	141
Toronto Blue Jays	140
Tampa Bay Rays	128

National League

Team	MR
Atlanta Braves	186
Los Angeles Dodgers	186
San Diego Padres	173
Cincinnati Reds	172
New York Mets	169
Washington Nationals	163
Philadelphia Phillies	162
Florida Marlins	161
Houston Astros	161
St Louis Cardinals	156
San Francisco Giants	154
Chicago Cubs	143
Milwaukee Brewers	143
Colorado Rockies	136
Pittsburgh Pirates	123
Arizona Diamondbacks	114

National League Opponents

Team	MR
Pittsburgh Pirates	200
Milwaukee Brewers	181
Chicago Cubs	181
Florida Marlins	177
Arizona Diamondbacks	177
Washington Nationals	175
Los Angeles Dodgers	168
Colorado Rockies	165
Houston Astros	153
Atlanta Braves	149
St Louis Cardinals	143
Cincinnati Reds	142
New York Mets	133
Philadelphia Phillies	129
San Francisco Giants	127
San Diego Padres	116

2010 Manufactured Runs

American League Leaders

Player	Tm	MRC
Pierre, Juan	CWS	51
Jackson, Austin	Det	42
Andrus, Elvis	Tex	40
Gardner, Brett	NYY	37
Suzuki, Ichiro	Sea	34
Davis, Rajai	Oak	33
Crawford, Carl	TB	31
Span, Denard	Min	31
Borbon, Julio	Tex	30
Crisp, Coco	Oak	29
Upton, B.J.	TB	29

National League Leaders

Player	Tm	MRC
Bourn, Michael	Hou	44
Reyes, Jose	NYM	39
Morgan, Nyjer	Was	33
McCutchen, Andrew	Pit	31
Pagan, Angel	NYM	30
Stubbs, Drew	Cin	30
Victorino, Shane	Phi	29
Ramirez, Hanley	Fla	29
Torres, Andres	SF	26
Furcal, Rafael	LAD	25
Phillips, Brandon	Cin	25

MRC = Manufactured Runs Contribution

Top Three From Each Team

Arizona Diamondbacks

Player	MRC
Young, Chris	21
Johnson, Kelly	15
Drew, Stephen	13

Atlanta Braves

Player	MRC
Prado, Martin	23
Heyward, Jason	22
Cabrera, Melky	21

Baltimore Orioles

Player	MRC
Patterson, Corey	19
Markakis, Nick	18
Izturis, Cesar	17

Boston Red Sox

Player	MRC
Scutaro, Marco	18
Youkilis, Kevin	14
Beltre, Adrian	14
Drew, J.D.	14

Chicago Cubs

Player	MRC
Theriot, Ryan	22
Castro, Starlin	14
Soriano, Alfonso	14

Chicago White Sox

Player	MRC
Pierre, Juan	51
Rios, Alex	25
Ramirez, Alexei	23

Cincinnati Reds

Player	MRC
Stubbs, Drew	30
Phillips, Brandon	25
Votto, Joey	20

Cleveland Indians

Player	MRC
Choo, Shin-Soo	19
Brantley, Michael	19
Crowe, Trevor	13

Colorado Rockies

Player	MRC
Fowler, Dexter	17
Gonzalez, Carlos	17
Tulowitzki, Troy	15

Detroit Tigers

Player	MRC
Jackson, Austin	42
Damon, Johnny	19
Cabrera, Miguel	14

Florida Marlins

Player	MRC
Ramirez, Hanley	29
Coghlan, Chris	18
Sanchez, Gaby	14
Uggla, Dan	14

Houston Astros

Player	MRC
Bourn, Michael	44
Pence, Hunter	24
Lee, Carlos	15

Kansas City Royals

Player	MRC
Podsednik, Scott	21
Betancourt, Yuniesky	21
Aviles, Mike	19

Los Angeles Angels

Player	MRC
Aybar, Erick	25
Kendrick, Howie	18
Hunter, Torii	16

Los Angeles Dodgers

Player	MRC
Furcal, Rafael	25
Carroll, Jamey	20
DeWitt, Blake	17

Milwaukee Brewers

Player	MRC
Braun, Ryan	22
Weeks, Rickie	18
Gomez, Carlos	17

Minnesota Twins

Player	MRC
Span, Denard	31
Hudson, Orlando	21
Cuddyer, Michael	19

New York Mets

Player	MRC
Reyes, Jose	39
Pagan, Angel	30
Wright, David	16

New York Yankees

Player	MRC
Gardner, Brett	37
Jeter, Derek	28
Granderson, Curtis	18

Oakland Athletics

Player	MRC
Davis, Rajai	33
Crisp, Coco	29
Pennington, Cliff	25

Philadelphia Phillies

Player	MRC
Victorino, Shane	29
Werth, Jayson	22
Utley, Chase	19

Pittsburgh Pirates

Player	MRC
McCutchen, Andrew	31
Tabata, Jose	18
Milledge, Lastings	10
Cedeno, Ronny	10

San Diego Padres

Player	MRC
Venable, Will	21
Headley, Chase	20
Gwynn, Tony	18

San Francisco Giants

Player	MRC
Torres, Andres	26
Huff, Aubrey	19
Sanchez, Freddy	14
Sandoval, Pablo	14

Seattle Mariners

Player	MRC
Suzuki, Ichiro	34
Figgins, Chone	28
Gutierrez, Franklin	23

St Louis Cardinals

Player	MRC
Rasmus, Colby	23
Schumaker, Skip	20
Pujols, Albert	18

Tampa Bay Rays

Player	MRC
Crawford, Carl	31
Upton, B.J.	29
Bartlett, Jason	28

Texas Rangers

Player	MRC
Andrus, Elvis	40
Borbon, Julio	30
Kinsler, Ian	27

Toronto Blue Jays

Player	MRC
Lewis, Fred	20
Wells, Vernon	13
Buck, John	9
Hill, Aaron	9
Overbay, Lyle	9
Escobar, Yunel	9

Washington Nationals

Player	MRC
Morgan, Nyjer	33
Desmond, Ian	23
Bernadina, Roger	16

The Manager's Record

Bill James

Managerial strategy is in constant search of equilibrium.   The purpose of this section is to document and quantify, as much as we can, the objective differences between managers.   Is a manager quick to go to his bullpen, or slow? Is he willing to bring back a reliever he used yesterday, or not so much?   Does he like to have runners in motion, or not?

The problem with measuring the differences between managers is that the things you are trying to measure tend to evaporate faster than the paying customers in a cathouse raid.   At one point in baseball history we could have sorted managers based on whether they liked to use a five-man rotation or a four-man rotation.   But after a few years, the four-man rotations disappeared, and this was no longer a relevant metric.

At one point in baseball history, we could have divided managers into those who liked to use a "closer", and those who did not.   That lasted about three years (1979-1982).   After that, everybody used a closer.

For many years we could have split managers based on how much they liked to platoon.   But with the expansion of the bullpens, teams no longer platoon, basically, and that's a less relevant divider than it once was.

For many years we could have divided managers based on how willing they were to use their best starting pitcher in relief, but nobody has really done that since about 1960.

We still measure how often managers will use their closer for more than one inning.   We still measure it, but the numbers are heading rapidly toward zero.

Whatever differences we can identify among managers will *tend*, over the period of a decade or so, to disappear.   At one point we set up standards to measure "Quick Hooks" and "Slow Hooks" by managers.   We set up the standards so that there were as many of one as there were of the other.   Ten years later, "Slow Hooks" (as we had originally defined them) had entirely disappeared.

To measure the differences between managers, then, requires constant innovation, and constant questioning.   We have to keep asking ourselves what it is, in our game, today, that distinguishes managers.   Here's what we have:

LUp—the number of lineups used.   Per 162 games, Tony LaRussa uses 135 different lineups, on average (ignoring the starting pitcher.)   Charlie Manuel uses 90, Bobby Cox, 95.

Pl%—Platoon Percentage.   The percentage of players in the starting lineup who have the platoon advantage.   68% of Willie Randolph's starting

players had the platoon advantage; for John McLaren, 49%. But this is heavily influenced by how many switch hitters the manager had.

PH—Pinch Hitters Used. Per 162 games, Clint Hurdle used 282 pinch hitters. Cito Gaston used 73.

Of course, there is a big difference between the number of pinch hitters used in the National League and in the American. Last year the norm was 260 in the National League, 87 in the American.

PR—Pinch Runners Used. Per 162 games, John McLaren used 58 pinch runners, Sam Perlozzo 54, and Grady Little 50. John Russell used 11, Willie Randolph 13.

DS—Defensive Substitutes Used. Per 162 games, Sam Perlozzo used 57 defensive substitutes, Brad Mills has used 51, and Manny Acta 50. John Russell used 9, and Cito Gaston 17.

Quick Hooks (Quick). We figure for each pitcher each game a "Damage Score", which is his pitches thrown, plus 10 times his runs allowed. The bottom 25% of the games in each league are Quick Hooks. If the manager takes his pitcher out after 92 pitches and 1 run allowed (102), that will be a quick hook. The top 25% are Slow Hooks. If a pitcher throws 114 pitches and gives up 4 runs (154), that will be a Slow Hook.

Ron Gardenhire has a Quick Hook/Slow Hook ratio of 51-27. Brad Mills' ratio was 29-52.

Sparky Anderson was known as "Captain Hook" because of his willingness to go to his bullpen early in his career. But if measured by the standards of today, Anderson would be by far the slowest "hook" in the major leagues.

LO—Long Outings. If a pitcher throws more than 110 pitches in a start, that's a Long Outing. Yes, this *is* redundant of Slow Hooks; thanks for noticing.

Dusty Baker with the Cubs in 2003 had 65 Slow Hooks—and the standard of a Slow Hook at that time was 120 pitches, not 110. The second highest total on record is 53, also by Dusty Baker, with the Giants in 2002. But Dusty has taken heavy criticism on this account, and has largely reformed. In 2010 he had only 22 long outings, which was actually below the league average of 26.

RCD—Relievers used on Consecutive Days. Manny Acta in 2007 used a reliever who had pitched the previous day 183 times. Eric Wedge in 2006, managing 162 games, did this only 48 times. Based on career averages, the norms range from 134 (Acta) to 60 (Cito Gaston).

LS—Long Saves. Saves of more than one inning. Jerry Manuel and Tony LaRussa in 2000 had 18 saves (each) of more than one inning. Many managers have had zero in a season, including John Russell, Jim Tracy and Mike Scioscia in 2010.

Rel—Relievers Used. John Russell used the most relievers in 2010, 517. Ozzie Guillen used the fewest, 407.

SBA—Stolen Base Attempts. Per 162 games, Willie Randolph's teams averaged 206 stolen base attempts. Ken Macha's teams averaged 80.

SacA—Sacrifice Bunt Attempts. Per 162 games, Clint Hurdle's teams averaged 108 sacrifice bunt attempts, which was necessary because it is so difficult to score in Colorado. John Gibbons' teams averaged only 29.

RM—Runners Moving with the Pitch. Per 162 games, Mike Scioscia's teams average 151 runners moving with the pitch, which is one reason his teams have such an exceptional record at going first to third on a single. Bobby Cox's teams averaged only 69.

PO—Per 162 games, Dusty Baker has ordered 53 pitchouts. John Russell ordered only 8.

But in this respect, as well, Dusty Baker has changed. He ordered only 13 pitchouts in 2010, well below the National League average of 18.

IBB—# (Meaning the number of Intentional Walks). Per 162 games, Bobby Cox ordered an average of 62 Intentional Walks. Terry Francona has ordered only 27, and there are some managers (who have had shorter careers) who are even lower than Francona.

Good—Intentional Walks leading to a Good Result. A good result is
1) The next hitter grounds into a double play, or
2) The team in the field gets out of the inning without additional runs scoring.

Bomb—A "Bomb" means that *Multiple* runs score in the inning after the intentional walk. If the hitter after the IBB grounds into a double play, then we count that intentional walk as a success, even if multiple runs score after the IBB.

Brad Mills last year had a 6-to-1 ratio between Good Intentional Walks (30) and Bombs (5). Tony LaRussa, in a long career, has a 4.2-to-1 ratio. Don Wakamatsu, on the other hand, had a 1-to-1 ratio—as many Bombs as good outcomes—and Ron Washington has a ratio of just 1.78 to 1.

But Washington, again, has changed. Washington in 2008 ordered 20 intentional walks that blew up in his face, one of the highest totals we have seen. But in 2009 this happened to him only 3 times, and, in 2010, zero. He became the

first manager since we started counting this to make it through the season without an Intentional Walk blowing up on him. Tony LaRussa has never hit zero, but he has been at 1 or 2 in four different seasons.

W and L—Wins and Losses.

Hey, I've never done this before, but I'm going to use this space to endorse a book, sort of. Chris Jaffe has written a book, *Evaluating Baseball Managers,* available from McFarland & Company, which uses methods not unlike these, but more complicated and more varied, to evaluate managers across history.

It has long been my argument that it is not our place, as sabermetricians, to stand in judgment on the performance of managers. People are careless about doing that; they pick factoids out of lists and use them to beat up on managers. Talk shows can become managerial bombing runs, often citing the information that we create. I think it is unwise for us to get into that; it creates an antagonistic relationship between managers and analysts, and frankly, 99% of the information that is cited in that context is BS anyway (Baseless Speculation).

On the other hand

1) Jaffe's research is quite outstanding, and

2) The fact that I choose not to get involved in rating or ranking managers doesn't mean that nobody else can do it, either.

I don't know Jaffe from a hole in the wall; he's not like a friend of mine or something, and also, I have to warn you that he is not a compelling writer. He does really good research. He develops a wide range of metrics by which to compare managers, like "Ballpark Adjusted Bullpen ERA" and "Leverage Points Average" and "Average Opponent Winning Percentage" (for pitchers), and I learned a great deal from reading his book. I hope you learn something from this data.

Categories of this record are Games Managed (G), Number of Different Lineups Used (LUp), the percentage of players who had the platoon advantage at the start of the game (PL%), Pinch Hitters Used (PH), Pinch Runners Used (PR), Defensive Substitutes Used (DS), Quick Hooks (Quick), Slow Hooks (Slow), Long Outings by Starting Pitchers (LO), Relievers Used on Consecutive Days (RCD), Long Saves (LS), Relievers Used (Rel), Stolen Base Attempts (SBA), Sacrifice Bunts Attempts (SacA), Runners Moving with the Pitch (RM), Pitchouts ordered (PO), Intentional Walks issued (#), Intentional Walks resulting in a Good Outcome (Good), Intentional Walks resulting Not in a Good Outcome (NG), Intentional Walks Blowing up on the Manager (Bomb), Wins (W), Losses (L) and Winning Percentage (Pct.).

Manny Acta

Year	Team	Lg	G	LUp	PL%	PH	PR	DS	Quick	Slow	LO	RCD	LS	Rel	SBA	SacA	RM	PO	#	Good	NG	Bomb	W	L	Pct
2007	Nationals	NL	162	101	.65	295	32	78	53	28	5	183	1	588	92	86	70	28	44	28	16	8	73	89	.451
2008	Nationals	NL	161	133	.62	293	31	39	38	46	6	119	4	517	124	95	63	24	44	27	17	8	59	102	.366
2009	Nationals	NL	87	66	.62	145	11	20	14	25	1	91	1	282	54	43	62	5	26	13	13	6	26	61	.299
2010	Indians	AL	162	142	.63	79	20	39	44	49	18	81	6	470	124	41	142	20	36	17	19	10	69	93	.426
	162-Game Average			125	.63	230	27	50	42	42	8	134	3	526	112	75	95	22	42	24	18	9	64	98	.395

Dusty Baker

Year	Team	Lg	G	LUp	PL%	PH	PR	DS	Quick	Slow	LO	RCD	LS	Rel	SBA	SacA	RM	PO	#	Good	NG	Bomb	W	L	Pct
1994	Giants	NL	115	76	.53	177	16	9	29	25	2	86	12	288	154	88		78	40	24	16	8	55	60	.478
1995	Giants	NL	144	96	.41	230	36	13	32	50	8	90	8	381	184	101		77	51	32	19	14	67	77	.465
1996	Giants	NL	162	129	.51	250	17	15	24	58	15	94	8	425	166	103		96	60	37	23	15	68	94	.420
1997	Giants	NL	162	114	.71	212	17	22	46	25	17	132	4	481	170	85		93	57	36	21	12	90	72	.556
1998	Giants	NL	163	130	.62	224	20	12	43	38	8	113	5	433	153	111		41	68	42	26	9	89	74	.546
1999	Giants	NL	162	120	.62	233	16	16	30	51	27	111		450	165	113		40	41	25	16	10	86	76	.531
2000	Giants	NL	162	82	.56	233	26	22	38	50	25	91	3	384	118	86		37	26	17	9	2	97	65	.599
2001	Giants	NL	162	122	.48	261	22	19	40	48	10	114	4	439	99	95		45	49	33	16	6	90	72	.556
2002	Giants	NL	162	118	.43	223	32	38	29	56	53	106	8	417	95	89	42	41	44	28	16	10	95	66	.590
2003	Cubs	NL	162	114	.49	272	25	43	24	58	65	111	3	420	104	93	31	24	36	23	13	4	88	74	.543
2004	Cubs	NL	162	113	.44	254	16	19	37	41	42	129	8	460	94	108	71	62	33	22	11	7	89	73	.549
2005	Cubs	NL	162	121	.59	240	21	29	40	46	36	103	2	457	104	88	107	70	48	27	21	7	79	83	.488
2006	Cubs	NL	162	133	.56	271	9	26	45	39	22	165	2	542	170	108	139	46	44	28	16	11	66	96	.407
2008	Reds	NL	162	119	.58	285	28	27	26	63	39	124	2	507	132	100	101	37	40	28	12	4	74	88	.457
2009	Reds	NL	162	130	.45	252	15	35	30	62	35	115	1	478	136	120	118	23	36	29	7	4	78	84	.481
2010	Reds	NL	162	120	.46	258	19	49	36	41	22	140	0	502	136	91	157	13	32	22	10	9	91	71	.562
	162-Game Average			118	.53	248	21	25	35	48	27	117	4	453	140	101	96	53	45	29	16	8	83	79	.512

Buddy Bell

Year	Team	Lg	G	LUp	PL%	PH	PR	DS	Quick	Slow	LO	RCD	LS	Rel	SBA	SacA	RM	PO	#	Good	NG	Bomb	W	L	Pct
1996	Tigers	AL	162	128	.50	123	29	17	17	27	26	82	8	426	137	63		13	63	29	34	19	53	109	.327
1997	Tigers	Al	162	116	.61	163	19	22	24	7	12	113	11	417	233	44		32	33	17	16	10	79	83	.488
1998	Tigers	AL	137	88	.58	102	25	7	15	15	10	89	4	362	143	24		38	45	24	21	15	52	85	.380
2000	Rockies	NL	162	106	.64	285	21	8	12	18	10	106	8	480	192	100		40	72	39	33	16	82	80	.506
2001	Rockies	NL	162	116	.61	314	27	14	18	30	8	117	6	476	186	108		43	71	40	31	13	73	89	.451
2002	Rockies	NL	22	15	.55	42	1	5	5	11	3	21	0	69	17	10	8	5	11	5	6	4	6	16	.273
2005	Royals	AL	112	93	.61	97	18	8	32	23	3	50	4	310	48	38	80	25	17	9	8	5	43	69	.384
2006	Royals	Al	152	132	.57	87	27	25	40	37	13	86	6	439	95	63	84	13	40	20	20	10	58	94	.382
2007	Royals	AL	162	141	.55	119	30	28	49	28	10	74	10	440	122	60	126	26	64	33	21	9	69	93	.426
	162-Game Average			120	.58	176	26	18	28	26	13	97	7	450	154	67	107	31	53	28	25	13	68	94	.420

Bud Black

Year	Team	Lg	G	LUp	PL%	PH	PR	DS	Quick	Slow	LO	RCD	LS	Rel	SBA	SacA	RM	PO	#	Good	NG	Bomb	W	L	Pct
2007	Padres	NL	163	115	.62	279	18	13	63	28	13	122	0	485	79	85	73	56	48	28	20	11	89	74	.546
2008	Padres	NL	162	113	.63	286	25	20	55	36	17	109	0	491	53	75	78	31	61	30	31	17	63	99	.389
2009	Padres	NL	162	137	.64	264	8	34	50	37	8	118	5	527	111	99	84	55	58	42	16	6	75	87	.463
2010	Padres	NL	162	135	.61	285	16	45	55	33	10	132	7	499	174	99	135	31	51	35	16	8	90	72	.556
	162-Game Average			125	.63	278	17	28	56	33	12	120	3	500	104	89	92	43	54	34	21	10	79	83	.488

Bruce Bochy

Year	Team	Lg	G	LUp	PL%	PH	PR	DS	Quick	Slow	LO	RCD	LS	Rel	SBA	SacA	RM	PO	#	Good	NG	Bomb	W	L	Pct
1995	Padres	NL	144	96	.59	262	30	23	44	41	17	38	3	337	170	68		38	37	19	18	11	70	74	.486
1996	Padres	NL	162	114	.52	289	29	15	51	33	10	67	12	411	164	73		65	47	29	18	12	91	71	.562
1997	Padres	NL	162	111	.60	291	26	9	45	45	3	81	11	426	200	84		58	37	20	17	11	76	86	.469
1998	Padres	NL	162	110	.65	280	62	44	44	45	9	81	12	369	184	84		27	45	31	14	10	98	64	.605
1999	Padres	NL	162	137	.60	298	51	21	44	36	4	68	5	403	241	60		29	48	29	19	13	74	88	.457
2000	Padres	NL	162	134	.52	285	44	14	41	47	14	105	5	443	184	52		27	50	21	29	11	76	86	.469
2001	Padres	NL	162	116	.60	255	54	27	32	47	6	85	10	422	173	43		23	54	31	23	13	79	83	.488
2002	Padres	NL	162	123	.66	259	44	56	39	40	17	106	4	459	115	63	74	14	61	38	23	14	66	96	.407
2003	Padres	NL	162	134	.58	339	20	29	34	43	16	100	3	413	115	63	41	6	52	33	19	12	64	98	.395
2004	Padres	NL	162	96	.54	261	28	47	47	32	15	76	3	437	77	75	96	14	39	24	15	10	87	75	.537
2005	Padres	NL	162	128	.58	285	31	49	46	36	23	87	1	456	143	89	111	16	45	33	12	8	82	80	.506
2006	Padres	NL	162	111	.60	264	64	48	43	42	24	111	2	475	154	77	110	21	63	43	20	10	88	74	.543
2007	Giants	NL	162	128	.72	264	50	45	26	50	36	132	2	496	152	86	119	10	41	29	12	3	71	91	.438

Year	Team	Lg	G	LUp	PL%	PH	PR	DS	Quick	Slow	LO	RCD	LS	Rel	SBA	SacA	RM	PO	#	Good	NG	Bomb	W	L	Pct
				LINEUPS		**SUBSTITUTION**			**PITCHER USAGE**						**TACTICS**				**INTENTIONAL BB**				**RESULTS**		
2008	Giants	NL	162	134	**.68**	276	32	39	24	59	**42**	97	6	478	154	77	**155**	5	59	40	19	8	72	90	.444
2009	Giants	NL	162	134	.65	231	21	52	42	40	32	84	8	457	106	93	118	5	49	32	17	10	88	74	.543
2010	Giants	NL	162	126	.55	224	45	70	29	37	40	118	12	477	87	102	144	12	58	41	17	8	92	70	.568
	162-Game Average			122	.60	275	40	37	40	42	19	90	6	442	148	75	108	23	49	31	18	10	80	82	.494

Daren Brown

Year	Team	Lg	G	LUp	PL%	PH	PR	DS	Quick	Slow	LO	RCD	LS	Rel	SBA	SacA	RM	PO	#	Good	NG	Bomb	W	L	Pct
2010	Mariners	AL	50	39	.60	9	12	2	15	8	6	14	2	104	52	19	71	9	8	5	3	2	19	31	.380
	162-Game Average			126	.60	29	39	6	49	26	19	45	6	337	168	62	230	29	26	16	10	6	62	100	.383

Dave Clark

Year	Team	Lg	G	LUp	PL%	PH	PR	DS	Quick	Slow	LO	RCD	LS	Rel	SBA	SacA	RM	PO	#	Good	NG	Bomb	W	L	Pct
2009	Astros	NL	13	9	.63	28	1	4	3	5	0	15	0	48	7	5	8	0	3	1	2	1	4	9	.308
	162-Game Average			112	.63	349	12	50	37	62	0	187	0	598	87	62	100	0	37	12	25	12	50	112	.309

Cecil Cooper

Year	Team	Lg	G	LUp	PL%	PH	PR	DS	Quick	Slow	LO	RCD	LS	Rel	SBA	SacA	RM	PO	#	Good	NG	Bomb	W	L	Pct
2007	Astros	NL	31	26	.42	63	8	23	10	5	2	11	0	88	19	16	20	4	14	8	6	4	15	16	.484
2008	Astros	NL	161	115	.58	252	16	47	60	35	14	108	2	488	166	81	112	5	53	35	18	11	86	75	.534
2009	Astros	NL	149	94	.54	238	26	36	48	34	14	116	6	449	150	86	77	8	53	30	23	12	70	79	.470
	162-Game Average			112	.55	263	24	50	56	35	14	112	4	487	159	87	99	8	57	35	22	13	81	81	.500

Bobby Cox

Year	Team	Lg	G	LUp	PL%	PH	PR	DS	Quick	Slow	LO	RCD	LS	Rel	SBA	SacA	RM	PO	#	Good	NG	Bomb	W	L	Pct
1994	Braves	NL	114	64	.60	163	30	25	22	31	5	60	5	244	79	83		44	52	33	19	9	68	46	.596
1995	Braves	NL	144	59	.56	224	48	40	41	34	13	80	6	339	116	77		41	46	31	15	4	90	54	.625
1996	Braves	NL	162	89	**.62**	254	32	27	48	43	19	110	9	408	126	90		34	64	38	26	14	**96**	66	.593
1997	Braves	NL	162	87	.64	276	**58**	29	40	37	**23**	90	4	374	166	**112**		13	56	42	14	10	**101**	61	.623
1998	Braves	NL	162	80	.64	245	28	25	44	33	14	70	1	354	141	97		40	37	22	15	8	**106**	56	.654
1999	Braves	NL	162	76	.58	272	**51**	34	44	39	13	99	6	394	214	89		**54**	**55**	35	20	11	**103**	59	.636
2000	Braves	NL	162	103	.59	252	**72**	11	**52**	41	6	81	13	376	**204**	**109**		**59**	52	35	17	5	95	67	.586
2001	Braves	NL	162	113	.57	278	50	23	49	40	4	93	8	412	131	84		**90**	**77**	49	28	13	88	74	.543
2002	Braves	NL	161	105	.48	282	33	44	60	30	20	113	9	469	115	89	47	51	63	41	22	12	**101**	59	.631
2003	Braves	NL	162	69	.52	262	49	45	40	45	23	113	10	489	90	85	23	49	69	**51**	18	11	**101**	61	.623
2004	Braves	NL	162	105	.70	243	57	28	**50**	34	25	128	**16**	483	118	105	87	25	50	30	20	14	96	66	.593
2005	Braves	NL	162	110	**.69**	247	**54**	35	46	27	20	125	7	484	124	104	93	11	52	34	18	11	90	72	.556
2006	Braves	NL	162	85	.58	299	24	35	44	38	24	144	3	522	87	99	58	24	69	48	21	12	79	83	.488
2007	Braves	NL	162	86	.68	290	33	21	60	24	10	143	1	528	94	77	68	28	**89**	**58**	**31**	**16**	84	78	.519
2008	Braves	NL	162	117	.67	**294**	31	17	59	34	6	**134**	6	**545**	85	90	77	23	**80**	45	**35**	**20**	72	90	.444
2009	Braves	NL	162	112	.62	252	37	32	48	34	19	**142**	1	488	84	**125**	47	21	59	35	24	14	86	76	.531
2010	Braves	NL	162	109	.65	263	51	50	49	31	9	140	1	490	92	89	121	**48**	64	36	**28**	14	91	71	.562
	162-Game Average			95	.61	265	45	31	48	36	15	112	6	446	125	97	69	40	62	40	22	12	93	69	.574

Terry Francona

Year	Team	Lg	G	LUp	PL%	PH	PR	DS	Quick	Slow	LO	RCD	LS	Rel	SBA	SacA	RM	PO	#	Good	NG	Bomb	W	L	Pct
1997	Phillies	NL	162	98	.66	288	19	28	28	**54**	22	102	9	409	148	91		30	42	23	19	9	68	**94**	.420
1998	Phillies	NL	162	84	.53	256	20	19	34	**57**	20	88	7	385	142	85		16	27	10	17	8	75	87	.463
1999	Phillies	NL	162	85	.51	239	13	31	29	41	16	111	7	441	160	81		27	24	14	10	6	77	85	.475
2000	Phillies	NL	162	108	.53	278	17	14	38	43	**25**	102	5	414	132	89		16	32	22	10	7	65	**97**	.401
2004	Red Sox	AL	162	141	.65	116	65	**58**	41	48	32	105	8	437	98	18	91	28	28	22	6	4	98	64	.605
2005	Red Sox	AL	162	104	**.67**	110	46	37	25	55	30	99	3	442	57	21	79	11	28	18	10	5	95	67	.586
2006	Red Sox	AL	162	116	.59	93	54	49	36	43	14	94	9	454	74	33	98	16	25	11	14	7	86	76	.531
2007	Red Sox	AL	162	109	.60	84	34	23	41	35	32	89	4	451	120	45	90	14	20	14	6	4	**96**	66	.593
2008	Red Sox	AL	162	131	.59	62	40	40	50	30	20	90	**11**	466	155	40	87	8	17	10	7	4	95	67	.586
2009	Red Sox	AL	162	113	.58	85	47	28	36	50	30	84	6	463	165	29	68	9	24	15	9	6	95	67	.586
2010	Red Sox	AL	162	**143**	.62	125	48	34	32	**63**	**49**	84	3	443	85	36	125	26	30	17	13	4	89	73	.549
	162-Game Average			112	.59	158	37	33	35	47	26	94	7	437	121	52	91	18	27	16	11	6	85	77	.525

Ron Gardenhire

Year	Team	Lg	G	LUp	PL%	PH	PR	DS	Quick	Slow	LO	RCD	LS	Rel	SBA	SacA	RM	PO	#	Good	NG	Bomb	W	L	Pct
2002	Twins	AL	161	111	**.69**	141	36	42	54	25	10	84	1	435	141	48	44	11	24	16	8	4	94	67	.584
2003	Twins	AL	162	126	.63	144	50	26	49	33	13	85	2	399	138	59	37	14	35	16	19	6	90	72	.556
2004	Twins	AL	162	131	.59	129	45	29	56	21	20	106	4	435	162	66	121	18	27	15	12	7	92	70	.568
2005	Twins	AL	162	**135**	.58	104	45	26	50	21	5	87	1	396	146	59	138	16	38	**28**	10	3	83	79	.512
2006	Twins	AL	162	97	.62	93	36	21	60	31	3	82	5	421	143	48	130	11	25	14	11	4	96	66	.593
2007	Twins	AL	162	139	.63	104	42	25	45	30	8	99	4	438	142	45	148	11	33	14	19	9	79	83	.488
2008	Twins	AL	163	103	.64	109	26	12	47	29	5	115	3	485	144	73	143	17	38	25	13	8	88	75	.540
2009	Twins	AL	163	129	.63	83	54	34	43	25	12	115	3	480	117	**62**	100	21	20	9	11	6	87	76	.534
2010	Twins	AL	162	112	.62	86	**55**	30	57	28	5	106	1	465	96	47	140	14	19	12	7	4	94	68	.580
	162-Game Average			120	.62	110	43	27	51	27	9	98	3	439	136	56	111	15	29	17	12	6	89	73	.549

Phil Garner

Year	Team	Lg	G	LUp	PL%	PH	PR	DS	Quick	Slow	LO	RCD	LS	Rel	SBA	SacA	RM	PO	#	Good	NG	Bomb	W	L	Pct
1994	Brewers	AL	115	94	.53	53	33	24	31	35	4	44	5	252	96	46		23	28	18	10	9	53	62	.461
1995	Brewers	AL	144	120	.58	83	67	52	42	42	10	52	4	321	145	64		52	39	18	21	12	65	79	.451
1996	Brewers	AL	162	114	.58	115	48	46	50	36	13	61	12	385	149	72		**82**	33	14	19	11	80	82	.494
1997	Brewers	AL	161	128	.59	190	42	36	51	34	6	93	6	367	158	65		55	25	15	10	6	78	83	.484
1998	Brewers	NL	162	125	.59	265	54	**46**	52	43	6	90	9	416	140	85		**59**	29	20	9	4	74	88	.457
1999	Brewers	NL	112	69	.57	182	15	5	28	26	4	45	5	294	75	85		57	22	13	9	8	52	60	.464
2000	Tigers	AL	162	120	.53	126	30	25	35	38	8	109	3	429	121	58		26	22	14	8	6	79	83	.488
2001	Tigers	AL	162	116	**.64**	93	40	14	25	**51**	9	81	3	391	194	58		36	**56**	37	19	11	66	96	.407
2002	Tigers	AL	6	3	.63	1	1	0	1	3	3	2	0	15	4	2	3	0	2	0	2	2	0	6	.000
2004	Astros	NL	74	31	.54	142	20	35	27	15	14	71	4	241	78	40	40	7	24	20	4	1	48	26	.649
2005	Astros	NL	163	101	.48	251	40	**63**	55	34	21	118	3	434	159	99	148	10	29	17	12	7	89	73	.549
2006	Astros	NL	162	111	.47	287	17	47	55	36	18	157	2	497	115	123	114	26	65	31	34	17	82	80	.506
2007	Astros	NL	131	99	.52	230	14	36	31	44	17	120	0	388	79	80	84	23	48	27	21	11	58	73	.443
	162-Game Average			117	.55	191	40	41	46	41	12	99	5	418	143	84	118	43	40	23	17	10	78	84	.481

Cito Gaston

Year	Team	Lg	G	LUp	PL%	PH	PR	DS	Quick	Slow	LO	RCD	LS	Rel	SBA	SacA	RM	PO	#	Good	NG	Bomb	W	L	Pct
1994	Blue Jays	AL	115	59	.55	41	16	21	7	14	2	23	5	221	105	44		48	23	15	8	6	55	60	.478
1995	Blue Jays	AL	144	82	.65	85	24	7	15	27	40	29	10	265	91	47		57	42	24	18	10	56	88	.389
1996	Blue Jays	AL	162	87	**.70**	126	23	11	12	27	23	41	4	300	154	63		34	37	23	14	9	74	88	.457
1997	Blue Jays	AL	157	90	.59	71	19	6	13	22	36	74	6	322	177	50		30	29	20	9	2	72	85	.459
2008	Blue Jays	AL	88	65	.59	36	18	30	18	19	25	40	0	216	37	41	37	11	16	8	8	6	51	37	.580
2009	Blue Jays	AL	162	105	.49	48	36	18	36	47	25	83	3	445	96	32	64	25	20	15	11	6	75	87	.463
2010	Blue Jays	AL	162	103	.45	40	40	13	51	33	12	77	4	455	78	22	88	23	36	19	16	6	85	77	.525
	162-Game Average			97	.57	73	29	17	25	31	27	60	5	364	121	49	74	37	34	20	14	7	77	85	.475

Bob Geren

Year	Team	Lg	G	LUp	PL%	PH	PR	DS	Quick	Slow	LO	RCD	LS	Rel	SBA	SacA	RM	PO	#	Good	NG	Bomb	W	L	Pct
2007	Athletics	AL	162	140	.57	64	31	24	39	43	14	112	9	446	72	31	91	22	**60**	38	22	10	76	86	.469
2008	Athletics	AL	161	133	.59	91	**57**	37	49	32	5	87	8	441	109	44	62	18	45	25	20	10	75	86	.466
2009	Athletics	AL	162	129	.59	77	27	40	**54**	40	5	108	11	488	181	37	71	5	30	15	15	7	75	87	.463
2010	Athletics	AL	162	126	.63	108	28	20	57	30	19	81	8	423	194	58	138	11	29	16	13	3	81	81	.500
	162-Game Average			132	.60	85	36	32	50	36	11	97	9	450	139	43	91	14	41	24	18	8	77	85	.475

John Gibbons

Year	Team	Lg	G	LUp	PL%	PH	PR	DS	Quick	Slow	LO	RCD	LS	Rel	SBA	SacA	RM	PO	#	Good	NG	Bomb	W	L	Pct
2004	Blue Jays	AL	50	36	.68	42	3	2	16	8	7	22	1	130	34	2	47	21	11	5	6	3	20	30	.400
2005	Blue Jays	AL	162	124	.66	**148**	11	37	**55**	18	9	77	12	432	107	28	128	45	29	13	16	9	80	82	.494
2006	Blue Jays	AL	162	120	.53	112	32	40	59	33	17	94	**16**	482	98	20	127	40	56	32	**24**	12	87	75	.537
2007	Blue Jays	AL	162	131	.46	**139**	48	33	45	37	31	75	9	420	79	35	99	37	34	17	17	6	83	79	.512
2008	Blue Jays	AL	74	60	.48	53	15	18	12	20	12	43	0	205	70	23	39	10	26	16	10	6	35	39	.473
	162-Game Average			125	.56	131	29	35	50	31	20	83	10	443	103	29	117	41	41	22	19	10	81	81	.500

Kirk Gibson

Year	Team	Lg	G	LUp	PL%	PH	PR	DS	Quick	Slow	LO	RCD	LS	Rel	SBA	SacA	RM	PO	#	Good	NG	Bomb	W	L	Pct
2010	Diamondbacks	NL	83	57	.64	154	7	11	25	21	8	43	1	247	69	28	62	19	19	13	6	2	34	49	.410
	162-Game Average			111	.64	301	14	21	49	41	16	84	2	482	135	55	121	37	37	25	12	4	66	96	.407

Joe Girardi

Year	Team	Lg	G	LINEUPS		SUBSTITUTION			PITCHER USAGE						TACTICS				INTENTIONAL BB				RESULTS		
				LUp	PL%	PH	PR	DS	Quick	Slow	LO	RCD	LS	Rel	SBA	SacA	RM	PO	#	Good	NG	Bomb	W	L	Pct
2006	Marlins	NL	162	117	.50	250	44	**66**	46	40	28	76	3	438	168	97	108	42	58	37	21	7	78	84	.481
2008	Yankees	AL	162	114	.63	97	37	42	**60**	37	12	88	10	475	157	38	**173**	**36**	37	22	15	8	89	73	.549
2009	Yankees	AL	162	106	**.73**	97	61	42	36	45	27	88	**13**	461	139	44	83	33	28	14	14	9	**103**	59	.636
2010	Yankees	AL	162	114	**.72**	117	44	31	43	39	33	76	3	430	133	47	152	20	37	26	11	6	95	67	.586
	162-Game Average			113	.64	140	47	45	46	40	25	82	7	451	149	57	129	33	40	25	15	8	91	71	.562

Fredi Gonzalez

Year	Team	Lg	G	LINEUPS		SUBSTITUTION			PITCHER USAGE						TACTICS				INTENTIONAL BB				RESULTS		
				LUp	PL%	PH	PR	DS	Quick	Slow	LO	RCD	LS	Rel	SBA	SacA	RM	PO	#	Good	NG	Bomb	W	L	Pct
2007	Marlins	NL	162	96	.50	284	29	34	33	**56**	20	138	5	560	139	91	79	22	60	36	24	**16**	71	91	.438
2008	Marlins	NL	161	106	.51	255	38	49	38	39	8	120	3	511	104	61	75	17	66	42	24	14	84	77	.522
2009	Marlins	NL	162	97	.58	281	28	49	48	26	12	116	0	**530**	110	86	88	20	60	38	22	15	87	75	.537
2010	Marlins	NL	70	31	.41	104	12	16	14	13	11	35	1	193	56	33	64	10	18	11	7	5	34	36	.486
	162-Game Average			96	.52	270	31	43	39	39	15	119	3	524	119	79	89	20	60	37	22	15	81	81	.500

Ozzie Guillen

Year	Team	Lg	G	LINEUPS		SUBSTITUTION			PITCHER USAGE						TACTICS				INTENTIONAL BB				RESULTS		
				LUp	PL%	PH	PR	DS	Quick	Slow	LO	RCD	LS	Rel	SBA	SacA	RM	PO	#	Good	NG	Bomb	W	L	Pct
2004	White Sox	AL	162	134	.58	**132**	35	15	28	**65**	48	86	8	399	129	**84**	97	17	36	15	**21**	8	83	79	.512
2005	White Sox	AL	162	112	.51	100	32	21	31	**56**	35	114	5	412	204	68	148	15	**42**	27	15	6	**99**	63	.611
2006	White Sox	AL	162	87	.60	**135**	42	38	28	**68**	35	83	7	398	141	61	85	27	**59**	**39**	20	9	90	72	.556
2007	White Sox	AL	162	124	.56	100	26	23	26	53	**33**	131	2	463	123	54	92	13	50	24	**26**	15	72	90	.444
2008	White Sox	AL	163	100	.52	75	49	37	42	48	14	100	3	463	101	44	98	8	42	29	13	6	89	74	.546
2009	White Sox	AL	162	124	.52	105	48	19	50	37	16	70	4	415	162	45	114	15	41	23	**18**	**10**	79	83	.488
2010	White Sox	AL	162	115	.51	85	46	36	41	51	24	61	**8**	407	**234**	60	220	25	**41**	26	15	**10**	88	74	.543
	162-Game Average			114	.54	104	40	27	35	54	29	92	5	422	156	59	122	17	44	26	18	9	86	76	.531

Mike Hargrove

Year	Team	Lg	G	LINEUPS		SUBSTITUTION			PITCHER USAGE						TACTICS				INTENTIONAL BB				RESULTS		
				LUp	PL%	PH	PR	DS	Quick	Slow	LO	RCD	LS	Rel	SBA	SacA	RM	PO	#	Good	NG	Bomb	W	L	Pct
1994	Indians	AL	113	53	.67	79	18	31	23	31	3	41	4	222	179	43		40	28	14	14	7	66	47	.584
1995	Indians	AL	144	64	.66	101	34	21	36	23	12	61	3	335	185	40		22	16	9	7	3	**100**	44	.694
1996	Indians	AL	161	96	.56	115	20	25	39	31	14	70	5	382	210	58		41	42	22	20	11	**99**	62	.615
1997	Indians	AL	161	109	.58	86	17	14	34	46	14	101	9	429	177	60		37	53	30	23	10	86	75	.534
1998	Indians	AL	162	108	**.62**	88	21	32	29	39	19	104	9	423	203	53		47	**48**	26	22	13	89	73	.549
1999	Indians	AL	162	123	**.66**	99	25	22	41	44	15	100	3	**466**	199	**82**		28	**55**	33	22	13	97	65	.599
2000	Orioles	AL	162	107	.54	77	42	19	25	**55**	24	84	2	396	**191**	36		31	32	21	11	2	74	**88**	.457
2001	Orioles	AL	162	**139**	.53	82	27	20	39	42	3	74	10	392	186	57		**71**	28	18	10	7	63	**98**	.391
2002	Orioles	AL	162	125	.52	127	22	22	36	46	32	74	6	407	158	54	26	42	34	22	12	6	67	95	.414
2003	Orioles	AL	163	120	.52	78	37	22	29	52	48	74	6	425	125	45	16	43	20	**23**	11		71	91	.438
2005	Mariners	AL	162	97	.52	125	24	18	30	45	31	73	1	433	149	61	120	36	32	21	11	7	69	93	.426
2006	Mariners	AL	162	84	.51	121	21	20	24	52	24	81	14	429	143	40	124	17	50	26	**24**	**16**	78	84	.481
2007	Mariners	AL	78	48	.47	41	18	21	20	26	9	44	7	209	55	22	58	13	20	12	8	4	45	33	.577
	162-Game Average			106	.57	101	27	24	34	44	21	83	6	411	179	56	83	37	40	23	17	9	83	79	.512

Trey Hillman

Year	Team	Lg	G	LINEUPS		SUBSTITUTION			PITCHER USAGE						TACTICS				INTENTIONAL BB				RESULTS		
				LUp	PL%	PH	PR	DS	Quick	Slow	LO	RCD	LS	Rel	SBA	SacA	RM	PO	#	Good	NG	Bomb	W	L	Pct
2008	Royals	AL	162			71	44	34	35	48	19	78	2	439	117	50	96	15	15	9	6	3	75	87	.463
2009	Royals	AL	162	141	.63	90	34	38	41	**54**	34	72	7	426	117	51	110	27	28	13	15	**10**	65	97	.401
2010	Royals	AL	35	24	.57	12	12	1	9	13	4	21	2	109	38	25	41	8	3	2	1	1	12	23	.343
	162-Game Average			135	.59	78	41	33	38	52	26	77	5	440	123	57	111	23	21	11	10	6	69	93	.426

A.J. Hinch

Year	Team	Lg	G	LINEUPS		SUBSTITUTION			PITCHER USAGE						TACTICS				INTENTIONAL BB				RESULTS		
				LUp	PL%	PH	PR	DS	Quick	Slow	LO	RCD	LS	Rel	SBA	SacA	RM	PO	#	Good	NG	Bomb	W	L	Pct
2009	Diamondbacks	NL	133	115	.63	222	10	13	24	50	24	61	5	392	113	64	41	5	24	12	12	6	58	75	.436
2010	Diamondbacks	NL	79	56	.53	120	7	4	12	40	21	39	1	207	58	19	51	7	19	9	10	9	31	48	.392
	162-Game Average			131	.59	261	13	13	28	69	34	76	5	458	131	63	70	9	33	16	17	11	68	94	.420

Clint Hurdle

Year	Team	Lg	G	LUp	PL%	PH	PR	DS	Quick	Slow	LO	RCD	LS	Rel	SBA	SacA	RM	PO	#	Good	NG	Bomb	W	L	Pct
				LINEUPS		SUBSTITUTION			PITCHER USAGE						TACTICS				INTENTIONAL BB				RESULTS		
2002	Rockies	NL	140	100	.52	274	28	41	33	45	17	104	3	437	139	46	50	13	38	22	16	11	67	73	.479
2003	Rockies	NL	162	108	.47	317	17	32	35	40	5	87	4	500	100	82	26	16	51	31	20	13	74	88	.457
2004	Rockies	NL	162	131	.57	289	18	35	36	63	20	74	1	473	77	128	67	12	84	54	30	12	68	94	.420
2005	Rockies	NL	162	135	.60	273	21	40	42	60	17	89	2	459	97	114	119	22	54	28	26	15	67	95	.414
2006	Rockies	NL	162	111	.49	259	17	22	34	52	17	107	2	499	135	156	114	28	81	45	36	23	76	86	.469
2007	Rockies	NL	163	96	.51	283	32	29	45	37	13	112	1	529	131	112	109	26	61	30	31	14	90	73	.552
2008	Rockies	NL	162	131	.49	253	20	31	40	43	16	85	2	485	178	111	116	43	49	31	18	6	74	88	.457
2009	Rockies	NL	46	42	.60	73	8	10	11	14	3	31	0	135	45	26	34	3	11	8	3	1	18	28	.391
	162-Game Average			119	.52	282	23	34	39	49	15	96	2	492	126	108	89	23	60	35	25	13	75	87	.463

Tony LaRussa

Year	Team	Lg	G	LUp	PL%	PH	PR	DS	Quick	Slow	LO	RCD	LS	Rel	SBA	SacA	RM	PO	#	Good	NG	Bomb	W	L	Pct
				LINEUPS		SUBSTITUTION			PITCHER USAGE						TACTICS				INTENTIONAL BB				RESULTS		
1994	Athletics	AL	114	97	.62	89	28	14	43	21	5	60	4	308	130	31		32	30	20	10	4	51	63	.447
1995	Athletics	AL	144	120	.54	113	38	24	33	38	19	46	7	358	158	42		42	26	18	8	4	67	77	.465
1996	Cardinals	NL	162	120	.52	246	25	13	32	48	24	90	8	413	207	117		41	43	28	15	7	88	74	.543
1997	Cardinals	NL	162	146	.54	307	17	18	34	42	16	81	2	399	224	77		79	34	26	8	2	73	89	.451
1998	Cardinals	NL	162	146	.52	259	7	18	62	31	13	82	14	429	174	85		34	38	25	13	8	83	79	.512
1999	Cardinals	NL	161	138	.47	264	32	28	50	41	13	96	14	454	182	103		30	38	20	18	11	75	86	.466
2000	Cardinals	NL	162	137	.53	240	35	25	40	31	11	63	18	386	138	107		34	28	21	7	6	95	67	.586
2001	Cardinals	NL	162	117	.47	256	26	13	46	36	7	140	7	485	126	102		25	36	21	15	4	93	69	.574
2002	Cardinals	NL	162	117	.52	340	27	41	58	33	23	110	6	472	128	106	75	13	39	25	14	8	97	65	.599
2003	Cardinals	NL	162	126	.50	352	28	51	38	49	36	113	9	460	114	108	56	9	36	28	8	2	85	77	.525
2004	Cardinals	NL	162	119	.53	275	25	69	30	48	31	120	16	469	158	88	158	9	24	17	7	4	105	57	.648
2005	Cardinals	NL	162	138	.55	270	25	48	40	38	22	88	4	436	119	92	153	9	27	16	11	7	100	62	.617
2006	Cardinals	NL	161	131	.56	272	11	53	50	34	21	95	6	469	91	86	123	13	35	21	14	3	83	78	.516
2007	Cardinals	NL	162	150	.60	317	19	37	46	44	8	102	5	516	89	85	120	23	25	10	15	11	78	84	.481
2008	Cardinals	NL	162	163	.64	275	26	57	52	40	16	96	14	506	105	87	114	18	21	13	8	1	86	76	.531
2009	Cardinals	NL	162	131	.52	289	12	51	66	39	17	102	8	481	106	93	91	17	23	16	8	1	91	71	.562
2010	Cardinals	NL	162	147	.55	292	18	20	52	40	16	80	5	455	120	87	151	22	32	17	15	8	86	76	.531
	162-Game Average			135	.54	269	24	35	46	39	18	95	9	452	143	90	116	27	32	21	12	5	87	75	.537

Jim Leyland

Year	Team	Lg	G	LUp	PL%	PH	PR	DS	Quick	Slow	LO	RCD	LS	Rel	SBA	SacA	RM	PO	#	Good	NG	Bomb	W	L	Pct
				LINEUPS		SUBSTITUTION			PITCHER USAGE						TACTICS				INTENTIONAL BB				RESULTS		
1994	Pirates	NL	114	94	.56	170	16	13	12	9	1	48	4	285	78	48		38	52	29	23	15	53	61	.465
1995	Pirates	NL	144	124	.56	282	0	4	13	12	11	71	4	391	139	69		51	50	30	20	10	58	86	.403
1996	Pirates	NL	162	117	.53	209	18	14	27	8	11	60	11	422	175	101		46	50	23	27	13	73	89	.451
1997	Marlins	NL	162	105	.59	258	36	31	21	12	18	65	2	404	173	91		38	41	25	16	0	92	70	.568
1998	Marlins	NL	162	98	.59	277	13	15	18	24	31	73	8	420	172	91		31	61	36	25	11	54	108	.333
1999	Rockies	NL	162	124	.56	294	11	12	11	29	21	72	5	421	113	88		11	46	24	22	14	72	90	.444
2006	Tigers	AL	162	120	.53	81	34	38	52	32	16	52	3	390	100	57	128	9	35	23	12	9	95	67	.586
2007	Tigers	AL	162	108	.53	77	31	49	46	43	14	70	5	443	133	35	123	20	41	24	17	13	88	74	.543
2008	Tigers	AL	162	131	.51	66	25	50	29	47	20	72	7	440	94	40	114	10	63	37	26	13	74	88	.457
2009	Tigers	AL	163	126	.55	125	52	50	47	47	38	86	3	439	105	60	132	19	42	26	16	6	86	77	.528
2010	Tigers	AL	162	129	.50	130	11	47	36	54	45	70	6	416	99	54	174	31	29	14	15	9	81	81	.500
	162-Game Average			120	.55	194	24	30	29	30	21	70	5	422	130	69	134	29	48	27	21	12	78	84	.481

Grady Little

Year	Team	Lg	G	LUp	PL%	PH	PR	DS	Quick	Slow	LO	RCD	LS	Rel	SBA	SacA	RM	PO	#	Good	NG	Bomb	W	L	Pct
				LINEUPS		SUBSTITUTION			PITCHER USAGE						TACTICS				INTENTIONAL BB				RESULTS		
2002	Red Sox	AL	162	120	.59	127	51	23	63	28	18	53	11	338	108	35	38	50	29	18	11	3	93	69	.574
2003	Red Sox	AL	162	118	.64	130	80	32	43	36	19	78	8	437	123	32	42	28	41	22	19	13	95	67	.586
2006	Dodgers	NL	162	118	.67	291	34	37	56	29	11	106	9	454	177	82	144	63	40	22	18	7	88	74	.543
2007	Dodgers	NL	162	112	.61	273	35	61	44	31	11	125	4	483	187	77	133	45	34	21	13	7	82	80	.506
	162-Game Average			117	.63	205	50	38	52	31	15	91	8	428	149	57	89	47	36	21	15	6	90	72	.556

Ken Macha

Year	Team	Lg	G	LUp	PL%	PH	PR	DS	Quick	Slow	LO	RCD	LS	Rel	SBA	SacA	RM	PO	#	Good	NG	Bomb	W	L	Pct
				LINEUPS		SUBSTITUTION			PITCHER USAGE						TACTICS				INTENTIONAL BB				RESULTS		
2003	Athletics	AL	162	111	.57	140	29	23	44	38	30	72	12	364	62	31	28	9	42	25	17	10	96	66	.593
2004	Athletics	AL	162	119	.60	123	14	14	37	47	39	94	5	414	69	30	63	2	49	31	18	9	91	71	.562
2005	Athletics	AL	162	127	.62	83	17	11	43	36	30	79	13	410	53	29	53	13	42	27	15	6	88	74	.543
2006	Athletics	AL	162	121	.58	62	33	23	39	47	28	104	8	444	81	29	70	22	47	26	21	11	93	69	.574

Year	Team	Lg	G	LINEUPS		SUBSTITUTION			PITCHER USAGE						TACTICS				INTENTIONAL BB				RESULTS		
				LUp	PL%	PH	PR	DS	Quick	Slow	LO	RCD	LS	Rel	SBA	SacA	RM	PO	#	Good	NG	Bomb	W	L	Pct
2009	Brewers	NL	162	111	.48	267	7	32	35	51	19	120	1	512	105	70	90	12	60	35	**25**	**17**	80	82	.494
2010	Brewers	NL	162	95	.47	226	14	22	42	**55**	27	102	9	495	107	52	138	5	42	27	15	11	77	85	.475
	162-Game Average			114	.55	150	19	21	40	46	29	95	8	440	80	40	74	11	47	29	19	11	88	74	.543

Pete Mackanin

Year	Team	Lg	G	LINEUPS		SUBSTITUTION			PITCHER USAGE						TACTICS				INTENTIONAL BB				RESULTS		
				LUp	PL%	PH	PR	DS	Quick	Slow	LO	RCD	LS	Rel	SBA	SacA	RM	PO	#	Good	NG	Bomb	W	L	Pct
2005	Pirates	NL	26	24	.52	54	1	5	11	4	1	22	0	94	19	19	20	2	5	2	3	1	12	14	.462
2007	Reds	NL	80	57	.59	130	10	26	20	22	9	58	3	266	62	44	36	12	18	10	8	3	41	39	.513
	162-Game Average			124	.57	281	17	47	47	40	15	122	5	550	124	96	86	21	35	18	17	6	81	81	.500

Joe Maddon

Year	Team	Lg	G	LINEUPS		SUBSTITUTION			PITCHER USAGE						TACTICS				INTENTIONAL BB				RESULTS		
				LUp	PL%	PH	PR	DS	Quick	Slow	LO	RCD	LS	Rel	SBA	SacA	RM	PO	#	Good	NG	Bomb	W	L	Pct
1996	Angels	AL	22	19	.64	21	5	0	7	6	6	10	3	48	11	20		6	4	3	1	1	8	14	.364
1998	Angels	AL	8	4	.57	2	4	0	1	5	3	5	3	12	2	7		0	1	0	1	0	6	2	.750
1999	Angels	AL	29	19	.58	29	4	1	6	0	4	20	0	85	23	12		7	3	1	2	1	19	10	.655
2006	Devil Rays	AL	162	**145**	.54	81	26	51	41	39	16	79	10	444	186	51	132	48	39	19	20	13	61	**101**	.377
2007	Devil Rays	AL	162	122	.53	80	19	16	31	**56**	19	113	1	483	179	40	118	**50**	31	18	13	4	66	**96**	.407
2008	Rays	AL	162	115	**.69**	**133**	16	39	48	37	14	112	7	448	**192**	31	113	26	29	15	14	8	97	65	.599
2009	Rays	AL	162	123	.66	**140**	21	18	28	51	23	**139**	3	510	**255**	29	99	15	22	10	12	7	84	78	.519
2010	Rays	AL	162	129	.67	**174**	31	18	41	34	26	135	2	491	219	45	166	12	34	**28**	6	3	96	66	.593
	162-Game Average			126	.62	123	23	27	38	43	21	114	5	470	199	44	126	31	30	18	13	7	81	81	.500

Charlie Manuel

Year	Team	Lg	G	LINEUPS		SUBSTITUTION			PITCHER USAGE						TACTICS				INTENTIONAL BB				RESULTS		
				LUp	PL%	PH	PR	DS	Quick	Slow	LO	RCD	LS	Rel	SBA	SacA	RM	PO	#	Good	NG	Bomb	W	L	Pct
2000	Indians	AL	162	102	.64	73	40	26	21	12	20	104	7	462	147	59		30	45	28	17	9	90	72	.556
2001	Indians	AL	162	114	.61	105	30	49	28	17	**10**	120	3	484	120	67		43	44	30	14	11	91	71	.562
2002	Indians	AL	86	67	.61	57	10	19	14	17	25	47	0	222	57	21	34	3	21	12	9	4	39	47	.453
2005	Phillies	NL	162	80	.64	265	36	19	42	28	13	119	6	442	143	86	76	11	51	35	16	9	88	74	.543
2006	Phillies	NL	162	81	.65	301	42	49	28	43	22	126	2	500	117	79	74	16	63	35	28	12	85	77	.525
2007	Phillies	NL	162	87	.64	264	**56**	75	40	40	19	128	6	498	157	84	90	30	62	41	21	**16**	89	73	.549
2008	Phillies	NL	162	77	.65	291	**62**	60	33	42	24	124	1	468	161	88	92	34	64	**46**	18	11	92	70	.568
2009	Phillies	NL	162	68	.67	283	20	16	32	55	32	107	3	459	147	74	65	3	31	19	12	3	93	69	.574
2010	Phillies	NL	162	94	.64	276	17	19	37	50	39	114	1	451	129	64	120	3	42	27	15	6	**97**	65	.599
	162-Game Average			90	.64	224	37	39	32	36	24	116	3	467	138	73	84	20	50	32	18	9	90	72	.556

Jerry Manuel

Year	Team	Lg	G	LINEUPS		SUBSTITUTION			PITCHER USAGE						TACTICS				INTENTIONAL BB				RESULTS		
				LUp	PL%	PH	PR	DS	Quick	Slow	LO	RCD	LS	Rel	SBA	SacA	RM	PO	#	Good	NG	Bomb	W	L	Pct
1998	White Sox	AL	162	110	.56	65	19	31	43	35	6	72	14	405	173	54		26	20	14	6	4	80	82	.494
1999	White Sox	AL	161	109	.58	79	35	39	35	42	9	78	8	409	160	69		22	31	20	11	7	75	**86**	.466
2000	White Sox	AL	162	84	.53	84	35	20	41	31	8	91	18	466	161	75		32	27	16	11	10	**95**	67	.586
2001	White Sox	AL	162	115	.53	104	34	50	45	39	5	93	16	406	182	**95**		41	38	24	14	9	83	79	.512
2002	White Sox	AL	162	104	.55	86	10	39	50	44	17	86	10	423	106	**73**	38	18	31	17	14	**11**	81	81	.500
2003	White Sox	AL	162	105	.55	146	40	**71**	39	36	27	74	10	361	106	66	39	20	30	18	12	7	86	76	.531
2008	Mets	NL	93	58	.76	167	7	31	12	20	33	95	2	324	89	54	81	6	37	18	19	6	55	38	.591
2009	Mets	NL	162	117	**.72**	**289**	11	37	34	51	22	137	2	511	**166**	112	104	3	60	38	22	14	70	92	.432
2010	Mets	NL	162	124	**.67**	290	19	25	39	47	32	**145**	5	491	174	100	169	9	55	42	13	6	79	83	.488
	162-Game Average			108	.60	153	25	40	39	41	17	102	10	443	154	81	94	21	38	24	14	9	82	80	.506

John McLaren

Year	Team	Lg	G	LINEUPS		SUBSTITUTION			PITCHER USAGE						TACTICS				INTENTIONAL BB				RESULTS		
				LUp	PL%	PH	PR	DS	Quick	Slow	LO	RCD	LS	Rel	SBA	SacA	RM	PO	#	Good	NG	Bomb	W	L	Pct
2007	Mariners	AL	84	52	.48	55	40	18	17	23	19	49	6	247	56	20	76	18	19	10	9	5	43	41	.512
2008	Mariners	AL	72	48	.50	31	16	4	17	24	9	45	1	197	65	17	63	11	12	6	6	5	25	47	.347
	162-Game Average			104	.49	89	58	23	35	49	29	98	7	461	126	38	144	30	32	17	16	10	71	91	.438

Bob Melvin

Year	Team	Lg	G	LINEUPS		SUBSTITUTION			PITCHER USAGE						TACTICS				INTENTIONAL BB				RESULTS		
				LUp	PL%	PH	PR	DS	Quick	Slow	LO	RCD	LS	Rel	SBA	SacA	RM	PO	#	Good	NG	Bomb	W	L	Pct
2003	Mariners	AL	162	111	.62	81	62	33	27	46	43	56	6	366	145	44	37	5	24	14	10	4	93	69	.574
2004	Mariners	AL	162	**151**	.59	109	**66**	26	26	63	43	82	5	414	152	56	123	24	32	18	14	8	63	99	.389
2005	Diamondbacks	NL	162	120	.68	**310**	26	38	26	56	36	123	**11**	458	93	93	101	30	43	27	16	9	77	85	.475

Year	Team	Lg	G	LINEUPS LUp	PL%	SUBSTITUTION PH	PR	DS	PITCHER USAGE Quick	Slow	LO	RCD	LS	Rel	TACTICS SBA	SacA	RM	PO	INTENTIONAL BB #	Good	NG	Bomb	RESULTS W	L	Pct
2006	Diamondbacks	NL	162	114	.72	278	11	35	37	42	15	86	0	461	106	83	61	30	44	28	16	8	76	86	.469
2007	Diamondbacks	NL	162	146	.57	243	11	61	35	42	31	96	2	469	133	74	70	25	38	30	8	4	90	72	.556
2008	Diamondbacks	NL	162	134	.57	263	27	30	41	39	16	102	0	444	81	87	79	28	41	27	14	9	82	80	.506
2009	Diamondbacks	NL	29	29	.62	47	6	8	7	4	3	17	0	91	29	17	13	3	3	1	2	2	12	17	.414
	162-Game Average			130	.62	215	34	37	32	47	30	91	4	437	120	73	78	23	36	23	13	7	80	82	.494

Brad Mills

Year	Team	Lg	G	LINEUPS LUp	PL%	SUBSTITUTION PH	PR	DS	PITCHER USAGE Quick	Slow	LO	RCD	LS	Rel	TACTICS SBA	SacA	RM	PO	INTENTIONAL BB #	Good	NG	Bomb	RESULTS W	L	Pct
2010	Astros	NL	162	128	.50	280	17	51	29	52	41	121	1	507	136	90	122	8	39	30	9	5	76	86	.469
	162-Game Average			128	.50	280	17	51	29	52	41	121	1	507	136	90	122	8	39	30	9	5	76	86	.469

Jerry Narron

Year	Team	Lg	G	LINEUPS LUp	PL%	SUBSTITUTION PH	PR	DS	PITCHER USAGE Quick	Slow	LO	RCD	LS	Rel	TACTICS SBA	SacA	RM	PO	INTENTIONAL BB #	Good	NG	Bomb	RESULTS W	L	Pct
2001	Rangers	AL	134	94	.66	92	14	19	9	18	6	60	5	340	106	29		5	24	10	14	8	62	72	.463
2002	Rangers	AL	162	128	.52	154	59	30	33	54	26	121	5	487	96	58	58	6	32	19	13	3	72	90	.444
2005	Reds	NL	93	73	.61	156	9	14	13	22	12	71	5	287	50	45	53	7	25	21	4	2	46	46	.500
2006	Reds	NL	162	140	.56	273	23	46	33	47	41	121	2	476	157	86	91	11	55	38	17	9	80	82	.494
2007	Reds	NL	82	63	.58	135	6	26	11	33	21	74	8	256	66	56	45	8	29	16	13	7	31	51	.378
	162-Game Average			128	.58	208	28	35	25	45	27	115	6	473	122	70	80	9	42	27	16	7	75	87	.463

Sam Perlozzo

Year	Team	Lg	G	LINEUPS LUp	PL%	SUBSTITUTION PH	PR	DS	PITCHER USAGE Quick	Slow	LO	RCD	LS	Rel	TACTICS SBA	SacA	RM	PO	INTENTIONAL BB #	Good	NG	Bomb	RESULTS W	L	Pct
2005	Orioles	AL	55	47	.61	28	23	26	15	11	5	46	2	180	41	24	25	8	3	1	2	1	23	32	.418
2006	Orioles	AL	162	124	.56	72	46	49	29	47	14	102	10	472	153	58	79	30	26	15	11	7	70	92	.432
2007	Orioles	AL	69	48	.60	29	26	25	16	15	13	64	1	211	62	30	29	13	8	3	5	5	29	40	.420
	162-Game Average			124	.58	73	54	57	34	41	18	120	7	489	145	63	75	29	21	11	10	7	69	93	.426

Lou Piniella

Year	Team	Lg	G	LINEUPS LUp	PL%	SUBSTITUTION PH	PR	DS	PITCHER USAGE Quick	Slow	LO	RCD	LS	Rel	TACTICS SBA	SacA	RM	PO	INTENTIONAL BB #	Good	NG	Bomb	RESULTS W	L	Pct
1994	Mariners	AL	112	98	.49	113	24	8	30	35	4	54	9	252	60	54		37	30	21	18	9	49	63	.438
1995	Mariners	AL	145	98	.56	137	41	22	37	39	30	58	20	324	151	66		40	37	18	19	12	79	66	.545
1996	Mariners	AL	161	99	.55	190	28	14	56	21	15	91	14	403	129	65		40	52	31	21	13	85	76	.528
1997	Mariners	AL	162	84	.57	147	35	27	38	47	25	79	11	392	129	61		32	36	18	18	10	90	72	.556
1998	Mariners	AL	161	111	.53	99	38	43	38	54	32	81	4	368	154	58		20	23	8	15	7	76	85	.472
1999	Mariners	AL	162	130	.48	122	30	30	31	40	21	61	10	346	175	49		31	39	15	24	8	79	83	.488
2000	Mariners	AL	102	100	.50	100	43	52	51	37	1	64	11	383	178	73		22	37	20	17	0	91	71	.562
2001	Mariners	AL	162	115	.64	121	44	64	55	33	5	62	9	392	216	62		33	28	19	9	3	116	46	.716
2002	Mariners	AL	162	129	.64	95	129	50	49	39	34	52	7	343	195	61	43	25	34	15	19	11	93	69	.574
2003	Devil Rays	AL	162	124	.60	188	43	26	38	41	29	59	5	372	184	53	52	20	37	21	16	10	63	99	.389
2004	Devil Rays	AL	162	137	.63	97	25	36	51	34	23	57	15	401	174	45	104	16	35	16	19	9	70	91	.435
2005	Devil Rays	AL	162	135	.54	127	18	52	38	54	32	67	10	401	200	53	128	16	41	19	22	13	67	95	.414
2007	Cubs	NL	162	125	.51	263	52	51	35	38	33	98	3	478	119	60	89	17	46	28	18	4	85	77	.525
2008	Cubs	NL	161	112	.47	286	22	31	42	37	27	111	3	478	121	93	98	15	45	28	17	9	97	64	.602
2009	Cubs	NL	161	131	.57	277	14	55	47	40	20	127	3	480	90	81	92	23	46	21	25	13	83	78	.516
2010	Cubs	NL	125	101	.53	192	10	37	31	41	32	93	6	371	68	65	103	16	33	17	16	9	51	74	.408
	162-Game Average			121	.55	167	39	39	44	41	24	79	9	403	153	65	91	26	40	21	19	10	83	79	.512

Mike Quade

Year	Team	Lg	G	LINEUPS LUp	PL%	SUBSTITUTION PH	PR	DS	PITCHER USAGE Quick	Slow	LO	RCD	LS	Rel	TACTICS SBA	SacA	RM	PO	INTENTIONAL BB #	Good	NG	Bomb	RESULTS W	L	Pct
2010	Cubs	NL	37	32	.52	44	1	15	10	11	6	20	3	111	18	14	16	4	9	8	1	0	24	13	.649
	162-Game Average			140	.52	193	4	66	44	48	26	88	13	486	79	61	70	18	39	35	4	0	105	57	.648

Willie Randolph

Year	Team	Lg	G	LINEUPS LUp	PL%	SUBSTITUTION PH	PR	DS	PITCHER USAGE Quick	Slow	LO	RCD	LS	Rel	TACTICS SBA	SacA	RM	PO	INTENTIONAL BB #	Good	NG	Bomb	RESULTS W	L	Pct
2005	Mets	NL	162	105	.64	222	10	51	47	34	20	74	5	392	193	89	118	18	43	28	15	9	83	79	.512
2006	Mets	NL	162	101	.68	247	9	24	40	40	15	119	4	474	181	102	106	16	39	25	14	9	97	65	.599
2007	Mets	NL	162	102	.68	269	21	28	26	44	27	122	3	499	246	97	100	10	40	26	14	7	88	74	.543
2008	Mets	NL	69	46	.77	104	3	11	12	20	11	73	1	233	85	44	48	4	16	10	6	2	34	35	.493
	162-Game Average			103	.68	246	13	33	36	40	21	113	4	466	206	97	109	14	40	26	14	8	88	74	.543

Jim Riggleman

Year	Team	Lg	G	LINEUPS LUp	PL%	SUBSTITUTION PH	PR	DS	PITCHER USAGE Quick	Slow	LO	RCD	LS	Rel	TACTICS SBA	SacA	RM	PO	INTENTIONAL BB #	Good	NG	Bomb	RESULTS W	L	Pct
1994	Padres	NL	117	93	.63	184	28	19	11	5	3	53	10	273	116	80		52	62	34	28	11	47	70	.402
1995	Cubs	NL	144	92	.56	196	9	30	15	8	13	119	12	414	142	90		53	68	45	23	12	73	71	.507
1996	Cubs	NL	162	87	.54	326	34	21	17	11	7	114	11	439	158	79		65	55	33	22	10	76	86	.469
1997	Cubs	NL	162	127	.50	280	40	44	13	5	2	113	9	441	176	103		74	51	38	13	6	68	94	.420
1998	Cubs	NL	163	104	.60	273	26	35	16	14	20	133	6	449	109	89		26	48	22	26	15	90	73	.552
1999	Cubs	NL	162	122	.61	312	25	30	16	19	8	105	4	441	104	94		20	48	21	27	15	67	95	.414
2008	Mariners	AL	90	70	.60	75	30	22	21	25	19	50	4	272	57	27	88	10	25	17	8	3	36	54	.400
2009	Nationals	NL	75	60	.51	115	15	33	24	16	4	63	6	250	59	44	36	8	33	17	16	8	33	42	.440
2010	Nationals	NL	162	131	.58	271	33	67	50	32	9	101	5	494	151	101	158	13	57	37	20	10	69	93	.426
	162-Game Average			116	.57	266	31	39	24	18	11	111	9	455	140	93	140	42	59	35	24	12	73	89	.451

Edwin Rodriguez

Year	Team	Lg	G	LINEUPS LUp	PL%	SUBSTITUTION PH	PR	DS	PITCHER USAGE Quick	Slow	LO	RCD	LS	Rel	TACTICS SBA	SacA	RM	PO	INTENTIONAL BB #	Good	NG	Bomb	RESULTS W	L	Pct
2010	Marlins	NL	92	60	.42	152	12	20	22	23	13	72	1	288	62	37	69	9	24	17	7	3	46	46	.500
	162-Game Average			106	.42	268	21	35	39	41	23	127	2	507	109	65	122	16	42	30	12	5	81	81	.500

John Russell

Year	Team	Lg	G	LINEUPS LUp	PL%	SUBSTITUTION PH	PR	DS	PITCHER USAGE Quick	Slow	LO	RCD	LS	Rel	TACTICS SBA	SacA	RM	PO	INTENTIONAL BB #	Good	NG	Bomb	RESULTS W	L	Pct
2008	Pirates	NL	162	128	.51	290	17	13	29	47	15	111	0	497	76	92	54	19	31	21	10	4	67	95	.414
2009	Pirates	NL	161	121	.60	251	3	5	44	45	12	89	0	456	122	78	97	15	37	20	17	10	62	99	.385
2010	Pirates	NL	162	119	.60	275	13	10	48	44	8	122	0	517	123	81	124	32	40	26	14	4	57	105	.352
	162-Game Average			123	.57	273	11	9	40	45	12	108	0	491	107	84	92	22	36	22	14	6	62	100	.383

Juan Samuel

Year	Team	Lg	G	LINEUPS LUp	PL%	SUBSTITUTION PH	PR	DS	PITCHER USAGE Quick	Slow	LO	RCD	LS	Rel	TACTICS SBA	SacA	RM	PO	INTENTIONAL BB #	Good	NG	Bomb	RESULTS W	L	Pct
2010	Orioles	AL	51	39	.63	27	14	3	11	17	6	33	0	157	40	18	39	2	18	12	6	5	17	34	.333
	162-Game Average			124	.63	86	44	10	35	54	19	105	0	499	127	57	124	6	57	38	19	16	54	108	.333

Mike Scioscia

Year	Team	Lg	G	LINEUPS LUp	PL%	SUBSTITUTION PH	PR	DS	PITCHER USAGE Quick	Slow	LO	RCD	LS	Rel	TACTICS SBA	SacA	RM	PO	INTENTIONAL BB #	Good	NG	Bomb	RESULTS W	L	Pct
2000	Angels	AL	162	75	.62	110	41	4	56	42	6	95	9	441	145	63		40	44	28	16	7	82	80	.506
2001	Angels	AL	162	130	.62	118	30	8	29	41	5	81	9	384	168	66		47	22	25	12	75	87	.463
2002	Angels	AL	162	102	.64	162	57	26	36	33	34	88	8	400	168	62	52	30	24	15	9	5	99	63	.611
2003	Angels	AL	162	130	.64	134	54	40	50	48	11	60	4	375	190	64	79	25	38	26	12	3	77	85	.475
2004	Angels	AL	162	126	.57	94	32	44	37	40	22	61	11	343	189	70	229	33	27	18	9	3	92	70	.568
2005	Angels	AL	162	124	.65	92	37	37	47	37	24	88	9	379	218	55	160	43	24	15	9	4	95	67	.586
2006	Angels	AL	162	114	.63	103	45	38	38	49	21	99	9	380	205	37	166	22	27	18	9	6	89	73	.549
2007	Angels	AL	162	127	.66	103	26	19	39	40	14	94	4	396	194	41	166	44	22	12	10	5	94	68	.580
2008	Angels	AL	162	125	.63	74	30	36	37	48	21	87	1	383	177	39	151	31	32	22	10	6	100	62	.617
2009	Angels	AL	162	123	.69	80	26	37	47	47	33	91	1	434	211	55	137	40	35	22	13	6	97	65	.599
2010	Angels	AL	162	133	.59	96	31	23	41	52	48	76	0	410	156	58	223	28	33	17	16	8	80	82	.494
	162-Game Average			119	.63	106	37	28	42	43	22	84	6	393	184	56	151	35	32	20	13	6	89	73	.549

Buck Showalter

Year	Team	Lg	G	LINEUPS LUp	PL%	SUBSTITUTION PH	PR	DS	PITCHER USAGE Quick	Slow	LO	RCD	LS	Rel	TACTICS SBA	SacA	RM	PO	INTENTIONAL BB #	Good	NG	Bomb	RESULTS W	L	Pct
1994	Yankees	AL	113	79	.59	95	31	3	24	30	0	38	7	241	95	34		22	24	13	11	4	70	43	.619
1995	Yankees	AL	145	107	.68	124	30	20	29	42	37	57	6	302	80	27		29	21	14	7	1	79	65	.549
1998	Diamondbacks	NL	162	124	.62	252	17	15	34	40	7	43	6	368	111	68		13	32	16	16	9	65	97	.401
1999	Diamondbacks	NL	162	97	.63	220	20	17	37	48	25	74	3	382	176	75		15	48	29	19	8	100	62	.617
2000	Diamondbacks	NL	162	99	.60	250	32	11	46	26	18	74	12	390	141	89		10	53	28	25	16	85	77	.525
2003	Rangers	AL	162	133	.61	88	51	41	35	33	12	93	7	494	90	35	80	12	45	24	21	14	71	91	.438
2004	Rangers	AL	162	120	.64	86	15	24	52	30	12	82	10	468	105	30	88	5	29	19	10	3	89	73	.549
2005	Rangers	AL	162	98	.59	57	22	11	42	39	17	79	8	454	82	11	103	5	31	10	21	16	79	83	.488
2006	Rangers	AL	162	95	.57	39	34	22	41	27	10	85	4	489	77	30	72	8	18	11	7	5	80	82	.494
2010	Orioles	AL	57	42	.74	20	11	13	23	9	10	24	1	144	38	13	31	1	10	9	1	1	34	23	.596
	162-Game Average			111	.62	138	29	20	41	36	17	73	7	418	111	46	86	13	35	19	15	9	84	78	.519

Dale Sveum

Year	Team	Lg	G	LUp	PL%	PH	PR	DS	Quick	Slow	LO	RCD	LS	Rel	SBA	SacA	RM	PO	#	Good	NG	Bomb	W	L	Pct
2008	Brewers	NL	12	3	.48	32	2	1	7	2	1	12	0	46	5	13	6	1	2	1	1	0	7	5	.583
	162-Game Average			41	.48	432	27	14	95	27	14	162	0	621	68	176	81	14	27	14	14	0	94	68	.580

Joe Torre

Year	Team	Lg	G	LUp	PL%	PH	PR	DS	Quick	Slow	LO	RCD	LS	Rel	SBA	SacA	RM	PO	#	Good	NG	Bomb	W	L	Pct
1994	Cardinals	NL	115	79	.68	192	9	0	36	29	6	106	4	330	122	57		33	28	18	10	6	53	61	.465
1995	Cardinals	NL	47	36	.51	99	6	4	17	11	1	41	2	146	42	26		14	16	10	6	2	20	27	.426
1996	Yankees	AL	162	131	.57	92	62	55	59	23	22	97	10	411	142	53		19	35	17	18	14	92	70	.568
1997	Yankees	AL	162	118	.61	75	70	23	35	41	19	84	14	368	157	54		14	41	23	18	10	96	66	.593
1998	Yankees	AL	162	96	.62	94	36	28	43	38	27	71	17	334	216	44		9	25	17	8	4	114	48	.704
1999	Yankees	AL	162	95	.63	114	63	10	29	51	26	80	12	359	161	31		12	27	17	10	8	98	64	.605
2000	Yankees	AL	161	112	.63	86	49	27	43	53	27	92	16	382	147	22		8	23	9	14	7	87	74	.540
2001	Yankees	AL	161	94	.56	76	33	14	37	45	10	77	17	362	214	41		21	29	20	9	6	95	65	.594
2002	Yankees	AL	161	108	.58	89	53	31	39	49	44	86	13	334	138	35	46	18	44	33	11	4	103	58	.640
2003	Yankees	AL	163	104	.65	118	48	18	26	51	52	75	10	367	131	39	69	33	36	21	15	8	101	61	.623
2004	Yankees	AL	162	116	.65	86	35	46	48	35	29	129	10	436	117	50	126	36	32	16	16	9	101	61	.623
2005	Yankees	AL	162	117	.64	94	65	47	44	45	28	92	7	418	111	40	123	50	25	11	14	9	95	67	.586
2006	Yankees	AL	162	120	.66	108	50	59	50	30	9	109	7	489	174	48	118	50	41	22	19	4	97	65	.599
2007	Yankees	AL	162	102	.68	99	34	22	51	29	10	113	13	522	163	51	152	41	33	17	16	7	94	68	.580
2008	Dodgers	NL	162	124	.53	277	43	66	61	30	17	94	8	461	169	75	133	38	58	46	12	5	84	78	.519
2009	Dodgers	NL	162	113	.59	263	22	22	62	23	18	125	8	526	164	107	163	17	68	45	23	12	95	67	.586
2010	Dodgers	NL	162	127	.55	255	18	47	42	37	30	92	5	475	142	108	192	8	75	53	22	11	80	82	.494
	162-Game Average			112	.61	139	44	33	45	39	23	90	11	421	167	55	125	26	40	25	15	8	94	68	.580

Jim Tracy

Year	Team	Lg	G	LUp	PL%	PH	PR	DS	Quick	Slow	LO	RCD	LS	Rel	SBA	SacA	RM	PO	#	Good	NG	Bomb	W	L	Pct
2001	Dodgers	NL	162	111	.50	204	34	20	46	34	8	84	4	409	131	81		10	37	19	18	9	86	76	.531
2002	Dodgers	NL	162	102	.52	317	39	37	49	36	21	118	9	423	133	81	46	18	45	31	14	5	92	70	.568
2003	Dodgers	NL	162	103	.64	269	22	64	52	29	22	148	11	438	116	97	32	10	35	23	12	8	85	77	.525
2004	Dodgers	NL	162	94	.70	295	25	19	49	34	16	128	16	459	143	81	93	7	47	32	15	8	93	69	.574
2005	Dodgers	NL	162	129	.64	303	31	37	44	40	20	126	2	459	93	76	97	17	34	21	13	6	71	91	.438
2006	Pirates	NL	162	121	.43	264	22	22	37	43	12	156	5	505	91	80	75	12	62	39	23	15	67	95	.414
2007	Pirates	NL	162	124	.49	240	12	26	33	40	13	113	0	495	98	80	90	12	55	30	26	11	68	94	.420
2009	Rockies	NL	116	87	.63	186	25	28	28	27	27	83	3	349	116	73	82	9	40	28	12	7	74	42	.638
2010	Rockies	NL	162	135	.65	257	30	41	38	40	34	128	0	513	141	64	135	11	54	34	20	10	83	79	.512
	162-Game Average			115	.58	275	28	34	43	38	20	124	6	465	122	82	84	12	47	29	17	9	82	80	.506

Dave Trembley

Year	Team	Lg	G	LUp	PL%	PH	PR	DS	Quick	Slow	LO	RCD	LS	Rel	SBA	SacA	RM	PO	#	Good	NG	Bomb	W	L	Pct
2007	Orioles	AL	93	71	.60	63	29	16	21	25	16	47	3	279	124	32	83	32	29	15	14	8	40	53	.430
2008	Orioles	AL	161	119	.58	117	36	25	41	44	11	87	4	492	118	38	143	11	44	18	26	12	68	93	.422
2009	Orioles	AL	162	132	.68	99	26	21	43	39	11	66	4	484	113	20	86	6	45	28	17	9	64	98	.395
2010	Orioles	AL	54	50	.62	24	14	7	6	16	10	33	1	153	32	10	24	2	17	7	10	5	15	39	.278
	162-Game Average			128	.62	104	36	24	38	43	17	80	4	485	133	34	116	18	47	23	23	12	64	98	.395

Don Wakamatsu

Year	Team	Lg	G	LUp	PL%	PH	PR	DS	Quick	Slow	LO	RCD	LS	Rel	SBA	SacA	RM	PO	#	Good	NG	Bomb	W	L	Pct
2009	Mariners	AL	162	138	.51	58	31	19	50	27	18	76	1	410	122	61	91	4	13	3	10	6	85	77	.525
2010	Mariners	AL	112	93	.61	49	21	12	37	21	20	39	2	254	129	40	124	17	25	11	14	7	42	70	.375
	162-Game Average			137	.55	63	31	18	51	28	22	68	2	393	148	60	127	12	22	8	14	8	75	87	.463

Ron Washington

Year	Team	Lg	G	LUp	PL%	PH	PR	DS	Quick	Slow	LO	RCD	LS	Rel	SBA	SacA	RM	PO	#	Good	NG	Bomb	W	L	Pct
2007	Rangers	AL	162	139	.60	89	30	53	47	46	4	78	9	467	113	76	67	13	38	19	19	11	75	87	.463
2008	Rangers	AL	162	129	.64	118	16	14	31	53	11	85	3	458	106	53	74	20	44	19	25	20	79	83	.488
2009	Rangers	AL	162	123	.55	48	11	11	39	47	28	80	9	436	185	44	80	5	14	9	5	3	87	75	.537
2010	Rangers	AL	162	112	.52	86	39	31	46	42	35	110	4	481	171	68	160	10	24	15	9	0	90	72	.556
	162-Game Average			126	.58	85	24	27	41	47	20	88	6	461	144	60	95	12	30	16	15	9	83	79	.512

Eric Wedge

Year	Team	Lg	G	LINEUPS		SUBSTITUTION			PITCHER USAGE						TACTICS				INTENTIONAL BB				RESULTS		
				LUp	PL%	PH	PR	DS	Quick	Slow	LO	RCD	LS	Rel	SBA	SacA	RM	PO	#	Good	NG	Bomb	W	L	Pct
2003	Indians	AL	162	145	.67	117	43	27	47	34	18	89	5	428	147	67	54	12	37	22	15	8	68	94	.420
2004	Indians	AL	162	114	.72	91	34	20	44	38	22	121	0	479	149	57	129	28	47	26	21	18	80	82	.494
2005	Indians	AL	162	111	.66	88	18	16	45	45	15	90	3	409	98	53	79	9	20	11	9	7	93	69	.574
2006	Indians	AL	162	111	.59	98	13	13	31	52	27	48	1	377	78	40	83	15	35	21	14	11	78	84	.481
2007	Indians	AL	162	117	.60	116	41	25	34	38	20	79	2	395	113	40	108	16	42	24	18	9	96	66	.593
2008	Indians	AL	162	136	.54	112	31	18	40	35	17	78	4	399	106	56	98	5	28	6	22	11	81	81	.500
2009	Indians	AL	162	148	.59	63	28	11	32	41	21	67	3	445	115	52	74	8	31	14	17	9	65	97	.401
	162-Game Average			126	.63	98	30	19	39	40	20	82	3	419	115	52	89	13	34	18	17	10	80	82	.494

Ned Yost

Year	Team	Lg	G	LINEUPS		SUBSTITUTION			PITCHER USAGE						TACTICS				INTENTIONAL BB				RESULTS		
				LUp	PL%	PH	PR	DS	Quick	Slow	LO	RCD	LS	Rel	SBA	SacA	RM	PO	#	Good	NG	Bomb	W	L	Pct
2003	Brewers	NL	162	97	.44	304	22	39	23	59	18	90	6	460	138	85	40	23	43	28	15	9	68	94	.420
2004	Brewers	NL	161	131	.60	283	25	20	39	41	27	63	2	423	178	79	108	8	27	16	11	8	67	94	.416
2005	Brewers	NL	162	99	.46	259	18	35	26	41	42	71	2	395	113	89	97	50	52	23	29	10	81	81	.500
2006	Brewers	NL	162	106	.48	238	12	14	33	44	18	77	4	427	108	80	82	16	34	14	20	12	75	87	.463
2007	Brewers	NL	162	109	.60	259	11	41	37	42	18	117	7	492	128	74	94	19	37	28	9	9	83	79	.512
2008	Brewers	NL	150	93	.48	217	5	16	37	39	23	69	5	399	141	61	105	31	30	17	13	7	83	67	.553
2010	Royals	AL	127	80	.57	56	25	6	22	39	20	65	0	332	127	40	128	18	25	16	9	5	55	72	.433
	162-Game Average			107	.52	241	18	26	32	45	25	82	4	437	139	76	98	25	37	21	16	9	76	86	.469

Categories of this record are Games Managed (G), Number of Different Lineups Used (LUp), the percentage of players who had the platoon advantage at the start of the game (PL%), Pinch Hitters Used (PH), Pinch Runners Used (PR), Defensive Substitutes Used (DS), Quick Hooks (Quick), Slow Hooks (Slow), Long Outings by Starting Pitchers (LO), Relievers Used on Consecutive Days (RCD), Long Saves (LS), Relievers Used (Rel), Stolen Base Attempts (SBA), Sacrifice Bunts Attempts (SacA), Runners Moving with the Pitch (RM), Pitchouts ordered (PO), Intentional Walks issued (#), Intentional Walks resulting in a Good Outcome (Good), Intentional Walks resulting Not in a Good Outcome (NG), Intentional Walks Blowing up on the Manager (Bomb), Wins (W), Losses (L) and Winning Percentage (Pct.).

2010 American League Managers

Manager	G	LUp	PL%	PH	PR	DS	Quick	Slow	LO	RCD	LS	Rel	SBA	SacA	RM	PO	#	Good	NG	Bomb	W	L	Pct
Manny Acta, Cle	162	142	.63	79	20	39	44	49	18	81	6	470	124	41	142	20	36	17	19	10	69	93	.426
Terry Francona, Bos	162	143	.62	125	48	34	32	63	49	84	3	443	85	36	125	26	30	17	13	4	89	73	.549
Ron Gardenhire, Min	162	112	.62	86	55	30	57	28	5	106	1	465	96	47	140	14	19	12	7	4	94	68	.580
Cito Gaston, Tor	162	103	.45	40	40	13	51	33	12	77	4	455	78	22	88	23	35	19	16	6	85	77	.525
Bob Geren, Oak	162	126	.63	108	28	26	57	30	19	81	8	423	194	58	138	11	29	16	13	3	81	81	.500
Joe Girardi, NYY	162	114	.72	117	44	31	43	39	33	76	3	430	133	47	152	20	37	26	11	6	95	67	.586
Ozzie Guillen, CWS	162	115	.51	85	46	36	41	51	24	61	8	407	234	60	220	25	41	26	15	10	88	74	.543
Jim Leyland, Det	162	129	.58	130	11	47	36	54	45	70	6	416	99	54	174	31	29	14	15	9	81	81	.500
Joe Maddon, TB	162	129	.67	174	31	18	41	34	26	135	2	491	219	45	166	12	34	28	6	3	96	66	.593
Mike Scioscia, LAA	162	133	.59	96	31	23	41	52	48	76	0	410	156	58	223	28	33	17	16	8	80	82	.494
Ron Washington, Tex	162	112	.52	86	39	31	46	42	35	110	4	481	171	68	160	10	24	15	9	0	90	72	.556
162-Game Average		124	.60	87	37	24	43	43	27	84	4	438	145	53	154	19	33	20	13	7	77	85	.475

Manager	G	LUp	PL%	PH	PR	DS	Quick	Slow	LO	RCD	LS	Rel	SBA	SacA	RM	PO	#	Good	NG	Bomb	W	L	Pct
Daren Brown, Sea	50	39	.60	9	12	2	15	8	6	14	2	104	52	19	71	9	8	5	3	2	19	31	.380
Trey Hillman, KC	35	24	.57	12	12	1	9	13	4	21	2	109	38	25	41	8	3	2	1	1	12	23	.343
Juan Samuel, Bal	51	39	.63	27	14	3	11	17	6	33	0	157	40	18	39	2	18	12	6	5	17	34	.333
Duck Showalter, Bal	57	42	.74	20	11	13	23	9	10	24	1	144	38	13	31	1	10	9	1	1	34	23	.596
Dave Trembley, Bal	54	50	.62	24	14	7	6	16	10	33	1	153	32	10	24	2	17	7	10	5	15	39	.278
Don Wakamatsu, Sea	112	93	.61	49	21	12	37	21	20	39	2	254	129	40	124	17	25	11	14	7	42	70	.375
Ned Yost, KC	127	80	.57	56	25	6	22	39	20	65	0	332	127	40	128	18	25	16	9	5	55	72	.433

2010 National League Managers

Manager	G	LUp	PL%	PH	PR	DS	Quick	Slow	LO	RCD	LS	Rel	SBA	SacA	RM	PO	#	Good	NG	Bomb	W	L	Pct
Dusty Baker, Cin	162	120	.40	250	10	40	36	41	22	140	0	502	136	91	157	13	32	22	10	9	91	71	.562
Bud Black, SD	162	135	.61	285	16	45	55	33	10	132	7	499	174	99	135	31	51	35	16	8	90	72	.556
Bruce Bochy, SF	162	126	.55	224	45	70	29	37	40	118	12	477	87	102	144	12	58	41	17	8	92	70	.568
Bobby Cox, Atl	162	109	.65	263	51	50	49	31	9	140	1	490	92	89	121	48	64	36	28	14	91	71	.562
Tony LaRussa, StL	162	147	.55	292	16	28	52	40	10	80	5	466	120	87	151	22	32	17	15	8	86	76	.531
Ken Macha, Mil	162	86	.47	226	14	22	42	55	27	102	9	495	107	52	138	5	42	27	15	11	77	85	.475
Charlie Manuel, Phi	162	94	.64	276	17	19	37	50	39	114	1	451	120	64	120	3	42	27	15	6	97	65	.599
Jerry Manuel, NYM	162	124	.67	290	19	25	39	47	32	145	5	491	174	100	169	9	55	42	13	6	79	83	.488
Brad Mills, Hou	162	128	.50	280	17	51	29	52	41	121	1	507	136	90	122	8	39	30	9	5	76	86	.469
Jim Riggleman, Was	162	131	.58	271	33	67	50	32	0	101	6	494	151	101	158	13	57	37	20	10	69	93	.426
John Russell, Pit	162	119	.60	275	13	10	48	44	8	122	0	517	123	81	124	32	40	26	14	4	57	105	.352
Joe Torre, LAD	162	127	.55	255	18	47	42	37	30	92	5	475	142	108	192	8	75	53	22	11	80	82	.494
Jim Tracy, Col	162	135	.65	257	30	41	38	40	34	128	0	513	141	64	135	11	54	34	20	10	83	79	.512
162-Game Average		119	.55	260	21	39	41	44	26	111	4	484	125	79	135	18	46	31	15	8	80	82	.494

Manager	G	LUp	PL%	PH	PR	DS	Quick	Slow	LO	RCD	LS	Rel	SBA	SacA	RM	PO	#	Good	NG	Bomb	W	L	Pct
Kirk Gibson, Ari	83	57	.64	154	7	11	25	21	8	43	1	247	69	28	62	19	19	13	6	2	34	49	.410
Fredi Gonzalez, Fla	70	31	.41	104	12	16	14	13	11	35	1	193	56	33	64	10	18	11	7	5	34	36	.486
A.J. Hinch, Ari	79	56	.53	120	7	4	12	40	21	39	1	207	58	19	51	7	19	9	10	9	31	48	.392
Lou Piniella, ChC	125	101	.53	192	10	37	31	41	32	93	3	371	68	65	103	16	33	17	16	9	51	74	.408
Mike Quade, ChC	37	32	.52	44	1	15	10	11	6	20	3	111	18	14	16	4	9	8	1	0	24	13	.649
Edwin Rodriguez, Fla	92	60	.42	152	12	20	22	23	13	72	1	288	62	37	69	9	24	17	7	3	46	46	.500

2010 Park Indices

The closing of the Humpdome in Minnesota left Tropicana Field (Tampa Bay) as the only domed stadium in baseball. The Twins began the 2010 season in a brand new park, Target Field, and it played like a pitcher's park. Home runs were down 35% in games at Target Field last year, making it the most difficult home run park in all of baseball.

In the following pages, as we did last year with the two new ballparks in New York, the historical data for the Twins' new home shows only one-year data instead of three, but three years of the old Metrodome are shown for comparison.

Park indices are calculated in a way that neutralizes the effect of a team's makeup and isolates the effects of the park. The isolation is figured by comparing what both the team and its opponents accomplished at home, and comparing that to what the same team and its opponents accomplished on the road.

To calculate the park index for home runs in a given ballpark, we take the total home runs of both the home team and its opponents at the ballpark and compare it to the total home runs of the home team and its opponents in other games. We then divide each of those totals by the at-bats in the equivalent situations, so that if there are more at-bats in either situation the index is not skewed. The result is then multiplied by 100 to yield the familiar form.

The park indices for doubles, triples, walks, strikeouts and home runs by lefties and righties are determined like home runs above—relative to at-bats. Indices of at-bats, runs, hits, errors and infield fielding errors (E-Infield) are calculated relative to games. The three batting average indices are calculated as is, since these are already relative to at-bats.

A park with an index of exactly 100 is neutral and can be said to have had no effect on that particular stat. An index above 100 means the ballpark favors that statistic. For example, if a park has a home run index of 120, it was 20% easier to hit home runs in that park then the rest of the parks in that team's league.

This year, due to the G-8 Summit in Toronto, the Blue Jays played home games in Citizens Bank Park in Philadelphia against the Phillies. As far as the park indices are concerned, those were home games for the Phillies. The games in the series during which the Marlins hosted the Mets in Puerto Rico are treated as road games for both teams.

Arizona Diamondbacks - Chase Field

	2010 Season							2008-2010						
	Home Games			Away Games				Home Games			Away Games			
	D'Backs	Opp	Total	D'Backs	Opp	Total	Index	D'Backs	Opp	Total	D'Backs	Opp	Total	Index
G	81	81	162	81	81	162		243	243	486	243	243	486	
Avg	.262	.267	.264	.238	.276	.256	103	.267	.262	.264	.236	.264	.250	106
AB	2697	2857	5554	2776	2684	5460	102	8081	8550	16631	8366	8063	16429	101
R	384	409	793	329	427	756	105	1162	1206	2368	991	1118	2109	112
H	706	763	1469	660	740	1400	105	2154	2244	4398	1975	2132	4107	107
2B	154	146	300	147	138	285	103	503	461	964	423	384	807	118
3B	25	21	46	9	11	20	226	88	56	144	38	48	86	165
HR	98	103	201	82	107	189	105	262	271	533	250	254	504	104
BB	316	234	550	273	314	587	92	898	708	1606	849	816	1665	95
SO	744	568	1312	785	502	1287	100	1934	1802	3736	2180	1655	3835	96
E	52	34	86	50	37	87	99	168	123	291	171	142	313	93
E-Infield	24	15	39	24	17	41	95	76	43	119	64	57	121	98
LHB-Avg	.280	.278	.279	.251	.256	.253	110	.282	.263	.272	.250	.266	.258	106
LHB-HR	36	47	83	45	43	88	94	90	113	203	103	95	198	102
RHB-Avg	.245	.258	.252	.225	.291	.259	97	.254	.262	.258	.225	.263	.244	106
RHB-HR	62	56	118	37	64	101	113	172	158	330	147	159	306	106

Atlanta Braves - Turner Field

	2010 Season							2008-2010						
	Home Games			Away Games				Home Games			Away Games			
	Braves	Opp	Total	Braves	Opp	Total	Index	Braves	Opp	Total	Braves	Opp	Total	Index
G	81	81	162	81	81	162		243	243	486	243	243	486	
Avg	.270	.237	.253	.247	.255	.251	101	.268	.248	.258	.260	.260	.260	99
AB	2664	2739	5403	2799	2657	5456	99	8156	8404	16560	8450	7979	16429	101
R	391	295	686	347	334	681	101	1107	1018	2125	1119	1030	2149	99
H	719	648	1367	692	678	1370	100	2189	2086	4275	2195	2078	4273	100
2B	148	129	277	164	133	297	94	433	442	875	495	440	935	93
3B	19	8	27	6	24	30	91	48	56	104	30	67	97	106
HR	74	60	134	65	66	131	103	205	197	402	213	204	417	96
BB	300	245	545	334	260	594	93	931	831	1762	923	790	1713	102
SO	534	666	1200	606	575	1181	103	1565	1887	3452	1662	1662	3324	103
E	61	53	114	65	50	115	99	178	155	333	151	140	291	114
E-Infield	30	24	54	23	21	44	123	89	71	160	58	59	117	137
LHB-Avg	.265	.241	.253	.247	.269	.258	98	.264	.250	.257	.267	.268	.268	96
LHB-HR	42	21	63	33	30	63	99	123	80	203	121	91	212	95
RHB-Avg	.274	.233	.253	.247	.245	.246	103	.273	.247	.259	.252	.254	.253	102
RHB-HR	32	39	71	32	36	68	107	82	117	199	92	113	205	96

Baltimore Orioles - Oriole Park at Camden Yards

	2010 Season							2008-2010						
	Home Games			Away Games				Home Games			Away Games			
	Orioles	Opp	Total	Orioles	Opp	Total	Index	Orioles	Opp	Total	Orioles	Opp	Total	Index
G	81	81	162	81	81	162		242	242	484	243	243	486	
Avg	.269	.271	.270	.250	.269	.259	104	.277	.279	.278	.253	.277	.265	105
AB	2750	2913	5663	2804	2679	5483	103	8263	8696	16959	8468	8123	16591	103
R	322	414	736	291	371	662	111	1131	1269	2400	1005	1261	2266	106
H	740	788	1528	700	720	1420	108	2292	2425	4717	2142	2254	4396	108
2B	137	145	282	127	153	280	98	447	460	907	446	473	919	97
3B	7	15	22	14	17	31	69	28	37	65	42	46	88	72
HR	72	106	178	61	80	141	122	264	323	587	201	265	466	123
BB	215	259	474	209	261	470	98	732	843	1575	742	910	1652	93
SO	498	544	1042	558	463	1021	99	1436	1497	2933	1623	1365	2988	96
E	52	43	95	53	54	107	89	143	116	259	152	165	317	82
E-Infield	29	19	48	24	19	43	112	68	49	117	60	74	134	88
LHB-Avg	.281	.277	.279	.257	.285	.270	103	.283	.275	.279	.264	.286	.274	102
LHB-HR	40	47	87	26	35	61	136	138	146	284	106	110	216	126
RHB-Avg	.257	.265	.261	.243	.256	.249	105	.271	.282	.277	.242	.271	.257	108
RHB-HR	32	59	91	35	45	80	112	126	177	303	95	155	250	121

Boston Red Sox - Fenway Park

	2010 Season							2008-2010						
	Home Games			Away Games				Home Games			Away Games			
	Red Sox	Opp	Total	Red Sox	Opp	Total	Index	Red Sox	Opp	Total	Red Sox	Opp	Total	Index
G	81	81	162	81	81	162		243	243	486	243	243	486	
Avg	.275	.254	.264	.261	.251	.256	103	.283	.257	.270	.262	.256	.259	104
AB	2756	2837	5593	2890	2710	5600	100	8137	8451	16588	8648	8175	16823	99
R	419	393	812	399	351	750	108	1361	1081	2442	1174	1093	2267	108
H	757	722	1479	754	680	1434	103	2306	2170	4476	2265	2095	4360	103
2B	189	177	366	169	131	300	122	598	536	1134	448	373	821	140
3B	7	10	17	15	15	30	57	37	33	70	43	38	81	88
HR	98	71	169	113	81	194	87	291	211	502	305	255	560	91
BB	301	288	589	286	292	578	102	961	810	1771	931	848	1779	101
SO	558	604	1162	582	603	1185	98	1587	1797	3384	1741	1825	3566	96
E	62	48	110	49	37	86	128	147	153	300	131	139	270	111
E-Infield	21	21	42	19	18	37	114	56	63	119	55	58	113	105
LHB-Avg	.255	.257	.256	.240	.270	.256	100	.270	.263	.266	.245	.262	.254	105
LHB-HR	42	28	70	43	43	86	86	113	91	204	118	121	239	88
RHB-Avg	.288	.252	.271	.275	.232	.256	106	.294	.252	.273	.275	.251	.264	103
RHB-HR	56	43	99	70	38	108	88	178	120	298	187	134	321	93

Chicago Cubs - Wrigley Field

	2010 Season							2008-2010						
	Home Games			Away Games				Home Games			Away Games			
	Cubs	Opp	Total	Cubs	Opp	Total	Index	Cubs	Opp	Total	Cubs	Opp	Total	Index
G	81	81	162	81	81	162		242	242	484	242	242	484	
Avg	.265	.266	.266	.248	.243	.246	108	.273	.251	.262	.253	.244	.249	105
AB	2722	2880	5602	2790	2642	5432	103	8087	8435	16522	8499	7984	16483	100
R	352	431	783	333	336	669	117	1194	1114	2308	1053	996	2049	113
H	721	767	1488	693	642	1335	111	2211	2120	4331	2153	1947	4100	106
2B	159	132	291	139	131	270	105	459	404	863	461	375	836	103
3B	15	18	33	12	14	26	123	37	50	87	40	55	95	91
HR	74	87	161	75	67	142	110	262	245	507	232	229	461	110
BB	235	312	547	244	293	537	99	859	862	1721	848	877	1725	100
SO	576	666	1242	660	602	1262	95	1673	1986	3659	1934	1818	3752	97
E	67	57	124	59	46	105	118	173	142	315	157	143	300	105
E-Infield	31	24	55	25	18	43	128	79	63	142	65	57	122	116
LHB-Avg	.253	.266	.260	.218	.244	.233	112	.249	.256	.253	.232	.249	.241	105
LHB-HR	17	27	44	22	27	49	95	69	101	170	70	70	140	120
RHB-Avg	.269	.266	.268	.261	.242	.252	100	.264	.248	.267	.264	.241	.253	105
RHB-HR	57	60	117	53	40	93	117	193	144	337	162	150	312	105

Chicago White Sox - U.S. Cellular Field

	2010 Season							2008-2010						
	Home Games			Away Games				Home Games			Away Games			
	White Sox	Opp	Total	White Sox	Opp	Total	Index	White Sox	Opp	Total	White Sox	Opp	Total	Index
G	81	81	162	81	81	162		244	244	488	243	243	486	
Avg	.272	.264	.268	.263	.264	.263	102	.265	.254	.260	.260	.269	.265	98
AB	2669	2827	5496	2815	2754	5569	99	8089	8538	16627	8411	8197	16608	100
R	403	371	774	349	333	682	113	1242	1101	2343	1045	1064	2109	111
H	727	745	1472	740	726	1466	100	2147	2172	4319	2188	2208	4396	98
2B	130	160	290	133	125	258	114	383	456	839	422	434	856	98
3B	10	8	18	11	12	23	79	21	32	53	33	42	75	71
HR	111	79	190	66	57	123	157	357	251	608	239	210	449	135
BB	260	256	516	207	234	441	119	817	776	1593	724	681	1405	113
SO	448	605	1053	474	544	1018	105	1431	1858	3289	1529	1557	3086	106
E	48	49	97	55	60	115	84	161	151	312	163	130	293	106
E-Infield	16	20	36	22	26	48	75	71	60	131	65	46	111	118
LHB-Avg	.265	.273	.269	.270	.257	.263	102	.267	.260	.263	.266	.265	.266	99
LHB-HR	14	25	39	10	29	39	104	89	101	190	60	100	160	117
RHB-Avg	.277	.256	.267	.259	.269	.263	101	.264	.251	.258	.257	.272	.264	98
RHB-HR	97	54	151	56	28	84	179	268	150	418	179	110	289	145

Cincinnati Reds - Great American Ballpark

| | 2010 Season | | | | | | | 2008-2010 | | | | | | |
| | Home Games | | | Away Games | | | | Home Games | | | Away Games | | | |
	Reds	Opp	Total	Reds	Opp	Total	Index	Reds	Opp	Total	Reds	Opp	Total	Index
G	81	81	162	81	81	162		243	243	486	243	243	486	
Avg	.278	.255	.266	.265	.254	.260	102	.261	.260	.261	.250	.265	.257	101
AB	2720	2828	5548	2859	2697	5556	100	8059	8478	16537	8447	8161	16608	100
R	399	341	740	391	344	735	101	1105	1101	2206	1062	1107	2169	102
H	756	720	1476	759	684	1443	102	2104	2207	4311	2111	2159	4270	101
2B	144	131	275	149	145	294	94	411	441	852	431	430	861	99
3B	14	10	24	16	8	24	100	41	35	76	38	35	73	105
HR	102	82	184	86	76	162	114	299	286	585	234	261	495	119
BB	252	275	527	270	249	519	102	824	829	1653	789	829	1618	103
SO	582	604	1186	636	526	1162	102	1682	1817	3499	1790	1609	3399	103
E	27	52	79	45	55	100	79	109	147	256	166	146	312	82
E-Infield	13	20	33	15	19	34	97	40	58	98	58	58	116	84
LHB-Avg	.275	.258	.264	.311	.252	.276	96	.262	.263	.263	.269	.259	.264	100
LHB-HR	39	34	73	31	35	66	103	132	124	256	122	104	226	111
RHB-Avg	.279	.252	.267	.251	.255	.252	106	.261	.258	.259	.240	.268	.253	102
RHB-HR	63	48	111	55	41	96	120	167	162	329	112	157	269	125

Cleveland Indians - Progressive Field

| | 2010 Season | | | | | | | 2008-2010 | | | | | | |
| | Home Games | | | Away Games | | | | Home Games | | | Away Games | | | |
	Indians	Opp	Total	Indians	Opp	Total	Index	Indians	Opp	Total	Indians	Opp	Total	Index
G	81	81	162	81	81	162		243	243	486	243	243	486	
Avg	.249	.258	.254	.248	.280	.263	96	.259	.268	.263	.258	.280	.269	98
AB	2688	2810	5498	2799	2684	5483	100	8126	8543	16669	8472	8162	16634	100
R	326	354	680	320	398	718	95	1110	1098	2208	1114	1280	2394	92
H	669	726	1395	693	751	1444	97	2101	2289	4390	2184	2288	4472	98
2B	146	165	311	144	142	286	108	461	481	942	482	427	909	103
3B	13	13	26	7	16	23	113	31	31	62	39	46	85	73
HR	64	70	134	64	77	141	95	219	207	426	241	293	534	80
BB	285	268	553	260	304	564	98	881	792	1673	806	822	1628	103
SO	589	486	1075	595	481	1076	100	1741	1537	3278	1867	1402	3269	100
E	57	60	117	53	35	88	133	151	169	320	150	132	282	113
E-Infield	29	28	57	26	15	41	139	80	69	149	71	48	119	125
LHB-Avg	.263	.264	.264	.264	.277	.270	98	.269	.269	.269	.263	.286	.274	98
LHB-HR	28	42	70	34	25	59	116	104	100	204	109	119	228	89
RHB-Avg	.235	.253	.244	.232	.283	.257	95	.250	.267	.259	.254	.276	.265	98
RHB-HR	36	28	64	30	52	82	79	115	107	222	132	174	306	73

Colorado Rockies - Coors Field

| | 2010 Season | | | | | | | 2008-2010 | | | | | | |
| | Home Games | | | Away Games | | | | Home Games | | | Away Games | | | |
	Rockies	Opp	Total	Rockies	Opp	Total	Index	Rockies	Opp	Total	Rockies	Opp	Total	Index
G	81	81	162	81	81	162		243	243	486	243	243	486	
Avg	.298	.263	.280	.226	.251	.239	118	.288	.270	.278	.237	.260	.248	112
AB	2775	2826	5601	2755	2633	5388	104	8192	8574	16766	8293	7966	16259	103
R	479	379	858	291	338	629	136	1354	1178	2532	967	1076	2043	124
H	828	743	1571	624	662	1286	122	2356	2311	4667	1966	2068	4034	116
2B	153	161	314	117	128	245	123	486	477	963	394	418	812	115
3B	38	14	52	16	15	31	161	91	66	157	41	56	97	157
HR	108	79	187	65	60	125	144	298	235	533	225	193	418	124
BB	299	232	531	286	293	579	88	926	761	1687	889	854	1743	94
SO	587	634	1221	687	600	1287	91	1681	1749	3430	2079	1680	3759	88
E	39	49	88	62	45	107	82	133	166	299	151	151	302	99
E-Infield	17	15	32	22	21	43	74	52	61	113	63	67	130	87
LHB-Avg	.305	.272	.291	.234	.247	.240	121	.287	.277	.282	.243	.262	.252	112
LHB-HR	63	27	90	34	21	55	166	140	90	230	104	75	179	128
RHB-Avg	.292	.258	.272	.219	.254	.238	115	.288	.265	.276	.233	.258	.245	112
RHB-HR	45	52	97	31	39	70	128	158	145	303	121	118	239	121

Detroit Tigers - Comerica Park

	2010 Season							2008-2010						
	Home Games			Away Games			Index	Home Games			Away Games			Index
	Tigers	Opp	Total	Tigers	Opp	Total		Tigers	Opp	Total	Tigers	Opp	Total	
G	81	81	162	81	81	162		243	243	486	244	244	488	
Avg	.282	.252	.267	.255	.274	.264	101	.280	.259	.269	.254	.275	.264	102
AB	2782	2843	5625	2861	2662	5523	102	8243	8469	16712	8581	8167	16748	100
R	411	329	740	340	414	754	98	1249	1110	2359	1066	1235	2301	103
H	785	716	1501	730	729	1459	103	2306	2193	4499	2181	2242	4423	102
2B	159	112	271	149	131	280	95	427	403	830	419	445	864	96
3B	17	21	38	15	22	37	101	59	52	111	49	55	104	107
HR	70	71	141	82	71	153	90	274	248	522	261	248	509	103
BB	275	246	521	271	291	562	91	824	836	1660	834	939	1773	94
SO	507	540	1047	640	516	1156	89	1509	1626	3135	1828	1523	3351	94
E	63	65	128	46	49	95	135	156	173	329	154	121	275	120
E-Infield	21	23	44	19	23	42	105	56	67	123	61	53	114	108
LHB-Avg	.274	.245	.257	.246	.264	.256	101	.266	.256	.260	.249	.276	.265	98
LHB-HR	28	33	61	18	43	61	94	85	107	192	73	123	196	98
RHB-Avg	.287	.259	.274	.261	.282	.270	102	.287	.262	.276	.257	.273	.264	105
RHB-HR	42	38	80	64	28	92	88	189	141	330	188	125	313	106

Florida Marlins - Sun Life Stadium

	2010 Season							2008-2010						
	Home Games			Away Games			Index	Home Games			Away Games			Index
	Marlins	Opp	Total	Marlins	Opp	Total		Marlins	Opp	Total	Marlins	Opp	Total	
G	78	78	156	84	84	168		240	240	480	245	245	490	
Avg	.247	.255	.251	.259	.266	.262	96	.256	.258	.257	.261	.260	.260	99
AB	2503	2720	6020	2928	2774	5702	101	8022	8434	16456	8580	8104	16684	101
R	343	353	696	376	364	740	101	1105	1104	2209	1156	1086	2242	103
H	644	696	1340	759	737	1496	96	2055	2176	4231	2238	2103	4341	99
2B	139	146	285	155	136	291	105	415	450	865	477	384	861	102
3B	18	16	34	19	19	38	96	52	40	92	38	64	102	91
HR	64	58	122	88	76	164	80	244	217	461	275	238	513	91
BB	278	289	567	236	260	496	122	857	908	1765	768	828	1596	112
SO	711	638	1349	664	530	1194	121	2039	1938	3977	1933	1605	3538	114
E	62	49	111	61	60	121	99	190	153	343	156	149	305	115
E-Infield	19	22	41	25	25	50	88	64	52	116	65	64	129	92
LHB-Avg	.228	.253	.245	.255	.257	.256	96	.249	.261	.256	.256	.253	.255	101
LHB-HR	5	24	29	3	29	32	92	50	101	151	67	95	162	91
RHB-Avg	.252	.257	.254	.260	.273	.265	96	.260	.256	.258	.263	.264	.264	98
RHB-HR	59	34	90	85	47	132	77	194	116	310	208	143	351	92

Houston Astros - Minute Maid Park

	2010 Season							2008-2010						
	Home Games			Away Games			Index	Home Games			Away Games			Index
	Astros	Opp	Total	Astros	Opp	Total		Astros	Opp	Total	Astros	Opp	Total	
G	81	81	162	81	81	162		240	240	480	245	245	490	
Avg	.248	.244	.246	.247	.279	.263	94	.265	.259	.262	.249	.275	.262	100
AB	2673	2786	5459	2779	2754	5533	99	7923	8356	16279	8416	8203	16619	100
R	297	324	621	314	405	719	86	997	1029	2026	969	1213	2182	95
H	662	679	1341	686	767	1453	92	2096	2166	4262	2099	2254	4353	100
2B	120	143	263	132	146	278	96	393	445	838	413	458	871	98
3B	16	19	35	9	18	27	131	48	48	96	31	60	91	108
HR	63	66	129	45	74	119	110	233	250	483	184	263	447	110
BB	199	281	480	216	267	483	101	651	779	1430	661	807	1468	99
SO	500	654	1154	525	556	1081	108	1457	1837	3294	1609	1612	3221	104
E	50	61	111	53	45	98	113	118	142	260	130	130	260	102
E-Infield	19	29	48	29	19	48	100	53	67	120	65	61	126	97
LHB-Avg	.243	.262	.254	.233	.246	.240	106	.261	.272	.267	.246	.263	.255	105
LHB-HR	13	30	43	8	24	32	127	59	99	158	53	98	151	104
RHB-Avg	.250	.232	.241	.252	.298	.273	88	.266	.251	.259	.251	.283	.266	97
RHB-HR	50	36	86	37	50	87	104	174	151	325	131	165	296	114

Kansas City Royals - Kauffman Stadium

	2010 Season							2008-2010						
	Home Games			Away Games				Home Games			Away Games			
	Royals	Opp	Total	Royals	Opp	Total	Index	Royals	Opp	Total	Royals	Opp	Total	Index
G	81	81	162	81	81	162		243	243	486	243	243	486	
Avg	.280	.275	.277	.267	.277	.272	102	.277	.272	.274	.258	.267	.262	105
AB	2757	2923	5680	2847	2709	5556	102	8247	8638	16885	8497	8100	16597	102
R	360	403	763	316	442	758	101	1065	1212	2277	988	1256	2244	101
H	773	803	1576	761	750	1511	104	2285	2347	4632	2188	2165	4353	106
2B	139	165	304	140	156	296	100	440	469	909	418	407	825	108
3B	25	14	39	6	9	15	254	67	56	123	43	46	89	136
HR	60	82	142	61	94	155	90	175	224	399	210	277	487	81
BB	229	254	483	242	297	539	88	684	794	1478	636	872	1508	96
SO	445	539	984	460	496	956	101	1384	1638	3022	1617	1635	3252	91
E	59	47	106	62	42	104	102	168	138	306	165	130	295	104
E-Infield	32	23	55	24	22	46	120	82	59	141	63	57	120	118
LHB-Avg	.284	.274	.279	.261	.280	.270	103	.280	.275	.277	.253	.266	.260	107
LHB-HR	23	37	60	31	39	70	85	74	91	165	96	131	227	72
RHB-Avg	.277	.275	.276	.273	.274	.274	101	.274	.269	.272	.261	.268	.265	103
RHB-HR	37	45	82	30	55	85	93	101	133	234	114	146	260	87

Los Angeles Angels - Angel Stadium of Anaheim

	2010 Season							2008-2010						
	Home Games			Away Games				Home Games			Away Games			
	Angels	Opp	Total	Angels	Opp	Total	Index	Angels	Opp	Total	Angels	Opp	Total	Index
G	81	81	162	81	81	162		243	243	486	243	243	486	
Avg	.247	.243	.245	.250	.270	.260	94	.271	.259	.265	.264	.268	.266	99
AB	2680	2852	5532	2808	2704	5512	100	8112	8539	16651	8538	8150	16688	100
R	319	322	641	362	380	742	86	1146	1062	2208	1183	1098	2281	97
H	662	692	1354	701	730	1431	95	2197	2208	4405	2256	2182	4438	99
2B	131	135	266	145	178	323	82	409	413	822	434	470	904	91
3B	6	10	16	13	21	34	47	30	32	62	47	52	99	63
HR	69	68	137	86	80	166	82	231	254	485	256	234	490	99
BB	232	276	508	234	289	523	97	716	739	1455	778	806	1584	92
SO	525	600	1125	545	530	1075	104	1468	1688	3156	1643	1610	3253	97
E	60	52	112	53	55	108	104	145	162	307	144	178	322	95
E-Infield	22	20	42	21	23	44	95	53	58	111	57	75	132	84
LHB-Avg	.263	.236	.248	.253	.273	.263	94	.288	.257	.271	.267	.277	.272	100
LHB-HR	29	24	53	31	34	65	82	87	108	195	85	120	205	95
RHB-Avg	.238	.248	.243	.248	.268	.257	94	.260	.260	.260	.263	.260	.261	99
RHB-HR	40	44	84	55	46	101	83	144	146	290	171	114	285	102

Los Angeles Dodgers - Dodger Stadium

	2010 Season							2008-2010						
	Home Games			Away Games				Home Games			Away Games			
	Dodgers	Opp	Total	Dodgers	Opp	Total	Index	Dodgers	Opp	Total	Dodgers	Opp	Total	Index
G	81	81	162	81	81	162		243	243	486	243	243	486	
Avg	.258	.234	.246	.246	.254	.250	98	.263	.231	.247	.262	.256	.259	95
AB	2650	2778	5428	2776	2644	5420	100	8035	8312	16347	8489	8030	16519	99
R	322	336	658	345	356	701	94	1038	878	1916	1109	1073	2182	88
H	684	651	1335	684	672	1356	98	2114	1917	4031	2220	2052	4272	94
2B	132	118	250	138	124	262	95	389	372	761	430	384	814	94
3B	10	7	17	19	33	52	33	37	23	60	60	75	135	45
HR	61	67	128	59	67	126	101	202	173	375	200	211	411	92
BB	271	270	541	262	269	531	102	799	746	1545	884	857	1741	90
SO	554	665	1219	630	609	1239	98	1574	1991	3565	1710	1760	3470	104
E	41	50	91	57	65	122	75	122	165	287	160	169	329	87
E-Infield	12	18	30	27	28	55	55	46	65	111	68	71	139	80
LHB-Avg	.265	.226	.245	.260	.259	.260	94	.270	.233	.252	.269	.262	.265	95
LHB-HR	26	22	48	21	31	52	90	77	72	149	73	75	148	101
RHB-Avg	.253	.240	.246	.237	.251	.244	101	.258	.229	.243	.256	.251	.254	96
RHB-HR	35	45	80	38	36	74	110	125	101	226	127	136	263	87

Milwaukee Brewers - Miller Park

| | 2010 Season | | | | | | | 2008-2010 | | | | | | |
| | Home Games | | | Away Games | | | | Home Games | | | Away Games | | | |
	Brewers	Opp	Total	Brewers	Opp	Total	Index	Brewers	Opp	Total	Brewers	Opp	Total	Index
G	81	81	162	81	81	162		243	243	486	243	243	486	
Avg	.259	.267	.263	.265	.267	.266	99	.256	.259	.257	.262	.269	.265	97
AB	2724	2881	5605	2882	2693	5575	101	8078	8534	16612	8573	8154	16727	99
R	365	414	779	385	390	775	101	1103	1128	2231	1182	1183	2365	94
H	706	768	1474	765	719	1484	99	2066	2209	4275	2250	2191	4441	96
2B	140	170	310	153	159	312	99	430	467	897	468	455	923	98
3B	13	8	21	20	15	35	60	53	37	90	52	40	92	99
HR	100	96	196	82	77	159	123	300	273	573	262	282	544	106
BB	280	293	573	266	289	555	103	877	875	1752	829	842	1671	106
SO	584	670	1254	632	588	1220	102	1796	1881	3677	1854	1591	3445	107
E	54	48	102	47	55	102	100	148	143	291	152	158	310	94
E-Infield	26	18	44	16	26	42	105	70	51	121	64	75	139	87
LHB-Avg	.244	.263	.254	.253	.276	.265	96	.259	.264	.262	.257	.268	.263	100
LHB-HR	29	43	72	27	28	55	128	94	135	229	75	103	178	126
RHB-Avg	.266	.269	.267	.271	.262	.267	100	.255	.255	.255	.265	.269	.267	96
RHB-HR	71	53	124	55	49	104	120	206	138	344	187	179	366	96

Minnesota Twins - Target Field

| | 2010 Season | | | | | | | 2007-2009 | | | | | | |
| | Home Games | | | Away Games | | | | Home Games | | | Away Games | | | |
	Twins	Opp	Total	Twins	Opp	Total	Index	Twins	Opp	Total	Twins	Opp	Total	Index
G	81	81	162	81	81	162		244	244	488	244	244	488	
Avg	.282	.263	.272	.265	.270	267	102	.277	.261	.269	.269	.283	.276	97
AB	2583	2942	5525	2885	2761	5646	98	8194	8678	16872	8577	8288	16865	100
R	399	313	712	382	358	740	90	1190	1045	2235	1174	1190	2364	95
H	756	748	1504	765	745	1510	100	2267	2266	4533	2304	2349	4653	97
2B	166	161	327	152	146	298	112	417	435	852	425	447	872	98
3B	27	14	41	14	21	35	120	70	37	107	55	44	99	108
HR	52	64	116	90	91	181	65	200	257	457	201	296	497	92
BB	296	189	485	263	194	457	108	796	610	1406	830	682	1512	93
SO	425	530	955	542	518	1060	92	1334	1671	3005	1505	1470	2975	101
E	41	44	85	37	53	90	94	122	148	270	157	179	336	80
E-Infield	16	18	34	8	23	31	110	44	53	97	57	69	126	77
LHB-Avg	.288	.269	.279	.269	.260	.265	105	.284	.264	.274	.282	.293	.287	96
LHB-HR	30	23	53	50	33	83	65	112	103	215	113	123	236	93
RHB-Avg	.275	.259	.266	.260	.277	.270	99	.269	.259	.264	.261	.276	.266	99
RHB-HR	22	41	63	40	58	98	66	88	154	242	88	173	261	91

New York Mets - Citi Field

| | 2010 Season | | | | | | | 2009-2010 | | | | | | |
| | Home Games | | | Away Games | | | | Home Games | | | Away Games | | | |
	Mets	Opp	Total	Mets	Opp	Total	Index	Mets	Opp	Total	Mets	Opp	Total	Index
G	81	81	162	81	81	162		162	162	324	162	162	324	
Avg	.255	.243	.249	.243	.276	.259	96	.265	.246	.255	.254	.279	.266	96
AB	2648	2777	5425	2817	2760	5577	97	5312	5585	10897	5606	5443	11049	99
R	334	282	616	322	370	692	89	677	632	1309	650	777	1427	92
H	676	676	1352	685	762	1447	93	1407	1373	2780	1426	1517	2943	94
2B	125	130	255	141	152	293	89	269	282	551	292	311	603	93
3B	25	13	38	15	14	29	135	57	23	80	32	32	64	127
HR	63	47	110	65	88	153	74	112	128	240	111	165	276	88
BB	263	285	548	239	260	499	113	523	579	1102	505	582	1087	103
SO	498	568	1066	597	538	1135	97	956	1132	2088	1067	1005	2072	102
E	48	53	101	39	57	96	105	89	100	189	95	112	207	91
E-Infield	19	22	41	17	26	43	95	39	40	79	42	50	92	86
LHB-Avg	.258	.241	.251	.251	.259	.254	99	.265	.237	.253	.261	.274	.266	95
LHB-HR	28	21	49	25	31	56	91	46	56	102	42	69	111	95
RHB-Avg	.252	.245	.248	.236	.285	.264	94	.265	.252	.257	.248	.282	.266	97
RHB-HR	35	26	61	40	57	97	64	66	72	138	69	96	165	83

New York Yankees - Yankee Stadium

| | 2010 Season | | | | | | | 2009-2010 | | | | | | |
| | Home Games | | | Away Games | | | | Home Games | | | Away Games | | | |
	Yankees	Opp	Total	Yankees	Opp	Total	Index	Yankees	Opp	Total	Yankees	Opp	Total	Index
G	81	81	162	81	81	162		162	162	324	162	162	324	
Avg	.279	.249	.264	.256	.250	.253	104	.281	.249	.265	.269	.251	.261	102
AB	2710	2762	5472	2857	2649	5506	99	5474	5599	11073	5753	5335	11088	100
R	473	366	839	386	327	713	118	933	725	1658	841	721	1562	106
H	755	688	1443	730	661	1391	104	1540	1394	2934	1549	1341	2890	102
2B	146	122	268	129	124	253	107	296	240	536	304	280	584	92
3B	16	3	19	16	11	27	71	21	13	34	32	25	57	60
HR	115	108	223	86	71	157	143	251	209	460	194	151	345	134
BB	318	269	587	344	271	615	96	666	570	1236	659	544	1203	103
SO	544	581	1125	592	573	1165	97	1027	1230	2257	1123	1184	2307	98
E	35	49	84	34	47	81	104	70	102	172	85	91	176	98
E-Infield	15	23	38	8	18	26	146	25	43	68	30	40	70	97
LHB-Avg	.280	.257	.270	.256	.249	.253	107	.285	.247	.269	.267	.254	.261	103
LHB-HR	78	56	134	46	31	77	170	168	98	266	120	65	185	141
RHB-Avg	.277	.243	.258	.255	.250	.253	102	.276	.250	.261	.272	.250	.260	100
RHB-HR	37	52	89	40	40	80	116	83	111	194	74	86	160	124

Oakland Athletics - McAfee Coliseum

| | 2010 Season | | | | | | | 2008-2010 | | | | | | |
| | Home Games | | | Away Games | | | | Home Games | | | Away Games | | | |
	Athletics	Opp	Total	Athletics	Opp	Total	Index	Athletics	Opp	Total	Athletics	Opp	Total	Index
G	81	81	162	81	81	162		241	241	482	244	244	488	
Avg	.261	.225	.243	.252	.264	.258	94	.254	.242	.248	.253	.267	.260	96
AB	2650	2711	5361	2798	2667	5465	98	7979	8244	16223	8504	8134	16638	99
R	354	276	630	309	350	659	96	1072	934	2006	996	1143	2139	95
H	691	610	1301	705	705	1410	92	2030	1995	4025	2148	2170	4318	94
2B	139	102	241	137	130	267	92	424	371	795	429	450	879	93
3B	19	9	28	11	8	19	150	40	33	73	34	43	77	97
HR	46	62	108	63	91	154	71	176	197	373	193	247	440	87
BB	271	245	516	256	267	523	101	824	763	1587	804	848	1652	99
SO	516	564	1080	545	506	1051	105	1603	1675	3278	1730	1580	3310	102
E	51	60	111	48	64	112	99	145	165	310	157	142	299	105
E-Infield	16	20	36	19	25	44	82	53	60	113	51	54	105	109
LHB-Avg	.257	.225	.242	.253	.284	.266	91	.250	.245	.248	.248	.280	.262	95
LHB-HR	16	18	34	28	39	67	50	87	87	174	97	99	196	88
RHB-Avg	.264	.225	.243	.251	.253	.252	96	.258	.240	.248	.256	.259	.258	96
RHB-HR	30	44	74	35	52	87	89	89	110	199	96	148	244	86

Philadelphia Phillies - Citizens Bank Park

| | 2010 Season | | | | | | | 2008-2010 | | | | | | |
| | Home Games | | | Away Games | | | | Home Games | | | Away Games | | | |
	Phillies	Opp	Total	Phillies	Opp	Total	Index	Phillies	Opp	Total	Phillies	Opp	Total	Index
G	84	84	168	78	78	156		246	246	492	240	240	480	
Avg	.264	.246	.255	.256	.262	.259	98	.263	.257	.260	.253	.262	.257	101
AB	2831	2919	5750	2750	2606	5356	100	8247	8647	16894	8421	8032	16453	100
R	410	319	729	362	321	683	99	1230	1024	2254	1161	1005	2166	102
H	747	718	1465	704	684	1388	98	2167	2221	4388	2130	2104	4234	101
2B	148	147	295	142	136	278	99	446	452	898	447	433	880	99
3B	19	9	28	15	15	30	87	56	26	82	49	47	96	83
HR	94	89	183	72	79	151	113	311	268	579	293	249	542	104
BB	282	211	493	278	205	483	95	885	709	1594	850	729	1579	98
SO	495	645	1140	569	538	1107	96	1597	1810	3407	1739	1607	3346	99
E	42	44	86	41	52	93	86	119	147	266	130	149	279	93
E-Infield	20	17	37	20	21	41	84	58	59	117	65	56	121	94
LHB-Avg	.261	.250	.256	.241	.268	.253	101	.267	.263	.265	.255	.261	.258	103
LHB-HR	60	33	93	36	39	75	118	183	102	285	173	99	272	103
RHB-Avg	.266	.243	.254	.271	.259	.264	96	.259	.253	.256	.251	.262	.257	99
RHB-HR	34	56	90	36	40	76	108	128	166	294	120	150	270	105

Pittsburgh Pirates - PNC Park

| | 2010 Season | | | | | | | 2008-2010 | | | | | | |
| | Home Games | | | Away Games | | | | Home Games | | | Away Games | | | |
	Pirates	Opp	Total	Pirates	Opp	Total	Index	Pirates	Opp	Total	Pirates	Opp	Total	Index
G	81	81	162	81	81	162		243	243	486	242	242	484	
Avg	.254	.268	.261	.231	.296	.263	99	.262	.272	.267	.240	.292	.265	101
AB	2629	2825	5454	2757	2736	5493	99	8117	8577	16694	8314	8084	16398	101
R	333	403	736	254	463	717	103	1054	1162	2216	904	1356	2260	98
H	667	758	1425	636	809	1445	99	2128	2331	4459	1993	2358	4351	102
2B	146	190	336	130	170	300	113	448	547	995	431	523	954	102
3B	15	20	35	12	15	27	131	49	46	95	33	69	102	91
HR	64	66	130	62	101	163	80	213	213	426	191	282	473	88
BB	230	267	497	233	271	504	99	707	875	1582	729	883	1612	96
SO	540	512	1052	667	514	1181	90	1524	1462	2986	1864	1446	3310	89
E	65	51	116	62	40	102	114	150	149	299	157	123	280	106
E-Infield	32	27	59	26	23	49	120	74	75	149	66	56	122	122
LHB-Avg	.236	.275	.253	.228	.296	.257	99	.262	.275	.268	.237	.293	.262	102
LHB-HR	40	29	69	36	40	76	94	118	79	197	96	98	194	101
RHB-Avg	.269	.265	.267	.233	.295	.267	100	.262	.270	.266	.242	.291	.268	100
RHB-HR	24	37	61	26	61	87	70	95	134	229	95	184	279	80

San Diego Padres - PETCO Park

| | 2010 Season | | | | | | | 2008-2010 | | | | | | |
| | Home Games | | | Away Games | | | | Home Games | | | Away Games | | | |
	Padres	Opp	Total	Padres	Opp	Total	Index	Padres	Opp	Total	Padres	Opp	Total	Index
G	81	81	162	81	81	162		243	243	486	243	243	486	
Avg	.242	.223	.232	.251	.256	.253	92	.233	.234	.234	.258	.273	.266	88
AB	2633	2747	5380	2801	2699	5500	98	7941	8403	16344	8486	8137	16623	98
R	322	262	584	343	319	662	88	889	915	1804	1051	1199	2250	80
H	636	613	1249	702	692	1394	90	1851	1969	3820	2192	2224	4416	87
2B	101	112	213	135	128	263	83	324	333	657	441	418	859	78
3B	14	12	26	10	10	20	133	45	36	81	37	48	85	97
HR	59	66	125	73	73	146	80	186	204	390	241	267	508	78
BB	293	266	559	245	251	496	115	907	832	1739	735	849	1584	112
SO	592	695	1207	591	600	1191	110	1809	1931	3740	1815	1651	3466	110
E	39	42	81	33	52	85	95	131	119	250	120	134	254	98
F-Infield	14	14	28	11	25	36	78	45	45	90	41	60	101	89
LHB-Avg	.236	.224	.230	.274	.236	.255	90	.235	.243	.239	.276	.272	.274	87
LHB-HR	21	19	40	42	23	65	64	73	72	145	139	107	246	59
RHB-Avg	.245	.222	.234	.236	.270	.252	93	.232	.228	.230	.245	.274	.259	89
RHB-HR	38	47	85	31	50	81	106	113	132	246	102	160	262	96

San Francisco Giants - AT&T Park

| | 2010 Season | | | | | | | 2008-2010 | | | | | | |
| | Home Games | | | Away Games | | | | Home Games | | | Away Games | | | |
	Giants	Opp	Total	Giants	Opp	Total	Index	Giants	Opp	Total	Giants	Opp	Total	Index
G	81	81	162	81	81	162		243	243	486	243	243	486	
Avg	.265	.225	.245	.250	.246	.248	99	.266	.240	.252	.252	.247	.250	101
AB	2668	2742	5410	2820	2682	5502	98	7993	8317	16310	8531	7970	16501	99
R	347	274	621	350	309	659	94	1019	967	1986	975	986	1961	101
H	706	618	1324	705	661	1366	97	2123	1992	4115	2151	1971	4122	100
2B	146	116	262	138	130	268	99	437	411	848	433	379	812	106
3B	18	14	32	12	26	38	86	67	50	117	43	55	98	121
HR	75	64	139	87	70	157	90	185	203	388	193	218	411	96
BB	238	292	530	249	286	535	101	675	867	1542	656	947	1603	97
SO	512	689	1201	587	642	1229	99	1543	1976	3519	1758	1897	3655	97
E	47	50	97	26	47	73	133	153	153	306	104	138	242	126
E-Infield	19	15	34	11	17	28	121	75	51	126	45	55	100	126
LHB-Avg	.260	.227	.243	.261	.247	.254	96	.273	.237	.255	.259	.245	.252	101
LHB-HR	28	23	51	35	31	66	78	70	62	132	74	85	159	85
RHB-Avg	.268	.224	.246	.243	.246	.245	100	.260	.241	.250	.247	.249	.248	101
RHB-HR	47	41	88	52	39	91	99	115	141	256	119	133	252	102

Seattle Mariners - Safeco Field

| | 2010 Season | | | | | | | 2008-2010 | | | | | | |
| | Home Games | | | Away Games | | | | Home Games | | | Away Games | | | |
	Mariners	Opp	Total	Mariners	Opp	Total	Index	Mariners	Opp	Total	Mariners	Opp	Total	Index
G	81	81	162	81	81	162		243	243	486	243	243	486	
Avg	.235	.238	.237	.236	.272	.253	94	.254	.250	.252	.252	.270	.261	97
AB	2642	2803	5445	2767	2703	5470	100	8138	8489	16627	8457	8100	16557	100
R	239	304	543	274	394	668	81	889	1017	1906	935	1184	2119	90
H	622	668	1290	652	734	1386	93	2069	2119	4188	2133	2186	4319	97
2B	107	142	249	120	151	271	92	389	422	811	403	481	884	91
3B	9	6	15	7	16	23	66	31	22	53	24	36	60	88
HR	35	69	104	66	88	154	68	170	225	395	215	265	480	82
BB	237	224	461	222	228	450	103	668	817	1485	629	795	1424	104
SO	598	510	1108	586	463	1049	106	1588	1619	3207	1579	1413	2992	107
E	48	50	98	62	54	116	84	133	154	287	181	152	333	86
E-Infield	23	16	39	37	24	61	64	63	58	121	91	73	164	74
LHB-Avg	.235	.240	.238	.242	.269	.254	94	.264	.249	.257	.259	.282	.270	95
LHB-HR	20	29	49	34	29	63	77	83	103	186	87	119	206	92
RHB-Avg	.236	.237	.236	.230	.274	.253	93	.247	.250	.248	.247	.261	.254	98
RHB-HR	15	40	55	32	59	91	61	87	122	209	128	146	274	75

St Louis Cardinals - Busch Stadium

| | 2010 Season | | | | | | | 2008-2010 | | | | | | |
| | Home Games | | | Away Games | | | | Home Games | | | Away Games | | | |
	Cardinals	Opp	Total	Cardinals	Opp	Total	Index	Cardinals	Opp	Total	Cardinals	Opp	Total	Index
G	81	81	162	81	81	162		243	243	486	243	243	486	
Avg	.270	.243	.256	.256	.270	.263	98	.273	.253	.263	.265	.270	.268	98
AB	2686	2780	5466	2856	2726	5582	98	8071	8417	16488	8572	8172	16744	98
R	386	280	666	350	361	711	94	1101	951	2052	1144	1055	2199	93
H	726	675	1401	730	737	1467	96	2203	2127	4330	2274	2209	4483	97
2B	142	124	266	143	142	285	95	413	425	838	449	467	916	93
3B	11	12	23	7	16	23	102	43	34	77	30	58	88	89
HR	67	55	122	83	78	161	77	212	191	403	272	228	500	82
BB	312	216	528	229	261	490	110	850	708	1558	796	725	1521	104
SO	471	564	1035	556	530	1086	97	1437	1591	3028	1616	1509	3125	98
E	53	59	112	46	49	95	118	144	148	292	136	137	273	107
E-Infield	28	23	51	20	21	41	124	65	59	124	55	58	113	110
LHB-Avg	.257	.253	.255	.269	.274	.271	94	.268	.259	.263	.267	.267	.267	98
LHB-HR	18	23	41	20	28	48	91	55	91	146	68	98	166	91
RHB-Avg	.277	.236	.257	.249	.268	.258	100	.276	.248	.262	.264	.273	.268	98
RHB-HR	49	32	81	63	50	113	72	157	100	257	204	130	334	77

Tampa Bay Rays - Tropicana Field Surface: FieldTurf

| | 2010 Season | | | | | | | 2008-2010 | | | | | | |
| | Home Games | | | Away Games | | | | Home Games | | | Away Games | | | |
	Rays	Opp	Total	Rays	Opp	Total	Index	Rays	Opp	Total	Rays	Opp	Total	Index
G	81	81	162	81	81	162		240	240	480	246	246	492	
Avg	.243	.232	.237	.251	.256	.253	94	.263	.237	.250	.251	.261	.256	98
AB	2607	2779	5386	2832	2737	5569	97	7832	8226	16058	8610	8307	16917	97
R	351	294	645	451	355	806	80	1167	935	2102	1212	1139	2351	92
H	633	646	1279	710	701	1411	91	2059	1950	4009	2161	2167	4328	95
2B	124	140	264	171	146	317	86	404	407	811	472	455	927	92
3B	19	22	41	18	12	30	141	60	52	112	50	38	88	134
HR	78	84	162	82	91	173	97	268	233	501	271	291	562	94
BB	330	234	564	342	244	586	100	958	740	1698	982	779	1761	102
SO	613	626	1239	679	563	1242	103	1781	1788	3569	1964	1669	3633	103
E	29	44	73	56	71	127	57	124	137	261	149	178	327	82
E-Infield	11	17	28	22	29	51	55	45	53	98	57	81	138	73
LHB-Avg	.232	.229	.231	.257	.267	.262	88	.262	.236	.250	.249	.262	.255	98
LHB-HR	46	34	80	43	46	89	95	149	92	241	147	131	278	92
RHB-Avg	.254	.235	.244	.244	.246	.245	99	.264	.238	.249	.254	.260	.257	97
RHB-HR	32	50	82	39	45	84	99	119	141	260	124	160	284	96

Texas Rangers - Rangers Ballpark in Arlington

| | 2010 Season | | | | | | | 2008-2010 | | | | | | |
| | Home Games | | | Away Games | | | | Home Games | | | Away Games | | | |
	Rangers	Opp	Total	Rangers	Opp	Total	Index	Rangers	Opp	Total	Rangers	Opp	Total	Index
G	81	81	162	81	81	162		243	243	486	243	243	486	
Avg	.288	.247	.267	.265	.244	.255	105	.286	.266	.276	.260	.263	.262	106
AB	2770	2846	5616	2865	2671	5536	101	8297	8605	16902	8592	8142	16734	101
R	430	339	769	357	348	705	109	1341	1217	2558	1131	1177	2308	111
H	798	704	1502	758	651	1409	107	2375	2292	4667	2236	2142	4378	107
2B	136	141	277	132	128	260	105	478	477	955	462	440	902	105
3B	13	7	20	12	14	26	76	55	46	101	32	38	70	143
HR	93	81	174	69	81	150	114	322	271	593	258	238	496	118
BB	264	264	528	247	287	534	97	841	825	1666	737	882	1619	102
SO	453	592	1045	533	589	1122	92	1633	1617	3250	1813	1543	3356	96
E	63	66	129	42	54	96	134	186	180	366	157	146	303	121
E-Infield	31	33	64	15	14	29	221	81	85	166	55	57	112	148
LHB-Avg	.303	.246	.272	.277	.237	.256	106	.284	.264	.273	.265	.265	.265	103
LHB-HR	38	28	66	25	25	50	133	141	118	259	112	99	211	124
RHB-Avg	.280	.248	.265	.258	.248	.253	104	.288	.268	.278	.257	.262	.259	107
RHB-HR	55	53	108	44	56	100	105	181	153	334	146	139	285	114

Toronto Blue Jays - Rogers Centre Surface: FieldTurf

| | 2010 Season | | | | | | | 2008-2010 | | | | | | |
| | Home Games | | | Away Games | | | | Home Games | | | Away Games | | | |
	Blue Jays	Opp	Total	Blue Jays	Opp	Total	Index	Blue Jays	Opp	Total	Blue Jays	Opp	Total	Index
G	78	78	156	84	84	168		240	240	480	246	246	492	
Avg	.254	.254	.254	.243	.257	.250	102	.259	.248	.254	.260	.265	.262	97
AB	2594	2725	5319	2901	2783	5684	101	8065	8353	16418	8629	8213	16842	100
R	387	348	735	368	380	748	106	1135	1007	2142	1132	1102	2234	98
H	660	602	1262	704	715	1419	103	2092	2070	4162	2241	2176	4417	97
2B	146	145	291	173	165	338	92	469	456	925	492	458	950	100
3B	10	16	26	11	15	26	107	39	48	87	27	40	67	133
HR	146	81	227	111	69	180	135	319	227	546	273	238	511	110
BB	224	249	473	247	290	537	94	768	769	1537	772	788	1560	101
SO	534	610	1144	630	574	1204	102	1528	1870	3398	1602	1679	3281	106
E	43	35	78	49	45	94	89	110	141	251	142	133	275	94
E-Infield	13	16	29	13	17	30	104	36	58	94	51	58	109	88
LHB-Avg	.246	.226	.236	.247	.249	.248	95	.267	.242	.253	.255	.272	.265	95
LHB-HR	42	24	66	27	27	54	130	92	90	182	86	105	191	100
RHB-Avg	.259	.271	.265	.240	.262	.261	106	.265	.252	.254	.262	.259	.261	97
RHB-HR	104	57	161	84	42	126	137	227	129	356	187	133	320	116

Washington Nationals - Nationals Park

| | 2010 Season | | | | | | | 2008-2010 | | | | | | |
| | Home Games | | | Away Games | | | | Home Games | | | Away Games | | | |
	Nationals	Opp	Total	Nationals	Opp	Total	Index	Nationals	Opp	Total	Nationals	Opp	Total	Index
G	81	81	162	81	81	162		242	242	484	243	243	486	
Avg	.260	.260	.260	.241	.271	.256	102	.256	.264	.260	.250	.277	.263	99
AB	2678	2835	5513	2740	2694	5434	101	8032	8559	16591	8370	8064	16434	101
R	327	359	686	328	383	711	96	1012	1211	2223	994	1230	2224	100
H	696	738	1434	659	731	1390	103	2058	2262	4320	2089	2236	4325	100
2B	135	136	271	115	139	254	105	388	486	874	402	455	857	101
3B	16	13	29	15	22	37	77	57	39	96	38	59	97	98
HR	74	76	150	75	75	150	99	201	259	460	221	255	476	96
BB	254	242	496	249	270	519	94	846	822	1668	808	907	1715	96
SO	566	590	1156	654	478	1132	101	1658	1569	3227	1865	1473	3338	96
E	63	40	103	64	51	115	90	197	139	336	196	146	342	99
E-Infield	22	16	38	32	21	53	72	77	61	138	82	59	141	98
LHB-Avg	.250	.269	.259	.230	.276	.252	103	.254	.276	.265	.242	.277	.259	102
LHB-HR	33	26	59	34	35	69	85	76	108	184	85	106	191	94
RHB-Avg	.268	.254	.261	.249	.268	.259	101	.258	.256	.257	.255	.278	.266	97
RHB-HR	41	50	91	41	40	81	110	125	151	276	136	149	285	97

2010 American League Ballpark Index Rankings - Runs

Home Park	Avg	AB	R	H	2B	3B	HR	BB	SO	E	E-Inf	Avg	HR	Avg	HR
					TOTALS							LHB		RHB	
Yankees (Yankee Stadium)	104	99	118	104	107	71	143	96	97	104	146	107	170	102	116
White Sox (U.S. Cellular Field)	102	99	113	100	114	79	157	119	105	84	75	102	104	101	179
Orioles (Oriole Park at Camden Yards)	104	103	111	108	98	69	122	98	99	89	112	103	136	105	112
Rangers (Rangers Ballpark in Arlington)	105	101	109	107	105	76	114	97	92	134	221	106	133	104	105
Red Sox (Fenway Park)	103	100	108	103	122	57	87	102	98	128	114	100	86	106	88
Blue Jays (Rogers Centre)	102	101	106	103	92	107	135	94	102	89	104	95	130	106	137
Royals (Kauffman Stadium)	102	102	101	104	100	254	90	88	101	102	120	103	85	101	93
Tigers (Comerica Park)	101	102	98	103	95	101	90	91	89	135	105	101	94	102	88
Twins (Target Field)	102	98	96	100	112	120	65	108	92	94	110	105	65	99	66
Athletics (McAfee Coliseum)	94	98	96	92	92	150	71	101	105	99	82	91	50	96	89
Indians (Progressive Field)	96	100	95	97	108	113	95	98	100	133	139	98	116	95	79
Angels (Angel Stadium of Anaheim)	94	100	86	95	82	47	82	97	104	104	95	94	82	94	83
Mariners (Safeco Field)	94	100	81	93	92	66	68	103	106	84	64	94	77	93	61
Rays (Tropicana Field)	94	97	80	91	86	141	97	100	103	57	55	88	95	99	99

2010 National League Ballpark Index Rankings - Runs

Home Park	Avg	AB	R	H	2B	3B	HR	BB	SO	E	E-Inf	Avg	HR	Avg	HR
					TOTALS							LHB		RHB	
Rockies (Coors Field)	118	104	136	122	123	161	144	88	91	82	74	121	166	115	128
Cubs (Wrigley Field)	108	103	117	111	105	123	110	99	95	118	128	112	95	106	117
Diamondbacks (Chase Field)	103	102	105	105	103	226	105	92	100	99	95	110	94	97	113
Pirates (PNC Park)	99	99	103	99	113	131	80	99	90	114	120	99	94	100	70
Marlins (Sun Life Stadium)	96	101	101	96	105	96	80	122	121	99	88	96	92	96	77
Braves (Turner Field)	101	99	101	100	94	91	103	93	103	99	123	98	99	103	107
Reds (Great American Ballpark)	102	100	101	102	94	100	114	102	102	79	97	96	103	106	120
Brewers (Miller Park)	99	101	101	99	99	60	123	103	102	100	105	96	128	100	120
Phillies (Citizens Bank Park)	98	100	99	98	99	87	113	95	96	86	84	101	118	96	108
Nationals (Nationals Park)	102	101	96	103	105	77	99	94	101	90	72	103	85	101	110
Giants (AT&T Park)	99	98	94	97	99	86	90	101	99	133	121	96	78	100	99
Dodgers (Dodger Stadium)	98	100	94	94	95	33	101	102	98	75	55	94	90	101	110
Cardinals (Busch Stadium)	98	98	94	96	95	102	77	110	97	118	124	94	91	100	72
Mets (Citi Field)	96	97	89	93	89	135	74	113	97	105	95	99	91	94	64
Padres (PETCO Park)	92	98	88	90	83	133	88	115	110	95	78	90	64	93	106
Astros (Minute Maid Park)	94	99	86	92	96	131	110	101	108	113	100	106	127	88	104

2010 AL Home Runs

Home Park	Index
White Sox	157
Yankees	143
Blue Jays	135
Orioles	122
Rangers	114
Rays	97
Indians	95
Tigers	90
Royals	90
Red Sox	87
Angels	82
Athletics	71
Mariners	68
Twins	65

2010 AL LHB Home Runs

Home Park	Index
Yankees	170
Orioles	136
Rangers	133
Blue Jays	130
Indians	116
White Sox	104
Rays	95
Tigers	94
Red Sox	86
Royals	85
Angels	82
Mariners	77
Twins	65
Athletics	50

2010 AL RHB Home Runs

Home Park	Index
White Sox	179
Blue Jays	137
Yankees	116
Orioles	112
Rangers	105
Rays	99
Royals	93
Athletics	89
Red Sox	88
Tigers	88
Angels	83
Indians	79
Twins	66
Mariners	61

2010 NL Home Runs

Home Park	Index
Rockies	144
Brewers	123
Reds	114
Phillies	113
Cubs	110
Astros	110
Diamondbacks	105
Braves	103
Dodgers	101
Nationals	99
Giants	90
Padres	88
Pirates	80
Marlins	80
Cardinals	77
Mets	74

2010 NL LHB Home Runs

Home Park	Index
Rockies	166
Brewers	128
Astros	127
Phillies	118
Reds	103
Braves	99
Cubs	95
Diamondbacks	94
Pirates	94
Marlins	92
Mets	91
Cardinals	91
Dodgers	90
Nationals	85
Giants	78
Padres	64

2010 NL RHB Home Runs

Home Park	Index
Rockies	128
Reds	120
Brewers	120
Cubs	117
Diamondbacks	113
Dodgers	110
Nationals	110
Phillies	108
Braves	107
Padres	106
Astros	104
Giants	99
Marlins	77
Cardinals	72
Pirates	70
Mets	64

2010 AL Avg	
Home Park	Index
Rangers	105
Yankees	104
Orioles	104
Red Sox	103
Royals	102
Blue Jays	102
Twins	102
White Sox	102
Tigers	101
Indians	96
Angels	94
Athletics	94
Rays	94
Mariners	94

2010 AL LHB Avg	
Home Park	Index
Yankees	107
Rangers	106
Twins	105
Orioles	103
Royals	103
White Sox	102
Tigers	101
Red Sox	100
Indians	98
Blue Jays	95
Angels	94
Mariners	94
Athletics	91
Rays	88

2010 AL RHB Avg	
Home Park	Index
Blue Jays	106
Red Sox	106
Orioles	105
Rangers	104
Yankees	102
Tigers	102
White Sox	101
Royals	101
Rays	99
Twins	99
Athletics	96
Indians	95
Angels	94
Mariners	93

2010 NL Avg	
Home Park	Index
Rockies	118
Cubs	108
Diamondbacks	103
Reds	102
Nationals	102
Braves	101
Pirates	99
Brewers	99
Giants	99
Phillies	98
Dodgers	98
Cardinals	98
Mets	96
Marlins	96
Astros	94
Padres	92

2010 NL LHB Avg	
Home Park	Index
Rockies	121
Cubs	112
Diamondbacks	110
Astros	106
Nationals	103
Phillies	101
Mets	99
Pirates	99
Braves	98
Brewers	96
Giants	96
Marlins	96
Reds	96
Dodgers	94
Cardinals	94
Padres	90

2010 NL RHB Avg	
Home Park	Index
Rockies	115
Cubs	106
Reds	106
Braves	103
Dodgers	101
Nationals	101
Giants	100
Brewers	100
Pirates	100
Cardinals	100
Diamondbacks	97
Marlins	96
Phillies	96
Mets	94
Padres	93
Astros	88

2010 AL Doubles	
Home Park	Index
Red Sox	122
White Sox	114
Twins	112
Indians	108
Yankees	107
Rangers	105
Royals	100
Orioles	98
Tigers	95
Mariners	92
Athletics	92
Blue Jays	92
Rays	86
Angels	82

2010 AL Triples	
Home Park	Index
Royals	254
Athletics	150
Rays	141
Twins	120
Indians	113
Blue Jays	107
Tigers	101
White Sox	79
Rangers	76
Yankees	71
Orioles	69
Mariners	66
Red Sox	57
Angels	47

2010 AL Errors	
Home Park	Index
Tigers	135
Rangers	134
Indians	133
Red Sox	128
Yankees	104
Angels	104
Royals	102
Athletics	00
Twins	94
Blue Jays	89
Orioles	89
Mariners	84
White Sox	84
Rays	57

2010 NL Doubles	
Home Park	Index
Rockies	123
Pirates	113
Nationals	105
Marlins	105
Cubs	105
Diamondbacks	103
Giants	99
Phillies	99
Brewers	99
Astros	96
Cardinals	95
Dodgers	95
Braves	94
Reds	94
Mets	89
Padres	83

2010 NL Triples	
Home Park	Index
Diamondbacks	226
Rockies	161
Mets	135
Padres	133
Astros	131
Pirates	131
Cubs	123
Cardinals	102
Reds	100
Marlins	96
Braves	91
Phillies	87
Giants	86
Nationals	77
Brewers	60
Dodgers	33

2010 NL Errors	
Home Park	Index
Giants	133
Cubs	118
Cardinals	118
Pirates	114
Astros	113
Mets	105
Brewers	100
Braves	99
Diamondbacks	99
Marlins	99
Padres	95
Nationals	90
Phillies	86
Rockies	82
Reds	79
Dodgers	75

2008-2010 American League Ballpark Index Rankings - Runs

Home Park	Avg	AB	R	H	2B	3B	HR	BB	SO	E	E-Inf	Avg	HR	Avg	HR
					TOTALS							**LHB**		**RHB**	
Rangers (Rangers Ballpark in Arlington)	106	101	111	107	105	143	118	102	96	121	148	103	124	107	114
White Sox (U.S. Cellular Field)	98	100	111	98	98	71	135	113	106	106	118	99	117	98	145
Red Sox (Fenway Park)	104	99	108	103	140	88	91	101	96	111	105	105	88	103	93
Orioles (Oriole Park at Camden Yards)	105	103	106	108	97	72	123	93	96	82	88	102	126	108	121
Yankees (Yankee Stadium) **	102	100	106	102	92	60	134	103	98	98	97	103	141	100	124
Tigers (Comerica Park)	102	100	103	102	96	107	103	94	94	120	108	98	98	105	106
Royals (Kauffman Stadium)	105	102	101	106	108	136	81	96	91	104	118	107	72	103	87
Blue Jays (Rogers Centre)	97	100	98	97	100	133	110	101	106	94	88	95	100	97	116
Angels (Angel Stadium of Anaheim)	99	100	97	99	91	63	99	92	97	95	84	100	95	99	102
Twins (Target Field) *	102	98	96	100	112	120	65	108	92	94	110	105	65	99	66
Athletics (McAfee Coliseum)	96	99	95	94	93	97	87	99	102	105	109	95	88	96	86
Indians (Progressive Field)	98	100	92	98	103	73	80	103	100	113	125	98	89	98	73
Rays (Tropicana Field)	98	97	92	95	92	134	94	102	103	82	73	98	92	97	96
Mariners (Safeco Field)	97	100	90	97	91	88	82	104	107	86	74	95	92	98	75

2008-2010 National League Ballpark Index Rankings - Runs

Home Park	Avg	AB	R	H	2B	3B	HR	BB	SO	E	E-Inf	Avg	HR	Avg	HR
					TOTALS							**LHB**		**RHB**	
Rockies (Coors Field)	112	103	124	116	115	157	124	94	88	99	87	112	128	112	121
Cubs (Wrigley Field)	105	100	113	106	103	91	110	100	97	105	116	105	120	105	105
Diamondbacks (Chase Field)	106	101	112	107	118	165	104	95	96	93	98	106	102	106	106
Marlins (Sun Life Stadium)	99	101	103	99	102	91	91	112	114	115	92	101	91	98	92
Reds (Great American Ballpark)	101	100	102	101	99	105	119	103	103	82	84	100	111	102	125
Phillies (Citizens Bank Park)	101	100	102	101	99	83	104	98	99	93	94	103	103	99	105
Giants (AT&T Park)	101	99	101	100	106	121	96	97	97	126	126	101	85	101	102
Nationals (Nationals Park)	99	101	100	100	101	98	96	96	96	99	98	102	94	97	97
Braves (Turner Field)	99	101	99	100	93	106	96	102	103	114	137	96	95	102	96
Pirates (PNC Park)	101	101	98	102	102	91	88	96	89	106	122	102	101	100	80
Astros (Minute Maid Park)	100	100	95	100	98	108	110	99	104	102	97	105	104	97	114
Brewers (Miller Park)	97	99	94	96	98	99	106	106	107	94	87	100	126	96	96
Cardinals (Busch Stadium)	98	98	93	97	93	89	82	104	98	107	110	98	91	98	77
Mets (Citi Field) **	96	99	92	94	93	127	88	103	102	91	86	95	95	97	83
Dodgers (Dodger Stadium)	95	99	88	94	94	45	92	90	104	87	80	95	101	96	87
Padres (PETCO Park)	88	98	80	87	78	97	78	112	110	98	89	87	59	89	96

2008-2010 AL Home Runs

Home Park	Index
White Sox	135
Yankees **	134
Orioles	123
Rangers	118
Blue Jays	110
Tigers	103
Angels	99
Rays	94
Red Sox	91
Athletics	87
Mariners	82
Royals	81
Indians	80
Twins *	65

2008-2010 AL LHB Home Runs

Home Park	Index
Yankees **	141
Orioles	126
Rangers	124
White Sox	117
Blue Jays	100
Tigers	98
Angels	95
Rays	92
Mariners	92
Indians	89
Athletics	88
Red Sox	88
Royals	72
Twins *	65

2008-2010 AL RHB Home Runs

Home Park	Index
White Sox	145
Yankees **	124
Orioles	121
Blue Jays	116
Rangers	114
Tigers	106
Angels	102
Rays	96
Red Sox	93
Royals	87
Athletics	86
Mariners	75
Indians	73
Twins *	66

2008-2010 NL Home Runs

Home Park	Index
Rockies	124
Reds	119
Astros	110
Cubs	110
Brewers	106
Diamondbacks	104
Phillies	104
Nationals	96
Braves	96
Giants	96
Dodgers	92
Marlins	91
Pirates	88
Mets **	88
Cardinals	82
Padres	78

2008-2010 NL LHB Home Runs

Home Park	Index
Rockies	128
Brewers	126
Cubs	120
Reds	111
Astros	104
Phillies	103
Diamondbacks	102
Pirates	101
Dodgers	101
Mets **	95
Braves	95
Nationals	94
Cardinals	91
Marlins	91
Giants	85
Padres	59

2008-2010 NL RHB Home Runs

Home Park	Index
Reds	125
Rockies	121
Astros	114
Diamondbacks	106
Phillies	105
Cubs	105
Giants	102
Nationals	97
Braves	96
Brewers	96
Padres	96
Marlins	92
Dodgers	87
Mets **	83
Pirates	80
Cardinals	77

* Data since 2010   ** Data since 2009

2008-2010 AL Avg	
Home Park	Index
Rangers	106
Orioles	105
Royals	105
Red Sox	104
Tigers	102
Twins *	102
Yankees **	102
Angels	99
White Sox	98
Indians	98
Rays	98
Blue Jays	97
Mariners	97
Athletics	96

2008-2010 AL LHB Avg	
Home Park	Index
Royals	107
Twins *	105
Red Sox	105
Rangers	103
Yankees **	103
Orioles	102
Angels	100
White Sox	99
Indians	98
Rays	98
Tigers	98
Blue Jays	95
Mariners	95
Athletics	95

2008-2010 AL RHB Avg	
Home Park	Index
Orioles	108
Rangers	107
Tigers	105
Red Sox	103
Royals	103
Yankees **	100
Angels	99
Twins *	99
Mariners	98
Indians	98
White Sox	98
Blue Jays	97
Rays	97
Athletics	96

2008-2010 NL Avg	
Home Park	Index
Rockies	112
Diamondbacks	106
Cubs	105
Reds	101
Giants	101
Phillies	101
Pirates	101
Astros	100
Braves	99
Nationals	99
Marlins	99
Cardinals	98
Brewers	97
Mets **	96
Dodgers	95
Padres	88

2008-2010 NL LHB Avg	
Home Park	Index
Rockies	112
Diamondbacks	106
Cubs	105
Astros	105
Phillies	103
Pirates	102
Nationals	102
Giants	101
Marlins	101
Reds	100
Brewers	100
Cardinals	98
Braves	96
Dodgers	95
Mets **	95
Padres	87

2008-2010 NL RHB Avg	
Home Park	Index
Rockies	112
Diamondbacks	106
Cubs	105
Reds	102
Braves	102
Giants	101
Pirates	100
Phillies	99
Cardinals	98
Marlins	98
Astros	97
Nationals	97
Mets **	97
Dodgers	96
Brewers	96
Padres	89

2008-2010 AL Doubles	
Home Park	Index
Red Sox	140
Twins *	112
Royals	108
Rangers	105
Indians	103
Blue Jays	100
White Sox	98
Orioles	97
Tigers	96
Athletics	93
Rays	92
Yankees **	92
Mariners	91
Angels	91

2008-2010 AL Triples	
Home Park	Index
Rangers	143
Royals	136
Rays	134
Blue Jays	133
Twins *	120
Tigers	107
Athletics	97
Mariners	90
Red Sox	88
Indians	73
Orioles	72
White Sox	71
Angels	63
Yankees **	60

2008-2010 AL Errors	
Home Park	Index
Rangers	121
Tigers	120
Indians	113
Red Sox	111
White Sox	106
Athletics	105
Royals	104
Yankees **	98
Angels	95
Twins *	94
Blue Jays	94
Mariners	86
Orioles	82
Rays	82

2008-2010 NL Doubles	
Home Park	Index
Diamondbacks	118
Rockies	115
Giants	106
Cubs	103
Pirates	102
Marlins	102
Nationals	101
Phillies	99
Reds	99
Astros	98
Brewers	98
Dodgers	94
Cardinals	93
Braves	93
Mets **	93
Padres	78

2008-2010 NL Triples	
Home Park	Index
Diamondbacks	165
Rockies	157
Mets **	127
Giants	121
Astros	108
Braves	106
Reds	105
Brewers	99
Nationals	98
Padres	97
Pirates	91
Marlins	91
Cubs	91
Cardinals	89
Phillies	83
Dodgers	45

2008-2010 NL Errors	
Home Park	Index
Giants	126
Marlins	115
Braves	114
Cardinals	107
Pirates	106
Cubs	105
Astros	102
Rockies	99
Nationals	99
Padres	98
Brewers	94
Phillies	93
Diamondbacks	93
Mets **	91
Dodgers	87
Reds	82

* Data since 2010   ** Data since 2009

2010 Lefty/Righty Statistics

The following section contains lefty/righty splits for all batters and pitchers who appeared during the 2010 season. The batting side of each hitter is shown below his name; for pitchers, the hand that he throws with is indicated.

For each batter, we show his batting average, on-base percentage, and slugging percentage along with a count of his at-bats, hits, doubles, triples, home runs, RBI, walks, and strikeouts. The results of opposing batters, broken out into the same categories, are displayed for pitchers.

Batters vs. Left-Handed and Right-Handed Pitchers

Batter	vs	Avg	AB	H	2B	3B	HR	RBI	BB	SO	OBP	Slg
Abreu,Bobby	L	.228	184	42	9	0	4	25	18	51	.296	.342
Bats Left	R	.267	389	104	32	1	16	53	69	81	.377	.478
Abreu,Tony	L	.257	70	18	5	0	1	6	1	12	.264	.371
Bats Both	R	.220	123	27	6	1	0	7	3	35	.233	.285
Aldridge,Cory	L	.000	0	0	0	0	0	0	0	2	.000	.000
Bats Left	R	.111	9	1	0	1	0	1	0	3	.111	.333
Alfonzo,Eliezer	L	.188	16	3	0	0	1	3	0	3	.188	.375
Bats Right	R	.240	25	6	1	0	0	1	0	7	.240	.280
Allen,Brandon	L	.143	7	1	0	0	0	0	3	4	.400	.143
Bats Left	R	.289	38	11	3	0	1	6	7	16	.391	.447
Alonso,Yonder	L	.111	9	1	0	0	0	0	0	3	.111	.111
Bats Left	R	.250	20	5	2	0	0	3	0	7	.250	.350
Alvarez,Pedro	L	.228	114	26	5	1	2	15	13	45	.302	.342
Bats Left	R	.270	233	63	16	0	14	49	24	74	.339	.519
Anderson,Bryan	L	.500	4	2	0	0	0	1	0	0	.600	.500
Bats Left	R	.250	28	7	2	0	0	3	1	7	.267	.321
Anderson,Garret	L	.133	30	4	1	0	1	2	2	9	.182	.267
Bats Left	R	.192	125	24	5	1	1	10	3	25	.209	.272
Anderson,Lars	L	.000	0	0	0	0	0	0	2	1	.333	.000
Bats Left	R	.219	32	7	1	0	0	3	5	7	.324	.250
Andino,Robert	L	.300	20	6	3	0	1	1	0	2	.300	.600
Bats Right	R	.293	41	12	1	0	1	5	3	11	.348	.390
Andrus,Elvis	L	.268	153	41	1	0	0	9	16	24	.341	.301
Bats Right	R	.264	435	115	10	3	0	26	48	72	.343	.301
Ankiel,Rick	L	.164	55	9	1	0	0	4	6	23	.270	.182
Bats Left	R	.256	156	40	12	1	6	20	20	48	.339	.462
Arencibia,J.P.	L	.000	12	0	0	0	0	0	1	6	.077	.000
Bats Right	R	.217	23	5	1	0	2	4	1	5	.250	.522
Arias,Joaquin	L	.333	33	11	2	0	0	4	2	5	.371	.394
Bats Right	R	.232	95	22	4	1	0	9	2	18	.247	.295
Atkins,Garrett	L	.204	49	10	0	0	0	2	7	11	.304	.204
Bats Right	R	.220	91	20	7	0	1	7	5	19	.260	.330
Ausmus,Brad	L	.154	13	2	1	0	0	0	1	2	.267	.231
Bats Right	R	.240	50	12	1	0	0	2	6	13	.321	.260
Avila,Alex	L	.182	33	6	1	0	0	3	3	9	.289	.212
Bats Left	R	.234	261	61	11	0	7	28	33	62	.320	.356
Aviles,Mike	L	.263	114	30	3	1	1	8	8	8	.300	.333
Bats Right	R	.319	310	99	13	2	7	24	12	41	.345	.442
Aybar,Erick	L	.252	155	39	8	0	1	6	8	20	.287	.323
Bats Both	R	.253	379	96	10	4	4	23	27	61	.314	.332
Aybar,Willy	L	.246	138	34	8	0	4	25	12	26	.305	.391
Bats Both	R	.212	132	28	5	0	2	18	18	35	.314	.295
Baker,Jeff	L	.350	140	49	12	2	4	18	10	21	.395	.550
Bats Right	R	.106	66	7	1	0	0	3	6	29	.181	.121
Baker,John	L	.125	8	1	0	0	0	1	0	2	.125	.125
Bats Left	R	.229	70	16	3	1	0	5	9	16	.325	.300
Baldelli,Rocco	L	.278	18	5	1	0	1	5	1	3	.316	.500
Bats Right	R	.000	6	0	0	0	0	0	0	2	.000	.000
Barajas,Rod	L	.190	79	15	1	0	3	7	4	18	.235	.316
Bats Right	R	.256	234	60	13	0	14	40	9	36	.300	.491
Bard,Josh	L	.283	46	13	5	0	1	4	4	13	.340	.457
Bats Both	R	.167	66	11	2	0	2	6	6	14	.233	.288
Barden,Brian	L	.200	10	2	0	0	0	0	0	4	.200	.200
Bats Right	R	.167	18	3	0	0	0	0	3	8	.318	.167
Barmes,Clint	L	.280	125	35	10	0	2	18	12	17	.340	.408
Bats Right	R	.214	262	56	11	0	6	32	23	49	.287	.324
Barney,Darwin	L	.280	25	7	1	0	0	1	4	5	.379	.320
Bats Right	R	.222	54	12	3	0	0	0	2	7	.250	.278
Bartlett,Jason	L	.273	165	45	11	1	1	11	20	26	.355	.370
Bats Right	R	.244	303	74	16	2	3	36	25	57	.307	.340
Barton,Daric	L	.310	155	48	12	2	4	19	24	32	.404	.490
Bats Left	R	.259	401	104	21	3	6	38	86	70	.389	.372
Bautista,Jose	L	.222	108	24	0	0	8	17	17	24	.333	.509
Bats Right	R	.269	461	124	28	3	46	107	83	92	.388	.642
Baxter,Mike	L	-	0	0	0	0	0	0	0	0	-	-
Bats Left	R	.125	8	1	0	0	0	1	0	2	.111	.125
Bay,Jason	L	.259	81	21	4	0	2	15	15	21	.367	.383
Bats Right	R	.258	267	69	16	6	4	32	29	70	.340	.408
Beckham,Gordon	L	.224	107	24	5	0	3	11	11	23	.311	.355
Bats Right	R	.261	337	88	20	2	6	38	26	69	.319	.386
Bell,Josh	L	.217	46	10	1	0	3	7	0	12	.217	.435
Bats Both	R	.212	113	24	4	0	0	5	2	41	.226	.248
Belliard,Ronnie	L	.167	66	11	4	0	2	7	6	11	.236	.318
Bats Right	R	.250	96	24	6	1	0	12	12	24	.333	.333
Beltran,Carlos	L	.292	48	14	5	0	4	6	5	11	.364	.646
Bats Both	R	.244	172	42	6	3	3	21	25	28	.335	.366
Beltre,Adrian	L	.328	183	60	19	0	8	27	15	32	.380	.563
Bats Right	R	.318	406	129	30	2	20	75	25	50	.358	.549
Berkman,Lance	L	.171	82	14	4	0	1	5	10	15	.261	.256
Bats Both	R	.267	322	86	19	1	13	53	67	70	.393	.453
Bernadina,Roger	L	.250	56	14	2	1	2	5	6	16	.328	.429
Bats Left	R	.246	358	88	16	2	9	42	29	77	.304	.377
Betancourt,Yuniesky	L	.289	128	37	8	1	3	14	10	14	.341	.438
Bats Right	R	.250	428	107	21	1	13	64	13	50	.271	.395
Betemit,Wilson	L	.312	77	24	5	0	4	12	11	21	.398	.532
Bats Both	R	.291	199	58	15	0	9	31	25	53	.370	.503
Blake,Casey	L	.314	140	44	9	0	6	17	15	32	.388	.507
Bats Right	R	.222	369	82	19	1	11	47	33	106	.294	.369
Blalock,Hank	L	.143	7	1	0	0	0	1	0	3	.143	.143
Bats Left	R	.268	56	15	3	0	1	6	6	12	.339	.375
Blanco,Andres	L	.220	50	11	3	0	0	1	3	9	.259	.280
Bats Both	R	.302	116	35	7	1	0	12	8	15	.359	.379
Blanco,Gregor	L	.179	56	10	0	0	0	2	7	11	.270	.179
Bats Left	R	.315	181	57	9	4	1	12	22	39	.387	.425
Blanco,Henry	L	.167	42	7	3	0	0	3	3	8	.213	.238
Bats Right	R	.239	88	21	2	0	2	5	8	18	.299	.330
Blanks,Kyle	L	.174	23	4	1	0	2	6	7	10	.387	.478
Bats Left	R	.152	79	12	5	1	1	9	8	36	.247	.278
Bloomquist,Willie	L	.289	83	24	6	0	2	8	5	10	.330	.434
Bats Left	R	.250	104	26	4	1	1	9	4	18	.275	.337
Blum,Geoff	L	.138	29	4	1	0	0	0	4	8	.242	.172
Bats Both	R	.289	173	50	9	1	2	22	11	25	.335	.387
Bocock,Brian	L	-	0	0	0	0	0	0	0	0	-	-
Bats Right	R	.000	5	0	0	0	0	0	0	3	.000	.000
Boesch,Brennan	L	.337	104	35	7	3	3	15	10	27	.403	.548
Bats Left	R	.233	360	84	19	0	11	52	30	72	.295	.378
Boggs,Brandon	L	.000	6	0	0	0	0	0	0	4	.000	.000
Bats Both	R	.000	1	0	0	0	0	0	1	0	.500	.000
Bogusevic,Brian	L	.000	2	0	0	0	0	0	0	1	.000	.000
Bats Left	R	.192	26	5	3	0	0	3	3	11	.276	.308
Bonifacio,Emilio	L	.348	46	16	2	1	0	1	4	5	.392	.435
Bats Both	R	.231	134	31	4	2	0	9	13	37	.295	.291
Borbon,Julio	L	.247	93	23	1	1	1	5	6	17	.297	.312
Bats Left	R	.284	345	98	10	3	2	37	13	42	.312	.348
Boscan,J.C.	L	-	0	0	0	0	0	0	1	0	1.000	-
Bats Right	R	-	0	0	0	0	0	0	0	0	-	-
Bourgeois,Jason	L	.250	60	15	2	0	0	2	4	5	.297	.283
Bats Right	R	.190	63	12	2	1	0	1	9	11	.292	.254
Bourjos,Peter	L	.182	55	10	3	1	0	2	1	8	.207	.273
Bats Right	R	.214	126	27	3	3	6	13	5	32	.250	.429
Bourn,Michael	L	.229	118	27	1	0	1	8	10	34	.292	.263
Bats Left	R	.276	417	115	24	6	1	30	49	75	.354	.369
Bowker,John	L	.133	15	2	1	0	0	1	1	5	.188	.200
Bats Left	R	.228	136	31	7	0	5	20	13	28	.291	.390
Bradley,Milton	L	.235	81	19	4	1	2	13	11	19	.323	.383
Bats Both	R	.190	163	31	5	0	6	16	17	56	.277	.331
Brantley,Michael	L	.172	64	11	0	1	3	4	10	21	.217	.250
Bats Left	R	.266	233	62	9	2	2	19	18	28	.317	.348
Branyan,Russell	L	.190	100	19	2	0	6	14	5	39	.236	.390
Bats Left	R	.254	276	70	17	0	19	43	41	92	.352	.522
Braun,Ryan	L	.271	155	42	12	0	5	29	17	24	.341	.445
Bats Right	R	.315	464	146	33	1	20	74	39	81	.374	.519
Brignac,Reid	L	.227	44	10	1	1	0	4	5	15	.314	.295
Bats Left	R	.261	257	67	12	0	8	41	15	62	.305	.401
Brown,Domonic	L	.077	13	1	0	0	0	2	0	5	.071	.077
Bats Left	R	.245	49	12	3	0	2	11	5	19	.304	.429
Brown,Dusty	L	.143	7	1	1	0	0	2	0	2	.143	.286
Bats Right	R	.400	5	2	0	0	0	0	0	0	.400	.400
Brown,Jordan	L	.300	10	3	2	0	0	0	0	2	.300	.500
Bats Left	R	.221	77	17	5	0	0	2	4	8	.268	.286
Bruce,Jay	L	.277	159	44	7	0	12	26	19	44	.352	.547
Bats Left	R	.283	350	99	16	5	13	44	39	92	.353	.469
Buck,John	L	.409	88	36	8	0	6	22	1	23	.411	.705
Bats Right	R	.246	321	79	17	0	14	44	15	88	.288	.430
Buck,Travis	L	.200	10	2	1	0	0	0	0	5	.200	.300
Bats Left	R	.156	32	5	1	0	1	2	4	9	.270	.281
Budde,Ryan	L	1.000	3	3	1	0	0	2	1	0	1.000	1.333
Bats Right	R	.143	7	1	0	0	1	1	0	5	.143	.571
Burke,Jamie	L	-	0	0	0	0	0	0	0	0	-	-
Bats Right	R	-	0	0	0	0	0	0	0	0	-	-
Burrell,Pat	L	.213	89	19	5	0	3	14	16	22	.324	.371
Bats Right	R	.264	284	75	14	0	17	50	41	83	.356	.500

Batters vs. Left-Handed and Right-Handed Pitchers

Batter	vs	Avg	AB	H	2B	3B	HR	RBI	BB	SO	OBP	Slg
Burriss,Emmanuel	L	.000	1	0	0	0	0	0	0	0	.000	.000
Bats Both	R	.500	4	2	0	0	0	0	0	1	.500	.500
Butera,Drew	L	.183	60	11	4	0	0	4	1	14	.203	.250
Bats Right	R	.207	82	17	2	1	2	9	3	11	.261	.329
Butler,Billy	L	.267	116	31	7	0	2	17	15	9	.348	.379
Bats Right	R	.330	479	158	38	0	13	61	54	69	.398	.491
Byrd,Marlon	L	.357	171	61	14	0	5	26	7	22	.390	.526
Bats Right	R	.267	409	109	25	2	7	40	24	76	.328	.389
Byrnes,Eric	L	.000	13	0	0	0	0	0	1	5	.071	.000
Bats Right	R	.158	19	3	2	0	0	0	5	4	.333	.263
Cabrera,Asdrubal	L	.264	121	32	9	0	0	7	8	15	.308	.339
Bats Both	R	.281	260	73	7	1	3	22	17	45	.335	.350
Cabrera,Everth	L	.214	42	9	2	1	0	2	5	7	.298	.310
Bats Both	R	.206	170	35	4	2	1	20	14	47	.274	.271
Cabrera,Melky	L	.233	146	34	9	1	1	9	16	18	.313	.329
Bats Both	R	.266	312	83	18	2	3	33	26	46	.320	.365
Cabrera,Miguel	L	.313	128	40	13	0	6	28	34	29	.446	.555
Bats Right	R	.333	420	140	32	1	32	98	55	66	.411	.643
Cabrera,Orlando	L	.326	135	44	11	0	1	9	10	10	.374	.430
Bats Right	R	.240	359	86	22	0	3	33	18	43	.275	.326
Cain,Lorenzo	L	.289	45	13	3	0	0	7	2	8	.313	.356
Bats Right	R	.314	102	32	8	1	1	6	7	20	.364	.441
Cairo,Miguel	L	.262	65	17	3	0	0	5	8	13	.351	.308
Bats Right	R	.304	135	41	9	0	4	23	9	17	.353	.459
Callaspo,Alberto	L	.233	116	27	6	0	1	10	6	9	.266	.310
Bats Both	R	.274	446	122	21	2	9	46	25	33	.311	.390
Cameron,Mike	L	.357	42	15	5	0	3	7	6	9	.438	.690
Bats Right	R	.225	120	27	6	0	1	8	8	35	.288	.300
Cano,Robinson	L	.285	214	61	8	1	13	43	17	31	.343	.514
Bats Left	R	.337	412	139	33	2	16	69	40	46	.400	.544
Cantu,Jorge	L	.234	141	33	12	0	2	13	10	25	.286	.362
Bats Right	R	.266	331	88	17	1	9	43	19	70	.311	.405
Carlin,Luke	L	.500	4	2	0	0	0	0	1	1	.600	.500
Bats Both	R	.300	10	3	0	0	0	2	1	1	.391	.000
Carp,Mike	L	.222	9	2	1	0	0	0	0	0	.222	.333
Bats Left	R	.179	28	5	1	0	0	0	4	8	.281	.214
Carroll,Brett	L	.154	26	4	1	0	1	3	4	10	.353	.308
Bats Right	R	.220	50	11	3	0	1	4	2	19	.286	.340
Carroll,Jamey	L	.295	95	28	4	1	0	7	14	11	.375	.358
Bats Right	R	.289	256	74	11	0	0	16	37	53	.380	.332
Carson,Matt	L	.167	60	10	1	0	4	7	2	15	.188	.383
Bats Right	R	.211	19	4	1	0	0	2	0	8	.211	.263
Carter,Chris	L	.200	20	4	0	0	0	1	4	4	.320	.200
Bats Right	R	.100	50	9	1	0	3	6	3	17	.226	.380
Carter,Chris	L	.143	7	1	0	0	0	0	0	1	.143	.143
Bats Left	R	.269	160	43	9	0	4	24	12	16	.324	.400
Cash,Kevin	L	.250	28	7	1	0	0	1	2	9	.300	.286
Bats Right	R	.140	86	12	1	0	2	4	9	20	.229	.221
Casilla,Alexi	L	.364	33	12	2	0	0	6	2	2	.389	.424
Bats Both	R	.252	119	30	5	4	1	14	11	15	.315	.387
Castillo,Luis	L	.243	70	17	2	1	0	5	7	6	.308	.300
Bats Both	R	.232	177	41	2	1	0	12	32	19	.348	.254
Castillo,Welington	L	.250	8	2	1	0	0	0	1	3	.333	.375
Bats Right	R	.333	12	4	3	0	1	5	0	4	.333	.833
Castro,Jason	L	.070	43	3	1	0	0	0	3	16	.130	.093
Bats Left	R	.243	132	37	7	1	2	8	10	26	.327	.342
Castro,Juan	L	.233	30	7	0	0	0	6	2	8	.273	.233
Bats Right	R	.182	99	18	5	0	0	7	6	17	.226	.232
Castro,Ramon	L	.286	35	10	0	0	4	5	2	8	.324	.629
Bats Right	R	.275	80	22	2	0	4	16	7	18	.330	.450
Castro,Starlin	L	.339	127	43	14	2	1	7	12	15	.393	.504
Bats Right	R	.286	336	96	17	3	2	34	17	56	.329	.372
Catalanotto,Frank	L	.000	1	0	0	0	0	0	0	1	.000	.000
Bats Left	R	.167	24	4	1	0	0	1	1	4	.200	.208
Cedeno,Ronny	L	.291	110	32	8	1	2	12	7	23	.331	.436
Bats Right	R	.246	358	88	21	2	6	26	16	83	.281	.366
Cervelli,Francisco	L	.322	87	28	3	2	0	10	18	13	.443	.402
Bats Right	R	.246	179	44	8	1	0	28	15	29	.315	.302
Chavez,Eric	L	.111	9	1	1	0	0	1	0	3	.100	.222
Bats Left	R	.245	102	25	7	0	1	9	8	28	.292	.343
Choo,Shin-Soo	L	.264	193	51	10	0	1	17	18	44	.338	.332
Bats Left	R	.319	357	114	21	2	21	73	65	74	.433	.566
Church,Ryan	L	.122	41	5	1	0	1	3	1	15	.163	.220
Bats Left	R	.219	178	39	15	1	4	22	15	50	.287	.382
Ciriaco,Pedro	L	-	0	0	0	0	0	0	0	0	-	-
Bats Right	R	.500	6	3	1	1	0	1	0	3	.500	1.000

Batter	vs	Avg	AB	H	2B	3B	HR	RBI	BB	SO	OBP	Slg
Clement,Jeff	L	.257	35	9	2	0	2	4	0	9	.257	.486
Bats Left	R	.183	109	20	1	0	5	8	6	28	.231	.330
Clevlen,Brent	L	.000	3	0	0	0	0	0	0	1	.000	.000
Bats Right	R	1.000	1	1	1	0	0	0	0	0	1.000	2.000
Coghlan,Chris	L	.261	88	23	5	0	1	6	11	18	.356	.352
Bats Left	R	.270	270	73	15	3	4	22	22	66	.328	.393
Colvin,Tyler	L	.250	108	27	5	3	6	15	5	26	.302	.519
Bats Left	R	.256	250	64	13	2	14	41	25	74	.321	.492
Conger,Hank	L	.000	2	0	0	0	0	0	1	1	.333	.000
Bats Both	R	.185	27	5	1	1	0	5	4	8	.290	.296
Conrad,Brooks	L	.278	36	10	3	0	1	9	5	11	.366	.444
Bats Both	R	.242	120	29	8	1	7	24	11	34	.311	.500
Cora,Alex	L	.161	31	5	0	0	0	4	1	3	.229	.161
Bats Left	R	.221	145	32	6	3	0	16	9	13	.274	.303
Counsell,Craig	L	.206	34	7	1	0	0	1	5	6	.308	.235
Bats Left	R	.259	170	44	7	0	2	20	16	23	.324	.335
Cousins,Scott	L	.500	4	2	0	0	0	1	1	1	.600	.500
Bats Left	R	.273	33	9	2	0	0	1	0	12	.273	.455
Craig,Allen	L	.208	48	10	3	0	2	9	5	11	.278	.396
Bats Right	R	.273	66	18	4	0	2	9	4	15	.314	.424
Crawford,Carl	L	.256	203	52	8	3	4	33	16	46	.312	.384
Bats Left	R	.332	397	132	22	10	15	57	30	58	.379	.552
Crisp,Coco	L	.329	79	26	5	1	4	15	7	13	.379	.570
Bats Both	R	.261	211	55	9	3	4	23	23	36	.328	.389
Crosby,Bobby	L	.217	69	15	7	0	0	8	8	15	.295	.319
Bats Right	R	.222	99	22	3	0	1	5	9	23	.294	.283
Crowe,Trevor	L	.202	104	21	3	0	0	7	8	16	.259	.231
Bats Both	R	.266	338	90	21	3	2	29	21	57	.315	.364
Cruz,Luis	L	.091	11	1	0	0	0	1	0	2	.091	.091
Bats Right	R	.500	6	3	0	1	0	0	0	0	.500	.833
Cruz,Nelson	L	.330	109	36	12	2	4	21	11	22	.390	.507
Bats Right	R	.314	290	91	19	1	18	57	27	59	.368	.572
Cuddyer,Michael	L	.286	179	51	14	1	6	23	23	35	.400	.475
Bats Right	R	.265	430	114	23	4	8	58	24	70	.307	.393
Cunningham,Aaron	L	.364	44	16	5	1	1	6	3	9	.431	.591
Bats Right	R	.250	88	22	7	0	0	9	4	19	.277	.330
Curtis,Colin	L	.222	9	2	1	0	0	0	1	4	.300	.333
Bats Left	R	.180	50	9	2	0	1	8	3	11	.241	.280
Cust,Jack	L	.221	68	15	3	0	1	5	10	26	.329	.309
Bats Left	R	.285	281	80	16	0	12	47	58	101	.410	.470
Damon,Johnny	L	.275	120	33	10	1	0	1	17	15	.365	.375
Bats Left	R	.270	419	113	26	4	8	50	52	75	.352	.408
Davis,Brad	L	.160	25	4	2	0	1	4	3	7	.267	.360
Bats Right	R	.226	84	19	5	1	2	12	6	30	.272	.381
Davis,Chris	L	.148	27	4	1	0	0	1	3	13	.226	.185
Bats Left	R	.204	93	19	8	0	1	3	12	27	.295	.323
Davis,Ike	L	.205	122	36	9	0	3	16	14	36	.362	.443
Bats Left	R	.254	401	102	24	1	16	52	58	102	.348	.439
Davis,Rajai	L	.304	138	42	10	1	2	15	10	13	.349	.435
Bats Right	R	.276	387	107	18	2	3	37	16	65	.309	.357
De Aza,Alejandro	L	.250	4	1	0	0	0	0	1	0	.400	.500
Bats Left	R	.308	26	8	2	0	0	2	0	4	.308	.385
DeJesus,David	L	.258	93	24	5	0	2	11	11	12	.349	.376
Bats Left	R	.340	259	88	18	3	3	26	23	35	.396	.467
Denorfia,Chris	L	.295	105	31	7	1	0	11	15	13	.382	.381
Bats Right	R	.257	179	46	8	1	9	25	12	38	.306	.464
DeRosa,Mark	L	.280	25	7	1	0	1	4	5	4	.400	.440
Bats Right	R	.162	68	11	2	0	0	6	4	12	.230	.191
Descalso,Daniel	L	.429	7	3	1	0	0	2	0	1	.429	.571
Bats Left	R	.222	27	6	1	0	0	2	2	5	.300	.259
Desmond,Ian	L	.300	140	42	11	3	1	17	10	29	.342	.457
Bats Right	R	.257	385	99	16	3	7	48	18	80	.295	.369
DeWitt,Blake	L	.253	79	20	3	1	1	6	5	17	.306	.354
Bats Left	R	.263	361	95	21	4	4	46	42	69	.342	.377
Diaz,Argenis	L	.000	4	0	0	0	0	0	1	2	.000	.000
Bats Right	R	.276	29	8	1	0	0	2	3	8	.323	.310
Diaz,Matt	L	.273	121	33	12	1	5	15	7	26	.318	.512
Bats Right	R	.223	103	23	5	1	2	16	6	18	.283	.350
Dickerson,Chris	L	.000	8	0	0	0	0	1	0	1	.000	.000
Bats Left	R	.225	89	20	2	0	0	4	6	33	.274	.292
Dobbs,Greg	L	.188	16	3	1	0	0	0	0	8	.188	.250
Bats Left	R	.197	147	29	6	0	5	15	12	31	.268	.340
Donald,Jason	L	.286	70	20	5	0	2	7	9	16	.390	.443
Bats Right	R	.243	226	55	14	3	2	17	13	54	.285	.358
Donaldson,Josh	L	.250	20	5	1	0	1	4	2	4	.318	.450
Bats Right	R	.000	12	0	0	0	0	0	0	8	.000	.000

Batter	vs	Avg	AB	H	2B	3B	HR	RBI	BB	SO	OBP	Slg
Doumit,Ryan	L	.186	129	24	3	1	2	10	12	22	.261	.271
Bats Both	R	.282	277	78	19	0	11	35	29	65	.363	.469
Downs,Matt	L	.256	43	11	3	0	1	5	1	9	.304	.395
Bats Right	R	.185	54	10	4	0	0	2	8	11	.286	.259
Drew,J.D.	L	.208	149	31	3	0	4	19	19	44	.302	.309
Bats Left	R	.277	329	91	21	2	18	49	41	61	.358	.517
Drew,Stephen	L	.255	161	41	9	4	5	18	20	37	.341	.453
Bats Left	R	.287	404	116	24	8	10	43	42	71	.356	.460
Duda,Lucas	L	.158	19	3	2	0	0	1	0	7	.158	.263
Bats Left	R	.215	65	14	4	0	4	12	6	15	.288	.462
Duncan,Shelley	L	.264	87	23	7	0	5	14	10	24	.340	.517
Bats Right	R	.211	142	30	3	0	6	22	16	52	.302	.359
Dunn,Adam	L	.199	166	33	7	1	9	24	20	63	.304	.416
Bats Left	R	.286	392	112	29	1	29	79	57	136	.379	.587
Durango,Luis	L	.182	11	2	0	0	0	0	3	2	.357	.182
Bats Both	R	.270	37	10	0	0	0	4	1	5	.289	.270
Dyson,Jarrod	L	.091	11	1	1	0	0	0	0	3	.091	.182
Bats Left	R	.239	46	11	3	2	1	5	6	13	.327	.457
Eckstein,David	L	.265	136	36	6	0	1	12	10	10	.327	.331
Bats Right	R	.268	306	82	17	0	0	17	17	25	.318	.324
Edmonds,Jim	L	.239	46	11	3	0	2	4	4	11	.300	.435
Bats Left	R	.285	200	57	20	0	9	30	19	49	.351	.520
Eldred,Brad	L	.333	12	4	0	0	1	2	2	5	.467	.583
Bats Right	R	.167	12	2	1	0	0	1	0	5	.167	.250
Ellis,A.J.	L	.250	20	5	0	0	0	2	6	5	.423	.250
Bats Right	R	.284	88	25	5	0	0	14	8	13	.347	.341
Ellis,Mark	L	.330	106	35	10	0	1	14	10	14	.387	.453
Bats Right	R	.279	330	92	14	0	4	35	30	42	.349	.358
Ellsbury,Jacoby	L	.235	17	4	0	0	0	1	0	4	.235	.235
Bats Left	R	.180	61	11	4	0	0	4	4	5	.242	.246
Encarnacion,Edwin	L	.234	64	15	2	0	6	14	14	12	.367	.547
Bats Right	R	.246	268	66	14	0	15	37	15	48	.288	.466
Escobar,Alcides	L	.236	127	30	4	2	0	6	15	23	.315	.299
Bats Right	R	.235	379	89	10	8	4	35	21	47	.279	.335
Escobar,Yunel	L	.274	106	29	2	0	2	10	17	16	.379	.349
Bats Right	R	.251	391	98	17	0	2	25	39	41	.325	.309
Espinosa,Danny	L	.200	25	5	1	1	2	4	3	7	.286	.560
Bats Both	R	.218	78	17	3	0	4	11	6	23	.274	.410
Esposito,Brian	L	.000	2	0	0	0	0	0	0	1	.000	.000
Bats Right	R	.000	1	0	0	0	0	0	0	0	.000	.000
Ethier,Andre	L	.233	159	37	7	0	3	19	13	36	.292	.333
Bats Left	R	.318	358	114	26	1	20	63	46	66	.396	.564
Evans,Nick	L	.333	21	7	3	0	1	4	1	5	.364	.619
Bats Right	R	.267	15	4	0	0	0	1	0	5	.267	.267
Evans,Terry	L	-	0	0	0	0	0	0	0	0	-	-
Bats Right	R	.000	1	0	0	0	0	0	0	1	.000	.000
Everett,Adam	L	.231	26	6	2	0	0	4	4	5	.323	.308
Bats Right	R	.164	55	9	3	0	0	0	0	13	.164	.218
Feliciano,Jesus	L	.200	15	3	0	0	0	0	0	4	.200	.200
Bats Left	R	.237	93	22	4	1	0	3	6	8	.287	.301
Feliz,Pedro	L	.240	121	29	2	0	2	10	7	10	.279	.331
Bats Right	R	.208	288	60	10	2	2	30	6	31	.223	.278
Fielder,Prince	L	.226	199	45	6	0	5	19	24	58	.336	.332
Bats Left	R	.280	379	106	19	0	27	64	90	80	.412	.544
Fields,Josh	L	.364	22	8	0	0	3	5	0	4	.364	.773
Bats Right	R	.259	27	7	0	0	0	1	1	5	.286	.259
Figgins,Chone	L	.286	189	54	8	0	1	8	24	35	.364	.344
Bats Both	R	.247	413	102	13	2	0	27	50	79	.329	.288
Flowers,Tyler	L	.000	3	0	0	0	0	0	0	0	.000	.000
Bats Right	R	.125	8	1	0	0	0	0	4	4	.417	.125
Fontenot,Mike	L	.214	14	3	1	0	0	1	1	2	.267	.286
Bats Left	R	.288	226	65	12	3	1	24	14	39	.335	.381
Ford,Darren	L	-	0	0	0	0	0	0	0	0	-	-
Bats Right	R	-	0	0	0	0	0	0	0	0	-	-
Fowler,Dexter	L	.260	154	40	9	2	2		26	34	.374	.370
Bats Both	R	.260	285	74	11	10	6	27	31	70	.332	.432
Fox,Jake	L	.209	110	23	4	0	2	11	5	26	.256	.300
Bats Right	R	.227	88	20	6	1	5	11	3	23	.266	.489
Francisco,Ben	L	.284	88	25	6	0	6	18	8	15	.344	.557
Bats Right	R	.253	91	23	7	0	0	10	6	20	.310	.330
Francisco,Juan	L	.222	9	2	0	0	0	1	0	5	.222	.222
Bats Left	R	.283	46	13	3	0	1	6	4	15	.340	.413
Francoeur,Jeff	L	.300	120	36	5	0	4	18	12	18	.363	.442
Bats Right	R	.231	334	77	13	2	9	47	18	63	.277	.362
Frandsen,Kevin	L	.226	53	12	5	0	0	4	3	2	.268	.321
Bats Right	R	.262	107	28	6	0	0	10	6	8	.307	.318

Batter	vs	Avg	AB	H	2B	3B	HR	RBI	BB	SO	OBP	Slg
Frazier,Jeff	L	.167	12	2	0	0	0	0	0	5	.167	.167
Bats Right	R	.273	11	3	1	0	0	1	1	1	.333	.364
Freeman,Freddie	L	.667	3	2	1	0	0	0	0	1	.667	1.000
Bats Left	R	.095	21	2	0	0	1	1	0	7	.095	.238
Freese,David	L	.357	70	25	4	0	1	9	7	18	.416	.457
Bats Right	R	.271	170	46	8	1	3	27	14	41	.339	.382
Fukudome,Kosuke	L	.262	42	11	2	0	3	11	5	11	.327	.524
Bats Left	R	.263	316	83	18	2	10	33	59	56	.377	.427
Fuld,Sam	L	.333	3	1	0	0	0	0	0	0	.333	.333
Bats Left	R	.120	25	3	1	0	0	3	3	5	.214	.160
Furcal,Rafael	L	.277	112	31	7	1	3	12	11	21	.336	.438
Bats Both	R	.310	271	84	16	6	5	31	29	39	.379	.469
Gamel,Mat	L	.500	2	1	0	0	0	0	0	1	.500	.500
Bats Left	R	.154	13	2	1	0	0	1	1	7	.267	.231
Gardner,Brett	L	.252	139	35	4	2	2	17	25	34	.373	.353
Bats Left	R	.287	338	97	16	5	3	30	54	67	.387	.391
Garko,Ryan	L	.095	21	2	0	0	0	1	2	3	.174	.095
Bats Right	R	.083	12	1	0	0	0	2	1	1	.154	.083
Gentry,Craig	L	.174	23	4	0	0	0	2	0	8	.174	.174
Bats Right	R	.300	10	3	0	0	0	1	1	3	.333	.300
German,Esteban	L	.500	2	1	0	0	0	0	0	0	.500	.500
Bats Right	R	.182	11	2	0	0	0	1	3	2	.357	.182
Gerut,Jody	L	.350	20	7	2	0	1	3	1	4	.381	.600
Bats Left	R	.137	51	7	2	1	1	5	2	13	.170	.275
Getz,Chris	L	.304	46	14	1	0	0	4	4	8	.373	.326
Bats Left	R	.219	178	39	8	0	0	14	15	20	.284	.264
Giambi,Jason	L	.277	47	13	4	0	2	11	5	13	.390	.489
Bats Left	R	.233	129	30	5	0	4	24	30	34	.374	.364
Gibbons,Jay	L	.333	15	5	0	0	1	2	0	3	.333	.533
Bats Left	R	.267	60	16	2	0	4	15	4	11	.308	.500
Gillespie,Cole	L	.204	49	10	3	0	0	2	2	16	.250	.265
Bats Right	R	.255	55	14	5	2	2	10	5	13	.311	.455
Gimenez,Chris	L	.250	20	5	2	0	0	3	3	8	.348	.350
Bats Right	R	.158	38	6	3	0	1	5	5	14	.256	.316
Glaus,Troy	L	.234	128	30	5	0	5	21	29	32	.371	.391
Bats Right	R	.243	284	69	13	0	11	50	34	68	.330	.405
Gload,Ross	L	.273	11	3	1	0	0	4	1	4	.385	.364
Bats Left	R	.282	117	33	7	0	6	18	7	11	.323	.496
Golson,Greg	L	.353	17	6	2	0	0	1	0	2	.353	.471
Bats Right	R	.000	6	0	0	0	0	0	0	1	.000	.000
Gomes,Jonny	L	.285	165	47	10	2	6	35	22	31	.378	.479
Bats Right	R	.257	346	89	14	1	12	51	17	92	.301	.408
Gomez,Carlos	L	.196	97	19	5	0	2	7	8	26	.271	.309
Bats Right	R	.273	194	53	6	3	3	17	9	46	.312	.381
Gonzalez,Adrian	L	.337	199	67	11	0	8	33	29	34	.424	.513
Bats Left	R	.278	392	109	22	0	23	68	64	80	.377	.510
Gonzalez,Alberto	L	.254	67	17	4	0	0	2	3	13	.282	.313
Bats Right	R	.244	119	29	4	1	0	3	4	17	.274	.294
Gonzalez,Alex	L	.224	152	34	12	0	6	19	9	36	.270	.421
Bats Right	R	.260	443	115	30	3	17	69	22	82	.302	.456
Gonzalez,Carlos	L	.320	222	71	8	3	14	42	11	56	.353	.572
Bats Left	R	.345	365	126	26	6	20	75	29	79	.389	.614
Gordon,Alex	L	.200	60	12	3	0	3	7	9	18	.304	.400
Bats Left	R	.220	182	40	7	0	5	13	25	44	.319	.341
Granderson,Curtis	L	.234	158	37	5	1	4	12	13	41	.292	.354
Bats Left	R	.253	308	78	12	6	20	55	40	75	.340	.526
Green,Nick	L	.167	12	2	0	0	0	1	1	4	.286	.167
Bats Right	R	.111	9	1	0	0	0	0	0	1	.111	.111
Greene,Tyler	L	.208	48	10	1	1	1	5	8	10	.345	.333
Bats Right	R	.232	56	13	2	0	1	5	5	14	.313	.321
Griffey Jr.,Ken	L	.250	12	3	1	0	0	0	0	2	.250	.333
Bats Left	R	.174	86	15	1	0	0	7	9	15	.250	.186
Gross,Gabe	L	.167	36	6	1	1	0	6	7	13	.302	.250
Bats Left	R	.253	186	47	10	0	1	19	10	26	.288	.323
Grudzielanek,Mark	L	.286	42	12	0	0	0	2	1	5	.302	.286
Bats Right	R	.265	68	18	0	0	0	9	7	5	.342	.265
Guerrero,Vladimir	L	.338	151	51	9	0	7	31	14	15	.395	.536
Bats Right	R	.287	442	127	18	1	22	84	21	45	.328	.482
Guillen,Carlos	L	.234	64	15	2	1	1	12	5	16	.286	.344
Bats Both	R	.286	189	54	15	0	5	22	16	25	.341	.444
Guillen,Jose	L	.215	107	23	5	0	2	14	14	19	.315	.318
Bats Right	R	.269	417	112	17	2	17	63	18	94	.314	.441
Gutierrez,Franklin	L	.248	141	35	10	0	3	12	16	33	.321	.383
Bats Right	R	.244	427	104	15	3	9	52	34	104	.297	.356
Guzman,Cristian	L	.317	120	38	5	1	1	11	5	15	.352	.400
Bats Both	R	.241	245	59	7	3	1	15	15	48	.292	.306

Batters vs. Left-Handed and Right-Handed Pitchers

Batter	vs	Avg	AB	H	2B	3B	HR	RBI	BB	SO	OBP	Slg
Gwynn,Tony	L	.325	40	13	3	2	0	5	3	6	.372	.500
Bats Left	R	.185	249	46	6	1	3	15	38	44	.294	.253
Hafner,Travis	L	.273	99	27	6	0	1	11	7	24	.342	.364
Bats Left	R	.279	297	83	23	0	12	39	44	70	.385	.478
Hairston,Jerry	L	.244	123	30	4	1	3	19	13	13	.312	.366
Bats Right	R	.244	307	75	9	1	7	31	18	41	.293	.349
Hairston,Scott	L	.233	103	24	4	0	3	17	10	13	.296	.359
Bats Right	R	.198	192	38	6	0	7	19	21	56	.294	.339
Hall,Bill	L	.199	146	29	7	1	7	16	16	50	.276	.404
Bats Right	R	.283	198	56	9	0	11	30	18	54	.346	.495
Halman,Greg	L	.286	14	4	1	0	0	2	1	6	.333	.357
Bats Right	R	.000	15	0	0	0	0	0	1	5	.000	.000
Hamilton,Josh	L	.271	166	45	5	1	8	23	13	41	.331	.458
Bats Left	R	.401	352	141	35	2	24	77	30	54	.447	.716
Hamilton,Mark	L	-	0	0	0	0	0	0	0	0	-	-
Bats Left	R	.143	14	2	0	0	0	0	1	5	.200	.143
Hanigan,Ryan	L	.291	55	16	4	0	3	11	16	3	.466	.527
Bats Right	R	.304	148	45	7	0	2	29	17	18	.379	.392
Hardy,J.J.	L	.210	105	22	5	2	1	7	12	18	.291	.324
Bats Right	R	.294	235	69	14	1	5	31	16	36	.333	.426
Harris,Brendan	L	.178	45	8	1	0	0	1	2	11	.213	.200
Bats Right	R	.143	63	9	2	0	1	3	7	12	.247	.222
Harris,Willie	L	.222	18	4	1	0	1	2	3	6	.333	.444
Bats Left	R	.180	206	37	5	2	9	30	30	54	.288	.354
Hart,Corey	L	.318	148	47	10	2	9	23	12	23	.378	.595
Bats Right	R	.271	410	111	24	2	22	79	33	117	.327	.500
Hatcher,Chris	L	.000	3	0	0	0	0	0	0	2	.000	.000
Bats Both	R	.000	3	0	0	0	0	0	2	3	.400	.000
Hawpe,Brad	L	.258	89	23	9	0	4	16	8	26	.327	.494
Bats Left	R	.239	209	50	12	2	5	28	34	59	.343	.388
Hayes,Brett	L	.143	14	2	2	0	0	2	1	5	.200	.286
Bats Right	R	.222	63	14	4	1	2	4	5	21	.279	.413
Hoadley,Chase	L	.217	189	41	6	2	2	18	19	36	.287	.302
Bats Both	R	.285	421	120	23	1	9	40	37	103	.345	.409
Heisey,Chris	L	.169	89	15	3	0	3	9	6	24	.242	.303
Bats Right	R	.321	112	36	7	1	5	12	10	33	.389	.536
Helms,Wes	L	.324	71	23	9	1	1	17	12	15	.420	.521
Bats Right	R	.180	183	33	3	3	3	22	14	61	.246	.279
Helton,Todd	L	.272	136	37	7	0	2	16	18	40	.340	.368
Bats Left	R	.248	202	50	11	1	6	21	51	50	.369	.366
Hermida,Jeremy	L	.176	34	6	2	0	0	3	3	13	.243	.235
Bats Left	R	.223	188	42	10	0	6	29	13	45	.272	.372
Hernandez,Anderson	L	.143	21	3	0	0	0	1	3	4	.250	.143
Bats Both	R	.239	88	21	5	0	0	7	7	15	.295	.295
Hernandez,Diory	L	.200	5	1	0	0	1	1	0	2	.200	.800
Bats Right	R	.000	4	0	0	0	0	0	0	2	.000	.000
Hernandez,Luis	L	.500	6	3	0	0	1	2	0	0	.500	1.000
Bats Both	R	.211	38	8	1	0	1	4	2	7	.268	.316
Hernandez,Ramon	L	.303	76	23	2	1	2	14	9	11	.376	.434
Bats Right	R	.295	237	70	16	0	5	34	20	38	.360	.426
Horrera,Jonathan	L	.292	72	21	3	2	0	8	5	11	.333	.389
Bats Both	R	.280	150	42	3	0	1	13	20	25	.360	.320
Hessman,Mike	L	.185	27	5	2	1	1	6	5	9	.313	.444
Bats Right	R	.071	28	2	0	0	0	3	3	14	.212	.071
Hester,John	L	.220	41	9	2	0	1	3	6	13	.319	.341
Bats Right	R	.204	54	11	5	0	1	4	5	19	.271	.352
Heyward,Jason	L	.249	173	43	6	1	6	20	24	47	.356	.399
Bats Left	R	.291	347	101	23	4	12	52	67	81	.411	.484
Hicks,Brandon	L	.000	1	0	0	0	0	0	1	1	.500	.000
Bats Right	R	.000	4	0	0	0	0	0	0	1	.000	.000
Hill,Aaron	L	.125	120	15	3	0	3	9	16	21	.226	.225
Bats Right	R	.228	408	93	19	0	23	59	25	64	.285	.444
Hill,Koyie	L	.297	37	11	3	0	0	5	1	8	.316	.378
Bats Both	R	.197	178	35	10	1	1	12	11	53	.242	.281
Hill,Steven	L	-	0	0	0	0	0	0	0	0	-	-
Bats Right	R	.333	3	1	0	0	1	1	0	1	.333	1.333
Hinske,Eric	L	.381	21	8	3	0	2	6	1	6	.409	.810
Bats Left	R	.246	260	64	18	1	9	45	32	69	.332	.427
Hoffpauir,Jarrett	L	.308	13	4	0	0	0	1	1	1	.357	.308
Bats Right	R	.143	21	3	1	0	0	0	1	4	.182	.190
Hoffpauir,Micah	L	.286	7	2	1	0	0	1	2	4	.444	.429
Bats Left	R	.156	45	7	2	0	0	4	3	11	.208	.200
Holliday,Matt	L	.344	154	53	11	0	7	27	23	23	.430	.552
Bats Right	R	.301	442	133	34	1	21	76	46	70	.375	.525
Hoover,Paul	L	.300	10	3	0	0	0	0	1	3	.364	.300
Bats Right	R	.167	12	2	2	0	0	2	2	4	.286	.333
Howard,Ryan	L	.264	193	51	8	0	12	39	17	61	.333	.492
Bats Left	R	.283	357	101	15	5	19	69	42	96	.364	.513
Hu,Chin-lung	L	.286	7	2	0	0	0	0	0	1	.286	.286
Bats Right	R	.063	16	1	1	0	0	1	0	4	.111	.125
Hudson,Orlando	L	.261	188	49	9	0	5	15	17	27	.319	.388
Bats Both	R	.272	309	84	15	5	1	22	33	60	.349	.362
Huff,Aubrey	L	.296	162	48	7	3	7	27	17	31	.378	.506
Bats Left	R	.287	407	117	28	2	19	59	66	60	.388	.506
Huffman,Chad	L	.091	11	1	0	0	0	0	0	3	.167	.091
Bats Right	R	.286	7	2	0	0	0	2	2	2	.444	.286
Hughes,Luke	L	.250	4	1	0	0	0	0	0	2	.250	.250
Bats Right	R	.333	3	1	0	0	1	1	0	1	.333	1.333
Hughes,Rhyne	L	.250	4	1	0	0	0	1	1	1	.400	.250
Bats Left	R	.209	43	9	2	0	0	3	3	18	.261	.256
Hundley,Nick	L	.274	62	17	7	0	1	8	13	13	.395	.435
Bats Right	R	.242	211	51	11	2	7	35	12	53	.279	.412
Hunter,Torii	L	.257	179	46	13	0	7	25	19	33	.328	.447
Bats Right	R	.292	394	115	23	0	16	65	42	73	.366	.472
Iannetta,Chris	L	.222	63	14	3	0	3	9	10	17	.324	.413
Bats Right	R	.184	125	23	3	1	6	18	20	31	.315	.368
Ibanez,Raul	L	.268	179	48	11	2	4	23	11	44	.309	.419
Bats Left	R	.277	382	106	26	3	12	60	57	64	.366	.455
Infante,Omar	L	.276	152	42	5	1	1	9	11	23	.323	.342
Bats Right	R	.342	319	109	10	2	7	38	18	39	.376	.451
Inge,Brandon	L	.254	130	35	9	1	7	20	15	36	.331	.486
Bats Right	R	.245	376	92	19	4	6	50	39	98	.317	.364
Inglett,Joe	L	.105	19	2	1	0	0	1	4	10	.261	.158
Bats Left	R	.276	123	34	7	5	1	7	11	24	.343	.439
Ishikawa,Travis	L	.111	18	2	0	0	0	2	1	5	.158	.111
Bats Left	R	.286	140	40	11	0	3	20	12	24	.340	.429
Iwamura,Akinori	L	.100	40	4	1	0	0	4	6	11	.213	.125
Bats Left	R	.192	156	30	6	1	2	9	25	30	.304	.282
Izturis,Cesar	L	.205	132	27	3	0	1	5	7	10	.254	.250
Bats Both	R	.240	341	82	10	1	0	23	18	43	.286	.276
Izturis,Maicer	L	.280	50	14	3	0	0	7	5	6	.357	.340
Bats Both	R	.241	162	39	10	1	3	20	16	21	.309	.370
Jackson,Austin	L	.226	164	37	7	0	2	11	14	48	.295	.305
Bats Right	R	.317	454	144	27	10	2	30	33	122	.364	.434
Jackson,Conor	L	.243	37	9	4	0	0	2	9	4	.391	.351
Bats Right	R	.234	171	40	9	0	2	14	22	23	.323	.322
Jacobs,Mike	L	.000	1	0	0	0	0	0	0	1	.000	.000
Bats Left	R	.217	23	5	1	0	1	2	3	6	.308	.391
Janish,Paul	L	.308	65	20	3	0	2	9	8	10	.392	.446
Bats Right	R	.237	135	32	7	0	3	16	14	20	.311	.350
Jaramillo,Jason	L	.238	21	5	0	0	1	1	1	3	.260	.381
Bats Both	R	.121	66	8	2	0	0	5	4	12	.181	.152
Jaso,John	L	.191	47	9	1	0	1	6	10	10	.333	.277
Bats Left	R	.274	292	80	17	3	4	39	49	29	.379	.394
Jay,Jon	L	.308	65	20	3	0	0	7	7	13	.387	.354
Bats Left	R	.297	222	66	16	2	4	20	17	37	.350	.441
Jennings,Desmond	L	.273	11	3	1	1	0	1	1	0	.333	.545
Bats Right	R	.100	10	1	0	0	0	1	1	4	.250	.100
Jeter,Derek	L	.321	212	68	12	2	6	24	25	28	.393	.481
Bats Right	R	.246	451	111	18	1	4	43	38	78	.315	.317
Johnson,Chris	L	.286	91	26	4	0	3	18	4	27	.306	.429
Bats Right	R	.316	250	79	18	2	8	34	11	64	.348	.500
Johnson,Dan	L	.235	17	4	1	0	1	7	5	4	.391	.471
Bats Left	R	.191	94	18	2	0	6	16	20	23	.333	.404
Johnson,Kelly	L	.310	184	57	11	2	12	33	15	46	.366	.587
Bats Left	R	.272	401	109	25	3	14	38	64	102	.371	.454
Johnson,Nick	L	.190	21	4	3	0	0	4	3	6	.346	.333
Bats Left	R	.157	51	8	1	0	2	4	21	17	.403	.294
Johnson,Reed	L	.301	103	31	9	1	2	9	3	24	.324	.466
Bats Right	R	.222	99	22	2	1	0	6	2	26	.257	.263
Johnson,Rob	L	.184	38	7	3	0	0	2	9	7	.347	.263
Bats Right	R	.193	140	27	7	0	2	11	16	39	.277	.286
Jones,Adam	L	.259	158	41	5	1	4	16	6	34	.287	.380
Bats Right	R	.293	423	124	20	4	15	53	17	85	.338	.466
Jones,Andruw	L	.256	86	22	2	0	8	23	15	19	.373	.558
Bats Right	R	.219	192	42	10	1	11	25	30	54	.327	.453
Jones,Chipper	L	.245	110	27	5	0	4	9	21	14	.366	.400
Bats Both	R	.275	327	90	16	0	6	37	40	33	.388	.440
Jones,Garrett	L	.220	214	47	10	1	6	27	12	52	.261	.360
Bats Left	R	.262	378	99	24	0	15	59	41	71	.330	.444
Joyce,Matt	L	.080	25	2	1	0	0	3	2	13	.143	.120
Bats Left	R	.262	191	50	14	3	10	37	38	42	.386	.524

Batter	vs	Avg	AB	H	2B	3B	HR	RBI	BB	SO	OBP	Slg
Ka'aihue,Kila	L	.250	44	11	2	1	2	8	2	7	.277	.477
Bats Left	R	.206	136	28	4	0	6	17	22	32	.316	.368
Kalish,Ryan	L	.233	43	10	3	1	0	3	1	12	.250	.349
Bats Left	R	.258	120	31	8	0	4	21	11	26	.323	.425
Kapler,Gabe	L	.206	97	20	2	0	2	13	7	16	.271	.289
Bats Right	R	.222	27	6	2	0	0	1	4	8	.344	.296
Kearns,Austin	L	.252	147	37	7	1	4	12	19	38	.345	.395
Bats Right	R	.270	256	69	14	0	6	37	27	78	.355	.395
Kelly,Don	L	.217	23	5	0	0	0	2	1	4	.269	.217
Bats Left	R	.247	215	53	4	0	9	25	7	38	.272	.391
Kemp,Matt	L	.295	156	46	7	1	6	20	12	36	.341	.468
Bats Right	R	.233	446	104	18	5	22	69	41	134	.299	.444
Kendall,Jason	L	.323	96	31	5	0	0	6	9	11	.381	.375
Bats Right	R	.237	338	80	13	0	0	31	28	34	.301	.275
Kendrick,Howie	L	.264	182	48	10	2	2	18	9	27	.299	.374
Bats Right	R	.286	434	124	31	2	8	57	19	67	.320	.422
Kennedy,Adam	L	.316	38	12	2	0	0	2	4	6	.435	.368
Bats Left	R	.240	304	73	14	1	3	29	33	38	.313	.322
Keppinger,Jeff	L	.304	138	42	17	1	0	10	14	5	.368	.442
Bats Right	R	.282	376	106	17	0	6	49	37	31	.344	.375
Kinsler,Ian	L	.376	93	35	7	0	1	11	15	13	.473	.484
Bats Right	R	.258	298	77	13	1	8	34	41	44	.353	.389
Konerko,Paul	L	.339	121	41	10	1	9	31	21	19	.441	.661
Bats Right	R	.304	427	130	20	0	30	80	51	91	.379	.562
Kotchman,Casey	L	.179	106	19	1	1	0	8	10	21	.252	.208
Bats Left	R	.231	308	71	19	0	9	43	25	36	.290	.380
Kotsay,Mark	L	.000	25	0	0	0	0	0	2	2	.074	.000
Bats Left	R	.258	302	78	17	2	8	31	30	34	.325	.407
Kottaras,George	L	.200	55	11	3	0	2	4	14	16	.362	.364
Bats Left	R	.204	157	32	9	1	7	22	19	28	.283	.408
Kouzmanoff,Kevin	L	.261	138	36	12	0	3	14	8	19	.311	.413
Bats Right	R	.242	413	100	20	1	13	57	16	77	.274	.390
Kratz,Erik	L	.143	7	1	0	0	0	0	0	1	.143	.143
Bats Right	R	.111	27	3	0	0	0	1	2	8	.172	.111
Kubel,Jason	L	.225	160	36	9	2	2	21	20	40	.311	.344
Bats Left	R	.260	358	93	14	1	19	71	36	76	.328	.464
Laird,Gerald	L	.183	109	20	5	0	1	10	8	25	.244	.257
Bats Right	R	.224	161	36	6	0	4	15	10	32	.276	.335
Lamb,Mike	L	-	0	0	0	0	0	0	0	0	-	-
Bats Left	R	.184	38	7	1	1	0	4	2	6	.225	.263
Langerhans,Ryan	L	.091	33	3	0	0	0	1	6	15	.231	.091
Bats Left	R	.243	74	18	2	1	3	3	18	36	.391	.419
LaPorta,Matt	L	.216	102	22	3	0	2	10	18	24	.331	.304
Bats Right	R	.223	274	61	12	1	10	31	28	58	.296	.383
Larish,Jeff	L	.091	11	1	0	0	0	0	0	5	.167	.091
Bats Left	R	.196	56	11	3	0	2	9	7	19	.286	.357
LaRoche,Adam	L	.264	182	48	16	1	6	34	8	56	.297	.462
Bats Left	R	.259	378	98	21	1	19	66	40	116	.331	.471
LaRoche,Andy	L	.256	86	22	6	0	1	9	9	16	.323	.360
Bats Right	R	.180	161	29	2	0	3	7	10	27	.237	.248
LaRue,Jason	L	.250	12	3	0	0	1	2	2	1	.357	.500
Bats Right	R	.182	44	8	1	0	1	3	3	6	.250	.273
Lee,Carlos	L	.274	135	37	5	0	6	23	11	9	.327	.444
Bats Right	R	.238	470	112	24	1	18	66	26	50	.281	.409
Lee,Derrek	L	.270	152	41	11	0	4	23	21	29	.356	.421
Bats Right	R	.256	395	101	24	0	15	57	52	105	.343	.430
Lewis,Fred	L	.247	93	23	5	1	0	7	6	26	.314	.323
Bats Left	R	.266	335	89	26	4	8	29	32	78	.337	.439
Lillibridge,Brent	L	.303	33	10	2	1	2	10	2	10	.343	.606
Bats Right	R	.185	65	12	3	1	0	6	1	26	.197	.262
Lind,Adam	L	.117	137	16	1	1	2	10	5	52	.159	.182
Bats Left	R	.275	432	119	31	2	21	62	33	92	.327	.502
Lindsey,John	L	.000	5	0	0	0	0	0	0	2	.000	.000
Bats Right	R	.143	7	1	0	0	0	0	0	1	.250	.143
Loney,James	L	.222	176	39	8	1	2	27	7	31	.262	.313
Bats Left	R	.286	412	118	33	1	8	61	45	64	.356	.430
Longoria,Evan	L	.324	176	57	24	0	5	31	25	35	.411	.545
Bats Right	R	.281	398	112	22	5	17	73	47	89	.355	.490
Lopez,Felipe	L	.258	128	33	6	0	4	16	11	20	.319	.398
Bats Both	R	.221	263	58	12	1	4	21	33	61	.306	.319
Lopez,Jose	L	.277	155	43	6	0	3	17	7	19	.307	.374
Bats Right	R	.226	438	99	23	0	7	41	16	47	.257	.326
Lowell,Mike	L	.224	98	22	5	0	3	12	7	15	.274	.367
Bats Right	R	.250	120	30	8	0	2	14	16	19	.333	.367
Lowrie,Jed	L	.338	71	24	4	0	5	13	10	10	.420	.606
Bats Both	R	.250	100	25	10	0	4	11	15	15	.353	.470

Batter	vs	Avg	AB	H	2B	3B	HR	RBI	BB	SO	OBP	Slg
Lucroy,Jonathan	L	.284	74	21	2	0	3	11	2	15	.303	.432
Bats Right	R	.241	203	49	7	0	1	15	16	29	.299	.291
Lucy,Donny	L	.400	10	4	2	0	1	1	1	2	.500	.900
Bats Right	R	.200	5	1	1	0	0	1	1	3	.333	.400
Ludwick,Ryan	L	.194	144	28	4	1	5	23	16	31	.268	.340
Bats Right	R	.275	346	95	23	1	12	46	32	90	.349	.451
Lugo,Julio	L	.306	98	30	3	1	0	8	7	21	.358	.357
Bats Right	R	.210	143	30	1	1	0	12	8	29	.257	.231
Luna,Hector	L	.167	12	2	0	0	1	1	0	7	.167	.417
Bats Right	R	.118	17	2	1	0	1	3	0	6	.111	.353
Maier,Mitch	L	.221	77	17	3	1	3	10	4	17	.256	.403
Bats Left	R	.274	296	81	12	5	2	29	37	51	.352	.368
Maldonado,Carlos	L	.000	4	0	0	0	0	0	1	2	.200	.000
Bats Right	R	.429	7	3	0	0	1	3	0	0	.429	.857
Mangini,Matt	L	.133	15	2	0	0	0	0	0	7	.133	.133
Bats Left	R	.261	23	6	0	0	0	1	2	6	.320	.261
Manzella,Tommy	L	.290	69	20	4	0	0	6	5	11	.338	.348
Bats Right	R	.201	189	38	3	0	1	15	8	60	.241	.233
Markakis,Nick	L	.361	191	69	17	1	2	23	18	30	.414	.492
Bats Left	R	.269	438	118	28	2	10	37	55	63	.351	.411
Marson,Lou	L	.286	70	20	5	0	1	7	8	13	.359	.400
Bats Right	R	.161	192	31	10	0	2	15	18	42	.243	.245
Marte,Andy	L	.290	62	18	3	1	0	4	6	15	.353	.371
Bats Right	R	.194	108	21	4	1	5	15	11	20	.267	.389
Martin,Russell	L	.235	85	20	5	0	1	11	16	19	.353	.329
Bats Right	R	.252	246	62	8	0	4	15	32	42	.345	.333
Martinez,Fernando	L	-	0	0	0	0	0	0	0	0	-	-
Bats Left	R	.167	18	3	0	0	0	2	1	5	.273	.167
Martinez,Osvaldo	L	.250	16	4	1	1	0	0	2	1	.333	.438
Bats Right	R	.370	27	10	3	0	0	2	2	5	.414	.481
Martinez,Victor	L	.400	155	62	17	0	12	39	10	14	.431	.742
Bats Both	R	.257	338	87	15	1	8	40	30	38	.315	.379
Mather,Joe	L	.219	32	7	1	0	2	1	4	4	.242	.250
Bats Right	R	.214	28	6	3	0	0	1	1	7	.241	.321
Mathis,Jeff	L	.204	54	11	3	1	1	5	1	16	.228	.352
Bats Right	R	.192	151	29	3	0	2	13	5	43	.215	.252
Matsui,Hideki	L	.236	140	33	5	0	7	20	7	36	.270	.421
Bats Left	R	.289	342	99	19	1	14	64	60	62	.394	.474
Matsui,Kaz	L	.000	3	0	0	0	0	0	0	0	.000	.000
Bats Both	R	.147	68	10	0	0	1	4	10	20	.205	.162
Matthews Jr.,Gary	L	.143	14	2	0	0	0	0	2	8	.250	.143
Bats Both	R	.205	44	9	3	0	0	1	4	16	.271	.273
Mauer,Joe	L	.272	206	56	14	0	2	25	20	25	.342	.369
Bats Left	R	.365	304	111	29	1	7	50	45	28	.442	.536
Maxwell,Justin	L	.155	58	9	3	0	3	9	20	25	.367	.362
Bats Right	R	.130	46	6	3	0	0	3	5	18	.212	.196
May,Lucas	L	.100	10	1	0	0	0	0	0	4	.100	.100
Bats Right	R	.222	27	6	1	0	0	6	0	6	.241	.259
Mayberry,John	L	.500	6	3	0	0	1	3	0	1	.500	1.000
Bats Right	R	.167	6	1	0	0	1	3	1	3	.286	.667
Maybin,Cameron	L	.222	81	18	2	0	1	7	7	30	.300	.284
Bats Right	R	.238	210	50	5	3	7	21	17	62	.303	.390
McAnulty,Paul	L	-	0	0	0	0	0	0	0	0	-	-
Bats Right	R	.136	22	3	0	0	1	1	1	11	.208	.273
McCann,Brian	L	.263	137	36	8	0	5	21	15	37	.353	.431
Bats Left	R	.272	342	93	17	0	16	56	59	61	.383	.462
McCoy,Mike	L	.276	29	8	2	0	0	1	6	6	.400	.345
Bats Right	R	.151	53	8	2	0	0	2	2	14	.182	.189
McCutchen,Andrew	L	.324	145	47	11	0	5	15	18	22	.400	.503
Bats Right	R	.273	425	116	24	5	11	41	52	67	.353	.431
McDonald,Darnell	L	.294	153	45	10	2	4	14	15	37	.357	.464
Bats Right	R	.247	166	41	8	1	5	20	15	48	.317	.398
McDonald,John	L	.250	40	10	3	0	2	3	1	2	.268	.475
Bats Right	R	.250	112	28	6	2	4	20	5	24	.275	.446
McGehee,Casey	L	.316	158	50	17	1	8	30	13	18	.358	.589
Bats Right	R	.274	452	124	21	0	15	74	37	84	.330	.420
McKenry,Michael	L	-	0	0	0	0	0	0	1	0	1.000	-
Bats Right	R	.000	8	0	0	0	0	0	0	5	.000	.000
McLouth,Nate	L	.135	52	7	1	0	0	2	3	14	.224	.154
Bats Left	R	.205	190	39	11	1	6	22	30	43	.317	.368
Mench,Kevin	L	.111	9	1	0	0	0	1	1	0	.200	.111
Bats Right	R	.111	18	2	0	0	0	1	1	6	.158	.111
Michaels,Jason	L	.275	91	25	8	1	5	15	6	11	.327	.549
Bats Right	R	.232	95	22	6	0	3	11	6	18	.295	.389
Miles,Aaron	L	.281	57	16	1	0	0	4	4	11	.317	.298
Bats Both	R	.280	82	23	4	0	0	5	2	3	.306	.329

Batters vs. Left-Handed and Right-Handed Pitchers

Batter	vs	Avg	AB	H	2B	3B	HR	RBI	BB	SO	OBP	Slg
Milledge,Lastings	L	.320	125	40	10	1	4	17	19	16	.414	.512
Bats Right	R	.256	254	65	11	2	0	17	9	46	.287	.315
Miller,Corky	L	.179	28	5	1	0	0	3	1	7	.258	.214
Bats Right	R	.283	46	13	4	0	2	6	1	9	.298	.500
Miller,Jai	L	.292	24	7	2	0	0	2	2	11	.370	.375
Bats Right	R	.194	31	6	1	0	1	2	2	12	.242	.323
Miranda,Juan	L	.167	6	1	1	0	0	1	2	1	.375	.333
Bats Left	R	.224	58	13	1	1	3	9	5	11	.286	.431
Mitchell,Russ	L	.188	16	3	0	0	2	3	0	3	.188	.563
Bats Right	R	.115	26	3	0	0	0	0	0	5	.111	.115
Moeller,Chad	L	.400	5	2	2	0	0	0	0	1	.400	.800
Bats Right	R	.111	9	1	1	0	0	0	1	3	.200	.222
Molina,Bengie	L	.350	100	35	4	0	1	11	11	8	.412	.420
Bats Right	R	.213	277	59	8	1	4	25	13	26	.253	.292
Molina,Gustavo	L	.000	3	0	0	0	0	0	0	1	.000	.000
Bats Right	R	.250	4	1	0	0	0	0	0	0	.250	.250
Molina,Jose	L	.174	46	8	0	0	1	1	2	14	.224	.239
Bats Right	R	.273	121	33	4	0	5	11	7	22	.333	.430
Molina,Yadier	L	.217	138	30	4	0	2	11	12	14	.280	.290
Bats Right	R	.281	327	92	15	0	4	51	30	37	.350	.364
Montanez,Lou	L	.053	19	1	0	0	0	2	1	2	.100	.053
Bats Right	R	.184	38	7	0	0	0	1	0	7	.184	.184
Montero,Miguel	L	.213	80	17	7	0	2	17	7	22	.286	.375
Bats Left	R	.286	217	62	13	2	7	26	22	49	.350	.461
Moore,Adam	L	.212	52	11	2	0	2	6	4	19	.263	.365
Bats Right	R	.190	153	29	4	0	2	9	4	44	.219	.255
Moore,Scott	L	.000	5	0	0	0	0	0	2	3	.286	.000
Bats Left	R	.222	81	18	2	0	3	10	6	16	.273	.358
Mora,Melvin	L	.296	135	40	6	2	3	17	15	19	.364	.437
Bats Right	R	.276	181	50	6	3	4	28	16	34	.351	.409
Morales,Jose	L	.250	4	1	0	0	0	3	0	1	.200	.250
Bats Both	R	.188	32	6	2	0	0	4	6	13	.308	.250
Morales,Kendry	L	.208	72	15	0	0	2	9	4	10	.256	.292
Bats Both	R	.339	121	41	5	0	9	30	8	21	.398	.603
Morel,Brent	L	.375	16	6	0	0	1	3	1	3	.412	.563
Bats Right	R	.184	49	9	3	0	2	4	3	14	.226	.367
Moreland,Mitch	L	.200	20	4	2	0	0	4	3	5	.300	.300
Bats Left	R	.264	125	33	2	0	9	21	22	31	.373	.496
Morgan,Nyjer	L	.200	135	27	3	2	0	4	10	34	.280	.252
Bats Right	R	.273	374	102	14	5	0	20	30	54	.333	.337
Morneau,Justin	L	.325	120	39	9	0	7	20	13	25	.391	.575
Bats Left	R	.358	176	63	16	1	11	36	37	37	.465	.648
Morrison,Logan	L	.342	73	25	7	1	0	7	15	17	.461	.466
Bats Left	R	.257	171	44	13	0	2	11	26	34	.359	.439
Morse,Mike	L	.295	88	26	3	1	8	18	11	25	.374	.625
Bats Right	R	.287	178	51	9	1	7	23	11	39	.340	.400
Moss,Brandon	L	.000	1	0	0	0	0	0	0	1	.000	.000
Bats Left	R	.160	25	4	1	0	0	2	1	5	.192	.200
Murphy,David	L	.272	114	31	8	0	1	15	10	22	.328	.368
Bats Left	R	.298	305	91	18	2	11	50	35	49	.368	.479
Murphy,Donnie	L	.500	2	1	0	0	0	2	2	5	.571	1.000
Bats Right	R	.250	32	8	3	1	2	7	0	14	.250	.594
Nady,Xavier	L	.242	128	31	9	0	2	12	9	33	.290	.359
Bats Right	R	.265	189	50	4	0	4	21	8	52	.317	.349
Napoli,Mike	L	.305	141	43	7	0	10	17	20	39	.399	.567
Bats Right	R	.208	312	65	17	1	16	51	22	90	.277	.423
Nava,Daniel	L	.207	29	6	2	0	0	3	6	10	.361	.276
Bats Both	R	.250	132	33	12	1	1	23	13	36	.349	.379
Navarro,Dioner	L	.184	49	9	3	0	0	3	5	2	.273	.245
Bats Both	R	.200	75	15	2	0	1	4	7	18	.268	.267
Navarro,Oswaldo	L	.000	7	0	0	0	0	0	2	2	.222	.000
Bats Right	R	.077	13	1	0	0	0	0	3	2	.250	.077
Navarro,Yamaico	L	.200	15	3	0	0	0	1	2	3	.294	.200
Bats Right	R	.111	27	3	0	0	0	4	0	14	.103	.111
Nelson,Chris	L	.444	9	4	0	0	0	0	1	1	.444	.444
Bats Right	R	.188	16	3	1	0	0	0	1	3	.235	.250
Nickeas,Mike	L	.000	3	0	0	0	0	0	0	2	.000	.000
Bats Right	R	.286	7	2	0	0	0	0	0	3	.286	.286
Nieves,Wil	L	.212	33	7	2	0	1	2	2	8	.257	.364
Bats Right	R	.200	125	25	6	0	2	14	6	21	.241	.296
Nix,Jayson	L	.233	90	21	3	0	4	9	5	15	.281	.400
Bats Right	R	.220	241	53	12	0	10	25	15	72	.280	.394
Nix,Laynce	L	.313	16	5	1	1	0	2	2	5	.389	.500
Bats Left	R	.289	149	43	10	1	4	16	13	34	.346	.450
Nunez,Eduardo	L	.269	26	7	1	0	1	4	0	0	.269	.423
Bats Right	R	.292	24	7	0	0	0	3	3	2	.370	.292
Oeltjen,Trent	L	.000	1	0	0	0	0	0	0	1	.000	.000
Bats Left	R	.227	22	5	1	1	0	1	4	7	.370	.364
Ojeda,Augie	L	.258	31	8	1	0	0	2	3	3	.324	.290
Bats Both	R	.146	48	7	2	0	0	3	5	5	.218	.188
Olivo,Miguel	L	.295	112	33	4	2	3	17	11	31	.355	.446
Bats Right	R	.259	282	73	13	4	11	41	16	86	.299	.450
Ordonez,Magglio	L	.371	70	26	4	1	6	19	11	6	.457	.714
Bats Right	R	.285	253	72	13	0	6	40	29	32	.356	.407
Ortiz,David	L	.222	185	41	13	0	2	24	13	57	.275	.324
Bats Left	R	.297	333	99	23	1	30	78	69	88	.416	.643
Overbay,Lyle	L	.222	126	28	5	0	6	18	11	33	.295	.405
Bats Left	R	.250	408	102	32	2	14	49	56	98	.340	.441
Pagan,Angel	L	.261	142	37	10	0	3	20	8	18	.298	.394
Bats Both	R	.300	437	131	21	7	8	49	36	79	.353	.435
Pagnozzi,Matt	L	.286	14	4	1	0	1	4	0	2	.286	.571
Bats Right	R	.400	25	10	1	0	0	6	2	6	.464	.440
Parra,Gerardo	L	.283	60	17	4	1	0	9	2	11	.317	.383
Bats Left	R	.257	304	78	15	5	3	21	21	65	.306	.368
Patterson,Corey	L	.207	82	17	3	0	1	5	3	23	.235	.280
Bats Left	R	.292	226	66	13	1	7	27	17	52	.343	.451
Patterson,Eric	L	.219	32	7	1	0	0	3	3	11	.286	.250
Bats Left	R	.213	155	33	7	5	6	13	11	51	.269	.439
Paul,Xavier	L	.238	21	5	1	0	0	2	2	5	.304	.286
Bats Right	R	.230	100	23	7	1	0	9	6	19	.271	.320
Paulino,Ronny	L	.358	95	34	6	0	3	17	4	12	.380	.516
Bats Right	R	.217	221	48	12	0	1	20	21	39	.283	.285
Payton,Jay	L	.200	15	3	2	1	0	0	0	3	.200	.467
Bats Right	R	.450	20	9	2	0	0	1	1	1	.476	.550
Pearce,Steve	L	.294	17	5	2	1	0	3	5	2	.435	.529
Bats Right	R	.250	12	3	0	0	0	2	2	4	.333	.250
Pedroia,Dustin	L	.236	72	17	5	1	0	3	15	10	.307	.333
Bats Right	R	.304	230	70	19	0	12	38	22	28	.367	.543
Pena,Brayan	L	.204	49	10	2	0	0	2	3	7	.264	.245
Bats Both	R	.275	109	30	8	0	1	17	9	20	.325	.376
Pena,Carlos	L	.179	156	28	4	0	8	32	28	60	.318	.359
Bats Left	R	.204	328	67	14	0	20	52	59	98	.329	.430
Pena,Ramiro	L	.161	31	5	0	0	0	3	1	6	.182	.161
Bats Both	R	.244	123	30	1	1	0	15	5	21	.277	.268
Pence,Hunter	L	.292	137	40	8	0	6	20	10	21	.338	.482
Bats Right	R	.279	477	133	21	3	19	71	31	84	.322	.455
Pennington,Cliff	L	.258	124	32	5	1	2	10	5	17	.292	.363
Bats Both	R	.247	384	95	21	7	4	36	45	79	.327	.370
Peralta,Jhonny	L	.241	145	35	8	0	6	27	25	32	.351	.421
Bats Right	R	.251	406	102	22	2	9	54	28	71	.295	.382
Petersen,Bryan	L	.000	1	0	0	0	0	0	0	0	.000	.000
Bats Left	R	.087	23	2	0	0	0	2	1	6	.125	.087
Phillips,Brandon	L	.291	182	53	10	1	8	18	7	24	.321	.489
Bats Right	R	.268	444	119	23	4	10	41	39	59	.336	.405
Phillips,Paul	L	.107	6	1	0	0	0	1	1	2	.286	.167
Bats Right	R	.235	17	4	0	0	0	0	1	5	.278	.235
Pie,Felix	L	.230	61	14	3	0	2	6	5	13	.299	.377
Bats Left	R	.286	227	65	12	5	3	25	0	39	.307	.423
Pierre,Juan	L	.297	158	47	2	0	0	8	16	13	.390	.310
Bats Left	R	.268	493	132	16	3	1	39	29	34	.324	.318
Pierzynski,A.J.	L	.250	112	28	5	0	2	12	3	13	.294	.348
Bats Left	R	.276	362	100	24	0	7	44	12	26	.302	.401
Plouffe,Trevor	L	.200	5	1	0	0	0	1	0	1	.200	.200
Bats Right	R	.139	36	5	1	0	2	5	0	13	.135	.333
Podsednik,Scott	L	.289	142	41	4	0	0	12	7	25	.322	.317
Bats Left	R	.300	397	119	10	7	6	39	33	58	.349	.406
Polanco,Placido	L	.280	157	44	7	0	1	12	12	17	.324	.344
Bats Right	R	.305	397	121	20	2	5	40	20	30	.346	.403
Posada,Jorge	L	.257	136	35	8	0	8	25	14	38	.340	.493
Bats Both	R	.243	247	60	15	1	10	32	45	61	.366	.433
Posey,Buster	L	.309	97	30	9	0	6	20	8	11	.367	.588
Bats Right	R	.304	309	94	14	2	12	47	22	44	.353	.479
Powell,Landon	L	.167	30	5	1	0	1	3	7	8	.324	.300
Bats Both	R	.232	82	19	3	0	1	8	8	21	.297	.305
Prado,Martin	L	.275	171	47	8	1	5	18	14	23	.326	.421
Bats Right	R	.320	428	137	32	2	10	48	26	63	.360	.474
Presley,Alex	L	.500	2	1	1	0	0	0	0	1	.500	1.000
Bats Right	R	.238	21	5	0	0	0	0	1	7	.273	.238
Pujols,Albert	L	.306	170	52	11	0	18	38	24	17	.388	.688
Bats Right	R	.314	417	131	28	1	24	80	79	59	.425	.559
Punto,Nick	L	.253	83	21	3	0	0	7	9	13	.319	.289
Bats Both	R	.231	169	39	8	1	1	13	19	37	.311	.308

Batters vs. Left-Handed and Right-Handed Pitchers

Batter	vs	Avg	AB	H	2B	3B	HR	RBI	BB	SO	OBP	Slg
Quentin,Carlos	L	.211	109	23	4	0	6	18	19	22	.351	.413
Bats Right	R	.253	344	87	21	2	20	69	31	61	.338	.500
Quinlan,Robb	L	.250	12	3	1	0	0	2	1	2	.308	.333
Bats Right	R	.048	21	1	1	0	0	0	1	4	.091	.095
Quintero,Humberto	L	.165	79	13	2	0	0	5	2	17	.185	.190
Bats Right	R	.263	186	49	8	0	4	15	6	42	.294	.371
Quiroz,Guillermo	L	.333	3	1	1	0	0	0	0	0	.333	.667
Bats Right	R	.250	4	1	0	0	0	0	0	1	.250	.250
Raburn,Ryan	L	.295	129	38	12	1	7	26	11	27	.363	.566
Bats Right	R	.273	242	66	13	0	8	36	16	65	.327	.426
Ramirez,Alexei	L	.278	151	42	5	1	5	18	5	18	.301	.424
Bats Right	R	.283	434	123	24	1	13	52	22	64	.317	.433
Ramirez,Aramis	L	.259	116	30	9	0	7	26	6	25	.298	.517
Bats Right	R	.235	349	82	12	1	18	57	28	65	.292	.430
Ramirez,Hanley	L	.286	133	38	5	1	6	20	16	23	.364	.474
Bats Right	R	.305	410	125	23	1	15	56	48	70	.382	.476
Ramirez,Manny	L	.260	50	13	4	0	1	8	15	4	.431	.400
Bats Right	R	.307	215	66	12	0	8	34	31	57	.404	.474
Ramirez,Max	L	.158	19	3	0	0	1	1	0	9	.200	.316
Bats Right	R	.240	50	12	3	0	1	7	12	13	.385	.360
Ramos,Wilson	L	.563	16	9	4	0	0	1	0	2	.563	.813
Bats Right	R	.206	63	13	3	0	1	4	2	10	.242	.302
Ransom,Cody	L	.194	31	6	0	0	0	1	1	7	.219	.194
Bats Right	R	.182	11	2	0	0	2	4	2	4	.308	.727
Rasmus,Colby	L	.270	115	31	8	1	4	14	14	34	.349	.461
Bats Left	R	.278	349	97	20	2	19	52	49	114	.365	.510
Raynor,John	L	.143	7	1	0	0	0	0	0	3	.143	.143
Bats Right	R	.333	3	1	0	0	0	0	0	0	.500	.333
Reddick,Josh	L	.400	5	2	1	0	0	1	0	2	.400	.600
Bats Left	R	.175	57	10	2	1	1	4	1	13	.190	.298
Redmond,Mike	L	.250	12	3	1	0	0	0	0	0	.250	.333
Bats Right	R	.196	51	10	3	0	0	5	2	10	.241	.255
Reed,Jeremy	L	.000	1	0	0	0	0	0	1	1	.500	.000
Bats Left	R	.150	20	3	0	0	0	1	3	7	.190	.300
Reimold,Nolan	L	.265	49	13	4	0	1	7	5	10	.327	.408
Bats Right	R	.164	67	11	1	0	2	7	7	16	.250	.269
Renteria,Edgar	L	.286	70	20	3	1	2	9	7	11	.351	.443
Bats Right	R	.272	173	47	8	1	1	13	14	32	.324	.347
Repko,Jason	L	.196	51	10	3	0	0	2	4	16	.268	.255
Bats Right	R	.250	76	19	3	0	3	7	9	22	.360	.408
Revere,Ben	L	.154	13	2	0	0	0	1	1	1	.214	.154
Bats Left	R	.200	15	3	0	0	0	1	1	4	.250	.200
Reyes,Jose	L	.309	139	43	5	0	2	11	8	10	.356	.388
Bats Both	R	.274	424	116	24	10	9	43	23	53	.309	.441
Reynolds,Mark	L	.218	133	29	6	0	12	30	33	56	.379	.534
Bats Right	R	.191	366	70	11	2	20	55	50	155	.297	.396
Rhymes,Will	L	.351	37	13	3	1	0	1	1	1	.368	.486
Bats Left	R	.292	154	45	9	2	1	18	13	15	.345	.396
Rios,Alex	L	.259	139	36	9	1	4	20	7	20	.293	.424
Bats Right	R	.292	428	125	20	2	17	68	31	73	.347	.467
Rivera,Juan	L	.264	148	39	8	0	5	15	15	16	.327	.419
Bats Right	R	.246	268	66	12	0	10	37	20	42	.304	.403
Rivera,Mike	L	.000	3	0	0	0	0	0	0	1	.000	.000
Bats Right	R	.000	11	0	0	0	0	0	2	2	.214	.000
Roberts,Brian	L	.288	59	17	2	0	2	4	9	8	.377	.424
Bats Both	R	.275	171	47	12	0	2	11	17	32	.346	.380
Roberts,Ryan	L	.143	42	6	1	0	1	2	2	12	.182	.238
Bats Right	R	.292	24	7	3	0	1	7	1	5	.308	.542
Rodriguez,Alex	L	.217	143	31	12	1	6	35	22	25	.314	.441
Bats Right	R	.290	379	110	17	1	24	90	37	73	.352	.530
Rodriguez,Ivan	L	.292	96	28	5	1	1	15	4	15	.320	.396
Bats Right	R	.258	302	78	13	0	3	34	12	51	.285	.331
Rodriguez,Sean	L	.292	120	35	10	1	2	15	14	37	.375	.442
Bats Right	R	.229	223	51	9	1	7	25	7	60	.270	.372
Rohlinger,Ryan	L	.333	6	2	0	0	0	1	2	1	.500	.333
Bats Right	R	.111	9	1	0	0	0	0	0	4	.111	.111
Rolen,Scott	L	.260	146	38	11	1	5	21	28	23	.388	.452
Bats Right	R	.295	325	96	23	2	15	62	22	59	.343	.517
Rollins,Jimmy	L	.297	111	33	3	0	3	18	13	9	.348	.405
Bats Both	R	.218	239	52	13	3	5	23	27	23	.297	.360
Romero,Niuman	L	-	0	0	0	0	0	0	0	0	-	-
Bats Both	R	.000	4	0	0	0	0	0	0	0	.000	.000
Romine,Andrew	L	.000	1	0	0	0	0	0	0	0	.000	.000
Bats Both	R	.100	10	1	0	0	0	0	0	4	.100	.100
Rosales,Adam	L	.289	90	26	0	1	4	14	9	19	.350	.444
Bats Right	R	.261	165	43	8	1	3	17	10	46	.305	.376
Ross,Cody	L	.287	129	37	10	1	7	18	11	25	.340	.543
Bats Right	R	.263	396	104	18	2	7	47	26	96	.315	.371
Ross,David	L	.308	78	24	7	2	2	20	7	19	.360	.526
Bats Right	R	.256	43	11	6	0	0	8	13	9	.439	.395
Rowand,Aaron	L	.211	95	20	5	0	4	9	8	15	.292	.389
Bats Right	R	.237	236	56	7	2	7	25	8	59	.276	.373
Ruiz,Carlos	L	.327	110	36	8	0	4	15	18	15	.431	.509
Bats Right	R	.291	261	76	20	1	4	38	37	39	.386	.421
Ruiz,Randy	L	.176	17	3	1	0	0	0	0	6	.176	.235
Bats Right	R	.130	23	3	1	0	1	1	0	5	.130	.304
Russo,Kevin	L	.222	27	6	1	0	0	1	0	5	.222	.259
Bats Right	R	.136	22	3	1	0	0	3	3	4	.269	.182
Ryal,Rusty	L	.274	106	29	5	0	3	7	3	37	.306	.406
Bats Right	R	.248	101	25	2	1	0	4	5	30	.309	.287
Ryan,Brendan	L	.224	152	34	6	0	1	7	12	16	.285	.283
Bats Right	R	.223	287	64	13	3	1	29	21	44	.276	.300
Ryan,Mike	L	.000	1	0	0	0	0	0	0	0	.000	.000
Bats Left	R	.211	38	8	0	0	0	2	1	5	.225	.316
Salazar,Oscar	L	.235	68	16	2	0	1	6	8	8	.316	.309
Bats Right	R	.238	63	15	2	0	2	13	8	15	.319	.365
Saltalamacchia,J	L	.143	14	2	2	0	0	0	5	3	.368	.286
Bats Both	R	.200	10	2	1	0	0	2	1	2	.273	.300
Sanchez,Angel	L	.284	74	21	2	0	0	6	3	15	.321	.311
Bats Right	R	.274	179	49	7	4	0	19	8	30	.309	.358
Sanchez,Freddy	L	.343	108	37	6	1	3	13	8	14	.388	.500
Bats Right	R	.276	323	89	16	0	4	34	24	27	.327	.362
Sanchez,Gaby	L	.324	142	46	10	1	6	27	15	22	.390	.535
Bats Right	R	.256	430	110	27	2	13	58	42	79	.324	.419
Sandoval,Pablo	L	.227	141	32	6	1	1	15	12	25	.284	.305
Bats Both	R	.282	422	119	28	2	12	48	35	56	.336	.443
Santana,Carlos	L	.146	48	7	3	0	1	5	12	12	.311	.271
Bats Both	R	.314	102	32	0	0	5	17	25	17	.443	.559
Santiago,Ramon	L	.313	67	21	1	0	1	7	6	8	.390	.373
Bats Both	R	.249	253	63	8	1	2	15	24	50	.323	.312
Sardinha,Dane	L	.222	9	2	2	0	0	3	0	4	.222	.444
Bats Right	R	.200	30	6	0	0	3	5	1	9	.226	.500
Saunders,Michael	L	.202	84	17	1	1	3	7	6	27	.256	.345
Bats Left	R	.215	205	44	10	1	7	26	29	57	.311	.376
Scales,Bobby	L	1.000	1	1	0	0	0	2	0	0	1.000	1.000
Bats Both	R	.250	12	3	0	0	0	0	7	5	.526	.250
Schierholtz,Nate	L	.294	51	15	1	0	0	3	3	10	.357	.314
Bats Left	R	.227	176	40	12	3	3	14	17	28	.297	.381
Schmidt,Konrad	L	.000	4	0	0	0	0	0	0	0	.000	.000
Bats Right	R	.250	4	1	0	0	0	0	1	0	.400	.250
Schneider,Brian	L	.056	18	1	0	0	0	0	0	5	.105	.056
Bats Left	R	.271	107	29	4	1	4	15	19	20	.381	.439
Schumaker,Skip	L	.211	76	16	1	1	0	5	7	17	.291	.250
Bats Left	R	.275	400	110	17	0	5	37	36	47	.336	.355
Scott,Luke	L	.240	100	24	3	0	7	19	11	26	.307	.480
Bats Left	R	.297	347	103	26	1	20	53	48	72	.385	.550
Scutaro,Marco	L	.282	181	51	12	0	3	14	17	21	.345	.398
Bats Right	R	.273	451	123	26	0	8	42	36	50	.328	.384
Shealy,Ryan	L	.000	3	0	0	0	0	0	0	1	.000	.000
Bats Right	R	.000	4	0	0	0	0	0	0	1	.000	.000
Shoppach,Kelly	L	.261	88	23	5	0	4	11	12	33	.369	.455
Bats Right	R	.114	70	8	3	0	1	6	8	38	.232	.200
Sizemore,Grady	L	.122	49	6	0	0	0	2	3	14	.204	.122
Bats Left	R	.266	79	21	6	2	0	11	6	21	.314	.392
Sizemore,Scott	L	.224	49	11	2	0	2	5	4	13	.283	.388
Bats Right	R	.223	94	21	5	0	1	9	11	27	.302	.309
Smith,Seth	L	.154	52	8	3	0	0	4	1	11	.182	.212
Bats Left	R	.261	306	80	16	5	17	48	34	56	.335	.513
Smoak,Justin	L	.215	121	26	8	0	4	18	10	29	.271	.380
Bats Both	R	.220	227	50	6	0	9	30	36	62	.326	.366
Snider,Travis	L	.254	59	15	4	0	2	5	2	22	.279	.424
Bats Left	R	.255	239	61	16	0	12	27	19	57	.310	.473
Snyder,Brad	L	.000	4	0	0	0	0	0	0	3	.000	.000
Bats Left	R	.217	23	5	1	0	0	5	1	9	.250	.261
Snyder,Brandon	L	.400	10	4	2	0	0	3	0	0	.400	.600
Bats Right	R	.200	10	2	0	0	0	0	0	3	.200	.200
Snyder,Chris	L	.192	78	15	3	0	6	19	11	25	.289	.462
Bats Right	R	.212	241	51	6	0	9	29	41	69	.330	.349
Sogard,Eric	L	1.000	2	2	0	0	0	0	0	0	1.000	1.000
Bats Left	R	.200	5	1	0	0	0	1	1	1	.333	.200
Soriano,Alfonso	L	.295	146	43	17	1	7	27	19	27	.376	.568
Bats Right	R	.243	350	85	23	2	17	52	26	96	.298	.466

Batters vs. Left-Handed and Right-Handed Pitchers

Batter	vs	Avg	AB	H	2B	3B	HR	RBI	BB	SO	OBP	Slg
Soto,Geovany	L	.367	109	40	8	0	6	20	22	20	.466	.606
Bats Right	R	.235	213	50	11	0	11	33	40	63	.354	.441
Span,Denard	L	.279	215	60	9	3	0	25	22	30	.347	.349
Bats Left	R	.256	414	106	15	7	3	33	38	44	.322	.348
Spilborghs,Ryan	L	.257	152	39	10	1	3	15	27	37	.379	.395
Bats Right	R	.296	189	56	10	1	7	24	12	46	.343	.471
St. Pierre,Max	L	.333	6	2	1	0	0	0	0	1	.333	.500
Bats Right	R	.000	3	0	0	0	0	0	0	0	.000	.000
Stairs,Matt	L	.000	3	0	0	0	0	0	1	1	.250	.000
Bats Left	R	.240	96	23	6	0	6	16	10	31	.308	.490
Stanton,Mike	L	.218	87	19	6	0	3	14	4	33	.253	.391
Bats Right	R	.272	272	74	15	1	19	45	30	90	.348	.544
Stavinoha,Nick	L	.262	61	16	3	0	0	5	2	10	.297	.311
Bats Right	R	.250	60	15	1	0	2	4	2	18	.274	.367
Stern,Adam	L	.000	5	0	0	0	0	1	0	2	.000	.000
Bats Left	R	.000	0	0	0	0	0	0	0	0	.000	.000
Stewart,Chris	L	-	0	0	0	0	0	0	0	0	-	-
Bats Right	R	-	0	0	0	0	0	0	0	0	-	-
Stewart,Ian	L	.231	91	21	2	1	2	14	12	31	.343	.341
Bats Left	R	.264	295	78	12	1	16	47	33	79	.336	.475
Stubbs,Drew	L	.240	167	40	6	2	10	23	17	51	.310	.479
Bats Right	R	.262	347	91	13	4	12	54	38	117	.338	.427
Sullivan,Cory	L	.000	3	0	0	0	0	0	0	1	.000	.000
Bats Left	R	.197	61	12	1	1	0	4	6	17	.269	.246
Sutton,Drew	L	.429	7	3	0	0	2	7	0	0	.429	1.286
Bats Both	R	.219	32	7	1	0	0	1	3	13	.286	.250
Suzuki,Ichiro	L	.309	230	71	6	1	0	15	9	24	.340	.343
Bats Left	R	.318	450	143	24	2	6	28	36	62	.369	.420
Suzuki,Kurt	L	.213	127	27	4	0	2	21	10	11	.284	.291
Bats Right	R	.253	308	93	14	2	11	50	23	38	.310	.391
Sweeney,Mike	I	.224	76	17	3	0	4	12	5	13	.280	.421
Bats Right	R	.280	75	21	2	0	4	14	9	8	.360	.467
Sweeney,Ryan	L	.246	65	16	4	0	0	7	7	10	.315	.308
Bats Left	R	.307	238	73	16	2	1	30	17	31	.350	.403
Swisher,Nick	L	.294	180	53	13	0	4	16	32	29	.415	.433
Bats Both	R	.285	386	110	20	3	25	73	26	110	.330	.547
Tabata,Jose	L	.247	97	24	2	0	3	10	11	16	.321	.361
Bats Right	R	.315	308	97	19	4	1	25	17	41	.355	.412
Tatis,Fernando	L	.250	44	11	4	0	1	4	4	12	.313	.409
Bats Right	R	.048	21	1	0	0	1	2	2	7	.130	.190
Tatum,Craig	L	.214	42	9	1	0	0	3	4	8	.283	.238
Bats Right	R	.319	72	23	3	0	0	6	8	13	.388	.361
Taveras,Willy	L	.389	18	7	0	1	0	4	1	3	.421	.500
Bats Right	R	.000	17	0	0	0	0	0	1	3	.056	.000
Teagarden,Taylor	L	.185	27	5	1	0	2	3	2	13	.241	.444
Bats Right	R	.136	44	6	0	0	2	3	6	21	.269	.273
Teahen,Mark	L	.162	37	6	1	0	0	2	4	9	.244	.189
Bats Left	R	.276	196	54	12	2	4	22	21	52	.342	.418
Teixeira,Mark	L	.278	180	50	15	0	10	39	38	33	.413	.528
Bats Both	R	.247	421	104	21	0	23	69	55	89	.344	.461
Tejada,Miguel	L	.282	174	49	10	0	9	30	15	16	.342	.494
Bats Right	R	.264	462	122	16	0	6	41	15	51	.300	.338
Tejada,Ruben	L	.296	54	16	3	0	0	1	6	8	.377	.352
Bats Right	R	.185	162	30	9	0	1	14	16	30	.282	.259
Thames,Marcus	L	.300	130	39	5	0	5	14	9	34	.352	.454
Bats Right	R	.268	82	22	2	0	7	19	10	27	.347	.549
Theriot,Ryan	L	.286	161	46	6	0	0	9	16	14	.350	.323
Bats Right	R	.264	425	112	9	2	2	20	25	60	.309	.308
Thole,Josh	L	.143	28	4	0	0	0	0	2	3	.200	.143
Bats Left	R	.299	174	52	7	1	3	17	22	22	.381	.402
Thome,Jim	L	.241	87	21	2	0	6	14	7	32	.298	.471
Bats Left	R	.302	189	57	14	2	19	45	53	108	.455	.698
Tolbert,Matt	L	.056	18	1	0	0	0	1	2	7	.143	.056
Bats Both	R	.275	69	19	4	3	1	17	7	11	.333	.464
Tolleson,Steven	L	.375	24	9	3	0	1	4	2	3	.423	.625
Bats Right	R	.200	25	5	0	0	0	2	2	6	.259	.200
Torrealba,Yorvit	L	.227	88	20	5	0	2	9	15	19	.346	.352
Bats Right	R	.287	237	68	9	0	5	28	18	48	.341	.388
Torres,Andres	L	.226	133	30	10	0	2	9	12	29	.313	.346
Bats Both	R	.283	374	106	33	8	14	46	41	99	.354	.527
Towles,J.R.	L	.111	9	1	0	0	0	1	1	2	.200	.111
Bats Right	R	.211	38	8	3	0	1	7	1	10	.244	.368
Tracy,Chad	L	.200	5	1	0	0	0	0	1	1	.333	.200
Bats Left	R	.248	141	35	8	0	1	15	10	35	.305	.326
Treanor,Matt	L	.137	73	10	1	0	2	11	4	9	.175	.233
Bats Right	R	.244	164	40	5	1	3	16	18	34	.335	.341
Trumbo,Mark	L	.000	5	0	0	0	0	0	1	3	.167	.000
Bats Right	R	.100	10	1	0	0	0	2	0	5	.100	.100
Tuiasosopo,Matt	L	.133	45	6	0	0	2	2	4	17	.220	.267
Bats Right	R	.195	82	16	5	0	2	9	5	32	.241	.329
Tulowitzki,Troy	L	.342	146	50	8	1	8	28	17	20	.415	.575
Bats Right	R	.302	324	98	24	2	19	67	31	58	.365	.565
Turner,Justin	L	.000	6	0	0	0	0	0	1	0	.143	.000
Bats Right	R	.091	11	1	0	0	0	0	0	3	.091	.182
Uggla,Dan	L	.306	134	41	9	0	9	28	24	29	.409	.575
Bats Right	R	.281	455	128	22	0	24	77	54	120	.357	.488
Upton,B.J.	L	.278	169	47	17	3	7	20	28	38	.381	.538
Bats Right	R	.218	367	80	21	1	11	42	39	126	.294	.371
Upton,Justin	L	.276	127	35	5	1	2	13	25	36	.390	.378
Bats Right	R	.272	368	100	22	2	15	56	39	116	.344	.465
Uribe,Juan	L	.231	108	25	5	1	2	14	15	25	.331	.352
Bats Right	R	.252	413	104	19	1	22	71	30	67	.304	.462
Utley,Chase	L	.294	136	40	9	0	10	27	22	26	.422	.581
Bats Left	R	.266	289	77	11	2	6	38	41	37	.371	.381
Valaika,Chris	L	.400	15	6	1	0	1	1	1	4	.438	.667
Bats Right	R	.174	23	4	0	0	0	1	0	5	.174	.174
Valbuena,Luis	L	.318	44	14	2	0	1	6	8	11	.423	.432
Bats Left	R	.169	231	39	10	0	1	18	20	50	.242	.225
Valdez,Wilson	L	.242	95	23	5	1	0	7	7	13	.294	.316
Bats Right	R	.265	238	63	11	2	4	28	14	30	.311	.378
Valencia,Danny	L	.374	99	37	7	1	2	16	12	12	.411	.525
Bats Right	R	.280	200	56	11	0	5	24	8	34	.303	.410
Van Every,Jonathan	L	.000	4	0	0	0	0	0	0	3	.000	.000
Bats Left	R	.267	15	4	1	0	1	1	2	6	.353	.533
Varitek,Jason	L	.222	27	6	1	0	3	5	2	10	.276	.593
Bats Right	R	.235	85	20	5	0	4	11	8	25	.298	.435
Velez,Eugenio	L	.167	12	2	1	0	0	1	1	4	.231	.250
Bats Both	R	.163	43	7	1	0	2	7	5	5	.250	.326
Venable,Will	L	.154	52	8	0	0	2	7	6	20	.254	.269
Bats Left	R	.259	340	88	11	7	11	44	39	108	.334	.429
Viciedo,Dayan	L	.340	50	17	5	0	3	7	0	8	.340	.620
Bats Right	R	.278	54	15	2	0	2	6	2	17	.304	.426
Victorino,Shane	L	.321	165	53	10	4	6	22	15	21	.381	.539
Bats Both	R	.235	422	99	16	6	12	47	38	58	.306	.386
Vizquel,Omar	I	.207	58	12	5	0	0	5	5	11	.266	.293
Bats Both	R	.290	286	83	6	1	2	25	29	34	.356	.339
Votto,Joey	L	.283	198	56	13	0	8	32	33	47	.393	.470
Bats Left	R	.347	349	121	23	2	29	81	58	78	.442	.673
Walker,Neil	L	.295	112	33	10	0	3	21	9	20	.344	.464
Bats Both	R	.296	314	93	19	3	9	45	25	63	.351	.462
Wallace,Brett	L	.240	25	6	1	0	0	2	0	9	.290	.200
Bats Left	R	.218	110	26	5	1	2	11	8	41	.295	.328
Watson,Matt	L	-	0	0	0	0	0	0	0	0	0	
Bats Right	R	.200	30	6	2	0	1	4	3	5	.273	.367
Weeks,Rickie	L	.329	152	50	10	2	8	18	27	33	.446	.579
Bats Right	R	.251	499	125	22	2	21	65	49	151	.340	.429
Wells,Casper	L	.265	49	13	3	0	1	7	3	12	.308	.388
Bats Right	R	.386	44	17	3	1	3	10	3	7	.426	.705
Wells,Vernon	L	.195	113	22	6	0	4	11	15	18	.289	.354
Bats Right	R	.291	477	139	38	3	27	77	35	66	.342	.553
Werth,Jayson	L	.287	167	48	14	0	6	18	31	42	.402	.479
Bats Right	R	.290	387	116	32	2	21	67	51	105	.382	.556
Whiteside,Eli	L	.172	29	5	0	0	1	1	1	4	.226	.276
Bats Right	R	.258	97	25	6	1	3	9	7	31	.321	.433
Wieters,Matt	L	.210	119	25	8	0	2	9	4	35	.236	.328
Bats Both	R	.263	327	86	14	1	9	46	43	59	.347	.394
Wigginton,Ty	L	.237	152	36	10	1	2	14	17	25	.324	.355
Bats Right	R	.252	429	108	19	0	20	62	33	91	.307	.436
Willingham,Josh	L	.277	94	26	3	0	6	15	20	20	.409	.500
Bats Right	R	.264	276	73	16	2	10	41	47	65	.382	.446
Willits,Reggie	L	.255	51	13	1	0	0	5	8	6	.356	.275
Bats Both	R	.259	108	28	6	0	0	3	11	20	.333	.315
Wilson,Bobby	L	.250	24	6	1	0	3	8	1	4	.280	.667
Bats Right	R	.222	72	16	0	0	1	7	7	19	.291	.333
Wilson,Jack	L	.264	53	14	2	0	0	3	3	5	.298	.302
Bats Right	R	.243	140	34	9	1	0	11	4	30	.275	.321
Wilson,Josh	L	.196	97	19	4	0	0	4	6	31	.271	.237
Bats Right	R	.239	264	63	10	2	2	21	8	43	.281	.314
Winn,Randy	L	.184	49	9	2	0	0	2	2	9	.216	.224
Bats Both	R	.256	156	40	6	2	4	23	19	28	.333	.397
Wise,DeWayne	L	.231	13	3	1	0	0	2	1	3	.333	.308
Bats Left	R	.253	99	25	2	2	3	12	3	26	.275	.404

Batters vs. Left-Handed and Right-Handed Pitchers

Batter	vs	Avg	AB	H	2B	3B	HR	RBI	BB	SO	OBP	Slg
Wood,Brandon	L	.169	77	13	1	0	0	2	4	21	.210	.182
Bats Right	R	.134	149	20	1	0	4	12	2	50	.156	.221
Woodward,Chris	L	.333	6	2	0	0	0	0	0	3	.333	.333
Bats Right	R	.077	13	1	1	0	0	0	3	6	.250	.154
Worth,Danny	L	.283	46	13	3	0	1	3	5	5	.353	.413
Bats Right	R	.233	60	14	2	0	1	5	1	8	.246	.317
Wright,David	L	.339	127	43	9	2	9	26	18	26	.412	.654
Bats Right	R	.267	460	123	27	1	20	77	51	135	.337	.461
Youkilis,Kevin	L	.404	89	36	9	1	8	23	19	16	.513	.798
Bats Right	R	.275	273	75	17	4	11	39	39	51	.376	.487
Young,Chris	L	.264	144	38	7	0	6	16	29	35	.389	.438
Bats Right	R	.255	440	112	26	0	21	75	45	110	.324	.457
Young,Delmon	L	.312	173	54	13	0	10	30	13	25	.366	.561
Bats Right	R	.292	397	116	33	1	11	82	15	56	.317	.463
Young,Delwyn	L	.333	21	7	1	0	2	7	0	2	.333	.667
Bats Both	R	.224	170	38	10	1	5	21	13	50	.281	.382
Young,Michael	L	.322	171	55	12	0	6	25	16	25	.374	.497
Bats Right	R	.270	485	131	24	3	15	66	34	90	.314	.425
Young Jr.,Eric	L	.238	63	15	0	0	0	4	7	8	.314	.238
Bats Both	R	.248	109	27	5	1	0	4	10	24	.311	.312
Zaun,Gregg	L	.161	31	5	2	0	0	4	4	5	.297	.226
Bats Both	R	.310	71	22	5	0	2	10	7	7	.375	.465
Zawadzki,Lance	L	.278	18	5	1	0	0	1	3	4	.381	.333
Bats Both	R	.118	17	2	1	0	0	0	2	3	.211	.176
Zimmerman,Ryan	L	.331	121	40	9	0	4	22	27	27	.453	.504
Bats Right	R	.300	404	121	23	0	21	63	42	71	.367	.512
Zobrist,Ben	L	.247	166	41	8	0	3	27	26	39	.345	.349
Bats Both	R	.235	375	88	20	2	7	48	66	68	.346	.355
AL	L	.256	-	-	-	-	-	-	-	-	.325	.393
	R	.262	-	-	-	-	-	-	-	-	.328	.412
NL	L	.258	-	-	-	-	-	-	-	-	.330	.404
	R	.254	-	-	-	-	-	-	-	-	.321	.398
MLB	L	.257	-	-	-	-	-	-	-	-	.328	.399
	R	.258	-	-	-	-	-	-	-	-	.325	.404

Pitchers vs. Left-Handed and Right-Handed Batters

Pitcher	vs	Avg	AB	H	2B	3B	HR	RBI	BB	SO	OBP	Slg
Aardsma,David	L	.244	86	21	4	0	1	5	14	27	.363	.326
Throws Right	R	.148	81	12	2	0	4	13	11	22	.247	.321
Abad,Fernando	L	.179	28	5	1	1	1	5	2	5	.226	.393
Throws Left	R	.214	42	9	1	0	2	3	3	7	.267	.381
Accardo,Jeremy	L	.462	13	6	1	1	0	7	2	1	.563	.692
Throws Right	R	.353	17	6	1	0	0	3	1	2	.389	.412
Aceves,Alfredo	L	.235	17	4	0	0	0	2	2	1	.350	.235
Throws Right	R	.194	31	6	1	0	1	4	2	1	.242	.323
Acosta,Manny	L	.163	43	7	1	0	1	4	3	12	.217	.256
Throws Right	R	.245	94	23	2	0	3	19	15	30	.345	.362
Adams,Mike	L	.185	119	22	3	2	1	7	14	40	.271	.269
Throws Right	R	.206	126	26	3	0	1	7	9	33	.259	.254
Affeldt,Jeremy	L	.290	69	20	4	1	1	13	11	17	.395	.420
Throws Left	R	.290	124	36	7	0	3	12	13	27	.364	.419
Albaladejo,Jonathan	L	.222	18	4	0	0	0	2	4	4	.364	.222
Throws Right	R	.238	21	5	1	0	1	5	4	4	.393	.429
Albers,Matt	L	.297	118	35	5	1	4	24	12	19	.362	.458
Throws Right	R	.250	172	43	6	0	2	20	22	30	.342	.320
Ambriz,Hector	L	.324	105	34	4	0	4	16	8	21	.368	.476
Throws Right	R	.354	96	34	9	2	6	21	9	16	.407	.677
Anderson,Brett	L	.299	107	32	6	0	0	7	3	13	.330	.355
Throws Left	R	.243	329	80	18	0	6	31	19	62	.293	.353
Arrieta,Jake	L	.315	222	70	19	1	7	40	29	27	.394	.505
Throws Right	R	.213	169	36	5	1	2	9	19	25	.304	.290
Arroyo,Bronson	L	.285	393	112	19	1	15	51	29	45	.333	.453
Throws Right	R	.185	411	76	17	0	14	39	30	76	.248	.328
Atchison,Scott	L	.290	107	31	6	0	5	12	11	21	.353	.486
Throws Right	R	.220	123	27	3	2	4	19	8	20	.271	.374
Atilano,Luis	L	.275	149	41	12	3	5	20	23	19	.370	.497
Throws Right	R	.286	192	55	13	0	6	26	9	21	.322	.448
Atkins,Mitch	L	.375	16	6	1	0	2	6	4	3	.500	.813
Throws Right	R	.231	26	6	1	0	0	1	2	7	.310	.269
Axford,John	L	.225	102	23	8	1	1	7	17	37	.339	.353
Throws Right	R	.183	104	19	5	0	0	10	10	39	.252	.231
Badenhop,Burke	L	.238	105	25	8	2	1	16	13	18	.319	.381
Throws Right	R	.252	147	37	5	0	4	17	8	29	.299	.367
Baez,Danys	L	.306	72	22	4	2	3	9	13	14	.407	.542
Throws Right	R	.297	111	33	5	1	3	19	10	14	.365	.441
Bailey,Andrew	L	.195	77	15	5	0	1	4	8	15	.271	.299
Throws Right	R	.202	94	19	2	0	2	10	5	27	.235	.287
Bailey,Homer	L	.238	151	36	10	1	2	9	18	40	.320	.358
Throws Right	R	.272	268	73	16	2	9	39	22	60	.333	.448
Baker,Scott	L	.277	328	91	31	2	12	38	25	81	.336	.494
Throws Right	R	.277	343	95	18	3	11	44	18	67	.313	.443
Balester,Collin	L	.257	35	9	1	0	2	3	4	10	.333	.457
Throws Right	R	.154	39	6	1	0	0	3	7	10	.313	.170
Balfour,Grant	L	.207	[illegible]	24	11	1	1	7	8	23	.327	.444
Throws Right	R	.174	109	19	4	0	2	13	9	33	.230	.266
Banks,Josh	L	.200	5	1	1	0	0	0	2	0	.429	.400
Throws Right	R	.467	15	7	2	0	1	5	2	1	.529	.800
Bannister,Brian	L	.273	256	70	16	2	5	24	26	43	.342	.410
Throws Right	R	.330	267	88	16	0	18	57	24	34	.388	.592
Bard,Daniel	L	.141	135	19	3	0	2	15	19	29	.255	.207
Throws Right	R	.215	121	26	5	0	4	15	11	47	.272	.355
Bass,Brian	L	.429	7	3	1	0	0	3	2	1	.556	.571
Throws Right	R	.273	22	6	0	1	0	7	8	1	.460	.364
Bastardo,Antonio	L	.200	35	7	2	0	1	4	6	14	.317	.343
Throws Left	R	.300	40	12	0	0	0	3	3	12	.378	.300
Batista,Miguel	L	.243	111	27	1	1	4	19	24	16	.380	.378
Throws Right	R	.229	192	44	7	1	5	28	15	39	.297	.354
Bautista,Denny	L	.204	49	10	2	0	1	7	13	21	.365	.306
Throws Right	R	.205	73	15	1	0	3	8	14	23	.352	.342
Beachy,Brandon	L	.273	33	9	1	0	0	2	4	7	.351	.303
Throws Right	R	.259	27	7	3	0	0	4	3	8	.333	.370
Beckett,Josh	L	.310	297	92	23	4	15	46	28	66	.374	.566
Throws Right	R	.267	221	59	13	0	5	29	17	50	.332	.394
Beimel,Joe	L	.221	95	21	4	1	3	10	7	15	.275	.379
Throws Left	R	.329	76	25	5	0	2	12	8	6	.388	.474
Belisario,Ronald	L	.257	74	19	4	0	3	8	12	11	.360	.432
Throws Right	R	.246	134	33	5	0	3	18	7	27	.299	.351
Belisle,Matt	L	.232	112	26	3	1	2	9	9	35	.289	.330
Throws Right	R	.253	229	58	14	0	5	26	7	56	.279	.380
Bell,Heath	L	.200	120	24	6	0	0	9	17	45	.304	.250
Throws Right	R	.241	133	32	7	0	1	7	11	41	.297	.316
Bell,Trevor	L	.308	133	41	10	1	2	18	13	26	.367	.444
Throws Right	R	.316	114	36	10	0	0	15	8	19	.366	.404

Pitcher	vs	Avg	AB	H	2B	3B	HR	RBI	BB	SO	OBP	Slg
Beltre,Omar	L	.333	15	5	0	0	2	4	3	7	.444	.733
Throws Right	R	.308	13	4	0	0	1	3	4	2	.526	.538
Benoit,Joaquin	L	.144	97	14	1	1	4	6	6	44	.192	.299
Throws Right	R	.150	107	16	3	0	2	5	5	31	.186	.234
Benson,Kris	L	.310	29	9	1	1	1	2	4	5	.394	.517
Throws Right	R	.300	30	9	1	0	1	1	2	3	.364	.433
Berg,Justin	L	.235	51	12	3	0	0	7	12	3	.400	.294
Throws Right	R	.300	110	33	3	0	3	25	8	11	.347	.409
Bergesen,Brad	L	.303	343	104	32	4	13	55	34	35	.368	.534
Throws Right	R	.266	335	89	21	0	13	39	17	46	.307	.445
Bergmann,Jason	L	.200	5	1	0	0	1	2	0	1	.200	.800
Throws Right	R	.400	5	2	1	0	1	4	1	1	.500	1.200
Berken,Jason	L	.253	83	21	5	0	0	9	8	18	.319	.313
Throws Right	R	.279	154	43	8	2	5	20	11	27	.325	.455
Betancourt,Rafael	L	.279	86	24	2	1	5	14	5	31	.319	.500
Throws Right	R	.187	150	28	7	0	4	19	3	58	.201	.313
Billingsley,Chad	L	.252	369	93	25	5	2	35	49	101	.340	.363
Throws Right	R	.236	351	83	11	4	6	34	20	70	.288	.342
Bisenius,Joe	L	.167	6	1	1	0	0	2	4	2	.500	.333
Throws Right	R	.357	14	5	1	0	1	3	2	3	.438	.643
Blackburn,Nick	L	.285	319	91	20	4	14	46	26	29	.338	.505
Throws Right	R	.318	324	103	17	2	11	46	14	39	.352	.485
Blanton,Joe	L	.266	331	88	14	2	14	42	29	68	.327	.447
Throws Right	R	.314	376	118	19	2	13	55	14	66	.336	.479
Blevins,Jerry	L	.231	91	21	3	0	2	11	4	27	.268	.330
Throws Left	R	.311	106	33	3	1	5	13	14	19	.392	.500
Boggs,Mitchell	L	.253	79	20	6	0	2	10	14	10	.358	.405
Throws Right	R	.238	168	40	9	1	3	20	13	42	.306	.357
Bonderman,Jeremy	L	.303	340	103	13	6	17	52	38	54	.378	.526
Throws Right	R	.250	336	84	12	2	8	45	22	58	.304	.369
Bonine,Eddie	L	.275	120	33	4	1	3	15	10	7	.326	.400
Throws Right	R	.329	155	51	11	2	4	30	12	19	.386	.503
Bonser,Boof	L	.346	52	18	0	0	1	7	5	9	.404	.404
Throws Right	R	.306	49	15	3	0	1	8	3	8	.346	.429
Bowden,Michael	L	.379	29	11	4	1	0	2	3	5	.438	.586
Throws Right	R	.273	33	9	2	0	2	10	1	8	.294	.515
Bowers,Cedrick	L	.333	18	6	2	0	2	8	2	4	.429	.778
Throws Left	R	.162	37	6	0	0	2	3	4	14	.244	.324
Boyer,Blaine	L	.352	105	37	7	0	2	16	12	7	.419	.476
Throws Right	R	.198	111	22	6	0	1	16	17	22	.305	.279
Braddock,Zach	L	.151	53	8	1	0	0	4	8	22	.270	.170
Throws Left	R	.284	74	21	8	0	1	13	11	19	.379	.432
Braden,Dallas	L	.271	181	49	7	0	4	22	13	23	.330	.376
Throws Left	R	.242	542	131	32	0	13	48	30	90	.282	.373
Bray,Bill	L	.106	47	5	0	0	3	8	0	10	.200	.290
Throws Left	R	.271	59	16	3	1	1	6	4	20	.317	.407
Breslow,Craig	L	.181	94	17	6	0	3	9	8	26	.245	.340
Throws Left	R	.201	179	36	7	1	6	19	21	45	.285	.352
Broxton,Jonathan	L	.243	107	26	5	0	0	11	14	37	.336	.290
Throws Right	R	.292	130	38	4	1	4	24	14	36	.363	.431
Bruney,Brian	L	.219	32	7	3	0	1	7	5	7	.316	.406
Throws Right	R	.389	36	14	1	0	0	6	15	9	.558	.417
Buchholz,Clay	L	.230	344	79	13	2	7	22	40	58	.311	.340
Throws Right	R	.221	285	63	10	0	2	21	27	62	.294	.277
Buchholz,Taylor	L	.250	20	5	2	0	1	2	0	4	.250	.500
Throws Right	R	.227	22	5	2	0	1	2	6	5	.393	.455
Buckner,Billy	L	.273	22	6	0	0	0	1	2	2	.320	.273
Throws Right	R	.476	42	20	4	0	4	14	3	9	.532	.857
Buehrle,Mark	L	.275	233	64	16	1	6	28	16	31	.320	.429
Throws Left	R	.303	601	182	34	0	11	66	33	68	.337	.414
Buente,Jay	L	.227	22	5	0	1	0	2	6	5	.393	.318
Throws Right	R	.440	25	11	0	0	0	6	5	4	.533	.440
Bulger,Jason	L	.250	40	10	4	0	2	7	10	7	.412	.500
Throws Right	R	.283	53	15	3	0	1	12	5	18	.356	.396
Bullington,Bryan	L	.330	94	31	5	1	3	15	11	15	.402	.500
Throws Right	R	.256	78	20	6	0	3	14	6	14	.330	.449
Bumgarner,Madison	L	.243	115	28	6	0	3	9	7	30	.304	.374
Throws Left	R	.283	322	91	19	2	8	28	19	56	.323	.429
Burnett,A.J.	L	.286	385	110	24	2	11	57	48	73	.376	.444
Throws Right	R	.285	330	94	18	1	14	46	30	72	.355	.473
Burnett,Alex	L	.351	57	20	4	0	1	5	14	10	.472	.474
Throws Right	R	.258	124	32	8	2	5	16	9	27	.319	.476
Burnett,Sean	L	.273	99	27	5	0	2	10	7	29	.327	.384
Throws Left	R	.182	137	25	4	0	1	8	13	33	.253	.234
Burres,Brian	L	.308	78	24	9	1	2	11	8	13	.386	.526
Throws Left	R	.265	238	63	23	2	7	34	26	32	.343	.466

Pitchers vs. Left-Handed and Right-Handed Batters

Pitcher	vs	Avg	AB	H	2B	3B	HR	RBI	BB	SO	OBP	Slg
Burton,Jared	L	.000	5	0	0	0	0	0	0	0	.000	.000
Throws Right	R	.000	5	0	0	0	0	0	0	1	.000	.000
Bush,Dave	L	.277	311	86	20	0	15	47	47	61	.372	.486
Throws Right	R	.293	382	112	29	1	13	50	18	46	.323	.476
Byrdak,Tim	L	.213	75	16	6	0	2	10	7	19	.271	.373
Throws Left	R	.333	72	24	3	2	2	15	13	10	.435	.514
Cabrera,Fernando	L	.000	1	0	0	0	0	1	1	0	.500	.000
Throws Right	R	.500	4	2	0	0	1	4	1	0	.600	1.250
Cahill,Trevor	L	.237	397	94	14	1	7	29	34	72	.300	.330
Throws Right	R	.198	308	61	6	0	12	39	29	46	.270	.334
Cain,Matt	L	.225	408	92	20	4	12	42	32	79	.280	.382
Throws Right	R	.217	410	89	19	4	10	35	29	98	.273	.356
Camp,Shawn	L	.299	107	32	7	1	3	12	11	12	.364	.467
Throws Right	R	.234	167	39	8	1	5	18	7	34	.278	.383
Capps,Matt	L	.248	133	33	8	0	2	14	10	31	.301	.353
Throws Right	R	.280	150	42	7	0	4	14	7	28	.312	.407
Capuano,Chris	L	.224	67	15	2	0	3	8	7	23	.297	.388
Throws Left	R	.272	184	50	14	1	6	26	14	31	.323	.457
Caridad,Esmailin	L	.400	5	2	1	0	0	1	0	1	.400	.600
Throws Right	R	.167	12	2	0	0	1	6	5	3	.389	.417
Carlson,Jesse	L	.158	19	3	1	0	0	2	1	3	.238	.211
Throws Left	R	.303	33	10	2	0	3	6	4	5	.378	.636
Carmona,Fausto	L	.269	435	117	22	4	8	53	39	56	.328	.393
Throws Right	R	.244	352	86	11	2	9	34	33	68	.317	.364
Carpenter,Chris	L	.239	385	92	23	1	7	36	30	84	.300	.358
Throws Right	R	.248	492	122	23	3	14	52	33	95	.303	.392
Carpenter,Drew	L	.600	5	3	0	0	1	2	0	1	.600	1.200
Throws Right	R	.250	8	2	1	0	0	0	0	1	.250	.375
Carrasco,Carlos	L	.193	83	16	7	1	0	6	10	18	.280	.301
Throws Right	R	.356	87	31	6	1	6	11	4	20	.387	.655
Carrasco,D.J.	L	.260	104	27	6	0	2	11	11	24	.333	.375
Throws Right	R	.227	181	41	9	1	3	31	23	41	.324	.337
Cashner,Andrew	L	.300	80	24	4	0	4	12	12	20	.404	.500
Throws Right	R	.246	126	31	3	1	4	13	18	30	.345	.381
Casilla,Santiago	L	.203	59	12	2	1	1	3	14	31	.356	.322
Throws Right	R	.211	133	28	5	0	1	10	12	25	.293	.271
Cassevah,Bobby	L	.386	44	17	6	0	0	6	5	1	.440	.523
Throws Right	R	.154	39	6	3	0	0	2	3	7	.233	.231
Castillo,Alberto	L	.391	23	9	1	0	4	6	1	7	.417	.957
Throws Left	R	.318	22	7	2	0	1	7	5	4	.444	.545
Cecil,Brett	L	.224	152	34	7	1	3	14	6	37	.255	.342
Throws Left	R	.275	512	141	38	0	15	68	48	80	.335	.438
Ceda,Jose	L	.333	18	6	1	0	1	3	3	3	.455	.556
Throws Right	R	.133	15	2	0	0	0	2	8	6	.435	.133
Chacin,Gustavo	L	.323	62	20	4	0	0	6	9	18	.403	.387
Throws Left	R	.310	100	31	5	0	3	18	11	13	.378	.450
Chacin,Jhoulys	L	.266	203	54	8	2	2	23	27	45	.350	.355
Throws Right	R	.201	299	60	10	0	8	36	34	93	.297	.314
Chamberlain,Joba	L	.246	126	31	8	1	3	16	13	39	.317	.397
Throws Right	R	.258	155	40	9	0	3	22	9	38	.301	.374
Chapman,Aroldis	L	.154	13	2	0	0	0	0	1	5	.214	.154
Throws Left	R	.212	33	7	1	0	0	7	4	14	.297	.242
Chavez,Jesse	L	.260	104	27	4	1	8	16	11	15	.336	.548
Throws Right	R	.292	144	42	15	0	3	28	12	30	.340	.458
Chen,Bruce	L	.259	139	36	9	0	4	9	18	24	.346	.410
Throws Left	R	.253	396	100	23	0	13	51	39	74	.318	.409
Chico,Matt	L	.500	2	1	0	0	0	0	0	0	.500	.500
Throws Left	R	.263	19	5	2	0	0	1	0	3	.300	.368
Choate,Randy	L	.202	124	25	5	0	1	16	8	36	.263	.266
Throws Left	R	.410	39	16	3	0	2	6	9	4	.521	.641
Cishek,Steve	L	.000	5	0	0	0	0	1	1	2	.167	.000
Throws Right	R	.111	9	1	1	0	0	0	0	1	.111	.222
Clippard,Tyler	L	.242	149	36	8	2	3	20	20	53	.326	.383
Throws Right	R	.188	176	33	6	1	5	25	21	59	.276	.318
Coello,Robert	L	.444	9	4	0	0	0	1	2	2	.545	.444
Throws Right	R	.000	12	0	0	0	0	1	3	3	.200	.000
Coffey,Todd	L	.275	69	19	7	0	3	13	12	17	.386	.507
Throws Right	R	.267	172	46	8	2	5	43	11	39	.312	.424
Coke,Phil	L	.273	110	30	4	0	1	16	8	32	.344	.336
Throws Left	R	.276	134	37	8	0	1	16	18	21	.355	.358
Coleman,Casey	L	.278	79	22	5	0	2	8	14	9	.389	.418
Throws Right	R	.250	136	34	9	0	1	13	11	18	.305	.338
Colome,Jesus	L	.294	34	10	4	0	1	5	6	4	.390	.500
Throws Right	R	.179	28	5	1	0	0	6	5	12	.306	.214
Colon,Roman	L	.250	4	1	0	0	0	0	1	1	.400	.250
Throws Right	R	.571	7	4	2	0	0	4	1	0	.667	.857

Pitcher	vs	Avg	AB	H	2B	3B	HR	RBI	BB	SO	OBP	Slg
Contreras,Jose	L	.253	87	22	5	0	3	8	12	21	.340	.414
Throws Right	R	.256	121	31	4	1	2	14	4	36	.302	.355
Cook,Aaron	L	.337	208	70	11	0	5	41	32	17	.420	.462
Throws Right	R	.258	299	77	11	1	6	30	20	45	.309	.361
Cordero,Chad	L	.294	17	5	1	2	0	4	4	5	.429	.588
Throws Right	R	.333	15	5	1	0	1	6	1	1	.368	.600
Cordero,Francisco	L	.274	117	32	6	0	1	13	23	25	.393	.350
Throws Right	R	.226	159	36	6	0	4	17	13	34	.291	.340
Cormier,Lance	L	.252	139	35	8	0	3	14	20	22	.344	.374
Throws Right	R	.320	103	33	8	1	4	19	14	8	.402	.534
Corpas,Manuel	L	.326	86	28	9	2	3	17	11	10	.408	.581
Throws Right	R	.239	159	38	8	0	4	25	11	37	.287	.365
Correia,Kevin	L	.248	254	63	10	3	9	32	39	52	.351	.417
Throws Right	R	.290	307	89	14	1	11	43	25	63	.345	.450
Cortes,Dan	L	.222	9	2	1	0	0	2	2	3	.364	.333
Throws Right	R	.100	10	1	0	0	0	1	1	3	.167	.100
Crain,Jesse	L	.196	102	20	5	0	3	16	12	23	.281	.333
Throws Right	R	.228	145	33	7	1	2	15	15	39	.304	.331
Cramer,Bobby	L	.313	16	5	1	0	1	1	0	2	.313	.563
Throws Left	R	.214	70	15	3	0	4	6	6	11	.276	.429
Cruz,Juan	L	.333	9	3	1	0	0	2	2	2	.455	.444
Throws Right	R	.429	14	6	1	0	0	6	2	5	.500	.500
Cueto,Johnny	L	.234	312	73	18	1	11	40	32	82	.306	.404
Throws Right	R	.276	391	108	25	2	8	35	24	56	.329	.412
Daigle,Casey	L	.632	19	12	3	1	1	9	4	4	.696	1.053
Throws Right	R	.342	38	13	4	0	2	8	2	2	.375	.605
Daley,Matt	L	.345	29	10	4	0	0	2	3	3	.406	.483
Throws Right	R	.270	63	17	4	1	2	7	7	15	.365	.460
Danks,John	L	.273	242	66	10	3	2	26	19	46	.331	.364
Throws Left	R	.221	557	123	25	0	16	58	51	116	.289	.352
Davies,Kyle	L	.279	376	105	30	2	13	59	49	76	.363	.473
Throws Right	R	.288	351	101	19	0	7	43	31	50	.344	.402
Davis,Doug	L	.265	34	9	2	0	0	4	4	9	.375	.324
Throws Left	R	.351	131	46	7	0	6	24	17	25	.430	.542
Davis,Wade	L	.260	354	92	16	2	15	45	38	63	.333	.444
Throws Right	R	.250	292	73	17	3	9	25	24	50	.310	.421
de la Rosa,Jorge	L	.206	97	20	7	0	3	9	13	31	.300	.371
Throws Left	R	.244	349	85	27	0	12	42	42	82	.331	.424
Deduno,Sam	L	.200	5	1	0	0	0	0	0	2	.200	.200
Throws Right	R	.333	6	2	0	0	1	3	1	1	.429	.833
Del Rosario,Enerio	L	.500	16	8	1	0	0	5	3	1	.550	.563
Throws Right	R	.346	26	9	4	0	0	9	1	3	.393	.500
Delaney,Rob	L	.000	1	0	0	0	0	0	1	0	.500	.000
Throws Right	R	.667	3	2	0	0	1	1	0	0	.667	1.667
Delcarmen,Manny	L	.194	93	18	5	0	1	8	16	23	.312	.280
Throws Right	R	.255	106	27	2	0	7	19	16	15	.355	.472
Demel,Sam	L	.237	59	14	2	2	3	13	5	13	.292	.492
Throws Right	R	.304	92	28	10	0	2	15	7	20	.360	.478
Dempster,Ryan	L	.234	346	81	18	3	8	33	46	106	.332	.373
Throws Right	R	.252	465	117	16	1	17	59	40	102	.317	.400
Dessens,Elmer	L	.232	56	13	4	0	1	5	6	6	.306	.357
Throws Right	R	.243	115	28	6	1	3	16	10	10	.318	.391
Detwiler,Ross	L	.381	21	8	1	1	0	1	5	3	.500	.524
Throws Left	R	.268	97	26	2	0	5	16	9	14	.336	.443
Diamond,Thomas	L	.268	41	11	1	0	1	11	8	12	.388	.366
Throws Right	R	.310	71	22	5	0	4	14	10	24	.395	.549
Dickey,R.A.	L	.226	274	62	10	2	4	18	25	51	.292	.321
Throws Right	R	.269	383	103	13	3	9	38	17	53	.304	.389
Donnelly,Brendan	L	.389	36	14	2	0	1	6	11	5	.521	.528
Throws Right	R	.160	75	12	2	0	5	14	14	21	.293	.387
Dotel,Octavio	L	.301	93	28	8	6	2	18	18	19	.412	.581
Throws Right	R	.166	145	24	3	0	7	19	14	56	.245	.331
Doubront,Felix	L	.189	37	7	0	0	2	6	2	11	.225	.351
Throws Left	R	.317	63	20	5	2	1	6	8	12	.403	.508
Downs,Scott	L	.152	79	12	1	0	2	9	7	20	.247	.241
Throws Left	R	.243	144	35	7	3	1	10	7	28	.283	.354
Drabek,Kyle	L	.292	48	14	1	1	1	5	3	9	.327	.417
Throws Right	R	.308	13	4	0	0	1	3	2	3	.375	.538
Duchscherer,Justin	L	.192	52	10	1	0	2	4	9	10	.306	.327
Throws Right	R	.320	50	16	1	0	1	5	3	8	.370	.400
Duensing,Brian	L	.162	142	23	6	1	1	3	7	34	.217	.239
Throws Left	R	.282	351	99	13	2	10	35	28	44	.335	.416
Duke,Zach	L	.328	137	45	7	0	9	21	7	26	.370	.577
Throws Left	R	.319	523	167	37	3	16	86	44	70	.370	.493
Dunn,Michael	L	.211	38	8	2	0	0	6	6	18	.318	.263
Throws Left	R	.212	33	7	1	0	1	4	11	9	.409	.333

Pitchers vs. Left-Handed and Right-Handed Batters

Pitcher	vs	Avg	AB	H	2B	3B	HR	RBI	BB	SO	OBP	Slg
Durbin,Chad	L	.324	102	33	11	2	2	16	14	22	.407	.529
Throws Right	R	.195	154	30	6	0	5	17	13	41	.273	.331
Ekstrom,Mike	L	.185	27	5	0	0	0	2	6	4	.353	.185
Throws Right	R	.241	29	7	1	0	0	1	3	6	.324	.276
Elbert,Scott	L	1.000	1	1	0	0	0	3	3	0	1.000	1.000
Throws Left	R	.000	2	0	0	0	0	0	0	0	.000	.000
Ely,John	L	.240	146	35	8	4	4	21	18	39	.317	.432
Throws Right	R	.299	234	70	17	0	8	35	22	37	.363	.474
English,Jesse	L	.188	16	3	1	0	0	1	1	3	.235	.250
Throws Left	R	.467	15	7	2	0	0	1	1	1	.500	.600
Enright,Barry	L	.241	170	41	4	2	10	18	15	25	.301	.465
Throws Right	R	.279	201	56	15	1	10	23	14	24	.329	.512
Escalona,Edgmer	L	.400	5	2	0	0	0	0	3	0	.625	.400
Throws Right	R	.125	16	2	1	0	0	1	1	2	.167	.188
Estrada,Marco	L	.429	21	9	2	0	2	7	4	7	.538	.810
Throws Right	R	.172	29	5	2	0	1	4	2	6	.226	.345
Eveland,Dana	L	.319	47	15	2	0	0	7	11	8	.441	.362
Throws Left	R	.326	175	57	16	0	4	29	21	16	.404	.486
Farnsworth,Kyle	L	.264	110	29	7	0	3	13	11	23	.336	.409
Throws Right	R	.202	129	26	5	1	1	11	8	38	.259	.279
Feldman,Scott	L	.302	278	84	18	3	4	41	25	40	.358	.432
Throws Right	R	.323	300	97	18	2	14	46	20	35	.368	.537
Foliciano,Pedro	L	.211	123	26	8	0	0	8	10	35	.297	.276
Throws Left	R	.336	119	40	4	0	1	11	20	21	.436	.395
Feliz,Neftali	L	.127	118	15	5	0	1	10	10	40	.214	.195
Throws Right	R	.220	127	28	3	0	4	10	8	31	.277	.339
Fien,Casey	L	.400	5	2	0	0	1	1	0	0	.400	1.000
Throws Right	R	.333	6	2	1	0	1	3	0	0	.333	1.000
Figaro,Alfredo	L	.304	23	7	2	0	0	4	5	0	.429	.391
Throws Right	R	.314	35	11	3	1	1	7	3	5	.359	.543
Figuoroa,Nelson	L	.280	143	40	8	4	6	22	21	22	.372	.517
Throws Right	R	.217	203	44	5	0	4	20	13	51	.207	.300
Fisher,Carlos	L	.286	35	10	1	0	1	5	6	9	.390	.400
Throws Right	R	.235	51	12	5	0	0	3	7	12	.339	.333
Fister,Doug	L	.274	361	99	20	0	8	42	19	54	.313	.396
Throws Right	R	.279	315	88	14	0	5	33	13	39	.313	.371
Flores,Randy	L	.295	61	18	4	0	3	10	8	10	.300	.508
Throws Left	R	.246	57	14	4	0	3	11	7	10	.328	.474
Floyd,Gavin	L	.259	402	104	13	2	8	45	31	91	.312	.361
Throws Right	R	.292	325	95	22	1	6	36	27	60	.354	.422
Fox,Matt	L	.200	10	2	0	0	0	2	2	0	.308	.200
Throws Right	R	.353	17	6	1	0	0	3	0	0	.333	.412
Francis,Jeff	L	.309	68	21	4	1	2	7	3	18	.338	.485
Throws Left	R	.290	338	98	21	1	9	48	20	49	.330	.438
Francisco,Frank	L	.206	78	16	0	1	0	0	13	21	.319	.231
Throws Right	R	.275	120	33	5	1	5	13	5	39	.307	.458
Franklin,Ryan	L	.250	104	26	6	2	4	14	6	20	.288	.462
Throws Right	R	.215	144	31	7	1	3	11	4	22	.257	.340
Frasor,Jason	L	.248	101	25	5	0	2	11	17	26	.361	.356
Throws Right	R	.247	146	36	11	0	2	17	10	39	.308	.363
French,Luke	L	.256	82	21	4	1	4	17	12	10	.354	.476
Throws Left	R	.264	254	67	15	2	9	29	17	27	.316	.445
Frieri,Ernesto	L	.176	34	6	4	0	1	4	9	13	.349	.382
Throws Right	R	.156	77	12	3	0	1	6	8	28	.235	.234
Fuentes,Brian	L	.128	47	6	1	0	0	6	4	18	.222	.149
Throws Left	R	.202	124	25	10	0	5	12	16	29	.293	.403
Fulchino,Jeff	L	.257	70	18	0	1	3	11	15	21	.402	.414
Throws Right	R	.292	120	35	6	0	4	21	7	25	.333	.442
Gabino,Armando	L	.571	7	4	1	0	1	2	3	0	.700	1.143
Throws Right	R	.313	16	5	0	0	2	5	0	2	.313	.688
Galarraga,Armando	L	.241	282	68	20	4	11	37	37	39	.327	.457
Throws Right	R	.276	272	75	10	1	10	30	14	35	.315	.430
Gallagher,Sean	L	.208	101	21	5	0	1	10	22	23	.355	.287
Throws Right	R	.333	123	41	9	0	6	32	19	20	.431	.553
Gallardo,Yovani	L	.280	318	89	24	2	5	34	43	96	.366	.415
Throws Right	R	.228	391	89	20	0	7	42	32	104	.287	.332
Garcia,Freddy	L	.271	317	86	21	2	11	38	28	47	.329	.454
Throws Right	R	.287	296	85	18	4	12	40	17	42	.329	.497
Garcia,Jaime	L	.211	123	26	4	0	1	11	10	37	.281	.268
Throws Left	R	.251	499	125	17	1	8	42	54	95	.323	.337
Garland,Jon	L	.254	339	86	16	4	8	42	34	58	.322	.395
Throws Right	R	.228	395	90	12	0	12	40	53	78	.325	.349
Garza,Matt	L	.241	369	89	20	2	13	31	39	66	.318	.412
Throws Right	R	.255	408	104	21	2	15	52	24	84	.299	.426
Gaudin,Chad	L	.283	127	36	9	0	9	20	13	24	.357	.567
Throws Right	R	.287	129	37	5	0	7	24	12	29	.372	.488

Pitcher	vs	Avg	AB	H	2B	3B	HR	RBI	BB	SO	OBP	Slg
Gee,Dillon	L	.170	47	8	3	0	2	4	8	5	.291	.362
Throws Right	R	.239	71	17	5	0	0	6	7	12	.308	.310
Germano,Justin	L	.213	61	13	3	0	1	3	6	15	.294	.311
Throws Right	R	.200	70	14	2	0	5	12	2	14	.273	.443
Gervacio,Sammy	L	.143	7	1	0	0	1	1	1	0	.250	.571
Throws Right	R	.375	8	3	1	0	0	3	4	3	.583	.500
Gomez,Jeanmar	L	.268	138	37	9	2	3	16	12	25	.325	.428
Throws Right	R	.360	100	36	6	0	4	20	10	9	.421	.540
Gonzalez,Enrique	L	.214	42	9	2	0	3	6	13	5	.400	.476
Throws Right	R	.255	47	12	2	0	1	9	4	8	.308	.362
Gonzalez,Gio	L	.209	177	37	5	1	5	14	18	38	.282	.333
Throws Left	R	.235	571	134	21	1	10	54	74	133	.326	.327
Gonzalez,Mike	L	.324	34	11	5	0	0	5	3	9	.378	.471
Throws Left	R	.130	54	7	2	0	1	3	11	22	.273	.222
Gorzelanny,Tom	L	.286	126	36	2	5	4	18	14	37	.347	.476
Throws Left	R	.251	398	100	26	1	7	43	54	82	.342	.374
Grabow,John	L	.294	34	10	1	1	0	4	7	7	.429	.382
Throws Left	R	.333	75	25	5	0	5	16	6	13	.383	.600
Gray,Jeff	L	.455	11	5	0	0	0	1	4	0	.600	.455
Throws Right	R	.259	27	7	1	2	1	5	1	4	.310	.556
Green,Sean	L	.333	6	2	0	0	0	1	5	2	.636	.333
Throws Right	R	.172	29	5	1	0	1	7	3	10	.333	.310
Gregerson,Luke	L	.180	122	22	4	1	3	17	8	39	.237	.303
Throws Right	R	.162	154	25	6	0	5	14	10	50	.212	.299
Gregg,Kevin	L	.225	102	23	6	2	2	13	20	35	.350	.382
Throws Right	R	.248	117	29	6	2	2	15	10	23	.308	.385
Greinko,Zack	L	.280	460	129	26	4	12	59	40	96	.341	.433
Throws Right	R	.235	383	90	14	3	6	46	15	85	.267	.334
Guerrier,Matt	L	.236	89	21	5	0	1	12	11	14	.324	.326
Throws Right	R	.210	167	35	3	1	6	21	11	28	.264	.347
Guthrie,Jeremy	L	.253	400	101	24	7	16	45	33	65	.315	.468
Throws Right	R	.234	394	92	22	1	9	40	17	54	.280	.363
Gutierrez,Juan	L	.286	91	26	3	1	6	16	15	17	.389	.538
Throws Right	R	.228	127	29	4	0	7	18	8	30	.290	.425
Haeger,Charlie	L	.354	48	17	2	2	2	14	10	8	.458	.604
Throws Right	R	.257	74	19	2	2	2	9	16	22	.396	.419
Halladay,Roy	L	.259	459	119	22	3	12	37	14	95	.283	.399
Throws Right	R	.231	404	112	19	1	12	32	10	124	.260	.349
Hamels,Cole	L	.196	153	30	7	0	5	13	20	45	.305	.340
Throws Left	R	.247	627	155	35	1	21	59	41	166	.298	.407
Hammel,Jason	L	.282	301	85	12	2	10	41	21	76	.328	.405
Throws Right	R	.291	399	116	23	0	8	46	26	65	.341	.409
Hampton,Mike	L	.333	9	3	0	0	0	2	0	0	.333	.333
Throws Left	R	.000	5	0	0	0	0	1	1	3	.143	.000
Hanrahan,Joel	L	.219	96	21	3	2	4	18	16	37	.333	.417
Throws Right	R	.222	167	37	9	0	2	8	10	63	.278	.311
Hanson,Tommy	L	.220	361	80	16	0	5	33	27	86	.282	.314
Throws Right	R	.251	407	102	18	3	9	46	29	87	.309	.376
Happ,J.A.	L	.179	67	12	1	0	1	2	10	14	.313	.239
Throws Left	R	.244	250	61	16	0	7	34	34	56	.332	.392
Harang,Aaron	L	.283	198	56	17	1	5	22	17	37	.346	.455
Throws Right	R	.323	257	83	10	1	11	39	21	45	.375	.498
Harden,Rich	L	.273	187	51	10	1	11	28	35	42	.402	.513
Throws Right	R	.238	168	40	6	1	7	29	27	33	.348	.411
Haren,Dan	L	.258	427	110	23	2	18	49	37	96	.313	.447
Throws Right	R	.274	492	135	26	2	13	54	17	120	.303	.413
Harrell,Lucas	L	.396	53	21	5	0	1	8	11	7	.500	.547
Throws Right	R	.271	48	13	2	0	1	9	6	8	.352	.375
Harrison,Matt	L	.235	85	20	4	1	2	17	14	16	.340	.376
Throws Left	R	.273	220	60	10	0	8	36	25	30	.343	.427
Hawkins,LaTroy	L	.269	26	7	2	0	1	8	2	9	.321	.462
Throws Right	R	.359	39	14	3	0	1	7	4	9	.444	.513
Hawksworth,Blake	L	.304	161	49	4	1	9	26	18	26	.377	.509
Throws Right	R	.315	203	64	10	0	6	22	17	35	.365	.453
Heilman,Aaron	L	.229	140	32	7	1	3	16	12	28	.289	.357
Throws Right	R	.291	141	41	6	2	6	27	14	27	.370	.489
Hellickson,Jeremy	L	.301	73	22	6	0	4	13	6	14	.358	.548
Throws Right	R	.154	65	10	0	0	1	3	2	19	.191	.200
Hendrickson,Mark	L	.317	120	38	6	0	3	18	9	27	.366	.442
Throws Left	R	.311	190	59	11	0	6	30	11	28	.351	.463
Hensley,Clay	L	.216	134	29	6	1	1	7	18	40	.314	.299
Throws Right	R	.184	136	25	5	0	2	8	11	37	.250	.265
Hernandez,David	L	.198	121	24	7	0	6	14	24	32	.338	.405
Throws Right	R	.271	177	48	9	1	3	24	18	40	.342	.384
Hernandez,Felix	L	.213	470	100	15	2	8	42	48	120	.289	.304
Throws Right	R	.212	444	94	19	1	9	30	22	112	.256	.320

Pitchers vs. Left-Handed and Right-Handed Batters

Pitcher	vs	Avg	AB	H	2B	3B	HR	RBI	BB	SO	OBP	Slg
Hernandez,Livan	L	.295	373	110	29	0	10	43	33	48	.350	.453
Throws Right	R	.248	428	106	16	3	6	39	31	66	.299	.341
Herndon,David	L	.328	64	21	7	0	1	12	9	5	.421	.484
Throws Right	R	.317	145	46	12	0	1	22	8	24	.351	.421
Herrera,Daniel Ray	L	.316	38	12	3	0	0	8	2	6	.333	.395
Throws Left	R	.328	58	19	2	0	2	8	4	8	.371	.466
Herrmann,Frank	L	.310	87	27	7	1	4	15	8	15	.368	.552
Throws Right	R	.241	87	21	1	2	2	12	1	9	.261	.368
Hill,Rich	L	.125	8	1	0	0	0	1	0	2	.125	.125
Throws Left	R	.444	9	4	0	0	0	1	1	1	.500	.444
Hill,Shawn	L	.302	43	13	2	0	1	4	4	9	.354	.419
Throws Right	R	.262	42	11	2	0	0	1	0	5	.279	.310
Hochevar,Luke	L	.288	205	59	12	2	5	27	20	39	.357	.439
Throws Right	R	.255	200	51	10	3	4	27	17	37	.317	.395
Hoffman,Trevor	L	.298	84	25	9	2	2	17	10	17	.368	.524
Throws Right	R	.242	99	24	5	0	6	14	9	13	.306	.475
Holland,Derek	L	.130	46	6	3	0	0	4	2	14	.167	.196
Throws Left	R	.277	177	49	13	0	6	22	22	40	.366	.452
Holland,Greg	L	.278	36	10	4	0	1	6	5	9	.366	.472
Throws Right	R	.310	42	13	1	0	2	7	3	14	.356	.476
Houser,James	L	1.000	1	1	1	0	0	1	1	0	1.000	2.000
Throws Left	R	.400	5	2	0	0	1	3	0	1	.500	1.000
Howry,Bob	L	.296	54	16	3	0	3	12	3	7	.333	.519
Throws Right	R	.320	97	31	9	3	5	23	10	7	.380	.629
Hudson,Daniel	L	.203	153	31	3	1	3	10	16	39	.276	.294
Throws Right	R	.201	184	37	8	0	5	13	11	45	.260	.326
Hudson,Tim	L	.233	400	93	18	1	11	32	38	69	.302	.365
Throws Right	R	.225	426	96	10	2	9	33	36	70	.295	.322
Huff,David	L	.342	73	25	5	1	4	12	12	12	.437	.603
Throws Left	R	.300	253	76	22	2	10	40	22	25	.358	.522
Hughes,Dusty	L	.260	96	25	3	0	1	11	13	15	.351	.323
Throws Left	R	.283	120	34	7	2	2	13	11	19	.350	.425
Hughes,Phil	L	.235	345	81	12	0	17	42	39	77	.311	.417
Throws Right	R	.253	320	81	15	1	8	36	19	69	.292	.381
Humber,Philip	L	.275	40	11	1	0	1	8	3	7	.318	.375
Throws Right	R	.244	45	11	1	0	0	3	4	9	.320	.267
Hunter,Tommy	L	.272	279	76	12	2	10	19	22	39	.328	.437
Throws Right	R	.231	216	50	9	1	11	26	11	29	.273	.435
Igarashi,Ryota	L	.279	43	12	4	2	1	8	7	7	.380	.535
Throws Right	R	.239	71	17	2	0	3	15	11	18	.329	.394
Infante,Gregory	L	.286	7	2	0	0	0	0	3	2	.500	.286
Throws Right	R	.000	8	0	0	0	0	0	1	3	.111	.000
Jackson,Edwin	L	.271	447	121	20	7	11	56	33	93	.322	.421
Throws Right	R	.258	361	93	14	0	10	39	45	88	.345	.380
Jackson,Steven	L	.273	22	6	0	0	2	5	2	6	.333	.545
Throws Right	R	.440	25	11	0	0	2	6	4	1	.500	.680
Jakubauskas,Chris	L	1.000	2	2	0	0	0	0	0	0	1.000	1.000
Throws Right	R	.000	2	0	0	0	0	0	0	0	.000	.000
James,Justin	L	.333	9	3	0	0	0	3	3	3	.538	.333
Throws Right	R	.444	9	4	0	0	0	1	1	2	.500	.444
Jansen,Kenley	L	.205	44	9	3	0	0	2	7	18	.314	.273
Throws Right	R	.063	48	3	0	0	0	2	8	23	.211	.063
Janssen,Casey	L	.283	113	32	1	1	4	18	16	27	.382	.416
Throws Right	R	.264	159	42	8	2	4	23	5	36	.293	.415
Jeffress,Jeremy	L	.273	11	3	1	0	0	0	3	3	.429	.364
Throws Right	R	.208	24	5	1	1	0	2	3	5	.286	.333
Jenks,Bobby	L	.243	107	26	8	0	1	9	8	38	.302	.346
Throws Right	R	.277	101	28	1	0	2	16	10	23	.342	.347
Jepsen,Kevin	L	.239	117	28	6	0	1	15	19	33	.353	.316
Throws Right	R	.263	99	26	4	0	1	16	10	28	.327	.333
Jimenez,Ubaldo	L	.191	397	76	24	3	4	28	51	121	.284	.297
Throws Right	R	.227	388	88	16	2	6	37	41	93	.314	.325
Joaquin,Waldis	L	.400	5	2	1	0	0	2	4	1	.667	.600
Throws Right	R	.308	13	4	0	0	0	1	3	1	.471	.308
Johnson,Jim	L	.264	53	14	1	1	1	4	2	9	.291	.377
Throws Right	R	.327	55	18	1	0	1	10	3	13	.373	.400
Johnson,Josh	L	.223	328	73	16	2	4	18	29	88	.292	.320
Throws Right	R	.235	349	82	16	4	3	29	19	98	.272	.330
Jones,Hunter	L	.000	1	0	0	0	0	1	0	0	.500	.000
Throws Left	R	.000	4	0	0	0	0	0	1	3	.200	.000
Jurrjens,Jair	L	.294	197	58	11	6	6	26	25	32	.371	.503
Throws Right	R	.250	248	62	16	3	7	28	17	54	.301	.423
Karstens,Jeff	L	.364	217	79	21	3	10	39	14	26	.400	.627
Throws Right	R	.249	269	67	9	0	11	27	13	46	.278	.405
Kawakami,Kenshin	L	.299	157	47	13	5	4	20	16	23	.358	.522
Throws Right	R	.271	188	51	16	1	6	27	16	36	.325	.463
Kazmir,Scott	L	.274	124	34	2	2	4	11	17	11	.371	.419
Throws Left	R	.271	458	124	31	3	21	82	62	82	.366	.489
Kelley,Shawn	L	.261	46	12	3	0	0	6	8	12	.370	.326
Throws Right	R	.269	52	14	4	0	5	10	4	14	.333	.635
Kendrick,Kyle	L	.312	346	108	24	4	15	53	31	37	.367	.535
Throws Right	R	.254	358	91	25	1	11	40	18	47	.291	.422
Kennedy,Ian	L	.218	348	76	15	0	15	37	29	88	.283	.391
Throws Right	R	.238	366	87	20	2	11	40	41	80	.323	.393
Kershaw,Clayton	L	.200	160	32	11	0	7	22	13	67	.273	.400
Throws Left	R	.218	588	128	21	4	6	45	68	145	.301	.298
Kilby,Brad	L	.154	13	2	0	0	1	1	0	1	.154	.385
Throws Left	R	.263	19	5	2	0	1	1	0	7	.263	.526
Kimbrel,Craig	L	.176	34	6	1	0	0	2	7	18	.317	.206
Throws Right	R	.079	38	3	1	0	0	0	9	22	.255	.105
Kintzler,Brandon	L	.300	10	3	0	0	1	1	1	2	.364	.600
Throws Right	R	.389	18	7	1	0	1	6	3	7	.476	.611
Kirkman,Michael	L	.214	28	6	1	0	0	1	4	10	.313	.250
Throws Left	R	.107	28	3	0	0	0	3	6	6	.250	.107
Kohn,Mike	L	.325	40	13	1	0	0	7	6	11	.413	.350
Throws Right	R	.114	35	4	1	0	0	0	10	9	.311	.143
Kroenke,Zach	L	.143	7	1	1	0	0	0	0	2	.143	.286
Throws Left	R	.400	20	8	0	0	2	7	4	0	.500	.700
Kuo,Hong-Chih	L	.095	63	6	1	0	0	3	5	28	.159	.111
Throws Left	R	.159	145	23	5	1	1	7	13	45	.233	.228
Kuroda,Hiroki	L	.245	339	83	17	3	6	33	26	69	.298	.366
Throws Right	R	.241	402	97	12	0	9	43	22	90	.284	.338
Lackey,John	L	.298	466	139	37	2	8	53	47	74	.364	.438
Throws Right	R	.251	374	94	22	4	10	45	25	82	.307	.412
Laffey,Aaron	L	.308	78	24	7	1	0	13	7	15	.356	.423
Throws Left	R	.270	141	38	7	1	1	17	21	13	.370	.355
Lannan,John	L	.287	150	43	1	3	4	17	9	27	.333	.413
Throws Left	R	.307	430	132	30	1	10	58	40	44	.366	.451
Latos,Mat	L	.220	350	77	15	1	6	24	18	91	.260	.320
Throws Right	R	.214	341	73	13	0	10	33	32	98	.283	.340
League,Brandon	L	.243	136	33	4	0	5	28	16	20	.331	.382
Throws Right	R	.218	156	34	5	0	2	15	11	36	.268	.288
Leake,Mike	L	.292	253	74	15	1	11	42	19	39	.342	.490
Throws Right	R	.291	289	84	13	0	8	26	30	52	.360	.419
LeBlanc,Wade	L	.308	146	45	15	2	4	18	6	26	.340	.521
Throws Left	R	.269	417	112	15	3	20	49	45	84	.340	.463
LeCure,Sam	L	.304	69	21	4	0	3	10	15	14	.435	.493
Throws Right	R	.252	115	29	5	1	3	11	10	23	.328	.391
Ledezma,Wil	L	.367	30	11	3	1	0	5	2	6	.424	.533
Throws Left	R	.255	55	14	3	0	2	7	4	16	.305	.418
Lee,Cliff	L	.281	192	54	9	2	4	17	4	35	.294	.411
Throws Left	R	.227	621	141	37	1	12	57	14	150	.243	.348
Lerew,Anthony	L	.277	47	13	0	0	1	3	5	9	.345	.340
Throws Right	R	.356	59	21	5	0	8	18	4	9	.400	.847
Leroux,Chris	L	.263	38	10	3	0	0	8	9	9	.396	.342
Throws Right	R	.360	50	18	5	1	1	14	5	13	.404	.560
Lester,Jon	L	.226	186	42	9	1	4	25	19	54	.301	.349
Throws Left	R	.219	572	125	22	2	10	50	64	171	.304	.316
Lewis,Colby	L	.239	377	90	18	3	9	36	42	94	.319	.374
Throws Right	R	.216	388	84	21	0	12	39	23	102	.264	.363
Lewis,Jensen	L	.264	53	14	3	0	1	4	7	10	.350	.377
Throws Right	R	.182	77	14	5	0	0	7	12	19	.286	.247
Lewis,Rommie	L	.233	30	7	2	0	3	9	3	7	.303	.600
Throws Left	R	.295	44	13	1	1	1	9	5	8	.367	.432
Lidge,Brad	L	.214	84	18	2	0	3	9	16	28	.340	.345
Throws Right	R	.173	81	14	5	0	2	8	8	24	.256	.309
Lilly,Ted	L	.301	133	40	5	1	9	21	3	28	.331	.556
Throws Left	R	.213	587	125	27	4	23	58	41	138	.266	.390
Lincecum,Tim	L	.254	426	108	15	7	12	37	46	121	.324	.406
Throws Right	R	.229	376	86	13	1	6	43	30	110	.293	.316
Lincoln,Brad	L	.299	97	29	6	1	6	24	8	15	.355	.567
Throws Right	R	.319	116	37	10	1	3	17	7	10	.370	.500
Lincoln,Mike	L	.222	27	6	2	0	0	6	3	5	.323	.296
Throws Right	R	.352	54	19	4	0	1	9	7	7	.429	.481
Lindstrom,Matt	L	.268	97	26	5	1	3	15	10	19	.336	.433
Throws Right	R	.336	125	42	3	1	2	13	10	24	.385	.424
Linebrink,Scott	L	.288	118	34	4	1	9	24	6	28	.333	.568
Throws Right	R	.234	107	25	5	0	2	12	11	24	.311	.336
Link,Jon	L	.385	13	5	1	0	0	0	3	3	.500	.462
Throws Right	R	.304	23	7	1	0	0	2	1	1	.333	.348
Liriano,Francisco	L	.218	165	36	4	2	0	15	4	52	.250	.267
Throws Left	R	.262	565	148	34	3	9	55	54	149	.333	.381

Pitchers vs. Left-Handed and Right-Handed Batters

Pitcher	vs	Avg	AB	H	2B	3B	HR	RBI	BB	SO	OBP	Slg
Litsch,Jesse	L	.276	105	29	5	0	5	15	14	9	.367	.467
Throws Right	R	.300	80	24	5	2	2	8	1	7	.317	.488
Loe,Kameron	L	.274	84	23	1	0	4	10	5	11	.311	.429
Throws Right	R	.228	136	31	7	0	2	13	10	35	.289	.324
Logan,Boone	L	.190	79	15	0	1	0	6	10	30	.286	.215
Throws Left	R	.279	68	19	4	0	3	9	10	8	.372	.471
Lohse,Kyle	L	.344	163	56	18	2	5	35	20	26	.414	.571
Throws Right	R	.330	221	73	17	1	4	33	15	28	.375	.471
Lopez,Javier	L	.162	99	16	0	1	2	7	11	28	.250	.242
Throws Left	R	.306	111	34	11	0	0	10	9	10	.361	.405
Lopez,Rodrigo	L	.293	365	107	24	4	15	50	34	53	.351	.504
Throws Right	R	.280	429	120	25	1	22	66	22	63	.316	.497
Lopez,Wilton	L	.284	102	29	3	1	2	8	3	11	.302	.392
Throws Right	R	.245	151	37	9	2	2	12	2	39	.253	.371
Lowe,Derek	L	.287	369	106	20	2	5	33	33	49	.348	.393
Throws Right	R	.259	378	98	13	1	13	51	28	87	.313	.402
Lowe,Mark	L	.440	25	11	2	0	0	2	3	5	.483	.520
Throws Right	R	.241	29	7	1	0	2	6	3	7	.313	.483
Luebke,Cory	L	.333	15	5	0	0	1	3	0	5	.333	.533
Throws Left	R	.222	54	12	2	1	2	5	6	13	.311	.407
Lyon,Brandon	L	.195	128	25	3	1	1	9	22	27	.318	.258
Throws Right	R	.257	167	43	13	0	1	11	9	27	.303	.353
MacDougal,Mike	L	.433	30	13	8	0	1	11	8	4	.553	.800
Throws Right	R	.208	48	10	1	0	0	8	4	10	.283	.229
MacLane,Evan	L	-	0	0	0	0	0	0	1	0	1.000	-
Throws Left	R	.333	3	1	0	0	1	1	0	0	.333	1.333
Madson,Ryan	L	.217	92	20	4	0	2	7	7	28	.287	.326
Throws Right	R	.208	106	22	3	0	2	9	6	36	.263	.292
Mahay,Ron	L	.219	64	14	1	0	1	6	2	12	.239	.281
Throws Left	R	.284	67	19	1	0	4	14	6	13	.342	.478
Maholm,Paul	L	.231	117	27	5	0	3	16	10	27	.295	.350
Throws Left	R	.316	636	201	54	1	12	91	52	75	.372	.470
Maine,John	L	.200	60	12	2	0	3	12	9	21	.304	.383
Throws Right	R	.357	98	35	7	0	5	14	16	18	.453	.582
Maine,Scott	L	.300	10	3	2	0	1	2	2	4	.385	.800
Throws Left	R	.158	38	6	1	0	0	0	3	7	.220	.184
Majewski,Gary	L	1.000	1	1	0	0	0	0	1	0	1.000	1.000
Throws Right	R	.364	11	4	1	0	1	5	0	1	.364	.727
Maloney,Matt	L	.148	27	4	1	0	2	2	2	10	.233	.407
Throws Left	R	.314	51	16	2	0	0	5	3	3	.352	.353
Manship,Jeff	L	.236	55	13	3	0	2	4	3	11	.276	.400
Throws Right	R	.344	61	21	2	2	1	10	3	10	.369	.492
Manuel,Robert	L	.150	20	3	1	0	1	2	5	3	.320	.350
Throws Right	R	.259	27	7	2	0	4	8	2	2	.310	.778
Marcum,Shaun	L	.190	385	73	14	2	8	28	20	95	.233	.299
Throws Right	R	.298	362	108	24	3	16	50	23	70	.345	.514
Marinez,Jhan	L	.333	9	3	0	0	1	5	0	1	.333	.667
Throws Right	R	.000	2	0	0	0	0	1	3	2	.600	.000
Marmol,Carlos	L	.130	123	16	4	1	1	15	25	67	.287	.203
Throws Right	R	.161	149	24	5	0	0	15	27	71	.313	.195
Marquez,Jeff	L	.500	2	1	0	0	0	0	0	0	.500	.500
Throws Right	R	.333	3	1	0	0	1	2	0	0	.333	1.333
Marquis,Jason	L	.336	116	39	4	0	7	21	16	13	.425	.552
Throws Right	R	.296	125	37	9	0	2	16	8	18	.367	.416
Marshall,Sean	L	.196	102	20	3	0	2	10	0	27	.255	.284
Throws Left	R	.218	174	38	8	1	1	14	19	53	.292	.293
Marte,Damaso	L	.146	41	6	2	0	1	8	3	11	.200	.268
Throws Left	R	.190	21	4	0	0	1	4	8	1	.419	.333
Marte,Victor	L	.292	48	14	3	0	3	19	8	5	.404	.542
Throws Right	R	.338	71	24	6	0	5	17	7	14	.405	.634
Martin,J.D.	L	.337	89	30	3	2	4	11	7	13	.384	.551
Throws Right	R	.245	106	26	5	1	5	17	4	18	.268	.453
Martinez,Cristhian	L	.326	46	15	4	0	2	8	2	6	.347	.543
Throws Right	R	.228	57	13	2	1	1	6	4	16	.279	.351
Martinez,Joe	L	.250	36	9	2	0	0	4	5	5	.357	.306
Throws Right	R	.370	46	17	5	0	1	7	4	4	.423	.543
Masset,Nick	L	.196	97	19	3	0	4	11	8	30	.257	.351
Throws Right	R	.242	186	45	5	1	3	23	25	55	.332	.328
Masterson,Justin	L	.290	389	113	18	0	10	43	46	58	.370	.414
Throws Right	R	.263	320	84	14	1	4	48	27	82	.331	.350
Mata,Frank	L	.346	26	9	3	0	0	6	5	5	.452	.462
Throws Right	R	.313	48	15	4	0	2	10	3	4	.370	.521
Mateo,Marcos	L	.273	33	9	1	0	3	7	3	10	.324	.576
Throws Right	R	.229	48	11	2	0	3	6	6	16	.321	.458
Mathieson,Scott	L	.500	4	2	0	0	0	1	0	1	.500	.500
Throws Right	R	.600	5	3	0	0	0	0	2	0	.714	.600
Mathis,Doug	L	.293	41	12	2	0	2	5	4	3	.356	.488
Throws Right	R	.375	48	18	1	0	5	12	7	7	.455	.708
Matsuzaka,Daisuke	L	.265	310	82	22	0	6	42	52	68	.376	.394
Throws Right	R	.211	261	55	16	0	7	33	22	65	.273	.352
Matusz,Brian	L	.218	147	32	3	1	2	11	11	51	.288	.293
Throws Left	R	.266	531	141	29	2	17	64	52	92	.332	.424
Maya,Yunesky	L	.333	54	18	3	0	2	8	4	6	.383	.500
Throws Right	R	.250	48	12	3	1	1	8	7	6	.357	.417
Mazzaro,Vin	L	.289	239	69	5	1	10	29	24	33	.353	.444
Throws Right	R	.246	236	58	11	0	9	36	26	46	.326	.407
McClellan,Kyle	L	.204	108	22	5	0	2	6	13	21	.287	.306
Throws Right	R	.214	168	36	5	0	7	18	10	39	.271	.369
McClendon,Mike	L	.194	31	6	1	0	2	2	1	6	.219	.419
Throws Right	R	.196	46	9	3	0	0	5	6	15	.288	.261
McCutchen,Daniel	L	.315	124	39	8	2	5	15	16	12	.394	.532
Throws Right	R	.286	154	44	12	0	8	27	12	26	.335	.519
McDonald,James	L	.250	140	35	14	0	2	8	19	31	.340	.393
Throws Right	R	.271	129	35	5	1	2	18	10	37	.317	.372
McGee,Jake	L	.222	9	2	1	0	0	0	2	3	.364	.333
Throws Left	R	.000	8	0	0	0	0	1	1	3	.111	.000
Meche,Gil	L	.273	121	33	5	2	2	16	18	21	.371	.397
Throws Right	R	.274	117	32	5	0	7	20	20	20	.381	.496
Medders,Brandon	L	.393	28	11	1	1	2	7	3	4	.452	.714
Throws Right	R	.385	39	15	5	0	1	9	3	4	.429	.590
Medlen,Kris	L	.281	178	50	13	1	5	20	9	39	.316	.449
Throws Right	R	.257	226	58	5	1	8	22	12	44	.299	.394
Meek,Evan	L	.168	125	21	1	0	1	7	14	18	.262	.200
Throws Right	R	.199	161	32	7	1	4	21	17	52	.282	.329
Mejia,Jenrry	L	.203	59	12	1	0	1	5	9	13	.319	.271
Throws Right	R	.340	100	34	7	0	2	12	11	9	.412	.470
Melancon,Mark	L	.167	30	5	1	0	0	2	4	4	.257	.200
Throws Right	R	.280	50	14	3	0	2	9	4	18	.345	.460
Mendez,Adalberto	L	.315	54	17	2	1	3	4	7	6	.403	.556
Throws Right	R	.268	41	11	2	0	4	8	5	5	.362	.610
Mendoza,Luis	L	.429	7	3	0	0	1	1	1	0	.500	.857
Throws Right	R	.467	15	7	3	0	3	8	2	1	.529	1.267
Meredith,Cla	L	.333	18	6	0	0	1	3	2	2	.381	.500
Throws Right	R	.286	42	12	5	0	3	8	2	5	.333	.619
Meyer,Dan	L	.400	15	6	0	0	1	5	4	3	.550	.600
Throws Left	R	.346	26	9	1	1	0	5	8	1	.500	.462
Mickolio,Kam	L	.250	8	2	2	0	0	2	1	2	.333	.500
Throws Right	R	.375	8	3	0	0	1	3	2	2	.500	.750
Mijares,Jose	L	.268	56	15	8	0	1	10	3	14	.311	.464
Throws Left	R	.268	71	19	3	0	3	8	6	14	.325	.437
Miller,Andrew	L	.405	37	15	1	1	3	8	10	10	.532	.730
Throws Left	R	.360	100	36	8	0	3	21	16	15	.445	.530
Miller,Justin	L	.286	28	8	1	0	0	4	5	7	.432	.321
Throws Right	R	.226	62	14	4	0	4	11	3	23	.258	.484
Miller,Trever	L	.203	74	15	1	0	1	7	9	16	.294	.257
Throws Left	R	.273	55	15	2	1	1	6	7	6	.359	.400
Mills,Brad	L	.273	33	9	2	1	1	6	4	5	.351	.405
Throws Left	R	.220	50	11	3	0	1	4	9	13	.344	.340
Millwood,Kevin	L	.307	394	121	11	3	14	55	43	79	.379	.457
Throws Right	R	.276	369	102	20	1	16	54	22	53	.322	.466
Minor,Mike	L	.293	41	12	4	1	0	5	3	13	.356	.439
Throws Left	R	.320	128	41	12	0	6	25	8	30	.353	.555
Misch,Pat	L	.294	34	10	1	0	2	6	1	4	.314	.500
Throws Left	R	.280	118	33	5	0	2	11	3	19	.298	.373
Mitre,Sergio	L	.226	106	24	6	0	3	12	5	17	.261	.368
Throws Right	R	.218	87	19	3	0	4	11	11	12	.317	.391
Mock,Garrett	L	.000	4	0	0	0	0	0	3	0	.429	.000
Throws Right	R	.400	10	4	0	0	2	2	2	3	.500	1.000
Moehler,Brian	L	.282	103	29	3	0	4	15	13	14	.362	.427
Throws Right	R	.314	118	37	8	1	1	18	13	14	.383	.424
Monasterios,Carlos	L	.242	161	39	7	0	5	19	21	28	.330	.379
Throws Right	R	.313	192	60	4	2	10	22	8	24	.359	.510
Morales,Franklin	L	.171	35	6	0	0	2	6	7	10	.310	.343
Throws Left	R	.293	75	22	4	0	3	13	17	17	.433	.467
Morrow,Brandon	L	.245	319	78	27	1	6	45	49	103	.348	.392
Throws Right	R	.253	229	58	15	0	5	24	17	75	.320	.384
Mortensen,Clay	L	.125	8	1	0	0	0	0	1	2	.222	.125
Throws Right	R	.313	16	5	0	0	1	3	1	5	.353	.500
Morton,Charlie	L	.329	143	47	6	1	8	28	11	26	.384	.552
Throws Right	R	.335	194	65	11	0	7	45	15	33	.387	.500
Moscoso,Guillermo	L	-	0	0	0	0	0	1	2	0	1.000	-
Throws Right	R	.500	4	2	1	0	0	1	0	2	.500	.750

Pitchers vs. Left-Handed and Right-Handed Batters

Pitcher	vs	Avg	AB	H	2B	3B	HR	RBI	BB	SO	OBP	Slg
Moseley,Dustin	L	.281	128	36	5	0	8	22	14	14	.354	.508
Throws Right	R	.256	117	30	4	0	5	15	13	19	.328	.419
Mota,Guillermo	L	.247	81	20	5	3	2	13	12	17	.337	.457
Throws Right	R	.240	121	29	8	2	2	16	10	21	.293	.388
Motte,Jason	L	.267	60	16	2	0	2	9	12	15	.389	.400
Throws Right	R	.198	126	25	4	0	3	10	6	39	.230	.302
Moyer,Jamie	L	.194	72	14	4	0	6	11	4	16	.256	.500
Throws Left	R	.249	358	89	17	1	14	45	16	47	.288	.419
Moylan,Peter	L	.308	52	16	3	0	2	11	22	3	.507	.481
Throws Right	R	.214	173	37	7	0	3	25	15	49	.283	.306
Mujica,Edward	L	.202	109	22	2	2	5	10	4	25	.230	.394
Throws Right	R	.243	152	37	6	1	9	23	2	47	.253	.474
Mulvey,Kevin	L	.200	5	1	0	0	0	0	1	0	.333	.200
Throws Right	R	.444	9	4	0	0	2	2	1	1	.545	1.111
Myers,Brett	L	.240	366	88	22	4	8	36	30	78	.300	.388
Throws Right	R	.254	488	124	18	2	12	43	36	102	.306	.373
Narveson,Chris	L	.226	164	37	7	0	2	16	13	37	.293	.305
Throws Left	R	.280	483	135	31	3	19	66	46	100	.342	.474
Nelson,Joe	L	.440	25	11	3	0	2	10	1	4	.462	.800
Throws Right	R	.214	14	3	1	0	0	1	5	5	.421	.286
Neshek,Pat	L	.286	7	2	0	0	0	1	2	2	.444	.286
Throws Right	R	.185	27	5	1	0	1	5	6	7	.353	.333
Ni,Fu-Te	L	.306	36	11	1	2	0	10	6	12	.432	.444
Throws Left	R	.281	57	16	4	0	2	11	13	10	.408	.456
Niemann,Jeff	L	.244	328	80	17	2	13	40	38	70	.322	.427
Throws Right	R	.239	330	79	14	1	12	39	23	61	.301	.397
Niese,Jonathon	L	.266	124	33	5	1	6	21	13	29	.364	.468
Throws Left	R	.283	562	159	39	1	14	66	49	119	.341	.431
Nieve,Fernando	L	.240	50	12	3	1	6	12	5	10	.316	.700
Throws Right	R	.231	108	25	3	1	4	16	17	28	.341	.389
Nippert,Dustin	L	.305	82	25	3	1	2	14	22	16	.448	.439
Throws Right	R	.261	138	36	8	0	5	13	12	31	.342	.428
Nolasco,Ricky	L	.283	304	86	14	3	8	28	22	73	.330	.428
Throws Right	R	.263	316	83	20	1	16	48	11	74	.288	.484
Norberto,Jordan	L	.235	34	8	1	0	1	7	10	7	.409	.353
Throws Left	R	.216	37	8	1	0	2	4	12	8	.408	.405
Norris,Bud	L	.241	274	66	18	1	12	46	47	85	.354	.445
Throws Right	R	.269	316	85	14	2	6	44	30	73	.338	.383
Nova,Ivan	L	.276	98	27	3	0	3	11	10	18	.349	.398
Throws Right	R	.258	66	17	5	0	1	7	7	8	.324	.379
Nunez,Leo	L	.214	131	28	8	0	1	13	11	33	.275	.298
Throws Right	R	.291	117	34	5	2	4	16	10	38	.346	.470
O'Day,Darren	L	.229	70	16	3	0	0	3	5	8	.289	.271
Throws Right	R	.181	149	27	4	0	5	17	7	37	.233	.309
O'Flaherty,Eric	L	.231	78	18	4	0	1	8	5	19	.277	.321
Throws Left	R	.229	83	19	5	1	1	11	13	17	.340	.349
Ogando,Alexi	L	.229	48	11	2	0	1	8	9	6	.345	.333
Throws Right	R	.198	101	20	1	0	1	7	7	33	.255	.238
Ohlendorf,Ross	L	.273	172	47	11	2	7	24	19	36	.351	.483
Throws Right	R	.250	236	59	16	3	5	24	25	43	.324	.407
Ohman,Will	L	.229	83	19	4	0	1	10	13	25	.323	.313
Throws Left	R	.288	73	21	4	0	3	14	10	18	.376	.466
Okajima,Hideki	L	.284	88	25	2	0	2	16	10	16	.357	.375
Throws Left	R	.340	100	34	6	1	4	13	10	17	.396	.540
Oliver,Andy	L	.269	26	7	2	0	2	5	6	7	.406	.577
Throws Left	R	.328	58	19	3	1	1	10	7	11	.412	.466
Oliver,Darren	L	.200	105	21	4	0	2	13	3	43	.234	.295
Throws Left	R	.281	114	32	10	0	2	12	12	22	.344	.421
Olsen,Scott	L	.289	90	26	2	1	2	7	6	18	.337	.400
Throws Left	R	.289	232	67	12	3	8	37	21	35	.348	.470
Olson,Garrett	L	.245	53	13	4	0	1	7	6	14	.322	.377
Throws Left	R	.284	102	29	6	0	5	13	9	17	.339	.490
Ondrusek,Logan	L	.205	78	16	6	1	1	7	1	15	.215	.346
Throws Right	R	.236	140	33	3	1	6	22	19	24	.325	.400
Ortiz,Ramon	L	.357	56	20	5	1	4	18	11	11	.463	.696
Throws Right	R	.220	59	13	2	0	1	6	5	10	.277	.305
Ortiz,Russ	L	.308	13	4	0	0	0	2	2	3	.375	.308
Throws Right	R	.375	16	6	1	0	0	2	3	3	.474	.438
O'Sullivan,Sean	L	.247	194	48	6	1	9	24	23	25	.323	.428
Throws Right	R	.302	139	42	11	0	6	22	8	18	.345	.511
Oswalt,Roy	L	.232	357	83	19	4	7	27	23	89	.286	.367
Throws Right	R	.196	404	79	17	0	12	36	32	104	.253	.327
Ottavino,Adam	L	.390	41	16	5	2	2	6	5	3	.457	.756
Throws Right	R	.356	59	21	4	0	3	12	4	9	.397	.576
Owings,Micah	L	.357	42	15	5	0	1	10	12	9	.500	.548
Throws Right	R	.163	80	13	2	1	2	12	13	26	.295	.288

Pitcher	vs	Avg	AB	H	2B	3B	HR	RBI	BB	SO	OBP	Slg
Padilla,Vicente	L	.167	144	24	4	0	7	19	15	32	.250	.340
Throws Right	R	.267	206	55	8	1	7	23	9	52	.314	.417
Palmer,Matt	L	.268	56	15	5	0	0	7	14	7	.414	.357
Throws Right	R	.291	79	23	8	1	1	13	6	10	.349	.456
Papelbon,Jonathan	L	.255	141	36	7	0	4	16	15	47	.327	.390
Throws Right	R	.189	111	21	7	0	3	15	13	29	.286	.333
Park,Chan Ho	L	.270	111	30	7	1	4	16	9	15	.325	.459
Throws Right	R	.246	142	35	5	0	5	22	10	37	.308	.387
Parnell,Bobby	L	.327	52	17	3	0	1	3	3	10	.364	.442
Throws Right	R	.276	87	24	2	0	0	7	5	23	.315	.299
Parra,Manny	L	.326	132	43	7	0	9	26	17	48	.400	.583
Throws Left	R	.264	349	92	16	3	9	47	46	81	.348	.404
Parrish,John	L	.300	10	3	0	0	1	3	2	2	.417	.600
Throws Left	R	.091	11	1	0	0	1	1	3	2	.286	.364
Patton,Troy	L	.333	3	1	1	0	0	0	0	1	.333	.667
Throws Left	R	-	0	0	0	0	0	0	1	0	1.000	-
Pauley,David	L	.247	186	46	4	0	6	23	14	23	.303	.366
Throws Right	R	.261	165	43	7	0	7	17	16	28	.332	.430
Paulino,Felipe	L	.306	134	41	7	3	0	16	26	30	.414	.403
Throws Right	R	.248	218	54	18	0	4	31	20	53	.318	.385
Pavano,Carl	L	.292	411	120	28	4	10	46	19	55	.325	.453
Throws Right	R	.242	442	107	21	0	14	42	18	62	.276	.385
Peavy,Jake	L	.275	204	56	11	1	4	26	18	39	.332	.397
Throws Right	R	.209	201	42	9	0	9	22	16	54	.278	.388
Pelfrey,Mike	L	.279	402	112	26	1	11	33	41	59	.346	.430
Throws Right	R	.272	372	101	21	5	1	45	27	54	.327	.363
Pena,Tony	L	.244	180	44	11	0	3	20	30	25	.354	.356
Throws Right	R	.308	208	64	10	1	7	40	15	31	.346	.466
Penn,Hayden	L	.833	6	5	0	0	0	2	1	0	.857	.833
Throws Right	R	.429	7	3	1	1	0	3	2	0	.556	.857
Penny,Brad	L	.360	86	31	6	0	1	5	5	9	.415	.465
Throws Right	R	.248	129	32	8	0	3	19	4	26	.265	.380
Peralta,Joel	L	.212	66	14	4	0	1	2	6	21	.278	.318
Throws Right	R	.145	110	16	3	1	4	11	3	28	.174	.300
Perdomo,Luis	L	.000	2	0	0	0	0	0	0	0	.000	.000
Throws Right	R	.500	2	1	0	0	1	1	0	0	.500	2.000
Perez,Chris	L	.216	97	21	7	1	3	12	18	23	.350	.402
Throws Right	R	.154	123	19	4	0	1	7	10	38	.234	.211
Perez,Oliver	L	.214	42	9	1	0	3	4	11	10	.411	.452
Throws Left	R	.317	142	45	5	3	6	29	31	27	.435	.521
Perez,Rafael	L	.306	111	34	3	0	2	9	9	14	.358	.387
Throws Left	R	.295	129	38	8	0	1	13	16	22	.370	.380
Perkins,Glen	L	.241	29	7	1	1	0	2	2	3	.313	.345
Throws Left	R	.386	57	22	4	1	3	15	3	11	.431	.649
Perry,Ryan	L	.167	78	13	1	0	1	6	11	17	.267	.218
Throws Right	R	.284	148	42	6	1	5	21	12	28	.353	.439
Pestano,Vinnie	L	.375	8	3	0	0	0	2	2	0	.500	.375
Throws Right	R	.100	10	1	0	0	0	0	3	8	.308	.100
Pettitte,Andy	L	.186	129	24	3	0	2	10	7	39	.226	.256
Throws Left	R	.283	350	99	20	0	11	38	34	62	.348	.434
Pineiro,Joel	L	.239	305	73	16	8	7	38	21	51	.288	.413
Throws Right	R	.284	289	82	11	2	8	28	13	41	.314	.419
Pinto,Renyel	L	.364	22	8	2	0	1	6	2	6	.481	.591
Throws Left	R	.190	42	8	2	0	0	4	7	10	.320	.238
Porcello,Rick	L	.303	340	103	16	2	8	41	22	37	.351	.432
Throws Right	R	.272	312	85	7	2	10	43	16	47	.313	.404
Price,David	L	.211	175	37	8	3	0	8	15	44	.277	.291
Throws Left	R	.224	595	133	25	4	15	56	64	144	.302	.355
Proctor,Scott	L	.182	11	2	1	0	0	0	0	4	.182	.273
Throws Right	R	.222	9	2	1	0	1	2	4	2	.462	.667
Purcey,David	L	.163	43	7	1	0	0	7	10	13	.309	.186
Throws Left	R	.235	81	19	6	0	3	6	5	19	.279	.420
Putz,J.J.	L	.253	91	23	5	2	2	15	6	31	.303	.418
Throws Right	R	.164	110	18	1	0	2	11	9	34	.227	.227
Qualls,Chad	L	.392	120	47	8	0	5	33	12	20	.448	.583
Throws Right	R	.292	130	38	8	2	2	23	9	29	.336	.431
Ramirez,Edwar	L	.267	15	4	0	0	0	1	6	3	.476	.267
Throws Right	R	.192	26	5	0	0	1	6	4	7	.290	.308
Ramirez,Ramon	L	.231	104	24	7	0	3	7	9	20	.292	.385
Throws Right	R	.190	147	28	6	1	4	15	18	26	.272	.327
Ramos,Cesar	L	.316	19	6	0	0	0	2	2	7	.381	.316
Throws Left	R	.500	24	12	4	0	1	8	2	2	.538	.792
Rapada,Clay	L	.053	19	1	0	0	0	0	2	4	.143	.053
Throws Left	R	.385	13	5	0	0	2	4	5	1	.556	.846
Rauch,Jon	L	.288	111	32	4	0	3	7	7	24	.333	.405
Throws Right	R	.248	117	29	8	0	0	14	7	22	.290	.316

Pitchers vs. Left-Handed and Right-Handed Batters

Pitcher	vs	Avg	AB	H	2B	3B	HR	RBI	BB	SO	OBP	Slg
Ray,Chris	L	.279	86	24	5	0	4	17	8	11	.340	.477
Throws Right	R	.203	118	24	8	1	1	13	17	20	.304	.314
Ray,Robert	L	.333	3	1	1	0	0	0	3	0	.667	.667
Throws Right	R	.100	10	1	0	1	0	1	2	3	.250	.300
Resop,Chris	L	.281	32	9	0	1	1	6	9	7	.429	.438
Throws Right	R	.140	43	6	4	0	0	7	4	19	.208	.233
Reyes,Dennys	L	.307	75	23	5	0	2	13	11	20	.409	.453
Throws Left	R	.177	62	11	1	0	0	5	10	5	.288	.194
Reyes,Jo-Jo	L	.333	6	2	1	0	1	4	1	1	.429	1.000
Throws Left	R	.571	14	8	1	0	1	7	2	1	.625	.857
Reynolds,Matt	L	.152	33	5	1	0	1	6	1	6	.216	.273
Throws Left	R	.179	28	5	1	0	1	1	4	11	.281	.321
Rhodes,Arthur	L	.214	84	18	6	0	3	9	1	26	.230	.393
Throws Left	R	.182	110	20	4	0	1	7	17	24	.289	.245
Richard,Clayton	L	.228	206	47	10	0	1	19	14	41	.283	.291
Throws Left	R	.281	565	159	28	1	15	59	64	112	.356	.414
Richardson,Dustin	L	.360	25	9	0	0	2	6	8	8	.529	.600
Throws Left	R	.240	25	6	2	0	0	3	6	4	.375	.320
Rincon,Juan	L	.250	4	1	1	0	0	1	2	1	.500	.500
Throws Right	R	.400	5	2	0	0	0	1	0	2	.400	.400
Ring,Royce	L	.375	8	3	0	0	0	1	1	2	.444	.375
Throws Left	R	.000	2	0	0	0	0	0	1	0	.333	.000
Riske,David	L	.133	30	4	1	0	0	2	2	6	.188	.167
Throws Right	R	.333	63	21	6	0	2	12	6	10	.403	.524
Rivera,Mariano	L	.214	103	22	3	0	2	12	6	14	.264	.301
Throws Right	R	.155	110	17	4	1	0	5	5	31	.217	.209
Rivera,Saul	L	.500	6	3	0	0	0	1	0	0	.429	.500
Throws Right	R	.571	14	8	0	0	2	8	3	1	.647	1.000
Robertson,David	L	.268	97	26	4	0	2	11	18	34	.388	.371
Throws Right	R	.250	132	33	4	1	3	17	15	37	.329	.364
Robertson,Nate	L	.269	78	21	5	0	0	4	11	14	.370	.333
Throws Left	R	.295	319	94	27	1	12	67	31	49	.359	.498
Rodney,Fernando	L	.273	132	36	9	0	1	16	18	28	.364	.364
Throws Right	R	.254	134	34	10	0	3	17	17	25	.355	.396
Rodriguez,F. (K-Rod)	L	.245	94	23	6	0	2	11	8	24	.308	.372
Throws Right	R	.188	117	22	5	0	1	9	13	43	.275	.256
Rodriguez,Francisco	L	.338	77	26	6	0	3	14	16	18	.452	.532
Throws Right	R	.192	104	20	2	0	2	12	10	10	.270	.260
Rodriguez,Henry	L	.283	46	13	1	0	1	8	7	13	.389	.370
Throws Right	R	.207	58	12	3	0	1	6	6	20	.277	.310
Rodriguez,Rafael	L	.250	8	2	1	0	0	0	0	1	.400	.375
Throws Right	R	.273	11	3	0	0	1	3	3	2	.429	.545
Rodriguez,Wandy	L	.247	168	39	8	1	2	11	6	43	.294	.348
Throws Left	R	.250	575	144	30	4	14	70	62	135	.326	.390
Roenicke,Josh	L	.219	32	7	1	0	0	1	6	6	.342	.250
Throws Right	R	.250	44	11	3	1	1	12	7	12	.377	.432
Rogers,Esmil	L	.370	127	47	5	4	1	19	13	24	.423	.496
Throws Right	R	.278	169	47	11	1	4	31	13	42	.346	.426
Rogers,Mark	L	.000	8	0	0	0	0	1	0	5	.000	.000
Throws Right	R	.091	22	2	0	0	0	1	3	6	.231	.091
Romero,J.C.	L	.217	83	18	2	0	1	7	11	20	.323	.277
Throws Left	R	.231	52	12	1	0	2	11	18	8	.452	.365
Romero,Ricky	L	.276	196	54	13	0	5	29	18	49	.350	.418
Throws Left	R	.231	584	135	29	0	10	57	64	125	.309	.332
Romo,Sergio	L	.241	79	19	3	1	1	7	7	16	.310	.342
Throws Right	R	.185	146	27	7	0	5	21	7	54	.234	.000
Rosa,Carlos	L	.414	29	12	2	0	1	8	4	5	.457	.586
Throws Right	R	.195	41	8	0	0	0	6	8	4	.302	.195
Rosales,Leo	L	.357	28	10	2	1	1	4	3	7	.406	.607
Throws Right	R	.366	41	15	3	0	1	9	6	5	.438	.512
Rosario,Sandy	L	.800	5	4	0	0	1	3	1	0	.833	1.400
Throws Right	R	.833	6	5	1	0	1	2	0	0	.833	1.500
Ross,Tyson	L	.258	66	17	4	0	1	11	6	10	.311	.364
Throws Right	R	.282	78	22	1	1	3	12	14	22	.383	.436
Rowland-Smith,Ryan	L	.342	114	39	5	2	6	23	10	17	.385	.579
Throws Left	R	.304	335	102	33	0	19	60	34	32	.378	.573
Runzler,Dan	L	.260	50	13	3	1	0	4	5	14	.339	.360
Throws Left	R	.232	69	16	2	0	1	9	15	23	.369	.304
Rupe,Josh	L	.278	18	5	1	0	0	1	2	2	.350	.333
Throws Right	R	.391	23	9	2	0	1	6	5	6	.500	.609
Russell,Adam	L	.143	21	3	0	0	0	3	3	12	.250	.143
Throws Right	R	.324	34	11	2	0	0	6	2	6	.351	.382
Russell,James	L	.238	80	19	2	0	5	16	4	29	.276	.450
Throws Left	R	.308	117	36	6	1	6	27	7	13	.357	.530
Rzepczynski,Marc	L	.262	61	16	1	0	1	6	7	17	.343	.328
Throws Left	R	.298	188	56	15	2	7	29	23	40	.384	.511

Pitcher	vs	Avg	AB	H	2B	3B	HR	RBI	BB	SO	OBP	Slg
Sabathia,CC	L	.261	203	53	8	0	4	13	14	62	.318	.360
Throws Left	R	.232	673	156	30	2	16	69	60	135	.295	.354
Saito,Takashi	L	.244	86	21	2	0	2	5	10	21	.323	.337
Throws Right	R	.172	116	20	8	0	2	12	7	48	.220	.293
Salas,Fernando	L	.250	48	12	0	2	3	8	7	12	.345	.521
Throws Right	R	.235	68	16	5	0	1	8	8	17	.312	.353
Sale,Chris	L	.290	31	9	1	0	0	1	4	9	.371	.323
Throws Left	R	.120	50	6	0	0	2	5	6	23	.214	.240
Samardzija,Jeff	L	.103	29	3	0	1	0	1	8	4	.297	.172
Throws Right	R	.367	49	18	4	0	4	16	12	5	.508	.694
Sampson,Chris	L	.306	49	15	0	1	1	8	4	9	.370	.408
Throws Right	R	.354	79	28	5	1	6	15	4	7	.386	.671
Sanabia,Alex	L	.204	137	28	2	1	3	11	14	25	.276	.299
Throws Right	R	.313	147	46	10	1	3	15	2	22	.336	.456
Sanches,Brian	L	.192	99	19	3	1	3	12	15	19	.302	.333
Throws Right	R	.195	123	24	4	0	4	13	12	35	.263	.325
Sanchez,Anibal	L	.262	367	96	12	3	4	35	42	80	.343	.343
Throws Right	R	.252	381	96	20	3	6	43	28	77	.307	.367
Sanchez,Jonathan	L	.181	138	25	5	0	5	7	22	44	.323	.326
Throws Left	R	.210	558	117	27	1	16	55	74	161	.303	.348
Sanchez,Romulo	L	.143	7	1	0	0	0	0	2	4	.333	.143
Throws Right	R	.000	7	0	0	0	0	0	1	1	.125	.000
Santana,Ervin	L	.271	457	124	26	3	16	54	46	83	.346	.446
Throws Right	R	.246	395	97	22	1	11	41	27	86	.297	.390
Santana,Johan	L	.273	198	54	8	1	4	20	13	36	.322	.384
Throws Left	R	.229	547	125	24	2	12	46	42	108	.282	.346
Santos,Sergio	L	.207	82	17	1	0	0	5	9	26	.293	.220
Throws Right	R	.298	121	36	9	0	2	15	17	30	.390	.421
Saunders,Joe	L	.259	193	50	7	2	5	24	15	37	.321	.394
Throws Left	R	.301	604	182	40	3	20	80	49	77	.352	.477
Sborz,Jay	L	.667	3	2	0	0	0	3	0	1	.667	.667
Throws Right	R	.500	2	1	0	0	0	2	0	0	.750	.500
Scherzer,Max	L	.239	376	90	8	4	9	40	39	96	.313	.354
Throws Right	R	.250	336	84	19	2	11	32	31	88	.320	.417
Schlereth,Daniel	L	.310	29	9	2	0	2	3	5	7	.412	.586
Throws Left	R	.244	45	11	1	0	0	4	5	12	.327	.267
Schlichting,Travis	L	.171	35	6	2	0	0	1	3	5	.237	.229
Throws Right	R	.275	51	14	2	0	0	12	7	9	.356	.314
Schlitter,Brian	L	.579	19	11	2	0	1	5	3	2	.636	.842
Throws Right	R	.304	23	7	2	0	1	10	2	5	.385	.522
Schoeneweis,Scott	L	.346	26	9	1	0	1	3	3	10	.414	.500
Throws Left	R	.323	31	10	3	0	1	9	7	3	.436	.516
Seddon,Chris	L	.276	29	8	3	0	1	8	4	9	.364	.483
Throws Left	R	.236	55	13	4	1	3	6	6	7	.306	.509
Sheets,Ben	L	.255	231	59	14	6	8	32	27	45	.330	.472
Throws Right	R	.278	230	64	17	2	10	33	16	39	.325	.500
Sherrill,George	L	.192	73	14	4	0	1	12	10	19	.206	.288
Throws Left	R	.427	75	32	8	2	3	30	14	6	.516	.707
Shields,James	L	.286	454	130	24	3	10	55	33	105	.338	.468
Throws Right	R	.304	382	116	26	3	18	54	18	82	.337	.529
Shields,Scot	L	.172	87	15	3	0	3	12	17	22	.308	.310
Throws Right	R	.333	90	30	3	0	3	14	17	17	.440	.467
Silva,Carlos	L	.259	162	42	8	1	4	18	12	33	.313	.395
Throws Right	R	.282	277	78	12	4	7	33	12	47	.320	.430
Simon,Alfredo	L	.269	93	25	4	0	1	12	11	16	.340	.344
Throws Right	R	.284	102	29	4	0	9	19	11	21	.365	.588
Sinkbeil,Brett	L	.333	3	1	0	0	0	4	3	1	.667	.333
Throws Right	R	.200	5	1	1	0	0	2	2	0	.429	.400
Sipp,Tony	L	.212	99	21	5	0	7	14	17	30	.331	.475
Throws Left	R	.223	121	27	6	0	5	17	22	39	.345	.397
Slama,Anthony	L	.333	9	3	2	0	1	4	3	3	.500	.889
Throws Right	R	.273	11	3	0	0	0	0	2	2	.385	.273
Slaten,Doug	L	.151	73	11	0	0	0	2	7	24	.235	.151
Throws Left	R	.295	78	23	5	0	2	12	12	12	.409	.436
Slowey,Kevin	L	.275	316	87	23	3	6	28	18	67	.310	.424
Throws Right	R	.284	299	85	16	1	15	44	11	49	.313	.495
Smith,Chris	L	.667	3	2	1	0	0	2	0	0	.667	1.000
Throws Right	R	.200	10	2	1	0	0	0	1	4	.273	.300
Smith,Greg	L	.179	28	5	2	0	0	5	6	9	.324	.250
Throws Left	R	.355	124	44	7	4	8	19	18	22	.432	.669
Smith,Joe	L	.342	38	13	1	1	1	6	9	2	.479	.500
Throws Right	R	.160	106	17	3	0	3	12	15	30	.264	.274
Smith,Jordan	L	.333	57	19	2	0	3	8	5	7	.387	.526
Throws Right	R	.241	108	26	5	0	4	16	6	19	.293	.398
Snell,Ian	L	.302	96	29	6	3	6	17	15	13	.393	.615
Throws Right	R	.313	99	31	4	2	4	17	10	13	.375	.515

Pitchers vs. Left-Handed and Right-Handed Batters

Pitcher	vs	Avg	AB	H	2B	3B	HR	RBI	BB	SO	OBP	Slg
Sonnanstine,Andy	L	.267	146	39	9	0	3	16	17	24	.348	.390
Throws Right	R	.253	174	44	11	1	8	32	10	26	.314	.466
Soria,Joakim	L	.231	143	33	6	0	2	9	8	36	.273	.315
Throws Right	R	.196	102	20	3	0	2	6	8	35	.257	.284
Soriano,Rafael	L	.196	107	21	6	1	2	11	10	22	.263	.327
Throws Right	R	.132	114	15	7	1	2	9	4	35	.168	.263
Sosa,Jorge	L	.286	56	16	3	1	3	14	13	7	.408	.536
Throws Right	R	.261	88	23	4	0	1	5	5	12	.301	.341
Springer,Russ	L	1.000	1	1	0	0	0	0	0	0	1.000	1.000
Throws Right	R	.167	6	1	0	0	0	0	0	1	.167	.167
Stammen,Craig	L	.291	227	66	13	2	4	35	12	26	.324	.419
Throws Right	R	.301	282	85	21	5	9	40	29	59	.364	.507
Stange,Daniel	L	.111	9	1	0	0	0	1	1	1	.200	.111
Throws Right	R	.429	7	3	1	0	1	6	5	1	.667	1.000
Stauffer,Tim	L	.197	132	26	8	0	1	3	9	29	.248	.280
Throws Right	R	.236	165	39	10	0	2	11	15	32	.308	.333
Stetter,Mitch	L	.357	14	5	0	0	1	3	2	3	.438	.571
Throws Left	R	.500	4	2	0	0	0	0	1	0	.667	.500
Stevens,Jeff	L	.385	13	5	1	1	2	5	3	2	.500	1.077
Throws Right	R	.267	60	16	3	1	2	11	7	13	.338	.450
Stokes,Brian	L	.382	34	13	3	1	2	12	9	5	.500	.706
Throws Right	R	.342	38	13	4	0	2	11	7	11	.457	.605
Stoner,Tobi	L	.000	2	0	0	0	0	0	0	0	.000	.000
Throws Right	R	.375	8	3	2	0	0	0	1	0	.444	.625
Storen,Drew	L	.247	77	19	4	0	0	6	8	20	.326	.299
Throws Right	R	.238	122	29	5	0	3	17	14	32	.321	.352
Strasburg,Stephen	L	.241	108	26	3	0	4	9	10	36	.300	.380
Throws Right	R	.207	145	30	7	1	1	12	7	56	.243	.290
Street,Huston	L	.208	72	15	4	0	1	6	5	24	.269	.306
Throws Right	R	.238	101	24	4	1	4	13	6	21	.284	.416
Strickland,Scott	L	.200	5	1	1	0	0	0	0	0	.200	.400
Throws Right	R	.800	5	4	1	0	0	4	1	0	.833	1.000
Strop,Pedro	L	.368	19	7	2	0	1	5	4	2	.500	.632
Throws Right	R	.357	28	10	4	0	1	7	7	9	.486	.607
Suppan,Jeff	L	.302	159	48	7	2	5	20	18	21	.370	.465
Throws Right	R	.339	242	82	17	1	8	40	19	30	.389	.517
Sweeney,Brian	L	.308	52	16	1	0	2	10	3	7	.339	.442
Throws Right	R	.198	86	17	3	0	3	6	3	7	.222	.337
Takahashi,Hisanori	L	.217	115	25	6	0	0	4	9	37	.274	.270
Throws Left	R	.264	345	91	22	0	13	48	34	77	.327	.441
Talbot,Mitch	L	.255	290	74	18	0	5	31	45	44	.356	.369
Throws Right	R	.295	322	95	21	1	8	44	24	44	.353	.441
Tallet,Brian	L	.176	102	18	3	1	4	19	6	28	.228	.343
Throws Left	R	.320	206	66	11	1	16	41	32	25	.415	.617
Tankersley,Taylor	L	.200	30	6	1	0	2	11	3	7	.286	.433
Throws Left	R	.333	18	6	2	0	2	6	4	0	.455	.778
Taschner,Jack	L	.286	28	8	3	0	1	7	3	9	.355	.500
Throws Left	R	.273	55	15	5	0	2	11	8	8	.365	.473
Tejeda,Robinson	L	.252	103	26	9	0	1	15	12	17	.328	.369
Throws Right	R	.234	124	29	6	0	4	16	14	39	.307	.379
Texeira,Kanekoa	L	.300	110	33	9	0	1	18	17	16	.388	.409
Throws Right	R	.308	130	40	7	0	2	25	8	17	.352	.408
Thatcher,Joe	L	.197	66	13	3	0	1	13	4	28	.239	.288
Throws Left	R	.172	58	10	0	0	0	4	3	17	.222	.172
Thayer,Dale	L	.500	4	2	0	0	0	2	0	0	.500	.500
Throws Right	R	.556	9	5	1	0	1	4	0	2	.556	1.000
Thomas,Brad	L	.252	115	29	3	0	1	16	11	22	.328	.304
Throws Left	R	.322	149	48	15	1	3	21	18	8	.389	.497
Thomas,Justin	L	.533	15	8	1	0	1	4	0	2	.533	.800
Throws Left	R	.317	41	13	1	1	2	8	5	3	.383	.537
Thompson,Brad	L	.382	34	13	3	0	3	5	3	4	.447	.735
Throws Right	R	.250	48	12	4	0	1	9	1	6	.260	.396
Thompson,Rich	L	.100	30	3	0	1	0	1	1	5	.129	.167
Throws Right	R	.225	40	9	1	0	2	4	3	10	.279	.400
Thornton,Matt	L	.175	97	17	4	0	2	10	6	44	.221	.278
Throws Left	R	.203	118	24	5	1	1	8	14	37	.296	.288
Threets,Erick	L	.286	14	4	0	0	0	0	3	2	.412	.286
Throws Left	R	.185	27	5	0	0	0	2	0	4	.179	.185
Tillman,Chris	L	.274	95	26	8	4	3	18	19	13	.393	.537
Throws Right	R	.238	105	25	1	0	6	17	12	18	.314	.419
Todd,Jess	L	.333	12	4	1	0	0	2	3	2	.467	.417
Throws Right	R	.333	15	5	2	0	0	3	0	7	.333	.467
Tomlin,Josh	L	.236	148	35	9	0	5	15	9	23	.283	.399
Throws Right	R	.296	125	37	12	1	5	18	10	20	.353	.528
Torres,Carlos	L	.400	30	12	5	0	0	7	5	5	.472	.567
Throws Right	R	.355	31	11	2	0	2	6	4	8	.429	.613

Pitcher	vs	Avg	AB	H	2B	3B	HR	RBI	BB	SO	OBP	Slg
Troncoso,Ramon	L	.244	86	21	7	0	5	22	10	20	.323	.500
Throws Right	R	.274	124	34	1	0	2	20	8	14	.328	.331
Uehara,Koji	L	.263	76	20	2	0	4	5	4	29	.300	.447
Throws Right	R	.185	92	17	1	2	1	7	1	26	.194	.272
Valdes,Raul	L	.330	88	29	10	2	4	16	3	27	.366	.625
Throws Left	R	.216	139	30	5	1	3	17	24	29	.335	.331
Valdez,Cesar	L	.351	37	13	2	1	1	7	5	6	.429	.541
Throws Right	R	.327	49	16	2	0	1	10	5	7	.400	.429
Valdez,Merkin	L	.333	3	1	0	0	0	0	3	0	.667	.333
Throws Right	R	.333	3	1	0	0	0	1	0	0	.333	.333
Valverde,Jose	L	.165	115	19	6	1	5	22	21	36	.297	.365
Throws Right	R	.204	108	22	1	0	0	3	11	27	.289	.213
VandenHurk,Rick	L	.346	26	9	3	0	1	7	6	7	.469	.577
Throws Right	R	.179	39	7	0	0	1	3	2	11	.250	.256
Vargas,Claudio	L	.250	36	9	1	0	1	5	4	8	.325	.361
Throws Right	R	.404	47	19	3	0	2	10	6	10	.472	.596
Vargas,Jason	L	.200	180	36	5	2	3	11	11	30	.250	.300
Throws Left	R	.268	564	151	43	2	15	60	43	86	.316	.431
Varvaro,Anthony	L	.200	5	1	0	0	1	1	3	1	.500	.800
Throws Right	R	.385	13	5	0	0	1	3	3	4	.500	.615
Vasquez,Esmerling	L	.224	98	22	6	0	2	12	20	32	.356	.347
Throws Right	R	.247	97	24	4	0	4	18	18	23	.393	.412
Vazquez,Javier	L	.275	302	83	18	3	19	56	44	59	.367	.543
Throws Right	R	.240	300	72	17	0	13	35	21	62	.297	.427
Venters,Jonny	L	.198	96	19	3	0	1	13	10	46	.310	.260
Throws Left	R	.207	203	42	5	0	0	14	29	47	.312	.232
Veras,Jose	L	.155	84	13	4	0	1	6	20	27	.317	.238
Throws Right	R	.221	86	19	2	0	4	9	9	27	.302	.384
Verlander,Justin	L	.230	474	109	15	5	9	44	44	127	.296	.340
Throws Right	R	.225	360	81	22	2	5	32	27	92	.284	.339
Villanueva,Carlos	L	.232	99	23	3	1	5	18	12	41	.333	.434
Throws Right	R	.243	103	25	3	0	2	9	10	26	.307	.330
Villar,Henry	L	.000	5	0	0	0	0	0	1	1	.167	.000
Throws Right	R	.294	17	5	0	0	0	3	2	2	.381	.294
Viola,Pedro	L	.000	4	0	0	0	0	0	1	3	.200	.000
Throws Left	R	1.000	1	1	0	0	1	3	0	0	1.000	4.000
Volquez,Edinson	L	.229	105	24	4	1	1	14	25	33	.377	.314
Throws Right	R	.273	128	35	6	0	5	15	10	34	.338	.438
Volstad,Chris	L	.292	322	94	12	3	11	45	25	49	.344	.450
Throws Right	R	.263	353	93	22	1	6	36	35	53	.337	.382
Wagner,Billy	L	.071	56	4	0	0	0	0	6	25	.175	.071
Throws Left	R	.186	183	34	6	1	5	14	16	79	.257	.311
Wainwright,Adam	L	.226	367	83	16	1	2	24	29	113	.283	.292
Throws Right	R	.222	464	103	17	4	13	41	27	100	.267	.360
Wakefield,Tim	L	.273	256	70	21	3	7	33	18	36	.321	.461
Throws Right	R	.271	306	83	18	0	12	47	18	48	.318	.448
Walden,Jordan	L	.214	28	6	0	0	0	0	4	12	.313	.214
Throws Right	R	.233	30	7	3	1	1	4	3	11	.303	.500
Walker,Tyler	L	.245	49	12	1	0	0	8	4	9	.296	.265
Throws Right	R	.277	83	23	3	2	5	20	4	21	.307	.542
Walters,P.J.	L	.264	53	14	2	0	3	10	7	14	.344	.472
Throws Right	R	.286	63	18	2	0	2	10	3	8	.313	.413
Weaver,Jeff	L	.321	56	18	4	0	2	11	12	6	.423	.500
Throws Right	R	.275	109	30	5	2	3	21	8	20	.325	.440
Weaver,Jered	L	.223	430	96	18	2	8	31	24	122	.263	.330
Throws Right	R	.220	414	91	22	0	15	39	30	111	.271	.382
Webb,Ryan	L	.333	93	31	8	0	1	11	9	15	.394	.452
Throws Right	R	.239	138	33	5	0	0	13	10	29	.291	.275
Weinhardt,Robbie	L	.214	42	9	1	0	1	7	6	6	.306	.310
Throws Right	R	.388	80	31	4	2	1	16	2	15	.424	.525
Wellemeyer,Todd	L	.316	95	30	2	2	7	20	19	15	.427	.600
Throws Right	R	.216	125	27	5	0	5	11	16	26	.313	.376
Wells,Randy	L	.261	306	80	14	1	4	28	38	49	.347	.353
Throws Right	R	.280	460	129	32	1	15	63	25	95	.323	.452
West,Sean	L	.500	6	3	0	0	0	0	0	3	.500	.500
Throws Left	R	.353	34	12	3	0	2	9	4	5	.421	.618
Westbrook,Jake	L	.268	343	92	15	3	9	43	45	54	.359	.408
Throws Right	R	.256	433	111	23	2	11	50	23	74	.299	.395
Wheeler,Dan	L	.154	39	6	2	0	3	7	4	8	.227	.436
Throws Right	R	.222	135	30	8	2	4	12	12	38	.287	.400
White,Sean	L	.357	56	20	6	1	2	11	6	4	.394	.607
Throws Right	R	.321	78	25	4	0	2	13	5	11	.361	.449
Williams,Randy	L	.327	49	16	6	0	0	11	9	11	.441	.449
Throws Left	R	.362	58	21	8	0	2	14	12	11	.479	.603
Willis,Dontrelle	L	.216	74	16	2	0	1	9	8	30	.298	.284
Throws Left	R	.322	174	56	10	0	5	26	48	17	.472	.466

Pitchers vs. Left-Handed and Right-Handed Batters

Pitcher	vs	Avg	AB	H	2B	3B	HR	RBI	BB	SO	OBP	Slg
Wilson,Brian	L	.206	126	26	4	1	2	7	18	48	.306	.302
Throws Right	R	.231	156	36	6	2	1	12	8	45	.273	.314
Wilson,C.J.	L	.144	153	22	5	0	0	12	12	46	.224	.176
Throws Left	R	.236	590	139	31	2	10	57	81	124	.333	.346
Wolf,Randy	L	.286	182	52	9	1	12	32	16	45	.345	.544
Throws Left	R	.250	643	161	36	4	17	68	71	97	.330	.398
Wolf,Ross	L	.318	22	7	0	1	1	5	3	6	.400	.545
Throws Right	R	.192	26	5	2	0	0	4	3	3	.300	.269
Wood,Blake	L	.286	91	26	5	0	3	19	17	14	.387	.440
Throws Right	R	.286	98	28	7	0	3	18	5	17	.318	.449
Wood,Kerry	L	.211	76	16	0	0	1	5	23	27	.406	.250
Throws Right	R	.209	91	19	4	1	3	12	6	22	.265	.374
Wood,Tim	L	.261	46	12	4	0	0	6	8	4	.370	.348
Throws Right	R	.339	62	21	4	0	2	14	7	6	.394	.500
Wood,Travis	L	.136	66	9	0	0	2	5	6	14	.219	.227
Throws Left	R	.240	317	76	16	1	7	33	20	72	.289	.363
Worley,Vance	L	.100	20	2	0	0	1	1	4	6	.250	.250
Throws Right	R	.240	25	6	1	0	0	1	0	6	.240	.280
Wright,Jamey	L	.227	97	22	4	1	1	13	13	17	.321	.320
Throws Right	R	.280	118	33	9	0	2	23	12	11	.351	.407
Wright,Wesley	L	.206	34	7	3	1	0	1	4	9	.325	.353
Throws Left	R	.316	95	30	8	0	6	23	9	20	.377	.589
Wuertz,Michael	L	.265	49	13	4	0	3	6	10	14	.390	.531
Throws Right	R	.227	97	22	3	0	3	12	11	26	.306	.351
Young,Chris	L	.167	24	4	1	0	0	0	3	6	.259	.208
Throws Right	R	.130	46	6	0	0	1	1	8	9	.259	.196
Zagurski,Mike	L	.308	13	4	1	0	1	4	1	6	.357	.615
Throws Left	R	.333	12	4	2	0	0	6	4	5	.526	.500
Zambrano,Carlos	L	.279	208	58	11	1	4	22	37	52	.389	.399
Throws Right	R	.221	276	61	8	0	3	30	32	65	.311	.283
Ziegler,Brad	L	.317	60	19	4	1	3	13	17	5	.468	.567
Throws Right	R	.213	164	35	9	0	1	11	11	36	.274	.287
Zimmermann,Jordan	L	.276	58	16	1	0	3	11	8	12	.364	.448
Throws Right	R	.238	63	15	4	0	5	8	2	15	.279	.540
Zito,Barry	L	.232	168	39	7	3	4	19	25	48	.337	.381
Throws Left	R	.255	569	145	31	2	16	63	59	102	.327	.401
Zumaya,Joel	L	.215	65	14	3	1	1	7	6	16	.278	.338
Throws Right	R	.240	75	18	3	0	0	8	5	18	.280	.280
AI	L	.259	-	-	-	-	-	-	-	-	.332	.405
	R	.257	-	-	-	-	-	-	-	-	.319	.400
NL	L	.257	-	-	-	-	-	-	-	-	.333	.405
	R	.257	-	-	-	-	-	-	-	-	.321	.397
MLB	L	.258	-	-	-	-	-	-	-	-	.333	.405
	R	.257	-	-	-	-	-	-	-	-	.320	.401

2010 Leader Boards

Many of our leader boards are derived from the complex pitch data we collect. Our pitch charting data is the most complete and thorough in baseball, and the information found in these leader boards cannot be found anywhere else. We track which pitchers threw the highest percentage of changeups, for example, and Bill James offers his own leader boards for categories like Runs Created, Tough Losses, and Power/Speed Numbers.

For the second consecutive season, our home run distance leader boards are fueled by Hit Tracker data. Please check out www.hittrackeronline.com and thank you Greg Rybarczyk.

In the past we measured hitter performance against various pitch types by result only. The problem with that approach was that if a hitter regularly looked silly on non-result-pitch curveballs, but mashed just a few along the way, he could look like a great curveball hitter, even though nothing was further from the truth. Bill James designed a formula to rate hitters not only on the result pitches, but on every pitch the batter faced. The hitters you'll now see in these leader boards are a much better representation of the guys who mastered each pitch type this past year.

Here are some definitions to help clarify parts of the leader boards that may not be familiar to all readers:

BPS stands for "Batting Average plus Slugging Percentage." We feel that BPS makes more sense than OPS for some leader boards because we wanted to know who was having success putting those balls in play, not just drawing walks.

OutZ is "Pitches Outside the Strike Zone."

Holds Adjusted Saves Percentage is calculated by dividing holds plus saves by holds plus save opportunities.

2010 American League Batting Leaders

Batting Average (minimum 502 PA)		On Base Percentage (minimum 502 PA)		Slugging Average (minimum 502 PA)		Home Runs	
Hamilton,Josh, Tex	.359	Cabrera,Miguel, Det	.420	Hamilton,Josh, Tex	.633	Bautista,Jose, Tor	54
Cabrera,Miguel, Det	.328	Hamilton,Josh, Tex	.411	Cabrera,Miguel, Det	.622	Konerko,Paul, CWS	39
Mauer,Joe, Min	.327	Mauer,Joe, Min	.402	Bautista,Jose, Tor	.617	Cabrera,Miguel, Det	38
Beltre,Adrian, Bos	.321	Choo,Shin-Soo, Cle	.401	Konerko,Paul, CWS	.584	Teixeira,Mark, NYY	33
Cano,Robinson, NYY	.319	Barton,Daric, Oak	.393	Beltre,Adrian, Bos	.553	Hamilton,Josh, Tex	32
Butler,Billy, KC	.318	Konerko,Paul, CWS	.393	Scott,Luke, Bal	.535	Ortiz,David, Bos	32
Suzuki,Ichiro, Sea	.315	Butler,Billy, KC	.388	Cano,Robinson, NYY	.534	Wells,Vernon, Tor	31
Konerko,Paul, CWS	.312	Gardner,Brett, NYY	.383	Ortiz,David, Bos	.529	Rodriguez,Alex, NYY	30
Crawford,Carl, TB	.307	Cano,Robinson, NYY	.381	Wells,Vernon, Tor	.515	3 tied with	29
Martinez,Victor, Bos	.302	Bautista,Jose, Tor	.378	Swisher,Nick, NYY	.511		

Games		Plate Appearances		At Bats		Hits	
Suzuki,Ichiro, Sea	162	Jeter,Derek, NYY	739	Suzuki,Ichiro, Sea	680	Suzuki,Ichiro, Sea	214
Bautista,Jose, Tor	161	Pierre,Juan, CWS	734	Jeter,Derek, NYY	663	Cano,Robinson, NYY	200
Figgins,Chone, Sea	161	Suzuki,Ichiro, Sea	732	Young,Michael, Tex	656	Beltre,Adrian, Bos	189
Cano,Robinson, NYY	160	Young,Michael, Tex	718	Pierre,Juan, CWS	651	Butler,Billy, KC	189
Markakis,Nick, Bal	160	Teixeira,Mark, NYY	712	Scutaro,Marco, Bos	632	Markakis,Nick, Bal	187
Pierre,Juan, CWS	160	Markakis,Nick, Bal	709	Markakis,Nick, Bal	629	Hamilton,Josh, Tex	186
Barton,Daric, Oak	159	Span,Denard, Min	705	Span,Denard, Min	629	Young,Michael, Tex	186
Butler,Billy, KC	158	Figgins,Chone, Sea	702	Cano,Robinson, NYY	626	Crawford,Carl, TB	184
Kendrick,Howie, LAA	158	Cano,Robinson, NYY	696	Jackson,Austin, Det	618	Jackson,Austin, Det	181
Teixeira,Mark, NYY	158	Scutaro,Marco, Bos	695	Kendrick,Howie, LAA	616	Cabrera,Miguel, Det	180

Singles		Doubles		Triples		Total Bases	
Suzuki,Ichiro, Sea	175	Beltre,Adrian, Bos	49	Crawford,Carl, TB	13	Bautista,Jose, Tor	351
Pierre,Juan, CWS	157	Longoria,Evan, TB	46	Jackson,Austin, Det	10	Cabrera,Miguel, Det	341
Andrus,Elvis, Tex	138	Young,Delmon, Min	46	Span,Denard, Min	10	Cano,Robinson, NYY	334
Jeter,Derek, NYY	136	Butler,Billy, KC	45	Pennington,Cliff, Oak	8	Hamilton,Josh, Tex	328
Jackson,Austin, Det	133	Cabrera,Miguel, Det	45	Gardner,Brett, NYY	7	Beltre,Adrian, Bos	326
Figgins,Chone, Sea	132	Markakis,Nick, Bal	45	Granderson,Curtis, NYY	7	Konerko,Paul, CWS	320
Butler,Billy, KC	129	Wells,Vernon, Tor	44	Maier,Mitch, KC	6	Wells,Vernon, Tor	304
Span,Denard, Min	129	Mauer,Joe, Min	43	Podsednik,Scott, KC	6	Crawford,Carl, TB	297
Cano,Robinson, NYY	127	3 tied with	41	11 tied with	5	Guerrero,Vladimir, Tex	294
Markakis,Nick, Bal	127					2 tied with	291

Runs Scored		RBI		Walks		Strikeouts	
Teixeira,Mark, NYY	113	Cabrera,Miguel, Det	126	Barton,Daric, Oak	110	Jackson,Austin, Det	170
Cabrera,Miguel, Det	111	Rodriguez,Alex, NYY	125	Bautista,Jose, Tor	100	Upton,B.J., TB	164
Jeter,Derek, NYY	111	Bautista,Jose, Tor	124	Teixeira,Mark, NYY	93	Pena,Carlos, TB	158
Crawford,Carl, TB	110	Guerrero,Vladimir, Tex	115	Zobrist,Ben, TB	92	Ortiz,David, Bos	145
Bautista,Jose, Tor	109	Young,Delmon, Min	112	Cabrera,Miguel, Det	89	Lind,Adam, Tor	144
Cano,Robinson, NYY	103	Konerko,Paul, CWS	111	Abreu,Bobby, LAA	87	Swisher,Nick, NYY	139
Jackson,Austin, Det	103	Cano,Robinson, NYY	109	Pena,Carlos, TB	87	Gutierrez,Franklin, Sea	137
Young,Michael, Tex	99	Teixeira,Mark, NYY	108	Choo,Shin-Soo, Cle	83	Napoli,Mike, LAA	137
Gardner,Brett, NYY	97	Longoria,Evan, TB	104	Ortiz,David, Bos	82	Inge,Brandon, Det	134
2 tied with	96	2 tied with	102	Gardner,Brett, NYY	79	Abreu,Bobby, LAA	132

2010 American League Batting Leaders

Intentional Walks

Cabrera,Miguel, Det	32
Cano,Robinson, NYY	14
Mauer,Joe, Min	14
Ortiz,David, Bos	14
Suzuki,Ichiro, Sea	13
Longoria,Evan, TB	12
Choo,Shin-Soo, Cle	11
Beltre,Adrian, Bos	10
Hafner,Travis, Cle	10
Markakis,Nick, Bal	9

BA Bases Loaded
(minimum 10 PA)

Guerrero,Vladimir, Tex	.647
Cano,Robinson, NYY	.611
Cervelli,Francisco, NYY	.545
Scutaro,Marco, Bos	.538
Teixeira,Mark, NYY	.533
Choo,Shin-Soo, Cle	.500
Pierre,Juan, CWS	.500
Raburn,Ryan, Det	.500
Guillen,Carlos, Det	.455
Rodriguez,Alex, NYY	.450

Sacrifice Hits

Andrus,Elvis, Tex	17
Figgins,Chone, Sea	17
Pierre,Juan, CWS	15
Barton,Daric, Oak	12
McDonald,Darnell, Bos	12
Pennington,Cliff, Oak	12
Aybar,Erick, LAA	11
Bartlett,Jason, TB	11
Cabrera,Asdrubal, Cle	11
3 tied with	10

Sacrifice Flies

Zobrist,Ben, TB	12
Rodriguez,Alex, NYY	11
Young,Michael, Tex	11
Longoria,Evan, TB	10
Peralta,Jhonny, Cle-Det	10
Butler,Billy, KC	9
Wigginton,Ty, Bal	9
Young,Delmon, Min	9
Cabrera,Miguel, Det	8
Gutierrez,Franklin, Sea	8

BA Close & Late
(minimum 50 PA)

Mauer,Joe, Min	.397
Hamilton,Josh, Tex	.383
Youkilis,Kevin, Bos	.370
Cabrera,Miguel, Det	.367
Pierre,Juan, CWS	.353
Young,Delmon, Min	.348
Cano,Robinson, NYY	.347
Choo,Shin-Soo, Cle	.342
Lopez,Jose, Sea	.333
Patterson,Corey, Bal	.333

Batting Average w/ RISP
(minimum 100 PA)

Hamilton,Josh, Tex	.369
Crawford,Carl, TB	.359
Young,Delmon, Min	.355
Andrus,Elvis, Tex	.347
Cabrera,Asdrubal, Cle	.342
Ellis,Mark, Oak	.339
Markakis,Nick, Bal	.338
Beltre,Adrian, Bos	.338
Cruz,Nelson, Tex	.336
Podsednik,Scott, KC	.330

SLG vs. LHP
(minimum 125 PA)

Martinez,Victor, Bos	.742
Konerko,Paul, CWS	.661
Morneau,Justin, Min	.575
Napoli,Mike, LAA	.567
Raburn,Ryan, Det	.566
Beltre,Adrian, Bos	.563
Young,Delmon, Min	.561
Cabrera,Miguel, Det	.555
Longoria,Evan, TB	.545
Upton,B.J., TB	.538

SLG vs. RHP
(minimum 377 PA)

Hamilton,Josh, Tex	.716
Cabrera,Miguel, Det	.643
Ortiz,David, Bos	.643
Bautista,Jose, Tor	.642
Choo,Shin-Soo, Cle	.566
Konerko,Paul, CWS	.562
Wells,Vernon, Tor	.553
Crawford,Carl, TB	.552
Scott,Luke, Bal	.550
Beltre,Adrian, Bos	.549

Leadoff Hitters OBP
(minimum 150 PA)

Jaso,John, TB	.380
Upton,B.J., TB	.367
Suzuki,Ichiro, Sea	.359
Roberts,Brian, Bal	.355
Podsednik,Scott, KC	.350
Jeter,Derek, NYY	.348
Jackson,Austin, Det	.341
Pierre,Juan, CWS	.339
Andrus,Elvis, Tex	.338
Crisp,Coco, Oak	.338

Cleanup Hitters SLG
(minimum 150 PA)

Morneau,Justin, Min	.626
Cabrera,Miguel, Det	.622
Konerko,Paul, CWS	.577
Youkilis,Kevin, Bos	.567
Longoria,Evan, TB	.558
Ortiz,David, Bos	.522
Wells,Vernon, Tor	.517
Rodriguez,Alex, NYY	.508
Matsui,Hideki, LAA	.507
Scott,Luke, Bal	.505

BA vs. LHP
(minimum 125 PA)

Martinez,Victor, Bos	.400
Markakis,Nick, Bal	.361
Konerko,Paul, CWS	.339
Guerrero,Vladimir, Tex	.338
Beltre,Adrian, Bos	.328
Morneau,Justin, Min	.325
Longoria,Evan, TB	.324
Young,Michael, Tex	.322
Jeter,Derek, NYY	.321
Cabrera,Miguel, Det	.313

BA vs. RHP
(minimum 377 PA)

Hamilton,Josh, Tex	.401
Cano,Robinson, NYY	.337
Cabrera,Miguel, Det	.333
Crawford,Carl, TB	.332
Butler,Billy, KC	.330
Choo,Shin-Soo, Cle	.319
Suzuki,Ichiro, Sea	.318
Beltre,Adrian, Bos	.318
Jackson,Austin, Det	.317
Konerko,Paul, CWS	.304

Home BA
(minimum 251 PA)

Hamilton,Josh, Tex	.390
Konerko,Paul, CWS	.342
Cabrera,Miguel, Det	.342
Scott,Luke, Bal	.338
Martinez,Victor, Bos	.335
Choo,Shin-Soo, Cle	.335
Longoria,Evan, TB	.324
Wells,Vernon, Tor	.321
Butler,Billy, KC	.320
Guerrero,Vladimir, Tex	.315

Away BA
(minimum 251 PA)

Cano,Robinson, NYY	.341
Mauer,Joe, Min	.339
Beltre,Adrian, Bos	.327
Hamilton,Josh, Tex	.327
Suzuki,Ichiro, Sea	.317
Ellis,Mark, Oak	.316
Cabrera,Miguel, Det	.315
Butler,Billy, KC	.315
Crawford,Carl, TB	.313
Hunter,Torii, LAA	.311

OBP vs. LHP
(minimum 125 PA)

Cabrera,Miguel, Det	.446
Konerko,Paul, CWS	.441
Martinez,Victor, Bos	.431
Swisher,Nick, NYY	.415
Markakis,Nick, Bal	.414
Teixeira,Mark, NYY	.413
Longoria,Evan, TB	.411
Barton,Daric, Oak	.404
Cuddyer,Michael, Min	.400
Napoli,Mike, LAA	.399

OBP vs. RHP
(minimum 377 PA)

Hamilton,Josh, Tex	.447
Choo,Shin-Soo, Cle	.433
Ortiz,David, Bos	.416
Cabrera,Miguel, Det	.411
Cano,Robinson, NYY	.400
Butler,Billy, KC	.398
Matsui,Hideki, LAA	.394
Barton,Daric, Oak	.389
Bautista,Jose, Tor	.388
Gardner,Brett, NYY	.387

2010 American League Batting Leaders

Stolen Bases

Pierre,Juan, CWS	68
Davis,Rajai, Oak	50
Crawford,Carl, TB	47
Gardner,Brett, NYY	47
Figgins,Chone, Sea	42
Suzuki,Ichiro, Sea	42
Upton,B.J., TB	42
Rios,Alex, CWS	34
Andrus,Elvis, Tex	32
Crisp,Coco, Oak	32

Caught Stealing

Pierre,Juan, CWS	18
Andrus,Elvis, Tex	15
Figgins,Chone, Sea	15
Rios,Alex, CWS	14
Hunter,Torii, LAA	12
Podsednik,Scott, KC	12
Davis,Rajai, Oak	11
Abreu,Bobby, LAA	10
Crawford,Carl, TB	10
3 tied with	9

Highest SB Success Pct
(minimum 20 SBA)

Crisp,Coco, Oak	91.4
Gutierrez,Franklin, Sea	89.3
Zobrist,Ben, TB	88.9
Span,Denard, Min	86.7
Pennington,Cliff, Oak	85.3
Patterson,Corey, Bal	84.0
Gardner,Brett, NYY	83.9
Crawford,Carl, TB	82.5
Suzuki,Ichiro, Sea	82.4
Upton,B.J., TB	82.4

Lowest SB Success Pct
(minimum 20 SBA)

Hunter,Torii, LAA	42.9
Ramirez,Alexei, CWS	61.9
Andrus,Elvis, Tex	68.1
Borbon,Julio, Tex	68.2
Abreu,Bobby, LAA	70.6
Rios,Alex, CWS	70.8
Podsednik,Scott, KC	71.4
Aybar,Erick, LAA	73.3
Figgins,Chone, Sea	73.7
Lewis,Fred, Tor	73.9

Steals of Third

Pierre,Juan, CWS	16
Davis,Rajai, Oak	15
Upton,B.J., TB	12
Suzuki,Ichiro, Sea	10
Pennington,Cliff, Oak	7
Crawford,Carl, TB	6
Crisp,Coco, Oak	6
Hall,Bill, Bos	6
Andrus,Elvis, Tex	5
Podsednik,Scott, KC	5

Grounded Into DP

Butler,Billy, KC	32
Cuddyer,Michael, Min	26
Beltre,Adrian, Bos	25
Wigginton,Ty, Bal	23
Callaspo,Alberto, KC-LAA	22
Hunter,Torii, LAA	22
Jeter,Derek, NYY	22
Suzuki,Kurt, Oak	22
Rios,Alex, CWS	21
Young,Michael, Tex	21

Grounded Into DP Pct
(minimum 50 GIDP Ops)

Crawford,Carl, TB	1.52
Rosales,Adam, Oak	1.72
Pena,Carlos, TB	1.79
Kelly,Don, Det	1.85
Saunders,Michael, Sea	2.00
Granderson,Curtis, NYY	2.13
Hafner,Travis, Cle	2.56
Suzuki,Ichiro, Sea	3.45
Maier,Mitch, KC	3.66
Damon,Johnny, Det	4.17

Hit By Pitch

Pierre,Juan, CWS	21
Quentin,Carlos, CWS	20
Jones,Adam, Bal	13
Teixeira,Mark, NYY	13
Hafner,Travis, Cle	12
Suzuki,Kurt, Oak	12
Wilson,Josh, Sea	12
Choo,Shin-Soo, Cle	11
Napoli,Mike, LAA	11
3 tied with	10

Pitches Seen

Barton,Daric, Oak	3015
Figgins,Chone, Sea	2905
Bautista,Jose, Tor	2880
Abreu,Bobby, LAA	2866
Markakis,Nick, Bal	2864
Teixeira,Mark, NYY	2817
Scutaro,Marco, Bos	2808
Pierre,Juan, CWS	2785
Suzuki,Ichiro, Sea	2738
Young,Michael, Tex	2730

At Bats Per Home Run
(minimum 502 PA)

Bautista,Jose, Tor	10.5
Konerko,Paul, CWS	14.1
Cabrera,Miguel, Det	14.4
Hamilton,Josh, Tex	16.2
Ortiz,David, Bos	16.2
Scott,Luke, Bal	16.6
Pena,Carlos, TB	17.3
Rodriguez,Alex, NYY	17.4
Napoli,Mike, LAA	17.4
Quentin,Carlos, CWS	17.4

Highest GB/FB Ratio
(minimum 502 PA)

Jeter,Derek, NYY	3.60
Andrus,Elvis, Tex	3.13
Pierre,Juan, CWS	2.60
Suzuki,Ichiro, Sea	2.26
Span,Denard, Min	1.97
Gardner,Brett, NYY	1.91
Kendrick,Howie, LAA	1.90
Jackson,Austin, Det	1.77
Mauer,Joe, Min	1.61
Hudson,Orlando, Min	1.57

Lowest GB/FB Ratio
(minimum 502 PA)

Bautista,Jose, Tor	0.57
Hill,Aaron, Tor	0.65
Granderson,Curtis, NYY	0.70
Quentin,Carlos, CWS	0.74
Konerko,Paul, CWS	0.78
Teixeira,Mark, NYY	0.78
Peralta,Jhonny, Cle-Det	0.79
Swisher,Nick, NYY	0.79
Pennington,Cliff, Oak	0.83
Inge,Brandon, Det	0.84

Pitches Per Plate App
(minimum 502 PA)

Gardner,Brett, NYY	4.62
Barton,Daric, Oak	4.40
Ortiz,David, Bos	4.37
Abreu,Bobby, LAA	4.30
Bautista,Jose, Tor	4.22
Gutierrez,Franklin, Sea	4.21
Figgins,Chone, Sea	4.14
Granderson,Curtis, NYY	4.12
Zobrist,Ben, TB	4.11
Damon,Johnny, Det	4.11

Pct Pitches Taken
(minimum 1500 Pitches)

Gardner,Brett, NYY	68.6
Abreu,Bobby, LAA	67.3
Jaso,John, TB	67.1
Barton,Daric, Oak	65.6
Andrus,Elvis, Tex	63.2
Scutaro,Marco, Bos	62.9
Youkilis,Kevin, Bos	62.5
Drew,J.D., Bos	62.3
Podsednik,Scott, KC	62.2
Zobrist,Ben, TB	62.1

Best BPS on OutZ
(minimum 502 PA)

Beltre,Adrian, Bos	.709
Hamilton,Josh, Tex	.678
Mauer,Joe, Min	.630
Martinez,Victor, Bos	.617
Bautista,Jose, Tor	.613
Cabrera,Miguel, Det	.605
Crawford,Carl, TB	.588
Scott,Luke, Bal	.576
Rios,Alex, CWS	.574
Guerrero,Vladimir, Tex	.570

Worst BPS on OutZ
(minimum 502 PA)

Overbay,Lyle, Tor	.204
Gutierrez,Franklin, Sea	.278
Jeter,Derek, NYY	.283
Kouzmanoff,Kevin, Oak	.299
Inge,Brandon, Det	.320
Hill,Aaron, Tor	.327
Abreu,Bobby, LAA	.329
Andrus,Elvis, Tex	.333
Choo,Shin-Soo, Cle	.339
Bartlett,Jason, TB	.346

2010 American League Batting Leaders

Best OPS vs Fastballs
(minimum 251 PA)

Hamilton,Josh, Tex	1.173
Bautista,Jose, Tor	1.090
Konerko,Paul, CWS	1.080
Scott,Luke, Bal	1.036
Cabrera,Miguel, Det	1.028
Youkilis,Kevin, Bos	.992
Swisher,Nick, NYY	.936
Butler,Billy, KC	.934
Martinez,Victor, Bos	.931
Beltre,Adrian, Bos	.916

Best OPS vs Curveballs
(minimum 50 PA)

Guerrero,Vladimir, Tex	1.214
Wells,Vernon, Tor	1.129
Beltre,Adrian, Bos	1.088
Cano,Robinson, NYY	1.031
Jones,Adam, Bal	.975
Bautista,Jose, Tor	.943
Hamilton,Josh, Tex	.923
Crawford,Carl, TB	.898
Young,Delmon, Min	.892
Kendrick,Howie, LAA	.873

Best OPS vs Changeups
(minimum 50 PA)

Konerko,Paul, CWS	1.112
Drew,J.D., Bos	1.103
Morneau,Justin, Min	1.097
Cabrera,Miguel, Det	1.091
Guerrero,Vladimir, Tex	1.073
Upton,B.J., TB	1.044
Hamilton,Josh, Tex	1.021
Ortiz,David, Bos	1.019
Longoria,Evan, TB	1.007
2 tied with	1.001

Best OPS vs Sliders
(minimum 32 PA)

Morneau,Justin, Min	1.154
Cano,Robinson, NYY	1.116
Thames,Marcus, NYY	1.111
Jaso,John, TB	1.088
Choo,Shin-Soo, Cle	1.055
Cruz,Nelson, Tex	1.052
Matsui,Hideki, LAA	1.050
Bautista,Jose, Tor	1.022
Teixeira,Mark, NYY	1.016
Napoli,Mike, LAA	.988

OPS
(minimum 502 PA)

Hamilton,Josh, Tex	1.044
Cabrera,Miguel, Det	1.042
Bautista,Jose, Tor	.995
Konerko,Paul, CWS	.977
Beltre,Adrian, Bos	.919
Cano,Robinson, NYY	.914
Scott,Luke, Bal	.902
Ortiz,David, Bos	.899
Choo,Shin-Soo, Cle	.885
Longoria,Evan, TB	.879

OPS First Half
(minimum 260 PA)

Cabrera,Miguel, Det	1.074
Morneau,Justin, Min	1.055
Hamilton,Josh, Tex	1.014
Boesch,Brennan, Det	.990
Youkilis,Kevin, Bos	.981
Ortiz,David, Bos	.945
Cano,Robinson, NYY	.944
Konerko,Paul, CWS	.942
Guerrero,Vladimir, Tex	.919
Beltre,Adrian, Boo	.907

OPS Second Half
(minimum 201 PA)

Bautista,Jose, Tor	1.099
Hamilton,Josh, Tex	1.098
Konerko,Paul, CWS	1.017
Cabrera,Miguel, Det	1.000
Mauer,Joe, Min	.974
Cruz,Nelson, Tex	.957
Matsui,Hideki, LAA	.955
Scott,Luke, Bal	.935
Beltre,Adrian, Bos	.933
Choo,Shin-Soo, Cle	.908

OPS by Catchers
(minimum 251 PA)

Mauer,Joe, Min	.909
Martinez,Victor, Bos	.884
Posada,Jorge, NYY	.844
Buck,John, Tor	.807
Cervelli,Francisco, NYY	.704
Jaso,John, TB	.699
Pierzynski,A.J., CWS	.695
Wieters,Matt, Bal	.687
Suzuki,Kurt, Oak	.670
Avila,Alex, Det	.669

OPS by First Basemen
(minimum 251 PA)

Morneau,Justin, Min	1.069
Cabrera,Miguel, Det	1.040
Konerko,Paul, CWS	.989
Youkilis,Kevin, Bos	.963
Teixeira,Mark, NYY	.871
Butler,Billy, KC	.869
Barton,Daric, Oak	.802
Napoli,Mike, LAA	.792
Cuddyer,Michael, Min	.781
Overbay,Lyle, Tor	.758

OPS by Second Basemen
(minimum 251 PA)

Cano,Robinson, NYY	.921
Pedroia,Dustin, Bos	.860
Kinsler,Ian, Tex	.793
Rodriguez,Sean, TB	.766
Aviles,Mike, KC	.764
Ellis,Mark, Oak	.754
Roberts,Brian, Bal	.748
Kendrick,Howie, LAA	.714
Hudson,Orlando, Min	.712
Beckham,Gordon, CWS	.701

OPS by Third Basemen
(minimum 251 PA)

Beltre,Adrian, Bos	.919
Longoria,Evan, TB	.879
Rodriguez,Alex, NYY	.835
Valencia,Danny, Min	.814
Encarnacion,Edwin, Tor	.776
Young,Michael, Tex	.769
Peralta,Jhonny, Cle-Det	.727
Inge,Brandon, Det	.719
Vizquel,Omar, CWS	.716
Tejada,Miguel, Bal	.673

OPS by Shortstops
(minimum 251 PA)

Gonzalez,Alex, Tor	.793
Ramirez,Alexei, CWS	.742
Scutaro,Marco, Bos	.727
Hardy,J.J., Min	.714
Jeter,Derek, NYY	.713
Escobar,Yunel, Tor	.696
Betancourt,Yuniesky, KC	.692
Pennington,Cliff, Oak	.689
Cabrera,Asdrubal, Cle	.671
Bartlett,Jason, TB	.666

OPS by Left Fielders
(minimum 251 PA)

Hamilton,Josh, Tex	1.131
Murphy,David, Tex	.892
Crawford,Carl, TB	.848
Young,Delmon, Min	.819
Raburn,Ryan, Det	.814
Gardner,Brett, NYY	.799
Lewis,Fred, Tor	.781
Kearns,Austin, Cle-NYY	.769
Podsednik,Scott, KC	.754
Rivera,Juan, LAA	.737

OPS by Center Fielders
(minimum 251 PA)

Hunter,Torii, LAA	.876
Wells,Vernon, Tor	.868
Granderson,Curtis, NYY	.802
Rios,Alex, CWS	.798
Crisp,Coco, Oak	.786
Jones,Adam, Bal	.767
Jackson,Austin, Det	.741
Upton,B.J., TB	.739
Davis,Rajai, Oak	.686
Span,Denard, Min	.679

OPS by Right Fielders
(minimum 251 PA)

Cruz,Nelson, Tex	.995
Bautista,Jose, Tor	.964
Swisher,Nick, NYY	.894
Choo,Shin-Soo, Cle	.884
Ordonez,Magglio, Det	.878
DeJesus,David, KC	.845
Quentin,Carlos, CWS	.830
Abreu,Bobby, LAA	.808
Markakis,Nick, Bal	.805
Drew,J.D., Bos	.794

OPS by Designated Hitters
(minimum 125 PA)

Thome,Jim, Min	1.046
Scott,Luke, Bal	.962
Ortiz,David, Bos	.909
Thames,Marcus, NYY	.875
Guerrero,Vladimir, Tex	.850
Cust,Jack, Oak	.843
Hafner,Travis, Cle	.826
Branyan,Russell, Cle-Sea	.822
Butler,Billy, KC	.815
Matsui,Hideki, LAA	.789

2010 American League Batting Leaders

OPS Batting Left vs. LHP
(minimum 125 PA)

Morneau,Justin, Min	.966
Markakis,Nick, Bal	.906
Barton,Daric, Oak	.895
Cano,Robinson, NYY	.857
Hamilton,Josh, Tex	.789
Damon,Johnny, Det	.740
Gardner,Brett, NYY	.725
Mauer,Joe, Min	.711
Pierre,Juan, CWS	.700
Overbay,Lyle, Tor	.700

OPS Batting Left vs. RHP
(minimum 377 PA)

Hamilton,Josh, Tex	1.163
Ortiz,David, Bos	1.059
Choo,Shin-Soo, Cle	.998
Cano,Robinson, NYY	.944
Scott,Luke, Bal	.935
Crawford,Carl, TB	.930
Swisher,Nick, NYY	.877
Matsui,Hideki, LAA	.868
Abreu,Bobby, LAA	.856
Lind,Adam, Tor	.829

OPS Batting Right vs. LHP
(minimum 125 PA)

Martinez,Victor, Bos	1.173
Konerko,Paul, CWS	1.102
Cabrera,Miguel, Det	1.000
Napoli,Mike, LAA	.966
Longoria,Evan, TB	.956
Beltre,Adrian, Bos	.943
Teixeira,Mark, NYY	.940
Guerrero,Vladimir, Tex	.932
Raburn,Ryan, Det	.929
Young,Delmon, Min	.927

OPS Batting Right vs. RHP
(minimum 377 PA)

Cabrera,Miguel, Det	1.054
Bautista,Jose, Tor	1.030
Konerko,Paul, CWS	.941
Beltre,Adrian, Bos	.908
Wells,Vernon, Tor	.895
Butler,Billy, KC	.888
Rodriguez,Alex, NYY	.883
Longoria,Evan, TB	.845
Quentin,Carlos, CWS	.838
Hunter,Torii, LAA	.838

OPS vs. LHP
(minimum 125 PA)

Martinez,Victor, Bos	1.173
Konerko,Paul, CWS	1.102
Cabrera,Miguel, Det	1.000
Morneau,Justin, Min	.966
Napoli,Mike, LAA	.966
Longoria,Evan, TB	.956
Beltre,Adrian, Bos	.943
Teixeira,Mark, NYY	.940
Guerrero,Vladimir, Tex	.932
Raburn,Ryan, Det	.929

OPS vs. RHP
(minimum 377 PA)

Hamilton,Josh, Tex	1.163
Ortiz,David, Bos	1.059
Cabrera,Miguel, Det	1.054
Bautista,Jose, Tor	1.030
Choo,Shin-Soo, Cle	.998
Cano,Robinson, NYY	.944
Konerko,Paul, CWS	.941
Scott,Luke, Bal	.935
Crawford,Carl, TB	.930
Beltre,Adrian, Bos	.908

RC Per 27 Outs vs. LHP
(minimum 125 PA)

Konerko,Paul, CWS	10.3
Martinez,Victor, Bos	9.0
Cabrera,Miguel, Det	8.9
Guerrero,Vladimir, Tex	8.0
Markakis,Nick, Bal	7.4
Upton,B.J., TB	7.0
Teixeira,Mark, NYY	7.0
Jeter,Derek, NYY	6.9
Morneau,Justin, Min	6.7
Longoria,Evan, TB	6.6

RC Per 27 Outs vs. RHP
(minimum 377 PA)

Hamilton,Josh, Tex	11.8
Ortiz,David, Bos	9.1
Choo,Shin-Soo, Cle	9.1
Bautista,Jose, Tor	8.7
Crawford,Carl, TB	8.6
Cano,Robinson, NYY	8.0
Cabrera,Miguel, Det	8.0
Matsui,Hideki, LAA	7.6
Rodriguez,Alex, NYY	7.4
Konerko,Paul, CWS	7.3

Highest RBI %
(minimum 502 PA)

Bautista,Jose, Tor	13.19
Rodriguez,Alex, NYY	12.79
Cabrera,Miguel, Det	12.15
Konerko,Paul, CWS	11.76
Hamilton,Josh, Tex	11.44
Guerrero,Vladimir, Tex	10.89
Young,Delmon, Min	10.81
Quentin,Carlos, CWS	10.78
Ortiz,David, Bos	10.46
Cano,Robinson, NYY	9.90

Lowest RBI %
(minimum 502 PA)

Figgins,Chone, Sea	3.38
Aybar,Erick, LAA	3.43
Izturis,Cesar, Bal	3.56
Andrus,Elvis, Tex	3.71
Suzuki,Ichiro, Sea	4.32
Jackson,Austin, Det	4.33
Hudson,Orlando, Min	4.53
Pierre,Juan, CWS	4.64
Gardner,Brett, NYY	5.38
Pennington,Cliff, Oak	5.39

Highest Strikeout per PA
(minimum 502 PA)

Pena,Carlos, TB	.271
Napoli,Mike, LAA	.269
Upton,B.J., TB	.269
Jackson,Austin, Det	.252
Ortiz,David, Bos	.239
Lind,Adam, Tor	.235
Inge,Brandon, Det	.231
Granderson,Curtis, NYY	.220
Swisher,Nick, NYY	.219
Gutierrez,Franklin, Sea	.218

Lowest Strikeout per PA
(minimum 502 PA)

Pierre,Juan, CWS	.064
Callaspo,Alberto, KC-LAA	.070
Pierzynski,A.J., CWS	.078
Suzuki,Kurt, Oak	.090
Mauer,Joe, Min	.091
Guerrero,Vladimir, Tex	.093
Martinez,Victor, Bos	.097
Scutaro,Marco, Bos	.102
Izturis,Cesar, Bal	.103
Span,Denard, Min	.105

Home Runs At Home

Bautista,Jose, Tor	33
Konerko,Paul, CWS	26
Hamilton,Josh, Tex	22
Wells,Vernon, Tor	20
Quentin,Carlos, CWS	19
Scott,Luke, Bal	19
Teixeira,Mark, NYY	19
Pena,Carlos, TB	18
Cabrera,Miguel, Det	17
3 tied with	16

Home Runs Away

Bautista,Jose, Tor	21
Cabrera,Miguel, Det	21
Branyan,Russell, Cle-Sea	18
Ortiz,David, Bos	17
Beltre,Adrian, Bos	15
Hunter,Torii, LAA	15
Rodriguez,Alex, NYY	15
Young,Delmon, Min	15
5 tied with	14

Longest Avg Home Run
(min 10 over the wall)

Hamilton,Josh, Tex	421
Crawford,Carl, TB	412
Boesch,Brennan, Det	409
Guerrero,Vladimir, Tex	407
Murphy,David, Tex	407
Hunter,Torii, LAA	407
Rodriguez,Alex, NYY	407
Abreu,Bobby, LAA	406
Smoak,Justin, Tex-Sea	406
Encarnacion,Edwin, Tor	405

Shortest Avg Home Run
(min 10 over the wall)

Scutaro,Marco, Bos	365
Callaspo,Alberto, KC-LAA	368
Pedroia,Dustin, Bos	370
Barton,Daric, Oak	371
Zobrist,Ben, TB	376
Duncan,Shelley, Cle	377
Lopez,Jose, Sea	378
Gonzalez,Alex, Tor	381
Ramirez,Alexei, CWS	381
Joyce,Matt, TB	382

2010 American League Batting Leaders

Under Age 26: AB Per HR
(minimum 502 PA)

Longoria,Evan, TB	26.1
Young,Delmon, Min	27.1
Jones,Adam, Bal	30.6
Boesch,Brennan, Det	33.1
Butler,Billy, KC	39.7
Wieters,Matt, Bal	40.5
Barton,Daric, Oak	55.6
Jackson,Austin, Det	154.5

Under Age 26: OPS
(minimum 502 PA)

Longoria,Evan, TB	.879
Butler,Billy, KC	.857
Young,Delmon, Min	.826
Barton,Daric, Oak	.798
Jones,Adam, Bal	.767
Jackson,Austin, Det	.745
Boesch,Brennan, Det	.736
Wieters,Matt, Bal	.695
Andrus,Elvis, Tex	.643

Under Age 26: RC/27 Outs
(minimum 502 PA)

Longoria,Evan, TB	6.1
Young,Delmon, Min	5.9
Barton,Daric, Oak	5.7
Butler,Billy, KC	5.4
Jackson,Austin, Det	5.0
Boesch,Brennan, Det	4.6
Andrus,Elvis, Tex	4.5
Jones,Adam, Bal	4.3
Wieters,Matt, Bal	3.5

Longest Home Run

Hamilton,Josh, Tex, 6/27	485
Cabrera,Miguel, Det, 4/21	468
Cruz,Nelson, Tex, 9/8	467
Thome,Jim, Min, 6/19	466
Wells,Vernon, Tor, 5/29	460
Wieters,Matt, Bal, 7/26	460
Hamilton,Josh, Tex, 5/25	459
Ortiz,David, Bos, 5/14	459
Guerrero,Vladimir, Tex, 9/7	458
Young,Delmon, Min, 7/28	458

Swing and Miss %
(minimum 1500 Pitches Seen)

Branyan,Russell, Cle-Sea	34.0
Cust,Jack, Oak	32.1
Pena,Carlos, TB	30.8
Napoli,Mike, LAA	30.5
Buck,John, Tor	29.2
Upton,B.J., TB	27.6
Hall,Bill, Bos	26.6
Scott,Luke, Bal	26.5
Jones,Adam, Bal	26.2
Cruz,Nelson, Tex	26.0

Highest First Swing %
(minimum 502 PA)

Guerrero,Vladimir, Tex	46.4
Boesch,Brennan, Det	42.8
Kouzmanoff,Kevin, Oak	41.5
Young,Delmon, Min	40.2
Hamilton,Josh, Tex	38.9
Pena,Carlos, TB	37.8
Wells,Vernon, Tor	37.0
Upton,B.J., TB	36.6
Cabrera,Miguel, Det	35.1
Quentin,Carlos, CWS	33.3

Lowest First Swing %
(minimum 502 PA)

Gardner,Brett, NYY	4.8
Abreu,Bobby, LAA	8.0
Mauer,Joe, Min	8.4
Pierre,Juan, CWS	8.8
Gutierrez,Franklin, Sea	8.9
Scutaro,Marco, Bos	12.8
Granderson,Curtis, NYY	13.7
Martinez,Victor, Bos	14.1
Andrus,Elvis, Tex	15.5
Markakis,Nick, Bal	16.7

Home RC Per 27 Outs
(minimum 251 PA)

Hamilton,Josh, Tex	11.0
Konerko,Paul, CWS	10.8
Bautista,Jose, Tor	10.2
Cabrera,Miguel, Det	9.4
Choo,Shin-Soo, Cle	8.4
Teixeira,Mark, NYY	8.3
Rodriguez,Alex, NYY	8.2
Scott,Luke, Bal	8.1
Quentin,Carlos, CWS	7.6
Wells,Vernon, Tor	7.6

Road RC Per 27 Outs
(minimum 251 PA)

Mauer,Joe, Min	8.7
Crawford,Carl, TB	8.2
Hamilton,Josh, Tex	7.7
Hunter,Torii, LAA	7.5
Cabrera,Miguel, Det	7.2
Cano,Robinson, NYY	7.0
Ellis,Mark, Oak	6.7
Matsui,Hideki, LAA	6.5
Beltre,Adrian, Bos	6.3
Bautista,Jose, Tor	6.3

2010 National League Batting Leaders

Batting Average
(minimum 502 PA)

Gonzalez,Carlos, Col	.336
Votto,Joey, Cin	.324
Infante,Omar, Atl	.321
Tulowitzki,Troy, Col	.315
Holliday,Matt, StL	.312
Pujols,Albert, StL	.312
Prado,Martin, Atl	.307
Zimmerman,Ryan, Was	.307
Braun,Ryan, Mil	.304
Castro,Starlin, ChC	.300

On Base Percentage
(minimum 502 PA)

Votto,Joey, Cin	.424
Pujols,Albert, StL	.414
Fielder,Prince, Mil	.401
Heyward,Jason, Atl	.393
Gonzalez,Adrian, SD	.393
Holliday,Matt, StL	.390
Zimmerman,Ryan, Was	.388
Werth,Jayson, Phi	.388
Utley,Chase, Phi	.387
Huff,Aubrey, SF	.385

Slugging Average
(minimum 502 PA)

Votto,Joey, Cin	.600
Gonzalez,Carlos, Col	.598
Pujols,Albert, StL	.596
Tulowitzki,Troy, Col	.568
Dunn,Adam, Was	.536
Werth,Jayson, Phi	.532
Holliday,Matt, StL	.532
Hart,Corey, Mil	.525
Gonzalez,Adrian, SD	.511
Zimmerman,Ryan, Was	.510

Home Runs

Pujols,Albert, StL	42
Dunn,Adam, Was	38
Votto,Joey, Cin	37
Gonzalez,Carlos, Col	34
Uggla,Dan, Fla	33
Fielder,Prince, Mil	32
Reynolds,Mark, Ari	32
Gonzalez,Adrian, SD	31
Hart,Corey, Mil	31
Howard,Ryan, Phi	31

Games

Kemp,Matt, LAD	162
Fielder,Prince, Mil	161
Headley,Chase, SD	161
Loney,James, LAD	161
Gonzalez,Adrian, SD	160
Weeks,Rickie, Mil	160
Pujols,Albert, StL	159
Uggla,Dan, Fla	159
3 tied with	158

Plate Appearances

Weeks,Rickie, Mil	754
Fielder,Prince, Mil	714
Pujols,Albert, StL	700
Gonzalez,Adrian, SD	693
Phillips,Brandon, Cin	687
Braun,Ryan, Mil	685
Holliday,Matt, StL	675
Headley,Chase, SD	674
Uggla,Dan, Fla	674
Johnson,Kelly, Ari	671

At Bats

Weeks,Rickie, Mil	651
Phillips,Brandon, Cin	626
Braun,Ryan, Mil	619
Pence,Hunter, Hou	614
Headley,Chase, SD	610
McGehee,Casey, Mil	610
Lee,Carlos, Hou	605
Kemp,Matt, LAD	602
Prado,Martin, Atl	599
Holliday,Matt, StL	596

Hits

Gonzalez,Carlos, Col	197
Braun,Ryan, Mil	188
Holliday,Matt, StL	186
Prado,Martin, Atl	184
Pujols,Albert, StL	183
Votto,Joey, Cin	177
Gonzalez,Adrian, SD	176
Weeks,Rickie, Mil	175
McGehee,Casey, Mil	174
Pence,Hunter, Hou	173

Singles

Theriot,Ryan, ChC-LAD	139
Polanco,Placido, Phi	130
Prado,Martin, Atl	126
Infante,Omar, Atl	125
Gonzalez,Carlos, Col	120
Pagan,Angel, NYM	119
Headley,Chase, SD	118
Braun,Ryan, Mil	117
Byrd,Marlon, ChC	117
2 tied with	116

Doubles

Werth,Jayson, Phi	46
Braun,Ryan, Mil	45
Holliday,Matt, StL	45
Torres,Andres, SF	43
Loney,James, LAD	41
Prado,Martin, Atl	40
Soriano,Alfonso, ChC	40
Byrd,Marlon, ChC	39
Pujols,Albert, StL	39
McGehee,Casey, Mil	38

Triples

Fowler,Dexter, Col	14
Drew,Stephen, Ari	12
Escobar,Alcides, Mil	10
Reyes,Jose, NYM	10
Victorino,Shane, Phi	10
Gonzalez,Carlos, Col	9
Torres,Andres, SF	8
5 tied with	7

Total Bases

Gonzalez,Carlos, Col	351
Pujols,Albert, StL	350
Votto,Joey, Cin	328
Holliday,Matt, StL	317
Braun,Ryan, Mil	310
Gonzalez,Adrian, SD	302
Weeks,Rickie, Mil	302
Dunn,Adam, Was	299
Uggla,Dan, Fla	299
2 tied with	295

Runs Scored

Pujols,Albert, StL	115
Weeks,Rickie, Mil	112
Gonzalez,Carlos, Col	111
Votto,Joey, Cin	106
Werth,Jayson, Phi	106
Braun,Ryan, Mil	101
Huff,Aubrey, SF	100
Phillips,Brandon, Cin	100
Prado,Martin, Atl	100
Uggla,Dan, Fla	100

RBI

Pujols,Albert, StL	118
Gonzalez,Carlos, Col	117
Votto,Joey, Cin	113
Howard,Ryan, Phi	108
Uggla,Dan, Fla	105
McGehee,Casey, Mil	104
Braun,Ryan, Mil	103
Dunn,Adam, Was	103
Holliday,Matt, StL	103
Wright,David, NYM	103

Walks

Fielder,Prince, Mil	114
Pujols,Albert, StL	103
Gonzalez,Adrian, SD	93
Heyward,Jason, Atl	91
Votto,Joey, Cin	91
Huff,Aubrey, SF	83
Reynolds,Mark, Ari	83
Werth,Jayson, Phi	82
Johnson,Kelly, Ari	79
Uggla,Dan, Fla	78

Strikeouts

Reynolds,Mark, Ari	211
Dunn,Adam, Was	199
Weeks,Rickie, Mil	184
LaRoche,Adam, Ari	172
Kemp,Matt, LAD	170
Stubbs,Drew, Cin	168
Wright,David, NYM	161
Howard,Ryan, Phi	157
Upton,Justin, Ari	152
Uggla,Dan, Fla	149

2010 National League Batting Leaders

Intentional Walks

Pujols,Albert, StL	38
Gonzalez,Adrian, SD	35
Fielder,Prince, Mil	17
Ruiz,Carlos, Phi	13
Ramirez,Hanley, Fla	12
Sandoval,Pablo, SF	12
Cabrera,Melky, Atl	11
Ethier,Andre, LAD	11
Howard,Ryan, Phi	11
Ibanez,Raul, Phi	11

BA Bases Loaded
(minimum 10 PA)

Desmond,Ian, Was	.545
Gonzalez,Adrian, SD	.545
Lee,Derrek, ChC-Atl	.533
Molina,Yadier, StL	.533
Denorfia,Chris, SD	.500
Stubbs,Drew, Cin	.444
Loney,James, LAD	.438
Victorino,Shane, Phi	.429
Walker,Neil, Pit	.429
Young,Chris, Ari	.429

Sacrifice Hits

Kershaw,Clayton, LAD	18
Dempster,Ryan, ChC	16
Morgan,Nyjer, Was	15
Zito,Barry, SF	14
Lincecum,Tim, SF	13
Eckstein,David, SD	12
5 tied with	11

Sacrifice Flies

Wright,David, NYM	12
Francoeur,Jeff, NYM	10
Gomes,Jonny, Cin	9
Kemp,Matt, LAD	9
Werth,Jayson, Phi	9
Jones,Garrett, Pit	8
McGehee,Casey, Mil	8
Polanco,Placido, Phi	8
Rolen,Scott, Cin	8
8 tied with	7

BA Close & Late
(minimum 50 PA)

Fowler,Dexter, Col	.418
Braun,Ryan, Mil	.382
Votto,Joey, Cin	.370
Torres,Andres, SF	.360
Sanchez,Gaby, Fla	.359
Schierholtz,Nate, SF	.346
Rolen,Scott, Cin	.342
Hernandez,Ramon, Cin	.333
Holliday,Matt, StL	.330
Pujols,Albert, StL	.329

Batting Average w/ RISP
(minimum 100 PA)

Gonzalez,Adrian, SD	.407
Votto,Joey, Cin	.369
Gonzalez,Carlos, Col	.350
Infante,Omar, Atl	.345
Ludwick,Ryan, StL-SD	.345
Pujols,Albert, StL	.343
Pagan,Angel, NYM	.339
Gomes,Jonny, Cin	.338
Utley,Chase, Phi	.333
Loney,James, LAD	.327

SLG vs. LHP
(minimum 125 PA)

Pujols,Albert, StL	.688
Wright,David, NYM	.654
Soto,Geovany, ChC	.606
Hart,Corey, Mil	.595
McGehee,Casey, Mil	.589
Johnson,Kelly, Ari	.587
Utley,Chase, Phi	.581
Weeks,Rickie, Mil	.579
Tulowitzki,Troy, Col	.575
Uggla,Dan, Fla	.575

SLG vs. RHP
(minimum 377 PA)

Votto,Joey, Cin	.673
Gonzalez,Carlos, Col	.614
Dunn,Adam, Was	.587
Ethier,Andre, LAD	.564
Pujols,Albert, StL	.559
Werth,Jayson, Phi	.556
Fielder,Prince, Mil	.544
Torres,Andres, SF	.527
Holliday,Matt, StL	.525
Braun,Ryan, Mil	.519

Leadoff Hitters OBP
(minimum 150 PA)

Young,Chris, Ari	.376
Drew,Stephen, Ari	.374
Fowler,Dexter, Col	.371
Furcal,Rafael, LAD	.370
Johnson,Kelly, Ari	.366
Weeks,Rickie, Mil	.363
Prado,Martin, Atl	.362
Infante,Omar, Atl	.349
McCutchen,Andrew, Pit	.348
Victorino,Shane, Phi	.345

Cleanup Hitters SLG
(minimum 150 PA)

Ramirez,Manny, LAD	.576
Tulowitzki,Troy, Col	.665
Uggla,Dan, Fla	.564
Holliday,Matt, StL	.514
Dunn,Adam, Was	.513
Howard,Ryan, Phi	.505
Posey,Buster, SF	.490
Huff,Aubrey, SF	.486
McCann,Brian, Atl	.478
Ramirez,Aramis, ChC	.471

BA vs. LHP
(minimum 125 PA)

Soto,Geovany, ChC	.367
Byrd,Marlon, ChC	.357
Baker,Jeff, ChC	.350
Holliday,Matt, StL	.344
Tulowitzki,Troy, Col	.342
Castro,Starlin, ChC	.339
Wright,David, NYM	.339
Gonzalez,Adrian, SD	.337
Zimmerman,Ryan, Was	.331
Weeks,Rickie, Mil	.329

BA vs. RHP
(minimum 377 PA)

Votto,Joey, Cin	.347
Gonzalez,Carlos, Col	.345
Prado,Martin, Atl	.320
Ethier,Andre, LAD	.318
Braun,Ryan, Mil	.315
Pujols,Albert, StL	.314
Ramirez,Hanley, Fla	.305
Polanco,Placido, Phi	.305
Holliday,Matt, StL	.301
Pagan,Angel, NYM	.300

Home BA
(minimum 251 PA)

Gonzalez,Carlos, Col	.380
Prado,Martin, Atl	.353
Castro,Starlin, ChC	.340
Tulowitzki,Troy, Col	.339
Pujols,Albert, StL	.335
Sandoval,Pablo, SF	.330
Werth,Jayson, Phi	.320
Pagan,Angel, NYM	.320
Zimmerman,Ryan, Was	.317
Sanchez,Gaby, Fla	.312

Away BA
(minimum 251 PA)

Votto,Joey, Cin	.349
Braun,Ryan, Mil	.336
Holliday,Matt, StL	.318
Byrd,Marlon, ChC	.315
Gonzalez,Adrian, SD	.315
Huff,Aubrey, SF	.315
Uggla,Dan, Fla	.308
Polanco,Placido, Phi	.306
Rasmus,Colby, StL	.306
Infante,Omar, Atl	.297

OBP vs. LHP
(minimum 125 PA)

Soto,Geovany, ChC	.466
Zimmerman,Ryan, Was	.453
Weeks,Rickie, Mil	.446
Ruiz,Carlos, Phi	.431
Holliday,Matt, StL	.430
Gonzalez,Adrian, SD	.424
Utley,Chase, Phi	.422
Tulowitzki,Troy, Col	.415
Milledge,Lastings, Pit	.414
Wright,David, NYM	.412

OBP vs. RHP
(minimum 377 PA)

Votto,Joey, Cin	.442
Fielder,Prince, Mil	.432
Pujols,Albert, StL	.425
Heyward,Jason, Atl	.411
Ethier,Andre, LAD	.396
Gonzalez,Carlos, Col	.389
Huff,Aubrey, SF	.388
McCann,Brian, Atl	.383
Ramirez,Hanley, Fla	.382
Werth,Jayson, Phi	.382

2010 National League Batting Leaders

Stolen Bases

Bourn,Michael, Hou	52
Pagan,Angel, NYM	37
Morgan,Nyjer, Was	34
Victorino,Shane, Phi	34
McCutchen,Andrew, Pit	33
Ramirez,Hanley, Fla	32
Reyes,Jose, NYM	30
Stubbs,Drew, Cin	30
Venable,Will, SD	29
Young,Chris, Ari	28

Caught Stealing

Morgan,Nyjer, Was	17
Kemp,Matt, LAD	15
Bourn,Michael, Hou	12
Phillips,Brandon, Cin	12
Wright,David, NYM	11
McCutchen,Andrew, Pit	10
Ramirez,Hanley, Fla	10
Reyes,Jose, NYM	10
3 tied with	9

Highest SB Success Pct
(minimum 20 SBA)

Gomez,Carlos, Mil	85.7
Victorino,Shane, Phi	85.0
Furcal,Rafael, LAD	84.6
Stubbs,Drew, Cin	83.3
Bourn,Michael, Hou	81.3
Gwynn,Tony, SD	81.0
Venable,Will, SD	80.6
Pagan,Angel, NYM	80.4
Young,Chris, Ari	80.0
Torres,Andres, SF	78.8

Lowest SB Success Pct
(minimum 20 SBA)

Kemp,Matt, LAD	55.9
Phillips,Brandon, Cin	57.1
Rasmus,Colby, StL	60.0
Fowler,Dexter, Col	61.9
Wright,David, NYM	63.3
Johnson,Kelly, Ari	65.0
Morgan,Nyjer, Was	66.7
Pence,Hunter, Hou	66.7
Theriot,Ryan, ChC-LAD	69.0
Upton,Justin, Ari	69.2

Steals of Third

Reyes,Jose, NYM	8
Victorino,Shane, Phi	8
Bourn,Michael, Hou	6
Morgan,Nyjer, Was	6
Torres,Andres, SF	6
Cabrera,Orlando, Cin	5
McCutchen,Andrew, Pit	5
Pujols,Albert, StL	5
4 tied with	4

Grounded Into DP

Sandoval,Pablo, SF	26
Rodriguez,Ivan, Was	25
Lee,Derrek, ChC-Atl	23
Pujols,Albert, StL	23
Lee,Carlos, Hou	20
Upton,Justin, Ari	20
Uribe,Juan, SF	20
Valdez,Wilson, Phi	20
Molina,Yadier, StL	19
3 tied with	18

Grounded Into DP Pct
(minimum 50 GIDP Ops)

Morgan,Nyjer, Was	2.74
Bernadina,Roger, Was	2.83
Gomes,Jonny, Cin	3.03
Utley,Chase, Phi	3.77
Venable,Will, SD	3.80
Weeks,Rickie, Mil	4.46
Walker,Neil, Pit	4.55
Rasmus,Colby, StL	4.67
McLouth,Nate, Atl	4.92
Gwynn,Tony, SD	5.45

Hit By Pitch

Weeks,Rickie, Mil	25
Fielder,Prince, Mil	21
Utley,Chase, Phi	18
Byrd,Marlon, ChC	17
Gomes,Jonny, Cin	12
Heyward,Jason, Atl	10
Morgan,Nyjer, Was	10
6 tied with	9

Pitches Seen

Weeks,Rickie, Mil	2956
Werth,Jayson, Phi	2849
Uggla,Dan, Fla	2830
Pujols,Albert, StL	2821
Fielder,Prince, Mil	2775
Young,Chris, Ari	2775
Johnson,Kelly, Ari	2765
Gonzalez,Adrian, SD	2668
Dunn,Adam, Was	2663
Wright,David, NYM	2658

At Bats Per Home Run
(minimum 502 PA)

Pujols,Albert, StL	14.0
Dunn,Adam, Was	14.7
Votto,Joey, Cin	14.8
Reynolds,Mark, Ari	15.6
Gonzalez,Carlos, Col	17.3
Tulowitzki,Troy, Col	17.4
Howard,Ryan, Phi	17.7
Uggla,Dan, Fla	17.8
Hart,Corey, Mil	18.0
Fielder,Prince, Mil	18.1

Highest GB/FB Ratio
(minimum 502 PA)

Schumaker,Skip, StL	2.99
Bourn,Michael, Hou	2.56
Morgan,Nyjer, Was	2.07
Theriot,Ryan, ChC-LAD	2.06
Heyward,Jason, Atl	2.03
Molina,Yadier, StL	1.83
Castro,Starlin, ChC	1.76
Keppinger,Jeff, Hou	1.72
Byrd,Marlon, ChC	1.71
Desmond,Ian, Was	1.67

Lowest GB/FB Ratio
(minimum 502 PA)

Ramirez,Aramis, ChC	0.48
Soriano,Alfonso, ChC	0.54
Gomes,Jonny, Cin	0.58
Reynolds,Mark, Ari	0.58
Rasmus,Colby, StL	0.66
Dunn,Adam, Was	0.67
Young,Chris, Ari	0.68
Ludwick,Ryan, StL-SD	0.71
Sanchez,Gaby, Fla	0.80
Werth,Jayson, Phi	0.81

Pitches Per Plate App
(minimum 502 PA)

Werth,Jayson, Phi	4.37
Reynolds,Mark, Ari	4.31
Blake,Casey, LAD	4.26
Lee,Derrek, ChC-Atl	4.24
Uggla,Dan, Fla	4.20
Upton,Justin, Ari	4.20
Young,Chris, Ari	4.18
Heyward,Jason, Atl	4.15
Johnson,Kelly, Ari	4.12
Dunn,Adam, Was	4.11

Pct Pitches Taken
(minimum 1500 Pitches)

Carroll,Jamey, LAD	65.0
Soto,Geovany, ChC	63.2
Snyder,Chris, Ari-Pit	62.6
Young,Chris, Ari	62.5
Keppinger,Jeff, Hou	62.0
McCutchen,Andrew, Pit	61.7
Willingham,Josh, Was	61.7
Utley,Chase, Phi	61.6
Ruiz,Carlos, Phi	61.6
Heyward,Jason, Atl	61.4

Best BPS on OutZ
(minimum 502 PA)

Zimmerman,Ryan, Was	.648
Tulowitzki,Troy, Col	.630
Ramirez,Hanley, Fla	.624
Sandoval,Pablo, SF	.613
Gonzalez,Carlos, Col	.595
Ibanez,Raul, Phi	.589
Ramirez,Aramis, ChC	.561
Pagan,Angel, NYM	.558
Pujols,Albert, StL	.546
Holliday,Matt, StL	.537

Worst BPS on OutZ
(minimum 502 PA)

Reynolds,Mark, Ari	.220
Headley,Chase, SD	.274
Ethier,Andre, LAD	.291
Weeks,Rickie, Mil	.299
Upton,Justin, Ari	.302
Cedeno,Ronny, Pit	.325
Ludwick,Ryan, StL-SD	.333
Young,Chris, Ari	.344
Fielder,Prince, Mil	.351
Desmond,Ian, Was	.357

2010 National League Batting Leaders

Best OPS vs Fastballs
(minimum 251 PA)

Votto,Joey, Cin	1.090
Tulowitzki,Troy, Col	1.067
Pujols,Albert, StL	1.029
Dunn,Adam, Was	1.019
Hart,Corey, Mil	.982
Torres,Andres, SF	.982
Fielder,Prince, Mil	.961
Howard,Ryan, Phi	.960
Werth,Jayson, Phi	.960
Braun,Ryan, Mil	.958

Best OPS vs Curveballs
(minimum 50 PA)

Huff,Aubrey, SF	1.266
Drew,Stephen, Ari	1.077
Sanchez,Gaby, Fla	1.019
McCutchen,Andrew, Pit	1.010
Howard,Ryan, Phi	.989
Soriano,Alfonso, ChC	.959
Holliday,Matt, StL	.919
Castro,Starlin, ChC	.915
Desmond,Ian, Was	.907
Gonzalez,Carlos, Col	.877

Best OPS vs Changeups
(minimum 50 PA)

Holliday,Matt, StL	1.179
McGehee,Casey, Mil	1.179
Rolen,Scott, Cin	1.166
Venable,Will, SD	1.143
Gonzalez,Carlos, Col	1.101
Weeks,Rickie, Mil	1.082
Gonzalez,Adrian, SD	1.053
Phillips,Brandon, Cin	1.029
Zimmerman,Ryan, Was	1.028
Ramirez,Aramis, ChC	.970

Best OPS vs Sliders
(minimum 32 PA)

Heisey,Chris, Cin	1.173
Hanigan,Ryan, Cin	1.156
Stubbs,Drew, Cin	1.150
Fukudome,Kosuke, ChC	1.103
Fielder,Prince, Mil	1.071
Pujols,Albert, StL	1.054
Jay,Jon, StL	1.043
Burrell,Pat, SF	1.032
Votto,Joey, Cin	1.013
Guzman,Cristian, Was	.995

OPS
(minimum 502 PA)

Votto,Joey, Cin	1.024
Pujols,Albert, StL	1.011
Gonzalez,Carlos, Col	.974
Tulowitzki,Troy, Col	.949
Holliday,Matt, StL	.922
Werth,Jayson, Phi	.921
Gonzalez,Adrian, SD	.904
Zimmerman,Ryan, Was	.899
Dunn,Adam, Was	.892
Huff,Aubrey, SF	.891

OPS First Half
(minimum 260 PA)

Votto,Joey, Cin	1.011
Pujols,Albert, StL	.992
Dunn,Adam, Was	.959
Ethier,Andre, LAD	.932
Gonzalez,Adrian, SD	.930
Huff,Aubrey, SF	.929
Wright,David, NYM	.924
Hart,Corey, Mil	.918
Rasmus,Colby, StL	.914
Willingham,Josh, Was	.913

OPS Second Half
(minimum 201 PA)

Gonzalez,Carlos, Col	1.091
Votto,Joey, Cin	1.042
Pujols,Albert, StL	1.033
Tulowitzki,Troy, Col	1.020
Werth,Jayson, Phi	.966
Bruce,Jay, Cin	.951
Holliday,Matt, StL	.944
Braun,Ryan, Mil	.917
Uggla,Dan, Fla	.907
Lee,Derrek, ChC-All	.888

OPS by Catchers
(minimum 251 PA)

Soto,Geovany, ChC	.900
Posey,Buster, SF	.860
Ruiz,Carlos, Phi	.853
McCann,Brian, Atl	.824
Hernandez,Ramon, Cin	.815
Doumit,Ryan, Pit	.774
Montero,Miguel, Ari	.769
Olivo,Miguel, Col	.766
Barajas,Rod, NYM-LAD	.737
Torrealba,Yorvit, SD	.723

OPS by First Basemen
(minimum 251 PA)

Votto,Joey, Cin	1.024
Pujols,Albert, StL	1.011
Gonzalez,Adrian, SD	.910
Dunn,Adam, Was	.901
Fielder,Prince, Mil	.874
Huff,Aubrey, SF	.850
Howard,Ryan, Phi	.855
Berkman,Lance, Hou	.808
LaRoche,Adam, Ari	.799
Sanchez,Gaby, Fla	.791

OPS by Second Basemen
(minimum 251 PA)

Uggla,Dan, Fla	.877
Johnson,Kelly, Ari	.869
Utley,Chase, Phi	.834
Weeks,Rickie, Mil	.832
Prado,Martin, Atl	.830
Walker,Neil, Pit	.818
Phillips,Brandon, Cin	.763
Infante,Omar, Atl	.753
Keppinger,Jeff, Hou	.736
Sanchez,Freddy, SF	.731

OPS by Third Basemen
(minimum 251 PA)

Zimmerman,Ryan, Was	.900
Wright,David, NYM	.863
Rolen,Scott, Cin	.842
Johnson,Chris, Hou	.822
McGehee,Casey, Mil	.810
Jones,Chipper, Atl	.801
Alvarez,Pedro, Pit	.786
Stewart,Ian, Col	.783
Freese,David, StL	.770
Reynolds,Mark, Ari	.756

OPS by Shortstops
(minimum 251 PA)

Tulowitzki,Troy, Col	.949
Ramirez,Hanley, Fla	.855
Furcal,Rafael, LAD	.838
Drew,Stephen, Ari	.808
Castro,Starlin, ChC	.758
Uribe,Juan, SF	.754
Reyes,Jose, NYM	.747
Carroll,Jamey, LAD	.725
Renteria,Edgar, SF	.718
Desmond,Ian, Was	.707

OPS by Left Fielders
(minimum 251 PA)

Holliday,Matt, StL	.924
Braun,Ryan, Mil	.877
Burrell,Pat, SF	.869
Willingham,Josh, Was	.853
Morrison,Logan, Fla	.837
Soriano,Alfonso, ChC	.830
Smith,Seth, Col	.811
Ibanez,Raul, Phi	.800
Gomes,Jonny, Cin	.772
Bay,Jason, NYM	.748

OPS by Center Fielders
(minimum 251 PA)

Rasmus,Colby, StL	.845
McCutchen,Andrew, Pit	.812
Torres,Andres, SF	.810
Pagan,Angel, NYM	.802
Young,Chris, Ari	.789
Byrd,Marlon, ChC	.778
Stubbs,Drew, Cin	.767
Kemp,Matt, LAD	.764
Fowler,Dexter, Col	.761
Victorino,Shane, Phi	.759

OPS by Right Fielders
(minimum 251 PA)

Werth,Jayson, Phi	.902
Hart,Corey, Mil	.867
Ethier,Andre, LAD	.863
Bruce,Jay, Cin	.853
Heyward,Jason, Atl	.845
Stanton,Mike, Fla	.837
Fukudome,Kosuke, ChC	.804
Upton,Justin, Ari	.790
Pence,Hunter, Hou	.785
Hawpe,Brad, Col	.756

OPS by Pitchers
(minimum 50 PA)

Haren,Dan, Ari	.870
Gallardo,Yovani, Mil	.863
Leake,Mike, Cin	.798
Narveson,Chris, Mil	.712
Zambrano,Carlos, ChC	.625
Dickey,R.A., NYM	.590
Wolf,Randy, Mil	.566
Niese,Jonathon, NYM	.531
Garland,Jon, SD	.527
Kennedy,Ian, Ari	.513

2010 National League Batting Leaders

OPS Batting Left vs. LHP
(minimum 125 PA)

Utley,Chase, Phi	1.003
Johnson,Kelly, Ari	.953
Gonzalez,Adrian, SD	.937
Gonzalez,Carlos, Col	.925
Bruce,Jay, Cin	.899
Huff,Aubrey, SF	.884
Votto,Joey, Cin	.863
Howard,Ryan, Phi	.826
Rasmus,Colby, StL	.810
Davis,Ike, NYM	.805

OPS Batting Left vs. RHP
(minimum 377 PA)

Votto,Joey, Cin	1.115
Gonzalez,Carlos, Col	1.003
Fielder,Prince, Mil	.975
Dunn,Adam, Was	.965
Ethier,Andre, LAD	.960
Heyward,Jason, Atl	.895
Huff,Aubrey, SF	.894
Gonzalez,Adrian, SD	.887
Torres,Andres, SF	.881
Howard,Ryan, Phi	.876

OPS Batting Right vs. LHP
(minimum 125 PA)

Pujols,Albert, StL	1.076
Soto,Geovany, ChC	1.072
Wright,David, NYM	1.066
Weeks,Rickie, Mil	1.025
Tulowitzki,Troy, Col	.990
Uggla,Dan, Fla	.983
Holliday,Matt, StL	.982
Hart,Corey, Mil	.973
Zimmerman,Ryan, Was	.957
McGehee,Casey, Mil	.947

OPS Batting Right vs. RHP
(minimum 377 PA)

Pujols,Albert, StL	.983
Werth,Jayson, Phi	.937
Holliday,Matt, StL	.900
Braun,Ryan, Mil	.893
Zimmerman,Ryan, Was	.879
Ramirez,Hanley, Fla	.858
Uggla,Dan, Fla	.845
Prado,Martin, Atl	.834
Hart,Corey, Mil	.827
Upton,Justin, Ari	.808

OPS vs. LHP
(minimum 125 PA)

Pujols,Albert, StL	1.076
Soto,Geovany, ChC	1.072
Wright,David, NYM	1.066
Weeks,Rickie, Mil	1.025
Utley,Chase, Phi	1.003
Tulowitzki,Troy, Col	.990
Uggla,Dan, Fla	.983
Holliday,Matt, StL	.982
Hart,Corey, Mil	.973
Zimmerman,Ryan, Was	.957

OPS vs. RHP
(minimum 377 PA)

Votto,Joey, Cin	1.115
Gonzalez,Carlos, Col	1.003
Pujols,Albert, StL	.983
Fielder,Prince, Mil	.975
Dunn,Adam, Was	.965
Ethier,Andre, LAD	.960
Werth,Jayson, Phi	.937
Holliday,Matt, StL	.900
Heyward,Jason, Atl	.895
Huff,Aubrey, SF	.894

RC Per 27 Outs vs. LHP
(minimum 125 PA)

Weeks,Rickie, Mil	9.4
Soto,Geovany, ChC	9.2
Utley,Chase, Phi	8.9
Zimmerman,Ryan, Was	8.7
Holliday,Matt, StL	8.3
Uggla,Dan, Fla	8.2
Wright,David, NYM	8.1
Rollins,Jimmy, Phi	8.0
Milledge,Lastings, Pit	8.0
Victorino,Shane, Phi	8.0

RC Per 27 Outs vs. RHP
(minimum 377 PA)

Votto,Joey, Cin	10.4
Pujols,Albert, StL	8.4
Gonzalez,Carlos, Col	8.2
Ethier,Andre, LAD	7.7
Heyward,Jason, Atl	7.3
Gonzalez,Adrian, SD	7.2
Fielder,Prince, Mil	6.9
Torres,Andres, SF	6.8
Dunn,Adam, Was	6.8
Braun,Ryan, Mil	6.6

Highest RBI %
(minimum 502 PA)

Gonzalez,Carlos, Col	12.05
Votto,Joey, Cin	12.00
Tulowitzki,Troy, Col	11.50
Pujols,Albert, StL	11.14
Howard,Ryan, Phi	10.68
Hart,Corey, Mil	10.45
Dunn,Adam, Was	10.27
LaRoche,Adam, Ari	10.24
Wright,David, NYM	10.20
Ramirez,Aramis, ChC	10.17

Lowest RBI %
(minimum 502 PA)

Morgan,Nyjer, Was	3.11
Theriot,Ryan, ChC-LAD	3.18
Escobar,Alcides, Mil	4.71
Bourn,Michael, Hou	4.75
Cedeno,Ronny, Pit	4.90
Cabrera,Melky, Atl	5.09
Fowler,Dexter, Col	5.37
Cabrera,Orlando, Cin	5.41
Castro,Starlin, ChC	5.47
Headley,Chase, SD	5.56

Highest Strikeout per PA
(minimum 502 PA)

Reynolds,Mark, Ari	.354
Dunn,Adam, Was	.307
Stubbs,Drew, Cin	.288
LaRoche,Adam, Ari	.280
Rasmus,Colby, StL	.277
Upton,Justin, Ari	.266
Kemp,Matt, LAD	.254
Howard,Ryan, Phi	.253
Weeks,Rickie, Mil	.244
Blake,Casey, LAD	.242

Lowest Strikeout per PA
(minimum 502 PA)

Keppinger,Jeff, Hou	.063
Polanco,Placido, Phi	.078
Lee,Carlos, Hou	.091
Molina,Yadier, StL	.098
Cabrera,Orlando, Cin	.099
Reyes,Jose, NYM	.104
Pujols,Albert, StL	.109
Theriot,Ryan, ChC-LAD	.116
Phillips,Brandon, Cin	.121
Schumaker,Skip, StL	.121

Home Runs At Home

Gonzalez,Carlos, Col	26
Reynolds,Mark, Ari	21
Dunn,Adam, Was	20
Young,Chris, Ari	20
Bruce,Jay, Cin	19
Fielder,Prince, Mil	18
Votto,Joey, Cin	18
Werth,Jayson, Phi	18
Pujols,Albert, StL	17
5 tied with	16

Home Runs Away

Pujols,Albert, StL	25
Gonzalez,Adrian, SD	20
Uggla,Dan, Fla	19
Votto,Joey, Cin	19
Dunn,Adam, Was	18
Wright,David, NYM	17
Zimmerman,Ryan, Was	16
4 tied with	15

Longest Avg Home Run
(min 10 over the wall)

Davis,Ike, NYM	415
Byrd,Marlon, ChC	415
Reynolds,Mark, Ari	415
Jones,Chipper, Atl	414
Gonzalez,Carlos, Col	414
Upton,Justin, Ari	413
Dunn,Adam, Was	411
Stewart,Ian, Col	410
Fielder,Prince, Mil	410
Tulowitzki,Troy, Col	409

Shortest Avg Home Run
(min 10 over the wall)

Victorino,Shane, Phi	376
Hairston,Jerry, SD	378
Reyes,Jose, NYM	380
Berkman,Lance, Hou	382
Hairston,Scott, SD	382
Edmonds,Jim, Mil-Cin	383
Lee,Carlos, Hou	384
Uggla,Dan, Fla	385
3 tied with	386

2010 National League Batting Leaders

Under Age 26: AB Per HR
(minimum 502 PA)

Gonzalez,Carlos, Col	17.3
Tulowitzki,Troy, Col	17.4
Rasmus,Colby, StL	20.2
Bruce,Jay, Cin	20.4
Stubbs,Drew, Cin	23.4
Davis,Ike, NYM	27.5
Heyward,Jason, Atl	28.9
Upton,Justin, Ari	29.1
McCutchen,Andrew, Pit	35.6
Sandoval,Pablo, SF	43.3

Under Age 26: OPS
(minimum 502 PA)

Gonzalez,Carlos, Col	.974
Tulowitzki,Troy, Col	.949
Rasmus,Colby, StL	.859
Heyward,Jason, Atl	.849
Bruce,Jay, Cin	.846
McCutchen,Andrew, Pit	.814
Upton,Justin, Ari	.799
Davis,Ike, NYM	.791
Stubbs,Drew, Cin	.773
Fowler,Dexter, Col	.757

Under Age 26: RC/27 Outs
(minimum 502 PA)

Gonzalez,Carlos, Col	7.6
Tulowitzki,Troy, Col	6.8
Heyward,Jason, Atl	6.5
Rasmus,Colby, StL	5.7
McCutchen,Andrew, Pit	5.3
Fowler,Dexter, Col	5.3
Davis,Ike, NYM	5.0
Upton,Justin, Ari	4.9
Bruce,Jay, Cin	4.9
Stubbs,Drew, Cin	4.9

Longest Home Run

Rasmus,Colby, StL, 6/27	483
Dunn,Adam, Was, 9/14	479
Heyward,Jason, Atl, 4/5	476
Dunn,Adam, Was, 5/15	471
Braun,Ryan, Mil, 5/8	467
Reynolds,Mark, Ari, 4/20	466
Mora,Melvin, Col, 9/22	464
Byrd,Marlon, ChC, 4/30	463
Weeks,Rickie, Mil, 5/7	459
4 tied with	458

Swing and Miss %
(minimum 1500 Pitches Seen)

Reynolds,Mark, Ari	39.3
Olivo,Miguel, Col	35.0
Dunn,Adam, Was	32.7
Howard,Ryan, Phi	32.5
Stanton,Mike, Fla	31.4
Alvarez,Pedro, Pit	31.0
Kemp,Matt, LAD	29.5
Stubbs,Drew, Cin	28.9
Hart,Corey, Mil	28.8
Venable,Will, SD	28.5

Highest First Swing %
(minimum 502 PA)

Sandoval,Pablo, SF	40.1
Uribe,Juan, SF	37.9
Reynolds,Mark, Ari	37.2
Votto,Joey, Cin	37.2
Molina,Yadier, StL	36.1
Gomes,Jonny, Cin	35.3
Byrd,Marlon, ChC	34.3
Ramirez,Aramis, ChC	33.9
McGehee,Casey, Mil	33.8
Ludwick,Ryan, StL-SD	33.6

Lowest First Swing %
(minimum 502 PA)

Prado,Martin, Atl	9.3
Young,Chris, Ari	11.0
Utley,Chase, Phi	11.6
Pujols,Albert, StL	12.1
Ibanez,Raul, Phi	14.2
Blake,Casey, LAD	14.4
Zimmerman,Ryan, Was	14.7
Victorino,Shane, Phi	15.7
Polanco,Placido, Phi	16.4
Drew,Stephen, Ari	17.0

Home RC Per 27 Outs
(minimum 251 PA)

Gonzalez,Carlos, Col	10.5
Tulowitzki,Troy, Col	8.4
Pujols,Albert, StL	8.4
Utley,Chase, Phi	8.2
Votto,Joey, Cin	7.6
Holliday,Matt, StL	7.4
Prado,Martin, Atl	7.3
Johnson,Kelly, Ari	7.0
Werth,Jayson, Phi	7.0
Ethier,Andre, LAD	7.0

Road RC Per 27 Outs
(minimum 251 PA)

Votto,Joey, Cin	10.5
Gonzalez,Adrian, SD	8.9
Huff,Aubrey, SF	8.5
Pujols,Albert, StL	7.5
Braun,Ryan, Mil	7.2
Zimmerman,Ryan, Was	7.0
Rasmus,Colby, StL	7.0
Heyward,Jason, Atl	6.6
McCann,Brian, Atl	6.2
Uggla,Dan, Fla	6.1

2010 American League Pitching Leaders

Earned Run Average
(minimum 162 IP)

Hernandez,Felix, Sea	2.27
Buchholz,Clay, Bos	2.33
Price,David, TB	2.72
Cahill,Trevor, Oak	2.97
Weaver,Jered, LAA	3.01
Lee,Cliff, Sea-Tex	3.18
Sabathia,CC, NYY	3.18
Gonzalez,Gio, Oak	3.23
Lester,Jon, Bos	3.25
Wilson,C.J., Tex	3.35

Winning Percentage
(minimum 15 Decisions)

Hunter,Tommy, Tex	.765
Price,David, TB	.760
Sabathia,CC, NYY	.750
Buchholz,Clay, Bos	.708
Cahill,Trevor, Oak	.692
Hughes,Phil, NYY	.692
Slowey,Kevin, Min	.684
Cecil,Brett, Tor	.682
Lester,Jon, Bos	.679
2 tied with	.667

Opponent Batting Average
(minimum 162 IP)

Hernandez,Felix, Sea	.212
Wilson,C.J., Tex	.217
Cahill,Trevor, Oak	.220
Lester,Jon, Bos	.220
Price,David, TB	.221
Weaver,Jered, LAA	.222
Buchholz,Clay, Bos	.226
Lewis,Colby, Tex	.227
Verlander,Justin, Det	.228
Gonzalez,Gio, Oak	.229

Baserunners Per 9 IP
(minimum 162 IP)

Lee,Cliff, Sea-Tex	9.07
Weaver,Jered, LAA	9.67
Hernandez,Felix, Sea	9.81
Cahill,Trevor, Oak	10.25
Marcum,Shaun, Tor	10.60
Braden,Dallas, Oak	10.65
Verlander,Justin, Det	10.71
Price,David, TB	10.96
Lewis,Colby, Tex	10.97
Sabathia,CC, NYY	10.98

Games

Choate,Randy, TB	85
Breslow,Craig, Oak	75
Coke,Phil, Det	74
Guerrier,Matt, Min	74
Bard,Daniel, Bos	73
Chamberlain,Joba, NYY	73
O'Day,Darren, Tex	72
Rodney,Fernando, LAA	72
Crain,Jesse, Min	71
5 tied with	70

Games Started

Hernandez,Felix, Sea	34
Sabathia,CC, NYY	34
Weaver,Jered, LAA	34
10 tied with	33

Complete Games

Lee,Cliff, Sea-Tex	7
Pavano,Carl, Min	7
Hernandez,Felix, Sea	6
Braden,Dallas, Oak	5
Carmona,Fausto, Cle	4
Santana,Ervin, LAA	4
Verlander,Justin, Det	4
6 tied with	3

Shutouts

Braden,Dallas, Oak	2
Pavano,Carl, Min	2
19 tied with	1

Wins

Sabathia,CC, NYY	21
Lester,Jon, Bos	19
Price,David, TB	19
Cahill,Trevor, Oak	18
Hughes,Phil, NYY	18
Verlander,Justin, Det	18
Buchholz,Clay, Bos	17
Pavano,Carl, Min	17
Santana,Ervin, LAA	17
5 tied with	15

Losses

Millwood,Kevin, Bal	16
Burnett,A.J., NYY	15
Kazmir,Scott, LAA	15
Shields,James, TB	15
Braden,Dallas, Oak	14
Carmona,Fausto, Cle	14
Fister,Doug, Sea	14
Greinke,Zack, KC	14
Guthrie,Jeremy, Bal	14
5 tied with	13

No Decisions

Davies,Kyle, KC	12
Bonderman,Jeremy, Det	11
Galarraga,Armando, Det	11
Masterson,Justin, Cle	11
Millwood,Kevin, Bal	11
7 tied with	10

Wild Pitches

Romero,Ricky, Tor	18
Burnett,A.J., NYY	16
Hernandez,Felix, Sea	14
Shields,James, TB	13
Garza,Matt, TB	12
Masterson,Justin, Cle	12
5 tied with	11

Strikeouts

Weaver,Jered, LAA	233
Hernandez,Felix, Sea	232
Lester,Jon, Bos	225
Verlander,Justin, Det	219
Liriano,Francisco, Min	201
Sabathia,CC, NYY	197
Lewis,Colby, Tex	196
Price,David, TB	188
Shields,James, TB	187
Lee,Cliff, Sea-Tex	185

Walks Allowed

Wilson,C.J., Tex	93
Gonzalez,Gio, Oak	92
Lester,Jon, Bos	83
Romero,Ricky, Tor	82
Davies,Kyle, KC	80
Kazmir,Scott, LAA	79
Price,David, TB	79
Burnett,A.J., NYY	78
Matsuzaka,Daisuke, Bos	74
Sabathia,CC, NYY	74

Intentional Walks Allowed

Ziegler,Brad, Oak	9
Frasor,Jason, Tor	6
League,Brandon, Sea	6
Niemann,Jeff, TB	6
Pena,Tony, CWS	6
Pineiro,Joel, LAA	6
Robertson,David, NYY	6
Sabathia,CC, NYY	6
Williams,Randy, CWS	6
11 tied with	5

Hit Batters

Burnett,A.J., NYY	19
Guthrie,Jeremy, Bal	16
Kazmir,Scott, LAA	12
Santana,Ervin, LAA	12
Masterson,Justin, Cle	11
Bonderman,Jeremy, Det	10
Lester,Jon, Bos	10
Liriano,Francisco, Min	10
Wilson,C.J., Tex	10
4 tied with	9

2010 American League Pitching Leaders

Runs Allowed

Shields,James, TB	128
Burnett,A.J., NYY	118
Millwood,Kevin, Bal	116
Davies,Kyle, KC	114
Greinke,Zack, KC	114
Lackey,John, Bos	114
Bonderman,Jeremy, Det	113
Masterson,Justin, Cle	107
Buehrle,Mark, CWS	105
2 tied with	104

Hits Allowed

Buehrle,Mark, CWS	246
Shields,James, TB	246
Lackey,John, Bos	233
Pavano,Carl, Min	227
Millwood,Kevin, Bal	223
Santana,Ervin, LAA	221
Greinke,Zack, KC	219
Sabathia,CC, NYY	209
Davies,Kyle, KC	206
Burnett,A.J., NYY	204

Doubles Allowed

Lackey,John, Bos	59
Bergesen,Brad, Bal	53
Buehrle,Mark, CWS	50
Shields,James, TB	50
Baker,Scott, Min	49
Davies,Kyle, KC	49
Pavano,Carl, Min	49
Santana,Ervin, LAA	48
Vargas,Jason, Sea	48
2 tied with	46

Home Runs Allowed

Shields,James, TB	34
Vazquez,Javier, NYY	32
Millwood,Kevin, Bal	30
Garza,Matt, TB	28
Santana,Ervin, LAA	27
Bergesen,Brad, Bal	26
8 tied with	25

Run Support Per Nine IP
(minimum 162 IP)

Hughes,Phil, NYY	7.45
Sabathia,CC, NYY	6.13
Price,David, TB	6.00
Cecil,Brett, Tor	5.94
Lester,Jon, Bos	5.71
Buchholz,Clay, Bos	5.65
Lackey,John, Bos	5.53
Verlander,Justin, Det	5.46
Bonderman,Jeremy, Det	5.42
Garza,Matt, TB	5.41

% Pitches In Strike Zone
(minimum 162 IP)

Lee,Cliff, Sea-Tex	54.8
Baker,Scott, Min	49.8
Niemann,Jeff, TB	48.9
Fister,Doug, Sea	48.8
Hughes,Phil, NYY	48.3
Matusz,Brian, Bal	48.0
Pavano,Carl, Min	47.2
Shields,James, TB	46.9
Price,David, TB	46.8
Porcello,Rick, Det	46.7

Pitches Per Start
(minimum 30 GS)

Verlander,Justin, Det	113.5
Hernandez,Felix, Sea	109.7
Weaver,Jered, LAA	109.2
Lackey,John, Bos	109.1
Santana,Ervin, LAA	107.9
Price,David, TB	107.8
Scherzer,Max, Det	106.4
Danks,John, CWS	105.9
Sabathia,CC, NYY	105.5
Lester,Jon, Bos	104.9

Pitches Per Batter
(minimum 162 IP)

Pavano,Carl, Min	3.46
Bergesen,Brad, Bal	3.50
Lee,Cliff, Sea-Tex	3.53
Niemann,Jeff, TB	3.60
Bonderman,Jeremy, Det	3.63
Braden,Dallas, Oak	3.65
Romero,Ricky, Tor	3.67
Buehrle,Mark, CWS	3.69
Baker,Scott, Min	3.69
Sabathia,CC, NYY	3.70

Quality Starts

Hernandez,Felix, Sea	30
Weaver,Jered, LAA	27
Sabathia,CC, NYY	26
Price,David, TB	25
Gonzalez,Gio, Oak	23
Carmona,Fausto, Cle	22
Verlander,Justin, Det	22
7 tied with	21

Batters Faced

Hernandez,Felix, Sea	1001
Sabathia,CC, NYY	970
Santana,Ervin, LAA	954
Lackey,John, Bos	930
Verlander,Justin, Det	925
Greinke,Zack, KC	919
Pavano,Carl, Min	906
Weaver,Jered, LAA	905
Shields,James, TB	899
Buehrle,Mark, CWS	897

Innings Pitched

Hernandez,Felix, Sea	249.2
Sabathia,CC, NYY	237.2
Verlander,Justin, Det	224.1
Weaver,Jered, LAA	224.1
Santana,Ervin, LAA	222.2
Pavano,Carl, Min	221.0
Greinke,Zack, KC	220.0
Lackey,John, Bos	215.0
Danks,John, CWS	213.0
Lee,Cliff, Sea-Tex	212.1

Most Pitches in a Game

Morrow,Brandon, Tor	137
Jackson,Edwin, CWS	129
Hernandez,Felix, Sea	128
Meche,Gil, KC	128
Harrison,Matt, Tex	127
Verlander,Justin, Det	127
Hernandez,Felix, Sea	126
Saunders,Joe, LAA	126
3 tied with	125

Stolen Bases Allowed

Burnett,A.J., NYY	37
Santana,Ervin, LAA	36
Carmona,Fausto, Cle	33
Pavano,Carl, Min	31
Weaver,Jered, LAA	27
Lackey,John, Bos	26
Matsuzaka,Daisuke, Bos	25
Verlander,Justin, Det	24
Wakefield,Tim, Bos	24
Lester,Jon, Bos	22

Caught Stealing Off

Scherzer,Max, Det	13
Greinke,Zack, KC	11
Talbot,Mitch, Cle	11
Lackey,John, Bos	10
Morrow,Brandon, Tor	9
Sheets,Ben, Oak	9
6 tied with	8

Stolen Base Pct Allowed
(minimum 162 IP)

Baker,Scott, Min	33.3
Braden,Dallas, Oak	33.3
Fister,Doug, Sea	40.0
Romero,Ricky, Tor	44.4
Marcum,Shaun, Tor	46.7
Buehrle,Mark, CWS	50.0
Danks,John, CWS	50.0
Greinke,Zack, KC	52.2
Millwood,Kevin, Bal	54.5
Scherzer,Max, Det	56.7

Pickoffs

Buehrle,Mark, CWS	11
Braden,Dallas, Oak	8
Chen,Bruce, KC	8
Lester,Jon, Bos	6
Sipp,Tony, Cle	6
Cahill,Trevor, Oak	5
Saunders,Joe, LAA	5
5 tied with	4

2010 American League Pitching Leaders

Strikeouts Per 9 IP
(minimum 162 IP)

Lester,Jon, Bos	9.74
Liriano,Francisco, Min	9.44
Weaver,Jered, LAA	9.35
Verlander,Justin, Det	8.79
Lewis,Colby, Tex	8.78
Scherzer,Max, Det	8.46
Hernandez,Felix, Sea	8.36
Shields,James, TB	8.28
Price,David, TB	8.11
Lee,Cliff, Sea-Tex	7.84

Opp On-Base Percentage
(minimum 162 IP)

Lee,Cliff, Sea-Tex	.255
Weaver,Jered, LAA	.267
Hernandez,Felix, Sea	.273
Cahill,Trevor, Oak	.287
Marcum,Shaun, Tor	.288
Verlander,Justin, Det	.291
Lewis,Colby, Tex	.292
Braden,Dallas, Oak	.294
Price,David, TB	.296
Guthrie,Jeremy, Bal	.298

Opp Slugging Average
(minimum 162 IP)

Wilson,C.J., Tex	.311
Buchholz,Clay, Bos	.312
Hernandez,Felix, Sea	.312
Lester,Jon, Bos	.325
Gonzalez,Gio, Oak	.329
Cahill,Trevor, Oak	.332
Verlander,Justin, Det	.339
Price,David, TB	.340
Romero,Ricky, Tor	.354
Liriano,Francisco, Min	.355

Opponent OPS
(minimum 162 IP)

Hernandez,Felix, Sea	.585
Buchholz,Clay, Bos	.615
Lee,Cliff, Sea-Tex	.618
Cahill,Trevor, Oak	.619
Weaver,Jered, LAA	.622
Wilson,C.J., Tex	.622
Lester,Jon, Bos	.628
Verlander,Justin, Det	.630
Price,David, TB	.637
Gonzalez,Gio, Oak	.644

Home Runs Per Nine IP
(minimum 162 IP)

Liriano,Francisco, Min	0.42
Wilson,C.J., Tex	0.44
Buchholz,Clay, Bos	0.47
Verlander,Justin, Det	0.56
Lester,Jon, Bos	0.61
Hernandez,Felix, Sea	0.61
Romero,Ricky, Tor	0.64
Price,David, TB	0.65
Floyd,Gavin, CWS	0.67
Gonzalez,Gio, Oak	0.67

Batting Average vs. LHB
(minimum 125 BF)

Feliz,Neftali, Tex	.127
Bard,Daniel, Bos	.141
Wilson,C.J., Tex	.144
Duensing,Brian, Min	.162
Valverde,Jose, Det	.165
Pettitte,Andy, NYY	.186
Marcum,Shaun, Tor	.190
Hernandez,David, Bal	.198
Vargas,Jason, Sea	.200
Choate,Randy, TB	.202

Batting Average vs. RHB
(minimum 225 BF)

Cahill,Trevor, Oak	.198
Matsuzaka,Daisuke, Bos	.211
Hernandez,Felix, Sea	.212
Lewis,Colby, Tex	.216
Lester,Jon, Bos	.219
Weaver,Jered, LAA	.220
Danks,John, CWS	.221
Buchholz,Clay, Bos	.221
Price,David, TB	.224
Verlander,Justin, Det	.225

Opp BA w/ RISP
(minimum 125 BF)

Buchholz,Clay, Bos	.161
Price,David, TB	.187
Lewis,Colby, Tex	.187
Garza,Matt, TB	.197
Weaver,Jered, LAA	.205
Hernandez,Felix, Sea	.211
Davis,Wade, TB	.218
Vargas,Jason, Sea	.218
Cahill,Trevor, Oak	.220
Lester,Jon, Bos	.225

OBP vs. Leadoff Hitter
(minimum 150 BF)

Weaver,Jered, LAA	.204
Gonzalez,Gio, Oak	.234
Lee,Cliff, Sea-Tex	.240
Pineiro,Joel, LAA	.244
Verlander,Justin, Det	.251
Cahill,Trevor, Oak	.252
Fister,Doug, Sea	.257
Marcum,Shaun, Tor	.261
Hernandez,Felix, Sea	.262
Bonderman,Jeremy, Det	.274

Strikeouts / Walks Ratio
(minimum 162 IP)

Lee,Cliff, Sea-Tex	10.28
Weaver,Jered, LAA	4.31
Marcum,Shaun, Tor	3.84
Shields,James, TB	3.67
Liriano,Francisco, Min	3.47
Baker,Scott, Min	3.44
Hernandez,Felix, Sea	3.31
Greinke,Zack, KC	3.29
Pavano,Carl, Min	3.16
Verlander,Justin, Det	3.08

Highest GB/FB Ratio
(minimum 162 IP)

Masterson,Justin, Cle	2.41
Romero,Ricky, Tor	2.08
Liriano,Francisco, Min	1.96
Cahill,Trevor, Oak	1.93
Lester,Jon, Bos	1.81
Hernandez,Felix, Sea	1.81
Carmona,Fausto, Cle	1.81
Pavano,Carl, Min	1.66
Buchholz,Clay, Bos	1.61
Porcello,Rick, Det	1.57

Lowest GB/FB Ratio
(minimum 162 IP)

Weaver,Jered, LAA	0.75
Hughes,Phil, NYY	0.76
Vargas,Jason, Sea	0.77
Garza,Matt, TB	0.80
Matusz,Brian, Bal	0.80
Baker,Scott, Min	0.82
Santana,Ervin, LAA	0.83
Lewis,Colby, Tex	0.84
Marcum,Shaun, Tor	0.89
Davis,Wade, TB	0.90

Sacrifice Flies Allowed

Slowey,Kevin, Min	11
Burnett,A.J., NYY	10
Carmona,Fausto, Cle	10
Guthrie,Jeremy, Bal	9
Feldman,Scott, Tex	8
Harrison,Matt, Tex	8
Matsuzaka,Daisuke, Bos	8
Sabathia,CC, NYY	8
Santana,Ervin, LAA	8
Verlander,Justin, Det	8

Sacrifice Hits Allowed

Romero,Ricky, Tor	9
Pettitte,Andy, NYY	8
Santana,Ervin, LAA	8
Aardsma,David, Sea	7
Burnett,A.J., NYY	7
11 tied with	6

GIDP Induced

Carmona,Fausto, Cle	30
Cahill,Trevor, Oak	27
Sabathia,CC, NYY	27
Burnett,A.J., NYY	25
Danks,John, CWS	25
Floyd,Gavin, CWS	25
Hernandez,Felix, Sea	25
Romero,Ricky, Tor	25
Buchholz,Clay, Bos	24
Cecil,Brett, Tor	24

GIDP Per Nine IP
(minimum 162 IP)

Carmona,Fausto, Cle	1.28
Cecil,Brett, Tor	1.25
Buchholz,Clay, Bos	1.24
Cahill,Trevor, Oak	1.24
Burnett,A.J., NYY	1.21
Floyd,Gavin, CWS	1.20
Romero,Ricky, Tor	1.07
Danks,John, CWS	1.06
Porcello,Rick, Det	1.05
Sabathia,CC, NYY	1.02

2010 American League Pitching Leaders

Saves

Soriano,Rafael, TB	45
Soria,Joakim, KC	43
Feliz,Neftali, Tex	40
Gregg,Kevin, Tor	37
Papelbon,Jonathan, Bos	37
Rivera,Mariano, NYY	33
Aardsma,David, Sea	31
Jenks,Bobby, CWS	27
Valverde,Jose, Det	26
Bailey,Andrew, Oak	25

Blown Saves

Papelbon,Jonathan, Bos	8
Bard,Daniel, Bos	7
Rodney,Fernando, LAA	7
Gregg,Kevin, Tor	6
Guerrier,Matt, Min	6
League,Brandon, Sea	6
Tejeda,Robinson, KC	6
Aardsma,David, Sea	5
Johnson,Jim, Bal	5
Rivera,Mariano, NYY	5

Save Pct
(minimum 20 Save Ops)

Soriano,Rafael, TB	93.8
Soria,Joakim, KC	93.5
Feliz,Neftali, Tex	93.0
Valverde,Jose, Det	89.7
Bailey,Andrew, Oak	89.3
Jenks,Bobby, CWS	87.1
Rivera,Mariano, NYY	86.8
Aardsma,David, Sea	86.1
Gregg,Kevin, Tor	86.0
Fuentes,Brian, LAA-Min	85.7

Save Opportunities

Soriano,Rafael, TB	48
Soria,Joakim, KC	46
Papelbon,Jonathan, Bos	45
Feliz,Neftali, Tex	43
Gregg,Kevin, Tor	43
Rivera,Mariano, NYY	38
Aardsma,David, Sea	36
Jenks,Bobby, CWS	31
Valverde,Jose, Det	29
2 tied with	28

Easy Saves

Soriano,Rafael, TB	28
Papelbon,Jonathan, Bos	27
Soria,Joakim, KC	22
Gregg,Kevin, Tor	20
Feliz,Neftali, Tex	19
Rivera,Mariano, NYY	19
Valverde,Jose, Det	17
Bailey,Andrew, Oak	16
3 tied with	14

Regular Saves

Soria,Joakim, KC	21
Feliz,Neftali, Tex	20
Soriano,Rafael, TB	17
Aardsma,David, Sea	16
Gregg,Kevin, Tor	16
Rivera,Mariano, NYY	14
Rauch,Jon, Min	11
Jenks,Bobby, CWS	10
3 tied with	9

Tough Saves

Perez,Chris, Cle	4
Jenks,Bobby, CWS	3
Thornton,Matt, CWS	3
Bailey,Andrew, Oak	2
League,Brandon, Sea	2
Uehara,Koji, Bal	2
21 tied with	1

Holds Adjusted Saves %
(minimum 20 Save Ops)

Soriano,Rafael, TB	93.8
Feliz,Neftali, Tex	93.5
Soria,Joakim, KC	93.5
Valverde,Jose, Det	89.7
Bailey,Andrew, Oak	89.3
Perez,Chris, Cle	88.9
Fuentes,Brian, LAA-Min	87.1
Jenks,Bobby, CWS	87.1
Rodney,Fernando, LAA	87.0
Rivera,Mariano, NYY	86.8

Relief Wins

League,Brandon, Sea	9
Coke,Phil, Det	7
Hernandez,David, Bal	7
Putz,J.J., CWS	7
Francisco,Frank, Tex	6
O'Day,Darren, Tex	6
Perez,Rafael, Cle	6
Thomas,Brad, Det	6
6 tied with	5

Relief Losses

Guerrier,Matt, Min	7
League,Brandon, Sea	7
Papelbon,Jonathan, Bos	7
Ziegler,Brad, Oak	7
Aardsma,David, Sea	6
Gregg,Kevin, Tor	6
8 tied with	5

Relief Games

Choate,Randy, TB	85
Breslow,Craig, Oak	75
Guerrier,Matt, Min	74
Bard,Daniel, Bos	73
Chamberlain,Joba, NYY	73
O'Day,Darren, Tex	72
Rodney,Fernando, LAA	72
Crain,Jesse, Min	71
5 tied with	70

Holds

Bard,Daniel, Bos	32
Jepsen,Kevin, LAA	27
Chamberlain,Joba, NYY	26
Downs,Scott, Tor	26
Benoit,Joaquin, TB	25
Guerrier,Matt, Min	23
O'Day,Darren, Tex	22
Crain,Jesse, Min	21
Rodney,Fernando, LAA	21
Thornton,Matt, CWS	21

Relief Innings

Pena,Tony, CWS	81.2
League,Brandon, Sea	79.0
Albers,Matt, Bal	75.2
Bard,Daniel, Bos	74.2
Breslow,Craig, Oak	74.2
Camp,Shawn, Tor	72.1
Chamberlain,Joba, NYY	71.2
Guerrier,Matt, Min	71.0
Hendrickson,Mark, Bal	70.1
Feliz,Neftali, Tex	69.1

Inherited Runners Scrd %
(minimum 30 IR)

Thornton,Matt, CWS	12.9
Wheeler,Dan, TB	18.2
Frasor,Jason, Tor	19.4
Smith,Joe, Cle	19.4
Perry,Ryan, Det	20.0
Sipp,Tony, Cle	20.0
Breslow,Craig, Oak	21.2
Atchison,Scott, Bos	21.9
Oliver,Darren, Tex	22.0
Guerrier,Matt, Min	22.2

Relief Opp On Base Pct
(minimum 50 IP)

Benoit,Joaquin, TB	.189
Soriano,Rafael, TB	.215
Rivera,Mariano, NYY	.239
Feliz,Neftali, Tex	.246
O'Day,Darren, Tex	.251
Putz,J.J., CWS	.261
Bard,Daniel, Bos	.263
Thornton,Matt, CWS	.264
Soria,Joakim, KC	.266
Downs,Scott, Tor	.270

Relief Opp Slugging Avg
(minimum 50 IP)

Rivera,Mariano, NYY	.254
Benoit,Joaquin, TB	.265
Feliz,Neftali, Tex	.269
Bard,Daniel, Bos	.277
Thornton,Matt, CWS	.284
Valverde,Jose, Det	.291
Soriano,Rafael, TB	.294
Perez,Chris, Cle	.295
O'Day,Darren, Tex	.297
Soria,Joakim, KC	.302

2010 American League Pitching Leaders

Relief Opp BA Vs LHB
(minimum 50 AB)

Duensing,Brian, Min	.116
Feliz,Neftali, Tex	.127
Bard,Daniel, Bos	.141
Benoit,Joaquin, TB	.144
Downs,Scott, Tor	.152
Hernandez,David, Bal	.160
Delcarmen,Manny, Bos	.165
Valverde,Jose, Det	.165
Perry,Ryan, Det	.167
Shields,Scot, LAA	.169

Relief Opp BA Vs RHB
(minimum 50 AB)

Sale,Chris, CWS	.120
Gonzalez,Mike, Bal	.130
Soriano,Rafael, TB	.132
Aardsma,David, Sea	.148
Benoit,Joaquin, TB	.150
Perez,Chris, Cle	.154
Rivera,Mariano, NYY	.155
Germano,Justin, Cle	.159
Smith,Joe, Cle	.160
Putz,J.J., CWS	.164

Relief Opp Batting Average
(minimum 50 IP)

Benoit,Joaquin, TB	.147
Soriano,Rafael, TB	.163
Feliz,Neftali, Tex	.176
Bard,Daniel, Bos	.176
Perez,Chris, Cle	.182
Rivera,Mariano, NYY	.183
Valverde,Jose, Det	.184
Thornton,Matt, CWS	.191
Breslow,Craig, Oak	.194
O'Day,Darren, Tex	.196

Relief Earned Run Average
(minimum 50 IP)

Benoit,Joaquin, TB	1.34
Perez,Chris, Cle	1.71
Soriano,Rafael, TB	1.73
Soria,Joakim, KC	1.78
Rivera,Mariano, NYY	1.80
Bard,Daniel, Bos	1.93
O'Day,Darren, Tex	2.03
Balfour,Grant, TB	2.28
Oliver,Darren, Tex	2.48
Downs,Scott, Tor	2.64

Rel OBP 1st Batter Faced
(minimum 40 BF)

Duensing,Brian, Min	.125
Benoit,Joaquin, TB	.127
Uehara,Koji, Bal	.140
Soriano,Rafael, TB	.156
Rivera,Mariano, NYY	.197
Breslow,Craig, Oak	.200
Feliz,Neftali, Tex	.200
Gaudin,Chad, Oak-NYY	.214
Jenks,Bobby, CWS	.218
Choate,Randy, TB	.224

Rel Opp BA w/ Runners On
(minimum 50 IP)

Benoit,Joaquin, TB	.111
Perez,Chris, Cle	.133
Bard,Daniel, Bos	.159
Rivera,Mariano, NYY	.163
Soria,Joakim, KC	.171
Thornton,Matt, CWS	.184
Breslow,Craig, Oak	.196
Hughes,Dusty, KC	.197
Crain,Jesse, Min	.198
3 tied with	.200

Relief Opp BA w/ RISP
(minimum 50 IP)

Perez,Chris, Cle	.085
Benoit,Joaquin, TB	.107
Soria,Joakim, KC	.130
Thornton,Matt, CWS	.130
Camp,Shawn, Tor	.139
Nippert,Dustin, Tex	.145
Balfour,Grant, TB	.161
Sipp,Tony, Cle	.167
Atchison,Scott, Bos	.172
Rivera,Mariano, NYY	.176

Fastest Avg Fastball-Relief
(minimum 50 IP)

Bard,Daniel, Bos	97.9
Feliz,Neftali, Tex	96.3
Thornton,Matt, CWS	96.1
Santos,Sergio, CWS	95.9
Jepsen,Kevin, LAA	95.7
Rodney,Fernando, LAA	95.6
League,Brandon, Sea	95.5
Perry,Ryan, Det	95.4
Valverde,Jose, Det	95.2
Jenks,Bobby, CWS	95.0

Fastest Average Fastball
(minimum 162 IP)

Verlander,Justin, Det	95.4
Price,David, TB	94.6
Buchholz,Clay, Bos	94.1
Hernandez,Felix, Sea	94.1
Liriano,Francisco, Min	93.7
Greinke,Zack, KC	93.5
Sabathia,CC, NYY	93.5
Garza,Matt, TB	93.3
Lester,Jon, Bos	93.3
Burnett,A.J., NYY	93.2

Slowest Average Fastball
(minimum 162 IP)

Buehrle,Mark, CWS	86.0
Braden,Dallas, Oak	86.7
Vargas,Jason, Sea	86.8
Marcum,Shaun, Tor	87.1
Fister,Doug, Sea	88.4
Millwood,Kevin, Bal	89.0
Bonderman,Jeremy, Det	89.8
Matusz,Brian, Bal	89.9
Weaver,Jered, LAA	89.9
Bergesen,Brad, Bal	90.0

Pitches 100+ Velocity

Zumaya,Joel, Det	223
Rodriguez,Henry, Oak	125
Walden,Jordan, LAA	53
Bard,Daniel, Bos	49
Feliz,Neftali, Tex	45
Verlander,Justin, Det	26
Farnsworth,Kyle, KC	7
Sale,Chris, CWS	6
Rodney,Fernando, LAA	4
4 tied with	2

Pitches 95+ Velocity

Verlander,Justin, Det	1490
Price,David, TB	1458
Jackson,Edwin, CWS	876
Hernandez,Felix, Sea	812
Bard,Daniel, Bos	781
Thornton,Matt, CWS	749
Feliz,Neftali, Tex	677
Greinke,Zack, KC	638
Rodney,Fernando, LAA	629
Buchholz,Clay, Bos	623

Pitches Less Than 80 MPH

Wakefield,Tim, Bos	2098
Weaver,Jered, LAA	1241
Braden,Dallas, Oak	1030
O'Sullivan,Sean, LAA-KC	834
Gonzalez,Gio, Oak	693
Vazquez,Javier, NYY	684
Garcia,Freddy, CWS	668
Buehrle,Mark, CWS	663
Vargas,Jason, Sea	624
Chen,Bruce, KC	583

Lowest % Fastballs
(minimum 162 IP)

Marcum,Shaun, Tor	44.6
Shields,James, TB	45.6
Davies,Kyle, KC	46.3
Liriano,Francisco, Min	48.1
Wilson,C.J., Tex	48.5
Romero,Ricky, Tor	48.5
Lester,Jon, Bos	49.9
Cecil,Brett, Tor	51.3
Buehrle,Mark, CWS	52.1
Danks,John, CWS	53.1

Highest % Fastballs
(minimum 162 IP)

Masterson,Justin, Cle	78.1
Price,David, TB	74.0
Davis,Wade, TB	71.6
Garza,Matt, TB	71.5
Porcello,Rick, Det	70.5
Burnett,A.J., NYY	69.0
Carmona,Fausto, Cle	67.8
Fister,Doug, Sea	67.0
Bonderman,Jeremy, Det	65.2
Scherzer,Max, Det	65.0

Highest % Curveballs
(minimum 162 IP)

Gonzalez,Gio, Oak	30.3
Burnett,A.J., NYY	27.4
Lackey,John, Bos	20.8
Verlander,Justin, Det	19.6
Baker,Scott, Min	17.0
Hughes,Phil, NYY	16.5
Lester,Jon, Bos	16.0
Price,David, TB	15.6
Niemann,Jeff, TB	15.4
Floyd,Gavin, CWS	15.1

2010 American League Pitching Leaders

Highest % Changeups
(minimum 162 IP)

Vargas,Jason, Sea	28.8
Braden,Dallas, Oak	25.9
Marcum,Shaun, Tor	25.8
Shields,James, TB	25.0
Cecil,Brett, Tor	23.5
Pavano,Carl, Min	21.9
Romero,Ricky, Tor	21.4
Buehrle,Mark, CWS	20.2
Scherzer,Max, Det	19.8
Matusz,Brian, Bal	18.7

Highest % Sliders
(minimum 162 IP)

Santana,Ervin, LAA	36.9
Liriano,Francisco, Min	33.8
Bonderman,Jeremy, Det	30.7
Lewis,Colby, Tex	27.2
Floyd,Gavin, CWS	24.1
Bergesen,Brad, Bal	23.3
Guthrie,Jeremy, Bal	21.6
Millwood,Kevin, Bal	21.6
Sabathia,CC, NYY	21.5
Pavano,Carl, Min	20.5

Balks

Buehrle,Mark, CWS	5
Vargas,Jason, Sea	4
Bergesen,Brad, Bal	3
Fister,Doug, Sea	3
Galarraga,Armando, Det	3
Porcello,Rick, Det	3
Price,David, TB	3
8 tied with	2

Strikeout/Hit Ratio
(minimum 50 IP)

Benoit,Joaquin, TB	2.50
Thornton,Matt, CWS	1.98
Bard,Daniel, Bos	1.69
Feliz,Neftali, Tex	1.65
Putz,J.J., CWS	1.59
Soriano,Rafael, TB	1.58
Valverde,Jose, Det	1.54
Perez,Chris, Cle	1.53
Sipp,Tony, Cle	1.44
Lester,Jon, Bos	1.35

Opp OPS vs Fastballs
(minimum 251 BF)

Cahill,Trevor, Oak	.595
Buchholz,Clay, Bos	.600
Lee,Cliff, Sea-Tex	.607
Hernandez,Felix, Sea	.631
Wilson,C.J., Tex	.633
Braden,Dallas, Oak	.642
League,Brandon, Sea	.646
Price,David, TB	.647
Guthrie,Jeremy, Bal	.653
Niemann,Jeff, TB	.660

Opp OPS vs Curveballs
(minimum 100 BF)

Weaver,Jered, LAA	.509
Verlander,Justin, Det	.554
Gonzalez,Gio, Oak	.558
Lester,Jon, Bos	.590
Floyd,Gavin, CWS	.606
Shields,James, TB	.646
Price,David, TB	.664
Feldman,Scott, Tex	.695
Baker,Scott, Min	.768
Sheets,Ben, Oak	.777

Opp OPS vs Changeups
(minimum 100 BF)

Lester,Jon, Bos	.405
Verlander,Justin, Det	.455
Hernandez,Felix, Sea	.485
Marcum,Shaun, Tor	.490
Vargas,Jason, Sea	.537
Weaver,Jered, LAA	.573
Fister,Doug, Sea	.577
Wilson,C.J., Tex	.581
Buchholz,Clay, Bos	.589
Braden,Dallas, Oak	.592

Opp OPS vs Sliders
(minimum 64 BF)

Westbrook,Jake, Cle	.412
Crain,Jesse, Min	.424
Guerrier,Matt, Min	.443
Hernandez,Felix, Sea	.443
O'Day,Darren, Tex	.462
Duensing,Brian, Min	.468
Sabathia,CC, NYY	.471
Jackson,Edwin, CWS	.519
Talbot,Mitch, Cle	.527
Scherzer,Max, Det	.536

Earned Runs

Shields,James, TB	117
Burnett,A.J., NYY	109
Davies,Kyle, KC	109
Millwood,Kevin, Bal	108
Bonderman,Jeremy, Det	105
Lackey,John, Bos	105
Greinke,Zack, KC	102
Buehrle,Mark, CWS	100
Kazmir,Scott, LAA	99
2 tied with	97

Hits Per Nine Innings
(minimum 162 IP)

Hernandez,Felix, Sea	6.99
Cahill,Trevor, Oak	7.09
Wilson,C.J., Tex	7.10
Lester,Jon, Bos	7.23
Price,David, TB	7.33
Buchholz,Clay, Bos	7.36
Weaver,Jered, LAA	7.50
Verlander,Justin, Det	7.62
Gonzalez,Gio, Oak	7.67
Lewis,Colby, Tex	7.79

2010 National League Pitching Leaders

Earned Run Average
(minimum 162 IP)

Johnson,Josh, Fla	2.30
Wainwright,Adam, StL	2.42
Halladay,Roy, Phi	2.44
Garcia,Jaime, StL	2.70
Oswalt,Roy, Hou-Phi	2.76
Hudson,Tim, Atl	2.83
Dickey,R.A., NYM	2.84
Jimenez,Ubaldo, Col	2.88
Kershaw,Clayton, LAD	2.91
Latos,Mat, SD	2.92

Winning Percentage
(minimum 15 Decisions)

Jimenez,Ubaldo, Col	.704
Halladay,Roy, Phi	.677
Gallardo,Yovani, Mil	.667
Hudson,Tim, Atl	.654
Johnson,Josh, Fla	.647
Zambrano,Carlos, ChC	.647
Wainwright,Adam, StL	.645
Carpenter,Chris, StL	.640
Myers,Brett, Hou	.636
Cueto,Johnny, Cin	.632

Opponent Batting Average
(minimum 162 IP)

Sanchez,Jonathan, SF	.204
Jimenez,Ubaldo, Col	.209
Oswalt,Roy, Hou-Phi	.213
Kershaw,Clayton, LAD	.214
Latos,Mat, SD	.217
Cain,Matt, SF	.221
Wainwright,Adam, StL	.224
Kennedy,Ian, Ari	.228
Hudson,Tim, Atl	.229
Johnson,Josh, Fla	.229

Baserunners Per 9 IP
(minimum 162 IP)

Oswalt,Roy, Hou-Phi	9.44
Halladay,Roy, Phi	9.59
Wainwright,Adam, StL	9.61
Latos,Mat, SD	9.84
Cain,Matt, SF	9.91
Lilly,Ted, ChC-LAD	9.94
Johnson,Josh, Fla	10.19
Arroyo,Bronson, Cin	10.56
Santana,Johan, NYM	10.67
Kuroda,Hiroki, LAD	10.68

Games

Feliciano,Pedro, NYM	92
Moylan,Peter, Atl	85
Masset,Nick, Cin	82
Gregerson,Luke, SD	80
Marshall,Sean, ChC	80
Lyon,Brandon, Hou	79
Venters,Jonny, Atl	79
Clippard,Tyler, Was	78
Lopez,Javier, Pit-SF	77
Marmol,Carlos, ChC	77

Games Started

Carpenter,Chris, StL	35
Dempster,Ryan, ChC	34
Hanson,Tommy, Atl	34
Hudson,Tim, Atl	34
Wolf,Randy, Mil	34
16 tied with	33

Complete Games

Halladay,Roy, Phi	9
Wainwright,Adam, StL	5
Cain,Matt, SF	4
Jimenez,Ubaldo, Col	4
Santana,Johan, NYM	4
10 tied with	2

Shutouts

Halladay,Roy, Phi	4
Cain,Matt, SF	2
Gallardo,Yovani, Mil	2
Jimenez,Ubaldo, Col	2
Oswalt,Roy, Hou-Phi	2
Santana,Johan, NYM	2
Wainwright,Adam, StL	2
20 tied with	1

Wins

Halladay,Roy, Phi	21
Wainwright,Adam, StL	20
Jimenez,Ubaldo, Col	19
Arroyo,Bronson, Cin	17
Hudson,Tim, Atl	17
Carpenter,Chris, StL	16
Lincecum,Tim, SF	16
Lowe,Derek, Atl	16
Dempster,Ryan, ChC	15
Pelfrey,Mike, NYM	15

Losses

Lopez,Rodrigo, Ari	16
Duke,Zach, Pit	15
Maholm,Paul, Pit	15
Wells,Randy, ChC	14
Zito,Barry, SF	14
Bush,Dave, Mil	13
Kuroda,Hiroki, LAD	13
Oswalt,Roy, Hou-Phi	13
10 tied with	12

No Decisions

Blanton,Joe, Phi	13
Hanson,Tommy, Atl	13
Kennedy,Ian, Ari	13
Bailey,Homer, Cin	12
Cueto,Johnny, Cin	12
8 tied with	11

Wild Pitches

Jimenez,Ubaldo, Col	16
Kennedy,Ian, Ari	16
Sanchez,Jonathan, SF	15
Parra,Manny, Mil	14
Hammel,Jason, Col	13
Jackson,Edwin, Ari	13
Kuroda,Hiroki, LAD	12
Dickey,R.A., NYM	11
Casilla,Santiago, SF	10
3 tied with	9

Strikeouts

Lincecum,Tim, SF	231
Halladay,Roy, Phi	219
Jimenez,Ubaldo, Col	214
Wainwright,Adam, StL	213
Kershaw,Clayton, LAD	212
Hamels,Cole, Phi	211
Dempster,Ryan, ChC	208
Sanchez,Jonathan, SF	205
Gallardo,Yovani, Mil	200
Oswalt,Roy, Hou-Phi	193

Walks Allowed

Sanchez,Jonathan, SF	96
Jimenez,Ubaldo, Col	92
Garland,Jon, SD	87
Wolf,Randy, Mil	87
Dempster,Ryan, ChC	86
Zito,Barry, SF	84
Kershaw,Clayton, LAD	81
Richard,Clayton, SD	78
Norris,Bud, Hou	77
Lincecum,Tim, SF	76

Intentional Walks Allowed

Kuroda,Hiroki, LAD	13
Lyon,Brandon, Hou	12
Kawakami,Kenshin, Atl	10
Lowe,Derek, Atl	10
Garland,Jon, SD	9
Kershaw,Clayton, LAD	9
Batista,Miguel, Was	8
Hudson,Tim, Atl	8
6 tied with	7

Hit Batters

Hanson,Tommy, Atl	14
Carpenter,Chris, StL	13
Billingsley,Chad, LAD	10
Dempster,Ryan, ChC	10
Kennedy,Ian, Ari	10
9 tied with	9

2010 National League Pitching Leaders

Runs Allowed

Lopez,Rodrigo, Ari	126
Maholm,Paul, Pit	119
Duke,Zach, Pit	115
Dempster,Ryan, ChC	110
Bush,Dave, Mil	108
Wolf,Randy, Mil	107
Blanton,Joe, Phi	104
Kendrick,Kyle, Phi	103
Carpenter,Chris, StL	99
4 tied with	97

Hits Allowed

Halladay,Roy, Phi	231
Maholm,Paul, Pit	228
Lopez,Rodrigo, Ari	227
Hernandez,Livan, Was	216
Carpenter,Chris, StL	214
Pelfrey,Mike, NYM	213
Wolf,Randy, Mil	213
Duke,Zach, Pit	212
Myers,Brett, Hou	212
Wells,Randy, ChC	209

Doubles Allowed

Maholm,Paul, Pit	59
Bush,Dave, Mil	49
Kendrick,Kyle, Phi	49
Lopez,Rodrigo, Ari	49
Pelfrey,Mike, NYM	47
Carpenter,Chris, StL	46
Wells,Randy, ChC	46
Hernandez,Livan, Was	45
Wolf,Randy, Mil	45
3 tied with	44

Home Runs Allowed

Lopez,Rodrigo, Ari	37
Lilly,Ted, ChC-LAD	32
Arroyo,Bronson, Cin	29
Wolf,Randy, Mil	29
Bush,Dave, Mil	28
Blanton,Joe, Phi	27
Hamels,Cole, Phi	26
Kendrick,Kyle, Phi	26
Kennedy,Ian, Ari	26
2 tied with	25

Run Support Per Nine IP
(minimum 162 IP)

Cueto,Johnny, Cin	6.01
Wolf,Randy, Mil	6.01
Blanton,Joe, Phi	5.94
Kendrick,Kyle, Phi	5.93
Volstad,Chris, Fla	5.86
Jimenez,Ubaldo, Col	5.56
Wainwright,Adam, StL	5.55
Gallardo,Yovani, Mil	5.50
Garcia,Jaime, StL	5.34
Kennedy,Ian, Ari	5.34

% Pitches In Strike Zone
(minimum 162 IP)

Lilly,Ted, ChC-LAD	52.8
Oswalt,Roy, Hou-Phi	51.4
Dickey,R.A., NYM	50.7
Blanton,Joe, Phi	49.8
Santana,Johan, NYM	49.6
Niese,Jonathon, NYM	49.3
Kershaw,Clayton, LAD	48.9
Lopez,Rodrigo, Ari	48.6
Hammel,Jason, Col	48.3
Sanchez,Anibal, Fla	48.2

Pitches Per Start
(minimum 30 GS)

Jimenez,Ubaldo, Col	109.1
Halladay,Roy, Phi	108.1
Cain,Matt, SF	106.1
Kershaw,Clayton, LAD	105.9
Dempster,Ryan, ChC	105.8
Wolf,Randy, Mil	105.1
Myers,Brett, Hou	104.8
Lincecum,Tim, SF	104.2
Gallardo,Yovani, Mil	103.3
Pelfrey,Mike, NYM	102.7

Pitches Per Batter
(minimum 162 IP)

Lopez,Rodrigo, Ari	3.53
Blanton,Joe, Phi	3.59
Halladay,Roy, Phi	3.59
Hernandez,Livan, Was	3.62
Hudson,Tim, Atl	3.63
Maholm,Paul, Pit	3.65
Wells,Randy, ChC	3.66
Dickey,R.A., NYM	3.66
Carpenter,Chris, StL	3.66
Kendrick,Kyle, Phi	3.67

Quality Starts

Cain,Matt, SF	25
Carpenter,Chris, StL	25
Halladay,Roy, Phi	25
Hudson,Tim, Atl	25
Jimenez,Ubaldo, Col	25
Wainwright,Adam, StL	25
Myers,Brett, Hou	24
Oswalt,Roy, Hou-Phi	24
4 tied with	23

Batters Faced

Halladay,Roy, Phi	993
Carpenter,Chris, Stl	969
Myers,Brett, Hou	936
Wolf,Randy, Mil	930
Hudson,Tim, Atl	920
Dempster,Ryan, ChC	918
Wainwright,Adam, StL	910
Lincecum,Tim, SF	897
Cain,Matt, SF	896
Hernandez,Livan, Was	896

Innings Pitched

Halladay,Roy, Phi	250.2
Carpenter,Chris, StL	235.0
Wainwright,Adam, StL	230.1
Hudson,Tim, Atl	228.2
Myers,Brett, Hou	223.2
Cain,Matt, SF	223.1
Jimenez,Ubaldo, Col	221.2
Arroyo,Bronson, Cin	215.2
Wolf,Randy, Mil	215.2
Dempster,Ryan, ChC	215.1

Most Pitches in a Game

Jackson,Edwin, Ari	149
Halladay,Roy, Phi	132
Narveson,Chris, Mil	130
Wells,Randy, ChC	129
Jimenez,Ubaldo, Col	128
Jimenez,Ubaldo, Col	128
Dickey,R.A., NYM	127
Hamels,Cole, Phi	127
3 tied with	126

Stolen Bases Allowed

Hanson,Tommy, Atl	33
Volstad,Chris, Fla	29
Lincecum,Tim, SF	27
Bush,Dave, Mil	22
Lopez,Rodrigo, Ari	22
Lilly,Ted, ChC-LAD	20
Cain,Matt, SF	19
Gorzelanny,Tom, ChC	18
Hammel,Jason, Col	18
Lannan,John, Was	18

Caught Stealing Off

Jimenez,Ubaldo, Col	13
Hudson,Tim, Atl	11
Lowe,Derek, Atl	11
Rodriguez,Wandy, Hou	11
Cain,Matt, SF	10
Carpenter,Chris, StL	9
Hernandez,Livan, Was	9
LeBlanc,Wade, SD	9
Sanchez,Jonathan, SF	9
Zito,Barry, SF	9

Stolen Base Pct Allowed
(minimum 162 IP)

Niese,Jonathon, NYM	0.0
Carpenter,Chris, StL	25.0
Hernandez,Livan, Was	30.8
Cueto,Johnny, Cin	42.9
Garland,Jon, SD	42.9
Lowe,Derek, Atl	47.6
Jimenez,Ubaldo, Col	48.0
Hudson,Tim, Atl	50.0
Kendrick,Kyle, Phi	50.0
Kershaw,Clayton, LAD	50.0

Pickoffs

Kershaw,Clayton, LAD	8
LeBlanc,Wade, SD	8
Richard,Clayton, SD	6
Sanchez,Jonathan, SF	5
9 tied with	3

2010 National League Pitching Leaders

Strikeouts Per 9 IP
(minimum 162 IP)

Lincecum,Tim, SF	9.79
Gallardo,Yovani, Mil	9.73
Sanchez,Jonathan, SF	9.54
Kershaw,Clayton, LAD	9.34
Latos,Mat, SD	9.21
Johnson,Josh, Fla	9.11
Hamels,Cole, Phi	9.10
Dempster,Ryan, ChC	8.69
Jimenez,Ubaldo, Col	8.69
Wainwright,Adam, StL	8.32

Opp On-Base Percentage
(minimum 162 IP)

Oswalt,Roy, Hou-Phi	.268
Halladay,Roy, Phi	.271
Latos,Mat, SD	.272
Wainwright,Adam, StL	.274
Cain,Matt, SF	.276
Lilly,Ted, ChC-LAD	.278
Johnson,Josh, Fla	.282
Arroyo,Bronson, Cin	.289
Kuroda,Hiroki, LAD	.291
Santana,Johan, NYM	.292

Opp Slugging Average
(minimum 162 IP)

Jimenez,Ubaldo, Col	.311
Kershaw,Clayton, LAD	.320
Garcia,Jaime, StL	.323
Johnson,Josh, Fla	.325
Wainwright,Adam, StL	.330
Latos,Mat, SD	.330
Hudson,Tim, Atl	.343
Sanchez,Jonathan, SF	.343
Oswalt,Roy, Hou-Phi	.346
Hanson,Tommy, Atl	.347

Opponent OPS
(minimum 162 IP)

Latos,Mat, SD	.601
Wainwright,Adam, StL	.604
Johnson,Josh, Fla	.607
Jimenez,Ubaldo, Col	.610
Oswalt,Roy, Hou-Phi	.614
Kershaw,Clayton, LAD	.615
Garcia,Jaime, StL	.638
Hudson,Tim, Atl	.641
Kuroda,Hiroki, LAD	.642
Halladay,Roy, Phi	.645

Home Runs Per Nine IP
(minimum 162 IP)

Johnson,Josh, Fla	0.34
Billingsley,Chad, LAD	0.38
Jimenez,Ubaldo, Col	0.41
Sanchez,Anibal, Fla	0.46
Garcia,Jaime, StL	0.50
Pelfrey,Mike, NYM	0.53
Kershaw,Clayton, LAD	0.57
Gallardo,Yovani, Mil	0.58
Wainwright,Adam, StL	0.59
Hanson,Tommy, Atl	0.62

Batting Average vs. LHB
(minimum 125 BF)

Marmol,Carlos, ChC	.130
Padilla,Vicente, LAD	.167
Meek,Evan, Pit	.168
Hudson,Daniel, Ari	.174
Gregerson,Luke, SD	.180
Sanchez,Jonathan, SF	.181
Adams,Mike, SD	.185
Jimenez,Ubaldo, Col	.191
Lyon,Brandon, Hou	.195
Hamels,Cole, Phi	.196

Batting Average vs. RHB
(minimum 225 BF)

Arroyo,Bronson, Cin	.185
Oswalt,Roy, Hou-Phi	.196
Chacin,Jhoulys, Col	.201
Venters,Jonny, Atl	.207
Sanchez,Jonathan, SF	.210
Lilly,Ted, ChC-LAD	.213
Latos,Mat, SD	.214
Cain,Matt, SF	.217
Kershaw,Clayton, LAD	.218
Zambrano,Carlos, ChC	.221

Opp BA w/ RISP
(minimum 125 BF)

Halladay,Roy, Phi	.173
Johnson,Josh, Fla	.181
Oswalt,Roy, Hou-Phi	.186
Sanchez,Jonathan, SF	.194
Santana,Johan, NYM	.199
Kershaw,Clayton, LAD	.199
Gallardo,Yovani, Mil	.200
Wainwright,Adam, StL	.200
Hamels,Cole, Phi	.202
Hudson,Tim, Atl	.207

OBP vs. Leadoff Hitter
(minimum 150 BF)

Latos,Mat, SD	.237
Oswalt,Roy, Hou-Phi	.248
Lilly,Ted, ChC-LAD	.260
Sanchez,Anibal, Fla	.261
Hanson,Tommy, Atl	.263
Dempster,Ryan, ChC	.266
Johnson,Josh, Fla	.274
Nolasco,Ricky, Fla	.280
Kuroda,Hiroki, LAD	.282
Cueto,Johnny, Cin	.284

Strikeouts / Walks Ratio
(minimum 162 IP)

Halladay,Roy, Phi	7.30
Johnson,Josh, Fla	3.88
Wainwright,Adam, StL	3.80
Latos,Mat, SD	3.78
Lilly,Ted, ChC-LAD	3.77
Oswalt,Roy, Hou-Phi	3.51
Hamels,Cole, Phi	3.46
Kuroda,Hiroki, LAD	3.31
Blanton,Joe, Phi	3.12
Hanson,Tommy, Atl	3.09

Highest GB/FB Ratio
(minimum 162 IP)

Hudson,Tim, Atl	2.87
Lowe,Derek, Atl	2.61
Garcia,Jaime, StL	2.19
Dickey,R.A., NYM	1.97
Halladay,Roy, Phi	1.72
Garland,Jon, SD	1.71
Maholm,Paul, Pit	1.69
Wainwright,Adam, StL	1.68
Kuroda,Hiroki, LAD	1.59
Carpenter,Chris, StL	1.58

Lowest GB/FB Ratio
(minimum 162 IP)

Lilly,Ted, ChC-LAD	0.56
Santana,Johan, NYM	0.76
Cain,Matt, SF	0.78
Zito,Barry, SF	0.80
Kennedy,Ian, Ari	0.84
Lopez,Rodrigo, Ari	0.92
Bush,Dave, Mil	0.94
Wolf,Randy, Mil	0.94
Narveson,Chris, Mil	0.95
Sanchez,Jonathan, SF	0.95

Sacrifice Flies Allowed

Billingsley,Chad, LAD	11
Bush,Dave, Mil	10
Hernandez,Livan, Was	10
Karstens,Jeff, Pit	9
Johnson,Josh, Fla	8
Ohlendorf,Ross, Pit	8
10 tied with	7

Sacrifice Hits Allowed

Hernandez,Livan, Was	17
Pelfrey,Mike, NYM	17
Lilly,Ted, ChC-LAD	14
Lopez,Rodrigo, Ari	14
Sanchez,Anibal, Fla	13
Wainwright,Adam, StL	13
Zito,Barry, SF	13
Gallardo,Yovani, Mil	11
Hammel,Jason, Col	11
Kennedy,Ian, Ari	11

GIDP Induced

Hudson,Tim, Atl	32
Pelfrey,Mike, NYM	26
Richard,Clayton, SD	26
Carpenter,Chris, StL	25
Garland,Jon, SD	25
Halladay,Roy, Phi	25
Jimenez,Ubaldo, Col	25
Wainwright,Adam, StL	25
Lowe,Derek, Atl	22
3 tied with	21

GIDP Per Nine IP
(minimum 162 IP)

Hudson,Tim, Atl	1.26
Richard,Clayton, SD	1.16
Pelfrey,Mike, NYM	1.15
Garland,Jon, SD	1.13
Lowe,Derek, Atl	1.02
Maholm,Paul, Pit	1.02
Jimenez,Ubaldo, Col	1.02
Garcia,Jaime, StL	0.99
Wainwright,Adam, StL	0.98
Hammel,Jason, Col	0.96

2010 National League Pitching Leaders

Saves			Blown Saves			Save Pct			Save Opportunities	
						(minimum 20 Save Ops)				
Wilson,Brian, SF	48		Clippard,Tyler, Was	10		Bell,Heath, SD	94.0		Wilson,Brian, SF	53
Bell,Heath, SD	47		Cordero,Francisco, Cin	8		Franklin,Ryan, StL	93.1		Bell,Heath, SD	50
Cordero,Francisco, Cin	40		Heilman,Aaron, Ari	8		Lyon,Brandon, Hou	90.9		Cordero,Francisco, Cin	48
Marmol,Carlos, ChC	38		Nunez,Leo, Fla	8		Wilson,Brian, SF	90.6		Wagner,Billy, Atl	44
Wagner,Billy, Atl	37		Broxton,Jonathan, LAD	7		Axford,John, Mil	88.9		Marmol,Carlos, ChC	43
Nunez,Leo, Fla	30		Wagner,Billy, Atl	7		Marmol,Carlos, ChC	88.4		Nunez,Leo, Fla	38
Franklin,Ryan, StL	27		Dotel,Octavio, Pit-LAD-Col	6		Capps,Matt, Was	86.7		Lidge,Brad, Phi	32
Lidge,Brad, Phi	27		Lindstrom,Matt, Hou	6		Lidge,Brad, Phi	84.4		Capps,Matt, Was	30
Capps,Matt, Was	26		Meek,Evan, Pit	6		Wagner,Billy, Atl	84.1		Rodriguez,Francisco, NYM	30
Rodriguez,Francisco, NYM	25		8 tied with	5		2 tied with	83.3		3 tied with	29

Easy Saves			Regular Saves			Tough Saves			Holds Adjusted Saves %	
									(minimum 20 Save Ops)	
Bell,Heath, SD	28		Marmol,Carlos, ChC	18		Wilson,Brian, SF	7		Lyon,Brandon, Hou	95.1
Cordero,Francisco, Cin	28		Wilson,Brian, SF	15		Bell,Heath, SD	5		Bell,Heath, SD	94.0
Wagner,Billy, Atl	27		Bell,Heath, SD	14		Marmol,Carlos, ChC	5		Franklin,Ryan, StL	93.1
Wilson,Brian, SF	26		Axford,John, Mil	12		Rodriguez,Francisco, NYM	4		Wilson,Brian, SF	90.6
Nunez,Leo, Fla	22		Cordero,Francisco, Cin	12		Axford,John, Mil	2		Axford,John, Mil	90.0
Capps,Matt, Was	16		Broxton,Jonathan, LAD	11		Casilla,Santiago, SF	2		Marmol,Carlos, ChC	88.4
Lidge,Brad, Phi	16		Franklin,Ryan, StL	11		18 tied with	1		Capps,Matt, Was	86.7
Lindstrom,Matt, Hou	16		5 tied with	10					Lidge,Brad, Phi	84.4
3 tied with	15								Wagner,Billy, Atl	84.1
									Cordero,Francisco, Cin	83.7

Relief Wins			Relief Losses			Relief Games			Holds	
Clippard,Tyler, Was	11		Clippard,Tyler, Was	8		Feliciano,Pedro, NYM	92		Gregerson,Luke, SD	40
Axford,John, Mil	8		Heilman,Aaron, Ari	8		Moylan,Peter, Atl	85		Adams,Mike, SD	38
Belisle,Matt, Col	7		Burnett,Sean, Was	7		Masset,Nick, Cin	82		Rhodes,Arthur, Cin	26
Casilla,Santiago, SF	7		Gregerson,Luke, SD	7		Gregerson,Luke, SD	80		Venters,Jonny, Atl	24
Marshall,Sean, ChC	7		Hoffman,Trevor, Mil	7		Marshall,Sean, ChC	80		Betancourt,Rafael, Col	23
Wagner,Billy, Atl	7		6 tied with	6		Lyon,Brandon, Hou	79		Clippard,Tyler, Was	23
8 tied with	6					Venters,Jonny, Atl	79		Feliciano,Pedro, NYM	23
						Clippard,Tyler, Was	78		Hensley,Clay, Fla	22
						Lopez,Javier, Pit-SF	77		Loe,Kameron, Mil	22
						Marmol,Carlos, ChC	77		Marshall,Sean, ChC	22

Relief Innings			Inherited Runners Scrd %			Relief Opp On Base Pct			Relief Opp Slugging Avg	
			(minimum 30 IR)			(minimum 50 IP)			(minimum 50 IP)	
Belisle,Matt, Col	92.0		Lopez,Wilton, Hou	3.0		Kuo,Hong-Chih, LAD	.211		Kuo,Hong-Chih, LAD	.192
Clippard,Tyler, Was	91.0		Casilla,Santiago, SF	12.8		Gregerson,Luke, SD	.223		Marmol,Carlos, ChC	.199
Venters,Jonny, Atl	83.0		Wilson,Brian, SF	13.3		Wagner,Billy, Atl	.238		Venters,Jonny, Atl	.241
Meek,Evan, Pit	80.0		Rhodes,Arthur, Cin	13.9		Mujica,Edward, SD	.243		Wagner,Billy, Atl	.255
Carrasco,D.J., Pit-Ari	78.1		Lopez,Javier, Pit-SF	15.8		Betancourt,Rafael, Col	.245		Adams,Mike, SD	.261
Gregerson,Luke, SD	78.1		Miller,Trever, StL	17.1		Romo,Sergio, SF	.261		Meek,Evan, Pit	.273
Lyon,Brandon, Hou	78.0		Feliciano,Pedro, NYM	18.0		Saito,Takashi, Atl	.265		Hensley,Clay, Fla	.281
Batista,Miguel, Was	77.2		Gregerson,Luke, SD	18.4		Adams,Mike, SD	.265		Bell,Heath, SD	.285
Marmol,Carlos, ChC	77.2		Marshall,Sean, ChC	19.0		Rhodes,Arthur, Cin	.265		Casilla,Santiago, SF	.286
Masset,Nick, Cin	76.2		Thatcher,Joe, SD	19.4		Franklin,Ryan, StL	.270		Marshall,Sean, ChC	.290

2010 National League Pitching Leaders

Relief Opp BA Vs LHB
(minimum 50 AB)

Wagner,Billy, Atl	.071
Kuo,Hong-Chih, LAD	.095
Marmol,Carlos, ChC	.130
Slaten,Doug, Was	.151
Braddock,Zach, Mil	.151
Veras,Jose, Fla	.155
Stauffer,Tim, SD	.155
Lopez,Javier, Pit-SF	.162
Meek,Evan, Pit	.168
Takahashi,Hisanori, NYM	.172

Relief Opp BA Vs RHB
(minimum 50 AB)

Ramirez,Ramon, SF	.119
Peralta,Joel, Was	.145
Frieri,Ernesto, SD	.156
Kuo,Hong-Chih, LAD	.159
Donnelly,Brendan, Pit	.160
Marmol,Carlos, ChC	.161
Gregerson,Luke, SD	.162
Owings,Micah, Cin	.163
Dotel,Octavio, Pit-LAD-Col	.166
2 tied with	.172

Relief Opp Batting Average
(minimum 50 IP)

Kuo,Hong-Chih, LAD	.139
Marmol,Carlos, ChC	.147
Wagner,Billy, Atl	.159
Gregerson,Luke, SD	.170
Meek,Evan, Pit	.185
Sanches,Brian, Fla	.194
Rhodes,Arthur, Cin	.196
Adams,Mike, SD	.196
Hensley,Clay, Fla	.200
Saito,Takashi, Atl	.203

Relief Earned Run Average
(minimum 50 IP)

Kuo,Hong-Chih, LAD	1.20
Wagner,Billy, Atl	1.43
Adams,Mike, SD	1.76
Wilson,Brian, SF	1.81
Bell,Heath, SD	1.93
Casilla,Santiago, SF	1.95
Venters,Jonny, Atl	1.95
Takahashi,Hisanori, NYM	2.04
Meek,Evan, Pit	2.14
Burnett,Sean, Was	2.14

Rel OBP 1st Batter Faced
(minimum 40 BF)

Romo,Sergio, SF	.176
Saito,Takashi, Atl	.179
Street,Huston, Col	.182
Gregerson,Luke, SD	.188
Marshall,Sean, ChC	.190
Acosta,Manny, NYM	.200
Kuo,Hong-Chih, LAD	.200
Lopez,Wilton, Hou	.212
Wilson,Brian, SF	.214
Ondrusek,Logan, Cin	.217

Rel Opp BA w/ Runners On
(minimum 50 IP)

Wagner,Billy, Atl	.098
Kuo,Hong-Chih, LAD	.128
Rhodes,Arthur, Cin	.163
Marmol,Carlos, ChC	.163
Venters,Jonny, Atl	.169
Hensley,Clay, Fla	.176
Casilla,Santiago, SF	.176
Sanches,Brian, Fla	.177
Burnett,Sean, Was	.184
Madson,Ryan, Phi	.185

Relief Opp BA w/ RISP
(minimum 50 IP)

Wilson,Brian, SF	.105
Wagner,Billy, Atl	.106
Kuo,Hong-Chih, LAD	.122
Motte,Jason, StL	.131
Hensley,Clay, Fla	.135
Casilla,Santiago, SF	.136
Madson,Ryan, Phi	.143
Rhodes,Arthur, Cin	.145
Burnett,Sean, Was	.167
Lyon,Brandon, Hou	.167

Fastest Avg Fastball-Relief
(minimum 50 IP)

Casilla,Santiago, SF	96.6
Cashner,Andrew, ChC	96.3
Boggs,Mitchell, StL	96.1
Hanrahan,Joel, Pit	96.0
Wilson,Brian, SF	95.9
Motte,Jason, StL	95.8
Wagner,Billy, Atl	95.7
Lindstrom,Matt, Hou	95.7
Broxton,Jonathan, LAD	95.3
Meek,Evan, Pit	95.1

Fastest Average Fastball
(minimum 162 IP)

Jimenez,Ubaldo, Col	96.1
Johnson,Josh, Fla	94.9
Latos,Mat, SD	93.7
Cueto,Johnny, Cin	93.2
Hammel,Jason, Col	93.1
Hanson,Tommy, Atl	92.7
Oswalt,Roy, Hou-Phi	92.6
Gallardo,Yovani, Mil	92.6
Halladay,Roy, Phi	92.6
Kershaw,Clayton, LAD	92.5

Slowest Average Fastball
(minimum 162 IP)

Dickey,R.A., NYM	83.9
Hernandez,Livan, Was	84.4
Zito,Barry, SF	85.7
Bush,Dave, Mil	86.5
Lilly,Ted, ChC-LAD	86.7
Arroyo,Bronson, Cin	88.0
Lopez,Rodrigo, Ari	88.2
Narveson,Chris, Mil	88.3
Maholm,Paul, Pit	88.3
Wolf,Randy, Mil	88.3

Pitches 100+ Velocity

Chapman,Aroldis, Cin	84
Parnell,Bobby, NYM	27
Jimenez,Ubaldo, Col	20
Strasburg,Stephen, Was	17
Cashner,Andrew, ChC	15
Farnsworth,Kyle, Atl	7
Boggs,Mitchell, StL	5
Broxton,Jonathan, LAD	4
Casilla,Santiago, SF	4
2 tied with	2

Pitches 95+ Velocity

Jimenez,Ubaldo, Col	1783
Johnson,Josh, Fla	1149
Jackson,Edwin, Ari	876
Boggs,Mitchell, StL	689
Paulino,Felipe, Hou	673
Wilson,Brian, SF	667
Hanrahan,Joel, Pit	628
Wagner,Billy, Atl	623
Strasburg,Stephen, Was	604
Latos,Mat, SD	598

Pitches Less Than 80 MPH

Dickey,R.A., NYM	1868
Lilly,Ted, ChC-LAD	1484
Zito,Barry, SF	1451
Rodriguez,Wandy, Hou	1136
Arroyo,Bronson, Cin	1069
Wolf,Randy, Mil	1044
Wainwright,Adam, StL	951
Carpenter,Chris, StL	945
Moyer,Jamie, Phi	910
Oswalt,Roy, Hou-Phi	870

Lowest % Fastballs
(minimum 162 IP)

Dickey,R.A., NYM	16.0
Halladay,Roy, Phi	37.1
Arroyo,Bronson, Cin	38.9
Myers,Brett, Hou	43.1
Narveson,Chris, Mil	45.2
Wainwright,Adam, StL	45.8
Lopez,Rodrigo, Ari	47.9
Carpenter,Chris, StL	48.7
Zito,Barry, SF	49.7
Sanchez,Anibal, Fla	50.0

Highest % Fastballs
(minimum 162 IP)

Kershaw,Clayton, LAD	71.6
Pelfrey,Mike, NYM	68.9
Sanchez,Jonathan, SF	65.0
Lowe,Derek, Atl	63.9
Hudson,Tim, Atl	63.8
Cain,Matt, SF	63.2
Johnson,Josh, Fla	61.9
Hernandez,Livan, Was	61.4
Jimenez,Ubaldo, Col	61.4
Richard,Clayton, SD	61.1

Highest % Curveballs
(minimum 162 IP)

Rodriguez,Wandy, Hou	36.4
Wainwright,Adam, StL	28.7
Carpenter,Chris, StL	27.0
Bush,Dave, Mil	22.6
Gallardo,Yovani, Mil	20.4
Myers,Brett, Hou	20.2
Zito,Barry, SF	19.4
Narveson,Chris, Mil	19.3
Billingsley,Chad, LAD	19.1
Maholm,Paul, Pit	17.5

2010 National League Pitching Leaders

Highest % Changeups
(minimum 162 IP)

Santana,Johan, NYM	26.5
Arroyo,Bronson, Cin	25.0
Lincecum,Tim, SF	23.0
Hamels,Cole, Phi	22.8
Narveson,Chris, Mil	21.3
Kennedy,Ian, Ari	18.4
Wells,Randy, ChC	17.5
Blanton,Joe, Phi	16.5
Sanchez,Jonathan, SF	16.0
Zito,Barry, SF	15.5

Highest % Sliders
(minimum 162 IP)

Dempster,Ryan, ChC	35.1
Kuroda,Hiroki, LAD	31.8
Hanson,Tommy, Atl	28.0
Myers,Brett, Hou	27.9
Johnson,Josh, Fla	27.7
Wells,Randy, ChC	27.2
Cueto,Johnny, Cin	26.7
Sanchez,Anibal, Fla	25.2
Latos,Mat, SD	22.9
Lilly,Ted, ChC-LAD	20.4

Balks

Duke,Zach, Pit	3
Hawksworth,Blake, StL	3
Maya,Yunesky, Was	3
15 tied with	2

Strikeout/Hit Ratio
(minimum 50 IP)

Marmol,Carlos, ChC	3.45
Wagner,Billy, Atl	2.74
Kuo,Hong-Chih, LAD	2.52
Gregerson,Luke, SD	1.89
Axford,John, Mil	1.81
Hanrahan,Joel, Pit	1.72
Betancourt,Rafael, Col	1.71
Saito,Takashi, Atl	1.68
Strasburg,Stephen, Was	1.64
Clippard,Tyler, Was	1.62

Opp OPS vs Fastballs
(minimum 251 BF)

Jimenez,Ubaldo, Col	.590
Venters,Jonny, Atl	.590
Hudson,Tim, Atl	.594
Wood,Travis, Cin	.595
Johnson,Josh, Fla	.598
Sanchez,Jonathan, SF	.605
Santana,Johan, NYM	.616
Kershaw,Clayton, LAD	.620
Latos,Mat, SD	.630
Lilly,Ted, ChC-LAD	.637

Opp OPS vs Curveballs
(minimum 100 BF)

Oswalt,Roy, Hou-Phi	.512
Myers,Brett, Hou	.528
Arroyo,Bronson, Cin	.535
Marshall,Sean, ChC	.550
Wainwright,Adam, StL	.551
Carpenter,Chris, StL	.558
Kennedy,Ian, Ari	.589
Narveson,Chris, Mil	.607
Halladay,Roy, Phi	.630
Cain,Matt, SF	.644

Opp OPS vs Changeups
(minimum 100 BF)

Kennedy,Ian, Ari	.488
Oswalt,Roy, Hou-Phi	.556
Cain,Matt, SF	.592
Nunez,Leo, Fla	.611
Lowe,Derek, Atl	.616
Takahashi,Hisanori, NYM	.624
Lincecum,Tim, SF	.645
de la Rosa,Jorge, Col	.665
Jimenez,Ubaldo, Col	.668
Heilman,Aaron, Ari	.676

Opp OPS vs Sliders
(minimum 64 BF)

Wagner,Billy, Atl	.425
Hanrahan,Joel, Pit	.428
Contreras,Jose, Phi	.452
Paulino,Felipe, Hou	.454
Marmol,Carlos, ChC	.463
Kershaw,Clayton, LAD	.475
Lidge,Brad, Phi	.475
Stauffer,Tim, SD	.482
Olsen,Scott, Was	.515
Latos,Mat, SD	.517

Earned Runs

Lopez,Rodrigo, Ari	111
Maholm,Paul, Pit	105
Duke,Zach, Pit	101
Wolf,Randy, Mil	100
Hammel,Jason, Col	95
Kendrick,Kyle, Phi	95
Blanton,Joe, Phi	94
Arroyo,Bronson, Cin	93
Narveson,Chris, Mil	93
3 tied with	92

Hits Per Nine Innings
(minimum 162 IP)

Sanchez,Jonathan, SF	6.61
Jimenez,Ubaldo, Col	6.66
Oswalt,Roy, Hou-Phi	6.89
Kershaw,Clayton, LAD	7.05
Wainwright,Adam, StL	7.27
Cain,Matt, SF	7.29
Latos,Mat, SD	7.31
Hudson,Tim, Atl	7.44
Kennedy,Ian, Ari	7.56
Johnson,Josh, Fla	7.60

2010 American League Fielding Leaders

2B Pivot %
(minimum 98 G)

Beckham,Gordon, CWS	0.678
Figgins,Chone, Sea	0.667
Ellis,Mark, Oak	0.662
Cano,Robinson, NYY	0.642
Kinsler,Ian, Tex	0.616
Hudson,Orlando, Min	0.612
Kendrick,Howie, LAA	0.608
Hill,Aaron, Tor	0.594

SS Pivot %
(minimum 98 G)

Pennington,Cliff, Oak	0.667
Scutaro,Marco, Bos	0.659
Ramirez,Alexei, CWS	0.617
Izturis,Cesar, Bal	0.606
Jeter,Derek, NYY	0.583
Andrus,Elvis, Tex	0.580
Aybar,Erick, LAA	0.557
Wilson,Josh, Sea	0.547
Hardy,J.J., Min	0.534
Bartlett,Jason, TB	0.531

Highest Pct CS by Catchers
(minimum 600 INN or 50 SBA)

Marson,Lou, Cle	33.8
Avila,Alex, Det	31.7
Laird,Gerald, Det	29.3
Wieters,Matt, Bal	28.4
Buck,John, Tor	24.2
Kendall,Jason, KC	24.1
Mauer,Joe, Min	22.1
Napoli,Mike, LAA	20.0
Treanor,Matt, Tex	20.0
Jaso,John, TB	18.0

Lowest Pct CS by Catchers
(minimum 600 INN or 50 SBA)

Posada,Jorge, NYY	12.2
Cervelli,Francisco, NYY	12.7
Suzuki,Kurt, Oak	13.2
Mathis,Jeff, LAA	14.0
Martinez,Victor, Bos	14.7
Pierzynski,A.J., CWS	17.6
Jaso,John, TB	18.0
Napoli,Mike, LAA	20.0
Treanor,Matt, Tex	20.0
Mauer,Joe, Min	22.1

2B Double Play %
(minimum 98 G)

Beckham,Gordon, CWS	0.599
Ellis,Mark, Oak	0.563
Hill,Aaron, Tor	0.563
Figgins,Chone, Sea	0.559
Cano,Robinson, NYY	0.533
Kendrick,Howie, LAA	0.508
Hudson,Orlando, Min	0.503
Kinsler,Ian, Tex	0.488

3B Double Play %
(minimum 98 G)

Longoria,Evan, TB	0.500
Peralta,Jhonny, Cle-Det	0.481
Young,Michael, Tex	0.480
Rodriguez,Alex, NYY	0.432
Inge,Brandon, Det	0.423
Callaspo,Alberto, KC-LAA	0.407
Beltre,Adrian, Bos	0.382
Kouzmanoff,Kevin, Oak	0.356
Lopez,Jose, Sea	0.302

SS Double Play %
(minimum 98 G)

Ramirez,Alexei, CWS	0.612
Pennington,Cliff, Oak	0.604
Izturis,Cesar, Bal	0.602
Jeter,Derek, NYY	0.590
Andrus,Elvis, Tex	0.583
Wilson,Josh, Sea	0.554
Hardy,J.J., Min	0.545
Aybar,Erick, LAA	0.520
Scutaro,Marco, Bos	0.515
Bartlett,Jason, TB	0.486

Errors

Pennington,Cliff, Oak	25
Wilson,Josh, Sea	22
Aybar,Erick, LAA	21
Wigginton,Ty, Bal	21
Ramirez,Alexei, CWS	20
Scutaro,Marco, Bos	20
Beltre,Adrian, Bos	19
Figgins,Chone, Sea	19
Young,Michael, Tex	19
3 tied with	18

Fielding Errors

Figgins,Chone, Sea	18
Wigginton,Ty, Bal	18
Wilson,Josh, Sea	14
Aybar,Erick, LAA	12
Cabrera,Miguel, Det	12
Ramirez,Alexei, CWS	12
Nix,Jayson, CWS-Cle	11
Pennington,Cliff, Oak	11
5 tied with	10

Throwing Errors

Pennington,Cliff, Oak	14
Encarnacion,Edwin, Tor	11
Kendall,Jason, KC	10
Lopez,Jose, Sea	10
Scutaro,Marco, Bos	10
Aybar,Erick, LAA	9
Beltre,Adrian, Bos	9
Betancourt,Yuniesky, KC	9
Young,Michael, Tex	9
7 tied with	8

Range Factor for 2B
(minimum 98 games)

Hudson,Orlando, Min	5.31
Beckham,Gordon, CWS	5.02
Cano,Robinson, NYY	4.99
Ellis,Mark, Oak	4.98
Hill,Aaron, Tor	4.69
Kinsler,Ian, Tex	4.65
Kendrick,Howie, LAA	4.50
Figgins,Chone, Sea	4.37

Range Factor for 3B
(minimum 98 games)

Lopez,Jose, Sea	3.08
Peralta,Jhonny, Cle-Det	2.90
Beltre,Adrian, Bos	2.84
Inge,Brandon, Det	2.83
Longoria,Evan, TB	2.73
Kouzmanoff,Kevin, Oak	2.69
Callaspo,Alberto, KC-LAA	2.56
Rodriguez,Alex, NYY	2.45
Young,Michael, Tex	2.36

Range Factor for SS
(minimum 98 games)

Pennington,Cliff, Oak	4.93
Ramirez,Alexei, CWS	4.89
Hardy,J.J., Min	4.60
Wilson,Josh, Sea	4.59
Betancourt,Yuniesky, KC	4.56
Andrus,Elvis, Tex	4.48
Izturis,Cesar, Bal	4.28
Aybar,Erick, LAA	4.14
Scutaro,Marco, Bos	3.83
Jeter,Derek, NYY	3.78

2010 National League Fielding Leaders

2B Pivot %	
(minimum 98 G)	
Utley,Chase, Phi	0.759
Weeks,Rickie, Mil	0.714
Walker,Neil, Pit	0.712
Johnson,Kelly, Ari	0.690
Schumaker,Skip, StL	0.676
Keppinger,Jeff, Hou	0.623
Eckstein,David, SD	0.613
Phillips,Brandon, Cin	0.606
Prado,Martin, Atl	0.606
DeWitt,Blake, LAD-ChC	0.592

SS Pivot %	
(minimum 98 G)	
Tulowitzki,Troy, Col	0.711
Ryan,Brendan, StL	0.701
Cabrera,Orlando, Cin	0.673
Ramirez,Hanley, Fla	0.671
Desmond,Ian, Was	0.653
Drew,Stephen, Ari	0.631
Reyes,Jose, NYM	0.594
Escobar,Alcides, Mil	0.585
Castro,Starlin, ChC	0.563
Uribe,Juan, SF	0.561

Highest Pct CS by Catchers	
(minimum 600 INN or 50 SBA)	
Molina,Yadier, StL	44.4
Olivo,Miguel, Col	40.0
Quintero,Humberto, Hou	32.7
Posey,Buster, SF	31.6
Rodriguez,Ivan, Was	31.1
Martin,Russell, LAD	30.6
Lucroy,Jonathan, Mil	28.8
Hernandez,Ramon, Cin	28.6
Paulino,Ronny, Fla	28.4
McCann,Brian, Atl	27.0

Lowest Pct CS by Catchers	
(minimum 600 INN or 50 SBA)	
Doumit,Ryan, Pit	7.1
Barajas,Rod, NYM-LAD	12.8
Snyder,Chris, Ari-Pit	18.2
Soto,Geovany, ChC	19.6
Molina,Bengie, SF	20.3
Hundley,Nick, SD	21.2
Montero,Miguel, Ari	25.4
Torrealba,Yorvit, SD	25.5
Ruiz,Carlos, Phi	26.5
McCann,Brian, Atl	27.0

2B Double Play %	
(minimum 98 G)	
Walker,Neil, Pit	0.566
Schumaker,Skip, StL	0.549
Johnson,Kelly, Ari	0.536
Utley,Chase, Phi	0.534
Eckstein,David, SD	0.508
Weeks,Rickie, Mil	0.506
Keppinger,Jeff, Hou	0.489
Prado,Martin, Atl	0.473
Phillips,Brandon, Cin	0.471
DeWitt,Blake, LAD-ChC	0.465

3B Double Play %	
(minimum 98 G)	
Polanco,Placido, Phi	0.527
Feliz,Pedro, Hou-StL	0.444
Sandoval,Pablo, SF	0.404
McGehee,Casey, Mil	0.377
Rolen,Scott, Cin	0.373
Headley,Chase, SD	0.350
Wright,David, NYM	0.349
Zimmerman,Ryan, Was	0.333
Stewart,Ian, Col	0.327
Reynolds,Mark, Ari	0.322

SS Double Play %	
(minimum 98 G)	
Tulowitzki,Troy, Col	0.674
Ryan,Brendan, StL	0.648
Reyes,Jose, NYM	0.613
Drew,Stephen, Ari	0.609
Ramirez,Hanley, Fla	0.605
Desmond,Ian, Was	0.589
Escobar,Alcides, Mil	0.587
Cabrera,Orlando, Cin	0.571
Cedeno,Ronny, Pit	0.561
Castro,Starlin, ChC	0.543

Errors	
Desmond,Ian, Was	34
Castro,Starlin, ChC	27
Escobar,Alcides, Mil	20
Wright,David, NYM	20
Furcal,Rafael, LAD	19
Cedeno,Ronny, Pit	18
Johnson,Chris, Hou	18
Reynolds,Mark, Ari	18
Uggla,Dan, Fla	18
4 tied with	17

Fielding Errors	
Desmond,Ian, Was	21
Castro,Starlin, ChC	16
Schumaker,Skip, StL	15
McGehee,Casey, Mil	13
Blake,Casey, LAD	12
Alvarez,Pedro, Pit	11
DeWitt,Blake, LAD-ChC	11
7 tied with	10

Throwing Errors	
Desmond,Ian, Was	13
Escobar,Alcides, Mil	13
Castro,Starlin, ChC	11
McCann,Brian, Atl	11
Wright,David, NYM	11
Zimmerman,Ryan, Was	11
Cantu,Jorge, Fla	10
Furcal,Rafael, LAD	10
5 tied with	9

Range Factor for 2B	
(minimum 98 games)	
Utley,Chase, Phi	5.14
Schumaker,Skip, StL	5.05
Prado,Martin, Atl	4.95
DeWitt,Blake, LAD-ChC	4.83
Phillips,Brandon, Cin	4.81
Keppinger,Jeff, Hou	4.77
Johnson,Kelly, Ari	4.74
Uggla,Dan, Fla	4.70
Weeks,Rickie, Mil	4.67
Walker,Neil, Pit	4.59

Range Factor for 3B	
(minimum 98 games)	
Polanco,Placido, Phi	2.90
Rolen,Scott, Cin	2.87
Wright,David, NYM	2.83
Stewart,Ian, Col	2.64
Reynolds,Mark, Ari	2.60
Blake,Casey, LAD	2.52
Zimmerman,Ryan, Was	2.47
Feliz,Pedro, Hou-StL	2.45
Headley,Chase, SD	2.40
McGehee,Casey, Mil	2.37

Range Factor for SS	
(minimum 98 games)	
Tulowitzki,Troy, Col	5.07
Ryan,Brendan, StL	5.01
Desmond,Ian, Was	4.49
Cedeno,Ronny, Pit	4.43
Castro,Starlin, ChC	4.33
Drew,Stephen, Ari	4.27
Escobar,Alcides, Mil	4.16
Reyes,Jose, NYM	4.16
Cabrera,Orlando, Cin	4.06
Ramirez,Hanley, Fla	4.01

2010 Active Career Batting Leaders

Batting Average (minimum 1000 PA)	
Pujols,Albert	.331
Suzuki,Ichiro	.331
Mauer,Joe	.327
Helton,Todd	.324
Guerrero,Vladimir	.320
Holliday,Matt	.317
Votto,Joey	.314
Jeter,Derek	.314
Cabrera,Miguel	.313
Ramirez,Hanley	.313

On Base Percentage (minimum 1000 PA)	
Pujols,Albert	.426
Helton,Todd	.424
Ramirez,Manny	.411
Berkman,Lance	.409
Mauer,Joe	.407
Jones,Chipper	.405
Giambi,Jason	.405
Thome,Jim	.404
Johnson,Nick	.401
Votto,Joey	.401

Slugging Average (minimum 1000 PA)	
Pujols,Albert	.624
Ramirez,Manny	.586
Howard,Ryan	.572
Rodriguez,Alex	.571
Guerrero,Vladimir	.563
Thome,Jim	.559
Votto,Joey	.557
Helton,Todd	.555
Braun,Ryan	.554
Cabrera,Miguel	.552

Home Runs	
Griffey Jr.,Ken	630
Rodriguez,Alex	613
Thome,Jim	589
Ramirez,Manny	555
Guerrero,Vladimir	436
Jones,Chipper	436
Giambi,Jason	415
Pujols,Albert	408
Jones,Andruw	407
Edmonds,Jim	393

Games	
Vizquel,Omar	2850
Griffey Jr.,Ken	2671
Rodriguez,Ivan	2499
Thome,Jim	2392
Rodriguez,Alex	2303
Ramirez,Manny	2297
Jeter,Derek	2295
Damon,Johnny	2276
Jones,Chipper	2261
Anderson,Garret	2228

At Bats	
Vizquel,Omar	10266
Griffey Jr.,Ken	9801
Rodriguez,Ivan	9468
Jeter,Derek	9322
Damon,Johnny	8947
Rodriguez,Alex	8826
Anderson,Garret	8640
Ramirez,Manny	8227
Jones,Chipper	8142
Thome,Jim	7982

Hits	
Jeter,Derek	2926
Rodriguez,Ivan	2817
Vizquel,Omar	2799
Griffey Jr.,Ken	2781
Rodriguez,Alex	2672
Ramirez,Manny	2573
Damon,Johnny	2571
Anderson,Garret	2529
Jones,Chipper	2490
Guerrero,Vladimir	2427

Total Bases	
Griffey Jr.,Ken	5271
Rodriguez,Alex	5043
Ramirez,Manny	4825
Thome,Jim	4463
Rodriguez,Ivan	4411
Jones,Chipper	4365
Guerrero,Vladimir	4272
Jeter,Derek	4218
Anderson,Garret	3984
Damon,Johnny	3903

Doubles	
Rodriguez,Ivan	565
Ramirez,Manny	547
Helton,Todd	527
Abreu,Bobby	524
Griffey Jr.,Ken	524
Anderson,Garret	522
Jones,Chipper	493
Damon,Johnny	487
Rolen,Scott	480
Rodriguez,Alex	474

Triples	
Crawford,Carl	105
Damon,Johnny	100
Rollins,Jimmy	98
Guzman,Cristian	89
Reyes,Jose	83
Pierre,Juan	82
Vizquel,Omar	75
Suzuki,Ichiro	71
Beltran,Carlos	67
Furcal,Rafael	65

Runs Scored	
Rodriguez,Alex	1757
Jeter,Derek	1685
Griffey Jr.,Ken	1662
Damon,Johnny	1564
Ramirez,Manny	1544
Thome,Jim	1534
Jones,Chipper	1505
Vizquel,Omar	1414
Abreu,Bobby	1358
Rodriguez,Ivan	1340

RBI	
Griffey Jr.,Ken	1836
Rodriguez,Alex	1831
Ramirez,Manny	1830
Thome,Jim	1624
Jones,Chipper	1491
Guerrero,Vladimir	1433
Anderson,Garret	1365
Giambi,Jason	1365
Rodriguez,Ivan	1313
Abreu,Bobby	1265

Walks	
Thome,Jim	1679
Jones,Chipper	1404
Abreu,Bobby	1341
Ramirez,Manny	1329
Griffey Jr.,Ken	1312
Giambi,Jason	1297
Helton,Todd	1197
Rodriguez,Alex	1119
Berkman,Lance	1057
Vizquel,Omar	1012

Intentional Walks	
Guerrero,Vladimir	247
Griffey Jr.,Ken	246
Pujols,Albert	236
Ramirez,Manny	216
Helton,Todd	178
Thome,Jim	166
Jones,Chipper	161
Suzuki,Ichiro	155
Berkman,Lance	137
Cabrera,Miguel	122

Hit By Pitch	
Kendall,Jason	254
Giambi,Jason	170
Jeter,Derek	152
Rodriguez,Alex	152
Guillen,Jose	145
Eckstein,David	143
Utley,Chase	125
Rolen,Scott	120
Tejada,Miguel	118
Rowand,Aaron	117

Strikeouts	
Thome,Jim	2395
Cameron,Mike	1842
Rodriguez,Alex	1836
Ramirez,Manny	1809
Griffey Jr.,Ken	1779
Edmonds,Jim	1729
Abreu,Bobby	1650
Dunn,Adam	1632
Jones,Andruw	1615
Jeter,Derek	1572

2010 Active Career Batting Leaders

Sacrifice Hits		Sacrifice Flies		Stolen Bases		Seasons Played	
Vizquel,Omar	251	Griffey Jr.,Ken	102	Pierre,Juan	527	Moyer,Jamie	24
Pierre,Juan	125	Rodriguez,Alex	93	Crawford,Carl	409	Griffey Jr.,Ken	22
Castillo,Luis	123	Ramirez,Manny	90	Vizquel,Omar	400	Vizquel,Omar	22
Hernandez,Livan	108	Vizquel,Omar	90	Damon,Johnny	385	Rodriguez,Ivan	20
Eckstein,David	106	Jones,Chipper	88	Suzuki,Ichiro	383	Thome,Jim	20
Oswalt,Roy	98	Anderson,Garret	87	Abreu,Bobby	372	Rhodes,Arthur	19
Vazquez,Javier	96	Giambi,Jason	87	Castillo,Luis	370	6 tied with	18
Wilson,Jack	95	Rolen,Scott	87	Rollins,Jimmy	343		
Renteria,Edgar	93	Lee,Carlos	86	Reyes,Jose	331		
2 tied with	83	2 tied with	84	Jeter,Derek	323		

At Bats Per Home Run (minimum 1000 AB)		Grounded Into DP		Highest SB Success Pct (minimum 100 SBA)		Lowest SB Success Pct (minimum 100 SBA)	
Howard,Ryan	12.8	Rodriguez,Ivan	331	Beltran,Carlos	88.1	Edmonds,Jim	57.3
Thome,Jim	13.6	Tejada,Miguel	261	Utley,Chase	88.1	Kotsay,Mark	61.3
Pujols,Albert	14.1	Guerrero,Vladimir	254	Kinsler,Ian	85.5	Guillen,Carlos	61.3
Dunn,Adam	14.1	Ramirez,Manny	243	Gardner,Brett	85.1	Anderson,Garret	63.0
Rodriguez,Alex	14.4	Jeter,Derek	235	Ellsbury,Jacoby	85.0	Mora,Melvin	63.3
Ramirez,Manny	14.8	Renteria,Edgar	234	Matsui,Kaz	85.0	Guzman,Cristian	64.8
Branyan,Russell	14.9	Konerko,Paul	233	Byrnes,Eric	84.9	Ordonez,Magglio	65.2
Fielder,Prince	15.4	Ordonez,Magglio	232	Rollins,Jimmy	83.1	Ausmus,Brad	65.8
Griffey Jr.,Ken	15.6	Jones,Chipper	228	Bourn,Michael	82.4	Guerrero,Vladimir	66.1
Thames,Marcus	15.6	Rodriguez,Alex	209	Weeks,Rickie	82.0	Berkman,Lance	66.1

Strikeouts / Walks Ratio (minimum 1000 AB)		At Bats Per GIDP (minimum 1000 AB)		OPS (minimum 1000 PA)		Secondary Average (minimum 1000 PA)	
Pujols,Albert	.707	Iwamura,Akinori	171.7	Pujols,Albert	1.050	Thome,Jim	.494
Mauer,Joe	.806	Matsui,Kaz	164.4	Ramirez,Manny	.998	Dunn,Adam	.482
Helton,Todd	.813	Bourn,Michael	157.7	Helton,Todd	.979	Pujols,Albert	.466
Keppinger,Jeff	.825	Suzuki,Ichiro	147.4	Thome,Jim	.963	Berkman,Lance	.451
Pedroia,Dustin	.856	Granderson,Curtis	145.0	Rodriguez,Alex	.958	Howard,Ryan	.441
Jones,Chipper	.910	Taveras,Willy	141.9	Votto,Joey	.958	Ramirez,Manny	.440
Kendall,Jason	.951	Morgan,Nyjer	113.2	Berkman,Lance	.954	Giambi,Jason	.436
Ojeda,Augie	.966	McCutchen,Andrew	111.4	Guerrero,Vladimir	.946	Rodriguez,Alex	.430
Ruiz,Carlos	.974	Drew,Stephen	107.0	Howard,Ryan	.944	Cust,Jack	.422
Pierre,Juan	.997	Andrus,Elvis	106.8	Jones,Chipper	.941	Jones,Chipper	.421

Highest Strikeout per PA (minimum 1000 PA)		Lowest Strikeout per PA (minimum 1000 PA)		Plate Appearances		At Bats Per RBI (minimum 1000 AB)	
Reynolds,Mark	.336	Pierre,Juan	.056	Vizquel,Omar	11668	Howard,Ryan	4.3
Shoppach,Kelly	.333	Keppinger,Jeff	.063	Griffey Jr.,Ken	11304	Ramirez,Manny	4.5
Branyan,Russell	.331	Polanco,Placido	.066	Jeter,Derek	10548	Pujols,Albert	4.7
Cust,Jack	.317	Eckstein,David	.073	Rodriguez,Alex	10206	Rodriguez,Alex	4.8
Stewart,Ian	.280	Pedroia,Dustin	.074	Rodriguez,Ivan	10133	Ortiz,David	4.9
Howard,Ryan	.275	Callaspo,Alberto	.076	Damon,Johnny	10046	Thome,Jim	4.9
Dunn,Adam	.269	Kendall,Jason	.079	Thome,Jim	9803	Giambi,Jason	5.0
Mathis,Jeff	.265	Molina,Yadier	.085	Ramirez,Manny	9757	Cabrera,Miguel	5.1
Gomes,Jonny	.264	Cabrera,Orlando	.088	Jones,Chipper	9654	Teixeira,Mark	5.1
Pena,Carlos	.263	2 tied with	.090	Anderson,Garret	9177	Morneau,Justin	5.1

2010 Active Career Pitching Leaders

Earned Run Average (minimum 750 IP)		Winning Percentage (minimum 100 Decisions)		Opponent Batting Average (minimum 750 IP)		Baserunners Per 9 IP (minimum 750 IP)	
Rivera,Mariano	2.23	Halladay,Roy	.663	Wagner,Billy	.187	Wagner,Billy	9.31
Wagner,Billy	2.31	Santana,Johan	.658	Rivera,Mariano	.210	Rivera,Mariano	9.37
Hoffman,Trevor	2.87	Hudson,Tim	.655	Hoffman,Trevor	.211	Hoffman,Trevor	9.60
Wainwright,Adam	2.97	Wainwright,Adam	.653	Wood,Kerry	.216	Santana,Johan	10.25
Lincecum,Tim	3.04	Oswalt,Roy	.644	Dotel,Octavio	.218	Hamels,Cole	10.78
Santana,Johan	3.10	Sabathia,CC	.641	Young,Chris	.220	Lincecum,Tim	10.85
Oswalt,Roy	3.18	Pettitte,Andy	.635	Lincecum,Tim	.224	Halladay,Roy	10.87
Hernandez,Felix	3.20	Lee,Cliff	.626	Harden,Rich	.224	Oswalt,Roy	10.97
Webb,Brandon	3.27	Weaver,Jered	.621	Santana,Johan	.226	Peavy,Jake	10.97
Halladay,Roy	3.32	Carpenter,Chris	.616	Cain,Matt	.229	Haren,Dan	10.99

Games		Games Started		Complete Games		Shutouts	
Hoffman,Trevor	1035	Moyer,Jamie	628	Halladay,Roy	58	Halladay,Roy	19
Rivera,Mariano	978	Pettitte,Andy	479	Hernandez,Livan	49	Carpenter,Chris	13
Wagner,Billy	853	Hernandez,Livan	445	Moyer,Jamie	33	Hudson,Tim	11
Rhodes,Arthur	850	Wakefield,Tim	440	Wakefield,Tim	32	Sabathia,CC	11
Hawkins,LaTroy	771	Suppan,Jeff	411	Sabathia,CC	30	Moyer,Jamie	10
Howry,Bob	769	Vazquez,Javier	411	Carpenter,Chris	29	Burnett,A.J.	9
Springer,Russ	740	Millwood,Kevin	406	Buehrle,Mark	27	Hampton,Mike	9
Farnsworth,Kyle	713	Hampton,Mike	355	Vazquez,Javier	26	Wolf,Randy	9
Moyer,Jamie	686	Zito,Barry	353	Pettitte,Andy	25	7 tied with	8
Cordero,Francisco	685	Hudson,Tim	344	Hudson,Tim	23		

Wins		Losses		Innings Pitched		Batters Faced	
Moyer,Jamie	267	Moyer,Jamie	204	Moyer,Jamie	4020.1	Moyer,Jamie	17102
Pettitte,Andy	240	Wakefield,Tim	172	Wakefield,Tim	3071.2	Wakefield,Tim	13262
Wakefield,Tim	193	Hernandez,Livan	163	Pettitte,Andy	3055.1	Pettitte,Andy	12987
Halladay,Roy	169	Vazquez,Javier	149	Hernandez,Livan	2946.1	Hernandez,Livan	12773
Hernandez,Livan	166	Suppan,Jeff	143	Vazquez,Javier	2647.1	Vazquez,Javier	11137
Hudson,Tim	165	Pettitte,Andy	138	Suppan,Jeff	2512.0	Suppan,Jeff	11002
Millwood,Kevin	159	Millwood,Kevin	137	Millwood,Kevin	2505.0	Millwood,Kevin	10705
Lowe,Derek	157	Lowe,Derek	129	Lowe,Derek	2328.2	Lowe,Derek	9831
Sabathia,CC	157	Zito,Barry	120	Halladay,Roy	2297.1	Hampton,Mike	9824
Vazquez,Javier	152	Weaver,Jeff	119	Hudson,Tim	2288.1	Hudson,Tim	9524

Strikeouts		Walks Allowed		Hit Batters		Wild Pitches	
Moyer,Jamie	2405	Wakefield,Tim	1158	Wakefield,Tim	178	Wakefield,Tim	119
Vazquez,Javier	2374	Moyer,Jamie	1137	Moyer,Jamie	144	Burnett,A.J.	99
Pettitte,Andy	2251	Hernandez,Livan	1004	Park,Chan Ho	138	Batista,Miguel	98
Wakefield,Tim	2063	Pettitte,Andy	962	Wright,Jamey	137	Suppan,Jeff	89
Millwood,Kevin	1940	Park,Chan Ho	910	Weaver,Jeff	124	Lackey,John	86
Santana,Johan	1877	Zito,Barry	910	Padilla,Vicente	106	Garcia,Freddy	80
Hernandez,Livan	1829	Hampton,Mike	901	Suppan,Jeff	94	Hampton,Mike	75
Sabathia,CC	1787	Wright,Jamey	868	Wood,Kerry	94	Park,Chan Ho	75
Park,Chan Ho	1715	Ortiz,Russ	860	Burnett,A.J.	89	Contreras,Jose	72
Halladay,Roy	1714	2 tied with	858	Oliver,Darren	89	2 tied with	71

2010 Active Career Pitching Leaders

Saves	
Hoffman,Trevor	601
Rivera,Mariano	559
Wagner,Billy	422
Cordero,Francisco	290
Rodriguez,Francisco	268
Nathan,Joe	247
Lidge,Brad	222
Valverde,Jose	193
Papelbon,Jonathan	188
Fuentes,Brian	187

Save Pct	
(minimum 50 Save Ops)	
Soria,Joakim	91.0
Nathan,Joe	89.5
Rivera,Mariano	89.3
Hoffman,Trevor	88.8
Bailey,Andrew	87.9
Papelbon,Jonathan	87.9
Wilson,Brian	87.0
Jenks,Bobby	86.9
Saito,Takashi	86.6
Valverde,Jose	86.5

Home Runs Allowed	
Moyer,Jamie	511
Wakefield,Tim	393
Vazquez,Javier	352
Suppan,Jeff	333
Hernandez,Livan	331
Millwood,Kevin	274
Pettitte,Andy	263
Lilly,Ted	258
Buehrle,Mark	253
Garland,Jon	248

Strikeouts Per 9 IP	
(minimum 750 IP)	
Wagner,Billy	11.92
Dotel,Octavio	10.95
Wood,Kerry	10.35
Lincecum,Tim	10.07
Hoffman,Trevor	9.36
Harden,Rich	9.13
Perez,Oliver	9.12
Farnsworth,Kyle	9.04
Peavy,Jake	8.93
Santana,Johan	8.85

Opp On-Base Percentage	
(minimum 750 IP)	
Wagner,Billy	.262
Rivera,Mariano	.263
Hoffman,Trevor	.267
Santana,Johan	.282
Hamels,Cole	.294
Lincecum,Tim	.295
Halladay,Roy	.296
Weaver,Jered	.296
Haren,Dan	.296
Peavy,Jake	.297

Opp Slugging Average	
(minimum 750 IP)	
Rivera,Mariano	.290
Wagner,Billy	.296
Lincecum,Tim	.330
Hoffman,Trevor	.342
Zambrano,Carlos	.350
Webb,Brandon	.352
Harden,Rich	.356
Wood,Kerry	.358
Hernandez,Felix	.360
Wainwright,Adam	.361

Hits Per Nine Innings	
(minimum 750 IP)	
Wagner,Billy	5.99
Rivera,Mariano	6.94
Hoffman,Trevor	6.99
Wood,Kerry	7.02
Dotel,Octavio	7.22
Young,Chris	7.35
Harden,Rich	7.39
Lincecum,Tim	7.39
Santana,Johan	7.59
Cain,Matt	7.60

Home Runs Per Nine IP	
(minimum 750 IP)	
Rivera,Mariano	0.49
Lincecum,Tim	0.57
Webb,Brandon	0.63
Wainwright,Adam	0.66
Billingsley,Chad	0.66
Zambrano,Carlos	0.71
Hudson,Tim	0.72
Lowe,Derek	0.73
Cook,Aaron	0.76
Hernandez,Felix	0.76

Strikeouts / Walks Ratio	
(minimum 750 IP)	
Wagner,Billy	3.99
Rivera,Mariano	3.94
Haren,Dan	3.86
Shields,James	3.70
Hoffman,Trevor	3.69
Sheets,Ben	3.62
Hamels,Cole	3.62
Oswalt,Roy	3.57
Santana,Johan	3.55
Halladay,Roy	3.53

Stolen Base Pct Allowed	
(minimum 750 IP)	
Carpenter,Chris	36.6
Buehrle,Mark	43.0
Zambrano,Carlos	50.0
Capuano,Chris	51.9
Garland,Jon	52.1
Greinke,Zack	52.2
Santana,Johan	52.6
Rodriguez,Wandy	53.0
Duke,Zach	53.2
Franklin,Ryan	54.5

GIDP Induced	
Pettitte,Andy	339
Moyer,Jamie	324
Hampton,Mike	287
Hernandez,Livan	274
Lowe,Derek	269
Suppan,Jeff	269
Buehrle,Mark	259
Hudson,Tim	249
Wright,Jamey	245
Garland,Jon	240

GIDP Per Nine IP	
(minimum 750 IP)	
Cook,Aaron	1.28
Wright,Jamey	1.25
Maholm,Paul	1.24
Westbrook,Jake	1.23
Silva,Carlos	1.17
Saunders,Joe	1.15
Hampton,Mike	1.14
Schoeneweis,Scott	1.09
Duke,Zach	1.07
Robertson,Nate	1.07

Complete Game %	
(minimum 100 GS)	
Halladay,Roy	0.18
Hernandez,Livan	0.11
Carpenter,Chris	0.10
Sabathia,CC	0.09
Lee,Cliff	0.09
Buehrle,Mark	0.08
Willis,Dontrelle	0.08
Burnett,A.J.	0.08
Webb,Brandon	0.08
Hernandez,Felix	0.08

Quality Start Pct	
(minimum 100 GS)	
Lincecum,Tim	73.8
Wainwright,Adam	69.7
Oswalt,Roy	69.0
Johnson,Josh	67.3
Hernandez,Felix	66.9
Webb,Brandon	66.7
Jimenez,Ubaldo	66.4
Santana,Johan	66.2
Halladay,Roy	65.9
Peavy,Jake	65.5

Walks Per 9 IP	
(minimum 750 IP)	
Silva,Carlos	1.73
Halladay,Roy	1.90
Haren,Dan	1.99
Shields,James	2.00
Buehrle,Mark	2.06
Sheets,Ben	2.07
Oswalt,Roy	2.09
Rivera,Mariano	2.09
Baker,Scott	2.10
Lee,Cliff	2.24

Games Finished	
Hoffman,Trevor	856
Rivera,Mariano	828
Wagner,Billy	703
Cordero,Francisco	494
Rodriguez,Francisco	409
Nathan,Joe	375
Lidge,Brad	360
Valverde,Jose	352
Fuentes,Brian	338
Howry,Bob	295

2010 American League Bill James Leaders

Top Game Scores

Pitcher	Date	Opp	IP	H	R	ER	BB	SO	GS
Morrow,Brandon, Tor	8/8	TB	9.0	1	0	0	2	17	100
Braden,Dallas, Oak	5/9	TB	9.0	0	0	0	0	6	93
Garza,Matt, TB	7/26	Det	9.0	0	0	0	1	6	92
Hernandez,Felix, Sea	6/30	NYY	9.0	2	0	0	3	11	91
Danks,John, CWS	7/8	LAA	9.0	2	0	0	0	7	90
Lewis,Colby, Tex	4/30	Sea	9.0	3	0	0	1	10	90
Wilson,C.J., Tex	8/20	Bal	8.2	3	0	0	1	12	89
7 tied with									88

Worst Game Scores

Pitcher	Date	Opp	IP	H	R	ER	BB	SO	GS
Kazmir,Scott, LAA	7/10	Oak	5.0	11	13	13	3	2	-8
Bannister,Brian, KC	6/12	Cin	3.0	10	11	9	2	2	-1
Hochevar,Luke, KC	4/29	TB	2.2	11	9	9	2	1	-1
Wakefield,Tim, Bos	5/28	KC	3.2	12	9	9	3	1	-1
Rowland-Smith,R., Sea	7/27	CWS	5.0	11	11	11	2	1	0
Lester,Jon, Bos	8/20	Tor	2.0	8	9	9	3	1	2
Pineiro,Joel, LAA	4/30	Det	3.1	10	10	9	1	1	2
Niemann,Jeff, TB	8/25	LAA	3.1	8	10	10	3	2	3
Pineiro,Joel, LAA	5/21	StL	3.0	9	9	9	3	1	3
Santana,Ervin, LAA	8/4	Bal	3.2	12	9	9	2	4	3
Shields,James, TB	6/11	Fla	3.1	9	10	10	3	4	3

Runs Created

Bautista,Jose, Tor	132
Cabrera,Miguel, Det	122
Hamilton,Josh, Tex	121
Crawford,Carl, TB	120
Cano,Robinson, NYY	118
Konerko,Paul, CWS	118
Teixeira,Mark, NYY	110
Choo,Shin-Soo, Cle	106
Beltre,Adrian, Bos	103
Swisher,Nick, NYY	100

Runs Created Per 27 Outs

Hamilton,Josh, Tex	9.3
Cabrera,Miguel, Det	8.2
Bautista,Jose, Tor	8.1
Konerko,Paul, CWS	8.0
Crawford,Carl, TB	7.4
Choo,Shin-Soo, Cle	7.0
Cano,Robinson, NYY	7.0
Mauer,Joe, Min	6.5
Matsui,Hideki, LAA	6.5
Ortiz,David, Bos	6.4

Offensive Winning %

Hamilton,Josh, Tex	.805
Cabrera,Miguel, Det	.782
Crawford,Carl, TB	.768
Bautista,Jose, Tor	.754
Konerko,Paul, CWS	.744
Choo,Shin-Soo, Cle	.727
Matsui,Hideki, LAA	.710
Longoria,Evan, TB	.694
Mauer,Joe, Min	.688
Cano,Robinson, NYY	.672

Secondary Average

(minimum 502 PA)

Bautista,Jose, Tor	.548
Cabrera,Miguel, Det	.462
Ortiz,David, Bos	.417
Konerko,Paul, CWS	.403
Pena,Carlos, TB	.401
Upton,B.J., TB	.390
Scott,Luke, Bal	.387
Teixeira,Mark, NYY	.379
Choo,Shin-Soo, Cle	.375
Abreu,Bobby, LAA	.373

Isolated Power

(minimum 502 PA)

Bautista,Jose, Tor	.357
Cabrera,Miguel, Det	.294
Hamilton,Josh, Tex	.274
Konerko,Paul, CWS	.272
Ortiz,David, Bos	.259
Scott,Luke, Bal	.251
Wells,Vernon, Tor	.242
Quentin,Carlos, CWS	.236
Rodriguez,Alex, NYY	.236
Beltre,Adrian, Bos	.233

Power / Speed Number

(minimum 502 PA)

Crawford,Carl, TB	27.1
Rios,Alex, CWS	26.0
Upton,B.J., TB	25.2
Choo,Shin-Soo, Cle	22.0
Abreu,Bobby, LAA	21.8
Longoria,Evan, TB	17.8
Gutierrez,Franklin, Sea	16.2
Granderson,Curtis, NYY	16.0
Bautista,Jose, Tor	15.4
Ramirez,Alexei, CWS	15.1

Speed Scores (2009-2010)

Crawford,Carl, TB	8.34
Granderson,Curtis, NYY	7.87
Span,Denard, Min	7.51
Upton,B.J., TB	7.50
Davis,Rajai, Oak	7.46
Andrus,Elvis, Tex	7.37
Suzuki,Ichiro, Sea	7.02
Podsednik,Scott, KC	6.98
Roberts,Brian, Bal	6.88
Damon,Johnny, Det	6.81

Cheap Wins

Lackey,John, Bos	6
Hughes,Phil, NYY	5
Bannister,Brian, KC	4
Cecil,Brett, Tor	4
Chen,Bruce, KC	4
11 tied with	3

Tough Losses

Hernandez,Felix, Sea	6
Pavano,Carl, Min	6
Lewis,Colby, Tex	5
Verlander,Justin, Det	5
Weaver,Jered, LAA	5
11 tied with	4

2010 National League Bill James Leaders

Top Game Scores

Pitcher	Date	Opp	IP	H	R	ER	BB	SO	GS
Halladay,Roy, Phi	5/29	Fla	9.0	0	0	0	0	11	98
Cain,Matt, SF	5/28	Ari	9.0	1	0	0	0	9	94
Cueto,Johnny, Cin	5/11	Pit	9.0	1	0	0	0	8	93
Wood,Travis, Cin	7/10	Phi	9.0	1	0	0	0	8	93
Lilly,Ted, LAD	8/19	Col	9.0	2	0	0	2	11	92
Sanchez,Anibal, Fla	7/29	SF	9.0	1	0	0	1	8	92
Dickey,R.A., NYM	8/13	Phi	9.0	1	0	0	1	7	91
Latos,Mat, SD	5/13	SF	9.0	1	0	0	0	6	91
Niese,Jonathon, NYM	6/10	SD	9.0	1	0	0	0	6	91
Oswalt,Roy, Hou	7/8	Pit	9.0	1	0	0	2	8	91

Worst Game Scores

Pitcher	Date	Opp	IP	H	R	ER	BB	SO	GS
Jackson,Edwin, Ari	4/27	Col	2.1	11	10	10	2	2	-5
Wolf,Randy, Mil	7/21	Pit	5.2	13	12	12	2	4	-3
Hanson,Tommy, Atl	6/22	CWS	3.2	13	9	9	1	0	-2
Moyer,Jamie, Phi	6/11	Bos	1.0	9	9	9	1	1	-1
Olsen,Scott, Was	9/1	Fla	1.2	8	9	9	2	1	2
Blanton,Joe, Phi	6/12	Bos	4.0	13	9	9	1	4	3
Latos,Mat, SD	9/17	StL	1.1	9	8	8	2	1	3
Santana,Johan, NYM	5/2	Phi	3.2	8	10	10	2	1	4
5 tied with									5

Runs Created

Votto,Joey, Cin	132
Pujols,Albert, StL	131
Gonzalez,Adrian, SD	122
Gonzalez,Carlos, Col	118
Weeks,Rickie, Mil	110
Huff,Aubrey, SF	108
Holliday,Matt, StL	107
Braun,Ryan, Mil	104
Uggla,Dan, Fla	101
2 tied with	97

Runs Created Per 27 Outs

Votto,Joey, Cin	9.1
Pujols,Albert, StL	8.0
Gonzalez,Carlos, Col	7.6
Gonzalez,Adrian, SD	7.5
Utley,Chase, Phi	7.0
Tulowitzki,Troy, Col	6.8
Huff,Aubrey, SF	6.8
Zimmerman,Ryan, Was	6.7
Holliday,Matt, StL	6.7
Heyward,Jason, Atl	6.5

Offensive Winning %

Votto,Joey, Cin	.822
Pujols,Albert, StL	.786
Gonzalez,Adrian, SD	.769
Utley,Chase, Phi	.726
Huff,Aubrey, SF	.722
Holliday,Matt, StL	.717
Zimmerman,Ryan, Was	.705
Gonzalez,Carlos, Col	.700
Heyward,Jason, Atl	.693
Ethier,Andre, LAD	.688

Secondary Average

(minimum 502 PA)

Pujols,Albert, StL	.484
Votto,Joey, Cin	.472
Reynolds,Mark, Ari	.415
Dunn,Adam, Was	.414
Fielder,Prince, Mil	.408
Werth,Jayson, Phi	.408
Rasmus,Colby, StL	.384
Tulowitzki,Troy, Col	.379
Heyward,Jason, Atl	.375
Gonzalez,Carlos, Col	.375

Isolated Power

(minimum 502 PA)

Pujols,Albert, StL	.284
Votto,Joey, Cin	.276
Dunn,Adam, Was	.276
Gonzalez,Carlos, Col	.262
Tulowitzki,Troy, Col	.253
Hart,Corey, Mil	.242
Soriano,Alfonso, ChC	.238
Werth,Jayson, Phi	.236
Reynolds,Mark, Ari	.234
Howard,Ryan, Phi	.229

Power / Speed Number

(minimum 502 PA)

Gonzalez,Carlos, Col	29.5
Young,Chris, Ari	27.5
Stubbs,Drew, Cin	25.4
Ramirez,Hanley, Fla	25.4
Victorino,Shane, Phi	23.5
Wright,David, NYM	23.0
Kemp,Matt, LAD	22.6
Votto,Joey, Cin	22.3
McCutchen,Andrew, Pit	21.6
Pujols,Albert, StL	21.0

Speed Scores (2009-2010)

Bourn,Michael, Hou	8.66
Victorino,Shane, Phi	8.05
Pagan,Angel, NYM	7.91
Morgan,Nyjer, Was	7.86
Fowler,Dexter, Col	7.79
McCutchen,Andrew, Pit	7.69
Gonzalez,Carlos, Col	7.57
Rollins,Jimmy, Phi	7.29
Drew,Stephen, Ari	7.02
Utley,Chase, Phi	6.94

Cheap Wins

13 tied with		3
Correia, Kevin, SD	Dempster, Ryan, ChC	
Duke, Zach, Pit	Garland, Jon, SD	
Hamels, Cole, Phi	Jackson, Edwin, Ari	
Kuroda, Hiroki, LAD	Lowe, Derek, Atl	
Moyer, Jamie, Phi	Myers, Brett, Hou	
Richard, Clayton, SD	Volstad, Chris, Fla	
Wolf, Randy, Mil		

Tough Losses

Kuroda,Hiroki, LAD	8
Hanson,Tommy, Atl	6
Kershaw,Clayton, LAD	6
Lopez,Rodrigo, Ari	6
Oswalt,Roy, Hou-Phi	6
de la Rosa,Jorge, Col	5
Dempster,Ryan, ChC	5
Hamels,Cole, Phi	5
Jimenez,Ubaldo, Col	5
Wells,Randy, ChC	5

Additional Bill James Leaders

AL Batters Win Shares
(2010)

Bautista,Jose, Tor	34
Cano,Robinson, NYY	34
Crawford,Carl, TB	32
Cabrera,Miguel, Det	30
Hamilton,Josh, Tex	30
Konerko,Paul, CWS	29
Longoria,Evan, TB	28
Choo,Shin-Soo, Cle	27
Mauer,Joe, Min	27
Beltre,Adrian, Bos	26

NL Batters Win Shares
(2010)

Gonzalez,Adrian, SD	35
Votto,Joey, Cin	33
Pujols,Albert, StL	32
Weeks,Rickie, Mil	29
Huff,Aubrey, SF	28
Braun,Ryan, Mil	25
Gonzalez,Carlos, Col	25
Holliday,Matt, StL	25
Tulowitzki,Troy, Col	25
Utley,Chase, Phi	25

AL Pitchers Win Shares
(2010)

Hernandez,Felix, Sea	23
Sabathia,CC, NYY	19
Weaver,Jered, LAA	19
Buchholz,Clay, Bos	18
Lester,Jon, Bos	17
Price,David, TB	17
Verlander,Justin, Det	17
Cahill,Trevor, Oak	16
Danks,John, CWS	16
Lee,Cliff, Sea-Tex	16

NL Pitchers Win Shares
(2010)

Halladay,Roy, Phi	25
Jimenez,Ubaldo, Col	22
Hudson,Tim, Atl	20
Wainwright,Adam, StL	20
Oswalt,Roy, Hou-Phi	18
Myers,Brett, Hou	17
Wagner,Billy, Atl	17
Wilson,Brian, SF	17
3 tied with	16

Batters Win Shares
(Career)

Rodriguez,Alex	443
Ramirez,Manny	408
Griffey Jr.,Ken	403
Jones,Chipper	382
Jeter,Derek	368
Thome,Jim	366
Pujols,Albert	347
Rodriguez,Ivan	334
Abreu,Bobby	332
Guerrero,Vladimir	318

Pitchers Win Shares
(Career)

Rivera,Mariano	241
Moyer,Jamie	224
Pettitte,Andy	206
Halladay,Roy	194
Hoffman,Trevor	188
Wagner,Billy	182
Hudson,Tim	178
Wakefield,Tim	173
Santana,Johan	170
Lowe,Derek	168

AL Component ERA
(minimum 162 IP)

Lee,Cliff, Sea-Tex	2.31
Hernandez,Felix, Sea	2.39
Weaver,Jered, LAA	2.59
Verlander,Justin, Det	2.79
Cahill,Trevor, Oak	2.81
Buchholz,Clay, Bos	2.88
Price,David, TB	2.91
Lester,Jon, Bos	3.00
Wilson,C.J., Tex	3.03
Sabathia,CC, NYY	3.11

NL Component ERA
(minimum 162 IP)

Wainwright,Adam, StL	2.36
Oswalt,Roy, Hou-Phi	2.37
Johnson,Josh, Fla	2.44
Latos,Mat, SD	2.52
Jimenez,Ubaldo, Col	2.57
Cain,Matt, SF	2.65
Halladay,Roy, Phi	2.69
Kershaw,Clayton, LAD	2.72
Kuroda,Hiroki, LAD	2.87
Hudson,Tim, Atl	2.95

AL Highest Avg Game Score
(minimum 30 GS)

Hernandez,Felix, Sea	63.44
Weaver,Jered, LAA	59.76
Price,David, TB	59.19
Lester,Jon, Bos	58.75
Verlander,Justin, Det	58.45
Sabathia,CC, NYY	57.59
Cahill,Trevor, Oak	56.83
Liriano,Francisco, Min	55.74
Lewis,Colby, Tex	55.56
Wilson,C.J., Tex	55.55

AL Lowest Avg Game Score
(minimum 30 GS)

Davies,Kyle, KC	45.09
Millwood,Kevin, Bal	45.90
Burnett,A.J., NYY	46.33
Shields,James, TB	46.79
Buehrle,Mark, CWS	47.97
Lackey,John, Bos	49.48
Matusz,Brian, Bal	50.78
Floyd,Gavin, CWS	51.19
Carmona,Fausto, Cle	51.67
Vargas,Jason, Sea	51.87

AL Lowest Offensive Win %

Izturis,Cesar, Bal	.189
Lopez,Jose, Sea	.255
Kouzmanoff,Kevin, Oak	.311
Callaspo,Alberto, KC-LAA	.365
Hill,Aaron, Tor	.368
Aybar,Erick, LAA	.370
Wigginton,Ty, Bal	.373
Pierzynski,A.J., CWS	.374
Wieters,Matt, Bal	.374
Betancourt,Yuniesky, KC	.384

NL Highest Avg Game Score
(minimum 30 GS)

Halladay,Roy, Phi	63.00
Wainwright,Adam, StL	62.48
Oswalt,Roy, Hou-Phi	60.91
Jimenez,Ubaldo, Col	60.64
Kershaw,Clayton, LAD	59.19
Latos,Mat, SD	58.74
Cain,Matt, SF	58.42
Hamels,Cole, Phi	58.30
Hudson,Tim, Atl	57.62
Sanchez,Jonathan, SF	57.30

NL Lowest Avg Game Score
(minimum 30 GS)

Maholm,Paul, Pit	44.13
Lopez,Rodrigo, Ari	45.94
Bush,Dave, Mil	46.03
Kendrick,Kyle, Phi	46.29
Volstad,Chris, Fla	47.63
Hammel,Jason, Col	48.50
Niese,Jonathon, NYM	49.03
Wells,Randy, ChC	50.13
Wolf,Randy, Mil	50.29
Lowe,Derek, Atl	50.48

NL Lowest Offensive Win %

Cedeno,Ronny, Pit	.362
Theriot,Ryan, ChC-LAD	.370
Escobar,Alcides, Mil	.371
Cabrera,Melky, Atl	.379
Morgan,Nyjer, Was	.380
Sandoval,Pablo, SF	.384
Cabrera,Orlando, Cin	.386
Desmond,Ian, Was	.427
Jones,Garrett, Pit	.437
Castro,Starlin, ChC	.464

Win Shares

Bill James initially devised Win Shares as a way to relate a player's individual statistics to the number of wins he contributed to his team. As a single number, Win Shares allows us to easily compare the accomplishments of each player and to compare players across positions.

We credit a team with three Win Shares for each win. If a team wins 100 games, the players on the team will be credited with 300 Win Shares—or 300 thirds-of-a-win. If a team wins 70 games, the players on the team will be credited with 210 Win Shares, and so on.

The following pages contain the sum of a player's Win Shares prior to 2001, followed by his individual season totals from 2001 through 2010. Career totals are also included for each player.

The quality of the team does not affect an individual player's Win Shares. A great player on a bad team will rate just as well as a great player on a good team.

Win Shares are also a great tool for evaluating award voting and Hall of Fame credentials. Generally, 30 Win Shares indicates an MVP-caliber season; 20 Win Shares indicates a season worthy of the Cy Young Award.

Win Shares also adjusts for offensive environment, so it is a great tool to use for looking at the greatest individual seasons in baseball history, as well as the greatest players of all time. For a complete description of how Win Shares are calculated as well as countless essays using Win Shares to analyze various facets of the game, check out Bill James' book, *Win Shares*.

WIN SHARES BY YEAR

Player	<01	01	02	03	04	05	06	07	08	09	10	Career
Aardsma,David					0		4	1	1	16	8	30
Abad,Fernando											2	2
Abreu,Bobby	81	26	29	28	33	25	27	18	22	23	20	332
Abreu,Tony								4		1	1	6
Accardo,Jeremy						2	4	14	0	2	0	22
Aceves,Alfredo									3	7	2	12
Acosta,Manny								2	4	1	4	11
Adams,Mike				5	1	0			6	5	10	27
Affeldt,Jeremy			5	12	4	1	3	5	6	10	3	49
Albaladejo,J								2	1	1	1	5
Albers,Matt							0	0	4	2	5	11
Aldridge,Cory											0	0
Alfonzo,Eliezer							9	1	0	1	0	11
Allen,Brandon										1	1	2
Alonso,Yonder											0	0
Alvarez,Pedro											14	14
Ambriz,Hector											0	0
Anderson,Brett										8	9	17
Anderson,Bryan										0	1	1
Anderson,Garret	82	17	23	25	14	16	14	13	19	7	0	230
Anderson,Lars											1	1
Andino,Robert						0	0	0	1	3	0	4
Andrus,Elvis										17	20	37
Ankiel,Rick	17	0		0				8	13	5	4	47
Arencibia,JP											1	1
Arias,Joaquin						1		3	0		1	5
Arredondo,Jose								11	1			12
Arrieta,Jake											5	5
Arroyo,Bronson	0	3	2	2	11	11	20	11	10	13	14	97
Atchison,Scott					2	0		2			2	6
Atilano,Luis											1	1
Atkins,Garrett				0	2	13	23	18	13	7	0	76
Atkins,Mitch										0	0	0
Ausmus,Brad	89	10	10	12	7	15	7	7	8	3	1	169
Avila,Alex										3	7	10
Aviles,Mike									17	2	10	29
Axford,John										1	11	12
Aybar,Erick							1	2	15	20	9	47
Aybar,Willy						6	6		6	7	6	31
Badenhop,Burke									0	5	4	9
Baez,Danys		6	11	9	10	10	6	1		5	0	58
Bailey,Andrew										17	11	28
Bailey,Homer								2	0	5	5	12
Baker,Jeff						1	3	1	7	7	4	23
Baker,John									9	13	1	23
Baker,Scott						4	0	8	13	12	8	45
Baldelli,Rocco				14	14		12	2	2	2	1	47
Balester,Collin									1	0	2	3
Balfour,Grant		0		2	3			0	11	5	6	27
Banks,Josh								0	2	0		2
Bannister,Brian							3	11	2	6	1	23
Barajas,Rod	1	1	3	5	9	11	7	3	10	12	13	75
Bard,Daniel										4	11	15
Bard,Josh			1	7	2		2	10	16	2	4	46
Barden,Brian									0	0	1	2
Barmes,Clint				1	3	9	6	0	12	13	10	54
Barney,Darwin											1	1
Bartlett,Jason					0	6	13	16	14	23	16	88
Barton,Daric								3	9	6	21	39
Bass,Brian									3	4	0	7
Bastardo,Antonio										0	1	1
Batista,Miguel	12	11	9	14	11	8	10	12	0	5	5	97
Bautista,Denny					0	1	1	0	3	1	3	9
Bautista,Jose					0	0	9	12	8	6	34	69
Baxter,Mike											0	0
Bay,Jason				5	15	30	21	12	24	29	11	147
Beachy,Brandon											0	0
Beckett,Josh		3	5	11	9	12	11	18	11	16	2	98
Beckham,Gordon										12	11	23
Bedard,Erik			0		6	8	13	17	6	8		58
Beimel,Joe		4	3	2	0	1	7	6	7	4	4	38
Belisario,Ronald										7	3	10
Belisle,Matt				0		4	3	5	0	1	11	24

WIN SHARES BY YEAR

Player	<01	01	02	03	04	05	06	07	08	09	10	Career
Bell,Heath					2	0	1	13	6	12	15	49
Bell,Josh											1	1
Bell,Trevor										0	2	2
Belliard,Ronnie	32	13	1	12	18	18	11	15	11	7	3	141
Beltran,Carlos	25	27	20	28	29	21	34	25	29	14	8	260
Beltre,Adrian	41	12	16	13	33	13	17	16	13	10	26	210
Beltre,Omar											0	0
Benoit,Joaquin		0	3	5	4	6	4	10	2		9	43
Benson,Kris	26		5	2	10	10	8			0	0	61
Berg,Justin										2	1	3
Bergesen,Brad										9	6	15
Bergmann,Jason						2	0	5	2	2	0	11
Berken,Jason										1	6	7
Berkman,Lance	11	32	29	25	30	20	31	24	36	22	14	274
Bernadina,Roger									1	0	10	11
Betancourt,Rafael				4	5	7	5	16	3	8	8	56
Betancourt,Yuniesky						3	13	19	8	8	12	63
Betemit,Wilson		0			1	7	9	8	2	0	12	39
Billingsley,Chad							6	12	16	9	11	54
Bisenius,Joe								0				0
Blackburn,Nick								0	10	12	3	25
Blake,Casey	1	1	0	11	17	9	11	11	18	19	13	111
Blalock,Hank		1	17	24	14	13	8	6	6	1		90
Blanco,Andres					3	1	2			2	4	12
Blanco,Gregor									11	0	6	17
Blanco,Henry	15	6	4	2	5	5	6	0	3	6	3	55
Blanks,Kyle										5	2	7
Blanton,Joe					0	13	10	13	7	11	4	58
Blevins,Jerry								0	3	1	3	7
Bloomquist,Willie			3	3	2	4	5	2	5	7	3	34
Blum,Geoff	13	8	15	5	3	7	9	9	9	6	7	88
Bocock,Brian									1	0		1
Boesch,Brennan											11	11
Boggs,Brandon									5	0	0	5
Boggs,Mitchell									0	2	4	6
Bogusevic,Brian											0	0
Bonderman,Jeremy				2	8	9	13	7	4	0	3	46
Bonifacio,Emilio								1	2	7	5	15
Bonine,Eddie									1	2	3	6
Bonser,Boof							6	4	0		1	11
Borbon,Julio									0	5	11	16
Boscan,J.C.											0	0
Bourgeois,Jason									0	0	0	0
Bourjos,Peter											3	3
Bourn,Michael							0	4	7	23	18	52
Bowden,Michael									1	0	0	1
Bowers,Cedrick										0	0	0
Bowker,John									7	1	2	10
Boyer,Blaine						4	0	0	1	3	3	11
Braddock,Zach											3	3
Braden,Dallas								0	4	8	12	24
Bradley,Milton	3	3	6	18	16	10	13	11	19	11	3	113
Brantley,Michael										3	5	8
Branyan,Russell	6	10	8	5	5	9	6	5	5	14	8	81
Braun,Ryan								22	23	36	25	106
Bray,Bill							3	1	4		1	9
Breslow,Craig						1	1		6	6	8	22
Brignac,Reid									0	2	10	12
Brown,Domonic											0	0
Brown,Dusty										0	0	0
Brown,Jordan											0	0
Broxton,Jonathan						0	9	10	10	16	6	51
Bruce,Jay									7	9	16	32
Bruney,Brian				2	0	3	2	6	3	0		16
Buchholz,Clay								3	0	6	18	27
Buchholz,Taylor							1	5	9		1	16
Buck,John					4	10	8	7	8	6	17	60
Buck,Travis								10	5	1	0	16
Buckner,Billy								1	1	1	0	3
Budde,Ryan								0	0	0	1	1
Buehrle,Mark	4	18	17	13	17	22	9	17	16	16	12	161
Buente,Jay											0	0
Bulger,Jason						1	0	1	0	7	0	9

WIN SHARES BY YEAR												
Player	<01	01	02	03	04	05	06	07	08	09	10	Career
Bullington,Bryan					0		0	0	0	0		0
Bumgarner,Madison										1	8	9
Burke,Jamie		0		1	5	0		6	2	1	0	15
Burnett,A.J.	8	9	14	0	7	11	9	11	14	12	4	99
Burnett,Alex											1	1
Burnett,Sean					2				2	5	7	16
Burrell,Pat	12	17	25	8	14	24	15	20	20	6	14	175
Burres,Brian							1	3	2	0	2	8
Burriss,Emmanuel								4	2	0		6
Burton,Jared							5	6	3	1		15
Bush,Dave					7	6	12	6	8	0	4	43
Butera,Drew											3	3
Butler,Billy							7	8	18	20		53
Byrd,Marlon			0	16	5	6	2	13	12	20	19	93
Byrdak,Tim	0				1	0	4	4	5	3		17
Byrnes,Eric	0	1	2	16	17	9	13	24	2	3	0	87
Cabrera,Asdrubal							7	12	18	9		46
Cabrera,Everth									14	3		17
Cabrera,Fernando				0	4	2	1	1	0			8
Cabrera,Melky					0	13	12	5	14	8		52
Cabrera,Miguel			12	19	27	33	29	20	25	30		195
Cabrera,Orlando	23	26	14	19	11	15	18	25	19	14	9	193
Cahill,Trevor										7	16	23
Cain,Lorenzo											6	6
Cain,Matt					5	11	12	14	20	15		77
Cairo,Miguel	30	4	3	3	14	5	5	4	4	0	5	77
Callaspo,Alberto						1	1	6	17	11		36
Cameron,Mike	61	29	18	21	15	11	25	20	17	17	4	238
Camp,Shawn					4	0	5	0	3	5	7	24
Cano,Robinson					12	17	21	12	18	34		114
Cantu,Jorge					4	18	5	1	19	17	9	73
Capps,Matt					0	7	14	7	2	13		43
Capuano,Chris				2	4	10	14	0			2	41
Caridad,Esmailin										3	0	3
Carlin,Luke									1	0	1	2
Carlson,Jesse									9	3	1	13
Carmona,Fausto							1	22	3	0	12	38
Carp,Mike										2	0	2
Carpenter,Chris	27	13	3		12	20	10	0	1	21	14	130
Carpenter,Drew								0	0	0		0
Carrasco,Carlos									0	3		3
Carrasco,D.J.				6	1	4			3	7	4	25
Carroll,Brett							0	0	6	0		6
Carroll,Jamey			3	3	6	9	13	5	10	8	14	71
Carson,Matt									1	1		2
Carter,Chris							0	0	5			5
Carter,Chris									0			0
Cash,Kevin			0	1	3	0		0	1	1	2	8
Cashner,Andrew										2		2
Casilla,Alexi					0	1	9	4	6			20
Casilla,Santiago					0	0	0	4	3	0	8	15
Cassevah,Bobby										1		1
Castillo,Alberto									2	1	0	3
Castillo,Luis	41	14	20	23	22	18	18	16	8	16	5	201
Castillo,Welington											1	1
Castro,Jason											4	4
Castro,Juan	9	1	2	7	5	7	6	1	2	2	2	44
Castro,Ramon	4	0	4	2	1	7	2	6	6	4	5	41
Castro,Starlin											12	12
Catalanotto,Frank	18	17	7	15	5	16	14	9	4	4	0	109
Cecil,Brett									3	10		13
Ceda,Jose										0		0
Cedeno,Ronny					2	5	1	5	7	9		29
Cervelli,Francisco								0	3	7		10
Chacin,Gustavo					1	14	5	1			2	23
Chacin,Jhoulys										0	10	10
Chamberlain,Joba								5	11	6	5	27
Chapman,Aroldis											2	2
Chavez,Eric	27	26	24	23	18	20	16	6	3	0	0	163
Chavez,Jesse								0	4	0		4
Chen,Bruce	13	4	1	0	4	13	0	0		1	9	45
Chico,Matt							5	0			0	5
Choate,Randy	1	4	0	0	3	0	1	0		5	2	16

WIN SHARES BY YEAR												
Player	<01	01	02	03	04	05	06	07	08	09	10	Career
Choo,Shin-Soo						0	4	1	16	23	27	71
Church,Ryan			1	8	9	16	10	7	3			54
Ciriaco,Pedro										1		1
Cishek,Steve										1		1
Clement,Jeff						2	3		0			5
Clevlen,Brent						2	0	0		0		2
Clippard,Tyler							1	1	5	9		16
Coello,Robert										0		0
Coffey,Todd					3	9	1	1	7	1		22
Coghlan,Chris									21	8		29
Coke,Phil								3	5	6		14
Coleman,Casey										3		3
Colome,Jesus		4	0	4	5	2	0	5	3	0	0	23
Colon,Roman					2	1	2			3	0	8
Colvin,Tyler										0	9	9
Conger,Hank										1		1
Conrad,Brooks								0	1	8		9
Contreras,Jose			7	6	17	13	5	7	4	6		65
Cook,Aaron		2	3	6	6	12	9	15	11	4		68
Cora,Alex	7	6	13	12	17	5	6	4	5	5	3	83
Cordero,Chad				2	12	15	12	10	0		0	51
Cordero,Francisco	5	0	8	12	17	11	12	12	11	13	10	111
Cormier,Lance				0	4	2	0	4	6	3		19
Corpas,Manny					3	15	6	1	5			30
Correia,Kevin			3	0	2	6	8	0	8	1		28
Cortes,Dan										0		0
Counsell,Craig	28	14	15	5	10	22	9	6	6	15	6	136
Cousins,Scott										1		1
Craig,Allen										2		2
Crain,Jesse					4	10	7	0	5	4	6	36
Cramer,Bobby										2		2
Crawford,Carl			6	13	20	22	21	20	11	19	32	164
Crisp,Coco			3	8	14	20	9	16	11	4	14	99
Crosby,Bobby			0	14	12	8	4	10	2	2		62
Crowe,Trevor									2	7		9
Cruz,Juan	4	3	0	7	0	6	6	6	2	0		34
Cruz,Luis								1	1	0		2
Cruz,Nelson					0	3	4	7	16	19		49
Cuddyer,Michael	0	3	1	10	7	22	16	7	17	15		98
Cueto,Johnny								6	7	12		25
Cunningham,Aaron								3	0	3		6
Curtis,Colin										0		0
Cust,Jack	0	0	4	0		0	19	17	14	12		66
Daigle,Casey				0		1			0	1		1
Daley,Matt									4	1		5
Damon,Johnny	87	17	22	19	26	25	21	15	23	21	10	306
Danko,John							4	17	16	16		53
Davies,Kyle					4	0	1	7	5	4		21
Davis,Brad										2		2
Davis,Chris								8	7	1		16
Davis,Doug	5	8	3	7	16	12	8	11	7	10	0	87
Davis,Ike											16	16
Davis,Rajai						0	5	5	13	14		37
Davis,Wade										2	8	10
De Aza,Alejandro							1		1	1		3
de la Rosa,Jorge					0	2	2	3	5	12	8	32
Deduno,Samuel									0			0
DeJesus,David				0	9	16	14	15	22	16	11	103
Del Rosario,Enerio										1		1
Delaney,Rob										0		0
Delcarmen,Manny					1	3	6	7	4	2		23
Demel,Sam										1		1
Dempster,Ryan	23	7	4	0	2	14	6	8	18	12	12	106
Denorfia,Chris						0	2		2	0	10	14
DeRosa,Mark	1	6	7	5	2	4	14	16	23	13	1	92
Descalso,Daniel											1	1
Desmond,Ian										2	11	13
Dessens,Elmer	13	10	15	7	5	4	5	0	0	2	5	66
Detwiler,Ross							0		2	0		2
DeWitt,Blake									12	0	15	27
Diamond,Thomas										0		0
Diaz,Argenis										0	0	0
Diaz,Matt			0	0	2	7	11	1	15	6		42

447

WIN SHARES BY YEAR												
Player	<01	01	02	03	04	05	06	07	08	09	10	Career
Dickerson,Chris									5	7	0	12
Dickey,R.A.		0		7	4	0	0		3	3	15	32
DiFelice,Mark									2	3		5
Dobbs,Greg				1	2	1	7	8	2	1		22
Donald,Jason											6	6
Donaldson,Josh											0	0
Donnelly,Brendan			6	11	5	6	5	2	0	4	1	40
Dotel,Octavio	10	12	17	12	14	2	0	3	6	6	6	88
Doubront,Felix											1	1
Doumit,Ryan					6	2	6	20	4	9		47
Downs,Matt									1	2		3
Downs,Scott	3		0	0	5	6	8	11	6	8		47
Drabek,Kyle										0		0
Drew,J.D.	31	22	15	13	31	12	19	12	16	18	13	202
Drew,Stephen							6	16	21	16	20	79
Duchscherer,Justin		0		1	9	11	10	1	13		2	47
Duda,Lucas											0	0
Duensing,Brian										6	13	19
Duke,Zach					10	10	2	3	12	1		38
Dukes,Elijah								2	9	7		18
Duncan,Shelley								3	0	0	6	9
Dunn,Adam		10	20	13	29	25	18	18	21	24	18	196
Dunn,Michael										0	2	2
Durango,Luis										1	0	1
Durbin,Chad	0	8	0	0	1		1	6	8	3	5	32
Dye,Jermaine	46	18	13	2	12	17	25	11	17	14		175
Dyson,Jarrod										2		2
Eckstein,David		12	21	10	10	27	13	12	8	17	13	143
Edmonds,Jim	124	30	29	21	33	25	11	9	11		8	301
Ekstrom,Mike									0	0	1	1
Elbert,Scott									0	1	0	1
Eldred,Brad					1		0			0		1
Ellis,A.J.									0	0	4	4
Ellis,Mark			14	18		21	14	20	13	11	19	130
Ellsbury,Jacoby							6	16	21	1		44
Ely,John											0	0
Encarnacion,Edwin					4	14	16	14	6	8		62
English,Jesse											0	0
Enright,Barry											6	6
Escalona,Edgmer											1	1
Escobar,Alcides									0	4	12	16
Escobar,Kelvim	28	11	9	12	14	5	12	18		0		109
Escobar,Yunel							12	13	24	14		63
Espinosa,Danny											4	4
Esposito,Brian							0					0
Estrada,Marco									0	0	0	0
Ethier,Andre							11	13	23	21	22	90
Evans,Nick								1	1	1		3
Evans,Terry							0		0	0		0
Eveland,Dana					0	0	0	8	0	0		8
Everett,Adam		0	1	11	12	14	13	4	4	6	1	66
Farnsworth,Kyle	5	9	0	7	3	14	5	3	3	2	5	56
Feldman,Scott					1	3	1	4	14	2		25
Feliciano,Jesus											1	1
Feliciano,Pedro		0	3	1		8	6	3	7	4		32
Feliz,Neftali										6	15	21
Feliz,Pedro	0	0	2	7	9	9	13	12	8	18	3	81
Fielder,Prince						2	16	27	23	36	23	127
Fields,Josh					0	12		0	3	1		16
Fien,Casey									0	0		0
Figaro,Alfredo									0	0		0
Figgins,Chone		0	9	20	22	17	21	12	26	11		138
Figueroa,Nelson	0	6	1	3	0			2	4	8		24
Fisher,Carlos									2	0		2
Fister,Doug										4	7	11
Flores,Jesus								6	9	3		18
Flores,Randy		1		2	3	1	3	0	1	3		14
Flowers,Tyler										0	0	0
Floyd,Gavin			2	0	0	2	15	13	12			44
Fontenot,Mike				0		5	12	7	7			31
Ford,Darren										0		0
Fowler,Dexter								0	15	13		28
Fox,Jake								0	6	1		7

WIN SHARES BY YEAR												
Player	<01	01	02	03	04	05	06	07	08	09	10	Career
Fox,Matt										0		0
Francis,Jeff			2	6	13	14	5		4			44
Francisco,Ben						1	9	10	5			25
Francisco,Frank		6		0	3	6	9	5				29
Francisco,Juan								2	0			2
Francoeur,Jeff			12	15	20	5	9	7				68
Frandsen,Kevin				0	4	0	1	3				8
Franklin,Ryan	1	5	6	13	6	6	4	8	14	10		81
Frasor,Jason			9	6	4	3	2	10	5			39
Frazier,Jeff									0			0
Freeman,Freddie									0			0
Freese,David									1	8		9
French,Luke									2	3		5
Frieri,Ernesto									0	4		4
Fuentes,Brian		1	2	10	2	14	12	10	12	9	9	81
Fukudome,Kosuke								15	17	13		45
Fulchino,Jeff				0		0	7	1				8
Fuld,Sam					0		4	1				5
Furcal,Rafael	17	9	20	26	20	26	27	15	8	17	19	204
Gabino,Armando									0	0		0
Galarraga,Armando						0	13	3	5			21
Gallagher,Sean						0	2	1	0			3
Gallardo,Yovani						9	2	10	11			32
Gamel,Mat						0	5	0				5
Garcia,Freddy	24	18	11	8	15	17	14	1	1	4	9	122
Garcia,Jaime							1		12			13
Gardner,Brett							3	9	17			29
Garko,Ryan			0	6	12	15	11	0				44
Garland,Jon	1	8	8	10	11	20	15	13	9	10	12	117
Garza,Matt					1	4	12	12	10			39
Gaudin,Chad			3	1	0	7	9	5	3	2		30
Gee,Dillon									3			3
Gentry,Craig									0	0		0
German,Esteban		0	0	2	1	11	8	5	1	1		29
Germano,Justin		0		0	4	0		2				6
Gerut,Jody			14	10	3		13	2	0			42
Gervacio,Sammy							3	0				3
Getz,Chris						0	10	4				14
Giambi,Jason	129	38	34	27	8	24	22	6	14	7	6	315
Gibbons,Jay	4	12	18	4	15	9	1			3		66
Gillespie,Cole									1			1
Gimenez,Chris								1	1			2
Glaus,Troy	44	21	22	10	8	23	16	14	20	0	11	189
Gload,Ross	0		0	7	0	4	7	5	4	5		32
Golson,Greg							0	0	1			1
Gomes,Jonny		0	0	14	6	8	2	10	18			58
Gomez,Carlos					2	13	6	4				25
Gomez,Jeanmar								2				2
Gonzalez,Adrian			1	1	16	25	24	34	35			136
Gonzalez,Alberto					0	3	5	2				10
Gonzalez,Alex	15	10	3	20	15	14	10	10		8	19	124
Gonzalez,Carlos							6	9	25			40
Gonzalez,Enrique					3	0	0	0	1			4
Gonzalez,Gio							0	2	15			17
Gonzalez,Mike		0	8	6	11	3	9	3				43
Gordon,Alex					12	15	2	3				32
Gorzelanny,Tom			0	3	11	0	2	7				23
Grabow,John		0	1	2	5	3	6	7	0			24
Granderson,Curtis			0	6	20	25	20	20	16			107
Gray,Jeff						0	1	0				1
Green,Nick		8	6	2	0		6	0				22
Green,Sean				2	5	4	3	0				14
Greene,Tyler							1	2				3
Gregerson,Luke							5	9				14
Gregg,Kevin		2	6	2	4	10	11	7	9			51
Greinke,Zack		9	3	1	9	15	26	11				74
Griffey Jr.,Ken	299	14	5	6	15	19	9	14	15	7	0	403
Gross,Gabe			2	2	10	4	10	8	5			41
Grudzielanek,Mark	75	17	12	18	8	18	13	12	10		3	186
Guerrero,Vladimir	96	23	28	18	27	27	24	29	22	7	17	318
Guerrier,Matt			0	5	5	9	2	11	7			39
Guillen,Carlos	10	14	12	12	22	8	25	19	13	6	5	146
Guillen,Jose	27	2	2	20	20	15	3	18	10	4	13	134

Player	<01	01	02	03	04	05	06	07	08	09	10	Career
Guthrie,Jeremy					1	0	0	12	13	7	15	48
Gutierrez,Franklin						0	1	6	5	21	14	47
Gutierrez,Juan								0		7	3	10
Guzman,Angel						0	2	0	7			9
Guzman,Cristian	17	18	14	14	16	6		7	20	9	9	130
Gwynn,Tony							1	3	0	13	6	23
Haeger,Charlie								2	0	0	1	3
Hafner,Travis		1		7	21	26	24	16	2	8	11	116
Hairston,Jerry	9	10	12	7	8	9	1	2	12	8	13	91
Hairston,Scott				3	0	0	7	9	14	5		38
Hall,Bill			1	3	7	17	20	10	8	4	11	81
Halladay,Roy	12	9	21	23	9	15	20	16	23	21	25	194
Halman,Greg											0	0
Hamels,Cole							8	15	18	10	16	67
Hamilton,Josh								11	26	11	30	78
Hamilton,Mark											0	0
Hammel,Jason							0	2	3	10	8	23
Hampton,Mike	93	11	5	11	10	6			3	4	1	144
Hanigan,Ryan								1	4	8	13	26
Hanrahan,Joel								2	7	3	7	19
Hanson,Tommy										10	12	22
Happ,J.A.								0	2	15	6	23
Harang,Aaron			4	3	5	11	18	17	6	7	1	72
Harden,Rich				4	14	12	4	2	16	7	2	61
Hardy,J.J.						11	3	19	20	6	10	69
Haren,Dan				1	2	13	14	17	19	20	14	100
Harrell,Lucas											1	1
Harris,Brendan					0	1	0	13	11	7	1	33
Harris,Willie		0	2	2	10	4	1	9	10	9	4	51
Harrison,Matt									3	1	3	7
Hart,Corey					0	0	5	21	16	9	18	69
Hatcher,Chris										0		0
Hawkins,LaTroy	23	3	11	13	16	5	4	5	6	10	0	96
Hawksworth,Blake										5	1	6
Hawpe,Brad				1	8	15	20	16	19	5		84
Hayes,Brett										0	2	2
Headley,Chase								0	8	16	15	39
Heilman,Aaron				0	0	10	8	8	2	5	4	37
Heisey,Chris											4	4
Hellickson,Jeremy											3	3
Helms,Wes	1	5	1	14	4	5	10	2	5	5	7	59
Helton,Todd	67	26	27	35	30	25	21	22	8	23	7	291
Hendrickson,Mark			4	5	7	4	8	3	3	6	2	42
Hensley,Clay						5	11	0	0		11	27
Hermida,Jeremy						3	8	13	13	11	4	50
Hernandez,And						0	1	0	4	7	1	13
Hernandez,David										3	6	9
Hernandez,Diory										1	0	1
Hernandez,Felix						8	8	14	13	26	23	92
Hernandez,Livan	38	5	7	22	19	13	10	10	3	3	11	141
Hernandez,Luis								1	1	1	2	5
Hernandez,Ramon	16	13	12	18	13	10	21	11	11	11	13	149
Herndon,David											2	2
Herrera,Daniel Ray									0	5	1	6
Herrera,Jonathan									1		6	7
Herrmann,Frank											2	2
Hessman,Mike				1	0			1	2		0	4
Hester,John										1	2	3
Heyward,Jason											23	23
Hicks,Brandon											0	0
Hill,Aaron						9	14	20	5	25	12	85
Hill,Koyie					0	1	1	1	0	7	3	13
Hill,Rich					0	5	13	1	0	1		20
Hill,Shawn					0		1	6	0	0	2	9
Hill,Steven										0		0
Hinske,Eric			22	12	6	11	7	3	10	5	8	84
Hochevar,Luke								1	3	1	4	9
Hoffman,Trevor	105	9	8	1	11	10	14	11	7	11	1	188
Hoffpauir,Jarrett										1	0	1
Hoffpauir,Micah									3	4	0	7
Holland,Derek										2	3	5
Holland,Greg											0	0
Holliday,Matt					9	17	19	27	21	25	25	143

Player	<01	01	02	03	04	05	06	07	08	09	10	Career
Hoover,Paul		0	0				0	0	0	1	0	1
Houser,James										0		0
Howard,Ryan					1	10	29	26	24	26	20	136
Howell,J.P.						1	2	0	11	11		25
Howry,Bob	26	5	3	0	4	11	9	11	3	5	0	77
Hu,Chin-lung								1	1	0	0	2
Hudson,Daniel										1	9	10
Hudson,Orlando			7	17	16	15	20	21	17	20	14	147
Hudson,Tim	27	17	23	23	16	14	7	17	10	4	20	178
Huff,Aubrey	3	5	12	21	20	14	9	12	21	8	28	153
Huff,David										3	0	3
Huffman,Chad											0	0
Hughes,Dustin										0	3	3
Hughes,Luke											0	0
Hughes,Phil								4	0	10	11	25
Hughes,Rhyne											1	1
Humber,Philip							0	0	0	0	2	2
Hundley,Nick									3	10	10	23
Hunter,Tommy									0	8	10	18
Hunter,Torii	13	19	20	16	13	11	17	22	21	20	23	195
Iannetta,Chris							1	5	17	10	3	36
Ibanez,Raul	6	9	12	15	12	17	25	23	21	17	19	176
Igarashi,Ryota											0	0
Infante,Gregory											1	1
Infante,Omar			3	3	12	7	5	4	9	7	19	69
Inge,Brandon		3	4	4	13	17	17	12	10	13	13	106
Inglett,Joe							6	1	12	2	4	25
Ishikawa,Travis							1		4	9	4	18
Iwamura,Akinori								13	21	6	2	42
Izturis,Cesar		4	4	10	25	6	3	5	9	8	6	80
Izturis,Maicer					1	6	13	16	11	17	7	71
Jackson,Austin											18	18
Jackson,Conor						0	12	13	17	1	4	47
Jackson,Edwin			2	0	0	1	2	10	17	9		41
Jackson,Steven									3	0		3
Jacobs,Mike						5	12	7	14	5	1	44
Jakubauskas,Chris										3	0	3
James,Justin											0	0
Janish,Paul									1	4	8	13
Jansen,Kenley											6	6
Janssen,Casey							4	10		0	5	19
Jaramillo,Jason										2	0	2
Jaso,John									0		16	16
Jay,Jon											8	8
Jeffress,Jeremy											1	1
Jenks,Bobby						6	12	16	13	8	7	62
Jennings,Desmond											0	0
Jepsen,Kevin									0	4	5	9
Jeter,Derek	123	28	24	19	26	26	32	24	18	28	20	368
Jimenez,Ubaldo							0	4	11	19	22	56
Joaquin,Waldis										1	0	1
Johnson,Chris										0	15	15
Johnson,Dan						9	5	10	1		4	29
Johnson,Jim							0	0	8	7	3	18
Johnson,Josh						1	12	0	6	19	16	54
Johnson,Kelly						9		19	19	6	21	74
Johnson,Nick		0	11	14	6	20	25		4	18	2	100
Johnson,Reed				11	9	10	16	3	13	3	3	68
Johnson,Rob								0	0	9	3	12
Jones,Adam							1	0	9	13	15	38
Jones,Andruw	100	22	27	23	17	21	22	15	2	6	9	264
Jones,Chipper	157	29	31	26	18	18	22	25	23	20	13	382
Jones,Garrett								0		10	13	23
Jones,Hunter										0	0	0
Joyce,Matt									6	1	10	17
Jurrjens,Jair								2	11	17	4	34
Ka'aihue,Kila									1		1	2
Kalish,Ryan											5	5
Kapler,Gabe	18	13	7	4	5	1	2		8	5	2	65
Karstens,Jeff							3	0	1	2	3	9
Kawakami,Kenshin										7	0	7
Kazmir,Scott					1	10	13	13	12	6	0	55
Kearns,Austin			16	12	5	10	17	20	3	2	10	95

WIN SHARES BY YEAR

Player	<01	01	02	03	04	05	06	07	08	09	10	Career
Kelley,Shawn										3	2	5
Kelly,Don								0		1	5	6
Kemp,Matt							3	10	19	26	15	73
Kendall,Jason	97	9	14	21	25	14	23	7	19	9	7	245
Kendrick,Howie							6	9	15	15	19	64
Kendrick,Kyle								9	3	2	5	19
Kennedy,Adam	13	8	17	13	13	17	15	2	8	18	7	131
Kennedy,Ian								2	0	0	11	13
Keppinger,Jeff				2		1	9	10	5	21		48
Kershaw,Clayton									5	12	15	32
Kilby,Brad										2	1	3
Kimbrel,Craig											4	4
Kinsler,Ian							12	17	24	24	13	90
Kintzler,Brandon											0	0
Kirkman,Michael											2	2
Kohn,Michael											3	3
Konerko,Paul	31	17	17	4	20	24	21	16	10	18	29	207
Kotchman,Casey					2	4	0	15	14	10	6	51
Kotsay,Mark	32	16	22	13	21	19	11	3	9	4	4	154
Kottaras,George									0	1	4	5
Kouzmanoff,Kevin							1	15	14	16	7	53
Kratz,Erik											0	0
Kroenke,Zach											0	0
Kubel,Jason				3			1	12	12	19	12	59
Kuo,Hong-Chih						0	3	0	10	3	15	31
Kuroda,Hiroki									10	5	11	26
Lackey,John			7	7	10	16	16	21	13	12	11	113
Laffey,Aaron								3	4	5	2	14
Laird,Gerald				1	3	1	5	10	9	14	6	49
Lamb,Mike	6	8	7	0	12	6	9	10	5		0	63
Langerhans,Ryan		0	0		12	8	5	4	2	2		33
Lannan,John								2	9	9	4	24
LaPorta,Matt										3	6	9
Larish,Jeff									2	0	0	2
LaRoche,Adam					7	11	16	16	16	17	16	99
LaRoche,Andy								2	2	12	2	18
LaRue,Jason	5	9	11	10	15	17	5	2	4	1	0	79
Latos,Mat										1	13	14
League,Brandon					1	0	5	0	4	3	8	21
Leake,Mike											7	7
LeBlanc,Wade									0	2	6	8
LeCure,Sam											2	2
Ledezma,Wil				2	3	0	4	2	2	0	0	13
Lee,Carlos	24	15	17	20	22	21	22	21	22	18	15	217
Lee,Cliff			1	3	6	13	10	1	24	17	16	91
Lee,Derrek	29	16	22	25	19	34	4	21	17	24	13	224
Lerew,Anthony					0	0	0			0	0	0	0
Leroux,Chris										0	0	0
Lester,Jon							5	4	18	17	17	61
Lewis,Colby			0	1	1	0	0				13	15
Lewis,Fred							1	5	13	7	10	36
Lewis,Jensen								4	6	3	4	17
Lewis,Rommie										0	0	0
Lidge,Brad			1	8	22	15	7	10	15	0	8	86
Lillibridge,Brent									1	1	2	4
Lilly,Ted	0	3	6	10	15	4	11	15	12	14	11	101
Lincecum,Tim								8	25	22	14	69
Lincoln,Brad											1	1
Lincoln,Mike	1	4	6	2	1				4	0	0	18
Lind,Adam							3	7	7	21	9	47
Lindsey,John											0	0
Lindstrom,Matt								5	6	2	4	17
Linebrink,Scott	1	1	0	6	10	11	8	5	5	3	3	53
Link,Jon											0	0
Liriano,Francisco						0	16		4	2	14	36
Litsch,Jesse								7	12	0	0	19
Loe,Kameron					0	8	2	3	2		5	20
Logan,Boone							0	3	1	0	4	8
Lohse,Kyle		3	11	11	6	10	4	9	12	3	0	69
Loney,James							3	16	14	18	18	69
Longoria,Evan									19	24	28	71
Lopez,Felipe		5	6	3	9	21	16	11	10	23	9	113
Lopez,Javier			6	0	0	2	4	6	0		6	24

WIN SHARES BY YEAR

Player	<01	01	02	03	04	05	06	07	08	09	10	Career
Lopez,Jose					3	5	16	10	18	12	7	71
Lopez,Rodrigo	0	15	2	14	8	4	4			0	3	50
Lopez,Wilton										0	8	8
Lowe,Derek	46	11	22	12	6	11	15	11	16	7	11	168
Lowe,Mark							3	0	1	8	1	13
Lowell,Mike	28	20	19	22	22	8	16	23	12	13	2	185
Lowrie,Jed									7	1	8	16
Lucroy,Jonathan											4	4
Lucy,Donny								0			1	1
Ludwick,Ryan			0	6	0	0		10	24	19	17	76
Luebke,Cory											1	1
Lugo,Julio	9	9	9	15	20	24	13	11	2	9	3	124
Luna,Hector					4	5	9	0	0		0	18
Lyon,Brandon		4	0	5		0	6	11	6	11	14	57
MacDougal,Mike		1	0	9	0	8	5	0	2	5	0	30
MacLane,Evan											0	0
Madson,Ryan				0	9	6	4	5	8	10	8	50
Mahay,Ron	9	2	0	5	8	0	4	7	6	2	2	45
Maholm,Paul						4	7	5	9	8	4	37
Maier,Mitch								0	1	9	11	21
Maine,John					0	0	6	11	7	4	0	28
Maine,Scott											1	1
Majewski,Gary			1	8	4	0	0					13
Maldonado,Carlos							0	0			1	1
Maloney,Matt										1	2	3
Mangini,Matt											0	0
Manship,Jeff										1	1	2
Manuel,Robert										1	1	2
Manzella,Tommy										0	3	3
Marcum,Shaun						1	3	10	12		14	40
Marinez,Jhan											0	0
Markakis,Nick							12	20	23	16	22	93
Marmol,Carlos							1	11	12	10	16	50
Marquez,Jeff										0		0
Marquis,Jason	1	8	3	1	14	12	2	8	8	15	0	72
Marshall,Sean							2	6	4	5	10	27
Marson,Lou									1	1	5	7
Marte,Andy						0	4	0	2	3	3	12
Marte,Damaso	0	1	9	15	9	4	4	5	6	0	1	54
Marte,Victor										0	0	0
Martin,J.D.										3	1	4
Martin,Russell							14	22	20	16	9	81
Martinez,Cristhian										1	1	2
Martinez,Fernando										0	0	0
Martinez,Joe										0	0	0
Martinez,Osvaldo											2	2
Martinez,Victor			1	3	20	22	18	29	7	21	17	138
Masset,Nick							1	0	4	10	7	22
Masterson,Justin									7	5	5	17
Mata,Frank										0	0	0
Mateo,Marcos											0	0
Mather,Joe									4		0	4
Mathieson,Scott							0				0	0
Mathis,Doug									0	4	0	4
Mathis,Jeff						0	0	2	7	4	3	16
Matsui,Hideki				19	28	23	6	16	10	18	20	140
Matsui,Kaz					13	5	7	14	12	16	1	68
Matsuzaka,Daisuke								12	16	2	7	37
Matthews Jr.,Gary	2	10	10	9	11	11	21	14	8	10	0	106
Matusz,Brian										3	10	13
Mauer,Joe					6	22	30	21	30	32	27	168
Maxwell,Justin								1		3	2	6
May,Lucas											0	0
Maya,Yunesky											0	0
Mayberry,John										1	1	2
Maybin,Cameron								0	3	2	8	13
Mazzaro,Vin										2	4	6
McAnulty,Paul						0	1	0	4		0	5
McCann,Brian						6	22	15	18	20	19	100
McCarthy,Brandon						5	5	3	1	5		19
McClellan,Kyle									4	6	8	18
McClendon,Mike											2	2
McCoy,Mike										0	1	1

Player	<01	01	02	03	04	05	06	07	08	09	10	Career
McCutchen,Andrew										18	22	40
McCutchen,Daniel										2	0	2
McDonald,Darnell				0				0		1	10	11
McDonald,James									1	3	4	8
McDonald,John	0	0	5	3	1	4	3	8	1	3	5	33
McGee,Jake											0	0
McGehee,Casey									0	17	23	40
McKenry,Michael											0	0
McLouth,Nate						1	2	10	24	19	4	60
Meche,Gil	12		9	5	5	8	13	14	5	0		71
Medders,Brandon						5	6	2	1	7	0	21
Medlen,Kris										3	7	10
Meek,Evan								0		4	9	13
Mejia,Jenrry											1	1
Melancon,Mark										1	2	3
Mench,Kevin			10	4	13	12	9	8	2		0	58
Mendez,Adalberto											1	1
Mendoza,Luis							2	0	0		0	2
Meredith,Cla				0		9	5	3	4	0		21
Meyer,Dan				0			0	0	6	0		6
Michaels,Jason		0	3	4	10	12	9	7	7	3	6	61
Mickolio,Kam								0	1	0		1
Mijares,Jose									1	8	2	11
Miles,Aaron				1	12	8	10	10	9	2	3	55
Milledge,Lastings							4	6	11	4	10	35
Miller,Andrew							0	2	0	2	0	4
Miller,Corky		2	5	1	0	0	0	1	1	3	3	16
Miller,Jai								0		0	0	0
Miller,Justin			3		2	0		5	3	5	1	19
Miller,Trever	6		4	4	2	6	2	3	6	2		35
Mills,Brad										0	1	1
Millwood,Kevin	45	5	19	12	5	14	13	5	6	15	5	144
Miner,Zach							4	5	8	6		23
Minor,Mike											0	0
Miranda,Juan									1	0	1	2
Misch,Pat							0	2	1	3	1	7
Mitchell,Russ											0	0
Mitre,Sergio				0	0	2	0	4		0	3	9
Mock,Garrett									2	0	0	2
Moehler,Brian	46	1	2	0		5	0	3	7	2	1	67
Moeller,Chad	2	0	6	6	5	3	1	0	3	1	0	27
Molina,Bengie	16	7	10	16	11	15	11	13	19	12	7	137
Molina,Gustavo							0	0	0		0	0
Molina,Jose	0	1	2	2	6	7	5	4	9	4	4	44
Molina,Yadier					5	14	9	12	15	20	17	92
Monasterios,Carlos											2	2
Montanez,Lou									3	1	0	4
Montero,Miguel							0	3	4	13	9	29
Moore,Adam										1	3	4
Moore,Scott								1	1	0	1	3
Mora,Melvin	12	11	16	15	24	20	18	10	17	7	0	150
Morales,Franklin								4	0	4	0	8
Morales,Jose								1		4	1	6
Morales,Kendry							2	2	0	23	8	35
Morel,Brent											0	0
Moreland,Mitch											6	6
Morgan,Nyjer								4	3	15	9	31
Morneau,Justin				1	9	7	26	18	28	18	17	124
Morrison,Logan											9	9
Morrow,Brandon								5	7	4	7	23
Morse,Mike						5	2	2	0	2	9	20
Mortensen,Clay										0	0	0
Morton,Charlie									0	4	0	4
Moscoso,Guillermo										1	0	1
Moseley,Dustin						0		6	0	1	2	9
Moss,Brandon								1	5	5	0	11
Mota,Guillermo	6	2	2	14	12	3	3	1	4	4	2	53
Motte,Jason									2	2	6	10
Moyer,Jamie	118	15	16	18	5	12	10	8	13	6	3	224
Moylan,Peter							1	9	1	7	6	24
Mujica,Edward							1	0	0	4	4	9
Mulvey,Kevin										0	0	0
Murphy,Daniel										6	10	16

Player	<01	01	02	03	04	05	06	07	08	09	10	Career
Murphy,David							0	5	11	11	15	42
Murphy,Donnie							0	0	3	1	3	7
Myers,Brett			3	9	4	14	12	9	7	3	17	78
Nady,Xavier	0			7	1	8	12	10	20	0	5	63
Narveson,Chris							0			2	7	9
Nathan,Joe	7		1	11	19	17	20	16	16	16		123
Nava,Daniel											5	5
Navarro,Dioner					0	4	5	6	17	5	2	39
Navarro,Oswaldo								0			0	0
Navarro,Yamaico											0	0
Nelson,Chris											0	0
Nelson,Joe		0		0		5		6	3	0		14
Neshek,Pat							6	8	1		0	15
Ni,Fu-Te										3	0	3
Nickeas,Mike											0	0
Niemann,Jeff									0	12	7	19
Niese,Jonathon									0	1	6	7
Nieve,Fernando							6		0	4	0	10
Nieves,Wil			1			0	0	1	4	4	2	12
Nippert,Dustin						1	0	1	1	5	3	11
Nix,Jayson									1	6	6	13
Nix,Laynce				4	7	4	0	0	0	6	4	25
Nolasco,Ricky							5	0	14	6	7	32
Norberto,Jordan											0	0
Norris,Bud										3	3	6
Nova,Ivan											2	2
Nunez,Eduardo											2	2
Nunez,Leo						0	1	3	5	9	10	28
O'Day,Darren									2	9	9	20
Oeltjen,Trent										0	0	0
O'Flaherty,Eric							0	4	0	4	5	13
Ogando,Alexi											6	6
Ohlendorf,Ross								1	0	11	4	16
Ohman,Will	0	0				4	5	2	5	0	4	20
Ojeda,Augie	2	2	1	0	3		4	6	5	0		23
Okajima,Hideki								11	8	7	2	28
Oliver,Andy											0	0
Oliver,Darren	50	3	3	10	1		6	5	9	9	6	102
Olivo,Miguel			1	8	7	7	13	7	7	9	11	70
Olsen,Scott						1	10	1	8	1	0	21
Olson,Garrett								0	1	1	1	3
Ondrusek,Logan											5	5
Ordonez,Magglio	58	25	25	23	8	10	19	34	16	13	11	242
Ortiz,David	19	7	11	14	24	30	27	27	15	11	18	203
Ortiz,Ramon	7	12	14	5	7	3	3	3			0	54
Ortiz,Russ	22	15	13	16	12	0	1	1		1	0	81
O'Sullivan,Sean										2	2	4
Oswalt,Roy		15	20	10	18	21	20	17	16	9	18	164
Ottavino,Adam											0	0
Outman,Josh									1	4		5
Overbay,Lyle		0	0	6	17	17	17	6	14	12	15	104
Owings,Micah								13	2	4	1	20
Padilla,Vicente	6	3	14	13	5	6	12	2	8	8	5	82
Pagan,Angel							3	5	3	12	23	46
Pagnozzi,Matt										0	2	2
Palmer,Matt										10	1	11
Papelbon,Jonathan						4	19	15	15	15	10	78
Park,Chan Ho	57	16	5	0	4	5	4	0	6	4	3	104
Parnell,Bobby									0	2	3	5
Parra,Gerardo										9	6	15
Parra,Manny								2	8	0	2	12
Parrish,John	0	0		2	6	2		2	2		1	15
Patterson,Corey	0	3	8	13	17	4	13	8	2	0	7	75
Patterson,Eric								0	2	3	4	9
Patton,Troy								1				1
Paul,Xavier										0	0	0
Pauley,David							0		0		4	4
Paulino,Felipe									0	0	1	1
Paulino,Ronny						0	14	10	3	8	8	43
Pavano,Carl	17	0	3	9	19	3		1	1	7	15	75
Payton,Jay	14	3	15	15	15	12	15	7	6		1	103
Pearce,Steve								2	2	2	1	7

Player	<01	01	02	03	04	05	06	07	08	09	10	Career
Peavy,Jake			3	7	15	16	12	21	13	6	6	99
Pedroia,Dustin							2	18	26	24	12	82
Pelfrey,Mike							0	1	12	4	12	29
Pena,Brayan						0	1	0	0	2	4	7
Pena,Carlos		3	11	9	11	7	0	28	22	17	16	124
Pena,Ramiro										4	3	7
Pena,Tony							1	11	6	6	4	28
Pence,Hunter								18	19	17	21	75
Penn,Hayden						0	0			0	0	0
Pennington,Cliff									3	7	19	29
Peralta,Jhonny				5	0	25	15	21	19	10	16	111
Peralta,Joel						2	5	6	0	0	5	18
Perdomo,Luis										1	0	1
Perez,Chris									4	3	13	20
Perez,Oliver			4	1	16	2	0	10	8	1	0	42
Perez,Rafael							1	9	8	0	6	24
Perkins,Glen							1	2	7	2	0	12
Perry,Ryan										4	5	9
Pestano,Vinnie											0	0
Petersen,Bryan											0	0
Pettitte,Andy	86	13	11	14	5	21	12	13	11	11	10	206
Phillips,Brandon			1	4	0	0	14	17	19	19	18	92
Phillips,Paul				0	2	2	0	0		3	0	7
Pie,Felix								5	2	5	6	18
Pierre,Juan	3	17	15	20	22	14	15	12	9	12	14	153
Pierzynski,A.J.	4	15	18	22	12	11	14	8	8	10	12	134
Pineiro,Joel	0	7	14	13	5	3	0	5	3	13	10	73
Pinto,Renyel							2	4	3	5	1	15
Plouffe,Trevor											0	0
Podsednik,Scott		0	1	22	13	12	9	1	2	15	15	90
Polanco,Placido	16	14	16	18	17	22	14	24	15	21	16	193
Porcello,Rick										13	5	18
Posada,Jorge	60	23	22	28	21	19	24	24	5	19	10	255
Posey,Buster										0	20	20
Powell,Landon										5	2	7
Prado,Martin							2	1	9	12	22	46
Presley,Alex											0	0
Price,David									1	6	17	24
Proctor,Scott					1	0	9	6	0	0		16
Pujols,Albert		29	32	41	37	34	37	32	34	39	32	347
Punto,Nick		0	0	1	4	6	12	5	10	11	5	54
Purcey,David									1	0	2	3
Putz,J.J.				0	3	5	17	20	5	1	8	59
Qualls,Chad					4	7	9	9	11	8	0	48
Quentin,Carlos							5	5	23	8	15	56
Quinlan,Robb				1	8	2	8	1	3	2	0	25
Quintero,Humberto				0	1	1	0	1	3	4	6	16
Quiroz,Guillermo					0	0	0	1	1	0	0	2
Raburn,Ryan					0			4	3	9	11	27
Ramirez,Alexei									18	15	20	53
Ramirez,Aramis	5	27	6	20	19	18	21	21	25	15	13	190
Ramirez,Edwar								0	5	0	0	5
Ramirez,Hanley						0	25	27	32	34	22	140
Ramirez,Manny	167	25	29	28	25	33	27	14	31	18	11	408
Ramirez,Max									2		1	3
Ramirez,Ramon							7	0	9	8	7	31
Ramos,Cesar										1	0	1
Ramos,Wilson											3	3
Ransom,Cody		0	0	0	2			2	3	1	1	9
Rapada,Clay								0	2	0	1	3
Rasmus,Colby										13	17	30
Rauch,Jon			0		4	2	8	10	9	7	9	49
Ray,Chris							4	12	6	0	5	27
Ray,Robert										1	0	1
Raynor,John											0	0
Reddick,Josh										0	1	1
Redmond,Mike	21	6	13	1	6	7	6	11	3	1	1	76
Reed,Jeremy					3	9	1	0	4	1	0	18
Reimold,Nolan										10	0	10
Renteria,Edgar	69	13	26	25	16	15	19	19	11	10	6	229
Repko,Jason						5	4		0	0	2	11
Resop,Chris							0	1	0	0	2	3

Player	<01	01	02	03	04	05	06	07	08	09	10	Career
Revere,Ben											0	0
Reyes,Anthony						1	3	0	5	0		9
Reyes,Dennys	11	1	4	0	4	1	9	2	6	3	3	44
Reyes,Jo-Jo								0	0	0	0	0
Reyes,Jose				12	4	16	28	24	28	5	18	135
Reynolds,Mark								14	17	20	16	67
Reynolds,Matt											2	2
Rhodes,Arthur	41	12	11	4	2	6	3		6	7	8	100
Rhymes,Will											6	6
Richard,Clayton									0	8	10	18
Richardson,Dustin										1	1	2
Rincon,Juan		0	0	7	12	10	8	2	1	1	0	41
Ring,Royce						0	1	2	0	0		3
Rios,Alex					7	9	18	22	20	11	18	105
Riske,David	0	3	2	10	7	5	4	8	1	0	0	40
Rivera,Juan		0	1	4	12	9	18	1	4	16	10	75
Rivera,Mariano	82	19	9	17	18	19	16	12	20	15	14	241
Rivera,Mike		0	1	0			4	0	4	4	0	13
Rivera,Saul							5	7	6	0	0	18
Roberts,Brian		3	2	14	16	28	13	22	20	20	7	145
Roberts,Ryan							0	0	0	8	1	9
Robertson,David									2	3	4	9
Robertson,Nate			0	1	8	7	14	8	1	1	1	41
Rodney,Fernando			0	1		6	8	3	4	10	6	38
Rodriguez,Alex	148	37	35	31	29	34	25	37	23	23	21	443
Rodriguez,Francisco			1	9	17	14	17	15	16	10	11	110
Rodriguez,Francisco											2	2
Rodriguez,Henry										0	1	1
Rodriguez,Ivan	188	18	11	25	22	10	24	12	11	5	8	334
Rodriguez,Rafael										0	0	0
Rodriguez,Sean									3	0	9	12
Rodriguez,Wandy						2	2	7	9	16	11	47
Roenicke,Josh									0	1	0	1
Rogers,Esmil										0	0	0
Rogers,Mark											1	1
Rohlinger,Ryan									0	0	0	0
Rolen,Scott	94	29	26	24	35	5	21	11	11	17	18	291
Rollins,Jimmy	1	20	17	18	24	21	25	28	24	19	14	211
Romero,J.C.	1	1	14	3	8	5	0	8	7	1	3	51
Romero,Niuman										0	0	0
Romero,Ricky										10	14	24
Romine,Andrew											0	0
Romo,Sergio									4	4	8	16
Rosa,Carlos									0	1	1	2
Rosales,Adam									0	3	8	11
Rosales,Leo									2	2	0	4
Rosario,Sandy											0	0
Ross,Cody			1			0	6	10	16	16	14	63
Ross,David			1	4	2	3	13	7	5	6	6	47
Ross,Tyson											0	0
Rowand,Aaron		5	7	6	20	18	7	21	14	15	7	120
Rowland-Smith,Ryan								2	9	7	0	18
Ruiz,Carlos							2	13	6	13	19	53
Ruiz,Randy									2	3	0	5
Runzler,Dan									1	3		4
Rupe,Josh							1	2	3	0	0	6
Russell,Adam									2	1	0	3
Russell,James										1		1
Russo,Kevin										0		0
Ryal,Rusty										2	1	3
Ryan,Brendan								5	2	14	8	29
Ryan,Mike			0	4	0	1						5
Rzepczynski,Marc										4	2	6
Sabathia,CC		12	13	13	11	12	15	24	23	18	19	160
Saito,Takashi							18	17	9	6	5	55
Salas,Fernando											1	1
Salazar,Oscar			1						3	7	3	14
Sale,Chris											5	5
Saltalamacchia,J.								5	6	6	0	17
Samardzija,Jeff									3	0	0	3
Sampson,Chris							4	5	7	3	0	19
Sanabia,Alex											4	4
Sanches,Brian							0	0	0	6	6	12

WIN SHARES BY YEAR

Player	<01	01	02	03	04	05	06	07	08	09	10	Career
Sanchez,Angel						0					7	7
Sanchez,Anibal							10	1	0	5	11	27
Sanchez,Freddy			0	1	0	12	23	21	11	13	14	95
Sanchez,Gaby									1	1	17	19
Sanchez,Jonathan							2	0	6	7	14	29
Sanchez,Romulo									1	1	1	3
Sandoval,Pablo									6	27	9	42
Santana,Carlos											7	7
Santana,Ervin						6	12	3	19	6	14	60
Santana,Johan	2	2	10	16	26	23	24	17	21	14	15	170
Santiago,Ramon			4	5	0	0	1	2	6	7	9	34
Santos,Sergio											5	5
Sardinha,Dane				0		0			1	1	1	3
Saunders,Joe				0	4	7	18	11	6			46
Saunders,Michael										1	6	7
Sborz,Jay										0		0
Scales,Bobby										2	1	3
Scherzer,Max									4	9	13	26
Schierholtz,Nate								2	3	8	5	18
Schlereth,Daniel										0	2	2
Schlichting,Travis										0	1	1
Schlitter,Brian											0	0
Schmidt,Konrad											0	0
Schneider,Brian	1	2	7	13	17	16	9	11	10	4	4	94
Schoeneweis,Scott	7	9	5	3	4	6	6	2	4	0	0	46
Schumaker,Skip						0	0	7	16	18	14	55
Scott,Luke							11	11	11	11	14	58
Scutaro,Marco			0	2	11	11	11	8	15	21	15	94
Seay,Bobby		0		1	2	0	0	6	3	6		18
Seddon,Chris								0			0	0
Shealy,Ryan						2	6	1	3		0	12
Sheets,Ben		6	8	10	21	11	7	10	15		3	91
Sherrill,George					1	2	3	8	7	13	0	34
Shields,James							6	12	15	11	3	47
Shields,Scot		2	6	12	11	13	11	8	8	0	0	71
Shoppach,Kelly						0	3	7	14	7	4	35
Silva,Carlos			7	5	14	14	2	11	0		7	60
Simon,Alfredo									0	0	4	4
Sinkbeil,Brett											0	0
Sipp,Tony										3	4	7
Sizemore,Grady					5	24	24	29	26	13	1	122
Sizemore,Scott											2	2
Slama,Anthony											0	0
Slaten,Doug						1	4	1	0		3	9
Slowey,Kevin								3	10	5	8	26
Smith,Chris									0	2	0	2
Smith,Greg									9	0		9
Smith,Joe								3	6	2	3	14
Smith,Jordan											3	3
Smith,Seth								1	3	14	9	27
Smoak,Justin											7	7
Snell,Ian					0	1	8	11	2	5	0	27
Snider,Travis									3	4	8	15
Snyder,Brad											0	0
Snyder,Brandon											1	1
Snyder,Chris					2	4	7	16	15	3	8	55
Sogard,Eric											0	0
Sonnanstine,Andy								3	10	0	3	16
Soria,Joakim								13	17	12	15	57
Soriano,Alfonso	0	16	28	27	16	16	26	20	16	10	15	190
Soriano,Rafael			1	7	0	1	7	9	2	12	14	53
Sosa,Jorge			2	5	3	14	2	6	0	0	1	33
Soto,Geovany						0	0	3	21	8	15	47
Span,Denard									16	21	20	57
Spilborghs,Ryan						0	3	9	8	7	9	36
Springer,Russ	23	0		0	1	3	5	8	6	3	0	49
St. Pierre,Max											0	0
Stairs,Matt	71	11	7	12	11	14	7	13	6	3	3	158
Stammen,Craig										3	3	6
Stange,Daniel											0	0
Stanton,Mike											13	13
Stauffer,Tim						0	1	0		3	9	13
Stavinoha,Nick									0	1	1	2

Player	<01	01	02	03	04	05	06	07	08	09	10	Career
Stern,Adam						0	0	0		0		0
Stetter,Mitch								1	3	4	0	8
Stevens,Jeff										0	0	0
Stewart,Chris						0	1	0		0		1
Stewart,Ian								1	9	11	8	29
Stokes,Brian							1	0	3	4	0	8
Stoner,Tobi										1	0	1
Storen,Drew											5	5
Strasburg,Stephen											5	5
Street,Huston						16	14	10	10	15	9	74
Strickland,Scott	8	10	5	2	0						0	25
Strop,Pedro										0	0	0
Stubbs,Drew										5	18	23
Sullivan,Cory						10	6	4	0	4	0	24
Suppan,Jeff	31	12	9	13	9	13	12	9	5	2	3	118
Sutton,Drew										3	2	5
Suzuki,Ichiro		36	26	23	27	22	24	33	19	28	23	261
Suzuki,Kurt								7	17	17	10	51
Sweeney,Brian				1	0		5				2	8
Sweeney,Mike	59	18	18	14	14	16	5	5	3	6	4	162
Sweeney,Ryan							0	0	12	12	8	32
Swisher,Nick					1	12	20	18	12	18	22	103
Tabata,Jose											14	14
Takahashi,Hisanori											9	9
Talbot,Mitch									0		6	6
Tallet,Brian			2	0		0	4	4	5	4	0	19
Tankersley,Taylor							5	4	0	0	0	9
Taschner,Jack						3	0	2	2	1	0	8
Tatis,Fernando	46	2	6	1			2		13	8	0	78
Tatum,Craig										1	3	4
Taveras,Willy					0	13	13	11	6	5	1	49
Teagarden,Taylor									4	3	1	8
Teahen,Mark						9	18	15	11	9	3	65
Teixeira,Mark				12	24	33	21	25	28	26	24	193
Tejada,Miguel	51	25	32	26	28	26	23	14	14	22	18	279
Tejada,Ruben											3	3
Tejeda,Robinson						5	4	0	3	6	4	22
Texeira,Kanekoa											2	2
Thames,Marcus			0	0	6	1	11	6	7	4	7	42
Thatcher,Joe								2	0	3	5	10
Thayer,Dale										0	0	0
Theriot,Ryan						0	6	11	16	17	11	61
Thole,Josh										2	8	10
Thomas,Brad		0		0	0						5	5
Thomas,Justin								0		0	0	0
Thome,Jim	161	31	33	29	20	4	26	21	17	11	14	366
Thompson,Brad						5	5	4	3	2	0	19
Thompson,Rich								0	0	1	3	4
Thornton,Matt					2	1	7	4	10	12	12	48
Threets,Erick									0	1	2	3
Tillman,Chris										2	1	3
Todd,Jess										0	0	0
Tolbert,Matt									3	5	3	11
Tulleson,Steven											2	2
Tomlin,Josh											4	4
Torrealba,Yorvit		1	4	7	4	4	6	6	4	9	12	57
Torres,Andres			0	0	0	0				8	23	31
Torres,Carlos										0	0	0
Towles,J.R.								3	2	0	2	7
Tracy,Chad					11	19	14	6	4	3	2	59
Treanor,Matt					1	2	5	6	5	0	3	22
Troncoso,Ramon									2	8	2	12
Trumbo,Mark											0	0
Tuiasosopo,Matt									0	0	1	1
Tulowitzki,Troy							1	24	9	24	25	83
Turner,Justin										0	0	0
Uehara,Koji										4	9	13
Uggla,Dan							23	16	24	18	24	105
Upton,B.J.					4		2	22	23	13	18	82
Upton,Justin								1	8	19	14	42
Uribe,Juan		7	10	9	18	17	11	13	11	13	16	125
Utley,Chase				5	8	25	27	28	30	32	25	180
Valaika,Chris										0		0

Player	<01	01	02	03	04	05	06	07	08	09	10	Career
Valbuena,Luis									1	6	4	11
Valdes,Raul										2		2
Valdez,Cesar											0	0
Valdez,Merkin				0				2	1	0		3
Valdez,Wilson				1	2		2		1	9		15
Valencia,Danny											12	12
Valverde,Jose				11	3	13	4	14	14	11	10	80
Van Every,Jonathan									1	1	0	2
VandenHurk,Rick								0	0	3	0	3
Vargas,Claudio				7	3	6	7	5	2	4	0	34
Vargas,Jason						4	1	0		3	10	18
Varitek,Jason	24	8	12	16	18	18	7	14	8	7	3	135
Varvaro,Anthony											0	0
Vasquez,Esmerling										3	1	4
Vazquez,Javier	22	21	13	21	9	12	11	18	11	16	5	159
Velez,Eugenio								1	4	6	1	12
Venable,Will									3	8	15	26
Venters,Jonny											9	9
Veras,Jose						1	1	5	2	4		13
Verlander,Justin						0	15	16	8	21	17	77
Viciedo,Dayan											3	3
Victorino,Shane				0		1	11	11	20	22	23	88
Villanueva,Carlos							4	8	6	2	2	22
Villar,Henry											0	0
Viola,Pedro										0	0	0
Vizquel,Omar	154	12	21	5	18	20	20	12	5	6	7	280
Volquez,Edinson						0	0	2	16	2	3	23
Volstad,Chris									7	4	6	17
Votto,Joey								3	19	24	33	79
Wagner,Billy	51	13	16	19	10	18	14	12	10	2	17	182
Wainwright,Adam						0	9	13	11	21	20	74
Wakefield,Tim	75	11	15	12	8	15	7	10	10	8	2	173
Walden,Jordan											2	2
Walker,Neil										0	16	16
Walker,Tyler			0		4	7	3	3	4	3	2	26
Wallace,Brett											1	1
Walters,P.J.										0	0	0
Wang,Chien-Ming						7	16	15	7	0		45
Watson,Matt				0	1					0		1
Weaver,Jeff	19	13	14	2	11	13	3	1		5	1	82
Weaver,Jered							14	12	11	17	19	73
Webb,Brandon			17	11	17	20	22	21	0			108
Webb,Ryan										1	4	5
Weeks,Rickie				0		9	10	14	16	7	29	85
Weinhardt,Robbie										0		0
Wellemeyer,Todd				0	1	0	4	4	12	0	0	21
Wells,Casper											4	4
Wells,Randy									1	13	9	23
Wells,Vernon	1	3	18	26	13	20	24	15	15	8	21	164
Werth,Jayson			1	1	11	9		13	17	26	22	100
West,Sean										4	0	4
Westbrook,Jake	0	2	1	6	15	8	13	9	3		9	66
Wheeler,Dan	2	0		3	3	10	12	4	12	6	4	56
White,Sean									1	8	0	9
Whiteside,Eli					0					3	2	5
Wieters,Matt										9	12	21
Wigginton,Ty			3	14	10	4	13	11	14	4	8	81
Williams,Randy				0	1					1	0	2
Willingham,Josh					0	0	14	19	13	11	14	71
Willis,Dontrelle			14	9	22	13	7	0	0		1	66
Willits,Reggie							1	14	1	0	4	20
Wilson,Bobby									0	0	3	3
Wilson,Brian							1	5	9	15	17	47
Wilson,C.J.						0	3	9	2	11	15	40
Wilson,Jack		5	12	12	22	14	12	19	7	9	4	116
Wilson,Josh							0		3	3	7	13
Winn,Randy	11	10	23	21	17	22	13	16	19	16	3	171
Wise,DeWayne	0	1		3			0	0	2	2	4	12
Wolf,Randy	17	11	15	12	6	4	2	5	7	14	9	102
Wolf,Ross								0			1	1
Wood,Blake											2	2
Wood,Brandon								0	2	0	2	4
Wood,Kerry	21	13	12	18	9	4	2	2	12	6	4	103
Wood,Tim										2	0	2
Wood,Travis											6	6
Woodward,Chris	2	1	10	9	4	4	3	1		1	0	35
Worley,Vance											2	2
Worth,Danny											3	3
Wright,David					9	26	30	34	27	20	24	170
Wright,Jamey	32	7	2	2	5	4	4	5	3	4	3	71
Wright,Wesley									3	1	0	4
Wuertz,Michael					2	6	4	6	3	10	3	34
Youkilis,Kevin					8	3	22	20	27	28	19	127
Young,Chris			2	10	12	12	5	1	3			45
Young,Chris							2	14	17	8	19	60
Young,Delmon							2	17	13	7	22	61
Young,Delwyn							0	2	1	8	3	14
Young,Michael	0	7	11	22	25	29	26	23	20	17	16	196
Young Jr.,Eric										0	2	2
Zagurski,Mike								1		0		1
Zambrano,Carlos		0	5	18	20	18	17	16	16	10	11	131
Zaun,Gregg	30	4	2	2	11	14	8	9	8	7	2	97
Zavada,Clay										4		4
Zawadzki,Lance											1	1
Ziegler,Brad									12	7	5	24
Zimmerman,Ryan						2	24	20	9	21	23	99
Zimmermann,Jordan										3	1	4
Zito,Barry	9	15	25	18	12	13	17	8	5	10	7	139
Zobrist,Ben							2	1	8	27	21	59
Zumaya,Joel							12	3	1	2	5	23

Instant Replay

Established just before the end of the season in 2008, instant replay has become a big part of baseball. Umpires review disputable home run calls to determine whether the ball left the playing field, was fair or foul, or was interfered with by a fan. Since its inception two years ago, 35% of the 133 reviewed calls have been overturned.

The chart below summarizes the results. The next page provides the details of every instant replay review since 2008.

Instant Replay Summary

Season	Instant Replays	Calls Overturned	Percentage
2008	7	2	29%
2009	59	22	37%
2010	67	23	34%
Totals	133	47	35%

Date	Matchup	Pitcher	Hitter	Inning	Outs	Men On	Score	Initial Ruling	Video Ruling
9/3/2008	NYA@TB	Troy Percival	Alex Rodriguez	9	2	_2_	6-3	HR	HR
9/9/2008	PIT@HOU	Jesse Chavez	Hunter Pence	6	2	12_	8-2	2B	2B
9/19/2008	MIN@TB	Boof Bonser	Carlos Pena	4	2	12_	6-0	Fan Int	HR
9/23/2008	CIN@HOU	Chris Sampson	Joey Votto	7	2	1__	2-1	1B	1B
9/24/2008	LAA@SEA	Felix Hernandez	Vladimir Guerrero	5	1	___	2-2	Foul	Foul
9/26/2008	LAN@SF	Scott Proctor	Bengie Molina	6	1	1__	0-2	1B	HR
9/26/2008	WAS@PHI	Joe Blanton	Kory Casto	6	2	___	3-7	HR	HR
4/19/2009	CLE@NYA	Jensen Lewis	Jorge Posada	7	1	1__	2-3	HR	HR
4/22/2009	OAK@NYA	CC Sabathia	Kurt Suzuki	2	0	12_	0-0	HR	HR
4/24/2009	SF@ARI	Tim Lincecum	Eric Byrnes	3	2	___	0-1	2B	2B
4/25/2009	SEA@LAA	Carlos Silva	Gary Matthews Jr.	3	0	___	0-3	Fan Int	Fan Int
4/29/2009	FLA@NYN	Josh Johnson	Fernando Tatis	6	0	___	2-2	HR	HR
5/13/2009	FLA@MIL	Braden Looper	Ross Gload	6	2	_2_	5-8	HR	Foul
5/13/2009	STL@PIT	Joel Pineiro	Adam LaRoche	1	2	__3	0-0	HR	2B
5/23/2009	TEX@HOU	Scott Feldman	Miguel Tejada	1	1	___	0-0	HR	HR
5/23/2009	NYN@BOS	Jonathan Papelbon	Omir Santos	9	2	1__	1-2	2B	HR
5/24/2009	NYN@BOS	Tim Redding	Kevin Youkilis	5	0	___	3-5	Foul	Foul
5/25/2009	WAS@NYN	John Lannan	Gary Sheffield	6	0	12_	1-1	HR	HR
5/27/2009	WAS@NYN	Jordan Zimmermann	Daniel Murphy	6	0	1__	3-3	2B	2B
5/28/2009	TB@CLE	Jensen Lewis	Willy Aybar	6	1	___	0-2	HR	HR
6/3/2009	BAL@SEA	Jason Vargas	Aubrey Huff	1	2	1__	0-0	HR	Foul
6/4/2009	BOS@DET	Tim Wakefield	Jeff Larish	6	1	1__	3-6	Foul	Foul
6/6/2009	TEX@BOS	Derek Holland	Mike Lowell	2	1	___	0-0	2B	2B
6/9/2009	LAA@TB	James Shields	Howie Kendrick	5	0	___	2-0	3B	3B
6/9/2009	SEA@BAL	Jason Vargas	Melvin Mora	1	2	1__	1-0	HR	Fan Int
6/10/2009	PIT@ATL	Jeff Karstens	Brian McCann	6	2	_2_	0-2	2B	2B
6/13/2009	CIN@KC	Bronson Arroyo	Billy Butler	4	0	___	5-3	Foul	Foul
6/19/2009	MIL@DET	Braden Looper	Dusty Ryan	4	2	1__	3-4	HR	2B
6/19/2009	MIL@DET	Braden Looper	Miguel Cabrera	3	2	___	2-3	1B	HR
6/21/2009	LAN@LAA	John Lackey	James Loney	8	2	__3	2-0	HR	HR
6/25/2009	PHI@TB	Jack Taschner	Pat Burrell	7	2	1__	10-4	GR 2B	GR 2B
7/1/2009	SEA@NYA	Jarrod Washburn	Melky Cabrera	5	1	___	1-1	HR	HR
7/3/2009	HOU@SF	Felipe Paulino	Travis Ishikawa	2	2	1_3	6-0	2B	HR
7/6/2009	PIT@HOU	Virgil Vasquez	Geoff Blum	1	2	12_	0-0	3B	3B
7/12/2009	WAS@HOU	Jordan Zimmermann	Carlos Lee	4	0	1__	1-0	2B	2B
7/17/2009	LAA@OAK	Trevor Cahill	Kendry Morales	2	1	___	0-0	HR	HR
7/19/2009	MIN@TEX	Francisco Liriano	Andruw Jones	4	1	___	1-3	HR	Foul
7/20/2009	CIN@LAN	Jason Schmidt	Willy Taveras	1	0	___	0-0	3B	3B
7/22/2009	MIL@PIT	Jeff Suppan	Ryan Doumit	3	1	___	4-2	2B	HR
7/29/2009	PHI@ARI	Tyler Walker	Gerardo Parra	8	0	___	3-0	2B	2B
7/29/2009	WAS@MIL	Garrett Mock	Ryan Braun	3	1	1__	0-4	HR	3B
7/31/2009	BOS@BAL	John Smoltz	Nolan Reimold	3	1	_2_	1-3	HR	HR
8/2/2009	LAA@MIN	Shane Loux	Joe Mauer	8	2	___	4-13	2B	2B
8/10/2009	CHN@COL	Esmailin Caridad	Troy Tulowitzki	2	2	123	4-0	Foul	Foul
8/11/2009	PHI@CHN	Angel Guzman	Carlos Ruiz	9	2	___	3-2	HR	HR
8/11/2009	TOR@NYA	Jesse Carlson	Jorge Posada	8	0	___	4-4	HR	HR
8/14/2009	NYA@SEA	R. Rowland-Smith	Jorge Posada	2	0	___	0-2	2B	2B
8/16/2009	HOU@MIL	Braden Looper	Hunter Pence	6	1	___	4-2	HR	Foul
8/20/2009	MIN@TEX	Bobby Keppel	Michael Young	6	1	_2_	7-1	2B	2B
8/25/2009	DET@LAA	John Lackey	Curtis Granderson	7	0	___	3-3	3B	3B
8/25/2009	TEX@NYA	Kevin Millwood	Robinson Cano	4	0	___	4-7	HR	HR
8/26/2009	OAK@SEA	Luke French	Jack Cust	6	1	___	3-4	Foul	Foul
8/28/2009	NYN@CHN	Pat Misch	Aramis Ramirez	6	0	___	1-1	Foul	Foul
8/28/2009	OAK@LAA	Craig Breslow	Kendry Morales	6	2	1__	1-6	Foul	Foul
8/31/2009	PIT@CIN	Paul Maholm	Brandon Phillips	5	0	___	4-0	HR	Foul
9/5/2009	NYA@TOR	Andy Pettitte	Randy Ruiz	2	0	___	0-1	HR	Foul
9/10/2009	DET@KC	Eddie Bonine	Alberto Callaspo	8	1	___	6-4	HR	HR
9/10/2009	ATL@HOU	Derek Lowe	Lance Berkman	3	1	12_	1-6	HR	HR
9/12/2009	SEA@TEX	Brandon Morrow	Chris Davis	5	0	___	2-5	HR	GR 2B
9/22/2009	SF@ARI	Matt Cain	Gerardo Parra	3	1	1__	5-4	HR	2B
9/23/2009	SF@ARI	Jonathan Sanchez	Rusty Ryal	6	1	1__	0-3	3B	3B
9/27/2009	SD@ARI	Edward Mujica	Chad Tracy	6	1	___	2-3	HR	HR
9/29/2009	ARI@SF	Jonathan Sanchez	Ryan Roberts	4	2	___	1-2	HR	GR 2B
9/30/2009	NYN@WAS	John Lannan	Jeff Francoeur	2	0	1__	0-0	2B	2B
9/30/2009	HOU@PHI	Pedro Martinez	J.R. Towles	2	0	___	1-1	2B	HR
10/31/2009	NYA@PHI	Cole Hamels	Alex Rodriguez	4	1	1__	0-3	2B	HR
4/06/2010	SF@HOU	Barry Zito	Jeff Keppinger	6	1	___	0-3	2B	2B
4/11/2010	WAS@NYN	Johan Santana	Josh Willingham	1	1	123	0-0	3B	HR
4/12/2010	BOS@MIN	Carl Pavano	Mike Cameron	5	0	___	1-4	Foul	Foul
4/13/2010	CIN@FLA	Nate Robertson	Jay Bruce	2	0	___	3-0	HR	1B

Date	Matchup	Pitcher	Hitter	Inning	Outs	Men On	Score	Initial Ruling	Video Ruling
4/20/2010	CLE@MIN	Kevin Slowey	Austin Kearns	5	1	___	1-5	2B	2B
4/23/2010	CHN@MIL	Ryan Dempster	Prince Fielder	1	2	1__	0-2	2B	2B
4/28/2010	CLE@LAA	Ervin Santana	Lou Marson	6	0	___	1-0	2B	2B
5/03/2010	STL@PHI	Jaime Garcia	Chase Utley	1	2	___	0-0	Foul	Foul
5/04/2010	NYN@CIN	Fernando Nieve	Scott Rolen	8	2	___	3-4	HR	HR
5/07/2010	CHN@CIN	Carlos Fisher	Marlon Byrd	8	1	1__	10-4	2B	2B
5/10/2010	TOR@BOS	John Lackey	Alex Gonzalez	2	0	1__	0-2	2B	2B
5/11/2010	WAS@NYN	Miguel Batista	Ike Davis	8	2	123	8-6	Foul	Foul
5/16/2010	TEX@TOR	Colby Lewis	John Buck	4	2	123	1-1	2B	2B
5/18/2010	CHA@DET	Freddy Garcia	Brandon Inge	6	1	___	2-4	HR	Foul
5/19/2010	MIN@BOS	Scott Baker	David Ortiz	4	1	_2_	0-1	3B	HR
5/21/2010	LAA@STL	Joel Pineiro	Felipe Lopez	3	2	___	8-4	HR	HR
5/23/2010	NYA@NYN	Johan Santana	Francisco Cervelli	7	2	1__	0-6	1B	1B
5/27/2010	WAS@SF	Barry Zito	Adam Dunn	7	1	1__	3-2	2B	2B
5/28/2010	LAN@COL	Carlos Monasterios	Clint Barmes	4	1	___	3-0	HR	HR
5/28/2010	TEX@MIN	Kevin Slowey	Ian Kinsler	4	1	___	0-1	HR	Foul
5/29/2010	TEX@MIN	C.J. Wilson	Delmon Young	3	0	___	0-1	Foul	Foul
6/01/2010	LAA@KC	Brian Bannister	Hideki Matsui	6	1	1__	3-5	2B	2B
6/03/2010	OAK@BOS	Jerry Blevins	Marco Scutaro	8	0	___	6-9	HR	HR
6/05/2010	BOS@BAL	Jeremy Guthrie	Marco Scutaro	6	1	___	0-0	Foul	Foul
6/08/2010	BOS@CLE	David Huff	Kevin Youkilis	4	2	_2_	0-1	2B	2B
6/08/2010	SD@NYN	Clayton Richard	Jose Reyes	7	2	___	0-1	2B	HR
6/16/2010	SEA@STL	Jason Vargas	Albert Pujols	4	1	___	0-1	2B	2B
6/18/2010	LAN@BOS	Carlos Monasterios	J.D. Drew	1	2	___	2-0	2B	HR
7/01/2010	NYN@WAS	Johan Santana	Ian Desmond	5	0	___	0-1	2B	2B
7/03/2010	NYN@WAS	Francisco Rodriguez	Adam Dunn	9	1	123	3-5	2B	2B
7/03/2010	PHI@PIT	Paul Maholm	Jayson Werth	4	0	1__	7-1	2B	2B
7/03/2010	BAL@BOS	Robert Manuel	Jake Fox	9	2	1__	1-9	2B	HR
7/05/2010	CLE@TEX	Joe Smith	Nelson Cruz	7	1	1_3	3-9	HR	Foul
7/07/2010	KC@SEA	Chad Cordero	Billy Butler	9	2	___	6-3	2B	HR
7/10/2010	SF@WAS	Miguel Batista	Buster Posey	9	0	1__	8-5	HR	HR
7/11/2010	CIN@PHI	Matt Maloney	Carlos Ruiz	3	0	___	0-0	2B	2B
7/11/2010	CIN@PHI	Matt Maloney	Jayson Werth	4	0		1-0	2B	2B
7/16/2010	COL@CIN	Bronson Arroyo	Miguel Olivo	8	0	___	1-3	HR	HR
7/19/2010	CLE@MIN	Aaron Laffey	Delmon Young	4	0	_2_	0-2	1B	1B
7/22/2010	WAS@CIN	Edinson Volquez	Willie Harris	3	1	___	5-0	3B	3B
7/24/2010	TB@CLE	Mitch Talbot	Ben Zobrist	5	2	12_	0-3	3B	HR
7/26/2010	BOS@LAA	Scott Atchison	Hideki Matsui	8	2	1__	1-4	HR	HR
7/26/2010	FLA@SF	Taylor Tankersley	Aaron Rowand	7	1	1__	0-3	HR	HR
7/30/2010	SEA@MIN	Doug Fister	Alexi Casilla	5	2	__3	3-0	3B	HR
8/01/2010	SEA@MIN	Francisco Liriano	Josh Wilson	2	2	___	0-0	Foul	Foul
8/05/2010	PHI@FLA	Will Ohman	Ben Francisco	10	1	___	5-4	Foul	Foul
8/06/2010	COL@PIT	Joel Hanrahan	Dexter Fowler	9	0	___	4-3	HR	3B
8/06/2010	MIN@CLE	Chris Perez	Jim Thome	9	0	1__	4-6	2B	2B
8/07/2010	COL@PIT	Huston Street	Andrew McCutchen	10	0	___	5-7	HR	2B
8/12/2010	FLA@WAS	Livan Hernandez	Mike Stanton	2	1	1__	0-0	3B	HR
8/13/2010	PHI@NYN	Cole Hamels	Mike Hessman	5	0	___	0-0	HR	3B
8/16/2010	TEX@TB	David Price	Bengie Molina	7	0	___	0-2	2B	2B
8/23/2010	MIN@TEX	Nick Blackburn	David Murphy	1	2	12_	0-0	3B	3B
8/25/2010	ARI@SD	Wade LeBlanc	Stephen Drew	1	0	___	0-0	2B	HR
8/29/2010	FLA@ATL	Leo Nunez	Brian McCann	9	2	___	6-6	2B	HR
9/02/2010	DET@MIN	Scott Baker	Austin Jackson	2	2	___	2-0	3B	3B
9/04/2010	COL@SD	Jason Hammel	Adrian Gonzalez	1	2	1__	0-0	2B	2B
9/04/2010	TB@BAL	James Shields	Luke Scott	5	1	___	5-2	2B	2B
9/06/2010	CHA@DET	Chris Sale	Brandon Inge	8	2	1__	4-4	HR	Foul
9/07/2010	CLE@LAA	Trevor Bell	Travis Hafner	6	0	___	1-1	HR	HR
9/07/2010	TEX@TOR	Scott Feldman	John Buck	2	2	___	0-0	2B	HR
9/14/2010	DET@TEX	Jeremy Bonderman	David Murphy	4	0	___	1-4	HR	HR
9/15/2010	DET@TEX	Colby Lewis	Ryan Raburn	1	2	1__	1-0	2B	2B
9/20/2010	KC@DET	Zack Greinke	Will Rhymes	6	2	1__	4-5	3B	HR
9/28/2010	OAK@LAA	Dallas Braden	Peter Bourjos	7	0	_23	3-2	HR	Foul
10/02/2010	MIL@CIN	Brandon Kintzler	Jay Bruce	5	0	___	3-1	HR	HR
10/03/2010	PIT@FLA	Brian Burres	Wes Helms	6	2	12_	2-2	HR	GR 2B

457

The Hall of Fame Monitor
A New Feature of the Book

Bill James

The purpose of this section is to summarize as tersely and impartially as we can where players from our generation stand with respect to the Hall of Fame, as nearly as we are able to see that in mid-career.

If a player is listed at "100" or above in the charts that accompany this article, that means that he is a fully-qualified Hall of Famer at this point, as best we are able to determine. If he is at "73", or "64" or "57", then he *may* be a Hall of Famer, either because of things that he has not yet done but will do in the future or because one set or another of Hall of Fame voters may take a liking to him. Many players are in the Hall of Fame who have scores short of 100, and some are in who have scores less than 60. We are not suggesting that this is wrong; merely, that it is difficult to anticipate.

There are, however, very few players in history who have scores over 100 and who are eligible for the Hall, but have not been selected. There are a handful, and it is likely that most of those will eventually be selected. I'm not going to get into names, because then it becomes a Hall of Fame argument, and this isn't a place for arguments; this is a place for objective information.

These estimates are based on a combination of two unrelated and very dissimilar systems. The question we ask in both cases is "Has this player done the things that Hall of Fame players have done?" OK, maybe it is "How many of the things that Hall of Fame players have done has this player done?", but. . .same concept.

One system is based on the Hall of Fame monitor that I first published almost 30 years ago, in one of the old Abstracts. I modified that system a little bit. The old system was originally set up so that a player at 100 was not a fully-qualified Hall of Famer, but rather, was in the middle of the gray area. The original theory was "Over 130—Hall of Famer, Under 70—Not a Hall of Famer, 70 to 130— Gray Area." I wanted a system here in which a player was either fully qualified—100 points—or could be said to be some percentage qualified, and so we took a few points out of the system to make it a little bit more conservative.

But basically, when we took the old system out of storage and dusted it off and tightened up a few of the riggings, we found that the old system still worked extremely well. There is very little evidence that the Hall of Fame standards have changed meaningfully in the last 30 years; mostly what has happened since then has been that many of the players who were outliers at that time have since been inducted. When I say "we", who I mean is myself, Rob Burckhard, Damon Lichtenwalner, and Jeff Spoljaric. The old system, as currently modified, consists of 32 "rules", which are as follows:

1) For each season that the player has hit .300 in 100 or more games, give him 2.5 points.   If he hit .350, make it 5 points; if .400, make it 15.

2) Give the player 4 points for each season in which he has had 200 or more hits.

3) Give the player 2 points for each season of 100 RBI and 2 points for each season of 100 runs scored.

4) Give the player 5 points for hitting 50 home runs in a season, 3 points for 40 home runs, 1 point for 30 home runs.

5) Give the player one point for hitting 40 doubles in a season.

6) Give the player 8 points for winning an MVP Award. . . 8 points for each MVP Award.

7) Give the player 3 points for each All-Star game appearance in a season in which the player played primarily shortstop, catcher or second base.

8) Oh, hell, let's give him 1 point for winning the Rookie of the Year Award, too; what harm can it do?

9) Give the player one point for winning a Gold Glove.

10) Give the player 5 points for being the regular shortstop or catcher on a World Championship team, 4 points for being the regular second baseman or center fielder, 3 points for third base, 2 points for being a regular wing outfielder, 1 point for being a regular first baseman.

11) Give the player 4 points for being the regular shortstop or catcher on a *league* championship team—a team that loses in the World Series--3 points for being the regular second baseman or center fielder, 1 point for third base.

12) Give the player 5 points for winning a batting title, 3 points for leading in home runs or RBI, 2 points for runs scored, 1 for hits, stolen bases, doubles or runs scored.   If he led in OPS, you can salute, but no points.

13) Give the player 30 points if he had 3,500 career hits, 20 points if 3,000, 10 points if 2,500, and 4 points if 2,000.

14) Give the player 20 points if he had 600 career homers, 15 points for 500, 10 points for 400, 3 points for 300.

15) Give the player 20 points if he played 1800 games in his career at catcher, 10 points if 1600.

16) Give the player 10 points if he played 2100 games in his career at second base or shortstop, or 5 points for 1800 games.

17) Give the player 10 points if he played 2000 games at third base.

18) Give the player an additional 5 points if his combined games played at second, shortstop and third base are 2500 or more.

19) Give the player 15 points for each season of 30 or more wins (as a pitcher), 8 points for 25 wins, 6 points for 23 wins, 4 for 20 wins, 2 for 18 wins, and 1 for 15 wins.

(For 19th century pitchers, subtract 10 wins from each season before awarding these points; in other words, 30 wins in 19th century baseball is counted as 20. Also, pay no attention to anything done in the National Association, 1871-1875. However, we don't believe there are any pitchers remaining in the game who were active in the 19th century. We're still doing research on Moyer.)

20) Give the player 5 points for 300 strikeouts, 3 points for 250 strikeouts, and 1 point for 200 or more strikeouts (as a pitcher. Mark Reynolds does not get points under this rule.)

21) Give the pitcher 5 points for 40 or more saves, 3 points for 30 or more, and 1 point for 20 or more.

22) A pitcher gets 8 points for winning an MVP Award, as a position player does, and 1 point for winning a Gold Glove and 1 point for a Rookie of the Year Award, the same as a position player. A pitcher also gets 5 points for winning a Cy Young Award, and 2 points for appearing in an All Star game.

23) Give the pitcher one point for throwing a no-hitter, even against Seattle.

24) Give the pitcher 2 points for leading the league in ERA, 1 point for leading in games, wins, innings, winning percentage, strikeouts or saves.

25) Give the pitcher 25 points if he has 300 or more wins, 15 if 275 wins, 10 if 250 wins, 5 if 225.

26) Give the pitcher 8 points if his career winning percentage was .625 or better, 5 points if it is .600 or better, 3 points if over .575 and 1 point if over .525, minimum, 190 decisions.

27) Give the pitcher 10 points if his career ERA was under 3.00, minimum 200 decisions.

28) Give the pitcher 20 points if he had (or has) 400 career saves, 10 points for 300 saves.

29) Give the pitcher 30 points if he appeared in 1000 career games, 20 points if 850 games, 10 points if 700 games.

30) Give the pitcher 20 points if he had more than 4,000 strikeouts, and 10 if he had 3,000 strikeouts.

31) When couples are seated together on the bus to the game, there must be at least three feet on the ground at all times. . .wait a minute, that's the wrong list.

32) Give the pitcher 2 points for each World Series start, 1 point for each World Series relief appearance, and 2 points for each win.

OK, that's one system. . .those 32 rules are one system. Total up the points under those 32 rules, and set that aside.

The other system—the new system—is much simpler. It is based on Win Shares, or actually, Win Shares with a caveat for relievers and one for catchers. But basically, for a season of 30 or more Win Shares, the formula is Win Shares, divided by 30, times 10, converted to the nearest integer. For a season of 10 to 29 Win Shares, the formula is Win Shares, divided by 30, SQUARED, times 10, converted into the nearest integer. For a season of less than 10 Win Shares, no points.

That's basically all. That's the whole system; add them up and if the total is 100 or more, Hall of Famer. These two formulas translate Win Shares for a season into Hall of Fame monitor points in the following way:

Win Shares Zero to 9	10	11	12	13	14	15	16	17	18	19	20	21	22	23	24
Points	0	1	1	2	2	2	3	3	3	4	4	4	5	5	6	6

Win Shares	25	26	27	28	29	30	31	32	33	34	35	36	37	38
Points	7	8	8	9	9	10	10	11	11	11	12	12	12	13

Win Shares	39	40	41	42	43	44	45	46	47	48	49	50	51	52
Points	13	13	14	14	14	15	15	15	16	16	16	17	17	17

Albert Pujols Win Shares by season are:

Year	2001	2002	2003	2004	2005	2006	2007	2008	2009	2010
Win Shares	29	32	41	37	34	37	32	34	39	32

We convert those into Hall of Fame points by the scale above:

Year	2001	2002	2003	2004	2005	2006	2007	2008	2009	2010
Win Shares	29	32	41	37	34	37	32	34	39	32
Hall of Fame Points	9	11	14	12	11	12	11	11	13	11

That's 115 points total; he's had a Hall of Fame career. Essentially, the new system says that if you have 10 seasons as an MVP candidate of some sort, you're a Hall of Famer. 30 Win Shares is an MVP candidate; 30 Win Shares is 10 points. Ten seasons of that, you're a Hall of Famer. The two problems with that system are relievers and catchers. The Win Shares system hates relievers. . .let's not get into that. . .so, to avoid infecting this system with the problems of the other one, we count each Save as one-fourth of a Win Share before doing the calculations above. Also, since catchers' careers are generally too short for them to meet Hall of Fame standards, even if they are great players, we divide their totals by .75.

We add the points awarded under the two systems together, divide by two, and round down. Those are the points accounted for in the Hall of Fame monitor, shown below.

The idea is that by looking at the question in two entirely different ways, we can avoid the weaknesses of either approach. One system probably underrates relievers; the other one probably overrates them, but when you put them together, you're OK. One system ignores park effects and changes in league standards; the other system meticulously adjusts for them. Hall of Fame voters *partially* adjust for them, so having a system part of which adjusts for them and part of which doesn't, that works. The system mirrors the process. Let's do a little Q and A about the system, to try to clear up some questions you might have:

Q. If a player is at 94, could we say that he has a 94% chance to be in the Hall of Fame?

A. Definitely not. A player at 94 certainly has some chance to be selected, but if a player retires at 50, he has very little chance to be selected to the Hall of Fame, and certainly not a 50% chance. A player at 94 is in a good position and is fairly likely to be elected, but is not an obvious Hall of Fame player, and doesn't have a 94% chance. Maybe 80, 85.

Q. Doesn't the system discriminate against starting pitchers? How come Tim Lincecum is listed below Joakim Soria, Josh Beckett is below Jon Papelbon, and Roy Halladay is listed below Carlos Beltran?

A. The system for starting pitchers is more back-loaded than the other positions, so that a pitcher earns big numbers of points for passing career markers like 250 wins, 300 wins, 3000 strikeouts, etc. A Hall of Fame starting pitcher will pick up a lot of points late in his career—if he lasts long enough to be a Hall of Famer.

Q. Aren't you concerned about this system having an adverse impact on the Hall of Fame voting?

A. How so?

Q. Well, you know. . .voters might tend to look at your system and say, "OK, this guy's qualified, this guy's not," rather than using their own judgment.

A. Well, a, I'm pretty certain that we don't have that kind of impact on people's opinions. Trust me; I've been writing for a long time. Not that much of it gets through. Everybody has their own opinion about who is qualified and who isn't, and certainly the voters have strong opinions about it. They're not going to set aside their own judgment in deference to ours. And b, to the extent that people pay attention to our research, we tend to think that that's a good thing, rather than a problem.

But having said that, we're not trying to lead the voters. We're trying to reflect the patterns of the voting, so as to anticipate the voting. That's all.

Q. Isn't a system like this inherently incapable of dealing with real-life factors in the voting, such as Mark McGwire's steroid abuse?

A. One of the interesting things we noted in doing the research is that . . .you know, our system is a combination of two different lines of analysis, and Mark McGwire actually doesn't show as a fully qualified Hall of Famer by either approach. Leaving the issue of steroids entirely out of it. He's in the 90s by both systems, in the area where a lot of guys get in, but. . .he's not an overwhelmingly qualified immortal.

When McGwire wasn't elected to the Hall of Fame, many people interpreted that as proof that the steroid guys won't be elected, but it's not clear that that's an accurate perception even of the transient mood, and, if it is, it's still a transient mood. There's no evidence that steroid users won't be elected in five years or ten or twenty, if they are clearly qualified.

Q. Do these points include the 2010 season?

A. They include the 2010 regular season, but not the post-season, and not the post-season awards. Which should be obvious to many of you, because many of you will have the book in your hands before the Awards are announced.

LEADING HALL OF FAME CANDIDATES BORN SINCE 1968 OR STILL ACTIVE

Only Player Born In the Year 1990 Who Has Yet Shown Up in the System:

Player	Points
Starlin Castro	2

Leading Hall of Fame Candidates Born in 1989

Player	Points
Jason Heyward	3
Michael Stanton	1

Leading Hall of Fame Candidates Born in 1988

Player	Points
Neftali Feliz	7
Elvis Andrus	5
Trevor Cahill	4
Clayton Kershaw	4
Rick Porcello	1

Leading Hall of Fame Candidates Born in 1987

Player	Points
Justin Upton	4
Buster Posey	3
Austin Jackson	3
Mat Latos	1
Jay Bruce	1
Ike Davis	1
Pedro Alvarez	1

Leading Hall of Fame Candidates Born in 1986

Player	Points
Felix Hernandez	15
Billy Butler	7
Phil Hughes	4
Yovani Gallardo	3
Jair Jurrjens	2
Colby Rasmus	2
Dexter Fowler	2

Leading Hall of Fame Candidates Born in 1985

Player	Points
Evan Longoria	15
Carlos Gonzalez	10
Delmon Young	6
John Danks	5
Asdrubal Cabrera	4
J. Chamberlain	3
Adam Jones	3
Chris Perez	3

Leading Hall of Fame Candidates Born in 1984

Player	Points
Prince Fielder	30
Joakim Soria	24
Brian McCann	23
Tim Lincecum	22
Troy Tulowitzki	16
R. Zimmerman	16
Jon Lester	12
Andrew Bailey	11
B.J. Upton	11
Ubaldo Jimenez	10
Jonathan Broxton	10

Leading Hall of Fame Candidates Born in 1983

Player	Points
Joe Mauer	57
Miguel Cabrera	55
Hanley Ramirez	43
Dustin Pedroia	32
Ryan Braun	28
Jose Reyes	28
Justin Verlander	19
Nick Markakis	17
Joey Votto	15
Cole Hamels	12
Russell Martin	12
Zack Greinke	11
Matt Capps	11

Leading Hall of Fame Candidates Born in 1982

Player	Points
Fr. Rodriguez	45
David Wright	41
Robinson Cano	32
Adrian Gonzalez	30
Grady Sizemore	23
Brian Wilson	21
Yadier Molina	19
Chad Cordero	17
Ian Kinsler	16
Dontrelle Willis	12
Aaron Hill	12
Andre Ethier	12

Leading Hall of Fame Candidates Born in 1981

Player	Points
Carl Crawford	29
Justin Morneau	26
Bobby Jenks	24
Carlos Zambrano	22
Josh Hamilton	21
Jake Peavy	18
Adam Wainwright	16
C.Granderson	16
Brandon Phillips	13
Alex Rios	12

LEADING HALL OF FAME CANDIDATES BORN SINCE 1968 OR STILL ACTIVE

Leading Hall of Fame Candidates Born in 1980

Player	Points
Albert Pujols	146
Mark Teixeira	55
Matt Holliday	41
CC Sabathia	39
J. Papelbon	37
Dan Uggla	22
Josh Beckett	17
Dan Haren	15
Shane Victorino	15
Nick Swisher	13
Jose Bautista	12

Leading Hall of Fame Candidates Born in 1977

Player	Points
Andruw Jones	63
Carlos Beltran	57
Roy Halladay	52
Roy Oswalt	33
Juan Pierre	32
J.J. Putz	29
Freddy Sanchez	27
Brian Roberts	26
Travis Hafner	23
A.J. Burnett	22
Bronson Arroyo	22

Leading Hall of Fame Candidates Born in 1975

Player	Points
Alex Rodriguez	188
Vladimir Guerrero	105
Scott Rolen	58
David Ortiz	49
Edgar Renteria	49
Derrek Lee	43
Luis Castillo	36
Brian Fuentes	36
Placido Polanco	33
Tim Hudson	32
Chris Carpenter	27
Torii Hunter	26
J.D. Drew	25

Leading Hall of Fame Candidates Born in 1979

Player	Points
Ryan Howard	51
Johan Santana	45
Adam Dunn	42
Adrian Beltre	36
Kevin Youkilis	27
Mark Buehrle	25
Brandon Webb	22
Jayson Werth	20
Garrett Atkins	19
Jason Bartlett	19
Michael Cuddyer	19
David DeJesus	19

Leading Hall of Fame Candidates Born in 1976

Player	Points
Lance Berkman	64
Michael Young	60
Alfonso Soriano	50
Carlos Lee	45
Paul Konerko	37
Eric Gagne	36
Brad Lidge	35
Troy Glaus	34
Aubrey Huff	24
A.J. Pierzynski	22
Pat Burrell	21

Leading Hall of Fame Candidates Born in 1974

Player	Points
Derek Jeter	138
Miguel Tejada	83
Bob Abreu	77
Magglio Ordonez	62
Jason Kendall	55
Joe Nathan	51
Jose Vidro	33
Jermaine Dye	32
Orlando Cabrera	27
Mike Lowell	27
Darin Erstad	25
Hideki Matsui	25
Kevin Millwood	18

Leading Hall of Fame Candidates Born in 1978

Player	Points
Chase Utley	53
Jimmy Rollins	50
Victor Martinez	35
Vernon Wells	32
Aramis Ramirez	32
Jason Bay	30
Jose Valverde	31
Cliff Lee	29
Carlos Pena	28
Barry Zito	23
John Lackey	22

Leading Hall of Fame Candidates Born in 1973

Player	Points
Ichiro Suzuki	110
Todd Helton	92
N. Garciaparra	70
Johnny Damon	60
Edgardo Alfonzo	37
Derek Lowe	31
Bartolo Colon	27
Mike Sweeney	26
Jason Schmidt	21

LEADING HALL OF FAME CANDIDATES BORN SINCE 1968 OR STILL ACTIVE

Leading Hall of Fame Candidates Born in
1972

Player	Points
Manny Ramirez	125
Chipper Jones	107
Carlos Delgado	76
Andy Pettitte	53
Shawn Green	46
Armando Benitez	45
Garret Anderson	43
J. Isringhausen	34
Keith Foulke	34
Raul Ibanez	22
Jason Varitek	21

Leading Hall of Fame Candidates Born in
1971

Player	Points
Ivan Rodriguez	99
Billy Wagner	92
Pedro Martinez	87
Jason Giambi	75
Jorge Posada	64
Brian Giles	52
Ryan Klesko	30

Leading Hall of Fame Candidates Born in
1970

Player	Points
Jim Thome	91
Jim Edmonds	64
Javier Lopez	41

Leading Hall of Fame Candidates Born in
1969

Player	Points
Mariano Rivera	150
Ken Griffey Jr.	114
Juan Gonzalez	68
Robb Nen	58
Troy Percival	57
Bret Boone	42
Arthur Rhodes	13

Leading Hall of Fame Candidates Born in
1968

Player	Points
Frank Thomas	121
Mike Piazza	120
Jeff Bagwell	107
Roberto Alomar	105
Gary Sheffield	101
Sammy Sosa	100
Bernie Williams	83
Jeff Kent	77
Mike Mussina	60
John Olerud	59

Leading Hall of Fame Candidates Born in
1967

Player	Points
Trevor Hoffman	106
Omar Vizquel	48

Leading Hall of Fame Candidates Born in
1966

Player	Points
Tim Wakefield	15

Leading Hall of Fame Candidates Born in
1962

Player	Points
Jamie Moyer	28

Leading Hall of Fame Candidates Born in
1960

Player	Points
Steve Moyer	0

The Player Projections Section
Bill James

As Fantasy Baseball is now America's fourth-largest business, this section of the book could be considered business consulting. Got a hot tip for you, boss: This Albert Pujols, he's pretty good. Albert's gold brick is easy to project, because he does the same thing every year. This little chart compares how he did in 2010 with how we had projected that he would do in these pages one year ago, published November 2009:

	Similarity	G	AB	R	H	D	T	HR	RBI	BB	SO	SB	Avg	Slg
Actual	938	159	587	115	183	39	1	42	118	103	76	14	.312	.596
Projected		158	579	121	193	45	1	44	129	106	63	11	.333	.642

That was not our best projection of the year. It was actually our 88th best, as we score those things. A lot of players, it turns out, are pretty consistent; it's just more notable for Albert because he is consistent and a beast.

As long as a player is consistent, we'll get his projection right, because . . .well, how would we miss? A guy hits .275, .280, .270, we're not going to project that he's going to hit .330. We had projected that Ross Gload would hit .281, and he did:

Ross Gload

	Similarity	G	AB	R	H	D	T	HR	RBI	BB	SO	SB	Avg	Slg
Actual	938	94	128	16	36	8	0	6	22	8	15	1	.281	.484
Projected		99	228	28	64	13	1	5	29	16	29	1	.281	.412

We were going to put Ross Gload on the cover, but the publisher wouldn't go along. We had projected that J.D. Drew would hit 22 homers, and he did:

J.D. Drew

	Similarity	G	AB	R	H	D	T	HR	RBI	BB	SO	SB	Avg	Slg
Actual	952	139	478	69	122	24	2	22	68	60	105	3	.255	.452
Projected		142	498	90	134	30	3	22	76	91	119	3	.269	.474

We did better overall on J.D.'s brother, Stephen:

Stephen Drew

	Similarity	G	AB	R	H	D	T	HR	RBI	BB	SO	SB	Avg	Slg
Actual	979	151	565	83	157	33	12	15	61	62	108	10	.278	.458
Projected		151	585	80	161	35	10	17	71	52	92	5	.275	.456

That was our third-best projection of the year. The other Albert Pujols is Cabrera. You just project big numbers for Cabrera, you should be OK:

Miguel Cabrera

	Similarity	G	AB	R	H	D	T	HR	RBI	BB	SO	SB	Avg	Slg
Actual	941	150	548	111	180	45	1	38	126	89	95	3	.328	.622
Projected		160	617	101	196	43	2	36	124	73	118	5	.318	.569

Switching to the other end of the spectrum. . . .when we get a projection wrong, it falls into one of three categories:

a) we projected that a player would play, and he didn't,
b) we didn't project that a player would play much, but he did, and
c) we just missed on his numbers.

More than seventy percent of our big misses are in the (a) group. Our worst projection of 2010 was for Ryan Garko:

Ryan Garko

	Similarity	G	AB	R	H	D	T	HR	RBI	BB	SO	SB	Avg	Slg
Actual	468	15	33	0	3	0	0	0	3	3	4	0	.091	.091
Projected		130	419	53	118	22	1	16	69	37	64	0	.282	.453

Followed by Tyler Flowers (who?), Jacoby Ellsbury, Chris Davis and Nolan Reimold. Here's the data for Ellsbury and Reimold:

Jacoby Ellsbury

	Similarity	G	AB	R	H	D	T	HR	RBI	BB	SO	SB	Avg	Slg
Actual	592	18	78	10	15	4	0	0	5	4	9	7	.192	.244
Projected		157	635	106	192	32	8	9	62	52	73	64	.302	.420

Nolan Reimold

	Similarity	G	AB	R	H	D	T	HR	RBI	BB	SO	SB	Avg	Slg
Actual	612	39	116	9	24	5	0	3	14	12	26	0	.207	.328
Projected		152	538	82	157	34	2	29	84	68	102	13	.292	.524

Ellsbury, of course, broke more ribs than a barbeque contest, whereas Reimold—projected to hit 29 homers, actually hit 3—was sent to the minors after hitting .205 through May 11. Which, you know, I don't mean to editorialize, but sometimes you've got to let a young player work through his issues.

Anyway, most of these are just guys who got hurt, like Ellsbury, Sizemore, Nick Johnson, Pedroia, Morneau and Mark DeRosa. Here's the data for DeRosa:

Mark DeRosa

	Similarity	G	AB	R	H	D	T	HR	RBI	BB	SO	SB	Avg	Slg
Actual	685	26	93	9	18	3	0	1	10	9	16	0	.194	.258
Projected		140	507	76	132	27	1	17	71	51	115	3	.260	.418

Our 17 worst projections of the season were for players who got much less playing time than we had projected for them, either because they were hurt or because they were young players and a job didn't open up for them.

My philosophy. . .just me. . .is that if we think that a young player *might* play, we project that he will play. As I see it, we don't have any way of knowing whether a job will open up next year for Mike Moustakas or Jesus Montero, so it is foolish for us to assume that we can figure those things out. What we should do is to say instead "*If* this player plays, this is how we think he will hit." In 2010, this philosophy led us to project playing time that didn't materialize for Kyle Blanks:

Kyle Blanks

	Similarity	G	AB	R	H	D	T	HR	RBI	BB	SO	SB	Avg	Slg
Actual	619	33	102	14	16	6	1	3	15	15	46	1	.157	.324
Projected		142	524	79	145	23	3	25	93	66	140	3	.277	.475

And for Micah Hoffpauir:

Micah Hoffpauir

	Similarity	G	AB	R	H	D	T	HR	RBI	BB	SO	SB	Avg	Slg
Actual	712	24	52	5	9	3	0	0	5	5	15	0	.173	.231
Projected		74	156	22	43	10	1	7	28	12	27	1	.276	.487

But it also allowed us to put on record our projections for young, previously untested players like Reid Brignac, Jason Heyward, Trevor Crowe and Ian Desmond.

Reid Brignac

	Similarity	G	AB	R	H	D	T	HR	RBI	BB	SO	SB	Avg	Slg
Actual	970	113	301	39	77	13	1	8	45	20	77	3	.256	.385
Projected		104	294	37	76	19	2	7	33	20	57	5	.259	.408

Jason Heyward

	Similarity	G	AB	R	H	D	T	HR	RBI	BB	SO	SB	Avg	Slg
Actual	950	142	520	83	144	29	5	18	72	91	128	11	.277	.456
Projected		146	542	86	164	27	5	17	78	59	64	11	.303	.465

Trevor Crowe

	Similarity	G	AB	R	H	D	T	HR	RBI	BB	SO	SB	Avg	Slg
Actual	947	122	442	48	111	24	3	2	36	29	73	20	.251	.333
Projected		93	311	46	81	18	2	3	30	35	55	17	.260	.360

Ian Desmond

	Similarity	G	AB	R	H	D	T	HR	RBI	BB	SO	SB	Avg	Slg
Actual	942	154	525	59	141	27	4	10	65	28	109	17	.269	.392
Projected		145	518	66	146	33	3	13	52	44	102	25	.282	.432

We are proud of those projections. Those were all young players getting significant major league playing time for the first time in 2010, yet we were able to make projections for them a year ago that met a very high standard of accuracy. There are many more of those that I won't bore you with. . .Logan Morrison, Darnell McDonald, Francisco Cervelli.

Minor league hitting stats *do* predict major league performance, if you understand them. People think that minor league hitting stats don't predict major league performance essentially because they don't know how to translate them from the minors to the majors. Adam Rosales prior to 2010 had a major league batting average of .212 in 259 at bats, but we were confident, based on his minor league stats, that he was a better hitter than that, and our projection for him was on target.

Adam Rosales

	Similarity	G	AB	R	H	D	T	HR	RBI	BB	SO	SB	Avg	Slg
Actual	960	80	255	31	69	8	2	7	31	19	65	2	.271	.400
Projected		81	219	32	57	13	2	7	25	20	40	3	.260	.434

But getting back to the three categories of players for whom we make mistakes, 70% of whom are players who don't get the playing time that we project for them. Occasionally the opposite happens: a player has gotten playing time that we did not anticipate. I believe that in 2010 there were 13 players whose playing time we dramatically under-projected, starting with Austin Jackson:

Austin Jackson

	Similarity	G	AB	R	H	D	T	HR	RBI	BB	SO	SB	Avg	Slg
Actual	893	151	618	103	181	34	10	4	41	47	170	27	.293	.400
Projected		97	282	40	83	15	3	4	37	27	65	14	.294	.411

See, that's the kind of projection that I beat myself up for, because our system worked perfectly; we knew exactly what kind of player Austin Jackson was. The only thing was, we had a bad projection for him because we outsmarted ourselves. We "knew" that he wouldn't get playing time in 2010, but he did. The same thing with Cliff Pennington:

Cliff Pennington

	Similarity	G	AB	R	H	D	T	HR	RBI	BB	SO	SB	Avg	Slg
Actual	878	156	508	64	127	26	8	6	46	50	96	29	.250	.368
Projected		60	207	29	52	10	1	2	18	26	33	13	.251	.338

And Alex Avila:

Alex Avila

	Similarity	G	AB	R	H	D	T	HR	RBI	BB	SO	SB	Avg	Slg
Actual	893	104	294	28	67	12	0	7	31	36	71	2	.228	.340
Projected		57	168	25	43	11	0	7	28	25	39	1	.256	.446

The other players who got much more playing time in 2010 than we had projected were Angel Pagan, Jose Tabata, Jonny Gomes, Daric Barton, Michael Stanton, Lou Marson, Andres Torres and Tyler Colvin and Alex Gonzalez. In most of those cases, we were basically right about how the player would hit, but just didn't foresee the openings for playing time.

Alex Gonzalez:

Alex Gonzalez

	Similarity	G	AB	R	H	D	T	HR	RBI	BB	SO	SB	Avg	Slg
Actual	818	157	595	74	149	42	3	23	88	31	118	1	.250	.447
Projected		80	230	25	57	14	0	6	28	14	42	1	.248	.387

Andres Torres:

Andres Torres

	Similarity	G	AB	R	H	D	T	HR	RBI	BB	SO	SB	Avg	Slg
Actual	846	139	507	84	136	43	8	16	63	56	128	26	.268	.479
Projected		87	292	45	77	12	5	6	25	29	75	14	.264	.401

Michael Stanton:

Michael Stanton

	Similarity	G	AB	R	H	D	T	HR	RBI	BB	SO	SB	Avg	Slg
Actual	858	100	359	45	93	21	1	22	59	34	123	5	.259	.507
Projected		65	162	26	37	8	1	9	28	16	55	1	.228	.457

I'll leave it to you to decide whether we were basically right about Stanton or basically wrong.   We were 30 points off on his batting average, but we had his power right and his strikeout/walk ratio pretty much right.

The third category of bad projections are those about which we are just wrong.   The champion of those in 2010, of course, was Jose Bautista:

Jose Bautista

	Similarity	G	AB	R	H	D	T	HR	RBI	BB	SO	SB	Avg	Slg
Actual	700	161	569	109	148	35	3	54	124	100	116	9	.260	.617
Projected		121	369	51	89	21	1	13	48	48	90	3	.241	.409

I don't how that happened; everybody else knew he would hit 54 homers. Why didn't we?   Joshua Bell got some at bats; he just didn't hit what we thought he would hit:

Joshua Bell

	Similarity	G	AB	R	H	D	T	HR	RBI	BB	SO	SB	Avg	Slg
Actual	756	53	159	15	34	5	0	3	12	2	53	0	.214	.302
Projected		91	347	51	100	21	2	11	61	45	71	2	.288	.455

We didn't foresee Andy LaRoche having the bad year that he had:

Andy LaRoche

	Similarity	G	AB	R	H	D	T	HR	RBI	BB	SO	SB	Avg	Slg
Actual	777	102	247	26	51	8	0	4	16	19	43	1	.206	.287
Projected		150	523	71	133	28	2	15	69	63	81	4	.254	.402

Or Mark Reynolds:

Mark Reynolds

	Similarity	G	AB	R	H	D	T	HR	RBI	BB	SO	SB	Avg	Slg
Actual	809	145	499	79	99	17	2	32	85	83	211	7	.198	.433
Projected		153	559	103	150	32	3	40	107	72	191	18	.268	.551

Or Adam Lind:

Adam Lind

	Similarity	G	AB	R	H	D	T	HR	RBI	BB	SO	SB	Avg	Slg
Actual	810	150	569	57	135	32	3	23	72	38	144	0	.237	.425
Projected		153	590	90	180	43	2	31	113	52	107	2	.305	.542

We didn't foresee Carlos Gonzalez emerging as a national figure:

Carlos Gonzalez

	Similarity	G	AB	R	H	D	T	HR	RBI	BB	SO	SB	Avg	Slg
Actual	811	145	587	111	197	34	9	34	117	40	135	26	.336	.598
Projected		143	515	78	144	35	7	19	73	41	107	18	.280	.485

Or Adrian Beltre competing for a batting championship:

Adrian Beltre

	Similarity	G	AB	R	H	D	T	HR	RBI	BB	SO	SB	Avg	Slg
Actual	811	154	589	84	189	49	2	28	102	40	82	2	.321	.553
Projected		131	483	61	130	29	1	17	68	32	82	10	.269	.439

Matt Wieters and Pablo Sandoval had disappointing seasons:

Matt Wieters

	Similarity	G	AB	R	H	D	T	HR	RBI	BB	SO	SB	Avg	Slg
Actual	812	130	446	37	111	22	1	11	55	47	94	0	.249	.377
Projected		148	547	75	170	29	3	20	92	61	112	0	.311	.484

Pablo Sandoval

	Similarity	G	AB	R	H	D	T	HR	RBI	BB	SO	SB	Avg	Slg
Actual	812	152	563	61	151	34	3	13	63	47	81	3	.268	.409
Projected		153	556	86	182	45	4	24	97	46	70	4	.327	.552

To balance out Josh Hamilton and Paul Konerko:

Josh Hamilton

	Similarity	G	AB	R	H	D	T	HR	RBI	BB	SO	SB	Avg	Slg
Actual	822	133	518	95	186	40	3	32	100	43	95	8	.359	.633
Projected		131	501	75	147	29	3	23	91	48	101	11	.293	.501

Paul Konerko

	Similarity	G	AB	R	H	D	T	HR	RBI	BB	SO	SB	Avg	Slg
Actual	857	149	548	89	171	30	1	39	111	72	110	0	.312	.584
Projected		148	539	74	143	27	0	29	90	67	96	1	.265	.477

Of the 414 projections in the 2010 Handbook, 54 score at 950 or better. This is a 950:

Jhonny Peralta

	Similarity	G	AB	R	H	D	T	HR	RBI	BB	SO	SB	Avg	Slg
Actual	950	148	551	60	137	30	2	15	81	53	103	1	.249	.392
Projected		146	531	74	143	33	2	15	72	50	124	1	.269	.424

And Jason Heyward, shown above, was a 950.   Of the 414 projections, 224 score at 900 or above.   These two are 900s:

Edgar Renteria

	Similarity	G	AB	R	H	D	T	HR	RBI	BB	SO	SB	Avg	Slg
Actual	900	72	243	26	67	11	2	3	22	21	43	3	.276	.374
Projected		138	507	69	140	28	1	8	59	44	76	8	.276	.383

Justin Smoak

	Similarity	G	AB	R	H	D	T	HR	RBI	BB	SO	SB	Avg	Slg
Actual	900	100	348	40	76	14	0	13	48	46	91	1	.218	.371
Projected		108	365	48	100	20	0	10	45	64	75	0	.274	.411

A "900" score generally means either that we missed on the player's playing time or that we missed on one element of his production, like his batting average. Of the 414 projections, 111 score below 850. These two are 850 projections:

Eliezer Alfonzo

	Similarity	G	AB	R	H	D	T	HR	RBI	BB	SO	SB	Avg	Slg
Actual	850	13	41	4	9	1	0	1	4	0	10	0	.220	.317
Projected		64	189	19	49	10	0	7	25	6	48	1	.259	.423

Aaron Hill

	Similarity	G	AB	R	H	D	T	HR	RBI	BB	SO	SB	Avg	Slg
Actual	850	138	528	70	108	22	0	26	68	41	85	2	.205	.394
Projected		138	540	78	153	35	1	20	76	40	78	5	.283	.463

Hill's Ball-in-Play batting average (what my friends refer to, horribly, as BABIP) was .197, which is ridiculously low, and basically guarantees that Hill will have a better season in 2011 than he did in 2010. We "missed" on his projection because we couldn't anticipate that everything he hit would be hit at somebody.

58 of the 414 projections score below 800. This is a '799' projection:

Brad Hawpe

	Similarity	G	AB	R	H	D	T	HR	RBI	BB	SO	SB	Avg	Slg
Actual	799	103	298	31	73	21	2	9	44	42	85	2	.245	.419
Projected		151	543	79	152	36	3	26	97	81	153	1	.280	.501

And 31 of the 414 projections score below 700. The Jose Bautista projection, presented earlier, was our only "700" projection of the season.

Our *best* projections come about when

a) we get the playing time right,

b) the player hits what we thought he would hit, and

c) there is a "coincidental match" between the numbers we picked and the numbers that occurred.

These were the ten best predictions of the 2010 Handbook (not repeating the numbers for 3. Stephen Drew, which were given earlier.)

1. Raj Davis

	Similarity	G	AB	R	H	D	T	HR	RBI	BB	SO	SB	Avg	Slg
Actual	985	143	525	66	149	28	3	5	52	26	78	50	.284	.377
Projected		138	496	74	141	27	4	4	44	37	77	50	.284	.379

2. Matt Holliday

	Similarity	G	AB	R	H	D	T	HR	RBI	BB	SO	SB	Avg	Slg
Actual	980	158	596	95	186	45	1	28	103	69	93	9	.312	.532
Projected		155	605	105	191	43	3	27	109	66	112	14	.316	.531

4. Russell Branyan

	Similarity	G	AB	R	H	D	T	HR	RBI	BB	SO	SB	Avg	Slg
Actual	978	109	376	47	89	19	0	25	57	46	131	1	.237	.487
Projected		112	412	56	98	21	1	27	67	57	155	2	.238	.490

5. Torii Hunter

	Similarity	G	AB	R	H	D	T	HR	RBI	BB	SO	SB	Avg	Slg
Actual	976	152	573	76	161	36	0	23	90	61	106	9	.281	.464
Projected		146	556	82	151	33	1	24	92	48	113	16	.272	.464

6. Alexei Ramirez

	Similarity	G	AB	R	H	D	T	HR	RBI	BB	SO	SB	Avg	Slg
Actual	974	156	585	83	165	29	2	18	70	27	82	13	.282	.431
Projected		147	527	75	150	19	2	18	78	42	58	12	.285	.431

7. David Eckstein

	Similarity	G	AB	R	H	D	T	HR	RBI	BB	SO	SB	Avg	Slg
Actual	973	116	442	49	118	23	0	1	29	27	35	8	.267	.326
Projected		128	444	57	120	21	1	3	35	34	40	4	.270	.342

8. Jason Kendall

	Similarity	G	AB	R	H	D	T	HR	RBI	BB	SO	SB	Avg	Slg
Actual	972	118	434	39	111	18	0	0	37	37	45	12	.256	.297
Projected		128	409	43	104	19	1	2	35	37	44	5	.254	.320

9. Emilio Bonifacio

	Similarity	G	AB	R	H	D	T	HR	RBI	BB	SO	SB	Avg	Slg
Actual	971	73	180	30	47	6	3	0	10	17	42	12	.261	.328
Projected		90	231	33	62	8	3	1	15	17	43	12	.268	.342

10. David Ortiz

	Similarity	G	AB	R	H	D	T	HR	RBI	BB	SO	SB	Avg	Slg
Actual	971	145	518	86	140	36	1	32	102	82	145	0	.270	.529
Projected		138	484	79	128	34	1	29	99	77	112	0	.264	.519

2011 Hitter Projections

Hitter	Team	Age	G	AB	H	2B	3B	HR	R	RBI	RC	RC27	BB	SO	SB	CS	SB%	Avg	OBP	Slg	OPS
Abreu,Bobby	LAA	37	157	600	161	38	1	18	96	94	95	5.50	97	136	23	10	.70	.268	.372	.425	.797
Abreu,Tony	Ari	26	85	229	63	15	1	3	27	25	27	4.18	9	45	3	2	.60	.275	.303	.389	.691
Ackley,Dustin	Sea	23	64	226	54	14	2	3	29	19	27	4.03	29	36	5	2	.71	.239	.325	.358	.684
Allen,Brandon	Ari	25	143	494	124	26	3	24	72	78	77	5.32	65	124	14	6	.70	.251	.338	.462	.800
Alonso,Yonder	Cin	24	130	493	133	36	1	13	56	58	70	5.00	46	91	12	4	.75	.270	.332	.426	.758
Alvarez,Pedro	Pit	24	149	537	149	35	2	27	78	103	94	6.25	62	154	4	3	.57	.277	.352	.501	.853
Anderson,Garret	LAD	39	80	206	54	11	0	5	22	29	24	4.08	11	35	1	1	.50	.262	.303	.388	.691
Anderson,Lars	Bos	23	37	104	27	9	0	2	12	13	14	4.73	12	26	1	0	1.00	.260	.336	.404	.740
Andrus,Elvis	Tex	22	148	533	146	17	4	2	82	43	62	4.04	53	82	34	12	.74	.274	.344	.332	.676
Ankiel,Rick	Atl	31	109	332	81	17	1	14	46	48	43	4.42	28	86	3	2	.60	.244	.307	.428	.734
Arias,Joaquin	NYM	26	55	105	28	4	1	1	13	10	11	3.67	4	13	3	1	.75	.267	.294	.352	.646
Avila,Alex	Det	24	117	349	87	19	0	12	43	48	48	4.75	48	79	2	1	.67	.249	.342	.407	.749
Aviles,Mike	KC	30	147	558	160	30	4	11	74	58	73	4.70	26	65	12	6	.67	.287	.320	.414	.734
Aybar,Erick	LAA	27	139	508	139	22	5	5	71	45	58	3.99	30	63	19	9	.68	.274	.320	.366	.687
Aybar,Willy	TB	28	78	178	45	10	0	5	19	24	23	4.50	20	31	0	0	.00	.253	.338	.393	.732
Baker,Jeff	ChC	30	115	366	103	24	2	11	51	51	55	5.42	29	82	2	1	.67	.281	.336	.448	.784
Barajas,Rod	LAD	35	118	395	92	21	0	16	45	56	43	3.69	20	72	0	0	.00	.233	.279	.408	.686
Bard,Josh	Sea	33	66	167	39	10	0	3	14	19	17	3.45	16	34	0	0	.00	.234	.301	.347	.648
Barmes,Clint	Col	32	137	449	113	26	2	12	55	50	52	3.98	27	80	5	4	.56	.252	.301	.399	.700
Bartlett,Jason	TB	31	146	534	149	30	3	6	79	51	69	4.56	48	92	17	8	.68	.279	.345	.380	.725
Barton,Daric	Oak	25	154	541	142	34	4	12	83	66	82	5.30	95	89	5	3	.62	.262	.375	.407	.781
Bautista,Jose	Tor	30	143	534	134	32	2	34	88	90	95	6.13	80	119	7	3	.70	.251	.355	.509	.864
Bay,Jason	NYM	32	133	465	124	26	3	21	75	78	80	6.05	69	129	10	3	.77	.267	.369	.471	.839
Beckham,Gordon	CWS	24	146	553	151	41	2	15	81	77	80	5.11	52	98	6	5	.55	.273	.343	.436	.779
Bell,Josh	Bal	24	143	528	144	36	1	21	65	74	78	5.24	39	130	3	3	.50	.273	.323	.464	.787
Belliard,Ronnie	LAD	36	83	177	46	11	0	4	22	22	22	4.33	15	35	1	1	.50	.260	.325	.390	.715
Beltran,Carlos	NYM	34	116	441	121	26	2	20	74	74	78	6.26	64	77	12	4	.75	.274	.369	.478	.847
Beltre,Adrian	Bos	32	154	579	164	38	1	24	77	88	91	5.67	40	91	2	5	.71	.283	.335	.477	.812
Berkman,Lance	NYY	35	138	459	126	29	1	22	72	79	87	6.73	87	100	5	3	.62	.275	.393	.486	.879
Bernadina,Roger	Was	27	78	194	53	9	2	5	27	20	28	5.02	18	38	11	4	.73	.273	.341	.418	.759
Betancourt,Yuniesky	KC	29	152	557	147	32	3	12	61	63	64	4.04	22	57	3	2	.60	.264	.293	.397	.690
Betemit,Wilson	KC	29	151	582	152	38	2	21	71	86	85	5.13	61	158	1	1	.50	.261	.332	.442	.774
Blake,Casey	LAD	37	147	511	127	28	1	17	66	66	66	4.46	51	133	1	1	.50	.249	.326	.407	.733
Blanco,Andres	Tex	27	86	237	61	11	1	2	23	20	24	3.51	14	29	2	2	.50	.257	.302	.338	.639
Blanco,Gregor	KC	27	55	187	49	7	2	1	27	13	23	4.21	28	38	9	4	.69	.262	.361	.337	.698
Blanco,Henry	NYM	39	75	193	43	9	0	4	17	19	18	3.12	16	41	1	0	1.00	.223	.282	.332	.614
Blanks,Kyle	SD	24	53	115	29	5	1	5	17	20	17	5.08	15	34	1	1	.50	.252	.353	.443	.797
Bloomquist,Willie	Cin	33	90	221	57	7	1	2	31	16	22	3.38	16	38	10	5	.67	.258	.311	.326	.637
Blum,Geoff	Hou	38	77	162	39	8	0	3	15	18	16	3.38	12	27	0	0	.00	.241	.301	.346	.647
Boesch,Brennan	Det	26	133	454	124	25	4	18	59	75	68	5.31	34	96	8	3	.73	.273	.328	.465	.793
Bonifacio,Emilio	Fla	26	53	105	28	4	1	0	15	6	11	3.62	8	21	6	2	.75	.267	.319	.324	.642
Borbon,Julio	Tex	25	104	323	96	10	3	3	49	30	41	4.56	19	39	16	7	.70	.297	.338	.375	.713
Bourjos,Peter	LAA	24	102	265	69	9	4	6	39	26	33	4.27	16	50	19	5	.79	.260	.305	.392	.697
Bourn,Michael	Hou	28	149	570	152	21	7	4	89	38	72	4.34	62	124	51	13	.80	.267	.341	.349	.690
Bowker,John	Pit	27	92	254	70	15	2	10	34	37	40	5.62	23	49	2	1	.67	.276	.338	.469	.807
Bradley,Milton	Sea	33	95	268	69	14	1	10	39	36	41	5.28	41	73	6	3	.67	.257	.366	.429	.795
Brantley,Michael	Cle	24	148	555	149	22	3	5	81	46	67	4.20	57	60	32	9	.78	.268	.337	.346	.683
Branyan,Russell	Sea	35	117	383	91	20	0	24	49	60	60	5.32	51	141	1	1	.50	.238	.332	.478	.810
Braun,Ryan	Mil	27	159	633	196	46	4	33	108	114	128	7.53	56	116	15	5	.75	.310	.372	.551	.923
Brignac,Reid	TB	25	113	339	87	20	2	9	44	43	42	4.28	23	73	5	3	.62	.257	.306	.407	.713
Brown,Domonic	Phi	23	152	548	158	33	4	26	84	94	96	6.22	48	131	28	11	.72	.288	.346	.505	.851
Brown,Dusty	Bos	29	41	113	28	8	0	2	12	14	13	3.98	12	28	0	0	.00	.248	.320	.372	.692
Bruce,Jay	Cin	24	153	540	151	27	4	31	87	83	97	6.42	58	127	7	4	.64	.280	.352	.517	.868
Buck,John	Tor	30	115	403	100	24	1	17	47	60	52	4.46	26	109	0	0	.00	.248	.302	.439	.741
Burrell,Pat	SF	34	126	397	94	20	1	20	51	67	61	5.23	68	116	0	0	.00	.237	.351	.443	.795
Butler,Billy	KC	25	156	590	181	44	1	18	78	89	105	6.67	63	80	0	0	.00	.307	.377	.476	.853
Byrd,Marlon	ChC	33	152	566	159	35	3	14	76	72	79	5.01	40	103	6	3	.67	.281	.339	.428	.767
Cabrera,Asdrubal	Cle	25	141	524	153	33	2	8	78	59	75	5.17	47	83	13	6	.68	.292	.354	.408	.762
Cabrera,Everth	SD	24	80	216	53	9	3	1	31	20	23	3.54	24	52	13	6	.68	.245	.329	.329	.658
Cabrera,Melky	Atl	26	136	329	88	17	2	6	41	39	42	4.49	30	44	6	2	.75	.267	.332	.386	.718
Cabrera,Miguel	Det	28	158	603	194	44	1	37	105	126	141	8.92	82	112	4	2	.67	.322	.406	.582	.988
Cabrera,Orlando	Cin	36	150	604	162	35	1	7	77	61	69	4.01	40	67	13	5	.72	.268	.316	.364	.680
Cain,Lorenzo	Mil	25	135	512	143	24	6	5	75	46	70	4.83	50	109	33	8	.80	.279	.345	.379	.723
Cairo,Miguel	Cin	37	72	132	34	7	0	2	17	13	14	3.68	8	19	3	1	.75	.258	.319	.356	.676
Callaspo,Alberto	LAA	28	134	455	128	25	3	7	56	47	60	4.74	34	32	4	2	.67	.281	.333	.396	.728
Cameron,Mike	Bos	38	121	452	108	26	2	18	63	58	62	4.65	54	135	7	3	.70	.239	.327	.425	.752
Cano,Robinson	NYY	28	161	627	193	44	3	24	95	95	110	6.56	42	73	3	2	.60	.308	.356	.502	.858
Cantu,Jorge	Tex	28	128	448	121	31	1	14	53	68	62	4.91	30	81	1	1	.50	.270	.324	.438	.762
Carroll,Jamey	LAD	37	135	444	118	18	2	1	68	32	50	3.92	55	84	10	6	.62	.266	.352	.322	.674
Carter,Chris	Oak	24	137	487	122	28	1	24	78	79	74	5.24	58	139	4	2	.67	.251	.330	.460	.790
Carter,Chris	NYM	28	82	191	55	12	0	7	23	29	31	5.93	17	23	1	0	1.00	.288	.346	.461	.807
Casilla,Alexi	Min	26	73	168	45	6	1	1	24	16	19	3.92	16	21	8	3	.73	.268	.335	.333	.668
Castillo,Luis	NYM	35	107	320	88	9	2	1	46	23	38	4.17	42	36	10	5	.67	.275	.361	.325	.686
Castro,Jason	Hou	24	113	395	94	15	1	5	52	32	40	3.44	45	68	1	1	.50	.238	.316	.319	.635
Castro,Juan	LAD	39	62	120	26	5	0	1	10	10	9	2.49	6	23	0	0	.00	.217	.254	.283	.537
Castro,Ramon	CWS	35	85	285	68	12	0	15	33	47	38	4.53	27	76	1	1	.50	.239	.304	.439	.743
Castro,Starlin	ChC	21	153	565	175	39	8	4	68	60	85	5.53	39	74	15	10	.60	.310	.359	.428	.787
Cedeno,Ronny	Pit	28	129	388	97	19	2	8	40	38	42	3.70	22	85	8	4	.67	.250	.294	.371	.665
Cervelli,Francisco	NYY	25	93	300	83	14	2	2	34	40	37	4.41	32	45	1	1	.50	.277	.352	.357	.709
Choo,Shin-Soo	Cle	28	149	548	164	33	3	20	88	85	102	6.78	77	116	19	7	.73	.299	.393	.480	.873

480

2011 Hitter Projections

PLAYER			BATTING												BASERUNNING			AVERAGES			
Hitter	Team	Age	G	AB	H	2B	3B	HR	R	RBI	RC	RC27	BB	SO	SB	CS	SB%	Avg	OBP	Slg	OPS
Church,Ryan	Ari	32	112	242	60	17	1	6	31	32	31	4.40	24	61	2	1	.67	.248	.323	.401	.724
Clement,Jeff	Pit	27	49	100	25	7	0	4	12	14	13	4.51	8	24	0	0	.00	.250	.312	.440	.752
Coghlan,Chris	Fla	26	135	532	158	34	5	9	90	58	85	5.80	58	93	19	7	.73	.297	.369	.430	.800
Colvin,Tyler	ChC	25	149	514	133	25	6	24	76	75	74	5.01	35	116	9	3	.75	.259	.307	.471	.778
Conger,Hank	LAA	23	110	369	100	19	2	8	43	45	50	4.81	41	57	1	1	.50	.271	.344	.398	.742
Conrad,Brooks	Atl	31	70	119	28	7	1	5	18	17	16	4.52	12	31	3	1	.75	.235	.311	.437	.748
Cora,Alex	Tex	35	73	165	39	6	1	1	16	13	14	2.84	12	17	3	2	.60	.236	.311	.303	.615
Counsell,Craig	Mil	40	85	169	40	7	1	1	19	12	17	3.40	20	25	2	1	.67	.237	.332	.308	.639
Craig,Allen	StL	26	44	152	43	9	0	6	21	26	24	5.72	12	29	1	0	1.00	.283	.335	.461	.796
Crawford,Carl	TB	29	149	570	171	27	9	14	93	71	92	5.82	40	94	42	12	.78	.300	.350	.453	.803
Crisp,Coco	Oak	31	106	373	102	20	3	7	58	40	52	4.83	36	59	27	9	.75	.273	.339	.399	.738
Crosby,Bobby	Ari	31	55	111	26	7	0	2	13	12	12	3.63	11	23	1	1	.50	.234	.309	.351	.660
Crowe,Trevor	Cle	27	102	328	84	18	2	3	43	30	37	3.85	29	53	16	6	.73	.256	.318	.351	.669
Cruz,Nelson	Tex	30	126	474	141	28	2	28	74	88	93	7.11	49	101	18	7	.72	.297	.365	.542	.907
Cuddyer,Michael	Min	32	135	471	130	28	3	16	73	70	73	5.53	50	84	5	2	.71	.276	.352	.450	.802
Cunningham,Aaron	SD	25	52	103	27	7	1	2	14	14	13	4.39	9	25	2	1	.67	.262	.333	.408	.741
Cust,Jack	Oak	32	134	430	104	20	0	20	66	64	69	5.49	91	160	1	1	.50	.242	.377	.428	.805
Damon,Johnny	Det	37	140	501	136	28	2	12	82	57	72	5.07	60	84	11	4	.73	.271	.352	.407	.759
Davis,Brad	Fla	28	54	149	34	10	0	4	15	18	16	3.59	14	37	1	1	.50	.228	.294	.376	.670
Davis,Chris	Tex	25	61	172	46	12	1	9	25	28	27	5.53	15	48	2	1	.67	.267	.330	.488	.818
Davis,Ike	NYM	24	147	523	148	36	1	23	78	80	95	6.55	75	128	3	2	.60	.283	.374	.488	.862
Davis,Rajai	Oak	30	135	404	116	22	2	4	57	37	53	4.58	26	58	39	13	.75	.287	.336	.381	.718
DeJesus,David	KC	31	157	606	175	35	5	11	86	68	88	5.25	59	88	6	5	.55	.289	.360	.417	.777
Denorfia,Chris	SD	30	83	223	60	12	1	5	30	25	29	4.54	19	34	7	3	.70	.269	.329	.399	.728
DeRosa,Mark	SF	36	129	458	118	25	1	14	66	63	61	4.65	46	100	2	1	.67	.258	.332	.408	.740
Desmond,Ian	Was	25	154	561	157	32	4	13	69	66	77	4.86	38	108	21	8	.72	.280	.328	.421	.748
DeWitt,Blake	ChC	25	113	341	86	17	3	6	40	40	41	4.16	36	56	2	1	.67	.252	.327	.372	.700
Diaz,Matt	Atl	33	130	339	99	21	2	10	42	47	51	5.46	20	73	6	3	.67	.292	.341	.454	.795
Dickerson,Chris	Mil	29	71	258	70	12	3	7	39	27	40	5.39	36	76	16	5	.76	.271	.363	.422	.785
Dobbs,Greg	Phi	32	73	103	25	5	0	3	11	13	11	3.62	7	22	1	1	.50	.243	.297	.379	.676
Donald,Jason	Cle	26	88	307	80	20	2	5	42	29	39	4.41	28	71	10	3	.77	.261	.326	.388	.714
Doumit,Ryan	Pit	30	121	443	118	30	1	15	56	61	63	5.02	37	88	2	1	.67	.266	.331	.440	.771
Drew,J.D.	Bos	35	145	513	135	29	3	22	86	77	86	5.88	84	120	3	2	.60	.263	.370	.460	.830
Drew,Stephen	Ari	28	152	606	101	37	9	16	82	67	89	5.27	59	109	8	4	.67	.270	.338	.443	.781
Duncan,Shelley	Cle	31	81	217	55	12	0	12	32	40	34	5.42	26	53	1	1	.50	.253	.336	.475	.811
Dunn,Adam	Was	31	160	567	140	31	1	39	90	102	106	6.44	107	197	2	1	.67	.247	.373	.511	.884
Durango,Luis	SD	25	120	271	67	8	0	0	46	20	38	3.41	46	62	39	16	.71	.261	.343	.280	.623
Eckstein,David	SD	36	123	416	111	20	1	2	50	30	44	3.71	29	36	6	3	.67	.267	.330	.334	.664
Ellis,A.J.	LAD	30	68	207	55	11	1	1	24	25	26	4.42	31	36	1	1	.50	.266	.361	.343	.704
Ellis,Mark	Oak	34	130	464	122	25	1	9	57	53	57	4.28	41	67	7	4	.64	.263	.331	.379	.710
Ellsbury,Jacoby	Bos	27	157	624	187	32	6	8	102	58	95	5.48	50	69	50	14	.81	.300	.355	.409	.763
Encarnacion,Edwin	Tor	28	122	430	111	26	1	22	61	67	67	5.44	44	82	2	1	.67	.258	.335	.477	.812
Escobar,Alcides	Mil	24	140	497	135	19	6	5	69	46	58	4.09	32	68	20	7	.74	.272	.318	.364	.682
Escobar,Yunel	Tor	28	147	558	159	28	1	8	79	60	76	4.90	65	68	6	4	.60	.285	.366	.382	.747
Espinosa,Danny	Was	24	134	424	108	16	4	21	69	60	60	4.79	35	100	19	10	.66	.255	.312	.460	.771
Ethier,Andre	LAD	29	153	577	166	39	3	24	86	90	102	6.42	67	110	3	2	.60	.288	.367	.490	.857
Evans,Nick	NYM	25	94	235	61	18	1	9	33	31	34	5.08	20	48	0	0	.00	.260	.318	.460	.777
Feliz,Pedro	StL	36	56	155	38	7	1	4	16	20	17	3.78	8	20	0	0	.00	.245	.287	.381	.667
Fielder,Prince	Mil	27	161	601	166	34	1	41	100	112	125	7.45	105	139	2	1	.67	.276	.390	.541	.931
Fields,Josh	KC	28	119	436	117	24	1	19	63	65	60	5.47	47	117	8	4	.67	.268	.341	.459	.800
Figgins,Chone	Sea	33	146	528	146	21	4	3	77	42	67	4.40	67	94	32	14	.70	.277	.360	.348	.709
Flores,Jesus	Was	26	93	312	82	17	2	9	33	55	41	4.63	24	76	0	0	.00	.263	.310	.417	.734
Flowers,Tyler	CWS	25	124	447	108	29	1	21	65	63	70	5.34	72	153	3	2	.60	.242	.347	.452	.799
Fontenot,Mike	SF	31	130	356	99	23	2	6	44	40	49	4.92	34	63	3	2	.60	.278	.344	.404	.749
Fowler,Dexter	Col	25	145	506	144	32	12	7	88	40	82	5.75	69	113	18	9	.67	.285	.373	.437	.809
Fox,Jake	Bal	28	88	248	68	17	1	13	35	42	40	5.75	16	52	1	1	.50	.274	.326	.508	.834
Francisco,Ben	Phi	29	107	303	82	21	1	10	42	38	45	5.20	27	55	10	4	.71	.271	.336	.446	.782
Francisco,Juan	Cin	24	86	189	53	12	1	10	25	32	30	5.69	9	48	1	1	.50	.280	.313	.513	.826
Francoeur,Jeff	Tex	27	128	419	112	23	2	13	53	63	54	4.53	24	74	5	3	.62	.267	.318	.425	.743
Freeman,Freddie	Atl	21	148	511	144	34	1	16	68	83	76	5.34	41	93	6	3	.67	.282	.335	.446	.781
Freese,David	StL	28	136	522	154	32	1	16	70	65	83	5.83	45	119	3	2	.60	.295	.353	.452	.805
Fukudome,Kosuke	ChC	34	146	490	129	34	3	14	70	60	76	5.38	78	106	8	6	.57	.263	.367	.431	.797
Furcal,Rafael	LAD	33	128	510	142	26	4	10	83	46	73	5.06	54	76	20	7	.74	.278	.349	.404	.753
Gamel,Mat	Mil	25	116	356	102	24	1	13	52	61	59	5.99	39	95	3	2	.60	.287	.359	.469	.828
Gardner,Brett	NYY	27	151	509	140	20	7	5	101	46	76	5.19	80	96	50	12	.81	.275	.377	.371	.748
Getz,Chris	KC	27	86	239	63	10	1	2	31	21	28	4.04	23	28	13	4	.76	.264	.333	.339	.672
Giambi,Jason	Col	40	105	277	63	11	0	15	38	50	42	5.08	56	75	1	1	.50	.227	.359	.430	.806
Gillespie,Cole	Ari	27	84	199	50	13	2	5	26	26	27	4.62	23	42	6	3	.67	.251	.332	.412	.744
Glaus,Troy	Atl	34	118	394	96	20	0	18	54	65	59	5.15	60	101	1	0	1.00	.244	.348	.431	.779
Gload,Ross	Phi	35	101	136	38	8	0	4	17	18	19	5.04	9	17	1	0	1.00	.279	.329	.426	.755
Gomes,Jonny	Cin	30	123	355	92	20	1	17	52	57	53	5.18	35	99	5	3	.62	.259	.339	.465	.804
Gomez,Carlos	Mil	25	108	295	76	13	3	4	44	29	33	3.81	19	66	19	6	.76	.258	.311	.363	.674
Gonzalez,Adrian	SD	29	161	600	171	35	1	33	92	102	115	6.97	87	119	0	0	.00	.285	.378	.512	.890
Gonzalez,Alex	Atl	34	121	407	98	26	1	13	46	53	46	3.86	23	81	1	1	.50	.241	.291	.405	.697
Gonzalez,Carlos	Col	25	144	582	179	38	8	28	101	101	113	7.13	44	122	22	9	.71	.308	.357	.545	.902
Gordon,Alex	KC	27	135	497	131	34	2	19	80	65	79	5.55	67	119	9	4	.69	.264	.356	.455	.810
Granderson,Curtis	NYY	30	152	580	153	27	9	25	95	73	93	5.60	66	139	14	5	.74	.264	.341	.471	.812
Greene,Tyler	StL	27	84	257	64	12	2	6	38	23	30	3.98	20	65	11	3	.79	.249	.311	.381	.692
Gross,Gabe	Oak	31	93	188	47	11	1	4	24	23	24	4.36	24	43	3	2	.60	.250	.338	.383	.721
Grudzielanek,Mark	Cle	41	49	128	36	7	0	1	15	11	14	3.91	7	16	1	1	.50	.281	.333	.359	.693
Guerrero,Vladimir	Tex	36	143	543	165	29	1	26	80	98	97	6.62	43	65	4	3	.57	.304	.363	.505	.867

481

2011 Hitter Projections

Hitter	Team	Age	G	AB	H	2B	3B	HR	R	RBI	RC	RC27	BB	SO	SB	CS	SB%	Avg	OBP	Slg	OPS
Guillen,Carlos	Det	35	113	423	118	26	3	12	60	59	65	5.49	47	75	4	3	.57	.279	.354	.440	.794
Guillen,Jose	SF	35	121	401	102	20	1	14	45	59	49	4.25	24	84	1	1	.50	.254	.316	.414	.730
Gutierrez,Franklin	Sea	28	151	559	146	32	2	14	77	63	73	4.52	49	131	20	7	.74	.261	.323	.401	.724
Guzman,Cristian	Tex	33	129	476	131	21	4	5	61	40	54	4.03	24	71	5	3	.62	.275	.314	.368	.682
Gwynn,Tony	SD	28	92	214	54	7	2	1	28	14	23	3.65	25	33	11	4	.73	.252	.333	.318	.651
Hafner,Travis	Cle	34	114	373	100	24	0	16	52	61	63	5.98	57	89	1	1	.50	.268	.377	.461	.838
Hairston,Jerry	SD	35	112	416	104	21	1	9	57	44	46	3.77	32	57	9	5	.64	.250	.311	.370	.681
Hairston,Scott	SD	31	98	266	66	15	1	11	34	34	36	4.63	23	60	4	2	.67	.248	.315	.436	.751
Hall,Bill	Bos	31	147	515	122	33	1	21	67	67	66	4.31	47	160	9	5	.64	.237	.302	.427	.729
Hamilton,Josh	Tex	30	131	481	156	32	2	26	80	91	103	8.16	44	87	7	3	.70	.324	.386	.561	.947
Hanigan,Ryan	Cin	30	100	334	94	17	0	5	39	37	46	4.98	45	37	0	0	.00	.281	.370	.377	.747
Hardy,J.J.	Min	28	131	480	126	26	2	16	64	62	66	4.83	46	80	1	1	.50	.263	.328	.425	.753
Harris,Brendan	Min	30	73	186	49	12	1	3	23	21	23	4.36	15	34	1	0	1.00	.263	.325	.387	.712
Harris,Willie	Was	33	99	186	42	8	2	5	28	18	22	3.89	27	43	6	3	.67	.226	.333	.371	.704
Hart,Corey	Mil	29	146	558	152	38	4	24	86	88	88	5.57	45	128	11	5	.69	.272	.332	.484	.816
Hawpe,Brad	TB	32	124	393	104	25	2	14	53	66	63	5.65	58	112	2	1	.67	.265	.362	.445	.807
Headley,Chase	SD	27	145	507	142	31	3	13	67	62	77	5.43	55	114	11	4	.73	.280	.355	.430	.785
Heisey,Chris	Cin	26	117	291	80	18	1	13	44	37	46	5.62	24	62	6	2	.75	.275	.336	.478	.814
Helms,Wes	Fla	35	107	204	49	11	1	4	19	27	22	3.69	17	58	0	0	.00	.240	.311	.363	.674
Helton,Todd	Col	37	124	406	116	27	1	11	58	53	70	6.28	74	75	0	0	.00	.286	.400	.438	.838
Hermida,Jeremy	Oak	27	97	279	71	16	1	9	35	37	38	4.73	32	69	2	1	.67	.254	.338	.416	.753
Hernandez,Ramon	Cin	35	117	420	111	22	1	11	42	62	54	4.54	36	63	0	0	.00	.264	.330	.400	.730
Herrera,Jonathan	Col	26	73	229	58	8	2	1	28	17	23	3.44	20	30	5	3	.62	.253	.313	.319	.632
Heyward,Jason	Atl	21	156	572	169	35	6	22	101	88	114	7.23	105	121	13	7	.65	.295	.411	.493	.904
Hill,Aaron	Tor	29	142	531	138	31	1	22	76	73	74	4.87	41	80	3	2	.60	.260	.319	.446	.765
Hill,Koyie	ChC	32	74	181	42	11	0	3	17	18	18	3.37	14	45	1	0	1.00	.232	.287	.343	.630
Hinske,Eric	Atl	33	126	269	64	17	1	10	38	38	36	4.54	33	72	2	1	.67	.238	.328	.420	.748
Holliday,Matt	StL	31	157	603	189	45	3	28	103	109	124	7.69	67	103	11	5	.69	.313	.390	.537	.928
Hosmer,Eric	KC	21	54	173	49	11	2	6	23	22	27	5.62	13	23	3	1	.75	.283	.333	.474	.807
Howard,Ryan	Phi	31	156	601	166	30	2	43	98	133	119	7.10	81	187	2	1	.67	.276	.368	.547	.915
Hudson,Orlando	Min	33	143	551	152	31	4	9	77	57	76	4.90	61	98	8	4	.67	.276	.351	.396	.747
Huff,Aubrey	SF	34	143	494	133	30	2	19	68	75	76	5.44	54	81	3	2	.60	.269	.348	.453	.802
Hundley,Nick	SD	27	101	332	79	19	1	11	38	50	40	4.09	31	77	1	1	.50	.238	.305	.401	.706
Hunter,Torii	LAA	35	149	569	155	34	1	23	81	92	86	5.31	53	113	11	7	.61	.272	.340	.457	.797
Iannetta,Chris	Col	28	95	324	82	19	2	16	46	55	54	5.80	50	73	1	0	1.00	.253	.363	.472	.835
Ibanez,Raul	Phi	39	146	538	145	31	2	20	75	83	81	5.33	58	109	3	2	.60	.270	.343	.446	.789
Infante,Omar	Atl	29	129	454	134	22	3	7	60	49	62	4.98	31	65	6	4	.60	.295	.342	.403	.745
Inge,Brandon	Det	34	136	434	100	20	2	14	48	57	50	3.87	44	121	3	2	.60	.230	.313	.382	.695
Inglett,Joe	Mil	32	92	218	62	11	2	2	28	20	29	4.77	20	35	4	2	.67	.284	.347	.381	.728
Ishikawa,Travis	SF	27	100	213	57	12	1	7	29	33	30	4.97	21	45	1	1	.50	.268	.336	.432	.768
Izturis,Cesar	Bal	31	134	413	103	15	2	1	41	28	36	2.97	24	42	10	5	.67	.249	.297	.303	.600
Izturis,Maicer	LAA	30	100	320	89	18	2	5	49	39	43	4.74	32	36	10	5	.67	.278	.347	.394	.741
Jackson,Austin	Det	24	151	607	180	35	8	6	95	62	90	5.38	54	147	28	8	.78	.297	.356	.410	.766
Jackson,Conor	Oak	29	56	142	38	9	0	3	20	19	20	4.95	18	18	3	1	.75	.268	.362	.394	.756
Janish,Paul	Cin	28	100	272	63	16	0	4	33	26	28	3.47	28	43	2	1	.67	.232	.308	.335	.643
Jaso,John	TB	27	120	369	98	19	2	7	54	48	52	4.97	58	44	3	1	.75	.266	.367	.385	.752
Jay,Jon	StL	26	105	339	95	20	1	6	48	37	45	4.70	27	47	12	5	.71	.280	.335	.398	.733
Jennings,Desmond	TB	24	134	522	146	31	8	6	92	50	80	5.37	59	81	54	11	.83	.280	.354	.404	.758
Jeter,Derek	NYY	37	158	641	189	31	2	13	101	68	95	5.39	62	105	17	6	.74	.295	.365	.410	.775
Johnson,Chris	Hou	26	146	506	145	31	3	18	59	71	75	5.39	24	112	3	1	.75	.287	.320	.466	.787
Johnson,Dan	TB	31	116	318	81	16	0	18	48	59	55	6.03	54	62	0	0	.00	.255	.365	.475	.839
Johnson,Kelly	Ari	29	146	522	140	33	5	19	83	65	84	5.64	67	121	10	5	.67	.268	.354	.460	.813
Johnson,Nick	NYY	32	98	337	89	23	1	10	53	47	58	6.06	78	74	2	1	.67	.264	.411	.427	.838
Johnson,Reed	LAD	34	91	215	57	12	1	3	29	23	24	3.90	11	47	2	2	.50	.265	.328	.372	.700
Johnson,Rob	Sea	28	73	193	44	11	0	2	20	17	18	3.12	18	39	2	1	.67	.228	.297	.316	.613
Jones,Adam	Bal	25	146	560	161	27	5	21	87	77	84	5.39	32	109	9	6	.60	.288	.335	.466	.801
Jones,Andruw	CWS	34	108	310	70	15	1	18	45	52	45	4.81	43	82	5	3	.62	.226	.330	.455	.784
Jones,Chipper	Atl	39	119	399	115	24	1	17	65	66	77	7.00	74	67	4	2	.67	.288	.401	.481	.882
Jones,Garrett	Pit	30	151	551	147	35	1	23	71	87	82	5.23	47	108	8	4	.67	.267	.326	.459	.785
Joyce,Matt	TB	26	129	388	100	28	3	18	61	63	66	5.88	59	93	5	4	.56	.258	.359	.485	.843
Ka'aihue,Kila	KC	27	144	461	117	23	1	22	75	76	78	5.88	89	87	1	1	.50	.254	.375	.451	.826
Kalish,Ryan	Bos	23	151	582	150	30	3	20	94	82	93	5.60	59	114	43	8	.84	.271	.340	.452	.791
Kapler,Gabe	TB	35	78	156	39	9	0	4	22	20	19	4.19	14	30	2	1	.67	.250	.320	.385	.704
Kearns,Austin	NYY	31	92	240	59	14	1	7	32	32	32	4.57	31	64	2	1	.67	.246	.351	.400	.751
Kelly,Don	Det	31	71	127	33	6	1	2	16	13	15	4.11	10	17	3	1	.75	.260	.319	.370	.689
Kemp,Matt	LAD	26	161	618	173	33	6	27	98	95	100	5.70	53	160	24	11	.69	.280	.339	.484	.823
Kendall,Jason	KC	37	119	385	97	17	0	1	39	32	37	3.29	34	41	7	4	.64	.252	.332	.304	.636
Kendrick,Howie	LAA	27	142	543	160	40	3	10	71	73	79	5.16	24	88	13	5	.72	.295	.329	.435	.764
Kennedy,Adam	Was	35	122	333	88	16	1	4	40	33	39	4.07	30	50	10	4	.71	.264	.334	.354	.689
Keppinger,Jeff	Hou	31	139	501	147	29	2	6	60	51	69	5.04	45	33	3	2	.60	.293	.354	.395	.749
Kinsler,Ian	Tex	29	137	545	150	33	2	20	98	74	88	5.71	64	79	21	6	.78	.275	.358	.453	.811
Konerko,Paul	CWS	35	151	556	152	28	0	32	78	96	98	6.31	70	109	0	0	.00	.273	.361	.496	.857
Kotchman,Casey	Sea	28	96	256	65	16	1	6	28	35	32	4.36	24	30	0	0	.00	.254	.327	.395	.722
Kotsay,Mark	CWS	35	76	187	48	10	1	3	19	20	22	4.09	16	21	1	1	.50	.257	.315	.369	.684
Kottaras,George	Mil	28	86	286	68	21	1	10	38	38	41	4.87	42	64	2	1	.67	.238	.335	.423	.758
Kouzmanoff,Kevin	Oak	29	139	518	137	32	1	18	57	77	67	4.56	27	98	1	1	.50	.264	.312	.434	.747
Kubel,Jason	Min	29	147	507	140	30	3	23	74	92	86	6.09	57	106	1	0	1.00	.276	.352	.483	.835
Laird,Gerald	Det	31	97	275	64	15	1	5	33	28	27	3.30	21	56	3	2	.60	.233	.297	.349	.646
Langerhans,Ryan	Sea	31	69	131	31	8	1	3	19	14	17	4.33	20	43	4	2	.67	.237	.342	.382	.724
LaPorta,Matt	Cle	26	143	537	138	29	1	22	74	77	78	5.07	62	101	1	1	.50	.257	.335	.438	.773
LaRoche,Adam	Ari	31	149	536	140	38	1	24	71	86	83	5.45	56	151	0	0	.00	.261	.333	.470	.803

2011 Hitter Projections

Hitter	Team	Age	G	AB	H	2B	3B	HR	R	RBI	RC	RC27	BB	SO	SB	CS	SB%	Avg	OBP	Slg	OPS
LaRoche,Andy	Pit	27	90	218	54	10	1	6	28	26	27	4.25	25	34	2	1	.67	.248	.333	.385	.719
Lee,Carlos	Hou	35	154	592	165	34	0	27	74	101	91	5.50	43	63	5	3	.62	.279	.331	.473	.804
Lee,Derrek	Atl	35	147	543	151	36	1	23	80	84	93	6.14	71	127	3	2	.60	.278	.365	.475	.840
Lewis,Fred	Tor	30	127	410	113	25	4	8	68	38	59	5.03	44	93	17	8	.68	.276	.353	.415	.768
Lind,Adam	Tor	27	149	551	155	37	2	26	72	92	92	6.04	44	115	1	0	1.00	.281	.338	.497	.835
Loney,James	LAD	27	157	571	160	36	3	12	68	85	82	5.14	55	85	8	4	.67	.280	.346	.417	.762
Longoria,Evan	TB	25	154	583	172	44	2	31	102	115	118	7.39	74	122	13	4	.76	.295	.379	.537	.916
Lopez,Felipe	Bos	31	134	463	125	25	2	9	64	46	62	4.70	50	90	10	5	.67	.270	.344	.391	.735
Lopez,Jose	Sea	27	133	471	125	28	1	12	51	60	56	4.18	20	54	3	2	.60	.265	.301	.406	.707
Lowrie,Jed	Bos	27	144	482	130	38	3	17	75	75	81	5.95	68	86	4	2	.67	.270	.361	.467	.828
Lucroy,Jonathan	Mil	25	107	338	87	18	0	6	37	40	40	4.11	35	50	3	2	.60	.257	.329	.364	.693
Ludwick,Ryan	SD	32	144	505	132	30	1	23	70	85	76	5.28	48	131	1	1	.50	.261	.333	.461	.794
Lugo,Julio	Bal	35	98	268	68	13	1	3	32	25	29	3.70	24	52	8	4	.67	.254	.320	.343	.663
Maier,Mitch	KC	29	120	389	104	21	3	6	48	42	49	4.42	36	65	5	3	.62	.267	.331	.383	.714
Manzella,Tommy	Hou	28	73	197	50	10	1	2	19	17	20	3.51	12	41	2	1	.67	.254	.300	.345	.645
Markakis,Nick	Bal	27	161	629	189	47	2	17	92	87	109	6.40	74	99	7	3	.70	.300	.377	.463	.839
Marson,Lou	Cle	25	76	212	51	12	0	3	28	21	24	3.83	28	42	6	2	.75	.241	.335	.340	.674
Marte,Andy	Cle	27	83	210	53	13	1	8	25	31	29	4.80	19	40	0	0	.00	.252	.317	.438	.755
Martin,Russell	LAD	28	130	467	124	24	1	9	68	56	64	4.78	69	78	10	5	.67	.266	.367	.379	.746
Martinez,Victor	Bos	32	134	517	154	33	0	19	69	88	89	6.37	55	63	1	0	1.00	.298	.369	.472	.841
Mathis,Jeff	LAA	28	65	146	31	7	0	3	17	16	12	2.69	11	38	1	1	.50	.212	.277	.322	.599
Matsui,Hideki	LAA	37	146	512	137	27	1	21	69	85	81	5.62	67	95	0	0	.00	.268	.355	.447	.802
Mauer,Joe	Min	28	141	535	181	38	2	15	93	87	114	8.33	80	58	3	2	.60	.338	.426	.501	.927
Maxwell,Justin	Was	27	65	125	30	6	1	4	20	13	18	4.78	19	40	9	3	.75	.240	.340	.400	.740
Maybin,Cameron	Fla	24	150	523	145	23	6	14	85	60	78	5.27	55	136	20	7	.74	.277	.349	.424	.774
McCann,Brian	Atl	27	143	515	144	38	0	24	68	94	91	6.34	64	90	4	2	.67	.280	.366	.493	.859
McCutchen,Andrew	Pit	24	154	593	170	34	6	16	99	63	97	5.80	69	89	33	12	.73	.287	.364	.445	.809
McDonald,Darnell	Bos	32	107	336	91	21	2	8	42	39	46	4.80	27	75	10	4	.71	.271	.327	.417	.744
McDonald,John	Tor	36	91	220	51	10	1	4	27	22	19	2.89	9	35	3	2	.60	.232	.265	.341	.606
McGehee,Casey	Mil	28	152	579	163	36	1	20	72	94	88	5.49	49	93	1	1	.50	.282	.339	.451	.789
McLouth,Nate	Atl	29	131	447	110	27	2	15	72	54	62	4.71	53	88	16	5	.76	.246	.335	.416	.751
Michaels,Jason	Hou	35	96	174	44	10	0	5	23	23	22	4.37	16	36	1	1	.50	.253	.326	.397	.723
Miles,Aaron	StL	34	82	173	46	7	1	1	20	13	18	3.66	10	20	1	1	.50	.266	.310	.335	.645
Milledge,Lastings	Pit	26	99	310	88	18	2	6	38	35	43	4.95	24	52	8	4	.67	.284	.347	.413	.760
Molina,Bengie	Tex	36	126	428	112	19	0	12	36	60	49	4.06	19	45	0	0	.00	.263	.301	.392	.693
Molina,Jose	Tor	36	76	195	44	9	0	4	18	17	18	3.10	11	44	1	0	1.00	.226	.279	.000	.611
Molina,Yadier	StL	28	138	493	134	23	0	7	41	62	59	4.23	45	49	0	4	.60	.272	.339	.361	.700
Montero,Jesus	NYY	21	126	403	115	29	1	21	51	67	73	6.59	39	75	0	0	.00	.285	.348	.519	.867
Montero,Miguel	Ari	27	110	403	110	28	1	14	51	58	61	5.41	41	77	0	0	.00	.273	.343	.447	.790
Moore,Adam	Sea	27	118	409	104	23	1	10	40	44	47	3.99	26	88	1	1	.50	.254	.300	.389	.689
Mora,Melvin	Col	39	104	298	81	14	1	8	38	40	40	4.77	27	49	2	1	.67	.272	.346	.406	.752
Morales,Kendry	LAA	28	146	544	161	32	1	27	75	95	93	6.30	36	87	1	1	.50	.296	.343	.507	.850
Morel,Brent	CWS	24	141	516	150	36	3	13	62	60	75	5.26	28	97	10	5	.67	.291	.327	.448	.775
Moreland,Mitch	Tex	25	64	178	50	11	1	7	25	30	30	6.05	20	32	2	1	.67	.281	.357	.472	.829
Morgan,Nyjer	Was	30	119	389	111	15	4	1	65	24	46	4.10	30	59	29	14	.67	.285	.347	.352	.700
Morneau,Justin	Min	30	132	506	149	34	1	27	81	101	100	7.28	67	91	0	0	.00	.294	.379	.626	.905
Morrison,Logan	Fla	23	137	515	144	39	8	9	80	65	83	5.79	73	89	3	2	.60	.280	.370	.439	.809
Morse,Mike	Was	29	96	284	79	17	1	11	36	44	44	5.58	23	68	1	0	1.00	.278	.337	.461	.798
Moustakas,Michael	KC	22	147	549	163	39	0	26	74	98	94	6.32	31	72	2	1	.67	.297	.334	.510	.845
Murphy,Daniel	NYM	26	123	431	121	33	3	12	59	64	66	5.46	38	54	8	4	.67	.281	.339	.455	.794
Murphy,David	Tex	29	106	412	117	28	2	12	56	61	65	5.65	42	70	10	4	.71	.284	.350	.449	.799
Nady,Xavier	ChC	32	83	226	60	12	0	7	26	31	29	4.54	14	54	0	0	.00	.265	.320	.412	.739
Napoli,Mike	LAA	29	129	411	101	22	1	24	62	66	64	5.32	49	125	4	3	.57	.246	.336	.479	.816
Nava,Daniel	Bos	28	61	137	38	11	1	3	19	22	21	5.46	15	30	1	1	.50	.277	.369	.438	.807
Navarro,Dioner	TB	27	86	250	60	13	0	5	26	26	27	3.68	23	38	2	1	.67	.240	.309	.352	.661
Nelson,Chris	Col	25	69	215	57	11	1	5	30	25	27	4.39	16	37	5	2	.71	.265	.316	.395	.711
Nieves,Wil	Was	33	69	163	39	7	0	2	14	16	15	3.15	9	25	0	0	.00	.239	.283	.319	.602
Nix,Jayson	Cle	28	96	262	62	14	0	9	32	28	30	3.86	20	57	5	2	.71	.237	.298	.393	.691
Nix,Laynce	Cin	30	90	168	45	10	1	7	23	26	25	5.24	13	40	1	1	.50	.268	.324	.464	.788
Nunez,Eduardo	NYY	24	88	220	65	11	1	3	29	24	30	4.94	13	26	12	3	.80	.205	.335	.395	.730
Olivo,Miguel	Col	32	123	450	110	22	3	17	53	62	53	4.02	22	136	6	3	.67	.244	.284	.420	.704
Ordonez,Magglio	Det	37	131	497	152	30	1	17	70	82	88	6.61	53	67	2	1	.67	.306	.374	.473	.847
Ortiz,David	Bos	35	151	564	147	39	1	33	91	112	104	6.48	91	146	0	0	.00	.261	.366	.509	.875
Overbay,Lyle	Tor	34	149	501	127	36	1	17	65	65	74	5.13	68	118	1	1	.50	.253	.345	.431	.776
Pagan,Angel	NYM	29	141	540	156	29	7	10	77	58	79	5.20	42	86	28	11	.72	.289	.340	.424	.764
Parra,Gerardo	Ari	24	141	405	117	22	7	5	49	45	57	5.08	30	70	8	4	.67	.289	.339	.415	.754
Patterson,Corey	Bal	31	87	302	76	16	1	8	38	31	35	3.92	17	70	16	6	.73	.252	.296	.391	.687
Patterson,Eric	Bos	28	72	153	40	8	2	4	23	16	22	4.93	14	35	12	3	.80	.261	.323	.418	.742
Paul,Xavier	LAD	26	50	101	28	6	0	2	14	11	13	4.51	7	21	4	2	.67	.277	.324	.396	.720
Paulino,Ronny	Fla	30	103	349	96	20	0	7	37	43	45	4.61	29	57	1	1	.50	.275	.331	.393	.723
Pedroia,Dustin	Bos	27	158	632	188	51	1	17	108	77	108	6.24	70	59	16	6	.73	.297	.372	.462	.834
Pena,Brayan	KC	29	84	240	67	15	1	4	24	25	31	4.61	17	27	3	2	.60	.279	.327	.400	.727
Pena,Carlos	TB	33	138	469	107	23	1	30	73	86	76	5.43	84	156	3	2	.60	.228	.354	.473	.827
Pence,Hunter	Hou	28	159	611	174	34	5	26	87	90	99	5.77	49	112	16	9	.64	.285	.339	.484	.823
Pennington,Cliff	Oak	27	150	499	124	25	5	5	67	44	59	4.01	58	83	29	8	.78	.248	.329	.349	.678
Peralta,Jhonny	Det	29	155	599	158	35	2	18	79	84	83	4.88	59	126	1	1	.50	.264	.333	.419	.752
Phillips,Brandon	Cin	30	156	615	166	31	3	20	88	76	83	4.71	43	89	17	9	.65	.270	.324	.428	.751
Pie,Felix	Bal	26	94	249	70	13	3	6	36	29	35	5.00	17	46	6	3	.67	.281	.330	.430	.759
Pierre,Juan	CWS	33	157	636	180	22	5	1	87	42	73	4.00	41	45	52	19	.73	.283	.337	.338	.675
Pierzynski,A.J.	CWS	34	132	496	137	27	0	12	53	59	61	4.41	21	53	2	1	.67	.276	.315	.403	.718
Podsednik,Scott	LAD	35	138	523	145	23	4	5	69	42	64	4.26	43	84	29	13	.69	.277	.335	.365	.700

483

2011 Hitter Projections

Hitter	Team	Age	G	AB	H	2B	3B	HR	R	RBI	RC	RC27	BB	SO	SB	CS	SB%	Avg	OBP	Slg	OPS
Polanco,Placido	Phi	35	148	601	177	30	2	8	83	62	79	4.82	35	48	5	2	.71	.295	.342	.391	.733
Posada,Jorge	NYY	39	111	361	94	22	0	16	49	60	58	5.63	53	93	2	1	.67	.260	.363	.454	.817
Posey,Buster	SF	24	137	510	157	32	3	21	74	83	94	6.90	47	72	1	1	.50	.308	.370	.506	.876
Powell,Landon	Oak	29	62	163	36	6	0	6	21	22	19	3.89	23	39	1	0	1.00	.221	.317	.368	.685
Prado,Martin	Atl	27	154	581	177	40	3	12	87	65	91	5.81	44	73	4	3	.57	.305	.356	.446	.801
Pujols,Albert	StL	31	159	587	192	44	1	43	120	126	158	10.27	107	70	11	5	.69	.327	.436	.625	1.061
Punto,Nick	Min	33	89	223	54	10	1	1	29	17	23	3.48	28	44	6	3	.67	.242	.329	.309	.639
Quentin,Carlos	CWS	28	137	505	132	32	2	28	84	92	84	5.82	57	79	3	2	.60	.261	.354	.499	.853
Quintero,Humberto	Hou	31	76	185	45	9	0	3	14	18	17	3.16	7	35	0	0	.00	.243	.278	.341	.619
Raburn,Ryan	Det	30	148	532	151	34	3	23	83	87	89	6.01	50	119	7	4	.64	.284	.349	.489	.837
Ramirez,Alexei	CWS	29	155	578	162	26	2	18	80	78	78	4.78	36	78	12	8	.60	.280	.325	.426	.750
Ramirez,Aramis	ChC	33	129	472	130	28	1	25	68	89	79	6.01	42	81	1	0	1.00	.275	.342	.498	.840
Ramirez,Hanley	Fla	27	153	590	184	40	4	25	108	80	119	7.42	68	104	33	11	.75	.312	.389	.520	.910
Ramirez,Manny	CWS	39	128	455	132	28	0	23	74	84	90	7.22	77	106	1	1	.50	.290	.401	.503	.904
Rasmus,Colby	StL	24	130	417	109	25	2	19	73	54	66	5.48	51	104	10	5	.67	.261	.343	.468	.811
Reimold,Nolan	Bal	27	144	526	142	28	1	22	72	70	84	5.63	66	97	11	4	.73	.270	.352	.452	.805
Renteria,Edgar	SF	35	122	441	121	24	1	7	58	49	56	4.51	38	71	6	3	.67	.274	.333	.381	.714
Revere,Ben	Min	23	92	341	96	9	3	1	33	18	39	3.93	26	39	34	13	.72	.282	.332	.334	.667
Reyes,Jose	NYM	28	128	532	152	28	9	11	85	52	80	5.32	42	62	36	11	.77	.286	.339	.434	.773
Reynolds,Mark	Ari	27	150	529	123	27	2	35	89	94	85	5.38	77	212	9	5	.64	.233	.337	.490	.826
Rhymes,Will	Det	28	71	225	62	11	2	1	29	21	26	4.05	17	23	9	4	.69	.276	.326	.356	.682
Rios,Alex	CWS	30	149	567	159	36	4	18	81	77	84	5.21	40	100	25	11	.69	.280	.333	.453	.787
Rivera,Juan	LAA	32	121	381	103	21	0	15	48	58	54	5.03	28	50	1	1	.50	.270	.324	.444	.767
Roberts,Brian	Bal	33	130	513	143	37	2	9	80	49	77	5.30	62	88	24	8	.75	.279	.359	.411	.770
Rodriguez,Alex	NYY	35	144	545	155	27	1	35	95	116	108	7.13	76	118	10	4	.71	.284	.381	.530	.911
Rodriguez,Ivan	Was	39	119	399	106	20	1	7	43	45	44	3.88	18	75	3	2	.60	.266	.301	.373	.674
Rodriguez,Sean	TB	26	118	385	101	22	2	16	66	57	56	5.04	34	103	12	5	.71	.262	.329	.455	.783
Rolen,Scott	Cin	36	131	469	130	34	1	16	69	75	74	5.64	50	79	3	2	.60	.277	.356	.456	.812
Rollins,Jimmy	Phi	32	136	556	148	33	5	15	87	61	79	4.96	49	59	25	6	.81	.266	.329	.424	.753
Rosales,Adam	Oak	28	107	347	91	19	2	10	47	40	46	4.64	29	72	4	2	.67	.262	.323	.415	.738
Ross,Cody	SF	30	147	491	130	30	2	18	65	70	68	4.86	36	115	6	3	.67	.265	.321	.444	.765
Ross,David	Atl	34	92	281	66	16	1	11	33	40	39	4.72	40	80	0	0	.00	.235	.332	.416	.749
Rowand,Aaron	SF	33	127	412	106	24	1	13	53	50	51	4.29	26	96	5	3	.62	.257	.322	.415	.737
Ruiz,Carlos	Phi	32	124	385	104	26	1	9	46	51	56	5.16	50	48	1	1	.50	.270	.360	.413	.773
Ryan,Brendan	StL	29	133	398	101	18	3	3	53	31	41	3.53	29	52	11	5	.69	.254	.308	.337	.644
Salazar,Oscar	SD	33	77	142	41	9	0	5	18	23	22	5.61	12	20	1	1	.50	.289	.344	.458	.802
Saltalamacchia,Jarrod	Bos	26	110	334	83	20	1	12	45	43	45	4.64	37	88	1	1	.50	.249	.323	.422	.746
Sanchez,Angel	Hou	27	79	271	71	13	2	1	31	24	28	3.60	20	40	3	2	.60	.262	.315	.336	.651
Sanchez,Freddy	SF	33	133	519	148	32	2	8	65	54	67	4.67	31	78	3	2	.60	.285	.330	.401	.731
Sanchez,Gaby	Fla	27	148	566	157	38	2	20	73	89	91	5.74	63	89	7	3	.70	.277	.353	.458	.810
Sandoval,Pablo	SF	24	143	530	163	38	3	18	71	78	94	6.62	44	68	3	2	.60	.308	.363	.492	.855
Santana,Carlos	Cle	25	149	528	148	32	1	22	83	91	95	6.43	88	101	7	4	.64	.280	.384	.470	.854
Santiago,Ramon	Det	31	123	389	95	15	2	5	47	34	39	3.43	32	71	3	2	.60	.244	.310	.332	.641
Saunders,Michael	Sea	24	114	322	78	13	2	10	43	34	39	4.07	34	83	10	5	.67	.242	.315	.388	.703
Schierholtz,Nate	SF	27	105	226	63	15	3	5	30	26	32	5.04	14	35	4	2	.67	.279	.326	.438	.764
Schneider,Brian	Phi	34	88	263	62	12	0	5	23	31	28	3.62	31	44	0	0	.00	.236	.321	.338	.659
Schumaker,Skip	StL	31	146	505	144	25	2	5	71	40	65	4.64	45	67	5	3	.62	.285	.346	.372	.718
Scott,Luke	Bal	33	142	493	131	31	2	27	70	80	86	6.16	62	114	2	1	.67	.266	.351	.501	.852
Scutaro,Marco	Bos	35	153	602	160	33	1	10	85	60	76	4.44	64	77	6	3	.67	.266	.339	.374	.713
Shoppach,Kelly	TB	31	97	288	69	19	0	13	39	43	40	4.75	30	101	0	0	.00	.240	.326	.441	.767
Sizemore,Grady	Cle	28	158	627	166	38	6	23	105	81	100	5.53	81	141	23	9	.72	.265	.355	.455	.810
Sizemore,Scott	Det	26	103	365	101	25	2	10	54	41	55	5.38	37	83	5	2	.71	.277	.343	.438	.782
Smith,Seth	Col	28	134	371	103	24	3	15	56	54	62	5.97	40	63	4	2	.67	.278	.350	.480	.829
Smoak,Justin	Sea	24	149	502	125	26	0	19	67	70	73	5.03	79	114	1	0	1.00	.249	.351	.414	.765
Snider,Travis	Tor	23	97	311	85	21	0	16	46	48	51	5.79	29	84	6	3	.67	.273	.337	.495	.832
Snyder,Chris	Pit	30	111	352	77	19	0	15	40	52	45	4.25	53	99	0	0	.00	.219	.326	.401	.727
Soriano,Alfonso	ChC	35	134	483	124	31	1	24	68	66	71	5.10	38	121	9	3	.75	.257	.317	.474	.792
Soto,Geovany	ChC	28	124	434	120	29	1	20	56	72	78	6.46	66	100	0	0	.00	.276	.373	.486	.859
Span,Denard	Min	27	142	531	156	21	7	5	85	58	77	5.21	59	69	24	9	.73	.294	.369	.388	.757
Spilborghs,Ryan	Col	31	132	365	100	23	2	10	52	46	54	5.22	41	83	6	4	.60	.274	.352	.430	.782
Stanton,Mike	Fla	21	152	522	140	32	2	38	85	104	102	6.89	69	162	5	3	.62	.268	.355	.556	.910
Stavinoha,Nick	StL	29	69	130	35	6	0	3	14	18	15	4.11	7	22	1	0	1.00	.269	.307	.385	.691
Stewart,Ian	Col	26	142	534	139	30	4	26	84	86	85	5.54	61	142	7	4	.64	.260	.342	.478	.819
Stubbs,Drew	Cin	26	150	545	143	26	4	20	90	71	82	5.19	59	153	35	9	.80	.262	.338	.435	.773
Suzuki,Ichiro	Sea	37	159	665	210	23	3	7	87	47	95	5.32	43	80	30	9	.77	.316	.361	.391	.752
Suzuki,Kurt	Oak	27	140	522	139	28	1	13	65	73	66	4.46	40	53	4	2	.67	.266	.329	.398	.728
Sweeney,Mike	Phi	37	43	131	35	7	0	5	15	21	19	5.09	12	17	1	1	.50	.267	.342	.435	.778
Sweeney,Ryan	Oak	26	124	437	128	25	2	6	61	53	61	5.08	39	58	4	3	.57	.293	.352	.400	.753
Swisher,Nick	NYY	30	153	534	137	32	1	27	87	83	89	5.81	80	136	1	1	.50	.257	.359	.472	.831
Tabata,Jose	Pit	22	155	568	163	30	3	7	83	52	77	4.80	44	76	37	12	.76	.287	.339	.387	.727
Tatum,Craig	Bal	28	50	108	25	5	0	1	9	12	10	3.13	9	22	0	0	.00	.231	.291	.306	.596
Teahen,Mark	CWS	29	126	443	119	28	3	9	59	51	60	4.77	44	108	5	3	.62	.269	.337	.406	.744
Teixeira,Mark	NYY	31	159	609	172	42	1	36	106	120	121	7.20	89	121	1	0	1.00	.282	.383	.532	.915
Tejada,Miguel	SD	37	159	638	178	34	1	17	80	84	83	4.67	33	68	3	2	.60	.279	.324	.415	.739
Thames,Marcus	NYY	34	103	295	73	13	0	17	39	46	43	5.04	28	84	0	0	.00	.247	.317	.464	.781
Theriot,Ryan	LAD	31	145	531	147	20	2	3	70	38	61	4.05	48	69	18	8	.69	.277	.340	.339	.679
Thole,Josh	NYM	24	73	241	67	16	1	2	23	24	32	4.75	26	28	2	1	.67	.278	.351	.378	.728
Thome,Jim	Min	40	96	249	61	12	0	17	39	47	47	6.50	53	80	0	0	.00	.245	.384	.498	.882
Torrealba,Yorvit	SD	32	106	381	97	21	1	8	39	48	45	4.08	34	79	5	3	.62	.255	.321	.378	.699
Torres,Andres	SF	33	152	521	141	30	8	14	84	53	78	5.20	54	125	25	10	.71	.271	.340	.440	.780
Tracy,Chad	Fla	31	103	287	79	19	1	9	35	40	42	5.25	23	49	0	0	.00	.275	.333	.443	.776

2011 Hitter Projections

Hitter	Team	Age	G	AB	H	2B	3B	HR	R	RBI	RC	RC27	BB	SO	SB	CS	SB%	Avg	OBP	Slg	OPS
Treanor,Matt	Tex	35	52	107	24	4	0	2	10	11	10	3.13	10	19	0	0	.00	.224	.308	.318	.626
Tulowitzki,Troy	Col	26	142	537	159	34	4	27	96	93	103	6.97	60	95	11	6	.65	.296	.371	.525	.896
Uggla,Dan	Fla	31	159	590	155	35	1	31	96	94	99	5.89	76	155	3	2	.60	.263	.352	.483	.835
Upton,B.J.	TB	26	149	534	136	34	3	16	87	63	79	5.00	72	152	40	13	.75	.255	.345	.419	.765
Upton,Justin	Ari	23	143	534	153	32	6	23	86	82	98	6.55	69	144	18	8	.69	.287	.371	.498	.869
Uribe,Juan	SF	32	145	502	127	27	2	20	62	73	66	4.55	36	95	2	2	.50	.253	.307	.434	.741
Utley,Chase	Phi	32	146	555	160	34	2	26	99	94	102	6.65	70	97	13	4	.76	.288	.387	.497	.884
Valaika,Chris	Cin	25	82	178	47	10	0	3	18	18	19	3.74	8	33	1	1	.50	.264	.296	.371	.666
Valbuena,Luis	Cle	25	132	494	121	28	2	11	66	51	59	4.07	53	98	7	4	.64	.245	.319	.377	.696
Valdez,Wilson	Phi	33	84	215	56	8	1	2	26	16	22	3.53	15	26	6	3	.67	.260	.312	.335	.647
Valencia,Danny	Min	26	137	479	139	35	2	10	61	62	70	5.32	34	78	3	2	.60	.290	.337	.434	.771
Varitek,Jason	Bos	39	72	246	56	12	0	9	28	33	30	4.11	32	70	0	0	.00	.228	.324	.386	.710
Venable,Will	SD	28	109	321	80	12	3	10	45	40	41	4.33	32	86	16	5	.76	.249	.321	.399	.720
Viciedo,Dayan	CWS	22	52	121	32	5	0	6	16	16	16	4.67	4	25	1	0	1.00	.264	.288	.455	.743
Victorino,Shane	Phi	30	155	612	171	31	7	16	97	66	90	5.19	52	81	30	10	.75	.279	.343	.431	.774
Vizquel,Omar	CWS	44	88	227	56	8	1	1	23	18	21	3.14	21	29	5	3	.62	.247	.316	.304	.620
Votto,Joey	Cin	27	151	555	177	40	2	33	96	105	131	8.87	85	113	13	6	.68	.319	.413	.577	.990
Walker,Neil	Pit	25	154	560	151	40	3	16	73	83	79	4.96	44	99	11	5	.69	.270	.324	.438	.761
Weeks,Rickie	Mil	28	133	522	134	27	4	21	94	61	80	5.31	67	143	11	4	.73	.257	.358	.444	.802
Wells,Vernon	Tor	32	152	587	158	37	2	25	81	85	88	5.28	48	84	7	4	.64	.269	.328	.467	.794
Werth,Jayson	Phi	32	157	560	154	34	2	28	98	91	103	6.53	84	156	14	4	.78	.275	.375	.493	.868
Whiteside,Eli	SF	31	68	170	39	8	1	5	18	20	17	3.35	9	40	1	1	.50	.229	.276	.376	.653
Wieters,Matt	Bal	25	130	482	139	25	2	16	55	74	78	5.91	54	94	0	0	.00	.288	.361	.448	.809
Wigginton,Ty	Bal	33	120	377	97	21	1	14	43	50	51	4.72	31	74	1	1	.50	.257	.324	.430	.753
Willingham,Josh	Was	32	136	475	123	28	2	22	71	72	79	5.79	73	115	7	3	.70	.259	.369	.465	.834
Wilson,Jack	Sea	33	105	349	91	19	1	4	35	30	37	3.70	19	47	3	2	.60	.261	.305	.355	.660
Wilson,Josh	Sea	30	93	262	64	15	1	3	25	23	26	3.38	15	48	4	2	.67	.244	.298	.344	.641
Winn,Randy	StL	37	97	250	67	15	1	4	31	25	32	4.50	22	42	6	2	.75	.268	.335	.384	.719
Wise,DeWayne	Tor	33	89	212	54	11	3	6	29	22	26	4.20	11	42	7	3	.70	.255	.295	.420	.714
Wood,Brandon	LAA	26	63	136	32	7	0	6	17	17	16	3.96	9	37	2	1	.67	.235	.288	.419	.707
Worth,Danny	Det	25	56	141	34	6	1	1	14	11	13	3.10	10	27	5	2	.71	.241	.291	.319	.611
Wright,David	NYM	28	157	601	177	43	2	27	99	104	116	6.98	82	147	20	8	.71	.295	.383	.507	.890
Youkilis,Kevin	Bos	32	151	562	165	41	2	25	103	95	110	7.15	87	119	5	3	.62	.294	.398	.507	.906
Young Jr.,Eric	Col	26	131	440	114	18	4	3	69	25	51	3.90	42	80	46	14	.77	.259	.324	.339	.662
Young,Chris	Ari	27	154	569	140	38	3	25	86	78	86	5.13	68	148	22	7	.76	.246	.330	.455	.785
Young,Delmon	Min	25	147	539	165	34	2	19	77	93	88	6.05	27	90	8	4	.67	.306	.345	.482	.827
Young,Delwyn	Pit	29	84	145	38	10	0	4	18	19	19	4.62	11	34	1	0	1.00	.202	.318	.414	.732
Young,Michael	Tex	34	154	629	184	36	2	17	80	82	94	5.47	48	110	5	2	.71	.293	.345	.437	.782
Zaun,Gregg	Mil	40	73	164	40	9	0	4	20	20	20	4.19	22	27	0	0	.00	.244	.340	.372	.712
Zimmerman,Ryan	Was	26	149	580	169	40	2	27	94	95	107	6.74	67	108	4	2	.67	.291	.368	.507	.875
Zobrist,Ben	TB	30	134	432	116	23	3	13	66	61	69	5.57	71	78	16	6	.73	.269	.374	.426	.800

Pitcher Projections

Bill James

This year, we're hoping to at least get everybody's won-lost record projected right. Last year we were exactly right on 8 out of 387; that's a start. It's a cornerstone. We projected Wandy Rodriguez' won-lost record right, and Joe Smith's:

Wandy Rodriguez

	G	IP	W	L	Pct	H	HR	SO	BB	ERA	Sv
Actual	32	195	11	12	.478	183	16	178	68	3.60	0
Projected	33	212	11	12	.478	214	24	179	75	4.12	0

Joe Smith

	G	IP	W	L	Pct	H	HR	SO	BB	ERA	Sv
Actual	53	40	2	2	.500	30	4	32	24	3.83	0
Projected	32	32	2	2	.500	30	2	28	15	3.94	0

We got Matt Thornton right (his won-lost record), Jorge Sosa, Francisco Cordero, Tony Sipp, Leo Nunez, and Dustin Nippert. Of course, none of those guys other than the Wandster won more than six games or lost more than five, but . . .hey, it's a cornerstone. We were one off on 25 pitchers. This is one off:

Matt Cain

	G	IP	W	L	Pct	H	HR	SO	BB	ERA	Sv
Actual	33	223	13	11	.542	181	22	177	61	3.14	0
Projected	33	225	14	11	.560	194	21	194	80	3.36	0

Or this:

Jason Hammel

	G	IP	W	L	Pct	H	HR	SO	BB	ERA	Sv
Actual	30	178	10	9	.526	201	18	141	47	4.81	0
Projected	32	182	10	10	.500	200	20	144	63	4.55	0

Or this:

Craig Breslow

	G	IP	W	L	Pct	H	HR	SO	BB	ERA	Sv
Actual	75	75	4	4	.500	53	9	71	29	3.01	5
Projected	72	77	5	4	.556	68	6	69	32	3.39	0

We had 46 projections that were two off in wins and losses—that is, two wins, or two losses, or one of each.   Like this:

Luke French

	G	IP	W	L	Pct	H	HR	SO	BB	ERA	Sv
Actual	16	88	5	7	.417	88	13	37	29	4.83	0
Projected	19	91	3	7	.300	102	11	57	33	5.14	0

Or this:

Mark Buehrle

	G	IP	W	L	Pct	H	HR	SO	BB	ERA	Sv
Actual	33	210	13	13	.500	246	17	99	49	4.28	0
Projected	33	216	12	12	.500	232	25	122	48	3.96	0

Or this:

Arthur Rhodes

	G	IP	W	L	Pct	H	HR	SO	BB	ERA	Sv
Actual	70	55	4	4	.500	38	4	50	18	2.29	0
Projected	64	53	4	2	.667	45	3	52	21	2.89	0

Or Gavin Floyd:

Gavin Floyd

	G	IP	W	L	Pct	H	HR	SO	BB	ERA	Sv
Actual	31	187	10	13	.435	199	14	151	58	4.08	0
Projected	30	190	9	12	.429	196	27	144	72	4.59	0

Or Brett Cecil:

Brett Cecil

	G	IP	W	L	Pct	H	HR	SO	BB	ERA	Sv
Actual	28	173	15	7	.682	175	18	117	54	4.22	0
Projected	19	98	4	7	.364	103	10	85	40	4.87	0

Wait a minute; hold on. That one didn't look right.

Yeah; sometimes it turns out we're off by quite a bit.   Like Kevin Millwood:

Kevin Millwood

	G	IP	W	L	Pct	H	HR	SO	BB	ERA	Sv
Actual	31	191	4	16	.200	223	30	132	65	5.10	0
Projected	29	175	9	10	.474	190	19	126	55	4.37	0

Which actually wasn't that bad a projection; we just didn't anticipate the ugly W and L. Bruce Chen, now; that was a bad projection:

Bruce Chen

	G	IP	W	L	Pct	H	HR	SO	BB	ERA	Sv
Actual	33	140	12	7	.632	136	17	98	57	4.17	1
Projected	23	78	3	6	.333	81	14	56	29	4.96	0

Bruce Chen also pitched well in 2000 (7-4, 3.29 ERA) and 2005 (13-10, 3.83). Make a note; sign Bruce Chen for 2015. Every fifth year, he's pretty good. We were closer on Bruce Chen than we were on Gio Gonzalez:

Gio Gonzalez

	G	IP	W	L	Pct	H	HR	SO	BB	ERA	Sv
Actual	33	201	15	9	.625	171	15	171	92	3.23	0
Projected	22	155	6	11	.353	145	21	168	86	4.76	0

Didn't do a real good job on David Price:

David Price

	G	IP	W	L	Pct	H	HR	SO	BB	ERA	Sv
Actual	32	209	19	6	.760	170	15	188	79	2.72	0
Projected	30	180	10	10	.500	166	24	157	78	4.30	0

David Price; you can pick on us for that one, because people *did* anticipate that David Price would be really good, so. . .why didn't we?   Bruce Chen; that just happens.   David Price, we should have done better.   Same with Jon Lester:

Jon Lester

	G	IP	W	L	Pct	H	HR	SO	BB	ERA	Sv
Actual	32	208	19	9	.679	167	14	225	83	3.25	0
Projected	31	206	13	10	.565	200	19	184	80	3.84	0

We should have done better.   We didn't have a real good projection for Tommy Hunter:

Tommy Hunter

	G	IP	W	L	Pct	H	HR	SO	BB	ERA	Sv
Actual	23	128	13	4	.765	126	21	68	33	3.73	0
Projected	28	170	8	11	.421	191	22	103	49	4.82	0

And we mis-projected Chad Qualls' ERA by more than 100%:

Chad Qualls

	G	IP	W	L	Pct	H	HR	SO	BB	ERA	Sv
Actual	70	59	3	4	.429	85	7	49	21	7.32	12
Projected	48	50	3	2	.600	48	5	41	13	3.42	39

We were over the hill on Trevor Cahill:

Trevor Cahill

	G	IP	W	L	Pct	H	HR	SO	BB	ERA	Sv
Actual	30	197	18	8	.692	155	19	118	63	2.97	0
Projected	31	185	8	13	.381	189	25	104	78	4.62	0

And no better on Ricky Romero:

Ricky Romero

	G	IP	W	L	Pct	H	HR	SO	BB	ERA	Sv
Actual	32	210	14	9	.609	189	15	174	82	3.73	0
Projected	30	190	7	14	.333	217	20	147	96	5.59	0

We had A. J. Burnett's won-lost record backward:

A.J. Burnett

	G	IP	W	L	Pct	H	HR	SO	BB	ERA	Sv
Actual	33	187	10	15	.400	204	25	145	78	5.26	0
Projected	35	223	15	10	.600	205	23	217	90	3.75	0

R. A. Dickey, we found him tricky:

R.A. Dickey

	G	IP	W	L	Pct	H	HR	SO	BB	ERA	Sv
Actual	27	174	11	9	.550	165	13	104	42	2.84	0
Projected	21	37	1	3	.250	43	6	22	14	5.35	0

And failed to anticipate the change of roles for C. J. Wilson:

C.J. Wilson

	G	IP	W	L	Pct	H	HR	SO	BB	ERA	Sv
Actual	33	204	15	8	.652	161	10	170	93	3.35	0
Projected	78	78	5	4	.556	72	7	76	36	3.92	0

Next year, let's just skip projections for guys who have initials rather than names.   We missed on J. A. Happ, too:

J.A. Happ

	G	IP	W	L	Pct	H	HR	SO	BB	ERA	Sv
Actual	16	87	6	4	.600	73	8	70	47	3.40	0
Projected	31	188	10	11	.476	182	25	171	77	4.31	0

We did OK for CC Sabathia, but I don't know if that counts because that's his actual name now:

CC Sabathia

	G	IP	W	L	Pct	H	HR	SO	BB	ERA	Sv
Actual	34	238	21	7	.750	209	20	197	74	3.18	0
Projected	34	238	18	9	.667	224	20	202	67	3.40	0

Projecting Mariano Rivera is kind of like projecting whether the sun will rise in the east or the west:

Mariano Rivera

	G	IP	W	L	Pct	H	HR	SO	BB	ERA	Sv
Actual	61	60	3	3	.500	39	2	45	11	1.80	33
Projected	65	68	5	2	.714	55	4	66	12	2.12	44

We got to be good, on Garza and Gallardo:

Matt Garza

	G	IP	W	L	Pct	H	HR	SO	BB	ERA	Sv
Actual	33	205	15	10	.600	193	28	150	63	3.91	1
Projected	31	201	12	10	.545	193	20	175	73	3.85	0

Yovani Gallardo

	G	IP	W	L	Pct	H	HR	SO	BB	ERA	Sv
Actual	31	185	14	7	.667	178	12	200	75	3.84	0
Projected	31	186	12	8	.600	157	17	205	84	3.53	0

We came pretty close, on Coffey and Coke:

Todd Coffey

	G	IP	W	L	Pct	H	HR	SO	BB	ERA	Sv
Actual	69	62	2	4	.333	65	8	56	23	4.76	0
Projected	81	87	4	5	.444	96	10	66	26	4.45	0

Phil Coke

	G	IP	W	L	Pct	H	HR	SO	BB	ERA	Sv
Actual	74	65	7	5	.583	67	2	53	26	3.76	2
Projected	70	56	4	3	.571	53	6	52	20	3.86	1

We regret that there were no pitchers named Milk or Juice. There was a Sipp:

Tony Sipp

	G	IP	W	L	Pct	H	HR	SO	BB	ERA	Sv
Actual	70	63	2	2	.500	48	12	69	39	4.14	1
Projected	46	35	2	2	.500	29	4	44	17	3.34	0

Take it for what it's worth; you can't sue us. The courts have ruled on that. And, of course, there is always a Joaquin Benoit:

Joaquin Benoit

	G	IP	W	L	Pct	H	HR	SO	BB	ERA	Sv
Actual	63	60	1	2	.333	30	6	75	11	1.34	1
Projected	45	50	3	3	.500	45	6	47	24	3.96	0

Who saw that one coming? Next year there will be another Joaquin Benoit, another R. A. Dickey and another Bruce Chen, and trust us, we're not going to project them right, either. There isn't a crystal ball in the office, but as long as a pitcher has a season that is a natural outgrowth of his previous performance, we should do fairly well. Thanks.

2011 Pitcher Projections

Pitcher	Team	Age	G	GS	IP	H	HR	BB	SO	HB	W	L	Pct	Sv	BR/9	ERA
Aardsma,David	Sea	29	50	0	49	42	4	26	48	2	2	3	.400	28	12.9	3.49
Acosta,Manny	NYM	30	53	0	54	49	6	32	48	1	3	3	.500	0	13.7	4.17
Adams,Mike	SD	32	74	0	71	57	5	25	74	0	5	3	.625	0	10.4	2.54
Affeldt,Jeremy	SF	32	49	0	48	46	4	22	38	2	3	3	.500	4	13.1	4.13
Albaladejo,Jonathan	NYY	28	42	0	50	43	5	17	44	3	4	2	.667	0	11.3	3.24
Albers,Matt	Bal	28	59	0	73	78	6	34	51	3	3	5	.375	0	14.2	4.68
Ambriz,Hector	Cle	27	31	0	46	54	7	15	36	1	2	3	.400	0	13.7	5.09
Anderson,Brett	Oak	23	27	27	171	169	15	40	140	6	10	9	.526	0	11.3	3.53
Arredondo,Jose	LAA	27	39	0	41	37	4	19	38	1	2	2	.500	0	12.5	3.73
Arrieta,Jake	Bal	25	20	20	122	125	12	57	94	7	6	8	.429	0	13.9	4.57
Arroyo,Bronson	Cin	34	32	32	209	206	28	60	137	9	12	11	.522	0	11.8	3.92
Atchison,Scott	Bos	35	50	0	64	62	6	20	55	1	4	3	.571	0	11.7	3.52
Atilano,Luis	Was	26	8	8	43	54	6	14	21	1	2	3	.400	0	14.4	5.44
Axford,John	Mil	28	55	0	66	54	3	34	83	1	5	3	.625	26	12.1	3.00
Badenhop,Burke	Fla	28	66	0	84	85	6	29	59	4	5	4	.556	0	12.6	3.86
Baez,Danys	Phi	33	42	0	41	40	5	16	26	3	2	2	.500	0	13	4.17
Bailey,Andrew	Oak	27	57	0	58	45	5	21	56	1	4	2	.667	30	10.4	2.64
Bailey,Homer	Cin	25	24	24	142	148	16	62	119	4	7	9	.438	0	13.6	4.50
Baker,Scott	Min	29	26	26	152	159	20	37	121	4	9	8	.529	0	11.8	4.03
Balester,Collin	Was	25	30	0	38	43	5	15	27	2	1	3	.250	0	14.2	5.21
Balfour,Grant	TB	33	46	0	46	33	3	21	55	1	4	1	.800	0	10.8	2.54
Bannister,Brian	KC	30	16	14	77	85	10	25	47	2	4	5	.444	0	13.1	4.68
Bard,Daniel	Bos	26	71	0	76	54	7	34	90	4	6	3	.667	0	10.9	2.72
Batista,Miguel	Was	40	57	0	81	87	9	37	51	3	3	6	.333	0	14.1	4.78
Beckett,Josh	Bos	31	26	26	168	165	20	49	155	7	10	9	.526	0	11.8	3.86
Bedard,Erik	Sea	32	12	12	66	58	6	26	65	2	4	4	.500	0	11.7	3.55
Beimel,Joe	Col	34	72	0	43	44	3	16	24	1	2	2	.500	0	12.8	3.98
Belisario,Ronald	LAD	28	63	0	57	55	5	24	43	4	3	4	.429	5	13.1	4.11
Belisle,Matt	Col	31	77	0	88	97	9	21	66	3	5	5	.500	0	12.4	4.09
Bell,Heath	SD	33	66	0	74	61	4	25	80	1	5	3	.625	40	10.6	2.55
Bell,Trevor	LAA	24	24	12	86	94	5	26	56	2	5	5	.500	0	12.8	3.98
Benoit,Joaquin	TB	33	65	0	65	50	7	24	67	2	4	3	.571	0	10.5	2.91
Berg,Justin	ChC	27	46	0	45	48	3	23	23	4	2	3	.400	0	15	5.00
Bergesen,Brad	Bal	25	30	29	198	217	24	52	98	7	10	12	.455	0	12.5	4.27
Berken,Jason	Bal	27	26	0	38	43	4	13	26	2	2	2	.500	0	13.7	4.74
Betancourt,Rafael	Col	36	74	0	67	57	7	16	72	0	5	2	.714	0	9.8	2.69
Billingsley,Chad	LAD	26	31	31	201	182	15	84	189	8	11	11	.500	0	12.3	3.63
Blackburn,Nick	Min	29	27	24	166	194	21	38	81	4	9	10	.474	0	12.8	4.55
Blanton,Joe	Phi	30	31	29	192	208	24	53	127	5	10	11	.476	0	12.5	4.22
Blevins,Jerry	Oak	27	55	0	45	42	4	14	45	2	3	2	.600	0	11.6	3.40
Boggs,Mitchell	StL	27	57	0	65	70	6	30	45	3	3	4	.429	0	14.3	4.85
Bonderman,Jeremy	Det	28	30	30	179	192	24	61	136	7	9	11	.450	0	13.1	4.58
Bonine,Eddie	Det	30	44	0	62	73	8	14	30	3	3	4	.429	0	13.1	4.65
Boyer,Blaine	Ari	29	58	0	60	65	4	29	44	3	3	4	.429	0	14.6	4.65
Braden,Dallas	Oak	27	32	32	214	213	19	60	145	4	12	12	.500	0	11.6	3.66
Bray,Bill	Cin	28	50	0	42	38	4	16	46	1	3	2	.600	0	11.8	3.43
Breslow,Craig	Oak	30	72	0	77	62	7	31	70	2	5	4	.556	2	11.1	3.04
Broxton,Jonathan	LAD	27	60	0	60	48	3	24	77	1	4	2	.667	33	11	2.70
Buchholz,Clay	Bos	26	29	29	193	173	17	74	168	5	13	9	.591	0	11.8	3.54
Buchholz,Taylor	Tor	29	35	0	35	35	4	11	25	1	2	2	.500	0	12.1	3.86
Buehrle,Mark	CWS	32	33	33	222	244	24	49	121	4	12	13	.480	0	12	4.01
Bullington,Bryan	KC	30	19	10	78	89	9	27	56	4	3	5	.375	0	13.8	4.85
Bumgarner,Madison	SF	21	31	31	188	185	15	51	137	6	12	9	.571	0	11.6	3.54
Burnett,A.J.	NYY	34	33	33	191	182	21	77	177	12	12	9	.571	0	12.8	4.01
Burnett,Alex	Min	23	29	0	34	35	3	16	29	1	2	2	.500	0	13.8	4.24
Burnett,Sean	Was	28	71	0	71	73	7	33	46	2	3	5	.375	0	13.7	4.44
Burres,Brian	Pit	30	24	15	96	109	12	42	65	5	4	7	.364	0	14.6	5.25
Bush,Dave	Mil	31	30	29	174	185	26	48	116	11	9	11	.450	0	12.6	4.50
Byrdak,Tim	Hou	37	67	0	40	35	5	22	37	1	2	3	.400	0	13	4.05
Cahill,Trevor	Oak	23	32	32	218	196	25	81	129	7	12	12	.500	0	11.7	3.67
Cain,Matt	SF	26	33	33	217	185	21	80	183	5	14	10	.583	0	11.2	3.36
Camp,Shawn	Tor	35	69	0	69	73	7	20	50	4	4	4	.500	4	12.7	4.17
Capps,Matt	Min	27	73	0	76	78	8	16	61	2	4	4	.500	38	11.4	3.55
Capuano,Chris	Mil	32	29	14	100	102	13	32	80	4	5	6	.455	0	12.4	4.23
Carmona,Fausto	Cle	27	33	33	224	233	21	82	139	13	11	14	.440	0	13.2	4.26
Carpenter,Chris	StL	36	34	34	235	206	17	53	183	10	18	8	.692	0	10.3	3.06
Carrasco,Carlos	Cle	24	17	17	89	92	12	34	79	4	4	6	.400	0	13.1	4.45
Carrasco,D.J.	Ari	34	55	0	72	78	5	30	50	4	4	4	.500	0	14	4.50
Casilla,Santiago	SF	30	63	0	77	70	7	37	76	4	4	4	.500	0	13	3.86
Cecil,Brett	Tor	24	28	28	177	183	18	63	140	5	9	11	.450	0	12.8	4.12
Chacin,Gustavo	Hou	30	47	0	37	42	5	14	22	1	1	3	.250	0	13.9	5.11
Chacin,Jhoulys	Col	23	27	23	151	133	14	70	138	9	9	8	.529	0	12.6	3.75
Chamberlain,Joba	NYY	25	76	0	76	71	7	30	81	3	5	3	.625	6	12.3	3.79
Chavez,Jesse	KC	27	58	0	70	77	10	27	56	1	3	5	.375	0	13.5	4.76
Chen,Bruce	KC	34	33	29	177	179	27	64	125	6	9	11	.450	0	12.7	4.37
Chico,Matt	Was	28	17	17	97	112	13	37	58	1	4	7	.364	0	13.9	5.10
Choate,Randy	TB	35	89	0	51	50	3	20	41	2	3	3	.500	0	12.7	3.71
Clippard,Tyler	Was	26	75	0	88	78	11	43	87	3	5	5	.500	0	12.7	3.99
Coffey,Todd	Mil	30	68	0	64	70	8	20	50	3	3	4	.429	0	13.1	4.50
Coke,Phil	Det	28	69	2	63	60	5	23	56	1	4	3	.571	1	12	3.57

2011 Pitcher Projections

Pitcher	Team	Age	G	GS	IP	H	HR	BB	SO	HB	W	L	Pct	Sv	BR/9	ERA
			HOW MUCH			WHAT HE WILL GIVE UP					THE RESULTS					
Coleman,Casey	ChC	23	23	15	114	119	8	44	59	3	6	7	.462	0	13.1	4.11
Contreras,Jose	Phi	39	67	0	59	60	6	21	43	3	3	3	.500	3	12.8	4.12
Cook,Aaron	Col	32	25	25	136	155	12	42	60	4	7	8	.467	0	13.3	4.43
Cordero,Francisco	Cin	36	72	0	73	64	5	33	75	2	4	4	.500	38	12.2	3.33
Cormier,Lance	TB	30	62	0	70	77	8	32	40	1	3	5	.375	0	14.1	4.89
Corpas,Manuel	Col	28	40	0	43	45	4	12	31	1	3	2	.600	0	12.1	3.77
Correia,Kevin	SD	30	25	21	124	128	14	49	91	4	5	8	.385	0	13.1	4.35
Crain,Jesse	Min	29	73	0	71	67	5	28	55	3	5	3	.625	0	12.4	3.55
Cueto,Johnny	Cin	25	29	29	176	174	23	57	146	13	9	10	.474	0	12.5	4.14
Danks,John	CWS	26	31	31	216	210	26	77	173	5	12	12	.500	0	12.2	3.92
Davies,Kyle	KC	27	33	33	197	213	23	92	140	4	8	13	.381	0	14.1	4.89
Davis,Wade	TB	25	27	27	163	158	18	67	132	7	9	9	.500	0	12.8	4.09
de la Rosa,Jorge	Col	30	27	27	178	177	20	84	161	7	9	11	.450	0	13.6	4.45
Delcarmen,Manny	Col	29	55	0	49	45	4	24	43	2	3	3	.500	0	13	3.86
Demel,Sam	Ari	25	47	0	45	42	3	18	40	1	3	2	.600	4	12.2	3.40
Dempster,Ryan	ChC	34	34	34	214	199	21	89	192	8	12	11	.522	0	12.4	3.83
Dessens,Elmer	NYM	40	60	0	56	57	6	17	34	1	3	3	.500	0	12.1	3.86
Detwiler,Ross	Was	25	13	7	46	53	3	19	33	1	2	3	.400	0	14.3	4.70
Diamond,Thomas	ChC	28	31	6	58	55	6	35	56	3	3	4	.429	0	14.4	4.66
Dickey,R.A.	NYM	36	32	30	209	227	23	69	124	9	11	12	.478	0	13.1	4.44
DiFelice,Mark	Mil	34	34	0	31	28	4	6	29	1	2	1	.667	0	10.2	3.19
Dotel,Octavio	Col	37	72	0	68	57	10	32	84	0	4	4	.500	0	12.2	3.84
Downs,Scott	Tor	35	60	0	58	53	5	19	47	3	4	3	.571	0	11.6	3.26
Drabek,Kyle	Tor	23	6	6	34	31	3	14	27	1	2	2	.500	0	12.2	3.71
Duensing,Brian	Min	28	43	22	180	199	18	55	111	6	10	10	.500	0	13	4.30
Duke,Zach	Pit	28	31	31	172	209	19	47	89	4	7	12	.368	0	13.6	4.92
Dunn,Michael	Atl	26	64	0	68	53	4	50	90	2	4	4	.500	0	13.9	3.84
Durbin,Chad	Phi	33	70	0	73	71	9	30	55	5	4	4	.500	0	13.1	4.32
Ely,John	LAD	25	14	14	80	80	8	31	63	2	4	5	.444	0	12.7	4.05
Enright,Barry	Ari	25	24	24	144	159	22	36	93	4	7	9	.438	0	12.4	4.50
Farnsworth,Kyle	Atl	35	62	0	62	58	8	24	64	2	4	3	.571	0	12.2	3.92
Feldman,Scott	Tex	28	27	14	105	111	12	38	59	5	5	7	.417	0	13.2	4.46
Feliciano,Pedro	NYM	34	92	0	62	59	5	27	57	3	4	3	.571	0	12.9	3.77
Feliz,Neftali	Tex	23	67	0	71	56	4	26	75	4	4	3	.571	39	10.9	2.66
Figueroa,Nelson	Hou	37	35	20	138	139	15	46	108	6	7	9	.438	0	12.5	4.04
Fister,Doug	Sea	27	29	29	183	209	19	42	121	8	8	13	.381	0	12.7	4.33
Floyd,Gavin	CWS	28	29	29	179	186	22	66	136	8	9	11	.450	0	13.1	4.42
Francis,Jeff	Col	30	18	16	87	95	10	27	59	3	4	5	.444	0	12.9	4.45
Francisco,Frank	Tex	31	37	0	35	28	3	15	40	1	2	1	.667	0	11.3	3.09
Franklin,Ryan	StL	38	57	0	66	66	8	19	37	3	4	3	.571	28	12	3.95
Frasor,Jason	Tor	33	60	0	67	59	5	29	65	3	4	3	.571	4	12.2	3.49
French,Luke	Sea	25	25	24	156	170	17	49	89	6	6	11	.353	0	13	4.38
Frieri,Ernesto	SD	25	55	0	55	41	5	27	56	2	3	3	.500	0	11.6	3.11
Fuentes,Brian	Min	35	40	0	49	41	5	21	51	4	3	2	.600	32	12.1	3.31
Fulchino,Jeff	Hou	31	55	0	51	56	5	23	40	3	2	4	.333	0	14.5	4.94
Galarraga,Armando	Det	29	29	29	178	178	26	67	122	8	9	11	.450	0	12.8	4.46
Gallagher,Sean	Pit	26	57	0	67	68	6	37	58	3	3	5	.375	0	14.5	4.70
Gallardo,Yovani	Mil	25	31	31	190	160	16	81	207	4	12	9	.571	0	12	3.60
Garcia,Freddy	CWS	34	27	27	148	155	21	42	99	4	7	9	.438	0	12.2	4.20
Garcia,Jaime	StL	24	30	30	175	165	15	74	148	6	11	9	.550	0	12.6	3.86
Garland,Jon	SD	31	33	33	210	222	21	66	113	6	10	14	.417	0	12.6	3.81
Garza,Matt	TB	27	32	31	206	194	23	71	171	9	12	11	.522	0	12	3.80
Gaudin,Chad	NYY	28	45	0	67	68	8	29	54	4	4	4	.500	0	13.6	4.57
Gee,Dillon	NYM	25	16	16	99	99	13	30	89	7	6	5	.545	0	12.4	4.09
Germano,Justin	Cle	28	43	2	67	72	8	16	44	3	3	4	.429	0	12.2	4.16
Gomez,Jeanmar	Cle	23	20	20	105	117	13	42	77	2	4	7	.364	0	13.8	4.89
Gonzalez,Gio	Oak	25	33	33	212	192	21	97	212	6	13	10	.565	0	12.5	3.99
Gonzalez,Mike	Bal	33	44	0	38	30	3	18	45	2	3	2	.600	0	11.8	3.08
Gorzelanny,Tom	ChC	28	26	23	133	133	12	56	106	4	7	8	.467	0	13.1	4.06
Gregerson,Luke	SD	27	75	0	72	55	5	23	81	2	6	0	.923	4	10	2.50
Gregg,Kevin	Tor	33	64	0	58	52	6	25	54	2	3	3	.500	28	12.6	3.57
Greinke,Zack	KC	27	32	32	222	219	19	56	193	7	14	11	.560	0	11.4	3.57
Guerrier,Matt	Min	32	75	0	74	69	9	24	49	3	5	3	.625	0	11.7	3.65
Guthrie,Jeremy	Bal	32	31	31	201	201	27	63	123	11	11	12	.478	0	12.3	4.12
Gutierrez,Juan	Ari	27	56	0	56	61	7	22	45	2	3	4	.429	9	13.7	4.82
Guzman,Angel	ChC	29	33	0	37	35	4	16	34	2	2	2	.500	0	12.9	4.14
Halladay,Roy	Phi	34	32	32	245	234	21	38	190	7	18	9	.667	0	10.2	3.16
Hamels,Cole	Phi	27	33	33	219	199	28	58	209	5	15	9	.625	0	10.8	3.45
Hammel,Jason	Col	28	30	30	179	199	19	58	140	7	9	11	.450	0	13.3	4.53
Hanrahan,Joel	Pit	29	71	0	71	70	8	38	73	3	3	5	.375	24	14.1	4.56
Hanson,Tommy	Atl	24	34	34	219	190	18	71	207	14	15	10	.600	0	11.3	3.41
Happ,J.A.	Hou	28	25	25	143	139	18	66	125	3	6	10	.375	0	13.1	4.28
Harang,Aaron	Cin	33	26	26	159	173	23	42	133	5	8	10	.444	0	12.5	4.42
Harden,Rich	Tex	29	18	14	76	63	10	36	80	3	5	4	.556	0	12.1	3.67
Haren,Dan	LAA	30	34	34	238	230	28	52	209	6	15	12	.556	0	10.9	3.52
Harrell,Lucas	CWS	26	14	4	39	44	4	22	24	1	1	3	.250	0	15.5	5.31
Harrison,Matt	Tex	25	45	3	66	76	7	25	41	1	3	4	.429	0	13.9	4.91
Hawksworth,Blake	StL	28	45	4	76	84	10	29	53	4	4	5	.444	0	13.9	4.97
Heilman,Aaron	Ari	32	69	0	72	68	8	29	62	4	4	4	.500	0	12.6	4.00
Hellickson,Jeremy	TB	24	26	26	161	143	18	46	170	9	11	7	.611	0	11.1	3.47
Hendrickson,Mark	Bal	37	53	0	65	76	8	19	39	2	3	4	.429	0	13.4	4.85

2011 Pitcher Projections

PLAYER			HOW MUCH			WHAT HE WILL GIVE UP					THE RESULTS					
Pitcher	Team	Age	G	GS	IP	H	HR	BB	SO	HB	W	L	Pct	Sv	BR/9	ERA
Hensley,Clay	Fla	31	72	0	78	76	6	33	58	3	5	4	.556	4	12.9	3.92
Hernandez,David	Bal	26	33	4	55	53	8	27	53	2	3	4	.429	0	13.4	4.58
Hernandez,Felix	Sea	25	32	32	223	197	17	72	204	7	13	11	.542	0	11.1	3.31
Hernandez,Livan	Was	36	33	33	218	250	25	70	119	5	10	15	.400	0	13.4	4.71
Herndon,David	Phi	25	44	0	52	62	6	15	28	2	2	3	.400	0	13.7	4.85
Herrmann,Frank	Cle	27	45	0	56	61	5	15	35	1	3	3	.500	0	12.4	4.02
Hill,Shawn	Tor	30	16	16	86	93	6	23	50	3	5	5	.500	0	12.5	3.87
Hochevar,Luke	KC	27	16	14	89	98	11	31	63	4	4	6	.400	0	13.4	4.65
Hoffman,Trevor	Mil	43	47	0	45	40	4	12	37	0	3	2	.600	11	10.4	3.00
Holland,Derek	Tex	24	20	14	86	84	12	30	73	3	5	5	.500	0	12.2	4.08
Holland,Greg	KC	25	29	0	37	36	3	19	36	0	2	2	.500	0	13.4	4.14
Howell,J.P.	TB	28	57	0	56	53	6	23	55	3	3	3	.500	5	12.7	4.02
Hudson,Daniel	Ari	24	32	32	201	192	24	79	183	10	14	9	.609	0	12.6	3.85
Hudson,Tim	Atl	35	34	34	226	216	18	66	137	8	15	10	.600	0	11.5	3.50
Huff,David	Cle	26	10	10	54	59	7	18	37	1	2	4	.333	0	13	4.67
Hughes,Dustin	KC	29	51	0	55	60	5	26	39	2	2	4	.333	0	14.4	4.75
Hughes,Phil	NYY	25	32	29	177	160	20	60	166	4	12	7	.632	0	11.4	3.56
Humber,Philip	KC	28	15	2	43	48	7	14	31	2	2	3	.400	0	13.4	5.02
Hunter,Tommy	Tex	24	29	27	158	171	21	46	91	4	8	10	.444	0	12.6	4.39
Jackson,Edwin	CWS	27	31	31	202	211	24	86	152	5	9	13	.409	0	13.5	4.54
Janssen,Casey	Tor	29	53	0	64	71	6	17	45	3	3	4	.429	0	12.8	4.36
Jenks,Bobby	CWS	30	47	0	49	44	4	17	48	1	3	2	.600	32	11.4	3.12
Jepsen,Kevin	LAA	26	71	0	64	63	4	32	62	1	3	4	.429	0	13.5	3.94
Jimenez,Ubaldo	Col	27	33	33	216	188	14	102	194	10	14	10	.583	0	12.5	3.63
Johnson,Jim	Bal	28	36	0	38	42	4	14	26	2	2	3	.400	0	13.7	4.74
Johnson,Josh	Fla	27	29	29	189	175	11	62	174	5	14	7	.667	0	11.5	3.38
Jurrjens,Jair	Atl	25	28	28	172	171	14	62	125	3	10	9	.526	0	12.3	3.82
Karstens,Jeff	Pit	28	21	16	102	115	14	29	65	1	5	7	.417	0	12.8	4.59
Kawakami,Kenshin	Atl	36	12	9	50	52	6	18	35	1	3	3	.500	0	12.8	4.32
Kazmir,Scott	LAA	27	29	29	162	153	20	75	151	7	8	10	.444	0	13.1	4.22
Kendrick,Kyle	Phi	26	32	31	179	200	21	50	82	8	9	11	.450	0	13	4.47
Kennedy,Ian	Ari	26	31	31	194	172	21	75	176	10	12	9	.571	0	11.9	3.66
Kershaw,Clayton	LAD	23	31	31	213	168	13	97	221	4	14	9	.609	0	11.4	3.13
Kimbrel,Craig	Atl	23	63	0	63	34	2	47	100	4	5	2	.714	25	12.1	2.57
Kirkman,Michael	Tex	24	27	0	33	31	3	18	28	1	2	2	.500	0	13.6	4.09
Kuo,Hong-Chih	LAD	29	60	0	66	50	4	25	78	2	5	2	.714	4	10.5	2.45
Kuroda,Hiroki	LAD	36	31	31	209	204	24	56	144	3	12	12	.500	0	11.3	3.66
Lackey,John	Bos	32	33	33	227	230	22	68	179	11	13	12	.520	0	12.3	3.89
Laffey,Aaron	Cle	26	20	2	35	40	2	14	20	2	2	2	.500	0	14.4	4.89
Lannan,John	Was	26	28	28	174	187	18	62	90	7	8	11	.421	0	13.2	4.40
Latos,Mat	SD	23	32	32	193	166	16	61	185	2	14	7	.667	0	10.7	3.26
League,Brandon	Sea	28	67	0	78	77	7	28	60	5	4	5	.444	2	12.7	3.92
LeBlanc,Wade	SD	26	28	28	157	153	24	54	132	4	7	10	.412	0	12.1	4.13
LeCure,Sam	Cin	27	20	3	46	49	6	18	39	3	2	3	.400	0	13.7	4.70
Ledezma,Wil	Pit	30	49	0	37	39	3	18	32	1	2	2	.500	0	14.1	4.62
Lee,Cliff	Tex	32	29	29	216	215	19	49	169	5	14	10	.583	0	11.2	3.50
Lester,Jon	Bos	27	31	31	204	178	15	82	193	7	14	9	.609	0	11.8	3.53
Lewis,Colby	Tex	31	33	33	208	199	23	73	178	7	12	11	.522	0	12.1	3.85
Lewis,Jensen	Cle	27	38	0	36	33	4	15	35	2	2	2	.500	0	12.5	3.75
Lidge,Brad	Phi	34	62	0	60	49	6	28	76	3	4	3	.571	30	12	3.45
Lilly,Ted	LAD	35	32	32	212	190	32	66	180	5	12	12	.500	0	11.1	3.65
Lincecum,Tim	SF	27	32	32	207	168	13	74	233	5	15	8	.652	0	10.7	3.00
Lindstrom,Matt	Hou	31	56	0	47	52	4	22	40	2	2	3	.400	6	14.6	4.79
Linebrink,Scott	CWS	34	56	0	64	63	10	21	56	2	3	4	.429	0	12.1	4.08
Liriano,Francisco	Min	27	31	31	190	181	17	66	195	7	13	8	.619	0	12	3.69
Loe,Kameron	Mil	29	65	0	69	78	8	25	41	2	3	4	.429	0	13.7	4.83
Logan,Boone	NYY	26	67	0	45	45	5	20	43	4	2	3	.400	0	13.8	4.40
Lohse,Kyle	StL	32	22	22	113	127	13	34	69	6	6	7	.462	0	13.1	4.54
Lopez,Javier	SF	33	76	0	57	58	3	25	36	3	3	3	.500	0	13.6	4.11
Lopez,Rodrigo	Ari	35	15	15	84	99	13	24	52	2	4	6	.400	0	13.4	5.04
Lopez,Wilton	Hou	27	71	0	73	85	6	11	47	1	4	4	.500	0	12	3.82
Lowe,Derek	Atl	38	32	32	193	203	16	57	123	3	11	10	.524	0	12.3	3.87
Lyon,Brandon	Hou	31	76	0	76	74	6	26	52	2	4	4	.500	23	12.1	3.55
MacDougal,Mike	StL	34	29	0	33	33	2	19	28	1	2	2	.500	0	14.5	4.64
Madson,Ryan	Phi	30	77	0	77	75	7	23	68	4	5	4	.556	3	11.9	3.62
Maholm,Paul	Pit	29	31	31	183	205	16	62	113	8	8	12	.400	0	13.5	4.52
Maloney,Matt	Cin	27	18	18	107	110	14	28	91	6	6	6	.500	0	12.1	4.04
Manship,Jeff	Min	26	18	0	36	45	3	11	26	1	2	2	.500	0	14.2	5.00
Marcum,Shaun	Tor	29	31	31	203	193	29	55	168	7	12	11	.522	0	11.3	3.77
Marmol,Carlos	ChC	28	79	0	83	56	6	51	105	8	6	4	.600	42	12.5	3.14
Marquis,Jason	Was	32	21	21	105	111	12	40	57	5	5	7	.417	0	13.4	4.46
Marshall,Sean	ChC	28	75	0	68	65	7	25	56	2	4	4	.500	0	12.2	3.84
Martin,J.D.	Was	28	14	14	70	74	8	17	47	3	4	4	.500	0	12.1	3.99
Masset,Nick	Cin	29	80	0	82	86	8	35	67	2	4	5	.444	0	13.5	4.39
Masterson,Justin	Cle	26	35	26	175	173	14	73	147	12	9	10	.474	0	13.3	4.11
Mateo,Marcos	ChC	27	41	0	43	44	6	17	38	3	2	3	.400	0	13.4	4.67
Mathieson,Scott	Phi	27	52	0	55	50	8	23	58	2	3	3	.500	2	12.3	3.93
Matsuzaka,Daisuke	Bos	30	27	27	173	159	17	73	158	8	10	9	.526	0	12.5	3.85
Matusz,Brian	Bal	24	31	31	181	179	19	62	154	6	10	10	.500	0	12.3	3.89
Mazzaro,Vin	Oak	24	26	19	131	131	12	48	95	9	6	8	.429	0	12.9	4.05
McCarthy,Brandon	Tex	27	25	25	143	137	20	48	108	4	8	8	.500	0	11.9	3.97

496

2011 Pitcher Projections

PLAYER			HOW MUCH			WHAT HE WILL GIVE UP					THE RESULTS				
Pitcher	Team	Age	G	GS	IP	H	HR	BB	SO	HB	W	L	Pct	Sv	BR/9	ERA
McClellan,Kyle	StL	27	68	0	74	66	7	26	59	3	5	3	.625	0	11.6	3.41
McClendon,Mike	Mil	26	33	0	42	42	2	11	34	2	3	2	.600	0	11.8	3.43
McCutchen,Daniel	Pit	28	43	7	84	92	12	23	55	3	4	5	.444	0	12.6	4.50
McDonald,James	Pit	26	23	22	132	120	11	54	129	6	8	7	.533	0	12.3	3.68
Meche,Gil	KC	32	26	4	50	52	6	21	37	1	2	3	.400	0	13.3	4.32
Meek,Evan	Pit	28	66	0	72	62	4	35	62	2	4	4	.500	12	12.4	3.38
Melancon,Mark	Hou	26	40	0	37	35	3	16	36	3	2	2	.500	0	13.1	3.89
Mendez,Adalberto	Fla	29	10	10	49	47	7	26	44	2	3	3	.500	0	13.8	4.59
Mijares,Jose	Min	26	44	0	30	26	4	15	28	1	2	1	.667	0	12.6	3.90
Miller,Andrew	Fla	26	17	14	65	73	6	43	54	4	3	5	.375	0	16.6	5.68
Miller,Trever	StL	38	52	0	32	28	3	13	29	2	2	1	.667	0	12.1	3.66
Mills,Brad	Tor	26	12	4	34	33	4	14	31	1	2	2	.500	0	12.7	3.97
Millwood,Kevin	Bal	36	31	31	202	225	25	65	143	7	9	13	.409	0	13.2	4.63
Miner,Zach	Det	29	30	4	58	62	5	27	37	2	3	4	.429	0	14.1	4.66
Misch,Pat	NYM	29	23	12	75	82	9	18	50	4	4	4	.500	0	12.5	4.20
Mitre,Sergio	NYY	30	32	1	61	67	7	19	38	4	3	3	.500	0	13.3	4.57
Mock,Garrett	Was	28	26	7	56	62	6	24	46	2	2	4	.333	0	14.1	4.82
Morrow,Brandon	Tor	26	27	27	162	140	15	86	173	5	9	9	.500	0	12.8	3.78
Morton,Charlie	Pit	27	18	18	94	101	8	38	68	5	4	6	.400	0	13.8	4.50
Moseley,Dustin	NYY	29	24	16	106	128	16	36	67	5	5	7	.417	0	14.3	5.52
Mota,Guillermo	SF	37	47	0	49	45	5	19	38	1	3	3	.500	0	11.9	3.49
Motte,Jason	StL	29	54	0	53	46	6	21	62	1	4	2	.667	0	11.5	3.40
Moyer,Jamie	Phi	48	9	9	56	59	8	15	33	3	3	3	.500	0	12.4	4.34
Moylan,Peter	Atl	32	83	0	63	57	3	32	51	3	4	3	.571	0	13.1	3.71
Mujica,Edward	SD	27	56	0	67	68	10	13	60	1	4	4	.500	0	11	3.76
Myers,Brett	Hou	30	33	33	215	212	29	71	183	6	10	14	.417	0	12.1	4.02
Narveson,Chris	Mil	29	34	29	180	181	24	74	149	6	9	11	.450	0	13	4.45
Nathan,Joe	Min	36	67	0	68	47	5	22	82	2	6	1	.857	34	9.4	1.99
Neshek,Pat	Min	30	62	0	57	49	7	20	61	2	4	2	.667	0	11.2	3.32
Niemann,Jeff	TB	28	28	26	147	142	19	56	119	7	8	8	.500	0	12.6	4.10
Niese,Jonathon	NYM	24	32	32	186	198	18	67	159	7	10	11	.476	0	13.2	4.31
Nippert,Dustin	Tex	30	33	1	50	52	6	23	41	2	2	3	.400	0	13.9	4.68
Nolasco,Ricky	Fla	28	30	30	179	183	24	44	164	5	11	9	.550	0	11.7	3.92
Norris,Bud	Hou	26	30	30	187	188	20	90	186	9	8	13	.381	0	13.8	4.52
Nova,Ivan	NYY	24	16	14	80	86	7	36	57	2	4	5	.444	0	14	4.61
Nunez,Leo	Fla	27	65	0	64	61	8	21	53	2	4	3	.571	28	11.8	3.80
O'Day,Darren	Tex	28	71	0	62	54	5	17	40	5	4	2	.667	0	11	2.90
O'Flahorty,Eric	Atl	26	49	0	41	40	2	17	33	3	2	2	.500	0	13.2	3.73
Ohlendorf,Ross	Pit	28	17	17	93	103	12	30	66	4	4	6	.400	0	13.3	4.74
Ohman,Will	Fla	33	57	0	39	35	4	19	38	1	2	2	.500	0	12.7	3.92
Okajima,Hideki	Bos	35	52	0	44	42	5	15	30	1	3	2	.600	0	11.9	3.68
Oliver,Darren	Tex	40	60	0	58	56	5	17	44	3	4	3	.571	0	11.8	3.41
Olsen,Scott	Was	27	20	16	88	95	13	35	65	1	4	6	.400	0	13.4	4.81
Olson,Garrett	Sea	27	42	0	47	48	6	21	38	2	2	3	.400	0	13.6	4.00
Ondrusek,Logan	Cin	26	68	0	69	64	4	22	48	2	5	3	.625	0	11.5	3.13
O'Sullivan,Sean	KC	23	27	23	131	147	20	43	80	3	6	9	.400	0	13.3	4.00
Oswalt,Roy	Phi	33	32	32	221	209	20	52	176	8	16	9	.640	0	11	3.38
Outman,Josh	Oak	26	20	15	86	79	8	38	60	2	5	5	.500	0	12.5	3.77
Padilla,Vicente	LAD	33	23	23	118	122	16	42	85	8	5	8	.385	0	13.1	4.50
Palmer,Matt	LAA	32	14	0	33	33	3	14	23	2	2	2	.500	0	13.4	4.36
Papelbon,Jonathan	Bos	30	66	0	69	55	6	20	76	3	5	3	.625	41	10.2	2.61
Park,Chan Ho	Pit	38	63	0	74	81	10	28	58	4	3	5	.375	0	13.7	4.99
Parnell,Bobby	NYM	26	50	0	42	45	4	19	35	1	2	3	.400	0	13.9	4.71
Parra,Manny	Mil	28	39	14	114	125	12	53	104	2	5	7	.417	0	14.2	4.82
Pauley,David	Sea	28	27	23	146	172	18	48	94	10	5	11	.313	0	14.2	5.18
Paulino,Felipe	Hou	27	22	22	124	133	13	60	112	4	5	9	.357	0	14.3	4.86
Pavano,Carl	Min	35	31	31	199	221	25	40	121	8	12	11	.522	0	12.2	4.16
Peavy,Jake	CWS	30	25	25	149	127	16	48	148	5	10	7	.588	0	10.9	3.50
Pelfrey,Mike	NYM	27	34	33	220	237	16	81	133	11	12	12	.500	0	13.5	4.25
Pena,Tony	CWS	29	48	6	120	128	12	40	80	4	6	7	.462	0	12.9	4.28
Peralta,Joel	Was	35	54	0	68	62	8	18	58	2	4	3	.571	0	10.9	3.31
Perez,Chris	Cle	25	59	0	64	46	7	35	72	5	4	3	.571	31	12.1	3.23
Perez,Oliver	NYM	29	14	3	31	29	5	19	30	2	1	2	.333	0	14.5	4.94
Perez,Rafael	Cle	29	70	0	66	68	5	23	55	2	4	4	.500	0	12.7	3.82
Perkins,Glen	Min	28	25	2	43	52	6	16	29	2	2	3	.400	0	14.7	5.23
Perry,Ryan	Det	24	67	0	77	70	8	37	65	3	4	4	.500	1	12.9	3.97
Pettitte,Andy	NYY	39	23	23	140	144	14	42	107	3	9	7	.563	0	12.2	3.86
Pineiro,Joel	LAA	32	29	29	193	209	20	50	110	5	10	11	.476	0	12.3	4.06
Porcello,Rick	Det	22	29	29	188	204	21	52	102	6	10	11	.476	0	12.5	4.21
Price,David	TB	25	32	32	217	189	22	87	191	7	14	10	.583	0	11.7	3.57
Purcey,David	Tor	29	36	0	36	36	4	19	33	2	2	2	.500	0	14.2	4.75
Putz,J.J.	CWS	34	59	0	50	42	4	17	53	1	4	2	.667	0	10.8	2.88
Qualls,Chad	TB	32	73	0	61	63	6	17	50	3	4	3	.571	0	12.3	2.84
Ramirez,Ramon	SF	29	70	0	75	66	7	31	61	1	5	4	.556	4	11.8	3.36
Rauch,Jon	Min	32	60	0	58	57	6	18	48	1	4	3	.571	0	11.8	3.57
Ray,Chris	SF	29	54	0	49	44	6	21	40	1	3	3	.500	0	12.1	3.86
Resop,Chris	Pit	28	43	0	39	36	2	10	38	1	2	2	.500	0	12.7	3.69
Reyes,Anthony	Cle	29	16	16	81	79	10	31	63	4	4	5	.444	0	12.7	4.22
Reyes,Dennys	StL	34	46	0	32	30	2	16	26	1	2	2	.500	0	13.2	3.94
Reynolds,Matt	Col	26	41	0	36	31	3	11	38	1	3	1	.750	0	10.8	3.00
Rhodes,Arthur	Cin	41	63	0	48	39	3	19	46	1	4	2	.667	0	11.1	2.81

2011 Pitcher Projections

Pitcher	Team	Age	G	GS	IP	H	HR	BB	SO	HB	W	L	Pct	Sv	BR/9	ERA
Richard,Clayton	SD	27	33	33	205	205	15	74	148	5	10	12	.455	0	12.5	3.60
Rivera,Mariano	NYY	41	61	0	62	47	3	11	58	3	5	2	.714	33	8.9	1.89
Robertson,David	NYY	26	69	0	68	53	4	35	89	2	5	2	.714	0	11.9	3.04
Robertson,Nate	Phi	33	13	9	52	59	7	19	35	2	2	3	.400	0	13.8	5.02
Rodney,Fernando	LAA	34	74	0	74	68	6	39	67	5	4	4	.500	6	13.6	4.14
Rodriguez,Francisco	LAA	28	47	0	49	48	5	24	38	2	2	3	.400	0	13.6	4.22
Rodriguez,Francisco	NYM	29	69	0	67	50	5	30	81	1	5	2	.714	35	10.9	2.69
Rodriguez,Henry	Oak	24	44	0	41	33	2	30	52	1	2	2	.500	0	14	3.95
Rodriguez,Wandy	Hou	32	31	31	206	196	22	65	184	8	12	11	.522	0	11.8	3.71
Rogers,Esmil	Col	25	35	13	100	113	8	35	81	6	5	6	.455	0	13.9	4.59
Romero,J.C.	Phi	35	64	0	38	32	3	25	30	3	2	2	.500	0	14.2	4.26
Romero,Ricky	Tor	26	31	31	213	211	20	91	176	10	12	12	.500	0	13.2	4.31
Romo,Sergio	SF	28	66	0	59	45	4	15	64	4	5	2	.714	0	9.8	2.29
Rowland-Smith,Ryan	Sea	28	20	11	71	74	9	26	48	3	3	5	.375	0	13.1	4.44
Russell,James	ChC	25	61	0	52	62	11	15	39	3	2	4	.333	0	13.8	5.71
Rzepczynski,Marc	Tor	25	21	20	110	112	10	52	111	6	5	7	.417	0	13.9	4.50
Sabathia,CC	NYY	30	34	34	236	215	19	65	202	8	18	8	.692	0	11	3.32
Saito,Takashi	Atl	41	50	0	50	42	4	15	54	2	4	2	.667	0	10.6	2.88
Salas,Fernando	StL	26	38	0	44	38	6	14	48	1	3	2	.600	0	10.8	3.27
Samardzija,Jeff	ChC	26	8	6	34	34	4	18	26	1	1	2	.333	0	14	5.03
Sanches,Brian	Fla	32	63	0	74	67	9	29	71	4	5	4	.556	0	12.2	3.77
Sanchez,Anibal	Fla	27	33	33	204	202	17	84	169	8	12	10	.545	0	13	3.97
Sanchez,Jonathan	SF	28	34	33	204	170	21	102	215	10	12	11	.522	0	12.4	3.71
Santana,Ervin	LAA	28	33	33	211	213	27	67	169	12	11	13	.458	0	12.5	4.14
Santana,Johan	NYM	32	28	28	195	167	21	49	181	3	15	7	.682	0	10.1	3.09
Saunders,Joe	Ari	30	33	33	215	229	26	68	129	5	11	13	.458	0	12.6	4.27
Scherzer,Max	Det	26	31	31	205	180	19	78	209	10	13	10	.565	0	11.8	3.56
Schlereth,Daniel	Det	25	29	0	32	27	1	23	38	2	2	2	.500	6	14.6	3.94
Seay,Bobby	Det	33	40	0	36	36	3	14	30	2	2	2	.500	0	13	3.75
Sherrill,George	LAD	34	66	0	37	32	3	18	37	1	2	2	.500	0	12.4	3.41
Shields,James	TB	29	34	33	204	217	27	47	170	7	11	11	.500	0	12	4.06
Shields,Scot	LAA	35	35	0	39	34	3	17	36	1	2	2	.500	0	12	3.46
Silva,Carlos	ChC	32	24	24	133	163	17	25	61	5	6	9	.400	0	13.1	4.80
Simon,Alfredo	Bal	30	50	0	50	62	10	19	33	3	2	4	.333	0	15.1	6.12
Sipp,Tony	Cle	27	71	0	68	54	10	36	81	1	4	4	.500	0	12	3.71
Slaten,Doug	Was	31	53	0	48	45	3	19	43	2	3	2	.600	0	12.4	3.56
Slowey,Kevin	Min	27	26	24	132	143	19	24	102	4	8	7	.533	0	11.7	4.02
Smith,Joe	Cle	27	62	0	48	42	3	25	41	2	3	3	.500	0	12.9	3.56
Smith,Jordan	Cin	25	47	0	54	64	7	17	31	2	2	4	.333	0	13.8	5.00
Snell,Ian	Sea	29	21	7	47	50	5	21	37	1	2	3	.400	0	13.8	4.79
Sonnanstine,Andy	TB	28	36	8	88	98	12	22	60	3	4	5	.444	0	12.6	4.40
Soria,Joakim	KC	27	65	0	67	52	5	18	74	3	4	3	.571	46	9.8	2.42
Soriano,Rafael	TB	31	63	0	62	43	5	18	68	2	4	2	.667	42	9.1	2.03
Sosa,Jorge	Fla	34	28	0	32	35	4	13	23	0	2	2	.500	0	13.5	4.78
Stammen,Craig	Was	27	42	11	106	117	11	31	61	2	5	7	.417	0	12.7	4.33
Stauffer,Tim	SD	29	39	12	116	119	10	39	78	4	6	7	.462	0	12.6	3.96
Street,Huston	Col	27	62	0	69	60	7	20	70	1	4	3	.571	35	10.6	2.61
Suppan,Jeff	StL	36	25	14	94	110	12	33	50	4	4	6	.400	0	14.1	5.17
Sweeney,Brian	Sea	37	28	0	43	42	4	10	28	2	2	2	.500	0	11.3	3.35
Talbot,Mitch	Cle	27	25	25	137	154	12	53	102	8	6	9	.400	0	14.1	4.73
Tallet,Brian	Tor	33	40	2	83	86	12	37	61	4	4	6	.400	0	13.8	4.88
Tejeda,Robinson	KC	29	45	0	51	45	5	29	46	2	3	3	.500	0	13.4	4.06
Texeira,Kanekoa	KC	25	37	0	55	60	5	26	41	2	2	4	.333	0	14.4	4.75
Thatcher,Joe	SD	29	76	0	37	33	2	12	41	2	2	2	.500	0	11.4	2.92
Thomas,Brad	Det	33	53	1	71	79	5	29	46	3	3	4	.429	0	14.1	4.56
Thornton,Matt	CWS	34	57	0	61	50	5	25	68	1	4	3	.571	2	11.2	2.95
Tillman,Chris	Bal	23	13	13	70	73	9	27	58	2	3	4	.429	0	13.1	4.37
Tomlin,Josh	Cle	26	20	20	128	129	19	35	95	5	7	8	.467	0	11.9	4.08
Troncoso,Ramon	LAD	28	44	0	53	55	4	21	38	3	2	3	.400	0	13.4	4.25
Uehara,Koji	Bal	36	58	0	64	59	8	8	57	0	4	3	.571	31	9.4	2.81
Valdes,Raul	NYM	33	31	2	53	60	6	20	45	3	2	3	.400	0	14.1	4.92
Valverde,Jose	Det	33	49	0	57	44	6	25	64	2	4	2	.667	26	11.2	3.00
VandenHurk,Rick	Bal	26	14	2	33	31	4	14	30	2	2	2	.500	0	12.8	4.09
Vargas,Jason	Sea	28	31	31	195	205	24	67	135	4	8	14	.364	0	12.7	4.29
Vasquez,Esmerling	Ari	27	58	0	52	48	5	31	44	5	2	3	.400	0	14.5	4.67
Vazquez,Javier	NYY	34	30	30	198	188	27	55	183	7	13	9	.591	0	11.4	3.73
Venters,Jonny	Atl	26	74	0	74	73	3	40	61	4	4	4	.500	0	14.2	4.14
Veras,Jose	Fla	30	65	0	66	57	7	34	69	4	4	3	.571	0	13	3.95
Verlander,Justin	Det	28	33	33	226	207	19	74	209	10	15	10	.600	0	11.6	3.46
Villanueva,Carlos	Mil	27	58	0	69	67	10	26	63	2	4	4	.500	0	12.4	4.17
Volquez,Edinson	Cin	27	32	32	182	157	18	94	181	10	10	10	.500	0	12.9	3.91
Volstad,Chris	Fla	24	30	30	186	192	19	69	119	6	11	10	.524	0	12.9	4.21
Wainwright,Adam	StL	29	32	32	211	197	16	59	175	5	15	8	.652	0	11.1	3.37
Wakefield,Tim	Bos	44	31	14	115	114	15	37	72	7	6	6	.500	0	12.4	4.07
Walters,P.J.	StL	26	6	3	32	33	4	12	28	2	2	2	.500	0	13.2	4.50
Wang,Chien-Ming	NYY	31	25	25	140	149	8	39	66	4	9	7	.563	0	12.3	3.99
Weaver,Jeff	LAD	34	33	0	36	42	5	11	24	2	1	3	.250	0	13.8	5.00
Weaver,Jered	LAA	28	34	34	222	205	25	61	199	3	14	10	.583	0	10.9	3.45
Webb,Brandon	Ari	32	28	28	179	166	12	58	142	7	12	8	.600	0	11.6	3.42
Webb,Ryan	SD	25	52	0	55	61	5	19	42	1	2	4	.333	0	13.3	4.42
Wells,Randy	ChC	28	31	31	201	211	20	65	152	6	11	12	.478	0	12.6	4.12

498

2011 Pitcher Projections

PLAYER			HOW MUCH			WHAT HE WILL GIVE UP					THE RESULTS					
Pitcher	Team	Age	G	GS	IP	H	HR	BB	SO	HB	W	L	Pct	Sv	BR/9	ERA
Westbrook,Jake	StL	33	33	33	214	224	19	68	122	7	13	11	.542	0	12.6	4.00
Wheeler,Dan	TB	33	63	0	47	38	7	14	42	1	3	2	.600	0	10.1	2.87
White,Sean	Sea	30	37	0	37	43	3	15	19	2	1	3	.250	0	14.6	4.86
Willis,Dontrelle	Ari	29	7	6	33	35	3	15	23	2	2	2	.500	0	14.2	4.64
Wilson,Brian	SF	29	71	0	80	68	4	35	87	3	5	4	.556	48	11.9	3.04
Wilson,C.J.	Tex	30	33	33	208	180	14	95	186	12	13	10	.565	0	12.4	3.59
Wolf,Randy	Mil	34	34	34	229	223	29	83	173	10	13	13	.500	0	12.4	4.05
Wood,Blake	KC	25	52	0	52	61	5	22	36	3	2	4	.333	0	14.9	5.19
Wood,Kerry	NYY	34	57	0	62	51	6	28	69	4	4	3	.571	25	12	3.48
Wood,Travis	Cin	24	24	24	149	135	13	52	126	8	9	7	.563	0	11.8	3.56
Wright,Jamey	Sea	36	53	0	70	74	6	33	42	5	3	5	.375	0	14.4	4.76
Wright,Wesley	Hou	26	15	5	37	37	5	21	34	2	1	3	.250	0	14.6	5.11
Wuertz,Michael	Oak	32	48	0	44	35	4	20	49	0	3	2	.600	0	11.2	3.07
Young,Chris	SD	32	20	20	112	91	13	46	95	3	7	6	.538	0	11.2	3.46
Zambrano,Carlos	ChC	30	33	33	221	195	17	100	188	11	14	11	.560	0	12.5	3.67
Ziegler,Brad	Oak	31	56	0	55	54	3	19	36	2	3	3	.500	0	12.3	3.44
Zimmermann,Jordan	Was	25	23	23	132	123	16	45	120	5	8	7	.533	0	11.8	3.75
Zito,Barry	SF	33	34	32	183	173	20	78	131	7	10	11	.476	0	12.7	3.98

Career Targets

This section is designed to give probabilities on players achieving important career milestones. The method (formerly under the name of "The Favorite Toy") was developed by Bill James and takes into account a player's age and performance level in predicting the probability that he will accumulate certain career stats. A detailed explanation of how the system works can be found in the glossary.

Congratulations to Alex Rodriguez, who became the seventh member of the 600 home run club this season. In 2010, Jim Thome moved into the all-time top 10 in home runs and Ken Griffey, Jr. ended his storied career with 630 home runs.

Aside from home run milestones, this season served as a bridge to the possibility of even more milestones next year.

- A healthy 2011 and 74 hits means that Derek Jeter becomes the first Yankee to reach 3,000 hits.

-Brandon Morrow tops our "Most Likely No-Hitter" chart. He came close this past August with a 17-strikeout one-hitter. Despite the abundance of great pitching performances in 2010, no pitcher is currently over 25% to twirl a no-no in his future.

-Injury-shortened seasons in 2009 and 2010 mean that A-Rod has dropped to a 33% chance to break the home run record.

-Manny Ramirez's quest for 600 home runs has dropped from 67% to 26%.

3,000 Hits	
% chance to reach milestone	
Jeter,Derek	99%
Rodriguez,Alex	93%
Damon,Johnny	57%
Pujols,Albert	51%
Guerrero,Vladimir	44%
Rodriguez,Ivan	37%
Cabrera,Miguel	37%
Suzuki,Ichiro	36%
Crawford,Carl	30%
Beltre,Adrian	29%
Tejada,Miguel	26%
Cano,Robinson	26%
Young,Michael	21%
Markakis,Nick	21%
Wright,David	19%
Ramirez,Hanley	18%
Braun,Ryan	17%
Butler,Billy	16%
Abreu,Bobby	14%
Pierre,Juan	13%
Zimmerman,Ryan	13%
Holliday,Matt	11%
Lee,Carlos	11%
Lopez,Jose	10%
Fielder,Prince	9%
Kemp,Matt	9%
Teixeira,Mark	9%
Polanco,Placido	9%
Wells,Vernon	9%
Young,Delmon	8%
Longoria,Evan	6%
Gonzalez,Adrian	6%
Loney,James	4%
Vizquel,Omar	4%
Konerko,Paul	4%
Lee,Derrek	4%
Pence,Hunter	4%
Rios,Alex	4%
Sandoval,Pablo	3%
Rollins,Jimmy	3%
Votto,Joey	3%
Cabrera,Orlando	3%
Jones,Adam	2%
Upton,Justin	2%
Tulowitzki,Troy	1%
Phillips,Brandon	< 1%
Reyes,Jose	< 1%
Francoeur,Jeff	< 1%
Renteria,Edgar	< 1%
Gonzalez,Carlos	< 1%

Career Targets

762 Home Runs
% chance to break record

Rodriguez,Alex	33%
Pujols,Albert	23%
Dunn,Adam	6%
Cabrera,Miguel	3%
Fielder,Prince	2%

2,298 RBI
% chance to break record

Rodriguez,Alex	47%
Pujols,Albert	19%
Cabrera,Miguel	13%

2,296 Runs Scored
% chance to break record

Pujols,Albert	12%
Rodriguez,Alex	10%
Jeter,Derek	2%

4,257 Hits
% chance to break record

900 Home Runs
% chance to reach milestone

Pujols,Albert	2%

2,000 RBI
% chance to reach milestone

Rodriguez,Alex	96%
Pujols,Albert	46%
Cabrera,Miguel	29%
Ramirez,Manny	23%
Teixeira,Mark	13%
Howard,Ryan	10%
Fielder,Prince	8%
Dunn,Adam	5%
Guerrero,Vladimir	5%
Longoria,Evan	5%

6,857 Total Bases
% chance to break record

Pujols,Albert	15%
Cabrera,Miguel	8%
Rodriguez,Alex	7%

4,000 Hits
% chance to reach milestone

Cabrera,Miguel	4%
Jeter,Derek	3%
Pujols,Albert	3%

800 Home Runs
% chance to reach milestone

Rodriguez,Alex	16%
Pujols,Albert	16%
Dunn,Adam	2%

600 Home Runs
% chance to reach milestone

Griffey Jr.,Ken	done
Rodriguez,Alex	done
Thome,Jim	99%
Pujols,Albert	84%
Dunn,Adam	43%
Cabrera,Miguel	28%
Ramirez,Manny	26%
Fielder,Prince	23%
Howard,Ryan	17%
Teixeira,Mark	15%

793 Doubles
% chance to break record

Pujols,Albert	18%
Markakis,Nick	12%
Cabrera,Miguel	10%
Butler,Billy	10%
Cano,Robinson	7%
Longoria,Evan	7%
Wright,David	3%
Beltre,Adrian	3%
Braun,Ryan	2%

Most Likely No-Hitter
% chance to reach milestone

Morrow,Brandon	22%
Lester,Jon	19%
Sanchez,Jonathan	18%
Lincecum,Tim	17%
Kershaw,Clayton	17%
Strasburg,Stephen	16%
Jimenez,Ubaldo	16%
Gallardo,Yovani	16%
Hamels,Cole	15%
Latos,Mat	15%

700 Home Runs
% chance to reach milestone

Rodriguez,Alex	92%
Pujols,Albert	38%
Dunn,Adam	16%
Cabrera,Miguel	10%
Fielder,Prince	8%
Howard,Ryan	2%

500 Home Runs
% chance to reach milestone

Griffey Jr.,Ken	done
Rodriguez,Alex	done
Thome,Jim	done
Ramirez,Manny	done
Pujols,Albert	94%
Dunn,Adam	89%
Guerrero,Vladimir	81%
Cabrera,Miguel	58%
Konerko,Paul	46%
Fielder,Prince	46%

1,000 Stolen Bases
% chance to reach milestone

Crawford,Carl	6%
Pierre,Juan	4%

Pitchers on Course
For 300 Wins

Bill James

Name	2010 Age	R/L	W	L	EWL	Momentum	Chance
Halladay, Roy	33	R	169	86	17.8	.888	.42
Sabathia, CC	29	L	157	88	17.6	.889	.38
Moyer, Jamie	47	L	267	204	8.3	.635	.16
Pettitte, Andy	38	L	240	138	10.2	.722	.15
Haren, Dan	29	R	91	74	13.1	.886	.14
Verlander, Justin	27	R	83	52	16.4	.842	.10
Hernandez, Felix	24	R	71	53	14.1	.857	.08
Hudson, Tim	34	R	165	87	11.9	.745	.04
Lowe, Derek	37	R	157	129	13.1	.733	.03
Oswalt, Roy	32	R	150	83	12.2	.747	.03
Lee, Cliff	31	L	102	61	12.3	.800	.03
Santana, Johan	31	L	133	69	11.0	.787	.03
Buehrle, Mark	31	L	148	110	10.7	.745	.02
Carpenter, Chris	35	R	133	83	13.1	.722	.02
Arroyo, Bronson	33	R	103	93	13.2	.756	.02
Vazquez, Javier	33	R	152	149	10.2	.757	.02
Garland, Jon	30	R	131	114	11.6	.747	.01
Dempster, Ryan	33	R	102	102	13.3	.735	.01
Lackey, John	31	R	116	82	12.3	.708	.01
Wakefield, Tim	43	R	193	172	6.2	.608	< .01
Lilly, Ted	34	L	113	96	10.9	.727	< .01
Zito, Barry	32	L	142	120	9.4	.711	< .01
Myers, Brett	29	R	87	71	11.2	.734	< .01
Wolf, Randy	33	L	114	97	11.2	.700	< .01
Hernandez, Livan	35	R	166	163	9.1	.604	< .01
Pavano, Carl	34	R	97	89	12.1	.695	< .01
Millwood, Kevin	35	R	159	137	7.1	.659	< .01

Note: EWL = Established Win Level

The two pitchers in baseball today who have the best chance to win 300 games are Roy Halladay and the artist formerly known as Carsten Charles Sabathia. This statement was true a year ago; however, the situation is very different now than it was a year ago. A year ago, the no-hit pitcher and the Big Lefty were first and second on a list of contenders. Now they have separated themselves from the field.

It is likely that one or two pitchers now active will win 300 games, and two is more likely than one.

Baseball Glossary

% Inherited Scored
The percentage of inherited baserunners a relief pitcher allows to score.

% Pitches Taken
The percentage of pitches that a batter does not swing at out of the total number of pitches thrown to him.

1st Batter Average
The Batting Average that a relief pitcher allows to the first batter he faces when he enters a game.

1st Batter OBP
The On-Base Percentage that a relief pitcher allows to the first batter he faces when he enters a game.

1st to 3rd (Baserunning)
"Moved" is the number of times a runner goes from 1st base to 3rd base on a SINGLE. "Chances" are the number of times a runner is on 1st base and a batter is credited with a SINGLE.

1st to Home (Baserunning)
"Moved" is the number of times a runner goes from 1st base to home on a DOUBLE. "Chances" are the number of times a runner is on 1st base and a batter is credited with a DOUBLE.

2nd to Home (Baserunning)
"Moved" is the number of times a runner goes from 2nd base to home on a SINGLE. "Chances" are the number of times a runner is on 2nd base and a batter is credited with a SINGLE.

Active Career Batting Leaders
A list of batting leaders among active (appearing in the most recent season) players. An active player is eligible when he meets the minimum requirements for the following categories:

> 1,000 At Bats—Batting Average, On-Base Percentage, Slugging Average, At Bats Per HR, At Bats Per GDP, At Bats Per RBI, Strikeout to Walk Ratio
> 100 Stolen Base Attempts—Stolen Base Success Percentage

Active Career Pitching Leaders
A list of pitching leaders among active (appearing in the most recent season) players. An active player is eligible when he meets the minimum requirements for the following categories:

750 Innings Pitched—Earned Run Average, Opponent Batting Average, all "Per
9 Innings" categories, Strikeout to Walk Ratio
250 Games Started—Complete Game Frequency
100 Decisions—Win-Loss Percentage

AVG Allowed ScPos
The Batting Average allowed by a pitcher while pitching with runners in scoring position.

AVG Bases Loaded
The Batting Average of a hitter while batting with the bases loaded.

Base Taken
A player is credited with a Base Taken whenever he moves up a base on a Wild Pitch, Passed Ball, Balk, Sacrifice Fly, or Defensive Indifference.

Batting Average
Hits divided by at bats.

Blown Save
When a relief pitcher enters a game in a Save Situation (see definition for Save Situation) and allows the other team to score the tying or go-ahead run.

Bomb (Intentional Walk)
An Intentional Walk is counted as a "Bomb" if
1) The next batter, after the IBB, does not ground into a double play, and
2) Multiple runs are scored in the inning, after the intentional walk.

BR Gain (Baserunning)
BR Gain (or Loss if a negative number) is the total of all the types of extra baserunning advances minus the (triple) penalty for all the BR Outs compared with what would be expected based on the MLB averages.

BR Outs (Baserunning)
BR Outs include the sum of Outs Advancing, Doubled Offs, and when a runner is tagged out on the bases when another runner moves up on a Wild Pitch, Passed Ball, or scores on a Sacrifice Fly.

BS Win
A Blown Save Win is a "win" credited to a reliever who has blown a save opportunity.

Career Targets
This method, once called the Favorite Toy, is a way to estimate the probability that a player will achieve a specific career goal. In this example, 3,000 hits will be used. The four components of the formula are Needed Hits, Years Remaining, Established Hit Level and Projected Remaining Hits.

Needed Hits. This is the number of Hits (or any statistic) that a player needs to reach a desired goal.

Years Remaining. This is the estimated number of years remaining in the player's career. It is determined using the player's age (on June 30th of the previous year; use 2010 when making the calculation after the 2010 season is complete). The formula is (42 - age) divided by two. This means a player who is 20 years old will have 11 remaining seasons, a player who is 25 years old will have 8.5 remaining seasons and a player who is 35 years old will have 3.5 remaining seasons. If the player is a catcher, then multiply his remaining seasons by .7. The only stipulation is that years remaining must always be greater than or equal to 1.5.

Established Hit Level. The Established Hit Level is a weighted average of the player's hits over the past three seasons. To calculate the Established Hit Level after the 2010 season is complete, add 2008 Hits, (2009 Hits multiplied by two) and (2010 Hits multiplied by three), then divide by six. If the Established Hit Level is less than 75% of the most recent performance (2010 Hits in this case), then the Established Hit Level is equal to .75 times the most recent performance.

Projected Remaining Hits. This is calculated by multiplying Years Remaining by the Established Hit Level.

The probability of achieving the specified goal is found by dividing Projected Remaining Hits by Needed Hits, then subtracting .5. The maximum that any player has of achieving a goal is .97 raised to the power of (Need Hits / Established Hit Level). This prevents the possibility of a player reaching a goal from being higher than 100 percent, which is impossible.

Catcher's ERA
The ERA for a catcher is equal to the ERA of pitchers pitching while the catcher is playing behind the plate. It is calculated exactly like ERA for pitchers. Take the number of earned runs allowed while the catcher is playing, multiply it by 9 and then divide it by the total number of defensive innings that the catcher was behind the plate.

Cheap Win
A starting pitcher who wins the game with a game score under 50 gets credit for a cheap win. See Game Score.

Clean Outing
A Clean Outing is a game in which the reliever is not charged with a run (earned or otherwise) AND does not allow an inherited runner to score.

Cleanup Slugging Average
The Slugging Average of a batter when he bats in the cleanup spot, or fourth, in the batting order.

Close and Late
A situation in a game that is very similar to a Save Situation. The following requirements are necessary for a Close and Late game:
   1.The game is in the seventh inning or later AND

2.The batting team is either leading by one run or tied OR

3.The tying run is on base, at bat, or on deck.

Component ERA (ERC)

A statistic that estimates what a pitcher's ERA should have been, based on his pitching performance. The ERC formula is calculated as follows:

1.Subtract the pitcher's Home Runs Allowed from his Hits Allowed.

2.Multiply Step 1 by 1.255.

3.Multiply his Home Runs Allowed by four.

4.Add Steps 2 and 3 together.

5.Multiply Step 4 by .89.

6.Add his Walks and Hit Batsmen.

7.Multiply Step 6 by .475.

8.Add Steps 5 and 7 together.

This yields the pitcher's total base estimate (PTB), which is:

$$PTB \ = \ 0.89 \times (1.255 \times (H - HR) + 4 \times HR) + 0.475 \times (BB + HB)$$

For those pitchers for whom there is intentional walk data, use this formula instead:

$$PTB \ = \ 0.89 \times (1.255 \times (H - HR) + 4 \times HR) + 0.56 \times (BB + HB - IBB)$$

9.Add Hits and Walks and Hit Batsmen.

10.Multiply Step 9 by PTB.

11.Divide Step 10 by Batters Facing Pitcher. If BFP data is unavailable, approximate it by multiplying Innings Pitched by 2.9, then adding Step 9.

12.Multiply Step 11 by 9.

13.Divide Step 12 by Innings Pitched.

14.Subtract .56 from Step 13.

This is the pitcher's ERC, which is:

$$\frac{(H + BB + HB) \times PTB}{BFP \times IP} \times 9 - 0.56$$

If the result after Step 13 is less than 2.24, adjust the formula as follows:

$$\frac{(H + BB + HB) \times PTB}{BFP \times IP} \times 9 \times 0.75$$

Consecutive Days

A count of how many times the pitcher was used after having pitched on the previous day or (in a few cases) in an earlier game on the same day.

Defensive Runs Saved (Runs Saved, for short) is the innovative metric introduced by John Dewan in *The Fielding Bible—Volume II*. The Runs Saved value indicates how many runs a player saved or hurt his team in the field compared to the average player at his position. A player near zero Runs Saved is about average; a positive number of runs saved indicates above-average defense, below-average fielders post negative Runs Saved totals. There are eight components of Runs Saved:

Plus Minus Runs Saved (all positions except Catcher)
Earned Runs Saved (Catchers)
Stolen Base Runs Saved (Catchers)
Stolen Base Runs Saved (Pitchers)
Bunt Runs Saved (Corner Infielders)
Double Play Runs Saved (Middle Infielders)
Outfield Arm Runs Saved (Outfielders)
Home Run Saving Catch Runs Saved (Outfielders)

Double Play %
Successful Double Plays divided by the number of Double Play opportunities. This statistic includes both the fielder who started the play and the pivot man.

Double Play Opportunity
A fielder is considered to have a double play opportunity when a ground ball is hit with a runner on first base and less than 2 outs and that fielder is involved in the play. This is used to calculate Double Play % and Pivot %.

Doubled Off
A runner is Doubled Off when he is out for failing to get back to his base before he, or the base, is tagged after a ball hit in the air is caught.

Early Entry
A count of the number of times the reliever entered the game in the sixth inning or earlier.

Earned Run Average
The number of earned runs that a pitcher surrenders per nine innings that he pitches. It is calculated by multiplying the total earned runs allowed by nine and dividing by the total number of innings pitched.

Easy Save
This label is used to separate Saves by difficulty level (Easy or Tough). A Save is considered Easy if the relief pitcher enters the game, pitches one inning or less, and the first batter he faces does not at least represent the tying run.

Fielding Percentage
The percentage of plays a player makes in the field without making an error out of the total number of opportunities. It is calculated by adding (Putouts plus Assists) and dividing by (Putouts plus Assists plus Errors).

Games Finished
The relief pitcher who is in the game for each team when the game ends is credited with a Game Finished.

Game Score
To determine the starting pitcher's Game Score:
Start with 50.
Add 1 point for each out recorded by the starting pitcher.
Add 2 points for each inning the pitcher completes after the fourth inning.
Add 1 point for each strikeout.
Subtract 2 points for each hit allowed.
Subtract 4 points for each earned run allowed.
Subtract 2 points for an unearned run.
Subtract 1 point for each walk.

GDP
Grounded into Double Play

GDP Opportunity
This is a situation where the batter has a chance to ground into a double play. It occurs with at least a runner on first base and less than two outs.

Ground / Fly Ratio (Grd/Fly, GB/FB)
Calculated for both batters and pitchers. For batters, it is the number of groundballs hit divided by the number of flyballs hit. For pitchers, it is exactly the same but uses the number of groundballs and flyballs allowed. Every fair batted ball is included except for bunts and line drives.

Hold
A relief pitcher is given a Hold anytime he enters the game in a Save Situation (see definition for Save Situation), records one out or more, and exits the game without giving up the lead. If the pitcher finishes the game, then he will only earn credit for a Save. He cannot receive credit for both a Hold and a Save.

Holds Adjusted Saves Percentage (same as Save/Hold Percentage)
Holds plus Saves divided by Holds plus Saves Opportunities.

Inherited Runner
When a relief pitcher enters the game, any runner who was on base at the time is considered an Inherited Runner.

Isolated Power
Slugging Average minus Batting Average.

K/BB Ratio
Strikeouts divided by Walks.

510

Leadoff On-Base Percentage
The On-Base Percentage of a batter when he bats leadoff, or first, in the batting order.

Leverage Index
Leverage is the amount of swing in the possible change in win probability, compared to the average swing in all situations. The average swing value, by definition, is indexed to 1.00.

If the score of the game is 12-0 or 14-1 the possible changes in win probability will be very close to negligible. Whether the pitcher gives up a home run or gets a double play ball doesn't really change the outcome of the game. There won't be much swing in either direction for the probability of the win. But in the late innings of a close game, the change in win probability among the various events will have rather wild swings. With a runner on first, two outs, down by one, and in the bottom of the ninth, the game can hinge on one swing of that bat. A home run and an out will both end the game, but with different outcomes for the teams involved. The Leverage Index we use (LI) was developed at the website Tangotiger.net, and compiled at the website Fangraphs.com.

Long Outing
A Long Outing is one in which the starting pitcher throws more than 110 pitches. Prior to 2002, we used 120 pitches as the cutoff in the Manager's Record section.

Long Save
A Long Save is when the pitcher credited with a save pitches more than one inning.

Manufactured Runs
1) A run that scores without a hit, or a run on which the only hit(s) is/are infield hits, is always scored as a Manufactured Run.
2) A run which is driven in by a home run is never scored a Manufactured Run, under any circumstance.
3) A run which is driven in by a double or a triple is scored as a Manufactured Run only if *two* of the four bases result from advancing on one of these four acts: a sacrifice bunt, a stolen base, a hit and run, or a bunt single.
4) Otherwise, a run is considered to be a Manufactured Run if two of the four bases do not result from the runner being forced along by a walk, a hit batsman, or a safe hit reaching the outfield.
5) A forceout or fielder's choice which does not improve the position of the base runners should not be counted as contributing toward a Manufactured Run. Advancing on a forceout or a fielder's choice DOES count toward a manufactured run, if the play is one which improves the position of the baserunners.
6) A base "gained" on a double play does not count as a contribution to a Manufactured Run. A run scored on a double play is a Manufactured Run only if two of the OTHER bases are not attributable to forced advancement.

Not Good Outcome (Intentional Walk)
A Not Good Outcome (NG) for an Intentional Walk occurs when one run scored in the inning after the intentional walk (and the next batter after the intentional walk did not ground into a double play).

Offensive Winning Percentage (OWP)

A player's Offensive Winning Percentage is the winning percentage of a hypothetical team which has an offense consisting of nine of that player, and pitching and defense which is average for the player's league. It is calculated by taking the square of RC/27 (see the definition for Runs Created per 27 Outs), dividing it by the sum of the square of RC/27 and the square of the average runs scored per game in the league.

On-Base Percentage

(Hits plus Walks plus Hit by Pitcher) divided by (At Bats plus Walks plus Hit by Pitcher plus Sacrifice Flies).

$$\frac{H + BB + HBP}{AB + BB + HBP + SF}$$

Opponent Batting Average

Hits Allowed divided by (Batters Faced minus Walks minus Hit Batsmen minus Sacrifice Hits minus Sacrifice Flies minus Catcher's Interference).

$$\frac{H}{BFP - BB - HBP - SH - SF - CI}$$

Opposition OPS

The OPS of the hitters facing the pitcher.

Out Advancing

A runner is out advancing when he is tagged out attempting to score from 2nd base on a single or from 1st base on a double, or attempting to go from 1st base to 3rd base on a single.

PA*

Used in the denominator for the calculation of On-Base Percentage. It is calculated by subtracting (Sacrifice Hits plus Times Reached Base on Defensive Interference) from Plate Appearances (see definition for Plate Appearances).

Park Index

To calculate the park index for home runs in a given ballpark, we take the total home runs of both the home team and its opponents at the ballpark and compare it to the total home runs of the home team and its opponents in other games. We then divide each of those totals by the at-bats in the equivalent situations, so that if there are more at-bats in either situation the index is not skewed. The result is then multiplied by 100 to yield the familiar form.

The park indices for doubles, triples, walks, strikeouts and home runs by lefties and righties are determined like home runs above—relative to at-bats. Indices of at-bats, runs, hits, errors and infield fielding errors (E-Infield) are calculated relative to games. The three batting average indices are calculated as is, since these are already relative to at-bats.

PCS (Pitchers' Caught Stealing)

The number of runners officially scored as Caught Stealing where the pitcher initiated the play. The normal Caught Stealing is when a runner is out attempting to steal a base but the play was initiated by the catcher. PCS plays are often referred to as pickoffs, but differ when the runner breaks towards the next base as opposed to returning to the base he was currently on. Pickoffs occur when the pitcher throws to a base that a runner is leading from, and the runner is out attempting to return to that base. Pickoffs are not an official statistic.

Pitches per PA

The total number of pitches a hitter sees divided by his total Plate Appearances.

Pivot %

Successful Double Plays turned by pivot man divided by the number of Double Play opportunities with that pivot man involved.

Plate Appearances

At Bats plus Total Walks plus Hit By Pitcher plus Sacrifice Hits plus Sacrifice Flies plus Times Reached on Defensive Interference.

Platoon Advantage %

Platoon Advantage % is the percentage of players in the starting lineup who have the platoon advantage (i.e. bats right against a left-handed pitcher or bats left against a right-hander) against the starting pitcher, e.g. If the opposing starting pitcher is right handed and the batting team has six left-handed batters in its lineup, the platoon advantage for that game would be 67%.

Plus/Minus System

The Plus/Minus System is a method for evaluating defensive play on batted balls. It is made possible by a game scoring system in which each batted ball is rated for type (line drive, grounder, etc.), velocity within its type (hard, medium or soft), and location on the field. A player gets credit (a "plus" number) if he makes a play that at least one other player at his position missed during the season and he loses credit (a "minus" number") if he misses a play that at least one player made. The size of the credits are proportional to the percentage of times all players make the play. All plays for each player at his position are summed to get his total plus/minus for the season. A total of zero would be average and any other number would approximate how many plays more or less the player made than the average player at the position for the number of chances the player had to field batted balls.

Power/Speed Number

A single number that reflects a combination of power and speed. To achieve a high Power/Speed Number, a player must score high in both power and speed. To calculate the Power/Speed Number, multiply Home Runs by Stolen Bases by two, and divide by the sum of Home Runs and Stolen Bases.

$$\frac{2 \times HR \times SB}{HR + SB}$$

PPO (Pitcher Pickoff)

The number of baserunners thrown out when a pitcher throws to a base with a leading baserunner, and the runner is tagged out attempting to return to the base. PPO is not an official statistic and does not count toward Caught Stealing totals.

Quality Start

A game where the starting pitcher pitches for at least six innings and allows no more than three earned runs.

Quality Start Percentage

Quality Starts divided by Games Started (see the definition for Quality Start).

Quick Hooks

Used in the Manager's Record. For Quick Hooks and Slow Hooks a score is calculated for each game that is the sum of the number of Pitches plus 10 times the number of Runs Allowed. The bottom 25% of scores in the league are considered to be Quick Hooks.

Range Factor

The number of Successful Chances (Putouts plus Assists) times nine divided by the number of Defensive Innings Played. The average for a player at each position in 2010:

        Second Base: 4.79
        Third Base: 2.59
        Shortstop: 4.35
        Left Field: 1.94
        Center Field: 2.65
        Right Field: 2.10

RBI %

The percentage of all potential runs driven in by a certain hitter. Simply put, it's RBIs divided by RBI Opportunities. An RBI Opportunity is any runner on base when the hitter steps up to the plate. We also count the hitter himself, as he can drive in a runner with no one on base via the solo home run. Here's the full formula:

A = Runs Batted In
B = Men On Base + Plate Appearances – Walks – Hit By Pitch – Reaches on Catcher's Interference + C
C = Walks, Hit By Pitch, or Reaches on Catcher's Interference with the bases loaded (resulting in a Run Batted In)

Regular Saves

Any save which does not meet the definition either of an Easy Save or a Tough Save is a "Regular" Save.

Run Support Per 9 IP

The total number of runs scored by a pitcher's team while he is in the game multiplied by nine and divided by total Innings Pitched.

Runs Created

"Runs Created" is an estimate of the number of a team's runs which are created by each individual hitter. The Cincinnati Reds scored 820 runs last year, let us say. How many of those were created by Joey Votto? How many by Brandon Phillips? How many by Jay Bruce?

There are many different formulas for estimating runs created. . .did you want the one that involves swinging a dead cat in the cemetery under a full moon? Yeah, I don't blame you. . .worm-eaten persimmons are so hard to find in the modern world.

This is the one we use now; it is complicated enough. First, there is an "A" Factor in the formula, a "B" Factor, and a "C" factor. The "A" Factor, which represents the number of times the hitter is on base, is Hits, Plus Walks, Plus Hit Batsmen, Minus Caught Stealing, Minus Grounded Into Double Play. The "B" Factor, which represents the hitter's ability to advance other runners, is 1.125 times the player's Singles, plus 1.69 times his Doubles, plus 3.02 times his Triples, plus 3.73 times his Home Runs, plus .29 times his Walks and Hit Batsmen, not counting intentional walks, plus .492 times Sacrifice Hits, Sacrifice Flies and Stolen Bases, minus .04 times Strikeouts. The "C" Factor, which represents opportunities, is At Bats, Plus Walks, Plus Hit By Pitch, Plus Sacrifice Hits, Plus Sacrifice Flies.

Having made these initial calculations of the A, B and C factors, we then change the "A" factor to "A plus 2.4 times C".

We change the "B" factor to "B plus 3 times C".

We change the "C" factor to "9 times C".

Multiply A times B, divide by then new C ("9 times C"), and subtract .90 times by the original C.

This is our first, temporary estimate of the player's runs created. We what we have done here is to ask these questions:

> 1. How many runs would a team probably score that consisted of eight "ordinary" type of hitters, plus this particular hitter?
> 2. How many of those runs would be created by the eight ordinary type of hitters?
> 3. What is the difference-and thus, how many runs did our player create?

To estimate this, we have placed our player in the context of eight hitters with a .300 on base percentage (2.4 divided by 8) and a .375 advancement percentage (3 divided by 8). For each trip through the batting order, the eight ordinary-type hitters would produce 9/10 of a run (2.4 times 3, divided by 8). The "9" in the denominator is eight ordinary hitters plus our man. The "-.9" being subtracted at the end is the runs created by the "ordinary" hitters. In essence, we have placed the hitter in a neutral solution, measured the neutral solution without our hitter, measured it with our hitter, and then estimated the contribution of this hitter as being the difference between the two.

We're not quite done. After that, we adjust the player's runs created estimate for his performance in two "run-sensitive" situations. Suppose that a player whose overall batting average is .250 has batted 100 times with runners in scoring position, and has gone 30-for-100. That's five hits better than expected, 30 hits where we would have expected 25. His team will score an extra five runs because he has done that, and so we increase the player's runs created estimate by five runs. If the player has hit poorly with runners in scoring position, we decrease it by the shortfall in the same way.

Suppose that a player has batted 250 times with runners on base, 250 times with the bases empty, and that he has hit 20 home runs overall. We would expect him to have hit 10 with men on base, 10 with the bases empty, right?

Suppose that he didn't. Suppose that he hit 12 with the bases empty, 8 with men on base. His team would score two runs less than expected because he did this, and we would thus penalize him two runs for the shortfall.

This is our second runs created estimate-the player's runs created, adjusted for his batting performance in run-sensitive situations.

Suppose, however, that we figure the runs created for all of the individuals on a team, and we add them up, and it doesn't match the runs actually scored by the team? What if the formulas say that the team should have scored 800 runs, but they actually scored 820?

Then obviously, the formulas missed. We're trying to measure the runs ACTUALLY created by each hitter as best we can, in the real world, not the theoretical impact of some combination of singles, doubles, triples and walks. If the actual number is different than the estimates, we have to adjust the estimates to fit the facts. In this case-820 runs scored with only 800 runs created-we would multiply each runs created estimate by 820/800, or 1.025. Then we round it off to an integer, and that's the player's estimated runs created.

Let go of that cat, Arthur. Heck, the moon isn't full for three weeks, anyway.

Runs Created per 27 Outs (RC/27)
This statistic estimates the number of runs per game that a team made up of nine of the same player would score. To calculate RC/27, multiply Runs Created by league outs per team game, divide the result by outs made by the player (the sum of at bats plus sacrifice hits plus sacrifice flies plus caught stealing plus grounded into double plays, minus hits). The formula written out is:

$$\frac{\frac{RC \times 3 \times LgIP}{2 \times LgG}}{AB - H + SH + SF + CS + GDP}$$

Runs Saved
See Defensive Runs Saved.

Save Opportunities

The sum of Saves and Blown Saves (see Save Situation).

Save/Hold Percentage (same as Holds Adjusted Saves Percentage)

The sum of Saves and Holds, divided by the sum of Saves, Holds, and Blown Saves.

For several years we figured "Save Percentage", which is simply Saves divided by Save Opportunities, and this stat has some currency in the game. But the Save Percentage severely discriminates against middle relievers, who have no real chance to be credited with the Save, since they will be taken out of the game and replaced by the Closer even if they throw 110 miles an hour and strike out everybody they see. Middle relievers typically have Save Percentages of zero, even if they pitch well. The Save/Hold Percentage is a much more realistic evaluation of a pitcher's success in Save situations.

Save Percentage

A pitcher's Saves divided by the total number of Save Situations he faces (see definition for Save Situation).

Save Situation

A relief pitcher is in a Save Situation when he enters the game with his team in the lead, has the opportunity to finish the game, is not the winning pitcher of record at the time, and meets any one of the three following conditions:

> 1. The pitcher's team is leading by no more than three runs and the pitcher has the chance to pitch for at least one inning,
>
> OR
>
> 2. The pitcher enters the game with the potential tying run on base, at bat, or on deck,
>
> OR
>
> 3. The pitcher pitches three or more effective innings regardless of the lead. The determination of a save in this situation is made by the official scorer.
>
> It is not possible to have more than one save credited to a single team in a game.

SB Gain (Baserunning)

Stolen Base attempts must be successful greater than about two thirds of the time to have a positive result on the number of runs scored. SB gain is therefore the number of bases stolen minus two times the number of caught stealing (SB Gain = SB - 2CS). For example, a runner steals 30 bases and is caught stealing 7 times. His SB Gain would be 30 - 2*7 = +16. Another runner steals 10 bases and is caught stealing 6 times. His SB Gain (actually a loss) would be 10 - 2*6 = -2.

SB Success Percentage

Stolen Bases divided by the number of Stolen Base attempts (Stolen Bases plus Caught Stealing).

$$\frac{SB}{SB + CS}$$

Secondary Average
A number meant to reflect everything else except for batting average. A player will have a high Secondary Average if he hits for power, takes walks and steals bases. It is calculated with the following formula:

$$\frac{TB - H + BB + SB}{AB}$$

Similarity Score
A number which reflects the similarity between two different statistical lines, either for a player or for a team. A score of 1,000 means that the statistical lines are identical.

Slow Hooks
Used in the Manager's Record. For Quick Hooks and Slow Hooks a score is calculated for each game that is the sum of the number of Pitches plus 10 times the number of Runs Allowed. The top 25% of scores in the league are considered to be Slow Hooks.

Slugging Average
Total Bases divided by At Bats.

$$\frac{TB}{AB}$$

Speed Score
Speed Score is a number which evaluates how fast a player is. To calculate the Speed Score, start with the player's statistics over the last two seasons combined. A value will be found for each of the following six categories and will be combined for a final score at the end:

1.Stolen Base Percentage. The value of this category is:

$$\left(\frac{SB + 3}{SB + CS + 7} - 0.4\right) \times 20$$

2.Frequency of Stolen Base Attempts. The value of this category is:

$$\frac{\sqrt{\dfrac{SB + CS}{Singles + BB + HBP}}}{0.07}$$

3.Percentage of Triples. This is calculated by taking the percentage of triples out of the number of balls put in play. To get the percentage, use this formula:

$$\frac{3B}{AB - HR - SO}$$

From this assign an integer from 0 to 10, based on the following chart:

Less than .001	0
.001 - .0023	1
.0023 - .0039	2
.0039 - .0058	3
.0058 - .0080	4
.0080 - .0105	5
.0105 - .013	6
.013 - .0158	7
.0158 - .0189	8
.0189 - .0223	9
.0223 or more	10

4. Runs Scored Percentage. This is calculated by taking the percentage of times the player scores a run out of the number of times the player is on base. To get the percentage, use this formula:

$$\frac{\left(\dfrac{R - HR}{H + HBP + BB - HR} - 0.1\right)}{0.04}$$

5. Grounded Into Double Play Frequency. To get the frequency, use this formula:

$$\frac{0.055 - \left(\dfrac{GIDP}{AB - HR - SO}\right)}{0.005}$$

6. Range Factor. The value of this category depends on the players position:

Catcher—1
First Baseman—2
Designated Hitter—1.5
Second Baseman—1.25 x Range Factor
Third Baseman—1.51 x Range Factor
Shortstop—1.52 x Range Factor
Outfield—3 x Range Factor

For an explanation on Range Factor, consult the definition in this glossary. Remember to figure range factors over a two-year period.

If any category value is greater than 10, then reduce it to 10. If any value is less than zero, then increase the value to zero. All category values must fall within the zero to 10 range. The Speed Score is then calculated by discarding the lowest of the six values, and taking the average of the remaining five.

Total Bases
Hits plus Doubles plus (2 times Triples) plus (3 times Home Runs).

$$H + 2B + (2 \times 3B) + (3 \times HR)$$

Tough Loss
A starting pitcher who loses the game with a game score over 50 gets credit for a tough loss. See Game Score.

Tough Save
This label is used to separate Saves by difficulty level (Easy or Tough). A Save is considered Tough if the relief pitcher enters the game with the tying run on base.

Win Probability
The probability of a team winning the game determined at any time during the game based on the score, inning, outs and base situation.

Winning Percentage
Wins divided by (Wins plus Losses).

Baseball Info Solutions

What will box scores look like in a hundred years? What did they look like a century ago? Whatever the difference, it can almost be entirely attributed to advances in baseball statistics analysis.

But analysis alone is not responsible for the prevalence of advanced statistics now in broadcasts and bar-room arguments across the world; you need to have high quality, innovative data or you may draw the wrong conclusions. Baseball Info Solutions has been supplying top notch, timely, and in-depth baseball data to its customers since 2002.

BIS collects a statistical snapshot of every important moment of ever Major League Baseball game with the most advanced technology, resulting in a database that includes traditional data, pitch-by-pitch data, and defensive positioning data. The company also has the highest quality pitch charting data available anywhere, including pitch type, location, and velocity.

BIS provides comprehensive services to about half of the 30 Major League Baseball teams, as well as many sports agents, media, fantasy services, game companies and private individuals.

John Dewan, the principal owner of BIS, has been on the cutting edge of baseball analysis for over 25 years. His experience goes all the way back to his days as Executive Director of Project Scoresheet, the Bill James-led effort that pioneered the new wave of baseball statistics that are now common terminology.

President Steve Moyer brings 20 years of baseball industry experience to BIS. His hands-on, can-do business demeanor helps set BIS apart from its competition.

The rest of the BIS team includes former professional and collegiate baseball players as well as programming and database management experts. Over the last five seasons, BIS has more than tripled its full-time staff.

BIS continues to grow within the industry while emphasizing personal attention to its customers. This focus on personal attention is evidenced by the fact that if you contact the office with an inquiry you may very well find yourself speaking directly to the company president.

To contact BIS:

Baseball Info Solutions
41 S. 2nd Street
Coplay, PA 18037
610-261-2370
www.baseballinfosolutions.com

Acknowledgements

Bill James is the brains behind the majority of what you see in this book, thus the title.

John Dewan is the primary owner of Baseball Info Solutions and is also a pioneer in the analysis of baseball data. John's specialty is defensive data.

The leaders of the Operations department at Baseball Info Solutions are Dan Casey, Mike Piekarski and Todd Radcliffe. The volume and accuracy of our data can be attributed in great part to these three.

The leaders of the IT department are Damon Lichtenwalner and Jeff Spoljaric. They keep the BIS databases in good hands.

Rob Burckhard and Ben Jedlovec form the R&D department. I like to call them the BIS "baseball scientists." Eric Heckman interned for them during the season.

Jim Swavely and Jon Vrecsics are the primary caretakers of our invaluable Minor League operation.

Abe Bakre, Paul Boye, Dedan Brozino, Jake Charlson, Ryan Clancy, Cale Cox, Rick Daniels, Scott Gregory, Matt Hamilton, Dana Hegman, Derek Henson, Ken Hoffman, Matt Horn, David Ireland, David Jeffrey, Christopher Jones, Matt Kaufman, Doug Kopf, Mark Layman, Kevin Macios, Jack Mengel, Thomas Michael, Evan Schaffer, Michael Schatz and Jeff Ward were the 2010 Video Scout crew. I doubt anyone watches more major league baseball over the course of a season than these guys.

Jim Capuano is the head of Business Development.

The ACTA Publications crew is headed by Greg Pierce, along with Andrew Yankech, Donna Ryding, Mary Eggert, Richard Struben and Brendan Gaughan.

Our friends in the baseball industry include: Greg Ambrosius, Andy Andres, Matthew Berry, Jim Callis, Mike Canter, Doug Dennis, Jeff Erickson, Peter Gammons, Jason Grey, Durward Hamil, Joel Kammeyer, Peter Kreutzer, Michael Lehrer, Chris Liss, Gene McCaffrey, Deric McKamey, Sig Mejdal, John Menna, Bob Meyerhoff, Lawr Michaels, Mike Murphy, Patrick Newman, Rob Neyer, Mat Olkin, Alex Patton, Scott Pianowski, Mike Phillips, David Pinto, Joe Posnanski, Nate Ravitz, Hal Richman, Steve Ruskowski, Greg Rybarczyk, Mike Salfino, Peter Schoenke, Ron Shandler, Joe Sheehan, John Sickels, Dave Studenmund, Tom Tango, Sam Walker, Mark Watson, Rick Wilton, Trace Wood, Todd Zola and Don Zminda.

We thank all of you for the things you have done, over the years, to make our book the industry standard.

Sincerely,
Steve Moyer
President
Baseball Info Solutions

NOTES

NOTES

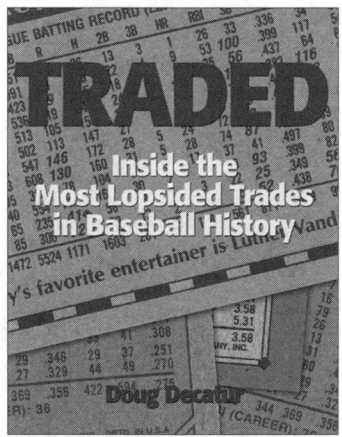